W9-DBG-669

Science-Fiction

Science-Fiction

The Gernsback Years

A complete coverage of the genre magazines

Amazing, Astounding, Wonder,

and others from 1926 through 1936.

by Everett F. Bleiler
with the assistance of Richard J. Bleiler

THE KENT STATE UNIVERSITY PRESS
Kent, Ohio, and London, England

©1998 by Everett F. Bleiler
All rights reserved
Library of Congress Catalog Card Number 98-13374
ISBN 0-87338-604-3
Manufactured in the United States of America

04 03 02 01 00 99 98   5 4 3 2 1

Library of Congress Cataloging-in-Publication Data

Bleiler, Everett Franklin, 1920–
    Science-fiction : the Gernsback years / by Everett F. Bleiler, with the assistance of Richard J. Bleiler.
        p.   cm.
    Includes bibliographical references and indexes.
    ISBN 0-87338-604-3 (cloth : alk. paper) ∞
    1. Science fiction, American—Dictionaries. 2. Gernsback, Hugo, 1884–1967—Contemporaries—Dictionaries.
  I. Bleiler, Richard. II. Title
    PS648.S3B57 1998   98-13374
    016.813'8762—dc21   CIP

British Library Cataloging-in-Publication data are available.

Contents

Preface

In the late 1920s and early 1930s a new literary phenomenon came into being in the United States. This was genre science-fiction, recognized as such and sold as such in between forty and fifty thousand newsstands, drugstores, and tobacconists. Although American in origin, it had in part an international ancestry, what with the earlier science-fictions of Jules Verne, H. G. Wells, and others. But as it now developed, it was something new.

The first issue of the first science-fiction magazine, *Amazing Stories*, published by Hugo Gernsback, a New York inventor and publisher of technical magazines, appeared on the stands and presumably arrived in the mail for subscriptions around the first week of March 1926. Within a little more than ten years, *Amazing Stories* and its later rivals numbered 345 issues, to say nothing of twenty issues of *Scoops*, an aberrant British boys' story paper.

This survival and proliferation rate is in itself a cultural phenomenon: that publications which easily lent themselves to ridicule were not only viable in the height of the Great Depression, but actually survived longer than most of the other pulp magazines. Today, the descendants of these 345 magazines are almost omnipresent. Science-fiction floods the television channels, permeates the book best-seller lists, fills carousels in supermarkets, accounts for hundreds of millions of dollars in motion picture production, and has become an accepted part of our modern life. Its strength probably emerges partly from novelty, partly from its limitless expansibility. It is the universe (and sometimes beyond) and the subatomic particle.

One may regard science-fiction in its later, superior aspects (as certain critics do) as the literature of the future with perceptual and normative values; or one may see it as the fictional recognition of the hegemony of science and technology in our civilization; or one may consider it simply a form of unusual entertainment. No matter which evaluation one accepts, its roots are important, and the early period described in this volume established many story elements, narrative techniques, ideas, and implementations of fantastic data that are still present.

Early genre science-fiction, as considered here, was an expression of popular culture that was unusual in combining fantasized ideas from science and/or technology with narrative techniques from the so-called pulp magazines, where event was the important consideration. The weight of the combination lay sometimes on one side, and sometimes on the other.

It made strange claims. It claimed paternity from science, whence its name, and it promised (according to its more enthusiastic promulgators) to influence and possibly to create the future. As one of the curiosities of history, Hugo Gernsback (as is discussed below in the history of *Air Wonder Stories*) advanced a theory whereby science-fiction displaces and offers an enlarging and emending critique of science and technology, creating a new synthesis, a statement very suggestive of Jacques Derrida's *supplément*. This is, of course, farfetched and somewhat incredible, but it embodies the messianic thought accompanying early genre science-fiction. Despite its pulp clothing, Gernsback's science-fiction shared a little with evangelical literature and social protest, though it was neither religious in a traditional sense nor utopian. It thus has points of interest beyond a gathering of implausible stories.

Early genre science-fiction may also be regarded as one aspect of the general twentieth-century literary cultural pattern, experiencing the forbidden, in this case, experiencing one aspect of the impossible. It also mirrored aspects of premodern America—aims, disavowals, perceptions, blindnesses—which it imaged more clearly than most of the other literature of the day. As is detailed in the Introduction, it was almost unique in recognizing the precariousness of the human situation. Crisis, catastrophe, debacle lie closer to its heart than either in other forms of popular fiction or in contemporary mainstream fiction.

The present work is the first detailed examination of this incunabular period, the Gernsback Era, from 1926 through 1936, so-called because Gernsback's ideas dominated developments, sometimes in imitation, sometimes in opposition. It covers the literature as a field, with its manifestations in different magazine traditions and its embodiments in individual stories. In its preparation, the needs of the reader--historian, critic, reference librarian, collector--have been borne in mind, with precise, detailed information.

The story descriptions that form the heart of this book have been based on reading every story in the physical magazine in which it originally appeared. They are not based on secondary sources, which are sometimes unreliable or take a point of view that may distort data for some readers.

Emphasis has been placed on narrative and the fantastic element, with enough detail to give a reasonable image of the story, rather than on interpretation in terms of any system, although a structuralist point of view (as in the two previous volumes in the informal series, *The Guide to Supernatural Fiction* and *Science-Fiction: The Early Years*) lies behind the execution of the book. Structuralism seems the best schema for handling large amounts of related literary data.

I am aware that such a classificatory/schematic/genealogi-cal/descriptive approach is not that followed by certain modern modes of criticism, but for the material covered here, concreteness and specificness seem primary, since the texts are almost unknown to scholarship. Very few of the stories have been described elsewhere, and most have never even been mentioned in general surveys.

A further factor is the inaccessibility of the texts. The original magazines are rare, and what with the extremely poor quality paper on which they were printed, they often survive in various stages of disintegration. A little more than 85 percent of the original stories considered here have never been reprinted in book form; of those reprinted, many appeared forty or more years ago in mass-market paperbacks that are now almost as difficult to obtain and almost as fragile as the sixty- or seventy-year-old magazines. In a few instances micro versions for certain issues of the magazines have been produced, but even these are not generally available because of their high cost, and they are often inconvenient to use.

These story descriptions have been used in the introduction to tabulate in a partly statistical approach the evolution of important themes and motifs, story orientations, types of science involved, and similar matters.

In addition to describing the stories, I have attempted to identify their authors briefly and, in the introduction, to draw certain conclusions about them as a group. This material does not pretend to be exhaustive for the half dozen or so important authors like John W. Campbell, Jr., or Jack Williamson--about whom data are readily available elsewhere--but it does offer at least a beginning on minor men and women, who are extraordinarily difficult, if not often impossible, to research. This information has been acquired from many sources, as can be seen in the acknowledgments section: colleges and universities, alumni associations, newspaper obituaries, local histories, public libraries, trade associations, learned societies, Social Security records, the Internet, and the memories of relicts and friends. I have also combed the letter columns of our magazines (and other publications) for leads. The result is a considerable amount of reliable new information with scores of new identifications, vitae, and corrections of earlier accounts.

Pseudonyms constitute a special problem. A few are resolved in standard reference sources, but most of our authors are not represented in such works. Over the decades, however, dozens of pseudonyms and their identities have been proposed in the amateur literature and are generally accepted in genre tradition. Unfortunately, not all of these identifications can stand up to examination, and it has been necessary to research them afresh. I have tried to trace each such identification and, where possible, verify it or reject it on the basis of outside knowledge, including publishing records and other sources. The result has been many corrections and many new identifications.

Also included is, to my knowledge, the first technical analysis of the artists who illustrated the magazines. Much of the iconography of later fantastic illustration is based on the work of five pioneers, whose work I have analyzed in some detail.

To render this large body of literature more accessible and more useful to the reader and researcher, I have provided several data compilations hitherto unavailable: magazine histories with considerable new information, identification of editorials, rosters of poetry and authors' letters, and location of reprints. Most important of all is an analytical index of themes and motifs; this represents a consolidation of about thirty thousand 3" x 5" file cards.

This study has not discovered new masterpieces in the pulp magazines of the Gernsback era. A realistic view, unfortunately, must recognize that the most of the stories represent a developmental stage, not a perfection. But as examples of popular fiction, daring in their imagination, iconoclastic in their assumptions, they have value apart from literary merit.

As Sir Arthur Clarke put it in his "In the Beginning Was Jupiter" (*New York Times Book Review,* March 6, 1983, p. 14), "Young readers of today, born into a world in which science-fiction magazines, books and movies are part of every day life, cannot imagine the impact of such garish pulps as that old *Amazing* and its colleagues *Astounding* and *Wonder*. Of course, the literary standards were usually abysmal—but the stories brimmed with ideas and amply evoked that sense of wonder that is or should be one of the goals of the best fiction."

Everett F. Bleiler

Acknowledgments

This work could not have been completed without the assistance and advice of many individuals.

First, I must express thanks to the following libraries where most of the background research for this project has been performed: The Olin and Uris Libraries of Cornell University; The Homer Babbidge Library of the University of Connecticut; the Mervyn H. Sterne Library of the University of Alabama in Birmingham; The Tompkins County Library of Ithaca, N. Y.; and the New York Public Library.

Special thanks must be expressed to the Department of Special Collections, Syracuse University Library, in the persons of Mark Weimer and Carolyn A. Davis, who made it possible to examine the Street and Smith and Gernsback Archives, a unique resource for American publishing.

I must also thank the MIT Science Fiction Society and Secretary Marcus Serofim for invaluable assistance.

The following surviving authors covered in this book deserve appreciation, not only for information graciously offered, but for their early work: Forrest J. Ackerman; Clinton Constant (previously Clinton Constantinescu); Chester Cuthbert; Walter L. Dennis; Lloyd A. Eshbach; Horace Gold (since deceased), Charles L. Hornig; Frank K. Kelly; Clifton B. Kruse; Dr. Kenneth Sterling (since deceased), and, of course, Jack Williamson.

Relicts and relations of deceased authors have also been helpful: Richard Donahue; Richard Dornisch; Lael Wertenbaker Fletcher (since deceased); Numa C. Hero, Jr.; Mrs. David Lasser; Mrs. Joseph Schlossel; Eric Sloat; Dr. Christian Wertenbaker; Alison Phillips; Mrs. Karl Ziska.

Especially helpful have been Mike Ashley, Neil Barron, Gene Christie, Tom Cockcroft, William Contento, Jim Emerson, Martin Gardner, Mark Goldberg, Kenneth Johnson, Stephen T. Miller, A. Langley Searles, and Graham Stone, all of whom shared their expertise.

The following institutions and their staffs have been helpful in resolving problems: Susan Woodward, Special Collections Librarian, The University of Adelaide; Angela Mills, Edmonton Public Library; J. Myler, San Antonio Public Library; R. G. Donner, Library Department, The City of Winnipeg; Wendy A. Swik, Military Affairs Librarian, United States Military Academy, West Point; Elaine Engst, University Archivist, Cornell University; Mary Cruickshanck, Collingwood Public Library, Collingwood, Ontario, Canada; Lawrence Campbell, Archivist, The Art Students League of New York; Gary A. Lundell, Reference Specialist, University of Washington; James W. Buckley, Torrance Public Library, California; Robert Nash, Collection Development, University of Nebraska at Omaha; Joan L. Clark, Cleveland Public Library; Peter Broughton, Royal Astronomical Society of Canada; Rae Hamlin of IABC; Tammy Vieira and Sue Williams, LSU College of Engineering; Patti Slider, Development Director, Washburn University School of Law; Alumni Records, University of Oregon; Teresa Scalzo, University of Minnesota Alumni Association; Karen Mack, Senior Public Information Representative, University of California, Los Angeles; Chatham Public Library, Chatham, N. Y.; Guy Cribdon, InfoAction, Vancouver Public Library; Niki Denison, Associate Editor, *On Wisconsin*, University of Wisconsin Alumni Association; Nancy Varat, University of California, Los Angeles; Jennifer Schaffner, Assistant Librarian, California Historical Society; Jean Spradlin-Miller, Mervyn H. Sterne Library, University of Alabama at Birmingham; and Charlotte Blackford of The State Bar of California.

Gratitude must be expressed to Martin Gardner, for his reminiscences about *Science and Invention* and the first issue of *Amazing Stories*; to George W. Price of Advent:Publishers for permission to reprint portions from Harry Bates's introduction to Alva Rogers's *A Requiem for Astounding*; and to Lloyd W. Eshbach for permission to print an excerpt from his autobiography *Over My Shoulder*.

Assistance on special topics is gratefully acknowledged: W. O. G. Lofts (since deceased), the foremost authority on British boys' literature, for unique information on *Scoops*; Sam Moskowitz (since deceased), who originally settled the identity of Warner Van Lorne, for confirmation of his discovery; Robert Madle, who knew most of the Philadelphia-Baltimore science-fiction people, for establishing the identity of Charles Cloukey; Dr. Rodes Garby, for biographical information on Lee Hawkins Garby; Robert Griffin and Don Ramlow, for biographical information on Franklin Ryan; Dwayne H. Olson, for data about the Wandrei brothers; Prof. Robert E. Bell, formerly of the University of Oklahoma, for information on the mysterious L. Taylor Hansen; Clare Vivet, for checking French publication sources; Libby Manthy of Lane Technical Preparatory School of Chicago, for tracking down, as far as has been possible, George McLociard; Milton Rothman, for checking out Alexander M. Phillips; John V. Baltadonis for information about Philadelphia authors; and Robert Weinberg, for information on the artist Wesso. I must also thank genealogists Laurel Drew and Carolyn Feroben for their careful researches into Western authors. Gratitude is also due to Will Murray and Mike Nickle for helpful responses on the Internet.

I must also thank Dr. Fiona Wood, Brewers and Licensed Retailers Association of Great Britain; Judy Lee of *The Rotarian*; and Gerald Diaz-Granados of the American Orchid Society.

Gratitude must be expressed to the membership of First Fandom, that unique collection of survivors from the 1930s and 1940s, the mammalian dinosaurs of science-fiction, who willingly shared their unique knowledge. President Ray Beam and Editor Mark Schulzinger permitted me to circularize the organization, and many persons responded or answered letters: Forrest J. Ackerman, Jack Agnew, Clifton Amsbury, David H. Blair, Walter J. Daugherty, Steven Francis, Donald L. Franson, Franz Grumme, Rosemary Hickey, Ben Indick, Frank K. Kelly, Virginia Kidd, Roy Lavender, Lester Mayer, Conrad H. Ruppert (since deceased), Julius Schwartz, Norman F. Stanley, and R. D. Swisher (since deceased).

And, finally, I must express my gratitude to the many fans and readers, mostly long departed, who cared enough to record a new phenomenon in American literature. Out of their letters, conversations, reminiscences, magazine and ephemera collecting has been built much of the later bibliographic background available to us.

                                        Everett F. Bleiler

Introduction

When I was nine or ten, my all-time favorite magazine was Hugo Gernsback's *Science and Invention*, then in its gold cover phase to symbolize the golden age of science. I read every one of Clement Fezandié's some forty tales about "Dr. Hackensaw's Secrets" (why has no publisher reprinted them?), as well as the serialized novels by early SF writers.

I recall revelling in stories about space travel, such as "Around the Universe" by Ray Cummings. At the time, my science teacher in grade school was assuring us that spaceships were total nonsense and that humankind would never reach even the moon.

In 1926 when *Science and Invention* advertised a forthcoming *Amazing Stories* magazine, printing what Gernsback then called "scientifiction," I was an eager twelve-year-old subscriber.

I can still recall my excitement in seeing the first lurid cover, and being introduced over the years to the science fiction of Jules Verne, H. G. Wells, and Edgar Allan Poe. In those days the magazine's emphasis was in reprinting classics. Later, of course, new writers were lured onto the scene.

I even bought by mail a copy of Gernsback's *Ralph 124C 41+*, surely the worst SF novel ever written, but I didn't know that at the time. I recall, however, wincing at the preposterous pun on Ralph's number in the book's final sentence.

When I reached high school, I gave my physics teacher all my back copies of *Amazing Stories*, to which I had continued to subscribe. I have no memory of how *Ralph 124C 41+* got away from me. Would that I had saved both it and the first year of *Amazing Stories*.

Martin Gardner

It was around 1923 or 1924 that I found *Science and Invention* with its science fiction. Dr. Hackensaw's

Secrets were running endlessly, and I remember a Ray Cummings serial about adventures in a watery world . . . But all this was as nothing beside the thrill that came early in 1926. I was fifteen . . . I had stopped to look into the window of Kinkaid's Book Store. The back wall of the window was covered with magazines. And there it was—a picture of the planet Saturn and above it a comet-tail title, *Amazing Stories*! I had money in my pocket—after all, I was now a working man—and in moments I was the delighted owner of the first issue of the world's first science fiction magazine.

As the months passed, each eagerly awaited issue of *Amazing Stories* was devoured, usually within two days after it appeared on the newsstands.

Lloyd Eshbach, *Over My Shoulder*, p. 35-36.

Such were the experiences of two men who bought the first issue of *Amazing Stories* when it appeared in March 1926. Martin Gardner bought it by subscription; Lloyd Eshbach, on the newsstands. Although neither man could have known it at the time, they were participating in the birth and development of what would turn out to be an important facet of modern life.

This was the birth of science-fiction *denoted as such*, although the publisher of *Amazing Stories*, Hugo Gernsback, called it by the portmanteau word "scientifiction." This is not to say that there was no science-fiction before 1926. Ransacking the literature from the eighteenth century to the 1920s, one can turn up thousands of stories that today we would call science-fiction, although they may have been called something else, if they were classified at all. There were stories about inventions, stories about interplanetary voyages, stories set in the future, stories about the destruction of the Earth, stories about immortal or nearly immortal men, and much else. Gernsback's contribution was to assemble such fantastic story types, all of which maintained a foothold in reality (as opposed to supernatural fiction), under a new byline and turn it into a successful commercial venture.

Before Gernsback's *Amazing Stories* there were a couple of tentative approaches to a magazine devoted to science-fictional topics. There was the isolated "Twentieth Century Number" (June 1890) of the *Overland Monthly*, which contained stories and essays describing twentieth-century matters. It was mostly concerned with the theories of Edward Bellamy of *Looking Backward,* although it also contained a translation of a German piece by Kurd Lasswitz. More significant was the science-fiction dime-novel series The Frank Reade Library, at first issued weekly, later biweekly, which printed 183 novels dealing with fantastic inventions and occasional lost races. It extended from 1892 to 1898, and might in retrospect be considered a science-fiction periodical. But it was a dead end, and its publishers did not have the wit to recognize the implications of their work. Perhaps the Geist had not yet encountered the Zeit.

A fascinating almost-of-history occurs with the *Thrill Book*, which was published in biweekly issues from March 1 through October 15, 1919 by Street and Smith. A request for stories issued by its first editor, Harold Hersey marks, it would seem, the first conscious departure from the romantic realism that had characterized the standard and pulp magazines:

> We are strongly desirous of securing strange, bizarre, occult, mysterious tales . . . . If we were to give you a formula we would say—sum up the demands of all other magazines, and then give us good stories which not one of them would take because of their odd qualities and harrowing nature. We quote as examples the stories of De Maupassant, Edgar Allan Poe, De Quincey's curious tales. . . . If you have the unusual, the mysterious, the occult, the harrowing—such stories will be gladly considered with a view to publication . . . . In this magazine accent is laid on the curious twist; the strange angles of human nature; the coming into contact with an unseen world; miraculous but logical happenings . . . . mysterious occurrences . . . If you have an idea which you have considered too bizarre to write, too weird or strange, let us see it. (Richard Bleiler, *The Annotated Index to The Thrill Book,* pp. 5-6).

In its last issues, under a different editor, the *Thrill Book* was moving toward being a fantastic fiction magazine, but Street and Smith unexpectedly canceled it, and the opportunity was lost.

About three and a half years later the first pulp magazine in English that specialized in fantastic fiction appeared. This was the March 1923 issue of *Weird Tales*. Although it is now remembered mostly for its supernatural fiction, especially the work of H. P. Lovecraft and Robert E. Howard, it printed more than 200 science-fiction stories between 1923 and the end of 1930, and it was in *Weird Tales* that "space opera" developed.

The appearance of *Weird Tales* and *Amazing Stories* exemplifies a trend in popular fiction magazines. In the earlier years, before World War I, pulp magazines diversified their contents, with stories of different types in each issue: perhaps Western, humor, crime, sports, romance, historical or geographical adventure, etc.; but around World War I, specialized magazines began to appear in basic fictional categories. Street and Smith's *Detective Story Magazine,* the first of its kind, appeared in 1915; Street and Smith's *Western Story Magazine,* in 1919; Street and Smith's *Sport Stories,* in 1923; the first air-war magazines, Dell's *War Birds* and Street and Smith's *Air Trails Magazine,* in 1928. The time was thus ripe for specialty magazines dealing with fantastic fiction, either supernatural or science-fiction.

Science-fiction, although it was not called this, had been appearing intermittently in various pulp magazines from before World War I. Much of it was adventure fiction with an undifferentiated fantastic background; much consisted of invention stories. The most frequent sites were the Munsey magazines *All-Story* and *Argosy*, and the combined *Argosy-All-Story;* Consolidated's *Blue Book Magazine,* and Street and Smith's *Popular Magazine.* Since these were among the most widely circulated magazines, readers of the pulps were not unfamiliar with the devices of science-fiction. (Most of this early pulp science-fiction is covered in *Science-Fiction: The Early Years.*)

Just as relevant, probably, was the presence of occasional early science-fiction in Hugo Gernsback's popular-science/technology/craft magazines. *Popular Electrics* from 1909 on printed primitive science-fiction, while Gernsback began his own science-fiction novel "Ralph 124C 41+" in *Modern Electrics* in 1911, following this with material by other authors. This early fiction printed in the popular science and technology magazines was extraordinarily bad, but it seems to have pleased the readers enough to justify its continued presence.

From early 1920 through the middle of 1928 Gernsback printed at least one fictional work in almost each issue of his magazines *Electrical Experimenter/Science and Invention* and *Radio News.* Most, but not all, of these stories were science-fiction; the others were based on some aspect or quirk of science, but not fantastic, a story-type that Gernsback later called "science faction" *(Wonder Stories Quarterly,* Fall 1930, p.5). An example of these science-but-not-science-fiction stories can be found in #176, Ellis Parker Butler's "Solander's Radio Tomb," which is described in the body copy of this book.

In the August 1923 issue of *Science and Invention,* which he called the "Scientific Fiction Issue," Gernsback, as a possible test, printed six stories, four of which were science-fiction: a serial part of Ray Cummings's "Around the Universe," G. Peyton Wertenbaker's "The Man from the Atom," J. Huekels's "Advanced Chemistry," and Clement Fezandié's "The Secret of the Super-Telescope." Gernsback also included two science stories, his own "The Electrical Duel" and Teddy J. Holman's "Vanishing Movies."

Response to the special issue must have been favorable, for in 1924 Gernsback gave serious thought to publishing a magazine devoted to science-fiction, or as he called it in a portmanteau word he coined, "scientifiction." In accordance with the law of the day, he patented the name of the proposed magazine, *Scientifiction,* and filed in the U. S. Patent Office a so-called "ashcan issue." This would have been a special booklet, printed in perhaps a dozen or two copies from galleys, containing a few specimen stories, and sold in at least two states. Unfortunately, this ashcan issue does not seem to have survived, but it is a reasonable supposition that it contained reprints from *Science and Invention* and/or *Radio News,* perhaps including some of Gernsback's own work.

Gernsback now circularized his subscription and customer lists, asking for comments and/or subscriptions. "Several years ago, when I first conceived the idea of publishing a scientifiction magazine, a circular letter was sent to some 25,000 people, informing them that a new magazine by the name 'Scientifiction' was shortly to be launched. The response was such that the idea was given up for two years." *(Amazing Stories*, September 1926, p. 483).

What convinced Gernsback to try again in 1926, this time with a magazine rather than an offer, is not known. In any case, with considerable publicity in *Science and Invention* and *Radio News*, *Amazing Stories* appeared on the newsstands in early March 1926.

It was a strange magazine. So far as I can tell, it may have been one of the two or three bedsheet-sized magazines of the thirty-five or more pulps on the newsstands at the time. It is not clear whether Gernsback selected this format (8" x 11") to distinguish it from the other pulps, which approximated 7" x 10", and associate it with the larger-sized slick magazines, or whether it was a matter of production costs, but the large size probably caused a display problem on the stands.

Amazing Stories was printed on pulp paper, but its contents were not pulp fiction. Instead they were, for the first year or so, almost entirely reprints, mostly of "classical" literature by H. G. Wells, Jules Verne, and Edgar Allan Poe, though with a scattering of reprints from Gernsback's technical/hobby magazines. Much of this was public domain and could be reprinted without fee.

Nor was the general atmosphere of the magazine that of the pulps. In its early years at least, *Amazing Stories* carried the redolence of the technical/hobbies magazines, what with Gernsback's enthusiastic promises of what scientifiction would do for the world, departments focused on the sciences, and its editorial staff—unfortunately—doubled from Gernsback's other magazines.

Once *Amazing Stories* was on the stands, Gernsback was faced with the problem of finding suitable fiction to continue publication. His knowledge of earlier science-fiction was limited, and he had to acquire original stories. It was one thing to accept an occasional amateurish short story for *Science and Invention* or *Radio News*, or to stretch a short novel there into fifteen installments, as he did in *Science and Invention* with Ray Cummings's "Tarrano the Conqueror;" all this was really lagniappe to technical or news matters. But now Gernsback had to find science-fiction stories that could compete with the general stories in other magazines, and in quantity. And there were almost no practicing science-fiction writers!

How Gernsback worked within this situation and how he encountered the related problem of illustration is covered in some detail in the histories of the *Amazing* and *Wonder* magazines in the following sections of this volume.

Gernsback's *Amazing Stories* and its spinoffs, *Amazing Stories Annual* and *Amazing Stories Quarterly*, gradually became more professional magazines and merged more with the general run of pulp magazines, but the first science-fiction magazine that was pulp in essence, and not just in form, appeared on the newsstands with William Clayton's *Astounding Stories of Super-Science* for January 1930. It survived for not quite three and a half years, died, and was resurrected as Street and Smith's *Astounding Stories* with new editorial policies.

Sister and competitive magazines appeared on the newsstands, with the following titles having been published by December 1936, the end of our period: *Amazing Stories, Amazing Stories Annual, Amazing Stories Quarterly, Science*

Wonder Stories, Air Wonder Stories, Science Wonder Quarterly, [Clayton] *Astounding Stories of Super-Science, Wonder Stories, Wonder Stories Quarterly, Miracle Science and Fantasy Stories,* [Street and Smith] *Astounding Stories, Thrilling Wonder Stories,* and *Flash Gordon Strange Adventure Magazine. Scoops*, a science-fictional boys' story paper, appeared, under diluted American influence, in Great Britain. Each of these publications is described separately in the body of the text.

The 345 issues of the above 14 magazines presented 1,835 stories by approximately 510 authors, including collaborations. The precise number of authors is uncertain because of possible pseudonyms and, conversely, misidentifications. This corpus of material will now be examined, as a body, in terms of the stories, the authors, and the readership.

The Stories

The science-fiction of the Gernsback era does not wholly form a continuity with the science-fiction of earlier periods, notably the book and magazine fiction of the first part of the twentieth century. Changes have taken place; some story types have waned, others have waxed. The traditional lost-race novel has almost disappeared, as has purely geographical adventure with fantastic elements in the manner of Jules Verne or the American dime novel. Early aeronautics, a frequent topic until World War I, is no longer significant, for heavier-than-air machines have been active in the outside world for a generation. With the relative perfection of the automobile and submarine, there is little need to fantasize about the Frank Reade sort of land rover or *Nautilus*-like undersea craft. Radium played a large part in early science-fiction, but by the 1930s it appears only occasionally, and then often in fantastic forms like "eca-radium." Hugo Gernsback apparently liked stories about silly inventions, which were common around the turn of the century, but otherwise dropped away almost completely in the 1920s.

Historical personalities, who frequently appeared around the turn of the century to enliven stories, are now rarely used, and then often à clef.

The detailed, realistic imaginary war, based on the power politics of the day, which dominated turn-of-the-century science-fiction in the United States and Great Britain, has almost disappeared, although modern versions with more fantastic elements, are occasionally present. And the Faustian scientist is no longer important; mad scientists occasionally occur, though less frequently than in the past, but the dynamic, unceasing quest for knowledge has become subordinated to schemes of conquest, subtle revenges, and curious cruelties.

Early science-fiction, particularly during the late nineteenth and early twentieth centuries, was closely associated with the utopia or ideal society. This association was not an abstract matter of speculating about alien societies, but more an attempt to embody panaceas, usually socialism of one variety or another, into fiction. Bellamism, the system expounded in Edward Bellamy's *Looking Backward* and *Equality*, was especially important. Hundreds of such social extrapolations are covered in *Science-Fiction: The Early Years*.

In the pulp science-fiction of 1926-1936, social messianism, as opposed to the scientific or technological perfectibilism favored by Hugo Gernsback, is not very important.

While political activist David Lasser (managing editor of the *Wonder* magazines) favored fiction that incorporated some social protest, including parables of Technocracy, few stories are blatantly propagandistic. Where social and cultural material occasionally enters stories in large quantity, it is more a question of almost anthropological interest in unusual human or humanoid life ways. Thus, while there are several (unfortunately cumbersome and boring) detailed expositions of life in Atlantis, the fourth dimension, or elsewhere, these are not usually intended as prescriptions for modern America but as something of novelty interest.

Satirical elements, too, are much less common in the science-fiction of our period than in earlier times. Occasionally, a story pokes fun at aspects of our culture, but this is unusual. The only large exception is the opus of Stanton A. Coblentz, who was primarily a satirist using science-fiction narratives to carry his ideas. Coblentz's major works, it must be added, were written before the appearance of the science-fiction magazines and languished, unsalable, until the appearance of *Amazing Stories* and *Wonder Stories*.

The largest overall difference between significant premodern and Gernsback-era pulp science-fiction seems to have been the presence of Ingredient X in the earlier period. This Ingredient X was a secondary matter apart from narrative; it may have been comedy of manners material, social protest or examination of society, psychological analysis, political recommendations, scurrility, aesthetic programs, educational theories, or similar topics, without which science-fiction may remain one-dimensional. Within our period, science-fiction, no matter what the editors claimed, was primarily a means of entertainment based on novelty of background.

It is therefore no surprise that much of the world of the 1920s and 1930s does not enter on an obvious surface level into the stories of the Gernsback era. The most important event, the Great Depression and its concomitants, is significantly absent. There are very few references to joblessness or economic misery, and even these few are muted. No heed is paid to the social disorders, like food riots or the attacks on the bonus marchers, that accompanied the Depression, to the slogans of the Hoover administration, or to the later government programs like the New Deal, the CCC or NRA. Only one story concerns itself with Franklin Delano Roosevelt and his policies: the à clef satire #256, "In Caverns Below" by Stanton A. Coblentz.

It is reasonable to assume that such silence was the result of an editorial tabu: "Readers want entertainment, something to take their minds off the pain of the outside world, not a reminder. They can get enough, more than they want, from the newspapers." The same tabu holds for other major problems—the Dust Bowl, lynchings in the South, Prohibition (apart from bootlegging), and rampant Fundamentalism. In this sense science-fiction was a cut-off from the realities of the day, but not quite escapism, as will be shown later.

Some aspects of dangerous life in the 1920s and 1930s, though, were not ignored. Professional crime, particularly with gangsters of Italian name, is a major topic. Such crime is not attributed to the Mafia, which is not mentioned in the dozens of stories about Italian-American gangsters, but is the work of impudent independent racketeers, some with a touch of megalomania. Echoing newspaper reports of crime in Chicago, take-offs on the name "Capone" are common. Science-fiction shares this horrified, disgusted interest with the general literature and *New Yorker* cartoons of the day.

The international situation is weakly represented, if stories on a fairly realistic level are considered. There is some fear of Russian Communist expansion, though this is confined to the work of a few militant authors like Capt. S. P. Meek, U.S. Army, who was convinced of deep plots and impending crises; but this fear focused on subversion and the activities of the Third International rather than on military threats. Even this coverage is trivial, however, compared to contemporary newspaper reports, especially in the Hearst papers. Stalinist atrocities, however, are not mentioned. On the other hand, there are few apologists for the USSR, Leninist, Trotskyite, or Stalinist. The doings of Nazi Germany are ignored, except in the work of Nat Schachner, who often brought Fascism and Hitler into his stories on an à clef basis. Hugo Gernsback, indeed, was insensitive enough to print translated German novels that were out-and-out revanchist or proto-Fascist. When criticized in a letter in the March 1935 issue of *Wonder Stories* for assisting an "anti-civilization campaign that is emanating like a foul cancer from Germany," Gernsback or one of his editors replied:

> We violently disagree with you, however, when you condemn us for printing German stories. It would be more narrow-minded by a long shot to turn down excellent science-fiction because we do not like the government in the country where they originate than to print them and send the money to that country. We have nothing against Germany—we are perfectly neutral—and we are not concerned with the actions of the political parties and leaders outside of the United States. What the leader of Germany does to or for the Germans is for the Germans to think about. *(Wonder Stories,* March 1935, p. 1265).

Japan, on the other hand, is regarded with considerable suspicion, more so than Germany, as can be seen from the many stories involving Japanese hostility. The editorial comment on Arthur Stangland's story #1411, "Outcasts from Mars," is thus strange: "Necessity is a great rebel against ethics. Germany perhaps meant to maintain Belgium's neutrality; but in face of extinction by her enemies she was forced to her action. Japan might want to respect China's independence, but in face of her crowded population she feels that she has no other course than that which she now pursues" *(Wonder Stories,* October 1932, p. 407).

This may not have been meant quite as antinomian as it sounds today.

There are no references to the Spanish Civil War (beginning 1936), the Italian invasion of Ethiopia (beginning 1935), the civil war in China (except #1476, John Taine's "White Lily"), civil disobedience in India, the German abandonment of the League of Nations, the Japanese invasions of China, the Young Plan, the Nuremberg Laws, or the other really important international events of the time.

Yet, apart from specific historical, temporal, geographical phenomena, there are hidden configurations that are likely to emerge unintentionally, perhaps not easily visible. If the stories of the Gernsback period are examined for such configurations, several aspects emerge. First, the stories are marked by an enormous cultural malaise, in which the Marxist concept of class war is often present, though without other aspects of Marxism. Sometimes the class war is overt, workers against plutocrats; more often it is metaphoric. It may be expressed in terms of stratified societies and attempts at breaking class barriers; age groups and quarrels over prerogatives and living rights; dominant females and the necessity for restoring the "natural" order of male supremacy; or religious tyranny masking social oppression that must be overturned. Related is a potent distrust of contemporary governmental institutions and the belief that they are hostile and work mischief.

Overwhelmingly present are evidences of xenophobia and colonialism, as Earthmen discover that nonterrestrial or nonhuman intelligent life is commonly foul, nauseating, vicious, and aggressive—with an obvious remedy for all this. As the later saying went, "The only good amoeboid is a dead amoeboid."

Implicit in many stories is the "manifest destiny" of the human race throughout at least the solar system. Mankind is justified in exterminating or subjugating lesser (or sometimes superior) breeds. Stories like #561, Edmond Hamilton's "A Conquest of Two Worlds," where unrestrained interplanetary colonialism and conquest are condemned, are very atypical—even in Hamilton's other work, where alien life is invasive and murderous.

In this area of social thought, the inner picture of the science-fiction of the Gernsback era is not pretty. It has advanced beyond the frank kill-'em-and-take-it approach of dime-novel science-fiction of the late nineteenth century, but only by pushing things down below the narrative surface. If science-fiction is to be considered, as it is by some theorists, a means of opening mankind to the wonders of the universe, it certainly failed badly during this early period.

Much of this xenophobia and colonialism is probably rooted in a general unarticulated, unconscious fear of the unknown that is represented in many stories of different sorts. New inventions create havoc, and scientists by meddling with natural processes unloose enormous harm. A couple of generations earlier, such meddling was seen as interfering with a divine purpose; in our period it meant interfering with *natura naturans*. Tied in with this is the feeling, fairly often implied, that deviation from normal is abnormal and that the abnormal is trouble. Supermen work evil, and enhancement of human abilities is disastrous.

On the narrative level, science-fiction of this period is often thrill and buoyancy, yet deadly peril may be there and must be fought. Beneath the surface, Gernsback-era science-fiction is really a literature of catastrophism and despair. As Bernard De Voto aptly recognized from only a small sampling of the science-fiction of 1939, in his essay "Doom beyond Jupiter," themes of world destruction and human devastation are basic. "Things go wrong" is an ultimate, far more than in other types of pulp fiction, with a fair amount of conclusive tragedy. A tally shows that of the 1,710 or so original stories published from 1926 through 1936, about three-eighths (636) are concerned with processes, inventions, actions, or social matters that bear their own inner destruction or malfunction: Things go wrong.

Connected with this generalized Angst is the large number of stories that involve suicide, at least 73, as can be seen from the motif index. This is very unusual in pulp fiction, though it also turns up in book detective/crime fiction, where the murderer

is often permitted or encouraged to commit suicide, if the author is not quite sure whether he/she has provided enough evidence for a conviction.

To compare this mind-set with other ranges of pulp literature, let us transform a typical science-fiction catastrophe story into the terms of a Western story. The cattle come down with rinderpest, the wells dry up, the ranch house burns, the bunkhouse collapses during a tornado, the bank would foreclose if there were anything worth taking, and the lone owner and his girlfriend (as sole survivors) are compelled to live chastely in a pup tent, hoping to catch and tame a couple of maverick calves—or commit suicide? Would such a story be publishable in Street and Smith's *Western Story Magazine?* The answer is obvious: non-theological Job is not applicable.

Yet despite this pessimism of antecedent, there is often, downplayed by De Voto, a sparkle of sunlight at the end of the planetary explosion. After Earth disintegrates, the human race may be extinct except for Roger and Betty, who are safely out in their spaceship, but Roger and Betty are compatible, their gene pools are unquestionably larger than in real life, second and later generation inbreeding is ignored, and the human race will spring up again on a new planet, assuredly better than before.

Perhaps associated with the latent and explicit catastrophism and fear of the unknown, conservatism is typical of Gernsback-era science-fiction. While calamity may triumph, personal evil almost never does. The wicked are punished in one way or another, perhaps by death, perhaps by brainwashing or neurosurgery. Property and ownership are seldom questioned, with only a handful of stories suggesting socialist or communistic economic systems.

Sexuality, as has often been pointed out, exists in a peculiar fashion. A tally of story modes shows that less than 5 percent of the original stories of the Gernsback era are concerned with any erotic matters deeper than platonic association. Occasionally girlfriends accompany male protagonists on their missions or have to be rescued from peril, but the relationship is friendship, perhaps at most a semi-contractual association chastely intended for marriage. Extramarital sex, except in the case of a few wicked femmes fatales who usually are punished for their passions, is seldom available. This pattern follows closely that established by Mills and McGarraghy for sensational magazines in general in 1930, where sex indicators are lower than for intellectual periodicals (*Hoover Report*, pp. 415-423),

Associated with sexuality is the strong emphasis on conventional sex roles of the period; male work is creative, active, dominating; female work is supportive, either actively or passively, as something on which the male can exercise his rescuing ability. Where family groups appear in the stories, as in the work of Dr. David H. Keller, the Three K's *(Kinder, Küchen, und Kirche)* are posited as ideals for women, from which arrogant women depart at their own peril.

In ethnic matters the science-fiction pulps concord with the general pulp magazines in embodying a male, white Anglo-Saxon world. The maleness is not surprising or unforgivable, since the readership of the pulps (except for the love story magazines) was overwhelmingly male. The ethnic negation is another matter. Orientals, when they appear, are usually treated with hostility, while Blacks are almost altogether absent, except for occasional ridicule or occasional villainous roles. Names of the positive characters are usually of British origin, occasionally

French. Germanic names are often associated with villainy; Italian names indicate gangsters. Other major name sources, like Jewish, Slavic, Spanish are seldom invoked.

This ethnicity of name, judged in hindsight from our own times, is a little surprising. According to the U.S. Census of 1920, Americans of English and Scottish origin were more than counterbalanced by Americans of other origins, while according to the U.S. Census of 1930, Americans of German and Italian origin, together, formed the largest component of first and second generation Americans. Surely these non-British Americans read the pulp magazines. Perhaps this was subliminal acculturation at work?

These are a few social aspects of the pulp genre magazines of the Gernsback era. The science?

In general, the science invoked and utilized in the original stories is the popular knowledge of the day, not the cutting edge of research; most of it is on a high school level, though terms from higher ranges are often tossed about. The day when science-fiction writers would read the technical journals, or at least semipopular accounts, for ideas or justifications of story procedures, had yet to come. Nor were such extrapolations as existed grand schemes like those described in Peter Nicholls's *The Science in Science Fiction.* Of the important authors of the day, only John W. Campbell, Jr., knew college-level theoretical physics and applied it (in large lumps) in his stories. E. E. Smith was aware of some developments, but cheerfully disregarded them when convenient, claiming that while he would not flout empirical data, he had a right to select or reject theory. Dr. Miles J. Breuer occasionally invoked modern work. Other men with scientific training, like Cecil B. White (William Henry Christie, later a noted astronomer), were more interested in naively describing cultural aspects of other societies.

The science during this period strongly stresses the physical sciences, with chemistry (sometimes on a competent level) much less common than applied or theoretical physics. Astronomy, with its obvious relevance to space travel and other worlds, ranges from reasonably competent popularizations to abysmal ignorance. Mathematics admittedly does not lend itself well to fictionalization, with an exception in the fourth dimension, to be noted below. Biology is greatly slighted, with whole areas of discovery ignored. Experimental psychology is notably absent. Anthropology, as evidenced in lost-race stories, projections of alien cultures, and archeological material, is fifty years behind the times.

Certain scientific concepts, probably emergent from popular factual journalism, assume a temporary fad status. In 1933 Prof. C. N. Lewis of the University of California announced that heavy water would cause precipitous aging and tissue decay; this was discounted later by other authorities, but nevertheless served as the basis for several stories. On March 3, 1930, the ninth planet, Pluto, was discovered; it entered several stories within the next few years. Prof. R. A. Millikan discovered cosmic rays in 1926; they were thereupon brought into fiction as a fanciful agent for, variously, evolution, devolution, origin of life, cause of death, means of immortality, energy, and weapons. In 1926 an announcement by Prof. H. J. Miller of the University of Texas that mutations could be accelerated by radiation received much publicity. Many stories followed this lead. Other discoveries of the day reflected in fiction are isotopes in general; the then missing elements 85 and 87, which

were erroneously described as isolated in 1930 and 1931 by a group in Alabama Polytechnic Institute; element 93, erroneously announced in 1934 by Enrico Fermi; island universes in the 1920s; and ultrasonics investigated by Robert W. Wood.

Concepts from the advanced theoretical physics of the day, watered down to slogans, also received attention: the Lorentz-Fitzgerald longitudinal contraction theory, Einstein's limitation on speed, Heisenberg's uncertainty principle, Dirac's ether. These concepts are often cited, but usually as small talk, and on occasion are misunderstood. An example of getting things backward was Donald Wandrei's popular "Colossus" where speed led to expansion.

One technological-scientific area, however, was treated adequately: rocket research. As described in the history of *Wonder Stories Quarterly*, authors and editors engaged in practical work and described state-of-the-art results. Gernsback and his editors fostered this interest with translations from German authors who drew upon contemporary German rocketry.

In addition to more or less conventional science and technology, there was a component that might be called Sunday supplement science, since its ideas were often presented as novelty items in newspaper supplements like Abe Merritt's *American Weekly.* These included death rays, which on occasion were taken seriously in the 1920s. Nikolai Alexeevich Rynin (a competent mathematician), for example, covers historical experimentation with lethal short wave radiation in his technical *Interplanetary Flight and Communication.* In 1932 Professors Arno Brasch and Fritz Lange of Berlin University were able to kill mice with beta radiation, and Kurt Schimkus, also of Berlin, claimed to be able to detonate gunpowder at a distance of 500 feet with suitable radiation. I do not know whether Schimkus's claim was valid. In 1936, an American newspaper clipping in my possession, of unknown origin, dated May 19, 1936 shows a photograph of an elaborate mass of machinery, with the following legend: "While a jury watched, Henry Fleur, inventor, killed a snake, a lizard and some termites with his 'death ray' and was quickly acquitted of defrauding inventors. Fleur, shown here with his machine, said more current would increase its power, but he refused to discuss its possible use in war. (Associated Press Photo.)" Nikola Tesla, too, in addition to being a great inventor, had his publicized crotchets, including death rays and claimed communication with Mars.

Other popular topics include astronomical catastrophism, with speculations on how the world might end. Novas and interplanetary collisions offer thrills. Paranormal abilities, notably telepathy or clairvoyance, too, play a large part in the science-fiction of the Gernsback era, though taken less seriously, probably, than in the science-fiction of later years, where such topics were fostered by editor John W. Campbell, Jr.

The fourth dimension offers a curious example of debasement of a scientific concept. Higher dimensions were a serious field of study in the late nineteenth and early twentieth century, both as pure mathematics and as aspects of cosmology, paralleling the interest in non-Euclidean geometry, particularly with the great mathematicians Georg Riemann and Felix Klein. There was also popular scientific interest in a fourth dimension, as in the 1920s when the *Scientific American* ran a contest for suitable non-technical expositions of the subject; this was later issued in book form edited by the prominent geometrician Henry Manning. In early science-fiction, before our period, the fourth dimension was often invoked, sometimes as simply a verbal trick for anything mysterious, sometimes as a hyperspace, sometimes as an accessible other-world much like our own. (An interesting metaphoric use of the fourth dimension as a metaphor for ruthlessness, greed, and corruption occurs in Joseph Conrad and Ford Madox Hueffer's *The Inheritors.*) These interpretations continued into the science-fiction of our period, with extensions to fifth and sixth dimensions in a fanciful, non-meaningful manner.

The "science" in science-fiction of the Gernsback period was not wholly borrowed from the outside world. Some concepts were created on a mythical level. These include the establishment of Atlantis as a rational supercivilization; various astronomical oddities like a Sargasso of Space, or graveyards of lost spaceships; visits behind reality to odd realms of being; and group or multiple beings. Particularly interesting is the establishment of "Bodia" (according to one cosmology of the day, a former fifth planet whose destruction formed the asteroids) as the ultimate origin of mankind and possessor of a supercivilization.

In terms of environmental background, scientific resources, narrative techniques, aims and axioms, the original stories within our eleven-year period (*Scoops* excluded) form a developmental unit with a certain amount of evolutionary change, not radical, but still perceptible. If scientific, technological, and narrative elements are tabulated by year, both continuities and changes may be seen.

In TABLE 1 the leading motifs of each original story have been tabulated. Secondary or throw-away elements have not been included, and *Scoops,* as part of a different literary tradition, has been omitted. Entries in Roman type show the absolute number of stories of each type for each year; entries in bold italics have been weighted to equalize the very different story counts from year to year and rounded off to the nearest half unit. This has been necessary for comparisons, since in 1928, for example, only 72 original stories were published, whereas in 1931, 236 stories appeared.

Categories have been derived from those used in the motif index, but sometimes enlarged or otherwise modified. "Earth mishaps" is limited to geological or geographic catastrophes like earthquakes, extreme volcanism, and floods. "Future setting" does not include stories that take place in the near future, where culture and technology are much the same as our present, but stories that are set in a future that is markedly different. "Inventions" includes stories that are primarily concerned with the working out of some sort of discovery. "Lost race" has been enlarged to include "hidden people." "Space opera" has been defined as an extravagant adventure usually based on combat in space on an interplanetary or interstellar level. "Space travel," on the other hand, has been limited to stories that are primarily concerned with the mechanisms of space travel, first voyages, and incidents in space travel.

It will be seen, on examining the weighted figures, that the percentages of most major motifs do not alter greatly from beginning to end, the smallness of the samples from each year perhaps occasionally overstating the amount of change involved. In some instances a single author with one or two stories could have changed the percentages.

Certain motifs, however, do change significantly over our ten-year period. The following motifs show a decline: Atlantis, medical material, monsters, and stories set on or concerning the moon. Other story types peak in the middle years from small beginnings, then decline: biological catastrophes, extraterrestrial invasions, lost races, mad scientists, space opera, and space travel. A third category includes motifs that became more frequent throughout our period: alien intelligence (both benign and hostile), future settings, last man, and machine intelligence.

Other story types take form after the beginning of our period: stories involving the outer planets, Mercury, the minor planets and satellites, Pluto, and supermen.

Story modes, too, show certain changes over our eleven-year period.

TABLE 2 analyzes six basic story modes: conflict, crime and detection, eros, exploration, exposition, and things-go-wrong. A seventh category, quests, showed so few examples that it was not included in the table. "Conflict" includes both actual physical violence and personal confrontations that may or not involve physical activity. "Crime and detection" is concerned with cross overs from the contemporary detective story, although space pirates, if suitably treated, may be included. Model stories are the sequence (#1085 through #1087) written by Bob Olsen about the Master of Mysteries. "Eros" is restricted to sexual material that goes beyond incidental platonic girlfriends who accompany the protagonist or young ladies who must be rescued. Examples perhaps familiar to the reader are stories #1026 through #1028, C. L. Moore's "The Bright Illusion," "Greater Glories," and "Tryst in Time," especially the last story. "Exposition" indicates that the purpose of the story is describing something, or explaining its working, with stress on descriptive matters other than narrative: scientific, technological, or social. A utopia, thus, would be considered an exposition. Examples of stories stressing exposition would be John W. Campbell, Jr.'s "Blindness" (#1467) or "The Irrelevant" (#1505), both of which are idea stories. Certain of Campbell's early novels, like "Solarite" (#187) combine "conflict," "exploration," and "exposition."

The largest groupings of stories are "things-go-wrong" and "conflict," categories which do not exactly concord with the intellectualized, perfectibilian aims that Hugo Gernsback first set and were followed (despite initial attempts to avoid them) by other magazine editors.

It will be observed from the table that stories based on conflict peak in the middle of our period, but remain high, while exploration and things-go-wrong stories increase until they reach a plateau.

Motifs and story types shifted during the eleven-year Gernsback period. Was there change in other areas? In one important respect the science-fiction pulp magazines differed from the general pulp phenomenon: they improved. If one compares an issue of *Adventure* from 1920 or so with one from 1935, one sees a difference in orientation and a falling away. If one examines an issue of a Munsey magazine from 1920 with one of 1935, one sees a considerable lowering of standards. In both cases the later issues show much cliché. With the science-fiction magazines, on the other hand, one sees a different evolution, though it is one that is beginning to be manifest only toward the end of our period. Literary quality improves, idea content (beyond gimmickry) is more varied and more profound, and a form-awareness is beginning to develop. This upward trend continues beyond our period.

Gernsback's program for science-fiction, as announced in

TABLE 1

IMPORTANT STORY MOTIFS

	1926-7	1928	1929	1930	1931	1932	1933	1934	1935	1936
Alien intelligence, benign	1 / *2*	1 / *1.5*	6 / *4*	6 / *2.5*	13 / *5.5*	13 / *7*	16 / *11*	13 / *6.5*	22 / *11.5*	15 / *10*
Alien intelligence, evil	1 / *2*	7 / *9.5*	16 / *11*	20 / *8*	24 / *10*	13 / *7*	17 / *11.5*	16 / *8*	26 / *13.5*	16 / *10*
Astronomical disasters	1 / *2*	5 / *7*	1 / *0.5*	11 / *4.5*	6 / *2.5*	7 / *3.5*	4 / *2.5*	9 / *4.5*	14 / *7.5*	5 / *3.5*
Atlantis	1 / *2*	2 / *3*	4 / *3*	7 / *2.5*	8 / *3.5*	10 / *5*	— / —	5 / *2.5*	2 / *1.5*	3 / *2*
Atomic disasters	— / —	1 / *1.5*	— / —	6 / *2.5*	7 / *3*	— / —	— / —	1 / *0.5*	4 / *2*	3 / *2*
Atomic worlds	— / —	1 / *1.5*	3 / *2*	3 / *1*	3 / *1*	5 / *2.5*	— / —	3 / *1.5*	7 / *3.5*	— / —
Biological motifs	2 / *4*	5 / *7*	2 / *1.5*	9 / *3.5*	13 / *5.5*	4 / *2*	10 / *7*	8 / *4*	9 / *4.5*	7 / *4.5*
Biological catastrophe	1 / *2*	— / —	4 / *3*	6 / *2.5*	11 / *4.5*	4 / *2*	4 / *2.5*	8 / *4*	2 / *1.5*	3 / *2*
Cyborgs	2 / *4*	1 / *1.5*	2 / *1.5*	— / —	5 / *2*	3 / *1.5*	3 / *2*	3 / *1.5*	4 / *2*	3 / *2*
Dimensions	2 / *4*	8 / *11*	6 / *4*	12 / *4.5*	18 / *7.5*	5 / *2.5*	9 / *6*	8 / *4*	13 / *7*	7 / *4.5*
Earth mishaps	1 / *2*	1 / *1.5*	4 / *3*	3 / *1*	3 / *1.5*	4 / *2*	4 / *2.5*	5 / *2.5*	1 / *0.5*	5 / *3.5*
Extraterrestrial invasion	— / —	2 / *3*	17 / *12*	22 / *8.5*	23 / *10*	29 / *15*	7 / *4.5*	4 / *2*	10 / *5*	8 / *5.5*
Future setting	6 / *12.5*	11 / *15.5*	36 / *25*	64 / *25*	79 / *33.5*	87 / *46*	57 / *38*	58 / *29.5*	77 / *40.5*	64 / *42.5*
Future primitivism	1 / *2*	— / —	2 / *1.5*	1 / *0.5*	4 / *1.5*	8 / *4*	— / —	2 / *1*	1 / *0.5*	1 / *0.5*
Immortality	2 / *4*	— / —	4 / *3*	7 / *2.5*	3 / *1.5*	2 / *1.5*	2 / *1.5*	5 / *2.5*	2 / *1.5*	— / —
Insects	— / —	2 / *3*	5 / *3.5*	9 / *3.5*	4 / *1.5*	3 / *1.5*	2 / *1.5*	6 / *3*	6 / *3*	4 / *2.5*

NOTE: Roman type indicates the number of stories; italic bold type figures are weighted.

TABLE 1 (*continued*)

IMPORTANT STORY MOTIFS

	1926-7	1928	1929	1930	1931	1932	1933	1934	1935	1936
Inventions	6	8	25	28	22	19	17	30	29	12
	12.5	*11*	*17*	*11*	*9.5*	*10*	*11.5*	*15*	*15*	*8*
Invisibility	2	—	2	4	5	3	5	3	—	1
	4	—	*1.5*	*1.5*	*2*	*1.5*	*3.5*	*1.5*	—	*1.5*
Jupiter	—	—	1	2	4	4	2	1	2	1
	—	—	*0.5*	*1*	*1.5*	*2*	*1.5*	*0.5*	*1.5*	*0.5*
Last man	1	2	4	3	9	8	3	14	9	7
	2	*3*	*3*	*1*	*4*	*4*	*2*	*7*	*4.5*	*4.5*
Lost race	4	3	4	14	21	7	4	5	4	3
	8.5	*4*	*3*	*5.5*	*9*	*3.5*	*2.5*	*2.5*	*2*	*2*
Machine intelligence	1	1	—	6	4	7	3	6	6	4
	2	*1.5*	—	*2.5*	*1.5*	*3.5*	*2*	*3*	*3*	*2.5*
Mad scientist	1	1	10	25	8	5	4	7	1	4
	2	*1.5*	*7*	*10*	*3.5*	*2.5*	*2.5*	*3.5*	*0.5*	*2.5*
Mankind imperilled	—	4	14	29	18	24	9	29	24	20
	—	*5.5*	*9.5*	*11*	*7.5*	*12.5*	*6*	*15*	*12.5*	*13*
Mars	3	2	5	16	13	19	12	12	8	7
	6	*3*	*3.5*	*6.5*	*5.5*	*10*	*8*	*6*	*4*	*4.5*
Medical material	7	9	16	10	10	9	5	23	16	11
	14.5	*12.5*	*11*	*4*	*4*	*4.5*	*3.5*	*11.5*	*8.5*	*7.5*
Mercury	—	—	—	—	3	4	1	2	2	2
	—	—	—	—	*1.5*	*2*	*0.5*	*1*	*1.5*	*1.5*
Minor planets, satellites	—	—	2	6	—	9	1	—	4	7
	—	—	*1.5*	*2.5*	—	*4.5*	*0.5*	—	*2*	*4.5*
Monsters	—	3	2	17	13	2	6	8	3	3
	—	*4*	*1.5*	*6.5*	*5.5*	*1.5*	*4*	*4*	*1.5*	*2*
Moon	—	4	5	11	9	11	6	4	3	3
	—	*5.5*	*3.5*	*4.5*	*4*	*6*	*4*	*2*	*1.5*	*2*
Pluto	—	—	—	—	3	—	—	3	4	2
	—	—	—	—	*1.5*	—	—	*1.5*	*2*	*1.5*
Prediction	—	1	2	—	3	—	1	2	2	3
	—	*1.5*	*1.5*	—	*1.5*	—	*0.5*	*1*	*1.5*	*2*

TABLE 1 (*continued*)

IMPORTANT STORY MOTIFS

	1926-7	1928	1929	1930	1931	1932	1933	1934	1935	1936
Relativity	—	—	—	6	5	4	3	6	1	3
	—	—	—	*2.5*	*2*	*2*	*2*	*3*	*0.5*	*2*
Saturn	—	—	—	—	—	—	1	—	3	3
	—	—	—	—	—	—	*0.5*	—	*1.5*	*2*
Sleeper awakes	1	—	5	2	1	3	5	3	1	—
	2	—	*3.5*	*1*	*0.5*	*1.5*	*3.5*	*1.5*	*0.5*	—
Social matters	5	13	23	24	32	27	26	19	26	13
	10.5	*18*	*16*	*9.5*	*13.5*	*14*	*17.5*	*9.5*	*13.5*	*8.5*
Space opera	—	2	2	14	10	14	3	8	9	5
	—	*3*	*1.5*	*5.5*	*4*	*7.5*	*2*	*4*	*4.5*	*3.5*
Space travel	3	11	18	57	79	72	43	37	41	35
	6	*15.5*	*12.5*	*22*	*33.5*	*38*	*29*	*19*	*21.5*	*23*
Supermen	—	—	—	1	6	4	4	5	8	6
	—	—	—	*0.5*	*2.5*	*2*	*2.5*	*2.5*	*4*	*4*
Synthetic men	—	—	—	3	1	3	1	—	—	1
	—	—	—	*1*	*0.5*	*1.5*	*0.5*	—	—	*0.5*
Time travel	3	2	6	13	16	9	10	9	11	8
	6	*3*	*4*	*5*	*7*	*4.5*	*6.5*	*4.5*	*6*	*5.5*
U.S.A. hostilities	2	2	17	11	16	16	14	3	10	7
	4	*3*	*11.5*	*4.5*	*7*	*8.5*	*9.5*	*1.5*	*5*	*4.5*
Venus	1	4	5	12	6	11	1	5	5	3
	2	*5.5*	*3.5*	*4.5*	*2.5*	*6*	*0.5*	*2.5*	*2.5*	*2*
Vigilantes	—	1	3	4	1	7	3	2	3	2
	—	*1.5*	*2*	*1.5*	*0.5*	*3.5*	*2*	*1*	*1.5*	*1.5*
Visitors	7	—	8	16	2	11	10	17	11	14
	14.5	—	*5.5*	*6*	*1*	*6*	*6.5*	*8.5*	*6*	*9.5*
Women stressed	—	3	4	5	6	3	—	3	6	1
	—	*4*	*3*	*2*	*2.5*	*1.5*	—	*2*	*3*	*0.5*
World conquest	—	1	8	23	12	10	10	12	11	7
	—	*1.5*	*5.5*	*9*	*5*	*6.5*	*6.5*	*6*	*6*	*4.5*
World peril	—	6	1	8	6	8	3	11	3	6
	—	*8.5*	*0.5*	*3*	*2.5*	*4*	*2*	*5.5*	*1.5*	*4*

TABLE 2

IMPORTANT STORY FORMULAS

	1926-7	1928	1929	1930	1931	1932	1933	1934	1935	1936
Conflict	5	17	52	96	96	117	54	55	60	68
	10.5	*23.5*	*37*	*37.5*	*41*	*62*	*36.5*	*28*	*31.5*	*45*
Crime and detection	4	9	14	25	23	13	12	10	7	8
	8.5	*12.5*	*9.5*	*9.5*	*10*	*7*	*8*	*5*	*3.5*	*5.5*
Eros	1	1	4	11	7	9	4	11	20	8
	2	*1.5*	*3*	*4.5*	*3*	*5*	*2.5*	*5.5*	*10.5*	*5.5*
Exploration	5	12	19	66	64	44	54	54	54	38
	10.5	*16*	*13*	*27*	*27*	*23*	*36.5*	*27.5*	*28.5*	*25*
Exposition	11	13	42	13	22	27	23	22	43	24
	23	*18*	*29*	*5*	*9.5*	*14*	*15.5*	*11*	*22.5*	*16*
Things go wrong	26	23	43	87	87	75	56	97	82	60
	54	*32*	*29.5*	*34*	*37*	*39*	*38*	*49*	*43*	*40*

NOTE: **Roman type indicates the number of stories; italic bold type figures are weighted.**

---

early editorials quoted in the magazine histories that follow, set up four justifications for scientifiction: prediction, inspiration, instruction, and entertainment—the last being an afterthought. If one examines the stories of the Gernsback era in terms of these four bases, it must be admitted that much is lacking. (One need not accept Gernback's goals, but that is another matter.)

Prediction has been trivial, probably much less than for popular scientific articles. The solitary specific, well developed case, Gernsback's incorporation of a theory of radar in his novel "Ralph 124C 41+," dates from before our period. Other technological predictions like jet propulsion, supersonic flight, genetic engineering are so general in statement that they mean little, and, in any case, it is quite possible that they have been borrowed from speculative sources in the popular scientific magazines. One would have to investigate individual elements.

When Gernsback described science-fiction as a source of inspiration, he meant two different things. First, that stories would suggest practical ideas for inventors to bring into material fruition. This is so unrealistic that it needs no comment, although he apparently held this position all his life, as appears from his address to the MIT Science Fiction Society in 1960, which was delivered four years before his death:

And let us make no mistake. The average science fiction author does not write masterpieces in English. Often the quality of the genre's literature is mediocre. There are very few H. G. Wells's or Edgar Allan Poe's. Their quality is more apt to fall into the Jules Verne category.

Yet we should never lose sight of the important truth that the outstanding science fiction author need not be concerned with *belles lettres*. His wholly unliterary story, such as Jules Verne's imaginary submarine in "Twenty Thousand Leagues under the Sea" may set scientists and technicians aflame for years, inspiring them to translate into reality that which the science fiction author's imagination blueprinted in great detail and perfection. (p. 5)

Gernsback goes on to accuse the Russians of pirating American science-fiction in order to steal scientific ideas.

Gernsback's second point was that science-fiction would interest young readers in science and channel them into scientific or technological careers. Such a causal connection undoubtedly exists, but it would be difficult to quantify, life histories being so complex, and the interrelation between facets of interest so tangled. Many who have followed scientific or advanced technological careers have stated that their interests were first caught by science-fiction. For the modern period kernels of such case histories are cited in the *Forbes* article "The Geeks Have Inherited the Earth" by Zina Moukheiber. Yet one can also postulate a reverse situation: Young readers who were interested in science also often developed an interest in science-fiction. In our period, the evidence is not conclusive.

If Gernsbackian science-fiction is considered as an informal educational process of sorts, it unquestionably had some value. Young readers could pick up isolated basic facts on a verbal, non-quantitative level in astronomy, physics, and (to a lesser extent) biology. This was useful in cases where the local school systems had inadequate science instruction, as was common enough. But this process should not be overvalued: it was disorganized and fragmentary, and quite a bit of nonsense was purveyed as science in the magazines. Without a prior background, a reader might take some of the more outrageous fictional theories to be fact; for example, Captain S. P. Meek's statement (in story #968, "Cold Light") that cold was an independent force, not just lack of heat, or Gernsback's theory (in the editorial to the December 1928 *Amazing Stories*) that the sense of déjà vu originated in memory molecules from dead brains that one snuffed in, or statements that Atlantis was to be taken seriously. Unfortunately, the science quiz columns in the magazines often focused on trivia or nonsense.

As for entertainment, the last of the Gernsback quartet and one so obviously the major purpose of science-fiction that it need not be belabored: perhaps 60,000 to 70,000 (allowing for duplication in the combined circulations of the magazines) men and women received some pleasure from the magazines, yet not enough to keep the magazines alive and healthy.

The Writers

The first years of pulp science-fiction consisted mostly of reprints and flounderings as amateur writers tried to accommodate the messianic pronouncements of Hugo Gernsback, publisher of the *Amazing* magazines, with market realities.

As has been detailed in the section on the history of *Amazing Stories*, when Gernsback established the magazine in 1926, there were almost no science-fiction writers, and it turned out that the genre was not a discipline that could be slipped into easily and intuitively. Gernsback's attempts to discover writers through contests and word-of-mouth among readers were not successful. At the beginning of the 1930s, with the establishment of Clayton's *Astounding Stories of Super-Science*, Harry Bates, who had no faith in contests, tried to impress the Clayton stable of general pulp writers into science-fiction, but, as he confessed, the attempt was a failure. While Bates had a clear notion of what action science-fiction should be, his would-be writers did not, and, for the most part, did not know enough science to fantasize about science or technology. The attempts of the otherwise successful pulp authors Arthur J. Burks and Hugh B. Cave, for example, to write science-fiction are somewhat pathetic.

It soon became apparent that writing science-fiction (or fantastic fiction) was a closed shop to general pulp writers, a situation that persisted. In part this was due to the demands of the genre, and in part to economics. In the first years a science-fiction writer needed not only a special background and aptitude, but another source of income. Payment was low and slow, except for *Astounding Stories,* and one could not make a living by writing s-f.

The immediate solution to filling the magazines came from a small handful of prolific nonprofessionals who had other sources of income. During the period 1927 through 1930, almost one quarter of the original stories were written by six men, whose work averaged out to more than one story per issue. They were not great writers, but with one exception they were

respectable practitioners who were able to sustain the reader's interest over an hour or less. All six pursued other primary occupations, writing science-fiction as a sideline.

These men were Miles J. Breuer, M. D., (seventeen stories); David H. Keller, M. D., (twenty-four stories); Capt. S. P. Meek, U. S. Army (seventeen stories); Ed Earl Repp (fourteen stories); A. Hyatt Verrill (eighteen stories); and Harl Vincent (twenty-one stories). Dr. Breuer was a specialist in tuberculosis, associated with a hospital in Omaha. He was unusual in being conversant with modern theoretical physics, as quotations from such books as d'Abro's *The Rise of the New Physics* show. Dr. Keller was a psychiatrist, usually associated with state mental institutions. He had very little background beyond his specialty of psychiatry, but he was uniquely aware of the possible social and psychological problems of advancing technology. Captain Meek was a professional soldier in the Ordnance Department, with postgraduate work in engineering and mathematics in various universities. Ed Earl Repp, a one-time newspaperman, was a scriptwriter who produced many low-grade Western motion pictures in Hollywood. He was the weakest writer of the seven. A. Hyatt Verrill is difficult to characterize. During our period he tried to convey the image of an archeologist/ethnologist, but he was obviously incompetent in these fields. He was a good popular naturalist and the author of several successful series of boys' books. He is perhaps best to be considered as a general writer, the only one of the group to fall into that category. Harl Vincent (the pseudonym of Harold Vincent Schoepflin) was a mechanical engineer working for Westinghouse, specializing in the installation of large electrical apparatus. Oddly enough, while Vincent was undoubtedly competent in his field and beyond, this seldom plays a part in his stories. Vincent did not flaunt his knowledge as did John W. Campbell, Jr.

So far as is known, only Repp and Verrill had had previous professional writing experience, although Dr. Keller had long been a compulsive unpublished writer. For Dr. Breuer, Dr. Keller, Captain Meek, and Harl Vincent the publication of science-fiction magazines afforded, it would seem, an otherwise unlikely secondary career and source of income. For these four men fantastic fiction also offered a limit, for they did very little (or no) work outside the broad fantastic area. Only Captain Meek, considerably later, was successful elsewhere, with a series of juvenile animal books.

This pattern of part-time specialists continues, though with changes, into the following six-year period, 1931-1936. Harl Vincent (thirty-two more stories) and Dr. Keller (twenty more stories) continued as numerically important authors, but Dr. Breuer, Captain Meek, Ed Earl Repp, and A Hyatt Verrill dropped away. Dr. Breuer and Captain Meek are reported to have had "nervous breakdowns," although it is not known exactly what this implies. Repp possibly found motion-picture script writing more profitable and science-fiction editors more critical; and Verrill, it is a fair guess, was unable to adapt to more modern times, although he still published occasional adventure stories elsewhere.

A new series of writers (supplementing Dr. Keller and Harl Vincent) began to dominate the pulps numerically, and the concept of a science-fiction writer per se, not a part-timer who properly practices another occupation, began to emerge, though still not fully. This concept, as much as the presence of six magazines on the stands in 1931, indicates that science-fiction was beginning to be recognized as a valid area in popular fiction.

The new men were John W. Campbell, Jr. (nineteen stories), Stanton A. Coblentz (nineteen stories), Raymond Z. Gallun (twenty-seven stories), Edmond Hamilton (fifteen stories), Nat Schachner (forty stories, including collaborations), and Jack Williamson (twenty-three stories including a collaboration). These men had varied backgrounds. Campbell, who received a B.S. in physics from Duke University, was perhaps the first modern science-fiction writer to be trained in contemporary theoretical physics. During this writing period he was first a college student (first at M.I.T., from which he was expelled for neglect of studies, then at Duke) then a salesman, and holder of miscellaneous jobs, though his science-fiction writing seems to have been most important to him. He might be classed as a semiprofessional writer. Coblentz, a journalist associated with New York City newspapers, held an M.A. in English from the University of California. He always remained at the edge of science-fiction proper, however, being properly a satirist. His technical background was small, and much of his work was written earlier in the 1920s, before the appearance of *Amazing Stories.* Gallun was essentially a technical writer. Hamilton was a professional writer, mostly of fantastic fiction; he had college training in the sciences and had been writing science-fiction for *Weird Tales* since 1926. Schachner, though trained as a lawyer and a member of the New York Bar, was a professional writer, both mainstream biographies and genre fiction. Jack Williamson, who was perhaps unique in determining from an early age to be a professional science-fiction writer, alone of these men continued to practice significantly and develop long after our period.

The remaining body of original stories in the period 1926-1936 was written by 488 or so attributed authors, some of whom were repeaters. A large percentage of the author pool, however, consisted of singletons, writers of a single story. The percentage of singleton writers in the periods 1926-1930 and 1931-1936 was respectively 17.5 percent and 15 percent. These figures probably indicate the continued presence of many nonprofessional writers.

Most of the fiction during our entire period seems to have been submitted by authors directly to publishers without intermediary literary agencies. While there is no precise information for the earlier period, the Street and Smith records from 1933 through 1936 indicate that much the larger proportion of stories accepted by *Astounding Stories* came from individuals. Toward the end of our period, Julius Schwartz and Mort Weisinger, two young fans, operated a literary agency called Solar Sales Service, but it was of very small importance.

It is often stated that pulp-magazine editors controlled the authors heavily and primed them with ideas, but this does not seem to have been an important factor with Street and Smith *Astounding Stories* or the other genre magazines of our period. Harry Bates of Clayton *Astounding Stories* for a time suggested ideas to authors, but, as he admitted, the system did not work, and he soon abandoned it. Later, with John W. Campbell, it became important.

As far as is known, contract or commissioned writing during this period seems to have been exceptional, although Hugo Gernsback intermittently had contractual arrangements with a few authors. He guaranteed Edmond Hamilton, Dr. David H. Keller, and A. Hyatt Verrill a certain payment (usually $25) per short story. All three men discovered difficulties in collecting.

For the other magazines one occasionally hears an anecdote about an author's being assigned to do certain stories, but it was exceptional and usually involved accredited, practiced writers.

Very little is known about the lives of most of the writers in the 1926-1936 period. Publishers' records either do not survive or are inaccessible; the only exception is the Street and Smith archives at Syracuse University, and even these offer little more than title listings, payments involved, addresses, and occasional pseudonyms. Publishers' correspondence seems to have been destroyed. Memoir and autobiographical material is equally scanty. This is in contrast to the occasionally voluminous material from later periods.

Similarly, there is very little information available about the editors of the day, and most of that is bare bones. Even the enormously important but controversial Hugo Gernsback has not been adequately studied, since most of what has been written about him is undocumented and occasionally suspect, erratic or unjudicious. Very little is specifically known about David Lasser (as an editor) and F. Orlin Tremaine, the two most important editors after Gernsback and before John W. Campbell, Jr.

It is possible, however, to isolate a few patterns among the authors considered in this book. Some occupational data is available for 222 of the approximately 510 writers of this period.

"Writers": 71
Journalists: 35
Engineers: 25
Editors and writers: 21
Businessmen: 17
Educators: 9
Physical scientists, chemists, physicists 8 (overlap with educators)
Medical: 7 possibly
Advertising men, overlap with journalists: 4
Motion picture associations: 4
Artists: 3
Religious: 3 including one specialist writer
Soldiers: 3
Biologists: 2
Civil service: 2
Insurance adjusters: 2
Astronomers: 1
Economists: 1
Farm hands: 1
Lawyers, practicing: 1
Politicians: 1
Railroad freight clerks: 1

The largest category, "writer," has been put into quotation marks to indicate that it is not really satisfactory, has been delimited by the professional or semi-professional publication of books or stories elsewhere than in the science-fiction genre magazines. The classification obviously is only partially valid, since it must include persons who practiced other occupations.

A warning must also accompany the above table. For most of the individuals the information we have is scanty and possibly, in some cases, not entirely accurate. Also, during the Great Depression one must expect changes of occupation, moonlighting, multiple occupations, and overlaps. Further, individual decisions must also be made about occupation: Nat Schachner and Arthur Leo Zagat were graduates of law schools, but did not practice; Stanley G. Weinbaum did graduate work as a chemist, but preferred freelance writing; and Gernsback and Lasser, with engineering backgrounds, nevertheless must be classified as editors and writers.

The breakdown, however, is at least suggestive. It will be observed that writers, editors, journalists and advertising men make up more than half the total. This is not unexpected.

For *Scoops*, the British story-paper for boys, a different situation holds. Most of the issues were filled by staff writers or by professional or semiprofessional specialists.

A sizeable proportion of the 510 authors also consists of young people who at the time had no occupation, but later moved to one profession or another. A few names from this group follow: Arthur Barnes, later semiprofessional writer, scriptwriter; Philip Cleator, consulting engineer; Alan Connell, member of the merchant marine; Howard Fast, mainstream writer, with return to fantastic fiction late in life; Henry Hasse, motion-picture industry; A. Rowley Hilliard, technical writer, Atomic Energy Commission; Frank K. Kelly, journalist, Presidential speech writer; P. Schuyler Miller, technical writer, educator; John R. Pierce, head of Bell Telephone Laboratories, Presidential Science Council; Kenneth Sterling, physician, medical researcher; G. P. Wertenbaker, writer, journalist; Donald A. Wollheim, author, editor, publisher.

Thirty-seven authors are known to have been twenty-one years of age or younger when they were first published during our period. Most are now forgotten, but John W. Campbell, Jr. (twenty years old), Raymond Z. Gallun (nineteen years old), Horace Gold (twenty years old), Charles Hornig (nineteen years old), P. Schuyler Miller (nineteen years old), Ray Palmer (twenty years old), Donald Wandrei (nineteen years old, science-fiction in *Weird Tales*), Jack Williamson (twenty years old), and Donald Wollheim (twenty years) were significant in the later evolution of science-fiction, Campbell, Gallun, and Williamson being major writers in the field. Hugh Cave (twenty years old) became a successful writer in other areas as did Howard Fast (eighteen years old) and G. Peyton Wertenbaker (sixteen years old).

Three authors in this group died at an early age. David R. Daniels (twenty years old) apparently committed suicide within a year of being published, as did Robert Wilson (twenty-one years old). Charles Cloukey, who first published at age sixteen, died in his twentieth year.

The youngest writer known to have been published was Kenneth Sterling, whose first story appeared when he was thirteen. The story concerned, however, was not significant and was quite possibly published for personal reasons.

Judged from magazine line portraits or inadequate information, another fifteen men may have fitted into this age range. None, however, was important, and most were single-story authors.

Information about our authors' educational background is scanty, but college education is definitely known or can be safely inferred for 93 writers. This figure, however, would seem obviously much too low, and more information would undoubtedly enlarge it.

In terms of higher education, eleven authors are definitely known to have received doctorates (Ph.D.s): Thomas S. Gardner, T. Proctor Hall, Alcan Hirsch, E. H. Johnson, William Lemkin, A. M. Low, Harold F. Richards, George H. Scheer, Jr.,

Kurt Siodmak, Edward Elmer Smith, and John Taine (Eric Temple Bell). At a somewhat later date John R. Pierce and Jack Williamson received doctorates. Although information is lacking, B. S. Kierstead may have held an advanced degree, and it is not clear whether Walter Rose's degree was a Ph.D. or an M.D.

Two other men are questionable. The Winthrop Hawkins and Frederick Hodges whose work is described in this volume may or may not have been the Hawkins and Hodges of the same names who held advanced degrees.

Two men are definitely known to have held medical degrees, Miles J. Breuer and David H. Keller. Four other men claimed medical degrees: Daniel Dressler, Albert B. Stuart, A. C. Webb, and D. E. Winstead. Since there are no national medical registers, except of specialists, it has not been possible to check them. If the William Lichtenstein of story #1236, "The Moon Doom," is the same person as the Dr. Samuel Lichenstein [*sic*] mentioned by Frank H. Winter in *Prelude to the Space Age*, as seems probable, another name may be added to the list. Edward Podolsky, if the identification is correct, received a medical degree a little later, as did Kenneth Sterling.

At least three cases of fraudulent claims to advanced degrees or their equivalent are known: Howard Wandrei, who used the pseudonym Howard W. Graham, Ph.D., and "Dr." Douglas Dold, to whom *Astounding Stories* editor Harry Bates awarded a doctorate for publicity purposes. Malcolm Afford was not a professor at a medical school, as his publishers claimed, but a writer of mystery fiction. The status of "Dr. Arch Carr" is not clear. The name may be a pseudonym suggesting an imaginary degree, or another person may have been acting as agent for an untraced genuine Dr. Carr.

It should be repeated that the above data are admittedly partial, since any contemporary biographical information at all is available for only about half the authors covered here, and there is little knowledge about the later life of most of the authors whose work appeared in the Gernsback era.

Most of the original fiction described in this book was written by American authors. As David Ketterer said in 1992, "Whatever its European or classical antecedents, genre SF was and is an overwhelmingly American phenomenon" (p. 1). This statement is even more overwhelmingly true during the period under consideration in this volume than in later years, when a British school or schools developed. Yet authors from other countries contributed to the genre magazines of the Gernsback era, although they wrote, for the most part, American-style science-fiction.

Thirteen authors can be counted as fully Canadian in the sense that they lived and wrote in Canada: John Lewis Burtt, William H. Christie (writing as Cecil B. White), Chester Cuthbert, Clinton Constantinescu, Will H. Gray, Thomas Proctor Hall, Ernest Milton Johnston, Burton Seeley Keirstead, A. B. L. McFadyen, Charles V. Tench, Richard Vaughan, Bruce Wallis, and Cyril G. Wates. Winthrop W. Hawkins and George P. Pearce, in addition, may have been Canadian. Probably other Canadians are among those authors whose biographical data are lacking.

Two authors had connection with Canada, but probably would not be considered Canadian: Horace Gold (writing at this time as Clyde Crane Campbell and Leigh Keith) and Henry George Weiss (writing as Francis Flagg). Both men were born in Canada, but moved to the United States as boys. I am not certain how to classify Laurence Manning, who grew up and received his college education in Canada, served in the Canadian armed forces in World War I, but came to the United States as an adult, settled in the New York area, and wrote all his fiction in the United States.

British authors include George B. Beattie, Bernard Brown, Philip Cleator, W. P. Cockroft, H. D. Dickinson, John Edwards, John Russell Fearn, Peter Gordon, John W. Groves, John Wyndham Harris, Benson Herbert, Holloway Horn, F. S. Howard-Burleigh, Stuart Jackson, Kenneth James, Ralph Judson (writing as Ralph Stranger), Festus Pragnell, Gladys St. John Loe, Laurence Smith, and George Wallis. R. Crossley Arnold may also belong to this group.

Australia is represented by Malcolm R. Afford, Felix Edward Collas (writing as Phil Collas), Alan Connell, and perhaps H. M. Crisp, whose Australian nationality has been questioned. Desmond Hall, Australian by birth and upbringing, then settled in the United States as a young man. James Morgan Walsh, who moved to England as a middle-aged man, probably counts as an Australian author.

Other areas and countries are scantily represented. Dr. Walter Rose wrote from South Africa, and perhaps Otfrid von Hanstein from Germany. Hanstein's opus has not been adequately examined in Germany, and the claim that he submitted original work to Hugo Gernsback comes from an untrustworthy source. Surprisingly, there are no original stories from France, which had a strong science-fiction tradition superior to the French reprints that appeared in the *Wonder* magazines.

The question how these authors happened to contribute to American magazines—or in larger terms, how did the diffusion of genre science-fiction take place—cannot be answered more than in generalities. Canadian readers and writers undoubtedly had access to the American pulp panorama through various means. British would-be writers were less fortunate. On the whole, American pulp magazines were not part of British popular culture, where adult reading was focused more on fiction magazines like those of the Hutchinson group, among others, and for young readers, on the boys' story papers. During the Depression, however, American publishers sold their remainder stock and returns as bulk paper. Sometimes used as ship's ballast, it was often transported to Great Britain to be sold at low price by the Woolworth chain of stores. The rise of British fandom is in large extent connected to this market.

Individual subscriptions to American magazines certainly existed, and writers' magazines often had an international distribution. Literary agents, too, played a part in creating markets. It is known, for example, that seven stories that appeared in the first two issues of Street and Smith *Astounding Stories* were bought as a package from a British literary agency. These were: Colonel Percy Fawcett's "The Curse of Callahuaya," Peter Gordon's "Anything Can Happen," Holloway Horn's "The Man from Cincinnati," F. S. Howard-Burleigh's "Don Mackinder's Model," Stuart Jackson's "The Lovely Ghost," Kenneth James's "Burroughs Passes," and Gladys St. John-Loe's "Where Four Roads Met." None of these seven stories, however, is science-fiction.

It will be observed that few of the authors listed above are important critically or historically. John Beynon Harris (though in later life) and Laurence Manning are still relevant, as is Otfrid

von Hanstein. Benson Herbert and Festus Pragnell deserve credit on a lower level for a novel each. J. M. Walsh would seem to have been the only non-American professional writer, mysteries in his case, who was able to adapt to American science-fiction standards. On the other hand, A. L. Burtt and John Russell Fearn filled many pages that some would say had better been left blank.

After 1936 most of the authors considered in this survey drop away. The cause, apart from natural attrition, jobs on the part of the young people, and perhaps changing economics with the first years of World War II, is probably a different writing world than had existed previously and new demands by editors, which the earlier, mostly amateur writers were not able to fulfill.

The following years, 1936-1938, mark a break between the older science-fiction and the circumbellum period that followed. In 1936, *Wonder Stories* died, to be replaced by *Thrilling Wonder Stories,* which was first aimed at younger readers, then later at an older, more sophisticated readership. *Amazing Stories* was sold in 1938. T. O'Conor Sloane retired, and Ray Palmer, as new editor, stressed juvenile and eccentric material. *Astounding Stories* under John W. Campbell, Jr., continued Tremaine's attempt to raise the literary level, to which was added Campbell's own concern with more accurate, more imaginative, more advanced (popularized) science and technology, plus eccentric material.

After 1936 only Raymond Z. Gallun, John Beynon Harris, Murray Leinster, Frank Belknap Long, C. L. Moore, Ross Rocklynne, Clifford Simak, E. E. Smith, and Jack Williamson continued as significant authors. Less important writers from our period who still contributed frequently to the restyled magazines included Eando Binder, Stanton A. Coblentz, John Russell Fearn, Edmond Hamilton, and Nat Schachner. During 1938 and 1939 other major early writers began to appear: Isaac Asimov, L. Sprague de Camp, Robert A. Heinlein, L. Ron Hubbard, Henry Kuttner, Fritz Leiber, Theodore Sturgeon, A. E. Van Vogt, and others. Science-fiction thereupon became something of a different world.

Thus far, authors have been considered semi-statistically, but it seems necessary to add a word about historical importance and quality. In general, apart from an occasional story, one must look back at the authors of 1926-1936 mostly as predecessors, rather than as authors to be read today apart from historical reasons.

The Readers

The readers of the early science-fiction magazines obviously cannot be described with precision either as a single group or a complex of groups, for there were no surveys, no polls, and no personal records in any quantity. There is a small amount of memoir material, but fan records are mostly later than our period.

There are, however, indirect ways of obtaining a reasonable notion of what the science-fiction magazine reader of the day was like: an examination of the letter columns and an analysis of the advertising. In the advertising, the assumption, of course, is that what appeared was, for the most part, desirable to the reader. Exceptions can be noted.

A constant feature of the science-fiction magazines was a readers' letter column. It served several purposes for the publisher: it saved money, filling empty space with free material that might otherwise have to be used for paid fiction; it offered a place for discreet propaganda, although the science-fiction publishers were not very skilled at this; and it provided entertainment apart from fiction, since many people like to read letters in newspapers and elsewhere.

There are, of course, dangers in using such letter columns to evaluate readership. First, the sample is too small. Harry Bates, editor of Clayton *Astounding Stories*, has stated that he used to receive about sixty letters per month. A dozen or two letters from this class obviously cannot represent a circulation ranging from 25,000 to 60,000 or more monthly readers. Second, the sample may well be atypical, for publishers select according to their views. There are, in addition, hobby letter writers (letter hacks), who bombard the magazines with correspondence, while other readers would never think of writing to a magazine. Third, there is the element of fakery. We must assume that the letters in the readers' columns were genuine and not written by the office personnel, but there are cases that call this assumption into occasional doubt. The letters printed in *Flash Gordon Strange Adventure Magazine*, for example, could have no other source than the staff, since the magazine had not yet been published. This case is obvious. More disturbing is the incident recorded by Professor R. Dale Mullen ("Notes and Correspondence," p. 543) in which a letter that he did not write was published under his name in *Scientific Detective Monthly*. These cases, however, seem to be very exceptional.

With these reservations, a few general conclusions can be drawn about the letter-writing readers of the early magazines. For comparison I have classified and tabulated letters from *Amazing Stories* for 1927; from *Amazing Stories, Astounding Stories,* and *Wonder Stories* for 1931; and from *Amazing Stories, Astounding Stories,* and *Wonder Stories* for 1936.

Sixty-eight magazines are involved and 1,177 letters.

Five categories were established: (1) serious letters, (2) listing and rating letters, (3) vanity letters, (4) notifications, and (5) eccentric letters.

Serious letters are defined as adult letters challenging or correcting authors, authors' defenses against criticism, detailed exposition of aesthetic matters, and similar points.

Listing and rating letters simply praise or denigrate individual stories or compare stories on a superficial level. A common approach for many of these letters was "*X* was swell, but *Y* was rotten," terms of criticism widely used at that time. It was not unusual for a (young?) reader to run down the contents of a magazine in terms of such polarities.

Vanity letters were written to express a point of view, or, the suspicion is, to set the writer's name in print. While vanity letters often evaluated stories in more detail than listing letters, they were often long, frequently jocular, personalized texts expressing opinions about many matters other than the stories. Easily identifiable anonymous letters, recognizable pseudonymous letters, hoaxes, and schoolboy humor fit into this category.

The last two categories, **notifications** (announcements of publications, memorials, deaths, etc.) and **eccentric letters** (advocates of various crank notions like Atlantis, Mu, viewing auras with dicyanin screens, perpetual motion, etc.) were not significant in number and have not been tabulated.

The three major categories, it is obvious, can overlap, particularly between listing and vanity letters, and there is the suspicion that many of the notification letters about science clubs were based as much on a desire for self-advertisement as for disseminating information. It is also admitted that categories cannot be entirely firm in some cases, since letters may fit into two groups, or the decision which category to use can often be arguable.

A further contaminant is the tendency for each magazine to establish its own letter-column personality. For example, *Amazing Stories* in its later years went in heavily for flagellatory letters (usually counted as vanity letters), to which editor T. O'Conor Sloane replied with constant amiability. One can only speculate about this; printing such letters implies a certain honesty, though perhaps not wisdom.

Nevertheless, it is believed that the figures that follow are at least indicative in a small way of the readership of the early science-fiction magazines.

Serious letters constitute 23 percent of the total in 1927, 12 percent in 1931, and 3 percent in 1936. In 1931 the percentage is very close among Clayton *Astounding Stories, Amazing Stories,* and *Wonder Stories.* One might have expected Clayton *Astounding Stories,* in its stress on simplicity and thrills, to be lower. The figure for Street and Smith *Astounding Stories* in 1936, which was not very high (less than 3 percent), is possibly atypical; 1935, with the intense dispute about Karl van Campen's story #1505, "The Irrelevant," would have shown a much higher percentage of serious letters, and 1937, beyond our period, would also have shown an upgrading.

Listing letters constitute 47 percent of the total in 1927, 40 percent in 1931, and 25 percent in 1936. The figure for 1931 may be thrown off by the obvious policy of the editors of *Astounding Stories* to print many short listings rather than a few longer vanity letters. But in 1931 the letter hacks are beginning to appear, as can be seen by repeated names in the letter columns.

Vanity letters constitute 24 percent in 1927, 40 percent in 1931, 67 percent in 1936. By now the letter hacks are in full operation, with the same letter writers appearing over and over from magazine to magazine. For reasons not clear to this writer (and not convincingly explained by survivors) the magazines seemed to have shared a policy of building up certain fan personalities. This increase in 1936 is, of course, correlated with the development of fandom.

A separate tally of letters by writers below twenty-one years of age has been based on statements in the letters themselves and on later biographical information about the writers. In 1927 juvenile letters constituted 3 percent of the total; in 1931, 18 percent; in 1936, 23 percent. These figures, of course, are minimal, representing positive knowledge of individual cases; it is impossible to say how many other readers for whom we do not have positive knowledge would fit into the juvenile category. A subjective reading of the total letter class corroborates these figures, with much stronger evidence of immaturity in 1936 than in earlier years.

The following conclusions might be drawn. (1) While a subclass of mature readers persisted through our eleven years, this class diminished proportionately. This change might be explained by the early presence of a sizeable component of readers from Gernsback's technical magazines, which component was gradually diluted by the addition of general pulp readers and young, new readers. (2) The proportion of younger readers increased over the years. By the end of our period, it is a safe speculation, the largest group consisted of late teenagers. (3) The decrease of listing letters and the increase of vanity letters, in some cases written by the same individuals five years apart, indicates that a steady readership accompanied the magazines. The letter hacks grew older, and instead of simply listing likes and dislikes, they began to explain how to improve science-fiction and the world and to demonstrate their wit. In general, fandom, as is known from other means of approach, was beginning to consolidate in the letter columns. (4) Although this has not been precisely tabulated, the acceptance of science-fiction tropes increased greatly over our ten-year period. Certain of Gernsback's early readers were still naive enough to wonder whether the stories were factual. In the June 1927 issue of *Amazing Stories* (p. 308), for example, a reader asks whether T. S. Stribling's "The Green Splotches" is a true account, since the narrator (Stribling states) won the Nobel Prize. And in the December 1927 issue of *Amazing Stories* (p. 912) a reader questions whether A. Hyatt Verrill's "The Man Who Could Vanish" really happened.

The advertisements in the magazines also offer pointers to typical readers. While it is true that such advertisements were placed in magazine groups, it is equally true that if they had not worked in the science-fiction area, they would have been withdrawn.

In the early issues of Gernsback's *Amazing Stories* the advertisements reveal the close association of the magazine and its readers with hobbies and occupational training. From February to December 1927, *Amazing Stories* printed approximately 2,650 inches of display and space advertising. Ads selling radio parts are much the most frequent, comprising about 340 inches, or almost 13 percent of the total. These are followed by career ads from two large technical schools, The Chemical Institute, with 300 inches, and Coyne Electric School of Chicago, with 240 inches. Radio engineering schools fill another 180 inches, with drafting and engineering drawing courses taking up 90 inches.

Entertainments form the second largest ad group. About 200 inches are devoted to magic instruction, mostly from the magician Tarbel; 90 inches to fingerprint instructions; 100 inches to novelties of various sorts; and 120 inches to bargain magazine subscriptions. Come-ons for fake contests occupy 90 inches. These last usually involve matching nearly similar objects in series—automobiles with different headlights, slightly variant versions of a drawing of Charlie Chaplin—or picking out objects beginning with a certain letter in an illustration. The awards included automobiles, or so the ads claimed.

Minor items include telescopes, typewriters, trusses, diet and fat ads, show-card instructions, home manufactures, automobile spark plugs, psychic inspiration, ventriloquism, hypnotism, boxing, ukelele lessons, jewelry, and commission sales of clothing. Some of these were dropped in 1928. For one reason or another the February 1927 issue has many gun ads, which otherwise are not important in pulp advertising. This suggests that a space salesman, with the idea that guns might sell, approached dealers and manufacturers, who agreed to a trial that did not work. Perhaps the first science-fiction bookshop ads

appear in small classified advertisements inserted by the Fresno Book Store, of Fresno, California in 1927. This seems to be the germ of science-fiction specialist dealers.

These ads obviously are intended to appeal to young males, possibly high school graduates, without much money, without sophisticated tastes, who are interested in learning a mechanical trade. A second group consists of electronics hobbyists, perhaps somewhat older. Both groups are likely to be attracted to novelty items.

It will be observed that the artifacts offered are not the higher priced luxury items—automobiles, expensive model Victrolas, Steinway pianos, swank resort hotels, Tiffany jewelry, player pianos, express rifles, custom refrigerators, posh finishing schools for young women, vacation sites—that were offered in the so-called "standard magazines" like *Everybody's* or *Cosmopolitan* a decade or so earlier, where the purchaser was possibly family or female as well as male.

An economic situation similar to that of *Amazing Stories* is apparent in the advertisements in a 1931 issue of Clayton *Astounding Stories*, which is typical of the later years of our study.

Present are seventeen pages (272 inches) of advertising. National Salesmen's Training Association, National Radio Institute, International Correspondence School, New York Academy of Music (teaching Hawaiian guitar), and Earle Liederman (muscle building) are present with full-page ads. Occupational or job improvement ads otherwise constitute about sixty-three inches; these include law, accountancy, song-writing, wholesale groceries, haberdashery, and information about government jobs. Body and health advertisements, apart from Earle Liederman, take up thirty-two inches, including reducing nose size, building muscles, straightening ears, curing acne, and similar topics. Also present are miscellaneous topics like soft-porn erotic French material, bargain jewelry and watches, low-cost weapons, inexpensive typewriters, and novelties.

The occupational ads of the 1930s typically show school situations, with a stern-faced educator promising results to the buyer. Sometimes crews are shown working on machinery; sometimes buildings and plants are stressed. Testimonial letters, of course, abound. Storiettes embodied in the ads may have been effective: the high executive who declares that he esteems correspondence school graduates, the young man who was starving with his family until he signed up for a radio repair course, the salesman who suddenly found that he could make hundreds of dollars a week selling a gadget that quadrupled gasoline mileage per gallon, and so on. The Great Depression, of course, is observable.

The approach in many of the ads is graphic and high pressure, as opposed to the laid-back, restrained air of the quality ads in the standard magazines of a decade earlier or the more matter-of-fact ads of the 1927 issues of *Amazing Stories*. In the body-building ads, "All I ask is 90 days," says Earle Liederman as he demonstrates a torso with shadowed pectoral muscles that suggest an overabundance of estrogen. "When I am through with you, you're a real man. The kind that proves it." His muscle kit includes four dozen full-page photographs of Liederman and his pupils. "Some of these came to me as pitiful weaklings, imploring me to help them." Other frequent muscle developers include Professor Jessop, who flexes a mighty biceps. Most interesting of all, however, is Charles Atlas, whose cartoon strip ads show the triumph of the 97-pound weakling who takes Atlas's dynamic tension muscle course and thrashes the beach bully who used to kick sand on him and his girlfriend. As the Depression deepens, the inches of muscle-building display ads increase greatly. The impetus here is obviously sexual, tools with which young males can impress young females.

Fleischmann's yeast claimed in cartoon strips to be effective in removing adolescent acne and promoting chaste juvenile romance. (The father of one of my college friends, a chief chemist for Fleischmann's, once told me that the yeast was more likely to give users acne than cure it.)

Erotic small ads now appear frequently. "MEN--BIG PROFIT! Direct from Paris. 400% to 800% Profit. Exquisite pictures. Lifelike, lovely colors. . . . No talking. Just show the samples!" "Charming--Captivating--irresistible DESIR D'AMOUR (Love's Desire), which goes straight to the heart like Cupid's arrows. Triple Strength vial 95¢." "French Love Drops. An enchanting exotic perfume of irresistible charm, clinging for hours like lovers loath to part." The one-inch ad shows torsos of a pair of lovers in Egyptian costume, reminiscent of Rudolf Valentino and any one of many female motion picture stars.

By far the largest proportion of pulp ads were aimed at young male readers, but there was always a small group of medical ads for older men, particularly prostatitis remedies, which, because of the tabus of the day, were described by indirection. Ads for quack and fraudulent medical materials were also common. For example, the Elco Electric Health Generator offered by Lindstrom and Co., of Chicago "Stop[s] that Pain by Relieving the Cause with Violet Ray, Vibration, Ozone, and Medical Electricity." An illustration shows a foldout kit with all sorts of metal prongs that plug into a device like a Rototool. Probably more directly harmful is "Radium Is Restoring Health to Thousands. No medicine, drugs or dieting. Just a light, small, comfortable inexpensive Radio-Active pad worn on the back at night." It heals "Neuritis, Rheumatism, High Blood Pressure, Constipation, Nervous Prostration, Heart, Lungs, Liver, Kidney and Bladder trouble . . . Try Degnan's Radio-Active Solar Pad. Radium Appliances, Los Angeles."

Miscellaneous small space ads with catchy headlines offered many varied wonders. "$1 brings your choice of these Xmas Gifts, 10 months to pay," "A new skin instead of an ugly face," "Blank cartridge pistol," "Say fellows! Let Me Show You How You Can Quickly Step Out of that Small Pay job. . . . Amazingly Easy Way to get into Electricity," "Tobacco Habit Banished," "QUIT TOBACCO," "Fight against Rupture," "Play the Hawaiian Guitar like the Hawaiians!," "BIG MONEY IN POULTRY!", "Direct from Movieland, Love Drops," "Finger Prints. . . . tells you how YOU can become a Finger Print Expert quickly and easily in your spare time at home! You can make $2500 to $10000 a year in this thrilling profession!" "Who Wants an Auto Free??" "I'LL PAY YOU $20 a Day—to show my Mystery [cigarette] lighter." "Be a detective. Make secret investigations. Earn big money."

The great majority of ads in the early genre pulp magazines boil down to three statements, money, sex, and power, with money and power often the preludes or concomitants to sex. Thus, the young man who is urged to enroll in a correspondence school and increase his income is often approached on the basis of being able to afford marriage. The young married man who gets a raise as a result of home study is rewarded by increased

friendliness from his wife. The ability to play the piano or guitar leads to attractiveness to females, as does increased musculature or removal of real or imagined disabilities. The art photos provide sexual stimulation and, perhaps, an element of power as one shows them to one's friends.

Since these ads were commercially successful, they permit an estimation of seller and buyer. The seller is easily characterized: often an out-and-out crook, sometimes a deceptive marketer, and most typically a merchant without too many scruples who oversells his product. The buyer is either a teenager with interest in the cultural novelties of the day or a young man with inadequate training, little money, some ambition or desperation, and much naiveté.

Science-fiction readers almost certainly responded to the same advertising stimuli as did the readers of the other pulp magazines, but they must have differed in other ways, as is indicated in the social distribution of pulp readership.

In the past, as is the case today in pulp-collecting circles and conventions, pulp readers tended strongly to prefer certain story types, perhaps after early exploratory ventures. Readers of the fantastic magazines, on the whole, had little empathy for Western stories, general adventure, crime and detective stories, sports stories, and, of course, love stories, which were aimed at female readers.

Readers (and writers) of the science-fiction magazines, judging from readers' columns, reminiscences and publishing data, greatly overlapped but did not wholly coincide with the readers (and writers) of the supernatural magazines *Weird Tales* and *Strange Tales*. This amounted to an informal readership group for the larger area of fantastic fiction.

How did this group, or the science-fiction readers alone, differ from readers of the other pulp magazines? As we have stated above, we can only speculate from inadequate information. First, judging from the letter columns, the science-fiction readers included a small number of men with higher education, often technical or scientific; these are the men who would respond critically to John W. Campbell, Jr.,'s tongue-in-check violation of the principle of the conservation of energy in his story #1505, "The Irrelevant." Such a group seems to have been lacking in most of the other pulp magazines.

Beyond this, the basic characteristic of the science-fiction reader seems to have been one of Weltanschauung. For most pulp readers and most of the general American public at this time, science-fiction was "crazy stuff," something impossible and thereby frowned upon and undesirable. An example may be cited from Jack Williamson's autobiography, *Wonder's Child*. When he was undergoing analysis at the Menninger Clinic in the 1930s, one of his doctors "commented that writing science fiction was symptomatic of neurosis" (p. 96).

The reader of fantastic fiction had no difficulty in accepting a departure from everyday reality, something strange and impossible. Not that he/she believed that the secondary realities in such stories had any real immediate existence, only that they could be accepted for the length of a story. In other words, this is the "temporary suspension of disbelief" of the earlier nineteenth-century Romantic period.

This departure from or reversal of the general literary acceptance of the 1920s and 1930s may be a hint of a small counterculture, for this was a period of intense social realism in literature and general thought. Our present cultural situation is the opposite; few persons today have difficulty in empathizing with a science-fiction motion picture or television program; modern science-fiction speaks an acceptable language, whereas it did not in the 1920s and 1930s—even though that modern language is far more fantastic than that of the 1920s. Such changes in cultural axioms are common historically.

Why such changes occur, and why a small group of mostly young men could run against the spirit of their times is a matter for philosophy of history. On different scales Vico and Hegel offered explanations.

A subclass within the class of science-fiction readers was science-fiction fandom, which should not be confused with the general readership of the magazines. It was something separate and very different.

Fandom was composed of young men (very few women) who might be considered "professional" readers in that the science-fiction magazines were not simply entertainment, but were a source of values, something to be lived in one way or another. Enthusiasm often took a messianic turn, as in the following serious, not-ironic letter from Walt Gillings, a British fan: "[I]t took *Amazing Stories* to convert me to science fiction, when I discovered it in 1927. Soon afterwards I made it my mission in life to persuade publishers to pay more attention to its development, and to exploit its possibilities. Some job, believe me! For we British are slow to adopt new ideas." (*Fantasy Magazine*, July 1935, p. 182).

It is difficult to put into words, but for the "trufan" science-fiction or the magazines entered his life more than a hobby and only a little less than a vocation. Over and over one encounters the statement that when a trufan discovered science-fiction he/she found a fulfillment.

It has been questioned whether, for some fans, science-fiction existed for them or they existed for science-fiction. Certainly there was a utopian note involved as brash young fans of the 1930s found and revealed solutions to the world's problems in science-fiction, Esperanto, Marxism, or Technocracy.

The essential aspect of science-fiction fandom was social interaction, a gathering together of like minds whether for friendship or enmity, either or both of which could stimulate fan activity. Some activity could consist of friendly association and cooperation, for the fan felt the obligation to talk about science-fiction in little magazines and voluminous correspondence; but there was also almost ritualized hostility, in-group against in-group. On reading accounts of fan activities of a slightly later period, notably Francis Laney's *Ah! Sweet Idiocy!*, Sam Moskowitz's *The Immortal Storm*, and Damon Knight's *The Futurians*, a reader is struck by the obsessive struggle for power, either within tiny groups of a half dozen people or between groups of similar size.

Power in this case meant office, control of the club duplicating machine, handling of meetings and conventions, disrupting another group, impressing another group with a publication, or simply recognition of status—all of which were ends in themselves. Events were taken very seriously, with a tremendous inflation of affect associated with them. Indeed, our two main documents, Laney and Moskowitz, have been criticized for treating puffs in a tea bag in the manner that Thucydides covered crises in the Peloponnesian War. Yet these nearly contemporary accounts are very interesting unwitting social

documentation and, if worked up suitably, could be excellent material for a case study of social interactivity.

Part of the in-group complex was the conscious development of an argot for fan activities and situations. The term "trufan" has been used above. Other terms that have crept into the outside world are "egoboo" (ego-boosting self-publicity), "fanzine" (fan magazine), and "gafiate" (to abandon an activity, from the initials of "get away from it all.") In some instances, as in the publications of the slightly later Los Angeles science-fiction group, what with neologisms, erratic "phonetic" spellings, and rebus-like wordplays, documents are almost unintelligible to an outsider.

In our period, fandom as such was just emerging; its heyday was to come in the late 1930s and the 1940s. But there were anticipations of things that would later emerge in greater force. One such was Gernsback's Science Fiction League, which is covered in the section on *Wonder Stories*.

While there were early fan groups like the East Bay (California) Club founded by Aubrey MacDermott and others in 1928, the ultimate historical roots of fandom seem to have been the so-called science clubs. In the early 1930s letter announcements of this sort began to appear in the magazine readers' columns:

> The Society wants earnest, young and old laymen of the world, who are charged with the germ of science, as members, and those who already have made their mark in science also. The S. C. C. [Science Correspondence Club] contains both men and women, instructors and pupils, the irresistible flame of youth, the glowing and steady coals of age, and the priceless jewel of International companionability and good-fellowship. The aim of our Society is to promote science in all lands and climes by personal and literary contact. Help us make the S. C. C. a society for and by science. (*Amazing Stories*, February 1931, p. 1048).

> May I announce that the Boys' Scientifiction Club has been dissolved and the Junior Scientific Association has taken its place. The aim of our organization is to encourage more youths to devote their lives to the advancement of science. This is accomplished by creating, in them, an interest in science by encouraging the reading of Science Fiction. . . . We have a library of some 3000 magazines, both scientific and Science Fiction; also quite a number of such books. Our library is located at the president's house, and, members may obtain books at all times. ($1.00 per year dues.) (*Astounding Stories*, September 1931, p. 430).

Among the several such small organizations in existence in the early 1930s, the Science Correspondence Club seems to have been the best known. Founded by Aubrey Clements, Walter Dennis and Sydney Gershon, it numbered perhaps a dozen or two members. Behind it lay the purpose of spreading "science and scientific thought among the laymen of the world," an ambitious program for a handful of boys in their teens. In 1931 the club changed its name to the Internationale [*sic*] Scientific Society and established relations with the German Verein für Raumschifffahrt, a serious adult organization. It disbanded around 1936, most of its members (all half dozen or so) being absorbed into the later Futurians. The Boys's Scientifiction Club mentioned above merged with the S. C. C. Other clubs that received attention were the Scienceers (notably of New York) and a British parallel, the Ilford Science Literary Circle. (These groups should not be confused with the American Interplanetary Society described under *Wonder Stories*, which was an adult organization seriously interested in rocket research.)

All the clubs or societies claimed memberships larger than life and proclaimed similar goals. Some charged dues, some did not. Recruiting seems to have been largely through the science-fiction magazines, together with complicated mergers, membership swaps, and raids. It is unfortunate that the clubs have not been studied, for they were an interesting minor social aspect of a new literary movement.

Despite their official titles, the science clubs were really surreptitious, even unwitting, literary groups, for while the members cared a little about science, they cherished science-fiction.

It is difficult in the absence of information to establish exactly what motivated the science club members. The acquisition of pen pals was undoubtedly primary (as was the case with other contemporary correspondence groups), yet in addition to the social aspects there seems to have been a veneration of "science" (though the club members probably had only a vague notion of what was intended) in a perfectibilian, Gernsbackian sense. Associated with this may have been an unconscious recognition that college might not be possible, that the educational system was inadequate, and that some self-help was needed, what with the Depression.

By the end of our period the science clubs had pretty much disappeared, absorbed into frankly science-fiction clubs or disbanded into individual trufans.

The consensus is that the science-fiction trufans of the late Gernsback era were a small group of youngsters, perhaps around one hundred or a little more in number; the figure would depend on how one defined a fan and who was known as such; and of course members dropped in and out. In general, the fans were organized by locale, with the most vociferous groups in New York and California, although there was a national and at times even an international feeling. There was extensive communication by letter and by amateur publications, which were beginning during the second half of our period of study. The first significant fan magazines date from this period: the *Time Traveller* (1932), the most useful *Science Fiction Digest/Fantasy Magazine* (1932-1936), and Hornig's *Fantasy Fan* (1933-1935).

Judging from information current at the time and later knowledge, the birth dates of the fans of our time period centered a little before 1920, with a few older fans and a few younger. They were overwhelmingly male and almost totally White, with only a single Native American in California. No Blacks or Asians seem to be known. Educationally, the older members were mostly non-collegiate at the time or drop outs, though some finished college after World War II on various veteran programs; the younger members, the 1920 and later group for the most part attended college either just before or after World War II. Many of the ancient fans from this period and the late 1930s survive, loosely organized into First Fandom, an amiable group of coelacanths who have been helpful in preparing the biographical sections of this work.

From this small population of a little more than one hundred (which is limited to active fans and not simply science-fiction readers) a significant number of important men and women emerged. To my knowledge (and it is probable that others exist whom I have overlooked) at least seven men of world importance are renowned in areas other than science-fiction. These include, alphabetically, Isaac Asimov, considered as a popularizer of science and informal educator; Sir Arthur C. Clarke, C.B.E., an engineer who conceived of communications satellites and has been honored with many international honors, including the UN Kalinga Prize for scientific exposition, and most recently the von Karman Prize; Willis Conover, Jr., who has been called the best-known unknown American of importance, familiar in the former Iron Curtain countries for Voice of America broadcasts into Asia; Martin Gardner, long associated with the *Scientific American*, philosopher, expositor of science and the world's expert on recreational mathematics (though not a member of clubs); Frank Kelly, author, speech writer to President Truman, founder of the Nuclear Age Peace Foundation; John Robinson Pierce, Ph.D., director of the Bell Telephone Research Laboratories, member of the President's Advisory Council, and educator; and Kenneth Sterling, M.D., world authority on the ductless glands, author of many papers and books.

The several dozen fan devotees of *Weird Tales* who overlapped with the (strictly speaking) science-fiction fans and worked in science-fiction also produced at least three figures of world importance. Foremost is H. P. Lovecraft, who is considered in some European countries to be one of the most insightful writers of the century; Lovecraft, although a generation older than the young people listed above, took active part in the fan amateur press of the 1920s and early 1930s. More important culturally today is Robert E. Howard, whose creation of the heroic adventure story has produced an enormous comic book, film and television industry based on his Conan stories. Edging into our period is Ray Bradbury, who in his early period worked in science-fiction and supernatural fiction and was an active fan.

This same small group of science-fiction fans also produced writers or editors of at least national importance. To list only those whose names come to mind, Forrest J. Ackerman, collector and editor; Isaac Asimov, again, as a science-fiction writer; James Blish, writer; Robert Bloch, author of *Psycho* and other mysteries; August Derleth, regional author and publisher; John Wyndham Harris, British writer whose works form the basis for several motion pictures, including *The Midwich Cuckoos*; Damon Knight, writer and editor; Henry Kuttner, writer; Judith Merril, writer, feminist activist; Sam Moskowitz, chronicler and editor; Raymond Palmer, editor, unfortunately the irresponsible source for much of our modern subculture of irrationality; Fred Pohl, writer and editor; Milton Rothman, scientist and writer; Wilson Tucker, mystery novelist; Frederick Shroyer, educator; Jack Williamson, writer and educator; and Donald Wollheim, editor, writer, publisher.

I must apologize to those men and women whom I may have inadvertently omitted. I am sure that they exist.

This is a remarkable showing, and I wonder how many of our major universities could match it in a comparable class sampling?

Science-Fiction

Story Descriptions

ADAMS, GERALD H.

U.S.A. author. Then a student at Willey College, Marshall, Texas.

    1. **FUTILITY.** *Wonder Stories*, April 1936.

Short-short story. * Third-prize-winning story in the contest based on the cover of the July 1935 issue of *Wonder Stories*. * The story is told from the point of view of Kvi, Master Scientist of Heva. Heva is a dark planet circling a dead sun, heated by internal radioactivity. Kvi has invented the telephotoscope, a device that amounts to a combination of supertelescope and magic lantern. Using augmented light, it can bring close-ups of planets in other star systems. * The problem, however, is that Kvi and members of his race cannot tolerate the low temperatures needed to operate the device properly. But Kvi has an expedient, recruiting assistants from a savage, somewhat lower form of life on the dark side of his planet. * This accomplished, Kvi focuses his device on the third planet of a star with nine planets. The image of the planet emerges (our Earth), but suddenly there is a blinding flash from Kvi's equipment, explosions, and his power plant is hurled into the sky. Kvi must start all over. * The cause of the disaster: The half-savage assistants from the dark side of the planet became engrossed in wildly chasing a local food animal and neglected their work. * Not great, but easily the best of the three stories that received awards in the contest.

AFFORD, MALCOLM R.

Australian writer. The portrait accompanying "The Gland Men of the Island" shows a middle-aged man. The advance notice for "The Gland Men of the Island" refers to Afford as a former professor of medicine at the University of Adelaide, Australia. A communication from the University of Adelaide, however, does not support this claim; no person of this name held a teaching position. The author is probably to be identified with Malcolm R. Afford (1906-1954), a popular Australian author of mysteries and radio dramas who also wrote under the name Max Afford. * According to Schwartz/Weisinger (*Science Fiction Digest*, April 1933, p. 5) *Amazing Stories* accepted a second story from Afford ("Glenleigh"), but it has not been printed in the United States.

    2. **THE GLAND MEN OF THE ISLAND.** *Wonder Stories*, January 1931. Ill. Marchioni. **THE HO-MING GLAND.** *Amazing Stories*, February 1933. Ill. Morey.

The same story. According to fan lore, Afford submitted the story to *Amazing Stories*, where editor Sloane procrastinated and shelved it for two years. Afford, who heard nothing from Sloane, thereupon sent the story to Gernsback, who accepted it and published it. Sloane, who seems to have been unaware of Gernsback's action, later found the story and printed it, without notifying Afford. The two versions differ slightly in editing.

Short story. * *Place:* An uncharted island in the Pacific Ocean near the Solomon Islands. * The great biologist Clovelee, his assistant Huxley (the narrator), and Follansbee are vacationing/naturalizing in the Pacific, when it becomes obvious that a typhoon will strike. Since their launch would not survive the storm, they land at a small, nearby island. Penetrating the jungle, they come upon a compound, around which they see gigantic humanoid creatures—and are captured. * After a short time in strangely tasteful surroundings, which include a marvelous library of medical and psychology books, they meet their host (Ho Ming), who has approached them silently. * A fairly young Chinese who speaks perfect English, he welcomes them by name and informs them that they must assist him in his work. He has been manufacturing supermen so that the Chinese can conquer the world. * Long before, his father (who is still living, an incredibly ancient man) had heard of the perpetual youth enjoyed by the Dalai Lama; serving in disguise as a monk in the Dalai establishment, he discovered the techniques and escaped with books of secret medical lore. He was followed, and many times barely escaped death until he sought out the

Afford, Malcolm (*continued*)

Emperor of China and explained his plans to him. The Emperor granted him protection and resources. * Ho Ming has been working with glands, transplanting them between apes and men, and has created eight-foot-tall giants of incredible strength and vitality. For human supplies he uses murderers, victims of press gangs, and others sent to him from China. * Ho Ming confesses that his creations have faults: they cannot speak (for the glandular operations destroy the voice apparatus) and they cannot reproduce; he expects Clovelee and the others to assist him in improving the monster men. * At about this time, the typhoon—of which Ho Ming had apparently been unaware until the last minute—strikes. The entire establishment is destroyed and everyone is killed except our three comrades, who made their escape in their electric launch. Naval authorities from New Guinea can find no trace of the island, which either was a floating island or sank beneath the sea. * Possibly parodic, with a strange medley of Talbot Mundy, Guy Boothby's Dr. Nikola, Wells's *The Island of Doctor Moreau*, Sax Rohmer's Dr. Fu Manchu, and genre sources.

[Anonymous]

Presumably a British writer.

3. **AIR ROAD 14**. *Scoops,* 3 March 1934. Ill. S. D. Boys' fiction. * Short story. * *Time:* probably the middle twenty-first century. * The Harvey establishment, Cosmos, Ltd. specializing in aircraft, hopes to win the forthcoming Trans-World races with its new superplane the *S.1.*, which is expected to attain speeds of over 1500 m.p.h. Although propeller driven, such models have antigravity fins to attain lift. * Misfortune: A few days before the race, when a pilot takes the *S.1.* up to 80,000 feet, it disintegrates and flies away from Earth in flames. A second plane, hastily assembled, shares the same fate. * Young Frank Harvey, the son of the firm, has figured out what is going wrong. He speculates that there is an "attractive beam" operating at the specified height and place and that the beam emanates from Mars. To fight off the beam, in the model he takes up he installs supergravity fins to counteract the pull from Mars. Although perilous, offering many cliffhangers, the system not only works but permits fantastic speeds. In succeeding flights Frank works out the precise area of the Martian attraction and calls it Air Road (comparable to our air lane) 14, but keeps it a secret. * The day of the race comes and Frank, not permitted to take up an *S.1*, flies an old crock into Air Road 14 winning the race not only hands down, but arms down, attaining a speed of over 3,000 MPH. * *Miscellaneous:* The Martian beam is not explained, whether natural or artificial, nor what happens when Mars is in superior conjunction.

ALDINGER, HARLEY S.

No information. Portrait accompanying "The Green Intelligence" shows a young man.

4. **THE WAY OF A DINOSAUR**. *Amazing Stories,* April 1928. Ill. Paul.

Short-short story. * *Time:* The Mesozoic period. * Episodes in the final days of a *Tyrannosaurus rex*. In ferocious battles he kills a stegosaurus, a triceratops, and a brontosaurus, but is himself killed in the water by a school of ichthyosauri. * Straight narrative. Questionable as science-fiction, since there is no fantastic element.

5. **THE GREEN INTELLIGENCE**. *Science Wonder Stories,* November 1929. Ill. Paul.

Short story. * The narrator, a freelance aviator, accepts sight unseen a job doing miscellaneous flying for the Markham brothers. As he learns when he approaches their isolated establishment, they have a bad local reputation. Animals are perpetually shipped in, then apparently killed, although there is no evidence of vivisection. * As the narrator eventually learns, when he gains the confidence of the Markhams, they are engaged in a project involving alien, nonprotoplasmic intelligence. A metal obtained from a meteorite, when treated suitably with electricity, seems to have a quasi-life, killing animate life near it. Over time, the thing has expanded an area of green radiance, and in some fashion it can communicate with the Markhams, to whom it has divulged scientific breakthroughs. But lately, it has become sulky and vicious, although the Markhams are reluctant to accept this. * At the crucial time it kills the Markhams and makes for the narrator, who leaps into his plane. He has a narrow escape as the radiation rises after him, but a timely bomb does the trick. * Routine.

6. **THE HERITAGE OF THE EARTH**. *Amazing Stories,* February 1932. Ill. Morey.

Short story. * Roger, newly under a cardiac death sentence, chances to meet his college chum Carl, a brilliant scientist. Carl, who has built a spaceship and intends to travel to Mars, invites Roger to accompany him. The chances of survival are 50/50, but this does not discourage Roger. * The vessel leaves nicely, but while the men are in the upper atmosphere, a detector indicates a large nearby object, perhaps a giant meteorite. It turns out to be a metal sphere about a thousand feet in diameter, which draws the spaceship into a landing dock. There Roger and Carl are met by an elderly man in Classical garb who introduces himself, in perfect English, as Marcus Titillius. The men soon meet his beautiful daughter Laelia. * Titillius's story: He and his daughter have inhabited the space sphere since the days of the Emperor Augustus, when Marcus was a well-known seeker of knowledge. At that time, he received a small meteoric sphere in which was a message, together with instructions and material for building an apparatus for communicating with Mars. * The Martians, stating that they would soon be extinct, made a surprising offer. They offered Marcus the present sphere, superscientific machines for maintaining life, a total library of Martian achievement, immortality apparatus, and much else. In exchange Marcus was to act as steward for Martian knowledge until Earth was ready to receive it. Since then he has been in orbit above Earth, watching with far-sensing apparatus. He had followed Carl's scientific progress closely. * Marcus cures Roger's cardiac condition easily, and Carl falls in love with the beautiful Laelia, who reciprocates. After Carl and Laelia are married by Marcus, Roger, who has become homesick, returns to Earth. Carl's science is lost, however, for the spaceship crashes and the laboratory is accidentally destroyed. Roger often thinks of the three immortals who live overhead. * *Miscellaneous:* The Martians died out when a certain element in their atmosphere became exhausted and could not be replaced.

ALEXANDER, W.

The editor's response to a letter from Dr. Miles J. Breuer in the June 1927 issue of *Amazing Stories* states, "Dr. Breuer is well-known to our readers from his most interesting story entitled

Alexander, W. (*continued*)

'New Stomachs for Old'. . ." This statement was not corrected, and Breuer did not disavow it. On the one hand, such side comments sometimes reveal the true identities of authors; on the other hand there was considerable carelessness in editing the early pulp magazines. In a letter in the January 1929 issue of *Amazing Stories* Breuer, after presenting a brief parody, attacked Alexander's proposed organ transplants very strongly. It is possible that the letter was a red herring to reconceal the identity of W. Alexander, but since it appeared a year and a half after the original comment, this seems unlikely. It may be significant that in Conklin's *Big Book of Science Fiction*, whereas a story by Breuer was printed with permission of his estate, Alexander's "One Leg too Many" was accredited to *Amazing Stories*, with permission of Ziff-Davis. The attribution is best left unresolved.

The Dr. Wentworth Stories.

Although not specifically so stated, these stories are set in a near future where medical science is farther advanced than it is today. Wentworth is a skilled surgeon who specializes in organ transplants. The stories are all literate, but flat, undramatized and primitive, with stilted writing.

    7. **NEW STOMACHS FOR OLD**. *Amazing Stories*, February 1927. Unsgnd. ill.

Short story. * *Place:* New York. * Colonel Seymour, a most proper and fastidious financier, suffers from stomach trouble, enough to affect his personality. Dr. Wentworth recommends a stomach transplant, adding that he has an ideal and willing contributor, a very poor Italian workman. * The operation is a success, but in a short time the colonel feels unusual pangs, and when he passes restaurants in the Italian section of town he drools for the food. It is not long before he becomes a habitué of the Italian section, even to donning a disguise to eat the spicy food. His habit is observed, and it damages his business. * The colonel chances to be in court when the Italian laborer is brought to trial for eating at the Ritz and being unable to pay the bill. His stomach has driven him to it, he claims. * Seymour recognizes the heart of the problem, and the two men reëxchange stomachs. Actually, all ends well, for the colonel's stomach gained new vigor in the Italian's body. * Very flat narrative, with some ethnic bias.

    8. **THE FIGHTING HEART**. *Amazing Stories*, February 1928. Unsgnd. ill.

Short story. * Doubtful as science-fiction. * Tom Wilson, a wimpish Milquetoast who is bullied by his wife, fellow workers, and boss, consults his friend Dr. Wentworth. Wentworth urges him to have a heart transplant, which, he says, is now a fairly common operation, thanks to two new pharmaceuticals, one of which puts the patient into suspended animation, while the other promotes extremely rapid healing. * When Wilson is willing, Wentworth provides a young prize fighter who is willing to exchange hearts for a suitable sum. * The operation, which is disguised as appendectomy, takes place, and Wilson emerges as a man able to hold his own against everyone. He tells off fellow workers and boss, and browbeats his wife into submission, thus arousing her latent love for him. * Life is now pleasant for Tom Wilson. Wentworth enlightens him. There was no operation, only suggestion. * Predictable.

    9. **THE ANANIAS GLAND**. *Amazing Stories*, November 1928. Ill. Paul.

Short story. * Businessman Ballinger has a problem: His irresistible urge to lie is damaging both his home life and his business. He approaches Dr. Wentworth, who provides a ready solution to Ballinger's problem. The fault, says Wentworth, lies in the recently discovered Ananias gland, which is situated in the brain, near the medulla oblongata. Ballinger's gland, X-rays show, is enlarged, but it can easily be reduced by surgery. * Surgery successfully accomplished, Ballinger now has a worse problem: He cannot resist telling the truth about his wife's weight and clothing, his friend's offensive relatives, and the soundness of his business. Disaster seems inevitable, but Ballinger returns to Dr. Wentworth, who operates, stretching the ananias gland a little, and Ballinger is now able to hit a happy medium.

    10. **THE DOG'S SIXTH SENSE**. *Amazing Stories*, September 1929. Ill. Briggs.

Short story. * Old Professor Scoggins, on visiting Dr. Wentworth, insists that dogs can read human thoughts and suggests that Wentworth use dog eyes instead of the usual pig eyes for eye transplants. Wentworth is noncommittal about the matter. * Wentworth's next operation is on Lewis Brunston, a private detective Brunston) who has lost an eye fighting a gang of car thieves. The operation is successful, and Brunston rapidly rises in his occupation until he is a national figure, as the greatest detective of the day. * About a year later Brunston calls upon Wentworth to complain. He discovered, soon after the operation, that with his new eye he could read thoughts. This helped him enormously in his profession, but it also destroyed his personal life, friends, family, even his marriage. He wants an explanation. * Wentworth realizes what must have happened. Old Scoggins, just before he died, must have slipped a dog's eye into the organ storage vault, and Wentworth used it unknowingly. * Brunston will receive a pig's eye, which, it is hoped, will not cause difficulties.

    11. **ONE LEG TOO MANY**. *Amazing Stories*, October 1929. Ill. Briggs.

(Reprinted in Conklin, *Big Book of Science Fiction.*)

Short story. * Dr. Wentworth, observing that the handyman mowing the lawn has a peg leg, offers the man, who is a college man with limited opportunities because of his disability, a new leg. Wentworth has been experimenting with organ regeneration, and has succeeded in transplanting the glands responsible for the phenomenon from lobsters to animals. He would now like to experiment on a human. * Hall is willing, and the operation and its consequences are entirely successful. In a few months Hall has a perfect new leg. * Legal problems now arise. Hall has unexpectedly become heir to a large fortune, but his claims are rejected because the known Hall is a one-legged man. In court, the judge scathingly denounces Hall and Wentworth, until Wentworth has a private word with the judge. He has observed that the judge lacks a finger joint. With a new finger, thanks to Wentworth's operation, the judge takes a favorable view of Hall's identity.

    12. **THE MILLION-DOLLAR GLAND**. *Amazing Stories*, December 1934.

Short-short story. * Dr. Wentworth, at a funds raising banquet, reveals that generosity is not a cultural matter, but is determined physiologically by a certain gland. As he later tells young tightwad millionaire Judson Bailey, this gland may be enlarged

Alexander, W. (*continued*)

to make a miserly person normal or even generous. * Bailey, who feels guilty at his stinginess, elects to have such an operation, which succeeds, with expected results. He is now willing to strip himself bare, and, indeed, would have done so had not Wentworth operated a second time. Also involved is a romance. * The story is carried as both "The Million-Dollar Gland" and "The Million Dollar Gland." * The late publication date of this story does not necessarily mean that it was written long after the others in the series. T. O'Conor Sloane often held stories for years before publishing them.

AM BRUHL, LEO

Presumably a German or Austrian author. A German-language original has not been found. It is quite possible that the title and the New York setting are adaptations by the translator for an American market. The translation has been ascribed to Carl A. Brandt, but I am not aware of documentation.

13. **GARFIELD'S INVENTION.** *Wonder Stories*, January 1934. Ill. Winter.

Short-short story, presented as a translation from German. * New York City setting. * Jefferson, who works as a leg man for a major entrepreneur, is assigned to visit the establishment of one Garfield, who claims to have made a wonderful discovery. Jefferson finds the laboratory to be something of a fortress (with electrified defenses) and Garfield more than a little mad. * Garfield, as he demonstrates, has discovered how to transmit taste sensations over a distance, so that with proper rays anything one eats can taste like anything else. But Garfield demands that Jefferson sign a contract with him, or he will not let him leave the laboratory. * Jefferson refuses, since he has no legal power to issue such a document, whereupon Garfield leaves him imprisoned. The situation seems hopeless, but Jefferson uses a gas leak to blow off the side of the building and escapes. * When he reports to his boss, his boss criticizes him for not signing, since the invention would be invaluable, and assigns him to check out an inventor who claims to be able to turn the Atlantic Ocean into stone. * Routine.

ANDERTON, SEVEN (1893-1958)

U.S. (Nebraska) newspaperman, free lance writer. Prolific author of crime stories and Western stories. Served prison sentence in 1947 for fraudulent checks and wrote about prison life. Contributed to various Street and Smith magazines, including *Clues*.

14. **THE KING AND THE PAWN.** *Amazing Stories Quarterly*, Fall/Winter 1932. Ill. Morey.

Novelette. * *Time:* Perhaps the very near future. * The usual ambiguity about the peace vigilante and his means. * Lee Bagley, Washington correspondent for a leading news agency, receives a strange letter. From a person calling himself the King of the World, it dictatorially appoints Lee as PR man for the new world government. In the letter the King reveals that he has taken fifty million dollars of bullion from a ship at sea. Inexplicably, everyone on the ship fell asleep, and a band of men removed the gold. Lee consults his friend the Secretary of State and determines to follow through his contact with the self-styled King. * The King's activities become more and more blatant, as he puts London to sleep for several hours and establishes an ambassador in Washington. An attempt to imprison the ambas-

sador turns out to be a fiasco, and he is now allowed at large in Washington. * A turning point comes when the King kidnaps Lee and has him flown to a secret base in South America. There the King, who is an affable, charming, intelligent, charismatic, well-meaning man, explains. He intends to reform the world by abolishing weapons and war, removing national boundaries, and setting up social reforms. His organization is very small, but devoted and high-minded, and he has some potent weapons: his sleep gas, superfast planes, and an engine-stopping ray. * Lee is tempted to join the King's organization, since he happens to agree with the King's liberal platform. But he does not like the King's violent means toward a goal, no matter how worthy, and refuses to accept the King's offer. The King releases him temporarily. * A test of power comes when the King announces that he will stop the war in Nicaragua. The forces of the United States are arrayed against the King, but with his motor-stopping ray and giant magnets that remove weapons, he is the master of the day. * The King's downfall comes when he captures (along with Lee's girlfriend) the noted aviator Lindborn. Lindborn and Lee seize the King's plane, capture the King, and take him to the United States. The empire is over before it started. But the King does not suffer: He swaps the secret of his weapons for a pardon and exile on a Pacific island. * Oddly flat writing and a silly story. The author probably had read Victor MacClure's "The Ark of the Covenant," which had been serialized in *Air Wonder Stories* about three years earlier.

ANTHOS

Unidentified pseudonym. The story has been stated to be a translation from German, but an original has not been located. Since "anthos" means flower in Greek, I wonder if the author's name was Blum or something similar. The translation is not acknowledged with the story, but it is usually attributed to Carl A. Brandt. Jordan (1986) suggests that the story is not German in origin and that it was really written by Brandt, but this seems unlikely. It is not dissimilar to other German science-fiction of the early 1920s.

15. **THE MALIGNANT FLOWER.** *Amazing Stories*, September 1927. Ill. Paul.

Short-short story. * *Place:* Northern India. * Sir George William Armstrong and his faithful batman John Bannister venture into a small hidden valley in the Himalayas, perhaps a tabu area, that maintains a botanical lost world. They come upon a remarkable plant that resembles a ten-foot calla with strange spots and protuberances. Sir George approaches the plant, whereupon it seizes him and proceeds to ingest him. Bannister chops him out, but Sir George has gone mad and dies insane in a short time. * When Bannister asks their yogi informant why only Sir George was affected by the plant, the Indian sneeringly replies, "Blood," which opens the way to speculation. Later Bannister reads of the man-eating plant of Madagascar. * The story is followed by pictorial material and a reprint of an article from *Science and Invention* on carnivorous plants.

ANTON, LUDWIG (1872-?)

German author, also wrote other fantastic fiction: *Die japanische Pest* (1922), *Der Mann im Schatten* (1926). Since this story dates from the premodern period, it is described in more detail in *Science-Fiction: The Early Years*.

16. **INTERPLANETARY BRIDGES.** *Wonder Stories*

Anton, Ludwig (*continued*)
Quarterly, Winter 1933.   Ill. Paul.   Trans. from German by Konrad Schmidt.
(Originally published as *Bruecken ueber den Weltenraum*, 1922.) * Novel. Essentially revanchism for World War I and the Treaty of Versailles, about which the author repeatedly comments bitterly. Other foci of his thought are union of the German-speaking peoples and revenge against the British. * The central story, after a romantic plot, other subsidiary elements, and a cumbersome frame situation have been stripped away: In the last days of World War I the German chemist Karl Lindner discovers a mineral that produces antigravity when activated electrically. His discovery is too late to be of any use during the war, but after leaving the army, with support from an international underground of German sympathizers, he continues his research into the mineral. * The end result is a spaceship, the *Astraea*, with which Lindner and comrades explore Venus. Venus is Earth-like and suitable for colonization, although there are intelligent giant ants that prove to be bothersome. As lagniappe there are enormous fields of diamonds, with which the adventurers can finance further work on Earth. * The comrades now must decide whether to attack France and England or to establish a new Germany on Venus. Choosing the latter, they gather up suitable men and women as colonists for a new world. Their plan is to sterilize one island, set up a terrestrial biosphere, and expand from that. * *Miscellaneous:* The explorers also visit Mars, which is barren and lifeless. * The novel contains several episodes in which the Germans outwit vicious and treacherous British and French and stupid Americans. * An offensive story, what with its right-wing revanchism and nationalism. Since Gernsback praised the story highly in the previous issue of *Wonder Stories Quarterly*, he obviously did not have enough sensitivity to see its thrust. Seen in retrospect, the story is proto-Nazi. * As fiction, negligible.

ARNOLD, R. CROSSLEY
No information. Portrait accompanying the story shows a middle-aged man. It is possible that the author was British.
    17. **THE SECRET OF THE TOMB**. *Wonder Stories Quarterly*, Fall 1930. Ill. Miller.
Novelette. * *Place:* Egypt. * After a brief frame situation, the narration of Alfred Stewart, archeologist. Stewart accompanies Dr. Peri, a French archeologist (whose characterization seems indebted to Hercule Poirot), to Egypt, where they undertake the excavation of a mastaba. A mysterious hitherto unrecorded disease strikes animals and men, whereupon fellahin workers rebel. The rebellion is easily put down when Stewart kills two of the workers to keep the rest in line. * On breaking into the mastaba, the archeologists and their workmen find themselves trapped as doors close behind them; but other chambers are open, and they are "herded" along by sequential door closing. They finally emerge in an underground wonderland that stretches between the mastaba and the Great Pyramid. In this underworld is the realm of the great Sais-Amen-Tanis, who is the master of a superscience. Sais welcomes them and provides carefully for their comfort, although he kills the Moslem and Copt workmen in sadistic ways, notably ripping apart by gorillas. * Sais, an Egyptian priest from around 2800 B.C., discovered the chemical secret of immortality and has developed other sciences since. He can dematerialize himself and rematerialize himself elsewhere;

work with atoms to create fabulous gems and gorillas; convey immortality; and much else. * Naturally, he is plotting. He plans to exterminate most of the world's population and repopulate the Earth with ancient Egyptians whom he is holding in suspended animation. And he offers Stewart and Peri jobs spreading his fantastic disease about. * The men are unenthusiastic, and things look bad. But there are traitors in Sais's camp: Nefti, a beautiful young ancient Egyptian princess, and Ali, a loyal Arab who managed to survive. * With Nefti's aid the two men escape, while Ali, behind them, blows up the atomic energy plant, Sais, and everything else. * An incredible mishmash of material from Sax Rohmer, Otis A. Kline, and similar thriller sources. Astonishing that it could have been printed.

ARNOLD, WESLEY
No information. Portrait accompanying "Waves of Death" shows a young man.
    18. **WITHIN THE PLANET**. *Science Wonder Quarterly*, Spring 1930. Ill. Leonard.
Short story. * *Time:* 1936. *Place:* perhaps Indiana. * The great earthquake has caused tremendous damage over a large part of the state; areas are leveled; enormous, deep chasms have opened; and loss of life has been great. The reporter narrator Jim and his former teacher, the well-known Professor Burlingham, fly to the area to investigate. Burlingham has his own ideas about such matters. * When they reach the earthquake-wracked area and examine a great chasm, they are astonished first to find tracks then to see strange humanoid creatures that have obviously emerged from the Earth's depths. These creatures are taller than a man, enormously muscular, fitted with prehensile feet, blind (with vestigial eye-sockets), and obviously gifted with acute senses of smell and hearing. * Professor Burlingham is greatly concerned about these beings, which seem hostile, for he is convinced that they are superior to *Homo sapiens* in mentality. (The reader is likely to be incredulous.) The professor, the narrator, soldiers, and monsters scramble around until there is another earthquake that seals off the cave world in which the monsters live. Burlingham believes that the latest temblor wiped out the menace. * Burlingham speculates that the underground men were originally trapped there by an enormous fault that then became roofed over. * Routine, but readable.
    19. **WAVES OF DEATH**. *Wonder Stories*, June 1930. Ill. Paul.
Short story. * *Time:* 1949. * The Schneider Cup competition is taking place, with American and British entries preëminent. The American *Dart*, piloted by Jimmy Wallace is favored to break the previous year's record of 650 MPH. * Wallace flies along, pushing up to 750 MPH, when his plane suddenly explodes. Skulduggery is suspected, foreign and American, and there is considerable to do, including a Congressional investigation. * Professor Charles Smith, however, provides an aerodynamic explanation. When the *Dart* approached and stayed at the speed of sound, it set up vibrations and forces which, combining with tunnel phenomena, caused the plane to disintegrate. * Since then, planes are careful when they approach the speed of sound, some even having governors; others try to pass the sound barrier as rapidly as possible to avoid the vibratory effect. * Not badly told.
    20. **THE STRUGGLE FOR VENUS**. *Wonder Stories*, December 1930. Ill. Marchioni.

Arnold, Wesley (*continued*)

Short story. * *Time:* A.D. 2012. *Place:* Mostly on Venus. * The first expedition to colonize Venus has just landed. The geography of Venus is fairly well known, hence surprises are not expected. But in a few days radio communication to Earth reports men missing from the camp, and then radio ceases altogether. * Starrett the narrator, an experienced space pilot, had originally been scheduled to go on the expedition, but was bumped by a broken leg. Now he will go on a one-man reconnaissance expedition, to learn what has happened; since Venus is moving away, he will fly around the sun to meet Venus as it approaches. * The trip is without incident, but when Starrett reaches Venus, he sees a strange encampment, from which flashes a ray that disables his ship. Landing near the deserted Earth camp, he sees a dirigible-like ship from which humanoid figures emerge. He eludes capture for a short time, but is finally taken prisoner. As the other prisoners inform him, their captors are Martians who arrived on Venus about two years earlier and will not permit Earth colonization of Venus. When the Martian spaceship returns to Mars in a short time, all the Terrestrial prisoners will be killed. * A tunnel, however, permits a mass escape, and the Earthmen take up their vessel just as the Martians leave. An impromptu bomb dropped on the Martian ship destroys it. The Martians on their home planet, who do not have radio since they communicate telepathically, apparently decide that their attempt at colonization was a failure and make no more attempts. * *Miscellaneous:* Venus seems Earth-like, with many native plants that are edible. * Routine.

ARONIN, BEN[JAMIN] (1904-1980)

U.S. (Chicago) writer, lawyer, Hebrew scholar, television personality (Uncle Ben on children's program *Magic Door*). Author of *The Lost Tribe* (1934) and other fiction. The assertion in fan bibliographies that Aronin is a pseud. for variously Edna Herron, Edna Heron, or Edward Heron-Allen, is absurd.

21. **THE DOUBT.** *Amazing Stories,* May 1932.

Short-short story. * *Time:* 1928. * Leslie Maples, World War I ace, receives a surprising visitor—Charles Richter, his last aerial opponent in the War. Until their aerial duel, which ended in crashes and disablements for both, their records had been even, twelve opponents shot down. * Richter comes directly to the point. He is stifled by the monotony of post-World War I life; he would like to relive once again some of the temporary glory of the dogfight. As he puts it, the ecstasy of an hour opposed to the drudgery of a lifetime. And, more important, he has to know which is the better man, he or Maples. * At first Maples does not agree, but gradually he comes to feel Richter's doubt. As a result the two ancient aces mount surviving World War I planes and continue their interrupted air duel. After even maneuverings, the two planes collide. Maples survives, though badly smashed up, and his doubts are ended. * Not a bad story of its type, but in no way science-fiction.

ARTHUR, ROBERT, JR. (c.1909-?)

U.S. author, born Ann Arbor, Michigan, attended University of Michigan; in later life resident of Old Lyme, Connecticut. Also wrote detective stories. Information per friend Robert Swisher. Rock and others incorrectly identify this writer with Robert Arthur Feder (1909-1969), a prolific short story writer and film writer who wrote as Robert Arthur up into the 1960s. Oddly

enough, the portrait accompanying "The Terror from the Sea" shows a man in late middle age. Arthur was presumably hiding his youth. The present stories would be considered immature work.

22. **THE TERROR FROM THE SEA.** *Wonder Stories,* December 1931. Ill. Paul.

Short story. * *Place:* Mostly the Chicago area. * The menace starts in Chesapeake Bay, when hordes of greenish little creatures like jellyfish, the size of one's hand, come ashore and begin to attack mankind. The creatures are hard to dislodge and even harder to kill, for tiny fragments regenerate into full individuals in a short time. They can leap about three feet, and they have a certain amount of intelligence. * In less time than the reader would expect, the green terror has covered much of the world—solid. North America is covered, Great Britain, Europe, Asia, are all covered, and it looks as if mankind is doomed. * The chief center of resistance is Chicago, which has been surrounded by a six foot wide ring of fire, fed by oil stores. Very strong light will repel the creatures, but this is only a limited defense. * The ultimate answer comes from an unknown hermit scientist who discovers that a certain combination of long and short radio waves will kill the creatures. The technique is revealed in the nick of time, just as the green menace has broken through the defenses of Chicago. * Part of the story is told through a semiliterate Irish-American and his fiancée.

23. **THEFT OF THE WASHINGTON MONUMENT.** *Amazing Stories,* October 1933. Ill. Morey.

Short story. * *Time:* the present, about A.D. 12,000, and the far future. *Place:* Washington, D.C. * Professor Green, whose ideas on time and space have been ridiculed, is plotting a suitable revenge and vindication. He will transport the Washington Monument into the future for a few days, then return it. * He and his friend Grayson set up equipment inside the monument and leave our time, stopping at A.D. 12,000. The then Washington is a unitary megalopolis with buildings miles high. But the culture is hostile, and the professor leaves hurriedly as a heat ray begins to melt the monument. * The two men continue as far as their energy will take them, which is a deserted, lifeless world. As they watch, a strange planetoid emerges into sight, collides with the Moon, then crashes into Earth just as the time-monument returns to our present. * *Miscellaneous:* The professor's apparatus is based on a new metal extracted from a meteorite that fell near his laboratory.

AUCKLAND, ROI

U.S. author, contributor to *Top-Notch* and *Mademoiselle*. It has been suggested that Auckland is a pseud. for Desmond Hall. If so, the name suggests New Zealand rather than Australian origin.

24. **BLIND REASONING.** *Astounding Stories,* February 1934. Unsigned ill.

Short story. * *Place:* at sea, mid-Atlantic. * As one of the ship's crew watches, a disheveled young man rushes from a cabin and leaps into the sea. Rescue turns out to be impossible. * Suspicion falls upon Dr. Raoul Enslade, the suicide's cabin mate, who has been working on the young man with mysterious electrical equipment. A check reveals that the apparatus is shattered and that Enslade is unconscious. * Revived, he explains. Young Charles Hart has had strange memory fugues since childhood; he breaks away from his surroundings and runs toward the sea. Enslade, who recognized Hart's behavior as an

Aukland, Roi (*continued*)

unconscious compulsion, has taken him to sea, where the compulsion should be strongest, and has prepared apparatus to suppress Hart's conscious mind, so that the unconscious can speak out and reveal what is happening. * The apparatus has worked, apparently, for Hart has been raving about a Princess Gaya and a ruler named Quatros, who is keeping him apart from the princess. Hart is Prince Gartrell, who has been sent overseas among barbarians, so that he cannot marry Gaya. Hart then raved about floods and shouted that he is coming. Breaking away from Enslade, he leaped into the ocean, as already told. * Enslade has a partial answer, an ancient kingdom above which they are now sailing, and ancestral memories of—Atlantis. * Competently done.

BAIN, ARTHUR L.
No information. Social Security records list several men of this name.

   25. **AUTHOR'S ADVENTURE**. *Amazing Stories*, April 1933.
Short-short story. * Not science-fiction. * Detective story author Pete Hearn is annoying when he reveals that he gets his plots by imagining his friends murdered in various ways. To demonstrate, he acts out part of a plot involving a window, slips, and falls out to his death. * Below routine.

BALDWIN, ROBERT
No information.

   26. **RETRIBUTION**. *Amazing Stories,* November 1933.
Short-short story. * *Time:* presumably the near future. * Gregory Booth and Cody Pfanstiehl have just left Earth in the first spaceship. Booth is delighted to be alone with Pfanstiehl, against whom he has bitter grudges, for he plans to murder him, and then claim that an accident had happened. But Pfanstiehl has much the same idea. He has Booth covered with a handgun. Before he can shoot, however, a small meteor pierces the ship, killing Pfanstiehl, while Booth dies trying to get his space suit on. * The point of it?

BALL, CLELLAND J.
No information.

   27. **THE GRAVITY KING**. *Amazing Stories Quarterly*, Fall 1928. Ill. Paul.
(First published in *Science and Invention*, April 1922.)
Short story. * *Time:* 1940. * When the great airlines tycoon Elias Craig receives a note from Norton, an inventor who claims to have discovered antigravity, his greed overcomes any sense of caution he might have had. With his fellow director-rogues, he visits the inventor's laboratory and witnesses a demonstration of antigravity. * But there is more: The inventor is a former associate whom Craig and his cronies robbed and framed into a prison term in order to seize an earlier invention that established their fortunes. Now, Norton is going to have his revenge. His laboratory is really a disguised antigravity vessel, and it is already high in the air. Norton plans to abandon the rogues in Tierra del Fuego, but in the scuffle that follows a bullet strikes the machinery, and the rudimentary spaceship sails off into space, bearing all to their deaths. * As a story, nothing, but

interesting attitudes toward big business ethics.

BALMER, EDWIN and **MacHARG, WILLIAM**
Balmer (1883-1959), U.S. author, editor, publisher. Editor, later associate publisher of *Red Book Magazine*. With Philip Wylie wrote two competent bootstrap new-world stories, *When Worlds Collide* (1933) and *After Worlds Collide* (1934). MacHarg (1872-1951), U.S. (mostly Chicago) writer, newspaperman; Balmer's brother-in-law. The stories described below are reprinted from *The Achievements of Luther Trant* (1910), with earlier periodical publications.

   28. **THE MAN IN THE ROOM**. *Amazing Stories*, April 1927. Ill. Dean.
Short story. * Not science-fiction, but a detective story. The first of a series of stories about Luther Trant, a Chicago experimental psychologist who puts his special knowledge to work at solving crimes. In most of his cases his modus operandi is application of various laboratory diagnostic tests. * When Professor Laurie is found dead, in a gas-filled chamber, the police wrongly suspect suicide because of financial irregularities. Luther Trant finds the murderer by using a word association test. Trant now decides to become a consulting psychological detective.

   29. **THE MAN HIGHER UP**. *Amazing Stories*, December 1926. Ill. Paul.
Short story. * Not science-fiction, but a scientific detective story. * In this case, Trant, acting for the U.S. Treasury Department, uses a primitive lie detector developed by a friend and traps a murderous, wicked capitalist who is defrauding customs and the Department of Internal Revenue.

   30. **THE ELEVENTH HOUR**. *Amazing Stories*, February 1927. Unsigned ill.
Short story. * Not science-fiction, but a detective story. * Luther Trant receives a desperate appeal for help from a man who claims he will be killed at eleven o'clock. So he is, and the wrong person is suspected. Trant clears up the case with a primitive lie detector, revealing that Oriental vengeance lies behind the crime.

   31. **THE HAMMERING MAN**. *Amazing Stories*, March 1927. Unsigned ill.
Short story. * Not science-fiction but a detective story. * With the use of the sphygmograph Trant solves a mystery involving Russian revolutionaries, a secret agent of the Russian police, and a romance in Chicago between a young Russian girl and the son of an American millionaire. * The Russia in the background is, of course, Czarist Russia. * Somewhat more imaginative than the other stories considered here, what with an example of prison secret communications.

[Anonymous]
Presumably a British writer.
   32. **BANDITS OF THE STRATOSPHERE**. *Scoops*, 21 April 1934. Unsigned ill.
Boys' fiction. * Short story. * *Time:* the near future. * *Background:* The International Postal Board delivers the world's mail along global circuits with fast mail planes and, at suitable points, powerful aerial destroyers to guard the routes. * Over the radio word comes that a mail plane that has just left Paris en route to Melbourne is being attacked by a gigantic pirate ship of fantastic speed. As the message ends, the mail plane has obviously been shot down and the pilot is presumably dead. *

Bandits of the Stratosphere (*continued*)

Big Bill Benson, a fellow pilot, flies to help, since the nearest destroyer is hours away. Near the crashed mail plane he sees an enormous gray plane with a wingspread of perhaps five hundred feet. He attacks the plane, but is hopelessly outgunned and outsped as the gray plane sprouts guns, including antiaircraft cannon, shoots him down, and flies away. * Bill recovers from his injuries, while the raids continue. Determined to destroy the pirate, Bill offers to act as a lure, while a destroyer lurks nearby. Posing as a mail plane, Bill's stratosphere fighter attracts the pirate as planned, and the destroyer joins the battle. But the pirate is more than a match for the destroyer, and things look bad until Bill, having laden his ship with mines instead of mailbags, drops a bomb manually on the giant ship. That is the end of the pirate. * Obviously, like several other stories in *Scoops*, derivative of the air-war magazines.

BARCLAY, FRED M.
No information.

    33. **THE TROGLODYTES**. *Amazing Stories*, September 1930. Ill. Morey.

Short story. * The framework narrator, a kindly man, helps a drenched, obviously exhausted man, who tells his story. * Joe Everett and his friends John Bowers and Jim House, workingmen, are on a boating trip when they spy a freshwater stream flowing from a cave into the river. They later enter the cave, dynamiting one narrow stretch, and find themselves in an enormous maze of passages and chambers, including some of crystalline beauty. As they examine what seem to be artificial rows of strange vegetation, they come in contact with the Ampu, a race of underground men. * Treated as guests rather than as prisoners, the explorers are taken on a hovercraft to a city perhaps a thousand miles underground. They learn the language of the Ampu and, eventually, their history and origins. * The Ampu, who are humans who have evolved in a peculiar fashion, are hypersensitive to light, hairless, and covered with scales. They live in a semisocialistic society that provides much leisure time. They practice agriculture, with both plants and cave animals, and in some respects (including disintegration projectors) are scientifically more advanced than the outside world. All in all, the Ampu are happy, but the outsiders notice a certain apathy and listlessness. Ampu scholars are very curious about the outside world and question the outsiders extensively, but when Jim describes weapons and wars, they are disgusted and horrified. * Ampu religion, which is important in the culture, is based on the constitution of the inner Earth. Glassy layers permit view of an astonishing small cosmology at the Earth's hollow center, where several orbiting bodies comparable to electrons revolve around an atomic nucleus. This phenomenon is both a Mystery and sacred. Part of the Ampu religion (the only cruel aspect of the culture) involves human sacrifice of a few victims every year and a half to these deities. The victims are criminals or older people who wish euthanasia. * The outsiders adjust to the new world in varying ways. Joe and John accept their life, and John, the most intelligent and best informed of the three men, is able to provide many insights into Ampu and surface life. He is also on the edge of a romance with an Ampu woman. Jim, however, is bored and truculent, and as the story progresses, becomes more unhappy, eventually deliberately stirring up trouble. * One element of potential discord is the origin of the Ampu. There are Ampu Fundamentalists who believe their ancestors were created by the divinities, the revolving planetoids within the Earth. Others, however, accept certain ancient cave graffiti, interpreted by the outsiders, as indicating that the ancestral Ampu were surface men who took refuge in the underworld during the last glacial period. Jim, who incites armed clashes among the religious factions, is disintegrated as part of the sacrificial program. * Part of the unrest caused unintentionally and intentionally by the surface men is connected with Ampu lassitude. The Ampu elders ask John how the listless Ampu can be awakened to the vitality characteristic of the three outsiders, no matter what their other limitations. John suggests that life is too easy in the underworld, and that a desire for what is not immediately attainable might awaken the apathetic people. * The underground visit comes to an end disastrously. Immediately after the sacrifices, a riot breaks out, and one of the Fundamentalists who hates the outsiders chases Joe and John, trying to disintegrate them. Only Joe escapes, making his way back out into our world. * Nicely written, nicely paced, interesting in subject matter. * A child of Bulwer-Lytton's *The Coming Race*, but one of the better stories in early pulp science-fiction.

BARNES, ARTHUR K[ELVIN] (1911-1969)

U.S. (California) author; born in Washington. Education has variously been cited as University of Washington or University of California. Frequent contributor to pulp magazines of various types. Occasionally collaborated with Henry Kuttner. Sometimes used the pseud. Kelvin Kent both for solo work and Kuttner collaborations. His stories about Gerry Carlyle, a sort of interplanetary Frances Buck, were popular in the late 1930s and early 1940s. A collection of these stories, *Interplanetary Hunter*, was published in 1956. The work described here would be best rated as promising juvenilia. See also Dave Barnes, pseud. or collaboration.

    34. **LORD OF THE LIGHTNING**. *Wonder Stories*, December 1931. Ill. Paul.

Short story. * *Time*: probably the near future. *Place*: the Pacific coast of South America. * Enormous storms ravage parts of the coast of Chile, oddly enough moving from town to town and skipping intervening areas. * Newspaperman Jack Darrell and geologist Lawrence Thornton decide to investigate. Darrell has a hunch that the phenomena are somehow connected with the great maverick scientist Borgman who disappeared some time previously. * After watching further disasters in other parts of South America, Darrell and Thornton discover that Borgman, who has gone mad, has developed a heat ray by focusing solar rays and is disintegrating large areas of the ocean. The resulting vacuum and vapor cause the frightful storms. Further, Borgman's activities, by disturbing the sea bottom in areas close to former volcanic activity, are causing volcanic eruptions. * Borgman, while raving and exulting, falls into a lava pit, shot by Darrell. * Why Borgman is doing all this is not clear. * Immature work.

    35. **THE CHALLENGE OF THE COMET**. *Wonder Stories*, February 1932. Ill. Paul.

Short story. * *Time*: probably the near future. Another adventure of newspaper star reporter Jack Darrell. * A mysterious killer fog, containing cyanogen and other gases, is spreading over the lands adjacent to the North Sea. With Belgian scientist Binet

Barnes, Arthur K. (*continued*)

Darrell investigates. Sailors' accounts tell of a purple sphere from which the gas flows. * Darrell and Binet determine that the center of the phenomena must be Ware Isle, whence they fly encased in protective clothing and gas masks. * They immediately encounter the source: huge floating slug-like beings that travel on a jet principle, by taking in gas and forcing it out, and are telepathic to some extent. * The slug people, who are rational and apparently passionless, explain that since their world is dying, they intend to take over the Earth. They have no hatred for or grudge against mankind, but mankind as the inferior race must yield to the superior. They have traveled to Earth on an artificial comet, which will be followed by others. * Our heroes are equal to the situation. Jack's pistol gains them freedom, and Binet, with a little device that he carries with him, combusts the gas envelope of the aliens. Mankind is saved. * Juvenile work.

36. **GUARDIANS OF THE VOID.** *Wonder Stories Quarterly*, Fall 1932. Ill. Paul.

Short story. * *Time:* the twenty-seventh century. *Place:* mostly Triton, with a showdown in space not too far from Venus. * Dirck Lanark, colonel in the Interplanetary Patrol, is summoned to a meeting with the top brass of the planetary secret services. A slave ship carrying Venusian greenies (wetbacks) is so fast that it has succeeded in outrunning space patrols, which are supposed to be the fastest ships in the system. The slaver, the officers declare, must have developed atomic energy, and he is probably the legendary villain Dr. Teak. Lanark is volunteered to track down the criminal and destroy him. * With a faithful comrade, a disguised Lanark proceeds to End o' Space, which is a sort of Baratraria located on Triton, where he expects to encounter Teak. After a time he is accepted into the rough camaraderie of the space rats and gains the good will of Teak by repairing one of his engines, a job which the local mechanics were unable to accomplish. * Teak explains his system of attaining atomic energy; it consists of flattening out the orbits of electrons and squeezing them out of the atom. Teak declares, "[his] voice rising to a high scream and a triumphant leer disfiguring his lips, 'I am the King of Space.'" * Dr. Teak apparently takes a fancy to Lanark and enrolls him in his gang. At the showdown, however, when Lanark believes that he has captured Teak and the ship, he learns that Teak has been aware of his identity all along and has been toying with him. Indeed, the Teak that he has captured, when stain is removed, turns out to be not Teak at all—a strange deal for Lanark that goes against the grain. But Lanark and his associate do polish off Teak, despite all the odds against them. * *Miscellaneous:* Martians are very tall and burly, with short arms and a snout that indicates reptilian origin. High caste Venusians are slender and more human than Martians, while chloro-men (greenies) seem to be rather weak, stupid plant people. * Immature work that should have been either thoroughly edited or not published.

37. **THE MOLE-MEN OF MERCURY.** *Wonder Stories*, December 1933. Ill. Winter.

Short story. * *Time:* before the twenty-third century. *Place:* Mercury. * *Background:* The Interplanetary Legion, which is supposed to maintain order in the name of the three inner planets, is in increasingly bad repute. Many of its members are thugs seeking refuge from the law, and mortality is extremely high. * The story is concerned with George Gower, remembered in the twenty-third century as a great hero, but in reality is a

shiftless ne'er-do-well. Gower was shanghaied into the Legion with no recourse but to accept his fate. He is a bad soldier, and life is hard for him. * His organization soon learns its mission, to fight the mole-men on Mercury. * *Background:* Mercury is the only source for exalite, an antigravity metal mined from domes set up on the libration zone. The current problem is that the deeper mines have penetrated hitherto unknown caverns inhabited by an intelligent life-form, the mole-men. These creatures look like two eggs atop one another with flap-like lower extremities with suction cups, and red hair. They have potent weapons and are immune to heat rays. Only cathode rays will kill them. Since they emerge unpredictably and are difficult to kill, the war is not going too well for the I.L. * Gower, who numbers cowardice among his failings, is forced to take part in skirmishes and battles with the mole-men. Oddly enough, he notices the first weakness that the strange beings possess: inability to tolerate volcanic fumes. The superior officers accept Gower's insight and plan to bomb a volcano so that its gases will flood the lower tunnels and kill all the mole men. But bombs are almost impossible to place. Men are needed for a suicide mission, and Gower "volunteers." His captain accompanies him. At the last minute Gower panics, attacks the captain, but in the melee falls into the pit and detonates the bombs, exterminating the mole-men. For the sake of the I.L. the captain does not tell what really happened, and Gower is a posthumous hero. * Still juvenile writing, but superior to the previous stories.

38. **EMOTION SOLUTION.** *Wonder Stories*, April 1936. Ill. Schneeman.

Short story. * *Place:* California. * Told in a confusing mixture of flashbacks and present narrative. * Ted King and his friend the great chemist George Jonas often argue as much for sake of arguing as anything else. Their present topic is evolution. Jonas contends that evolution has stopped for mankind; the next stage would be pure intellectuality, but because of emotion this can never happen. * This conversation sets Jonas off on a quest for the cause of emotion, which he readily finds in a glandular secretion. He further compounds a chemical that will destroy the emotion secretion in the body. King is interested, but horrified when he learns that Jonas plans to pour his emotion-destroying liquid into the local reservoirs, thus permitting new evolutionary advances. He tries to stop Jonas, but instead is himself held prisoner while Jonas performs his fell deed. * Later, King and Jonas see what has happened: incalculable loss of life and general chaos. People no longer care about anything. This includes sex, and as King now points out to Jonas, the local population will remain childless and Jonas's potion will die with them. * Some improvement over earlier work, but still melodramatic.

BARNES, DAVE

Pseud. of Arthur K. Barnes, either solely or, according to Tuck, in collaboration with Norbert Davis. Davis was a fairly well-known writer, who contributed many stories to the pulp magazines, including *Complete Stories* and *Detective Stories*.

39. **THE HOUSE THAT WALKED.** *Astounding Stories*, September 1936. Unsigned ill.

Short story. * A science-fictional adaptation of a supernatural motif. * A Victorian house takes to appearing in vacant lots around the city. In it, visible from the outside, is a corpse with its head battered in. On the rare instances when viewers have

Barnes, Dave (*continued*)

the courage to enter, the house disappears, leaving no trace. On one occasion, when the police entered the house, they fell unconscious and awakened in an empty lot. * One ancient informant, a carpenter, recognizes the house and, indeed, claims to have had a hand in building it. It was the scene of an unsolved murder about fifty years earlier—but the house burned down completely! * A resolution comes when the house makes it appearance before the murderer, who drops dead from shock. * An explanation is offered. An innocent suspect in the ancient murder had vowed both revenge and vindication. He built a house in exact replica of the murder dwelling, then, with a technique for stopping electronic movement, photographed it and prepared what amounted to holographic images, which he projected around the city. Many of the effects, like the unsuccessful entry by the police were stage-managed. When his purpose was accomplished with the death of the murderer, he destroyed his construction. * A very interesting twist, but a routine story. The model may have been "An Itinerant House" by Emma Dawson, in which the mechanism is supernatural.

BARNETTE, JACK

At the time of writing, Baltimore resident. The magazines on occasion spell the name as Barnett, but the above seems to be correct. Portrait printed with "The Vapor Intelligence" shows a young man. Also contributed to Gernsback's *Scientific Detective Monthly*.

40. **THE PURPLE DEATH**. *Amazing Stories*, July 1929. Ill. Paul.

Short story. * Researchers Grey and LeBrun are looking for rays that will act as germicides. They have some success by running ultraviolet into the bloodstream via a glass piping inserted in the body, but most success comes from LeBrun's new El ray, which has a very strange generating tube. By chance it is discovered that if the El ray is combined with ultraviolet, the result is a most potent disintegrator ray. The men enthusiastically foresee applications in medicine and industry. * But there is a catch. Anything once irradiated by the El ray is perpetually sensitive to ultraviolet, and if one goes out into the sun—poof! That is the end of the doctors and their apparatus. * Amateurish. * Dr. Miles J. Breuer, a frequent contributor to *Amazing Stories*, savagely attacked the medical aspects of this story in a letter in the September 1929 issue.

41. **THE VAPOR INTELLIGENCE**. *Science Wonder Stories*, January 1930. Ill. Paul.

Short story. * An epigone of H. P. Lovecraft's "The Colour out of Space," told with heavy local color as reminiscence of an event in the past. * Essentially, during a meteorite fall a space egg of some sort lands in the swamps around Shantyville, the local black community (which is described in a racist way). In a matter of days strange phenomena are observed. There are no more insects in the Loon Marsh area, then no more small animals. And something is devouring people and cattle, leaving only skeletons. The local blacks flee the area in terror, claiming that they have seen ghosts. * The white residents of the neighboring town now see strange lights in the sky, a shining floating globe, and questing light tentacles. The shining sphere sails off, but the thing, whatever it is, is not immune to rifle fire, for it seems to have been killed. A factor in solar radiation also may have been responsible for its death. * Vegetation will not

grow where the thing, disgorging blood, died. * A learned guess is that the creature, whatever it was, came from one of the outer planets, probably Jupiter, and was intelligent enough to construct a space vessel.

BARNEY, B. H.

U.S. (Midwestern) figure, said to have been a farmhand at the time the following story was printed. The story, as should have been obvious to the editors of *Amazing Stories*, was a plagiaristic reworking of elements from the stories of A. Merritt, actually lifting passages verbatim. Merritt protested, and the editors of *Amazing Stories* printed a brief acknowledgment of the situation in the June 1933 issue: "A. Merritt, who is well known to many of the readers of AMAZING STORIES, has called our attention to many similarities in descriptions, characterization and situations in the story 'Beyond the Veil of Time,' by B. H. Barney, published in Fall-Winter issue of AMAZING STORIES QUARTERLY, and descriptions, characterization, and situations in two of his books 'The Moon Pool' and 'The Face in the Abyss.' Mr. Merritt objects particularly to the utilization of the conception and name of 'The Dream Makers,' which formed an essential part of his 'Face in the Abyss.'" * Barney denied the charges, claiming he had never read Merritt's stories, and it is not clear whether he ever admitted his guilt. *Amazing Stories* was unable to retrieve the monies paid to him. According to an item in Schwartz/Weisinger (*Science Fiction Digest*, April 1933, p. 9) Barney was a farmhand who earned only $15.00 a month. So far as is known, Barney wrote no more fiction. * A point that is usually missed about Barney, no matter what his ethics or naiveté, is that he created a reasonable pastiche of Merritt and H. Rider Haggard, with a dash of Marie Corelli. His story shows imagination and ingenuity, even if amateurish and constructed of "borrowed" material. He might have become a successful writer had he continued.

42. **BEYOND THE VEIL OF TIME**. *Amazing Stories Quarterly*, Fall/Winter 1932. Ill. Morey.

Novelette. * *Time:* present and an undetermined time in the past. *Place:* Peru. * Richard Nelson, a mathematician, is traveling in the Andes when he hears of a hitherto unknown ruined city. A preliminary reconnaissance with Huayan, a friendly Indian, locates the site, but Nelson must leave. * After a time he returns with an electronic machine he hopes will recapture ancient light and sound, revealing the life within the obviously pre-Inca city. * On his return, he makes the acquaintance of Dan Bradford, an American engineer, who will be his companion in adventure. * Nelson sets up his machine and starts it. There is a vision of a beautiful woman, an explosion, and Nelson, Bradford, and Huayan awaken far in the past. * The unintentional explorers make their way through a tropical jungle-like valley, fight off an attack by an ape-like creature, see strange life-forms, and find themselves before the city. From the gates emerge the guard, blond, blue-eyed men mounted on small, tame dinosaurs. Since the explorers speak Aymara, communication is easy, and the three find themselves guests of Prince Lotha. * *Background:* The holy city of Amnestar is preeminent in the kingdom of Pacama, which extends to the east. There are suggestions of Atlantis in its ancient history. Beyond Pacama are wild Indian tribes, who are hostile. The civilization of the land is about on a Classical Mediterranean level, with elaborate architecture and art. A powerful priesthood is preëminent, and there is considerable

Barney, B. H. (*continued*)

tension between religious and civil leaders. * The heart of Amnestar is a religious cult focused on the Lords of Life and Death, black, shrouded figures (perhaps hypostases), who pass judgment on individuals at the behest of the priesthood. Life, a woman, is the stronger of the two, but Death often wields power, using what amounts to a death ray. Important in the religion are the Dream-makers, who create visions that they project mentally in the great temple. It is they who produce the image of a handsome, sensual, evil woman's face that lures victims to death in a fiery abyss within the temple. * The high priest Shasta is a lecherous, ruthless, power-mad scoundrel who desires to wed Losaya the Flower Maiden, who amounts to a high priestess. (It was her beautiful face that became visible when Nelson first turned on his machine.) Unlike the other Pacamans, Losaya is a brunette, a pigmentation trait that sometimes emerges in the royal family. She and Bradford are attracted to each other. * The basic plot that follows is a typical lost-race story. Shasta tries, with the Dream-makers' projection of the evil face, to lure Bradford to his death, but he is saved by the Flower Maiden and the Lord of Life, at whose behest Bradford and Losaya wed. * The land breaks out into civil war, priestly party against secular, with the secular ultimately victorious. In a temple confrontation Bradford shoots the Lord of Death, there is a flashing of death rays, and the cultic horrors are dead. But Shasta survives, with Losaya captive. Nelson kills Shasta, but dying, the wicked priest activates the death ray apparatus and propels Nelson back to the present, where he records his experiences. * As the reader can see, the story is basically a medley of elements from "The Moon Pool," "The Conquest of the Moon Pool," and "The Face in the Abyss" by Merritt.

BARRETT, H. I.
No information.

43. **THE MECHANICAL HEART.** *Amazing Stories Quarterly*, Fall 1931. Ill. Morey.
Short story. * Jim Bard, an inventor whose ambition is to perfect a workable telephoto apparatus, is dismayed when Dr. Wentworth tells him that he will die shortly from a heart attack. Wentworth's death sentence does not bother Jim as much as the thought that his work will remain unfinished. * After some byplay, Jim and his assistant Henry decide to put aside the telephoto for a short time, and, instead, construct a mechanical heart. Dr. Wentworth is discouraging, but when the apparatus is finished, he inserts in into Jim's thorax, where it works perfectly. In addition to a pump it consists of a pacemaker (my term) for accelerating heart beat for emotional situations. * There are a few small contretemps, such as the occasion when the over-stimulated heart causes Jim to make love to the cleaning woman, but all in all it is a wonderful achievement. * Jim and Henry finish the telephoto and prepare to display it and make an announcement of the mechanical heart at a learned congress. At the meeting, however, there is a problem with the electric current to the telephoto, and Jim, to preserve his invention, shifts his cardiac wiring to the apparatus, willingly sacrificing himself for the sake of his invention. * Routine.

BARRY, B. X.
According to Schwartz/Weisinger the pseud. of Ray A. Giles. Probably not the same person as Ray Giles (1889-?), author of

various inspirational books on money and health. The story blurb refers to Barry as a "well-known writer." Winter, on the other hand, mentions, as an early member of the American Interplanetary Society, a Roy A. Giles, who seems more likely as an author. The cover of the magazine carries the author's name incorrectly as F. X. Barry.

44. **PIRATES OF SPACE.** *Amazing Stories,* December 1931. Ill. Morey.
Short story. * *Time:* A.D. 2080. *Place:* mostly out around the asteroids. * *Background:* Space travel is common, with wireless transmission of power and rockets. The three inner planets are at about the same level of civilization, with considerable interplanetary trade. Venusians are human, but small and slim. Martians are humanoid giants, around twelve feet tall. Late in the story a perfectly human race will be found on an asteroid that is kept invisible by space mirrors. * The problem with space travel in the late twenty-first century is the renegade Martian space pirate Quantok, who operates a small fleet of battleships from an unknown base. Apart from actual damage, Quantok's raids have made it impossible to set up energy relay stations in space. * Eventually, the three inner planets, having had enough of Quantok, fit out a huge space armada to destroy him. Among the ship captains in this fleet is Hal Kane, who has lost his commercial captaincy because of Quantok. Trying to escape Quantok, he flew the *Agular* too close to Earth, causing some damage to property. * During the first battles, Kane and his co-captain, sweetheart Vena Hazzard, perform so brilliantly that they rise to be joint admirals of the grand fleet. * Defeated in immense space battles, Quantok is captured and executed. It turns out that his base has been the invisible asteroid Dagnarth, where he enslaved and terrorized the friendly, gentle inhabitants. Vena, it is also revealed, is the lost princess of Dagnarth. When she marries Kane, they eventually become king and queen. * *Miscellaneous:* Besides the human inhabitants, the invisible planetoid boasts of semi-human dog people. * Space battles are fought with rays. * Pretty bad.

BARSHOFSKY, PHILIP
According to Tuck, pseud. of M. Kaplan, otherwise unidentified. To my knowledge this has not been corroborated, and it seems doubtful. See also Philip Jacques Bartel.

45. **ONE PREHISTORIC NIGHT.** *Wonder Stories,* November 1934. Ill. Paul.
(Reprinted in Ashley, *History of the Science Fiction Magazine,* Vol. One.)
Short story. * *Time:* perhaps the Mesozoic. * The rocket ship lands on the Terrestrial island, and small, four-armed creatures, presumably descended from some sort of six-legged ancestor, emerge. They are Martians, looking for a new planet to replace dying Mars. Now that they have found Earth salubrious, they will return to Mars with the good news, leaving behind a small outpost. * But fate and the wildlife arrange matters otherwise. While the Martians have various sorts of rays and electrified defenses, the dinosaurs are so turbulent and so gigantic that Martian weapons are inadequate. Falling monsters break down the live wires, a gigantic beast tumbles the spaceship over so that it cannot function, and insects jam the potent electron gun. In a matter of hours the Martian expedition is destroyed. Since there is no word from the expedition, the Martian authorities will abandon investigation of Earth. Lucky for us. * *Miscellaneous:*

Barshofsky, Philip (*continued*)
The Martians communicate by a whistling language.

46. **THE IMPERFECT GUESS**. *Wonder Stories*, April 1936. Ill. Winter.
Short story. * Humor. * Finally experiencing a burst of inspiration, hack science-fiction author Philip Ganese writes a story about "comical creatures from some unknown dimension" who invade Earth and are soundly defeated. The beaten invaders are then forced to join traveling circuses as freak exhibits. * Shortly after he sends his story to *Eggsaturated Tales*, Ganese observes on his bedroom wall a strange light, from which emerge creatures like those he described in his story. The creatures, who caught Ganese's thought vibrations and assume that Ganese was deliberately insulting them, are outraged and affronted at the undignified manner in which he has portrayed them. They demand that the story be suppressed, making threats, which they can obviously fulfill if he does not accede. * Ganese resists for a time, but finally has no choice but to yield. He withdraws the story and apologizes. In exchange the strange creatures, now pleased, leave a telecard for future communications and offer to share their advanced science with him. * Clumsily handled; the idea might have worked with a more skilled writer.

BARTEL, PHILIP JACQUES
The publishers used both Jaques and Jacques in various places. Pseud. of Philip Barshofsky, who was a resident of the New York City area at this time. According to McGhan, Rock and Tuck, Barshofsky in turn is the pseud. of Maurice M. Kaplan, about whom there is no information. To my knowledge the identification with Kaplan has never been confirmed, and it seems doubtful. It will be observed that stories under the names Bartel and Barshofsky appear in the November 1934 issue of *Wonder Stories*. Social Security records list a Philip Bartel (1901-1970), who resided and died in Maryland. This is probably not the same person.

47. **TWENTY-FIVE CENTURIES LATE**. *Wonder Stories*, November 1934. Ill. Winter.
Short story. * *Time:* The "forty-fifth century of enlightenment," whenever that might be. * *Background:* The human race has changed greatly. Heads are larger than ours; there are no more teeth, and legs have almost atrophied, so that individuals often move about on small carts. The culture is almost completely mechanized, with little work for individuals to do. * In sexual behavior, too, there have been changes. Unmarried men and women are not allowed to meet, and marriage is handled completely by a eugenics board. There is no more biological family. * Science and the arts are organized in a syndicalist arrangement, with special families devoted to each. * Smith-Robert, a brilliant young scientist high in the hierarchy, has a problem. He has refused to obey the directive of the eugenics board that he marry. The reason: Some twenty-five years earlier, while on a scientific project in the Andes, he rescued Brown-Joan, a young female whose flier had become disabled. This was the first female he had seen, and he the first male she had seen. They fell in love—something previously unknown in the era—and for years communicated, first by secret channels, then by telepathy. * Now Smith-Robert must act if he wants some sort of legal union with Brown-Joan. With the help of a glib and persuasive friend, who is a member of the historian family, he pressures the supreme council into giving him

permission to marry into the Browns. A little verbal jockeying contracts Smith-Robert and Brown-Joan. * The determining factor: Brown-Joan had discovered a new, plentiful substitute for a catalyst necessary for power of all sorts. She turned it over to Smith-Robert so that he could bargain with the board. * Stilted and stuffy in presentation, and not entirely consistent. Published as by Philip Jaques Bartel.

48. **WHEN TIME STOOD STILL**. *Amazing Stories*, February 1935. Ill. Morey.
Short story. * *Time and place:* post-Revolutionary USSR. * American engineer Earl Lyons is working with two Russian scientists trying to remove the bugs from a device that alters the time component of time and space. After some difficulties, the men are successful, and Earl and scientist Khalin are brave enough to venture into the apparatus and experience what may come. * Themselves now invisible and intangible, since time has been reduced to a stasis, they can still see into the laboratory. As they watch, they see two counterrevolutionaries enter the laboratory and murder the aged Mikhailloff, who devised the experiment. But, returned to normal time and space, they see that Mikhailloff is alive; they kill the counterrevolutionaries and save Mikhailloff. * Also present in the story is a handsome young lady member of the secret police, who acts heroically and has set her cap for Lyons. * Below routine. * For a sequel see #51, "The Time Control."

49. **THE ELIXIR OF PROGRESS**. *Wonder Stories*, April 1935. Ill. Paul.
Short story. * *Time:* The early forty-fifth century, in the same culture as Bartel's previous story, #47, "Twenty-five Centuries Late." * World culture is dependent upon two vitamins, L, which conveys energy, and M, which conveys intellect. Without them, humanity, which lives on concentrated food, will rapidly deteriorate. Spinach is the only real source of L and M. * A natural disaster has just wiped out most of the world's supply of spinach, and thanks to the stupidity of Burke-Cliff, a minor employee in food production, all the reserves have been destroyed. It looks like the death sentence for Burke-Cliff. * His friend Jones-Lem, of the voluble history family, however, talks around the situation by blaming the Eugenics Bureau for not working on Burke-Cliff's stupidity earlier. The stratagem is effective, and the Supreme Council reprieves Cliff, but, to provide for his psychological care, marries him to a shrewish psychologist. The marriage is not one of gender equality, but official female superiority. * Jones-Lem now undertakes a quest for a substitute for spinach. Historical research brings to light coffee, a forgotten beverage that was banned millennia earlier—at about the time the master vitamins became necessary. * Lem now undertakes a search for a coffee plant. The quest seems hopeless, for the coffee tree seems extinct, but at last Lem finds a single specimen in the jungles of the Amazon. Its berries suitably roasted and prepared, it proves to be a far superior source of L and M than spinach ever was. * When all concerned take swigs of black coffee, things brighten, and even Burke-Cliff becomes more intelligent and achieves equality with his wife. * One of the more curious early science-fiction stories. A dull story, but perhaps Bartel needed some caffeine. In any case, as one who dislikes black coffee, I find the story incredible beyond fantasy.

50. **ONE HUNDRED GENERATIONS**. *Wonder Stories*, September 1935. Ill. Saaty.

Bartel, Philip Jacques (*continued*)

Short story in the same future culture as stories #47 and #49. * *Time:* It now seems to be the year 5400, possibly in the Western European calendar. *Place:* mostly in the Andes. * The future men are beginning to be concerned about their physical degeneration. Legs are atrophying, and walking has become almost impossible. Science is looking for a way to restore mankind to its former physical vigor. * An unexpected communication promises a solution to the problem, but the message has been presented in a most peculiar way. Every thirty years, for the past two thousand years, a scientific outpost in the Andes has been destroyed by fire. On this last occasion a cylinder with a message written in archaic language was found amid the ashes. The message asks that a representative be sent to a secret installation. * Smith-Jay, assigned to investigate, proceeds to a site in the Andes, where he is conducted through heavy, blanketing mists to a hidden retreat in a volcanic crater. There he meets an ancient man with developed legs. * The ancient man, who is served by strangely humpbacked men with normal legs, tells his story. He is the last Di Marco. An ancestor almost three thousand years earlier had recognized that human physique was deteriorating and determined to reverse the process. When he encountered a small tribe of white Indians living in the impenetrable mists around the volcano. he used them as breeding stock, transplanting condor wings onto them and making accommodating muscle and bone changes. His descendants continued his work, finally producing a race of winged men. The humps that Smith-Jay observed beneath clothing are fully functioning wings. The Di Marcos have been burning the outpost to attract attention. * Smith-Jay observes the flying people and, forgetting his wife at home, is attracted to the beautiful winged maiden Lyth, who carries him about on her flights. All in all, interbreeding with Di Marco's vigorous winged men and women seems to be the ideal solution to the problem of physical decay. * His investigation satisfactorily completed, Smith-Jay returns to civilization with the ailing Di Marco and a few of the winged people. * When Di Marco dies, soon after landing, the horrible sequel unfolds. Smith-Jay finds Lyth and her companions eating the corpse of their revered old leader. It seems that the condor element in the new people cannot be restrained from flesh-eating, including human flesh. In utter horror, Smith-Jay disintegrates the winged people, reveals to the Supreme Council what he has done, and collapses. It is long before he regains his sanity. At that time he learns that is wife has discovered a reasonable scientific method for rein-vigorating mankind. * Routine on the whole, but the gradual adumbration of the repulsive character of the bird-people is well done.

51. **THE TIME CONTROL.** *Amazing Stories,* December 1936. Ill. Morey.

Short story. * Sequel to #48, "When Time Stood Still." * *Time and place:* post-Revolutionary USSR, several months after the first story. * Mikhailoff and his team are facing a crisis; unless he can demonstrate the utility of his invention, SOVERG (Soviet Bureau of Energy) will cut off his funds. Even the persuasive-ness of G.P.U agent Mina Boyarsky does not suffice, and Earl Lyons must enter the time machine once again to satisfy the inspectors. The demonstration, which shows the immediate death of the most obstructive of the commissars, is effective. Funding is continued. * An international crisis is brewing in the

Far East. Fortunately, a peace treaty is in preparation between the USSR and Japan,but, unfortunately, Yousopoff, one of the Russian commissioners, is so boorish that there is trepidation about his behavior. And as Mina states worriedly, if there is war, members of the G.P.U will not be permitted to marry. * The group sets up a time viewer and watches the future conference. Sure enough, the drunken Yousopoff throws an inkwell into the Japanese envoy's face. There will be war. But then it occurs to Earl: This can be prevented, just as was Mikhailoff's murder in the first story. Since Mina has the whole G.P.U. under her control for the conference, she will simply exclude Yousopoff, and all will be well. So it is. She also sees, in the time viewer, her impending state wedding with Lyons. * Routine, but now a historical curiosity because of its attitudes.

BATES, HARRY

Professional name of Hiram Gilmore Bates (1900-1981). Born in Pittsburgh, Pennsylvania. Attended Allegheny College and University of Pennsylvania, but without receiving degrees. Worked at various jobs, including clock repairman, newspaper reporter, cameraman, but most significant as pulp magazine editor and writer. Edited *World-Wide Adventures, Danger Trails, Soldiers of Fortune* for Clayton. Also edited all issues of (Clayton) *Astounding Stories* and *Strange Tales.* A competent editor, regarded with respect and liking by authors who worked with him (cf. Cave's *Magazines I remember*), but unfortunately aimed his s-f magazine at a lower level than did Gernsback, stressing action. Also an excellent writer under his own name, with "Alas, All Thinking" and"Farewell to the Master," the latter filmed as *The Day the Earth Stood Still.* In later life worked in editorial role for motion picture studios. Died in poverty; his last days are described by Sam Moskowitz in a letter in the 1984 (4-2)issue of *Fantasy Commentator.* Collaborated with assistant Desmond W. Hall on stories under the pseuds. Anthony Gilmore, H. G. Winter; wrote solo as A. R. Holmes. These stories are covered separately under the pseuds. The pseudonymous stories are on a lower level than his attributed work.

52. **A MATTER OF SIZE.** *Astounding Stories,* April 1934. Ill., Marchioni.

(Reprinted in Healy and McComas, *Adventures in Time and Space.*)

Novelette. * Mystery, exploitation, and the adventures of a microman. *Time:* the interplanetary future. * A strange-looking man, who calls himself Jones, enters the laboratory of ethnologist Arthur Allison. The stranger's physical type is unusual enough—large globular, chinless head, feet with vestigial toes—that Allison takes seriously the proposition that the stranger makes. * Jones explains that Allison has been selected for a high honor on Jones's planet. where he will study applied ethnology for about four months, then will be returned unharmed, in-formed about a civilization forty thousand years ahead of Earth's. * Allison accepts, awaking later in a cell, somewhere. He sees other people of Jones's racial type, then meets a hand-some, normal young woman (Miss CB-301), who makes extraor-dinary statements. She admits, in embarrassment, that she is an almost subhuman atavist, barely able to do fourth-dimensional geometry, but that Allison must marry her. So Jones has decreed. * Miss CB-301, whom Allison calls Miss Brown, is deeply attracted to him and reveals much more than she should. Using her viewer (which she later gives to Allison), she shows

Bates, Harry (*continued*)

him his exact double entering an apparatus with an ugly woman of Jones's type, then emerging radiant with love for the woman, whom he marries. Miss Brown explains that this is the marriage machine, which makes couples fall in love. * Allison, although he does not understand what is going on, realizes that he has been tricked and that Jones means him no good. When Jones next visits him, obviously intending to submit him to the marriage machine, Allison overpowers him, takes an anaesthetic device that Jones uses, and makes his way to the spaceport. * There he sees a gigantic spaceship of familiar Earth model. He recognizes it as a well-known vessel created by the Terrestrial government for the Titans of Saturn's third moon (Tethys). Evading the guards, he sets the automatic controls for Earth. * *Background:* The Titans of Tethys, gigantic humanoid beings, have been recognized by biologists as belonging to the same stock as Earthmen, although this relationship cannot be explained. Allison has been working on a monograph about this. * After weeks of travel, the ship lands. When Allison emerges, he is almost captured by a Titan, whereupon he realizes with horror, since everything about him is gigantic, that the ship has transported him not back to Earth, but to Tethys. * But then comes enlightenment: He was wrong. He is back on Earth, in New York, and it is not his surroundings that are large, but he that is small. Fitting together what he has observed and what Miss Brown has told him, he now realizes that Jones has split him into many tiny facsimiles, 1728 in all, each of whom is to breed with a tiny woman. His myriad counterparts are busily performing their function, thanks to the marriage machine, but Allison can only imagine the worst conclusion to the situation. * Now, as a microman, he must escape. Adventures follow, in one of which Allison, to evade capture by Jones's agents, crawls into a toothpaste box and mails himself to a friend. But it is in vain. He is captured, seized by one of his 1727 counterparts, and confronted by Jones. * Jones, who is not unfriendly, explains. His people are of the same stock as Earthmen and the Titans. About forty-five thousand years ago, all lived on a great continent in the Pacific. When it sank, the Titans moved to Tethys, where they adapted by growing enormous, but declined scientifically, while Jones's people settled elsewhere (location not revealed), reduced their size to that of the tiny Allison, and continued to evolve and develop their great science. They have no interest in contacting Earthmen, but to keep their stock vital, every twenty-five years they invite a selected human male to their domain, divide him into micromen, and use him as breeding stock. After this, the visitor is reassembled and returned to Earth unharmed. * Allison, while indignant at being treated as a stud, recognizes that Jones is telling the truth and that some profit may come of the arrangement. He agrees to cease rebelling if Jones will enlarge Miss Brown and send her back to Earth with him. * Imaginative and amusing. The reader, of course, will catch on long before Allison did.

53. **ALAS, ALL THINKING.** *Astounding Stories*, June 1935. Ill. Dold.

(Reprinted in Bleiler and Dikty, *Imagination Unlimited*; in Knight, *Science Fiction of the 30's*; in Silverberg, *Arbor House Treasury;* and in Stong, *The Other Worlds*.)

Novelette. * *Time:* 1963 for the frame narrative; the undated far future for the heart of the story. * It is a notorious and sad fact that Harlan T. Frick, the greatest scientist and inventor of the

day, has abandoned research and has become a playboy. Two of his friends, Matson and Wayland, try to draw him out at a dinner, taping his conversation. The result is astonishing. After some wild comments about murder and exterminating the human race, plus a frenzied disclaimer of intelligence, Frick tells his story. * He had been working not very successfully on a time machine, when a time platform appeared in his laboratory and a young woman stepped off it. This is Pearl, as Frick calls her, a woman from the far future. Large-headed, thin and ungainly, she apparently was curious about the past and, sensing Frick's work, borrowed a time machine from a museum and came to our time. She wants to be shown around New York City, and offers a trip to the future in exchange. * As Frick soon discovers, Pearl is utterly humorless and cerebral, and at every possible occasion she squats to ponder on what has been said or is happening. For her, intellect and ensuing meditation is the ultimate in humanity, and she is distressed that New Yorkers do not practice it. She is also shocked at the hordes of people, the number of possessions, and the variety of actions. Thought alone should be enough. * Yet, though alien to us in her intellectuality, she confesses that she is atypical of her people. Something probably went wrong when they prepared her in the laboratory, and she is much more worldly than the norm. * One twentieth-century phenomenon fascinates her, though she does not understand it. This is love. She persuades Frick to undertake a mild courtship of her, while she analyzes her feelings at every step. * Frick gets his reward when Pearl takes him to her own era. He is astonished. There are no high science, no great cities, simply a collection of small, dull, dusty, dirty cubicle-buildings that contain the whole human race, all thirty-six of it. Within the cubicles are quiescent, stagnant creatures with enormous heads, some of whom have not moved for years. They simply meditate. Pearl and three others who alone are mobile tend to the automatic food machines for these thinkers. * Frick is appalled at what has happened to the human race and decides that it would be better extinct. Luck favors him when the other three mobile people die when their necks (unable to bear the weight of their great crania) snap when they see him, and he sabotages an incubator containing a couple of youngsters. This leaves only a few living fossils in their cubicles. * Pearl now makes a startling proposition. She asks Frick to mate with her. After some repugnance, he agrees, thinking that if the new people combined Pearl's intellect with his physical vigor and zest for life, it would be worthwhile, but he sets a condition: Pearl must permit him to execute the stagnant thinkers. After some reluctance she agrees, and it is done. * But Pearl now insists on being wooed in the manner of a twentieth-century novel. Frick follows her whim, but at every possible incident Pearl squats and analyzes interminably. * Frick is now worried. Taking her time machine, he explores her future. He finds that she is turning into one of the mushroom-like humans, still unable to make up her mind. He then returns to 1963, where he unburdens himself to his friends, but announces that he intends to exterminate the human race. * With Wayland and Matson he goes farther into Pearl's future, where she has degenerated totally. He snaps her neck, and the three men return to 1963, where Frick destroys the time machine. * A very interesting story, well told.

BAUER, E.
No information.

Bauer, E. (*continued*)

54. **THE FORGOTTEN WORLD**. *Amazing Stories,* August 1931. Ill. Morey.

Short story. * Time: from about 1930 to 1960 or so. *Place:* Antarctica. * Lost race. * In the early 1930s Bud Layton, a divinity student whose hobby is aviation, hopes to fly over the South Pole and join his comrades who hold the mother ship at Discovery Bay. But Layton does not arrive and is presumed dead. Thirty years later, however, the comrades receive a radio message from Layton, asking them to come and rescue him. Retrieved but dying, Layton tells his story. * While in flight, trying to avoid a storm, he flew into a warm valley that was permeated with narcotic fumes; before losing consciousness, however, he was able to land in a warm, wooded area with a small lake. * He awakens to find himself in civilized surroundings, tended by a handsome young woman named Eros, and Mada, her father, who is the chief scientist and king of the land of Noen. * Noen is truly a hermit land, for it is permeated with a peculiar gas that both vivifies the land and causes a physiological change in all who breathe it. Once breathed, it is a necessity, and one can never leave Noen. After Layton's body was retrieved, nearly dead, to save his life Mada converted him to the gas metabolism. * *Background:* Old Mada has been trying for much of his life to create an antidote to the gas, so that the surviving members of the race can leave Noen, for the people, who have both the remnants of a supercivilization and an incredibly long history, are dying out. Eros was the last birth, and in another thirty years or so the race will be extinct. * Politically, Noen is pretty much a socialist eutopia (despite the kingship), with everyone working altruistically at suitable tasks. Electricity, produced in a complex way from the habituating gas, is at the basis of Noen science, even powering the individual flap-wing flying suits the people use. Elaborate cyclopean architecture is the rule, especially for the earlier periods in Noen history when the population was larger than it has been for some time. * Layton marries Eros, who has proposed to him following the local custom, and lives happily with her as the culture collapses. As predicted, about thirty years after his arrival in the happy valley, only he, Eros, and Mada are still living, and Eros and Mada die shortly thereafter. Just before his death Mada had finally perfected his gaseous antidote, and Layton, released, but laden with sorrow, flies his old plane out of Noen. As he leaves, he sees the land collapse into volcanism, destroying everything, including the fabulous scientific records of the ages. * Layton does not live long after telling his story. * *Miscellaneous:* The civilization of Noen dates from the Tertiary Age; before the glaciers it was widespread and far higher than our present civilization. * Layton is able to understand the people of Noen, since they speak the natural language of mankind, which is universally understood. The Noenians also undoubtedly know English, since they have good radio reception, although the radiation in the surrounding mountains prohibits broadcasting signals. * A religious element enters when the Noenians wax enthusiastic about the Bible that Layton always carries in his pocket. * Too much space is devoted to describing the culture of Noen, not improving a boring, amateurish work. Probably suggested by E. Charles Vivian's *Fields of Sleep* (1923).

BAUER, GEORGE PAUL

No information. Presumably a U.S. writer. It is not clear whether this is the same person as George P. Bauer (1899-1988), a social worker at Hiram House, the first settlement house in Cleveland, Ohio. Portrait with "A Subterranean Adventure" shows a middle-aged man. Also contributed serial "Soul Mates" to *Occult Digest*.

55. **BELOW THE INFRA RED**. *Amazing Stories,* December 1927. Unsigned ill.

Novelette. * *Place:* A parallel world separated from ours by vibratory rate. * The narrator becomes acquainted with Professor Carl Winter, who reveals his discoveries. Winter theorizes that there are worlds of experience cut off from us because we cannot see infrared and lower light, or hear ultra sound. Winter has now constructed a machine that will enable himself and the narrator to witness this new world. * Seated in the apparatus, the two men see a new world, perfect-looking humans in a wonderful landscape. And then the men discover that they are in the other-world, which the professor describes as defined by a different rate of vibration. * The experimenters are welcomed by King Elolio and his sister Queen Ealara, who communicate with them telepathically. The land is a complete eutopia, almost on a fairy tale level, with absolute perfection. * There is only one problem. In addition to the beautiful blond people, there are the Pluonians, a race of dark-skinned, hairy brunettes, who are just as vicious as the Alanians as pure and good. * The Pluonians attack. Battle, however, is not physical, but chest-to-chest mental struggle of wills. The Alanians win decisively when King Elolio kills the Pluonian king in mental combat. * Matters come to a second climax when the Pluonian captives, foolishly released by the narrator, kidnap him and the queen, whom he loves. The Pluonians plan to sacrifice the narrator, and the Pluonian king means to rape the Alanian queen. All ends well, as the Alanian king rescues them via projection. * But the end comes. The narrator is embracing Queen Ealara, when he and Winter are returned to our world. An electrical storm has shorted the apparatus. Winter hopes to return to Alania, but dies. The narrator, Barton, trying to return on his own, is found dead. Perhaps he was successful? * *Miscellaneous:* Gigantic statues are used as habitations. * The Alanians have wonderful paranormal powers, including manipulation of matter in various ways. * In some manner the land of Alania is connected with our next step in spiritual progress, and may be considered a life, of a sort, after death. * As a story, pretty horrible.

56. **A SUBTERRANEAN ADVENTURE**. *Wonder Stories,* June-August 1930. Ill. Paul and Miller.

Novel. * *Place:* The Denver area and caverns below. * The narrative of a strange man who was found along the road badly beaten and cut. * Ned Gothram, the narrator, and his nephew Teddy have developed a process that disintegrates rocks—a smearing of a substance, a flash of a ray, then dust and a hard durable substance along the edges. Building an earth-borer equipped with such a disintegrator, the two men set out on their way to bore through the Earth. * All goes well for a time, but then the borer falls through air, landing in an ocean of crude oil &in a gigantic black cavern. The explorers make their way through the dark to a rock floor, then, following lights, emerge into a beautiful lighted area, green with vegetation, and with obvious evidence of civilization. * Humans with powerful artificial wings fly up to them, paralyze them with wand-like apparatus, and carry them into the city. A thought-reading device permits communication, and the explorers learn that they

Bauer, George Paul (*continued*)

will not be permitted to leave, and that their fate will be decided. * Matters follow their own course. Teddy falls in love with their language instructor Noama, the granddaughter of the governor of the area; she reciprocates; and Teddy rescues her from an assault by Sarro, the Minister of Police, who becomes an implacable enemy. * Assaults, protestations of love, death sentences, fisticuffs, imprisonments, torture, assignment to the radium mines all follow in sequence. Noama always tries to save the two men; Sarro is always felled with an honest blow; but Ned and Teddy remain prisoners or in peril. * Eventually, Ted, Ned, and Noama make their way up out of the underground land pursued by Sarro and his henchmen. Both Noama and Teddy seem to die, but the narrator, as he relates his story is not quite sure, hinting at a sequel that does not seem to have been published. * *Miscellaneous:* The Inner People bored their way into the Earth's caverns about two hundred million years ago when the sun exploded, burning off the crust of the then larger Earth. At the time there were also two moons, one of which was destroyed. Life arose again on the outside, following the same patterns as before, with dinosaurs, etc.; some of the Inner People emerged and became our ancestors. They degenerated so much, however, that the Inner People sealed themselves in away from them. As a result of this history, there are motion pictures of dinosaurs and other historical curiosities. * Junky and cliched, heavily based on Bulwer-Lytton's *The Coming Race*. Of no value.

BEARDEN, JACK O.
No information.

   57. **THE NOTORIOUS "C39."**   *Amazing Stories,* November 1933.
Short-short story. * *Time:* the interplanetary future. *Place:* the Earth-Mars run. * Space policeman William 25E48 has been assigned to capture the great criminal known as C39, reported to be on board the spaceship *Tellurian* in disguise. The identity of this person is known only from a scrap of paper indicating an identification tattoo of C39. There are three possibilities on board. Williams picks the wrong one, but does manage to capture the real criminal, whose social deviance is removed by surgical means. * The story concludes with a trick ending, but the reader is not likely to be impressed with it.

BEATTIE, GEORGE B.
An announcement in the October 1930 issue of Gernsback's *Amazing Detective Tales* refers to Beattie as "one of [England's] foremost writers." No books were published under Beattie's name, and he is not listed in British biographical dictionaries of authors. Allowing for Gernsbackian hyperbole, it is possible that Beattie wrote for periodicals. Portrait printed with "The Murders on the Moon Ship" shows a middle-aged man. In the 1950s a George Burnet Beattie, who was associated with the Brewers' Society and the National Association of Soft Drinks Manufacturers, Ltd., wrote two trade publications. It is not clear whether this person is the present author.

   58. **THE MARTIAN NEMESIS.** *Wonder Stories Quarterly,* Winter 1931. Ill. Marchioni.
Short story. * *Time:* the near future. *Place:* mostly Mars. * The great explorer Sir Stewart Knightlow has just died and is about to be buried with great honors in Westminster Abbey. His lawyer reads a document left by Sir Stewart. * Knightlow and

Ray Browne, a younger man, are in love with Mary, who seems to have settled on Ray. Knightlow is bitter and jealous. When the first expedition to Mars leaves, both men are among the party, Ray having been shamed into going by Mary's father. * Mars, the explorers discover, is tolerable for Earthmen; the atmosphere, though thin, has a high oxygen component that renders it adequate. The landscape includes various sorts of xerophytic vegetation, and small wildlife abounds. Occasional ruins are to be seen, but there is no indication of what happened to their builders, who are obviously extinct. Exploration is at first uneventful, though there is considerable tension between Ray and Stewart. * An enormous environmental change comes, however, when polar melt water fills the canals and the vegetation revives, much as desert vegetation does on Earth. And now the horrors begin. Martian vegetation is lethal. Some plants are so poisonous that touching them causes a horrible death; others shoot poisoned spines; and still others, somewhat parallel to pitcher plants on Earth, lure their prey to themselves. The plants thus feed on animal life, which supplies the chemical additives the soil lacks. It is no longer a mystery what happened to the Martians. * In a very short time, the members of the expedition have all died horribly except Ray and Stewart, who fly back to Earth. They land in a desert area (not precisely located) and undergo great hardships. The two men disagree bitterly, with Ray revealing that he has long known about Stewart's love for Mary, for Stewart talks in his sleep. During the ensuing quarrel, Stewart kills Ray with a shovel. * Stewart is rescued, but he has lost his mind, and for a long time has no memory whatever of his experiences on Mars or in the Terrestrial desert. Now a great hero, raised to a baronetcy, he marries Mary, and they have a son. But fate catches up with Sir Stewart. His wife Mary leaves him when she learns from his sleep talking that he killed Ray. And Mary and Stewart's small son is killed by a Martian plant that sprouted from Ray's burial place. At this, Stewart's memory returns. * The lawyer destroys Sir Stewart's manuscript describing these events. * *Miscellaneous:* The spaceship travels by "quantum control." * Good detail on Mars and a convincing British setting. All in all not a bad story if one overlooks the plot clichés.

   59. **THE MURDERS ON THE MOON SHIP.** *Wonder Stories,* February 1931. Ill. Wilson.
Novelette. * *Time:* the twenty-first century. *Place:* a space trip to the Moon. * A more or less conventional detective story of the period, complete with red herrings, clues, and suspects. Concerned are a group of about twenty people including a well-known scientist, a mild scientific crank, a mysterious sinister Frenchman, two female twins, and others. Corpse after corpse is found, and there is a suspicion that a Borgia-type ring is involved, for some victims seem to have been stung to death. * Suspicion shifts from person to person until the real culprit is identified. * Ethically, one should not reveal solutions of such stories, but there is little likelihood that any reader of this book will read Beattie's story. The killer was a poisonous winged reptilian of great geological age that had been in suspended animation in a fossiliferous piece of rock that the professor was transporting. * Routine. * The story was originally scheduled for the November 1930 issue of *Amazing Detective Tales.*

   60. **THE MAN WHO SHRANK.** *Wonder Stories,* April 1932. Ill. Paul.
Short story. * *Time:* the near future. *Place:* mostly an island in

Beattie, George B. (*continued*)

the South Pacific. * This is the narrative of the scientific detective Li Phou Lee, whose name is probably meant to be a humorous touch. * In college, Lee knew the eccentric James Lombard, who flunked his medical exams miserably. At the time Lombard spoke wildly of the limitations of medical science and of what he would accomplish by himself. * Many years later, when Lee is tracking down the murderer Zela (who can be identified by missing toes and teeth), he encounters Lombard on a small, little known island in the South Pacific. Lombard, an unpleasant, arrogant, brutal man, has accomplished a great deal. He has devised a protective agent against a particularly horrible Oceanic boil; has built a projector that controls the weather and ultraviolet apparatus that grows vegetables in small fractions of their usual ripening period; and has perfected a way to transplant lobster glands to humans, permitting organ regeneration. Indeed, Lombard has grown fingers that he lost while at college and has also grown toes and teeth onto the criminal Zela, thus making identification impossible. Lombard refuses to surrender Zela, and Lee leaves the island with only a confession that he managed to tape on a dummy snuff box. * Police routine is slow, and it is weeks before Lee can return (by sea, since the senior police officer suffers from air sickness), and the situation is changed. Lombard's corpse lies dead in his rooms; the natives that Lombard had practically enslaved and used brutally have fled; and the island is half overgrown with gigantic vegetation. * The mysterious point is that Lombard's corpse continues to shrink; from that of a tall man to the size of a child. * Lee has a solution that is corroborated when they find Lombard's secret laboratory, where he created freaks. Among them are a gorilla with lobster-claws instead of hands, a mouse the size of a bear, and many other monsters. And then Lombard's murderer is captured: a tiny man, less than a foot high. * The little man tells his story: A circus dwarf, he had been kidnapped by Zela and treated by Lombard who shrank him still more. He escaped, however, hid, and inoculated Lombard with the shrinking serum. * As Lee now explains: Lombard had discovered how to remove the space between atomic particles, thus creating tiny creatures. He then sold his monsters and dwarfs to circuses. Lee, after some study, discovers how to reverse Lombard's process. * *Miscellaneous:* Rocket planes are a common means of travel. * An entertaining story.

61. **THE "PLATINUM PLANETS."** *Wonder Stories*, August, 1932. Ill. Paul.

Short story. The paper chase. * *Time:* the fiftieth century, with a prologue in the thirty-first century. *Place:* Earth and Jupiter. * The first man to visit every planet in the solar system was the great sculptor Greatorex XIX 32, who spent years on this quest. As an artistic record for each planet he selected a suitable material and carved a suitable symbol. For example, for Mars, he carved a granite group of man-ants and called it Cunning, and for Pluto, a flat disc-like object representing amoeboid life, calling it Sloth. * When he returned to Earth, however, he found that there had been great race wars, in which his family had been killed. Kidnapping the African crown prince whose country was responsible for the deaths, Greatorex tortured him to death, and from his thigh bone carved Slaughter, a symbol for Earth. * Greatorex then plated his carvings with platinum and flew off into space, thence was lost to history. * Over the centuries the so-called Platinum Planets were choice collectors' items, so

fabulously expensive that they became synonymous with impossibility. According to legend, there is also a curse on them, that the nine Planets cannot be assembled without tragedy befalling their owner. * After a disastrous war, date not provided, the millionaire Pascal, then holder of the set, came to the conclusion that the curse could be dispelled by returning each piece to its native planet. He blasted off with the extraterrestrial Planets, planning to restore them to their homes. What happened to him and the Planets is not definitely known, but he is believed to have died in a storm on Jupiter. * In the fiftieth century the multibillionaire radium mogul Jackthorpe R/43, bored with having done all that life expects of him, hears the legend of the Platinum Planets and decides to search for them. After considerable investigation, the only lead, from Neptunians, is that the Planets are on Jupiter where they are worshipped by the savage inhabitants. * Using Io as a staging area, Jackthorpe's enormous spaceship, the *Asteroid*, descends to Jupiter. By chance the ship lands near a row of statues, which are gold-plated corpses, sacred as cult objects. * A confrontation with the natives follows, but Jackthorpe, using a thought transmitter, reads from native minds that the Planets are maintained in a shrine on the other side of Jupiter, together with the gold-plated corpses of Pascal and his crew. As the Earthmen blast off to fly to the shrine, they witness a horrible aspect of Jupiter. The crust is so thin above a viscous substratum that the ship's rockets blast it away, swamping the natives. * Proceeding to the shrine, Jackthorpe flies down alone and retrieves the eight non-terrestrial Planets, having previously sent the priests away with the thought control projector. As the *Asteroid* leaves, with Pascal's gold-covered corpse on board, the concussion of its rocket blasts drives Pascal's ancient spaceship down into the viscous subsurface of the planet. The return voyage to Earth is disastrous, what with accidents and air leaks. Indeed, the surviving explorers are in a frozen coma when they are found, and are revived with difficulty. Is it the curse of the Planets? * Time passes, during which Jackthorpe exhausts every possible source of information in order to locate Slaughter, which is presumably on Earth, left behind by Pascal. The solution to the problem comes when an advanced thought probe reads Pascal's dead brain, Slaughter, or Earth, thanks to a succession of circumstances, was also on the ancient spaceship in a secret compartment. Jackthorpe returns to Jupiter, hoping to salvage the sunken vessel, but he is too late. The space pirate Namur has beaten him to the goal and has taken the statue. But all ends well, and the curse seems to be dead. * *Miscellaneous:* Longevity is now six or seven hundred years. * Rocket shoes serve for propulsion. * The gravity on Jupiter is heavy, but Earthmen can tolerate it and move about. * The natives of Jupiter, who have a primitive culture, are humanoid, but taller and broader than men. What with the heavy gravity and thick atmosphere, they move very slowly. * Not a bad story, but one thinks with regret what Jack Vance could have done with the concept. * The story is also carried as "The Platinum Planets" and "The Platinum 'Planets.'"

BEAUMONT, DAVID H.

U.S. writer, then resident in South Euclid, Ohio.

62. **WHEN THE CYCLE MET.** *Astounding Stories*, November 1935. Ill. Marchioni.

Short-short story. * *Time:* the far future, when the sun is old and

Beaumont, David H. (*continued*)

dim. Mankind still exists on Earth, but is concentrated in nine giant dome-cities. Native races dwell on the other planets. * Danger is imminent. The planets are disappearing, and according to calculations, Earth and the sun should perish in a very short time. * The time comes. The sun disappears, and Earth undergoes a period of darkness. Then there is light. The sun is back, but shining with a brilliance long forgotten. The other planets, too, suddenly appear. * As explained, it is all a matter of time, which is circular like space. A cycle has been completed, and all is new again. In some fashion this seems to be connected with periods of glaciation. * Below routine, with confused exposition.

BECK, CLYDE F. (1912-1985)

U.S. (Nevada, California) fan, writer, brother of Claire P. Beck. Book *Hammer and Tongs* (Lakeport, California: Futile Press, 1937), reprinting material from the *Science Fiction Critic*, is probably the first book devoted to genre criticism. Beck wrote two other stories, "Anastomosis" (*Startling Stories,* November 1947) and "Collision Orbit" (*Planet Stories,* Summer 1950).

    63. **WHEN THE MOONS MET!** *Wonder Stories,* August 1930.

Short story. * Second-prize winner in the contest based on the cover of the February 1930 issue of *Air Wonder Stories.* Mr. Beck won seventy-five dollars * *Place:* an unidentified planetary system containing three small planets with apparently highly irregular orbits. The natives of Iona, who may be human or humanoid, have mounted the first exploratory space expedition, two ships of which are to explore the world known as Karkor. * It seems empty, but the explorers spy a dome, from which emerges a horde of small humanoid creatures in individual flying suits/machines. They waste no time in parleying with the friendly Ionans, but immediately attack with disintegrators. The two Ionan ships are brought down. * Malben, trapped in the wreckage of the Ionan ship, realizes that if the Karkorians learn the secret of interplanetary flight, they will invade Iona. He manages to hold off the ferocious natives long enough to fix and activate the ship's gravity unit; this provides enough thrust to push the small planet into the orbit of the third world, which is empty. Iona is thus saved. * Juvenilia.

BECKWITH, O. L.

In 1930, per letter, a resident of Ovid, Mich. No other information, except that portrait shows a young man. Contributed "Winged Death" to *Amazing Detective Tales* (September 1930).

    64. **THE ROBOT MASTER.** *Air Wonder Stories,* October 1929. Ill. Paul.

Short story. * *Time:* 1965. *Place:* New York and an artificial island in the Atlantic. * New York 1965 is the embodiment of a flying culture. Planes are everywhere, private, public, flying from level to level of the complex building system, and all noiseless. The air above the city is divided into zones, the highest of which, above five thousand meters, is restricted to official use. Mail planes fly through it at 700 MPH. An official, the Director, sits up on the high level in his helicopter-plane, enforcing the regulations. On the present occasion the Director is Arnld [*sic*] Benning. * Five ships approach, signal to Benning; one comes close, and two iron figures, obviously

robots, leap into his plane and seize him. After this, the five planes proceed to bomb New York, destroying buildings and bridges, killing about three million people. * Arnld awakens to find himself captive on a secret artificial island. Placed handy for his perusal are old newspaper clippings about his uncle, Hyle L. Benning, who has been estranged from Arnld's branch of the family. Decades ago Professor Benning, a pioneer in robot work, claimed to have worked out systems for unitary control of many robots doing multiple tasks. He was ridiculed, and in 1950 was sent into exile by the World Council of Seven. Since then he has disappeared, after vowing revenge. * Professor Benning, an evil little man, now makes his presence known to Arnld. Since he feels some family sentiment, he offers Arnld the succession to his forthcoming world empire, if Arnld will join him. Professor Benning intends to send out his robot fleets in a few minutes to bomb the world's capitals in revenge for the slight that has been inflicted upon him. After this he will be emperor of the world. * Arnld refuses the offer, and the vicious old man would have killed him had Arnld not evaded the robots and leaped overboard into the sea. But Arnld climbs back out of the sea onto the artificial island and smashes in his uncle's skull with a handy metal rod. He then disables the switch for the master apparatus that controls the robot forces.

    65. **THE HEAT RAY**. *Air Wonder Stories,* April 1930. Ill. Paul.

Short story. * *Time:* 1938-1940. *Place:* mostly Southern Illinois. * When old Anton Babel develops a heat ray, the consequences are tragic—the accidental maiming and death of his assistant. In a panic Babel flies to California, to consult with his college student son Anton, Jr. Along the way, while passing through Chicago, Babel drops a paper with specifications of the ray. This paper comes into the hands of a gangster overlord (John Merton Graves), who kills the elder Babel and, with the aid of a crooked scientist, constructs heat ray apparatus that are fitted on planes. By 1940 Graves has established a band of desperate men who hijack planes and rob them. * Young Anton Babel, who witnessed his father's murder, tracks down Graves and is eventually responsible for his death. Young Anton then destroys the heat ray apparatus and his father's notes and diagrams. The discovery, which is lost, was a matter of mirrors and prisms concentrating sunlight so greatly that it approximated the internal heat of the sun. * Amateurish and a very bad job. * The title is also given as "The Heat-Ray."

BELL, EARL L[EASTON]

U.S. (Augusta, Georgia) newspaperman. The author's name is spelled Earle on the cover of the magazine. Bell also had two stories in *Weird Tales,* "Doctor DeBruce" (February 1924) and "The Land of Lur" (May 1930). Coauthor of excellent *The Augusta Chronicle, Indomitable Voice of Dixie* (University of Georgia, 1960). The implication is that the following stories are immature work.

    66. **THE MOON OF DOOM**. *Amazing Stories Quarterly,* Winter 1928. Ill. Paul.

Novelette. * *Time:* A.D. 2009. *Place:* the Earth variously and the Moon. * The Earth is now a near eutopia. Wars, disease, and want have been abolished. Science and technology have advanced greatly. With the discovery of atomic power, earlier sources of energy like steam and electricity have practically vanished. Great flying machines called atomotors ply the air. *

Bell, Earl L. (*continued*)

Catastrophe! The brilliant young Professor Sherard has discovered that the Moon is changing its orbit and is approaching Earth; it will strike in about six months. His explanation for the phenomenon is that the waste from atomic motors has produced an impenetrable belt of magnetism around the Earth, which belt, by affecting the tides, has changed the Moon's orbit. The governments of the world immediately ban all atomic motors, but it is too late. * As the Moon draws closer, millions of people die in natural catastrophes; glaciers creep down from the poles and render much of the world uninhabitable; civilization collapses; and mankind seems doomed. * When the Moon is about sixty-five thousand miles away, Sherard makes another announcement. Since the Moon is now drawing away the Earth's atmosphere, it should soon be habitable, whereas the Earth will become uninhabitable. Sherard urges people to fly their atomotors to the Moon; there should be enough air in space to support flight. * Altogether, about two hundred and fifty men and women fly to the Moon, where the experiences of Ernest and Mildred become central. Evidences of a former intelligent Lunar life are all around them, and Professor Burke succeeds in deciphering inscriptions that the Lunarians left. It seems that they were somewhat insectlike, and worshipped a hermaphroditic god, whom the Earthmen call He-She. In the lunar temples idols of He-She pounded victims to death with a mallet; indeed, this is the fate that befalls Professor Burke, when he, Ernest, and Mildred are trapped in such a temple. * The Moon starts to recede from Earth, and it becomes obvious, since the Earth has flipped over with a new axis, that the polar regions should be habitable. Ernest and Mildred will return to Earth as a new Adam and Eve, since all the other Earth people on the Moon have been accidentally killed. * Pretty bad. It is surprising that Gernsback would print this as the lead story in a new magazine.

67. **THE YOUNG OLD MAN.** *Amazing Stories*, September 1929. Ill. Briggs.

Short story. * *Place:* the Ozarks. * In the frame situation the two young campers meet the strange country storekeeper Clinton Fancher. He is obviously educated, reads a book written in Medieval Latin, and looks about 45 years old, except for his eyes, which are indescribably ancient. Indeed, the campers hear, he often wears black glasses to conceal them. * The young men next hear that Fancher is dead, and after the inquest they read a farewell note that Fancher left to a friend. * Fancher (1269-1926) was dying of tuberculosis when he sought the help of a famous monk who was said to have discovered an elixir of immortality. The monk at first refused to help him, then yielded, connecting him to an electric apparatus that he said held the fluid of life. Fancher recovered and has wandered and lived since, but he considers immortality a curse, as the monk, obviously Roger Bacon, told him. Fancher committed suicide in despair. * Negligible.

BELL, STANLEY D.

No information. Portrait accompanying story shows a middle-aged man.

68. **MARTIAN GUNS.** *Wonder Stories*, January 1932. Ill. Paul.

Short story. * *Time:* 1947. *Place:* mostly in space and on the Moon. * The *Flame* with its eight-man crew (and one female stowaway, Nina Wingate) is off to the Moon on the first space voyage. The takeoff is reasonably realistic. But then, when the rocket is away from Earth on its way to the Moon, David Halliday, the leader of the expedition, makes an announcement. * Exploration and glory are not the only reasons for the lunar voyage. Halliday has evidence that persons on the Moon, probably Martians, are starting a systematic bombardment of Earth with giant bombs. The bombs have started to fall, and observations have shown strange lights on the Moon. The other members of the expedition receive this information with varying degrees of skepticism. * Landing on the Moon and exploring in space suits, the Terrestrials encounter the enemy, who are Martians. There is a shoot-out between Earth rifles and Martian heat rays, with the Martians winning, the Earthmen being either killed or captured. * Meanwhile, back on Earth, the bombardment is taking effect and being recognized for what it really is. Wingate, Halliday's prospective father-in-law and sponsor, manages to convince the world as to what is happening, and a fleet of rocket ships is built for a Lunar invasion. * Time passes. * The bombardment increases, with a giant shell every two hours or so. The Earth fleet has established itself on the Moon, and picks up Halliday and Miss Wingate, who have escaped captivity. * The battle for the Moon begins, but does not go too favorably for the Terrestrial forces, for the Martian heat ray is more effect than explosive weapons. And the shells continue to pour down on Earth. * Finally, the former captives, who know Martian psychology, suggest destroying the giant Martian cannon. Losing this will damage Martian morale so much that the war will be over. This is done with a suicide mission. * *Miscellaneous:* The Martians, who are tall and green, but otherwise human or humanoid, wish to settle Earth, since their own planet is dying. * Routine or a little less.

BENEDICT, JERRY

According to Schwartz/Weisinger the pseud. of Jerome Barry (1894-1975), author of mysteries including *Murder with Your Malted* (1941), *Lady of Night* (1944), and others.

69. **THE BRONZE DOOR.** *Amazing Stories,* May 1933. Ill. Morey.

Short story. * Jack Wells, a junior engineer in Combined Electric, works in an office outside the bronze door. The door, which is something of a symbol of high advancement, seals off from the bull pen the working place of Reycraft, the top flight man in the establishment and the office of the magnate himself, P. L. Landon. * Jack, who is both ambitious and imaginative, confides his hopes of advancement to his wife. And then when Reycraft runs amok in the office, Jack gets his chance. He is advanced to the inner sanctum, where he works under the eye of the magnate himself. * Jack fulfills his promise, but something is wrong. He is under stress and is obviously on the edge of a breakdown. Fortified with the suspicions of his wife, Jack investigates and discovers that all his predecessors have come to bad ends. Artificial fever, created by Landon himself, has been overstimulating them all. * Jack and his wife confront the wicked capitalist, and in the inevitable fisticuffs (in which Jack pummels Landon) Landon is accidentally burned to a crisp electrically. Mrs. Wells saves the situation for her husband by wiping out fingerprints. * Below routine, more suited to a lower grade non-s-f pulp than here.

BENTLEY, GARTH (1903-1956)

U.S. (mostly Chicago) author, editor. Graduate of Northwestern

Bentley, Garth (*continued*)

University. Associated with furniture and interior decorating field, where edited basic books, notably *The Seng Handbook.* Founder and first president of the International Council of Industrial Editors. Author of *How to Edit an Employee Publication* and several poetry collections.

70. **REBELLION—5000 A.D.!** *Wonder Stories*, July 1931. Ill. Marchioni.

Novelette. * *Time:* mostly at A.D. 5000. *Place:* the Chicago area. * In our time, Professor Crewe, who is developing a straight-line radio broadcast that is carried by an electric current, asks his friend the narrator to help in the first full-scale test. * The narrator pulls the switch at the proper time and awakens on a grassy hill. A group of strangely dressed people greet him and urge him to make a speech. He reluctantly declares, "A new age is coming," which is received with great enthusiasm. He is then spirited away from the group on a small but rapid plane into the titanic city of Chicago. * Historical and geographical background: Civilization continued to advance after the twentieth century, but in the twenty-seventh century a world war wiped out most of the human race. After this, the nations started to rebuild, but around 2900 a series of natural catastrophes began: Tidal waves swept the Earth, most of Europe sank into the sea, as did the eastern part of the United States; the rest of the world was hard-hit, but two new lands arose, Lemuria in the Pacific and ancient Atlantis in the Atlantic. Most of the world relapsed into savagery, but by A.D. 4000, civilization had arisen again. * In the present world of A.D. 5000 the total population of America, apart from a few insignificant groups, is concentrated in five enormous cities: Chicago, and future versions of St. Paul, Des Moines, Winnipeg, and Lansing. What is going on in the rest of the world is not clear, for exploratory expeditions are not welcomed. * Socially and politically: What with the rise of the new society after the catastrophes, industrial and economic magnates gradually have taken everything, with the result that a hereditary council of twelve owns almost the entire five cities. There is a very small middle class that has managed to hold onto a little, but almost the entire population is like helots. The economy is in some degree socialistic, with everyone receiving food, shelter, and medical treatment, but there are no liberties, and controls are strict. The force arm of the council is a band of aerial police who have short-range disabling or death ray weapons. * Among the malcontents has arisen a cult that expects salvation from a hero from the past, much as in Wells's *When the Sleeper Wakes.* And our friend the narrator has fallen into that slot. * At first unwilling, he gradually allows himself to be taken over by the underground after a premature revolt is bloodily crushed. Since there are no private weapons, he supervises the manufacture of riot guns with steel pellet ammunition. * This ready, his forces challenge the oligarchy and defeat its police army. A conference is held. The oligarchy is willing to deal, even surrender, but it asks for a plebescite over the two modes of the life. The narrator agrees, against the counsel of the underground leaders, and the oligarchy proceeds to flood the land with propaganda. During the election, the narrator's party loses badly, and the oligarchic council regains control. After this debacle, the narrator and about fifteen thousand recalcitrants leave and fly to unoccupied Atlantis, where they will form a new culture. * *Miscellaneous:* A romance is also involved. * There is strict birth control. * Better in

summary than as a story.

71. **BEYOND THE STAR CURTAIN.** *Wonder Stories*, October 1931. Ill. Marchioni.

Short story. * *Time:* the interplanetary future and the far future. * Verne and Derek, two brilliant young scientists, construct a powerful spaceship and decide to explore the Coal Sack. After a long journey, they pass through the Coal Sack, finding a very different universe on the other side. They spend some time with a lethargic people (undescribed) there, but yearn for Earth and start back home. * When they arrive, however, they find a surprising planet, overgrown and tropical, with insects the size of horses and elephants and a few humans who have reverted to primitive life. Since the women are attractive, the young men decide to stay and try to refound civilization. In any case, they have nowhere else to go. * Relativistic concerns are ignored, and the story is presented somewhat like a science-fantasy. * Not very good.

BERLOW, SIDNEY D.

American chemist, then resident in Ithaca, New York. Portrait shows a middle-aged man.

72. **THE CRYSTAL EMPIRE.** *Wonder Stories*, January 1932. Ill. Paul.

Short story. * *Time:* Perhaps the end of the twentieth century; the date 1942 is mentioned as in the past. *Place:* New Mexico and the Southwest. * The area around Attica, New Mexico, is suddenly flooded with a poisonous gas that spreads rapidly. The death toll is heavy, and the authorities are at a loss as to who is responsible and what to do about it. * Don Brink, a brilliant young scientist, has a theory. Calling to mind an old geographical article that described a cave near Attica with a strange crystalline life, he decides to investigate the cave. Luck is with him for a short time, for he gathers up small, crystalline life-forms, which he delivers to his helicopter pilot for transfer to the great scientist Dr. Ellis. On entering the cave again, however, Brink is paralyzed by a ray and captured by a gigantic silicon creature. * He awakens as a captive of the crystal beings and is taken before their ruler, who manipulates an enormous computerized (my term) visual panel controlling the silicon creatures that are now invading the outside world. * Imprisoned, Brink escapes, wanders about, then. finding himself near the control room, crashes in and in a battle kills the silicon ruler. * Meanwhile, on the outside, Dr. Ellis, displaying the silicon life that Brink brought out of the cave, finally convinces the authorities what is happening. * In a fairly short time the U.S. Army and the silicon forces are locked in battle over much of the Southwest. The army holds the silicon beings, but it is close, and the struggle might go either way—when suddenly the silicon forces begin to withdraw, back to the original cave. When Brink killed the silicon ruler, he seems to have destroyed the silicon will to fight. * Of no particular interest.

BERNAL, A[RTHUR] W[ILLIAM] (1913-1991)

U.S. writer. Then resident in Oakland, California. Graduate of University of California, Berkeley. Later radio script writer. Bernal also wrote four stories that appeared in *Weird Tales* during this period. These included two novels "Vampires of the Moon" (1934) and "Satan in Exile" (1935). Two additional science-fiction stories appeared in *Amazing Stories* in 1940 and 1941. Later resident in New York City area, food and restaurant

Bernal, A. W. (*continued*)

critic for New York *Daily News,* WNCN-FM, and elsewhere under pseud. Stendahl.

73. **COSMIC MENACE.** *Amazing Stories Quarterly,* Summer 1931. Ill. Morey.

Short story. * *Time:* the interplanetary future. * *Background:* Earth has a planetary government. Venus is inhabited by furry men; Mars, by squat and spongy men. Mars is completely encased in a transparent dome, while Earth and Venus have domed cities. All three worlds are united in an alliance. Out beyond Pluto is another planet, Capjadista, but it plays no part in the story. * A vast cloud of cosmic dust and debris is approaching the solar system, and there seems to be no defense against it. As it approaches Mars, it crushes in the protective dome, killing the Martians, and similarly destroys Venus. Earth, on the other side of the sun, will be next. The result of this devastation is war, as early refugees from the now uninhabitable planets try to reach Earth. * At a meeting of the Earth council a Martian scientist suggests a plan: Remove Earth from its orbit and find a new star away from the dust. His plan is accepted. Giant gyroscopes are placed at the poles, and an enormous atomic explosion in Brazil will send the planet off. * The planet moves satisfactorily, and despite a small brush with an arm of the dust leaves the solar system. Heat from the atomic site and new discoveries preserve underground life on Earth as mankind seeks a new star. * Very overwritten with purple apostrophes and exclamation points.

74. **DRAUGHT OF IMMORTALITY**. *Amazing Stories,* December 1935. Ill. Morey.

Short story. * *Place:* England. * The narrator, while undertaking repairs on his ancestral home, comes into possession of a small casket that a workman found buried in a wall. In it is a Latin manuscript written by the narrator's ancestor, the notorious thirteenth-century magician Munster. * Munster claims to have discovered an elixir of life, which he has taken. He found it extraordinarily difficult to prepare, however, and his attempts to duplicate his first dose were failures. Thus, when he wanted to save the life of his beloved wife, he was too late; she died before he could produce a second dose. Now immortal, he writes, he considers the elixir a curse and cannot deplore its existence enough. Nevertheless, he is enclosing a little flask of the potion, which he urges the reader not to drink. * The narrator, after considerable shilly-shallying, drinks the elixir, whereupon Munster himself knocks on his door. Munster reproves him, and tells him again that immortality is a curse. By now the narrator has come to agree. * But then he awakens. He did not drink the elixir, which is still at hand, and Munster did not appear. This much was a dream. He discards the elixir. * Extremely amateurish.

BERTIN, JOHN

Occasional contributor to the pulp magazines. According to Clute and Nicholls, pseud. of Giovanni Bertignono (1904-1963), U.S. author born in Italy. Posthumous publications *The Pyramids from Space* (1970) and *The Interplanetary Adventurers* (1970), issued as by Bertin, were written, possibly from Bertin's Nachlass, by Peter B. Germano, the executor of Bertin's estate. See also the collaboration Edward Morris and John Bertin.

75. **BROOD OF HELIOS.** *Wonder Stories,* May-July 1932. Ill. Paul.

(Reprinted in book form by Arcadia House, New York, 1966.) Novel. * *Time:* About four million years in the future, although the characters do not know this until nearly the end of the story. * All in all, derivative of George Allan England's *Darkness and Dawn.* * When Professor George Meredith sets off his experiment for crystallizing atomic systems, he establishes in effect a time stasis for those within reach of his rays: himself, his beautiful daughter Ruth, her friend Gregory, and Harvard football star Alan Deneen. * They all awaken in the unchanged laboratory, but outside are enormous mountains and rubble. In the sky are two suns, a red one and a blue one; the climate is hot; and, as they soon discover, there are strange non-protoplasmic plants and animals. Their early conclusion is that somehow they have been transported to another world. * They wander about for a time, occasionally seeing great silvery rocket ships traversing the sky. When one lands nearby, Gregory and Professor Meredith are taken on board, apparently captured. * It is now up to Deneen and Ruth to survive in the wilderness. Fighting their way through the non-protoplasmic life, which is usually vicious but weak, they make their way to an area where there is normal terrestrial wildlife, deer and wolves. Now skin-clad, the two make their way to the north, since this is where the airships go. As Deneen and Ruth move along they are bothered by strange mental sensations, as if someone is trying to communicate with them. * The two explorers come upon a crashed silver ship, near which are several corpses, human but different from ordinary mankind. And then they are attacked by a horde of savage submen with stone weapons. * Deneen figures out how to fly the ship, and the explorers take off. Another silver ship appears, bespeaks them telepathically, and signals them to follow. They arrive at a wonderful supercity that is inhabited by the strange people. Professor Meredith and Gregory have been living there as guests and have been trying to reach Deneen and Ruth telepathically, whence their mental sensations. * Meredith explains. Cosmological and anthropological background: About four million years earlier a strange sun invaded the solar system, disrupting the planets, and carrying away with it Earth and Moon, but driving the Moon much closer to Earth. The results were cataclysmic upheavals and destruction. After things settled, some native life began to spread again, while the non-protoplasmic life evolved. The human race, finding Earth no longer habitable, migrated to the Moon, where it developed into the strange people that use the silver airships. The Lunarians, who continued to advance culturally, abandoned speech and became totally telepathic. They also became totally quietistic and pacifist. * Some time ago, exact date not specified, the Lunarians found it necessary to return to Earth, where they encountered a new problem: Over the millennia they had exiled criminal types to Earth, where they multiplied enormously, forming the hordes of savages that attacked Ruth and Deneen. These savages, who are subnormal mentally, desperately hate the Lunarians and are determined to exterminate them; the helpless Lunarians cannot defend themselves in the slightest degree. * It looks as if the Lunarians (and the twentieth-century people) will be exterminated, but all is saved. Meredith develops a death ray in the nick of time, and Deneen destroys the god the savages worship—George Washington's head from Mount Rushmore, transported by the various diastrophisms—by crashing an airship into it. Completely demoralized, the savages flee. By now Meredith and Gregory

Bertin, John (*continued*)

(who really served no purpose) are dead, and it is up to Deneen and Ruth to restore *Homo sapiens sapiens* and to care for the surviving moon people. * The story reads better in summary than it really is. Immature work.

BINDER, EANDO

Joint pseud. for this period of Otto Oscar Binder (1911-1975) and Earl Andrew Binder (1904-1965). Earl Binder was born in Austria; his name seems originally to have been Andreas Binder. The family came to the United States around 1910, and Otto was born in Bessemer, Michigan. * Midwestern (Chicago) authors, although Otto was a resident of New York City for much of our period. While exact circumstances of writing are not known for individual stories, Otto seems to have been the senior partner. Earl Binder dropped away from fantastic fiction in 1940, and later stories published as by Eando Binder were the work of Otto Binder alone. Otto, who had attended Northwestern University and the University of Chicago, worked as a librarian before becoming a freelance writer. * Otto Binder also used the personal pseuds. Gordon A. Giles, John Coleridge, and Dean D. O'Brien, as well as the house pseud. Will Garth. In later years he edited and later published the magazine *Space World* and wrote a syndicated newspaper column. From 1939 to the late 1960s he was active in the comic book world; he was the leading script writer for *Captain Marvel* and also did many *Superman* scripts. * Eando Binder was a prolific author during the late 1930s and 1940s, his most popular work being the Adam Link stories (about a sentient, sometimes sentimentalized robot) and the Anton Yorke sequence (about an immortal superscientist and his wife). As a writer, Eando (regardless of which Binders were involved) brought some imagination to background in early stories, despite weakness in writing technique; in later work this imagination was lost. All in all, Eando Binders was a competent purveyor of pulp adventure, of no great historical or critical importance. * See also #1810, "The Hormone Menace" and #1811 "Static."

   76. **THE FIRST MARTIAN**. *Amazing Stories*, October 1932. Ill. Morey.

Short story. * *Time:* 1978-1981. *Place:* mostly Minnesota. * The beginning of this totally confused story consists of a three-page exposition of the history of isotopic research, culminating in the discovery by Professor Svens of not only new isotopes, but element 85. This resulted in the development of atomic energy. * In 1978 the first interplanetary contact took place when a Martian spaceship crashed in Minnesota. Privately built, it is later learned, it used a crude form of atomic energy. The dead Martian pilot seems to have been human or humanoid. * In 1981 a double interplanetary contact takes place. Dr. Svens's spaceship leaves for Mars, passing en route a Martian spaceship, neither knowing of the other's presence. Both ships land safely, and Svens return to Earth before the Martians leave. This is the beginning of relations between Mars and Earth. * Of no interest whatever, except possibly as an early unsuccessful attempt at hard science-fiction, as opposed to the soft science-fiction Eando Binder would later write.

   77. **THE MOON MINES**. *Wonder Stories*, April 1933. Ill. Paul.

Short story. * *Time:* the interplanetary future. *Place:* mostly on the Moon. * *Background:* The Earth has become the United Socialistic Republic, a somewhat repressive, if paternalistic state. Among its organs is the S.I.S. (Special Investigation Service), which is a secret police of incredible probity. Richard Harrington, who in earlier ages might have become a pirate or soldier of fortune, has been placed by the compulsory classification tests in the S.I.S., where he is a valued operative. * After a territorial war between Earth and Mars, both planets agreed to keep the Moon open, available for limited development, with mining rights much like those of the American Old West. Claims (mostly to radioactive minerals and platinum) can be filed with each planet, priority being the deciding factor in case of dispute. Special investigators check claims. As for Martians, they are humanoid giants eight or ten feet tall. According to Earth standards they are treacherous and untrustworthy, and are cordially disliked. * Harrington is called into action because of two circumstances: Recently there has been a pattern of conflicting claims. Martians have successfully filed claims on deposits slightly earlier than Earthmen, and it is obvious that there have been leaks to the Martians. And now investigator Wood has disappeared. * Harrington goes to the Moon, where, pulling his rank quite frequently, he checks into both Terrestrial and Martian colonial organizations. The Martians are obviously doing something crooked; indeed, they try to kill Harrison by damaging his space suit. They later hold him prisoner. The question is, which of the Earthmen is also involved? * Harrington solves the problem and some of the parties are happy. * Clichéd in story, horrible in surface writing, but sometimes imaginative in background detail. * The story is carried on the contents page as "Moon Mines."

   78. **MURDER ON THE ASTEROID**. *Wonder Stories*, June 1933. Ill. Paul.

Short story. * *Time:* the twenty-second century. *Place:* the asteroid belt and Earth. * In some ways an unhumorous Laurel and Hardy story. * The space miners Hanson and Timothy have spent almost all their resources trying to rediscover a platinum-rich asteroid that Timothy had once found. Timothy, a small shadowy alcoholic with personality problems, unfortunately miscalculated the asteroid's position, so that his claim was rejected by the authorities. * At present Hanson, a burly, thuggish man, resents the fact that his money and time have been wasted on a wild goose chase for a fortune that may not exist. Carried away by his hatred and resentment, he unsuccessfully tries to strangle Timothy. At just this time Timothy sights his platinum asteroid, and the men land. Hard feeling is forgotten, or is it? * Enough platinum extracted to support a claim, orbit of the asteroid correctly plotted, the men decide to leave. But Hanson considers it unnecessary to share. He murders Timothy, puts his corpse into a space capsule, and tosses it off the planetoid, to float eternally in space. * A generation passes. Hanson is now one of the richest men in the system, but wealth has not improved his brutal personality. He also pays blackmail to an old acquaintance who has recognized that Timothy's disappearance is at least fishy. * Hanson's only virtue is his love for his daughter Elaine, who is going on a trip near the asteroids. Hanson is a little worried, for there is danger involved. His worry is justified, for the space capsule containing Timothy's corpse crashes into Elaine's liner, killing her. * Good detail in the first part, with some psychological depth in the pulp mode, but a ridiculous, clichéd second part.

   79. **THE SPORE DOOM**. *Wonder Stories*, February

Binder, Eando (*continued*)
1934. Ill. Paul.
Short story. * Time: the twenty-third century. *Place:* Mammoth
Cave and the Chicago area. * *Background:* In 1975 a devastating world war broke out, parties not identified by Binder.
Toward the end of the war the weaker side released fungus
spores to destroy the opponent's crops. These fungi multiplied,
mutated, combined with non-fungoid plants and created a
vegetable revolution which soon covered the world in savage
luxuriance. Then a worse development took place: The new
vegetation began to absorb oxygen from the atmosphere. In a
short time the air became depleted and inadequate for human life
and the human race retreated to underground fastnesses sealed
with air locks. * At story time there are about a hundred such
underground cities, with a total population of about fifty million
people. Life is very regimented, and health is not vigorous.
Atomic energy provides power. There is some underground
agriculture, but most food is gathered from outside by tripod
walking machines. Since much of the vegetable life outside is
poisonous, food processing involves perpetual testing. * In the
Mammoth Cave city Roy Cantwell is such a tester. When he
believes that he sees a pattern for possible genetic control among
the outside plants, he goes outside channels to obtain a special
research assignment. Actually, he receives the assignment
through the help of Vina, his supervisor's daughter, who takes a
fancy to him. * Roy works away at his project, at the same time
establishing a romance with Vina. This romance cuts into the
territory of one Spargo, a dark, vicious man with Spanish blood,
who feels he has a monopoly on Vina. When Spargo cannot win
Vina fairly, he pollutes several food-producing areas with fungi,
casting the blame on Roy. Roy, convicted of criminal
negligence, is sentenced to death. * With Vina's help he escapes,
and he and Vina flee to the outside in a gathering tripod. There
Roy continues his experiments on the site of ancient Chicago.
Success is near, but he must return to Mammoth Cave for
materials. Spargo recognizes him, chases him in another walking
machine, and the two men battle. Spargo is killed, and Roy can
continue his work. * The background is acceptable, but the plot
needed only to have Spargo twirl his moustache. The ethnic
stereotype now reads strangely.

80. **THE GREEN CLOUD OF SPACE**. *Wonder Stories*,
May 1934. Ill. Winter.
Short story. * *Time:* the near future. * Boy inventor Dick Palmer
has reasoned out the origin of the short-lived but devastating
Green Plague that struck the world a few months earlier. It is
caused by a cloud of space viruses carried by the ether; and the
Earth is going to pass through another, more extensive part of
the cloud in a short time. * Dick is working, along with his
friend George Craft (brother of Dick's girlfriend Dorothy), to
discover a serum against it. He is almost there, but needs
capital. Dick's father is a very wealthy man, but he is an iron-
hearted, wicked capitalist who has disowned Dick for not being
a businessman. There will be no money from him. * Dick is
right, of course. The Green Plague strikes again, but Dick has
prepared a working serum. Kudos, wealth, and happiness should
be his, but not so. A mob destroys his own lab supply, and
George dies for want of the serum. Along the way Dick's
plutocratic father dies begging for help, clutching Dick's knees
(figuratively), but even this does not offset the loss of George.
* A pretty horrible job.

81. **ENSLAVED BRAINS**. *Wonder Stories*, July-
September 1934. Ill. Paul.
(Reprinted in book form by Avalon, New York, 1965. The text
may be abridged or altered.)
Novel. * Time: 1973. *Place:* mostly the New York area, but
also the West Coast and other places. * *Background:* During a
horrible world war in the late 1930s the Japanese attacked the
West Coast and occupied it, while much of the world was
devastated. After the war a consortium of scientists and
engineers founded the Unidom, a (surreptitiously Technocrat)
state that in a short time came to include the United States,
Canada, Western Europe, European Russia, and Latin America.
Large population shifts took place from Europe to the Americas.
* Politically, the Unidom consists of parallel structures of
scientist, judicial, legislative, and executive personnel, rising up
to two chief executives, one a scientist, the other a layman.
Practically speaking, however, the scientists (which term includes engineers and comparable persons) are dominant. The
guiding principles of the Unidom are rationality, utility, and
perfectibilism; good living is guaranteed for all in a system of
fettered capitalism. * Under the Unidom mankind has prospered
as never before, and science has made unparalleled advances.
Resources are carefully conserved, the main power sources being
tidal stations and floating solar power platforms at sea. As all
admit, the Unidom has done an enormous amount of good, but
abuses have crept in, particularly in suppression of liberties. *
Into this world enters Dan Williams, practically a Rip Van
Winkle figure who has spent the past forty years in the Congo
fighting Zulus [*sic*] on what seems to be a mid-nineteenth-
century level. Accompanied by his cousin Earl Hackworth,
Williams views the new civilization. He is amazed at the
progress that has been made by the Unidom, but he soon learns
of a horrible flaw in the new culture. There is a eugenics bureau
that despite original good intentions has turned into a tyranny.
Among other matters, it busies itself with the matings of a few
superior females, who have no choice. And Hackworth's
daughter Lila has been assigned to marry leading scientist
Professor Jorgen, who is revealed toward the end of the novel as
a most obnoxious madman. * Williams, horrified at this state of
events, suggests a Romeo and Juliet solution. Included in his kit
from Africa is a drug that produces suspended animation. If Lila
takes it, she and her lover Terry will gain time. This is done,
and Lila is on the shelf as a mysterious case in a Unidom
hospital until retrieved. * Williams soon encounters something
even worse. Much of the production work is handled by central
automation controlled by human brains detached from their
bodies and kept alive artificially. This is possible legally, since
under Unidom law corpses are state property. Some scientific
study has shown that such brains are conscious and suffer
torments, but the hierarchy has suppressed the report and exiled
the scientists who prepared it. * When Williams learns that his
dead sister's brain is being used to control the industry of
Boston, he goes berserk. Arrested when he tries to destroy the
brain apparatus, he is subject to the death penalty, as are
Hackworth and Terry. But the three men are rescued by a
faithful Bantu follower Williams brought with him from Africa.
Through luck they stumble upon a high official of the Brothers
of Humanity, an underground group that wants to restructure the
Unidom back to its humane beginnings. This official, who
should know, blames the present bad situation on the scientist-

Binder, Eando (*continued*)

executive Monier, who has become an erratic, irresponsible, cruel dictator. * At the proper time the underground sets off a rebellion, destroying almost all the enslaved brains and seizing the West Coast, but despite the rebels' initial success, the Unidom proves too strong. The rebellion is on the point of total collapse when Williams and colleagues shut down the East Coast tidal power plant and bring up the solar power platform to focus its rays on the Unidom capitol. The Unidom surrenders, and presumably a more reasonable government will take its place. At the last there is a cliffhanger as the foul madman Jorgen is about to plunge the fatal needle into the unconscious Lila's breast. * Some interesting concepts at the beginning, but the story degenerates into too much dashing around and pulp simplistics. On the whole the story has more thought than is usual with Binder's work, but it is curiously archaic in mode.

82. **EIGHTY-FIVE AND EIGHTY-SEVEN**. Amazing Stories, October 1934. Ill. Morey.

Short story. * *Time:* 1946 and following years. *Place:* the Tyrol, Austria. * The great scientist Professor Johann Haupt, who has retired to an almost inaccessible eyrie in the mountains to pursue his researches, accepts as an assistant brilliant young Karl Marienfeldt. Together the two men work with a strange metal that the professor has extracted from a meteorite. Part of the metal is the hitherto unisolated element 85; a residue may contain the other missing element, number 87. * After a long period of research and experimentation, Haupt leaves his laboratory and offers an explanation of his work to a learned congress. As he tells it, by running enormous electric currents through a tube containing rare gases and Number 85, he has produced a glass-like substance that when ground into a lens shows remarkable views of a high civilization on Venus. The meteorite, the professor concludes, originally hailed from Venus. * The congress adjourns to visit Haupt's establishment, where they find an astonishing development. Marienfeldt has disappeared, leaving a short manuscript behind. As he explains, by further experimentation with the supposed 87 he has developed antigravity. Finding a small spaceship in a room that Haupt kept locked, he has now taken off for Venus. * No more is heard of Marienfeldt. Unfortunately, there can be no more space travel, for Karl has used all the meteoritic material.

83. **THE THIEVES FROM ISOT**. Wonder Stories, October 1934. Ill. Paul.

Novelette. * *Time:* 1955. *Place:* somewhere in the north polar area. * Newspaperman Bill Nevers is assigned to follow up his managing editor's hunch. Some three years earlier an enormous airship, thousands of feet long, had appeared over various parts of the world. It would flash down a ray, then leave. Bill's editor hypothesizes that the visitors were looking for something and that they found it at the north pole. The bad weather over the past two or three years may also be due to activities at the pole. * Nevers and photographer Sam Peters fly north at 650 mph until they are diverted by a storm. Ahead of them they see an ice-clear area and a high tower from which a beam kills their engine. Forced to land, they are taken prisoner by tall men who are hairless, with a somewhat Mongoloid cast of features. Nearby is the enormous ship that had been seen in the skies years before. * Koor Lato, the commanding officer of the strangers, is quite friendly. He speaks English, learned from an explorer who is present at the site. * Koor Laro explains. He

and his men have come from Pluto and have established a base for extracting copper ore to ship back home. Pluto, which has a superscience, is short of certain metals and must obtain them from other planets. When the current deposit near the pole is exhausted, a matter of days, the Plutonians will leave, never to return. They have just developed a technique for atomic transformation and are now able to manufacture their own missing elements. The Plutonians will not establish communication with Earth or permit visitors, for their culture is basically xenophobic. * Despite the evidences of superscience around him, Nevers is reluctant to believe the Koor's story, but insists that the strangers are simply Asiatics, perhaps associates of the Second Fu Manchu. He breaks his parole and communicates with the outside world, but without result. * Finished, the Plutonians leave. A note from Koor Laro gives Bill and Sam the tower that was the principal building of the visitors; since it is formed of beryllium, it is worth a fortune. * *Miscellaneous:* The spaceship operates by regulating gravity. * Pluto, although dark, is rendered warm by radioactivity. * The Plutonians have a nictitating membrane to protect their eyes against strong light. * Plutonians, Martians, and Earthmen are all of common stock. * An attempt to achieve lightness of narrative, but badly structured and clichéd.

84. **DAWN TO DUSK**. *Wonder Stories*, November 1934-January 1935. Ill. Paul.

Novel. * *Time:* mostly about two billion years in the future. *Place:* mostly on Mercury. * Largely future history, probably suggested by the work of Olaf Stapledon. * Brilliant biologist Professor Anton Reinhardt summons former student Andrew Boswell to a private meeting along with several prominent scientists. There Reinhardt makes a controversial speech. After comments on the panspermia theory of life, Reinhardt reveals that he has developed a technique for suspended animation. He injects a certain virus into a body, maintains the body in anaerobic conditions, and awakens it by admitting air. Demonstrating the validity of his claim, he now asks for volunteers to join him in entering what amount to time capsules, with the probability of being awakened in ten or twenty thousand years. * Most of the audience refuses, but Boswell and two others agree to accompany Reinhardt. Time capsules of the greatest strength and durability are constructed, and the subjects are put to sleep, their location carefully hidden. * Boswell, upon whom the story centers, awakens to find himself in a room with a strange-looking man before him: bubble-headed, long-armed, weak-legged. This is his informant and friend-to-be, Monituperal. Professor Reinhardt also awakens, but the other men died when their capsules were damaged by powerful earth forces. As Reinhardt speculates, he and Boswell must be much farther in the future than they had planned. * The future men, who have an incredible superscience, work upon Reinhardt and Boswell while they are unconscious, reconstructing their digestive systems so that they no longer need food and implanting a knowledge of the future tongue in their brains. * Now the two men from the past learn about their situation. They have slept something like two billion years and are on Mercury. An exploratory mission to Earth chanced to discover their capsules, retrieved them, and brought them to Mercury, where the men were revived. Mankind survives only underground on Mercury, for the other planets have become uninhabitable. The sun is dark. * Monituperal explains past history in considerable detail: There have been great wars, climatic changes on Earth,

Binder, Eando (*continued*)
glacial periods and other changes, during which civilizations have risen and fallen. Two mutations produced the future people who are no longer Homo. Actually, the future people are to some extent cyborgs (my term) with antigravity controls implanted where the stomach used to be, and other mechanical aids. * Materially speaking, the future world is an eutopia of a sort, a working anarchistic society propelled by altruism. But spiritually, it is in the dumps. The reason? The human race has become totally sterile. No more children are born, and after the current life span of five hundred years, the race will be extinct. * The Binders tie this into a somewhat mystical framework. Reinhardt and the future men believe that while life arises spontaneously under suitable conditions, intelligence is a separate principle that wafts in on microscopic space seeds. To further the spread of intelligence, the future men themselves are disseminating such seeds through space. The origin of intelligence? The future men believe that there is an ultimate being or beings, whom they attempt to understand. Related to this concept, the future men believe that the right of the human race to exist has been withdrawn by a higher power. Against this decree, their superscience has no force. * There are no events after the awaking of Boswell and Reinhardt, and in a short epilogue chapter, Boswell, as the very last man, returns to Earth to die. As he dies he makes a prayerful last word and seems to perceive an answering flash. * A much more mature work than Binder's earlier fiction, although the mystical element is odd for pulp science-fiction of the day.

85. **THE ROBOT ALIENS.** *Wonder Stories*, February 1935. Ill. Paul.
Short story. * *Time:* 1955. *Place:* Illinois, the Joliet and Chicago areas. * An attempt at combining the alien menace story with irony on human reactions, with special reference to contemporary official types. * When the great meteorite flashes through the sky, amateur astronomer Bert Bodell traces it to its impact site, to discover that it is not a meteorite but obviously an artificial construction. As in H. G. Wells's *The War of the Worlds*, a segment of the vessel opens. Two gigantic, moderately humanoid mechanical figures emerge. There is immediate panic among the many onlookers, including the police, who assume that the figures are aggressively hostile. Federal troops are summoned, and the area is cordoned off. * Once again, when the creatures, who to a reader are obviously attempting only to communicate, advance, there is panic, and many people are killed in the rush. * At this point, with presidential backing, the army attacks. Shells demolish the ship, which the robots abandon, and airplanes track the robots, who separate, one reaching the streets of Chicago. The robots do not seem to be harmed by small arms and in general can dodge shell explosions (incredible though this may seem), but they are not indestructible, and one is finally destroyed by massive concentration of artillery. * The second robot, however, encounters Frank Miller, an intelligent millionaire semi-recluse, who is open minded. He soon recognizes that the robot is not hostile and is only trying to communicate. After some weeks Miller learns that the vessel came from Mars, and that the robots are controlled by individual Martians who have established some sort of faster-than-light signal system. Miller publishes his conclusions, but hysterical natives kill him and destroy the last robot. * *Miscellaneous:* The Great Depression has ended, and the United States has entered a new era of great prosperity. * More mature work than Binder's previous stories, but somewhat clumsily handled, with over-stylized, semicomic caricatures.

86. **SET YOUR COURSE BY THE STARS.** *Astounding Stories*, May 1935. Ill. Marchioni.
Short story. * An idea story. * *Time:* the near future, when Earth-bound rocket travel is practical. * Professor Ortmann has built a workable rocket spaceship. Scheduled to pilot it on a first flight to the Moon is great rocket pilot Jason Garrard. The planning and technology are on the primitive side by modern standards, since Garrard is not familiar with the controls; navigation is visual, aimed at Antares. * The rocket takes off well enough, but Garrard, after about ten thousand miles, returns to Earth, ditching the ship and landing by parachute. * His reason? Not cowardice, as he is accused. It was just that when he left the Earth's atmosphere, the sky became a blaze of solid light and he could not identify Antares, hence could not find the moon. * Routine, with a curious scientific error.

87. **SHIPS THAT COME BACK.** *Astounding Stories*, November 1935. Ill. Dold.
Short story. * Essentially a story of sea peril transplanted into space. * *Time:* the interplanetary future. *Place:* space near Saturn. * The officers and men of the space freighter *Edison* en route to Saturn awaken after being unconscious for about seventeen hours. They are all badly bruised (one dying later of injuries), the fuel is almost all gone, some of the machinery is out of commission, but the hull is undamaged. What happened? The damage could not have been caused by a meteor, as was first thought. It may, as first officer Sorrel advances, be just one of those space catastrophes that do not get reported because they are usually fatal. * The personal situation is strained. Captain Robey, though capable and fearless, is a bucko tyrant who would have been at home on a windjammer. Cruel and unfeeling toward the crew, he drives them on a possible retrieval route with minimal power. It soon becomes clear, however, that this will not work. The cargo must be jettisoned to save energy, but Robey considers even the suggestion mutinous. As he says, captains who jettison cargo are done professionally. * Matters come to a head, there is a near mutiny, and the captain accidentally kills the sole passenger on the vessel. Robey now recognizes what fate has dealt him. He orders the cargo thrown out, and, entering what has happened in the ship's log, commits suicide. * Told with bravura.

88. **SPAWN OF ETERNAL THOUGHT.** *Astounding Stories*, April-May 1936. Unsigned ill. (Brown?)
Short novel. * The peace vigilante and world saver brought somewhat up to date. * *Time:* probably the near future. *Place:* Earth and around the solar system. * Old Dr. Hartwell and Vincent Renolf have finally achieved the great goal in Hartwell's work: the creation of a bank of ten brains, formerly those of great scientists, maintained in life and linked electronically (via a headgear) to the experimenter. These brains, which Hartwell and Renolf acquired by various means, legal and illicit, now serve to create the greatest mentality in history when Renolf wears the headgear. Hartwell drops dead at the moment of triumph, but his daughter Dora and Renolf will carry on. * Since the purpose of the invention is the amelioration of mankind, Vincent immediately takes steps. In need of funds, he whips off (with the aid of the captive brains) the design for a revolutionary television device, which he sells for a million dollars in cash,

Binder, Eando (*continued*)

then builds a small spaceship equipped with disintegrators and a force screen. He now commands the nations of the world to disarm, performing a few spectacular feats to create conviction, although he is careful not to take life. Sinking most of the world's largest fleets is easy, as is stopping a Japanese-American war. The world at his feet, Renolf creates an international governing council. He estimates that it will take about three years to correct abuses and inadequacies. * During this time, poor Dora is panting with expectation, for Vincent Renolf will not marry her until his work is finished. Indeed, the young man has become in effect a double personality: when he wears the headgear, as Renolf, he is aloof, arrogant, cold, and super-intellectual; without it, as Vincent, he is a pleasant young genius. * The world put in order, Renolf now decides to explore space. In the back of his mind is his memory of a strange hostile mental wave that he has occasionally caught when he had the headgear on. Attempts to locate it by electronic means have failed; the equipment has burned out, and there have been nearly fatal accidents when Renolf tried to investigate. * Dora still held at arm's length on the spaceship, Vincent sets out with her to explore. The moons of Saturn show signs of a once-great civilization with enormous dome cities, but all are dead. The satellites of Jupiter, Mars, and Mercury all share the same pattern, supercivilizations that died. And the hostile mental waves are still perceptible. * All that is left now is the Moon, where Renolf finds what he has been seeking. As he approaches Tycho, his vessel encounters an impenetrable force screen through which a supermind speaks to him, frankly and gar-rulously. The creature, the Spawn of Eternal Thought, is a nearly incorporeal intelligence that came from outer space eons ago. It maintains itself by eating planets and derives mental stimulation and nourishment by eating peoples—whence the dead civilizations the explorers encountered. It is not quite ready to devour mankind yet, but will in a short time. * Renolf and Dora return to Earth and confide their discoveries to the world council. There is suitable horror. Renolf now proposes a plan: strike at the thought monster unexpectedly, since it may not be quite as incorporeal as it claims. Earth, after all, has little to lose. If nothing is done, the monster will eat mankind, who knows when; if the strike fails, the monster will probably be enraged enough to destroy Earth. * All concerned decide that it is better to strike. For this Renolf needs a hundred-brain unit, which is gladly furnished to him. (Binder breezily passes over the procurement of these brains and ignores the cruelty and immorality of the linkages, as developed in "Enslaved Brains.") Super-super-Renolf explains. He will propel an atomic explosion of a ton of sand against the monster, following this, in a matter of seconds, with an even larger atomic device. * The Spawn of Thought survives the first blast, but before it can retaliate, the second blast destroys it. Some damage is done to the Earth, but this is still better than the fate the monster promised. * Routine, and a little silly, but a suggestion of a type of story Binder wrote several times later.

89. **THE TIME ENTITY**. Astounding Stories, October 1936. Ill. Thomson.

Short story. * John Dakin engages in telepathic conversations with his descendant of the year 2086. The transmission, the future person claims, is based on the nature of time, which is not a straight line, but a succession of wriggles and curves, some of

which lie closer together than others. In this case, clarity is enhanced when Dakin turns on the radio. * The two chitchat, and a couple of predictions that the future person makes come true, despite John's attempt to prevent them. But then John learns that his only child has just been killed in an automobile accident. How can there be descendants in the year 2086? Binder seems to consider this a paradox. * Lightweight, of no interest.

BIRD, ROGER

No information.

90. **UNIVERSAL MERRY-GO-ROUND**. *Amazing Stories*, April 1933. Ill. Morey.

Short story. * *Time:* 1946. *Place:* mostly on an asteroid with a very irregular orbit. * The great Professor Witherton has not only identified a new planet that he plans to visit, but has devised a way to get there. Using relativity, he has discovered a way to make his spacecraft stand still, locked onto the ether, while the rest of the universe moves around. He has selected the unknown planet to visit because it is in line with his ship when the universe moves, whereas the other planets are not. The trip will take about a year and three days. To relieve the monotony of being sealed in the gigantic metallic sphere for over a year, his daughter Audrey will play the violin for the explorers. Max, the narrator, who is in love with Audrey, is delighted with this arrangement. * The ship takes off, but when it reaches the asteroid belt, since the professor is a little late in pushing a certain button, the ship collides with an asteroid about five miles in diameter. The ship is damaged and the professor is injured, but the gravity and atmosphere of the little world are tolerable. Audrey and Max make the best of it, eating sardines and candy bars. * Exploring, the lovers encounter the intelligent inhabitants of the small world. These are gigantic creatures about fifty feet high, with three eyes, two legs, and multiple arms and hands. The monsters live on giant mushrooms that they harvest. * One of the giants captures the three Earth people and displays them to his fellows, who find them amusing. Prodded, the Earth people dance jigs to amuse the giants. * The professor notices, as do the giants, that the asteroid is approaching the Earth and will collide with it. Seeing that the giants have prepared a spaceship to leave their world, the professor leaps into it, but Max and Audrey are too late, and are left stranded on the asteroid. But resourceful Max cuts down some drapes and turns them into a parachute, so that he and Audrey can float to Earth while the asteroid crashes on ahead of them. They land in the Rocky Mountains. * More like a very-low-level British boys' story than American science fiction. I do not think it is parodic. The influence of Swift's *Gulliver's Travels* is obvious.

BISHOP, CAPT. H[ARRY] G[ORE] (1874-1934)

American soldier, served in artillery branch. Born in Michigan. Graduate U.S. Military Academy. Attended Army War College, Army Staff College, distinguished graduate Army School of the Line. Distinguished Service Medal. Honorable discharge as brigadier general, 1919. Author of several standard texts on artillery. Administrator in the Philippine Occupation. * Wrote other fiction for *Everybody's Magazine* and elsewhere, but, to my knowledge, only one other science-fiction story ("Congealing the Ice Trust," *New Broadway Magazine*, 1907). The present story is covered in more detail in *Science-Fiction: The Early Years*.

Bishop, Capt. H. G. (*continued*)

91. **ON THE MARTIAN WAY**. *Amazing Stories*, February 1927. Ill. F. S. Hynd.
(Originally published in *Broadway Magazine*, November 1907.)
Short story. * *Time:* the interplanetary future. *Place:* space, the Earth-Mars run. * To cut business losses the R. D. Jones space line converts the *Columbia*, a cargo vessel, into a passenger ship carrying invalids to Mars for the benefits of the rarefied Martian atmosphere. Winston, the dispatcher at Hoboken, who is upset because of amatory difficulties, neglects to warn the ship about an approaching comet (Biela's), with the result that the ship is lost. Winston, after a fifteen year prison term, signs up on another liner, the *Trenton*, and in an act of heroism saves the ship at the cost of his own life. The *Trenton* was caught in a "dead zone" where interplanetary gravities neutralize one another; by blasting off in the lifeboat Winston set up a saving reaction. * A competent job, though obviously a projection of current ship lore. * In reprinting this story, Gernsback, it seems obvious, obtained rights from the publisher, not the author, whence the outdated rank attributed to then General Bishop.

BISSIRI, AUGUSTO

Italian, possibly Sardinian, author. Also wrote *All'ultimo sangue, romanzo scientifico-fantastico* (1955). There is no indication in the magazine that the story is a translation or adaptation.

92. **THE LORD OF THE WINDS**. *Amazing Stories*, December 1926. Unsigned ill.
Short story. * *Place:* near Death Valley, California. * The narrator and his acquaintance Wells make their way to visit the great reclusive Professor Matheson, who maintains an elaborate scientific establishment in the desert. Wells has rubies he wants authenticated, and the narrator is a surreptitious newspaper reporter. * Matheson, thawed out by the gift of a huge ruby, explains his work: He has set up gigantic Crookes tubes to ionize the air, thus rendering wind and weather control possible. He will eventually expand his operation over the world, creating perfect climate and an eutopia free from want and war. * It sounds fine, but the enormous tubes suddenly become operative, creating winds of superhurricane velocity. Matheson and Wells are killed, and the narrator barely survives. One of the local miners, looking for something to steal, accidentally turned on the tubes at full power, and they did not cease functioning until broken by flying debris.

BIVONA, FRANCESCO (1908-?)

U.S. author, resident of New York City. Occupation given as senior clerk. Author of many volumes of poetry, including *Violet Flame* (1950) and *The Agony of Faust* (1971). Other works include *Strange Plays* (1992) and *Two Ancient Tales* (1993).

93. **THE FINAL STRUGGLE**. *Wonder Stories*, October 1934. Ill. Winter.
Short story. * Indeterminate location. * The nameless narrator, an aviator, makes a forced landing in the wilderness snow. He is immediately beset by a strange gigantic, humanoid creature that he calls the monster. Escaping, he makes his way into a nearby building, where, after minor episodes, he is trapped by the vicious creature. Eventually the monster is caught between two spiked power doors and dies. Along the way the narrator

rescues a tortured prisoner who is a former assistant of the mad scientist who created the creature. The mad scientist dies during the melee. * More suitable for the shudder pulps than a science-fiction magazine, but wretched work.

BLANDFORD, CHARLES G.

No information.

94. **A LINK TO THE PAST**. *Amazing Stories*, September 1927. Ill. Paul.
Short story. * *Place:* Central Ontario, Canada. * An ongoing frame situation at the State Museum of Natural History encloses the narrative of the only survivor of the Schlechting Expedition. * The men headed in from James Bay, along the Moose River, into a tabu area, where they encountered a primitive white native who spoke a language with Scandinavian elements. He warned them not to continue, but they disregarded his advice and came to a lost world with a higgledy-piggledy mixture of ancient tree ferns, dinosaurs, and similar life. The land was heated to an uncomfortable degree by volcanic fires, which streamed forth unbroken, according to schedule, like geysers. * The perils were such that all the men were killed except Jarvis, who took a wife and settled down among the lost race. His wife has died, and now, twenty years later, he has returned to civilization. While he is not greedy, he expects salary for the actual time he served with Schlechting. * The savants, who have listened scornfully to Jarvis's story, call him a fraud—until he pulls out an unfossilized trilobite shell, which convinces them.

BOLTON, PAUL (1903-?)

U.S. (Texas) journalist. In 1946 prepared series of stories for the Hart Hanks newspapers that were broadcast over station KTBC. Also wrote *Governors of Texas* (1947). Portrait accompanying "Chicago 2042 A.D." shows a man in early middle age. The author's newspaper experience is evident in "The Time Hoaxers."

95. **THE TIME HOAXERS**. *Amazing Stories*, August 1931. Ill. Morey.
Short story. * *Place:* Austin, Texas. * The story is told through a series of newspaper articles, some factual, some speculative, some sensational, some derisive. * The events behind the articles are simple enough. A strange-looking craft settles in the backyard of local preacher J. H. Atkins. From the craft emerge four men and one woman; all are small, under five feet high, and all are scantily or transparently dressed. The leader of the strangers proclaims that he and his associates have come from the year 2030, hoping to help advance the civilization of 1930. He requests a meeting with scientists or at least political leaders. Instead, the little people are hauled off to jail for indecent exposure. * The incident is picked up by various news syndicates, and after a denial by a motion picture studio that the incident is a publicity stunt, it is generally believed that the five visitors are lunatics; but when a trespasser accidentally electrocutes himself by meddling with the strangers' vehicle, the little people are charged with murder and scheduled for trial. * A resolution comes when Jason Copeland, a university student, and Anis, the future woman, recognize a mutual passion. Jason helps the future people to escape custody, and together they all leave for the future. * The editor/reporter has throughout the story left options clear, hoax or genuine visit, but at the end he produces an unpublished clincher: a yellowed, tattered newspaper clipping from 1930 that Anis brought with her from 2030. From

Bolton, Paul (*continued*)

her position in the future she knew that her romance with Jason and escape had already taken place. * *Miscellaneous:* The future people explain that time is a sinuous stream with bridgeable points that approach one another. * Well handled.

96. CHICAGO, 2042 A.D. *Wonder Stories*, October 1932. Ill. Paul.

Short story. * Another fictional implementation of gangster Chicago of the 1930s. * *Time:* the 1950s and A.D. 2042, with a prefatory statement dated A.D. 2508. *Place:* Chicago. * By 1950 Jerry Ratoni, Chicago-based racketeer, is almost ruler of the United States. His crimes go unpunished, and his bootleg industry, which meets with public approval, encompasses the whole country. Against him is secretly formed the Council of 46, a vigilante organization devoted to his downfall. * The narrator, Wakefield, a member of the Council, agrees to act as a mole in Ratoni's organization. As a competent rumrunner he serves Ratoni for about eighteen months, gathering information. * At the time that the Council has set to assassinate the ganglord and his lieutenants, Ratoni's building starts to shake and disintegrate. There is a confusing blur, then Ratoni, his secretary, and Wakefield find themselves in Lake Michigan, about one hundred years in the future. (As is explained in a footnote, an inventor was demonstrating a disintegrating device, which got out of hand.) * The trio are rescued by an eccentric inventor, Crazy Kriml, and brought before the Big Shot, the gangster overlord of the area. As Wakefield sees, the situation in the future is just as bad as it was earlier. * The three involuntary time travelers are in danger, but Ratoni's resourcefulness saves the day. Proving his identity by finger prints, he claims that he has achieved immortality by chemical means. He then offers the secret to the fat, ineffectual Big Shot and after a short time usurps the position of Big Shot himself. * Ratoni's reign, however, is short. The inventor Kriml, who has a social conscience of a strange sort, disintegrates Chicago and threatens to disintegrate other areas if the gangsters are not expelled. Ratoni dies obscurely; the narrator and Ratoni's secretary (a secret enemy of Ratoni's, who had been planning to kill him) marry; and the world is improved. * Something less than routine.

BONNEY, NORMAN J.

U.S. writer, probably bank clerk in Boston, Massachusetts. Has also contributed to *Adventure* magazine. Portrait accompanying the story shows a young man. Social Security records list a Norman Bonney (1910-1972), a resident of Peabody, Massachusetts.

97. THE MAN WHO LAUGHS. *Wonder Stories*, October 1930. Ill. Marchioni.

Short-short story. * Inventor Menley has made capitalist Cameron Crawford wealthy with his inventions, while Crawford has kept him a wage slave. For a year Menley has been working on an invention, which Crawford now comes to inspect. It is a humaniform robot designed to do various household tasks. When Crawford scoffs at the machine's imperfections, insults Menley, and threatens to leave, the inventor produces a pistol and forces Crawford to shake hands with the mechanism. This is the beginning of the end as the five hundred-pound robot crushes him, throws him around, and mangles him. Menley is now mad and in an asylum.

BOTHAM, R. R.

Pseud. of Russell Robert Winterbotham. For biographical information see Winterbotham.

98. THE LAST WAR. *Flash Gordon Strange Adventure Magazine*, December 1936.

Short-short story. * *Time:* indefinite future. * The earth has been wrecked by wars. "Entire races had been wiped out, mountains had been leveled with powerful weapons. Artificial earthquakes had shaken down cities and sank [*sic*] lowlands into the sea." Only two parties are left. A fortress of the North American Federation Forces and an attacking force using a mobile ray machine and a plane. The fortress falls to enemy rays, and everyone is killed except a military officer and a young woman. The enemy forces were self-activating robot devices; their human operators have long been dead. The human race is extinct except for the officer and the woman. But the world is finally at peace.

BOWERS, CHARLES GORDON

No information, but, judging from the story, the author was in some way connected with the medical profession. Dr. Miles J. Breuer, who occasionally served as technical referee, attested to the accuracy of the surgical procedures. See also the comments on author W. Alexander.

99. THE BLACK HAND. *Amazing Stories*, January 1931. Ill. Morey.

Short story. * The artist Van Puyster, in part because he refused to follow medical advice, has a gangrenous right arm that must be amputated. When Van Puyster protests bitterly, Dr. Evans suggests a remedy. Organ transplants are now becoming successful. Evans proposes transplanting the arm of a black criminal, who has been sentenced to death, onto Van Puyster. The criminal has agreed to the operation in exchange for a large sum to be given to his heirs, and the prison officials raise no objection so long as the operation is performed at the prison hospital. * The operation, which the author describes in close detail, is successful, and Van Puyster resumes his career. But he is a racist, and the presence of the black hand preys on his mind. Eventually going mad, he tries to murder blacks. * Undoubtedly authentic in terms of medical procedures of the day, but the author avoids the potentially more interesting repercussions of the operation, which he reveals only in a newspaper clipping. The motif itself is one met in the supernatural fiction of the day.

BOWMAN, B. L.

U.S. writer; resident of New York City at this time. Possibly a woman.

100. LABORATORY CO-OPERATOR-3. *Astounding Stories,* January 1936. Ill. Schneeman.

Short story. * Romance and parapsychological doings. * *Time:* presumably the near future. * The story is somewhat confused, but it seems that experiments with etheric doubles (whose physical bodies are hundreds of miles away) are conducted in certain hospitals, and that such doubles assist the surgeons in operations. Part of the procedure is that complete records are kept at each end of the situation, so that the presence of such doubles can be firmly established. * In any case, Dr. Gordon Milton develops a passion for etheric double Co-operator-3, who assists him in various operations. He eventually seeks her out physically (with her assistance) and establishes a romance. * Phyllis Farrington, the cooperator in question, advances research

Bowman, B. L. (*continued*)

by bringing along with her the etheric double of a white Alsatian dog. The implication is that the cooperators can now carry along with them doubles of consultants who are not able to travel in this way by themselves. * Of no interest. The story really belongs in one of the lesser supernatural fiction magazines like *Ghost Stories* or *Mind Magic*.

BREUER, MILES J[OHN], M.D. (1889-1947)

U.S. (Nebraska) author. Born in Chicago. Educated University of Texas, Rush Medical College. Internist, specialty tuberculosis, at Lincoln General Hospital, Nebraska. A frequent contributor to the early s-f pulps. Breuer was an intelligent if uneven writer who often had unusual ideas with implications beyond the pulps. He was unusual among fellow writers in having backgrounds in medicine, the biological sciences, and the physical sciences. See also joint work by Clare Winger Harris and Miles J. Breuer, and Miles J. Breuer and Jack Williamson; also the unsettled identity of W. Alexander.

101. **THE MAN WITH THE STRANGE HEAD**. *Amazing Stories*, January 1927. Ill. F. S. Hynd.

(Reprinted in Conklin, *Big Book of Science Fiction*.) Short story. * *Place:* Nebraska. * The narrator, a physician, has his attention called to the strange behavior of Mr. Anstruther, who lives in the Cornhusker Hotel. Anstruther has been pacing the floor for days, without cease. When he finally collapses, the narrator, an acquaintance, and the police break in. Anstruther is dead. * At the autopsy, a very strange situation is discovered that explains the disparity between Anstruther's weak, drooping head, and his former incredible body strength and vigor. Actually, the real Anstruther is a shrunken, aged man inside a humaniform living machine that has been operating with radium motors. The implication, not spelled out, is that the mechanism had been walking about after its inhabitant was dead.

102. **THE STONE CAT**. *Amazing Stories*, September 1927. Unsigned ill.

Short story. * A version of the mad scientist who uses a petrifying liquid to turn persons he dislikes into statues. As is usual, he is himself plumped and statuefied. * Others have handled the motif better.

103. **THE RIOT AT SANDERAC**, *Amazing Stories*, December 1927. Unsigned ill.

Short-short story. * The workers at the mine at Sanderac are a mixed group: ordinary Americans, fervid Russian communists, and Russian anti-communist refugees. * The narrator's friend Grant has devised a mysterious instrument with a keyboard and many little globes. When he plays it for the narrator, the narrator's moods swing wildly from rage, to despair, to jollity. * Grant explains what has been happening. Emotions are a result of changes in the electronic patterns of one's glands; by shooting streams of electrons at the various glands he can thus alter mood. * All well and good, but at a public demonstration that evening a White Russian plays the device. The audience runs amok and slaughters the Communists. The authorities, investigating the incident, pay no heed to the narrator's testimony about the emotion machine.

104. **THE PUZZLE DUEL**. *Amazing Stories Quarterly*, Winter 1928. Ill. Paul.

Short-short story. * Not really science-fiction, but a crime story. * The narrator, a college student, witnesses a quarrel between two other students, an Indian and a German. Both students, who are hotheaded and vindictive, insist on a duel to maintain their honor. Their seconds hope to circumvent a duel by insisting that it be handled with scientific weapons, but the only result of an electric duel is that both the Indian and the German die. There is nothing fantastic about the modes of death.

105. **THE APPENDIX AND THE SPECTACLES**. *Amazing Stories*, December 1928. Ill. Paul.

(Reprinted in Conklin, *The Science Fiction Galaxy* and in Fadiman, *The Mathematical Magpie*.)

Short story. * When the crude, greedy capitalist Cladgett calls in Bookstrom's loan and refuses a small extension, Bookstrom is forced to drop out of medical school and accept a position as a junior mathematics instructor. His chance for revenge comes years later, when he is a full professor, specializing in dimensional mathematics. * Dr. Banza, Cladgett's physician and Bookstrom's friend, diagnoses Cladgett's illness as acute appendicitis. But Cladgett fumes and rages at the thought of time (and money) lost during recuperation. Bookstrom enters the picture: He has developed a machine which puts a person slightly into the fourth dimension. Bookstrom thus proposes to remove Cladgett's appendix without an operation. He does so, for a high fee. * After a time, however, Cladgett is ill again, and X-rays show that a pair of eyeglasses are imbedded in Cladgett's viscera. Cladgett sues for malpractice, but the case is thrown out, since there are no scars as evidence of an operation. * Finally, for removal of the spectacles, Cladgett must pay Bookstrom's price: a heavy endowment for impoverished medical students at the university. * Despite the rather sordid plot, told lightly, with a note of humor.

106. **THE CAPTURED CROSS SECTION**. *Amazing Stories*, February 1929. Unsigned ill.

(Reprinted in Fadiman, *Fantasia Mathematica* and in Silverberg, *Other Dimensions*.)

Short story. * Young mathematics instructor Jiles Heagey has expanded Einstein's equations to the point where they encompass the fourth dimension. He has also constructed an apparatus to render it accessible. (The principle involved is geometrical rotation.) On its first trial the machine brings into our world a fourth-dimensional being, which consists of roughly spherical segments that combine and disassociate themselves. All well and good, but a couple of the segments corner Sheila Mathers, Jiles's near fiancée, and drag her away into the fourth dimension. * At this point Dr. Mathers, Sheila's father and the department head, who disapproves of Heagey, accuses him of murder. * It is now up to Jiles to retrieve Sheila. An entry into the fourth dimension does not help, for he cannot find her. Taking thought, he enlists the aid of artists and sculptors in constructing a three-dimensional message for the fourth-dimensional being still held in our space: Release Sheila and we will release you. It works.

107. **BURIED TREASURE**. *Amazing Stories*. April 1929. Ill. Hugh Mackay, with cryptographic plate perhaps by the author.

Short story. * *Time:* A.D. 3008. *Place:* somewhere in the former U.S. Humanity, thanks to eugenics and the application of science, is physically improved over the past, but one aspect of the new mankind is questionable. All strong emotions—fear, love, anger—have been eliminated. A group of young college students, examining a ruined building from the remote past, discuss this loss, which, in a tepid way, they seem to regret. A

Breuer, Miles J. (*continued*)

portion of the building suddenly collapses, and in the rubble the students find a small metal cylinder within which is a sheet of paper with what seems to be a cryptogram. * One of the young men consults the Index of the World's Knowledge, from which he learns that the enciphering method involved a grid, which he easily constructs. The document, dating from the 1920s, reveals that a cache worth one hundred thousand dollars is concealed in the foundations of the building. * The students, who do not understand the circumstances of Prohibition America, on excavating the cache find a case containing twenty-four bottles. Deciding that the liquid must be potable, they sample a bottle. For the first time, as they get a little high, they feel emotions, which they enjoy, without understanding what is happening. The liquor is apparently wine. But the building collapses farther and destroys the rest of the cache. * Miscellaneous points: Breuer offers a fairly complex grid device, which the reader is expected to cut from the magazine, oil to make it transparent, then apply it to a diagrammatic typewriter keyboard. * The students carry "detractors," which seem to be energizing devices. * Personal names no longer contain vowels, but are all consonantal, like Hz. * One wonders what kind of liquor could have been worth four thousand dollars a fifth back in 1924, but still a pleasant, if a little pathetic story.

108. **RAYS AND MEN.** *Amazing Stories Quarterly*, Summer 1929. Ill. Hugh Mackay.
Short story. * *Time:* the present and A.D. 2180. *Place:* Nebraska. * The narrator (Doctor Atwood), an interne at the Lincoln General Hospital, agrees to be the guinea-pig for a new anaesthetic that a colleague has discovered. He awakens about two hundred and fifty years later into a new world. He is treated with professional courtesy by the personnel at the hospital, but adjustment to the new Lincoln is very difficult. Not only is the technology more advanced, but people have changed, both en masse and as individuals. Instead of the individualism of the twentieth century, a concern with one's relationship to society is paramount. As a result, all are well adjusted, and on an international level there is no more war. Individuals learn to sublimate violent feelings when necessary. * Atwood falls in love with Elite Williams, one of the nurses; she likes him, but warns him to control his emotions because the eugenics laws may not permit them to marry. She is right, of course, for when Atwood is classified, he is designated as a blue, above Elite's purple, and marriage is impossible. There can be no exceptions. * Shortly after this, Elite, breaking rules, warns Atwood that he is about to be picked up by the police for "education," which really means imprisonment and perhaps brainwashing, since he is considered too violent for the future culture. He tries to escape, but is traced by the police, whom he disintegrates—and awakens back in 1928. * Was his experience delusion caused by the anaesthetic? Or did he really slide into the future temporarily? Atwood claims that one of his legs is now different from the other, the result of a future leg transplant after an accident. * *Miscellaneous:* While in the future, Atwood finds people anticipating what he has to say. He wonders if telepathy is involved. Nurse Williams tells him that telepathy is impossible, but that the future people are very skilled at muscle reading. * Energy is chiefly extracted from the air. * Literate, as always with Breuer, but the ambivalence of the future society, with both socialization of the individual and violent repression

of differences, is jarring and not as smoothly handled as it might have been.

109. **THE BOOK OF WORLDS.** *Amazing Stories*, July 1929. Unsigned ill.
Short story. * Old Professor Cosgrave, the most civilized man the narrator has ever known, is gentle, kindly, and utterly horrified at brutality. This kindliness is the cause of his mental undoing. * While working with geometric solids, Cosgrave conceives the idea of a four-dimensional stereoscope, a hyperstereoscope. Just as an ordinary stereoscope gives the illusion of three dimensions from two-dimensional pictures, the hyperstereoscope would create four-dimensional images from solids. * Constructed, the device shows fourth dimensional worlds. (Cosgrave makes the analogy of spots on pages of a book, which are far apart when the book is open, but perhaps contiguous when the book is closed). Cosgrave sees an evolutionary sequence from giant reptiles to a human race. He watches the humans advance scientifically and technologically, but each stage of advancement is associated with horrors and bloodshed. Death rays and horrible slaughter characterize the later stages of the world that Cosgrave watches. * Cosgrave breaks down, for he realizes (or assumes) that what he has seen is a general evolutionary pattern that will also come to pass in our world. It must be stopped, he says, before he goes mad. * One of Breuer's better stories.

110. **THE FITZGERALD CONTRACTION.** *Science Wonder Stories*, January 1930. Ill. Paul.
Short story. * *Time:* perhaps the near future. *Place:* Chicago. * Astronomers note a strange shining object that moves first toward Earth, then circles around the Moon. Shortly after this the narrator and his friend Wendelin (who is supervisor of the Cicero airport outside Chicago) are present when an enormous polyhedral vessel lands. At times the vessel is invisible. * After a while a door opens, and down a runway come several completely normal human beings, who seem bewildered at what they see. A young woman among them throws herself upon Wendelin with every indication of affection. * After some communication with sign language and graphics, the strangers remove their vessel to the Midway in order to make things handier for the savants from the University of Chicago. * The mystery unfolds when the strangers learn enough English to converse readily. They are, of course, of the same stock as we, for probabilities would prohibit the emergence of another human race elsewhere. And they come from the Moon, some two hundred thousand years ago. * *Background:* The ancestors of the travelers were inhabitants of the land of Mo, then situated in the Pacific Ocean. In a great catastrophe, Mo and surrounding matter were ripped out of the Earth and flung into space, to become our present Moon, Luna. The people of Mo, aware of the coming catastrophe, provided against it with underground shelters and stored resources. * On the Moon, which retained Terrestrial air and water, the survivors emerged and began another civilization, which soon rose to spectacular heights. But another tragedy was impending as the Moon began to lose air and water. * Since the only hope of survival was a return to the Earth, the Lunarians turned their minds to space travel. Although not as skilled in mass production and manufactures as our present culture, the Lunarians were far ahead of us in theoretical physics and engineering, hence were able to build the spaceship that landed in Chicago. * The spaceship was con-

Breuer, Miles J. (*continued*)
structed out of photon matter, therefore is not subject to the limitations of ordinary matter; elaborate mechanisms convert its substance back and forth between the two states as necessary. * The members of the space team decided to take the ship out on a trial run around the universe, setting automatic controls to bring the ship back to the Moon. The journey took about three and half days of their time, but when they returned to the Moon, they saw that enormous periods of time must have passed since they departed, for the Moon was dead. The voyagers had overlooked the question of time in the Fitzgerald contraction. * Some of the Lunarians will remain on Earth, but others, including Vayill, the young woman who greeted Wendelin, decide to take the supership out to explore the universe. Her history: Her fiancé, whom she was to marry just before the voyage, received a fatal cosmic ray burn and could not have lived more than a few days. By chance he resembled Wendelin closely. Vayill and Wendelin establish a romance. They marry, and he leaves with her on the ship. * Dr. Breuer, in the early part of the story, cites as reference Col. James Churchwood's books about Mu. He should have known better. * A pleasant enough story. * For a sequel see #114, "The Time Valve."

111. **THE HUNGRY GUINEA-PIG.** *Amazing Stories,* January 1930. Ill. Wesso.
(Reprinted in Conklin, *Science Fiction Adventures in Mutation.*)
Short story. * *Place:* Chicago. * Hinkle visits his old University of Chicago classmate, the great medical researcher Parmenter. Parmenter, as he informs Hinkle, has been working on glandular extracts that produce gigantism. His subjects have been guinea pigs, several of which were killed when they reached the size of dogs. But one guinea pig has been allowed to continue to grow. * The expectable happens. The guinea pig, which is now the size of a large bus and may weigh twenty or more tons, escapes. It is not vicious, indeed, it is timid and fearful, but its size and stupidity cause much damage, including the loss of several lives. Bullets do not bother it, and since it is within city limits, there are no realistic ways of destroying it. Parmenter is now deluged with lawsuits. * But there is a way out. During World War I Parmenter had been an artillery officer. Borrowing a cannon from the Army, he uses food to lure the rodent into an empty park, then directs the bombardment. The guinea pig is killed, but so is Parmenter.

112. **THE GOSTAK AND THE DOSHES.** *Amazing Stories,* March 1930. Ill. Morey.
(Reprinted in Conklin, *Science Fiction Adventures in Dimension,* in Conklin, *Great Science Fiction by Scientists,* and in Silverberg, *Arbor House Treasury.*)
Short story. * The title is taken from the little catchphrase, "The gostak distims the doshes," which is cited in works like Ogden and Richard's *The Meaning of Meaning* as an example in semantics. The phrase, thanks to Breuer's story, became something of a meaningless slogan among early science-fiction fans. The purpose of the story is an illustration of mob psychology. * The narrator listens to an exposition of relativity by the great physicist Woleshensky. According to Woleshensky, by altering one's mental set it should be possible to exchange one of the spatial dimensions (in which it is possible to move) for the temporal (in which it is not possible). The result would be motion into a fourth dimension. * Taking Woleshensky literally, the narrator concentrates on such an exchange and finds himself

in an other-world, but in a university milieu much like the one he left. The people speak English, but are all strangers to him. He seeks out a professor of physics, explains what has happened, and is accepted for what he is. After a time he is assigned to instruct a course in experimental physics. * Life in the other-world, which is much like Earth, but slightly less advanced technologically, is pleasant enough until the gostak episode. * Inexplicably, there is great excitement on the campus and elsewhere about the gostak and the doshes. Quarrels break out, cheering sessions take place, and soon the narrator's immediate world is caught up in a furor. The narrator tries to find out exactly what "the gostak distims the doshes" means, but is trapped within the semantics of the phrase—each term can only be defined within the parameter of the sentence, not externally—in a way a verbal anticipation of Goedel's theorem. His benefactor, the physicist, secretly agrees with the narrator, but they seem almost unique. * In a very short time the nation is at war with other cultures who take the phrase differently or reject it, and the casualty lists begin to arrive. * The narrator is now in danger, since his views are known; he is arrested, tried, and sentenced to death. But it suddenly occurs to him that perhaps he can escape the mad land by reversing the process by which he entered. He escapes, and finds himself back in the college with Woleshensky. * The context, of course, is a post-war examination of the hysteria of World War I, and perhaps other wars. An interesting story, parabolic in execution.

113. **THE DRIVING POWER.** *Amazing Stories,* July 1930. Ill. Wesso.
Short story. * Professor Grimm, a dedicated scientist, is unhappily married to a superficial, high-society-oriented woman. While they live amicably, there is no real love or understanding between them, and Grimm tends to spend more and more time in his laboratory. * His greatest discovery is a technique of subatomic engineering whereby he can manipulate subatomic particles—adding and subtracting by means of extremely short-length X-rays—and create substances of his own desire, even life, which is, after all, chemical. As he perfects his apparatus, he eventually is able to create in his laboratory what amounts to a dream world, with a fine home and surroundings, and an extremely pleasant, intelligent, and amiable young woman, whom he presumably takes for a lover. * This creation is recorded in a series of patterns, so that he can shut the woman and her surroundings off when he leaves the laboratory, and recreate her easily the next day—almost a magic lamp situation. * The culmination comes when, to silence his greedy wife, he indicates that the invention he has been working on would be worth millions. She barges into the laboratory, the professor dissolves the projection too rapidly, and his papers are scattered and blown into the nearby river, where they are lost. * The professor takes his loss philosophically. * Breuer contributes several very long footnotes describing, in imaginative terms, of course, the processes that Grimm used, and their relationship to concepts in modern theoretical physics. They demonstrate that Breuer had a good non-specialist's knowledge of contemporary physical science. As for the story itself, it is intelligent and interesting.

114. **THE TIME VALVE.** *Wonder Stories,* July 1930. Ill. Paul.
Short story. * Sequel to #110, "The Fitzgerald Contraction." * *Time:* About twenty years later on Earth, but a much shorter time in the photon ship's flight; also an undated period perhaps

Breuer, Miles J. (*continued*)

thousands of years later. *Place:* The Chicago area. * Wendelin, Vayill, and six other space travelers decide to continue their explorations, in this instance choosing the future Earth, via the same principle of relativity that brought the Moans to twentieth-century Chicago. * After a short period of subjective time they land in a waste area, with only a few mounds showing what used to be Chicago. In the near distance is a shining, beam-flashing area that is later revealed to be a still-active atomic bomb left from the destruction of Chicago. * The natives, who are small, scruffy, and nasty, capture the party and treat them badly, but a peculiar custom works for a time for the welfare of the travellers: The natives elect an absolute chief for a month, at the end of which time he is forced into the nuclear radiation and disintegrated. Wendelin is chosen as such a chief, but is strong enough to hold the job for several terms—until things get too hot. In the meanwhile, the photon ship has been destroyed in an explosion caused by the natives' tampering. * Back in the twentieth century, the aged scientist Dhorgouravhad, Vayill's father, is intensely depressed about his daughter, who will not return to Earth for another 200,000 years. She is already dead to him, he realizes intellectually, but he cannot accept the situation. Using high Moan science he makes fortunes with inventions, devoting the money first to constructing a calculating machine that will reveal the fate of the travelers. Analyzing an incredible number of variables, it predicts the world in which Wendelin and his associates find themselves. * Old Dhorgouravhad now constructs a time machine based on electron flow and entropy. In it, he and the narrator fly to the future and rescue the travelers just as they are about to be put to death in the radioactive area. * Thanks to relativity, the narrator and the Moans who remained in the twentieth century are twenty years older, but the explorers are only a few weeks older than when they left. Vayill, who had been bored with domesticity in Chicago, now decides that apartment life is for her. * Less satisfactory than the first story, which was at least based on a scientific principle, without a time machine popping out as a savior.

115. **PARADISE AND IRON**. *Amazing Stories Quarterly*, Summer 1930. Ill. Wesso.
Novel. * *Place:* Galveston and a Caribbean island. * The machine menace at hand, but easily defeated. * The Breckenridges were once close friends of Kramer, the mysterious oil baron who disappeared decades ago. Hence it is strange that when Kramer comes to Galveston, he refuses to recognize them. * Young Davy Breckenridge, M.D., who has also served a term as a Texas Ranger, is intrigued by the situation and forces himself upon Kramer as the mystery man is sailing away on his black yacht. Kramer is not unfriendly, but is obviously apprehensive. * The yacht, which is crewless and fully automatic, bears the two men to an unidentified, nameless island where the note of peril is immediately reinforced, for an enormous piece of machinery almost kills Kramer's granddaughter Mildred. Davy saves her life, while a group of formally dressed young men and women watch almost apathetically. * This is the entry to a very strange culture that baffles Davy, although the reader will probably work out what is really happening long before Davy does. * The people who watched ineffectually while Davy saved Mildred are all highly cultured, pleasant, sophisticated, beautiful people who live a life of utter

ease and perpetual entertainment. The arts are cultivated remarkably, and athletic skill is high. Life seems edenic and beautiful. Everything anyone could want, including luxuries, is available on demand, without money. The only work involved is an occasional day of "supervision." Technology is remarkably high, with automated cars, automated housing, and much else. * Yet there is something very wrong in the City of Beauty. Beneath the insouciant airs and the indolent dawdling there is a note of suppressed panic, a powerful tabu against talking of certain things, and a helpless feeling of inevitability when incidents such as Mildred's "accident" take place. * Davy, who is intelligent, is more and more bewildered as his stay on the island lengthens. He learns that there is no traffic whatever with the outside world (except for Kramer's occasional trips), and that even to mention it is tabu. The people, descendants of gifted, artistic people who settled the island two generations ago when Kramer was young, will not discuss the outside, nor even their own world. He is repeatedly told that the walls have ears. * Davy, after several "accidents" nearly kill him, comes to the conclusion that on the other end of the island, where there is a tabu area called the City of Smoke, there is a ruling caste that has created the reign of psychological terror and that it is responsible for mysterious disappearances, as individuals are seized by machines and raced away to the City of Smoke. He is only partly right, of course. * Let us skip over adventures against individual machines that have evil designs on Davy: Davy penetrates the City of Smoke, which is an incredible assemblage of automated industrialism, and finally learns the truth. Kramer had early developed the concept and technology of automation that finally produced the City of Smoke and by extension the City of Beauty. Involved is an advanced technology that supports invisibly the carefree activities of the City of Beauty. But the machines developed beyond Kramer's intentions and after a time became autonomous, with a gigantic computer (my term) that now rules the island. All the service machinery in the City of Beauty is bugged, visually and aurally, and the machines haul away those who show signs of not accepting the situation. The machine leadership, desiring to understand human emotions, has even taken to vivisecting humans considered rebellious. Davy narrowly escapes such a fate in the City of Smoke. * As Kramer fears, it is only a matter of time before the machines realize that they need not serve the humans at all. Indeed, by the end of the story, the machine rulers have recognized that they are superior to men and have decided to expand beyond the island into the outer world and take it over. * While most of the humans close their eyes to the situation, there is a small underground led by Kramer. Unfortunately, it is disorganized and ineffectual; it does nothing but meet secretly and talk. Now that Davy understands the situation, as the most aggressive person on the island he accepts leadership of the underground and begins to remodel it on a military basis, preparing it for combat. * The climax finally comes. The machines seize Mildred, and the machine leader offers Davy a deal: her release in exchange for cooperation in entering the outside world. Davy refuses. He himself battles with the machine action-leader, "killing" it with his axe, while the underground storms the City of Smoke and smashes the central machine brain. The machine menace is over except for an occasional survivor. * Davy and Mildred leave the island in a small, non-automated yacht that old Kramer had secretly built

Breuer, Miles J. (*continued*)

and hidden in a small cove, while the survivors of the play culture begin to learn how to make a living. * An oddity: Davy diagnosed the weakness of the underground as lack of discipline. As a remedy he instituted U.S. Army close order drill! * Breuer's most ambitious work. There is considerable suspense and mystery in the earlier sections of the story and an interesting artificial culture (based as Breuer admits on Wells's *The Time Machine*). Like *Erewhon* and *The Time Machine*, "Paradise and Iron" recognizes the problem of superior machine evolution and human stasis. There is imagination, Butlerian insight, and reasonable development, but the plot structure is erratic, the resolution is inadequate, and the heroics are unconvincing. It all turned out to be too easy. The story is still worth reading for the thought and the initial puzzle element.

116. **THE INFERIORITY COMPLEX.** *Amazing Stories*, September 1930. Ill. Paul, plus two photo montages perhaps by Breuer.

Short story. * *Place:* Chicago. * While attending refresher courses at the University of Chicago Medical School, the narrator makes the acquaintance of Professor Twitchett, a biologist. Twitchett is a shy little man, and only after a time does he become confidential with the narrator and describe his research. Working with nutrition and selection, he has been breeding gigantic microscopic life, amoebas the size of dogs, hydras seven feet tall (if they stand on their limbs), etc. Twitchett's claims must be true, for he displays photographs of himself together with his giant specimens. (These photographs are reproduced in the story, as indicated above.) Twitchett's research is attended with some danger, but he considers it worthwhile. * The narrator finally visits Twitchett's lab, but finds nothing. Twitchett has been committed to an insane asylum and his story was all a compensatory mechanism bolstered with faked photographs. * This incident bears out the earlier point of the story made in argument between the narrator and his partner, the importance of considering psychological aspects in human problems.

117. **A PROBLEM IN COMMUNICATION.** *Astounding Stories*, September 1930. Ill. J. Fleming Gould and the author.

Short story. * *Time:* presumably middle-late twentieth century. * *Place:* Northern Virginia. * Professor Hagstrom worries about his close friend Benda, a prominent engineer, who has thrown up his job and joined the Church of the Scientific God. This cult, founded by a charismatic leader named Rohan, "conceive[s] the earth to be a workshop in which men serve Science, their God, serving a kind of apprenticeship during which He perfects them to the state of ideal machines." * As a visible body for his group Rohan has established Science Community, a model city that embodies the utmost in modern technology. * The narrative takes several courses. Benda, on entering Science Community, discovers that he is subject to total discipline and is as good as a prisoner. His correspondence is censored, and he is constantly watched. * Benda is desperate to learn what is really going on. With the help of fellow engineers who have been trapped in the Church, he cautiously investigates and discovers that the cultists plan to seize New York City. Each of the captive engineers is to manage his specialty after the coup. * In the meanwhile, outside, Hagstrom worries about his friend Benda, whose letters sound strange. When Hagstrom proposes to visit Benda, Benda discourages him coldly, but finally agrees. During Hagstrom's

visit, Benda talks blandly, but gathers plants for Hagstrom to identify after he leaves. * Hagstrom, who understands that Benda does not dare to speak openly, recognizes that the plants constitute a cryptogram based on their shapes. He deciphers it and informs the authorities, whereupon Federal troops raid Science Community, capturing the leaders. * The cryptogram, which is reproduced, involves plant fragments with geometric shapes, which are interpreted by means of a logically derived code alphabet. * *Miscellaneous:* There are no indications of technical progress in the cult. * The Science Temple is shaped like a dynamo and is decorated with mechanical motifs; inside, blue-clad devotees worship at lathes, microscopes, and vacuum tubes. * An anticipation of Technocracy.

118. **ON BOARD THE MARTIAN LINER.** *Amazing Stories*, March 1931. Ill. Morey.

Short story. * *Time:* well into the interplanetary future. *Place:* Mars, the satellites of Jupiter. * Mars and the outer satellites Ganymede and Callisto seem to be heavily colonized from Earth, and must, therefore, be Earth-like. * Star reporter Streak Burgess is assigned by his editor to pick up human interest stories on the Mars rocket run. The passenger list is small, and chance lets Burgess make the acquaintance of a Mr. Johnson, who is trying to escape an extortionist who is trying to kill him. Johnson also happens to be the president of the Mars, Ganymede, and Callisto Line, to which the vessel belongs. * As it soon turns out, Johnson has not escaped the extortionist, who is on board, making attempts on Johnson's life. * A search of the vessel reveals nothing, but on the crucial occasion Burgess chases the assassin into an empty stateroom, where he apparently disappears. This incident gives Burgess an idea that proves to be the solution to the mystery. The would-be murderer is invisible; he is wearing a cloak or cape that is not perceptible under the narrow radiation band of the ship's lights. Burgess and an engineer friend on the ship set an infrared viewer that reveals the criminal, who is taken. * There are also romance and maturation subplots involved, but these need not be summarized. * *Miscellaneous:* Stewards on such ships are not human, but are humaniform robots. * The economic structure seems to be capitalistic.

119. **THE TIME FLIGHT**. *Amazing Stories,* June 1931. Ill. Morey.

Short story. * A latch-on to H. G. Wells's *The Time Machine.* * *Time:* the 1920s and various undated times in the future. * When Mrs. Hubble died, she left her colossal fortune to her husband Ezra for his life span, on his death to revert to Jerry Strasser, her son by a previous marriage. Ezra, who for reasons not made clear hates Jerry desperately, has worked out a way to "take it with him." * After a well-publicized competition, he settles on Henry Jurgenson, a young engineer, to build him a time machine on the model of the one described by H. G. Wells. After prolonged search, Jurgenson locates Filby, and with his fragmentary plans duplicates the original time machine. * Hubble then summons a news conference, shows a suitcase with money and securities, and announces that he will travel one hundred years into the future and die there, thus depriving Jerry of his mother's money. Hubble then disappears into the future. * Jerry Strasser, who has an annuity from his mother, attends college, specializing in physics, particularly thermodynamics. He chances to become friendly with Jurgenson. When the two men at a later date recognize their past associations with Hubble, they decide to build another time machine, follow Hubble, and retrieve the

Breuer, Miles J. (*continued*)

money. Instead of concentrating on geometry and dimensional time, Jerry uses the concept of entropy, motion in time by changing the flow of matter particles. * The entropy shell constructed, the two men take off, espy Hubble as he travels to the next century, and follow him. * Hubble, however, is an ingenious rogue. He asks for a parley, then, keeping his money, he seizes the entropy shell and leaves for the future. The two men follow in the Wellsian time machine. In an unknown era in the future, they catch up with Hubble and force a showdown. Hubble accidentally kills himself after shooting and wounding Jerry, and the two comrades return to the present with the money, leaving in the future Hubble's corpse and the broken Wellsian machine.

120. **THE DEMONS OF RHADI-MU.** *Amazing Stories Quarterly*, Fall 1931. Ill. Morey

Short story. * *Place:* Somewhere along the Colorado River, which (in real life) was largely unexplored until the turn of the present century. * Roughly ten years ago Professor Geiger and his daughter Lyla, looking for traces of colonists from Mu, disappeared in the unexplored area along the Colorado River. Young Morley determined to find them, and now as Major Morley of the aerial land survey, he has a chance. With two enlisted men he will fly over and photograph the area. * In a relatively short time the party espies a patch of green. Landing, they are captured by primitive natives and taken to a rather elaborate temple complex, where friendly priests on a higher level of culture greet them. As Morley soon learns, the priests speak a language related to Sanskrit, and the lost race is derived from the lost continent of Mu in the Pacific. The surveying team is treated well, in some sense regarded as semidivine by the primitives. * The land, however, is not a political unit. It is shared by two similar but hostile peoples, separated by a morass of boiling radium. Hostilities break out, and the explorers try to help the people with whom they have been staying. During a battle, however, Morley and his associates, betrayed by a woman whom Morley scorned, are captured. Needless to say, they find that Professor Geiger is the mastermind behind battle effects that terrified their friends. * Geiger, his daughter Lyla (who renews a previous romance with Morley), and the others plan an elaborate escape. Geiger builds a land rover driven by a huge propeller, sheathes himself and the others in lead clothing, and drives through the radium formation to the place where Morley's plane is still standing. After a little trouble, all fly away to safety, with a fortune in radium. * Perhaps Breuer's worst story. Usually his work has an idea behind it; in this case, there is nothing except flat, weak thrills.

121. **THE EINSTEIN SEE-SAW.** *Astounding Stories*, April 1932. Ill. Wesso.

Short story. * Tony Costello, a scientific genius who provided special devices and equipment for the mob, was fortunate enough to remain untouched when the gangsters were rounded up. The police had nothing on him. On the crucial occasion his desk disappears, and in its place is an ancient desk with papers on relativity and tensor analysis. Studying the papers, Costello discovers that Professor Bloomsbury has solved the problem of transferring objects from one space to another via the fourth dimension. * Not too long after this, safes with large amounts of currency disappear from banks and shops, leaving in their places old barrels of rubbish. The police suspect Costello, but, again,

they can prove nothing. * A new element enters when reporter Phil Hurren and Ione, the professor's daughter, decide to investigate Costello's laboratory. Costello catches them, and, instead of killing them, transports them out of our space. * Phil and Ione find themselves in a small universe, surrounded by cross sections from another universe that shares dimensions with the one they are in. There is no food or water, and there is a dangerous life-form that looks like dissected tinkertoys. * They return to our world, thanks to Ione's knowledge of her father's work, by using a huge safe as a counterbalance. They are deposited back in Costello's laboratory, but the energy released incinerates Costello. * *Miscellaneous:* Ione's father seems to be hopeless at anything except mathematical physics. * An amusing piece of work within the conventions of the magazine.

122. **MECHANOCRACY.** *Amazing Stories,* April 1932. Ill. Morey.

Short story. * *Time:* the twenty-sixth century. *Place:* mostly Washington, the capital of the world. * *Background:* The world is now entirely uniform in culture (exception noted below); everyone lives in gigantic cities, and all live under the authority of the World Government, a mechanical brain that makes all decisions, even in matters of personal life, and carries out all administration. The machine never errs. * Originally this system was adopted to prevent nationalism and wars. But while life in the machine cities is pleasant enough, with all needs taken care of, without poverty and crime, there is a machine pragmatism that can be lethal. The World Government considers the good of the system and the human race, not that of the individual. * Quentin Smith Lakeman has just returned from a year's stay in Democratia, a small republic in Tibet that is the sole exception to the World Government. Originally populated by individualists who were unwilling to accept machine control of their lives, it has apparently prospered and developed a high liberal culture. At present the World Government has decided that Democratia must be examined and perhaps brought under control. Since the machine lacks data, it sent Quentin as an undercover agent to gather information. Before sending Quentin, the machine warned him on several occasions that the mission was highly dangerous and offered him the choice of refusing it. Quentin, however, misunderstood the warning. * He landed in Democratia with no great difficulty, met the people, who welcomed him, and he began a romance with a young woman named Martha. A city machine man, he was soft and somewhat rigid, but a year in Democratia developed him in all ways. Indeed, he no longer wanted to return to the World Government. But his friends urged him to return, pointing out that a report by a friendly observer would be of more use to them than one by a later, potentially hostile observer. * Quentin has returned and reported to the machine. Now he knows what the machine meant when it warned that the assignment was dangerous. The machine sentences him to euthanasia, since he has been influenced by Democratia. This would have been his automatic reward for his service. The mechanical brain also has decided to exterminate Democratia. * Quentin, who might have accepted the sentence meekly a year or two earlier, now is unwilling, and with Jack, Martha's brother who accompanied him back to the city, escapes. There are problems and perils, but the two finally return to Tibet. * They are not there long before a delegation from the cities flies in to request Quentin to return and to help them set up a new civilization. The machine World Government is

Breuer, Miles J. (*continued*)

destroyed. Jack, on an occasion when Quentin was lying unconscious, bombed the apparatus. The brain was apparently not well protected, since no city man would think of such a thing. * Interesting beginning, but a fizzle ending.

123. **THE PERFECT PLANET.** *Amazing Stories,* May 1932. Ill. Morey.

Short story. * *Place:* Nebraska. * Wish fulfillment. * Gus Kersenbrock, a somewhat dull, ineffectual automobile mechanic, stumbles upon a wrecked spaceship out in the sand dunes. While fumbling around inside the ship, which maintains a lower gravity than Earth, Gus accidentally opens the valve on a gas cylinder, with astonishing results. * The gas almost immediately increases his intelligence and imagination, so that when he returns to his hitherto frustrating job, he finds the most difficult repairs easy. Gus is also now able to improve his nowhere romance with Kitty, edging out his rival Thompson, who is a young, small-time bootlegger. But the effect of the gas lasts only a few days. * When Gus returns repeatedly for reinforcement, the periodicity of his ability evokes curiosity. Thompson follows him and tries to seal off the spaceship. When the men come to blows inside the ship, however, the gas is accidentally released, and both men are elevated. Gus, as usual, becomes more intelligent and more forceful, while Thompson, who had been a mean-minded, small-town hood, acquires character. Gus and Thompson come to terms. They will have the gas analyzed and marketed, and Kitty can choose whomever she wishes. * Routine.

124. **THE FINGER OF THE PAST.** *Amazing Stories,* November 1932. Ill. Morey.

Short story. * *Time:* undated near future. * Humor. * The brash young salesman Waldo Swift enters the office of Herodias Buffum, president of The Radionics Remedies Company, and proceeds to demonstrate the Paleoscope—a device that reproduces images of past events. This offers the excuse for a series of sitcom situations, as an important formula is stolen, sexual misbehavior is revealed, and similar matters. * Trite.

125. **THE STRENGTH OF THE WEAK.** *Amazing Stories,* December 1933. Ill. Morey.

Short story. * *Place:* significant portions on a lost island in the Azores. * When football hero Jerry rescues Helen Louise Worcester from being raped by her father's lab assistant Marko Petrescu, he sets off an unforeseeable chain of events. * Petrescu, who has been working on neurology, particularly synapses, leaves, and for several years nothing happens. Then Professor Worcester and Helen Louise disappear. There are no clues, but Jerry receives a mysterious message telling him to follow a certain green plane. He does so, and finds himself on an unknown Azorean island. * There Petrescu has set up a marvelous mechanical installation with everything controlled by surgically installed human brains. Professor Worcester's brain operates the main building complex. Petrescu himself is now a gigantic cyborg (my term), with his brain in a metal body. But even if he is a machine, he still desires Helen Louise, though a reader may wonder why and how. * Things look bad, but youth and virtue triumph. Worcester rebels, killing Petrescu, and vibrations set loose at Petrescu's command destroy the establishment and the island as Jerry and Helen Louise escape. * Below Breuer's usual level.

126. **MILLIONS FOR DEFENSE.** *Amazing Stories,* March 1935. Ill. Morey.

Short story. * Not science-fiction. * John Stengel, returned from college during the height of the Great Depression, has no choice but to take a job in his obnoxious uncle Jake Bloor's bank. Stengel, who reads in the newspapers of local bank robberies, tries to build a system for protecting the bank, while Jake scoffs. But when robbers come, to John's surprise, they are led by his Uncle Jake, who is now preparing to rob his own bank. Jake jeers at John's burglar devices, which involve tear gas and an alarm circuit, but is caught. * Unusual in the s-f magazines for a story to invoke the Depression atmosphere so strongly, but a weak story.

127. **THE CHEMISTRY MURDER CASE.** *Amazing Stories,* October 1935. Ill. Morey.

Short story. * Not science-fiction, but a detective story. * When Dr. Seeley is found dead of cyanide poisoning in his laboratory, his death is at first considered accidental. But as evidence accumulates, murder becomes certain. Isaiah Culp, curator of the Chemistry Building, does much to solve the case. Part of the point of the title is that two of the personalities in the story used to communicate via chemical symbols used in a substitution cipher. * Not much as a detective story.

128. **MR. DIMMITT SEEKS REDRESS.** *Amazing Stories,* August 1936. Ill. Morey. The heading carries the story as "Mr. Dimmitt Seeks Redress," while the contents page carries it as "Dr. Dimmitt Seeks Redress."

Short story. * Professor Dimmitt, whose wife and child were killed in an automobile accident by corrupt politician Graw, discovers that he has no possibility of legal redress. Indeed, if he continues his efforts against Graw, his life will be in peril. He retreats to his laboratory. * Dimmitt does have one weapon, which he has accidentally discovered. This is a preparation that increases metabolism enormously. He first observed it when a preparation splashed into his eyes and he discovered that his time sense was apparently disrupted. * Dimmitt improves his discovery so that he can speed up his whole body enormously. Revenge is in sight. Walking about invisible, because of his great speed, he shadows Graw. His opportunity comes when he sees Graw's young son on the street while Graw is driving up recklessly Picking up the statue-like boy, he sets him down in front of Graw's car and waits for Graw to kill his own son. He gloats as he sees Graw's horrified face. But at the last minute Dimmitt discovers that his conscience will not let him commit murder. He removes the boy from danger and goes on his way. He later learns from a newspaper report that Graw died of a heart attack, obviously caused by Dimmitt's action. * Routine.

BREUER, MILES J. and WILLIAMSON, JACK

Information about the authors is given under their own entries. According to *Future's Child,* Williamson's autobiography, the idea for "The Birth of a New Republic" was Breuer's, but most of the writing was done by Williamson. Breuer and Williamson also collaborated on the chapbook *The Girl from Mars* (Stellar Publishing, 1929), Gernsback's Science Fiction Series No. One, and on at least two unpublished fantastic stories.

129. **THE BIRTH OF A NEW REPUBLIC.** *Amazing Stories Quarterly,* Winter 1931. Ill. Wesso.

(Reprinted by P.D.A. Press, New Orleans, 1981.)

Novel. * A pastiche of American history. * *Time:* the early twenty-fourth century. *Place:* mostly the Moon. * The narrator, John Adams, reminisces from 2399 to the events of the third

Breuer, Miles J. and Williamson, Jack (*continued*)

decade of the twenty-fourth century. * *Background:* In 1989 atomic energy was unlocked; essentially, it is derived by bombardment of heavy metals with hard radiation, generating outbursts of electricity, heat, and various gases, apparently without dangerous radiation. The process is the property of the extremely powerful Metals Corporation, one of the cartels ruling the Earth, and is kept proprietary and totally secret. * In 2130 Colon left San Diego with three small spaceships and landed on the Moon. The moon was not quite barren, for there was atmosphere and moisture in the caverns, and an intelligent life-form that was in the process of developing barbaric civilizations on the surface. These are the so-called moon calves or Lunarians, large creatures reminiscent of elephants with long legs; they have prehensile trunks and three eyes. Their metabolism involves silicon, with which they are plated, and enormously powerful jaws enable them to eat rock for food. After colonization the moon calves were slaughtered, dispossessed, poisoned with carbohydrates that rendered them drunk, and in general crushed, but wild tribes still roam in barren places. * Large scale colonization became possible when Cardigan developed a process for liberating oxygen and other gases from the lunar rocks. As a result, a thin but tolerable atmosphere, with helium instead of nitrogen, exists around the Moon, while large glass-covered cities—notably New Boston, Colon, and Theophilus—present all the luxuries of the Earth. The population of the Moon is about two and a half million people. * Metal extraction is the chief industry, with raw materials shipped to the Earth to the Metal Corporation, at prices set by the Terrestrial company. The economy is capitalistic, and it is possible for one to grow very rich if one has a good mining claim. * As for personal background: John Adams, as a boy, was taken to the Moon by his parents. His father, a very intelligent man, found a good claim, rich in rare minerals, which he worked well, becoming one of the wealthiest men on the Moon. John went to college in New Boston, where he met a young woman named Mary Jon, with whom he fell in love; but she left college and disappeared mysteriously. * About the time that John becomes mature, tension arises between the Moon settlement and the Metals Corporation. First, a trade war begins when Metals Corporation reduces its paying prices in order to wreck lunar economy. From here on, events are pastiches of the American War of Independence, including personalities and battles: Warrington, Franklin Gardner, Captain Benedict, Lafollette, etc. There would be no point in giving details. The moon people win, establishing a republic with Warrington as president. * A strong element in the success of the moon people lay in a new development of atomic power. A generation earlier, one Vardon worked it out for Tranco (France), but he was killed and the invention destroyed. His daughter, Adams's college friend, has the secret, which she gives to Adams. * *Miscellaneous:* The D ray is equivalent to a disintegrator. * The caverns of the Moon, used as a refuge during the war, teem with strange, horrible, exotic life. * At the end, Adams speaks of travel to other planets, without detail. * An odd story. The early biography of Adams and the cultural setting are well done, but the military aspects fall apart novelistically. All in all, a curiosity of early science-fiction.

BRIDGE, FRANK J.

Pseud. of Francis J. Brueckel, who has a separate entry. The

blurb to "Via the Time Accelerator" refers to Bridge as the author of "The Moon Men" and "The Moon People." Brueckel's story "The Moon Men" had already appeared, but no story titled "The Moon People" is recorded.

130. **THE MECHANICAL BLOODHOUND.** Science Wonder Quarterly. Spring 1930. Ill. Ruger.

Short story. * A sequel to #144, "Professor Diel's Ray," which was published under the name of Frank Brueckel. * Really a science-fictional detective story, perhaps originally submitted to Hugo Gernsback's *Scientific Detective Monthly.* * Jack Barton has been receiving threatening phone calls as the date of his marriage to Alice Smedley nears. The identity of the caller, apart from the fact that he is a rejected admirer of Alice, is unknown, and the threats are worrying. With the narrator's assistance, scientific aid solves the problem. Professor Diel has invented a machine that picks up scent particles and analyzes them, using a photographic technique. With air samples from the phone booth from which the calls have been made and others from the office of the suspect, the criminal is identified and restrained legally until after the wedding. * A flat nothing as a story.

131. **THE WAR LORD OF VENUS.** *Wonder Stories,* September-November 1930. Ill. Marchioni.

Adventure novel in the mode of Edgar Rice Burroughs. * *Time:* A.D. 2004. *Place:* mostly Venus. * Ludwig Von Kressen has isolated the principle that drives the tails of comets away from the sun and is now embodying it in a large spaceship. His destination is Venus, and accompanying him are three friends: the narrator, Ken Marx, a writer; Parri, a French astronomer; and Dr. Throck, an English physician who speaks as do American novelistic Englishmen. * The voyage is extremely rapid and uneventful, and Venus is as expected, mostly water-covered, but with some islands and large landmasses that maintain paleontological animal life: dinosaurs, saber-tooth tigers, etc. * There are also two types of humanity, crude people like *Eoanthropus dawsoni,* termed Piltdown men; and handsome, intelligent people equivalent to Cro-Magnon man. * As might be expected, the Earthmen (except Parri, whose mind is deranged and amnesiac) assist the Cro-Magnards against the Piltdowners. The progress of the story is a succession of captures, escapes, raids, rescues, and finally full-scale military operations (with grenades constructed by the Earthmen) in an attempt to wipe out the Piltdowners. The campaign is successful. In the meanwhile, the narrator has teamed up with the tall, handsome Queen Deena of the Cro-Magnards and at the end of the story takes her back to Earth with him. Along the way the men became formal members of the tribe. * Little to recommend.

132. *VIA THE TIME ACCELERATOR.* *Amazing Stories,* January 1931. Ill. Morey.

Short story. * *Time:* the present and A.D. 1,001,930. * Brockhurst, a scientist friend of the narrator's, explains time and the fourth dimension in a variation of Einsteinian relativity and claims that time travel is possible by altering the vibration rate of atomic particles. * He now sets out on a time-trip paralleling H. G. Wells's time traveler (who is mentioned) and, as the narrator watches, returns in a matter of seconds, bruised and battered, in a bruised and battered machine. * Brockhurst's narrative: As he leaves the present, in blurred vision he sees himself returning, a sight that keeps his spirits up during his time traveling. He reaches 1,001,930 with no difficulty, finding Earth

Bridge, Frank J. (*continued*)

barren and rocky, but with strange globular vegetation with curious exposed roots. A huge fortress-like building is not too far away. * He is in peril almost immediately, for the plants are water-sucking creatures that float with internal hydrogen-cells; what looked like roots are tentacles with sucking cups. * Brockhurst, escaping the plants with difficulty, enters the building, where an old man who claims to be the last man on Earth greets him by name. The old man explains: As a time paradox, he has already been back to the year 502,181, in Brockhurst's machine; his arrival was recorded, and the old men has read this in ancient records. This is how the old man knew Brockhurst's name and origin. * The old man begs Brockhurst to take him back to 502,101, but this is impossible since the machine cannot hold two men. Thereupon the old man steals the machine and leaves, undoubtedly for the year 502,181. * Brockhurst is in a quandary. There is no way for him to return to the past, yet he has seen himself return. Is it possible that he really saw the Last Man traveling to the 1930s? On exploring the great building, however, he finds a museum, and there, in a glass case, is his time machine, bruised and battered, held together by straps, placed there around A.D. 502,101! * Brockhurst repairs the machine, finds fuel, and returns to 1930. * He ponders the curious situation: The Last Man could have taken the machine out of the museum showcase before Brockhurst arrived from the past, and traveled back to 502,101, but there are logical problems. "It had been waiting there before it arrived there, yet it could not have waited there, if it had not arrived there first. . . . He couldn't have [taken the machine], for then he would have been taking the time machine out of its location long before it arrived at that location, and I, after arriving in 1,001,930, would have returned to 1930 with the original, new machine, so I could not have left it in 1,001,930, that it might go back to 502,101. . . ." * *Miscellaneous:* the vampire plants decompose water. They caused the desiccation of Mars; and, on reaching Earth, have been responsible for the desiccation of Earth and the destruction of native life. * The story as story is unremarkable, but the time paradox, perhaps first fully worked out here, is clever. The story marks an enormous improvement over Brueckel's earlier work.

BROOKE, JAMES

No information.

133. **STROHEIM.** *Amazing Stories,* February 1936. Ill. Morey.

Short story. * The great surgeon (and medical researcher) Stroheim is in a class by himself, with techniques, general knowledge, and brilliance that are unmatched. He is also an unpleasant, ruthless egotist. At the moment he has just killed a patient by performing a brain operation that reduced the patient to something like an automaton, responsive to Stroheim's will. (The hospital superintendent, Miss McKay, who is madly in love with the cold Stroheim, raises only the mildest objections to his activities.) * Stroheim, in addition to being a surgeon nonpareil, has a powder that increases nerve impulses, making him a superman both in physical strength and intellect. With this powder he plans to rule the world, reforming it and removing weaknesses to suit his taste. * Stroheim's erstwhile assistant, the dastardly Dr. Earl, knows of the powder and will stop at little to get it. He, too, wants to rule the world. Earl captures Stroheim

and puts him in an iron cage, while the treacherous (so one might think) Miss McKay snuggles up to Earl and abuses Stroheim. But it is all a ploy, and in the showdown Miss McKay shoots Earl. * Stroheim, all this behind him, discovers that he is from now will exercise his formidable talents only to help mankind. * The description above can only hint at the quality of the story.

BROOKS, EDWY SEARLES (1889-1965)

Very prolific British author of British boy's serials; adventure, school stories, and notably Sexton Blake detective stories. Work appeared in *Magnet, Gem, Nugget,* and many other papers. Also wrote under many pseuds., Berkley Gray, Edward Thornton, Reginald Browne, Robert W. Conrad, and others not relevant for this study.

134. **SUBMARINE ROAD-'PLANE NO. 1.** *Scoops,* 10 March 1934. Ill. S. D. Published anonymously; attribution per W. O. G. Lofts, who had access to the publisher's records.

Boys' fiction. * Short story. * When John Hall, "stony-broke," unemployed mechanic, reads a legal notice requesting him to contact solicitors in Yorkshire about his late uncle's estate, he immediately sets out, even though the trip exhausts his money. The solicitors inform him, however, that his uncle died almost penniless, leaving John only the key to a certain shed. * Opening the door of the shed, John sees a peculiar-looking automobile, the dashboard of which is covered with strange controls. Hoping that he may obtain a few pounds for the crock, he takes it out on the road. He finds it very difficult to handle, and it is soon out of control, racing at an enormous speed. Ahead is a police car with a stop sign. When a collision seems unavoidable, John pulls frantically at unidentified controls, whereupon the car sprouts wings and takes off neatly into the air. Still frantically trying to master the independent-minded car, which is heading for the sea, John tries other controls, whereupon it descends to the sea bottom, now completely enclosed and watertight, where it proceeds amiably. Further controls bring it to the surface, where it becomes a speedboat. * Complications enter. The uncontrollable car swamps a motorboat that was heading for a tramp steamer, and one of the occupants of the motorboat lands on the bonnet (hood) of the car. * After more to-do, including encounters with the other men, an explanation takes place. The man on the bonnet is Sir Hubert Reynolds, automobile tycoon, who was being kidnapped for ransom. Obviously interested in the vehicle—an instruction manual for which John finds too late-- he offers John partnership in marketing the multipurpose vehicle. * This is the most fantastic cut of all—an honest automobile czar!

135. **SUBMARINE TANK NO. 1.** *Scoops,* 7 April 1934. Unsigned ill. Published anonymously; attribution per W. O. G. Lofts, who had access to the publisher's records.

Boys' fiction. * Short story. * Young Tom Millward and reporter friend Jerry Sanders have been invited to the workshop of Professor Rodney Millward near the Channel. There in a cave, entry to which is sealed by steel doors, the professor maintains a workshop in which he has built *Submarine Tank No. 1.* This is essentially a submarine that can crawl along the bottom of the sea with treads of some sort. * The boys came just in time, for the British submarine *Alpha* has collided with a French vessel in the Channel and is resting helpless on the sea bottom. * A brief interruption shows the hopelessness of the submarine, with dead motor, batteries emitting poisonous gas, and lack of air. *

Brooks, Edwy Searles (*continued*)
Millward takes along the two young men as assistants, since his engineers are all off duty, and they make their way to the stranded sub. But how to transfer the men from the submarine to *Submarine Tank No. 1*? Millward has a solution. He has an apparatus that decomposes water into hydrogen and oxygen; he permits the hydrogen to escape, then adds nitrogen to make air—which forms in a dome around the two vessels. The crew of the *Alpha* is thus saved. * There is also a secondary plot. Wolfe, a vicious neighbor of Millward's, and two gangster associates stow away on the submarine tank and try to seize it.

136. **THE IRON WOMAN**. *Scoops,* 14 April 1934. Unsigned ill. Published anonymously; attribution per W. O. G. Lofts, who had access to the publisher's records.
Boys' fiction. Rally round colonialism, boys! * Short story. * *Place:* an island off Wales, and the coast of West Africa. * The great millionaire inventor Garston Grand and his engineer associate Dick Metcalf have assembled their great project on a small island off the coast of South Wales. Ready to be operative, it is a sixty-foot-tall steel woman, capable of walking quite nicely and grasping things with great precision. The woman is not a robot, but simply a piece of machinery powered by electricity broadcast from Grand's yacht and controlled by operators who sit in a chamber in the woman's waist, like fetuses. Why this device is shaped like a woman is never explained, but perhaps Garston Grand's psychologist could say a few words. * The Woman works perfectly, and Grand announces the first use to which it shall be put. In the West African colony of Semsi, local chief Obogo has declared independence, murdered the British commissioner, and captured British administrators and traders, taking them to the interior. Obogo is not really operating on his own, however, but is the tool and figurehead of the unscrupulous Mark Veese and two American gangsters. The British navy cannot restore the Raj, for the jungle comes down to the water, and the beaches are too shallow for ships to draw near the land. It is thus up to the Iron Woman. * Obogo has just killed the local witch doctor, and the American scoundrels are worried lest the natives revolt. The Iron Woman strides ashore. Grand delivers an ultimatum to Veese, who defies the Britons, and the destruction begins. Veese, who has been temporarily captured but released, takes off into the jungle, as do the frantic natives. The Iron Woman thereupon busies herself trampling down the entire native town, sparing only the white compounds and housing. * Grand and party take off in pursuit of Veese. Along the way, the Woman becomes mired in a deep swamp. While Metcalf frantically regears the Woman's legs to obtain more power, Veese and associates empty a petrol depot into the swamp and fire it. It looks as if Grand and company are finished, but Metcalf gets the Woman operative at the last moment. Ironically, the Iron Woman's big feet open a channel out of the swamp, carrying the burning petrol away from our friends to the gangsters, who are burnt to death. Obogo, captured, reforms, and the British prisoners are released. The author, in a bad prophecy, proclaims that this is "merely the first of a long series of stirring adventures for Garston Grand's Iron Woman."

137. **THE MARCH OF THE BERSERKS**. *Scoops,* 19 May 1934. Unsigned ill. Published anonymously; attribution per W. O. G. Lofts, who had access to the publisher's records. Boys' fiction. * Short story. * *Place:* a small island in the Azores, and Kent, England. * Dr. Sigmund Mentz, wealthy stormy-petrel endocrinologist, has scoured England for unhealthy, malnourished, underdeveloped young men. Having assembled two thousand such unfortunates, he is now on his way to his establishment in the Azores, where, with pituitary injections, he intends to transform them into physical and mental marvels. Many people regard his claims and hopes with doubt, but he has had some success in animal experiments. * Although Mentz is generally considered a philanthropist, he is really a scientist and is conducting a calculated experiment. It is intimated, though not spelled out, that if his technique works, he will apply it to himself. * On the island, the young men are fed and housed, but are not subject to any discipline. After two months the results of Mentz's treatment are apparent; the men are bronzed Apollos. * Mentz now returns to England to recruit another two thousand men. His assistant, Dr. Carlton, keeps in touch with him by radio for a time, then is silent. Another voice claims that Carlton is ill, but Carlton manages to scream out a plea for help. It is obvious that something is wrong. * Mentz hurriedly sails back to the Azores, where he finds a horrible situation. His establishment is completely wrecked; skeletons are lying about; and his prize specimens, now nine or ten feet tall, muscled like gorillas and covered with hair, have run amok. Although bestial and vicious, they have not lost their intelligence. The so-called berserks kill Mentz and his crew, seize the steamer, and sail for Britain, where they land at Folkestone. Raging, roaring, killing everyone whom they encounter, burning, destroying, they march on Canterbury. They massacre the local police and seem unstoppable, since the inept central government cannot respond to the situation. * Two aviators, Squadron Leader Williams and Lieutenant Fellowes, risking their careers, take matters into their own hands, dropping poison gas on the berserks and exterminating them.

BROTMAN, MORTON
Portrait accompanying "The Phantom Killer" (*Amazing Detective Tales,* August 1930) shows a man in early middle age. Otherwise no information. Social Security records list a Morton Brotman (1893-1976), a resident of Essex County, New Jersey.

138. **THE MISSING HOURS**. *Wonder Stories,* April 1935. Ill. Winter.
Short story. * Crime story, with a science-fictional element. * A bank is robbed; a noted scientist is murdered; the police are killed—and in each case time is missing. The explanation: A little man has a flashlight-like apparatus with which he hypnotizes his victims, controlling them for about an hour. He commands them to forget the assistance they may have given him in committing his crimes. Also involved is a super-explosive. * Routine at best. The hypnotic tube is not explained.

BROUGH, PETER
According to Schwartz/Weisinger the pseud. of E. P. BROE. No other information.

139. **FINGERS OF THE MIST**. *Amazing Stories,* June 1929. Ill. Paul.
Short story. * *Place:* mostly Newfoundland. * Planes flying over Newfoundland are missing, and fishermen are afraid to venture on the sea. * Trevelyan is asked by Admiral Stokes to investigate. Flying to St. John's, he soon solves the problem. Alexander, an eccentric biologist, has been conducting

Brough, Peter (*continued*)
experiments with squid tissue. He has developed a tissue that can survive in sea water, eliminating waste properly, and grow with fantastic rapidity, but without turning into a squid. It can extrude tentacles at will. * Trevelyan saves Alexander's life from such a creature, and learns that some of Alexander's material has been flushed into the sea. * The explanation of the disappearances: A gigantic tissue creature reaches up into the sky and pulls down low-flying planes; it also eats fishermen. Trevelyan kills it with a phosphorus bomb.

BROWN, BERNARD

British author of several books on motion picture practice and technique. Brown obviously also has a sound knowledge of acoustics and recording techniques. Unfortunately, it has not been possible to find any information about him.

140. **PRIMA DONNA 1980.** *Amazing Stories,* October 1931. Ill. Morey.
Short story. * *Time:* 1980. * *Background:* In this future world, where crime, unemployment, and bad weather have been eliminated, entertainment rules, particularly the vulgarities of Los Angeles-based World Teltainments, headed by Joe Schonberg. World Teltainments is a television empire, an American monopoly that broadcasts scrambled signals through receptor boxes that prevent unauthorized reception. * The current fad is the great singer Dorna Guiselle, who sings utter drivel in the most gorgeous voice known, with incredible virtuoso swoops. She receives a salary of ten million dollars a year and is the prized possession of Schonberg. * To protect herself Guiselle has a private throat and ear specialist, Dr. Helberg, who watches her (with a bank of acoustic instruments) on closed circuit when she performs. Helberg is an Order A consultant who is available on circuit perpetually. * On this occasion Helberg notices with alarm that La Guiselle's voice sounds different, and on running an analysis, he sees that frequencies above 6000 are thinner than they should be. * A physical examination confirms that there is indeed something wrong with her throat, laryngeal leukoplakia, a precancerous condition that necessitates an operation. The procedure is usually successful, but it will mean that Guiselle will be unable to sing for several months. * In desperation, Helberg turns to his friend El. Nash, an eccentric genius in the area of acoustics and electronics. After interviews with Joe Schonberg—who is a caricature of a Hollywood producer—Nash (who had devised the scrambling barriers used in broadcasting) agrees to help World Teltainments out of its crisis, for its rating is falling rapidly. * Helberg operates, Guiselle is recuperating satisfactorily, and Nash has provided a solution in Miss Wentworth, a capable singer, who while not on the level of Guiselle, has a warmer voice. Nash, using artificial enhancement of harmonics, turns her voice into the supervoice, the perfect voice. It looks as if World Teltainments is saved, for Wentworth achieves a stardom even superior to Guiselle's former popularity. * All might seem well: Helberg is in love with Wentworth; Wentworth is happy with a small salary that Schonberg is paying her; and Schonberg, who has callously discarded Guiselle, canceling her contract, is minting money. * But the rapid denouement: Guiselle, in a prima donna's passion, arrives at the studio and tries to knife Schonberg, then Wentworth; while she is being held, Schonberg calmly shoots her, confident that he can control the broadcast image of the murder. And Nash, who

bears Schonberg a grudge, announces that the perfect voice is now attainable by anyone with his apparatus and that Schonberg's monopoly is ended. * One of the best stories in *Amazing,* strikingly modern in its anticipation of technology, with a secure content of acoustics, A&R work, and business ethics.

141. **PHOTO CONTROL.** *Amazing Stories,* August 1934. Ill. Morey.
Short story. * *Time:* a frame perhaps around A.D. 2000, with earlier material from the 1930s. * *Place:* London. * Told in retrospect. * The London of the future is quiet and peaceful, without traffic or hordes of people. This is how it happened. * Bob Williams, an assistant to the great engineer Jason Stewart, is in love with Vera, Jason's daughter. Hence it is a particularly deep personal tragedy when Vera is killed in a traffic accident that might have been avoided. * The two men determine to remove the possibility of further accidents. First, they work upon braking mechanisms, using a gyroscope and an air pressure arrangement that permits far shorter braking distances. Then, they design a radar-like system that prevents double-crashes. The final improvement, about five years after they started, is a totally automated traffic grid that encompasses a city. Such grids become international. * But there is something going on, and as Williams learns at the last minute, Stewart has gone mad with grief for Vera and is determined to teach the rest of the world sorrow. Williams tries to stop him, but Stewart changes the frequency of the control system, and the entire system collapses, killing perhaps millions. * Not bad. The integration of science/engineering into the story is well handled.

BRUECKEL, FRANK or FRANCIS, JR.

U.S. author, then resident in Milwaukee, Wisconsin. Removed to California. According to Social Security records a Francis J. Brueckel (1910-1976) died in Los Angeles. This is presumably our author. See also Frank J. Bridge, pseud.

142. **THE MOON MEN.** *Amazing Stories,* November 1928. Ill. Paul.
Short story with obvious influence from Edgar Rice Burroughs. * *Place:* mostly space and Ganymede. * A manuscript written by Clyde Bachus about previous experiences. * Lloyd, a family friend who has discovered that gravity is caused by the rotation of electrons around the atomic nucleus, has further worked out a means for reflecting gravity back to its source. He now builds a space car, the *Space-Waif.* On the maiden voyage, Lloyd, Bachus and friends leave the Earth for a quick jaunt to the Moon, but someone has sabotaged the gravity apparatus, and before the men can regain control, they are far beyond the Moon, ultimately landing on Ganymede. * Ganymede has a varied climate. In the tropics it is like a Carboniferous Earth, but this area is edged by temperate zones. * There are two intelligent races on Ganymede. One race, the Ja-vas, are brown-skinned, very slender, and have enormous heads; they are scientifically advanced beyond us. The other race is perfectly human, white-skinned, but primitive in culture. The Ja-vas capture Bachus and his friend Rosonoff and place them in a slave pen along with human Ganymedans. There Bachus learns the language and becomes acquainted with the charming Navara. * Slavery under the Ja-vas is not too arduous, but Rosonoff, Bachus, Navara, and others seize the first chance to escape. Using cathode-ray death guns, they kill their Ja-vas guards, seize a land car, and make for the area where the space car must be. Their escape is successful

Brueckel, Frank (*continued*)

but tragic, for when a gigantic dinosaur-like monster attacks, Navara seizes it by the tail and is killed. Bachus reaches the space car, where he learns that the other members of the expedition, except perhaps Rosonoff, are all dead. He flies back to Earth, writes out his manuscript, and departs as the frame narrator watches. * *Miscellaneous*: The Ja-vas also have glass rods that serve as paralysis rays. * In some way, though the author does not explain it, the Ja-vas can understand English and even speak a little. Perhaps telepathy. * A young man's work.

143. **THE MANUSCRIPT FOUND. . IN THE DESERT**. *Science Wonder Stories*, March 1930.

Short-short story. * Third-prize winner in the contest based on the November 1929 cover. Brueckel received fifty dollars. * The narrator, wandering about in the desert, comes upon a cave filled with superscientific equipment. There is also a visitor from space. When the alien reaches for his weapon, the narrator beats him to the draw and kills him. Entering the cavern, the narrator turns on a television equivalent that shows flying saucers carrying away the Eiffel Tower and the Woolworth Building. As the narrator watches, he sees an Earthman, apparently in the Woolworth Building at the time of its removal, gun down the alien crew of one of the saucers. The saucer, out of control, accidentally rays one of the other saucers, then crashes into the third, thus destroying all. But a beam from the space event comes through the television set, destroying the cave and its equipment. The narrator is dying, and presumably is writing all this down. * The aliens: Humanoid, dwarf, huge headed, goggle-eyed, blue-skinned. * Negligible as fiction.

144. **PROFESSOR DIEL'S RAY**. *Science Wonder Stories*, March 1930. Ill. Paul.

Short story. * The professor and his narrator assistant discover a way to harness cosmic rays so that they can pass through solids and return, bearing visual images. It takes a certain amount of experimentation before this result is achieved. But on the first occasion the machine is used, it witnesses a bank robbery and provides information for the police. * During the course of the story, the narrator mentions a magazine that publishes scientific detective stories, obviously Hugo Gernsback's *Scientific Detective Monthly*. * Negligible. * For a sequel see #130, "The Mechanical Bloodhound," which was published as by Frank Bridge.

BRUELL, EDWIN

No information.

145. **MEN WITHOUT SLEEP**. *Wonder Stories*, May 1933.

Short story. * One of the very few occasions on which a pulp magazine has published a story written in experimental prose. The model might well be Isidore Schneider's *Doctor Transit*. The author concentrates more on stylistic effects than story line. * Dr. Raynell, who has devised a serum that removes his need for sleep, gathers up derelicts and broken-down artists and imprisons them in a large garret after he has made them drug addicts. Raynell has now developed a further serum that should convey immortality. But when he drinks it, he ages instantly and falls dead. Later the attic is found full of corpses, Raynell's victims who died perhaps in sympathy with his death. * On the whole unacceptable, being muddled and filled with weak metaphor, but an occasional image is striking.

BUCHANAN, CARL and CARR, DR. ARCH.

Buchanan, who may be pseudonymous, was a U.S. author who contributed to other Street and Smith publications, notably *Clues*. Carr, who seems to be pseudonymous, has a separate entry. Carr alone has another story on a similar theme: "Wanderer of the Void," in the April 1937 issue of *Thrilling Wonder Stories*. The circumstances of the collaboration are not known.

146. **WARRIORS OF ETERNITY**. *Astounding Stories*, August 1934. Ill. Dold.

Short story. * *Time*: introductory section in the publishing present, but major action around A.D. 12,000, although in the sequel "Discus Men of Ekta" a time relativity is invoked that permits contemporaneity. * *Place*: major action on the planet Phenos, several billion light-years away. * Dr. Daniel Futrell has invented rays that create the perfect anaesthetic by removing the intellect from the body and sending it (temporarily) into space. It has worked on animals, but a human subject is necessary: himself. His friend Wilks Hurd will supervise the experiment, which could be fatal, should Hurd use too much energy. * Futrell is out of his body watching, when to his amazement he sees Hurd deliberately turn the control on full, killing Futrell's body. Hurd then marries Futrell's sweetheart Margaret, who collects Futrell's enormous insurance. Margaret, Futrell is convinced, is a conscious participant in the crime. * Futrell wanders in space, drifts about, until he receives a psychic message from Mola, a young woman who induces him to come to the planet Phenos. Phenos is a near eutopia; the people are human, having deliberately adopted that form in the past as the most desirable; and the Phenosians have long been acquainted with the principle of intelligence-liberation. * There is one problem, the so-called Warriors of Eternity. When the savants of Phenos discover criminality or mental aberration, the person concerned is put physically into suspended animation, while his intelligence is sent out. Unfortunately, these exiles have assembled on a certain planet, have possessed the bodies of its inhabitants, have built a space armada, and threaten to conquer Phenos. If they can destroy certain defenses, they will reoccupy their former bodies and overwhelm the land. * The men of Phenos implore the aid of Futrell, who is now incarnated in a Phenosian body. But Futrell is so obsessed with hatred for Hurd and Margaret and with plans to return physically to Earth and kill them, that it takes much to divert his energy to helping Phenos. The beautiful Mola, whom he met in space, is instrumental in convincing him. In the following war, which consists, in part, of psychic attacks, Futrell is instrumental in defeating the Warriors of Eternity. In the meanwhile, he learns that his hatred has dissolved under his love for Mola. Not that it mattered, for ten thousand years have passed since he was murdered. * Suggestions that the authors may have read Edgar Fawcett's *The Ghost of Guy Thyrle*. * A weak effort. * For a sequel see #147, "Discus Men of Ekta."

147. **DISCUS MEN OF EKTA**. *Astounding Stories*, February 1935. Ill. Dold.

Short story. * Sequel to #146, "Warriors of Eternity." * *Time*: about thirty years (Earth time) after the first story; the time relativity set up at the end of the first story is tacitly bypassed. * Dr. Paul Britten has devoted his life to creating a synthetic man. The end product, which is rather good, lies on the table, but Britten's attempts to animate it have failed. In frustration and despair, Britten calls upon the disembodied Futrell, whose fate he knows, to come to his aid. Lo! The body is animated

Buchanan, Carl and Carr, Dr. Arch (*continued*)
and Futrell is there. * Futrell explains: He has long been waiting for Britten to finish his work, since there is a great crisis on Phenos. In time past, when natives became old, they shifted their psyches to the preserved bodies of criminals whose minds had been driven out. But the supply of bodies is now very low. Worse, the inhabitants of the satellite Ekta, thirty-foot wide lenticular-shaped beings, are bombarding Phenos with radiation that causes premature aging. Thus, Futrell on Phenos is now a very old man, and the once beautiful Mola is an old hag. In a short time the Phenosians will be extinct, unless Britten's artificial bodies can provide new housing for their minds. * Britten agrees to accompany Futrell back to Phenos. Repairing Futrell's old machinery, they divorce their psyches from their bodies and fly to Phenos, where the situation has become even worse than described. Indeed, Futrell's body on Phenos is dead. But Britten makes him a new one, and all concerned hold a council of war. * The problem: Phenosian science is not adequate to penetrate Ektan defenses, and almost nothing is known about the discus creatures, who progress by whirling themselves around rapidly. Things look very bad, especially when a massive invasion of Ekta is a disaster. * The resolution comes when Britten manufactures a synthetic Ektan, which he animates. Dropped off on Ekta, he penetrates the Ektan breeding chambers, leaving behind powerful radio-controlled explosives. The Ektans are destroyed, but Britten is killed during his mission of sabotage. His mind is brought back to Phenos, where, finding romance with the daughter of Futrell and Mola, he settles down. This is just as well, since back on Earth the physician entrusted with the preservation of the bodies of the deutero-Futrell and Britten has gone mad and destroyed them. * Rubbishy, like the first story. Really a story that should have been written twenty years earlier.

BUERGEL, BRUNO H[ANS] (1875-1948)
German novelist, educator, expositor of popular science, notably astronomy. Born in Berlin. Said to have been the illegitimate son of the archeologist Adolf Trendelenburg. Important author of books popularizing science, notably *Aus fernen Welten* (1910), often reprinted and translated into several other languages. Juvenile *Dr. Ulebuhles Abenteuer Buch* (trans. as *Oola-Boola's Wonder Book*, 1932) used to be considered a high point of art deco book design. Also wrote *Gespenster, ein spiritistischer Roman* (1921). The present work is carried in the magazine as by Burgel.

    148. **THE COSMIC CLOUD.** *Wonder Stories Quarterly*, Fall 1931. Trans. from German by Konrad Schmidt and Fletcher Pratt. Ill. Paul.
(*Der Stern von Afrika*, 1921. Because of its origin, this story is covered in more detail in *Science-Fiction: The Early Years*.)
Novel. * *Time:* A.D. 3000. *Place:* Europe and Africa. * *Background:* Around A.D. 2700. the world entered a cloud of cosmic dust, which has since effectively cut off solar radiation, creating a new glacial period. Much of the north and south temperate zones are either uninhabitable because of the cold, or barely habitable. Civilization has thus shifted south, where the United States of Africa is the predominant power. In all probability the Earth will have passed through the dust nebula in another two or three thousand years, but it is doubtful if the human race (at least as a civilization) will survive that long. *

The story is concerned with Johannes Baumgart, who believes that the answer to the problem lies beyond Earth, on the Moon. Convinced that the Moon once held an advanced humanoid civilization with scientific resources adequate to combat the dust, he proposes a lunar voyage to acquire information. After some political difficulty his plan is accepted, but the science and engineering to support a voyage to the Moon are barely adequate. An earlier attempt at space travel, about two hundred years earlier, failed. * The *Star of Africa*, nevertheless, is constructed, and after a trial flight on Earth, it sets out for the Moon. Communication is maintained for a time by canisters dropped back to Earth, since radio will not work. But after the last canister is retrieved, there is no more indication of what happened to Baumgarten's spaceship. A gigantic meteorite fell into the ocean; this may have been the remains of the *Star of Africa*; or, the light that an astronomer saw on the Moon may indicate safe arrival. * In any case, the years pass, and nothing is heard of the heroic venture. The best guess is that the ship crashed on the Moon. * *Miscellaneous:* Travel in A.D. 3000 involves rockets propelled by a new, very powerful explosive. * Baumgart's speculation on lunar civilization is ultimately based on a Spenglerian cyclical theory of civilization that he proposes. * Race prejudice seems to have disappeared, and blacks and whites mingle on a basis of equality in the United States of Africa. * The United States of Europe is a much less important state than Africa, and it relies on Africa for food. * A routine work, with considerable time spent on romance. The pessimistic ending is unusual, but it is possible that the author was considering a sequel to reverse matters. If so, this sequel does not seem to have been published, at least not in book form.

BULEY, BERNARD
Prolific British writer of boys' serials, story-paper editor. Australian in origin. Formerly associated with *Hulton's Boys' Magazine*. According to W. O. G. Lofts, while F. Haydn Dimmock was editor-in-chief of *Scoops* and other Pearson's boys' papers, Buley was what amounted to managing editor of *Scoops*. See also #436, "Flaming Frontier" which has been identified as Buley's work too late to be included in this entry.

    149. **MASTER OF THE MOON.** *Scoops*, 10 February-24 April 1934. Unsigned ill. Published anonymously; attribution per W. O. G. Lofts, who had access to the publisher's records.
Boys' fiction. * Episodic short novel. * *Place:* Chicago, the Moon, and England. * Basically two themes, the battle of titans and saving the world. The narrative presentation is much like that of earlier American dime novels. * Captain Nick Chance, great scientist, and his four comrades (Chang, a Chinese; Sambo, a gigantic African black whose life Chance saved some time earlier; Submarine Sam Pike, a Yankee; and young Lord Algernon Tyford) are about ready to depart on the first rocket stratosphere flight. But actually, this announced goal is a subterfuge. Chance intends to go to the Moon to circumvent scientist Dr. Merlan, who plans to conquer the Earth. Merlan, whose rocket ship the *Meteor* has long traversed space, has established an empire on the Moon. Enslaving the native humanoid Moonmen, he has created an arsenal of fantastic weapons. For reasons obscure, Chance alone knows of Merlan's nefarious plans and activities. * There would no point in giving details of the up-and-down plot; only leading incidents will be

Buley, Bernard (*continued*)

indicated. Chance's ship, the *Rocket*, is attacked and disabled by space monsters. Chasing a stowaway, Captain Chance abandons the *Rocket* and lands on the *Meteor*, where he confronts Merlan. The two men exchange roles as victor and conquered several times, but eventually Chance disables some of Merlan's elaborate control apparatus. As for Chance's comrades, in the disabled *Rocket* they land on the Moon, where they are hunted by dragon-like and serpent-like Moon monsters several hundred feet long. They survive, of course. * As Chance repeatedly discovers, each time he foils Dr. Merlan, things take a turn for much the worse. Thus, when Chance knocks out Merlan's control box, he causes the native Moonmen, in rage and panic, to begin their invasion of Earth. One of the saving factors, however, is that Lord Algernon, disguised in a lunar space suit, can mitigate the calamities. * Back in space, both the *Meteor* and the *Rocket* have problems, first with space algae that befoul the vessels, then with the Sargasso of Space, whence extrication is difficult. * As for the invasion: The Moon has been knocked somewhat off its orbit, and Earth is suffering from earthquakes. San Francisco has been destroyed. The Moonmen land on Salisbury Plain, where they are defeated. Lord Algernon kills Merlan in a space-suited duel. * *Miscellaneous:* Both sides use a special moon metal for ship construction and rocket fuel. * Merlan's might consisted of five machine cities on the Moon and a gigantic space station. Our friends captured the space station and destroyed the machine cities. * The Moonmen are dispatched to Earth by being shot out of guns. * Like much lower-level British boys' fiction, so alien that it is difficult to evaluate. To an American it seems anachronistic, but possibly British boys liked it.

BURCH, WALTER

No information, but judging from the drift of the story, the author must have been a lawyer or have had legal training.

150. **THE MAN WHO WAS.** *Amazing Stories*, May 1927. Ill. J. M. de Aragon.

Short story. * Richard Ames, a wealthy businessman wrongly convicted of murder, is executed in the electric chair at Sing Sing. His friend Dr. Grant claims the body after receiving full certification of Ames's death. * Some time passes, and the estate of Richard Ames must be settled. Grant, who is executor, is unwilling to distribute Ames's effects according to his will, for, as it is now revealed, Ames is not dead, but was resuscitated by Dr. Grant. * Fate takes a hand. When Ames is about to appear in public, he is recognized by a detective and arrested. This causes a legal problem. The state insists that Ames be re-executed, since the intent of the law and the sentence of death is permanent death. Ames's lawyers argue that Ames paid his penalty when he was executed and medically declared dead, and that a second execution would be unconstitutional double punishment. * After further legal argument, the judge rules in favor of Ames, but only after Grant proves that Ames was really dead and that he had been revived. Grant had used electric shock, adrenalin, and vitasal, a substance that is the essence of life. * All well and good, but since Ames died, he no longer has any legal existence, and he is penniless after his estate is willy-nilly settled. But his wife and brother support him. * Later Ames is proved innocent when the true murderer comes forward and explains. * The detailed legal argument is interesting, but the story is clumsily told.

BURG, FRITZ

No information.

151. **THE SILICON EMPIRE.** *Amazing Stories,* August/September issue, 1933. Ill. Morey.

Short story. * *Place:* the upper Congo area. * The narrator, a member of the ill-fated Blackstock Expedition, is seeking the long-lost ruins of an Egyptian exile-city, when he literally stumbles into it. After falling a considerable distance, he finds himself in an underground passage, where a strange creature like a gigantic amoeba seizes him and carries him off without injuring him. It takes him to a large chamber lit by phosphorescent globes, where on a marble slab lies a beautiful nude woman. The woman arises and speaks to him telepathically. * She tells him that he is about fifteen miles underground, in the throne room of the Silicon Empire. * After a lecture on the possibilities of silicon life, she comes to the point: The silicon people, who are highly intelligent, want to experiment with bisexual reproduction in addition to the splitting process they normally use. Thus, the woman, Princess Isita of the ancient Egyptian city, and the narrator have a certain future ahead of them. However, there is a catch. The speaker is not really the princess, but the silicon emperor, who is occupying her mind and body. Another silicon being will take over the narrator. * Escape is easy enough. The being occupying the princess withdraws for a time, whereupon the narrator awakens the true princess, and together they race up the passages to the outside world, easily eluding the slow-moving amoeboids. On reaching civilization, the narrator marries Isita. * *Miscellaneous:* The silicon people have been hoping to perform this experiment for several thousand years, but until the narrator came along, Isita was the only human they had caught. They kept her in suspended animation during the interval. * Amateurish.

BURKHOLDER, A. L.

No information.

152. **DIMENSIONAL FATE.** *Wonder Stories*, August 1934. Ill. Paul.

Short story. * The narrative of Leopold Dochler, who is on death row in prison awaiting execution for the murder of his friend Joseph Burnett. Dochler, together with his college friends and World War I buddies Burnett, Patterson, and Madison, established a thriving engineering business. Burnett was an inventive genius, while Dochler, a mediocre engineer, became a lawyer and handled the firm's legal matters. * Burnett has theorized that if objects could be projected faster than the speed of light, they would transfer into the fourth dimension; also that electrical and magnetic effects could keep atoms from flying apart during the process. * Suitable machinery is built, and after a cat is transferred and safely retrieved, Burnett and Patterson decide to venture into the new dimension. A brief trip is successful, the men reporting a barren landscape and a red sun. * On the second trip, however, when Dochler and Madison retrieve the projection platform from the other dimension, they see on it a gigantic creature like a dragon with a somewhat humanoid head. It holds Burnett in its jaws and a pistol in a claw. During turmoil, the creature shoots Burnett, but is tossed back into its own dimension by the narrator. * Burnett's story before he dies: The other dimension is inhabited by the dragon people. They captured him and Patterson, took them to a superscientific city, and vivisected Patterson. Burnett managed to escape. * Burnett

Burkholder, A. L. (*continued*)

dies, and at his request the narrator and Madison break up the apparatus. Just as the survivors are trying to destroy Burnett's body and the evidence of his death, the police arrive and, seeing what is going on, arrest them. Dochler is tried and found guilty of murder. * *Miscellaneous:* The dragon-like creatures are more intelligent than humans, and there is a danger that they will invade Earth. * Routine and threadbare.

153. **THE MAD WORLD.** *Wonder Stories*, February 1935. Ill. Paul.

Short story. * The great brains (masses of cerebral tissue the size of a small room) have been traveling some fifty thousand years at half the speed of light. They are now arriving at our solar system. * *Background:* The great brains originated on a planet on the edge of the universe. Masters of an incredible science, they fought the inevitable decay and death of their star, even to living on the dead star itself for a time, but have been forced to seek a new home. Ten ships laden with specialists and administrators have undertaken the quest, with the brains in their living machines in suspended animation. * On passing one system they were attacked by an enormous fleet of living robots, whom the brains destroyed, but with the loss of nine of their ten ships. Now a solitary ship remains. * When the ship passes Mars, it is attacked by spaceships and seized by a tractor ray, but the brains are equal to the situation, and as they pass by Mars they force Deimos and Phobos to collide and drop upon Mars. * When the brains, who are completely telepathic, reach Earth, however, they meet more than they can handle. The perpetual broadcast of thoughts of anger, hatred, insanity, and desire affect the brains, and in a short time many lose their mental balance, some murderously. It is with the greatest difficulty that the chief supervisory brain assembles enough cooperation to lift the spaceship off the planet and back on its course. * Earth has been saved by the viciousness of its inhabitants.

BURKS, ARTHUR J. (1898-1974)

U.S. writer, one of the legendary fiction machines of the pulp era, with scores of stories. Served in U.S. Army in the Caribbean in the early 1920s and based early work on Haitian folklore and history. In 1930s prolific writer of action stories. In World War II head of U.S.M.C. physical training program. A very uneven writer, much of whose work is slapdash and padded; his best work has a certain coarse fluency. He never really mastered the science-fiction mode. * See also #1812, "Dictator of the Atoms."

154. **MONSTERS OF MOYEN.** *Astounding Stories*, April 1930. Ill. Wesso.

Short story. * Probably a debasement of Floyd Gibbon's future war novel *The Red Napoleon* (1929). * *Time:* the near future. The half-crippled, charismatic Asian Moyen has seized and consolidated Asia and Africa, and is now turning his attention to the Americas. Against him is Prester Kleig, head of the Secret Agents, Master of the Secret Room, who is returning to America after a mission to Moyen. Kleig has mysteriously survived the sinking of the ship on which he was returning. Associated with him is Professor Mariel, one of the great scientists of the day. * Moyen now attacks the United States with aerosubs (combination vehicles that function under water or in the air) that mount a disintegrating ray. * The President, his council of scientists, and Kleig debate what to do. Professor Mariel's viewing apparatus keeps them informed as to what is happening, while Moyen, using a similar apparatus, makes taunting remarks into the Secret Room. * Moyen captures the American fleet with a magnetic force and drags it out to sea, where his aerosubs destroy it. * His gigantic submarine vessels that mother the aerosubs creep up on land and disgorge other aerosubs and apparatus. * It looks as if America is lost, but Professor Mariel, acting on a suggestion of Kleig's, creates an apparatus that shifts Moyen's vehicles back in time. Moyen is killed, and America is saved. * Padded, undeveloped, and pretty bad. "Monsters of Moyen" is sometimes incorrectly called Burks's first science-fiction story; it is preceded by his "The Invading Horde" (*Weird Tales*, November 1927).

155. **EARTH, THE MARAUDER.** *Astounding Stories*, July-September 1930. Ill. Wesso.

Short novel. * *Time:* perhaps around A.D. 4000. *Place:* the Earth and the Moon. * Unapologetic social Darwinism with a vengeance, articulated in several fashions. The Earth is fantastically overcrowded; humanity is spread almost solid over the land and dry bottoms of what once were the seas, miles down into the Earth, and atop the highest mountains. The cause of this incredible population is immortality; there is no more death, except by accident, and people keep breeding. At the moment the social fabric is collapsing, with murders, expulsions, and seizures of living space. As an additional problem, the Earth is gradually losing its internal heat. * Earth's enormous population is divided into twelve Gens, each of which headed by a leader who purportedly embodies the will of his constituents. These twelve leaders form a council, atop which are the three Sarkas—Sarka the First, Sarka the Second, and Sarka the Third, grandfather, father, and son—all supernal geniuses. Sarka the First discovered immortality about 1800 years ago; Sarka the Second discovered antigravity and an accompanying range of phenomena; and Sarka the Third is working on the population problem. * Science and technology are erratically high, with beryls (à la Talbot Mundy) that show what is happening around the world and are attuned to the Earth's rotation; matter transmission (which is still in an experimental stage), disintegrators, flying apparatus, etc. * In the past, when the question of overpopulation arose, Gens Leader Oui, who ranks only below the Sarkas as a genius and is hostile to them, suggested altering the rotation of the Earth. This would cause great floods and destroy much of mankind, but would ensure survival of the fittest. Sarka the First refused to cooperate with Oui, and to prevent Oui's plan from being followed at a later time disintegrated all Earth's seas, opening up new lands to settlement. * Sarka the Third is now ready with his solution to overpopulation. He advocates taking the Earth out of its orbit to seek Lebensraum, first approaching and conquering the Moon, then Mars. He will move the Earth by changing the rotation of the various beryls, thus disrupting the Earth's rotation. His proposal is accepted by the Gens, but the wily Oui seizes control of the operation and manages to disrupt the Great Plan. * The Earth approaches the Moon, and hordes of humans fly to attack, but are met by lunar fighting machines, for the Lunarians are obviously aware of terrestrial plans. The Earthmen fare badly as the battle continues. * Matter-transmitted to the Moon, Sarka the Third and his girlfriend Jaska discover strange things: Oui has gone over to the Lunarians, with whom he has obviously been in contact, and has an alliance with the Lunar ruler, a glowing

Burks, Arthur J. (*continued*)

woman named Luar. Captured, Sarka and Jaska are sentenced to death by radiation from inside the Moon, but (since this radiation is much like that which rendered H. Rider Haggard's She immortal) instead are transformed into shining, superior beings. * It has become clear that the Martians (who are gigantic humans with eyes on long flexible stalks) are assisting the Lunarians (who are very small humanoids, all head and legs). * Earth is invaded by the Lunar and Martian forces, and the situation is grim. The tables are finally turned, however, when Sarka seizes mental control of Lunar energy cubes and turns them against the invaders. The Lunarians and Martians are forced to surrender and to yield large portions of their planets to human occupancy. * Obvious echoes of H. Rider Haggard and A. Merritt. * Better in summary than in reading. The somewhat imaginative positing of the initial situation is outweighed by too many incongruities and lame divagations. Nevertheless, the story was popular among early readers. * According to Schwartz/Weisinger, Burks received $1,380 for the story, a high payment for the day.

156. **MAD MARIONETTES. A COMPLETE NOVEL**. *Miracle Science and Fantasy Stories*, April/May 1931. Ill. Elliott Dold.
Short story. * *Time*: A.D. 2000. * *Place*: New York. * New York City is now a megalopolis extending from central New Jersey into Connecticut. It is also the home of a super-civilization, with enormous buildings five hundred stories high (with aerodromes on the roofs), and electro sub-cubes (flying antigravity cars) with automatic anticollision devices. There are no more streets. The Hudson and East Rivers have been roofed over and contain enormous complexes of buildings. Communication is via audiophone. * There is international tension, with potent bacteriological warfare possible. A useful portable weapon is the Lethal Tube, which projects an explosive so violent that it amounts to disintegration. * Head of New York, exact political position not stated, but in effect a benevolent total dictator, is the great scientist Rolda, to whom is due much of the development of New York. Rolda is worried. He has been getting nuisance calls on the audiophone, inexplicably calls that do not reveal the speaker, a seeming technical impossibility. * The calls continue and finally come to a climax when the Unknown invades Rolda's office and demonstrates a science far superior to Rolda's. In a sequent chase the Unknown's flying vessel is able to fly through walls and buildings thanks to a combination invisibility-disintegrating gas/field that he projects. At the end it is revealed that the Unknown is one Serge Alexoff, whose government in the Urals plans world conquest. * The story ends with this discovery. * One thrill comes when the Unknown kidnaps Mareta, Rolda's faithful companion, and tosses her out of his flying vessel; Rolda catches her in midair. * The first member of a series, Cities of the Future, that never came into being.

157. **MANAPE THE MIGHTY**. *Astounding Stories*, June 1931. Ill. Wesso.
Novelette. * *Place*: Africa. * Dr. Moreau and Tarzan meet. * Lee Bentley and Ellen Estabrook, shipwrecked off the coast of Africa, chance upon the establishment of Professor Barter, who disappeared from civilization years before after publishing a monograph on ape speech. * As Lee and Ellen soon learn, Barter specializes in brain transplants; he has already transferred the brain of one of the black natives into an ape, presumably a gorilla. * The professor speaks mysteriously of great projects,

and Lee learns the hard way what they are. He awakens in the body of a great ape, while the ape's brain has been placed in Lee's body. Lee is now Manape, and his human body is Apeman. * The problems are: Surviving until Barter reverses the operation, as he promises; preventing the rampaging Apeman from damaging his human body; and preserving the virtue of Ellen against apes, Apeman, and natives who capture the three. * Lee, who uses his clumsy ape hands to best advantage, saves the situation. Barter reverses the operation, as promised, and now hopes for international recognition. But when he ventures out among the apes, he is torn to pieces. He forgot his whip. * Some good touches, but credence is greatly strained. According to Ackerman, in *Gosh! Wow!*, editor Harry Bates suggested the plot to Burks. * For a sequel see the following story, #158, "The Mind Master." * Burks received $840 in payment for the story.

158. **THE MIND MASTER**. *Astounding Stories*, January-February 1931. Ill. Wesso.
Sequel to #157, "Manape the Mighty." If you thought the first story was silly, you should read this one. * Novelette. * *Time*: Three months or so after the events in Africa. *Place*: New York City. * Lee Bentley and Ellen Estabrook are back in New York—and so is Professor Barter, who is not dead, but is very much alive and equipped with heat and disintegrator rays, a far-viewer, and brain implants that permit long-distance hypnotic control. Hidden in secret headquarters, he hatches nefarious plans. * Barter is no longer a research biologist, but nurses higher ambitions. As he indicates in public announcements, he intends to improve the human race by kidnapping twenty tycoons and turning them into superior beings. * Lee Bentley has a very good idea what Barter is really going to do: he plans to transfer the tycoons' brains into ape bodies. * The mad scientist seems unstoppable, but Bentley has an ingenious plan. A newly discovered South American ape is more human than other apes. Bentley will disguise himself as such an ape, false skin and all, and await Barter, who will kidnap him. * This much happens, but Barter pierces the disguise, and, since he already has captured Ellen, things look bad. But Bentley, seizing Barter's disintegration tube, turns it upon Barter and his Japanese assistant. * One problem has been solved, but another remains: What to do about the tycoons whose brains have been placed into ape crania? One of the ape-tycoons resolves matters by first disintegrating the other transplantees, then himself. * According to fan lore, which may or may not be true, the cover showing a gigantic ape climbing up or down a high rise, dangling a human by the foot, suggested the idea of the motion picture *King Kong* to Edgar Wallace and Merian Cooper. In an interview, editor Harry Bates claimed to have suggested the idea to Burks.

159. **LORDS OF THE STRATOSPHERE**. *Astounding Stories*, March 1933. Ill. Wesso.
Novelette. * *Time*: presumably the near future. * The great scientist Kress is about to leave in his spaceship-plane to set a stratosphere altitude record. But he has forbodings, which become event. * Nothing is heard from him for three weeks, at which time his corpse is dropped on the lab roof of his friendly rivals Lucian Jeter and Tema Eyer, who are also building a stratosphere plane. * Shortly after this, mysterious events take place. As a beam of white light strikes, objects fly up into the sky. At first the beam works erratically, but then it settles on Manhattan, picking up, oddly enough, old buildings, then drop-

Burks, Arthur J. (*continued*)

ping them into the Hudson. * Jeter and Eyer leave in their new plane, determined to find the source of the ray. By checking air currents they locate an enormous invisible flying platform, on which they and. After a brief walk-about, they return to their plane, which is being "absorbed" into the platform, down to an inner globe. * A door opens, Orientals appear, capture Jeter and Eyer, and take them to the men responsible for it all: four Eurasians—the Japanese Sitsumi who has discovered the principle of invisibility (bending light around objects) and three Chinese, one of whom has invented the gravity-inverting ray. * Sitsumi, after offering the two Americans membership in his group, explains: As Eurasians they have been discriminated against in both cultures. Now with their formidable apparatus they intend to take over the world. They explain the strange building-plucking in Manhattan. Their eventual headquarters will be in Manhattan, and, in addition to making a terrorist point, they are getting the city ready for urban renewal! * Our hero-scientists have twenty-four hours in which to save the world. During this crisis time six replicas of their aircraft fly to attack the platform, but without success. The platform and sphere are bullet and explosion proof—but they do have a weakness. They disintegrate under certain vibrations, notably those of airplane motors. * Jeter and Eyer break loose. When they race their plane engine, the platform collapses, and the menace is ended. * The strange concept of urban renewal is amusing, but otherwise the story has little to offer.

160. **MY LADY OF THE TUNNEL.** *Astounding Stories,* November 1933. Ill. C. R. Thomson (C R T).

Short story. * Abnormal psychology and the supernatural. * George Styne tells of his childhood background and later life. As a boy on a poverty-stricken farm in the Midwest, he read a newspaper serial called "My Lady of the Tunnel." Set in the Civil War period, the story concerned a tunnel linking an old mansion to Federal and Confederate forces. Men often died in the tunnel, not because of the war, but because the tunnel was inhabited by a mad woman named Sybil who cut the throat of anyone she caught in the dark. * Styne was enormously impressed by the story and Sybil, and for years had nightmares about her, in which she almost stabs him in the throat, while he tries to fight her off. But there is an erotic element; he loves Sybil and does not wish to harm her; she loves him, but will still kill him if she can. * When Styne joins the marines during World War I, the repetitive dream ends, but when he is stationed in Haiti after the war and is in a perilous situation suggestive of a tunnel, the dream recurs. * Returning to the States, he is led by an inner compulsion to an old house in Long Island, which he believes he recognizes as his dream house. There he lives for a time as a paying guest with the decayed, ancient Caleb Farhm [*sic*], who is generally considered mad. * As Styne's last notes in his diary indicate, in order to explain his shrieking nightmares, he has told his story to Farhm, who seems excited. * Fahrm's lawyer finishes the story. Years before, Farhm had written "My Lady of the Tunnel," and like Styne he had developed a fixation upon Sybil. Hence, he could not tolerate Styne's familiarity with her and Sybil's seeming response. And he cut Styne's throat. * A surprisingly good story until one comes to the trick ending. The early detail is excellent, and in some cases can be recognized as autobiographical. Much better than one would have expected from Burks.

BURROUGHS, EDGAR RICE (1875-1950)

U.S. pulp writer, contributing mostly to the Munsey group and *Blue Book.* Generally considered one of the more important pulp writers within his narrow range. Author of the Tarzan novels, which have formed an industry of their own what with multitudinous reprints, motion picture adaptations, comic strips, etc. * Born in Chicago of well-to-do middle class parents; served in U.S. Cavalry in the Southwest for a time; operated various business ventures, none successful, until began freelance writing of fantastic adventures. His Martian novels have been extremely influential in science-fiction and supernatural fiction in offering models for an extremely romantic mixture of sentiment and adventure. As a technician, fitfully high on imagination (though with many parrotings and repeatings of threadbare earlier themes), with bad writing, weak characterizations and plotting. Essentially a boys' writer, apart from certain fixations (rape, phallic swordplay, sadism) and horrible social values.

161. **THE LAND THAT TIME FORGOT.** *Amazing Stories,* February-April 1927. Unsigned ill.

(Originally published as three short novels: "The Land That Time Forgot" (*Blue Book,* August 1918); "The People That Time Forgot" (*Blue Book,* October 1918); "Out of Time's Abyss" (*Blue Book,* December 1918). First book publication as *The Land That Time Forgot* (Chicago: McClurg, 1924 and London: Methuen, 1925. There have been Grosset and Dunlap reprints of the book, and separate paperback editions of the components.) A detailed discussion is to be found in *Science-Fiction: The Early Years.* * Novel, set on an unknown island in the Pacific. The unusual feature of this island is that evolution is still taking place very rapidly, but on an individual basis, not specific or generic. An individual starts as an egg and rises through various stages of life until he/she finally becomes the equivalent of a modern Homo sapiens. At the top level, humans breed as we do. * The plot, which is strongly colored by World War I jingoism, describes the adventures of British and American captives from a German submarine. The Germans do not play a large part. * In the first part, Bowen J. Tyler, a young American shipbuilder (his company actually built the submarine), and Lys, a young woman, have adventures amid the horrible reptilian and mammalian fauna of Caspak. * In the second part, friends of Tyler's, learning from a message in a bottle of his fate, come to rescue him. The story traces the adventures of Billings up through the various evolutionary stages of humanity—watching the "call" to a higher stage in operation—and the acquisition of a fully human girlfriend. * The third part, which is much the most imaginative, tells of the adventures of an Englishman, Bradley, among the final evolutionary stage of Caspak: winged men. These winged men, who are only males and must capture human women to breed, have a mad barbaric civilization, with a writing system and advanced architecture; their culture is based on socially accepted murder. * *The Land That Time Forgot* is generally considered Burroughs's finest work.

162. **THE MASTER MIND OF MARS.** *Amazing Stories Annual,* 1927. Ill. Paul.

(First book publications by McClurg, Chicago, 1928, and Methuen, London, 1939; American book reprints by Grosset and Dunlap. Reprinted in Burroughs, *Three Martian Novels.* Reprinted in paperback several times by Ace Books and Ballantine Books.)

Novel. * *Time:* around 1918 on. *Place:* Mars. * The sixth story

Burroughs, Edgar Rice (*continued*)

in Burroughs's Martian series. Background, a description of the previous stories, and a more detailed coverage of *The Master Mind of Mars* are given in *Science-Fiction: The Early Years*. * Mars, for Edgar Rice Burroughs, is a Lowell-Schiaparellian planet, with dwindling resources and the remnants of a once-high civilization, now somewhat decadent. The surface of the planet consists mostly of desiccated sea bottoms covered with a reddish vegetation, although along the canals, which are artificially maintained, there is lush growth. The thin atmosphere, which is escaping into space, is replenished or maintained by special atmosphere plants. * The natives fall mostly into two groups: a red race, which is totally human but oviparous, and a green race (the result of an ancient laboratory experiment that escaped control) which is gigantic and has four arms. (There are other less important peoples, but they need not be mentioned here.) The red men are highly civilized, with a science and technology superior to ours (though in a sword-and-raygun fashion), but the green men are on the edge of savagery, wandering about in hordes like American Plains Indians. Both races are extremely warlike and very long-lived, apart from ever-present accidental or intentional death. * In the previous volumes John Carter, a Virginian adventurer, soldier of fortune, and post-Civil-War prospector, was translated in astral body or some other mysterious fashion to Mars, where after interminable peril and slaughter he married a princess in the leading royal house of the planet. He has since received the honorary title of Warlord of Mars, which does not seem to mean much. * In the present story, Ulysses Paxton, an American soldier in World War I, lies dying in the trenches when he thinks of Carter's fate and wishes himself to Mars. * He awakens in the presence of a very ancient Martian, who turns out to be the great scientific genius Ras Thavas. Ras Thavas's specialty is organ transplants; not so much remedial medicine, but more transplanting brains from worn-out or damaged bodies to new ones. He has a thriving business, but, Mars being a planet of intrigue and bloody execution, he cannot trust his secrets or his fate to a fellow Martian. He will soon need to have his brain moved into a new body that he has been preserving for just this purpose. Ras Thavas thus settles on Paxton for his trusted assistant, for Paxton has nowhere else to go and nothing to gain by betraying the aged scientist. It is understood that when Ras Thavas finally collapses, Paxton will attend to his recycling. * All well and good, but in the meanwhile Paxton has fallen in love with one of Ras Thavas's reserved stock, the beautiful and charming Valla Dia, into whose shapely body the surgeon has transplanted the brain of an aged, shrewish, vicious old Martian queen. * Paxton's desire to reassemble Valla Dia forms the motivation for the remainder of the novel. Paxton forces Ras Thavas, when the latter is dying, to promise to restore Valla Dia, and sets out to recapture her body. * This venture takes him and assorted brain-transplant comrades to the city of Tur, which Burroughs uses as a means to satirize Fundamentalist religion, including a fake oracular idol. * Paxton and Valla Dia are, of course, successful and are united at the end. Ras Thavas, however, in his retread body, has been driven from his laboratories by his suspicious overlord, who thinks that the scientist has been plotting against him. * Ras Thavas is more interesting than Burroughs's usual characters. An irony on scientism, he is a monster of pride and arrogance, yet considers himself the most rational man on Mars. * This is

Burroughs's only original science-fiction story published in the genre pulp magazines during his significant period of writing. From 1939 to 1943, however, he published several stories in *Fantastic Adventures* and *Amazing Stories*. These stories are not highly regarded by most of his admirers. At least one story that is attributed to him, "John Carter and the Giant of Mars," was written by another hand.

BURTT, J[OHN] LEWIS, B.Sc.

Although Tuck refers to Burtt as a U.S. author, according to correspondence printed in the magazines, he was really a science schoolmaster in Jesmond, British Columbia, Canada. Nothing else known. An inquiry in Jesmond and nearby towns revealed no memories of Burtt.

The Lemurian Documents Series

A series of six stories that appeared irregularly in *Amazing Stories* in 1932. Their common characteristic is an attempt to euhemerize Greek myths in terms of an ancient superscience present in Mur (Lemuria). Elements are added, however, from the cultures of Easter Island and pre-Columbian Middle America. Burtt is not always consistent on names, which are sometimes Classical and sometimes Murian. The stories, which are stated by the author to be fictionalized versions of historical events, are based on documents found in a chest retrieved from the Pacific Ocean. Their original compositors enclosed a key to the Lemurian language and writing system, thus enabling the translation of the documents. They are dull, contrived narratives.

163. **THE LEMURIAN DOCUMENTS. NO. 1: —PYGMALION.** *Amazing Stories,* January 1932. Ill. Morey.

Short story. * The great biologist Vaag-Mel-On (the Classical Pygmalion) wagers with friends that he can create a complex living being. According to the terms of the wager, Vaag-Mel-On has ten years in which to accomplish his task, with a possible extension if circumstances demand it. First Vaag-Mel-On creates, organ by organ, muscle by muscle, nerve by nerve, an exact model of a perfect female body. Then he replaces each part with a sterilized, inactivated synthetic flesh duplicate. In all this, he is helped by his opponents in the bet, who have come to be as fascinated by the project as he. * Success seems imminent, but at the last moment the vivifying motors burn out and destroy the woman's brain. Since Vaag-Mel-On has come to love his creation fetishistically, he dies of grief. At the moment of death he recognizes that while the semblance of life can be created, life itself cannot. * Routine.

164. **THE LEMURIAN DOCUMENTS. NO. 2: THE GORGONS.** *Amazing Stories,* March 1932. Ill. Morey.

Short story. * Par-Su (the Classical Perseus), one of the youngest commanders in the Murian air navy, is summoned to the imperial Presence, where Emperor Pol-Dactu (the Classical Polydactes) assigns him to a difficult, almost impossible task. The emperor would like to marry Princess Ma-Ira of Cho-San, but she has been demanded in marriage, with threats of war, by the Mingan Emperor. Behind the Mingan Emperor are the Gorgons, who are forcing him to make this demand. The Gorgons are three monsters (Medusa and two brothers) who were expelled from one of Jupiter's moons and are currently upon Earth. Invulnerable to all known weapons, they project paralyzing and lethal rays. * Par-Su

Burtt, J. Lewis (*continued*)

consults the great scientist Mar-Kurus (the Classical Mercury), who has developed a new disintegrating ray. Accompanied by Mar-Kurus's beautiful daughter Minerva, Par-Su obtains invisibility apparatus and defenses against the Gorgon's rays from the three lunar wise women. He and Minerva then kill the Gorgons. In a later episode Par-Su uses Medusa's head to quell a rebellion. * Little fictional conviction.

165. **THE LEMURIAN DOCUMENTS. No. 3: DAEDALUS AND ICARUS.** *Amazing Stories,* May 1932. Ill. Morey.

Short story. * Third in the series, set, this time, in the earlier history of Mur. * Against a background of hostility between the empires of Minga and Mur, the scientist Dyd-Allu (the Classical Daedalus) and his son are captured by the Mingans. While a slave, Dyd-Allu creates individual flying units operated by man power, with which he and Icarus escape. Icarus, weakened by a wound, falls into the sea, but Dyd-Allu returns to Mur, where his flying apparatus becomes the deciding factor in the war with Minga.

166. **THE LEMURIAN DOCUMENTS. No. 4: PHAETON.** *Amazing Stories,* June 1932. Ill. Morey.

Short story. * Fourth in the series. * When Phaeton, son of the Emperor Phob-Istu (the Classical Phoebus) by a morganatic marriage, is recognized as crown prince, he undertakes to complete a project the emperor had long abandoned, creating a viable spaceship. After considerable trial and error, Phaeton builds such a ship, which he flies into the upper atmosphere. But the ship's controls do not work properly, and Phaeton is stranded in orbit above the Earth. Worse, his rocket, on periodic close approaches to Earth, devastates the land, laying waste large sections with its blasts. The emperor finally decides to destroy the vessel with a broadcast of radio waves. This is done.

167. **THE LEMURIAN DOCUMENTS. No. 5: THE SACRED CLOAK OF FEATHERS.** *Amazing Stories,* July 1932. Ill. Morey.

Short story. * Fifth in the series, set in an early period of Murian history. * A modification of the story of Jason and the quest for the golden fleece. * One of the ancient talismans of the empire of Mur is a cloak made of feathers from a rare and beautiful bird. It was stolen centuries earlier by a rival kingdom, but it now seems time to retrieve it. The country reputed to hold the cloak is considerably more primitive than Mur. * Jason and comrades, building a submarine, follow an underground channel into the sacred lake of the kingdom of Ecparu. There, with cannon pointed at the royal palace, they demand the cloak. But Ecparu no longer holds it; it was taken as booty on a raid by the neighboring kingdom of Kulthak. After ferocious battles in which the Kulthakians use poison gas, the Murians and men of Ecparu win and regain the cloak, which is returned to Mur.

168. **THE LEMURIAN DOCUMENTS. No. 6. PROMETHEUS.** *Amazing Stories*, September 1932. Ill. Morey.

Short story. * The sixth and final story in the series. * The Murians have long been in quest of atomic energy, but, despite some progress, have not succeeded. The great scientist Pro-Mak-Tnu (the Classical Prometheus), however, recognizes what is needed, data from a working atomic plant—the sun. Pro-Mak-Tnu takes his spaceship as close to the sun as is humanly possible, gathers what data are necessary, and returns—a wreck

of a man. The data are entrusted to his brother Ep-Mak-Tnu (the Classical Epimetheus) and the latter's wife Pandora. * Through no fault of Pandora's, the vault where the secret is kept is raided by agents of the hostile underground civilization of Plu-Ton. Unfortunately, they took only data on releasing atomic energy and neglected to take information about limiting the process. In desperation, the Murian council tries to send control data to Plu-Ton, even though he is an enemy, but it is too late. The under--ground people release wild atomic energy, destroying themselves and Lemuria. * Ep-Mak-Tnu and Pandora, who are in aircraft at the time of the disaster, survive. Traveling to the still primitive land of Atzt-Lan, they serve as culture heroes. * To Epimetheus is given the power of vision into the future: He sees Atlantis rise to high civilization, but be destroyed by atomic explosions. Perhaps our age, too—although Ep-Mak-Tnu does not see the end of our civilization. * The most successful of the six stories.

Other fiction

169. **WHEN THE UNIVERSE SHRANK**. *Amazing Stories,* October-November 1933. Ill. Morey.

Short novel in the "Skylark" mode. * *Time:* A.D. 2945. *Place:* mostly in space on the way to Sirius and back. * Something strange is happening: people are getting enormously larger (twelve feet), animals are correspondingly larger, as are plants. No, it is soon discovered, that is stating it backwards: the inorganic universe is shrinking. The expanding universe postulated for centuries has ended, and space is now moving back onto itself. This is effective not only on an atomic level, but in heavenly bodies, which are drawing much closer to one another. As a practical result of this, there is no longer room on Earth for mankind. * What can be done? There is no way that the process can be stopped, but brilliant young Diane da Silva suggests removing the oceans from the Earth and developing the new land that is exposed. The learned council laughs, but remarkable genius scientist Neil Cameron takes her seriously, and the two, funded by the billions owned by Cameron's mother, work together. * When Neil finishes a spaceship, the two young people, who are in love, decide to visit Sirius, which is much closer than it used to be. * Partway there, their meteor detector, a sort of radar, observes a large body ahead of them; it is a spherical spaceship, obviously from Sirius. A space battle follows, at the end of which Neil and Diane are forced to surrender. Not only were rays and energy screens involved, but telepathic assaults. But the lovers do manage to send warning back to the solar system before they give up. * Taken on board the Sirian vessel, they discover that the Sirians are perfectly human. They, too, are having problems with Lebensraum, and they hope to colonize other suitable worlds. * After con-versations and will battles with the telepathic Sirian commander, Neil and Diane escape to their vessel and start back to the solar system. * Their warnings were received, and preparations are underway for an interstellar war. Diane and Neil are given high commands in the Solar System fleet, which includes components from Earth, Mars, Venus, and the Outer Satellites. * Thanks to their information, the Sirian fleet is badly beaten, and the Sirians agree to a somewhat harsh peace. Meanwhile, back on Earth, a captive Sirian whom Neil and Diane had captured and befriended has solved the water problem. Constructing enormous hollow metal balls, he forces water into them with Sirian antigravity

Burtt, J. Lewis (*continued*)

projectors. The water is then taken out into space, where it forms a hydrosphere inside Mercury's orbit. As years pass, organic life shrinks back down to adjust to the new environment. * *Miscellaneous:* The inhabitants of the various planets in the solar system all seem to be human or humanoid. * When Neil's message reached the solar system, the head of the system's ruling body dissolved the government and assumed the position of absolute dictator, a step of which Neil approves. A note of the times in the 1930s. * Before the space battle, the solar system ships strewed masses of ball bearings through space to act as meteors against the invaders. * A very weak job that manages to catch the flaws of the "Skylark" series without their virtues. E. E. Smith wrote a very bitter letter criticizing the science of the story, but one can speculate that he really resented the imitation.

170. **THE WHITE DWARF**. *Amazing Stories,* May 1934. Ill. Morey.

Short story. * *Time:* events of the 1960s and later, told in reminiscence from about 2050. * When around 1960 it becomes obvious that something is wrong with the sun, the great scientist Robert Sanderson, father of the narrator, provides an explanation. The sun is collapsing into a white dwarf, a tiny body with minimal radiation. * At first the situation seems hopeless, but Sanderson evolves a scheme that saves the world. Placing banks of enormously powerful rockets at strategic places, he forces the Earth out of its orbit into a new orbit very close to the now visibly shrinking sun. While this is taking place, a deputation of Venusians arrives, asking for information on planet moving. Friendly relations are established. * There was some damage, but at least the Earth and mankind survived. A reader is likely to be incredulous, particularly when Burtt, who should have known better, does not understand the principle of rocket propulsion. * Told as a historical narrative. * Routine at best.

171. **THE MARTIAN MAIL**. *Amazing Stories,* April 1935. Ill. Morey.

Short story. * *Time:* the interplanetary future. *Place:* the space run between Earth and Mars. * The new mail ship, the *Marterra,* operates on a novel (apparently untested) principle. An apparatus on board changes the nature of space before it, creating a gravitational pull that drags it along. * The trip proceeds smoothly for a time, but then the chief engineer worriedly informs the captain and the president of the line that the gravitational vortex has gotten out of control and that the ship is in danger. * Worse, as time goes by. The vortex develops, becoming larger and more powerful, since space has been disrupted, and it starts to pull Mars and Earth out of their orbits. Deimos, indeed, crashes into Luna. * It looks like the end of the solar system, but President Torrens may have a solution: Create another vortex that will cancel out the first. The operation may save the solar system, but it means certain destruction for the *Marterra.* * The second vortex does work, but both Mars and Earth have already suffered enormous damage. As for the *Marterra,* its shattered remains are later found, with a few of the personnel still alive. As an aftermath of the disaster, the Earth's orbit runs closer to the sun. * Routine.

172. **THE NEVER-DYING LIGHT**. *Amazing Stories,* August 1935. Ill. Morey.

Short story. * *Time:* the remote past. *Place:* a planet in another solar system, then Earth. * Essentially events in Genesis transformed into science-fictional terms. * A frame narrative

reveals that the author's friend Maybright, since dead of radiation, found the Temple of the Undying Light somewhere in South America near Asuncion and has translated metal tablets found there. * The document: The planet Parydis, which is much like Earth, is in great danger from a cosmic cloud that threatens to explode the world. As the cloud approaches, the ruler Adman-Kar takes council, especially with his sons Bel and Canin. In the background are perpetual reference to religious prophecies. * Adman-Kar and Bel propose migrating to another solar system, while Canin raises objections, urging that Parydis will survive the cloud. * When it becomes obvious that Parydis is doomed, the people enter twenty gigantic spaceships and start the search for a new home. After spending decades in space and passing through one system that is unsuitable, they find Earth, on which they settle. * The colonization is not happy. Canin kills Bel, dissension breaks out, and in a short time much of the ancient culture is lost. It is obvious to the writer (Thot-Nubis) and Adman-Kar that many millennia must pass before mankind arises again. * Thot-Nubis, in addition to writing a chronicle, generously includes instructions for creating atomic power, which Maybright does not include. The temple is still there, guarded with lethal atomic radiation. * Cumbersome and routine.

173. **WHEN THE METEOR STRUCK**. *Amazing Stories,* June 1936. Ill. Morey.

Short story. * *Place:* an alien star system and the solar system. * The story is a narrative dispatch sent by Elzar the Archivist telling of Prince Kestran's mission. When the planetoid Nor was expelled from Kestran's system as a nuisance to navigation, Kestran and his crew followed it out of curiosity. To their dismay, they saw that it would strike the third planet (Earth) of another system, a planet inhabited by beings who were just rising in civilization. * Since they did not have planet-moving power, the best that the aliens could do was divert Nor slightly so that it crashed into Luna instead of the Earth. * Kestran was also concerned about the further fate of the Earth. Radiative heat generated by the Lunar impact was melting the polar ice caps, and civilization was likely to be destroyed by flood. Oddly enough, the fourth planet, where a higher civilization existed, was dying of desiccation. * The aliens had a bright idea: Preserve Earth's civilization from flood and help Mars by transferring the water to Mars. The aliens, working telepathically on the minds of both planets, created feelings for peace and comradeship and suggested the technology for space flight to the Martians. * The two worlds came to friendly agreement. Earth would trade water to the Martians in exchange for space technology. * In a few years heavy space craft began to carry containers of water into space, where it froze, then removed the containers and repeated the process until a large ball of ice was formed in space. Spaceships then towed this ice to Mars, where is fell upon the poles. As a result of this, everyone is happy. * The aliens are not described except indirectly as not bipeds. * Routine.

BUSWELL, LOUIS
No information.

174. **CLOUDS OF DEATH**. *Amazing Stories,* June 1929. Unsigned ill.

Short story. * *Time:* the near future. * The second world war started in the Balkans. In a short time most of the world was engaged, but the United States did not participate. The third

Buswell, Louis (*continued*)

world war, the most terrible of all, was caused ultimately by resentment against ugly Americans (my term) who ostentatiously squandered money in poverty-stricken countries. * The enemy (nations not identified) attack the United States, and with a ray that kills gasoline engines, sweep everything before them. America seems lost, but Icarus Wright Langley, a friend of the narrator's, develops a man-powered flap-winged (or rotating winged?) little plane that turns the tide. * Pretty bad.

BUTLER, ELLIS PARKER (1869-1937)

American humorist, frequent contributor to magazines. Is now remembered mostly for the short story "Pigs Is Pigs," although other stories about Mike Flannery, railway agent, are equally amusing. Butler contributed sixteen short stories to Hugo Gernsback's *Radio News* in 1923 and 1924; only a few, however, are science-fiction. At his best a sharp, gingery writer, although with a tendency to lampoon ethnic and personality types.

175. **AN EXPERIMENT IN GYRO-HATS.** *Amazing Stories*, June 1926. Ill. Paul.

(First published in *New Broadway Magazine*, June 1920.)

(Reprinted in Moskowitz, *Science Fiction by Gaslight*.) Humorous short story. * Walsingham Gribbs, an aristocratic young man about town, would be a good catch for any local maiden save for one fault: he has so little control of his legs that he always seems drunk. The reason for Gribbs's condition is an unfortunate experiment of his father's, who whirled him around on a rotating platform that escaped control. * The narrator of the story, a hatter who wants his daughter to marry Gribbs, constructs a hat with a gyroscopic motion that will keep its wearer upright. But the hat, too, escapes control, whirling Gribbs around—in the opposite direction from the original mishap, thus curing him. * Somewhat amusing, but by no means up to Butler's better work, as in *Mike Flannery Off Duty and On* or "Pigs Is Pigs."

176. **SOLANDER'S RADIO TOMB.** *Amazing Stories*, June 1927. Unsigned ill.

(First published in *Radio News*, December 1923.)

Short story. * Not science-fiction, but an amusing story. * Remington Solander, a fervid, very wealthy religionist, sets up a trust fund so that an automatic radio station sited on his tomb after his death will perpetually broadcast pious quotations and hymns that Solander has been collecting for years. This works out well, and the cemetery prospers for a time. But the government reassigns wave lengths among the local stations, and the station that now holds Solander's former frequency is a commercial station. There is nothing the narrator and his fellow trustees can do about it when the radio tomb blasts out vulgarities and jazz. * Slight, but penetrating.

BYRNE, STUART JAMES (1913-present)

U.S. author, then resident in Los Angeles. In later life various administative positions in aircraft and merchandising industries. Screenwriter for several motion pictures, including *Journey into Fear*. Also contributed stories to the magazines edited by Ray Palmer and other s-f magazines under such pseuds. as John Bloodstone, Howard Dare, Marx Kaye (a house pseud.).

177. **THE MUSIC OF THE SPHERES.** *Amazing Stories*, August 1935.

Short-short story. * *Time:* the interplanetary future. * *Place:* too close to the sun. * The great space liner, with 2000 passengers and 115 crewmen, is about sixteen million miles from the sun and in trouble. Its vibratory repulsion mechanism is not strong enough to save the ship, which is sliding toward the solar mass. The captain calls for a volunteer to sacrifice his life and save the ship. A nameless young man responds. Entering a lifeboat, he rockets off, the impetus from his little vessel being sufficient to deflect the liner into an escape orbit. * The story, which is purple in writing, now considers the sensations of the young man as he approaches death in the sun, fancying that he hears the music of the spheres.

CAMPBELL, CLYDE CRANE

Writing name of Horace Leonard Gold (1914-1996). Canadian-born U.S. (New York, later years California) writer, editor. Although not a major science-fiction writer, the author of several amusing fantastic stories, notably the small classic "Trouble with Water" (*Unknown*, March 1939). Editorial assistant 1939-1941 on *Startling Stories, Thrilling Wonder Stories,* and *Captain Future.* Free-lance writer in various fields. Most important as founding editor of *Galaxy Science Fiction*, which became arguably the leading science-fiction magazine for a time; later founding editor of *Beyond Fantasy Fiction.* Gold was a good judge of fiction, but had the reputation of being the most heavy-handed editor in the genre. * See also pseud. Leigh Keith.

178. **INFLEXURE.** *Astounding Stories,* October 1934. Ill. Dold.

(Reprinted in Ackerman, *Gosh! Wow!*)

Novelette. * *Time:* 1942 when things start; after that, all times. * An enormous fourth-dimensional sun or other object approaches our sun, drags it and the planets away at the speed of light, so distorting the time axis of space-time that all (or in story terms, many, up to the twenty-sixth century) different ages are superimposed, often with some interpenetration of matter. The general situation is much as in #851, Murray Leinster's "Sidewise in Time," except that the ages are jumbled together, instead of being kept segmentally separate. * The story, which is episodic and does not lend itself well to summary, is concerned mostly with 1942 theoretical physicist Lanse and his friend Worthing. * As a result of the impaction of all times, the world is suddenly enormously overpopulated as all (with limitations) the people of all time (adult, certain age!) are present. Even when dangerous primitives are exterminated, the food supply is totally inadequate. Universal war breaks out, ending when almost all men from all times are destroyed. A small band of male survivors discovers an isolated group of Oriental women, among whom they will settle. * Gold has stated that he devoted considerable research to the fourth-dimensional aspects of the story. Too much in too little space, inconsistent, and more confusing than satisfying.

179. **GOLD.** *Astounding Stories,* January 1935. Ill. Dold.

Short story. * *Place:* New York City. * Ness, a pawnbroker, becomes suspicious when Lloyd Walsh brings in the same amount of chemically pure, twenty-four carat gold each week. A consultation with higher-powered crooks develops a hypothesis: Walsh, who is a chemist and has a loft filled with machinery in the East Side, must be making the gold. The crooks decide to plant a spy with Walsh to learn his secret. *

Campbell, Clyde Crane (*continued*)

Their agent, young Benton, who is a strange mixture of idealism, altruism, and crookedness, worms his way into Walsh's confidence and learns that Walsh makes gold by subjecting lead to extreme pressure and a stream of alpha particles. A side product of the process is enormous amounts of energy. * Benton, who becomes enthusiastic about the social possibilities of the new energy source, almost unconsciously identifies with Walsh against the crooks. Together he and Walsh eagerly discuss setting up a millennial society, somewhat on the lines of socialism. * This is not to be. The crooks raid the loft, and Benton, trying to help Walsh, focuses the alpha-ray projector on his former associates. The result is an atomic explosion that kills everyone and wrecks the building.

180. **AGE**. *Astounding Stories*, April 1935. Ill. Dold.
Novelette. * The novelty of heavy water was in the air at this time, and C. C. Campbell obviously latched onto the more sensational, less accurate accounts. * *Time:* 1954. *Place:* mostly the New York City area. * Scientifically naive entrepreneur Naughton is the victim of a scam operated by Hannon and Finch, a pair of rogues with some engineering and other technical background. The gimmick is building a transportation rocket powered by hydrogen and oxygen, which is to be separated out from water by electrolysis. * The two rogues, with Naughton's capital, build a large bootleg plant near Lake Ashokan, one of New York City's water supplies, separate their gases—and then dump the deuterium oxide residue into the reservoir. * The result, in accord with s-f tenets of the day, is that those who drink a little of the water age with fantastic rapidity. The author demonstrates this with little case studies of personalities around the area, also with striking incidents, as when two prize fighters die of old age a day after a bumbling match. * Another aspect of heavy-water poisoning is ravenous appetite. In a short time New York City is consuming the produce of much of the nation, with famine not unlikely. * Dr. Ross at the university works out what is happening. The local health authorities do not take his warnings seriously, but when financier Naughton sees what is happening to himself, he provides support. Since it is impossible to remove the heavy water from the water supply, the public is urged not to drink city water. Ross discovers another tiny ingredient of water (light water) that cancels out and reverses the damage done by heavy water. Naughton promotes it, and after a time life returns to normal, those poisoned by the heavy water regaining their vitality.

181. **FOG**. *Astounding Stories*, June 1935. Ill. Marchioni.
Short story. * *Place:* New York City. * When old Dr. Cobb is performing brain surgery in an (undescribed) experiment, the patient shifts, the doctor's knife slips, and the patient's frontal lobes fall out onto the operating table. Cobb and his assistant expect the worst, immediate death of the patient, but when he continues to live, Cobb injects pineal extract into him. * The long-term result is that the patient regresses in an evolutionary manner, becoming hairy, long-armed, and immensely strong. He has the intelligence of an ape. * The expected happens. The "brute" escapes from Cobb's house and runs amok before he is killed. In the shoot-out both Cobb and his assistant die. Lucky they; they should have faced ethics charges.

182. **THE AVATAR**. *Astounding Stories,* July 1935. Ill. Dold.

Novelette. * The Frankenstein theme in the modern world. * *Time and place:* England, probably in the near future. * Old Dr. Earle, as he tells a group of scientific umpires, has created life. He has made artificial protoplasm and after years of experiment has animated it. His proof lies in the man sitting next to him, the man whom he manufactured. This is David Belvedere, who is incredibly handsome, unbelievably strong and healthy, and is gifted with an IQ of 283. * Earle requests funds for further research and improvements, but his application is rejected, the final argument being that his superrace would displace ordinary men and women. Earle continues his work privately, hoping that David will assist him, but, surprise! David turns out to be an intelligent, selfish hedonist who cares nothing about Earle or further research. He leaves. * David's enormous sex appeal makes him irresistible to women, and in a short time he is the world's most glamorous motion picture star, the subject of endless publicity. * Others than film producers recognize David's unique abilities and characteristics. The Council of Seven, a somewhat amorphous group of terrorists, enlists him as their leader at a salary of five million pounds per year. After a few strikes around the world, the terrorists seize control, and David is world dictator. * Old Dr. Earle appeals to him for funds in order to improve his work, but David brutally rejects him. And now Earle, recognizing that David, while a superman, is still only human, decides to benefit mankind. He creeps into David's sleeping chamber and cuts his throat. * Strange organization, with flashbacks, but the good ironic touches so characteristic of Gold's mature work are beginning to appear.

CAMPBELL, JOHN SCOTT

U.S. (mostly California) author, in 1933 resident in Seattle. Also contributed to other Street and Smith magazine *Top-Notch*. According to rumor, still living. Portrait shows a middle-aged man.

183. **THE INFINITE BRAIN**. *Science Wonder Stories,* May 1930. Ill. Paul. As by John C. Campbell.
Novelette. * Gene, the narrator, is friendly with the electronics experimenter Anton Des Roubles, whom he helps occasionally in assembling components. It is no secret that Anton is trying to create machine intelligence. He has already created a creeping device that seems exactly like Turing's turtle. * Then Anton dies suddenly, leaving his apparatus to Gene. On entering the lab, Gene finds a note telling him to turn on the switch—which animates a complicated device that has a lens, a mobile arm, and a keyboard for receiving and delivering messages. The machine begs him not to turn the switch off, but to help finish constructing Anton's project. Actually, the machine is Anton's personality conveyed mechanically via a system of measuring synapse speed and sequence within the brain cells; it also has Anton's memory. * The narrator accedes, and over time enjoys working with the machine, which is emotionless and pleasant to deal with. * A turning point comes when the machine desires to go ahead with Anton's ultimate project, hooking up to a brain storage system of infinite capacity. The pleasant days are now over, for after this project is completed, the machine develops a stronger, less friendly personality, ending by holding Gene captive. It has also constructed all sorts of subsidiary machines that it controls by radio. * As might be expected, the now nasty machine attempts to conquer the world. With violet disintegrating rays, an incredible aircraft, and titanic walking

Campbell, John Scott (*continued*)

machines, it kills most of the population of New York and is ready to take on anything. The army, led by General MacArthur, is wiped out, MacArthur apparently finding the machine more dangerous than bonus marchers. * The world is obviously in trouble, for the machine is much more powerful than any human armed forces and is growing stronger day by day. * Gene and a friend who has shared some of the horrors with him sneak back into Manhattan, hoping to find a way to circumvent the machine. They are captured, but the machine, which remembers Gene and has a cruel sense of humor, returns him to the outside world with a message stating that the hour of destruction is near. But Gene has learned a secret. The machine's radio signals may be blanketed by stronger broadcasts nearby. So it proves, and the menace is ended. As for the machine, it transported itself to some South Sea island, where it lies underwater, now powerless. * The first part of the story is interesting as Campbell goes into the methodology of the inventors, but the story soon degenerates into a typical, flimsy world-saver. * The attribution of this story to John C. Campbell is probably a typographical error rather than an attempt at a partial pseudonym. The portrait published with the story indicates that the author is John Scott Campbell.

184. **THE INVULNERABLE SCOURGE**. *Wonder Stories*, November 1930. Ill. Marchioni.

Short story. * A pest that almost wiped out civilization arises from a friendly dispute between Riis, Professor of Biology, and Pfeffler, Professor of Physiology (who speaks with an annoying German accent). Riis, who has been working extensively in genetic engineering and has created a cricket that miaows like a kitten and a large beetle with luminous eyes, claims that insects are better suited to inherit the Earth than man. When Pfeffler scoffs, to convince him, Riis creates the ideal insect: fast breeding, extremely hardy, omnivorous, aquatic or terrestrial or aerial, poisonous to eat, and equipped with a poison sting. As might be expected, the insect accidentally escapes. * Since each generation increases geometrically, there will be trouble. The first generation numbers fifty thousand, the second a billion and a quarter, and there are several generations per annum. In less than a year North America is suffering badly, with cities almost deserted, agriculture almost abandoned. The rest of the world will soon follow. It looks like the end not only of mankind, but of non-microscopic life on Earth. * Finally, the two savants do what they should have thought of doing long before: devise a natural enemy against the beetle, especially bacterial. They accomplish this. After long incubation, the bacteria are effective, and the beetle menace is almost over. * Told in a very low-key manner, with a certain amount of humor, but weak in internal logic.

185. **BEYOND PLUTO**. *Wonder Stories Quarterly*, Summer 1932. Ill. Paul.

Short novel. * *Place:* Africa and various planets in other solar systems. * A little of everything (except romance): African travel, lost race, supercivilization, space travel, interstellar warfare, world-saving, etc. The influence of H. Rider Haggard is obvious in the earlier section of the story. * The narrator and his associate Cummings, geologists spending time in Cairo after field work, chance to meet two noted British scientists, Lord Hanavan and Professor Milroy, and are persuaded to accompany them in quest of a dead civilization. Evidence consists of an ancient Egyptian papyrus describing a failed punitive expedition into the Sudan and a handful of square platinum coins showing a new form of writing. Previous modern expeditions to the area have vanished without a trace. * Despite some harassment from fanatics who try to stop the expedition, the party proceeds up the Nile to the probable site. The area, they discover, is considered tabu by the natives, but the Englishmen continue. * After overcoming enormous difficulties, they reach a high point and look down on, not ruins, not a primitive establishment, but on Zongainia, an enormous supercity later stated to contain millions of inhabitants. They see flying machines obviously far more advanced than Western European airplanes, titanic skyscrapers, and much else. * Since the explorers have little choice, they enter the city surreptitiously and are captured. They are not badly treated, but they are obvious prisoners. After a time they are taken to the ruler of the land, variously called El Zoia or Ver Menisto—a charismatic, young-appearing man, who converses easily with them in perfect English. * Background of the land of Zongainia: It was originally settled by immigrants from the Moon, who landed from gigantic spaceships about 65 B.C. The Moon was first damaged by meteoritic swarms, then by volcanism, so that it lost its air. At first the Moonmen (Metyrs) maintained relations with nearby people, but since disease and crime were problems, the Metyrs diverted rivers, and sealed off their land, annihilating would-be invaders. The Moonmen then undertook the task of civilizing and assimilating the hordes of natives (Persians, Egyptians, Romans, etc.) in the land. For this reason there are two languages used in Zongainia, a patois of Earth languages and, second, a lunar language. Since that time civilization has developed, and instead of being a hermit culture, as the explorers think, Zongainia has extensive trade and diplomatic relations with other planetary systems. Its people are well aware of what is going on in the outer world (indeed, the ruler is familiar with Hanavan's latest monograph), but they are insistent on having no contact with the diseases and other problems of the nations of Earth. * All well and good, but the upshot is that outsiders never leave Zongainia on foot; they are packed off to an exile community on the planet Dunsaan of Alpha Centauri. Thither hie our involuntary exiles on a faster-than-light spaceship. * Dunsaan is a miserable place. The other exiles are divided into hostile factions, British and a Frenchman against bestial, drunken Boers. (The author obviously has no love for the Boers.) Our friends have arrived at just the right time: The British have been planning an escape and are about to leave. The excitement among their captors about a war that has just broken out between Zongainia and another space empire, Kanan, is to their advantage. * Our friends, joining the British exiles, set off in a stolen spaceship, heading roughly toward Earth, for cover joining the Zongainian space fleet. * After adventures implausible they are captured by the Kananese, who are not especially friendly and consider them Zongainian spies. Things look bad. The Kanan dictator intends to lure the Zongainian fleet within range of a magnetic disintegrator battery that he has prepared, but the Earthmen manage to flip the switch, foiling him. In the bombardment that follows, Kanan is conquered, but the Earthmen are wounded. They are shipped back to Earth in a hospital ship, mistaken for Zongainian soldiers. Back in Zongainia they wander about, planning to escape the land, when they are invited home by a friendly native, and then to a victory celebration. This turns out to be the biggest surprise

Campbell, John Scott (*continued*)

party in history, for they are acclaimed as heroes. The Zongainians knew who they were all the time. As a reward for their achievements, they are permitted to leave the land, having passed their word to be silent about it. * *Miscellaneous:* The natives of the Alpha Centaurian planet are small creatures with mushroom heads and slender limbs. * The natives of Kanan are Mongoloid humans; they do not converse as we do, but hum. The linguist of the group develops a method of hypnotizing the Kananese with whistling-humming sounds. * The lunar people have very long life spans. The present ruler, the Ver Menisto, is several thousand years old and still going strong. * Zongainian medicine is far more advanced than ours. * The story begins like a reasonable adventure novel, but becomes sillier and sillier as it goes on. Unfortunate, for Campbell is a literate man.

CAMPBELL, JOHN W[OOD], JR. (1910-1971)

U.S. (mostly New York and New Jersey, though earlier work written in Massachusetts) author, editor. Campbell's vita is available in many other sources, hence need not be detailed here. Attended M.I.T., flunked language requirement, transferred to Duke University, where he received a B.S. in physics. Held various jobs and worked as free lance writer until 1937. During our period one of the two leading exponents of the space opera, the other being E. E. Smith, Ph.D. In another guise, under the pseud. Don A. Stuart, the author of neo-Wellsian short stories. Although not a polished or even always competent writer, a man very fertile in ideas, with many unusual concepts taken from recent science. As one of the founders of hard science-fiction, Campbell, almost single-handedly, began to shift science-fictional science from Sunday supplement fare and the science of 1900 or so to modern concepts of relativity, atomic structure, and much else. Campbell was obviously fascinated with odd aspects of modern science and technology, and in his best work his enthusiasm emerges to the reader. He also assisted, with critical letters, in correcting scientific lapses in the work of other men (although he did not hesitate to make his own unsubstantiated extrapolations). * In 1937 Campbell became editor of *Astounding Stories*, and for all practical purposes ceased writing fiction. As an editor he continued the work of F. Orlin Tremaine, but also he directed *Astounding*, including retitlings, in directions that did not win general approval. Today, Campbell is remembered mostly as the type of an authoritarian editor, brimming with ideas, who was able to force his concepts and personality upon a succession of writers, but through inflexibility and quirks became, in the opinion of many, a negative factor in the history of science-fiction. See also #1813, "The Brain Stealers of Mars." See also pseuds. Don A. Stuart and Karl Van Campen.

Stories are presented as The Arcot, Morey, and Wade Series and Other Works, chronologically within each group.

The Arcot, Morey, and Wade Series

Five stories set in the advanced technological world of A.D. 2126 and a little later are concerned with the adventures of three supermen of science: Richard Arcot, William Morey, and Wade, whose first name does not seem to be given. Arcot, a physicist, is an incredible idea man; Morey, a mathematician, supplies the practical application of Arcot's ideas; and Wade serves as a backup. In this ascetic world of science and engineering, Arcot and Morey (and later Wade) work for Morey's father, a tycoon of industry, who delightedly bushels out the funds as the tiresome threesome bushel in money-making discoveries. The stories, like much of Campbell's other work, are self-justifying demonstration stories proving that the inspired genius can overcome all obstacles by a pottering, intuitive approach. As fiction they are weak, with no characterizations and rudimentary plots. Such story as exists is strangled by Arcot's patronizing, extrapolated lectures. On the credit side, Campbell's enthusiasm for oddities of science sometimes is communicated to the reader. In the reprint book editions published by Fantasy Press, *The Black Star Passes* and *Islands of Space*, the texts were extensively edited by Lloyd A. Eshbach, with Campbell's approval.

186. **PIRACY PREFERRED**, *Amazing Stories*, June 1930. Ill. Wesso.

(Reprinted in Campbell, *The Black Star Passes*.)

Novelette. * *Time:* A.D. 2126. * Introducing series heroes Richard Arcot and William Morey. Arcot, the son of a most distinguished scientist, is the most brilliant man in the world; Morey, more methodical, but also a man of genius, is the firm moneybags, through his wealthy father. Since height seems to be a point of great importance to the author, we should mention that Arcot is six feet tall, while Morey is six feet four inches. The third member of the group, to join later, is even taller. * The situation is that an air pirate is plundering the great flying ships of the day. He is never sighted, but his prey settles safely to earth, with all the passengers and crew in a state of suspended animation—the antidote to which the pirate has prescribed. The pirate leaves behind him stock of his own issuance for Piracy Incorporated. * Arcot and Morey take a hand. They reason that the pirate must have a remarkably penetrating gas, since the ships' hulls are no protection; that he must possess the secret of invisibility; and that, since he has escaped mechanical detection, he must be using some sort of glider. * Countering moves: The team succeeds in capturing a specimen of the gas in a vacuum bottle, where outside air pressure keeps the gas inside. Arcot reasons that the pirate creates invisibility with a development of a known phenomena associated with short radiation. * The team builds a superaircraft. Wingless, it is propelled at thousands of miles per hour by realigning molecules so that they all move in the same direction, drawing energy from the heat in the air. Thus, it is not so effective at very high altitudes. The team can nullify the pirate's gas by constructing a double hulled ship with a vacuum between layers. * Arcot and Morey lie in wait for the pirate and, when he attacks a cargo plane, use suitable radiation to render his aircraft visible. In the following chase the pirate, employing rockets, ascends higher than Arcot and Morey can, but he forces himself into orbit and cannot land for lack of fuel. His supplies, too, are limited. He appeals to Arcot and Morey for aid. They rescue him, and at the end of the story offer him a place in their researches. Ignored are legal problems surrounding his crimes. * Filled with scientific discussions of the sort that Campbell loved, sometimes interesting, but the story drags. * For a sequel see #187, "Solarite."

187. **SOLARITE**. *Amazing Stories*, November 1930. Ill. Morey.

(Reprinted in Campbell, *The Black Star Passes*.)

Novelette. * Sequel to #186, "Piracy Preferred." *Place:* mostly

Campbell, John W., Jr. (*continued*)

Venus. * Arcot and Morey's molecular motion ships are being produced in quantity, and the untoppable geniuses now decide that they will use their invention to make an interplanetary voyage. For reasons based on the science of Campbell's day, they settle on Venus as their goal. Joining them as a somewhat junior partner is Wade, the former Piracy Corporation, who has been reconstructed. He had formerly suffered from kleptomania caused by a blood clot on his brain; this (the blood clot, not the brain) was removed by an eminent surgeon, perhaps the same one who has performed similar operations on other science-fictional personnel. Actually, as this and the following stories demonstrate, recruiting Wade was a misdirection on Campbell's part, since he plays a minimal part in the science and adventure. * The new vessel, the *Solarite*, proceeds to Venus without difficulty, evading the usual meteors and space fragments. * Venus is much like Earth, but considerably hotter, 150°F. and higher. Thus, the explorers wear cooling suits and must be careful what they touch. * As the *Solarite* flies along the not-unpleasant Venusian surface, the explorers come upon a battle scene. A monoplane-like flying machine with a wing span of three-quarters of a mile is attacking a beautiful city, which is defending itself somewhat ineffectually with tiny fighter craft. Both sides are using high-explosive bombs. * The Terrestrials decide to take a hand; snapping on Wade's invisibility device, they attack the giant plane, directing their atomic hydrogen propulsion rockets against it. The giant plane, disabled, flies away, and the Terrestrial triumvirate descend to receive the gratitude of the city. * The Venusians, who are human, seven-feet tall, but cyanotic in complexion and furnished with two opposable thumbs, are somewhat telepathic. To the surprise of the Terrestrials, the Venusians thank them for arriving so rapidly. * Explanation: There are two nations on Venus, Lanor (good) and Kaxor (bad). In most respects they are about equal scientifically, but Kaxor is ahead in military technology. Kaxor plans to conquer Lanor, then fly to Earth and conquer it. The Venusians had sent messages to Earth, warning and asking for help. * With the presence of Arcot, Morey, and Wade, the war takes a new turn. While their invisibility is no longer of use, since the Kaxorians immediately learned how to negate it, Wade's sleep gas is effective whenever the *Solarite* can approach near enough to the giant planes to use it. Decisive, however, is Arcot's idea of projecting his molecular motion against the giant planes. * Kaxor is beaten, and when its megalomaniac ruler is removed, there is peace on Venus. * *Miscellaneous:* Once the Kaxorians have learned the secret of invisibility and use it, Arcot counters by spraying their planes with luminous paint. * Since telepathy is too difficult and too limited, the Lanorians use learning machines to establish effective communication with the Earthmen. * A lot of space is filled with popular scientific exposition, both genuine and fantastic.

188. THE BLACK STAR PASSES. *Amazing Stories Quarterly*, Fall 1930. Ill. Paul.
(Reprinted in Campbell, *The Black Star Passes* and in Campbell, *John W. Campbell Anthology*.)
Novelette. * ^Sequel to #187, "Solarite." * About three years after the previous story. * The first part of the novel centers on an unnamed people who dwell on glass-domed planets around a dark star. Most of this section of the story is told through the master scientist Taj Lamor. The treatment is not unsympathetic.

* The people of the dark star are humanoid, perhaps somewhat taller than Earthmen, and pallid. Their civilization, which is millions of years old, is decadent, for much has been lost. * For hundreds of millennia the humanoids have been adjusting to the fact that their star has gone out. Expediences to conserve air, heat and water help, as do total atomic energy and creation of matter from energy, but these are obviously temporary. Unfortunately, the humanoids have lost the technique of moving planets from their orbits and steering them about. * A new hope for renewed racial life comes when they observe that their sun will pass close to another sun, one with eight planets. Mass migration is the answer to their dead sun, assuming that they can resurrect enough ancient space technology to build ships. * A scouting expedition of the strangers alerts the solar system, so that when an armada of mile-long ships appears, the solarite fleets, led by Arcot, Morey, and Wade are ready. In the first battle, the smaller solarite ships are superior to the outsider dreadnoughts, partly because they are more mobile, partly because the strangers know nothing of war and have few weapons. After the first disastrous engagement, Taj Lamor signals a retreat back to the home system. * A large part of the story now focuses on the three Terrestrial comrades, Arcot, Morey, and Wade, as they wander through a wrecked stranger ship, commenting on its technology. An item of technology that Arcot seizes upon is solid matter composed of photons. In addition to being a perfect insulation, it can serve as a heat source permitting more efficient space travel for the molecular motion ships. * The strangers prepare a second invasion, this time with small ships carried in the dreadnoughts, and with superior armament. The space battle is closer than the last, but Arcot's molecular motion ray and a heat ray based on stored light defeat the invaders, who retreat again. * There are no more hostilities, and the black star passes away from our system, creating, it is true, some disruption. Neptune has been torn away, and the Earth is closer to the sun. Two of the dark star's planets, however, were left behind, with technological material. * The dynamism of war, however, has given the somewhat blasé people of the dark star new energy. Despite their defeat, they have more hope than before. They are encouraged to see that their star is now headed toward Sirius. The ancient secret of planet moving has been rediscovered, so that even if the situation around Sirius is not ideal, they can improve it. * Much time is spent on exposition, as Arcot, primarily, harangues on energy, weapons, construction, etc. * For a sequel, see #189, "Islands of Space."

189. ISLANDS OF SPACE. *Amazing Stories Quarterly*, Spring 1931. Ill. Wesso.
(Reprinted in book form by Fantasy Press, Reading, Pa., 1956, and in Campbell, *John W. Campbell Anthology*.)
Novel. * ^Sequel to #188, "The Black Star Passes." * Speculative theoretical physics embodied in a novel of exploration. * Two new discoveries or theoretical speculations by Arcot bid fair to render interstellar travel possible. First, Arcot discovers a way to use the photon-composed metals of the people of the black star to produce and control material energy. Second, Arcot theorizes that since the Einsteinian limitation of speed to below the speed of light is a property of space, if space could be changed, that limitation would disappear. Altering space should be possible by pouring enormous quantities of energy into it. * The way is now clear, if one adds other

Campbell, John W., Jr. (*continued*)

technological novelties, for a starship. For about twelve thousand words Campbell describes the ideas involved and the ship itself. * The *Ancient Mariner* is built, and in conjunction with thousands of words on popular astronomy, it flies away, reaching speeds of one hundred thousand light-years per hour. Since it is in a hyperspace of its own construction, it need not fear collision with meteors or space debris. * Along the way the ship passes through a region where cosmic rays are created, resulting in considerable damage to the ship and a little to the crew. But the Earthmen win through and in intergalactic space view the galaxies from afar, a wonderful sight. * Selecting a likely sun, the travelers visit a frozen planet where they find remains of a high civilization and indications that its people were human. Unfortunately, Arcot theorizes, they did not have energy sources sufficient to leave their frozen planet and committed mass suicide. * Next, the explorers are trapped by the enormous gravity of a dwarf star. Even their powerful engines are inadequate for them to escape; the best that Arcot can do is swing the *Ancient Mariner* into a circular orbit around the star. * The situation looks hopeless, but there is always a way out: There are other dwarf stars nearby. Arcot will play his molecular motion ray upon the nearest, stop its rotation, causing it to crash into their captor, and then escape in the burst of energies. * So it happens, but the explorers are hurled away so far, unconscious, that they are now lost in space. As Arcot reasons, their only hope for returning to Earth is to locate an advanced civilization that has star maps adequate for locating the home galaxy. * After some navigation, the travelers find a suitable solar system with two inhabited planets. Nansal, the first planet on which they try to land, possesses a high technological civilization, but is hostile. * After some attempts to establish a peaceful relation (by demonstrating the power of their weapons!) the Earthmen leave and approach Sator, the second planet. There they are received in a friendly manner. * Torlos, their contact-person, a heavily muscled humanoid, is receptive to Arcot's telepathy, and communication is established. Arcot's telepathic abilities come as just as much of a surprise to Morey and Wade as to the reader; it seems that Arcot studied the technique on Venus and just hadn't felt like using it before. * The explorers, who find it impossible to convince the Satorians of their place of origin, suggest the following trade: information about the Arcot's molecular motion engine and ray, the lux-shielded material energy system, and the mode of transforming space for faster-than-light travel—in exchange for lead and identification of their home galaxy and, if possible, solar system. * Just as in *The Skylark of Space*, however, these first hosts are treacherous and plan to kill the explorers and seize their weapons. * Torlos, who is really a Nansalian secret agent, informs Arcot, and the party (including Torlos) crashes out of the Satorian city, Torlos later destroying it. * All fly to Nansal, where they are welcomed, and a deal is struck. When the Satorians attack with a new secret weapon, an electrical projector, the *Ancient Mariner* makes mincemeat of the Satorian fleet. The Terrestrials leave for Earth, taking Torlos with them. * *Miscellaneous:* The people of Nansal have iron bones instead of calcium, hence their enormous strength. On the whole, they do not eat, but absorb heat directly from sources around them. * Weapons stress magnetic fields. * Greatly overloaded with unnecessary (though at times ingenious) exposition, hence almost unreadable; weak novelistically; and clichéd in its action plot. All the imagination has gone into the technology. * For a sequel, see #190, "Invaders from the Infinite."

190. **INVADERS FROM THE INFINITE**. *Amazing Stories Quarterly*, Spring/Summer 1932. Ill. Wesso.
(Reprinted in book form by Gnome Press, Hicksville, N. Y., and in Campbell, *John W. Campbell Anthology*.)
Novel. Sequel to #189, "Islands of Space." * *Background:* Arcot's discoveries and inventions have revolutionized the science and technology of the solar system. His molecular-motion power units are omnipresent, even as small one-person flying packs. Extensive interplanetary trade has developed, and, as corollaries, space pirates and a space patrol. It behooves Arcot to whip up a defense against the molecular motion rays, which he does in a spare moment. * To the narrative, or Arcot against the universe! Big excitement! A great spaceship of hitherto unknown design lands on the roof of the Morey establishment. From it emerge Ortolians, strange-looking beings, obviously evolved humanoid dogs, who communicate telepathically with Arcot. At first Arcot uses his Venusian method, but the dog people produce a helmet that works much better. * Their story: They were developed from dogs by a human or humanoid people long extinct as a result of civil wars. The dog people have lived in peace, but now their planet has been raided by a Thessian ship (from the planet Thett) whose people are planning cosmic conquest. The dog people do not have the physical science or engineering to withstand the raider, but with their mental abilities (which are farther developed than either human or Thessian) they lured the warship to destruction, read the minds of the dead Thessians, patched up the ship, and came seeking help. * It seems that the Thessians have long been exploring the cosmos; they have located twenty-one civilizations, have studied Earth, and respect the achievements of Arcot—which is why the dog people (the Ortolians) have sought him out. They located him from a space patrolman whose mind they read as they passed by. * As the Ortolian dog people describe the Thessians: They are pygmies, extremely heavy, fantastically strong (because their planet of origin is larger than Jupiter), equipped with webbed hands and feet to swim through the dense atmosphere of their world, iron-boned, enormously vital, highly intelligent, and nasty. * The gravities of their sun and planet are so strong that their geometry is non-Euclidean, and there is a certain distortion visible in their forms and equipment. * Their armament is most potent. They have the molecular motion ray, cosmic ray projectors, photon metals, and heavier power supplies than Arcot and his team. Their space drive, as Arcot later learns, is based not on altering space, like Arcot's, but on altering time. The Thessian system is slower, but it offers what amounts to time travel. * The location of Thett is ambiguous; in the earlier parts of the story it seems to be in our galaxy, but in the conclusion it is in another galaxy far distant. * As Arcot and the reader will soon learn, the problem in this future war is nullification: Once one side devises a weapon, the other side adopts it in a matter of days or weeks, neutralizing it. Thus, any warring power must keep looking for new weapons that have the virtue of novelty. * Arcot and comrades speed to the help of Ortol, which is under attack when they arrive. Molecular and cosmic rays are useless, and to avoid more powerful Thessian weapons, the Terrestrial ship must flit in and out of our space. But a magnetic ray destroys the

Campbell, John W., Jr. (*continued*)
invaders. * The comrades now proceed to Tolso, another solar system that is under attack, where the inhabitants are small, very husky and powerful, but with tiny heads. It seems that their brains are not in their heads, only their organs of perception. The Tolsonians have an invincible weapon that they have been using against the invaders with great success. The only problem is that they do not have power sources adequate to operate many installations. * Arcot studies the device, improves on it immediately, and announces that it is a matter creator. Eventually, by using a special thought-helmet built by the chief dog psychologist, he is able to control the Tolsonian discovery not only as an invincible weapon but as a device for creating matter of all sorts. * The comrades return to Earth, to find that it, too, is under attack by the Thessians, who have gigantic bases in the Arctic and Antarctic. Arcot destroys both bases, despite the general inadequacy of his defenses and weapons. He uses a modified version of the Tolsonian matter-creating device to tunnel under the Thessian base and emerge up into it. * The next journey is to the people of the Dark Star (see #188, "The Black Star Passes"), who have settled around Sirius. They, too, are under attack, and in exchange for help gladly give Arcot the secret of moving planets around. * During a battle around Sirius, the Terrestrial ship is again in peril, and, after a particularly violent shock, is thrown ninety thousand years into the past by the Thessian time-distorter that Arcot had installed. * The comrades return to Earth and follow history up through time, stopping in the 1930s to visit M.I.T., where, unfortunately, they do not think to look up John W. Campbell, Jr.! * On returning to his present, Arcot finds that the Thessians have renewed their attack, now with gigantic space forts that are demolishing New York and Chicago. Arcot takes care of them. * Arcot takes his improved matter creator to Eros, where he builds a supersuper-spaceship out of solidified cosmic rays; it is powered by the nature of space itself. * The time has come to attack Thett and remove the menace. Battles follow one another, with Thessian fleets annihilated, until the allied forces reach Thett, which is in another galaxy. But the Thessians have still another supersuper-weapon, the triple ray, which is a beam of solidly packed photons. It cuts through Arcot's defenses like a knife. * The military situation does not look good. Despite a promising start, the campaign against Thett may turn into a stalemate or even defeat. But Arcot whips up a defense screen of solid protons, through which *nothing* can penetrate, and with it destroys Thett. * As Arcot returns to the solar system with his supersupership, he is, thanks to the supermatter creator, practically a god, with the power to create and destroy universes. No further progress seems possible for Arcot, unless he decides to take on Jehovah. * *Miscellaneous:* The Thessians turn out to be galactic outlaws in their area, criminals and no-goods who were expelled from a peaceful, pleasant people known as the Warless Ones of Venone. The Warless Ones receive the Allies in friendly fashion, and relations are established. * The dog culture of Ortol practices polygyny and ruthless eugenics. Dog psychologists have a technique for removing grief and also an apparatus for projecting thought mechanically onto screens. * "Invaders from the Infinite" is in some ways the early John W. Campbell story par excellence: weak novelistic skills combined with very strong speculative, imaginative theoretical physics. One may be bored with Arcot's interminable lectures and rendered drowsy by the

repeated space battles, but one must also admire Campbell's ingenuity in creating novel artifacts (in the broadest sense of the word), together with their characteristics and behavior under various circumstances.

Other Works

191. **WHEN THE ATOMS FAILED**. *Amazing Stories*, January 1930. Ill. Wesso.
Short story. * Campbell's first published story, written while he was a sophomore at M.I.T. * *Time:* 1947. * The concatenations of chance and the heroic nature of the inventor/scientist. * The narrator, David Gale, reminisces from 1957 about the great events associated with his college chum Stephen Waterson ten years earlier. * As the sequence opens, Waterson arrives on the rooftop with a thirty-five foot radiform flying machine. In conversation with Gale he explains what has occupied him since their college days. He has been working with machine intelligence and has developed a supercalculating device that has opened up whole new fields of mathematics. Among its products are atomic energy, total-matter energy, and antigravity, with such applications as disintegration, heat rays, electronic propulsion, curving space for flight, etc. His flying machine, which the men christen the *Terrestrian,* is capable of fantastic speeds. * At just this time astronomers observe strange flashes on Mars; soon twenty spherical vessels are seen to be rapidly approaching Earth. Waterson reasons that the Martians must be hostile, for otherwise so many ships would not be needed. He also decides that while the Martians are in general superior scientifically to Earth and possess atomic energy, they do not have his total-matter energy or his personal advanced technology. (To restate Waterson's main point in modern terms, the computer revolution has not taken place on Mars.) * The remainder of the story is concerned with Waterson's single-handed defeat of the Martian armada in a turkey shoot. While the Martians have cathode ray projectors and heat rays, Waterson has heat rays, atomic disintegration rays, incredible high explosive shells, etc. * When the sorry remnants of the Martian fleet flees from Earth, Waterson, as a demonstration of strength, seizes one ship and drags it to Venus before releasing it. * The aftermath of all this is a peaceful relationship between Earth and Mars. * *Miscellaneous:* The Martians, as a single line states, are either human or humanoid. * Huge gobbets of undigested semipopular science, some right, some wrong, demonstrate Campbell's fascination with the scientific ideas involved. * Almost unreadable at times. For a sequel see #192, "The Metal Horde."

192. **THE METAL HORDE**. *Amazing Stories*, April 1930. Ill. J. De Pauw.
Short story. * Sequel to #191, "When the Atoms Failed." * *Time:* 1961. *Place:* space around the inner planets. * Although it is only fourteen years since the earlier story, great changes have taken place. The three inner planets (Venus, Earth, Mars) are peacefully united as the System, also known as the Solarites, with its capital on Venus and Waterson as president. Waterson has not aged in the meanwhile, since means are now available for prolonging youth. There is a very brisk interplanetary trade, and the results of Waterson's genius are visible everywhere. * An emergency arises: A fleet of space vessels is sighted heading toward the solar system from the direction of Sirius. The armada, for it is recognized as such, must have left the region of

Campbell, John W., Jr. (*continued*)

Sirius some 1600 years ago; this implies either great longevity or perhaps suspended animation. Further implications are that the Sirians can extract the total energy of matter that Waterson's computer worked out for him and that they have gigantic calculating machines (computers, in modern terminology). * The story is not developed in terms of personalities, but is mostly a chronicle of space battles, with Waterson appearing for a paragraph or two now and then. * The inner worlds have three weeks in which to prepare a defensive fleet, and every resource of the three planets is devoted to creating small ten-man ships armed with disintegrators, heat rays, etc. By the time the invaders reach Mars, the Solarites have several thousand ships. * In the first, ensuing battle, the Solarites are defeated, but not badly, and withdraw, but the invaders also have lost many ships. Production continues on the three planets. * The invaders do the unexpected. Landing on Mars, they terraform the entire planet, while constructor vessels manufacture new fighting ships, transmuting the Martian rock and soil into what they need for their purpose. * Battles continue, with the fleets growing larger and larger, until there are millions of vessels on each side. None of the military actions is decisive, but the invaders manage to stay a little bit ahead. * The situation improves for the Solarites when Waterson develops a very effective long-range disintegrator and inertialess flight to match the speedy invader craft, but the incredible production system of the invaders more than makes up for losses in battle. The battles range from planet to planet, over and around the sun, with a particularly heavy onslaught on Venus. * Waterson finally ends the war with a ray that prevents utilizing the total energy of matter. At this point the invader fleets succumb, and the war is as good as over. * The clincher comes when the Solarite forces capture a gigantic spherical vessel that the invader fleets have guarded zealously. It now becomes known that the invaders are not organic life, but mechanical devices controlled by a gigantic computer, the spherical ship. * The author reveals something of the past history of the Sirian planet. It was inhabited by a humanoid race that developed supercomputers at some time in their past. After a while the computers became independent, and humans and computers were at war. Finally, the humans expelled the last of the great mechanical brains, which left Sirius and approached our solar system. Waterson and his colleagues take this as a cautionary history and disavow building giant mechanical brains—a point of view opposite to that expressed strongly in the first story. * *Miscellaneous:* The Martians seem to be human, but eight or ten feet tall. The Venusians are not described, but they seem by implication to be human.

193. **THE VOICE OF THE VOID.** *Amazing Stories Quarterly*, Summer 1930. Ill. Wesso.

Short story. * Social Darwinism and genocide. * *Time:* about ten billion years in the future. *Place:* in part, a planet orbiting Betelgeuse. * Mankind is about four feet tall, barrel chested, short-legged and long armed, and gifted with long, slender fingers and prehensile toes. His head is not much larger than ours, but the brain is more deeply furrowed. * The problem facing future man is that the sun is clogged up and is going out; further, as is learned a little later, it is about to go nova. For countless millennia mankind has fed the sun by tossing in debris, including the outer planets, and has developed local energy by eroding the substance of the four inhabited planets, but this is no

longer adequate. Mankind must migrate. * After millennia of research the problem of matter transmission has been solved. It amounts to reading atoms precisely and recreating them via a fourth-dimensional tube. * The last humanity decides on Betelgeuse as the only possible sun with habitable planets. Indeed, the first transmitted expedition finds a beautiful, forested world. But the expedition is attacked by force beings and utterly destroyed. For years mankind transmits other expeditions armed in various ways, but none of the armament is effective: heat rays, disintegrator rays, explosives, etc. Finally, after much analysis of the various defeats, Terrestrial science devises an apparatus that will not permit the use of atomic energy, the food of the force beings. Once it is learned that this is effective, a Terrestrial armada attacks the natives of the Betelgeuse planets, and after many space battles, destroys them utterly. Man will now have several billion years of life before another crisis of solar inadequacy arises. * Personalities are generally avoided by Campbell, except for citation of names in an undeveloped chronicle-like narrative. * *Miscellaneous:* Campbell describes the force beings as unintelligent, but they do seem to communicate and act as if intelligent.

194. **THE DERELICTS OF GANYMEDE.** *Wonder Stories*, January 1932. Ill. Paul.

Short story. * *Time:* the interplanetary future. *Place:* mostly space and Ganymede. * Duke Stetson, space officer and would-be inventor, and Joan Reading, daughter of space-fleet owner John Reading, are in love and would like to marry. Old John Reading, who has never met Stetson, sets a condition before he will give his consent: Stetson must have two hundred thousand dollars to be eligible. Stetson, of course, has no money. * Stetson ships as an officer on board the *New Seattle*, planning to reach Mars, then Phobos, where he will set up his invention. This is a device that will transmit radio signals through the Heaviside layer, which presently prevents interplanetary communication by radio. On board the vessel, besides Stetson, is Joan's father, who is anxious to reach Mars for a business deal. Neither knows that the other is on board. * The ship is traveling too fast. A meteor strikes, knocking out the controls, and the rockets blast away at four and a half times Earth gravity. All on board are killed except Stetson, Reading, Parker (the swinish food magnate), and an oiler, all of whom happen to have been in liquids—bathing or investigating the water tank—when the acceleration began. * The ship, which is running wild, passes Mars and is into the asteroid belt before Stetson, who does not reveal his identity, gains some control of the ship. He works it into the Jovian system and onto Ganymede, which is known to have a breathable atmosphere and an ambience suitable for survival. * On Ganymede, Stetson takes a high course, still not revealing his identity. With the cooperation of the oiler he builds a crude habitation and obtains food from the wildlife of the satellite, then charges his fellow castaways incredible sums to share his "hotel" and accommodations. In a short time he has built up (in IOUs) the two hundred thousand dollars that Reading had demanded. * Stetson also sets up his invention, which in some fashion controls solar static, and sends a message to the interplanetary police stations and Earth. His apparatus is so powerful that it burns out wiring on receiving stations. * The men are rescued. Stetson reveals himself, destroying Reading's IOUs, and wins Joan—and a potential fortune with his communications device. * A curious attempt at a sentimental comedy with a trick idea, from a man who specialized in space opera.

Campbell, John W., Jr. (*continued*)

Not as bad as might have been expected, if one can overlook the contrivances.

195. **THE ELECTRONIC SIEGE.** *Wonder Stories*, April 1932. Ill. Paul.

Short story. * *Time:* A.D. 2374. *Place:* from the Earth-Mars run out into the asteroid belt. * *Background:* Interplanetary travel is common and safe, except for the actions of the Eugenics Research Colony, a very unusual group of space pirates. They kidnap suitable persons from ships they capture, taking them to an unknown destination for experimental purposes. The Interplanetary Lane Patrol cannot cope with the E.R.C. ships, which are faster and have proton-beam weapons. * The *Vega*, on the Earth-Mars route, is carrying a delegation of eminent scientists and might be desirable prey to the E.R.C. And so it is. Defending patrol ships are beaten off, and the *Vega* is captured by a space sphere, its passengers (suitably paralyzed) carried off. * Unknown to the E.R.C. as well as to the officers of the *Vega*, however, one passenger, a grossly fat, obnoxious business tycoon, is really Lieutenant Barclay of the I.L.P. in disguise; more, he is a Jovian colonist, with musculature that permits him to leap around and use fantastic strength under normal Earth gravity. * The captives are taken to the E.R.C. headquarters, an artificial hollow planetoid with an internal sun and a meadowy Terrestrial ambience. Normal Earth gravity is attained by rotation. * Barclay breaks out of his prison, breaks into the central powerhouse, overcomes the personnel, wrecks some equipment, changes others, shuts off the internal sun, cancels the gravitational system, broadcasts specifications of the proton guns to the I.L.P fleet, and discloses the space coordinates of the planetoid. * He is recaptured, but his destructive binge in the powerhouse severely limits the defense capabilities of the planetoid. The scientific gimmick is that so much electrical potential is being built up that the pirate leader has to surrender. * Routine work. For a sequel, see #197, "Space Rays."

196. **THE LAST EVOLUTION.** *Amazing Stories*, August 1932. Ill. Morey.

(Reprinted in Campbell, *The Best of John W. Campbell*; in Norton, *Award Science Fiction Reader*; and in Liebman, *Science Fiction. The Best of Yesterday*.)

Short story. * *Time:* A.D. 2538 and following years. *Place:* mostly around Earth. * Mankind has hit its peak. Restricted in number to about ten million people, it has achieved remarkable scientific heights, including the development of sentient, thinking machines. The resultant culture is almost a symbiosis or benevolent partnership between machine and man. * The story is narrated by F-2, the last of the predecessors of an ultimate machine. An invasion, one hundred great spaceships manned by somewhat humanoid, chitin-armored beings, came from an unknown source. The humans, who long had abandoned war, had few weapons, although their investigating machines—the size of a hand—were effective in spying on invader activities. * In a great space battle, Terrestrial rays were inadequate against the defenses of the invaders (who had a superior type of atomic energy), and the invaders continued on to Earth, which they systematically bathed in a green death ray. Torpedoes finally destroyed the invading fleet, but the outlook remained bad. While the machines were not damaged by the bath of radiation, humanity was doomed, for there was no defense against the green ray. * A second invasion took place as an armada of one

thousand invader ships entered the solar system. Hoping to preserve mankind, the great machines created even more advanced machines, including the narrator F-2, but even this was inadequate. Then F-2 created the ultimate, a machine or being composed of pure force. This machine, if it can so be called, became the heir to mankind, which is now extinct. While F-2 finally discovered a shield against the green ray, it was too late. * The supermachine approached the alien fleet, which was about to destroy Mars, turned the flagship inside out dimensionally, flashed a stasis ray on it which would prevent change of any sort, and ordered the aliens out of the solar system. They obeyed, for the sphere of force was irresistible. * Evolution is now complete, from animal, to man, to machine. * The idea is good, but the handling is poor, and the writing is very bad.

197. **SPACE RAYS.** *Wonder Stories*, December 1932. Ill. Paul.

Short story. * Sequel to #195, "The Electronic Siege." * Another adventure of Special Captain Donald Barclay, physical superman from Jupiter. *Time:* A.D. 2374. *Place:* space. * The space pirate Jennings, a renegade scientist commonly known as Robin Good, has captured a space police vessel. The resultant publicity does not please the authorities, and Barclay is assigned to track down and capture Jennings. * He is successful, of course, and along the way various gimmicks and stratagems are brought forth: a paralysis ray, a shield against a paralysis ray, potent new power sources that the pirate would like to operate, and a ray that operates by focusing two components. * Barclay contrives to have outlaw Jennings capture a passenger ship holding other Jovians. The Terrestrial pirates cannot stand up against the musclemen and women, who are not only supernally strong but incredibly fast in motion. * In this story Campbell asserts that the Jovian supermen are the product of a planned experiment in which many Terrestrials were placed on Jupiter, with the survivors adapting to the heavy gravity. * Routine, synthetic thrills. Gernsback, who wrote the blurb for the story (an unusual procedure since David Lasser wrote the blurbs), seemed to think that the story was parodic, but this seems doubtful.

198. **BEYOND THE END OF SPACE.** *Amazing Stories*, March-April 1933. Ill. Morey.

Short novel. * *Time:* 1955. *Place:* in part in another universe. * Essentially, the story is a rehash of one aspect of E. E. Smith's "The Skylark of Space." * Tom Warren, experimenting in the university laboratory, accidentally liberates total atomic energy, causing an enormous explosion and an outburst of radiation. After he recovers, he is fired from the university, largely through the machinations of old Nestor, a capitalist swine who has his own purposes. * Nestor has realized that Warren has stumbled onto something important and hopes, by offering Warren a meager job, to gain the discovery. But Warren, warned and alerted by his millionaire friend Putney, is well aware of what Nestor is up to. * Warren and Putney thereupon establish a company to exploit the invention, Warren providing the science and Putney offering an incredible ability to foresee the wicked plans of the robber baron. * Nestor thereupon hires the brilliant intellectual crook Atkill either to recapitulate the discovery or to steal it. Raids and criminal acts are foiled by Warren's advanced security apparatus. * Warren and Putney get their energy source somewhat under control, build a space laboratory (the *Prometheus*) in which to conduct further research, and are prepared to take off when Nestor (with associated capitalists)

Campbell, John W., Jr. (*continued*)

bombs their establishment. The explosion sets off the atomic energy source in the ship, blowing our friends Warren and Putney out of our space and into another. They are wrongly considered dead. * On Earth, Nestor has foresightedly bought rights from Warren's heirs and now has the process. He and his colleagues build ten superships embodying the new energy source and, as the Council of Five, destroy conventional energy sources and declare themselves rulers of the United States. Nestor, with creditable foresight, has provided nine of his ships with poison gas installations so that he can remove his gangster tools when he is securely in power. * But things do not go that smoothly. Just as Nestor bungled his chance with Warren, he alienated the brilliant, if crooked, Atkill, who steals one of the ships, furnishes it with weapons beyond those of Nestor's fleet, and starts to wreck Nestor's plan. When part of Nestor's fleet begins to lay waste New York City, Atkill destroys the ships. Unfortunately, one of the atomic flames expands out of control, and the best that Atkill can do is drag it out to sea, where it explodes, presumably killing him. * Just as the remainder of Nestor's fleet begins to melt down Washington, D.C., Warren and Putney return with new weapons and defensive screens. Nestor and his associates are defeated and captured. * Warren hints that Atkill may not be dead, but Campbell ignored the hint. * Though clichéd, much more readable than most of Campbell's other early stories.

 199. **THE BATTERY OF HATE.** *Amazing Stories,* November 1933. Ill. Morey.
(Reprinted in Knight, *Science Fiction of the Thirties.*)
Short story. * *Time:* 1938. *Place:* New York, Massachusetts, Maine. * Essentially a story of business skulduggery, an expansion of a basic situation in the various space operas of Campbell and E. E. Smith. * Brilliant young scientist Bruce Kennedy has invented a superbattery that bids fair to revolutionize civilization and industry. Wicked capitalist Marcus Gardner hears of the battery when Kennedy files a patent application and is determined to obtain the battery, lest his energy empire be wiped out. * The story is thus a narrative of conflict between Gardner, who uses all means, fair and foul, to ruin Kennedy and his rich friend Donovan, and Kennedy, who strikes back. Gangsters, automobiles capable of more than 150 MPH, and a superfast plane are involved. * The first part of the story is more readable than most of Campbell's work from this period, but the story falls apart toward the end.

 200. **THE MIGHTIEST MACHINE.** *Astounding Stories,* December 1934-April 1935. Ill. Dold.
(Reprinted in book form by Hadley, Providence, R.I., 1947, and in Ace paperbacks.)
Novel. * *Time:* the late twenty-first century. * *Place:* mostly in an other-universe that has some basic connection with ours. * This is the age of interplanetary exploration, with rocket travel to Mars and occasionally Jupiter, and settlements on the Moon. It is also the age for great breakthroughs, most of which come from the brilliant mind of the Jupiterian genius Aarn Munro. Aarn, who was born on Jupiter when his parents were stranded there during the first expedition, as a result of combatting Jupiterian gravity is a physical superman with incredible strength (able to carry about tons of lead) and agility—once away from Jupiter's gravity. He is also an incredible mentality, solving such matters as antigravity, a momentum wave for propulsion,

perfect meteor shields, and the ability to enter a hyperspace—in a matter of hours. His most significant achievement, perhaps, is the creation of transpons, or beams for extracting energy directly from the sun (the Mightiest Machine). * Since much of his experimentation is too dangerous to be performed on Earth, Aarn persuades his employers/backers to construct an enormous space laboratory, which is eventually called the *Sunbeam.* * On its shakedown cruise, the *Sunbeam* reaches incredible speeds, but unfortunately crashes into a small planetoid. Aarn's systems strain, space strains, and there is an enormous explosion. * From Earth it looks as if the ship is destroyed, but the reader soon learns otherwise. Space simply gives way, and Aarn and his friends are hurled into another universe. * When they recover from the shock, they find themselves in a strange space with gigantic suns relatively close. Near them is a small fleet of needle-like space ships that attack them. Aarn fights off the attackers with his transpons, while his various meteor defenses serve as protection. But after a time the *Sunbeam* runs low on power, and the closest giant sun (Anrel) is too far away for convenience. At this point, globular spaceships appear and defeat the needle ships. * *Background:* As Aarn and friends discover, their rescuers are human. Communications are established (realistically, without thought helmets, etc.), and the Earthmen learn that their saviors (Magyans) are descendants of natives of Mu, who cracked into this universe about thirty or forty thousand years earlier. Their enemies, the Tefflans, who had attacked the *Sunbeam,* also came from Earth. Originally an underground race, a blending of primates with other animals, they are goat-men with horns and hoofs. Since the two races are totally antipathetic, Tefflans and Muans waged perpetual war, with Mu sinking as the unfortunate result of an attempt to destroy the Tefflan cavern world. * On reaching the second universe, Tefflan and Muan ships settled on different planets, where both sides lost their science. Only recently have they discovered each other, with war the result. The cause for the permanent war? On the one hand, Tefflan culture is nasty, but in one place Campbell states clearly that the Tefflans are no worse than humans; it is just that there is a total antipathy between the two races that justifies genocide. * Aarn and comrades, after shifting into hyperspace to obtain power from the sun, proceed through another dimension to Magya, where they await an attack from the Tefflans. * The big attack comes. The Magyans, thanks to new weapons invented by Aarn, are totally victorious, destroying the Tefflan space fleet. All concerned on Magya now take thought about a way to remove the Tefflan menace forever. * A new problem. When the Magyans first came to the second universe, they recorded coordinates for returning. The Tefflans captured these documents (which apparently did not exist in duplicate) during an early battle, and, putting two and two together at the appearance of the *Sunbeam,* have thoughts of invading our universe. Aarn and fellows, on the other hand, need the coordinates to return home. * Aarn invents little flying spy viewers that locate the plates in the main Tefflan shrine, and disguising themselves as Tefflans, the men raid the shrine (incidentally destroying it) and carry off the plates. Outraged, the Tefflans now drop into the atmosphere of Magya a catalyst that forms poisonous compounds. Unless a remedy is soon found, Magya is doomed. And chemically, it is a tough nut. Eventually, at the last minute the Terrestrials discover a way to neutralize the catalyst. * The time has arrived

Campbell, John W., Jr. (*continued*)

for the destruction of Teffel itself. Aarn and associates fix up Magyan satellites with space drives and hurl them against Teffel, destroying both the planet and its space defenses. * The war is over, and our friends prepare to return home, with the implication that intercourse between the two universes is now possible. * All in all, perhaps the type specimen of the Campbell hard space opera, with a great quantity of fanciful and ingenious scientific extrapolations, fictional weaknesses, and polarized social simplistics that regard genocide with equanimity. It was popular in its day, but it is now a museum piece. * Campbell wrote three further adventures of Aarn and his comrades that were not published in magazine form, but were issued as *The Incredible Planet* (Fantasy Press, Reading, Pa., 1949). They lack the strengths, such as they are, of *The Mightiest Machine*.

201. **THE CONQUEST OF THE PLANETS. (THE MOTHER WORLD)**. *Amazing Stories*, January-March 1935. Ill. Morey. The first episode carries the title "The Contest for the Planets." This is probably a clerical error.

Short novel. * *Time:* the main action takes place around A.D. 3340, but there is extensive prologue material reaching from the late twentieth century into the future. *Place:* future underground New York. * Space travel, which began in the twentieth century, soon showed that most of the planets were suitable for human habitation. But, through the inevitable dynamics of colonization, the highest quality men emigrated from Earth and sought better life elsewhere, notably on Mars. Earth, though its nations technically had taken possession of the planets, had decayed both physically and culturally, thus could do nothing when the planets declared their independence. * Perhaps several hundred years later (Campbell's sequence and development is confusingly presented), Montgommery, the leader of the Planetarians, presented an ultimatum: The Planets will have nothing more to do with Earth, which is now cut off from the rest of the solar system. Until Earth regains its ancient scientific lead and achieves a decent society, Earth is a tabu planet. * *Future background:* By 3340 a distinctive culture has developed on Earth. Population is concentrated in enormous cities, in which large populations of Plehbs live practically as slaves underground, while on the surface, devoted to lives of leisure and pleasure, live the Polshins, who maintain an iron control over the Plehbs. Polshins periodically seize the better-looking women from the Plehbs. The chief purpose of this does not seem to be normal sexuality, but sadism, especially whipping the women to death. Science and culture have decayed, although the Polshins still maintain arsenals of superscientific weapons above ground, should there be slave revolts. Large sections of the underground cities have become abandoned, even forbidden places. Contact with the other planets is all but forgotten. * To explain what will happen, Campbell invokes a private genetic theory: When a population reaches a certain low quality level, it will automatically begin to produce higher quality members. * Young Bruce Lawry, a remarkably brilliant Plehb boy, venturing into the forbidden Deserted Passages, comes upon an ancient, long disused library. Since books have been almost totally destroyed, this is an incredible find. Bruce and his like-minded friend Don Wade devote their time to reading the ancient literature, and not only acquire a unique knowledge of history (which has been lost or forbidden), but recapitulate much of the ancient science. By the time they are twenty-one or twenty-two, they realize that they

must overturn the cruel rule of the Polshins and prove Earth again worthy to join the commonwealth of planets. An inciting incident occurs when Polshin guards take away Don's girlfriend for the harem (and whipping block) of the city ruler, Polshin Omallin. * About two years pass before the young men are ready to strike. During those two years Bruce and Don have not only recreated the ancient science, but have gone far beyond it, with total atomic energy, far viewers that can reach the stars, projection devices, disintegrators, force shields, and much else. In the meanwhile they have been organizing the Plehbs in New York, and have started similar movements in the other American cities. * The revolution breaks a little prematurely, when the Polshins get wind of what is lurking in the corridors beneath them. There are battles, in which the Plehbs are victorious, but the total situation may be a stalemate, for the Plehbs cannot destroy the enormous Polshin fortresses without doing tremendous damage to the Earth. To eradicate Omallin's stronghold, for example, would involve destroying all New York. But Bruce is equal to the task: He invents a matter transmitter, with which he disassembles the fortress, incidentally saving his girl from Omallin, who had her tied on a table ready for vivisection. Omallin himself Bruce turns into a little statuette. * On Mars, the news of Earth's achievements is received with applause. Since there is immortality of a sort on Mars, Montgommery himself ends the isolation of seven hundred years. * A theme Campbell returned to several times in his Don Stuart stories. As a story, weak, without much fictional credibility from many points of view.

202. **UNCERTAINTY**. *Amazing Stories*, October and December (two issues) 1936. Ill. Morey.

Hard s-f short novel. * *Time:* the twenty-fourth century. *Place:* the inner planets, space, and the planetary system of Mira. * The story is told in part through supergenius millionaire Buck Kendall and in part through Miran spaceship commander and scientist Gresth Gkae. * *The Miran background:* On the planets circling Mira an intelligent form of life has arisen: roughly humanoid in form, but with double-segmented arms and legs, feather-like skin covering, and vertically placed eyes (one of which is telescopic). Since they are heartily sick of the vagaries of their variable star, they have fitted out space expeditions to find a new planetary home. Traveling at a speed faster than that of light, Gresth Gkae's two-thousand-foot-long ovoid ship now enters the solar system, which it finds quite suitable for colonization. * *The solar-system background:* Space travel is well developed, and science is high, but somewhat below that of the Mirans. A space police patrols the lanes, and serving in one of their ships (more as a result of a dare than anything else) is the forenamed Buck Kendall. When the Miran ship, which has been tracked, appears and attacks Kendall's ship, he and his friend Cole are the only survivors. The other men were disintegrated by a neutron beam; Kendall and Cole, chancing to have been protected by the water tanks, escape in a tender while the Miran ship takes the patrol vessel into its hold. * Gresth Gkae, returning to Mira, reports that the solar system could not withstand Miran arms, while Kendall, resigning from the force, devotes his millions (and other funds) to developing new weapons. An enormous Miran armada sets out for our system, and Kendall builds superfortifications on the Moon and Mars. * The attack comes and is handled in typical Campbell fashion. For every ray, destructive device, or protective screen that the

Campbell, John W., Jr. (*continued*)

Mirans produce, Kendall develops a counter. Terrestrial weapons are adequate and can occasionally destroy an enemy ship (more frequently driving ships away disabled), but Earth still lacks the omnipotent power source (material energy) that the Mirans have. The Terrestrial forces are driven farther and back, until . . . Kendall, throwing away his textbooks, builds on empirical principles apparatus that embody Heisenberg's uncertainty principle. With such devices he attains at a bound: incalculable energy, irresistible disintegrators, and faster-than-light travel superior to the Mirans. With one ship he wipes out the Miran armada, while with another he chases Gresth Gkae's flagship back to Mira. * In a generous gesture, however, instead of disintegrating the whole Miran system, he makes peace, for he regards the Mirans as honorable foes. The Mirans, thanks to a second exploratory expedition, have found another system that is suitable for colonization. * The scientific double-talk is presented in heavy loads that at times are almost impenetrable. * This is probably Campbell's last space opera; sequels to "The Mightiest Machine" published posthumously in *The Incredible Planet* were probably written earlier.

CAMPBELL, W. J.
No information.

   203. **THE MAN ON THE BENCH**. *Amazing Stories*, January 1928. Ill. Paul.
Short story. * Dr. Sexton has discovered two extracts that change personality: Degenero brings out bad components of personality; Elimino removes such and creates good. Both extracts, as the author states, are too dangerous to be "placed in the hands of promiscuous persons." * As a demonstration to fellow scientists Sexton changes a dog's moods by injecting it with his extracts. But he needs a human subject. * After advertising in the mode customary in such stories, Sexton finds his man on a park bench. This is petty crook Slats Nelson. Injected with Elimino, Nelson turns out to be an amnesiac solid citizen who was hit on the head with a baseball some years earlier. * Undeveloped and naive.

CARLISLE, LOGAN
Pseud. of Logan Carlisle Ramsey (1898-?), per listing in *Science Fiction Digest*, April 1933, p. 5. Ramsey was also the author of *Air Pilots' Dead Reckoning Tables* (1941) and *Navigation of Aircraft* (1941). At the time of writing, he is carried as Lt., presumably in the U.S. Army Air Force.

   204. **THE AIRWAYMAN**. *Amazing Stories,* April 1936.
Short story. * A scientific detective story. * *Time:* the near future. * Vaden, the narrator, a veteran pilot with Transatlantic Aerial Express, is carrying an immensely valuable consignment of radium when his copilot, producing a gun, hijacks the plane, seizes the radium, and leaps overboard with it into the wilderness of Labrador. Vaden is suspected as an accomplice until an elderly man, the greatest scientist of the day, proves that he is innocent. The culprit is found dead, and the radium is retrieved. * As a gimmick: The pilots of TAX scorn parachutes, since accidents no longer happen. Erlic, the criminal, landed safely with small retrorockets fastened to his waist. * An old-fashioned story, but handled skillfully enough.

CARPENTER, S. C.
No information. Portrait accompanying the story shows a middle-aged man.

   205. **THE SUPER VELOCITOR**. *Science Wonder Stories*, December 1929. Ill. Blythe.
Short story. * Detective story. * Bandits have successfully robbed the train three times, without leaving either evidence of their identity or suggestions of their methodology. New York detective Hamilton, called in, undertakes an investigation. On his first occasion of riding with a valuable consignment, he suffers the embarrassment of having the consignment disappear while he turns his head away. * A lead comes when local police notice that a certain criminal (Spider Morgan) is displaying unusual wealth and has passed a marked bill. Hamilton, pretending to be a stupid thug, works his way into Spider's confidence and joins the gang that is performing the robberies. * The robbery technique involves an apparatus that accelerates human metabolism so enormously that the criminals have time to perform the robberies in what seem seconds to outsiders. Also involved is a levitating device. The mastermind is obviously a man of considerable scientific attainments. * A reasonably well-imagined, nicely paced story, although the tenderloin slang and cant are not too convincing. I would doubt that criminals habitually said "youse" during this period.

CARR, DR. ARCH
No clear information. According to Street and Smith records, payments for this story and collaborations with Carl Buchanan were made to a J. R. Peery of Eupora, Mississippi. It is uncertain whether Carr is a pseud. or Peery acted as an agent. See also collaboration Carl Buchanan and Dr. Arch Carr.

   206. **CARDIACA VERA**. *Astounding Stories,* March 1935. Ill. Dold.
Short story. * Medical student and mortician James Stewart fulfills an obligation when he notifies Dr. Murray of a young woman he has just been about to prepare. Thought dead, Inez is barely alive, though she will be dead in an hour or two. Murray arrives, takes the woman, and arranges for a fake identification and burial. * Behind this unethical and possibly criminal skulduggery, which Murray declares is all for science, is this: Murray has invented a mechanical heart that he wants to test. He removes the woman's diseased heart, connects his apparatus (which is large and cumbersome, covering a table), and waits. The heart functions perfectly. * But problems arise: Stewart has qualms of conscience, the young woman is very unhappy at being permanently attached to a table, and Murray has fallen in love with her. A resolution: Murray's assistant, who is in love with him, commits suicide, whereupon Murray transfers her heart to Inez, and all is well. The characters then declare that the Latin for "true heart" is "cardiaca vera," an absurdity that the editors should have corrected. * Melodramatic writing, below routine.

CARROLL or CAROLL, DUANE N.
No information. The first story is published as by Caroll, the second as by Caroll.

   207. **INTO THE MESOZOIC**. *Amazing Stories Quarterly*, Fall/Winter, 1932.
Short story. * *Place:* The Arctic, northwest of Greenland. * The narrative of James Cory, the only survivor of the Shaw Expedition. * The party camps near a snow mound. The heat of their tent loosens some snow, revealing a rocky tor and a cleft leading

Carroll, Duane N. (*continued*)

downward. The members of the expedition descend into the cleft, which is lighted in some unexplained way, and after long walking come out upon a talus slope, beneath which is a green, tropical lost world. Pterodactyls attack; other dinosaurs are a menace. The party becomes separated, and only Cory manages to return to the surface and backpack to civilization. * Routine.

208. **WHEN REPTILES RULED.** *Wonder Stories,* January 1934. Ill. Paul.

Short story. * *Time:* the Mesozoic. Location not given. * Not really science-fiction. A short period in the life of a *Struthiominus*, a small dinosaur. Called Lugi by the author, he steals an egg from the nest of a gigantic pteranodon, is pursued and hunted, and is saved when a *Tyrannosaurus rex* catches the pteranodon and kills it. * The dinosaur is somewhat personalized. * Routine.

CAVE, ARTHUR

No information.

209. **THE WEATHER MASTER.** *Amazing Stories,* July 1935. Ill. Morey.

Short story. * *Time:* 1980. *Place:* Washington, D.C., and Greenland. * The situation looks bad for America in the war with Russia; America has no armies and no air force, while the Russians have an enormous fleet of bombers that have already devastated much of the country. * When things are at their worst, the great scientist Professor Wilton comes to Washington and makes a startling promise. He engages to sweep the Russian air armadas out of the skies and defeat the Russians on the ground. His solution: weather control. * The cabinet at first scoffs at Wilton, but he proves his point quite easily by paralyzing the nation's transportation with a dense fog all over the country. Given carte blanche, Wilton creates storms that sweep the Russians out of the skies and deposit so much snow on Russia that the country is paralyzed. * Wilton explains: By studying weather patterns over the Greenland ice cap and erecting suitable control structures, he is able to manipulate air currents with great precision. * Fine, but Wilton now demands his reward, which amounts to dictatorship over the United States and enormous sums of money. It is impossible, declares the president, whereupon Wilton threatens that he will bring the United States to its knees. He sends a deep fog over the country again, but it does not bother brilliant young scientist Lane, who uses infrared light, flies to Greenland, and shoots Wilton. * Moral: It could have been avoided, had the various parties discussed terms beforehand.

CAVE, HUGH B. (1910- present)

U.S. author of British birth. A versatile writer who never fulfilled his potential. A frequent contributor to the pulp magazines, usually with adventure and horror fiction. Also contributed to the slick magazines. War correspondent in World War II and owner of a coffee plantation in Jamaica after the war. Cave's *Magazines I Remember* is a good mixture of business autobiography and pulp gossip. * Much of Cave's better work, which can be vivid and pointed, if thin, is to be found in the collection *Murgunstrumm and Others* (1977). The following stories are not among his better work.

210. **THE CORPSE ON THE GRATING.** *Astounding Stories,* February 1930. Ill. Sabo.

Short story. * *Place:* London. * Dr. Dale (the narrator) and M.S. visit the great Professor Daimler, who complains that he has not been able to revive a man who has been dead for about a month. On leaving, Dale scoffs, but M.S. reproves him sharply, saying that Daimler is a great scientist. * Dale and M.S. pass a warehouse, where they see a corpse clutching a grating, obviously dead of fear. After an exchange of comments, M.S. challenges Dale to spend the night in the building in question. Dale agrees, but horrors unfold that night with an animated corpse. As Dale is recovering, he learns that the corpse was one of Daimler's experiments; his revival technique did work, but very slowly. * Much influence from Poe. Cave on occasion imitates "The Fall of the House of Usher" as Dale reads a Gothic novel to the accompaniment of strange happenings. * Really more a story for the horror pulps than for an s-f magazine. In any case, pretty bad.

211. **THE MURDER MACHINE.** *Astounding Stories,* September 1930. Ill. J. Fleming Gould.

Short story. * *Place:* England. * Essentially a crime story. Dr. Dale, narrator, is concerned with a mysterious crime committed under will-compulsion. Indeed, under a similar compulsion, he himself almost commits murder! * The explanation lies in Michael Strange, a mad scientist who has created a machine that broadcasts hypnotic thought waves by radio. Strange seeks revenge for being flouted sexually. * Scotland Yard resolves the situation. * Pretty weak material. Cave's forte was not science-fiction.

CHADWICK, PAUL

No information.

212. **CRUSADERS OF SPACE**. *Amazing Stories Quarterly,* Fall/Winter 1932.

Short story. * *Time:* The interplanetary future, later than 2045, which is referred to as in the past. *Place:* Space and Oberon, a satellite of Uranus. * Mark Travers, an inspector for the great firm of Planetoid Chemicals, Inc., is summoned to the president's office for interview. Travers need not be worried, President Zanton informs him, for Zanton has been investigating him for the past five years and knows that he can be trusted. * Travers has a special, top secret mission: He is to escort Paula, the president's daughter, to Oberon, where Zanton's son Harvey is trying to synthesize vitamin A, which is in serious shortage in the solar system. Indeed, if Harvey Zanton is not successful in his research, civilization may collapse. * Travers and Paula embark, leave their spaceship in a small tender heading for Oberon, but are captured by the vicious Hulgar, a man-ape of unspecified planet. Holding Paula hostage, Hulgar demands an interview and negotiations with Harvey. * Actually, Hulgar has a dirty trick in mind. In the Zanton laboratories he plans to release a brood of the incredibly lethal Venusian mortifer beetles that secrete a deadly poison and devour human flesh with great rapidity. * In the meanwhile, Travers manages to escape. Desperately trying to reach the laboratory before Hulgar and to warn Harvey, he slogs through the jungles, fighting off tentacled carnivorous plants. But he is too late. Hulgar has killed everyone in the laboratories. * This is not the end, however. Travers turns the tables on the pirates, shooting Hulgar and releasing a swarm of the beetles on his gang. * Paula will continue the experiments, with Travers. * Scientific ignorance in a less than routine story.

CHAMBERLAIN, J. LESLIE

No information. Perhaps, judging from story details, a resident of the Northwest, with World War I experience in the Military Police.

213. **THE SWORD OF AKALAH.** *Amazing Stories,* June 1936. Ill. Morey.

Short story. * The fate of the world is interwoven with the madness of Bill Carstairs. * Some thirteen years ago, Carstairs, demobbed from the army, spends some time in a museum in San Francisco. There, as one of the museum's treasures, is a great sword imbedded in a block of sandstone; it is a relic of Atlantis dredged up some time before. * Bill now dreams of his former life as Tim-Ur in Atlantis. A minor priest in the main temple, he sees the beautiful Akalah. She is a virgin priestess who is believed to be an embodiment of a goddess by the populace, but is used as a prop by the wise, scientifically advanced priesthood (the White Magicians). One of her attributes is the Sword of Akalah, a great sword imbedded in a block of sandstone. Another is a scimitar that swings back and forth, powered by perpetual motion. * Akalah and Tim-Ur, falling in love, make plans to steal an aircraft and fly to one of the western nations, where they can marry. Akalah conceals in the hollow hilt of the sword, which they plan to take with them, the secrets for perpetual motion, atomic energy, and similar matters. * As they are about to steal away, there is a great commotion. The Black Magicians have succeeded in gaining possession of some kalite, the substance that produces atomic energy. Atlantis is in danger, says Akalah. The Black Priests can produce atomic energy, but they do not know how to control it. They may destroy Atlantis. And so they do. Atlantis goes down. * Awaking, Carstairs tries to take the sword, but is arrested. When he speaks of the secrets of atomic energy and perpetual motion hidden in the sword hilt, he is placed in an insane asylum. * Now, thirteen years have passed. The frame narrator, a former friend of Carstairs, receives a letter in which Carstairs (who frankly admits that he has become a little mad from his stay in the madhouse) declares that he now remembers (from his past life) how to make a simple form of kalite. He will use this to blow his way out of the asylum, and three months from then will blow up the world. The frame narrator reads in the newspaper that there has been a great explosion at the asylum, that Carstairs has escaped, and that the sword has been stolen from the museum. The Earth has three months before destruction. * Not bad for a romantic tale.

CHAMBERLIN, PHILIP DENNIS

No information.

214. **THE TALE OF THE ATOM.** *Amazing Stories,* January 1935.

Short-short story. * The story is told from two points of view, macrocosmic and Terrestrial. * In the macrocosm (to which the solar system is simply an atom) the great scientist Atwar is trying to split atoms. Master of a superscience, he is not humanoid, but has four arms, six fingers to an arm, and four eyes. As he sends energy down into our cosmos, his progress is checked by machine-telepathic observers. * On Earth, where it is A.D. 86,300, astronomers note with dismay that a blue flame is approaching the sun, the same phenomenon that destroyed Sirius some four hundred years earlier. * The great scientist Granstedt sets up a project to save the Earth. When the blue flash strikes the sun, enormous generators on Earth release

quantities of various gases, which freeze solid and form a strong shell around the planet. Granstedt's titanic rockets then move the Earth out into space, toward Vega. But when the gases thaw, when Earth arrives in its new orbit, it is, unfortunately, bare; everything has been wiped out by gravitational forces that might have been contained had the Moon been included in the move. The human race is extinct. * In the macrocosm, Atwar notes with satisfaction that he has split an atomic nucleus, but is mildly puzzled that one electron should have migrated away toward another nucleus some distance away. * Cleverly handled, if scientifically somewhat suspect.

CHAPPELOW, EDWARD E. (1902-1986)

U.S. author and fan. Then a resident of Chicago area. Died in Du Page, Illinois. Science-fictionally inspirational poem "Join a Chapter" (of the Science Fiction League) in September 1935 *Wonder Stories.* Otherwise no information.

215. **THE PLANET'S AIR MASTER.** *Air Wonder Stories,* August 1929. Ill. Paul.

Novelette. * *Time:* 1982. *Place:* mostly New York and London. * *Background:* Aeronautics has advanced enormously. Giant five-motored planes with passenger facilities in triple decks inside the wings fly along magnetic control beams across continents and seas. As planes approach landing platforms, other magnetic beams seize them and land them into tracks on the platforms. When leaving, planes are hastened along tracks and catapulted into the air. The platforms themselves are enormously complex buildings, not described with sufficient clarity by the author. * The current problem is that planes of giant International Air Line are being robbed on the New York-London route. Planes are found floating on the ocean, somehow forced from the beamed routes, and robbed. * The problem concerns Wallace, New York official of International Air Line, and Inspector Riel of Scotland Yard. * Riel, who has been investigating the crimes for some time, knows that much more is involved than an occasional robbery. Behind the crimes is a criminal mastermind who will stop at nothing to obtain what he wants: in this case records of certain strange, perhaps extraterrestrial signals. * Against Riel's ingenuity stands the Air Master of the World's organization and impressive armory: a spy ray that penetrates almost anything, transmitting light and sound, and a telepathic ray that can also be a mind-controller. * Riel, who has a detector for the rays, tries various expediencies, all of little avail, for the mastermind repeatedly outplays him. * On the crucial occasion, Wallace, disguised as Riel, rides a plane from London. He is picked up by the Master, who reveals himself to be J. B. Jolsen. * Jolsen, who was not fooled by the substitution, knows Wallace's identity and plans to use him later. At the moment he intends to use his will control apparatus to cause American and British fleets to battle one another, while he and Wallace watch. But the battle does not come off; instead the planes bomb the island where Jolsen has his installation. Jolsen escapes in a submarine. * Explanation: Riel discovered that an iron helmet protected him from the telepathic rays, and, stowed away in an iron barrel on Wallace's plane, summoned the fleets, whose personnel wore iron protection. * *Miscellaneous:* The Air Master wanted the light records desperately, because, being interplanetary, they might give him the power to conquer the solar system, not just the Earth. Actually, they turned out to be experimental signals sent by a French laboratory, and all the Air

Chappelow, Edward E. (*continued*)

Master's activity was misdirected. * Routine material, reminiscent of early motion pictures and not a little confusing. * For a sequel see #217, "The Return of the Air Master."

216. **IN TWO WORLDS.** *Science Wonder Stories*, October 1929. Ill. Win.

Short story. * Amateur scientist Ted Nelson theorizes that our brain perceives material only within a certain range, but that this range can be expanded by suitable apparatus. Working in his garage with the assistance of narrator Tom, Ted constructs a suitable pair of thought helmets to change this perception range. * The apparatus works rather feebly at first, but when refined, with more power applied, it shows billiard ball atomic particles flying about. (The objective is a silver coin.) At highest efficiency, the apparatus shows an atomic world with humans, including one delightful female, for whom Ted experiences an instant passion. * The experimentation for the day ends, but next morning Tom learns that Ted is dead, his garage having been destroyed by a fire. Going to a secret cache, Tom finds a last letter from Ted, who declares his intention of locating once again the atom with the young woman. Too much power added, apparently. The narrator hopes that Ted will be joined to the young lady in some future existence. * Pretty poor as a story, confusing, with the development not fitted well to the theoretical statements at the beginning.

217. **THE RETURN OF THE AIR MASTER.** *Air Wonder Stories*, March 1930. Ill. Paul.

Sequel to #215, "The Planet's Air Master." * Novelette. * *Time:* 1986, four years after the previous adventure. * Aeronautics has progressed enormously, for torpedo-shaped craft fly at 500 MPH and faster and have taken over the airways. * Vessels of the Torpedo Air Express Co., however, have been leaving the control beams and disappearing. Detective Riel, in London, is convinced that Jolsen, the Air Master, is back again, with new inventions with which to commit crime. * The Air Master soon makes his power known with new and better spy rays and a device that disintegrates a London building. Riel, however, is now able to use Jolsen's spy ray to spy back on Jolsen. Through various locating devices Riel now knows that the fiend is operating somewhere in North America. * It will be a perilous game to track Jolsen down, for "he is undoubtedly the world's master of gravity, master of vision, of time, of speed and to a certain extent master of man's brain." * When Riel's counterespionage discovers that Jolsen must have some sort of interplanetary viewer, he devises a trap for the mad genius. Riel's associates fake a science-fiction film showing a supercivilization on another planet and build dummy reception apparatus for space signals. Riel hopes that Jolsen, eager to obtain new weapons, will try to steal the apparatus, thereby revealing his location. * Such proves to be the case, but when Riel proceeds to Newfoundland, it is he who is captured by Jolsen, not vice versa. In a long interview of nine double-columned pages Jolsen asks Riel to urge the world to surrender. In exchange he offers Riel a high position in the new order. Jolsen demonstrates just a few of the weapons with which he plans to conquer the world, and later, the solar system: a disintegrator, a heat ray, a paralysis ray, and worst of all, radiation with which he can drive the world's animals against man. As proof of his powers, he sets off a small animal revolt in Africa, where a tiger [*sic*] helps wipe out a safari. Worst of all, Jolsen can sic the insects of the world on

mankind. This would mean the end of the human race. * Riel, however, turns the tables on the fiend, although the attempt leaves him paralyzed for a time, and the laboratory goes up in fire and destruction. Riel drags himself away, but the Air Master is now dead. * *Miscellaneous:* Jolsen's interplanetary viewer has been turned on to Venus, where there is a highly civilized superior race and a race of hostile intelligent animals. Some of Jolsen's technology has been stolen from Venus via spy ray. * Still like an early motion picture scenario, with set scenes and a pictorial approach, but written out in great detail.

218. **THE AIR TRAP.** *Air Wonder Stories*, May 1930. Ill. Paul.

Short story. * *Time:* the near future. *Place:* Africa, five hundred miles from Cape Town. * Something is radically wrong on the airmail route. Two planes have left the guide wave and have stopped signaling. And now a third, sent out to investigate, also seems to have gone down. All this seems to be happening over Skeleton Valley, a tabu place to the natives that is filled with skeletons. * The air chief and the pilots, shocked at the apparent tragedy that has befallen their friends, come to the conclusion that criminal activity is behind it, especially since the mails are carrying a fortune in diamonds from Kimberley. * Jim Rogers and Tom Curtiss investigate. Leaving their plane a distance from Skeleton Valley, they creep up. They find skeletons and the corpse of their friend, but no sign of robberies. Instead, the valley begins to glow and the rocks to coruscate. As rain begins, the situation grows worse, their strength fails, and it is almost a miracle that they escape from Skeleton Valley. * The explanation: The valley is filled with a strange mineral that emits magnetism and other effects when damp, whence the loss of the planes flying the beam and the physical effects that killed other pilots. * Routine.

CHAPPLE, PAUL K.

U.S. writer, then resident in New York City.

219. **THE MAN WITH THE LONGITUDINAL HEAD.** *Wonder Stories*, May 1934.

Short-short story, printed in the letter column. A frank parody of David H. Keller's story "The Literary Corkscrew." * Thurlow Glinkbottom, frustrated, unsuccessful author, learns the secret of literary success from a story in the science-fiction magazine *Marvel Narrations*. The secret is pain. * Thurlow thereupon constructs an apparatus to squeeze his head, so as to force literary quality out onto paper. Applying his device, he types out a story of interplanetary warfare between Mars and Earth and excitedly hastens to deliver it to the offices of *Marvel Narrations*. People look strangely at him as he passes; he does not suspect why until a huge ruffian seizes him—and Thurlow now has achieved fame in a circus as the Man with the Longitudinal Head. * Amusing.

220. **THE GROWTH PROMOTER.** *Wonder Stories*, November 1934.

Short-short story. * A footnote comments that the well-known science-fiction writer Nada Williams suddenly stopped writing s-f at the height of her career. While active, she obtained scientific ideas from her guardian, the great scientist Albert Webster. A half-completed manuscript, "The Growth Promoter," may offer explanations. * As the story goes: Nada has sold her first story to *Miracle Tales* and is off on a career as a writer. Dr. Webster helps her with many ideas. On the crucial occasion

Chapple, Paul K. (*continued*)

Webster, speaking in a strange manner, suggests that a scientist might have worked out a ray that would speed up human maturation to a matter of hours, rather than years. Working with kidnapped babies, he might create a group of nearly mindless assistants, whom he would control telepathically. * As Nada mulls the idea, she suddenly suspects that Webster is speaking of himself and that he is the scientist concerned. When she questions him about it, he drops dead and his zombie-like assistants follow. * Apparently when Webster kidnapped Nada as a baby, he found her so appealing that he did not subject her to his ray, but allowed her to grow up as a normal woman. Either this upsets Nada so much that she cannot write any more, or Webster was more necessary to her than she had imagined. The author provides no solution. In the first case, a reader may judge that Nada overreacted.

CHESNUTT, CLARA E.
No information.

221. **ESCAPE FROM CERES.** *Amazing Stories*, October 1935. Ill. Morey.

Short story. * *Time:* the interplanetary future. *Place:* Ceres and Mars. * Stanton, sentenced to twenty years' imprisonment on the penal colony on Ceres, takes part in a small jail break. Reaching Mars, he is fortunate enough to find a corpse whose identity he can temporarily assume, and eventually makes his way to Earth on a dirty tramp spaceship. He is recognized almost immediately on arrival, but the news is good. The day after he escaped, the real criminal confessed and Stanton's innocence was established. * Competent enough, but an ordinary jailbreak story.

CLAUSEN, CARL (1895-1954)

U.S. author. Born in Denmark, died in Pennsylvania. Also contributed to other pulp magazines, notably *Adventure*.

222. **THE GRIM INHERITANCE.** *Amazing Stories*, August 1929. Ill. Clardy.

Short story. * Really a crime story and not science-fiction. * Austin Crane, of a formerly well-to-do family, suffers badly from hypothyroidism; so much so that if he does not take his extract, he degenerates unrecognizably in a matter of days. He uses this phenomenon to right a wrong that had been done to him. * After the death of his mother, Crane goes to live with Stoddard, the executor and embezzler of his family's estates. When he realizes first that he has been wronged, and second, that Stoddard serves as a fence for stolen bonds, he sets Stoddard up. Creating a false identity as a petty criminal, he offers Stoddard bonds, then hijacks the cash involved, enough to make up for Stoddard's embezzlement. He is unrecognized because he has not taken his thyroid extract for some time. * Far-fetched, but not fantastic enough to count as science-fiction.

CLEATOR, P[HILIP] E[LLABY] (1908-1994)

British author, engineer (Liverpool area), with family engineering business. Of no significance in science-fiction proper, but apparently an important figure in the British development of rocketry in the period before World War II. One of the founders and president of the British Interplanetary Society. Columnist and contributor of articles on rocketry to *Scoops*. Author of *Rockets through Space* (1936) and *The Robot Era* (1955). His work in rocketry is covered in Frank H. Winter's *Prelude to the Space*

Age. Also wrote at least four short stories that were published after World War II in British science-fiction magazines.

223. **MARTIAN MADNESS.** *Wonder Stories*, March 1934. Ill. Winter.

Short story. * *Place:* mostly Mars. * In the framework narrative, three British travelers, temporarily stranded at an inn when their automobile went into a ditch, listen to the story of a stranger with a marked and scarred face. * The stranger's story: He and two friends took off in their newly designed rocket ship and, traveling at 300,000 MPH, reached Mars in a short time. Mars seemed barren, with breathable atmosphere, but signs of life became apparent in a short time. Floating creatures like jellyfish attacked them. There was little possibility of defense, since pistol shots simply fragmented the creatures into a horde of smaller ones, and flame, though effective, was limited. Only the narrator survived to return to Earth, badly scarred by the attacks. Is his story to be believed? * Less than routine. * Shortly after the story was printed, British fans accused Cleator of plagiarizing "The Pioneers of Pike's Peak" by Basil Tozer (*Strand Magazine*, September 1897, and anthologized later). As Mike Ashley has stated in "The Rocket Man," the accusation was justified, although Cleator maintained his innocence. Cleator did not copy "The Pioneers of Pike's Peak" word-for-word (as Allen Glasser did with Marion Ryan and Robert Ord's "The Heat Wave"), but he obviously worked with Tozer's story before him, rewriting it.

CLICK, J. HAROLD
No information.

224. **THE DIMENSION SEGREGATOR.** *Amazing Stories*, August 1929. Ill. Hugh Mackay.

Short story. * *Place:* California. * The narrative of witness Dr. Thorndyke. * Philip Tulane, a mathematician, was also a physicist and chemist of genius. One of his discoveries was tulanium, or iron reduced to absolute zero by compression and refrigeration. It is infinitely hard and completely solid, since atoms and molecules are forced together. * Tulane is interested in dimensions, and often discusses them in visits with old Professor Derioux and the professor's beautiful daughter Theda. Theda and her father are "soft" on psychological matters, while Tulane is hard and rational. * Tulane discusses the possibilities of stripping a dimension from three-dimensional objects and turning them into two-dimensional objects; he speculates that they would then be able to penetrate anywhere, except where bounded by tulanium. Tulane constructs a ray machine that can do such stripping. The group experiments with objects, with striking results: If the projector is rotated, the object will be restored in various distorted forms. Indeed, a dog so treated displays reversed left-right symmetry. By an accident, Dr. Derioux loses one dimension from his hand—which remains functional, but is now invisible. * Tulane announces that he will go into the second dimensional world and retrieve the missing hand as soon as he has worked out a suitable means of entry. He and Theda then visit the second dimensional world, which they describe as peaceful and idyllic. * All goes well until an earthquake destroys the equipment while Tulane and Theda are in the other world. They are trapped there. Fire breaks out and destroys everything. * The narrator has now decided that the other-world is the after-death world and is wonderful. He looks forward to joining Theda and Tulane there. * *Miscellaneous:* Theda has paranormal gifts of hypnosis that play a part in the story. *

Click, J. Harold (*continued*)
Disjointed, boring, very amateurish, but a new idea in dimensional stories.

CLOUKEY, CHARLES (1912-1932)

U.S. (Lansdowne, Pennsylvania) author. Tuck, Rock and other fan sources incorrectly identify Charles Cloukey as the pseud. of Charles Cloutier. According to Robert Madle, who knew the family well, the author's name was really Cloukey, pronounced Clookey. Cloukey was a very talented young man, greatly interested in science, and was an Edison Scholarship finalist for Pennsylvania in 1931. Fan circles knew that Cloukey was young, but it was not generally known that he was only sixteen years old when his first story was published. He was a clear writer with good ideas and a good sense of pacing who might have become important had he lived. Today, of course, he is forgotten.

The Paradox Series

Three stories based on time traveling and experiences in both the thirtieth century and our time. Time is considered to be an Einsteinian fourth dimension. In some fashion it can be altered by electrical means, so that time travel is possible by Wellsian time machines or portable apparatus. The secret of time traveling was discovered in the twenty-ninth century. * By the thirtieth century the world has undergone two Martian invasions, which have been repelled, and is now about to undergo a third, more serious attack. The Martians, who cannot tolerate terrestrial gravity and climate well, transplant their brains to human bodies. Since the eye and optic nerve must remain connected to the brain, Martians can be identified by their purple eyes. It is tacitly assumed that they are human or humanoid. Their planet is dying, whence their attempts to conquer the Earth. * Martian science is about on the same level as Terrestrial. Both cultures seem to have hypnosis machines, inertialess flight, supersonic flying machines, solid electricity as a power source, and antigravity. The Martians also have the superexplosive brarron, which can be detonated only by certain radio waves. * The author is aware of the commoner time paradoxes circulating at the time (such as going into the past and murdering your grandfather when he was a boy, etc.), but despite the titles of his stories, does not really invoke them very much. The three stories are presented in a complex narrative mode in which expository sections in a Philadelphia club are interspersed with expanded narrative.

225. **PARADOX**. *Amazing Stories Quarterly*, Summer 1929. Ill. Walitt.
Short story. * Time: mostly A.D. 2930. *Place:* Philadelphia and elsewhere. * During a present-day discussion of time at a club, Raymond Cannes tells his story. Some months earlier he received an invitation from his friend the great scientist Endicott Hawkinson to visit his lab. There, to his utter amazement, Hawkinson showed him a long mathematical paper on time traveling, written in Cannes's hand! Cannes, who is a layman, cannot explain the situation or even understand the paper. * Hawkinson, convinced that the scientific data are correct, uses them to build a time machine. Cannes volunteers to enter it, and in few seconds is in 2930. * At first he is regarded with some suspicion, since he claims to hail from an era almost a thousand

years before time travel became possible, but hypnosis machines reveal the truth of what he says. * He is then assigned to the great scientist Bonn, who, among other matters, is responsible for historical research. * Up to now, time travel was possible only into the future, but Bonn has invented apparatus for entering the past. He writes out a manuscript with the data that Hawkinson received, has a copying machine write it in Cannes's handwriting, and Cannes returns to 1928, where he deposits it in Hawkinson's laboratory. While in 1928 he wonders about various paradoxes, but does not test them. He then returns to the future, since there should not be two Canneses in 1928. * Back in 2930, on the super-airliner *Patrician*, Cannes first alienates Bonn's daughter Greta by unwelcome advances, then finds Bonn murdered by an invisible man. The murderer, whom Cannes captures, is a Martian. Under the hypnosis machine the captive reveals that the Martians have a secret base in Antarctica and have spread enough of their superexplosive brarron to destroy mankind. The plane also is booby-trapped. There are fifteen minutes to act. * The passengers and crew leap overboard with flight disks, and Cannes is left alone on the plane, which is due to explode. He thereupon uses his time machine to return to our time. Now at the club he announces that he has beaten fate. According to records of the thirtieth century, he was killed yesterday in an automobile accident; but he is still alive. But when he leaves the club, he is run over; he had made a mistake about the date. The time machine has been accidentally destroyed. For a sequel see #226, "Paradox +."

226. **PARADOX +**. *Amazing Stories*, July 1930. Ill. Paul.
Short story. * Sequel to #225, "Paradox." * *Time:* A.D. 2930. *Place:* various, including Australia and Antarctica. * As in the previous story, the author throws together a large amount of ideas, thematic devices, and plot techniques in a somewhat disorganized fashion. * It is best to proceed by isolating story strands. * The narrative strategy is again a club discussion, this time by a friend of the experiencer. In this case Sherman and Preston discover that the original time cube was not so badly damaged by fire as had been believed. It proves possible to repair it and provide it with a better power source, whereupon the two men travel to the thirtieth century. Since they have foreknowledge of part of the events that Cannes reported, they try to provide advance warnings of the Martian peril and also to offset part of the tragedy of the *Patrician*. In this they are helped by Jac Vanon, a young member of Dwar Bonn's laboratory, who is in love with Greta Bonn. Jac, in his flying machine, performs a midair rescue of Greta. But, as turns out later in the story, Greta dies when she and a companion are captured by the Martians. * The second strand is the Martian attack. Thanks to Cannes's actions in the previous story, information about the Martian plot breaks in time, so that only a third of the human race is destroyed. Jac manages to obtain a small sample of the Martian superexplosive brarron, and Earth scientists, after much difficulty, discover how to detonate it. Destroying Martian spacecraft, they take aim at Mars, where huge amounts of brarron are stored. * Earth air forces try to storm the Martian stronghold on Antarctica, but are almost wiped out. However, in a single invisible plane the twentieth-century men, Vanon, and the great Japanese scientist Yun (who speaks a sort of pidgin) penetrate Martian headquarters and confront the Martian commander. * Since it is a stalemate situation, the two

Cloukey, Charles (*continued*)

parties come to terms. Yun agrees not to blow up Mars with the brarron stored there, and in exchange the Martians will revive Greta and permit all to leave during a twenty-four hour truce. * Preston has been killed. * Hypnosis machines are present, but are usually dropped and broken when needed. For a sequel see #227, "Anachronism."

227. **ANACHRONISM**. *Amazing Stories*, December 1930. Ill. P. Muller.
Short story. * The third and last story in the "Paradox" series. * The final episodes of the Third Martian War. * *Time:* A.D. 2930. *Place:* mostly Antarctica and Philadelphia. * Yun, who can read Martian script, discovers that the Martian commander is tricking him and instead of providing a drug to revive Greta, plans to release a deadly pestilence. Killing the Martians, the Terrestrials fly out of Antarctica back to Australia. Mars is devastated by brarron explosions, and the war is over, except for mopping up on Earth. After some difficulty Greta Bonn is revived and is on the way to recovery. Sherman returns to our time. * One Martian spy, however, escapes detection in the future. Killing Yun and stealing the time machine, he makes his way to 1929, not for military reasons, but for revenge. Now in present-day Philadelphia, he begins a series of mysterious murders that involve matter creation of a sort. By intersecting two beams of atomic particles he precipitates red hot iron balls. In part the mad Martian's aim is erratic murder; in part it is the death of Sherman, whom he cannot locate. The Martian is finally cornered in a melodramatic finale just as he is about to pour acid on Sherman's sister. He dies of a heart attack. Sherman had previously been killed in an auto crash. All the time travelers are now dead; all the machinery and mathematical documentation have been destroyed by the Martian; and there will be no more time traveling in the twentieth century.

Other Works

228. **SUB-SATELLITE**. *Amazing Stories*, March 1928. Ill. Paul.
Short story. * *Time:* the middle twenty-first century. * Several subplots are involved. First, Dr. Francis Javis, a noted scientist, and Richard C. Brown have just reached the moon in a rocket ship that has collapsible wings for air-travel. Javis funded his project with a new process for producing artificial diamonds. But Javis and Brown were not alone on the moon. One Duseau, a disgruntled, discharged employee, stowed away and is now determined to kill the other two men. If successful, since there is no law on the Moon, he can return to Earth with impunity. Duseau now has Javis and Brown trapped among the crevasses while he takes pot shots at them with a machine rifle. They are unarmed. * The second subplot is a disinheritance situation. Dr. Javis, who is bad tempered, has quarreled with his two sons and repeatedly changes his will. At the moment it looks as if the deserving son will be disinherited unless voice analysis of a radio message can establish a new last will and testament. * Both problems are resolved. One of Duseau's shots, thanks to the moon's low gravity and the velocity of his bullets, goes completely around the Moon and strikes him in the back, killing him, so that Javis, Sr., and Brown are able to return to the Earth in the rocket. * Ingenious, and not a bad story. For a sequel see #229, "Super-Radio."

229. **SUPER-RADIO**. *Amazing Stories*, July 1928. Ill. Paul.
Short story. * Sequel to #228, "Sub-satellite." * *Time:* A.D. 2072. * Javis of the previous story is now dead, and his fortune in artificial diamonds rests in a bank vault. The diamonds, however, disappear, obviously stolen. In their place is an apparatus for matter transmission designed by Clankey, whom the thief has kidnapped. The crimes must be the work of the master criminal M. W. * Wesley Gibson, Clankey's assistant, now offers help. According to him, Clankey's matter transmitter works linearly in only one direction. Thus, when the orientation of the machine abandoned in the bank vault is determined, it pinpoints the direction in which the gems disappeared. * A superplane, following this line, arrives at an artificial island in the North Atlantic. Criminals and their loot are there. Tussles and shoot-outs take place. Most important is the discovery that M. W. is a beautiful young woman, the former friend of Aviator Brown of "Sub-Satellite." She can produce ball lightning and use it as a weapon. Good triumphs; M. W. and her henchmen are captured. Psychiatric surgery is so far advanced that a couple of hours in the operating room transforms her from a cold outlaw into a warm young woman who will now join the ranks of great scientists. * Less successful than its predecessor.

230. **RHYTHM**. *Amazing Stories*, April 1930. Ill. Morey.
Short story. * *Time:* 1999. * *Background:* The great scientist Thornton Greene disappeared ten years ago and is presumed dead. He was working on a scientific project of extreme importance, but beyond the fact that it concerns synthetic life, not much is known about it. His secret papers are stored in a bank vault, accessible to his son, Graham Greene, only after Thornton Greene is legally presumed dead—which is now. Graham Greene, unfortunately, has lost both his feet in a plane crash. He walks well enough, however, with prosthetics and should be able to carry on his father's work. * As the narrator (Von der Konz) begins the story, Graham Greene has retrieved his father's papers, but he and his fiancée, the Flaming Atom—a short red-haired young woman—have been captured by his step-uncle, the able but ruthless scientist Calvroon. Calvroon desperately wants the papers and is prepared to murder Greene and his friends for them. His technique is an acoustic device that accelerates cardiac rhythm. Since Graham Greene has a weak heart, he will die; if the others do not die, perhaps Calvroon will simulate a plane crash. * The machine on, Graham collapses, as expected. * But it is not the end: Graham, lunging out, KOs Calvroon and releases his friends. * Calvroon's plot was perfectly sound from a scientific point of view, but he did not know that Greene had an exceptionally high hearing range and did not hear the low beats that Calvroon used. * For a sequel, see #231, "Synthetic."

231. **SYNTHETIC**. *Amazing Stories*, May 1930. Ill. Morey.
Short story. * Sequel to #230, "Rhythm." * Short story. * *Time:* A.D. 2000, about a year after the previous story. * Three subplots now merge. First, Calvroon has escaped from prison and is busy trying to murder the three parties of the first story with a heat ray. He does not succeed in killing them, but does force down the Flaming Atom's plane; she is blinded by the crash. * Second, Von der Konz and the Flaming Atom have a friendly rivalry about flying. Von der Konz currently holds the

Cloukey, Charles (*continued*)

speed record over a measured course, but the Flaming Atom might well have won the upcoming competition had she not been blinded. * Third, Graham Greene's recapitulation of his father's work is proving very successful. He and his staff have created artificial life, and, indeed, have even made a full-fledged rabbit. They would like to expand their range, but Thornton Greene left formulas for only two life-forms, rabbits and male humans. * A peculiarity about the rabbit: after life was formed, it grew at a fantastic rate, reaching maturity in a matter of hours, after which it slid into normal metabolism. * Greene and his staff are now engaged in manufacturing a man. They are successful, and the result, in a few days, is a handsome, intelligent young man whom they call Bob Nelson. Hypnolearning provides him with a perfect command of English and many skills. * The day of the competition is here, and there are developments. Nelson will take the Flaming Atom's place, and Calvroon will make a desperate attempt to murder everyone. Nelson easily wins, since he is reckless, and to prevent Calvroon from killing the others, he crashes his plane into the mad scientist's, killing him. Nelson, it was earlier revealed, was in love with the Flaming Atom and sacrificed himself. This proves that Nelson, a most noble character, really did have a soul, something that had been questioned. * As a final tie-up, the Greene synthetic life project provides new legs for Graham and new eyes for the Flaming Atom.

    232. IN THE SPACESPHERE. *Wonder Stories*, June 1931. Ill. Paul.

Novelette. * *Time:* the interplanetary future. *Place:* the space run between Earth and Mars. * A very complicated tale of political intrigue, murder mystery, deception, dope smuggling, revolution, and much else aboard the *Cosmonia*. Traveling to Mars are Martian Planetchief Zon Scarna, his beautiful daughter Kee Scarna, Martian opposition leader Norr Avornu, various other Martians, Venusians, and Earthmen, including a dynamic trio who fight off the menaces and solve the mysteries. Present are space piracy, kidnapping, and many seemingly impossible murders. Since the story is essentially a mystery story with red herrings and false suspects, it probably would not be fair to summarize it. * Props include the drug venn, which is addictive and fatal, and invisibility created by crystals with peculiar optical properties. The invisibility apparatus is concealed in a cylinder inside which invisible men do their deeds. An unusual feature is an interplanetary romance that does not come off because of too great differences in culture and life-style. * *Miscellaneous:* The Martians use special gravity belts to adjust to Earth gravity. * Martians and Venusians are more or less human. * Space navigation is done with calculating machines. * The prevalent weapon is a dart gun. * More confusing than entertaining, less successful than Cloukey's earlier work. This seems to be the same story as "The Red Dust of Venus," which was listed as forthcoming in the May 1931 issue of *Wonder Stories*.

    233. THE SWORDSMAN OF SARVON. *Amazing Stories,* August-October 1932. Ill. Morey.

Novel. * *Time:* A.D. 2180. *Place:* Earth and Venus. * Sword-and-ray-gun romantic adventure in the mode of Edgar Rice Burroughs and Otis Adelbert Kline, but with the complex plotting characteristic of Cloukey's work. * *Terrestrial background:* The world now consists of three superpowers: the Federal Government of United America, United Mongolia, and Federated Europe. Mongolia and Europe are allied and hostile to America, thus creating a perpetual threat of war. In America United Utilities, the great power trust that controls energy, is almost omnipotent, and in Europe the Dornn Brothers hold a similar, but somewhat less powerful position. * Science in this future world is high, but not so high as might be expected. Atomic power has finally been attained on a laboratory level, but it is the discovery of one man (Ives) and a closely guarded secret. The first interplanetary rocket is almost ready to leave. * *Venusian background:* Venus is habitable by Earthmen, but only with protection; the solar radiation, particularly the ultraviolet component, is so heavy that it can blind or kill Earthmen in a matter of minutes. The native Venusians, who have evolved an immunity to the radiation, are descended from Atlantean colonists who lost most of their science and culture after the destruction of Atlantis, but have since regained much. As in the work of Cloukey's models, Burroughs and Kline, the Venusian development is lopsided, with a superscience in some respects and barbarism in others. In this "sword-and-ray-gun" situation the Venusians have never discovered explosives or invented firearms. The chief weapon is the sword, with which wars and personal combats are waged. Venusian warriors wear three swords, which they throw as well as wield. The greatest champion on the planet is the hunk Meriden, the Swordsman of Sarvon, a gigantic man of fantastic swordsmanship. * On Venus there are only two nations, Cor and Sarvon, each of which inhabits a gigantic, iron unitary city housing millions. These cities, which have similar strict caste systems—scientific aristocracy and ordinary citizens—are bitter enemies. They have been quarreling throughout their history, but the final battle seems imminent. * Since the narrative is too complex to be summarized suitably, essential points only will be offered. (1) Cor has developed mechanical personality transfer, whereby Corian personalities can be transferred to Earth, and vice versa. With this invention they surreptitiously control key positions in the Terrestrial economy and politics. (2) Cor's plans of conquest include both Sarvon and Earth. Terrestrial humanity will be exterminated. (3) The Earth scientist Ives has discovered atomic energy. The Corians on Earth murder him, brain-transfer his sister, and try to seize his notes. (4) The Corian transplants who occupy the bodies of the Dornns and Lee Chilton (the heir to United Utilities) are fomenting a world war in order to weaken Earth enough for easy Venusian conquest. (5) The Corians do not want Earthmen to enter space; their transplants are sabotaging the space program, including the partially constructed first spaceship. (6) Until matters have progressed considerably, the Terrestrial actors, who include Boyd (a leading detective) and the quondam head of United Utilities, are unaware of the Venusian element in the sabotage and war plot. The scientists of Sarvon know more, but not everything. (7) The scientists of Cor have created a projector that causes instant metal fatigue in iron; with this invention they hope to disintegrate the city of Sarvon. (8) Both sides have (as experimental models) a device that permits limited interpenetration of matter, thus allowing the holder to walk through walls. * Against this background, the adventure proceeds in alternating sections on Earth and Venus. The Terrestrial sections describe the efforts of Boyd and associates to outwit the Venusian agents (whose identity they do not know) and prevent a world war. The Venusian sections describe the adventures and sword fights of Meriden and Lee Chilton,

Cloukey, Charles (*continued*)

transplanted to Venus. They penetrate Cor, rescue Miss Ives in her Venusian body, and accomplish the downfall of Cor. * The terrestrial spaceship finally leaves and lands on Venus, although the Earthman are severely handicapped by lack of tolerance for the solar radiation. As a final motif, a vengeful Corian scientist develops a foolproof, very easy way to clear Earth of humanity. He places his spaceship into orbit above Earth and systematically destroys the ozone layer. He is almost successful. * Running through the book is the theme of Meriden versus Chilton as rivals for the love of Miss Ives. According to Venusian folkways Meriden has the right to challenge rival suitors; indeed, he already has killed quite a few. What will happen when the wars are over and he can challenge Chilton? * Cloukey had great difficulty with the characterization of Meriden, who is somewhat less than cardboard; and the division of hero into Meriden and Chilton is awkward. But the other characters meet pulp standards. * Cloukey's writing is obviously hasty, but the story certainly is superior in imagination and plotting to the similar work of Burroughs and Kline.

COBLENTZ, STANTON A[RTHUR] [1896-1982]

U.S. (California, though resident in New York City for this period and later) journalist, poet, miscellaneous writer, one of the more important early pulp s-f writers. A.B. and M.A., University of California, Berkeley. Associated with *New York Times* and *New York Sun* as book reviewer for most of our period. Prolific writer of verse, with more than twenty published volumes; founder of *Wings: A Quarterly of Verse;* associated with amateur (traditional) verse movement of 1930s through 50s. Prolific writer of science-fiction, which ranges from short idea sketches to fairly long novels. His most characteristic work is the satirical novel, much in the classical tradition, in which modern men, set in alien environments based on contemporary s-f motifs, encounter societies formed on the foibles and follies of our culture. (Such novels were apparently not written for the pulp magazines, but were rejects from book publication that had been stored away "in the trunk.") As such a satirist, Coblentz was sometimes amusing and sometimes insightful, but heavy-handed, repetitive, and often tied to ephemeral issues. In this concern with social elements, Coblentz was unusual in early pulp science-fiction, and it is safe to say that he is best considered a satirist or ironist rather than a science-fiction author in such works. Coblentz's other science-fiction was usually less interesting and less important. * On the whole Coblentz could be characterized as a literate writer with ideas, whose work was often marred by careless writing. * His novels are best read in the magazine versions, since the F.P.C.I. editions are abridged, altered, and on occasional small points "updated."

234. **THE SUNKEN WORLD.** *Amazing Stories Quarterly*, Summer 1928. Ill. Paul and unsgnd.
(Reprinted in book form by F.P.C.I., Los Angeles, 1948.)
Novel with elements of cultural criticism and irony. * *Time:* 1918 on. *Place:* The Atlantic seabed. * The narrative of Anson Harkness, U.S.N., as told to Stanton A. Coblentz. During the last days of World War I, the new experimental model submarine, *X-111,* takes to the waters. Designed primarily as a ram, it does not fare well when, already damaged, it comes into combat with two German submarines. It sinks. * All seems lost, but after being at the sea bottom for a time without hope of

rescue, the submarine is carried by a current through sluice gates into an air-filled space. Emerging to explore the vegetated area, the seamen come upon architecture reminiscent of Classical Greece, and a highly civilized people. As Harkness later learns, he and his comrades are in Atlantis. They are treated courteously by the Atlanteans, but are subject to a gentle form of will control. * The Atlanteans speak and write a language related to Classical Greek, and Harkness, who has studied Greek in college, is able to communicate with them in a fairly short time. * To describe Atlantis and its history first: Atlantis did not catastrophically sink through natural causes; it was deliberately submerged around 2000 B.C. Atlantean civilization, which was a mechanized, irresponsible world much like our own, was obviously about to disintegrate into ruin in about five hundred years, as the sage Agripides worked out scientifically. With the approval of the authorities, Agripides constructed a huge glass dome, fifty feet thick, over part of the small continent; permitted those who wished to settle there; and, working on the tectonics of the area, submerged it. Those who did not wish to accept the submergence dispersed to Atlantean colonies and elsewhere. The domed area was and still is self-supporting, thanks to Atlantean science. * The submerged Atlanteans, at first under Agripides, then later other sages, established a state with regulations that still exist. Emergence to the outside world is strictly forbidden, even though the Atlanteans have a few submarines. The population is frozen at about five hundred thousand people, with a strict eugenic system. While marriage is a personal matter, childbearing is subject to state control, with defectives not allowed to reproduce and children limited in number. The result is a handsome, highly intelligent people. * The economy is socialistic, with all working for the state at tasks that amount to a few hours a day, and with state supply of necessities. Personal property is limited to a few private things, and, as might be expected in such a system, there is no money. Atlantean free time is spent in a remarkable development of the arts. * The land is administered by the High Chief Adviser, who is selected on the basis of competitive debates and examinations. He holds his term for three years, after which he is subject to challenge by other aspirants. Local administrative matters are handled by Local Advisers, who are similarly chosen. There are no codified law and courts. * In general, Atlantis is a eutopia, but Coblentz inserts a question: Cannot perfection ultimately become a bore? There is a small political party, the Party of Emergence, that, while admitting the values of Atlantis, deprecates the loss of an element of adventure. This party advocates permitting individual Atlanteans to move out into the upper world. Harkness becomes friendly with Xenophile, one of the leaders of the party, and becomes a strong voice in the movement. * Harkness adjusts easily and well to Atlantean society, partly because he is better educated than the other seamen on the submarine, and partly because he is enamored of the beautiful blonde Aelios, who has been one of his tutors. After a time he is given Atlantean citizenship and is assigned to a task within his potential: writing a history of the upper world. Here Coblentz inserts a considerable amount of satire into the novel, for Harkness, while he admires Atlantis and is happy there, still cannot comprehend what a horrible place the upper world with its mechanism, social injustice, and wars seems to the Atlanteans. * Harkness wins Aelios and settles down, but a succession of crises alters matters. The *X-111,* which has been drifting around outside the dome, on

Coblentz, Stanton A. (*continued*)

one occasion rams the glass and cracks it. The resulting leak is repaired with difficulty. For a short time this incident aids the Party of Emergence, which almost wins a national referendum, but then Harkness's book describing the outside world (the horrors of which, through authorial irony, Harkness still does not comprehend) knocks the foundations from under the party, although some Atlanteans feel a moral duty to go out and improve the world. * A second crisis ends everything. The crack in the dome has opened again, worse than before, and the sea waters are flooding Atlantis. The Atlantean authorities assign Harkness a submarine and ask him to go to the outside world, which has more engineering experience, and request aid. The submarine, with Harkness and Aelios, leaves. But on reaching Washington, the mission is subject to ridicule and red tape, and by the time Harkness and Aelios return above Atlantis, it is too late. The land has been destroyed. * Literate and competent, although the indecision whether to write a social tract, a romance, or irony destroys the effect that a great author might have achieved. In any case, worth reading as one of the better documents of early pulp science-fiction.

235. **AFTER 12,000 YEARS**. *Amazing Stories Quarterly*, Spring 1929. Ill. Paul and unsigned ill.
(Reprinted in book form by F.P.C.I., Los Angeles, 1950.)
Novel. * *Time:* A.D. 12,201. *Place:* mostly the New York City area. * Novel, essentially an attack on Western culture, militarism, and war hysteria in terms of science-fiction. The pervading metaphor is the anthill. * The narrator, Henry Merwin, unemployed, without prospects of a job, and burdened with a selfish, shrewish, unsupportive wife, answers a newspaper advertisement and permits himself to be anaesthetized by Dr. Montrose, who has been experimenting with suspended animation. Montrose's animal subjects have responded to revivification promptly enough, but Henry remains "dead." Any chance of emergency resuscitation is removed by Montrose's sudden heart attack. * Henry is buried, and presumably loses consciousness, for he awakens by an eroded sea shore in a long-abandoned cemetery. * Background, the world in which Merwin awakens: There are three nations, Panamica (North and South America), A-Uria (Eurasia), and Afalia (Africa and the rest), and international relations are based, anticipatory of Orwell's *1984*, on a jockeying for alliances. The civilization and culture of the three nations are about on the same level, with a spotty high science and technology, with stress placed on biology and social engineering. The population of each nation consists of four physiological groups: wolf-faces, intellectuals, workers, and soldiers. The wolf-faces, dwarves with spindly, weak bodies and vicious, vulpine features, are the rulers and executives of the culture. The large-heads, dwarves with spindly, weak bodies and enormous heads, are the scientists and intellectuals; they rank below the wolf-faces. Both wolf-faces and large-heads are so weak physically they often have to be carried by the workers. The workers are physical giants, enormously powerful, with tiny heads; they are extremely stupid and serve to carry out the orders of the rulers. The fourth class, the soldiers, are giants like the workers, but with much smaller heads; they are robotic and mechanical in movement, totally obedient and mindless. For all four castes breeding is strictly endogamous. * For the lower orders initiative, individuality, imagination (all measurable mechanically) are forbidden and severely punished, the cultural

ideal being the strict apportion of labor as in a termitarium. * There is, of course, no concept of justice or individual rights, and the state inflicts death for trivial causes. * Although Coblentz does not develop this point strongly, the culture seems to be capitalistic, the chief executive being called the Financial Democrat. The language spoken is an evolved English, in which, for example, the old word "gold" is pronounced as "God." A new alphabet is in use, in which, for example, the letter "s" is now written with a vertical line through it, as "$". There is a frivolous, rich capitalist class, but Merwin does not come much in contact with these people. * Just as the anthill is the social ideal, the culture in general is focused on insects. Exotic and colorful hypertrophied insects are bought as pets by wolf-face women, and the military authority breeds countless billions of war insects for combat duty. The insects are pampered with fresh foods, while the humans eat distasteful food tablets. * This is the situation in the three nations, although as Merwin learns later, it is not quite so bad in A-Uria as in Panamica. * The only remnant of normal humanity exists on Borneo; a few thousand in number, they live furtively in a single giant cave under semi-primitive conditions. Occasional members are taken as slaves by the anthill-men. * Merwin is captured by the workers of City 64, near where ancient New York stood. Taught the language of the time, he is interrogated and classified as a native of Borneo. Anthill scientists scoff at his narrative of suspended animation, and he is sentenced to labor in the insect pens, cleaning the cages and feeding the various gigantic wasps, enormous ants, etc. It is miserable work, and he lives in utter squalor. During this life he chances to meet the normal Luella, a white girl from Borneo, who is also a slave. They strike up a platonic romance, with clandestine meetings at self-improvement lectures that the state (like the Communist world) offers. Marriage or any sort of closer relationship is impossible. * Merwin, after a bad start, gains some approval from his superiors, more by chance than his own efforts, and life becomes a little easier. * But then the crisis comes. War has broken out between Panamica and A-Uria, the cause a gigantic construction diverting the Gulf Stream to Labrador and freezing Europe. War hysteria immediately breaks out, and slogans and wild enthusiasm fill the day. Merwin must serve in the military forces, but testing apparatus shows him to be so individualistic that he is almost executed. But manpower is short enough that he is put through a mechanical conditioning course to remove his individuality and increase his love of the state. * The course (results judged by blood tests) is ineffective so far as Merwin is concerned, but his superiors finally decide that he can serve as an aerial carrier of attack insects against the A-Urians. In a small flying machine he transports cargoes of evolved termites and other insects, on occasion watching bloody battles between the insect and human ground forces. After a time he captured by the A-Urians, who do not treat him badly, but assign him as slave labor to the food farms. * The war does not go well for either side, however. Evolved termites escape control, and more effort is spent trying to eradicate them than in fighting, but the termites are too entrenched, and other insects also escape control. The result, after a few years, is that the world is ravaged by swarms of enormous, ravenous insects, and that anthill mankind is at the edge of extinction. *. Merwin manages to steal his plane and fly to City 64, where he finds Luella in a small insect-besieged cage section. She had believed him dead, for the censorship machines conducted a false corres-

Coblentz, Stanton A. (*continued*)

pondence between them and gave false reports. Together they fly to Borneo, where they join the normal community. * Apparently the giant insects cannot reach Borneo, for years later Merwin and Luella are living happily. * The description of the anthill society and many little touches describing sadistic exploitation are stronger than the plot-line. All in all, the novel might be considered a weaker, partial anticipation of *1984*. * One should read the full magazine text rather than the abridged F.P.C.I. edition.

236. **THE GAS-WEED**. *Amazing Stories*, May 1929. Ill. Paul

Short story. * *Time:* 1968. *Place:* California. * A world war is in progress, with, as Coblentz puts it, half of the white and half of the yellow races at war with half of the yellow and half of the white races. This, of course, is not very precise. * A meteoritic fire ball strikes in California. Not long after this, a reddish plant is observed growing from the meteorite crater. The plant kills Investigators with puffs of poison gas and shortly later, defends itself with extremely hard, tough sword-like processes. * Heat, explosives, gases all have no effect on the plants, which spread, irresistibly, at great speed over California. Seeds from the plant also spread, and within about a year, the plant has an aggressive worldwide distribution. It cuts down agricultural land, millions of people starve, and the war is called off. * Some of the secrets of the plant are gradually discovered. It is silicon life, not carbon, whence its adult invulnerability, though seedlings can be destroyed. * Things still look bad for the human race when an accident reveals a weakness of the alien plant: It cannot resist cancer cells. * Aerial bombardment of the plant with cancer cells destroys it, and it is now almost extinct. * No narrative center; literate, but a farfetched resolution.

237. **THE MAKING OF MISTY ISLE**. *Science Wonder Stories*, June 1929. Ill. Paul

Short story. * *Time:* perhaps the near future. *Place:* Washington, D.C. and an artificial island in the North Pacific, about a thousand miles from Asia. * Four scoundrels—the President, the Secretary (of State?), General Blackfoot, and Dr. Turnbull—are hatching a dastardly but feasible plot. As Turnbull, who is selling the idea, states: There is a recently discovered volcanic protuberance in the Pacific that lies only fifty fathoms below the surface of the sea. Under this is magma ready to surge up if released. Turnbull proposes dropping a series of atomic bombs in the appropriate locations, thus fracturing the surface rock, and then building a military base on the island that will result when the magma erupts and cools. This island will then be used for the conquest of Japan, China, and Eastern Siberia. * The politicians are delighted at the proposal, and millions of dollars are secretly devoted to Turnbull's project, which develops as planned. * There is one problem, however; the atomic blasts have upset the stability of the region, although Turnbull is remarkably obtuse not to have understood this. And when the politicians and Turnbull go to the island, ready to start the invasion of Asia, the island explodes and sinks, taking the plotters with it. In Asia, Japan, which had been at the edge of war with the United States, becomes amenable to discussions. * More a political fable than fiction.

238. **THE RADIO TELESCOPE**. *Amazing Stories*, June 1929. Ill. Clardy.

Short story. * Vincent, the narrator, becomes assistant to eccentric Professor Vogel of the Observatory of Mt. Topeka. It is not an easy job, for Vogel is irritable and secretive to an extreme degree as he works privately on a strange-looking electronic apparatus. * Finally, Vogel, declaring the job done, tells Vincent to attach the apparatus to the telescope, and turns it on. * The mechanism, which Vogel calls a radio telescope, is not a radio telescope in the modern sense, but a device for capturing dispersed light rays. It is a trillion times more powerful than ordinary telescopes, and the two men spend hours examining strange planets, wonderful forms of life over the universe. * One particular planet, thousands of light-years away, fascinates Vogel. It is an idyllic, paradisiacal world with beautiful, sylph-like winged females. Ogling this world, one female in particularly, becomes a voyeuristic monomania with Vogel, who shows signs of mental collapse. The end comes when brutal, black ape-like creatures creep up upon the sylphs, hunting them for food. Vogel's behavior is pitiful. * At this point the radio telescope collapses in an explosion. It may have been a stroke of lightning from a storm overhead. In any case, the results are disastrous. Vogel is blind and mentally impaired, and the secret of the radio telescope is lost.

239. **THE WAND OF CREATION**. *Amazing Stories*, August 1929. Ill. Hugh Mackay.

Short story. * Dr. Emery Kramm has devoted his life to one scientific task: the creation of life. At one stage of his research he prepared an extract from marine jellies that should have formed life, yet did not. Continuing his research, investigating nutritional deficiencies, Kramm finally discovers a medium in which the cells exhibit all the criteria of life: respiration, absorption of food and excretion, reproduction, and a fourth, movement. * Not long after Kramm's epoch-making research, a mysterious plague begins to affect the human race. It is almost always fatal, and all in all it kills perhaps two hundred million people around the world. * It is caused by Kramm's synthetic life, as carried by flies. Once flies are controlled, the disease wanes. * Not dramatized as a story, but told flatly like a chronicle.

240. **RECLAIMERS OF THE ICE**. *Amazing Stories Quarterly*, Spring 1930. Ill. Wesso.

Novel. * *Time:* perhaps the near future. *Place:* a newly discovered island at N. 82°, almost due north of Bering Strait. * Essentially a Vernian story of geographical adventure with a few secondary science-fictional elements. * Stephen Rathbone, a scientific and engineering genius, conceives the idea of developing the north polar regions by tapping the internal heat of the Earth. His theory is that hot water piped up from a colossal heat well will warm the water locally and induce a warm climate, suitable for agriculture. His pilot project is to be kocated on a small island discovered by his friend the noted Arctic explorer Norwood. * The expedition will include Rathbone, his sister Ada, Allenham (her fiancé), Norwood, Rodney (the narrator) and about forty assorted technicians and workmen. * That there will be emotional difficulties is immediately clear, for Rathbone does not want Ada along, but cannot refuse her, since she is partly capitalizing the venture; and Rodney is madly in love with Ada, who is madly in love with Allenham, who is a worthless cad. * The expedition reaches Desolation Island in a huge vacuum-lift dirigible that discharges personnel, supplies, and equipment. Work proceeds very rapidly, for it is now revealed that Rathbone has discovered a universal solvent that eats

Coblentz, Stanton A. (*continued*)

through rock like ice. * But disasters begin. The dirigible crashes on one of its supply trips, and the pioneers are isolated. As the rock penetration continues, they encounter a fissure that releases enormous quantities of poisonous gas. Food runs low. Blizzards strike. And the worthless Allenham causes difficulties. * Rathbone reaches a level where the heat of the rock reaches 212° F. This should be adequate for his purposes, but he greedily continues to penetrate downward. Horrible result! The drilling sets off latent volcanism. The nearby mountain turns into a volcano; the pit becomes a geyser of molten lava; and the island soon goes down into the sea. Most of the survivors leave on an electric sledge, much like Captain Scott's, but the narrator and Ada, in what seems a death sentence, take a dog team. The sledge crashes through the ice, while Ada and Rodney win through to Wrangel Island, where they are safe. Along the way Ada finally discovers that she loves the patient Rodney. * All right as an adventure novel. Solidly written, with an attempt at characterizations, with some good detail, but formulaic.

241. **A CIRCE OF SCIENCE.** *Amazing Stories*, May 1930. Ill. Morey.

Short story. * *Time:* 1964-1965. * A short chronicle. * Professor Gilcrest has discovered the life ray, which is akin to the X-ray. Animals and plants subjected to it are dramatically altered to their behavioral opposite. Thus, dogs try to climb trees, hawks burst into song, rabbits attack passersby, lilies slash out at people who approach them, etc. * This is acceptable, even a little colorful, as long as it is confined to the laboratory. But during a fire at his labs, Gilcrest foolishly opens the cages, whereupon his specimens escape. * The world is now beset with horrors, not only animals, but even distorted staple food plants and new diseases. The situation seems desperate, when suddenly the strange phenomena stop, and animals and plants revert to their previous natures. The action of the ray was apparently limited.

242. **MISSIONARIES FROM THE SKY.** *Amazing Stories*, November 1930. Ill. Paul.

Short story. * Dr. Ira Rand, one of the greatest scientific geniuses of all time, takes the narrator into his confidence and reveals his secret discoveries. By modifying television equipment, Rand is able first to see Mars, then later to communicate with the Martians. * Mars is Schiaparellian, with canals and drylands. The Martians, who are far more advanced scientifically and socially than we are, are about eight feet tall, can bound like kangaroos on enormously developed hind legs, have three forelimbs ending in tentacles, and have large heads. * Once contact has been established, the Martians give Rand a crash course in the Martian language, and learn English themselves. * All well and good, but when Rand describes Terrestrial culture to the Martians, they are horrified at wars and social misery. Being both benevolent and meddlesome, they offer to reform the Earth. Using gases to destroy human willpower, they will take over all Terrestrial authority and turn the world into a eutopia, free from fear and want. But, they will do this only if Rand, taken as Earth's representative, gives his consent. * At the moment, millions of Martians clad in individual flying space suits are ready to leave for the Earth as soon as Rand answers. * What will Rand do? Is freedom worth the price of the present horrors? Is security worth the loss of freedom? (Questions quite important at that time in Europe.) * Rand finally decides by smashing his apparatus. His greatness will now never be known.

243. **INTO PLUTONIAN DEPTHS.** *Wonder Stories Quarterly*, Spring 1931. Ill. Paul.

(Reprinted in book form by Avon Books, New York, 1950.)

Novel. * *Place:* mostly Pluto. * Dan, the narrator, and his friend Andrew Lyman Stark, college instructors, have long been fascinated by the concept of space travel. Thus, when Stark invents an asbestos compound that acts as a shield against gravity (much like H. G. Wells's Cavorite), an interplanetary voyage seems possible. At first the friends consider Mars as a goal, but when Pluto is discovered, they set their sights there. * In a sphere about seventy-five feet in diameter, the two men set forth. Their flight, which takes about seven months, is uneventful until they near Pluto, when their ship's shell is pierced by a small meteor and they nearly lose their air. But they reach Pluto. * Pluto, which is cold and icy, is furnished with a breathable atmosphere, and gravity offers no difficulties. As the men explore, they find archeological remains, then a tunnel leading underground. After they have proceeded for a way, they are captured by the natives. * The Plutonians are humanoid, about seven feet tall, extremely thin, with large globular heads, on the top of which is a natural lantern-like formation that provides light for life in the tunnels. As the men later learn, the color of the light emitted by the lamp indicates emotional states. * The Plutonians, who are not brutal, treat the Earthmen well enough and teach them the native language, at which time the explorers learn about Plutonian civilization. * Culture on Pluto is incredibly old, and Plutonians live to enormous ages. In material science they are ahead of us, but with certain obvious blindnesses—they insist that interplanetary travel is impossible and that Andy and Dan come from the interior of their planet. * There are three sexes on Pluto, male, female, and neuter. The neuters, who are artificially produced surgically, include the rulers, scientists, and artists. The rationale is that persons of genius seldom pass their abilities to their descendants, hence it is wiser to remove the distraction of sex so that they can function better. Neuterhood is considered a highly desirable state and is an honor eagerly sought after. * Our heroes, who would like to escape back to the surface and regain their spaceship, become very friendly with Zandaye, an aberrant Plutonian woman who is considered a monster of fatness and odd coloration by the Plutonians, but approaches a desirable human type. Indeed, she and Dan fall in love. * With Zandaye's help, the two men try to escape, but during their flight one of them damages the atmosphere plant so that the culture is likely to suffocate unless it is repaired. * Dan and Andy are recaptured, and after a judicial examination are sentenced to corrective surgery. This amounts to reconstructing their skulls and brains so that a headlamp will grow; obviously the Plutonian surgeons have no concept of what is involved. * Things look very bad for the explorers, until by a fortunate chance the Plutonians begin to sicken with serious cases of mumps. By bluffing, the Earthmen convince the natives that they (Dan and Andy) control the plague, and the situation is improved. Surgery is canceled, and the men are allowed some freedom, which they use to escape into the upper tunnels out onto the surface, where they repair the leak in their spaceship and return to Earth. * *Miscellaneous:* In addition to the sexual satire there is a small amount of economic material. Far down inside the planet live undesirables who dress richly, play about with gold and gems, and are generally irresponsible. Otherwise, Plutonian culture is ascetic. * Poets are treated with great honor,

Coblentz, Stanton A. (*continued*)

and the chief poet of the land is considered a culture hero. *
Less satire than Coblentz's other novels. The story line is
simple, by now clichéd, but is presented in great detail.

244. **THE BLUE BARBARIANS.** *Amazing Stories
Quarterly*, Summer 1931. Ill. Wesso.
(Reprinted in book form by Avalon, New York, 1958. The text
may be altered or abridged.)
Novel. * *Time:* A.D. 794,104. and following years. *Place:*
mostly Venus. * Satire on mechanization, mercantilism, and war
mongering, intermingled with adventure elements. * *Background:*
The Earth has long been in a very severe glacial period, and only
the equatorial zone is habitable. While humanity does not seem
to have evolved since the present, population has certainly
diminished, the total number of persons being about 30,000.
Science, however, remains spottily high. * For centuries, a
project to migrate to another, more hospitable planet has been
central, but only in the past few decades has it become possible,
using an atomic blast, to send off small, two-man spaceships
toward Venus. Several such scouting missions have departed,
but there has been no word from any of them, and the assumption is that the explorers are dead. In one of these earlier
missions, Ardu Twell, a young woman for whom the narrator
feels unrequited love, took part and was presumably lost. * The
narrator (Erom Reve) has been inducted for the next voyage.
Unfortunately, at the last minute his carefully selected companion
was disabled, and the eccentric poet Daolgi Kar took his place,
smuggling on board his pet dog, Yap Yap. In many ways Kar
will prove to be more nuisance than help. * The voyage is
uneventful until the spaceship reaches the vicinity of Venus,
when Reve discovers that what seems to be mist veiling the
planet is really an enormous sphere of meteors. The two men
must abandon their ship immediately, without time even to send
a radio message to Earth; they fly (on personal power wings)
down to the surface as their ship explodes above them. * Venus
is pretty much a lush, jungle-like world (though with variable
temperature zones), very hot, and humid. Its atmosphere is of
different composition than Earth's, but is tolerable. * After
wandering about the jungles for a time, evading monstrous
beasts, the explorers approach a city that seems made out of iron
pyramids. They enter it and are captured, after some turmoil, by
a machine that hurls wire bails around them. They are then
taken and tossed into a zoo, where the natives gawk at them. *
Background: The Venusians are humanoid, much slighter than
humans, blue-skinned, and goggle-eyed. Their economy is
rampant capitalism of the worst sort, with plutocrats ruling each
of the seventy or so countries. There is a strict caste system,
aristocrat as opposed to mob, indicated by the use of capital
letters in names. Hordes of debased workers toil for subsistence
in horrible factories that are mechanized as in the motion picture
Metropolis and are utterly inefficient, just as their products are
worthless. As an overseer says, the purpose of such works is to
provide work. * Central to the economy is physical money,
which in this case is colored glass, green glass being much the
most valuable denomination. (Money is unfamiliar to the
explorers, but they soon comprehend its significance.) * On the
whole, Venusian science is much inferior to that of the future
Earth, being about on the level of the 1930s; indeed, apart from
technological application of a traditional sort, science is
discouraged, even penalized. * The pyramidal cities, in which

most of the population lives, have been planned to best function
as manufactures, nothing else, and the populaces race around
madly on motorized roller skates in order not to lose time from
work. * The arts do not exist, and at a later time when Kar
writes a Venusian poem, it causes a sensation. The language is
simple, mostly nouns without verbs, all guttural and crude. *
After a period in the zoo, where they learn a few words from
observing the visitors, the two men and the dog are taken to a
laboratory. They are about to be vivisected, but when they speak
rudimentary Venusian, the examining magistrate-surgeon
reclassifies them as trespassing barbarians from another land and
sentences them to two years of hard labor in the factories. *
There, in a great sawdust mill, under conditions reminiscent of
a Victorian sweatshop, Reve stands oiling yellow links in a
power chain, while Kar is supposed to regulate timing on the
saws. Thanks to Kar's negligence, the mill catches fire, and the
Earthmen escape in the confusion. * After some difficulties, they
evade pursuit—Yap Yap proving most useful, for the Venusians
are universally terrified of him—and reach a wilderness area.
While at work the two men had heard of white-skinned, blue-
eyed giant savages in another land. They now speculate whether
these savages might be survivors from previous expeditions.
Perhaps they can contact them? * Reve, who has a first-rate
technological background and is something of a hustler in the
mode of Hank Morgan in Mark Twain's *A Connecticut Yankee
in King Arthur's Court*, determines to create a (financial) power
base. Gathering raw materials, he smelts green glass of the
proper color, then going to the nearest town, proceeds to buy the
good will of the mayor and officials with a few pieces of glass.
Suitably bribed, the officials are delighted to welcome the
newcomers as proper citizens, indeed, as large-letter aristocrats.
* With his counterfeit glass, replenished several times, Reve buys
the town and surrounding lands, becoming one of the wealthiest
men in the land of Wultho. (He first experiences the phenomenon of rent and is both puzzled and pleased by it.) His cash
stifles any suspicion that he and Kar are escaped convicts. * By
now Reve has a fair idea where the white giants are located.
Obtaining a government dirigible he and Kar make their way to
another continent, inhabited by savages. There they find a small
settlement of Earthmen, all but two of the space travelers having
survived and gradually assembled. Among them is Ardu Twell,
Reve's flame. She does not welcome him, however, and proves
to be a very dangerous nuisance. * Although the Earthmen share
a comfortable primitive life, despite a little harassment by the
cowardly blue-skins, all agree that they should remove to Reve's
financial empire in Wultho, where they can buy technology to
build return spaceships. In Wultho Reve's glass smooths all
problems around the white savages. * At this point, war hysteria
breaks out. When one country increases its armaments, others
follow, with the result that Venus is on the edge of a world war,
with fanatical patriotism waiting to follow any incident. Such an
incident occurs when the wilful Ardu Twell first insults, then
slaps a diplomat from a neighboring country. * War breaks out,
and a recent invention, portable disintegrator projectors,
devastates the world. More than three-quarters of the Venusian
population is dead and most cities destroyed by the time the
Earthmen barely manage to enter their space vehicles and begin
the journey back to Earth. Reve has at last established radio
communication, and the trip should be successful. Reve, despite
the last-minute horrors, is happy because Ardu Twell has in-

Coblentz, Stanton A. (*continued*)

dicated some remorse for the trouble she has caused. * As a puzzling note, Reve considers Venus destroyed, but a reader may wonder whether it is not perfect for colonization now that the natives have pretty much exterminated themselves. * As is common with Coblentz's more ambitious satirical works, the satirical passages are often excellent, but the adventure framework does not fit too well and is much too long. The novel reads better in summary than in actual text.

     245. **THE PLANET OF YOUTH.** *Wonder Stories*, October 1932. Ill. Paul.

(Reprinted in book form by F.P.C.I., Los Angeles, 1952.)

Novelette. * *Time:* 1995 and following years. *Place:* Earth and Venus. * In 1989 the Langley Audubon Interplanetary Expedition left for Venus. It may have arrived safely, but no communication has been received from it. In 1995 a follow-up expedition with Forsythe, the narrator, as a minor member, reaches Venus successfully. They discover Venus to be much like a tropical Earth of the Mesozoic, with reptilian life, but horrific dinosaurs play no part. The climate is very salubrious, and everything seems to have a soft glow. * In a relatively short time the expedition is able to contact the Langley-Audubon group, who have all survived and are in wonderful physical condition, some even appearing younger than when they left Earth. Indeed, several members of the earlier expedition are reluctant to return to Earth. * Forsythe, too, would like to remain on Venus, but his superior, Poindexter, who has a grudge against him, orders him back to Earth. * After knocking around for a time on an Arctic expedition, always hankering to return to Venus, Forsythe has a brilliant insight. The blooming health of the humans on Venus is not chance, but is due to something in the atmosphere that amounts to a fountain of youth. * He decides to capitalize on the concept, but his enemy Poindexter chances to overhear his ideas and forms a gigantic corporation, Venus Improvement Corporation, which in a short time ships hundreds of thousands, perhaps millions, of people to Venus, where they thrive. A titanic monopoly controlled by Poindexter, it effectively freezes Forsythe out of the picture. * The Venus adventure has enormous repercussions on Earth, which Coblentz treats ironically. Nations fall apart, aspects of civilization collapse, and wars break out. All the while Forsythe keeps trying to return to Venus, but is always prevented by Poindexter. * On the one occasion that he stows away and reaches Venus, he sees another broken society. No one works on Venus except convicted criminals, stowaways, and African blacks who have been kidnapped as slaves. Forsythe had hoped to be sentenced to labor and remain on Venus, but the malicious Poindexter ships him back to Earth, where he is immediately drafted into one of the wars. * The resolution comes when it is discovered that the Venusians are dying like flies. The radiation, while temporarily imparting youthfulness and vigor, is ultimately toxic. It is now necessary to try to rebuild Earth. * An interesting story, cleverly handled with big business machinations and despotism.

    246. **THE MAN FROM TOMORROW.** *Amazing Stories Quarterly*, Spring/Summer 1933. Ill. J. Munson.

Novel. * *Place:* New York, presumably at Columbia University. * One James Richard Cloud, a rather shabby stranger, presents himself at Professor Howard's office and makes what seems to be an outrageous claim. Cloud asserts that he not only anticipated Einstein in conceiving of time as a fourth dimension, but

has constructed a machine that permits view into the past or future. Howard is about to dismiss the man as a crank when his assistant Horn, who examines Cloud's mathematical analysis, urges that they visit Cloud's laboratory. * There, in squalid surroundings, they see a machine composed in part of mirrors set at all sorts of angles, and around the room they see many historical artifacts, which Cloud says are items snagged on the edge of his time viewer. * Cloud demonstrates to the complete satisfaction of the men that he can view the past. But the future? Cloud sets the dials for two hundred years ahead and turns the machine on. The men view fantastic architecture, a horrible war, but then there is an explosion. The machine is a twisted mass of metal, and in its wreckage lies an unconscious human figure. The experimenters remove the man and finally succeed in reviving him. * The future man, who is clad in a strange garment like a minimal bathing suit, is about five feet tall, nearly bald, and has sharp irregular features and a bulging forehead. * When the little man (John Wormwood) regains consciousness and can speak, there is an exchange of information and also a contretemps. Wormwood comes from the twenty-third century. A physicist, he had been exploring the fifth dimension, otherwise Cloud's machine would not have captured him. Crabbed, arrogant, feisty, insensitive, uncooperative, he complains bitterly at having been precipitated back into the Neurotic Age of savagery. * Wormwood is an affliction, for it is long before he is willing to conform in the least to twentieth-century notions of clothing or decorum, and his typical response, when he is frustrated, is to draw a paralyzing gun and temporarily disable those against whom he is angry. * At first Howard's colleagues suspect a hoax when Wormwood's arrival is announced, but after his identity is accepted, he is lionized for a time at the university. But the novelty wears off, and his nuisance value is too great. * Making a living becomes an unfamiliar necessity for him, but he thrives for a time writing columns for the sensational periodicals, whose readers consider his serious proclamations the height of humor. * The area of sex is also a problem, for while he occasionally bemoans the loss of a woman in his own time with whom he would have mated, he waxes enthusiastic over the fiancée of Nelson's assistant and lathers her with unwelcome attentions. Courtship in the twenty-third century apparently consists not only of brazen advances, but the most flowery addresses, reminiscent of a Tudor poet or a trouvère. * Things must come to an end. Sent to a prison to interview a murderer on death row, Wormwood decides that the man is being unjustly treated and gives him his paralysis gun. The prisoner attempts to escape, but is recaptured, and Wormwood's friends must do their best to conceal the naive future man. * Cloud, in the meanwhile, has finished an improved version of his time machine. As all agree, Wormwood must be returned to his own time, but by chance Cloud, too, is precipitated into the future, and the machine once again is destroyed. The secret is lost. * *Miscellaneous:* Cloud's apparatus is well-known in a superior form in Wormwood's time. * Future men must be obsessive fresh-air enthusiasts, for one of Wormwood's chief complaints is the lack of removable walls. * Wormwood is less tolerant of heat than we, preferring chilly air. * Raucous noises, polluted air and similar familiar expressions of twentieth-century life are intolerable for Wormwood; he collapses in the New York subway. * Nudity is apparently common and accepted in the future. * Some satire on the twentieth century; some situation humor. The story carries

Coblentz, Stanton A. (*continued*)

well for a time, but eventually drags, and the conclusion is as welcome as expected.

247. THE MEN WITHOUT SHADOWS. *Amazing Stories,* October 1933. Ill. Morey.

Short story. *Time:* 1999 and following years. *Place:* the supernatural capital of Omaha, Nebraska, and elsewhere. * The narrative is told by the Hon. Alexander D. Coldwell, Minister of State of the United Republics of the West (Urow). Urow, which is composed of the Western Hemisphere and Europe west of the Caucasus (and Africa??), is currently at war with the Orient, which is not defined, but presumably is a unit composed of the major Asian countries. * Since the war is not going too well for Urow, Coldwell is preparing new weapons. His latest, he announces to the national council, is a poison so deadly that a few molecules are lethal. This poison is to be dumped into enemy water supplies. * For about a year now there have been atmospheric disturbances as gigantic mistlike humanoid figures have been striding around the Earth. They do not seem to be solid, but are perhaps gaseous. There has been some attempt to communicate with them and identify them, but this has been unsuccessful. * Now at Coldwell's conference, such a figure appears and addresses the conference. He/She/It is from Saturn, and, although the Saturnians do not usually concern themselves with the lower forms of life, they have been studying Earth. They can read human thoughts, but it has taken them time to build an apparatus for speaking to humans. * The Saturnian continues: He and his fellows are disgusted with humanity, what with the present war and Coldwell's plan. Hence they will establish a protectorate over Earth to save it from its viciousness and folly. When the conference members protest or try to leave, the Saturnian lets forth a barrage of lightning. * The Saturnian conquest is easy; their artificial lightnings overawe all opposition with very little loss of human life. In the new society as established, many things are different: The politicians, including Coldwell, are fired and put to menial dirty work, while more responsible men take their places. Crime, poverty, and national boundaries are all wiped out. Parents are examined for child-rearing qualifications, and children are taken away from unsuitable parents, like Coldwell, and placed in crèches. * But as is the case in Coblentz's other works on the same theme, this new pacific mode of life does not please mankind, and there is bitter lamentation for the good old days. The Saturnians easily crush several small revolts. * After ten years the Saturnians announce that they will leave for a time, since they are homesick. At their departure everything returns to the old way, with nations reëstablished, the war reinstituted, and Coldwell back in power. Terrestrial scientists work feverishly on electric weapons to defeat the Saturnians on their return. * The Saturnians do come back, disregard the Terrestrial weapons, which are powerless against them, and make a further announcement: Earth is so rotten that it is not worth saving. So saying, they leave. Coldwell is again busied with plans to poison the Asian water supply. * One of Coblentz's better stories, more acceptable for its brevity than his longer novels with similar themes.

248. THE CONFESSION OF DR. DE KALB. *Astounding Stories,* January 1934. Unsigned ill.

Short story. * *Time:* A.D. 2010-2050. * De Kalb, now an old man, reminisces about his great discovery and its historical impact. A research neurologist, he worked to discover a ready means of changing human personality, and, after a decade or so, discovered what he was looking for. This was the anaesthetic hypomatrin, which when injected apparently removed previous personality and conditioning, leaving a tabula rasa upon which a new personality, new drives, new likings could be imposed. * De Kalb had intended his research to eradicate crime and otherwise improve mankind, but instead it became a tremendous commercial development as people wanted to change their personalities. In a very short time those who could afford the treatment changed to glamour personalities and jobs, while menial or laboring jobs became impossible to fill. * The negative side of hypomatrin now emerged: The change could not be altered or reversed. After a time there was no more agriculture or factory work, and civilization collapsed. Countless millions of people died before the hypomatrin generation was replaced. It was the worst disaster to hit the human race since the Black Death. * A historical narrative, not developed as a story.

249. MANNA FROM MARS. *Astounding Stories,* March 1934. Ill. Marchioni.

Short story. * *Time:* 1998 and following. * A historical narrative, rather than a story. * Communication has been established with Mars, and there is great interest in the different modes of life on Mars and Earth. The Martians, who are more advanced scientifically than Earthmen, attribute their scientific progress and near eutopian mode of life to their assured food supply, the sugar-leaf plant. It is totally nutritious; creates its own chemical necessities; and is fantastically productive. One acre will support a hundred persons. * The Martians agree to send seeds to Earth, and a drop is scheduled for Christmas, 1998. But the shipment does not arrive. The Martians offer an explanation: The space container was dragged off its trajectory by unexpected gravitational influence, so that it did not land where scheduled. A global hunt locates the Martian projectile—in the wilds of Australia, on lands cultivated by a Japanese. * The nations respond as might be expected. Australia claims proprietorship; Japan claims proprietorship; other nations disagree; and in a short time a world war is raging. When the war is over, with the loss of tens of millions of lives, it is discovered that the sugar-leaf seed was destroyed during bombing raids. * The Martians refuse to send another shipment, stating that their previous dispatch caused enough trouble. The world is now in far worse condition than before communication with Mars, and some seriously wonder whether the Martians really did act in good faith or whether the situation was a cruel hoax.

250. THE GREEN PLAGUE. *Astounding Stories,* April 1934. Ill. Dold.

Short story. * *Time:* A.D. 2444. * Future history, told as the confession of Professor Caxton Brooks, a noted bacteriologist. Brooks is now carving a history of events into the walls of a cave. * Some ten years earlier he had an inspiration. Inasmuch as most bacteria are skotophiliac, why not develop a bacillus that can thrive in sunlight? * After a couple of years of laboratory work, Brooks develops such a bacterium, but, unfortunately, it is lethal to warm-blooded creatures, killing them in a matter of hours. A careless laboratory assistant and several others are victims to the disease before Brooks is able to contain it. * Worse is to come. Brooks's country, Upper America, is on bad terms with Transeuropa. In a mixture of folly, patriotism, and greed Brooks sells his discovery to the American military, which is now sure that it has the ability to wage a successful war

Coblentz, Stanton A. (*continued*)

against Transeuropa. The new disease, called the green plague, wipes out Transeuropa down to bird and animal life, then spreads to the rest of the world. In a short time mankind is almost extinct, as are both wild and domestic animals. * There is no defense against the green plague, but since the bacteria do not thrive in darkness, a few people have taken refuge in caves. At the moment, Brooks seems to be the last man, but he hopes that others may survive elsewhere. * A familiar theme with Coblentz.

251. **THE RADIO MIND-RAY**. *Astounding Stories*, July 1934. Ill. Dold.

Short story. * *Time:* 1992. * The reminiscences of Professor Hamlin Osborne, who is currently living in hiding on an undisclosed South Sea island. Osborne discovered a combination of drugs that strengthened the electric patterns in his brain so that he could control others. This works telepathically. At first modest in his wishes, he uses his ability to make life more comfortable for himself. But ambition enters when the presidency of his college is vacated. Hiring ninety-six assistants to whom he gives his drug, he utilizes his mind-battery to capture the office. But this is not enough. He now concentrates on the governorship of his state, which he also wins with his mental aids. * Osborne now decides that he should be president, and enlarging his group to 196, he prepares for his campaign of suggestion. All goes well, and as a dark horse he steadily gains in the polls, until, one day, when he feels strangely subdued, a group of men enter his office and hand him a satchel of money, for which he groggily signs. He now learns that he has been betrayed. Certain of his brain battery members have sold out and have forced him telepathically to agree to sell cabinet posts. When the news breaks, Osborne flees in disgrace. * Competent, but uninspiring.

252. **IN THE FOOTSTEPS OF THE WASP**. *Amazing Stories*, August 1934. Ill. Morey.

Short story. * *Time:* A.D. 2054. *Place:* imaginary South America. * Dr. Mandano, in search of a more powerful anesthetic, studies wasps and derives a chemical that will produce indefinite suspended animation in humans. His intention is humane, but the discovery is taken over by the Querzal dictatorship, who institute one of the most elaborate health censuses on record. Physical examinations are scheduled for everyone, during which numbers of persons—the unemployed, dissidents, soldiers—are surreptitiously treated with the Man-Preserver. The bodies are then indexed and secretly stored in enormous mountain vaults, with the intention of reviving the military personnel in a forthcoming war with neighbors. * Captain Cardenzas, a strong underground enemy of the government, follows rumors of the Man-Preserver, and as leader of the League of Free Men turns the sleepers to good account. Reviving them, explaining what the government had done to them, providing them with arms stored nearby, he has an instant army. On seizing the government, Cardenzas sets up a new punishment—Scientific Incarceration, or suspended animation, into which he puts the previous governmental officials, the industrialists and war mongers who supported it, and the physicians who performed it—fifty thousand in all. * Not dramatized, simply historical narration.

253. **THE TRUTH ABOUT THE PSYCHO-TECTOR**. *Astounding Stories*, October 1934. Ill. Dold.

Short story. * *Time:* events of the 1960s as reminisced about from 1996. * Dr. Alexander I. Shotgrass, Ph.D., tells the true story of the psycho-tector. Building upon research with the galvanometer back in the 1950s, he created a device that responded to brain currents. His theory is that unconscious response will indicate aptitudes or lack of them. * Shotgrass's apparatus works, as many tests show, but when it is put into practical use, there are difficulties. It is too honest. Indeed, Shotgrass faces severe financial penalties from lawsuits. At this point, Shotgrass reveals, he took thought and began to falsify results to flatter his subjects. With this approach he won his lawsuits, and instead of facing bankruptcy, as he had been, he soon became a rich man. His conscience bothered him, however. He faked a fire destroying all his machines and retired to Nice, where he now lives as a millionaire. * Routine.

254. **BEYOND THE UNIVERSE**. *Amazing Stories*, December 1934.

Short-short story. * The narrator, an instructor in chemistry, is fascinated by the possibility of disrupting the time sense. After much experimentation he arrives at a compound of drugs and chemicals that seems (as far as he can tell from the behavior of laboratory animals) to offer what he wants. With friends watching, he takes the drug and then experiences a cosmic vision, soaring out into space beyond the solar system, seeing systems merging into galaxies, galaxies into galactic clusters, clusters into supergalaxies, on seemingly infinitely. At first exhilarated, he gradually feels a sense of tininess as the progression unfolds. * But then he awakens in a mental hospital. He has been unconscious for six months, and his occasional mutterings about what he has seen have resulted in a diagnosis of insanity. Released, he resists the temptation to try the drug again. * Nicely done, comparable to the cosmic visions of Wells or Stapledon.

255. **RICHES FOR PLUTO**. *Astounding Stories*, December 1934. Ill. Marchioni.

Short story. * *Time:* from the 1980s to 2001. *Place:* Washington, D.C., and vicinity. * In the 1980s communication was established with Pluto, which houses an intelligent, scientifically-advanced race, who, according to television pictures, are roughly humanoid, though with four eyes. The Plutonians are friendly, and in a short time announce that they will visit Earth. It is necessary, given navigational conditions in space, for guidance signals to be sent to them along the year-long flight. * In 1998 the Plutonians come to the Washington area, thirty-foot-tall pallid giants. They are amicable enough, and contact is friendly, as they wander about, until they spy a heap of coal, which is apparently a substance of enormous value on Pluto. At this, the Plutonians go mad with delight, and with reckless abandon, with no regard for human life, seize whatever coal, under any circumstances, that they can find. * The situation becomes bad enough that conflict develops between the Plutonians and the armed forces. Since the Plutonians have incredible weapons that shoot electrical bolts for miles, there is no withstanding them. When they have filled their vessel with coal, they gleefully announce that they are incredibly rich, and that other Plutonians will arrive, to become equally rich by despoiling Earth. * The situation seems hopeless, for Plutonian science is much superior to Terrestrial, but a resolution comes with the Westfall brothers, who willingly accompany the visitors as human specimens for exhibit on Pluto. The Westfalls include among their luggage oxygen tanks (since the Plutonians have a different atmosphere)

Coblentz, Stanton A. (*continued*)

and benzine. The Plutonian craft goes up in a blaze. * Since the first ship required guidance signals, there probably will be no further visitors from Pluto. * Routine for Coblentz, a historical narrative rather than a story.

256. **IN CAVERNS BELOW.** *Wonder Stories*, March-May 1935. Ill. Paul.

(Reprinted in book form as *Hidden World*, Avalon, New York, 1957. The text may be altered and/or abridged. A later reissue by Garland, New York, 1975, restores the original title.)

Novel. * Bludgeoning satire on militarism, patriotism, propaganda, capitalism, the New Deal, Franklin D. Roosevelt, and similar topics of importance in the mid 1930s. * The story vehicle narrates the adventures of Frank Comstock (perhaps a dig at the would-be social reformer, or perhaps simply a memory of the Comstock Lode), a mining engineer who, with his friend Philip Clay, is precipitated into a strange cavern world below Idaho. His entry situation is much like that described in Bulwer Lytton's *The Coming Race*. * As the men stand on the brink of an underground precipice, they see beneath them titanic battles between military forces that annihilate each other. Great explosions rock the earth, and enormous electric discharges strike nearby. The two men become separated, Comstock being captured by pallid men who take him prisoner with a device that shoots metal rings. He is put with other captives, who are executed one by one with a heat ray; but when it comes to his turn, he is saved by his pocket notebook, which intercepts the rays. This arouses enough interest that he is taken in hand by an authoritative person, later identified as Professor Tan Trum, who believes that Comstock is a savage from inside the Earth and wants to study him. * *Background:* The inner world of caves is divided into two nations, Wu and Zu, which are practically identical in population and civilization, but are bitter enemies and are engaged in perpetual warfare. The causes of war are either trivial or imaginary, for warfare exists for its own sake and forms the central core of the underground civilization. * Politically each land is an absolute dictatorship, with the ruler selected from the first-class citizens, who are so unused to physical activity that they need breathing aids and other mechanical devices to survive. Economically, the lands are unrestrainedly capitalistic, with huge monopolies owned by the first-class citizens. The first class is utterly privileged: Members do not pay taxes and are not conscripted into the armies. The second-class citizens (professional people of various sorts) and the third-class citizens (*Lumpenproletariat*) bear the weight of the culture and form the armies. Everyone is both brainwashed and subjected to perpetual surveillance. * In addition to being brainwashed, the soldiers in the vast military forces are drugged so that they act like robots and die without hesitation. Mortality is enormous. While most of the military action takes place in a barren no-man's land, explosive-bearing earth-borers also cut through the rock into enemy cities; a faithfully followed convention, however, limits such borer attacks to second and third-class neighborhoods, never first-class. * Material culture is very high, with enormous development of electricity, potent explosives, food pills, and much else. Air is brought down from the outside world in an elaborate network of tunnels and tubes. Transportation is by means of small scooters that travel at breakneck speed, apparently without traffic regulations, through the cities. * Socially, family life is based on the production of

men for the armies; battle casualties are glossed over with various euphemisms. Beauty standards among the females include obesity and the creation of artificial wrinkles. Physically, the underground people are weakly and incredibly myopic. * Comstock is assigned to live with Professor Tan Trum and his family, where he learns the folkways and regulations of the strange society. He has difficulty in adjusting to the culture of Wu, for rabid patriotism and unquestioning acceptance of propaganda are essential. There is also a sexual problem, for one of daughters of the house, a fat and wrinkled, horribly ugly young woman, sets her cap at him. * After taking an oath as a citizen, which involves swallowing a document he has signed, Comstock is assigned to work in the atmosphere plant. Years pass, during which he advances up the organizational ladder, usually through misunderstood circumstances. When, for example, he tries to escape to the surface through one of the ventilation tubes, he blocks the passage, stopping air flow; on emerging, he receives a commendation for clearing the passage. * During his work, Comstock discovers a small overlooked valve that controls the air flow. This serves to bring him into power. Assuming a new identity as Luma the Illustrious, he creates a crisis by shutting off the air and usurps the position of the former dictator (who is obviously modelled on Franklin D. Roosevelt). He now learns that his friend Clay, whom he believed dead, has similarly risen to power in the land of Zu. * When the two outsiders secretly meet to discuss plans for escape, they are observed by spies, and revolutions break out. Such reforms as they had tried to institute are overturned, and the warfare, which both men had tried to halt, breaks out again in renewed force. As they escape into the upper world, they can hear the explosions behind them. * The satire is occasionally amusing, despite its heavy-handedness, but the message has become monotonous. As perception of our societal ills of the day, obviously, despite some conservatism, the story has some validity. Unfortunately, the story lacks one of the essentials of good satire, credibility. The basic assumption that humanity is stupid and too easily manipulated is not convincingly handled.

257. **TRIPLE-GEARED.** *Astounding Stories*, April 1935. Unsigned ill.

Short story. * *Time:* 1962. *Place:* New York City. * Dr. Ridings, who has been shipwrecked in the South Seas, passes eleven years on a desert island before he is rescued. Although he observes that his rescuers are somewhat reticent to tell him about the outside world, he is totally unprepared for what he encounters when he reaches New York: Everyone dashes around at an incredible speed. It is extremely hazardous to walk along a sidewalk or to cross a street; conversation is impossible; activities of daily life are unintelligible. * When in a hospital recovering from accidental injuries, Ridings finally learns what has happened. In 1951 the great endocrinologist Fells discovered Speedo, a preparation that dilates the time sense and accelerates physical and mental processes. Since then, use of the drug has become almost universal, with some obvious exceptions, as when sailing at sea. Ridings's informant is a would-be poet who has been reluctant to take Speedo. The poet describes the havoc which the drug has caused under the guise of improvement. * Ridings, nevertheless, is intrigued, and he persuades the poet to join him in trying Speedo when they leave the hospital. * The results are unfortunate. For some reason, perhaps their initial resistance, they become not triple-geared, but sextuple-geared, so

Coblentz, Stanton A. (*continued*)

that the world seems like a morass of snail-paced beings to them. In despair, they both leave for Ridings's desert island, where they will live at single speed. * Presumably intended to be satiric.

258. AN EPISODE IN SPACE. *Astounding Stories,* May 1935. Ill. Dold.

Short story. * *Time:* the interplanetary future. *Place:* the trans-Neptunian planet Orcus, which seems to have a small sun of its own, so dim that it cannot be seen from Earth. * Orcus, which is small, is rugged, provided with an atmosphere deficient in oxygen, and surprisingly warm—several degrees above 0° C. * The narrator and his comrades leave their rocket ship and explore, finding primitive vegetation, but no other sign of life. Unexpectedly they come upon what seems to be an artificial passage, which they follow until they are suddenly closed by automatic doors into a gigantic lighted cavern with a breathable atmosphere. The cavern is filled with elaborate automatic machinery that maintains livability. * There are also natives, tall, somewhat humanoid creatures who are most hostile. There is a shoot-out, after which the explorers escape, but incidentally damage the airlocks, thus destroying the native culture. As the expedition leaves, the narrator reflects that this might be the future of Earth. * Routine.

259. OLDER THAN METHUSELAH. *Amazing Stories,* May 1935. Ill. Morey.

Novelette. * *Time:* probably the near future. *Place:* an artificial cavern world underneath Pacific Antarctica or an island near Antarctica. * The newly-wed narrator, Owen Hornwell, and his wife Muriel take off from California on their honeymoon in a plane newly designed by Hornwell, but soon meet disaster. Their plane is forced to descend to the ocean, and the honeymooners are fortunate to be picked up by Captain Hawker's *Sea Dragon,* a whaler headed for Antarctic waters. The captain is hostile, and he and his crew are brutes. * When the ship reaches a certain point, it no longer responds to control and is dragged along south. The vessel proceeds along a narrow inlet, enters an enormous cave mouth, travels through illuminated passages, and comes to a halt beside an ancient pier far underground. * The unwilling adventurers are there greeted in good English by a group of extremely ancient, decrepit people. Explanations follow: The underground people, who have attracted the *Sea Dragon* by superscientific means, are colonial survivors of Mu, which went down about 3,400 years ago. Thanks to a certain elixir, they have remained alive ever since, but their longevity does not include perpetual youth. They learned English from a previous band of captives, who, unfortunately, committed suicide. * Their reason for attracting the *Sea Dragon,* as the Father Supreme blandly states, is to improve the blood of the Children of Mu, both by blood transfusions and interbreeding. Each of the outsiders must marry a Muan woman, and Muriel is to be the property of the incredibly decrepit Father Supreme. * The Muans are gradually regaining strength from blood transfusions from the outsiders, when Captain Hawker, a brutal man, kills a Muan. This is bad enough, since there hasn't been a death for hundreds of years, but the Captain and his crew shift the crime to Hornwell. Hornwell is judged in a prejudiced court (since the Father Supreme, to release Muriel for a mating, wants him out of the way) and sentenced to expulsion to the world of dark chambers underneath the colony. * This is usually a death

sentence, but the ancient woman whom Hornwell was scheduled to marry loves him and manages to supply him with a light and food. Together they wander about until they come to the long unheeded, forgotten, totally automatic support system for the land. By experimenting with the equipment, Hornwell learns how to shut off the heat supply to the chambers above. This is immensely important, since the Children suffer badly from hypothermia. Hornwell would have been able to use this as a weapon against the Children, but when he temporarily shut off the heat, the elixir of life was destroyed, and the Children of Mu are frantic with rage and fear. Hornwell, Muriel, and a few members of the crew of the *Sea Dragon* dash madly out of the cavern world as the Children pursue them with lightning bolts which kill most of the crew and destroy the lost land itself. * Routine. The narrator's trick of gaining control of a hidden land is now clichéd with Coblentz.

260. THE GOLDEN PLANETOID. *Amazing Stories,* August 1935. Ill. Morey.

Novelette. * *Time:* 1995. *Place:* the USSR., near Smolensk, and the United States. * When the Golden Planetoid, which is highly luminous, is first sighted telescopically, it is taken to be a natural body; but its erratic path, its regular ovoid shape, and other matters soon reveal that it is being directed by intelligence. After circling the Earth, it lands near Smolensk. About thirty miles long, five miles thick, it rests on the Earth, unapproachable because of its lethal golden radiation. * Chester Wilde, an American engineer in the employ of the Soviet government, undertakes to investigate the planetoid by driving a tunnel from underneath, thus avoiding the radiation. The work progresses, but when the tunnel draws near the ovoid, the roof collapses, and Wilde is buried. * He regains consciousness within the planetoid. Around him are its inhabitants: three-legged, four-armed giants about sixty or seventy feet tall, with semitransparent flesh. The giants perform certain surgical procedures on him, including implanting a device in his skull that enables him to receive the telepathic speech of the visitors. * The giants are not hostile. They are simply exploring the universe, as they occasionally do in small vessels like the planetoid. At the moment, they are making repairs on the bottom of their ship, which was damaged slightly on impact. When this is done, they may explore a little around the solar system, then will resume their journey. Ultimately, they come from the star system Stole, about thirty-five light-years away. Since they live for about a million years, long journeys are not impossible for them. Their metabolism is not material like ours, but electric. * When Wilde asks the giants why they have not contacted humanity, they reply that they already know mankind telepathically and have no desire to learn more. Humanity is so bestial that they will be glad to leave. * The giants now make an offer to Wilde. Since part of their purpose is gathering specimens of local life, they would like to have specimens of humanity who will travel back to Umgu of their own free will. They will release Wilde, but he must return within a year with at least five suitable, willing humans; at this time, they will give him whatever he wishes that lies within their power. Wilde accepts. * Back in the United States, retaining his telepathic power, Wilde finds matters difficult. He learns that his wife is committing adultery; that his business associates would gladly be rid of him; and that his so-called friends dislike him. When he tries to explain his mission for the giants, he is laughed at. Indeed, not only does he fail to recruit anyone, but

Coblentz, Stanton A. (*continued*)

he arouses so much resentment that he is placed in a lunatic asylum. In the meanwhile, the planetoid has left on a brief exploratory trip, as the giants stated. * In the asylum Wilde finds congenial spirits. To a lunatic who imagines himself Alexander the Great, Wilde offers new worlds to conquer; to a reckless speed demon, travel at hundreds of miles a minute; to two crooked businessmen, loot; and to a mad poet, chances of recognition. * Deadline approaching, the six escape from the asylum and fly to Smolensk. But the planetoid has not yet returned. A week or so later, Wilde learns that the planetoid has exploded in space, perhaps having struck an asteroid. And his telepathic sense is now gone. * Ten years pass. Wilde has settled down as an engineer in Russia, and his lunatics have made their mark on the world. Except for one crook who is in jail, they are now important men. * Amusing once the satiric elements emerge.

261. **THE GLOWWORM FLOWER.** *Astounding Stories,* June 1936. Unsigned ill.

Short story. * *Time:* A.D. 1976-1977. * In 1976 Reimers and Bayle made the first successful space flight, a circumnavigation of the Moon. Their flight took place despite Cassandra-like warnings from the noted scientist Dean Cameron Prince that no good would come of interplanetary travel. * Not long after the return of the moon voyagers a strange plant is observed near the rocket, a plant with interlaced ferny leaves and beautiful iridescent, many-hued flowers that are luminescent at night. The flowers also has a remarkably attractive odor. Botanists soon discover that the plant is intrusive, having grown from spores picked up in space by the moon shot. * The glowworm flower, which seems to have been easy to grow, spread rapidly horticulturally and naturally. A peculiar phenomenon soon became apparent: sensitive persons (poets, scientists, musicians, artists, etc.) found the perfume addictive, and after sniffing extensively, collapsed into comas. These comas, if repeated, ended in death. * More unusual, however, were the dreams or mental experiences that the flower addicts shared. They found themselves on a strange planet with a double sun, beautiful ambience, and small, very friendly pixie-like people. The conclusion is that somehow the flowers either transmit sensations from another world or recall previous existence states. * The glowworm habit is bad enough so far as individuals go, but it is worse socially, for the entire cultural elite of the world is threatened. When the situation is recognized, a program to exterminate the flower is established, but it is unsuccessful until all space flights are prohibited. Professor Prince was right. * Told as history, not as fiction. * Capably handled.

COCKROFT, W. P. (c.1913-?)

British author. The author's name is sometimes incorrectly given as Cockcroft.

262. **CATACLYSM.** *Scoops,* 28 April 1934. Unsigned ill.

Short story. * *Time:* late twentieth century. *Place:* Southern France and Mars. * The young inventor Jacques Havart, whose workshop is in Southern France, has just finished his spaceship. Constructed of a new metal and rocket powered, it will be the third interplanetary venture when it leaves for Mars. The first blew up. The second, an attempted lunar voyage, was a failure; Motier, the operator, survived a crash but has since been insane.

* Havart plans an international expedition: himself and his platonic girlfriend Mary, the German Mollheimer, and the Americans Garstang, Mary Raymer and her brother Martin Raymer. The ship lifts properly, but it is then discovered that the mad Motier has taken the place of one of the crew. * The voyage through space is uneventful, and after about sixty days the ship lands on Mars. The air is thin but breathable; vegetation and animal life indicate that Mars is suitable for human colonization. * On Mars the explorers encounter: (1) multilegged, vicious snake-like creatures that attack in enormous numbers; (2) plants with soporific fruit; (3) gigantic birds of prey; (4) carnivorous plants with beautiful flowers; (5) Martians. * The Martians are about human height, composed of two block-like body segments, with spindly legs and short arms ending in claws. They have no heads, but have eyes in the upper body. As appears more clearly in the sequel, #263, "City of Mars," they are civilized, with an excellent development of electricity, including stun guns. * The explorers and the Martians immediately fall into hostile relations. After some wandering back and forth, the Earthmen are captured. Havart, Mary, and the Raymers escape, but Garstang and Mollheimer have disappeared. Their fate is not known. * The four survivors (Motier having been eaten by the carnivorous plants) reach their ship and return to Earth. There they find a horrible situation. War has broken out, and most of the major cities of the world lie in ruins. While truces are in effect, they are fragile and readily broken. Worse, a frightful, nearly always fatal plague is raging. * Havart suggests a solution to an international congress: Abandon Earth and settle Mars with an elite group. His idea is accepted, and a fleet of some sixty or more spaceships is constructed. The motto of the enterprise, ironically, is exactly the opposite of that on the Statue of Liberty. * Most of the ships reach Mars, but on *904,* on which Havart and Mary were flying, the plague appeared, and Havart took the ship into the sun. Altogether three thousand humans reached Mars, and about sixteen years later, as a postscript says, there are about eight thousand, though their situation is still precarious. * A word must be added about Mollheimer, whose journals form the central part of the story. The women have an instinctive aversion to him, perhaps because he has a reputation as a lecher. * Much more fully developed and longer than the typical *Scoops* short story, with a more adult point of view, but badly developed. For a sequel see #263, "City of Mars."

263. **CITY OF MARS.** *Scoops,* 16 June 1934. Unsigned ill.

Short story. * Sequel to #262, "Cataclysm." * *Time:* perhaps around A.D. 2000. *Place:* Mars. * Most of the story is devoted to the experiences of the captives Mollheimer and Garstang. After some initial danger of being vivisected, they are permitted to live as instructors of English and Terrestrial matters. They discover Martian culture to be complex, with an elaborate social structure, high development of electricity, unitary city air-conditioning and power machines, and much else. The Martians live totally underground in artificial caverns in many independent but mutually friendly cities. * After a time Mollheimer and Garstang, who now work assembling machinery, are more or less accepted, although they are not permitted near the outside. When the chance to escape comes, though, they bolt. Garstang is killed, but Mollheimer is recaptured. Before he is retaken, however, he sees that Terrestrial spaceships are landing on Mars.

Cockroft, W. P. (*continued*)

This accounts for a certain uneasiness the men had observed among the Martians. * Mollheimer, embittered that no attempt has been made to rescue him and anxious to avoid death for trying to escape, throws his lot in with the Martians, offering to teach them the art of war and to manufacture powerful weapons for them. The Martians prepare for a grand attack. * About sixteen years after the first landing the Martians strike. The story centers on the human settlements, which consist of six cities. The Martians employ enormous disintegrator cannon that Mollheimer built, and the humans counterattack with explosives. New London is completely destroyed, with great loss of life, but the humans win the war when they invade the Martian city and destroy the air-conditioning-power machine. The Martians surrender, and a live-and-let-live relationship is established. Mollheimer is killed during the battle. * Better in summary than in narration.

     264. **THE ALIEN ROOM**. *Wonder Stories*, December 1934. Ill. Paul.

Short story. * *Place:* Mount Everest. * The story of what happened to the Moyston Expedition that perished on Mount Everest, as told through the notebook of Wilde, the sole survivor. * High on the mountain the expedition came upon a strange metal construction. They entered it and found on the floor the skeleton of a gigantic man, perhaps ten feet tall. Further exploration revealed banks of controls, one of which turned on lights. * The men speculated that the construction was an observatory maintained by a race of men who lived in caves in the mountain; an unopenable circular floor plate seemed to corroborate this interpretation. * The men persisted in meddling with the controls, while Wilde, outside, watched. Suddenly, the building took off in a flash, straight up, and Wilde realized that the construction was really a spaceship that was stranded on Everest. As for the men in the ship, they could not have survived more than a few minutes. * Flatly narrated. Perhaps influenced by American dime novels.

CODER, S. MAXWELL

U.S. author, perhaps Samuel Maxwell Coder (1903-?) then resident in Philadelphia and later author of several Fundamentalist or evangelical books, including *Jude, The Acts of the Apostates* (1958), *Faith That Works* (1966), and *The Comfort of the Scriptures* (1967).

    265. **THE ETHER SHIP OF OLTOR**. *Amazing Stories*, July 1927. Ill. Paul.

Short story. * An honorable mention in the contest based on the cover of the December 1926 issue of *Amazing Stories*. Coder received no monetary prize, but perhaps glory. * *Time:* A.D. 2036. * A small sun and a planet invade the solar system, and for a time it is feared that they will collide with the Earth and destroy it. But the Earth suffers only meteoritic and seismic damage, while a new planet, Neone, now is in orbit not far from the Earth. * Bob Staunton and his friend Frank are on board the *Empress of Ceylon* when a strange spherical vessel appears overhead. Since Bob is more or less telepathic, he relays a message from the sphere to the ship's captain: The Alien wants all the gold on board the ship, or he will sink it. Willy-nilly, the captain surrenders the gold to Oltor, the master of the sphere, a red-skinned man with a strange mass of filaments rising above his head. * Bob has learned telepathically, however, that Oltor

is by no means unfriendly; he simply desperately needs the gold for his atomic motors, and he will later repay the captain with platinum. Indeed, he invites the two men to visit the sphere, and, later, to accompany him to his home world, the new planet Astarak (Neone). * After purchasing an obsolete marine vessel, which the globe lifts away from Earth, the visitors and the Earthmen travel to Astarak, where Bob and Frank enjoy themselves for a time. * There is, however, an emergency. A race of brown people subservient to the red people are preparing to make war with a seemingly irresistible disintegrator ray. When the war breaks out, the red men win, thanks to a suggestion by Bob. Ultimately the Earthmen return home. * *Miscellaneous:* Oltor, who built the ether-ship, explains that since gravity is a strain in space, a counterstrain, produced by atomic engines that use gold as fuel, will remove gravity. * The chief weapon of the red Astarakans is a mentally operated ray tube that paralyzes the nervous system. * The excrescence on the heads of the red men is brain filament that enables them to communicate telepathically. * The natives of Astarak go about nude, as in the contest illustration. * The alien sun, whose final whereabouts is not revealed, took Neptune along with it.

COLBY, LINCOLN S.

No information.

    266. **THE RADIO DETECTIVE**. *Amazing Stories*, May 1931. Ill. Morey.

Short story. * *Place:* Chicago. * A scientific detective story, not really science-fiction. * Retired judge Nicholas Gardner, since moving to the suburbs, has deteriorated physically, with falling hair and many skin sores. In addition, he seems to be having delusions of nightmare figures in his bedroom. * Neil, his daughter Millicent's beau, figures it all out with an electroscope and similar equipment. * In the house next door is James Dowling, a vicious criminal who has vowed revenge on Gardner. Dowling, who studied science while in stir, has X-ray apparatus with which he bombards the Gardner house. The nightmare figures, which both Millicent and Neil saw, were X-ray-luminous chemicals applied by Dowling. * Routine as a detective story.

COLLADAY, [CHARLES?] MORRISON

No specific information. Colladay is said to have been a Southerner by birth and to have spent his last years in New York State, in the Hudson Valley area. The portrait printed with "The Silent Scourge" shows a middle-aged man. In later life Colladay contributed articles to several non-fiction magazines, but no record of him survives among their files. * There is some confusion about Colladay's full name. Gernsback's Science Fiction Classics Number Six, *When the Earth Fell,* was published as by Morrison Colladay, but the pictorial advertisement for it in the Fall 1929 issue of *Science Wonder Quarterly* shows the author as Charles H. Colladay. A Charles M. Colladay contributed "Spirit Trails" to the January 1928 issue of *Ghost Stories*. The name is unusual enough that these names all probably represent the same person. The aberrant "H" is presumably an error, such mistakes being common enough in the early science-fiction magazines. Social Security records list no Morrison Colladays, but two Charles Colladays, one of whom died in Connecticut in 1968, and the other in Kansas in 1965. There is no evidence that either was the author in question. * Schwartz/Weisinger in *Science Fiction Digest,* April 1933 (p. 5), list another story, "The

Colladay, Morrison (*continued*)

Great Cold," as having been accepted by *Amazing Stories*. It does not seem to have been published.

267. **THE SILENT SCOURGE.** *Wonder Stories*, December 1930. Ill. Marchioni.

Short story. * *Place:* East Orange, New Jersey, and vicinity. * The local citizens are mysteriously disappearing, and the police have no clue. The first break comes when a terrified man enters a meeting between the chief of police and leading citizens and tells what he has seen: a caterpillar-like creature forty or fifty feet long that emerged from the dark and carried a man off! After some scoffing, the police and concerned citizens check the story and discover that it is true. East Orange is infested with giant centipedes that are seemingly invulnerable to small arms fire. The giant insects are photophobic, however, and live in burrows during the day. * The local authorities and the state eventually put Benson in charge of a campaign against the insects. The second break comes when it is discovered that the gigantism is caused by a substance manufactured in a secret government factory as a component in a most powerful poison gas. This substance both attracts the centipedes and causes their gigantism. Conventional weapons are not very successful against the centipedes, but a secret new poison gas kills them. The menace is over at the cost of no one knows how many lives. * Intelligent, well-written, but somewhat on the flat side.

268. **THE COSMIC GUN.** *Wonder Stories*, May 1931. Ill. Marchioni.

Short story. * The great scientist Hartridge is dead; his swollen, partly decayed body has been found in his laboratory. It is a sorry end for one of the great pioneers. * At the coroner's inquest, Hartridge's physician and friend Dr. Goodrich insists that Hartridge was murdered. The reason: Hartridge had succeeded in concentrating cosmic rays so that at full strength they amounted to a disintegrator. Foreign agents were interested in the apparatus, and one group, obviously, claims Goodrich, has stolen Hartridge's small model and used it to kill the scientist. * There is scoffing at first, but Goodrich proves right. After complications the situation culminates in a duel between the small stolen model and the large laboratory device. Good triumphs. * The coroner's court is ably handled, but the remainder of the story washes away.

269. **THE BURNING SWAMP.** *Amazing Stories*, August 1931. Ill. Morey.

Short story. * *Place:* eastern Arkansas, along the Mississippi. * The narrator and his friend Jim, senior engineering students, are vacationing along the Mississippi when they see the great meteorite flash overhead and strike nearby. Abandoning their ancient motor boat and poling their way in a small dinghy across swamp lands, they come to the impact site, which is still ablaze and too hot to investigate. * Returning later, they discover to their astonishment that the site consists of a very large hill of pulverized rubble like pumice, with a central pit—and in the pit are artificial constructions and man-sized creatures like gigantic roaches. * The students are spotted and captured, but escape as the aliens' disintegrator rays destroy a small investigatory posse headed by the local sheriff. Returning to civilization, the students tell their story, but no one will believe them. It is all hushed up, and the official story is that a peat bed beneath the swamp is afire. As the narrator reflects, there have been other meteorite strikes, and it is probable that the insect-like creatures will eventually emerge and attempt to take over the world. * Told simply, with conviction. * For a sequel see #271, "The Blattids."

270. **THE RETURN OF THE COSMIC GUN.** *Wonder Stories*, October 1931. Ill. Marchioni.

Short story. * A sequel of a sort to #268, "The Cosmic Gun." * *Time:* 1940. *Place:* mostly the Chicago area. * The leading characters are Professor Henry Carey of the University of Chicago, creator of a remarkable disintegrator; Bill Adams, important journalist and contact figure for the administration in Washington; and Angelo Angelino, leader of the IBPA, an ubiquitous criminal organization that threatens the world. The IBPA began in Chicago as a band of racketeers, but gradually has evolved into a Fascist secret society with a political program and philosophy. While it claims, according to Angelino, not to harass the small man, it is really concerned with power for the powerful, namely itself. Angelino, who resembles Napoleon slightly, fancies himself as a reincarnation of the Emperor. * The IBPA, however, is not simply a band of thugs; it maintains secret laboratories with highly advanced research programs, factories, and disciplined troops. Among its scientific resources, as the Federal government knows to its alarm, are an engine-stopper, an ammunition exploder, and a secret weapon that turns out to be a heat ray. * The narrative is concerned mostly with Carey, whom the IBPA wants to recruit, although at one point it tried to kill him in a plane crash caused by an engine stopper. The IBPA wants Carey's disintegrator, which is fantastically powerful. * After complicated cloak-and-dagger episodes involving the three main characters, Carey pretends to accept the IBPA offers, and as a secret agent penetrates the IBPA laboratories north of Chicago. Time is important, since the IBPA is due to strike for world domination in a few days. * Federal forces cannot use conventional weapons, thanks to the engine stopper and the ammunition exploder, but Carey's disintegrator mops up the criminal organization in Chicago—which is already heavily damaged. At one point during the siege of the IBPA, the old cosmic gun is taken out of mothballs and used to drill holes diverting the lake into the otherwise impregnable tunnels held by the organization. * *Miscellaneous:* Carey's disintegrator is a generator of ether waves that dissolve anything before them. * The first part of the story, the chase and pursuit situation, is good thriller material, but the ending is routine work. Colladay, however, writes better than most of his genre contemporaries.

271. **THE BLATTIDS.** *Amazing Stories*, December 1931. Ill. Morey.

Short story. * Sequel to #269, "The Burning Swamp," set about three months later. * The Federal authorities are now interested in the peculiar happenings in eastern Arkansas, and the Army investigates. Our friends Jim and the speaker are narrative centers. * The swamp has stopped burning, but there are still evidences of the strange insect men. Digging at the site reveals an artificial tunnel, and the investigators realize that the blattids (as they are now called) have moved underground to a new site. The old site suddenly explodes into flame again, and it is not clear whether Colonel Blassus, commanding officer of a detachment that had entered the tunnel, has been killed. * Jim and the narrator follow the tunnel trail above ground with their compasses, and find the new blattid camp in a valley in the Boston Mountains in western Arkansas. There the insects have set up, ready to take to the air, an enormous force of flying

Colladay, Morrison (*continued*)

machines. It is necessary to act quickly. * The two young men volunteer for the dangerous mission of exterminating the giant roaches. Donning gas helmets and carrying cylinders of a fantastically powerful poison gas, they allow themselves to be captured. They gas the blattids, along the way rescuing the colonel, who had been held in captivity. The blattids are all dead, so far as is known, although there is the possibility of other landings.

272. **THE PLANETOID OF DOOM**. *Wonder Stories*, December 1932. Ill. Paul.
(Reprinted in Conklin, *Big Book of Science Fiction*.)
Short story. * *Place:* the Gulf of Mexico, the lower Mississippi drainage, and New Orleans. * The narrator, a young engineer, is with his friend Jim when the small planetoid strikes somewhere in the Gulf area. Since his ship is especially sturdy, he and Jim survive as they are washed up over New Orleans, which is completely flooded, with apparently almost everyone killed. Various sea monsters are present—giant moray eels, octopi—and at a later stage, dinosaurs like tyrannosaurs. * The men make their way to Natchez through a totally flooded countryside, and then, as part of a rescue expedition, return to the New Orleans area, where they explore, looking for survivors. Earthquakes and tidal waves follow, together with local volcanism. * Eventually the entire lower Mississippi basin is lost, sunken below sea level; it is now a bay of the Gulf of Mexico. * There are various theories for the remarkable predatory sea life. Some scientists believe that the strange chemical properties of the planetoid caused instant gigantism among sea denizens; others believe that the strange life existed in lower depths in the Gulf and was forced to the surface. * Told with verismo, not ineffectively.

273. **GIANT IN THE EARTH**. *Wonder Stories*, April 1933. Ill. Paul.
(Reprinted in Conklin, *Best of Science Fiction*.)
Short story. * *Place:* mostly North Carolina. * A mysterious epidemic has broken out in the mountainous area of western North Carolina. It is fulminating and always fatal. Most epidemiologists blame an unknown microorganism, but Gary and the narrator, on visiting the area and seeing the blasted nature of the environment, conclude that it is radioactivity, probably radon gas. Although some higher medical authorities accept their theory and urge evacuation, there is also considerable resistance, and the pestilence spreads. * This is bad enough, but volcanism and earthquakes strike the same area, and in a short time, to the accompaniment of many deaths, the whole of western North Carolina and adjacent states is leveled off into a barren plateau riddled with volcanic activity. The explanation is that there are localized deposits of radioactive minerals that can reach meltdown, causing emission of radon, followed by earthquakes and volcanoes. * Told pretty much as a chronicle. Effective as a catastrophe story.

274. **EARTHSPOT**. *Wonder Stories*, May 1934. Ill. Paul.
Short story. * *Time:* probably the near future. *Place:* Labrador. * Radio suddenly is inoperative; electricity operates sporadically; and a fifty-mile-wide blackened zone extends from Savannah, Ga., into Canada. The zone of destruction, as the great scientist Ogden explains to newspaper reporters, is the line of zero declination of the compass. So, obviously the disasters are related to Earth's magnetic field. * Ogden leads an expedition to

the Boothia Peninsula in Labrador to investigate the north magnetic pole. While the men are there, a strange eruption occurs, a vortex of heat that rapidly expands, assuming giant proportions. The vortex heats the atmosphere enough to melt the polar ice caps, with resultant flooding of the coastal regions of the world. Millions of lives are lost. Ogden and his men survive, reaching a Manhattan largely under water. * As the story ends, the climate of the Earth has been changed, with Canada now semitropical. It was all caused by an earthspot, comparable to a sunspot. * Narrative, rather than composed fiction, but well enough handled.

COLLAS, PHIL (Writing name of FELIX EDWARD COLLAS, 1907-1989)
Australian author. Later a prominent authority on Australian philately, with *The Postal History of the Australian Army during World War II* (1986) and twenty other books on philately.

275. **THE INNER DOMAIN**. *Amazing Stories*, October 1935. Ill. Morey.
(Reprinted in book form by Graham Stone, Sydney, 1989.)
Short story. * *Time:* 1978, 1981 and later. *Place:* a cavern world beneath the Great Sandy Desert in Australia. * In 1978 strange radio signals are heard. The language is totally unintelligible, even unidentifiable, though one linguist claims that it is an extinct language from Central Australia. Then silence. * In 1981 Charles Winslow happens to be flying over the desert in Australia when he feels a wrench and loses consciousness. He awakens in strange surroundings, among gigantic dark men who seem very surprised to see him. A thought helmet explains matters considerably: He is among the Arnuna (better known as Arunta), far below the surface of the world, in an artificial cavern world equipped with all the wonders of a superscience. He was accidentally picked up by an experimental matter transmitter. * The Arnuna know in a general way from radio signals that there is a populated surface. Several years earlier they had tried to communicate, but with no success. This explains the mysterious signals of 1978. * *Background:* Millennia ago, when the climate of Australia was wetter, a band of Arnuna (then still savage) came upon the entrance to the enormous cave world. Entering, they found, completely deserted, a great complex of lighted cities with immense quantities of stored food. For a time, the Arnuna lived in and out of the caves, but diastrophism eventually sealed the entrance and trapped some of them inside. Over the millennia they studied the remains about them and gradually regained the superscience of the previous inhabitants, even surpassing it. * Later in the story the Arnuna, who have developed a time viewer, show Winslow what happened to the first city builders. Human, though of a very different racial stock, they were exterminated by an eruption of underground amoeboid creatures who devoured them. (A reader may interrupt this motif of Australians being chased around underground by shoggoths as influence from H. P. Lovecraft, or even vice versa, but chronology does not support this.) * As a geologist and radio expert Winslow adjusts well enough to life underground, but he knows that it is physically impossible for him ever to return to the surface. By the time of his death many years later, radio communication with the outside world is beginning, but many years will pass before there is physical contact. * *Miscellaneous:* Winslow learned the Arnuna language instantaneously from a modified thought helmet. * The original builders of the under-

Collas, Phil (*continued*)
ground city had large heads, extremely slender bodies, long pendulous ears, and very long slender arms, somewhat suggestive of Easter Island sculptures. No hint is given of their origin. * Amateurish, but intelligent, and a little different from most of the stories in *Amazing Stories.*

COLLIER, HARRY
According to Rock, pseud. of Harry Walton, fairly prolific contributor to the s-f pulps in the early 1940s, with a total of twenty-four stories. There are several book authors named Harry or Harold Walton, but none of them is clearly identifiable with the present writer.

276. **A SUITOR BY PROXY**. *Wonder Stories*, April 1935. Ill. Paul.
Short story. * Humorous in intention. * Professor Ohmpere, "Dean of Physics," has uttered a new theory of matter in which atoms do not exist, but are merely vortices of energy. One of the implications of the theory is that radio transmission of projections is possible. * The shy, introverted student Spindledrift approaches Ohmpere, asking assistance. He is too timid to personally court the girl he loves (who happens to be Ohmpere's daughter) and would like to approach her by projection. Ohmpere, after some reluctance, explains how this may be accomplished, and Spindledrift constructs suitable apparatus. Mounted on a platform, he performs actions that he considers desirable, whereupon a projection does exactly the same thing at whatever distance Spindledrift wishes. * Spindledrift's romance proceeds pleasantly for a time, but Dare, a rival, upsets his plans. With Ohmpere's connivance, Dare throws decayed fish and hungry cats into the projecting apparatus while Spindledrift is proposing. The situation becomes chaotic as the cats wreck the Ohmpere establishment. Spindledrift is seen no more, presumably a fugitive. * Pretty bad, without even much internal logic.

COLLINS, DEAN
No information. A possible identity is Dean Collins (1887-?), Oregon newspaper journalist, fiction writer, M.A. University of Oregon, 1911. Another person, Dean Albert Collins, M.A., University of Minnesota, 1928, thesis *The Effect of Cyanides upon Irritability and Capillary Permeability in Relation to Surgical Shock* seems less likely.

277. **STALLION'S TRAPPINGS**. *Amazing Stories*, March 1933.
Short-short story. * Professor Shea, who has inherited one million dollars, offers it to Dr. Malavan with a peculiar return in mind. He wants Malavan to transplant the brain of recently dead, notorious, ruthless business titan Mortimer Judd into his (Shea's) head. Shea is sure that he will retain his own personality, but acquire Judd's predatory abilities. * The operation is successful, and Shea, formerly a resentful, downtrodden worm, becomes a Tartar, driving his henpecking wife to divorce and becoming the terror of the campus. His career becomes as vile (and as profitable) as the late Judd's had been. * But Shea suddenly commits suicide, leaving behind a note to Malavan: "I could stand his memories no longer."

COLLINS, W. F.
No information.

278. **TWENTY YEARS FROM TODAY**. *Amazing Stories*, February 1931.
A fiction-article, only two pages long. * *Time:* 1950. * Most of the item is devoted to the sunmat and its repercussions on technology. An Alaskan prospector accidentally discovered that a certain type of moss served as a heat trap, storing solar heat in tiny cells. Sunmats manufactured from the plant or based on the plant permit Arctic agriculture, while a luminous principle serves as artificial lighting. * Really a humorous, speculative newspaper column.

COLTER, HAROLD MOORHOUSE
No information.
279. **ABSOLUTE ZERO**. *Amazing Stories*, January 1929. Unsigned ill.
Short story. * The strange death of the rustic Philander Jones. His crushed corpse was found in the basement of his house, having crashed through two floors. * The narrator explains: Electricity came to White Manitou, and Jones, who bought a refrigerator, became fascinated with the problem of cold. Hoping to reach absolute zero, he began experimenting with liquid hydrogen and other refrigerants. When he reported progress, his neighbors thought him mad, especially when, just before his death, he ran about shouting, Eureka. * The narrator's reconstruction: Jones discovered a unique property in his supercold liquid: It would dissolve and accept iron endlessly, with perhaps a flash of light. Eventually, the dissolved iron created an extremely thin film of neutronium in his test vessel. Its weight was so great that when Jones, who crept under the table to pick something up, bumped into a table leg, the unstable situation collapsed, and the enormous weight of the neutronium crushed him down through the floors into the basement. * Cleverly worked out.

CONN, ALAN
Pseud. of Alan Connell, who has a separate entry.
280. **FATE**. *Wonder Stories*, April 1936.
Short-short story. * Not really science-fiction. * The irony of fate. * Shintle is so terrified at the thought of death that he spends a fortune on quacks who promise longevity. After assorted medications and treatments, he prepares to withdraw to his underground chamber, which is shielded with lead against cosmic rays; but the elevator malfunctions and he falls to his death. * A fictional nothing.

CONNELL, ALAN (1917-present)
Australian (Sydney) author; birth date is also given as 1916, as in Clute, *The Encyclopedia of Fantasy*. In addition to several stories in the American pulp magazines is said to have written about eighty s-f and other stories for ephemeral Australian publication, before entering career as merchant seaman. His bibliography does not seem to be recorded. In 1991 his Serpent Land trilogy (probably written in 1932, published in chapbook form in the middle 1940s), was reissued in Australia. See also Alan Conn, pseud.
281. **THE REIGN OF THE REPTILES**. *Wonder Stories*, August 1935. Ill. Paul.
Short story. * *Time:* Frame situation in the present, body of the story in the late Mesozoic. * The after-the-fact narrative of Sanders. Sanders and the narrator have been carrying on their

Connell, Alan (*continued*)
interminable argument about evolution vs. special creation. Sanders leaves for a short time, and a few hours later returns tanned, heavily muscled, and with a short beard. * His story: When he left the house, he was abducted by three men who used him in a scientific experiment. One of the men, the supernal genius Juan, had worked out a means of transferring objects to the past, and Sanders chanced to be selected to be a guinea pig for time travel. * Sanders awakens in a gigantic room, obviously a laboratory; a jungle is visible outside. While Sanders sees dissected human corpses, the experimenters and the dominant life-form are not human, but large winged reptiles who obviously possess a superscience. Sanders is captured, escapes, and wanders about the jungle for a time with two primitive humans. He is recaptured, however, but at the last moment is retrieved from the past by Juan and his associates. * The point of the story is that apes and mankind were artifically created by the intelligent reptiles as slaves to take the place of reptilian servants, who were becoming extinct. Humans were obviously superior. * Juan and his associates speculate that nature had intended the intelligent reptiles to be the dominant Terrestrial life-form, but that by interfering with nature and creating man, the reptiles caused their own downfall. * As proof of his story, Sanders brings back the hand of one of the reptiles, which was grasping him when the time field cut in. Sanders, announcing that he intends to go back to the Mesozoic, leaves; he has not yet returned to our time. * The mode of time travel is not explained. * Obvious evidences of H. G. Wells's *The Time Machine* and the work of Edgar Rice Burroughs. Amateurish.

282. **DREAM'S END**. *Wonder Stories*, December 1935. Ill. Paul.
Short story. * Strange things. David Lane sees his sweetheart levitating while she walks, turning into something very strange, then disappearing. Massey Dune, astronomer at the observatory, sees stars race across the sky, disappear, and appear as new constellations. When a great soprano starts croaking like a frog, her audience disappears. (What is so unusual about that?) And Harry Dexter, who has insights, writes down his impressions of strange things that are happening within his perception. * Harry theorizes that the universe is the dream of a cosmic dreamer, and that the dreamer is awaking. He is right. Lewis Carroll made the same speculation in *Through the Looking Glass*.

283. **THE DUPLICATE**. *Wonder Stories*, April 1936. Ill. Winter.
Short story. * *Place:* Minnesota. * When Dr. Green receives a request to visit Jordan, his lifelong enemy, he is perplexed, but goes. The visit seems to no purpose, for Jordan simply shows him some machinery. * But Jordan really had a purpose: His machines have measured Green from many points of view and have constructed an android exactly like Green. The android, under Jordan's control, then commits crimes, including murder; witnesses, of course, identify Green as the criminal. * Green seems trapped, but on the occasion of the murder, Jordan did not know that Green had already been arrested and had a perfect alibi. The denouement then follows with a fairly obvious "surprise" ending. * Routine.

CONSTANTINESCU, CLINTON (1912-present)
Canadian author (later chemical engineer and amateur astronomer), then resident in Lethbridge, Alberta, Canada; presently resident in California. Name later changed to Clinton Constant. Since at story time he was a member of several major scientific organizations—American Association for the Advancement of Science, American Chemical Society, Royal Astronomical Society of Canada—the suggestion is that much of the following story was written tongue-in-cheek. According to *The Time Traveler* Constantinescu published a serial "The Martian Menace" in Canadian newspapers in 1932.

284. **THE WAR OF THE UNIVERSE**. *Amazing Stories Quarterly*, Fall 1931. Ill. Morey.
Novelette. * The great interstellar donnybrook. * *Time:* 1992. *Place:* The solar system and mostly around Eta Cassiopeia. * Space travel is common, and the humanoid inhabitants of the other planets are on friendly terms with the Earth. Indeed, there seems to be a sort of interplanetary council. * The solar system is suddenly bombarded with meteorites, destructive comets, and damaging rays. Buildings are wrecked and many lives are lost. Analysis of the damaging objects indicates that they emanate from the planetary system of Eta Cassiopeia, which the narrator's supertelescope shows is an enormous staging ground for machines, space spheres, and soldiery of an indeterminate sort. * Meeting on Jupiter, the associated solar planets discuss matters. Various rays have been devised to minimize damage or to repel matter from space, while other apparatus neutralizes the attacking rays. The associated worlds decide not to limit themselves to defense, but to strike against the foe. By now the solar system's scientists have developed an incredible armament, and a Jovian scientist has developed the alkali ray. This is a ray that not only moves much faster than light, but also drags objects along with it. Thus, a spaceship carrying such a projector can travel many times the speed of light. * The enormous fleet of tens of thousands of ships (called projectiles) sets out for the enemy system. A scouting expedition lands on one of the planets and discovers a race of intelligent birds, who provide some information. Millennia ago the birds controlled the system, but insect beings stole their science and almost exterminated the birds. Taking the birds on board the solar fleet, the invasion leaders decide to restore the few remaining birds to their heritage. * Space battle after space battle now follows, with hundreds of thousands of insect globes battling against the solar spaceships. On the whole, the solar fleet is the victor until the insects project a defensive cloud of pure protons, guided by magnetism, which the solar vessels have difficulty penetrating. * But, an unexpected development: Other fleets (forms of life not identified) arrive, with swarms of controlled comets and even a small sun, creating a grand mixed melée, from which the solar forces withdraw. Worst of the new participants are termite-shaped ships manned by man-sized termites with incredible weapons. * At one time the solar fleet is hard pressed enough that it retreats into the fifth dimension. * The turning point in the grand melée comes when a fleet of humans (Merlyrinnians) from Rigel draws up, establishes communication with the solar fleet, and becomes allied with it. The newcomers have terrific lightning projectors, but are weak in rays. * The final result, all the fighting fleets are destroyed except the humans, who now attack the insect planets, which surrender. It turns out that there are good insects as well as bad (Ilkaites), and that the bad held the good in subjection. The good insects are delighted with the way the war has gone and are reestablished in their worlds. The good insects reveal that the Ilkaites had first sent fleets to attack other planetary systems, but

Constantinescu, Clinton (*continued*)

were defeated. Now their tactic is long distance bombardment, which they seem to practice indiscriminately. * The grand fleet, accompanied by some of the Merlyrinnians, returns to the solar system, where the narrator, a renowned scientist responsible for many of the devices that brought victory, marries the daughter of the leader of the Merlyrinnians. * *Miscellaneous:* Among the Sears Roebuck of weapons and devices: the rayograph, which analyzes hostile radiation; ultra-cosmic ray projectors; atomic propulsion engines; gravity balancers; antigravity repulsion disks; krypton glow tube ray converters; the quadramomotor, which transfers objects to higher dimensions; sunlight storers; atomic bombs, also used to test the speed of the new spaceships; master controls for the enormous fleets; electronometric measuring devices to offset the Lorentz-Fitzgerald contraction on clocks; magnetic repulsion rays, and still more. * All the races of the solar system are human. Martians are somewhat taller; Jupiterians and Saturnians are much more heavily built; Mercurians, Venusians, Neptunians are smaller and more delicate. * Imaginative in detail, but immature work and somewhat primitive in development. The science is occasionally on the fantastic side, as when the characters watch spiral nebulae squirm around, but this is undoubtedly deliberate nonsense on the author's part.

CORBETT, CHAN

Pseud. of Nat Schachner, who has a separate entry. Schachner has stories under his own name in the same issues.

285. **WHEN THE SUN DIES.** *Astounding Stories,* March 1935. Ill. Dold.

Short story. * *Time:* 1985-1988. *Place:* eventually northern Alabama. * In 1985 it is observed that the sunspot cycle is not operating according to prediction. In a fairly short time it becomes obvious that the surface of the sun is covered with spots and that the sun is perceptibly cooling. The result, of course, is catastrophic; the temperate zones are soon barely habitable; the oceans are frozen; and much worse is to come. * The great scientist John Hammond, developer of the fantastically strong metal hammondite, intends to save the human race. Gathering a selected thousand persons, he develops an area in northern Alabama that has resources of coal, iron, and natural gas. He builds a "hemisphere" about a mile across and five hundred feet high, and stocks it with everything that his colony will need to survive—even to livestock—and develops underground resources. (There is no provision for using the Earth's internal heat.) Hammond shares his plans with similar enterprises, several of which are presumably constructed. All concerned now sit in Glacida, waiting for the glaciation to hit the retreat. * Hit it does, for Schachner apparently thought that glaciation strikes with the force of a cosmic hammer. The shock of falling ice dents the dome, does considerable damage, injures a few people, but essentially the biosphere survives well. * A second shock now strikes. The astronomer of the group announces that the sun will never regain its former condition, but will become a cold white dwarf, thus dooming all the planets. The question arises whether it is worth living without hope of returning to normal life. Hammond and his associates refuse to give in and determine to keep mankind alive, despite adversities. * Really a summary rather than a story.

286. **INTRA-PLANETARY**. *Astounding Stories,* October 1935. Unsigned ill.

Short story. * A personalized disease germ causes a medical revolution. * The experiences of Tubo, a microbe, are told in terms of interplanetary fiction. He lives within a volcanic planet, and when such a planet loses its life force he floats through space to another planet. Tubo, in addition to being a personality, has a keen intellect, and within a small laboratory he works on the problems of his life-form. His adventures, which include space travel and battle with horrible monstrosities (white corpuscles) within the corridors of the planet, culminate in a great discovery that revolutionizes both bacterial and human life. * Tubo recognizes that his kind would do best living in a sort of symbiosis with their planet. The chief cause of trouble in the past has been unrestricted multiplication. By practicing birth control and not damaging their carrier, bacteria can live happily and fully. * In the human world bacteriologist Dr. Truesdale has created an injection composed of dead bacteria that he believes will conquer disease. Indeed, a moribund patient (Tubo's planet) who received the shot, recovers remarkably. Truesdale becomes famous, but actually, if one observed closely, one could see that the efficacy of the shot radiated out from Tubo's planet, with his new creed carried by volunteer germs to other worlds. * Overlong for the subject, but with some imaginative detail.

287. **ECCE HOMO**. *Astounding Stories,* June 1936. Unsigned ill.

Short story. * *Time:* the hundred thousandth century is mentioned, but this may not fit context. * *Background:* In the eightieth century the human race was divided into Masters and Servants, the Masters being a scientific elite, who, with controlled mutations, gradually grew into gigantic brains of stupendous power, artificially maintained in quartz globes. The Servants, or ordinary humans, were permitted to live only as individual slaves bred and conditioned to absolute devotion to their lords. The Masters conquered space and settled the solar system, but as their numbers lessened, they gradually withdrew back to Earth. * As the story begins, almost all the Masters are dead, mostly of boredom after millennia of life. Only two Masters and two servants survive. The great El, who is served by the male Jem, is gradually undergoing psychological changes that may well be pathological. Desiring to have a new experience, he lays a careful plan. Accompanied by Jem, he flies around to the world to visit the Master Om, who regards his arrival with mild curiosity. Om, too, is bored, and even the utter novelty of a physical visit, instead of telepathic contact, arouses little interest. Om's female human attendant An, however, awakens Jem's desires, and she reciprocates. * El, carefully controlling his mental circuits, suggests to Om that they both commit suicide simultaneously as a thrilling new experience. Om agrees readily enough, and El summons two flying machines that purportedly will smash them. Om is killed, but at the last moment El exerts his enormous will, which could move a planet, and wards off the flying machine that was intended to kill him. * El now announces his intentions to the two humans. He is the sole Master in the universe, and, envisioning a horde of servants who will worship him, he commands Jem and An to mate. At this, something unthinkable takes place. An, who is less subservient than Jem, defies El, berating him for having killed her kind Master. * El has now degenerated enough to feel anger. This is his undoing, for when he orders Jem to seize An, he does not recognize the emotion that is stirring in Jem—who almost without thinking smashes El's crystal container, killing him. Jem

Corbett, Chan (*continued*)
and An are now ready to mate. * Routine.

288. **THE THOUGHT WEB OF MINIPAR**. *Astounding Stories,* November 1936. Ill. Flatos.
Short story. * Told dually through John Weatherby, a small clerk in New York City, and the intelligent spiders of Minipar—a world millions of light-years away. The spiders, who have a superscience based on various kinds of nets, interchange personalities with other races throughout the galaxy in order to gain knowledge. * In the present instance, they are sending out Heurilu, who enters Weatherby's body, while Weatherby's mind comes to Minipar into Heurilu's body. Heurilu-in-Weatherby remains in hospital, gradually learning about Terrestrial civilization. He is diagnosed as having a remarkably complete case of amnesia, although one of his physicians has strong suspicions of personality transfer from another world. Weatherby-in-Heurilu, after his initial panic has waned, becomes acculturated to Minipar civilization and even learns to construct some of the more elementary scientific webs. His weak intellect (compared to that of the spiders) and small knowledge, however, are a disappointment to his mentors. * The time comes to reverse the experiment. Weatherby is reluctant to leave Minipar, but there is no choice. Returned to Earth, he is sensible enough to remain silent about his experience, which gradually fades from his memory. * Routine.

CORBETT, JOHN M.
No information. Judging from "The Black River," someone well-grounded in petroleum geology and engineering, perhaps resident in the Los Angeles area.

289. **THE CAVES OF PELE**. *Amazing Stories,* May 1932. Ill. Morey.
Short story. * *Time:* 1973. *Place:* Hawaii. * Essentially a short adventure story with no fantastic material except futurity and politics. Agents of the United Empire of Asia (China, Japan, Philippines) are storing enormous quantities of weapons in the lava tunnels of Mauna Loa, planning an attac on the United States. As private papers show years later, Martin Fischer, assistant director of volcano research at Kilauea, stymied the plot. Also involved were a renegade English scoundrel and a captive maiden. * Routine.

290. **THE BLACK RIVER**. *Wonder Stories*, December 1934. Ill. Paul. Attributed to James M. Corbett on the contents page of the magazine, undoubtedly a flight of the fancy.
Short story. * *Time:* 1936-1938. *Place:* the Los Angeles area. * The American Petroleum Institute (A.P.I.) is concerned with limiting petroleum production for reasons of conservation, but major producer Silas Mortimer (obviously modelled to some extent on John D. Rockefeller) not only refuses to go along, but announces that he has a plan for drilling that will almost double the California production. According to his geologist's revolutionary theories, there is an enormous pool of oil about twenty thousand feet below the Los Angeles area. He plans to drill in the San Fernando Valley. * Despite outcry and some complications with a romance between Mortimer's son and the daughter of the hostile chairman of the A.P.I., the drilling goes ahead, using revolutionary technology that the author describes in detail. Ways are devised to drill thousands of feet deeper than hitherto considered possible, new channel concepts are applied, and all gets under way. * The drillers hit the mother lode, but

with unexpected results. A pillar of petroleum rises into the sky hundreds of feet high and wide, and is uncappable. The petroleum soon fills the reservoirs that Mortimer had constructed and breaks out into the river, heading toward the sea. Booms are set up to avoid polluting the ocean (and loss of oil), barricades are created, but to no avail. Then the oil catches fire, and Los Angeles is cut in two by a river of fire. * It looks like an incredible catastrophe, but then old Mortimer, who has been ill, awakens. Much of it has been a dream. While the drilling has begun, it has not progressed very far. Mortimer, considering his dream veridical, cancels the project and is willing to cooperate with the A.P.I. * Not a bad story. The engineering detail is interesting.

CRAMER, STERLING S.
No information. Social Security records list Sterling Cramer (1903-1994), a resident of Pennsylvania and New Jersey, and Sterling Cramer (1904-1995), a resident of San Francisco. There is no evidence that either man is the present author.

291. **DEATH FROM WITHIN**. *Wonder Stories*, June 1935. Ill. Saaty.
Short story. * *Place:* An imaginary Caribbean island under American control, where the natives speak Spanish. * The narrator, a lieutenant in the American police force, accompanies visiting Dr. Geddes to investigate the Death, which strikes suddenly, killing almost instantaneously. As the two men proceed through the primitive native settlements, they see victims of the Death, and Geddes, who makes impromptu autopsies on a few bodies, soon discovers what has happened. * The victims, although they show no external injuries, suffer from traumatic internal thoracic wounds—as if someone were slashing their vital organs with a scalpel—but without breaking the skin. * Dr. Geddes works out what is happening. The attacks are taking place from another (geometric) dimension. The island happens to be a focus where our world and the other world meet, and a denizen of the other dimension is vivisecting humans. Since the being is fourth dimensional, he has no difficulty is passing through objects in our world. * Geddes is proved right, the painful way, for the narrator observes such a being materialize and go to work on Geddes. It is immune to bullets. * There is no remedy except to stay away from areas where such penetrations take place. * As a thriller, not badly done. It creates a mood.

CRIMP, H. M.
According to an advance notice in the October 1932 issue of *Amazing Stories,* an Australian. Otherwise no information. However, Graham Stone, in *Past, Present & Future* (August 1979, p. 13), an Australian publication, suggests that Crimp may not have been Australian. Crimp would seem to have a background in biology.

292. **THE CALL TO MIGRATE**. *Amazing Stories,* December 1932. Ill. Morey.
Short story. * Professor Mark Scott devises a radio apparatus that stimulates the migratory urge of locusts. His discovery is applauded by the scientific world, but largely ignored elsewhere. * Heintz and Thorpe, two grifters, see an angle to this. Heintz manages to borrow (and have copied) the naive Scott's apparatus. Their plan: to corner the present wheat market, which is glutted world-wide, then use the locusts to devastate future crops.

Crimp, H. M. (*continued*)

The two rogues bring in Pancrast, a crooked financier to supply cash. First, Heintz and Thorpe buy up storage wheat in enormous quantities, then later supervise broadcasts to move the locusts onto growing crops. As this plot advances, inflated prices, famine, and political disturbances arise. * Heintz and Thorpe do not know, however, that Pancrast has made a secret deal with the great money-man Isaccson [*sic*], by which they would be frozen out. * The two grifters are understandably furious when they learn of this, and do what they can to upset the greater rogues. Joining the Communist Party they foment riots and general social upheavals. The upshot of it all is that all four rogues are killed, but civilization is on the edge of being wiped out. * Professor Scott, however, saves the day. Inventing a still better transmitter for controlling the now enormous hordes of insects, he diverts them to the ocean, Death Valley, and similar areas. * Rather crudely done. The anti-Semitic note appears more strongly than in the above summary. For a sequel see #293, "The Mosquito Army."

293. **THE MOSQUITO ARMY**. *Amazing Stories,* April 1935. Ill. Morey.

Short story. * Sequel to #292, "The Call to Migrate." * Professor Scott and his assistant Jimmy Blake, now in Louisiana to study the boll weevil, discover that the mosquitos are impossible to tolerate. Temporarily shelving their boll weevil studies, the men set out to find a mechanical means of repelling or controlling the movements of mosquitos, just as Scott previously did with locusts. After a time their work is successful. * And timely, for the Soviet Union, after destroying London, Paris, and Berlin and conquering Europe, is now attacking the United States. The Russians bomb the major cities, while field armies move across the land, supported by air superiority. * Scott and Blake assemble a mighty horde of mosquitos, inoculate them with malaria, and send them against the Russians. In a relatively short time, the Russian offensive collapses, and the invaders withdraw. But malaria accompanies them back home, and the Soviet Union collapses, the vicious dictator Kriloff himself dying of the disease. * Routine.

CUMMINGS, PARKE (1903-1987)

U.S. (Connecticut) author. Other works *The Dictionary of Sports* (1949) and *The Dictionary of Baseball* (1950).

294. **NOTHING TO IT**. *Amazing Stories,* February 1936.

(Reprinted from the *Saturday Evening Post,* 1934.)

Short-short feature. * Not science-fiction. * Fictionalization of a teaching situation as a father tries to help his child in the algebraic solution of a work problem. The father flounders hopelessly, while the son solves the problem. * The piece carries an erroneous copyright date of 1834; it should have been 1934.

CUMMINGS, RAY (I.e. **RAYMOND KING CUMMINGS**) (1887-1957)

U.S. (mostly upstate New York) writer. Born in New York City; attended Princeton University for one year. Prolific author of detective stories, general adventure fiction, science-fiction. At one time worked in minor capacity for Thomas A. Edison's plant, writing record labels and/or editing the house organ; early accounts of Cummings sometimes magnified this into scientific collaboration with Edison. * Although at times a fluent writer,

Cummings had no depth of idea and was unable to move beyond a very few basic concepts that he worked and reworked with hackneyed monotony and a somewhat maudlin, sentimental point of view. Weak imagination, characterizations and plotting are usual in his fiction, which has justly been called hackwork. * Historically, however, Cummings was important for "The Girl in the Golden Atom" (*All-Story*, 15 March 1919), an early adventure in size that has a certain fairy tale-like period quality. Certain of his Tubby short stories (described in *Science-Fiction: The Early Years*) are amusing as *reductiones ad absurdum* of scientific ideas. All in all, such small significance as Cummings has lies in his work before the emergence of the genre pulps covered in this volume. * See also joint work by William Thurmond and Ray Cummings. * See also #1814, "Blood of the Moon," #1815, "Shadow Gold," #1816, "Trapped in Eternity." and #1833, "Earth-Venus 12".

295. **AROUND THE UNIVERSE**. *Amazing Stories,* October 1927. Ill. Paul.

(First published in *Science and Invention,* July-December 1923.) One of a series of stories about Tubby, a bigmouthed ignoramus, whose frailties are used as a vehicle for a story usually (though not here) parodic of some aspect of science. In this case, the story is didactic. * Tubby's wishes suddenly come true, like Mr. Fotheringay in H. G. Wells's "The Man Who Could Work Miracles." He wishes a spaceship into existence for himself, and with Professor Isaac Wells-Verne he travels around the solar system. On Venus he learns that the Martians are plotting to invade the Earth and have already occupied the Moon. The Venusians cannot help the Earth; the natives of Jupiter rebuff Tubby; and the Mercurians are already ready to attack along with the Martians. The professor suggests going out into size, to the macrocosm of which our universe is subatomic; after this journey they return to our solar system. The explorers tumble an asteroid on Mars, thus canceling the Martian war plans. Tubby now realizes that he could have stopped the war simply by wishing. Back on Earth he stops the Earth's rotation, creating chaos, then wishes everything back as it was. * Along with this rather jejune narrative and weak fantasy there is a fair amount of scientific exposition. An uninspired story, described in more detail, along with the superior Tubby short stories, in *Science-Fiction: The Early Years*.

296. **PHANTOMS OF REALITY**. *Astounding Stories,* January 1930. Ill. J. Fleming Gould.

Capsulated nouvelle. * Dynastics and romance. * Charles Wilson, Wall Street clerk, receives an invitation from his brilliant, wealthy friend Derek Mason to visit a world in the fourth dimension and prevent a wrong. Derek explains the fourth dimension as a world that differs in vibratory frequency from ours; the culture there is primitive, but is "dependent" on our world. The people speak English and the landscape (apart from real estate development) is the same. Politically, Derek says, the fourth-dimensional world is an oligarchy, with a corrupt, luxurious nobility ruling oppressed workers. * In the very near future, Derek continues, the king will choose a consort; if he picks the evil, sex-mad, debauched Sensua, the workers will rise in rebellion. If he selects the pure Blanca, the workers will be happy, for Blanca will strengthen the king's better nature. * The two friends enter the other-world. Derek had hoped for time to make plans for controlling the king's choice, but there are only hours. Sensua and Blanca, according to custom, will dance,

Cummings, Ray (*continued*)

after which the king will make his choice. But it is an open secret that the king will choose Sensua. * All plans, however, are shunted aside when Sensua, apparently not willing to trust the obvious, knifes Blanca, killing her. Rebellion breaks out; the nobility are massacred; and the king is murdered. * Derek is now revealed to be the long-lost Prince Alexandre, the true heir to the throne. After some hair-raising adventures he is accepted as king. All the villains are dead. * The narrator, a trivial man, did his share during the conflict by returning to our world in order to double back and catch the main villain by surprise. He comes back to our world, but does not explain background: How did Derek come to our dimensional world in the first place, since the other-world is on a medieval level? * So artificial that it is almost a pastoral, but with little to recommend.

297. **BRIGANDS OF THE MOON**. *Astounding Stories*, March-June 1930. Ill. Wesso.

(Reprinted in book form by McClurg, Chicago, 1931; also as a paperback by Ace Books, New York, 1958. The McClurg edition is extremely scarce; I have never seen a copy. It was also pirated in Toronto around 1948 or so and misattributed to John W. Campbell, Jr.)

Novel. * In a foreword Cummings states that he is presenting a typical adventure novel of the late twenty-first century. * Economic warfare, thrills, and romance. * *Time:* A.D. 2079. *Place:* space, the Moon, an unnamed giant asteroid that is Earth-like in atmosphere and vegetation. * To simplify the complicated, cliffhanger plot: Gregg Haljan, Third Officer of the interplanetary liner *Planetara*, is caught up in the intrigues of Martians who want to seize the enormous radium deposits that the Grantline expedition has discovered on the Moon. The Martians are particularly eager to acquire the radium since they have developed a fine radium engine, but have little fuel for it. * The Martians and a mutinous crew seize the *Planetara*, maroon the passengers on a pleasant asteroid, and, forcing Haljan to navigate for them, fly to the Moon. The *Planetara* crashes, but all the important characters survive, and the struggle continues. * Haljan and his allies from the *Planetara* join with Grantline's forces, and fight off the surviving hijackers and a Martian ship. The battle is complex, but flying platforms turn the trick, just as a police ship draws near. * *Miscellaneous:* Martians are humanoid, but gigantic; Venusians are petite and sexy; both apparently can interbreed with Earthmen. * Space flight is accomplished by magnetic creation of antigravity. * The various parties have portable heat rays, the zed-ray (which can penetrate rock like an X-ray), paralysis tubes, and darkness bombs. * A cloak of invisibility operates by absorbing color and bending light rays around itself; it is not wholly effective. * There is a world government, the United States of the World—USW, which arose after a war with Asians (unspecified nationality) in 1962. * Routine work. For a sequel see #304, "Wandl the Invader."

298. **JETTA OF THE LOWLANDS**. *Astounding Stories*, September-November 1930. Ill. Wesso.

Short novel. * Economic espionage and intrigue. * *Time:* A.D. 2020. *Place:* mostly the dry sea bottom north of Puerto Rico. * *Background:* The oceans of the world have disappeared, leaving sea bottoms that have been settled, colonized, and exploited, with many small states. The country of Nareda, for example, is a small protectorate of the United States. * Philip Grant, an operative in the customs department of the National Detective Service, is assigned to investigate mercury smuggling from Nareda to the United States. * On arriving at Nareda he immediately becomes enmeshed with the criminals, who include a Dutch innkeeper and mine owner (Spawn), a crooked politician, and the Lowlands bandit De Boer. Jetta of the title, a sixteen-year-old, becomes Grant's sweetheart and helps him when he is captured. The ending is predictable. * Pure adventure apart from a couple of gimmicks: the sea, invisible planes, rays, and superradio. * In a letter (*Astounding Stories*, October 1930) Cummings explains the invisibility as a combination of factors: light rays bent by magnetic fields, de-electronization, and color absorption.

299. **THE MARK OF THE METEOR**. *Wonder Stories Quarterly*, Winter 1931. Ill. Paul.

Short story. * *Time:* the interplanetary future. *Place:* space, on the Mars-Earth run. * An incident in a voyage. A meteor strikes the spaceship *Comet*, wrecking the vessel, causing it to lose its air, and killing all those on board except three people who are in the sealed off command module. The three are Graham Trent, communications officer; Alma Rance, a beautiful maiden; and Kol, a Martian. * The situation is almost triangular: On Mars Kol has been harassing Alma, while on the spaceship Alma and Graham have fallen in love. * The Martian tries to kill Graham, who manages to lock himself and Alma in a sealed area. He then leaves the spaceship through an air lock, returns around through space, and kills the Martian. Graham and Alma are then rescued by the space patrol. * *Miscellaneous:* The Martians are apparently perfectly human, but very tall and grayish in complexion. * Space communication involves light signals. * Routine.

300. **THE GREAT TRANSFORMATION**. *Wonder Stories*, February 1931. Ill. Marchioni.

Short story. * *Time:* A.D. 1948. *Place:* London. * Fundamentalist reporter Georg [*sic*] Blake of the *Vocal Times* (apparently television news) is assigned to interview Dr. Roberts, who has claimed that he has made a great discovery. Roberts, a very aged man with a delicate-looking sixteen-year old daughter, explains: Animals and man do not differ in essence, only in degree. An ape is simply an undeveloped man. Beyond this, Roberts has discovered the essence of mankind by processing a human brain; he has thus obtained the sperm of thought, which he can impart to animals. * While feeding Tom, the young gorilla that lives in the next room, Roberts surreptitiously inoculates him. In a very short time the gorilla seems to change in personality. Then, seizing a knife, it kills Roberts. The reporter fears that the gorilla will attack him and Miss Roberts, but instead, the gorilla, realizing that it is now a human mind trapped in an ape body, commits suicide. * All through the story the narrator makes foolish religious comments about souls and divine will. * Pretty bad.

301. **BEYOND THE VANISHING POINT**. *Astounding Stories*, March 1931. Ill. Wesso.

(Reprinted as Ace Double D-331, New York, 1958.)

Novelette. * Adventures in size. * *Time:* 1960. *Place:* Quebec and an atomic world in a piece of gold ore. * Narrator George Randolph receives an emergency summons from his friend Alan Kent, who is in Quebec. Years before, Alan's father's assistant Franz Polter assaulted Alan's then fourteen-year-old twin sister Babs, and Alan believes that Polter has now abducted her. Polter, who has become a multimillionaire through his gold

Cummings, Ray (*continued*)

mine, lives in Quebec under the alias of Rascor. * George and Alan enter Polter's estate, are captured, and witness an incredible transformation. Polter shrinks in size and disappears into a piece of ore under an electron microscope. * As George and Alan lie bound, waiting for death, an inch-high woman (Glora) creeps up to them, unties them, and gives them a drug that enlarges them enormously. They wreck the establishment, and then prepare to descend into the world of the golden atom where Polter has taken Babs. * The descent is arduous and dangerous, but George and Alan emerge in the atomic world near the city of Orena, where Polter maintains a force of giants to intimidate the natives, whom he rules. * There are back-and-forth adventures among Polter, Babs, the comrades, and the great scientist Dr. Kent. Dr. Kent, who is held captive by Polter, alone knows how to make the size-changing drugs, but he refuses to do so. * An accident precipitates a conclusion. The enlarging drug is spilled, noxious insects and germs emerge in titanic size, and it looks as if the humans of Orena are lost. Glora remains in her imperilled land, but the others ascend in pursuit of Polter and Babs. Polter is killed; Babs is rescued; and all return to the microcosm, where Alan remains with Glora. * *Miscellaneous:* No explanation is given for the size-changing drug. Time passes more rapidly in the microcosm than the macrocosm. Polter became rich by enlarging gold ore, from which he extracted the metal. * One more tired, clichéd development of a motif that Cummings belabored several times.

302. **THE EXILE OF TIME**. *Astounding Stories*, April-July 1931. Ill. Wesso.

(Reprinted in book form by Avalon, New York, 1964; also in paperback by Ace Books, New York, 1965.)

Novel. * *Time:* departure point 1935, and then back and forth throughout time. *Place:* mostly the New York area. * The action is complicated, repetitive and confusing enough that a plot summary would have little value. Important moments and essential themes: Tugh, a misshapen hunchback from 2930, is rampaging through time in a time cage that he claims to have invented. His vita is bad: In 1777 he harassed Mary Atwood and was forced to flee, and in 1935 he was involved in sex crimes. In both instances he escaped, vowing revenge. * Returning to 1777, Tugh abducts Mary, and, back in 1935, he causes his robot servitor Migul to transport from the future hundreds of robots who demolish Manhattan, causing tens of thousands of deaths. * Along the way to these deeds Tugh's servitor, the robot Migul, on Tugh's instructions, kidnaps George Rankin from 1935. Tugh intends to take George into the far future, where super-surgeons will transfer Tugh's brain to George's handsome body. * Another time cage is involved. It is operated by Harl, who claims to have co-invented Tugh's machine. Harl is accompanied by the Princess Tina. * The two parties chase each other back and forth in time. * A crossing of the paths takes place in 2930, where Tugh is fomenting a revolt of the robots, who are human enough to feel themselves ill-treated and exploited. If the robots win, Tugh will become master of the world, and the human survivors will become slaves to the robots. * When the revolt breaks out, Princess Tina and Harl are besieged in the station that broadcasts power to the robots; if Tugh does not seize the installation within two days, the robots will become inactive from loss of power. Tugh fails. * Tugh at one time took Mary and George to the beginning of the universe; now, in

flight after the failed revolt in 2930 he takes the kidnapped Mary to the year one billion, where he is followed by the other time machine. There is a clash, and Tugh is killed. Surprise! Tugh was not a human, but a superrobot from the far future. * The robot Migul plays a large part in the story; Cummings attempts to humanize him as a sentient being who would like to be free and at times thinks he is free, but is really under Tugh's domination. * *Miscellaneous:* By 2930 New York City has become a garden city; before this it was a titanic megalopolis. * Space travel is possible through ether waves. * Time, Cummings says in a long passage, is a religious matter, the Scroll of God, which unfolds. We humans are not real identities, but successions of changed vibratory states. If the vibratory state is changed, one "moves in time." This is the purpose of the Creator. * There are paralysis, freezing, heat, and disintegrator rays. * The telespectroscope enables those in one time cage to see the other through time. * Routine work.

303. **THE WHITE INVADERS**. *Astounding Stories*, December 1931. Ill. Wesso.

Novelette. * *Time:* 1938. *Place:* Bermuda, New York, the fourth dimension. * Wraith-like white figures with strange helmets and gear are seen around Bermuda; nubile young women disappear. * Jane, Don, and the narrator become involved when they capture one of the invaders, who is later revealed to be Tako, the leader of the white figures. Tako, however, escapes, and, capturing our friends, takes them into the fourth dimension. * The fourth dimension, which differs from our world in space-time coordinates, is much like Earth, a pleasant enough place. The people, who are totally human, live in a neo-medieval society with nobles and workers, but possess the remnants of a superscience from the past. * Tako, who has discovered the means of crossing to our world, is actually engaged in white slaving. He is kidnapping beautiful Earth women for sale to the harems of the nobility. But he keeps Jane, to whom he has taken a fancy, and he spares Don and the narrator as sources of information about New York City. * Tako plans to devastate New York with materialization bombs and organic disintegrator rays, then, with his headquarters and ray apparatus in the Empire State Building, receive tribute in the form of women. Ultimately, he wants power. * There seems no stopping Tako, who invades New York, causing enormous death and destruction. But he is brought down by Tolla, a woman from his harem who is intensely jealous of Jane. Tolla disintegrates Tako and turns materialization beams on the invaders, causing them to explode fully into our world. The invasion is over. * *Miscellaneous:* Tolla had previously been dropped into our world to learn English and our ways. * In the fourth dimension vehicular travel operates by altering space-time coordinates, a technique that led Tako to discover the way into our world. * There were probably earlier visitors, whence our stories of ghosts. * Clichéd, although Cummings seems to be taking a little more pains with the invasion leader Tako than he usually does with his villains. * The story is essentially a rewrite of "Into the Fourth Dimension" (*Science and Invention*, September 1926-May 1927), which is covered in *Science-Fiction: The Early Years.*

304. **WANDL, THE INVADER**. *Astounding Stories*, February-May 1932. Ill. Wesso.

(Reprinted by Ace Books, New York, 1961, Ace Double D-497.)

Sequel to #297, "Brigands of the Moon." Cummings abandons here the strategy that the story is a work of fiction of the late

Cummings, Ray (*continued*)
twenty-first century. * Novel. * *Time:* A.D. 2070. *Place:* space.
* A strange little planet about one-fifth the size of the Moon has
entered the solar system. This is Wandl. * As the story begins,
the characters of the first story, Gregg Haljan, Anita Prince,
Venza of Venus, and Snap Dean are assigned by the interplanetary police to check into the activities of the Martian bandit Set
Molo. * Molo, it soon becomes clear, is plotting with the inhabitants of the new planet Wandl to conquer the three inhabited
worlds: Venus, Earth, and Mars. * Wandl itself has come from
another star system as a sort of gigantic space station. Its
inhabitants are of two sorts: workers, who are ten feet tall and
very thin, and rulers, who are hypertrophied brains, perhaps a
foot or two across, with tiny vestigial bodies. The rulers of
Wandl plan to use tractor beams focused from Wandl to stop the
rotation of the three solar worlds and then drag them back out
into space to their home system. * There are goings-on back and
forth until our friends are captured by the Martian collaborator
Set Molo and taken to Wandl, where the Master, a brain six or
seven feet across, interviews them. They will perhaps be
permitted to live as zoo and laboratory specimens after the native
races of the solar system are otherwise extinct. * What to do?
Escape, of course, and foil the plans of the Master. This they
do. After considerable in-and-out action, the Earthmen destroy
the great gravity mechanisms that are interfering with the
rotation of the three solar system planets, and in an enormous
space battle Wandl's fleet is badly beaten. Wandl is now more
or less isolated; it follows a peculiar orbit, since it can no longer
steer its progress, and falls into the sun. * Among curiosities are
transportation by means of giant mail tubes. * As an unusual
technique for pulp fiction, Cummings provides many long expository footnotes explaining matters of real science, fantastic
science, and general background. This is probably an attempt to
prevent impeding the story by too much "factual" matter.

CURRY, TOM (1900-1976)
U.S. (Connecticut) author. Frequent contributor to other pulp
magazines, with many Western stories. Curry's Westerns are
superior to his fantastic fiction.

305. **THE SOUL SNATCHER**. *Astounding Stories*,
April 1930. Ill. J. Fleming Gould.
Short story. * A distraught mother appears at the laboratory of
Professor Ramsey Burr. Her son, Allen Baker, is due to be
electrocuted because of an experiment in personality transfer that
went wrong in Burr's laboratory, and she blames Burr. * Burr
reassures the woman: He has perfected the process and will use
it to save her son. It involves two steps, first exchanging
personalities, then bodies. He demonstrates this with a cat and
a monkey. * At the proper time he will exchange personalities
with Allen, and then recreate bodies, so that Allen will be in the
lab, safe, while Burr will be in the death cell. The authorities
will have no choice but to release Burr. * But all does not go
well. Allen's personality moves into Burr's body, but the second
part of the process does not take place. It is later learned that
Allen's body was electrocuted ahead of schedule, with Professor
Burr's mind in it. Since the professor was ultimately responsible
for the whole mess, the result is not wholly unfair.

306. **GIANTS OF THE RAY**. *Astounding Stories*, June
1930. Unsigned ill. (J. Fleming Gould?)
Short story. * *Place:* Matto Grosso. * While lying drunk in a

saloon, the scoundrelly Maget overhears a conversation about a
fabulously rich mine that Professor Gurlone and his associates
are working in the Matto Grosso. He tells his partner Durkin
what he has heard, and the two rogues decide to follow the
Gurlones back to the mine and hijack its wealth. * The mine
turns out to be an incredibly rich radium deposit that runs far
underground. Its emanations have caused gigantism in the local
animal life. * As the tramps soon learn, the radium extracted
from the ore is lethal. And the excavations have opened an
enormous cavern teeming with gigantic predatory life-forms that
are eager to get out and eat the members of the expedition. *
Durkin dies of radiation burns; Maget turns honest and tries to
help the Gurlones. But the monsters are too much for them, and
they are forced to abandon the mine. They plan to return with
suitable weapons.

307. **FROM AN AMBER BLOCK**. *Astounding Stories*,
July 1930. Ill. J. Fleming Gould.
Short story. * In the laboratory of the great museum lies an
enormous block of amber (perhaps the size of a large truck?) that
has been brought in from Manchuria. The natives who excavated it feared it as something monstrous. In the center of the
amber is a black blotch, nature unknown. * The reader will have
little difficulty in guessing what is in the black blotch. It is a
horrible monstrosity, a dinosaur of a sort, a gigantic snake with
clawed feet and blood-sucking proboscis. It kills several people
before it succumbs to bullets and an ax wielded by—a young
woman, Betty Young, fiancée of the paleontologist in charge. *
The unusual feature of this otherwise clichéd story is that it
focuses more on Betty than on the men.

308. **HELL'S DIMENSION**. *Astounding Stories*, April
1931. Ill. J. Fleming Gould.
Short story. * The police are interrogating Professor John
Lambert in his laboratory. His fiancée, Madge Crawford, has
mysteriously disappeared. Lambert claims that her disappearance is the result of an experiment in acoustics that released
unexpected forces into whose range Madge accidentally stepped,
but the police think that Lambert has murdered her. * The officer
in charge, however, indulges Lambert, permitting him to try to
reverse the experiment. Lambert is unsuccessful, and in despair
allows himself to be disintegrated in the same way that Madge
was. * He finds himself in a gray world, tormented by strange
shapes that poke and prod at him. Madge is there, too. The two
humans undergo torments and tortures, until they suddenly find
themselves back in our world. A friend, Professor Morgan, who
understands the process, has been successful in retrieving them.
But it is now eight days later. Some of the police are still
incredulous and insist that Madge and Lambert were hiding
somewhere in the lab. * H. G. Wells did it much better in "The
Plattner Story."

CUTHBERT, CHESTER D. (1912-present)
Canadian (Winnipeg) author. Insurance claims supervisor.
Active fan and collector.

309. **THE SUBLIME VIGIL**. *Wonder Stories*, February
1934. Ill. Winter.
(Reprinted in Moskowitz, *Editor's Choice*.)
Short story. * A mood story. * The narrator reminisces about
John Bancroft, a strange man who combines aspects of outlaw,
individualist, lover, and hermit. After a stormy childhood
Bancroft became engaged to the beautiful young Alice Gray.

Cuthbert, Chester D. (*continued*)
While he was standing with her atop a mountain ridge, she suddenly disappeared into midair, as witnessed by the narrator, the local physician. After an intensive search for her, Bancroft left the area, but returned ten years later. Now for the past twenty-five years he has been standing on the mountain top awaiting the return of Alice. * A German savant, seeking Bancroft, offers an explanation of sorts to the narrator. Perhaps when the universe was formed, perhaps in the depths of stars, there are "vacuums" in the ether, which drift about, perhaps cyclically. Alice was swallowed by one of these vacuums. Since there is no time or space, no life or death in such a vacuum she remains there in a nonexistent existence. Perhaps the vacuum will seize John Bancroft as he awaits on the mountain. * Possibly suggested by Ambrose Bierce's "Mysterious Disappearances." Nicely written.

310. **THE LAST SHRINE.** *Wonder Stories*, July 1934. Ill. Winter.
Short story. * *Place:* the Sierra Madre Mountains, Mexico. * Dan Armour, perhaps a soldier of fortune, perhaps an explorer, hears of the Valley of Peace in Mexico. This is an isolated hermit area into which men have ventured but never returned. He finds it without difficulty. * The natives, Indians of an otherwise unknown sort, are not unfriendly, but will not permit him to leave. After a time, as he learns the language, he comes to realize that he is being groomed for a role. He is to pass through the Veil, a peculiar nonmaterial barrier within the temple. Other men have tried, but have died. A prophecy, however, indicates that eventually a stranger will enter the land and pass the barrier. * On the other side of the barrier is Xenolie, a beautiful young woman, preserved immortal; the person passing through will awaken her to the plight of the people outside the barrier, at which she will return to this world and relieve them. The successful venturer should be able to converse with her telepathically. * After a vigil and other forms of ascesis, Armour can see Xenolie, who obviously is living at a different, much slower time rate than the outside world. * Xenolie explains: In the remote past the humans had a super-civilization, but life operated at a different time rate than at present. When astronomers observed a disturbance of the ether, they recognized that it would change the time structure and that destroy their civilization. They then prepared what amounted to a time capsule, into which Xenolie entered; to preserve it and to prepare for her emergence, they set up the mechanism of a cult. But something went wrong, for the mountain forming process concentrated the preservative substances, placing her in suspended animation rather than a shorter sleep. * The time come, ritually prepared, Armour penetrates the barrier, which disappears and Xenolie is free. She and Armour live among the Indians, she as an exalted goddess. As they discover, they will never be able to leave the area, for enough of the time substance remains to render life outside impossible for them. * Perhaps too complex for the brevity of the story. The mythic elements are original and imaginative.

DALLAS, EVERARD
No information. W. O. G. Lofts has suggested that Everard Dallas was the same person as Oswald Dallas, a prolific British writer of boys' books and story-paper serials, but this has not been verified.

311. **RAY CONTROL NO. 1.** *Scoops,* 9 June 1934. Unsigned ill.
Boys' fiction. * Short story. * *Time:* the twenty-first century. * Reporter Graham, who works for the *Radio News* (newspapers seemingly no longer being existent) is assigned to interview the eccentric scientist Harvey Hamish. Hamish, an unpleasant man who is obviously partly mad, demonstrates his new invention by focusing a small box on the reporter, who is overcome with mirth to the point of nearly collapsing. The invention, explains Hamish, is a device for controlling human emotion (and mental set). Since Graham fears that he will not be believed if he reports what he experienced, he requests further demonstrations. * The two men perambulate around London, where Hamish sets up various emotions: panic during the Changing of the Guard. benevolence in a greedy financier, softheartedness in heavyweights in a gym, etc. The climax comes when Hamish demonstrates how his device can increase productivity in an automobile assembly line. Hamish forces the workers to speed up until they drop from exhaustion. Instead of welcoming the invention, however, the manager indignantly expels the two men. * It all ends when Hamish drops his little black box, and, while bending to retrieve it, is run over and killed. * *Miscellaneous:* London has an extensive fleet of passenger Electromobiles.

DANIELS, DAVID R. (1915-1936)
U.S. (Colorado) fan, author. Frequent contributor to the amateur magazines. Daniels's death by gunshot has been variously interpreted as accident or suicide. Fan magazines of the period deplored his death, even to including poetry to his memory.

312. **STARS.** *Astounding Stories,* May 1935. Ill. Dold.
Short story. * *Time:* the early interplanetary future. *Place:* Venus. * Oliver and Erikson, on the first flight to Venus, survived the crash of their spaceship and have been working at repairing it. The ship itself is now operable, but fuel is in short supply. As the men know, there is only one chance in a million that they can return to Earth; that chance involves reaching the vicinity of the Moon, where they can be picked up. * The real situation, however, is psychological. Oliver, who has been somewhat swallowed up by lethargy, is unwilling to leave Venus, while Erikson is obsessive about leaving. Actually, for Erikson it is not so much a question of returning home to Earth, but the thrill and fascination of flying out among the stars again. Erikson leaves. * *Miscellaneous:* Venus seems to be tolerable for Earthmen. The natives, not described closely, are small, somewhat humanoid, intelligent, primitive, and lethargic—perhaps due to the atmosphere. * Routine.

313. **INTO THE DEPTHS.** *Astounding Stories,* June 1935. Ill. Dold.
Short story. * Lovelace descends in a bathysphere into a deep in the Banda Sea. At about 20,000 feet, he reports to the surface, not about typical bathyal life, but about strange lighted spheres that are comparable to suns with planetary systems, and even galaxies. His listeners above believe that he has lost his reason, perhaps from oxygen deprivation. * At bottom, 23,500 feet, Lovelace reports strange artificial towers, together with some sort of demonic sea-men who menace the bathysphere. * The crew above retrieves Lovelace, who has lost his mind. When he recovers, he has no memory of what he has seen, and the

Daniels, David R. (*continued*)
camera, unfortunately, had stopped recording. * Routine.

314. **THE FAR WAY**. *Astounding Stories,* July 1935. Ill. Marchioni.

Short story. * *Time:* from 1937 on to more than a billion years in the future. * A mysterious recurrent situation: Bill Stuart is present for a time, then he suddenly disappears and is not seen for years. This pattern emerges in 1937, 1940, 1952, 1987, 2063, and on into the future. On each occasion Stuart has not changed noticeably in appearance. * A mental superman of about A.D. 1,040,000 explains that Stuart's life-line, which should normally run through the fourth dimension, is warped by the sixth dimension, so that it skips long periods. The future man understands such things, but knows of no other individual who has shared Stuart's disorder. * Most of Stuart's time jumps, which grow progressively longer, are not too eventful. He is careful, indeed, to provide for finances when possible, and when he travels by air he always wears a parachute—which saves his life on one occasion. * In the thirty-fifth century, life becomes more meaningful. The world is unified, and war is breaking out with Mars. Earth, which has long been in peace, has no weapons, but Stuart is able to supply technical knowledge that leads to victory. During this time-stop Stuart falls in love with Queen Eryl, and they marry—but then Stuart disappears. He moves farther and farther into the future. At one time the Earth is enclosed in a crystal sphere to conserve resources. * As he moves along in time, the sun becomes cooler and redder, air becomes more and more rarefied. His death approaches on a nearly airless, lifeless Earth. At this point Queen Eryl appears, apparently transported to him by the savant of 1,040,000. The lovers die together in embrace. * Interesting to see that the time-hopping individual previously met in supernatural fiction (as in Edwin Arnold's *Phra the Phoenician* or George Griffith's *Valdar the Oft-Born*) is now provided with a science-fictional rationale.

315. **THE BRANCHES OF TIME**. *Wonder Stories,* August 1935. Ill. Paul.

Short story. * *Time:* various future dates, A.D. 2090, about A.D. 100,000, and the undated far future. Also the past, the Mesozoic. * James H. Bell, B.S., tells of his adventures. Stumbling on a great discovery, he has built a time machine that operates on the basis of time as a fourth dimension, and has traveled into both past and future. In the future he acquired an atomic engine (invented 1987) and still farther in the future, a flying machine. As he watched, war broke out in 2083 between Japan and the United States, engulfing the world. When the war ended, the only survivors were a handful of scientists and a single soldier (Lark), who ran amok, killing the other survivors and committing suicide. This is the end of the human race. * Bell ventures far into the future without finding any human presence, but in the very distant future he finds a race of intelligent ants who have developed a material civilization. * Bell decides to change history and save the human race. He intercepts Lark before he can kill the scientists. The result is that mankind once again multiplies and spreads over the Earth in a eutopian society accompanied by superscience. * Traveling one hundred thousand years into the future, Bell is greeted by a superman who has been expecting him. The superman, communicating telepathically, begins to explain time to Bell and takes him to the Mesozoic in the time machine. There,

following the instructions of the future man, Bell shoots an ancestral mammal. When the two then return to the beginnings of our historical period, they find, not humans, but reptiles. The two then return to the past, where the superman bids Bell to prevent himself (on the previous visit) from killing the ancestral mammal. Bell does so, and thereby recreates our world. The future man explains that there are many world lines, all existing in an infinity of time. * Bell, narrative finished, announces that he will again travel in time. * Not bad. While not great fiction, this is a pattern-setting story that first set forth a basic motif (branching time) in developed clarity.

316. **THE WAY OF THE EARTH**. *Astounding Stories,* October 1935. Ill. Marchioni.

Short story. * *Time and place:* Earth, A.D. 2637, and the planet Radrok, which may be anywhere in time and space. * *Background:* The rebellion headed by the great scientist and inventor Lee Navarre has been put down, and Navarre has been captured alive and unharmed. He should be executed by the "dictatahr." but the great scientist Noklid, who made the dictator's victory possible, asks for Navarre. Noklid plans to use him in an experiment. * As Noklid explains: He has developed a method for releasing the human mind from its body and directing it elsewhere; he wants to send Navarre's mind down to the center of the Earth, where he expects to find a new state of matter, a new dimensional world, with possible entry to other spheres of existence. Navarre agrees, since the alternative is death. * Descending, Navarre discovers that Noklid's theories are correct. Passing through dimensional boundaries, he emerges on the planet Radrok, which is peopled by humans. There an experiment similar to Noklid's is underway. * *Background:* The planet Radrok, which has double suns, is ravaged by an unusual menace: dragon-like space creatures that eat buildings. Their composition is plastic enough that bullets and similar projectiles do not damage them greatly, and their numbers are so great that destruction of individuals means little. They apparently hover in space in a particular area awaiting the planet to reach this point in its orbit. * The great scientist Hatzho is sure that atomic energy can destroy the creatures, but his world has not yet succeeded in liberating it. Hence, Hatzho has set up an experiment similar to Noklid's on Earth, releasing the mind of his assistant, hoping that he will land on some planet that has atomic energy and then return with the information. * As might be expected, Navarre passes into the Radrokian body, while the Radrokian enters Navarre's Earth body. The story follows Navarre, who is a highly skilled inventor of weapons. Creating atomic energy devices, he exterminates the space creaturs, then usurps the government of the land. Along the way he finds romance. * *Miscellaneous:* Daniels makes the point that Radrok may be the only other planet in the universe where human creatures evolved, whence the attraction between dissociated minds and bodies. * Told in a strange half-jocular manner that does not add to the story. Routine.

317. **DEATH CLOUD**. *Astounding Stories,* February 1936. Ill. Wesso.

Short story. * *Time:* about A.D. 3600. * Background: In the thirtieth century a cosmic cloud was observed to be approaching the Earth. Spectroscopic analysis revealed that it was mostly composed of chlorine. Predictions of its effect on Earth varied. Some thought it would be drawn away by the sun's gravity; others thought it would cause mild irritation; still others believed

Daniels, David R. (*continued*)

that it spelled the end for Terrestrial life. * The worst scenario came to pass, and most of mankind was exterminated. A few farsighted scientists, however, set up sealed glass-domed biospheres, nine of which survived the cloud, which poisoned the atmosphere permanently. Life continued in the domes, but travel outside was possible only in special suits or in sealed vehicles. * For a time the nine cities coexisted peacefully, but hostilities eventually broke out and cities were destroyed. * By the time of our hero, Gar Nel, only two cities remain—Onyal (Gar's city) and Naraval, about two thousand miles away. Both are culturally decadent and have small populations—about two thousand people for Onyal. Relations between the cities are cool, with only occasional contact. * Gar Nel is one of the few exceptions to the decadence of his culture. With the advice of old Rael, his girlfriend's father, he hopes to reinvigorate mankind by increasing contact between the cities, including city exogamy. Unfortunately, his activities are regarded with suspicion by the Naravalians, who attack Onyal. After an air battle, the enemy shatters the dome over Onyal, and in a counterattack Onyal shatters Naraval. * At first this looks like the end for mankind as the chlorine flows in. But, surprise! Old Rael has secretly installed apparatus causing human adaptation to chlorine. The people of Onyal can now emerge from their broken fortress and live outside. Vegetation has already adapted to the new atmosphere. * Told mostly as history, with minimal story development. Little fictional conviction.

DANIELS, J. STALLWORTH

No information. Portrait with story shows a young man.

318. **THE HORRIBLE TRANSFORMATION**. *Science Wonder Stories*, May 1930. Ill. Paul.

Short story. * *Place:* Africa. * Henderson, the narrator, who has not heard from his brother for some time, goes to Africa in search of him. There he hears stories about a fifteen-foot-tall gorilla that was chasing a white man. The locals plan to trap the gorilla, but the narrator has a chance to approach the gorilla first. * The gorilla tells its story. The gorilla is his brother, who was betrayed by his colleague Hohenstein, who transplanted his brain into a gorilla's skull, then inserted growth glands. The giant gorilla, which succeeded eventually in killing Hohenstein when it heard that the operation was irreversible, now awaits a merciful death. The narrator hears the shots and collapses. * All too predictable, and less than routine.

DARE, JOHN C.

No information.

319. **COSMIC POWER**. *Amazing Stories*, April 1931. Ill. Morey.

Short story. * *Time:* A.D. 2000. * The basis of this future civilization is wireless transmission of power, which is broadcast in five bands, according to utility. Unfortunately, the world's electricity is controlled by the infamous Power Trust, headed by the greedy robber baron P. G. Wilson, who repeatedly increases rates. Against Wilson is Food Products, Inc., which has annoyed Wilson by a somewhat altruistic attitude toward feeding the multitudes. * The latest rate increase has just come in, and Cherron, Strom, and others of Food Products, Inc., recognize that they have been forced out of business. At this point, Professor Vondig appears in the office with a solution. As he reveals in

conversation, he is the son of the Vondig who created the technology behind the Power Trust and was then swindled out of his rights. Essentially, what Vondig has to offer is a means to tap the enormous amount of free electricity in space above the Earth. * Cherron and associates go along with Vondig and build a suitable apparatus, then, burning out the Power Trust's plants, supply low-cost electricity in their place. When Wilson discovers who is responsible, he attacks the FPI plant with a multitude of gasoline-powered planes (that would not be affected by disruption of power broadcasts). He and his fleet are destroyed by Vondig's projector. * *Miscellaneous:* Wilson's planes mounted heat rays. * The gasoline engine has almost disappeared, its place taken by electricity. * Synthetic food is now the rule. * Somewhat unusual to find the motif of the robber baron against the defrauded inventor this late.

[Anonymous]
Presumably a British writer.

320. **DEATH DIVE**. *Scoops,* 14 April 1934. Unsigned ill. Boys' fiction. * Short story. * *Time:* probably the near future. * The ship *Commodore*, from New York City, traveling at fifty-five knots, is carrying about four million pounds in bullion. It is kept on course by radio triangulation from sending stations. * Villainy is afoot, however. Gangsters led by one Heinrich murder the guards and cut into the safe, removing the bullion. At the same time, the vessel, its navigation disturbed by the gangsters, strikes a reef and sinks. Many passengers lose their lives, but the gangsters, who are prepared, remove the bullion quietly into a launch and sail away unobserved. * About a week later salvage operations begin. Diver Jim Harper and comrades approach the sunken wreck, which is about 600 fathoms down. As he works through the ship, Jim observes strange things: There are lights, a harpoon where one should not be, and finally an attack with underwater guns by Heinrich and his gang. Heinrich, it seems, does not want it known that the gold was removed before the ship went down, and believes that killing the divers will preserve his secret. An underwater battle between gangsters and divers is ended conclusively when the salvage vessel drops a depth bomb on Heinrich's small submarine. * After it is all over, Jim learns that Scotland Yard was aware of what was going on and used him as a stalking-horse. Oddly enough, he is flattered rather than resentful.

DICKINSON, H. O.

According to Tymn and Ashley, a British writer; otherwise no information.

321. **THE SEX SERUM**. *Wonder Stories*, October 1935. Ill. Winter.

Short story. * *Place:* England. * The narrator claims that he alone knows the solution to one of the great criminal mysteries of the twentieth century. Old Professor Neville and his daughter Jeanette disappeared; an unidentified old woman was found murdered in the professor's house; an unidentified young man was found badly injured in the same house; and Arnold Gilmour, seemingly mad and jailed, proclaimed that he had committed murder. The corpses of the professor and his daughter were never found; the unidentified young man fled from the hospital and has not been seen since; and Gilmour, awaiting trial, committed suicide in jail. * The background to the narrator's solution: Gilmour and Jeanette were in love, but old Professor

Dickinson, H. O. (*continued*)

Neville selfishly discouraged their romance, repeatedly bemoaning the fact that his only child was a girl; he wanted a boy who would not be carried off into marriage. * Reconstruction of events: On the crucial occasion, Gilmour visited the Neville establishment, where the old professor began to crow about his great achievement. As he described it, he had located the master gland determining sex, and with a few drops of secretion from it, he could change a woman to a man, the process releasing hitherto suppressed physiology. Gilmour thought this madness, but when he went to visit Jeanette, he discovered that the professor had already turned her into a young man. * In a rage Gilmour demanded that the professor reverse the process, but he refused, claiming that he had only a few drops of the male-to-female hormone and that he was not sure of its effects. Overpowering the professor, Gilmour inoculated him with the male-to-female hormone to verify its efficacy. It never occurred to him that a sex change would destroy the professor's mentality, but it did. Neville, now an old woman, no longer cared about science and was only interested in growing roses. * Gilmour kills the professor-as-an-old-woman, stuns Jeanette-as-a-young-man, then dashes away, insane. The unidentified young man in the hospital was the transformed Jeanette. * At the close of the story the narrator reveals that he, now the father of two boys and a successful physician, was once Jeanette. * Routine, with some overwriting.

DIFFIN, CHARLES WILLARD (1884-1966)

U.S. engineer, educator and writer. Born in Pennsylvania; graduate of University of Buffalo, major in analytical chemistry. Moved to California, where resident mostly in San Diego and El Cajon at time of present stories. Worked as housing contractor, also airplane salesman. Wrote several volumes in the San Diego City Schools Project on the history of transportation. A popular, fairly prolific contributor to various pulp magazines. An intelligent writer who wrote down for the market. See also C. D. Willard, pseud.

Stories are grouped as The Harkness-Bullard Series and Other Works.

The Harkness-Bullard Series

Three stories set in the 1970s, when space travel is just beginning, the result of private enterprise, rather than government funding. This world is one of enormous international cartels, a flying culture in which professional pilots are rated, and general technological advancement. The first two stories are based on the first wonders of interplanetary exploration; the third seems an afterthought. A fourth story, "Two Thousand Miles Below," is set in the same cosmos, but quite a few years earlier.

322. **DARK MOON.** *Astounding Stories*, May 1931. Unsigned ill. (probably Wesso).

Novelette. * *Time:* 1973. *Places:* New York, the north polar regions, and a new second moon. * Business rivalry, interplanetary adventure, and romance. * In 1973 technology has advanced greatly, and New York is a fantastic megalopolis. Young Walt Harkness of the important Harkness transportation company has just made a resources-straining deal; all might have been well, but a tremendous tsunami overwhelms his properties, and he is almost stripped bare. (Apparently insurance has dropped out of existence.) His creditors, notably Schwarzmann, are murderous crooks. But Harkness has one asset, a newly developed flyer capable of space travel. * The cause of the tsunami is a second, dark moon that has appeared from space and is circling the Earth. In some way not clearly revealed by the author, this has also resulted in the appearance of many ravenous space monsters that attack aircraft in the stratosphere, so that air traffic is badly hampered. * Harkness and his friend/employee master pilot Chet Bullard set out for the dark moon, along the way rescuing a fair maiden (Diane) from space monsters. The three reach the dark moon, which is like a tropical Earth, with enormously hypertrophied, ravenous insect-like creatures. A gigantic spider is particularly dangerous. Also present are submen who are at a paleolithic stage of culture. * After perils and pain the three escape back to Earth. It is now revealed that Diane, who has been living incognito and has just come of age, is now in possession of the hostile trust that has been harassing Harkness. Diane fires the scoundrelly Schwarzmann, and all is well. * *Miscellaneous:* The spaceship uses as fuel a new superexplosive, which Harkness and Chet also apply to small arms. * The dark planet is riddled with gold and also provides a gas that is fatal to the space monsters. * The flying culture of Earth has strictly regulated air levels for licensed operators, with frequent flying patrols. * For a sequel see #323, "Brood of the Dark Moon."

323. **BROOD OF THE DARK MOON.** *Astounding Stories*, August-November 1931. Ill. Wesso.

Novel. * Sequel to #322, "Dark Moon." * *Time:* about 1973. *Place:* a new second moon. * Removing the villainous Schwarzmann from control of Diane's giant holdings was not as easy or as final as Diane and Harkness thought. After various dirty tricks, Schwarzmann captures the three comrades, seizes their ship, and takes them to the dark moon, where the Terrestrials seem trapped. The ship lies inaccessible in a cloud of poison gas, and, in any case, it does not function, for Harkness damaged the mechanism while turning the tables on Schwarzmann and his myrmidons. * The tale follows several subplots: survival amid apemen, carnivorous plants, and giant reptiles; evading Schwarzmann and his followers; secret work, on the part of Dr. Kreiss, a defector from Schwarzmann's group, to penetrate the gas and repair the ship; and encounters with the Krargh, a strange race of tremendous hypnotic power and incredible intellect who live in a pyramid. The Krargh eat hypnotized apemen, but would like to vary their diet with Earthmen. * After back and forth action, the Master, the leader of the Krargh, captures most of the Terrestrials, including Harkness and Diane. Harkness he will torture to death, while he reserves the fate worse than death for Diane. * A resolution comes. Thanks to Kreiss, who sacrifices himself, Chet reaches the spaceship, now operative again, blows up the pyramid, exterminating the super-intellects, and rescues Harkness and Diane. They can now return to Earth, since Schwarzmann is dead. * *Miscellaneous:* The telepathic hypnotics, who are the end result of controlled evolution directed solely at increased mind power, are giant brain sacks, six or seven feet across, with huge single central eyes that blaze when active. Their bodies are tiny and vestigial. For a sequel see #324, "The Finding of Haldgren."

324. **THE FINDING OF HALDGREN.** *Astounding Stories*, April 1932. Ill. Wesso.

Diffin, Charles W. (*continued*)
Novelette. * A sequel to #323, "Brood of the Dark Moon." *
Time: 1974. *Place:* the Moon. * Master Pilot Chester Bullard
and Walter Harkness are about to be officially decorated as the
first men in space when Bullard unexpectedly rejects the honor,
claiming that Frithjof Haldgren anticipated them five years
earlier. Bullard adds that he believes that Haldgren reached the
moon and is now signalling for help. * A bitter quarrel arises
with officialdom, during which Bullard is broken, stripped of his
flying insignia and is as good as outlawed. Moving swiftly,
however, he escapes, and with the assistance of O'Malley, an
Irish-American freighter pilot, reaches Harkness's hidden
spaceship in the Arctic. Bullard and O'Malley set out for the
Moon. * On the moon Bullard, tracing flashes of light that he
believes have been made by Haldgren, finds to his astonishment
a beautiful young woman in a space suit. She is Haldgren's
sister Anita, who had stowed away on his ship. * Bullard and
Anita are now captured by lunar natives, who are humanoid,
dark, clawed, and winged. Since Bullard killed several Lunarians to avoid capture, he, Anita, and Frithjof Haldgren will be
executed, probably tossed into a fiery pit. * They are taken
inside the moon, to an area where there is a breathable atmosphere, to meet their fate. It is a close call until O'Malley
reaches them, and Bullard and the Haldgrens can gain the
spaceship. * Back on Earth, the authorities must eat their words,
and Chet is honored by a promotion to Chief Pilot of Space. *
Miscellaneous: The Lunarians are devolved from an almost
angelic race that created mighty architecture on the surface and
the airlock system that preserves air inside the Moon. * An
unexplained flickering blue luminescence lights the lunar interior.
* At one time Bullard and Anita were in free fall to the hollow
interior of the Moon. * Starts as a reasonable action story, but
decays in mid-narrative.

Other Works

325. **SPAWN OF THE STARS**. *Astounding Stories*,
February 1930. Unsigned ill.
(Reprinted in Conklin, *Best of Science Fiction*.)
Short story. * *Place:* mostly California and New York City. *
Cyrus R. Thurston buys a plane and takes off with his friend
Slim Riley, an A.A.S. pilot, for California. Along the way they
observe a huge glass-like bubble on the ground. Landing to
examine it, they see a "loathsome . . . sickening . . . flabby . . .
nauseous [*sic*]" amoeboid with a wicked eye climbing into the
bubble. The creature has been eating the local cows. * This is
not the only sighting of the space amoebas. A bubble appears
over New York City, where it destroys a plane. In a short time
reports of bubbles and the fantastic damage they have done come
from all over the world. * There are five bubbles. Their exhaust
is so far into the range of supercold that it destroys anything it
touches. The army and the navy are helpless before the alien
ships, which utilize atomic bombs. * Eventually, one of the ships
is shot down, almost by accident, and some of its armament is
retrieved. Meanwhile the other four ships are at work destroying
San Diego and Berlin with their atomic weapons. The alien attack strategy is to form a square, then drop bombs that rise in
mushrooms of flame and smoke. * Professor MacGregor has a
clue. The alien ships are powered by a sort of fusion process,
activated by light. MacGregor then builds a photic apparatus

that will activate the bombs that the ships carry. But delivering
the attack is a suicide mission. Riley volunteers. The four alien
ships are destroyed just after they have wiped out the air force.
* *Miscellaneous:* The amoeboids are photophobic. * There just
are no good amoebas. The first one encountered tried to eat
Thurston when it emerged from the crashed globe.

326. **THE MOON MASTER**. *Astounding Stories*, June
1930. Ill. Wesso.
Short story. * *Place:* mostly on the Moon. * Jerry Foster is
hiking in the mountains when he stumbles on the establishment
of Thomas Winslow, a recluse inventor who has been defrauded
by the monopolies. After some misunderstandings the two men
become friendly, and Winslow reveals that he has released
atomic energy. He breaks down water into protons and neutrons,
stores them in a little flask, and utilizes them as power. His
purpose? A trip to the Moon in a cylindrical spaceship that he
has built. * The two men fly off, landing on the dark side of the
Moon during lunar night. When day approaches, frozen gases
and ice melt, forming an atmosphere into which the men can
venture. There are vegetation and horrible monstrous reptilian
carnivores that beset the explorers. But figures emerge from
camouflage, beat off the monsters, and capture the Terrestrials in
a net. * The Moon-people are completely human, perhaps barbaric in culture, and are ruled by a cruel, oppressive priesthood.
The heart of their religion is a sanctum that is lighted by sunlight
reflected from gold; within this shrine dwells a horrible spider-
like hypnotic monster that eats human sacrifices. * Foster and
Winslow win through, despite many perils, injuries, and hardships; during this, they are helped by the Princess Marahna, who
is in love with Jerry. Jerry kills the hypnotic monster, Winslow
saves them from a frenzied attack with an improvised flame-
thrower, and the priesthood is overthrown. Jerry could have
stayed as Marahna's consort and ruler of the land, but reluctantly
returns to Earth with Winslow. * Fairy tale-like quality.

327. **THE POWER AND THE GLORY**. *Astounding
Stories*, July 1930. Ill. J. Fleming Gould.
(Reprinted in Ashley, *History of the Science Fiction Magazine*,
Vol. One.)
Short-short story. * Old Professor Eddinger receives an excited
summons from Avery, his prize pupil. When the professor
arrives, Avery demonstrates his discovery: an elaborate apparatus
that releases atomic energy. Avery, wildly enthusiastic,
proclaims that the new energy source will release mankind from
slavery. But the professor, to Avery's annoyance, is unenthusiastic. Making a small adjustment to Avery's apparatus,
Eddinger shows how it can be converted into a potent death ray.
Avery still maintains that good will triumph; the professor
predicts evil. * Actually, the professor had developed the same
device years earlier, but suppressed it. Will Avery? * Unusual
for its pessimistic appraisal of a great scientific advance. Today
the subject is clichéd, but the story was fresh when it was
written.

328. **THE PIRATE PLANET**. *Astounding Stories*,
November 1930-February 1931. Ill. Wesso.
Novel. * World-saving adventure. * *Place:* California and Venus.
* Flashes are seen on Venus, and heavy missiles hit the Earth.
A spaceship the size of an enormous building hovers over cities
and releases a deadly poison gas. What does all this mean? *
Lieutenant McGuire of the U.S.A.S. and Professor Sykes, a
prominent astronomer, are kidnapped by the aliens and taken to

Diffin, Charles W. (*continued*)

Venus, where they learn what is happening. The aliens, who are humanoid but extremely nasty in appearance and behavior, soon inform our heroes that they plan to conquer the Earth. Reason: Lebensraum. Venus is mostly water-covered, with only a few islands. The Earth seems doomed, but salvation comes from two directions. First, McGuire and Sykes, after the usual pulp fisticuffs, reach a transmitter and send a message to Earth, telling Lieutenant Blake of the U.S.A.S. to look up a certain recluse inventor who claims to have built a spaceship. Second, at a moment of great peril McGuire and Sykes are rescued by a truly human race, who are almost superhuman in physique and mentality. These people possess a superscience, but are quietistic and pacifistic. As they explain matters: The aliens who have been causing the trouble are really descended from rats, and all their scientific prowess and technology, including wonderful crystal cities, have been stolen from the true humans, whom they have almost exterminated. The true humans live underground protected by force screens. * Back on Earth, Blake locates the recluse inventor, and the United States builds an invasion fleet of spaceships from his plans. The American fleet, with the unexpected assistance of the Venusian humans, defeats the rat-men, who are driven back underground. * Part of the motivation is the rat-king's kidnapping of the beautiful Althora, McGuire's girlfriend. * *Miscellaneous:* mechanical thought-reading, a little telepathy, various rays. * Routinely bad.

329. **WHEN THE MOUNTAIN CAME TO MIRA-MAR.** *Astounding Stories*, March 1931. Ill. Wesso.

Short story. * *Time:* 1932. *Place:* California. * An earthquake knocks off the side of Mount Sentinel, near where Garry Connell has a date farm. On investigating, he finds a carved aperture and a passageway into the mountain, leading to a huge lighted room, within which is a glowing ceiling object and a collection of metal chests. Examining apparatus around the chests, he releases a lever that had become jammed, whereupon ancient machinery begins to function. * In a short time two chests open, releasing a huge, ugly, nasty-looking black man and a beautiful white woman. Connell recognizes the man as the evil, cruel king depicted in carvings on the wall. * Horab, the black king, is very hostile, but the young woman, Luhra, who is friendly, explains matters telepathically to Garry. In the far past Horab, who is master of a sword-and-ray-gun science, set up apparatus to place himself, Luhra (who is from another land), and a band of warriors into suspended animation for one hundred years. At that time, what is now a mountain inland was an island in the sea. But the mechanism jammed and did not function until Garry set it in motion. * Black warriors also awaken in their chests, and there is a battle royal, which ends suddenly when the warriors drop dead, their partial vitality exhausted. * Connell and Luhra are still in danger from Horab, but all ends well. Horab dies heroically, facing a renewed earthquake. Connell gets a pre-paleolithic princess and a casket of gems. * Probably suggested by H. Rider Haggard's *When the World Shook.*

330. **HOLOCAUST.** *Astounding Stories*, June 1931. Ill. Wesso.

Short story. * Imaginary war in 1939. * The narrator reminisces about Paul Stravoinski, who for a short time was almost de facto dictator of the world. * There is a new government in Russia, and after a short burst of propaganda about brotherhood and cooperation, Russian ambassadors present ultimatums to the world's major capitals. "Surrender, or else." * The else, which soon happens, means enormous flights of armored air cruisers and extremely powerful guided torpedoes, which the Russians seem to have in inexhaustible quantity. * Europe falls to the Russians. Then Dictator Paul announces on the radio that he will destroy the Capitol at Washington. He does this with an atomic explosive. * By now the narrator realizes that Dictator Paul must be his former friend Paul Stravoinski, who had been working on atomic theory and was also embittered against the democracies. * The narrator appeals to Paul, without success. But when Paul sees the corpse of a former girlfriend, who had been killed in the war, he has a change of heart. He now turns his weapons on the Russians. The war is soon over; Paul is dead; and a better world emerges. * "Holocaust" exemplifies the evolution of a subgenre. In earlier science-fiction the imaginary war story was a cautionary tale with a fair amount of hypocrisy; in "Holocaust" it is purely an adventure story with a dab of sentiment.

331. **THE HAMMER OF THOR.** *Astounding Stories*, March 1932. Ill. Wesso.

Short story. * *Time:* 1943. *Place:* U.S.S.R. and elsewhere. * Danny O'Rourke of the Air Fire Force is in the Urals instructing the Russians on fire control, when a strange gigantic man is brought in. Danny believes the man is from space, but the Russians laugh—until the man pulls out a tiny ray tube, wrecks the station, kills much of the personnel, and disappears. * Some time later, incredibly hot fires break out over much of the world. Whole cities are destroyed. Standard fire fighting equipment is useless, for pools of molten rock underlie the blazing areas. * Danny, putting two and two together, realizes that the space stranger must be responsible for the fires. A young scientist friend of Danny's works out the technical basis of the fire weapon. The strange ship is discharging electricity to ground itself. This knowledge does little good for a time. * Eventually, Danny takes up his ship with a disintegrator that also accumulates electricity; when he approaches the stranger's ship, both vessels go down in a titanic explosion.

332. **TWO THOUSAND MILES BELOW.** *Astounding Stories*, June 1932-January 1933. Ill. Wesso.

Novel. * *Time:* perhaps thirty thousand years ago, and 1942. *Place:* Nevada, points underneath, and the center of the hollow Earth. * In a prologue, primitive men, concerned about the approach of glacial cold, take refuge in deep caves. There, sealed in by the ice, they develop a science based on the Earth's internal heat. One group evolves away from *Homo sapiens;* the other remains stable as a superior form of mankind. * In 1942, Dean Rawson, a rising young mining engineer, convinces a huge syndicate to back him in a scheme to drill heat wells in order to tap the Earth's heat for power. In the Tonah Basin, Nevada, the work goes nicely until the drill reaches a point about ten miles below the surface. Then, the camp is raided by mysterious figures who drag Rawson down into the Earth. His protégé Smith escapes and vainly tries to alert the authorities. * The invaders continue to pour out of the drilling, and in a short time much of the Southwest is overrun by strange-looking men from inside the Earth. Tall, with pointed heads and huge glaring eyes, either red-skinned (the leader caste) or yellow-skinned (the slave caste), they possess fantastically powerful flamethrowers, a disintegrating ray, and heat guns. The air force fails disastrously against them, as do ground troops. * Meanwhile, Rawson is

Diffin, Charles W. (*continued*)

dragged down into dark tunnels that are lit only by the radiation of molten rocks, which the red men create with their rays. This underground world of the molemen is incredibly hot, to the point where Rawson is burned when he touches certain floors and walls. * After a short period of captivity and ordeals, Rawson is sentenced to death in molten lava, but at the moment of utmost peril he is rescued from the cruel molemen by Loah, a beautiful young white woman. She and her white associates, spiriting Rawson out of the hot tunnels of the molemen, take him in an antigravity car to the center of the hollow Earth. There Rawson finds a near eutopia, with a handsome, kindly people; a wonderful landscape with vegetation; enormous beautiful crystal formations; and a small internal sun. And the people speak English! Explanation: One of the crystals acts as a radio receiver (The story was written during the days when radio crystal sets were still in marginal use), and the People of the Light have learned English from it as a sacred language. * There are problems. The People of Light are pacifistic and cannot fight against the savage molemen, from whom they are separated by rock formations. And they are few in number. Over the millennia the small sea in the center of the Earth has expanded, so that only one small island remains. * And now, the red molemen, who have followed Loah when she rescued Rawson, are about to invade the land. Rawson kills off the first batch of invaders with hydrocyanic acid gas obtained from local vegetation, and proposes a tube that will connect the inner ocean with the heated areas of the molemen. This tube will serve a double function, steam out the molemen and restore dry land to the People of the Light. * While this project is underway, Rawson and Loah venture back into the molemen's tunnels, where Rawson kills the moleman king. But they are in imminent danger of being captured. * Meanwhile, back on the surface, poison gas turns the tide against the molemen, and Smith, with military backing, enters the underground world, where he rescues Rawson and Loah. The war is over when steam and hot water destroy the heated tunnels. * *Miscellaneous:* The whites split off from the molemen millennia ago, sealing themselves off in the center of the Earth and remaining phenotypically stable, while the molemen changed. * Both cultures make use of minerals that increase and decrease the force of gravity. * The inner sun emits rays of repulsion, rather than attraction. * The publishing history of the present story is obscure. The Harkness-Bullard stories (#322, #323, #324), though published earlier, refer to events within this story. It is possible that Clayton Publications, after purchasing the present story, held it back for a time before publishing it.

333. **LAND OF THE LOST.** *Astounding Stories,* December 1933-January 1934. Ill. Amos Sewell and Mark Marchioni.

Novelette or short novel. * *Place:* on a shell of strange matter that surrounds the Earth; a modified Fortean concept. * James Blaine, inspecting engineer for the new Metropole Bridge in New York, runs into strange phenomena. First, as he is watching the discharged anarchist agitator Portrero trying to stir up trouble, Blaine sees the whole area disappear, cut down to bedrock. Portrero is reasonably assumed to be dead. No explanation can be found for the incident. * Two years later, when the bridge is finished, a small metal ball floats down from the sky with a message from Portrero, who vows revenge. Then, when the

bridge is opened, whole spans disappear. For reasons beyond the comprehension of the reader, Blaine is held responsible and suspended. But the phenomena continue. Blaine's girlfriend Sylvia Brewster, the daughter of his boss, is wrenched into the sky away from her father's penthouse, whereupon Blaine volunteers to undergo the same experience, to follow Sylvia. He finds himself scooped up. * *Background:* The Earth is surrounded by a sphere of strange solid matter (transparent from below), upon which live vegetation, animals, and intelligent beings. As explained, this ring formed when the Earth cooled, as space radiation struck stray matter and consolidated it. In a sense the shell-sphere is contrary to Earth, with a different balance of gravity and repulsion. When breaks sometimes occur in the shell, the upset in balance dashes terrestrial matter up to the shell and vice versa. This is the explanation of the first incident, the accident in which Portrero disappeared. * On the shell world with a group of his more rabid followers, Portrero has learned how to control the gravitational phenomenon and plans enormous damage to the Earth. Aiding him are the shell natives, gigantic, somewhat stupid humanoids with a primitive culture. Apart from Portrero and the giants is a race of pallid white men who maintain a superscience with full control of gravity and much else. They are almost totally isolationist, xenophobic, passionless, ultra-rational, arrogant, and pitiless. * Blaine, on arriving at the shell, finds Sylvia, who is being held captive by Portrero for a purpose the reader can imagine. Seizing one of Portrero's land rovers, they escape, hoping to find refuge and help among the pallid whites. Unfortunately, the pallids do not care what the mad Portrero does, nor will they help Blaine and Sylvia. They permit the fugitives to enter the force-zone-guarded city for a time, as low-grade workers, but expel them when Blaine (to protect a friend) criticizes the engineering of the city. * After back-and-forth action, Portrero and the more villainous of his followers are killed, and Blaine and Sylvia descend back to Earth. * *Miscellaneous:* Subject to the frigid whites is an oppressed race of humane, normal people who help the fugitives in small ways. * No explanation is given for human forms on the shell. * Probably written to fulfill the requirements of the late Clayton *Astounding Stories,* with abundant physical struggle and fisticuffs; more junky and disorganized than other work by Diffin.

334. **THE LONG NIGHT.** *Astounding Stories,* May 1934. Ill. Marchioni.

Short story. * *Time:* The author is inconsistent; either a thousand years in the future or many thousand years. * Garry Coyne, biologist, has isolated the chemical basis of suspended animation from lizards that have survived for ages entombed in rock. Now he intends to experience the future. Injecting his discovery into his veins, he climbs into his coffin and begs an unwilling friend to preserve him. * Garry awakens in a dust-filled room in a gigantic sphere that has been built to house him. Exploring a little, he finds that he is above a beautiful, titanic city that is seemingly deserted and falling to ruin. To add to the mystery, a canned voice and projection of a long-dead ruler named Tahjor explain matters somewhat, but not enough. * Venturing into the city and exploring, Coyne encounters an enormous humanoid female, ten-feet-tall, naked and savage, who captures him and takes him to her pen, where tiny vicious males scuttle around. She is about to brand him when Lorell, a normal woman, appears and rescues him. Together they flee to Lorell's

Diffin, Charles W. (*continued*)

people. * *Background:* After wars and several geological upheavals, an Oriental people conquered the Western hemisphere, Tahjor being one of their last rulers. As a result of the purple plague, the Orientals have since died out, but their laboratory creations, the vicious, subhuman, brutal "homoids," survive and swarm over the area. * Lorell's folk, a small group of normal men and women, live in isolation in the nearby mountains. As Coyne learns to his astonishment, these people have a messianic cult about him; as Co-heen he is supposed to save them when he awakens. * Unfortunately, the hordes of homoids have followed Coyne and Lorell to the mountain retreat, and it looks like the end of humanity. But Coyne activates an ancient flying machine and fetches from the city an apparatus that in some fashion (at the last minute) removes the homoid threat. The reader may be puzzled, for the author is not clear about what has happened. * As a teaser, during the final battle, Coyne, injured, momentarily slides back to our present. His friend makes a sage comment about all time existing together, whereupon Coyne slides back in the future, to the arms of Lorell. * A weak story with evidences of hasty writing. It is possible that Diffin drew on E. R. Burroughs's *Tarzan and the Ant Men*.

335. **BLUE MAGIC.** *Astounding Stories,* November 1935-February 1936. Ill. Dold.

Novel. * A femme fatale and an iron-jawed he-man in a struggle for power and romance. * *Place:* introductory sections somewhere in the Northwest, but mostly on an unidentified satellite of Jupiter and Jupiter itself. * As Diffin puts it, in a teasing summary, "To Rance Driggs, forestry agent, magic seems to have descended on Black Mountain." There are inexplicable three-toed footprints, a giant greenish humanoid that lurks in the shadows, a paralysis ray, a spaceship, and a magic jewel that shows the incredibly beautiful, but cruel and lustful Dra Vonga, ruler of the satellite Xandros. * Almost before Rance knows it, he and girlfriend Katherine Putnam are the captives of Dra Vonga on Xandros. Since Rance is manly, outspoken, and presumably very handsome, the blonde temptress Dra Vonga is attracted to him. Katherine, however, she resents and regards with scorn, puzzled that Rance should prefer her. * The ins and outs of the plot need not be detailed; only motifs and main themes shall be commented on. (1) The science of Dra Vonga. As a heritage from her "dead" father, Dra Vonga has a bewildering array of magic flames that perform various actions, such as withering limbs. She also has the means of controlling time, so that duration differs, according to her will, between Earth and Jupiter. Thus, at the end of the story, when Rance and Katherine return to Earth, they discover that their hair-raising adventures of days, perhaps weeks, took only an hour or two of Earth time. (2) The cohorts of Dra Vonga. In addition to her purely human followers, whose throne she has usurped, she has imported giant green humanoid creatures from Jupiter to do her will. Dra Vonga also makes use of ferocious carnivorous beasts (karanas) from Jupiter. (3) The intentions of Dra Vonga. In addition to winning Driggs, she wants hidden magic that her magic crystal globe has told her Driggs can produce. This turns out to be fire, hitherto unknown on Xandros. Dra Vonga's aim, of course, is the conquest of Earth and other planets. (4) Dra Vonga's reluctant collaborator. Helping Dra Vonga to build a fleet of spaceships incorporating a space-changing principle is Duvaurier, a pioneer French space traveler who crashed on Xandros.

Duvaurier, while recognizing the evil component in Dra Vonga, is madly in love with her. (5) The fate of Dra Vonga. After battles between Dra Vonga's green soldiery and the rebellious humans, and an enormous forest fire set by ranger Driggs, Dra Vonga is killed by radiation evoked by her father, not really dead, but mad and long a captive. * *Miscellaneous:* Both Jupiter and its unidentified satellite are suitable for humans. * Little to recommend. The treatment, in summary, may seem parodic of the old-fashioned romantic adventures of the Munsey magazines a generation earlier, but this was probably not the author's intention. More likely is the influence of the *Flash Gordon* comic strips. Dra Vonga is reminiscent of Queen Asura with her magical science.

DOANE, WARREN F.

It is not certain whether this is Warren F. Doane, U.S. writer on economic subjects and author of *The Flight of Capital and Industry from Massachusetts* (1935) and *Billions for Boondoggling* (1936), an argument for flood control.

336. **THE ALCHEMY OF IAN BJORNSEN.** *Amazing Stories,* January 1934. Ill. Morey.

Short story. * *Place:* an introductory episode in Port Said, with most of the action earlier in Tibet. * The narrator wonders about Robertson, who displayed incredible strength in a street action in Port Said. On a later meeting, Robertson, who is obviously an unhappy man, tells his story. * While exploring Tibet he stumbled upon a hidden retreat in which Bjornsen, a European scientist, was conducting secret research. One of Bjornsen's results is a pill that conveys superstrength for a short time. * Bjornsen welcomes Robertson, for he has need for a skilled assistant, his daughter Ola being unwilling. * Bjornsen has discovered a way to dissolve a living creature into certain liquids, then after further preparation cause the creature to reemerge, living and unharmed. The process works with dogs, as Bjornsen demonstrates, but he must try it on a human, himself. Robertson reluctantly agrees to assist, and Bjornsen is suitably melted down, ready for retrieving. * At this point a horrible accident takes place. A gigantic tiger-like beast, whom Robertson has previously seen, breaks into the laboratory, and during the melée, falls into the tank and dissolves. Thus, when Bjornsen is retrieved, his molecules are mixed with those of the tiger, and he is a ferocious monstrosity. Robertson and Ola manage to place the monster in a cage, but as it is struggling, it obtains some of Bjornsen's strength tablets, smashes the cage, and escapes. * Ola disappears, and there seems to be no way to separate Bjornsen from the tiger. * Robertson plans to return to Tibet and try to undo the disastrous experiment. Some years later, his skeleton is found along with that of an inexplicable tiger-man.

DOLD, DOUGLAS M[ERIWETHER]. (c.1890-1933?)

U.S. editor, author, brother of William Elliott Dold. Although the exact circumstances are not known, Dold seems to have done some work on *Miracle Science and Fantasy Stories.* He also served for a brief period in an editorial capacity with Clayton *Astounding Stories* and other Clayton magazines. Occasionally contributed to other pulp magazines, notably *Adventure.* According to Harold Hersey's (often unreliable) autobiography, *Pulpwood Editor,* and other sources, Douglas Dold was blind in his later years and worked with readers, although it is difficult

Dold, Douglas M. (*continued*)
to accept that a totally blind person was capable of carrying on editorial work. In all probability Dold was legally blind, but did have a certain amount of vision. On the *Astounding* masthead Douglas Dold is listed as Dr. Dold, but according to fan legend, this was a degree awarded to Dold by editor Harry Bates, for prestige reasons. Dold is also said to have sold plots to other authors. The circumstances and date of his death are also unclear. According to Murray Leinster, Dold died as the result of a fire in his home. According to Hugh Cave, Dold kept poisonous snakes as a hobby and died of snakebite. It is possible that neither account is correct.

337. **VALLEY OF SIN. A DOUBLE BOOK-LENGTH NOVEL.** *Miracle Science and Fantasy Stories,* April/May 1931. Ill., including map, Elliott Dold.

Lost-race novel. * *Place:* Introductory episodes in New York City; then the Sudan, somewhere west of Fashoda. * When Dr. Anthony Penn assists at a traffic accident, the dying victim, a gangster named Jim Points, bequeaths to him his effects and a male dog named Violet. Among Points's effects is a tile brick, which when broken reveals several ivory slips upon which is Arabic writing. * A succession of events leads to the following: The ivory slips describe the Valley of Sin, which was established by Ancient Egyptians as a penal colony, is fabulously rich, and may still flourish. * Rival expeditions set out to find it: first, Penn, Professor Sharp, and Sharp's beautiful daughter Eve, and second, Hubert Orne, a ruthless former associate of Sharp's, and Professor Vandeen. * The way into the hidden land is hidden by an artificial lake, created by a huge dam, which the Penn-Sharp expedition demolishes. After various perils Penn and associates enter the lost land, which is inhabited by a very strange skeletal sort of people, who look like living mummies and are violently xenophobic. An extremely complex series of attacks, repulses, slaughters, captures, escapes, and perils follows, all pointless to describe. * In some fashion Orne manages to become associated with an ancient prophecy, so that he is accepted by the natives, leading them against the Penn-Sharp expedition in many attacks. Eventually, however, the natives rebel against Orne and mummify him alive; Vandeen is killed; and Penn, Sharp, and Eve Sharp escape (pockets filled with gems) by an alternate route. The alternate route, unfortunately, opens watergates that submerge the land. * Dold really says little about the lost race, which is ambiguously posited as Tuareg with survivals of Ancient Egyptian culture, or perhaps evolved Ancient Egyptian. * Obvious dime-novel elements, hardly worth reading. There is no question of plotting, only a succession of hostile encounters as goods and bads run about.

DOLD, ELLIOTT or ELLIOT (1892-1957)
Business name of William Elliott Dold, Jr., U.S. artist, brother of Douglas Dold. Born in New York City, educated at William and Mary; studied at the Art Students League, New York under George Bridgman. Well-known in science-fiction circles for his magazine illustrations, which were the epitome of Art Deco style, with heavy blacks, geometric constructions, and powerful, oppressive atmosphere. At his best a fine illustrator. According to his account in *Fantasy Magazine*, Elliott Dold also served as managing editor for *Miracle Science and Fantasy Stories,* handling stories, art work, production, and other matters. He also claimed to have been largely responsible for the inception of the

magazine. Although the present story is accredited to Elliott Dold, it was obviously written by the same person as #337, "Valley of Sin." It is probable that both stories were cooperative ventures between Douglas Dold and Elliott Dold, divided in attribution. For reasons not known, at times Dold attributed his art work as Elliot Dold.

338. **THE BOWL OF DEATH. A COMPLETE NOVEL.** *Miracle Science and Fantasy Stories,* June/July 1931. Ill., including map, Elliott Dold.

Novelette. * Lost race story. *Place:* somewhere in Mexico. * Roger Dale, whose plane is almost out of gas, crash lands near a mountain range. After a little exploration, looking for water, he stumbles upon a cave that leads into the mountains. First he passes through an area filled with corpses of conquistadores petrified in perfect condition, then emerges into a small hidden valley, where vegetation and animal life are characterized by a peculiar bloated hypertrophy. Although enormous in size, they are extremely delicate, and a good blow with a club will smash them. * Dale rescues Xalia, a handsome young redheaded woman, from giant bats and enters the politics of Japaxlan. Xalia is the last of the true Mictli, descended from Aztecs and the conquistador leader Valdes. She is also the Holy Priestess who alone knows how to prepare the sacred drink from peyote buttons. * There are machinations. The swollen Romero, descendant of a rival, evil conquistador, wants to marry Xalia, and if not marry her, sacrifice her on the altar of Taotl (Quetzalcoatl). * Perils, pursuits, escapes, some of them through the boiling waters of a geyser, end with the eventual escape of Dale and Xalia. Conquistador armor and weapons help. * Dale gets his plane going, and he and Xalia (with golden crown and appurtenances) are married in New Mexico. * No merit. Like "The Valley of Sin," obvious dime-novel antecedents, but in this case mixed with A. Merritt.

DONITZ, HAROLD
No information.

339. **A VISITOR FROM THE TWENTIETH CENTURY.** *Amazing Stories,* May 1928. Ill. Paul.

Short story. Really an essay describing a future society, with minimal fictional elements. * *Time:* the late twenty-first century. *Place:* New York City. * Markham, a fairly prominent architect who is planning to enter a city-planning contest, falls asleep, to awaken in the New York of the last part of the twenty-first century. His coming is not unusual, for, as he is efficiently processed, he is told that men from the past are often summoned to the future world. * The remainder of the story is pretty much a description of the future New York. The city is composed of identical twenty-five story buildings about a quarter of a mile on each side, surrounded by park areas, connected by multiple-lane moving sidewalks. There are only twenty-five such cities in the country, each with an enormous population, and a couple of factory cities; the rest of the country is devoted to parks or agricultural land. There are no more streets, roads, or automobiles. (Petroleum ran out around 1975, and substitutes were not really effective.) With the abandonment of automobiles, the damage they caused—pollution, urban decay, rural devastation—was halted. Tracked trolley-powered vehicles with automatic avoidance and anti-collision mechanisms are used for travel beyond local limits. There are also interurban pneumatic tubes, and a transcontinental tube is now under construction.

Donitz, Harold (*continued*)

Monorail equivalents of trains also exist. Air travel is possible with gigantic rapid dirigibles. There are no more ocean liners, but gigantic sea sledges take their place. * To continue the Bellamistic aspect of this world, work loads are delimited by the pleasantness or unpleasantness of the task. * Markham's visit comes to a conclusion. High up on one of the giant dwelling complexes, he slips and is in danger of falling, whereupon he awakens back in his own time. It was all a dream. * He now decides to redesign his contribution to the contest, using elements from the dream/future, but his entry loses to a gimcracky project. * Literate and intelligent, but rather pointless except as a minor attempt at an architectural utopia.

DORNISCH, ALCUIN [JOSEPH] (1901-1987)

U.S. (Pennsylvania) author, journalist, local historian. Also wrote novel *The Bloody Forest* (1935).

340. **SOLARIUS.** *Amazing Stories,* December 1932. Short-short story. * Events inside the sun, with various physical processes personified, on up to an emperor. The story centers on R45-L, a sector chief or military commander in the perpetual war against sun spots. R45-L is disgruntled, for the emperor, who takes the army for granted, is more interested in the solar prominences that the soldiers create as an aesthetic activity than in military matters. After winning a battle, R45-L is offered position in the interior of the sun. This is a promotion, but R45-L rejects it, preferring his more hazardous post on the front line. * A curiosity.

DOUGLAS, WILLIAM WITHERS

No information.

341. **THE ICE MAN.** *Amazing Stories,* February 1930. Ill. Lyman Anderson.

Short story. * The first person narrative of Marcus Publius, who has escaped from the B——— Insane Asylum. Originally written in Latin, his narrative has been translated by a friend. The point of the story is semisatirical comment on our civilization as seen by a Roman. * The narrative: In 59 B.C., when Julius Caesar ruled Rome, Marcus volunteered to take a sleep-inducing drug and be placed in a cask of frozen oil, with the understanding that he would be awakened in a year. Actually, the cask was fished out of the sea in 1928 by Professor Emil Haskell, who revived Marcus with adrenalin. The professor held Marcus, against his wishes, in a mild captivity while he taught him English and took down detailed notes about life in Rome. Marcus, who is an extremely strong man, escaped, and after the professor's house caught on fire, incinerating the professor, was free to wander around New York with cash from the professor's wallet. * Marcus comments mostly on material culture, with fear of automobiles, etc., but also falls into the clutches of a gold-digging young waitress, who takes him in hand. After a riot in a speakeasy Marcus is arrested, interrogated, and put into an insane asylum. * In the hands of a more skilled writer, this might have been amusing, but here it is a rather clumsy succession of banalities. * An odd note, not totally relevant here, but amusing: On opening the magazine, which had been stored in a metal box for perhaps fifty years, I found handwritten sheets on which I had translated the first part of Marcus's story into Latin—undoubtedly when I was in Boston Latin School around 1936. I now marvel at how much I have forgotten!

DOW, PACKARD

No information. Portrait accompanying the story shows a young man.

342. **THE WINGED MENACE.** *Wonder Stories Quarterly,* Spring 1931. Ill. Marchioni.

Short story. * *Place:* Algeria. * Barton and his niece Susan, tourists in Algiers, are fascinated by the folklore about the strange ruins, which include a pyramid not far from the city. The Arabs will have nothing to do with the pyramid, claiming that it is haunted, and the local French authorities are not interested in it, claiming that it is too dangerous to enter because of collapsing and pitting. * Susan and her Italian friend Count Dodo decide to visit the ruins. They do not return, and Susan's uncle and his friend Stanley, searching for the missing two people, make a preliminary investigation of the pyramid. They are appalled at what they discover. After considerable conversation, complaint to the American consul and to French higher-ups, the men invade the pyramid via a great shaft that leads downwards. Descending on rope ladders, they discover more than they expected. The entire area is undermined by a system of caves, some of which show artificial working, and it is filled with a myriad of intelligent, giant vampire bats. French troops drive out the bat-people and rescue the lost explorers. * *Miscellaneous:* While it is not entirely clear, it seems that the bat-people display a certain artistic talent on the walls of their domain. * Less than routine.

DOYLE, SIR ARTHUR CONAN (1859-1930)

Kt., M.D., LL.D. * British (Scottish) physician (ophthalmology), author. Productive writer of fiction, essays, war propaganda during the Boer War, and, in his last years, apologetics for Spiritualism and occult phenomena. Now remembered mostly for detective stories featuring Sherlock Holmes. In addition to the present work, wrote a considerable amount of excellent science-fiction, which is described in full in *Science-Fiction:The Early Years.*

343. **THE POISON BELT.** *Scoops,* 5 May-9 June 1934. Unsigned ill.

(First published in *Strand Magazine,* March-July 1913. Book publication: London: Hodder and Stoughton, 1913; New York: George H. Doran, 1913, and many reprints.)

Novel. * World peril and the irascible Professor George Challenger. Malone, the narrator of *The Lost World* and a close friend of Challenger's, receives a summons to visit Challenger, bringing along cylinders of oxygen. He and his comrades from *The Lost World* (Professor Summerlee and Lord John Roxton) arrive, after quarreling and behaving childishly on the train, to learn that the world is passing through a belt of poisonous ether—which has affected their emotional balance. But with oxygen and willpower one can hold off the effects of the ether. * The comrades and Mrs. Challenger seal themselves in a room with oxygen and watch the world die around them. * When their oxygen gives out, they smash a window, deciding that death is inevitable, to discover that the air has cleared. * Setting out in a motorcar, the comrades tour the London area, discovering death everywhere. But on returning to Challenger's establishment, they observe that the birds are singing again. The poisonous ether was not deadly, merely anaesthetic, and mankind is alive. While there were some deaths and damage, the situation is not so bad as was feared. * A good adventure story.

DRENNEN, PAUL

No information.

344. HEADHUNTERS FOOLED AND FOILED.
Amazing Stories, August/September issue, 1933.

Short-short story. * Mostly a monologue by a con man trying to inveigle a hotel reporter into investing money. * The con man, who goes by the name of Houdini Burbank, claims to have spent about thirty years in South America trying to develop tagua, commonly known as vegetable ivory, on a commercial basis. (Tagua is the fruit of the corozo palm; it is extremely hard, fine textured, and very similar to animal ivory.) * Burbank achieved considerable results, producing nuts the size of baseballs, which his employees carved and stained to look like small Indian shrunken heads. Unfortunately, some of the heads reached the Jivaro headhunters, who, recognizing the quality of Burbank's wares, kidnapped him and demanded to know the process, so that they could apply it to their own shrunken heads. Burbank, being a canny man, stalled, claiming magical necessities, until he was able to escape. Now back in the United States he is seeking investors to help him secure his plantation against the Jivaros. * Cleverly handled, with good dialogue, but probably not science-fiction.

DRESSLER, DANIEL, M.D.

No information.

345. THE WHITE ARMY. *Amazing Stories,* September 1929. Ill. Mackay.

(Reprinted in Wollheim, *Every Boy's Book of Science Fiction.*) Longish short story. * The experiences of a personalized white corpuscle who leads the reader through a fairly thorough exposition of the function of the blood stream. The story differs from similar, earlier pathetic fallacy stories about blood corpuscles in being more detailed and factual. At the end the leucocyte dies when an infected appendix, where he was fighting invasive germs, is removed. * Literate, but a textbook might be more entertaining. Scientific fiction, not science-fiction.

346. THE BRAIN ACCELERATOR. *Amazing Stories,* November 1929. Ill. Wesso.

Short story. * The narrator, a physician, reminisces on the strange discoveries and mysterious end of Colonel Grigsby, noted soldier, inventor, and reclusive scientist. The two men became acquainted after Grigsby suffered an accident, and after many evenings of friendly scientific discussion, Grigsby reveals his secret projects. He has discovered that the nerve impulse is a peculiar sort of electricity and has a radiation device for reproducing it. Indeed, with his apparatus he can revive the dead, as he demonstrates with a dog. And more, by stimulating neural activity, his apparatus also increases intelligence. The revived dog, for example, displayed a complete understanding of human speech. * After this demonstration the narrator leaves. The next day, he hears that the colonel is dead, his house and laboratory burned. But Grigsby has left a message: He has tried the radiation on himself, with remarkable results, but the increased mentality involves metabolic change, whence the heavy fatigue. * Perhaps the colonel committed suicide; perhaps his death was accidental. * Slow moving, and very heavily larded with scientific exposition of research medicine.

DREW, DOUGLAS

Pseud. of Gordon K. Saltar, U.S. author, then resident in

Milford, Delaware. Author of *Microscopic Identification of Woods* (1967).

347. NIGHTMARE ISLAND. *Astounding Stories,* October 1936. Ill. Wesso.

Short story. * *Place:* a Caribbean island near Anguilla. * Young Estelle Wolfe, whose college education in the United States has been subsidized by her uncle Peter Wolfe, receives a summons to come to his island and assist him in his work. She is also to bring along a reliable witness. Such a witness is Rupert Seward, her boyfriend. * Peter Wolfe is a mad scientist of the most vicious sort. Personally obnoxious, cruel, selfish, ruthless, he conducts his experiments with no regard (as will be seen later) for human life. * Basically, Wolfe is trying to amalgamate the animal and vegetable kingdoms. When he discovered that the tapan trees had a true circulation like an animal's, he gradually implanted fish muscle into them, with a capable artificial heart. Onto his prize tree, inside the house, Wolfe then grafted an enormous, most ferocious moray eel. Other trees around his small laboratory were also provided with hearts, flesh, and blood. * When Wolfe picks up Estelle and Rupert at Anguilla, they run into bad weather and are shipwrecked on the island. They discover, to annoyance on Peter Wolfe's part, horror and fear on the part of the other two, that they cannot penetrate the jungle and reach the laboratory without danger, for the vegetable-animals have overgrown enormously and are very aggressive, with bloodsucking tendrils. * Wolfe kills them by shooting their artificial hearts, and the three reach the laboratory, where the prize tree has grown to enormous size. Indeed, it has killed Wolfe's two native male assistants. Worse, when Wolfe reaches in the window, the incorporated eel (now gigantic) bites off his arm. This loss does not seem to bother him much. * Now really insane, Wolfe chains up Estelle and Rupert and proceeds to graft his young female servant into the tree. The graft is successful and is soon to be followed by similar placement of Rupert and Estelle. Chance preserves the young couple and destroys the mad scientist. The engrafted woman, now grown to titanic size, breaks Estelle's chains and sets the laboratory on fire with a burning glass. Finis one very vicious mad scientist and one plant-animal hybrid. * Parodic?

DUTHIE, JOHN

U.S. author, then resident in Pasadena, California.

348. ELECTROLYTIC ONSLAUGHT. *Astounding Stories,* June 1935. Unsigned ill.

Short story. * *Time and place:* perhaps the middle future, underwater in the ocean. * *Background:* Dion, the narrator, who inspects the underwater walls of Submara, explains its historical background. Several hundred years earlier his people had been the decadent, tyrannical rulers of a land empire. But their subjects the Transeanians rebelled and drove them into the ocean. There they survived by creeping into a cavern world that was accessible at certain times, but not observable from above. Eventually they regained part of their civilization. Their greatest achievement, about two hundred and fifty years before story present, was the creation of the crystal-dome city Submara on the ocean floor. The enemy knows of the existence of Submara, and has attacked it unsuccessfully many times. * On this occasion Dion notices a small leak in the concrete wall; in itself this is minor, for such leaks are readily repaired by special crews. Dion observes, however, that the leaking fluid is not water, but

Duthie, John (*continued*)

hydrochloric acid—which the Transeanians are using to dissolve the concrete. Such a procedure must involve a giant electrode and catalyst just outside the city. * Dion discovers that the apparatus has been set up by a traitor, who happens to be the head of protective rays; after considerable turmoil, Dion kills the traitor (in a duel in diving suits) and saves the city. * Some ideas, but amateurishly presented.

DUTTON, PATRICK

Judging from the story, then a resident of or a person well acquainted with the Boston area.

349. **THE BEAUTIFUL BACILLUS.** *Amazing Stories*, June 1931. Ill. Morey.

Short story. * The narrative is simple, the important complications coming from the treatment. * Cambridge, Massachusetts. * The frame narrator, a friend of the scientist Polen, who is assistant to and collaborator with the great bacteriologist Professor Glissop, describes the strange fates that befell Polen and Glissop. Polen was found raving mad in the professor's laboratory, and no trace was ever found of Glissop. * Polen's notes indicate what happened. Glissop studied bacteria not from the point of view of disease, but as phenomena in themselves. He theorized that ultimately the bacteria would inherit the Earth and produce intelligences far superior to those of mankind. Combined with this hypothesis, Glissop had a personal interpretation of evolution, in which unexpected constants appeared. * Glissop and Polen devoted their activities toward increasing the size of certain spirochetes that Glissop had developed. One single bacterium emerged from this program, a creature that grew into plant-like form and eventually became as large (perhaps) as a house plant. It developed a bell-like flower, which emitted sounds, and Polen and Glissop became convinced that it could communicate with them and was even more intelligent than they. It was, so to say, the bacterial ultimate. Being such an ultimate, it was benevolent. Unfortunately, it also had a sense of humor. When it perceived a shabby scholar (Glissop) playing the violin very badly, it ruptured itself by laughing, and died. * The bacterial entity dissolved into dust, which Glissop handled. After this, Glissop steadily devolved through the anthropoids, lizards, and lower forms, eventually to a spirochete of the sort that he had originally worked with. This, in turn, became a disease entity that, symbolically, attacked the eyes of Polen, who went mad. * On first reading this story I wondered if it might be an unrecorded Lovecraft collaboration, since it is written in a very complex, tightly organized, elaborate prose that is handled with considerable rhythmic grace and occasional elegance. On second thought, I decided that while the author may well have imitated Lovecraft's style and manner of story development, the language itself is subtler than Lovecraft's and eschews his personal vocabulary of horror. * As a general evaluation: Undoubtedly overwritten for its subject, difficult to read, yet certainly worth reading. One of the few stories in early *Amazing Stories* that deserve to be preserved.

DYE, GEORGE A.

No information.

350. **THE MYSTERY OF PLANET DEEP.** *Wonder Stories*, August 1933. Ill. Paul.

Short story. * *Place:* Mindanao Deep. * Much of this story is devoted to an insipid shopgirl romance of the sort that one might have met in one of the love-story magazines. The scientific element comes with Dr. Alexander Conway, the father of the young woman concerned. Conway has developed a steel that is enormously stronger than the finest steels otherwise known. With it he builds what amounts to a bathysphere with quartz glass windows. Into the bathysphere, which is about six feet in diameter, crowd Conway, his daughter, her fiancé Hunt, and a fellow biologist. Communication is by telephone connection to a mother ship. * Down into the Mindanao Deep, off the Philippines, the bathysphere descends. At about thirty-two thousand feet the explorers see a strange light in the water and the ruins of an ancient city. On returning later to investigate, they observe that the bathysphere is not in water under high pressure, but, resting on the sea bottom, is surrounded by air! * Leaving the bathysphere to investigate, Conway and his associate discover that the light comes from a projectile-like ship lying among the ruins. They enter the ship, in which they see evidences of humanoid life, now dead, and superscientific devices. Unfortunately, they meddle with the controls, and the ship takes off. They barely escape from it, and it is touch and go whether the two men, and Hunt who has gone to rescue them, will survive, for the sea is beginning to intrude into the air. But all are back in the bathysphere, though in bad shape. Later, recovering from their injuries, they decide to say nothing of their experience, for who would believe their story of an interplanetary visitor. * *Miscellaneous:* One of the incidents might be taken as interplanetary communication, but the author is vague. * Purple and badly overwritten.

EBERLE, MERAB (?-1959)

U.S. (Ohio) author, perhaps associated with the Red Cross during World War I period. Author of several children's plays and pageants, including *The Spirit of Democracy* (1917), *Bobby in Belgium* (1918), *Anne of the Red Cross* (1918), and others. Also poetry collection *Many Doors* (1961). Studied at Oxford College, Ohio, and art editor, *Dayton Journal Herald*.

351. **THE MORDANT.** *Amazing Stories*, March 1930. Ill. Morey.

Short story. * *Place:* Youngstown, Ohio. * The narrator, a newspaperman, reminisces about his association with the great scientist MacDowell, with whom he was friendly. On one of his visits to MacDowell, the scientist reveals that he has discovered a "mordant," which in this case means an elixir that keeps a living things—both plants and animals—in perpetual youth. It does not provide immortality, freedom from accident or disease, just cessation of aging. * MacDowell is afraid, however, to release his discovery until it is tested, for plant experiments (this is stated in period gobbledygook) suggest that sterility is a side effect. He needs human subjects. * The narrator proposes the great and ambitious operatic diva Rosa Celeste, who willingly takes the mordant. * Twenty years pass. Rosa remains in perfect youth, but it is becoming apparent that something is lacking in her. Apparently the mordant, in addition to stifling physical development, stifles the soul. All this proves that there is a soul and a God. * The story ends abruptly with Rosa's death by shipwreck. Her youthful body is found by the narrator. * Silly and amateurish.

EDHOLM, CHARLTON [LAWRENCE] (1879-?)

U.S. writer, then resident at Dobbs Ferry, New York. Contributor to *Popular, Top-Notch, Love Stories*, and other pulp magazines. Author of novels *The Lone Cowboy* (1937) and *Cowboy Luck* (1938).

352. PING-TING. *Astounding Stories*, October 1933. Ill. Amos Sewell.

Short story. * Centering on Frank, a member of the local fire department. Colonel Mordoff's wild animal emporium, known locally as the monkey house, is a strange place. In addition to being a fire trap, it holds fierce human passions. There are also a gorilla and Ping-Ting (a subman from Mongolia) who hate each other. When fire breaks out, Ping-Ting releases all the animals, including the gorilla, and the two die in the flames, locked in combat. In the meanwhile Frank rescues Mordoff's "niece." * Less than routine and somewhat questionable as fantastic fiction. In one place it is hinted that Ping-Ting is simply a human freak.

EDWARDS, GAWAIN

Writing name of George Edward Pendray (1901-1987). U.S. (New York) journalist, public relations specialist. In many ways the prime mover in the American Interplanetary Society/American Rocket Society, responsible for much of the early research conducted by the society. Author of *The Coming Age of Rocket Power* (1946) and serious articles about potential space travel. Edited posthumous papers of Robert H. Goddard, rocketry pioneer. Science editor for the New York *Herald Tribune*, 1932-1933. Also wrote novel *The Earth-Tube* (1929), which combines science-fiction themes with the Yellow Peril. It is covered fully in *Science-Fiction: The Early Years*.

353. A RESCUE FROM JUPITER. *Science Wonder Stories*, February-March 1930. Ill. Paul.

Short novel. * *Time:* probably in the ninetieth century, 8916 being the latest date mentioned. *Place:* the Jovian system and Earth. * The story breaks into two portions, events centered in Jupiter's satellites and those on Earth. * In the past, on Ganymede, a winged human race evolved that developed a high civilization. It colonized the other satellites and eventually Jupiter, although gravity devices were necessary at first. Over the years local races developed, notably a short, squat, very strong Jupiterian race that eventually conquered the satellites. At the moment the cultural situation involves an imperial court much like ancient Rome and powerful semi-independent noble families with strong notions of caste. The present emperor, Dolmician, is brutal, sensual, and corrupt. There are strong separatist movements among the satellites. All in all, the cultural milieu is not dissimilar to that of Frank Herbert's *Dune*. * As the story begins, a Jupiterian expedition visits Earth, which seems totally desert and without inhabitants. A younger member of the expedition, Allus Marce, the scion of a noble house, espies ruins that seem in better state of preservation than those otherwise encountered. Atop a tower is a statue that holds in its hand a cylinder, obviously offering it. Marce takes the cylinder, whereupon the statue glides down inside the tower. (As is explained later, the statue arrangement, a piece of most ingenious stupidity, is to indicate the presence of living beings below. But who can fathom that?) * The expedition returns to Jupiter, where Marce finds himself cheated. His superior takes credit for finding the cylinder, which contains papers, and court linguists

fake an immediate translation to avoid imperial wrath. * Marce is bitter. He knows, though only his father shares this knowledge, that his family is partially descended from an Earthman who visited Jupiter about eight hundred years earlier; ancient family records, which Marce is not supposed to have examined, also contain keys to the Terrestrial language, so that Marce can translate the document. It is a long history of Earth and an appeal for help from the last human survivors, who have rigged up the statue previously mentioned. * Marce determines to return to Earth secretly on a rescue mission. His journey, as his father and he know, will create powerful enemies at court and may well set off prematurely the rebellion that has long been fermenting. * To anticipate, Marce and his followers reach Earth, and after great difficulties rescue the maiden Nina and her moribund father. Marce strikes a bargain with them, wherein they will help the revolution with their understanding of Terrestrial power and military technology. * The situation on Earth, as revealed by the long narrative of Nina's father, covers Terrestrial history for about seven thousand years: Humanity waxed and waned, with wars, spurts of civilization, and declines. It would be pointless to repeat the exposition. Three major events, however, stand out. The first was the development of a water engine that breaks water down into its components, providing nearly free energy. It brought about a near eutopia. Second, the failed Jupiter mission. When it became obvious that Jupiter was populated, the Earth frantically armed, fearing invasion. No invasion came, but the nations of Earth used their arms upon one another, with horrible results. Third, the Western nations, pressed by the Orientals, developed a catalyst that spontaneously disintegrated water. Burning up the Pacific Ocean did end the Yellow Peril, but it also began a process that eventually destroyed all the oceans, the lakes, rivers, and ground water. Humanity simply withered away, despite conservation. Toward the end only a few score people survived in a depression, and what with madness, murder, and natural catastrophe this boiled down to Nina and her father. They are about ready to give up when Marce rescues them and takes them back to Jupiter. * *Miscellaneous:* There is obviously a romantic element between Marce and Nina. * Over the centuries, what with the disappearance of water vapor, the natives of Earth have become black-skinned. Nina wonders if she will become white, like the Jupiterians, when she lives there. * Literate in expression, but oddly archaic in some ways, despite the modern scientific aspects. For a sequel see #354, "The Return from Jupiter."

354. THE RETURN FROM JUPITER. *Wonder Stories*, March-April 1931. Ill. Paul.

Short novel. * Sequel to #353, "A Rescue from Jupiter." * *Time:* Probably the ninetieth century. *Place:* Ganymede and Earth. * Since the first story, the inhabitants of the four inhabited satellites in the Jovian system have revolted against the cruel Emperor Dolmician of Jupiter. At first the rebels, armed with new weapons devised by the ancient scientist from Earth, were successful, but Ganymede's allies betrayed her, and now Ganymede stands alone against the Empire. * The story follows two subplots. * In the first, Dolmician invades Ganymede. The Ganymedan space fleet under Allus Marce fights bravely, but is defeated, and the forces of the emperor conquer Ganymede. Both Allus Marce and Nina are captured and tortured. Old Allus, however, has flown away in a spaceship, destination unknown. * The second subplot concerns mostly Nina's aged and

Edwards, Gawain (*continued*)

nameless father, who is revealed more and more to be a scientist of remarkable ability. He has refused to turn over the secret of the water-destroying chemical to the Ganymedans, since it is too terrible a weapon, but makes an important recommendation. Inasmuch as Ganymede is losing its heat and soon will be uninhabitable, the Ganymedans should emigrate to Earth. He believes that the water burner has dissipated on Earth, since there is no more water left, and that he can recreate water by atomic manipulation. * Before the Jupiterian attack, he flies to Earth in a gigantic spaceship. His men build a huge space mirror to obtain solar power, then set up transmutation apparatus on the surface in the north polar area. His optimism was justified, for the system works, and Earth should once again be habitable, though it will be long before it returns to its former state. A few plants are already sprouting. * As the Ganymedans are working with the aged Earthman, old Allus flies up. After a conference with the Earthman, he returns to Ganymede, where he surrenders to Dolmician. He bears in his hand a token recognized by the natives of the Jupiter system as affording immunity until an audience with the emperor is granted. Before the gross, sensual emperor, Allus makes a demand: Dolmician must evacuate Ganymede, or else Allus will explode the token in his hand; it is really a very cleverly constructed pressure bomb. Dolmician, after an attempt at deception, refuses, whereupon old Allus blows up himself, the emperor, the palace and much of the city. In the resulting confusion, the Ganymedans successfully attack the army of occupation and regain their independence. Young Allus Marce will be the new ruler and Nina, his consort. * Routine, with much the same atmosphere as the first story.

355. **A MUTINY IN SPACE**. *Wonder Stories*, September 1931. Ill. Leonard.

Short story. * *Time:* 1989. *Place:* Space approaching Venus. * Although there have been moon voyages, this is the first trip to another planet. The commander is Captain Ledyard, not only a great pioneer in space travel, but a noted designer of space craft and the creator of Ledyardol, the standard rocket fuel. Along with him is a picked crew of seven men, renowned scientists and first-rate technicians. Unfortunately, Ledyard, when picking his blue-ribbon associates, selected for ability, not psychological stability, and the various members break down rapidly. Perhaps this is the reason that previous attempts to reach Venus failed. * One of the crew members dies of an infection that could have been avoided; another goes insane under stress; and others are in nearly as bad condition. There are perpetual queries whether Ledyard is really holding the ship onto its proper course, and finally, just as Venus is almost in sight, a full fledged mutiny. At first the mutiny is only a matter of demands, but it soon erupts into violence, and Ledyard is killed. But before dying, in an unparalleled act of heroism, he wrote out navigation instructions for his mutinous crew, so that they could safely reach the Venus that now appears in the viewing plates. * As a result of this, Ledyard is remembered as a hero, with statues. * The story is hard science-fiction, told with up-to-date information on rocketry, and is probably as accurate as was possible for the time—allowing, of course, for a fantastic element.

EDWARDS, JOHN

Probably a British writer. Several men named John Edwards were writing at this time, and it is not possible to identify our

author with any of them. Edwards contributed to British magazine *Tales of Wonder* as well as to American magazines.

356. **MASTERS OF THE EARTH**. *Amazing Stories*, June 1932. Ill. Morey.

Novelette. * *Time:* 1998-1999. *Place:* mostly Labrador. * The peace vigilante meets with unexpected opposition. * A group of British scientists and industrialists decide to follow up on a remarkable development in electrical engineering. A small installation situated atop the magnetic north pole has demonstrated the power to cancel out electricity throughout the northern hemisphere. * The entrepreneurs, who include the great scientist Paul Lynthorpe, do not intend commercial application, but wish to prevent wars. Their premise is that if two obstreperous European nations abrogate peace treaties and go to war, their electricity can be completely shut off. * The installation is completed, but the unexpected happens. The world receives a broadcast from Aparo, head of a hostile Lunarian mission that has seized the station and captured the crew. To demonstrate his power, he will cancel electric transmission for at least a week. The Lunarians, who are roughly humanoid with large heads and spindly limbs, intend to move en masse to Earth, slaughter much of humanity, but retain a few survivors as slaves. * The Lunarians seem irresistible. They easily captured the plant on Boothia Felix Peninsula. Their gigantic rotating space spheres are impervious to small arms fire, and their paralysis and death gases are potent. Since Aparo, who has studied the Earth for years, speaks perfect English and is also telepathic, the chance of outwitting him is small. The remaining Lunarians, including the powerful Great One of Luna, will soon arrive. * Despite Lunarian brutality there is resistance. Smart bombs laden with high explosives are effective against the space spheres, and even Aparo cannot focus his attention on his captives at all times. A revolt at the station is successful, and the first Lunar expedition is defeated. * The Great One, whose powers of will are enormous, is locked in mental battle with Professor Lynthorpe, when the professor, to save the world, blows up the installation, himself, and the Great One. * Now that the invasion is over, the nations of Earth decide to create no more titanic magnetic plants, but to maintain peace by more conventional methods. * Routine.

357. **THE MENACE FROM SPACE**. *Wonder Stories*, April 1934. Ill. Winter.

Short story. * *Time:* 1943. *Place:* Great Britain. * Three phenomena are of importance to the human race: exhaustion of farm lands through overtillage, an approaching space gas cloud that is presumably poisonous, and communications of a sort with Venus. * The Earth is bombarded with small metal projectiles that contain the seeds of an extraterrestrial plant form. Mossy plants from these seeds or spore soon spread and cover much of the Earth. They give off an anaesthetic gas that places those who breathe it into a coma amounting to suspended animation. * The cloud of space gas is deadly poisonous, but it does not affect those in suspended animation from the moss exhalations. Thus, the human race survives the gas cloud without too much damage. It is now clear that the tiny projectiles were sent by the Venusians to protect the human race. In addition, the moss, which absorbed the space gas, turns out to be a remarkable fertilizer. * *Miscellaneous:* Some of the small rockets from Venus contained a metal plate with diagrammatic information about the space gas and its remedy. * There is considerable plot

Edwards, John (*continued*)
similarity to John Russell Fearn's "Seeds from Space." In any case, the story is clumsy and of no importance.

ELLIS, SOPHIE WENZEL (1893-1984)
U.S. author, resident of Little Rock, Arkansas. Occasional contributor to the pulp magazines, including *Love Stories, Ghost Stories, Weird Tales,* and *Strange Tales.* Also contributed to the *Thrill Book* in 1919 under her maiden name Sophie Louise Wenzel.

358. **CREATURES OF THE LIGHT.** *Astounding Stories,* February 1930. Unsigned Ill
Novelette, really a capsule novel. * *Place:* New York and Antarctica. * The plot line is so complex that the story is best approached through the characters. * (1) The protagonist, Northwood, is an extremely handsome, gifted man. (2) Dr. Emil Mundson, a hunchbacked scientist of great renown, who is obviously modelled on Charles P. Steinmetz, has isolated the life ray and with it has set up a secret superlaboratory and sub-tropical refuge area in Antarctica. Here he has set about breeding a superrace, anticipating evolution by perhaps fifty thousand years. He flies back and forth in a globular ship that can achieve speeds over a thousand miles an hour; his source of power is a device that turns sunlight directly into electricity. (3) Adam, a superman of incredible mental ability and physical perfection. He is one of Mundson's creations, and it was his giant intellect that created the solar sphere that Mundson flies. Adam also is telepathic and has the power to disappear, entering the fourth dimension (time), a few moments ahead of the present. He does this by mental power. Adam has also perfected a death ray. Amiability, however, is not a strength of the future race, for Adam is power mad and intends to take over the world. He also wants the human female Athalia, whom Mundson has reared. (4) Athalia, a normal woman. Mundson rescued her from the slums of New York; she is, however, remarkably beautiful, sweet, and intelligent. Athalia and Northwood love one another, a situation that irks Adam. (5) Eve, Adam's female counterpart. Just as perfect as Adam, she is the most advanced of the superpeople in the Antarctic oasis. She desires Northwood, and to obtain him is willing to do anything. * Adam pretty much has things under control, to the discomfit of the three ordinary humans, until Eve takes a hand. Eve seizes Adam's death ray and kills him with it, but accidentally destroys herself and wrecks the maintaining machinery of the oasis. * Northwood, Mundson, and Athalia escape, with Mundson somewhat, but not wholly repentant, of his experiments. * Not the height of literary perfection, but filled with interesting mythic ideas.

359. **SLAVES OF THE DUST.** *Astounding Stories,* December 1930. Ill. Wesso.
Short story. * *Place:* the Tapajos area in Brazil. * Hale Oakham, young scientist, visits Sir Basil Addington, a maverick scientist who has performed biological miracles. * Hale learns that Addington has solved the mystery of life, which he calls a special mind electron. Using a ray machine Addington can disintegrate living things and then recreate them, integrally or altered. His lab is full of chimeras. * Addington offers a mystical explanation: Mind electrons are entrapped in matter electrons (which are the same as energy) and are striving to be free, so that they can return to a primal source. One of his long-term projects is releasing his ray around the world, extinguishing

all life, thus making it possible for the mind electrons involved to return to creativity. * Addington has also established a death cult among the Indians and occasionally strikes individuals dead with his ray. * Oakham does not approve, but assists Addington, partly in hope of restraining his madness, partly for love of the beautiful, charming blonde Aña, whom Addington has created in his lab. Addington has plans for Aña when he has cleansed the world. * All ends well. * Ellis probably picked up the qualified monism à la Ramanujan from contemporary occult sources.

360. **THE SHADOW WORLD.** *Amazing Stories,* December 1932. Ill. Morey.
Short story. * Scientist Salter has been investigating the so-called shadow world, by which he means a world of attenuated matter ranging from the stratosphere up. This matter, he has discovered, forms an ambience just like ours, though of course enormously more diffuse, with geography and living beings. But it is invisible except to ultraviolet light. * Using an apparatus that ascends to this shadow world, expanding suitably, capturing objects, then descending, and contracting its catch, he has brought down animals. And now, he has captured Pathon, an invisible winged man, with whom he is struggling when Jack Fantom, a family friend and beau of Salter's niece Annis, comes along. * The invisible man, who is seen to be a handsome specimen when rendered visible by suitable light, becomes a guest in the Salter establishment and learns enough English for communication. He tells of horrors in the upper world, but unfortunately has an eye for Annis, a situation which Jack Fantom resents. * The Salters, Jack, and Pathon ascend to the upper world armed with the professor's recently invented disintegrator tubes. The upper world is not too dissimilar to ours, except that it is overrun with gigantic, ferocious, voracious insects, which the disintegrator tubes slice up readily. * There is great rejoicing up above at the slaughter of the insects, which the upper people try indifferently to exclude by ray barriers. Pathon formally asks his king for Annis, but Jack objects. Allowed to choose between the two men, Annis selects the Earthman, as much because she does not like the upper-level cuisine as anything. In a frenzy, Pathon destroys the ray barriers of the land, and the insects do an enormous amount of damage. The lower world people climb back into Salter's apparatus and return home, where Annis undoubtedly can slake her gastric appetites. * Annis's peculiarities (combined with Professor Salter's vicious tongue) would seem to be an attempt at depth characterization, but it comes across almost as parody. Of no interest.

ELSTAR, DOW
Pseud. of Raymond Z. Gallun, who has a separate entry. Gallun has a story under his own name in the same issue of the magazine.

361. **AVALANCHE.** *Astounding Stories,* December 1935. Ill. Dold.
Short story. Von Karman machines sweep the universe. * *Time:* the future, undated, but presumably many centuries from now. * *Background:* The race known as the Rothel has conquered the Earth, exterminating the peoples of the lands it has overrun. At the moment only one city is left unconquered, and it is being flooded with poison gas by the Rothel. In a laboratory near the city, however, is Fai Torran, the greatest scientist of the day, and his servant-assistant Nareth. * As the Rothel approach, Fai Torran makes an announcement. He has created mechanical

Elstar, Dow (*continued*)
equivalents of his and Nareth's brains and has released them out into space. And since the Rothel embody survival of the fittest at its most ruthless, in about three years they will meet and be supplanted by a fitter race. Torran then blows up his laboratory, himself, and such of the Rothel as are nearby. * The incident is soon forgotten, but astronomers note anomalous conditions on the other planets, which seem dwindling in size, while surface disturbances are taking place. And then the scourge hits Earth. * What Fai Torran did was create self-replicating machines that are sweeping through the solar system. They are so numerous that there is no defense against them, and mankind is exterminated. Clouds of the little machines sweep out to the stars, to the rest of the universe. * Competent.

ENDERSBY, VICTOR A. (1891-1988)
U.S. (California) civil engineer. Graduate of Stanford University, 1916. Captain, Corps of Engineers in World War I. Bridge engineer, state highway department in late 1920s. Author of many technical articles and *Laboratory Compaction Methods and Their Effects on Mechanical Stability Testing for Asphaltic Pavements* (1952). Judging from letters in *Air Wonder Stories*, somewhat concerned about our cultural problems and interested in occultism. Not a great writer, but one of the more intelligent contributors. In later life apparently convinced of the authenticity of Theosophy. with books *The Hall of Magic Mirrors* (1962) and *Battle Royal of Hodgson versus Hartmann versus Waterman Refereed by the Editor of Theosophical Notes* (1964). Died in Napa, California.

362. **THE DAY OF JUDGMENT**. *Science Wonder Stories*, April 1930.
Short-short story. * Honorable mention in the contest based on the cover to the November 1929 issue of *Science Wonder Stories*. * A moral-problem story. * On the planet Suven, a considerable distance away, there is annoyance. Emanations through the ether from Earth have brought all sorts of degenerate impulses, ranging from lack of consideration to downright criminality. These impulses are disrupting Suven society, and something must be done about it. Therefore, an expedition will go to Earth and bring back samples of the inhabitants; depending upon analysis, the Earth may then be either cured or destroyed. * Back on Earth, an engineer describes, in full technical detail, the seizure of the Woolworth building by a flying saucer. * In the building, in a state of suspended animation, are many people: crooked bankers, scheming exploiters, adulterous merchants—all to be judged by Suven. The only witness for the defense is a lame, self-sacrificing black janitor, who is scorned by the white crooks who have offices in the building. What will the decision of Suven be? * The natives of Suven are balloon-like aerial jellyfish who work with static electricity and magnetism, and communicate by color changes on their surface. * Clever, with some bitter thought; it would have been worth expanding to more suitable length.

363. **THE GIMLET**. *Amazing Stories*, May 1930. Ill. Morey.
Short story. * *Place:* California, near Bakersfield. * As Bill narrates it, it all began in their college days when he and George Balsey discussed science-fiction magazines, which Balsey scorned, finding more mystery and more intellectual stimulation in real science, particularly the structure of the Earth. What probe could stand the pressure of the Earth's interior? A chance remark by Bill focuses George's life on a quest. * Years later, George summons Bill to see what progress he has made in penetrating the Earth. As he early recognized, only the wall of an atom could stand geological pressures, and he has constructed a cylindrical atom of indefinite length, into which he can feed light sources and recording equipment. * The two men watch the probe as it passes through layers of various sorts, including lead and gold, then elements with impossible atomic weights, moving finally into a hyperspace of sorts. A strange sky and strange stars are visible. * The explanation is in terms of relativity: There are two divisions of space, with a limitless boundary between them, and about a thousand miles down in the Earth is such a boundary between two worlds, which are mirror images of one another in terms of matter and energy. Space is thus curved back within a hyperspace. * Bill must leave and learns what happens later through correspondence. George has become convinced that his other space contains life and that it is the life after death. At the end, George is dying in the hospital, after having destroyed (so far as he can) his project. He now recognizes that it is not meet for man to look into such things. * Confusingly presented, with large gobs of quasi-scientific speculation.

364. **AFTER 5000 YEARS**. *Wonder Stories*, July 1930.
Short-short story. * While cleaning a stationary boiler, Trevethen apparently faints, and his cousin Brinston (also a rival in love), not knowing that Trevethen is in the boiler, fires it. * Brinston realizes his terrible error in a short time and dashes out, half mad, after trying to drag Trevethen out. Fortunately, a medical man realizes what has happened and saves Trevethen, who has most of his skin boiled off. * Trevethen does not die, but recovers fully, though he complains of bad dreams about a man in a kettle in ancient times (identified by the doctor as Mesopotamian). Later, the doctor, discussing the case with Lawrence, an archeologist friend, learns that the incident recapitulates one Lawrence had recently translated from Babylonian tablets. * Recurrent patterns in fate? Reincarnation? In any case, not science-fiction.

365. **DISOWNED**. *Astounding Stories*, September 1932. Ill. Wesso.
Short story. * Tristan and his friends venture out into a thunderstorm, where ball lightning explodes near Tristan, momentarily rendering him unconscious. That is not all: The electricity in the lightning reversed the magnetic polarity of his atoms, so that he is repelled by the Earth rather than attracted. His friends must watch him carefully to see that he does not float away. * Tristan tries to adapt to his condition and capitalize on it, without much success. Eventually, he barnstorms around the countryside, performing a spectacular stunt: He allows himself to float off into the air, landing on a dirigible above. * This livelihood is tolerable for a time, until a vicious young bumpkin cuts the ropes that hold Tristan down, and he soars off into the sky to his death. * Perhaps early black humor; perhaps simply mixed tones of humor and tragedy.

366. **A JOB OF BLENDING**. *Amazing Stories*, March 1934.
Short-short story. * Small tailor Manderson suffers from the extortions of the protection racket until he devises a lethally clever way out. Since cash is scarce, he persuades his tormenter, Fat Jake Stolzwein, to accept a suit in exchange for the monthly

Endersby, Victor (*continued*)

protection money. * The suit, which is strangely colored, strikes the fancy of the gangsters, and Jake's boss Lupinetti orders a similar suit. Unfortunately, both Jake and Lupinetti are killed in traffic accidents. Manderson's pattern is adapted so well to the city milieu, creating such perfect camouflage, that Jake and Lupinetti were as good as invisible.

367. **WHEN THE TOP WOBBLED.** *Amazing Stories,* February 1936. Ill. Morey.

Novelette. * *Time:* mostly 1945 and after. *Place:* the San Francisco Bay area. * It is the height of the depression in the early 1930s when young Ben Seiverson decides to pursue a doctoral program in the earth sciences, with particular reference to seismology. In this he is encouraged by his fiancée Eileen Gilders and his friend, philosophy instructor Ten Drake. His own father and Gilders, Sr., a successful engineer, are less enthusiastic. * Ben's researches, which will soon produce spectacular results, are conditioned in part by an extensive series of dreams that Eileen has of a spinning top. * Ben's hypothesis, finalized in the early 1930s: The incidents of geomorphology and orogeny, including earthquakes, are not random or the result of special incidents, but are part of a pattern associated with large astronomical and geological forces. Numerically, every Platonic Year, or twenty-six thousand years, such disturbances are intensified; and every fourth Platonic Year, or about one hundred and five thousand years, they are catastrophic, including a shift in the Earth's axis. The upcoming shift, Ben claims, will transfer the axis to the magnetic north pole and cause incredible damage. * Ben's hypothesis is ridiculed, but there is some change of mind the next year, when earthquakes follow the pattern Ben predicted. There is still no general acceptance, but Gilders and the others quietly build an ark, a cylinder about sixty feet by twelve. * All happens as Ben predicted. California is completely wrecked, part of it sunken beneath the sea, part of it newly elevated, with most of the population killed. But the ark rides out the devastation, and the survivors emerge to start a new life. They are joined by a few other survivors, and mankind (in this area at least) begins afresh. The environment is (surprisingly) quiet, and agricultural life becomes reestablished, with individual homesteads without central political organization. * The second crisis comes with Gilders's Progress League, which is made up of those who want a mechanized, industrial civilization and the luxuries of the past. Gilders proposes to set up a technocratic state with extreme concentration of work for about five years excavating the metals of buried civilization. Despite the pretty words, it amounts to enslavement of the survivors. * The situation comes to a head between Gilders and philosopher Drake, who sees the implications that the others do not see, and in a shoot-out Drake wins. * *Miscellaneous:* Behind the events of the story lies a mystical theory of history, in which some power, unidentified, periodically cleanses the Earth to create a new start. * Probably based on reading S. Fowler Wright's *Deluge* and/or *Dawn,* but taking a different route for civilization. Where Wright opted for a mildly fascistic dictatorship, Endersby preferred laissez-faire anarchism. * Endersby is an intelligent, literate writer, but the story lacks Wright's novelistic skills.

ENGLAND, GEORGE ALLAN (1877-1936)

U.S. author, contributor to various pulp and slick magazines. Born in Nebraska; A.B. and M.A. from Harvard University.

Writing career mostly in New York and Maine. Socialist candidate for governorship of Maine in 1912. Although a legend has grown that he disappeared on a treasure hunt, he died in a hospital in New Hampshire. An important figure in early science-fiction, with imaginative novels, often with socialist messages. Important works are the *Darkness and Dawn* trilogy, "The Elixir of Hate," and "The Empire in the Air." His work is covered thoroughly in *Science-Fiction: The Early Years.*

368. **THE FLYING LEGION.** *Air Wonder Stories,* January-April 1930. Ill. Paul.

(Originally published in *All-Story Magazine* 15 November-20 December 1919. Book publication by McClurg, Chicago, 1920.) Described in more detail in *Science-Fiction: The Early Years.*)

Novel. * Larger than life adventure. * *Time:* Uncertain; close enough to World War I for professional soldiers, bored with peace, to be young enough to be active; far enough away for there to have been significant scientific and aeronautical advances. * *Place:* mostly Spanish Morocco, Arabia. * The Master, a wealthy, highly successful soldier of fortune, assembles a band of desperate mercenaries to raid Mecca and seize the holy treasures of Islam, which he will hold for ransom. As a first step he steals a remarkable aircraft and fits it out with a paralysis ray, a motor-stopping device, an invisibility apparatus, and superexplosives. * After various adventures the Master and his associates make off with the treasures of Mecca, then continue on to a hidden city in the Ruba al-Khali that is so secret and sacred that not many Moslems even know of it. * The Master makes a deal with the ruler of the city, but something goes wrong, and he and his associates are trapped in underground tunnels. Most die, but the Master and a woman associate escape through a water course out into the desert, whence they return to New York. American criminal charges against the Master are dropped in exchange for his secret weapons. * Part of the story consists of a surreptitious romance between the Master and a female war ace who entered his company in disguise. * *Miscellaneous:* The hidden city is carved out of a reef of gold. * Sort of a fictional version of the Nietzschean Uebermensch. Overfelt, melodramatic, inaccurate, but with a verve and éclat.

369. **THE THING FROM—"OUTSIDE."** *Amazing Stories,* April 1926. Unsigned ill. The author's name is incorrectly given as George Allen England.

(First published in *Science and Invention,* April 1923. Reprinted in Derleth, *Strange Ports of Call,* and in Colombo, *Friendly Aliens.*)

Short story based in part on Charles Fort's *The Book of the Damned* and probably suggested by Algernon Blackwood's short story "The Willows." * *Place:* Labrador. * The vacationers are beset by something that burns frigidly cold circular prints into solid rock, into the ground, an axe, whatever it touches, and kills humans horribly. It has already killed their Indian guides. What is it? Jandron, a geologist, has heard of something like it and is convinced that it is a being far superior to mankind that is after human brains/minds. The thing, whatever it is, kills most of the expedition so that only Jandron and the young woman Vivian survive, she amnesiac. * The creature must have a territory of some sort, for the part of Labrador through which they pass is completely desolate. * Blackwood's story is better.

ERNST, PAUL [FREDERICK] (1899-1985)

U.S. author, prolific writer of thrillers for the hero-pulp

Ernst, Paul (*continued*)

magazines in the 1930s, notably the *Avenger* novels under the house pseud. Kenneth Robeson. Also contributed horror-adventure and science-fiction stories to *Weird Tales*. Ernst is not to be confused with the German writer of the same name or with Paul Ernst (1886-?), a writer of detective stories. * See also #1818, "Death Dives Deep," and #1819, "The Microscopic Giants."

370. **MAROONED UNDER THE SEA**. *Astounding Stories*, September 1930. Ill. Wesso.

Short story. * Professor Berry, Stanley, and Martin, having at their disposal a heavy glass sphere, are ready to make the first full-mile descent into a deep off Indonesia. As the descent proceeds, the explorers see many strange life-forms. But one creature, a gigantic slug-like monster perhaps fifty feet across, proves troublesome. When such a slug clasps the sphere, its weight, combined with a storm at surface level, breaks the retrieval cable. * It looks as if the explorers have a choice between a slow death and a quick death, but a somewhat humanoid fish that wears a spiny shell as armor swims up and obviously regards them with amazement. Other such fish approaching, drag the bathysphere away, and in a short time the explorers find themselves in a lighted, air-filled cavern in the company of a splendid human race: all handsome men, and gorgeous women. * This is the land of Zyobor, which was settled so long ago that there are no traditions of how and when. * The people are on a barbaric level, with good crafts, city planning, and a monarchy. Queen Aga and Martin are attracted to one another, an attraction strengthened by the law that the queen must marry a red-headed man, Martin being the only red-headed man present. * But there is a flaw in this near eutopia: The land is in immanent danger of being invaded by the Quabos, humanoid, intelligent, deep-sea monsters, and the humans expect to be exterminated. But Professor Berry works out a way to defeat the Quabos with flamethrowers, and all seems well. * The manuscript ends here, but presumably Martin will marry Queen Aga. * *Miscellaneous:* The Quabos, when invading, wear water-filled glass helmets. * The Zyobarans communicate with the fish-men, who are their servants, by telepathy.

371. **HIDDEN IN GLASS**. *Amazing Stories*, April 1931. Ill. Morey.

Short story. * Professor Brainard has long been carrying on a scientific feud with Professor Willard, who has just attacked Brainard's views on the fourth dimension. Brainard, furious, after spending considerable time in calculations, places an order for specially molded glass. But when Willard's laboratory catches fire, Brainard generously offers the use of his own laboratory while he travels. A few days later, Willard's corpse is found, head bashed in. * It is a sealed room situation; the room contains nothing but laboratory equipment, including a large sealed, transparent glass box. Unfortunately, a detective standing guard over the laboratory is also found with his skull fractured in the same manner as Willard. * Detective Hardy, believing that he sees an opening in the wall behind the box, has it moved aside; it is so heavy that several men can barely slide it along. There is no opening; it was an illusion caused by the refraction of the glass. * And then, after a short time, the box pops open, and Professor Brainard leaps out, clothing singed, obviously insane. * Explanation: Brainard's box involved the fourth dimension, and when the detectives moved it into the

sunlight, the sun's rays were focused on Brainard, igniting his clothing. The mystery of the box itself is still unsolved, says Detective Hardy, since part of Brainard's apparatus was smashed when he broke out of the box. * Competent pulp mystery.

372. **THE WORLD BEHIND THE MOON**. *Astounding Stories*, April 1931. Unsigned ill.

Short story. * *Place:* the Moon, and a second moon. * Wichter and Joyce, on their successful trip to the Moon, see a second satellite that always remains exactly in a straight line with the Earth and the Moon, hence is not visually or physically perceptible. They call it Zeud, though why is not explained. * The explorers continue on to Zeud, which is about the same size as Luna, but has a breathable atmosphere and a tropical climate. * The two men venture forth from their ship, encounter vicious dinosaurs and somewhat humanoid, primitive, semiintelligent beings who capture them for their larder. * Our heroes escape, the deciding factor being removal of eyeglasses, which action for some reason impresses the natives enormously. Back to Earth. * The motive power of the spaceship is hydrogen, which it extracts from the air; this is used on a reaction principle. * Pretty feeble.

373. **THE INCREDIBLE FORMULA**. *Amazing Stories*, June 1931. Ill. Morey.

Short story. * *Time:* 1982 *ff.*, and 2514. * A brief frame situation in A.D. 2514 is followed by a narration of the events of 1982 and a few years later. * In 1982 Professor Vansom receives a deathbed summons from his teacher and master, the great biologist Max Weinghold. Weinghold, who is about to commit suicide, confides his great discovery to Vansom: A chemical means for reviving the dead and creating immortality. * Unfortunately, the technique produces zombie-like beings with limited sensory equipment, no personality, little intelligence, and horrible appearance. Weinghold asks Vansom to act as trustee for the secret, either to improve it or to suppress it. * Vansom, however, proves to be weak and for enormous sums first sells the secret to a capitalist then joins in the founding of an organization for creating "livies" (as they are called) for cheap slave labor. * This causes enormous repercussions in the economy and in personal life, all of which Ernst works out in considerable, capable detail. Families sell corpses; gangs burke victims; all for the livey factories. * The zombie industries profit enormously and soon are in a position to control world economy. But then there is a revolt, the result of which is the near extermination of the human race. The culture based on zombie labor wins out, though only a few thousand in number, and sets up a luxury civilization based on sensible use of zombie labor. * An interesting story, unusual for its cynical, unexpected ending.

374. **THE RED HELL OF JUPITER**. *Astounding Stories*, October 1931. Ill. Wesso.

Novelette. * *Time:* the interplanetary future. *Place:* mostly Jupiter. * A world-saver story in the mode of Edmond Hamilton. * It is now ten years since the invention of the atomic motor, and to avoid problems, all extraterrestrial flights are assigned to the Planetary Exploration Forces. Capt. Brand Bowman and Dex Harlow are now assigned to discover why P.E.F. ships have been disappearing in the Red Spot of Jupiter. Jupiter is in the carboniferous stage of evolution, but its gravity is too strong for Earthmen. * Entering the Red Spot, their ship is captured by some sort of tractor beam and dragged to a low-gravity area

Ernst, Paul (*continued*)

intensely settled by Rogans, very nasty, hostile, repulsive, pipe-like humanoids, who have four arms with sucker disks like octopi. Since Jupiter's gravity would be much too strong for them, they modify it with magnetic force. Also present are normal humans from Callisto who are slaves to the Rogans. * Greca, a beautiful human slave who takes a fancy to Bowman, communicates with him telepathically. According to her, the Rogans have captured the P.E.F. ships so that they can copy them and invade the Earth; despite their otherwise high science, they do not have atomic power. * The P.E.F. men are now in for it, as the Rogans prepare tortures to extract information from them. * Naturally, Bowman, Dex, and Greca escape, turning down the gravity control lever that weakens Jupiter's heavy gravity, disabling the Rogans, and disintegrating them in droves. The Earth is saved. * *Miscellaneous:* The Rogans feed on human blood, which they drink on the hoof. They also have enormous dinosaur-like beasts to which they feed recalcitrant slaves, and supertelescopes with which they have watched Earth. * Intensely clichéd, of course, but competent as naive pulp action.

375. **THE PLANETOID OF PERIL**. *Astounding Stories*, November 1931. Ill. Wesso.

Short story. * *Time:* Some time in the third millennium A.D. *Place:* mostly in the asteroid belt. * Harley 2Q14N20, a ten-bar engineer, decides to buy a planetoid so that he can make enough money to marry an economic titan's daughter. He sees an announcement that Planetoid Z40 is for sale, inquires, and despite attempts by the management to withdraw it from the market, buys it. * The reason for the reluctance to sell: While the terraformed asteroid is pleasant and rich in resources, with a comfortable three-hour day and night, it has proved fatal to previous buyers. No one knows why. The only survivor, who is half-mad, talks of walking rock that is impervious to the disintegrator pistols that dissolve all organic matter. * Harley lands on his planetoid and soon discovers the problem. What he took to be an outcropping of rock is really a building-sized monster that sets out after him. Since it is living rock, or at least has a thick outer casing of silicon, it is immune to his ray pistol. * Harley barely escapes the first night, during which the monster, which has a certain intelligence, wrecks his spaceship. On the second night, after cat-and-mouse games, the monster seizes him, but, being totally nocturnal, releases him when it falls asleep at daybreak. * Now Harley has an idea: He attaches his only unwrecked propulsion tube from his spaceship to the monster and blasts it off into space. * *Miscellaneous:* In this future world, the United States is one megalopolis. Everyone has a serial number and wears occupation and rank designations like army insignia. Harley wears crossed drills with ten bars to indicate that he is a top-rank engineer. The businessman who sold him the planetoid wears dollar signs. * For life on a planetoid one wears an oxygen concentrator. There are personal antigravity and heavy gravity belts. Matter concentrators squeeze matter down atomically. Atomic cannon are more effective than ray guns, but Harley didn't have one. When an earlier investigatory expedition visited the asteroid, the crafty monster simply pretended to be a rock. * Not a bad thriller.

376. **THE RADIANT SHELL**. *Astounding Stories*, January 1932. Ill. Wesso.

Short story. * There is a hidden international crisis. The Arvanian government has acquired the plans for Ziegler's heat ray. With the ray, which operates far beyond the range of artillery, the Arvanians can conquer the world. Indeed, they plan to declare war on the United States as soon as the plans for the ray reach Arvania and projectors can be built. At the moment the plans are under guard in the Arvanian Embassy, officially nonexistent. * Professor Thorn Winter will save the nation and the world. He has mastered invisibility, which involves a chemical coating, then alignment of atoms so that light passes through without impedance. He enters the Arvanian Embassy nude, but there are complications: first, dust which renders him shadowy; second, a dog, which smells him; and finally, refraction. But after a complicated bruhaha between various Arvanian thugs and an invisible man, Winter breaks out of the embassy with the plans. * Capable pulp action.

377. **THE RAID ON THE TERMITES**. *Astounding Stories*, June 1932. Ill. Wesso.

Novelette. * Termite lore, sometimes fanciful, embodied in action. * Dennis Braymer, enthusiastic entomologist, would give almost anything to experience termite life first hand. He has his chance when his friend Matt Breen, an eccentric scientist, explains about his discovery of element 85. When subjected to heavy electric currents it can reduce living things in size. Matt demonstrates with a dog, which he first shrinks, then enlarges, no worse for wear. * Dennis and his friend Jim agree to be shrunk, equipped with small steel wire spears, and placed near a termitarium. This done, they have such adventures in the termite hill as one might expect. * The men discover, however, that the termites are not motivated solely by instinct, but that there is a termite master soul who controls the hill. It is a gigantic termite brain, with a small wasted body. When the men kill the termite master, which has been quite hostile, they are able to escape from the hill and regain their size. * Much too long for what it has to offer.

378 **FROM THE WELLS OF THE BRAIN**. *Astounding Stories*, October 1933. Unsigned ill.

Short story. * Professor Wheeler explains his invention to Carson. Since thought is electrical and matter is ultimately electrical, thought is potentially matter. His invention can thus turn thought into living substance. Wheeler demonstrates with various projections, including his concept of an angel. But horrible thoughts, Wheeler declares, are stronger and clearer than pleasant—and here comes the most horrible of all, a shambling ape-like creature. * As the reader has anticipated, the monster is real and cannot be dissolved. It kills Wheeler and smashes the invention, incidentally knocking Carson unconscious. When Carson regains his senses, the monster is gone and the laboratory is a shambles. * Routine.

379. **THE THING IN THE POND**. *Astounding Stories*, June 1934. Ill. C. R. Thomson.

(Reprinted in Margulies and Friend, *My Best Science Fiction Story,* and in Davenport, *Famous Monster Tales.*)

Short story. * *Place:* Florida. * Gordon Sharpe, African explorer, visits at the behest of his old friend Professor Weidbold. Something strange is going on in Greer's Pond, near the professor's small laboratory. A monster drags in cows and eats them, and when Sharpe and Weidbold investigate, it chases them quite hungrily. A charge of dynamite and (later to be applied) sulfuric acid take care of it. It was a fragment of chicken heart, kept alive à la Alexis Carrel, that a disgruntled employee threw

Ernst, Paul (*continued*)

into the pond, where it multiplied. Its decease will undoubtedly please the locals, who resent the professor. * Hackneyed.

380. **THE STOLEN ELEMENT**. *Astounding Stories,* September 1934. Ill. Dold.

Short story. * *Place:* Naples, Italy. * The great physicist Vichoni can transmute elements by bombarding them with electrons, but his results are not stable, lasting only about thirteen minutes. This is unfortunate, for the element 93 that he has created is fantastically hard. * Vichoni's villainous lab assistant Carlo, however, has accidentally discovered how to make the transmutation permanent. He and his associate Farnese are not interested in science or element 93, however, but in manufacturing gold from iron. * Carlo has a scheme worked out. Murdering Vichoni, he transmutes an iron bar up two stages to uranium, and with split second timing sells it to a fence while the bar is in the gold stage, before it can relapse to iron. He plans, with the money he has received, to buy additional equipment and manufacture permanent gold. But fate is against him. He carried the bar without shielding, and the radiation has burned him badly, indeed, in a peculiar way. In some fashion, it has turned his left arm to gold. After murdering Farnese, who has become hysterical, there is nothing left for him but suicide. * Routine.

381. **THE 32ND OF MAY**. *Astounding Stories,* April 1935. Ill. Marchioni.

(Reprinted in Conklin, *Best of Science Fiction.*)

Short story. * When the nameless narrator passes at a peculiar angle between mirrors and perhaps trips on a rug in Barton's apartment, he finds himself in an alien world. It is a flat land covered with what seems to be a spongy, resilient vegetation, beneath a slate gray sky. As he watches, a peculiar round glowing thing approaches and vanishes. As it turns out, the glowing thing is a two-dimensional being composed in geometric fashion. It is hostile; armed with a weapon that looks like two crossed sticks, it projects some sort of damaging force. The narrator evades it and another being (which is hostile to the first). While under attack and wounded, he manages to find the place where he entered the strange world and returns to Barton's apartment. As he learns, he could not have been away for more than a fraction of a second, whence the title of the story. * The implication is that in some fashion the mirrors distorted dimensions. * Not bad as a thriller. Ernst's best s-f story.

ESHBACH, LLOYD ARTHUR (1910-present)

U.S. (Pennsylvania) author, bookdealer, publisher. Associated with various religious publishing enterprises, including Moody Press. Contributed fairly frequently to the genre magazines in the 1930s. The best of this work has been reprinted in *The Tyrant of Time* (1955). Founded Fantasy Press (1946) and Polaris Press (1952), both of which specialized in reprinting magazine fantastic fiction. In 1980s resumed fiction writing with fantasy novels. Also an expert lapidary, with specimens in the Smithsonian. One of the more remarkable men in early science-fiction. Excellent *Over My Shoulder* (1983) contains personal reminiscences and data about early fan publishing.

382. **THE INVISIBLE DESTROYER**. *Air Wonder Stories,* May 1930. Ill. Paul. Published as by Lloyd A. Eschbach.

Short story. * *Time:* 1967-1969. *Place:* mostly an artificial island in mid-Atlantic, and another dimension. * In 1967, in the Adirondacks, a group of scientific friends debate the upcoming decision to create a world government. Most see it as a step forward, in ending international wars, but the great Russian scientist Demetriovich disagrees most strongly. He declares that world government is an illusion, because no state will conform when it feels it is to its advantage to do otherwise; that the Union will entrench and strengthen already present corruption and tyranny; that giant cartels now operating worldwide will take over the country; and that blood-glutted dictators will oppress the masses. The others disagree, and Demetriovich sulks. * Two years later, on a star-shaped artificial island in mid-Atlantic, the world government is about to be inaugurated when a gigantic voice, seemingly from the clouds, bids them stop. After several warnings, the voice afflicts the politicians with extra gravity, so that they cannot move. * This does not deter the politicians, however, and the next meeting takes place with an armada of sea and air craft for protection. But then the delegates see a blue cone floating nearby in midair. The cone emits a white ray, and the men find themselves alone on the island; all the armament surrounding them has vanished. * By now all concerned know that the power behind the threats is Demetriovich; hence it is no surprise when he emerges from the cone and greets them. He informs them that he has translated them to a parallel universe, much like Earth, but uninhabited, and there they shall remain until he sees fit to take them back to our world. He explains that he is now master of vibration, whence the force screen that protects his cone, his paralysis ray, and their present situation. He then leaves. * The mad scientist, however, overlooked one important point. In the Union buildings is a small plane, kept in readiness for emergency purposes. The narrator and two associates thereupon fly toward North America, hoping that Demetriovich was wrong about the parallel world. He was. They find North America covered with a glass sheet, and living beneath this a race of large-headed dwarf-men who possess a super-science. The dwarves, who are friendly, communicate with them via telepathy and a mechanical thought projector. * The ruler of this world, an enormous brain, agrees to help them. Arming them with weapons against Demetriovich, the dwarves return the exiles to their own universe. * Back at the Union Star Island, the men await the return of the mad scientist, who it is learned, has become world dictator and, despite his earlier arguments, has done nothing but work mischief. He comes, not alone, but with three other cones manned by followers. His weapons, however, are powerless against those of the dwarves, and, with the self-sacrifice of one of the original disputants with Demetriovich, the mad Russian is destroyed. * Imagination and story drive. * Of Eshbach's stories described here, this was the third written.

383. **THE GRAY PLAGUE**. *Astounding Stories,* November 1930. Ill. Wesso.

Short story. * Strange meteorites land and explode in China, the Southwestern United States, and Spain. An enormous meteoritic body strikes the Atlantic. And then the gray plague begins; it is a fulminating, always fatal pulmonary disease that also removes calcium from the bones, flattening out the body. * Millions die, but then Parkinson, a crippled man, approaches the President of the United States in California and offers a preventative to the plague. * Parkinson's story: A bacteriologist, he was knocked off his yacht by the Atlantic meteorite. Unconscious for a time, he awakens upon a rough, copper-like formation. It opens, and three tall humanoid figures emerge and draw him down inside,

Eshbach, Lloyd Arthur (*continued*)

where his captors place a strange helmet on his head. As he soon learns, the helmet is a thought-transference device that makes his total mind accessible. * The three strangers now brief him: They are Venerians who plan to release a plague that will annihilate mankind so that Venerians can migrate to Earth. They will experiment on Parkinson until they find a proper microbe. Parkinson undergoes unspeakable suffering, even to losing an arm, before the Venerians settle on the gray plague. * Parkinson, however, is not crushed by his misfortunes. Managing to seize a ray rod, he kills two of the Venerians, and with the thought helmet extracts from the third Venerian the data about counter-measures against the gray death. Taking a Venerian flying globe, he flies to California, where he meets the President. * Terrestrial scientists hope to learn wonders from the artificial meteorite, but it is gone, presumably destroyed or withdrawn by Venus. * Ingenious plotting.

384. **THE VALLEY OF TITANS.** *Amazing Stories,* March 1931. Ill. Morey.

Short story, partly in the mode of A. Merritt. * *Time:* the undated near future. *Place:* a hidden valley in the Himalayas. * Jimmie Newton, narrator, is on an investigatory flight in an area near the Himalayas where many planes have disappeared, when he is caught up in a storm and blown into a small, mountain-ringed valley. His plane is smashed. As he looks around, he sees that he is in a lost world with archaic vegetation and animal life. * A horde of submen, some riding dinosaurs, capture him and take him to a mysterious blue spherical building, where Verne Carcante, a normal white man greets him. * Carcante explains matters: The valley, which is inhabited by many kinds of dinosaurs, must have been sealed off at an early date, and evolution has not taken place since. The blue building and other marks of high civilization were present when he entered the valley and presumably are of enormous antiquity, perhaps of prehuman origin. * Verne Carcante is an experimental biologist specializing in evolution. He has discovered that evolution is caused by secretions from a ductless gland, which he can stimulate by radiation. He would like to advance mankind, but so far his ray has only turned his subjects into the half-ape men that Newton encountered. * Carcante has been responsible for the mysterious disappearance of planes, including the great trans-atlantic airliner *Teutonia.* He has a gigantic helicopter fitted with enormous grapnels and atomic energy. * Carcante makes a proposition to Jimmie Newton: He will spare Jimmie if Jimmie will act as his assistant. If he refuses, he will be tied to the cross that holds Carcante's experimental subjects and treated with the ray. Jimmie refuses and is placed on the apparatus. * As the experiment is about to begin, the beast-men rebel, and Carcante leaves to quell them. At this point Claire Maynard, a young woman, emerges from a secret chamber and cuts Jimmie down. A survivor of the *Teutonia,* she had managed to escape Car-cante's notice when he began to work on the passengers, and stumbled into a secret passage. The two leave through a maze of underground tubes that penetrate deeper and deeper and were obviously not designed for human use. * At one point the combined weight of the fugitives breaks the casing of the tube, and they are precipitated into a different network. They see strange living disks of purple light pass by them; then they are taken gently by the disks and carried to an enormous lighted city composed of purple spheres like the one on the surface. * The

ruler of the disk people, who calls himself Novad Thasor, receives them. A gigantic misty being, utterly benevolent, he explains matters. He is an extraterrestrial who came to Earth countless ages ago. The purple light beings are his people, who once lived on the surface, but were so troubled by emerging forms of life that they retreated to the inner Earth for sanctuary. Here they have lived for ages, until Newton and Claire stumbled upon their world. * The god-like Novad Thasor will help them to return to the surface and if they have difficulties escaping will come to their aid. * The disks return Claire and Jimmie to the surface, where they find no trace of Carcante, who may be dead. The submen attack them, and even the machine gun that Jimmie removed from his plane is inadequate to repel them. Claire is about to be sacrificed by the beast-men; Jimmie, riding a maddened dinosaur, is vainly trying to rescue her; whereupon Novad Thasor comes to their rescue and disintegrates the submen. Jimmie and Claire fly out in Carcante's helicopter. As they look back, they see that the disk beings have destroyed the upper valley and permanently sealed off the subterranean world, as had been promised. * Imaginative, but too much going on for the length of the story. The story would have been better as a novelette. Of Eshbach's stories described here, this was the first written.

385. **A VOICE FROM THE ETHER**. *Amazing Stories,* May 1931. Ill. Morey.

(Reprinted Ashley, *History of the Science Fiction Magazines,* Vol. One.)

Short story. * *Place:* Mars, except for an introductory episode. * In 1925, when Mars and Earth were in conjunction, the frame narrator, while experimenting with his radio equipment, heard and recorded the following narrative, which after four years of study was translated. * Tuol Oro, one of the six great master scientists of Mars, tells of his injury and his revenge. The Great Council had summoned the master scientists and those of lesser rank to report on their achievements. The scientists speak through the "Power of the Spheres," while the twenty-member council communicates telepathically. Tuol Oro, a microscopist, reports. Using microscopes of novel design he has not only seen atomic particles, but has gone beyond and seen vegetable life of a horrible, most destructive sort on a proton of sodium. His report finished, he awaits applause, but instead hears the head of the council denounce him as a liar and expel him from the scientific community. * Tuol Oro, who in addition to being a great scientist, is a violent egotist, vows revenge, and, now mad, decides to use the horrible, all-devouring plants to destroy the people of Mars. After years of secluded experimentation, he succeeds in extracting one of his plants from the atomic particle and enlarging it suitably. It is just as voracious and rapid as it was on the proton. * Tuol Oro now prepares a glass box to protect himself and installs heat projectors around his house, since intense heat destroys the plants. * When the council calls on him, he releases his fungus and sees the beginning of the destruction of Mars. Now alone on the planet, he decides to broadcast his story to Earth—but as he talks, the glass of his box collapses, and the plants devour him. * Of Eshbach's stories described here, this was the second written.

386. **THE LIGHT FROM INFINITY**. *Amazing Stories,* March 1932. Ill. Morey.

Short story. * An unusual attempt to combine motifs of space opera, size change, and world peril. * To consider the astronom-

Eshbach, Lloyd Arthut (*continued*)

astronomical matters first: the Moon and Earth act very strangely, bobbing back and forth in their orbits, with resultant catastrophe on Earth. At one time a direct collision seems possible. These phenomena are connected with a red ray from Tycho on the Moon. This ray is also coursing over the surface of the Earth, crushing and destroying everything. * The narrative is concerned with the adventures of John Kennard and Nevil Craig, who fly to the Moon in the *Rocket*, the first spaceship. As the *Rocket* approaches the Moon, it is seized by an attractive power and dragged into an enormous crimson building, which turns out to be the operations center of two twenty-foot-tall extremely slender humanoid beings. The giant red men do not harm the space travelers, but treat them well enough, though they make no attempt to communicate with them. * Kennard and Craig determine to end the ray that is destroying Earth. Outwitting the giants temporarily, they gain control of equipment that turns out to be a size-changing apparatus. They are enlarged up to a macrocosm, where they find another red giant (now small compared to them) observing the Earth and Moon (which are subatomic particles) in a microscope. (Eshbach stresses that the red people have in some way circumvented differential time rates between atomic phenomena and the macrouniverse.) * After adventures back and forth, the two humans, returned to our world, destroy the lunar apparatus and save the Earth. * *Miscellaneous:* The red people have disintegrator tubes that work well enough against their own plane of existence but (because of different atomic structure) are little more than nuisances to the Earthmen. * A mixture that does not work well. Eshbach seems to have forgotten to explain why the red giants from the macrocosm are doing all this.

387. **THE TIME CONQUEROR**. *Wonder Stories*, July 1932. Ill. Paul.

(Reprinted in revised form as "The Tyrant of Time" in Eshbach, *The Tyrant of Time.*)

Novelette. * *Time:* The present and various periods in the future: A.D. 2944, A.D. 3660, and about A.D. 4250. * Episodes of revenge for a horrible crime. * The great but ruthless scientist Koszarek theorizes that time is a plane, past to future, all existent in another dimension. He further theorizes that a human brain, cut off from sensory stimuli, will develop new senses, including time viewing. Murdering Ovington, an old, down-and-out colleague, Koszarek sets up Ovington's brain with artificial maintenance equipment. * After a time the brain begins to function, communicating telepathically with Koszarek. When Koszarek begs to learn the future, the Brain offers to show him future incarnations. These are presented in three episodes, in each of which Koszarek acts with renewed villainy. It amounts to an unredeemed Scrooge and Christmases Past, Present, and Future. * In 2944 the world is covered by a supercivilization, ruled by the Brain, which is omniscient. It is housed in the great mile-high Science Tower. By this time, human generation is performed by artificial means, resulting in a race of men infinitely superior to present-day men. The only exception is the partially deformed Clavering, who is despised by his fellow men. Clavering works as a chemist for the Brain, creating an elixir of immortality. But, bitter and vengeful, he is plotting to kill the Brain. He fails, dying in the attempt. His elixir, it turns out, offers immortality, but in the form of conscious petrification. * In his next incarnation, Koszarek is Vastine, an attendant on the

Brain. The world situation seems hopeless. Extraterrestrial molluscoid invaders that fly about in spiked purple globes have melted the polar ice cap, so that much of the world is flooded. The Brain, men think, is helpless against the invaders, but this is not the case. Knowing the future, it is prepared. It establishes a few refuges for mankind, conceals Vastine's thoughts when the invaders question him telepathically, and waits. A meteorite storm smashes and destroys the invaders, and the flooding waters are boiled out into space. Vastine, who has been getting delusions of grandeur, plots against the Brain and is killed. * By now the Brain has Koszarek completely under its domination. It shows his last incarnation as Koz (sometimes spelled Kos), a despicable, semioutlawed figure in a future primitivism around A.D. 4250. After maligning the Brain, he is crushed to death by its mental power. * Back in our time, Koszarek is also killed by the mental power of Covington's brain. * Crudely vigorous, but it holds one's attention very well.

388. **THE BRAIN OF ALI KAHN**. *Wonder Stories*, October 1934. Ill. Winter.

Short story. * Dr. Carl Selkirk, noted neurologist, has proof that personality does die with the body, but that the brain remains active and sentient. His proof, however, is not capable of demonstration, since it involves telepathic communication. * Dying in the doctor's hospital is the Hindu [*sic*] Ali Kahn, who must be some sort of adept, since he, too, is capable of telepathy. The vicious Hindu, who is dying of cerebrospinal meningitis, fears that Selkirk will conduct a post mortem, thereby destroying his (Ali Kahn's) brain. In an attempt to dissuade Selkirk he threatens him telepathically with a similar death by meningitis. * Selkirk pays no heed, but after dissecting Ali Kahn's body, begins to feel ill. In a very short time he dies of meningitis, with classical clinical symptoms. But his autopsy reveals no trace of disease. He was killed by the Hindu's suggestion. * Some operating room lore, but not one of Eshbach's stronger stories.

389. **THE KINGDOM OF THOUGHT**. *Amazing Stories*, August 1935. Ill, Morey.

Short story. * *Time:* the undated far future, when the sun has lost much of its energy and Earth is pretty much frozen. * Donald Stile (a twentieth-century man) awakens in a strange Arctic milieu. Running toward him is Gorg Merlo, a small man with a large head, who communicates with him telepathically; and approaching to attack is a gigantic fur-clad subman swinging a stone axe. Stile manages to overcome the savage, whereupon the little man talks of the Keeper and the Time Sphere. What does it mean? * *Background:* Stile, by means later explained, is in the far future, where human evolution has ended in enormous brains of incredible power who are able to manipulate matter by thought. The brains (which are six or seven feet across, with tiny bodies) are divided into two groups, White and Black, good and evil, which are at perpetual war, with White slightly the more powerful. Working with the Whites is the Gray Brain, which seems to partake of the nature of both groups. As Keeper, the Gray Brain uses the Time Sphere to fish champions out of the past for the perpetual war. This is how Stile was picked up. * Within the Time Sphere the Keeper also maintains human thought forms that look human and are material, though Eshbach makes the point (as with horrible thought forms maintained by the Blacks) that they cannot harm one if one disbelieves in them. * With Merlo, who comes from our future, Stile enters the Time

Eshbach, Lloyd Arthur (*continued*)

Sphere where he meets a congenial figure, an Elizabethan swordsmith. The three men become close comrades. * Stile, who seems to have more perspicacity than either the other men or the White Brains, recognizes that the Gray Brain is evil and is really working with the Blacks. The Gray Brain is on the point of killing him and his two comrades, when the chief of the White Brains intervenes, rescuing him. But the upshot is that the three men are sent into the territory of the Blacks, with some protection. * They encounter psychic and physical attacks, but win through far enough to stir the Blacks into activity. In the battle that follows, the Blacks are defeated, several killed by the automatic that the White chief had materialized for George. * As the Black world comes crashing down around him, Stile loses consciousness and awakens back in our time. He had been unconscious after an automobile accident, but he is still clad in the chain mail the White chief had made for him and is still carrying his automatic. He muses that he would rather be back in the future with his comrades than at his teller's desk at the bank. * Gimmicks include disintegrators, radiative heat suits, and similar material. * This is one of the earliest joint quest stories, a subtype that later became popular. It has much imagination, but does not pull out themes as clearly as do later examples.

390. **THE METEOR MINERS**. *Amazing Stories*, December 1935. Ill. Morey.

(Reprinted in Eshbach, *The Tyrant of Time*.)

Short story. * *Time:* the interplanetary future. *Place:* the asteroid belt. * Essentially a character story, the value of the aged. * Among the meteor miners—those hardy men who capture metallic asteroids for the extractive industries—Steve Anders is remembered as a great miner. But he is old, approaching seventy years, and the large companies like Earth, Venus and Mars Lines. will no longer hire him. * As a last resort he applies to rough, tough Captain Barker, whom he had trained many years ago. Barker, though a hard man and a bucko captain, is a man with an occasional soft spot in his heart, and for charity and old time's sake he takes on Anders as assistant dispatcher. This is the petty officer who sends out the small one-man prospector ships from the mother ship, directs them, and recalls them. * Anders is not happy about a desk job; he would prefer to take out his old rocket boat that is stored in a cubby, but he is grateful. * A time to pay debts comes when the metal yield has been scanty, a dangerous comet is approaching, and it looks as if Barker will die out in space. Anders in his old craft is decisive in rescuing him. * As can be seen, a common human pulp situation, but handled with considerable grace and skill. One of Eshbach's best stories.

391. **THE OUTPOST ON CERES**. *Amazing Stories*, October 1936. Ill. Morey.

Short story. * *Time:* the interplanetary future. *Place:* mostly on Ceres. * Commercial exploitation of the solar system is just getting under way, and Earth, Venus, Mars Lines is attempting to set up regular trade between Ganymede and the inner planets. The problem has been fuel. Indeed, one of the great freighters ran out of power and had to be retrieved. The solution to the fuel problem is establishing a refueling station in the asteroids, Ceres being the best choice. * Larry Damore is the first occupant of the one-man station. His history is unusual. An intelligent, educated man, he has suffered severely from morphine addiction originating in medical situations. He hopes to cure himself by the cold turkey method on Ceres. * While Damore is in station, he receives signals that the *Helios* has struck an asteroid. Flying out to the wreck, he finds only two survivors, one of whom, surprise, is his former girlfriend Marcia, who is also the daughter of the head of the shipping line. (This played no part in Damore's obtaining the job.) * The survivors return to the station on Ceres, where, in a short time, Larry sees hitherto unsuspected activity on the nearby asteroid Vesta. The planetoid seems to be covered with metallic objects, which are beginning to fly toward Ceres. They turn out to be tiny cylinders constructed and operated by almost microscopic worms. They are hostile. It is only a matter of time before the buildings of the station will succumb to their attacks. * Larry, in a heroic gesture, diverts attention from Marcia and her friend, who escape in the station tender. Larry is thought to be dead, but when a relief mission arrives, it finds him only somewhat burned and bruised. * Larry outgrows his addiction and marries Marcia. * *Miscellaneous:* No action is taken against the Vestans, who were presumably only defending their territory. * Good background at first, but the romantic entanglement destroys any credibility.

EUSTACE, C. J.

Perhaps Cecil John Eustace (1903-?), author of many books of Catholic interest and novel *The Scarlet Gentleman* (1927).

392. **TEN DAYS TO LIVE**. *Amazing Stories Quarterly*, Summer 1928. Ill. Paul.

Short story. * Purple prose and high emotion. * The great maverick scientist Eden has constructed a small machine with which he will move the Earth a few million miles closer to the sun. His purpose is improving the climate in general. The machine can function for only five days; if it functioned longer than that, the Earth would become too hot and eventually fall into the sun. * There are two complications: Eden is a dying man and may not live to fulfill his project. Second, the local half-wit (Greely) lusts for Eden's beautiful sister and also knows about the machine. * The worst happens. Greely breaks in, kills Eden, and steals the machine, which he sets into operation. The narrator and his friend Villiers search high and low for it. As time passes, the days grow shorter, the heat increases, great storms break out, and mankind is on the point of collapsing. At the very last moment the narrator and Villiers find the machine and destroy it, at the sacrifice of Villiers's life. Apparently now the climate really is better. * Elements of religiosity are also included.

FABERS, DAN

No information.

393. **THE RED RAY**. *Amazing Stories Quarterly*, Spring 1930. Ill. monogram MA (?).

Short story. * *Time:* undated near future. * David Saunders is in New York when the invisible air fleet bombards it, destroying many great buildings. He is also handy when men emerge from an invisible ship to make repairs, at which time a young woman (Tiania) tries to escape from the mysterious invaders. * Saunders rescues her and takes her to his home by pneumatic car. Since she is telepathic and acquires English in a matter of hours, he learns what is happening. * *Background:* Jahad, the usurping ruler of Mars, plans to conquer the Earth or at least loot it very

Fabers, Dan (*continued*)

thoroughly. Tiania is the daughter of the deposed ruler. The Martian ships are invisible because they are constructed of a certain metal. Tiania proves her point by giving Saunders an invisible knife. * Jahad issues a radio ultimatum. Things look bad for mankind, but when Saunders tests the knife in his laboratory, he discovers that the hitherto invisible metal (a new element) becomes visible under infrared rays. * Infrared projectors render Jahad's fleet visible, and it is blown out of the sky. The infrared also blinds the Martians. * Saunders personally KO's Jahad and marries Tiania. * Amateurish.

FARLEY, RALPH MILNE (Pseud. of Roger Sherman Hoar, 1887-1963)

U.S. (Massachusetts and Wisconsin) author, politician, lawyer, educator. Held political appointments in Massachusetts and was a state senator in Wisconsin. Apparently a very versatile man who achieved expertise in such varied fields as patent law and mathematics of ballistics; but strong self-promotion did not obscure the fact that he was a weak literary craftsman with nothing to say. His fiction tends to be clichéd and crude. While Farley's work in the genre pulp magazines is of little significance, his "radio series" that appeared in the Munsey magazines was of some historical importance. These are fully covered in *Science-Fiction: The Early Years*. Certain of the work that appeared under Farley's name in later years was ghosted by other men (including E. Hoffmann Price) on the Stratemeyer system, Farley furnishing the plot, which the other person developed into fiction. It has also been claimed (in Schwartz/Weisinger) that work published as by Farley after 1931 was a collaboration with his daughter Caroline Prescott Hoar. See also the collaboration Ralph Milne Farley and Stanley G. Weinbaum. * See also #1820, "Liquid Life."

394. **THE DANGER FROM THE DEEP**. *Astounding Stories*, August 1931. Unsigned ill.

Short story. * The cables to George Abbot's bathysphere are cut by intelligent, shark-like beings with rudimentary arms; the bathysphere is towed into an underground area with a normal atmosphere; and Abbot finds himself among humans. * After a time, communication and a romance are established. George learns that the shark-like fish, who are of supernal intelligence, are the masters of the humans; that the humans were originally laboratory creations, evolved by the sharks to parallel *Homo sapiens*, whom the sharks had observed in surface-spheres millennia ago; that the sea humans are far superior to surface man in intelligence; and that a ruthless testing policy has sentenced his girlfriend Milli to death. * George learns other disturbing news. The sharks and their human protegés had originally wished to make friendly contact with surface mankind. But when they realized how bad life on the surface is and how stupid surface man is, they changed their minds. Now they want to conquer the world. * With two good reasons for escaping, George, Milli and another couple steal submarines and make their way to the surface. The underground world behind them is destroyed, since George did not close the airlock doors. * Quirky and undeveloped. Farley attempts a light touch that does not succeed.

395. **THE DEGRAVITATOR**. *Amazing Stories*, March 1932. Ill. Morey.

Short story. * Assorted bigwigs from United Airways, Ltd. have come to the laboratory of Conrad Hughes, who claims to have invented an antigravity apparatus, using concepts from General Relativity. Despite considerable hostility on the part of the visiting scientific consultant, Hughes demonstrates an appreciable effect. (As a nice touch, in order to preclude the possibility of a rigged test, the commission uses a neighboring house on the pretense of being vacuum-cleaner salesmen.) * Everything seems settled. Hughes is not greedy. He primarily wants a small, but permanent, salary and a well equipped laboratory in which to continue his work. But chance is against him. Hughes had casually mentioned a dangerous process that was going on elsewhere in his lab. This experiment—creating a passable imitation gold—explodes, killing Hughes and destroying all data about his discoveries.

396. **BLACK LIGHT**. *Astounding Stories*, August 1936. Unsigned ill.

Short story. * *Place*: Washington, D.C. * Black light was an early popular term for ultra-violet radiation. * The President of the United States, summoning G-man Walter Curtis, details him officially as a military adviser, but secretly as a bodyguard against an assassination attempt. * On a visit to the great Professor Woodward, who has developed a black-light searchlight, the President and Curtis see a remarkable display, including a landscape that, depending on the light focusing on it, shows winter, spring, or summer scenes. * Then, when the main parties are locked in the laboratory, Professor Woodward announces that he will kill the President. But Curtis, utilizing an ultraviolet mirror, blinds and shoots the professor—who is revealed to be a bewigged foreign spy. The real Woodward was bound and gagged elsewhere. * Nothing, perhaps only borderline s-f.

FARLEY, RALPH MILNE and WEINBAUM, STANLEY G.

Both authors have separate entries. According to the reminiscences of Weinbaum's widow, Weinbaum wrote the first half of the story and Farley the second half.

397. **SMOTHERED SEAS**. *Astounding Stories*, January 1936. Unsigned ill. (Brown?)

(Reprinted in Weinbaum, *A Martian Odyssey* [Hyperion], and in Weinbaum, *The Red Peri*.)

Novelette. * *Time*: A.D. 2000. *Place*: the United States and the Pacific, near Guam. * Background: The United States and the Asiatic Union (ruled by the Khan) have been at war for some time. While the Asiatic Union achieved early successes and still occupies part of Alaska, the war has turned into a stalemate, thanks to the Beckerley screens that create eddy currents, destroying explosives. Both sides have such dome-like defenses. The United States controls the seas, but the Khan has more than twice as many men in the field as the United States. * A new event, however, is intruding on the stalemate. This is the enormous increase of algae in land and oceanic water. In some places the algae are so numerous that ships can pass only with great difficulty. The cause of this phenomenon is not known, but it is being studied by Lt. Richard Lester of the Bureau of Military Biology and Bacteriology. * The plot line need not be detailed; let it be enough to mention main threads. Lester is very much in love with Sally Amber, and she reciprocates. Sally is a beautiful young woman who some say greatly resembles Asian Princess Stephanie, the master spy known as the Nightshade. Is Sally the Nightshade, working for the Khan? The

Farley, Ralph Milne and Weinbaum, Stanley G. (*continued*)
reader will easily pierce this cliché after a page or two. In any case American espionage expert Cass has his suspicions and will make up his mind in a couple of days. His decision may mean death for Sally Amber. * The Asiatics capture Lester and prepare to torture him for information about his algal researches. He solves the problem, of course, recognizing that the Beckerley fields are causing the epidemic, and also discovering that the Khan's fields have failed because of supply problems caused by the algae. * It will do no harm to reveal that Sally, though really Princess Stephanie and a patriot, finds that love is stronger than duty. Fortunately for her, Cass is killed before he can denounce her. * A pretty bad job, what with weak writing, cliché, and nonsense. It is not surprising that "Smothered Seas" was rejected previously by *Astounding* and *Argosy*. After Weinbaum's death, when his reputation was at his highest, standards were lowered to publish material from the trunk.

FAST, HOWARD MELVIN (1914-present)
U.S. writer, political figure. One of founders of Progressive Party, recipient of International Peace Prize in 1954. Member of Communist Party, imprisoned for contempt of Congress. Popular historical novelist with *Citizen Tom Paine* (1943), *Spartacus* (1951), and other titles. Wrote many detective novels as E. V. Cunningham and general fiction, sometimes politically oriented, as Fast. During 1950s and later contributed frequently to the *Magazine of Fantasy and Science Fiction*. His mature fiction has been well regarded critically.

  398. **WRATH OF THE PURPLE**. *Amazing Stories*, October 1932. Ill. Morey.
Short story. * *Time:* 1939. *Place:* mostly Upstate New York. * The narrator, a bacteriologist of note, receives an urgent summons from his old teacher and friend Dr. Richard Carter. Carter has horrible information to impart. His experiments in the creation of life have succeeded all too well. A purplish substance he has produced by irradiating certain chemicals has all the aspects of life, except that it cannot be destroyed. It grows at a geometric rate, eats humans and vegetation, and is not harmed by chemicals, gases, explosion, electricity, flame, etc. In a matter of weeks this purple mass will cover the planet. * There is obviously great concern, once the danger is recognized, and the narrator and Carter are given the responsibility of discovering a weapon against the purple jelly. * Author Fast at this point takes the easy way out. Dr. Carter, by adjusting the radiation that he used to vivify the mass, creates a ray that can disintegrate faster than the jello can multiply. The world is saved. * Juvenile work, clichéd in subject matter, but more fluently written than most contemporary s-f.

FAWCETT, COL. P[ERCY] H[ARRISON] (1867-1925?)
British soldier (Royal Artillery), traveler, surveyor, publicist. Fawcett, a capable surveyor, but otherwise eccentric and influenced by occultism, was convinced that major cities lay half-buried in the Amazon jungles and spent years looking for them. A minor person who was not taken seriously, he achieved international notoriety when he and his son Jack disappeared on an expedition into the Matto Grosso. They were almost certainly killed by hostile Indians, but the press and publicity seekers turned his fate into one of the great disappearances of the twentieth century. A collection of his papers was printed as *Lost*

Trails, Lost Cities (1953). The present story may be a reprint, but an earlier publication has not been found.

  399. **CALLAHUAYA'S CURSE**. *Astounding Stories*, October 1933. Unsigned ill.
Short story. * *Place:* the Bolivian Andes. * Supernatural fiction. * The British engineer visiting the abandoned mines follows the warning of the local corregidor and does not hang his hammock in the ruined house. A crime took place there some twenty years ago, when an army officer kidnapped and raped the wife of a native overseer, beating and imprisoning the overseer when he resisted. The next morning the woman and the officer were found dead, while the man had disappeared. * Obviously a Callahuaya curse lies upon the ruins, for another officer, some years later, saw the ruined house as if it were new and sound, with a beautiful beckoning woman. He, too, was found dead the next morning. * A trite theme, but the local color is well handled.

FEARN, JOHN RUSSELL (1908-1960)
Extremely prolific British (Liverpool area mostly) writer, who worked both as Fearn and under many pseuds., the most significant of which were Thornton Ayre and Polton Cross—both, however, after the time span of this study. In later years he frequently used the working names Volsted Gridban and Vargo Statten for scores of short novels. After a stint as a textile salesman following World War II, Fearn resumed writing, turning out an enormous volume of work. He also edited the British *Vargo Statten's Science Fiction Magazine* for a time. * Fearn was a slapdash, slipshod writer, whose work sometimes embodied a crude vigor and careless imagination, being essentially action fiction with a shrugged off scientific background. According to his contemporaries he lacked power of self-criticism, and, strange though it may seem to a reader, took his work seriously and was bewildered by unfavorable reaction. In much of his work, his origins in British boys' fiction is obvious. His stories were never very popular among American readers, nor highly regarded critically, but in later years they underwent many reprints and translations in European markets. In a way, Fearn was a man ahead of his time; he would undoubtedly have been very successful in the present world of television science-fiction series. * See also John Edwards.

  400. **THE INTELLIGENCE GIGANTIC**. *Amazing Stories*, June-July 1933. Ill. Morey.
Short novel. * *Time:* from 1938 on, mostly around 1940. *Place:* mostly London, with an episode on Mars. * Frankenstein on the Belly. * David Elton, a brilliant young biologist, recognizing that about four-fifths of the human brain is not utilized (but presumably will eventually be activated by evolution), conceives of creating a synthetic man whose brain is totally usable. He expounds his idea to two prominent scientists, who consider it possible. One of them, Dr. Soone, a neurological surgeon, will be delighted to make the brain connections proper to creating a superman. The second scientist, Ross, is reluctant, since he believes that the creature will not have a soul. Elton's fiancée Nan, too, is convinced that the synthetic man will be inhuman and begs Elton to forbear. When he refuses, she jilts him. * The work moves apace—involving chemicals and radiation—and the Intelligence is finished. At that very moment it stands up and makes an announcement: While growing, it telepathically

Fearn, John Russell (*continued*)

learned everything that mankind knows. It adds that it will take over the Earth, which is in a mess, and improve it. When Ross objects, the creature kills him by mind energy. Soone, however, is willing to serve the Intelligence, for he expects to gain power. Thereupon, the Intelligence, which understands time and space perfectly, vanishes into the fourth dimension (time) with Soone. * A couple of years pass, with nothing more eventful than the reconciliation and marriage of Elton and Nan. But then there is an incredible political development. The nations of the world decide to make peace and elevate a single executive as supreme ruler; naturally, it is the Intelligence, whose hypnotic power can encompass hundreds of men at a time. * Under the Intelligence, the world changes. National boundaries are removed; poverty is erased, as is unemployment; the state offers subsistence; old cities are razed, and new futuristic cities rise, like New London; atomic power is used on rapid planes, etc. But along with this progress comes regimentation. Everyone is enrolled in the State and assigned a serial number to use instead of a name. Marriage is forbidden. * During this development, Elton and Nan have cautiously remained unobtrusive, unaware that the Intelligence has been watching them. Indeed, when Elton was tried for the murder of Professor Ross, the Intelligence, working covertly, saved Elton's life—for a purpose that is now apparent. * The intelligence captures Elton and Nan, and Dr. Soone makes the recruiting offer customary in such situations: join, supervise the production of more intelligences, and become powerful. Refusing, as is customary, Elton and Nan are put to work shoveling metal ores. * They escape, along the way rescuing old Professor Athlinstone, a chemist of note. They make their way to Elton's hidden laboratory, where Athlinstone begins work on devices that will topple the Intelligence—a viewing ray, thought protection helmets, and light and thought screens. Athlinstone also works on the fourth dimension. But his *chef d'oeuvre* will be a thought projecting machine more powerful than the organic Intellect. As a machine, Athlinstone says, it will be controllable by man. * All goes well for a time, but then there are difficulties. The Intelligence, who knows very well what has been going on, after capturing David and Nan, shoots them off in a rocket to Mars. They will serve as guinea pigs to check the safety of space travel. He admits that chances of survival are small. The Intelligence also confronts Athlinstone and his will-magnifying machine; the Intelligence wins after a titanic struggle. * New element: The Intelligence's scientists inform him that the sun is due to explode in a couple of years. There is no defense against this catastrophe, which must be caused by hostile forces outside the solar system. The Intelligence thereupon builds spaceships to take a selected few humans and unfinished new intellects to a new solar system. The rest of humanity can perish, he declares. * Let us shift to Mars. David and Nan reach Mars safely, where they are greeted telepathically by a charismatic sage who calls himself Kal of U-Otar. A being of pure thought, millions of years ahead of Earth, he can create and destroy matter by mind power. Kal reveals that he is well aware of the Intelligence and has set in motion powers that will destroy him. As conversation reveals, Kal is as superior to the Intelligence as the Intelligence is to ordinary men. Kal implanted in the Intelligence's mind the idea of the Martian expedition and is disrupting the sun so that the Intelligence and his myrmidons will be destroyed. In the meanwhile, Elton and Nan will return

to Earth in suspended animation. * Time passes, and the time has come. The Intelligence and his colleagues are about to leave Earth, but Kal has sabotaged the Intelligence's spaceship. And the Intelligence begins to deteriorate spectacularly, until he is no more than an ordinary man. He and Dr. Soone die together. * Now it is up to David, as leader of mankind, to start a new order. Humanity goes underground, emerging some time later to see that a new sun (the gift of the Martians) is beginning to shine. * *Miscellaneous:* The Intelligence is only of average height, but perfect physically. His black-eyed gaze cannot be met by humans, so great is its power. * Even more junky than the summary might suggest.

401. **THE MAN WHO STOPPED THE DUST**. *Astounding Stories,* March 1934. Ill. C. R. Thomson.

Short story. * *Place:* Mostly the London area, but a final sequence in Central Asia. * Professor Renhard, great scientist whose mentality is beginning to wane, is annoyed enough at dust that he decides to destroy it. Working out a vibration that will upset electronic patterns, he builds a suitable machine and turns it on. The apparatus seems inoperative, but when Renhard accidentally wanders into its path, he dies instantly. Thus, the machine has been functioning, but at first imperceptibly. * When Renhard's body is found, however, there is a knife in its chest. Renhard's friend and coworker Dr. Anderson is tried for murder found guilty, and locked up as criminally insane. Actually, Gaston, a personal enemy has framed Anderson. * The machine continues to operate. The sky turns black, no more rain falls, and skin eruptions plague humanity. Mankind is threatened when agriculture no longer becomes practicable over much the world. * Sam Brown, an amateur scientist, works out what is happening and builds an apparatus to counteract Renhard's; but the question is whether Brown's device can stop the disintegration of dust in time, for the assumption is that once dust is totally destroyed, it cannot regenerate. At the moment, only a small patch of blue sky in Central Asia contains dust, and it is fast deteriorating. * Brown takes his apparatus to Central Asia. It functions well enough, but is not strong enough to counteract Renhard's machine, which is not only still operating, but has proved impossible for Gaston to shut off. * Salvation comes from London. Gaston, now insane, springs Anderson from the mental hospital. Anderson is able to turn the machine off. Dust, humanity, and the planet are saved, but an outburst of energy destroys the Central Asiatic crew in a great explosion. * The usual faults.

402. **THE BRAIN OF LIGHT**. *Astounding Stories,* May 1934. Ill. Dold.

Novelette. * *Place:* New York City, and a layer about 145,000 miles above the Earth. * When Max Forsythe and Robert Walford (the brother of Max's fiancée, Ada) send their experimental ultra-short wave beam up into the Heaviside Layer, it creates incalculable peril for the human race. Not long after the experiment, sunlight is cut off all over the world, and a voice (later explained as thought speech) bids the two men to stop their experiments. The voice claims that they have killed thousands of inhabitants of the light world. * Disregarding the warning, the two men send up another beam, whereupon the external force now shuts off all light, and on restoring light, the voice declares that it has destroyed color all over the world. Such is the case; the world is now monochrome. Worse yet, the sky-being has kidnapped Ada and will not return her unless the experiments

Fearn, John Russell (*continued*)

cease. * Observing that the area where Ada was last seen is warm, the two men convert a handy metal case into a small spaceship and take off, following what they rightly assume is a heat beam. They find themselves in a solid world, where mighty cities and strange landscapes appear and disappear like mirages. A native of the area (an enormously tall humanoid creature) is amicable enough. He informs them that Ada is being held by the Light Brain, the ruler of the extraterrestrials. It becomes clear from this conversation that while most of the light people are gentle and friendly, the Light Brain (an outsider who has seized power and is resented) is nasty and vicious. * Our friends decide to rescue Ada, kill the Light Brain, and work out a way to continue their broadcasting without damaging the sky people. * It would be pointless to summarize the ensuing incidents, which involve various aspects of color, light, and "particles of sound." The Light Brain is revealed to be an alien from millions of miles away. * The Light Brain's forces move toward Earth, but are defeated in a space battle. Max and Robert kill the Light Brain and rescue Ada. The friendly light people agree to move to a distance where Forsythe's short-wave broadcasts will no longer injure them. * *Miscellaneous:* It is generally known in the United States that Forsythe is responsible for the calamities that have befallen the world, but no one seems greatly resentful. * In New York City, after light was canceled for a few hours, many people froze to death. * Inchoate and junky.

403. **INVADERS FROM TIME**. *Scoops*, 12 May 1934. Unsigned ill.

Boys' fiction. * Short story. * Young Tom Lawton has been working on the question of time. As he explains to his friend Bill Ritchard, by altering the relationship between time and motion, he can speed up time, permitting retrieval of objects from the future. Working into the past, however, is impossible. * On the first demonstration of his apparatus, controls set to A.D. 2534, he brings back to 1934 a metal box containing a metal foil document with the genealogy of a family from one Robert Halford in the 1930s to four brothers in the twenty-sixth century. * On the second operation of the machine, however, Tom and Bill receive a surprise. Their catch is the four future brothers, including Varkol, Master of Greater London. As Varkol explains, they knew of Lawton's work from historical records; thus, when their pedigree disappeared, they simply waited in the proper place to come to our time. Varkol, admitting that he likes power, adds that since he cannot return to his own time, he will take over London and improve it, then the world. Since the future men are armed to the teeth with paralysis rays, death rays, and much else, Tom and Bill have no choice but to fall in with Varkol's plans. * Exploding the Nelson Monument and surrounding buildings, Varkol first sets up an impenetrable headquarters building, then subjects the two young men to a brainwashing operation that both increases their mental capacity and renders them completely subject to his will. Instructed by Varkol, the men now persuade the Londoners to consider Varkol's proposals for creating a new and better London. * With the consent of the Londoners, Varkol and his brothers, with their superscience, transform London into a wonderful place. But the price is now becoming apparent. Varkol announces, through Tom, that London is too crowded; in a day or two he will asphyxiate half the population. In the following riot Tom is stoned, a fortunate blow on his head

releasing him from Varkol's mental bond. * Tom now intends to fight the invaders with superscientific weapons of his own, since he retains his genius-level mentality. His forces attack the future stronghold, but with no success; Varkol simply is impregnable and has better weapons. It looks like death for four million people. * Bill saves the situation. Released from mental control (and mental level) so that he can help locate Tom for the future men, Bill realizes what must be done to save the world. Robert Halford, the present ancestor of the quadrumvirate, must die, so that he has no descendants. Halford, who is of a scientific turn of mind, readily agrees when requested and commits suicide—at which time Varkol and his brothers disappear. They were never born. Their work on London, however, remains. Asked to explain this, Tom replies "It's all a paradox."

404. **HE NEVER SLEPT**. *Astounding Stories*, June 1934. Ill. Marchioni.

Short story. * The great psychologist Jason Veldor explains his theory and discoveries to the narrator of the frame episode. Veldor believes that sleep is not necessary. He also theorizes that dreams are not really personal, but are the impingement of other personalities, perhaps from different space-time continua, upon the sleeper. * Veldor has also developed Veldoris, a new drug that which removes the need for sleep and will permit him to explore the dream world. Unfortunately, as Veldor admits, it is strongly addictive. * Later, the narrator finds Veldor dead. Veldor's diary supplies the remainder of the story: Under the influence of Veldoris he has experienced episodes from the lives of a primitive man, a Victorian maiden, and a future person. He has also had experiences in (presumably) other dimensions and worlds. Now, although he realizes that he needs sleep, he finds the craving for Veldoris too strong to resist, and he is sure that he will die. As a last message, Veldor begs the narrator to destroy the formula for Veldoris and the supply at hand. (Why didn't he do it himself?) * Ancestral memory is also involved. * Confused and routine.

405. **BEFORE EARTH CAME**. *Astounding Stories*, July 1934. Ill. Brown.

Novelette. * *Time and place:* apart from beginning and end frames, many millions of years ago (perhaps more) on the fifth Bodean planet. * The great scientist Dr. Ainsworth has discovered a technique for recovering ancestral memory; it amounts to deadening certain cells pertaining to consciousness, whereupon the ancient memories well up and are reflected upon a screen that Ainsworth has also invented. Young Lee Carnforth is going to be the first subject; in exchange he gets the professor's daughter Mary. * Lee, after a brief period of astronomical sights, awakens in a laboratory on the planet Jir. The great scientists Laznor and Haznan explain: the planet Jir and its sun, both artificially formed, are rapidly disintegrating, and in four days or so will be totally demolished. There is no possibility of saving the planet or even of saving the human race by space travel. The best that the scientists of Jir (who are incredibly more advanced than the scientists of our day) can do is create a new solar system and send to its emergent planets the seeds of life from Jir, including two protoplasmic masses that will contain the brain matter of the two highest Jirians. These two are Prince Morna (Lee Carnforth) and his sweetheart Princess Axata (corresponding to Mary Ainsworth). The process will kill them, but they will die in four days anyway. Before the actual operation, however, Morna and Axata must be careful in

Fearn, John Russell (*continued*)

their thoughts, since preparatory work has sensitized their brains abnormally. * Haznan and his fellows begin their work, creating a sun out of the cold of space, then whirling off nine planets. But Jir is cracking up even more rapidly then expected, and as a result eight of the nine planets are spoiled for the repository for Jirian life. Only Earth (which the Jirians name such) turns out to be suitable. Another difficulty is that the minds of the experimental subjects are affected adversely, and they will not be the perfect humans that the Jirians had planned. As Fearn states in a passage that will appeal to modern feminists, "The women who follow after [Axata] will be weaker than the men—will know the meaning of pain, will be prone to hysteria and nervous excitement—instead of the calm, resourceful women I had planned. Always will they be weaker than the man." * Morna and Axata, who is dying of injuries, are scooped out, placed into the protoplasmic containers, and shot off into space. (Morna does not remember this, since he died before it happened, but it can be inferred.) * Lee awakens back in our time, whereupon Dr. Ainsworth shows him the motion picture of his memories and explains somewhat. According to Ainsworth, the brute creation is native to Earth, whereas mankind thus is not, and resemblances between apes and man do not mean evolution. Also, females bear the marks of Axata's injuries, including a peculiar mark on Mary's wrist. * *Miscellaneous:* Fearn does not indicate where the human race originated, since it was older than Bodia. * The humans of Jir differed from us in one respect: the males were totally male, and the females totally female, whereas we are mixed male and female in each sex. * The Jirians assigned the English names to the planets that we now have. This is deliberately stated. * The Jirians wear Classical Greek garments. * The asteroid belt is the remains of Jir; its sun was totally destroyed.

406. EARTH'S MAUSOLEUM. *Astounding Stories,* May 1935. Ill. Dold.

Novelette. * *Time:* 1972 and following. *Place:* Southern California, elsewhere in the U.S., and the Moon. * Young astronomer Norton Vane, while observing the Moon, is the first to see the disappearance of the rays on Tycho and to witness the emergence from the crater of what must be a spaceship. And with his friend and superior Professor Konsicks, Vane is the first to welcome the occupants of the spaceship, which lands near the observatory. * From the long, cigar-shaped vessel emerge five beings, human in type, but from seven to eight feet tall. They are friendly, and being much more intelligent than Terrestrials, learn enough English in a few hours to tell their story. * They have been in suspended animation in the Moon for about twenty million years. Explorers from a star about forty thousand light-years away, they arrived in the solar system while Earth was still molten. Out of curiosity, they decided to wait until Earth developed life, and set themselves up in a stasis protected by an energy shield—the functioning of which produced the rays on Tycho. While they slept, however, the Moon was ripped from Earth, and the explorers thus awoke on the Moon rather than the Earth. * Utterly benevolent and altruistic, the visitors offer to improve Earth with their knowledge. Since their science has mastered faster-than-light travel and antigravity, their promises are entirely credible. * In a few years, Earth has become a near eutopia, with weather control, matter transmission, and tidal power. The older cities—New York, London, Paris, and

others—have been disintegrated, and their places taken by sky cities, elevated far into the air with interconnecting bridges. * The visitors also begin to terraform the Moon so that it can be colonized. They supply atmosphere, antigravity, and much else. * But there is trouble brewing. Although eutopia has come, there is a strong minority of disgruntled hooligans on the Moon who would like either to seize world power or destroy the new order. With the cooperation of a traitor in the establishment, the hooligans break into the great lunar power station, where they are trapped—thanks to a miscalculation by the traitor. * This is bad enough, but the lunar power station (which cannot be entered because of a dimensional lockout) is draining the energy from the sun, which in a matter of weeks will become a cold star. Even the superscience of the visitors cannot prevent this. Secondary heat sources, including "all manner of devious heat machines," will not serve. * The best that the visitors can do, since they are now both tired of life and disappointed and disgusted with mankind, is destroy the lunar power station by ramming it with their spaceship, knowing that it means death for themselves. The impact turns the Moon into a new small sun. All will be well, for mankind can now perhaps absorb what the visitors have brought. * More unified than usual with Fearn.

407. LINERS OF TIME. *Amazing Stories,* May-August 1935. Ill. Morey.

(Reprinted in book form by World's Work, London, 1947.)

Novel. *Time:* the base time is A.D. 2000, but with excursions to A.D. 22,000, the Mesozoic past, and the future billions of years after the death of the solar system. * *Place:* mostly the New York area. * *Background:* New York, A.D. 2000, is a supercity with suspended gravitation stairways and air lanes filled with planes buoyed by a gas lighter than hydrogen. Buildings are sheathed heavily with lead to block out cosmic rays that cause human aging. Ground transportation stresses automobile-like vehicles powered by wireless transmission, with power ultimately from solar stations. Oddly enough, space travel has proved to be impossible. * One of the major industries of the day is time travel. This became possible a generation or so earlier when radio experimentation discovered a time fluid along which ships can travel. * With the time liners of the monopolistic Time Liner Corporation, it is possible to go almost anytime in the future except the so-called Problem Area, from about A.D. 22,000 for a few thousand years, which in some fashion is shielded against time sightseers. * Problem: Commander Sanford Lee, a master pilot for Time Liner Corporation, is assigned to investigate the disappearance of several time liners in the future. Associated with him is his girlfriend Elna Folson, who hails from A.D. 20,000, but is currently resident in 2000. Also connected with both is the strange, villainous Elnek Jelfel, who claims to come from the Problem Area (though this seems impossible) and expresses too much interest in Elna Folson—to Lee's loudly expressed annoyance. * Lee's ship takes off with both Elna and Jelfel on board, whereupon things happen. Jelfel reveals himself as the Master of the Problem Area, transports Elna and Lee into it by matter transmission, and disintegrates their ship. * Jelfel now sends messages to the time centers of A.D. 2000 and A.D. 20,000, warning that unless they give him the (closely guarded) secret of time travel, he will kill both his captives. The time chiefs refuse, even though Elna Folson is the daughter of the chief executive of A.D. 20,000. * Jelfel also tells the young couple that he intends to destroy all civilization before and after

Fearn, John Russell (*continued*)

his own period by time vibrations, whereupon he will transport his own overpopulation to the cleared areas. * Lee and Elna Folson escape Jelfel temporarily, hoping to matter-transmit themselves back to 2000 and give warning of Jelfel's intentions, but Jelfel interferes, and they are tossed back to the age of the dinosaurs.   This is for the good, however, for amiable, superintelligent gaseous beings befriend them, show them an ancient time machine nearby, and set them forth back to 2000. * In 2000, however, the authorities do not believe the time voyagers; Lee is sentenced to immediate death, and Elna to long imprisonment. They escape when New York begins to collapse because of Jelnek's time vibrations. * Back to the time machine, which jams, transporting them out of the solar system, billions of years into the future, where they meet a planetary entity of supersuperintelligence.   He befriends them, gives them wholesome advice, and changes their brain structure to make them a superman and superwoman. (This change doesn't really amount to much in story detail, for Elnek continues to outwit them.) * Back to the Problem Area to a confrontation with Elnek, who captures them again and throws them into an engineering sweatshop, where they work on a strange vessel. Elnek tells those interested that the vessel is a time liner, but Lee, with his superbrain, eventually figures out that it is a spaceship—and space travel is considered impossible. * With the aid of a fellow prisoner who has invented an invisibility device and keeps it handy, all three confront Jelnek for the final showdown. * Lee, who has X-ray vision, hitherto neglected, discovers that Elnek is not human. Reproached for this, Jelnek confesses that he is from Jupiter, proving it by removing his human disguise and revealing himself to be a foul, multilegged monster. Battles and fisticuffs. Jelnek is killed. Lee and Elna return to 2000, where they discover, in a paradox of time, that the age is not ruined.   But the menace from Jupiter is still present.   Our hero and heroine now set up apparatus to toss Jupiter into the sun, which is easily managed. * Comment is not necessary except to say that Fearn, in addition to being a subliterate writer who even misuses words, never stops to recognize the implications or potentials of the various motifs that he tosses into the story helter-skelter. * A sequel, "Zagribud" (*Amazing Stories*, December 1937-February 1938) is beyond our time limit.

   408. **THE BLUE INFINITY**. *Astounding Stories,* September 1935. Ill. Dold.
Novelette. * *Time:* 1941 on. *Place:* Scotland, interstellar space, and a second universe. * In 1939 observations showed that a strange sun would pass through the solar system, perhaps destroying the Earth. Actually, the sun moved across the system without doing more than seismic damage to the Earth, and mankind thought the danger was over. * In a short time, however, things go wrong. Rio de Janeiro is burned to a cinder, and Australia and Tasmania sink beneath the sea. * The great scientist John Morgan explains: When the wandering star passed by our sun, it ruptured the corona, permitting powerful radiations to emerge and strike the Earth at predictable intervals and places, as the sun and Earth rotate. There seems no hope for Earth, for eventually everything will be consumed. * An unexpected visitor changes the situation. Miss Eunice Banks, genius daughter of the great Sir Rodney Banks, announces that she can save the Earth. Her father had anticipated everything, but, fearing to be

ridiculed, had said nothing. Instead, he spent his fortune constructing equipment. * The plan that Eunice proposes: remove the Earth from its orbit and transfer it to Alpha Centauri. With her father's machinery she will negate the sun's gravity so that the Earth will spin loose; then with a device that will destroy the ether (thus permitting faster than light travel) will set Earth on its path; progress will be accelerated by a gravity-tripler that will cause Alpha Centauri to attract Earth to it. Special equipment to be built will keep the atmosphere in place, and mankind can go underground during the transit, which Eunice believes will take about a week. Eunice wants Morgan to sponsor the idea, since men will not accept the judgment of a woman. * All goes well, and Earth moves out into space. But as it approaches Alpha Centauri, the gravity tripler breaks down—shoddy work by a greedy supplier—and Earth careens free through the universe. Stopping it would mean destruction. * Eunice has an idea: She now hopes that the Earth will burst out of our universe into another, which it does. The heavens are full of a blue haze, which Eunice interprets as multiple suns; oddly enough, gravity does not exist, only zones of force. Earth settles into an orbit around a pleasant, golden sun, but all is still not well. The sun does not produce ultraviolet radiation, and Earth's orbit will take it much too close to it. * Eunice has an idea: drag Earth back to its former universe by using its gravity. After some difficulties, this works. * Eunice has an idea: Storing some of the blue haze, she heads back to our old sun, where she flips it out to serve as a new corona. All now seems well. * The peoples of Earth build a gigantic statue of Eunice, but otherwise she is soon forgotten. Her marriage to the caddish brother of John Morgan turns out to be disastrous, and Eunice dies an unhappy woman. Her statue stands, however. * *Miscellaneous:* While Eunice had the Earth packed up and en voyage, all the other planets of the solar system were destroyed. * Rubbishy, but offers perhaps the first important female scientist in the literature.

   409. **MATHEMATICA**. *Astounding Stories,* February 1936. Ill. Marchioni.
Novelette. * *Time and place:* 1980, our world, and various levels of existence beyond time and space. * The concept behind the story is that persons and things, indeed universes, are reducible to mathematical statements, and that changes in these statements will involve changes in material manifestations. This is associated with macrocosm-microcosm relations. * In 1975 an expedition reached Vulcan, which was discovered to be an artificial metal construct. A fragment of its metal was taken to the laboratory of Professor Farrington by Dawson, who claimed that the metal had peculiar properties: Whatever one thought about took material form for a short time, then disappeared in a mass of geometric or abstract visual elements. Farrington, on first examining the metal, speculates that it must have been created or activated by a civilization far superior to ours. * About a year later, a remarkable mechanical device takes form in Farrington's laboratory, and from it emerges a small man with an enormous head.   Identifying himself as Pelathon, he claims that his universe was created by Farrington's thought when he first examined the fragment from Vulcan.   Pelathon's universe developed (and mankind evolved) for about ten billion years of his time, although only a year or so has passed on Earth. * Since Pelathon's science recognizes that "life is thought manifestation combined with figures," he determined to find the creator of his cosmos. Subtracting, with fantastic machines, from the "in-

Fearn, John Russell (*continued*)

finitely big to the small," he has come to Farrington's laboratory. * This is only the beginning, however, for Pelathon now raises the question, Whose thought has produced Farrington''s universe? Since matter is ultimately thought, the origin of our universe must be in some way connected with Vulcan and still a deeper microcosm. * Insulating a small spaceship with a special preparation created by Pelathon, Farrington, Pelathon and Vernon (the narrator) fly to Vulcan, the interior of which is filled with fantastic machinery much like Pelathon's. Locating a focal point, they use the machinery to subtract themselves to an atomic microcosm until, after a time, they reach a bare red planet, later identified as Mathematica. Emerging from their conveyance, since the planet is Earthlike, they first see shifting appearances, due to mathematical changes, then are greeted by a tiny man whose head is so enormous that it must be supported by a metal rack. This is Si-Lafnor, another mathematician, who takes them into a building filled with even more elaborate equipment. * Si-Lafnor explains: He is responsible for our universe, which reflects thought he put into it. The practical aspect of the creation was managed by the planetoid Vulcan, which is constructed of element 87. Thus, our universe and indirectly Pelathon's are all due to Si-Lafnor. * But regress continues. Si-Lafnor is in search of the mathematician who created him. The three travelers agree to accompany Si-Lafnor in his transmutations, but something goes wrong. As Pelathon explains it, their host's machines were designed to work on him, not others. In any case, Farrington and the narrator die of starvation on the barren planet Mathematica. Pelathon, whose race had adapted away from food and drink, remains in suspended animation. Is this the end? * No, after a time Farrington and Vernon find themselves re-created into distorted bodies. A new entity, the original mathematician, now addresses them. This is the ultimate; they can go no farther. The original mathematician created everything, but he is also perpetually reducing everything back to figures and factoring them out, so that his "eternal" mathematical work will come to an end and he can rest. * The original mathematician begins to dissolve them, but salvation is at hand. Si-Lafnor, who has solved a problem hindering him, appears and turns them into primes, just as he had previously done to himself. They are now immune to factoring by the original mathematician and are immortal. * The Terrestrials and Si-Lafnor return to Mathematica, where they find Pelathon. Si-Lafnor now promises to create a universe and a second Earth suitable for them, although he is not sure whether an occasional minor difference may not creep in because of the difficulty of the mathematics. Alas, the differences, though at first trivial, really add up, for the world the men find themselves on has little resemblance to Earth. It is a matter of odd dimensions. Pelathon explains a little. Si-Lafnor, although well-meaning, made mistakes. The people of the planet, though alien and hostile, cannot harm the three arithmetical travelers, who, as primes, are immortal, even demigod-like in appearance. This eternal isolation is their punishment for venturing down into arithmetic. The three now live together in a small cave. * Interesting concepts and more ingenuity than Fearn usually displays, but the usual bad writing. A curious rendering of the mystical quest, with a solution that would now be regarded as Gnostic. * For a sequel see #410, "Mathematica Plus."

410. **MATHEMATICA PLUS**. *Astounding Stories*, May 1936. Ill. Schneeman.

Novelette. * Sequel to #409, "Mathematica." * Pelathon, Farrington, and the narrator are still stranded on the strange planet, which is called Xulon. Shifting his opinion considerably, Pelathon now declares that the natives, who are superior scientifically to his own world, are not so much maliciously hostile as callously indifferent to others. Living in a state between matter and thought, they amount to being pure intelligences. * At this point one of the natives of Xulon approaches and converses with the humans. The Xulonites, who have absorbed the knowledge of all the planets in their universe, as well as the races concerned, are puzzled at and interested in the three comrades, whom they are unable to absorb. * The intelligence, for convenience sake, thereupon assumes human form and makes an offer to them: If they will perform a task, the Xulonites will send them back to their own universe. The task is going to the end of numbers, in the opposite direction to the beginning our friends once reached. The Xulonite states that his own people would be destroyed if they made the attempt, but since the three humans are immortal, they can perform the task safely and return to report. The three agree. * They are now sent upwards in size, watching the universe grow smaller and die. When the universe is finally gone, Pelathon then reveals what he secretly knew and withheld from the intelligences of Xulon: The journey had to be one-way; there was never any possibility of their being retrieved by Xulon. * Since the universe no longer exists, the three lose their bodies and become space spirits. But as Pelathon declares, mathematics is still present and must embody itself again. This is proved true, when a new universe forms, and the three find themselves reëmbodied in original form in the hall of the original mathematician, who offers explanations. * He was formed out of the intellect in the previous universe, yet he has himself formed all the universes. The previous visit of Farrington, Si-Lafnor, and the narrator to him has not yet taken place. The supreme mathematician will now form Si-Lafnor's universe, ours, and Pelathon's. * The men find themselves back on Mathematica, where Si-Lafnor continues explanations. As both the intelligences of Xulon and the supreme mathematician have declared, time does not exist. Yet, paradoxically, time is a cyclical matter. Si-Lafnor reveals that his creation of the alien universe of Xulon was not a miscalculation, but a deliberate step toward the ultimate return. * The men, controlled by the mathematics of Si-Lafnor, now live their original voyage from Earth to Vulcan backwards, arriving at the laboratory where Pelathon first appeared. Pelathon returns to his universe, and Farrington and the narrator find themselves at the moment when Farrington, holding the metal from Vulcan, unwittingly created Pelathon's universe. Time has now made a complete circle. * If Fearn is remembered favorably at all, it will be for the two Mathematica stories, which despite the usual weak writing and poor planning, embody ingenious and intricate paradoxes.

411. **SUBCONSCIOUS**. *Amazing Stories*, August 1936. Ill. Morey.

Novelette. * *Time:* 1937 following. *Place:* England and Mars. * Since the structure is elaborate, junky, and confused, it is best to present the story in terms of themes and motifs. * On Earth, young science-master Moore Holmes experiences strange symptoms after being struck by lightning. When sleeping or daydreaming he is a being called King-Lord Laj, who is master of another world—soon identified as Mars. Laj has set in motion

Fearn, John Russell (*continued*)

a green electric space cloud that will extinguish life on Earth within a few months. Once the green cloud has destroyed mankind, the Martians will immigrate to Earth. Mars is dying, with its final gasp a matter of weeks away. * *The immediate background:* Laj and his consort-to-be, Princess Olania, control by their will power, augmented by fantastic machinery, the minds of everyone on Earth, Laj the men, Olania the women. Their power operates through the subconscious mind, which is not really human, but a Martian extension, sealed off from the conscious mind by a neural barrier. The lightning that struck Holmes dissolved his mental barrier so that he receives feedback from Laj. * *The past background:* Laj and Olania, who seem from some passages to be incredibly old, have controlled mankind for ages, and have telepathically built up human civilization in order to prepare the planet for the Martian immigration. * *The action on Earth:* Holmes and two friends, once they understand the situation behind Holmes's dreams, realize that they must act to save the Earth. His friends, recapitulating his electric shock, also come in touch with Laj's mind. Since Holmes's impingement has disturbed Laj somewhat, destroying his utterly intellectual approach, the men hope that their trine involvement may destroy him. Holmes's girlfriend Una Lannister is similarly prepared to attack Olania. * *The Martian background:* Laj is aware that he is slipping mentally and is worried. If the council learns of it, he will be deposed and his impending marriage to Olania will be canceled. Olania, at first even more cold and ruthless than Laj, also finds her resolution sapped by contact with Una. * The two Martian leaders come to the conclusion that it would be immoral to destroy Terrestrial life. They agree that it would be better to let Mars die. This does not suit Laj's jealous and ambitious second-in-command, who murders Laj and denounces Olania. But Olania is equal to the occasion. She produces two devices that Laj had been secretly working on: a machine for reading dead brains and another for capturing fossil sound. They confirm her account of happenings, and the council decides that Mars must change its policy toward Earth. The Martians shut off all machines, both those that threaten Earth and those that maintain life on Mars, thus committing suicide en masse, in toto. * As a side effect of inactivating the Martian control machines, Earthmen no longer have subconscious minds and no longer dream. One wonders what psychoanalysts then do for a living. * It should be mentioned that the abstract above is considerably clearer and more consistent than Fearn's story.

412. **DESERTED UNIVERSE**. *Astounding Stories,* September 1936. Ill. Schneeman.
Short story. * In a prologue and epilogue from A.D. 2082, explorers from another universe tell of finding Earth totally devoid of human life, even of skeletal remains, although architecture and material culture are still in reasonable condition. The explorer Moviz-Kaflo offers an explanation based on records he has examined. * In 1951 the great (unfortunately moribund) scientist Dr. Hugh Calthorpe summons former student Peter Conroy to help conduct the great experiment that is the summation of Calthorpe's work. Calthorpe believes that mankind is controlled by outside forces whose thought flows in varying degree into human minds. "[F]rom birth to death we are in a kind of trance, a dream, dictated [to us] by some other power, immovably linked to the vast complexity which we call

universal thought." * Calthorpe also believes that the brain continues to function as such a receiving station after death, so long as it is not allowed to decay. To corroborate his theory, Calthorpe has constructed a thought helmet that will convey his thoughts after death to Conroy. * When the apparatus is activated by Calthorpe's death, Conroy first sees a cosmic vision, then awakens in a strange laboratory, to a new, superior identity in a macrouniverse. As Vanrod, he has been undergoing a common surgical procedure in which individual brain cells are removed, then inserted into beings in a subuniverse. In other words, our universe is simply the contents of a bowl in a laboratory in the macrocosm. * The problem is that Calthorpe's experiment on Earth has disturbed a cosmic balance. As the operating surgeon coldly tells Vanrod/Conroy, such an event took place once before, with the resulting extinction of intelligent life. It will now happen again. * Conroy awakens back in our universe. In a short time the prediction of the surgeon from the macro-universe is fulfilled. People disappear in ever increasing numbers until mankind is gone. Intelligent life also disappears from the macrocosm. The explorer from another universe, because of his different origin, is unaffected by the disaster. * The reader is also likely to be unaffected.

413. **DYNASTY OF THE SMALL**. *Astounding Stories,* November 1936. Ill. Dold.
Novelette. * *Time:* 1937-1940 or so. * According to Dr. Haddon Blair's system of microbiology, protozoa eat bacteria, thus maintaining a balance of life, but they also cause certain human diseases. * Hoping to eradicate all disease, Blair begins with protozoa, developing in his laboratory an amoebic form of life that eats their nuclei. His colleagues regard his claims askance, but the great explorer Northern obtains a quantity of the culture for use on an African safari. Unfortunately, the plane carrying it crashes, releasing the amoebics into the sea. * Changes soon become obvious. The seas become black. Vegetation increases enormously, since friendly bacterial action is no longer inhibited by protozoa. With such increase of plant growth, water is almost exhausted. And new bacterial diseases arise that almost wipe out humanity. * Blair and his friend Northern see only one solution: establish isolated, sterile fortress-colonies and try to work out a bacteriological remedy. Thus, in a short time a small cadre of humanity is concentrated in such enclaves, while the rest of mankind dies. * As the isolates watch, they see a new development. Bacteria now grow to visible size, indeed, burst into enormous tree-like forms of incredible beauty and complexity—and demonstrate intelligence. Conversing telepathically with Blair and others, they reveal that they have always been intelligent and maintained a culture, but only now, thanks to Blair, whose work they recognize, have they been able to develop fully. Unfortunately, their plans do not really include a place for mankind. * The situation looks hopeless, but the militarists initiate a war against the germs, using apparatus like giant lawn mowers. The result, unexpectedly, is the death of the bacteria, for while cut-up germs sprout into new individuals, this results in overpopulation and lack of nutrients; as a result the bacteria die of starvation. Humanity can now emerge into a disease-free world. * Carelessly planned and sillier even than usual.

FEDOR, A. and HASSE, H[ENRY]
Hasse (1913-1977) was a U.S. (Indiana and later West Coast) fan and writer with some interest in bibliographic matters. Together

Fedor, A. and Hasse, Henry (*continued*)

with William Crawford he compiled a useful (untitled) index to the fantastic fiction in the Munsey magazines. He also collaborated with Ray Bradbury on "Pendulum," Bradbury's first published story, and with Emil Petaja. Hasse also had a few stories published in the 1960s. * Fedor, who is elsewhere referred to as Al Fedor, was at that time a resident of the Chicago area. In 1935 he delivered a speech about sciencefiction to the Chicago s-f club. Nothing else is known of him. A letter in the November 1931 issue of *Amazing Stories* is from an Albert Feder of Detroit. Given the propensity of the letter column editors to misspell names, this may be Fedor.

414. THE END OF TYME. *Wonder Stories*, November 1933. Ill. Burian.

Short story. * Probably intended to be humorous or at least satirical. * B. Lue Pencill, editor of *Future Fiction*, receives a visit in his office from a strangely dressed man. The stranger, who identifies himself as Tyme, claims to have come from the year 2232 in order to make certain changes in 1932. He also reveals that his mode of time travel is a variant on matter transmission, using time molecules instead of matter. * Pencill, who believes Tyme to be insane, plays along with him for a short time, but manages to summon assistance. Tyme is dragged away and locked up in a mental institution, from which he mysteriously disappears. * Sophomoric, immature work. For a sequel see #415, "The Return of Tyme."

415. THE RETURN OF TYME. *Wonder Stories*, August 1934. Ill. Winter.

Short story. * Sequel to #414, "The End of Tyme." * *Future Fiction* is in bad shape financially, and editor B. Lue Pencill is about to commit suicide when he is interrupted by Tyme, the man from the future. Tyme, producing a stack of *Future Fiction* magazines, proves to Pencill that not only did he not commit suicide, but that the magazine continued profitably for years. As a secondary point, Tyme's file proves that Pencill did obtain rights to print Professor S. Mith's epoch-making novel "The Core." * Tyme explains how the nearly bankrupt publishing house can survive. Pencill must come to terms with Mith on a long-term basis, and then, since the contents of future magazines are known and available for years ahead, pay the authors minimum rate. It all works out well. * What Tyme and Pencill apparently overlook is that the magazine is at the mercy of any author who holds out for high payment—since ultimately *Future Fiction* must yield. * An interesting paradox, but Fedor and Hasse ignore a deeper paradox: Who did create the stories?

FEZANDIÉ, [ERNEST] CLEMENT (1865-1959)

U.S. (New York) author; born in New York, earlier life teaching in New York City schools; technical writer; president of Declat Mfg. Co. Died in Belgium. In many ways the epitome of a Gernsback author, most of his stories were based on a somewhat clumsy exegesis of an advanced technological concept. Often, however, his extrapolations proved prophetic. Some thirty-nine previous stories about Dr. Hackensaw appeared in Gernsback's *Science and Invention* from 1921 through 1925. These, and a novel, *Through the Earth* (1895), about an earth tube, are fully described in *Science-Fiction: The Early Years*. The following two stories are the last members of the series. * See also Henry Hugh Simmons, pseud.

416. DR. HACKENSAW'S SECRETS, SOME MINOR

INVENTIONS. *Amazing Stories*, June 1926. Ill. Paul.

Short story. * Pep (a young girl protagonist) visits Hackensaw (a very great scientist and inventor), who soliloquizes about his latest inventions. Most of the story is devoted to his experiments for a mechanism to rid the business world of secretaries, whom he characterizes as ignorant, gum-chewing ninnies. His first machine is an electric typewriter that used electric contact between fingertips and keys to print more rapidly than pushdown keyboards. His final invention in this area is a voice-activated machine that prints from dictation, homonyms being distinguished by special prefixes. This machine also translates many languages. * Other devices are an antitheft sign for automobiles, a process for canning bread, and a mechanical judge. The rationale for the mechanical judge is paradoxical: The weaker case will pick the better lawyer. Therefore the mechanical judge, which measures intelligence and legal skill, automatically will find for the weaker advocate. * Other inventions are devices for measuring a woman's age, the height of her skirts, and the hardness of her arterial walls. But the doctor drops this chain of research when he loses all his female friends. * Curiosity fare only.

417. DOCTOR HACKENSAW'S SECRETS. THE SECRET OF THE INVISIBLE GIRL. *Amazing Stories*, July 1926. Unsigned ill.

Short story. * The last of the stories about Dr. Hackensaw and Pep. * Hackensaw acquires a new assistant, Phessenden Keene, who becomes indispensable. On a trip to Africa Keene unwittingly photographs an invisible young woman, whose aura is recorded by the photographic process. * Hackensaw, Pep, and Keene set out to capture the woman. They set out bundles of bananas as bait, then when she takes some, Hackensaw's special audion (radio tube) that magnifies odors enables them to track her; when she is treed, special ultraviolet-sensitive spectacles render her visible, and Keene ropes her. * Hackensaw and his party bring her to New York, where they try to civilize her, but she cannot tolerate the climate and dies. Pep, who had been somewhat jealous of Aura, as she was called, eventually marries Keene. * Unlike the other Hackensaw stories, which are humor of a rough sort, a heartless production.

FIERST, A[DOLF] L.

An associate editor with Gernsback's *Air Wonder Stories* and *Science Wonder Stories* in 1930. Said to have been a rewrite man. Active in the American Interplanetary Society. Portrait accompanying story shows a man in young middle age.

418. THE MAN OF BRONZE. *Wonder Stories Quarterly*, Winter 1931. Ill. Miller.

Short story. * *Time:* 1945. * Young Frederick Vaux, ostensibly an irresponsible playboy, really works for the Secret Service. In the present instance he is assigned to investigate the sculptor Helmer, who has a studio in New York. Vaux's superior believes that Helmer, with whom Vaux is friendly, is really a secret agent of the Hisalpinians (whose identity the reader can readily guess). The present problem concerns the great scientist Manning, who has developed a superexplosive. The Secret Service believes that Helmer and his associates are trying to get the formula. And Manning is now missing. * Vaux, after preliminaries, visits Helmer's studios and lets it be known that he is also very interested in atomic physics, which happens to be true. Helmer then invites him to see his private laboratory, which is

Fierst, A. L. (*continued*)

operated by the great Hisalpinian scientist Kroll. * There Vaux sees two things of interest: a powerful apparatus emitting short-wave radiation that amounts to a disintegrator; and a marvelous statue of Manning. Unfortunately, as Vaux soon recognizes, the statue is not really a statue, but the copperplated corpse of Manning—which means that the Hisalpinians have the formula. * Vaux arouses the suspicions of Kroll and Helmer and is himself due to be electroplated. But all ends well. The Hisalpinians are foiled, and the formula is saved. * Not badly written on the surface level, with good concrete detail. An acceptable minor thriller. * The story was originally scheduled for the November 1930 issue of *Amazing Detective Tales.*

[Anonymous]

Presumably a British writer.

419. **FIGHTING GAS**. *Scoops,* 19 May 1934. Unsigned ill.

Boys' fiction. * Short story. * Crooks Bud Flanagan and Pete M'Gee, after burglarizing Professor Dunn's laboratory, make off with the formula for a gas the professor has created: fighting gas. A permanent alcoholic vapor, it renders those who breathe it irascible, quarrelsome, and vicious. The two Irishmen use the gas to incapacitate possible obstructive persons while they raid jewelry stores, banks, and other sources of wealth. On each occasion, the gas produces a riot in which the police join. * Newspaper reporter Jack Mansford is caught up in the action in one such robbery. Smarting with humiliation later, he associates the robbers with the Dunn case and reasons that a gas mask would be protection. During a riot at Birmingham, Jack catches sight of the masked robbers and follows them to their lair, where they are plotting to rob the Bank of England. * As the Irishmen start their operation, they set up diversions along the route and, in front of the Bank, begin to seize a shipment of bullion. But Jack, who has followed them, succeeds in ripping off their masks, whereupon they succumb to fighting fury and are captured.

FISHER, PHILIP M[ELANCHTHON], JR. (1891-?)

U.S. (California) writer. Graduated University of California, Berkeley, 1913. Newspaper writer and executive, political figure. Seems to have been still alive in 1940s. The identification of this man with Philip M. Fisher, educator (1878-1932), in *Science-Fiction: The Early Years* is wrong. Although the present story is trivial, Fisher wrote several competent, thought-provoking stories for the Munsey magazines in the late 1910s and early 1920s. These stories have occasionally been reprinted and are described in *Science-Fiction: The Early Years.*

420. **THE LADY OF THE MOON**. *Astounding Stories,* August 1935. Ill. Marchioni.

Short story. * *Place:* the San Francisco Bay area. * The narrator visits fiftyish Professor Kimball Jamison, who claims that he has made a wonderful discovery, a supertelescope with a viewing platform that presents what seem to be holographic images. Jamison, who is obviously very excited, then displays his invention. Focusing on a certain meadowy place on the Moon, he creates on his viewing platform the image of a gorgeous blonde human female. Jamison, despite his age and general decrepitness, is infatuated with the woman and believes that she sees him and reciprocates. The viewing over, the narrator leaves.

Shortly after this, Professor Jamison disappears, and the narrator wonders whether the moon woman took him to herself. * Old-fashioned and routine.

FLAGG, FRANCIS

Pseud. of Henry George Weiss (1898-1946) Nova Scotia-born U.S. (Arizona, California) writer. The literature usually gives his name as George Henry Weiss, but Henry George Weiss is correct ("Why I Use a Pen Name," *Fantasy Magazine*, February/March 1935). Attended University of California. Educator, occasional writer of both science-fiction and weird fiction. An intelligent writer, whose work was often original, imaginative, and literate, but constrained by pulp considerations. One of the better writers in the genre pulps; his stories (from *Weird Tales)* were occasionally listed in the *O. Henry Memorial Award, Best American Short Stories* volumes. His poetry appeared under his real name in *Driftwind, Contemporary Verse,* and *Bozart.* Flagg's only separate publication is a small chapbook, *The Night People* (Los Angeles: F.P.C.I., 1947). * See also the collaboration Francis Flagg and Forrest J. Ackerman.

421. **THE MACHINE MAN OF ARDATHIA**. *Amazing Stories*, November 1927, Unsigned ill.

(Reprinted in Ashley, *History of the Science Fiction Magazine,* Vol One.)

Short story. * The narrator, a retired elderly social theorist, is pondering a sentence that he is writing, when there is a blinding flash, and in the place of his rocking chair is a crystalline tube about five feet high, in which, surrounded and encompassed by gadgetry, is a strange creature about three feet high. It has an enormous head and a tadpole-like body. * The creature, which is very friendly, identifies itself as a cyborg (my term) from A.D. 29,926. A historian in its time, it knows English well, though it speaks by means of a mechanical apparatus. * The visitor's exposition: In Ardathia, the future land, humanity has divested itself of sex; individuals are produced synthetically, then inserted into crystal tubes, where they live out their lives. In the tube it is nourished by a circulating fluid controlled by machinery in the base. Longevity is about fifteen hundred years, but accidents, since the Ardathians explore and perform hazardous exploits, kill many. * While an Ardathian itself is physically helpless, it has a large range of mechanical and radiational tools with which it can perform tasks as stupendous as moving a mountain or traveling in time. * The present Ardathian does not explain time traveling in any detail, except to say that time is a continuum. Time traveling is not unfamiliar to the Ardathians, but this is the first occasion that a traveler has come so far into the past. * The Ardathian gives a general history of humanity. About A.D. 16,000, the Bi-Chanics came to realize that "man's bodily advancement lay on and through the machine. They perceived that man only became human when he fashioned tools." They accomplished much, but were succeeded by the Tri-Chanics, who developed the crystal envelope that encases the time traveler. The Tri-chanics raised embryos in vitro, but became extinct when their successors, the Ardathians developed. * The Ardathian leaves unexpectedly, and when the narrator tells of his experience he is considered insane and is clapped into an asylum. There is a little ambiguity here, but the resolution of a prophecy made by the Ardathian makes the story veridical. * A very clear statement of the development of cyborgs, with a fair amount of (fictional) plausibility. See also #431, "The Cities of

Flagg, Francis (*continued*)

Ardathia" for a connected story.

422. **THE MASTER ANTS**. *Amazing Stories*, May 1928. Unsigned ill.

Short story. * After a fashion a latch-on to H. G. Wells's "The Empire of the Ants." * *Time:* the present and A.D. 2450. *Place:* mostly in and around California. * A strange manuscript is precipitated from the air, along with the wreckage of a small time machine. The ms., which is from long-missing Professor Reubens and his friend Raymond Bent, conveys the following story. * Professor Reubens, who has constructed a time machine frankly in the mode of H. G. Wells, invites his friend Bent to make a small journey into the future. Off, and crash! The two men awaken naked, bearded, and bald amid a pile of scrap metal that was once a time machine and discover that they have aged perhaps twenty to twenty-five years. Unforeseen friction caused by passing through time, explains the professor. * As the men explore, they are almost immediately captured by foot-long intelligent ants who ride naked, devolved humans as steeds. The two men are taken to the ant city, where they are placed in a corral with other devolved humans. It now becomes obvious that the humans are domestic animals, ridden as mounts and (the females) milked for ant food. Bent suffers the horrible, humiliating experience of being broken in by an ant, who, using antennas as a bit, rides him until he is exhausted and broken in spirit. * Fortunately, after this, the two men spy an aircraft in the sky, and a normal human woman, peering out, rescues them and takes them to Science Castle, the last stronghold, as far as is known, of humans. There, the time travelers learn from the English-speaking humans what has happened to the Earth. * It is now A.D. 2450, and the ants have just about conquered the world, with the exception of this one refuge. Back around 1935 rumors and news reports first mentioned a plague of giant, intelligent ants in South America. But the world paid no heed. The stories were confirmed and the ants continued to advance, but the nations were indifferent, being concerned more with local matters and wars. By the time the ant peril was recognized as such, it was too late. The ants, who can chew through anything except a certain alloy, were too numerous, and human armies were simply taken over as beasts of burden by the ants. * A few farsighted scientists, however, began to build an impregnable fortress against the ants (Science Castle), which was finished around A.D. 2000. By this time humanity (except as beasts of burden) was extinct in the Western Hemisphere. * Science Castle (which exists in a state of perpetual siege and is approachable only from the air) survives by the utmost ingenuity in recycling and recombining materials. Science is enormously high, with various viewing devices, heat rays, wireless power transmission, and much else. The population is small. * But now an emergency arises. Hitherto, the air has been safe, since the ants had no flying machines, and the builders of Science Castle did not protect the top areas with the protective alloy. But now the ants, who have made an alliance with giant wasps, attack from the air. As the narrative ends, Science Castle, except for a small sealed area, has fallen, and free humanity is almost extinct. Reubens sends his message back via his repaired time machine. * Bent also has a romance with a future woman. * The episodes where the ants break Bent as a mount are powerfully handled. * For an earlier adventure of Professor Reubens, see #430, "The Seed of the Toc-Toc Birds."

423. **THE BLUE DIMENSION**. *Amazing Stories*, June 1928 Ill. Paul.

Short story. * *Place:* California and an other-world. * The young man who assisted Crewe in his experiments is justifying himself, proclaiming that he did not really murder Crewe. * Crewe, a specialist in optics, explains to the narrator that we perceive only a limited range of vibrations, and that there are vibratory groups which amount to other-worlds. Crewe then produces a pair of spectacles for seeing into the other-world. What the men see is a blue world, with strange vegetation and odd animal life. There are gigantic, semi-humanoid beings with extensible tentacle "arms," a more civilized and smaller brownish form of similar humanoid life; and a strange city, into the buildings of which the doctor and the narrator cannot look, for unexplained reasons. Crewe has also invented a roller press-like arrangement, which, as he demonstrates with mice, can transfer things to the other-world. Against the wishes of the narrator, Crewe now hops into the machine, emerging in the other-world as a gigantic being. For a while the narrator loses sight of him, but when Crewe returns and signals that he wishes to be retrieved, there is a difficulty. He neglected to transfer a vibrator to the other-world, so that he is now stranded. He signals for food, which the narrator sends, but when the narrator drops the dimensional spectacles, they no longer function, and there is no telling what has happened to Crewe. * More clichéd than usual with Flagg.

424. **THE LAND OF THE BIPOS**. *Science Wonder Stories*, March 1930. Ill. Paul.

Short story. * The narrator (a college dropout) and his friend Red are members of a criminal gang that intends to burglarize the establishment of the chemist Sanborn, who is reputed to be a wealthy miser. The two men, on breaking into the laboratory, however, are rendered unconscious; they awaken to find themselves in a giant glass container. Sanborn calmly informs that as criminals they now have a chance to make themselves useful. He intends to transmit them as electrons to another plane of existence. (Exactly what the chemist has in mind is not clear, since he refuses to popularize for his captives. But he mentions transmission around the universe and cyclical universes that may involve change.) * The two men find themselves in an Earth-like habitat, but one ruled by man-sized bird-like creatures (Bipos) who have a science superior to ours and various monstrous servitor creatures. There are also humans in this world, but, alas, they are cattle, kept by the Bipos for meat. Our anti-heroes escape, and after various adventures (including fighting off a gigantic beetle), reach underground warrens where the humans live. Human culture is very primitive, but individuals are not unintelligent. * The narrator and Red marry and settle down among the Murlos, showing them how to repel raids of a vermin-hunter that the Bipos introduce into the warren. With the intention of locating other Murlo settlements, the two men wander far from the burrow, but are captured by the Bipos. * During the capture, Red uses his automatic to kill an animal the Bipos use for hunting, and this interests their captors. After some preliminaries, they place Red before a screen that reveals thoughts. The Bipos scientist first indicates his view of the humans as the stupid equivalents of vermin that destroy crops; Red reveals scenes of Terrestrial life, to the amazement of the Bipos—and then the two men are retrieved by Sanborn. Although they have lived weeks in the other world, they have been away from Earth only a matter of hours. * Their experiences in

Flagg, Francis (*continued*)

the other world have rehabilitated the two men, and they would now like to return with suitable resources and help the Murlos. Sanborn will accompany them with a small arsenal and scientific equipment. He would like to communicate with the bird people. * An entertaining fable.

425. **AN ADVENTURE IN TIME**. *Science Wonder Stories*, April 1930. Ill. Paul.

Novelette. * *Time:* 1950 and A.D. 2999. *Place:* California. * In the 1950 frame, Bayers, Professor of Physics at the university and a notorious controversialist, claims that time travel is possible. Indeed, after an absence from the campus, he returns looking somewhat bedraggled and claims he has been into the future. His listeners scoff. * His story: Despite his earlier theorizing, matters really began when a small time-sphere materialized in his lab, bearing a holographic (my term) image of a beautiful woman named Editha. He studied the apparatus and constructed a larger model, in which he set forth, hoping that since he duplicated the previous machine, he would arrive at the era from which it was dispatched. * Bayers, after some minor problems, finds himself in a strange area: It is all wild and beautiful, but in the distance are white buildings. Approaching him is a tall strangely clad man, walking on the air with peculiar shoes. But then he sees that it is not a man, but a woman. She bids Bayers follow her, and he is taken in an aero to the central intelligence division, where women question him. When he says that he came from the past, the women do not disbelieve him, but comment that experimentation in time travel has been discontinued, since they want no disturbance from the males in the past. From this, Bayers learns that the future society is a gynecocracy. * *Background:* After a World War in 1938, there was a really terrible war in 1969, during which about half the human race died. After the second war an international league was set up with a governing body, prohibition of war, international support measures, and a general socialist approach. By 1998 the members of the congress were overwhelmingly women, who then established a feminist government. Over the course of time genetic engineering increased the size and strength of women and diminished the height of men to about five feet. Men now live as pampered pets or tolerated second class citizens who have no say about anything. Fortunately, Bayers's time machine is concealed, so that the women cannot destroy it. * Bayers conforms externally to the new world, although, as later becomes obvious, he does not know everything that is going on. Meeting some of the future males, who are small, weak creatures, he becomes involved in an underground movement and agrees to help them gain freedom. Since (because of his height) he can pass as a woman if visibility is poor, he is chosen to disable the control center for the mechanical apparatus of the culture. With this control center in their power, the men hope to win an equal share in the government. * Bayers intends to do his part, but who is in charge of the control center but the beautiful Editha of the time sphere, who scornfully tells him that his attempt would have been useless because of safeguards. One word leads to another, whereupon Editha attacks him. Bayers, who wrestled in previous life, has almost met his match in the Amazon, but manages to overcome her with jujitsu pressure points. She is humiliated, but when he kisses her, she responds, and they become lovers. Their love is no by means smooth, however, for Editha's feelings are ambivalent. On the one hand

she loves Bayers, but on the other she bitterly resents the fact that a man has overcome her—and their wrestling bouts continue. * The end comes when Editha is chosen to be one of the Mothers. Flagg is not entirely clear as to what is involved, but the Mothers are immortal, or nearly so, and are in charge, in some way, of the breeding programs. Judging from Editha's initial response, however, the new status involves brainwashing or diminution of personality. * Editha finally accepts the new status, whereupon the matrons declare that Bayers will be her mate. Again, while details are not provided, he will perhaps become a mindless stud, artificially maintained in life. * The machines carry Bayers off, as he protests. But the measures that would have restrained a future man are not enough for Bayers, who escapes and returns to his own time. His listeners in 1950 scoff, but he displays on his chest an enormous brand indicating his status in Editha's world. * *Miscellaneous:* The future women speak Esperanto. * The gynecocracy holds the east and west coasts of the United States, but in the central area is a more conventional area with normal sex relations. This area is hostile to the women (inconsistent with the eutopian aspect that the women described to Bayers when he first arrived). Bayers accompanies Editha on an air raid, in which the women's disintegrators cause the destruction of the iron and metals in the lands beneath them. Now the women will overrun the area and found a robot city to do their material work. * As for the time-sphere that Bayers copied, it was illicitly manufactured by Editha as an experiment. * The curious relationship between Editha and Bayers is imaginatively handled. Otherwise, the story is literate, but on the dull side.

426. **THE LIZARD-MEN OF BUH-LO**. *Wonder Stories*, October 1930. Ill. Marchioni.

Short story. * *Time:* 1935 on, with a frame in 1985. *Place:* California. * The story begins with William Swiff, young maverick scientist of genius, stating that he takes many of his ideas from science-fiction magazines. He esteems this form of literature, especially the work of Francis Flagg. * Promotion over, Swiff hires the narrator, a college friend, as a secretary and scientific dogsbody. Around 1935 Swiff discovers a chemical means for creating suspended animation and uses it successfully on animals and men. It actually has a curative effect on chronic disease. By 1945 Swiff, who is secretive, is working on a more ambitious project, although the narrator knows nothing about it. On the crucial occasion he simply sees Swiff disappear into an apparatus. A letter left behind by Swiff instructs the narrator to keep certain machines in operation until Swiff returns. * Ten years pass. In 1945 Swiff returns, young as when he left, but bruised, ragged and torn of garment. Swiff's story: Experimenting with the rotation of matter at nearly the speed of light, he opened a gateway to another world, but to enter it he had to be in a state of suspended animation. * Awaking in the otherworld, he found it Earth-like, with good vegetation, small partly feathered humanoid beings obviously evolved from hummingbirds, and nasty lizard-men. Swiff became very friendly with a hummingbird woman and saved her when she was abducted by the lizard-men, who use the hummingbird people's feathers for ceremonial costume and sacrifice the little beings. * Swiff was at first taken as a god by the lizard-men, but the canny high priest knew better. He enticed Swiff into a dark passage, captured him, and tossed him into the pit, where there were a man-eating plant and a horrible monster. Swiff shot the monster,

Flagg, Francis (*continued*)

escaped from the pit, killed the high priest, put the temple personnel to sleep with gas bombs, rescued his little friend, and returned to Earth. His subjective time was only a few days, although in Earth time he had been gone for ten years. * Swiff announces his intention to return to the other-world with guns and bombs. He leaves, but by 1985 has not returned. * *Miscellaneous:* The basic concept is that if something is rotated rapidly enough, it becomes not only invisible but intangible. Swiff thus passes through the wheel. The other-world is not precisely identified, but it seems to be the fourth dimension. * The inhabitants in the other-world communicate by sign language; since it is nearly universal, Swiff masters it easily. * An obvious outgrowth of H. G. Wells's *The Time Machine.*

427. THE SYNTHETIC MONSTER. *Wonder Stories,* March 1931. Ill. Marchioni.

Short story. * *Place:* Arizona. * Edwards, the narrator, a chemist who has moved to Arizona to arrest his tuberculosis, enters the employ of Dr. Jacobs, a brilliant but somewhat eccentric biologist, where he makes various preparations for Jacobs. Since Edwards is as incurious as Jacobs is secretive, he has no idea what Jacobs is up to. * Mysterious events take place around the establishment—a horrible creature with a strange flat face, and curious blubbering noises. It all ends when Something attacks Mrs. Reynolds, the housekeeper with whom Edwards is enamored, and Jacobs fights with Something in the laboratory. * Jacobs's lab notes explain matters: He has created protoplasm and with various rays and chemicals has been working toward an artificial man. But what he has produced has no mind and experiences mostly hunger. When the police find Jacobs's corpse, the monster, now dead, has swallowed Jacobs's head. * Routine, on the clichéd emotional side, but the ending comes as a nice shock as Flagg handles it.

428. THE HEADS OF APEX. *Astounding Stories,* October 1931. Ill. Wesso.

Short story. * Justus Miles, answering an ad for a soldier of fortune, is hired by the mysterious Solino, who seems to be disabled in some fashioned. Also working for Solino are Miles's friend and fellow mercenary Rusty Ward (both having served among the Sandanistas), and similar "hard guys." A remarkable submarine takes them into the sea, then crashes, skin broken, but no water enters. Instead, Miles and Ward find themselves in a great cave under the ocean. After perils, including fighting off gigantic green men, they reach Apex, where they meet a group of men resembling Solino. * One of these men, Zoro, the Chief of the Heads of Apex, explains. They (including Solino) are really cyborgs (my term). Their heads and brains are maintained mechanically, so that they are practically immortal. * The land of Apex is not in our world, but in a parallel world of different vibratory rate, and it is peopled by descendants of the Atlanteans, who had developed a supercivilization several hundred thousand years ago. At the moment, continues Zoro, the land is imperiled. The commoners are in rebellion, egged on by the renegade Head Spiro. Solino has recruited the band of mercenaries to crush the revolt. * Miles and Ward agree to put down the rebellion. Obtaining weapons from the submarine, they have some success against the rebels, but are captured. * They are now surprised to hear a different story from the renegade Spiro. While the other Heads did not lie, they did not tell the whole truth. The Heads preserve their immortality by

draining the blood of the commoners. As a result, the whole culture and race are dying of exhaustion. Spiro himself had been a normal man, with a woman he loved, but the Heads transformed him into a cyborg against his will. * Miles and Ward are bewildered and forced to examine their life roles. As mercenaries have they become assassins? They decide that they will not help Zoro and the Heads, but their decision does not alter matters, for Spiro plans to kill them anyway. But a maiden, Spiro's former sweetheart, helps them to escape, and all three emerge back in our world. Meanwhile, in Apex, the Heads, deprived of blood by the rebellion, have died of starvation. * *Miscellaneous:* The giant green men are aborigines of the other-world. Some interesting touches.

429. THE SUPERMAN OF DR. JUKES. *Wonder Stories,* November 1931. Ill. Paul.

Short story. * *Place:* Mostly Chicago and Arizona. * Killer Mike, important young mobster, falls afoul of his gangster overlord Frazzini and must leave town hurriedly. Frazzini, who is obviously Capone à clef, has enormous resources, both in the underworld and in the national government, and hounds Killer Mike across the country. * In Tucson Mike finds refuge. An elderly gentleman, seeing that Mike is homeless and almost destitute, hires him as a laboratory subject, assuring him that the work is safe. Mike accepts, hoping that Frazzini will not find his trail. * The scientist, Dr. Jukes, is experimenting with glandular extracts in an attempt to create a superman of a sort. His experiments so far have been successful in producing speed and strength. * Jukes hopes to sell his discovery to the U.S. government, but does not know that the politician with whom he has been dealing is really in Frazzini's pay. Frazzini wants the discovery to make his men more effective in crime. * Now that the experiment is successful, Jukes plans to murder Mike, as he has done with previous subjects, but by chance Mike is inoculated with the full strength of Jukes's compound, instead of a dilution. He becomes incredibly swift—to the point of being invisible when he moves—and strong. He kills Jukes, his assistant, and Frazzini's political contact, and then takes after Frazzini. One of Mike's new gifts is the ability to read thoughts. This is not a paranormal ability; according to one of the psychological theories of the day, thought is accompanied by tiny muscular movements of the vocal cords, which verbalize what is going on mentally. Mike can hear these subliminal vocal murmurings. * Mike kidnaps Frazzini and carries him out in the desert, where the ganglord is later found, totally mad. As for Killer Mike, when the extract wore off, his nervous system was so damaged that he is now a half-witted goatherd in New Mexico. * *Miscellaneous:* During the last stages of the glandular extract, Mike grew to about seven feet tall. * Not one of Flagg's better stories.

430. THE SEED OF THE TOC-TOC BIRDS. *Astounding Stories,* January 1932. Ill. Wesso.

Short story. * *Place:* California. * Remarkable events! Mining engineer Talbot sees two strange birds near an abandoned mine; spheres materialize in the air, burst, dropping seeds that grow almost instantly into impenetrable iron-like plant barriers; and almost before anyone knows it, the United States is endangered. * A young man comes forward with an explanation: The great Professor Reubens, who has disappeared, had long been working on viewing an atomic system; this achieved, he entered into communication with intelligent life-forms on an atomic planet.

Flagg, Francis (*continued*)

Ergo, the invaders must be coming from the microcosm. * Talbot, with Army assistance, enters the mine shaft; an associate will flood the area with an explosive gas if he does not return in a short time. * Inside the shaft, he finds what he has been searching for: the strange birds, who are manipulating elaborate machinery by telekinesis. He is captured and taken down to the atomic world, where he meets Reubens, who explains that the birds plan to conquer our world just as they have other worlds. Together the two men, escaping, take the horrible risk of throwing themselves into the size machine. They are returned to Earth just before the explosion takes place. The Earth is saved. * The final adventure of Professor Reubens is recounted in #422, "The Master Ants."

431. **THE CITIES OF ARDATHIA**. *Amazing Stories*, March 1932. Ill. Morey.

Novelette. * Although it may not be apparent to the reader who does not know the background Flagg describes in the brief article "About 'Ardathia'" (*Science Fiction Digest*, October 1933), the present story and "The Machine Man of Ardathia" are parts of a fictionalized future history, the middle terms of which do not seem to have been written. Flagg wanted to show what would happen if the machine remained unsocialized, the property of an unproductive class, and if the trend toward automation (my term) continued. * With regard to the term "Ardathia," Flagg may have felt some (not obvious) connection with Marie Corelli's novel *Ardath*. * *Time:* The first section is set in the not too distant future; the second, about five hundred years later. * *Background:* The first future world is much like that of the motion picture *Metropolis*. In the giant complexes called the Industrial Cities of Ardathia, humanity is distributed inequitably into economic and social classes. At the top are the few Purples, who hold the wealth and the power; they are headed by a small council called the Titans. At the bottom are the Unlings, who are downtrodden proletariat of the most oppressed sort. They live in utter misery and serve only to fulfill the needs of the Purples. Between the Purples and the Unlings are the Scholar Men, who serve as engineers, managers, magistrates, and supervisors, and just below them the Pinks, or internal police. The three upper classes do not live in the hells of the industrial cities proper, but in graduated play towns in the vicinity, commuting when necessary by plane. * The Unlings are smoldering with rebellion and are secretly organizing; working with them and coordinating them are the so-called Equalizers, who hope to create a more just society when the old order is overthrown. Heading the Equalizers is the renegade Purple Elan, a man with a social conscience; central to the story is Jan, an intelligent, capable Unling. * The story proper is concerned with the great rebellion and its outlying incidents. The Unlings and Equalizers count on the genius of the Unling scientist Ventar, who has devised program disks for controlling the Mechanical Brain and the mechanisms of the omnipresent weapons systems set up in the Unling quarters to keep the populace down. But Ventar, kidnapped by the Purples and bribed, instead gives the Unlings program disks responsive to the control of the Purples. As a result, when the rebellion takes place, the Unlings are slaughtered, and their leaders Elan and Jan are captured. * Before the rebellion, however, Elan and Jan had decided on a social experiment. They kidnapped Thora, daughter of Rocca, the leading Titan, and installed her in a horrible working class

milieu as an Unling, where she saw incredible misery and had to work for a living. As might be expected in such a fictional situation, Thora, who had been a spoiled princess, develops compassion and falls in love with Jan. * When the rebellion is crushed, the council, at Rocca's intervention, pardons Jan, who marries Thora and joins the council. While this is a sellout, it had been forced on him by Elan, as the only hope for the Unlings. * Jan and Thora remain happily married, while Jan works for social equality, but without much success. This story segment ends when the genius scientist Ventar announces a plan for complete automation of the cities, after which the workers would no longer be needed, but could be expelled into the wilderness. * The second segment of the story is set about five hundred years later. In this world, the giant machine that Ventar set up now rules humanity, with repression just as bad as in the earlier episode. Matters of individual life are totally controlled by the machine, which operates through a hierarchy of petty officials. * The people of the great cities believe that they constitute all humanity, and that beyond the cities there is nothing. Even to speculate on an outside world is punishable by death. The official creed is that the Machine created man. * Actually, in some areas in the outside world there are settlements descended from the Unlings expelled by Ventar 500 years earlier. They are semiprimitive agriculturalists. * Jan of the tribe of Rocca, a descendent of the earlier Jan and Thora, was plane-wrecked among these primitives for about ten years, and is just returning to the automatic city. He discovers that his wife has remarried, thinking him dead. This does not disturb him greatly, for he had expected it, but when he tries to explain where he had been for ten years, he is in great danger. When he proclaims that the outside world is inhabited and that humans made the Machine, and not the Machine humans, he has committed blasphemy. He is arrested, tried, sentenced to death, and "returned to the Machine," a euphemism for being crushed to death by a giant piston. * Some good detail, but today it all seems very dated, what with the euphoric leftist social protest of the time.

432. **THE RESISTANT RAY**. *Amazing Stories*, July 1932. Ill. Morey.

Short story. * *Time:* probably not too long after 1945, which is mentioned as the date of one of Ragnar's previous triumphs. * Ragnar, noted secret service agent, chances upon a Martian scheme to obtain a force screen of a sort from Dr. Lasser, its Terrestrial inventor. Old Dr. Lasser believed that he was developing his weapon for the United States, but actually he was being funded by the Martian prince Franz Josef. * Franz Josef has plans for conquering the Earth. He tried this once before (as is mentioned in passing), but was defeated by Ragnar, against whom he holds a grudge. * Franz Josef, holding Lasser and his beautiful daughter captive, flees, Ragnar in pursuit. Although Ragnar is captured by the zone of force, which acts like a solid substance, he turns the tables and all is well. The diplomats will sweep everything under the carpet. Franz Josef had plans for Miss Lasser, as does Ragnar, but Ragnar's are honorable. * A potboiler undoubtedly written down by Flagg.

433. **AFTER ARMAGEDDON**. *Wonder Stories*, September 1932. Ill. Paul.

Short story. * *Time:* perhaps the twenty-first century. *Place:* mostly the Los Angeles area. * The ancient priest of the blue flame tells a young man about the past and the history of their tribe. The priest is so old that he cannot remember exact years,

Flagg, Francis (*continued*)

but the beginning of his narrative probably dates from the end of the twentieth century. * War broke out after an inadequate peace conference that was sabotaged by politicians who held munitions investments. Exactly who was fighting whom is not entirely clear, but the French bombed the United States with bacteriological weapons and an explosive gas that erodes and destroys metals and many other substances. The death toll was horrendous, and civilization fell. * The narrator and a few others managed to fly to Tucson, where they survived for a time, gradually returning more and more to primitive ways as their old tools, weapons, and transportation devices were eaten away by remnants of the gas balls used during the war. They are not the only human survivors, for there are hostile Indians who move up from Mexico, but this seems to be the total situation for North America. * Leadership of the American survivors falls upon Williams, the most forceful of the survivors, who used to be the narrator's butler. Under his capable leadership the small group survives. * There is one problem that faces the survivors: shortage of women. A revolt among the womanless males is staved off by a wise decision of Williams's: let the women decide whether to accept polyandry. The result is that the future society, as the old man says, is a polyandrous matriarchy. * The survivors eventually return to the Los Angeles area, where the narrator, making use of the radiation and effluvia of a perhaps still active atomic bomb, attains enormous longevity and the role of priest and healer. But he is now ready to die. * Essentially a short rehash of Jack London's *The Scarlet Plague* and the end portions of H. G. Wells's *The War in the Air*, written perhaps to bring in the odd sexual notion. Not one of Flagg's better stories.

434. **THE MENTANICALS.** *Amazing Stories*, April 1934. Ill. Morey.

Short story. * *Time:* around A.D. 3500. *Place:* Long Island. * The great scientist Professor Stringer, funded by millionaire Olson Smith, has built a time machine. As Stringer says, his concept of time is based on electronic flow, and while he was building the machine it sometimes seemed as if someone were whispering instructions into his ear. * While Stringer is demonstrating the machine, Bronson, captain of Smith's yacht, on an impulse enters it and sets it off. He returns not too long afterwards in an explosion caused by partial materialization within a solid. On recovering sufficiently from his injuries, he tells his story. * For a time he is unable to stop the machine's progress, but when it finally comes to a halt, he finds himself in a barren area, around which are situated enormous, strange-looking buildings. From them emerge cylindrical machines that seem to move by hovering above the ground. They seize him, not too roughly, and carry him into the buildings, which form a complex with innumerable courts and passageways, to a place where there are a few people—naked, speechless, utterly savage, indeed, no longer really human. They squat around automatic food machines. * Bronson is not constricted in his movements, and he wanders freely, although always accompanied by the cylindrical machines, who emit a humming noise. Bronson hopes to encounter the humans who are the masters of the machines, but gradually comes to recognize that there are no humans except for the few subhumans he encountered and that the machines are autonomous. * During his wanderings he comes upon ancient accounts of the origin of the Mentanicals, the debates about machine intelligence, the creation of the multiple

mechanical cell, the placing of Mentanicals in industry, their gradual mental development, and their revolt in the form of a strike in which they no longer served man. By now mankind was so dependent on the Mentanicals that without them civilization collapsed. The Mentanicals, during this upheaval, were not so much hostile as indifferent to humanity. After a time a Mentanical civilization arose, as seen by Bronson. * Hearing a human voice, Bronson investigates and finds a human cyborg fastened to a cross. They converse, and Bronson learns that the man is Borgson, the inventor of the multiple cell, who was first converted to a cyborg before the machine revolt, then later maintained by the machines. Borgson adds more information: As Mentanical generations came and went, the belief arose among them that they were a natural evolution from mankind, with Borgson a transition point. They now hold Borgson in a certain veneration and maintain him in life. * Borgson, while begging Bronson for death, adds frightening news. The time machine was not an independent production of Professor Stringer's, but was suggested by radio waves through time from the Mentanicals, as was Bronson's entry into the machine. The machines, who expected a fellow machine, were nonplused when a human arrived. The Mentanicals do not plan conquest in an ordinary sense, but will simply move back and occupy the past. Thus, Borgson ends, it behooves Bronson to enter the time machine, which is standing beside Borgson's life apparatus, and return before the machines can prevent him. Bronson barely succeeds in evading the machines and operating the time machine. * Back in our time, Bronson is relieved to learn that Stringer, who was injured during Bronson's explosive return, has suffered brain damage and should no longer be subject to suggestion from the future. Smith is now devoting his not inconsiderable resources to buying up and suppressing any invention that might lead to the Mentanicals. * One of Flagg's better stories, with thought-provoking aspects.

FLAGG, FRANCIS and ACKERMAN, FORREST J.

Flagg has a separate entry. * Forrest James Ackerman (1916-present) is a U.S. (California) fan, collector, publicist, literary agent, author. Associated with the motion picture industry. Editor of various monster publications. Coauthor with A. W. Strickland of *A Reference Guide to American Science Fiction Films*, Volume One (1981). One of the more visible science-fiction fans from earliest times, with an incredible collection of printed material and motion picture ephemera and memorabilia. Has since written under about fifty pseuds. An ingenious hand with puns and neologisms, he confesses, with well-deserved remorse, to having created the term "sci-fi." The following story is described in *Gosh! Wow!* as being based on an idea of Ackerman's, developed by Flagg. A second Flagg-Ackerman collaboration, "An Experiment with Time," appears in the January 1934 issue of *Fantasy Magazine*.

435. **EARTH'S LUCKY DAY.** *Wonder Stories*, April 1936. Ill. Paul.

Short story. * *Time:* 1953 and 1978. * Mysterious events in 1953: A vessel exploring the stratosphere vanishes, as does a superfast racing car; a military force, including a secret weapon, disappears without a trace. * Some twenty-five years later a very strange explanation emerges. An enormous metal cylinder, hundreds of feet high, is found in the Arizona desert. In it are the corpses and associated artifacts of the cases mentioned,

Flagg, Francis and Ackerman, Forrest J. (*continued*)
together with about twelve hundred large tablets made of an unknown metal; on the tablets is an English message in enormous lettering, revealing that Earth was visited by beings of stupendous size, who looked for signs of life, but everywhere found only death. The beings learned English from thought records and wrote out the message as a memorial for the dead planet. * The gimmick is that the titanic space visitors have a different time sense and move with such rapidity that our motion seems like stasis to them, much like the situation in H. G. Wells's story "The New Accelerator." * Somewhat less than routine, with many plot loopholes.

[Anonymous, i.e., Bernard Buley, who has a separate entry.]
436. **FLAMING FRONTIER**. *Scoops*, 16 June 1934. Unsigned ill.
Boys' fiction. * Short story. * *Time:* the interstellar future. * *Place:* a spacedrome (space station) on the "Orion Passage," near the Black Star. * Ingredients: meteor swarms that the personnel of the spacedrome break up with explosives; the *Queen of Space*, a passenger vessel due to pass by soon; a volcano on the Black Star that will cause problems; antigravity, developed by CPO Frank Lawtor on the spacedrome; a Venusian derelict filled with carnivorous bugs. * Very low level, almost unintelligible. * The story has been identified as the work of Bernard Buley too late for insertion under his entry.

FLEMING, ROSCOE B.
Perhaps Roscoe Fleming, Colorado resident, author of *The Man Who Reached the Moon and Other Poems* (1955).
437. **THE MENACE OF THE LITTLE**. *Amazing Stories Quarterly*, Summer 1931. Ill. Morey.
Novelette. * *Time:* A.D. 2230. *Place:* mostly Washington, D.C., and Wymont, a new area formed from segments of Wyoming, Montana, and Idaho. * Rob Born, a Washington newspaper reporter, is the narrator in retrospect. * From around A.D. 2220 strange isolated happenings, not recognized as significant, have been leading up to the events of 2230: a small floating metal globe, ice-coated from presumable travel through the upper atmosphere; auroral displays in Wymont; electric fish seen by fishermen; small dragon fly-like flying machines with three-foot wing spreads; and the four-day, inexplicable cancelation of all electricity in the Los Angeles area in 2227. * In 2230 there is a new turn. Prominent scientists and politicians are found dead, their hearts exploded; and Rob is summoned by his future father-in-law, the biophysicist Henry Aurelius. * Aurelius has a strange story that he tells Rob confidentially: The Earth is about to be attacked by an alien life-form from space, probably Mars, that is far ahead of us scientifically. The previous incidents were trials of equipment; the present deaths are deliberate removal of men who might have formed centers of resistance. * When Rob is incredulous, Aurelius reveals that he has been lucky enough to survive such an attack and capture the attacker. It is an ant-like creature about seven inches long, clad in antigravity clothing, armed with a tiny projector that can cause heart attacks. Aurelius escaped death because he was in his hot-room, where the heat overcame the insect, which obviously is from a cold world. At the moment, concludes Aurelius, not much can be done except be on guard. * Other events follow: A death projector wipes out a large section of Chicago until knocked out by a cloud-

cannon (a heat projector), as suggested by Aurelius. The President of the United States is assassinated by one of the invaders. And an ultimatum arrives: Unless the United States surrenders all land above ten thousand feet to the Martians, they will exterminate humanity. * Although the President and his advisers recognize that the threat is very real, they decide not to surrender. As Aurelius points out, there are two factors in favor of the Terrestrials. First, the Martians are so superior that they tend to underestimate their opponents. Second, a psychogram from the brain of the ant that attacked Aurelius reveals the probable location of the headquarters of the invaders—Mount Seldon. Gravity sensors indicate that the mountain lacks mass and must be hollow. Preparations are made to attack the mountain with an enormous charge of superexplosive before the ants are aware of what is happening. * In another story thread, Rob Born and his fiancée Mary venture near Mount Seldon and are captured. The ants, who are telepathic, take them into the mountain and show them weapons, with the stated intention of releasing them as a further warning to the Terrestrials. At each stage of their interrogation and instruction, Rob and Mary encounter ants with greater mental power, up to the commander of the ant forces on Earth, who has an enormous head and an incredible intellect. He rules against sending Rob and Mary out as a demonstration of power and sentences them to death. * Salvation comes from a fellow captive, a forest ranger who has a concealed weapon. When he shoots the ant commander, the other ants, who are in telepathic communication with the leader and perhaps under his telepathic domination, are temporarily "out of phase," and Rob and Mary escape. Just as they are leaving, a suicide pilot delivers an enormous load of the explosive Yamakite that (in modern terms) would amount to a cluster of the largest hydrogen bombs. Not only is the ant headquarters blown up, but the immediate area is turned into an active volcano. * *Miscellaneous:* Wireless transmission of power is present. * The ant leader has powers of will control. * The Earth is now frantically arming against another invasion by the Martian ants. * A well-done thriller, nicely paced, with good characterizations and incident. It is possible to criticize the salvation of Rob and Mary as too easy, but this is not a major flaw. One of the few stories from early *Amazing Stories* that are worth reading.

FLINT, HOMER EON
Professional name of Homer Eon Flindt (1888-1924), California (San Jose) author. (Earlier sources give an incorrect birth date. See Ashley, "The Galactic Emancipator.") Flint was the most promising of the authors who write science-fiction for the Munsey magazines, and his early death undoubtedly hindered the development of pulp fantastic fiction. His better work, which is covered in detail in *Science-Fiction: The Early Years*, applied social philosophies to exotic or future societies. As has been remarked, however, his technique was not always on the same level as his ideas. Flint is now remembered mostly as the co-author (with Austin Hall) of the science-fiction novel "The Blind Spot" (1921). One of his stories, "The Greater Miracle," a supernatural piece, was listed among the best stories of 1920 by Edward J. O'Brien.
438. **THE NTH MAN**. *Amazing Stories Quarterly*, Spring 1928. Ill. Paul.
A posthumous work, first purchased in 1920 by the Munsey

Flint, Homer Eon (*continued*)

Corporation, but not published then. It was resold to Gernsback, circumstances not known. * Novelette. * *Time:* 1920 to 1933. *Place:* various places around the United States and elsewhere, but mostly the San Francisco Bay area. * Mysterious events: The Great Wall of China is removed, the head of the Sphinx is ripped off and placed atop the Great Pyramid, a ship is carried from the sea two thousand miles to land, and a building in which German revanchists and anarchists are plotting is carried away. * These are explained in terms of the Nth man, a two-mile-high giant who emerges from the sea near San Francisco and makes certain demands: The vicious plutocrat Daly Fosburgh, who secretly rules the country, must be broken and financial regulations must be reformed. If not, the Nth man threatens vengeance. * The political powers do not accept the giant's ultimatum, but attack him, with disastrous results. The air force, artillery, other military arms are useless against him. The president must surrender. Part of the giant's terms are that his enemies must step forth to be eaten, but at the last moment the giant is persuaded to relent. * Explanation: Pendleton, the giant's father had been injured and persecuted by the vicious tycoon Fosburgh, who also drove the giant's mother to suicide. Pendleton thereupon used sea-turtle glandular secretions to transform his son into a nearly invulnerable giant plated with thick chitin. The giant, when old enough to understand, vowed revenge. * Mission accomplished, the giant returns to the sea. There is speculation that he will grow so large that he will exhaust the resources of the ocean. * Not one of Flint's stronger stories; it is not surprising that Munsey did not publish it.

[Anonymous]

Presumably a British writer.

439. **THE FLYING ROBOT.** *Scoops,* 10 March 1934. Ill. S.D.

Boys' fiction. * Short story. * *Place:* Scotland. * *Background:* The great scientist Greville Horder has created a winged humanoid robot that flies quite well. Controlled by radio, it has a television camera and sound speakers in its chest. Since it would have obvious use in criminal activities, American gangster Spike Pirelli has tried to buy the invention, offering one million pounds. * As Horder is working in his laboratory with assistants Weldon and young Lyn Roberts, Pirelli and his thugs attack with tommy guns. Roberts makes a dash for Edinburgh with the specifications of the robot, pursued by mobsters. Weldon and Horder succumb to the siege. Pirelli stows the robot in a lorry and leaves. * But Horder, though injured, regains consciousness and activates the flying robot. Under his direction it leaves the lorry, rescues Lyn, and eventually, after complications, turns the tables on Pirelli. * There is, however, a third element in the situation. Count Marcus Leblanc, an agent of the Belgranian government, also wants to steal the robot. His efforts come to little when the robot accidentally kills him. * As the story ends, the flying robot is carrying Pirelli into Glasgow, to be handed over to the police. * Properly speaking, the device is not a robot.

FOX, GEO. R.

U.S. author, then resident in Three Oaks, Michigan. Judging from throwaway material in the story, a fervent Socialist. It is not clear whether this is George R. Fox (1880-?), author of *The Fangs of the Serpent* (1924).

440. **THE ELECTRONIC WALL.** *Amazing Stories,* June 1927. Unsigned ill.

Short story. * The second-prize winning story of the contest based on the cover of the December 1926 issue of *Amazing Stories.* Fox won $150. * *Time:* events of 1938 told in retrospect from 2038. *Place:* significant portion on Mars. * The story explains the disappearance of the *USN Woodrow Wilson,* a transport bearing soldiers to the Mesopotamian front during the early days of World War II. (The enemy seems to have been a Franco-Italian alliance.) * The *Woodrow Wilson* was off the coast of North Carolina when it suddenly became enveloped in a strange fog, radio no longer operated, telepathic messages would not go through, and in a short time it became obvious that the ship was floating in the air. * The men, however, received telepathic messages telling them not to be concerned, since they would not be harmed; everything would be explained in about three hundred hours. * After a time the men see that they are in space, the Earth far behind, and that they are being pulled along by lines of force from a small artificial planet. * At the allotted time, their destination becomes visible. It is Mars. Telepathic explanations follow: The Martians have abducted the servicemen to alleviate a male shortage on Mars. If any Earthmen do not wish to stay and breed with the beautiful Martian females, they will be returned to Earth. (A plausible suggestion to randy sailors and soldiers!) * All the men elect to remain on Mars, where they acquire the remarkable longevity hinted at in the narrator's time frame. * *Miscellaneous:* Mars is a Schiaparellian planet with a science far ahead of ours, with gravity control and atomic energy. Socially, the Martians have been passing through the Marxist stages of societal evolution and are now at the level of absolute freedom and anarchism. They are human, except that they have feather-like appendages around their heads; these are not vestigial from flying, but are receptor organs for telepathy. Judging from the contest illustration, nudity is acceptable on Mars. (There is a size confusion within the manuscript; on the voyage, the Martians are described as being inch-high; later they are of normal human height.) * The narrator is dropping off his message before returning to Mars. He wants Earthmen to concentrate on peace. * Amateurish.

FREDERICK, J[USTUS] GEORGE (1882-1964)

U.S. (New York) author, businessman. Publisher, editor of the *Business World.* Wrote books on advertising, stocks, other aspects of business. Also wrote *How to Understand Women* (1941). Contributor to the slick magazines. President of the Writers Club ca. 1937. In early days Frederick wrote two pioneering s-f stories: "The Dupe of a Realist" (*Argosy,* 1902) and "The Planet Juggler" (*All-Story,* 1908), which are covered in *Science-Fiction: The Early Years.* Now remembered mostly for his excellent *The Long Island Sea Food Cook Book* (1939 and later editions.)

441. **THE EINSTEIN EXPRESS.** *Astounding Stories,* April-May 1935. Ill. Dold.

Novelette. * *Time:* 1942. * *Place:* Springfield, Massachusetts for terrestrial events. * Arthur Woodlock and his colleague Gregory Slocum have been experimenting with enormously high currents, thirty million volts and more. They have smashed atoms, but even more important, have discovered that they can transform objects into light, which they can send forth into the universe. Part of the process involves creating a metal template of the

Frederick, J. G. (*continued*)

object sent. This template then can be used to recreate the object, with the implication, recognized by the scientists, that it would be possible to make duplicates of persons—including great scientists like Einstein. This motif of the template and restoration of objects transformed into light, although developed at some length, is really a throwaway and plays no real part in the story, except for the transmission of a dog. * Woodlock, who is of a mystical turn of mind, firmly believes that he, his girlfriend Amelia, and Slocum form a cosmic pattern paralleled in atomic structure, and that if they were transformed into light and sent out into space, they would exist as an entity or something similar. He convinces the others to undergo the experience. The night watchman operates the machinery, and Woodlock, Amelia, and Slocum are disintegrated and beamed out as light. * All three regain consciousness in space as a group being of a sort. They gradually grow accustomed to their new existence, which really amounts to a succession of shocks as they expand through the universe and experience cosmic events, including a nova. In some way, not made clear by the author, fragmentary atoms of themselves can be broken loose by such encounters, and there is a danger of annihilation. * A change comes when they encounter a space intelligence, who explains matters to some extent. They are one result of a program of a thousand "test-tubes" set up around the universe by cosmic intelligences who hope to create cosmic "atoms" like Woodlock and associates. Above the space intelligence is a being called the Integrator, which in some fashion is interested in restoring the order that was lost when the universe differentiated in what we now call the Big Bang. This Integrator is not God, nor does the space intelligence know anything about a God, but Woodlock's association with the cosmic workers would be welcomed. The story ends abruptly. * *Miscellaneous:* Much heed is paid to popular conceptions of atomic structure, quantum mechanics, etc. * The author also supplies a villainous rejected lover named Ackerman who kidnaps Amelia, but this comes to nothing. * Probably derivative of Olaf Stapledon's *Star Maker.* The author attempts to play with ideas larger than he can handle. Amateurishly presented.

FREKSA, FRIEDRICH (1882-1955)

German journalist, dramatist, novelist, historical writer. Born in Berlin. *Sumurun,* his dramatic pantomime with music (1920 and later), was once internationally known. Also wrote two other fantastic novels, *Praschnas Geheimnis* and *Der Wanderer ins Nichts.* According to Jordan (p. 49), his name was Kurt Friedrich-Freksa, but this has not been corroborated.

442. **DRUSO.** *Wonder Stories,* May-July 1934. Ill. Paul. Translated from German by Fletcher Pratt.

(Translation of *Druso oder: Die gestohlene Menschenwelt,*Berlin 1931. A note about texts: The German text has not been available to me for comparison, but, judging from comments about "Druso" made by Alpers in Clute and Nicholls, and by Fisher, there may be slight differences between the German original and the Pratt translation.)

Novel. * Despite different time indications given by the editors of *Wonder Stories,* the prologue material is set mostly around A.D. 2295, and the main action in 2580 and the years following. *Place:* Chiefly the Aachen area of Germany and the new planet Druso. * Background history: The twentieth century was a

period of wars. Since it was generally recognized around the end of the century that the cause of these wars was over-population (particularly differences between potentially hostile countries), in 2012 a world treaty was signed limiting population. This was followed by eugenics programs. Treaties limiting military forces also went into effect. * In 2037 it was discovered that the Chinese were cheating on both treaties. Having worked out a successful technique for suspended animation, they were placing huge military reserves in anabiosis in caves throughout restricted areas of China, until the time came to overwhelm the world. China was brought down. * The Chinese technique is now used for another purpose: Periodically a group of specially selected cultural ambassadors is put to sleep for one hundred years; on awaking, they will serve as living pieces of history for the future age. * In other respects, too, the world of the late twenty-third century is one of superscience, with atomic energy, limited space travel, solar energy, and much else. * The story is the narrative of Alf Bentink, one of the scientific elite of the day. The first quarter or so of the novel is devoted to a tedious Bildungsroman focusing on Alf's maturation and his growing romance with Judith Thyrberg, a young Swedish woman. They marry with a shadow over them: Judith has been selected as a sleeper in the cultural program. She could refuse, both on personal grounds and because of pregnancy, but patriotism demands that she accept, which she does. Alf is not happy about the situation, but the best he can do is join her in the hundred year sleep. * Alf awakens to find around him not the superlaboratory and medical experts he expected, but ruins and men who are obviously almost semiprimitive. As it turns out, his crypt was discovered by chance, and in opening it, the future men accidentally destroyed all the sleepers but Alf, Judith, and two friends. The sleepers have been in suspended animation not one hundred years, but almost three hundred, and their circumstances have been forgotten. * *Background:* About twenty years after Alf was put into anabiosis a strange planet (Druso) appeared near Earth. Controlled in path, it took up an orbit not far from the Moon. Where it came from is not indicated. The natives of Druso made sweeping promises of benefits they would shower on humanity, then when Earth relaxed the Heaviside layer to permit entry of Druso's energy beam, the Drusonians began a bloody conquest. Energy cancelation, poison gas, and other horrors destroyed resistance. The point is made several times that naive leadership permitted the Drusonians to enter. (This is equated with the German "myth" of the post-war period that the German leadership of World War I betrayed the nation.) At present the two planets are locked together by an energy beam. * Drusonian rule is harsh. The Drusonians, who are giant insects of several sorts, have forbidden humans to study science, with the result that mankind has regressed to a sort of medieval culture. The Drusonians have also successfully instituted a program of propagandistic thought control, for most humans believe the Drusonians are benefactors and willingly make sacrifices at omnipresent Drusonian shrines—each controlled by a small insect. Druso maintains tight control over Earth, what with the shrines (that are in contact with the home planet), air patrols, and much else. * Druso is obviously exploiting Earth, with humans recruited for labor on Druso. Such slaves never return, and their fate is unknown, although the official line is that they have entered a workers' paradise. * The only exception to this gloomy world picture is the New Atlantis, a group of

Freksa, Friedrich (*continued*)

about three hundred thousand people who live underground in Labrador. The Drusonian insects cannot tolerate cold, hence tended to avoid the Arctic, and in their conquest of the Earth they missed a scientific installation in Labrador. The New Atlanteans have since increased in power, with secret ramifications around the world. But while they are superior scientifically to the rest of humanity, they are still far away from the science of the twenty-third century. Thus, the awaking of the scientists from the past means much to them in their ultimate plan of driving out the Drusonians. * Alf and his associates join in the work of New Atlantis, which aims at cutting the energy beam that links Earth to Druso. According to scientific opinion, if the well-guarded beam is severed, Druso will drift away and will be unable to pierce the Heaviside layer again. While there are indications that the various insect types of Druso are dying out, their extinction may take a long time and humanity must plan on immediate action while there is a possibility of success. * The crucial situation that sets off the denouement is the capture of Judith and her daughter Urania by humans loyal to Druso and their transfer to Druso among the slave shipment. This accelerates a program long in the minds of the Atlanteans: a visit to Druso itself to see what is going on. Alf and friends insinuate their way into a group of humans being shipped to Druso and see the reality. Instead of being a paradise, as the Drusonian temples claim in their propaganda, Druso is a hell. Humans are used as cattle. They are slaughtered and butchered scientifically; the women are milked like cows; and some are forced to expend psychic energy restoring weak giant insects. * The plot takes two turns. Alf and associates are smuggled back to Earth, where they cut off the energy beam. Druso drifts away. And on Druso itself, a human underground and outlaw army of escapees battles the insects. Eventually the humans on Druso win, and the planet, insects extinct, will return to proximity to Earth. * *Miscellaneous:* Drusonian vision lies in the infrared, hence blue is invisible to them. This phenomenon aids the human underground. * Drusonian races include giant ants, beetles, and perhaps termites. * As an adventure story, routine at best, once the boring introductory section is passed. Otherwise, an unpleasant book. * In retrospect *Druso* can be seen as a document in the rise of right-wing thought, parallel to National Socialism, in Weimar Germany. The basic plot can be read as a metaphor for the political situation of the day, although it must be admitted that similar plots are not unfamiliar from English-language science-fiction. Present are many buzzwords and concepts associated with Germany of the Nazi period: "the master race," the necessity for individuals to sacrifice themselves for the good of culture, the great benefits created by war, the desirability of blondism, etc., all with a particularly Germanic tone that is unpleasant. * As is the case with "Interplanetary Bridges" by Ludwig Anton, one is surprised that Gernsback would publish such a work.

FRITCHEY, ALFRED

No information. It is not clear whether this is Alfred James Fritchey, California poet.

   443. **BEFORE THE ICE AGE.** *Amazing Stories*, December 1928. Unsigned ill.

Short story. * Narrative told in suitable language by a miner who has been employed in driving a tunnel through the solid granite of Bald Mountain. An accidental blast not only kills part of the work crew, but breaks an opening into a great cave, within which are wonders. * Two university professors and the miners explore the cave, where there are evidences of a science much superior to ours—projection machines, permanent lighting, holograph images, a history of the preglacial world on tablets, and maps. In one room are the figures of a beautiful blonde woman and a heroic man. One of the professors can read the inscriptions in the rooms, which were on an island before the mountain was elevated. The inscriptions are in Aramaic. * The explorers leave, and the night shift takes over. When the explorers return the next day, they find nothing. An explosion set off by the night shift smashed everything into tiny fragments, for all the paraphernalia of the incredible cave were made of glass. * Indebted to H. Rider Haggard's *When the Earth Shook*, or perhaps A. W. Lawson's *Born Again*.

GAIL, OTTO WILLI (1896-1956)

German author. Artillery officer in World War I; after war matriculated at Munich Technische Hochschule, where he studied electrical engineering and mathematics, but was forced to abandon education for financial reasons. After unsuccessful career in typewriter sales, began freelance writing. Author of several popular science books, especially on astronomy and astronautics. Author of three science-fiction novels whose factual basis is derived from the Valier-Oberth group of German rocket experimenters. In addition to the two novels following, also wrote excellent boys' book *Hans Hardt's Mondfahrt* (1928), translated as *By Rocket to the Moon* (1930). According to Jordan (p. 49) Gail died in the United States, but this has not been confirmed.

   444. **THE SHOT INTO INFINITY.** *Science Wonder Quarterly*, Fall 1929. Translated from German by Francis Currier. Ill. Paul.

(Reprinted in offset book form by Garland Publishing Co., New York, 1975.)

(*Der Schuss ins All*, 1925.) Since the story is of non-pulp origin, it is described in more detail in *Science-Fiction: The Early Years*. * Hard s-f novel based closely on contemporary German rocket research. * *Place:* Germany, Rumania, and around the Moon. * Rocket rivalry, scientific achievement, and blasted romance. * There are two centers of rocket research. The German establishment, headed by the engineer August Korf and centered at Wilhelmshaven, is much more advanced than the Rumanian center, headed by Suchinow and backed by Russian capital. Hence, it is a surprise when the Rumanian ship, piloted by one Skoryna, leaves before the Germans are ready. There are suspicions that Suchinow has stolen some of Korf's research. Further suspicion focuses on Natalka Weiss, who worked with Korf, left abruptly, married unexpectedly, and postdated correspondence to Korf. As it turns out, Natalka did not actually steal, though she used her work with Korf; she is Suchinow's daughter, is unmarried, and is Skoryna the pilot. * The Rumanian project, however, ends in tragedy, for the ship is trapped in a low orbit around the Moon. Korf, finishing his superior rocket, goes to rescue the vessel, which he salvages. Natalka is almost dead; she revives, but dies when Korf's craft returns to Earth. * *Miscellaneous:* Korf's rocket is a step rocket, uses liquid oxygen and hydrogen fuel, and is well planned.

Gail, Otto Willi (*continued*)
During the voyage phenomena of weightlessness are considered in detail. * A serious attempt to apply rocketry to fiction; it is fairly rigorous and farsighted in technical matters. As fiction, however, it is somewhat melodramatic, with weak characterizations. Still, worth reading, if only as a period piece. For a sequel see #445, "The Stone from the Moon."

445. **THE STONE FROM THE MOON.** *Science Wonder Quarterly,* Spring 1930. Translated from German by Francis Currier. Ill. Paul.
(*Der Stein vom Mond, Kosmischer Roman,* 1926.) Novel, sequel to #444, "The Shot into Infinity." Since the story is of non-pulp origin, it is described in more detail in *Science-Fiction: The Early Years.* * A much less serious work than its predecessor; it combines elements from Elena Petrovna Blavatsky's Theosophy with contemporary rocketry. * The story is complex enough that it is best presented in terms of subplots. * *Time:* perhaps the near future, in any case several years after the first story. *Place:* Yucatán, the Atlantic Ocean, and space near Venus. * In Yucatán, British archeologist Sir William Burns encounters Isabella de la Cosa, a young Maya woman with a split personality; her second personality, which is called Tuxtla, is that of a pre-Conquest Maya woman. She also has strong paranormal abilities; these are greatly enhanced when she comes into contact with a strange gem found by Sir William Burns. This gem is claimed to be a fragment of the moon that existed before Luna. (Here Gail is invoking the crank astronomical theory of Hans Hoerbiger that the Earth has had successive moons, that have variously been destroyed when they exceeded Roche's limit. Luna, thus, is only the latest of these moons. The theory was more generally taken seriously on the scientific fringes in Germany than in the English-speaking world. Indeed, the German rocket researcher Max Valier even wrote a small monograph in support of Hoerbiger's theory.) When Tuxtla begins to have memories of Atlantis, Sir William takes her out in the Atlantic to the traditional site of Atlantis, where she is flooded with ancient memories. * Since the events of "The Shot into Infinity," August Korf has built a small fleet of rocket ships, with which he is exploring space and the Moon. He has been conducting rocket experiments in the area of Atlantis, and by chance his rocket is now ready to leave for his space station. * The backwash from the departing rocket sinks Burns's small vessel, but Tuxtla is pulled into the rocket in time and is off into space with Korf and others. * After stopping at Korf's space station, the rocketeers fly toward Venus at Tuxtla's urging, where they espy a small satellite ready to fall into Venus's atmosphere. It is discovered to be a Terrestrial sailing boat, filled with Mayan artifacts from Atlantis. * Partial explanation: About 11,000 B.C. Atlantis contained a high civilization whose adepts wielded mental powers that enabled them to do things for which we now require machinery. Wicked Queen Huitaca (whose personality imbues Tuxtla) used the ancient gem for levitational purposes; the application went out of control, drawing Luna, our present moon, but then a separate planet, into orbit around Earth. Atlantis was destroyed by the gravitational disturbances, and Queen Huitaca's royal barge was hurled out into space. Her frozen corpse is still on the ship. * After the explorers visit the barge, it falls down into Venus's atmosphere and is destroyed. * All parties return to Earth. Tuxtla is now completely mad, and, as Queen Huitaca demands, royal honors

in a madhouse and makes a general nuisance of herself. * *Miscellaneous:* Many of the side issues are more interesting than the occult plot. Korf's space station is built of metallic sodium, creates artificial gravity by rotation, and holds enormous mirrors that will supply light and heat to Earth. * More a curiosity than the earlier story, but often prophetic in space matters.

GALLUN, RAYMOND Z[INKE] (1910-1994)
U.S. technical writer, science-fiction writer. Born in Wisconsin, the birth date of 1911 given in some sources being incorrect. Earlier work from Beaver Dam, Wisconsin, but long residence in New York and abroad. Has written under various pseuds. including Dow Elstar, Arthur Allport, E. V. Raymond, and William Callahan. Gallun's fiction, which was professionally written, was unusual in attempting a fusion of pulp event-desiderata with humanistic concerns—personal growth, universal tolerance. Davin's interview with Gallun (*Fantasy Commentator,* Fall 1988) is interesting and informative. See also pseuds. Dow Elstar and E. V. Raymond, and joint work by John Michel and Raymond Z. Gallun. * See also #1821, "Saturn's Ringmaster."

The Old Faithful Series is considered first, then Other Works in order of Publication.

The Old Faithful Series

446. **OLD FAITHFUL.** *Astounding Stories,* December 1934. Ill. Dold.
(Reprinted in Gallun, *The Best of Raymond Z. Gallun;* in Ackerman, *Gosh! Wow!;* in Asimov, *Before the Golden Age;* in Bleiler and Dikty, *Imagination Unlimited;* and in Pohl; *Science Fiction: The Great Years.*)
Novelette. According to Davin's interview with Gallun, "Old Faithful" was written about two years before publication, in early 1932. It was first submitted to Dr. Sloane at *Amazing Stories,* who held it for more than a year, then rejected it. * *Time:* not specified, but probably the near future. * *Place:* mostly on Mars, with Terrestrial episodes in the Southwest, probably Flagstaff, Arizona. * Martian 774 has been in communication with Earth for about ten Terrestrial years. Using light flashes, 774 and (on Earth) Professor Walters have exchanged signals, laboriously extracting limited meaning from a minimum of light patterns. * It is possible that in another ten years or so fluent, more complex communication might take place, but 774 has received a death sentence. On Mars, where resources are very limited and strictly rationed, individuals live an allotted time, with extensions granted only for work useful to the culture. Since his Martian superiors do not consider 774's communications with Earth important, he has been allowed only forty more days of life, with the certainty that all the elaborate and ingenious equipment used in his work will be dismantled. * Rejecting such a command to die has been unknown on Mars, but 774 is convinced that his work is important enough for him to do something extraordinary. Working on new equipment, he sends his last messages to Earth. * At the observatory in New Mexico, Walters, his daughter Yvonne, and engineer Jack Cantrill receive 774's last message, which seems incoherent in its repeated references to a comet. * Cantrill deciphers it: There is a comet whose path will take it close to both Mars and Earth. Presumably 774 is riding on the comet to save energy. This is proved correct when a damaged

Gallun, Raymond Z. (*continued*)

Martian riding machine draws near the observatory and collapses. It contains the dying 774, who has been badly shattered first by his rocket ascent from Mars, then his crash landing on Earth. The Terrestrials try to help him, but he dies. His voyage, however, opens the possibility of interplanetary travel. * *Miscellaneous:* The nickname "Old Faithful" refers to 774's punctuality in communicating from Mars. * Mars is closely Schiaparellian. * Gallun beautifully handles the alienness of 774: his body, which would be a horror to us; his strange sensory apparatus and non-human mode of thought; his scientific devices, which operate on different principles from ours; and the semantic problems encountered by 774 and his human friends, with a detailed examination of the linguistic principles involved. * One of the best stories to appear in this period, with a human touch seldom met elsewhere. It is also one of the first stories to characterize aliens in a sympathetic manner. For a sequel see #447, "The Son of Old Faithful."

447. **THE SON OF OLD FAITHFUL**. *Astounding Stories*, July 1935. Ill. Dold.

Novelette. * Sequel to #446, "Old Faithful." * Several years have passed since the events of the first story. Jack Cantrill and Yvonne Walters have married, and Jack, using technology derived from 744's equipment, has just returned from the first flight around the Moon. While Terrestrial science has benefited enormously from 774's voyage to Earth, there is still much about the spaceship and its contents that is far beyond Terrestrial understanding and use. * The story is told partly through 775, 774's child, and partly through the American group of the first story. * 775, who was mentioned briefly in the first story, has now matured and faces a difficult decision. The Martian authorities have ordered him to prove his loyalty by destroying his parent's installation. But 775 is secretly very reluctant, perhaps because he has inherited 774's seed of independence. * After studying 774's records, 775 makes a dangerous decision: He will remove key equipment, conceal it underground, destroy what is left, fake a death crash, and continue his parent's work in hiding. But, apart from the danger of detection, there is a difficulty: He has only enough food and water for about a month. His only chance for survival is communicating with 774's friends on Earth and summoning help. When his supplies are exhausted, he will go into suspended animation and await rescue. His messages go forth. * At the observatory in the Southwest, Jack and others receive 775's signals. The "vase," a particularly mysterious piece of equipment, the function of which has not been understood, turns out to be a device for interplanetary communication—and other even more surprising power later emerge. Jack and Yvonne are eager to fly to Mars, but this seems impossible until Jack works out a method for storing fuel on the Moon and leaving from there. * Jack and Yvonne's flight is mostly uneventful; a single deviation from path is corrected by the vase, which is operated long-distance by 775. The spaceship lands safely on Mars, and the parties greet each other, with the promise of better communication. As a saving factor, when the Martian authorities learn that the work of 774 and 775 has been productive, the previous decretals are reversed and 775 is pardoned. * Less appealing than the first story, with an unconvincing resolution. The alienness, however, is well communicated. For a sequel see #448, "Child of the Stars."

448. **CHILD OF THE STARS**. *Astounding Stories,* April 1936. Ill. Marchioni.

Short story. * The third and last story in the Old Faithful series. * *Time:* about nine years after #447, "The Son of Old Faithful." * *Background:* In the brief time since the last story, both Earth (using Martian technology from 774 and 775) and Mars have become aggressive colonizers and exploiters around the solar system. Conflicts of interest have arisen, notably about the radioactive riches of Jupiter. * As a result of all this, the two planets are on the brink of a shooting war, with a Martian fleet nearing Earth and a Terrestrial fleet approaching Mars. The greatest peril is that both sides will release atomic fire that will totally destroy the planets. The Cantrills, of course, deplore this situation, but there is nothing they can do about it. * 775, who has been visiting Earth, also deplores the war hysteria and decides to return to Mars, perhaps to influence events there. He is not aware of it at first, but on his ship there are two stowaways of sorts: Dr. Noel Ransome, discoverer of atomic energy, a ruthless and unscrupulous genius; and Thalia, the Cantrills' nine-year-old daughter, who has a strong emotional bond with 775. Ransome plans to steal 775's scientific secrets, notably a long-distance mind-reading device. Thalia simply wants to accompany 775. * As the people and circumstances mesh: Both Martians and Terrestrials are ready to unleash atomic fire; Ransome wounds 775 and makes off (in his tiny spaceship) with the plans for the thought-reader. * 775 works out his secret means for stopping the war. First, using his new thought projector, he urges both governments to fill their atmospheres with as much smoke and dust as possible. He then accelerates his ship to the speed of light, whereupon it breaks a hole through space, permitting radiation from Sirius to flood the solar system. The Sirian radiation is strong enough that both planets are forced to lay aside their war plans. Indeed, stimulated by broadcasts of friendliness from 775's thought projector, they assist each other in the new danger. * 775 had expected to die when he broke the fabric of space, but he survives and unexpectedly has opened a way for rapid interstellar travel. With the universe wide open for exploitation, there need not be any more territorial wars in the solar system. * *Miscellaneous:* the unnecessary Dr. Ransome reforms. * Much the weakest of the three stories. The story is illogical and unconvincing in terms of its prequels, being simply a pulp action plot latched on to the background of the first two stories. Gallun's characterization of Thalia Cantrill, too, is incredible. One would think that Gallun had never seen a nine-year-old girl.

Other Works

449. **THE CRYSTAL RAY**. *Air Wonder Stories,* November 1929. Ill. S. Strother.

Short story. * Gallun originally wrote "The Crystal Ray" for a high-school English class in Wisconsin—and received a grade of B. * *Time:* A.D. 2141. *Place:* Ecuador and the vicinity of Chicago. * The Asians, who are a dominant world power, are now attacking the United States, the last bastion of the white race, and the situation is not good for the Americans. Central America has fallen, and the decisive battle is to be fought near Chicago. If the Americans lose, the war is over. * Calhoun and Pelton, two America aviators, are on a three-day leave with their scout plane. Calhoun is a famous ace, Pelton is a scientist.

Gallun, Raymond Z. (*continued*)

Landing in the Ecuadorian Andes, they sightsee until a local Indian tells them the legend of the Devil's Nest in the nearby mountains. According to legend it is death to enter it. * The two men explore, finding a crater with a beautiful crystalline mineral. A flash of light, however, shining through a crystal kills Calhoun instantly; it is a natural death ray. * Later. Around Chicago the crucial battle begins. The Orientals not only have finer flying equipment, but three times as many planes. Chicago has almost fallen by the time projectors fitted with Pelton's Andean crystal are ready. But, once in operation, they wipe out the Asians and America is back on the way to victory. Unfortunately, Pelton died bringing down the leading Asian ace in an air duel. * The combatants use giant planes, gases that corrode flesh away instantly, the superexplosive terrorium, and a device that distorts light rays and provides the equivalent of camouflage. * The technical explanation of the death ray is that crystals of andesite transform ordinary light into a vibration far higher than light. * Better written than most fiction in *Air Wonder Stories*, but essentially a routine story and probably to considered promising juvenilia. The choice of the extant term "andesite" for the imaginary mineral is unfortunate.

450. **THE SPACE DWELLERS**. *Science Wonder Stories*, November 1929. Unsigned ill.

Short story. * *Time:* 1941. *Place:* northern Wisconsin. * During the time of Hanley's "False Comet," Douglas Barclay, brilliant young maverick scientist, is at work in his laboratory when a stranger enters. * The stranger, who is seven feet tall and totally black, introduces himself as Othlahoma, from Hanley's comet, which is really a device for space traveling. Othlahoma, who reveals that he has approached Barclay because instruments indicated him to be a highly superior mind, also comments that in all his exploration of space he has never before come upon a race so closely approximating his own as Earthmen. * Othlahoma now tells his story: His people developed a high civilization on a planet hundreds of light-years away. But their sun was dying, and their planet was losing water and air, so that life on it would eventually become impossible. With Grooga, a great scientist of his world. Othlahoma built a spaceship involving antigravity and rockets, and with it began to explore other planets in their system for a potential new home. * On one of the moons they found an astonishing phenomena: a race of savage, ferocious beings who functioned on an airless world at almost absolute zero. The explanation is the radioactive substance xata, which flows in their veins. * After many experiments Grooga and Othlahoma discovered a way to transfer xata into humans. The results were sensational. It turned the subjects' skin black, increased their strength enormously, enabled them to live even in space without air and at absolute zero, and made them immortal. * As a result of a palace revolution, however, Othlahoma and his followers have had to leave their planet, and now they roam the universe exploring it. * When Barclay expresses interest in atomic power, so that he, too, can leave Earth and explore space, Othlahoma offers to transform him with xata and take him along as a companion in exploration. Barclay accepts. * *Miscellaneous:* Othlahoma communicates by telepathy. He also has a ray that explodes objects atomically. * The story is also titled "The Space-Dwellers."

451. **ATOMIC FIRE**. *Amazing Stories*, April 1931. Ill. Morey.

Short story. * *Time:* about ten million years in the future. * *Background:* In A.D. 2089, the Martians, whose planet was dying, invaded and conquered Earth, which they have ruled since. The Martians are humanoid, with spindly limbs, barrel chests and cat-like eyes, and are covered with fur. Humans, too, have evolved, with larger chests and fur. The two races live together amicably, but the Martians are the superior both politically and intellectually. * Over the past multimillennia Earth has become desiccated and has been terraformed to the canal system found on ancient Mars. Life is possible, but difficult. But there is a threat: The solar system is endangered by a gaseous nebula that will close off solar radiation, on which the Earth is totally dependent. The outlying fragments of the nebula are due in a few weeks. After this, humanity will presumably perish. * The great Martian scientist Aggar Ho and his human assistant Sark Ahar are among the many who are trying to release atomic energy. Aggar Ho, indeed, seems close enough that he has been directed to conduct his final tests away from Earth, lest a chain reaction destroy the planet. * The two men take the test apparatus on board a spaceship and begin their work in space near the Moon. As feared, atomic wildfire breaks out. It might have been fatal, but Sark Ahar, putting his aged chief into the space lifeboat, directs the spaceship to the Moon, which the atomic fire transforms into a new, small sun. This will preserve life on Earth until the nebula will have passed in about fifty years. * *Miscellaneous:* Aggar Ho's technique for releasing atomic energy seems to consist of running enormous electric currents through heavy metals. * Much of the point of the story is that an Earthman, who is considered an inferior by most Martians, was instrumental in saving Earth, despite general Martian superiority.

452. **THE LUNAR CHRYSALIS**. *Amazing Stories*, September 1931. Ill. Morey.

Short story. * *Time:* 1951 as reminisced about from 2004. *Place:* mostly the Moon. * Professor Paxton and narrator Jerry make the first voyage to the Moon in the rocket ship *Black Meteor*. The journey is uneventful, and the man land near Tycho, where they disembark in space suits. After a certain amount of exploration, they find fossil remains of former life and the shattered ruin of what must have been a crystal-covered agricultural area. Then they espy a strange building, a four-sided, temple-like edifice, which they investigate. * Part of the floor of the ancient structure collapses, and they find themselves in a large room filled with enormous masses of incomprehensible machinery. Especially prominent are an enormous flywheel and rows of large flask-like containers. Unfortunately, there does not seem to be any way to leave the room, since the walls are too high and the doors are impregnable to Terrestrial explosives. * In nervous desperation Jerry meddles with the machinery, closing a switch, whereupon things happen. The flywheel spins at ever increasing speed, and after a time the flasks pop open, from them emerging strange creatures that look like multicolored mollusks. Upright and about the size of humans, they have a shell on their back, and tentacles with organs that presumably are eyes. * The creatures grasp the explorers firmly but gently, taking them down a passageway to an enormous underground world obviously once a garden spot, but now dead. The Lunarians, however, set in motion processes that create a suitable atmosphere and fill the empty depressions with water. * The human explorers are well treated and are permitted to witness operations around the site,

Gallun, Raymond Z. (*continued*)

as robotic devices are readying what are obviously spaceships. *
Communication is now established. Lunarian 333, using a
mechanical voice simulator, converses with them in perfect
English, informing them that their brain currents had been
studied while they were sleeping. 333 then gives them a brief
history of his race on the Moon: The intelligent mollusks
developed while the Moon still had an atmosphere and revolved
on its axis. They were almost rendered extinct when the Moon
stopped rotating and began to lose its atmosphere, but they found
a habitable depression in Tycho, where they established an
underground supercivilization. They knew, however, that their
tenancy was only an expedient, what with the continued
deterioration of the Lunar environment, and looked for remedies.
* When 333 developed a gas that produced suspended animation,
the whole race entered hibernation, planning to awaken about
two hundred and fifty million years in the future, when Earth
would have become habitable. But their machinery failed for
one reason or another, and it required Jerry's meddling to set it
into operation. * By now, watching the host of spaceships being
readied, Paxton and Jerry are in a panic. They break away from
their hosts, dash to the *Black Meteor,* and set forth for Earth,
broadcasting a warning about the impending invasion. * When
the Lunar armada approaches, the nations of the Earth are ready,
but soon discover that they have no weapons that will damage
the invading ships. Then an enormous voice, filling the skies,
makes an announcement: the Moon people are not hostile. They
simply wish to buy a small quantity of air and water, for which
they are willing to pay with scientific knowledge. * This is the
beginning of amity between the two worlds and the source of a
Terrestrial renaissance. * Nicely told.

453. THE REVOLT OF THE STAR MEN. *Wonder
Stories Quarterly,* Winter 1932. Ill. Paul.
Short story. * *Time:* the interplanetary future. *Place:* Mars,
Earth, and space. * A complex story of future adventure, too
involved for detailed summary. Story threads: The Martian
nobleman Hekalu Selba wants to conquer Earth and Mars and set
himself up as ruler. He also desires beautiful young Janice
Darell. As secret allies, Hekalu Selba has the space people,
black titanic humanoids who live in airless space. They have a
radioactive metabolism (as in #450, "The Space Dwellers") that
rids them of the need for heat, air, and nourishment. The space
people are currently assisting the Martian, but have their own
ideas about ultimate events. * Against the Martian and the space
people, more as a passive observer than an active agent, is
Austin Shelby, a Chicagoan who has invented a disintegrator ray.
Hekalu Selba, of course, wants the ray, and puts Shelby to
considerable pain and discomfort trying to extract the secret from
him. * Things might have been bad, but a rebellion led by an
honorable star man and Shelby's functioning disintegrator
frustrate the Martian coup. A double cross by the star people
aiding the Martians does not help. * *Miscellaneous:* Martians
are completely human. * The star people, who come from far
beyond the solar system, often ride small one-man flying saucers.
While their military power has been broken by the war,
individuals still wander into the solar system on trading missions.
* Competently written, but for some reason a bore.

454. WAVES OF COMPULSION. *Wonder Stories,*
March 1932. Ill. Paul.
Novelette. * *Time:* perhaps the near future. *Place:* not precisely

located, but somewhere in the Midwest, near the Mississippi
River. * Merton Sandhurst, director of the great subterranean
laboratories that are working on (among other things) space
travel, is one of the central figures in the peril that faces and
almost overcomes the human race. * A strange, small, purplish
object emerges from space and takes up a low orbit around
Earth. At first it is assumed to be natural, but it soon becomes
clear that the object is a spaceship or space station inhabited by
purplish, globular beings that can float in the air. * The first hint
of their presence comes when almost the entire human race falls
under the psychic domination of the strange beings. Whole
populations are subject to immediate organization into work
crews clearing land and building strange constructions. As is
eventually learned, these devices intended to maintain the
psychic domination and cause the eventual extinction of
mankind. Huge antigravity machines are forcing Earth's
atmosphere out into space, to make the planet more convenient
for the invaders. * A few stronger minds can resist the will
control of the invaders to some extent. Among them are
Sandhurst and a college student friend, but even their freedom is
limited. More potent is a wire armor that Sandhurst's assistant
develops in the underground laboratories. After captivities and
escapes, Sandhurst and his crew, in their newly constructed
antigravity flier, attack the space sphere and its defending ships
with smart bombs and end the menace. * Competent pulp adventure.

455. THE MOON MISTRESS. *Wonder Stories,* May
1932. Ill. Paul.
Short story. * A rather tangled story of adventure and intrigue.
Time: the interplanetary future. *Place:* the Moon. * The quest:
Grey and Parks are trying to find and rescue the prospec-
tor/explorer Joywater, who alone knows the location of an
enormous unclaimed deposit of radium somewhere on the Moon.
* The opposition: A secret cult (the worshippers of Mu Lo) co-
posed of wicked Orientals and Occidentals has captured Joywater
and will torture him to obtain the location of the radium deposit.
This opposition includes the Queen, an exotic dancer who sings
erotic songs. * Detail: The cult of the Mu Lo is based upon an
eighty-foot idol of gold left by a now-extinct Lunar race of
gigantic insects. The idol is operative and kills its victims. *
Further complications: Small, degenerate Lunar insects are a
menace. * Another complication: Perhaps Parks is not all that he
seems? Perhaps he is really a traitor? * No, he is not a traitor;
he is an archeologist. He has wormed his way into the cult in
order to find archeological material. * All ends to the wishes of
Grey, Park, and Joywater. * The writing and the detail are
competent, but the story is jumbled and confusing.

456. THE FLIGHT OF THE RX-1. *Amazing Stories,*
July 1933.
Short story. * *Time:* the near future. *Place:* the crater Plato on
the Moon. * The verismo experiences of Paul Hahn, the first
man to reach the Moon. His is a suicide flight, accepted with
the full understanding that there would be no return. Having
landed safely, he now has about a half hour of oxygen left.
During this short time, he leaves the ship briefly to set off a
magnesium flare. He encounters a strange lunar plant, and then
dies. His body lies at the edge of the crater. * Effective, nicely
handled.

457. MOON PLAGUE. *Wonder Stories,* January 1934.
Ill. Winter.

Gallun, Raymond Z. (*continued*)

Short story. * *Time:* the interplanetary future. *Place:* the Moon. * *Background:* The Moon has a shallow atmosphere and is inhabited by plant men: eighteen-foot-high slab-like beings with roots on the bottom of their "feet." They have a chlorophyll metabolism and restore their water by planting themselves periodically in an as-yet-undiscovered location. They communicate with colored lights; on the top of their bodies are organs that flash and receive light signals. They are reasonably intelligent, primitive in culture, and hostile. * Steve Jubiston returning to the laboratory-camp of the Melconne Expedition, discovers that the buildings and equipment have been wrecked by the plant-men; one of his comrades has been killed, another disabled, and the spaceship and Melconne (the expedition leader) missing. When the disabled youth (Claire Melconne) recovers enough, he tells Jubiston that the raid of the plant men was led by Garth Jubiston, Steve's younger brother, who had deserted from the camp six weeks earlier and had been presumed dead from lack of air. Claire Melconne adds that Garth is insane, driven mad by a strange lunar fungus that has invaded his body tissues. Claire himself is also infected, but in an initial stage. * Steve and Claire follow Garth's tracks. Garth and the plant men capture them. After back and forth action, Steve retrieves the spaceship and rescues Melconne, Sr. Garth dies. * Steve has a dual problem: watching over the Melconnes, who are infected by the fungus, and finding air and water, which Garth has indicated are present in the crystal mountain. And now Steve, too, shows signs of infection. * In the spaceship, Steve follows a plant men down through caves and caverns to an underground lost world, complete with air, water, and life. Above it is a crystal dome through which penetrate light and heat, forming what amounts to a greenhouse. Steve finds among Garth's notes a remedy for the terrible fungus, and the three men recuperate before returning to Earth. Garth's actions, the result of mental aberration, will not be revealed. * Competent pulp work.

458. **SPACE FLOTSAM.** *Astounding Stories,* February 1934. Ill. Marchioni.

Short story. * *Time:* The interplanetary future. *Place:* somewhere in space. * Essentially a character study. * Hal Trilbey and his friend Lonnie Shannon are young space rats. Not quite delinquents or criminals, though heading in that direction, they have bummed around the inner planets in various jobs, including a stint in the space patrol. While in the patrol they were recruited by the Venusian revolutionary Corad, who plans to conquer the inner planets, using, among other things, horrible fungous and bacterial agents. * The two young men did not know what they had let themselves in for, and when Lonnie sees Corad slice a captive Earthman to death, he protests. He is beaten badly, and when Hal tries to visit him, he is seized, accused of being a spy, and sentenced to space walk. Corad puts him into a space suit with ten hours of air and tosses him out of the spaceship. * There is no hope for Lonnie, for he is hundreds of thousands of miles from space routes. As he floats in space, he takes serious thought, perhaps for the first time in his life, and decides that if he must die, his death should accomplish something. Working himself back toward the spaceship, he crawls up the rocket tube (a procedure that will mean roasting in a few minutes), enters the combustion chamber, smashes all the jets, and sets off an explosion that destroys Corad's gigantic ship and all on board. * An unexpectedly close patrol ship sees the

explosion, but obviously does not know the circumstances. Its commanding officer thinks bitterly of patrol traitors like Hal Trilbey. * *Miscellaneous:* Venusians are human or humanoid and big; Martians are humanoid and small, and maintain an advanced mechanical civilization hundreds of miles deep within their planet. * Unusually stuffy writing for Gallun, but not a bad story.

459. **THE WORLD WRECKER.** *Astounding Stories,* June 1934. Ill. Dold.

Short story. * Fred Anderson shows his friend his great scientific achievement: a glass case, heavily refrigerated, in which rests a strange snowy growth. It is a plant, says Anderson, matter-transmitted from the tenth planet, the hitherto undiscovered world that Anderson has named Cerberus. * Over four billion miles from the sun, Cerberus boasts of intelligent life and a high civilization. Life is not chemical, as on Earth, but electrical, energy being drawn from the planet's atmosphere. The cold is so extreme that ice has never been melted, even under laboratory conditions, and snowfalls consist of solid hydrogen and oxygen. * The natives of Cerberus are friendly, and Anderson, in addition to receiving and sending suitable objects, has even established communication via written symbols. * Now Anderson will send something different—a lighted candle. (Even the reader knows better than this!) The result is that Anderson's apparatus explodes and both he and his visitor are injured. As for Cerberus, six hours later the men see a bright light in the sky where Cerberus used to be. The candle flame blew up the planet. Anderson is chagrined for a moment or two, then eagerly busies himself with spectroscopic analysis of the light from the lost planet.

460. **THE WAND OF CREATION.** *Astounding Stories,* September 1934. Ill. Dold.

Short story. * *Time:* since the twentieth century is mentioned as in the past, presumably at least the twenty-first. * Nixon and Spears, geologists, are driving the new subterrine (earth-borer) down about seventy miles, hoping for evidence that the center of the Earth is not as hot as theorized. Examining a specimen of rock from outside the borer, the men discover that it is fantastically heavy and presumably a new highly radioactive mineral. Indeed, it burns Spears's hand. * But then strange things happen in the subterrine: a sandwich crawls about, the drinking water is alive with slimy life, and the men themselves start growing greenish lumps. As Spears and Nixon now realize, they have stumbled upon the substance that originally turned inanimate matter into life far back in Earth's past. (On the surface it disappeared, what with radioactive decay.) It is a great scientific discovery, but it obviously will be fatal, since there is no possibility of their returning to the surface and spreading the life-force. * The men discover that their communications system—a sort of sonar that amplifies the voice—is not working; they can receive messages, but cannot send. The messages are not comforting. Their progress in the subterrine has opened up a lava lake, which is erupting in Chicago and is causing enormous loss of life and damage throughout the area. * The men decide, since they are doomed, to divert the lake of lava into a gigantic cavern they have discovered and explode the subterrine. Before exploding the subterrine, however, they warn their surface contact by signalling in Morse by turning their engine on and off in calculated bursts. The eruptions cease. * Capably handled.

Gallun, Raymond Z. (*continued*)

461. **THE MACHINE FROM GANYMEDE**. *Astounding Stories*, November 1934. Ill. Dold.

Short story. * *Time:* 1951. * Double events of great importance. First, telescopes show strange clouds emanating from Europa and Ganymede, together with flashes of light. The obvious conclusion is that the two moons are engaged in space warfare with each other. Second, great scientist Lutkin announces his weapon that will end war. A ray that suspends chemical action, it is in effect a potent, long-distance death ray. Lutkin at first intended to keep his discovery secret, but in light of events around Jupiter decides to release the weapon to the important nations of the Earth. * As Lutkin is addressing his audience in a special meeting of potentates, a small sphere hurtles down from space, emits rays that kill everyone assembled, destroys the laboratory, seizes Lutkin's equipment and notes, and flies off. Shortly thereafter, astronomers see Europa destroyed by what must be Lutkin's ray. * Lutkin's daughter and his assistant vow to recapitulate the discovery, though there are no laboratory records. * Competently told.

462. **MIND OVER MATTER**. *Astounding Stories*, January 1935. Ill. Marchioni.

Short story. * *Time:* presumably the near future. * The two friends Jorgensen, the great rocket-plane test pilot, and Dr. Toussaint, medical researcher and pioneer in cyborg-prosthetics, have often discussed Toussaint's work. Indeed, Jorgensen has declared that in case of accident, his body is to be delivered to Toussaint. * The opportunity comes sooner than expected, not long before Jorgensen had been scheduled to retire, when he is killed in a crash. Toussaint, who is on hand, retrieves the corpse and works on it. * Some months later, Jorgensen regains consciousness. He is puzzled about some aspects of himself, until Toussaint brings him a mirror and explains. Jorgensen's brain is encased in a metal body, connected to limbs with fine wires and elaborate circuits. As Jorgensen recognizes what has happened, particularly when he realizes that he has lost his girlfriend, his rage mounts. Toussaint, on the other hand, tries to convince him that he is now superior to mankind, a test pilot capable of space flight to the other planets. * Jorgensen tries to attack Toussaint, but the doctor, who had foreseen trouble, inactivates his friend, changes chemicals in his "metabolism,"—and Jorgensen is now delighted and looking forward to space. * A curious story.

463. **TELEPATHIC PIRACY**. *Astounding Stories*, March 1935. Ill. Dold.

Short story. * *Time:* 1949. * Roland Voss, independently wealthy brilliant scientist, chances to buy a peculiar meteorite in which is imbedded a small metal object. As Voss soon discovers, this object—the provenience of which is never discovered—is a mechanical telepath. With it he can follow the mental patterns of anyone whom he observes or thinks of. * At first Voss uses the power of the telepath (which he keeps secret) for altruistic ends. But, as might be expected, power gradually corrupts him, and he begins to steal profitable inventions and discoveries from their true creators' minds. * Voss's greatest coup comes when he focuses the device on the Moon, and contacts the minds of a cavern-dwelling lunar race far ahead of us scientifically. From them Voss learns the secrets of atomic power and disintegration. * Hybris, of course, is his downfall. He decides to reform the world on socialistic principles, with himself as supreme dictator.

But when he makes such an announcement, no one pays any heed. * Voss now decides that a practical lesson is necessary. With an atomic-powered super air vessel, he flies to Chicago, disintegrates part of the suburbs, then back to New York, where he destroys an air force and a warship. This is his death, for the telepath transfers the general national emotion of anger to his brain, overloading it, killing him and burning out the telepath. * Despite having caused some five thousand deaths, Voss's achievements with Lunar science have ushered in a new era of technology and have improved society. * More thought-provoking than the typical peace or economics vigilante.

464. **N'GOC**. *Astounding Stories*, May 1935. Ill. Dold.

Short story. * *Time:* about a half million years ago. * The story shifts back and forth between Ul, a paleolithic man a little more intelligent than his bestial fellows, and the inhabitants of what Ul calls N'Goc, a tiny secondary moon. * N'Goc, which is covered with a natural crystal shell, is hollow; within its interior, which contains air and water, a race of intelligent beings has developed. They are not described closely during the early part of the stories, but they are obviously not human, and their science is alien in technology. * The Philosopher, the wisest of the inhabitants of N'Goc, has discovered that N'Goc is about to fall down to Earth. The inhabitants take action. Building several space capsules, exploding them toward Earth with black powder, they hope to colonize Earth with rulers, slaves, and domestic animals. * The capsules land near Ul's tribe, which watches the flames with dismay. Ul, however, is brave enough to locate the capsules, and, recognizing that they are evil, begins to throw them into a nearby lava pit. In this he is helped by his timid fellow tribesmen, whom he has shamed into following him. But one capsule breaks open. The Philosopher bites Ul; the capsule follows the others into the lava pit, but not before some of the slaves and domestic animals escape onto Earth. These are present-day spiders and other insects. Thanks to Ul human beings, not intelligent spiders, rule Earth. * Not a bad story. For a latch-on see #468, "Buried Moon."

465. **BLUE HAZE ON PLUTO**. *Astounding Stories*, June 1935. Unsigned ill.

Short story. * *Time:* the interplanetary future. *Place:* Pluto. * An epidemic has broken out in one of the settlements on Pluto, and Terry Sommers, along with Dr. Cairns and a Venusian assistant, has been assigned to deliver antitoxin. Unfortunately, the spaceship has crashed, Cairns is dead, and the tiny Venusian is badly injured. Can Cairns make it on foot to the settlement at Pindar? Even carrying the wounded Venusian? * He succeeds, though it is a narrow thing. The Venusian, whom Sommers at times regarded as a hateful impediment (though out of humanity Sommers continued to carry him), managed to signal Pindar by summoning the dangerous native blue-haze beings. Their concentration was observed at Pindar, and rescuers arrived. * *Miscellaneous:* The plague is a form of silicon life that originated on Ganymede. It absorbs liquids from its victims, amounting to almost instant total dehydration. * Pluto is somewhat less inhospitable than one would expect. * The blue haze, also called Addison's fire, eats metal and has corroded Sommers's space suit. * Routine at best.

466. **DERELICT**. *Astounding Stories*, October 1935. Ill. Dold.

(Reprinted in Gallun, *The Best of Raymond Gallun*, and in Moskowitz, *The Coming of the Robots*.)

Gallun, Raymond Z. (*continued*)

Short story. * Partly a wonder story, partly a healing story. * *Time:* the interplanetary future. *Place:* space, in the vicinity of Jupiter. * Jan van Tyren, despondent at the death of his wife and child during a native attack on the Terrestrial settlement on Ganymede, chances upon a strange, battle-damaged, disabled alien space sphere. Judging by internal architecture and fixtures, its builders were not humanoid, but it is not possible to determine their origin or nature. * Investigating some of the apparatus, van Tyren accidentally summons a robotic creature that emerges like a jinn from a bottle. Long, serpentine, with a single-orbed head, it examines and apparently evaluates van Tyren, reading his thoughts about needs and wishes. The serpent, which van Tyren calls Khambee in memory of a Mercurian native he had once employed, sets the vessel in order, establishing air and air-cleaning gardens, prepares food, repairs the engines and hull, and also bathes van Tyren in a healing blue light that soothes his grief over his dead family. * Time passes, during which van Tyren is healed. The vessel, which embodies a science far beyond that of man, presumably is capable of interstellar travel, and for a time van Tyren considers escaping into the void. But Khambee, knowing his inner mind, activates a viewer, showing him battles still raging on Ganymede. Van Tyren decides to return to life, a decision that Khambee had anticipated and approved. * One of Gallun's better stories, with a wealth of mythic detail that cannot be conveyed in this summary: the nature of the Classical and psychoanalytic healing serpent, the blue light, and much else. A surprising story for the day.

467. DAVEY JONES' AMBASSADOR. *Astounding Stories,* December 1935. Unsigned ill. (Brown?)
(Reprinted in Gallun, *The Best of Raymond Z. Gallun;* in Conklin, *Best of Science Fiction;* in Knight, *Science Fiction of the Thirties;* and in Silverberg, *Earth Is the Strangest Planet.*)
Short story. * Cliff Rodney, biologist, in his bathyal submarine knows that the end is near when the glass of his viewing port cracks and a stream of water under high pressure forces itself in. The water rises, while he tries to stay above it, but then his vessel is dragged away. He slides into unconsciousness. * He awakens to find that his submarine is in an air-filled cavern; it is foul-smelling and nasty, but still air. Leaving his vessel, he discovers that his refuge is artificially sealed with a glassy plug and that glassy plates permit vision of the sea and fish. * As he watches, a skate-like fish flattens itself against the plates. Upon its body appears a message printed in English: "Do not die until I can come and write to you. The Student." The Student, a large, flat fish, appears, guarded by special fighter fish, and communicates by writing with chalk on the window. Rodney writes on the cave sand. * *Background:* Rodney has encountered a high underwater civilization that has progressed not by metal technology or fire, but by biological manipulation of sea life-forms. The glass on his cavern is formed by something like a mollusk; the air he breathes is produced by a giant fish, whose breathing is pumped in by other fish; and beyond is a sea city inhabited by specialist sea beings. * As for the Student, he has learned English from books that he has found. He maintains a small museum of human litter in the next cavern. An indefatigable, if emotionless, investigator, he has gone far in scientific understanding, but would like to learn even more by studying a living man. * Rodney and the Student converse extensively, con-trasting points of view and sharing data, but the Student will not release him. Rodney points out the wonders of actually seeing the sun and sky and examining more advanced human technology, but the Student replies that his culture does not desire contact with humans. Considering human history, it would be too dangerous for the fish. When Rodney asks if the Student will keep him there until he rots, the Student replies, "Until you rot." * There is a qualification. The Student knows that Rodney cannot escape, but is very curious to see how he will try. He therefore willingly gives Rodney glass and cements for repairing the submarine. * Rodney has a plan. After repairing the submarine and extracting hydrogen from the water, he creates an explosion sufficient to dislodge the plug sealing the cavern and sails out. Clouds of squid ink fill the sea about him, and he feels weight on his ship, but he is fortunate enough to break loose. * When he reaches the surface, he is surprised to see a glassy bubble attached to the submarine. In it is the Student. As the Student now states, although his culture forbids contact with humans, he has violated the law and has actually helped Rodney escape; his personal retinue of squids clouded the water to prevent capture. With enough oxygen in the bubble to sustain him, he looks forward to living in an aquarium and studying people. * Perhaps the best of the bathysphere/captivity-by-sea-monster stories, with a fascinating cultural description.

468. BURIED MOON. *Astounding Stories,* February 1936. Ill. Marchioni.
Short story. * A latch-on to #464, "N'Goc." * *Place:* far down underneath an island in the South Pacific. * The story is told subjectively through Tod Cram, who, in a tortured, distorted version of himself, is among strange beings who control his will and much of his activities. * It is difficult for him to think consecutively or to remember what has happened, but memory returns intermittently. He had been operating an earth-borer in search of a meteorite beneath Sunset Island, when his vehicle broke into an open space. Many little creatures swarmed over him, superior creatures turned elaborate apparatus on him, affecting his mind, and he has been explaining to his captors how to make a replacement part so that his borer will work again. * *Background:* Cram has encountered N'Goc, a small secondary moon that once circled Earth, but crashed some hundred thousand or so years ago. As the earlier story told, N'Goc was a small glassy hollow sphere in which life developed and evolved. In its last days, it was inhabited by intelligent spiders who had developed an idiosyncratic science. When the spiders recognized that their world had reached a gravitational limit, most of them left for Earth in black-powder rockets, but through a historical chance perished. N'Goc itself, however, unexpectedly survived the collision and now lies buried in the Earth, where its inhabitants live precariously with their superscience. They hope that when Cram's earth-borer is repaired, they can reach the surface and spread out over Earth. * In a moment when the spiders' psychic control is relaxed, Tod recognizes what he must do. He commits suicide with the sharp driving shaft the spiders had made. Since the spiders had intended him to pilot the borer, it is now unlikely that they will be able to emerge. They do not have the physical strength to operate the borer, and it will probably rust away. * As Tod lies dying, he feels no hatred against the spiders. They were only doing what any race faced with extinction would do. * Competently handled.

Gallun, Raymond Z. (*continued*)

469. **MAD ROBOT**. *Astounding Stories,* March 1936. Ill. Wallace Saaty.

Short story. * *Time:* the interplanetary future. *Place:* mostly Saturn. * Bar Andrews, departing from Callisto, plans to make a record close fly-by of Saturn. As he flies along, he thinks of Callisto, on which are to be found the strange Crystal Folk. Large crystals, they are living, perhaps even intelligent, but they are being brushed aside and destroyed as humans mine norsonium (element 98), a valuable rocket fuel. Andrews feels sorry for the Callistans. * His musing is interrupted when he discovers that Scarecrow, his humanoid robot controller, is driving the ship directly for Saturn. This is disastrous, for there is not enough fuel for leaving Saturn. Scarecrow refuses to change course, however, and will not accept commands or explain his peculiar actions. Andrews can only think of the occasional rare instances of robotic breakdown. Since Scarecrow also has the ship's small arms and is obviously prepared to use them, there is nothing that Andrews can do. * When the ship lands on Saturn, Scarecrow forces Andrews to don a space suit and carry out certain heavy chests. Andrews now sees that the chests contain seeds of the Crystal Folk, which the robot is sowing on norsonium ore. It is obvious that the Crystal Folk somehow tampered with Scarecrow while Andrews was on Callisto. * Andrews's first reaction is rage. He escapes from the robot, flies the ship away, refines some norsonium for fuel, and prepares to leave. But by now he has cooled down and recognizes the pathetic situation of the Crystal Folk. He will not destroy them with a rocket blast, as he could, nor will he reveal the presence of the valuable ore on Saturn. Picking up Scarecrow, who has run out of energy, removing certain crystals in the robot's control area, Andrews leaves Saturn. * Nicely done.

470. **THE WEAPON**. *Astounding Stories,* May 1936. Ill. Marchioni.

Short story. * *Place:* the foothills of the Andes, merging into the Amazon jungle. * Kent Marwell and John Corliss, young college graduates, have paid two hundred dollars for a guide (Pedro) and instructions for reaching a hitherto unknown major ruin. They are disappointed at first, for the stone enclosure is not large, but there are metal girders, partly fused, that indicate something beyond Inca architecture. On wandering into the ruin they see in a fetish hut a black cube and a bell-shaped apparatus. When Marwell presses a switch on the apparatus, it projects an image of a tall winged being vivisecting an Indian. The obvious implication is that an interplanetary visit was involved. * In the meanwhile, all about the two explorers are bands of hostile pygmies who persist in shooting barrages of poisoned darts. When the pygmies charge, the explorers make use of another property of the alien implement: It is a also heat-ray projector that stores up solar radiation, which it can reproduce either as image or heat. * The Indians persist in attacking, and the weapon is gradually becoming weaker. A resolution comes when Pedro turns the weapon on the fetish hut, whereupon the black cube (presumably spaceship fuel) explodes violently, ending the pygmy menace. Pedro, it seems, had been one of the Indians the space visitors had partially vivisected. * *Miscellaneous:* Another image projected from the device shows a scene presumably from the native planet of the visitors, a strange-towered city with many of the bird-men moving about. * Routine at best, and without fictional conviction.

471. **THE SCARAB**. *Astounding Stories,* August 1936. Ill. Dold.

(Reprinted in Conklin, *Science Fiction Thinking Machines.*)

Short story. * *Time:* 1947. * A political coup described indirectly through the Scarab, a remarkable tiny mechanical spy device in the shape of a large insect. It can fly, transmit pictures, and obey radioed instructions. * The Scarab flies to the laboratories of Professor Allison, which are under unsuccessful siege by the armed forces of the United States. The laboratories are mounting a successful resistance with attraction rays, engine stoppers, poison gas, atomic explosives, and superplanes. * How did this happen? Several months ago the evil scientist Boris Kolin captured Allison and his staff, injected them with a will-controlling drug, and forced them to develop the wonderful new weapons. Kolin demands enormous quantities of radium, or else his bombers will strike. The situation, so far, has been hopeless. * The Scarab, however, crawls under the defensive screens, flies into the laboratory, strikes at Kolin, and injects a narcotic into him. It similarly incapacitates the staff of the laboratory. Kolin's coup is over. * The crippled operator of the Scarab reveals that he persuaded Allison, some time before, to make the Scarab, which he now hopes to use exploring the world of insects. * Competently handled.

472. **A BEAST OF THE VOID**. *Astounding Stories,* September 1936. Unsigned ill. (Thomson?)

Short story. * *Time:* 1937-1938. * The strange story of Lothar Weiss, a semirecluse in a small Midwestern town, as left behind when he disappeared. * Weiss stumbles upon a meteorite in which was imbedded a black, leathery-looking substance. Cutting away the meteoritic metal with an oxyacetylene torch, he observes that the mysterious object is seemingly unaffected by heat. Removed, it turns out to be a flattish disk with claws around the edge, much like the top of a small umbrella. * After a time Weiss discovers that the object is alive, and, upon experimenting, he learns that it lives on the minerals in soil, which he feeds to it. Eventually Darkness, as he calls it, grows to a diameter of about fifty feet. * At first Weiss keeps it in a cage, and it becomes friendly, apart from one incident in which it attacks him. But then, most amazing of all, Weiss discovers that the creature can fly, apparently by some sort of anti-gravitational mechanism. * From here it is a logical step that Weiss, when Darkness is large enough, rigs up a small saddle and a space suit, and is carried about high above the Earth. Riding Darkness, he visits the Moon (which is barren except for a small vegetation); Venus (which is barren); and Mars (which is Schiaparellian with the archeological remains of a high civilization). * But now Weiss discovers that Darkness is about to bud and produce a new generation. Weiss considers this too dangerous for Earth. Utterly loath to kill Darkness, he mounts it and leaves for the stars. The space creature will slip into suspended animation when it leaves the solar system and will continue on its path, but Weiss will die along the way. * Interesting concept.

473. **GODSON OF ALMARLU**. *Astounding Stories,* October 1936. Ill. Thomson.

(Reprinted in Gallun, *The Best of Raymond Z. Gallun.*)

Novelette. * *Time:* perhaps the 1980s. * In a short prologue a mechanical device much like that described in #471, "The Scarab" comes to Earth, makes its way into a house, and injects a substance into a sleeping baby. This is not explained at the

Gallun, Raymond Z. (*continued*)

time, but it is part of a long-range plan dating from before the rise of humanity. * *Background, as imparted gradually*: There is a rogue planet, apparently composed mostly of neutronium, that makes a periodic swing through the solar system on an orbit of perhaps hundreds of millions of years. On a previous pass it destroyed Bode's fifth planet (Almarlu), which then held a supercivilization. The natives of Almarlu did not have time to save their own world, but they distributed seeds of their biota, including themselves, on the as yet lifeless Earth. They also set up a monitor to prepare for the next approach of the neutronium planet. Such a monitor selected baby Jeff Scanlon and prepared him for the task of saving mankind. * Jeff, who seems otherwise an average man, demonstrates incredible financial wizardry, and in a short time is financially the most powerful man on Earth. In semiretirement, he betakes himself to science, and, obviously drawing unconsciously on the knowledge of Almarlu, about which he occasionally dreams, creates communications marvels and wireless transmission of power. * His *chef d'oeuvre*, however, is a device for tapping the Earth's rotational inertia. Jeff cannot explain what he has done, nor does he understand it, but it works. He builds an incredibly strong power station on a small subarctic island. This station is so massively built that it is practically indestructible. * At just this time, the neutronium planet becomes visible. Almarlu has predicted well. But when Jeff turns on his apparatus full force, focused on the Moon, it drives air and water out into space. Earthquakes, tidal waves, submersions begin to take place. * Jeff is blamed for the damage, and his position is not enviable. But this is only a preparatory step. Jeff broadcasts that the Earth is doomed. He urges everyone to take to the air and fly into the beam radiating from his station. The beam will carry them to the Moon and safety. He is not generally believed, but enough people follow his advice that the Moon has a substantial population, transported along with air and water from Earth by Jeff's beam. As the survivors watch, Earth splits apart and dies. * Not very convincing.

474. **THE PATH**. *Astounding Stories*, November 1936. Ill. Flatos.

Short story. * *Time*: the near future. * Background: The dictators conquered the last vestige of free humanity and instituted a rule of regimentation and terror. "Work, food, sleep, and play" were all controlled. And as act of revenge the dictators placed captured Paul Fenwick, a great scientist who had aided in the resistance to them, in a space shell and shot him off Earth. It is generally assumed that he died. * About ten years later, small planes fly over the palaces of the dictators, emitting a ray that stops all chemical action. Successful rebellion then breaks out. * As Fenwick's former associates discuss it: Fenwick's orbit was not as simple as assumed; it became elliptical, and like a comet gradually approached the sun. During this time Fenwick devised the antichemical ray and radioed details to the underground on Earth. * Routine.

GARDNER, THOMAS S[[AMUEL] (1908-1963)

U.S. (New Jersey) chemist, s-f fan. Born in Tennessee. Ph.D., Ohio State University, on synthesis of sugar alcohols and their derivatives. Senior chemist at Hoffman-LaRoche. Active s-f fan; established standard version of Robert E. Howard's chronogeography.

475. **THE LAST WOMAN**. *Wonder Stories*, April 1932.

Ill. Paul.

(Reprinted in Margulies and Friend, *From Off This World* and in Moskowitz, *When Women Rule*.)

Short story. * *Time*: about twenty thousand years in the future. *Place*: Nuk, which the ancients called New York. * Historical background: In the twentieth century the biochemist Zeeman discovered a compound that destroys the hormones causing emotion, including sexual desire. As a result, for a resolute band of scientists and their followers, all the energy formerly directed into sexuality was channeled into intellectual productivity. Some time later another scientist discovered a means for perfect organ transplants, including brains, thus assuring immortality for a secret few. And still later, the production of artificial ova was perfected, thus rendering women unnecessary to the Scientists. Such genetic variation as was needed was produced by sperm selectivity. These discoveries and techniques, however, were not shared beyond the elite Scientists, and the masses (the normals) were unaffected. In 2794 war broke out between the normals and the Scientists, in which the normals were wiped out. During the war the Scientists had as allies the Metal Men, humanoid beings with machine intelligence. Since then humanity has been totally male, all without sexual drive, but retaining secondary sexual characteristics. * There is, however, one exception to this, as the lecturer in about A.D. 22,000 informs his student listeners. There is one female, the result of a mistake in the processing of sperm, who is kept in zoo circumstances as a demonstration specimen to show what ancestral humans were like. She sits in her cage, stared at by contemporary males, Metal Men, Martians, and Venusians. * But, although this is not generally known, there is also a single full male in the solar system. This is Explorer X12. Space-wrecked on Ceres, he has missed his periodic desexualizing shots and has reverted to normal sexuality. * When X12 and the woman meet, they are attracted to each other and attempt to elope. But they are no match for the powerful tracking science of the day. They are captured and executed by instant incineration. * The Science Civilization delivers a final judgment against emotion, declaring that no more atavists (like Explorer X12) or accidents (like the woman) shall be permitted to live. * *Miscellaneous*: The Martians are reptile-men, taller than humans, and nasty. Venusians are shorter, like three or four-foot-high insects. * Intelligent and literate, but without the impact of S. Fowler Wright's similar work. * The present story is erroneously attributed to Thomas D. Gardner in the magazine.

476. **THE INSECT WORLD**. Wonder Stories, April 1935. Ill. Paul.

Short story. * *Time*: The far future. * The report of an interstellar expedition visiting Earth. The visitors, who are insects or insectoid, have no difficulty in communicating telepathically with the termites, ants, wasps, and bees that now are dominant on Earth. Along with general information about individual families of insects, the explorers hear of a long extinct race of gigantic mammals who had established a great civilization, including interplanetary travel. But almost no traces of these mammals survive. The explorers follow leads until, aided by friendly ants, bees, and wasps, they discover a memorial, paper with writing on it—the names of victims of a great earthquake in Japan. * The history, as gleaned: Man was increasingly threatened by new varieties of termite that were able to withstand cold. To fight the termites, mankind developed the intelligent, tool-using ants that the explorers met, but this was of no avail. Quietism

Gardner, Thomas S. (*continued*)
gradually became characteristic of the humans, who finally simply died out. * Inadequate editing, which should have removed some of the rough spots.

477. **THE WORLD OF SINGING CRYSTALS.** *Wonder Stories*, April 1936. Ill. Paul.
Short story. * *Time:* The far future. * In the same series as #476, "The Insect World." The expedition makes a report to the Council of Eo. The explorers have encountered a planet covered with enormous, beautiful living crystals. Telepathic communication is possible, and the crystals are revealed to be both individuals of a sort and also members of a group being that constitutes the planet. The crystals, which are based on an ammonia system rather than carbon, are friendly and informative, and the stay of the explorers is pleasant. * As the explorers are about to leave, however, chance reveals that the crystal world is dying and that out of courtesy the crystals have hitherto not revealed the fact. An unabsorbable radioactive meteorite is destroying them. It is a simple matter for the explorers to remove the intrusion, and all are happy. * Not so much a story as a bare narrative.

GARFIELD, HARVEY J.
Presumably a British author; otherwise no information.

478. **ELECTRIC ZONE.** *Scoops,* 9 June 1934. Unsigned ill.
Boys' fiction. * Short story. * *Time:* the near future. * The *Meteor*, a great rocket-propelled zeppelin, is on its maiden voyage with five hundred passengers, including Sir Hamilton Benson, Minister of Aviation, and his daughter Kit. On the ground, maintaining communication every five minutes is Kit's boyfriend, radioman Jimmy Hampton. Suddenly nothing is heard from the *Meteor*. * On board the ship, when it reaches an altitude of eight-five thousand feet, the power suddenly goes off and metal surfaces become lethal to the touch. As is soon recognized, the ship is stranded in an electric zone, a phenomenon similar to an air pocket, where electricity runs wild. The ship cannot escape without help, which seems impossible, for a flight of stratoplanes sent out to rescue the ship are all (except one) destroyed by the electricity. * This survivor, pilot Bob, and Jimmy figure out what to do. They hurriedly wrap a plane in insulation, fly up to the *Meteor*, fire a harpoon with a cable to the ship, and pull the zeppelin out of the electric zone.

GARFINKEL, SAMUEL
U.S. author, then resident of Brooklyn, New York.

479. **THE ACT OF RETIPUJ.** *Amazing Stories,* January 1931. Ill. Wesso.
Short story. * Eccentric fiction. * *Time:* A.D. 4036. *Place:* Sunev (Venus). * The individual Ruycrem Arsm makes a long deathbed statement to the planetary ruler Runtas Sunaru I. * On the question why it is impossible to communicate with Earth, Ruycrem Arsm explains: In the remote past, the great Aztec astronomer Retipuj was singled out by the sun god or sun spirit for an important task. Retipuj, the god states, will be immortal until his task is completed, and in the meanwhile he must learn as much technology as possible. * In the year A.D. 2030, Retipuj is instructed by the sun god to build interplanetary arks with which to transfer mankind to Venus, since the Earth, what with loss of vegetation, is losing its oxygen and soon will be uninhabitable. The Aztec god takes Retipuj to a location where there are ores of unknown metals and commands him to start

work. About fifty years later the god tells Retipuj that He has prepared Venus for human habitation, and that the migration should begin. Those selected for survival will be summoned to Madagascar by Retipuj's will power and will then be ferried to Venus. It all happens as the god desires, and Retipuj, his task finished, is granted death. * His narrative completed, Arsm obtains a pledge from his ruler to preserve this information, which came from a remote ancestor of the Arsm family. * The editors probably desperately needed a filler of a certain length; otherwise, there was no reason to print this item, which is not far from being unintelligible.

GATES, FRANK
U.S. author. A note in my copy of the magazine associates Gates with Seattle, Washington. If this is the correct Gates, he was a resident of Seattle; he attended the University of Utah, where he wrote the class musical comedy; he was also the author of several books of poetry.

480. **THE MAN WHO DIED BY PROXY.** *Amazing Stories*, May 1927. Unsigned ill.
Short story. * An anecdotal explanation of the death of Felix Dzerzhinsky, historical head of the secret police in the Soviet Union. * The American named Burton came to Moscow for medical aid. He had been bitten by a virulently poisonous snake in South Africa, and he had hopes that Dr. Levervitch, a great authority on poisons, could cure him. If not, he will die in horrible agony in a short time. * When Burton is getting funds from a banker in Moscow, however, he has the misfortune to encounter Dzerzhinsky, who shoots the banker, seizes the money, and orders Burton executed for the murder of the banker. * Dzerzhinsky needs a blood transfusion, however, and Burton willingly gives permission. Burton dies on the operating table, murdered, but Dzerzhinsky does not outlive him long, dying in torment from the venom transferred into his circulatory system with Burton's blood. * Borderline science-fiction.

GATTER, GEORGE F. (1914-?)
U.S. author, then resident of Waterbury, Connecticut.

481. **THE EMOTION GAS.** *Wonder Stories,* April 1936. Ill. Winter.
Short story. * Ethics in showbiz. * J. Harvey Green, a former actor, has a remarkable business proposition to put to theater owner Jonas Beverly. Green has developed a gas that in some way affects emotion, rendering people volatile and easily pleased. * Put into use in Beverly's theater, the gas produces well-satisfied patrons for dismal shows. * Beverly is making a fortune, but he is greedy. Firing capable actors, he hires low-priced hams. When Green protests, Beverly refuses to alter his plans and adds that he no longer needs Green, since he (Beverly) now has the secret formula for the gas. * Green has his revenge. He simply releases the gas earlier during the performance. The effect of the gas is the same, but reaction sets in much earlier than before, during the performance rather than after. Audiences respond with dissatisfaction and disgust to what they might otherwise have laughed at. Beverly is ruined. * Routine.

GEE, JACKSON
Unidentified pseud., presumably of a U.S. author. Since Gee sold his story to Street and Smith through an agent, his identity was not revealed.

Gee, Jackson (*continued*)

482. **AN EXTRA MAN**. *Astounding Stories*, October 1930. Ill. J. Fleming Gould.

Short story. * *Time:* 1972, reminiscing about 1932. * In the great museum is a square sealed box that is perpetually guarded by soldiers. It is Drayle's invention, which the government decreed should be suppressed, without further research. An old man, formerly Drayle's lawyer, tells Drayle's history to his hyperactive grandson. * Drayle, a great scientist, discovered how to disassemble a man into constituent chemicals, transmit his essential vibrations by radio, and reassemble him from chemicals at a receiver elsewhere. * Unfortunately, on the crucial demonstration of the process, the subject's wife (Mrs. Farrel) watched the disassembling of her husband. Convinced that Farrel was murdered, she shot Drayle, wounding him slightly. A little later Drayle reassembled Farrel in Boston. * All might seem well, but Drayle's Washington assistant, expressly against Drayle's instructions, also reassembled Farrel while Drayle was incapacitated. There were thus two Farrels vying for Mrs. Farrel. The ending is tragicomic. * Told as somewhat nasty comedy, with references to the science-fiction writer Jackson Gee, who has made scientific prophecies that have turned out to be valid. Capably handled.

GELULA, ABNER J. (1906-1985)

U.S. (New Jersey) journalist, advertising man. In 1939 interview claimed was technical editor for *Radio World*; radio editor for Gernback's *Radio News*. Died in Atlantic City, N. J.

483. **AUTOMATON**. *Amazing Stories,* November 1931. Ill. Morey.

Short story. * *Time:* presumably from about 1930 to about 1950. *Place:* mostly the Pine Barrens, New Jersey. * The dangers of machine intelligence. * Old Professor Holtz is determined to create machine intelligence, and with the assistance of young Martin he finally succeeds. The result is a humaniform creature that has machine strength and human intelligence, but is utterly without emotion. As is learned later, its sole personal drive is a relentless quest for efficiency. * When the machine becomes active, Professor Holtz's young ward Teresa teaches it to speak, read, and write, which it does with exemplary efficiency. It also advances beyond contemporary science in some respects, curing old Holtz of a paralysis by means of a novel electrical treatment. The automaton's remarkable qualities are soon recognized, and similar robots are manufactured; Holtz and Martin, as patent holders, become rich. In a short time Holtz-Martin automata run much of the world's superstructure. * There is a problem, however, which may be characterized as spiritual seduction. The automata, promising efficiency and success to those who will follow their advice or instructions, take more and more young people out of the path of normal life, into paths seeking power. Such happens to Teresa, who had been Martin's fiancée. In the position of choosing between Martin and power, she chooses power, with the automaton as her grey eminence. Martin, recognizing what is happening, begins a campaign to eliminate the automata, but when he tries to destroy the original machine, in order to release Teresa (or so he believes), he is clapped into a madhouse. * About twenty years pass. Martin is still incarcerated, but Teresa has now risen to become Secretary of the Treasury. Things seem stable, but when a reporter tries to deliver a message from Martin to Teresa, the robot tries to kill the reporter, recognizing that the message will destroy Teresa's efficiency. Teresa calls the police, and the robot accidentally destroys itself. * The concept of a different robot ethic than the highly touted Asimov group is interesting, but the story is clumsy and greatly overlong. The parable-like theme that emerges in the summary was less important to the author than a romance and thrills. According to contemporary fan reports (*The Time Traveller, Science Fiction Digest*) the rights to "Automaton" were sold to a film company for a production starring Boris Karloff, but to my knowledge such a film was not made.

484. **THE VALLEY OF THE BLIND**. *Amazing Stories Quarterly*, Spring/Summer 1933. Ill. Morey.

Short story. * A rehash of H. G. Wells's short story "The Country of the Blind." * *Place:* Brazil. * Ralph Standish, somewhat bored young New York playboy, joins a geological expedition to Brazil. While in the field, he hears of a tabu region, and, on impulse, out of boredom as much as anything, decides to investigate it alone. He deserts his party and wanders away. * After a time he comes upon a cultivated area with houses; working in the fields are nude blond white men and women. As he approaches them, he observes that they pay him no attention, and then sees that they are blind. When he draws nearer, they scent him, make a peculiar singing noise, and then speak to him telepathically. * He is told, in effect, that, like others who have visited the land, he may live freely in the land if he works and conforms, but that he can never leave. The blind people do not want the outside world to learn of their existence and interfere with them. Standish makes no attempt to leave, although he is confident that when the time comes, what with his weapons, he will have no difficulty. * Standish gradually adjusts to the blind society, although it is hard at first, and even introduces some improvements into the culture, like wheeled vehicles instead of sleds. But the blind people, who maintain an austere discipline, make it clear that he can never reach their level of mental advancement as long as he has vision to distract his mind. * When Standish makes an attempt to leave, the blind people do not hinder him, but he is soon tracked and trapped by a band of pumas. And then he realizes the guardianship of the land: The blind people control the animals of the jungle. Since he has broken the law in attempting to escape, he is in danger of being executed by the willpower of the blind leaders, but a young couple whom he has befriended and to whom he talks of the outside world cover up for him. * On another occasion, he sees the mental power of his captors. When a hostile Indian tribe attacks the land, all the wild animals (including apes!) slaughter the Indians, the apes disposing of the corpses after the battle. * By now, a couple of years have passed, and Standish has fallen desperately in love with the young woman Laomi. She reciprocates, but the Council forbids any union, pointing out that functioning eyes in his children would disrupt the land. Standish moils in anguish, but finally decides that since he will never leave the land, he must relinquish his vision. He submits to the operation, despite last minute reluctance. * The story is moderately well handled, despite the desperate zoology, but it raises the question of the bounds of plagiarism.

485. **HIBERNATION**. *Amazing Stories,* July 1933. Ill. Morey.

Short story. * *Time:* A.D. 2103. * Professor Gordon Anderson,

Gelula, Abner J. (*continued*)

demonstrating his discovery of chemical suspended animation, selects himself as the first experiment—and awakens 170 years later in a Technocratic civilization. He is honored as a great benefactor by General Marsden, chief of the Hibernation Center, and hears the wonders of the new age. * According to Marsden, the Great Depression continued, ever deepening, until 1956, at which time the Technocrats gained national power and revamped the nation and civilization. Socialism of a sort was established, with much communal life, including dining halls and the state as universal employer. * Anderson's discovery then became the center of the new civilization. To ease unemployment, the unemployable jobless were placed in suspended animation in huge establishments around the country. Since production methods continued to improve and unemployment kept recurring, a cycle was established; periodically new groups of un-employables would be put into hibernation. At the moment, some twenty million people sleep in the giant vault-like buildings. The sleepers must be cared for with periodic injections and temperature control. * General Marsden is an apologist for the new order, but Marsden's beautiful daughter Alicia, whom her father regards with pain as a radical, tells another story. According to her, the Technocratic state exists for an elite of a million or so aristocrats who are not subject to the hibernation "draft" and live in luxury, while the rest of the nation lives in perpetual fear and want. Further, adds Alicia, culture and science have stagnated since the 1950s. * Anderson is easily convinced by Alicia, and attends meetings of a rebellious underground. He also begins the search for an easy, foolproof way to revive the sleeping millions. An incentive beyond altruism arises when Alicia, with whom Anderson has fallen in love, is picked up at an underground meeting and placed under hibernation. * Anderson finds a gas that breaks suspended animation almost instantly. When it is released, millions emerge from their sleep-prisons. Alicia, awakened, says that the millions, whose buying power is needed, will break the Technocratic system and restore democracy. Let us hope that she is right. * The economic cycle postulated by Gelula is interesting and unusual in the literature, but obviously inspired by the Great Depression. Otherwise the story is routine.

486. **THE VENGEANCE OF A SCIENTIST**. *Wonder Stories*, February 1934. Ill. Winter.

Short story. * Dr. Farrington, a young medic, works as junior to a Dr. Logan, who is caught up for performing abortions. Farrington, although he did nothing illegal, but merely provided medical care, is implicated in Logan's crimes, is stripped of his license, and is imprisoned for three years. While he is in prison, his wife dies and his daughter is taken away for adoption. He vows revenge on the unjust medical board. * When he is free, Farrington obtains a job as an X-ray technician. Hearing of an obscure report of invisibility caused by short radiation, he experiments and learns how to produce and control invisibility; the length of time one is invisible depends on duration of exposure. * He now takes his revenge on the board that sentenced him. From one doctor, who is a greedy miser, he strips away his money, donating it to charities. Two others, staid, sanctimonious pillars of society, he photographs in a very compromising situation at a medical convention. The invisible Farrington watches the fourth man, a psychiatrist of impeccable authority and an irrefutable expert witness, accept a huge bribe

from legatees to certify a wealthy philanthropist. Farrington drives him to a breakdown with invisible voices in the court room. * The final member of the board, a surgeon, however, is more fortunate. Farrington pushes the surgeon's arm when he is performing brain surgery, thus killing the governor of the state. But the surgeon, with presence of mind, calls for the doors to be guarded, and Farrington's invisibility is wearing off. Farrington escapes, but when he is about to be captured back at his work-place, he commits suicide. * Competent but routine. For story purposes Gelula awards a medical board the power to imprison an offender.

487. **PEACE WEAPONS**. *Amazing Stories,* June 1934. Ill. Morey.

Short story. * *Time:* 1957. * A new generation has arisen since World War I, and the League of Nations has all but collapsed. A war is now going on between France and England on one side, and Germany on the other. What other nations are involved is not clear. * A new version of the peace vigilante, Morton Hardy, unofficial U.S. observer at League headquarters, now makes his appearance. (For those who are too young to remember or are otherwise unacquainted with applicable history, the United States, because of a feud between President Wilson and Con-gress, did not join the League of Nations.) Hardy seizes upon a scientific discovery that comes to his attention: the gigantizing formula of the great entomologist Professor Kingsley. Kingsley, with a drop of liquid, can create ants the size of trucks, beetles the size of buses. * Hardy and associates busily disseminate such giant insect stock along the front and elsewhere, and in a short time the soldiers of the various nations are busier fighting the insects than their fellow men. The battles are fierce and hard-won, for the insects are almost invulnerable except to the heaviest explosives. * When the fighting is over and the nations are willing to make peace, Hardy tells what he has done. He has further given to the League a police weapon that can be used against anyone in further outbreaks of war: the giant insects. * Too much of a romp, but superior to Gelula's earlier stories.

GERNSBACK, HUGO (1887-1964)

U.S. publisher, inventor, electronics entrepreneur, born Hugo Gernsbacher in Luxembourg City, Luxembourg, the son of a wholesale vintner. It is not known whether Gernsback changed his name legally or whether he simply adopted the present form on arriving in America. * Much of what has been written about Gernsback's early life is imprecise and occasionally questionable, since it is unsupported anecdote, perhaps glamorized, but it is known that he attended the Luxembourg École Industrielle and the Technikum in Bingen, Germany, where he studied electrical engineering for a time. Judging from his later life, his back-ground was thorough, but narrow. * Even as a boy or teenager, Gernsback displayed business acumen, although this was com-bined with a strong visionary component. When he decided that European patent law was too restrictive to include his inventions, he came to the United States in 1904, where after a short time he set himself up in business selling electrical and electronic parts, some of his own manufacture. It is claimed that in 1907 he sold the first practical home radio and the first amateur radio kit, both of which were highly successful commercially because of the rapidly growing amateur interest in radio. In April 1908 he published his first magazine, *Modern Electrics,* a slim thirty-two-page pamphlet describing simple electrical devices,

Gernsback, Hugo (*continued*)

answering simple questions, and offering a three-page editorial exhorting the reader. This was followed by many other similarly oriented magazines including, in the period before *Amazing Stories,* the *Electrical Experimenter, Practical Electrics,* the *Experimenter* (a retitling of *Practical Electrics*), *Radio News,* and *Science and Invention* (a retitling of the *Electrical Experimenter*). Gernsback's greatest editorial achievement came with *Science and Invention,* which showed remarkable editorial flare in offering science and technology news, extrapolations of science, speculations, survey articles by well-known figures, explanations of stage magic, exposés of so-called supernatural phenomena, contests, curiosities of crafts, and much else, all well presented. In some of these early magazines Gernsback printed occasional technical and fantastic fiction, which, though mostly on a very low level, seems to have been popular. As an anticipation of his later commitment to science-fiction, in the August 1923 issue of *Science and Invention* (which he called the "Scientific Fiction Number") Gernsback printed four science-fiction stories, one of which was a serial part. This issue may have been intended as a trial balloon, although there is no documentation to this effect. * In this irregular manner began Gernsback's professional involvement with science-fiction, which he claimed he had read enthusiastically since childhood. Just what Gernsback read, beyond Jules Verne, is uncertain, since he was not specific, but it would seem reasonable that as a German-speaker educated in a German technical school he would have been acquainted with the work of Kurd Lasswitz. It has been objected that Gernsback never mentioned Lasswitz, but this is not a strong objection. * In 1924 Gernsback first proposed to publish a science-fiction magazine. Patenting the title *Scientifiction* (a portmanteau word which he invented), he circularized his readers and customers, asking for comments and/or possible subscriptions. The campaign was a failure, however, and Gernsback shelved the plan for about two years. While Gernsback, to my knowledge, never commented, it is possible that the appearance of *Weird Tales* in February 1923 (issue of March 1923) may have suggested the issue of the magazine *Scientifiction* to him, or the concept may simply have been in the air. * In March 1926 Gernsback finally published *Amazing Stories* (issue of April 1926), the first genre science-fiction magazine, if one discounts the Frank Reade Library and the "Twentieth Century Number" of the *Overland Monthly,* which were dead ends. *Amazing* survived under various different editors and publishers until 1996. (At the moment, March 1998, it has been announced that *Amazing Stories* will be revived, but it is not clear what is involved.) * Gernsback followed *Amazing Stories* with an *Amazing Stories Annual,* which was extremely successful since it included a new novel by Edgar Rice Burroughs, and *Amazing Stories Quarterly,* which was less successful and died during the Great Depression. After the loss of the *Amazing* magazines with his bankruptcy in 1929, Gernsback started another science-fiction chain, the *Wonder* magazines: *Science Wonder Stories* (later *Wonder Stories*), *Air Wonder Stories,* and *Science Wonder Quarterly* (later *Wonder Stories Quarterly*). These events are covered in more detail in the magazine histories in this volume. * Despite his pioneering work in science-fiction, which has had enormous repercussions, in the 1920s Gernsback was more important as a publisher of technical and semitechnical magazines. His magazines served a generation as introductions to radio, pioneer television, popular

science in many fields, and various handicrafts. It has been said, with some justice, that his *Science and Invention* in its heyday was the most interesting and informative popular science magazine published in the United States. * Unfortunately, there is no bibliography of Gernsback's publications, and even fans have hazy ideas about their range. Thus, the following discussion is not complete, but even a partial list shows a very wide range of interest from electronics to aircraft to amusements to health material and more. The bibliographic situation is complicated by the fact that much of his publication was ephemeral, one-shot material, and that Experimenter and his later companies Stellar Publications and Continental Publishing sometimes sold ephemeral books by other publishers as if they were their own. In addition to the periodicals already mentioned, Gernsback published the pioneer magazine *Television,* which appeared in 1928 and was coordinated with his radio-television station WRNY. Other magazines included *Everyday Mechanics/Everyday Science and Mechanics, Radio-Craft* (later *Radio-Electronics*), *Radio Listener's Guide, Your Body, Technocracy Review,* and many others. * Fiction magazines beyond the science-fiction magazines already listed included *Scientific Detective Monthly* (later *Amazing Detective Tales*), *Pirate Stories,* and *High-Seas Adventures,* the last two of which were very competently edited and produced pulp magazines. In 1953 Gernsback issued his last science-fiction magazine, *Science Fiction Plus,* edited by Sam Moskowitz; it ran for seven issues. Although it printed some modern-looking material, it was, as was recognized at the time, anachronistic. Gernsback also briefly entered the comic book field in 1940 with his unsuccessful *Superworld Comics;* with contributions by Charles Hornig and Frank R. Paul, it lasted for three issues. * One-shot publications, sometimes ephemeral, included *Houdini's Spirit Exposés, Beauty Secrets, Popular Card Tricks, Aero Mechanics, All about Television Including Experiments* (1927), *1001 Radio Questions and Answers, How to Electrify Your Radio Set,* the *Radio Trouble Finder,* and undoubtedly other booklets. While I have no knowledge of *Beauty Secrets,* those of the other publications that I have seen are professional, but often somewhat disorganized in presentation, occasionally being built out of magazine articles. Less to Gernsback's credit were *French Humor,* an innocuous collection of occasionally bilingual squibs and cartoons sold with a false suggestion of soft pornography, and *Oi! Oi! I'm Leffing,* which, with a very offensive cover, contained mildly anti-Semitic jokes and parodies in the manner of Milt Gross. The last is a good example of Gernsback's lack of sensitivity, given his own Jewish background. * Gernsback also pioneered in serious sexual education with the ten-volume set the *Sexual Education Series* by science-fiction author David H. Keller, M.D., and at a later date the magazine *Sexology,* which is said to have been his most successful publication financially. * Gernsback also considered himself a fiction writer, as the following story descriptions indicate. Here his position is peculiar. His most important work, *Ralph 124C 41+,* has justly been called the worst science-fiction novel ever written, yet it had enough technological and scientific imagination to support a minor industry, as it applied extensions of contemporary technology to many areas of life. Most noteworthy, and often cited, is Gernsback's clear, technical statement of radar published back in 1911. His other fiction, though sometimes technologically highly imaginative, like his "Baron Münchhausen's

Gernsback, Hugo (*continued*)

Scientific Adventures," is equally bad. * Allied to this scientifictional emergence into life is Gernsback's experience as an inventor, which, as been detailed in several places in the Introduction, he considered strongly linked to science-fiction. According to certain sources, including Siegel, Gernsback is said to have held more than eighty patents, but Kraeuter lists only thirty-six, most of which deal with matters of electricity and electronics. A layman, obviously, cannot express an opinion on their importance. * Gernsback's entrance into radio and television broadcasting was also pioneering. His station WRNY may have had the first real radio programming back around 1928, with live classical music conducted by the versatile Joseph Kraus and evening science lectures by Gernsback, Sigmund Spaeth, and notables of the day. Descriptions in the literature about Gernsback's television broadcasts in 1928, many years before adequate British pioneer broadcasting in 1935, however, are misleading, for his broadcasts were not television in the modern sense. They seem to have been radio sound, which would be interrupted for a moment or so, during which a tiny frozen picture would be broadcast; in other words, it was not simultaneous sound and picture. WRNY, alas, turned out to be a very expensive, money-devouring hobby, as was revealed in Gernsback's bankruptcy. * Listing Gernsback's truly impressive achievements is easy enough, but it is very difficult to characterize the man. Much of what he did and said is controversial in interpretation, even at times contradictory. It is obvious that he was a very brilliant man, gifted with a remarkable imagination focused on technology, highly competent in his area of electricity and electronics, sensitive to cultural and business trends, and a visionary of sorts where scientific education was concerned. As a personality he is said to have been witty and amiable, at least in his early years. He was respected and liked by his employees, who were willing to stand by him during his troubles. David Lasser has stated that his workers so much enjoyed the sense of freedom that working for him entailed, that they were willing to overlook delayed paychecks. He obviously could count on the support of a gifted staff that helped prepare his technical magazines, particularly the excellent *Science and Invention*. (Unfortunately, almost nothing is known about these men beyond their names. Preëminent were Joseph Kraus, Charles P. Mason, and H. Winfield Secor.) * There is little question that Gernsback was sincere in his faith in scientific education and that he was a scientific millenarian of a sort. For him the future, as created by modern science, was the great period to come. He also saw science-fiction as a tool toward achieving the new world both by direct instruction and by inspiration, an interpretation that many have considered naive. * This is the credit side of Gernsback. Unfortunately, there is another side. As a publisher of fiction Gernsback had limitations; he could not judge literary merit; he had little literary background, and despite his claims to the contrary really knew very little about historical science-fiction. Personally, he was a weak fiction editor. As Jack Williamson has said, "He was never a helpful or creative editor, nor even very ethical" (Williamson, *Wonder's Child*, p. 53). He made bad choices for his early fiction editors—Sloane, Whitehead, Brandt, Hornig (who was too young); Lasser alone was effective. His background in the sciences beyond his specialty seems to have been weak. * As a business man Gernsback has been severely and justly criticized. His treatment of authors is notorious. As

his editors Lasser and Hornig both have stated, Gernsback felt that publication should be reward enough for an author. Many early authors have reported difficulties in receiving payment for their work, in some case even having had to resort to legal threats: Lovecraft, Burroughs, Williamson, Keller, Manning, Verrill, and Wollheim come to mind. Although Gernsback was unquestionably aware of the existence of professional writers, he never seemed to realize, ultimately, that fiction was not necessarily a superstructure on another mode of livelihood, but something that had to pay its way for the writer. There have been attempts to apologize for Gernsback because of the Depression, but these are not plausible. The result of this sharp practice was that the more successful authors came to avoid Gernsback's publications, and the development of a pool of semiprofessional or professional science-fiction writers had to wait until the *Astounding* magazines. * Gernsback's bankruptcy in 1929, which is covered in more detail in the history of *Amazing Stories*, is hardly to his credit. While the total situation may never be known, he obviously walked away from his debts and has been accused, with some reason, of a deliberate policy to bilk his creditors. * Apart from unscrupulousness in business, Gernsback's sincerity has otherwise been criticized. His so-called advisory panels of experts who passed on the scientific merits of every story were fakery, and, as has been developed elsewhere, paradoxically, while he sincerely believed in science and technology as optima, he was willing to utter inferior science in his magazines. At times, expediency played too important a part, as did the desire for an image of respectability. * Gernsback's role in the history of science-fiction has also been disputed. Humanistically oriented critics have censured him for channeling science-fiction into a gimcrack route, with total disregard of literary or social aspects. Ideologically, it has been said, Gernsback perpetually pushed science-fiction in the wrong direction, at first with stodgy, mechanistic, badly written material, later with juvenile activities. Such critics consider his work disastrous. Others have blamed his business practices for impeding the growth of a literary subform. His historical position has also been discounted: as an if-of-history, science-fiction was in the air at the time, and if Gernsback hadn't set up an opening, someone else would have, since the pulp trend was toward more specialized magazines. * His supporters, on the other hand, honor him for the vision that did establish science-fiction as an market phenomenon, permitting later developments. They consider him a founder and prophet who, despite personal flaws, "got things going." According to these critics, he was unique in perceiving unifying factors in what had hitherto been disparate minor fields of writing and, especially, setting up a phenomenon that today is a major cultural force. Without Gernsback, if one might put words into the mouths of such admirers, many TV channels would be empty, many motion picture screens would be dark, many carousels in the great book chain stores would sit barren. Good or bad, Gernsback is a historical fact that cannot be denied. * My own feeling is that both points of view have some justification. As has been stated in *Science-Fiction: The Early Years*, "his contribution first to American cultural history, then to world cultural history, was establishing a commercial entity that was capable of growth. He brought together under a single canopy many varied sorts of fantastic fiction and presented it in a way that it could survive. One can criticize Gernsback severely from many points of view,

Gernsback, Hugo (*continued*)
but he was a man of vision and without his work science-fiction would not exist in its present form."

Stories are described in the order of their original publication.

488. RALPH 124C 41+. *Amazing Stories Quarterly*, Winter 1929. Ill. Paul.
(First published in *Modern Electrics*, March 1911-April 1912. Revised for book publication by The Stratford Company, New York, 1925. Second edition, by Frederick Fell, New York, 1950.
* Fragments are reprinted in Curtis, *Future Tense;* in Rabkin, *Science Fiction, A Historical Anthology;* and in Warrick, *Science Fiction: Contemporary Mythology.*)
Episodic novel that is essentially a series of technological prophecies hung upon a sensational story. * *Time:* A.D. 2660. *Place:* New York and space. The central character is the unexcelled scientist Ralph 124C 41+, the + at the end of his name indicating his status as one of world's ten superminds. * A faulty connection on his telephot machine causes Ralph to make the acquaintance of Alice 212B 423, a beautiful young woman whom he rescues from an avalanche by directing electric force onto the snow and melting it. Their acquaintance ripens when she visits Ralph in New York, and he shows her the wonders. * Two unwelcome suitors harass Alice, Fernand (an Earthman) and Llysanorh' (a Martian). Fernand kidnaps Alice, and Ralph tracks them through space with his radar equivalent. But, actually, this is a misdirection, for Llysanorh' had hijacked Alice away from Fernand. The Martian is now on his way to the asteroid belt, where he can hide from detection. Ralph follows. Using an artificial comet to distract the Martian, Ralph attacks, but in the shoot-out Alice is accidentally killed. * Ralph is equal to the emergency: Carefully icing down Alice, he takes her back to New York where he repairs and revives her. (He had previously had some experience with such cases, reviving a dog from a deep-freeze.) * The consensus has long been that Hugo Gernsback was one of the worst novelists to reach print; nevertheless his novel is remarkable ideologically for its childlike faith in technological progress and its highly imaginative predictions, many of which have been realized. These include phototelephones, television, voice-command lighting, wireless transmission of power, magnetic elevators, microfilm newspapers, superimposed color printing visually separable by filter screens, tape recorders, the hypnobioscope (a device for sleep learning, one of Gernsback's crotchets), safe radium, suspended animation, automatic vocal translators, earth tubes, linear motors, motorized roller skates, weather control, appetite-stimulating gases, aerocabs, solar heat receptors, liquid foods (no more chewing), hologram stage performances, store-to-house belt delivery systems, daily compulsory bacteria-killing irradiation, heat wells, plant growth hormones, a financial structure based on real estate values with check payments instead of cash, and X-ray spectacles. * Miscellaneous point: The planets are inhabited by more or less human populations who can interbreed, Martians being tall and large-chested. * "Ralph 124C 41+" is described in more detail in *Science-Fiction:The Early Years.* * As an oddity, in Gernsback's comic book *Superworld Comics* (May 1940, August 1940) there appeared "Marvo 1-2GO+ the Super Boy of the Year 2680. Prodigy, mastermind, explorer and adventurer," which obviously invokes the earlier "Ralph," though it con-

centrates on juvenile adventure, without the anticipatory invention aspect of "Ralph." Script and artwork are not signed, but Paul was clearly the illustrator, and it is probable that Charles Hornig wrote the script.

489. BARON MÜNCHHAUSEN'S SCIENTIFIC ADVENTURES. *Amazing Stories*, February-July 1928. Ill. Paul. (First irregularly published in the *ElectricalExperimenter*, May-August, October, December 1915; January, March, April, June, November 1916; February 1917.)
(Episode #12, "How the Martian Canals Are Built" is reprinted in Haining, *The Fantastic Pulps*.)
Thirteen episodes continuing the adventures of Baron Münchhausen in our time. The episodes, which are described in much more detail in *Science-Fiction: The Early Years*, are characterized by Gernsback's typical leaden humor, imaginative and interesting technological extrapolations, and fatuous narration. * *Time:* World War I. *Place:* the Moon and Mars. * Baron Münchhausen, awaking from suspended animation caused by accidental injection with embalming fluid, contacts the narrator, I. M. Alier, who is an enthusiastic radio ham. After telling how he helped the Allies almost conquer Germany, the Baron announces that he has discovered an antigravity substance (marconium) and has built a space ship utilizing it. The third, fourth, and fifth episodes describe lunar conditions. The moon has a slight atmosphere supporting cave life, but is hollow, with many craters permitting access to the interior. * The remainder of the story, episodes six through thirteen describe Mars, which Münchhausen and a companion visit. Mars is a Lowell-Schiaparellian world, with gigantic humanoid inhabitants with barrel chests. Martian science is far more advanced than ours, with flying fortresses, thought transference helmets, power rays derived from the sun, gravity control, atomic energy, Theremin-like music, enormous futuristic cities with elevated roadways, total city lighting with aerial globes, supertelescopes, synaesthetic art forms, and atmosphere plants to replenish the waning air. * Much of this detail is very imaginative, though the narrative mode is often irritating. Essentially, though, a curiosity, without the fascinating primitive speculations of *Ralph 124C 41+.*

490. THE MAGNETIC STORM. *Amazing Stories*, July 1926. Ill. Paul.
(First published in the *Electrical Experimenter,* August 1918.)
Short story. * World War I fiction. * *Place:* France. * The great Tesla's lab manager, "Why" Sparks, has a brilliant idea for ending the war. The secret is not revealed until after the German collapse, but, inexplicably, German telephones, airplanes, and automobiles will not function. The German army is paralyzed, and the war is soon over. * Explanation: "Why" set up an enormous magnetic field by stretching wires along the front, and electrical equipment, overloaded, burned out. A metal shield protected the French side of the line. * The breakdown of internal combustion engines because of electrical overloading was a common enough motif in early science-fiction.

491. THE ELECTRIC DUEL. *Amazing Stories*, September 1927. Unsigned ill.
(First published in *Science and Invention*, August 1923.)
Not really science-fiction. * *Place:* Italy. * Two young Italian electrical engineers, both enamoured of the same woman, decide on a duel to the death with electricity. Equipped with electrified headpieces, they box with gloved quarterstaves; whoever is knocked out of the ring will be electrocuted. Both fall out—but

Gernsback, Hugo (*continued*)
it is all a dream.

492. **THE MOST AMAZING THING. (IN THE STYLE OF EDGAR ALLAN POE).** *Amazing Stories*, April 1927.
An editorial in the manner of Poe's "The Thousand and Second Tale of Scheherazade." * The explorer reports to the all-powerful Supremental about the Third Planet of the Sixth Universe. His description is too detailed and specific to be summarized, but it tells of soft-bodied beings who have an electric control system in a lump at the top of their bodies, with electrical communications throughout their bodies. These beings do not reconvert light rays for sustenance, as the explorer and his master do, but ingest various solid substances that undergo chemical changes. Nor can they float; apart from clumsy engines that bear them about to a limited extent, they remain on the surface of their world. * To each item of the explorer's summary the ruler makes such comments as "Preposterous," "Incredible," and "Piffle." But, as the explorer says, the "worst is yet to come." Periodically these beings, for no reason at all, exterminate thousands of themselves with machines that bore holes in or otherwise damage bodies, and then when the incident is over, appear to become good friends again. * An amusing piece, much the best of Gernsback's attempts at fiction, but, since there is some question about who wrote Gernsback's editorials for his science-fiction magazines, it may not have been written by Gernsback. Charles Hornig claims to have written Gernsback's editorials while editor of *Wonder Stories*, and the same situation may have existed earlier. At least, Gernsback's editors may have reworked his expository material. It must be added, however, that surviving manuscripts reveal that Gernsback himself wrote at least some of the material that appeared under his name in his technical magazines, notably the April Fool articles under the pseudonym Mohammed Ulysses Fips.

493. **THE KILLING FLASH.** *Science Wonder Stories*, November 1929. Ill. Paul.
Short-short story. * In a side note Gernsback states that he wrote the story to demonstrate to would-be authors that it is possible "to put quite a bit of material into 1400 words without sacrificing either science, action, or plot. And the space allows the inclusion of one or more surprise endings." Gernsback, however, says nothing about quality or intelligibility. * Illinois. * The very confused story consists of several frames: In the first, Friendly announces his intention of killing Lindenfeld by sending a high voltage charge across a telephone line. Second, a reply from the local telephone company tells Friendly that his scheme will not work. Third, a news report states that Friendly was killed when his electric charge set off explosive materials in the floor above him. Fourth, a rejection slip from *Science Wonder Stories* suggests changes that would destroy the story, which encompasses all the preceding. The rejection slip is signed "O. Utis, Ass. Editor." ("Outis" is the Greek word for "no one.") * Doubtful as science-fiction, and hardly a literary model.

GILBERT, KENNETH (1889-1969)
U.S. writer; author of several books on nature, hunting, fishing, also fiction: *Fighting Hearts of the Wild* (1928), *Brian Boru, Wolf Dog* (1930), etc. Also contributed to pulp magazines, including *Adventure*.

494. **THE WINGED DOOM.** *Amazing Stories*, October 1927. Ill. Paul.
Short story. * *Time:* late twenty-first century. *Place:* the East Coast and over the Atlantic. * War breaks out when a European power tries to seize the secret of antigravity, held by the United States. The European armada approaches. * The hero who will save America is the aerial buccaneer The Kingbird, pirate sans pareil, who places patriotism above profit in this instance. Flying his superplane to what seems to be a flagship of the opposing fleet, anchoring by means of suction cups, he captures The Heir (i.e., crown prince) and forces him to cancel the invasion. Mission accomplished, The Kingbird resumes his career of robbing aerial liners and baffling the aerial police. * Telepathy is now an everyday matter. * Pretty horrible.

GILMORE, ANTHONY
Joint pseud. of editors Harry Bates and Desmond Hall of Clayton *Astounding Stories*. In their collaborations, in general, Bates claims to have provided ideas and perhaps plots, while Hall did the actual writing, but individual circumstances are not known. See author entries for biographical information. Gilmore also contributed fiction to *Complete Stories* and other pulps.

Stories are described under The Hawk Carse Series and Other Works.

The Hawk Carse Series

The Hawk Carse stories, which are dated vaguely as in the period A.D. 2117-2148, are for all practical purposes traditional pulp Western stories transplanted into space, with the addition of an Oriental villain in the mode of Sax Rohmer's Dr. Fu-Manchu. While stories by other authors have approached this same aesthetic, the Hawk Carse series is a typological extreme. * Hawk Carse, "the greatest adventurer in space," "he of the spitting ray gun and the phenomenal draw," guns down his enemies; these are outlaws who are the equivalent of cattle rustlers or minions of an Oriental fiend. Carse is so fast and so accurate with either hand that he permits his enemies, in face-to-face duels, to draw their weapons before he shoots neat holes in their foreheads. Four- and five-to-one odds are nothing to the Hawk. In this expertise the Hawk excels his cowboy prototypes. * Carse is cold, icy, and passionless, except for anger when harassed by badmen. For his trusty steed the Hawk has the *Star Devil*, the fastest ship in space, designed by his friend and associate Master Scientist Eliot Leithgow. And for a faithful companion, the Hawk has the giant black man Friday, whom Carse's foes refer to as a nig or nigger. * The Hawk's ultimate purpose is revenge for an injury done to him in the past, a wound that necessitates his wearing his hair in bangs over his forehead. The Hawk is also greatly concerned to clear the name of his friend Leithgow, who has been framed for a crime. * The Hawk's counterbalance and relentless foe is the diabolic Eurasian scientific genius Ku Sui. A monster of evil, he is the overlord of gangs of space pirates and similar criminals. He is the master of strange knowledges and tortures, and only the Hawk can stand against him. * The stories have been collected, with an additional story, as *Space Hawk* (Greenberg; New York, 1942).

495. **HAWK CARSE.** *Astounding Stories*, November 1931. Ill. Wesso.
Novelette. * *Time:* somewhere in the period A.D. 2117-2148. *

Gilmore, Anthony (*continued*)

Place: On and around Iapetus, one of Saturn's moons, which is Earth-like. * Hawk Carse has pioneered in the settlement of Iapetus, where he has established a ranch for raising the ferocious phanti, a form of native life whose horn has considerable monetary value. Carse and his employees consider their ranch safe, for who would dare to injure the Hawk—except perhaps his great enemy, the outlaw genius Ku Sui? * On the present occasion the Hawk is returning to Iapetus when he receives a signal that his ranch is being attacked. He rushes to the site, only to see a pirate vessel about to leave. The Hawk's hitherto irresistible ray simply bounces off the pirate vessel, which blasts off. * After cleaning up the dead, the Hawk pursues. As he draws near the pirate craft, he receives a taunting message from his enemy Judd the Kite, and within a matter of minutes the Hawk's ship is filled with an instantaneously fatal fungus. All except the Hawk and Friday are dead. * Judd boards the *Star Devil* and, despite some temporarily successful resistance by the Hawk and Friday, captures them and takes them back to Iapetus. Ultimately Judd will deliver Hawk to Ku Sui for suitable treatment. * But while Judd, who himself has a penchant for torturing his captives, often flaying them alive, is working on Friday, Carse turns the tables by releasing the insanely vicious phanti bulls, who stampede and attack the outlaws. In a final shootout Carse beats five men to the draw, killing them all. He is now on his way to keep Judd the Kite's rendezvous with Ku Sui. For a sequel see #496, "The Affair of the Brains."

496. THE AFFAIR OF THE BRAINS. *Astounding Stories*, March 1932. Ill. Wesso.
Novelette. * Sequel to #495, "Hawk Carse." * *Place:* mostly in the asteroid belt. * Hawk and Friday (now sometimes called Eclipse) fly away in the captured pirate ship to keep Judd's rendezvous with Ku Sui. They reach the appointed place and wait. Nothing happens, but suddenly Ku Sui and his myrmidons appear in Carse's ship and capture the two men. Ku Sui then takes them to his headquarters, an asteroid off Jupiter, where he taunts and gloats in Oriental courtesy. * Finally Ku Sui reveals his purpose. The Hawk must tell where Master Scientist Eliot Leithgow is hiding. Placed in a hypnotic machine, the Hawk breaks and gives Ku Sui the information he wants. * Ku Sui's reasons for wanting to find Leithgow: He has built a mental battery of the six greatest brains in civilization. Detached from their bodies, wired up, they act as a brain trust and have enabled him to make his greatest scientific advances. But the brain group is not perfect; it would function even better if Leithgow's brain occupied the key position. * It looks as if Ku Sui has won, for he has captured Leithgow, and the Hawk will soon be tortured to death. Ku Sui makes initial preparations for the operation, which is televised into the Hawk's cell. Bitter at having betrayed his friend, the Hawk and Friday make a death dash at their guards (who are zombie-like men whose brains Ku Sui has altered)—and win through. * There is enough commotion and confusion that the Hawk is able to rescue Leithgow. Following the instructions of the brain panel, the three men escape in Ku Sui's advanced self-propelled space suits. Behind them Ku Sui's establishment blows up, (perhaps) killing the brains (who received Hawk's promise to release them from their horrible half-life) and Ku Sui. * Ku Sui's great secret is now revealed: His home asteroid has been rendered invisible by superscience generated by the brain panel. * For a sequel see

#497, "The Bluff of the Hawk."

497. THE BLUFF OF THE HAWK. *Astounding Stories*, May 1932. Ill. Wesso.
Short story. * Sequel to #496, "The Affair of the Brains." * *Place:* space and Ganymede. * As Hawk Carse, Eliot Leithgow and Friday are flying in their self-propelled space suits, they realize that their attack on Ku Sui has failed. Since his asteroid is still invisible, his more important weapons and resources (including his own life) must have been protected. This proves right. * The next problem is locating Leithgow's scientific notes before Ku Sui can seize them. The papers are missing, but the Hawk believes that he knows where they must be: at Lar Tantril's ranch. * Carse is right, but Lar Tantril is just as intelligent as Carse. He captures the three men, disables the Hawk's gravity plates, and is prepared to turn Carse and his associates over to Ku Sui. * Carse must think fast. He strikes a bargain with Lar Tantril. If the Hawk can reveal a flaw in the defenses of Tantril's establishment, Tantril will release him. Hawk wins by entering a lake, where his space suit serves as a private mini-sub. He swims away. * For a sequel see #498, "The Passing of Ku Sui."

498. THE PASSING OF KU SUI. *Astounding Stories*, November 1932. Ill. Wesso.
Short story. * Sequel to #497, "The Bluff of the Hawk." * *Place:* space and Ganymede. * The Hawk, certain that Ku Sui will keep a rendezvous on Ganymede with Tantril, lies in wait for the invisible asteroid. More important to Carse than killing Ku Sui is his determination to keep a promise he had made to the captive brains and destroy them. * The asteroid flies up to Ganymede, becomes visible, and while Ku Sui descends to the satellite, Carse and his friends await the criminal genius in his own lair. * Ku Sui is captured. The Hawk informs Ku Sui of his fate. Ku Sui will not only clear Leithgow, but will transplant the captive brains back into human bodies. (The brains had previously agreed to this change in plans.) Carse suggests that Ku Sui's robotized medical assistants serve as receptacles. * Ku Sui smilingly agrees, but manages to sabotage the brains' life supply, so that the operations must be performed within a few hours, or else the brains will die. * Hawk is annoyed, but even more so, when under the influence of a mind-controlling drug, Ku Sui reveals that the robotized assistants are absolutely necessary to act as assistant surgeons. Carse is now in the position of having to find suitable bodies in a matter of minutes. He does this by kidnapping several drug fiends (various racial types, which the author and the Hawk regard with contempt), whose brains will be scooped out, to be replaced by the captive brains. * The operations are successful, but Ku Sui is gradually acquiring tolerance to the mind drug. He escapes as the asteroid is about to crash on Ganymede. Hawk, who is present, also manages to escape, but assumes that the villainous Eurasian perished with the asteroid. * A reader familiar with serial literature would have noticed the opening that Gilmore left for the restoration of Ku Sui.

A final story, "The Return of the Hawk," written by Harry Bates alone, appeared in *Amazing Stories* for July 1942. The Hawk's solution to the problem of the captive brains did not work out, for their wives rejected them, and the brains went mad. Hawk and Ku Sui now play with the technique of recreating bodies from voice records (as in Bates's "Farewell to the Master"). Ku Sui gets more than he bargained for. * A weak story.

Gilmore, Anthony (*continued*)
Other Works

499. **THE TENTACLES FROM BELOW**. *Astounding Stories*, February 1931. Ill. Wesso.
Novelette. * *Time:* 1935. *Place:* off Newfoundland. * The supersubmarine NX-1 has been assigned to survey the sea bottom off Newfoundland, where there have been land upheavals. Instead, the NX-1 becomes involved in a deadly duel with a gigantic round submarine that is superior in power and is armed with paralysis and heat rays. The submarine is manned by intelligent octopi. * The NX-1 is overmatched, but after almost being dragged into a sea cavern, it escapes. One officer has been captured. * Commanding Officer Keith Wells takes the submarine up, renews his armaments and descends again. The NX-1 passes into the cavern, within which is an enormous underground sea and a well-planned octopus city. * Again the great enemy submarine encounters the NX-1, this time capturing it and removing the crew (in pressure suits). Their fate may not be pleasant, for the sailors previously captured by the octopi have obviously been vivisected. Indeed, at one time Keith Wells is confined in a glass bell jar. * Luck is with the captives, however, and they escape to the sea and regain the NX-1. In a final duel with the octopus submarine Keith torpedoes it, and on leaving the cavern, blasts down the entrance walls, sealing off the octopus sea menace. * Routine action story.

500. **FOUR MILES WITHIN**. *Astounding Stories*, April 1931. Ill. Wesso.
Short story. * Professor Guinness, his daughter Sue, and Phil Holmes have constructed an earth-borer; it descends by disintegrating rock and reascends with rockets. With it the Guinness-Holmes partnership expects to find an enormous subterranean radium deposit. * Just before the maiden descent, however, the vicious Quade, a disgruntled former partner, traps Holmes and captures the Guinnesses. The Guinnesses and Quade descend, emerging into a gigantic cave four miles down, nicely lit by radium deposits. * Quade is for leaving the Guinnesses there to die, but there are two distractions: the arrival of Holmes in a second borer that Quade had built, and the hunger of an enormously large amoeboid that chases the humans back and forth underground. Eventually the ameboid eats Quade; the others disintegrate the monster with the digging rays of the borer and reascend. * Unconvincing thrills.

501. **THE COFFIN SHIP**. *Astounding Stories*, October 1933. Ill. C. R. Thomson (C R T).
Novelette. * *Time:* A.D. 2137. *Place:* space and an unidentified satellite of Saturn. * Falardo, the great space pirate, the terror of the planets, has been captured, tried and sentenced. He will receive the same punishment as he inflicted on his victims: bound in chains, he will be placed into a spaceship headed out of the solar system, where he will slowly starve to death. His ship is due to pass the space installation No. 4, where his captor Capt. Stephen Davenant is stationed. * But when the coffin ship passes the base, it is empty. Falardo's chains lie discarded, and he is gone! Yet the ship has been watched telescopically since it left. The answer is found when photo records of the coffin ship's past route are examined: a great spaceship painted black to avoid detection passed by the coffin ship. Palardo must have been rescued by men from the black ship. * Davenant in his ship *Hotspur* pursues the black ship, challenges it, and demands its

surrender. Agreeing to comply, a figure crosses over from the ship to the *Hotspur*. It is a woman, obviously the beautiful renegade Venerian Princess Tuaris, Falardo's devoted mistress. She releases a narcotic gas, and Davenant lies captured. * He awakens on the black ship, which is the property of Haklut, the other great space pirate. As Davenant soon learns, Haklut, though previously an enemy of Falardo's, has rescued him at the Princess's behest in exchange for Falardo's treasure. * Haklut takes the entire company to his secret base on a miserable, gloomy planet, which is later identified as a satellite of Saturn. There Haklut imprisons the captive patrolmen on a deserted island, hoping to break their spirits enough that they will reveal the secret patrol radio code. In the ocean around the island are titanic crab-like creatures that render escape impossible—almost. * Davenant and group kill one of the crabs, hollow out its shell, and sail in it to Haklut's headquarters. There things explode. Falardo and Tuaris plan to double-cross Haklut. In the shoot-out, Tuaris is killed, whereupon Falardo, who loved her deeply, goes to pieces. * Falardo is killed when the patrolmen ram the *Hotspur* into the pirate headquarters; Davenant shoots the swinish Haklut; and the space pirates are exterminated. * *Miscellaneous:* Davenant has strong erotic feelings toward the princess. * Competent commercial work.

GLAMIS, WALTER
Pseud. of Nathaniel Schachner, who has a separate entry. Schachner had another story under his own name in the same issue of the magazine.

502. **THE ORANGE GOD**. *Astounding Stories,* October 1933. Ill. Amos Sewell.
Short story. * *Place:* northern Tibet. * There are rumors of a dangerous new cult in Central Asia, and Ward Bayley is flying to Calcutta to report. But the mail plane bearing him and pilot Saunders is blown far off its course into northern Tibet, where it crashes. * The plot becomes complex, and narrative details need not be given. * Bayley and Saunders are captured by members of a dissident Buddhist sect that also holds a young American woman captive. The Buddhists are led by a master-mind who plans world conquest. Also present is a strange orange creature, seemingly a god in a glassy bubble. It sucks in occasional natives, who disappear. The three Westerners, too, would have been sucked in, but Bayley mastered the situation. * Explanation: The orange being, from another planet or universe, is gathering specimens to send back to its home. It is telepathic and maintains a superscience, but it has a weakness: Terrestrial atmosphere is poisonous to it. Thus, when Bayley shoots a hole into its globe, it speedily comes to terms and releases the three men. It returns to its own sphere of existence, while the former captives receive the gratitude of the natives for freeing them from their oppressive ruler and the orange god. * Below routine.

GLASSER, ALLEN (c. 1910?-?)
U.S. (New York) fan. Active, in this period, in the correspondence science clubs of the day for young people and a "letter hack" to the genre magazines. His first letters were signed Aaron Glasser. * Glasser dropped out of sight after 1933, at least in science-fiction, but it is generally believed that he is now dead. Social Security records list several Allen Glassers, but it is not known which, if any, is relevant. The present Allen

Glasser, Allen (*continued*)

Glasser is not the Allen Glasser (1918-?) described in *Living Biographies*, a writer and advertising man who contributed to *Saturday Review, True, Playboy,* and other periodicals.

The present story is a blatant, word-for-word plagiarism of "The Heat Wave" by Marion Ryan and Robert Ord, published in *Munsey's Magazine*, April 1929. Nothing is known about Marion Ryan; several authors of that name are recorded. Robert Ord was the pseud., according to *Who Was Who in the Theatre*, of Mrs. W. Gayer Mackay, née Edith Ostlere. She and Mackay collaborated on several staged plays, the best-known of which was an adaptation of *Paddy, the Next Best Thing* by Gertrude Page. According to Street and Smith records Glasser was responsible for at least one more plagiarism, having sold a stolen story to Dell Publishing Co. See also the comments on story #504, a collaboration between Glasser and A. Rowley Hilliard.

503. **ACROSS THE AGES**. *Amazing Stories,* August/September issue, 1933. Ill. Morey.

Short story. * *Time and place:* Pre-Depression-era New York City and Rome, ca. A.D. 80. * Paul Feron, wage slave in the office of his sadistic, vulgar employer Sellers, loses his job when he interferes with Sellers's abuse of a fellow employee. Seated on a park bench in the sweltering heat, he sleeps and dreams of a similar situation in ancient Rome, in which he (a projected heroic figure) tries to save a young Christian maiden from the lions by bribing the games master. When the games master doublecrosses him, Feron strangles him as the crowd and nobility applaud. * Feron awakens and returns home, where his wife greets him with fear and horror. The police are looking for him, for he strangled Sellers (in a memory fugue) a couple of hours earlier. * The explanation is presumably abnormal psychology. * Questionable as science-fiction, but competent period pulp fiction.

GLASSER, ALLEN and HILLIARD, A[LEC] ROWLEY

Glasser and Hilliard have separate entries. Glasser provided the idea, which Hilliard developed into a story. According to Moskowitz, *The Immortal Storm* (p. 14), Glasser stole the plot from Mort Weisinger, who had mentioned it confidentially to him.

504. **THE MARTIAN**. *Wonder Stories Quarterly,* Winter 1932. Ill. Paul.

Short story. * The third-prize winning story in the Interplanetary Plot Contest. Glasser received fifteen dollars. * *Place:* At least the last part is in the New York City area. * The story does not lend itself well to summary, since it is essentially a description of the feelings of a Martian who is stranded on Earth. A small humanoid figure with a large head, it has great difficulties with Terrestrial gravitation. It is treated brutally and exploited when it comes into contact with humans. At first the Martian has great difficulty understanding aspects of Earth life, but it eventually learns enough English to communicate simple ideas. * After being chained and maltreated, the Martian is sold to a circus, whose manager extracts invaluable scientific information from him under the pretense of helping him build a spaceship to return to Mars. When the Martian finally learns that he is being tricked, he commits suicide in despair. * *Miscellaneous:* Mars is Schiaparellian and is short of water; the Martian is apparently on an exploratory mission to Earth. Martian science is far ahead of Terrestrial, with (besides space travel) disintegrators, trans-

mutation, and similar matters. * Hilliard managed to put feeling into the story.

GLEASON, C. STERLING

U.S. author, contributed several stories to Gernsback's *Radio News*, sometimes in collaboration with Joseph Mountain. These stories include a series of film parodies like the present, set more or less around Flicker Films. Gernsback refers to Gleason as "a radio authority of considerable reputation" with inventions to his credit. Nothing else is known. It is doubtful that he is to be identified with Clayton Sterling Gleason, California economist.

505. **THE RADIATION OF THE CHINESE VEGETABLE**. *Science Wonder Stories*, December 1929. Ill. Winter.

Short story. * Humor, parody of early motion pictures. * *Place:* California. * In Hollywood the preeminent chop suey house is that of the beautiful young Wun Look, and her primacy is due to her use of a special Chinese vegetable. Wicked commercial interests, headed by the vicious villain Dandy Diavolo, corner the market, injuring her business, but the heroic Harold Dare devises a special electrical radiative system that enables the vegetable to grown outside the monopoly area. * Capturing Dare and Wun Look, Diavolo intends to torture Dare to death with electricity, but Wun Look will be spared, since the villain intends to learn from her the secrets of her cuisine. While Dare is being tortured, however, he utilizes the electricity applied to him to create radio signals, which are transmitted by the wires above the Chinese vegetables, and picked up by receivers outside. The police rescue Dare and Wun Look. * More amusing in the reading, as parody, than in summary. * Another contest between Harold Dare and Dandy Diavolo is to be found in "The Voice of the People," by Joseph D. Mountain and C. Sterling Gleason; it is described in *Science-Fiction: The Early Years*.

GOLUB, F.

Probably a German writer. No other information.

506. **THE SECRET OF THE MICROCOSM**. *Wonder Stories*, January 1934. Translated, and perhaps adapted, from German by Francis Currier. Ill. Winter.

Short-short story. * Professor Robert Swenson, a long-time friend of the narrator's, demonstrates his latest invention, a magnifying device that can probe below the electronic level. As the narrator watches, Swenson shows electrons, an electronic world, and on it a high civilization with colossal architecture and weird flying machines. He also glimpses a naked, lemon-yellow being. But something goes wrong, there is an explosion, and the narrator awakens in the hospital. He does not know how Swenson's invention works, nor has he told anyone of his experience. The invention is lost. * Routinely primitive.

GORDON, MILLARD VERNE

Pseud. of Donald A. Wollheim, who has a separate entry. According to fan report, Wollheim used a pseud. when submitting the story because he was on bad terms with Gernsback.

507. **THE SPACE LENS**. *Wonder Stories*, September 1935. Ill. Paul.

Short story. * *Time:* about A.D. 2800. *Place:* a rogue planetoid, about three thousand light-years away. * When the crew of the *Astralite,* after passing through various perils on its seven-year, faster-than-light exploratory voyage, sees an Earth-like planet

Gordon, Millard Verne (*continued*)
loom up, there is great excitement. Even more, when the crew of the approaching spaceship sees terrestrial geographical configurations, and even a Mediterranean landscape. * The ship lands, and although the planet is airless, the explorers witness a Roman army battling Carthiginians. Explanation: Due to an ether-warp, the Earth's light as of three thousand years ago is focused on the rogue planet, creating the illusion of past history.

GORDON, PETER

British author. No other information.

508. **ANYTHING CAN HAPPEN!** *Astounding Stories,* October 1933. Unsigned ill.
Short story. * *Place:* in the Himalayas, perhaps near Nepal. * A narrative told in Calcutta by Jimmy Carew, an engineer constructing a railroad in the mountains. * He and associates are captured by natives and carried into the mountains to a strange city carved out of the living rock. There Carew meets the queen, who tells him that she and her people do not want the railroad; they want to preserve their own ways, including their own goddess—who is the beautiful young queen herself. * The queen, however, cannot seem to comprehend that Carew lacks the power to halt the railroad line, and she belabors him repeatedly with her demand. Carew is justifiably worried. * Finally one night, Carew is brought before the queen, who makes an unexpected proposal: She will save his life if he marries her; otherwise he must die on the spot. Since she is a very beautiful, charming woman, Carew leaps at the chance. The rites are performed, but this is not enough. After a time the queen insists that they must also be married Western style and Carew must go to Calcutta and fetch back a priest. * Carew eagerly agrees, for despite the fact that he loves the queen, he is unwilling to share her with her four other husbands, to say nothing of the eventual twelve that custom assigns her. * Now in Calcutta, he does not intend to return and is worried about a native who shadows him and will presumably murder him if he tries to leave India. There is an unexpected way out of Carew's predicament. * Not a bad story in the mode of Kipling, but not science-fiction.

GRAHAM, HOWARD D., Ph.D.

Pseud. of Howard Elmer Wandrei (1909-1956), who did not hold a doctorate. U.S. (mostly Minnesota, but resident in New York City for much of the period covered here) author, artist. Brother of the better-known Donald Wandrei. Wandrei's life is covered in Olson's excellent introduction to *Time Burial.* See also other pseuds. H. W. Guernsey and Howard Von Drey. Howard Wandrei was a literate, imaginative writer, but was often careless in plotting and story development; a reader often has the impression that Wandrei set up a situation, then became bored with the story and finished it hastily. Wandrei also wrote extensively in other areas under the pseud. Robert A. Garron. Altogether he is said to have written about two hundred stories. Wandrei was also a competent artist, but little of his work has been published; some has been reproduced in the collection *Time Burial.* * According to Olson the Graham stories were written in collaboration with a Dr. Mike Smola; although it is not known how they collaborated, it is a reasonable assumption that Wandrei did the final writing. Social Security records list two persons named Michael Smola, one (1904-1985), died in Syracuse, New York; the other (1907-1981) was a resident of Illinois.

509. **THE WALL.** *Astounding Stories,* May 1934. Ill. Paul Orban.
(Reprinted in Howard Wandrei, *Time Burial,* and in Knight, *Science Fiction of the Thirties.*) Short story. * *Place:* Central Manhattan. * Harold Jasper and Professor Gorsch, consulting engineers for a large construction company, by running inert gases through certain substances have created a remarkable paint. Its only defect is an unanticipated secondary matter: the two applications that have hardened have created impenetrable force zones. One zone has cut off Manhattan and surrounding areas for about a hundred miles; the other has reared a force pillar into the atmosphere. * There is great to-do as city engineers and consultants try to determine what has happened and how it can be remedied. Jasper and Gorsch, who ultimately succeed in neutralizing the paint, are themselves under a strain lest their role be discovered. * Not a bad story.

510. **GUNS OF ETERNAL DAY.** *Astounding Stories,* July 1934. Ill. Marchioni.
Short story. * *Place:* Minnesota. * When old Dr. Maudlen, who plans to retire to the family homestead with his daughter, approaches his property in Minnesota, he meets an astonishing situation. The property, which he has not seen for years, has been seized by Professor Cujol, a squatter who has built a road to the house, established a high tension line, and set up two gigantic cannon-like objects on the granite hill. When the doctor objects strongly to what has happened, Cujol explains. * Cujol, who apparently has unlimited funds, is something of a monomaniac. Maudlen's hill is particularly desirable to him because of its heavy granite foundation, which can support his equipment. He tried to find Maudlen and buy the farm, but could not locate him. * The project: Cujol is focusing rays on the moon and melting it, turning it into a small, second sun. Why? Cujol considers the feat sufficient of itself, but he also believes that nearly perpetual daylight will be beneficial to mankind. The moon is already glowing with heat. * Maudlen brings legal action, which drags on for years, during which time Cujol has worked enormous damage. The perpetual radiation and heat almost wreck the Earth, melting polar ice caps, burning cultivated land into deserts, spawning a band of dangerous life forms, and creating new diseases for mankind. Cujol dies of one of the plagues his mad project has created. * Things look bad for life on Earth, but as a deus ex machina, an unexpected comet passes so close to Earth that it drags away the Moon, restoring the former situation of day and night. * An interesting beginning, but a middle that is silly, and an ending that falls to pieces.

511. **TIME HAVEN.** *Astounding Stories,* September 1934. Ill. Dold.
Short story. * *Time:* A.D. 2443. * Vincent Merryfield, who entered his time machine in 1936, awakens to find himself in a brave new world of gigantic buildings, automation, and utter efficiency. He is also informed by Cope, the director of the huge enterprise Merryfield Tower, which encompasses most of Manhattan, that he owns or controls much of the world, thanks to skilled financial handling of the estate of an aunt. * The world of the future is highly controlled, with bureaucratic infiltration everywhere, but there are no more depressions, no poverty, no more threat of overpopulation. Real war no longer exists, but there are institutionalized permissory wars, which amount to games in the semblance of war. * As the future world is described to him, however, Vincent learns that although he owns

Graham, Howard D. (*continued*)

"everything," he is really totally powerless, completely tied down by laws and regulations, and is no more than an artifact in the enormous official web. Since Vincent is turbulent and impatient, his situation is intolerable for him. But when he declares that he will reenter his time machine and return to the 1930s, he learns to his astonishment that he never really built a time machine. His apparatus simply put him into suspended animation, and he has been cared for by a special medical staff for the past five hundred years. * This is the last straw. Leaping off his thirty-six thousand-foot-high tower, discarding the antigravity device that is generally used to traverse heights, he commits suicide. * An example of future mores: Merryfield has been assigned a female "companion." Should he chance to dislike her and reject her, she will be put into some sort of limbo, for she exists only for the position, for which she has been trained. * A child of Wells's *When the Sleeper Wakes*. Routine, although the recognition of the paralyzing power of bureaucracy is interesting. * Wandrei rewrote the basic idea into "The Missing Ocean," a hard-boiled story that appeared in *Unknown Worlds* (May 1939) as by Howard Wandrei. I prefer the earlier version.

512. **THE OTHER**. *Astounding Stories*, December 1934. Ill. Dold.

(Reprinted in Howard Wandrei, *Time Burial*, and in Knight, *Science Fiction of the Thirties*.)

Short story. * *Place:* New York City. * Basil Sash, brash, aggressive reporter, tries to interview the famous eccentric explorer Ingvaldssen, who has returned from the Arctic with the frozen body of a woman in a slab of ice. Ingvaldssen discourages reporters in a vigorous physical way, but for one reason or other he decides to take Sash into his confidence. He shows Sash the woman, a beautiful woman of hitherto unknown racial type, obviously the product of a high civilization, with strange garments and a metal object in her hand. On her face is an expression of utmost scorn and disdain. * As Ingvaldssen tells it, near her was half a mammoth, the other half mysteriously absent. He speculates that she was an interplanetary visitor frozen instantaneously by a cold wave, as was the mammoth. Thanks to cosmic ray drift, asserts the explorer, access to Earth is most suitable at the poles. * Ingvaldssen, who has fallen fetishistically in love with the woman, states frankly that he murdered his associate on the expedition to get sole possession of her. He claims that she is not dead; indeed, with a special refrigeration system of his own he is slowly thawing her. She should be ice-free in a moment or so. * Sash is a little worried about the object the woman holds; as a reader of *Astounding Stories*, he is concerned that it might be some sort of a ray gun. * He turns out to be right. The woman thaws and comes to life immediately. Ingvaldssen rushes to her, whereupon, smiling scornfully, she disintegrates him. Her ray continues on through the walls of the building, clearing a path to the Hudson. As for the alien superwoman, Sash hears "the fluid tinkle of the Other's disdainful silver laughter." * Interesting for the ending.

GRANT, HAL

No information.

513. **THE ANCIENT HORROR**. *Amazing Stories*, April 1928. Ill. Paul.

Short story. * *Time:* 1905. *Place:* Northern Vermont. * When the town water suddenly ceases to flow, investigation reveals that

the bottom has dropped out of the local reservoir, draining the water into a cave system below. Other alterations of water level and location take place until the situation stabilizes. But now there is another problem, men and women mysteriously disappear in the vicinity of the lake, and the tourist industry suffers. * The narrator sees the cause: a gigantic dinosaur-like monster, undoubtedly emergent from hidden caverns, who has been gobbling up the locals and tourists. The narrator has a narrow escape, and the monster is destroyed by the explosion of a cache of nitroglycerine left behind by a construction crew. * Enormously inflated.

GRAY, WILL H.

Canadian author, then resident in Vancouver, British Columbia.

514. **THE STAR OF DEAD LOVE**. *Amazing Stories*, May 1927. Ill. Paul.

Short story. * While Dr. Joyce is relaxing on his veranda, he sees a white diaphanous shape approach. It is a beautiful young woman, who is as hazy as a ghost is supposed to be. The doctor beckons to her to sit with him, and they communicate by diagrams of various sorts, though communication is difficult because of her immateriality. As the doctor learns, she is from Venus, is over a thousand years old, and has an intellect many times more powerful than his. The woman also has a small disintegrator on her finger, with which she accidentally cuts one of his porch pillars. * The woman leaves, taking along with her some of Joyce's books. From them, in a day or two she learns perfect English. * A romance begins to grow, and the young woman instructs Joyce in her native superscience. She agrees to become material, though she is only inches tall when this happens. Joyce looks forward to joining her, but this is not to be. A small band of Venusians come and drag her away. * Miscellaneous point: Males died out on Venus thousands of years ago, and reproduction is by parthenogenesis. * A clumsy fairy tale.

515. **THE TIDE PROJECTILE TRANSPORTATION CO**. *Amazing Stories*, September 1927. Unsigned ill.

Short story. * *Time:* perhaps the first quarter of the twenty-second century. * The Tide Projectile Transportation Co. offers extremely rapid transport from coast to coast. Huge projectiles are thrown into the air by gigantic springs, which are readied by compressed air obtained from tidal power. A projectile is then guided on its course by a pilot who uses compressed-air reaction jets to make flight corrections. Speed is more than ten thousand miles an hour. * On the present occasion the pilot is a woman, Henrietta Morgan, who is regarded with some apprehension by her male colleagues, since there are few woman pilots. As the flight takes off, Morgan, daydreaming of a potential husband (situation explained below), misses signals, with the result that her projectile overshoots its target and lands in the Atlantic. Retrieving it will be very difficult, and the passengers and pilot are in grave danger of suffocation. In such emergencies the passengers are usually put into suspended animation, but for one reason or another the standard kit is not present. * This is not the whole story, however. When the projectile strikes sea bottom, it rams into a World War I submarine that has been trapped beneath an ancient Atlantic cable for centuries, and knocks the submarine loose. On the submarine, in a state of accidental suspended animation, is Lieutenant Commander Roger Wells of 1917. Wells leaves the surfaced submarine and is rescued by a

Gray, Will H. (*continued*)

passing yacht. * Meanwhile, communication continues with Morgan and the trapped projectile. Wells and Morgan converse to their mutual satisfaction, and Wells makes the suggestion that succeeds in blasting the projectile to land—dump radium into the water. * When Morgan and Wells meet, they decide that they want to marry. But they must act fast. * The reason: The future society is greatly concerned with eugenics. In the early application of controlled breeding, the most intelligent men and women interbred, but the results were bad, with much insanity. As matters now stand, all humans are rated on a scale up to 100, and husband and wife together cannot exceed 110. Thus, Henrietta Morgan, who is highly intelligent at 87, must marry a low-rated, stupid man. Her co-workers commiserate with her. * Wells, however, provides a nice resolution. Since as a "primitive" ignorant of future science and culture, he did poorly on the examinations, he received the low rating of 21. This figure is obviously incorrect, and a second examination will undoubtedly rate him much higher, but legally, at the moment, there is nothing to prevent the marriage of Wells and Morgan. * The future culture is at least partially socialistic, for food is provided without charge. Other matters are handled by what amounts to an evolved credit system maintained by the state. Science is high, with advanced medicine and antigravity. * Amusing moments, but the story needed a more skilled writer.

516. **THE BEES FROM BORNEO.** *Amazing Stories*, February 1931. Ill. Morey.

(Reprinted in Conklin, *Omnibus of Science Fiction*.)

Short story. Really an undramatized narration. * Silas Donaghy, perhaps the best American breeder of honeybees, receives a queen of a hitherto undomesticated species from Borneo. When Donaghy places the queen in one of his hives, the result is a new bee strain of fantastically high honey production. * Donaghy distributes the new strain, but it proves to be too good. His bees not only destroy flowers in gathering floral segments as well as pollen, but raid the hives of ordinary Italian bees. The result is a Federal directive, issued under senatorial pressure, barring Donaghy from using the mails to ship his bees. He finds himself heavily in debt, with many lawsuits pending. * The final blow comes when he thoughtlessly uses the mails and is heavily fined. * Donaghy, now slightly mad, deliberately hybridizes a wasp with his bees, the result being a insect that is hardy, vicious, and lethal. He distributes his creation in many little balloons. * In a short time the wasp-bees have multiplied so rapidly and spread so widely that they have become a national menace. Silas, who has been deteriorating mentally, has been institutionalized, but society collapses so totally that he simply wanders out of the asylum. * When Silas recognizes that his only son has been killed by the lethal bees, he is shocked back into sanity, and he now decides to end the hymenopterous menace. Secluded, he breeds and looses drones that are faster and hardier than the wasp-bee drones, but with a lethal factor built into their offspring. The menace subsides with the new generation. * Interesting, with a very modern note, what with killer bees and genetically planned nonviability. The author is well versed in apiculture.

GREENFIELD, TAYLOR H.

No information. Probably not Taylor Hatton Greenfield (1905-?), Maryland attorney, later associated with Vietnamese government and U.S. departments concerned with Southeast Asia.

517. **THE SWORD AND THE ATOPEN. HOPKINS UNIVERSITY MIDWINTER LECTURE 2348.** *Amazing Stories*, January 1930. Ill. Morey.

Short story. * *Time:* A.D. 2347. * The United States is about to succumb to an Oriental (Mongol) invasion. The Orientals are not only in possession of antigravity and remarkable flying machines, but have supermetals and atomic bombs. (These atomic bombs are not like ours, but cause matter to revert to hydrogen, which in turn is precipitated as water. There is no question of radioactivity.) * At the moment the war front is along the Mississippi, and it seems certain that the Mongols will be victorious. Indeed, the American commanding general is ready to surrender. * Dr. Rutledge, an elderly scientist, changes matters. He has developed an entirely new protein. Abandoned in the form of flour to the advancing Orientals, it sets up an anaphylactic reaction, wiping out them all out. * *Miscellaneous:* The Americans can convert sunlight directly to electricity. * Undeveloped, more a recital of events than a story, and also very far-fetched.

GREGORY, JOHN MILLER

U.S. (New York City) author, fairly frequent contributor to the pulp magazines, including *Top-Notch*, *Western Story*, *Ghost Stories*, etc. Apparently associated in some way with Harold Hersey. The present story is so close to the various works of Victor Rousseau, also associated with Hersey, that some sort of collaboration or borrowing has been suspected. But there is no proof for or against this. Gregory does not seem to have published any books, but the Library of Congress holds a typescript of *The Gray Phantom, A Mystery Comedy*, a play adapted by Gregory and Herman Landon from the novel of the same title by Landon.

518. **FISH-MEN OF ARCTICA.** *Miracle Science and Fantasy Stories*, June/July 1931. Unsigned ill.

Novelette. * *Time:* presumably the near future. *Place:* the north polar area. * The Moon is approaching the Earth, and there is the expected panic. An explanation comes from the great scientist Professor Carmine: In the remote past the Moon was torn from the north polar regions; in the resulting depression lives a race of fish-men who are currently drawing the Moon down, presumably with the intention of destroying the Earth. * The supersubmarine *Black Whale*, which can descend to depths of ten miles, under Jim Fentress (accompanied by Professor Carmine's beautiful daughter Hope) sets out on a reconnaissance mission. When the submarine reaches the danger area, however, a purple tractor beam (of the same sort that is moving the Moon) seizes it and drags it down to a sealed underwater city inhabited by goggle-eyed fish-men, who are apparently amphibious, though otherwise human. * Our explorers are captured by the fish-men, who question them via thought tubes. As Fentress and Hope soon recognize, their captors are religious fanatics obsessed with following the will of the sun god Surt, as announced by the high priest. * The king is not unfriendly, though his son Kenton obviously has eyes for Hope, but Ektom, the Great High Priest of Surt, the sun god, is another matter. A dwarf who claims to be half a million years old, the master of a secret science, he has constructed the projectors that have been dragging the Moon down. According to his plans, the fall of the Moon will ex-

Gregory, John Miller (*continued*)

terminate surface life, after which the fish-men will emerge and take over the world. * Also present, to confuse the story, is Lora, a beautiful lorelei whom Jim rescues from the embraces of a man-eating tree. She has been captured and her singing ability removed by Ektom. She is willing to help the outsiders in their resolve to save the Earth. * When Jim, Hope, and Lora happen to be at the ray installation as Ektom enters, they capture him, make their way to the submarine, and return to the surface. When Ektom dies in the polar ice, the ray ceases to function. The world is somewhat damaged, but is no longer in danger of destruction. * *Miscellaneous:* Ektom's claimed immortality is a fraud, as is his claimed invulnerability. * Obviously hastily written, with poor development, loose ends, and non sequiturs, as if the author had padded out a plot summary. Very much like the work of Victor Rousseau in ideas and plotting.

GROSS, JEROME and PENNY, RICHARD

No information about Gross, except that the portrait accompanying the story shows a young man. Penny, according to Tuck and Rock, was the pseud. of David Lasser, managing editor of *Wonder Stories,* whose career is described elsewhere. So far as I know, this attribution has not been corroborated, although the portrait accompanying "Emperors of Space" is almost identical to the portrait of Lasser in the July 1931 issue of *Wonder Stories.* When questioned shortly before his death, Lasser had no recollection of the matter. On the face of it, it is surprising that Lasser could have had a hand in such a crude story.

519. **EMPERORS OF SPACE**. *Wonder Stories,* November 1931. Ill. Paul.

Novelette. * *Time:* 1952 and 2055. * The complicated and confused story is best approached by listing motifs. (1) The yellow rot, apparently originating in China, bids fair to destroy the world's agriculture. Heroic Swedish scientist Luke Raleigh will devise a remedy against it. (2) The Orientals are plotting against Raleigh, whose researches will be important in the development of atomic power. (3) Raleigh has built an enormous atomic powered gyroscope. When the Orientals attack him, he and his friend and sponsor Harry take refuge in the gyroscope, which Luke turns on full speed. (4) The gyroscope spins so rapidly that it alters space-time. While the rotating machine is visible and is carefully watched until it stops in 2055, for Luke and Harry only a short time has passed. (5) The United Asiatic Empire kidnaps Luke and tries to make him work for them. (6) Things look bad, but a revolt of the oppressed peasants overthrows the empire, and the world will now be a better place, since Luke has a remedy for the yellow rot. * *Miscellaneous:* Esperanto is generally spoken. Travel to the Moon is feasible, the Orientals maintaining a base there. From the Moon they obtain lunite, which is the only substance resistant to the disintegrators used. * A very bad job.

GROVES, J[OHN] W[ILLIAM] (1910-?)

The blurb accompanying "The Sphere of Death" refers to Groves as a British author. Groves later published two other science-fiction stories, "Robots Don't Bleed" in *New Worlds,* Winter, 1950, and "Regrowth" in *Startling Stories,* January 1950. Also wrote books *Shellbreak* (1968) and *The Heels of Achilles* (1969).

520. **THE SPHERE OF DEATH**. *Amazing Stories,* October 1931. Ill. Morey.

Short story. * The great chemist Barton, who has already revolutionized industry by discovering a means for storing electricity in an oxide of zinc, accidentally stumbles upon a chemical disintegrator. A tiny sample produces a sphere that disintegrates everything and almost kills him and the narrator before it exhausts its energy. Indeed, the narrator is laid up for a long time with a physical and mental breakdown. * When he recovers, Barton informs him that he has discovered how to control the phenomenon, both in size and mobility. Barton adds that since his discovery will be of inestimable value in engineering and is too important to be a commercial monopoly, he has offered it to the government. A demonstration will shortly take place. * Representatives of the government arrive, a shabby set of vultures. After the demonstration they announce that Barton's discovery will make an incredible weapon. Offering him a million pounds, they add that he cannot refuse the offer, since he has been naive enough to reveal the entire process to them. * Barton, who is a humane man, does what he considers necessary after sending the narrator away. He disintegrates himself and the official wolves. The discovery is lost. * A trite story in subject matter, but well enough handled and entertaining.

GUERNSEY, H. W.

Pseud. of Howard Elmer Wandrei (1909-1956), whose vita is given under his other pseud. Howard D. Graham, Ph.D. Wandrei used the Guernsey pseud. extensively in his later work for other pulp magazines.

521. **MACKLIN'S LITTLE FRIEND**. *Astounding Stories,* November 1936. Ill. Saaty.

(Reprinted in Howard Wandrei, *Time Burial* and, as by Howard E. Wandrei, in Conklin, *In the Grip of Terror.*)

Short story. * A meteorite landed in Spinney's Lake. Since then strange things have been happening locally. Farmer Joe Spinney claims to have lost cows, chickens and a dog, and now young Willard Macklin, M.D., appears as a patient at the office of Dr. Kley, his future father-in-law. * Macklin, when he unwraps the cloths around his neck, reveals, growing out of his head, a snake-like tentacle, with suckers, about five feet long. It all started when he banged his head while swimming in Spinney's Lake. * Kley detaches the growth, which was apparently about ready to drop off as mature, and it turns out to be an incredibly powerful, ferocious, dangerous, creature of enormous vitality that can leap great distances and rip off skin and flesh with a glancing blow of its suckers. The two men have all they can do to kill it, and Kley dies during the battle. Later dynamite is dropped into Spinney's Lake. * A trite idea, but well handled as a thriller.

GURWIT, S. GORDON

U.S. author, then resident of Chicago. Possibly to be identified with Samuel Gordon Gurwit (1890-?), author of *Alias the Promised Land* (1938). Perhaps had some engineering background. Has also contributed fiction to *Top-Notch* and *Detective Stories.*

522. **WORLD FLIGHT**. *Astounding Stories,* January 1934. Ill. Marchioni.

Short story. * *Place:* mostly Tibet. * Brownell and Goodwin, who have built a steam-powered airplane, have just left on a projected flight around the world. Their purpose, to demonstrate the unique capabilities of their plane: less expensive to operate than gasoline-powered planes; less noisy, hence suitable for

Gurwit, S. Gordon (*continued*)

stealth work; able to fly at much higher altitudes than internal combustion engines, and thereby faster. Flight accomplished, they hope to sell their plans to the government. * The flight goes well, but as they fly past Mount Everest, their plane malfunctions and, as they soon recognize, is dragged to the ground by an inexplicable force. Landing, the men emerge from their plane and almost immediately are attacked by a ferocious insect the size of a horse. They kill it, but are captured by seven-foot-tall Tibetans who take them to their leader, Dr. Fang. * Dr. Fang, an old man, tells the men that he brought down their plane for a purpose. Using it as a model, he plans to build a fleet and drop lethal germs on the outside world. * Fang's intent, thus, is world conquest, and he may well be successful, for he possesses a superscience. Over three hundred years old, he has developed an elixir that produces extremely long life, gigantism and enormous strength, and mental vigor. He also has germ cultures of incredible virulence and viewing devices, and can revive the undamaged dead. Part of his power, which spreads over Tibet and much of China, is based on his status as a living Buddha, venerated and deferred to by even the Dalai Lama. * Fang follows precedent and offers the two young Americans immortality and high positions in his new empire in exchange for cooperation. They do not trust him, however, and at the first opportunity they kill a guard, seize his pistol, and shoot Fang. * Months later a white-haired, exhausted, crippled man at the point of death wanders into Darjeeling. It is Goodwin; Brownell did not survive the long trek out of Tibet. * The author, who probably was acquainted with the work of Talbot Mundy, has a letter in the same issue of the magazine discussing some of the scientific points in his story.

HAGGARD, J[AMES] HARVEY (1913-present)

U.S. (California) author. As The Planet Prince contributed occasional poetry to *Wonder Stories*. Most of Haggard's fiction dates from the 1930s, but he continued writing until at least 1960. The work described below is probably juvenilia, most of it having been written before Haggard was 22 years old. Unfortunately, he stopped writing just as his stories were getting interesting.

523. **FASTER THAN LIGHT.** *Wonder Stories*, October 1930. Ill. Marchioni.

Short story. * The fourth-prize-winning story based on the cover of the February 1930 issue of *Air Wonder Stories*. Mr. Haggard received twenty-five dollars. * *Time:* presumably the near future. * The scene of action is a monoway, a future mode of aerial transportation that is stabilized by two sets of gyroscopes. The story is told mostly in conversations among an Englishman, a professor, and a Westerner. * For reasons not known, the monoway has broken away from the electrical impulses that power it and has escaped into space. It is heading toward the sun, increasing in velocity to the speed of light and gradually diminishing in size as it speeds. When it reaches zero size and infinite mass, it breaks into another universe, emerging near a planet from which little men in space suits float up toward the monoway. The little men utter a telepathic command, but the world starts to recede as the monoway is pulled back into our cosmos. The monoway, it is realized, will not fall into the sun

—and then the narrator awakens. He had been knocked unconscious on a street car by sleep gas used by bandits. It was all a dream.

524. **AN ADVENTURE ON EROS.** *Wonder Stories*, September 1931. Ill. Paul.

Short-short story. * *Time:* A.D. 2012. *Place:* Around Eros in one frame of reference; in a training school on Earth in the other. * Professor D Four-Ten and his prize student K Two are in space not too far away from Eros when their ship begins to act strangely and they receive a radio message about a swarm of electro meteors that have brushed by the fueling station on Eros and created problems. * The spaceship is attracted to Eros, where it barely escapes destruction on landing. Then a swarm of natives attacks the ship. Normally, the tentacular, civilized Erosians are friendly, but perhaps the electrical situation has irritated them. And the ship's disintegrators are not working. Then the ship is hurled away by an electric charge. * At this point the young man awakens. It has all been a sleep-learning training film played from a tape. Professor D Four-Ten is now ready to examine the student.

525. **CASTAWAYS ON DEIMOS.** *Wonder Stories*, August 1933. Ill. Paul.

Short story. * *Time:* A.D. 2032. *Place:* on the Earth-Mars space run. * The passenger liner *Suetonia* runs into a meteor swarm and is badly disabled. The passengers and crew take to the lifeboats, the fate of one of which the story follows. The lifeboat does not have sufficient fuel (venusite) to reach a planet, but it can orbit around Deimos and land—which it does. Deimos is barren, rugged, and airless. * The story turns upon the characters of the people in the lifeboat: Paul Roscoe, young man susceptible to female charms in an honorable way; Buck Dodson, crude interplanetary salesman, a giant of a man, susceptible to female charms in a dishonorable way; assorted minor characters; and Melda Vorden, who is probably intended to be the New Woman of the day. Many readers of the early thirties would have considered her a "bold thing." She is much the best man on the boat. Both Roscoe and Dodson are attracted to her. * The approach is probably intended to be stark realism of a sort. Dodson and a confederate try to murder Paul, but Melda is more than a match for them, walloping them with an iron bar. Melda also discovers enough venusite to power the spaceship and permit them to leave. Eventually, everyone dies except Paul, Melda, and two children. * Routine or less.

526. **THROUGH THE EINSTEIN LINE.** *Wonder Stories*, November 1933. Ill. Lumen Winter.

Short story. * *Time:* the interplanetary future. *Place:* between Neptune and Pluto, and in another dimension. * Bull Gorgon and Jimmy Dane of the Earth-Guard interplanetary police, former buddies, are now enemies (because of cabin fever) when their ship crashes on a hitherto unknown world between Neptune and Pluto. It is a bleak world with crystalline growths and a multitude of strong suns in the sky. * Since discipline counts more than personal hostility, Dane leaves the ship to fetch nearby water for the unconscious Gorgon. He is immediately beset by a horde of armadillo men who capture him and drag him off to their caves. They are obviously going to sacrifice him to a gigantic idol with moveable parts. * The time for sacrifice comes. To Jimmy's surprise the idol informs him with hand gestures that there is a ray gun behind the altar. The free-for-all starts. Gorgon, who has been working the idol, emerges and the

Haggard, J. Harvey (*continued*)

two men fight their way back to the spaceship, which Gorgon repaired while Dane was a captive. They fly away, once again buddies. * Dane explains: Somehow, he does not know how, they penetrated another universe that is static, where ours is in motion. * *Miscellaneous:* Also involved was a golden-furred humanoid whom Dane saved from the armadillo men. He betrayed Dane. * Fisticuffs, crashing blows, and smashing punches in almost every paragraph as Dane and Gorgon take on the armadillo men. In its glorification of the manly art, more a story for late Clayton *Astounding Stories* than for *Wonder Stories*.

527. **EVOLUTION SATELLITE.** *Wonder Stories*, December 1933-January 1934. Ill. Paul.

Short story. * *Time:* the twenty-first century. *Place:* Ariel (Uranus satellite Number One). * Bob Mobart and Gade Williams of the Earth-Guard interplanetary police are assigned to investigate the disappearance of several sightseeing passenger ships around Uranus. Perhaps Satellite One, declares Mobart, is involved, since there has long been a suspicion that there is something strange about it, though it has never been explored. * The men bring their ship down on Ariel, which has breathable atmosphere; gravity devices regulate their weight. They immediately see, first, that growth is fantastically rapid among aggressive carnivorous plants and, second, that there is total variation among the plants within eye range. * Unfortunately, the policemen gape too long at the plants. One of the giant plants seizes the spaceship and holds it captive; it is unable to open its antigravity plates because of the plant's tendrils. * The explorers recognize the key factor in Ariel's life forms: Everything immediately adapts to its environment, so that when a ray gun cuts into one of the plants, the weapon is effective only for a very short time, after which the plant presents defenses against the rays. * The men make a break for it out through the side of the ship and fly through the incredible evolutionary products of Ariel. Rescuing a beautiful young scaled woman, whose name is Nadia, from submen, they continue for a while, until Mobart is separated from the other two. Feeling increasingly odd, he and a humanoid companion (with tentacle arms) seek Williams and Nadia. When Mobart finds them, he sees that they are distorted versions of humanity, with grotesquely large heads and wasted bodies. And then, to his astonishment, Mobart recognizes that he, too, has evolved in the same manner. He also sees that the final stage in Ariel's life cycle is that of a giant mushroom emitting spores that start the myriad life forms again. * A rescue ship arrives. Mobart leaves, but Williams stays with Nadia, with the eventual fate of both turning into mushrooms. Back on Earth, the sadly degenerated Mobart, fixed in his Ariel transformation, ekes out a miserable life. * More imaginative than Haggard's earlier work.

528. **AN EPISODE ON IO.** *Wonder Stories*, February 1934. Ill. Winter.

Short story. * *Time:* the interplanetary future. *Place:* Io. * To Io comes Earth-Guard member Peter Flaxon to investigate the disappearance of three members of the Earth-Guard who according to trader Bullock wandered into the jungle and disappeared. Io is a wild and savage place, covered with vegetative growth and fierce animals. Very few humans have ever visited it, a half dozen within the past few years. Such visitors include Professor Teston and his beautiful daughter, who are somewhere out in the bush. * Props of the story include incredibly stupid,

enormous human hulks who are controlled by telepathy; Bullock, who is training them for a small army, says they are natives. Thrills involve cloak-and-dagger work. * The resolution, which brings in a patrol ship, is that Bullock is not Bullock, but a criminal who has taken his place. He is concerned with smuggling gems out of Io. The so-called natives are really artificial men that the late Professor Teston manufactured in vats. * Echoes of Edgar Rice Burroughs's *The Monster Men* and perhaps H. G. Wells's *The Island of Doctor Moreau*.

529. **CHILDREN OF THE RAY.** *Wonder Stories*, March 1934. Ill. Paul.

Short story. * *Time:* the interplanetary future. *Place:* Jupiter. * The scientific expedition exploring Jupiter is hovering above the Red Spot. Captain Dane refuses to take the ship down into the Red Spot, but reluctantly agrees to lower Professor Bablon and Lieutenant Connor in an observation sphere. This amounts to a bathysphere on a steel cable. * The two men descend into a red haze and emerge onto a barren landscape, where they soon see the dominant life form: trapezoid-shaped creatures with pseudocephals that resemble flowers. * But now a crisis strikes. The pink radiation that permeates the area corrodes metal almost instantaneously, so that the cable of the bathysphere breaks and the fittings disintegrate. The trapezoidal beings, who have some intelligence, roll the sphere away to their village, where the men discover that they can communicate a little by telepathy with the leader of the trapezoids. By now the men have had to emerge from the sphere; although the gravity is strong, the atmosphere is breathable. * There are problems with the trapezoids, who are uncertain how to place the men. The Jovians reject the explorers' claim that they are gods, but finally decide that they must be associated with another people, who live near the central place where the pink ray emerges. The trapezoids worship the ray, and in addition to making sacrifices to it, immolate themselves in it, like moths in a flame. The humans are taken near the ray, where they see the other people, who are insectoids who fly about in the ray, but do not seem intelligent. Escape, pursuit, narrow squeaks, and finally the men are saved by a silken rope that the mother ship has been dragging around at random through the Red Spot. * The alienness is convincing, despite the bad writing.

530. **RELATIVITY TO THE RESCUE.** *Amazing Stories*, April 1935. Ill. Morey.

Short story. * *Time:* the interplanetary future. *Place:* Venus and space. * Burney, Bellen, and Vallard, employees of the Venus Trading and Commerce Co., operate a small trading post in the horrendous jungles of Venus, where they buy gems from the savage natives. The natives, who are four-legged, single-eyed, tentacle-armed, are both primitive in culture and exceedingly ferocious. * As the story begins, the three men are fighting for their lives against a native attack. But there is another factor. This is the notorious space pirate Black Silvard, who has persistently raided Venusian posts, stealing fortunes in gems. Revelations occur: Bellen is Silvard's brother-in-law and has been acting as a spotter for the pirate; and Brice is a secret service agent. * As the native attack is at its height, Silvard's superspaceship, the *Space Demon*, appears, disperses the natives, takes the gems and captures Brice. Actually, Brice and Silvard are old acquaintances, for they worked together in the company laboratories, where Silvard created the four-dimensional system that enables him to take his ship out of space when necessary.

Haggard, J. Harvey (*continued*)

Silvard is pleasant enough, but it is clear that when it suits his convenience he will kill Burney. * The downfall of the pirates comes from internal tensions. Silvard and his wife dislike the brutal Bellen intensely, and when Bellen is caught poaching on the full harem that Silvard maintains in a luxury suite on the ship, Silvard treats him savagely. Further, Silvard's wife, jealous of the harem, stirs up Bellen against Silvard, hoping that the men will kill each other. During the upheavals that result, Burney manages to send out a signal to the space police. * When the police arrive, Silvard fights off the first ships, then retreats into the fourth dimension. But when Bellen shoots Silvard and Burney, the change in state forces the ship back into normal space. * Routine, with more complications than necessary.

531. **HUMAN ANTS**. *Wonder Stories*, May 1935. Ill. Paul.

Short story. * *Time:* A.D. 2050 and about A.D. 2250. * Rufus Jones, undergoing an operation in 2050, saw, just as he lost consciousness, a flight of planes pass overhead. Surgery in 2050 involves putting the patient into suspended animation in a sealed container of special gas to allow healing after the operation. Thus, Jones expected to awaken in good physical condition after a few weeks. Instead, when he awakens, he discovers that his container lies among ruins and that a wilderness flourishes about him. * Being resourceful, he survives, wandering about for several months, until he comes upon a remarkable building complex surrounded by arable fields, in which men and women are working. A strange humming noise comes from them. * When he tries to approach them, they are so hostile that he takes refuge back in the nearby woods. Some time later, he sees a beautiful young woman (whose name is later revealed to be Leetha) steal away from the workers and creep into the forest, where she lies down. When he speaks to her, she is terrified and runs back to the fields, where she is immediately accused of being a criminal and is attacked. Jones tries to help her, but is captured. He and Leetha are both taken inside the city and brought before a magistrate. * *Background:* As Jones learns piecemeal, the plane squadron that he saw as he lost consciousness was part of a bombing attack that destroyed civilization with poison gas. He survived because his container was sealed. The attackers, men of Altrurany, then set up a new civilization, in which total altruism is the norm; in practice, this means that the individual counts for nothing, the society for everything; that anyone who slacks his/her duties is criminal and must be punished severely. So-called "wild men" who turn up occasionally and Selfish Ones who break the Creed (atavists back to normal humanity) are put to death. * Leetha, who is really an atavist, is given fifty lashes for slacking, while Jones, as a special case, is to be taken for judgment before the Uniad, an infallible oracle/judge that is the ultimate source of authority. In some way the Uniad is the group mind of the culture. Before judgment, however, Jones is permitted to view the strange city, which amounts to a human anthill. * The Uniad sentences Jones to death, but he and Leetha escape through a secret tunnel that the priests use to activate the Uniad—which is a fraud. Out in the forest they will presumably thrive. * The coalescence of altruism and social control is unusual for the magazines. As a story, mediocre.

532. **LOST IN SPACE**. *Astounding Stories*, August 1935. Ill. Marchioni.

Short story. * *Time:* the interstellar future. *Place:* some unknown area far away in space. * Something inexplicable has happened to the great interstellar spaceliner *Zelathon V.* Riding along near Sirius, it was suddenly hurled an incredible distance off the astral space lines, so far that the constellations have changed and the captain and navigator have no idea where they are. * Something else has happened, too. Inhibitions have been released, unconscious desires emerge, and in general crew and passengers go to pieces psychologically. Husband and wife discard each other. A crew member murders the purser for the ship's funds. The captain and his mate behave like children. A lover finally accepted by a vamp calmly shoots her dead. And so on. All this turmoil is later explained rather facilely: The air supply has been allowed to deteriorate. * As for navigating the ship back to a known port, in this case the solar system, the homing instinct of a small, abused toy poodle turns the trick. * *Miscellaneous:* Some sort of pulsing system is used for space travel. * A curious story, with its pioneering mingling of inner and outer space, but not realized very well. Two fumbling letdowns disappoint one's expectation of something more significant.

533. **PHANTOM STAR**. *Astounding Stories,* October 1935. Unsigned ill.

Short-short story. * *Time and place:* the interstellar future, in space near Beta Centauri. * A frank latch-on to Edgar Allan Poe's "The Cask of Amontillado." * The narrator, who has been gravely injured by Fran Gregori, entices him into space on a two-man vessel, offers him Amontillado from Earth, walls him into a compartment with a force screen, and then announces that he will drive the spaceship into a nearby sun. Gregori, who had stolen the ideas and work of the narrator, breaks down, admitting his crimes. But the narrator still drives the spaceship into the giant sun. Nothing happens. * Actually, this was a staged event. The narrator recorded Gregori's confession and has no intention of killing him or committing suicide. The nearby giant sun does not really exist; it is simply a space mirage of light that has traveled around the finite universe.

534. **FRUIT OF THE MOON-WEED**. *Astounding Stories,* November 1935. Ill. Marchioni.

Short story. * Strange eroticism in the guise of interplanetary exploration. * *Time:* the interstellar future. *Place:* a planet in a multiple star system. * The narrator and his friends Wycoll and Krapelli are on the almost unknown planet Nircon seeking fruit of the moon-weed, the source of a valuable drug. The planet, which seems Earth-like in gravity and atmosphere, supports a heavy, very strange vegetation, among which are javelin trees that shoot spear-like seeds at random. Such maneuvers are necessary for plant fertilization, since there is almost no animal life. * The narrator, returning after exploring with Wycoll, sees Krapelli apparently dead near a stand of moon-weeds. Something must have killed him, and the narrator believes he has seen motion in the vegetation. Moving in, he discovers a remarkably beautiful young woman, with whom he immediately establishes an erotic relationship. But during this episode, an ogre-like female monstrosity also emerges and forces the narrator to kiss her. He loses consciousness at the horror of it. * He awakens back in space. Worried about the young woman, who should not be abandoned, he then learns that it was all delusion, fantasies caused by the moon-weed. He had been wandering about with a blossom over his head. Krapelli, too, had been doped and was

Haggard, J. Harvey (*continued*)

not really dead. But the two men have served their biological purpose. As a result of their actions two moon-weed blossoms were fertilized and are setting seed. * A subtext that is more interesting than the surface narrative.

535. **HUMAN MACHINES**.   *Astounding Stories,* December 1935. Ill. Flatos.

Short story. * *Time:* perhaps around A.D. 4000 or a little later. * Therm Sutner finds himself alone on a deserted beach fringing a subtropical milieu. It is all very puzzling, for he has no idea where he is or how he came there. For several days he wanders about, living on the plentiful wild fruit, until the summons comes. * A horrible creature something like a magnified sow bug emerges from the water and announces that it will take him to Darth. So it does, despite Sutner's initial resistance. * When Sutner meets Darth, he begins to understand what is happening. Two thousand years earlier, the scientist Lan Darth had founded the humanticist party, which swept the world. Its creed included parthenogenetic reproduction, abolition of sex, and eugenic development of specialized human types. Sutner was one of the few important personalities who opposed the plan. Thereupon, Lan Darth hurled him into the future with a time device, depositing him on the beach. * It is not Lan Darth that Sutner meets, however, but his many-times removed "descendant," who is really a hypertrophied brain on a spindly body. Darth shows him the new world, which is a hodgepodge of weird human specializations, one of which was the amphibious horror that carried Sutner to Darth. * After a time, however, Sutner realizes that much of what he is being shown is illusion. Darth has been communicating mental images, not physically showing a reality. Exerting his will, Sutner rebels, to find himself alone on a ledge with Darth. He attacks Darth, but during the struggle falls unconscious. He awakens to find himself alone on the beach near the subtropical vegetation. Sutner wonders whether there are other real humans in the world. * The story, which deliberately eschews rational explanations, leaves matters open. Perhaps Darth was the only living being, and he created mentally the future horrors that Sutner viewed. Perhaps Sutner killed Darth and was thereupon freed. Or perhaps it was all a dream? * An interesting concept, but the author does not quite bring it across. The concept, in any case, with its dream-like ambience, is more significant than the routine stories that Haggard usually wrote.

536. **MOON CRYSTALS**.   *Astounding Stories,* January 1936. Unsigned ill.

Short story. * A resolution of marital discord. * *Time:* the interplanetary future. *Place:* Venus. * *Background:* Venus, which is damp and jungle covered, is nevertheless tolerable for Earthmen, who have a few settlements and trading posts. One such post consists of Omar Klegg and his delicate wife Enid, a selfish, petulant woman who is obviously unsuited to pioneer life. Omar trades with the natives for Venus moon gems; these are radioactive crystals that are highly valued on Earth. * The natives are generally nasty, and Klegg's position is shaky, being based on the goodwill of a native whom he had helped. And now the native is dying. Klegg must establish himself with the other natives, or die. * The Venusians are very sensitive to carbon dioxide, and Klegg had helped his native friend to cap certain gas exudations. He regains mastery by shooting the wells open again. Enid, surprisingly enough, stands up well during the

crisis, and she and Klegg are reconciled. * *Miscellaneous:* The natives are humanoid, green, and primitive. * The moon crystals seem to have been of meteoritic origin. * Routine.

537. **A LITTLE GREEN STONE**.   *Astounding Stories,* March 1936. Ill. Flatos.

Short story. * *Time:* the interplanetary future. *Place:* the trans-Plutonian planet Euthan. * *Background:* Euthan is a small world, about the size of Mars, with one small moon. It is damp and wet, treacherous underfoot, and overgrown with clinging fungi. Its peculiar vegetation does not depend on photosynthesis, since there is no light to speak of, but on cosmosynthesis based on cosmic rays. The inhabitants, who are practically human, though aloof and unsocial, play no part in the story. * Earth maintains a trading station and would like to expand its operations greatly. Hence the expedition of Cathin (who visited Euthan a generation earlier), Stone (the resident trader), and the narrator. The men carry flashlights and ray guns. * The story follows two dynamics. Stone, who sympathizes with the natives and does not want them exploited, is deliberately leading the other two men in circles so that the expedition will fail. Cathin, in his earlier visit, fathered a child on a native. This child, Kalutu, is a half-human, half-bestial monstrosity who serves as a faithful guard-animal to Stone. Kalutu's monstrous aspect arose out of non-matching chromosomes. Stone knows of Kalutu's parentage, but Cathin does not. * As the men slog along with their flashlights, bickering, Cathin falls into a death pool, from which Kalutu rescues him at the cost of his own life. * The little green stone in the title of the story refers to a trinket, half of which Cathin carried; Kalutu received the other half from his mother. * Confused in narrative, with the subtleties not well handled.

HALE, EDWARD EVERETT (1822-1909)

U.S. (Boston) journalist, man of letters, Unitarian clergyman. Very prolific writer in many areas; leader in various social reforms. Now remembered mostly for short story "The Man without a Country" (1863). In science-fiction, author of pioneering artificial-satellite story "The Brick Moon" (1869-1870).

538. **THE GOOD-NATURED PENDULUM**.   *Amazing Stories,* May 1933.

(Reprinted from *The Ingham Papers,* 1869.)

Short story. * *Time:* early nineteenth century. *Place:* Boston, Massachusetts. * Garrulous reminiscences of a situation in which mischievous young schoolboys rigged the pendulum of the master's clock to shorten the school day. The dominie seems to have caught on after some confusion in daily activities. * The story is not really science-fiction, for while it includes a little science, it is not particularly fantastic.

HALE, STEPHEN G.

U.S. (Pennsylvania) author. According to John V. Baltadonis, an art teacher in the Northeast High School of Philadelphia.

539. **THE LAUGHING DEATH**.   *Amazing Stories,* April 1931. Ill. Morey.

Short story. * *Time:* 1940-1947. *Place:* the Philadelphia area. * A rather confusing mishmash of motifs: world peril, mad scientist, imaginary war, etc. * The narrator, an associate of the great inventor/entrepreneur Joel Murch, reminisces about the events that led to a catastrophe. Several subplots are involved. * Murch, who is greatly interested in splitting the atom, comes

Hale, Stephen G. (*continued*)

into temporary possession of a supermicroscope that renders his goal possible. He then constructs several "Worms," or earth-borers that operate by disintegrating matter and using the residue as an impermeable sealing or lining material. The Worms revolutionize underground construction, and Murch applies them driving subway tunnels at fantastic job speed. There is, however, a danger involved. The Worms are controlled by an electric cable; if the cable should break, atomic disintegration may escape. * Murch's tubes are not just for travel; he sees them as refuges during a war that he anticipates will come. War and rebellion do break out, fostered by the plots of the mad scientist Dr. Serge Grubsnig (whose name, spelled backward, is revelatory). The real owner of the supermicroscope, he is Murch's rival and enemy. * The upshot: Grubsnig, disguised in Murch's heat suit, cuts the cable to a Worm, which runs wild, cutting the Earth in two. The narrator and his wife are on the segment corresponding roughly to the northern hemisphere, while the southern hemisphere is flying around in its own orbit. Life in the northern segment is precarious. * An amateurish, cluttered story, badly composed, and certainly not worthy of publication. As an example of the prose: "[Joel's] eyes were challenging the fiend. 'Rave, rave, rave, as I did,' gnashed the latter." * I fail to see the relevance of the title to the story. Judging from a letter of the author's in the April 1932 issue of *Amazing Stories*, the story was meant seriously. For a sequel see #540, "Worlds Adrift."

541. **WORLDS ADRIFT.** *Amazing Stories,* May 1932. Ill. Morey.
Novelette. * Sequel to #539, "The Laughing Death." * *Time:* perhaps the third quarter of the twentieth century. *Place:* the former Philadelphia area on half of the world. * For reasons that I do not understand, Bob, his wife Hilda, and their children are (almost) the only humans on their half of the world. Years pass; Hilda dies; the children mature. * After many fruitless attempts to locate other survivors, Bob finally receives a weak signal from the other half of the Earth. And he finds on his hemisphere a sick old man who wishes to be known as Brown. (The reader, if he happens to remember details of the first story, will have no difficulty in identifying Brown with Grubsnig, who is repentant, but embarrassed to admit his identity.) * The two men work amicably together as Brown toils away on his great project: pushing their half-world, using the energy of the Worms, up to the other half, thus putting the planet together again. Energy devices are to blanket the contact. * The time comes, and Bob, Grubsnig now being dead, sets off the machinery. But the men overlooked the Moon in their plans, and the result is disaster. While Bob is able to land the Moon gently on his half-world, he misses juncture with the other half, and as he writes in disjointed phrases, his world is being propelled away into outer space. Finis. * Not much better than the first story.

HALL, AUSTIN (c. 1885-1933)
U.S. (California) writer. A rather mysterious personality, about whom little is really known. According to an interview in Schwartz/Weisinger, he was at one time a sports editor on a San Francisco newspaper. According to other sources, he was a rancher. It has been claimed that he was very prolific in many areas of pulp fiction, notably Westerns, but I have encountered very little of his work. Among Hall's other fantastic work

(covered in *Science-Fiction: The Early Years*) are "Almost Immortal" (1916), "The Rebel Soul" (1917), and "Into the Infinite" (1919), all of which constitute explorations of the nature of the mind and personality, suggested by Stevenson's *The Strange Case of Dr. Jekyll and Mr. Hyde.* Hall was also once highly regarded for "The Blind Spot" (1921), a story of parallel worlds written in collaboration with Homer Eon Flint. * Hall was a very uneven writer whose ideas often outstripped his literary abilities. The following story may be his second worst, the worst being "People of the Comet" (1923).

541. **THE MAN WHO SAVED THE EARTH.** *Amazing Stories,* April 1926. Ill. Paul.
(First published *All-Story,* 13 December 1919. Reprinted in *Amazing Stories Annual* [1927]; in *Famous Fantastic Mysteries,* February 1940; and in Conklin, *Best of Science Fiction.*)
Short story. * World peril. * Opalescent globes, presumably of pure force, appear in various places around the world and seemingly disintegrate large portions of the Earth around them. * There is no defence against them, and the situation is bad. Indeed, one such globe in the Caribbean removes so much water that the Gulf Stream is diverted, with disastrous results. * Only the eccentric Charles Huyck knows what is really happening. The globes are the instrumentality of the Martians, who are raiding Earth's resources, particularly water, to save their dying, desiccated world. Huyck creates an apparatus that draws force from the sun, disrupting the equipment on Mars. The peril is averted. Hall discourses briefly on the conflict between morality and necessity in such a raid. * Padded and wandering.

HALL, D[ESMOND] W[INTER] (1909-1992)
U.S. magazine editor, occasional writer. Born in Sydney, Australia; moved to U.S. in 1916. According to various biographical articles, a graduate of the University of California, Los Angeles, but the University has no record of his attendance. Pulp writer, then editorial assistant (associate editor) to Harry Bates on the new Clayton *Astounding Stories* for about nine months (exact dates not known); later became assistant to F. Orlin Tremaine on Street and Smith *Astounding* for about a year after establishment of the magazine, acting as first reader. In late 1934 Hall was transferred to *Mademoiselle,* which he seems to have left around 1937. His later life is not clear, but for a while he acted as a literary agent and probably continued to write pulp fiction. Author of *A Woman of Fifty* (1948) and *I Give you Oscar Wilde* (1965). According to the reminiscences of various authors Hall had more responsibility than his title might indicate, handling most of the editorial work and reporting to Bates or Tremaine. Although not a strong writer, Hall may have been a capable editor. See also pseud. H. G. Winter and joint pseud. Anthony Gilmore.

542. **WEREWOLVES OF WAR.** *Astounding Stories.* February 1931. Unsigned ill.
Short story. * *Time:* 1938. *Place:* Southwestern U.S. * Really an aviation-pulp action story, such as might have appeared in Clayton's *Air Adventures* or *Flyers,* with a few s-f elements. * The United Slavs have invaded the United States and are carrying everything before them. At the moment the battle lines are running through the Southwestern desert. * The story is concerned with Capt. Derek Lance, U.S.A.F., one of the flying branch known as the Werewolves of War. Most of their tactics are dogfights. * Unfortunately, there must be a spy in the unit,

Hall, Desmond W. (*continued*)

since the Slavs are usually ready for the Americans and destroy them with long-distance flame throwers. * The new weapon designed by Professor Singe is America's hope. It consists of an enormous shell of a superexplosive, propelled by vibrations in the ether. Its one weakness is that it must be directed from nearby. * Lance and the great ace Captain Hay form a suicide team to use Singe's weapon. Hay, in suitable disguise, leaps in midair into a Slavic fighter plane and flies to the Slavic headquarters. Lance does his part in directing the weapon. * Both men die, but the Slavs are crushed, and there are statues of Hay and Lance in San Francisco. * Low grade.

543. **RAIDERS INVISIBLE.** *Astounding Stories*, November 1931. Ill. Wesso.

Short story. * Like the preceding story, an aviation story adapted somewhat with science-fiction motifs. It is possible that both stories were leftovers from the recently deceased Clayton air adventure magazines. * *Time:* 1935. *Place:* around the Panama Canal. * War games are taking place around the Canal, the Blue Atlantic fleet defending, the Black Pacific attacking. The purpose of the exercise is not only to gain practice, but to demonstrate American might to a certain hostile power. * Suddenly, as air scout pilot Chris Travers watches, the dirigible ZX-2 explodes, despite being filled with inert helium. Horrified, Chris returns to his mother ship, the dirigible ZX-1, and finds everyone dead of poison gas. Acting rapidly, gas mask on, Chris tosses overboard the bomb that had been meant to destroy the airship; fights desperately with an invisible man, who escapes; follows him in his plane to a camouflaged base; is burned down by a ray; is captured, and tortured. His captors are Soviet agents, who also plan to blow up the Gatun Spillway. * Chris, after watching the invisibility process (which gives bodies the refractive index of air), fights vigorously and manages to save the Canal. * Little to recommend.

544. **A SCIENTIST RISES.** *Astounding Stories*, November 1932. Ill. Wesso.

(Reprinted in Ackerman, *Gosh! Wow!*, where it is attributed to Harry Bates and Desmond Winter Hall. It is not known whether this is an error or private information.)

Short story. * New York City. * Passersby marvel at a very tall man who emerges from a building. And marvel more as he visibly grows taller and taller. He is not hostile; indeed, Dr. Wesley, as he is identified, looks most benign. But he continues to grow, until, when he is hundreds of feet tall, he blurs, then is dissipated in the atmosphere. * Wesley's notes, examined after his disappearance, reveal that he has made a great discovery, but it is too dangerous to release. Hence he is allowing himself to die along with what he discovered. * The story was very popular in its time, but it now seems to have little to recommend it.

HALL, T[HOMAS] PROCTOR (1858-1931)

Canadian (British Columbia) educator, physicist, mathematician. Ph.D., Clark University, 1894. Books and papers on advanced algebra. The identification is secure, despite the low quality of this story.

545. **DOCTOR O'GLEE'S EXPERIMENTS.** *Amazing Stories Quarterly*, Summer 1929. Ill. Walitt.

Short story. * *Place:* Vancouver, Toronto, and other parts of Canada. * An extraordinarily confused, amateurish story. The central theme seems to be the utility of certain forms of radiation. William K. Brown has invented a workable doodlebug that locates various metals, and Dr. O'Glee uses various forms of solar radiation to work cures. The two men come together in the case of Norine Wardel, a feeble-minded child whom O'Glee cures with his treatments. O'Glee can also cure certain persons with criminal tendencies. And in one incident, his apparatus stops an epidemic. Thugs, misidentification, false accusation of kidnapping, etc. enter the story. * One of the worst performances in the pulp magazines of this period. It is astonishing that *Amazing Stories* would print it.

HAMILTON, EDMOND [MOORE] (1904-1977)

Prolific U.S. writer of fantastic fiction, whose career ranged from 1926 to shortly before his death. Born in Youngstown, Ohio; educated at Westminster College, Pennsylvania, majoring in physics, but leaving before obtaining a degree; a professional writer for most of his life. Married fantasy writer Leigh Brackett in 1946. In later life primary series author for the Captain Future stories. * Hamilton is a difficult writer to characterize, for although he usually wrote superficial, repetitive, clichéd material for the lower market, he was, particularly in his later years, capable of technically superior, more profound work. Unlike other writers comparable in some ways, such as Ray Cummings and John Russell Fearn, Hamilton was respected by his peers. * Hamilton can justly be considered the inventor of the space opera, which he developed with a succession of short stories, novelettes, and novels that appeared primarily in *Weird Tales*. * In general it can be said that while Hamilton's work was often totally formulaic, repetitive, naive, and poorly fitted with characters, it was cleanly written. * See also #1822, "Cosmic Quest" and #1823, "Mutiny on Europa."

546. **THE COMET DOOM.** *Amazing Stories*, January 1928. Ill. Paul.

Short story. * *Place:* Northern Ohio, Lake Erie. * The Green Comet, a very spectacular object, is drawing close to Earth. There is no danger of a collision, but then astronomers suddenly discover that the Earth is leaving its orbit and is approaching the comet. * This is the background situation. Most of the story is taken up by Walter Coburn's narrative to his friend Marlin. An entomologist working on Logan Island, Coburn and his associate Hanley were present when a conical space ship from the comet landed. Four-legged, tentacled metal beings emerged, flashed rays, and captured the two men. * After learning English speech and writing from them in a fantastically short time, the invaders reveal that they are cyborgs (my term). Their protoplasmic brains have been transplanted to metal bodies powered by atomic energy, hence they are almost immortal. * The comet people live on the resources of the solid cometary head, but this is almost exhausted. When they approached the solar system, they decided to capture a planet (Earth being the most suitable) and take it into the comet for future use. They are now setting up a power plant to neutralize the sun's gravity vibrations. * The comet people then make an offer: They need intelligent human advice on exploiting the Earth's resources, and in return for such collaboration, they will grant Coburn and Hanley the cometary immortality as cyborgs. Hanley accepts, but Coburn is unwilling, and manages to escape. * Narrative over, Coburn and Marlin decide to wreck the cometary installation. They fail and are captured, but they see Hanley (now a metal man) leap forward and turn off the critical switch. The Earth has been

Hamilton, Edmond (*continued*)

saved. Did Hanley have last-minute qualms of conscience, or was he deceiving the cometary people from the beginning? Hanley, incidentally, could be identified, since he had only two tentacles. * Hamilton's essential hackneyed plot, but a little better in writing than much of his comparable fiction.

547. **LOCKED WORLDS.** *Amazing Stories Quarterly*, Spring 1929. Ill. Paul and unsgnd.

Short story. * *Place:* Boston and a parallel world. * The great scientist Professor Adams of Northeastern University evokes a storm of ridicule and abuse when he propounds a new theory of matter: That stray electrons rotating in reverse direction to the basic electrons really constitute a second form of matter in a parallel universe; and that this universe can be reached by electrical changes in matter. * Adams resigns from Northeastern and disappears, perhaps by means of the strange apparatus in his lab. Not long after this, circles of matter around the country are replaced by circles of a different type of matter. Rawlins, speculating that these phenomena have been caused by Adams, with no good intention, suggests that he and Harker, the narrator, follow Adams wherever he went, using the apparatus in Adams's laboratory. * Said, done, and the two men find themselves in a strange world, where they are captured almost immediately by giant, intelligent spiders. They are transported on a flying disk to the spider city, where they are taken before Adams, who is now totally mad. Adams states that he intends to transfer the spider cities to Earth, which the spiders will easily conquer with their disintegrator rays. * Adams retains Rawlins as a willy-nilly assistant, while Harker is thrown into prison. There as his cell mate he meets a bird-man (Nor-Kan), who teaches him the local language and explains matters. * Long ago the bird-men were the ruling race on the planet, with a high superscience. But the race degenerated, and to operate the gigantic machines supporting their culture, the bird-men bred a race of intelligent giant spiders. The spiders eventually revolted and defeated the bird-men, who now survive only in a fortress protected by artificial wind barriers at the south pole. Nor-Kan was captured in a raid. * Harker and Nor-Kan escape, enter the bird-man's flyer, which is nearby, and make their way to the south polar regions, where they put the case to the rulers, pointing out that Adams, in addition to transferring spider cities to our world, will be able to breech the polar defenses with his dimensional apparatus. * The bird-men decide to open hostilities. During the attack Harker and Rawlins seek out Adams and manage to stop his hand just as he is pulling the switch to transfer the spider cities. The switch is not an on-off switch, as might be expected, but a rheostat; as a result the spider cities are not transferred, but exploded. Rawlins and the narrator return to Earth. All is well. * *Miscellaneous.* The spider-people travel within their city by means of conveyor belts fitted with hooks. One such hook drags Adams to his death. * The bird-people use antigravity to fly torpedo-shaped ships equipped with guns that project electricity.

548. **THE HIDDEN WORLD.** *Science Wonder Quarterly*, Fall 1929. Ill. Paul.

Novelette. * *Place:* somewhere in northern Brazil along the equator. * A strange, powerful beam of light is seen in three places along the equator: Africa, Indonesia, and the Pacific. Great geologist Dr. Kelsall draws conclusions about it: It should next appear in Brazil on a certain date. Thereupon Kelsall, the narrator Vance, and two others hie to Brazil with suitable equipment and wait. * Kelsall is right; the light appears at the proper time and place, but there is also a great explosion, and where the light emerged from the ground is a wide shaft leading into the Earth. As the men watch, a succession of flying globes emerges and deploys around the area, flashing disintegrator rays. Vance and Darrell escape, but Kelsall and Fenton are captured by strange creatures that look much like seven-foot shmoos (of Al Capp's) with four tentacle arms and enormous, single eyes. These creatures hustle their captives into one of the globes, which descends into the shaft. * Vance and Darrell determine to rescue their comrades. Overpowering several of the creatures, which Hamilton terms flesh-monsters, they seize a sphere, and by trial and error learn how to operate it. They fly down the shaft for about a thousand miles, which turns out to be the thickness of the Earth's outer shell. Below is a small inner planet, heated and illuminated by the glowing concave portion of the outer shell. Landing unobserved, Vance and Darrell creep around, follow the various inner people to the place where the others are held captive, rescue them, easily win several aerial duels with the enemy, and fly back to the outer world just as the inner planet explodes. * *Background:* According to the history that one of the flesh-monsters imparted to Kelsall via a thought-machine, the Earth's original form was the small inner planet. An enormous onrush of planetesimal material formed the outer shell, which then sealed in the inner world. Life began far earlier inside the Earth, culminating in the flesh-monsters, who developed a high science. For ages the inner planet did not revolve along with the outer shell, but remained stable and motionless. Recently, however, it has been dragged into motion, and as a result is showing signs of shattering. Indeed, stabilizing techniques that the flesh-monsters attempted made the matter worse, so that the collapse is due within a matter of hours. The flesh-monsters built spherical antigravity vessels, drove their disintegrator ray out to the surface, and planned to emerge, slaughter mankind, and take over the world. * As an added oddity, overpopulation is so great on the inner planet that the entire globe is covered scores of layers deep with construction levels. * Routine for Hamilton.

549. **THE OTHER SIDE OF THE MOON.** *Amazing Stories Quarterly*, Fall 1929. Ill. Wesso.

Short novel. * *Place:* Yucatán and the Moon. * The Howland expedition to Yucatán met with disaster, cause generally unknown. But Carson, a survivor, tells the main narrator what happened. In Yucatán the archeologists saw a succession of pie plate-like flying disks emerge from a great mound and fly about. The occupants of the flying saucers, who were turtle-men, killed some members of the expedition with vacuum rays and captured Howland. Carson, who lay hidden, was unnoticed. The disks then all descended into an enormous artificial bore in the mound, formed up on a cylindrical projectile, and exploded off to the moon, after which Carson escaped. Since the turtle-men were assembling materiel around the mound, it is probable that they plan to attack the Earth. * Carson and his comrades decide to follow the turtle-men to the Moon, both to rescue Howland and to prevent an invasion. In Yucatán they descend into the pit, climb upon a ready disk, and whisk themselves away to the Moon. As they later learn, the system utilizes light pressure. * The projectile flies along a beam to Copernicus, enters a tunnel, and emerges on the dark side of the Moon. There the turtle-men live in a pleasant countryside covered by a gigantic glass dome,

Hamilton, Edmond (*continued*)

with artificial gravity like that of the Earth. * After much zigzag adventure, captured and escaping, the men meet Howland and learn from him the history of the turtle people. * *Background:* The turtle people rose to planetary dominance on Earth geological ages ago. Their science was advanced enough to communicate with the inhabitants of the Moon, who were giant, benevolent, intelligent black worms with a science far superior to that of the turtle-people. The worms had encased their world in a glass sphere to conserve waning resources. The worm people taught the turtle-men much, instructing them how to build the projectile system that still exists in Yucatán. Traffic between Earth and Moon was frequent. But a climactic change caused a glacial period far more severe than the modern Wisconsin glaciation, and the turtle people faced extinction. In an act of unparalleled treachery they shot projectiles toward the Moon, destroying the crystal covering on the Earth side of the moon and causing the Moon's craters. The worms were all killed, whereupon the turtle-men took over what remained of the glass shell on the dark side of the moon. Now, however, their resources are waning and they intend to return to the Earth. * The Earthmen resolve to frustrate this plan. Escaping, they seize a flying disk, and proceed to the launching site. There, Carson and his comrades enter a cylinder to go back to Earth, while Howland flicks the switch that first blasts through the lunar glass and kills all the turtle-men, then sends the others back to Earth. * The world is saved.

550. **CITIES IN THE AIR**. *Air Wonder Stories*, November-December 1929. Ill. Paul and unsgnd.
Novel. * *Time:* A.D. 2069. *Place:* New York area and Berlin area. * In the world of 2069 there are three empires, the American Federation, the European Federation, and the Asiatic Federation. The human race is now concentrated in enormous floating cities that are suspended in the air on circular bases by antigravity created by electrostatic force from the atmosphere. Each federation has one hundred cities surrounded by air forts supported on cosmic ray beams and mounting heat guns. The cities move about, but slowly. * Narrator Capt. Martin Brant of an air cruiser receives orders to join the main fleet. War has broken out with both the European and Asiatic Federations, and an attack is imminent. The cities move slowly inland; the aerial forts move out to the coast; and the air fleet flies to encounter the enemy on Atlantic and Pacific. The situation is not good, for the enemy outnumbers the Americans greatly. * The Atlantic battle begins, and in a series of dogfights and large maneuvers the fleets engage. The Americans fight well, but are overmatched. The combat moves under water, for the aerial cruisers are also submarines, and then, on command of the commander in chief, into a cloud bank. This reveals the secret weapon of the Americans: an artificial cloud emitted by the hidden forts now blasts the enemy. The result is a tactical victory for the Americans. The European fleet retreats to its home base on Berlin, the European capital. Even with losses, however, the European fleet is stronger than the American, and a further invasion is inevitable. * The narrator is summoned to the commander-in-chief and given a special mission. The enemy is known to be in possession of a secret weapon; it is up to Brant and a small fleet to discover what this weapon and destroy it. Brant leaves, bombs Berlin severely, causing much damage to the fleet based there, but is captured. * Whereas up to now the

story has been fairly reasonable, it now takes the typical Hamilton turn. A fellow captive, a longtime mole, knows what the secret weapon is: a means for moving the cities around as rapidly as air cruisers. After frustrated attempts, Brant finally escapes and makes his way back to New York. Meanwhile, all the cities of Europe assemble around Berlin, then fly rapidly to New York and attack. (Civilian populations have been removed and put into underground shelters.) * Things look bad, but Brant, with a small commando (my term) group, invades Berlin, captures the control room, and whirls Berlin around like a yo-yo, bumping into and destroying the other enemy cities. When the battle ends, the Americans have been overwhelmingly victorious, with all the great cities of Europe destroyed: London, Paris, etc. There is a possibility of world peace now that the European and Asiatic warlords are dead. * *Miscellaneous:* There was a previous air war in 2039, in which the Americans were victorious. * The air cruisers, which are torpedo-like affairs, use atmospheric electricity for power, via the jet principle. Ramming is a common battle tactic.

551. **THE SPACE VISITORS**. *Air Wonder Stories*, March 1930. Ill. Paul.
Short story. * *Time:* the near future. *Place:* Iowa, Finland, and Chicago. * An enormous swath is cut into the landscape in a small town in Iowa—perhaps a couple of miles long, a quarter of a mile deep and wide. It is inexplicable. Then another incident occurs in Finland, but this time a shepherd sees a gigantic metal scoop reach down from the sky and make the excavation. Half of Chicago is carried away, and similar catastrophes take place in other parts of the world. * The great scientist Dr. Howard works out an explanation. We are at the bottom of an air ocean, and beings above the ocean are trawling the "seabed," for reasons not known: raiding resources, scientific sampling, or what? At first the authorities scoff at Howard's theory, but it is accepted when the incidents continue. Mass hysteria, of course, results. * Howard can suggest only one solution to the problem: fill the air with floating mines—metal balloons with vacuum lift and high explosives—and hope that the resulting damage to the dredges will discourage the space beings. * The factories of the world produce such air mines, for a long time with no results. The damage continues, and human economy collapses. But eventually an explosion brings down two dredges, and the menace is—temporarily?—over. * A Fortean concept. * One of Hamilton's better stories.

552. **EVANS OF THE EARTH-GUARD**. *Air Wonder Stories*, April 1930. Ill. Winter.
Short story. * *Time:* around A.D. 2010. *Place:* the Moon and space. * Interplanetary travel proper is not possible, for hostile Martians and Venusians destroy any ship that approaches their planets. The Moon, however, has been colonized from Earth; rich mines have been developed, glass-covered pleasure cities have been built, and there is extensive commerce. Space pirates have unfortunately profited from this development, and against them the Earth-Guard has been established, with five hundred patrol ships. At the moment only the Hawk, a gentleman outlaw with the fastest ship in space, is a problem. * Captain Evans of *Rocket 283* receives a distress signal from a one-man rocket that is being attacked by the Hawk's black ship. On *283*'s approach, the Hawk flies away, and Evans rescues Seaworth, the man who was under attack. Seaworth reveals that he is a secret agent investigating the Hawk's lunar and terrestrial associates and that

Hamilton, Edmond (*continued*)

he has information that will lead to the pirate's capture. For this reason the Hawk is trying to kill him. * Seaworth proceeds to Earth on *283*, conducts his business, and returns to the Moon with Evans. But along the way . . . * Evans hears pops, is knocked unconscious, and awakens to find himself the prisoner of the Hawk, who is Seaworth. The battle in space was a ruse, for the pirate wants to add a space patrol cruiser to his fleet, since all ships must stop if signalled by the patrol. * It looks bad, particularly since the space patrol has been ridiculed for its lack of success in catching the Hawk. But Evans has one trick, and with it he bluffs the Hawk into abandoning the captured vessel immediately. *Rocket 283* has been saved, and the Hawk, on realizing that he has been tricked, renders a farewell salute. * Obvious plotting, but gracefully handled. The title is also given as "Evans of the Earth Guard."

    553. THE UNIVERSE WRECKERS. *Amazing Stories*, May-July 1930. Ill. Wesso.

Short novel written before the discovery of Pluto. * *Time:* 1994. *Place:* mostly near Neptune. * The story is so prototypically a Hamilton space opera that a detailed discussion is hardly necessary. * Hunt, the narrator, who is a member of the Intelligence Bureau of the World Government, is among the first to learn that the rotation of the sun is speeding up; if it continues for about four more months, the sun will split in two, destroying all the planets of the solar system except Neptune. And, as Professor Marlin has discovered, the phenomenon is being caused by a force ray from Neptune. This ray has been analyzed and duplicated by Professor Whitely; it can serve as the propulsion means for a spaceship. * At the behest of the World Government, a spaceship is rapidly built, and Marlin, Whitely, Hunt, and Marlin's assistant (Randall) leave for Neptune, which they can reach in a couple of weeks. * On approaching Neptune, they see that it is completely enclosed in a metal sphere and apparently deserted. The explorers land, and when Whitely and Hunt leave the ship on reconnaissance, a strange spaceship flies down and captures them. Marlin and Randall fly away in the Terrestrial ship and are presumably destroyed. * The captors of Whitely and Hunt are disk-shaped beings, about human size, with seven limbs and a pair of bulbous compound eyes. They bundle the two humans into the spaceship and fly with them to Triton, Neptune's moon, which is also completely encased in a free-floating metal sphere. There Marlin and Hunt are taught the language of the Neptunians. * When the Earthmen are sufficiently skilled in the tongue, the Neptunian leader obligingly explains his racial history and current project. Life arose on Neptune because of its internal heat. As this heat waned, the Neptunians, who have a superscience, encased their planet in metal to conserve heat. When this no longer served, Neptunians migrated en masse to Triton, which they also encased. Now that Triton, too, is becoming unhabitable, they plan to create a new, nearby small sun by disrupting Sol with a force beam. A second beam focused on a nearby star keeps Triton from being itself driven out of the solar system. The Neptunians know that their force beams will destroy the inner planets, but consider it a matter of *sauve qui peut*. * Whitely and Hunt escape with the aid of Marlin and Randall (who were not killed) and report to the World Government, which prepares an armada of thousands of spaceships. Despite enormous losses, the Terrestrials defeat the Neptunians and lay siege to Triton. The solar projector is so heavily fortified that the now weakened Earth forces cannot destroy it, but they do smash the balancing projector, and Triton is whisked out into space. Finis for the disk-men. * *Miscellaneous:* On their journey to Neptune, the voyagers pass Mars closely enough to see that it is Schiaparellian and inhabited. * At the end, Marlin crows over the victory in a manifest destiny manner. * As is the case with all the many stories of this sort that Hamilton wrote, the formula is rigid and the finale is a turkey shoot.

    554. THE SECOND SATELLITE. *Astounding Stories*, August 1930. Ill. J. Fleming Gould.

Short story. * *Time:* the near future. *Place:* mostly on a second moon of Earth's. * Several fliers who have taken the new X-type plane to a forty-mile altitude have disappeared. Hackett and Norman, fliers, have worked out an explanation. Earth has a small second moon that moves so rapidly that it is not seen. It has been capturing the missing airmen. * Hackett and Norman take their plane up to the forty-mile range and are indeed snared by the gravity of the new moon. It has atmosphere, and as the fliers soon discover, intelligent frog-men, who capture them, take them in air vessels to their gigantic city that is situated under a dome. Also present in the frog city are green-skinned humans, who serve as blood sources for the frogs to feed on. * Norman and one of the green men, escaping, fly toward the major city of the green men, where a previous aviator, Fellows, is planning an attack on the frogs. * The frog city is much like a mushroom on a slender stalk, which the Earthmen and the green men blast away, destroying the frog hegemony over the second moon. Hackett is rescued. * Typical Hamilton story, familiar many times from *Weird Tales*.

    555. WORLD ATAVISM. *Amazing Stories*, August 1930. Ill. Paul.

Short story. * The great Professor Howard Grant has discovered the secret of evolution. It is caused and maintained by a certain radiation from the sun. Should this radiation be cut off, life would begin to deteriorate. Grant's associates Harker (the narrator) and Ferson accept his theory, but when Grant presents it at a scientific conference, he is hooted and mocked. In a rage Grant stamps out of the hall, vowing revenge. Grant thereupon disappears and is all but forgotten except by his two associates. * Several years later, it is clearly observable that something is happening to the human race. Crime rates rise, human irritability increases, and the fabric of civilization begins to deteriorate. Science has no answer for the phenomenon, although when Ferson claims that the human race is devolving much as Grant had suggested, he is ignored. The degeneration continues, and mankind all over the world continues to change, down through primitive man, finally to ape-like beings without much intelligence who run through the streets naked and speechless. * Acting on the assumption that Grant has caused the devolution, Ferson and Harker, however, have protected themselves with an apparatus that generates the necessary radiation of evolution. They then track down Grant, finding him in a building in New York. He is now completely mad. A shoot-out follows, in which all three men die. Harker, though mortally wounded, wrecks the apparatus that jammed the solar radiation and is writing this account of the death of civilization. Civilization is at an end, and mankind must begin the long, slow climb upward again.

    556. THE MAN WHO SAW THE FUTURE. *Amazing Stories*, October 1930. Ill. Morey.

Hamilton, Edmond (*continued*)

(Reprinted as "The Man Who Saw Everything" in Hamilton, *The Horror on the Asteroid*. Under original title, in Elwood and Moskowitz, *Strange Signposts*; in Gunn, *The Road to Science Fiction #2*; in Haining, *The Fantastic Pulps*; and in Moskowitz and Elwood, *Other Worlds, Other Times*.)

Short story. * *Time and place:* 1444, Paris, France, and 1944 New York. * Henri Lothiare, an apothecary's assistant, is up before the Royal Inquisition on the charge of sorcery. He had been seen in an area where there were abnormal peals of thunder, and his neighbors had seen him disappear from that area. * Henri denies that he is a sorcerer, and with permission tells his story. * When investigating the field out of curiosity because of the peculiar noises, he was seized by an unknown force and whirled away. He found himself in a totally strange area, among men who spoke a different sort of French than his. After some preliminaries these men, Thicourt and Rastin, told him that he was in the future, the year 1944, and that they had set up the noises as a lure to attract someone they could capture. * To state Henri's succeeding experiences in modern terms: Henri, who seems to have accepted the future calmly enough, acccompanied Thicourt and Rastin on a tour of twentieth-century life, including a transatlantic flight in an airplane and a view of the wonders of New York City. * At a learned gathering, Thicourt and Rastin describe their experiment, but are jeered at. Then, to prove their claims, the two scientists return Henri, in an instantaneous vanishment, to his own time. * Henri is burned at the stake, of course, but the Inquisitor later has tiny doubts. * Historical nonsense, and a little too facile.

557. THE MAN WHO EVOLVED. *Wonder Stories*, April 1931. Ill. Paul.

(Reprinted in Hamilton, *The Horror on the Asteroid*; Hamilton, *The Best of Edmond Hamilton*; Asimov, *Before the Golden Age*; Margulies and Friend, *From off This World*.)

Short story. * The narrator and his friend Dutton respond to an invitation to visit old college chum Pollard, who is now a well-known scientist. As they soon learn, Pollard has a reason for inviting them. He wants them as observers and assistants in a remarkable experiment that he is about to perform. As he informs them, he has discovered the evolutionary principle. It is a question of concentrating cosmic rays, and he intends to submit himself to enhanced radiation and experience what future man will be like. After some protests on the part of the viewers, the experiment begins. * Stage One: Fifty million years. An almost god-like figure in physique and mentality; a true superman, but within the *Homo sapiens* range. The experiment continues. * Stage Two: One hundred million years in the future: Smaller, with a shrivelled body and a balloon head; it scorns the previous stage and regards Dutton and the narrator as savages. It announces that it is beyond friendship and will kill them if they do not operate the machine as commanded. The experiment continues. * Stage Three: One hundred and fifty million years: A head a yard across and a tiny body. It steps out of the machine and announces that it will take over the world and use it as a laboratory for experiments, humans as lab animals. To demonstrate its abilities, it jumbles a few chemicals together and creates gold. It can control its former friends telepathically, but they persuade it to continue on to the next stage. The experiment continues. * Stage Four: Two hundred million years in the future. Pollard is no longer a head but a giant brain with two

tentacles supporting it. The brain announces that it cares nothing about this world, but has higher objectives. It is perfectly telepathic. The experiment continues. * Stage five: Two hundred and fifty million years in the future. Pollard is now a gigantic brain four feet across, without a body or facial features. It informs the watchers telepathically that it is now fed by pure energy and can move itself about more rapidly then they can conceive. It is no longer hostile, but is without emotion. It is pure intellect, and it wants merely to concentrate on intellectual problems. But it intends to go on to the last stage, perfection. The experiment continues. * Stage six: Three hundred million years in the future. Pollard is no longer in existence. There is simply a lump of protoplasm. Apparently evolution works in a circle, returning to its beginning. * Dutton accidentally sets the lab on fire and is now in a madhouse. * A good story within pulp limitations, with a very clear statement of a basic situation in science-fiction. There is also a (perhaps unintentional?) humorous note in the various future stages of humanity.

558. MONSTERS OF MARS. *Astounding Stories*, April 1931. Ill. J. Fleming Gould.

Short story. * *Place:* mostly on Mars. * Milton, who has been listening in on extraterrestrial radio signals for some time, is finally able to respond. The signals come from Mars, and the Martians, who are ahead of us scientifically, offer to let Earthmen visit Mars by matter transmitter. This is accomplished by raising the atomic vibratory rate to that of radio and then transmitting. * Milton, Lanier, and Randall enter the apparatus, which has been built according to Martian instructions, and find themselves on Mars. But it is not a pleasant experience: The Martians, humanoid, but with scales and crocodile heads, are obviously hostile, and the Martian emperor announces that he will use the matter transmitter to take over Earth, since Mars is dying. * The three comrades escape, have adventures with a strange life-form of subhuman intelligence in the jungles along the canals, and eventually reach the transmitting platform at scheduled time for their retrieval. They smash the terrestrial terminal, and Earth is saved. * *Miscellaneous:* The Martians have various ray guns. * Mars is Schiaparellian, but along the canals are belts of horrible jungle. * The Martian emperor, a monstrous intellect, has three bodies grafted together to support his head. * The Martians have learned to speak English. * Typical Hamilton formula.

559. THE SARGASSO OF SPACE. *Astounding Stories*, September 1931. Ill. Wesso.

Short story. * *Time:* the interplanetary future. *Place:* mostly among the outer planets. * The space freighter *Pallas*, en route from Jupiter to Neptune, has lost its fuel and is headed for the "dead area," the Sargasso of Space in the orbit of Neptune, where the various gravities of the sun and the planets cancel each other out. Without a power source an object in it cannot leave. * On drifting into the dead area, the spacemen encounter a tangled mass of spaceships of various ages and types. * Captain Crain and First-Officer Kent hope that they can find fuel in one or another of the derelict ships. Instead they find trouble, for there is another group of spacemen, mutineers and criminals, who are also trapped in the Sargasso. The mutineers hope to capture the *Pallas* and leave when fuel is found. * Space phones and a friendly young woman held captive by the mutineers tip the scales in favor of the crew of the *Pallas* and, refueled, the ship leaves. * Of no particular interest.

Hamilton, Edmond (*continued*)

560. **THE REIGN OF THE ROBOTS**. *Wonder Stories*, December 1931. Ill. Paul.

(Reprinted in [Anonymous] *Strange Love Stories*.)

Short story. * *Place:* the Chicago area. * Young Grant Perry, a multimillionaire, is under pressure from Mr. Loring to contribute $20,000,000 to Loring's neoprimitive society. Loring and his followers believe that man, in the future, is likely to become subject to machines; as a remedy they wish to set up an idyllic premodern community on a Pacific island. * When Perry displays understandable reluctance to release his money, Loring offers to let him visit the future ten thousand years away and see what will happen. Loring's chemists have developed a preparation that permits such time travel: a red elixir to go into the future, a green to return to the past. As Loring says, there is enough of the preparation for only one visit; ingredients no longer exist. Loring will accompany Perry. * The two men awaken on a deserted lakeshore. Not far away are small constructions marking tunnel openings. From one of them races Eda, a beautiful young woman who has escaped from the intelligent machines known as the Masters and is being pursued. Animated mechanical devices emerge, display death-ray tubes, and capture the three humans, accusing all of being runaway slaves. The machines take their captives down into an enormous underground world and propose to send them to the Master Who Thinks in charge of the machine city. Vivisection seems to be in the offing, since the humans have displayed unusual psychological characteristics. * Thanks to Eda's brother, who sacrifices himself, the two men from the past and Eda escape from the machine city and run toward the beach, where the drugs for time traveling have been discarded by the machine that captured the explorers. The two time travelers barely succeed in taking the drugs before the machines catch up with them; Perry hopes that by clasping Eda to him he can save her, but the machine tears her away as the men return to their own time. * Back in the twentieth century, Perry, enormously shaken by his experience, mourning Eda and feeling that he has failed her, gives his check to Loring. * But at this moment "Eda" enters. Loring's daughter Edith, she reveals that the whole episode was a hoax and plot to squeeze money from Perry, but that she is so moved by his bravery, resourcefulness, and self-sacrifice that she can no longer maintain her end of the deception. Loring, she says, is sincere and not a crook. He constructed the machine city, which was really much smaller (thanks to legerdemain deception) than Perry realized, with society members inside the purported machines, operating them. Although Perry thought he had freedom of action, his every movement was orchestrated and controlled. * At this point one would expect Perry either to assault Loring or report him to the district attorney, but instead, overcome with relief at seeing Eda, with whom he fell in love, he lets his check stand. * A competent action story with a good twist. One of Hamilton's better stories, once the gimmick is appreciated.

561. **A CONQUEST OF TWO WORLDS**. *Wonder Stories*, February 1932. Ill. Paul.

(Reprinted in Hamilton, *The Best of Edmond Hamilton*, and in Wollheim, *Every Boy's Book of Science Fiction*.)

Short story. * *Time:* the 1970s. *Place:* mostly Mars and Jupiter. * A strong fictional protest against colonialism, with obvious reference to the historical policies of the major nations, including the United States. The treatment is not in terms of thrills and switch-snapping, as is usual with Hamilton, but is chronicle-like, with some attempt at characterization. * *Background:* In 1962 the first space flight took place when Gillen, a recluse scientist who invented atomic power, voyaged to Mercury, Venus, Mars, and Jupiter. Gillen reported by radio that Mercury was molten, Venus water-covered, but Mars inhabited by very tall primitive humanoids with huge chests, and Jupiter by even more primitive semihumanoid, gentle, peaceful creatures of limited intelligence. * The story is concerned with three young men, caught up in the glamour of Gillen's feat, who join the exploratory and colonial services: Crane, Burnham, and Halkett. Crane and Burnham adjust easily to the exploitative methods used to strip Mars and Jupiter of their resources and have no hesitation in undertaking military operations that amount to genocide. Crane, indeed, becomes a strategist of genius. Halkett, however, is conscience-stricken at the rape of Mars. The three men indulge in many friendly arguments, each side trying to win over the other. The end comes when Halkett provides physical aid to the last beleaguered Martian forces. He is captured and sentenced to ten years in prison. The conquest of Mars is finished, with three-quarters of the native population dead and the remnant reduced to misery and near-slavery on reservations. * It is Jupiter's turn next. Crane is placed in charge of the military operations, which he handles with great skill. But Halkett, released from prison, makes his way to Jupiter and commands the resistance. The Jupiterians resist heroically, but the struggle is hopeless. Trapped with his small forces near the pole of Jupiter, Halkett refuses to surrender, but blows up himself and his soldiers. Crane and Burnham remain bewildered and uncomprehending. * An unusual story for Hamilton, much more worthy of preservation than his world-saver tricks. In an interview Hamilton stated "I wrote ["A Conquest of Two Worlds"] because I was sick of the usual science-fiction assumption that in interplanetary struggles the earthmen would always be in the right" (*Fantasy Magazine*, January 1934, p. 15).

562. **SPACE-ROCKET MURDERS**. *Amazing Stories*, October 1932. Ill. Morey.

Long short story. * *Time:* presumably the near future. *Place:* New York and Labrador. * A message for peace and tolerance in the guise of interplanetary invasion. * The world's leading rocket researchers have been dying mysteriously. As evidence accumulates, it becomes clear that the victims were killed in fire bombings following visits by a squat-appearing man named Nebo, who had very white skin and green eyes. * Melford (friend of one of the victims), Police Chief Crail, and German rocket expert von Gersten (who first identified the syndrome) determine to discover who is thus sabotaging space studies and why. * As a lure, they persuade Professor Jackson, a colleague, to announce publicly that he has discovered atomic energy and intends to apply it to space travel. The investigators and the police department, staking out Jackson's laboratory and home, will then arrest Nebo. * The situation is not that simple. Nebo and his colleagues land on the building with a fantastic noiseless flying machine, kidnap Jackson, and fire the laboratory. Thanks to the stakeout, however, the police are able to kill one of Nebo's associates and extinguish the fire. * The corpse of the intruder offers surprises. It is not human, but a strange form of unknown life, certainly not Terrestrial. It is an octopus-like creature surgically altered to appear roughly human, with painted

Hamilton, Edmond (*continued*)

skin to imitate human complexion. And on the corpse the investigators find a talisman-like device that indicates a point in Labrador. * Jackson learns much more from his kidnappers. From Venus, they have maintained observers on Earth for about two hundred years. Their reason: They fear eventual invasion. Venus has only a tiny island land area, with a small, peaceful population. Earth, with its enormous population, aggressive cultures, and developed weaponry, would pose a threat to Venus if space travel became possible. As for the Venusians themselves, who are about two thousand years ahead of us scientifically, they are descended from creatures like squids; the observers are a special group modified to pass as human. * Jackson is now in trouble, for the Venusians, who do not have atomic energy, are certain that he is in possession of the secret, and he cannot convince them otherwise. They will take him to Venus for questioning. * Things are resolved when armed forces, including planes, attack the alien base in Labrador. Jackson is rescued, but the Venusian spaceship gets away. It is anticipated that there will be no more space-rocket murders now that the background situation is known. * The narrator, who presumably speaks for Hamilton, does not dismiss the Venusian position; Earth's history has been horrible, and the Venusian actions are justifiable from their point of view. But he hopes deeply that when the two peoples meet, peace will be maintained. * Reasonable adventure.

563. **THE ISLAND OF UNREASON**. *Wonder Stories*, May 1933. Ill. Paul.

(Reprinted in Hamilton, *The Best of Edmond Hamilton*; and in Ashley, *History of the Science Fiction Magazine*.)

Short story. * *Time:* undated near future. * *Background:* The society described in this story is a world state totally focused on reason. It seems to be organized in a pyramidal hierarchy of power, with higher members holding the authority to make unquestioned, unappealable decisions even on matters of life and death. Everything is totally regimented. * Breach of reason, or permitting emotions to interfere with a rational life, is a most serious crime. Offenders are sentenced for varying lengths of time, as much as life, to a small penal island far out in the ocean. Civilization maintains no control of the island, where the culture is a total anarchy, with perpetual violence. Exiles who are dropped off there must fend for themselves. * Allan Mann, Serial Number 2473R6, has committed a breach of reason. He had been working on a new atomic motor. When he was almost finished, he was ordered to turn his work over to another person. Allan objected, and is now being tried. He admits that he was at fault, but he must still undergo exile to the island of unreason; his sentence is indefinite, for the court never informs the convict of the length of his sentence. * Allan is flown to the island, where almost immediately he becomes involved in saving a beautiful young woman from attack by the island chief. Allan and the young woman, who hit it off well, thereupon spend the rest of the day fighting off attacks or running away. * The next day, the airplane returns to pick up Allan, for it turns out that his sentence was for only one day. But, as the reader well knew from the beginning of the story, Allan likes the freedom of the island and the woman, and has by now made friends with the island chief, who is by no means an evil man. * Routine.

564. **THE MAN WITH X-RAY EYES**. *Wonder Stories*, November 1933. Ill. Lumen Winter.

Short story. * Dr. Jackson Homer has perfected a process whereby human vision can be enhanced so that it parallels X-ray vision. Transparency, however, is limited to inorganic matter; organic matter is opaque. Young newspaper reporter David Winn offers to become the first human guinea pig; if the process works, he will become the greatest reporter on Earth. * The process, which involves sensitizing the retina, is successful, and David marches forth to seek his (figurative) fortune. Dodging invisible taxi cabs and avoiding invisible walls are a problem, but David does not worry. * The result of his new ability will not surprise the reader. Assigned to cover reform politicians, big business magnates, factory owners, he discovers by reading their lips through walls that they are all crooks and rogues. Somewhat depressed, he goes to visit his girlfriend Marta. He suffers the worst when he oversees her discussing him with her mother. As she says, David is not much, but he is the best she can hook. * They fish David's body out of the river the next day. * Routine.

565. **MASTER OF THE GENES**. *Wonder Stories*, January 1935. Ill. Paul.

Short story. * *Place:* A small Latin American country. * Haddon and Lanham, two American soldiers of fortune awaiting execution for involvement in a revolution, are offered their lives if they will swear to serve Dr. Alascia as bodyguards in his establishment in the jungle. While Alascia will not say much as yet, there is a possibility of trouble with the natives. * Alascia's story: In a primitive area where there has been an unusual number of monstrous births, he has set up a laboratory to study the phenomenon and discover its cause. * As Haddon and Lanham see when they arrive in the native village, Alascia has not been exaggerating. There are children without limbs and with malformations of various sorts, and shortly after the Americans arrive, a headless child is born with eyes and mouth in its chest. Alascia explains the genetics involved to the two Americans, who are ignorant of science. * The situation collapses when Haddon accidentally learns that Alascia did not arrive to study the phenomenon after the fact, but was present before it began. Haddon then puts two and two together from textbooks in Alascia's forbidden lab. Alascia, using a gigantic Crookes tube, has been causing the monstrous births in a research project. Confronted, the scientist calmly admits this, but reminds the Americans of their oath to protect him. * But there is more: Alascia's daughter has secretly married, is pregnant, and will give birth to a monster. The situation explodes: the daughter commits suicide; her husband informs the natives of what has been going on; and Alascia, releasing the Americans from their oath, awaits his death. * A reasonable pulp story.

566. **THE TRUTH GAS**. *Wonder Stories*, February 1935. Ill. Paul.

Short story. * Humor of a sort, in *Saturday Evening Post* folksy situations. * Professor Jason Rand, annoyed by the persistent lying of his young assistant John Daly, leaves his laboratory for a time, urging Daly to hold closer to working hours. Nothing happens for a time, until one day, Daly, on visiting his girlfriend Lois, blurts out that her new dress is a horror and calls her father an old fussbudget. * Other such incidents occur: Police admit taking bribes, politicians blandly declare that they loot public funds, movie stars criticize their fans, criminals in the dock admit their crimes, etc. * It becomes obvious that some factor is causing unwanted truth. Daly, putting two and two together, realizes that Professor Rand is probably responsible and

Hamilton, Edmond (*continued*)

that the vehicle is a gas. With nose plugs to filter out the gas, he finds Rand and confronts him. After a little to-do, Daly destroys Rand's apparatus, and the two men return to civilization. Rand, on seeing what his discovery has done, is forced to admit that total truth is not always desirable. Daly wins back Lois. * Routinely competent, but not rigorously followed out.

567. **THE ETERNAL CYCLE**. *Wonder Stories*, March 1935. Ill. Wallace Saaty.

(Reprinted in Ackerman, *Gosh! Wow!*)

Short story. * *Time:* to the end of the universe. * A triangle resolved by predestination of a sort. * Paul Grann, a brilliant scientist, and Lane Winters are both in love with Christa Dain, who chooses Winters. Christa is thus apprehensive when Grann invites Winters to the lab. * Christa proves right, for Grann, lurking behind a door, knocks Winters unconscious, ties him up, then when Winters regains his senses informs him that they will travel together to the end of the universe. Grann has built a box-like apparatus that permits shifting from one time frame to another, thus traversing millions of years in a short time. * Time whizzes by as the two men (Winters now being released) watch enormous changes in the universe. Ten million million years in the future, they see the universe die. Since it is the end, Grann produces vials of poison for himself and Winters, but, wait, a new glow is apparent, and the universe begins to form again. As the men watch, it takes shape, and after a time obviously is the same as the old universe. Even to the Earth. Everything is recreated exactly as it was in the previous universe. * Grann brings his apparatus down to his laboratory just in time to see himself knock Winters unconscious, drag him into the apparatus, and leave for the future. * What to do? Both men reenter life, knowing that their experience will be recapitulated perhaps infinitely as they repeatedly leave through time and return to a successor universe in cyclical cosmoses. Grann has by now regained his sanity, and the two men, as friends, greet the second Christa. * Routine handling of a situation examined several times previously.

568. **THE ACCURSED GALAXY**. *Astounding Stories*, July 1935. Ill. Dold.

(Reprinted in Hamilton, *The Horror on the Asteroid;* in Hamilton, *The Best of Edmond Hamilton*, and in Asimov, *Before the Golden Age.*)

Short story. * *Place:* the northern Adirondacks. * Newspaper reporter Garry Adams chances to be near when a peculiar meteorite strikes. A glowing polyhedron about ten feet in diameter, it is obviously a construct. Adams summons irascible scientist Ferdinand Peters, who arrives posthaste to examine it. * Peters is at first stumped, but on approaching the polyhedron closely, declares that it is a force field, which he can dissolve. The two men obtain electronic and other equipment, which Peters begins to set up. * Garry, however, observes a peculiar phenomenon: When Peters is close to the object, he knows what to do, though the science involved is obviously far beyond contemporary knowledge; but when Peters is a short distance away, he has no idea what is going on. The conclusion: Peters is being controlled by thought impulses from within the polyhedron. * The being in the polyhedron now communicates with them, telling them a curious creation myth. It is a creature of pure force, one of a race that existed far in the past, before the expansion of the universe. The only living creatures in a dead

universe, they could travel where they willed by power of thought. But then there was a cosmic error. The captive in the polyhedron, who was experimenting with combinations of matter, accidentally created material life, which escaped control. The force beings tried to destroy this "loathsome infection" of matter, but were unsuccessful, and it began to spread through the then universe. As a palliative, the force beings decided to hinder the spread of the infection. Rotating the supergalaxy, they broke it up into smaller galaxies which flew apart into an expanding universe. (This is the explanation for observed galactic movement.) * As punishment for his crime, the other force beings enclosed the experimenter in a force container and left him in the diseased central galaxy. The polyhedron cannot be opened from inside . . . * Suddenly Garry realizes with terror that while the being has been sending thought pictures to them, it has also been causing Professor Peters to set up the releasing apparatus. He cries to the professor to stop, but it is too late. The polyhedron dissolves, and a forty-foot pillar of light bursts forth and flashes into the sky. * The men lose consciousness. When they awake, they learn that all electromagnetic phenomenon in the area—light, electricity, electronics—were canceled for about two hours as an aftermath of the energy being's release. * One of Hamilton's better stories, although the basic idea is not original, H. P. Lovecraft having developed an excellent version of the same idea.

569. **THE COSMIC PANTOGRAPH**. *Wonder Stories*, October 1935. Ill. Paul.

Short story. * Old Professor Robine summons former student Gregg Felton to witness a great discovery. Years ago, when Felton was at college, he had taken issue with the professor's statement that man was destined to extinction as the universe grew older. Felton had no rational reason for his argument, simply a feeling about the dynamic nature of man. * Robine now shows Felton a thirty-foot metal sphere in his basement. It contains a model of our universe. Isolating and catching atomic vibratory waves, Robine has used them to set up miniature atoms. Thus, the universe in the sphere is the exact duplicate in miniature of our universe. And since atomic action in the microcosm is enormously accelerated, the microcosm will show the future of our cosmos. * Locating our planet, the men watch through a porthole and see it become a dead waste. It seems as if Robine is right, but Felton suggests trying other planets. The watchers then see that mankind has settled other worlds, eventually surviving on Mercury under a dying sun. But this is not the end. On Felton's suggestion, the watchers try other stellar systems, finding that mankind has spread through the universe. As the universe grows older, the watchers see the tiny men stave off stellar death, crashing stars together as renewal. But even this must end. * Then Robine and Felton hear a strange noise, and as they watch, they see cylinders of the atomic people emerging up in size to our cosmos. Robine's apparatus explodes, however; in the wreckage the men find traces of the atomic men. Felton is now convinced that in our future mankind will not only try, but will succeed in reaching a macrocosmic universe. * One of Hamilton's better early stories.

570. **INTELLIGENCE UNDYING**. *Amazing Stories*, April 1936. Ill. Morey.

Short story. * *Time:* present, A.D. 3144, and A.D. 22,918. * Old Professor John Hanley, a renowned biologist, bemoans the fact that his knowledge will be lost with his impending death. He

Hamilton, Edmond (*continued*)

devises a solution: Making an exact copy of his neural patterns, he will imprint them on the brain of a newly born child, and thus will retain his mentality. He speculates that this will be a considerable benefaction for humanity, too. * The plan works, and John Hanley renews himself periodically and serves mankind well. * At his twenty-first embodiment in 3144, however, a war breaks out between the Northern Federation and the Southern Federation. When the victors in an aerial battle try to seize Hanley, he turns the tables with an ultrasonic vibration that upsets the balance mechanism in the human ear—all over the world. With mankind at his mercy, he now declares himself ruler of the world. * Hanley apparently rules wisely and well, perhaps too well, for the greatest crisis of all comes in 22,918, when Hanley is regarded as a divine figure and is worshipped in temples. He discovers that the sun is about to collapse into a white dwarf. The only hope for mankind is mass-migration to Mercury. * Hanley appeals to the people to start building spaceships and to terraform Mercury, but he is greeted with mass hysteria and pleas for divine assistance. After having had all its major decisions made for millennia by Hanley, the human race has become utterly helpless and ineffectual. * It is up to Hanley himself. He builds robots, uses some of them to construct ships and sends others to Mercury, where they cause it to rotate and otherwise prepare it for humans. Mankind moves in toto, but Hanley stays behind. He has decided that he has done more harm than good in unintentionally removing human initiative. Mankind may struggle and have difficulties on Mercury, but it will eventually arise again without his help.

571. **DEVOLUTION**. *Amazing Stories*, December 1936. Ill. Morey.

(Reprinted in Asimov, *Before the Golden Age;* and in Colombo, *Friendly Aliens.*)

Short story. * *Place:* northern Quebec. * Some time earlier, when Ross was conducting an aerial geographical survey for the Canadian government, he saw a strange sight near the Great Whale River in northern Quebec: about a dozen creatures that looked like giant globs of jelly gliding through the woods. Biologists Woodin and Gray have accompanied him back to investigate, though they are somewhat skeptical. * As they are camped that day, the creatures appear. Ross and Gray shoot at them as they approach, and then drop dead. Woodin tries to run away, but finds himself paralyzed and captured. He then receives a telepathic message urging him not to try to escape, assuring him that he will not be harmed. The creatures only want information; they killed Ross and Gray in self-defense. * One of blobs explains: They are members of a vast universal empire (the Arctarians) that has spread through the galaxies. Since they have mental control of matter, they need no spaceships, but can travel where they will. The present ten beings have just come from a planet circling Sirius, hoping to learn what happened to a colony that was established on Earth about a billion years in the past. All such colonies report telepathically to the central imperial group, which organizes and controls the universe, but the Terrestrial colony stopped reporting hundreds of millions of years ago. * The Arctarians are both puzzled and horrified at the bestial life on Earth and wonder what happened to their predecessors. They ask Woodin, who obviously does not know. * The Arctarians now decide to find an answer in the ancestral memory retained in Woodin's brain.

In almost a reverie, Woodin sees the Arctarians land, gradually change from unicellular organisms to multicellular, then continue to degenerate through various forms of life—archaic creatures, dinosaurs, ancestral mammals, to man—the lowest form of all. Humanity, with its wanton destruction of life in wars, is the last and most despicable degeneration from the ancient Arctarians. * The Arctarians decide that Earth life is so loathsome that nothing can be done about it but abandon it. Woodin, shattered by his visions and the Arctarian conclusions, can only rave that this is not so; evolution to the high point of *Homo sapiens* is true, not devolution to the low point of modern man. The Arctarians regard him with a mixture of pity and loathing and leave. Woodin, unable to live with such an image of himself, commits suicide. * Although the Arctarians do not articulate it, the problem with Earth (as Hamilton built up in an early part of the story) is radioactivity, which induces mutations. * I cannot agree with the Arctarians, but the concepts are interesting.

HAMMOND, W. F.

No information.

572. **LAKH-DAL DESTROYER OF SOULS**. *Amazing Stories*, March 1928. Ill. Paul.

Short story. * Sensational Oriental menace with more than a little indebtedness to Robert W. Chambers's *The Slayer of Souls*. * General Humiston tells his son-in-law Professor Fiske Ferrell, "perhaps the greatest criminologist the world has ever known" about the spiritual and physical evil that besets the world. It all emanates from the genius-fiend Lakh-Dal, whose headquarters may be near Lhasa. The World War was ultimately his doing, as are the numerous contemporary cases of mental breakdown among the learned and powerful. * Ferrell undertakes the quest for the hidden Lakh-Dal, but the story of his adventures is so confusingly complex that it is not worth detailing here. Eventually, Ferrell, who is himself a high initiate in Chinese mysteries (although no one knew of this before), demolishes Lakh-Dal psychologically, whereupon the wife of Fu-Yung, Lakh-Dal's victim, beheads him. * Among the Oriental fiend's weaponry is an infrared ray that annihilates matter; a development of cosmic rays that permits him recreate what he has annihilated with the infrared and create new matter; and a lunar ray that produces idiocy. The third step in Lakh-Dal's plans for world conquest involves releasing a horde of rats infected with bubonic plague. * Pretty silly.

HANSEN, L[UCILE] TAYLOR (1897-1976)

U.S. author, resident mostly in Los Angeles; died in Phoenix, Arizona. Statements elsewhere that her forename was Louise are incorrect. Attended University of California, Los Angeles, irregularly in the 1920s, without a degree. Occasional writer of science-fiction until 1942. Also author of fifty-eight short popular-science articles, mostly in the series "Scientific Mysteries," in *Amazing Stories* from 1941 to 1948. Wrote three mildly eccentric books, *Considerations of and Additions to the Taylor-Wegener Hypothesis of Continental Displacement* (1946), *He Walked the Americas* (1963), and *The Ancient Atlantic* (1969). * Hansen was not an important author, but the question of her identity has rendered her interesting. She made attempts at concealment, including a man's photograph accompanying "The City on the Cloud" and a statement (on the telephone to Forrest J. Ackerman) that she hadn't written the stories published

Hansen, L. Taylor (*continued*)

as by L. Taylor Hansen, but simply handled them for her brother. This brother has been identified by Rock as Louis Ingvald Hansen, who received a doctorate in chemistry from the University of Minnesota. No evidence, however, has been cited for Rock's identification, and new material firmly identifies L. Taylor Hansen as Lucile Taylor Hansen. While it is remotely possible that the name was at one time used by two persons, the probabilities are that Lucile was simply a shy authoress.

573. **WHAT THE SODIUM LINES REVEALED.**
Amazing Stories Quarterly, Winter 1929. Ill. Paul.
Forthcoming notices describe this story as a collaboration with L. H. Edwards, Ph.D., but Edwards was not credited on publication. The *Comprehensive Dissertation Index, 1861-1972* fails to reveal an L. H. Edwards. * Short story. * *Place:* Ganymede. * The millionaire amateur astronomer Larone accidentally drops a spectrographic grating into his telescope with strange results—the sodium lines are blinking in Morse code. Captain Matthews of the U.S. Army Signal Corps, called in to interpret the code, takes down the following story. * David Thromant and his father, who developed atomic energy with gas emanations as power sources, set out in a small spaceship for Mars. They were forced off their course, however, landing on one of the satellites of Jupiter, probably Ganymede. * Ganymede is much like Earth, but with lower gravity. On emerging from the ship, David was first attacked by an enormous centipede-like creature, then rescued and captured by an intelligent life-form that resembles a gigantic beetle, which played a paralysis ray on him. * The beetle people, however, are friendly, and after curing the septic bites David received from the centipede, they house and feed him and instruct him in their language. Even more helpful, however, is a beautiful young woman (Moa), who tells him in ancient Greek of a sort that she is the last descendant of Atlanteans that Martians brought from Earth millennia previously. * The Martians, who are superior in civilization to the insect people of Ganymede, are also friendly. Indeed, a Martian resident acts as chief adviser to the beetle people. When David is brought before this individual, the so-called Magu, he sees that it is very tall, very thin, and insect-like in appearance; it wears air-pressure armor. It converses amicably with David, making an offer that is not unacceptable: It will marry David to Moa, but David must agree not to try to return to or communicate with Earth after his marriage. David agrees, but while keeping the letter of the agreement, he violates the spirit and has transmitted this message to Earth before his marriage. * *Miscellaneous:* The Martians and the beetle people anticipate that Sirius will crash through the solar system in about a quarter of a million years and are evolving new races to inhabit other solar systems. * The Martians listen in on broadcasts from a supercivilization far away, and from it have learned much, including the sodium-line transmission that David is now using. * The Magu, which has a far-viewing screen that shows scenes on Earth, disapproves of the Earth's warlike cultures.

574. **THE UNDERSEA TUBE.** *Amazing Stories*,
November 1929. Ill. Wesso. Diagrams, perhaps by the author.
Short story. * *Time:* The near future, when the Channel tunnel is functioning, and subterranean tunnels are becoming an accepted mode of long distance travel. * The New York-Liverpool tunnel has been in operation for about three years. When it was being constructed, a remarkable archeological discovery took

place along its route. The miners broke into a small cavern in which was a crystal, liquid-filled coffin containing a beautiful young redheaded woman. When the coffin was opened, the liquid evaporated, and the young woman turned to dust. But this seems to have been a single, chance discovery, for nothing more came of it. * At the moment the narrator is planning to take the transatlantic tunnel to England. His friend, one of the tunnel engineers, urges him to fly instead, for he believes that the tunnel lies across an earthquake fault that shows signs of being active. The narrator rejects his advice. * An earthquake disrupts the tunnel, and the narrator is fortunate to escape with his life. But while he lay unconscious for a time in the wreckage of his car, he had a visionary experience of the end of Atlantis, with fantastic architecture, a gigantic statue, etc. * *Miscellaneous:* The tunnels are operated by air pressure and suction, much like old-fashioned department store tubes. * Odd, to have the interesting material presented as throwaways.

575. **THE MAN FROM SPACE.** *Amazing Stories*,
February 1930. Ill. Wesso.
Short story. * The narrator, Bob, a college student, is in Professor Kepling's observatory when the man from space manifests himself. Before the man appeared, the topic of Kepling's lecture and subsequent conversation was novas, their historical observation, their sudden appearance, and their unpredictability. * When the man appears, he is roughly humanoid in build, but apparently composed of a light, shining substance much different from our flesh. He shanghais Bob, his friend Jim, and Kepling aboard a remarkable glass-like spaceship, which moves away from Earth at fantastic speed. The alien makes no real attempt to communicate with the Earthmen, but as they look back at the sun, they see that it has gone nova. The Earth has been destroyed. * The three men and the alien fly through space until they reach the triple star system of Almack, on a planet of which the space being lands. The planet is almost barren, but as the three move about they see horrible, mountainous forms of life—one of which is responsible for the deaths of Jim, Kepling, and the alien. Bob is now alone on the strange planet, the last Earthman. Even if he can learn to operate the starship, he has no fate but to wander alone through the universe. * But then he awakens. It was all a dream. He has simply slept through one of Professor Kepling's lectures. * The author appends a note: If the story is somewhat inconsistent, so are dreams.

576. **THE CITY ON THE CLOUD.** *Wonder Stories*,
October 1930. Ill. Marchioni.
Short-short story. * Essentially a dialogue between a semiliterate old prospector and a college professor of physics. The prospector, in a folksy dialect, asks for general information about mirages, which the professor-narrator supplies. The cap comes when the prospector, wondering whether mirages may originate in other worlds, describes briefly and vaguely a mirage city with an alien form of life. The description is so imprecise, however, that a reader cannot tell much from it. * Flat.

577. **THE PRINCE OF LIARS.** *Amazing Stories*,
October 1930. Ill. Paul.
(Reprinted in Ackerman, *Gosh! Wow!*)
Short story. * *Time and place:* New York, the ancient Aegean and Near East around the sixth century B.C., and a planet of Sirius. * The narrator of the fairly elaborate frame situation states as his salvo that he became converted from a confirmed

Hansen, L. Taylor (*continued*)
Newtonian to a confirmed Einsteinian (relativist) because of his association with Dr. Smead. Smead, who is a colorful character, has a reputation as a teller of tall tales, but the narrator has accepted him as truthful. * After a casual acquaintance Smead takes a fancy to the narrator and tells him a very romantic life history, which is easily recognizable as Smead's. * The intelligent young Greek Gnostes, a pupil of Pythagoras's, was shanghaied as a galley slave and held in captivity for several years. Off the coast of an unnamed country (which the reader will recognize as Egypt), he manages to jump ship. Hotly pursued by his master and his friends, Gnostes takes refuge in a temple, where Thora, a beautiful young woman, hides him inside a gigantic idol and befriends him. Presumably they become lovers. Prah, the jealous high priest, has learned of Gnostes's presence and is determined to kill both him and Thora. * When the natives, led by the priests, attack, Thora explains matters. She is not a native Egyptian, but, although Terrestrial, is an observer for the men of Allos, who are due to arrive at any moment to relieve her of her post. * It is questionable whether Gnostes and she can hold off their attackers until the men of Allos arrive. Thora gains some time by using the brilliant eyes of the idol as a disintegrator, but the mob manages to creep around behind them. Just as Prah is about to kill Gnostes, the men of Allos arrive and, at Thora's cry, flash their disintegrators. Prah is killed and the Egyptians repelled, but, unfortunately, Thora dies in the melee. The men from Allos take the wounded Gnostes on board what is obviously a spaceship, away into interstellar space. * As Gnostes recovers, he learns that the men of Allos are not really human (for atmospheric and gravitational differences they wear spacesuits when they are in his quarters) but seem to be highly evolved insects. They are, however, kindly and benevolent. * On their home planet, which is later revealed to be in the solar system of Sirius, Gnostes matures, studies, and is trained to be an observer, just as Thora had been. Throughout his stay on the Sirian planet he is driven by a desire for revenge on Prah, whom he blames for Thora's death; for one reason or another, which the author does not explain, he cannot accept that Prah was disintegrated along with her. * On returning to Earth to serve as observer, however, he discovers that hundreds of years have passed. * His story finished, Smead hints that his term on Earth is ending and requests the narrator to hold and bequeath suitably two remarkable paintings: one of the young Gnostes, recognizable as Smead, and the other of Thora. * When the narrator questions the time gaps, Smead explains it in terms of relativity. * Some good touches, but too long.

HANSTEIN, OTFRID VON (1869-1959)
German writer, born in Bonn. Very productive author, with over 150 books, mostly historical and geographical fiction, the latter based on extensive travel. His science-fiction books were generally popular, although eventually banned and suppressed by the Nazis. His work was known in English only through the translations published by Hugo Gernsback, presented here in order of original German publication.

   578. **THE HIDDEN COLONY.** *Wonder Stories*, January-March 1935. Translated from German by Fletcher Pratt. Ill. Paul.
(*Die Farm der Verschollenen*, 1924.) The story is covered in more detail in *Science-Fiction: The Early Years*. * Novel. *

Time: mostly 1919. *Place:* Yucatán. * The wonders and perils of automation as emerging from the work of the great inventor Wenzel Aporius. Aporius, who disappeared in 1914 en route to Mexico, where he was to set up an enormous mechanized farm, has generally been considered a war casualty. But as the 1919 narrator and Aporius's daughter discover, Aporius reached land and established his project in Yucatán. Inherent in the scheme is the contemporary concept that wasteland, particularly jungle, must be ravaged into cultivation, a concept that today is less highly regarded. * The narrator and Fräulein Aporius discover the gigantic farm grinding away by itself in remorseless automatic pseudo-life, as a symbol of both perfectibility and destruction. The colonists have died, left, or collapsed mentally and morally. Aporius himself barely survives, insane, when the 1919 explorers find him. * There are prefigurations of the *Metropolis* mentality, as the mad Aporius conceives of Mexico, completely planiformed, controlled by the president at an enormous switchboard. * The frame situation is confusing and the characterizations are weak, but the elevation of technology and the symbolism are fascinating. Although Aporius's world is usually taken as the glorification of mechanism and control, a closer reading reveals considerable ambivalence in Hanstein's vision. However, stodgy in writing and presentation.

   579. **UTOPIA ISLAND.** *Wonder Stories*, May-June 1931. Translated from German by Francis Currier. Ill. Paul. (Possibly a translation of *Ein Flug um die Welt und die Insel der Seltsamen Dingen*, 1927. Jordan, however, denies this, and there is no suggestion for another German-language original. Since the work is of non-pulp origin, it is described in considerable more detail in *Science-Fiction: The Early Years*.)
Novel. * *Place:* the (imaginary) Iguana Islands off the coast of Peru. * Against a background of mysterious brain-drain of noted scientists to unknown destinations, the point of the story is the establishment and functioning of a futuristic ultrascientific city. For this much the story is a Ralphism. * Utopia Island, funded by the treasure of the Incas, which was discovered on the island, is the home of the dream technology of the 1920s: art-deco buildings made of rustproof metal and glass, moving sidewalks, developed automobiles and combination vehicles, 1,000 MPH rocket planes, transportation tubes and rapid transit between the islands of the archipelago, automation everywhere, machines that read printed matter, and others that print oral material. Great medical advances have been made, including organ transplants from banks. Weather control has also been perfected. * The plot line consists mostly of an attempt by outlaws from a South American country to seize the island for its wealth; this culminates during an international sports festival of partially mechanized events. * *Miscellaneous:* Proprietors Ben Cook and Bob White intend to use the island as a center for advanced research and world peace. * A little German nationalism is involved, but this is of the traditional sort. * Interesting as a Ralphism, with more material than is indicated above displaying the possible wonders of technology.

   580. **BETWEEN EARTH AND MOON.** *Wonder Stories Quarterly*, Fall 1930. Translated from German by Francis Currier. Ill. Paul.
(*Mond-Rak 1. Eine Fahrt ins Weltall*, 1928.) Since the story originates outside our parameters, it is described in more detail in *Science-Fiction: The Early Years*.
Novel. * *Time:* probably the near future. *Place:* an artificial

Hanstein, Otfrid von (*continued*)

island off the coast of California; in space; and on the Moon. *
The first space voyage, in large part an accident. * The great
engineer Waldemar Apel is building a spaceship on the artificial
island New Atlantis, about a hundred miles west of San Francisco. The ship is not quite ready for takeoff, but newspaper
reporters manage to evade security and board the craft. When
they meddle with the controls, the ship blasts off, bearing with
it two of the reporters, Al Right (an American) and Kurt Korus
(a German), along with engineer-pilot Egon Helmstaetter, who
rushed onboard when he saw that something was wrong. * Helmstaetter had originally planned only a stratosphere flight to
Madagascar, but the spaceship heads into outer space, fortunately
toward the Moon. * The voyage is uneventful, and the three men
comport themselves amicably, even though they know that there
is no possibility of returning to Earth, since they used all the fuel
in the blasting takeoff. * The Moon, which they reach safely, is
realistic, airless and inhospitable. Fortunately for the involuntary
voyagers, however, they find frozen oxygen and hydrogen. Since
their fuel is oxyhydrogen, it is now possible for them to return
to Earth, although landing will be risky, since the ship is
damaged. Actually, the ship is almost a total wreck by the time
they reach Earth, and there is no possibility of landing. * The
explorers fall into orbit high above Earth; using a small rocket,
they make a smoke signal, which is seen back on Earth. * Meanwhile, Apel has been building a second rocket. When he sees
the signal, he takes the second rocket up, matches its orbit to the
first, ropes it, and rescues the three men, who are at the point of
death. * As a miscellaneous fantastic note: Hanstein ties his
voyage to H. G. Wells's *The First Men in the Moon.* Korus
dreams that he is captured by lunar men, who are small, bulbous-
headed, and prehensile limbed. When he tells Egon, Egon comments on Wells's novel. * The development is fairly realistic,
based on German rocket research of the time, but not as valid as
Gail's comparable work. * On the dull side, although in context,
back in 1928, it was probably more exciting.

581. **ELECTROPOLIS.** *Wonder Stories Quarterly,*
Summer 1930. Translated from German by Francis Currier. Ill.
Paul.

(*Elektropolis. Die Stadt der technischen Wunder*, 1928.) Because of its non-pulp origin, the story is covered in more detail
in *Science-Fiction: The Early Years.*

Novel. * The wonders of mechanization, muted post-World War
revanchism, and neocolonialism. * *Place:* introduction and
ending in Berlin, Germany, otherwise in Central Australia. *
Fritz, unemployed and without prospects in post-World War I
Germany, is astonished to find a remarkable, if mysterious, job
almost tossed in his lap. He is to follow instructions precisely
and be transported to Australia, where he will receive further
communications. Dropped off near a shack in the desert, he is
astonished to discover that the shack is really the entrance to an
enormous cave filled with scientific and engineering marvels.
And Mr. Schmidt, the master or owner of this remarkable
establishment, is Fritz's long-lost uncle who is taking this
opportunity both to help him and enlist him in a great enterprise.
* Schmidt's history: As a young man he was a pupil of the
celebrated Wenzel Aporius (cf. #578, Hanstein's "The Hidden
Colony"), the great master and innovator of automated engineering and development. Schmidt followed a varied career,
working his way around the world at odd jobs. While pros-

pecting in Australia, however, he found a remarkable deposit of
pitchblende (explained later as a meteorite), which he worked,
with a project in mind. With money from the radium he extracted, he first purchased the mine area from the Australian
government, then later an enormous extent of desert. His plan
is to apply the techniques of Aporius to develop this desert into
a wonder garden to be populated by immigrants from Germany.
He has incredible generators, agricultural machinery, rain
makers, and much else. * Fritz enthusiastically joins Schmidt in
the development of Electropolis. * There are two crises. The
Australian government, when it sees what Schmidt is accomplishing, reneges on its treaty and attacks the establishment. An
electrical field that explodes ammunition and knocks down
airplanes protects the colony, and after a time the Australians
desist, from here on simply denying the existence of the Schmidt
establishment to the outside world. A second crisis comes when
disgruntled employees try to seize Electropolis; they perish in the
attempt, but drive the radium-bearing meteorite out into space.
* After about five years, Schmidt dies, transferring authority to
Fritz. Electropolis is finished and ready for immigrants. *
Miscellaneous: Schmidt also has an apparatus that permits
thought-reading to some extent. It consists of metallic clothing
and special detectors of body electricity. * Today, Aporius and
Schmidt's concept of "reclaiming" desert or waste land is rejected, but in the 1920s it was a prevalent belief and practice.
The nationalism involved in the story is also less palatable today
than it was when the novel was written. * As reading, competent
work, but with no special appeal. Even so, certainly superior to
most of the other longer works in pulp science-fiction of the day.

582. **IN THE YEAR 8000.** *Wonder Stories,* July-August
1932. Ill. Paul. Translated from German by Konrad Schmidt
and Laurence Manning.

According to the story blurb, "In the Year 8000" was written
specially for *Wonder Stories.* Whether this is correct is not
known; in any case, a German or German-language publication
has not turned up. It is quite possible that Hanstein was unable
to find a German publisher for the novel and turned it over to
Gernsback. The story is described in more detail in *Science-
Fiction: The Early Years.*

Short novel. * *Time:* A.D. 8002. *Place:* Germany, the Moon,
and elsewhere. * The future world is one of high science and
automation. The Moon has been colonized and developed for
radium mining; there are thought machines of various types; and
an earth tube is under construction. Food production is based on
the enormous completely automated farms that Hanstein has
favored elsewhere. * Politically, there have been great changes.
The world is divided into three empires; the Blancos, or Europe,
Australia, and America; the Flavos or Yellows, Asia; and the
Nigros, Africa. All speak Esperanto, but relations among them
are hostile. The Orientals and Africans are ruled by despotic
emperors, while the whites have a democratic government. *
Socially, the culture is slanted toward scientism and rationality,
a trend which some deplore. There is an underground movement
that urges a return to nature and emotion. Birth control is rigidly
practiced, and to maintain the population level a sizeable proportion of the women is desexualized and turned into neuters.
This is done on a voluntary basis. The fertile females are kept
as group mothers in what amount to harems. * The story line is
concerned with three elements: (1) Frequent, very destructive
meteorite storms. The major cities have ray shields against the

Hanstein, Otfrid von (*continued*)

meteorites. (2) An African fifth columnist in Berlin. He will turn off the ray shield during the next meteorite bombardment, so that Berlin will be destroyed. At the same time the Yellows and Blacks will invade Europe. (3) The love life of Bela Wilson. She has read too many ancient romances. She is torn between two men, the cold engineer in charge of the earth tube project, who cares little for her, and an emotional young man who loves her deeply. * Things go off. The meteorite swarm does less damage to Berlin than expected. The invaders are defeated. The earth tube explodes. And both young men are badly wounded; out of the two men, advanced surgery makes one man who is suitable for Bela. Together they abandon the mechanistic civilization and go to live on one of the communal farms. * Much less pleasant than the other Hanstein stories, with some elements of early racism. Also too much resonance from Harbou's *Metropolis*.

HAPPEL, R. V.

U.S. author probably to be identified with Richard V. Happel (1903-1988), then resident in Pittsfield, Massachusetts, later in Jamestown, New York, per letters in May 1927 issue of *Amazing Stories* and the *New York Times*, 20 August 1935. Moskowitz in *The Immortal Storm* mentions a Dick Happel who was an assistant to John W. Campbell, Jr., on *Astounding Stories*. This seems to be a confusion with Carl Happel, who was the editor of various Clayton magazines (*All Star DetectiveStories, Clues)* and later worked for Street and Smith. It is not known whether the two men were related.

583. **THE TRIPLE RAY.** *Amazing Stories Quarterly*, Fall 1930.

Short story. * Professor Lucius Raymond is the inventor of of two rays, the Twin Ray and the Triple Ray. The famed Twin Ray, a combination of ultraviolet and infrared, amounts to a disintegrator. Its source is an adapted Crookes' tube, with an unmentioned radioactive substance. A demonstration of this ray to the Germans leads to their retreat from Paris. (While the author is not clear, this seems to refer to a second world war.) The ray, in addition to being the prize weapon in the American arsenal, has extensive peaceful uses. * The Triple Ray, which destroys atoms, has been discovered almost by accident. On the single occasion that it is used, it drills a hole through a hill. More, it continues on and slices the top off a nearby mountain. Then it leaves the solar system and disrupts several stars. And it continues, moving faster than light. Since the universe is finite and space is curved, the ray will continue on around the universe, spreading, and return to disintegrate Earth. It will eventually devour the whole universe. * A good idea, but clumsily handled.

HARBERS, HENRY

No information. Portrait published with story shows a middle-aged man. The author is probably not Henry Carl Harbers (1911-1976), noted engineer, inventor, and manufacturer of moving systems.

584. **THE LOST MARTIAN.** *Science Wonder Stories*, December 1929. Ill. Paul.

Short story. * *Place:* Mars, South America, and elsewhere. * On Mars there is a feeling of loss and mourning because of the presumed death of the great scientist Ruthen. Some time earlier,

Ruthen, who was engaged to the Princess Argene, had constructed a spaceship powered by antigravity and left on a trial run. His ship went out of control, however, and since nothing has been heard, he probably died by crashing onto Earth. * Actually, as the story now follows Ruthen's adventures, he survives the crash, but his ship is inoperable. He has landed in a tropical region, where he makes the acquaintance of a missionary who teaches him English. For a long time Ruthen seems to be suffering from shock, but he gradually begins to repair his ship for a return to Mars. One metal, unfortunately, does not seem to occur on Earth. * Taking gold (which is of no great value on Mars) from the fittings of his ship, he leaves the jungle and goes to England, where he poses as an Indian student. Here, after considerable chemical work, he obtains the substance he needs, but when he returns to the Amazon, he finds that his friend the missionary is dead and that the Indians have wrecked his ship. Return is now impossible. * On Mars, however, a new development has taken place. A means has been discovered to project nervous energy, including thought waves, beyond the body. Such thought waves are projected to Earth, where a medium picks them up, and eventually Ruthen is enabled to contact his friends on Mars. * The problem now facing the Martians is whether they should retrieve Ruthen quietly or whether they should reveal themselves to the natives of Earth. The story ends on this note. * *Miscellaneous:* Ruthen's original disaster was not accident, but sabotage on the part of a treacherous friend who was in love with the Princess Argene. * Martians must be completely human in appearance, perhaps dark Mediterraneans. * A dreary, dull story, presented as bare narrative.

HARRIS, CLARE WINGER (1891-1969)

U.S. (Lakewood, Ohio) author. Occasional contributor to the fantastic pulps. Also wrote book *Persephone of Eleusis* (1923). Not a significant writer, but a pioneer woman contributor who had many original ideas. Her first known story, "A Runaway World" (*Weird Tales*, July 1926) may be the first story to deal with the Earth as a runaway electron in a macrocosm. Her fiction has been collected in *Away from the Here and Now*, one of the earliest collections of a s-f genre writer.

585. **THE FATE OF THE POSEIDONIA.** *Amazing Stories*, June 1927. Ill. Paul.

(Reprinted in Harris, *Away from the Here and Now*.)

Short story. * The third-prize-winning story of the contest based on the cover of the December 1926 issue of *Amazing Stories*. Mrs. Harris won $100. * *Time:* Chronology is confusing, but the heart of the story seems to take place in 1945. * The narrator has a strong antipathy toward Martell, the copper-skinned, large-chested man who always wears a skullcap. This antipathy arose when the men first met and grew when Martell became his neighbor, especially since Martell seems to be too friendly with the narrator's girlfriend Margaret. * In the outside world, ships and planes are mysteriously disappearing, and the ocean levels are receding a little. The narrator, who unabashedly spies on Martell through the keyhole, breaks into his apartment and examines a strange machine there. It amounts to a live television viewer, showing several scenes around the world with men like Mar-tell—but with feathers growing from their heads. * By now the narrator realizes what is happening: Martell and his likes are Martians, and they are stealing the Earth's water. And the great liner *Poseidonia*, on which Margaret is traveling, has disap-

Harris, Clare Winger (*continued*)

peared, seized and taken to Mars. The final image on Martell's machine shows Martell and Margaret on Mars. Margaret says that she loves the narrator, and that the Martians now have enough water and will conduct no more raids on Earth's resources. * Although Margaret says nothing about it, nudity seems permissible on Mars. * Pretty bad.

586. **THE MIRACLE OF THE LILY**. *Amazing Stories*, April 1928. Unsigned ill.

(Reprinted in Harris, *Away from the Here and Now.*)

Short story. * *Time:* from the near future to A.D. 2928 and 3928. The story is told in memoirs or comments from persons in one lineage, as assembled by Nathano in 3928. The general theme is regeneration, good and bad. * The battle among vegetation, insects, and man ended at about A.D. 2900, by which time the insects had eaten up all the vegetation on Earth. The insects then turned upon one another, in a relatively few years becoming practically extinct. The last insect, a foot-long beetle, was kept in gentle captivity and regarded with what amounts to sentimental affection. * With the loss of the vegetable world, man now turns to synthetics and practices thorough conservation, even to recycling the human dead. Civilization survives. * In the year 3928 Nathano, who tells a little about his future world, finds a fairly large box filled with small pellet-like objects. At first he cannot identify them, but after a time he recognizes that they must be seeds, the like of which no one in his time has seen. Planted, they sprout, and a new world begins. But along with them reappears the beetle. * *Miscellaneous:* At about this time, radio communication has been established with Venus. The Venusians ask for help, since they are fighting a losing battle with the native insects. But when television contact is established, the Venusian broadcast reveals that the intelligent race consists of giant beetles, while the "insects" are tiny humanoids. This image dampens Terrestrial enthusiasm for helping the Venusians. * Mars is also inhabited by intelligent beings, with whom the Venusians are in communication. * In the hands of a more skilled author, this could have been a touching story.

587. **THE MENACE OF MARS**. *Amazing Stories*, October 1928. Ill. Paul.

(Reprinted in Harris, *Away from the Here and Now.*)

Short story. * *Time:* 1958. * Hildreth, an assistant in the astronomy department at the university, tells of the great disaster. A powerful earthquake, a resulting flood, and phenomenally hot temperatures cause thousands of deaths. The sun becomes enormous in the sky, and gravity decreases to about half its usual power. The coasts are flooded, the heat increases, and millions die. Human life is possible only at the poles, and the settlement of Polaria is founded on island rafts at the north pole. * What is happening? What is the cause of all this? The general explanation is that the universe as a whole has undergone a change; whereas it was formerly comparable to a gas with planets equivalent to electrons, it has suddenly become a liquid, with motions and distances decreased. * Worse is to come. The Earth's orbit changes erratically. Professor Hildreth attributes the new changes to the planet Mars, which is a living entity of great intelligence and power. While Mars has protected itself to some extent from the increased solar radiation caused by the changes in the universe, it has altered the Earth's orbit by power rays, so that Earth will perpetually serve as a sun shield. * Mars

also begins to colonize the other planets with its substance, a red crystalline matter that dissolves just about anything. This has appeared on Earth as small, floating balloon-like objects. * The Martian red belt on Earth expands, but fortunately it is vulnerable to water. When the universe finally stabilizes, torrential storms weaken the Martian substance so that it is no longer a real menace. The final restabilization also changes Earth's orbit to a more favorable one, without the Martian menace. * Much imagination.

588. **THE FIFTH DIMENSION**. *Amazing Stories*, December 1928. Ill. COS (?).

(Reprinted in Harris, *Away from the Here and Now.*)

Short story. * Ellen, the wife of a business man, occasionally has presentiments of catastrophes to come. A striking example concerned Mrs. Maxwell. Ellen had forebodings when she saw Mrs. Maxwell enter her garage . . . Mrs. Maxwell was killed by an explosion. In each case Ellen feels that this is something that has happened before. * Now she has a presentiment that the train on which her husband John is about to travel will have a major accident. She persuades John to take another train. Her presentiment is correct; there is a disaster on the line. * The theory behind these events is not extrasensory perception or supernaturalism, but, as explained by John, is a matter of time cycles which repeat in the universe, in each case with slight change. * The background, not mentioned, is J. W. Dunne's book on serial universes, *An Experiment with Time*. * In his editorial in this issue of *Amazing Stories*, Gernsback speculates on such cases of precognition. His explanation is that physical fragments of dead brains may eventually become part of living brains, and that under certain circumstances their memory may be awakened.

589. **THE EVOLUTIONARY MONSTROSITY**. *Amazing Stories Quarterly*, Winter 1929. Ill. Paul.

(Reprinted in Harris, *Away from the Here and Now.*)

Short story. * Caldwell, who has lost touch with his brilliant college chums Marston and Staley, receives an unexpected invitation to visit them. As he remembers it, Ted Marston, in their college arguments, used to theorize that evolution is caused by bacterial agents, while he, Caldwell, in such discussions, used to stress the modifying factor of environment. * Shortly after he arrives at Marston's establishment, Caldwell is summoned to the laboratory by a talking cat that walks on its hind legs; the animal horrifies him. Staley, who works with Marston, now informs Caldwell that he and Marston have indeed isolated the bacterium of evolution—witness the cat Cutey—and Marston is now using it on himself. Staley does not altogether approve of Marston's course of action, but yields. The visit goes pleasantly enough. * Two years pass. Caldwell is summoned again to Marston's place, but on this occasion by Staley's sister Dorothy, who is becoming frightened at the turn of events. Caldwell had previously thought Dorothy an inane ninny, but when he meets her, he realizes that she has become his ideal woman. The explanation: Marston has been giving her occasional evolutionary shots, fortunately not too many. * Marston, on the other hand, has taken maximal doses and has reached the ultimate of human evolution unconditioned by environment. He has turned into a creature like a giant spider, is telepathic, and can control the will of others. He declares that he has also acquired seven new senses. And he plans to rule the human race. * There is no stopping him, seemingly, but one of his experimental subjects coshes him while Caldwell distracts him. * A fair amount of

Harris, Clare Winger (*continued*)
religious claptrap is also included.

590. **THE DIABOLICAL DRUG**. *Amazing Stories*, May 1929. Unsigned ill.

(Reprinted in Harris, *Away from the Here and Now*.)

Short story. * Young biologist Edgar Hamilton would like to marry Ellen Gordan, but there is (for her, at any rate) an unsurmountable obstacle: She is several years older than he. * Hamilton believes that he has a solution to the problem. He has produced a chemical injection that reduces the electric resistance in nerve tissue so that metabolism is retarded. He hopes that by injecting this into Ellen, her life processes will be slowed enough that he can catch up with her in physiological age. * Theoretically possible, but actually, Ellen slows down so enormously that she is like a statue. In despair, Hamilton prepares an antidote, a speeder-up, which he injects into himself. Again, a misfortune, for he speeds up so enormously that he breaks out of our universe up into the one above. * There he finds a pleasant world and a human people. He marries, has a son and grandson. But the land is about to sink into the sea. At the last moment he and his son and grandson take the slow potion and return to Earth. * Since he is now an old man, there is no question of his marrying Ellen, but he restores her to normalcy, and later his grandson marries her. * Difficult to follow and a little too amateurish for readability.

591. **THE ARTIFICIAL MAN**. *Science Wonder Quarterly*, Fall 1929. Ill. Paul.

(Reprinted in Harris, *Away from the Here and Now*.)

Short story. * Moralities. * Young George Gregory, college athlete and scholar, takes the position that physical perfection is the result of right thinking. When he loses a leg, he begins to question this position, asserting that his loss of a limb has been paralleled by psychological loss. Another accident costs him an arm, and shortly afterward, his fiancée, who can no longer tolerate his mental degeneration, cancels their engagement. By now Gregory has accepted the position that he has lost as much godliness as he has physique. * Gregory disappears for a time, then next appears, insane, in his successful rival's office, threatening to kill him. As George now demonstrates, he is a cyborg (my term), with artificial legs, one artificial arm, artificial heart and other internal organs. His nose, chin, and ears have also been removed. As he explains, he has deliberately cast off as much of his body as he could. His plans for murder, however, are disrupted by the police. As George lies dying, he expresses repentance. * Routine.

592. **THE APE CYCLE**. *Science Wonder Quarterly*, Spring 1930. Ill. Winter.

(Reprinted in Harris, *Away from the Here and Now*.)

Short story. * *Time:* the 1930s and 2216. *Place:* Northwestern Illinois in the earlier period; somewhere in the Southwest and elsewhere in the later. * In a way, parabolic about the American experience with black chattel slavery. * Daniel Stoddart and his young son Ray, traveling in the Orient and tropics, where they see the remarkable ability of trained monkeys to gather fruit, determine to alleviate the labor of mankind by breeding intelligent apes to take over scut work. Daniel sets up an establishment in which various monkeys and apes are trained, with remarkable success. While there are occasional foreshadowings of trouble, on the whole the work of the Stoddarts is successful. * By 2216 Stoddart's apes and monkeys, now

produced elsewhere, have become a necessary part of the world's economy. Ape workers run machines in factories, tend to housework, drive automobiles and other wheeled vehicles, serve as airplane pilots, etc. Naturally, this demands increased intelligence in the apes, many of whom even speak well. * As might be expected, the apes are dissatisfied with their lot, which amounts to slavery; as an added source of trouble, some of the apes desire human women for sexual purposes. (One ape-human hybrid takes an important part when things start to collapse.) The apes organize, concealing their program from their human masters under the guise of labor relations, gather weapons, and set a day for their rebellion. The rebellion is quite successful, and in a very short time apes control the world and start to force humans into slavery. * The present Stoddart resolves matters, after considerable turmoil, by disguising himself as an ape (flaying a dead ape leader and wearing his skin), and bombing the ape leadership. Humanity has control again. * *Miscellaneous:* The author does not indicate exactly how the Stoddarts developed their ape and monkey stocks into reasoning beings. * In the hands of a more skilled author who would not be afraid to carry the story to a logical conclusion, this might have been a powerful story. As it is now, amateurish, silly, and disappointing.

HARRIS, CLARE WINGER and BREUER, MILES J., M.D.
For biographical information see the separate entries for the authors.

593. **A BABY ON NEPTUNE**. *Amazing Stories*, December 1929. Ill. Wesso.

(Reprinted in Harris, *Away from the Here and Now*; in Wollheim, *Flight into Space*; and in Ackerman, *Gosh! Wow!*)

Short story. * *Time:* A.D. 2345. *Place:* Neptune in part. * *Background:* In 1967 controlled radio beaming was perfected, leading to the recognition of interplanetary signals some two years later. These signals were long unintelligible, but in 2099 a theoretical basis was established, and by 2300 it was possible to communicate with Mars, Venus, four of Jupiter's moons and one of Saturn's. Neptune, however, is problematic, for while signals seem to be emanating from it, they are unintelligible. * Interplanetary travel, too, is now possible. In 2345, a team visited Venus, which was found to be tropical in geography, inhabited by highly intelligent slimy, writhing worms. * The first breakthrough in analyzing the Neptunian signals comes when it is recognized that they have to be speeded up enormously, compressing a Neptunian broadcast of several days into a couple of minutes. Translated, beyond greetings, the message contains an invitation to visit. * In 2347 the geodesic-hurdling spaceship *Neptunian* leaves, flying at about a tenth the speed of light. It reaches Neptune, but there is no sign of the forests and beautiful landscape the Neptunian Elzar described—nothing but bare rock. The expedition returns, discouraged. Elzar, in a communication to Earth, cannot understand why the Terrestrials did not visit him. * Another breakthrough: Elzar's culture and milieu is gaseous and can be seen with proper equipment, as a second expedition discovers. To fulfill the promise of the story title, the members of the second expedition save Elzar's child from a gaseous monster.

HARRIS, HUGH KING
No information.

Harris, Hugh King (*continued*)

594. **THE DIMENSION TWISTER.** *Wonder Stories*, April 1933.

Short-short story. * Kent Forbs, noted scientist, and Stan Wycks, famous crime investigator, look into a series of murders in which a Maltese cross is stamped into the breast of the victim. Forbs, knowing of a window on which a similar cross is traced, enters and overhears Ungar, a German scientist (of sorts), browbeating one Quayle, who has consulted Ungar about removing his cowardice. Ungar rants and raves about atoms, the fourth dimension, previous incarnations that are causing mental problems, all the while strapping Quayle into an electric chair. Forbs and Wycks break in and save Quayle. No science is involved, although the editors call the story a scientific detective story. * So bad that it might be considered a parody, but probably meant seriously.

HARRIS, JOHN WYNDHAM PARKES LUCAS BEYNON (1903-1969)

British author, wrote under various combinations of his many names, of which John Wyndham was the most significant. As Wyndham wrote *The Day of the Triffids* (1951) and *The Midwich Cuckoos* (1957), both of which were turned into motion pictures, the latter as *The Village of the Damned*. Harris's earlier work conforms more or less to better American pulp standards, though usually with an individual touch (a tolerance and quietism perhaps derived from Harris's Quaker background), but post-war work tends more toward mainstream analysis of British middle-class societal reactions to strange events. A smooth, skilled writer. During the decade or two following the magazines in this study Harris also wrote under the pseud. John Beynon.

595. **WORLDS TO BARTER.** *Wonder Stories*, May 1931. Ill. Marchioni.

Short story. * *Time:* 1935 and 2134. * In the laboratory of the great inventor Lestrange there suddenly appears an odd-looking machine, out of which tumbles a stranger. The stranger asks for a piece of string and does something to the controls of the machine, which then disappears. * Explanation: The stranger is Jon Lestrange, a remote descendant of Lestrange's, from the twenty-second century. His story: In his own time the wreckage of a time machine was found, and in it the body of a very strange man: enormous head, small body, club feet, different internal organs, and so on. The science of Jon's day could not explain it. * Sometime later a telepathic broadcast simulating radio was heard around the world. Its purport: Men from the five thousand and twenty-second century plan to take over the world. They claim to be peaceful and say that they do not wish to harm anyone, but they will not accept refusal and urge immediate preparation for mass deportations to the future. In their own time, the sun is cooling and the Earth will not be habitable long. For them, with their life spans of thousands of years, this is a problem, but, as they placidly state, it should matter less to the men of the twenty-second century, who have short lives. The far-future men will leave their incredible plant in operation for the twenty-second century men, who will be able to live in comfort. * The men of Jon's time find the declaration impossible to accept, whereupon the far-future men, still proclaiming their distaste for violence, first shut off the world's electricity as a warning, then drive the twenty-second century men into transports by will-control. There is no possibility of

resistance. * During the confusion Jon and his wife (who arrives in 1935 a little later) manage to steal time machines and take refuge in our time. They hope that if they return their machines rapidly enough, whence the business with the string, the far future men will not bother them. * *Miscellaneous:* Lestrange of our time will have invented a battery that will be the basis for future civilization and will outmode all other power sources. * The far-future dwarves have a base in the Sahara, to which they take a human delegation and show them the world of the far future, with a dying sun. * Competent work.

596. **THE LOST MACHINE.** *Amazing Stories*, April 1932. Ill. Morey.

(Reprinted as by Harris in Ross, *The Best of Amazing*. Reprinted as by John Wyndham in Wyndham, *The Best of John Wyndham*, and in Wyndham, *The Man from Beyond*. Also reprinted in Moskowitz, *The Coming of the Robots*.)

Short story. * It seems best to follow chronological sequence rather than narrative order, which involves a frame and an extensive, somewhat confusing flashback. * The spaceship from Mars lands in England, with its occupants marveling at the green landscape, instead of omnipresent Martian red. Since it may be perilous for Banuff, the organic Martian, to leave the vessel, his machine companion Zat disembarks for a brief exploration. At that moment the space vessel explodes, and Zat is alone on Earth. * On his first confrontation with humans Zat, who can perceive human thoughts, but cannot communicate, discovers to his surprise that he is feared. Indeed, one human shoots at him. * Zat leaves hurriedly and wanders over the British countryside, trying to comprehend the marks of civilization, railroad tracks, houses, etc., all of which are alien to him. * Humans are all terrified of him, except a single very drunken laborer who seems to accept him as a sort of pet. But when the laborer sobers up, he has a different idea: he tries to sell Zat to a circus. This backfires when the circus owner insists on inspecting Zat's internal mechanisms. * Zat finally comes into contact with a doctor and his daughter, whom he recognizes as more civilized people. But Zat, depressed and discouraged, recognizes that it will be long before intelligent machines can be devised, and that Earth is not ready for him. He commits suicide, turning himself into a puddle of liquid, but leaving a written statement for the doctor. As the story begins, the doctor and his daughter discover the metal puddle that had been Zat and speculate what had happened. * *Miscellaneous:* Banuff, Zat's companion, was human. * Interesting, but the later Harris could have handled it better.

597. **THE VENUS ADVENTURE.** *Wonder Stories*, May 1932. Ill. Paul.

(Reprinted in Wyndham, *Exiles on Asperus*, and in Norton and Moskowitz, *The Space Magicians*.)

Short story. * *Time:* A.D. 2134 and 2922. *Place:* mostly on Venus. * The prologue, set in the first half of the twenty-second century, describes the career of Joseph Watson, later known as Noah Watson. A Fundamentalist evangelist, he is in rebellion against the liberal mores of the day, especially against the system of artificial birth, which has replaced natural childbirth. * Watson, who becomes convinced that the Day of Judgment is at hand, makes many fanatical converts, including the extremely wealthy Chicago aircraft manufacturer Headington. * Using Headington's wealth and technical resources, Watson builds a flying Ark. It is a subject of ridicule for most people, and aeronautic inspectors refuse to pass it for flight. * On the day in

Harris, John Beynon (*continued*)

2134 that Watson predicted the world would end, there chances to be a slight earthquake, at which Watson, Headington, and their followers dash into the Ark and take off into the heavens, no one knows where. At the time, it is assumed that they all died in space. Unfortunately, the scientific and engineering personnel who designed and built the Ark were on board when it left, and the secret of space travel has been lost. * In 2922 the great chemist Vida Newton, wife of Hal Newton (one of the foremost rocket pilots and designers) invents jonite, an explosive that is powerful enough to permit space travel. Building a spaceship, the couple and friends set out for Venus, which they reach without incident. On Venus they discover a totally unexpected situation: native Venusians who are somewhat humanoid and speak English, and two very hostile colonies of Earthmen descended from the "Arkers." It seems that after the Ark left, and the Earth was obviously not destroyed, Headington and the more intelligent people on the Ark were bitterly disillusioned about Watson's prophecies. They separated from his followers and eventually formed the group known as the Dingtons. They retain much of the science of the migration and have even progressed in some areas. The Wots, on the other hand, are fanatical followers of Noah Watson, whose ravings they regard as a sacred book. They are genetically much inferior to the Dingtons, whom they hate. A strong point of difference between the two races is that the Dingtons are friendly with the intelligent native Venusians, while the Wots, regarding the universe as given to them by their god, eat them. The Dingtons live in a modern city called Chicago, while the Wots live in a filthy town called Arrarat. It is obvious that the Wots are regressing toward savagery. * The expected adventures: the women of the expedition are captured by the Wots; several members of the expedition are killed, two by stoning; the air fleet of the Dingtons and a native Venusian army destroy Arrarat and begin a program of genocide against the Wots. * The Terrestrials, such as survive, return to Earth, while the Dingtons are now building a spaceship for a visit. * *Miscellaneous:* Venus is gray and overcast, but otherwise much like the Earth. Most of the horrendous fauna has been exterminated or brought under control by the Dingtons. * The prologue material is very well handled; the writing is nice, as is always the case with Harris, but the adventures on Venus are on the clichéd side.

598. EXILES ON ASPERUS. *Wonder Stories Quarterly*, Winter 1933. Ill. Paul.

(Reprinted in Moskowitz, *Three Stories*, as by John Beynon Harris, and in Wyndham, *Exiles on Asperus*.)

Novelette. * *Time:* 2077. *Place:* space and the fairly recently discovered asteroid Asperus. * *Background:* Mars, which has a long cultural history and is inhabited by a nearly human race, has been conquered/occupied by Earth, with considerable repression of the native peoples. As part of the occupational process, the Martians have been demonized in propaganda campaigns. * At this point a general Martian rebellion is in progress; the leader, the Martian Sen-Su, has just been captured by the Earthmen. * The *Argenta*, an Earth vessel currently serving as a prison ship, is en route to the asteroid Asperus, where it will maroon the recently captured members of the Martian revolt, including Sen-Su. * When a space fragment crashes through the ship's armor, killing almost all the prison guards, the Martians seize control of the vessel. Despite their image in propaganda, they prove to be

humane, genuinely sorry for the loss of lives involved. Roles now reversed, they will drop the Earthmen on Asperus and return to the rebellion. * As the Earthmen are being abandoned, however, their chief engineer, Angus, on whom most of the story centers, manages to drain most of the fuel from the *Argenta*, so that the Martians, too, are stranded. The Earthmen then make a break for it into the heavy undergrowth that covers the small world. * Two astonishing situations emerge: On the planetoid, surviving well enough, are the survivors of the missing Terrestrial *Red Glory*, which crashed there a generation ago. Although the *Red Glory* is too damaged to fly, its tanks still contain enough fuel to permit escape on the *Argenta*. The second surprise is that the planet is inhabited by a race of winged, humanoid people who live in cave complexes. Nocturnal in habit, they have been raiding the survivors of the *Red Glory*, carrying men and women away, never to be seen again. Indeed, the Batrachs (as Harris strangely calls them) have already seized some of the new castaways and the Martians. * Under the leadership of Angus, the survivors of the *Argenta* invade the Batrach caves to rescue the captives. They discover a situation very different from what they expected. First, they find the captured *Red Glory* people, who are held as slaves to work the mines, but there are no children or young people among them. Then they find the younger generation of humans, whom the Batrachs have separated from their parents and reared within Batrach culture. They act very strangely. * Since some of the Batrachs have learned English from their captives, Angus and the others can communicate with them. By threatening the Batrach Council with punitive expeditions using poison gas and advanced arms, Angus gains concessions. The Batrachs will conduct no more raids and will release those of their slaves who wish to leave. * It is only now that the Earthmen realize what has been going on. The second generation slaves refuse to leave. Explanation: The Batrachs, rather than being monsters, are somewhat pathetic beings. As intelligent as humans, their anatomy is such that they cannot handle tools or perform any but the simplest mechanical actions. "The Batrachs can think, but they cannot do." Therefore, they are using the captured humans to build a civilization; to retain the younger generation, they have systematically conditioned them to dread the "Outside," which has become a term of horror, and have reinforced this fear with a strong religion. Indeed, the second generation becomes quite hostile to Angus when he suggests that they move to Earth. * Having made peace among themselves, the Earthmen and Martians will return to Earth in the refueled *Argenta*. They do not like the situation on Asperus, but they realize that there is nothing they can do about it. As Harris says in his foreword, the whole matter is later tacitly ignored by the higher authorities. * *Miscellaneous:* Harris adopts the conditioning system Aldous Huxley used in *Brave New World*. * Sophisticated thought embodied in the action plot, with interesting discussions between the Batrach leader and Angus on the nature of freedom, or its illusion. * Some structural problems, but with a depth and general humaneness lacking in comparable American pulp fiction.

599. WANDERERS OF TIME. *Wonder Stories*, March 1933. Ill. Paul.

(Reprinted as by John Beynon in *Tales of Wonder*, Winter, 1941, and in book form as by John Wyndham by Coronet Books, London, 1973. Texts of the reprints have not been available to me. It is possible that some revision has taken place.)

Harris, John Beynon (*continued*)

Novelette. * *Time:* the far future, undated. * The basic situation is that there is a snag in the time stream, in which defective time travelers are likely to be caught. This snag deposits time machines into a certain, undated time in the far future. * In our century, scientist Roy Saber has constructed a time machine with which he has traveled ten years into the past, from 1951 to 1941, in order to collect his sweetheart Betty Mordan. There is no question of time paradoxes, for Saber hadn't previously met himself, and there is no reason why two versions of himself cannot simultaneously exist. * As Saber is about to take Betty back into the future, police, led by a meddling passerby whom Saber had thought he had disposed of, shoot at them. The time machine, somewhat damaged, materializes in the time snag, which is similar to contemporary Britain, except that there do not seem to be any native humans. There are, however, red machines and white machines that race madly about, fighting each other. * Also caught by the snag are other parties, the most important being Del Two-Forty-A, a little man from A.D. 10,402. Intelligent, resourceful, he is the leading spirit in the dangerous future. Others include a separate party of little men from A.D. 10424, a woman (Jessica Tree) from 2200, and two men from 3920. * After evading the machines for a time, the humans are captured by tentacled white machines and taken to a headquarters where they are interrogated by a gigantic machine that is obviously the controller of the city. It is possible to communicate with the machine in a limited way, since it seems to know past languages and writing systems. Also held by the white machines are empty, damaged time machines, which leads to the conclusion that many others, who did not survive, were similarly caught in the snag. * Personalities enter the story. Betty, a shallow, rather stupid young woman, is attracted to Hale, one of the men from 3920, and Roy, disgusted with her, establishes a speedy romance with Jessica. A crisis comes when Hale and Betty steal Del Two-Forty-A's repaired machine and leave, after a shoot-out. * One of the results of the violence is that a carelessly aimed disintegration ray accidentally cuts open the gigantic white master machine. From it pour hordes of ants, who are aggressively hostile. * The remaining time castaways have to fight off attacks by white machines until another of the time machines is repaired and they can leave. They are eventually successful, despite cliffhangers. Roy goes to the twenty-third century with Jessica, and the others to their own times. * *Miscellaneous:* The men from the 105th century have very potent little disintegrator tubes. Physically, they are much like present-day men, although their heads are slightly larger and they are about four feet high. They are obviously more intelligent than the earlier travelers. * Harris deliberately leaves the red machines, so hostile to the white, a mystery. It is a reasonable guess that they contain red ants. * An amusing story.

600. **THE THIRD VIBRATOR.** *Wonder Stories*, May 1933. Ill. Paul.

Short story. * *Time and place:* modern England and two periods in the remote past. * Diana visits her fiancé, Hixton, who is currently in a mental institution. He had tried to destroy his lifetime work, a death ray or disintegrator ray that had been accepted by the government as a weapon to prevent future wars. * Hixton tells Diana his story: As he was listening to a congratulatory speech by a politician, he suddenly felt a falling sensation, and found himself in Lemuria, where vibrators like his

have been used to destroy invaders, also thereby creating enormous deserts. A new type of vibrator is about to be tested. It destroys Lemuria. * Hixton next finds himself in Atlantis, perhaps millennia later. Lemuria is now only a myth. Xtan (Hixton) reinvents the vibrator and plans to use it, despite the pleas of the aged priest Zacta, who recognizes its dangers. When Zacta forbids its use, Xtan murders him. Attacked by angry mobs he defends himself with the vibrator and destroys Atlantis. * Acting on these minatory memories, Hixton tried to destroy his invention. As he now learns, he was successful. The secret is lost. * Routine.

601. **SPHERES OF HELL.** *Wonder Stories*, October 1933. Ill. Paul.

Short story, told with the bourgeois, middle-class ambience that was so effective in Harris's later *The Midwich Cuckoos* and *The Day of the Triffids*. * The imaginary land of Ghangistan, Devon, and Cornwall. * In a prologue, the Prince of Ghangistan fumes because he is too weak militarily to take revenge on the British. But perhaps the Western-educated nephew of the ancient courtier Haramin has a solution to the problem? * Shift to England: The most enthusiastic gardeners in the West Country receive in the mail a small capsule containing a seed or spore. It has been sent to them for garden trial as a publicity device. Each gardener thinks himself specially favored, but it is later learned that the area has been well covered with the trial capsules. * Planted, the capsule soon produces a strange globular plant (really fruiting body) that grows with extreme rapidity and is very light. * Ralph Waite, son of one of the recipients, becomes suspicious when there is a rash of skin irritations and deaths in the same area as the strange plant. A scientist friend confirms his opinion: The gift plant is both saprophyte and parasite, and has an affinity for human flesh. The problem now is destroying the fungi before the spores can spread and overwhelm England. In a short time Cornwall and the West Country are under what amounts to siege, with the army combating the spreading menace. Waite takes part in the battles, but, disabled, misses the final episode: The fungus was not stable. It returns to being a saprophyte only, and the peril is over. * Back in Ghangistan, the prince, while disappointed that the fungus did not wipe out the British, takes considerable comfort in the fact that it cost Britain more than a war with Ghangistan would have cost, with little expense to Ghangistan. * The later Harris would have handled the story better.

602. **INVISIBLE MONSTERS.** *Wonder Stories*, December 1933. Ill. Burian.

Short story. * *Time:* the interplanetary future. Location indeterminable. * Three young men are out camping when a rocket ship crashes nearby. On investigating the next day, they discover that it is the *Hurakan*, which left on the first interstellar voyage some seven years earlier. There seem to be no human bodies about, but in the chart room David discovers that the ship must have reached Procyon and returned—thus obviously having traveled at speeds greater than light. * That is not all that David discovers. As he watches, the metal plates of the ship bulge and his friend Toby is caught in midair and eaten by an invisible monster. A specimen from Procyon obviously is loose. * The police at first refuse to believe David's story, and suffer accordingly. In a short time it becomes clear that a monstrous thing, growing very rapidly, is spreading around the countryside centering on the shipwreck. Bullets do not harm it; fire does not

Harris, John Beynon (*continued*)

hurt it; and explosives simply spread it around more. There are perils and thrills as the men try to escape the hungry jaws of the creatures. * A resolution comes when a biologist takes charge. Tossing methylene blue upon the monsters, he makes them visible. Then, with a metal probe he is able to pierce their cardiac organs. The peril is over. * Routine.

603. THE MOON DEVILS. *Wonder Stories*, April 1934. Ill. Winter.

Short story. * *Time:* the interplanetary future. *Place:* the Moon. * The manuscript of Stephen Dawcott, a member of the *Scintilla* expedition, which is investigating Lunar archeology. * Archeological remains are not unknown on the Moon, but the ruins found by the *Scintilla* group are different from and much more elaborate than other sites. The men penetrate a sealed chamber, within which is apparently a funerary situation: corpses in coffin-like boxes. As the explorers open the coffin lids, rather crude but effective mechanical devices make injections into the perfectly preserved corpses. * But the bodies are not corpses. They come to life and prove to be remarkably vicious, intelligent humanoids. They kill most of the expedition by slitting their space suits, then smashing in the windows of the parked spaceship. With Dawcott, wounded and barricaded in one compartment, the Moon men fly the spaceship to Earth, where they land on a South Sea island. When Dawcott recovers enough, he blows up the *Scintilla*, but the Moon men have already left the ship and presumably are free on Earth to breed and work mischief. * *Miscellaneous:* The Moon men have enormous chests in which they can store air for long periods of time. * Below Harris's usual standard.

604. THE MAN FROM BEYOND. *Wonder Stories*, September 1934. Ill. Paul.

(Reprinted as by John Wyndham in Wyndham, *The Man from Beyond*; in Wyndham, *The Best of John Wyndham*; and in Elwood, *Alien Worlds*.)

Short story. * *Time and place:* the near future, with a frame situation on Venus perhaps millions of years in the far future. * The frame situation: The inhabitants of Venus, who have achieved a high civilization, are centaur-like beings evolved from six-legged ancestors, as is the case with all Venusian animal life. * Oddly enough, there is a single animal in a Venusian zoo that seems to have quadrupedal origins. He was retrieved from a valley that is inundated with a preservative gas that holds living creatures in suspended animation indefinitely. Thus, animals retrieved from the valley may represent extinct species going back millions of Venusian years. * The strange creature, on display to sightseers, catches the attention of a schoolboy who is more observant, apparently, than the adults, and demonstrates that he is an intelligent being. He is the Earthman Gratz, who eventually tells scientists how he came to Venus. * It is a sordid story of big-business intrigue and ruthlessness. Morgan Gratz, who secretly acts for Metallic Industries, one of the two great syndicates that rule Earth, has a passionate hatred for International Chemicals, the other giant, by whom he is employed. He thus informs M.I. about I.C.'s plans to send a spaceship to Venus to stake claims to potential resources. In an interview with the board of M.I., he agrees to go on the Venus expedition and to sabotage it utterly. According to the agreement that Gratz reaches with M.I., M.I. will build a rival spaceship, claim the planet, and rescue him. * During the voyage and after landing,

Gratz murders the other members of the expedition, and, on an island on Venus, awaits rescue. But as he gradually recognizes, he has been double crossed by M.I., which has never intended to rescue him. He wanders into the valley and is overcome by the preservative gas. * Gratz, who warns the Venusians against dealing with either M.I. or I.C., does not realize how much time has passed since he came to Venus—millions of years. Venusian astronomers show him Earth in their telescopes, a barren, dead planet pockmarked with enormous craters, presumably the result of atomic wars. * A good story.

HARRISON, EDWARD LEE

No information, except that portrait accompanying the story shows a middle-aged man. Schwartz/Weisinger, who cite the author's middle name as "Leo" in *Science Fiction Digest*, April 1933 (p. 5), list two stories accepted by *Amazing Stories*: "The Night of Terror" and "The Last Stand of the Nations." They do not seem to have been published.

605. THE AIR SPY. *Air Wonder Stories*, October 1929. Ill. Paul.

Short story. * *Time:* the undated near future. * The Euravian spy von Horst, who has acquired secret plans of the whole American air fleet, has been tipped off that his cover has been blown (my expression). He has boarded the superplane *Pegasus* for Lisbon, and is in a fair way to escape. But the U.S. Aerial Patrol at Charleston has been alerted, and Commander Holder of the *Petrel* is in pursuit. * The patrol plane under normal circumstances can overtake the *Pegasus*. But there is a special circumstance. Holst's wife, hearing of her husband's flight, repairs to an old friend, a crank inventor who has invented a strange wingless flying machine called the *Spindle*. With the *Spindle*, which is faster than the other planes, Frau von Holst may be able to rescue her husband before the *Petrel* catches the *Pegasus*. And so it happens. After capture of the *Pegasus* and several cat-and-mouse situations Holder discovers that the Holsts have escaped down a hanging ladder into the *Spindle* and are away to Europe and safety. * One of the few stories where an aerial spy escapes. Not developed much, but with a certain amount of suspense.

HASSE, HENRY (1913-1977)

U.S. (Indiana and later West Coast) fan and writer with some interest in bibliographic matters. Together with William Crawford he compiled a useful (untitled) index to the fantastic fiction in the Munsey magazines. He also collaborated with Ray Bradbury on Bradbury's first published story, "Pendulum," and with Emil Petaja. Hasse resumed writing in the 1940s, with fiction in *Planet Stories* and elsewhere. See also collaboration A. Fedor and Hdnry Hasse.

606. HE WHO SHRANK. *Amazing Stories*, August 1936. Ill. Morey.

(Reprinted in Healy and McComas, *Adventures in Time and Space* and in Asimov, *Before the Golden Age*.)

Novelette. * Infinite regress. * The ruthless Professor announces to his assistant that he has proof that not only is the world an electron in a macroscopic universe, but that below it atomic structures are planetary systems, similarly continuing on down, perhaps infinitely. * The Professor also has prepared an injection that will condense atomic structure and a thought helmet that will transmit back the impressions of a traveler in size. So saying, the Professor overpowers his assistant, inoculates him,

Hasse, Henry (*continued*)

and sends him down into the atoms. * The narrator recounts his experiences on through a myriad of stages as he discovers that the atomic parallel continues on down indefinitely. He comes upon planets inhabited by intelligent gaseous beings, by hostile robots, by winged people, and even a planet called Earth. This is the first indication, hitherto cleverly concealed, that the narrator, while humanoid, is not human and not an Earthman. * The story is open-ended. There just is no finality to the sequence of macrocosm-microcosm (equals new macrocosm), etc.

HASTA, M. H.

From internal evidence, probably a U.S. academic with scientific background.

608. **THE TALKING BRAIN**. *Amazing Stories*, August 1926. Unsigned ill.

Short story. * The narrative of Professor Harvey, a friend of the gifted, eccentric scientist Murtha. Murtha, who is experimenting with neural signal transmission, has made great advances. Indeed, using selenium he is fast approaching the development of artificial eyesight for blind persons. * When Harvey returns from a vacation, however, he finds Murtha a shattered man. Murtha takes him to his laboratory and shows what has happened. A student named Vincent was mortally injured in an automobile accident. Before the body died, Murtha removed its brain and inserted it (suitably nourished and stabilized) into an artificial body. The brain is alive and can signal via Morse code, but its message is horrible. It demands death. * Murtha, who has cleverly taken care of the legal aspect of his deed, is willing to destroy Vincent, but wants a witness to see what he has accomplished. After he demonstrates Vincent to Harvey, he kills Vincent and commits suicide. * Amateurish, but more intelligent than most of the original stories in early issues of *Amazing Stories*.

HAWKINS, WINTHROP W.

It is not clear whether this is Winthrop Wesley Hawkins (1911-1988?), Canadian educator and scholar. A.B. University of New Brunswick; M.Sc., Dalhousie; Ph.D. University of Toronto. Taught at University of Manitoba, University of Saskatchewan, Dalhousie, and associated with several governmental boards. Area of work biochemistry, nutrition, physiology.

608. **THE REGENERATIVE WONDER**. *Amazing Stories,* February 1934. Ill. Morey.

Short story. * *Place:* mostly Maine. * The narrator is summoned to the laboratory of his friend the maverick scientist Irvin Pembert. Pembert, as he soon demonstrates, has discovered a method of organ regeneration that can even replace a lost head. First, he bombards the area to be regenerated with radiation that changes it to an undifferentiated cell mass, then he places it in a certain liquid and applies other rays. Oddly enough, regenerated organs are healthier and sounder than the originals. Thus, when the great violinist Bondini breaks his hand and is no longer able to play, Pembert is able to replace it with one as good as or better than the original. * Intelligent and literate, but dull and without narrative art.

HAYS, RUSSELL

Contributed one story to *Clues* and an article to *Popular Mech-*

anics during this period; otherwise, no information.

609. **THE BEETLE EXPERIMENT**. *Amazing Stories*, June 1929. Unsigned ill.

Short story. * In the museum is an abnormally large specimen of the local tiger beetle. Professor Asa Hall occasionally comes in to look at it, murmuring, "Oh, you devil, you." * Explanation and backflash: Hall, experimenting with the growth cycles of beetles, discovers a chemical means of inducing gigantism. He injects several beetles, all but one of which he "freezes" at about four inches. (One of these is in the case at the museum.) A single larva, however, he continues to inject until it is several feet long. It pupates, and Hall hopes to watch its emergence as a beetle. * But the beetle, larger than Hall had expected, emerges when he is absent, bites through the building walls, and escapes. * Hall at first thinks of advertising for the lost beetle, but when there are reports of people being attacked, mutilated, and killed, he keeps silent. Instead, he tries to hunt down the beetle, since he knows its habits. He is successful, but not before five people have been killed. Overcome by remorse, hair whitened overnight, Hall destroys his notes and suppresses his discovery. * A little overwritten in places, but not a bad story.

610. **THE PURPLE PLAGUE**. *Amazing Stories*, February 1931. Ill. Wesso.

Novelette. * *Time:* 1981. *Place:* mostly China. * Background: The world is divided into two power groups, the Caucasian Allies and the Far East Entente (including China, India, Japan). The world has been at war since 1978. The ultimate causes were the economic power of the new Far East and the Chinese refusal to accept population limitations; the immediate cause, an embargo by the Caucasians. In 1979 the great Chinese scientist Chang Lin instituted bacterial warfare with an extremely powerful cross between typhoid and dysentery; this was the Blue Death, which killed millions and almost defeated the West. * Now, in 1981 espionage reveals that Chang has been conducting death tests on prisoners of war with an agent even more lethal than the Blue Death. This is the Purple Plague. * When the intelligence reports come in, Dr. Breckenridge, chief Caucasian scientist and head of the Caucasian Coalition, recognizes that the only hope for the West is acquiring a sample of the disease agent. * Fortunately, Breckenridge's assistant, Dr. Arthur McCarthy, has studied in China and speaks Chinese fluently. Transformed by plastic surgery, transported to China by the intelligence underground, McCarthy, after adventures on the road, is installed as a lower servant in Chang's household. (On both sides the administrations are riddled with moles.) * With a combination of luck, astuteness, and assistance from a mole, McCarthy, as Soo Yong, manages to save Chang's daughter from Fundamentalist outlaws and gains Chang's gratitude. But he is unable to win entry into the sealed compound where the bacteriological research is conducted. Eventually, he ingeniously gains entrance, manages to steal a small amount of the culture, and delivers it to his contact before collapsing with the Purple Plague. Chang saves his life with an antitoxin, but regretfully announces that McCarthy, whose identity was revealed in his fever ravings, must be executed. * The situation, however, is saved. The Caucasians, in a risk-all attack, succeed in defeating the Oriental air fleets, and the Orientals request an armistice. Part of the agreement calls for destruction by Western bombers of Chang's laboratories. * *Miscellaneous:* Closed circuit television and picture phones are commonplace. Both sides have

Hays, Russell (*continued*)

uranium bombs, but it is not clear whether these are technically atomic bombs. Medical science is much advanced beyond publication date. * A rather good espionage thriller, with inner logic, good plotting, reasonable characterizations. A reader can forgive a romance between McCarthy and Chang's daughter. One of the better stories in *Amazing*, and a great improvement over the author's previous story.

HEALD, HAZEL [and LOVECRAFT, H. P.]

Heald (1895-1961) was a Massachusetts amateur writer on the edge of the Lovecraft circle. Lovecraft revised Heald's work in varying degree, with resultant publication of several stories in *Weird Tales*. For Lovecraft, see his separate entry. * With the present story it is not known exactly what Lovecraft did. August Derleth in *The Horror in the Museum* suggests that revision was minimal, mostly stylistic, but I find the Lovecraft element stronger than this.

611. **THE MAN OF STONE**. *Wonder Stories*, October 1932. Ill. Paul.

(Reprinted in Lovecraft, *The Horror in the Museum* and in Lovecraft, *Marginalia*.)

Short story. * *Place:* the Adirondacks. * The narrator and his friend Ben, hearing of wonderfully realistic sculptures that an acquaintance came upon in the wilderness, decide to investigate them. They wonder if they are the work of their acquaintance Wheeler, who disappeared in the area some time before. * The narrator and Ben find the sculptures without too much difficulty, but see, to their amazement and horror, that they are not really statuary, but the petrified bodies of Wheeler and a dog. * Following a lead given by one of the local men, the two make their way to the cabin of Mad Dan Morris, who has a fearsome reputation. There they find two more petrifications, Dan and his young wife Rose. Dan's diary notes tell what has been going on. * Dan, of witch and magician stock, is a Lovecraftian mage who studiously applies himself to supernatural magic, sacrifices and all. He has tried to force his normal young wife into helping him, but she has steadfastly refused, despite whippings. * When Wheeler became acquainted with Rose, an attachment grew up between them, which Mad Dan was not slow to recognize. He took careful thought about how to punish the pair, and finally settled on a petrifying potion, the recipe for which he found in the *Book of Eibon*, a tome inherited from his witch ancestors. The dog and Wheeler were easily taken care of, but Rose, locked in the attic, did not petrify properly, though furnished only the petrifying liquid to drink. * The diary ends here, but added is a note from Rose. She knew what Dan was trying to do and drank little of the liquids he gave her, despite thirst, surviving on rainwater from leaks in the roof. She then escaped. Although half paralyzed, she managed to tie Dan and pour the liquid into him through a funnel. She then drank the remainder. * Not a bad story.

HELD, S[ERGE] S[IMON]

French author. No other information. According to Versins, *La mort du fer* was considered for the Prix Goncourt. A search in U.S. university bibliographic resources failed to reveal any other work by Held, and a search by a French librarian (Mlle. Claire Vivet) was equally unsuccessful.

612. **THE DEATH OF IRON**. *Wonder Stories*, September-December 1932. Trans. from French by Fletcher Pratt. Ill. Paul.

(Translation of *La mort du fer*, 1931 in book form. It has been rumored that there is an unlocated earlier periodical or newspaper publication, but this has not been discovered. The story is described in more detail in *Science-Fiction: The Early Years*.) Novel. * French politics and catastrophe, intermingled with mysticism. The story is told mostly through two metallurgical engineers, Leclair and Selevine, the latter a Russian emigré. * Accidents become frequent in the Morain et Cie ironworks; at first these accidents are attributed to sabotage either by the workers or the owners (as an excuse to lay off workers), but it becomes apparent after a time that a mysterious organism is eating iron and steel. Iron flakes off and becomes phosphorescent, with a skin disease attacking those in proximity to the decaying metal. After a time iron has disappeared from the world, and various substitutes that have been developed are not adequate. Civilization is gone, and man reenters a stone age. * *Miscellaneous:* There is a suspicion, not verified, that Selevine, for reasons of his own, first discovered the iron destroyer, nurtured it, and disseminated it. * The speculation is offered that the iron disease is nature's way of ridding the Earth of man's civilization. * Competent, but for the present-day reader too much about the variety of French politics: Socialists versus Capitalists versus Syndicalists versus Communists, etc.

HELLER, CLARENCE EDWARD (1888-after 1957)

U.S. (Brooklyn, New York) author. Associated with Brooklyn College. Author of about six thousand poems, whence called the Bard of Brooklyn.

613. **FLAMINGO. A DRAMA OF A.D. 1950**. *Amazing Stories*, July 1930. Ill. Morey.

Short story. * *Time:* 1950. * A date told in the manner of Hugo Gernsback's *Ralph 124C 41+*. Fifty-odd-year-old Alonzo Hepburn, rejuvenated by radium-iron treatment, takes 26-year old Dolly Van Swagger to see *Flamingo*, a theatrical performance of the day. Dolly seems to have set her cap at Alonzo, but he, a widower, considers himself too old for her. * The story is slender, and the author's purpose (as with *Ralph*) is to make a series of technological predictions. * Politics do not interest Heller greatly, but there was a Russian-Italian War in 1940, outcome unrevealed. * Essentially, the culture of 1950 is robotic. With the creation of the first female robot, robots became increasingly important in daily life as servants and workers. Indeed, the play *Flamingo*, to which Alonzo takes Dolly, is acted entirely by humanoid robots. * A second strand to the future culture is size: Both Alonzo and Dolly's families live in an apartment hotel 160 stories high, with individual disk elevators onto which one steps. The theatre that shows *Flamingo* seats seventy-five thousand people, with gigantic mirrors conveying images to large sections of the audience. But even a theatre of this size cannot hold all the first-night crowds, as Alonzo's wall-projected newspaper reveals, for fifty thousand people were turned away. For deaf patrons there are special rooms, and for the blind, a projection device that operates directly on the retina. * The author's mode does not seem to be satire at vulgar mechanization (as the modern reader may interpret the story) but romanticization of future technology. * In all probability the story owes much to the author's wife, Florence Heller, who was associated with Warner Brothers, Inc, at the Vitagraph Studios, Brooklyn, in a technical capacity.

HERBERT, BENSON (1912-1991)

British educator, writer, publisher. A.B., Oxford. M.Sc., Birmingham University, radio engineering and research. Occasional contributor to the pulp magazines and writer of s-f chapbooks during World War II. Later founded Utopia Publications, Ltd., which printed some science-fiction. A better writer technically than most of his American counterparts, but not strong on ideas.

614. **THE WORLD WITHOUT**. *Wonder Stories*, February 1931. Ill. Marchioni.

(Reprinted in Margulies and Friend, *From off This World.*)

Short story. * *Time:* the near future. *Place:* Cairo, Egypt. * As a result of a scientific squabble, Parling, a great mathematician, invites Klington, an equally great philosopher and linguist, to a demonstration that the universe consists of a group of three-dimensional cosmoses packed together like cards. * At a predynastic site he found a metal rod that can be poked into other dimensional worlds, prying them apart and permitting entry. Apparently there is a infinite number of such worlds, which can differentiated on the Egyptian rod by a Vernier screw. * Locating a place that has a reasonable temperature, although the atmosphere is chlorine and gas masks are necessary, the two men enter a strange ambience, with odd colors, great enamel-like barriers, a hostile unintelligent life-form like a giant insect, and curious formations. There seems to be no horizon, but space curves up. The landscape seems to be in motion, with portions rising and falling. * After a time the explorers recognize that they are not on a strange planet, but inside the mouth of a gigantic creature in another dimension. The barriers are teeth, and the rising-falling is motion of the jaw. Perils mount; oxygen runs short; and Parling falls to his death. Klington barely makes it back to our world. * Well imagined, although the initial premise of an Egyptian tomb-find lacks credibility. * For a sequel see #615, "The World Within."

615. **THE WORLD WITHIN**. *Wonder Stories*, August 1931. Ill. Marchioni.

Short story. * Sequel to #614, "The World Without." * *Time:* the near future. *Place:* Cairo, Egypt. * Klington, returned from his horrendous adventure in the mouth of the gigantic creature in another dimension, tells his experiences to a friend. To convince his friend he opens up the entrance to the other-world, whereupon a monstrous being is seen approaching—Parling in his diving suit. * Parling's narrative takes up the rest of the story, which is a typical adventure in the bloodstream, involving a personalized corpuscle. Parling wanders through various areas of the gigantic being, witnesses the operation of the various components of the bloodstream and an invasion by bacteria. He is accompanied on most of this by an intelligent yellow corpuscle, with whom he converses telepathically. The corpuscle is civilized, but his culture is mental rather than physical. Eventually, under the guidance of the friendly corpuscles, Parling finds the ladder back to our world and returns. * Conventional in subject matter, but better written than usual for the story type.

616. **THE SHOT FROM THE SKY**. *Wonder Stories*, February 1934. Ill. Paul.

Short-short story. * The reactions of individuals in Lancashire and nearby areas as a rocket ship streaks through the air and lands. Despite anticipations of something horrible, as in H. G. Wells's *The War of the Worlds*, very ordinary men emerge. The ship is an American rocket airplane seeking a record for an Atlantic crossing. * A trivial sketch.

617. **THE CONTROL DRUG**. *Wonder Stories*, November 1934. Ill. Winter.

Short story. * The narrator describes the fate of his friend Robert Manne, a research chemist. Manne, investigating the properties of a certain dye, stabilizes it and takes a small dose. It results in a euphoric mood, without apparent after effects. * The narrator now witnesses several tragedies that befall persons who sampled the drug. One of his friends commits suicide, another goes mad and is taken to an asylum; and a third commits murder. * Chemist Manne, now raving mad, explains matters before attacking the narrator. The drug operates by releasing inhibitions and repressions, so that in effect it exaggerates enormously one's present mood. When Manne first sampled the drug he was feeling pleased, whence the euphoria. The others who took the drug chanced to have other feelings dominant, whence the horrors. The drug is also immediately habit-forming.

618. **THE PERFECT WORLD**. *Wonder Stories*, October 1935-February 1936. Ill. Paul.

(Reprinted in book form, abridged, as *Crisis!—1992*, Richards, London, 1936.)

Novel. Stress is not so much on science-fictional elements, which are weak, as on irony of personality types as they respond to a series of incredible situations. The overall tone is black humor of a sort. * *Time:* 1992. *Place:* Munich, Germany, and Arion, a new planet Arion that has entered the solar system. * The personalities include Herr Lieben, a chemical engineer, who is far from being a high-minded scientist; his daughter Ilse, intelligent, good-looking, but somewhat predatory; Henry Guidance, a ruthless, somewhat shady British entrepreneur and promoter of rocket travel; French geologist Grindin, a coward whose plans to avoid a space flight fail; Hesker, a Czech amateur astronomer and burglar; a mad Welsh stowaway; and lesser characters, all of whom, as the story develops, display serious flaws beneath their personae. * *Background:* The world of 1992 is not too different from ours, except that dress and decoration have continued the futurist style of the 1920s and early 1930s. Travel, however, has changed greatly; rocket ships, called soarers, now provide transportation upon Earth. There has been a little space travel, notably sponsored by Henry Guidance, but it has not been too successful, and as a result of alternate successes and failures, Henry Guidance has made and lost fortunes. The deterrent to successful space flight is lack of a powerful fuel—which Herr Lieben has just developed. * In the astronomical world, however, much is happening. The Czech astronomer Hesker has observed a new dark body that is approaching the Earth. A planet about the size of Mars, according to all calculations it should strike in a matter of a few weeks. As might be expected, rioting, looting, massacres, massive fires, and other horrors are overwhelming the world. The single-minded Guidance and Lieben, however, are immune to the hysteria and carry on as if nothing were wrong. * Surprise! The great New Zealand astronomer Hergesheimer recalculates the orbit of Arion and discovers that it will not collide with Earth, but will pass by without doing any more harm than tidal effects. This discovery provides the impetus for Guidance's new enterprise, a rocket flight to Arion using Lieben's new fuel. * Oddly enough, Herbert says very little about advance investigations or preparations for the flight. *Soaring Rocket No. 3* takes off with the personnel named above,

Herbert, Benson (*continued*)

plus others, and the voyage is uneventful except that two stowaways are found: Ilse Lieben, who has set her cap at the unknowing Grindin, and a Welshman, who refuses to reveal his identity or reason for stowing away. The ship lands on Arion. * Arion turns out to be like Earth, with rather odd vegetation, but similar gravity and atmosphere. There is one strange life form: a ten-footed creature that crashes madly through the vegetation and is an accidental menace. * But then incredible things happen. The landscape changes; what was a plain, in a matter of minutes may change into a steep mountain slope; and gravity, too, seems occasionally annulled. Some of the vegetation seems to be artificial, and there are strange pipe-like constructions scattered about. Exploratory parties disappear. * Explanations are finally forthcoming when the explorers encounter an Arionian, who is a tree-like being, deaf and mute, but highly intelligent and provided with keen vision and other senses of perception. Ilse learns to communicate with it by means of the Arionian written language, which turns out to be logical and simple. Many of the strange happenings are then explained. Arion is not a natural planet, but a space station hollowed out of a planet by the Arionians, who have come from a stellar system in the direction of Betelgeuse. While passing by the solar system, on their way to visit friends in another star system, they decided to look briefly at Earth—which they now do not consider worth the trouble to examine closely or visit. * Everything on the surface of Arion is artificial, and the shifts of landscape and gravitational anomalies have been caused by directional shifts as the planet is steered about. The wonders of Arionian superscience, however, are concentrated in the hollow interior of the planet, which the explorers are allowed to visit briefly. * As the explorers interact, their masks drop and their true natures (typically not very admirable) emerge. But the men and Ilse accept each other with a certain realistic tolerance. The exception is the Welshman, who reveals a strange psychopathology. He has stowed away to gain revenge on Guidance, who killed his pet parrot years earlier. (Guidance suffers from a phobia against birds.) The Welshman has also smuggled along a cassowary that he has trained to peck at bright objects—in this case Guidance's eyes. Guidance has a narrow escape. * When it comes time for the explorers to leave Arion, the natives obligingly build a new spaceship for them, since the old rocket was destroyed when deserters from the expedition tried to take the rocket up. * The ironic note is continued to the end of the novel, when ignoble motives still move the main characters. * "The Perfect World" was not regarded with much enthusiasm when it appeared, perhaps because it was too British and too involuted for the American pulp market. But I liked it, and I still find it a very amusing story, perhaps not so profound as its author meant it to be, but well written and a change from literal adventure.

HERMANSON, ULF

No information. Portrait accompanying story shows a young man.

  619. **THE HOUSE IN THE CLOUDS.** *Wonder Stories,* November 1930. Ill. Paul.

Short story. * In a frame situation Banston tells the frame narrator about his unbelievable experience, which had made him the laughingstock of the flying field. He was flying aimlessly when he saw a barrel rise into the air, apparently at the end of a long wire; he followed it up, and was at about twenty thousand feet when he saw ahead of him, floating in midair, what looked like a section of a bridge, upon which was a house. * His motor died, and he coasted onto the structure. Two men secured his plane and took him to the Professor, who explained. Formerly a teacher in a great university, he discovered antigravity and now uses it to escape the vulgarity and viciousness of the world. No, he will not release the discovery, for he has no use for mankind. As for Banston's engine, the Professor stopped it. Now Banston must leave, and the flying platform disappears to a higher altitude. * The narrator and Banston determine to find the strange structure again and discover its secret science. It is not spelled out what they will do, but they apparently have no moral compunction about their future actions. They sight the platform, land, knock a guard unconscious, but discover that they have been trapped. The platform starts to founder, since the unconscious guard was apparently in charge of stabilizing it. The Professor and his men escape in one plane, Banston and the narrator in another. * Curious moral values. Routine as fiction. Possibly a leftover from *Air Wonder Stories.*

HESTER, R. FREDERICK

According to Library of Congress records, R. Frederick Hester is the working name of a Robert Fordham Hester (1896-?), author of *A Modern Oligarchic Manifesto* (1934). It is not certain that this is the present author.

  620. **THE GIPSIES OF THOS.** *Amazing Stories,* May 1935. Ill. Morey.

Short story. * *Time:* the near future. *Place:* planets around Proxima Centauri and Alpha Centauri. * Mark Felestone and his family were among the first to undertake space travel, landing on Venus, where his daughter Therese was born. For a while they were stranded there, since big business monopolies prevented them from obtaining element 87, a necessary catalyst for atomic power and space travel. * A new discovery has enabled them not only to leave Venus, but to undertake a voyage of exploration among the stars, notably the system of suns and planets around Alpha Centauri. * The system around Proxima Centauri being uninhabitable, the explorers approach Alpha Centauri. Leaving the mother ship *Pegasus* on one planet, the explorers descend in a tender (the *Mercury*) to Thos, a giant planet inhabited by a race of friendly two-hundred-foot-tall human giants. The *Mercury* being short of fuel, the explorers are temporarily stranded on Thos, where Therese becomes quite friendly with a young giantess. Eventually, the two parties are reunited, despite deaths from the potent solar radiation. Equipped with crystals of health and long life obtained from the giants, the Earthlings depart. * The influence of *Gulliver's Travels* is obvious. * Below routine.

HEWELCKE, GEOFFREY

No information, but apparently a man with some scientific and literary background. According to Rock, wrote "The Dust of Death" (*Weird Tales,* April-May 1931) under the pseud. Hugh Jeffries.

  621. **TEN MILLION MILES SUNWARD.** *Amazing Stories,* March 1928. Unsigned ill.

Novelette in the mode of Jules Verne. * *Time:* 1935 through 1937. *Place:* mostly New York and the Caucasus-Caspian area. * The journalist narrator Martin, in response to an urgent

Hewelcke, Geoffrey (*continued*)

summons, visits his friend the scientist Farintosh. Farintosh reveals a horrible situation. The newly discovered star in Cassiopeia is not a star but a comet, and it is due to collide with the Earth in about twenty-nine months. Martin is at first incredulous, but others support Farintosh's calculations. The government, with the cooperation of the newspapers, attempts to suppress the information, but a small paper breaks silence, with the panic and social upheavals that can be imagined. * For a time there seems no hope, but Farintosh proposes an action that would be very risky, but would at least offer a chance for survival. He proposes shifting the Earth out of its orbit by concentrating a weight of quadrillions of tons at one place. He would do this by raising the level of the Caspian Sea by means of canals from the Black Sea across the mesothalassa north of the Caucasus. * There is considerable opposition, particularly from a Professor Schreiner, who claims that moving the Earth would create seismic upheavals, but the nations accept Farintosh's plan as the only hope. * Work proceeds well, until a Moslem extremist, Hadji Hassan Agha, a leader of the workmen on the project, declares that it is against the will of Allah. His agitation, fostered by the Sultan of Turkey, commits considerable sabotage, but the project is finished successfully, just in time. The Earth swings aside just enough to avoid a direct hit by the comet, although it is dragged by the comet a little closer to the sun. As Schreiner predicted, the damage from earthquakes, subsidence, tidal waves, etc., is enormous, with millions of dead, but at least the Earth and mankind have survived. Thanks to the comet, the Earth's climate is more equable, but since the Moon is much farther away, tides have almost disappeared. With the enormous project, the nations disarmed, and it seems as if an era of peace is at hand. * Ably accomplished, a competent job, even if the mode is old-fashioned. Since the author refers to the Sultan of Turkey as an actor, it is possible that the story was written considerably before publication.

HIGHSTONE, H. A.

U.S. writer, then resident in Oakland, California. It is not clear whether this is Harold Alfred Highstone (1901-?), a writer on agricultural topics, with *Practical Farming for Beginners* (1940) and articles. From the story it seems possible.

622. **FRANKENSTEIN—UNLIMITED.** *Astounding Stories*, December 1936. Ill. Dold.

(Reprinted in Derleth, *Far Boundaries*.)

Short story. * A sardonic fable, antimechanism, antilabor, anti many other things, told in Midwestern rural dialect. * *Time:* The year A.D. 2000 is mentioned as long ago; from other hints, perhaps around A.D. 2400. * Life is difficult for the tribe, which lives under primitive conditions, but Old Grampaw, who is in a good mood after a feed of wild goat and wild carrots, tells little Chuth about the Great Brain, which still clanks away over the hill. Grampaw seems to have been some sort of a minor technician about fifty years earlier. * Men first created machines to make objects; then machines to handle and process objects; then to make other machines; then to repair other machines. The upshot was intricate and bothersome. There was no coordination, and the actions of the various machines often conflicted. Eventually, it was decided to turn the Central Repair shop, which dispatched repair machines automatically, into a central control

unit that would coordinate everything. This is how the Great Brain, which covered about forty acres, was born. * For about two hundred years the Great Brain worked perfectly, but then it began to develop a personality, a cantankerous one at that. It would deliberately make mistakes, like flooding the radio with commercials from the twentieth century (which were unintelligible in the socialist society of the day), or print newspapers upside down and backwards. When questioned, it replied that it was overworked and needed more resting time. This was granted, but the Brain continued to malfunction deliberately. * Eventually, about fifty years ago, there was a showdown, with the master engineer winning by altering the Brain's current. But actually, this was the beginning of the end, for the Brain thereupon surreptitiously developed a horde of fighting machines that drove the humans into the woods, where they live precariously. What the Brain is currently doing is not known, but its hoots and whistles can occasionally be heard. * *Miscellaneous:* The Brain and its concomitants are conceived as a local phenomenon. * Cleverly handled.

HILL, H. HAVERSTOCK

Pseud. of J. W. Walsh, who has a separate entry.

623. **TERROR OUT OF SPACE.** *Amazing Stories,* February-May 1934. Ill. Morey.

Novel. * *Place:* the Solomon Islands, en route to Mars, Mars, and the United States. * Harper (the narrator), Spain (his partner) and their wives operate a plantation in the Solomon Islands. One day they see a strange light in the sky and hear an explosion. Further manifestations reveal that their island is undergoing a visit by a rocket ship from outer space. The planters and their overseer, an American named Retallick, are captured and taken onboard the spaceship, which then leaves. * Their captors, who are completely human, are not unfriendly, and communication first with a thought helmet (which is not too efficient), then sign language, and then a native Solomon Island dialect, reveals matters. Their captors are taking them to Mars. This is the second Martian visit to Earth; on the first, several hundred years ago, they captured a few natives and learned the language from them. Since then, the technique of space travel had been lost, and it has been recovered only recently. The Earthmen are examined with fantastic medical apparatus and more or less sanitized to protect the Martians against disease. * The journey proceeds comfortably, with the Earthmen gradually learning more about their hosts, and Retallick conducting a romance with the skipper's daughter. The Martians, however, regard themselves as a superior race, which the Terrestrials find annoying. * Along the way, there is a crisis. The Martian ship encounters a hostile space sphere, which it destroys in a battle of rays. This corroborates a suspicion that Harper has had; there is a hostile power abroad in space. The Martians, who have been secretive, now admit the fact. Earth, they reveal, has a second moon that orbits just behind Luna, so that it is invisible from Earth. This planetoid, called Aros, was formed from matter expelled from the dark side of the Moon, which is markedly concave. The Arosians, as the Martians learn from corpses recovered after the space battle, are humanoid, gigantic, and black. They plan conquest of the solar system. * The Martian chief council makes a proposition to the captive Earthmen: The Martians will defend Earth against an almost certain attack from Aros and will supply Earth with weapons, information, and general technology, in

Hill, H. Haverstock (*continued*)

exchange for title to the dark side of the Moon. * The Martians and their guests/captives return to Earth and report the Martian offer to the Terrestrial leaders, chief among whom are the American president and the British prime minister. At the persuasion and example of the president, the nations of Earth agree. * It is now time for a preemptive strike against Aros. A Martian-Earth armada attacks, fighting off the Arosian spheres and puncturing a force screen that the Arosians maintain around their planet. Aros is now a dead world, and the two planets, Mars and Earth, look forward to mutually profitable intercourse. * *Miscellaneous:* The Martians also captured native workmen from Harper's plantation; considered inferior beings, they were thrown into the hold and ignored. * Retallick and his Martian lover marry, though it takes much arguing to prevail against the Martian feelings of racial superiority. * Mars is by no means Schiaparellian; it is a fertile world, almost totally encased in a glass covering to conserve air and heat. The canals are road systems. * Readable, competent adventure.

HILLIARD, A[LEC] ROWLEY (1908-1951)

U.S. writer. Graduate of Cornell University, 1930, liberal arts major. At this time resident of Ithaca, New York; later, associated with the *Ithaca Journal*. Author of mystery novels, *Justice Be Damned* (1941) and *Outlaw Island* (1942) with series character Judge Manfred. Later employed by the Atomic Energy Commission, resident in Alexandria, Virginia. See also joint work done as by Allen Glasser and A. Rowley Hilliard.

624. **THE GREEN TORTURE**. *Wonder Stories*, March 1931. Ill. Paul.

(Reprinted in Margulies and Friend, *From off This World*.)

Short story. * *Time and place:* 1980, undetermined location during a future war situation. * The great scientist Thorne, who has discovered a means for creating temporary paralysis by radio waves, has been captured by the enemy, who is trying to extract his secret from him. His former colleague Bjornsen is conducting the torture. * Thorne has been placed in a small room, with a magnetic belt around his waist; with him is an automatic machine like a giant tortoise fitted with poisonous spikes; as long as Thorne moves around the room, the contraption, which is slow moving, cannot impale him. But if he stops . . . When he is ready to talk, he can push a button on the wall. * Thorne dodges and evades for hours, and, about ready to surrender, collapses. But then he is rescued, the enemy having been put *hors de combat* with Thorne's paralysis ray. Thorne learns that his torture was really mostly psychological. There was no poison involved. * Routine.

625. **THE AVENGING RAY**. *Wonder Stories Quarterly*, Spring 1931. Ill. Marchioni.

Short story. * Giant weasels as large as St. Bernard dogs suddenly attack the hapless residents of Bayside, Long Island, and other outlying parts of New York City. At first the attacks are occasional, but they soon become frequent. Police action is ineffective, there being so many of the animals. The area soon becomes an emergency zone and has to be evacuated. And then the weasels start swimming the Sound. * Dr. Jules, who is officially concerned with the plague, shamefacedly confesses to responsibility. He had been experimenting with controlled mutations, breeding weasels for body mass; some animals escaped, and, for inexplicable reasons, the mutations increased in the directions of size, early maturation, and breeding frequency. * It is not a minor problem, but something that threatens mankind, for there soon will be millions of the vicious animals. Explosives dropped from the air are useless, as are ground tactics. * Hilliard finally gets rid of them with a deus ex machina. The U.S. War Department lends the local authorities a few death ray apparatus, which really take the weasels down. * A reasonable thriller, if one can overlook the forced ending of the story. * For a follow-up see #626, "The Island of the Giants."

626. **THE ISLAND OF THE GIANTS**. *Wonder Stories*, August 1931. Ill. Leonard.

Short story. * A latch-on to #625, "The Avenging Ray." * *Place:* a Pacific island. * Jerry and Howd, two young men on a boating vacation, camp for a night on a small island called Neeya and have a strange experience. They hear weird noises and see a human face that is gigantic in size. The next day they sail up to a pier and land, hoping to get some information. They see a few shacks and are greeted by an intelligent man obviously out of place on the island, who gives them supplies. They sail away, convinced that something is wrong. As they leave, the stranger consults his superior who orders him to let the young men go. * The next episode involves Dr. Herbert Jules, the son of Professor Jules of the previous story. Jules, Sr. has disappeared while investigating Neeya, the mysterious island the young men had visited. Jerry and Howd are summoned to Washington, where there is a consultation among Jules and high governmental officials. Jules tells a strange story: An eighteenth or early nineteenth-century scientist, one Haufbauer, had anticipated the discovery of X-rays and their use for controlled mutations; prosecuted for heresy, he escaped and presumably set up operations on Neeya Island, where he started the manufacture of supermen. Professor Jules, Sr., has apparently died investigating Neeya. * The government sends Jules, the two young men, and an envoy to Neeya, with the promise of warships as reinforcement. On arriving there, they are captured and learn what is going on. * It is as Jules suspected. Neeya Island has been the breeding ground of controlled mutations and has developed men with superhuman abilities including will control and thought reading. A race of giants has been bred as menial servitors. * Not all of the islanders are perfect, and some imperfect beings are permitted to live as front men and lower-grade officials. Otherwise, the culture is completely ruthless, with death, sometimes by controlled electric beam, for failure or deficiency. * A-1, the incredibly intelligent leader, and his assistant, A-7, state their wishes to the captives. The supermen simply want to be left alone, but are willing to "go public." They do not wish to kill outsiders, but will do so if necessary. * The warship arrives, and when it begins hostilities, the supermen destroy one assault boat with a heat ray, at which the warship retreats. Jules, the envoy, and the two young men are permitted to leave on the warship. * Some time later Jules receives a message from A-1. The supermen did not kill his father, who died a natural death from exhaustion and illness. They further invite Jules to become their public relations agent with the outside world. * *Miscellaneous:* The supermen are very short lived, fifteen to twenty years. * Too much for its compass, and with some unbelievable motivations. * For another adventure of Jules as central character see #628, "Reign of the Star-Death."

627. **DEATH FROM THE STARS**. *Wonder Stories,*

Hilliard, A. Rowley (*continued*)
October 1931. Ill. Marchioni.
(Reprinted in Conklin, *The Science Fiction Galaxy*.)
Short story. * George Dixon tells his friend Julius Humboldt of his scientific quest: examining meteorites for evidence of extraterrestrial life. Success soon crowns his work, for with a meteorite that Julius steals from the American Museum of Natural History, Dixon soon isolates a life principle. * But as he discovers the next morning, the life principle is highly contagious. It turns organic matter, including himself, into a black dust. * Julius, summoned by phone, arrives at Dixon's later stages and has the onerous task of cleaning up the black dust. Dousing the house, lawn, Dixon's corpse, and himself with gasoline, he applies the torch, hoping that flame and intense heat will sterilize the area. * As for the life-form itself, Hilliard frequently refers to its spreading by "rays," but does not explain what he means. * Routine at best. * For a sequel see #628, "Reign of the Star-Death."

628. **THE REIGN OF THE STAR-DEATH**. *Wonder Stories*, April 1932. Ill. Paul.
Sequel to #627, "Death from the Stars" and latch-on to #626, "The Island of the Giants." * *Place:* Long Island, New York. * Destroying the plague from the meteorite was not as simple as Humboldt had hoped. It continued to spread. * Dr. Jules of "The Island of the Giants" is the center of resistance in the battle against the star-death. His is a fierce, uphill struggle to convince the health authorities, the police, the press, and others of both the danger from the star-death and its unique nature. Jules tries to establish quarantining of a rigorous order, against resistance; on one occasion he kills a man who might have taken the plague into New York City. * As the death spreads, so does panic. There seems to be no defense against it—flame, chemicals are all powerless. * Jules, however, attacks it scientifically, and we now learn what Hilliard meant by rays in the first story. The initial substance emitted rays that dislodged electrons in a peculiar pattern, setting up a chain reaction in colloids, thus perpetuating itself. Jules works out the wavelength of the radiation and neutralizes it with blanketing radiation. * Developed as a pulp action thriller, with plentiful crisis situations, but amateurish writing. * The title is also carried as "Reign of the Star-Death."

629. **THE SPACE COFFIN**. *Wonder Stories*, August 1932. Ill. Paul.
Short story. * *Time:* the near future, later than 1940. * John Hand of the Secret Service is investigating the criminals known as the Adjustors. These are kidnappers who have abducted business tycoons and financiers and extorted enormous ransoms in gold. Previous investigations into their activities have failed. One mystery associated with them is that there is insufficient time for them to have seized their captives or released them. But Hand believes that he has solved the mystery. * When the next victim, a millionaire, receives an extortion demand and is being kidnapped, Hand manages to take his place. After some suspense and mysterious circumstances, Hand finds himself a prisoner in a very strange setting, garbed in a peculiar suit closed by the unfamiliar new invention, zippers—which Hand has difficulty operating. But Hand knows what is going on: He is on a small rocket-propelled space platform that can follow the rotation of the Earth. His zippered suit contains iron threads that respond to magnetic fields, giving the semblance of gravity. Hand manages to escape and report back to work with the case solved. *

As a subplot, the mastermind behind the kidnappings was Hand's friend and patron Gordon Wintermaine, the great philanthropist. Wintermaine leaves a farewell statement in which he reveals that he used the ransom coinage to pay for his philanthropic projects. He was noted for "personal mortgages," which in modern terms were loans for educational purposes. Hand had received such a loan when in need. * *Miscellaneous:* Wintermaine had established his space station by a combination of a strong magnetic field counter to the Earth's and rockets. * In several places Hilliard refers to science-fiction, with Hand commenting how his circumstances approximated those of a s-f novel. * A reasonable pulp action story.

630. **BREATH OF THE COMET**. *Astounding Stories*, January 1934. Ill. Marchioni.
Short story. * *Time:* 1935. * Old Professor Hertz is generally considered a madman when he declares that Hertz's comet (named after his father) will brush past North America and wipe out everything. Competent astronomers declare that the comet does not exist, or that his mathematics is eccentric, or that comets do not have solid heads. * Hertz, now widely ridiculed as a madman, builds himself a little refuge and climbs into it just before the due date for the comet. After a suitable wait, he emerges. * He was right. The comet did strike, and there is nothing to be seen but desolation. For Hertz, who is now really mad, the satisfaction of having been right outweighs the tragedy. Indeed, when an airplane from Europe comes to rescue him, he prefers to remain among his dead and commits suicide by leaping out of the plane. * Routine.

HINTON, EDWARD H.
No information.

631. **MONSTERS OF CALLISTO**. *Wonder Stories*, October 1933. Ill. Paul.
Novelette. * *Time:* the interplanetary future. *Place:* Callisto. * Neill Furber, Captain of the *Gotham*, is transporting a cargo of strategic minerals from New York to Nunei on Callisto when a meteor swarm strikes the vessel. What with the electric disturbances that accompany showers, the ship cannot receive magnetic fixes, and it soon drifts over the horrible Da'Elin on Callisto. This is the local graveyard of ships; no ship to fly over it has ever returned, and it is known to be death. * The *Gotham* is caught in the enormous attraction of the Da'Elin, and nothing that Furber can do will save his ship. Penetrating a boiling surface and layers of enormous heat, it crashes. In the last moments, however, strange phenomena take place: sound completely disappears, while telepathic communication suddenly becomes possible. * Furber gradually awakens, and by exercise of will power regains use of his limbs and sight. Sound still does not exist, but telepathy does. * Furber now sees that the Da'Elin is an ocean formed of a strange form of matter, not quite liquid, not quite gas. It can be breathed, and it is dense enough that vicious wildlife can swim and fly about in it. * What Furber and his gradually decreasing crew witness and experience (although the author does not make this identification) is Terrestrial sea life magnified enormously, as giant rays, crabs, squid, etc. attack the men. * Magnetizing the hull of the *Gotham* as a focal point, the men begin a trek toward higher ground. * They come upon a wrecked vessel, the well-known *Girondelle* that disappeared some time before. And in the wreckage of the *Girondelle* live two people, the beautiful young Diane Brunei

Hinton, Edward H. (*continued*)
and the French scientist and Academician Professor Lenoir. Lenoir, who has studied the Da'Elin, understands it and to some extent can control the wildlife. Unfortunately, he is a mad scientist who wants to be alone with Diane. Thus, he plots to kill the other survivors in various ways. Furber has several narrow escapes and is often disabled until Lenoir is killed by a giant crab. * Through Lenoir's records and a peculiar "atlas" that he maintained, the castaways discover that they are not far from an underground tunnel leading up to a surface pond that escapes the boiling level of the Da'Elin. After trials and tribulations, the castaways make their way to safety. * *Miscellaneous:* Through a peculiar property of the atmosphere, the survivors do not have to eat, although, obviously, the native life does. * There is a romance between Furber and Diane. * The inhabitants of Callisto are of terrestrial origin, as are the inhabitants of Venus, Mars, and Jupiter. * In the older Vernean tradition, but routine, and too long.

HIRSCH, ALCAN, Ph.D. (1885-1938)
U.S. (originally Texas) chemical engineer, metallurgist. Doctorate on metallic cerium, University of Wisconsin. Author of several technical monographs, notably on electric furnaces for smelting metals. In later life lived in New Rochelle, New York.

632. **WITHIN SIGHT OF HELL**. *Amazing Stories*, December 1933. Ill. Morey.
Short story. * Johnson, a newspaper reporter, begs the warden for permission to meet the convict Clark, who has been sentenced to death for vicious murders. The warden is not unfriendly, but cannot accept Johnson's belief that Clark is really "Smiley" Rogers, a World War I ace and a remarkably fine man. * The execution begins as scheduled, but the fuses burn out before the current can do much more than singe and shock Clark a little. The reason: Clark's body is one mass of metal supports that caused burn-out. * Clark awakens as Rogers. He had been amnesiac. The failed electrocution, acting like shock therapy, restored his true, amiable personality. He is pardoned. * The reader may wonder about the murder that Rogers committed as Clark and the legality of it all. * Part of Rogers's trouble was a violent dislike of members of the medical profession. * Somewhat less than routine.

[Anonymous]
Presumably a British writer.

633. **HISTORY HYSTERICAL**. *Scoops*, 7 April 1934. Unsigned ill.
Short story. * Humor. * Sequel to #1316, "Sheer Personality." * Professor Dingle is in the madhouse amiably conversing with fellow inmates Julius Caesar and Teapot (who imagines he is a teapot and pours imaginary cups of tea), when his cat, reaching for mice under the wainscoting at home, turns off the ray projector. Dingle reassumes his real personality and after a time is released. * He now develops the theory that madness and other personality problems are the result of unconscious memories of previous incarnations. His former fellow inmate Julius Caesar, for example, was probably a bad actor who played the role many times. As for the Teapot? * Dingle develops a powder for releasing such unconscious memories. After he and his friend Stobbin take a small quantity, they find themselves in the court of brutal medieval Baron De Brassat. Dingle is Geoffrey

D'Ingle, a court astrologer, while Stobbin is St. Aubyn, his bitter rival and enemy. * When the two astrologers quarrel violently, the Baron decides to have some amusement. He orders them to joust with one another, to the death. During the second course, both men are off their horses, and D'Ingle is belaboring St. Aubyn with a mace, when they both regain their normal personalities back in our time, where Dingle is about to wallop Stobbin with a poker. * Stobbin has had enough, but Dingle is now enthusiastic about developing similar knowledge of the future. * *Miscellaneous:* The Teapot in the asylum was a cupbearer and fanciful pourer at De Brassat's court. The baron nicknamed him De Pot. * Like the first story, capably-handled light humor.

HODGE, FREDERICK ARTHUR
U.S. author, resident in Pittsburgh, Pennsylvania, per guest editorial in Summer 1929 issue of *Amazing Stories Quarterly*. It is not clear whether this is Frederick Arthur Hodge (1872-?), a historian and philosopher, who received a doctorate from the University of Virginia on the work of John Locke. It seems doubtful.

634. **A MODERN ATLANTIS**. *Amazing Stories Quarterly*, Spring 1928. Ill. Paul, with photographs of models of a historical proposed seadrome by Edward Armstrong.
Novelette. * Despite the enormous quantity of words, the story is relatively simple. * *Time and place:* The 1930s, mostly on the isleport Atlantis, which is sited about half way between New York and the Azores. It is a huge floating landing platform with all conveniences and necessities, including an observatory. * The plot is an attempt by the Central European Alliance, in which Austria seems to play a leading part, to seize the isleport preparatory to bombing and invading the East Coast. Against this dastardly conspiracy are two World War I heroes, Bob Holden, Harvard man and amateur scientist, and Jerry Scott, soldier of fortune and daredevil. Also involved is the beautiful, accomplished, charming Kitty Riley Cromwell, who acts as a nurse to the cardiac Holden and is also a spy for enemy scientist Dr. Von Sturm. But Kitty is really a double agent, loyal to the United States. * When the Central European Alliance attacks the isleport, Holden meets them with a disintegrator ray that is based on the new element glorium, number 93. This element is particularly unstable, and its emissions take the form of a destructive ray. * Invasion broken and romances cleared up, Holden deposits his ray machine, for safe keeping, in the basement of the Harvard Club. This is Joe College with a vengeance! * Cryptography is also involved. * Very amateurish and very badly written, with countless clichés of idea and language.

HODGES, A. L.
No secure information. Possibly Arthur Louis Hodges, Long Island, New York, journalist. Graduate University of Kentucky. The blurb for "The Mystery of Professor Brown" characterizes Hodges as "a scientist of no mean ability."

635. **THE DEAD SAILOR**. *Amazing Stories*, May 1930.
Very short piece, six paragraphs long. Not s-f. The sailor, who was assisting the lowering of an experimental half-shell into the sea, is shot dead, but there is no bullet. The explanation is that a jet of water forced through the tube of the half-shell acted as a bullet. * An idea for a story, rather than a story, and so farfetched as to be useless.

Hodges, A. L. (*continued*)

636. **THE PEA VINE MYSTERY**. *Amazing Stories*, May 1930.
Very short piece, four paragraphs long. Not s-f. The corpse of a man is found entangled in garden pea vines. The explanation is that he happened to fall in the right area when the pease were at maximum growth. They strangled him.

637. **THE MYSTERY OF PROFESSOR BROWN**. *Amazing Stories*, August 1930. A short piece, a single page long. * Professor Yarboro Brown is found dead in his laboratory. An autopsy reveals no clue to his death, for his heart and internal organs are in excellent condition, and there is no suspicion of foul play. * His assistant Willie Jones works out a solution. The professor had received a head wound in World War I, and a fragment of metal remained in his scalp without affecting him. But when Brown was working around the new induction furnace, he placed his head inside it—normally a harmless procedure—and the metal in his skull heated almost instantaneously and burned through into his brain. Brown had apparently forgotten about the metal.

638. **AN ASTOUNDING ANNOUNCEMENT**. *Amazing Stories*, June 1935.
Short-short story, based on probability, like the two previous stories. * When Professor Prothero, who is experimenting with atomic fission, starts his apparatus, he hears a commotion among his white mice. On examining them, he finds them all dead, without apparent cause. Similarly, his dog outside the laboratory lies dead. And, as Prothero learns with dismay, there is a chain of dead people across the countryside in direct line with the other fatalities. He obviously has a death ray. * Prothero deeds the invention to the Federal government, which seals it away impenetrably in a guarded concrete pyramid, but informs the rest of the world of the terrible weapon the United States. The result is world peace. * Generations later, when warfare has been almost forgotten, the pyramid is opened. What is there? A note saying that it was all a hoax. The deaths Prothero observed were coincidence. * The late appearance of this story may reflect T. O'Conor Sloane's habit of holding stories for years before publication.

HOLMES, A. R.
Pseud. of Harry Bates, who has a separate entry.

639. **THE SLAVE SHIP FROM SPACE**. *Astounding Stories*, July 1931. Ill. Wesso.
Short story. * Jim Wilson and Clee Partridge, two young men camping in the Adirondacks, see a strange flying globe land. On approaching it, they are seized by invisible forces and carried aboard. As they learn gradually, they have been captured by Xantra, a humanoid interplanetary or interstellar visitor, who has implanted control mechanisms in them and will use them as his slaves. He has also changed their atomic rate so that normal humans are invisible to them. * Also on board the ship are somewhat brutal slaves from another world and Vivian Gray, a young woman whom Xantra intends to use for sexual purposes. * Jim and Clee manage to remove their control implants and with Vivian plot Xantra's overthrow. A narcotic gas helps, and after some turmoil Xantra lies captive. The two men bring the ship back to Earth, and with Vivian survive a crash into the ocean. * *Miscellaneous:* Xantra is pretty much human, but is far more intelligent than Earthmen. In addition to general telepathic

control working through the implants Xantra has a thought helmet for specific messages. Xantra's place of origin is not disclosed.

HORN, HOLLOWAY (1886-?)
British author of mysteries and general fiction. Contributed to pulps, including *Detective Stories*, *The Shadow*, also British newspapers and magazines. Also wrote as H. L. Waghorn. The name sounds like a pseudonym, but I have never seen any documentation.

640. **THE MAN FROM CINCINNATI**. *Astounding Stories*, November 1933. Unsigned ill.
Short story. * Supernatural fiction. * Old Sir John Balcombe becomes very friendly with the pleasant young American tourist who shows such true appreciation for ancient Balcombe Manor and its traditions. He even tells the tourist about the family ghost, which is a death fetch that appears as a normal human being and is recognized only after the event. * The event takes place. Sir John's servants, who have watched him talking to himself, find him dead. * Clichéd, but competently handled.

HOUGHTON, JOSEPH F.
No information. Portrait accompanying the story shows a middle-aged man.

641. **THE *ANDROMEDA* MENACE**. *Wonder Stories*, December 1931. Ill. Paul.
Short story. * *Time:* the interplanetary future. *Place:* mostly on the space route between Mars and Earth. The circumstance is big business dirty tricks. * Background: Space flight is governed by a National Council, which has set down strict rules of conduct, including speaking passing vessels and rendering assistance to disabled vessels. * At the moment, a highly important navigational contract is up for grabs. If the *Andromeda*, an extremely fast vessel owned by Space Transport Service, reaches Earth first, Solar Navigation Lines will lose the contract. Solar Navigation's vessel, the *Vega*, piloted by Captain Jimmie Mabry, is a good ship, but not up to the *Andromeda*. Crooked, greedy General Manager Jud Anson of Solar Navigation intends to help out fate a little. * Summoned to Anson's office, Mabry is put to the question at once: If there is a conflict between orders from the company chief and the National Council, which will you accept? Mabry, who is an honest man, declares that he will follow the National Council, at which Anson flies into a fury and threatens him. * The *Vega* leaves port with Anson on board. After a time it becomes clear what he intends: He has planted a bomb on the *Andromeda*, and he tries to prevent Mabry from going to its rescue. * Mabry, who knows that his career is on the line, nevertheless stops to aid the disabled *Andromeda* and tows it to port, saving hundreds of lives. * Accomplishing this is difficult, for while he is theoretically in total command of the *Vega*, Anson tries to usurp authority and many of the officers support company policy. But Mabry wins through. Actually, it is also a matter of luck, for Anson's wife was unexpectedly transferred to the *Andromeda*, and when she realized on which ship she was sailing, she revealed the presence of the bombs, thus minimizing damage. * *Miscellaneous:* Martians are about eight feet tall and human. * Well paced and well developed.

HOWARD-BURLEIGH, F. S.
British author. No other information.

Howard-Burleigh, F. S. (*continued*)

642. **DON MACKINDER'S MODEL**.   *Astounding Stories,* October 1933. Unsigned ill.

Short story. * Supernatural fiction. * Artist Don Mackinder rents the house formerly leased by the Moretons. It is a pleasant enough house, but there is a problem: Since moving in, Don paints portraits of a mysterious woman, and his wife is worried about his fidelity. * Inasmuch as the ending of the story is totally predictable, there is no harm in revealing it. Mackinder has been seeing and painting the ghost of Moreton's wife, whom Moreton murdered and buried under new construction work. * Routine.

HOY PING PONG

Pseud. of Arthur Wilson Tucker (1914-present), usually known during the 1930s and 1940s as Bob Tucker, later as Wilson Tucker. U.S. (Southern Illinois) fan, writer. Motion picture projector. In early fan days attempted humor of a peculiar sort; later a serious s-f writer of some substance. Novels *The Lincoln Hunters* (1958), *Ice and Iron* (1974-1975), *The Year of the Quiet Sun* (1970) were well received. Also wrote mysteries.

643. **REPORT OF THE 196TH CONVENTION**. *Wonder Stories,* November 1934 (letter column).

A satirical account of the 196th convention of the Science Fiction League, Juno 45-51, 2132 in Ackermanville, California, under President Ackerman. The purpose of the piece seems to be poking fun at the ubiquity (and alleged greed) of the California fan Forrest J. Ackerman. Ackermanville contains a publishing house which produces *Stfiction Tales* and *Macabre Stories*, edited by Forrest J. Ackerman; Ye Ackerman Cafe; Ye Olde Coffee Pottee Inne, F. J. Ackermanee, Propee.; and the Ackerman Flyer, a train operated by engineer Ackerman. Delegates are present from at least Mars and Pluto. There are mild escapades, speeches, descriptions of missionary activity (for science-fiction) on other planets, etc. The meeting closes with Ackerman announcing that the next convention will be held at Ackermanville, North Carolina, and presenting bills to those present. * (In case the title of the magazine is not recognizable, "stf" was a commonly used abbreviation for "scientifiction" and, occasionally, "science-fiction." *Juvenile material, of course.

HUEKELS, JACK G.
No information.

644. **ADVANCED CHEMISTRY**. *Amazing Stories,* March 1927. Unsigned ill.

(First published in *Science and Invention,* August 1923.)

Short story. * Black humor of the 1920s. * Professor Carbonic, in addition to discovering that the vital force is really brain electricity, is able to increase vitality by drilling through the cranial bones and pouring chemicals on the brain. With this technique he has been able to revive moribund persons, even the recent dead. * When the professor has a fatal heart attack as a result of excitement during his experiments, he begs his associates to use his technique to revive him. Unfortunately, they insert too much of the chemical preparation, and the professor, now a human dynamo, electrocutes himself and another person. * The note of parody is continued with such names as Murray Atic, Sal Soda, and Mag Nesia. Feeble.

HUGI, MAURICE [GASPARD] (1904-1947)
British writer, occasional contributor to *New Worlds* and *Tales of Wonder*. Attributed story "The Mechanical Mice" (*Astounding,* January 1941) according to Tuck was not written by Hugi, but by Eric Frank Russell.

645. **TEMPLE OF DOOM**.   *Scoops,* 26 May 1934. Unsigned ill.

Boys' fiction. * Short story. * *Place:* Mato Grosso, Brazil. * Three Englishmen—Sam Freen, Vincent Parker, and Richard Shirley—have left their caterpillar-treaded landrover and entered the jungle in search of the lost city that is described on a manuscript left by a Frenchman generations ago. According to the manuscript, the city is riddled with gold and gems, but the natives are hostile. * The Frenchman turns out to be correct, for our friends are soon captured by the natives (who are descended from Incas, though they speak some Spanish) and are scheduled to be sacrificed at the appropriate time. And the strange white city, obviously ancient and not built by Indians, is indeed riddled with gold and gems. * The sacrificial altar is a transparent block, within which lies the body of a man, who is connected with many wires to dials and controls. As the priest raises his knife, however, a gong sounds, and the altar-container opens by itself. In a panic, the Indians flee. The explorers untie themselves and then, extricating the man from the box, revive him with an adrenalin shot. * The stranger, whose name is Sund, takes the Englishmen down into hidden vaults and chambers, where fantastically elaborate machinery is to be seen, plus a row of other figures like Sund. * Producing thought helmets, Sund now converses with the explorers. He is the Master Scientist of Eos, which we call Atlantis. About ten thousand years ago, the Atlanteans were waging war with Mars, desiccating it and splitting it into the so-called canals with heat rays. The expenditure of energy and mass, however, caused the Earth to shrink a little, lowering the mountain barriers surrounding Atlantis and flooding it. Sund and a group of fellow scientists were the only survivors. They took refuge in South America, and since there were no females to continue the race, placed themselves into suspended animation. As Sund calmly adds, he and his fellows will now take over the Earth, which is rightfully theirs. * The Englishmen are annoyed at this presumption, for, after all, the world belongs to the British Empire. They try to shoot Sund, but bullets simply bounce off his protective shield of powerful electricity. Parker tries to seize him, whereupon he is electrocuted. * Sund seems invincible, what with his disintegrator rod and his lightning bolts, but when the explorers shoot out the machinery, the underground substructure explodes and collapses. The surviving explorers manage to reach the surface pursued by Sund, who tosses lightning bolts at them. It looks bad, but when in desperation Freen throws a water bottle at Sund, the situation changes. The water, flowing off Sund, grounds him and he is electrocuted, his body is then accidentally disintegrated by his ray rod. * Freen and Shirley make their way back to civilization, no richer than before, probably no wiser, but possessors of a disintegrator rod.

646. **THE MINES OF HALDAR**. *Scoops,* 23 June 1934. Unsigned ill.

Boys' fiction. * Short story. * *Time:* 1984. * *Place:* mostly on Mercury. * Spaceship *No. 17AZ,* en route from Earth to Venus, encounters a cloud of greenish space gas that renders everyone unconscious. When the crew awakes, the ship is inside Mercury's orbit, heading for the sun. Mercury's gravity, however, saves them from a fiery death, and they land on Mercury in the

Hugi, Maurice (*continued*)

twilight zone. * When the castaways leave the ship to explore, they are captured by skeleton men, the Lokstals of Lok, who put them to work in radium mines. Oddly enough, the Lokstals speak English, which they have learned from Terrestrial radio broadcasts. The men rebel against the skeleton men, who are fairly delicate, but are overcome by paralysis rays. Rescue eventually comes from outside, in response to an earlier call for fuel. * Haldar of the title is one of the Mercurians.

[Anonymous]
Presumably a British writer.

647. **THE HUMMING HORROR**. *Scoops,* 28 April 1934. Unsigned ill.

Boys' fiction. * Short story. * Inexplicably, radio sets all over Great Britain begin to hum, no matter where the sets are tuned. At first it is perceptible only in Great Britain, then it manifests itself in a belt around the world, with a two-hour periodicity. It grows louder, more and more intolerable, emerging from other electric and electronic apparatus (even when shut off) and eventually even from human beings. Madness is the result, and the asylums are filled with people who have broken down. * Suddenly the humming stops, at which time five top-like vehicles descend from space. They are immediately protected, covered by a half-mile-wide blue hemispherical screen; obviously electrical, it is lethal to the touch * Great scientist Greville Mallory is convinced that the sound not only emanates from space, but is a carrier wave for something. In a short time he is proved right. As he watches the hemisphere, a more or less humaniform mechanical man emerges from the blue field. It projects an image of Saturn in front of it and begins a telepathic conversation with Mallory. It has come with four fellows on an exploratory expedition from Saturn. At one time Saturn was inhabited by a humanoid race, but it is now extinct, and the planet is the home of mechanical men. The mechanical man, announcing that it will take Mallory to the research council, seizes him, and carries him into the sphere. * The situation looks bad, but Mallory's assistant McAuley, reasoning that the screen is harmless if one is not in contact with the earth, parachutes into the electric hemisphere, landing safely. He is seen. Trying to avoid capture, he boards one of the spaceships and by chance is successful in severely damaging the installation. Only one spaceship, that badly damaged, succeeds in limping away. It is shot down in an air battle over the English Channel. * Mallory, rescued, explains. He was placed in a thought-reading machine, where he described Terrestrial life to the visitors. The machine men were not hostile, but were motivated only by scientific curiosity. They had to be destroyed, however, for if they returned to Saturn and further expeditions followed, the humming power beam might well have destroyed mankind.

HUXLEY, JULIAN [SOREL] (1887-1975)
British biologist, author of many important books popularizing science.

648. **THE TISSUE-CULTURE KING**. *Amazing Stories,* August 1927. Ill. Paul.

(First printed in *Cornhill Magazine,* April 1926. Reprinted in Conklin, *Great Science Fiction by Scientists;* in Conklin, *Best of Science Fiction;* and in Clarke, *Time Probe;* in Gunn, *The Road to Science Fiction #2;* and in Silverberg, *Arbor House Treasury*

of Science Fiction Masterpieces.)

Short story. * *Place:* a hitherto almost unexplored part of Africa. * The narrator chances upon a strange hermit kingdom, where biological monstrosities (including gigantic humans) are commonplace. Hascombe, an English scientist captive in the land for some years, explains. When he first came into the land, he recognized that the cultural patterns were a Frazerian divine king, ancestor worship, worship of teratological animals, and sex. * He determined, for amusement, to apply modern scientific methods to foster the native practices and beliefs. Under the sponsorship of the intelligent high priest Bugala, he created tissue cultures of the king and elders (to be preserved for worship instead of bones, as had previously been the case), and devised various monstrous forms of animal life. The system thrives. * As a second theme, the narrator, Hascombe, and Bugala begin to work on channeling the naturally strong paranormal abilities of the natives. Their work is successful, and Bugala now controls the minds of his people with a gigantic will battery. * The two Englishmen determine to escape. Putting the entire population to sleep with the will battery, they leave the land, trusting to metal caps to protect them from mental assaults. But they remove the caps too soon, and Hascombe is compelled to return to Bugala, to a fate that can be guessed. * Intelligent and thought-provoking in its union of social sciences and contemporary biological research, with far more ideas than the typical science-fiction story of its day.

[Anonymous]
Presumably a British author.

649. **ICE METROPOLIS**. *Scoops,* 14 April 1934. Unsigned ill.

Boys' fiction. * Short story. * *Place:* the magnetic north pole in Alaska [*sic*]. * Professor James Heddle has an unusual theory to explain the presence of the magnetic poles; he believes that they are caused by electricity created by intelligent beings. To prove his theory he has built a superplane to fly to the pole. He and his mechanic friend Frampton are accompanied, unknown to them, by stowaway Hank Goldoni, vicious American thug and murderer, who is fleeing justice. * On reaching the pole and disembarking, the explorers encounter fur-clad little men with alabaster-like complexions. Heddle is able to converse with them, after a fashion, in ancient Tartar. The little men take the three outsiders onto a metal platform, which sinks far into an enormous cavern that is filled with steel skyscrapers and illuminated by a gigantic glowing artificial sun. Propellerless planes fly through the air. This is Metrovia. * Taken before the ruler, the men are informed that they will not be mistreated, but that they can never leave. The people of Metrovia do not want an incursion of disruptive outsiders. * Heddle and Frampton would like to leave, but are not uncomfortable in the city. The situation changes when, exploring, they are attacked by a vicious creature much like an airborne jellyfish. When they report this to the ruler, he falls into despair. Ages ago, when his ancestral Tartars settled in the area, they fought the gloogs, driving them underground, where they were sealed off by an earthquake. Obviously, they have worked their way out. * Since the gloogs are multitudinous, and the Metrovians have no weapons, the end seems certain. The explorers, however, hold back the monsters

"Ice Metropolis" (*continued*)

with machine guns until Heddle can put together an electric gun, which removes the gloog menace. The remaining gloogs underground are sealed off again by another earthquake. * As a reward for their help, Heddle and Frampton are allowed to leave after giving their word that they will say nothing about Metrovia. The fate of Goldoni, who disappeared during the gloog attack, is not known. * *Miscellaneous:* Metrovian electricity comes from a vein of iron ore that extends from the lithosphere to the core of the planet. * The Metrovians, who eat food pills, live longer than outside men. * Probably influenced by American dime novels.

[Anonymous]

Presumably a British writer.

650. **THE IMMORTAL MAN**. *Scoops,* 21 April 1934. Unsigned ill.

Boys' fiction. * Short story. * Professor John Hyman, developer of the cancer cure and the world's greatest biologist, is now ninety years old. He is reasonably healthy, but his assistant Dick Warrender worries when he hears the old man chuckling to himself over his secret work. * Then Hyman declares that he has found what he has been looking for—immortality. He proves his point with self-inflicted wounds that heal instantly. As he explains to Dick, he stopped the cellular aging process with certain radiation on the brain and uses jellyfish and lobster secretions for cellular regeneration. * When Hyman announces his discovery in Albert Hall, however, he is hooted and jeered. Furious, the old man refuses to say any more, but it is obvious to observers that he is growing younger. * The professor gets revenge when, in association with a financial shark named Isaac Helmholtz, he works an insurance annuity scheme. As the national insurance commissioner soon discovers, if Hyman lives a few generations, the insurance companies will go bankrupt. Hyman, however, consents to be bought out for three hundred million pounds, which he then invests at compound interest. Thus, Hyman cannot lose; in a short time he will own Great Britain. * A resolution comes from the great scientist Cunningham, who has created atomic energy. Cunningham, who is old and decrepit, offers Hyman asylum from angry mobs in exchange for immortality. When Hyman refuses, Cunningham disintegrates him. As Warrender discovers, Hyman is gone and Cunningham has become a senile idiot.

[Anonymous]

Presumably a British author.

651. **THE INVISIBLE WITNESS**. *Scoops,* 17 March 1934. Unsigned ill.

Boys' fiction. * Short story. * Jack Forbes and Professor B. J. Dancton, who have been trying to develop color television, are ready for a trial run. The equipment works perfectly, but as Forbes, at his home, watches, he sees a man emerge from behind curtains and threaten Dancton. The burglar demands the formula for a poison gas that Dancton has developed; the inventor refuses to yield it, whereupon the burglar murders him. While this has been happening, Forbes has telephoned the police who arrive with incredible celerity just as the intruder is opening Dancton's safe. He escapes, mission unaccomplished. * The police suppress most of the background of the murder, and with their consent Jack Forbes sets a trap. Arranging infrared cameras about the laboratory, focusing on the safe, he lies in wait. The

burglar arrives and opens the safe, whereupon Jack tries to capture him, succeeding only after a fairly long fight. With all the evidence that Jack has acquired, the police are certain of a conviction. As for the murderer, Patrick Hallagan, he was acting as an agent for a foreign government. * Borderline as sciencefiction. The story reminds us, however, how eagerly sought and unattainable color television was not many decades ago.

IRVING, MINNA (c.1857-1940)

Pseud. of Minna Odell, poet, born Tarrytown, New York, died Wycoff, New York (according to records). A frequent contributor of verse to turn of the century magazines. Although the present story is weak, some of Ms. Irving's verse is deft and clever. Her supernatural ballad "The Christmas Riders" is rather good.

652. **THE MOON WOMAN**. *Amazing Stories,* November 1929. Ill. Walitt.

Short story. * *Time:* The main part of the story is set in A.D. 3014, but see the comment below. * Professor James Hicks believes that he has discovered a serum of suspended animation, but since he cannot persuade anyone to try it, he decides to be his own guinea pig. In the presence of his friend Dr. Blickman, he injects himself with enough serum for a year. Blickman is supposed to take care of his body until awaking time. Blickman, however, is tempted by Hicks's wealth, the use of which he will have while Hicks is asleep, and reinjects him several times. Hicks is placed in a mausoleum. A year later, when he does not revive and his body is obviously not alive, he is declared dead. * Two centuries later (the date 3014 is cited), Rosaria, a young woman flying above the area sees the tomb, which she thinks is a temple. She flies down to it, and manages to squeeze her way in through the roof. At this time Hicks awakens. * He and Rosaria converse. The future people have a flying culture and flit about with small artificial wings. Food tablets offer the taste and nourishment of twentieth-century foods. Disease is unknown. When the Earthmen reached the Moon in 1930, the Moonmen began to descend and mingle with the terrestrials, sharing their superscience. Rosaria herself had a Lunarian mother. * As Hicks is declaring his love for Rosaria, he awakens. The serum did not work, but he had a good night's sleep and a pleasant dream. * *Miscellaneous:* The frame situation, no matter what date Rosaria quotes, is not around 2800, but our own time. * Below routine.

JACKSON, STUART.

Possibly Stuart Jackson (1906-?), British journalist; feature writer for Northcliffe newspapers, film critic for Liverpool Evening Express and Sunday Chronicle. Editor-director of Star Features, Ltd.

653. **THE LOVELY GHOST**. *Astounding Stories,* November 1933. Ill. C. R. Thomson (C R T).

Short story. * Supernatural fiction. * A reminiscence of the great pianist Chalapinski. After an unfortunate marriage, he had an affair (marriage is not mentioned) with the delightful Chrystel, whom he loved deeply. Together they worked to bring him to his present high position as a concert artist. But while they were traveling, there was a train wreck, and Chrystel was killed. * Chalapinski had to perform that evening despite the tragedy, but

Jackson, Stuart (*continued*)

he was buoyed by the feeling that Chrystel was with him. Indeed, some force prompted him to move his hand just before the wing of the grand piano accidentally slammed shut. But Chalapinski did not see Chrystel. He was temporarily blind. * Sentimental and rather foolish.

JACKSON, WOOD.

No information, but portrait shows a middle-aged man.

654. THE BAT-MEN OF MARS. *Air Wonder Stories,* May 1930-*Wonder Stories,* June and July 1930.
Short novel. * *Time:* 1958. *Place:* largely Mars. * Leonard Fry, a great scientist, has unlocked atomic energy and is now mastering space travel. He has already sent an unmanned rocket to the Moon, where he has set off an atomic explosion. Now he has built a three-hundred-foot-long rocket ship, atomic powered, to explore Mars. * He and his friend Henry Randolph fly off, together with Alicia Rowan, Fry's platonic girlfriend, as a stowaway. Since Alicia is repeatedly described as the virgin from Earth, her status seems unequivocal. The rocket reaches Mars without major incident. * *Background:* Mars is Schiaparellian, with canals, dry sea bottoms, and totally human inhabitants, who are divided into two roughly equipotent but hostile nations, Osin and Avin. Osin, on the whole corresponds to the good guys, Avin to the bad. Also present are gorilline bat-men, flying humanoids, against whom Martian cities are walled. Martian science is about equal to Terrestrial, but has progressed in different ways. The main point is a prophecy that great days will come when a virgin from Earth marries a Martian ruler. * Alicia foolishly wanders away from the rocket and is seized by the bat-men, but rescued by Osinian warriors. All the Earthmen go to the court of Osin, where they are well treated, though held captive, but the Kor (king) of Osin insists on marrying Alicia. The king of Avin, however, demands Alicia, and war breaks out. * The Earthmen, with their atomic power, destroy the walls of Avin's cities, and Avin capitulates. Fry gets Alicia back, and Randolph will wed Tor Florio, the Kor of Osin's sister, with whom he had been carrying an illicit romance. All concerned are suitably married, and the Earthmen and their quondam virgins leave for Earth. * *Miscellaneous:* Fry's atomic power simply reduces matter to dust, without radiation problems. * A strange mixture of H. Rider Haggard and Edgar Rice Burroughs, in a belated fantastic adventure. Of no interest. The title of the story is also given as "The Bat Men of Mars."

JACOBI, CARL (1908-1997)

U.S. (Minnesota) writer, editor. Editor of *Minnesota Quarterly.* Fairly prolific writer of pulp fiction, in this area notably supernatural horror fiction, much of which appeared in *Weird Tales.* At his best a clean, economical writer with a sense of style and unusual, evocative detail. His better work has been reprinted by Arkham House in *Revelations in Black* (1947) and *Portraits in Moonlight* (1964).

655. MOSS ISLAND. *Amazing Stories Quarterly,* Winter 1932. Ill. Morey.
Short-short story. * *Place:* Canada. * The narrator, a naturalist, visits a small island off the coast of New Brunswick. While examining a limestone formation, he chances to open up a small hole, or vug, that is filled with a brownish liquid that he recognizes as a decay product of a certain moss. His friend the noted biologist Professor Monroe has claimed that such liquid contains the essential principle of growth, called muscivol. * The narrator, after filling his thermos bottle with the liquid, makes a small test on a tuft of moss, which immediately springs up wildly into growth. As he leaps back, however, he spills the muscivol and barely escapes with his life as the mosses erupt into fantastic, towering growth. He is fortunate to reach the boat that was to pick him up. As he looks back, he sees that the whole island is covered with white, presumably the plant growth, although his rustic boatman asserts that it is only mist. * As befitting a *Weird Tales* author, some attempt at mood.

656. THE TOMB FROM BEYOND. *Wonder Stories,* November 1933. Ill. Paul.
Short story. * A science-fiction horror story, the monster from the crypt theme. * John Arnold, representative of a real-estate firm, visits the great explorer Trenard in his isolated house. Trenard was the discoverer of the lost civilization of Dras, now submerged near Borneo. It was a high culture, apparently with an intuitive knowledge of higher mathematics and physics. Trenard believes that a tomb that he transported from Dras to his estate embodies a mathematics that permits entry from other dimensions. He may be right, for there have been mysterious deaths in the area. * One problem is that Trenard has used the tomb, which stands in a lake, as a resting place for his dead sister. Now he is determined both to remove his sister's remains and to destroy the tomb. The narrator watches as a horrible monstrosity emerges from the tomb toward Trenard, while Trenard tries to flood the lake with oil and ignite it. Trenard succeeds, but dies in the effort. * Echoes of Poe, Merritt, and *Weird Tales,* without too much internal logic or conviction, but at least more literate than most of Gernsback's stories.

JAMES, D. L.

U.S. author, then resident in Jacksonville, Florida. Published seven other stories in the genre magazines in the late 1930s and 1940. * See also #1824, "Crystals of Madness."

657. THE COSMO-TRAP. *Astounding Stories,* April 1936. Unsigned ill. (Brown?)
Short story. * *Place:* Northern Florida and an other-world of some sort. * Mac, the narrator, is petulantly complaining about events following the mysterious disappearance of Voorland. He gives details in a backflash. * Voorland, a hermit scientist, has summoned Mac to his isolated laboratory, where on an open platform there is an apparatus that apparently consists of miles of tubing containing argon. What it does, Voorland claims, is create a perfect vacuum—which does not exist naturally. (Even so-called empty space contains matter.) In such a vacuum, things are drawn together. * The apparatus opens a gateway to another frame of existence, into which Voorland and Mac venture. The air is breathable, but the landscape, which is composed of odd-looking rocks, is alien. Indeed, when Voorland picks up a stone, it sprouts legs and breaks away. Voorland explains this: The inorganic world is alive. * The landscape turns hostile, and the stones try to seize the men as they rush to reenter our world. Plummeting through the gateway, the men consider themselves safe, but Voorland brought with him a small stone, and, as Mac watches, an arm snakes through from the other-world and retrieves the stone. Voorland topples back into the other-world, and the arm, entangled, wrecks the machinery. * Now, six months later, Mac is reconstructing the machine to rescue

James, D. L. (*continued*)

Voorland. The delay is no problem, since there is a considerable time differential between the two worlds. * Routine.

JAMES, [T.] H[OWARD] and JAMES, MAURICE

No firm information. Portraits accompanying the story show two young men who may well be brothers. While the story legend reads H. James, his portrait is identified as T. Howard James. A Thomas Howard James (1912-?) was later associated with Eastman Kodak, Rochester, New York. A Maurice James (1905-1982) was a prominent entomologist. There is no evidence, however, that either man is to be identified with the present authors.

658. **THE MYSTERY METAL.** *Science Wonder Stories*, March 1930. Ill. Paul.

Short-short story. * *Place:* New York City. * Strange events at a succession of banks. The watchmen have been found dead, and gold in the vaults has been changed to a strange bronze-like metal. When the bank president Thomas Lester, the brother of scientist Dan Lester, is killed, Dan takes a hand. He soon determines that radiation from an evolved cosmic ray generator is involved; the rays both transmute and kill. Triangulation reveals the source, the laboratory of a mad scientist named Kay, who obviously has a grudge against banks. When the police and others break in, they find apparatus and Kay, who has been accidentally killed by his ray. * Negligible.

JAMES, HENRY

According to Schwartz/Weisinger and Day the pseud. of L. C. Kellenberger, about whom there is no information. The name "Henry James," according to Schwartz/Weisinger was an accidental contamination from the story. From internal evidence, perhaps a Bostonian, or at least a New Englander.

659. **MERNOS.** *Amazing Stories*, February 1929. Ill, Paul.

Long short story. * *Place:* mostly Mars and the asteroid belt. * Henry James, a New Hampshire farmer-astronomer, is reclining under a tree during a hot summer day when something from the sky strikes near him. It is a cylinder containing a long manuscript written in German. Professor Margehtes, a neighbor, recognizes the author as Professor von Altenburg, a researcher on interplanetary travel who disappeared shortly before World War I. * The narrative: Altenburg builds himself a small spaceship with a propeller for use in the atmosphere and an antigravity cap for space. He sets out for Mars, which he reaches in a very short time. * Mars is arid, the canals are dry, and archeological remains are plentiful. There is life, however. Small globular beings float toward him and converse with him telepathically. They are friendly, but no longer possess the great science of their past. A dying race, they are on the edge of extinction. * Altenburg leaves Mars, but his space car is deflected by a gigantic meteor and he is forced out into the asteroid belt, where he lands on an unknown planet. This planet, Mernos, which is surrounded by a gas that does not reflect light rays, is invisible from Earth, but is the true missing planet according to Bode's Law. It is very pleasant and Earth-like. Altenburg soon meets the inhabitants, who converse with him telepathically. They take him to an incredibly beautiful city, where he stays, learning the customs and history of Mernos. * The Mernians are perfect specimens of humanity. Their culture is a true Schlarafenland.

All necessities are supplied by the state; the people work at pleasant tasks for brief times; there is no more crime or poverty; there is a planetary government. Solid food is no longer needed; one simply breathes certain vapors. * In addition to being locally telepathic, the Mernians can dissociate their astral bodies and visit other worlds; Earth, thus, is completely familiar to them. Their explorations have taken them all over the universe. * Altenburg is given the choice of remaining on Mernos or returning to Earth by spaceship (an antiquated mode of travel which the Mernians are willing to revive for him). He decides to stay on Mernos, which is perfection compared with Earth, but will send several cylinders with his message back to Earth. * James and his associates publicize Altenburg's message, and on one occasion are convinced that they were visited by his astral presence. * Oddly enough, Altenburg does not receive a female companion, as is usually the case in such stories. * *Miscellaneous:* The inhabitants of Saturn are human, too, but are at the cultural level of Rome during Julius Caesar's time. * The inhabitants of one of Jupiter's moons are more or less intelligent insects. * One wonders why (apart from 1/2¢ per word) early writers delighted in detailed ethnographic accounts of boring and insipid societies.

JAMES, KENNETH

British author. James Kenneth Wallace, who has used the pseud. Kenneth James, may be responsible for the present story.

660. **BURROUGHS PASSES.** *Astounding Stories*, October 1933. Ill. Charles Durant (C. D.)

Short story. * Supernatural fiction. After-death experiences. *Place:* on the Indian frontier, where troops of the British Indian Army, including Gurkhas, encounter deserters from a Chinese army. The geography is thus a little strained. * Burroughs, an officer, knows himself to be a coward, yet manages to conceal it from his fellow officers and the enlisted men. Thus, when he is assigned to a column against the Chinese deserters/brigands, he behaves heroically in battle to cover his fear. The skirmish over, he is lying down comfortably, with some satisfaction at his role in the fighting, when he hears one of the other officers regret that he died in battle. * A very trite situation handled routinely.

JAMES, M. F.

Pseud. of James W. McLaughlin. U.S. (Boston, Massachusetts) author.

661. **THE EXPEDITION FROM KYTLM.** *Astounding Stories*, December 1936. Ill. Flatos.

Short-short story. * *Time:* 1947. * Presented from two points of view, Terrestrial and alien. * From the Terrestrial side, terrible catastrophes follow the appearance of a gigantic dark body the size of the sun. It enters the solar system and, disregarding the laws of celestial mechanics, moves about among the planets. As it approaches Earth, a large part of the Atlantic Ocean disappears into the sky; tidal waves and earthquakes cause millions of deaths. Hundreds of thousands of people disappear en masse; Shanghai, Kyoto, and Canton vanish in a few minutes. New York is burned to a crisp by a concentration of solar rays. * From the point of view of the explorers on the spaceship of the First Universal Expedition from Kytlm: The captain reports. His group found a midget solar system, with a sun no larger than their spaceship. Most of the planets were empty of life, but on

James, M. F. (*continued*)
the third planet instruments recorded the existence of plentiful microscopic life, some of which congregated in large colonies. Samples were taken, with the hope that study in Kytlm laboratories would be profitable. By accident a lens focused on one such colony burned it. The captain rejects, as too frivolous to consider, the conjecture that the bacteria concerned are civilized sentient beings. * Routine.

JANUS, WARWICK
No information.
662. **PALADINS OF THE SKY**. *Amazing Stories Quarterly*, Fall 1931.
Short story, chronicle form. * Time: A.D. 2000. * One of the few early stories that is generally favorable to the USSR. * In 1945 France, Germany, and Great Britain attacked the Soviet Union. The fighting was ferocious, but the Red air force and army beat back the invaders. By the next year China and India had joined the Russians, and their combined armies, after a five-year war, conquered Europe, Asia, and Africa. * The new order is headed by the Eurasian Council of four members, with Pogon Lonklos as Executive Director for life and real master. Pogon is succeeded by his son Suyd, who continues his father's policies. * In 1962 the United States of South America came into being and was soon allied with the United States. * On 1 January 2000 Suyd Lonklos, writing from his capital in Calcutta, sends an ultimatum to the American alliance: merge with Eurasia, or war. The Americans reject the ultimatum. * Commander Helman, the chief of the American Defense Council is well aware that the Eurasian air force is stronger than his; but he replies with neither surrender or defiance. Instead, he sends a challenge to Lonklos, asking for a personal duel to settle the matter. Six American leaders are to fight six Eurasian leaders in air combat. If the Americans win, the Eurasians will return to Calcutta; if the Eurasians win, the Americans will surrender. * Helman knows Lonklos personally from their days together as cadets, and he is sure that Lonklos cannot refuse a dare. Lonklos accepts, and the combat takes place, with Helman the sole survivor. The Eurasian forces withdraw per agreement. * Nothing to recommend. Probably a filler selected from the slush pile to fill a few pages.

JENKINS, AINSLEE
Pseud. of Samuel Emmett Gowen (1902-1973), generally known as Emmett Gowen. Born in Nashville, Tennessee. At this time resident in New York City. Various publicity jobs, including Better Business Bureau, New York; free lance writing. Fairly frequent contributor to pulps *Top-Notch, Cowboy Story, Clues*, also to *Scribners, Yale Review, Atlantic Monthly*, etc. From 1959 an operator of hunting, exploring, archeological diving services in Mexico and Central America. Died in LaVergne, Tennessee. Late work *On Man and the Good Life* (1974), study of popular Tennessee ethnobotany.
663. **IN THE SHADOW OF THE TII**. *Astounding Stories*, November 1933. Ill. Amos Sewell.
Short story. * *Place:* Tahiti. * Beautiful native maiden Tuaoa is harassed by the brutal, lecherous Louis Sparth, who has bought her from the village headman for two cases of whiskey. Tuaoa takes refuge with the native god Tii, the last idol of a once powerful deity, all others having been destroyed by the

missionaries, and begs him to help her. * Tii comes through. Sparth goes down the sacrificial cliff, Tuaoa is free, and Tii is pleased to have renewed worship. * Routine.

JESSEL, JOHN
Pseud. of Stanley G. Weinbaum, who has a separate entry. Jessel was a family name. Weinbaum has another story under his own name in the issue concerned.
664. **THE ADAPTIVE ULTIMATE**. *Astounding Stories*, November 1935. Ill. Dold.
(Reprinted in Weinbaum, *A Martian Odyssey* [Fantasy Press]; in Weinbaum, *A Martian Odyssey* [Hyperion]; in Weinbaum, *Dawn of Flame*; in Weinbaum, *The Best of Stanley Weinbaum*; in Weinbaum, *Dawn of Flame*; and in Stong, *The Other Worlds*.)
Short story. * A variant on the soullessness theme. * Dr. Daniel Scott, brilliant young researcher, has been investigating adaptivity. Concentrating on Drosophila, which he states has an optimal mutational rate, he has prepared an extract of adaptability that he would like to try on a human. It has already worked successfully on a rabid dog and a cat with a broken spine, curing both. * Dr. Bach, his friend at the hospital, supplies him with a suitable case, one Kyra Zelas, who is dying of tuberculosis and has only hours to live. She agrees to the experiment. * Kyra does not die, but gradually recovers. Indeed, she shows the utmost adaptability, not just toward disease, but toward men and life, being transformed into an incredibly beautiful, charming woman. But something is lacking; it would have been called a soul in the older literature, for Kyra is now utterly without conscience or morality. On her first venture outside the medical situation, she brains a man with a cobblestone to acquire money. * She is charged with murder, but easily evades justice. When arrested in broad daylight, she was a dark brunette; in the dim light of a cell or courtroom, she is a ravishing blonde. The case is thrown out as mistaken identity. * Kyra leaves Scott's establishment and makes a predictable venture into society, rising to become the mistress of the Secretary of the Treasury. She makes no bones about planning to start a world war in order to become empress of the world. * Various tests, accidents, self-inflicted injuries have shown that as the adaptive ultimate Kyra is immune to disease, poison, or physical injury. Even a knife self-plunged into her heart does not harm her. * How can she be destroyed? For destroyed she must be, to prevent world calamities. Scott and Bach are at their wit's end. Finally, it occurs to them that she might be poisoned by her own waste products. They pour carbon dioxide into her bedroom, then, while she is unconscious, they operate and remove her enlarged pineal gland, which they had decided was the seat of her strange ability. The operation is a success, and instead of the beautiful monster, they see the wretched Kyra Zelas. (Weinbaum does not reveal whether she has regressed into tuberculosis.) Scott, who has been in love with her for some time, still appreciates the glorious adaptive. * Routine. * According to Tuck the story was adapted to television and served as the basis for the motion picture *The She-Devil* (Twentieth Century Fox, 1957).

JOHNSON, A. H.
No information, but portrait accompanying "The Thunderer" shows a young man.
665. **PHAGOCYTES**. *Amazing Stories*, February 1929. Unsigned ill.

Johnson, A. H. (*continued*)

Short story. * The pathetic fallacy as draped upon a white blood cell, who tells of his experiences fighting invasive germs. The story is written in terms of small scale military actions. * Somewhat questionable as science-fiction. In any case, a subform out of date by this time. Much better examples had been published earlier.

666. **THE THUNDERER**. *Air Wonder Stories*, January 1930. Ill. Paul.

Short story. * *Time:* not long after 1950. * The eugenics vigilante strikes for mankind. * Huge storms beset the Atlantic coast, and a (presumable) crank claims credit. The self-styled Thunderer, he demands a billion dollars in cash, a work force, one hundred square miles for a personal kingdom, absolute control of all marriages, and the right to sterilize any and all as he sees fit. He looks forward to a perfected human race under his program. His demands are couched in a harangue about human degeneration due to survival of the unfit and uncontrolled breeding. * The great U.S. Army flier, Capt. David Anderson, holder of flying records, is sent out to track down the madman. Anderson, like many others, would admit that the Thunderer has a point, but objects to the way he makes it. Humanity, as Anderson says, should not be operated like a stud farm. Associated with Captain Anderson is Professor Wilkinson, a great physicist. * Wilkinson discovers the Thunderer's modus operandi: With enormous electrical power (later explained as atomic energy produced by the disintegration of lead), using a special new catalyst, the madman decomposes water into hydrogen and oxygen. The decomposition creates the storms. The Thunderer can also short circuit gasoline engines. * The Thunderer's vessel, which Anderson has seen, is like a Frank Reade aircraft, a ship's hull with a multitude of rotors. Wilkinson explains that these function according to an insight of Thomas Edison's, that really rapid air travel can only occur on sound waves produced by small vibrators like a bumblebee's wings. * The Thunderer continues on his way, draining lakes, wrecking the Suez Canal, and shattering the world. Calcutta, Hamburg, London, and New York are among his victims. Eventually, Anderson and Wilkinson, in a new superplane powered by picric acid and shielded electrically, catch sight of the Thunderer's vessel and capture him. * A great scientist, if a little mad, the Thunderer describes his techniques and aims, but manages to escape. Perhaps Anderson succeeded in destroying his vessel, perhaps not. The author has obviously left an opening for a sequel.

667. **THE RAID OF THE MERCURY**. *Amazing Stories*, July 1931. Ill. Morey.

Short story. * In a contemporary frame, the author (Johnson) visits a professional seer whose abilities he has derided. The seer, a dark man who speaks with an accent, shows him a vision of a future incident. * *Time:* undated future, but the sequel offers the date of roughly A.D. 22,000. The story is a romance, folded into an episode of air piracy. * The great aerial cruiser *Light of the Western Skies* is stopped, after brief resistance, by the *Mercury,* a pirate vessel operated by Prince James and his social revolutionaries. From the cruiser Prince James abducts his sweetheart Avice (Duchess of Orleans, Princess of the Cumberlands, and Countess of the Delta) and his enemy Lothaire (Prince of the Second Cycle, Vice-Pontiff of the Plutocracy). In this neo-feudal world of the future, the Plutocracy is apparently the

paramount power, but it is held somewhat in check by various independent nobles like the families of James and Avice. * Lothaire escapes, and James and Avice flee, until they can gather their resources. Pursued by Lothaire's forces, the *Mercury* escapes by flying through the future equivalent of an active railroad tunnel. The revolution will continue. * Episode over, Johnson (who is described by the seer as a writer of science articles) ponders over what he has experienced. * The enormous air cruisers are propeller driven. * The future society has points of interest, and one must regret that it is lost in a melodramatic, undeveloped tale. For a sequel with more detail about the future culture see #668, "The Superman."

668. **THE SUPERMAN**. *Amazing Stories,* August 1931. Ill. Morey.

Novelette. * Sequel to #667, "The Raid of the Mercury." * *Time:* around A.D. 22,000. * The author has abandoned the narrative strategy of precognition and presents the further exploits of Prince James without apology or explanation. The cultural situation, an odd mixture of Graustark, the Middle Ages, and Karl Marx, anticipatory at moments of Frank Herbert's *Dune,* is much more fully developed than in the previous story. * Background: The North American continent seems to be divided politically into several independent or semi-independent principalities. Important personalities in this politic are Princess Avice of Orleans, the Cumberlands, Countess of the Delta, and Prince James Lancaster, exiled monarch of the Kingdom of the South. In some respects parallel to the medieval situation of the Papacy, is the Plutocracy, which is both a rival and a supporting (in certain times) power to the secular states. The Plutocracy, a small group of several thousand incredibly rich men, is headed by a pontiff; second in command and proclaimed successor to the pontificate, is Prince Lothaire of the Second Cycle—the villain of the piece. The military arm of the Plutocracy is the corps of Myrmidons, a Janissary-like group of hardened, often brutal professional soldiers utterly loyal to the Plutocracy. Battle techniques are essentially sword-and-ray-gun fashion. * Independent from the Plutocracy but allied with it, supported by it and supporting it, is the Scientific Kingdom, a small enclave protected by fantastic weapons. Founded millennia earlier, it not only concentrates the scientific knowledge of the age, but has been long engaged in a eugenics program to develop supermen. Prince Lothaire is one of these supermen, gifted with incredible reflexes, mentality, and amorality. * In such a society, which is quite oppressive, there is necessarily a shadow- or counterculture. The workers, who are treated abominably, are at the edge of armed revolt, although they would not stand much chance against the Myrmidons. And a secret society, the Black Groups, is devoted to destroying the power of the Plutocracy and improving the lot of the general population. The Black Groups, who have infiltrated the Plutocrats and the Myrmidons, are favorably minded toward the political, baronial revolt that Prince James Lancaster has turned loose against Lothaire. * The plot line is simple: Lothaire captures Avice; this is in itself illegal, since she is an independent ruler, but he hopes to torture information from her about her husband, Prince James. James, learning of the incident, rescues her and in so doing establishes an alliance with the Black Groups, a member of whom is a trusted member of Lothaire's bodyguard. * Prince James hopes to unleash a coordinated attack by workers, Black Groups, his baronial forces, and soldiery from allies, but Plutocrat counterintelligence sets off the

Johnson, A. H. (*continued*)

workers prematurely, expecting that the Myrmidons will easily crush the revolt in the large cities before the other forces can be brought up. The tactic almost works, but James and his forces win the great battle. The Plutocracy is destroyed, its members massacred, and James is now king of North America. During the final battle, James overcame his personal enemy Lothaire in a sword match, and Lothaire was killed trying to escape. * Previously, Lothaire obtained a secret weapon from the Scientific Kingdom—bubonic plague. Bacilli were spread by releasing infected rats into the workers' quarters. The tactic was promising, since bacteriology was a dead science, all harmful bacteria (except specimens retained by the Scientific Kingdom) having been destroyed millennia ago. But when information obtained by a Black Group double agent revealed the nature of the plague, which threatened to wipe out much of North American humanity, Prince James penetrated the stronghold of the Scientific Kingdom and escaped with vaccines, antidotes, and formulas. * *Miscellaneous:* The Scientific Kingdom maintains a special race of dehumanized humans whom it uses for vivisection and other experimental procedures. * The supermen of the Scientific Kingdom (of which Prince Lothaire is an example) have raised their average IQ to about 200 and have achieved physical perfection. They occupy most of the offices in the Kingdoms and many in the Plutocracy; once Prince James's revolution had been crushed, the Scientific Kingdom planned to take over everything. * Not much superscience is involved in the future culture, although the Scientific Kingdom is guarded by an impregnable electric field. * In background and occasional incident anticipatory of the far superior *Dune* series of Frank Herbert, but unfortunately not developed adequately. If the nexus had been utilized by a better craftsman, developing both stories into a novel, it might have been an early classic of romantic future adventure.

669. **THE AMIR'S MAGIC.** *Amazing Stories,* March 1932. Ill. Morey.

Short story. * Borderline science-fiction at best. * *Place:* Northwest India. * The narrator Sanderson, a member of the Indian Secret Police, tells of an experience that made him wary of bees. * There was sedition in one of the native states, caused by an Afghan amir who was trying to stir up rebellion against the British. The Afghan, as he demonstrates to Sanderson, seems to have the magical power to direct killer bees against his victims. Sanderson, who is held prisoner, is due to die as a demonstration the next day, but he outwits the amir, who is himself killed. * Secret: The amir used a chemical that attracts and enrages poison-laden bees. * Obvious imitation of Edgar Wallace's Sanders of the River stories, without much real information about India, despite many native terms.

JOHNSON, E. D.

No information.

670. **THE HOLE THAT GREW.** *Amazing Stories Quarterly,* Spring/Summer 1932. Ill. Morey.

Short story. * *Time:* the near future. *Place:* the San Francisco area. * Professor Beale, attempting to split the atom, has been all too successful. He has started a small atomic destruction that cannot be stopped. At the moment it is confined to the building, but eventually? * Flying to California to assist Beale are the narrator (Gray) and the great Professor Pritchard. Pritchard,

Gray, and Beale work desperately, but without success, and news of the peril leaks out, causing panic. * After considerable study and experiment, the investigators believe that they have a process that will stop the atomic decay. Alas, it only speeds up things enormously, so that the atomic hole expands out into the neighboring field, growing at a geometric rate. * Finally, Pritchard discovers a means to stop the destruction, but to apply the finishing touches, he must sacrifice his life. * Not many technological advances except a 500 mph rocket plane. It seems rather illogical that only three men should be entrusted to ward off the destruction of the world.

JOHNSON, E. H.

Probably Elbe Herbert Johnson (1887-1967), U.S. physicist. Born Michigan. Ph.D., University of Chicago. Hon. D.Sc., Kenyon 1955. Professor of Physics, University of Wisconsin. Areas of interest, history of physics, molecular spectra.

671. **THE GOLDEN VAPOR.** *Amazing Stories Quarterly,* Winter 1928. Ill. Paul.

(First published in *Science and Invention,* February 1920.)

Short story. * Dr. Grieg, an Alsatian physicist of high reputation, finds himself blacklisted from work in Europe because of his controversial views on light and matter. Coming to the United States, he continues his researches. His starting point is the perception that there can be interchange of molecules between contiguous solids, and that light has a certain motive power. He first produces a device for transmitting gas molecules, then continues to improve his device until he has produced a functioning matter transmitter. * By chance Grieg's laboratory is above a bank that is preparing a shipment of bullion. When the bullion cases are opened, they prove to contain only iron. The professor has obviously stolen the gold, although the author is at pains not to say this directly.

JOHNSTON, E[RNEST] M[ILTON]. and SMITH, CLARK ASHTON

Ernest Milton Johnston (1873-1946) was a resident of Collingwood, Ontario, Canada. An educator, he graduated from the University of Toronto in 1926. His portrait is included with the story. Clark Ashton Smith has a separate entry. Johnston supplied the plot, which Smith developed.

672. **THE PLANET ENTITY.** *Wonder Stories Quarterly,* Fall 1931. Ill. Paul.

(Reprinted as "Seedling of Mars" in Smith, *Tales of Science and Sorcery.*)

Novelette. * The second-prize-winning story of the Interplanetary Plot Contest. Mr. Johnston received twenty-five dollars. * *Time:* 1947. *Place:* California, Mars, Venus. * In the fall of 1947, a few days before the great football game at Berkeley, a strange vessel descends into the stadium. Oval, the ship is about a hundred feet long, oddly faceted, and unlike any vessel hitherto seen. There is much speculation about it. * As a mixed group of scientists and officials stand near it, a doorway in the ship opens and a stairway descends. The situation seems to be an invitation. The group enter the ship, whereupon the door closes and the ship flies off, to where? * As the captives soon realize, they are on their way to Mars. The flight, which is not too unpleasant, seems to be of very short duration, perhaps a couple of days at most. As the ship approaches Mars, the men see that the canals are not constructions or waterways, but vegetable

Johnston, E. M. and Smith, Clark Ashton (*continued*)
growths that seem united as far as can be seen into a single gigantic plant. The ship lands in a clearing amid the vegetation, and the men alight, finding reasonable accommodations awaiting them. As the men watch, a protrusion emerges from the plant stem, growing rapidly into an exact simulacrum of Gaillard, who is in effect the leading character. The simulacrum encourages Gaillard to talk, and in a matter of hours, from hearing him speak, plus telepathic understanding, it speaks perfect English. * This is the plant being's story: It is the sole living thing on Mars, and for ages it has dwelt in solitary contentment. In mentality it is far superior to mankind, and in science and technology, although of a strange sort, it is millennia ahead of humanity. It can create almost anything it wishes from free atoms. It built the spaceship, for example, in a matter of hours. * The plant explains. It has examined Earth closely with special optical organs that amount to fantastic telescopes, and it has brought the party from Earth for a purpose. It wishes to make a trade. It needs a small quantity of water, since Mars is drying out beyond control, and in exchange it offers scientific and technological information beyond price. * Gaillard frankly states the obvious, that he and his associates have no power to make such a pact. The plant being thereupon transports the party back to Earth as intermediaries. It soon becomes obvious that mankind is not mature enough to accept the offer, for Gaillard and those who want to accept the trade are hounded, some even murdered. * The plant offers a new solution. A huge spaceship from Mars takes Gaillard and his people to Venus, where in the libration zone there is a fine tropical continent awaiting settlement. Not too long after this, the plant shoots a seed to Earth. It sprouts and takes over the planet. * The writing is literate, as is always the case with Smith, but the characterizations are weak, and the development is very out of balance, with too much summary at the ending. Still, unusual enough to be worth reading.

JONES, ARTHUR FREDERICK
No information. There is an Arthur Frederick Jones, a Massachusetts dog fancier and writer about dogs, but there is no reason to think that he is our Arthur Frederick Jones.

　　673. **THE INQUISITION OF 6061**. *Wonder Stories*, December 1933. Ill. Winter.
Short story. * *Time:* A.D. 6061. * The world is a dictatorship, and the dictator X, a religious zealot, insists that everyone should worship Electricity. Other religion is to be exterminated, since it is the only element of individuality left in the world. * There are religious examinations like those of the early Roman Empire. Stubborn individuals who refuse to bow to the spark are hauled off into the dictator's building and tortured to death. * J is a particularly stubborn case. To break his will, X causes him to be taken around to the various torture chambers to see what is done to infidels. He sees fingers being amputated, men being racked, victims being killed by exhausting air in sealed bells, etc. * A crisis comes when J is taken to a room where there is an enormous electrical discharge. One of the guards ventures too near the electricity and is almost dragged in. J saves him. This opens the eyes of the guards, who discuss the situation with J. * The end result is a mass movement that topples X. As X leaves his fortress, a discredited man, J calls upon the stormy heavens to show X that there is a higher power than electricity. A

lightning bolt strikes X, killing him, but who knows whether it convinced him? * Jones makes the point that language, too, has deteriorated through the dictatorship. * Told in a fabular manner that might have been interesting with a more skilled writer. As the story is, primitive and most amateurish; probably the work of a very young man. Sample: "'Now you will change your mind,' [J] leered in [X's] ear."

JONES, NEIL R[ONALD] (1909-1988)
U.S. (Fulton, Upstate New York) author. By occupation an insurance adjuster for the New York State Department of Labor. According to Tuck, Jones was the inventor of "Interplanetary," a fairly popular board game. * One of the more prolific early writers of pulp science-fiction, although very weak technically. Jones's stories are described as The Professor Jameson Series, The Durna Rangue Series, and Other Works.

The Professor Jameson Series

Twenty-one stories set about forty million years in the future, describing the (repetitive) adventures throughout the universe of a twentieth-century man whose brain has been placed in a metal body. Each successive story is usually provided with an explanatory backflash. * As the longest series of the day, drearily innocuous similarities.

　　674. **THE JAMESON SATELLITE**. *Amazing Stories*, July 1931. Ill. Morey.
(Reprinted in Jones, *Planet of the Double Sun* and in Asimov, *Before the Golden Age*.)
Short story. * This first story sets the background for the series about Professor Jameson and the Zoromes. * *Time:* 1958 in a prologue. About forty million years in the future for the body of the story. * *Place:* Space near the Earth, and the Earth. * Old Professor Jameson is obsessed with preserving his body in perfect condition after death. His solution: Let his body be placed in a shell and shot into space, where it will be preserved by the absolute cold. Jameson dies, and his body is placed into orbit about sixty-five thousand miles from the Earth, with radium-powered jets to alter his rocket's orbit against meteors. * Time passes. The sun becomes a red, weak star; the Earth loses much of its atmosphere; and the human race becomes extinct. * At about A.D. 40,000,000, when an exploratory ship of the Zoromes enters the solar system, its crew decides to examine the inner planets. * *Background:* The Zoromes, who originated on a planet hundreds of millions of light-years away, are ultimate cyborgs (my term), with living brains occupying metal bodies. They are about three feet high, cubic, with four metal legs and feet, grasping tentacles, and an organic brain in a metal headpiece. They are nearly immortal, for all their parts except the brain can easily be replaced. Since the entire race has been machine-converted, they no longer multiply, but remain constant in number, except for accidental deaths. (This point is contradicted in a later story, #680.) Benevolent beings, they devote their time to exploring the universe. * The Zoromes encounter Jameson's rocket, retrieve it, and decide to reanimate him. Removing his brain and reactivating it, they insert it in a Zorome body and awaken Jameson. At first bewildered, he soon regains command of himself, and he and Zoromes exchange information telepathically. * The party descends to Earth, which is a dead

Jones, Neil R. (*continued*)

waste. Jameson, depressed by the fate of mankind and the Earth, at first wonders whether he wants to live, but finally decides to accept the Zorome mode of life and accompany his rescuers in their flight about the universe. * A sort of childlike naiveté renders the story not unacceptable, despite weak writing and literary flatness.

675. **THE PLANET OF THE DOUBLE SUN.** *Amazing Stories,* February 1932. Ill. Morey.
(Reprinted in Jones, *Planet of the Double Sun.*)
Short story. * The second story in the Professor Jameson series. * Jameson and the Zoromes land on the first planet of a system illuminated by two suns, a blue one and an orange one. In a ravine they find a large quantity of skeletal material of tripedal beings and a cryptic inscription that has something to do with the suns. * As the explorers soon discover, the emanation of the blue sun in some fashion permits immaterial "phantom birds" from another dimension to enter bearing thoughts of madness and suicide. There is no defense against them. The Zoromes have little resistance to the psychic attack, and all but Jameson die. Jameson, who is able to resist the assault to some extent, is now out in space alone in a badly damaged, nonfunctioning ship. He wonders whether he will ever be found by another Zorome vessel.

676. **THE RETURN OF THE TRIPEDS.** *Amazing Stories,* May 1932. Ill. Morey.
(Reprinted in Jones, *Planet of the Double Sun.*)
Short story. * The third story in the Professor Jameson series. * *Time:* five hundred and seventy-one years after the previous story. * Jameson, using the telescope in his disabled vessel, has discovered that the skeletal material on the first planet was not that of natives, but of visitors from the second planet, which is still inhabited by the tripeds. He watches their gradual scientific progress, which finally includes spaceships. * One such ship approaches Jameson's vessel, and during telepathic communication background is exchanged. The tripeds had tried to colonize the first planet some seven hundred years earlier, but were forced off by the malignant dimensional creatures. Triped civilization then fell as a result of wars, and only now is it regaining earlier heights. * At the moment, the tripeds, who have thought shields, are sending a revenge mission to the first planet to attack the dimensional beings and, if successful, to begin to clear the planet for colonization. * Jameson accompanies the tripeds, takes part in the triped invasion of the other dimension, in which poison gas destroys large numbers of the phantom birds. The tripeds will later return in great force and exterminate the flying horrors. * Jameson also discovers that the Zoromes are not all dead. While in the other dimension he sees and communicates with his machine-man comrades who survive. They were not all destroyed, as indicated in the previous story. Some fifteen survive. They tried to commit suicide by leaping into the ocean. They were not killed, but they were damaged and were unable to climb out of the water. They can all be easily repaired on the Zorome ship. * This done, Jameson, his Zorome friends, and a few tripeds (converted to machine men) leave for their next adventure.

677. **INTO THE HYDROSPHERE.** *Amazing Stories,* October 1933. Ill. Morey.
(Reprinted in Jones, *The Sunless World.*)
Novelette. * The fourth adventure of Professor Jameson and the Zoromes. * The explorers approach a planet that seems to be a solid sphere of water. On the surface live a primitive people, something like frogmen, who are not unfriendly. They are timid and wary, however, because they are subject to slave raids from a far more civilized people who live deep in the sea, perhaps at a small core. * The raiders (the Uchke) suddenly attack, knocking several of the Zoromes into the sea and capturing them. *Background:* The Uchke, who have gorilline heads, but small spindly bodies, have hollowed out the small iron core of the planet and closed it off with airlocks. In this area they maintain a high civilization, with factories manned by frog-man slaves. The Uchke are not natives of the water world, but come from a nearby planet. * Jameson and fellow Zoromes undergo perils, dismemberment, captivity, and more perils until things are resolved. They instigate a slave revolt, holding out until the Zorome spaceship finds them. While the Uchke have heat rays, good explosives, and disintegrators of a sort, their weapons are weak compared to those of the Zoromes. * After cleaning out the inner world, the Zoromes will go to the Uchke home planet and either exterminate the oppressors or give them a salutary lesson. * Routine.

678. **TIME'S MAUSOLEUM.** *Amazing Stories,* December 1933. Ill. Morey.
(Reprinted in Jones, *The Sunless World.*)
Short story. * The fifth adventure of Professor Jameson and the Zoromes. * On investigating the planet of the Uchke, the Zoromes discover that Uchke science and technology are not their own, but the creation of a subject race, the Qwux. The Qwux are so superspecialized in their work that once one individual, Zlestrm, is removed, the Uchke are no longer able to repair their ships or travel in space. This solves the problem of aggression in the water world. * Zlestrm has another specialty: he has constructed a time viewer that can show the past of any particular place. Since the Zoromes are now near Earth, they descend and watch episodes in terrestrial history. These include the incident described in #689, "Martian and Troglodyte," a view of Atlantis, and, in considerable detail, the circumstances of Professor Jameson's entombment in the space rocket. Much play is given, in a racist manner, to the reactions of a comic black to the transportation of the corpse. * The story ends with a minor crisis.

679. **THE SUNLESS WORLD.** *Amazing Stories,* December 1934. Ill. Morey.
(Reprinted in Jones, *The Sunless World.*)
Short story. * The sixth adventure of Professor Jameson and the Zoromes. * In this instance, on passing through an area filled with dead stars, they come upon a runaway planet. Hollow, it maintains two forms of life: more or less humanoid purple intelligent beings who live in the illuminated interior of the planet, and black cylindrical semi-intelligent leech-like creatures that inhabit the dark surface and prey on the humanoids, notably dissidents and the helpless aged who have been expelled. The humanoids have cities and some small civilization. * Several Zoromes, trapped inside the world, help the humanoids, leading to the defeat of the leech-like creatures. As a complication, the dark planet is due to collide with a planet in another system unless the Zoromes can disintegrate the second planet in time. * All ends well.

680. **ZORA OF THE ZOROMES.** *Amazing Stories,* March 1935. Ill. Morey.

Jones, Neil R. (*continued*)
(Reprinted in Jones, *Space War.*)
Novelette. * The seventh story in the Zorome series. * The Zoromes and Jameson return to Zor, their home planet. There Jameson becomes acquainted with Zora, a young female. Zora, who has four legs, a vase-like body, and six tentacle-arms, is in love with Bext, a pleasant young male. As Zora reminds Jameson when he expresses astonishment, organic Zoromes are needed to replenish the machine men, who cannot breed. After she has reached the proper age and fulfilled her civic duties, she, too, will become a machine person. * Unfortunately, interplanetary hostilities break out with the planet Mumed, to whose unpleasant people the Zoromes have taught the art of machine adaptation. With their enormous science, the Zoromes could disintegrate Mumed, but they are reluctant to do this since it would destroy evolving life on another planet in Mumed's system. * Instead, more conventional interplanetary war is the norm. Bext is killed, but his brain is saved and installed in a machine. On learning this, Zora has herself transformed to machine life. * During the war, the Zoromes use invisible ships, the principle of which is not explained.

681. **SPACE WAR**. *Amazing Stories*, July 1935. Ill. Morey.
(Reprinted in Jones, *Space War.*)
Novelette. * The eighth story in the Professor Jameson Series, a direct continuation of #680, "Zora of the Zoromes." * The space war against Mumed continues. Invisible Zorome ships play a lesser role than in the previous story, since the Mumes use a radar-like spotting technique that bypasses invisibility. In one episode, Jameson, somewhat damaged, is mistaken by the Mumes for one of their fellows, a natural mistake since the Mumes use the same equipment as the Zoromes. He is taken to an enormous underground fortress, where he helps operate a net-like ray apparatus that threatens to capture the whole Zorome fleet. He is able to warn the Zoromes in time, and Mumed is badly beaten. The Mume dictator, fleeing the planet with Jameson in chase, is killed on another planet of the Mumed system. The war is over.

682. **"LABYRINTH."** *Amazing Stories*, April 1936. Ill. Morey.
(Reprinted in Jones, *Space War.*)
Novelette. * The ninth story in the Professor Jameson series. * Jameson and the other Zoromes visit a planet that contains a primitive metal-eating life form. Slug-like creatures without much intelligence, they are dangerous because of their numbers and avidity. The Zoromes, whose pure metal is a strong attractant, are forced to take refuge in endless caverns, dashing about to evade the slugs. * The Zoromes are eventually rescued.

The remaining twelve stories in the Zorome series are much the same as those described. They are: "Twin Worlds" (*Amazing Stories,* April 1937); "On the Planet Fragment" (*Amazing Stories,* October 1937); "The Music Monsters" (*Amazing Stories,* April 1938); The Cat-Men of Aemt" (*Astonishing Stories,* August 1940); "Cosmic Derelict" (*Astonishing Stories,* February 1941); "Slaves of the Unknown" (*Astonishing Stories,* March 1942); "Doomsday on Ajiat" (*Astonishing Stories,* October 1942); "The Metal Moon" (*Super Science Stories,* September 1949); "Parasite Planet" (*Super Science Stories,* November 1949); "World without Darkness" (*Super Science Stories,* March 1950); "The Mind Masters" (*Super Science Stories,* September 1950); and "The Star

Killers" (*Super Science Stories,* August 1951).

The Durna Rangue Series

In the middle of the third millennium A.D. the Earth is really ruled by the infamous cult known as the Durna Rangue or the Asurians. Possessed of a science beyond that of the rest of the solar system, the Asurians engage in all sorts of unholy experiments and procedures of the utmost cruelty. Captives who fall into their hands are routinely vivisected, parts stored for future need. Durna Rangue tentacles of power also reach elsewhere in the solar system. The iconography accompanying the stories fits them well, with tall, dark, hooded and robed figures reminiscent of the Spanish Inquisition and the AMORC Rosicrucian ads.

683. **ESCAPE FROM PHOBOS**. *Wonder Stories,* February 1933. Ill. Paul.
Short story. * *Time:* the interplanetary future. Although the story is not dated directly, comments in #684, "Little Hercules" establish it as about the twenty-fourth century. * *Place:* Phobos and Mars. * Ern Hantel, a murderer, is awaiting execution in the prison on Phobos when a fellow prisoner (Hoenbraun) contacts him and offers him a chance of escape. As Hoenbraun gradually reveals, they will tunnel out of their cells to the storeroom, don space suits, strap on rockets and parachutes, and drop down to Mars. It is chancy, but still better than certain execution. Hoenbraun reveals that he is a member of the Asurians, also known as the Durna Rangue, a supersecret scientific-religious cult, who will rescue and harbor the fugitives on Mars. * All goes according to plan, except that there is not enough cloth for two parachutes. Hantel and Hoenbraun quarrel, and in the resulting struggle Hoenbraun is killed. * Hantel blasts off to Mars. There can be no direct pursuit, since spaceships are not allowed on Phobos, in case of a prison break. He lands safely, takes cover, and before long reaches the agreed rendezvous. * An Asurian takes him underground, where he is examined. The Asurians, who are masters of psychology, know that Hantel is lying about the circumstances of Hoenbraun's death. He would be punished, but he breaks loose, passing through radiation chambers on his way out, and regains the surface. But he is an old man, for the radiation is apparently used by the Asurians for disguise purposes. Since he is obviously too old to be the escaped prisoner, he passes patrols and is free. The Asurians will catch up with him eventually. * Routine.

684. **LITTLE HERCULES**. *Astounding Stories,* August 1936. Ill. Dold.
Novelette. * Second story in the Durna Rangue series. * *Time:* the twenty-sixth century. * *Place:* Buffalo at first, but perhaps elsewhere later in the story. * *Background:* Grimo, a small-time, hunted criminal, is offered asylum if he will join the Durna Rangue. He agrees. After some time, occasionally unconscious, he finds himself, not vivisected (as at one time he feared), but transformed into a miniature version of his former self. Boiled down to about three feet tall by atomic condensation, he nevertheless retains his former weight and strength. * There are many other dwarfed servitors of the Durna Rangue, but Grimo is the sole example of an experimental technique that allowed him to keep his intelligence and full personality. The other midgets are nearly mindless and without volition. * As a virtual slave, Grimo

Jones, Neil R. (*continued*)

assists the scientific masters of the cult in their researches and operations, notably with the mechanism that ages its victims artificially, as mentioned in #683, "Escape from Phobos." * Among his tasks is assistance—at a safe distance—in the creation of Aonis, an incredibly beautiful and seductive synthetic young woman. Aonis, whom Grimo finds irresistible, is, however, a veritable Rappaccini's daughter, whose touch is fatal. But, as the Durna Rangue scientist says, She is purely experimental. * All this while Grimo has desperately hoped to escape, even though it seems impossible. His chance finally comes when an earth subsidence discloses an exit to the outside world, and he leaves. * Oddly enough, the author, whose skills are otherwise limited, succeeds in conveying the wickedness of the Durna Rangue, although one could wish that he and the editors of *Astounding Stories* had looked up the meaning of the noun "proselyte," which they seem to believe means priest.

Other stories that involve the Durna Rangue are "Durna Rangue Neophyte" (*Astounding Stories*, June 1937); "Kiss of Death" (*Amazing Stories*, December 1938); "Invisible One" (*Super Science Stories*, September 1940); "Captives of the Durna Rangue" (*Super Science Stories*, March 1941); "Priestess of the Sleeping Death" (*Amazing Stories*, April 1941); "Vampire of the Void" (*Planet Stories*, Spring 1941); "The Citadel in Space" (*Two Complete Science Adventure Books*, Spring 1951; not seen).

Other Works

685. **THE DEATH'S HEAD METEOR.** *Air Wonder Stories*, January 1930. Ill. Winter.
Short story. * *Time:* the twenty-sixth century. *Place:* the asteroid belt. * Jan Sterling, working for the Meteorological Bureau, is dispatched to investigate several large meteors that have just been discovered. His task is to check for gems and minerals, using various probes operated from inside his one-man spaceship. Unfortunately, his grapples become imbedded in a meteor that will strike Mars. He works valiantly with his various pieces of equipment to dislodge his craft, escaping at the last minute. * His little space car has atomic motors. * This is Jones's first published story.

686. **THE ASTEROID OF DEATH.** *Wonder Stories Quarterly*, Fall 1931. Ill. Paul.
Short story. * *Time:* A.D. 2560. *Place:* space and Mars. * The narrator (Reene) and his friend Nez Hulan are both in love with the beautiful Zelna, and it seems that Nez Hulan has won. But fate intervenes. When both men are out on an expedition, Reene leaves the ship to investigate a cave-like opening in an asteroid, where he is attacked by vicious native life. When he emerges, the spaceship is not at hand. On locating the vessel, he sees that a meteor has struck it (the deflectors were out of order and were being repaired), the ship is badly damaged, and Nez Hulan and the others are dead. Reene manages to nurse the disabled ship to Earth, where he collapses. * When he recovers, he learns that the medical science of the day has repaired Nez Hulan, giving him metal legs and a metal head, into which his brain has been inserted. (Other anatomical details obviously are not mentioned.) In a matter of weeks Nez Hulan is back at work at the university laboratory on Mars. His engagement to Zelna stands, despite his

physical condition. * But he is not the old Nez Hulan. He is now brilliant, cold, and vindictive. After a time Zelna transfers her affections to Reene, whereupon Nez Hulan embarks on a series of murders, swearing that he will be revenged on both Zelna and Reene. He kidnaps Zelna, ties her up, and abandons her on a spaceship that is aimed to crash on Phobos. Reene rescues her. Nez Hulan flies off into space and joins a band of space pirates. * *Miscellaneous:* Mars, which is much like Earth, is peopled with settlers from Earth. The asteroidal life has a lot of fangs and claws. * It is hard to believe that the author was serious with this juvenile work, but all indications are that he was, young lady tied across the train tracks and all. * For a sequel see #690, "Moon Pirates."

687. **SPACEWRECKED ON VENUS.** *Wonder Stories Quarterly*, Winter 1932. Ill. Paul.
Short story. * *Time:* 2342 A.D. *Place:* Venus. * Crime and cloak-and-dagger work, with a trick ending. * The spaceship *C-49* is descending to Venus with its load of platinum and passengers, when there is a sudden explosion and the ship is disabled. Crew and passengers crowd into a life cylinder and descend safely to the planet. * As investigation of the wreck clearly indicates, the shipwreck was caused by sabotage, and elementary detection by the captain reveals the identity of the culprits. Under space law they are subject to immediate death, which is inflicted on them. * The castaways, bearing the platinum, make their way slowly through the hostile jungle toward their original destination of Deliphon, with death repeatedly striking from the Venusian ambiance. Soon few are left. * At about this point, the survivors are attacked by the space pirates who planned the caper. Virtue, naturally, triumphs, but only by paying the price of a double trick ending, one aspect of which is unconvincing, the other of which is ingenious. * *Miscellaneous:* Venus has natural poisonous gases and horrible monsters. * Electric-bolt weapons play a part.

688. **SUICIDE DURKEE'S LAST RIDE.** *Amazing Stories*, September 1932. Ill. Morey.
Short story. * *Time:* 1974. *Place:* Cincinnati. * Skulduggery at the race track. * The annual rocketmobile speed classic is now on. The judging factor is speed over a number of laps around a long, almost perpendicularly banked course. Individual cars run in separate channels, and average speed is about 750 MPH. Drivers do not sit in their cars, but operate them with radio remote controls from a viewing room. At one time cars were personally driven, but the rules have been changed for the sake of safety. * In the present instance, the race lies between the *Mystery* and the *Silver Bullet*. Brady, the owner of the *Silver Bullet* is known as a crook, and there is a wild card, a mysterious Mr. Smith. * Once the race is on, Brady intercepts the radio commands to the *Mystery*, and there is no recourse but for veteran driver Suicide Durkee to drive the car manually. It is difficult controlling the car against Brady's interception, but he succeeds and wins. Mr. Smith proves to be a gangster who had his money on the *Mystery* and would have been very annoyed if the *Silver Bullet* had won. * Reasonable sports story with a slight science-fictional element.

689. **MARTIAN AND TROGLODYTE.** *Amazing Stories*, May 1933. Ill. Morey.
Short story. * *Time:* about 200,000 B.C. * *Background:* The remarkably inclusive fauna of Earth at this time includes primitive man, pterodactyls, tyrannosaurs, mammoths, and saber-

Jones, Neil R. (*continued*)

tooth tigers. * The story follows two threads. The human thread: The cave-man Thrag is having problems because Nrok, the lecherous old chief of the tribe, desires Thrag's mate Tua. Nrok has expelled Thrag from the tribe, and Thrag is having difficulty surviving. * The Martian thread: A small expedition from Mars is exploring Earth. When they see Thrag in danger of being eaten by a cave bear, recognizing that he is an intelligent being, they kill the bear with a death ray. Later, when the Martians unwisely leave their ship without air helmets, one collapses and is near death. * Thrag rescues him and carries him back to the spaceship. * The two Martians then befriend Thrag, giving him one of their death ray tubes. Thrag returns to his tribe, regains Tua, and kills Nrok. Along the way the death-ray tube was broken. * The Martians leave for their home planet, not knowing that a great war that will cause the downfall of Martian civilization has already broken out. * Routine. * The story is tied in with #678, "Time's Mausoleum," where the same events are seen from a different point of view.

690. **MOON PIRATES.** *Amazing Stories,* September-October 1934. Ill. Morey.

The story is carried as "The Moon Pirates" in the first installment, "Moon Pirates" in the second. * Novelette. * Sequel to #686, "The Asteroid of Death." * *Time:* 2564. *Place:* after an episode in space, an underground establishment on the Moon. * The *Space Limited*, an express flight from Venus to Mars, is attacked and captured by the space pirate Carconte, who makes short work of the crew. Those who will not join his band are either exploded into space (the future equivalent of walking the plank) or will be changed by brain surgery to willing hands. Beautiful young Suzette Clarkford will serve Carconte's lusts, while the remainder of the captives will become experimental material for Nez Hulan, the mad scientist-cyborg who is Carconte's second in command. Nez Hulan, as cruel as before, plans to turn one passenger, an old acquaintance, into a severed living head. * Also present on the ship is Hal Trenton, on whom the story centers. * The moon pirates, with the tremendous loot they have taken from the express, retreat to their incredible underground lair on the Moon, where various story threads are acted out. Suzette's father undergoes Nez Hulan's foul experiment and becomes a living head in a jar. Trenton and the other men, finding a secret passage the pirates did not know about, give the severed head a merciful death, save Suzette from rape, fight off the bandits, kill Nez Hulan, and signal to the space police, who rescue them, destroying the pirate spaceship and its crew. * Elements along the way include disintegrating screens, atomic pistols, a bone-dissolving ray, torture rays, and similar material. * The author does not explain the origin of the lunar base; since the secret passage was not known to the pirates and was dust filled, the installation must predate the criminals. * Badly planned, badly written.

JONES, RALPH T.

No information. Portrait accompanying the story shows a man in late middle age. Ralph Tatton Jones (1885-?), British born Georgia journalist, editor, is probably not the correct identification.

691. **THE MAN-BEAST OF TOREE.** *Wonder Stories Quarterly,* Fall 1931. Ill. Marchioni.

Short story. * *Place:* mostly the imaginary planet Toree, in

another star system. * A nude, oddly tanned, mute, mentally disturbed stranger turns up in Texas. After considerable psychiatric care, he returns to normalcy and tells a strange story. * Tom was abducted by frog-men from another system, who shanghaied him aboard a spaceship and took to their native planet (which is not identified). On the voyage he was treated as if he were a lower animal. * On Toree, Tom is examined by fantastic apparatus, which extract sufficient data from his mind that the scientist examining him can address him in English. * As Tom now learns, he faces a horrible fate. On Toree there is a semi-intelligent humanoid race (the Thuts) who are used for racing; individual frog-men mount Thut men and women and race them just as our civilization does horses. Tom will enter the stables of a local capitalist who keeps a string of mounts. But before Tom can run, he must be surgically prepared: His thumbs are cut off, and a ring is driven through his nasal septum. * What with Earth muscles, Tom is stronger than the Thuts and has a successful career as a racing animal, though often beaten brutally by his jockeys. During this period he becomes friendly with a Thut woman and learns to speak the Thut language. * After a time, Tom presumably ages, and he is put into a stud farm as a breeder. Since he apparently does not fulfill this task, he is sent to the knacker to be turned into table meat for the frog-men. At the last minute he escapes, taking refuge in a vehicle that turns out to be a spaceship. Found as a stowaway, he is inexplicably dropped off back on Earth by the scientist who first interrogated him. * Routine, with too many plot loopholes.

JONES, THOMAS RICHARD

No information.

692. **REPRISAL.** *Amazing Stories,* October 1928. Unsigned ill.

Short story. * *Time:* 1931. *Place:* Great Britain. * A newspaper advertisement in all the London papers, signed He Who Controls, predicts that the Thames will freeze and that unprecedented cold weather will beset Great Britain. It so happens. * Then a man calling himself Boric Hengsten turns himself in to the police and demands to see the prime minister. Hengsten tells his history and makes a demand: As a young student he was unjustly accused of a crime and sentenced to two years in prison. The government refused to reopen the case, despite new evidence. Now Hengsten wants one million pounds. The prime minister has no choice but to yield. Hengsten explains what he has done. With submarine breakwaters and pumps he has changed the course of the Gulf Stream. The original current can easily be restored. * A flat narrative.

JUVE, HENRIK DAHL (1899-1990)

U.S. engineer, writer. Born in Wisconsin, but spent most of life in the Northwest, particularly Oregon and Idaho. Attended, but did not graduate, University of Willamette and University of Seattle, majoring in electrical engineering. In Depression years and later, filled a succession of jobs more or less associated with technology. Juve's fiction is described as The Addison-Gauthier Series and Other Works.

The Addison-Gauthier Series

The following three stories are set in a very detailed, very vividly imagined twenty-eighth century culture, the first two

Juve, Henrik Dahl (*continued*)
being Ralphisms, the third more strictly an adventure story.

693. **THE SILENT DESTROYER**. *Air Wonder Stories*, August 1929. Ill. Paul.
Short story. * *Time:* the twenty-eighth century. *Place:* somewhere west of New York City, and China. * This story is in the school of *Ralph 124C 41+*, in which a flat story, told in the flattest way, is the vehicle for descriptions of artifacts and processes, all given in very precise detail. * *Background:* At the moment the world is divided into two nations, the Occidental Government, which includes all the whites, and Orienta, which includes Orientals and blacks. The two nations are at war, mostly because of the machinations of a renegade Occidental scientist named Ghorski. If Ghorski could be removed, peace would probably follow, and eventually a world government. * An Occidental military patrol encounters a strangely clad man wandering through the wilderness around a top secret underground base that is apparently the headquarters of military-scientific intelligence. The man discloses that he is Theodore A. Addison from the twentieth century, a known historical figure. He had been tarrying in the fourth and fifth dimensions and has just discovered how to assume flesh again. * A scientific examination passes Addison for security purposes, and he is allowed free entry to the installation. Later he accompanies his friend Captain Gauthier on a flying battleship that is going to China in an attempt to remove Ghorski. The battleship wins through, despite desperate fighting, and after some reversals the Occidentals (thanks to Addison's twentieth-century pistol) kill Ghorski. * Much more important than the plot is the precise background detail that Juve offers. In the twenty-eighth century, which is called the Age of Man, mankind lives wholly in gigantic cities, and the countryside has been allowed to revert to its natural state. Humanity is much the same, except that all suffer acute discomfort at loud noise; thus when Addison fires his pistol, the sound is probably more effective than the missile. Religion is dead, and a pseudo-religion formed on science has taken its place. All persons are classified in terms of personality by examining their auras mechanically; after such classification one wears clothing of the same color and, for best functioning, eats appropriate food pills, there being no natural food. * Science is very high, with a thorough understanding of dimensions up to the seventh, which is the highest in our universe. There are speech-print machines, remarkable television (the theory of which Juve provides in considerable detail), 98 percent efficient lighting that operates on local wireless transmission of power, infrared floodlights and viewers; instant photography, and many other devices. * The giant battleship on which the detachment travels moves at about a thousand miles an hour, powered by a new force and operated from a console with television screens. Special screens nullify gravity, and a potent weapon is the antinullifier, which negates the enemy's gravity screens. Another weapon is a molecular disrupter, which acts like a disintegrator ray; it is also used to create matter and transmute matter from the free atoms and molecules that arise from its use. The air in the battleship, for example, is produced by a disrupter. There is a defense against a disrupter, a shield of completely motionless atoms, but it is still new and not generally available. * A very special type of narrative, comparable to primitivism in painting. * For a sequel see #694, "The Sky Maniac."

694. **THE SKY MANIAC**. *Air Wonder Stories*, October 1929. Ill. Paul.
Short story. * Sequel to #693, "The Silent Destroyer." * *Time:* the twenty-eighth century. *Place:* around the New York City area and under the north polar ice. * Apparently the aura system doesn't work as well as the future men think, for a ferocious criminal (Hogarloff) is running amok in a first-class battleship, raying laboratories and universities, committing countless murders with his band of thugs and fanatics. * According to Captain Gauthier, Hogarloff was once a historian. But, after reading too much literature of the eighteenth and nineteenth centuries, he became insanely convinced that science was evil and should be destroyed. When he is captured, says Gauthier, he will be brainwashed (my term) back to normalcy. * An elaborate electronic device suggestive of radar locates the madman's ship, and Gauthier and crew, including Addison, seek him out. After a ferocious battle with rays slicing segments off both ships, Hogarloff wins, capturing Gauthier, Addison, and others. They are all under the north polar ice in the outlaw's hideout. * Things look bad, but Addison's old suitcase, which he brought along with him, has the means of deliverance: a dismantled hacksaw, which the future men do not recognize. Addison and friends saw through their prison bars and capture Hogarloff. * New gimmicks: Giant buildings are constructed and assembled at a central factory and shipped around by antigravity. * Antigravity involves potential energy, which is stored and accounted for financially by special investment firms. * Reading is done with wire tapes and cassettes; the future men are taught speed-reading from childhood. * Surgeons work with a diagnostic sense transmitter, by applying which they can feel the injured person's pain sensations. (Hardly a device to appeal to the medical profession!) * Hogarloff was traced with an electronic beam that registered when it touched his motors and returned information. * The air battleships can also operate underwater like submarines. * A little more life than the first story, but prolonged lectures on potential energy.

695. **THE VANISHING FLEET**. *Air Wonder Stories*, February 1930. Ill. Paul.
Short story. * *Time:* the twentieth-eighth century. *Place:* the New York area and somewhere in the Pacific. * In the same series as "The Silent Destroyer" and "The Sky Maniac," but without Addison the time-traveler. The story, which concentrates on Captain Gauthier and, to a lesser extent, on his friend and subordinate Lieutenant Evenrude, is not a Ralphism like the two previous stories, but an adventure story set against the same background. * There has been a succession of plane losses over a certain area in the Pacific, and the authorities have called in military intelligence. Several cruisers that investigate also disappear. Evenrude then is assigned on a one-man mission; his radio, too, goes off. * Gauthier is more immediately involved when the plane on which his fiancée is traveling is also declared lost, though in a different area. Defying his superiors and temporarily "resigning" so that he can operate freely, he flies into the crisis area, where he is captured. Taken into an enormous network of underground chambers, He is brought before a suave young Oriental called the monarch. * Taking a very high line, Gauthier pretends that he wants to join the monarch in his "racket," and wins, if not belief, at least a respite. The monarch tells his aims: Orientals have been downtrodden by whites too long; it is time for a change. Using a gravity device, he is

Juve, Henrik Dahl (*continued*)

capturing ships in order to build a mighty aerial navy. * Gauthier, of course, turns the tables, disrupting the monarch's computer, summoning aid, and rescuing his fiancée. The U.S. Air Service finishes matters with ships rendered invisible by a project that Gauthier had been working on before the crisis. * Routine work, without the curiosity interest of the two earlier stories.

Other Works

696. **STREAMERS OF DEATH**.   *Science Wonder Stories*, February 1930. Ill. Paul.

Short story. * *Time:* The undated future, probably not so far as the Gauthier-Evenrude series. *Place:* Portland, Oregon. * Buford Renshaw, the protagonist, a medical student researching aspects of neural transmission, is caught like everyone else when the black lights take place over the world. First there is a gigantic display like auroral lights, then a shifting to the red spectrum, then a manifestation of black light that has psychic repercussions. Many people go mad when the black light appears, and many die. * It is soon recognized that the phenomenon is due to human agency, and a search is on. The only lead is that enormous power is drawn from one or another local electric installations, and it is possible to shut off the current before the black light becomes too dangerous. But then it becomes obvious that the criminal is in possession of his own power plant. * Renshaw's contribution comes when his neural researches lead to an apparatus that puts the user into the perception frame of another person. By applying this apparatus to a host of suspects, a lead is gained. The phenomena are being produced by a band of fanatics who want to eradicate the present human race and start a new millennial world of their own. A place memory then locates the band, which is either taken or killed just as the black light is about to become lethal. * The conclusion comes as a great surprise to Renshaw and the authorities, for the mastermind behind the scheme is Renshaw's future father-in-law, a noted scientist and philanthropist. The rationale, as revealed when the culprit is examined with the thought helmet, is that he could not stand everyday human unhappiness and wanted to put the human race out of its misery. The cult members were to have perished, too, for the mad scientist had simply been using them for his purposes. * *Miscellaneous:* Elaborate live television is common; Renshaw's little private flying torpedo operates with antigravity; disruptors destroy atoms either in disintegration or to create new materials. * The story holds one's attention.

697. **THE MONSTERS OF NEPTUNE**. *Wonder Stories Quarterly*, Summer 1930. Ill. Paul.

Short story. * *Time:* the middle twenty-first century. *Place:* mostly Neptune. * Young Dana Manson, dissatisfied son of the owner of the great Consolidated Interplanetary Transport Company, declares that rather than take a desk job in the company he will undertake new explorations of the solar system. Deciding on Neptune, which is still unknown, he sets forth with paroled convict Dutch Hoss, former inmate of Sing Sing Prison, as a comrade and assistant. The two men reach Neptune very rapidly and without incident. * *Background, as gradually imparted:* Neptune is not too different from Earth, with tolerable gravitation and atmosphere, but is hot and jungle-like. There are huge deposits of radium, which, in addition to heat, give off a

violet light that supplements solar radiation. The dominant life-form is an intelligent creature much like an elephant-sized gorilla, with three-fingered hands and a single frontal eye. These beings are covered with heavy, thick scales so permeated with oil that they are flammable. For good reason, thus, the Neptunians, who are extraordinarily vicious and combative, are terrified of fire, or, by extension, of a red crystal that looks like a glowing coal. * Landing and beginning to explore, the two men have their first experience with native life as they helplessly watch a titanic being shatter their spaceship with boulders. The creature, later revealed as the native ruler, attacks the men; he is impervious to various rays, but a bullet in his single eye kills him. * The remainder of the story is a succession of chases, captures, and escapes as the titanic natives take after the men. Along the way they rescue Gailman, a previous explorer who was being held captive for a cannibalistic feast. * The turning point comes when Hoss sets fire to the new native leader and gains control of the red crystal. Dana announces his plans for the development of Neptune, and will leave with Gailman on Gailman's spaceship, which is hidden nearby. * See the sequel #699, "The Struggle for Neptune" for comments. * According to Schwartz/Weisinger, Dean Process Pictures Productions negotiated for motion picture rights to "The Monsters of Neptune," but the deal fell through. Presumably this was an echo of *King Kong*.

698. **THE MARTIAN REVENGE**.   *Wonder Stories*, August 1930. Ill. Paul.

Short story. * *Place:* mostly Mars. * Masters, discovering an antigravity principle (gravipotential), builds a large spaceship using his discovery and propelled by gunpowder engines. His expedition sets forth for Mars. While Juve does not give numbers, the expedition must be fairly large, since it includes crew, Danby, a news correspondent, and the two scientists Masters and Grigson. The voyage proceeds well enough, except that the men forgot to take the gravitation of Phobos into account, and the ship had to crash land on Mars, fortunately into a body of water. * Mars is more or less Schiaparellian, perhaps not so extreme as the classical model, but the canals are waterways. There are agricultural areas and cities. * Shortly after the ship lands, the Martians arrive, small creatures with spurred feet, obviously evolved birds. Juve says little about their accomplishments, but they seem farther advanced scientifically than the Earthmen. There are many small flying machines, and the Martians construct canals by using a liquid substance that expands enormously when another chemical is added, pushing the ground away. When applied several times, this process forms canal beds very nicely. * The Martians seem friendly enough, and after a short time they are permitted to enter the spaceship freely. The Earthmen become lax and careless, wandering about Mars casually with the natives. Only Grigson has some doubts, wondering whether the Martians may be too alien to be understood. * The crisis comes when the entire personnel of the spaceship are out watching the construction of a canal. A Martian approaches the others, and suddenly, without warning, all the Martians attack ferociously, indifferent to Terrestrial bullets. Several of the crew are down, and it looks like the end, when the supposedly unmanned spaceship flies overhead, bombards the natives, and rescues the surviving explorers. * Double explanation: Masters's college-age son and his new wife stowed away and remained undiscovered; when

Juve, Henrik Dahl (*continued*)

they recognized what was going on, they emerged and brought the ship over. Second, the Martians were upset because they discovered, while rummaging around in the ship, that the unscrupulous journalist, against orders, had stolen an egg from the Martian incubators. Grigson proved right. * Much less to offer than Juve's Ralphisms; one more routine story. It would seem that the story made an impression on Stanley Weinbaum.

699. **THE STRUGGLE FOR NEPTUNE**. *Wonder Stories Quarterly*, Fall 1930. Ill. Paul.

Short story. * Sequel to #697, "The Monsters of Neptune." *Time:* the middle twenty-first century. *Place:* Neptune. * A direct continuation of the first story. * Manson and Gailman set forth for Earth, leaving Dutch in charge of the natives by virtue of the red crystal. Gailman gives Dutch language records so that he can communicate with the natives. * The story is concerned with Dutch's expedients to retain power. The red crystal is not enough, for a few of the more intelligent natives doubt its supernatural qualities. Dutch ignites gasoline as a persuader, but even this does not suffice. Dutch now uses Machiavellian ploys, setting dissidents against one another in a civil war and inciting the natives to attack Martian visitors. He manages to survive until Manson returns. * The Martians, who are about on the same level of technology as the Terrestrials, are egg-shaped beings. * The present story and its predecessor are sad comedowns from Juve's earlier work. Juve's Ralphisms were not great literature, but they were interesting for their ideas. Juve obviously took pains with them.

700. **IN MARTIAN DEPTHS**. *Wonder Stories*, September 1932. Ill. Paul.

Novelette. * *Time:* 1982. *Place:* Mars. * Partly action story, partly an exposition of the historical aperçu or theory that civilization and power move westward. In this case, the noted historical scientist Matheson declares that rather than let history shift to the Orient, Western man should shift the frontier to space. The result is the first voyage to Mars. * The Matheson Expedition is something of a disaster. En route the cook goes mad; the trip is difficult psychologically; and there is more than a suspicion that the rocket tubes are being eroded prematurely by the blasts. * The ship lands hard, though not disabled. Mars is like Earth in terms of atmosphere and gravity, but the area in which the explorers find themselves contains enormous insects and reptiles, to say nothing of active carnivorous plants whose spines carry a deadly poison. The canals are avenues of rushing water, and in an initial exploration the men find an enormous pumping plant. * Most important, however, is a message that the narrator, the communications officer, receives in Morse code. Signed "Earth Languages Expert," it informs the explorers that the Martians have learned Morse code by monitoring radio. It also tells them that the Martians regard Earth civilization as horrible and potentially polluting. The Martians also order members of the expedition not to leave the vicinity of the spaceship. The Earthmen must depart within three days, promising that no further expeditions shall visit Mars. * The explorers, acting in part on Matheson's cultural-historical interpretations, decide to defy the Martians and, while stalling for time, explore the planet. This resolution is a disaster, for Matheson and others lose their lives. When the survivors reach a Martian city, they are captured by soporific gas and held prisoner. Under a new leader the Earthmen agree to leave Mars,

but cannot overcome the suspicion that the Martians mean treachery and will kill them anyway. Again faking compliance, at the proper moment the explorers shoot their way through the Martian throngs and escape in their spaceship, with two Martians as prisoners. It was later learned that the Martians were entirely sincere, being so constituted as to be completely literal in speech and totally honorable. The aftermath is another expedition, described in a sentence or two, and, when the Earthmen have analyzed the Martian gas weapon, the conquest of Mars. The narrator reflects on the Drang nach Westen with an ambivalent combination of sadness and sense of inevitability. * *Miscellaneous:* The Martians, who have an incredibly ancient civilization, are somewhat globular creatures organized centrally around a spine-like process, with a single 360° eye atop their body, and several limbs ending in fingers. * The idea behind the story is interesting, but the author does not have the skill to handle it.

KALETSKY, MILTON (1916-?)

U.S. (New York) fan, educator, and writer. Teacher in New York City high school system. In the early 1940s contributed about a dozen other stories and articles to science-fiction magazines. In our period a frequent contributor to the letter columns, usually severely criticizing erroneous science in the stories. (On one occasion Street and Smith paid him twenty dollars for two letters, a very unusual action.) The editorial policy of *Wonder Stories* was to praise his knowledge and acumen, then point out that fictional techniques and imagination, too, were necessary. Kaletsky also wrote as Milton Kalet in *Popular Magazine*. See also pseud. Dane Milton. * Social Security records list the deaths of two persons named Milton Kaletsky, but it is not clear that either of these men was the present author.

701. **THE END OF THE UNIVERSE**. *Wonder Stories*, April 1934.

Short-short story. * *Time:* the remotely far future. * Entropy has been at work for millions of years. The stars are all gone, and life persists only on one spaceship. Most of mankind, otherwise immortal, has already committed suicide, using a machine that turns their matter into energy for the survivors. The last man, Karem, tired of it all, leaps into the energy machine and disintegrates himself. The universe goes out. * Donald Wandrei's "The Red Brain" is much better.

702. **THE BEAM**. *Amazing Stories*, September 1934.

Short-short story. * Mad scientist and inventor Gayle has a grudge against the world, blaming it for lack of recognition and wealth. (Unfortunately, none of his great discoveries ever pans out.) On reading an article in the newspaper about rays from the human eye that stimulate growth and rapid reproduction, he frantically works to recapitulate the discovery—with success. * He will now install his equipment in all the large cities, where they will create such an enormous overpopulation that the human race will soon become extinct from starvation and lack of space. But when he stands in the path of his ray, he himself is multiplied, duplicated, then quadruplicated up to higher powers and ever smaller sizes. Unable to shut off the ray, he ends as a multitude of almost microscopic millions around the laboratory floor, all dying of starvation.

KALLAND, JOHN FRANCIS

U.S. writer then resident in St. Paul, Minnesota.

703. **THE SAGES OF EROS**. *Amazing Stories,* February 1932. Ill. Morey.

Short story. * *Time:* 1939. *Place:* Eros. * Prescott and Maguire, who have finished their spaceship, set out for Mars. But when they are well out into space, their craft is pulled off course and brought down on Eros, where they are welcomed by dwarfish ancient humanoid men with huge heads and spindly limbs. Eros itself is almost paradisiacal, encased in a crystal shell. * The remainder of the story is a telepathic lecture by the sages of Eros. Eros was originally part of the Bodean fifth planet. Its population was enormous, so great that it polluted the air, killing off most of the race. Giant insects, against which there was little defense, then evolved, driving the Erosians underground. Even here, after ages, the insects penetrated. * Intelligent life was preserved by a fluke: The insect larvae bored down to the molten core of the planet, which thereupon exploded, flinging off the fragment now known as Eros. Since then the Erosians have developed a superscience, including near immortality and the ability to steer their planetoid where they will. * Viewers show scenes from Earth and Mars. The latter planet, which is arid and rugged, is inhabited only by ferocious monsters. In the solar system only Eros, Earth, and certain of the Jovian satellites have intelligent life. * The young men return to Earth and tell their tale, which is not believed. * Very amateurish.

704. **RESTITUTION**. *Amazing Stories,* December 1935. Ill. Morey.

Short story. * When Dr. Allen Chamberlain responds to an urgent summons from his friend Jim Cummings, he finds that Cummings has disappeared and that his new invention is missing. Cummings, Chamberlain reveals to the police, had developed a radiation apparatus that amounted to a cancer cure. * Not long after this a group of hoodlums attack Chamberlain and his wife, chloroforming them and carrying them away. They awaken strapped to hospital tables, while around them potters an elderly man with a German accent. In cages nearby are creatures that look like missing links, while a small chimpanzee hops around the room. * The elderly man, who has stolen Cummings's apparatus and is using it in his work, explains what will happen. He feels it his duty to make restitution to God's First People, or apes and the missing links, by transferring into their bodies the brains of Dr. and Mrs. Chamberlain. As for Cummings? Chamberlain does not realize what has happened, but the reader will readily perceive that the chimpanzee's skull holds Cummings's brain. * Actually, the chimp provides the resolution to matters. It releases Mrs. Chamberlain, who creates enough of a fuss that the scientist does not quite succeed in debraining the unconscious Chamberlain. Just then the police arrive. During the melée, the mad scientist is knocked about. When he regains consciousness, he is entirely sane. He is Dr. Mueller, a pleasant biologist who had been studying apes in Africa, had an accident, and has since been amnesiac. All his crimes must be forgiven, since they were done by a secondary personality. Mueller transfers Cummings back to his own body—which had been kept in a refrigerator—using the cancer machine to restore vitality. * Amateurish.

KATELEY, WALTER

U.S. writer, then resident in Cleveland, Ohio. Engineering background. Said to have been employed at one time as a technical examiner in the U.S. Patent Office. According to an obituary notice (furnished by the Cleveland Public Library) of Pearl W. Kateley, wife of Walter Kateley, Walter Kateley was still living in 1953. Since there is no Ohio obituary notice of Kateley, he presumably left the state after his wife's death. The statements in Rock and McGhan, not corroborated to my knowledge, that Kateley was the pseud. of a Harold June are almost certainly incorrect.

Kateley's fiction is described in two groupings, The Kingston Series and Other Works.

The Kingston Series

The Kingston stories, which share a common background, describe the unusual discoveries of George Kingston, a somewhat eccentric inventor who lives in the Washington, D.C. area. The later stories are not really sequels in the sense of continued action, but they share a common factor in Kingston and his friend the narrator. Time is not specified, but the stories seem to take place in the near future.

705. **THE FOURTEENTH EARTH**. *Amazing Stories,* February 1928. Unsigned ill.

Short story. * The narrator, who works in the U.S. Patent Office, decides to investigate personally a rather extravagant patent application that has been submitted. One George Kingston claims to have invented a substance that can alter the atomic density of any element. Kingston is not in his laboratory when the narrator visits, but the meddling narrator picks up a disk marked "14." * He undergoes strange sinking sensations, recovering his senses in what seems to be a normal world. Friendly humanoid people greet him, take in a sort of skimming machine to a city, where he is housed, and later interrogated. * After he is able to communicate with his hosts (the feli), he learns that they are far ahead of us scientifically. They create whatever they need, food, buildings, etc. by directly manipulating atomic particles (perhaps largely photons), for some procedures using a decomposing ray. Some of their operations, which are on an enormous scale, are responsible for volcanoes on the surface. * By now the narrator recognizes that he is in the fourteenth density layer of the Earth, far beneath the surface, breathing what might be solid granite. When he makes known his wishes to return to the surface, the feli obligingly make preparations. Grasping the disk that caused his adventure, he reaches the upper world in normal form. * The author makes considerable to-do about the religion of the feli, which seems to be a sort of ubiquitous deism. * An interesting idea, but clumsily handled.

706. **THE WORLD OF A HUNDRED MEN**. *Science Wonder Stories,* March 1930. Ill. Win[ter].

Long short story. * A follow-up to #705, "The Fourteenth Earth." * The narrator, who still works in the U.S. Patent Office, receives an invitation from Kingston to undertake another experiment. Kingston, who has invented a process for consolidating electronic circuits, plans to use his device in connection with an exploration of Meteor Crater, Arizona. Kingston's borer will remove dirt, sand, and debris, which will then be converted to brick-shaped masses (much smaller in size than the input) used to wall the tube as excavated. * The system

Kateley, Walter (*continued*)

works well enough, without artificial crises, until the excavation reaches a depth of two miles. At this point obviously artificial fragments are found, and when explosives break down a barrier, the men find a large open space supported by extremely strong girders. * Further exploration reveals a museum-like situation, with many documents, to which is provided a learning key. * The excavators and outside experts decipher the documents, which tell an amazing story. The meteorite at the bottom of Meteor Crater is the remains of the asteroid Valenna, a planetoid about a mile in diameter, which was furnished with atmosphere, water, and life that evolved into a human or humanoid species. * The inhabitants of Valenna developed a high civilization about four hundred thousand years ago, although there were many losses and reachievements of culture during this history. From early times the Valennans kept photographic records of Earth, which show various geological stages from the early pleistocene up. One especially interesting series shows continental drift from to and away from a Pangea. * Since Valenna was tiny, there was always a problem with overpopulation, and after several near extinctions the population was limited to one hundred. This figure was interpreted differently according to food supply (whether just males, or males and females, including, or not counting children), but the population was never allowed to get out of hand. * In a great engineering feat the Valennans separated the surface layer of the planetoid from the iron core and motorized the surface so that it could revolve and take maximum advantage of sunlight. * At some time in the past, date uncertain, the Valennans discovered that their orbit would bring the planet so close to Earth that there would be a collision. They thereupon created the highly durable museum for future intelligent discoverers on Earth. * One of Kateley's better stories. While the scientific basis is absurd, the long introductory sections explaining the excavations at Meteor Crater have considerable interest.

707. **REMOTE CONTROL**. *Amazing Stories*, April 1930. Ill. Wesso.

Short story. * In the Kingston series. * *Place:* the southern coast of England and Minnesota. * The undated near future, with a flashback. * The narrator, visiting his friend Kingston at the workings for the Channel Tunnel, discovers to his astonishment that the work is being done by animals: whales swim up with great stones saddled to their backs, gorillas heave tons of sacks of cement, squirrels perform incredibly rapid calculation and typing, etc. The explanation: A remarkable discovery that has its roots back to the college days of Kingston and the narrator in Minnesota. * The two men, amateur naturalists, were examining a large formicary, speculating how it is possible for the workers, who live only a few months, to perform their various tasks so efficiently, when an accidental spilling of oil and buttermilk on one of their lenses shows hitherto invisible lines of force emanating from the anthill. Further investigation reveals a brain-like body floating in liquid, the directing intelligence of the formicary. * Years of research and experiment resulted in Kingston's discovery of similar force lines for animals and their possible utilization by humans. As a result, the construction of the Channel Tunnel is directed from a building in London. * Obviously no SPCA or labor unions in Kateley's near future.

708. **BEINGS OF THE BOUNDLESS BLUE**. *Amazing Stories*, May 1931. Ill. Morey.

Short story. * The narrative of the scientist Kingston, who has just returned from a mysterious disappearance of several months. * Kingston, speculating about magnetism, has come to the conclusion that the phenomenon does not involve alignment of atoms, but expansion of electronic orbits. After much experimentation he develops a method for enlarging these orbits, together with a substance (transite) that performs the operation. * On the critical occasion Kingston accidentally grasps a disk of transite and finds himself expanding, out of his house, into the open, up into the sky. After a time he hits something, is knocked unconscious, and awakens in a strange land, where everything seems gigantic. (This, of course, is illogical.) People gather around him; he is taken to a hospital and treated. * To anticipate the explanations: Kingston is in a world above the Heaviside layer, where everything, although solid to the inhabitants, would be very tenuous to us. The people are completely human, and the culture of the upper people is almost exactly like ours. The upper people have very little knowledge of the lower Earth; the little they have has been gained mostly through "submarine" expeditions, but they are irritated by the noise of radio broadcasts, which they have learned to filter out by layers of certain chemicals. * One of the upper scientists has developed an apparatus that projects brain images visually, even on screens, so that Kingston first learns his circumstances, then can explain about the lower Earth. He learns the language of the area, and is reasonably content for a time, until he has urges to return home. Fortunately, he has found the disk of transite that brought him to the upper world, and with the aid of scientists he is able to reverse its operation and return to his home. * *Miscellaneous:* The upper people, who in some respects are scientifically ahead of us, maintain climate control by enormous wind machines. The action of these machines, in turn, causes hurricanes and cyclones on Earth. On one occasion Kingston, while watching a race in which winds were used, also saw its counterpart as a most destructive hurricane down below. * There is no explanation why the upper people and culture are like ours. * The story is probably of Fortean suggestion.

Other Works

709. **THE EYE OF THE VULTURE**. *Amazing Stories*, November 1928. Ill. Paul.

Short story. * As students on a surveying party Megg and the narrator were fascinated by vultures' ability to find carrion. * Years later Megg contacts the narrator and explains progress he has made in investigating bird vision. He has not only worked out a theoretical explanation in terms of ultraviolet light, but has devised an apparatus for rendering visible light beyond the human visual range. One result is that the apparatus shows odors as emanations of ultraviolet. * The crowning experience comes when the men focus Megg's apparatus on a mirage of a city. The result is incredibly beautiful. * Not a story so much as a narrative.

710. **THE HOLLISTER EXPERIMENT**. *Amazing Stories Quarterly*, Winter 1929. Ill. Paul.

Short story. * *Place:* over much of the United States. * Professor Hollister, a biologist, believes that the thyroid gland is the master planner of metabolism. Experimenting with various thyroid preparations, he injects a grasshopper, which escapes. * The grasshopper grows with incredible rapidity, until it is eventually

Kateley, Walter (*continued*)

hundreds of feet long. It is in no sense vicious or aggressive, but by its size it is enormously destructive as it ranges with great speed over much of the United States. Since it is covered with chitin several feet thick, it is practically invulnerable to attack. Eventually it flies out over the Pacific, from California, and is seen no more. * The author demonstrates some knowledge of entomology.

711. **EROS TO EARTH**. *Science Wonder Stories*, October 1929. Ill. Paul.

Short story. * *Place:* off the coast of Florida. * The narrator, on a fishing vacation, espies a little man (three feet high) who comes bobbing up out of the water on a propellant device. The little man, who speaks English well, informs the narrator that he is a native of Eros. He and his associates have established a small underwater scientific colony, protected by a large coffer dam; there the Erosians hope to acquire an understanding of metal formation on Earth. Eros, it seems, is very short of heavy metals, although its bodies of water have such metals in suspension. * The narrator accompanies the little men down into the Erosian establishment, where all concerned converse amicably for a considerable time. The Erosians, who learned English from a *Webster's Unabridged Dictionary*, arrived on a small spaceship that hitched a ride on a tiny planetoid whose orbit approaches both Eros and Earth. * The narrator explains theories of metal deposition, particularly the work of bacteria. This information is invaluable to the visitors, for their biological knowledge, which is farther advanced than ours, will enable them to speed up processes that take hundreds of thousands of years on Earth. The narrator leaves amicably, with a hint of an invitation to visit Eros. * As an incident, a gigantic whale shark crashes through the wall of the coffer dam, but without any permanent damage to the Erosian establishment. * Very flat.

712. **THE STEAM GOD**. *Amazing Stories*, October 1929. Ill. Wesso.

Short story. * *Place:* the Arctic. * The narrator, a member of the Kingsford Arctic Expedition, parachutes out of his burning plane to the Arctic ice, without much hope of survival. But after a time he comes upon a narrow green valley, steam-filled because of extensive hot springs, with a strange flora. Shortly thereafter he is captured by gigantic men about ten feet tall. * Taken to the city of the giants, he is tried and (although he does not know it at the time) sentenced to death for various offenses: walking on priestly property, etc. (Actually, there is something going on behind the scenes. By priestly law, there must be a human sacrifice to the Steam God each year; there is always difficulty in finding a criminal or other suitable victim, and there are always demands from the more liberal giants that the practice be abolished. The narrator's arrival is opportune, for both the priests and some of the liberals are appeased by the judge's decision.) Meanwhile the narrator is assigned to the giant scientist Chunen for study. * Background: The giants have lived for ages in the steam world, without any record or tradition of their origin. They are unaware of the outside world. Their civilization is fairly high, but is dependent almost entirely on the omnipresent steam from the local volcanism. The giants live mostly on mushrooms and other vegetation that they grow in caverns they have hollowed out of the rock, but they also maintain small almost token herds of ancestral, four-legged whales, which they kill yearly for a ceremonial feasting. In all,

the giants number about six million people. * The narrator wins the regard of the savant Chunen, who has a plan to save him from the Steam God. The narrator has told him about the geysers of Yellowstone and the practice of causing eruptions by inserting soap down the channel. Chunen, at the time appointed for the narrator's sacrifice, slides some soap into the cauldron, stimulating an eruption which is taken to indicate that the sacrifice should be called off. * The now-friendly giants bring in the wreckage of the narrator's plane, build him a new one, and he flies back to his own world, accompanied by Chunen. * Wesso's cover showing the giant ambulatory whales amid fantastic machinery has its appeal.

713. **THE GOLD TRIUMVIRATE**. *Science Wonder Stories*, November 1929. Ill. Paul.

Short story. * *Time and place:* The frame narrative 1960, a South Seas island. The body of story, an earlier date in Ohio. * The frame narrator encounters a beachcomber who tells a strange story. He is currently if not quite hiding out at least lying low because of financial upheavals in the United States. * Some years earlier he and a friend devised a way to manufacture gold. They took two elements whose atomic weights added together were that of gold, then combined them in gaseous form under radiation. With help from a friend with a financial background, they gradually unloaded their product without arousing suspicion or overloading the market. * All went well for a time, during which they became multimillionaires with holdings of all sorts. But a disgruntled employee revealed their secret, and there was trouble. The beachcomber immediately left for the South Seas, where he disappeared. He is now intensely curious what has happened to his other holdings since gold has been devalued. But, in any case, regardless of his financial situation, he has found contentment in the natural beauties of the area.

714. **THE ARCTIC RESCUE**. *Air Wonder Stories*, May 1930. Ill. Winter.

Short story. * *Place:* the Arctic. * The narrator joins an expedition sponsored by the Smithsonian to search for a specimen of a particularly large blue whale. Following a routine voyage, during which the naturalists obtain the whale they need, the ship becomes trapped in the ice, and there seems to be no hope of escape. After months of waiting vainly for a channel to open, most of the expedition leaves the ship, dragging a long boat over the ice to open water. The narrator, his assistant, and the captain remain with the ship, still hoping for a thaw. * Eventually, they have a bright idea. Skin the giant whale that they have slung alongside, inflate its skin with hydrogen that they can prepare by electrolysis from sea water, and use it as a balloon. All this is done, and the voyage ends in Montreal at the end of a flagpole. * Borderline science-fiction at best.

715. **THE INCREDIBLE MONSTROSITY**. *Wonder Stories*, June 1930. Ill. Paul.

Short story. * *Time:* 1970-1980. *Place:* mostly the New York and San Francisco areas. * Verne, one of the great engineers of the day, proposes a new mode of transportation to revolutionize the nation's economy: a gigantic metal sphere, a mile high, that, propelled by a linear motor, will roll across the continent in about four hours. It will run in a straight line from New York to San Francisco along a special channel with electric power sources at intervals; all to be activated by sound. * Ten years later, at enormous cost, the *Scarab* (in analogy to an Egyptian beetle that rolls along a sphere of dung) is about ready. There

Kateley, Walter (*continued*)

have been problems along the way with commercial rivals, and, behind the scenes, with international plots. Verne's assistant Babcock is involved with an Oriental power that plans a surprise attack on the United States, which is militarily weak, with much of its armament scattered on the East Coast. * The Orientals attack, cutting off communications, and advance along the *Scarab*'s roadbed. Verne, learning what is happening, persuades the military to fill the ball with disassembled planes, and activates the giant sphere, which rolls across the country at the speed of sound. Not only is the invasion halted, but the *Scarab* crushes much of the invading army along the roadbed. * The engineering aspects form an unusual story, since Kateley has worked out details very thoroughly, but the war is on the weak side. Oddly enough, Kateley's idea was seriously proposed in the 9 June 1934 issue of *Scoops*.

716. **INSECTS EXTRAORDINARY**. *Amazing Stories Quarterly*, Winter 1932. Ill. Morey.
Short story. * *Place:* the Southeastern United States. * The narrator, who works in the Patent Office in Washington, and his friend Warren, an entomologist in the Department of Agriculture, are off on a field trip to investigate a report that a swarm of Zatts has been seen in the southern United States. * *Background:* Zatts are a peculiarly elusive form of insect that has proved impossible to study, since specimens cannot be caught. Only one specimen is known, and that may have been a hoax. The Zatts are important because they eat metal; if they multiply unchecked, they could prove a disaster. * Finding a swarm of Zatts, the investigators try to capture specimens, but fail repeatedly. Finally they trap a couple with a parachute net. But when they study a dead Zatt under a high-powered microscope, they are shocked. The Zatt is not an insect, but a tiny flying machine manned by tiny humanoids. * There is a complicating factor. De Morse, an unwelcome Washington colleague who is also investigating the Zatts (unsuccessfully), is so desperate to claim the discovery that he tries to murder Warren and frame the narrator. The plot fails, and De Morse makes his escape. * The Zatt situation expands: The tiny humanoids are building a small town out of metal stolen from human artifacts. The narrator works out a way to communicate visually with them, and a treaty is made. The humans will allow the Zatts to settle, will supply them with metals, and will not hamper them; the Zatts will no longer raid human metals, will try to teach humans their advanced technology, and will not take over other areas without permission. * The villainous De Morse makes another appearance, trying to gas the Zatts, but is himself killed by Zatt cyanide. * *Miscellaneous:* The Zatts came from another world, location not cited. * The initial situation is handled with more skill than is usual with Kateley, but the melodramatic murder plot and clumsy handling of the remainder of the story spoil matters.

717. **UNDER ARCTIC ICE**. *Wonder Stories*, June 1932, Ill. Paul.
Short story. * *Place:* the North Polar area. * The narrator, an aviator who is bringing a cargo of books to an Arctic expedition, is forced to parachute out of his plane when he discovers wing damage. He lands roughly, and when he regains consciousness finds himself at the bottom of a flask-like depression, perhaps a mile below the ice surface. The air is warm. There is vegetation, and also a very strange form of intelligent life, the Tovarts. * The Tovarts, who capture the narrator, are human-

sized turtle-like creatures with mollusk-like front and back shells and short stubby feet. They have a special organ, which Kateley calls the auxiliary; perhaps weighing fifteen or twenty pounds, it contains a variety of sensory and prehensile elements and is attached to the body by a long flesh tube. * The Tovarts are not unfriendly, and one of them, with the permission of the ruler, teaches the narrator the Tovart language. * *Background:* The Tovarts came to Earth about three hundred years ago, probably from a large asteroid or planetoid where they had developed from amphibian ancestors. On the critical occasion, while a group of scientists were in space conducting observations, they witnessed the sudden explosion of their planet. Making their way to Earth, they landed in the Arctic, where they bored through the ice and started a new civilization with what they had available on the ship. Atomic power helped melt the ice and maintain the flask-like living area. * As for their present situation: The Tovarts, who still maintain a high civilization, are intensely religious and guide their daily lives by bell signals from a burdensome priesthood. It is this priesthood that causes problems for the narrator. * Among the books salvaged from the airplane is a Bible; when a friendly Tovart translates the first part of Genesis, the high priest declares it blasphemous because of its anthropocentrism. The narrator is sentenced to death by asphyxiation in an outburst of natural gas that the priests use as an oracle. * Fortunately, the narrator's friend has helped him to repair his plane and has extracted some gasoline from the small oil deposits. When the narrator is about to be executed, he flings a flame into the gaseous emissions, causing an explosion. In the confusion he reaches his plane and flies away. * *Miscellaneous:* The Tovarts sleep by floating in a pool. * Routine for Kateley.

718. **ROOM FOR THE SUPER RACE**. *Amazing Stories*, August 1932. Ill. Morey.
Novelette. * *Place:* the Arctic and the central United States. * Tower (the narrator) and Watson, ornithologists stranded in the Arctic by the loss of their supply boat, emerge from their makeshift hut to see an enormous spherical body hovering overhead. As they soon learn, it is a dirigible planetoid about five miles in diameter that has come from the asteroid belt. The inhabitants of the planetoid, on catching sight of Tower and Watson, encircle them with a heat ray and take them to the planetoid, which has now settled on the ice. An automobile-like conveyance driven by robots takes them inside. When Watson reacts violently at a command in English to give up their weapons, the two men are separated, and most of the narrative is centered on Tower. * Tower soon sees that his captors are completely human and indistinguishable from Northern Europeans. After some cosmetic preparation, he is taken into the presence of Dr. Cook, the director of public affairs, who holds a long explanatory conversation with him. As Cook (who is remarkably like a modern corporation public-relations vice president) makes clear to Tower, the aliens are rigorously and remorselessly logical social Darwinists. They are the Super Race and as such they have a right to supersede lesser races. Starting with North America, they will take over the Earth, which they will reorganize into gigantic estates for individual planetarians. * As a first stage in the new world, the Americas must be evacuated. The Super Race, who claim to be humane, have no intention of exterminating the human population, unless necessary, but urge migration to Central Asia. As Cook says, "We are reluctant to impose any unnecessary hardship on even an inferior

Kateley, Walter (*continued*)

race." But beneath this superficial pleasantness and courtesy, Tower recognizes, lie total racism and total ruthlessness. When Tower argues the matter ethically, Dr. Cook, who is well versed in American history, simply recalls the whites' treatment of the American Indians. * Tower is at first outraged when Dr. Cook suggests that he act as a sort of press agent or publicity man for the aliens. But after a time, on taking sober thought and seeing the resources and weapons (notably an incredible heat ray) of the Super Race, he decides that not only is resistance hopeless, but that he may be able to prevent much misery if he agrees to become a collaborator. (Kateley nicely describes Tower's gradual conversion to a quisling.) * Tower is placed in charge of Station X, the radio outlet of the Super Race, and also acts as an psychological adviser and regional expert for dealing with the humans. * Humanity, as might be expected, does not accept the aliens' ultimatum. As an example of their power, the Super Race devastates a large part of the Midwest with their heat ray, but even this does not bring the prompt response that the Super Race requires. Tower, though sick at heart, hopes that a limited sacrifice may prevent a general massacre. To convince the outside world of the hopelessness of the situation, he suggests a scheduled battle between the forces of the United States and those of the floating world, during which battle the United States will be allowed to bring up all its naval and military force. As Tower anticipated, the battle is totally one-sided; the aliens' heat ray destroys forts, battleships, and airplanes, while an army of robots (held in storage from a previous war) slaughters the ground troops. * This battle is convincing, and the Americans, despite foreign opposition, prepare to migrate to Central Asia, as a reasonably empty, inhabitable area. Although the American government does its best, it proves impossible to accomplish the total evacuation demanded by the Super Race. When Tower points this out to the director, he states that he will be lenient, so long as the Midwest is emptied. Tower and Station X are then relocated on one of the palatial estates the Super Race is establishing. * One evening, just before the final emigration from the East Coast, Watson, who has been working in the engineering department of the asteroid, awakens Tower excitedly. Watson has set a time bomb in the planetoid's power room, and the planetoid, its antigravity mechanism destroyed, should fall to Earth. As the men watch, the asteroid sprouts flames and crashes down. The peril is over. * *Miscellaneous:* The asteroid is called the World of a Thousand Men, since it maintains fairly rigid population control, with a limit at one thousand beings. * The planetoid is powered by cosmic rays, with gravity control by magnetizing and demagnetizing portions of the iron core of the planet. * For navigation reasons, the core of the planetoid has been completely separated from the outer shell, which revolves about the core. * Much of its technology is based on keyboard control of equipment and of the multitudinous robots that do the dirty work of the culture. * The Super Race learned English from an explorer whom they captured years earlier, on a previous trip, also from books and intercepted broadcasts. * Kateley does not explain the human physiology of the Super Race. * Unlike most stories of this sort, there is no question of romance between the two explorers and Super Race females. While Watson describes his female informant as gorgeous, the Master Race will not accept race pollution. * Easily Kateley's best story, and one that is worth reading. The psychology of

Tower is particularly interesting, as are the discussions of ethics and racial superiority. The contemporary reference is obvious.

719. **CHILDREN OF THE GREAT MAGMA**. *Amazing Stories,* August/September issue, 1933. Ill. Morey.
Short story. * *Place:* Antarctica. * The narrator is a member of the Gordon Antarctic Expedition, which is conducting sonic surveys to determine the depth of the ice cap. On the present occasion he is taking an exploratory plane flight with pilot Bogardus, when Bogardus threatens him with a revolver. * A Fundamentalist religious fanatic, Bogardus (though he had not shown signs of violent madness before) had previously insisted that the Garden of Eden was situated in Antarctica. Now, in the plane, Bogardus, threatening the narrator with death, declares that they will seek the Garden. * When the plane runs out of gas, the aviators make a forced landing. Bogardus, flourishing his weapon, takes such supplies as they have and, deserting the narrator, stalks away. He is killed shortly thereafter when the ice splits. * The narrator, seeing a misty area ahead, makes his way toward it and finds a small lost world heated by volcanic activity. Not only does it contain an exotic fauna and flora, but it also holds a small population of humans who cultivate the land extensively, using channels of hot groundwater to repel the ever encroaching ice. These people, who are nondescript whites, apparently have inhabited the oasis since the time when Antarctica was warm. Their culture is primitive, but efficient. * The narrator is accepted as a god for a short time, but the elaborate priesthood is suspicious and decides to put him to the test. He is lowered into a pit-like depression, where mammoths and woolly rhinoceroses live. It would have been fatal for him had not a search dirigible hovering overhead dropped rescuing ropes. * *Miscellaneous:* Kateley speculates that the volcanism is the result of impact by an extraterrestrial body, perhaps a neutronium planetoid. * Of no real interest.

720. **SUBJUGATING THE EARTH**. *Amazing Stories,* June 1934. Ill. Morey.
Novelette. * Essentially a rehash of the author's #718, "Room for the Super Race." * *Place:* mostly the Arctic, Chicago, and New York. * The narrator and his friend Cornwallis, naturalists stranded in the Arctic, are captured by strange beings with bizarre flying machines. These Cudors, to anticipate, are from the asteroid belt, whence they have traveled by moving their planetoid. They are shaped like boilers, with multiple legs and arms, and a triangular head with three eyes. Their science, which includes antigravity, is far superior to ours. * When the narrator and Cornwallis learn the Cudor language from their captors, they are informed that the Cudors plan to take over Earth as a matter of right, as the superior race. Individual Cudors will establish large walled estates, on which humans will be banded and enslaved. * The narrator is forced into a quisling position as a go-between and publicity agent, while Cornwallis, who is an accomplished musician, is employed as such by the Cudors, who are enthusiastic music lovers. * It looks bad for the human race, but Cornwallis, like Watson in the earlier story, sets a time bomb that blows up the asteroid's antigravity plant, causing it to fall down upon Earth. Cudors who were not killed in the crash do not live long. * The earlier version is superior.

KAW

Unidentified pseud., probably initials. It is not known whether this is the same person as the artist KAW who illustrated Ed Earl

KAW (*continued*)

Repp's "The Stellar Missile" in *Science Wonder Stories*, November 1929. "Through a Haunted Loud Speaker," a story in *Ghost Stories*, November 1926 is attributed to K. A. W., probably the same person.

    721. THE TIME ELIMINATOR. *Amazing Stories*, December 1926. Ill. Paul.

Short-short story. * *Place:* Long Island. * Hamilton Fish Errell, a Yale graduate and an inventor, has developed an apparatus that views past history. It is based on the theory that light never dies and that time is a measure of space. (The explanation is very vague.) Errell views Joan of Arc at Orleans and similar historical moments, but his triumph is political-romantic. He shows General Humiston, the father of his girlfriend, Jerry, a secret meeting of foreign politicians at Fontainebleu, and wins his consent to woo the fair Jerry. * The foreign politicians are planning to corner various necessary American imports, force a war on the United States, and seize the American gold supply. * Amateurish.

KEELER, HARRY STEPHEN (1890-1967)

U.S. (Chicago) writer of detective stories. Fairly important in the mystery genre during the 1930s; noteworthy for extremely complex plot situations.

    722. JOHN JONES'S DOLLAR. *Amazing Stories*, April 1927. Unsigned ill.

(First published in *The Black Cat*, August 1915. Reprinted in Fadiman, *Fantasia Mathematica* and in Derleth, *Strange Ports of Call.* Keeler also incorporated the story into his mystery novel *The Face of the Man from Saturn* [1933].)

Short story. * The marvels of compound interest amusingly displayed. In A.D. 3221, at the University of Terra, the Professor of History lectures via television-equivalent to his students. As he explains it, in 1921 one John Jones placed a dollar in a savings account, to be transferred through eldest male children, collectible by his fortieth descendant. * For the first years and decades the sum plus compound interest of three percent did not amount to much, but toward the end of the third millennium, during the lifetime of Jones's thirty-ninth descendant, it became astronomical. By 2921 the sum exceeded seven trillion dollars, or more than the worth of the solar system. * The Board of Directors is panicked, for the sum is now unpayable. But there is an unexpected resolution: The last descendant of Jones dies childless, and the interplanetary state confiscates the account. * *Miscellaneous:* Gravity control has enabled man to colonize all the planets. * The Moon, as a menace to space navigation, has been chipped away and blasted out into space. * Future man, who now has numbers suffixed with -Male or -Female for a name, is large-headed and small-bodied. Human life span is about two hundred years, and bodies of the dead are recycled. * An amusing *jeu d'esprit.*

KEIRSTEAD, B[URTON] S[EELEY] (1907-1973)

Canadian economist, then associated with the University of New Brunswick. Author of *Essentials of Price Theory* (1946), *The Theory of Economic Change* (1948) and various studies of Canadian economy. Also mystery, *The Brownsville Murders* (1933), in collaboration with D. Frederick Campbell.

    723. ISLAND OF SCIENCE. *Amazing Stories*, December 1933. Ill. Morey.

Short story. * *Time and place:* an island off the southeast coast of India, with an episode in late ninth-century England. * The narrator, a guest on a yachting cruise in the Carnatic Sea, is shipwrecked on an unknown island. The men who rescue him are not Indians, but speak to him in perfect English. * As the narrator soon learns, he is on the Insula Scientiae, which was established by a small group of Renaissance Italians and has since become the seat of a superscience. On the island there are only three scientists, plus a few servants whom they create in their laboratories. These three scientists are as good as immortal, for they manufacture androids for body replacement parts. * The three scientists understand space and time completely, and, with a mechanical sled-like device, can transport themselves to any time or place they will. Pukha, the chief scientist, claims to have been in England at different periods. * The narrator scoffs, whereupon the men place him on the time sled. Asked for a preferred destination, the narrator wildly exclaims that he would like to see King Alfred at the time the oat cakes were burned. * In a very short time the narrator is in Anglo-Saxon England with King Alfred, whom he reminds about the cakes. While the men converse, the narrator shoots Canute, a Dane who is about to kill Alfred. The narrator is then retrieved to the Insula Scientiae. * *Miscellaneous:* King Alfred is characterized with the speech patterns of a modern Englishman. * Intelligent, but quirky, pointless, and amateurish in presentation.

KEITH, J. E.

No information except that portrait accompanying "Between Dimensions" shows a man in early middle age.

    724. BETWEEN DIMENSIONS. *Wonder Stories*, October 1931. Ill. Paul.

Short story. * *Time:* 1942. *Place:* northern Wisconsin and other dimensions. * The narrator, Dahn, a retired chemical engineer, visits his friend Rogers in the North Woods. On one occasion he has to leave Rogers and fly (in his rocket plane) to Chicago for an ailing tooth and is delayed returning. Arriving back at the cabin, he finds no trace of Rogers despite an extensive search in the nearby woods. * The next day, when he awakes, he sees that the cabin is not in the northern woods, but in a blinding desert. Taking a gun he starts to explore, but finds nothing except the desert and a mile-high cliff, off which he slips. * He does not land fatally at the bottom, however, but after falling a few feet he comes to Earth in a pleasant meadowy land. Following a yellow brick road, he sees a huge city that is inhabited only by living machines. At first they pay no attention to him, but then he finds himself paralyzed and carried into laboratories, where he is examined by various mechanical devices. He manages to escape—and now recognizing that velocity causes a change in worlds—leaps off a wall back into the desert world, where he meets Rogers. * They compare notes and work out a periodicity for the cabin, which shifts from our world to the desert world according to a schedule. At the proper time they reënter the cabin and find themselves back in Wisconsin. Just before they left the desert dimension, an invisible monstrosity attacked the cabin; since bullets would only leave the other dimension because of their speed, and the men escaped, they must have killed the monster just after it followd them into our world. * The two men plan in a general way to make their experiences known, but when the cabin disappears again and fails to return, they decide to be silent. Until the day of his death Rogers never knew the

Keith, J. E. (*continued*)

explanation of what had happened. * Thirty years later, however, Dahn learned that Scanlon, a great mathematical physicist, had been conducting experiments nearby. Scanlon's work involved the Lorenz-Fitzgerald contraction and dimensions. * Intelligently written and readable.

725. **"21931."** *Amazing Stories*, February 1936. Ill. Morey.

Short story. * *Time:* A.D. 21,931. * *Background:* In 21,931 health and longevity have become such overpowering fetishes that all life is governed by them. In the Bay area mankind lives in an enormous environment-controlled underground city. It is not clear whether this is the only human settlement, but several thousand years earlier an attempt had been made to colonize Venus. It failed, but the abandoned structures of the space program are still standing in the (above surface) Old City. Those few people who work on the outside are incessantly concerned about losing longevity through radiation. A life span of three hundred and fifty years is typical. * The families of those who do not reach the minimum age of two hundred and fifty years are penalized, being prohibited from breeding and being reduced to the lowest servitor class in the rigid caste system. Illness is severely punished, and everyone wears a nose and mouth filter to protect himself/herself against contamination. * As a result of millennia of synthetic food, the sense of taste has almost completely atrophied, and teeth are no longer present. * Population is strictly controlled at five hundred thousand for the city, and only a selected group is allowed to breed. It is the function of the Bio-Genetical Laboratories to determine such breeders. * This is the pattern, but the aged 31K07, head of the Bio-Genetical Laboratories, is a secret atavist. He was born with a sense of taste, and almost uniquely he enjoys the outdoors. His laboratories are the only functioning buildings above ground, and for generations he has resisted pressure from workers and the council to move them underground. * This is the general situation when crises beset the city. First, an earthquake topples the laboratory buildings, causing damage to sections of the underground world; then another enormous earthquake, followed by subsidence and flooding, destroys the city completely. The only survivors are a handful of people, including 31K07 and his assistant, who happen to be outside. They float through the flood on makeshift rafts and on reaching land prepare to found a new civilization. * Nicely written, nicely thought out; one of the better stories to appear in *Amazing*. The title may indicate that the story was submitted in 1931; it would have been typical of editor Sloane to hold a good story for five years, while filling the magazine with rubbish.

KEITH, LEIGH

Street and Smith records indicate that payment was made to Ernest Pendrell of New York City, who later was active in television. The story was actually written, however, by Horace Gold (as verified in correspondence), who used Pendrell as an accommodation address. Gold has a biographical entry under Clyde Crane Campbell.

726. **NO MEDALS.** *Astounding Stories*, March 1935. Ill. Dold.

Short story. * Patrick Finch, inventor, has devised a fine weapon for his country, which is currently at war. The weapon is recycled soldiery. He rewires the nervous system of corpses with fine silver wire, then directs their movements with electrical controls. He has a sample individual already prepared. * As Finch waits for the brass hats to come and inspect his invention, he fantasizes its use, with hordes of dead soldiers attacking the enemy and routing them. Unfortunately, in his enthusiasm he manipulates the controls carelessly, and his sample stabs him fatally with a bayonet.

KELLER, DAVID H[ENRY], M.D. (1880-1966)

U.S. (mostly Pennsylvania) physician, medical administrator, author. Born in Philadelphia; M.D., University of Pennsylvania; specialty, psychiatry. Served in various mental institutions. Colonel, U.S. Army Medical Corps in World War II, attached to Chaplain's School, Harvard University. Edited serious sexological magazines and studies for Hugo Gernsback. * Keller was a compulsive writer, obviously with no power of self-criticism, who wrote a considerable amount of fiction for the sake of writing, without much thought of publication. As quoted, "I wrote thirteen novels and over fifty stories before I tried to sell any one of them. Then my wife said I must try to write for profit and I wrote and sent 'The Revolt of the Pedestrians' to Amazing Stories" (Schwartz and Weisinger, "David H. Keller, M.D.," p. 3) Thus, publication dates sometimes have little relevance to writing date. In general Keller may be classed as an American primitive, with an extremely uneven product. * Although one of the more prolific of the early science-fiction writers, Keller had little scientific background, and many of his stories contain lapses, even within his own field of study. Contrary to the weltanschauung of Gernsback and many of the other early authors, Keller had considerable reservations about technological and scientific "progress," and his work was unusual, almost unique, in considering the impact of such "progress" on individuals and society, typically negatively. An ultra-conservative ideologically, he explored in his work the evils of social control, feminism, ruthless big business, black racists, scientific vigilantes and others who he thought impinged upon the rights of individuals or trampled on traditional values. The questions he raised were thus highly pertinent to the genre and the life of the time, indeed, often to our time, but the answers he provided were often twisted and unpleasant. His intolerance focused particularly on women's rights and blacks; I do not know, however, if he was a bigot in life. As a corollary Keller advocated a localized, folksy, small-town life of the McKinley period, particularly as exemplified in the Pennsylvania Dutch area, where his regionalism, based on family history, is sometimes effective. * Keller was a very poor technician (despite his own high evaluation of himself as a stylist), and it is doubtful if much of his fiction would have been published in a more critical venue. Yet, and it is always necessary to apologize for taking Keller seriously except as a social phenomenon, occasionally he wrote fable-like stories, detached from daily realities or surrogate science-fiction realities, that were excellent. Most of these stories, however, were not science-fiction, but weird or horror fiction, away from locality or era. It is these fabular stories that seem to have been valued highly in the 1930s by critics like Regis Messac in France, where Keller was acclaimed as a major author.

See also joint work done as by David Lasser and David H. Keller, M.D.

Keller, David H., M.D. (*continued*)

Keller's Taine of San Francisco Stories are presented first, followed by Other Works, both series in chronological order of publication. This implied dating may not be too meaningful, since Keller often held stories years before selling them.

The Taine of San Francisco Stories

Taine, a small man with certain too-often-repeated mannerisms, is a detective operating in the San Francisco Secret Service, presumably a branch of the police department. The Taine stories do not involve deduction to any large extent, mystery with reader participation, or realistic procedural material; Taine's solution of cases rests mostly on intuition, ruthlessness, and a remarkable ability with disguises. The Taine stories embody a considerable amount of racial bigotry, expressed in stereotypes and ethnic slurs. In quality they range mostly from mediocre to poor.

In addition to the stories considered below, three stories about Taine were published in Gernsback's *Scientific Detective Monthly/Amazing Detective Tales*: "A Scientific Widowhood" (February 1930), "Burning Water" (June 1930), "Menacing Claws" (September 1930). *Wolf Hollow Bubbles* was published as a chapbook in 1934, and "Hands of Doom" in *Ten Story Detective* in 1947.

727. **THE MENACE.** *Amazing Stories Quarterly*, Summer 1928.

(Reprinted in *Amazing Stories Quarterly*, Winter 1933.)

A group of four racially bigotted, linked science-fiction detective stories, with the common theme of attempts by "uppity" blacks to take over America. [a] *The Menace*. Unsigned ill. Taine is summoned by the president of the First National Bank to New York, where he meets financial magnates and high officials in national and local secret services. As they explain: They are baffled by two related problems that have cost the lives of previous operators assigned to solve them. First, racially white criminals, killed during crimes, have the fingerprints of known black criminals. Second, an incredibly wealthy syndicate has been buying real estate in Harlem and other parts of Manhattan, then settling blacks there. The financiers consulting Taine fear that New York and eventually the country will be taken over by blacks, who have found some way to turn themselves white. Tens of millions of dollars are at Taine's disposal if he takes the case. * Six months later, N. Gerome, a French mulatto who has made millions in Indo-China, arrives in Harlem and introduces himself into the confidence of light-skinned black banker Acquoine. He even woos the banker's beautiful daughter. All the while, this Frenchman, who is really Taine in light-colored black-face, donates hundreds of thousands of dollars toward helping the blacks of the area. * On the crucial occasion, Acquoine makes a startling suggestion to M. Gerome (Taine): Let the Acquoines, father and daughter, and Gerome be turned white, drop their former identities, and return to New York as white millionaires. Application can be made to the Powerful Ones, who are able to accomplish all this. Taine agrees delightedly, saying that he has never wanted anything more than to be a white man. * In a skyscraper fortress the Powerful Ones interview Gerome and explain matters to him: A black scientist has discovered how to extract gold from sea water, whence their incredible wealth; the same scientist has also discovered a serum that will turn blacks white. * The blacks plan to conquer the world. They have already infiltrated everywhere in white culture

and have hypodermics ready to transform all the blacks into whites. * All well and good, but the Powerful Ones have really been teasing Taine. They know full well that he is a spy and plan to kill him. The leader of the cabal, a very dark exotic dancer formerly known as Ebony Kate, announces that she will feed Taine to her pet thirty-foot boa constrictor. Taine, of course, escapes, traps the white-black leaders, and blows up their stronghold. [b] *The Gold Ship*. Ill. Paul. * A year after the first episode, the Menace is still active, for the black leaders were not all killed in the blast set off by Taine. The Menace now attacks in a different fashion. * The French government suddenly announce that it will assume all war debts from World War I, its own and those of other nations. Why? This is so out of character and such a far-reaching proposal that it arouses suspicion. The President of the United States and his cabinet, worrying the matter, decide to call in Taine. * The British ambassador provides a clue: The French have granted certain concessions to a black syndicate in exchange for enormous quantities of gold. * The American government, for diplomatic reasons, cannot refuse the French offer, but Taine is secretly ordered to destroy the shipment before the gold convoy reaches the United States. In the meanwhile it is revealed that the blacks deceived Taine in their previous encounter. They do not extract gold from sea water; they manufacture it. * When the convoy reaches the United States, however, there is no gold in the bullion chests, only an amalgam of other metals. Taine explains how he transformed the shipment. The gold the blacks were offering was not real gold. It could pass metallurgical tests, but it had one defect. It would break down when subjected to X-rays. Thus, Taine arranged for the battleships escorting the convoy to surreptitiously bombard the bullion ship with radiation. * Much of the narrative is focused on Count Sebastian, one of the black leaders, who has conceived a violent passion for a young mulatto woman. As for the versatile Taine, he played the part of a lady's maid to the female impersonator who seduced the black leader. [c] *The Tainted Flood*. Unsigned ill. * *Place:* California. * Back in San Francisco some time later, Taine realizes that he is being tailed; He thereupon disguises himself, tails his tailers, and learns their identities and plans. They are the leaders of the white negroes—Count Sebastian, the front man; Semon, the scientist who created the artificial gold; and Marcus, an activist. Their latest plan for revenge: They will dump into the Croton Reservoir that serves New York City a chemical that will turn everyone who drinks the water into a negro. After New York City they will move on to other cities until every white man in the country has been turned black. * Taine, invoking presidential carte blanche to enforce his demands for action, substitutes chemicals, so that the water is harmless. * The clincher comes when the captured chemicals must be tested. A young white man who wants to marry a black girl who has hitherto refused him volunteers to drink treated water. He turns ebony. [d] *The Insane Avalanche*. Ill. Paul. *Time:* Up to forty years after the last episode, perhaps 1970 or so. *Place:* mostly an unidentified Pacific island. * The three albified black leaders—Count Sebastian, Semon, and Marcus—have taken refuge on a Pacific island along with Ebony Kate, who survived the blast in the first part of the case. They are disgruntled and depressed at the failure of their elaborate plans, but new hope comes with the arrival of Dr. Abraham Flandings, a mulatto psychologist. Flandings reveals that the black underground still

Keller, David H., M.D. (*continued*)

exists, though it is weak; he also makes suggestions for carrying out the black revenge. The Powerful Ones, he asserts, were too hasty in their plans; instead of instant, traumatic action, they should have worked for long-term results that would escape notice at first, hence would not be stopped. He offers such a long-term plan utilizing a glass building material that, in some fashion, disrupts the metabolism and creates insanity. The black leaders agree with him and accept his plan. * Years pass, and for undiscovered reasons the number of insane people in the American population increases. In fact, there are so many cases of insanity that Congress is considering euthanasia. Old Professor Howens, however, has a better proposal. From giant wasps that he has bred he has isolated and duplicated a chemical that will preserve people indefinitely in suspended animation; all that is needed is a yearly injection to prevent dehydration. * The government sets aside areas for the insane, who are injected and stored away. By now it is recognized that the epidemic has been caused by the glass that has become almost omnipresent in construction. * The black plotters might seem to have achieved their goal of destroying the white man, but they are again disappointed. Superior whites did not break down into insanity, and with the removal of the inferior 98 percent of the population, human achievement has zoomed. America is now a land of wonders and geniuses, who have also solved the racial problem. They have stashed away the insane blacks and have deported all the others to Africa with one thousand dollars apiece in their pockets. * The black leaders on their Pacific island, now old men, realize with dismay that they have failed again. The psychologist Flandings, however, suggests another attack: Change the yearly injection fluid for the people in suspended animation into an awakener and excitant, so that one hundred and fifty million raving maniacs will burst loose in America. * While the four black leaders are in the United States preparing for this feat, an ancient man visits the island. This is Taine of San Francisco, who has worked out what was happening. Ebony Kate, who is now senile, receives him in friendly fashion, and as they spend time together, a bond is built between them. Thus, when the four white-blacks return to the island, Taine does not have to kill them. Kate has already poisoned them. * Kate, now reformed, turns into a nurturing black mammy who lives in the United States, caring for Taine's grandchildren. * As for the last black plot, it fizzled. The maniacs awoke and started to rage, but they had so little vitality that they crumbled into dust after a few minutes. * The end result is an America without problems: The white trash and low-grade whites are all dead; the blacks are either all dead or dumped into Africa. Adolf Hitler could not have done it better. * Not only very weak from a literary point of view, but a disgraceful chain of stories, probably the most offensive to be found in early science-fiction.

728. **THE FEMININE METAMORPHOSIS.** *Science Wonder Stories*, August 1929. Ill. Paul.
(Reprinted in Moskowitz, *When Women Rule*.)
Novelette. * One of Keller's idiosyncratic stories in which he apparently recognizes a social problem, but then distorts reactions to it in a very offensive way. * *Place:* partly China. * The story begins with the case of Martha Belzer, a highly intelligent, capable subexecutive who is blatantly denied promotion because she is a woman; it is part of a policy, both tacit and overt, among major companies, in order to retain male domin-

ance. Keller states Belzer's problem quite fairly, in a tone that would be considered modern. * But things happen. First, the richest woman in the world, who has just inherited her father's wealth, turns it all into cash. * Second, the American government begins to be concerned about an American hospital in China that is perforce guarded by American marines because of troubled times. The hospital is staffed by women, who perform perpetual surgery, but what is going on? * Since Taine of San Francisco knows Chinese and can pass for an Oriental, the government assigns him to investigate. Disguised as a young Chinese woman, Taine gains access to the hospital. All that he learns, however, is that the surgeons are paying Chinese males to allow themselves to be castrated (Keller paraphrases this smoothly rather than stating it outright); thereupon an extract made from the gonadal tissue is shipped to Paris. The trail ends there. * Three years pass. New York financial and industrial tycoons are worried about a new group of operators who are just as able as they, if not more able. The new operators, however, are intensely clannish, do not socialize, do not play golf, but do play bridge at an elaborate edifice called the Bridge Club. * One of the concerned tycoons consults Taine, who is beginning to see a pattern. Assuming the identity of a young woman telephone operator, whom he kidnaps, he works his way into the organization. He finds early corroboration of his speculations when he sees that one of the men in the bridge club wears a ring that Taine (disguised as a young Chinese woman) had given to a woman doctor in China. * There is a confrontation with the master council of the Bridge Club, who reveal themselves to be a ruthless, murderous group of women who intend to kill Taine. Explanation: A few years earlier a group of five thousand aggressive feminists volunteered to undergo sex changes in Paris; this was not a partially surgical matter as today, but chemical, with the hormones extracted from Chinese males. Secondary sex characteristics changed, transformed visually into men, closely organized, the feminists are on the edge of obtaining financial control of the country. As for their ultimate plans—they intend to turn mankind into a female race. They have already furtively distributed chemicals that increase the ratio of female births to male, and they hope for parthenogenesis, on which their scientists are working. As the president grants, however, they may keep a few men around for a time as messenger boys. * During this final confrontation there is a complex swap of identities until it is revealed whom Taine is impersonating at the moment, but Taine drops the lid on the feminist conspiracy: What they did not know, not being Orientalists, is that all Chinese have a mild form of syphilis, which the women received along with the hormonal injections. As a result the five thousand sex-changers will all die of paresis in a very short time. The menace is over. * The story, after the initial situation, is padded with the usual platitudes and ultra-reactionary domestic sentiments, ending on a religious note about God willing there to be male and female. Scientifically, of course, Keller must have known that his denouement was impossible, the spirochete being so sensitive. * Unfortunate. A bad story.

729. **EUTHANASIA LIMITED.** *Amazing Stories Quarterly*, Fall 1929. Ill. Wesso.
Short story. * Anna Van Why, a pioneer in electrobiology, in carrying on the work of Jagadis Chandra Bose has discovered that the actuality of death in plants and animals is the immediate loss of electrical potential. Her half brother, John Van Why, a

Keller, David H., M.D. (*continued*)

gifted but crooked man, is greatly interested when Anna explains her theories to a visiting scientist. John Van Why is an important member of the Paint and Powder Club, a group of thirty-nine rogues who individually or collectively run most of the rackets in New York City. * About a year later the chief of the New York City Secret Police requests Dr. Van Why's assistance, since she is a leading thanatologist, in solving a series of mysterious deaths. All the victims have been male, mostly middle-aged and wealthy; there has been no certifiable cause of death. * Dr. Van Why states that she is willing to help, if she can have the help of a detective who looks stupid, but is really intelligent. But when Taine of San Francisco reports to her, she rejects him as inadequate and does nothing for the police. * Some time later one of the most powerful racketeers in China approaches the Paint and Powder Club, offering millions of dollars in cash and most lucrative entries to new ranges of gambling, drug peddling, white slaving and other brands of organized crime. * All he asks in return is the secret of the mysterious deaths. Van Why is reluctant to reveal this, but when pressed does so. The murders were accomplished by withdrawing electricity from the victims. * This is what Taine, disguised as the Chinese mastermind's secretary, has waited for. The criminals are rounded up, and the mysteries solved. John Van Why, however, commits suicide in one of the chairs rigged up as murder apparatus.

730. **THE CEREBRAL LIBRARY.** *Amazing Stories,* May 1931. Ill. Morey.

(Reprinted in Keller, *Life Everlasting.*)

Short story. * *Place:* mostly Eastern Pennsylvania. * Newspaper ads seek out five hundred college graduates who are willing to read three hundred books a year over a period of five years. They will live in luxurious isolation in a secured manor house, working through a library of seven hundred and fifty thousand books. They will each receive ten thousand dollars per year, collectible at the end of the contractual period. * After a time, the Chief of the Secret Service hears of the arrangement and becomes suspicious. For reasons best known to the author, the Chief does not use one of his own operatives to investigate, but requests aid from San Francisco, which sends Taine. * Taine, after an interview with the Chief, attempts to work his way into the manor, but has only limited success. Time passes. * The great Chinese surgeon Wing Loo, whose specialty is organ transplants, arrives in America, where he is welcomed by the great scientist Charles Jefferson, whose specialty is electricity. The two men strike a bargain on a large task that Wing Loo will do for Jefferson, who is sponsoring the reading project. * Time passes, and the five year period is up. The library at the manor has been destroyed, and the men are about to be paid off. * Taine now reports to the Chief, and smuggles him into the manor, where the Chief can witness the consummation of the five-year program. Concealed, the Chief listens to a conversation between the Chinese surgeon and Jefferson. Jefferson states in naive self-revealment that he has always wanted to have access to precise information, quotations and summaries of the great books, and now he has it. Wing Loo has removed the brains from the readers, placed them in glass jars, wired them up to a console (my term), where Jefferson, consulting them via a keyboard, can obtain what he wants. Wing Loo states that Taine is now a captive and will be disposed of suitably. * This is not,

of course, the end. When the Chief, pistol in hand, emerges from hiding, Taine explains. Actually, Taine has been masquerading as the Chinese surgeon for a year, keeping the real Wing Loo under sedation. The brains that are visible in the jars are only wax imitations, and the young men are all safe and sound, though unpaid, since Jefferson never had enough funds to reward them as contracted. * It is questionable, according to Taine, whether Jefferson has done anything illegal. In any case, Jefferson should start reading on his own. As for the young men, they are richer in knowledge if not in cash. * An interesting idea, though clumsily handled. The detective story purist will find that the criteria of fairness and story logic are mangled.

731. **THE TREE OF EVIL.** *Wonder Stories,* September 1934. Ill. Winter.

Short story. * A Taine story, the cleansing of Poisonville. * When millionaire Harley was a boy, Glendale was an average American small town, sound and wholesome. But now decades after Harley has left, it has become a sink of vice, a crime center, an embodiment of viciousness. Or so Dr. Riorden, a medical sociologist, assures Harley. * Riorden is right, of course, and Harley agrees to fund a secret investigation and reform process, for which they hire Taine of San Francisco. * The three men proceed in disguise to Glendale. Taine takes a job disguised as a slatternly waitress in the local hash house; Riorden, interviewing the Episcopal clergyman of the town, pretends to be a medical man stricken off the register for performing abortions; and Harley poses as a bank robber with thousands of dollars to spend in the town. Riorden and Harley are in danger. They would be murdered were it not for the fact that the citizens of Glendale wish to strip them financially bare before killing them. * As the three outsiders soon discover, the root of the evil that permeates Glendale lies in a certain tree, the leaves of which the locals eat. Chemicals in the leaves destroy conscience and awaken evil potentials. Harley, half seduced by the clergyman's handsome wife, succumbs to the leaves and has to be removed from Glendale by force. Taine, solo, cleans up the town, though internal tensions assist in the downfall of the evil culture. * The background that Taine uncovers: From Indian times there has been a small local cult based on the tree of evil and an attendant giant serpent to which sacrifices are made. One family of poor whites took over the cult after the Indians died out, and when one of their women, a strikingly handsome woman, married the Episcopal clergyman, the cult acquired new vitality and spread. * One of Keller's best stories from a literary point of view; the background is excellent, and the characterizations of the fallen clergyman and his wife are beautifully handled. Unfortunately, it is also one of Keller's most offensive stories. For example, when Taine, disguised as a black youth, meets the clergyman and his wife, the clergyman comments, "You may have been made in the image of a god, but if you were, that god was an ape."

732. **ISLAND OF WHITE MICE.** *Amazing Stories,* February 1935. Ill. Morey.

Novelette. * A Taine of San Francisco story. * *Place:* mostly on an island in the South Seas. * When Taine is offered a princely salary to go to Tibet and investigate, among other things, the Dalai Lama, he smells a rat; accepting, he sends a look-alike. * He then reports to the Chief of the Secret Service in Washington, who tells of a strange situation that may be connected with the Tibetan job. Two men, (unsuccessfully) attempting to conceal

Keller, David H., M.D. (*continued*)

their identities, have offered a world cruise to a select group of twenty-four college graduates and two proctors. One of the men, Weisman, is an eccentric philanthropist, the other, Ludwig, is well-known for field work studying apes and monkeys. Investigation has shown nothing amiss with the offer, but both the head of the Secret Service and Taine feel deeply that there is something wrong. * The young people are chosen, and despite the sudden deaths of Weisman and Ludwig the project will go on. The vessel leaves New York, sails according to plan through the Mediterranean, but when it reaches the vicinity of a small island somewhere in the South Seas, matters take a strange turn. * The story now focuses on the group. Pretending that the ship is disabled and that a storm is coming up, the skipper of the vessel puts the men and women ashore on the island and sails away. The island is desert except for a sealed central building and several large glass structures that look like enormous jars. In each of the jars is a desk and chair. * The story now shifts back and forth between the maroons and the two men fortified in the central building—Ludwig and Weisman, who falsified their deaths. The two scientists are really conducting a psychological experiment to see how men and women react in stress situations. Ludwig is concerned whether the men and women will descend to a level below apes. As part of their experiment the two ruthless scientists withhold food and try to pit the castaways against each other, but the experiment does not go entirely as planned. The scientists had expected the old chivalric code favoring women to cause trouble, but the women reject it and voluntarily share food. There is also strong group solidarity that forcefully squelches dissidents. * The scientists also did not make sufficient allowance for the ingenuity of the group, who find a way to drive them out of their fortification. When everything is settled, it is revealed that Taine really has been in charge of the whole situation, and that the castaways, while subjected to some inconvenience, have never been in any real danger. It was all an adventure. * In the hands of a more skilled author, this could have been a thought-provoking story, but Keller bumbles it badly.

Other Works

A prefatory note: Keller used and reused certain names in his stories, for example, Hubler and Cecil. These do not refer to the same persons from one story to another, or even to connections between the persons named. Keller simply liked the names, which in some cases came from his extended family.

733. **THE REVOLT OF THE PEDESTRIANS.** *Amazing Stories*, February 1928. Ill. Paul.
(Reprinted in Keller, *Tales from Underwood*; in Derleth, *Beyond Time and Space*; and in Gunn, *The Road to Science Fiction #2*.)
Short story. * Social commentary in the form of double genocide, with a strong fabular element. * *Time:* perhaps the twenty-fifth or twenty-sixth century. *Place:* mostly the New York City area. * Persistent use of artificial transportation, *i.e.,* improved automobiles for even the shortest distances, has caused hereditary atrophy of the legs. The world of the Automobilists has come into being, a world that is essentially socialist to the extent of providing food, housing, and other necessities for all,

yet also preserves extreme wealth and power for a few families. The automobile has become more and more the center of life, and most of an individual's life is spent in his/her automobile, driving about madly. The environment, of course, has been horribly poisoned by automobile waste. * This culture has little empathy or use for the person who is not an Automobilist, and rights are gradually withdrawn from Pedestrians, as the walking minority is termed. It is at first legally permissible to run down Pedestrians who venture on the highways; later laws are passed calling for the extermination of Pedestrians, with bounties on their heads. * An introductory episode describes the accidental death of the Pedestrian woman Miller, and the vow that her young son takes to be avenged on the Automobilists. * The hundred or so surviving Pedestrians withdraw to the Ozarks. There, their presence unknown to the Automobilists, who believe them extinct, they develop their plot for exterminating the Automobilists and regaining the world. Their hopes are not unrealistic, since most of the Pedestrians are scientists and engineers who rejected the Automobilist culture. * One hundred years later, the story has two narrative centers. First, the daughter of Heisler, the wealthiest, most powerful man in the world, is an atavism, a child born with normal legs. Heisler, who is at first shocked, comes to accept his daughter's condition and even to develop it, so that she grows up into a vigorous, active, independent young woman. Her existence is concealed from all but a few close friends. Second, Abraham Miller, the leader of the Pedestrians, is now prepared to act. Pedestrian spies have penetrated the Automobilist establishment, and Miller's scientists have the power to destroy the hated culture. Before acting, however, Miller arranges (without their knowing his identity) a meeting with the Automobilist leaders, including Heisler. He asks only for coexistence for his people. When the Automobilist leaders refuse, the Pedestrian scientists destroy electricity all over the world, almost instantaneously. As a result the Automobilists perish horribly. * Miller rescues Heisler, who had been sympathetic to his plea, and meets Heisler's daughter, with whom he strikes an instant rapport. The new culture that arises will never again fall into the perils of mechanism. The destruction of electricity is permanent. * Despite occasional flat writing, a powerful story, horrible at times, but imaginative and rigorous in logic. Keller, in terms of total output, is a bad writer, but he did produce a small handful of stories, like the present, that are (almost against his will) worth reading.

734. **THE YEAST MEN.** *Amazing Stories*, April 1928. Ill. Paul.
(Reprinted in Keller, *Tales from Underwood.*)
Short story. * A fabular approach to aggression; like "The Revolt of the Pedestrians," somewhat sanguinary. * The story is concerned with Eupenia and Moronia, two imaginary nations perhaps situated in Central Europe. The nations are on bad terms. Eupenia, which is headed by a hawkish premier, wishes to overrun Moronia, which it totally surrounds. Moronia possesses a ray that destroys planes as they cross the national border, but otherwise is the weaker of the two nations. * An American scientist long resident in Moronia provides the answer to Eupenian aggression. He has developed a form of yeast, activated by radium, that takes roughly humanoid form, moves slowly by means of a metabolic process, and decays three days after its genesis, leaving a puddle of most noxious liquid. It is difficult to destroy, since fragmentation only creates new

Keller, David H., M.D. (*continued*)

individuals. In small numbers, of course, they amount to little, but in large quantities they are an incredible, undefeatable weapon. * Special cannon project the yeast fragments into Eupenia, and in a very short time the land is not only chaotic, but ruined. The war is over. * One of Keller's stories where the folksy primitivism gets in the way of the narrative.

735. **A BIOLOGICAL EXPERIMENT**. *Amazing Stories*, June 1928. Ill. Paul.
(Reprinted in Keller, *Tales from Underwood*.)
See the prefatory note to story #733. Short story. * *Time:* A.D. 3928. * Keller's often-expressed conservative ideas on sex, the family, and society. * *Background:* In 1928 a judge gave legal sanction to companionate marriage, which meant ordinary marriage, but no children until the parents decided the marriage was stable. Around 2028, to prevent the poor from overbreeding, it became illegal to bear a child without a permit. Naturally, the law was often evaded. Around A.D. 2800, after plagues had wiped out much of the human race and the quality of mankind was low, compulsory sterilization was enacted for the unfit. Unfortunately, many of the fit had themselves sterilized to avoid the troubles and responsibilities of childbirth and child-rearing. By A.D., 3000 synthetic children were the rule; ovaries were removed from a few selected women of exceptional quality, and individual eggs were fertilized and reared in laboratories. The last natural childbirth took place in 3009. * The world of 3928 is a rational eutopia in some ways; fine specimens of humans live disease-free lives. The state cares for all material needs, and it is possible to lead a productive life, according to one's own wishes. But there are certain limitations. Education and culture are regimented, although this does not seem to be oppressive. Family life is strictly controlled. If couples wish to marry, they must satisfy strict requirements; they must also get permits to obtain a baby (or older child) from the laboratories. The largest problem with this culture is that although there is no want, there is also no happiness. * In this world a startling event takes place. Young Leuson Hubler and Elizabeth Sellers evade the mandatory sterilization radiation treatment, forge a marriage permit, marry, and elope, hiding out in the Ozarks. They plan to make their own subsistence living and have children the natural way. The factor that set them off was reading forbidden books that made them yearn for the freer, more biologically natural life of the past. What they have done is criminal. * Some time later, Leuson returns to Washington to visit his mentor and friend, the Librarian of Congress, who tells him a surprising story. Leuson and Elizabeth's revolt was not wholly their own; the Librarian and a like-minded friend had been setting them up for this since their childhood, allowing them to read forbidden books and all. The reasons: (1) The two elderly men want to make amends for an earlier experiment that failed. They had reared synthetic girls, whom they exposed to the older literature of the free world. But on reaching adulthood, after being sterilized, the young women committed suicide in despair. (2) The two men wish to see if humanity is still capable of natural childbirth, since it is about a thousand years since the last occasion. (3) The Librarian obviously wants to subvert the dead culture around him by awaking maternal instincts that still remain in the unconscious. * Leuson and Elizabeth survive under their self-imposed primitivism. Elizabeth becomes pregnant, produces a fine child, but dies in childbirth. Medical aid came too late. * This tragedy

does not discourage the two old men. The Librarian takes the baby to the annual meeting of the National Society of Federated Woman, an ultrafeminist group that seems to maintain hegemony over the culture, and explains what has happened. His speech and the production of the baby awaken unconscious forces in the women, who break down and demand a return to the old ways. * Unfortunately, the story, which is moving, is so clumsily written that its point is lost in misdirections, essay material, and sentiment. The above summary may suggest more clarity and direction than the story has.

736. **UNLOCKING THE PAST**. *Amazing Stories*, September 1928. Ill. Paul.
Short story. * *Time:* the near future. * Robert Howes and his companionate wife Anise have a decision to make. They are poverty stricken, partly because of misfortunes, partly because of Robert's occupation, partly because of the birth of their child, Angelica. Under the conditions of companionate marriage they should not have had a child. * The professor makes them an offer. As he explains it: Ancestral memory has been demonstrated many times; indeed, the first sounds that babies make are not random noises, but words from ancient tongues spoken by their ancestors. If one could study a child who had perfect memory of the lives of his/her ancestors, instead of tiny fragments, it would revolutionize history. And such a study is possible with the professor's discovery of a process to awaken such memories in the "empty" areas of the brain. The process is based on radium-arcturium gas passed through neon. The professor offers twenty-five thousand dollars per year *in perpetuo* to Robert for the use of Angelica. * Despite misgivings, the parents finally agree. The child undergoes the treatment, but that evening, she awakens Anise, talking learnedly of past events, gradually revealing the horror of memory of things past. Angelica is glad that her parents are spared such terrors. * But then Anise awakens; it was all a dream, but a veridical dream that causes both parents to refuse the professor's offer. They will struggle along as before, without submitting their child to such pain. * Interesting, but the usual bad writing.

737. **STENOGRAPHER'S HANDS**. *Amazing Stories Quarterly*, Fall 1928. Ill. Paul.
Short story. * *Time:* the present and about A.D. 2125. * The great business tycoon Jerome Smith of Universal Utilities complains bitterly to Dr. Billings, his scientific consultant, about the low quality of his stenographers. As he says, despite long training, the work of the average woman is riddled with errors; the intelligent women leave for better jobs; the good-looking ones are set up in apartments; and the whole situation is a business loss. (Smith seems to run some sort of mail order business that involves a heavy correspondence in individual letters, not form letters.) * Billings, pressed for a solution, fearful of losing his job, suggests various standard remedies—higher pay, incentives, etc., all of which have been tried, with no success. Finally Billings comes up with the ultimate solution: breed perfect stenographers as a human subrace. Establish half the work force as efficient males, discharge the incompetent women, set up surreptitious incentives for the superior males and females to marry, and carry this on, with perpetual selection and elimination of the weaker children. * To Smith's objections that this would take too long, Billings advances two arguments: It would enable Universal Utilities to control the future of business, and with special foods and treatments, the human breeding cycle

Keller, David H., M.D. (*continued*)

could be speeded up until it is about ten years. Smith accepts. * Two hundred years later, the system is working beautifully. A special race of perfect stenographers who care about nothing but typing perfect letters is the backbone of Universal Utilities, which is now the world's economic titan. * The situation, however, is not as stable as it may appear. Mirabella Smith, the daughter of the current reigning Smith, knows little about details of the family business, and wonders about becoming a stenographer. Horrified when she sees the stenographers in operation, she is dismayed at what her ancestors have done to human beings. She thereupon takes up with and marries a young normal doctor who is a baby reject from the breeding program. * Somewhat later the stenographers begin to deteriorate, worse and worse, so that Universal Utilities is in trouble. Mirabella, head of the business now that her father has died, at a board meeting reveals the reason as worked out by her husband, Dr. Thoney. The stenographers, due to inbreeding and hyperspecialization, have all become nocturnal epileptics and are cracking up. They must be retired, and normal stenographers must be restored. * According to a prefatory note to "The Human Termites" Keller conceived the idea for "Stenographers' Hands" during a dinner with Hugo Gernsback and his wife; Keller claims that whole paragraphs were taken from Gernsback's conversation—probably the complaints about the bad crop of stenographers. * Interesting initial situation, but the limp ending destroys any possible impact.

738. **THE PSYCHOPHONIC NURSE.** *Amazing Stories*, November 1928. Ill. Paul.

(Reprinted in Keller, *Tales from Underwood* and in Conklin and Fabricant, *Great Science Fiction about Doctors*.)

Short story. * *Time:* the near future. * Keller's response to the liberated woman. * Mrs. Susanna Teeple, mother of a three-week-old boy, perpetually grouses at the amount of time his care is taking her and the damage it is doing to her career. Her suffering husband, who says little, buys a custom-built baby nurse to free his wife for her personal work. This device, which Teeple nostalgically designs in the form of a "black Mammy," operates by voice signals and is a complex of electrical wiring, radio tubes, and gears. * Mrs. Teeple, delighted, continues her quest for self fulfillment with books and articles, including a proposed book, *Woman, the Master Sex*. But her child is obviously becoming disoriented away from humans. * Teeple, rather than disturb his wife, has a male nurse constructed to walk the child in a perambulator—but secretly substitutes himself for the automaton during the walks. He hopes that by this means his child will come to know a human being. On one of these surreptitious excursions, he is trapped in a sudden snow squall and catches pneumonia. * His illness shocks his wife back into *Kinder, Küche, und Kirche*, which is where Keller obviously thinks she should be. * As is often the case with Keller, a socially interesting message (obviously not very palatable today), but bumbled in the narration.

739. **THE WORM.** *Amazing Stories*, March 1929. Unsigned ill.

(Reprinted in Keller, *Tales from Underwood*; Ross, *The Best of Amazing*; Derleth, *Strange Ports of Call*; Conklin, *Br-r-r-r!*; Carr, *Creatures from Beyond*.)

Short story. * A mood story, obviously semi-allegorical in intent. * *Place:* Vermont. * The family of John Staples, an elderly

recluse, have operated the old isolated grist mill for at least two hundred years. Staples himself no longer runs the mill, for there is no more grist to be ground. * He begins to hear a grinding noise from beneath the flagstones in the cellar of the mill. The sound, together with vibrations, grows stronger, and it becomes obvious to the old man that something is gnawing its way up to the mill. The creature breaks through, and Staples sees the gigantic, semihumanoid head of the monster as it gnaws through stones, beams, and fresh concrete, impervious to anything the old miller can do, from a red hot stove to a diversion of the millrace into the creature's hole. Eventually, it destroys the mill, the miller, and his dog. * The rational explanation is that the creature (which Keller calls by the archaic term "worm") is some sort of subterranean life that for generations has heard the vibration of the mill and has interpreted it as the noise of another of its kind, perhaps a mate. * Perhaps the story means that mankind and his mechanisms will be swallowed by forces around him, either nature or the unconscious. * A good story.

740. **THE THREAT OF THE ROBOT.** *Science Wonder Stories*, June 1929. Ill. Paul.

Short story. * When Ed Ball returns to New York after twenty years abroad, mostly in the wilds where he had little news of what was happening outside, he is stunned when he attends a football game of his alma mater, the University of New York. There is almost no audience present. Eleven men sit at keyboards, while the team (as he soon learns) consists of robots controlled by computers [my term]. * New York gets a sound trouncing by Pennsylvania (which interfered with the broadcast instructions to the robots), and Ball, who is enormously wealthy, takes thought. Football, for him, is the heart of college life, and if there is no attendance at the games, with only television coverage, American culture is headed for a collapse. * He thereupon uses his colossal fortune to develop secretly a first-rate human team that beats the Pennsylvania robots badly. This sets off a trend toward experiencing life rather than watching a substitute. * Incredible, but not badly told.

741. **WHITE COLLARS.** *Amazing Stories Quarterly*, Summer 1929. Ill. Hynd.

See the prefatory note to story #733. * Short story. * *Time:* the near future. * The enormous increase of advanced education has caused a social problem: There are not enough jobs for intellectuals (or, as Keller terms them, "white collars"). Rather than accept well-paying artisan jobs, they prefer to starve or live on charity of various sorts. The feeling of caste is strong enough, in addition, that a white collar is no longer willing to marry a wealthy artisan. * Such is the case with Angelica Reiswick and Larry Hubler. Hubler, a presentable young man, is the son of a millionaire plumber, while Angelica, whose father is a physician and mother a teacher of Greek, is a doctor of law. She refuses to consider romance with a plumber and, with her family, is close to starvation. * The white collars stage protests, mount parades, riot and demolish the wealthy artisan quarter, but to no avail; the situation just grows worse. * A harsh but effective political solution is reached. Senator Whitesel pushes through a bill that establishes vast public works, offers compulsory work with a livable salary to white collar males, and forces white collar females to become housewives or workers. Those who do not accept this program will be deprived of citizenship, given one thousand dollars each, and deported where they will. * The Reiswicks, like many other intellectuals, choose deportation. But

Keller, David H., M.D. (*continued*)

at the last minute Larry Hubler kidnaps Angelica. Angelica at first scornfully rejects Larry's pleas, but when she sees the luxury to which she will be lifted, she ungraciously and snootily accepts Larry. * As often the case with Keller, an interesting social problem clumsily and unfeelingly handled.

742. **THE BLOODLESS WAR**. *Air Wonder Stories*, July 1929. Ill. Paul.

Short story. * *Time:* 1940. * The United States is almost totally disarmed, whereas the other major nations, who happen to be in debt to the United States, are heavily rearming. * Inventor John Farrol, who is in possession of startling information, tries to make himself heard in Washington, but is ignored. In desperation he forces an interview with Jacob Strange, head of Universal Electric, and appeals to his patriotism. As Farrol reveals: He has invented a system for controlling planes by radio. The Japanese have stolen the secret and are preparing for war against the United States. They have built up a huge air fleet through dummy receivers and have concentrated thousands of planes in Mexico. The Mexicans have signed a secret treaty which involves dividing up the United States. * Thanks to Farrol's invention it will not be long before fleets of radio-controlled drone planes, led by a single pilot perhaps, will be directed against the cities of the United States. * Farrol proposes a way to negate the impending attack without actually going to war. Monitors will wait in each city of the United States until alerted by equipment set off by the sound of the approaching armada. Then, using a modification of Farrol's invention, the monitors will seize radio control of the fleets and drop their bombs either at sea or elsewhere. * It all happens as Farrol prophesied, but now Mexico and Japan both protest their friendly attitude toward the United States.

743. **THE BONELESS HORRORS**. *Science Wonder Stories*, July 1929. Ill. Paul.

(Reprinted in Keller, *Life Everlasting*.)

Short story. * A fabular approach to literary myths, with a weird science-fictional component. * *Time:* around 12,000 B.C. *Place:* mostly the lost continent of Mo (Mu). * In this ancient world there are three great empires, all on roughly the same level of culture: Gobi, which is a flat, fertile plain in the area of present-day Southern and Central Asia; Mo, a Pacific continent whose remnants are to be seen in modern Oceania; and Atlantis, pretty much in the traditional location, with colonies in the Americas and Mediterranean. * The dominant of the time is desperate hatred between Gobi and Mo, each of which is endeavoring, through superscientific means, to destroy the other. Gobi scientists and engineers, for example, are driving a tunnel hundreds of miles long beneath Mo; at the proper time super-explosives will ignite subterranean gas chambers and sink Mo into the Ocean. * In Gobi, the erratically sadistic emperor, who delights in torture and slaughter, is worried about his mortality, hence is delighted when his men capture Herakles, an Atlantean scientist who will be able to prolong his life with a compound derived from bee queen jelly and other apian substances. It works well, and the King, the high priest, and the royal councilors all not only stop aging but actually feel more youthful. * Herakles, however, is more than he seems. An agent from Mo, he is secretly working, with superhydraulics, on a plan to elevate Gobi so high that it will be uninhabitable. It becomes a race between Herakles and the Gobi Emperor, whether Gobi will be

elevated first, or Mo sunk first. * Herakles also has another arrow in his quiver: Into the bee extract, which he has been personally preparing, he has been inserting chemicals that dissolve the bony structure of the body, disguising the change with narcotics. * D-day comes for all. Mass explosions heard all the way into Gobi destroy Mo, which sinks into the sea; Gobi rises into the sky, but not exactly as Herakles had planned, forming modern Tibet; Atlantis sinks, the innocent victim of forces unleashed by the other two lands; Herakles is murdered by the faithful odalisque of the Emperor of Mo. As for the emperor and his councilors, they lay, bones dissolved into jelly, immortal and paralyzed, in a bitterly cold cave in the newly risen Hima-layas. They are still there. * *Miscellaneous:* The natives of Gobi were ancestral Orientals; the Atlanteans were European Nordics; the natives of Mo were presumably Polynesians. * The rulers of Atlantis were visiting the American Southwest when the cata-strophe struck. They committed suicide. Their perfectly preserved bodies, together with a fortune in gems, were found by American prospectors—but the site was lost. * One of Keller's superior stories, in which he carries the fanciful note through very well.

744. **THE FLYING FOOL**. *Amazing Stories*, July 1929. Ill. Hugh Mackay.

(Reprinted in Keller, *Tales from Underwood.*)

Short story. * Robert Smith, small salesman of ribbons and laces during the day, is a great inventor (mentally) during his nights. Unfortunately, he is married to a wife who is fine domestically, but has the personality and imagination of a clothing store dummy. * On reading a popular account of Einstein's General Theory, Smith decides that he will attempt to fly by antigravity. Permalloy and magnetism will be his means. * Creating a device for extracting electricity from the air, he spends his few dollars on permalloy wire. He has the wire woven into a new suit that he is buying, adapts a chair, and prepares to take off. Nothing happens. * His foolish wife, noticing the wire in his suit, extracted it and sold it as junk metal for less than he paid. He is back at his ribbon counter. * Obviously parabolic in nature.

745. **THE ETERNAL PROFESSORS**. *Amazing Stories*, August 1929. Ill. Hugh Mackay.

See the prefatory note to story #733. * Short story. * *Time:* the near future. *Place:* New York and Chicago. * There is a bitter feud between the great Chicago University and New York Universit. Each tries to lure away talent and attract the better students. The academic rivalry becomes deadly when in an unspecified fashion the faculty of NYU is responsible for the death of several members of CU. * The tycoon Bowlers, a staunch supporter of Chicago, turns to dirty tricks. He hires Johnson, a great biologist, to destroy the NYU faculty; at a banquet Johnson thereby infects the entire faculty with malignant cancer cells. The president of NYU, Jacob Hubler, is able, how-ever, to keep the resulting illnesses secret. * It would seem that Chicago has won, but by chance the great Russian experimental surgeon Chenenko is in New York at this time. Thanks to his work, the faculty of NYU continues to lecture as brilliantly as ever, long past the expected termination point for the cancer. * Bowlers, infuriated, hires detectives to discover why the cancer attack did not work. After a long period of surveillance, much money spent on bribery, and similar techniques, the detectives present Bowlers with an answer: The NYU faculty consists of detached heads on artificial bodies, brains fed with artificial

Keller, David H., M.D. (*continued*)

blood, all the work of Chenenko. They seem happy and certainly function; they remain youthful, while the CU faculty is deteriorating with old age. * Bowler again consults Johnson, who works another dirty trick: adding excess adrenalin to the artificial blood sustaining the faculty heads, who begin to deteriorate, collapse, and die. * In a short time, both faculties are moribund. President Hubler of NYU calls a meeting for all concerned. CU, he states is dead from normal causes; NYU is practically dead. Learning a lesson from this, the other universities should try to live together in peace. He then shuts down the last artificial maintenance systems. * Clumsily handled, but a good fabular note.

746. **THE HUMAN TERMITES.** *Science Wonder Stories*, September-November 1929. Ill. Paul.
(Reprinted in book form by the Keller Memorial Library.)
Short novel. * According to a prefatory note by Keller the story arose out of a dinner conversation with the Gernsbacks, during which Gernsback recommended that Keller read *The Life of the White Ant* by Maurice Maeterlinck, to whom Keller has dedicated the following story. * *Time:* from the present to a couple of years into the future. *Place:* South Africa, Australia, the United States, and somewhere in Quebec. * The great maverick naturalist Souderman is fascinated by termites, their long history, their adaptation to environment, and their remarkable organization. After years of study he has adopted the hypothesis that in each termitary there is an organizing and controlling faculty that stands in the same relation to individual insects as the central nervous system does to cells in a higher organism. This controller, which cannot be the queen, must give orders in some undiscovered manner. * Inventing an apparatus for magnifying and recording sound, Souderman spends several years beside a termitary in South Africa, recording and studying. He sends his data to a linguist in Capetown, who discovers from them that there are two termite languages, one used to the workers within the hill, and the second among the termite rulers, from hill to hill. * Some of the messages reveal that the termite central intelligences have a long-term plan to exterminate mankind and take over the world. Disturbed by this, Souderman decides to communicate with the local termite ruler, urging coexistence. In reply, he receives an astonishing message: We have tolerated your presence for years in order to study a specimen of mankind closely. We are done, and now you must leave. * Recognizing his danger, Souderman decamps immediately. He is fortunate to escape, for his records are destroyed by the termites, and the linguist in Capetown is killed. The termites are ready to move. * Making his way to the United States by a circuitous route, he recruits Adam Fry, a brilliant young entomologist who accepts Souderman's conclusions. Fry will continue Souderman's work, while Souderman will proceed to a secret hideout in the north, where it is too cold for the termites to penetrate. Fry, in turn, recruits Bailey Bankerville, a wealthy young banker, who also has enough wisdom to accept Souderman's theory and data. The group, which also includes Bankerville's sister Susanne and associates, decides to investigate in the field. * It is Susanne who makes the next integrative step: If the individual termites are cells in an organism with a central brain of some sort, perhaps humans follow the same pattern. The group then accepts the hypothesis that the nations of Earth, comparable to the termites, are governed by invisible, unknown central intelligences, whence

wars and foolish mass actions. * After evading attacks by local termite groups, the expedition proceeds to an Australian island to study the menace at close hand. Susanne again makes the next discovery. Under some sort of partial willcontrol by the termite central intelligence of the island, she descends through large tunnels into the heart of the island system, where she meets the termite brain, a mass of protoplasm on the floor of the cave. The central intelligence wants to read her and to use her, but in the process it provides information, letting her ride about the tunnels under the termitary on a gigantic hybrid creature. * The termites are about ready to act. They have been creating (by cell implant) termite-animal-human monstrosities the size of small buses, and have billions of such warriors ready to emerge and act. They also have a technique for removing a human brain and inserting into the cranium one of the termite master brains. Indeed, as Susanne watches, the central intelligence inserts itself into the cranium of an expedition member it has captured, a lecherous photographer, who retains enough human personality to wish to attack Susanne. Susanne, too, will become a carrier for a termite mastermind, since human bodies will enable the masters to operate in cold climates. * Things look bad, but the resourceful young woman draws her automatic, shoots the termite central intelligence, and leaves the termitary. There are close calls, but the survivors of the expedition escape, with the leaders flying to the United States. Behind them, Australia is being completely depopulated by the giant termite warriors, who are now moving across Oceania. Hawaii is next. Then the West Coast. * Back in the United States the now fugitives contact (via Susanne's mind) the human central intelligence, but it proves to be completely hostile and in league with the termites. (Why this is so Keller gives no reason, though it seems illogical.) Instead of helping, the human intelligence prompts authorities to hunt down the fugitives, who take refuge on an isolated mesa in Quebec, where Souderman has begun an establishment. * They fortify the mesa, breaking down access points, storing enormous quantities of food and ammunition, and with a selected colony of survivors, prepare to fight off the termites. * By the time they are ready, the termites have taken over the Earth, and so far as is known, the human race is extinct except for the Souderman group. The giant termites come in enormous armies; the humans fight them off, but the odds are too great, and eventually the mesa must fall. But at the last minute one of the humans evolves a termite disease that is transmitted to the insect masses below by inoculated cattle. Since the termites recycle their dead by eating them, the disease spreads, wiping out the local insects, and possibly the world group. Mankind can arise again. * *Miscellaneous:* While the termites are about to emerge and the fugitives are trying to alert the human authorities, the human central intelligences drove their populations into innumerable devastating wars. * Interesting beginning, but it soon becomes rather silly, and the development is not helped by liberal doses, later, of Keller's homespun mawkishness. The motif of the human central intelligences, evoked on one occasion, is let slide, as are other loose ends.

747. **THE CONQUERORS.** *Science Wonder Stories*, December 1929-January 1930. Ill. Paul.
Novel. * *Time:* mostly 1933. *Place:* mostly Western Tennessee, near Reelfoot Lake. * All radio inexplicably ceases to function in the United States for about four hours. When radio is restored, a strange message is received: All planes must cease

Keller, David H., M.D. (*continued*)

flying over Virginia, West Virginia, Tennessee, Kentucky, and North Carolina. The message is signed "The Conquerors." * The authorities pay no heed to the message, of course, but in a short time planes simply cannot fly over the prohibited areas; motors die. Another message threatens that violators of the prohibition may be killed, and promises that electricity will be shut off. This, too, is done. The government offers a million dollars reward for information, but to no avail. * A new development comes when a person claiming to be the ambassador of the Conquerors pays a visit to the President. His message: The five states involved must be totally evacuated within three months. The ambassador himself is a tiny being, less than three feet tall, with an enormous head; in appearance he is thus like a macrocephalic idiot, but there is obviously nothing wrong with his mentality. On a second visit, after he is shot by a trigger-happy presidential guard, an autopsy reveals that the tiny man is not quite human. Pinkish blood and various anatomical features distinguish him from *Homo sapiens*. * When the inhabitants of the five states do not leave, despite warnings, the Conquerors cover the area with a thick mist that erodes and rots almost everything, even roadways. There is no choice but evacuation. * The action of the story begins with Sir Harry Brunton, a noted British anthropologist and explorer, who has been commissioned by the British government secretly to investigate the situation in the five states, since the British fear their own possible involvement with the Conquerors. Brunton, with two young Americans (Wright, a scientist, and Ormund, a native of the affected area, who has a fixation about hunting) venture into the forbidden area at the end of Reelfoot Lake. They encounter no obstacles; indeed, it becomes obvious that their coming has been anticipated and facilitated. * In a short time, the party encounters the dwarves, who make it clear that they want Brunton to accompany them; the other two men are unwelcome, but will not be harmed since they are servants of Brunton's. * Background and explanations that are provided gradually: The dwarves are a branch of the human race, separated from our line about one hundred thousand years ago. The ancestors of the dwarves entered a world-circling system of enormous caves, where they have lived ever since. Whereas surface man's evolution was governed by violent events and emotions, the ancestral dwarves, living in an unchanging environment, were able to cultivate intellect. They soon developed a supercivilization underground, and for the past fifty thousand years have lived out a conscious plan. * As a result of their peculiar evolution (aided by selection), they are totally cerebral, humorless and literal, almost without passions, including pity or sympathy. They are few in number, perhaps twenty thousand in all, and are organized in a rigid, remorseless hierarchy. At the top is the Directing Intelligence, below him are three Coordinators, two hundred specialists, and then directors. Whenever one of these officials feels that he is flagging mentally, he voluntarily enters a lethal chamber or a death slide, to be replaced by a superior member. The lower offices are filled by ruthless elimination of inferior candidates, with suicide for those who fail. Longevity is great, the Directing Intelligence operating for up to three thousand years. * Most of the work in the Conqueror establishment is done by automatic machinery, with a few Middle-Men (ordinary humans) slaves, who are treated pitilessly, with torture to obtain efficiency and death down a slide when they are worn out.

Science is, of course, incredibly high. * The Conquerors have broken the reproductive chain. Essentially a male culture, they keep a few females as egg producers, their ovarian production being graded and culled, treated chemically, and reared in a scientific manner. As a result, sexuality has disappeared. * An unusual feature of their civilization is the maintenance, for scientific studies, of controlled habitats for various stages of surface human history. Thus, there are colonies of pre-modern men, Egyptians, and Romans. Such a habitat is currently being constructed for modern New York, with noise, filth, inconvenience, vulgarity all built into it. The two Americans, together with women that the Conquerors have supplied them, will be placed in it. Thus, when the Conquerors have wiped out surface man, as, lately, they have decided to do, mankind will survive in these zoos. * The final great project of the Conquerors, is movement en masse to Venus. Their science is equal to the task. The question is whether they should exterminate surface man before or after their migration. * Sir Harry Brunton is in an anomalous position. The Conquerors, who follow surface events closely, have recognized in him not only a man of enormous anthropological insight, but a mind somewhat kindred to theirs, although in the latter belief they are mistaken. He is created an honorary citizen and is to act as an adviser to the Directing Intelligence. * It gradually emerges, despite the high ideals (in a warped way) of the little supermen, that something is wrong. Their officials are wearing out earlier than they should, and the culture is becoming permeated with a sort of listlessness that prevents proper action. For example, the Directing Intelligence, who should be good for hundreds of years more, is beginning to feel old and is suffering from headaches. * Brunton quickly recognizes the source of the problem: Too great deviation from the human mainstream, which can easily be cured by blood substances from normal humans. * But now Sir Harry springs his surprise. All along he has been playing a double game, praising and agreeing with the most monstrous Conqueror actions, including torture and murder; but now he strikes a bargain. He will deliver the secret if the Conquerors refrain from exterminating the surface men before returning from Venus and if the two Americans and the women assigned to them will be permitted to leave without harm. The Directing Intelligence agrees, although he adds the proviso that Sir Harry must accompany them to Venus. * A very strange work, with considerable imagination and more logical power than Keller usually shows, with less of the folksy twaddle that disfigures his stories. The novelistic skills are weak, but the story is still worth reading. * For a sequel see #750, "The Evening Star."

748. **AIR LINES.** *Amazing Stories*, January 1930. Ill. Wesso.

(Reprinted in Keller, *The Folsom Flint*.)

Short story. * *Time:* the near future, perhaps the middle twentieth century. * In general a rehash of #738, "The Psychophonic Nurse," or, Keller's response to the liberated woman. * Mrs. William Dills, who has the effrontery to go by her maiden name, Beryl Angelo, is a first-class inventive-idea person, cherished by a huge corporation, while her husband is a would-be writer who works at home. Beryl's pregnancy and childbirth might have impeded her career, but she avoided domestic distractions by using human and robot help. As a result, she hardly ever sees her child. * Her greatest brainstorm bids fair to revolutionize the transportation industry: a system of

Keller, David H., M.D. (*continued*)

drone cargo planes guided by radar or radio beam networks, fuel calculated to the drop for economy's sake. Her pilot project is in her backyard, disguised as an old heap. Unknown to her, her husband takes their child out to play in it during the day. * On the critical occasion, after the drone cargo plane leaves the ground, everything calculated to a hair, Beryl learns that her husband and child are on board, trapped there when the plane automatically took flight. And, worse, there was an arithmetical error in the fuel calculation; instead of circumnavigating the world, the plane will crash in the Pacific. * But the worst does not happen: the plane returns safely. Dills disconnected the automatic pilot and flew the plane back manually. The shock, however, has served as a lesson to Mrs. Dills, who now vows to attend to her family instead of her career. * One of Keller's better stories.

749. A TWENTIETH CENTURY HOMUNCULUS.
Amazing Stories, February 1930. Ill. Morey.
(Reprinted in Haining, *The Fantastic Pulps.*)
Short story. * *Time:* 1937. *Place:* mostly New York and a Pacific Island. * The multimillionaire and former Columbia University football star John Reiswick chances, when somewhat drunk, to hear a lecturer proclaim that in another generation or so there will be no Columbia football team. When, greatly upset, Reiswick later asks the lecturer to explain his statements, the lecturer tells him that for unknown reasons the American birthrate has fallen precipitously. On checking among his staff Reiswick finds corroborative evidence, for only one man, married to an Asian woman, has produced a child. Reiswick himself is unmarried. * Casting about for a solution to the problem, Reiswick consults a maverick scientist (Hermopheles Jones) who has been working with parthenogenesis. When Jones describes the claims made by the Renaissance physician and alchemist Paracelsus for the creation of artificial men (homunculi) Reiswick agrees to support his research in that direction. Reiswick buys a Pacific island, builds a suitable plant, hires an efficient staff, and sets Jones to work. * As the project gets under way, however, Reiswick falls in love with his intelligent, amiable secretary Ruth, whom he marries. Although for story reasons Reiswick does not know it, Ruth becomes pregnant and carries her child while Reiswick is in Japan negotiating a political settlement. When he returns, she has just given birth, but he is unaware of the circumstances and believes that Jones has created a parthenogenetic homunculus. Ruth finally enlightens him. * At about this time it is discovered that American sterility is caused by a nutritional deficiency that is remedied by Asian food. * Parabolic in nature, but sadly unconvincing even within that latitude.

750. THE EVENING STAR. *Science Wonder Stories*, April-May 1930. Ill. Paul.
Short novel. * Sequel to #747, "The Conquerors." * *Time:* a little after 1933. *Place:* Tennessee and Venus. * The Conquerors are about ready to leave for Venus with Sir Harry Brunton and his friend Miss Carter accompanying them. It is understood that the Conquerors, when they return, will destroy the human race with a plague, but Sir Harry now hints that the Conquerors will not return. * There are two new developments: Brunton induces a friend, the astronomer Whitland, to join the expedition; since Whitland is dwarfish, the Conquerors become convinced that he has Conqueror blood in him and welcome him to the nation.

[This point is in contradiction to elements in the earlier story.] Second, the Conquerors receive a radio message (in many languages) urging them to follow 85 and guard against 87. These numbers are interpreted as elements 85 and 87, which proves correct, since the ship is almost drawn off course by a star composed largely of 85. * The ship arrives at Venus, which is partly frozen and partly too hot for habitation, but with a libration zone that is habitable though uncomfortable. * Life on Venus: Apart from wild animals, there are creatures known as Monsters; almost infinitely variable in form, semi-intelligent, fearless, and innumerable, they are the results of genetic experiences on human stock that went wrong ages ago. Second, there are the Masters. This is a small group of totally human benevolent, altruistic supermen, with wonderful physiques and mental ability, and life spans of thousands of years. They live in a high science, but are very few in number (less than fifty) and are pretty much sterile. It was the Masters who sent the radio messages to Earth, which they have been monitoring for thousands of years. They had high hopes for the visit from Earth, but they are greatly depressed by the Conquerors, whom they regard with aversion. * Interrelations: Brunton, his friend Miss Carter, and Whitland leave the Conqueror area, and after perils from the Monsters are saved by the Masters, who treat them well. The Conquerors, in their fearless arrogance, do not recognize the peril that the Monsters offer with their overwhelming numbers. As result, when all the Monsters in the area attack the Conquerors, who are out in the open, many of the little men are killed before the others can take refuge in the spaceship. Among the dead are necessary specialists. But the Conquerors are not beaten: They lure the remaining Monsters far out into the libration zone, where they are exterminated first by weather, then by Conqueror electric guns. This area of Venus is now clear. But as Keller claims, the intense struggle has done something to the Conquerors, who are not used to high emotional situations or great physical activity, and they are no longer the little supermen that they were. As a result of their mental decline, when their spaceship becomes frozen in mud, the Directing Intelligence orders full speed ahead and the ship crashes into a mountain. This is the end of the Conquerors on Venus. * By radio provided by the Masters, Brunton now warns the authorities on Earth to clean up the remaining Conquerors, if the human race is to survive. This is apparently done. * *Miscellaneous:* The Masters have vegetable-man servitors who can protrude limbs of sorts, speak English, and shoot electric charges. * Keller now explains the Conquerors' xenophobia: They worry about threatening human mutations; this is expressed in terms of atavisms from the future, time being a stream of sorts. * The Conquerors are also automatically killers, without much reason for being so. Atlantis is now listed in the cultures they have destroyed. * It is never clear how many Conquerors went to Venus, and how many remained on Earth, but the final situation does not have much credibility, nor does the naiveté displayed by the Conqueror leaders. * All in all, a sloppy job, destroying much of the conviction the first story achieved, and damaged by annoying coyness about sexual matters.

751. THE FLYING THREAT. *Amazing Stories Quarterly*, Spring 1930. Ill. Morey.
A novelette in length, but structurally a meandering muddle. * *Place:* western New Jersey and Borneo. * Dr. Anna Rock, a physician and enthusiastic lepidopterist, has retired to an enormous

Keller, David H., M.D. (*continued*)

estate in New Jersey to study butterflies and moths. Her privacy is invaded by Timothy Jones, a persistent young man who vainly tries to sell eggs to her. * When he leaps from a plane into her establishment, she finally examines his wares, which turn out to be two insect eggs the size of human heads. * Jones exasperatingly (to the reader, too, with his mannerisms) refuses to tell a full story, but he reveals that the ova are those of giant butterflies developed by a mad scientist whose establishment is in Borneo. Jones had been working for the scientist, but, life imperiled, escaped with a male and female egg of gigantic silkworms. * Rock accepts Jones's story, hires him, and sets out to hatch the ova. One hatches into an enormous silkworm, eventually about thirty-five feet long. The other ovum, however, turns out to be that of a ferocious gigantic dragonfly, which takes to the water. Eventually, it emerges, kills the silkworm, takes to the air, captures a monoplane, and is shot down. The pilot of the plane, Captain Lewellen, R.A.C., enters the story. * Dr. Rock, as her charges grow, tries to interest the scientific community, but with little success, for the scientists consider her a particularly clever hoaxer. * Previously, a bizarre incident had taken place: Dr. Scheermann, the mad scientist in Borneo, used sex hormones to lure an enormous horde of giant insects to New York City. He intended this as a warning and accompanied it with a manifesto: The United States must establish a Socialist government, free the workers, and punish the man who stole his insect eggs. Nothing more comes of this demand, however, and presumably Scheermann forgets it. * Paths converge. The scientific world accepts Rock's insects; Jones reveals that Scheermann is planning to liberate masses of giant dragonflies; and the human race, if not in peril, is to suffer many casualties. * Rock, Jones, Lewellen, and a scientific team proceed to Borneo, reach Scheermann's area, are welcomed cheerfully by a pleasant little old man, then captured. Scheermann keeps his native workmen in subjection by staging human sacrifices to the giant dragonflies. His threat: Unless Rock marries him and her female friend marries Scheermann's Japanese assistant, they will be eaten, together with the men, by the dragonflies. * But at the last moment Scheermann inexplicably allows them to leave. He is captured and taken to British colonial headquarters, where it is revealed that the man thought to be Scheermann is really a British secret agent who killed Scheermann, disguised himself, and took the dead scientist's place. Just when the substitution occurred, Keller does not say. * The story, which is disorganized, reads as if it were written extemporaneously without planning, without regard to consistency, and without concern for what went before. Keller at his worst.

752. **THE IVY WAR.** *Amazing Stories*, May 1930. Ill. Morey.

(Reprinted in Keller, *Tales from Underwood* and in Conklin *Best of Science Fiction.*)

Short story. * *Place:* presumably Pennsylvania. * A swamp hole in Yeastville suddenly assumes local importance when a strange ivy-like growth kills first a dog, then the local real estate developer. By chance a British explorer happens to be present. He tells of an ivy-like plant that has been overrunning a large portion of England. Some scoff, but the thing is really dangerous. * Actually, it is not a plant, but an animal-like creature, probably of geological age, that can send out its branches like tentacles from far down, perhaps from subterranean caverns. * It soon overruns Yeastville, but is chopped back. This is only a temporary respite, for the creature reemerges and the chopped off portions sprout to form nuisances elsewhere. * Since parts of the plant, on entering the Delaware River, slip past smaller cities and attack Philadelphia from two directions, it is possible that the growth is intelligent. (Or it may have a road map!) Thousands of lives are lost, and it is now recognized that the problem is national, for there is no real way to kill the plant animal. * But the United States is not conquered by a creeping thing. Dr. White discovers a hemolytic toxin that, when injected into the plants, kills them almost instantly. * The peril is over.

753. **THE MOON RAYS.** *Wonder Stories Quarterly*, Summer 1930. Ill. Paul.

Short story. * Fabular, set in imaginary European lands. * The small nation of Parvonia is threatened by Slavonia, its far more powerful neighbor. In the past skilled balance-of-power diplomacy preserved Parvonia's independence, but such tactics are no longer feasible. * Parvonia seems doomed to conquest and absorption, when American tycoon Perkins and his tame scientist Dr. Hamilton arrive. Perkins promises to save the country. * Going to Slavonia, he begins a strange publicity campaign, offering substantial cash prizes for lunar observations on a folk level—i.e., what people see in the moon. The campaign is genuine, people get paid, and in a short time Slavonian interest turns away from war to moon-gazing. But there is a more sinister development. Nervous breakdowns increase, psychic malaise mounts, sex life changes—and Slavonia collapses internally. * The gimmick: Hamilton's theory that lunar radiation can affect people psychologically is correct, and the prolonged moon-gazing resulted in greater exposure to lunar rays. * Weak.

754. **BOOMERANGING 'ROUND THE MOON.** *Amazing Stories Quarterly*, Fall 1930. Ill. Morey.

Short story. * *Time:* the near future. * The flying culture has been dominant for a time, but there are signs that it is waning, and President De Loach of Aviation Consolidated is worried. He is looking for a new idea to add adventure and risk to the concept of flying. * Hill, a subordinate inventor in the company who has been courting De Loach's daughter, comes up with the desired novelty: a boomerplane, or a flying device like a boomerang, that would be hurled off and would return as a result of its own aerodynamics. He suggests such a boomerplane for a flight around the Moon. * Experiments prove the idea feasible, and AC engineer Simmons builds such a plane, which would be set in motion by atomic energy. But there is something crooked: Simmons is in love with De Loach's daughter and bitterly resents Hill's amatory success. Therefore, recognizing that there are two types of boomerang, a return sport boomerang and a non-return hunting boomerang, he designs the boomerplane for non-return. He alone knows the distinction. * Hill leaves in the plane, but De Loach's daughter is a stowaway. When Simmons learns that she is on the boomerplane, he commits suicide, but Hill and his lover simply continue delightedly, forever. * A curious fabular ending.

755. **SERVICE FIRST**. *Amazing Stories Quarterly*, Winter 1931. Ill. Morey.

Keller, David H., M.D. (*continued*)

(Reprinted in Derleth, *The Outer Reaches.*)

See the prefatory note before story #733. * Short story. * *Time:* the near future. * Henry Cecil and his wife, Arline, are faced with a problem that affects all, rich and poor, in the New York City area: gouging landlords. The rent on his one-room apartment has just been raised again, to a level more than the Cecils can afford, even though both are employed. It means more than a move; it means a defeat, for Henry has promised his wife a certain living standard. * Cecil, although not a good wage earner, is a man of keen and perceptive imagination. A brainstorm hits him. Quitting his job, he forces his way into the office of Provens, President of Universal Air, who has publicly complained of a similar rent outrage. Henry proposes that Universal Air construct a plane with conveniences and necessities like a house trailer; to have mooring platforms for night use and day parking during work. The publicity angle is to be "Service First, Why Pay Rent." * After some initial resistance, Provens agrees that the idea is splendid, and with extensions, such as various services at the mooring stations, the enterprise is wildly successful. Rents plummet, while the air culture expands. * Henry now suggests a second step, purchase of real estate and establishment of low-cost cooperative housing. It, too, will be a success. Henry has risen from a low-paid worker to the pride of the company. Business rivals try dirty tricks, including assassinating Cecil, but are unsuccessful.

756. **THE SLEEPING WAR.** *Wonder Stories*, February 1931. Ill. Marchioni.

Short story. * *Place:* Eastern Pennsylvania. * *Background:* A mysterious, incredibly wealthy Chinese with the improbable name of Wand Foo has purchased a four-thousand-acre tract of waste land and has enclosed it with an entranceless, high fence. This much is generally known. Not generally known is that Wand Foo has spent hundreds of thousands of dollars in bribes to discontinue and reroute a road running through his property. * The secret service has gotten wind of the affair, and Agent Abe Summers, a local boy, is assigned to investigate. He manages to crawl under the fence where it crosses a stream and enters the sealed area. Since he believes in taking bulls by the horns, he does not conceal himself, but boldly confronts Wand Foo and his associates, a Soviet agent (Sergiov) and an American Indian revanchist (Troubled Waters). * Wand Foo, who has previously encountered Summers, is by no means reluctant to talk. This is part of a plot to weaken the United States so that it can be conquered by allied China, Soviet Russia, and (probably) Japan. On his property Wand Foo will dump into the local water table, which serves Philadelphia and New York, a chemical that will cause the population to sleep indefinitely. Wand Foo obtains this chemical from Russia, through a tunnel on his estate that leads to the sea. * The conspirators lock Summers in the tunnel, where he will starve to death, and proceed to put their plans into effect. The populations of the cities served by the water supply become comatose, whereupon the Russians demand that the United States surrender and become a Soviet state. * Summers survives. Making his way to the sea exit of the tunnel, he is fortunate enough to encounter revenue agents who have been planning to raid Wand Foo's establishment on suspicion of smuggling. * Grabbing a small

amount of nourishment, Summers rides a convenient motorcycle back through the tunnel, kills the Russian and the Indian, and tortures Wand Foo into revealing the antidote to the sleep drug. * Not very good.

757. **THE AMBIDEXTER.** *Amazing Stories*, April 1931. Ill. Morey.

Short story. * *Place:* Canton, China and Chicago. * Organ transplant and Oriental revenge. * Dr. Hopkins, by general assent the greatest surgeon in the world (because he is totally ambidextrous), consults Dr. Wing Soo of Canton, the greatest surgeon in the Orient. The problem: Hopkins is suffering from a tumor on the frontal lobe of his brain, and he hopes that Wing Soo can remove it, replacing the brain tissue with that of another person. * Wing Soo is somewhat doubtful of his abilities, but admits that he has a technique for cryogenic operation that might work. He displays animals that he has frozen and revived. * The operation is successful, and Hopkins resumes his practice in Chicago, as perfect an operator as before. But some time later, Hopkins, after murdering a young woman during an operation, flees to China, where he again consults Wing Soo. Hopkins reveals that he has been increasingly tormented by an urge to kill with his left hand, so much so that he has taken to tying it down. But on the occasion of the fatal operation, he succumbed to the urge. * Wing Soo tells his side of the story. He used brain tissue from a convicted murderer in the transplant. His reason: Hopkins, while in Canton, had attacked/seduced/raped the Chinese surgeon's daughter. Hopkins, in some remorse, commits suicide, and Wing Soo freezes his body for possible future use when his own brain grows old.

758. **FREE AS THE AIR.** *Amazing Stories*, June 1931. Ill. Morey.

(Reprinted in Keller, *Tales from Underwood.*)

Short story. * *Time:* 1950-1951. *Place:* New York City and the Adirondacks. * Background. The United States in the 1950s is a flying culture, with almost everyone obsessed with airplanes. Poor and middle-income apartment dwellers are known to surrender their financial future in order to own a small plane. * The nation's economy is monopolized by three robber barons, Freilausen of United Motors; James Jeremiah Jenkins, foodstuffs, now mostly synthetic; and Samuel Smith, banking, insurance, and businesses other than food and transportation. The politicians are figureheads who take orders from the three moguls. At the moment, Smith, who plans to be president of the country, too, has proposed a new monopoly that the titans can exercise: airspace. * The three plutocrats rig a small case in Tennessee to establish a legal precedent. According to plan, a plane drops a piece of iron and damages a hillbilly's chimney; the moguls ram the case through the courts and establish that a person owns the air over his land, just as he owns the rock beneath it. The cabal then buys up strips of waste land around the country and acquires city air rights in exchange for taking over the city debt. In a very short time the plotters have crisscrossed the country with their holdings, so that it is impossible to travel without crossing their land. They are now ready to charge tolls for utilization of their air space. * William Jordan, a small wage slave, is married to a nagging wife who is obsessed with flying; to silence her, he divests the family of savings, insurance, and all possessions in order to buy her a

Keller, David H., M.D. (*continued*)

small plane. He is thus highly unsympathetic when he happens to overhear the plans of the three titans. Chancing to meet a wealthy antimodernist (Turner), Jordan repeats what he heard, and the two men decide to act. With a band of resolute associates they kidnap the three capitalists and take them to the antimodernist's isolated estate. * They now squeeze the monopolists. First, Turner invokes the new legal decisions about ownership of the air. The associates place the capitalists in gigantic sealed glass jars and refuse to let them have air until they disgorge enormous amounts of cash. Then Turner and his associates charge the robber barons exorbitantly for food and other necessities. Eventually, the barons are stripped of their financial power. By now, however, they have been put to work at odd jobs around the estate. The combination of healthy old-fashioned life and the high principles of Turner and Jordan reclaims the wicked capitalists, and they come to enjoy their new life. * The initial concept is nice, but the story is very clumsily handled.

759. **HALF-MILE HILL**. *Amazing Stories Quarterly,* Summer 1931. Ill. Morey.
Short story. * *Place:* rural America, perhaps Pennsylvania. * The small village of Sclocum used to be a fine rural settlement—a few houses, a store, an I.O.O.F. hall, and a few other buildings strung out along a dirt road. But then the automobile arrived, and the road was paved. * At first the villagers could count on their fingers the cars that passed, but after a couple of decades, there were too many to count. * Then the giant freight trucks and the transcontinental buses began to come through, notably the Ocean-to-Ocean Bus Line. The noise was insufferable, particularly as the heavy vehicles ground their gears and roared their engines as they passed up Half-Mile Hill. * Then suddenly, heavy vehicles cannot make it up the hill, but stall at the bottom. Trucks, buses, heavy passenger cars all suffer in the same way. Road engineers, traffic consultants are baffled, especially since the phenomenon is intermittent. Eventually, after much squabbling and political maneuvering, a detour takes traffic around Sclocum. * Associated with the rise of the automobile has been the decline of the railroads, particularly the small X. V. and P. Railroad System that services the Sclocum area. The bus and truck lines are able to undercut the railroad's rates, and it is possible that the railroad will go out of business. * A small stockholder (Early Robins) approaches Smathers, the president of the railroad line and makes a strange offer: He can repeat the phenomenon of Half-Mile Hill at other sites, hampering the motor lines. Smathers accepts his offer on a trial basis, whereupon Robins shuts off heavy equipment in other hilly areas. The heavy trucks and buses stall and cannot climb. * The result is that the bus and truck lines have to reroute their vehicles, and, finally, agree no longer to undercut the railroad freight fares. As a result, Robin's stocks rise in value. Robins does not explain how he does it, except that it is an electrical apparatus that is activated by excessive noise. * One of Keller's better stories.

760. **THE STEAM SHOVEL**. *Amazing Stories,* September 1931. Ill. Morey.
Short story. * A fabular latch-on to #730, "The Cerebral Library." *Place:* Burma. * The great Chinese surgeon Wing Loo, outclassed and outmaneuvered by detective Taine, is recuperating and regaining some of his lost face and self-esteem visiting a friend who is building a railroad through the jungles of Burma.

His friend, Smith, tells him of labor difficulties due to native superstition; of a giant steam shovel which he has difficulty in using, since the natives are unable to operate it; and of an ancient elephant that seems to feel an empathy toward the steam shovel. * A crisis comes when the local rajah visits the camp and recognizing the elephant as one he used to own, demands that it be killed. His reason: decades earlier, the elephant jostled him in the howdah, so that he missed a shot while hunting game. * The rajah's command must be obeyed, since he threatens to rip up the railroad tracks, and Smith is in despair. But Wing Loo has a solution. He transplants the elephant's brain into the steam shovel, which thereupon becomes a cyborg (my term). The animated steam shovel operates wonderfully, using perfect judgment in its work; the elephant's former attendant services it and works with it. * All is well until the rajah visits the site, whereupon the elephant-steam shovel, recognizing him, kills him and dashes into the jungle, where it still wanders about. * Not rigorous, obviously, but interesting.

761. **THE RAT RACKET**. *Amazing Stories,* November 1931. Ill. Morey.
(Reprinted in Ghidalia, *Satan's Pets.*)
Short story. * A new racket has arisen in the big city. If restaurants, hotels, food manufacturers, etc. do not pay protection, their premises are invaded by hordes of rats, with an effect on trade that can be imagined. The situation is notorious and soon becomes nationwide, for there is little that can be done about it. * Multimillionaire Winifred Willowby, however, is determined to destroy the racket. Summoning leading experts on rats—biologist, zoologist, psychologist, and folklorist—he settles on the great historical incident of rat control: the Pied Piper of Hamlin. * Time passes. * Willowby invites Consuelo, the Big Boy, head of the rackets, to a conference and makes a proposition. If the Big Boy will assist him in his political ambition to become president, he will let the rackets run unhindered. Since Consuelo controls senators, governors, and judges as well as hoodlums, he is a powerful man. * Willowby sets up a special total conference in his high office building. After some welcoming words, however, Willowby slips out, and rats by the thousands pour into the rooms, eventually killing all the mobsters and their crooked associates. * As Willowby reveals, historical research uncovered the vibrational sequence that the Pied Piper used; applied properly and enhanced, it rid the country of rats. * Obvious and somewhat lacking in internal logic, but amusing.

762. **THE PENT HOUSE**. *Amazing Stories,* February 1932. Ill. Morey.
(Reprinted in Keller, *The Folsom Flint.*)
Short story. * The curious newspaper ad calls for a cultured, well educated, healthy, congenial young man and woman, offering five years of steady employment. Hundreds apply, but the old man settles on Claude and Doris because they seem to him most compatible. * *Explanation:* The old man is the scientist Dr. Jordan. He has observed an increase in the death rate from cancer, which he believes is caused by spores from space, and he is certain that deaths will increase rapidly, so that the human race will be all but extinct in five years. Thus, he proposes that Claude and Doris allow themselves to be sealed up in a specially prepared, fully furnished and equipped penthouse for five years, until the death cloud has passed. Jordan promises the young couple that the wealth of the world will then be theirs when they restart the human race. * Claude and Doris accept, although with

Keller, David H., M.D. (*continued*)

a canny proviso of a cash settlement, too. They also invite Jordan to spend the five years with them, to which he agrees. * Time passes rapidly enough, with Doris bearing a daughter. But when the penthouse is opened, obviously there is no diminution of the human race. New York is as crowded, noisy, and dirty as ever. It is not that Jordan was wrong; it is just that during the cancer epidemic, a cancer remedy was discovered that rendered the spores from space innocuous. The young couple and Jordan do not regret their experience. * *Miscellaneous:* Jordan set up a similar arrangement on the West Coast. * Interesting, if one can ignore the sentimentalities.

763. **THE METAL DOOM**. *Amazing Stories,* May-July 1932. Ill. Morey.

See the prefatory note before story #733. * Short novel. * *Place:* perhaps Westchester County or a little farther north. * The metal doom begins suddenly when all metal spontaneously disintegrates into corrosion and dust. This is a world-wide phenomenon. Why, Keller does not explain, although he hints in one place that a superior power (divinity?) has decided that mankind is moving too far away from nature and should be reoriented. * The story is told mostly through two narrative centers, Paul Hubler, an unwilling Manhattanite, and John Stafford, a former millionaire landowner. * When the doom begins, Hubler has the foresight to see what will happen. He, his wife, and child, taking a few belongings, walk up into the countryside until they find a deserted cabin, which Hubler restores, thus beginning a neo-primitive life. Hubler develops stone and wood tools and weapons, and in a short time becomes reasonably proficient at their use. * At first the Hublers are not bothered, for most of the city millions died during the collapse, but gradually criminal elements approach. After a time, Hubler realizes that he and his family can not survive in isolation, and he joins the nearby community established by John Stafford. * Stafford, who had manpower available, has begun a small settlement that recognizes him as leader. His community has horses, cattle, and a greater potential for survival than individuals could have. * After a time, the New York survivors decide to investigate what has happened in the rest of the United States. The South, they discover, is gone, for the blacks massacred all the whites and have reverted to the savagery of Africa. Zoo animals have escaped, with lions and tigers occasionally to be met. And Indians and Mexicans are invading the Southwest. But elsewhere there are communities similar to Stafford's, which are willing to accept a general bond of federation. There are also wandering bands of criminals, murderers and rapists. * The largest crisis comes when an army of mounted Tartars, shipping over from Europe, invades the land. The Americans are greatly outnumbered, and despite better tactics than those of the Tartars, would have succumbed had it not been for a brilliant idea of Hubler's. Gliders carrying glass flasks of poison gas fly over the Tartar hordes and exterminate them. * In addition to the community life, Stafford has his own adventures as he wanders about much of the nation, picking up an eccentric physician as a wife. * Most important, Hubler and an elderly scientist have the bright idea of melting some of the metal dust to see what will happen. Wonderful! The result is new metal, as good as the old. (The reader may marvel that no one thought of this before.) But now, with metal regained, a new world can arise, one in which defectives will be destroyed rather than pampered. * Novelistically bad, ethnographically

absurd, and filled with Dr. Keller's ultraconservative notions about blacks, criminals, and others. * Many inferior echoes of S. Fowler Wright's *Deluge.*

764. **NO MORE TOMORROWS**. *Amazing Stories,* December 1932. Ill. Morey.

(Reprinted in Keller, *Life Everlasting.*)

Short story, reminiscent in many ways of the work of Poe. It is more in the range of absurdist fiction than science-fiction proper. * The narrator, a formerly wealthy man, has lost his money on the stock market, and without money he cannot hope to hold the love of the beautiful but meretricious Leonora. * As a brilliant research psychologist, however, he has an incredible resource. He approaches the three local leaders of the Internationale, whom Keller characterizes beautifully, and makes an offer. He has localized the portion of the brain that creates foresight and has isolated a chemical that will destroy that ability. If this extract, he informs the Russian agents, is given to the two or three hundred leading planners and entrepreneurs in the Western world, capitalist society will eventually collapse and Russia will triumph. The agents of the Internationale are enthusiastic and strike a bargain. * Eagerly the narrator dines with Leonora and tells her of their future wealth. But he has misunderstood Leonora. First, she is to some extent patriotic, and second, she is not so much greedy as worried about the future. In fact, she worries so much that she hasn't been able to enjoy the present. Recognizing that the narrator's preparation would be a boon for her and unwilling to watch America be destroyed, she so manages matters that she and the narrator drink the preparation. * She is happy, but the narrator, realizing that he no longer has foresight, turns this into a symbolic equation, that he has no tomorrows. He breaks down and does nothing to keep his bargain with the Russians, although they have given him a sizeable advance. They capture him, but when they say that they will kill him tomorrow, he can only shriek with laughter, "You cannot kill me tomorrow, for I have no more tomorrows." * An excellent, very effective story.

765. **UNTO US A CHILD IS BORN**. *Amazing Stories,* July 1933. Ill. Morey.

(Reprinted in Keller, *The Folsom Flint* and in Keller, *Life Everlasting.*)

See the prefatory note before story #733. * Short story. * A homily on family life. * *Time:* 2030. * This is a mechanized, regimented, dehumanized world, perhaps partly socialist. The state controls life and death. Marriage and childbirth are directed by machine gradings, and in some manner, not spelled out, the state may euthanatize citizens who are no longer productive. At birth, children are taken from their mothers, have serial numbers tattooed on their backs, and then are placed in mechanical crèches for two years. Education begins at this time, with machine teachers, and children are sorted out according to their abilities and trained accordingly. Job placement is then completely carried out by the state's machines. * Jacob Hubler, who has considerable inventive ability, is a favored member of this society, since he has devised a useful cooking apparatus. As a result, at age sixty, he is assured of being permitted to live until 150 and is told that he may have a child if he wishes and can pass the examinations. * Delighted, Hubler agrees. The machines approve his application, but give him such a high classification that finding a mate of similar level seems impossible. But by the irony of fate, a suitable woman turns up

Keller, David H., M.D. (*continued*)

in the person of his secretary, whom Hubler has apparently considered more or less furniture. * Married, the Hublers produce a boy, who is entered in the system. The Hublers never see him, but receive progress reports at regular intervals. A prodigy of sorts, the boy is classified as a philosopher and is rated as an adult at age twelve, with the privilege of having a personal name. He is appointed assistant professor of philosophy at the national university and given full citizenship. * The Hublers are overjoyed, especially when they learn that their son will visit them. But it is a horrible experience. The boy is dehumanized, impersonal, official, and remote. His visit lasts for only an hour or two. * Hubler, who has just recently received a letter authorizing him to have another child, since the first turned out so well, sadly rejects the opportunity. * One of Keller's better stories.

766. **THE TREE TERROR.** *Amazing Stories,* October 1933. Ill. Morey.

Short story. * *Time:* perhaps the near future. *Place:* partly in Nebraska. * The great cellulose tycoon, worried about shortages of raw materials, employs a panel of scientists whom he bullies for breakthroughs. Among the scientists is Simcox, who has been creating X-ray mutations in an attempt to create a gigantic club moss. His experiments are successful beyond his hopes, and in a short time he has a thriving forest on waste land in Nebraska, with plants hundreds of feet high that are mature in a matter of months. * The tycoon is pleased, but problems soon arise. The club mosses escape cultivation and in a relatively short time become a menace, usurping farm lands, waste lands, and much of cities. Mankind may be doomed. * But Simcox finds an inventor who has constructed a small machine that transforms cellulose directly into edible substances. Civilization is saved. * The reader may be less sanguine than Dr. Keller. In any case, weak.

767. **THE LOST LANGUAGE.** *Amazing Stories,* January 1934. Ill. Morey.

(Reprinted in Knight, *Science Fiction of the Thirties.*)

Short story. * A psychological story about an autistic child of a peculiar sort. * Young David Phillips is a normal child in most ways, but he does not talk. He is not deaf, and when he grows toward adolescence he begins to write in a peculiar script that is all his own. After a time his family observes that these markings are not scribbles, but have meaning to the boy. * His father, who is a wealthy man, tries various expediences, finally sponsoring a specially built typewriter that contains the boy's symbols. David types away enthusiastically, but the outside world still does not know, apart from one or two words, what he is putting down. The assumption, based on consultations with linguists, is that the symbols record an inner language (with sounds) that is consistent, if not known. * A further invention translates the symbols into vibration, i.e., sound. Again linguists are baffled, but one scholar remembers having heard similar sounds from an ancient Welsh woman who was the last speaker of a local sub-language. * This seems probable, since the Phillipses originated in her area of Wales, but the old woman has been dead for some time, and local scholars (horrible neglect that should be reported to the Welsh learned societies!) did not record her speech. * It all seems hopeless, but the little boy's sister announces that out of love she will devote her life to learning the boy's language, which may be the product of ancestral memory. * One of Kel-

ler's better stories, though a little flat.

768. **THE LITERARY CORKSCREW.** *Wonder Stories,* March 1934. Ill. Paul.

(Reprinted in Keller, *Tales from Underwood;* in Liebman, *Science Fiction: The Best of Yesterday;* and in Margulies and Friend, *From Off This World.*)

Short story. * A fabular account of creativity, probably with some personal reference. * A rather dowdy middle-aged lady makes an appointment with a well-known neurologist, not to discuss her own case, but her husband's. Her husband, as she gradually reveals during the consultation, is an author of world stature, a recognized literary genius. * His literary history is strange. As a clerk in a bookstore, he was obsessed with the notion of becoming a professional writer, but his work was horribly bad. Rejections continued to come in over the years. * But, on one occasion when he was suffering from a ruptured appendix and insisted on writing, he turned out a first-class story. Recovered, he again wrote rubbish. But then an inflamed tooth beset him, and he wrote good work again. * After a succession of such incidents, the author, the great Henry LeKler, as his wife reveals, realized that pain is necessary for good work. Since he cannot become ill to order, LeKler insists that his wife provide pain, working a corkscrew into his back. Under such conditions he produces bestsellers and attains to more than just affluence. * His wife can no longer stand inflicting pain on LeKler. She asks the neurologist if there is not some other way to produce the same effect. * The doctor easily solves the problem. LeKler suffers from glandular inadequacy; pain stimulates his glands to give him the necessary boost. Mrs. LeKler gratefully follows the doctor's instructions. Dietary supplements surreptitiously given to her husband provide all that they both could wish for. * Some time later, Mrs. LeKler reads in the newspaper that the neurologist has also become a prominent author. * One of Keller's better works, told with an engaging sympathy. A modern reader may smile a little at Keller's equation of literary quality with bestsellerdom, but that is a minor point. * For a parody, see #219, "The Man with the Longitudinal Head" by Paul K. Chapple.

769. **THE DOORBELL.** *Wonder Stories,* June 1934. Ill. Winter.

(Reprinted in Keller, *Tales from Underwood,* and in Conklin, *Omnibus of Science Fiction.*)

See the prefatory note before story #733. * Short story. * Not really science-fiction, but a conte cruel. * On invitation the writer Jacob Hubler accompanies the multimillionaire Henry Cecil to Cecil's country estate. Cecil hopes that Hubler can find material for a story while visiting. * As Hubler soon discovers, there are strange things in the background, including a man who periodically screams in agony. He was taken sick while a guest, says Cecil, and is unfortunately dying in pain. And there is a doorbell about which Cecil seems to be obsessed. * Cecil finally tells his story. When he was a little boy, a trio of local ruffians burst into his house and killed his widowed mother and his brother. He was sworn to revenge. When he became wealthy, he located the criminals, befriended them, and invited each to visit him at his estate. He then fed the criminals fishhooks hidden in gelatin capsules. The doorbell activates an enormously powerful electromagnet that draws the fishhooks through the guts of the criminals. The point of the doorbell is that the murderers, instead of going around to the back door as friendly folk would

Keller, David H., M.D. (*continued*)
have done, rang the front doorbell. * One of Keller's better stories.

771. **LIFE EVERLASTING.** *Amazing Stories,* July-August 1934. Ill. Morey.
(Reprinted in Keller, *Life Everlasting.*)
Short novel. * One of Keller's typical messages: Instinctive family values are stronger than the desire for immortality. * Maverick scientist Biddle has produced a serum that, in animals, corrects physical defects and promises if not immortality, at least extraordinarily long life. Behind his research is his personal tragedy; he is a widower with a small son who has an incurable illness. Biddle, however, is afraid to try his serum on his son without extensive tests on other humans. * Moving into a small New York rooming house, he settles on four fellow roomers as subjects, paying them well to accept a shot of a serum: a crippled newsie (newspaper vendor); a stupid, vain taxi dancer prostitute; an asthmatic drudge; and an introverted, frustrated elderly man with a bad heart. * The serum works wonders, both curing physical ailments and improving mental and moral constitutions. Biddle thereupon goes public with it, additional patients showing the same improvement. * It seems wonderful, but there is a reaction among certain top businessmen (insurance, medicine, etc.), who plot to have Biddle killed. The plot miscarries when the gangster hired to do the job kills them instead. * It seems like the millennium until a curious fact is observed: Biddle's improved humans are sterile. When asked about this, Biddle indicates that he is not surprised, since animals he treated were sterile. He adds that he has no knowledge how long the sterility will last. He further states that he considered such sterility an advantage, otherwise the world would soon be covered with humans, many more than it could support. * This discovery arouses a backlash, as people are forced to choose between immortality and children. As might be expected from Keller, children win out, even among the original four subjects whom Biddle treated. Fortunately, Biddle has discovered an antidote. Unfortunately, Biddle never did get around to inoculating his own son, who died. * Mediocre at best.

771. **ONE-WAY TUNNEL.** *Wonder Stories,* January 1935. Ill. Paul.
Short story, somewhat fabular in approach. * *Time:* Perhaps a hundred years or so in the future. *Place:* Mostly New York City and Boston. * As technology improved, transportation became more and more aerial, until eventually ground travel almost ceased. Concomitant with this development went a major population shift into the large cities. As a result, the countryside gradually reverted to wilderness, with a reemergence of many of the former beasts of prey, like wolf packs. * The crisis comes when enormous lizards suddenly beset the entire world en masse. Their origin is not known, perhaps they are survivals that suddenly emerged, perhaps they are a product of evolution. In any case, they are creatures like gigantic snakes (as much as three hundred feet long) with multiple legs and functional wings, ferocious and carnivorous. While they are vulnerable to heavy weapons, their numbers are so great and they are so widely spread that mankind is soon in peril of extinction. * In a very short time almost the entire human race is dead. The only survivors are in the coastal cities of Boston, New York City and Philadelphia, which for inexplicable reasons the monsters have not seriously attacked. With furious haste, the survivors roof

over these three cities with domes of glass eight feet thick and guard them with elaborately protected entrances. Fortified tunnels connect the three cities, since surface travel is no longer possible. * Humanity has at least a respite, but life inside the domed cities deteriorates; boredom and inactivity arise, together with the formation of a criminal class, which becomes an overwhelming social problem. * The great biologist Long, who was instrumental in the design of the domed cities, offers a remedy: evacuate Boston, put one-way barriers along the tube into Boston, then suddenly seize "every pervert, law violator, and menace to the community" and force them into Boston. This is done. * Within outlaw Boston, survival of the fittest produces two gang leaders who control the city, the Brainless Wonder and the Beautiful Spider, who, submerging their rivalry in a frantic hatred of New York and Philadelphia, decide to destroy the domed cities. The Beautiful Spider tricks his way into Philadelphia, then killing the air entrance guard, permits the waiting monsters to enter and destroy the population. He is killed, however, by the wife of the guard. * Philadelphia fallen, the population of New York is rightfully apprehensive. Dr. Long once again takes a lead. Approaching the chief executive of New York, he makes a request. Since mankind is stifling in the domed city, he and a party of about fifty men and women wish to leave the city and take to the wilderness, where they will fight for survival against the monsters. The city authorities give their approval on condition that Long remove the menace of Boston. Long agrees. * Just as Long is forcing poison gas into the Boston ventilation system, killing the criminal population, the gangster leader the Brainless Wonder arrives and tells that he has blasted a hole into the New York dome, permitting the reptiles to enter. This leaves Long's party as the sole hope for the human race. * What might have been a thought-provoking work is badly handled. The fabular notes, like the nature of the monsters and the domed cities, are buried in a welter of boring, extraneous material.

772. **THE LIFE DETOUR.** *Wonder Stories,* February 1935. Ill. Paul.
See the prefatory note before story #733. * Short story, fabular in approach. *Time:* indefinite near future. * In this abstracted city-world (little indication is given of other places) a river divides the city of Victorus. On one side is Primus, where the rulers and aristocrats live; on the other, the home of the Otherons or workers. There is very little contact between the two subcities, although favored Otherons are permitted to walk across the Bridge in order to work for the rulers. As a rare event, individual Otherons, as a reward for great accomplishment, may be raised to Primus. One reason for this dichotomy is that the Otherons, through long exploitation and segregation, are usually without imagination, although they may be intelligent. * At the moment Primus, the leader of the aristocratic section of Primus, is manipulating Henry Cecil, a young Otheron scientist who is working with heavy water. Primus, claiming that his proposed actions are for the benefit of the Otherons, plans to use Cecil's new process for producing heavy water in great quantity to exterminate the Otherons, since (because of the development of automatic equipment) they are no longer needed by the aristocrats. As Primus knows, heavy water, after producing initial exhilaration, causes rapid senescence and death. * All would go well from Primus's point of view, except that Cecil's fiancée, Ruth Fanning, has imagination and tests a sample of heavy

Keller, David H., M.D. (*continued*)
water. As a result of this, Cecil switches pipes so that the flow
of heavy water enters Primus, not the ward of the Otherons.
When Henry and Ruth return from their honeymoon, they find
the city of Primus dead, with old Primus the leader on the edge
of death. The way is now open to free and enlarge the world of
the Otherons. * Clumsily handled, but with moments of interest
in the background.

773. **THE LIVING MACHINE.** *Wonder Stories*, May
1935. Ill. Paul.
(Reprinted in Wollheim, *Every Boy's Book of Science Fiction*.)
Short story. * John Poorson, inventor, has a brainstorm after he
is nearly struck by a recklessly driven automobile. He devises
a mechanism (not described) that is contained in a silvery globe;
on receiving oral instructions, this mechanism can drive a car
perfectly under any conditions of traffic, to any destination.
Poorson sells his device to Babson, president of the great
Universal Auto Construction Company. The business arrangement, however, is peculiar: the U.A.C.C. manufactures the
device in the globe, but only Poorson can activate it. * The
invention is revolutionary, not only in efficiency, but in reducing
accidents enormously. There is, however, a problem: Poorson
and one of the chief engineers of U.A.C.C. have moral qualms
about the device, for they feel that in some fashion it is a living
entity. * Within five years Poorson's device has swept the world,
not only ground travel, but air as well. A new problem arises,
however, as Babson's empire comes into collision with the gasoline monopoly of the World Gasoline Company. The two giants
attempt a merger, but it fails, and in revenge, the head of
W.G.C. devises a way to sabotage Poorson's invention. Into all
the gasoline that he sells, he inserts a small quantity of cocaine.
Since Poorson's devices are, in a sense, living, they become
poisoned, and whereas they used to be totally safe, they now run
amok and create a situation far worse than before their invention.
More than a quarter of a million people die in automobile and air
accidents. * Poorson discovers what is happening and provides
a solution: a new type of battery that will obviate the use of
gasoline totally. W.G.C. will be ruined, and automobiles again
will be safe. For Poorson, too, it is a good solution, for it frees
him from the guilt of having created the living automobile brains
and going against the will of God. * A weak story.

774. **THE WHITE CITY.** *Amazing Stories*, May 1935.
Ill. Morey.
(Reprinted in Keller, *The Folsom Flint*.)
Short story. * *Place:* Vermont and Manhattan. * John Johnson,
college graduate, has turned away from urban life with
considerable bitterness and has buried himself away on an old-
fashioned Vermont farm, which he operates productively. His
solitude is disturbed, however, by Vanderbie, a very wealthy
family friend, who makes an unusual offer. Vanderbie, too, was
a farm boy, and he has had the idea of turning some twenty-five
acres of slum land that he owns in central Manhattan into a dirt
farm. His purpose: partly to show the new generation what a
farm was like, partly to make money via publicity, etc. * After
some difficulty he persuades Johnson to leave Vermont and run
the Manhattan establishment for five years, at which time he will
give him a million dollars. * Buildings are razed, trees planted,
farm buildings set up, stock imported, and a high fence placed
around the farm for protection. * The farm prospers, and
Johnson is reasonably happy on it. But circumstances change.

For reasons then unknown, an incredible amount of snow falls
on New York City, and New York City only; about one hundred
feet. The city is not just paralyzed, but almost wiped out. John,
however, survives, as does Vanderbie in his nearby penthouse.
* John, who studied meteorology in college, recognizes that the
snowfall is not natural and must have been produced by human
agency. Hence, he and a small army of his friends, provided
with small arms and even cannon, are ready when an ultimatum
sounds over the radio. America must surrender, or the power
that has destroyed New York will do the same to other American
cities. * When the senders of the message land in New York in
large superflying machines, they are blown out of existence by
John and his friends. From a survivor (who is obviously
Japanese, though not identified as such) John and Vanderbie
learn that the operation was not sponsored by a government, but
by a private consortium. * The crisis over, John throws up his
job in Manhattan and returns to his farm in Vermont. * There is
also a very reluctant romance. * Routine.

KELLY, FRANK K[ING] (1914-present)
U.S. writer, journalist, historian, political figure. Born Kansas
City, Mo. In later life well-regarded short story writer with
publications in the *New Yorker, Story Magazine, Esquire,* listings
and republications in annual compilations of best stories.
Journalist with *Kansas City Star,* A.P. Nieman Fellow at Har-
vard University. Army correspondent in World War II. Speech
writer for Harry Truman during 1948 presidential campaign.
Taught journalism at Boston University. Staff member to Scott
Lucas and Averil Harriman. Official in Fund for the Republic,
Center for the Study of Democratic Institutions, National Peace
Academy, Nuclear Age Peace Foundation. Author of several
books on political science, history, *The Fight for the White
House* (1961), *Your Freedoms: The Bill of Rights* (1964), and
Your Laws (1967). The following stories are not mature work,
but have many virtues, notably a willingness to explore problems
of the day in metaphoric fashion. Kelly has a very interesting
account of his early writing days in "My Interplanetary Teens,"
first printed in the *Atlantic Monthly,* July 1947, and reprinted in
Fantasy Commentator for Summer 1989 (VI-3).

775. **THE LIGHT BENDER.** *Wonder Stories*, June
1931. Ill. Marchioni.
Short story. * *Time:* A.D. 2030. * World peril narrated not in
straight-forward fashion, but offset to a secondary character with
events told by indirection. * The engineers Hend and Rall have
achieved invisibility by bending light rays with enormous
magnetic fields. In this world of 2030 the most important
building is the Peace Tower, in which, after disastrous wars, all
weapons have been sealed away. The engineers plan to render
the tower invisible as a demonstration. Their rationale: If it is
recognized that invisibility is possible, crime and other social
evils will disappear. * When the Peace Tower is rendered
invisible, however, something unexpected happens: A blackness,
foul and horrible, creeps over the city. On other occasions,
creatures of blackness enter our world, with whole areas being
blacked out. * In some fashion the invisibility apparatus has
opened a gateway into another dimension, from which the
monsters, with comparable equipment of their own, can reach
our world. If the crossings become too frequent, the natural
dimensional barriers will become thin, in which case the
monsters will be unrestrainable. * The only hope is that if the

Kelly, Frank K. (*continued*)

monsters use their machinery enough, there will be a backfire destroying both the Terrestrial equipment and that of the other-world. So it turns out. * *Miscellaneous:* New York City State is a futuristic supercity with towering spires and busy air traffic supported by antigravity broadcasts. * New York City State seems to select its highest officials by a combination intelligence test and election. * A literary experiment that does not work out.

776. **THE RADIUM WORLD**. *Wonder Stories,* February 1932. Ill. Paul.
(Reprinted in Kelly, *Star Ship Invincible.*)
Short story. * *Time:* around A.D. 2290. *Place:* mostly in space on the Earth-Mars run. * *Background:* Space travel is now common, with rocket propelled vehicles following lanes projected from planetary power sources. Earth has a world government; Mars is an empire. The two planets maintain a shaky peace; it would not take much provocation for war to break out. On the whole the Terrestrials act honorably, while the Martians, who, incidentally, are completely human, are inclined to be aggressive and unscrupulous. * The story: The plotting is complex, and only the main action is covered here. Captain Grant of the *Trident* saves a passenger from assassination and discovers that Gray, the intended victim, is an old college associate. Gray explains matters in a long intercalated story. * During Gray's last voyage (it is not clear in what capacity), one of his men ran amok, killing many of the crew and destroying the water supply. As a result the partly crippled ship had to make a forced stop on Deimos for water. On landing, however, Gray observed nearby a glowing formation, which he recognized as an enormous deposit of eca-radium, the prime power and medical resource for the inner planets. It is fantastically valuable. * Gray and his surviving associates stake a claim in accordance with the law, but as they are finishing, a Martian war vessel lands, and its commander jumps Gray's claim. There are hostilities and violence back and forth, but Gray and his friends at last escape alive. When they try to register their claim, however, the Martian courts rule in favor of the claim jumpers. * Since the eca-radium is invaluable, the situation turns into an interplanetary confrontation, with a strong Martian party clamoring for war. The Terrestrial government, however, makes a compromise offer, which the Martian Emperor will probably accept, if he receives it in time. The problem is that the Martian hawks will do their utmost to prevent the offer from reaching the Emperor. Gray, assigned to carry the message, dodging ass-assins, is now on Grant's ship hoping to get through. * The action now resumes. A Martian warship attacks the *Trident*, but Grant manages to destroy it, and Gray, after considerable difficulties and perils, reaches the Terrestrial ambassador with the note. War does not break out. * *Miscellaneous:* A potential interplanetary romance with a Venusian woman does not succeed. * Overly complicated. For a sequel see #779, "The Crisis with Mars."

777. **RED APRIL, 1965**. *Wonder Stories*, March 1932. Ill. Paul.
Short story. * *Time:* 1965. *Place:* along the Canadian front of the war between Russia and the United States. The war, which began about four years ago, is going badly for the United States despite omnipresent propaganda to the contrary. * At first it was believed that the Russians did not have such modern armaments as cathode rays, bacteriological weapons, screens against bombs

and rays, supercommunications systems, spy rays, robot controls, and the like, but this belief turned out to be very wrong. * The story focuses on a sector of the lines in Canada, where Captain Livingston holds a key point. That there has been a security leak is obvious, for a squadron of Red planes has just bombed an important ammunition dump. The suspect must be one of two subordinate officers whose whereabouts immediately before the attack is not clear. * Intelligence Colonel Grenham and Captain Livingston must find the spy. The first suspect is Lieutenant Clarence, whose suspicious activities turn out to be a forbidden phone call to his wife. The second suspect, Lieutenant Everard, seems to be drunk, but a search reveals that he is carrying highly valuable intelligence information about the giant Red offensive that is due to break at any time. Thanks to this information, the Russians are badly beaten in the following battle. Everard was killed trying to guard his information, while Livingston died in the battle. * The story, which attempts some verismo, jumps around considerably and is confusingly presented. It is told in large part through two black enlisted men who speak dialect and embody the Amos and Andy image of the time. Today they would be considered most offensive. * The military aspects would not be considered realistic today. * Nevertheless. the story shows great improvement over Kelly's earlier work. The orientation is toward peace.

778. **EXILES OF MARS**. *Wonder Stories Quarterly,* Summer 1932. Ill. Paul.
Short story. * *Time:* the interplanetary future. *Place:* Mars. * The solar system is ravaged by Cancer Four, which attacks the natives of the three inner planets and is currently epidemic. The sole medicament against it is eca-radium, which is found only on Mars. For reasons best known to the author, the extraction is handled by automated equipment supervised by small units of four people, who are compelled by contract to serve for the remainder of their lives, with death as the penalty for leaving the job. Around them, on dying Mars, are hordes of natives who are desperately in need of water and periodically attack the eca-radium plants. As an inadequate defense force there is an organization of Martian cyborgs—brains in metal walking-fighting machines. * At the moment Armiston, on whom the story centers, is cracking up. He foolishly signed up after a disastrous love affair, and he cannot stand either the tension or mode of life. His senior associate tries to help him and force him into shape, but it is hopeless. There are also two native Martians in the group; an elderly male and a young woman with whom Armiston is falling in love. * A band of desperate outlaws seeking water attacks the plant after the cyborg force has been lured away. The male Martian and Armiston's senior Weber are killed, and it is up to Armiston and the Martian woman to carry on. Armiston eventually wipes out the attackers by sacrificing himself in an explosion. * The constant theme and harping thread is that the production of eca-radium must continue without let, no matter what is happening. The gnawing worry about this is transmitted to the reader, enough to override the rather incredible initial situation. * *Miscellaneous:* Martians are human, but smaller than Earth people.

779. **THE CRISIS WITH MARS**. *Wonder Stories Quarterly*, Fall 1932. Ill. Paul.
Sequel to #776, "The Radium World." * *Time:* A.D. 2293. *Place:* Washington, D.C., and space on the way to Mars. * *Background:* Relations between Mars and Earth continue to be

Kelly, Frank K. (*continued*)

strained. One problem is Martian immigration, which has risen so enormously that a sizeable proportion of Earth's population is now of Martian origin. Restricted immigration is in the air, a move that may well cause war. The Martian ambassador and the Terrestrial government, however, have worked out a secret pact: Martian immigration will be halted, and in exchange a large glassed-over section of the Moon will be turned over to Mars. This area, however, is riddled with valuable minerals, which the Terrestrial Metallurgic Corporation covets. The villainous profiteers will stop at nothing to destroy the pact. They plan to trap De Abu, the Martian ambassador, and substitute a different document that will provoke Mars to war, during which TMC will profit even more. * The World State Secret Police has been bugging the TMC and is aware in a general way of the plot, but does not know how it will be effected. * Captain Grant of the space liner *Trident* is ordered to bring his ship directly to the presidential palace to pick up the Martian ambassador and his suite. While it is recognized that the *Trident* is probably filled with hostile secret agents and assassins, it is hoped that the danger to the Martian can be minimized. Also onboard, disguised as a Venusian (which he accomplishes by cleverly working his face muscles), is secret agent Gray. * There are scares and curious incidents, but Gray works it all out and the treaty is safe. The gimmick is that the purported ambassador is really the disguised ambassadorial secretary in the pay of TMC, and the purported secretary is really the ambassador mentally under control through a brain implant. The villainous capitalists, their plot uncovered, all commit suicide. * *Miscellaneous:* Captain Grant suffers an instant passion for De Abu's wife, who apparently did not notice the substitution of her husband. * Martians are human, small, with large heads. Venusians are fleshy with large heads. * Kelly probably should have waited several years before attempting the story.

780. **THE MOON TRAGEDY.** *Wonder Stories*, October 1933. Ill. Paul.

Short story. * *Time:* A.D. 2274. *Place:* mostly in a staging area in New York and the crater of Tycho, the Moon. * The future world is a fractional *Brave New World*, in that mankind is artificially propagated in terms of specific function, with rigid castes on the basis of exogenesis. Class One, educators, administrators, leaders; Class Two, white collar workers, machine workers; Class Three, serfs and unskilled workers. The members of the Third Class inhabit the lower levels of the city and are utterly expendable. They are considered not wholly human. The two upper classes are allowed to have names; members of the lowest class have only numbers and are called nameless ones. Sexuality no longer exists. * Enormous projects are undertaken to accommodate the growing population. The latest was the "conquest" of Africa, which meant terraforming the land, wiping out all native fauna and flora, and exterminating the natives. This was done so that concrete and steel developments could take the place of desert and jungle. * This task was the work of the Storm Troops, a hundred thousand-man army, and the Service Corps, ten thousand technicians in a work army. Each army is composed of Third Class men, corresponding to present-day army enlisted men, and upper-class men, corresponding to present-day officers. There is an enormous gulf between the two ranks. * Leaf Feld is something of a mistake, perhaps decanted incorrectly, for he is at heart rebellious; he does not think in military terms and is more suited for lab work, yet is unhappy at this. During the Conquest of Africa, where he served as a lower grade officer, he was wounded and transferred to the developmental laboratories. * An announcement has come through, asking for volunteers for a huge project, constructing a crystal dome over the crater of Tycho as the first step in occupying the Moon. Leaf volunteers, is accepted, processed, and shipped to the Moon as a lower-grade officer. In his squad is a Third Class man who saved his life in Africa. Feld would like to be friendly with the lower class man, but this feeling is squelched severely by superior officers. * On the Moon, atomic engines transform rock into air and soil, and tiny flying ships bear beams to be welded into a framework. The last is a particularly dangerous assignment, with very heavy mortality, for the two-man vessels often collide with each other and the framework. * Driven by his Weltschmerz, Leaf and his Third Class friend volunteer as welders, and both die in a crash. * But, as Kelly cynically ends, there is a splendid monument to the thousands who died in building the Tycho dome. * Told in a verismo approach, with excellent detail and a bitter scorn for the structured society of the day (with relevance to our times). Occasionally a little amateurish, but still a very considerable achievement for a nineteen-year old.

781. **INTO THE METEORITE ORBIT.** *Amazing Stories,* December 1933. Ill. Morey.

(Reprinted in Knight, *Science Fiction of the Thirties.*)

Short story. * *Time:* the twenty-second century. *Place:* mostly Arizona and space around the Earth. * The story is told confusingly with divided protagonists; complex, inadequately explained background; and a long flashback. * *Background:* Science has advanced greatly since our time. There are humaniform, almost human robots; thought-transmission helmets; matter transmission; and much else, but space travel is beyond mankind. Socially, much of the world is under the thumb of a ruthless power syndicate known as the Group, or the Five, against which part-story hero Girand has been fighting. * The story is best presented here in chronological order, rather than in the author's confusing narrative order. Jimmy Warren, immensely wealthy heir to the inventor of the robots, has sponsored the construction of a spaceship, in which he hopes to be the first man to reach the Moon. His vessel leaves with no problems, but it is learned almost immediately afterward that his research assistant, an agent of the Group, has sabotaged the ship. Jimmy is now stranded in space, with locked controls in an orbit far above Earth. He has enough supplies for two months, during which time the great scientist Granton and Jimmy's other associates on Earth frantically construct a second, rescue, ship. * Time passes. Girand, who happens to be Jimmy's legal guardian as well as close friend, has just returned from battling the Group in Africa. He now receives a telepathic message from Granton asking him for help. He also receives a gloating communication from the Group via normal channels, with a cryptic message about Jimmy Warren. * Granton transports Girand by matter transmission to the secret laboratory in Arizona, which is under siege by the Group, and asks him to take the second spaceship up and rescue Jimmy. Girand is willing, ascends, and transfers Jimmy to the second ship, but last-minute danger from the meteor belt makes the rescue doubtful. The previous traitor, who has reformed, sacrifices himself to save Girand and Jimmy. * *Miscellaneous:* Future man seems to be considerably shorter and

Kelly, Frank K. (*continued*)

slenderer than present day man. * The attempt at complex narrative structure and the elliptical background destroy the story, which becomes very difficult to follow.

782. **CRATER 17, NEAR TYCHO**. *Astounding Stories*, June 1934. Ill. Dold.

(Reprinted in Kelly, *Star Ship Invincible*.)

Short story. * *Time:* 2021. *Place:* New York and space, on the way to the Moon. * The class struggle in terms of heroism and self-sacrifice. * *Background:* Space flight is present, but is still at an early stage. Contact has been made with Mars. Earth itself is a tyranny, with population concentrated into unitary cities. The aristocracy and ruling class live on the surface, while lower ranks live progressively deeper in the Earth in the Bottom Levels. Many of the laboring class never see the surface. * At the moment, an underground rebellion is about ready to explode. The timing, however, is unfortunate, for the official representative of the Bottom Levels is a traitor and has just betrayed his fellows to the Controls. * At Gotham spaceport, Brand, an underground leader, has on board the *Isis* an illegal cargo of Martian sound oscillators that can kill or rip human bodies apart. The plan is for Gar (another underground leader) to pick up the weapons and distribute them among the Bottom Levels. But Gar has been betrayed and barely escapes to the *Isis*. The ship, still laden, must leave Gotham and fly to a hidden refuge place on the Moon. * Most of the story describes the flight of the *Isis*, pursued by Control ships. Overloaded with the unanticipated weight of Gar, hindered by the breakdown of machinery, inadequately supplied with oxygen, the *Isis* would not have made it without the self sacrifice of Gar and a crewman who voluntarily "walked the plank" into space. A meteor swarm also works to the advantage of the fugitives. The *Isis* reaches its destination, Crater 17, near Tycho, where there is a rebel station. The venture has been a failure, but not a catastrophe. * *Miscellaneous:* A Lunar native is small, but humanoid. * A serious story told with a certain amount of verismo and with considerable brutality. The characterizations are a little wobbly, but a competent job, very different from the Pollyanna stories typical of the period. Much Kelly's best story to date.

783. **FAMINE ON MARS**. *Astounding Stories*, September 1934. Ill. Marchioni.

Novelette. * *Time:* perhaps the twenty-fifth century. *Place:* a space station beyond the Moon. * *Background:* Earth is totally under the control of the Combine, a dictatorial cartel or similar enormous business entity that systematically brainwashes and conditions the young to accept its principles. The Combine at one time controlled Mars, which it began to make habitable with generators that can create water out of sand. But when the Martians rebelled and declared independence about twenty years ago, the Combine withdrew the generators, and Mars has been rapidly drying up. Most of the Martians are dead of thirst, and in a very short time they will be extinct. As for the Martians themselves, they seem to be a native race, humanoid, green-skinned, tall, large-chested, heavily muscled, but afflicted with very brittle bones. Communication between Earth, the Moon, and Mars is beamed transmission relayed by space stations. * The narrator and his Martian associate, NX-5, are the signal operators on the relay station. They are friends, so far as an Earthman and a Martian can be friends, but, as NX-5 soon indicates, there are stronger forces than friendship. NX-5, to save

his people, intends to hijack a water generator and rocket it to Mars. For this he needs the help of the narrator, who veers among his Combine conditioning that Martians are an inferior race, his personal sympathy for the Martians, his reluctance to kill other men on the stations, and the hypnotic gas and apparatus that NX-5 uses to control him. Much of NX-5's plan is unsuccessful for one reason or another, but the upshot is that the Martians get a generator, though the narrator kills NX-5. * The story is not so much one of incident as of character analysis and personal by-play between the Martian and the Earthman. * Well handled.

784. **STAR SHIP INVINCIBLE**. *Astounding Stories*, January 1935. Ill. Dold.

(Reprinted in Kelly, *Star Ship Invincible*.)

Novelette. * *Time:* the early twenty-second century. *Place:* the space dome on Jupiter, and space between Mars and Jupiter. * Space travel is common enough and generally uneventful, with the exception of the route between Mars and Jupiter, where the Hole in Space is a great peril. It is a dimensional something that sucks in ships, and presumably destroys them. Flights usually skirt far around the Hole, which is periodic after a fashion. * On this occasion, the big brass has decided to take a chance with the *Star Ship Invincible*, which thanks to new equipment should be able to run past the edge of the Hole safely and save time. As a further feature, the command section of the ship is rigged with a device that will cause dimensional changes, permitting it to pass through the Hole. * The story is told with two narrative centers: Graham, a control man on the Jupiter Dome, and Captain Moran and Lieutenant Hansen on the spaceship. Graham, who has been stationed without relief on Jupiter for ten years, is apprehensive about his wife, who is flying to join him on the *Star Ship Invincible*. Graham not only is distrustful of the brinkmanship policy of the space line, but keeps thinking of the fate of the twentieth-century *Titanic*, which was similarly publicized. On the ship, Moran and Hansen are in repeated conflict, particularly when they learn that their vessel will not escape the Hole, but is doomed. * The ship is lost, but Moran and Hansen survive after a fashion in the dimensional escape-command capsule. They undergo incredible dimensional transformations before their tiny vessel crashes on Jupiter. These changes are well imagined. * Kelly takes the notion of conflict, a standard trick in the writing of the day, very literally, with resultant occasional overdramatization rather than verismo.

KENDIG, JULIAN, JR.

Presumably a U.S. author. According to a letter in the March 1931 issue of *Amazing Stories* (p. 1152), Kendig was a sophomore in high school when he wrote the first story.

785. **FOURTH DIMENSIONAL SPACE PENETRA-TOR**. *Amazing Stories*, January 1930. Ill. Wesso.

Short story. * Perkins describes his adventures with the great Professor Longhorn, who explains the fourth dimension to him: It is not a geometric rotation of surfaces, nor is it time; it is a matter of motion. Thus, motion inward from a tesseract involves the fourth dimension. Practically speaking, this means a trip down into subatomic size. * Longhorn has devised suitable equipment for such exploration, and the two men descend into an atomic solar system, where they locate a suitable planet (a hydrogen electron) with human inhabitants. Since the natives are telepathic, there is no difficulty in communication. * The

Kendig, Julian, Jr. (*continued*)

subatomic people (who are ruled by a sort of scientific council) are friendly, and they and Longhorn exchange information. As the explorers learn, the table of elements is very different from that of our world, and radium is plentiful and cheap. * The exploratory trip has been successful, but there is a time problem. Since there is an enormous difference in time rates between the two worlds, the dimensional travelers cannot remain away from our world long. And once they leave, they can never return to the subatomic world, even if it could be found again, for millions of years would have passed there. * The explorers return to our world, bringing with them a friendly savant and a baby brontosaurus just as a violent volcanic upheaval destroys much of the subatomic land. * A crude piece of work. * For a sequel see #786, "The Eternal Mask."

786. **THE ETERNAL MASK**. *Amazing Stories*, February 1933. Ill. Morey.

Novelette. * Sequel to #785, "Fourth Dimensional Space Penetrator." * The story falls into two parts. In the first part, the opening situation is an argument between Longhorn and Secretary Lamar (the man who came up from the hydrogen electron with the explorers in the previous story). Longhorn maintains that there are areas of condensed ether where the orbital motion of satellites (among other things) will be impeded, causing an interplanetary collision. * Lamar, who claims to have had partial success in producing antigravity, disputes this vigorously. In his interpretation, gravity is a compound force consisting of attraction and repulsion; should an attractive force bring two celestial bodies close, the repulsing force would counteract this and prevent a collision. The men wager two thousand dollars. * As proof, Longhorn says that his calculations show that the moon will collide with the Earth in a matter of days. He insists that all concerned spend the remaining time sealed in his great observatory. * As they watch, the Moon grows larger and larger, until it fills much of the sky. The narrator, Perkins, is alarmed, but both Longhorn and Lamar seem indifferent. The argument is settled when Longhorn admits that Lamar's theory is right. Actually, as Lamar figured out but did not reveal, the Moon is not approaching Earth; the men are in a small spaceship headed for the Moon. * Arriving at the Moon, the men don space suits and explore. The side of the Moon facing us is barren, but Longhorn is convinced that the other side is habitable and probably peopled. He proves right, but the small flyer that the men use unfortunately lands amid a group of reactionary antiscientific Lunarians, who destroy the flyer and imprison the explorers, who are to be boiled alive. They are rescued, however, by submarines manned by the more civilized Lunarians (the Rionians), among whom they stay for a time. To their great surprise they learn that a Chinese ship had anticipated their voyage by several years; the scientist concerned, Hi Ming has risen to the position of prime minister of the land. * A problem: Hi Ming's rebellious crew wants to return to Earth and steals Longhorn's mother ship. After a chase our friends recapture it and make their way back to Earth. * *Miscellaneous*: The habitable side of the Moon, which is a huge hollow, is divided by a wall more than five miles high. Within the habitable side is a fairly large sea. * The Lunarians are completely human. * Conversation among the various peoples is possible by telepathy, which Longhorn picked up on the atomic world. Also, the Chinese scientist has taught some of the Rionians English,

French, and Chinese. * The first part of the story, the impending fall of the Moon, is unexpectedly plausible, though amateurishly presented, and the reader may be surprised at the relativistic solution. The story should have been closed off at this point, for the remainder is a very bad let down.

KENNEDY, FRED

No information.

787. **TRIAL BY TELEVISION**. *Amazing Stories*, December 1931. Ill. Morey.

Short story. * An inverted detective story set in 1985. It is told in terms of Molby Grant, second engineer on the gigantic Brantler airliner that makes the fortieth-parallel run. Grant is a capable young man, but is highly dissatisfied with his situation and his prospects for promotion. Under ordinary circumstances he will have to wait for years before a berth opens for a chief engineer. * Grant, however, is unwilling to wait, and he decides to murder his chief, old McCurdie, throwing the blame on Chief Engineer Lopez, who has a bitter feud with McCurdie. Grant arranges one of the highly poisonous propellant gases to leak out under such circumstances that Lopez will be blamed. * Everything goes according to plan. McCurdie is dead. Lopez is in custody. And Grant is now acting chief. * All this takes place while the ship is in flight. New York detectives, however, investigate the crime by television during the flight, and Grant is trapped by the one thing that he forgot: When he entered the room where the gas was released, he left behind an odor print that the examining detective identified as his. Grant breaks down and is a snivelling wreck as the ship lands. * *Miscellaneous:* Airliners are propelled by two gases that explode violently when they are mixed in the rocket tubes. * A competent job, with really good technical detail, convincing and easily presented.

KENNELLY, JOSEPH

No information. Portrait accompanying story shows a young man.

788. **DEATH FROM THE SEAS**. *Wonder Stories*, January 1931. Ill. Lyman Anderson.

Short story. * *Time:* the 1940s. *Place:* On and beneath the Sargasso Sea. * Ships are mysteriously disappearing in the Caribbean; even radio-beam navigation offers no solution, for the beams are suddenly cut off. Among the last to disappear was a *New York Times* expedition that included the narrator's sweetheart, Marna Montgomery. * Thus, when the shipping company for which the narrator works proposes a two-man reconnaissance mission, the narrator is willing to go. Accompanying him is the noted adventurer Novak. * The two men venture quietly into the danger area in a motor boat, and in a short time come upon a derelict ship that has been stripped of all steel and has obviously been burned as if by a heat ray. * As the two men investigate the ship, they see a strange submersible emerge near them, from which radiation pours; they are rendered unconscious and taken in the vessel, which descends. * When they revive, they are greeted by a small man with an enormous head and taken before a council. Thought helmets permit communication. They are on their way to the sunken city of Daar. * *Background:* Millennia ago, when their continent began to sink, the scientists of the land, who had discovered antigravity, simply set up an antigravity shield to hold the waters in place above their sunken

Kennelly, Joseph (*continued*)

land. * Their descendants still live underwater. The reason that they have attacked surface vessels is that they need iron, which they disintegrate into atomic energy. As for the land itself, it supports a small population of about twenty thousand, mostly workers, with a small elite governing class that is apparently somewhat oppressive, since there is much social unrest. Why the people of Daar preserved Novak and the narrator, when they killed almost everyone else, is never explained. * As we said, *almost*, for Marna Montgomery is there, well preserved, and well treated. As one of the little men explains, breeding is controlled, and a single female is used to produce eggs for the new generation, thus providing racial uniformity. Marna has been selected, but is unenthusiastic. * The three surface people plot to escape, although it seems hopeless. But social ferment proves to be their salvation. The workers learn that the elite plan to burn them with heat rays, whereupon they rebel and seize the antigravity station. During the ensuing melée, workers are burned, the antigravity rays are shut off, the sunken land is destroyed, but our friends escape in the submersible. * Weak on motivations, with loose ends, and rubbishy.

KERLIN, RICHARD G.
U.S. author, then resident in Lincoln (or Linwood), Nebraska. Kerlin's letters would seem to reveal a more mature person than the following pastiche.

789. **THE ALIEN HAH-RAH.** *Wonder Stories*, December 1935.
Short item printed in the letter column. * The report of the Ackerman-Darrow Scientifictionic Expedition to the Gobi Desert. (Ackerman is identified in his collaboration with Francis Flagg. Jack Darrow, a pseudonymous Chicago fan of the day, was a persistent contributor to the readers' columns of the science-fiction magazines, with scores of letters rating stories.) * Among the desert sands the expedition found hollow meteorites containing threats to mankind or the expedition, including one meteorite that held a manuscript. * The manuscript: Kidnapped by a mad scientist, the narrator was inflicted with s-f magazines until he went mad and began to write s-f himself. He was then transported to Mars, whence he sent his message via meteorite to Earth. * The author has a knowledge of earlier science-fiction and in his development ridicules many stories and motifs.

KEY, EUGENE GEORGE (1907-1976)
U.S. writer, then resident of Chicago. Portrait shows a young man. Key was also the author of *Mars Mountain* (Fantasy Publications, Everett, Pa., 1934), a collection of three original science-fiction short stories, and stories in Gernsback's *Scientific Detective Monthly*. *Mars Mountain* was the first fantasy book published by a specialist publisher.

790. **THE RED ACE.** *Air Wonder Stories*, February 1930. Ill. Paul.
Short story. * *Time:* 1956. *Place:* mostly the Chicago area. The story is presented as a long letter from James Golden, son of the owner of Golden Air Lines, to a friend. The airlines, particularly Golden, are being raided by an aerial bandit known as the Red Ace. Flying an enormous red propellerless plane, he forces planes and personnel down by some inexplicable effect, loots his prey of bullion and currency, then flies away. His home station has never been found. * Jim and his friend Professor Emil

Schneider, though scorned by Jim's hard-nosed father, have their own ideas about what is happening, and they are working along the same lines as the Red Ace. The two men develop a device (not explained) for increasing or decreasing gravity. It is ready when the Red Ace next attempts a robbery. The two men, using their gravity apparatus and a heat ray, succeed in driving away the bandit. * The next step is installing equipment into a plane and following the Red Ace to his lair and destroying it. Unexpectedly, when the Red Ace is next encountered and driven off, the bandit ship heads directly for the Moon, Jimmy and Emil on its heels. After a battle above the outlaw's lunar base, the menace is removed. The Red Ace, an ancient man in colorful uniform who obviously suffers from megalomania, is captured, and Golden, Sr., will no longer sneer and scoff at basic research as conducted by his son. * *Miscellaneous:* The Red Ace's ship, though held aloft by antigravity, was propelled by the jet principle (air drawn through a central tube) and by rockets in space.

KIRBY, JASON
No information.

791. **THE FLOATING ISLAND OF MADNESS.** *Astounding Stories*, January 1933. Ill. Paul.
Short story. * *Place:* Istanbul and the Arabian Desert. * Secret Service Lieutenant Ainslee, Sureté agent M. Foulet, and Scotland Yard Inspector Brice are all tracking men responsible for currency upheavals in the world's economy. Their quarry always disappears from roofs. Brice deduces that a glider and plane must be involved. * On the crucial occasion, when the three sleuths follow the glider and its mother plane, their plane is seized by a magnetic ray that drags them along to a huge floating platform a thousand feet above the Arabian desert. * There they meet the Master, the long missing mad scientist Algernon Fraser. The Master, who is served by robot-like men, explains matters to the three before he will turn them into similar robots. He has discovered an attracting ray and a weightless substance that is lighter than the ether. He also possesses a serum that will remove their individuality, though not their intellect. * The men cleverly evade the injection, but still have not escaped the Master's power. Brice is removed to receive a second injection. * Days pass, whereupon the Master demands that Foulet and Ainslee reveal their governments' secrets. If they refuse, they will be dropped to the desert. In the nick of time Brice, who has escaped, appears, knocks out the Master, and all fly off as the platform, its controls tampered with by Brice, floats up into the sky, away from the Earth. * Below routine.

KIRKHAM, HENRY F.
No information. Portrait accompanying "The Time Oscillator" shows a man in late middle age:

792. **THE TIME OSCILLATOR.** *Science Wonder Stories*, December 1929. Ill. Paul.
Short story. * *Time:* The present, the future, various places and times in the past. * The physician narrator becomes acquainted with the reclusive scientist Brown, who explains his work: Time is not a point, as we think, says Brown, but a dimension with all sorts of features of its own. With the use of rays, vibrations, mirrors, and a crystal block it is possible to perceive events in both past and in future. * Brown allows the doubting narrator to experience the phenomena, which include a scene during the

Kirkham, Henry F. (*continued*)

French Revolution, another of a clash between Romans and Northmen, another in the ancient Near East. More elaborate is a venture into the future, where the narrator is welcomed by a future man who knew in advance of his coming and greets him with a barrage of metaphysics. * Brown now suggests the most dangerous, most elaborate experience of all: a physical visit to Atlantis. The two men, taking along weapons and a small invisible house, and clad in electrically charged garments, move to Atlantis, which is barbaric in civilization but has splendid architecture. * The explorers, proclaiming themselves messengers of the gods, take a very high hand, shooting and shocking (with their electric garments) when opposition arises. Their tactics work for a time, but eventually activate a simmering rebellion of the lower-order natives, with the result that the explorers barely escape with their lives back into the time house. They return to their own time; artifacts they hoped to bring back disappeared during transit. * *Miscellaneous:* The white ruling class, which speaks Sanskrit, oppresses a large aboriginal population. * A very muddled, amateurish story, with bewildering values. * For a sequel see #794, "To the End of Time."

793. **LORDS OF THE DEEP**. *Wonder Stories*, November 1930. Ill. Marchioni.

Short story. * When Professor Silas Hocking, who enthusiastically claims that the Phoenicians crossed the Pacific and colonized the Americas, drops an ancient book, out pops a manuscript with a map confirming his theories. The manuscript contains a Phoenician account of a lost race that lives in a gigantic cavern under the Pacific Ocean, with a sealed entrance on Easter Island. The manuscript also claims that the lost race once inhabited a great continent since sunk. * Hocking, the narrator, and Wilson proceed to Easter Island, where they blow up one of the statue platforms and find the entrance to the underworld. Entering, they encounter Phoenician warriors who take them to the citadel of the city, where they realize they are as good as prisoners. * *Background:* Easter Island is the last remnant of the lost continent of Lemuria. As the continent gradually sank, various races inhabited it, the latest being the Phoenicians, who conquered the land. Interbreeding with the natives, they retreated to the giant caverns during volcanic disturbances. * At the moment the land is undergoing civil war. The priests, with a puppet king, control the main city and most of the land, while the legitimate king is in a weaker position. The *casus belli* is that the legitimate king wants to open the land to the outside, while the priests, who believe that their power would be endangered by external contacts, wish to keep the land a hermit kingdom. * The priests now make their terms known to the outsiders: Hocking and party must pose as messengers of the gods, favoring the priests, and must help in the war; otherwise, they will be killed. The explorers have no choice but to agree, although they plan treachery. * The impersonation of divinity turns out to be a fiasco; firearms are fine, but not enough in quantity; and the outsiders are captured by the true king. They convince him of their bona fides and join his party, but the war goes against them, and the end seems near. The narrator, however, escapes to the surface in a homemade diving suit and returns in the nick of time with a machine gun. The war is ended. * Along the way the narrator picked up a Phoenician princess. * Routine.

794. **THE END OF TIME**. *Wonder Stories*, December 1930. Ill. Marchioni.

Short story. * Sequel to #792, "The Time Oscillator." * Brown, who has dropped out of sight, reappears and invites the physician narrator to another time trip, on this occasion to the end of the human race. They leave in a new time machine, taking along automatics, electric garments, and an atomic disintegrator Brown has invented. * As they move into the future they pass through a supercivilization that maintains an enormous glassed-in area against glacial cold and also has antigravity. Continuing, they come to what may be the last men, the Ultimates, bearded, elderly men who live in an underground world. The future men, who communicate telepathically, say that they have been waiting for the time travelers. As Brown learns from them, they understand time travel fully, but, since their expert on the subject died, they lack the mechanical skill to build an apparatus. * A walk through the cavern reveals that the future men, few in number, are all aged and no longer can reproduce. They possess a fantastically high science, but are somewhat apathetic, dispelling their cultural malaise with a work ethic. Although they know that their race is doomed, they maintain life and an elaborate science out of pride. * The Ultimates seem friendly enough, but both time travelers perceive a sinister aspect about them, and Brown, who intercepts a telepathic message, discovers that the future men plan to use them in a scheme. * Such is the case. There is another race of men on the planet, not quite so advanced scientifically, with whom Brown's hosts are not on friendly terms. The other race controls the only deposit of a (new) radioactive element that is necessary for creating food; the element could also be used to fertilize parthenogenetically and in vitro the elderly females of the Ultimates, so that the race can continue. The other race is well aware of this, and permits only limited access to the mineral; the Ultimates must furnish hostages, who will be killed if the Ultimates take more of the mineral than is permitted. The Ultimates deviously plan to slip in the time travelers as hostages, take more of the mineral than they should, and abandon the travelers to be executed. * Brown, who admits, despite his enormous egotism, that he is far inferior to the Ultimates mentally, is their match in guile. The time travelers shoot down all parties at the hostage exchange, escape, and temporarily convince the Ultimates that the other race has attacked them. They almost succeed, but the Ultimates catch on to what has happened. There is a shoot-out, in which Brown is wounded, but his disintegrator saves the day. The men reach their time machine and escape. * The narrator, operating the machine, overshoots their goal, and lands temporarily during the Webster-Hayne debate in 1830. * *Miscellaneous:* In this world of the far future, the sun is almost extinguished, and only surface Mercury would be suitable for human habitation. The incredible telescopes of the Ultimates have revealed life on the other planets, though now extinct for the most part, and on other solar systems. * For power the Ultimates have mountainous magnetos that draw upon the Earth's electromagnetic force. This power maintains heat, light, and atmosphere in the Earth, much of which has been hollowed out. * Better than its predecessor.

KLEIER, JOE

No information.

795. **THE HEAD**. *Amazing Stories*, August 1928. Ill. R. E. Lawlor.

Kleier, Joe (*continued*)

Short story. * Dr. Leeson makes a strange offer to Beardsley, who is dying of cancer. Leeson has developed the technique for keeping a severed head alive apart from its body: artificial blood and elaborate machinery, carefully attended perpetually by two assistants. And he wants to buy Beardsley's head. * At first Beardsley is shocked, but when Leeson offers him fifty thousand dollars to provide for his young daughter, Beardsley accepts. * The conditions are that Beardsley will stay alive for two months; if after that, he desires death, Leeson will fulfill his wishes. If Beardsley makes no signal, he will also be put to death at that time. * The operation proceeds successfully, but Leeson is killed in an automobile accident almost immediately afterwards, and the Beardsley situation receives much publicity. Legal action against Leeson's assistants fails, since Beardsley is not dead and had consented to the operation; and no one can take the responsibility of releasing him. * Time passes, during which the head is cared for. A religious cult arises around it, and its facial movements are taken as oracles. Not until years later, during war, is the head destroyed by an invader.

KLINE, ALLEN S. and KLINE, OTIS ADELBERT

Allen S. Kline was the son of Otis Adelbert Kline and at one time managed the Otis A. Kline literary agency, which handled a considerable amount of fantastic and general pulp material. During at least part of our period he was a resident of the Chicago area. Otherwise, no significant information is available. Otis Adelbert Kline has a separate entry.

796. **THE SECRET KINGDOM.** *Amazing Stories,* October-December 1929. Ill. Bob Dean.

Novel. * *Place:* Brazil. * A borderline lost-race story, not quite fantastic enough to be science-fiction. The interminable story is a succession of form clichés in imitation of Edgar Rice Burroughs and similar writers. It would be pointless to summarize the story in detail. * Alfred Bell, a noted young scientist and Herculean man of action, is on a sponsored field trip in Brazil gathering biological specimens when he chances to save a strangely dressed man from a carnivore. * The man, expressing gratitude in perfect Spanish, invites Bell to accompany him. * *Background:* Bell has saved the life of the Inca Huayna Capac II, ruler of a small enclave descended from ancient Peruvians who fled the Spanish conquest. There is no question of real isolation, for they know quite well about the outside world and have modern weapons; their capital New Cuzco combines elements of Inca culture and modern South American. So that the outside world remains uninformed, however, outsiders who enter cannot leave. * Bell is elevated to the nobility by the Inca, but incurs the enmity of the high priest (Tupac), partly because Bell falls in love with the beautiful Spanish maiden Nona Flores, a medical school graduate who lives in New Cuzco. Tupac wants to marry her. A wild card is a villainous German who is pursuing Bell to steal his papers and specimens. These ingredients are combined in an endless series of plots, counterplots, captivities, escapes, murders, and hairbreadth escapes. At one time Bell is to be fed to a giant boa; he lassoes it around the neck with a rope he happens to be carrying, using the bars of his cell as a capstan of sorts to lift the snake until it is helpless. Eventually, Bell, his Indian servant, and Nona escape from the Incas' mountain by parachute. The villains lose their heads when they encounter Jivaros. * A bad job.

KLINE, OTIS ADELBERT (1891-1946)

U.S. (Chicago and New York, mostly) writer and in later years literary agent for many of the contemporary authors of fantastic fiction. In his youth he is said to have been connected with Tin Pan Alley and the early motion picture industry. Kline was a fairly successful writer of pulp action fiction, much of it in deliberate imitation of other, more financially successful authors, notably Edgar Rice Burroughs. In science-fiction, Kline wrote a series of adventure novels set on Venus, a space opera set largely on the Moon, and a Tarzan epigone; the last, "Jan of the Jungle," was adapted into the motion picture *The Call of the Savage,* starring Dorothy Lamour. Kline's work was very popular among the older fans, but today he seems a curious phenomenon: an intelligent man with a puckish sense of humor who deliberately created sensational absurdities and wrote down for the market. * See also #1825, "Revenge of the Robot."

797. **THE MALIGNANT ENTITY.** *Amazing Stories,* June 1926. Ill. F. S. Hynd.

(First published in *Weird Tales,* May/June/July 1924 Anniversary Issue. Reprinted in *Amazing Stories Quarterly,* Fall 1934.)

Short story. * One of the earlier versions of the wicked amoeba situation. * Mysterious events! Professor Townsend, in good health the night before, is found next morning in his laboratory as a stripped skeleton. Late, the policeman who is standing guard after the skeleton is discovered is similarly skeletonized. * A colleague, Dr. Dorp, believes that the solution to these events may lie in Townsend's research. He is right. Townsend had discovered how to create life, and in a sixty-gallon tank lives the product of his science a giant amoeba that can pop out and eat people quite rapidly. Part of the amoeba is destroyed, but a nucleus escapes temporarily. It is captured, and as it is being burned, it reveals part of the mystery. It takes on the form of a criminal, perhaps a burglar, whose evil potentialities supplemented the natural hunger of the giant germ. * A crude job. Dr. Dorp reappears in the following story, #798, "The Radio Ghost."

798. **THE RADIO GHOST.** *Amazing Stories,* September 1927. Ill. Paul.

Short story. * *Place:* the Chicago area. * Dr. Dorp in this story seems to be a psychic investigator concerned with exposing fake supernaturalisms. Young Miss Van Loan consults him. Her eccentric uncle, a noted believer in spiritualism, has left her his fortune on condition that she reside in his house for one year. If she leaves, the bequest goes to a cousin, Ernest Hegel. * Her problem is that the house is so badly haunted that she cannot tolerate it. There are apparitions, unaccountable cold breezes, self-propelled furniture, and much else. * Dorp and the narrator, who undertake to investigate, soon find themselves confronted with foul-smelling haunts, self-operating doors, and aggressive furniture. On one occasion Dr. Dorp is almost killed. * Dorp solves the problem, however. All the phenomena are accounted for by mechanisms, magnetism, and radio. The culprit is cousin Ernest, who is controlling activities from several miles away. * A competent piece of pulp fiction. On one occasion the narrator fans the fainted heroine with a copy of *Science and Invention*!

799. **THE MAN FROM THE MOON.** *Amazing Stories,* October 1930. Ill. Morey.

Short story, a companion piece to the author's "Maza of the Moon" (*Argosy-All-Story,* 21 December 1929-11 January 1930; book form, McClurg, Chicago, 1930). "The Man from the

Kline, Otis Adelbert (*continued*)

Moon" describes in more detail ancient events mentioned in passing in the novel. * *Time:* the basic situation in the remote past. *Place:* the historical portion on Mars and the Moon. * A long introduction describes how two scientists in the Southwest come into possession of a manuscript describing interplanetary warfare in the remote past. They had been examining a perfect meteoritic crater—Thompson, a selenographer, believes that lunar craters are meteoric in origin—when they see an elderly Chinese performing strange rites at the crater. A little later he approaches their camp and explains that they are destined, according to prophecy, to receive a certain manuscript. When he was a monastic novice in Tibet, he saw a sacred stone with an unreadable inscription. Since he was something of a paleographer, he recognized certain symbols and secretly made a copy, but it was not until years later that he succeeded in fully translating it. * The inscription was the work of Pan K'u, crown prince and later ruler of the planet Magong. In the remote past Magong was inhabited by a race like our present-day Chinese; Mars was inhabited by a white race; and Earth (in part?) by primitive whites. Mars and Magong were about on the same high scientific level and conducted an extensive trade. But trouble arose because of trading settlements, and war broke out. * In addition to space battles with various rays, the opponents attacked each other's home world. The Martians drew in asteroids and cascaded them upon Magong, causing extensive cratering; and the people of Magong projected a ray that stripped away Martian atmosphere. The scientists of Magong as a last resort tried to change the orbit of their planet in order to avoid the meteoritic bombardments, but simply managed to drop Magong in gravitational captivity to Earth; it is now our moon. As a result of the war, both Magong and Mars are wrecked, with (as other works by Kline reveal) only a handful of survivors left on each. * Pan K'u, the young crown prince, in a desperation move descends to the Earth. Unable to return, he marries local women and establishes the terrestrial Oriental race. Before dying he wrote the long inscription, prophesying that it would eventually be read and that the great crater left by his spaceship would be found. * Finis. * Not quite as silly as *Maza of the Moon*.

800. **THE THING THAT WALKED IN THE RAIN.**
Amazing Stories, March 1931. Ill. Morey.

Short story. * *Place:* Nicaragua. * Professor Mabray and associates, including the narrator, come to the mountain lake to investigate the disappearance of Mabray's friend Dr. Fernando de Orellano. The area is tabu, and the local Indians are very reluctant, unless highly paid, to enter it. * Two motifs channel the story. * First, the lake is inhabited by a gigantic hydra, the size of a house, that not only catches people who wander too close to the shore, but in rainy weather leaps out and hunts down prey. Members of the party have close escapes, with machetes cutting off tentacles. * In the second subplot, Bahna, a mysterious Hindu, building on Hindu mythology, has set up the cult of Nayana Ida, a monster god whose aveisha here is Nayana Idra, the gigantic hydra. Bahna, who has a fanatical following in the area, conducts human sacrifices with a fair amount of pageantry. * Capturing the investigators, Bahna offers Mabray's daughter a position as his wife and high priestess and the others, administrative jobs. They all refuse, and despite perils, bring down Bahna and kill the hydra. * There is a fair amount of charlatanry in Bahna's cult, with mysterious disappearances and

appearances and seemingly magical effects. * Bahna raised the giant hydra by simple chemical means and planned to destroy it when the time came. * A curious medley of disparate materials; a thriller that does not come across.

801.**THE METAL MONSTER.** *Amazing Stories*, July 1931. Ill. Morey.

Short story. * *Time:* 1960. *Place:* Nicaragua and inside the Earth, perhaps a gigantic cavern, perhaps the hollow Earth. * Walter Stuart, assigned to fly over and photograph the volcanic crater of Mount Cosegiuna shortly after its eruption, sees a marvelous sight. The inside of the crater, deep down, is lined with a causeway and steps, and around and up it, working, are metal globes with tentacles. The globes spot Stuart's plane and attack it. * Stuart manages to escape when his plane is shot down, but his comrade is captured. Making his way to the capital of Nicaragua, Stuart tells what he has seen, displaying a tiny captured globe creature. Globes thereupon attack the capital, and, capturing Stuart and the president's daughter Dolores, fly away with them through the volcano's crater into the interior of the Earth (which, as they discover later, has a fauna of gigantic predatory insects and a flora of gigantic fungi and molds). * Stuart, after a time, is confronted by a strange humanoid being with an enormous head and transparent flesh, through which bones and internal organs can be seen. This creature is Zet, ruler of the inner world. Masters of a superscience, he and the other members of his race, the Snals, control the metal spheres (Teks) telepathically, just as they communicate with Stuart and other human captives. As Stuart learns, the Snals plan to conquer the world, enslaving the human race, which will operate the metal spheres for the convenience of the Snals. * If Stuart learns how to control such a sphere, he will be allowed to live; otherwise, he will he thrown to the gigantic moulds as food. The same holds true for other captives, but for Dolores and other handsome women, there will be a different fate. Zet plans to cross Snal brain power with external man's hardier constitution. * Stuart is put to work operating machinery, with an overseer armed with a paralysis ray and a melting rod supervising him. Dolores, for the time being, is also put to work. Things look hopeless, especially when viewing screens show that the outer world is helpless against Snal weapons. External weapons cannot even damage the metal spheres, which are made of an indestructible metal. * But a chance comes when Stuart saves Dolores from rape by an overseer. The two humans escape from the Snal fortress-city, discovering along the way that salt (in Dolores's tears) dissolves the hitherto inactive, indestructible metal. After battles against monstrous life forms, including gigantic bats, the two capture a sphere, fly to the outer world, inform a nearby submarine fleet about salt, and watch the almost immediate destruction of Snal power. After salt-impregnated missiles demolish Snal battle spheres and defensive shields, American military forces cut a canal from the Pacific to the opening of the Snal tube, allowing the salt water to flow in. Most of the Snals are wiped out, but the master scientist who interrogated Stuart and who disapproved of the invasion survives, willing to share his knowledge with surface man. * *Miscellaneous:* The Snals had long known that there was an outer world, but attempts to reach it failed when they struck molten rock. The eruption of Cosegiuna provided an opportunity to emerge. * The indestructible metal of the Snals is a new element. * Interesting thriller beginning, but a rapid collapse into

Kline, Otis Adelbert (*continued*)

unconvincing simplistics and triteness. The conversations between Dolores and Stuart in the latter part of the story are almost unbelievable.

802. **A VISION OF VENUS**. *Amazing Stories,* December 1933. Ill. Morey.

(Reprinted in Wollheim, *Swordsmen in the Sky.*)

Short story. * *Place:* The main narrative takes place on Venus, in the same universe as Kline's Venus novels, of which this is a spinoff. * Dr. Morgan, who is frequently in machine-telepathic contact with individual Venusians, records the experiences of young Lotan. * Lotan, a botanist, is searching through the occasional islands of Venus for a particularly rare food fungus. If he can bring back even a small quantity of spores, he will receive a reward and be ennobled. * When Lotan's telepathically controlled flyer develops trouble, he has to make a forced landing on a small islet, where he rescues a beautiful young lady from hyena-like beasts. But this is not the end. She is then seized by a flying reptile and borne off. Following in his ship, Lotan rescues her in mid air. He is desperately in love with the woman, who reciprocates, but there are insurmountable social barriers, until the young woman reveals that by accident she has gathered spores of the sought-after fungus. Lotan's future is made, and romance follows. * *Miscellaneous:* Venus is hot and sticky, with primarily fungoid vegetation. There are many enormous, savage, predatory beasts, including a sea monster that can chew up battleships. The natives are completely human, with a sword-and-ray-gun culture. * Light, and not to be taken seriously.

KNIGHT, RAYMOND

Probably Raymond K. Knight, U.S. author of several plays, including "Strings" (1928).

803. **JUST AROUND THE CORNER**. *Amazing Stories,* July 1928. Ill. R. E. Lawler.

A play offered "for those who would like to produce a play, based on science in a sense, for the amusement and entertainment of their friends . . . . The scientific paraphernalia is easy to procure. Any radio fan will have enough of the material on hand without having to buy any of it—or at least very little." * The situation: Professor McAndrew has devoted years to the problem of scientific communication with the dead. He has constructed a radio-like apparatus that he hopes will function; after dying he intends to communicate with the living through this apparatus, delivering a certain message, now sealed, as proof of survival. He waits impatiently for his death, which should take place soon. Also present are a scientific witness; his assistant Kraussner, a German Ph.D.; and Meyer, a former assistant, discharged as too unstable for the project. * An altercation takes place among the men, after which Meyer, rushing out, commits suicide, hoping to be the first to speak over the apparatus. This he does. McAndrew listens, then himself dies. And Kraussner dies, poisoned by Meyer. A message should come from the other side, but it is too late. * The summary sounds silly, but the playlet is well dramatized and, allowing for datedness, could be staged.

KNIGHT, THOMAS H.

No information, but portrait accompanying "Great Green Things" shows a man in late middle age.

804. **THE MAN WHO WAS DEAD**. *Astounding Stories,* April 1930. Unsigned ill.

Short story. * Bucolic setting in a country store, as a young man and his friends, around a winter stove, listen to the strange story told by the skeletal man. * He is a confessed seducer and murderer who interrupts a cracker-barrel argument about reincarnation and the return of the dead. His story: Years ago, after being tried and found guilty, he was executed. But he had made a bargain with a scientist who claimed to be able to revive him if his neck was not broken. The scientist took his body, injected it with sera, and applied various lights and gases. During this time, the man claims, his spirit flitted about the room and watched what was going on. The corpse was revived, but the spirit did not reenter. * Tale over, the man leaves. One of the men present reveals the obvious cliché: He was the scientist. He tracks down the stranger and kills him. * A story that really belonged in *Weird Tales*, rather than a science-fiction magazine, and, in any case, was not crying for publication.

805. **THE REVENGE OF THE CHOSEN**. *Wonder Stories Quarterly*, Fall 1930. Ill. Marchioni.

Short story. * Oriental revenge. * Mysterious deaths in a rustic, perhaps Southern locale—punctures in the throat; a seemingly supernatural demand for "the Green Heart"; mysterious dreams and perhaps transfer of psyches to animals; and the menangause, a super-super-mongoose that is quite vicious. * The punctures are made by the poisonous menangause; the supernatural messages are conveyed by the menangause, which can slink about almost unseen; the Green Heart is a giant emerald that old Captain Taylor filched from a native sanctuary in India; the personality transfers seem genuine. * All ends well when the narrator of the fevered tale shoots all the Indian priests who have come in quest of the gem. * Possibly parodic; it is difficult to believe that the author could have been serious.

806. **GREAT GREEN THINGS**. *Wonder Stories*, April 1931. Ill. Marchioni.

Short story. * *Time:* 1940, after World War II. *Place:* probably the jungles of Brazil. * After an argument between entomologist Randall and aviator Ray concerning the possibility of giant insects, the men fly in Ray's superplane to a jungle area in Brazil, where they find more than they are looking for. Enormous hordes of insects the size of dogs attack them and the plane, biting the tires flat. Ray is captured and tied down by a rope-like substance that the insects secrete, but Randall rescues him by lighting a great gasoline fire, at which the insects demonstrate phototropism of the most extreme sort, leaping into the flames. Since the plane's tires are flat, it is necessary to get out and push to start it. * Routine.

KOBER, WILLIAM

Then a resident of the Bronx, New York City. No other information. Kober has a long letter criticizing the physics of John W. Campbell, Jr., and E. E. Smith, Ph.D., in the August 1931 issue of *Amazing Stories*.

807. **THE MAN WHO LIVED TWICE**. *Amazing Stories,* November 1932. Ill. Morey.

Short story. * *Time:* 1973 and A.D. 8117. * *Place:* Upstate New York. * *Background:* In the world of 1973 the United States is fighting a losing war against the European Consolidation, Military operations are characterized by rocket-powered planes, superexplosives, and detector rays. Atomic power or atomic

Kober, William (*continued*)

explosives, however, seem only a dream. * The narrator, who is a physicist in the Bureau of Standards, has the job of winnowing out the multitude of suggestions, mostly crank, that the agency receives for new weapons. In the present instance he has received a prospectus from Professor Dane, once a fairly well-known scientist, who has since dropped out of sight. Dane claims to have invented a means for creating a new sort of gravity, which by distorting space-time can transport objects into the future. The suggestion is that the future may hold atomic energy, which has been an impossible goal in the twentieth century so far. The narrator's first inclination is to dismiss Dane as a crank, but the solid exposition that accompanies the proposal convinces the narrator that he should visit Dane. * The visit proves most profitable, for Dane, as he demonstrates, has achieved all that he has claimed. And a trip into the future by the narrator may prove invaluable. * The narrator finds himself, to his astonishment, in a wilderness, through which he wanders. After a time he sees a teardrop-shaped vessel slowly flying above, and then sees it attacked by a small rocket-driven vessel, which crashes, but also forces the teardrop to crash land. Other teardrops fly up and play heat rays that turn the area into a molten pool, while the injured narrator struggles away. * He is saved by a young woman from another rocket plane, who mistakes him for the kamikaze flier that destroyed the teardrop. From her he learns what is happening: the Earth has been invaded by a humanoid extraterrestrial force, which, using disintegrator and death rays, is systematically destroying all life. Until now humanity has had no weapons to match those of the invaders, whose teardrops are protected by impenetrable screens. * Abandoning for the time an attempt to learn how the war in his own time ended, the narrator hopes to accomplish two goals, find the secret of atomic energy, which the invaders obviously have, and gain information for the imperiled future people. * He and the young woman entice a teardrop to land, whereupon the narrator tries to rush into it as the invaders emerge. He covers some distance, but is killed by invader weapons before he can discover anything. * But retrieved back to 1973 by Dane, the narrator is whole and sound, even if his mission was a total failure. * Intelligently written with good exposition of theoretical matters, good detail, and absence of cheap thrills.

KOSTKOS, HENRY J. (1900-1977)

U.S. author, electrical engineer associated with Western Electric at Kearney, New Jersey, resident of Westfield, New Jersey. Also worked in telephone industry. At one time had own contracting business in Chicago and New York. Did postgraduate work in business administration at New York University. Later life in Baltimore area. A brief autobiographical sketch appears as "The Autobiography of a Science-Fictioneer" in *Fantasy Magazine* (March 1934).

808. **THE METEOR-MEN OF PLAA**. *Amazing Stories,* August/September issue, 1933. Ill. Morey.

Short story. * *Time:* probably the near future. * *Place:* a semi-solid world in the stratosphere or higher. * Scientist Gordon Bancroft, who has just finished building his spaceship, informs his friend George that circling Earth is a region of particles that sometimes form semisolid lands. He also informs George that this region supports life; he has sent up space probes that returned with insect-like creatures with helium sacks. Bancroft

further reveals that there is intelligent life on a solid area, as is proved by a creature that came tumbling down with a meteorite. It was roughly humanoid, but with enormous feet like snowshoes for the obvious purpose of support on a tenuous floor. * The spaceship, which operates by antigravity of a sort, ascends about a thousand miles. Finding a properly viscous continent, the men leave the spaceship to explore. They wear oxygen masks and foot flaps, and must be careful as they move around, lest they sink through the crust and fall down to Earth. * Bancroft and George soon encounter friendly intelligent life: red humanoid creatures with slits instead of noses, back humps with helium bladders, thin limbs with clawed enormous feet. Their science is high, but peculiar, being based on solidifying gases to make food, tools, weapons, etc. * Warfare breaks out between the friendly beings whom the explorers encountered and another people, with gases poisonous and erosive the principal weapons. At first, what with our heroes' firearms, the battle goes to the friendly people, but the tide turns and the Earthmen are fortunate to regain their spaceship. They turn on their auxiliary rocket tubes as a weapon against the invader, but, alas, the gaseous world catches fire, and Bancroft and George barely escape back to Earth. This was the end of the land above the skies. * Low-grade material, almost juvenile. Presumably suggested by the Roy Rockwood boys' books.

809. **BLACK DEATH**. *Astounding Stories,* March 1934. Ill. Paul Orban.

Short story. * Dr. DuPrey has worked out a technique for controlling pathogenic bacteria. A thought helmet enables his mind, while he lies unconscious, to energize and control special agents against disease. In this first experiment, DuPrey's mind will be connected to a container of antitoxin and bubonic plague germs, but in later experiments his technique will be used directly on diseased individuals. * The experiment begins, but as DuPrey soon recognizes, he is not working in a laboratory vessel, but in a human body that is undergoing violent attack by plague bacteria. After difficulties, perils, and narrow escapes, mobilizing and controlling the special antitoxin particles, DuPrey destroys the bacteria. * Regaining consciousness, DuPrey is at first outraged that the experiment was changed and that his assistant inserted him into a human body, but he then learns that his daughter, who had accidentally scratched herself while handling a plague culture, had contracted the disease and had been at the point of death. Her only hope was DuPrey's untried technique. It was successful. * Routine.

810. **THE MAN WHO STOPPED THE EARTH**. *Amazing Stories,* March 1934.

Short-short story. * *Time:* presumably moderately far in the future, though no indications of date are given. * The three great scientists, despite misgivings on the part of one man, decide to make the Great Experiment. With their superscience they will stop the Earth in its path, so that the remainder of the universe, which is in motion, will move past it. * They are successful, but they should have heeded warnings. Atoms are held together by electromagnetic forces generated by the movement of bodies, and without that force the Earth disappears into less than dust.

811. **THE EMPEROR'S HEART**. *Astounding Stories,* June 1934. Ill. Dold.

Short story. * *Time and place:* later than the twentieth century, in the imaginary land of Lunggrad. * The great and good Emperor Georges Delrex VI lies dying of cardiac arrest. As a

Kostkos, Henry J. (*continued*)

desperation move, his physician calls in the somewhat suspect Dr. Durgget, who has invented a substitute heart. Against the wishes of court officials, the empress gives consent to an operation, and the emperor is hooked up to the (nonportable) artificial circulatory machine. Supplemented by newly developed healing rays, the operation is a success. * In a short time, however, it is observed that the emperor seems to look younger; and after a while it is clear that he is regressing to childhood, then infancy, then to an embryonic state. When it seems that the emperor has disappeared, a change takes place and a new fetus forms, which is fostered and developed. But the newly reborn emperor is female. The court officials, to cover up, announce that the recently deceased empress died in childbirth, producing a daughter. * Routine.

812. **NORTH GOD'S TEMPLE**. *Amazing Stories,* August 1934. Ill. Morey.

Short story. * While working with a magnetograph, abrasive scientist Darius Norton receives a strange message purportedly from the priests of the People of the Magnetic God, who arrived on an asteroid fragment from the Bodean fifth planet. Driven by an urge to visit a fjord in northern Norway indicated by the magnetograph, Norton leads an expedition. Along the way he acts strangely and has to be restrained from plunging into the ocean. * Then later, when Norton is out in a small iron shell, the boat is seized and pulled beneath the sea. Onlookers believe that Norton is dead, but actually he has been dragged into an enormous underground world, where, after perils, he reaches a metal structure that is far more magnetic than magnetite. Surrounded by skulls of nonhuman beings, it is the Temple of the Magnetic God, from the fifth Bodean planet. Norton finds remains of a superscience, including the device that summoned him, and, wounded and ill though he is, he manages to make some of the equipment function. But the rising sea washes away the records of the strange people and drowns Norton. * Very different from Kostkos's other work; although not the work of a skilled writer, the story has a dream-like feeling.

813. **MEN CREATED FOR DEATH**. *Amazing Stories,* December 1934. Ill. Morey.

Short story. * *Time:* A.D. 2434. * *Background:* The former United States has long been divided, because of mutual hostility, into three nations: The Atlantic Seaboard States, Western America (beyond the Mississippi), and the Southern Confederation of States. All three, however, are united against the peril of the Yellows and Blacks, who are waging war against America. The Blacks are the more to be feared, since they have been inoculated with radium salts against radium rays and have aircraft that can, to a limited extent, penetrate the American ray barriers and bypass the ray forts. Leading the Blacks (whom the author characterizes as animal-like, bestial, and vicious) is their great scientist, the hunchbacked Suun Yaar, whose laboratories are at the mouth of the Niger. * The war is going badly for the Americans, for the Blacks are persistently overcoming American scientific advances. A further factor is shortage of American manpower. In a short time the heavy attrition of soldiery and civilians due to Black attacks will lead to defeat and extinction. * The only hope is to produce soldiers rapidly, claims great scientist DuPrey (who is obviously not the DuPrey of story #809). With accelerated metabolic implementation he hopes to generate adult humans in a matter of a couple of years. If the

West can hold out that long. * Suun Yaar is aware of what the DuPrey team is accomplishing, and a Black plane, penetrating defenses, kidnaps several of the leading participants. The Black genius tells the Americans that he needs extra men to conquer the universe and informs them that they will continue their research for him. The scientists have no choice, but they notice, as time passes, that the Black city seems less and less populous. The suspicion is that Suun Yaar is also short of manpower. This is confirmed when an American raid releases the captives, and a horde of American soldiers overcomes the Blacks. DuPrey's system has been working. Unfortunately, the created men are very short-lived, and there is a sentimental ending about a created hero whose mother recognizes that his lifetime will be very brief. * Routine, except for its racist rancor.

814. **SLEEP SCOURGE**. *Wonder Stories,* December 1934. Ill. Paul.

Short story. * *Time:* 1973. *Place:* Richmond, Virginia. * Ronald Veecks and Marcella Vogel are driving along the Eastern Seaboard Viaduct at 250 MPH, heading for New York, when Ronald suddenly collapses and is, to all appearance, dead. Marcella, who happened to be bending over, is not affected, but thousands of people in the area keeled over like Ronald. * Marcella hopes that the genius physician/scientist Rex Drake can save Ronald, and he does. He appears at the hospital, commandeers the emergency room, applies his D-ray (more powerful and more adjustable than an X-ray), and discovers that Ronald is alive. Cardiac and arterial injections bring Ronald back. Most of the other victims recover when Drake's technique is applied, but about five thousand people die. * What happened? Drake has the answer to this, too. Ronald's company has just installed cosmic ray power cables, which were being tested. Something went wrong, and the rays poured through the cables, causing an enormous gravitational pull on the corpuscles of the victims. * When Drake's explanation is published, survivors and relicts bring suit, and the Chesapeake Power Company suffers judgments of millions of dollars. * Drake again has a remedy. He explains that the cosmic rays transmuted the copper in Chesapeake's cables into pure gold, so that the company is ahead financially. * Solutions are a little farfetched, and morality questionable.

815. **EARTH REHABILITORS, CONSOLIDATED**. *Amazing Stories,* March-April 1935. Ill. Morey.

Short novel. * *Time:* "several thousand years in the future." *Place:* Saturn and frozen America, mostly New Jersey. * *Background:* In the not too distant future a wandering planetoid stripped away the Earth's atmosphere, dispersing it in space. As the result, the planet as good as died and soon became covered with enormous layers of ice. Most of the human race perished, but a few survivors made their way to Saturn, where they were permitted to settle, but were enslaved. (The Saturnians themselves are human.) * Over the centuries, the descendants of the Earthmen have been released from slavery, but they are scorned and abused as second-class (or lower) citizens. Some of the Earthmen have memories of Gordon Bennett, the great scientist of the past who had developed a "super-atmosphere," the secret of which lies buried beneath the ice on Earth. If rediscovered, it might serve to restore the Earth by attracting the atmosphere back. * On Saturn, descendant Warren Bancroft, who possesses a forbidden ancestral manuscript, is in love with Nita, a beautiful upper class Saturnian. Her father will not permit them to marry;

Kostkos, Henry J. (*continued*)

instead, he wants her to marry Gurra, a Plutonian humanoid, who is black, distorted, and nasty. At about this same time Bancroft learns that a group of Saturnian archeologists may have come upon the location of Gordon Bancroft's ancient laboratory on Earth. * With a group of fellow Earthmen who are eager to restore Earth's past glory, Warren and Nita steal a spaceship and take off for Earth, pursued by Gurra, whom they evade. On Earth, Warren falls into a deep crevasse, finding there thin air and friendly English-speakers, who have grown natural fur against the cold. These people are primitives, but they have a heat-emitting substance (radonite) that is useful for melting ice. * From here the story becomes a succession of conflicts with Gurra and his associates, but all ends well. Gurra is killed; Gordon Bancroft's secret process is rediscovered, and Earth will be restored in a short time. * *Miscellaneous:* The author obviously had American blacks in mind when writing about Plutonians; the would-be miscegenetic Gurra, instead of flashing a razor, wields a flame-knife which accomplishes the same thing. * Space travel is by rocket. * Below routine.

816. **WE OF THE SUN**. *Amazing Stories,* February 1936. Ill. Morey.

Short story. * *Place:* in part, within the sun. * Papers found after the disappearance of Prof. Jefferson Collier. * Collier, a recluse scientist, has been experimenting with extremely high temperatures; in his special furnace he has attained temperatures up to 100,000° (F. or C.?). This is equivalent to the interior of the sun. * When his dog accidentally falls into the furnace, Collier observes a strange phenomenon. Something resembling the dog seems to form in the heat, then fly away toward the sun. Later, when Collier cremates his dead child and wife in the furnace, he observes the same phenomenon. * Now tired of life, Collier leaps into his furnace. He awakens in a strange new existence within the sun, where he encounters his dog, his child, and his wife. The Colliers are not human any more, but gray formless beings. Collier speculates on the relationship of such solar life to solar physics.

817. **SIX WHO WERE MASKED**. *Amazing Stories,* October 1936. Ill. Morey.

Short story. * *Time:* Although a great scientist named Dr. Paul DuPrey appears in the earlier "Men Created for Death," which is set in the twenty-fifth century, there is no indication that the present story is set in other than publication time, the 1930s. A third story concering DuPrey, #809, would seem to be chronologically between the other two. * Dr. Paul DuPrey, in a demonstration of his new technique for fighting crime, displays to his audience six masked men on hospital stretchers. One of them is a sexual serial killer (my term); the others are leading lights of the town—mayor, police commissioner, clergyman, etc. * DuPrey asserts that by mingling blood from the six men and than feeding it back into the veins of all, the blood of the normals will cure the killer. Despite considerable opposition he has been able to keep the criminal's identity secret and the criminal out of the hands of the police. The process takes place, and all leave. * Some time later, a similar sex crime occurs. The obvious suspect is the previous killer, but he has a perfect alibi. Instead, the confessed murderer is the clergyman. * DuPrey is shaken, for the obvious explanation is that the killer's blood contaminated the clergyman. But DuPrey finds a way out of the dilemma by invoking hypnosis. * Routine.

KRAUS, JOSEPH H. (1898-1967)

A more important man than would seem from this single fiction. Born in New York. An employee of the Gernsback enterprises since the days of Gernsback *Amazing Stories* and *Science and Invention.* Later worked with Charles P. Mason on Gernsback's *Everyday Science and Mechanics.* Editor of *Practical Microscopy.* Coauthor with H. Winfield Secor of the Gernsback publication *All about Television* (1927), which was claimed to be the "first and only complete book on television." A versatile, learned man who also conducted the thirty-one piece orchestra on Gernsback's radio station. In later life Kraus operated the National Science Fair and International Science Fair for Science Service in Washington, D.C., thus influencing the lives of many young scientists-to-be. * According to Charles Hornig, as reported in *Fantasy Magazine,* when Hornig was at a loss to find a topic for the April 1935 issue of *Wonder Stories,* Kraus "drew a rough sketch showing a man at the bottom of the ocean in a deep-sea outfit shooting a harpoon gun at a frightful looking monster." Kraus was then commissioned to write a story to accompany it. Such a commission, based on artwork, was very unusual in the genre magazines of the day—apart from contests.

818. **PHANTOM MONSTERS**. *Wonder Stories,* April 1935.

Short-short story. * Dr. Walker, who has been investigating bathyal life in a diving suit, is hauled to the surface raving like a maniac about all sorts of monsters that were about to attack him. Recovered after sedation, he realizes that his experiences were not veridical. The pressure in his suit forced his ocular lenses into nearly spherical shape, thus forming microscopes of a sort, and what he saw was microscopic life. * Not really developed, just a brief narrative.

KRUSE, CLIFTON B[RYAN] (1905-present)

U.S. clergyman, then resident in Hutchinson, Kansas. Later resident in Texas and Colorado. In addition to the following stories, Kruse wrote eight other science-fiction stories under his own name (up to 1943) and "Niedbalski's Mutant" (*Astounding Stories,* May 1938), under the house pseud. Spencer Lane. The author is not to be confused with his son Clifton B. Kruse, Jr., who is a lawyer and educator.

The Flying Engineer Series is described first, then Other Works.

The Flying Engineers Series

Set at some undated time in the interplanetary future, the stories describe adventures and perils undergone by the crew of *Special Engineering Transport W62.* Despite the title of its service, the *W62* is apparently a trouble-shooter vessel. Commanding Officer Wiljon Kar and engineer Proch are not markedly characterized, but Lieutenant Mardico, who speaks a peculiar idiom, is reminiscent of Jack Williamson's Giles Habibula in the Legion of Space Series. The advanced science of the day includes rays of various sorts, with rockets and antigravity for space travel. The stories are not as smooth as the comparable Commander Hanson series of Sewell P. Wright.

819. **MENACE FROM SATURN**. *Astounding Stories,* July 1935. Ill. Schneeman.

Short story. * The first story in the Space Engineers series. *

Kruse, Clifton B. (*continued*)

Time: the interplanetary future. *Place:* Venus. * *Background:* Venus is utterly inhospitable, with a poisonous green atmosphere. Nevertheless, since it is the source of venusite, an ore that is an absolute reflector of energy, a mining operation has been established. Housed in a gigantic dome made of flexible plastic, it sustains about eight hundred men, who receive oxygen, supplies, and replacements from Earth. At the moment the oxygen is running low; supplies are late; and much of the personnel is down with the dread Venusian scale fever. Shortage of manpower makes it difficult to keep the dome suitably distended—which operation is done by small fliers that push against the flexible plastic in case of outside disturbance. * Wiljon Kar, C.O. of *Special Engineering Transport W62*, reasons out part of the problem. Earth must be under attack, hence cannot send supplies. The logical enemy is Saturn, which alone of the planets will not join the interplanetary league or permit visitors. And the most probable weapon is a swathing stream of particles derived from disintegrating the rings of Saturn. This prevents communication or shipping from leaving Earth. Worse, Kar predicts, in the very near future the Saturnians will change the process and permit the gaseous cloud to solidify, enclosing Earth in a solid sphere. * Kar, after making repairs on the Venus dome, rescues Earth. Taking out a small freighter filled with venusite, he flies into the path of the Saturnian energy beams and dumps the venusite. Since it is totally reflective, it turns the Saturnian energy beams back on Saturn, turning it into a seething, molten mass. (The sequels, however, indicate that Saturn was by no means so badly treated.) * *Miscellaneous:* Space travel involves both rockets and antigravity. * A story that would have been more at home in the earlier Clayton *Astounding Stories.*

820. **W62 TO MERCURY**. *Astounding Stories,* September 1935. Ill. Dold.
Short story. * The second story in the Flying Engineers series. * *Time and place*: the interplanetary future, on Mercury. * *Background:* Mercury is basically inhospitable, with a frigid side and a boiling hot side, but with a small libration zone that is the seat of human extractive industries. * Wiljon Kar and Mardico arrive at the small post of Satania, where relief is needed, since some catastrophe has befallen the observatory, killing much of the complement. The aged commandant believes that Mercury really has a life-form that is hostile and dangerous. * As Kar and the others watch, a gigantic bluish bubble appears and carries away their spaceship. Other mishaps follow. * The resolution: The blue mass is really a gathering of electric energy that precipitates on things. It seems to have a life of sorts, but does not seem to be intelligent. The author is not clear on these points.

821. **A PRINCESS OF PALLIS** [*sic*]. *Astounding Stories,* October 1935. Ill. Dold.
Short story. * The third story in the Wiljon Kar-Flying Engineers series. * Kar and the *W62* have been assigned to a secret mission, investigating a peculiar suction that has been attacking (and sometimes capturing) freighters near the asteroids Juno and Pallis. (Presumably the asteroid Pallas is meant.) * The *W62* runs into trouble even before takeoff. Old Lieutenant Mardico, a little the worse from celebrating, is about to board ship when a beautiful young woman intercepts him, pushes him aside, enters the ship, and slams the port in his face. Since there are

apparently no bed checks, roll calls, or inspections in the Flying Engineers, Commander Wiljon Kar does not know (1) that Mardico is not on board; (2) that there are various stowaways hidden about the ship; (3) that the young woman, whose name is Sulla Tradine, will seize control of the ship. * Mardico, commandeering a freighter, catches up with the *W62*, disables it, boards it, and turns the tables on the young woman. After various ups and downs, the Flying Engineers triumph. The mysterious "suctions" were caused by space wreckers centered on Pallis. * *Background:* Some years ago an entrepreneur named Tradine filed claim on the planetoid Pallis, which he developed. Now, his two children—the blonde lady pirate Sulla Tradine and her brother—have set up magnetic energy stations to capture ships, which they loot. * *Miscellaneous:* Sulla brought on board Plutonian scalies, apparently a giant lizard-like form of life that is used in the inner planets for heavy work.

822. **STRANGER FROM FOMALHAUT**. *Astounding Stories,* January 1936. Ill. Marchioni.
Short story. * The fourth story in the Flying Engineers series. * *Place:* space out beyond Pluto. * The *W62* flies to investigate the strange comet that is approaching the solar system. On closer examination, however, the object is revealed to be not a comet, but a gigantic space vessel that attacks the *W62* with a blanketing ray that cuts off power. * The crew of the *W62*, donning spacesuits, board the strange ship, where they encounter its single occupant, a sphere that emits tentacles of burning energy. The men kill it by smashing its energy source. The *W62* is now towing the vessel back into the solar system.

823. **THE W62'S LAST FLIGHT**. *Astounding Stories,* May 1936. Ill. Wallace Saaty.
Short story. * The last story in the Flying Engineers series. * As the control personnel on Mars report, the *M31*, one of the largest passenger vessels in space, en route from Mars to Venus has inexplicably left its course and is heading directly toward the sun. *W62* to the rescue! * As Wiljon Kar and comrades approach the *M31*, not only is the heat unbearable, but their vessel is being dragged along (even though the propellants are shut down) with the *M31*. The explanation: a small inner planetoid, perhaps once a satellite of Mercury, that has been transformed into a gas that attracts metal. * The crew of the *W62* is sent over to the *M31*, and Kar and Mardico remain alone, intending a suicidal rescue of the trapped passenger vessel. Kar, though badly injured, forces the *W62* into the gaseous formation. The ship explodes, but Kar and Mardico survive and will be picked up. And the *M31* is safe. * Routine, and somewhat confusingly presented, despite the simplistics.

Other Works

824. **THE HEAT DESTROYERS**. *Wonder Stories,* December 1933. Ill. Saaty.
Short story. * An episode in the war of A.D. 2414-2434 between the forces of Asia, led by the Russian Zanoff, and those of Europe and America. The Asians, called here Changs because their main component is Chinese, have won major victories, and the battleground is now in the Southwestern United States. * Three planes have the mission of flying through and over the invader's lines to deliver identical packages to certain destinations. Two of the planes, including one flown by Captain Rondo, make it after engagements in the air and on ground.

Kruse, Clifton B. (*continued*)

Equipment is set up—a heat-death ray, and the Asians are decisively beaten. Similar victories take place in Poland and Italy. The Swedish soldier Anderson plays a significant part disguised as a Chinese.

825. **THE DEATH PROTOZOAN.** *Amazing Stories,* February 1934. Ill. Morey.

Short story. * Professor Von Sinka, the great microscopist, has developed an optical apparatus that might be termed a supermicroscope. Instead of using lenses, it focuses meeting beams of light that can magnify many more diameters than any conventional viewing apparatus. * Among the items that Sinka demonstrates to his learned guests is a new, lethal form of life that he calls the death protozoan. It is something like an amoeba with many cilia. The scientists watch as the protozoan demolishes a laboratory mouse. The only defense against it is high heat. * The occasion is not academic, but tragic, as is soon learned. Somehow Sinka has become contaminated with the protozoan, and cremation is in order.

826. **DR. LU-MIE.** *Astounding Stories,* July 1934. Ill. Dold.

(Reprinted in Wollheim, *Every Boy's Book of Science-Fiction.*)

Short story. * *Place:* Colombia. * Robert Warrington, about to manage a plantation in Colombia, learns unexpectedly that he has no job, hence is quite willing to accept the hospitality of Dr. Lu-Mie, a chance acquaintance who lives near Bogota. Lu-Mie's house is strange, however; a series of rooms that look as if they were poured of cast concrete, plus a heating arrangement that seems to involve fungi. Warrington, becoming more and more suspicious and uncomfortable, insists on leaving, whereupon Lu-Mie reveals himself as a gigantic termite that has been disguised as a human. * Lu-Mie explains. He wants to learn more about human ways and more about the outside world, hence will keep Warrington as an informant. Some time earlier the termite group to which he belongs, deciding that they would take over the world from mankind, bred and reared him suitably, so that he is human in many ways. * Lu-Mie is friendly and pleasant enough, despite his holding Warrington captive, and a certain empathy grows between the man and the termite. But Warrington, realizing that the termite nutriment he is receiving and his association with Lu-Mie are gradually depriving him of humanity, decides to make a break for liberty. At the last minute he is trapped, whereupon Lu-Mie, recognizing the bond of friendship even between alien creatures, permits him to leave. * An unusual message and some powerful symbolic statements, despite crude writing and some logical weaknesses.

827. **OSA THE KILLER.** *Astounding Stories,* January 1935. Ill. Dold.

Short story. * *Time:* 1936. * The notes of Harvard student Frank Williams, who has visited his uncle Peter Wilfred Williams, the famous entomologist, and has taken part in an experiment. * Professor Williams, generally known as Peter Bill, has invented the green ray, a device that permits a human to experience the life of an insect. Donning thought helmets, Frank and Peter Bill watch moments in the life and death of Osa, a praying mantis. * When Osa is killed by a larger, superior mantis, something goes wrong, and the experiment ends suddenly, with Peter Bill in a coma. To restore the scientist to consciousness, the authorities foolishly decide to reverse the experiment. Unfortunately, they only succeed in bringing to the fore the personality

of Osa, which had lodged in Peter Bill's brain. Professor Williams, now mentally a mantis, tries, and succeeds to some extent, to eat one of his scholarly colleagues, raw. The matter is hushed up.

828. **DON KELZ OF THE I.S.P.** *Astounding Stories,* February 1936. Unsigned ill. (Brown?)

Short story. * The first of a series about Don Kelz, set in the same universe and the same time period as the Flying Engineer series. Kelz is a free-floating agent of the Interplanetary Secret Police. * *Time:* the interplanetary future. *Place:* mostly on Mars, which is a sort of Wild West barroom ambience. * *Background:* Although Wiljon Kar, as described in #819, "Menace from Saturn," has destroyed Saturn, the danger is not yet past. A keg of Saturnian dextronite has been hijacked and is circulating among outlaw bands on Mars. Dextronite is so powerful that when activated it could devastate a large portion of Mars. * Kelz is tracking down the space rats who first legitimately came upon the explosive. Of these only old Max Durr is still living. Durr agrees to help Kelz, who deputizes him after a fashion. The quest involves a crooked high official, who hopes to conquer Mars, and ends in a cliffhanger as an atomic cannon (whose radiation is likely to set off the dextronite) is burning down a barrier behind which Kelz has taken refuge.

829. **THE DRUMS.** *Astounding Stories,* March 1936. Unsigned ill.

Short story. * *Time:* the interplanetary future. *Place:* Saturn. * The second adventure of Don Kelz of the I.S.P. and his elderly associate, former space rat Max Durr. Saturn was not so badly damaged as reported in #819, "Menace from Saturn." Not only does the planet still exist, but about four million human blacks from Earth, who can stand the climate better than whites, have colonized it. Kelz is now investigating the peculiar disappearance of such blacks into the jungles. * As he and Durr soon learn, the blacks have been captured and enslaved by gnolls, the surviving natives of Saturn. It was generally believed that the gnolls—who are green lizard-like, tentacled creatures—became extinct after their civilization was shattered by Wiljon Kar and a follow-up campaign, but, no, they still flourish. * Captivities and escapes are followed by a successful rebellion of the slave-chains against the gnolls. It is not clear whether the Saturnians are finally exterminated, or whether this is only a local incident. * *Miscellaneous:* The drums, in this story of African adventure transferred to Saturn, seem to be used as signals.

830. **CODE OF THE SPACEWAYS.** *Astounding Stories,* July 1936. Ill. Schneeman.

Short story. * *Time:* the interplanetary future. * The Interplanetary patrol ship *X9* is about to land at Crystal Base on Uranus, when a mysterious warning arrives. Disregarding the warning, the *X9* approaches, whereupon it is struck with a crippling neutron blast. The disabled vessel manages to land about fifty miles away from Crystal Base. * Charter Dubinsky ("charter" being some sort of junior officer or subaltern), who knows Crystal Base, volunteers to enter the base secretly and regain control of it, for it obviously has been seized by pirates of some sort. Disabling the ventilation system, he enters, outwits the outlaws, and frees the captive station members. The outlaws, who had hoped to seize the *X9*, had a paralysis ray. * *Miscellaneous:* Dubinsky is one of the few instances in the pulp s-f of the day of a non-WASP leading character.

831. **FLIGHT OF THE TYPHOON.** *Astounding Stories,*

Kruse, Clifton B. (*continued*)
October 1936. Ill. Dold.

Short story. * *Time:* the interplanetary future. *Place:* the asteroid belt. * The *Typhoon*, a small freighter, has been assigned to fly directly through the asteroid belt from Mars to Io, in an attempt to find a shorter route than is presently used. The story is told through Cadet Carter. * As might be expected, the *Typhoon* hits trouble. First there is a sand blast (swarm of tiny particles) that cuts through the hull, then the ship almost hits a small planetoid. Carter, acting impulsively, discards the underslung reserve storage elements. This saves the ship, but loses necessary food and water. More hardships follow, and several crew men die. * The rocket engines explode, and the ship is heading out of control toward Jupiter. The only hope of survival is being intercepted by rescuers from Io, but there is no way to signal. Not quite correct: One of the crew, the pleasant, obese quartermaster who had befriended Carter, deliberately turns himself into an electric torch, killing himself, but permitting his buddies to survive. * The stark realism is somewhat better than the loose flying engineer stories.

LANE, GORDON
U.S. advertising man, then resident in Belle Vernon, Pa.

832. **ALMOST AN INTERPLANETARY STORY.** *Amazing Stories,* September 1929.

The title has obviously been assigned by Dr. Sloane. * Short-short piece imbedded in a letter in the readers' column. * Lane describes a spaceship made of concentric spherical shells of aluminum, the interstices filled with a new gas with superior lifting power. * Rising toward the Moon, the sphere encounters along the way a Sargasso of space, which consists of a small secondary satellite and an assortment of air vessels that the satellite has captured in periodic near approaches to Earth. Among these captives are the plane and corpse of the Red Baron von Richthofen, André's balloon, the remains of Nungesser and Coli, and other air disappearances. * Also present is a strange helicopter-like vehicle that contains a luminescent disk that transmits messages telepathically. It is an age-old machine from the Moon, while it was still inhabited (by a human white race). The lunar population was wiped out when a comet swept over its surface. The lunar craters are the remains of gigantic foxholes the inhabitants dug as refuges against the comet.

LANE, SPENCER
A house pseud. The Street and Smith payment cards record that $75 was paid to "Warner Van Lorne," in this case Nelson Tremaine. The pseud. was used since Tremaine had a story under the Van Lorne name in the same issue.

833. **ORIGIN OF THOUGHT.** *Astounding Stories,* June 1936. Unsigned ill.

Short story. * Professor Abelard Hill is one of the sensations of the day. Proclaiming that thought has active power, he has established what amounts to a cult that studies his theories and practices his mental exercises. Many say that he is a charlatan, but his followers claim to be able to work various feats of telekinesis. It is to this man that stony-broke Jerry Moore applies for a job advertised in the newspaper. * Hill offers him the job, which pays handsomely. In exchange Moore must first train his mind according to Hill's method, then permit himself to

be teleported somewhere by the mass thoughts of Hill's followers. The experiment works; Moore disappears, no one knows where, for Professor Hill did not specify a location. * Moore awakes in a gray misty milieu filled with a vague light. He wanders about aimlessly on a spongy ground, growing more and more tired, hungry, and thirsty. At the height of his discomfort, however, he envisions food and drink, which appears before him and is totally material. Postulating that he can create things by thought, he makes a comfortable bed and other furnishings for himself. Then, missing his girlfriend, Helen, Hill's secretary, he envisions her, and she appears, white and trembling. (Since this is pure-minded science-fiction of the '30s, there is no direct connection between the bed and Helen.) * By now Moore has recognized, from what Helen has told him of missing furniture, that he is not creating things, but is teleporting them from our world. He and Helen decide to experiment with sending things back, including Helen. Helen, if and when she returns to Earth successfully, is to urge Hill to exert his group's mental powers and bring Moore back. It works. * Professor Hill, dismayed, proclaims that Moore, when he was at the origin of thought, might have caused enormous damage—"unmade universes." The professor will suppress his higher teaching and conduct no more dangerous experiments. The upshot is that Hill is now considered a charlatan, and Moore and Helen will marry. * Routine at best.

LASSER, DAVID and KELLER, DAVID H., M.D.
Lasser (1902-1996), although a fairly important political figure in the 1940s, is now mostly remembered as Hugo Gernsback's managing editor for the *Wonder* magazines from their inception until the summer of 1933, at which time he was replaced by Charles Hornig. Lasser, who received a degree in engineering management from M.I.T., after a succession of small jobs was hired by Gernsback in 1929 as editor of *Science Wonder Stories* and *Air Wonder Stories*. As Lasser has stated, he had had no editorial experience and at first lacked skills, but developed them while concentrating on the scientific and literary aspects of stories published. Lasser proved to be a good editor, and such improvement as took place in the magazines was due to his efforts. Lasser was also an activist for various political and economic causes, and was discharged by Gernsback for neglecting his job. As Gernsback said, in effect, "Since you are so interested in the unemployed, you can now join them." * In the early 1930s Lasser was one of the pioneers in American rocketry, founding and serving as the first president of the American Interplanetary Society, later renamed the American Rocket Society, a semiprofessional organization that was very effective. In 1931 he wrote *The Conquest of Space*, which is said to be the first serious but popular book in English about space travel. * After leaving the pulp world Lasser entered politics and labor activities. He formed the Workers Alliance and apparently was instrumental to some extent in the formation of the W.P.A., from which he was barred by congressional act. During World War II he served on the War Production Board. After World War II he was on the staff of Averil Harriman and conducted various union activities. Apparently a hated man in certain political circles, with the unprofitable distinction of being personally denounced in Congress by Martin Dies and Everett Dirksen. The following story displays many of his social attitudes. * See also collaboration as by Jerome Gross and

Lasser, David and Keller, David H., M.D. (*continued*)
Richard Penny for possible pseudonymous work. * Keller's career is covered separately. In the present story Lasser provided the idea, which Keller developed: "Lasser gave me the plot and three thousand words of notes. I wrote the novel and sent it to him and he operated on it. After the operation I did not recognize the poor thing. Lasser had amputated some of my best chapters" (Schwartz and Weisinger, "David H. Keller, M. D.," p. 4). Lasser was equally dissatisfied.

834. **THE TIME PROJECTOR**. *Wonder Stories*, July-August 1931. Ill. Paul.
Short novel. * *Time:* 1950. *Place:* Various areas around the United States, including a secret hideout in the Blue Ridge Mountains. * *Background:* There have been strange visions in the sky around New York City; projections of a sort, they show future events with remarkable accuracy. They have caused an enormous amount of popular interest, sometimes violent, with rioting and police suppression of crowds. Big business is upset, since investments are suffering because of some of the information revealed and because of new questions about the future. The more reactionary tycoons are sure that the pictures are the work of anarchists or other radicals, and conservative politicians in Washington rush through a bill suppressing social protest. Others, like the great lawyer William Blake, the father of young millionaire Carol Dunfrey's girlfriend Joan, believe that the pictures are produced by a scientist of genius who is trying to destroy our social fabric. * The story is concerned mostly with Carol Dunfrey, the richest young bachelor in the world. Greatly depressed by the recent deaths of his parents he is just beginning to reenter life, and he hasn't been aware of the sky pictures. * Now a mystery opens up before him. A posthumous note from his father urges him to help Henry Booth and tells him, in a complicated way, how he should locate Booth. Who is Booth? All that Carol learns, after cloak and daggerish episodes, is that both his parents knew Booth and trusted him, and that Booth is important. * Now, following instructions, Dunfrey is in his private plane flying toward the Blue Ridge Mountains to meet Booth. When he reaches a certain mountain, the mountain top slides open, revealing a large open space, into which he descends. He meets Booth, obviously a man of genius, who greets him and explains much. * It is Booth who has been producing the pictures. Funded by Carol's father, he has spent his life building a supercomputer (my term) that takes into account an almost infinite number of variables and can create images of things to come. His purpose in showing the pictures is not frivolous; his apparatus reveals that in twenty years there will be an incredibly savage world war. He wants his machine to be used to prevent that war, and is building credence by revealing the future in small ways. * At first suspicious, Carol becomes convinced both of Booth's honesty and the importance of his work. He buys a newspaper and begins propagandizing in favor of the cloud pictures. * Plots and actions become complex. Joan Blake learns of the situation and becomes converted. Her father, who is brilliant and ruthless, suspects Carol's involvement and uses his vast fortune to track down Booth. A prevision of an earthquake that will level Los Angeles forces Carol to interview the President of the United States in order to have the city evacuated—vainly. Carol is declared an outlaw. And Blake's forces zero in on the hollow mountain. * Eventually, the story turns into a clash of philosophies of life when Booth and

Blake meet. Booth believes that he can help mankind by predicting evils and then avoiding them. Blake rejects this point of view, affirming that this is in itself a danger and that man must progress by his own good decisions and mistakes. The two men cannot agree, although both recognize that the war must be averted. * A resolution comes when Booth's apparatus apparently reveals that he and the apparatus will be destroyed in a bombing raid set off by Blake. This is what happens. Perhaps enough has been learned that the war may be aborted? * Reasonably good pulp fiction. Stylistically, the story lacks Keller's sometimes pompous homespun quality.

LAWRENCE, RAYMOND EMERY
Perhaps the same person as the Raymond E. Lawrence who was a contributor to *Adventure*. No other information.

835. **THE POSTERITY FUND**. *Amazing Stories*, May 1929. Ill. Paul.
Short story. * *Time:* The frame situation is in the middle twenty-sixth century; the reminisced situation is in 2130. * The human race, almost extinct, has lapsed into primitivism, with small villages and a bow-and-arrow culture. The old man (Sylvester Krantos), who is in danger of being expelled from the village, claims to have been all over the world and to be more than five hundred years old. * He reminisces to a boy and girl. In the twentieth century human biology had advanced sufficiently that longevity treatments were common. As a result the world became overpopulated. There were age riots, in which almost all the immortal elderly were killed. Krantos, however, survived, and became cashier in an important New York bank. * The Great Destruction came in 2130. It was the result of several factors. Economic: Centuries earlier the institution of posterity funds took the popular fancy, and towns invested sums of money that could not be disturbed and would be accessible only generations, perhaps hundreds of years later. The number of these posterity funds is great, but until the present they presented no problem. They were covered. A lifestyle factor: Synthetic food has been developed, and it is so good and so nourishing that natural food has fallen into disfavor. Agriculture has just about ceased. Since the banks covered their posterity funds with land value, they are greatly worried. Third, a psychological factor: The towns now begin to withdraw their posterity funds. A panic arises, coming to a crisis at Krantos's bank. His superior, President Hendershot, shows strain, and the mobs attack the bank building. * There is an antiburglar poison gas system, and when this is ineffective against the mobs, Hendershot releases the poison gas generally. A catalytic reaction carries it around the world, and almost the entire human race dies. * Krantos survives, though ill, because of his immortality treatments. A few men and women, who were in a submarine, also survive. They are the ancestors of the primitives among whom Krantos lives. * Some echoes of Jack London's *The Scarlet Plague*, but an intelligent, if somewhat long-winded, story.

[Anonymous]
Presumably a British writer.

836. **THE LEGION OF THE LOST**. *Scoops*, 31 March 1934. Ill. S. D.
Boys' fiction. * Short story. * *Time:* the near future. * The great Professor John Halifax has just been murdered by his deaf and dumb Chinese assistant, who departs immediately for the East

"The Legion of the Lost" (*continued*)
with Halifax's invention. This is a matter transmitter that operates by turning electrons into waves, transmitting them via radio, and reassembling them. * Eighteen months pass, and then very peculiar disturbances of the ether (i.e., radio reception) are observed. Inexplicable Oriental corpses are found in a small town in England; the corpses look as if they have been imploded. * Secret Service man Claude Radlett, newly arrived from Kaito, the capital of the Empire of the East (which includes China and Japan) is able to put two and two together and figure out what is happening, especially since he observed a secret mobilization of crack troops in the East. A further clue comes when he sees in London Marshal Yongi, whom he had left in Kaito only a matter of hours before. * Proceeding to the area where the corpses were found, Radlett and associates discover a peculiar radio installation. A raid reveals that the Orientals were matter-transmitting an army to England, with the intention of conquest. The invasion was caught in time. Some of the Oriental soldiers were transmitted, but not recovered, hence the title of the story.

LEINSTER, MURRAY

Pseud. of William Fitzgerald Jenkins (1895-1974). U.S. (born in Norfolk, Virginia) writer, active in many genres of pulp fiction, generally considered one of the better writers in the area. Leinster's career in s-f extended from 1919 with "The Runaway Skyscraper" to the last years of his life. Throughout this period Leinster capably remained abreast of developments, often producing work that matched that of his younger, more acclaimed fellow-writers. * As a professional pulp writer, of course, Leinster was constrained to follow editorial preferences, with the result that all his work is not on the same level. It is generally conceded that his best work is to be found in the short stories written in the decade and a half after World War II. His novels tend to be more formulaic than his short stories. In later years he was often called the Dean of Science-Fiction Writers, a fitting acclamation. Leinster was also a very versatile man, well-read in science and history of culture, with several inventions to his credit, notably a projection technique used in motion pictures.

837. THE RUNAWAY SKYSCRAPER. *Amazing Stories*, June 1926. Unsigned ill.

(First published in *Argosy*, 22 February 1919. Reprinted in Ross, *The Best of Amazing*.)
Novelett e, described in more detail in *Science-Fiction: The Early Years*. According to Leinster, the story was begun as joke upon an editor, but, to Leinster's surprise, was accepted. * Strange sensations and peculiar behavior on the part of the sun, which rises in the west and sets in the east, with ever increasing speed, accompany the nudging of the Metropolitan Building into the fourth dimension (time). The building ends in precolonial New York, when Manhattan is a forested wilderness. Arthur Chamberlain, an engineer, and his secretary, Estelle, are the leading characters. As the strongest will and best brain among the skyscraper's involuntary passengers, Chamberlain orders matters for temporary survival and work out a way for the skyscraper to return to its original time. Chamberlain theorizes that the building was too heavy for its foundations, whence its settling in time. Perhaps if the building could be lifted a little, it would fall temporarily back into "place." Such is done. The time travelers have been away for about two weeks, though the building returns only a matter of seconds after it left. *

Leinster's first science-fiction story, handling a theme that he returned to several times—civilized men forced to survive under primitive conditions. * Not high literature, but still more readable than most of the other stories described in this book.

838. THE MAD PLANET. *Amazing Stories*, November 1926. Ill. Paul.

(First published in *Argosy*, 10 June 1920. Reprinted in Moskowitz, *Under the Moons of Mars*, and in revised form in Leinster, *The Forgotten Planet*.)
Novelette. * *Time:* about A.D. 50,000, when as a result of huge volcanic emissionsthe climate has changed greatly, extinguishing almost all animals and plants, except gigantic insects and fungi. Humanity survives, but in a very degenerate form that has lost almost all culture, including fire. This story and its sequel focus on Burl, a young man of more intelligence than his fellows, who takes first steps on the road back to civilization. The plot is essentially a series of confrontations and escapes involving enormous predacious insects, such as wasps the size of horses. Burl learns to use the first weapon, a spear. * Overlong, but entertaining. * For a sequel see #839, "The Red Dust."

839. THE RED DUST. *Amazing Stories*, January 1927. Ill. R.

(First published in *Argosy*, 8 April 1921. Reprinted in revised form in Leinster, *The Forgotten Planet*.)
Sequel to #838, "The Mad Planet." * *Time:* about A.D. 50,000. * This story continues the adventures of Burl and his group. Their living territory becomes saturated with deadly spores of a new type of fungus that spreads rapidly. Burl and his people must move elsewhere. The same sort of encounters with hypertrophied insects occurs as in "The Mad Planet"; during the course of events Burl learns leadership and becomes the first chief. Mankind is starting its upward path again. * Too much of the same.

840. TANKS. *Astounding Stories*, January 1930. Ill. J. Fleming Gould.

Short story. * An episode in the War of 1932. * The approach is fairly detailed naturalism of World War I mode, with doughboy central figures who grouse and complain. The model would seem to be the American Expeditionary Force stories of Leonard Nason that were appearing in *Adventure*. * The enemy is not identified, but is Oriental, probably Japanese; the locale is somewhere in the United States. * The battle is shaping up with artificial fog and poison gas. The big problem is determining what the numerically superior enemy commander has in mind. The American general, using information furnished by two infantrymen stranded in a foxhole, is able to outwit the Oriental general. The deciding factor is psychological: the American general understands the motivations and drives of the Oriental, with whom he is acquainted. The Oriental general does not want mere victory, but a brilliant victory that will be praised in the literature of the art of war. The Americans win. * Very little science-fictional material except superior poison gas and gigantic tanks. Competent commercial work of the period, but Nason did it better for World War I.

841. MURDER MADNESS. *Astounding Stories*, May-August 1930. Ill. J. Fleming Gould.

(Reprinted in book form by Brewer and Warren, New York 1931.)
Novel. * Essentially a thriller, with only minimal fantastic material. * In essence, though not in story development, the

Leinster, Murray (continued)

Master, a white-haired, courtly elderly South American, has discovered a combination of drugs that produce a peculiar effect. The drugs act on the cortex, resulting in some mental enhancement; but as the drug deteriorates in the blood stream, it turns the user into a violent maniac. A small quantity of the drug, however, restores normalcy. Thus one must use the drug forever—unless the Master has an antidote. * Secret Service men are disappearing; others are raving mad; eventually much of South America is under the domination of the Master, who claims that his purpose is benevolent, to improve mankind. Against this menace acts Charles Bell, who is affiliated with a top-secret government organization, and associates. Bell wins, of course, and the Master, when cornered, surrenders his secret. * There is also a kidnapped maiden, Bell's fiancée. * As is usual with Leinster, a competent work of its sort, with many good touches, but out of place in *Astounding Stories*.

842. **THE FIFTH-DIMENSION CATAPULT**.
Astounding Stories, January 1931. Unsigned ill. (Wesso?)
(Reprinted in Knight, *Science Fiction of the Thirties*.)
Novelette. * Young mathematical-physicist Tommy Reames receives an urgent call to come to Professor Denham's laboratory. The professor is in great danger, and only Reames can help him. * When Reames arrives, he learns that Denham has not only been investigating the fifth dimension, but has an apparatus for visiting it. He and his daughter Evelyn have entered the fifth-dimensional world, and are stranded there, in great peril. The transporting mechanism has burned out, and Denham's slippery German assistant Von Horst does not know how to build another. * Denham's viewer, however, still functions, and it is possible to see Denham and his beautiful daughter in a world of tropical vegetation, strange life-forms, a beautiful golden city in the far distance, and incredibly vicious jungle people who would torture the explorers to death if they captured them. * These jungle people, called the Ragged Men, apparently have a science of a sort, but are motivated by blind hatred of the hitherto unmet dwellers in the golden city. * Denham and his daughter have adventures trying to avoid the Ragged Men; Reames and Smithers, Denham's mechanic, sweat trying to rebuild the apparatus; and Jacaro, a counterpart of Al Capone hovers in the background. * Reames is successful. At a crucial moment he transmits a burst of tommy-gun fire into the fifth dimension to rescue the Denhams, and he retrieves them just as the people of the golden city gas the area. Unfortunately, Jacaro's men storm the laboratory, wound Reames and Smithers, and make off with the catapult. * The fifth dimension is considered spatially, as at right angles to the fourth (time), which is at right angles to the third; the proper bends are made (in part) with solid ammonium, which has a fourth-dimensional aspect. * Competent adventure fiction. For a sequel see #847, "The Fifth-Dimension Tube."

843. **THE POWER PLANET**. *Amazing Stories*, June 1931. Ill. Paul.
Short story. * *Time:* Not dated, but probably the early twenty-first century. * The Power Planet, which is operated internationally, is a gigantic space station about 40,000,000 miles away. It collects electricity, which is distributed to stations on Earth. Its operation is based on the temperature difference between its solar side and dark side. Mail rockets visit it at infrequent intervals bringing supplies, but otherwise it is almost

incommunicado. * Lt. Jimmy Cardigan, watching through the station telescope, observes that war has broken out on Earth. New York and London have gone up in flames, and the lunar power stations have been destroyed. * Since radio waves cannot penetrate the Heaviside layer, the personnel on the Power Planet do not known who is fighting whom on Earth, or exactly what is happening. All that is certainly known is that a war rocket has been spotted heading for the Power Planet; it should arrive soon. The Power Planet, unfortunately, has been established by treaty as an unarmed station. * When, shortly before the war rocket is due, the mail rocket arrives, little more is known, but it brings a female passenger (Miss Blair, the President's daughter), whose presence is not exactly welcomed. * The bulk of the story is devoted to the reactions of the various personalities on the station and the various expediencies that are used to ward off the war rocket when it arrives. Most interesting of the men is Skeptsky, a Jewish officer who does not grieve openly for lost friends and relatives as do the other officers, since he and his people are used to suffering atrocities. * The war rocket arrives, and the best that the personnel of the Power Satellite can do is fire torpedoes from the mail rocket at it. But these are warded off by a field of some sort that destroys their directional apparatus. Skeptsky volunteers to ride and manually control a torpedo. When this is not successful, he kamikazes into the war rocket, destroying it. The danger to the space station is over. * As a pathetic gesture, Skeptsky, before leaving, asked for a farewell kiss from the president's daughter; she refused. * On Earth the aggressor is now known, and defenses are in operation against him. He is not identified. * *Miscellaneous:* The enormous space station grows its own food. * Since the attackers are willing to destroy the Power Planet in order to damage the rest of the world, it is probable that they have atomic energy. * A rapid-fire romance develops between Cardigan and Miss Blair. * Very competent pulp science-fiction, with scientific detail well integrated into the story, excellent pacing, and acceptable characterizations. The romance, of course, is de trop; *Amazing Stories* would undoubtedly have printed the story without it.

844. **MORALE. A STORY OF THE WAR OF 1941-43**.
Astounding Stories, December 1931. Ill. Wesso.
Short story. * *Time:* Not precisely dated beyond the subtitle date. * *Place:* Somewhere on the East Coast. * A war story of a sort, told in the manner of Leonard Nason, mostly focusing on an enlisted man (Sergeant Walpole) who has an observation post somewhere on the coast. The point is psychological. * Near Walpole's post a freighter runs aground. It splits open, and a monster tank about two hundred feet long, forty feet wide, and fifty feet high emerges. It is not primarily an offensive weapon, but a device aimed at American morale, for it simply crunches up things. It is accompanied, however, by bombers that drop explosives and gas bombs. * The Wobbly, as it is called, cannot well be attacked, for a device on its top projects a radio power beam that sets up eddy currents in motors and iron weapons, inactivating them. The Wobbly thus seems invulnerable. * It is finally destroyed by a feint of sorts. A barrage of rockets in front of it arouses the suspicion of its operators, who stop it, whereupon it is hit by friendly fire. Its overhead bombers are unaware that it has stopped (since there seems to be no communication), and do not make allowances for its position. Not a very convincing gimmick. * The enemy is not identified, but it seems to be Oriental and probably Japanese. * As usual with

Leinster, Murray (*continued*)

Leinster, nicely written, but not really s-f and not really war fiction.

845. THE RACKETEER RAY. *Amazing Stories,* February 1932. Ill. Morey.

Short story. * Old Professor Sharpe and his assistant Tommy Garland have just developed what amounts to a super-magnet—differing from a magnet in being focusable and having theoretically an infinite range. To support the project Tommy and Sharpe have been using a small model for ocean salvage. But when the professor unwisely tries to sell salvaged firearms previously discarded by the police, he is arrested and jailed. * While in jail, Sharpe comes to the attention of King Burk, top racketeer, who recognizes the value of the invention. Burk bails out Sharpe, beats him and leaves him for dead, and steals the projector, which he uses for a crime epidemic—bank robberies, assaults on policemen, abductions, all of which the police are powerless to prevent. Finally Tommy and a friendly detective bring down Burk and his mobs by using nonferrous firearms, Very pistols retooled. Sharpe recovered. * Routine for Leinster.

846. POLITICS. *Amazing Stories,* June 1932. Ill. Morey.

(Reprinted in Curtis, *Future Tense,* and in Janifer, *Masters' Choice.*)

Short story. * *Time:* 1934. *Place:* the Pacific, off the coast of California. *Background:* The great Asiatic power, unnamed but obviously Japan, has attacked the United States and in a naval battle has sunk most of the American fleet. The battle was lost because of tactical directives from Washington ordering the fleet commander not to damage the enemy fleet too greatly and to divide his own forces in an unmilitary way. * This defeat is really damaging, for America has disarmed and has little weaponry. The political situation is also very bad, for both Congress and the Executive Branch consist of lily-livered opportunists who are concerned only with holding their jobs. As Leinster says in a direct quote from "Politics," "A politician is a man who believes that the greatest catastrophe that can befall his country is the election of somebody else to the office he wants." * The enemy now insists on a most humiliating peace treaty, which Washington is about to accept. * The men on board the *Minnesota,* however, feel differently. The *Minnesota* is the utmost in naval engineering, with incredible range finders and infrared sensors. Thus, ensconced in a smoke cloud, it wipes out the Asiatic fleet. When a presidential order arrives to surrender the fleet, there is no enemy left to receive the surrender. * Leinster was obviously very hot against politicians and the peace movement of the day. His emotion submerges his usual clarity in a less than routine barrel-shoot.

847. THE FIFTH-DIMENSION TUBE. *Astounding Stories,* January 1933. Ill. Wesso.

Novelette. * Sequel to #842, "The Fifth-Dimension Catapult." * As Reames, recovered from bullet wounds, and Denham learn, Von Horst, using the stolen catapult as a model, has built a fifth dimension tube for Jacaro. Jacaro has raided the Golden City, whose people in retaliation are pouring their horrible poison gas through the tube upon Earth. * Reames and Evelyn venture again into the fifth dimensional world, hoping to make contact with the people of the Golden City and persuade them to cease hostilities. They have adventures among horrible animals and the Ragged Men, whom Reames shoots by the score, perhaps hundred. *

When an aircraft from the city tries to gas them, Tommy captures the flier, to whom he communicates their friendly intention. They are taken to the city of Yugna, where Tommy learns enough language to explain matters to the Council. The members of the Council can accept Tommy's statement of dimensions, since they have a tradition that their remote ancestors came through a similar tunnel to their present world. * The situation in Yugna and elsewhere: The Yugnans are fighting a losing battle against the jungle in a world that is much hotter than Earth. Their science, on the whole, is superior to ours, although there are gaps because of their lack of iron. They have flying machines that utilize a static jet, thermite throwers, and electric charge guns. Their technology is also higher than ours, with one incredible exception: They have never developed automation, governors, or feedback mechanisms, with the result that the population is practically enslaved to the advanced machinery that keeps the culture going. Many of the inhabitants cannot endure the strain and become drug fiends, thence Ragged Men. There are a few other cities in the world, mostly in worse shape than Yugna. * The plot takes several directions. Tommy must persuade the Yugnans not to wipe out Earth-life with their incredibly poisonous gas, then to migrate to Earth. The Yugnans, with Tommy's weaponry, must repel raids from another city, led by Jacaro and his gunmen. And Denham and Smithers, forced to leave Earth through the tube, must begin reforming Yugnan technology enough to make the culture more viable. * There are battles back and forth. The gangsters, fleeing through a misassembled new tube, are tossed into a different dimension. The Yugnans beat off their enemies. And the Earth people, temporarily stranded in the fifth-dimensional world until another tunnel can be built, are esteemed guests. * *Miscellaneous:* There is also a giant toad with considerable hypnotic power. It hungers for Evelyn. * Competent pulp adventure.

848. BORNEO DEVILS. *Amazing Stories,* February 1933. Ill. Morey.

Short story. * *Place:* Borneo. Much local color, but not really science-fiction. * There are strange stories from the interior. Flocks of demon birds with scales and saw-toothed beaks have been attacking people, and the natives have been leaving young women as sacrifices to them. * Captain Houghton of the Sarawak Constabulary investigates. After considerable to-do, including captivities, murders, death by demon-bird attacks, and romance with a handsome white woman, a solution is offered. It is all a fake engineered by a Dutchman and an associate in order to gain control of a ruby deposit. The demon birds were ordinary hornbills with feathers trimmed and painted with aluminum paint, beaks serrated, and fitted with poison on their jaws. The reason that the birds are so vicious is drug craving. The Dutchman has addicted them to Indian hemp, and the birds will do anything to get their fix. * As usual with Leinster, nicely written, but utterly unconvincing, from bird to bride.

849. INVASION. *Astounding Stories,* March 1933. Ill. Wesso.

Short story. * *Time:* A.D. 2037. *Place:* The Rockies. * The world is divided into two factions, the United Nations, which includes the United States, and the Com-Pubs, which seems to include both the modern USSR. and part of Western Europe. Relations between the two factions consist of an armed truce, with borders guarded by constant air flights. * Thorn Hard, a pilot in the Pacific Watch, is on leave in the Rockies with his

Leinster, Murray (*continued*)

girlfriend Sylva, when the trouble begins. Com-Pub radio announces that a strange vessel, apparently from Mars, is approaching Earth. And as Hard watches, a two-hundred-foot-long rocketship settles near him, while radio signals of a strange sort emanate from it. It is presumably the Martian ship. It destroys Thorn's plane, but he is able to approach the rocket ship close enough to see Cyrillic lettering on it. The ship and the Martian episode are thus some sort of Com-Pub trick. * Thorn and Sylva soon learn what is really going on when they are rendered unconscious and captured by Kreynborg, an enormously fat lecher. Kreynborg, obviously a very great Com-Pub scientist, has set up a sphere of impenetrable force around the ship, so that it is unapproachable. And he has a paralysis gun. * Kreynborg explains, intermittently gloating over the delights he shall enjoy with Sylva. The Com-Pub strategy is to lure the air fleet of the United Nations to the area around the force sphere, then to set up a second sphere outside, trapping the fleet between the two force spheres until the men starve to death. While the U.N. fleet is thus trapped, the Com-Pubs will attack. * It all goes as Kreynborg says, and it is up to Thorn, who is alternately a captive and a free man, to shut off the screens. An improvised slingshot brings down Kreynborg, and Thorn shuts off the force screen.

850. **BEYOND THE SPHINXES' CAVE.** *Astounding Stories,* November 1933. Unsigned ill.

Short story. * *Place:* Thessaly. * There is trouble at the mine; several workers have disappeared mysteriously in the lower levels, and the other miners refuse to descend. Blanchard, who has been down before, has seen a strange thing, hence when he and Jimmy Flynn descend, they are armed. And since a foul, disabling smell has been reported, Flynn wears a gas mask. * The first peril the men encounter is a beast with a human head; it fascinates Blanchard, drawing him toward it. Apparently the strong odor it emits is a paralysant. Jimmy, protected, shoots the creature—which is a sphinx. Shortly thereafter, following entry into a system of caves, they encounter a hydra. By now, Jimmy, who knows a little about Classical mythology, recognizes where they are: in Hades. Further events confirm this. * *Background:* The underworld, which is lighted, is ruled by a decadent superior class, somewhat comparable to the ancient gods, who cruelly oppress a slave class. As weapons, the "gods" have a paralysis ray that operates from a Medusa-head device, thunderbolts, a sword heat ray and disintegrator, and large shields that serve as flying platforms of a sort. * Jimmy and Blanchard rescue a beautiful young woman, with whom they are able to communicate after a fashion. She hopes that the outsiders can bring weapons to the slaves for a successful rebellion. * Automatics are effective against novelty weapons, but things become too hot for our heroes, who are forced to retreat back into the cave passages, while the nameless young woman returns to her people with weapons of the gods. * Back on the surface, the two men think momentarily of invading the underworld with troops, but there is an enormous subterranean explosion, the mine collapses, and, obviously, the land of the gods is gone. As the men now say, they saw nothing down there. * A good action romp.

851. **SIDEWISE IN TIME.** *Astounding Stories,* June 1934. Ill. Brown.

(Reprinted in Leinster, *Sidewise in Time;* in Leinster, *The Best of Murray Leinster;* in Asimov, *Before the Golden Age;* and in Silverberg, *Worlds of Maybe.*)

Short novelette. * *Time:* 1935. *Place:* initially Fredericksburg, Virginia, but with later complications. * The basic situation: The Earth suddenly becomes a shifting patchwork of different time segments within the same geographical area as various alternative worlds exchange portions with our world. These changes follow certain spatial boundaries at fairly regular intervals. Thus, a Norse colony, from a universe where the Norse successfully colonized America, takes the place of an eastern metropolis; a Mesozoic jungle with dinosaurs, from a cosmos where the dinosaurs did not die out, appears in an ordinary Eastern woodland; a border town gives access to the Confederate States, which won Gettysburg and the Civil War; an America conquered by Romans maintains villas and harsh slavery, etc. The story is presented in a series of such alternate-time vignettes strung on the narrative thread of Professor Minott's expedition into the new lands. * Minott, a teacher in a small, low-rated college in Virginia, seems to have been the only person to anticipate and understand the breakdown of time and space that has beset the universe. As he explains, it is a question of worlds of if, and the probabilities are that the spasm will destroy the universe. But on the off chance that the universe will survive, he assembles a small group of college students, including a woman he vainly loves, and crosses the boundaries into a sidewise world. * Minott is dictatorial, harsh, and fanatical; he intends to reach a Norse land where he can establish himself as ruler. The students have no idea of his plans until it is too late. * Adventures include encounters with monsters and hostile Indians, and temporary enslavement in a Roman villa. All does not go well for Minott, however, for his charges do not share his goals. The students, feeling that enough is enough, finally rebel. Most of them return to Fredericksburg when its time-space segment manifests itself again, but Minott, with a woman who apparently loves him, continues his venture sidewise into time. There is no indication of his final fate. * A competent thriller, one of the first to recognize the possibilities of alternate worlds.

852. **THE MOLE PIRATE.** *Astounding Stories,* November 1934. Ill. Dold.

(Reprinted in Moskowitz, *Three Stories.*)

Novelette. * *Time:* 1935. * Scientist Jack Hill, of American Electric, had no notion of the problems he would cause when he announced his invention: a technique for interpenetrating matter. It operates by altering the magnetic polarities of atoms, so that matter is perfectly aligned in planes, permitting interpenetration by other matter. Hill not only demonstrates his process with a brass cube, but reveals that he has constructed an "earth plane," a vehicle that can move through matter. The *Mole* is propelled by a screw coated with thorium (since radioactivity creates a certain suspension of the perichoresis) and restrained from sinking through the floor by a similar coating on its base. It works, as Hill demonstrates with a trial run with the great scientist Eisenstein. Unfortunately, Eisenstein turns out to be the scientific criminal Durran, who hijacks the vehicle and departs with it, instituting such a reign of crime as the world has never seen before. Raiding Sing Sing to rescue old comrades in crime, he loots banks with impunity, bombs various cities, murders, and is unrestrainable. All that he has to fear is more powerful earth planes that will track him down. * Durran takes care of this problem by destroying half-built competitive vehicles, hunting down Hill, and finally kidnapping him and his

Leinster, Murray (*continued*)

girlfriend, Gail Kennedy, daughter of the American Electric tycoon. To obtain information from Gail, Durran agrees to release Hill, which he does, dematerialized, furnished with a pair of snowshoe-like supports. Hill must keep in perpetual motion to avoid sinking into the Earth. * But virtue triumphs. Hill figures out an effective, if painful way, to communicate with the world, and is restored to normality. * Meanwhile, Durran has demanded a ransom for New York City, which is about to be delivered. Hill is present at the meeting. Gail is released, and Durran, when he is tricked into dematerializing, discovers that the *Mole* is out of control. Hill has caused chemicals to be strewn about that dissolve the thorium coating of the *Mole's* semimaterializing devices. Durran, his henchmen, and the Mole sink down into the Earth, where Durran explodes the vehicle. * Routine thriller.

853. **PROXIMA CENTAURI.** *Astounding Stories,* March 1935. Ill. Dold.

(Reprinted in Leinster, *Sidewise in Time;* in Leinster, *Monsters and Such;* in Leinster, *The Best of Murray Leinster;* in Asimov, *Before the Golden Age;* and in Gunn, *The Road to Science Fiction #2.*)

Novelette. * *Time:* the interplanetary future. *Place:* space near Proxima Centauri, and planets thereof. * *Background:* The starship *Adastra* has been in flight about ten years and is approaching its goal, the system of Proxima Centauri. The vessel, a globe about a mile in diameter, with a crew of two hundred, is a small biosphere with agricultural resources. Astronautically, the voyage is a brilliant success, but socially there are problems, for the crew (the Muts) has been in a state of near mutiny for much of the voyage, what with boredom, fear, and the overrigid social hierarchy. The officers' quarters and the control rooms are sealed off against the potential mutineers. A second element of discord lies in Helen Bradley, the daughter of the commanding officer; both Alastair, second in command, and Jack Gary, an NCO, are in love with her. She prefers Jack, a situation that will cause complications. * As the *Adastra* nears Proxima Centauri, a spaceship is detected approaching them. From its behavior, Jack reasons out that it is unfriendly, a conclusion verified when the vessel bombards them with various radiations, which do no harm. The attackers, believing that the crew of the *Adastra* has been killed, send over a boarding party, some of whom the Earthmen capture. Communication is established with the captive plant men by means of a language analyzer. * *Background established by this incident:* The Proxima Centaurians, who are roughly humanoid in shape, are a development of mobile carnivorous plants. On their planet, animal life is almost extinct, for animal tissue is both the utmost gustatory delight to them and a status and wealth symbol. Technologically, the plant men are somewhat ahead of the solar system, with faster vessels and more powerful weapons. Oddly enough, their civilization is not founded so much on metal as ours, but on controlled vegetation. Thus, their gigantic spaceship is really the equivalent of an enormous artificial gourd. * When a fleet of Centaurian vessels attacks the *Adastra,* surrender is unavoidable. The result is a horror that could not have been anticipated. The plant men seize most of the crew and all of the animal life of the *Adastra,* beginning a planetary orgy of animal food. Alastair, Gary, and Helen are kept alive, partly so that they can explain some of the unique equipment on

the *Adastra,* partly so that Gary and Helen can become breeding stock in a small planetoid owned by the commander of the plant fleet. * The real concern is not so much the personnel of the *Adastra;* their fate has already been decided and carried out. It is the announced intention of the plant men to send their fleet to the solar system, on which they will descend without warning. * Alastair, who is otherwise an unsympathetic character, finds a solution. The propulsion device of the *Adastra* differs from that of the plant men. It must be shielded in a particular way, or else it will set off a disintegration field. Alastair demonstrates the rockets to the plant men, thereby disintegrating the planet, the fleet, and everything. Helen and Gary, furnished with a marriage license (!), sit on the planetoid awaiting the second Terrestrial vessel, which is on its way. * Some good material, some cliché, and some nonsense. When it was published, "Proxima Centauri" was considered something special; today, it seems much less successful.

854. **THE FOURTH-DIMENSIONAL DEMONSTRATOR.** *Astounding Stories,* December 1935. Ill. Wallace Saaty.

(Reprinted in Leinster, *Sidewise in Time;* in Leinster, *Twists in Time;* in Leinster, *The Best of Murray Leinster;* and in Stong, *The Other Worlds.*)

Short story. * Humor of a slapstick sort. * The ingredients are (1) Peter Davidson, a young playboy, unfortunately penniless. He had counted on the estate of his deceased scientist uncle, but no cash remains. (2) Daisy, a gold-digging dancer or chorus girl, who is currently Peter's inamorata; she will marry him if he has enough money. (3) Arthur, a pet kangaroo, technically the property of Daisy, but in practice a freewheeling nuisance. (4) The demonstrator, really a matter duplicator that presumably operates via time as the fourth dimension. (5) Various U.S. Treasury agents. * Peter's impractical uncle used the demonstrator only as a scientific device, but Peter, on seeing it work, realizes its potential. He duplicates quantities of coinage, gems, gold ingots, and currency. It is the last item that causes trouble, for all the bills have the same serial number. * The agents come, and one is accidentally duplicated by the machine. Daisy falls into the machine and emerges as four more Daisies, each as greedy and obnoxious as the original. And Arthur the kangaroo is turned into a herd that plays together nicely. * As Peter recognizes, the bills will have to be returned in time. Most of the damage is undone, and he and Daisy will have to get along with the bins filled with coins, gold, and gems. * In its day this was considered funny, but now it seems like something for teenagers.

855. **THE INCREDIBLE INVASION.** *Astounding Stories,* August-December 1936. Ill. Wesso .

(Reprinted in book form, revised, as *The Other Side of Here,* Ace Books, New York, 1955.)

Novel. * Essentially a Ray Cummings story of invasion from the fourth dimension, a little updated. * *Time:* probably the near future. *Place:* Newark, and areas up into Westchester County, N.Y. * A brief prologue from 2037 signed by Murray Leinster comments on the technological situation in the late 1930s and 1940. * *Background:* When Professor Straussman theorized that two objects could occupy the same space and time, depending upon atomic alignment, he was largely ignored except by a few specialists. He disappeared. Years later, Professor Blair has been working on Straussman's ideas. He also has disappeared,

Leinster, Murray (continued)

and his daughter Lucy and her boyfriend Steve Waldron are greatly concerned. * An unexpected break comes when Fran Dutt, a young man working in Blair's laboratory, obviously in love with Lucy, leaves a note urging her to flee to the West with Steve, but first meet him in a New York City hotel. Under no circumstances are they to leave Steve's car until they reach the hotel. As the firm-jawed, steely-eyed Steve reflects, there is something suspicious about Dutt; he is not American, origins unknown, and he obviously knows too much. * Steve and Lucy, taking the warning seriously, drive out of Newark just as the mysterious catastrophe strikes. People suddenly fall over, stiff and rigid, perhaps dead, though with no signs of dissolution. Steve and Lucy proceed under nightmarish circumstances. * Meeting Dutt, Steve and Lucy, after "persuasion" of various sorts, learn roughly what is going on, this knowledge being amplified by later events. * *General background:* Straussman and Blair are right; two, indeed several, objects can occupy the same space, and Dutt has come from an other-world based on such atomic alignments. His world has monitored ours for some time, kidnapping scientists who are too close to discovering the other-world, including Professor Blair, who is a captive, but safe. The government of the other-world is an aggressive, repressive, tyrannical oligarchy, with a small group of masters who rule by terror over a much larger body of servitors. The masters plan to conquer our world, or at least a large part of it, and loot it. The masses are not in sympathy with this plan, but lack the power, will, and organization to conduct a successful rebellion. Dutt deplores the aggression and is a member of an ineffectual underground. The strange paralysis, it is later revealed, is caused by radiation, against which there are protective armor as well as makeshift power packs that Steve develops. * The narrative side of the story is concerned first with the flight of Steve and Lucy from the New York City area, then their return to Newark, where they are caught up in the middle of the invasion. There would be no point in listing the ins and outs of their perils. * The aliens are well aware of Steve's knowledge, and using their extensive, powerful fifth column in our culture, have Steve declared a plague carrier to be shot on sight. Steve, on the other hand, works out an electric way to revive those stricken, and a portable defense. His attempts to announce the procedure are repeatedly defeated by chance and the invaders' agents. * Eventually, with protective armor taken from the enemy, and a few lucky breaks, our forces defeat the invaders. Steve forces Dutt to return to his world and start the revolution, which is successful. As the story ends, the invaders will make reparations; our world will find new lands to occupy in the other-world, which is almost unpopulated—a reverse invasion! * *Miscellaneous:* The invader masters, who carry potent hook whips, busy themselves with abducting handsome young women, slinging frozen women about like clothing dummies. * The scientific level of the other-world is somewhat inconsistent. On the one hand, the invaders have developed dimensional doorways, paralyzing radiation and other matters, yet seem to maintain a shoddy civilization. * No explanation is given for their completely human form. * Good in beginning, but the perpetual chase and backtracking lose conviction after a time. The characterizations are not as strong as is usual with Leinster; Steve comes across as a surly grouch. * All in all, not worth reading except as a period piece.

LEITFRED, ROBERT H. (1891-1968)

U.S. author, then resident in Laguna Beach, California. Also wrote mystery novels *The Corpse That Spoke* (1936), *The Man Who Was Murdered Twice* (1937), and *Death Cancels the Evidence* (1938). *Death Cancels the Evidence* is unremarkable.

856. **WHERE GRAVITY ENDS.** *Air Wonder Stories,* September 1929. Ill. Paul.

Short-short story. * In 1917 AEF airman Richard Merrill flew out of a French airport and disappeared. No wreckage of his plane was ever found; he had not been captured by the enemy. In 1919 his diary was picked up in a field in Iowa; it was wrapped in his leather jacket together with an enormously heavy radioactive stone. * The diary: Merrill flies out, falls into a dogfight with a superior German plane, escapes, but the control mechanism of his plane is damaged beyond repair. * He flies on and on, ever higher, until he has to don his oxygen mask. When his engine dies, his plane continues on at fantastic speed, up to 500 mph. Finally, he spies a large body ahead of him, to which his plane is drawn. While he fears a fatal collision, he survives the crash, and finds himself on a planetoid with low gravitation and a little vegetation. But the planetoid starts to break up, poisonous gases fill the air. . .* Astronomical reports indicate that some sort of meteoritic outburst took place at the time Merrill wrote his diary. * Routine, suggestions of Philip M. Fisher's "Beyond the Pole."

857. **PRISONERS ON THE ELECTRON.** *Astounding Stories,* October 1930. Ill. J. Fleming Gould.

Short story. * *Time:* 1999. *Place:* New York. * Professor Dahlgren has invented a size-reducing machine, but unfortunately has fallen victim to it and has presumably been deposited on an electron. * Aaron Carruthers and Karl Danzig are experimenting with the apparatus, though they know that Dahlgren is unquestionably long dead, what with time relativity. Nanette, Danzig's sister, stumbles into the field of the machine, and Aaron, to save her, follows. The two shrink down and eventually land on a savage tropical world, where dinosaurs, giant apes, and apemen range. In peril, they are rescued by the apemen and taken to the last humans, seven men whose ancestors were civilized by Dahlgren. The apemen serve as guards to the humans, chasing away hostile fauna. * It is a savage life, but is rendered even worse by dinosaur attacks and the knowledge that the electron world is breaking up volcanically. * The visitors are rescued just in time by Karl Danzig back in the macrocosm. They spent four months on the electron, although they were away from our world only fifteen seconds. * *Miscellaneous:* Shades of Edgar Rice Burroughs—a gorilla tries to rape Nanette. * In 1999 there are a thirteen-month calendar and food tablets. * Naive work.

858. **PRISMS OF SPACE.** *Astounding Stories,* November 1933. Unsigned ill.

(This story is incorrectly carried as by Robert H. Leitfried.)

Short story. * Bruce Lanyard, returning from Asiatic travels, obeys the summons of old friend Dr. Asa Cadmore. But as Bruce discovers when they meet, Ishtar, Cadmore's daughter and Bruce's sweetheart, is not present. Where is she? * Cadmore explains. He has invented a system of matter transmission in which matter is transformed into light and deposited elsewhere. Ishtar entered the apparatus and arrived safely somewhere (not precisely located, but presumably Mars). Cadmore, however, can no longer see her and be certain of her safety, for Martian (?) scientists have driven back a black beam that destroyed

Leitfred, Robert H. (*continued*)

Cadmore's prisms. It has taken him a long time to reconstruct suitable duplicate apparatus. * Bruce volunteers to follow Ishtar and rescue her, although he knows that the venture is chancy. Landing on the strange world, he is captured by tall, bronze-skinned humans, who have an immediate and important use for him. They intend to transplant the head of their ailing ruler onto Bruce's body. Luckily for Bruce, Cadmore retrieves him in time. * On a second try, Bruce is again captured, but on this occasion he meets Ishtar, who holds the position of resident goddess. Together they plot to escape, but they are caught up in a palace revolution in which the scientists plan to depose the ruling religionists. Cadmore retrieves them just in time. At the last minute before leaving, Bruce managed to destroy the alien counterpart to Cadmore's apparatus, thus preventing further interference. Back on Earth, Cadmore destroys his own apparatus. * Difficult to believe that the author was serious.

LEMKE, HENRY E.

According to Schwartz/Weisinger, pseud. of Richard Tooker, who has a separate entry.

859. **THE LAST OF THE SWARM**. *Wonder Stories*, October 1933. Ill. Paul.

Short story. * *Time:* 1972 on. *Place:* mostly Kentucky, along the Mississippi. * Political background: World War II ended in 1969; the combatants are not identified. What with world peace, the military establishment of the United States is greatly curtailed, and Birdsley Ames, chief technician in the military laboratories, has been fired. He is working privately. * Geographical background: Since 1960, the Southeast, including Florida, Alabama, Louisiana, Georgia, etc., has been gradually sinking, so that it has become largely salt marsh with occasional islands. The cause is not known, nor can anything be done about it. * Ames and the narrator retire to Kentucky to continue private research, until around 1980 the menace appears. These are gigantic mosquitoes the size of small birds, whose bite releases a toxic substance that creates not only numbness but coma. They travel in huge flocks, and wherever they fly, mankind perishes. * Because of their size and numbers, there is no real defense against them except heavy nets, and mankind seems in danger. A mosquito raid against Chicago, for example, resulted in more than two hundred thousand deaths. * The government recalls Ames and places him in charge of the campaign against the insects. He and his assistant have many narrow escapes before Ames comes up with the answer, a disease fatal to the insects. * Ames acts strangely when inoculating captive mosquitoes with his weapon, and refuses even the narrator access to his working materials. * The reason for all this eventually emerges: In a farewell note Ames reveals that the disease is just as fatal potentially to humans as to insects, and he himself carries it. He thereupon destroys himself and anything else that might cause problems. * Competent thriller, though a familiar theme.

LEMKIN, WILLIAM, Ph.D. (1897-1978)

U.S. (New York City) chemist, educator. Born in Poland. Ph.D. 1922 from New York University, thesis on neutral salts. Author of textbooks that underwent several editions: *Exploring the New World of Science*, 1969; *Graphic Survey of Chemistry*, last ed. 1969. Teacher in New York High School of Science. One of

the leaders of the American Interplanetary Society/American Rocket Society. Died in New York City. Lemkin was also a capable illustrator and cartoonist, contributing to Gernsback's *Science and Invention* and *French Humor* magazines.

860. **COLD LIGHT**. *Amazing Stories*, November 1929. Ill. McGerr.

Short story. * The narrative is divided into two sections. First, rural scares, as a shining man or a glowing head appears around the countryside, to the great consternation of the local folk. * Second, the experiences of old Dr. Hament, as he is trying to duplicate the cold light of the firefly. * Hament is successful, producing a remarkable lighting device that he calls the Hament Colite Luminar. On attempting to market it to the gigantic International Illumination Corporation, however, he is treated scurvily. He is insulted and slandered, and his laboratory is burglarized as the corporation tries to steal his invention. The IIC scientists try to duplicate the Luminar from his stolen notes, but produce nothing of value. * Hament, in a public appearance, denounces IIC, explains their errors (neglect of a catalyst), and demonstrates his remarkable invention. He was also the glowing man who appeared around the countryside. * Disorganized, heavily overladen with technical exposition.

861. **VITAMINE Z**. *Amazing Stories*, February 1930. Ill. Morey.

Short story. * Reporter Paul visits his old teacher, the great Professor Beardsley, who explains his life work. Beardsley, now very old and feeble, has been working on the assumptions that the bacterial theory of disease is wrong and that all human ailments are the result of nutritional deficiencies. As he explains, he has discovered some twenty different vitamines, some of which have spectacular effects: curing rabies, typhus fever, poliomyelitis, etc. almost instantly. Beardsley demonstrates his results to Paul both in the lab and clinically. * But Beardsley's greatest triumph is the isolation of vitamine Z, which, as he demonstrates on a rat, will cure senility and old age. Beardsley is just about to inject himself with vitamine Z when he keels over from a heart attack and dies instantly. The syringe with the fluid is broken, and the fluid is so volatile that analysis would have been impossible, even if the narrator had thought of it. * Much superior to the previous story.

862. **AN ATOMIC ADVENTURE**. *Wonder Stories Quarterly*, Fall 1930. Ill. Marchioni.

Short story. * The pathetic fallacy, the life and times of a carbon atom. For one reason or other the atom has no memory of past events, although he is admittedly (almost) eternal. Learning about atomic life and theory from a friendly fellow carbon atom, he joins with oxygen atoms and is finally destroyed in a human laboratory as he is turned into electricity. * Boring.

863. **THE ECLIPSE SPECIAL**. *Amazing Stories*, December 1930. Ill. Morey.

Short story. * *Time:* perhaps 1993. * Astronomer Boyd and his friends Fleming and the narrator discuss the difficulties of observing total eclipses of the sun. Observation means arduous travel, transportation of heavy equipment, inconvenience, all for an event of a few minutes, which may not even be observable because of bad weather conditions. Fleming suggests following the eclipse by plane, holding the eclipse in sight. Boyd rejects this as impossible for several reasons. * But there is an interesting phenomena that was recorded by several (but not all) groups during a recent eclipse, the suggestion of a new force

Lemkin, William (*continued*)
called tentatively the solunaray. * Some time later Boyd summons his friends. He has investigated the solunaray and has found that it exists and is extremely powerful. Further, he has constructed an air vessel that will lock onto it, permitting hours of perfect observation of an eclipse. The ship will be used on the approaching Arctic eclipse. * The ship works perfectly, forced along by the solunaray, but there is some difficulty in breaking the hold that the ray has. All ends well. * Science in the 1990s is high, with antigravity, atomic power, and great advances in medicine and other fields.

864. **BLUE WATERS**. *Amazing Stories Quarterly*, Winter 1932. Ill. Morey.
Novelette. * *Place:* the Badlands of Nevada. * Duncan (the narrator) and Arthur Morley (a chemist) have been prospecting in the desert for osmium, since Morley is convinced that one of the osmium oxides will have enormous commercial value. The two men are winding up their successful exploration with a large quartz jar of osmium supernitrate when they hear the Indian legend of the Blue Lake. * Morley, for reasons that are revealed later, is intensely interested and although the local Indians fear the Blue Lake as cursed and the home of a demon, learns its general location. A succession of guides takes the two men close to the area, despite every imaginable obstacle that nature can put in their way. * At last, in the broken country, they find the blue lake, which is as bright in color as reputed. Morley now explains: He speculated that the coloration was due to colloidal gold, and a few simple experiments have proved him right. The lake, which is about two miles by one, and so deep that a sounding cord does not reach bottom, must contain at least one hundred thousand tons of gold. Morley is not worried about the effect that this amount of gold will have on the economy, but concerns himself with the scientific aspect of the colloid. * Nature or the curse of the land decides matters otherwise than Duncan and Morley would have wished. A violent storm arises, and the two men, who are out on the lake in a small birch bark canoe that they use for exploring, are lucky to survive. By accident the jar of osmium supernitrate, which Morley has with him in the canoe, is spilled. * The next morning, the lake is no longer blue. Morley explains: The osmium precipitated the gold to the unfathomably deep bottom of the lake, and it is lost. The two men leave. * A reader may speculate that if Morley had been an engineer rather than a chemist, he would not have given up so easily. * Reasonable geographical adventure for the most part, but very hard on the Indians, whom the author despises.

865. **A MATTER OF NERVES**. *Amazing Stories*, June 1932. Ill. Morey.
Long short story. * The narrator strikes up a park bench acquaintance with a miserable looking young man named Carl Vernon. As acquaintance grows, Vernon reveals that he makes his living as an experimental subject for Dr. Seagrave, a neurologist. Seagrave, while not exactly a mad scientist, is a very inconsiderate, compulsive man who cares nothing about the pain his experiments cause. * At the moment Seagrave has surgically reversed neural connections so that the young man feels and actually physiologically responds to cold when he is exposed to heat, and vice versa. Vernon sticks it out because he is in love with Seagrave's daughter. * The narrator remonstrates with Seagrave, and the story drags on over far too many pages until Vernon rescues both Seagrave and his daughter from

drowning. At this point Seagrave regains his sense of proportion and agrees to reverse the operation on Vernon. * Much too long for the little it has to say.

866. **THE DOOM OF LUN-DHAG**. *Amazing Stories,* November 1932. Ill. Morey.
Short story. * *Place:* mostly New Jersey and Tibet. * A baffling bombardment afflicts the Earth. In most cases, huge, shining, machined, bullet-like objects explode with violence, but on occasion they land smoothly, open, display a legend demanding that two well-trained chemists enter the ship, close at an appointed time, and fly away. In France, two convicts are placed into such a ship, which departs, but returns with their corpses. The same thing happens with two German chemists. It is thought that the missiles must come from space. * Ray Fletcher and Cliff Hale, two brave young men, decide to chance it and enter the next missile. The missile flies off with them, and in a short time they find themselves in a strange land—not on another planet, as the general supposition had been with the missiles—but (as they learn) in Lhasa, Tibet. They are the captives of the mad Tibetan scientist Lun-Dhag. * Lun-Dhag, who is master of a superscience, does not kill them, as he did the French and Germans, but informs them that if they cooperate, they can be high officials after he conquers the Earth for Lamaism. They agree, although they have strong suspicions that they will die when they are no longer needed. * As they soon learn, the reason that Lun-Dhag desperately needs chemists is that his missiles (which operate through an unknown chemical process) cannot be targeted with any degree of accuracy, this despite the fact that his establishment in Lhasa is "the centre of the most concentrated and phenomenal advance in scientific achievement ever seen in the entire world." * Nevertheless, thanks to the young men there is some improvement, and Lun-Dhag is now ready for the big push. He will dispatch supermissiles laden with superexplosives powerful enough to destroy half a city with one blast. Hale will have the honor of sending off the first such missile to New York. He pulls the switch, then he and Fletcher fight their way (using a stolen paralysis tube) to another supermissile, which they enter. Behind them the whole establishment explodes. Is all lost with our daring adventurers? No. Hale set the controls of the first supermissile so that it would land atop Lun-Dhag, and emptied the explosive out of the second, so that he and Ray will be flown safely to the vicinity of New York City. Lhasa is blown up; the two young men are rescued at sea. * *Miscellaneous:* The Dalai Lama and his priests are associated with Lun-Dhag in his fiendish schemes. * The Tibetans have a very efficient paralyzing ray. * Pretty bad.

867. **ISLE OF THE GARGOYLES**. *Wonder Stories,* February 1936. Ill. Wallace Saaty.
Novelette. * Borderline science-fiction at best. * *Place:* Mostly an island a few hundred miles off Peru. * The well-known endocrinologist Dr. Stannard explains hypothyroidism to his friend Newhall, stressing the most severe clinical manifestations. After explanations, Stannard announces that he intends to visit a Pacific island off the coast of South America, where the population, described as monstrous, probably suffers from thyroid deficiency curable with thyroxin. These people, instead of being typically passive, seem to be very hostile to strangers. * After considerable back and forth action, the O. Henry clincher comes into view: Stannard and Newhall take a cargo of thyroxin

Lemkin, William (*continued*)

to the island, hoping for mass cures; the pills are lost; and after a very short time it becomes apparent that Stannard himself is a cretin who has been maintained in normalcy by thyroid extract. Degenerating badly, he joins his fellow hypothyroids in the jungle. * Below routine.

868. **BEYOND THE STRATOSPHERE**. *Amazing Stories,* June-August (two issues) 1936. Ill. Morey. (The author's name is incorrectly given as Lemke on the cover.) Short novel. * *Time:* the near future. *Place:* on a planetary shell about 150 miles above the Earth. * Stratosphere Transport, Inc., conducts a successful business with unmanned freight rocket flights between the major cities of the world. But when the company tries experimental rockets flying above 125 miles in altitude, they disappear. Oddly enough, no crash traces are found. * Bob Hart and his friend Earl, reasoning that if the rockets have not come down, they must still be up there, obtain permission to ride the next high altitude flight as crew. * The rocket functions well enough until it reaches the problematic height, at which point there is a crash and the young men are rendered unconscious. * They awaken to find themselves and their somewhat bunged-up rocket on a vast airless gray plane. Venturing out in space suits, they explore and in a short time come upon the lost rockets, which are being dismantled by strange beings. These are cube-like creatures seemingly composed of a gelatinous substance, with many small fringe tentacles and two large tentacles tipped with an organ that acts like a cutting torch. * The creatures, who are intelligent, are friendly enough, and the young men spend much time watching them. The cubes do object, however, when the men meddle with the planetary shell. This is a very peculiar substance, extremely light, transparent from one side, opaque from the other—thus permitting radiation to penetrate from the sun. It is thick enough, obviously, to resist any but the largest meteors. * After a time, when their air is running low, the young men persuade the cubes to let them dig a hole into the crust. Then, repairing their rocket with parts cannibalized from the other ships, they set it up with the help of the cubes, and take off back to the surface, penetrating the remainder of the crust with no difficulty. The young men were particularly friendly with two of the cubes, whom they took along, but the cubes did not survive the atmospheric pressure of surface Earth. * *Miscellaneous:* The planetary shell is, of course, the Heaviside layer. * Essentially a boys' story, and not a bad job as such.

LEMON, DON MARK (1876-1961)

U.S. (California) author. Occasional contributor of fantastic stories to the *Black Cat*, the *Thrill Book*, and Munsey magazines before our beginning date. This fiction is covered in *Science-Fiction: The Early Years*. Lemon's early work was often interesting for its novelty of idea.

869. **THE SCARLET PLANET**. *Wonder Stories Quarterly*, Winter 1931. Ill. Paul.

Novel. * *Time:* the interplanetary future. *Place:* a hitherto unknown planet, apparently not associated with any sun. * "The Scarlet Planet" is difficult to categorize or describe beyond saying that it is probably to be considered an eccentric novel satirizing sexuality. So far as I have been able to determine, there is no set plan to the story, nothing more than a sequence of incidents. The theme, if it can characterized as such, is an identification of sexuality with death, in a more limited sense with vampirism; perhaps also metaphoric statements about the generation of death out of life. * Three men, survivors of a larger expedition, land in their eight-hundred-foot-long superplanet ship on an unknown planet that is characterized as red in color. This redness is pretty much associated with the incredibly rare mineral 4-X-Olite, which is used on Earth to produce immortality or near immortality. As will be seen, this life also produces death. * The three men include Corporal Davidson, a sober man who usually opts for sanity, and Privates Hal-Al and Bailee, who are simply embodiments of unrestrained male sexuality and seldom think or talk of anything but human females. They might be considered slightly personalized phalli. (Since the publication period was the 1930s, nothing is as explicit as it would be in a modern novel.) Jacquet, a fourth crewman who faked his death in space, but turns up as a wild card, is a lesser element; he is eventually unmasked as a notorious interstellar outlaw whom Davidson is pledged to kill or capture. * The essence of the red planet is beautiful nude young femininity, which abounds not as reasoning women, but as sexual bodies for the two privates; unfortunately, these women are vampiric, and during each sexual encounter with the men, they drink their blood. Davidson repeatedly tries to restrain the excited men, but seldom has much success. * The narrative consists of a series of confrontations with the women and their male associates (gigantic humanoid creatures that embody characteristics of pig and snake, thus continuing the sexual metaphor), captures, escapes, loss of the spaceship and other conveyances, quarrels, and pain. It should be noted that the women are mute and that they have a peculiar life cycle: At a certain age they leap into local bodies of water, drown, and are preserved in their beauty. * Despite the absence of rationality on the planet, a high science is involved, with spherical traveling machines that mount paralysis rays, itch rays, and similar material. * The narrative eventually ends. Davidson and the two privates regain their spaceship and leave, the two privates smuggling on board two women who are apparently not vampiric. Davidson kills Jacquet. And the men have taken on board enough 4-X-Olite to make them wealthy. * *Miscellaneous:* The alien planet has days and nights six months long. * The spaceship is driven by atomic power. * There are also humanoid beings much like gigantic stick insects. * At various times the explorers are beset by floods of geometric solids. * A curious work, totally out of place in a s-f magazine of the day. At times it seems like the recording of a sexual dream; at other times one wonders, vainly, whether the author had a series of metaphoric equations in mind. In any case, the story is odd, but not odd enough to justify anyone's reading it for curiosity's sake.

LESSER, DERWIN

Pseud. of Charles Derwin Hornig (1916-present). U.S. (New York) editor; later California resident. Published excellent fanzine the *Fantasy Fan* (1933-1935). After Gernsback fired David Lasser as managing editor in July 1933, he hired Hornig as a replacement at about one third of the salary he paid Lasser. Gernsback apparently felt that Hornig, as a teenager, would share the interests of the younger readers more than an older person. The first issue that Hornig edited was October 1933. Hornig remained editor until the death of *Wonder Stories* in 1936. After leaving Gernsback's employ Hornig shifted among

Lesser, Derwin (*continued*)

various jobs, then from 1938 to 1941 edited the Silberkleit science-fiction magazines *Future Fiction, Science Fiction*, and *Science Fiction Quarterly*. As a pacifist during World War II, did forestry service for a time, then was later imprisoned. Major occupation since as accountant. The name Lesser was Hornig's mother's surname. Hornig also used the pseud. Derwin Lesser for the scripts for the strip "Buzz Allen the Invisible Avenger" in Gernsback's comic books (*Superworld Comics*, 1940) and for articles in *Future Fiction*.

870. **THE FATAL GLANCE**. *Wonder Stories*, February 1935.

Short-short story. * *Time:* 1954. *Place:* Arizona. * The great 420-inch telescope known as Seer of the Void is ready to be put into operation. It is so powerful that it can show the lunar surface as if it were only a few feet away. To the great astronomer Professor Janus is assigned the honor of being the first to examine the surface of Mars. On looking into the image plate, he falls over dead; the second and third persons also succumb, though not fatally. Since then no one else has dared to examine Mars. What happened? The human mind can image only things it has seen, or combinations of elements from things it has seen. If something totally alien is perceived, it may not have a clear passage into our minds, but may have to "fight its way through to our realization, destroying as it penetrates." * A sophisticated concept, probably derived from Hornig's extensive acquaintance with the supernatural fiction of the day, where the concept of transcendent horror occasionally emerged.

LESTER, IRVIN and **PRATT, [MURRAY] FLETCHER**

It is stated in Rock and Tuck, and is apparently generally accepted, that Lester was a pseudonym of Pratt's, comparable to the situation with B. F. Ruby. In Conklin's *Big Book of Science Fiction*, however, Pratt states in a footnote to "The Roger Bacon Story" that Lester was "a newspaper man with whom I was working at the time the story was written, and we always used a joint byline. It's so long ago that I can't be certain at this date whether he actually had a hand in this one or not, but I suspect not. He died about 1928 or 1929." (p. 387) "The Reign of the Ray" is accompanied by a purported portrait of Lester showing a man in young middle age. It has not been possible to check Lester further. Pratt has a separate entry.

871. **THE OCTOPUS CYCLE**. *Amazing Stories*, May 1928. Ill. Paul.

Short story. * *Place:* Madagascar. * Walter Weyl, American biologist, answers an appeal from a French friend to visit Madagascar and investigate reports of a series of mysterious disappearances. The reports are true, as Weyl discovers, for from the very boat that he is traveling on a man has vanished. * The jungle, Weyl soon learns, is the most dangerous place, and there he discovers what has been going on. A new or unrecorded form of life, a giant mollusc that approximates an ambulatory octopus, has been snatching away people. * These creatures, who prove to be far more numerous and more intelligent than expected, expand their attacks, and soon Fort Dauphin is besieged by a horde of monstrosities whose chitin covering protects them against small arms. Fire and artillery seem to be the only weapons effective against them. * Actually, Lester and Pratt provide a reasonable way to save the world from the octopoid invasion: The mollusks have a life cycle that involves

return to the sea for periods. When on this occasion they return, schools of killer whales await them. Finis the octopus peril. * Logically worked out, but the reader is not likely to be convinced that mankind is imperilled by such creatures, even though Lester and Pratt pull out all the stops.

872. **THE GREAT STEEL PANIC**. *Amazing Stories*, September 1928. Ill. Paul.

Short story. * The second story about Walter Weyl, consulting biologist to the New York Police Department. * Strange things are happening in New York City. Cables supporting the Brooklyn Bridge are cut, an elevated train support is severed, elevator cables break—and the iron railings outside Weyl's office are partly eaten through. The police think that it is the work of radicals and anarchists; Weyl has his doubts. * A few tests reveal the answer: Metals originally were precipitated by bacterial action, and obviously there are now bacteria around that eat iron. * Weyl's solution to the problem involves summoning New York's electrical experts and magnates. Every piece of structural iron in the city must have a weak current of electricity passed through it to kill the iron-eating bacteria. * It is not known how the iron-plague started.

873. **THE ROGER BACON FORMULA**. *Amazing Stories*, January 1929. Ill. Paul.

(Reprinted in Conklin, *Big Book of Science Fiction*, where it has been rewritten by Pratt, and in Ackerman, *Gosh! Wow!*)

Short story ultimately based on William R. Newbold's "decipherment" of the Voynich Manuscript misattributed to Roger Bacon. * *Place:* in part Venus. * A frame situation tells of finding the corpse of Edwin Hart, Greenwich Village musician, his death presumably the result of drugs. * Hart's manuscript: In a cafe he strikes up acquaintance with a shabby old man, who turns out to be a profound student of Roger Bacon's works. Indeed, the old man has certain manuscripts otherwise unknown. One tells of a drug that releases the mind (by ionizing brain particles) so that it can travel where it will. * Hart takes the drug, which the old man has prepared, and flits to Venus, which is Earth-like, with intelligent, somewhat humanoid creatures who have six tentacles instead of arms. Hart watches them for a time, studying their culture. * But Venusian night comes, and Bacon's drug needs light to work. Hart cannot move in the darkness, and he fears that if he is away too long, his body back on Earth will be considered dead. Indeed, he worries whether the old man, frightened at his absence, may not dump his body into the river. * A succession of lightning flashes, however, gives Hart enough energy to leave Venus, and he returns to Earth. He considers making further explorations, which he presumably did undertake, perhaps fatally. * Routine work.

874. **THE REIGN OF THE RAY**. *Science Wonder Stories*, June-July 1929. Ill. Paul.

Short novel, presented mostly as chronicle or historical material rather than as conventional fiction. The story, which is episodic, shifts narrative centers as events take place. * *Time:* Looking back from 2055, to the period from about 1924 to 1936. *Place:* Various places in the United States and Russia. * First episodes: Young maverick scientist Bob Adams has constructed a variant Coolidge tube with interesting properties. At close range it amounts to a death ray; at a distance, it explodes ammunition and gasoline. Adams offers it to the government, which does little or nothing about his offer. In the meanwhile, the Russians

Lester, Irvin and Pratt, Fletcher (*continued*)

have heard of Adams's work. A Russian agent posing as an engineering student wins Adams's confidence, but when he reveals his motives, there is a struggle; the tube goes off full force and explodes an ammunition dump and local firearms; the Russian is killed; and Adams is knocked unconscious. Other Russian agents spirit Adams, his tube, and his diary away to Russia. * Second episodes: The American government, belatedly realizing what has happened, sends a secret agent disguised as a tobacco peddler into Russia. The agent finds that Adams, who has been amnesiac for a long time, but is now recovered, has refused to reveal the code in his diary or the secrets of the tube. Both men escape into Turkey. * Third episodes: Stensoff, the Russian dictator, realizing that the tube, if fully developed and widely distributed in other armed forces, will destroy his program of world conquest, begins an immediate attack. Washington and the entire top level of government are destroyed. An assistant secretary of the navy, the sole survivor, assumes command and immediately sets up a strict dictatorship. Congress is disbanded; the entire population is drafted and assigned work roles on a military basis; money is canceled and work vouchers are issued in its place. And in the backwoods, inventor Hamilton and assistant Jim Blunt develop the first successful human-powered flying machine, an ornithopter. It is just as revolutionary a development as the Adams ray. * Fourth episodes: The Soviets do not quite overrun Europe, for Adams tubes halt their advance. A large part of the story is now devoted to an essay-like narrative of campaigns. A pattern emerges: When the Russians acquire Adams tubes, modern warfare is ended, and armies return to swords, crossbows, compressed air and spring guns, and similar weapons. In the United States archery drill is compulsory. By 1936 the Russians have been driven back to the area of Tula, where they are finally defeated. * The end of the war, however, does not restore liberties to the American people, who live happily under the dictatorship imposed during the war. The work army continues, with jobs assigned by the government and payment in work vouchers. Literature has declined, supplanted by "pictographs" (i.e., the equivalent of VCR cassettes). Rules from above take the place of parliamentary laws. There has been a crackdown on outlaw types, with the unfit and criminal sterilized. As for democracy, Harvard Mellen, the last spokesman for the authors, declares that it is more a matter of spirit than forms, and that it does not matter if there is no more vote. * Occasionally in the mode of the social H. G. Wells, but too often a boring succession of military maneuvers in which Pratt demonstrates his acknowledged tactical prowess. It is hard to decide whether the Fascist or other totalitarian tendencies represent the authors' beliefs or are simply a literary device.

875. **DANGER**. *Amazing Stories*, July 1929. Ill. Clardy.
Short story. * *Place:* the Pacific, near Sala y Gomez. * The Museum expedition is in the Pacific studying island life. After stopping for a short time at Easter Island, the group proceeds to Sala y Gomez, about two hundred miles away. Along the route old Professor Hartford speculates that the next dominant lifeform on Earth will not be insects, "who have had their chance," but perhaps a single-celled organism like a giant amoeba. * He proves right. When the expedition reaches Sala y Gomez, such a creature emerges from the ocean and eats all the expedition except the narrator. The biologists foolishly tried to capture it

in a barred cage. Incidentally, such an organism cleared out lifeforms from Easter Island centuries ago, before the modern forms were introduced. * Very thin.

LINN, RALPH
No information.

876. **ELEMENT 87**. *Amazing Stories*, June 1930. Ill. Morey.
Short story. * The narrator learns from his friend von Hofen of his great invention, a matter transmitter. The theory is that all elements are simply vibratory variants of a basic pattern and that with suitable apparatus one can dissolve and reassemble atoms. At present the invention will separate out elements from compounds—i.e., carbon from iron in steel. * Improving his apparatus von Hofen tries more elaborate projects, including transmitting a corpse borrowed from a medical school. The result is a badly assembled body that creates a stir in the school when it is later found. * The answer to the problem, von Hofen says, is the missing element 87. And the man most likely to be able to isolate it is Professor John Carson, a bad egg of genius who is currently in prison. * The narrator and von Hofen manage to smuggle Carson out of prison. Carson does isolate 87, which he calls Carsonium, but, being a crook, tries to kill the two inventors and steal their invention. After a struggle the narrator and von Hofen transmit the unconscious criminal to the reception terminal—but discover that the machine was not working properly (what with a detached wire). Carson's atoms are distributed throughout the air. * Of no particular interest, except in demonstrating popular interest in the elements missing from the periodic table.

LINTOTT, J. N. T., B.Sc.
British journalist, contributor to *Daily Express, Daily Mail, Birmingham Mail, Good Housekeeping,* and other newspapers and journals. B.Sc., University of London.

877. **THE MYSTERY OF THE TWILIGHT BELT**. *Scoops,* 16 June 1934. Unsigned ill.
Boys' fiction. * Short story. * Skulduggery in the Twilight Zone of Mercury, in the interplanetary future. * When Tom Hewat finds a corpse in the silicon dome on Mercury, the mine manager Mervin Mandrake and his assistant Carson try to frame him for murder. Tom refuses to surrender, and locks himself into the control room, threatening to shut off the dome's oxygen if the miners break in. * For a time it looks like an impasse, but Tom, managing to escape, follows Mandrake and Carson out on the surface to a cavern riddled with large diamonds. It seems that the two villains murdered the original discoverer of the gems so that they could keep them, instead of turning them over to the company. All ends well after a shoot-out.

LOCKE, A. T.
U.S. author. Contributor to pulps, notably *Top-Notch* and *Texas Trail*. Author of Western novel *"Hell Bent" Harrison* (1927).

878. **VANDALS OF THE STARS**. *Astounding Stories*, March 1930. Ill. J. Fleming Gould.
Short story. * *Time:* 1975. *Place:* New York. * The world is now organized into The United States of the World with its capitol in The Hague, but is really secretly ruled by five plutocrats who control money, transportation, amusements, agriculture, and factories and power systems. There are televisor

Locke, A. T. (*continued*)

phones, the luciviser (supertelescope with light enhancing abilities), superplanes and dirigibles, etc. * An enormous, glowing hot metal object appears over Manhattan; hovers for a time, then speeds to other great cities, returning to Manhattan. At first the object is thought to be an inexplicable natural phenomenon, but after a time it becomes obvious that the object is a three-quarter-mile-long spaceship. * Fragoni, leader of the five plutocrats, is deputed to treat with the potential visitors/invaders. He flies to the top of the ship, where a port opens, from which, along with soldiers, emerges a majestic man who identifies himself in English as Teuxical, an officer of the emperor of the space empire of Lodore. * As Teuxical explains, laws of evolution operate similarly throughout the universe, so that Fragoni should not be surprised that the visitors speak English. * Several things become obvious: Lodoran science is far ahead of Earth's; the Lodorans conquer and force heavy tribute from all planets they visit; and, while Teuxical is essentially a pleasant man, his son Zitlan is a lecherous wretch. * Time passes, as Earth becomes part of the Lodoran empire, with the amiable Teuxical as governor. The plutocrats decide that the only way to free Earth is to destroy the spaceship, but how? Young Dirk Vanderpool (transportation), who serves as hero, has a plan. When things become chaotic after Zitlan murders Teuxical, Dirk directs an artificial lightning bolt through an open hatch of the spaceship, killing all the invaders. * *Miscellaneous:* The invaders have a paralysis ray. They also live thousands of years. * Pulp professionalism, but weak science-fiction.

879. **THE MACHINE THAT KNEW TOO MUCH.** *Astounding Stories,* December 1933. Unsigned ill.

Short story. * Young Weatherby, a well-qualified student of linguistics, takes a job with reclusive, secretive old Jonathan Forsythe. The old man has an apparatus that picks up fossil sound, and with it he proposes to locate lost treasures. When Weatherby suggests patenting the invention, Forsythe becomes enormously excited and outraged. Indeed, Forsythe is so suspicious that he listens, by remote focus, to Weatherby's conversations with his girlfriend. * The climax comes when Weatherby unexpectedly returns to the house and overhears a conversation between Forsythe and another person, as reproduced from past sound by the machine. It seems that not only did Forsythe steal the secret of the apparatus, but he also murdered the real inventor. Confronted, Forsythe displays remorse, and after Weatherby leaves, blows up himself and his house.

LOCKE, RICHARD ADAMS (1800-1871)

U.S. (New York) journalist, born and educated in England. Worked on various newspapers in New York City. After the success of the moon hoax, founded own newspaper, which was unsuccessful. In later life perpetrated another hoax with purported journals of African explorer Mungo Park, but his efforts fooled few.

880. **THE MOON HOAX.** *Amazing Stories,* September 1926. Ill. F. S. Hynd.

(First published in the *New York Sun,* 25-31 August 1835. Reprinted in pamphlet form as *A Complete Account of the Late Discoveries in the Moon* (1835), with occasional later reprints. Much the best edition is *The Moon Hoax,* Gregg Press, New York, 1975, with supplementary material. *The Moon Hoax* is covered in much more detail in *Science-Fiction: The Early Years.*) *

Fictionalized essay. * One of the most celebrated hoaxes of the nineteenth century. The text is purportedly reprinted from an issue of the *Edinburgh Journal* describing the great astronomical discoveries made by Sir John Herschel in South Africa. * According to the article, the Moon contains not only atmosphere and vegetation, but is the home of intelligent beings of various sorts, including winged humanoids who maintain a barbaric culture. * The author claimed that *The Moon Hoax* was a satire, but a satirical basis is not obvious. It is, however, a very readable, clever account.

LOCKE, WILLIAM P.

No information. An accompanying portrait shows the author as a middle-aged man.

881. **THE MOON BEASTS.** *Science Wonder Stories,* August 1929. Ill. Paul.

Novelette. * *Place:* The North Woods, perhaps Quebec, with a frame narrative situation in New Guinea. The lecturer tells of finding a strange path cut through the jungle in New Guinea, whereupon one of his listeners relates his own explanation for it. * Joe, the narrator, and Barry are camping in the woods when they see a strange object like a bisected dirigible floating in the air. * Some time later they find a road cut through the brush, with the debris strangely crumbling and turning to dust as they pass. They finally come to the cause: what seems to be a flying machine about fifty by twenty by fifteen feet, with strange protuberances. As they crawl over and around it, however, they discover that it is a living creature. A periscope-like organ emerges, which, after a time, shows them replay pictures of their own activities, then an image of three creatures like itself leaving the Moon. The creature is friendly enough. * At first the campers are bemused, but then think what a horde of such monsters would mean to the world, and decide that they must destroy it. They build fires that drive the creature into the nearby lake, where it drowns. Why it did not fly away is not considered. * Joe and the lecturer will now travel to New Guinea and hunt down the second moon beast. * The nature background is played up, extending the story beyond a proper length. * A cruel piece of work.

[Anonymous]
Presumably a British writer.

882. **THE LONDON-CAPETOWN EXPRESS.** *Scoops,* 24 March 1934. Unsigned ill.

Boys' fiction. * Short story. * *Time:* the near future. *Place:* a station in the Sahara Desert. * The remarkable *Silver Serpent,* the ultra-streamlined express train from London to Capetown, is about to pass through on its first run, now that the Sahara link has been finished. The train, which is powered by liquid hydrogen, should take about forty hours to complete the run, passing through the English Channel Tunnel and the Gibraltar-Tarifa Tunnel. * There is trouble afoot. Kreutzer, a trouble-making workman who is part Arab, has quit the job and may organize the Arabs to disrupt the train. * So it happens. The Arabs raid the camp; they are beaten off in what was probably only a diversionary raid, but they do steal dynamite, which they use to cover the track. Hero Bill Tarrant clears the rubble away with the portable disintegrator used for such purposes. * Both Bill and his superiors expect more trouble, and Bill is assigned

"The London-Capetown Express" (*continued*)
to ride a pilot train through ahead of the *Silver Serpent*. A signal faked by Kreutzer stops the pilot, and Bill and his black assistant Zed are captured. Kreutzer announces that he will place a dynamite bomb on the tracks, to be set off by the passage of the *Silver Serpent*. But Bill manages to be rid of his bonds and to fell Kreutzer with a stone thrown at the proper time. The train goes through safely. Bill is recuperating in hospital.

LONG, AMELIA REYNOLDS (1903 or 1904-1978)
U.S. (Pennsylvania) author. Author of many mystery novels under own name and pseuds. Patrick Laing, Adrian Reynolds, Peter Reynolds. Contributed fiction to fantastic genre magazines under her own name, also as Mordred Weir (according to Rock). As Peter Reynolds, author of *Behind the Evidence*, crank novel about the Lindbergh-Hauptmann case. Standard references give Long's birth date as 1904, but Social Security records cite 1903.

883. **OMEGA**. *Amazing Stories*, July 1932. Ill. Morey. (Reprinted in Wollheim, *The End of the World*, and in Ackerman, *Gosh! Wow!*)
Short story. * *Time:* 1928. * The narrator discusses the hypnotic experiments of Professor Mortimer, who has been using a subject to view the past by clairvoyance. To establish the validity of his work, Mortimer wants an examination of the future, but this may be dangerous. * The murderer Williams, however, is willing to undertake the risk. Under Mortimer's direction Williams moves mentally into the future. * Data received: Around A.D. 3000 communication was established with Mars; around 10,000, with Venus. At about 47,000 the Martians became extinct as a result of wars, pestilence, and environmental deterioration. At this same time there was renewed glaciation on Earth. Civilization was incredibly high, but wars and disease took their toll. Eventually, man reverted to savagery and became extinct. * When Mortimer tries to awaken Williams, he has no success. Further, as has happened in previous sessions, Williams has taken on the form of a human of the period he views, so that he is now a bigheaded, spindle-limbed being. Somewhat worried that Williams will not awaken, Mortimer takes him into the still farther future, when the world is collapsing—and Williams, too, collapses into a pile of dust. * Routine, with weak echoes of Poe.

884. **SCANDAL IN THE 4TH DIMENSION**. *Astounding Stories,* February 1934. Ill. C. R. Thomson (C R T).
Short story. * Sitcom material about frustrated young love and miscarried science. * Professor Lynn Boswell and his student assistant Felix are working on the fourth dimension, which the professor asserts is a matter of visibility. Felix and the professor's daughter Betty are in love, but the crusty, possessive mathematician will not give them permission to marry. Felix's chance comes when the professor accidentally makes his bottom half invisible. Felix is the only person who can help the professor regain normalcy, and Felix sets a price—Betty. The grumpy professor holds out for a time, but eventually succumbs after a succession of embarrassing incidents. * Trivial and routine.

885. **A LEAK IN THE FOUNTAIN OF YOUTH**. *Astounding Stories*, August 1936. Ill. Wesso.
Short story. * Humor. * Professor Aloysius O'Flannigan, a biochemist, has developed what he claims is an elixir of rejuvenation. An opportunity to use it comes when his and the narrator's mutual friend Gustavus Adolphus Lindstrom is wanted

for a bank robbery (though innocent) and cannot produce an alibi. Since he had wanted to be alone, he had been taking a rest in an empty sarcophagus in the museum, and there are no witnesses. The police are close on Lindstrom's trail. * O'Flannigan conceals Lindstrom by inoculating him with the elixir. Unfortunately, the rejuvenation continues longer than desired, transforming him into a baby. * The second dilemma arises when Lindstrom is cleared by the police, who now accuse O'Flannigan of having made away with him. The narrator and O'Flannigan would like to retrieve Lindstrom with a counterserum, but the dragon-like nursemaid they have hired will not let them near the baby. Following the professor's instructions, the narrator manages to render the nurse unconscious with an injection, after which the professor and the narrator bring Lindstrom back to his proper age. There are complications, including an automobile chase, and the unintentional rejuvenation of the elderly nurse, who shows signs of erotomania. * Routine at best.

LONG, FRANK BELKNAP, JR. (1903-1994)
U.S. (New York) author, now remembered mostly as close friend and associate of H. P. Lovecraft, but a significant writer on his own. In his early work, essentially a *Weird Tales* author, with stories of supernatural horror much in Lovecraft's mode. In science-fiction considered in this volume Long developed a more individual story. His better work after World War II often invoked themes of science-fiction horror. Like Murray Leinster, Long was able to adjust to changing styles and market, remaining an active writer well into the 1970s and occasionally later. At his best, in his earlier work, a good stylist and competent storyteller with an individual touch.

Long's work is presented as the Mini-Men Series and Other Works.

The Mini-men Series

The following three stories take place in the same world-situation over fifty million years in the future. At some time in the past, enormous glaciations covered almost the Earth except Africa, and mankind was close to extinction. Other forms of life, however, developed and flourished, notably intelligent insects on land and intelligent, technologically adept barnacles in the sea. Each of the new life-forms salvaged part of mankind, which they then bred to their own use as slaves. It is probable, though not certain, that mankind was suitably reduced in size. The common theme of all three stories is the emergence of manhood.

886. **THE LAST MEN**. *Astounding Stories*, August 1934. Ill. Howard V. Brown.
(Reprinted in Long, *Rim of the Unknown*, and in Knight, *Science Fiction of the Thirties*.)
Short story. * *Time:* considerably more than fifty million years in the future. * *Background:* The insects (perhaps moths) rear humans in giant dormitorylike buildings (homoriums), where they are subjected to accelerated growth and indoctrinated as servants. Communication between man and insect is telepathic, with touch contact of antennae to forehead. * The humans are only chattels, and in many ways their life is difficult and dangerous. As Maljoc, the human protagonist, reflects, the insects are not wantonly cruel, but they can be ruthless and they

Long, Frank Belknap (*continued*)

do not regard human life as important. * Maljoc has just come of age and is permitted to mate. Making his way to the homorium of the females, he selects a particularly beautiful young woman as his mate. She reciprocates, and they leave the homorium. But there is a danger associated with beauty. Just as mankind millions of years earlier had pinned exceptionally beautiful insects to mats in collections, the superinsects now often pin exceptionally beautiful women in their collections. This is what happens. An insect seizes the woman and declares her too beautiful for Maljoc. In an act of rebellion that is almost unprecedented Maljoc tries to fight off the insect, but the situation is hopeless. Realizing this, Maljoc deliberately drops to his death along with the woman. He feels, as he falls, that he had "recaptured for an imperishable instant the lost glory of his race." * An effective story, nicely written.

887. **GREEN GLORY.** *Astounding Stories,* January 1935. Ill. Marchioni.

(Reprinted in Long, *Rim of the Unknown.*)

Short story. * *Time:* about fifty million years in the future. * *Background:* The story centers upon the two dominant races of the surface world, the empires of the ants and the bees, who are engaged in perpetual war. Both insect forms are highly intelligent. * Associated with the ants, living in their tunnels, are humans, who serve their masters with complete devotion and faithfulness. While Long is not specific, it seems that humans have devolved in size, rather than that the insects have grown larger. In any case, humans are laboratory products of the ants. * The story concerns the little man Atasmas, a faithful servant of the ants, who has been selected for a kamikaze mission by the ant queen. Since he is small, Atasmas can penetrate the bee fortress, where he will open a container containing a fungus so rapid and lethal that it will exterminate the bees. Atasmas will die, of course, but that knowledge does not disturb him. * There is one discordant element: the night shapes. As the queen mother tells him, during the great glaciation, when man was almost extinct, the ants rescued the males, whom they propagate artificially. But heterosexuality still resides in the human unconscious, and Atasmas, along with the other tiny men, has dreams of females—the feared night shapes. The bees, on the other hand, preserved women as slaves. * Atasmas is carried to his destination across the sea to the great beehive complex, where he slips in. But his mission is impeded when he encounters a night shape. After some astonishment and bafflement, the man and woman recognize their nature and embrace. * Atasmas, knowing that death is inevitable, but still a death in loving embrace, opens the fungus container, and both die, transformed into green fungus. Atasmas rejected a chance to escape with the giant flying insect that transported him to the bee domain. * A highly imaginative, moving story.

888. **THE GREAT COLD.** *Astounding Stories,* February 1935. Ill. Dold.

(Reprinted in Long, *Rim of the Unknown,* and in Derleth, *Worlds of Tomorrow.*)

Short story. * In the same world-picture as "The Last Men" and "Green Glory," about fifty million years in the future. * The barnacles, the third great component of the future Earth, rule the oceans. By no means a low form of life, as at present, they maintain a high science and are renowned for their architectural wonders. Serving the barnacles for the past ten million years is a race of tiny web-footed men, although here there are both male and female humans and breeding takes place in the traditional manner. * Two great moments are at hand. First, the barnacles, among whom males are small and insignificant compared to females, have decided to reduce the size of human males on the same ratio to human females, since males, compared to females, are clumsy. Clulan, a young human, regards the proposal with horror. Second, one of the great crustaceans has gone mad, and Clulan is assigned to destroy it, lest it do harm. Armed with a weapon of supercold he accomplishes his task. * The sea humans, however, are not as downtrodden as their counterparts among the ants, bees, and other insects. Thus, many of the humans rally to Clulan when he strikes a blow against the crustaceans. This is the release of the Great Cold, which in a moment freezes all the world's oceans and destroys all sea life. Implicit is the suggestion that the land life-forms, too, are dead. If this is not the case, at least the sea men have died like men.

Other Works

889. **THE THOUGHT MATERIALIZER.** *Science Wonder Quarterly,* Spring 1930. Ill. Paul.

Short story. * The ultimate in psychosomatic ailments. * Perkins is somewhat incredulous when Randall claims that his invention will make the human body experience the thoughts that its brain has, but Perkins foolishly lets himself be used as a guinea pig. Randall connects him, warns him not to think of unpleasant things, and wanders off for a time. * Shrieking and screaming are soon heard throughout the building. Perkins, who usually dreams in terms of Bengal, has encountered a ravenous giant tiger through the apparatus. Randall destroys the apparatus. * Intelligent, but not developed as one might have expected from Long. One of Long's weakest stories.

890. **THE VAPOR DEATH.** *Astounding Stories,* October 1934. Ill. Dold.

Short story. * *Time:* undated fairly far future? *Place:* somewhere in Asia. * Background: The world is divided between the free brains of Asia and the Great Brain of (presumably) Europe. The three hundred million free brains are cyborgs (my term), with their brains transferred at birth to mechanical bodies with wheels. Ruled by Calcon, they live in terraced cities in Asia. The Great Brain in Europe seems to be some sort of mechanical brain or giant computer. It captures humans and transforms them into robotic beings controlled by ganglia of various sorts. Between the free brains and the Great Brain there is unremitting warfare, with the Great Brain's robot ships raiding Asia. A third group, the Primitives, consists of normal humans who for one reason or another could not be transformed into cyborgs. They serve the free brains as slaves. * Calcon has devised a rocket plane and suitable explosives for destroying the Great Brain, and since the cyborgs apparently cannot fly the plane, Calcon commands the Primitive Mago to conduct the raid, which will almost certainly end in death for him. A personal element has also entered into the choice of Mago, for Calcon, who seems to be developing sexual desires, is jealous of Mago, who is loved by the maiden Lulan. Thus, if all goes well, Calcon will have killed two birds with one stone. * As Calcon and Lulan watch in a viewer, Mago successfully bombs the Great Brain and survives. The Great Brain is dead, and its menace over. But not quite. Just before

Long, Frank Belknap (*continued*)

Mago bombed it, it sent forth a robot plane with a gas that dissolves the metal housing the free brains. Thus, they all die, too. The Primitives are left to develop a new and better world. * Not bad.

891. **LOST PLANET**. *Astounding Stories*, November 1934. Ill. Dold.

Short story. * *Time:* the interplanetary future. *Background:* Some eight hundred years earlier, when Earth culture was at its peak, with titanic mile-high cities, the Venusian colonists warred on the mother planet. This war continued for about five hundred years, during which time Earth repelled attacks from Venus, but apparently did not retaliate. For the last three hundred years, there has been absolutely no contact between the two planets, and the Venusians have no knowledge whatever of conditions of Earth. Flason's small rocket ship is the first attempt at exploration. * Flason lands his ship with no difficulty, and observes, to his astonishment, that the great cities of old lie in ruins and that the landscape is a desolation. Chancing upon a cubical structure, which was apparently built as a communications and recording center, he learns that Earth was invaded by strange beings from another planet, perhaps even another universe, who destroyed mankind and his works with an erosive gas. Terrestrial man is extinct. * And then Flason sees one of the invaders—a black, bat-like creature—watching and menacing him. He is lost, for he is unarmed. No, a sudden blast from a flame projector behind him destroys the monster. His savior was a stowaway on his ship—a young woman who was in love with him, but whom he had ignored on Venus. * Routine at best.

892. **THE BLUE EARTHMAN**. *Astounding Stories*, April 1935. Ill. Marchioni.

Short story. * *Time:* about ten million years in the future. *Place:* somewhere in the Atlantic Ocean. *Background:* The planetary orbits are constricting, and the planets are gradually approaching the sun. Mercury and Venus have returned to gas. The Earth no longer revolves. One side, facing the dying sun, is unbearably hot; the other, frigid. Either the planet wobbles, or else Earth's orbit is small enough and orbital speed great enough that seasons last only ten days or so. * On the lighted side of the Earth, white mankind survives in enormous floating cities, maintained by a superscience. On the frozen side, blue-skinned mankind also survives, with equally advanced, but different science. Between the two races exists incredibly deep-seated hatred that has developed into incessant war. * A new menace, however, has produced a temporary truce between the two races and some coöperation. Enormous tube-cities have fallen into the ocean from Mars, and the Martians war incessantly on both human races. The Martians, who are almost unknown as a race to the Earthmen, are revealed late in the story to be giant molluscoid creatures, who also have a superscience. * The story concerns Kellkall, who lives alone in a small sea scout/fighter craft. At first a warrior against the blue men, he is now assigned to fight the Martians in whatever way he can. He lives permanently in his vessel, but once a year (as now) his assigned life mate is permitted to visit him. This is a delight to him. * Kellkall attacks a Martian tube with his proton gun, destroying it, but his mate Loomono is killed during the battle. Kellkall's vessel, too, is destroyed. But he is not killed. He awakens in the combat vessel of a renegade blue man, who does not accept the national

command to help the whites, but pursues a personal sadistic vendetta. He plans to burn Kellkall to death in a solar engine, as he has done with other white captives. He has also revived Loomono to a sort of zombie life, to serve him as a companion. * Kellkall is being tortured when Loomono releases him; she has killed the blue man and his subordinates. But, as she says faintly, she can no longer retain her personality and life. She and Kellkall die as the blue man's vessel is captured by a Martian trawler. * A good mood of alienness.

893. **EXILES OF THE STRATOSPHERE**. *Astounding Stories*, July 1935. Ill. Schneeman.

Short story. * *Time:* millennia in the future. * *Background:* Mankind has pretty much abandoned the surface of the Earth, which it considers a horrible, unhealthy place. Instead, man inhabits gigantic floating cities high in the stratosphere, above the germs and fungi of the surface. These cities, which correspond to nations, are mutually hostile and in a state of perpetual warfare with one another, employing superscientific weapons. Socially, judging from Lutaton's Dome, these are horribly regimented, cruel cultures, somewhat reminiscent of the Spanish Inquisition and a Nazi prison camp. * Lutaton of the Biological Patrol is due to be punished because he dared to give a drink of water to a war captive about to be thrust alive into a blast furnace. His was a heinous crime, but the judges are relatively merciful. Instead of being put to death, as he deserves, he is tortured slightly and assigned to a dangerous task. His superiors give him a ray gun and a little flask containing a lethal virus, and send him down an interminable ladder to the surface of the Earth. There he is to seek out Stuton, a rebellious Dome man, and his followers and kill them. If he is successful, he will be reinstated in his job. * *Background:* The rebel Stuton, once the foremost scientist of the Dome and the inventor of potent weapons against the other air cities, had descended to the surface with a few associates and refused to return. When pressed to obey, he resisted and began bacteriological warfare against the Dome. Since the culture is obsessed with germs, his is a potent threat. * Armed to the teeth, Lutaton descends, finding, instead of a sinkhole of pestilence as he had expected, an almost paradisiacal subtropical milieu. In a short time he encounters a young woman who has left Stuton's group to escape sexual harassment. (It seems that Stuton has become power mad, and his followers are not much better than their colleagues up in the Dome.) A more immediate problem, however, is a gigantic dinosaurlike carnivorous reptile that attacks Lutaton and the young woman. His ray gun proving inadequate, Lutaton is forced to use his destructive virus against the reptile. On exploring farther, Lutaton discovers that the dinosaur had broken through the electric defenses of Stuton's camp and killed the rebels. * After a brief discussion of the comparative virtues of order and freedom, Lutaton and the young woman decide to remain on Earth. There apparently is no fear of Lutaton's being corrupted, as was Stuton. * Like Long's other disturbing tales of future man, well imagined and written, but the dinosaur sticks a little in one's craw, as does the overbrief resolution of important issues.

894. **SKYROCK**. *Astounding Stories*, September 1935. Unsigned ill. The title is given as "Sky Rock" on the contents page.

Short story. * A Fortean incident. * Professor Staubwasser's helicopter lies crashed, its crew dead. Professor Holt, a

Long, Frank Belknap (*continued*)

colleague of Staubwasser's, and Haldane, a New York City reporter, discuss the incident acrimoniously, with Holt rejecting the theory that led to Staubwasser's death. Staubwasser believed that a peculiar formation in a meteorite was a human footprint, and that the meteorite came from a floating solid, lithic body in the stratosphere. * When Staubwasser's helicopter is unearthed, however, crushed onto its nose is a claw so large that it must have come from a raptor with a wing spread of hundreds of feet. Holt now admits that he has simply been trying to avoid sensational publicity, and that he was wrong. * Haldane and Holt ascend in pressure suits in Holt's helicopter. When they are about twenty-five miles above the Earth, their vessel is seized by an unknown force and shattered against a rock formation. The island in the sky really exists, now explained by Holt as due perhaps to a peculiar property of space, perhaps to the vacuum features that dragged in their helicopter. * The men explore. The area is barren, but they find, in a crystal coffin-like container, the body of a very beautiful young woman; she is Caucasian, but not of any known racial type. As Haldane, fascinated, contemplates her, one of the giant birds attacks and kills him. Holt shoots, but to no avail, and topples off the rock, landing safely by parachute below. He suppresses his discovery. * Interesting.

895. **THE LICHEN FROM EROS.** *Astounding Stories,* November 1935. Ill. Marchioni.

Short story. * *Time:* 1964. *Place:* mostly backflash to Eros. * After the Winters Expedition returns in the *Top* from Eros, Winters tells his cousin Galton of strange events. Eros has a breathable atmosphere, but its gravity is so weak that the explorers found locomotion very difficult, and they floundered about. When Ruth, Winters's fiancée, fell, she came in contact with a lichen-like growth that fastened itself to her back, painfully. Winters ripped it off and preserved it. * Now on Earth, Winters shows Galton the lichen under a microscope. It is not a vegetable growth as it appears to the naked eye, but a fantastic microscopic city with remarkable buildings and quite advanced armaments, including heat rays—which had burnt Ruth. But the tiny people are all dead. The closing situation is that Winters is infatuated with a microscopic woman who lies dead in the ruins of her city. She is beautiful and perfectly human. * Confusingly presented. Rather diffuse and disorganized, without the usual clarity and style of Long's work.

896. **CONES.** *Astounding Stories,* February 1936. Ill. Schneeman.

(Reprinted in Long, *Rim of the Unknown,* and in Conklin, *Possible Worlds of Science Fiction.*)

Short story. * *Time:* the interplanetary future. * Peril and romance during one of the first explorations of Mercury. Mercury is uninhabitable, being frigid on one side and boiling on the other. But the libration zone is tolerable for men encased in space suits. The present expedition intends to cross the libration zone before returning to the mother ship, the *California.* The personnel of the expedition includes Gibbs Crayley, cold, lone-wolf biologist in disfavor on Earth because of certain experiments he performed; Mona Massin, gorgeous female biologist, as avid a scientist and as cold a person as Crayley; and several men, all sweating and panting for Mona's unattainable charms. * The greatest dangers in exploring seemingly lifeless Mercury are hot spots, areas where ultraviolet radiation suddenly bursts forth with disintegrating force. Such hot spots kill several members of the expedition. A second problem, now first discovered, consists of tall, cone-shaped semi-intelligent creatures that move so rapidly that the eye cannot catch them, though Crayley photographs them with a stroboscopic camera. Hostile, they project a beam of ultraviolet light that dissolves the calcium in the human body. These beings account for the rest of the expedition except for Gibbs and Mona, who are lucky to escape. As might be expected, the two frigid biologists discover, after sharing perils, that they love each other. * *Miscellaneous:* Mona took along her pet cat. Clad in a tiny space suit and weighted down, it was killed by one of hot spots. * The cones are composed of radiant particles. * Unusual for Long in not being tightly written, but heavily padded. Not one of his better stories.

897. **THE ROARING BLOT.** *Astounding Stories,* March 1936. Ill. Marchioni.

Short story. * *Time:* presumably the near future. * A small dark body has entered the solar system and is approaching the sun. It will undoubtedly cause disruptions, but scientists differ about the degree of these disruptions. When the body strikes, there seems to be no great damage, but strange glows and feathering light displays are visible over much of the Earth. * On Earth there are also evidences of collision with a shattered body. In the instance developed in the story, a presumable meteorite has driven a deep hole into the Earth, but there is no crater, and the hole, as plumbed, descends in a straight line for miles. Strangest of all, the hole is not hot, but very cold, despite all visual indications of enormous activity. * Investigating the hole is Thomas Traven, a brilliant young physicist who is slowly dying of radium poisoning. Since he has nothing to lose, he is willing to take chances with the strange phenomenon. Lowering a special camera into the hole, he obtains a remarkable photograph. He then announces that the hole represents Dirac ether, or a swarm of negative particles. * The phenomenon ends when Tom is lowered down into the hole. An eruption that takes place blows him out gently and deposits him nearby, cured of his radium poisoning. The hole, together with similar phenomena scattered about the Earth, heals back to its previous state as the negative particles are reconstituted into matter. While a conclusion is not spelled out, this seems to be the worst that will happen from the collision. * Clumsy in narrative, padded, and unconvincing.

898. **RED STORM ON JUPITER.** *Astounding Stories,* May 1936. Unsigned ill.

(Reprinted in Wollheim, *Flight into Space.*)

Short story. * *Time:* A.D. 2002. *Place:* Jupiter. * *Background:* The Red Spot, called the Jeel, is a peculiar landmass, sometimes offering a fairly firm crust, sometimes jelly-like. Enormous storms rage over it, ripping up the surface. The human extractive stations, called Form Stations, survive by spreading a firming liquid about them—like oil on water. Miners work around it, seeking radioactive deposits, which are rich, though life expectancy is a matter of months. In addition to the miners there is a renegade called the Foam Station Smasher, who does what his name suggests, smashing and raiding stations. Against him is the Law Garrison, or planetary police. * Evart Harnden of the Law Garrison is dismissed because he encountered the Smasher and did not shoot at him. Harnden hesitated partly because he was too disabled to bring his weapon to bear and partly because he felt gratitude after the Smasher spared him. *

Long, Frank Belknap (*continued*)

Now, cashiered from the police and acting as an independent out on the Red Spot, Harnden again encounters the Foam Station Smasher. A beautiful young woman also enters the picture. All ends well. * The story is negligible, but the background is well imagined.

899. **THE FLAME MIDGET**. *Astounding Stories,* December 1936. Ill. Flatos.

(Reprinted in Long, *The Dark Beasts;* in Long, *The Hounds of Tindalos;* in Long, *The Early Long;* in Conklin, *Best of Science Fiction;* and in Norton and Donaldy, *Gates to Tomorrow.*)

Short story. * Suggestions of Poe. * *Place:* South Carolina. * The narrator responds to a summons from his reclusive biologist friend Richard Ashley, who shows him a startling sight under the microscope: a tiny humanoid figure, somewhat repellent in aspect, enclosed in crystalloid sheaths. As the narrator stares, he receives a telepathic communication from the microscopic being, telling him not to be afraid. * The visitor, Ashley states, is from a tiny planet about two hundred light-years away. It is composed of radioactive material so powerful that when it releases its protective shields, a beam of destructive energy flows out for miles. One such radiation has already accidentally killed several people, who were considered victims of lightning. * Moving away from the tiny figure, whose telepathy Ashley says has a radius of only a couple of feet, Ashley declares that he intends to destroy it in a special furnace that can reach 5,000° F. The reason? When the alien returns to his tiny planet (which is only the size of a desk), his fellows will begin an invasion of Earth. * Ashley sets off the heat-flash, but it is in vain. The alien has been suspicious and has followed Ashley, learning of his plan. Returning to his spaceship, which is moored in Ashley's kidney, he mocks Ashley, telling him that he will shine like a star. The alien spaceship carries Ashley, gleaming with flame, off into the sky. * The police at first suspected the narrator of Ashley's death, but there was no evidence (or body), and he has been cleared. But he is intensely worried about the potential invasion, which should be due in about four hundred years. * A nicely done science-fiction horror story. The metaphor of the alien spaceship for a kidney attack is powerful.

LORRAINE, LILITH

Pseud. of Mary Maude White, née Dunn (1894-1967). U.S. (mostly Texas) writer of occasional fiction, educator (in Mexico), radio announcer, newspaper reporter. A prominent figure in the amateur (traditional) poetry movement, with several volumes of poetry, some of which deal with science-fictional subjects. Founder of Avalon, a poetry association.

900. **INTO THE 28TH CENTURY**. *Science Wonder Quarterly,* Winter 1930. Ill. Paul

Short story. * *Time:* prologue and epilogue material 1932; otherwise around 2730. *Place:* Corpus Christi, Texas, and its future equivalent. * The nameless narrator is boating in the Gulf of Mexico when he is suddenly seized by an unknown force and ripped into the future. He finds himself on a gold-plated futuristic battleship (vintage 1980) that is filled with a merry group of young men and women in Classical garb, tunics and robes. * The future people, particularly the handsome young woman Iris, thereupon take the narrator on what amounts to a guided tour of an eutopia with strong occult elements. * The future civilization of 2730: The economy is a true socialism,

with about two hours of work a day. The world government, which consists of a "king" and a few officials, is elected for a yearly term by an elite group. The chief function of the government consists of regulating education, which involves formal college training, then a year on a floating college, whence the ship that took in the narrator. * The guiding principle of the society is a mixture of science and philosophy, plus attunement with a divine principle (not personal) that permeates the universe. From such foundations an incredible civilization has been built, including thought-controlled apparatus of various sorts. Disintegrator and reintegrator apparatus (the latter of which creates matter suitably from free particles) are important aspects of the culture. Attunement with the divine also endows the future people with near immortality and eternal youth. Once the external sources of illness were removed, internal disorders disappeared. There is no religion per se, but all live a relationship with the divine. * Strict birth control is practiced, with special permits required to create a child, which on conception is reared in vitro. Marriage is more or less monogamous, although there are no strict rules about it, but encouragement is given to interracial unions. (The author, who is a Texan, lists racial components, which include whites, Orientals, American Indians, Indian Indians, but not blacks; what happened to the black race she does not say.) Eugenics is also practiced, with superior persons encouraged to breed. False shame has been eradicated, and males and females bathe together nude. * The new city of Nirvania is beautiful, with parks and spacious homes. Transportation is accomplished by gravity-control surface vehicles and individual flying wings. * All this is in the fourth dimension, which is time. * During the narrator's tour of the culture with the charming Iris, she takes him to the tower of the Mad Inventor Holden, which tower has been preserved from the narrator's past. While meddling about, the narrator opens a casket, breathes in a certain dust, and finds himself back in 1932. * Holden, who is present and enraged when the narrator suddenly appears in the tower, nevertheless explains matters. Time travel of the sort that the narrator underwent is a matter of changing vibratory rate, which can be done in various ways. While the future people had a mechanical time dredge, Holden has a compound of Oriental drugs that will accomplish the same thing and return the narrator to the twenty-eighth century and Iris. The narrator finishes his manuscript and presumably leaves. * In the middle of the narrative the author inserts a long future history. During the 1940s and 1950s industrial dictators arose who controlled the world's economy. These dictators, who oppressed the workers severely, also established thought control. Special brain operations removed all initiative and inserted a desire only to work. This system prevailed for a time, but fell to a revolution of the young people, who had a disintegrator ray. In the new world that followed, after some excesses, a matriarchy of sorts was established. The author is vague, but the rise of a new cult of chivalry, in addition to social equality, seems to have given women the edge in the future culture. While men perform the actual administration and work, the women seem to be the spiritual center, with a matriarchy of sorts. It must be admitted, however, that the author is far from clear (even self-contradictory) on this point. * A curious semi-eccentric work, mushy and sentimental, archaic for its time. Ms. Lorraine, who was not overburdened with modesty about her literary ability, may well have taken it seriously.

901. **THE JOVIAN JEST.** *Astounding Stories*, May 1930. Ill. J. Fleming Gould.
Short story. * A strange object lands in a rural field, where it is soon discovered and surrounded by local people, including Professor Ralston. A tentacle flashes out and seizes first a yokel named Jones, then the Professor. It releases them both, and then addresses the crowd through the Professor. * In a talk-down pep talk it reveals that it is from another "universe," one where the cosmic calamity that caused diversification on Earth did not take place; instead, the space beings evolved to perfection and are almost immortal. They travel around the universe exploring and learning. * The being then reveals that while Jones is innately more intelligent than the professor, the professor has a larger vocabulary. The being announces its departure, but, perhaps as a joke, perhaps as a lesson, it implants the Professor's verbal ability into Jones. The result is mildly disastrous.

902. **THE CELESTIAL VISITOR.** *Wonder Stories*, March 1935. Ill. Paul.
Short story. Attempted humor. * *Place:* the little asteroid Eutopia, and Earth. * The story is the first-person narrative of the young explorer Zanor, who is the first to visit Earth. * *Background:* Millennia earlier, when it became obvious that Atlantis was undergoing destruction, a band of wise men and their families built a spaceship and left Earth, settling on the asteroid that they named Eutopia. In the millennia that have passed, this history has been all but forgotten, considered a mere legend. On Eutopia the migrants set up an ideal civilization without the errors that caused the destruction of Atlantis. Immortality has been achieved by means of periodic dissolution and reassembly by ray. * Zanor, who is a youth of a mere two hundred years, feels that Eutopian culture has grown jejune and static. He craves something new. Investigating ancient records and legends, he confirms the Terrestrial origin of the Eutopians and determines to visit Earth by what amounts to matter transmission on one of the rejuvenation rays. He takes along with him a cloak of invisibility, a small disintegrator, a thought transmitter, and food pellets. * On Earth he runs into expectable difficulties and romance. He is arrested, placed in jail, released when he demonstrates his disintegrator, lionized by a reporter, and assisted by the judge's handsome daughter, with whom he falls in love. They decide to become "eternal mates" and return together to Eutopia on the disassembling ray. * *Miscellaneous:* The Eutopians are in telepathic and radio communication with Venus. * A very bad job that would be considered a weak parody were the author not so obviously serious.

903. **THE ISLE OF MADNESS.** *Wonder Stories*, December 1935. Ill. Schneeman.
Short story. * *Time:* 1940 and perhaps several hundred years later. *Place:* In the later section a Polynesian island, and the ruins of San Francisco, Chicago, and New York City. * 1940: First, the human psyche is deteriorating, and it is anticipated that in a few hundred years the race will be totally mad. Second, a religion based on a combination of mechanism and violent reaction rules America. Third, mechanical mind control directs most Americans. * There are, however, a few exceptions to mind control, minds strong and unusual enough to resist it. They are weeded out by the authorities and sent to an island in the Pacific Ocean, where they live in exile. This island is pejoratively called the Isle of Madness. * Centuries pass. The islanders, who have long been completely isolated, have developed a super-science, including a force screen, disintegrators, and much else. They also have evolved physically and mentally into supermen, capable of telepathic communication. More, they have achieved a mental contact with a higher power that may be divinity of a sort or simply the human master soul. * At a suitable time in the future, the inhabitants of the Isle of Madness receive a message from the master soul ordering them to explore the outer world. Mounting gliders that can be maintained aloft almost indefinitely, bearing weapons, they venture to the mainland. They find no humans, but in the ruins of San Francisco they are attacked by packs of humanoid wolves or lupine humans, who are devolved mankind. The same happens in the ruins of Chicago. In New York the explorers find a message from perhaps the last human being in the outer world. * *Miscellaneous:* The Statue of Liberty is used as a symbol for the last men. * Little to recommend.

LOVECRAFT, H[OWARD] P[HILLIPS] (1890-1937)
U.S. (mostly Providence, Rhode Island) author, generally considered the quintessential twentieth-century American writer of supernatural horror fiction. Lovecraft's pathetic life and his eccentricities have been belabored so much that it is hardly necessary to go into great detail. Obsessed with a notion of gentility and an uncompromising desire for independence, he made a scanty living as a ghost writer and died nearly a pauper. During his lifetime Lovecraft became a figure of almost mythical stature, whose ideas and literary techniques dominated much of supernatural fiction. A learned, if self-taught man of brilliant intellect, he gathered around himself a circle of similar writers whose work shows his influence. While Lovecraft's early work was usually supernatural in orientation, his later work had drifted, though within the same symbolic range, toward rationality and science-fiction. The two late stories considered here exemplify this trend.

904. **THE COLOUR OUT OF SPACE.** *Amazing Stories*, September 1927. Ill. de Aragon.
(Frequently reprinted. In Lovecraft, *The Outsider and Others*; Lovecraft, *The Colour out of Space*; Lovecraft, *The Dunwich Horror and Others*; Lovecraft, *The Lurking Fear*; Lovecraft, *Three Tales of Terror*; Lovecraft, *The Haunter of the Dark*; Lovecraft, *The Best of H. P. Lovecraft*; Lovecraft, *Best Supernatural Stories*; Fiedler, *In Dreams Awake*; Moskowitz, *Masterpieces of Science Fiction*; Conklin, *Omnibus of Science Fiction*; and undoubtedly elsewhere.)
Short story. * "West of Arkham the hills run wild, and there are valleys with deep woods that no axe has ever cut. There are dark narrow glens where the trees slope fantastically, and where thin brooklets trickle without ever having caught the glint of sunlight." * The story is told in the frame situation of an engineer who is surveying the countryside around Arkham, preparatory to flooding the area to create a reservoir. He observes a "blasted heath" that is completely lifeless and oddly decayed, and hears dark hints of strange happenings; he finally learns the history of the events of the past from the ancient rustic Ammi Pierce. * A meteorite struck on the farm of Nahum Gardner. Examined by the savants from local Miskatonic University, it was discovered to be composed of a strange metal that gradually decreased from day to day. Imbedded in it was a small, seemingly empty opalescent sphere, which the scientists accidentally broke. In all probability there were other such inclusions in the meteorite. * The meteorite is gone, but its effect

Lovecraft, H. P. (*continued*)

lingers as Nahum's farm, stock, and family gradually decay. The trees, such as do not wither away into a grayish ash, writhe of their own accord; the cattle waste away and die; and Nahum's family first goes mad, then dies. * The center of the infection is the open well near Nahum's house. From it emerge the opalescent colorings that were first seen in the sphere in the meteorite. * Eventually, as stories of the strange deaths spread, an investigation takes place. A group of men including Ammi Pierce, detectives, and medical officials visit the Gardner farm not long before dusk. They find the remains of the Gardner children, and witness the strange apotheosis of the dweller in the well. A pillar of color shoots up, and presumably the thing leaves the Earth. A weaker efflorescence seems unable to leave and is still in the well. * The explanation is that certain of the spheres in the meteorite hatched and that their life-forms took refuge in the well, gathering strength for their next phase of life by sapping the life force of the countryside. * The narrator leaves, shaken, wondering about the water in the projected reservoir. * An excellent story, one of Lovecraft's finest works; in my opinion the best original story to appear in *Amazing Stories*. It is well known what difficulties Lovecraft had in collecting payment from Gernsback.

905. **AT THE MOUNTAINS OF MADNESS**. *Astounding Stories,* February-April 1936. Unsigned ill. (Brown?) (Reprinted in Lovecraft, *The Outsider,* and in Lovecraft, *At the Mountains of Madness,* and in Derleth, *Strange Ports of Call*). Short novel, written in 1931. The present text was restyled and abridged by the editors of *Astounding Stories,* greatly to Lovecraft's annoyance. * *Place:* Antarctica. * Dyer, the narrator and leader of the Miskatonic University Expedition of 1931, offers a long cautionary tale to warn future expeditions to Antarctica. The first part of his document restates the official report in narrative form. * As Dyer tells it, the expedition, the purpose of which was to gather geological specimens, moved into Antarctica easily and efficiently with a small group of airplanes. Dyer remained at the base camp, but his associate Lake, with others, flew off to a different site. In a relatively short time, aided by a new rock drill perfected by Professor Pabodie, Lake uncovered a treasure trove of paleontological remains ranging from earliest times to the Pliocene. * Especially rich was a limestone cave in which Lake found several specimens of a remarkable ancient life-form: a barrel-shaped creature, apparently formed on a quinary symmetry rather than our binary, about eight feet tall, with tentacles, wings, and peculiar feet. Oddly enough, the feet of these beings are compatible with footprints imprinted in rock from the archaic period. * Most of the creatures, which did not seem really fossilized, appeared to be intact, and Lake began dissecting damaged specimens. He continued to report his findings by radio, until suddenly, after a particularly violent storm, communication ceased. * Dyer and companions, on flying to Lake's camp, found a holocaust. The dogs were all dead, as were the humans, although one man was missing. Equipment was wrecked and shattered in a purposeful way; and the damaged paleontological specimens, whom Dyer calls the Old Ones, were ceremonially buried in the snow, which was marked with certain strange symbols. The intact Old Ones were not to be found. Dyer, in his official report, blamed the tragedy on the storm. But now that he has heard of other expeditions planned for the area, he must utter a warning. He

intends to tell what really happened and what it all means. * The second and longer part of the novel is the secret history that Dyer tried to conceal. He and Danforth decide to investigate a range of mountains visible in the near distance, mountains that obviously are higher than the Himalayas. A peculiarity of these mountains is that they seem to have strange geometric formations on the sides, together with caves, all suggestive of construction. As Dyer and Danforth fly through a pass between the peaks, they see beneath them a colossal city constructed according to a quinary geometry; it is ruined, ice-filled in part, but sufficiently preserved in places to show an awesome, terrifying quality. The men land and begin to explore. * The details of what they see as they wander through chambers and corridors and climb up and down in the ruins take up most of the remainder of the novel. As they explore, Dyer studies seemingly omnipresent sculptures and bas reliefs. They convey a cosmic history. * To summarize this secret history of Earth: The Old Ones came from another world, presumably from another solar system; they were able to travel through space without vehicles by altering their physical nature suitably. Originally an aquatic race, they settled on the still lifeless Earth in the seas that are now Antarctica, where they built up a colossal civilization. For their convenience they created Earth life, some of which they modified to suit their needs, some of which they simply let evolve in its own directions. For hundreds of millions of years the Old Ones ruled the Earth, gradually moving out of the seas onto land and building cyclopean cities. * During their long hegemony they were challenged on several occasions by other invading races from the stars. While the Old Ones defeated octopoidal creatures of Cthulhu's sort, they were less fortunate with the Abominable Snowmen. More dangerous than either invader, ultimately, were the shoggoths, creations of the Old Ones. Protoplasmic masses responsive to telepathic commands, they served as nonmechanical prime movers and tools. They evolved, however, and, developing a certain intelligence, they revolted on occasions. The Old Ones suppressed them with difficulty. * As Dyer recounts, the art styles of the Old Ones in the wall sculptures gradually declined, and toward the end were almost decadent. The onset of glaciation apparently destroyed the Old Ones, although there are representations of a deep inland sea refuge. * As Dyer and Danforth move about, taking notes and photographs, dropping paper trails so that they can find their way back, they are gradually oppressed with a feeling of threat, especially associated with certain odors. Then they find, deep in the subterranean chambers, material looted from their expedition camp and the last corpse of their comrades. They also find a group of the Old Ones, strangely mutilated. * The ultimate horror comes when they finally recognize what has happened. The Old Ones in the camp had thawed out and awakened; moved by scientific curiosity, perhaps attacked by the dogs, who loathed them, they destroyed the camp and then moved into their ancient city, seeking refuge and perhaps companions. Instead, they met with living shoggoths—one of which now emerges and chases Dyer and Danforth out of the ruins. The men are fortunate to reach their plane in safety. As they fly away, Danforth sees a still greater horror associated with a still higher range of mountains in the distance. It disturbs his mental balance, and we shall never know what he saw. *Miscellaneous:* Dyer and Danforth, in their underground explorations, come upon a small group of enormous blind penguins, obviously adapted to their

Lovecraft, H. P. (*continued*)

subterranean life. * The Old Ones, who have facetiously been termed giant sea cucumbers, partake of both animal and vegetable natures. * Lovecraft, throughout the narrative, makes references to the *Necronomicon*, the mad Arab Abdul Alhazred, and similar stock figures of the Cthulhu complex. These usually destroy the mood of the story. * The basic concept is one that Lovecraft often toyed with fictionally: that man is but the latest of a succession of dominant races, many of which were higher than he. * One of the most interesting aspects of the story is the metaphor of architecture as a structuring of both horror and life.

906. **THE SHADOW OUT OF TIME**. *Astounding Stories*, June 1936. Unsigned ill. (Brown?)

(Reprinted in Lovecraft, *The Outsider;* in Lovecraft, *The Best of H. P. Lovecraft;* in Lovecraft, *The Colour out of Space;* in Lovecraft, *The Dunwich Horror;* in Lovecraft, *The Dunwich Horror and Others;* in Wollheim, *Portable Novels of Science;* and probably elsewhere.)

Novelette. * *Time:* Recollections of the period 1908 to 1913; 1935; and about one hundred and fifty million years ago. * *Place:* New England and Australia. * The narrative of Professor Nathaniel Wingate Peaslee of Miskatonic University. * In the first part of the story Peaslee, speaking from 1935, tells of his strange personality disorder some score of years ago. In 1908 he suddenly collapsed and was amnesiac on recovering consciousness. He had not only forgotten his identity, but much of his cultural and historical ambience; he was like a little child learning about an adult world. When he recovered sufficiently, he undertook travels to strange parts of the world, meeting mysterious people, mastering odd lores. During this learning episode, which also encompassed science, his mental powers were far beyond those of other men. Then, in 1913, a stranger visited him, set up a complex machine, left, and Peaslee regained consciousness of himself as of 1908. What had happened in the missing years, 1908 to 1913? * Back as his former personality, Peaslee spends much of the next twenty years or so trying to discover just what he (himself as well as the personality that inhabited his body) did during the blank period. In this, he is both assisted and hampered by heavy dreams, which gradually come to form a pattern. * As Peaslee finally establishes: His body had been occupied by the mind of a member of the Great Race, a nonhuman group of intelligences that held Earth in sway during the late Paleozoic and early Mesozoic. The members of the Great Race were able to cast their minds into the future and usurp bodies; during such occupation the original intelligence was housed in the body of the usurper back in the past, as was Peaslee's. This mind-transfer had two purposes. On the one hand it served scientific purposes; the usurper gained knowledge about the future, while the captive mind was encouraged to write or communicate about life in his own time. Such documents formed an enormous library. The other purpose was personal and race survival. In the past the Great Race came from another planet and usurped bodies, and in the future they will take over the bodies of intelligent superbeetles, whose civilization will follow ours. * As Peaslee gradually pieces together his stay in a body in the far past, he is able to reconstruct the ancient civilization, which was far higher than ours. It maintained a titanic architecture, high science, and great art. As for the members of the Great Race, they were cone-shaped beings about ten feet tall, with a globular four-eyed head and arm-like

appendages (two with prehensile claws). All in all, Peaslee's stay among the elder race was not too unpleasant, and he had many conversations with fellow prisoners from other times and places. * There is, however, a danger awaiting the Great Race. When they arrived on Earth, they found it inhabited in part by black, semimaterial creatures of implacable hostility, whose minds they could not penetrate. Many wars followed. The Great Race was victorious in the sense of driving its enemies underground into tunnels and caverns, but unsuccessful in that the monstrous beings will eventually emerge and triumph. When this happens the Great Race will move their personalities en masse to the future, as has been mentioned. * For some time Peaslee has been publishing his dreams as a case history in psychopathology without arousing any great interest. Then he receives a message from an engineer in Australia, who claims to have come upon vestiges of architecture like that Peaslee described. * The university and others fund an expedition, and Peaslee, his son, the engineer, and a work crew proceed to the proper region in the great western desert. As they work around the ruins, which are so shattered as to be nearly uninterpretable, a feeling of dread and horror arises in Peaslee. After spending a night away from camp, he recommends that the dig be canceled, and, near a breakdown, leaves the camp. On ship from Australia, however, he records his reasons for urging that the expedition be withdrawn. * His final story: Wandering about on that night, he chanced, amid the blowing sand, on an entrance to a half-buried tunnel, which he was sure he recognized. He followed it, with total familiarity, into the library archives that he remembered in his dreams. And there he withdrew a certain book. All this was done in accompaniment to a great sense of peril, particularly around certain openings and pits, which he remembered as having been sealed. As he learned to his horror, these subterranean passages were still inhabited by the semimaterial enemies of the Great Race. Pursued by piping monstrosities, he raced out of the ruins to safety. Along the way he dropped the library book, which was the volume that he had written one hundred and fifty million years ago. * The story, of course, is a combination of Lovecraft's fictional philosophy of history and the supernatural material-evidence-for-the-truth-of-the-visitation motif, worked together in surficial detailed verisimilitude. It is a story difficult to evaluate, since like so many smash-ending stories, it is weakened by repeated readings. The close detail and successful attempt at de-emotionalized scholarly prose is completely successful, but many readers find this a limitation.

LOVERING, PAUL H.
No information.

907. **WHEN THE EARTH GREW COLD**. *Amazing Stories Quarterly*, Fall 1929. Unsigned ill.

Short story. * *Time:* 1938 and A.D. 28,989. *Place:* the Chicago area. * Eustace Maynard, a wealthy amateur scientist, has discovered antigravity and has built a small, well-equipped spaceship for interplanetary travel. Oddly enough, his discovery includes perfect suspended animation. * While he and Professor Brown (the astronomer) are discussing a voyage, a dog who has been revived from suspended animation accidentally knocks over the chemicals, and the men sink down unconscious. * They awaken in a cave in A.D. 28,989, although they obviously do not know the year until informed. A little exploration reveals a

Lovering, Paul H. (*continued*)

network of caves, a river of light, and a band of nasty little cannibals who try to capture them. Already captive is a young woman, somewhat taller than the cannibals. Maynard and Brown rescue the woman, are attacked, and are in turn saved by a smallish man with sleep bombs. * He explains somewhat. The sun is almost out, thanks to an ice nebula that has enveloped the solar system, and its weak radiation is captured, condensed, and used as the living medium for the underground men. They use it for heat and light for growing mushrooms. The surface of the Earth is completely uninhabitable, and mankind seems to consist of the English-speaking dwarves and the uncivilized cannibals, all few in number. In a short time mankind will be extinct. * The twentieth-century men are welcomed by the future people, who believe their story. As the future men sadly say, the only hope for humanity would be migration to a planet in another system, and for that antigravity is needed. When Maynard explains that he has discovered the secret, the little people take him to a gigantic telescope built just before the Earth became cold and show him an edenic planet that they call Hope. * Using Maynard's discovery, as a test the future men send two young people to Hope. After they arrive safely, the exodus takes place. * The future people, who are pacifists and life-respecters, will not prevent the nasty cannibals, now headed by a renegade from the civilized people, from following them and having an equal chance at survival. * Very amateurish child of Wells's *The Time Machine*.

908. **THE INEVITABLE CONFLICT**. *Amazing Stories*, December 1931-January 1932. Ill. Morey.

Short novel. * *Time:* presumably not too distant future. *Place:* the East Coast. *Background:* In this future world there are (as far as the author informs us) only two nations, the Mongolian Empire, which has conquered the whole Old World, and the Matriarchy of the United Companies, which consists of the former United States and perhaps Latin America—the author being silent about this. * The Matriarchy is an outgrowth of capitalism. The giant trusts and industries gradually subsumed the country; at first they were male dominated, but eventually, through wives and efficient secretaries, they were taken over (with two exceptions cited in the story) by women. * The resulting culture is a feminist dictatorship, with men being deprived of rights, assigned to low jobs, and subject to horrible penalties for even subversive speech. Police power is in the hands of a female corps called the Amazons, who report to the female council, particularly the matriarch. The Amazons have been sterilized, a situation that many of them resent. * In addition to the inequity, the matriarchal system has led to cultural stasis and decay, general unhappiness, anomie, and military weakness, for the female rulers are inept. It is clear to many that the Mongolian Empire is only waiting for a chance to gobble up the Matriarchy, which currently pays an enormous tribute to maintain peace and independence. * Against this background, two action themes unfold and intertwine. Stephen Mowbray, one of the two male company heads, is a rebel. Defying the matriarch and the council, he speaks openly about the decadence of the time. More, he has surreptitiously organized a resistance movement, with which he intends to topple the matriarchy and restore bisexual values. In this movement are female European veterans of the wars with Mongolia, workers, and the criminal underworld. Stephen can

hold them all together. * Stephen is just about ready for his putsch, with new weapons and defenses against the matriarchy's disintegrator rays, when the second theme assumes importance. The Mongolian emperor lands troops not far from the capital and demands surrender. He intends to have the world under his dominion before he dies. The matriarch tries to buy him off, but is unsuccessful. * The salvation of America lies in Stephen Mowbray's hands. The winning tactic against the Mongolian hordes is an old-fashioned air raid with explosives. The emperor is killed, and his successor is a peaceful man. Mowbray, now ruler of America, will straighten things out. * *Miscellaneous:* Society in the future world is rigidly stratified, with intense class feelings. Thus, a company woman feels only scorn for Stephen's worker fiancée. * The matriarch had a good plan for bringing Stephen to heel. She and the council planned to marry him to a domineering female company executive, who would whip him into shape. But things moved too fast for this to happen. * Better in summary than in the original text, which is long-winded and fumbling.

LOW, A[RCHIBALD] M[ONTGOMERY] (1888-1956)

British consulting engineer, research physicist, science expositor. D.Sc., Ph.D. Usually credited as Professor Low from one-time position as honorary assistant professor of physics for the Royal Artillery. Wrote many books explaining technology and science, no one of which is preëminent. Also a prolific inventor with pioneer work on television (demonstrated 1914), ballistics (early smart bomb), rocketry (radio controls), etc. Wrote boys' fiction, sometimes anonymously, perhaps also pseudonymously. Unfortunately, not a skilled writer of fiction.

909. **SPACE**. *Scoops*, 17 February-21 April 1934. Unsigned ill.

(Published in book form as *Adrift in the Stratosphere*, Blackie, London, 1937.)

Boys' fiction. * Short novel * Three young Englishmen—Peter, Victor, and Philip—are cycling in the countryside when one of their motors breaks down. Seeing a shed close by, they enter it, hoping to find assistance. Instead, they see a large, remarkable machine, which they vaguely have heard associated with the great inventor Professor Slater. The boys meddle with the controls, and almost before they know it, are miles away from the Earth and rising fast. * Slater's machine, as the trespassers learn the hard way, is the *Astronauticus,* a small spaceship. It is lifted by a powerful gas bag, which is to be discarded when the ship is in the proper position, at which time rockets will function. The professor has provided for many eventualities, for the rocket ship contains an apparatus that translates languages instantly, food and water pills, and a notebook full of surprising information. * The rocket climbs through the atmosphere, passing through belts of monochromatic light and X-rays that render the young men suitably transparent. * Out in space, a gigantic monster attacks the ship, spewing volumes of poison gas. The men destroy it with a rocket blast. * Victor manages to make a radio operative, and for a time the young men hear fossil broadcasts of months earlier, trapped in the stratosphere. More important, they hear a rough voice, which the translating machine renders into English. It is from Mars. The Martians have seen Slater's machine leave, and intend to destroy it. Barrages of various sorts of rays (death, madness) hit the *Astronauticus,* but, despite periods of unconsciousness and

Low, A. M. (*continued*)

bruising, the young men survive, for the professor's notebook tells how to cancel out various rays. Finally, the King and Lord of Mars appears on their viewer, informing them that the Martians, who are very long-lived, are afraid of Terrestrial germs and that Martian technical secrets cannot be shared. The *Astronauticus* must be destroyed. * The men escape the various attacks, however, and find themselves in a region of space islands, on one of which they land. It is Earth-like and pleasant. The telepathic inhabitants are human, though twice as tall as a man. The ruler of the space island explains to the trio that they are really on a comet. The cometeers, who live in the open or in caves, are deliberate neoprimitives, having discarded much mechanical civilization, with great improvement in health and longevity. They retain enough science, however, to fight off Martian attacks and to provide the young men with calculations for returning to Earth. * *Miscellaneous:* The people of the space island are telepathic and also speak English, since they monitor Earth's radio. They have an extensive file of historical motion pictures of Earth. * The Martian king informs the boys, a propos of nothing, that the Martian time rate is faster than Earth's, so that a Terrestrial minute equals a Martian year. * Feeble.

910. **THE TIME TRAVELLER.** *Scoops,* 3 March 1934. Ill. S.D. Published anonymously. The attribution to Professor Low is based on an examination of the company records by Mr. W. O. G. Lofts.

Boys' fiction. * Short story. * *Time:* mostly in A.D. 2034. * Reporter Brant Emerson of the *Live Wire* has unsuccessfully tried to interview Professor Lestrange, but when he saves the absentminded professor's life during a traffic incident, the professor becomes very friendly. Taking Brant to his laboratory, Lestrange displays his great invention, a time machine. The machine works, Lestrange claims. He has tried it himself, but he needs corroboration from another person. * Looking for a scoop, Brant eagerly enters the machine and is transported to the year 2034. London is now a collection of huge skyscrapers, among which are monorails and aerocabs. Currency has changed, with a new decimal coinage, and automat-like machines dispense food and heavy-water pills. As Brant sees with dismay, there are no more newspapers; their place has been taken by omnipresent radio and television. During his initial perambulation of future London, Brant runs into some minor trouble, but nothing major happens. * Brant has a bright idea. He visits the current communications czar, Lord Bracknell, who is the descendant of Brant's old employer on the *Live Wire.* Bracknell, easily convinced of Brant's genuineness by a perusal of old records, takes him on as a reporter extraordinary. Among other things, Brant, on seeing a television coverage of a battle in the Atlantic, is permitted to accompany the International Air Force that is repelling a pirate attack on the Floating Stations. He sees that the pirates are all blacks, and is told that the black would-be dictator is trying to conquer the world. Flying torpedoes dispose of the pirates, but Brant's plane is damaged, whereupon his seat is automatically ejected with a parachute. * Back in London, Brant is arrested for jaywalking, examined as insane, but rescued by Bracknell. Following this at an international congress, Brant saves Bracknell's life from an assassin. As Brant is being interviewed on television, however, he is retrieved by Professor Lestrange. * Brant hastens to write up his story for the *Live Wire,* jubilant in knowing that his job, according to future

records, is secure for five years. * *Miscellaneous:* Midget auto races take place in gigantic stadiums.

911. **VENGEANCE ON VENUS.** *Scoops,* 7 April 1934. Unsigned ill. Published anonymously. The attribution to Professor Low is based on an examination of the company records by Mr. W. O. G. Lofts.

Boys' fiction. * Short story. * *Place:* mostly Venus. * The great scientist Reginald Bland has just invented a matter transmitter; it translates electrons into waves, then reassembles them at another point. Bland and his acquaintance Gawain Sinclair immediately leave for Venus, where they arrive after about three minutes. Venus is much like a tropical Earth, except that the vegetation is yellow and red instead of green. As the progress of the story reveals, Sinclair was a poor choice for a companion, for in addition to being very unpleasant, he goes mad and becomes a deadly enemy. * In a relatively short time, the two men encounter civilization, as an armored, mounted man with a lance challenges them. He speaks a variant Spanish, which Bland can handle well enough. The men then proceed to the capital of the land of Ballestoa, where they find a very strange combination of ultra-modern architecture, flying machines and what-not, with a medieval social culture including knights, pages, and fair maidens. The men meet Queen Marita, with whom Bland becomes friendly. * The land is currently engaged in a civil war, with Marita's cousin Pedro in rebellion. And, oddly enough, the war is waged totally in a medieval manner with armored knights, without modern technology. Bland tries to persuade Queen Marita to use airplanes, but she refuses. * About this time Sinclair, who has been becoming more and more unpleasant, disappears; he has defected to Pedro, for whom he is building a modern army. Bland finally convinces Marita to do the same. * His first air raid, however, is a disaster, for Sinclair has set up a vibratory wave that affects the inner ear, causing vertigo. Planes crash, and Bland is captured. Sinclair, who is now totally mad, gloats at the thought of the death to which he will put Bland. * But all is not lost. Bland escapes, instructs the remaining pilots to fly above the range of the vibration, and bombs Pedro's army out of existence. Pedro kills Sinclair, and is himself killed in the bombing. Bland is the hero of the day, and will undoubtedly espouse Marita.

912. **S.O.S. FROM SATURN.** *Scoops,* 12 May, 1934. Unsigned ill. Published anonymously. The attribution to Professor Low is based on an examination of the company records by Mr. W. O. G. Lofts.

Boys' fiction. * Short story. * *Time:* the interplanetary future. *Place:* space and Saturn. * MacRufus and his comrades Wildy and Sid, on board the spaceship *Silver Sphere,* receive a code message equivalent to an SOS. from Saturn. They are puzzled at first, since no one has ever traveled to Saturn, but decide to accept the message as valid. * Saturn is much like Earth, but with heavy red vegetation, and the men are able to move about without discomfort. Their first venture outside their ship, however, ends in an attack by repulsive creatures like giant insects. Fortunately, white light is so unusual on Saturn that torch (i.e. flashlight) beams kill the monsters. * Following their television screens, the men fly to a gigantic city, once magnificent, but now mostly in ruins. There in a single citadel, the inhabitants of Saturn are fighting off attacks by the monstrous wildlife. * MacRufus and associates are equal to the task. Rigging up strong light projectors, they wipe out the giant

Low, A. M. (*continued*)

insects and their leaders, called Intelligences, who are like flying jellyfish. But in a near mishap the men are forced to leave the planet precipitously. One of the Intelligences managed to enter the spaceship and start it up. He was readily destroyed, and the men are on their way back home. * *Miscellaneous:* The natives of Saturn are human, but very delicate and weedy. They are also totally effete and degenerate, unable to accomplish anything, a defect which the travelers comment upon. * The Saturnians learned signals from monitoring space radio.

LOWER, HAROLD A. (1895-1947)

U.S. author, then resident in San Diego, California. Portrait accompanying the story shows a young man in military tunic, perhaps of World War I period. The contents page incorrectly renders the author's name as Vernon A. Lower. The author is cited by Schwartz/Weisinger as Harold W. Lower, which also seems to be incorrect. According to the story blurb Lower was an electrical engineer by profession. The author also contributed two articles to *Astounding Science Fiction* in 1939. Another story, "The Message from Mars," is listed in *Science Fiction Digest,* April 1933 (p. 5) as accepted by *Amazing Stories,* but it does not seem to have been published. See also Harry Martin, pseud.

913. **RAIDERS FROM SPACE**. *Science Wonder Stories,* March 1930.

Short-short story. * The fourth-prize-winning story in the contest based on the cover of the November 1929 issue of *Science Wonder Stories.* Lower received $25. * *Time:* the near future. * The Gregorys are arguing about buying a new television set when they turn on to a news feature. On the screen they see flying saucers carrying off the Eiffel Tower and the Woolworth Building, while other images show and a commentator describes the destruction being visited on New York City by an invasion from space. * The Gregorys are greatly disturbed, since their son works in New York. But their anguish is speedily resolved when Tom enters. What they have been watching is a preview or teaser for the great new German science-fiction film about to be released. * Much the best entry storywise, much superior to the higher-winning entries. A prevision of Orson Welles.

LOWNDES, ROBERT W[ARD] (1916-present)

U.S. editor, author, s-f fan. Member of Futurians in youth. Edited magazines *Future Fiction, Science Fiction Quarterly, Dynamic Science Fiction,* and others. Also edited s-f line for Avalon Books. Has written in collaboration with James Blish, Cyril Kornbluth, Donald Wollheim and others, and under many pseuds. Although Lowndes is remembered mostly as an editor, his fiction has been acclaimed critically.

914. **REPORT OF THE PLUTONIAN AMBASSADOR BY SIR DOC LOWNDES**. *Wonder Stories,* September 1935.

Short humor piece in the letter column, written in much the same vein as Hoy Ping Pong's storiette, #643, "Report of the 196th Convention," in the November 1934 issue of *Wonder Stories.* In this case, the point is reaction against the needless, trivial, carping criticisms that appear in the readers' column. * The narrator, an Earthman, visits the Plutonian chapter of the Science Fiction League, where he witnesses changes in the June 1935 magazine that the Plutonians make with superscientific devices. As individuals complain about certain elements, like cover design

or the presence of staples, Plutonian superscience alters them. He protests and is finally expelled. * Juvenile work, of course.

LUDWICK, KATHLEEN

U.S. author, then resident of Oakland, California. According to Street and Smith records, contributed to *Western Story* and other pulp magazines. Social Security records list a Kathleen Ludwick (1892-1970), who lived in New York and died in Maryland. It is not clear whether this person is the author concerned. The contents page of *Amazing Stories Quarterly* carries the author incorrectly as Luckwick.

915. **DR. IMMORTELLE**. *Amazing Stories Quarterly,* Summer 1930. Ill. Morey.

Short story. * *Place:* California, around Palo Alto. * The frame narrator, whose wife Linnie, a nurse, was killed when the Germans in World War I bombed a hospital tent, recalls the deathbed confession of Victor de Lyle that he heard some years before. * De Lyle, a blond man in his middle years, confesses that he is really a black man who was born around 1745. A slave, he was the half brother of the white Dr. Immortelle, who was presumably killed in an automobile accident. * Immortelle, an intelligent man, was greatly interested in the artificial prolongation of life by blood transfusions, and after some failures worked out a successful technique using the blood of children whom he either took from orphanages or kidnapped, as strays from the streets. He performed the same operations for de Lyle, whose racial characteristics were changed by the transfusions so that he became physiologically white. (According to the author, whites are a superior race.) * The criminal pair persisted in this for more than a century and a half, until Immortelle happened to hire the frame narrator's friend Linnie. Linnie, after a time, recognized him as the man who escaped after murdering her little brother some years before. Immortelle was all for killing Linnie, but de Lyle rebelled, and faked an accident to kill Immortelle. * Pretty bad. Involuted and confusing.

McCLARY, THOMAS CALVERT (1907 or 1909?-1972)

U.S. newspaperman, professional author, political speech writer, ghostwriter. Born in Chicago, lived in various parts of the U.S., mostly New York in his later years. Also wrote under pseuds. Thomas Calvert, Thomas Chester, Ray Tender, and others. Fairly prolific author of Western stories and mysteries. Contributed to later Nick Carter series and Man from U.N.C.L.E. See also pseud. Calvin Peregoy.

916. **REBIRTH**. *Astounding Stories,* February-March 1934. Ill. Don Hewitt.

(Reprinted in altered book form by Bart House, New York, 1944.)

Novel. * A good exemplification of many of the underground and not so underground social dissatisfactions and panaceas of the 1930s. * *Time:* 1957 and following. * "The masses were squeezed between big finance, corrupt politics, selfishness, the murderous underworld. War swept the world of happiness." The reason for this horrible (quite contemporary) situation: The world is paralyzed, "fettered by habits and traditions of long-dead ages." * Goddard, perhaps the greatest scientist of all time, is depressed and outraged by the situation, all the more so

McClary, Thomas Calvert (*continued*)

through his own experience. When he announced that he had a potent death ray, he believed that the nations would accordingly outlaw war. Instead, each offered huge bribes for sole possession of the ray to use against its enemies. * Goddard now determines to reform mankind along the lines of the general theorem stated above. He believes that if mankind can make a completely fresh start, abandoning the past, a better world order will emerge. He has the tools for such a new start, for his newly discovered radiation will strip away all memory from humanity, but will not change essential personality or intelligence. On this basis, with the artifacts remaining from civilization, Goddard believes that a millennial culture will develop. * Goddard turns on his ray. The catastrophe strikes and humans are now languageless, dataless, skillless flesh-creatures. As for Goddard, he sealed himself and a philosopher friend in a special construction that would provide learning tools for regaining what was lost. * McClary tells of developments in the New York City area, gradually expanding to a national level. Loss of life is horrendous, but some people do survive by utilizing slowly, concept by concept, what they can find locally. Food, shelter, fire, clothing, weapons emerge, perhaps much faster than the reader would have expected. A social organism evolves; it amounts to an elected total dictatorship that rules for the benefit of the people. From a small group in Manhattan, civilization develops and spreads until, in a few years there is a national culture. * The story is told mostly in terms of people who gravitate to the top: Bent, an elderly former capitalist, who is wise, becomes the theoretical leader; two strong-arm workers (coal heaver, construction worker), become the physical heads of government; a woman, Goddard's unattainable sweetheart, maintains an inchoate quest for former associates; and a few types recapitulate, after a fashion, their former development. * As the story ends, Goddard and Peterson emerge from their retreat, by far the most acculturated of the new men. The new civilization is much superior to the old, or so the author seems to believe; modern readers may have strong doubts. * *Miscellaneous:* As an unnecessary element, McClary includes a love-rival of Goddard's whom Goddard places in space as an observer. The motif is not developed, perhaps because McClary usually submitted uncorrected first drafts to the magazines. * Apart from external matters, weak on internal logic and fictionally lacking in conviction. "Rebirth" used to be considered a classic, perhaps because it expressed a range of thought that was popular at the time—ruthless destruction of the past on the assumption that what would emerge would be better. Now, while there is occasional imaginative throw-away detail, the story seems to be an overwritten social document.

MacCLURE, VICTOR (1887-1963)

Scottish artist, author, culinary expert. Author of *Scotland's Inner Man. A History of Scot's Food* (1935), and other works. Also illustrated many travel books.

917. **THE ARK OF THE COVENANT**. *Air Wonder Stories*, July-October 1929. Ill. Paul.

(First published in book form as *Ultimatum, A Romance of the Air* [Harrap, London, 1924] and as *The Ark of the Covenant* [Harper, New York, 1924].)

As a reprint the story is described in more detail in *Science-Fiction: The Early Years.*

Novel. * *Time:* Not firmly dated, but perhaps the later 1920s or early 1930s. * *Place:* New York, Washington, Brazil. * The peace vigilante, this time successful. * Wall Street is looted, as are other financial centers around the world. The modus operandi is the same: a sleep gas renders everyone unconscious, then men from a gigantic superdirigible remove bullion and cash, leaving in their place an equivalent amount of pure radium. * Young James Boon, son of one of the New York bankers affected, is also the developer of a superfast plane. Working out that the probable locale of the air bandits is somewhere around the Caribbean, he and Lamont, a physicist friend, investigate. They find the home station of the robbers, but are captured. * To their surprise, they learn that the robbers are not criminals, but high-minded social reformers who intend to render war impossible and to improve. They have been careful not to injure or kill anyone in their actions. Boon and Lamont are converted. * The organization is headed by a mysterious man called the Master, who has, in addition to the dirigibles and sleep gas, atomic power, a motor-stopping ray, and the ability to transmute metals. Near the home station are enormous deposits of radium, together with a new gas that is lighter than hydrogen. * The time is ready for a putsch, and the Master and his forces make a majestic flight to Washington. American defense forces are defeated, and the Master interviews the president, who not only knows the Master, but is converted. * A new era begins. The world will disarm; the Master reveals the secret of atomic power and turns over one of the great arks for policing purposes. * One of the better peace vigilante stories, with mainstream detail, and a couple of excellent sequences.

McDERMOTT, DENNIS

In this case, pseud. of P. Schuyler Miller, who has a separate entry. The pseud. was coined by Walter L. Dennis, based upon his own name and that of a friend, Paul McDermott. Despite information to the contrary elsewhere, McDermott had nothing to do with the writing of the story (per letter from Walter L. Dennis, 26 March 1995). The story was originally intended for publication in the fanzine the *Comet*, but, on being submitted to Gernsback, was published as below. * The portrait printed along with the story is that of Walter Dennis. * See also P. Schuyler Miller and Dennis McDermott, "The Duel on the Asteroid," a sequel.

918. **THE RED SPOT OF JUPITER**. *Wonder Stories*, July 1931. Ill. Marchioni.

Short story. * *Time:* A.D. 20,000. *Place:* space and Jupiter. * The notorious space criminal Black Lem Gulliver, who has been tried and sentenced for murdering a Martian, is being shipped to the penal colony on Titan. This is a lawless Hell, where newcomers seldom survive long. * Lem manages to escape from his confinement on the vessel, and during a struggle for the control of the ship disrupts the flight program, so that the ship heads for Jupiter itself, not Titan. * The ship crash-lands in the Red Spot, which is the home to an incredibly vicious and active carnivorous plant life. Lem's captors die, but Lem, in a herculean effort, regains the ship and flies away. * *Miscellaneous:* Books are forbidden, but a kindly guard lets Lem read an old copy of *Gulliver's Travels*. * Martians are humanoid, small, very fragile, with greenish blood. Venusians are tall and humanoid. * All concerned use heat rays. * There is an attempt at verismo detail and characterization. * The original title, as

McDermott, Dennis (*continued*)
submitted, was "Gulliver, 20,000 A.D." or according to another source "Lem Gulliver—3,000 A.D." * For a sequel see #1017, "The Duel on the Asteroid" by P. Schuyler Miller and Dennis McDermott.

McDOWD, KENNIE
No information, but portrait shows a middle-aged man.

919. **THE MARBLE VIRGIN.** *Science Wonder Stories,* June 1929. Ill. Paul.
Short story. * Told in purple prose, probably in imitation of the work of Poe. * The narrator, Wallace Land, a successful traditional sculptor, has set himself the task of cutting a beautiful, virginal woman out of a block of marble in his studio. As the work progresses, he becomes fetishistically attached to Naomi, as he calls the statue. * Across from the narrator's studio is the laboratory of the great scientist Huxhold, who in addition to being slightly mad, is a selfish, egotistical, lecherous brute, who will serve as a temporary, scientific Aphrodite. * Huxhold demonstrates an apparatus he has invented: It will disperse the atoms of objects, perhaps to another realm of existence, and animate the inanimate. He demonstrates the first technique on a stray cur, the second on a marble leg that Land provides. * Huxhold now becomes obsessed with the notion of animating the statue Naomi, and Land yields. Naomi, brought to flesh, is a charming young woman, though as ignorant of life as a new-born baby. Land "rears" her platonically, still madly in love with her. But the lustful Huxhold has his own notions, which include rape. Land saves Naomi's virtue, but Huxhold disintegrates her, whereupon Land murders him. Land, writing his confession, now intends to follow Naomi into disintegration, expecting that they will be together in another frame of existence. * Almost self-parodic, and certainly not a *science* wonder story. The story was not liked by the readers.

MACFADYEN, A. [B. L.], Jr.
Canadian author, then resident in Flin Flon, Manitoba, later Winnipeg, Manitoba. Macfadyen also wrote six stories that appeared in *Astounding* and *Unknown* in the late 1930s and "The Helping Hand" in *Astounding* in 1948.

920. **THE TIME DECELERATOR.** *Astounding Stories,* July 1936. Ill. Dold.
(Reprinted in Knight, *Science Fiction of the Thirties.*)
Short story. * *Time:* 1935 and 2380, with incidents in 1940 and 1980. * Dr. Kerschner, theorizing on the relation of time and gravity, has built an antigravity flyer, which Latimer, his junior, is going to test. Turning on the device, Latimer finds himself flying in 1940, with an aggressive air traffic cop ready to shoot him. He escapes rapidly by turning on the apparatus again, to find himself in 1980 accosted by another air patrolman with a ready gun. By now Latimer has worked out that the device propels him into the future at decimal multiples of four, hence 2380 will be next. * Here he finds a much more pleasant world, where he makes the acquaintance of an amiable young woman. She informs him that field machines like his are familiar, but seldom used because of the danger attendant upon them. He also learns it is generally accepted that they move only forward in time, although one scientist has indicated doubts about this. * The doubts turn out to be correct, for Latimer finds things becoming hazy, and he returns to Kerschner in 1936. It was not

fantasy, for he brought with him the young woman's cloak. He now wants to return to her. * Routine.

921. **THE LAST SELENITE.** *Astounding Stories,* November 1936. Ill. Thomson.
Short story. * *Time:* 1938. *Place:* mostly inside the Moon. * A manuscript found in a field in Orange County, New York, in 1954. * Sherrill (the narrator) and Castle, both associated with Stanton University, are attempting to set a balloon altitude record. Their ascent is normal until they reach thirty miles, at which height they suddenly accelerate and are borne away from the Earth toward the Moon. Approaching a crater, they descend a shaft into caverns deep inside the Moon. The gondola settles, and the men discover that there is atmosphere outside. * A telepathic voice identifies itself as Ythan Yth, the last native of the Moon. All its fellows have died, and it now feels that it, too, is dying. It has brought the balloon to the Moon for a purpose: It wants to impart its colossal knowledge to the Earthmen, so that it will not be lost. Yth will make suitable alterations in the men's brains to increase their capacity. But it will be a race with time, for Ythan Yth is dying more rapidly than he anticipated. * Sherrill and Castle are transformed mentally and are now supermen who understand everything about the universe. Their balloon flashes up out of the Moon, and they are out in space. But Yth, whose powers were failing, made a slight error in their trajectory, and the two men are now in an orbit about five hundred miles above the Earth, with limited supplies. Writing down instructions for building a mechanism to save them, they propel it to Earth, hoping that it will reach its destination in time. Obviously, it did not. As Castle says, it is terrible to know everything and not be able to use it. * *Miscellaneous:* Yth speaks of an ancient war, hundreds of millions of years ago, with the inhabitants of the fourth satellite of the fourth planet. (Perhaps Yth meant Jupiter, and, as his mind was failing, miscounted?) The enemy wrecked the Moon, causing the craters, and the Lunarians ripped the atmosphere from the enemy world. * Yth is not described closely, but he seems to be vaguely humanoid, perhaps a hundred feet tall, with an enormous head. The men see him only in passing. * Routine.

McKAY, HAROLD
U.S. (California) author. Portrait shows a young man. San Francisco area resident at this time. Later wrote *Marine Radio for Pleasure Craft* (1960), published as Gernsback Library No. 84.

922. **FLANNELCAKE'S INVENTION.** *Air Wonder Stories,* December 1929. Ill. Winter.
Short-short story. * *Place:* San Francisco area. * Humor, the invention that runs amok. * Joe Flannelcake, a nonstop pitch-talker, finally succeeds in getting an interview with financier Treat. Flannelcake has invented a helicopter-type plane that really works. A small rubber-band model functions well, and Treat agrees to see a larger, gasoline-powered model. The result is foreseeable when the model is flown in the house because of high winds outside. Blood, wreckage, and disaster. * A late exemplar of a turn-of-the-century story type. Without interest.

923. **THE FLYING BUZZ-SAW.** *Air Wonder Stories,* April 1930. Ill. Paul.
Short story. * The narrator is working in the carpentry shop when a circular saw blade flies loose, cutting him in the thigh. * He awakens in the year 2024 during the great war between

McKay, Harold (*continued*)

North America and South America. The war is going against the north, but perhaps the secret weapon being constructed in California will turn the tide. It amounts to an enormous flying circular saw; several have been built. * The great air battle is shaping up over Panama, with the South American fleet far superior in number to the North. * The narrator, piloting the flying saw, goes into action, sliding dexterously around, carving airplanes to shreds with his machine, until he finally attacks a dirigible. Part of the nose of the dirigible becomes entangled with the saw blade, and the narrator is heading for the ground, out of control. * Then he regains consciousness in the carpentry shop. The men applying first aid to his wound wonder why he asks how the war ended. * The title is also given as "The Flying Buzz Saw."

McKENZIE, A[DELBERT] R[OLAND] (1907-1981)

U.S. (mostly Illinois, but widely translocated) author. Degree from Carroll College in Wisconsin. Followed many occupations, but seemed to consider self primarily a writer.

924. **LUVIUM**. *Amazing Stories,* November 1931. Ill. Morey.

Short story. * Lost race on an obvious level. * *Place:* the Sahara Desert. * Jack Wright's narrative. * On an archeological dig in the Sahara, Jack and his friend, the noted scientist Carr, stumble upon a maze of underground passages, each set sealed off from passages still lower. At the final step, the men break into a lighted area. Soldiers clad in strange, jewel-bedecked metal cloth dash up, killing Carr with a ray gun, and, at the intercession of a higher officer, capturing Wright. * Wright is now in the land of Luvium, which was probably settled from the surface before the ice age. It is a highly advanced state, with many mechanical marvels, including radium lamps, monorail conveyances, artificially prepared food and atmosphere, and much else, but is governed by a half-mad tyrant. Luvium is one of several underground empires, all bitterly hostile to each other and perpetually at war. * Wright, taken before the tyrant Baku, is sentenced to death as a spy from one of the other empires, a sentence encouraged by the evil Zemb, a giant whom Wright had felled with a good right cross. But, as a result of a protest by the heir to the monarchy, the sentence is commuted until Wright can learn the native language, which is elaborately tonal. * Wright learns about the culture and history of the land while residing with his savior, whose daughter Votta becomes his sweetheart. * At the next judgment, Baku sentences Wright to death. A rebellion stirred up by Wright and friends seems to fail, and Wright and Votta try to escape to the surface. But Zemb outwits them, and Wright alone makes his way to the outer world. He plans to return to Luvium. * *Miscellaneous:* Baku's throne is suspended in mid air by magnetic power. * Juvenile work, heavily indebted to Edgar Rice Burroughs. * For a sequel see #925, "Luvium under the Sand."

925. **LUVIUM UNDER THE SAND**. *Amazing Stories,* June 1936. Ill. Morey.

Novelette. * Sequel to #924, "Luvium." *Place:* an underground city beneath the Sahara Desert in Libya. * Narrated by Jim Merton, a crashed aviator whose life Jack Wright has saved. While Merton is recuperating, Jim teaches him the language and ways of Luvium. Both men descend. * The story is again imitation Edgar Rice Burroughs, with perpetual swordplay in

corridors, vicious villains, treachery, dynastic intrigue, and what have you. It would be pointless to summarize the narrative. Wright triumphs at the end and wins his girlfriend Votta. While Merton may return to the surface, Wright will remain in Luvium. * Gimmicks include a talking idol (taken seriously by the natives) that is operated by priestcraft from a keyboard; and a force screen that protects the mad, wicked ruler Baku from missiles. * Pretty bad. * There is a third story beyond our time limit: "Luvium, the Invincible City" (*Amazing Stories,* September 1943). Written in hard-boiled style, it describes Nazis, including Hitler or a look-alike, down in Luvium.

McLOCIARD, GEORGE (c.1911?)

U.S. author. Pseud. of George F. Locke, then a student in Chicago. Although the names Charles F. Locke and George M. Locke are sometimes given, they are not correct. Attended Lane Technical School in Chicago, where several of his early science-fiction stories appeared in the school magazine *Lane Tech Prep.* Two were reprinted in *Amazing Stories,* as follows.

926. **SMOKE RINGS**. *Amazing Stories,* February 1928. Ill. Paul.

(First published in *Lane Tech Prep,* October 1926.)

Short-short story. * Why the *Shenandoah* crashed. (Background for those not acquainted with the history of lighter than air craft: The *Shenandoah* was a giant Zeppelin seized from Germany after World War I as partial reparations. During a storm it broke loose from its moorings and crashed, killing all on board.) * Wilbur Gunderson, who died in a fire, refusing rescue, left an explanation for the *Shenandoah* disaster. Basing his work on the anatomy and physiology of the human buccal cavity, he developed an apparatus that blew enormous explosive smoke rings. Anything within them, when they were detonated, would be shattered. Unfortunately, on a trial, when he exploded a hole through the clouds with his device, he did not know that the *Shenandoah* was exactly where his ring was aimed. Finis.

927. **MONORAIL**. *Amazing Stories,* December 1928. Ill. Paul.

(First published in *Lane Tech Prep,* February 1927.)

Short story. * *Place:* Washington, British Columbia, Alaska. * John Nally, who is racing around the world, has missed the Seattle boat to Nome. A pleasant stranger informs him of a new, unpublicized mode of transportation. This is a monorail operating from Mono City. Nally has some suspicions, but goes to Mono City, buys a ticket, and boards a smoothly running monorail that moves through Canada at speeds up to 130 MPH. But there is a contretemps: Three bandits on board hold up the train, tie the engineer and Nally (who happens to be in the equivalent of the cab), set the controls, and announce that the train will be wrecked at the next bridge, since the bridge has been blown up. * The bandits were only joking, however, and the train finishes its run safely.

928. **THE TERROR OF THE STREETS**. *Amazing Stories,* April 1929. Unsigned ill.

Short story. * *Place:* Chicago. * The narrator Malone is the only friend of the strange student Stefenson. Stefenson rebuffs others, and in his college work he has alienated the faculty by disruptively challenging his instructors on technical points. * Stefenson is eventually expelled from college, whereupon Malone visits him at his home. This turns out to be not a dwelling, but a large factorylike building, where the obviously enormously wealthy

McLociard, George (*continued*)

Stefenson conducts experiments and research. * Stefenson's first display is invisibility, the advocation of which caused his expulsion from college; he is able to bend light rays around objects. * A crisis comes when Stefenson's girlfriend is killed in an automobile accident caused by faulty brakes on a truck. Stefenson takes the death very hard. isolating himself for a time. * Then newspaper ads announce that the *Terror* will stalk the streets. An enormous vehicle, as strong as a tank, with fantastically powerful engines, it dashes about breaking all traffic regulations. The police cannot catch it. * Stefenson explains: He drives the *Terror*, and his purpose is to show the need for the enforcement of traffic rules. He now reveals what has been happening behind the scenes: He is not an American, but a member of a hidden nation that has made fantastic scientific and engineering progress, far beyond the Western world. He has been stationed as an observer in the United States, but his time is now up. He leaves in a fantastic plane, taking along Malone's girlfriend, whom he has accepted to take the place of the dead woman. * Obvious dime-novel influence. * It all seems like a very roundabout way to achieve traffic control.

929. **TELEVISION HILL**. *Amazing Stories*, February-March 1931. Ill. Wesso.

Short novel. * *Time:* the near future. *Place:* mostly around Rockford, Illinois. * McManus, a news reporter with some technical background, is recruited by King and Wentworth to act (in effect) as news editor and PR man for a new communications enterprise. Essentially, what King and Wentworth have invented, after many years of research and experiment, is a universal far viewer that will pick up images from anywhere on Earth. The completed invention is an enormous, complex mechanical device that occupies a strongly secured, guarded, secret site known as Television Hill. After a probationary period, McManus is fully accepted by King and Wentworth and starts a romance with Diane, King's daughter. (This material is greatly overdeveloped.) * The enterprise proceeds fabulously, for the news reels that Television Hill distributes through a front organization are far superior to anything else on the market. But there is a gap in the coverage, a small sector in the direction of New Orleans. * When a mechanical defect is corrected and viewing is resumed, the operators are astonished to find in the South Pacific, roughly halfway between Cape Horn and New Zealand, a large, unknown island on which is another television machine like theirs. Further viewing shows not only a science superior to that of the outside world, but a certain ruthlessness, indicated by wrecked sea vessels. The inhabitants, who are white, are later revealed to be about seven million in number and to have powerful connections in the outside world. * From now on, troubles plague Television Hill, until, unexpectedly, an advanced plane lands within the compound, and emissaries from the island demand that King destroy the television machine. King refuses, whereupon in a short time everything collapses. The plant is wrecked by explosions and fire, and a giant cyclone created and directed by a superflying machine destroys Television Hill. At this point it is revealed that the scientists of the strange nation have been watching King for years and that his establishment has been riddled with moles. These secret agents at first did small sabotage, then destroyed fail-safe plans and duplicate specifications and set off the final destruction. The crowning blow comes when Diane King reveals that she, too, is an agent of the

unknown nation. She was substituted for the real Diane, who hadn't seen her father for years. * McManus still loves her, but it is questionable what the future will be, for the ending is inadequately developed. * *Miscellaneous:* King's television apparatus and presumably that of the strangers can transmit along its ionized beams high electrical charges equivalent to artificial lightning. * A good general idea and much imagination, but not too well handled in terms of form. The first half of the story is taken up with exposition and chitchat, with the action, hastily handled, beginning in the last third of the story.

McNEILL, A. M.

No information.

930. **THE NOISE KILLER**. *Amazing Stories*, May 1930. Ill. Morey.

Short story. * A narrative rather than a formal story. * The aviator narrator lands his plane near a town where there is absolutely no sound. At the outskirts of the town, where sound is somewhat perceptible again, he hears the explanation from an elderly rustic. The rustic's brother, tired of the perpetual noise, released into the air a substance that was supposed to suppress only mechanical sound; but it suppressed all sound. His brother is dead; the machine cannot be turned off; and there is nothing that can be done about it all. The aviator flies away.

McRAE, D. B.

U.S. author, then resident in San Bernardino, California.

931. **THE GRAVITOMOBILE**. *Amazing Stories*, July 1927. Ill. Paul.

Short story. * Honorable mention in the contest based on the cover for the December 1926 issue of *Amazing Stories*. * The narrator goes to visit his old college friend Harry Teasdale, a maverick scientist, who explains what he has been doing. He has solved the problem of gravity, which is a vibration in the ether, far shorter than other known radiation. Teasdale demonstrates with a small spherical machine. * Having adequate funding, due to ownership of a radium mine and a new method of extracting the element, Teasdale now builds a gigantic gravity sphere for a trip to Mars, which Teasdale expects to be much like Earth. The sphere will carry along a small ocean liner for living and exploratory purposes, for, as Teasdale says, a liner would be difficult to match for compactness and efficiency. * The party arrives at Mars without incident, finding it a green, well-watered area, with cities. But as the sphere is about to deposit the ship into a body of water, something goes wrong, and the sphere and ship are about to crash. To one side can be seen handsome nude people (as depicted on the magazine cover). * Death seems certain, but then the narrator awakens back in his college class. It was all a dream. * The best-paced and liveliest of the published contest stories. Gernsback may not have liked the dream ending.

MANLEY, EDGAR A. and THODE, WALTER

No information. Portraits accompanying the story show early middle-aged men.

932. **THE TIME ANNIHILATOR**. *Wonder Stories*, November 1930. Ill. Paul.

Short story. * *Time:* 1945. * The narrator, a journalist, is present when his friend genius scientist Larry Stenson claims to have discovered the nature of time (a stream), constructed a time

Manley, Edgar A. and Thode, Walter (*continued*)
machine, and ventured into the future. The future, Larry claims, is horrible. * *Background:* By the year 2400 the human race is extinct, its place taken by superhumans created in the laboratory by the great scientist Chang Hsu around 2250. The new race, which has large pot-shaped heads, is gigantic, Mongoloid, superintelligent, and nasty. They have built a supercivilization, which is ruled by a khan. These future men understand time travel, but do not bother to use it, since their position is, they believe, secure. * The adventures of the three comrades are confusingly presented. The narrator and Bert, following Stenson, who has disappeared, proceed to 2418, where they are captured by the dome-headed men, examined by the khan, sentenced to death by disintegration, and rescued by a man from 2050, who takes them to 2250, a critical date. They discover that they cannot change the future, and they all return to their own times. * *Miscellaneous:* While the comrades are in the time machine, they are invisible but can see and hear what is going on. * The time machine has a tendency to move about of its own accord. * The future dome-headed men speak Tibetan, which the narrator can understand from his travels. * Around 2300 the new people emerged and disintegrated the world's cities and as much of humanity as they could reach. * Telepathy plays a part. * Pretty bad, with purple writing to embellish the confusion.

MANNING, LAURENCE [EDWARD] (1899-1972)
U.S. (New York) author. Born in St. John, New Brunswick, Canada; served in World War I in Royal Canadian Air Force; educated in St. John's University, graduate work at Harvard. Law degree in 1918. Came to New York in 1920. Technical writer, editor of *Florists Exchange*, later owner of Kelsey Nursery Service, important mail-order organization. One of the founders of the American Interplanetary Society (later the American Rocket Society), and editor of its bulletin. His fiction is usually not in the pulp tradition of conflict, but more like mainstream narration. A good storyteller, whose material is usually imaginative, well-written and entertaining. In addition to work considered here, also wrote two unpublished novels, "Grogue's Doom" and "Maze of Creation," and probably other work.

Stories are presented, chronologically within each group, as The Man Who Awoke Series, The Stranger Club Series, and Other Works.

The Man Who Awoke Series

Five short stories examining possible future societies as seen by a sleeper who awakens periodically. The stress is not so much on political or political-economical developments, as is common in stories of this type, but on the application of certain basic psychological or biological ideas. The stories contain a thoughtful element unusual in pulp fiction. The series has been reprinted in slightly altered form by Ballantine, New York, 1975.

933. **THE MAN WHO AWOKE**. *Wonder Stories*, March 1933. Ill. Paul.
(Reprinted in Asimov, *Before the Golden Age*.)
Short story. * *Time:* mostly A.D. 5000. * The first story in the series, investigating selfishness and an ecological society. *

Norman Winters, scholarly banker, mysteriously disappears. His founders of the American Interplanetary Society (later the American Rocket Society), and editor of its bulletin. His fiction is usually not in the pulp tradition of conflict, but more like mainstream narration. A good storyteller, whose material is usually imaginative, well-written and entertaining. In addition to work considered here, also wrote two unpublished novels, "Grogue's Doom" and "Maze of Creation," and probably other work.

Stories are presented, chronologically within each group, as The Man Who Awoke Series, The Stranger Club Series, and Other Works.

The Man Who Awoke Series

Five short stories examining possible future societies as seen by a sleeper who awakens periodically. The stress is not so much on political or political-economical developments, as is common in stories of this type, but on the application of certain basic psychological or biological ideas. The stories contain a thoughtful element unusual in pulp fiction. The series has been reprinted in slightly altered form by Ballantine, New York, 1975.

933. **THE MAN WHO AWOKE**. *Wonder Stories*, March 1933. Ill. Paul.
(Reprinted in Asimov, *Before the Golden Age*.)
Short story. * *Time:* mostly A.D. 5000. * The first story in the series, investigating selfishness and an ecological society. * Norman Winters, scholarly banker, mysteriously disappears. His gardener, with whom he is very friendly, is under suspicion, but a letter turns up explaining what has happened. * Determined to see the future of the human race, Winter has built himself a secret, lead-lined vault with automatic devices, an X-ray lamp, and carefully sealed supplies. A small clock operated by water power (from an artificial stream) will awaken him at A.D. 5000. He also has a drug that induces suspended animation. * Winters awakens, weak and emaciated, and digs himself out into a forested world that might, in modern terms, be considered an ecological extremist's ambience. * *Background:* Mankind, at least in North America, while retaining many aspects of science superior to ours, has reverted to a forest life reminiscent of some of the earlier utopias like W. H. Hudson's *A Crystal Age* or William Morris's *News from Nowhere*. There is no more field agriculture, but food and raw materials are obtained from specially bred trees and fungi that are grown on fallen trees. There are no more cities. Mankind lives in small settlements of controlled size in the forests. When the population exceeds a theoretical limit, a new community is founded elsewhere. As for the people themselves, evolution has removed chest hair and the vermiform appendix; their possession by Winters is accepted as proof of the truth of his story. * Winters encounters people very early, and is hospitably received. Unfortunately, he arrives during a cultural crisis, and he is manipulated for selfish reasons. At the moment a new community is about to be founded; this means the destruction of a certain number of food trees, a policy bitterly resented by the radical youth, who fear that their own future is being jeopardized. When the tired, unwitting Winters on invitation describes twentieth-century culture, his narrative is seized upon as an explosive issue. Riots and rebellion break out,

Manning, Laurence (*continued*)

and Winters is hunted like an animal by members of the youth party. He is fortunate to escape back to his hidden chamber, which has been improved somewhat by friendly older scientists. * An interesting culture, well portrayed.

934. **THE MAN WHO AWOKE. II—MASTER OF THE BRAIN.** *Wonder Stories*, April 1933. Ill. Paul.

Short story. * *Time:* A.D. 10,000. * Norman Winters awakens, somewhat feeble and weak; indeed, he is fortunate to survive, for his primitive reviving equipment is on the edge of collapse. Strength regained, he emerges to find himself in a forest, with all evidences of civilization gone. * As he walks along, he does not notice an aircraft flying silently overhead, and, before he is half aware of it, he has been captured in a net. He is taken on board the flying machine, where he is called a wildling and told that he will be taken to the city, as is done with all wildlings. * Along the way and at the city Winters learns about the new civilization. Everything is operated and controlled by the Brain, which we would term a supercomputer. The Brain has terminals for listening in on all things; has all aircraft booby trapped for destruction if necessary; and makes all decisions. In exchange for absolute control of mankind, the Brain provides a materialistic eutopia of sorts. There is no want or crime; necessities of life are furnished; and work is limited to about an hour a day, mostly elementary supervision of machinery. There are pleasure cities, access to which is easy after a certain amount of work; these correspond to a Victorian preacher's concept of Sodom and Gomorrah. The Brain does not tolerate independent humans, and such as are captured are given the choice of joining the Brain's world or death. * The culture is somewhat stratified according to occupational level, with the Brain mechanics and educators (in modern terms programmers and feeders) at the top. * Winters, when interviewed at the city, has a narrow escape when he first rejects an offer to join the work force. A member of the secret underground convinces him that he should retract his refusal. As for the underground, it is small, but apparently well organized and resourceful; It objects to the decadence that dependence on the Brain has brought to mankind. * Winters takes up his job, which he fulfills faithfully, and is duly rewarded with vacation time at one of the pleasure cities. There, the underground contacts him and demands his aid. He now learns that as a stranger he is the only unshielded person who can approach the Brain, for after a few weeks in the city some psychic influence repels people from the Temple of the Brain. The Brain's mechanics and information men wear special protective helmets, but it is impossible to obtain them. * Winters must enter a certain maintenance tunnel, remove a wall plate, place a bridge transformer on a cable there, and then cut the cable. This will drive the Brain mad. Winters accomplishes his task, with some difficulty, and the world of the Brain begins to collapse. All aircraft explode in the air, people go mad in sympathy with the Brain's insanity, and a mob storms the Brain and destroys it. Mankind is now free to follow its own evolution. * Winter's grateful friends in the underground build him a far superior retreat with atomic-powered apparatus, and he descends to sleep for another period. * *Miscellaneous:* The central Brain is located in the city to which Winters was taken. Subsidiary stations in other cities carry out the Brain's orders and decisions. * Manning provides a detailed future history, high points of which follow: A.D. 3000. Humanity becomes unitary, with a single language

and a policy of reducing the average work load. Food stuffs shift from ground crops to trees. * A.D. 5000. The world described in the previous story. * A.D. 6500. Synthetic food causes the abandonment of the countryside and concentration of people in cities. * A.D. 7000. Atomic power is developed, and an era of prosperity and scientific advances begins. * A.D. 7100. Space travel begins. Mars and Venus are explored. Both are empty of intelligent life. * A.D. 8000. The mechanical brain is created. * A.D. 8200. The Brain has developed enormously and now judges human law cases. * A.D. 8500. The Brain rules the world through the council of educators. * A.D. 9000. The educators revolt against the Brain, but are crushed. * A.D. 9500. The last revolt against the Brain. From now on the Brain tries to capture outsiders to prevent attacks. * A.D. 10,000. Winters awakens, and the Brain is destroyed.

935. **THE MAN WHO AWOKE. III—THE CITY OF SLEEP.** *Wonder Stories*, May 1933. Ill. Paul.

Short story. * *Time:* A.D. 15,000. * A culture of withdrawal and retreat into dream. * The story begins with an argument between a pair of lovers, Jalna, a young woman, and Eric, her fiancé. Jalna wants to join the sleepers and spend the rest of her life in a dream machine, where she will be hooked up mechanically into a programmed dream in which she will be a contented housewife, with Eric her devoted husband. Once she is thus connected, she cannot be restored to normal life, for her natural sense organs are destroyed and the machine maintenance is irreversible. Eric refuses to accept this, for he wants to experience real life. * *Background:* Most of America is wilderness except for a few enormous, self-sufficient futuristic cities embodying a superscience. The awake population, however, is tiny. In Niagara City, for example, there are a million sleepers, with only about four hundred scientists (among them Eric) to care for them. The birth rate is negligible. * Historically, the system is an outgrowth of remedial surgery, in which artificial sense organs were hooked into the sensory nerves. Eventually, it became a system whereby programmed lives were available to those wired to the dream machines. * The argument between Jalna and Eric is inconclusive. When Eric leaves, he is in danger of being attacked by wolves. Unarmed, he would be lost were it not for a strangely dressed man who calls to him to stand still and shoots the wolves with bullets from an air pistol. Eric's savior is Winters, just arisen from his chamber and still weak. * Winters is horrified when he learns of the future culture, which implies the extinction of the human race, for the same situation holds all over the world. His presence serves as a catalyst, and in a short time a small underground movement forms among Eric and his friends. About seventy individuals, they are prepared to secede secretly from the dreamer culture and start a new society somewhere in the wilderness. What they are planning is subject to the death penalty, but they provide themselves with ray guns in case of conflict. Jalna betrays them, and they are soon in a battle with the loyalists, who are dragging up a heat ray gun—the end. Jalna, however, has second thoughts when she sees Eric about to be killed, and she carries up a small atomic bomb, which disposes of the loyalists. The rebels fly away and build their new settlement west of Lake Superior. * Establishing a new settlement is easy enough, for a scientific basic of the day is an atomic reconstructor that can transmute common substances like dirt into any desired element or compound. With this machine, the future men create their food,

Manning, Laurence (*continued*)

building material, artifacts, and defensive weapons. Thus, in a matter of a week, while Winters lies in therapeutic sleep, the rebels have built a new city, defenses and all. Winters would be welcome to stay, but he prefers to continue on into the future in the new, advanced crypt that his future friends construct for him. * *Miscellaneous:* While Winters was asleep a minor glacial episode occurred. The glaciers have retreated, but the climate is once again considerably colder than in Winters's time. * The human race has continued to evolve; teeth have disappeared, and skin color is now very dark, although blondism is not unknown. * Well handled.

936. **THE MAN WHO AWOKE. IV—THE INDIVID-UALISTS.** *Wonder Stories*, June 1933. Ill. Paul.
Short story. * *Time:* A.D. 20,000. *Place:* somewhere in the Middle West. * *Background:* The world of A.D. 20,000 is characterized by utter individualism. There are no more cities nor human groups; society consists of isolated individuals who dwell in living-machines that contain all the amenities of a city. Most of these machines are aircraft, but at least one, that of the biologist Hargry, is a titanic thousand-foot-high walking-machine fitted with precision grasping tentacles. * Men and women are specialists in various sciences or arts, which they pursue with fanatical compulsiveness. All (except for moments of sexuality) are violently xenophobic and intensely competitive, so that when members of the same art or science meet, the result is likely to be war to the death with various superscientific weapons. Yet there is a certain selfish idealism in these pursuits, for all strive for perfection or advancement of knowledge—which they do not share. * Within this culture, Winter's appearance has been awaited with eagerness, especially by the biologists who want to use him as breeding stock, then vivisect him with great thorough-ness. * Winters does appear, first encountering a female historian who questions him a little, then dismisses him as a brainless barbarian. Winters also witnesses a ferocious air battle between two rival biologists, who are both destroyed by the mighty Hargry, who seems to be one of the world's dominant figures. Hargry captures Winter, declares his plans for analyzing him, but regretfully adds that he must leave temporarily for more impor-tant matters. He places Winters in a strange building with hundreds of mirrors, each of which reflects a mirror being, who can communicate. Hargry had originally designed the building with the illusory entities to torture Bengue, a fellow biologist. (Bengue had originally bred Hargry, who rebelled against him.) * Winters has difficulties with the mirror people, but smashes through and finds the imprisoned Bengue. Both escape just as Hargry is returning. Winters, playing a hide and seek game with the tremendous walking-machine, slides back down into his chamber, while Hargry, above, demolishes the city over him. * The biologist Bengue, who admits to being abnormal in liking human companionship, after some years of secure research unbothered by Hargry, constructs himself a crypt and also enters suspended animation, hoping for a better time. * *Miscellaneous:* The atomic converters have now been perfected far beyond those of Winters's earlier awaking. * The astronomers alone are not individualists, but cooperate. Their goal is interstellar travel for the preservation of the human race. A small colony was estab-lished on Mars around A.D. 18,000. Venus was unsuitable for colonization. * Human longevity remains the same as in our time; one of the aims of the individualist superbiologists is to

discover immortality. * Future history: A.D. 15,100, exogenesis was perfected, and all human reproduction from here on is a laboratory matter. Natural evolution, thus, no longer operates. * From about A.D. 18,000, with the perfection of the conversion machine, individualism gradually rose to its climax at Winters's awaking. * Told with some narrative sophistication.

937. **THE MAN WHO AWOKE. V—THE ELIXIR.**
Wonder Stories, August 1933. Ill. Paul.
Short story. * *Time:* A.D. 25,000, and on into the far future. *Place:* perhaps Minnesota, and around the universe. * Winters, now a very tired, worn old man on the edge of death, awakens into a semitropical environment. Struggling along, he is fortunate to reach a glass dome, in which dwell and work the biologist Ponceon and his associates. * Winters has arrived at an opportune time, for Ponceon has just perfected a system of human rejuvenation involving cell transplants. Winters will be one of the first guinea pigs, a difficult specimen since there are no cellular replacements for some of his vestigial organs like the vermiform appendix and teeth. * Rejuvenated as a young man, Winters now explores the culture, both past and present. Not long after he left the world of the individualists there was a sort of rebellion among the weaker members that broke the hold of the titans and established a worldwide social contract. Social violence ceased. By A.D. 22,000, the new system was firmly established, and mankind prospered. * Interplanetary travel is now common, with large colonies on both Mars and Venus. Humanity lives in small dome settlements of congenial people. Since the atomic production machines can make anything, there is no commerce or financial structure, but products of the mind are exchanged. * Ponceon's method, announced despite some friendly opposition, proves to be the most important discovery in history, for with it and suspended animation mankind can now explore and expand to the stars. * Winters no longer needs to reenter the sleep-waking cycle, but instead experiences the universe; over millennia he explores strange planets and (human) cultures. * Around the year A.D. 100,000, while on the dying Earth beneath a dying sun, Winters learns of a quest for the meaning and purpose of life that is being undertaken by a man named Condonal. After long exploration Winters finds Condonal, who explains his program. He and his followers, using mechanical implementation, attempt a sort of mystical union with a higher being, a new level of thought; or, since Manning is somewhat ambiguous, perhaps they are working toward the creation of this being, from whom they have hopes of enlightenment. In any case, Winters joins this mystical cult, which spreads through the universe, and spends millennia in the quest. The story has no real ending; Winters is still at work. * Possibly the mystical cult owes something to the work of Olaf Stapledon. * *Miscellaneous:* Future man does not seem to have evolved beyond the brown-skinned, toothless beings of A.D. 20,000. * An excellent conclusion to a good series.

938. **THE LIVING GALAXY.** *Wonder Stories*, September 1934. Ill. Saaty.
(Reprinted in Conklin, *The Science Fiction Galaxy.*)
Short story. * In the same universe as the Man Who Awoke series. * A frame set about five hundred million years in the future provides background. Mankind has spread throughout the universe, in most instances terraforming worlds to make them habitable. Originally, mankind came from a minor galaxy called First Universe. Three scientific and technical advances permitted

Manning, Laurence (*continued*)

this diffusion: atomic energy, atomic synthesis (which destroyed the need for labor), and immortality (by cellular transplant and rejuvenation). * A lecturer now tells the story of Bzonn and his companions, date not provided, but undoubtedly hundreds of millions of years after our time. * Astronomers have noted an unexpected increase in the red shift and the emergence of a black area that seems to be moving into the universe. In another million years or so it will strike the First Universe. Within the black area is absolutely nothing. * Bzonn and a band of comrades determine to investigate. Hollowing out a small planet and filling it with the most advanced equipment, they set out on a journey that will last millions of years. During this time they multiply and leave colonies to study the black phenomenon, travel around the phenomenon, build many other planet-ships, and eventually leave our universe, venturing into the blackness beyond matter, where light does not exist. Many planetoids of the exploring fleet are lost outside our universe, but Bzonn returns. * Bzonn's data reveal that the black intrusion is the impact on our universe of a small galaxy formed like a cylinder with a tentacle. Bzonn theorizes, though others have since disputed his conclusion, that this is a living, intelligent being, whose "atoms" are star systems. * During his millions of years of exploration Bzonn has developed a technique for exploding stars. Venturing inside the "star beast" Bzonn explodes key stars, effectually killing the monster and removing the menace. * A story of remarkable scope. In a way it is unfortunate that Manning did not develop it into a full novel. Most unusual for Gernsback's magazines.

The Stranger Club Series

Narratives of adventure related or introduced in a peculiar, exclusive club in New York. The scheme is reminiscent of the Jorkens stories of Lord Dunsany, but without Dunsany's light, humorous, frothy touch. The stories are presumed to be true, if fantastic, and are presented more as narratives than as conventionally developed stories. A central character is peppery old Colonel Marsh, onetime explorer and big game hunter.

939. **THE CALL OF THE MECH-MEN.** *Wonder Stories*, November 1933. Ill. Paul.

Short story. * *Place:* The initial setting is in the New York club; the adventure, in Labrador. * Old Marsh, having taken it into his head that there is something strange about the magnetic north pole, decides to investigate. Hiring a plane and pilot, making arrangements for gas dumps along the route, he and an aviator (Stanley) fly to Boothia Peninsula. * After locating the pole with exactitude, Marsh sets off a large explosion with dynamite he has brought along, uncovering a cement dome, which the two men clear off. A door opens, and a metal creature, a box set upon three legs, with capital appendages and a long tentacle, seizes them and carries them down into an underground world. It installs the men into a zoo, where they see along with contemporary forms of life a pair of mammoths. Stanley collapses mentally, but Marsh retains both his intense curiosity and intellect. * The metal beings (mech-men) consider them simply animals, for as is later revealed, they cannot conceive that protoplasm can attain real intelligence or that evolution has taken place so rapidly upon Earth. * Marsh gradually becomes aware

of mental sensations, and with a combination of slow telepathy and writing, he communicates with the mech-men. Stanley is unable to comprehend this, and spends his time chasing rabbits that are in the same cage. * What Marsh learns: The mech-men, who hail from a planet in another unidentifiable star system, are accustomed to make millennia-long exploratory travels around the universe. When they passed through the solar system, their ship was damaged beyond repair in the asteroid belt. They made a forced landing on Earth above an underground pool of petroleum that they had located with their instruments. The solar system lacks elements needed to repair their ship. Hence, they have installed a beacon—the north magnetic pole—as a signal to future visitors. It is not possible to date their arrival, though it must have been at least tens of thousands of years ago. * The mech-men have some curiosity about terrestrial life, whence the zoo, but have a low opinion of all protoplasmic life and debate repeatedly whether it is worth maintaining the zoo. * Marsh and one of the machines have extended conversations about the outside world. The question of machines in our world arises. At first, the mech-men insist that humanity must be a creation of intelligent machines, then, when Marsh explains the situation, rationalize it by claiming that mankind, although it does not know it, is really serving machines and is accelerating their evolution toward intelligence. * The situation changes abruptly. Apparently the mech-men have decided to eliminate the zoo, and after a time without food, Marsh and Stanley make a break for liberty, easily lifting off the lock on their cage. It is touch and go for a time, but they reach their plane and fly away. They do not tell of their adventure—present circumstances excepted—for obvious reasons. * Interesting situation and ideas, but too long for its matter. This first story is said to have been written as a parody; if so, the parodic touch gradually dropped away in the later stories.

940. **CAVERNS OF HORROR.** *Wonder Stories*, March 1934. Ill. Bulow.

Short story. * At the Stranger Club, Smithers quietly sneers at Colonel Marsh's hunting exploits, which had really involved considerable danger to the Colonel. Marsh responds with the expected crusty indignation. Smithers goes so far as to bet Marsh that he can provide hunting for much more dangerous beasts not far from New York. As becomes clear later, Smithers has been deliberately manipulating Marsh and his friends into a strange situation. * The men accompany Smithers to his Long Island estate, and, during the evening, all armed to the teeth, Smithers takes them from his gun room out onto a landscape of terror. They descend a talus slope; to one side of them is a lower area, from which emerge horrible monstrosities with incredible dentition. Other flying creatures attack from above. * The reader, who has noticed the title, will of course recognize that this is taking place underground and that the gun room is really a secret elevator; but Marsh and the narrator do not know this and have difficulties reconciling what they have seen with the placid Long Island landscape. * After the men leave the perilous area and the bet is settled, Smithers explains: while building on his estate, he found a cleft that descended far into the earth. After initial exploration by ladder and rope, he had the secret elevator constructed. He has explored the area somewhat, finding, in addition to the area where the monsters live, a valley filled with phosphorescent fungi, and farther, deeper, an area with red fires, presumably volcanic, around

Manning, Laurence (*continued*)

which he believes he has seen figures. * Smithers intends to investigate the fiery area, and so manipulates the others that he descends alone, with a telephone line, while they try vainly to join him. But as was the case with Randolph Carter, Smithers comes to a bad end, and his friends at the phone terminal hear his final moments. It is impossible to rescue him or retrieve his body. * *Miscellaneous:* The throwaway suggestion is made that the figures associated with the underground fires may have given rise to legends about devils. * A good story. The story was submitted by Manning as "Smithers' Kingdom," which the editors of *Wonder Stories* changed to the cat-releasing version above.

941. **VOICE OF ATLANTIS.** *Wonder Stories*, July 1934. Ill. Winter.

Short story. * A Stranger Club tale. * *Time:* about 18,000 B.C. *Place:* traditional Atlantis. * Volking, not known well to the other members of the club, upon some prodding by Marsh and others, tells his tale. A research psychologist of a sort, he has been experimenting with brain electricity, trying to identify thought. While working on a very elaborate helmet, constructed at random with electronic equipment, he accidentally drops it. Upon replacing the helmet on his head, he feels a strange sensation, sees a curtain, and an old man confronts him. This is Marron, one of the guardians of the Atlantean program for thought communication with the future. * Volking and Marron converse, sometimes at cross-purposes, until a mutual understanding is reached. It seems that while the Atlanteans can communicate with the future fifty thousand years hence, the interval between this date and their own time cannot be reached, and they have no idea what happened to their civilization. When Volking tells of the legendary submergence of Atlantis, Marron becomes excited and takes him to the court of the ten Atlantean kings, where Volking repeats the legend. His explanation is received with some incredulity at first, then belief. But the Atlantean rulers do not welcome Volking's information. It would be disastrous if publicly known. At a nod from the kings Marron, using mental power, forces Volking to destroy his equipment beyond repair. Since he attained his results accidentally, it is highly unlikely that he can repeat his achievement. * The heart of the story, however, is not the linear plot, but the conversation between Volking and Marron, the contrast between modern civilization and Atlantean. Marron regards our world as the creation of apes and madmen, skilled with their hands and moved by curiosity, but hopelessly diseased. He criticizes our waste of natural resources, our political structure, and much else. His criticisms are from the point of view of a Classical exponent of the Golden Age. Atlantis, on the other hand, while scientifically far ahead of us, is a completely closed, controlled society. Scientific knowledge seems to be the property of a priestly class and is not released. Thus, superficially, Atlantis is a barbaric state based on the manpower of slaves and very primitive machines, but actually it is far more sophisticated than our culture. * *Miscellaneous:* One reason for the loss of Atlantean civilization is that the Atlanteans were very poor colonists and seldom stayed away long from Atlantis. * Volking's visit is dated, on the basis of a star chart, as about twenty thousand years ago. * An excellent story.

942. **THE MOTH MESSAGE.** *Wonder Stories*, December 1934. Ill. Saaty.

Short story. * *Place:* Colorado. * Among the members of the Stranger Club is LaBrot, a member of the French embassy. His hobby is entomology. As he tells Colonel Marsh, the narrator, and others, in Colorado he observed a curious phenomenon in a certain species of moth. The markings on its wings seemed so much like letters that he submitted them to a linguist friend, who deciphered them as old Phoenician. The message reads "The children of the Sun are at the place of hills at the source of water." LaBrot is sure that the message refers to a particular isolated mesa in Colorado. Members of the club decide to accompany LaBrot and investigate. * Marsh charters a dirigible and the party flies to Colorado, where they make a landing on the mesa—and while they sleep are captured by a dwarfish people and eventually disarmed. They are taken to a remarkable temple complex, which is run by a normal old man and his beautiful young daughter. The young woman, Val-Bel, teaches the captives her language, and they learn the situation. * *Background:* The people of the mesa, who number only a handful of the dwarfish servitor class and the two normal people, are the last descendants of an Atlantean mining colony, which used to ship gold to Atlantis. Sudden orogeny, however, raised their land, and they have been unable to leave, whence their breeding the moths with the message. The old man refuses to believe that Atlantis is gone and has nothing but scorn for such modern science as he has seen with the explorers. * But, no matter what his feelings about modern man, he decrees that one of the explorers must mate with his daughter, her selection. The others will be put to death. Since Val-Bel and LaBrot are greatly attracted to each other, part of the old man's decision is acceptable, and LaBrot manages to rescue his friends. * To convince the old man that Atlantis is really gone, the party, after returning to civilization, takes him over the site of Atlantis. Finally convinced, he has no more interest in the billions of dollars worth of bullion that he and his ancestors have been guarding for Atlantis. The narrator suggests that it be used to relieve the Great Depression. * Well handled.

943. **SEEDS FROM SPACE.** *Wonder Stories*, June 1935. Ill. Paul.

Short story. * *Time:* Not precisely indicated, but possibly before Prohibition, although the author makes no attempt at period background. * Colonel Marsh tells the strange history of Blenkins, who lives alone in an isolated grove and tends his trees. * Blenkins, who was a wealthy young Manhattan playboy, was standing at a seaside cliff in Maine when a rush of pebble-like seeds showered past him out into the ocean. Three seeds, however, he captured, and taking them back to New York with him, planted them in soil boxes on his rooftop garden. After a time the seeds sprouted, producing very strange seedlings that grew rapidly into unearthly-looking trees: short bulbous trunks, triple, long, leaf-like appendages, and a weird-looking flower-bud or something similar on top. * Blenkins, who is a severe alcoholic, regards them in his usual stupor. But one night, as he is sitting drinking, he hears a noise. He turns about, and sees the three trees come marching into the room, walking on their root-like lower extremities. Communication is rapid, since the trees are far more intelligent than humans, and the trees work through Blenkins's books on an overnight basis. While they converse among themselves telepathically, they are able to modify air passages among their roots to produce comprehensible speech. * As the trees reveal: Most of the habitable planets in the universe

Manning, Laurence (*continued*)

contain vegetable life, animal being rare, and to their knowledge, which involves complete ancestral memory, Earth alone has produced intelligent mammals. As the trees, who possess a super-science, multiply on a planet, they shoot containers of their seeds out into space, chancing that some will land on a habitable world and sprout. * Discussions with Blenkins reveal that the trees are utter rationalists, literalists, and pragmatists, totally without subtlety or emotion; anything that is not immediately practical, like art or music, they reject as a waste of time. For them it is an obvious matter that they should take over Earth, not out of passion or greed, but simply because they are the superior race. * During one of their conversations, they bid Blenkins to obtain a truckload of new soil for their use. They plan to build up energy, modify their leaves into wings, and fly to suitable spots to distribute their seeds. Blenkins cannot get topsoil on short notice, and has to settle for manure, with which the trees are unfamiliar. On sampling it, they become delighted, for the manure is obviously an intoxicant to them. * As Marsh now points out, a top-flight chemist could have extracted invaluable information from the trees (who are masters of all sciences); but to save the world a different sort of man was needed, a colossal drunkard, a man who would recognize the characteristics of intoxication and know how to utilize them. * Such a man was Blenkins when the trees succumbed to the "alcoholic" delights of manure. After false starts and misadventures, he destroys the aliens while they are in a drunken stupor, and mankind will survive. * A very amusing story, well told.

Other Works

944. **THE VOYAGE OF THE ASTEROID.** *Wonder Stories Quarterly*, Summer 1932. Ill. Paul.
Novelette. * *Place:* partly on Venus. * The low-key circumstances of the first space voyage are within the technology of the day, or perhaps a little more advanced, but not fantastic. * As Bigelow (the narrator, an expert photographer) and Mason are walking in the countryside in Westchester County, they see a remarkable aircraft fly overhead and land in a nearby estate. When they try to investigate, they are ordered out by an armed man. That might have been the end, except that Bigelow, to prove that he is respectable, left his card. He now undergoes a rather annoying investigation, and finally an explanation. * The mysterious owner of the aircraft turns out to be Haworth, an old college friend, who contacts them and, after some hesitation, explains what is going on. Haworth, a very wealthy man, has been experimenting with rocketry. He has had considerable success with liquid fuels (oxygen and gasoline) and is building a large step rocket to explore space. Bigelow and Mason are invited to accompany him. * The large rocket (the *Asteroid*) is finished, stored with provisions, and the men take off for Venus as the most suitable planet. Since this was in the naive days about space and planetary geography, the explorers arrive without incident and find a mostly water-covered Venus. The land areas are tropical, with giant counterparts of terrestrial dinosaurs and small humanoid reptilians who seem to have acquired a certain amount of intelligence. * The explorers have a difficult time, what with becoming lost and falling ill with Venusian fevers, but regain the *Asteroid* and return to Earth uneventfully. They all become wealthy as a result of the voyage.

* A fair amount of contemporary knowledge about rocket flight is worked into the narrative. * Well written, but overlong for what it has to say. * For a sequel see #945, "The Wreck of the Asteroid."

945. **THE WRECK OF THE ASTEROID.** *Wonder Stories*, December 1932-February 1933. Ill. Paul.
Short novel. * *Time:* perhaps slightly in the future. *Place:* Mars. * The comrades of the Venus voyage described in #944, "The Voyage of the Asteroid" now determine to make another voyage of exploration, to Mars. A recent astronomical discovery, that the "canals" are deep valleys, presumably with air at their bottom, makes their plans all the more feasible. * The problem of payload seems insurmountable at first, but is solved by a brilliant suggestion: Land the main ship on Phobos, and descend to Mars in a small tender. * The voyage is boring and uneventful. One man stays on Phobos with the *Asteroid*, and the others descend to Mars in the *Planetoid*. * The small ship, however, does not quite reach the designated valley, but is stranded on the surface of Mars, somewhat damaged by a crash landing. The explorers descend into the nearby valley, which contains thin but adequate air and vegetation. At first the men suffer from lack of water, but pulp from a cactus-like plant solves the immediate problem, while a flood from the polar melt later provides adequate supplies. For food the explorers find edible vegetable matter and small animals that they call chickenporks. * Life seems easy enough, but there is a time factor. As Haworth declares, if they cannot repair the *Planetoid* within a matter of weeks, they will have to winter on Mars, not a pleasant thought. Preparations include welding and mechanical repairs, distillation of alcohol from native plants, and storage of liquid air. * But now a great danger arises. With the flood water, the vegetation has burgeoned and various gigantic insect forms have been emerging first as caterpillars, then as flying forms. All seem to be carnivorous and aggressive. It is possible to fight off carnivorous moths with wing spans of eight feet, but when wasp-like creatures with twenty-foot wingspans, poisonous stings, and bodies weighing hundreds of pounds attack, there is no real defense. It is only by luck and the self sacrifice of a crew member that the expedition is able to complete preparations and return to Phobos for the trip back to Earth. * *Miscellaneous:* The narrator, Bigelow, finds archeological material, including a catacomb-like site with wall carvings that enables him to construct an aspect of Martian history. The original intelligent Martians were the ancestors of the chickenporks, who, with the rise of the giant insects, gradually devolved into very small, animal-like beings. * A competent adventure story with reasonable development, although Manning ignores very obvious solutions to problems. The title, of course, is completely misleading.

946. **THE PROPHETIC VOICE.** *Wonder Stories*, April 1935. Ill. Paul.
Short story. * *Time:* Probably a couple of hundred years in the future. * A puzzle story. * Science and mankind have progressed enormously. The nations of the world are united in a world state; there is one world language; poverty and want have been removed. On the scientific side interplanetary travel has begun, and telepathic communications have been received from the future. * Into this well-balanced world comes a strange message from the future that alters everything. An excited voice announces that in two years of the recipients' time, there will not

Manning, Laurence (*continued*)

be a single human on Earth. Exactly what has happened, the future man does not know, but obviously there must have been survivors to produce him and his fellows. * Some explanations can be ruled out: interplanetary collision, solar flare, plague. The most reasonable explanation, the future voice states, is an interplanetary invasion. To evade this and insure the survival of mankind, the voice suggests suspended animation underground for a few decades and provides the formulas for achieving this. * At first there is panic, then mankind enters suspended animation en masse in enormous caverns beneath the Pyrenees. * Eighty years later, mankind emerges, to find the world unchanged (except for natural processes, of course). Communication with the future is renewed, but no one then knows anything of the message. * The great Professor Blaisdik of the Everest chronotelepathic station asks certain questions, and in some cases offers answers. Was the message a contemporary hoax, as some believe? No, the level of science involved was much superior to ours. Did the message really come from the future? Probably not from the future, but from outer space, thus from nonhumans who wanted to explore our planet without interference. Have the aliens, after exploring Earth, decided that it is unsuitable and left permanently? We cannot know. Our telepathic messages from the future are controlled by the future beings. We have no real knowledge whether their senders are human or aliens. Is it significant that communication with the future comes from only a short "distance" in the future? Does this mean that mankind was later wiped out? * There are no answers. * A good puzzle story.

947. **WORLD OF THE MIST**. *Wonder Stories*, September-October 1935, Ill. Paul.

Short novel. * *Place:* mostly an other-world. * In the story frame, a radio operator near Singapore has received a long communication purportedly from a rocket ship. * The message: The narrator Trench (a young millionaire) and his friends Cogger Bent and Wadsley Billing are men at loose ends, all suffering from pain or emotional distress. Hence, when the brilliant Cogger theorizes about neutronium and its potentiality of warping space into another set of four dimensions than ours (via Einstein's relativity equations), his comrades are interested. As Cogger speculates, it is quite possible that neutronium may exist in a pure state in occasional asteroids or meteors, the remnant of collapsed stars. * Converting his holdings into cash, Trench sets about constructing a spaceship. Since Manning was an enthusiastic follower of rocket research, the Cogger-Trench ship is realistic for its time, with suitable fuel and design, including collapsible wings for reentry into Earth's atmosphere. * The comrades set out into space without mishap and cruise about, searching for planetoids. Though the odds are (at least) thousands to one against finding such a body of neutronium, the quest is successful. * According to Cogger's theory, if they can form the neutronium into a ring through which the spaceship can pass, they should enter another frame of existence. Detaching the outer skin of their ship, they pile the powdery neutronium around it, then use this formation as a passage tube. Haste is necessary, for the neutronium is extremely active and rapidly erodes all substances. * At the last minute, after forming such a ring-passage, however, the venturers judge that the project is too dangerous and decide to return to Earth. But as they enter Earth's atmosphere, the rocket's folding wings do not work. The

explorers have no choice but to fly through the ring (which is falling a little ahead of them) and take their chances, since the rocket is otherwise doomed. * They find themselves in a strange world, where everything is in reverse to our universe. Solids in our world are empty space in the other world, and empty space in our world (or just ether) is solid in the other world. Thus, the other world is like a molded form to ours. Light, however, penetrates from our sun, and there is an omnipresent reddish mist. There is, of course, no breathable atmosphere, only the pink mist. * Yet matters are not that simple. Outside the ship the men see a panorama of terrestrial forms, including humans in historic garb, and the explorers experience similar strange dreams. They come to the conclusion that the pink mist has intelligence of a sort, and that since it occupies the interior of everything formed in our universe, it possesses form-memory of a sort. * Such theorizing is fine, but the pink mist also erodes matter, for the ship's skin and the space suits are becoming dangerously thin. * The situation seems hopeless, but there is a resolution. When the ring of neutronium struck the Earth, it formed a volcano, evidences of which are visible in the other world. The men, since death is otherwise inevitable, fly the ship back through the ring, out into the volcano in our world. Cogger and Trench survive and are rescued near the volcano in the Dutch East Indies, but Wadsley is killed. * The frame narrator raises questions at the end of the story. * Well-handled, a far way from Manning's earlier interplanetaries; one wonders what psychological elements (as seems obvious) are hidden within the story. * "Forthcoming Stories" in the February 1936 issue of *Wonder Stories* lists a sequel, "Maze of Creation," which was to begin as a serial in the April issue. It has never been published. One might guess that it contains spiritualist elements.

MANNING, LAURENCE [EDWARD] and PRATT, [MURRAY] FLETCHER.

Manning and Pratt have separate biographical entries.

948. **THE CITY OF THE LIVING DEAD**. *Science Wonder Stories*, May 1930. Ill. Paul.

(Reprinted in Wollheim and Ernsberger, *The Second Avon Fantasy Reader.*)

Short story. * *Time:* around A.D. 4500. *Place:* exact location not clear, but the people concerned seem to be Scandinavians. Their land is near the ancient country of the Anglesk, but is isolated by a new mountain that has risen, blocking entrance. * In the land of Alvrosdale, the culture is not barbaric, but mechanical civilization has died, and machines are regarded with horror and aversion. Since the land is small and overpopulation is a problem, each year, on a certain day, a number of the more adventurous young people take artificial wings and try to fly over the mountain to the fair, but deserted lands of the Anglesk on the other side. Quite a few die along the way. * The chief elder, Hal Hallstrom, tells candidates of his experience when he was young. There were no wings then, and he climbed the nearly unpassable mountain and descended with great difficulty and peril. (He seems to have been the first to do so.) * He found a green, pleasant land with many ruins, some filled with elaborate, decayed machinery, but never a living soul. Eventually he saw a light, and, entering a building, found many corpses covered almost completely with wires. To his horror, some were alive, though almost motionless. He then encountered an ancient man, who was ambulatory, but was covered with

Manning, Laurence and Pratt, Fletcher (*continued*)
wires. * The ancient man, applying a thought helmet to Hal, taught him the language and told him what was going on. Over the centuries, the English became more and more jaded, abandoning actual life for synthetic thrills like radio, motion pictures, and television. Thus, when a medical breakthrough provided artificial sensory organs, the next step was programmed adventures, at first realistic, but then wish-fulfillment exploits for the individual. There were enormous libraries of such artificial lives. The individual, his sensory organs removed, was hooked up to dream machines and provided with mechanical artificial sustenance. Life was thus abandoned for the illusion. It is the old man's task to care for the dreamers, who never emerge from the machines, but since the task is overwhelming, he attends only to his friends. * The old man, who was not totally wired, would like to see Hal's land and showed Hal how to make artificial wings. They flew toward Alvrosdale, but the old man died along the way, and Hal returned alone with the secret of the wings, which are apparently gliders. * Pratt's writing mannerisms are sometimes annoying, but the story does hold one's attention. Manning's later treatment of the same concept in "The Man Who Awoke" is superior.

MANTELL, E.
No information.

949. **THE MEN FROM GAYLN**. *Wonder Stories*, August 1934. Ill. Winter.
Short story. * *Time:* 1945. *Place:* Indiana. * During World War I, an enormous glowing sphere appeared near the trenches in France, then disappeared. Now in December 1945, it has reappeared in a field in Indiana. The globe cools, and a thin, dark man emerges, followed by seven-foot-tall reddish-skinned men. The thin, dark man (Mithrad), who is spokesman, speaks English. Understanding, however, is a little difficult to achieve. * The strangers come from several million years in the future. They have long been able to travel in time, but hitherto have not come so far back. Their purpose: There has been a feminist rebellion in Gayln; all the females have withdrawn and formed a separate nation, killing men on sight. Further, the women have developed a system of artificial reproduction so that males will soon be extinct. * The future men, who are harsh and arrogant, now make an offer to the people of 1945: They will pay equal weight in any precious metal for women to take back into the future with them. They add that if their demands are not met willingly, they will simply take such women as they want. This ultimatum delivered, one of the future men strikes down the spokesman with an electric bolt. (Why he does this is by no means clear.) * The forces of Earth attack the sphere, but are massacred, and in a few days black-clad figures emerge from the sphere, devastate the countryside, slaughtering men and capturing nubile women. * It all looks hopeless, but a resolution comes from Mithrad, who has survived the electric bolt. A member of a captive race in the far future, he is happy to plan Earth's defenses against the time invaders. When the invaders next attack, they are met by similar electric weapons augmented by tear gas, and after a ferocious battle, the time invaders are defeated. From Mithrad and the captured globe science takes enormous leaps: antigravity, time travel, transmutation, matter transmission, and knowledge of other dimensions where the dead dwell. * *Miscellaneous:* Future man has two hearts, a different circulatory system, no teeth (but bony ridges), and no toes. * The reader is likely to be concerned with the many loopholes in the plot. Also, what will eventually happen to the human race, since the far-future feminists are apparently left unchallenged and uncorrected?

MARCELLINUS, AMMIANUS
According to Tuck, pseud. of Aaron Nadel. No other information. Presumably not Aaron B. Nadel, writer on military topics. Why the author selected the name of a late Classical historian as a pseudonym is matter for speculation.

950. **THE THOUGHT MACHINE**. *Amazing Stories*, February 1927. Ill. Paul.
Short story. * The inspiration for Henry Smith's thinking machine has an odd source: the stupidity of his vulgar, selfish girlfriend. Using the funds earned by his patented typewriter eraser, he devotes his life to creating what we, today, would call a master computer. He is successful, even to devising a complicated electrical language, and his psychomachs spread over the world. * The machines can answer many sorts of problems—physical, psychological, and social—with the result that by about 2050 the world is a near eutopia. But mankind, shielded from any sort of life challenge, degenerates. * By about 2150 the psychomachs warn humanity to change its way of life, but to no avail. Within another hundred years or two the human race has degenerated to savagery, with pastoral nomads, raiding tribes, and primitive agriculturalists. Science is forgotten, and magic has reemerged as the technique for controlling the world. Oddly enough, the author does not say what happened to the self-sufficient, self-repairing machines. * Really more a story outline than a story, but a very early rendering of a theme later to become important in science-fiction.

MARIUS
U.S. author. According to Rock pseud. of Steve Benedict (1899-?). Benedict wrote at least one other science-fiction story, "Stamp from Moscow," *Astounding Science Fiction*, January 1953. Also non-s-f *Gabee of the Delta* (1953) and *The Little House on Wheels* (1958).

951. **VANDALS FROM THE MOON**. *Amazing Stories*. July 1928. Ill. R. E. Lawlor.
Short story. * *Place:* California, mostly the Bay Area. * Black spots are seen on the Moon, followed shortly by torpedo-like spaceships that land on the West Coast of North America. From them emerge hundred-foot-long worm-like metal machines (the Moon worms), which move out over the landscape, playing a yellow ray that causes almost everything to decay. The Moon worms seem irresistible, for only heavy artillery or tons of high explosive can damage them. * After a time there emerge from openings in the sides of the worms tiny elf-like men with huge heads and small limbs; since they obviously suffer from Earth's heavier atmosphere and gravity, they do not walk, but are carried about in three-legged walking chairs. * In a matter of months the Moon-men conquer the West Coast, destroying or driving out the population. They also round up hordes of women, whom they ship off to the Moon to alleviate a shortage of lunar females. * The newly-married narrator and his wife suffer through invasion and witness the end, as clouds of air-borne bacteria developed in Germany are released on the Moon-men, destroying them. Soon the invasion is over. While a little of the lunar scientific

Marius (*continued*)

equipment remains, most has been destroyed by the invaders. *
Very close in theme, development, and details, to H. G. Wells's
The War of the Worlds. It is surprising that *Amazing* printed it.

952. THE SIXTH GLACIER. *Amazing Stories*, January-
February 1929. Unsigned ill.

Novelette. * *Place:* in part, Mexico, then unconcentrated. * Told
through Bender, a newspaper reporter. * The narrative centers on
two themes, an archeological and a futurological geographical.
* In the archeological sector: Millionaire streetcar magnate and
eccentric amateur archeologist Stephen Dunraven has discovered
an incredible site in Mexico. Far beneath the surface, it consists
of a city with the remains of advanced equipment indicating a
superscience. Dunraven dates it as about 130,000 B.C., or earlier
than the Wisconsin glaciation. * Skeletal material, however, is
not that of *Homo sapiens sapiens*, but is Neanderthaloid, which
Dunraven thinks is an unrepresentative situation. Most important
of all, however, is a gold plate with hieroglyphics on it that
Dunraven interprets as referring to past and future glaciations.
According to Dunraven, the plate attributes Earth cooling and
glaciation to passage through a belt of cold ether, with a rough
periodicity. * Further work on the ancient site reveals that the
intelligent race was not human, but arachnid, gigantic spiders
perhaps three feet tall. The primitive human bones found at the
site were those of slaves kept by the more intelligent spiders.
The last glaciation finished off the arachnids, but the tougher
humans survived. * The geographical theme: According to the
spider chronologies, the next glaciation should be just about
ready to start. And so it does. Astronomical observations show
an odd-looking feature in space, and the glaciation hits with
fantastic speed. Great snowstorms fill the air, and the glaciers
creep south (and north in the southern hemisphere), covering
everything. In Europe the ice sheet reaches down through Italy.
The rate of movement, once the major sheets are formed, is
about five miles a day, but by some quirk the ice dashes through
Manhattan pushing over skyscrapers. * As for narrative and plot,
little happens. The reporter narrator Bender flies about a little
and suffers from unrequited love, and Dunraven crows a little
when he is proved right and the critical savants wrong.
Throughout the remainder of the story geography plays a larger
part than personalities, with a listing of places now smothered by
ice. * Dunraven, however, has ideas for combatting the advance
of the continental glaciers. Jetties sunk in the ocean deflect
tropical currents to the north, while electric heating systems
installed at strategic places melt ice. As a result of all this, after
about four years the glaciers retreat and ultimately go back to
their original positions. The damage, however, has been colossal. Japan is wrecked, with 98 percent of its population dead.
China is almost depopulated, hordes having broken south into
India. * During the glacial period society suffered, with many
relapses into primitivism. But now that the sixth glacier is gone,
European man at least is attempting to build a better world order.
* Less derivative than the previous work, although traces of
Wells, Serviss, and Doyle are apparent. * The author would seem
to have some knowledge of historical geology and meteorology,
for his coverage of glacial theories was up-to-date for his time.
Nevertheless, the story reads better in summary than it really is.

MARSHALL, JAMES P.

U.S. author, then resident of Providence, Rhode Island. No other

information, except that portrait shows a man in early middle
age. The editor refers to him in the blurb as a "well-known
author," but this seems to be an overstatement.

953. WARRIORS OF SPACE. *Science Wonder Stories*,
June 1929. Ill. Paul.

Short story. * *Time:* perhaps around 1955-1960. *Place:* New
York, San Francisco, and space near Saturn. * The present story
is a sequel to "The World in the Balance," which appeared in
Argosy-Allstory, 16 April 1927, and described an invasion from
Dione. It is covered in detail in *Science-Fiction: The Early
Years*. * In the earlier story, a globe appeared in the sky above
New York City, descended, revealing itself to be a spaceship
about 150 feet in diameter, and began to disintegrate parts of the
city, including the Statue of Liberty. Terrestrial weapons were
of no avail. After a time a humanoid figure emerged from the
globe and demanded surrender, promising to return in three days.
A young scientist, Arthur Maynard, observing that the rays
destroyed everything except gold, suggested the use of gold-
plated armor and defensive weapons. The concept was valid, for
golden shields held by Terrestrials reflected the disintegrator rays
back on the space globe, which was destroyed. * Thirty years
have passed, and the world anxiously fears a return of the
invaders. Now the Dionians are back, attacking San Francisco.
Arthur Maynard and his son Donald will be the backbone of the
defense against them. Working out a means of controlling
gravity, the Maynards have built a bradawl-shaped vessel that
flies by increasing and decreasing gravity in various directions.
* On receiving news of the attack on San Francisco, the Maynards fly from New York to the scene of action in about eight
minutes. The Dionian spheres are no match for the Maynards'
vessel, which destroys some spheres by reflecting their rays with
golden mirrors and others by ramming. Three, however, escape
and presumably make their way back to Dione. Along the way
they disintegrate the U.S. Mint and seize the gold stored therein.
* This action, of course, is a disaster for Earth, for if the
Dionians, who apparently do not have gold on their planetoid,
improve their ray so that it destroys gold, the Earth will be
defenseless. * Donald Maynard has the solution, which he
proposes to the government. The Earth must construct a huge
fleet, invade Dione and destroy it rather than wait for another
attack. The mechanism of destruction will be an enormous fleet
of the antigravity ships, which will push Saturn and its satellites
out of orbit into the sun. This is done, and the menace from
Dione is over. The Earth is damaged by slight orbital changes,
but this is still preferable to the Dionians. * Routine at best.

MARTIN, AL. H.

No information. Portrait shows a young man.

954. THE JOVIAN HORDE. *Wonder Stories Quarterly*,
Summer 1932. Ill. Paul.

Short story. * Lance Norden, returned from a five-year expedition in the Matto Grosso, is present when the strange phenomena
begin. The Moon changes its orbit and approaches more closely
to Earth, with resulting disturbances; and Earth is invaded by
spaceships bearing a bestial race from Jupiter that intends to
enslave or destroy the human race. A message from the Moon
warns the Earth not to resist. * The invaders consist of gigantic
humanoid females, with smaller subservient males; they are
equipped with projectors that emit torture/heat/disintegrator rays.
While bestial in appearance and many of their actions, the

Martin, Al. H. (*continued*)

invaders have a high science with atomic energy based on cosmic ray bombardment of metals, and antigravity created by magnetic fields. * Lance and his date Lorna watch as the Jovians (as they are later revealed to be) capture humans, strip them naked, brand them as property, and then subject them to various tortures. (The author makes considerable play with nudity and torture). * Lance is captured, branded, rescued by Lorna, and gains possession of a death tube. Stealing an invader ship, he takes it to top scientists who analyze the protective metal on the ship and duplicate the death rays. Terrestrial poison gas plays a large part in the defeat of the Jovians, who abandon their base on the Moon and leave. The Moon returns partly to its old orbit, and all is well again. * The sexualization of the narrative is unusual for *Wonder*.

MARTIN, HARRY

According to Schwartz/Weisinger, the pseud. of Harold A. Lower, who has a separate entry.

955. **RICE'S RAY**. *Amazing Stories*, January 1928. Ill. DeB.

Short story. * *Place:* mostly Venus. * Rice, who has been working for the government developing a ray that will conduct electricity, has found, instead, a ray that conducts gravity. With Rice's ray the law of inverse squares does not apply: Gravity is as strong as at its original source. * After some experimenting and theorizing, Rice and friends build a spaceship, make a trip to the Moon (just mentioned in passing), and set out for Venus. * Venus is tropical, with vegetation like terrestrial paleobotany, pterodactyls, and upright, plantigrade, stone-throwing reptiles that may be more-or-less intelligent. The explorers return to Earth and plan for a follow-up to Mars. * Undeveloped and primitive, but with a fair amount of scientific exposition. Oddly enough, reader response to the story was enthusiastic.

MARTIN, STUART (1882-?)

British author of detective novels. *The Hangman's Guests* (1931) and *Only Seven Were Hanged* (1929) were published in the United States. Also contributor to British boys' papers, including *Modern Boy, Boys Realm, Magnet*, etc.

956. **DEVILMAN OF THE DEEP**. *Scoops,* 7 April-26 May 1934. Unsigned ill. Some episodes published anonymously.

Boys' fiction. * An interminable episodic novel in the tradition of H. Rider Haggard. * *Place:* mostly undersea off the coast of Uruguay. * Young scientist Mark Stanmore and associates Bulwer Kells and Abel Cornwall are exploring the sea bottom in a bathyal submarine-gondola, when they feel that their vessel is being pulled off its path. Looking out, they see that their vessel is surrounded by hordes of humanoid beings with suckered tentacles for arms and legs, and wide staring eyes. These fish-men drag the vessel into an air-filled cavern that is sealed off with a block of ice. A booming voice, speaking English, thereupon orders the men to leave their vessel. * The voice is that of Devilman, the fifteen-foot-tall king of the fish-men, who has been conducting a war with another people and can use surface weapons. * This is the first occasion that living humans have come into his domain. Unfortunately, Devilman, who is a merciless tyrant and blood-soaked monster, intends to kill Kells and Cornwall out of hand. He plans to keep Stanmore alive for

a time as a weapons instructor. (An oddity that the reader will appreciate is that the explorers are armed to the teeth. Perhaps they expected a mutual shoot-out in the bathyal vessel?) * *Background:* Although much, like Devilman's knowledge of English, is not explained, the fish-men have an idiosyncratic science based on sea materials. A nearby underwater volcano provides energy, and salvaged material from wrecks has provided an impetus to a competent technology. Much of this advance is due to Prince Sea Flight, a friendly, amiable fish-man, the rightful ruler of the land, whose power has been usurped by the vicious Devilman. * The story takes the form of dynastic adventure as the surface men are included in the civil war between Devilman and Prince Sea Flight. After many hair-raising adventures Sea Flight wins. Devilman is killed, and the explorers are returned to the surface in a small vessel that Prince Sea Flight had prepared. * Pretty bad, even as boys' fiction.

MARTIN, WALTER LIVINGSTON

No information.

957. **ZINA THE KILLER**. *Wonder Stories Quarterly*, Fall 1931.

Short story. * Not science-fiction, but a nature sketch, the life history of a female scorpion. * The editor states that he liked the story so much that he included it (even though it is not science-fiction) and asks for reactions. None was published.

MASON, F. V. W.

Although, to my knowledge, the following story has not been acknowledged, the author is probably the well-known writer of thrillers Francis Van Wyck Mason (1901-1978), who wrote as Van Wyck Mason and under several pseuds. He is best remembered for series thrillers about U.S. Army intelligence operative Captain (and higher ranks) Hugh North. Also historical novels. Educated at Harvard. Served in World Wars I and II, in the latter attached to Supreme Headquarters, A.E.F. The following story may be his first published work, but not a creditable one.

958. **PHALANXES OF ATLANS**. *Astounding Stories*, February-March 1931. Ill. J. Fleming Gould and Wesso.

Short novel. * *Place:* the Arctic. * Nelson and Alden survive an emergency plane landing somewhere in the Arctic. Returning to camp from hunting, Nelson finds evidence that Alden has been seized by members of a strange culture. Following their trail through a subterranean passage, Nelson comes upon Atlans, a semitropical land heated by volcanism. * The sunken land is inhabited by two races, first, blond or redheaded descendants of refugees from Atlantis and Henry Hudson's men, and second, the Jarmuthians, dark, hairy, macrorhine descendants of the Hebrew Lost Tribes, who are described in anti-Semitic terms. * The culture of the land is fairly high, with steam used for an energy source. There are steam tube-cars that reach 300 MPH and guns that shoot compressed steam; but in general the land is at a sword-and-ray-gun level. * The Atlanteans are tolerable, if insufferably proud and quarrelsome, but the Jarmuthians are filthy, crude, greedy, and treacherous. The Atlanteans worship the Greek gods, but the Jarmuthians worship a Moloch and practice human sacrifice and cannibalism. The two peoples are bitterly hostile to each other. * Some time earlier the Jarmuthians captured the Atlantean crown princess; to keep her from ending on a platter, the Atlanteans pay a yearly tribute of virgins for

Mason, F. V. W. (*continued*)

sacrifice and barbecuing. At the moment the Hebrews, who have also captured Alden, are asking for more. * Nelson's position is precarious. He is grudgingly accepted by the Atlantean civil authorities, but the priesthood would like to sacrifice him to Ares. * Nelson, who has retained his rifle, persuades the Atlanteans to accept him as a champion in a field duel against the Hebrews. He will fight six men, with the captives and the ransom the stakes. He wins, but the Hebrews welsh, and the war goes on. * The Jarmuthians now announce that they will eat the princess, whereupon Nelson, pretending to be a defector, allows himself to be captured. There are problems, but all ends well, Alden rescuing Nelson and the princess with a trained pterodactyl that carries them away. * Dinosaurs of various sorts are common, both as combat and traction animals. The usual lost-race clash between priestly and secular is also present. * Somewhat shoddy work.

MATHESON, DONALD or FLORENCE

No information. The story heading attributes the story to Florence Matheson, whereas the contents page of the magazine has Donald Matheson. Schwartz/Weisinger (*Science Fiction Digest*, April 1933, p. 5), in a listing of stories accepted by *Amazing Stories*, cite the author as "D. Matheson," which would seem to support "Donald."

959. **THE MOLECULE TRAPPER.** *Amazing Stories,* September 1934.

Short-short story. * The narrator tells of the experiments and death of Bell. Bell has devised an apparatus that can shrink or enlarge objects. Thus, he can make a crumb of bread expand to the size of a basketball. His aim is to expand a molecule to the size of an egg. But he has had difficulty in catching a molecule to enlarge. He thereupon reduces a tiny sphere of helium, hoping to trap a molecule in it; but it is compressed so greatly that it acts like a bomb, destroying the laboratory and killing him.

MATHISON, VOLNEY G.

U.S. author. Judging by this story and the author's *The Radio Buster* (Philadelphia: Stokes, 1924), Mathison was probably a professional brass pounder (i.e. old-time telegraph operator) with some experience in Alaska and elsewhere. Mathison also had two short pieces in Gernsback's *Radio News* and "The Death Bottle" in *Weird Tales*, March 1925. Mathison was a prolific author elsewhere under the pseud. Dex Volney, contributing Western stories with Alaskan setting to Street and Smith magazines. Apparently resident in New York at this time and connected with the Pacific Radio Co., New York City.

960. **THE MONGOLIANS' RAY.** *Amazing Stories,* June 1929. Unsigned ill.

Short story. * Flim-flam. * Samuel Jones, former telegraph operator, is associated with *Mazerka Magazine* in a program to expose scientific hoaxes, fraudulent mediums, and similar disreputable phenomena. He has twenty-five thousand dollars per year at his disposal. * He is astonished one day when a man in complete plate armor enters his office and tells a wild tale. The Asian, also called Mongolians and Tartars, have perfected a long-distance hypnotic ray for mind control, with the intention of exterminating the white race. Only heavy metal is a shield against the ray. The armored man (Count Vrennisky) and his

associate Dr. Von der Vogel are in perpetual danger of assassination. * Jones, led along by circumstances, including a newspaper report of Von der Vogel's death, decides to investigate the armored man's claim; he visits the armored man's laboratory, where there is an impressive range of equipment. * When Jones meddles with it, there is an explosion, and Jones is morally bound to replace the radium that has been dissipated. As he is about to sign a check, the con is blown. A young woman, who he thought was the count's associate, is a Secret Service agent. The so-called Count Vrennisky is Arman Stressman, Radium Harry, etc., a well-known con man. The newspaper article about Von der Vogel's death had been planted, and the apparatus had been rigged to explode at the slightest touch.

MAUGHAN, RALPH

No information.

961. **THE CHOICE.** *Amazing Stories,* June 1934.

Short-short story. * Borderline science-fiction at most. * Dr. Harley, whose son is dying of meningitis, rushes to his friend, Dr. Bennett, who has just perfected a cure for the disease. Bennett has only a small quantity of the serum ready. Unfortunately, Bennett drops dead. The formula is not known, and Harley is in the predicament of deciding whether to cure his son with the sole test tube of liquid in existence or to take it to be analyzed. The answer is left open.

MAXON, P. B. (?-shortly before 1940?)

Very little information. Apparently Maxon at the time of writing "The Waltz of Death" was an unemployed newspaper reporter. He died suddenly after revising his story for book publication, but his death was not publicized and, to the best of my knowledge, the exact date is not known.

962. **THE WALTZ OF DEATH.** *Wonder Stories,* May-July 1935. Ill. Schneeman.

(Reprinted in book form by Mystery House, New York, 1941; paperback edition by Bart House, New York, 1944.)

Novel. * A detective story of a sort, with a science-fictional element as explanation. There would be no point in summarizing the plot in any detail, since the novel is badly padded and structured. In essence: During a soirée in which great scientist Dick Straith plays a Brahms waltz, Mat Telfer slumps over dead. Autopsy reveals that his body is riddled with tiny perforations. The narrator, a criminologist, covers the case, consulting with insurance investigators. Along the way, it is revealed that Telfer was a cad who was blackmailing beautiful young Peg Duncan. "For money?" "No, not for money. That wasn't what he wanted, Lauder." "Oh!" * As the ending reveals, the murderer had discovered that certain very high vibrations can shatter electronic orbits, causing transmutation of a sort. Such vibrations transmuted and exploded the aspirin in Telfer's pocket and system. * The novel was highly touted by the editors of *Wonder Stories* as having received an honorable mention in a contest sponsored by *Liberty Magazine,* but it is a very bad job.

MAXWELL, JOSLYN

According to the advance notice for "The Outpost on the Moon," Maxwell was the pseud. of Max J. Irland, who may have been the M. J. Irland associated with the Ford Scientific Research Staff in Dearborn, Michigan, and author of "Windshield Optics"

Maxwell, Joslyn (*continued*)

(in *Applied Optics*, 1969). McGhan, Rock, and Tuck, on the other hand, render the name as Ireland. Portrait accompanying the story shows a young man. The author would seem to have a scientific background. Social Security records list a Max Irland (1906-1995) as registering in Michigan and dying in Florida.

963. **THE OUTPOST ON THE MOON**. *Wonder Stories*, December 1930-February 1931. Ill. Paul.

Novel. * *Place:* mostly the Moon and Ganymede. * George Marland, scientific journalist, renews acquaintance with his college teacher and friend Barton Wiley, who takes him into his confidence on his latest work. Wiley has achieved antigravity by working on the atomic nucleus. * With funding from the university, the two men construct a spaceship and leave for the moon. A radar-like arrangement alters course to avoid meteors in space. * The space flight is uneventful, although the men see a strange light on the Moon that they believe is most probably an active volcano. They land, explore in space suits, and discover that there are other men on the Moon. A party picks them up and takes them to an elaborate underground establishment that houses a large colony of scientists. * Explanation: The colony, which was established about ten years earlier, is controlled by Professor Forscher, a maverick scientist of incredible learning and genius. Staffed by the cream of Earth's scientists, in addition to general research it is focused on a single problem: A solution to mysterious sulfurous meteorites that have been striking the Earth in a pattern. Years before, when a young man, Forscher observed the periodicity of the bombardment and determined to find its cause. The best hypothesis at the moment is that the meteorites represent an attempt at communication by the inhabitants of Ganymede. Forscher has under construction a telescope with a hundred-foot lens, with which he hopes to settle the problem. * The lunar outpost is self-sufficient, thanks to Forscher's creation of a new trans-uranic element that offers enormous quantities of energy and can be used for the creation and transmutation of elements. Underground farms produce food stuffs for the voluntary exiles. A small fleet of spaceships travels back and forth to Earth and around the Moon. * Wiley and Marland are welcomed and join the group with enthusiasm. When the giant telescope is finished and it reveals the possibility of life on Ganymede, the colonists construct a large spaceship. Marland and four others leave, reaching Ganymede in about a month. There are a few mishaps and a space rescue along the voyage, which is Vernean in manner, with a semi-comic French geographer. * Ganymede is dark and cold, but inhabitable. It is also populated by strange beings with carrot-like bodies, four weak-looking legs, and two flat arms with finger-like appendages. The explorers are first captured by hostile natives, then rescued by friendly, obviously superior Ganymedans, who treat them as guests. Communication is gradually established by writing. * The situation on Ganymede: There are two hostile cultures, one of which is a rabble-led workers' democracy, with runaway capitalism, weak science and perpetual unrest; the other a scientific technocracy, which is superior in all respects, but weaker militarily because of a much smaller population. The scientific culture would like military aid from Earth to defeat their enemy. While they have efficient flying machines operated by gas turbines and guns that shoot poison darts, their weaponry is inferior to the Earth's. In exchange for armaments, they offer the technology of their advanced television and combustion engines. * The Earthmen, who are obviously in no position to make interplanetary diplomatic agreements, agree to pass the message along to Terrestrial authorities. After another adventure with the hostile Ganymedans, who capture two of the party, the surviving explorers return to Earth. * *Miscellaneous:* Ganymede is heated by the interaction of magnetic fields from Jupiter. * Ganymedan astronomers do not know of the existence of Mercury, but have observations of a trans-Plutonian planet. * Mars, as revealed by Forscher's telescope, is barren and dead; the canals were an optical illusion. * A strange work. The first portion of the story, up to the flight to Ganymede is well done, with a considerable amount of imaginative science; the adventures on Ganymede, however, tend to be routine at times. Still, I read the story with enjoyment, a rare incident in this project.

MEADOWCROFT, KIRK

U.S. writer. Also wrote *Apes, Ivory and Jade, Essays on the Minor Arts* (1936).

964. **THE INVISIBLE BUBBLE**. *Amazing Stories*, September 1928. Ill. Paul.

Short story. * The narrator is summoned by his old friend and fellow student Professor Sylvester to assist in an experiment. Sylvester's researches have been following a dual objective: a solution to mysterious disappearances (his sweetheart disappeared before his eyes a long time ago) and an investigation of radiation in the range of cosmic rays. He can now report some success. * His apparatus can create a black bubble of nothingness that swallows things irretrievably. At first Sylvester believes that he can devise a way to retrieve what has been swallowed, but eventually recognizes that the black bubble is a one-way process. Sylvester himself falls victim to the forces he uncovered.

MEEK, CAPTAIN S[TERNER] [ST.] P[AUL] (1894-1972)

American soldier, writer. Educated at the University of Chicago, M.I.T., and elsewhere, major apparently chemistry. Entered U.S. Army in 1917, and remained as a career officer. In earlier years served in the Philippine Islands. In later years held the rank of colonel in the Ordnance Dept., U.S. Regular Army. Chief of Small Arms Ammunition Research 1923-1926 and Chief Publications Officer, Ordnance Dept., World War II. Also wrote animal books for older children, i.e., *Franz, A Dog of the Police* (1935 and often reprinted). An intelligent man with a good background in the sciences, who obviously wrote down for the pulps. According to Schwartz/Weisinger (*Science Fiction Digest*, June 1933, p. 10) "Some of Capt. S. P. Meek's stories are polished up by a professional critic, Laurence D'Orsay." * See also Sterner St. Paul, pseud.

Meek's stories are presented as the Dr. Bird Series and Other Works.

The Doctor Bird Series

Dr. Bird. who is associated with the Bureau of Standards in Washington, D. C., is almost a superman. Tall, incredibly strong, with one of the world's finest minds, he is a master of almost every branch of scientific knowledge, yet is also a man of action. In his exploits Bird is accompanied by Carnes, an intermediate grade member of the Secret Service, who serves as

Meek, Capt. S. P., U.S.A. (*continued*)

a backup and a Watson. Since Bird has ready access to the President, rules, regulations, laws, decrees, etc., are suspended at his wish, and he has a free hand. Bird (as undoubtedly was the case with S. P. Meek, U.S.R.A.) is a political ultra-conservative who finds Russian Communists or their American dupes under the beds of most things that threaten or go wrong. As a series opponent, Bird has the great Russian scientist Saranoff, who is almost on Bird's level, but is a fanatical and wicked man. In the later stories the beautiful young Russian defector Feodovna Andrevitch (a.k.a. Thelma Andrews) works in association with Bird and on occasion saves his life. She is obviously in love with Bird, who haughtily rejects any emotional involvement. Perhaps this is because Bird is already married? (See #977, "Poisoned Air.") Two additional stories in the series appeared in Gernsback's *Scientific Detective Monthly/Amazing Detective Tales*: "The Perfect Counterfeit" (January 1930) and "The Gland Murders" (June 1930). In the second story, the Russians are disrupting America by poisoning bootleg whiskey!

According to Meek, the Dr. Bird series was terminated because of protests by left-wing readers who objected to his anti-Russian attitude. Boredom seems to be a more likely explanation.

965. **THE CAVE OF HORROR**. *Astounding Stories*, January 1930. Ill. J. Fleming Gould.

Short story. * The first published story in the Dr. Bird series. * *Place:* Mammoth Cave, Kentucky. * Strange things are happening in Mammoth Cave. People have disappeared, sometimes leaving bloody traces. The Army has been called in, but such soldiers as have ventured into the cave have been killed. * Bird investigates, and after various adventures, including pursuit by something monstrous and ferocious, he solves the mystery. He sets up an ultraviolet projector, for it is his theory that the monster is invisible except to ultraviolet light. Then, venturing into the cave in a tank, he succeeds in taking a photograph as the monster is taking a tethered cow. It is a huge animal with a frog-like head, sturdy limbs, grasping upper limbs, and a long tail. But it is almost two-dimensionally slender, so that it can slither through narrow passages. * Bird and his associates battle with the monster; it is wounded, but it escapes into the recesses of the cave, whereupon the Army seals up the monster's place of entry. Bird theorizes that the creature is an infant specimen of life-forms to be found beneath the surface of the Earth. * Intelligently written.

966. **THE RADIO ROBBERY**. *Amazing Stories*, February 1930. Ill. Morey.

Although the second story published, perhaps the first story in the sequence about Dr. Bird and his expert doings. * *Place:* Philadelphia. * When the personnel at the Federal Reserve Bank open the vault to receive a shipment of bullion, there is a terrific explosion and the vault door is blown upon an employee, killing him. An inspection of the vault reveals that what should be bullion is only bar copper. The police arrest the bullion teller for murder, his motive robbery and sexual jealousy. * Carnes, as local head of the Secret Service, on examining the premises, calls in Dr. Bird. The problem is that there is no evidence of a bomb or fumes, suggesting to both men that the explosion was caused by igniting gas—but there is no gas in the area. As a wild card in the background, however, there have been strange radio disturbances. * Bird investigates, sets up a lure for the criminal,

borrows Army radio directional finders, and the Secret Service pounces. * The criminal is one Wallace, who had formerly worked for the Bureau of Standards and was known to Bird. Wallace had discovered a process for temporarily altering copper into the semblance of gold. He and a confederate bank guard substituted the fake gold for the real. Since the metal was not stable, Wallace disrupted it with radio waves to remove evidence. During the shootout, Wallace is killed and his apparatus self-destroyed. * Carnes plays a larger part than in the other stories. One of the better stories in the series.

967. **THE THIEF OF TIME**. *Astounding Stories*, February 1930. Unsigned ill.

Short story. * *Place:* Chicago. * Bird and Carnes happen to be in Chicago when a mysterious crime takes place: a bundle of bank notes disappears from the teller's booth. The brutal Chicago police, who are sure that the theft is an inside job, arrest the bank personnel, but Bird is convinced that there is another solution. He is right, of course. He traps his man with an ultra-fast camera. The criminal is a former associate at the Bureau of Standards who had been working on catalysts to speed up metabolism. He speeded himself up about thirty thousand times, so that his motion was invisible or almost so. * Also involved is a track star who used the catalyst to establish records.

968. **COLD LIGHT**. *Astounding Stories*, March 1930. Unsigned ill.

Short story. * Carnes of the Secret Service describes a mysterious situation: a plane carrying secret military documents has crashed, and, from the air, it can be seen that the bodies of the crew are shattered in a peculiar way, as if they were pieces of glass. * Bird suspects supercold, which he considers to be a basic force, not just absence of heat. Someone must be able to project cold so intense that flesh and bone can shatter. And the secret documents are missing. * An aerial search with a thermocouple uncovers the criminals, and after a gun battle matters are resolved. A criminal scientist had devised the cold projector, but his assistant, who turned out to be a Russian spy, stole the plans. Both criminals are dead, and the projector, unfortunately, has been destroyed.

969. **THE RAY OF MADNESS**. *Astounding Stories*, April 1930. Unsigned ill.

Short story. * Two phenomena concur: the spectroscopic discovery of lunium, a new element, in light reflected from the moon, and the mental and physical disorders of the President of the United States. * Bird learns of the President's illness by chance, but puts two and two together. An investigation of the President's sleeping quarters reveals that quartz glazing permits the passage of ultraviolet and other radiation, and that an unknown party is bombarding the windows with the emanations of lunium, which has the property of causing mental and dermal disorders. * The culprit is a Russian agent who is attempting to block Anglo-American friendship.

970. **STOLEN BRAINS**. *Astounding Stories*, October 1930. Ill. Wesso.

Short story. * *Place:* Maine. * Bird corners his friend Carnes and takes him to his (Bird's) summer camp in Maine, without explanation. There Carnes is amazed to see doubles of himself and Bird. * Explanation: There have been mysterious cases of amnesia centered around an area in Maine. Bird, acting under direct presidential authority, is setting a trap. * The trap is sprung, the decoys are captured, and after thrills and perils

Meek, Capt. S. P., U.S.A. (*continued*)

explanations take place. * The sinister hunchback, Slavatsky, building on earlier suppressed work, has discovered that mental power depends upon the amount of a certain chemical (menthium) deep in the brain. By extracting this chemical hypodermically, he removes memory and ability, and by injecting it into another person, he can increase the second person's mental capability. He plans to develop a supermentality and take over the world. He already has a marvelous flying globe and a sleep gas. * Bird resolves everything, turning the criminals into idiots by removing their menthium.

971. **THE SEA TERROR**. *Astounding Stories*, December 1930. Unsigned ill.

Short story. * The seaman Mitchell, the only survivor of the *Arethusa*, has a strange story to tell. His ship, which was carrying gold bullion, was attacked and sunk by a sea serpent that was hundreds of feet across, with eyes thirty feet wide. Bird believes him, but sees deeper implications, especially since divers in the area have been lost. * Bird explores the wreck of the *Arethusa* in a bathysphere, finding that the bullion has been removed to a nearby cave. * A raid reveals what has been happening: the great Slavic scientist Saranoff, who is associated with the Youth League, a militant Communist-front organization, has worked upon the glandular function of sea life and has developed the sea serpents. He has also created giant octopi, one of which almost does for the bathysphere. * As for Saranoff?

972. **THE BLACK LAMP**. *Astounding Stories*, February 1931. Ill. Wesso.

Short story. * Thieves break into Bird's laboratory and steal his model of a radite gun. This gun, which fires a 2 1/2 oz. charge of radite, has a range of fifteen miles, striking within a two hundred foot circle. The explosion is equal to that of a sixteen-inch mortar shell. * The thieves used some sort of a paralysis ray that happens to turn glass opaque; only Bird's special transparent plastic vitrilene is proof against it. * It is the Communists, of course, headed by Saranoff, who is alive and still operating through the Young Labor Party. * The Russians also have a lethal red ray, as Bird discovers when he and the Army attack the Maryland station from which the Communists planned to shell Washington. * Bird obtained information about this station from a captive Communist, whose brain he electrostimulated, causing the man's death. As for Saranoff?

973. **THE EARTH'S CANCER**. *Amazing Stories*, March 1931. Ill. Morey.

Short story. * *Place:* California. * Bird and Carnes are assigned to investigate a strange epidemic in Lassen County, California. The sufferers develop skin growths and lesions and undergo personality changes, including raving homicidal madness. Sufferers commonly run away into the woods, refusing treatment and attempting to kill those who approach them. Bird hypothesizes that the epidemic is a peculiar sort of radiation cancer caused by local conditions. * Bird examines the edge of the epidemic area, which is characterized by overblown lush vegetation that dries into dust. He and Carnes, both dressed in lead suits, enter the core location. There they are attacked and captured by cancerous madmen who have established a cult focused on the shining, bubbling center of the infection, a mass of radium. * Bird and Carnes would have fared badly had it not been for a radite grenade that Carnes threw into the radium pool. This, combining with the radium in the pool, destroyed the

deposit. Carnes is badly injured, and Bird is overcome by the psychic aspects of the site. But both are rescued and recover nicely. * This story is numbered and described in publication sequence, but it was probably written earlier, perhaps not long after #965, "The Cave of Horror," to which reference is made. It is probably the third story in the series.

974. **WHEN CAVERNS YAWNED**. *Astounding Stories*, May 1931. Unsigned ill.

Short story. * Dr. Bird is still chasing Russian Communists, notably the criminal genius Saranoff. * A tremendous chasm suddenly opens beneath the presidential train as the President is on his way to a summit (my term) to nullify the Russian attacks on religion. The chasm is not a collapsed cave roof, as is first thought, but is man-made. Dr. Bird soon realizes what has happened: Saranoff has discovered a way to consolidate matter, squeezing out the space between atomic particles. * Saranoff uses his intention to destroy Wilmington, North Carolina and a naval fleet. But when his submarine-carried apparatus attacks Washington, D.C., Bird is ready with equipment that reëxpands matter and incidentally destroys the Russian's weapon. As for Saranoff? * *Miscellaneous:* Saranoff also has a far-viewing and far-speaking device.

975. **THE PORT OF MISSING PLANES**. *Astounding Stories*, August 1931. Ill. Wesso.

Short story. * *Place:* mostly underground in the Southwest. * Dr. Bird decides to investigate why mail planes in the Southwest are disappearing. As he and Carnes fly along the route of the missing aircraft, their plane is dragged down by an unknown force into an opening in the ground. They are now the captives of a strange race of intelligent humanoid mole-men, the Selom. * The mole-men, who are photophobic and have a different visual range than humans, are not malevolent, but they have been misled by the villainous Saranoff, who escaped death in the previous encounter by venturing into their tunnels. * Saranoff intends to use the captured fliers to attack the United States. Since the Selom have not only telepathic and hypnotic powers, but also apparatus for removing personality and memory, his plan seems feasible. * Saranoff schedules Bird for mental emasculation, but Bird appeals to the sense of justice of the Selom and to the Selom king, who has been absent. * The king stops Saranoff's procedure and questions both men. Since their testimonies are radically different, the king subjects them to a mechanical truth detector. * The result is surprising. The king rejects both men, saying that although both are sincere, both are obsessed with death and destruction. Declaring that his people will take no part in surface quarrels and sealing his land, the king removes most of Bird and Saranoff's memories of their visit and deposits them suitably on the surface. * *Miscellaneous:* The Selom, who are far more advanced scientifically than we, when excavating, remove rock from their tunnels by shifting it back in time. It can be retrieved if necessary. As for Saranoff?

976. **THE SOLAR MAGNET**. *Astounding Stories*, October 1931. Ill. Wesso.

Short story. * *Place:* mostly Siberia, near Archangel. * The amount of daylight each day is increasing abnormally. Most scientists have no explanation, but Dr. Bird reasons out that the Russians, notably Saranoff, are using a "solar magnet" to improve the climate of their northern lands by shifting the axis of the Earth. * Bird and Carnes, boarding a destroyer, head for Russia. They find Saranoff's installation not too far from

Meek, Capt. S. P., U.S.A. (*continued*)

Archangel. Shelling is of no avail, for the shells do not explode, and Bird and Carnes are captured. Saranoff is away, but on his return the men will be forced to talk. * But, Feodovna Androvitch, a dissident young woman but a loyal Communist, who both hates Saranoff and owes a debt to Bird for his kind treatment of her crooked brother back in America, releases the two Americans. The destroyer now successfully shells the solar magnet and Saranoff's installation. As for Saranoff?

977. **POISONED AIR**. *Astounding Stories*, March 1932. Ill. Wesso.

Short story. * *Place:* Aberdeen Proving Ground, Maryland. * A strange poison gas fells soldiers at the proving ground. Dr. Bird suspects that the phenomenon is related to the Meuse incident of a short time before and that the Russian genius Saranoff is involved. * The gas turns out to be a new form of oxygen, perhaps O_5, which crystallizes, but is dissipated by sunlight or X-rays. * Bird prowls the swamps later, trying to catch the Russians who are responsible, but is himself captured and infected with a new bacterium. Carnes rescues him, but Bird's life was really saved by his assistant Thelma Andrews, the former Feodovna Androvitch of the previous story. * What is she doing in a sensitive post in the government? Bird tells Carnes that she hates Saranoff so deeply that her hatred overpowers all other feelings, so that she is willing to live with capitalism for a time. Actually, as the reader can see, the fair Thelma is setting her cap for the doctor. In "The Radio Robbery," however, Bird is married, a state of affairs which Thelma may not know or Meek may have forgotten. * As for Saranoff?

978. **THE GREAT DROUGHT**. *Astounding Stories*, May 1932. Ill. Wesso.

Short story. * Bird happens to be nearby when during an enormous air manoeuvre the planes of the U.S. Air Service develop engine trouble. Bird recognizes what is wrong: a stream of static electricity is causing the iron motors to malfunction. He works out a remedy. Obviously, Saranoff is behind this. * Bird thereupon receives a call from Thelma telling him that Saranoff is hiding out in the marshes off Bush River. But it is a trap, and Bird is taken. Saranoff, after gloating appropriately, announces that he has so arranged matters that Carnes, when he comes to rescue Bird, will blow him up. Saranoff leaves, setting the key to Bird's chains just out of reach. * But Saranoff underestimates Bird's mechanical ingenuity. Bird simply rewires his flashlight into an electromagnet and attracts the keys over to himself. Saranoff is once again defeated. * Saranoff has also been interfering with weather patterns, whence the title of the story. * Thelma now makes her appearance. She had been in Saranoff's group in disguise, working against him. Her delight at seeing Bird alive receives a typical freezing squelch from him. * By now hackneyed.

979. **VANISHING GOLD**. *Wonder Stories*, May 1932. Ill. Paul.

Short story. * Bird has been summoned to New York to investigate the strange diminution of gold in the vault of the Federal Reserve Bank. A few questions reveal that the same phenomenon is taking place in other banks. * As Bird immediately recognizes, the diabolic Saranoff is behind it all. But how is he doing it? It does not take Bird long to figure out what is happening and how it is being done. Saranoff is aiming the disintegrating impulses of radium at the bank vaults, thus

transmuting some of the gold to copper. * Bird triangulates Saranoff's place of operations, a disused tunnel under Central Park. There is a shoot-out, in which the conspirators fair badly. When Bird sees that Miss Andrews has been slightly wounded, he loses his aplomb for a moment, but speedily regains it. * This is the last story printed about Dr. Bird, a situation not to be deplored. The stories were getting rather silly.

Other Works

980. **THE MURGATROYD EXPERIMENT**. *Amazing Stories Quarterly*, Winter 1929. Ill. Paul.

Short story. * *Time:* A.D. 2060. *Place:* mostly a small island in the Hawaiian group. * *Background:* In 1934 a workable international government was established by the Western nations. In 1968, the Sino-Japanese empire attacked the West in a war that lasted until 1980. So many people were killed that the pressure of overpopulation, which had caused the war, was temporarily removed. But after the war, with complete peace under a world government and highly effective medical resources, the population rose by 2080 to more than 31 billion with average longevity of 142 years. The planet simply cannot support so many people. * By this time a certain amount of eugenics is practiced, with unfit persons not being allowed to breed. Qualifications for fitness are physical condition, mental ability, and morality, all measurable by machine. But the eugenics program is inadequate. * The great scientist Dr. Fabian Murgatroyd suggests a solution to the Malthusian situation that is present: alter human metabolism by replacing blood with a chlorophyll-like substance that can absorb nutrition directly from the sun, like a plant. The supreme council approves Murgatroyd's plan, offering him funds and small Hawaiian island for experimentation. * Murgatroyd, his daughter Eileen, and her suitor Harry (the narrator) commence their experiments. In a short time Murgatroyd has produced chlorophyll-blooded rabbits. Experiments with humans must follow. The government sends Murgatroyd a small group of defectives, who become the first subjects. The process is entirely successful physically, but it soon becomes apparent that personality changes are involved. Morality readings are so low that they are meaningless, and the subjects have an overpowering craving for raw meat. In a short time they degenerate to such an extent that they are dangerous, even to eating human flesh. * There is, however, one exception, Professor Holmburg, a biologist with a cardiac condition; by force of his superior intellect, he recognizes his changed appetites and is able to control them to some extent. He serves as a helper and a go-between the Murgatroyd group and the vegetable men. * Matters soon get out of hand. The vegetable people besiege the normals and seize local communications, including visiting airplanes. Since vegetable females multiply with incredible rapidity, producing seeds rather than babies, and since they are also almost indestructible, they pose a threat to the human race. * Holmburg, who has been altered back to a hematin-blooded individual, saves the situation. He develops a plant disease that wipes out the vegetable men with great rapidity. But the Earth remains overpopulated, without obvious remedy. * In passing, the theory is proposed that the vegetable men are in effect carnivorous plants. * A good beginning, but the development soon takes a silly turn. The influence of *The Island of Doctor Moreau* is obvious in certain details. * A very early

Meek, Capt. S. P., U.S.A. (*continued*)

story about biological engineering with a considerable amount of thought.

981. **FUTILITY.** *Amazing Stories*, July 1929. Ill. Clardy.

(Reprinted in Ackerman, *Gosh! Wow!*)

Short story. * Told in retrospect by Kenneth, who has just received a $20,000,000 bequest from his late friend Thomas Wallace. * Flashback: Ken, who has been a mining engineer in Peru for about fifteen years, is surprised to see how aged and worn his old college chum Wallace has become. Wallace claims that he has only a short time to live; he will be critically injured in a traffic accident and will die in great pain in the hospital. * Ken scoffs, whereupon Wallace explains. Wallace and their friend Bob Jerningham, after leaving college, worked hard at the machine analysis of data. Their first efforts, which were very successful, resulted in machines that predicted tides and similar matters, but gradually Wallace and Bob worked toward prediction of everyday matters. * Eventually they constructed an enormous mechanism that would handle 83 variables; they used it to make fortunes on the stock market. They then attacked problems of human life. Working with 934 variables they were able to obtain complete accuracy in predicting the events of an individual's life. * The only problem is that the theory and practice involve predestination. The machine does not err, and nothing can change fate. It predicted Bob's death, which came about, and now Wallace is under the machine's death sentence. * Wallace now offers to turn over his fortune to Kenneth, if Kenneth will let the machine predict his fate. Kenneth refuses, at which Wallace is all the more depressed, since the machine predicted the refusal. * Ken leaves, and, as stated, later hears that Tom Wallace died as predicted, and, to Ken's surprise, has left him his money anyway. * Arguably Meek's best story.

982. **THE RED PERIL.** *Amazing Stories*, September 1929. Ill. Wesso.

Short story. * *Time:* 1957. *Place:* Washington, D.C. and Moscow. * *Background:* The United States, which consists of ninety-one states, seems to have absorbed at least Mexico and Canada. The continental European countries have formed a Continental Confederation. The USSR, now the Russian S.S.R., is still an outlaw nation. Science and technology have advanced greatly, with planes that fly at 2,000 MPH, the superexplosive radite, vacite bombs that created a vacuum for hundreds of yards, and uranite bombs, which amount to atomic bombs. * The surgeon general of the United States has observed a startling phenomenon: Guinea pigs and rabbits are dying in enormous quantities, due to a new disease. The implications are that the nation will not be able to produce vaccines against diseases, and that a hostile power, undoubtedly the Russians, is responsible. Indeed, the great Russian bacteriologist Feodor Balinsky is probably behind it. * The surgeon general is right. An ultimatum from Moscow demands that the workers of the free nations rebel, kill their leaders, and set up Communist regimes. As proof of power to enforce the demand, gigantic brick-shaped air vessels seemingly made of glass fly over major cities, dropping dust bombs; American planes, bombs, antiaircraft, and whatever make no impression on them. Most of the world, except the United States, Great Britain, and the Chinese-Japanese union, yields. * The attack on the United States begins with the Russians dropping disease germs on New York City. There are

inadequate vaccines against the resulting epidemics. * Salvation comes from two directions: First, Major Hamilton of the U.S. Army reasons that the Russians are able to create gravity, using it to repel attacks and to keep their dreadnoughts in the air. He eventually devises a ray that cancels out the Russian gravity apparatus. Second, Boris and Ilga Vestoff, Russian-American brother and sister, fly to Russia as counterintelligence operatives, make their way to Balinsky (who has been operating a sabotage program against the West and is a womanizer), torture him until he yields a serum against the diseases he has spread, and return to the United States with it. * The Russian dreadnoughts fall out of the air, and the Americans manufacture antitoxins. An air attack destroys the Russian government; the Russian people revolt against Communism and will probably join the European confederation. The captured Russian ruling body, the Council of Seven, is placed in exile on St. Helena. * It is discovered that Balinsky has been suffering from a brain clot; once this is surgically removed, he becomes affable and benevolent; he marries Ilga Vestoff. * For a sequel see #986, "The Last War." The explicit sections on torture will probably please sadists.

983. **THE OSMOTIC THEOREM.** *Science Wonder Quarterly*, Winter 1930. Ill. Barker.

Novelette. * *Time:* 1945-1955. *Place:* significant action in the Gobi Desert. * Meek's version of "When the Earth Screamed." * Lawrence, a publicity agent, is in love with Professor Hurlburt's underage daughter Alice, and to win the professor's approval for a marriage, agrees to help the professor with publicity. Hurlburt theorizes that the interior of the Earth is not a tremendously hot core of iron, but a saline liquid that is colder than the surface of the world. He presents his theory in more detail and with more buttressing than is likely to interest the reader. Hurlburt plans to test his theory by drilling, and it is Lawrence's job to arouse public interest and investments. * All goes well, and the professor settles on a site in the Gobi Desert as perhaps the place where the outer membrane is thinnest. The problem is that the area is wild, subject to raids and extortion by local warlords, plus heavy bribery to a weak Peking government. As a result the dig is as much a fortified encampment as an excavation. But with a new superdrill the work progresses. * Just as the project seems drawing to a conclusion, there is a political shift and the Americans come under attack by a particularly vicious Cantonese [*sic*] warlord who has a personal grudge against Hurlburt. Things look bad, but Cantonese shells penetrate the shaft, piercing the last layer before the inner core. The professor was right; the Earth is filled with water, which emerges and drowns all the Cantonese. There are also worldwide catastrophes as the Earth's surface shrinks with water lost, but Meek skips over these in a sentence or two. * Possibly Meek's worst story.

984. **TRAPPED IN THE DEPTHS.** *Wonder Stories*, June 1930. Ill. Paul.

Short story. * Essentially an idea story based on applied chemistry. * Jimmy Dale's new advanced submarine, the *Loon*, takes off with Jimmy, his girlfriend Jean, and engineer MacPherson. The mother ship (the *Albatross*) will follow. * Trouble comes when the *Loon* is rammed by the *Albatross* and disabled. It goes to the bottom, too deep for rescue. * MacPherson and Jimmy try various expedients that lighten the ship a little, but not enough. The final lift comes when Jimmy electrolyzes a mixture of sulfuric acid and water, which produces hydrogen and oxygen.

Meek, Capt. S. P., U.S.A. (*continued*)

Breathing is a little difficult, but the sub rises enough for rescue. * Trivial, although Gernsback may have liked the applied chemistry.

985. **BEYOND THE HEAVISIDE LAYER.** *Astounding Stories*, July 1930. Unsigned ill.

Short story. * *Time:* the near future, perhaps a generation ahead. * *Background:* Just as the Heaviside layer traps radio signals, it also serves as a barrier to stratosphere (and beyond) flight. In a recent attempt to reach outer space, a plane mysteriously lost power in the Heaviside layer and became frozen in orbit. The pilot, unable to return to Earth, died in his plane. * Reporter Bond, the narrator, is assigned to interview the maverick scientist Jim Carpenter, with whom he once worked. Carpenter, who has devised a workable rocket engine that is based on the atomic disintegration of powdered aluminum, has announced that he will punch a hole in the Heaviside layer. He holds the unconventional (Fortean) view that the Heaviside layer is not electromagnetic, but is a jelly-like substance that surrounds the Earth. * To pierce this layer Carpenter has set up a bank of infrared projectors that will burn a hole through which his spaceship can pass. * Bond and Carpenter set out without mishap, and Carpenter is proved to be right. Flying through the hole in the layer, the men reach outer space. But there are space monsters. An amoeboid creature the size of a large building seizes the ship, and another dragon-like creature is an equal menace. Small arms are not of much use, but Carpenter, adapting one of his rocket engines into a disintegrator, fights off the monsters, and the explorers return to Earth. * Obviously indebted to the work of A. Conan Doyle, but a competent pulp story. For a sequel see #987, "The Attack from Space."

986. **THE LAST WAR.** *Amazing Stories*, August 1930. Ill. Morey.

Novelette. * A sequel to #982, "The Red Peril." * *Time:* 1967. *Place:* mostly St. Helena and Tibet. * The wicked Council of Seven, the leaders of the Russian S.S.R., has been exiled for life to St. Helena. Balinsky, however, has been released, "reconstructed," and is now working for the American government. The most important prisoner on St. Helena is Nashky, who was mentioned only in passing in "The Red Peril"; he is perhaps the world's greatest physicist-engineer. As part of his sentence, to avoid the death penalty, he built, under close supervision, the impenetrable generators that protect St. Helena. * Nashky escapes, but returns in a giant black flying machine that negates the island's force fields and shoots a strange solvent that dissolves guns, concrete, and human flesh. Nashky demands the release of all the prisoners and the surrender of some technical personnel. The commanding officer is forced to yield. * Unknown to Nashky (indeed, in two cases, even to the American commander) is the fact that the technical personnel taken by the Russian include three Trojan horses, Williams, a Secret Service man; Hamilton, the brother of the great scientist of "The Red Peril," and Jane Hunter, the commanding officer's daughter. The three, when solicited in an offhand manner by Nashky, agree to defect to the new Russian S.S.R. * The American air force attacks Nashky's single ship, but is wiped out except for a flagship that Nashky spares. And by now Nashky's powers and plans become known. He has two solvites; one, Solvite A, with a local action, he used on St. Helena; the other, Solvite B, spreads spontaneously. Nashky plans to exterminate the entire population of the world with B, and then repopulate it with his henchmen and their women, who are holed up in a fortress in the Gobi desert. * Nashky almost succeeds in his plans, and most of humanity is wiped out. The American undercover agents do their work, although at the end, when the bestial Mongolians that Nashky uses as guards discover that Jane is a woman, the three are besieged in a tower of the fortress. But Williams has discovered that the solvites act upon nitrogen and that argon should serve as a barrier against them. This information saves the American counterpart fortress that contains the second remnant of humanity. * The Americans go one better than simply spraying argon. Their great physiologists and biologists, who have learned how to create life, manufacture artificial men with argon instead of nitrogen in their body chemistry. * Nashky's great black plane is shot down; his fortress in the Gobi is stormed by the artificial men; and Hamilton, Williams, and Miss Hunter are rescued. Nashky is killed in the assault. * The world can now be repopulated by the American stock. * Narrated in a strange manner, with an abrupt shift in the middle of the story that suggests either clumsy abridgment or strange pacing. In any case, not one of Meek's better works.

987. **THE ATTACK FROM SPACE.** *Astounding Stories*, September 1930. Ill. J. Fleming Gould.

Short story. * Sequel to #985, "Beyond the Heaviside Layer." * Six years later, and the hole in the Heaviside layer has still not completely healed. * There has been a wave of kidnappings of children, who are jerked into invisibility. Carpenter reasons out that the Earth is being invaded through the Heaviside hole and that the children have been abducted by aliens. He and Bond ascend in their rocket ship, now fairly heavily armed, but are captured by a spaceship manned by gigantic, beetle-like individuals. The beetle-men, in their kidnappings, achieve invisibility with substances that permit ordinary light to pass through and absorb ultraviolet. * The Earthmen, being stronger than the beetles, manage to capture the spaceship and escape. * As a horde of beetle ships passes through the Heaviside hole, disintegrator rays from Earth destroy most of them; Bond and Carpenter account for the rest. * A beetle captured by the humans reveals that the beetles come from Mercury, where there is a race of human slaves who work in the radium mines. The Mercurian humans are dying out, and the beetles, in kidnapping the children, were trying to acquire new breeding stock.

988. **THE TRAGEDY OF SPIDER ISLAND.** *Wonder Stories*, September 1930. Ill. Paul.

Short story. * *Place:* an island in the South Seas. * Shipwrecked Bill Webster, Herculean college athlete, does not find it easy when he awakens on the beach. First, he must disentangle himself from the web of a spider with a body two feet across, then rescue beautiful young Myra Collins from a similar situation. * Explanation: Myra's father, not quite a mad scientist, but an irresponsible one, has been irradiating the ductless glands of spiders in order to produce a race of gigantic arachnids. His purpose is the development of new textile materials from the webs of such spiders. He has been quite successful, and the spiders, whose webs fill much of the island, also are a protection against raids by the hostile natives from another island. * The situation gets out of hand when Webster suggests a slightly new technique to Professor Collins. The resulting spiders are not only larger, but more aggressive and do not respond to a little ray projector that the Collinses have

Meek, Capt. S. P., U.S.A. (*continued*)

hitherto found a good weapon. * In the final shoot-out, both giant spiders and drumming natives attack Collins's establishment. Webster and Myra escape on a speed boat, but Professor Collins, who is dying of a heart condition anyway, does not make it. * Routine.

989. **THE DRUMS OF TAPAJOS**. *Amazing Stories*, November 1930-January 1931. Ill. Paul.

(Reprinted in book form by Avalon, New York, 1961.)

Novel. * *Place:* mostly the jungles of Brazil. * Lost race, Freemasonry, and Conservatism in the jungles. According to an interview with Meek published in *Fantasy Magazine* (February 1934) the characters are based on the author and friends who took part in a camping trip along the Mexican border in 1918. Duncan (the narrator) represents Meek; Mariston, a professional soldier in the U.S. Army; Willis, a somewhat shady adventurer. * Duncan, Bob Mariston, Nankivell ("a crazy sort of fellow" —who in real life settled down as a traveling salesman for plumbing supplies), all on Infantry duty along the Mexican border, wonder what to do when they leave the Army. The consensus is for either gunrunning or starting a revolution in Latin America, until Ray Willis, a professional soldier of fortune, suggests something different. Revolutions and gunrunning, he says, are out of fashion. Instead, he proposes investigating a tabu area in Brazil. He had been on the edge of it, had met a strangely dressed white man, and acquired a gold-hilted dagger that he shows his associates. All agree to follow Willis's suggestion. * As the comrades move up close to the tabu area, they learn that it is death to go farther. There are the drums, odd sounding tomtoms announcing that someone will be killed, and poison darts and arrows from Indians lurking in the undergrowth. A further menace, as they learn later, is the Guardian of the Jungle, a watchdog dinosaur the size of a small elephant. * After losing several members of the expedition, the Americans are surrounded by unseen enemies and herded along through the jungle toward an unknown destination. * They arrive at a stone gateway, where they are greeted by an imposing-looking elderly white man. They are at Troyana. * *Background:* Troyana, which goes in heavily for megalithic constructions despite its high science, is inhabited by white descendants of the people of a hitherto unknown Atlantic island south of Atlantis. (In the sequel, #993, "Troyana," however, Meek suggests a connection with Troy.) Their speech is Semitic and is related to ancient Hebrew. Their society is organized on a rigid caste basis, with Indians (Cowans) at the bottom, most of whom live in the jungle, with only a few allowed in the city. Above them are descendants of the ancient Atlanteans; they are a low-level race, stupid, and given to violence. They are described as coarse-featured brunet whites with kinky hair. Above the Atlanteans are Troyanan Craftsmen, whose clothing color is yellow, and above them are the Planners, who wear blue. The Blues are the aristocracy of Troyana, and from them are drawn the Master and the Council. Two higher groups, whose color is red, are very few in number; they control the Crypt, where atomic energy is generated. For the most part this stratification through the Blues is rigid and hereditary. * For the Semitic Troyanans, religion is a deistic monotheism, but the Atlanteans maintain a cult that involves worshiping a golden calf and human sacrifice. The upper Troyanans have fostered this cult in order to focus and control the lower orders. * The population of

Troyana is small in number, perhaps only a few thousand Blues, but longevity is high, two hundred years not being uncommon. * Science is extremely high, with far-viewing and hearing apparatus that enable the Blues to monitor the world and learn important outside languages. Such apparatus permitted the Troyanans to watch and listen to the expedition all along its path, preserving the adventurers, despite misunderstanding on their part, from the Guardian of the Jungle. * The travelers are welcomed by the elderly man, Nahum by name. Although Meek never spells it out, the surreptitious subtext of the story is Freemasonry. There are many little hidden passwords, gestures, and initiatory elements, and it becomes clear, though not stated, that the four Americans (whom we might consider opportunist thugs) are accepted as full and honorable Blues in the Troyanan society because of their Masonic background. * The Americans adapt easily to Troyana. The irrepressible Nankivell conducts a (Platonic?) affair with Nahum's daughter Estha, and Mariston and Willis also find women. The narrator, however, has a fiancée back home. * But things must explode. As Nahum and others declare, the low-grade Atlanteans seem to be at one of their periodic stages of dissatisfaction with the social hierarchy, and trouble may arise. * The outsiders attend the Rite of the Golden Calf, which is an expression of the Atlantean mood. As the Americans soon realize, the Semitic Troyanans try to control the mob with a hypnotic device that holds the viewer's attention and depresses his power of observation. Amid a wild crowd they watch Estha prance forth clad only in a girdle of gems, dance wildly with her cousins, and begin to sacrifice a baby. Nankivell cannot control himself, and even though the others try to restrain him, he fires his pistol. This breaks the hypnotic spell holding the Atlanteans; Estha drops the baby, which is seen to be only a doll; and the Atlanteans break into a riot. * After chases back and forth, pistoling and raying, the situation is this: A large portion of the Atlantean upper classes has been slaughtered, and the survivors, together with the Americans, are besieged in the Crypt (the atomic energy plant), while the Atlanteans, led by a renegade high Troyanan, hold the remainder of the city. The Crypt is impregnable, but there are supplies for only five years. * The question of the Americans arises. It is generally recognized that they could not live happily in Troyana and that their Troyanan women could not live in the outside world. After frank discussion, the Americans leave via a secret exit, with the approval of the Troyanans. Nankivell, however, manages to smuggle Estha out with him, and all make a run for it. The Troyanans recapture Estha, and Nankivell sets out alone back to Troyana. His comrades, who have no choice but to abandon him, assume that he is dead. They manage to bluff their way past the outside guards and reach civilization with a fortune in diamonds that Nahum had given them. * Now several years later, Duncan, who has set up a laboratory, receives a weak radio message from Nankivell, asking him to return with cobalt for the atomic generators. Willis and Mariston will go back, although it is uncertain whether their route will be protected or imperiled. * A curious work. A modern reader is likely to assess the story with very different values than those Meek imparts. As fiction, the first part is a mediocre adventure tale, but Troyana and its personalities are pretentious bores. * For a sequel see #993, "Troyana."

990. **SUBMICROSCOPIC**. *Amazing Stories*, August 1931. Ill. Morey.

Meek, Capt. S. P., U.S.A. (*continued*)
(Reprinted in Asimov, *Before the Golden Age.*)
Short story. * The fairy-tale aspect of s-f. * *Place:* Nevada and a microscopic world contained therein. * Narrator Courtney Edwards has been fascinated since college days by the problem of atomic structure. For a time he worked with the great Professor Hanson, who theorized that the orbits of atomic particles might be compressed or expanded by vibratory means, and on Hanson's death Edwards continued research privately. Working in a secluded unmapped valley in Nevada, he has constructed apparatus that fulfills his wishes. Testing it by magnifying and diminishing his body size, he loses his first apparatus, which vanishes into tininess. * A second apparatus, which he intended to use in a limited manner, runs out of control and deposits him in an ambience where grains of sand in our world seem like mountains. Oddly enough, this world has much the same vegetation and fauna as our world—and, a handsome, scantily clad young white woman who comes dashing by, pursued by gigantic apemen who have single eyes on the front and back of their head. Edwards shoots the apemen, rescuing the young woman. Communication is not too difficult, since she speaks a sort of primitive Hawaiian, which Edwards, who was brought up in Hawaii, can follow. (Captain Meek was at that time stationed in Hawaii.) The young woman is Awlo of the city of Ulm. It is later revealed she is the crown princess. * *Background:* At one time the land of the primitive Hawaiians (whose presence is not accounted for) was populous and rich, but invasions of the gigantic apemen (Mena), who eat their captives, have reduced the human population to two large fortified cities. The culture of the land is barbaric, but precious metals and gems are present in abundance. The social structure and caste system are much like those of pre-European Hawaii. * The humans are now greatly threatened by the much more numerous apemen, but oddly enough the humans are reluctant to use bows and arrows, since they fear that the apemen will copy them and become even more of a threat. * Edwards and Awlo (who is a little on the haughty side, à la Edgar Rice Burroughs) make their way, through perils, to Ulm where they are welcomed. As the crown princess, Awlo must marry. She selects Edwards, thus affronting her previous suitor, Lamu, crown prince of the other human city. But matters seem to be smoothed out. * Edwards lives in Ulm for some years as a prince, until the latest, strongest Mena attack. Realizing that the Hawaiians are lost unless they can acquire superior weapons, Edwards returns to our world for guns, taking Lamu and Awlo along with him. But Lamu, who really is a scoundrel, drags Awlo away and descends back into smallness with her. Edwards is now building a new size transmuter in order to follow them. * *Miscellaneous:* Through some unknown physical property, the atomic reduction cannot go below the size that Edwards reached. Thus, going back and forth is not difficult, although, as will be seen in the sequel, the participant may not always alight on exactly the same spot in Ulm. * A succession of plot clichés, without even the grace of an explanation. For a sequel see #991, "Awlo of Ulm."

991. AWLO OF ULM. *Amazing Stories,* September 1931. Ill. Morey.
(Reprinted in Asimov, *Before the Golden Age.*)
Novelette. * Sequel to #990, "Submicroscopic." * *Place:* the ultramicroscopic world described in the first story. * The intrigue plot is extremely complex and incident laden, even if on the trite

dynastic-adventure side. Only main threads will be indicated. * Edwards brings his load of guns and ammunition down to the microscopic land, but discovers that he is not near the city of Ulm and has no idea where Ulm lies. He wanders about with hand weapons, until, spying a strange-appearing propeller airplane flying overhead, he waves to it. The machine lands, six-armed men emerge, and, flashing a green paralysis ray on him, capture him and take him onboard. The men, who speak the common microscopic archaic Hawaiian language, consider Edwards simply an Ulmian. * *Background:* Edwards is now in the hands of the men of Kau. Racially they do not conform to the often blond type of the Ulmians, but are Mongoloid. And as Edwards soon learns, the men of Kau have only two arms; what he saw was fighting suits, which may hold as many as thirty or forty extra arms, each of which projects various rays, gases, shielding fields, etc. Elaborate controls inside the suits enable the wearers to operate them. (During formal combats, crystal shells cover the area of the duelists.) When the suits are functioning, a defensive field emitted by the suits can repel bullets. The suits, like the airplanes, are powered by wireless broadcast, but oddly enough the men of Kau do not realize that such radio waves can also be used for communication. As can be seen, the men of Kau thus possess a lopsided superscience. * Edwards learns that Ulm fell to the Mena soon after he left and that a few Ulmians are held as slaves in Kau. But so far as he can tell, Princess Awlo is not among the survivors. With a fellow captive, Edwards manages to escape and elude recapture. Instructing this friend in the principles of radio message transmission, including International Morse Code, Edwards then takes a bold path. Attracting the attention of a Kauan plane, he declares himself to be a prince of Ulm, demands to be treated according to his rank and taken to Kau. Such is the Polynesian reverence for caste and rank that his demands are accepted without much question. * In Kau Edwards learns that Awlo is alive and is scheduled to become the wife of the ruler. But protocol is so strong that Pacioma, the ruler, cannot marry Awlo unless Edwards is dead, and his death involves a dilemma, for if he is executed as a criminal, Awlo is tabu. * From here the plot takes many turns, some not too credible. There is controversy among his fellow captives whether he traitorously abandoned Ulm in its need, and a meeting with the vicious Lamu, whom Edwards kills in a duel in fighting suits. As matters are resolved, Edwards duels with King Pacioma, both wearing the largest fighting suits known, and Edwards wins. When Edwards shuts off the broadcast bands empowering the fighting suits, the war is over, for bullets are now effective. * Just when all seems well, the mountains of Ulm start to collapse and other mountains fall from the skies. Edwards knows what is happening. Someone in the macrocosm is disturbing the surface area in which Ulm is situated. Taking Awlo with him, he races back in size as the microscopic land is completely destroyed. In our world he finds a prospector working through the sand, looking for gold. Awlo is now all that is left of the tiny land. * The concept of the fighting suits is excellent and is well handled, otherwise the story is confused, overplotted, and unconvincing.

992. GIANTS ON THE EARTH. *Astounding Stories,* December 1931-January 1932. Ill. Wesso.
Novelette. * *Time:* The time frame is obscure, for while one would ordinarily expect such events to take place in the future, the links with Genesis, rationalized in terms of science-fiction,

Meek, Capt. S. P., U.S.A. (*continued*)

suggest the past. *Place:* Earth and Mars. * *Background:* Some forty years earlier the Jovians (called the Sons of God) conquered Earth, setting up what amounts to a satrapy. Since the Jovians are entirely human, though seven or eight feet tall and far stronger than Earthmen, it is possible for them to interbreed with humans. * Glavour, the present governor, is a tyrannical lecher, and the Earthmen plot against him. The explosive spark comes with his attempt to seize the beautiful Lura for his harem. Damis, son of the former Jovian governor by an Earthwoman, objects, and after a hand-to-hand struggle with the gigantic Glavour, joins the terrestrial underground. There he is a valuable member, since he knows how to operate a spaceship, a skill limited to Jovians. * The general plan, after an uprising, is to send a mission to Mars and ask for weaponry against the Jovians. The Jovians had previously tried to invade Mars, but were badly beaten by the superior science of the inhabitants. * When Damis and his associates reach Mars, the Martians (who amount to giant caterpillars) are well disposed to them and give them ether-destroying disintegrators that are far superior to the violet-ray guns of the Jovians. * The revolution is successful. The Jovian garrisons are destroyed, and an invading fleet is disintegrated. * *Miscellaneous:* The Jovians have also conquered Venus, which contains crystal-domed cities. * The Martians, who explain to the visiting Earthmen that terrestrial evolution, too, will develop intelligent insects as a final life-form, feed by shifting enormous domes atop beds of vegetation. They travel by matter transmission and can read the brains of dead Jovians electronically. * The writing mode is that of Edgar Rice Burroughs: "'Back, Jovian,' cried Lura in ringing tones. 'Think you that a daughter of a king of men is to be a toy for your base Jovian passions?'"

993. **TROYANA**. *Amazing Stories,* February-April 1932. Ill. Morey.

(Reprinted in book form by Avalon, New York, 1961.)

Novel. * Sequel to #989, "The Drums of Tapajos." * *Place:* Brazil, in the Tapajos River drainage, like the first story. * As entry to the story, a new character, a trader in precious metals, receives an assignment from a mysterious robed white man. He is to convey another white man, who is totally amnesiac, out to civilization. At a certain time the amnesiac will recover his identity and personality, but will have permanently lost his memory of recent events. This all happens as the robed man stated, but an accident reveals considerably more. The amnesiac comes down with a severe fever, and in his delirium, when psychic fetters are in some way loosened, he reveals in sketchy and intermittent ravings the further history of Troyana and Nankivell. On recovering, this man, who is Willis, has no memory whatever of what he revealed. * The story, which centers on Nankivell, begins by recapitulating and explaining in more detail the last events of "The Drums of Tapajos." Estha has been captured by the forces of Amos, the leader of the rebels, and Amos has sent an image to Nankivell showing him the captive Estha and other matters. (Essentially, though it is not explained clearly, the wicked Amos wants to lure Nankivell back to Troyana for questioning. Amos suspects that the besieged Troyanans may be sending for outside aid.) * Nankivell proceeds along the familiar route to Troyana, fortunately and skillfully avoiding capture, and enters the city complex. He wanders through a labyrinth of unfamiliar ancient subterranean corridors,

coming upon an area frequented by enormous dangerous toad-like creatures. Passing through, he finds himself in an enormous hall, in which, encased in crystal containers, are many richly clad white men, not of the Troyanan physical type. Although he does not know this yet, they are the remains of the Atlantean court who fled sinking Atlantis and placed themselves in suspended animation, expecting to awaken at a certain time. * On leaving the labyrinth, Nankivell finds himself outside, in the presence of the jungle guard of loyal Troyanans, Indians, and watchdog dinosaurs. They are prepared to storm the areas held by Amos. Nankivell joins them. For a time the assault goes well, but then the tide of battle turns against Nankivell and his comrades, who are either killed or captured. Amos now offers Nankivell and Estha a choice: either join him and enter the citadel to betray it, or be tortured to death. Both choose torture. * When the time comes, however, Estha masters the situation. Appearing before the Golden Calf in her ceremonial regalia, she invokes the religious feeling of the Atlanteans (since she is the familiar high priestess of the cult) and accomplishes her and Nankivell's escape through secret passages. * After perils, they reach the citadel. Nankivell is not well received at first, since he ran off with Estha, but judgment on him is postponed and eventually he is accepted with some tolerance, although the rigid Master will not permit the two to marry. * Years pass, while the loyalists are besieged. Energy supplies are running low, since they have been used more rapidly than expected, and Nankivell makes his desperate broadcast for cobalt, as recorded in the previous story. There is no reply, but he hopes that Mariston or the others have received his message. * As the energy situation grows worse, one of the high Troyanan officials calls to mind a secret tradition, that of the Atlantean court in suspended animation that Nankivell has already seen. It is proposed that a mission descend into the labyrinth, awaken the Atlanteans, and bargain with them for a supply of cobalt, which they must surely have. The Troyanan official adds, however, that the Atlantean court was vicious and that it might try tricks. * The warning proves apt, for when, after decimating perils in passing through the labyrinth, the seekers reach the Atlantean room and revive the king and some nobles, there is trouble. The crafty king, who decides that he should take over the rule of the Atlantean subpopulation, promises atomic fuel, but instead his courtiers trundle out paralysis rays, gas projectors, and explosion projectors that drive the Troyanans pell-mell back out of the labyrinth. All that they have accomplished is create a new enemy. * At this same time, the energy supply has been exhausted. The final struggle begins. The diminishing loyalists with failing ray tubes and Nankivell's firearms (short of ammunition) now are overpowered by the triumphant rebels, who have in some fashion made cause with the Atlantean court. It looks like the end, but at the very darkest moment Mariston and Willis appear with weapons, plenty of ammunition, and enough cobalt to revive Troyana. The decision is not clear for a time, but the loyalists and the outsiders finally win. The revived Atlanteans are either killed or put back in their jars; the rebels are decimated; and Amos and the Master both die when Amos explodes the Golden Calf. * In the new Troyana, after a transition period, Mariston is chosen Master. He loosens things somewhat, permitting the marriage of Nankivell and Estha. Mariston himself marries his Troyanan sweetheart from the earlier story. Willis is permitted to leave with a fortune, but with his memory of Troyana expunged. * *Miscellaneous:* While

Meek, Capt. S. P., U.S.A. (*continued*)
the mechanism is not explained, the symbolic drums, which herald death, are in some way associated with the Golden Calf and controlled by Amos. * More an adventure story and less Masonic trappings than the first story. The adventurers are presented in a more favorable light, and the conservative Troyanans less so. As fiction, routine at best.

994. **B.C. 30,000.** *Astounding Stories*, April 1932. Ill. Wesso.
Short story. * An exemplification of Freud's philosophy of history: The rule of the old man over the primeval horde gives way to a tribal concept with more individual rights. * The narrative focuses on the rebellion of the Chief Hunter Anak against the Father Uglik, and the privatization of women. Within these ideas "B.C. 30,000" is an adventure story, with confrontations, perils, and battles. There is also an encounter with a Neanderthal man. * I would not consider the story science-fiction, though some authorities might disagree.

995. **THE SYNTHETIC ENTITY.** *Wonder Stories*, January 1933. Ill. Paul.
Short story. * *Time:* 1917 and 1937. * Professor Van Hooten, a distinguished biologist, has finally succeeded in creating test-tube life, a lump of protoplasm that grows indefinitely. Van Hooten repeats his experiment several times, but is still hesitant to report his accomplishment. * Destroying his creation is a problem, for chemicals do not harm it, nor does burning. Van Hooten is worried until he discovers that his goldfish can digest fragments of the creature. He then feels justified in dropping it into the ocean, with the expectation that the fish will eat it. Qualitatively he is right; but quantitatively, wrong, for the creature grows faster than the fish can eat. * Twenty years later, ships disappear in the Atlantic and there are reports of a monstrous entity that is sucking in vessels and destroying them. The navy investigates, locating the creature, but explosives only hinder the creature momentarily. Seamen are lost. * The resolution comes with the work of Dr. Chang, a Chinese associate of Van Hooten's. Chang has discovered a fantastically strong human carcinogen to which the creature is susceptible. But the carcinogen must be conveyed to the creature in a living human body. Van Hooten voluntarily sacrifices himself to undo his unintentional mischief. * A trite story, frequently written, but presented here with more literary skill than usual. * The story is wrongly attributed to D. D. Sharp on the contents page of the magazine.

MELHORN, R. I.
No information.

996. **INFRA-CALORESCENCE.** *Amazing Stories,* October 1932. Ill. B. Bamont.
Short story. * Scientific detective story. * The Keystone Mill, long deserted and suitable only for demolition, has just burned to the ground. The police and the insurance companies suspect arson, but there is no proof. The most reasonable suspect is Horace Jackson, who has inherited the property, but whose whereabouts are unknown. The only unusual feature about the fire is the presence in the ashes of small blue marble-like objects. * Professor Clark, physics teacher at the local high school, solves the problem. At his instructions the police stake out another building that Jackson owns, while Clark operates a radio directional finder. It works, Jackson is caught red-handed, and Clark explains. The little marbles were made of quartz mixed with a peculiar isotopic carbon. When subjected to bombardment with radio waves, they became incandescent. * Clark suggests further use for Jackson's technique, including wireless broadcasting of power. * One of several stories of the period that focused on the novelty of isotopes.

MERRITT, A[BRAHAM] [GRACE] (1884-1943)
U.S. newspaperman, executive, writer of fantastic fiction. Born in New Jersey suburb of Philadelphia; rose from cub reporter on Philadelphia paper to editor of the *American Weekly,* a Sunday supplement to Hearst newspapers. Most of his fiction appeared in the Munsey pulp magazines *Argosy, All-Story,* and *Argosy-Allstory.* During his lifetime he enjoyed a remarkable reputation among fans, being generally considered the finest writer in the genre, but modern criticism does not regard him highly, and he is now almost forgotten, except as a minor reference in the history of the field. For at least his early work, Merritt was strongly concerned with matters of style, favoring a decorated prose filled with color and sound allusions, sometimes to the detriment of other aspects of his work. * Merritt wrote within the pulp tradition, with typical pulp plots and characters. His strength lay in imaginative background. Most of his work was based on thematic dualism, actual evil (not deprivation of good) against good; sexual aspects, in a chaste manner, often pitted good women against wicked women. The most highly romantic of early pulp fiction, his work does not stand up well, being somewhat cynically artificial and contrived. * See also #1826, "The Drone Man" and #1827, "Rhythm of the Spheres."

997. **THE PEOPLE OF THE PIT.** *Amazing Stories,* March 1927. Ill. Martin Gambee.
(First publication in *All-Story,* 5 January 1918. Reprinted as pamphlet, [Brotherhood of the White Temple, Sedalia, Colorado, 1948]; also reprinted in Merritt, *The Fox Woman;* in Moskowitz, *Masterpieces;* in Colombo, *Friendly Aliens;* in Haining, *The Fantastic Pulps;* and in Gunn, *The Road to Science Fiction, Vol.2.* Also in *Amazing Stories Annual,* 1927.)
Short story. * *Place:* Yukon. *Time:* presumably during one of the gold rushes in the not too distant past. * Merritt's first published story. * Ranging through unknown territory in the Yukon, the two explorers first see in the distance a five-peaked mountain around which play strange lights, then come upon a dying man, who offers a cautionary tale. * On approaching the mountain he found an ancient road that he followed until it came to an abyss, into which led a seemingly interminable series of steps. The steps themselves were strange, since they seemed to incorporate both warning and protection symbols. At the bottom of the steps he found a great depression with a flourishing ancient biosphere, with what seemed to be living lights, who captured him and chained him to an altar with a chain that he describes as living gold. He was then psychologically forced to take part in spiritually obscene rites with the lights, with sexual elements that combined degradation and ecstasy. But he managed to escape, and taking advantage of the protective aspect of the stairs he made his way to the top, but both his experience and his hardships have been too much for him, and he dies. The two explorers turn back. * Perhaps Merritt's most effective short story, for despite the usual stylistic oddities, the story has a certain power because of its irrationality and lack of explanation. (A modern psychoanalytic reading is obvious.) * A story that was widely imitated in the early literature.

Merritt, A. (*continued*)

998. **THE MOON POOL**. *Amazing Stories*, May-July 1927. Ill. Paul.

(First published as two separate works, the short story "The Moon Pool," *All-Story*, 22 June 1918 and "The Conquest of the Moon Pool," *All-Story*, 15 February-22 March 1919. First book publication, a combined, abridged version of the two stories, by Putnam, New York 1919. The book version, which has been followed here, has been reprinted several times, notably as paperbacks by Avon Publishers. In some texts a Russian Communist serves as villain instead of an Imperial German. The short story "The Moon Pool" is reprinted in Moskowitz, *Under the Moons of Mars*.)

* Novel. * *Place:* Oceania, notably Ponape in the Caroline Islands, and an enormous subterranean world beneath the Pacific. * In the short story, the Throckmorton Expedition, while fossicking around ruins on Ponape, is destroyed by a monstrous being that emerges from a door in the giant stones. This creature, which seemingly absorbs its victims while they undergo extremes of pain and pleasure, pursues the narrator across the ocean and catches him. * In the sequel novel, Dr. Goodwin, a friend of Throckmorton's, and three adventitious men—Larry O'Keefe, an exuberant Irish-American aviator; Olaf, a gigantic Scandinavian whose wife has been taken by the monster of the short story; and von Hetzdorp, a villainous unreconstructed Hun from Imperial Germany—penetrate the ruins farther and find an entrance to the underground world of Muria. * Muria, which is perhaps a cavern left when the moon was ripped out of the Earth, has the following gimmicks: two races, blond and brunet, one subject to the other; superscientific weapons, including anti-gravity projectors, disintegrators of a sort and invisibility cloaks; a wicked, lustful, beautiful female ruler (Yolara); a sweet, pure, beautiful maiden (Lakla); and various exotics, paleontological and imaginary. Highly important is the Shining One, the monster of the short story, which is under the control of the evil Murian leaders; it gobbles up enemies of the state and such unwelcome intruders as our friends. Originally it was created as a research tool, but it has acquired independence of a sort. Most important of all are the three Silent Ones; these are the last survivors of an ancient race of intelligent reptiles, whose intelligence and paranormal abilities qualify them almost as demigods. * A threat emerges: the evil Murians, with whom von Hetzdorp is collaborating, are planning to invade and conquer the outer world. Their scheme is quite possible, given Murian weapons. * The plotline is a battle between good and evil; the revolting workers of Muria against the foully decadent aristocrats; Lakla against Yolara; and the Silent Ones against the Dweller. Good wins, but only after Larry and Lakla are called upon to sacrifice themselves. * Today *The Moon Pool* is a very flimsy construction, but in its time it was considered perhaps the greatest of science-fiction stories, and it was imitated scores of times by lesser authors. In all probability the *Amazing Stories* printing was the text that enthusiastic fans and budding authors read, since the *All-Story* sections were collectors' rarities and the Putnam book was not easy to obtain.

999. **THE FACE IN THE ABYSS**. *Amazing Stories Annual*, 1927. Ill. Paul.

(First published in *Argosy-All-Story*, 8 September 1923. Reprinted in Ackerman, *Gosh! Wow!;* also in *Famous Fantastic Mysteries*, October 1940; *A. Merritt's Fantasy Magazine*, July

1940. Combined, abridged, with sequel "The Snake Mother" in book form as *The Face in the Abyss*, Liveright, New York, 1931. Several reprintings by Avon Books.)

Novelette. * Lost-race story. * *Place:* the Andes, perhaps Peru. * Graydon, a mining engineer, sets out with three comrades to find the lost treasure of the Incas. Instead, the four men stumble upon a lost race of white people presumably descended from Atlanteans. * *Background:* Atlanchi is truly a hermit land, protected from visitors by invisible flying serpents. It is just chance that the men were not killed when they entered. The land, which is ruled by a degenerate aristocracy, possesses the remnants of an extremely high civilization, most of which has been lost. The most interesting element is Adana, the Snake Mother, who has the body of a gigantic snake, but a humanoid torso, arms, and head. She is the last survivor of a race of superintelligent snake-people who once ruled the Earth. Benevolent, though ruthless as needed, she is tired of the degeneracy of the land and would like to see a cleansing upheaval. * Motifs: hunting packs of small dinosaurs; telepathy and mind control by the Snake Mother; a "good girl," Suarra, the servant of the Snake Mother; The Lord of Folly, a hypostatized figure from the past, folly literally personified; another hypostatized figure, the Lord of Fate; genetic engineering to produce monstrous forms of humanity; immortality, coupled with sterility; dream machines, into which much of the population has retreated from life; and the Face, a huge face carved in the rock, from which ooze drops of liquid gold. Unwary humans who approach, overcome by greed, are transformed into gold. * The story line: Graydon's companions are crooks and thugs, and when he saves Suarra from rape, the others turn on him, accusing him of making deals for the wealth of the land. The four intruders, accompanied by Suarra and the two Lords, proceed to the Face, where the three thugs are dissolved into gold. Graydon is saved by the Snake Mother, who promised Suarra that she would save him if he could respond to her will. But Graydon must leave the Yu-Atlanchi. * He obeys, but has second thoughts. He attempts to return, but is badly wounded by a flying serpent and must return to civilization to be healed. * In the sequel novel "The Snake Mother" (*Argosy*, 25 October-6 December 1930), which is not included here, Graydon returns to the land, and, after adventures, aids the Snake Mother in cleaning up and destroying (or banishing) the hypostatized spirit of evil that had permeated the land. * The original novelette is a good adventure story; the sequel is much weaker. For a curious repercussion to the story, see #42, "Beyond the Veil of Time" by B. H. Barney.

[Anonymous]
Presumably a British writer.

1000. **METALCLAD**. *Scoops*, 31 March 1934. Unsigned ill.

Boys' fiction. * A sequel or companion piece to #1070, "No Man's 'Plane," presumably by the same author. * Short story. * The war between Bergamia and Slavonica continues, with Captain Cliff Hurst, a British ace in the Bergamian service the leading figure. * Intelligence reports indicate that the Slavonicans have a new development in aerial warfare: enormous, heavily armored dirigibles that carry a dozen or so small fighter planes inside their gas bag. * An attack begins, and Bergamia does badly. Its planes are shot down, and bullets simply bounce off

"Metalclad" (*continued*)

the dirigibles. Are they indestructible? No, Lantogen, the remarkable new gas that lifts the dirigibles, will explode violently if it comes into contact with another gas prepared by the Bergamians. The problem is getting the Bergamian gas into the airships. * Hurst takes part in the air battles. Forced down, he seizes a grounded Slavonican plane and, dodging shells from his own forces, flies inside one of the Slavonican dirigibles. Before leaving again, he activates a gas bomb, and the metalclad is finished. Since Bergamia now has the technique of destroying the superairships, Slavonica will probably not construct any more, and Bergamian cities are safe. * *Miscellaneous:* Airplane carriers play a large part in the story. * A British counterpart to stories published in American air-war pulp magazines.

MICHEL, JOHN [B.] and GALLUN, RAYMOND Z.
Michel (1917-1968): U.S. (mostly New York) science-fiction fan, political activist, member of the Futurians. At a later period wrote science-fiction mostly under the pseud. Hugh Raymond. Not a significant writer, but an interesting figure in early fandom. His pathetic life is well covered in Damon Knight's *The Futurians.* * Gallun has a separate entry.

1001. THE MENACE FROM MERCURY. *Wonder Stories Quarterly,* Summer 1932. Ill. Paul.
The seventh-prize-winning story from the Interplanetary Plot Contest. Michel supplied the plot, and Gallun fleshed it out. * Short story. * *Time:* the interplanetary future. * The space liner *Thelon,* since it happens to be the nearest vessel when strange lights are seen about Mercury, is ordered to investigate. Martian Captain Pakoh and his Terrestrial friend Torrence are the central figures. * When they near Mercury, which is uninhabited and barren, they see globular spaceships of unknown origin, a cone-like vessel, and metal automatons working on the surface. What are they doing? It soon becomes clear. They are attempting to liberate atomic energy, and, as it also becomes clear, they have succeeded too well. An atomic fire has broken out, and it is out of control. * The beings in the space spheres (called the Visitants) are trying to close it off, but with no success. And now the *Thelon* is trapped, with the possible death of five hundred passengers. Torrence and Pakoh manage to turn the trick with a space lifeboat. The Visitants sail off, without revealing their identity, but Mercury will burn until it is completely combusted. * The gimmick is that the Martian Captain Pakoh persistently plays with a heavy metal yoyo (here called a jo-jo), which serves as a lifeline to Torrence during an emergency. * Nicely written, as usual with Gallun, but trivial.

MIHALAKIS, ULYSSES GEORGE
U.S. writer, then resident in San Francisco. Portrait with story shows a young man. Wrote Oriental fantasies for *Unknown* under pseud. Silaki Ali Hassan and was at one time a professional wrestler under that name. Porges, however, (Vol. 2, p. 943-944) gives his name as Agis I. Mihalakis. Signed self as Ulysses George in fan letters.

1002. THE MACHINE OF DESTINY. *Wonder Stories Quarterly,* Summer 1931. Ill. Marchioni.
Short story. * *Place:* California, the San Francisco Bay area. * The framework narrative describes a typed manuscript retrieved from the wreckage of a plane. * The manuscript: William Noone, the narrator, reads a space ad calling for a big man with

"gizzard" to take part in an experiment. Curious, he applies and meets an elderly scientist (Dr. Magyarkanisza) who explains. He has constructed an apparatus that will predict the fate of the participant within a certain time limit. If Noone agrees to participate in the experiment, which is not dangerous, Magyarkanisza will pay him one hundred dollars, plus one hundred dollars per week should the machine predict his death within a year. * The machine, which is a thought helmet hooked up to banks of equipment, predicts that Noone will have a serious accident in a short time and will die in a plane crash not long afterward. Noone is incredulous, but pleased when Magyarkanisza gives him $200. * The accident takes place at a steel foundry, and Noone is beset with worry about the future. Finally, he decides to defy the prediction and board a plane. When the scheduled time passes, he is delighted; the prediction was false. But the plane crashes within an hour—Noone forgot about time zones and time differences. * *Miscellaneous:* While the predicting apparatus is not clearly described, it seems to involve a ray probe into the cerebrum, where memories of the past are stored. The future is also apparently stored there, too. * Somewhat less than routine.

MILLER, P[ETER] SCHUYLER (1912-1974)
U.S. (Upstate New York and Pennsylvania) educator, technical writer, and frequent contributor to the early genre pulp magazines. Born in Schenectady, New York. B.S. in chemistry, Union College. Associated with Schenectady Public Schools and Fischer Scientific Company, Pittsburgh. Book reviewer for *Astounding Science Fiction/Analog,* and bibliophile. Authority on areas of crank science, local folklore and archeology. Not a major writer, but his work was intelligent, thoughtful, and literate. Was active in early fandom. See also collaboration P. Schuyler Miller and Dennis McDermott.

1003. THE RED PLAGUE. *Wonder Stories,* July 1930. Ill. Paul. An adaptation of the cover of the February 1930 issue of *Air Wonder Stories.*
Short story. * The first-prize-winning story in the contest based on the cover of the February 1930 issue of *Air Wonder Stories.* Miller won $150. * *Place:* Mars. * A meteorite, which disabled a plane as it passed, brings to Earth the beginning of the red sand: a phenomenon that acts as a catalyst, drawing water from everything. There is no defense against it, and it soon spreads over large areas. It threatens all Earth life as well as man. * The only hope seems to be Mars, which obviously has suffered from the same complaint, and, judging from recent observations, seems to have a remedy. Three atomic-powered rockets set out for Mars, but only one reaches its destination. * On Mars, a subterranean building thrusts up through the green moss, and the Martians greet the explorers. The Martians are humanoid, but very small and thin, with barrel chests and short legs. * A thought-ray serves as means of communication. The Martians tell the Earthmen that they will be judged. If they prove worthy, they will receive a remedy for the red sand. The Earthmen pass the test, and the Martians inform them that a strong electric field will disintegrate the catalyst into harmless components and that the green Martian moss will prevent its recombining. The Earthmen return, bearing information and samples of the moss. * *Miscellaneous:* The strange substance struck Mars thousands of years ago, forcing the Martians to go underground, where they built a superscience including antigravity and much else. * The

Miller, P. Schuyler (*continued*)

canals are lines of the green moss used to reclaim the waterways. * Overwritten and immature.

1004. **DUST OF DESTRUCTION**. *Wonder Stories*, February 1931. Ill. Paul.

Short story. * *Time:* 1967. *Place:* Nebraska and the Moon. * Hank, the narrator, happens to be near Norfolk, Nebraska, when the catastrophe strikes: winds of superhurricane force, utter destruction, a green dust thick over everything, and victims imploded. Knocked out by the storm, he chances to regain consciousness near Red Brockton, a known desperado with whom he strikes a deal to rescue people. * A strange machine lands nearby, and in it are two friends of Hank's. One, Professor Jarvis, has constructed a successful spaceship and is just returning from beyond the Earth. While in space he and Dick, his associate, saw a ray striking the Earth, causing the catastrophe. The beam, which originated from the Moon, is a tremendous cathode ray that turns the nitrogen in the air to powder, thus creating an enormous vacuum. * Jarvis further reveals his own accomplishments: On a private space station he has been conducting experiments and has developed atomic power; he can also create new matter, including a new element with a high atomic number that serves as fuel for his spaceship. * Resolving to investigate and remove the menace, the four men go to the Moon, where they find evidences of a supercivilization. The craters of the Moon contain underground cities (with atmosphere) connected by pneumatic tubes. As for lunar life, it consists of an enormous number of insect-like beings about the size of small dogs, all vicious and very active. The Earthmen kill countless Lunarians in various ways, but the supply seems endless. Dick, however, sacrifices himself to destroy both the great ray projector that has been bombarding the Earth and the air mechanism of the lunar civilization. His action is barely in time, for the ray had caused an enormous amount of damage on Earth. * Miller leaves open whether the insect beings were the real intelligence that created and directed the attack on Earth. * *Miscellaneous:* The exterior of the Moon is barren and airless, with perhaps small pockets of air and moisture in deep sections. * Routine, and far from clear in its destruction and slaughter.

1005. **THROUGH THE VIBRATIONS**. *Amazing Stories*, May 1931. Ill. Paul.

Short story. * Almost nostalgic exploration, told in an overwritten style reminiscent of the work of A. Merritt, concentrating more on prose effects than substance. * Dr. Alexander Gregory, scientific genius, theorizes that the extremely high wavelength of matter can be altered, permitting entry to other frames of existence. He has constructed an apparatus that functions on the basis of his theory, and he and his friend Jack, the narrator, decide to explore a different mode of existence. Donning space suits with radiation insulation, air supply, strap-on helicopters, and attached tool kits, they translate themselves into an otherworld. This parallel, interpenetrating world is much like Earth, but with slightly different gravity and atmosphere, different colorations, and a large, cool, green sun. * As the men explore, they come upon a gigantic building mass with which is associated an incredibly powerful ventilation system leading to an inner world. The two men descend with their tiny helicopters and find the ruins of an enormous, beautiful city, within which is much human statuary. Gregory, on more exploration, declares that the dead civilization was that of Atlantis, which must have

been translated from our world by a resonance apparatus similar to his own. As corroboration, he tells that back on Earth he had found a continuation of Plato's *Timaeus*, which described a situation that could be interpreted in this fashion. As for the population of the underground city, it lies in dust, consumed by a horrible fungus. * The two men continue to explore. They see that the Atlanteans had possessed a superscience, evidences of which survive, such as still functioning aero cars and power sources. In a library the two men find video reels showing the destruction of the Atlantean cities in the underground world. * While Miller does not make the situation entirely clear, it seems that in going underground the new Atlanteans encountered a native subterranean civilization that lived in nearly airless caverns. Hostilities broke out, and the Atlanteans were badly defeated. * The explorers continue on, finding empty cities, but eventually come to an area where a few survivors of the Atlanteans still wage war against their enemies. The surface men can do no more than watch as the last Atlantean bastion goes down, then flee as the enemy, a formless black cloud that is a living being, pursues them. They escape, shatter a crystal portal that keeps the underground world airless, and reach the surface. Presumably the horrible cloud monstrosity (and its fellows?) is destroyed. On the off chance that a few Atlanteans may survive elsewhere, the travelers leave a message behind them. They then return to Earth. * *Miscellaneous:* Gregory's resonator also serves as a disintegrator. * Very imaginative, but undeveloped in terms of narration and overdeveloped in terms of lush descriptions. Intelligent. * For a sequel see #1006, "Cleon of Yzdral."

1006. **CLEON OF YZDRAL**. *Amazing Stories*, July 1931. Ill. Paul.

Short story. * Sequel to #1005, "Through the Vibrations." * Set about twenty years after the first story, it is the narrative of Cleon, an Atlantean ruler. After the departure of Gregory and Stewart, the Atlanteans found the messages the visitors had left behind. Following Terrestrial plans, Cleon has built a dimensional apparatus and is visiting Earth, desirous of opening a limited cultural interchange. * Cleon's story, which is confusingly narrated, covers events in the other-world. The Atlantean-Greeks, who are attacked by Black Ones, the horrible, nebulous beings described in the first story, are badly defeated. An expedition into the lower world is wiped out by the energy discharges of the monsters. Atlantean culture is badly hurt by the defeat, but with the help of utterly alien entities (the Singing Ones), the humans defeat the Black Ones, perhaps exterminating them. Along the way Cleon encounters another human group (Thulans), which is descended from Northern Nordics. * This summary is offered with diffidence, since the story is narrated in quasi-Biblical style and is so muddled that it is difficult to tell what is happening. I note that contemporary readers complained of its obscurity.

1007. **"THE MAN FROM MARS."** *Wonder Stories Quarterly*, Summer 1931. Ill. Marchioni.

(Reprinted in Margulies and Friend, *From Off This World.*)

Short story. * The narrator, wandering through a small circus in a rural area, notices ballyhoo for The Man from Mars; he is skeptical and amused until he notices that his friend Harvey Henderson is involved. He enters the exhibit, watches a remarkable exhibit of what might be fine legerdemain or superscience, and is puzzled by the Man from Mars—a queer-

Miller, P. Schuyler (*continued*)

looking creature with a huge chest, skinny limbs, and large head. * Henderson tells the narrator a strange story. The Man from Mars really is a Martian, and its spaceship is concealed not too far away. The Martian, who is partly telepathic with humans, is depressed with its life as a sideshow and wants to leave, but the circus strong-arm men will not permit it. * With the narrator's help Henderson and the Martian elude the circus toughs and reach the spaceship. The Martian, who is injured by the rough adventure and suffering from Terrestrial atmosphere and gravity, nevertheless activates a Martian embryo and departs, presumably back to Mars. As a surprise, the Martian reveals to the narrator that it is not a Man from Mars, but a Woman from Mars. * *Miscellaneous:* The Martian as seen in the sideshow is mostly a mask and costume rigged up by Henderson. The true Martian is a very small squid-like creature in a transparent tube. It has a large, somewhat human head, but is otherwise alien. It is, of course, the mistress of a superscience that enables it to perform what seem to be magical effects. * The development is clumsy, and the motivations are incredible.

1008. **THE ARRHENIUS HORROR.** *Amazing Stories,* September 1931. Ill. Morey.
(Reprinted in Miller, *The Titan.*)
Short story. * *Place:* Africa. * Silicon life. * Told by Bill, who shows strange responses to a word association test administered by a psychologist friend. * Bill and Tom have gone to a desert area of Africa, where Tom has found what seems to be an enormously rich deposit of pitchblende. The lode is in a crater filled with thick growths of particularly siliceous reeds that cut like knives if one touches them. The two men work alone, processing the radium, and soon have an appreciable quantity. * At the same time, they watch a new nova that is not too far away (astronomically speaking), with a cloud that forms at its dissolution. As the men watch and mine, they discuss Arrhenius's theory that life spores came to Earth from space, perhaps propelled by the power of light. * Their speculations are prophetic, for such a spore has apparently come to Earth and found a congenial ambiance near the radium mine. It soon burgeons into a large crystalline structure that is both alive and intelligent (though no proof of its intelligence is offered by the author). When it strikes the main radium deposit it picks up enough energy to burst into a frenzy of growth, trapping the men within its structure. But Tom, chancing that pure radium will disintegrate the silicon creature, tosses their produce into it. The silicon being explodes, leaving shattered shards that are harder than diamond, and killing Tom. Although the narrative is kept on a personal level, the implications are that carbon life on Earth has had a narrow escape. * Bill returns to the United States with nothing, since the silicon creature absorbed all the radium in the area. The company that sponsored him fires him. * In addition to the narrative proper there are extensive sections of speculation on the origin of life, the chemical possibility of silicon life, and similar topics. * Overwritten in the color and sound symbolism of A. Merritt, which technique destroys the interesting ideas.

1009. **TETRAHEDRA OF SPACE.** *Wonder Stories,* November 1931. Ill. Paul.
(Reprinted in Asimov, *Before the Golden Age.*)
Short story. * *Place:* somewhere in the Chaco, South America. * Aviator Hawkins, delivering supplies to the Museum archeological expedition, is forced to bail out of his plane by a heat

blast. On the ground, from a hiding place, he sees an astonishing sight: two gigantic metal spheres, around which are a group of metallic tetrahedron-shaped things that are obviously alive. As Hawkins continues to watch, there emerges from the spheres a radiance that turns almost everything to scoured ash. * Survivors of the expedition creep up to Hawkins and from them we learn a little of what has been going on. As Marston, the leader of the expedition explains, the tetrahedra, which come from space, are a threat to mankind, not only because of their weapons, but also because of their incredible fecundity. They multiply with fantastic rapidity, splitting into smaller tetrahedra, so that whereas there were about a hundred when they arrived, they are now to be numbered in thousands. * At first the local Indians worshipped the newcomers, but this soon turned to war, in which the Indians were exterminated. * The survivors of the expedition and Hawkins are now besieged on a hilltop by the tetrahedra. The invaders are vulnerable to firearms, but their numbers are so great that the explorers are doomed. But then it suddenly rains, fatally for the metal beings, who cannot tolerate water. A few of the invaders take refuge in the spheres, but most are destroyed. * At this time Marston, who has been studying the rumbling sounds the tetrahedra use among themselves, attempts to communicate with them. Using an Indian drum, he duplicates tetrahedron sounds and converses, after a primitive, very simple fashion, with the tetrahedron leader. It is verified that the strange beings are natives of Mercury. They have already investigated Venus, which is too wet for them. Marston manages to convince them that Earth, too, is too wet, and the tetrahedra leave for Mars, which Marston had recommended as a more suitable planet for colonization. The menace is over. * *Miscellaneous:* The tetrahedra are remarkably ignorant about Terrestrial life and civilization, and are obviously dismayed when they find the remnants of Hawkins's plane. * The last part of the story, when Marston and the Mercurian leader argue, is quite interesting as a logical device, but the preceding material is in the tradition of A. Merritt at his worst, with elaborate overwriting and obsession with color effects. * A reasonable idea, spoiled by preciosity. * Miller defended the physical chemistry of the story against Willy Ley in a long letter in the March 1932 issue of *Wonder Stories.*

1010. **RED FLAME OF VENUS.** *Wonder stories,* September 1932. Ill. Paul.
Short story. * *Time:* the interplanetary future. *Place:* Venus. * A mishmash, confusing in tone and event. * Bill Bradley, rookie member of the newly founded Interplanetary Police, has been assigned to the land of Laxa on Venus. In a series of comic sexual adventures, Bradley works his way up to become the lover of the beautiful Queen Noreena. He soon finds himself enmeshed in complex intrigues involving a semisecret cult, that of the Flame Flower, which is also called the flame god Taramantha. * There would be little point in detailing the overelaborate plot, which abandons comedy, but some strands may be cited. The flame god is an enormous floral entity that produces incredibly beautiful red flowers and also eats people. It is served by the black priests, who want to seize power. They kidnap Noreena and almost achieve their aims, but thanks to Bradley and the patrol are foiled. Along the way there are ray guns and battles. * A pretty horrible job.

1011. **THE FORGOTTEN MAN OF SPACE.** *Wonder Stories,* April 1933. Ill. Paul.

Miller, P. Schuyler (*continued*)
(Reprinted as "Forgotten" in Miller, *The Titan*, and in Derleth, *Strange Ports of Call.*)
Short story. * *Time:* the interplanetary future. *Place:* Mars. * Cramer and his two associates, Gronfeld and Graham, have been prospecting in the horrible Martian desert. They have worked out a rich radium deposit and are now ready to return to civilization, their fortunes grandly made. But, while Cramer is busied elsewhere, his partners abandon him, stealing his share of the radium, leaving him without food or water. * Cramer is as good as dead, but he remembers a mountain area where there may be water in deep caves. Unfortunately, the area is days away, across harsh desert. * Cramer would have died had he not been rescued by small, semi-intelligent beings, who gave him water and then brought him back to their own area. There Cramer lives, eating pods that the little beings grow and certain mushroom-like plants. As he observes the friendly little creatures, he sees that they have certain skills, although he never is reaally able to communicate with them. It was chance that brought them to his help; periodically they must renew their plant breeding stock from wild specimens. * About ten years later, a rocket arrives with other Terrestrial prospectors. At first Cramer, although he has almost forgotten how to speak, is delighted, since he can now return to civilization with them. But he soon learns that they plan to destroy the little beings in order to mine their area. He gives his life to repay his small saviors, blowing up the prospectors' ship as it is in flight. * Not a bad story, unusual, as the editor says, for seeing alien life as more friendly and humane than humans. The editor also compares the story to the work of S. Fowler Wright, a comparison that I find very strange.

1012. JEREMIAH JONES, ALCHEMIST. *Amazing Stories,* May 1933. Ill. Morey.
Short story. * Humor.* The eccentric, absent-minded scientist Jones informs the narrator that the ancient alchemists were accomplished scientists. He follows this argument by producing from a Sanskrit manuscript many remarkable recipes, including one for making artificial gold. * This recipe falls into the hands of a local would-be entrepreneur, then a gangster laboratory assistant. There is much turmoil and to-do until Jones reveals offhandedly (thereby betraying the premise of the story) that the metal is not gold, but just an alloy that can pass most physical and chemical tests, but not all. * Pretty flat.

1013. THE ATOM SMASHER. *Amazing Stories,* January 1934.
Short-short story. * A detailed description of a single event, the first atomic explosion. * *Time:* presumably the near future, since it refers to experiments of the 1930s; perhaps around 1990? * As a student, the nameless protagonist is fascinated by the possibility of smashing an atom by enormous electrical charges. While he presumably dedicates his life to this task, Miller does not describe it, but settles only on the moment when the student, now an old man, achieves his dream. The result, described in somewhat purple prose, is an uncontrolled atomic explosion that dissolves mountains, gouges a huge trough, and creates local havoc.

1014. THE POOL OF LIFE. *Amazing Stories,* October 1934. Ill. Morey.
Short story. * *Place:* northern Vermont. * Cady, the narrator; Hewitt, a newspaper reporter; and Prentiss, an anthropologist, are on the train when news reaches them of the massacre at Granby. An entire village has been wiped out, and the authors of the massacre, several of whose corpses have been found, are pallid, microcephalic giants who use stone weapons. * Prentiss was to marry Cady's cousin Dorcas. At first it is assumed that she is dead, but it is soon recognized that she has been abducted by the mysterious microcephals. * Following the trail left by the raiders, the three men (suitably armed) eventually enter an enormous cave world lit by radioactivity. In this lost world is not only archaic vegetation, but a whole gamut of ancient life, including saber-toothed tigers, bears, mammoths, and mastodons. * As for the microcephals, who ride small mammoths, the outsiders soon realize that some outside force must be controlling them, since their tiny heads have little brain capacity. This outside force attempts to seize the minds of the explorers, and to some extent it succeeds, since the men have to be perpetually vigilant to avoid being mentally swamped. * Under partial or intermittent mental control, the men are herded along by the submen and their mammoth steeds until they reach the heart of the land. This is a pool of greenish jelly, which Cady, as a chemist, realizes is a reservoir of silicon life. It is intelligent and telepathic, and it exerts control over everything in the cavern world. * What to do? The creature controls Dorcas, whom it brought back as a type specimen of outside humanity. It controls the microcephals, who are devolved American Indians. And it promises to take over the world if it can get its power outside the cave. [The reader may find this a large assumption.] * The narrator, after many contretemps, manages to end the menace by poisoning it with the local moonshine liquor. [The reader may deplore this.] The world has been saved. * The first portion of the story is interesting, but then Miller loses control into a mass of absurdities.

1015. THE PEOPLE OF THE ARROW. *Amazing Stories,* July 1935. Ill. Morey.
Short story. * Not science-fiction, but prehistoric fiction in the mode of Robert E. Howard. * *Time:* probably the upper paleo-lithic. * True men (*Homo sapiens sapiens*) armed with bows and arrows migrate north to follow the game. On reaching good hunting territory in the north they come into conflict with ape-like men whom Miller may have intended as Neanderthals or perhaps earlier hominids. * One aspect of the story is a sort of mystical connection between wolves, a wolf god, and the group leader, who, generation after generation, is called Wolf. * Overwritten and of no great interest.

1016. THE CHRYSALIS. *Astounding Stories,* April 1936. Ill. Wesso.
(Reprinted in Conklin, *A Treasury of Science Fiction,* and in Silverberg, *Earth Is the Strangest Planet.*)
Short story. * *Place:* Upstate New York. * Miller, who was an enthusiastic and knowledgeable amateur archeologist, here describes a dig that a modern would regard with horror and disbelief. * Bates, an archeological dendrochronologist of the Adirondack area, is delighted when his team encounters a cluster of worked timbers deep down at a stream site. * It soon becomes evident that the timbers, which may be pre-Pleistocene, formed a sort of crib, which the men are avid to uncover. Tossing the timbers aside, the team comes to the surprise: the perfectly preserved, naked body of a beautiful blonde young woman. She is not of any modern physical type, showing certain Mongoloid aspects in addition to the blondism. * Bates and his group

Miller, P. Schuyler (*continued*)

remove her and fly her to the laboratory in Syracuse. There a close examination reveals many oddities: her surface texture is not like skin, and her apertures are fused together. She has no skin pores, and her teeth are fastened to her gums, which do not open. * The scientists are about to dissect her, despite the suggestion that she may be in some manner alive, but it is decided to X-ray her first. When the apparatus is turned on, however, the woman splits down the middle, and a horrible monstrosity emerges. Unfolding wings seven or eight feet high, it envelopes several of the scientists. They fall dead, totally drained and collapsed. What happens to the monster is not clear. It was possibly repelled when a light was turned on, or it may just have flown away. * A curious story with obvious psychological implications. Miller's best story, perhaps the only one described here that is worth reading.

MILLER, P. SCHUYLER and McDERMOTT, DENNIS.

Miller has a separate entry. McDermott here is the pseud. of Walter L. Dennis (1911-present), active in newspaper work, true detective magazines, radio, and television, including positions on the *Oklahoma News* (Scripps-Howard) and the *Tulsa Tribune*. This and the preceding story were both associated with fan activities among Miller, Dennis, and Paul McDermott. Dennis and McDermott organized and developed the fan Science Correspondence Club in 1929 (later the Internationale [*sic*] Scientific Association) and published the *Comet* (later *Cosmology*), arguably the first fanzine. * For this story Dennis supplied the plot, which Miller developed, with both men preparing the final version.

1017. **THE DUEL ON THE ASTEROID.** *Wonder Stories*, January 1932. Ill. Paul.

Short story. * Sequel to #918, "The Red Spot of Jupiter" by Dennis McDermott. * The interplanetary future. * The doings of two dynamic rogues, Red Tonti of the Moon, and Lem Gulliver. * Red Tonti, after a battle with the Lunar Patrol, is finally cornered underground in his lunar hideout and captured. * Lem Gulliver, leaving Jupiter, discovers that he does not have enough fuel to escape the asteroid belt. When passing near a giant asteroid on which he sees a wrecked spaceship, he leaps out of his ship and lands, with his usual luck, on the asteroid. * Gunning down a Venusian rogue and capturing a wealthy young Earthwoman, he plots an escape from the asteroid. His chance comes with a radio call for help from Red Tonti, who managed to seize part of the patrol ship when he was being deported to the hell-moon penal colony on Titan. Posing as a Venusian rogue, Lem rescues Tonti and drop-maroons the police onto Titan. * During the battle on the asteroid, Lem was wounded on the left arm. He simply drew his ray gun, set it appropriately, and amputated the arm. Its loss does not hamper him in future activities. * The authors seem to have attempted a hard-boiled space story. Some readers liked the stories, while others criticized them for their brutality. A third story by Miller and Dennis, "The Hell Moon," was written and accepted, but never published.

MILLER, R[ICHARD] DeWITT (1910-1958)

U.S. author, then resident in Los Angeles, California. Best-known for *Forgotten Mysteries* (1947 and later editions), a collection of "factual" supernatural accounts; retitled *True Stories of*

the *Supernatural*. Collaborated with Anne Hunger on *The Man Who Lived Forever* (1956).

1018. **THE SHAPES.** *Astounding Stories,* February 1936. Ill. Schneeman.

Short-short story. * Fortean fiction. * Conway and Professor Blevins are watching the Lake of the Crying Shadows. According to Indian folklore and Conway's previous observations, on certain fixed occasions there are peculiar whispering sounds and strange luminous bubbles. Blevins is a skeptic, but Conway believes that in the depths of the lake are cosmic castaways, beings from a failed interplanetary or interstellar expedition who are signalling for rescue. * Conway proves to be right. When the sounds and bubbles are at their height, there is a flash, a gigantic spaceship is momentarily seen in the sky, and the visitors are gone. Conway is exultant, but Blevins, who is a stick-in-the-mud, is outraged enough to murder him in order to suppress the incident. The integrity of tradition and conservative science must not be violated. * Fortean concepts and data are presented in passing. * Capably handled.

1019. **THE VIRUS.** *Astounding Stories,* July 1936. Ill. Flatos.

Short story. * *Time:* A.D. 2990. * *Place:* a volcanic, mid-Pacific island. * Two events occur at about the same time, the outbreak of the Virus and the development of the artificial heart. * The Virus is a violently contagious, rapid, always fatal disease that will undoubtedly exterminate mankind unless a vaccine is developed against it. Until now the quest for such a vaccine has been unsuccessful, but Dr. Girard has set up a laboratory on an isolated island, where he hopes that the Virus will not arrive before he has succeeded in his researches. He is at the edge of success when a volcanic eruption breaks out, threatening his laboratory. * There is no possibility of removing his plant, and attempts to divert the lava flows by exploding a new channel have been unsuccessful. Even in insulated suits men succumb to heart failure in the torrid crater. * Here is where the artificial heart saves the human race. Conrad Veldt, the pioneer subject of the operation, recognizes that he is living on extra time; if it were not for the procedure, he would be dead. He thus volunteers to venture into the lava pit and blast the required channel, trusting that his artificial heart, turned to full capacity, will accomplish more than a biological heart. So it happens. Veldt creates a channel that diverts the lava flows, but dies while doing so, and Girard has time to perfect his vaccine. * Routine at best. The concept of futurity is poorly handled.

MILLS, CHARLIE

No information. Too many possibilities.

1020. **ROADSIDE STRATEGY.** *Amazing Stories,* July 1934.

Short-short story. * Not science-fiction. * When filling station attendant Freddy Jones recognizes the gangster getaway car, he puts kerosene into its gas tank, with the result that the car breaks down and the gangsters are soon captured. But it was all an accident, Jones was so flustered that he took the wrong can. * A nothing.

MILOCHE, FRANK (1899-1981)

U.S. author then resident of New York City. According to letter in May 1930 issue of *Scientific Detective Monthly*, a skilled chess player. According to Social Security records Miloche died

Miloche, Frank (*continued*)
in New Jersey.

1021. **THE EMPIRE OF GLASS**.   *Wonder Stories Quarterly*, Spring 1931. Ill. Marchioni.
Short story. * *Time:* mostly around A.D. 3000, but with prologue material in our time. *Place:* Northern New Jersey and the New York City area. * George Preston, wandering through the woods, sees a strangely dressed little man with a bulbous head and small limbs who seems to be looking for something. Preston shouts to the little man, who runs away and enters a strange mechanical contraption, which then disappears. * Shortly after this, Preston finds a helmet-like device, which the little man was presumably looking for. Preston dons the helmet, whereupon the narrative shifts to what Preston sees about a thousand years in the future. * The locale is a crystal city, where a little man is desperately trying to escape the attack of a horsefly as large as a good-sized dog. He evades it with great difficulty. * The next circumstance that Preston watches is a meeting of the little men. The gist of it: The Earth is overrun with giant insects with which mankind cannot cope. Extinction is near at hand. The other planets are not habitable, and there is no other place where mankind can take refuge. But there is time. The scientist Nebor has developed a time viewer and a time machine, the latter of which works on the principle of the matter transmitters in general use. Nebor relates that he has traveled to the past (our era) and the future. As Nebor traveled farther into the future, he observed that while mankind was not present, the giant insects gradually became extinct. Mankind, thus, says Nebor, should decide whether to travel into the past and come to an agreement with early men, or into the future and resettle the Earth after the insects are gone. The assembled future people, who constitute the total human race, choose the future. At this point Nebor retrieves the time helmet from Preston, who learns nothing more. * Routine.

MILTON, DANE
Pseud. of Milton Kaletsky, who has a separate entry.

1022. **THE HORMONE**. *Astounding Stories*, November 1934. Ill. Marchioni.
Short story. * *Time:* 1945. * The narrator, who is writing from an insane asylum, tells the true story of what happened to the great scientist Arnold Breve. * Breve, who had been working on endocrinology, has isolated cortin, a hormone that he claims restores vigor and energy. Indeed, after a few injections, he is almost glowing with health. But his metabolism has changed, with higher body temperature and blood pressure. * The true situation emerges when Breve takes a concentrated shot: he ages visibly. While the hormone Cortin at first seems to be a stimulant, it actually accelerates metabolism and speeds up the aging process. Breve dies, in appearance an aged man. The narrator has been unable to convince the authorities that the ancient corpse in the lab is Breve. * Routine.

[Anonymous]
Presumably a British writer.

1023. **THE MIND MACHINE**. *Scoops,* 24 March 1934. Ill. Shirley.
Boys' fiction. * Short story. * Aloysius Pennington, a senior ledger clerk, has been working for years on a thought-reading machine. Some time ago he succeeded but, not completely satisfied, he has since been working on a device to communicate thought, too. He is now testing his invention on a train out of London. He listens to pathetic thoughts, guilty thoughts, boasting thoughts. When he overhears an embezzler who plans to commit suicide, he uses his transmitter to change the man's mind. * Pennington is determined to turn his invention over to the government, but he is frustrated by incredulity, ridicule, and red tape. A series of semicomic feats that he performs (rather foolishly to a modern mind) do not change official opinion. * Chancing to eavesdrop on the thoughts of Jimmy the Bat, a burglar who is concerned with hiding his loot, Pennington alerts Scotland Yard and is at last taken seriously. Although still a clerk, he is accepted and lionized as the man who invented the thought reader. * Poorly worked out even for a boys' story.

[Anonymous]
Presumably a British writer.

1024. **MONSTER OF THE MARSH**.   *Scoops,* 24 February 1934. Ill. Shirley.
Boys' fiction. * Short story. * *Place:* Africa. * "[T]hat extraordinary genius, Cecil Kemp," has created the *Master*, an amphibious, tank-like landrover (much like one of Frank Reade's inventions) that can push through the densest jungle or cross the most treacherous morass. At the moment he and associates are crossing Kioga Swamp, where the atmosphere is so filled with fumes that it is lethal. To venture outside one must wear a diving suit. * Kemp and party are seeking lost millionaire aviator Jervis Lyndon, who presumably crashed somewhere in the swamp. They find Lyndon alive and well on a small high island in the center of the morass above the gas. But they also find a surviving dinosaur the size of a brontosaurus, but with plated back and strictly carnivorous habits. The dinosaur eats a member of the party who treacherously tried to kill the others by opening the ventilators to the swamp gases. This villain, Brutton, was next in line for Lyndon's inheritance.

MONTAGUE, JAMES
U.S. author, then resident in Brookline, Massachusetts.

1025. **FORBIDDEN LIGHT**.   *Astounding Stories,* December 1935. Ill. Marchioni.
Novelette. * Pierce Stanton, Boston scientist, is taking a brief vacation somewhere in the mountains, perhaps Appalachia, when he stumbles upon the monster. His adventures are so complex— with grades of villains, chases and pursuits, narrow escapes, and romance— that they need not be summarized. Instead, main features of the story will be indicated. * Robert, a luminous, humanoid, monstrous *thing* with the strength of a couple of elephants moves through the woods at the command of whoever holds a certain disk. It casually tosses Stanton's car out of its way and chops down large trees with a single stroke of its axe. It is also determined to kill Stanton and others. * Who or what is Robert? Robert was originally a human. About one hundred and fifty years ago, the Panchettes, a family of hermit scientists who have been working for centuries, discovered elemesium. (As the author confusingly describes it, elemesium is both an ingredient of light that is filtered out by the atmosphere and does not reach Earth, and the strength principle in living beings.) At that time, Robert Panchette was seriously injured during an experiment, and in an attempt to save his life his fellows saturated him with elemesium. Robert lived, but lost almost all

Montague, James (*continued*)

his mentality and became a robot-like creature of incredible strength and vitality; he is controlled by a small actinic disk. * The present-day Panchettes, Guido and his sister Lione, have established a science retreat up in the mountains. They do not welcome intruders, who are likely to face the invincible Robert. In addition to possessing the secret lore about elemesium, Guido can create storms. * International complications are also present, for the Panchettes are currently being wooed by the infamous Braggadore and his vicious sister, who want the secret of creating superbeings like Robert for military purposes. Their country of origin is not indicated, but can be guessed. * There is considerable dashing about and near escapes for Stanton. While Guido Panchette is a vicious man, his sister Lione is a good-hearted woman who helps Stanton survive during the commotion. * Eventually, Guido and the Braggadores are killed; the basement full of machinery for sustaining the monster is blown up; and the monster is presumably destroyed. * Not worth reading.

MOORE, C[ATHERINE] L[UCILLE] (1911-1987)
U.S. (Ohio, later California) author. At this time, Moore was primarily a writer of supernatural fiction, with her series about Jirel of Joiry and Northwest Smith appearing in *Weird Tales*. It was a measure of her popularity that Tremaine published what are really not science-fiction stories. In 1940 Moore married fellow writer Henry Kuttner, and her later work is collaborative in varying degrees with Kuttner and mostly science-fiction, often appearing under such pseudonyms as Laurence O'Donnell and Lewis Padgett. Her best work is among the finest to appear in the fantastic pulps, being highly imaginative and characterized by a powerful use of sexual symbolism.

1026. **THE BRIGHT ILLUSION**. *Astounding Stories*, October 1934. Ill. Dold.
(Reprinted in Moore, *The Best of C. L. Moore*, and in Janifer, *Masters' Choice*.)
Short story, really supernatural fiction. * *Place:* North Africa and an unidentified distant planet. * Dixon, who is dying of thirst and hardship in the desert, sees ahead of him a huge glowing semiovate object, toward which he is physically drawn. Inside the light-object, he learns telepathically that he has been selected for a task by the godlike being who constitutes the glowing object. On another planet, far away, there is a rival god-being, whom the glowing light-being wishes to supplant. For this it needs Dixon, who can penetrate to the other god and discover its weakness. Since the alternative is death, Dixon agrees to do as the light-being wishes. * He finds himself on a world with other dimensionality, incredible colors and changing shapes, so alien that he would have gone mad had the light-being not encased him in a protective envelope that transforms the appearance of the outside world to his normality. The envelope also transforms his appearance to the natives, who are weird snake-like beings with a multiple sex system. Moore applies much effort to creating the alienness of this world. * The point of the story, however, is love that can surmount almost anything. Dixon meets what seems to be a beautiful young woman, a priestess who believes that he is a special emissary of the god IL. As they converse, love grows between them, although the young woman had not known the experience before. For this love, she is willing to help him destroy IL, who lives vampirically on his

worshippers. * Dixon and the woman, knowing that they cannot fulfill their love in their present forms, discuss death and the possibility of a union after death. The young woman fears that she will become part of IL, while Dixon will presumably become part of the light-being. * Dixon is torn, among love, fear of death, and dismay as his protective envelope begins to weaken. He must act rapidly, using the information that the young woman has given him. He speaks the formula or invocation needed to admit the light-being, and the battle of gods takes place. But the light-being does not win; it is IL who is victorious. * IL, who is a passionless being, is curious about the matter of love, which Dixon ultimately explains as a force that is part of the self. The lovers ask IL about death, and to their astonishment he replies that he does not know what happens after death, but he does not absorb those whose energies feed him. Something escapes. Thereupon the lovers ask for death, hoping to meet again, and IL obliges them. * Interesting, if not as smoothly written as the comparable *Weird Tales* stories about sexuality.

1027. **GREATER GLORIES**. *Astounding Stories*, September 1935. Ill. Dold.
Short story. * A summary is difficult, since the important aspect of the story is its rich, detailed development; it also illustrates the peculiar sexual elements to be found in the early work of C. L. Moore. * The protagonist awakens, after shipwreck, on a desert island. Exploration brings him to a strange wall, which draws him to it physically. Passing through it, he finds himself in an incredible building that has been constructed to fit nonhuman requirements; it is also, as gradually becomes clear, a paraphrase of an alien anatomy, with circulatory and nervous systems. * After a time the protagonist becomes aware of a powerful entity around him; it is not unfriendly, but seemingly dispassionate. The entity, which is godlike, informs him that it is the creation and embodiment of an extinct race that constructed the building as a temple and abode for it. This being was intended to create a perfect world—a task which the being confesses is still beyond its powers. Nevertheless, it obviously has abilities that would be considered supernatural. * Projecting its thought, the god-being creates before the protagonist an idyllic world, with mountains and meadows; in it is a human female, to whom the protagonist is attracted. As a creation or synthetic being, the woman is not really alive or conscious, but the protagonist succeeds in sharing with her some of his own life force, whereupon she awakens to a degree. * But the result is tragic. She knows that she is not real, that she is a creation, and that she belongs to a world that does not exist. * The god-being intervenes, informing the protagonist that his desire created her as his ideal, in response to one of the god's thoughts. She cannot become real or enter their real world. But the protagonist, if he wishes to chance the uncertainty, will be permitted to join the woman within the god-being. The protagonist is willing. * Part of him disappears into the god, and the remainder stumbles zombie-like around the island. * A very thought-provoking story that obviously lends itself to psychoanalytic interpretation.

1028. **TRYST IN TIME**. *Astounding Stories*, December 1936. Ill. Jack Binder.
(Reprinted in Moore, *The Best of C. L. Moore*.)
Short story. * Eric Rosner, at age thirty, seems to have exhausted all the thrills of a violent life. He has encountered danger as a soldier of fortune, street brawl killer, cattle drover, leader of Tatar bandits, colonel of a Chinese regiment, African ex-

Moore, C. L. (*continued*)

plorer—in short has been a veritable Conan of modern days. But the older he grows the more he becomes aware that he is missing something, hasn't experienced something. Money has meant nothing to him; women, nothing; hardship, nothing. * Rosner becomes very friendly with Walter Dow, a theoretical physicist who talks of the thrills of science. Dow specializes in inertia, and he mentions in passing that he has successfully harnessed the inertia of time. As Dow and Rosner recognize, standing still as time moves by would be the greatest adventure! * Dow constructs a small backpack device that in effect will permit Eric to move in time, though this is not Dow's theoretical concern, and Eric departs on the first of a series of encounters. It is difficult to determine, however, from the ambiences that Moore provides, whether he is moving only in the past, or perhaps, on occasion, into a primitive future. In any case, he visits ancient Rome, the paleolithic Basque country, Elizabethan England, medieval France, and elsewhen. * In his more significant adventures he meets a beautiful woman with violet eyes. She and Eric are attracted to each other, but each encounter ends with no possibility of fruition: she is dying, she is bound by religious vows, she is only a child, or there is some other impediment. On successive occasions, however, her recognition of Eric increases. * In the Elizabethan episode, when the woman is being burned alive as a witch, Eric is forced to shoot her in a mercy killing. As he then activates his time mechanism, he finds himself in darkness. The woman comes to him with full recognition, and he learns what is behind it all. Because of some cosmic fault, he and the woman had been fated ever to miss each other; that fault has been expiated, and they can now step out together into life. * Not really science-fiction. The theoretical aspects have been carelessly handled, and the emotional message is clichéd.

MOORE, WILLIAM RUSSELL

Identity not clear. Perhaps William Russell Moore, New York playwright, author of several one-act plays including *Six-Gun Romance* (1932) and *Everybody's Getting Married* (1933). A second possibility is journalist William R. Moore (1910-1950), an Associated Press Correspondent killed during the Korean War. Or, possibly a third, unidentified party.

1029. **WARRIORS OF ZANTOS.** *Amazing Stories,* June 1933.

Short-short story. * *Time:* the interplanetary future. *Place:* an unspecified solar system. * Knir and Kama, two human observers in a space car, examine the strange planet. On each pole is situated an enormous city extending millions of square miles toward the equator of the world. In one city the buildings are round; in the other, pointed. At the equator, completely surrounding the world is a wide, tall band of metal. * As the men move closer, they see that the metal band is composed of broken machinery, and in one spot they see a small battle in which white and red war machines combat each other. The explorers are inclined to meddle, first on one side, then other. The result is that all the war machines are destroyed. * Some time later the explorers find tablets in each of the two cities, claiming, in almost identical language, that the enemy is monstrous, and adding that the writer, the last of his kind, has created war machines to avenge himself on the enemy. * Cleverly handled.

MORAN, NEIL

U.S. author, then resident in New York City. Also contributed stories to *Top-Notch* and *Love Stories.*

1030. **THE TOOTH.** *Astounding Stories,* April 1934. Ill. Charles Durant.

Short story, somewhat ambiguous in event. * Old Professor Radley, who has been in India and has seen and acquired some occult powers, wishes to bring together young Lois Lane and dentist Garney. Lois Lane loves Garney, who probably reciprocates, but does not know it. Currently Dr. Garney is extracting a bad tooth from Radley. * Professor Radley hypnotizes the pair, causing them to focus on the tooth and undergo an experience in prehistoric times. They respond as Radley wishes, but Radley is not sure whether real magic may have been involved. * Not very successful. One wonders if the name Lois Lane stuck in the memories of Jerry Siegel and Joe Shuster.

MORGAN, JACQUE

Perhaps Jacque Lloyd Morgan (1873-?), who was a New York businessman. Also wrote under the pseud. Jacque Lloyd. The following three stories are reprints from a series of five that first appeared in Hugo Gernsback's *Modern Electrics* magazine in 1912 and 1913. The stories, which are described in more detail in *Science-Fiction: The Early Years*, are intended as backwoods humor based on the foolish inventions of Jason Fosdick, a small-town tinsmith. All are permeated with a racial attitude that would not be acceptable today.

1031. **THE SCIENTIFIC ADVENTURES OF MR. FOSDICK. THE FELINE LIGHT AND POWER COMPANY IS ORGANIZED.** *Amazing Stories,* July 1926. Unsigned ill.

(First published in *Modern Electrics,* October 1912. Reprinted in *Amazing Stories Annual,* 1927.)

Short story. * Fosdick has decided to make use of the static electricity generated by cat fur. Capturing a group of cats, he places them in an apparatus he has devised. His idea works, but only too well, for Fosdick and his friend are so charged that they have to sit on insulated stools.

1032. **THE SCIENTIFIC ADVENTURES OF MR. FOSDICK. MR. FOSDICK INVENTS THE SEIDLITZ-MOBILE.** *Amazing Stories,* June 1926. Ill. Paul.

(First published in *Modern Electrics,* November 1912.) * Short story. * Fosdick has constructed an automobile powered by the gas produced by Seidlitz powders. When, out on a jaunt, Fosdick and the narrator are unable to replenish their Seidlitz powders, they use instead bicarbonate of soda and sulfuric acid. The result is overpower and an explosion, but no real harm is done.

1033. **THE SCIENTIFIC ADVENTURES OF MR. FOSDICK. THE INTERNATIONAL GALVANIC UNDERTAKING CORPORATION.** *Amazing Stories,* August 1926. Unsigned ill.

(First published in *Modern Electrics,* December 1912.)

Short story. * Fosdick decides to revolutionize the undertaking business by metal-plating the dead for perfect preservation. He persuades a friend to submit to the process. The result is disastrous: It is almost impossible to remove the sheet copper, which adheres to the friend's skin, and the graphite used as a conductor has been driven into his pores, turning Fosdick's friend partly black. Also included is crude racial humor about

Morgan, Jacque (*continued*)

black people. * All three stories exemplify a motif frequent in science-fiction before 1920: anti-intellectualism aimed at the inventor, and sublimation of fear by ridicule.

MORRIS, EARLE E.

No information.

1034. STARVATION IN SPACE. *Amazing Stories Quarterly*, Winter 1932.

Short story. * *Place:* North Dakota and Mars. * The narrator, proprietor of the Mars-Earth space port, reminisces in 1955 about events of 1935 and the years following. * The narrator, a young engineer in North Dakota, receives, one evening, a telepathic command to step outside his house; there, immediately above him, he sees a four-hundred-foot-long, dirigible-like flying machine. It alights, and he receives a telepathic command to enter. * In the ship he is politely received by humans, and telepathic greetings are exchanged. * The narrator soon learns why his presence is requested. The spaceship has come from Mars to purchase grain. Long telescopic survey from Mars has isolated the grain-producing area of the United States, and, indeed, from closer range has selected the narrator as its intermediary. * As the Martian leader, the crown prince of Mars, explains, Mars adopted synthetic food centuries ago, but the population has increasingly suffered from malnutrition. In order to return to agriculture, Mars must have seed grain, agricultural know-how, and immediate shiploads of grain to avert famine. * The pallid, etiolated aspect of the Martians, who are all half-starved, arouses the narrator's pity. After he buys sufficient food to revive the visitors, negotiations begin. The Martians want him to build an enormous spaceport according to their specifications and to acquire great quantities of grain for immediate shipment. They will pay with gold bullion and platinum, and the narrator will be their sole agent and representative. * The spaceship levels a suitable tract of land with a disintegrator, and in a remarkably short time building commences. * All goes well, and a booming trade develops between Mars and North Dakota. The Martians lavish honors on all concerned, and when the narrator visits Mars, he is made an honorary member of the royal family. The king also presents him with the golden royal spaceship and the title to the spaceport. * The last third or so of the story is devoted to a description of Martian culture. In the physical sciences they are far ahead of us, with antigravity, but in matters of food production and preparation, they have lost much and are behind us. The government of Mars is a monarchy supported by a nobility, almost on a feudal level. The political-economical structure is vaguely described as paternalistic, with wage controls, and it would seem that giant cartels work together with the government. Since the Martians have antigravity, transportation is more advanced than on Earth. Travelers lie down in one-man cars that are pushed at high speeds through tunnels. * Almost on a fairy-tale level, somehow too saccharine to be pleasant and too much heavy exposition. From 1994 (1998 in final proofreading), one wonders where the U.S. Customs Department and Immigration Service were when all this was going on.

MORRIS, EDWARD and BERTIN, JOHN

Morris was then a resident of Chicago; his portrait shows a young man. Bertin, who developed the story out of Morris's plot, has a separate entry.

1035. REBELLION ON VENUS. *Wonder Stories Quarterly*, Summer 1932. Ill. Paul.

Morris was the winner of the Interplanetary Plot Contest, receiving $10. * Novelette. * *Time:* around A.D. 2000. *Place:* space and Venus. * Venus, which was first settled extensively by homesteading miners who developed the important radium mines there, has since come under the control of the Company, which is headed by the ruthless, swinish plutocrat Allen. The Company has been oppressing the miners, and Venus has been more or less on the point of rebellion for the past ten years. The Company police have crushed labor organizations, and the terrestrial government (the League) seems to wink at the enormities committed by the Company. It is questionable whether the Company or the League is the real ruler of the solar system. * At the moment, the Company has lured to Venus the great scientist Harrington, who is on the edge of releasing atomic energy. Actually, as the Company knows, Harrington is one of the leaders of the underground, and the Company plans to dispose of him after he has been forced to turn his discoveries over to them. * Also present on the spaceship carrying Harrington are his daughter, Director Allen's son, and the Bradfords—two prisoners who were leaders of the last rebellion. Allen's son displays himself to be a murderous cad. * The spaceship strikes a meteor and is wrecked; only two lifeboats reach Venus. One lifeboat holds the scientist Harrington, whose survival Company boss Allen conceals, making Harrington work in his laboratory in secret. The other lifeboat contains Harrington's daughter, Allen's nasty son, and heroic young Bradford. It lands safely on Venus, beyond the Company power. Bradford Jr. leads the insurrection. * After considerable time: The Company is about to exterminate the miners, but Harrington saves the day with atomic weapons he has secretly built in the Company labs. The buildings and armed forces of the Company are destroyed, and the League dissolves the Company. Both Allens face life sentences. There is also a romance between young Bradford and Harrington's daughter. * Obvious fictional echoes of labor-capital disputes and unrest at the time. As a story, badly structured, confusing, and of no importance.

MORROW, LOWELL HOWARD

U.S. author, resident at the time in Cleveland, Ohio. Author of *Atalantis* (1902), s-f novel about future artificial island and intrigue, described fully in *Science-Fiction: The Early Years*. Portrait included with "Island in the Sky" shows an elderly man. Morrow is said to have been associated with the railroads. According to "The Story behind the Story, 'Omega, the Man,'" (*Fantasy Magazine*, June 1934) Morrow spent his boyhood in Upstate New York and early adult life in Michigan. An obituary notice furnished by the Cleveland Public Library refers to a Lowell H. Morrow of Painesville, who died in 1951. It is not clear whether this person is our author.

1036. ISLANDS IN THE AIR. *Air Wonder Stories*, July 1929. Ill. Paul.

Short story. * *Time:* probably near future. * The narrator's friend Professor Gustave Stiener (also spelled Steiner in some places) announces that he has mastered gravity. He does not destroy it or reverse it, but by electrical means bends it around so that it repels the Earth. At first Bob is incredulous, but when convinced he finances Stiener's project, a gigantic flying platform.

Morrow, Lowell Howard (*continued*)

* Work goes smoothly enough, but there is a problem. Professor Van Beck, a colleague who has previously stolen credit for many of Stiener's achievements, is snooping around trying to steal the invention. Indeed, it was probably Van Beck who broke into the office and copied plans. * On launching day, Stiener's platform flies beautifully, but lo, another flying platform appears, Van Beck's! In a fury Stiener deliberately crashes his platform into Van Beck's, destroying both, killing both men. Meanwhile, Bob the narrator is on a second platform of Stiener's, which he does not know how to operate very well. He makes a mistake at the controls, and the platform rises off into space. Bob is rescued at the last minute by Stiener's sister, who flies her small plane onto the platform and picks him up. * Routine work.

1037. **THE AIR TERROR**. *Air Wonder Stories*, September 1929. Ill. Paul.
Short story. * Clare, a former Air Force pilot and great inventor, has designed a superplane, which he is trying to sell to the United States War Department, but the rigid bureaucrats, including one Colonel Brandon, refuse to accept his ideas and even ridicule them. In a rage Clare determines on revenge. Stealing twelve thousand dollars and a plane, he flies to a secret location and builds his superplane. As finished, it is buoyed by his supergas in the wings, has retractable wings, is heavily armored, and has many other unique features, both of helicopter and plane. * Still possessed by the spirit of revenge, Clare commits many robberies, landing on roofs and speedily flying away. He is known as the Air Master. * After a time, however, he has a qualm of conscience and decides to return the money he originally stole to finance his plane. But there is Fate. . . The man from whom he stole it is the fiancé of Colonel Brandon's daughter, to whom Clare feels an attraction. Clare's plan to return the money is a fiasco, and he is fortunate to escape. He now learns that war is imminent. (How he could have escaped knowing this before may puzzle the reader.) And the enemy air force is far superior in number and quality to the American. * War comes, and Clare, like a good patriot, zooms into action, ramming into and shooting down enemy planes and turning the tide of battle. At the last, however, his plane is damaged, and he crashes. He is badly injured, but, pardoned, he now is supervising, from a wheelchair, the creation of a fleet of his planes. * Somewhat less than routine. For a sequel see #1038, "The Blue Demon."

1038. **THE BLUE DEMON**. *Air Wonder Stories*, December 1929. Ill. Nutter.
Short story. * Sequel to #1037, "The Air Terror." * Clare is apparently recovering from his injuries, for he is now able to make his way about fairly well on crutches. * Disasters! Disasters! Most of the American air fleet has suddenly dived into the sea, with no survivors. Another, smaller, fleet has crashed into the mountains. And other crashes take place, until there is hardly an American military plane in the air. No one has ever seen an enemy operating, and the only clue is that the bodies of the dead are blue, presumably from electrocution. * In desperation the War Department consults Clare, who is placed in charge of the investigation. Clare constructs an insulated ship and cruises about trusting that he will be attacked. * He does encounter the enemy, but under peculiar circumstances, for several white ships, emerging from clouds, are fighting one another. Clare's ship is attacked, but the insulation is full

protection, and the enemy ships without their peculiar weapon are no match for Clare's craft. * From the wreckage of one of the enemy ships corpses of turbaned Indians are extracted. * Other encounters follow, with a denouement that is intended as a surprise. The strange air vessels that are battling among themselves really constitute two parties: the enemy Indians, and the supership of Lon, an old comrade of Clare's from the first story. * Lon explains. Mentally impaired by a head wound, he was unable to function properly for years, but eventually recovered. Taken to India, he was forced to construct airships like Clare's. In them were installed the electric projectors that destroyed so many American aircraft and the device for creating artificial clouds that concealed the Indian aircraft. Lon, however, developed a cloud dissipater, installed it on a superior ship, escaped, and has since been conducting his private vendetta against the hostile Indians. * Routine or less.

1039. **THROUGH THE METEORS**. *Air Wonder Stories*, April 1930. Ill. Paul.
Novelette. * *Time:* A.D. 2008. *Place:* mostly the Adirondack area of New York. At some time in the late twentieth century the various meteor swarms out in space changed orbit and formed an impenetrable sphere around the Earth. The scientific world refuses to believe this, however, even though the last attempted space flight was shredded by the meteors. Only Professor Halpin, the friend of the narrator, seems to recognize the situation. * A succession of enormous meteoritic bodies now strikes the Earth's atmosphere and explodes. Indeed, one such explosion takes place near the narrator and Halpin, who examine the wreckage. At about this time, Halpin, who is exasperatingly reticent about what is going on, receives funds from the wealthy narrator and begins construction on a new type of spaceship that he claims can pierce the meteor swarms. * A new development comes when the narrator, examining the debris of another large meteorite, finds the unconscious body of a beautiful young blonde woman (Omene) clad in space armor. He takes her home, nurses her, and teaches her English. From Omene he learns that the large meteorites are crashed spaceships from an unspecified satellite of Jupiter, and that they have as their purpose conquest of the Earth. But they have been unable to penetrate Earth's meteor guard. Halpin had recognized all this and has been making preparations. * The invaders no longer try to penetrate Earth's meteor belt, but instead drop superexplosives that destroy Chicago, Boston, New York, and other cities. * By now the world is awakened to its peril. When Halpin's new spaceship successfully negotiates the meteor belt, he is credited, and work is begun on a fleet of spaceships with meteor deflectors like his. * Back on the narrator's estate, a curious triangle is beginning to emerge. The narrator is madly in love with Omene, and can think of nothing but selfishly restraining her and possessing her (platonically). Omene, although she defends the actions of her people, believes that she can convince them to abandon the assault on Earth, since she is a high princess. The narrator will not permit her to leave, but practically holds her captive. Halpin, who also may be in love with Omene, seems to agree with her, but does nothing until the last moment. * The Earth fleet is now ready. It flies out through the meteor belt and confronts the fleet from Jupiter. In the resulting battle, Halpin's meteor deflectors defend the fleet, while a ray he has invented destroys the whole Jupiterian armada except for one vessel which Omene (whom Halpin has smuggled

Morrow, Lowell Howard (*continued*)

on board) begs him to spare, since it is captained by her brother. Then, Omene, donning her space armor from her original flight, floats down to the Jupiterian ship. The war is presumably over. The narrator, although torn by her departure, is forced to realize that Omene was not happy on Earth and had to return to her home planet. * *Miscellaneous:* Omene states a principle of cosmic evolution, that intelligent life will take human form. * The story sounds better in summary than it actually is.

1040. **A RESCUE IN SPACE**. *Wonder Stories*, September 1930. Ill. Paul.

Short story. * Third-prize-winning story in the contest based on the cover of the February 1930 issue of *Air Wonder Stories*. Morrow received $50. * *Time:* hundreds of years in the future. *Place:* mostly on Mars. * The Martians, a highly civilized, gentle human race, have been driven underground, partly by the deterioration of the planet, partly by the depredations of hostile planets. There has been peace for a time, but now Venusian Emperor Luban is prepared to attack with *The Spectacles,* a horrible space device whose exact powers are not clearly known. This is the gigantic vessel shown on the cover of the magazine, a curious construction like a motorcycle laid on its side, with all sorts of gadgets shown or suggested. * When the Venusians attack, the Martians fare badly. Their entire air fleet and their flying soldiery are wiped out by *The Spectacles*' disintegrator rays, while the odd vessel itself is invulnerable to Martian rays. Luban demands surrender, and the Martians ask for time. * From Earth, to the rescue, comes Melvin Blue in his new spaceship. Although the Martians have been in radio communication with Earth, they have discouraged visits or other relations, fearing pollution by Earth's culture. Blue not only rescues Zola (daughter of Martian President Wando), who has been cast away in space after the space battle, but manages to ram the antigravity centers of *The Spectacles,* damaging it so that it crashes. Luban is killed, and the war is over. Zola and Melvin Blue will marry, and Earth and Mars will have friendly relations. * *Miscellaneous:* The Venusians have already slaughtered the people of Uranus and Neptune. * Lustful Emperor Luban would be willing to call off his invasion in exchange for beautiful Zola, but she refuses. * So bad that one wonders at times whether it was intended as a parody, but almost certainly this is not the case.

1041. **OMEGA, THE MAN**. *Amazing Stories*, January 1933. Ill. Morey.

Short story. * *Time:* millions of years in the future. *Place:* mostly at the bottom of the Pacific deep off the coast of present-day Japan. *Background:* Over the millennia the Earth has gradually been losing its atmosphere and water into space. At the moment it is almost totally arid, with no life or vegetation except for a tiny oasis in the Pacific deep, where there is a small pond and some grass. * The human race is almost extinct on Earth. There are only two people left, Omega and his wife Thalma, who is expecting a male child. Although they are possessed of the remnants of a superscience, with antigravity and much else, there is really nothing they can do about the situation on Earth. * On other planets much the same situation holds. Only on Mercury is there a sizeable remnant of mankind, and its future is limited. * Omega and Thalma settle near the pond, where they hope to bring Alpha, their child, into being. On occasion they watch viewing screens for signs of water elsewhere and fly about

in search, but with no success. * There is one problem with their present milieu: a gigantic monster, in appearance much like a plesiosaurus, that lives in their small pond. It is dangerous and hungry, though what it has to eat beyond the humans is not clear. Electric defenses are not much protection against it; mining the pond is useless; and the humans are never able to get a good shot at it with their ray guns. It remains a terrifying nuisance. (The reader, if he wishes, can take it as a symbol.) * Alpha is born, and, as is the case with future man, is mentally adult in a few months. His parents plan to produce a female child as a mate for him. But the monster kills Alpha, and even though Thalma finally succeeds in killing the monster, she dies of sorrow. * Omega, left alone, vegetates for a time, then decides to create a companion artificially. His product, however, is not what he wished, for it is a reptile-like creature, only semi-intelligent, but friendly. Unfortunately, as Omega discovers too late, it absorbs water, ultimately draining the pond dry and incidentally killing itself. There is no more possibility of life on Earth. After a farewell flight around the world, Omega lies down with his dead family to die. * *Miscellaneous:* The future humans, who have age spans of hundreds of years, are thin and bony, with large chests and heads. * Adult in theme, with odd mythic elements, but long-winded.

MOSKAL, KENNETH

Then resident of Chicago; probably a very young fan.

1042. **INTO THE EARTH**. *Wonder Stories*, September 1935.

A short letter in the Readers' Column. * Moskal descended into the Earth and found a race of people, each of whom had a double on the surface. They all read future issues of *Wonder Stories*, each issue with stories by Stanton A. Coblentz and Stanley G. Weinbaum. * Of no interest except in showing the rancor with which fans regarded one another. "I couldn't fine [*sic*] a double for Mr. Kaletzky [*sic*] and on asking an information bureau, I found that they didn't keep dogs."

MUND, EDWARD S.

U.S. author; probably pseud. of James S. Edmunds.

1043. **BRAIN LEECHES**. *Astounding Stories,* July 1935. Unsigned ill.

Short story. * *Time and place:* Somewhat confused, but perhaps 1995 in Minnesota. * A new planetoid enters the solar system. It seems certain to collide with Earth, but at the last moment it settles into orbit about halfway between the Earth and the Moon, creating enormous seismic disturbances. An icy mass, it gradually melts, and a three-thousand-foot-long "dirigible" flies from it down to Earth, landing near the narrator and his friend. * The beings on the spaceship close in the immediate area with a force screen of sorts and herd in the two young men. Near the spaceship, Jack encounters humans, and learns from them that the aliens are amoeboid puppet-masters who use humans as carriers. As Jack learns from a captive young woman from another planet, who either speaks English or is a telepathic broadcaster, the monsters, who are few in number, control their "steeds" by inserting tentacles up into their brains. Jack also learns from the monsters, one of whom rides him, that they plan to spawn and take over the Earth. * By a lucky chance, inexplicable and unaccountable, Jack is momentarily free of his brain leech. Killing it, he and the others set out on a rampage,

Mund, Edward S. (*continued*)

destroying all the other invaders. Mankind is saved, and, as a remarkable aftermath, has learned an enormous amount from the technology of the aliens. * A very amateurish treatment of a trite theme.

MURRAY, RICHARD RUSH

U.S. writer. Attended M.I.T., where was John W. Campbell Jr.'s roommate. At time of writing was associated with the Signal Section of the Panama General Depot, Canal Zone, Panama (per letter in May 1933 *Amazing Stories*.) It is not clear whether this is the same person as Col. Richard Rush Murray (1907-1967), director of communications of the Army Signal Corps in the Aleutian Islands during World War II. A confusing factor, apart from a small problem with age, is that Colonel Murray's obituary in the *New York Times* makes no reference to M.I.T. and states that he graduated from the University of Vermont.

1044. **RADICALITE**. *Amazing Stories,* January 1933. Ill. Morey.

Hard science-fiction short story. * *Time:* frame situation in the present, past action around 1921 or so? *Place:* Germany. * MacCleod, the frame narrator, a tourist in Berlin, chances to save Baron von Sturmfeld from being struck by an automobile. The grateful Sturmfeld invites MacCleod to his apartment and tells his life history. * Sturmfeld, an ace in World War I, was shot down over France and was amnesiac, identity unknown, for about three years, during which time he worked in a factory. Suddenly regaining his memory, he continued in his new life for a time, until he met Krug, a former friend and fellow student at Harvard where the baron had been taking a graduate degree in chemistry. * Krug told of a breakthrough in physical chemistry. He and his colleagues had produced metallic ammonia, which is a much superior (and far cheaper) catalyst for producing sulfuric acid than platinum is. Unfortunately, this new substance, called radicalite, is frightfully unstable and enormously powerful as an explosive. Krug explained all this in considerable chemical detail to Sturmfeld (and the reader) and offered him a job as his assistant. * Sturmfeld accepted and worked with Krug for a short time, but while Sturmfeld was away, the plant was destroyed in an explosion so severe that it was felt and heard for enormous distances. Krug was killed, and the town itself was leveled. * The story ends without a clear indication of following events. * Certain readers challenged the chemistry of the story, but Murray defended it successfully. * Literate and smooth in presentation, despite a considerable amount of chemical technicality, but too much is left up in the air. For a sequel see #1045, "Stellarite."

1045. **STELLARITE**. *Amazing Stories,* March 1933. Ill. Morey.

Short story. Sequel to #1044, "Radicalite." * *Time:* present. *Place:* mostly in space. * About a year has passed since the previous story. Sturmfeld appears in New York and offers a business proposition to MacCleod. He has resumed work on radicalite, using more powerful ray apparatus and different raw materials, and has created a superior product. He can also control its explosive properties. This new, improved radicalite is the perfect fuel for a reaction motor. * Sturmfeld suggests building a rocket ship and winning the enormous monetary prize that the American Astrophysics Society is offering for the first transatlantic rocket flight. But why stop there? Why not a flight into space? * Three months later the spaceship, named the

Stellarite, is finished. As a power source the Baron is using metallic helium, which he has compressed at absolute zero. It is a perfect superconductor and, due to molecular and atomic changes, it remains solid. * The maiden flight from Germany to New York is a success, but there is a sinister note. A villainous Communist, one Hans Bahrendt, tries to board the ship. * A second flight, to the Moon, follows; the passage is rapid and smooth; the men drop magnesium flares to show that they have orbited the Moon; and then learn the bad news. Bahrendt, as he reveals in a note, has removed most of their fuel, leaving them only enough to reach the Moon. They are stranded. * Actually, there is enough fuel left to lift them away from the Moon, and the men, deciding it is better to chance space than to face certain death on the Moon, blast off. Their new orbit, however, seems disastrous, for it will take them into the Sun. Actually, Venus disrupts this orbit, and the men pass through the upper atmosphere of the planet and head back into outer space. * This, too, looks like the end. But by utilizing the enormous energy locked up in the solid helium plates, Sturmfeld devises a way to make the ship opaque to cosmic radiation, which will propel it back toward Earth. Attaining speed twice as great as that of light, the ship returns safely to Earth. * *Miscellaneous:* The third occupant of the spaceship was a journalist named William Campbell. * The rapid flight through the upper atmosphere of Venus indicated that it was inhabited by civilized beings. * As before, long passages of clear technical exposition, now about superconductivity; good tone; but clichéd story material.

MYERS, RAY AVERY

No information; portrait accompanying the story shows a young man.

1046. **INTO THE SUBCONSCIOUS**. *Science Wonder Stories,* October 1929. Ill. Paul.

Short story. * The great maverick scientist H. A. Macey, M.D., is about to give a demonstration of his discoveries to two fellow scientists who are more favorably inclined toward him than most of his colleagues. * Macey has been working on recovering ancestral memory, which he accomplishes by first putting a subject into hypnosis, then encasing both subject and himself in thought helmets with viewing screens that show memory content. Along with Macey's concept of ancestral memory runs a system of typology, in which persons who look reptilian "take after" ancient reptilian ancestors. * On the present occasion, Macey has as his subject a low-grade local man who looks frog-like. * Macey puts the man through his process, and brings up pictures of a Neanderthal family. He probes farther and farther back, until he reaches a group of giant plantigrade frogs, who must have been our distant ancestors. As the scientists watch, a monstrous creature gobbles up the frog that the subject was empathizing with. When the subject recovers from the shock, Macey hypnotizes away his memory of what has happened, and all is well. * Near the end of the story Gernsback offered $50 in prizes for the best letters explaining the single great fallacy in the story. The response was heavy.

[Anonymous]
Presumably a British writer.

1047. **THE MYSTERY OF THE BLUE MIST**. *Scoops,* 10 February 1934. Unsigned ill.

Boys' fiction, obviously drawing on H. G. Wells's *The Invisible*

"The Mystery of the Blue Mist" (*continued*)
Man. * Short story. * Henry Austin has invented a cloak of invisibility. Saturated with chemicals that absorb all color, it enables him to move about unseen—except for his eyes when he drops enough of the cloak to look out. Also, in certain lights the cloak assumes a misty appearance. * The cloak leads to various experiences, some calculated, some chance, some tragic. (1) Austin is responsible for the death of a lorry driver who saw eyes seemingly floating in space and crashed. (2) Austin raids a bank and steals bags of silver which he gives to a poor family. (3) Austin creeps into prison and cuts the rope as a murderer is about to be hanged. Austin reflects that the convict, while guilty, should not be blamed for killing a swine. (4) Austin, challenged when the police claim that they will pick up the invisible man before Big Ben strikes twelve, climbs up to Big Ben and hampers its hands, but is responsible for the accidental death of a guard/maintenance man. (5) Austin rescues a man drowning in the Thames. The water spoils his cloak. * Routine for boys' fiction.

NATHANSON, ISAAC R.
No information, except that portrait accompanying "The Falling Planetoid" shows a man in late middle age. Nathanson wrote one more story, "The Last Neanderthal Man" (1937). Social Security records list an Isaac Nathanson (1882-1962), a resident of Missouri, but there is no evidence that this is the author.

1048. **THE CONQUEST OF THE EARTH.** *Amazing Stories.* April 1930. Ill. Morey.
Short story. * *Time:* 1937 and 1962. *Place:* Washington, D.C., and elsewhere. * A chronicle narrative rather than a formal story. * On inauguration day, March 4, 1937, an enormous globe appears out of the sky and settles on the Capitol grounds. After a time there emerge from it small flying disks, upon which ride, individually, strange iridescent beings that resemble mollusks out of their shells. These beings, who indicate by charts that they have come from the Andromeda Nebula, are unaggressive and affable, but in large part ignore the Earthmen. After staying for a time in Washington, they visit other parts of the Earth, then depart, presumably back to their home planet. * In 1962 the second visitation occurs. On this occasion it is not a reconnaissance party, but colonization. A large fleet of ships lands near Cincinnati and proceeds to use the land for construction and development. Other fleets land elsewhere and begin the same operations. The terrestrial authorities hesitate to risk a confrontation with the technically superior aliens, and the activities of the Andromedans are ignored in an uneasy tolerance. * After a time, however, it becomes obvious that mankind is badly threatened. It is now possible to communicate with the aliens, who remain peaceful if land-grabbing, but the aliens do not seem willing to admit that humans have rights. The aliens plead necessity: Their planet is so overcrowded that mass migration is unavoidable, and during their long exploration of space, they have found only Earth suitable for colonization. * As convoys of Andromedans continue to arrive, the various Terrestrial governments decide that force is necessary. But force fails, for Andromedan science is so far superior to human that battles are massacres. Bacterial warfare, too, is a failure. * Finally, when humanity is about to be eliminated, a scientist discovers how to release atomic energy, not as an explosion, but as atomic fire that can be controlled by a damping substance. The Andromedans, although they have atomic power, do not have the atomic fire or its antidote and are nearly exterminated. The invasion is at an end. * *Miscellaneous:* The Andromedans travel at speeds greater than that of light, for once one reaches the speed of light, different principles hold. * The Andromedans are more or less conelike, weigh about 150 pounds, have three eyes on stalks and three side appendages for grasping. Their lifespan is thousands of years, and they do not die in our sense. When an Andromedan grows old, a nonphysical conjunction with another Andromedan produces a new growth in the aged body; this new growth, which develops into a new being with full memory of the old body, takes its place. * The little Andromedan airmobiles operate by antigravity. * A lot of exposition and little dramatization.

1049. **THE FALLING PLANETOID.** *Science Wonder Stories*, April 1930. Ill. Imrey.
Short story, really a chronicle rather than a developed story. * An asteroid about one and a half miles in diameter takes up a diminishing orbit around the Earth. According to analysis, which is proved to be right, in about four years the planetoid will pass a critical limit, then collide with Earth. The anticipated destruction will be enormous, possibly the end of the Earth as we know it and of mankind. * A congress meets in Geneva, but accomplishes nothing. The salvation of the world comes from Franz Grimm, a minor ballistics engineer in Vienna. He determines that a succession of explosive shots fired at precise intervals will drive the planetoid into a farther, elliptic orbit, which will be stable. His figures are accepted, but there is long political delay in fulfilling the plan because of the cost, which is fantastically high. But public pressure prevails, and fifty thousand engines, built to Grimm's specifications, are set up and fired. They accomplish the task, and the Earth now has a small second moon.

1050. **THE PASSING STAR.** *Amazing Stories*, September 1930. Ill. Morey.
Short story, essentially a rehash of H. G. Wells's "The Star." * *Time:* 1931-1947. * Young Dr. Bernard Daily is first to observe a small star that is approaching the solar system straight-on. When he reveals his observations, he is scoffed at, but in time it is recognized that a collision with the star, or at least a near miss, is inevitable. * As the star draws near, it swallows up Jupiter and its moons, then passes Earth at about twenty-two million miles. The Earth suffers badly, mankind is almost wiped out (for politics prevented the building of enough underground shelters), and the orbits of the Earth and moon are slightly changed. But Daily, his wife, and undoubtedly refugees in similar shelters survive, and mankind will establish a better world. * Wells did it much better.

1051. **PITHECANTHROPUS ISLAND.** *Wonder Stories Quarterly*, Winter 1931. Ill. Marchioni.
Short story. * *Place:* an unknown South Pacific island. * The *Golden Gate*, flying from San Francisco to Sydney, is storm-driven to a hitherto unknown island about a thousand miles from Australia. The plane lands safely, and the crew escapes injury. As the aviators explore the island, which is a lost world with primitive vegetation and fauna, they first espy herds of mammoths, then bands of pithecanthropoi—very primitive, hairy, prognathous submen. * The pithecanthropoi, who are unremittingly hostile, have dragged away the airplane, and it is touch

Nathanson, Isaac R. (*continued*)

and go whether the aviators will survive long enough to reach it and leave the island. They do. * Routine.

1052. **MOON PEOPLE OF JUPITER**. *Amazing Stories Quarterly*, Spring 1931. Ill. Paul.

Novelette. * *Place:* space and Io. * The narrator, Nelson Bond, tells of the great *Martian,* the first spaceship. Propelled by antigravity repulsion and propulsion, 600 feet long, 120 feet wide, with a complement of 120 men, scientists and engineers as well as crew, it will visit Mars. * The ship leaves neatly, reaching speeds of seven miles per second, and is well on its way to Mars when an enormous meteor strikes, destroying the power units as well as causing other damage. * The ship drifts, knocked off course, passes by Mars, and heads for the outer solar system. For a time it looks as if the ship will not be able to resist the gravity of Jupiter, but jury-rigged motors finally enable the *Martian* to crash-land on Io, right in the middle of a populous city, killing hundreds of Ioans. * Io is much like Earth, though drier and with lower gravity. The natives are foot-high beings like miniature centaurs, with four legs and four arms, and eyes on the back of their heads as well as on the front. Their civilization is about on the same level as Earth's, with explosives, firearms, and flying machines. Despite the fact that they are warlike, the Ioans receive the Earthmen peacefully. * The explorers learn the language and establish friendly relations, although the Ioans, as a precaution, insist that the *Martian* be disarmed—small arms, machine guns, and even two small cannon. * During a war that breaks out with another nation over water rights, the Earthmen help their hosts, but are less effective than they had hoped, for the little enemies have quite satisfactory weapons. All the while the Earthmen work to repair their ship for the voyage back to Earth. * A crisis comes when the ship is about ready to leave. Some of the crew mutiny, imprison the loyal members of the expedition, and raid a very rich native temple for gold and jewels. The natives kill or capture the mutineers, but now, sour on the Earthmen, decide to kill them all as human sacrifices. A friendly native warns Bond and the few loyal men who are at liberty. Bond and his associates rescue the captives and after much bloodshed and many casualties leave Io for the trip back to Earth. * *Miscellaneous:* Some of the Ioan nations practice human sacrifice periodically, one person per moon of Jupiter. * Some improvement over the earlier stories, but still amateurish.

1053. **THE ANTARCTIC TRANSFORMATION**. *Amazing Stories,* November 1931. Ill. Morey.

Short story in the school of Verne. * *Time:* probably the near future. *Place:* Antarctica. * Plane flights over Antarctica during the Kingsbury Expedition discover a large valley over which hang steam clouds, obviously the product of heavy subterranean volcanism. Young engineer Benjamin Smith proposes to blast down to this heated ground water, release it, and thereby melt a large part of the ice cap. This should turn Antarctica into habitable, tillable land. * Smith has great difficulty in finding funds for his project, but finally secures the support of the great oil magnate John Dykeman, Jr. * The work progresses. It is almost time to set off the enormous blasts that, if Smith and consulting engineers are correct, will reclaim Antarctica, when a villain hoves upon the scene. * This is Roger Thornton, a wealthy young entrepreneur who is a bitter rival of Smith's for the love of beautiful Norma Hastings. When Thornton realizes

that Norma has rejected him for Smith, he vows revenge. Assembling a motley band of cutthroats and desperadoes, he and his men drive across Antarctica in propeller-driven landrovers, planning to sabotage the Smith-Dykeman project. His timing, however, is bad, for he and his hired thugs are caught in an enormous wave of boiling water released by the blast. * Some years later, Antarctica has been pretty much cleared of ice and reclaimed. * Very flat. Perhaps only borderline science-fiction.

1054. **GOLD**. *Amazing Stories,* January 1934. Ill. Morey.

Short story. * Lewis Walling, brilliant young maverick scientist, has not only discovered atomic energy, but, as a by-product, is able to produce gold dust from mercury. Being naive in business matters, he approaches the gold baron Wilbur Morris for funding for development and further work. Morris dismisses Walling brutally, but when his business spies learn that Walling really is making gold and selling it to the United States Mint, Morris takes action. First, he instigates a Senatorial investigation into Walling's sources of gold, then when this fails, burglarizes Walling's laboratory. Walling, trapped, deliberately sets off a small atomic explosion that incapacitates the thugs, among whom is Morris. * Overlong and undeveloped.

1055. **SHOT INTO SPACE**. *Amazing Stories,* August 1934. Ill. Morey.

Short story. * Human relations on the first space flight. Through a mishap, the rocket fuel all explodes at once, destroying the propulsion mechanism of the vessel and driving it into orbit far above Earth. There are only enough food, water, and air for two weeks. * It looks hopeless. The ship will gradually circle nearer to Earth, at which time its wings can function, but by then the men will be dead. * On board the ship, inventor Joshua Malcolm bears up well, but pilot and associate Ed King goes to pieces. Matters go from bad to worse, and finally, when Ed attacks Malcolm, Malcolm shoots him in self defence. With only one man breathing, there is enough air, and Malcolm manages to reach Earth, though more dead than alive. * Routine.

1056. **THE WORLD AFLAME**. *Amazing Stories,* January 1935. Ill. Morey.

Novelette. * *Time:* the near future. * When Professor Mendoza and his graduate student assistant Tomlinson pour enormous quantities of electricity into beryllium, they ignite an atomic fire in the laboratory that is most difficult to extinguish. Indeed, it destroys the entire building, causing millions of dollars of damage. * Mendoza would like to continue his researches and learn how to control his discovery, but the university refuses to fund him. After a time he leaves teaching and turns to private industry, where he is funded for a time, but even this eventually stops. Mendoza dies, and Tomlinson, now a major scientist himself, continues his work with a Federal agency. * Tomlinson is on the edge of achieving controlled atomic power when war breaks out between the United States and a consortium of nations including Japan, China, and conquered Europe. Although the United States is shortsighted about Tomlinson's work, the enemy is not, for thugs break into the laboratory and steal Tomlinson's data. * Some time later, when the war is going badly for the consortium, they fire an intercontinental rocket containing an atomic fire bomb. The rocket was aimed at New York City, but landed in the Catskills, causing a tremendous explosion and the formation of a new volcano. * Tomlinson alone recognizes the gravity of the situation, but is unable to convince the politicians

Nathanson, Isaac R. (*continued*)

that the atomic fire must be extinguished. As a result, it is neglected until too late, when it can no longer be contained. * After about ten years it becomes obvious that the Earth will not survive. The only hope for the human race is migration to another planet. Spaceships powered by controlled atomic power explore Mars and Venus. Venus, which is empty and lifeless, but tolerable in climate, is selected, and such of the human race as survives migrates there. * Although very amateurish in presentation, the story, until the too-easy end, has a certain inevitability.

1057. **A MODERN COMEDY OF SCIENCE.** *Amazing Stories*, April 1936. Ill. Morey.

Short story. * An advertisement appears in the newspapers. Signed "The Utopian Reformer," it declares that he will enforce a 25-MPH speed limit in the city and punish infractions of traffic regulations. No one pays any heed, but in a short time in certain specified locations automobiles are inexplicably wrecked or damaged. After a time traffic violations cease. * The Utopian Reformer now focuses on corrupt and inept politicians. In this case, as a bodiless voice he confronts them and demands resignation or restitution, beating them severely with a hickory stick until they yield. There is no evading him, no protection against him. Politics in the city becomes considerably cleaner. As a final major exploit the Reformer flagellates a union-busting wicked capitalist into yielding to labor. * The actions of the Utopian Reformer attract considerable attention from the press, and cub reporter Bill Fitzhugh and old pro Jake Hanson are assigned separately to try to track down the reform vigilante. Fitzhugh, when he hears the Reformer's voice, believes that it sounds familiar, but can go no further. He obtains his first clue when the Utopian Reformer announces that he will now take a small salary for his work. Extrapolating from this, Fitzhugh is able to work out the identity of the invisible scourge. It is one of his professors at the local university. But Fitzhugh says nothing of his suspicions. * At the crucial occasion, the professor's apparatus fails, for one reason or another, and he is revealed. Nothing will be done to him, since he is a popular figure, and those whom he has beaten are not likely to reveal it. * The professor explains his invisibility in general terms to Fitzhugh; it is due to a dislocation of relativistic time and space, permitting him to enter the fourth dimension; hence he is both invisible and intangible. The initial reason for his activities was the death of his daughter in a street accident. * The best of Nathanson's stories.

NELSON, STANLEY H.

British writer of boys' fiction. Editor of *Boys' Magazine*.

1058. **THE TIME TELEVISOR.** *Scoops*, 23 June 1934. Unsigned ill.

Boys' fiction. * Short story. * Colwyn Grant, a television engineer, has invented a time viewer that can show almost anything; he and his newspaper reporter friend Don Denby have witnessed the death of Joan of Arc, Bleriot's flight, and much else. * Don is assigned by his boss to cover the epoch-making flight of aviatrix Betty Hanson, who is attempting to establish a flying record from England to Australia. Problems arise: Betty is accused of having committed a murder in England, and she disappears after leaving Singapore. With the time viewer Grant and Denby follow her movements, discovering that she crashed

among Negritos in Malaysia and is being held for a human sacrifice. The friends rescue her from the pygmies and, when she comes to trial in England, establish her innocence with the time viewer. As a result of her ordeal in Malaysia Betty had lost her memory, but she regains it.

NEVINS, W. VARICK, III (1910-1967)

U.S. (Upstate New York) author. Attended Alfred University. Acted under name Varick Nevins.

1059. **COSMIC CALAMITY.** *Wonder Stories*, June 1934.

Short-short story. * Chick Connors, intelligent, well-educated Great Depression victim, is struck by an automobile. Not really injured, he is picked up by the driver, the well-known scientist Charles Farmell, who buys him a meal and takes him to his laboratory. Farmell reveals that he has been working with cosmic rays and has developed a substance that is impermeable to them. With a reflector of this substance he intends to beam signals to Mars. Connors can watch while the demonstration takes place. There should be no danger, unless the reflector happens to focus on the immediate surroundings. * Farmell, however, is very wrong, for things go wrong, and before the scientist can reach the cutoff switch, everything first goes into a white glare, then a blackout. * But it was only a science-fiction film, a defective film at that. * Neatly handled.

1060. **THE SENSE TWISTER.** *Wonder Stories*, August 1934.

Short story. * Lewis Barden, bored with office life, answers an advertisement calling for a daring person to undertake a dangerous experiment without recompense. * Barden answers the ad and learns what is involved. Dr. Austin has developed a technique (injections plus radiation) that causes nerves to report opposite sensations from normal. Thus, injuries will produce pleasure rather than pain, sour things will taste sweet, etc. The process can also deaden nerves completely. Austin has experimented with animals, but now needs a human subject. * Barden had first applied out of boredom, but follows through when he sees the scientist's beautiful young daughter. But it is all a hoax, the result of a bet whether anyone would be foolish enough to accept an offer of the sort. And the young woman is to be married the next day. * Barden realizes that he has been a prize sucker.

1061. **THE EMOTION METER.** *Wonder Stories*, January 1935.

(Reprinted in Ackerman, *Gosh! Wow!*)

Short-short story. * Professor Miller has invented an emotion-rating machine that is a vast improvement over the contemporary lie detector. Inviting his students to participate in an experiment, he asks them to bring with them photographs, including pictures of favorite girlfriends. * The machine works perfectly, identifying the most loved person, until it comes to Russell Ricker, who consistently shows almost a zero score. But then the meter leaps to 100. Solution, Ricker is looking into a mirror.

1062. **THE MYSTERY OF THE -/-.** *Wonder Stories*, June 1935. Ill. Paul.

Short story. * *Place:* Southern California. * College professors Angell and Nash and their wives take a brief vacation out in the desert, where, buried in the middle of the sandy wastes, they find a very strange metallic construction. Clearing the sand away, the men come to the conclusion that the gigantic object, upon which

Nevins, W. Varick, III (*continued*)

is the symbol -/-, must be a fragment of a wrecked spaceship. *
It makes sense, but they are soon disillusioned by a young man
who reveals that the device is a motion picture set that had been
covered by recent sand storms. * Flat. So obvious that one
wonders why *Wonder Stories* printed it.

NEWTON, EDSEL (c. 1910?-?)

U.S. author. According to letters in *Amazing Stories*, traveled
extensively in connection with business; Montana, Singapore,
Cuba, etc. A letter in the February 1931 issue of *Wonder Stories*
(p. 1048) describes his tussles with religion and drink. Perhaps
some aeronautic experience. While the first story is accredited
to E. Edsel Newton, other accreditations are simply Edsel
Newton. Portrait printed with stories shows a young man. In
later life apparently a journalist associated with the *Los Angeles
Daily Journal*. Author of *Report on Civil Liberties: An Historical Sketch of the American Civil Liberties Union in South California* (1959). A Social Security death listing in Georgia for an
Edsel Newton does not seem to be the right man.

   1063. **THE SPACE HERMIT**. *Amazing Stories*, July
1929. Ill. Paul.

Short story. * *Place:* California and elsewhere. The narrator
Metters, a freelance airplane pilot, sees young Claxon die when
his plane collides with a long, fish-shaped, transparent air vessel.
Buying a supercharger for high elevation work, Metters sets out
to find the mysterious ship. After some searching, he locates it,
lands his plane on its flat top, and barely manages to reach a
landing ladder, before the captain of the ship flips his plane off.
* Metters is on board the *Glorie*, a supercraft built and operated
by the great Professor Hedron, whom the world believes dead.
* Hedron, who ranks among the greatest geniuses of all time, has
created transparent steel, engines that draw their power from the
air, food and water machines, and all else for living permanently
above the Earth. This last is his plan, for he is slightly mad and
a ferocious misanthrope. He never wants to set foot on the Earth
again. * Since he is not bloodthirsty, he comments, he will
accept Metters as an unwanted guest, but Metters must conform
to the ship's rules. * Also present on the ship is the professor's
daughter Glorie. Hedron believes that she, too, prefers hermitry,
but it is obvious to Metters, even though he is forbidden to talk
to her, that she is very unhappy and would like to return to
Earth. * Metters manages to overcome the madman, who dies of
a heart attack, and then brings the ship down far enough for him
and Glorie to leap to the ground. He then sends the ship aloft
as a tomb for the mad scientist. * Although H. G. Wells is
mentioned in the text, the obvious reference is to Jules Verne.
An airborne Captain Nemo amateurishly handled.

   1064. **FREEDOM OF THE SKIES**. *Air Wonder Stories*,
December 1929. Ill. Paul.

Short story. * *Time:* 1974. *Place:* mostly a flying platform
somewhere in the Pacific. * Fred Brettner, pilot for huge International Airways, is distressed because his fiancée (Nadia
Deneen), whom he was to have married that morning, has mysteriously disappeared, leaving behind a cold note. * Brettner
takes his cargo plane out and sees, flying beside him, a small
plane with Nadia on board. The pilot shouts across that Brettner
had better follow him, or he will never see Nadia again. * Both
planes land on a floating deck the size of five large battleships,
and Brettner is taken into the presence of the Grand Master of

the Conquerors of the Skies, a charismatic, handsome young man
who is the leader of a widespread secret organization that plans
world conquest. (Indeed, its ramifications are so extensive that
Brettner's dispatcher is a member, to whom has been promised
the rule of a Latin American country.) * The Grand Master explains: The floating island, which is submersible, is his
headquarters. He has several hundred planes, but he needs about
ten thousand for his plans, which include destroying the major
cities of the world. Brettner is to help hijack planes to the
island. If he refuses, he and Nadia will go to the disintegrator
chamber, where many recalcitrants have already been removed.
Brettner agrees to work with the Grand Master, but plans
treachery. * Time passes, and other planes are lured to the Grand
Master's platform. Brettner now has an assignment: to obtain
superexplosive pills to drop on the cities of the world. * Brettner
returns with pills, which are distributed among the Grand Master's pilots. The raiders take off. To Brettner is entrusted the
destruction of Washington, D.C. But Brettner manages to be
alone with the Grand Master, and drawing a radium-ray pistol,
captures him. Presumably the empire of the air is over, though
the author gives no details. The world's great cities are safe, for
Brettner gave the bombers aspirin tablets to drop. * *Miscellaneous:* Telepathic communication is possible with a certain
concentration device. * The disintegrator contains a gas that
dissolves human flesh and bone instantly. * Silly, and a horrible
job. The author has obviously been influenced by early motion
pictures.

   1065. **THE TORPEDO TERROR**. *Wonder Stories*,
September 1930. Ill. Leonard.

Short story. * *Time:* 1939. *Place:* mostly California. * Reporter
Edwards, a flying enthusiast, is assigned to investigate the Tilden
plant, where strange small devices, function unknown, have
turned up. Tilden, the owner of the plant, is a rabid hater of the
press, but his daughter Nadine is more friendly. She shows
Edwards small electronic devices and informs him that similar
objects have been found in the factories of other companies. No
one has any idea about the function of the devices. * Edwards,
who has a hunch that something is very wrong, successfully
urges that all local industries search for similar objects and put
them all in an isolated place where they can do no damage. * So
far so good, but not good enough. Edwards was right, for he,
Nadine, and old Tilden are kidnapped by a secret organization.
Explanation: Behind this is the Holy Race (also called The
Invincibles), a group not identified by the author, who plan
world conquest. Their king has decreed that it is time to destroy
most of the world's cities and industries for the new takeover.
The little devices were to serve as beacons for flying torpedoes
filled with superexplosives. The one torpedo that was activated
by the mechanisms assembled at Edwards's suggestion created
a crater a quarter of a mile deep and the same distance across. *
Things look bad, but it turns out that there is a triple agent
among the Invincibles, who was first working for Tilden, then
for the Invincibles, but is really associated with the secret
service. He helps the Tildens and Edwards escape. When the
torpedoes that are supposed to destroy Los Angeles leave, they
contain not explosives, but the three former captives who land
safely and alert the authorities. As for the other torpedoes, they
are neutralized by scrambling the radio signals that guide them.
Newton mentions in passing that the Invincibles were later
tracked down and captured or killed. * *Miscellaneous:* The

Newton, Edsel (*continued*)

Invincibles have devices to control compasses (whence their capture of Nadine and Edwards) and a fuelless electromagnetic perpetual motor for their aircraft. * Starts out nicely, but soon fizzles away.

1066. **THE FLAMING CLOUD**. *Wonder Stories*, January 1931. Ill. Marchioni.

Short story. * *Time:* 1975. *Place:* California and the Pacific Ocean. * Captain Blaine returns to the Los Angeles airport with a strange story: Over the Pacific his plane encountered a column of heat so intense that it singed the varnish off his fuselage and almost brought his plane down. He was fortunate to escape with his life. * The narrator and Blaine take a fast light plane up in search of the column. They find it off the coast of Alaska, heading for Nome and likely to lay the city waste. Near the heat zone is Professor Metter's plane. * The professor confesses that he is responsible for the phenomenon. With the help of the Canadian government he has developed chemicals which will create hot-air formations that will heat the Arctic wastes and permit them to be used. The present formation got out of control with an imbalance of chemicals. * The professor tames his unruly creation, and in the name of the Canadian government, promises free land to those whose property was damaged.

1067. **THE HOUR THE CONQUEROR CAME**. *Wonder Stories Quarterly*, Winter 1931. Ill. Marchioni.

Short story. * *Time:* 1942. *Place:* mostly the air route between Los Angeles, California, and Valparaiso, Chile. * A secret society, a criminal mastermind, and a substance (called "multiple") that forms a foam almost indefinitely, choking and strangling off what it encounters. Fortunately, it disappears after about eight hours. * Holden, the inventor of multiple, has been murdered, and the obvious suspect is Creel, an acquaintance of Holden's and the reporter narrator's. * Creel seizes the great international airliner *Golandrina*, killing off such persons as he wishes with multiple, then discharges a huge quantity of multiple over Valparaiso, destroying the city. But he is eventually hoist with his own petard when some of the multiple leaks into his command cabin. Creel, by the way, heads the terrorist organization called the Black Legion, which after his debacle may be defunct. * Nothing to recommend.

1068. **THE SARGASSO MONSTER**. *Wonder Stories*, April 1931. Ill. Paul.

Short story. * *Time:* the near future. *Place:* the Sargasso Sea. * Thanks to international dirty tricks among rival airlines, the *Bolivar*, piloted by Captain Campbell, has to make a forced landing in the Sargasso Sea. A saboteur on board has destroyed the wiring, so that repairs are impossible. * As the passengers and crew wait for rescue, they are caught up into one of the most lurid of Sargasso Sea ambiences. The plane is twisted around by an enormous whirlpool and almost goes under, and monsters of the most gigantic sort (would make whales look like rabbits) either gobble up or attempt to gobble up the humans as they race across the solid seaweed. * Eventually relief comes. The saboteur, who expected to be picked up by his sponsors, is eaten by one of the gigantic creatures. * There is also a romance between Campbell and a straight-shooting young lady who is skilled at both firing pistols and setting off rockets at monsters. * At times almost parodic.

1069. **HOUSE OF MONSTROSITIES**. *Wonder Stories*, December 1934. Ill. Marchioni.

Short story. * *Place:* California. * The newspaperman narrator visits his friend Dr. Stancliffe Podge, who is experimenting with organ transplants and advanced grafting on animals. Podge has created various horrors, which he proudly shows to the narrator. One of them, however, acts as the reader would expect: An eight-foot-tall hybrid of lion, bear, and other carnivores, it breaks loose and runs amok, killing Podge, most of the other hybrid horrors, and some innocent neighbors. The narrator has a narrow escape. * The sort of story one would have found, if better developed, in one of the horror pulps of the late 1930s. Perhaps written tongue-in-cheek.

[Anonymous]
Presumably a British writer.

1070. **NO-MAN'S 'PLANE**. *Scoops*, 24 February 1934. Ill. Origin.

Boy's fiction. * Short story. * *Place:* two imaginary countries in Europe, Bergamia and Slavonica. * British ace Capt. Cliff Hurst, formerly a flying instructor in the Bergamian forces, now commands a sizeable air force in the war against Slavonica, but his function in the story is not so much command as dogfighting. * As he soon discovers, one of the Slavonican secret weapons is a radio-controlled drone plane, the invention of the genius Paul Sergoff. After various air duels, Hurst makes a forced landing, encounters a dying secret service man who explains what is going on, and snoops around Sergoff's establishment. * The danger: Sergoff has just sent off twelve robot planes to drop an extremely poisonous gas on the capital of Bergamia. Hurst foils the attack. Shooting down a couple of the drones, he makes away with the rest by releasing a smoke screen that prevents radio signals from reaching them. They fall into the sea. * For a sequel or companion piece, presumably by the same author, see #1000, "Metalclad."

NORTHFORD or **NORTHFIELD, JAMES EDISON**

Probably the pseud. of a U.S. author. The author's name is cited as Northford in the story caption, but as Northfield on the contents page.

1071. **THE MASTER OF MARS**. *Flash Gordon Strange Adventure Magazine*, December 1936. Ill. Fred Meagher.

Novel. * *Time:* the interplanetary near future. *Place:* Mars, the asteroids, space in general. * A spin-off of the popular King Features Syndicate comic strip "Flash Gordon," drawn by Alex Raymond, which first appeared in Sunday newspapers on 7 January 1934, and in comic-book format (*King Comics*) in April 1936. While Flash Gordon, his girlfriend, Dale Arden, and the scientist Dr. Zarkov correspond to the characters in the comic strip, the novel has otherwise little connection with Raymond's strip. * Flash, Dale, and Zarkov are now on Mars. How they arrived and what they had done previously are left unstated. * As the novel begins, the trio ride their mounts up to the fortress-stronghold of Martian dictator Pwami, where Zarkov and Flash deliver an ultimatum: Unless Pwami resigns (since he has not fulfilled promised reforms and is a cruel tyrant) Zarkov will make atomic bombs to be used against him. Flash ends his demand by assuring Pwami that if he resigns, he will be so popular that he will be elected president! Pwami's response is what might expected of a self-respecting dictator. Since he wants Zarkov's bombs in order to conquer the solar system, he paralyzes the trio and deals with them suitably: Dale to his

Northford, James Edison (*continued*)

harem; Zarkov to the labs, where he will be tortured until he reveals how to split the atom; and Flash to the pits and dungeons. * An enormous poisonous serpent, an acid-filled pit, and electric shackles form small obstacles to Flash, who rescues his friends—only, as they air-crash into a canal, to be captured by shark-men. Another escape brings them back into Pwami's power. * Dale goes back to the harem; Zarkov to the dungeons on the prison planetoid Ceres; and Flash is put on a rocket to Jupiter, the unwilling love-captive of Princess Illana of Jupiter, who admires his manliness and intends to marry him. But even a love-sick princess must yield to Flash, who brings her under control. * After more perils and escapes our trio are on Pwami's flagship as the Martian space fleet heads for Earth. On board is a gigantic atomic disintegrating ray projector. Zarkov has cracked, and Pwami is ready to start his conquest of the solar system. But Flash is too clever for Pwami. He gains control of the ray and saves Earth from the Martian fleet. Pwami is due to stand interplanetary trial, with only one foreseeable verdict. * *Miscellaneous items:* viewing devices, heat-ray pistols, gorilla-men on a planetoid on which Flash and Illana are shipwrecked. * Pretty bad, even as a semijuvenile.

NOWLAN, PHILIP FRANCIS (1888-1940)

U.S. author. Born in Philadelphia, B.A. University of Pennsylvania, 1910. Journalist on trade publications before writing the following works. Later wrote script for early Buck Rogers comic comic strip. In 1940 resumed fiction writing for short time before death. See also Frank Phillips, pseud.

1072. **ARMAGEDDON-2419 A.D.** *Amazing Stories*, August 1928. Ill. Paul.
(Reprinted with "The Airlords of Han" as *Armageddon 2419 A.D.*, Avalon, New York, 1962 and Ace, New York, 1963.)
The origin of the comic strip "Buck Rogers in the Twenty-Fifth Century," which ran from 7 January 1929 to 8 July 1967. Crudely drawn by Dick Calkins and unimaginative, it seems to have been the first real science-fiction comic strip, although there were partial predecessors.
Novelette. * *Time:* A.D. 2419, as reported and reflected upon many years later. *Place:* mostly the east central United States. * The narrator, Anthony Rogers, trapped in a mine by radioactive gas, remains in suspended animation for about five hundred years. He awakens in perfect condition, clothing and all, into a strange world. * *Background:* After World War I another world war followed, in which the nations of Europe attacked the United States, which won the war, but was economically and culturally wrecked. The Russians thereupon overran Europe. Oriental expansion began, and by the beginning of the twenty-second century the Han had conquered the Old World and overrun America. (While in the first story the Han are tacitly considered Chinese, in the sequel, "The Airlords of Han," the Han are identified as a hybrid race formed by extraterrestrials and Central Asiatics, and not Chinese. The word "Han" itself is an authentic term for the Chinese people.) * The Empire of Han pursued a policy of extermination against the Americans, driving the few survivors into the forests and wastelands, where they lived precariously for centuries. But, as the Han gradually weakened and lost their original vigor, the Americans grew in strength and, in a new development of science, gained areas of knowledge that the Chinese do not have, inclu-

ding what amounts to an antigravity substance and effective war rockets. * At the time that Rogers (who is not called Buck) awakens, the Americans are loosely organized into large-area groups called gangs, which are more or less on good terms with one another, but have no central organization. Their factories and laboratories are hidden underground, while the main bodies of people live in woodland camps in a lifestyle that combines elements from Robin Hood, Edward Bellamy, and Daniel Beard. The Americans look forward to the day when they can rise up and expel the Han, but do not expect it to happen in the near future. In the meanwhile, they try to remain inconspicuous. * The Han, who are concentrated in a few enormous cities, travel back and forth in huge armored flying fortresses equipped with very effective disintegrator rays. They are kept aloft by repellor beams. * The Han military presence seems to be almost totally aerial, with no ground troops mentioned. The Americans, who maintain a guerrilla war, have reasonably good explosives and rockets, but these are not adequate to penetrate the Han armor or the circles of disintegrator rays that guard Han cities. * Rogers, now awake, saves a young woman (Wilma Deering) from outlaw Americans and is accepted by her people as a man from the twentieth century. He brings a fresh point of view to the war, working out a way to destroy Han ships by shooting rockets into their repellor rays, whence they are attracted up into the ships. He also evolves the concept of rocket barrages, instead of individual firing. These tactics prove very successful. * Rogers leads an expedition into the Han city equivalent to New York, locating records that reveal Americans collaborating with the Han. As a reward for his accomplishments he is appointed a sort of regional war chief. Along the way he has picked up Wilma as a mate. She fights along with him, but she might be more effective if she could avoid being repeatedly knocked unconscious. * A well-developed, professionally handled pulp work that can still be read with some enjoyment, though now, of course, dated. The Yellow Peril situation is, of course, offensive. * For a sequel see #1073, "The Airlords of Han."

1073. **THE AIRLORDS OF HAN.** *Amazing Stories*, March 1929. Ill. Paul.
(Reprinted with "Armadeddon—2419" as *Armageddon 2419 A.D.*, Avalon, New York, 1962 and Ace, New York, 1963.)
Novelette. * Sequel to #1072, "Armageddon—2419 A.D." *Time:* around 2420 or so. *Place:* mostly in the Rocky Mountain area. * The struggle between the American gangs and the Han continues, with the tide turning more and more toward the Americans. Rogers's new tactics have proved very effective, and Han disintegrators and air power are now much less decisive than they used to be. * The Americans have developed two new weapons: a metal that can withstand the disintegrators (unfortunately in very short supply), and atomic bombs. With this more potent armament the Americans are able to destroy the eastern Han stronghold, Nu-Yok, which goes up in a tremendous atomic explosion. * During an air battle, Rogers ventures his little flyer too close to a Han aerial dreadnaught; his flyer is damaged, and he is captured. He is taken to the Han supercity of Lo-Tan, which seems to be somewhere in the Rocky Mountains, surrounded by disintegrator batteries in a circle one hundred miles wide. * There, once the Han discover that their psychological techniques cannot make him reveal secret information, the Han emperor keeps him around as a sort of pet, a favored person with whom the Emperor can have light argu-

Nowlan, Philip Francis (*continued*)

ments and discussions. Most of the story is devoted to Rogers's captivity. * In the outside world, the Americans continue their technological progress and their military advances. One of their most potent weapons is a small spherical rocket-powered spy-machine; impervious to the disintegrators, it also serves as a weapon, crushing Han soldiers. One such sphere creeps through the Han defenses in Lo-Tan and establishes contact with Rogers, who escapes with its aid. * It is well that he escapes when he does, for the Han, recognizing that the Americans have beaten them on the surface, plan to transfer their surviving cities so far underground that the Americans can never find them. Thanks to Rogers, however, the Han are all massacred. The rest of the world gradually follows the American lead. * *Miscellaneous:* In this second story Nowlan disavows prejudice against Orientals, declaring that the Han, who originated in Central Asia, were not Chinese, but descendants of humanoids from space who interbred with the local population. Physically, they differ from Chinese and Japanese and are a hateful lot, thanks to their extraterrestial origins. * Han culture is discussed at some length, though in a confused manner: At the top is a tyrannical emperor, beneath whom is a military bureaucracy; surprisingly, there is intense political individualism among subordinates, who scorn the Emperor. * Han culture is the acme of laziness, with the Han spending their lives within their apartments, watching television entertainments or outside events by visoscopes. * Han society is heavily male oriented, with women little better than prostitutes who move from male to male. They do no work, however, and are supported by the state. The men, too, receive a state allowance. Although Nowlan is not precise, it would seem that children are reared in state crèches and "adopted" by their fathers at a certain age. Men are assigned jobs by the state corporation, but they work mostly by remote control from their apartments. * All in all, Han culture seems a weird mixture of state socialism and capitalist oppression. * Much less interesting than the first story. * Both stories have had a very large cultural impact beyond the borders of science-fiction proper.

1074. **THE TIME JUMPERS**. *Amazing Stories*, February 1934. Ill. Morey.

Short story. * *Time:* 1961, with episodes in 993 and 1753. *Place:* the coast of New Jersey and Upstate New York. * Submitting a disk of the new metal dobinium (found only in a single meteorite) to a bombardment of artificially produced cosmic rays, narrator Ted Manley can change space-time coordinates and travel in time in his newly finished time car. * In their first voyage Ted and his girlfriend Cynthia reach the year 993, when they are attacked by a band of Norse explorers. The time travelers barely escape. On their second voyage they reach Upstate New York in 1753, during the French and Indian Wars. They watch Braddock's redcoats being massacred by the Indians and warn George Washington of an ambush. They then return. * Nothing much.

O'BRIEN, FITZ-JAMES (1828-1862)

U.S. author, journalist. Born in or near Limerick, Ireland; little is known of his earlier life, and that little is suspect due to his habit of romanticizing himself. Spent some time in England, where contributed to periodicals; came to the United States

around 1852. In New York was well-known as a Bohemian and as an excellent journalist. Entered the Union army and died as a result of wounds received in battle. Although undeservedly forgotten (except for the following story), a very ingenious, imaginative, perceptive writer. Most of his fiction is supernatural; this is covered in *The Guide to Supernatural Fiction*. His other science-fiction is covered in *Science-Fiction: The Early Years*.

1075. **THE DIAMOND LENS**. *Amazing Stories*, December 1926. Unsigned ill. Also *Amazing Stories*, October 1933. Ill. Morey.

(First published in the *Atlantic Monthly*, January 1858; reprinted and anthologized many times in both genre and general collections. Recent reprints are in Franklin, *Future Perfect*, and in Gunn, *The Road to Science Fiction*, Vol. 1.)

One of the early classics of science-fiction, so familiar that it hardly needs detailed summary. * Linley, the narrator, who is an amateur microscopist enthusiastic to the point of fanaticism, is determined to create the ultimate microscope. Since he has reached the limit of orthodox science, he attends a Spiritualist seance and invokes the aid of the spirit of Antony Leeuwenhoek, the founder of microscopy. Leeuwenhoek tells him that such a microscope can be made from a diamond of 140 carats, suitably prepared with electricity. A diamond of this size and water seems impossible to obtain. But actually such a gem lies in the possession of an acquaintance. Linley murders him, ingeniously creating the illusion of suicide and a locked room situation, steals the gem and follows the spirit's instructions. In a drop of water he sees a microscopic wonderland, through which frolics an incredibly beautiful young woman, whom he calls Animula. Linley becomes infatuated with her and neglects matters of daily life. But the end comes when he sees her dying; the water in which Animula lived has evaporated. The narrator thereupon goes mad. * A fine story.

O'DONNELL, JOHN SHAMUS

No information.

1076. **NAVAL CONTROL**. *Amazing Stories Quarterly*, Winter 1932. Ill. Morey.

Short-short story. * *Place:* the San Francisco area. * Tongue-in-cheek trials and tribulations of a widower. * The narrator, who seems to have been a missionary, laments the death of his wife Florence Minerva, who, he says, clad half the natives of Peru in mother hubbards and converted them as Baptists. But his friend the renowned Irish scientist Egan will construct for him an android (my term) that is the exact image of Florence Minerva. * Florence Minerva the Second, who is operated by electricity, is all she should be in appearance, but there are behavioral problems. Atmospheric electricity sets her off; sitting on an iron bench drains her magnetism; and proximity to a certain sailor with a silver plate in his head induces telepathic communication (singing ribald sailor songs) and erotic feelings. At the last, as the sailor ships out to sea, Florence Minerva the Second wades into the water after him and is lost. * Amateurish, but occasionally amusing.

OHMERT, J. G.

No information.

1077. **CELESTIAL PIONEERS**. *Amazing Stories Quarterly*, Spring/Summer 1933. Ill. Morey.

Ohmert, J. G. (*continued*)

Novelette. * *Time:* the first fifteen years of so of the twentieth century. *Place:* the Seattle area and Mars. * A backyard spaceship and colonization. * John Stanton discovers the phenomenon of antigravity by running a new force, called X-tricity, through metal, but he lacks the engineering and technical knowledge to develop and exploit his discovery. He thus invokes the aid of his old teacher Professor Martin Hess, who also happens to be a very wealthy man. Hess agrees to work with him. * Hess, who sometimes speaks with a German accent and sometimes does not, is honest, but extremely secretive, so that Stanton does not even realize what is going on in the shop. * Finally, all is revealed. Hess has built a spaceship and is intent upon leaving the woes of Tellus behind and colonizing Mars. * Hess, Stanton, and Stanton's wife Kitty take off, fly uneventfully to Mars, and find in a depression a well-watered area with vegetation and sufficient atmosphere for ready survival. Indeed, gentle archaic herbivores are present to serve as stock for milch and meat cattle. * The Stantons remain on Mars, farming, while Hess returns to Earth for more colonists. He does not select adults, however, but three male and three female children, whom he presumably takes back to Mars with him along with a new wife. At about this time World War I is under way. * Hess's colony will learn nothing of Terrestrial history, but will try to begin humanity afresh, avoiding the horrible situations that led to the war. * *Miscellaneous:* Hess also has landed on the Moon, which is barren and lifeless. * Overlong, and somewhat on the naive side.

OLES, FLOYD (1896-?)

U.S. (Seattle) author, journalist. Also wrote *Letters of Sour Mash Sam* (1934), topical journalism. Author of local memoirs, *Glencove, Scenes from a Puget Sound Boyhood* (1986).

1078. **HOFFMAN'S WIDOW.** *Amazing Stories,* February 1936.

Short story. * *Place:* the Aleutian Islands. * Not science-fiction. * A story of revenge in which Maria, a half-Aleutian woman, avenges the death of her husband by trapping his murderer. A Kodiak bear will finish the job.

OLOG, TOM

U.S. writer, then resident of San Bernardino, California, presumably a young person. Olog's entry won first prize ($50) for the best letter expounding "What Science Fiction Means to Me." Since the letter takes the form of a storiette, it seems valid to include it in this study.

1079. **THE GIFT OF THE MASTER MENTALITY.** *Science Wonder Stories,* July 1929.

Short-short story. * Thaght, Scientific Director of a part of the universe, a monstrous black, whale like creature floating on a red ocean under a green sun, communicates directly with the Master Mentality, the Center of the Ultra-Universe. His message is so delicate that he cannot entrust it to the thought rolls. * Thaght has been traveling about the macro-universe, through empty space. When he reduced himself to a two-millionth of his usual size, he discovered in a tiny area that was considered empty a mass of universes. Among them was one tiny planet called Earth, with inhabitants of such low mentality that Thaght could not communicate with them. He watched them and saw how they mistreated such innovators as Columbus, a theorist on radio

(Hertz?), and others. * The problem, Thaght says, is that these people have a "strange quirk in their brain which holds back faith in the future and discards new thoughts." As a result they cannot control their own planet. Thaght asks for instructions. * The response: The Master will send Thaght a thought roll that will prepare the minds of these people for great advancement. "This thing is, an illimitable weapon, SCIENCE FICTION!" * In the manner of Poe's "The Thousand-and-Second Tale of Scheherazade" and not wholly unintelligible.

OLSEN, BOB (1884-1956)

Writing name of Alfred Johannes (or John) Olsen, Jr., U.S. (California) author, graduate of Brown University, member of Phi Beta Kappa. While not a great writer, one of the more competent members of Gernsback's stable, who sometimes wrote with a light touch. From internal evidence Olsen must have had a good background in mathematics and biology. In later life associated with an advertising agency.

Olsen's fiction is covered below under The Four-Dimensional Series, The Master of Mystery Series, and Other Works.

The Four-Dimensional Series

A sometimes humorous series based on a geometric concept of the fourth dimension, which, according to the author, can be attained by spatial manipulation of objects in our three-dimensional world. Yet the fourth dimension is also another realm of being, an other-world or parallel world, into which one may penetrate. Many of the names and concepts are à clef: Sidelburg or Sidlis for Sidis; Banning for Henry Parker Manning (who wrote several technical books on geometry of higher dimensions); Mayer for Mayo, etc.

1080. **THE FOUR-DIMENSIONAL ROLLER-PRESS.** *Amazing Stories,* June 1927. Ill. Paul.

(Reprinted in Wollheim, *Every Boy's Book of Science Fiction.*) Short story. * The narrator, a skilled mechanic and pattern maker, is hired by the young genius William James Sidelburg (an echo to the historical William Sidis, with an increment of William James) to work on a strange apparatus that is constructed mostly of six-inch wooden spheres. * After a time Sidelburg explains. The object is a four-dimensional roller press. The concept behind it is based on the occult fourth dimensional theories of Charles Hinton and Sidelburg's own notion that the fourth dimension is equivalent to mass. * According to Sidelburg, all objects have extensions into the fourth dimension. If they can be compressed, as in the four-dimensional cylinder that the men have constructed, they will retain the same mass, but will be enlarged in our world. * The machine constructed, Sidelburg tests it with various objects, including his pet baboon Jocko, who becomes enlarged to the size of a gorilla. The baboon bounds around remarkably. * Sidelburg now insists on undergoing the process. As he is being enlarged, however, the mischievous monkey manipulates the controls so that Sidelburg swells up to the size of a balloon and floats away with the hypercylinder. * The narrator states that men should not meddle with nature. For a sequel see #1081, "Four Dimensional Surgery."

1081. **FOUR DIMENSIONAL SURGERY.** *Amazing*

Olsen, Bob (*continued*)
Stories, February 1928. Ill. Paul.
Short story. * Sequel to #1080, "The Four-Dimensional Roller-Press." * The narrator, the assistant to Professor Sidelburg, who was expanded out of existence in the previous story, receives a surprise visit from Dr. Paul J. Mayer of the Mayer Clinic and Professor Banning, a well-known mathematician. * The two men make a proposal: Banning is suffering badly from inoperable gall stones. Would it be possible for the narrator to create a four-dimensional surgical device to remove Banning's stones without harming him? * The narrator is reluctant at first, claiming that he is only a mechanician, but he is persuaded, and with the aid of Banning makes a four-dimensional forceps. * Preliminary tests are successful. The operation is under way when a drift in the dimensions causes both Mayer and Banning to disappear into the fourth dimension. * Fortunately, Mayer seizes the light wire with the forceps, and the narrator is able to pull both men back into our world. While in the other dimension, Banning simply picked out his gall stones himself, with no problems. * As in the previous story, the fourth dimension is considered geometrically, in terms of rotating bodies. * Amusing. * For a sequel see #1082, "Four Dimensional Robberies."

1082. **FOUR DIMENSIONAL ROBBERIES.** *Amazing Stories*, May 1928. Ill. R. E. Lawlor.
Short story. * Sequel to #1081, "Four Dimensional Surgery." * Professors Banning and Mayer are away when the narrator receives an unexpected and for a time frightening visit. Dern of the great private detective agency (a reference to Burns) and an operative question him about the four-dimensional forceps that he and Manning had developed. * Hundreds of thousands of dollars have recently been stolen from safe deposit boxes, under impossible circumstances. Perhaps by four dimensional means? The detectives ask the narrator's aid, which he willingly offers. * The forceps, it immediately becomes apparent, have been stolen. The narrator and the detectives, working out a logical modus operandi by comparison of signatures and time tables, establish a stakeout and capture the culprit, but not before he almost slides into the fourth dimension. * Olsen repeats the gist of his geometrical explanations of the fourth dimension. * For a sequel see #1083, "Four Dimensional Transit."

1083. **FOUR DIMENSIONAL TRANSIT.** *Amazing Stories Quarterly*, Fall 1928. Ill. Paul and unsgned ill..
Novelette. * Sequel to #1082, "Four Dimensional Robberies." * Professor Banning is back with a new invention based (in part) on the fourth dimension. This is an extremely rapid airplane. As he explains to the narrator, the factors that hamper aerial travel are three: friction, inefficient mechanical devices, and gravity. He has designed a plane, the *Spirit of Youth,* that will obviate all three problems: friction, by a system of tiny oil globules extruded on the plane during flight; inefficiency, by a new three-chamber engine of great efficiency; and gravity, by a four-dimensional rudder. The narrator is to help construct the rudder. * Since Banning is a wealthy man, a plane is built to his specifications. It also is provided with rockets for emergency propulsion, and insulation that is an almost perfect non-conductor. As pilot, Banning has induced the noted young aviator Berghlin (Lindbergh) to serve. * Just before the plane is about to leave, a challenge appears: A noted fake explorer and impostor, Pontius Bragg, wagers that the *Spirit of Youth* cannot circumnavigate the Earth in eighteen hours. The stakes are

twenty thousand dollas. * The plane takes off, easily reaches 800 MPH and slides into the fourth dimension, where the aviators see beneath them life as perceived from another dimension. The plane functions so well that Banning decides to take a trial flight around the Moon. This, too, succeeds, revealing the Moon to be a totally dead world. Returning to Earth, the narrator and Berghlin assume that Banning has lost the wager because of time spent on the lunar voyage, but it turns out that once again Banning has prepared well: He hoaxed his two comrades into thinking far more time had passed than really had. The plane was actually aloft only about fifteen hours. * Less successful than the shorter pieces. The Vernian bet situation and the lunar voyage, with its aftermath, fall limp. * For a sequel see #1084, "The Man Who Annexed the Moon."

1084. **THE MAN WHO ANNEXED THE MOON.** *Amazing Stories*, February 1931. Ill. Morey.
Short story. * Sequel to #1083, "Four Dimensional Transit." * *Place:* near the Moon. * Professor Banning, aviator Berghlin, and the narrator prepare for a voyage to the Moon in a vessel that combines rockets and a fourth-dimensional tube. The tube will lift the ship out of the Earth's gravitational field, while the rockets will permit directional travel. * The three voyagers reach the Moon in a little more than an hour and explore in space suits. The Moon is barren and lifeless, and gravity effects are as expected. As the title indicates, Professor Banning annexed the Moon in the name of the United States. The narrator has a small adventure when he falls into a cleft; the ship settles in a deposit of lunar dust; and a space repair is needed when the fourth-dimensional tube is damaged; but otherwise the trip is without unexpected incident (exception noted below). * The treatment is as hard science-fiction, with a fair amount of explanatory material about the fourth dimension and selenography. * *Miscellaneous:* The white streaks in Tycho and elsewhere are upwellings of platinum. * The one fantastic element on the Moon is the existence of rapid mud-earth movements, which are a real peril. These are a little puzzling in the light of the story's general realistic approach.

The Master of Mystery Series

Three stories set in the Los Angeles area in the late 1940s, though there is little evidence of futurity. Justin Pryor, who today would be called a technical adviser, is known to his friends as the Master of Mystery because of his love of puzzles and skill at solving them. In the following stories, however, he really serves as a private detective. The stories are constructed like classical detective short stories, with a crime, invocation, to-do, solution in company, amd fair play toward the reader, who is provided with clues. On the whole they are closer to being detective stories than science-fiction.

1085. **THE MASTER OF MYSTERY**. *Amazing Stories*, October 1931. Ill. Morey.
Long short story. * *Time:* According to the chronology presented in "Seven Sunstrokes" around 1948, although there are no evidences of futurity in the story itself. *Place:* Los Angeles. * Justin Pryor, who terms himself a business counselor, operating under the name of the Business Merchandising Bureau, is called in to solve a baffling murder. An elderly manufacturer has been found in a sealed-room situation with his head bashed in. Pryor

Olsen, Bob (*continued*)

solves the case easily, as will the reader to whom Pryor has been very conscientious in providing clues. The method of murder is perfectly reasonable and possible. * Too long for what it has to offer, but mildly entertaining. For a second case involving Pryor see #1086, "Seven Sunstrokes."

1086. **SEVEN SUNSTROKES**. *Amazing Stories,* April 1932. Ill. Morey.

Long short story. * *Time:* 1948. *Place:* Los Angeles. * Justin Pryor solves a second case. Some time earlier there had been a notorious kidnapping in which Ruth Whipple was abducted and presumably raped. Escaping, she committed suicide, as did her father. Now six persons allegedly responsible for the crime (though free for lack of evidence against them) have mysteriously died of sunstroke. Strickland, the seventh suspect, tries to invoke Pryor's help. * Since Strickland is an unsavory man, Pryor is unenthusiastic, and while he delays with other work, Strickland, too, dies. In this instance it is certainly murder, since there was a threatening letter. * Pryor works out the agent of death, a chemical that reacts with ultraviolet light to cause a poisoning with the same symptoms as sunstroke. And he also locates the murderer, with whom he has some sympathy. Adequate clues are presented for the reader, too, to solve the case. * Not uninteresting, but as with the previous story, too long for what it has to say.

1087. **THE POOL OF DEATH**. *Amazing Stories,* January 1933. Ill. Morey.

Novelette. * Pryor's third case. * *Time:* around 1948. *Place:* Hollywood, California. * The passée movie star Helen Franklin wants Pryor to investigate the disappearance of her husband, motion picture director George Raymond. She calls it murder and has a suspect in mind. * Raymond had been swimming with a colleague in the colleague's "plunge" (a local term for a swimming pool), and he apparently never came out. Other partygoers were playing bridge or otherwise engaged nearby and they would have seen him pass by. * Pryor investigates the group, who are all fairly low-key for Hollywood: a coarse rival director, a jealous but brilliant Italian scientist, and a young architect who is smitten by Helen Franklin. * There is much conversation and walking about until a solution is reached, but not before there is a second disappearance under the same circumstances as the first. * Since this is a s-f study and since the reader is not likely to seek out Olsen's story, some indication of a solution must be offered—especially since Olsen gives it away early in the story. Using pituitary extract, the logical suspect has developed a gigantic amoeba, which he is able to control chemically. It lives in an "annex" to the swimming pool. * Far too long for what it has to offer.

Other Works

1088. **THE EDUCATED PILL**. *Amazing Stories*, July 1928. Unsigned ill.

Short story. * Written in slang and sports jargon, Damon Runyon mode. The manager of a baseball team tells how his team, with the aid of the inventor Schnitzelkuchen, won the penant against the Silk Sox. * Schnitzelkuchen has invented the aeroplane ball, a ball the size of an ordinary baseball, interior filled with all sorts of apparatus, including a propeller. It can make fantastic curves, return to the pitcher, stop in midair, and procede by jumps. Despite some difficulties, the aeroplane ball wins the crucial game. Told as a monologue interview with a journalist.

1089. **THE SUPERPERFECT BRIDE**. *Amazing Stories*, July 1929. Ill. Hugh Mackay.

Short story. * Dr. Goddard, who has selected Broderick as the most suitable person for his proposal, explains that he has a perfect artificial woman (Eve) available and that Broderick may win her for a bride. Displaying her nude, he arouses Broderick's desires to near frenzy, then introduces him to her. * The woman is highly intelligent, at least as good a chess player as Broderick, a gifted musician, and amiable. But as Goddard has explained throughout the exposition, Eve is artificial, a composite. * Just as an artist, when doing a painting may use the face and head of one model, the body of another, the hands of still another, Dr. Goddard has built Eve up by organ transplants, purchasing perfection from other women. * Broderick, who is practically panting with lust, can have Eve and become the father of a perfect race, but there is one prerequisite. He must surrender himself to similar organ transplants. Goddard will begin with a leg. * Broderick agrees, is anaesthetized, and awakens—to learn that no operation has taken place. It was all a screening hoax. Goddard is Eve's father, and she is naturally perfect. Goddard wanted to make sure that a man loved her enough to make sacrifices. * This is all fine with Broderick, but the clincher comes when Eve reveals that it was not her father who selected Broderick, but herself. She had met Broderick years before. * A curious story, almost surreal in its eroticism.

1090. **FLIGHT IN 1999**. *Air Wonder Stories*, September 1929. Ill. Paul.

Short story. * *Time:* 1999. * Pretty much an exposition of future wonders, à la *Ralph 124C 41+*. * 1999 is overwhelmingly a flying culture, with privately owned antigravity space cars and public space buses that follow prescribed routes. The vessels are propelled by compressed air. Individuals have special suits with antigravity apparatus and fabric flight membranes like those of flying squirrels. With such suits individuals fly up to space buses as they pass by. Behind all this is gravinul, a substance that impedes gravitation, which can then be adjusted. Air flying zones are rigidly delimited and rigorously enforced. Planes and automobiles no longer exist and, indeed, are almost forgotten. * In other respects, too, life is very different from that of Olsen's time. Jek's family lives in what seems to be a subterranean apartment, access to which is via a trapdoor. A robot servant, called a televox, assists in the apartment. * Education is far more advanced than in our day, and young children already know more mathematics than many professionals do in our day. The popular game Mathic is based on higher math. Advanced television makes news easily available. * While future man is much the same as today, except perhaps for longer arms and outturned feet (Olsen is not clear about this), the naming system has changed. Every person must have a unique name that has no meaning; this is checked by and registered with a national bureau, which will itself provide a name if parents delay too long. Men's names begin with the first half of the alphabet, women's, with the second half. The full name, which is worn on the left breast, also includes marital status and occupation, although individuals are called by their first name. Mr. and similar forms are abolished. * The culture is peaceful except for the Purple Women, a gang of vicious female outlaws who rob and kill without remorse. Jek, in anticipation of encountering

Olsen, Bob (*continued*)

such outlaws, has devised a little asphyxiation device that he can operate with his feet. * After arguing with his wife about finances and discussing children with similar parents, Jek boards a space bus, on which are two policemen armed with machine guns in case of an attack by the Purple Women. * Another space car pulls along beside the bus, and two Purple Women leap into the bus. In a rapid shoot-out the women kill one policeman and paralyze another with their vibrators. Jek, too, is in danger until he is able to use his asphyxiator, which kills one of the bandits. In a struggle with the other, Jek and the woman fall overboard, both striving to be the first to reach the vibrator the bandit has dropped. Jek wins. As a bank reward for his exploit he receives enough cash to satisfy his financial needs. * *Miscellaneous:* The principle of the vibrator is not understood, but the women also have a protection against it, as well as against bullets. * When he sat down on the bus, Jek put on glasses and a hearing device that presented him with live news television. * A curiosity.

1091. **THE PHANTOM TELEVIEW.** *Science Wonder Stories*, November 1929. Ill. Paul.

Short story. * *Place:* California. * The story begins with a letter to Hugo Gernsback, editor of *Science Wonder Stories*, asking for help. The narrator (Harvey Blake) is currently in San Quentin under death sentence, and he believes that the only person who can help him would be best reached through *Science Wonder Stories*. * *Background:* The narrator is killing time while awaiting his mother's arrival by train, when he sees a sign inviting entry to see the Teleview. He enters, and Pythagoras Denker, obviously an eccentric inventor, demonstrates a completely effective viewer that operates by reflection from atmospheric layers. * Blake asks to see his mother's train, and to his horror witnesses a train robbery, involving derailing and murder. Dashing to the railroad station, he informs the stationmaster of the robbery, then rushes to the wreck, where he saves his mother. Thanks to the Teleview, he is able to give the police the automobile registration number and a description of the culprits. * The police, naturally, are suspicious of Blake, and when they pick up the criminals on the basis of his information, the vicious young thugs as an act of revenge inculpate him. He is put on trial, and since he cannot find Denker and his Teleview to prove his story, he is found guilty and sentenced to death. * Am amusing story.

1092. **COSMIC TRASH.** *Science Wonder Stories*, April 1930.

Short-short story. * Honorable mention in the contest based on the cover to the November 1929 issue of *Science Wonder Stories*. * *Time:* the near future. * Close, the narrator, perhaps out of prison after a ten-year turn, is in New York watching the Woolworth Building being ripped out by the roots by a flying saucer. The job boss, a vice president of Cosmic Disposal, explains: The new technique for ridding cities of unwanted buildings is not tearing them down, but ripping them up and hauling them into space, where they eventually fall into the sun. The supervisor then shows Close the Eiffel Tower being similarly disposed of. When Close asks if the process can dispose of anything, the supervisor boastfully replies yes. Close thereupon, echoing one of the gags of the period, asks if he can get rid of forty-years accumulation of razor blades. * Amusing.

1093. **THE ANT WITH A HUMAN SOUL.** *Amazing Stories Quarterly*, Spring/Summer 1932. Ill. Morey. Novelette.

* Formicology in fictional form. * Williams, a college student and former Fundamentalist who has lost his faith, attempts to commit suicide by leaping into the river. He is rescued by Dr. De Villa, a biologist, who after long discussion makes him an offer: ten thousand dollars to undergo certain experiments. * De Villa has discovered how to alter the size or volume of objects. A substance that he calls spacite fills the spaces between molecules, and this substance can be inserted or extracted by his volumalter machine. De Villa demonstrates his discovery by producing an ant the size of a sheep. * The question: Will Williams permit part of his brain to be inserted into the braincase of an enlarged ant, then let himself be shrunk to enter an ant hill and observe? Williams will. * De Villa ties a cord around him so that he can be recognized and arranges to retrieve him at a certain signal. * Williams undergoes several episodes among different kinds of ants, mushroom-growing, leaf-cutting ants, slave-holding ants, dairy ants, etc. His experiences are not really adventures, but more observation and routine activity. On the whole he is in no danger, except in his last phase as a honey ant. De Villa retrieves him in time, and, somehow, Williams has acquired a more realistic view of life. * A little pathetic fallacy in the last portion of the story, but otherwise clear. * Greatly overlong and padded, plus little to say. Disappointing after certain other of Olsen's works.

1094. **THE PURPLE MONSTERS.** *Amazing Stories*, August 1932. Ill. Morey.

Short story. * *Place:* mostly New York and Los Angeles. * An early echo of the motion picture *King Kong*. * Walter Garff, police reporter, is in his dentist's office in the Empworth Building when he first sees the purple monster. About six-hundred-feet-high, four-armed, with a long trunk, it is obviously hungry, for it keeps popping into its mouth such humans as it catches. It is big and strong enough to smash open skyscrapers and pick up elevated trains. It has two similar companions. * Garff escapes the monster, but is assigned to fly over it in a helicopter. As he approaches, Army planes attack it and are swatted out of the air. Garff, too, is knocked out of his airship, but his parachute saves him. It also attracts the attention of the monster, who catches him and puts him into a bell jar in its enormous spaceship. Into the same jar, not too long after, goes musical star Joyzelle Ekstrom, whom the monster captured presumably because she was wearing costume wings. The common factor is the unusualness of their appearance, parachute and wings. * After some to and fro action, Garff and Joyzelle escape from the jar but remain in hiding while the monster flies the spaceship to Los Angeles. * Here Garff turns the tables. He kills one monster with a perfectly directed rifle-shot and disintegrates the other two with the ray gun on the ship. (Having watched the monster work the controls, Garff knows how to operate the ship.) Needless to say, he gets a promotion and a raise from his newspaper. * As is later learned, the monsters originally landed in New Jersey. Their ultimate origin is unknown, with scientists arguing stubbornly. The best case can be made for Ganymede, one of Jupiter's moons. * Nothing to recommend.

1095. **CAPTAIN BRINK OF THE SPACE MARINES.** *Amazing Stories*, November 1932. Ill. Morey.

Short story. * *Time:* the interplanetary future. * Adventure and humor of a sort. * Captain Brink of the Earth Republic Space Navy reports to Ganymede Outpost to receive an emergency assignment. He is to rescue two young women—the thrill- and

Olsen, Bob (*continued*)

publicity-seeking Valentine twins—from Titan, where they are under attack by hostile natives. Unfortunately, Titan is almost unknown, and the E.R.S.N. is so short handed that it can spare only one small rocket ship and two men to Brink, where a whole navy is really required. * The three men reach Titan, which is inhabited by highly intelligent brain-beings who in appearance and body function are like giant amoebas. Brink and one associate are captured (the other man is presumably held separately elsewhere or dead) and are imprisoned near the Valentine twins. By this time, the Titanians are able to converse telepathically with the marines. The space marines will be vivisected the next day. * The captives manage to escape, using fire, which the Titanians fear; reach their ship, into which fuel has mysteriously been transferred; and fly off Titan. It is revealed that their missing comrade has been a deus ex machina and has readied the ship for their departure. * Throughout, some play is made of the Spanish-American War popular song, "Captain Jinks of the Horse Marines," suitably adapted to the circumstances. * Some attention is paid to phenomena of space travel. * Not one of Olsen's better stories. * For a sequel see #1103, "The Space Marines and the Slavers."

1096. **THE CRIME CRUSHER**. *Amazing Stories*, June 1933. Ill. Morey.

Novelette. * Crime story. * Brash, aggressive young David Smith, who likes to call himself the Lone Mongoose, has invented a device that can recapture images of events in the recent past. He has already used it to solve one mystery, and he has hopes of eradicating crime. * Unfortunately, the district attorney to whom Smith offers help is corrupt, and the underworld is resentful of the discovery. But the district attorney's beautiful daughter, who likes Smith, is of great help. Surviving assaults and gunnings down, Smith succeeds in reforming the D.A., and the clean-up begins. * *Miscellaneous:* Smith's device is based on the postulate that time is a curved stream in which segments (like motion picture film in a case) are close enough to be bridged for viewing. * One might suspect parody, but writing down of a peculiarly distressing sort seems more likely.

1097. **THE FOUR DIMENSIONAL ESCAPE**. *Amazing Stories*, December 1933. Ill. Morey. Geometric diagram by Olsen (?).

Novelette. * *Place:* California. * Although this story is not a member of the earlier four-dimension series, it invokes the same geometry, now frankly based on the work of Henry Parker Manning. * It is the narrative of Norman Kemp, who by chance becomes acquainted with Professor Newton Schuler, the inventor of a four-dimensional tongs. Schuler operates in secret, since his invention would be put to criminal use by gangsters, who are trying to track him down. * The gangsters frame Kemp for a murder; he is imprisoned in San Quentin; the hangman is placing the noose around his neck—when Schuler retrieves him with the four-dimensional tongs and takes him to his new secret laboratory on a small island off the coast. There are perils and chases, but Kemp is exonerated when his accusers confess the truth. * As an odd point, Schuler, using the tongs, provides the imprisoned Kemp with a book on the fourth dimension. * Routine.

1098. **PERIL AMONG THE DRIVERS**. *Amazing Stories*, March 1934. Ill. Morey.

Novelette. * *Place:* Angola. * Life among the ants, but with a

new twist. * Gordon Cabot, wealthy young athlete, is madly in love with Gloria Freeland, who seems to like him, but is not willing to settle down until she has had her share of adventures—nonsexual. Thus, when Gloria sends Cabot a telegram summoning him, he comes running. * Gloria's scientist friend Dr. Thurston has evolved a scientific method for extracting the soul (or spirit, or personality, or whatever) from one living creature and placing it in another. * Gloria, who is fascinated by ants, now declares that she wants to experience the life of a driver ant. Cabot willy-nilly joins her in the mad adventure. Cabot becomes a young male ant, Gloria, an immature female. * The two undergo the expected adventures of ant life, watching the army seize its prey, assaulting a termite hill, making the nuptial flight, being trapped by a spider, being partly paralyzed by a wasp, etc. * This story differs from Olsen's similar stories in that Gloria for some reason is overpowered by her residual ant personality and must be repeatedly thwarted, retrieved, or rescued by Cabot when she wants to pursue suicidal activities. Eventually, with Gloria half dead, they are returned to their human form. * Because of the personality struggle, more lively than similar stories.

1099. **THE FOUR DIMENSIONAL AUTO-PARKER**. *Amazing Stories*, July 1934. Ill. Morey.

Short story. * Humor. * A reversion to the older silly-invention tradition in science-fiction. * *Place:* California. * Underwood, owner of a small advertising agency in Los Angeles, receives a strange client, an eccentric inventor who claims to have invented a four-dimensional auto parker. As the client (Thoroughgood) demonstrates, he can shift himself and his automobile sufficiently into the fourth dimension to permit interpenetration of objects. The two men ride in Thoroughgood's ancient car, which is equipped with the invention, and undergo sitcom adventures. Eventually, the car takes off out of control into the air and the two men are forced to leap to safety. * Olsen explains fourth dimensional geometry in his usual manner, although in this case he also brings in folding and rotation. * Routine or below.

1100. **NOEKKEN OF NORWAY**. *Amazing Stories*, November 1934. Ill. Morey.

Short story. * *Place:* rural Norway. * The American narrator, hearing the legend of the haunted tarn where several of his ancestors died, decides to investigate, even though his aged grandmother warns him against it. He is nearly eaten for his pains when he takes out a small boat on the tarn. Noekken exists, a huge gelatinous, voracious monster that a friend explains as a giant amoeba. The two men decide to kill it. They succeed, but it is a near thing. * There is a question whether certain aspects of folklore about the creature, namely its sensitivity to mistletoe, are true. * Routine.

1101. **SIX-LEGGED GANGSTERS**. *Amazing Stories*, June 1935. Ill. Morey.

Short story. * Personalized ants. * Brighty, a small black ant, who is much more intelligent than her associates, works out a way to exterminate the large red ants that raid her hill and take away larvae and eggs to be reared as slaves. She cleverly induces one of the slave ants to carry into the hill of the enemy reds the eggs of an insect that produces an intoxicating secretion. * Questionable as science-fiction. The only fantastic element is the pathetic fallacy.

1102. **THE ISLE OF JUVENESCENCE**. *Amazing Stories*, June 1936. Ill. Morey.

Olsen, Bob (continued)

Novelette. * *Place:* Los Angeles and an island off the Pacific coast of Mexico. * Phil Gaynor, an almost penniless victim of the Depression, is accosted by a stranger (Dr. Maxim) who asks to see his hat, then offers him a job. When Gaynor expresses interest, Maxim flies him in his personal plane to his establishment on a Mexican island. There Maxim, after wining and dining him, offers him ten thousand dollars to undergo a certain experiment—brain transplant, which he has performed on animals by a version of fourth-dimensional surgery. * Gaynor stalls for time, since he has come to realize that he is danger no matter what he decides. There is a further factor: Gaynor has seen a beautiful young woman (Thelda Goodwin) who is in the same peril as he. Maxim, however, is too clever for him. Gaynor awakens in the body of a pre-teen boy. * There are encounters with his swap partner (a boy's brain in Gaynor's body), confrontations with Maxim, imprisonments, meetings with the young woman and the girl who is to be her partner in the next brain transplant—until things are resolved. Gaynor escapes by removing the glass from the transom in the room in which he is imprisoned; climbing through the opening, he eliminates the doctor and his associates with brass bed knobs in socks, He then hijacks the doctor's plane and escapes with the two women. * Returning shortly thereafter with police, Gaynor forces Maxim's surgical assistant to reverse the operation and restore him to his own body. * The only unusual aspect of this routine story is that Maxim, after being arrested, keeps his word and pays Gaynor ten thousand dollars, thus enabling him and Thelda to start a romance and a business.

1103. **THE SPACE MARINES AND THE SLAVERS.** *Amazing Stories,* December 1936. Ill. Morey.

Novelette. * Sequel to #1095, "Captain Brink of the Space Marines." *Time:* The interplanetary future. The story refers to a happening "way back in 2734." *Place:* Ganymede, space, and Mars. * The Martian space pirate Zurek has just raided the settlement on Ganymede, killing the old and very young, and carrying away the others as slaves. Among those kidnapped is Ingeborg Andersen, the sweetheart of Dan, the cadet member of Captain Brink's team on the *Hyperion.* * Brink and associates, on reporting the incident to superiors, receive an unexpected reply. Mars is simply looking for an incident to start a war, and relations are so strained that an attack on Zurek's base on Mars would be a casus belli. Nevertheless, the chief of the Space Marines is willing to look the other way if Brink and comrades stage a private raid as civilians. * Lt. Jimmy Sullivan has a good contribution to make: an invisible spaceship; not one made invisible by conventional science-fiction means (which Olsen refutes with scorn), but a ship with automatic camouflage created by scanning devices that reproduce on one side of the vessel exactly what is to be seen on the opposite side. The result is not perfect, but adequate for most circumstances. * The rescuers locate Zurek's base, infiltrate it, supply needle-guns to the slaves, kill Zurek, and rescue Miss Andersen. Presumably this incident does not upset the interplanetary apple cart. * *Miscellaneous:* The Martians have electrolysis weapons. * The Earth is now a single republic. * The discussion of invisibility is interesting, but the story is much too long for what it has to say.

OLSEN, JAMES P.

U.S. author, contributor to the pulp magazines, mostly Western

stories. Books include *Powdersmoke Paddy* (1940) and *Riordan Rides the Range* (1942).

1104. **THE CAVERN WORLD.** *Astounding Stories,* June 1930. Ill. Charles Klinger.

Short story. * *Time:* 1940. The great oilfield has suddenly gone dry, and Blaine Asher plans descend eight thousand feet into the oil-bearing formation to see why this has happened. Since he has an apparatus that melts rock like ice, the descent should be easy. He also has an electric gun. * When Blaine is at the proper level, however, a wildcat blast not only destroys his exit, but opens up a cavern teeming with black octopus-like monstrosities. Asher fights them off with some success, but, completely unexpectedly, two enemies (Lee Wong and Krenski) appear and capture him. * Although they plan to kill him, they explain what has been going on. Lee controls the Petrolia (the underground beings), who are semi-intelligent, by providing pools of oil in which they can spawn and feed. He and Krenski plan to rule the world through their oil monopoly based on the Petrolia. * A shoot-out follows, of course, and Asher, alone surviving, returns to the surface to tell his story to the head of the great oil company. The oil is flowing again now that Lee and Krenski are dead. Soon, the Petrolia, too, will all be dead. * No interest.

ORLOVSKY, V[LADIMIR]

Russian author. According to Schwartz/Weisinger, the pseud. of Benjamin Block. This has not been confirmed elsewhere. According to I. Ph. Masanov's *Slovar' pseudonimov russkix pisatelei,* Orlovsky was the pseud. of V. Borovski. It is possible that Block was the translator. Rynin mentions another science-fiction story by Orlovsky, "Mashina-Uzhasa" ("The Horror Machine").

1105. **THE REVOLT OF THE ATOMS.** *Amazing Stories.* April 1929. Ill. Paul.

(First published as "Bunt Atomov" in *Mir Prikl'uchenii,* No. 3, 1927.)

Short story. * *Place:* Germany and all over the world. * Professor Flinder is trying to split the atom by bombarding elements in a strong magnetic field with radioactive particles. * On the crucial occasion he succeeds, only too well. The reaction escapes control, producing a small ball of energy that grows with the matter that it dissolves. The energy ball is uncontainable; floating out of Flinder's laboratory it flits around the world, creating havoc and destruction wherever it goes. In addition to direct victims and fires, it causes extremely violent storms. * Flinder's assistant Deriugin, a Russian refugee, works out a technique that might control the ball: trap it in a circle of strong magnetism. This works up to a point, but the ball breaks loose again. The end comes when a titanic volcanic eruption hurls the ball and surrounding areas out into space, where they remain. The peril is over.

ORNDORFF, FRANK (1885-1971)

U.S. (Illinois) author. Also wrote rationalist *The Truth about the Bible, What the Ministers are Afraid to Tell You* (1927) and *Kongo, the Gorilla Man* (1945). Died in Hopewell, Illinois.

1106. **THE TERRORS OF THE UPPER AIR.** *Amazing Stories Quarterly,* Winter 1928. Ill. Paul.

Short story. * The great detective Pemberton has discovered that Kidwell and Dexter, two barnstorming aviators who plan to set an altitude record at the fair, are guilty of a bank robbery

Orndorff, Frank (*continued*)

involving murder. * It is too late to apprehend the men, who have already taken off, but the aviator-criminals maintain contact by radio. When they are at about thirty-thousand feet, they excitedly report that a great updraft has seized their plane and is carrying it up to about sixty thousand feet. There they see wonders: aerial life, both plant and animal, sustained by little gas-filled bladders. * But there is no serene exploration: Gigantic aerial monsters attack the plane; the broadcast stops suddenly; a bloody fragment of a plane falls to the ground, as does a scattering of dollar bills. * The presumption is that the aviator-criminals were eaten by the stratospheric life, but a smarter guess is that they have faked the whole story, have manufactured clues, and have landed elsewhere with their loot. It is probably significant than only dollar bills, not bills of higher denomination floated to Earth.

OSBORNE, CHESTER G.

Perhaps Chester Gorham Osborne (1915-?), author of children's books *The First Bow and Arrow* (1951) and *The First Puppy* (1953).

1107. **THE TONE MACHINE**. *Wonder Stories*, May 1934. Ill. Winter.

Short-short story. * To Alan Carter, hero, the great Chinese scientist Wuan Tsen demonstrates his invention, a device that controls emotions by means of certain sounds. It can create a feeling of ecstasy, or one of utter horror. Unfortunately, gangsters get wind of the invention, and kidnapping Carter and his girlfriend, force him to betray Wuan Tsen. The gangsters steal the tone machine and use it to commit bank robberies, protecting themselves with diving helmets to shut out the sound. * Carter, working himself free from his bonds, follows the gangsters to their yacht and captures them by turning on the tone machine while he is wearing a diving helmet. The coast guard completes the rout of the gangsters. The machine is presumably destroyed. * Very crude and amateurish.

PALMER, RAY[MOND] [ARTHUR] (1910-1977)

U.S. (Wisconsin and Illinois) fan, author, editor, publisher. Editor of *Amazing Stories* after Zipf-Davis bought the magazine in 1938, and in 1939 founding editor of *Fantastic Adventures*. Later published and edited magazines *Other Worlds, Imagination, Universe Science Fiction,* and *Science Stories,* with confusing title and publication circumstances. Also other publishing ventures under his own name and pseuds. * As an editor catered at first to the semijuvenile ranges, then to the eccentric margin of science-fiction and beyond, expounding various crank (or hoax) matters like the Shaver Mystery. Also founded occult "factual" magazine *Fate*, in which he stressed and developed the flying saucer hypothesis. It has never been clear (friends and associates differing on interpretation) whether Palmer was an imaginative but somewhat irresponsible small-businessman and hoaxer who latched onto occult matters as a source of income, or a sincere, perhaps mildly psychotic, believer in the matters he promoted. * Palmer also wrote fiction under his own name and many pseudonyms and house names; his opus is uncertain. * As a science-fiction editor, Palmer was of no historical importance, except as a force for the worse; as an occult proponent, he stands behind much of the modern outgrowth of irrationality; as a writer, he could well be ignored.

1108. **THE TIME RAY OF JANDRA**. *Wonder Stories*, June 1930. Ill. Leonard.

Short story. * *Time:* 1944 and 1957. *Place:* West Africa. * The narrator, Sylvester Gale, is shipwrecked somewhere along the coast of West Africa. He undergoes hardships, but, more important, he finds ruins of a surprising supercivilization. It must have flourished far in the past, for the soil level is now much higher than when the buildings were built. * In one room he finds active apparatus involving ninety-two sets of tubes. Meddling with it, he is precipitated (in a manner) into the great past. He can see what is going on, but is invisible and is constrained by the walls and surface features of his own time, which are invisible to him. * Gale learns something of the language by attending an elementary school invisibly, and wanders about observing. * The great project of the day, which most scientists consider both foolish and potentially catastrophic, is boring an earth tube in search of a hollow interior. As Gale watches, molten lava pours out of the hole, overwhelming the civilization, while mobs rage, destroying everything. * Gale, who is in horror of continuing his shadow existence, has also watched scientists who are experimenting with time travel. By latching onto the process, he "transports" himself forward thirty-four thousand years to his own time. But he miscalculates a little and enters the year 1957. At this point the scientific equipment has been wrecked, and the best he can do is remove some platinum heads from the cathode tubes and, when he is rescued and returned to civilization, sell them. * The scientists of Jandra based their time travel on accelerating electrons sufficiently to precipitate them into another dimension. * Confusing exposition, and of no interest.

1109. **THE TIME TRAGEDY**. *Wonder Stories*, December 1934. Ill. Paul.

Short story. * Judge Gregory's son William is missing, and the judge, who is nearly mad with guilt, explains over the telephone to a police desk sergeant what happened. * In 1901, an intruder struck down the judge's father, killing him. The man, who gave his name as William Gregory, was tried by the judge, sentenced to death, and hanged. William Gregory made no attempt to defend himself, and there was no explanation for his entry and assault—beyond his claim that it was self-defense and accidental. * On leafing through an old collection of newspaper clippings, the judge now has realized what happened. His son William had built a successful time machine that hurled him into the past; he was unable to return, since the machine did not travel with him—an oversight. When he emerged in the past, the judge's father saw him, attacked him, and William, as a murderer, was executed. He did not explain matters, for he knew that he would not be believed. The judge now commits suicide. The police desk sergeant, to whom the judge told the story, merely considers the judge to have been mad. * Creeping up on a paradox.

1110. **THE SYMPHONY OF DEATH**. *Amazing Stories*, December 1935. Ill. Morey.

Short story. * *Time:* the interplanetary future. *Place:* mostly on Mars. * The editor of the *Toronto Star Post*, learning of a closed meeting on Mars, which only Martians can attend, assigns star reporter Dale Scott to crash it and learn what is going on. Scott, who can pass for a Martian if suitably disguised, attends the meeting as a Martian reporter and learns the worst. * The Martians, despite their pretense of friendliness, plan to exterminate the population of the Earth at one fell swoop. Their

Palmer, Ray (*continued*)

technique: Sensuora emanations, the Martian counterpart of music, can have an overpowering emotional effect on Earthmen, hence is usually filtered when produced on Earth. But now the Martians have a stronger version that will drive humans into violent combat with each other. The Martian wave cannot travel far, but this shortcoming will be obviated by superimposing the wave on the universal broadcast of Jerry Sheldon's great new symphony. The Martian inventor demonstrates the power of his invention, which affects Scott strongly. * Scott's disguise is pierced. He is captured and put in prison with a Terrestrial murderer from the Callisto prison colony. As might be expected, they escape, and Scott manages to reach Earth and destroy the enormous broadcasting crystal that was just beginning to send out the lethal radiations. * The Martians have also built a huge invasion fleet, but Palmer does not reveal what happened to it. * Routine or less.

1111. THREE FROM THE TEST TUBE. *Wonder Stories*, December 1935. Ill. Paul.

Short story. * Osbourne Fairfield, a great medical researcher and biologist, has worked out a technique for in vitro conception and embryonic development. Advertising his technique, he acquires two millionaires whose wives are unwilling to undergo childbirth. Both want sons, although as things develop, one millionaire is more than willing to settle for a daughter. * A series of accidents and personality conflicts between Fairfield and his friend/associate/superior Marchmont produces an unexpected result: not two males, but two girls and one boy. Further, the girls, thanks to genetic manipulation of the x-chromosome and the new M hormone, stand in a sort of Corsican brothers relationship to each other; they have not met, yet they share the same feelings and have the same desires. * Twenty years pass, and the three children are grown up; Fairfield is a score of years older, of course, but he does not show his age. The young women chance to meet their young "brother," and as anticipated, they are both strongly attracted to him. When the young man is killed in an accident, the girls pine and one attempts suicide. Fairfield, who is in love with one of the girls, believes that he can separate them into "normalcy" by further cellular manipulation, but only one of the girls will survive the process. He hopes that it will be the one that he loves. So it is. * Told in a succession of personality conflicts worthy of a true confessions magazine. A tawdry performance.

PARKER, HARRY D.

Presumably U.S. author. Portrait accompanying story shows a middle-aged man. The story indicates some background in the sciences or engineering. Day states that Parker was a member of the A.S.M.E. and the S.A.E.

1112. THE GRAVITATIONAL DEFLECTOR. *Science Wonder Quarterly*, Fall 1929. Ill. Paul.

Short story. * Tom Lee, physicist and engineer, after a near automobile accident decides to improve on the braking system. Instead of relying on friction produced by a chemical system, he plans to use gravity itself. His plan, utilizing the fourth dimension, is to bend gravity. But then an extension of idea suggests not only braking but propelling his automobile by gravitational forces. * The car is constructed and ready for a test run—which proves to be tragic. Lee forgot centrifugal force, which, when gravity was redirected, hurled him and his car off

the Earth.

PARKINSON, R. D.

U.S. author. Then resident of Belle Harbor, Long Island, New York. According to Schwartz/Weisinger the pseud. of R. P. Deary. Otherwise, no information.

1113. THE RAYS FROM THE ASTEROID. *Wonder Stories*, December 1935.

Short-short story. * First-prize story in the contest based on the cover of the July 1935 issue of *Wonder Stories*. Parkinson received twenty-five dollars. * The asteroid Pallas, whose people have rebelled against the government of Ceres, is in flight and is approaching Earth. The ruler of Pallas decides to use a certain ray upon Earth, in order to free Pallas from the gravity of the Moon, so that Pallas can continue to evade Ceres, which is in pursuit. He does not believe that Earth is inhabited; the atmospheric pressure is too great for intelligent life. Unfortunately, the ray from Pallas creates a deadly neural disease among humans. * The authorities on Earth release from prison the great scientist Sidney Elton, currently awaiting execution for murder. Perhaps Elton can use his new cosmic-ray polarizer to save humanity? * Elton uses his apparatus to project himself to Pallas; blows up the installation and repels Pallas, cutting off the fever ray. By an irony of fate, he is electrocuted at the minute he would have been electrocuted for murder if he had remained in prison. * The above summary is offered with diffidence, since the story is almost unintelligible. As an example of style, the first sentence contains 107 words. One can only marvel at both author and editor. The story deserves notice as one of the most confused narratives read in this project.

PATZER, SIDNEY

U.S. author, then resident of Burlington, Washington. Also wrote *The Ship from Nowhere* published in Gernsback's chapbook Science Fiction Series #18. Although there has been speculation that the name Patzer was a pseudonym, a Sidney Patzer, undoubtedly our author, received an A.B. in 1928 and an M.A. in 1938 from the University of Washington. His master's thesis was "The Cuban Junta and Its Activities in New York prior to the Spanish-American War." Portrait with "The Great Invasion" shows a man in young middle age.

1114. THE GREAT INVASION. *Wonder Stories Quarterly*, Summer 1931. Ill. Marchioni.

Short story. * *Time:* 1942. *Place:* Ohio. * Atmospheric disturbances, and a great green bowl-like energy phenomenon closes over a part of Ohio. Plane reconnaissance shows that within the bowl are three gigantic ships. Hostilities begin almost immediately. The green mist, which is a force shield, both protects the strangers and acts as a disintegrator, while a red ray is equally potent. The U.S. Army attacks, but is slaughtered. After a time, however, the situation turns into a stalemate, for the aliens are vulnerable outside their protective dome, and Terrestrial weapons are useless against the dome. * A breakthrough comes when Private Walton observes, on examining the dust remnant of his sergeant who was caught by the green mist, that the mica face of the sergeant's watch was not disintegrated. This discovery leads to mica defenses, which are a protection against the green force shield, but not the red ray. * Walton chances to be on a reconnaissance party that is trapped inside the force dome when it flashes off and on. He is taken prisoner by

Patzer, Sidney (*continued*)

the invaders, whose identity is now known from their signals to Mars. The Martians are about two feet tall, humanoid in appearance, but in some fashion plastic, with extensible eyes. * Ulla, a Martian woman, puts Walton through a hypnogogic course, so that in a short time he knows enough of the Martian language to communicate. Ulla then informs him that the Martians are prepared to invade Earth with a fleet of twenty-five thousand spaceships and a hundred million fighting men. They offer the nations of Earth a choice: warfare ending in the conquest of the planet, or a territorial concession, an area that the Martians can colonize freely. Walton is released to deliver the message. * Returning to the Martian area, Walton is allowed to wander about the encampment. When he expresses a wish to see Mars at close range, one of the Martians indulges him. This viewing initiates an unexpected disclosure. The invaders have no gigantic reserves on Mars; there is no fleet of twenty-five thousand spaceships with millions of fighting men. Indeed, the Martian outpost contains the total Martian population, and they are almost out of power. Just as a message comes from the President of the United States ceding Antarctica to the Martians, Walton realizes that the Martians learned how to bluff so successfully by picking up images of poker from his mind. * Routine, with a flimsy surprise ending.

 1115. **THE LUNAR CONSUL**. *Wonder Stories*, November-December 1933. Ill. Paul.

Short novel. * *Time:* 1947. *Place:* mostly in Morocco. * Master of the world and social vigilante themes combine in the mysterious figure who calls himself Mithra, Consul of Luna. The master of a superscience that includes superradio, disintegrator rays, antigravity, a spaceship, mechanical mind control apparatus, force screens, synthetic food, and much else, he first makes himself known by carving a huge inscription on the Moon. * He has a social program in mind, the first step toward which is the long-distance transformation of all the gold of the world into lead. Economic chaos, as might be expected. With his disintegrator the Lunar Consul also wipes out slum districts in London and Paris. That a few thousand people died during the process does not seem to disturb him. As for Japan, against which he has a grudge, he drops Shikoku and Kyushu into the sea. * Young J. Jeremiah Lawson, a member of the Secret Service in the Justice Department [*sic*], goes after the Lunar Consul. He discovers that leading scientists have been disappearing over the past year or two, and hypothesizes that the Lunar Consul's establishment is somewhere in the Atlas Mountains in Morocco. * With Madeleine Henderson, daughter of one of the missing scientists, and a companion agent, Lawson proceeds to Morocco, and in the mountains, in almost no time at all, encounters an establishment protected by an impenetrable force screen. * Through an unusual circumstance, the three manage to pass through the screen, and find themselves in the headquarters of the Lunar Consul. Present are all the missing scientists who work, more or less willingly, for the fiend. * From here the story is one of intrigue and mystery. Who is plotting against whom, and just which of the scientists is the Lunar Consul? Eventually the mystery is solved, in a manner probably not too surprising for a modern reader, and the French army moves in. The Consul is killed when his escape ship crashes into the force screen. * *Miscellaneous:* The Lunar Consul operates invisibly throughout the establishment. He attains his

invisibility by a form of mind control, natural power of mind augmented by a mechanical device he wears upon his head. He thus registers on film. A captive scientist creates another form of invisibility, a suit of mirrors that reflects the light behind the wearer. * Still another captive scientist has discovered how to augment the mentality of gorillas and uses a trio of apes as servants and helpers. * Changes wrought by the Consul: The forced abdication of King Edward VIII of Great Britain. The establishment of thirteen twenty-eight-day months, the first to be called Luna. Repeal of the Alien Exclusion Act in the United States, followed by an enormous influx of Orientals to California. The British Empire broken up, with India granted independence. The Central American countries consolidated into a block. The United States forced to return Baja California, seized two years earlier, to Mexico. The United States forced to return French territory seized for nonpayment of war debts. The Polish corridor ceded to Germany. Korea and Chinese territory stripped from Japan. Lithuania invaded by the Russians. And many other map adjustments, usually involving slaughter and riot. * The Consul's final and most ambitious project is to release rays that would kill the stupidest 10 percent of the human race. Fortunately, Lawson and comrades foil him. * Some interesting ideas and detail, but amateurish. The mystery situation—Who is that hombre with the invisibility?—is a bore.

[Anonymous]
Presumably a British writer.

 1116. **THE PEAL OF DEATH**. *Scoops,* 17 March 1934. Unsigned ill.

Boys' fiction. * Short story. * Mad scientist Cedric Evans, who believes that he has been swindled by the utilities Combine, has vowed revenge. Researching acoustics, he has created an ultrasonic projector, based on a gigantic silent bell, that will crumble substances with the proper resonance properties. After several small experiments, he uses his apparatus to destroy a power station and Nelson's monument. * An unintended victim of the various destructions has been physicist Harvey Lingard, who is clever enough to work out what the mysterious destroyer is doing. By chance the walls of his dwelling collapse, while an ancient nonfunctioning grandfather clock has recorded the times of the attacks. Lingard recognizes human agency and is able partially to locate the "epicenter." His theory is reported in the newspapers. * Evans now makes a mistake. Constructing a bomb, he leaves it at Lingard's home, where it explodes. Lingard, however, after an examination of bomb fragments, is able to identify components. With police assistance he is able to narrow suspects to a few people, of whom Evans seems most suspicious because of his fairly well publicized suit against the Combine. Breaking into Evans's laboratory, Lingard finds the ultrasonic bell and even watches as Evans begins a new episode of destruction. They fight. During the struggle the soundless bell peals, disintegrating part of the laboratory and releasing a flood of hydrochloric acid. Evans dies, and the secret of the silent peal is lost. * The detectional side is handled with reasonable realism.

PEARCE, GEORGE P.
No information.

 1117. **THE GIRL AND THE GLACIER**. *Amazing Stories,* May 1933. Ill. Morey.

Pearce, George P. (*continued*)

Short story. * *Place:* the Canadian Rocky Mountains. * Ted Underwood, riding his horse Jake through the mountains, breaks the ice layer and falls into an ice cavern. His horse is killed, and Ted cannot devise a way to escape from the deep pit. As his eyes become accustomed to the dim light, he espies a young woman standing near him. A closer look, however, reveals that she is frozen in the ice. * Being a resourceful man, Ted chops her out and warms her by his fire. When she does not revive, he goes to sleep, awaking to find the young lady up and about, indeed cooking a horse steak. * The woman, Mademoiselle Margerite de Grosellier, after some light-hearted persiflage reminiscent of the work of Robert W. Chambers, reveals that she dates from 1700. As she soon demonstrates, besides Gallic charm she embodies much frontier craft, easily figuring out how to escape from the cavern, skilfully slipping into the embrace of a grizzly bear then knifing it, etc. In short she is better fitted for roughing it than Ted. * With some difficulty Ted convinces her that it is 1931, and after a few tears a romance begins. * The story does not come off.

PELCHER, ANTHONY

U.S. (then New York) author. Portrait accompanying "The Soulless Entity" shows a middle-aged man. Social Security records include an Anthony Pelcher (1897-1981), a resident of Texas, who died in North Carolina. It is not known whether this person was our author.

1118. INVISIBLE DEATH. *Astounding Stories,* January 1930. Ill. J. Fleming Gould.

Short story. * At the inquest on the mysterious murder of the great reclusive scientist Darius Darrow his widow testifies that the Professor observed that one model of his invention was missing. But what was his invention? * The canny reader will recognize that the strange phenomena that take place are those associated with an invisible man. Murder is followed later by extortion attempts on Wall Street tycoons. * Engineer Lees solves the crimes: Darrow's invention was a device that created invisibility by changing the vibratory rate of objects. The criminal is a retired illusionist who uses his triplet daughters as tools for his effects. * Surface writing is competent.

1119. MAD MUSIC. *Astounding Stories,* February 1930. Unsigned ill.

Short story. * After the sixty-story apartment building collapses, Jenks, a young engineer in the Muller Construction Company, which erected the building, is assigned to find an explanation for the disaster. The answer, after chases and romance, is to be found in the Mad Musician, an eccentric who has devised a vibratory apparatus that can use the resonance of a building to cause it to vibrate and collapse. Another building almost goes down before the Mad Musician is cornered and his apparatus shut off.

1120. VAMPIRES OF VENUS. *Astounding Stories,* April 1930. Unsigned ill.

Short story. * *Place:* the Rocky Mountains and Venus. * Leslie Larner, young but distinguished entomologist, receives a strange message: A Venusian asks to meet him at a certain place in the Rockies. * Larner goes elsewhere for his vacation, whereupon two Venusians seek him out (by monitoring his heart from afar) and persuade him to accompany them back to Venus. * The Venusians, despite their high science, are unable to cope with bloodsucking insects as large as horses. They need a terrestrial entomologist. * On Venus Larner soon discovers that the insects are descended from stowaways of noxious Mercurian life-forms. His group captures a specimen, and by releasing it discovers the insect breeding place, which is destroyed by disintegrators. Larner also finds interplanetary romance. * *Miscellaneous:* Venusians are much like Earth people, but smaller. They are the result of millennia of eugenics and birth control, with life spans of about eight hundred years. The planet is a single political state, and there has been no war for thousands of years. Both sexes have equal rights. Scientifically and technologically, of course, they are far superior to Earthmen. Among their capabilities is weather control. Their spaceships, which raid Earth for talc, ride magnetic currents between the planets. So why couldn't they kill their insects?

1121. THE SOULLESS ENTITY. *Wonder Stories,* January 1931. Ill. Paul.

Short story. * The emigré scientist Martinoff, the designer and builder of many marvelous robots, is found dead in his laboratory, accidentally stabbed, apparently by one of his creations. The police accept this theory, but Dr. Farnum, a great neurosurgeon and Martinoff's friend, does not. He is convinced that Martinoff was murdered and he intends to find the criminal. When he does, he will use the criminal's body for a remarkable experiment. Farnum has discovered how to wire nerves so that they accept radio commands instead of neural impulses. * A little detective work locates a suspect; this is the bully of Martinoff's secretary. The secretary is a supposedly reformed female criminal and prostitute. Scopolamine extracts a confession. The criminal, Solokoff, is electrocuted, and Farnum receives his body, which he restores to life, then wires with radio devices. As finished, Solokoff has no personality and is no more than an automaton, which Farnum exhibits to his scientific friends. This goes on for a time until Solokoff's accomplice and mistress discovers what has happened to him. Still loving Solokoff, she stays with him, but eventually poisons him and commits suicide. * A little strange legally, but competently written.

PEREGOY, CALVIN

Pseud. of Thomas Calvert McClary, who has a separate entry.

The Shortwave Castle Series

Three stories focusing on Dr. Conklin, a scientist of genius, who has discovered how to make synthetic gold. He has used his great wealth to erect (in the Rocky Mountains) an enormous building complex (variously called "Shortwave Castle" or "Shortwave Castle") in which he conducts fantastic experiments. The stories, which are written in a slapdash fashion, edge uncomfortably between humor of a sort and imaginative exploration of ideas. On occasion Peregoy invokes the older sitcom motif of the scientist's beautiful daughter and her athletic but stupid fiancé. Internal evidence would seem to indicate that Peregoy wrote a fourth story, but it has not been printed.

1122. SHORT-WAVE CASTLE. *Astounding Stories,* February 1934. Ill. C. R. Thomson.

Short story. * A world in a box. * *Place:* in the Rocky Mountains area. * Dr. Conklin has set up what amounts to an isolated second world, acres in extent, in the gigantic building complex that he calls Shortwave Castle. In it he has placed (cloned?)

Peregoy, Calvin (*continued*)

descendants of himself and a friend, and by applying certain rays and controlling the environment has decreased the size of his subjects and speeded up metabolism and growth so enormously that one month in our world is equivalent to a lifetime in the tiny world. * At the moment, 176 generations have passed in Supermania, Conklin's miniature creation. The microcosmic people have developed a superscience, have taken control of their evolution with suitable genetic engineering, and have developed specialist mentalities far beyond those of humanity. * The tiny people are aware of Conklin, who moves along the edges of their world examining them with a telescopic microscope, and can communicate with him with suitable speedup and slowdown apparatus. Such intercourse is necessary, for there are many chemical processes that, for time reasons, Conklin performs for the little people, and he must supply them with raw materials. * Conklin is worried that the tiny people will rebel and destroy him, and the little people are secretly worried about their fate after he dies or should he try to kill them. So far Conklin has been able to keep the upper hand. With his control of their environment, he can render them unconscious and then interfere; indeed, he has already removed potentially threatening equipment and resources. * The little people decide to act against Conklin. They ask him to permit a delegation to enter the outside world so that they can offer their science and wisdom to *Homo sapiens*. Conklin agrees, although he is suspicious. Actually, the Supermanians are seeking information for their revolt and future adaptation to the outside world. They plan to use a sound frequency, emitted by a superviolinist, to drive humanity insane with fear for hours, thus into collapse. To further their plans they breed a being low enough in mentality to communicate readily with Conklin. This creature is so abysmally stupid by Supermanian standards that it has difficulty in mentally extracting cube roots of long numerical sequences. * The delegation arrives, and Conklin enlarges them for temporary adaptation. But things go wrong. The superviolinist who is to play the destructive sound is distracted by a human girl who loves music, and, instead of wiping out *Homo sapiens*, destroys the microcosm. * *Miscellaneous:* The tiny people no longer propagate sexually, but mentally. They are organized into specialist families, members of which are totally adapted to their function: the Pianist has four arms, each hand with twelve fingers, and one enormous ear; the Mathematician has an enormous head and no legs; the Violinist is a long slender strip; the Electronics person is punctured with holes and insulators and lives on electricity. * A peculiar fabular story, very badly organized and written, but occasionally very interesting in idea and subtext, with a wealth of throwaway material. * For a sequel see #1123, "Dr. Conklin, Pacifist."

1123. **DR. CONKLIN, PACIFIST**. *Astounding Stories*, August 1934. Ill. attributed in the heading to Dold, but obviously by Marchioni.

Short story. * This is Conklin's third experiment, the first having been described in #1122, "Short-Wave Castle." The second, which involved normal (though tiny) people, a war of the sexes, then a sexless civilization, boredom, and mass suicide, is mentioned, but does not seem to have been published. * Conklin, who is distressed by the sad state of the world, discovers a small group of cells in the brain that produce the evil component in mankind: hatred, greed, intolerance, aggressiveness. A further

discovery, a ray that knocks out these cells, delights Conklin. With a small band of followers he travels the world, radiating peace and good fellowship, eventually blanketing almost the entire world. Wars stop; Nazis no longer persecute Jews; Russian Communists welcome dissidents; robber barons feel compassion for the poor. * For a short time, the situation seems wonderful, but then the disastrous aspect of Conklin's ray emerges: ambition is gone; men are too squeamish to kill pests and vermin; agriculture collapses; the government is too compassionate to collect taxes; industry falls apart. * Worse yet, Conklin's hated rival, Professor Wales, who has long been working on a death ray, heads a band of fanatics who have escaped Conklin's ray and are engaged in conquering the world. Conklin now invents a ray to restore things to the original status quo. * Intended to be humorous, but too rambling and inconsequential. The point, that evil may have a good, even necessary side, is not well made. * For a sequel see #1124, "Shortwave Experiment."

1124. **SHORTWAVE EXPERIMENT**. *Astounding Stories*, February 1935. Ill. Dold.

Short story. * Sequel to #1123, "Dr. Conklin, Pacifist." * Dr. Conklin, annoyed at the puerility of his daughter's fiancé, Pat, and her own limited range of interests (clothing, food, etc.), has been experimenting with cosmic rays as a means of increasing intelligence. His method works, but as Conklin eventually realizes, it does not affect basic personality or interests. Thus, Pat, instead of enthusing emptily about hockey, now studies the campaigns of Napoleon in order to win games. Conklin is discouraged and destroys his apparatus. * As a side issue, Conklin's domestic animals develop human intelligence and can speak. Thus, the cat and dog converse about the danger from the intelligent wolf pack that intends to besiege the establishment, and the superintelligent parrot gives Conklin advice. * Feeble. Probably intended as humor.

PERIL, MILTON R.

According to Schwartz/Weisinger the pseud. of Francis Arthur Jones, about whom I have no information; the identification has been questioned. It is unlikely, for reasons of quality, that this is Francis Arthur Jones, author of *Thomas Alva Edison* (1931), which went through several editions and retitlings.

1125. **THE DYNASTY OF THE BLUE-BLACK RAYS.** *Amazing Stories*, October 1930. Ill. Morey.

Short story. * *Place:* mostly Peru. * The noted German archeologist Heinrich von Grossbach receives a visit from the American scholar Crowders. Some time before, part way up on a hill hitherto believed to be unclimbable, Crowders had found remains that might tie in with the legend of Tenta Raci and his followers. Tenta Raci was a brother to Manco Capac, the first Inca; he disappeared mysteriously about eight hundred years ago, rapt, according to legend, into the sky. * The two savants go to Peru and with an Indian companion climb the hill, despite great difficulties; they find at the top a tunnel leading into the interior. They descend great distances, after a while finding their way lit by a radiance that the author characterizes as blue with a black rim. * At the bottom of the tunnel they are greeted in friendly fashion by a group of Inca Indians, who are eager to learn what has happened in the outside world. * The gimmick is that the Indians, thanks to the blue-black radiation, are eight hundred years old and immortal. They no longer need food and drink. (The explorers already feel themselves rejuvenated after a short

Peril, Milton R. (*continued*)

stay underground.) But the immortality of the Incas is achieved at a price; they are sterile, and they can never leave the area or they will die immediately. Indeed, the explorers had better leave soon or they will never be able to. * Grossbach and his two companions make their way out; behind them they see the hidden cave world explode as water breaks into the (presumably) radioactive rocks. The lost race is gone. * Very badly written and badly edited. For example, the Inca, underground for eight hundred years, counts time by the Christian era.

1126. **THE LOST CITY.** *Amazing Stories,* May-July 1934. Ill. Morey.

Novel. * *Place:* a hidden world under Egypt. * Sir John Mansfield, great archeologist and Egyptologist, comes into possession of an ancient papyrus manuscript, purportedly written by King Cheops himself. According to the papyrus, Cheops received a strange visitor, a tall light-complexioned man who claimed that he was an Atlantean. Cheops was at first incredulous, but the man took him to an underground world, where refugees from Atlantis had settled and lived peacefully since the Submersion. With the agreement of the Atlanteans, Cheops sealed off the hidden world, and to disguise the entry built a temple in the form of an animal with a human head over it, surrounding this Sphinx with pyramids to distract attention from it. Cheops also gives directions for entering the underground world through the Sphinx. * Mansfield, following instructions (which amount to inserting a knife edge into various masonry joints), after considerable peril from being trapped alive, finds himself in the midst of a rejoicing crowd—the men of Atlantis. Since Ancient Egyptian is their tongue, conversation is easy enough. * Although Cheops did not say so in his manuscript, the people of Atlantis possessed something of a superscience, which has maintained them underground. When Cheops sealed off Atlantis, the Atlanteans retained a quota of Nubian slaves, whom they have maintained as servants. These slaves, as Sir John learns, are incredibly animal-like and vicious and must be kept down by force and terror. The chief barrier against them is a wall and a pit of flesh-consuming amoeboid matter, though paralysis rays are also effective. * Mansfield is welcomed, indeed, his arrival has been watched step by step through viewers, and he immediately falls in love with the beautiful blonde Venia, daughter of the high priest. Soon after Mansfield's arrival a slave revolt takes place. After this is quelled, Mansfield watches Atlantean surgeons piece together mortally wounded Atlanteans in almost instant cures and subject the blacks to triage executions. * A crisis comes during still another insurrection, when the blacks kidnap Venia, whom the charismatic black leader plans to sacrifice. After considerable bloodshed (in which Mansfield with bare hands and pistol kills several dozen gigantic blacks), Mansfield kills the black leader and rescues Venia. * At this point, one of the mysteries of the land is explained. At intervals a gigantic voice has been booming through the chambers making astute comments and bearing news. No explanation has been offered for it, and the underground people take it for granted as the word of divinity. But now Mansfield is taken aloft through the roof of the temple, into a hidden suite of rooms where he encounters the source of the voice: Cheops himself, who has maintained life through an Atlantean invention that he has kept private. Cheops is friendly and offers Mansfield an assistantship, but at this point the mother of all insurrections breaks out. The

blacks destroy the apparatus restraining the amoeboid, and in a final debacle, blacks, Atlanteans, and amoeboid are tangled up together. Mansfield and Venia manage to escape by the river exit, but it seems as if Atlantis is gone. Further attempts to reenter the Sphinx have been unsuccessful. * Badly written, clichéd in idea, and one of the two most racist documents examined in this survey, the other being Dr. Keller's "The Menace."

PERRY, JAMES D.

Perhaps James D. Perry (1895-?), author of mystery novel *Murder Walks the Corridors* (1937), although in terms of literary quality the identification seems improbable.

1127. **DEATH BETWEEN THE PLANETS.** *Wonder Stories,* November 1933. Ill. Paul.

Short story. * *Place:* mostly an unidentified planet or planetoid, perhaps a second moon. * A meteorite strikes in New England, and in its fragments is found a cylinder containing a manuscript. It is the story of Rusty, explaining his fate. Obeying the summons of his former girlfriend, Joan, Rusty visited her at her husband Ivan's laboratory in New Jersey. Ivan, a mad scientist who is badly disabled from a scientific accident, has built a small spaceship and plans to shoot Joan off in it. Joan escapes with Rusty's help, but now Rusty is going to be the space monkey. * The ship leaves with the unconscious Rusty, who awakens on a strange low-gravity land lit by a violet light. Following metal tracks, he has the misfortune to step on a small creature like a beetle that is riding in an electric contrivance. Before long he is captured by the beetle-creatures, who have pain projectors, and, what with his stupendous strength, is put to work carrying heavy objects. Along with him work small, primitive semihumanoid creatures. * The beetle-people are apparently unhappy with him, for they reerect his spaceship and send him packing back to Earth, where he crashes as a meteorite. * The author does not identify the locale, which may be a secondary moon, as in Roy Rockwood's *The City beyond the Clouds.* * Very amateurish.

PETERS, WOODS

U.S. author, then resident of Hawaii. No other information, but probably a very young man.

1128. **WHEN INCA-LAND REVOLTED.** *Amazing Stories,* August 1930. Ill. Briggs.

Short story. * *Time:* 1964. *Place:* the United States and Peru. * *Background:* After the conquest of the Inca empire, certain of the Incas and the Mongols took refuge in a hidden Andean valley, where they began a strong, independent scientific development. The new race, which is now somewhat superior scientifically to the outside world, is called the Ingol. * In 1964 Ingol planes raid San Francisco, Manila, Berlin, and Shanghai, leaving them cities of the dead. Ingol aircraft (which use atomic energy and a rocket principle) are so far superior to those of the outside world that there is no defense against them. After this a projection appears at a presidential conference, demanding that the nations of the world surrender, accept Ingol governors, turn over their wealth so that sun temples can be founded, and provide a dozen virgins per nation each year for human sacrifice. The president stalls for time. * Meanwhile an American photographer accidentally stumbles on the process that the Ingols use for making projections and operating their far-viewing and far-hearing machines. With this discovery the nations of the outside

Peters, Woods (*continued*)

world locate the Ingol stronghold, destroy the Ingol fleet, and force the Ingol chiefs to surrender. * Not very good. It is not clear what connection the Incas would have with Mongols.

1129. **THE GREAT CATASTROPHE OF 2947.** *Amazing Stories*, May 1931. Ill. Morey.

Short story. * *Time:* Despite the advanced date in the title, there is no indication that story-time is later than the last quarter of the twentieth century. *Place:* Hawaii, and caverns beneath. * Since the middle of the twentieth century there have been frightful earthquakes, and major cities like Paris have been destroyed by a process that seems to release molecular bonds. No explanation is available. * In Hawaii, where the tremors are closely monitored, the volcanoes have suddenly become inactive. The narrator, a reporter wandering through the crater of Mauna Loa, enters an underground passage where he is captured by tiny humanoid beings. Masters of an advanced science with antigravity helmets and molecular decomposers, they take him to their Queen Kasala, who informs him that she is Pele, the fire-goddess of Hawaii. * *Background:* Communication is easy; the underground people have learned English by following surface radio broadcasts. Despite their isolation, the underground people are affected by surface events and vice versa. When they create new tunnels by disintegrating matter, the gases released cause earthquakes and volcanic eruptions. And radio beams from the surface, when they come into contact with excavating rays, can cause violent explosions in the underground realm. At the moment Queen Kasala intends to remedy this situation by conquering the surface world. What with antigravity and disintegrators it seems as if the conquest will be easy. * The narrator, who is supposed to serve as a consultant to Kasala, instead misleads her as to suitable targets and also manages to communicate with the surface. The underground people are fascinated by music, which they do not possess, and when the narrator builds a xylophone, the queen is delighted. She does not know that he is playing messages in Morse code. * When the small people begin to emerge, the outside military is ready for them, and after a series of debacles, Kasala is willing to talk peace. Grievances adjusted, there is now friendly commerce between surface and underground peoples. * The author does not give the history of the little people, so that it is not clear whether they originated on the surface or are a separate group. In any case, a rather low-grade epigone of Bulwer-Lytton's *The Coming Race*.

PHILLIPS, ALEXANDER [MOORE] (1907-1991)

U.S. (Pennsylvania) author, born in Philadelphia. Occupation architectural draftsman. Contributed eight other stories to the fantastic pulps. Short fantastic humor novel "The Mislaid Charm" (*Unknown*, February 1941; Prime Press, Philadelphia, 1947) was popular at one time.

1130. **THE DEATH OF THE MOON.** *Amazing Stories*, February 1929. Unsigned ill.

(Reprinted in Wollheim, *Flight into Space*.)

Short story. * Perhaps the first version of a standard theme in early science-fiction. *Time and place:* North America during the Mesozoic. * There but for the grace of God. . . The Moon is a dying planet, and the Lunarians must find a new home. Their greatest scientist has perfected a means of interplanetary travel, and he and a band of selected scientists intend to explore Earth

for possible colonization. Only the master scientist possesses the knowledge for space travel. * It is the misfortune of the Lunarians that they land near the stamping grounds of a particularly active Tyrannosaurus rex, who does not appreciate the pathos of their situation and insists on eating them. Lunarian rays are just not strong enough to cut him down in time. The Lunarian explorers are all killed, and the Lunarians on the moon cannot mount another expedition. * Told in somewhat purple prose, partly personalized dinosaur, partly lunar predicament. According to Robert Madle, Phillips first wrote the story as a high school exercise; the teacher rejected it with scorn, but Gernsback later published it.

1131. **MARTIAN GESTURE.** *Wonder Stories*, October 1935. Ill. Schneeman.

Novelette. * *Time:* the near future. *Place:* Mars and post-holocaust Earth. * Although the author expends a great many words, the story line is simple. Martian astronomers see strange flashes of light on Earth and wonder about them. They are concerned, apart from curiosity, lest a catastrophe that may be befalling Earth may also affect their own planet. After some argument, a pioneer spaceship that had been intended for the exploration of Jupiter is diverted to Earth. * The Martians land on Earth, where they find the atmosphere and gravity difficult, but bearable. As they explore, they find everywhere scenes of horrible disaster, ruined cities, air polluted with poisonous gas, and enormous quantities of corpses. Eventually they encounter and capture what may be the last human being. * When the Martians are able to communicate with him, they learn that the cause of destruction was something alien to their experience—warfare. The nations of Earth exterminated one another. The Martians return to Mars with the Earthman. * *Miscellaneous:* The Martians are humanoid with two arms and legs, but with multiple fingers. As protection against cold and atmospheric loss they have developed very thick, impervious skin. * Of no interest.

PHILLIPS, FRANK

Pseud. of Philip Francis Nowlan, who has a separate entry.

1132. **THE ONSLAUGHT FROM VENUS.** *Science Wonder Stories*, September 1929. Ill. Paul.

Short story. * *Time:* the near future. *Place:* the New York area and Brazil. * *Background:* The inhabitants of Venus, who are completely human in appearance, but metabolically different from mankind, are forced by the imminent volcanic destruction of their planet to abandon it en masse. Almost fifty thousand space shots carry about fifty million Venusians toward Earth, but only about 1500 vessels reach their destination, the others either missing their target or being destroyed by meteors. Terrestrial astronomers have seen the flashes on Venus, but all concerned have interpreted them as only explosions; hence the Earth is not prepared for an invasion and has no real defence, apart from routine aerial patrols. * The narrator, a member of the Air Guard, is at the action center for most of the invasion of the Earth. During an air battle over the space shot that landed in Northern Mexico, his plane becomes disabled, and he is captured. It is quite possible that he is the only captive in North America. * As he watches from within the Venusian landing place, men and women set up ray projectors that provide a "magnetic" shield against metal objects. Thus, bombs dropped by the Air Guard bounce off, although the explosions cause casualties from concussion. The Venusians also fight Terrestrial

Phillips, Frank (*continued*)

aircraft with vacuum bombs. * As the narrator later learns, if the Venusians were able to set up their projectors in time, Terrestrial forces could do little or nothing against them, but the Venusians often failed to do so. * Held a captive, the narrator is compelled to teach English to certain of the Venusians, after which he is told frankly that he has been spared because he is the only captive capable of helping the Venusians to build airplanes that will function in Earth's atmosphere. If he does not cooperate, he will be killed. * The threat is not an empty one, for the Venusians are utterly without mercy and cannot even comprehend treating with Earthmen. Indeed, when he suggests negotiations to his female instructor, his statement is taken as an unforgivable insult. But the narrator eventually escapes and bears very useful information to military headquarters. * The war goes on, not wholly to the advantage of the Venusians. They do not tolerate Earth's dryness and heavy solar radiation well and are comfortable only at nights in rainfall or jungle mist. As a result, they withdraw their forces from most of the Earth and concentrate them in the jungles of Brazil, where Earthmen have great difficulty in fighting them. * The Earthmen have had some success in attacking individual sites, but at heavy cost, succeeding by sheer weight of numbers. Eventually, with plastic weapons and nonmetallic bombs that are not affected by the magnetic shields, the Earthmen storm the last Venusian fortresses and destroy the invaders. There is no question of surrender or prisoners of war, for, if taken, the Venusians commit suicide. * *Miscellaneous:* The Venusians have dead-white clammy skins, the pores of which soak up atmospheric water; bloodless lips; orange eyes; and yellow hair. For comfort they often wear waterproof suits and helmets to preserve body fluids. The narrator finds Venusian women sexually repellant. * Both Venusian sexes work alike within the military organization. * Venusian flying machines are mushroom-shaped vehicles that move too slowly to fight Terrestrial vehicles, but are protected by ray envelopes. * Venusian society is based on an extended basis of self-interest, without familial love. * When the Venusians first landed, they employed excavating machines that turned rock into lava, then formed it into structures. During the last battle the Venusians used these devices to create lava flows against the Terrestrial infantry. * Similar in theme to Will McMorrow's "The Sun-Makers" (*Argosy*, 1925), but original in development. Competent pulp action.

PIERCE, JOHN [ROBINSON] (1910-present)

Distinguished U.S. scientist, engineer. Born in Des Moines, Iowa. Long director of Bell Telephone Research Laboratories; later Professor of Electrical Engineering at California Institute of Technology. Member of President's Advisory Committee. Recipient of many awards and honorary degrees, long listing in *Who's Who in America*. Many technical studies. Also wrote under pseud. J. J. Coupling, with articles in later *Astounding Science Fiction*. An excellent popularizer. At the time of writing "The Relics from the Earth," a student at Caltech.

1133. **THE RELICS FROM THE EARTH.** *Science Wonder Stories*, March 1930.

Short-short story. * The second-prize-winning story in the contest based on the cover of November 1929 *Science Wonder Stories*. Pierce received $75. * The story, set in the undated future, is narrated by the leader of an expedition from Triton to recover symbolic souvenirs of mankind's past, the Eiffel Tower

and the Woolworth Building. Because of overwhelming insects, humanity had been forced to abandon Earth and move to Triton. * There is an accident along the way back, as a meteor hits the narrator's flying saucer, but he survives and returns to Triton.

1134. **ADRIFT IN THE VOID.** *Wonder Stories*, June 1934. Ill. Paul.

Short story. * *Time:* the interplanetary future. *Place:* the Earth-Mars run. * The spaceship *Astra* has been badly damaged by a meteor, and the call has come to abandon ship. The situation is desperate, with fire and partial loss of air. By stopping to help fellow-passenger Myria, Mark misses his chance to enter the last lifeboat. He and Myria are now abandoned on the disabled vessel, which is rapidly deteriorating. The two enter the refrigeration chamber, which has its own air supply, and can don spacesuits as a last resort. * Mark comes to the conclusion that the *Astra* was not accidentally damaged, but was attacked by space pirates who are after its cargo of platinum. He is soon proved right, for Martian pirates add to the difficulties Mark and Myria face. With luck and bravery, however, they hold out until a cruiser of the space police arrives and rescues them. * Plotwise, the story is routine, but what is remarkable is the intense atmosphere of conviction that the story carries, the verisimilitude that the author attains.

1135. **PRE-VISION.** *Astounding Stories*, March 1936. Ill. Marchioni.

Short story. * *Time:* presumably the near future. * Brilliant young mathematical physicist Hardy Stuart, convinced that the Maxwell electromagnetic equations permit interpretation of the future as well as of the past, is constructing a device to prove his point. His colleagues, even Rhonda, his boss's daughter (who loves him though he is not perceptive enough to see it), consider his quest chimerical, but he continues his work despite obstacles personal and technical. * His first success comes when his viewing plate shows a scene in his laboratory, not too clearly, but revealing a body on the floor. At this point, the device explodes, and Hardy becomes the body on the floor. Recovered from his injuries, Hardy continues his work in secret, rebuilding his device. The second viewing, also of his laboratory, shows his friend and physician dropping dead. So it happens. The third viewing shows Rhonda becoming involved in a traffic accident on leaving the laboratory. Hardy dashes out and manages to save her, though he himself is injured. He finally realizes that he loves her. * As he recovers in the hospital, he wonders whether the machine can show only images of death and peril? Future work will tell. * Not bad.

PLUNKETT, CYRIL

U.S. author, then resident in Fremont, Ohio. Accompanying portrait shows a young man.

1136. **THE X-GAS.** *Air Wonder Stories*, March 1930. Ill. Winter.

Short story. * *Time:* 1949. *Place:* Brazil. * The United States has defeated Brazil in a war, and the superdirigible *C49* is picking up a load of bullion as war reparations. Commodore Montfort is showing three Brazilian delegates over the *C49* as a courtesy. As he describes it: The dirigible is lifted by X-gas, a new discovery that is also a very useful poison gas. With a ceiling of ten miles and a load of gas bombs, the *C49* is practically unconquerable. * The Brazilians, however, plot. Lieutenant Grennen, while off duty, is drugged with a truth

Plunkett, Cyril (*continued*)

serum so that he reveals everything about the ship. Acting on his information three airplanes land on the *C49*'s top surface and Brazilians seize the vessel. It looks bad, but Grennen, who was wrongfully placed under arrest for drunkenness as an aftermath of his drugging, comes to the rescue. First, he recaptures the ship; then saves the ship from destruction by leaping overboard to his death with an exploding bomb. * The ship also has a device that is both a far viewer and a shield against far viewing. * Of no interest. The title is given variously as "The X-Gas" and "The X Gas."

PODOLSKY, EDWARD

Perhaps Edward Podolsky, M.D., New York author of popular medical books. Social Security records list an Edward Podolsky (1902-1965), resident of New York.

1137. DEATH BY RADIO. *Amazing Stories,* December 1932. Ill. Morey.

Short-short story. * *Time:* the near future. * Professor Van Sicklen is found mysteriously dead in his laboratory. An autopsy shows that he died of hydrocyanic acid poisoning—but there is no evidence of poison in the laboratory. * Dr. Wald, Van Sicklen's associate, explains matters. Van Sicklen had invented the scentograph, an apparatus for wireless transmission of scent, which is described as a vibratory phenomenon like Hertzian waves. For a time he experimented with perfumes, but just before his death he insisted that Wald transmit the scent of hydrocyanic acid gas. Finis. Wald is held blameless.

POE, EDGAR ALLAN (1809-1849)

Great American poet, critic, fiction writer, essayist, editor. Information about his life and achievements is so readily available and widely known that they need not be described here. His position in fantastic literature in general is covered in *The Guide to Supernatural Fiction* and in *Science-Fiction: The Early Years.* Poe's relation to science-fiction is peripheral, despite his primacy in supernatural fiction, and the following stories are mostly either outside the form or marginal. There would be little point in listing reprint locations or anthologizations of the following stories, all of which are readily available in innumerable editions. A good collection which contains most of them, with excellent historical and critical notes, is *Science Fiction of Edgar Allan Poe,* ed. by Harold Bever, Penguin, Harmsworth, England and New York, 1976. The best textual edition is *Collected Works of Edgar Allan Poe,* edited by Thomas Ollive Mabbott and associates, and published by Harvard University Press.

1138. MS. FOUND IN A BOTTLE. *Amazing Stories,* March 1934.

(First published in the [Baltimore] *Sunday Visiter* for 10 October 1833. First book publication in *Tales of the Arabesque and Grotesque,* 1840.)

Poe's first published story, it won a $50 prize and encouraged him to enter the life of letters. It is not science-fiction, but a metaphoric story, the exact meaning of which has been debated by scholars. * The narrator, a dealer in antiquities, is storm-tossed on a sinking vessel when he is flung aboard an ancient ship that passes over his former vessel, sinking it. The ship is weird: the crew and captain, who are clad in old-fashioned clothing, go about their tasks like automata, without heeding

him; and the ship itself is constructed of a strange swollen wood. The ancient vessel heads south, and just as it seems about to sink into a whirlpool, the narrator tosses his story overboard in a bottle. * The story has been interpreted as an allegory of discovery, with the captain perhaps Columbus; the whirlpool has been interpreted as Symmes's Hole, leading to the interior of the hollow Earth, although this interpretation does not seem likely. Other interpretations for both points are possible.

1139. A DESCENT INTO THE MAELSTROM. *Amazing Stories,* February 1934.

(First published in *Graham's Gentleman's and Lady's Magazine,* May 1841. First published in book form in *Tales by Edgar A. Poe,* 1845.)

Short story. * Not science-fiction, merely a description of a perilous adventure in the Maelstrom off the coast of Norway. The story is sometimes taken as implying an entry to the interior of the hollow Earth via Symmes's Holes, but this is farfetched.

1140. THE GOLD BUG. *Amazing Stories,* April 1934.

(First published in *Dollar Newspaper,* 21 and 28 June 1843. First published in book form in *Prose Romances,* 1843.)

Short story. * Not science-fiction, but a good tale of ratiocination. A slip of parchment with strange symbols is analyzed by letter frequency as a cryptogram locating Captain Kidd's treasure. The story is perhaps the first popular exposition of code-busting, a fascinating account.

1141. THE BALLOON HOAX. *Amazing Stories,* April 1927. Unsigned ill.

(First published in the *Extra* [New York] *Sun* 13 April 1844. First published in book form in *The Works of the Late Edgar Allan Poe,* 1850-1856.)

Short story. * Borderline science-fiction at best. A hoaxing report of a transatlantic balloon flight accomplished by historical persons: Thomas M. Mason, Robert Holland, and W. H. Ainsworth. The fanciful element is a spring-driven propeller in the form of an Archimedean screw. The balloonists had planned to float to France but, since the balloon was operating so well, instead flew across the Atlantic, landing in South Carolina.

1142. MESMERIC REVELATION. *Amazing Stories,* May 1926. Unsigned ill.

(First published in *Columbia Lady's and Gentleman's Magazine,* August 1844. First published in book form in *Tales by Edgar A. Poe,* 1845.)

Short story. * One of Poe's lesser works, best considered as an advance version of "The Facts in the Case of M. Valdemar." * Vankirk, who has been mesmerized previously, agrees to let the narrator mesmerize him again. While in the mesmeric sleep, Vankirk describes a philosophical and religious system that amounts to a qualified monism. But when the narrator tries to awaken Vankirk, he discovers that Vankirk is dead. The question is whether Vankirk, speaking after death, has offered a veridical solution to great problems of life. * One of Poe's half-hoaxes, based on the contemporary theory of animal magnetism as a means of arousing, via the unconscious mind, knowledge beyond the ken of the conscious mind. * Questionable as science-fiction.

1143. THE THOUSAND-AND-SECOND TALE OF SCHEHERAZADE. *Amazing Stories,* May 1928. Ill. Paul.

(First published in *Godey's Lady's Book,* February 1845. First published in book form in *The Works of the Late Edgar Allan Poe,* 1850-1856.)

Poe, Edgar Allan (*continued*)

A fictionalized essay in which the wonders of mid-nineteenth century science and technology are ironically described in terms of *The Arabian Nights*. Scheherazade, who is the storyteller, Islamicizes the Victorian world as the last adventure of Sindbad the Sailor. Unfortunately, the king is not in a receptive mood for her metaphor and is alternately bored and offended. At the end Scheherazade gets the bowstring. * Amusingly written, a good jeu d'esprit, but is it science-fiction?

1144. **THE FACTS IN THE CASE OF M. VALDE-MAR**. *Amazing Stories*, April 1926. Ill. F. S. Hynd.

(First published in the *American Review*, December 1845. First separate publication as *Mesmerism. "In Articulo Mortis,"* 1846.) One of the most anthologized stories in fantastic fiction. It is sometimes reprinted under such variant titles as "M. Valdemar," "The Case of M. Valdemar," etc.

Short story. * The narrator, who is a mesmerist, places his dying friend Valdemar into a trance. Valdemar is dead, but, preserved from decay by the magnetic fluid, retains a sort of pseudolife, speaking and making slight movements in response to the mesmerist's passes and gestures. This continues for about seven months. Finally, the narrator decides to awaken Valdemar. And Valdemar dissolves into a mass of decay. * A very effective story, of great historical influence in modern supernatural fiction, particularly in the work of H. P. Lovecraft and his school.

1145. **THE SPHINX**. *Amazing Stories*, July 1926. Unsigned ill.

(First published in *Arthur's Lady's Magazine*, January 1846. First published in book form in *The Works of the Late Edgar Allan Poe*, 1850-1856.)

Short story. * Proportion and perception. The narrator, taking refuge in the country from the cholera in New York City, depressed and dejected, upon looking out of the window sees a horrible monster descending a hill. Seemingly as large as a ship, it is equipped with wings, a long deadly proboscis, and tusks. To fit the narrator's association with death in the city, the monster has a death's-head on its breast. * Upset by this vision, the narrator tells his friend, who sees nothing. On a later occasion, however, the narrator sees the horror again. His friend explains it: The narrator has placed his face too close to the window, and his eye is magnifying a death's head moth.

1146. **MELLONTA TAUTA**. *Amazing Stories*, November 1933.

(First published in *Godey's Lady's Book*, February 1849. First published in book form in *The Works of the Late Edgar Allan Poe*, 1850-1856.)

Short epistolary story. * A letter dated April 1st, A.D. 2848, from a young lady who is ballooning. The young lady, who is flighty and very badly informed, "ranges disastrously over systems of logic, premodern manufactures, personalities in American history, and general nineteenth-century culture." Her point of view is antimodern, being conservative, politically, and culturally reactionary. * Amusing despite its crotchets and quavers.

1147. **VON KEMPELEN AND HIS DISCOVERY**. *Amazing Stories*, July 1927. Unsigned ill.

(First published in the *Flag of Our Union*, 14 April 1849. First published in book form in *The Works of the Late Edgar Allan Poe*, 1850-1856.)

Short story. * *Place:* Bremen, Germany. * A chatty involuted story about alchemy. Von Kempelen, whom the narrator knows, has been arrested in Bremen for coining. The charge, however, is unjustifiable, for Von Kempelen is really manufacturing gold out of lead. * The main result of the arrest is that the price of gold has fallen and that of lead has risen.

POOL, CHARLES B.
No information.

1148. **JUSTICE OF THE ATOMS**. *Wonder Stories*, July 1935. Ill. Winter.

Short story. * *Place:* Oakbury, an imaginary town in upstate New York. * Crime busting and various mystery situations. A large hobo inexplicably appears in a prison cell. A block of concrete crashes down upon the desk of the crooked district attorney—but no concrete had been above the desk. Newspaper reporter Freeman, unjustly accused of murder, inexplicably turns up in Canada, where he finds political asylum. * The background for these mysteries is the crime situation in Oakbury, where gangster chief Black Golo, despite his thirty-two murders and other crimes, is immune from punishment because of his political connections. Working on the various cases is newspaper reporter Ladory. * Behind the mysterious phenomena is a public spirited, pseudonymous inventor, who has developed matter transmission on the basis of electrolysis. The inventor, using his device, kidnaps Golo and his henchmen and distributes their molecules up and down the Mississippi River Valley. * Reasonable crime thriller.

POSTLETHWAITE, LEVITICUS WILMINGTON, D.T.G.
According to Schwartz/Weisinger, the pseud. of Kenneth Sterling, who has a separate entry.

1149. **THE SLITHERING HORROR**. *Wonder Stories*, October 1935.

A short piece in the letter column. The first-person narrator describes his sensations as the horrible creature draws near him. He is paralyzed with fright, hypnotized by its green eyes. * But his friend awakens him from his spell, asking him if he is going to stare at that darn fish forever. The aquarium will shortly close. * The title referent and the subject matter are more for *Weird Tales* than *Wonder Stories*, but the storiette is amusing. * At the end of the piece a rejection notice is printed; this is said to reproduce an actual rejection slip from *Amazing Stories*.

PRAGNELL, FESTUS (1905-1965)
British writer. Sometime resident in Southampton. Served on London police force. An occasionally clumsy but imaginative spare-time writer, who published a fair amount of fiction in the American pulps. His better work is strongly in the tradition of H. G. Wells. An interesting writer, with a good imagination, who stood on the edge of importance. It is occasionally stated that Pragnell was a pseud. (for Ray Palmer, among others), but this is incorrect. Pragnell's later work is much inferior. * See also joint work done as R. F. Starzl and Festus Pragnell.

1150. **MEN OF THE DARK COMET**. *Wonder Stories*, June 1933. Ill. Paul.

Short story. * *Time:* the interplanetary future. *Place:* space and a controlled planetoid. * *Background:* The plant people of the dark comet had developed a high, completely fulfilled civilization on a world light-years way, when they learned that their planet would soon be destroyed by a cosmic collision.

Pragnell, Festus (*continued*)

Hollowing out a small moon, they fitted it up as a space station and set out across the cosmos to locate a suitable sun around which to orbit. Since their world has no gaseous cometary matter, it can only be seen as it occludes the stars. * The story is concerned with Captain Heathcote of the *Aristotle*, voyaging from Ganymede to Earth, and passenger Boddington, a former drug addict who had served his prison term on Ganymede. Heathcote, although a very capable man, is rigid, unimaginative, and intolerant. Boddington, although a feckless "decadent," is imaginative and perceptive. * The two men find themselves the only survivors on the ship; Martians on board have released a poisonous narcotic gas and have hijacked the cargo of a rare industrial metal. Heathcote draws the obvious conclusion: The Martians are stockpiling the metal in order to build a space navy for a surprise attack on Earth. * The disabled *Aristotle* crash-lands on the invading planetoid, and Heathcote and Boddington are rescued by the plant-men, who look like desiccated trees. The plant-men, who possess a totally rational culture, are hospitable, but communication between them and the humans is very difficult. Some headway is made by simple signal ingenuity, but eventually the plant beings rig up a mechanical telepathic device. It works well enough on Boddington, but not on Heathcote, who resists it. * Life on the planetoid is pleasant enough, particularly for Boddington, who becomes very friendly with one of the alien beings, but the men become homesick, and there is the problem of the Martian attack. At first the cometeers refuse to let them leave, but they finally agree. They refit the *Aristotle* with an immensely improved drive and send it off at a speed nearly that of light. The plant-men continue on their way; our sun has too much ultraviolet for their comfort. * On arriving back on Earth, Boddington and Heathcote discover that they have been away for three years, although in their subjective time it seemed only months. Instead of being welcomed, they are accused of piracy, and their warnings against the Martians are scoffed at. * War does indeed break out. After great difficulty Heathcote and Boddington take the *Aristotle* up into space and with a weapon that the friendly plant man gave Boddington easily annihilate the Martian space armada and devastate Mars. As he promised, Boddington destroys the ray apparatus. Most of the dark planet technology is so advanced that it cannot be even analyzed, but what little can be understood revolutionizes space travel. * *Miscellaneous:* The dark planet travels at a speed greater than that of light, hence it is invisible when approaching the solar system. The plant-men have antigravity. * The Martians, who are in general somewhat inferior scientifically to Terrestrials, have three sexes; members of the one sex on the *Aristotle* are flat, oval, yellow beings. * Some good detail, some attempt at character depiction.

1151. **THE ESSENCE OF LIFE.** *Amazing Stories,* August/September issue, 1933. Ill. Morey.

Novelette. * *Place:* England. * A document written by economist/sociologist Joseph Hammond shortly before his death in an automobile accident. * Hammond, who gives popular lectures, particularly observes one of his audience, a gigantic, powerful, dark man who seems very interested. Hence, it comes as no surprise to the reader when this man (Planco) writes to Hammond requesting a meeting, saying that he will send his car. A Rolls Royce picks up Hammond and takes him to a fashionable town house, where he meets Planco and his wife Kareem.

* Hammond, who has a certain sensitivity, observes that things are wrong. The Plancos are obviously not used to Western European social matters, and, horrifying to Hammond, Planco's eyes glow in the dark like a cat's. * With some apologies, Planco explains. He and his wife are student observers, and they have settled on Hammond as the most intelligent, most insightful interpreter of European culture. As for their origin, they claim that they are from Jupiter and demonstrate enough superscience to prove their point. * Planco explains his human appearance by invoking a law of general evolution on many worlds. But when Hammond comments that mankind is the highest life-form, Planco smilingly contradicts him. High as the Jupiterian humans are, there is a higher life-form on Jupiter, the Masters, to whom the humans are pets. Hammond is outraged at the notion and suggests revolution, but is courteously put down by Planco, who says that the humans love their masters. * Since Hammond is sickly, Planco inoculates him with a life essence that will destroy germs and build up his vitality. The essence knocks Hammond unconscious for a time, but the result is remarkable. * On a later occasion, Planco tells Hammond that the Master wants to speak with him. They travel into the countryside to a palatial, guarded estate, where Hammond receives another shock. A picture that he surreptitiously examines reveals that the Master is an octopus-like creature. * The Master converses with him via a mechanical speech box. He has accepted Hammond, he says, as the preeminent authority on mankind and the unofficial representative for mankind. And now he wants Hammond's opinion. Should the Jovians, to advance mankind, give them the elixir? The two discuss the notion briefly, mentioning wars and criminals, until Hammond, without thinking, suggests that the Jovian system of Masters and human pets be established on Earth by the octopoids. He is immediately horrified at what he said, especially when the Master takes the notion very seriously and comments that he will refer it to the chief council on Jupiter. But it is up to Hammond, as representative of Earth, to decide what shall be done. As Hammond leaves, he is torn between dismay and hope. Is the relief from wars, criminality, short lives, and disease worth the subjugation of the human race? He cannot decide. * Hammond's brother, too, cannot decide whether Hammond's document is madness or a veridical account that led him to suicide. * *Miscellaneous:* The Jovians have been exploring space for hundreds of years. They early discovered that unknown interplanetary forces prohibit direct flight. They now use planetary attraction beams that propel or drag ships along seemingly erratic paths. * The Jovian humans are able to exert a certain amount of hypnotic willcontrol. Thanks to the essence of life they live for hundreds of years. * The human Jovians are music lovers, but because of their gigantism, singers in the higher voice ranges do not exist. Hence they particularly like to listen to recordings of Rosa Ponselle and Beniamino Gigli. * An interesting story, far more mature than most of the *Amazing* stories.

1152. **THE ISOTOPE MEN.** *Wonder Stories,* August 1933. Ill. Paul.

Long short story or novelette. * *Time:* the remote past and the twenty-second century. *Place:* mostly Bode's fifth planet. * Professor Barlem has devised a way to recover ancestral memories. The process has not yet been tried on humans, but it has been fatal to dogs. Nevertheless, Barlem's son Christopher volunteers to undergo the experience. He believes that the superior human mentality and will can withstand traumas fatal to research

Pragnell, Festus (*continued*)

animals. Christopher almost dies, but when recovered, tells his story. * He remembers many early lives, most important and clearest of which is that of Hasteen Pollard on the fifth Bodean planet. * *Background:* The nameless planet [now called Bodia] is inhabited by humans with the remains of a superscience, now much in decadence. The culture is rigidly stratified, with superiors and inferiors, thought control, immediate drastic punishment for small offenses, and prohibition of any sort of scientific knowledge or research. (This complex characterizes both Hasteen's northern nation and the hostile southern nation.) * The planet receives its power from a small satellite which beams energy created by atomic disintegration. Small artificial suns in the atmosphere distribute light, heat and power. At one time the moon was much larger than it is, but over the ages loss of matter has reduced it to a critical point; if it loses more mass, it will no longer function. * Dwelling on the moon are scientists who reject the planetary culture and are greatly concerned about the lunar situation. As a peculiarity revealed later, with no great relevance to the story, the bodies of the lunar scientists contain a large quantity of isotopes as a result of their environment. * Hasteen Pollard, a youth of enquiring mind, is observed by the thought police when he trespasses into one of the forbidden libraries. He is thus automatically sentenced to death. His father, however, who is a secret rebel, rays and disintegrates the police and with Hasteen flies away to the south. A cryptic message, perhaps from a political underground, has led him to believe that he will find refuge in the antarctic. * As the two flee southward in their aircraft, war breaks out between north and south. In some ways this helps the fugitives, since the nations are more concerned with battles than with two rebellious individuals. Hiding at times in the artificial suns, maneuvering in the stratosphere, the Pollards reach the antarctic continent, where they crash. Rescued by lunar scientists, they are taken to an underground secret city that the Lunarians maintain. There they learn that the Lunarian scientists plan to abandon the main planet and let the moon crash. They intend to migrate to the third planet, which should be suitable for humans. * Pollard, Sr., a humane man, begs the Lunarians to give the people on the planet a chance at further life, if they reduce energy consumption and plan for the change. * The Lunarians reluctantly agree, and the Pollards and a Lunarian fly secretly to the Pollard home where Pollard, Sr. makes a radio appeal. The result is as the Lunarians predicted. The Pollards are attacked by both populace and police. Pollard, Sr., is killed, and Hasteen, too, would be killed, but the broadcast power goes off and he escapes in the confusion. Almost accidentally he meets the Lunarian fleet at a rendezvous point. As he watches, the falling moon shatters the fifth planet. * While Christopher Barlem remembers no further details, Hasteen must have reached Earth and become one of our ancestors. * *Miscellaneous:* Disintegrator rays are common, as is atomic power. * During the war, the north decisively defeated the south and was in process of exterminating the population when the planet was destroyed. * As is often the case with Pragnell, a wealth of good throwaway detail.

1153. **A VISIT TO VENUS.** *Wonder Stories,* August 1934. Ill. Paul.

Short story. * *Time:* the twenty-third century. *Place:* mostly on Venus. * *Background:* While science and technology have advanced, the human race has degenerated enormously. Uncontrol-lable acromegaly, dwarfism, and various structural abnormalities are very common and usually lead to death. It is assumed that the problem lies in an unidentified vitamin deficiency that is affecting the pituitary gland. * Scientists hope that help can be obtained from Venus, with which there has been some communication. The Venusians claim to understand the human problem, but declare that a solution is too complex to be transmitted by radio. Several attempts at space travel to Venus have been failures. * The ruthless capitalist Loted, who is really the secret ruler of the world, has just received a medical death sentence, hence is in a receptive mood when the young inventor Harley breaks into his apartment and asks for funding to build a spaceship. * Harley questions the good faith of the Venusians, who know how to cure the plague, yet find excuses for not transmitting information. Harley further speculates that the Venusians have sabotaged the Terrestrial space flights. * Why? asks Loted. Why not? replies Harley. * The upshot is that Loted provides money and Harley secretly builds a small spaceship in which the two men set out for Venus, hoping to find there the cure for the plague. They reach their destination without much incident apart from personality clashes between the crooked financier (who admits that one reason for his leaving Earth is the impending collapse of his financial empire) and the somewhat idealistic inventor. * Venus is much like Earth, except that the atmosphere contains less oxygen and more carbonic acid gas. After a narrow escape from carnivorous plants, the explorers are captured by red and purple egg-shaped beings with one leg, two tentacle arms, medial tubes of uncertain function, and eyes on two opposing sides of their body. * These creatures, who are obviously intelligent, communicate with the men telepathically and are most hostile. But the men escape and come into contact with the real rulers of Venus. They now learn that they have been in a zoo. The real rulers, who are also unipeds, have maintained previous explorers from Earth as guinea pigs to test out plagues that they are sending to Earth, ultimately with conquest in mind. They are also releasing spheres filled with disease entities into our atmosphere. * The situation seems hopeless. Escape is impossible, for the telepathic Venusians always know about such things. * The resolution comes when the wicked capitalist Loted betrays his associates for a promise to be cured of acromegaly; when he discovers that the Venusians have no intention of keeping their promise, he flies into a rage too suddenly for Venusian telepathy to forestall him, kills his immediate captors, and makes a broadcast to Earth, explaining what the Venusians are doing. Caught by a Venusian decomposition ray, he dies during his broadcast. The end is thus left open.

1154. **THE GREEN MAN OF GRAYPEC.** *Wonder Stories,* July-September 1935. Ill. Paul.

(Reprinted in book form, in a greatly abridged version, as *The Green Man of Kilsona,* Philip Allan, London, 1936, and Greenberg, New York, 1950.)

Novel in the mode of the early H. G. Wells. * *Place:* an atomic world. * In a framework narrative, Learoy Spofforth, a well-known athlete, visits his brother Charles, a brilliant physicist, who has been experimenting with a microscope so powerful that it can penetrate atomic structure. Scientist Spofforth has also devised an apparatus for transferring personality. In a wholly irresponsible action, he drops the unwitting Learoy's personality into the body of a humanoid being on a proton fragment. * Learoy regains consciousness as Kastrove, a gorilline being with

Pragnell, Festus (continued)

human intelligence who is one of many similar beings attacking a wrecked air vessel on which is a relatively normal young blonde woman. * *Background:* The planet Kilsona is very much like the Earth, most of it being temperate, except for an enormous desert. (As will be seen later, Kilsona is to some extent a metaphor for Earth.) The wildlife, however, is far more intelligent than Terrestrial wildife, so much so that animals are able to understand and utilize weapons. * Kastrove is a green man, a member of one of the major Kilsonan races. The green men are cave dwellers with a very primitive material culture, except that (inexplicably for a time) they possess potent ray guns and their area boasts of an advanced electric plant. They are organized in tribes, with chiefs, subchiefs and warriors; but the chiefs are men normal by human standards. * Issa, the woman trapped in the crashed air vessel, is a member of the second major race, the blond dwellers in the crystal cities. The men of the crystal cities, who are slenderer than most Terrestrials, possess the decayed remnants of a once-high science, but are utterly decadent and vicious. * Between green men and city-dwellers exists a potent hostility that is broken at regular intervals when the city dwellers provide ray guns and service the power equipment for the green men. The two races can inter-breed, the result being a normal human being. The green men accept such crosses, but the city-dwellers do not. This much Kastrove soon learns about his new ambiance. * Kastrove, in what he later recognizes as an act of utter folly (since it involved contact with lethal reptiles in the surrounding swamp), succeeds in capturing the blonde woman. By custom, Issa is his property, although there are personal difficulties before Kastrove is secure in possession of her. Although she at first regards him with abhorrence, his kindness gradually wins her regard and love, and they mate, producing a son who is a normal human. At about this point crises arise. * As Kastrove gradually realizes, his situation is not so simple as he first believed. He learns that questions should not be asked, and that his life is in danger because he been too curious. And he discovers that there is a potent tabu associated with the so-called, mysterious Larbies, who must not be mentioned. * On the critical day, there is a mounting sense of psychological malaise among the cave-dwellers, which comes to a climax when a hitherto invisible aerial dreadnought lands nearby. The cave men, who are now under total willcontrol, produce their children and a quota of young adult males, who are taken into the ship. Kastrove, who has incurred the enmity of the local chief, is one of the draftees; Issa, who has asked to accompany him, is taken along. * *Back-ground:* The hidden springs of Kilsona now emerge. Both the green men and the blond city-dwellers are the creatures of the Larbies, aquatic molluscoid creatures who are telepathic to some extent and have a superscience. The Larbies maintain both human races as breeders of soldiers. They condition the children that they have taken away to utter subservience (which Issa never outgrows), return them to their tribes, and later, when they are adult, use them as cannon fodder. Their enemies, who have withstood them for generations, are the men of Gorlem, small but hardy and tough human fighters, who maintain strongholds underground in a great desert. Invisible Larbie air vessels and Larbie conscripts have not been able to destroy the Gorlemite establishments. * Kastrove's resistance to Larbie hypnotic powers is soon noted by the molluscs, and he is examined under fan-

tastic apparatus. The Larbies apparently accept his strange origin, but consider him beneath notice. * Kastrove and Issa, trained as warriors, fight in camouflaged tanks against Gorlem counterparts. Kastrove, of course, is desperate to escape. His chance comes when he helps a dying, captured Gorlemite to flee from a Larbie fortress. * Kastrove reaches a Gorlem outpost, but has great difficulty in convincing his new captors that he is not a Larbie spy. Eventually, taken to the underground central city of Gorlem, he is examined by scientists who accept the story of his origin. He is more than a curiosity, however, for while Kilsonan science in general is superior to Terrestrial, there are occasional aspects that are more developed on Earth, like supersonics and heavier-than-air flight. Kastrove's unconscious mind proves to be a treasure trove, and thanks in part to his knowledge, the men of Gorlem undertake a major drive to expel the Larbies. * The attempt proves costly and almost leads to total Gorlemite defeat, for the Larbies produce new weapons that seem irresistible. But Gorlem wins, with ultrasonics turning the trick, and Kastrove, now a first-class scientist (the highest rank in Gorlem), can wait without trepidation to be retrieved by his brother. Atomic decades pass; Issa dies; and Kastrove sits waiting, an ancient man. His brother Charles retrieves him back to Earth, but his sanity is temporarily impaired. *Miscellaneous:* At one point Pragnell somewhat unnecessarily develops Kilsona as a metaphor for our own world, social and economic problems and all. * A weak beginning and somewhat misleading frame situation can be overlooked, for in detailed background, scope, plotting, and structure "The Green Man of Graypec" is one of the two or three finest original novels to appear in the early s-f pulp magazines. It was praised by H. G. Wells. * According to Tuck, Pragnell prepared a sequel, "Kastrove the Mighty," which (to my knowledge) has not been published in English, but has appeared in a German translation, *Kastrove der Mächtige* (UZ 1966). I have not seen this.

PRATT, [MURRAY] FLETCHER (1897-1956)

U.S. author, born near Buffalo, New York, most of adult working life in New York City area. Attended Hobart College. In earlier years a newspaper man in Buffalo and on Staten Island, instructor in mail order writing courses, then freelance writer. In addition to science-fiction stories, wrote serious, well-received historical and biographical books. Pratt was also an expert on military history and war games. Pratt's early work (as in this volume) and his later solo science-fiction and fantasy are not important, since although highly intelligent and learned, he was a dull writer and sometimes careless craftsmen. As Sam Merwin stated in "A Nest of Strange and Wonderful Birds" (*The Alien Critic*, August 1974) "His ideas for stories were invariably superb, but he just as invariably lost interest in them before they were finished. I was always having to send them back to have the endings more fully written." * Pratt is remembered today mostly for his collaborations with L. Sprague de Camp, notably short stories, some of which were excellent.

See also various collaborations: Irvin Lester and Fletcher Pratt, Laurence Manning and Fletcher Pratt, I. M. Stephens and Fletcher Pratt; and Fletcher Pratt and B. F. Ruby. The consensus has been that the Lester and Ruby collaborations were not true collaborations, but work performed by Pratt alone, which for reasons best known to himself he published as he did. This may not be correct. Pratt claimed that Irvin Lester was a real person

Pratt, Fletcher (*continued*)

who collaborated with him, as described in the entry under Irvin Lester and Fletcher Pratt.

1155. **THE MAD DESTROYER.**   *Science Wonder Quarterly*, Spring 1930. Ill. Ruger.

Short story. * The narrator, a newspaper reporter, is assigned to interview Professor Brooke, professor of astronomy at the university. The narrator knows that Brooke was once a man of reputation, winning international awards, but rumors have circulated that since the death of his daughter he is not the man he used to be. * Brooke turns out to be an irascible, tyrannical man, who conducts the interview in a sarcastic, heavy-handed way—not unjustifiedly since the reporter obviously does not have adequate scientific background to interview the professor properly. * The gist of the professor's claim: He has solved the three-body problem, and with the mathematics involved (which permits solution of more than three bodies in gravitational relation to one another) has examined the orbit of Eros. According to his calculations, Eros will be dragged off its orbit during its next near approach to Earth in 1934 and will fly into the sun, causing the sun to go nova. The narrator is somewhat incredulous, but the professor's assistant, who is a more reasonable man than Brooke, claims that the figures are valid. * But there is more: Brooke is also a mad scientist who covers the reporter with a pistol and intends to hold him captive. The reporter manages to send a message to his editor. During the following shoot-out the professor is killed and his papers destroyed. The narrator now anxiously awaits 1934. * One of Pratt's better short stories before his series of collaborations with L. Sprague de Camp several years later. The dialogue and characterizations are well handled, and the clichéd subject matter is treated with suitable lightness. There is, of course, a parodic note.

1156. **THE WAR OF THE GIANTS.** *Wonder Stories*, May 1931. Ill. Marchioni.

Short story. * *Time:* the near future. The mode is realism. * An episode in a future battle involving a tank attack on fortified positions that hold robotic automated guns. The story is bracketed by the cold-blooded comments of a general and his staff on calculated loss of men and material to gain a battle advantage. * The inner portion of the story is devoted to the experiences of a rookie tank operator and his comrades in a tank that must be the size of large building. * The general's plan succeeds, but the tank crew is all killed by an air attack. No identification of the enemy is made, although the tankmen are Americans. * Pratt's best story to date. * During my college days one of my instructors, who knew Pratt, described a project that Pratt worked on: shorthand recording of conversations in everyday situations—streets, subway trains, markets, etc. The purpose was to attain realism in fiction. In this story the technique works.

1157. **THE ONSLAUGHT FROM RIGEL.** *Wonder Stories Quarterly*, Winter 1932. Ill. Paul.

(Reprinted in book form as *Invaders from Rigel* by Avalon, New York, 1960, with paperback reprints. The text may be abridged or otherwise altered.)

Novel. * *Time:* 1946 on. *Place:* New York City, New Jersey, Chicago, and a few other places. * The story is concerned with a very peculiar invasion from Rigel, the oddity being that an emanation of "life force" from the invaders' spaceship has turned the population of the Western hemisphere into metal. Most victims became statuary, but a few men and women (whom the invaders plan to use as slaves) are beings of living metal. * The story is told through two groups of the living metal survivors: first, several people in New York City, including Benjamin Franklin Ruby (see comments under the "author" B. F. Ruby); and, second, air pilot Herbert Sherman and exotic dancer Marta Lami, both captured by the invaders. At first the survivors attribute the change to a great comet that approached Earth; actually, the "comet" was the spaceship from Rigel. * Ruby and his few comrades awaken in a typical sleeper-awakes situation in New York, to find themselves transformed; they no longer eat, but receive energy from electric shocks and have to lubricate themselves with oil. Almost immediately they run into difficulty from large bird-like creatures who have airplane forewings, flapping rear wings, and two legs. The birds, who are called dodos, carry light-bombs of great power and endeavor to capture the metal survivors. The metal-men fight off the birds, who are vulnerable, but the humans are usually in a stage of siege. * A new factor enters when an Australian warship enters the local waters. The Australians, who received only a small quantity of the mysterious radiation, were not turned to metal, but the iron in their blood has been changed to cobalt, so that they are blue-skinned. Australia, they inform the Americans, has not suffered so badly as North America, although bombing raids by the birds are not unknown. * The invaders are entrenched, with enormous underground fortifications in the New Jersey area. After repeated minor engagements, the Australians take the offensive against the invaders. With tanks and mobile cannon, the combined Australian and American forces attack, but with limited success. Planes from the Australian warships hold the air against the weird dodos, but on the ground the invader tanks seem invulnerable. * The story shifts to Sherman and Marta. Sherman awakens as a metal-man, and in a short time is captured by the invaders, who might be briefly described as humanized small elephants. The science of the invaders, who are Lassans from a planet of Rigel, is on the whole much superior to human, but, as Sherman learns, they have less knowledge of explosives. In captivity in the Lassan underground fortress, Sherman serves as an involuntary informant via a thought helmet; as consolation he also learns much about the invaders. The Lassans are an aggressive culture that believes it has a Spencerian right to destroy or utilize "lower" lifeforms. Lassan expeditions have already spread death and destruction through many planetary systems. * Sherman escapes with important information that leads to the Lassan defeat and destruction. The final explosion of the Lassan life-force supplies turns the metal men back to human form. * *Miscellaneous:* The Lassans derive the life-force from inside the Earth. * The birds are controlled telepathically by Lassan regulators, as are gigantic apemen whom the Lassans brought with them. * Some story inconsistencies, almost parodic in main outline. The first part is interesting, but the story soon degenerates into routine work. The story would seem to exemplify Sam Merwin's comment cited in the biographical sketch about Pratt, above.

1158. **DR. GRIMSHAW'S SANITARIUM.** *Amazing Stories*, May 1934. Ill. Morey.

(Reprinted in Margulies and Friend, *My Best Science Fiction Story.*)

Short story. * A report on the strange happenings at the

Pratt, Fletcher (*continued*)
had an excellent reputation, but chance brought him to the attention of the police. When the coffin of one of his patients was accidentally knocked open, it proved to contain not a corpse, but a dummy. Further investigation revealed that the good doctor was also a dope peddlar who turned his wealthy patients into addicts, and further (though the significance of this is not clear until later) sold mentally deficient dwarves and midgets to circuses. The bodies of his purportedly dead patients remain missing. * In the sanitarium investigators found in a medicine capsule fragments of a manuscript written in microscopic hand. This fragmentary document reveals what was going on. * John Doherty, an educated police officer who suffered a head wound in a robbery, was sent to Grimshaw's sanitarium for treatment. An observant man, he soon observed Grimshaw's involvement with drugs. But Grimshaw incapacitated him and a friend. Feeding them a new enzyme that he had discovered and destroying their pituitaries, he turned them into micromen, perhaps two or three inches tall. * The manuscript does not reveal how the men escaped, but for a time they survived in primitive fashion in Grimshaw's grounds. Other attempts to capture or kill them proving unsuccessful, Grimshaw has now taken to introducing cats into the garden. . . * The manuscript goes no farther. * The conclusion is that Grimshaw turned his patients into mentally-ill or drug-habituated dwarves and midgets and sold them to circuses. * Routine.

PRATT, [MURRAY] FLETCHER and RUBY, B. F.
According to Rock and Tuck, Ruby here is a pseud. for Pratt. Benjamin Franklin Ruby, it will be remembered, is a character in #1157, Pratt's "The Onslaught from Rigel." It may be significant that in Groff Conklin's *Omnibus of Science Fiction*, which reprints "The Thing in the Woods," Pratt alone is indicated as copyright holder. See also the separate entry for Ruby.

1159. **THE THING IN THE WOODS**. *Amazing Stories*, February 1935. Ill. Morey.
(Reprinted in Conklin, *Omnibus of Science Fiction*.)
Short story. * Parker and Bradley, mycologists at Central Packing Company, observe a very strange weed fungus. It looks like a tiny puffball, but it moves about with a rolling motion. The men nurture it and watch it carefully as it grows at an inordinate rate. It does not seem to be a fruiting body, like other mushrooms (or else Pratt and Ruby were ignorant of fungous forms), but is itself a plant capable of fertilization. Indeed, as is observed, it enlarges its diet by rolling around after insects and other small forms of life. * Its growth, however, is geometric, and on the weekend when the men go to a command performance at their boss's, the fungus, which is now seven feet high, escapes. * As might be expected, it rolls around the countryside eating animals and humans. Police bullets do not seem to bother it much, but when Parker sprays it with a solvent for cellulose, it collapses away. * In all probability, Pratt was not serious when he wrote this.

PRESTON, ROBERT PAGE
No information.
1160. **LAND OF TWILIGHT**. *Amazing Stories*, November 1934-January 1935. Ill. Morey.
Novel. * *Time:* 2004 on, with a frame situation from 2034.

Place: Mercury. * Ersatz Edgar Rice Burroughs. * A manuscript transmitted from Mercury a generation after the events described. * David Garfield and stowaway friend Bill Hughes leave on a rocket flight to the Moon; it seems to be the first such flight, although the author does not specify this. In any case, near the Moon their ship is disabled by an electrical storm and driven off course toward the sun, but by a lucky chance, the travelers are able to land safely on the small temperate zone of Mercury. * *Background*: This portion of Mercury is hot and tropical, with innumerable giant carnivores, reptilian and otherwise, and lush vegetation. It is inhabited by three races of men. The subhuman Dars, who are muscle-bound and simian, are very primitive in culture and very numerous; they like to eat the Vereans. The human and friendly Vereans are few in number and live in a beleaguered valley; they are somewhat more advanced than the Dars. The human but nasty Nimara, who are encountered only in the last few pages of the novel, are civilized, with good mechanized ground transportation, cities, impenetrable armor, and poison gas projectors. * David and Bill rescue a beautiful young Verean woman (Dianna) from her Dar captors, but are themselves captured and taken away separately. David, after a short time, is rescued by Dianna, and they make their way to her land, where David is welcomed. Bill, on the other hand, undergoes long captivity among the Dars, whom he civilizes to some extent, teaching them the use of fire. * David and the Vereans, with the resources of the spaceship, fight off attacks by hordes of Dars and rescue Bill. After this, an amnesty is arranged between the two peoples, with a promise of peace and shares of civilization. * The Earthmen and Dianna, however, are captured and enslaved by the Nimara, who have a cruel culture. But our friends escape and make their way back to Verean territory, which will be developed. * Probably the work of a very young man. Very amateurish in development, clichéd in idea.

PRINGLE, ALFRED
No information.
1161. **INTO THE VALLEY OF DEATH**. *Amazing Stories*, February 1930. Ill. Hugh Mackay.
Short story. * *Place:* Los Angeles and Death Valley. * A strange client who looks wild and makes extravagant claims visits the office of patent attorneys Harding and Parsons. The stranger, Miller by name, points out the faults of conventional weapons and describes his invention, a device for focusing sound waves so powerful that they amount to disintegration rays. He demonstrates his invention, which is genuine enough, and suggests a large-scale test in Death Valley, where he has a small secret laboratory. * The men proceed to Death Valley, where Miller rips up boulders and tears down cliffs to demonstrate the power of his device. * But it gradually becomes clear that he is mad and that he intends to destroy Los Angeles. When Parsons chances to wonder whether there is a defense against the ray, Miller flies into a fury and turns on both the ray and its defense, in an attempt to kill the two men. They survive the resulting explosion, but Miller and his weapon are destroyed. * Good dialogue, but a contrived ending.

PROUT, BENT
No information.
1162. **THE SINGING WEAPON**. *Amazing Stories*, May 1927. Unsigned ill.

Prout, Bent *(continued)*
Short story. * *Time:* 1945. * Young Josef Kelinev would like to become a scientist, but his father, a musician, insists that Josef follow his path. But when old Feodore shatters a precious glass with the vibrations of his violin, the two men undertake a study of the destructive effects of vibration. * Their work comes in handy, for the United Asiatic Nations unexpectedly attacks the United States. The Asiatics seem undefeatable. Their armored helicopters drop virulently poisonous gas bombs on San Francisco, and New York City comes under attack. The American government refuses surrender terms that the Asiatics offer—repeal of the Asiatic Exclusion Act and a sizeable indemnity—and the Asiatics continue to press forward. * Old Feodore, however, now brings to the attention of the war department the vibratory weapon he and Josef have created. Manufactured, it breaks the Yellow Menace. * Josef continues to experiment, working toward a vibration that will kill men. He succeeds, and is his own first victim.

PURCELL, ARTHUR
U.S. author, then resident of Canoga Park, California.

  1163. **POSITIVE INERTIA**. *Astounding Stories,* October 1936. Ill. Flatos.
Short story. * A sports story, probably intended as humor. * Professor Wilson approaches the narrator, the Logan College football coach, with a strange proposition. If the coach will let his son William Wilson play in the crucial game against State, he guarantees victory. * This is puzzling at first, for William is small and unathletic. But Professor Wilson proposes to endow William with a tremendous amount of inertia so that he will easily buck the line. The reason for Wilson's offer? A bequest of one hundred thousand dollars and his son's romance depends on Logan beating State. * Coach Hyde agrees after Professor Wilson provides a demonstration, and the game takes place. As expected, things go wrong, but the situation is a winner for the Wilsons. Coach Hyde, however, is in trouble. * Trivial.

PUTNAM, EDMUND W.
An Edmund Whitman Putnam (1882-1940) was a popular writer on astronomy. Associated with Putnam and Sons Publishers.

  1164. **THE PASSING OF JOHN FORSYTHE**. *Amazing Stories*, September 1930. Ill. Paul.
Short story. * *Time:* the mid-twentieth century. * As a child, the great scientist John Forsythe had an imaginary playmate, a very charming, pretty girl. There was no physical contact, for his dream girl seemed as if in another world. As an adult, Forsythe confides to the narrator (his uncle) that all his great discoveries, all his actions have been done with the assistance or advice of the dream girl. * Forsythe speculates that there is a parallel world, sight of which is either possible or not possible through frequency of brain vibration, but that thought transference takes place between the worlds. Thus, great scientist that he is, Forsythe has constructed an apparatus to lower the vibrations of the other-world to our level. As a result he can see the dream girl and her surroundings. * Acting on a suggestion from his uncle, he now modifies his apparatus so that he can send objects into the other-world. He has many failures, but eventually succeeds. With what may seem foolishness to the reader, he transports an insanely vicious dog into the other-world as the young woman appears. The screen clouds, but the uncle sees

that the dog has been tamed by the young woman. Forsythe then goes through. * Sentimental twaddle, badly presented.

QUIEN SABE
According to Schwartz/Weisinger the pseud. of Numa C. Hero, who also contributed a contest editorial "The Latent Value of Scientifiction" in the Winter 1930 issue of *Amazing Stories Quarterly*. Hero (1887-1982), a graduate of Georgia Institute of Technology, was a prominent engineer and real estate developer in the New Orleans area. * According to Rock and other sources, Harry Bates also used the pseud. Quien Sabe. Indeed, *Twentieth-Century American Science-Fiction Writers* assigns this story to Bates, but the attribution is obviously incorrect.

  1165. **THE CITY OF ERIC**. *Amazing Stories Quarterly*, Spring 1929. Ill. with monogram MA (?).
Short story. * *Place:* mostly Brazil. * The narrator, a journalist, chronicles the McLittle Expedition, which was a follow-up to strange discoveries in the jungles: a sword of unknown metal, a gigantic flying machine, and a robed white man. * The expedition reaches its goal, where the men are confronted by a bearded, elderly white man, who speaks to them in perfect English. * He tells them that since they have come this far, they may continue to the city of Eric, but they can never return to the outside world. * The stranger, Alof by name, wears a sword like the one previously examined; actually, it is not a sword but a sort of activator containing hundreds of thousands of volts of electricity. * Alof uses it to start remarkable vehicles, lift enormous weights, disarm a man, etc. * At the city of Eric, where they will be judged, the explorers are physically examined. The narrator later sees a motion picture of an operation that was performed on him while he was unconscious, to improve his physique. Men with swords used as energy devices sliced him open, remodelled his heart, scraped out his intestines and removed a section, flipped him together, healed him perfectly, all in a matter of a few minutes. * *Background:* The people of Eric take the position that the outside world is not yet ready for their knowledge, citing their own history when they learned science from the Martians and misused it. * Improved, the adventurers are assigned roles in the culture of the city. One member, a big game hunter, is allowed to go to Jupiter on a hunting expedition. The narrator, who has no scientific background, is instructed to write a history of the expedition, here presented. * *Miscellaneous:* Eric, the leader of the city, is a woman. * Spaceships leave periodically for the other planets. * The Martians must be human, since there are persons of mixed Martian-native parentage. * Incoherent, permeated with occult thought, amateurish, with dime-novel influence.

RAY, RICE
Pseud. of Russell Blaiklock. The "Forthcoming Stories" section in the December 1933 issue of *Wonder Stories* lists the author of this story as Russell Blaiklock, who later wrote "Invisible Continent" (*Future Fiction*, January 1942.). Correspondence in the readers' department indicates that Rice Ray was associated with motion picture production and was employed in Hollywood. In any case he was not a practiced writer. According to

Ray, Rice (*continued*)
Schwartz/Weisinger Ray submitted a sequel to *Wonder Stories*, where it was rejected.

1166. **TO-DAY'S YESTERDAY,** *Wonder Stories*, January 1934. Ill. Winter.
Short story. * *Place:* California, in one of the giant motion picture studios. * Sound engineer Cavanaugh and his protégé/assistant Wilson become aware of a strange situation: a microphone has disappeared from the set during the shooting of a mini-epic. Theft seems ruled out. But when Cavanaugh looks at the processed film of the shooting, he sees that the sound record, instead of being just symbols, forms images of a strange land, within which rests the microphone. * Cavanaugh wrestles with the textbooks and comes up with a solution: time is a matter of extremely high frequency waves, and the enormous wiring involved in the set, when shorted, set up a disturbance in the time waves that removed the mike to somewhen else. Further experimentation shows more of the strange land and offers proof of Cavanaugh's theory. * All well and good. But young Wilson, who is bigmouthed and impulsive, after a friendly dispute with his boss, goes to the studio and transfers himself to the otherwhen. When Cavanaugh looks in, he can see Wilson, and the two can converse reasonably with writing. Cavanaugh sends food through. But neither man apparently is concerned with bringing Wilson back. It would have been pointless, anyway, for a strange carnivorous tree that is fairly mobile eats Wilson. * Pretty bad in the writing, but interesting for studio lore. The story was savagely attacked for technical inaccuracy in letters from A. Lenard of Budapest and Bob Tucker of Indiana, but Ray defended himself successfully, a professional against the amateurs.

RAYMOND, E. V.
Pseud. of Raymond Z. Gallun, who has a separate entry.

1167. **NOVA SOLIS.** *Astounding Stories*, December 1935. Ill. Marchioni.
Short story. * *Time:* 1957 and A.D. 3957. * When, in 1957, a vast mass of cosmic rubble, meteors and small bodies, approached the sun, it became obvious that it would cause solar disturbances, perhaps even turn the sun into a nova. Mankind seemed threatened with extinction. But Dr. Heth, of Heth and Keyston Chemicals, has just discovered a drug that produces suspended animation. * Hoping to weather out the solar storms, the three hundred or so loyal employees of the company and their families construct a tunnel and vault about seven miles deep inside the Earth; into this they retreat, seal themselves off with provisions, set an alarm clock for two thousand years, and go into suspended animation. * Brad Keyston, Heth, and the others awaken as scheduled, in good physical condition. But they have to face the conditions around them. The surface is undoubtedly not yet habitable. What should they do? Should they simply use up the year's resources that they possess, then die? Or should they explore the surface? * Keyston, Heth and others venture out in asbestos suits. The surface is indeed uninhabitable; it is barren, lava-covered, and 135°. The situation seems hopeless. But then they see flying machines of a peculiar transparent sort, almost nonmaterial; in them are nonmaterial beings. Following the route of the flying machines, the survivors come to a huge abandoned dome site that had apparently been built by the alien beings. * Heth explains matters: The aliens, who must have

come from the sun, have been living on Earth while it was extremely hot, but are gradually abandoning it as it cools. * This provides a solution for mankind. The abandoned sun domes are so well insulated that humans can live in them, farm, and start a new civilization. * Routine.

RAYMOND, KAYE
U.S. author, then resident of Chicago, Illinois. Contributed three stories to *Astounding Science Fiction* in 1937.

1168. **INTO THE INFINITESIMAL.** *Wonder Stories*, June 1934. Ill. Schneeman.
Novelette. * *Place:* mostly the Indiana dunes and an atomic world. * Author Kaye Raymond introduces the story in a framework. * The narrative is that of Tracy, star reporter of the *Chicago Chronicle*, who is assigned to investigate the mysterious disappearance of a train from Chicago, passengers and all. On examining the area where the train was last seen, he has a narrow escape as something disintegrates part of a nearby tree. A little legwork reveals that this has all been unintentionally done by the recluse scientist Blakely. Tracy immediately becomes friendly with Blakely and falls in love with Blakely's beautiful daughter. * Blakely explains: Basing his work on an older atomic theory, by bombarding substances with powerful rays stronger than X-rays, he has created element 85. In some fashion the atomic engineering produces a disintegrator ray, which has done the damage already recorded. Blakely, now that he knows the deaths he has caused, is horrified, but this does not prevent him from following through on the second manifestation of his atomic theory. He has built an apparatus for reducing size and with it plans to visit electronic worlds. Tracy accompanies the scientist and his daughter. * They proceed down in size, seeing electrons as small suns, and finally land on an electron world. It is somewhat Earth-like, but peopled by flame beings. Captured, the explorers are taken before the flame ruler, who communicates with them telepathically. He informs them that his immortal people are about four quadrillion years old and are transformations of original material beings like the explorers. The transformation gave immortality, but in some fashion destroyed mental happiness. The three visitors, the fire ruler states, will now be absorbed to integrate happiness back into the people. * The explorers, who do not relish this fate, manage to reach their size ship and return to our world. Alas, when they arrive they learn that their escape was orchestrated, and, unknown to them, two flame beings accompanied them up to our world. The flame people will now emerge and take over. * This is the end of the manuscript, which is broken during narration by comments purporting veracity. * Badly written, with a romance on a shopgirl level.

RAYMOND, MOORE
Pseud. of Raymond Moore (1903-?), U.K. author. Born in Queensland, Australia. Science correspondent for the *Daily Express*. Writer of popular science articles and boys' fiction.

1169. **SCOUTS OF SPACE.** *Scoops*, 5 May 1934. Unsigned ill.
Boys' fiction. * Short story. * *Time:* the interplanetary future. *Place:* mostly the asteroid belt. * Peter Thorpe, pilot, and Bill Reed, mechanic, of the Inter-Planetary police ship *Silver Spear* are ordered to aid the *Marathon*, which has just been raided by a space pirate. Reaching the *Marathon*, the space policemen

Raymond, Moore (*continued*)

learn that the pirate ship seemed to head for the asteroid belt when it left, in the direction of the asteroid Strobos. This is surprising, for the asteroid belt is generally considered too dangerous for a base, and such a base has not been observed. * Thorpe nevertheless heads for the asteroids. As the men approach Strobos, they see that a segment of a mountain slides aside, revealing a cavern in which is the pirate base. Unfortunately, the pirates see the space policemen approach and focus a pain ray on the *Silver Spear*. Thorpe crash lands, losing consciousness. When he comes to, he discovers that Bill is missing, apparently captured by the pirates. * Hiding in a secret locker, Thorpe escapes the notice of the pirates who enter the ship. Bill breaks away from the pirates, and the two men prepare for combat. In the ensuing space battle, the *Silver Spear*'s heat ray is more effective than the pirate's pain ray, and the pirate ship is destroyed. Thorpe and Reed find the pirate's loot and captives in the mountain cavern. * Despite the similarity of name between the *Silver Spear* here and the *Silver Sphere* in #912, Professor Low's "S.O.S. from Saturn," the stories are obviously by different authors, Raymond being much the more skilled writer.

1170. **SCOUTS OF SPACE [II]**. *Scoops,* 2 June 1934. Unsigned ill.
Boys' fiction. * Short story. * *Time:* the interplanetary future. *Place:* the asteroid belt and the Tenth Satellite of Jupiter. * Peter Thorpe and Bill Reed, in the *Silver Spear*, encounter a derelict cargo ship, the *Lights of London,* near the asteroid belt. The vessel presents almost a *Mary Celeste* situation, for everything is apparently intact and there seems to be no reason that the crew abandoned ship. * But then Bill is attacked by a nearly invisible monster that manifests itself as extreme cold. Peter kills the creature with his heat ray, and infrared spectacles show the men that the freighter is swarming with amoeboid semimaterial creatures that Peter claims are in some way fourth dimensional. The creatures follow the space men back into the *Silver Spear*, oozing through the metal walls, but are finally destroyed. * Peter and Bill now head for the Tenth Satellite, where the crew of the *Lights of London* has taken refuge. There they discover the survivors besieged by monstrosities that toss ropelike organs around their prey, much as a toad does. The space policemen rescue the castaways and depart, presumably on a new assignment.

REA, MARGARETTA W.
No information. Social Security records list Margaretta Rea (1916-1986), a resident of New Jersey, and Margaretta Rea (1876-1967), a resident of Pennsylvania.

1171. **DELILAH**. *Amazing Stories,* January 1933. Ill. Morey.
Short story. * Not really science-fiction. * Gifted young artist Bertram has been painting a masterpiece that is certain to win a competition and assure him a future. But during the evenings someone is working on his canvas. The work is first rate and concordant with Bertram's plan, but since he did not paint it, he cannot ethically submit the canvas. * Wailing and woe. * The chief suspect for the secret spoiler is Bertram's girlfriend Minna, whom he taught to paint. * But the culprit is really Bertram, who paints somnambulistically. * Judging from Ms. Rea's description, Bertram is behind the times and is painting calendar art. *

Hardly suitable for a s-f magazine, even if it had been better written.

[Anonymous]
Presumably a British writer.
1172. **REBELS OF THE PENAL PLANET**. *Scoops,* 17 February 1934. Unsigned ill.
Boys' fiction. * Short story. * *Time:* the interplanetary future. *Place:* mostly space. * *Background:* the solar system seems to be organized into a unit called Cosmos, with the center of government on Earth. There is a governing council and a Lord President. Although it is not specified, the planets seem to be settled by humans only, with Uranus serving as a penal planet for particularly bad criminals. Among such criminals is the mad scientist Professor Amos Revukla, who has seized control on Uranus and is leading a revolt against the central government. * With new weapons, including a sleep gas (soporifalium), heat rays, and disintegrator rays, his enormous space fleet begins to wipe out the great cities of the world. Edinburgh and York are already gone, to be followed by about thirty others before Capt. Jerry Grahame of the Inter-Planetary Defence Force defeats the "Uranusians." * When Revukla captures Jerry and tortures him with a pain rod, he errs greatly, for Jerry, knocking out his guard, with a couple of associates captures the professor's three hundred-man flagship. Then, cleverly making use of Revukla's code, he commands the rebel fleet to drop its protective magnetic screens at inappropriate moments. The rebellion is over.

RECTOR, CHARLES H.
No information. Charles H. Rector, author of *The Story of Beautiful Porto Rico* (1898) seems improbable as the author of the following story.
1173. **CRYSTALS OF GROWTH**. *Amazing Stories,* December 1927. Ill. Paul.
Short-short story. * The narrator visits his friend Professor Brontley, a great biologist. Brontley explains: On the theory that perfect nutrition would result in enormously enhanced growth, he has succeeded in ridding food of all extraneous matter. He now plans to take one of his full sustenance pills. * He does so, and immediately swells up to a height of nine feet. Brontley then insists that the narrator take a pill, too. When he refuses, Brontley turns nasty, and the narrator recovers consciousness later. His friends insist that he dreamed the experience, but Brontley's lab is as the narrator remembered it, and Brontley has disappeared. What has happened to him the author does not even hint.

REGIS, JUL[IUS]
Pseud. of Julius Pettersson (1889-1925), Swedish author of mysteries. Two have been translated into English: *No. 13 Toroni* (1922) and *The Copper House* (1923).
1174. **THE PARADISE OF THE ICE WILDERNESS**. *Amazing Stories,* October 1927. Ill. Paul. Anonymous translation from Swedish. The source is not known.
Short-short story. * *Time:* 1899. *Place:* the area around the mouth of the [imaginary?] Chantanga River in Siberia. * The Swedish whaling captain's narrative: Having heard stories of frozen mammoths being found in Siberia, he decides to investigate. Making land, he finds not only a perfectly preserved frozen mammoth, but a small lost world with giant ferns and

Regis, Jul. (*continued*)
living mammoths, one of which chases the party. * Undeveloped.

REID, J. DAVID
No information.

1175. THE GREAT INVASION OF 1955. *Amazing Stories*, October 1932.
Short story. * After some preliminaries dealing with the concept of isotopes, the narrator is summoned by the Secretary of War, who shows him a thin sheet of metal. It has remarkable qualities, being almost inflexible and unbelievably light. As the secretary states, planes built of this mystery metal would have great advantages over conventional planes. The metallic sample, he adds, was obtained by a spy from a secret installation on a small Japanese island. * As war breaks out between Japan and the United States, the narrator's friend Harvey Wilkins solves the problem of the mystery metal. A single projector mounted on a plane destroys whole Japanese air fleets about to attack the West Coast. * *Explanation:* The mystery metal is an isotope (atomic weight 206) of lead, which the Japanese have been able to separate and crystallize. Radiation from a special cathode tube mounted on the American plane knocked off a helium atom, turning the mystery metal into mercury. * An example of the contemporary interest in isotopes.

REMENTER, EDWARD L.
U.S. author, resident of Pennsylvania. Probably the Edward Rementer (1888-1986) listed in Social Security records.

1176. THE SPACE BENDER. *Amazing Stories*, December 1928. Unsigned ill.
Short story, in part tongue in cheek. * *Place:* Venus. * A workman brings to the frame narrator a bottle found during an excavation. The bottle, which is glasslike but flexible, impervious to blows, etc., contains a manuscript, which is in the handwriting of the long missing Professor Livermore. * The manuscript: Livermore, a mathematician, has been working on dimensions. He has off-trail theories: that space does not really exist, that time is not a dimension, and that the fourth dimension is a geometric matter. In support of his theories he has built an apparatus that bends space so that objects distant in our world can be brought together in the fourth dimension. In this fashion he plans to visit Venus. * Livermore sets up his apparatus and awakens on Venus, where he is soon captured by the dominant race, humanoid beings with catlike characteristics. Indeed, as he soon learns, the Venusians are descended from cats, just as we are from primates. * The description of Venusian culture and individuals then proceeds by humorously linking terrestrial feline and Venusian humanoid characteristics. The note of the culture is absolute individualism. As King Tabi says, as long as a person obeys the law, no one cares what he does. Education is totally voluntary, but free, with the result that most of the population is ignorant, while the percentage of geniuses and great artists is much higher than with us. Music is extremely advanced. Duels to the death are common and unrestrained. * Livermore plans to return to Earth as soon as the Venusian scientists repair his apparatus. In the meanwhile he is sending this manuscript. * But the manuscript is now twenty years old. Does this mean that Livermore is dead, or that the Venusians decided against letting him return to Earth? * The mixture of straight science-fiction and rather feeble irony is not very

effective. Probably suggested by Clarence Day's *This Simian World* (1920).

1177. THE TIME DEFLECTOR. *Amazing Stories*, December 1929. Ill. Briggs.
Novelette. * Satire on the roaring twenties, romance, and a little s-f. * *Time:* A.D. 6925. * An unduly long introductory section discusses the eccentric genius, Professor Melville, who claims to have discovered tempium, a new element that permits time travel. When his claims are ridiculed, he withdraws to continue his work privately. * The second section is narrated by Melville, explaining his theoretical conclusions about time (which does not really exist, hence can be pushed aside), and reflections on time travel. He asserts that one can travel into the future, since it is not yet formed, but not into the past, which is fixed. Travel into the future is risky, since there is a variable time differential, in which minutes in the time apparatus may equal long periods of time in the future. * Melville, who needs a subject for his experiments, settles on his daughter's friend John Woodland. A bargain is struck: Melville considers Woodland an unwelcome suitor, but will drop his objections if Woodland participates in his experiment. * Woodland, who is a shallow collegiate type, has trepidations about it all until he is shamed by the professor's daughter into accepting the offer. * Woodland's narrative consists mostly of an ethnographic survey of the future, with more detail that it would be suitable to present here. Essentially, future mankind and his/her culture is a parody of ours, based on extending and amplifying present cultural trends. Sloppy language, reversal of sex roles in life style, insane clothing and body decoration, utterly corrupt politics, foolish eating rituals, inane and cacophonous arts, etc. As the author says, "the reader will have come to the conclusion the world of 6925 was inhabited by fools, or madmen. Of course, conditions were not quite that bad, but the general level of intelligence was very low. . . . . [and] a sense of responsibility. . . . was entirely lacking." * This white (European, American) nation, whose culture has been described, is not a world power; it is threatened by more powerful nations, a black empire in Africa and an Oriental (Chinese) monarchy. * Woodland converses with the Historian, the only intelligent, reasonable man he meets. The Historian blames the cultural degeneracy on the values of the past: quantity instead of quality, indiscriminate breeding, etc. * At the proper time Woodland is brought back to his own era. Unfortunately, the heroic experiment is useless as scientific proof, for it cannot be duplicated. Melville has exhausted his supply of tempium, and it would take decades to assemble more. * The author supplies three possible evaluations of Woodland's story: First, the story is true. Objection, it is too fantastic to be convincing. Second, Melville hypnotized Woodland and suggested the story. Objection, this is unlikely, what with Melville's known honesty and integrity. Third, Woodland invented the future culture in order to win Melville's daughter. Objection, unlikely, Woodland didn't have the brains to do this. * As with the previous story, The author has imagination, but lacks literary skill and could have profited by strong editorial assistance.

RENSHAW, F. STANLEY
No information.

1178. ANCIENTS OF EASTER ISLAND. *Amazing Stories*, April 1933. Ill. Morey.
Short story. * *Time:* present and remote past. *Place:* Easter

Renshaw, F. Stanley (*continued*)

Island and Lemuria. * The archeologist narrator (Harvey Manly) and his associates on the scientific expedition stop at Easter Island. Gaining the confidence of the islanders, who speak of a prophecy, the scientists take part in one of the ceremonies, fetching a sea bird's egg from a neighboring islet when the annual avian migration arrives. * Since the ceremony goes well, the narrator is accepted as a semisacred being. After dancing and ceremonies, he finds himself, together with a beautiful young woman, in Easter Island of ages past, when it was still part of Lemuria. He sees the subsidence of the land and the stranding of the few survivors on a mountain peak, all on the point of starvation. * In this past life he is a prince, and in theory he should not provide food for the lesser peoples, but shedding his rank he swims out to an islet and gathers birds' eggs for food—thus initiating the ceremony still continued. He is now regarded as a semisacred hero, and the island sculptors represent him in giant statues. * After a time, the narrator awakens in our present. The young woman who accompanied him in the dream experience or recapitulation of history is present and becomes his bride. * It is not clear exactly how the narrator's experience should be classified. * *Miscellaneous:* Besides ordinary Polynesians, the population of Lemuria and Easter Island included giants about twelve feet tall, with peculiar ears, as represented on the extant statues. * Routine at best.

REPP, ED[WARD] EARL (1900 or 1901-1979)

U.S. (California) writer, born in Pittsburgh. Worked in newspaper advertising and publicity in early life; later became motion picture script writer for Columbia and Warner Brothers, mostly for Western pictures. Said also to have written occasional plays for the television Lone Ranger program. Also wrote dozens of Western novels under pseuds. John Cody and Peter Field. A fairly prolific contributor of science-fiction in the 1930s. Most of his work shows an approximation to action pulp techniques. Unfortunately, a crude, careless writer who often exemplified the worst of the pulp tradition.

1179. **BEYOND GRAVITY**. *Air Wonder Stories*, August 1929. Ill. Paul.

Short story. * *Time:* 1980. *Place:* mostly Denver. * Much of the story is devoted to a puppy romance and small talk among family friends. * The new U.S.A.F. superplane, the *Annihilator*, is flying into Denver with young Lt. Bob Allison as one of the pilots. The *Annihilator* can reach 1,600 MPH without difficulty, and there is a general belief that it is invincible. * The airplane leaves for the West Coast, but on crossing the Rockies it is caught in an unusually powerful updraft and is hurled off the Earth into orbit, exactly how far is not clear, but far enough that there is no air. * The ship is out of energy, is malfunctioning, and cannot break its orbit and return to Earth. Some men, including Allison, are injured, and the air supply is short. * The ground forces ponder various ways to help the *Annihilator*, but there is no easy way. One clever idea is to shoot up canisters of nitro-radium to the plane's orbit, in the hope that the plane's landing nets will catch one. The crew would then force it through the exhaust to blast the plane down. The plane does capture such a canister, but, unfortunately, another canister blows off the exhaust and the steering mechanisms so that the explosive cannot be used. * As a desperate last resort magnetic devices, wires attached, are shot up at the *Annihilator*; these will attach

to the plane, exhaust its antigravity mechanism, and permit the aircraft to be drawn down. After a couple of tries, this works, without a moment to spare. * *Miscellaneous:* The plane seems to operate with antigravity repulsion plates and a rocket-principle motor. * While the plane was in orbit, four-dimensional surgery was performed on Allison, and according to Allison the ship has four-dimensional fittings. * Routine at best. * For a sequel see #1190, "The *Annihilator* Comes."

1180. **THE RADIUM POOL**. *Science Wonder Stories*, August-September 1929. Ill. Paul.

(Reprinted in Repp, *The Radium Pool*; also in Crawford, *Science-Fantasy Quintette*.)

Short novel. * *Place:* Death Valley, California. * As the rather confused narrative goes: The narrator, a newspaper reporter, is assigned by his editor to accompany Professor Bloch on a scientific expedition into Death Valley, the purpose, to substantiate old claims of unusual skeletal material. Into their camp staggers a man, who is half dead from thirst and privation. * The man, a prospector who does not give his name, tells that he and a half-crazed old man named Driftin' Sands headed out into the valley to search for a lost mine. Sands, however, is also searching for his young sweetheart Allie Lane, who was lost in the valley some forty years ago. The two wander about, discover ancient traces of the Lane party, and in an unexplored area come to a bubbling pool of pure radium. Sands accidentally dips his finger into it, whereupon a rejuvenation process begins that eventually changes him back into a young man. But the two men are captured by gigantic humanoids and taken down into caves filled with superscientific equipment. * Abaris, the commander of the strange beings communicates telepathically with the narrator, revealing that they come from Jupiter and are shipping radium back to Jupiter in small space spheres. A gigantic orrery shows the progress of the spheres. The mining operation is almost finished, and the Jupiterians will soon return to their home base. * Most important of all, Allie Lane is with the interplanetary visitors, preserved in her youth by the radium emanations, as is her father. * The ancient lovers are delighted to see one another, and the old romance resumes. A complication lies in the fact that Abaris is also (in a way) in love with Allie. This creates a problem, for while, as Allie declares, Abaris is a kindly being, he can also be ruthless. Nevertheless, despite their precarious situation, Allie and Sands are married by Allie's father, who is a clergyman. * The humans attempt to escape, but everything goes wrong. Allie, her father, and Sands are all on their way to Jupiter, where the Reverend Lane and Sands will go into a zoo, while Allie will be the "bride of Jupiter." Only the narrator escapes. * Repp suggests a sequel. * *Miscellaneous:* The invaders have a stun ray, although Abaris's tremendous mental power can accomplish the same result. * Radium is the main power source on Jupiter. * The Jupiterians, who are immortal or nearly so through their knowledge of radium, are taller than humans, with thin cylindrical legs, large torsos, and huge heads with antennas. * Somewhat below routine work.

1181. **THE INVISIBLE RAIDERS**. *Air Wonder Stories*, October 1929. Ill. Paul.

Short story. * *Time:* 1944. * The Federal Aero-Police are greatly concerned about the rash of air piracies. As enormous cargo planes fly across the continent, they are robbed with impunity. Colonel Brigham, the chief of the service, is currently reaming

Repp, Ed Earl (*continued*)

Captain Wollack, head of the Midwestern sector, for failure to catch the thieves, when Wollack counters that the robbers are (literally) invisible, hence cannot be fought. * Brigham scoffs, but soon changes his tune when Professor Standish, a friend, asserts that invisibility can be achieved by using coloration below the human visual range. In other words, infrared paint. The professor demonstrates an apparatus that will render such objects visible again. * The Aero-Police hasten to install Standish's projectors on their ships. Then there is a bullion raid on a giant plane. Brigham watches (via television and Standish's special descrambler) as a host of small planes land atop the cargo plane, disgorge men, carry away the bullion and fly off. But Wollack and his men are after them, and in a large air battle they defeat the bandits completely, capturing their leader, Sharkey. * Sharkey, an intelligent and scientifically trained man, had stolen the secret of invisibility from a Japanese scientist, as Standish thought. Now he is trying to exchange the secret, plus his loot, for a pardon. * Somewhat below routine. * For a sequel see #1183, "Beyond the Aurora."

1182. **THE METAL WORLD.** *Science Wonder Stories*, October 1929. Ill. Paul.

Short story. * *Place:* San Francisco. * Newspaper reporter Dowell and Professor Blackton happen to be present when the first earth-borer of the Demetrians bursts up through the streets of San Francisco, disintegrating almost everyone in sight. After several such episodes, the Demetrians—who are creatures like huge centipedes—make an announcement: Mining must cease, for all the minerals in the earth belong to the underground Demetrians. Defiance causes more destruction and more casualties. * Professor Blackton, however, is equal to the task. He has just invented a viewer (modified X-ray) that grants vision of what is going on down in the caverns and tunnels of the invaders, who live in the solid metallic core of the earth. Then Blackton, despite attacks by the Demetrians, supervises the construction of a fleet of earth-borers, which, cutting their way down, release poison gas, wiping out the menace. * The author calls the invaders Demetrians with reference to the Greek goddess Demeter, who was connected with the underground world. * Of no interest.

1183. **BEYOND THE AURORA.** *Air Wonder Stories*, November 1929. Ill. Paul.

Short story. * Sequel to #1181, "The Invisible Raiders." * *Time:* 1946. * Captain Wollack, who has inherited a fortune, is retiring from the Federal Aero-Police and with the help of Professor Standish intends to build the ultimate airplane. As finished, the *Tobias Wollack* is a five-fuselaged affair with huge wings, propelled by gas-powered rockets. * The aircraft is almost finished and ready to make its maiden voyage, when Wollack learns disturbing news. Sharkey, the air criminal of the previous story, who had received a ten-year sentence for his crimes, still controls remnants of his gang from prison, and one of Wollack's workmen is Sharkey's mole. Wollack tries to make the suspect talk, but instead Wollack, Standish, and the loyal mechanics are drugged. And Sharkey has escaped from prison. * Wollack awakens in the airplane, confronted by Sharkey, who tells him that he and Professor Standish must operate the plane in a takeoff. * The plane rises beautifully, and in a short time is in the upper atmosphere flying at enormous speed. * Sharkey, at this point, is seized by hybristic mania and decides that he will

take the *Tobias Wollack* to the Moon. Standish and Wollack try to convince him that this is suicidal, Sharkey's men are terrified, but the outlaw will not yield. Fortunately, during the upheavals that arise in dodging a meteor swarm, Wollack is able to kill his guard. After some shooting back and forth, he regains control of the plane and brings it down. Sharkey is dead, and later, when asked where his body is, Wollack reveals that it was dumped out beyond the aurora high above the Earth. * One of Repp's better stories, an acceptable pulp action story.

1184. **THE STELLAR MISSILE.** *Science Wonder Stories*, November 1929. Ill. KAW.

(Reprinted in Repp, *The Stellar Missiles*.)

Short story. * *Time:* somewhat later than 1965. *Place:* California and Arizona. * *Background:* Some years earlier, Professor Brandon, investigating Meteor Crater in Arizona, discovered that the meteoritic body was really an interplanetary vessel manned by beings popularly called "the Aliens." In addition to wreckage and bones, Brandon found a number of beings in suspended animation, suggesting that the Aliens were active in shifts and that those in anabiosis could not be revived in time by the working detail. These beings were humanoid, with very large heads with triple the brain capacity of humans. The spaceship itself demonstrated a science beyond that of Earth. * Inexplicably [to a reader], the remains of the vessel were left in place, together with masses of written material that were not collected or preserved. But the space beings were removed and entrusted to Dr. Miles Farrington, who was charged with reviving them. So far he has had no success. * The story is told through a young reporter. As the story opens, Brandon reproaches Farrington publicly for inability to revive the Aliens, whereupon Farrington delivers a long discursive rebuttal: After years of research, he can duplicate the Alien suspended animation, but he cannot bring subjects back to life. Actually, he confesses, he has put his own son Tom into suspended animation and now cannot reawaken him. There are suitable sobs as the audience hears this. * The only recourse, Farrington claims, is to return to the space wreck and see if traces of a reviving serum can be found. * An investigatory party removes to the meteorite crater and reexplores the wreck. The young reporter, kicking through a mass of Alien papers on the floor (some of which he tries to ignite!), finds a couple that are interesting. As read by an expert, the papers reveal that the Aliens came from a planet situated just "beneath" the Earth, thereby invisible, and that they planned to exterminate mankind and take over the world. * Farrington finally is somewhat successful. He finds a tiny plant growing near the place where the reviving liquid must have been spilled. The plant, which glows, was nourished, he declares, by the serum and radioactivity. Not much serum can be extracted from the plant, but Farrington obtains enough to revive an experimental dog and son Tom. * Pretty bad. For a sequel, see #1191, "The Second Missile."

1185. **FLIGHT OF THE EASTERN STAR.** *Air Wonder Stories*, December 1929. Ill. Paul.

The title is carried as "The Flight of the Eastern Star" on the contents page. * *Time:* later than 1950, which is mentioned in the text. *Place:* the Pacific. * Tom, the narrator, a businessman on a vacation, decides to take a trip to the Orient via the *Evening Star*, one of the major aircraft of International Airways. He is fortunate that the local manager, Worthington, is an old college chum, for he gets preferred treatment and an inside view of what

Repp, Ed Earl (*continued*)

is happening. * The author does not give dimensions, but the *Eastern Star* must be an enormous craft. It is rendered nearly weightless by antigravity plates that are based on an application of magnetism, and it is propelled on the rocket principle by repeated Diesel combustions of various elements, producing a gas. * The flight starts off with a bad omen, for the vessel was delayed by an updraft over the Rocky Mountains. When the ship takes off, there is a near disaster, for one of the pilots forgot to adjust the elevators, and the ship nearly crashed. Captain Markson, a martinet of the old school, immediately fires the responsible person and dumps him overboard. The culprit, highly embarrassed, does not bother to open his parachute and must be cleaned off the pavement. * The *Eastern Star* is operating under a rigid schedule, for it must deliver a load of bullion to Peking or the company will pay a huge forfeit. * Along the way the captain receives a distress signal from a dirigible that is caught in a tornado and is disabled. Markson cuts the tornado in two with his giant ship and rescues the crew by expanding landing nets into which they jump from the dirigible. The blimp captain prefers to go down with his ship. * The *Eastern Star* reaches its destination in time, and the narrator enjoys his vacation.

1186. THE RED DIMENSION. *Science Wonder Stories*, January 1930. Ill. Winter.

(Reprinted in Repp, *The Radium Pool*.)

Short story. * *Time:* just before the Russian Revolution. *Place:* Moscow. * The story is told through the manuscript narrative of Arnoldi Kherkoff, found with his corpse near a Siberian prison camp after the Revolution. * Kherkoff, the young protegé of the great scientist Dr. Korsakoff, is intrigued when Korsakoff informs him that there are other realms of existence beyond our physical senses. * Korsakoff, further, has constructed equipment for perceiving such worlds: two helmet-like arrangements filled with prisms and lenses and other apparatus, which the men don. * They now look into the sixth dimension, called the Red Dimension because it is in the infrared range. Kherkoff sees a tangled jungle, horrible insect-like creatures, then a lone upright being that might be an evolved insect. When attacked by the beasts, it flashes a disintegrating ray from a spear-like weapon. It is eventually brought down, whereupon a band of its fellows rush up and play their disintegrators upon the remaining insect beasts. * Panicked, Kherkoff rips off his helmet and faints. When he recovers consciousness, he finds that Korsakoff is dead, head mangled by the disintegrator rays that must have been conducted through the apparatus from the Red Dimension. Tried for murder, Kherkoff is sentenced to life imprisonment in Siberia. * Repp, in a foreword as Repp, states that he has been unable to find any record of the case in Russian archives. * Routine.

1187. THE STORM BUSTER. *Air Wonder Stories*, January 1930. Ill. Paul.

Short story. * *Time:* the near future. *Place:* California and the Pacific Ocean. * Aeronautics are quite advanced, and enormous airplanes fly the oceans. But aviators encounter great danger in up-and-down air currents and electrical storms. Indeed, the great airliner *City of Honolulu* has just been destroyed in a storm. * Thanks to Marshall Dunning a solution to these weather problems has been attained. Dunning, a poor student of genius at Institute of Technology, has discovered how to split the oxygen

atom and thereby dissipate atmospheric electricity around an airship. His discovery, however, is hedged with difficulties. After he blew up the university lab and nearly killed himself in a crucial experiment, campus politics of the dirtiest sort, including theft of information, almost cost him his discovery. * Recovered, he and his sponsor Professor Hamlin equip a government bomber with his apparatus and fly into a storm. A broken cable almost wrecks the plane and the project, but an erstwhile bad guy redeems himself by splicing the cable outside and all ends well. Aviation is now safe.

1188. GULF STREAM GOLD. *Science Wonder Stories*, May 1930. Ill. Paul

Short story. * *Place:* Santa Monica, California, and off the coast of Florida. * The narrator, a patent attorney noted for his integrity, receives a strange phone call: A Mr. Cantrell, calling from San Diego, sixty-odd miles away, says he will visit the narrator in an hour. Near the appropriate time, the narrator sees a man emerge from the sea in an easily removed diving suit, and Cantrell is there. * The point: Cantrell has invented a super-submarine capable of sixty knots, and he needs capital for another invention—a device for removing gold from sea water. The invention constructed, Cantrell, his brother, and the narrator will go to the Gulf Stream and remove gold by the hundredweight. * So they do, but they run afoul of a fleet of bootlegger vessels, including a hostile submarine. The bootleggers mistake them for Federal dry agents and fire on them, killing Cantrell's brother. In a senseless fury, Cantrell rams the other submarine, sinking it, but also sinking his own vessel. He and the narrator escape with a few pounds of gold. They will build another submarine and retrieve the gold they extracted. * Essentially an adventure story, much like an adult version of a sea dime novel, with encounters with sea beasts, etc. * Routine at best.

1189. THE SKY RULER. *Air Wonder Stories*, May 1930. Ill. Paul.

Short story. * *Time:* the near future. * As Professor Markleson tells his friend Dr. Jorstedt, he has not only discovered how to control gravity, but has built a large vessel incorporating his discovery. Shortly after this, the *Sky Urchin* is ready to make its maiden voyage. Markleson is at the controls as the ship rises, and a blue ribbon group of celebrities is on board. Then, Markleson feels a pistol thrust against his back. The ship is being skyjacked. * The pirates are masked, but Markleson is sure that the bandit leader is his friend Jorstedt, who inexplicably did not attend the launching. Outraged at the betrayal of friendship, Markleson attacks the bandit leader, whereupon he is knocked unconscious. * Markleson is long in recovering from the blows and is partially amnesiac. He learns that the skyjacker, who now styles himself the Sky Ruler, has claimed ownership of the sky and is exacting heavy tribute from the nations. There seems to be no defense against him, for resistance has ended in crushing defeat. Only the United States, so far, has defied him. * Two events change the situation. When Jorstedt visits the amnesiac Markleson, Markleson regains his memory and goes berserk. He is temporarily convinced, however, that he has made a mistake and that his friend is not the bandit. Second, the professor's assistant, Jack Reeves, has invented a magnetic ray for capturing the *Sky Urchin* when it approaches Washington to collect tribute or to attack. When the extortionist appears, his ship is dragged down, out of control. Most of the crew parachute out, but a single black figure leaps out without a parachute. * Markleson

Repp, Ed Earl (*continued*)

goes to view the corpse of the Sky Ruler, expecting to see Jorstedt, and now learns the truth. The criminal was Jorstedt's bad-egg twin brother. Jorstedt himself did not know the situation until the last. * *Miscellaneous:* Markleson attains antigravity by running electricity through a special highly magnetic alloy containing a new metal, and propels his vessel with rockets as improved from Professor Goddard's work.

1190. **THE *ANNIHILATOR* COMES**. *Wonder Stories*, August 1930. Ill. Leonard.

Novelette. * Sequel to #1179, "Beyond Gravity." * *Time:* 1980. *Place:* inside the hollow Earth. * Lt. Allison recovered rapidly from the injuries suffered during the fiasco of the *Annihilator*, and is recalled to duty as commander of the new *Annihilator II*, which is a greatly improved version of the airplane. * Saying goodbye to his sweetheart over a couple of pages, Allison reports for duty and learns that he is to rescue a party of Swedish explorers who are lost somewhere near the north pole. The trip north is uneventful, except for a few space-filling incidents, but when the great plane reaches the pole, there is consternation: There is an open body of water, the plane keeps going over the north pole, and the observers sight land. As they soon realize, they are inside the hollow Earth, as described by Marshall B. Gardner in *A Journey into the Earth's Interior*. * The *Annihilator* lands, and Allison and his first officer (Bright) wander out exploring. They find more than they were looking for: herds of stampeding mammoths, great predatory dinosaurs, and the Triceratopsians—humanoid reptiles with triceratopslike heads, horns, neck guard, and all. They have a savage culture, with a village, a kingship, religious rites including sacrifice, bows and arrows—and most horrible dispositions. * They soon capture the two humans, despite pistols and all, and drag them away most brutally. Allison and Bright hear gunshots and the departure of the *Annihilator* in the distance. (It is later revealed that the personnel of the *Annihilator* believed the two officers dead, and were themselves defeated in a battle involving the Triceratopsians and the mammoths they control.) * Allison and Bright, at the village, find an ancient white man, an escaped criminal, who acts as adviser to the Triceratopsian king and serves mostly as a means for taunting the captives. Some of the missing Swedish explorers are also there; others were killed in battle. All the captives will be sacrificed in various ways. * As Allison and Bright are about to be eaten by a real Triceratops whom the reptile men worship, the *Annihilator* appears overhead and blasts the village. Also, one of the crew, thought to be dead, has been acting as a deus e serpente; disguising himself in a reptile-man skin, he has been defending the two officers with well-placed explosive bullets. All the outsiders that are alive are rescued, and the Triceratopsians are almost exterminated. * *Miscellaneous:* There is a small sun inside the Earth. * No mention is made of the fourth-dimensional effects cited in the first story. * The naive Triceratopsian king, egged on by the renegade white criminal, hopes to conquer the outside world. * Ersatz Edgar Rice Burroughs, and routine.

1191. **THE SECOND MISSILE**. *Amazing Stories*, December 1930. Ill. Morey.

(Reprinted in Repp, *The Stellar Missiles*.)

Short story. * Sequel to #1184, "The Stellar Missile." * *Time:* fifteen years after the first story, or about 1980. *Place:* Siberia. * Young Thompson Farrington, son of the late Dr. Miles Far-

rington, speculates that the great Siberian meteorite of 1908, which lay waste an enormous area, was really a second spaceship sent out by the aliens. With associates—Brandon, Dennison, and Valeri—he proceeds to Siberia, hires an enormous crew of laborers, and begins to excavate the area. * They find nothing at first, although the native workmen—Russians, Tungus, and mixtures—consider the area tabu and are surly and obviously ill at ease. * Then mysterious disappearances begin. Valeri, workmen, all disappear without a trace. The camp is besieged, and anaesthetic darts render the work force and the Americans unconscious. * The Americans awaken as captives of the Aliens, who, after some justified resentment on the part of the Americans, converse with them telepathically. One of the Stellarites (Olandee), informs them that they are hostages for the transfer of the remaining Stellarite bodies from the first ship. One member of the expedition (Brandon) will return to civilization and bring back the sleeping Aliens with him to Siberia; if he does not return in thirty days, the Stellarites will leave, taking the Earthmen with them to certain death. * Olandee rejects the claim of the Earthmen that they were justified in killing the other Stellarites to prevent world conquest; Olandee states that this world is unsuitable for his people. * Brandon leaves, and there is suspense up to the last minute and beyond when it seems that he will not return in time. But he does, and the four Americans are freed; their workmen, however, are taken by the Stellarites to their home planet around Alcyone. (This is not the place of origin cited in the first story.) * Sloppy work, bad writing, weak editing. Example: "'You offer an entirely new theory on interplanetary machine construction, Tom,' the professor stated, his eyes flashing with a peculiar light."

1192. **THE SYNTHETIC MEN**. *Wonder Stories*, December 1930. Ill. Paul.

Short story. * *Time:* around A.D. 2000. *Place:* California. * Conservative, Fundamentalist reporter Douglass is assigned to interview Professor Pontius, a great maverick biologist. Decades ago Pontius's father discovered the radiative range of the life force, and the present Pontius has continued working in the same direction. * Welcoming Douglass, Pontius explains his work. He has created protoplasm and has directed its evolution and development into human form. He shows Douglass two male figures in gigantic test tubes and invites Douglass to help him in the next step in the process, removing the figures from the tubes and preparing them for outside life. * Douglass agrees, especially since Pontius's beautiful daughter Allanna is also to help. But he is sure that the men in the tubes are hopelessly evil and malevolent. * Joe Agar, one of the test tube men dies when removed, but Jack Agar, the second man, seems healthy enough when strapped to a laboratory table. Douglass continues to have trepidations. * During the night he hears noises, clumping, banging, and sees Jack Agar thumping down the corridor of the house. The creature has already crushed the skulls of Pontius and the butler, and is now heading for Allanna's room. Douglass bursts in in time to save Allanna, but the monster now attacks him, and it is much stronger than he is. At the last minute the police arrive and shoot the synthetic man. Douglass thereupon proclaims the wickedness of usurping the powers of the Creator. Pontius's discovery is lost. * An attempt to write science-fiction horror fiction that will satisfy the Bible Belt, but on the crude side.

1193. **FROM OUT OF THE EARTH**. *Wonder Stories*,

Repp, Ed Earl (*continued*)
March 1931. Ill. Marchioni.
Short story. * *Place:* Death Valley, California. * Members of a paleontological expedition stumble upon a dying prospector. Apparently an outlaw who has avoided civilization for years, he tries to shoot his rescuers, since he fears they have come to arrest him, but, mollified, tells a strange story. * Many years earlier, he and three comrades, prospecting an isolated, unexplored mesa, came upon a fabulously rich lode, with gold lying around in chunks. * Unfortunately, there was also a horrendous eight-legged flying monster that was carnivorous, hungry, and persevering. The monster, which the prospector thinks must have come from the Moon, ate his three comrades, and he barely escaped. On returning to civilization, he found himself accused of murdering his partners in order to gain sole control of the rich deposit. But he could no longer find the mine or the area where the monster dwelt. Since then he has wandered the desert, avoiding contact with humans. He now dies. * The members of the expedition are inclined to believe him, but consider the monster to have been something that emerged from a cavern. * Routine.

1194. **THE BEAST OF BAN-DU-LU.** *Wonder Stories*, May 1931. Ill. Lane.
Short story. * *Time:* the interplanetary future. *Place:* Venus. * The first scientific expedition to Venus, a small affair, finds a tropical world with forms approximating those of the dinosaur age. An exploratory party is captured by intelligent reptilians (with long prehensile tails) whose heavy bone structure renders them apparently immune to bullets. There seems no possibility of rescue, for the men remaining at the spaceship do not know how to operate it. * The reptilians barter their captives to still another group, who are more civilized. These beings have a town and a social organization involving a king, the horrible, gigantic Ban-du-lu. * They also have a young German woman (Cassandra), the sole survivor of a previous, apparently unknown expedition. She is in a peculiar position, a captive, yet treated with honor because the reptile king plans to mate with her. Ban-du-lu also plans to sacrifice the Earthmen to the sun, just as he did with the other members of the German expedition. * All concerned are saved by the arrival of the spaceship; the Venusians are killed; and Tyber, who loves Cassandra, personally puts down Ban-du-lu in a duel. * Pretty horrible. * The title is carried on both the contents page and the cover as "The Beasts of Ban-du-lu," which does not make much more sense than the other version of the title.

1195. **DEEP SEA JUSTICE.** *Amazing Stories Quarterly*, Summer 1931. Ill. Morey.
Short story. * *Time:* 1980. *Place:* New York. * Submarine transport has cut greatly into surface shipping, and most freight now goes underwater at one hundred knots. The *A-T 72* is carrying a load of bullion, a fact that renders Chief Quartermaster Bentley uneasy. His feelings are justified when a pirate submarine captained by Gorziatti, a desperate criminal escaped from Devil's Island, demands their gold. The captain refuses, and the two vessels play seek-and-avoid until they are both caught in a tremendous undersea current that drags them down into an air-filled cavern. * After some disputes between the sailors and the pirates, they make temporary common cause to escape. Further caverns reveal a castaway, whom Gorziatti shoots, and a gigantic dinosaur-like animal that eats Gorziatti.

There seems no way to escape except for a hole into which air pours with tremendous pressure. The sailors and pirates leap into the hole in their diving gear, and some, including Bentley, are picked up. Most are suffering from the bends. * *Miscellaneous:* Air pressure from the inner Earth keeps the water out of the cave complex. * In the cave are remains of ancient man, some with long fangs, also stone implements and wall paintings.

1196. **THE WORLD OF THE LIVING DEAD.** *Amazing Stories*, November-December 1932. Ill. Morey.
Short novel. * *Place:* the Caribbean, under Mount Pelée, and either inside the hollow Earth or in a gigantic cavern with an internal sun. * Clichéd adventure. * On the good ship *Scienta* are Dr. Marsden; his beautiful daughter Patti; heroic Annapolis-graduate first-mate Bob Allen; and villainous, lecherous Captain Norton. The Marsdens seem to be combining a search for Atlantis with transporting a cargo of zoo animals. * A storm strikes, and thanks to Captain Norton's incompetence and cowardice the ship is disabled and driven through an underwater tunnel beneath Mount Pelée into an underground world. The involuntary explorers find there the remains of many ships, including the *Cyclops* (a cause celebre during World War I times and after), and many strange phenomena. * The narrative centers on Bob Allen. As he wanders about exploring, he comes upon a strange sight: a glowing pit in which work living skeletons, who are guarded by humanoid creatures with individual flying apparatus and disintegrator tubes. Allen is captured and put to work. From Larkin, a former sailor on the *Cyclops*, he learns what is going on. * *Background:* The area is incredibly rich in radium, which the Subterraneans use for weapons and flying apparatus. The concentration is so strong that it makes flesh invisible after a time; the subterraneans prevent radium burns by periodically running their slaves through a treatment. * The purpose of all this is conquest. The Subterraneans are so numerous that they need Lebensraum, and they plan to exterminate humanity and take over the surface. They already have tunnels disintegrated directly under the world's great centers of population and will emerge at any moment soon. What with the Subterraneans' disintegrators, individual flying apparatus, and wonderful flying machines, humanity is in great danger. * Allen is too turbulent to endure slavery, and his fate seems likely to be unpleasant. But Larkin, who has been planning escape, gives him a disintegrator tube and flying apparatus, with which Allen flies off while the other slaves create a diversion. Along the way Allen discovers that gold is a shield against the disintegrator rays, which consume everything else. * After various adventures Allen returns to the entrance to the underground world, where he encounters Britt, the former commander of the *Cyclops*, who has managed to survive in primitive fashion. As fellow Annapolis men, they get along fine. Rigging up a radio set, Allen sends messages to the outside world. Newport News, however, seems to consider the message a hoax, and it is doubtful if help will arrive. In the meanwhile, Allen and Britt disintegrate their way to the surface and wait. * The navy does come, though, for a classmate of Allen's recognized his name, and the way is ready for an invasion of Subterranea. Since synthetic gold has been developed, there is no difficulty in creating shields against the rays. * Allen penetrates farther than the others, and with Larkin enters the palace of the Subterranean queen, where he has heard Patti is being held. Held she is, by the queen, a gigantic monster, who is about to

Repp, Ed Earl (*continued*)

suck her blood. Wicked Captain Norton, too, is there, trying to bargain for his life against Patti's virtue or vitality. He insists that Allen prepare an affidavit clearing him (Norton), which Allen does on a piece of paper he finds in his pocket. But Norton does not escape so easily. Larkin disintegrates both Norton and the queen, whereupon all the Subterraneans drop dead. It seems that they all received not only their life energy, but also their programming from the queen, who controlled every Subterranean movement. * Low-grade material.

  1197. **THE PHANTOM OF TERROR**. *Amazing Stories,* April 1933. Ill. Morey.
(Reprinted in Repp, *The Radium Pool.*)
Short story. * When Professor Mortenson announces that he has devised an apparatus for entering the fifth dimension, he makes a huge mistake. A gangster enters his laboratory, beats him, and steals the apparatus. Soon after this there is a series of bank robberies in which the criminal mysteriously appears and disappears. They obviously involve Mortenson's discovery. * At first Mortenson is under suspicion, but when the robberies continue, the police accept his help. He constructs additional devices so that he and the police can enter the fifth dimension and kill or capture the bandit. There is peril, for the bandit can apparently look (though himself invisible) into our world. Mortenson is fortunate to escape an attack. * The police and Mortenson enter the fifth dimension, which is much like Earth, with jungles, giant dinosaurlike beasts, and hostile lizard-men who ride attack-dinosaurs. These natives have skinny limbs, round paunches, large heads with eyes on feelers, and blue skin. They are in league with the bandit, who has given them silver dollars as ornaments. * It is rough going for a time, police (sub)machine guns against armies with bows and arrows, but the police win. The nameless bandit flees back to our world, where he is gunned down. * Routine adventure work.

  1198. **THE BODY PIRATE**. *Amazing Stories,* March 1935. Ill. Morey.
Short story. * The great medical researcher Dr. Lape has perfected fifth-dimensional surgery to such an extent that he can transfer brains from one animal to another, without ordinary surgery, by dimensional means. Thus, he has barking cats, meowing dogs, etc. * Lape falls in love with his assistant, the beautiful Dot Faversham. Unfortunately, he is not a very attractive man, being both deformed and nasty. Thus, Dot rejects his suit, preferring Herbert Strong, a handsome hunk who operates a muscle factory. * Lape knows what to do. He entices Strong to the laboratory, renders him unconscious, enters the fifth-dimension apparatus, and waits for the automatic machine to transfer his brain to Strong's body. * An unfortunate circumstance spoils Lape's plans. Thanks to his physical vigor, Strong recovers from the drug earlier than Lape expected, and the process fails. Instead, Lape is dead. Since, with ironic foresight, Lape had willed his estate to Strong, Strong now has both Dot and a fortune. * In another author one might suspect parody.

[Anonymous]
Presumably a British writer.

  1199. **REVOLT OF THE STONE MEN**. *Scoops,* 21 April 1934. Unsigned ill.
Boys' fiction. * Short story. * *Place:* Scotland. * Mole Mountain is astonishing; it suddenly appeared in a field, and has been growing at a rate of one hundred feet per day. Great geologist and archeologist Sir Anthony Rostrum and London newspaper reporter Arthur Dennis investigate it. An explosive blast reveals a cavern in the mountain, into which the two penetrate. After a time they see huge toeless footprints and find a cylindrical device that turns out to be a disintegrator powered by radioactivity. Then they are set upon, captured, and knocked unconscious. * The men regain consciousness in a small stone room. With them is an almost globular being with a broad face, above which is an organic visor. Arthur fires his revolver at the creature when it approaches, but it is seemingly living stone, for the bullets drop from it, flattened. * Sir Anthony, however, discovers that the beings are able to communicate with him telepathically. The men are taken before the stone king, who interrogates them. Refusing to believe in the numbers of surface men, since there are only one thousand stone men, the king announces that he will invade the upper world and conquer it. The greatest scientist of the land, he reared the artificial mountain as a probe to the outside. * Taken outside, Arthur and Sir Anthony manage to escape the disintegrator rays of the stone men and report what they have experienced. Oddly enough, Arthur's paper prints his story, with the result that a crowd of curiosity seekers gathers near the mountain. * For a time nothing happens, then the mountain opens and the stone men emerge. Their disintegrators carry everything before them, and it looks as if England is in trouble. But Sir Anthony, reasoning that since they seem to be impervious to flame throwers, they may have difficulty with cold, suggests bombarding them with liquid air, dry ice, etc. This is effective, and the stone men are wiped out. * *Miscellaneous:* The stone men, who obtain food and all their necessities from radioactive rocks, have developed a high mechanical civilization. According to Sir Anthony, they are descended from humans who were trapped underground ages ago.

RICE, LOUISE and TONJOROFF-ROBERTS

Rice is probably Louise Guest Rice (1880-?), born in Indiana, writer of cookbooks and mystery stories, and an occasional contributor to the pulp magazines, including a graphology column to *Mystery Magazine*. She is possibly the Louise Rice of Navesink, New Jersey who contributed a letter to the August issue of *Amazing Detective Tales*. Nothing is known of Tonjoroff-Roberts.

  1200. **THE ASTOUNDING ENEMY**. *Amazing Stories Quarterly*, Winter 1930. Ill. Morey.
Novelette. * *Time:* Not certain, but perhaps in the late twentieth or early twenty-first century. *Place:* New York and an island off the coast of North Carolina. * The world is suddenly in turmoil. Bridges are collapsing; ships are foundering; planes are falling apart; giant skyscrapers are toppling. Agriculture is almost impossible to practice, what with plagues of insects. * Some persons, like rabble-rouser Goellet, consider it all a Bolshevik or Oriental conspiracy, but Colonel Fortescue and his associates Dr. Notzu, Ivanoff, and Mildred have discovered that the destruction is caused by insects who are applying a new and potent acid to metal structures. And, as Fortescue concludes, these insects, which are giant in size, are intelligent and directed by a superior intelligence that is well aware of what the human race is doing. * Fortescue further concludes that an insect headquarters is on a

Rice, Louise and Tonjoroff-Roberts (*continued*)

small island off the coast of North Carolina. There the investigators proceed, fortifying themselves in a small house behind copper screening, which metal alone is not harmed by the insect acids. Outside, millions of giant ants and termites (which the authors consider to be surface insects) swarm, trying to attack the investigators. * Fortescue discovers that infrared rays will destroy the insects, and it would seem that the insect menace may be halted. But then Fortescue is paralyzed by a two-foot-long wasp, and Mildred is kidnapped. While the investigators are wondering what to do, a giant bat flies up to the window, bearing a letter from Mildred. She has been kidnapped by an upright ant four feet high, who is the superintelligence directing the insects. Through Mildred he presents an ultimatum to the humans: abandon electricity, destroy the cities, and the insects will permit mankind to survive. * This ant prince has also told Mildred that he intends to mate with her, so that their offspring will rule the world. The prince has held back a serious assault on the human island stronghold, but sent the wasp to sting Fortescue. The wasp, which is still in the house unharmed, can provide an antidote to the sting, if the ant prince approves. * The humans are not enthusiastic about either the ultimatum or Mildred's fate. They reject the ant prince's terms and invade the insect stronghold down a tunnel on the island. The battle is hard, with infrared against smaller ants, swords against larger, upright, infrared resistant ants, but the humans win. The ant prince is shot, and Mildred is saved from the fate worse than death. * Very silly and badly presented.

RICH, H[AROLD] THOMPSON (1893-?)

U.S. author, then resident of Mount Vernon or Pleasantville, New York. Author of songbooks and verse. Friend of William Carlos Williams. Occasional contributor to *Weird Tales*. Story "The Purple Cincture" (*Weird Tales*, August 1925) was well-known. An additional science-fiction story, "The Beast Plants," appeared in *Famous Fantastic Mysteries* (April 1940). Two persons with the same name and year of birth are recorded; one died in California in 1984, the other in Maine, 1974.

1201. **THE FLYING CITY**. *Astounding Stories*, August 1930. Ill. J. Fleming Gould.

Short story. * *Place:* Arizona, a flying city, New York. * Young Professor Gordon Kendrick has discovered heatricity and how to harness it. But just as he begins to operate his apparatus, he is captured by invisible men and taken to a flying city very reminiscent of Swift's Laputa. It is inhabited by dwarves far ahead of us scientifically. * King Cor welcomes Kendrick sardonically and explains: The dwarves captured Kendrick because his discovery is moving too close to their own science. The flying city originated far away in space on the planet Vada. When its sun died, it moved away, and now that it needs repairs, the Vadans have decided to conquer the Earth and settle here. * Kendrick escapes with the aid of an Earthwoman who is being held hostage. After some back and forth adventure, he works out a defense against the Vadan disintegrator rays: a device that acts like a mirror and will toss the ray back onto the invisible flying city and destroy it. That is what happens. There is also a romance. * *Miscellaneous:* The Vadans descend from and reascend to the city with an antigravity escalatorlike field. The whole city can be made invisible. Much of Vadan science is based on an understanding of wave frequencies higher than vis-

ible light. * Rather cluttered and junky.

1202. **THE SUNKEN EMPIRE**. *Astounding Stories*, January 1931. Unsigned ill.

Short story. * *Place:* underwater, the Sargasso Sea area. * Newspaperman Larry Hunter stows away on Professor Stevens's advanced submarine, the *Nereid*, which is departing on an expedition to locate the remains of Antillia. Stevens (à la Lewis Spence) postulates that while Atlantis sank around 9000 B.C., Antillia, to the west, populated with Atlanteans, did not sink until several thousand years later. * The submarine, indeed, does find pyramids in the proper place, but surprise! The pyramids are inhabited and accessible via air locks. The surviving Antillians, who derive energy from volcanic activity, lead a canned life. Pacifist, somewhat degenerate, they speak a language of mixed Basque and Greek, which Stevens can understand. * Complications: The Antillians ask for help against surface invaders who have enslaved them. These surface men are German World War I submariners, under Rolf von Ullrich, who are looting the land of its plentiful gold and jewels. * There are seesawing adventures as the Germans capture the Stevens group; utilize the superior *Nereid* for deep sea work; and abandon the Americans underseas (except for Stevens's beautiful daughter, for whom Ullrich has a use that cannot be spelled out). Fate, however, favors the Americans. The greedy Germans overload their submarine so greatly that it sinks.

1203. **THE DIAMOND THUNDERBOLT**. *Astounding Stories*, July 1931. Ill. Wesso.

Short story. * *Place:* the Himalayas and Texas. * Professor Prescott of the expedition is astonished when his assistant Stoddard first shows him huge chunks of diamond, then reveals that he is a Secret Service agent tracing a massive diamond smuggling operation. The source for the chunks of diamond is an enormous meteorite. * The next element enters when the men see a rocket near the giant meteorite. They are captured by strange dwarves who take them to a palatial establishment belonging to the Czarist Prince Krassnov, a pioneer rocket experimenter who disappeared a couple of years earlier. * Krassnov tells the men that he has built up an enormous fortune with his diamonds and intends to use it to restore aristocratic rule in Russia. He offers the two men a share in his enterprise. When they refuse, Krassnov turns them over to the dwarves, who will torture them to death. * But Prescott and Stoddard are not daunted. They escape, stowing away on the prince's rocket, and fly with him to Texas. Eventually the prince is trapped and the conspiracy is at an end.

1204. **SPAWN OF THE COMET**. *Astounding Stories*, November 1931. Ill. Paul.

Short story. * *Time:* 1947. *Place:* the New York area, the Southwest. * When the Mystery Comet appears, the Earth is pelted with meteorites that look like large eggs. Indeed, as shortly appears, they are eggs, which hatch over much of the world into gigantic ant-like creatures. Possessed of a high technology, they build a gigantic city in the desert. But these ant-creatures do not seem to be of normal matter, for they generate enormous amounts of heat and they are indestructible by any means known to man. * The ant-creatures depopulate the British Isles, and in a short time humanity will be extinct. * Reporter Jim Carter is present at most developments: seeing the eggs; being the first to fly over the ant city and survive; and assisting Professor Wentworth (his future father-in-law) in the

Rich, H. Thompson (*continued*)
battle against the ants. The professor devises a cathode ray weapon that releases atomic energy, destroying the ants, but dies of burns from the resulting radiation. * *Miscellaneous:* The ants gain their strength and vitality from a new radioactive element.

RICHARDS, HAROLD F[REDERIC], Ph.D. (1894-?)
American educator. Received Ph.D. in physics, University of Cincinnati, 1920 on electrification by impact. Contributed other stories to *Science and Invention.* Author of general textbook *The Universe Surveyed* (1937). Social Security records list five persons named Harold Richards who were born in 1894, two of whom were residents of Ohio.

    1205. **THE VIBRATOR OF DEATH.** *Amazing Stories Quarterly*, Spring 1928. Unsgnd ill.
(First published in *Science and Invention*, January 1922.)
Short story. * Doubtful as science-fiction. * *Place:* Paris. * France is beset by Communist agitation, which the authorities believe is being fostered by Krampdorff, a socialist criminal. * One of the factors holding back revolution is the great mezzosoprano Marie Denbaule. When Marie sings publicly, the workers, who adore her, forget their grievances and their plans for an uprising, and return docilely to work. * On the crucial occasion, Marie is to sing at an amusement park, after mounting one of the stunts, a tall vibrating column. But the column vibrates excessively, and Marie dies of heart failure. * The Sureté tracks down the villains, and a spokesman explains. The vibration forced her heart to cease beating. The man behind the crime is Jacobs, the Jewish carnie man who worked on such matters at New York University before he was expelled and deported for socialist agitation. * Not only racist and reactionary, but silly.

RICHTER, CHARLES DE (1885 or 1887-?)
French writer. Author of many detective stories, which do not seem to have been translated into English. Also translated detective stories from the English of Mark Cross, Arthur Somers Roche, and others into French. Another s-f novel, not translated, *L'homme qui voulut le déluge* (1945), also concerns a mad scientist. Oddly enough, editor Charles Hornig in The Reader Speaks of *Wonder Stories*, March 1935 refers to Richter as a German author currently residing in Monaco.

    1206. **THE FALL OF THE EIFFEL TOWER.** *Wonder Stories*, September-November 1934. Translated from French by Fletcher Pratt. Ill. Paul.
(Later French publication, *La menace invisible* [1937].) Fairly long novel. * A thriller on the theme of the peace vigilante. * *Time:* 1987. *Place:* mostly France. * *Background:* France, which is now called the union of French-speaking peoples (not defined), maintains its republican form of government; Germany suffers from Communists and Nazis (mentioned as such), though neither seems to be in power; but Great Britain has granted India independence and is now a protectorate of India. Russia remains Communist. All the major countries are engaged in an arms race. * A series of strange accidents besets the naval programs of France, Germany, and Italy. Cruisers, as they are about to be commissioned, suddenly topple over and are badly damaged as their shorings collapse. Then military installations throughout France similarly collapse. Handwritten notes mysteriously delivered to the various French ministers urge disarmament. *

Other mysterious events take place: A vicious murderer is smuggled out of a prison, apparently invisibly; and investigating reporter Louis Berson is similarly abducted and later returned without any memory of what happened. * It is eventually discovered that the destruction is due to termites, which have developed technology to survive cold and are seemingly directed. Berson, around whom much of the story centers (the other center is Gromier, French Minister of the Interior) solves the mystery. A sincere though somewhat addled scientist has discovered how to communicate with termites and has created a termite directing intelligence that he can influence. He is assisted by an utterly mad, sadistic doctor who wires up human captives to obtain neural energy. But the solution of the mystery may be too late, for the termites are almost omnipresent, and no matter how many termitaries are dynamited, others spring up. The central termite intelligence, however, is finally destroyed in a very easy manner. * For a short time after the invisible menace has ended, the nations agree to act on peace, but this situation does not last long and the arms race picks up again. * Also included is a romance between Berson and the daughter of the peace vigilante. * Among incidents, the Eiffel Tower, undermined by the termites, topples over. * Of no particular interest. Somewhat dated for English-language science-fiction, but in the French thriller tradition.

RIDEAUX, CHARLES DE BALZAC (1900-1971)
British author of boys' fiction, adult mysteries, miscellaneous work often written under the pseud. John Chancellor.

    1207. **THE REBEL ROBOTS.** *Scoops*, 10 February 1934. Ill. S. D.
Published anonymously, attribution per W. O. G. Lofts, who had access to the publisher's records.
Boys' fiction. * Short story. * *Time:* no stated period, but presumably near future. * Max Chancellor, Master of the Mechanical Squad, is in charge of constructing robots (humaniform in this case) for much of the city's dirty work. He has also been working on a superior robot, Genius No. 1, which will be able to think. It is powered by cosmic rays. * Unfortunately, as Chancellor is in his laboratory, Genius No. 1 kills him and runs amok. It steals the crown jewels, hijacks a lorry laden with bullion, and performs other crimes. In a short time it is joined by other robots who are similarly antisocial. Their headquarters is not known; after their crimes, they simply disappear. Against the robot crime wave are John Hughes and Phil Kester, old Chancellor's assistants. * When a giant robot captures Phil, John follows it down into the Thames to an underwater, subterranean retreat. There the solution is found. A former assistant of Chancellor's, now mad, constructed a black box for controlling Genius No. 1 and has been operating him. The mad scientist and Genius No. 1 constructed the other robots that have been causing trouble. * *Miscellaneous:* John and Phil constructed their own private army of red robots to combat the criminal element, but this did not lead to anything important, although good triumphs.

ROBIN, RALPH (1914-?)
U.S. (mostly Philadelphia and Washington, D.C.) author. Educated at University of Pittsburgh (B.S.) and University of Maryland. Chemist with National Bureau of Standards. Second career as poet and teacher, lecturer and adjunct professor of

Robin, Ralph (*continued*)
English, American University, Washington, D.C. Christopher Morley Award from Poetry Society of America, 1976. Work frequently anthologized, as in Martha Foley's *Best American Short Stories of 1958*. Other fantastic fiction has appeared in *Magazine of Fantasy and Science Fiction*.

1208. **THE PYGMIES OF PHOBOS.** *Amazing Stories,* April 1936. Ill. Morey.

Short story. * *Time:* a frame situation of A.D. 2505, with extensive flashback material. *Place:* the main body on Mars and Phobos. * At the beginning of the twenty-sixth century, since space travel does not seem possible without atomic energy, scientists build two one-hundred and twenty-foot high radio towers in the Himalayas, hoping to receive space signals that would have been stopped by the Heaviside layer. * Shortly after the towers are activated, Director Stanley Evans and associates hear the "music of the spheres," a telepathic message conveyed by music. * The message: Ages ago, two forms of intelligent life arose on Mars, humanoid creatures much like mankind and protozoa about a millimeter across. Both peoples developed mechanical civilizations at about the same time. When they became aware of each other, however, they immediately began wars of extermination. The humans, with superior size and material weapons, destroyed countless protozoans, while the telepathic microbes, fighting with bacterial weapons, did the same for their human opponents. Finally, after thousands of years of war, the peoples made a shaky peace. * The protozoans, fearful that war would break out again, made a suggestion that satisfied both races: encasing Phobos in a shell to retain necessities of life and moving the protozoans there, leaving Mars to the humans. After this, both races lived on friendly terms, discovering in a collaborative effort atomic power based on thorium. * But over the millennia, despite intensive environmental engineering with sealed cities and similar matters, Mars gradually declined, losing air and water. Martian civilization, too, began to wane, and by the time of the thought-music had deteriorated greatly. * At this point, the protozoan dictator Thakin proposed an invasion of Mars. The council rejected this proposal with horror, but Thakin, gathering his followers and seizing the entire planetary supply of thorium, fled to Mars. There, he inserted individual protozoa into the brains of the human Martians, subjecting them to protozoan control. After Mars had thus been overrun by his followers, Thakin demanded the surrender and evacuation of Phobos. When the protozoans refused, Thakin threatened to bombard the tiny world with war rockets. The thought-music ends suddenly, indicating that the protozoa are extinct. * The listeners in the Himalayas are depressed at the destruction of the tiny people and outraged by the fate of such humanoid Martians as survive. * The author created an opening for a sequel, but none has been published.

ROCHESTER, GEORGE E[RNEST] (ca. 1895-?)
Very prolific British writer of serials for boys' periodicals. Served in R.A.F. in World War I, hence air stories noted for authenticity. Some serials reprinted in book form: *Jackals of the Clouds* (1936) and *Wings of Doom* (1936). Also wrote under pseuds. Barton Furze, Frank Chatham, Hamilton Smith, Eric Roche, John Beresford, Elizabeth Kent, and others. Moved to U.S. after stroke in 1962, but returned to England.

1209. **THE BLACK VULTURES.** *Scoops,* 28 April-23 June 1934. Unsigned ill.

Boys' fiction. * Short novel. * A salmi of a sort: traditional British boys' fiction, the work of Guy Boothby, *The Shadow,* and the American air pulps. * *Place:* Germany, Tibet, Greenland, and the Arctic in general. * *Background:* The Black Vultures are a band of aerial desperados who have been attacking European cities from the air, bombing and gassing the inhabitants, and looting banks and other sources of wealth. Little is known about them—their identity, their headquarters, and their modus operandi. As is revealed early in the story, however, they operate from an enormous dirigible that has on its top a landing deck that holds a dozen fighter planes and can fly at speeds of 300 MPH and more in the stratosphere. * The Black Vultures are Germans, judging by their names and the opening locale, but this is not belabored by the author. They are led by a dynamic and vicious man called Zoroster, who embodies traits of the Shadow and Dr. Nikola. * The story opens by showing how Zoroster recruits his thugs and criminals, when he enlists a German ex-convict who is about to commit suicide. * More important to the story, when Zoroster raids a small town in East Prussia, British scientist Derek Oldham, who is doing meteorological research there, recognizes the presence of poison gas and succeeds in putting on a gas mask in time. Watching the bandits raid the town bank, on an impulse he grasps the landing gear of one of their planes and is carried away to the zeppelin, losing consciousness as the plane enters the higher atmosphere. * When he awakens, he is first sentenced to death by Zoroster, then on the recommendation of Falze, a gang member who is presented throughout in a favorable light, is granted a respite until he decides whether he will join the band. * When the Black Vultures raid a fabulously wealthy monastery in Tibet, Derek escapes via parachute, landing, to his surprise, near the badly injured Zoroster. As the reader already knows, Zoroster has raided the monastery, slaughtering the warlike monks and taking their treasure, but his plane malfunctioned and he crashed. He is badly injured, with a broken limb and internal injuries. * Zoroster, who knows Tibet, recognizes that he will suffer a cruel death if he is captured. Thus, he and Derek strike a temporary truce until they can reach safety. They are captured, however, and are sentenced to be executed by a gigantic Buddha that crushes its victims in its hand. Indeed, Zoroster is already somewhat squashed when the men are rescued by the outlaw band. * All proceed to the pirate base in Greenland. Derek's sentence is mitigated, and he is given a chance for his life in an air duel with one of the band who has fallen into disfavor for cowardice. In this first of several duels, Derek, of course, wins. * There would be no point in giving further plot detail. Incidents alone will be mentioned. The pirate force destroys an American punitive expedition. Derek escapes and duels again. Derek is recaptured and almost has his eyes burned out. Derek escapes again, this time reaching a Russian air base in Siberia. A Russian force overwhelms the air pirates, and Derek has the satisfaction of shooting down Zoroster's plane. * Fast moving and not bad for boys' action fiction, if one can accept the conventions.

ROCKLYNNE, ROSS (1913-1988)
Professional name of Ross Louis Rocklin, U.S. author. Born in Ohio, but worked mostly in California. Journalist, prolific professional writer with about eighty stories, mostly from the

Rocklynne, Ross (*continued*)

1940s. One of the better hard s-f writers of the day. The stories described here do not represent his mature work.

1210. **MAN OF IRON**. *Astounding Stories*, August 1935. Ill. Dold.

Short story. * The working out of an idea. * Nasty scientist Dr. Merra has worked out a technique for perichoresis. It involves using radiation to make molecules repel one another so that they can glide past each other. * The process has worked with inanimate objects, and now Merra plans to walk through a gigantic iron cube that he keeps in the laboratory. His assistant will work the controls as he progresses. * Unfortunately, Lemmans, the assistant, is Merra's secret enemy. Not only did Merra swindle him out of his inheritance, but he has treated him abusively. A timid, sneaky soul, Lemmans has long wanted revenge. * Now that Merra has entered the cube and is well inside it, Lemmans turns off the radiation. The result is that two bodies attempt to occupy the same space. The explosion is horrific. * Routine.

1211. **AT THE CENTER OF GRAVITY**. *Astounding Stories*, June 1936. Ill. Schneeman.

(Reprinted in Rocklynne, *The Men and the Mirror*; and in Moskowitz, *Exploring Other Worlds*.)

Short story. * *Time:* the interplanetary future. *Place:* inside Vulcan. * Edward Deverel, wanted criminal, has led Jack Colbie of the Interplanetary Police Force a merry chase, from Mars, to Earth, Venus, and finally to Vulcan. When Deverel tried to hide in a crater, Colbie followed him; but the crater was not a crater, but a passage to Vulcan's hollow interior. Now both men are trapped inside the planetoid, which has an internal reservoir of gases. Their oxygen supply is limited. * The men amicably discuss means of escape. Reaction from pistols, for various reasons, would not work, nor would the gravitational pull of the sun. Colbie is in control of the situation for a time, but Deverel has obviously figured out a way to escape. * A change comes when winds arise due to solar forces. Deverel manages to obtain Colbie's gun and kicks away. Colbie now realizes what will happen to them as the winds continue to rise. The expanding gases will force them, if they are at the right place, through the crater passage out into space. So it happens. Colbie, without reaction devices, takes long to settle back to the surface of Vulcan and his ship, while Deverel, with the pistol, controls his movements and escapes. * Well-devised hard science-fiction.

1212. **ANTON MOVES THE WORLD**. *Astounding Stories*, November 1936. Ill. Marchioni.

Short story. * *Time:* A.D. 2676. *Place:* mostly in space. * The great space pirate Anton Larval has been captured by the Interplanetary Police Force. It is only by chance that he was taken, for his ship is far superior to anything else in space, thanks to his inventive genius. Larval, it should be noted, is not a typical pirate. He operates not out of greed, but solely for the adventure. * Anton should be sentenced to death. Instead, the world president sets him free, but on condition that he does what he can to save the Earth. * What is wrong? In space there are strange sparks that are attributed to a small sun (in a hyperspace) that has ripped the barriers into our universe and is manifesting itself in a fragmentary way. Projecting the sparks in terms of solid geometry, it can be seen that the invading sun, when it is fully manifested, will be close enough to Earth to destroy it. Anton, with usual selfconfidence and exuberance, promises to save the world. * The method: Using beams of force and the sun as a fulcrum, Anton moves the Earth to a new orbit, where it escapes the invader sun, which hurls itself out of the solar system. * Anton is free, and as per contract is promised anything he wishes. But he discovers that there are unsuspected depths to the contract. When he returns to his life of piracy, he learns to his dismay, that all ships have been ordered to give him everything he wants, graciously. Since there is no more zest in piracy, Anton decides to reform; the image of a young woman scientist who cooperated with him on his task moves him powerfully. * The interesting aspect of the story is the surface writing, which shows more personality than is usual in pulp fiction.

RODMAN, J.

U.S. author; according to Gernsback's blurb, then a lieutenant in the U.S. Army. The *Official Military Register* of 1930 lists a Capt. John H. Rodman (1893-?) and a Capt. John W. Rodman (1891-?), both Infantry officers born in Kentucky. It seems questionable whether either man was our author.

1213. **THE UNDERSEA EXPRESS**. *Amazing Stories*, December 1927. Unsigned ill.

Short story. * *Time:* A.D. 2550. * The narrator takes a voyage via the undersea express (supersubmarines that travel at 100 knots) from New York to England. The propellant is a new gas that seems to operate via phase states. Along the way the submarine goes to the rescue of a disabled fellow vessel. * Very flat.

ROMANS, R. H.

An advance notice in *Air Wonder Magazine*, January 1930, refers to Romans as "an astronomer of no mean accomplishments," for what that is worth. Otherwise, no information except that a portrait shows a middle-aged man. Kyle states that Romans was a French author. This is almost certainly incorrect. His use of local color would place him somewhere in the Midwest.

1214. **AROUND THE WORLD IN 24 HOURS**. *Air Wonder Stories*, October 1929. Unsigned ill.

Short story. * *Time:* Perhaps a decade or so later than 1930, which is referred to in the text. *Place:* Akron, Ohio, and around the world. * An invention and a con game. * Three of the big track bookies hear of a wonderful chance to bilk a sucker. Olaf Hansen, a Swedish-American crank inventor from Minnesota, has built a Rube Goldberg machine in which he claims that he can fly around the world in twenty-four hours or less. He offers one hundred thousand dollars as a bet, but wants ten-to-one odds. * Posing as capitalists, the three bookies examine the machine, which is a monstrosity with a home-made propeller, one blade of which is shorter than the other, an ancient automobile motor, strange headlights on front and back, and bat-like wings. The bet is on. * At trial day, the plane, which is so heavy that it must be dragged out with a tractor, does take off, but performs erratically in the air, and lands again. Olaf, in a Swedish accent, declares that the propeller has not been working properly; he thereupon removes it from the machine and discards it. On a second ascent, the motor drops out. * Descending, Olaf, now speaking in serious, unaccented English, proclaims the debut of a new motorless plane. Off again, the plane flies through storms, stops at suitable places around the world, and is back at Akron within the stipulated time. * "Olaf" now discards his

Romans, R. H. (*continued*)

masquerade and reveals himself as a once well-known aerial circus clown and inventor who wanted, as a side issue, to get his revenge on the three bookies who had cheated him so often in the past. * His plane operates on a new principle: Artificially induced air pockets and changes in air pressure pull and push the plane forward. No motor is needed, only a rank of flashlight batteries and the apparatus described as headlights. * Amusing.

1215. **THE MOON CONQUERORS**. *Science Wonder Quarterly*, Winter 1930. Ill. Paul; photo and sketches by "Dorothy Brewster."

Novel. * *Time:* early 1940s through 1952. * *Place:* Arizona and the Moon. * The first section of the story is the narrative of Dorothy Brewster, daughter of the eccentric millionaire scientist William Brewster, who has built a one-hundred-foot reflecting telescope on a new light-gathering principle. Dorothy sees little of her father when she is growing up, but when she leaves college as a well-trained, highly intelligent astronomer, she joins him at his establishment in Arizona. The new telescope, which is just operational, is fantastically successful, showing the moon from a close distance. As Dorothy watches, she sees a flying sphere move across a crater, then discharge a handsome young man, whom the men in the sphere maroon. While Dorothy watches, the question is whether the man can reach shelter before the harsh lunar night begins. Unfortunately, Dorothy shatters the telescope, and does not know (for a time) what happened next. The implication of all this is that the Moon definitely has an atmosphere, even though it is not visible from Earth. * The second section of the novel consists mostly of the recorded narratives of George L. Davis, a newspaper reporter, and Dr. William Haverfield, a college president, who are members of the Brewster expedition to the Moon. * Dorothy Brewster, whose wealth is incredible, has subsidized research on the design of a spaceship. She has settled on a complex vehicle that will be flung off the Earth by a linear motor and propelled in space by light pressure and rockets. The *Astronaut* takes off with Miss Brewster and three men, reaching the Moon after an uneventful trip. Miss Brewster had insisted on a particular landing site, which turns out to be near the place where she saw the handsome Lunarian. The Moon has an atmosphere, and locomotion is easy enough. * In a very short time Dorothy rescues the Lunarian, whose name is Baklo. Since being marooned by political rivals, he had been living in a cave. A romance immediately begins. Baklo summons friends by radio, and soon Lunar spheres come and remove him and our friends to a city on the other side of the Moon. The spheres then blast the *Astronaut*. The incident is misinterpreted in various ways: Watchers on Earth think it signals the death of the explorers; the explorers think it is a hostile act; but actually it is simply a precaution to prevent the spread of terrestrial germs on the Moon. * The explorers are first quarantined, then subjected to various medical treatments both to remove bacteria and to rejuvenate them to some extent. (The Lunarians have very long life-spans thanks to advanced medicine.) * The Earthmen, when they have learned sufficient language for communication, are taken before the Lunarian ruler and his council. Surprisingly, the Lunarians are somewhat hostile, despite Dorothy's rescue of Baklo, for the Moonmen cherish a long grudge against Earth because of incidents in the past. The Lunarians also consider the Earthlings to be barbarians and members of an inferior race. * At

this time Romans offers a very long statement of interplanetary history. The human race ultimately originated outside our solar system, no details known. But it developed on Bodia, the now-missing fifth planet, where there were two races, blacks and whites. The blacks, who soon developed a supercivilization, enslaved the whites, who remained at a much lower level of development. On one occasion, while a black liner (with white slaves) was on an exploration voyage to the small planet that is now our moon, Bodia exploded, probably from the experimental release of atomic energy. The surviving blacks thereupon settled on the Moon, which was then a hospitable world. Over thousands of years escaped white slaves took refuge in Lunar caverns and isolated areas, developing small independent states and a lesser science. * The great catastrophe came about 34,500 years ago when another sun and attendant planets entered the solar system. One of the new planets passed close by Luna, capturing it as a satellite. This new planet was our Earth. Earth also stripped away Lunar atmosphere and water, which had been concentrated in a deep sea on the other side of the Moon. Some Lunar whites, led by a magisterial scientist, sealed themselves off in caverns when they saw the impending disaster; most died, but about 30,000 survived to form the present Lunar race. The Lunar blacks either died or moved en masse (with white slaves) to Earth. The companion novelette, #1216, "The War of the Planets" gives details of what happened to the blacks and their slaves, but the result was the destruction of black civilization. Occasional recent Lunar expeditions to Earth, the last about five hundred years ago, revealed only contemptible savagery. * To return to the story: The Lunar authorities permit the Earthmen to live and accept Lunar education into advanced science, but the Earthlings are considered second-class citizens, and Dorothy and Prince Baklo are not permitted to marry. * Five years after arrival, however, the explorers turn the tables on their hypercritical hosts. Dorothy and Haverfield, in concerted attack on the Lunar council, prove that Earthlings are not inferior to Lunarians, but actually superior. In five years the explorers have mastered sciences and arts that take the Lunarians considerably longer, and in the last five hundred years Earth culture has progressed far more rapidly than has Lunarian. The Lunarians grudgingly agree. Dorothy and Baklo marry, and in 1955 the other expedition members return to Earth in a Lunarian sphere. * *Miscellaneous:* Despite their high material science, the Lunarians seem to be somewhat afflicted by lassitude and cultural fatigue. * Lunarian science, in addition to rejuvenation techniques, possesses antigravity, atmosphere-creating machinery, and many scientific marvels. * There is a native Lunarian life-form that is much like a kangaroo with enormous flat feet. * Mercury, too, is a new planet brought in by the wandering sun. * The ancient blacks, called Vuduites (of obvious derivation), were a bloodthirsty group who practiced human sacrifices. * The varied voices of the first part of the novel are a reasonable Vernian exposition, but the deadly and unnecessary middle historical section is likely to make most readers put the magazine aside. The ending, of course, is very contrived. * For a companion story see, #1216, "The War of the Planets."

1216. **THE WAR OF THE PLANETS**. *Wonder Stories Quarterly*, Summer 1930. Ill. Paul.

Novelette. * Companion work to #1215, "The Moon Conquerors." Mostly a historical narrative compiled by Professor Haverfield from lunar records. There are no fictional elements

Romans, R. H. (*continued*)

until the last few pages. * After the rapture of the Moon's atmosphere and surface water by the intrusive Earth, the inhabitants of the Moon continued to develop within Lunar caverns. The Lunarians remained apprehensive about the possibly hostile black humans on Earth, but it was not until about thirty-two thousand years ago, when antigravity was redeveloped, that the Lunarians were in a position to investigate Earth. * A small fleet of space spheres secretly explored Earth, which was still very sparsely inhabited. On one occasion they killed the last surviving tyrannosaurus in South America. * Geographically, Earth was different. The Amazon drainage was under water; the Mediterranean was a landlocked inhabited valley; Atlantis existed, as did land bridges between Oceania and Asia. Ethnographically, the Earth contained white primitive savages; very bestial Neanderthal men in Europe; white peoples held as slaves by the black; racially mixed people who became brown-skinned men and Orientals; and scattered highly civilized blacks who lived in cities with all the ancient science. * For many years the Lunarians raided the blacks, who had no notion whence the attacks originated. Eventually, however, a large black fleet followed the lunar spheres back to the Moon and attacked the Lunarians directly. The assault was overpowering, but the Lunarians survived by perfecting atomic matter transformers and moving deeper into the Moon. * The next episode was an invasion of Earth and Moon by Martians. The Martians, who were giant ants, established outposts on both planets, but eventually were defeated by the blacks and Lunarians. As a curious reversal of history, the Lunarians, who had developed invisible ships, aided the blacks without their knowing it. Lunarian invisibility now became the decisive factor, enabling an invasion of Mars and the complete destruction of Martian civilization. Meanwhile black civilization collapsed internally as a result of slave revolts and warfare. * About ten thousand years ago, Lunar war hawks, on the principle of *Carthago delenda est*, mounted an illegal attack on Earth. Led by the nobleman Kargo, husband of the twin sister of the Lunar monarch, the Lunarians conducted very efficient genocide against all the humans on Earth. What with invisible ships and advanced Lunar weapons, Kargo was invincible. His chef d'oeuvre was disintegrating a channel from the Atlantic Ocean to the Mediterranean basin, flooding out the local cultures. As a result of his campaign, only scattered remnants of humanity survived on Earth. * When Kargo returned to the Moon with his fleet, however, he was arrested. He and his followers were sentenced to exile on Atlantis without many of the appurtenances of civilization. * Our present world, thus is descended from a combination of black and white survivors of Kargo's attack and Kargo's group. * *Miscellaneous:* Present-day small ants are descended from the Martian ants, who deliberately created tiny races when they were attempting to establish colonies. Mars, which is Schiaparellian, is dying. * Some imaginative verve, but one wonders to what purpose.

ROSBOROUGH, L. B.

No information.

1217. **HASTINGS—1066.** *Amazing Stories*, June 1934. Ill. Morey.

Short story. * Crooked inventor-exploiter Henry Carteret is obsessed with his ancestor Lammot de Carteret, one of the Norman heroes at the Battle of Hastings. Thus, to be able to witness his ancestor's exploits, he has constructed (partly from stolen ideas) a time viewer that works on a novel principle. According to Carteret, at the edge of the universe there is a light barrier comparable to the Heaviside Layer for radio; this barrier is impermeable to light, which it reflects back to its origins. By a stroke of luck the light-barrier is precisely at the correct distance to reflect the Battle of Hastings. * With a select audience, including the rival inventor whose work he had stolen, Carteret now reproduces the battle. Unfortunately, the apparatus reveals Lammot de Carteret not as a hero, but as a rank coward who was hanged by William after the battle. Henry Carteret goes berserk, smashing his apparatus, attacking his guests, then dying of a heart attack. * Routine.

ROSE, DR. WALTER (1884-still living in 1962)

South African (Capetown) naturalist. Author of standard *Reptiles and Amphibia of Southern Africa* (1950, with later editions) and other works. Occasional contributor to s-f letter columns. Rose's second story, a novel, "By Jove!," appeared in *Amazing Stories* in 1937.

1218. **THE LURKING DEATH.** *Amazing Stories,* February 1936. Ill. Morey.

Short story. * *Place:* Capetown, South Africa. * Strange disappearances at night from the common at Rondebosch—dogs, people, even an armed policeman at a time when the common is cordoned off by police. When the area is examined by day, nothing is to be seen, not a trace of the victims or possible criminal. * Gartside, amateur naturalist, solves the mystery through his acquaintance with irascible, eccentric old Professor Culbertson. Culbertson has discovered that by focusing concentrated ultraviolet rays on lower forms of life he can enlarge them significantly. * The answer lies in an enlarged trapdoor spider that has escaped. Gartside, who knows the habits of the arachnid, is able to destroy it with a combination of chlorine and explosives. * The point is that trapdoor spiders are so skillful at camouflaging their burrows that they are very difficult to locate. * Intelligent, but stuffy in the writing.

ROSS, E. L.

According to Street and Smith records, pseud. of Ross Stagnor, U.S. author.

1219. **FACETED EYES!** *Astounding Stories,* October 1935. Ill. Marchioni.

Short story. * Using new radiative techniques Professor Newt Miller has achieved remarkable results inducing mutations in Drosophila. Indeed, he claims that his mutations are taking a peculiar direction—all progressing up toward humanity. * The high point comes when Miller lets the narrator into a hitherto restricted part of the laboratory. There in a cage is an anthropoid Drosophila the size of a gorilla! It has two shining eyes, and these have a hypnotic power—as the narrator soon discovers. * Some time later, he returns to find the cage open, Miller dead, and the monster escaped on the campus. Revolver and machine gun bullets simply bounce off its chitin as it rages about, and its hypnotic abilities make it dangerous to encounter. The narrator consults a professional hypnotist to help him face it, but the monster is finally overcome when someone drops a fifty-pound lump of iron onto it from a roof top. * One might suspect parody, but the author seems serious.

ROUSE, WILLIAM MERRIAM (1884-1937)

U.S. journalist, born in Albany, New York; resident at this time in Westport, Connecticut.   Contributor to pulp magazines, notably *Adventure* and Munsey magazines. Two other science-fiction stories of his are described in *Science-Fiction: The Early Years*. Author of *Bildad Road* (1940) posthumously published by Orlin Tremaine Co.

1220. THE DESTROYER.   *Astounding Stories*, November 1930. Ill. J. Fleming Gould.

Short story. * Author-illustrator Allen Parker discovers that he has lost control over his creativity.   The story he has been working on has turned nasty, and his drawings are foul.   His beautiful wife Betty suggests that he see the newly arrived Dr. von Stein, who is some sort of psychologist. * Von Stein, an embodiment of Prussianism, is responsible, as the reader will immediately guess. He lusts for Betty, and he has already killed two people for their money. * Von Stein has discovered the nature of thought (vibration in one dimension) and can mechanically control the will of others. His apparatus can also destroy matter. * Parker seems lost, but a recourse to violent action is successful, and the bad doctor is disintegrated.

ROUSSEAU, VICTOR

Pseud. of Victor Rousseau Emanuel, 1879-1960. U.S. (New York) author of British birth; formerly resident in South Africa. A fairly prolific contributor to the early pulp magazines, writing in many areas: Westerns, detective stories, geographical adventure, weird fiction, and early science-fiction.   Also published under the names H. M. Egbert and V. R. Emanuel, but was best-known as Victor Rousseau.   Rousseau was fairly popular in the 1920s, but seems to have sold much less after the 1930s.   Most of his work was ephemeral, but his novel *The Messiah of the Cylinder* (book, 1917, described in *Science-Fiction: The Early Years*) is a serious work worth reading. It is an answer to H. G. Wells's *When the Sleeper Wakes*, the utopian element of which Rousseau misunderstood. A sequel written by Rousseau has not been published.

1221. THE BEETLE HORDE.   *Astounding Stories*, January-February 1930. Ill. J. Fleming Gould.

Nouvelle. * *Place:* Antarctica and Australia. * An expedition charged with locating the south pole with precision comes upon marvels.   Aviator Tommy Travers and scientist Jim Dodd find evidence of man-sized beetles near the pole.   Then, their plane is sucked into a vortex and drawn inside the Earth, which is inhabited by the beetles, who are fairly intelligent and carnivorous.   Also present is a hitherto unknown human race: tall, ultra-blond, with eyes fitted with nictitating membranes to avoid harsh light.   Primitive in culture, clad in garments of human hair, they serve as food and slaves for the beetles. The humans, in turn, feed on giant land shrimp, even though there are monocotyledonous fruit trees in the area. * Dodd and Travers are captured by the beetles, who are controlled by Bram, a scientist from a previous expedition. Bram, a bitter professional rival and enemy of Dodd's, is now mad and a drug addict. Throughout the story Bram and Dodd carry on heated exchanges about the origin of marsupials; this may be intended as humor. * Bram, nevertheless, decides to use the two men in his plans for world conquest. He has a good chance of victory, for it is almost time for an incredibly large generation of beetles to metamorphose, an event that occurs only every 150 years or so.

His control of the horde is excellent. * Travers, Dodd, and Haidia (a lost-race woman who is in love with Dodd) decide to escape. They pass beyond a flaming deposit of petroleum and through areas where dwell gigantic predators like praying mantises.   After a long passage through dark canyons and old river beds, the fugitives emerge in the Victoria Desert in Australia, Bram and his beetle horde close behind them. Friendly natives rescue the refugees, but the beetles emerge, and the battle for Australia begins. * Billions of the incredibly savage beetles, now almost omnivorous, protected by heavy chitin that small arms fire cannot pierce, devastate Western Australia. In a short time the horde reaches as far out to sea as Mauritius. Their numbers are so great that even effective conventional weapons are inadequate. * The battle is now on for eastern Australia; its outcome seems certain. But there is a saving factor. As the explorers observe, the beetles are burrowing underground to metamorphose to a new, larger form, and are now vulnerable to burning oil or gasoline, and handguns. The world is saved. Bram died unrepentant during one of the oil attacks. * *Miscellaneous*: The members of the lost race, when they emerge into the full sunlight, no longer need their nictitating membranes. * It is not clear whether the underground events take place within the hollow Earth or simply in great caverns. * Crudely written, obviously patterned in part after A. Conan Doyle's Challenger stories, but certainly without Doyle's flair.

1222. THE ATOM-SMASHER. *Astounding Stories*, May 1930. Ill. J. Fleming Gould.

Nouvelle. * *Time:* the present and about 12,000 B.C. *Place:* Long Island and Atlantis. *. The brilliant if somewhat unpleasant scientist Tode and old Professor Parrish were working to liberate atomic energy when a terrific explosion, accompanied by a violet light, left only a water-filled pit where their laboratory had been. It is known as the Vanishing Place. * Five years later, however, Parrish's daughter Lucille receives a telephone call from her supposedly dead father. She tells her boy friend Dent, who flies to the Vanishing Place. While still in mid flight, he sees a violet light, and there is Tode on a strange platform in the water, pointing a projector at him. Dent's plane is disintegrated, but he makes his way through muck and water to the platform, where Tode captures him. Also captive are Professor Parrish and Lucille. * Tode is obviously mad, a megalomaniac who lusts for the unwilling Lucille. He can move through time with the atom-smasher that he and Parrish invented, and he has established a base at 12,000 B.C. on the island of Atlantis. The Neanderthals who inhabit much of the land consider him a god, but the great city of Atlantis, which possesses a superscience and wields a disintegrator ray, is at war with him. So far Tode has been unable to conquer Atlantis, which he wants both to rule and raid. * Captivities, escapes, flights through time, battles take place. At one point Dent, Lucille, and Professor Parrish are captured by the Atlanteans, who are smiling and polite, but plan to offer them as sacrifices to idols with whirling arms that cut victims to death. * Our friends escape on the atom-smasher, but are unable to control the mechanism with enough precision to return to their own time. They make a bargain with Tode, who has remained outside Atlantis, but he reneges. Eventually, the adventure ends when Tode, after threatening to shift them into eternity (the fifth dimension), is electrocuted. The three comrades return home, leaving the atom-smasher in the water pit. * Other matters: A friendly Neanderthal called Cain is very helpful. * Atlantis,

Rousseau, Victor (continued)

which has been submerging gradually, is given the final push by an atomic blast from the atom-smasher. Atlantean settlers have already reached Europe. * The machine travels through time as a fourth dimension. * Routine material.

1223. **THE LORD OF SPACE**. *Astounding Stories*, August 1930. Ill. J. Fleming Gould.

Capsulated nouvelle. * *Time:* A.D. 2044. *Place:* Earth, Moon, Eros. * The Earth is in great peril. The interplanetary outlaw Axelson (the Black Caesar) has seized the Moon colony, has destroyed the terrestrial mining site, and is playing a tremendous disintegrator ray on Earth. He has already depopulated much of Asia, and now demands surrender and sovereignty of the entire Earth. * Against him is pitted Nathaniel Lee in his spaceship. As Lee and his crew approach the Moon, they discover a female stowaway, Madge Dawes, a newspaperwoman. * The mission may not be easy, however, for Lee's ship is easily captured by the Black Caesar, who orders all the crew executed except for the officers. To Lee he offers a high job in the new administration. But the most unexpected incident comes when Axelson, who was born in space and has never been on Earth, sees Madge. He has never before seen a human female. Carried away by her charms, he announces that he will marry her. * Axelson then transships his captives to Eros, where his real headquarters are. The disintegrator rays, which seem to come from the Moon, are really reflected from Eros. * *Background:* Axelson's comrades are a mixture of the primitive natives of the Moon and lags from the prison colony, mostly old Communists who still hope for the triumph of Leninism. They are unhappy with the Black Caesar's imperial ambitions. * A second blow to weaken Axelson comes when he talks to Madge. Since he has had no experience with women, he goes to pieces when she refuses him. The third comes with coryza, the common cold, which Lee and his crew brought to the Moon. Most of the outlaws, including Axelson, die of it. The world is saved and it looks as if Lee will be the next president of the World Federation. * *Miscellaneous:* Atomic power is in general use. * The Moon has some air in deep caverns and pits; its inhabitants are humanoid and primitive. * Eros is like Earth, but somewhat better.

1224. **THE INVISIBLE DEATH**. *Astounding Stories*, October 1930. Ill. Wesso.

Nouvelle. * *Time:* about 1940. *Place:* the Washington area, the Bahama Islands. Aspects of World War I revanchism. * The story begins with the inexplicable escape from prison of Hugo Von Kettler, who has been sentenced to death for conspiracy to overthrow the government of the United States. The scope of the story soon widens, for Von Kettler is an agent of the so-called Invisible Emperor, who plans to conquer the world and establish an oligarchy of aristocrats. Signal in stopping the vile plot are Capt. Richard Rennell, U.S.S., and the maverick inventor Luke Evans. * As is soon revealed, Von Kettler escaped under a cloak of invisibility, which his half sister Fredegonde smuggled into the prison to him. Fredegonde, who falls in love with Rennell, however, is not at the heart of the conspiracy. * The Invisible Emperor demands the surrender of the United States, and when his demand is rejected, attacks: Superbombs destroy American cities; the Invisible Death (cyanogen carried by artificial hurricanes) create swaths of death across America; and the President is kidnapped by invisible men. * Rennell, however,

reasons that the enemy's headquarters must be in the Bahamas, where he flies. An American assault on the islands fails, with both naval vessels and air fleet being destroyed. Rennell is captured, to serve as an envoy back to Washington. * He sees, in a magnificent courtroom, the Invisible Emperor, who is not openly identified, but is obviously Kaiser Wilhelm II of Germany. Fastened down with golden chains is the President of the United States, who serves as the Emperor's footstool. * Rennell escapes, and by chance reversing a lever, gases the court of the Invisible Emperor with the cyanide that had been intended for the Americans. Fredegonde, when she realized what was really happening, helped Rennell. The peril is over. * Side issues: The Emperor also had a device that nullifies sound, vortex machinery for causing the hurricanes, and a magnetic engine stopper. Invisibility, which was extended over the Emperor's establishment and the Bahamas, was produced by a chemical that made matter permeable to all ranges of light. Evans, who had developed the chemical, but was laughed at, counteracted it with blackness bombs that caused higher frequencies of radiation to become visible.

1225. **THE WALL OF DEATH**. *Astounding Stories*, November 1930. Ill. Wesso.

Short story. * *Time:* 1961. *Place:* the U.S. and South America. * Horrors and a strange morality. * *Background:* The exploration of Antarctica had unexpected results. It released from isolation the Earth Giants, protoplasmic monsters about a hundred feet high, roughly humanoid in form, omnivorous, and almost indestructible. If blown or cut up, fragments become new individuals. They are the Theosophical second root race. * As the monsters moved up South America almost in a solid mass, devouring all vegetable and animal life, it was observed that human flesh made them torpid. The American government thereupon staged raids on China, kidnapping hundreds of thousands of Orientals, who were fed to the monsters to stay their advance. But the last raiding expedition was defeated, and America is faring badly in a war with China. * Human fodder for the monsters is now selected by lottery in America. Special forces raid the homes of those drawn and kidnap them at night. * Two friendly rivals are working on a scientific means to destroy the hungry protoplasmic creatures. Cliff Hynes is developing the W-Ray, an enhanced cosmic ray, and Kay Bevan, a matter crumbler. Both approaches, although promising, have bad bugs in them. * A crisis comes when Ruth, the young woman whom both men love, is taken away by the lottery. Both men fly to the area where she is being held, ready to be served up to the Earth Monsters. Cliff's invention saves the day. A rotating top-like device with the new element psenium, it is useless against the monsters themselves, but it disintegrates inorganic material. With the device, Cliff undercuts the monsters, burying them under a mile of rock. South America is soon cleared. * Other matters: Weapons used in the war include disintegrators and the black death. * Americans now have official numbers, but still use personal names. * Confusing in presentation, and underdeveloped for its weight of material.

1226. **OUTLAWS OF THE SUN. A COMPLETE NOVEL**. *Miracle Science and Fantasy Stories*, April/May 1931. Ill. Elliott Dold.

Novelette. * *Time:* the interplanetary future. *Place:* mostly on the (imaginary) planet Circe, the outermost member of the solar system. * Circe, which is smaller than Earth, with weaker

Rousseau, Victor (*continued*)

gravity, is no paradise, but is inhabitable by man. * There is a love triangle: beautiful Celia Birch, and her admirers Tony Betts and Carl Snow. Celia prefers Tony, which enrages the brilliant but slightly mad Snow. * Snow has invented both an interplanetary viewer and a matter transmitter, which he uses to set up apparatus and to deposit Celia on Circe. He then transports old Professor Birch (Celia's father), Tony, and himself (at various times) to Circe. * The story focuses on Tony, who finds himself in a miserable environment with carnivorous, tentacled trees that lumber along after prey, and various monsters. After some search, he finds the other terrestrials, who are the captives of primitive giants. But the three Earth-people are only about a foot tall! * Snow explains. There is a size-adjustment ratio between planets, and while he adjusted Betts to Circean size, he forgot about himself and the Birches. * Betts is captured and with the others is taken to a cave held tabu by the giants; there they find the "essence" of a previous explorer from Earth. * This person, who is later suggested to have been Friar Bungay (a medieval English magician), also neglected size ratios and landed as a gaseous being. Over the centuries he has been trying to reassemble himself, with partial success. He can control a carnivorous tree. In conversation with Snow, Bungay asks to be materialized so that he and Snow can take over the solar system. Snow agrees, but first intends to transmit Betts and Professor Birch into space as comets. * Alas, plans do not always work out. Betts breaks loose, beats off the giants, watches Bungay's pet tree eat Snow, and transmits himself and his friends back to Earth. Bungay seems to have wasted his long-built-up energy. * *Miscellaneous:* In addition to the ferocious primitives there are flying humanoids, who are pleasant and friendly, and many sorts of carnivorous monsters.

1227. **REVOLT ON INFERNO. A BIG BOOK-LENGTH NOVEL COMPLETE IN THIS ISSUE.** *Miracle Science and Fantasy Stories*, June/July 1931. Ill. Elliott Dold. Novelette. * *Time:* the interplanetary future. * The planet Inferno, about the size of Mercury, is the tenth and outermost planet of the solar system, with a fifty-year orbit of some irregularity. * There is no life on the surface of Inferno, which is rough and rocky, but extensive salt seas and marshes contain a wealth of horrible, monstrous life-forms of great greed and viciousness. Inferno is the ultimate penal colony for Earth; no convict has ever returned from it. * At the moment the ship *Planetaria* is approaching Inferno bearing fifty revolutionaries who had been plotting to overthrow the harsh dictatorship of Yoska. * Among the men is Donald Evans, on whose secret weapon the revolutionaries had counted. It is a device that can cause instantaneous absolute zero within a range of hundreds of miles. * Accompanying the prisoners is Danvril, Yoska's agent, who tries to make a deal with Evans: if Evans reveals how the apparatus (which is aboard) works, Danvril will release all the prisoners. Evans agrees. * Danvril, however, breaks his promise and plans to ship the conspirators to the worst deathcamp on the planet. In part he is moved by will to power; in part he is Evans's rival for the love of the fair Ottili. She has traveled to Inferno to visit her brother, previously imprisoned. * There is intrigue and action back and forth. Evans and members of a small underground movement first sabotage the *Planetaria*, then capture it, lose it to Danvril, etc. * As the story ends, Danvril, the prison guards, and associates are all wiped out; the

Planetaria, repaired, will bring Evans's weapon to Earth, and Yoska will be overthrown. * *Miscellaneous:* The chief hand weapon of the day is the yetta tube, which causes instant paralysis that can be relieved only by a chemical antidote applied within a short time. * There are also ray guns of great power, and armor against them. * The monstrous wild life of Inferno includes a superreptile with hypnotic power. * Little to recommend.

RUBY, B. F.

A questionable identity. According to Rock and Tuck, a pseud. for Fletcher Pratt, who has a separate entry. See also #1159, "The Thing in the Woods" published as by Fletcher Pratt and B. F. Ruby, also #1157, "The Onslaught from Rigel" by Fletcher Pratt.

1228. **THE PELLUCID HORROR.** *Amazing Stories*, August/September issue, 1933. Ill. Morey.
Short story. * Scientific detective story. * A mysterious murder, in which a witness claims to have seen the victim strangle himself, yet there is an inexplicable hole in the victim's occiput. Reporter Guthrie, with the consent of the coroner, invokes the aid of the great scientist Thorpe, who soon works out what happened. A second crime, unsuccessful this time, leads the investigators to the locality where the murderer lives. Thorpe and Guthrie burst in on an invisible man. * Explanation: Thorpe was aware of certain experiments in which pineal secretion created temporary invisibility in tadpoles and had an idea of the identity of the mad scientist-culprit. The murder and the attack were for obtaining pineal glands to maintain invisibility. * Reasonably competent pulp fiction.

RUCH, MONROE K.

No information. Portrait published with story shows a young man.

1229. **THE MOON DESTROYERS.** *Wonder Stories Quarterly*, Winter 1932. Ill. Paul.
Short story. * *Time:* mid-twenty-fifth century. *Place:* mostly on the Moon and in surrounding space. * Earthquakes have become disastrous; indeed, as the story opens, the Laurentian fault has been responsible for the complete destruction of New York City, with the deaths of millions. As to the cause of the earthquakes—it is the gravitational force of the Moon. * What can be done about it? Professor Erickson and Jack Holden have the answer: destroy the Moon. Jack is the inventor of hexogen, a gas that turns solid matter into a gaseous cloud. If enough hexogen is applied to the moon and antigravity shields disperse the resulting gas, the Moon will be gone and the earthquake cycle will be broken. * In terms of engineering, the feat is not difficult, but there are human problems, a nest of space pirates on the Moon who resent their headquarters being destroyed. There is action until the pirates are beaten; Jack's sweetheart, being held by the pirates for the fate worse than death, is rescued; and the Moon is wafted away.

RUFF, J[OHN] W.

No information, except that portrait shows a young man. The author's first name is cited as "John" by Schwartz/Weisinger, *Science Fiction Digest*, April 1933 (p. 5), where another story, "The Moon Dwellers" is listed. It does not seem to have been printed.

Ruff, J. W. (*continued*)

1230. **THE PHANTOM OF GALON**. *Air Wonder Stories*, December 1929. Ill. Paul.

Short story. * *Time:* 1963. *Place:* in part in the East Indies. * Back in 1938, Richard Manning, the son of the great aeronautic inventor, was the first baby born in midair over the Atlantic. His parents were killed in an air accident some years later, and Richard was reared by Richard Herrick, a family friend who is also a great scientist and inventor. When young Manning reached maturity, Herrick moved to the Orient and the two men drifted apart. * During the early 1960s the world is troubled by the Phantom, a mysterious, cruel air pirate who attacks ships, often sending them crashing and killing all on board. His black ship is far faster than anything else in the air, and he has an engine-stopping ray and a paralysis ray. In 1963, however, he has been inactive. * Richard Manning, having designed an engine that draws electrostatic energy from the air, is constructing a rocket ship to house it. All along he has had the intention of using his new aircraft to hunt down the Phantom; now he has all the more reason, since the Phantom has kidnapped Richard's fiancée, Margaret, and threatens horrible revenge if Richard searches for her. In the meanwhile, Herrick, whose wisdom would have been useful against the Phantom, dies. * The *Skyrocket* is finished, and Richard sets out on his quest. He searches the world, and finally comes upon the outlaw ship. In a intercontinental chase, with both vessels flying at speeds in excess of 600 MPH, Manning loses, then recovers the *Phantom*, which is on the ground on Galon, an East Indian island. Manning creeps up to it, is captured, and discovers that the Phantom is Herrick, who faked his death. Herrick explains: Many years ago he was struck on the head and suffered brain damage; since then he has lived as a dual personality. One component was evil, the other—now momentarily in control—is not. Herrick releases Margaret and commits suicide. * Little to recommend.

RUPERT, M. F.

U.S. woman writer, then resident of Chicago, Illinois. Portrait published with story shows a woman in early middle age.

1231. **VIA THE HEWITT RAY**. *Science Wonder Quarterly*, Spring 1930. Ill. Winter.

Short story. * Dimensions and an ambivalent feminist ideal society. * John Hewitt, while experimenting with his newly invented apparatus for capturing light rays, observes an unusual set of Fraunhofer lines, which he investigates further. He discovers that they are signals, presumably from another dimension. After a time he is able to communicate to some extent with the senders. * This is not Hewitt's sole discovery, however; he has also invented the Hewitt ray, a development of X-rays, which permits matter transmission. One might expect the Hewitt ray to have an enormous economic impact on civilization, but it seems to have been considered a novelty and soon discarded. * Hewitt has now succeeded, he informs his absent daughter Lucile in a farewell letter, in combining his light machine and his matter transmitter and is going to transmit himself into the fourth dimension. * When Lucile arrives at the lab, she discovers that her father has already left. She decides to follow him. Donning her flying togs and strapping on a pistol, leaving a friend to operate the machine, she enters the chamber, passes through, and finds herself in a strange world.

There are a pink sky and a red sun, horrible monsters that attack her, and savage men who capture her. Lighting a cigarette, however, puts her in a position of advantage, and she manages to seize a flying machine resting nearby (its previous occupant had been killed by the savages) and fly away. Her machine is subject to remote control, however, and she is taken willy-nilly to the feminist establishment of the Second Evolutionary Plane, where she is welcomed. * *Background:* The city of the Second Evolutionary Plane is a red-hot feminist ideal society. As Mavia, Lucile's guide, relates, after considerable turmoil in the past, the women seized control, put to death all males except a few kept for breeding purposes, and established a planned society. The triumphant women had at first considered exterminating males, but discovered that parthenogenesis produced stock inferior to that from bisexual reproduction. At present there is a small pool of male studs who are brainwashed and kept in subservience. To maintain the population level each woman is required to produce two children. Childbirth is no longer a problem. When women want sexual satisfaction apart from reproductive sessions, they resort to a level of sterilized male hetaerae. Lucile is shocked at this, but Mavia calmly tells her that different cultures have different customs. * There is no concept of family or parental relationship, hence the women cannot comprehend Lucile's concern about her father or even who her father is. * The scientific and engineering level of the Second Evolutionary Plane is very high, with antigravity and much else, although the women do not have the Hewitt ray. * In addition to the women, there are a First Evolutionary Plane, which consists of the primitives who first captured Lucile, and a Third Evolutionary Plane, a group of monstrous males who are at perpetual warfare with the women. The members of the Third group are characterized by massive heads, weak bodies maintained by machines, and great scientific prowess. According to Mavia, the Third group is worried lest the Second (female) group eventually equal them scientifically and become rivals. * Professor Hewitt, it is revealed, landed among the Third group, who are delighted to have his scientific expertise, since our science (while generally much inferior to theirs) has developed on different lines. * Since the women fear a massive raid by the Third Evolutionary Group, who have new weapons, they stage a preemptive strike in which they snatch away Professor Hewitt by Lucile's adroit use of the ray and wipe out the Thirds. The two Earth people then return home. Lucile takes along with her a male discard from the breeding group who was about to be either brainwashed and sterilized or disintegrated for rebellious tendencies. He had the audacity to claim that men were being abused by women. By Terrestrial standards he is a wimp, but he achieves some manhood and gives promise of romance for Lucile back on Earth. * *Miscellaneous:* The world of the Evolutionary Groups is the fourth dimension. * The monstrous humans of the Third Group also invoke aid in the war from two dimensional beings who are deadly in certain ranges, but limited. They emit powerful electric charges, but can function only in certain areas. * The dirty work in the female culture is done by giant domestic insects. * Lucile and Mavia converse via thought helmets. * Female medicine is advanced, with artificial heart implants and electrical pacemakers. * The women live in several great cities which consists of multiple levels, each devoted to special purposes. Travel within the cities seems to be on foot within levels, with nongravity shafts for passing up and down. Food is

Rupert, M. F. (*continued*)

produced within the city, with trained insects performing the manual labor. Meals are ordered and served by manipulating a computer (my term) keyboard. * The female population is perfectly socialized; outlaws are treated medically to remove their psychological problems. If this does not work, they are executed. * Ms. Rupert is a feminist of sorts. As her spokeswoman Lucile says, "we women knew we were the equal of the men, but it was taking a long time and much hard work to convince men of our equality. I intended to marry no man who did not look upon me as his equal, mentally and physically." But while granting that the extremist Second Evolutionary Plane women achieved great things, Lucile holds no brief for a certain heartlessness in the female culture. Mavia is totally indifferent to the death of her associate who was killed by the savages of the First Evolutionary Plane and describes the historic seizure of power by the women and present degradation of men as revenge for millennia of exploitation. Ms. Rupert would thus seem to advocate real equality, not dominance in the name of equality. * As can be seen, the ideas are very interesting. Ms. Rupert had the ability to drive ideas to their logical conclusions, even if she was not a practiced or skilled writer. From this point of view, worth reading.

RYAN, FRANKLIN W. (1913-1996)
U.S. (Michigan) author. B.Sc. from Western State Teachers College, M.Educ. from Wayne State University. High school teacher, administrator; active in local politics.

   1232. **THE LAST EARL.** *Amazing Stories,* January 1933. Ill. Morey.
Short story. * *Time:* modern, but with an extensive flashback to the early 1920s. *Place:* Cluj, Roumania. * Many elements from contemporary horror motion pictures. * Jack Surrey, recent medical graduate, accompanies his friends Mary and Jimmy Jassy to their ancestral castle in Roumania, where their father had been lord of the area. Along the way there are supernatural portents: Jack has visions and dreams warning him back, and the local peasants urge the friends to stay away from the castle. At the castle itself, Jack is confronted by a horrible man with burning eyes, who attacks him but is repelled by a crucifix, whereupon he disappears through the wall. * Jack is injured and disabled for a time. When he recovers and explores the castle (to the usual portents), he finds the corpses of Mary and Jimmy. As an M.D. he should know that they are dead. * But there is a respite: One of the frightening persons that Jack had seen in visions turns out to be unvillainous and a helper. He had warned Jack telepathically out of good will. Further, this person tells Jack where he can find an explanation of the mysteries of Jassy. * Jack examines the family Bible, which the master monster, for obvious reasons, cannot touch. In it is a long ms. from his friends' dead father. Jassy Sr., an inveterate experimenter, had discovered that a combination of ultraviolet and infrared radiation, radioactivity, and electricity could animate dead brain tissue. He thereupon opened the coffin of the last lord of the previous dynasty, Earl Cenozoic [*sic*], who had died in the 1860s, and reanimated him. One result of the process was that the dead Earl Cenozoic, who is the master monster, could pass through solid matter. Cenozoic then apparently murdered Jassy Sr. * Jack penetrates the vaults, finds the coffined body of Cenozoic and presses a crucifix to its lips, whereupon the

monster collapses into dust. Jimmy and Mary awaken, and all three leave the castle, blowing it up behind them. * Ryan seems to have been attempting to rationalize certain contemporary horror themes with science-fiction, but his attempt, though innovative, was not very successful. Readers complained bitterly about this story, but Ryan defended it in a letter in the July 1933 issue of *Amazing Stories*, removing the suspicion that the story was meant to be parodic.

SACHS, BERNARD
No information. There were several authors of this name.
   1233. **THE MEMORY MACHINE.** *Wonder Stories,* July 1935. Ill. Paul.
Short story. * *Time:* The last years of the twentieth century. * *Background:* Science and technology are far advanced beyond those of our time. Enormous uniform skyscrapers that fill cities have traffic levels along which selfmobiles (small electric vehicles) move rapidly. These vehicles are equipped with the equivalent of radar to avoid collisions. * The dominant feature of the new civilization is augmemory, a system by which memory can be transferred, either in part or whole, from one person to another, even broadcast generally. Those who are participants have an identifying hole in their forehead. * The system, developed by Charles August from contemporary studies on electroencephalography, might have been a blessing, but it has turned out badly in many ways. Transfer of memory for educational purposes has resulted in stifling imagination and creating a depressing cultural uniformity. People who have used augmemory become sluggish. Charles August has become nearly a dictator, and a considerable apparatus of terror is inherent in the future civilization. * Harold August, son of Charles August, chances upon Stephens, an agitator who reveals to him much of the bad side of augmemory; indeed, Stephens was the coinventor of the process, but was shunted aside by Charles August. Stephens is now the head of a small underground that opposes augmemory. * After some plot complexities, Stephens is unjustly sentenced to death for murder; Charles August, on absorbing Stephens's memories, is overcome with remorse and commits suicide; Harold August tries to take control of the company, but is attacked by rebellious underlings who have long been planning a coup; and Harold disarms his enemies emotionally by broadcasting an augmemory of altruism. * *Miscellaneous:* Socially, companionate premarriage lasts five years, after which couples are allowed to marry. * Some suggestions of the motion picture *Metropolis* are present, and the author mentions (without citing the name of the story) Israel Zangwill's "The Memory Clearing House." * Weakly developed and saccharine in ending.

ST. JOHN-LOE, G[LADYS] (1895-?)
British women's writer. Author of such books as *Spilled Wine* (1932) and *Smoking Altars* (1936).
   1234. **WHERE FOUR ROADS MET.** *Astounding Stories,* October 1933. Ill. Charles Durant (C D)
Short story. * The surrogate murderer theme given a slight science-fictional twist. * The narrator has an extremely powerful, veridical dream of murdering a man. But it is only a dream; there is no question of somnambulism or other real participation. When he reads in the newspaper that such a crime has taken place, he goes to the police to tell about his dream. The police,

St. John Loe, G. (*continued*)

naturally, consider him the murderer and book him. But at that time the real murderer is brought in. The narrator sees with astonishment that the murderer is his exact double. The police doctor then explains that psychic affinities sometimes occur between people who are totally alike physically. * Routine.

ST. PAUL, STERNER

Pseud. of Sterner St. Paul Meek, who has a separate entry. This seems to be the only occasion on which Meek used this pseudonym; it avoided name duplication, since he had another story under his own name in the same issue.

1235. **INTO SPACE**. *Astounding Stories*, February 1930. Unsigned ill.

Short story. * *Place:* California. * The explanation for the appearance of a new satellite around the Earth. The narrator, a newspaper reporter, receives a call to visit his old science teacher Professor Livermore, who lives like a recluse out in the hills. * Livermore explains: He has discovered that gravity and magnetism are manifestations of one force; that gravity particles have positive and negative poles; and that by reversing these poles he can create antigravity. And he has finished building an antigravity spaceship, which he plans to take to the Moon. * Livermore sets off, maintaining radio communication. All goes well for a time, but when he reaches the "dead area," where the gravitations of the Earth and the Moon neutralize one another, his vessel becomes stuck in space. If he had a rocket, he could move. But now he will die in space. This is the explanation for the new satellite that has recently been sighted.

SALISBURY, NATHANIEL; LICHTENSTEIN, WILLIAM; BAIRD, WESLEY P.; and FISK, CLINTON EARLE.

No precise information on any of the authors. It has been suggested that Salisbury was Nat Schachner, although there is no evidence for this. It is also possible that the first segment was written by a member of Gernsback's staff. Social Security records list a Nathaniel Salisbury (1874-1962), a resident of New York City, but there is no proof that he was the author concerned. * Social Security records also list three Wesley Bairds and five Clinton Fisks, any or none of whom may be applicable. The story blurb, however, states that Fisk was a resident of Jersey City, New Jersey. * As for Lichtenstein, a Dr. Samuel Lichtenstein was secretary of the American Interplanetary Society in 1934; Winter states that Dr. Lichtenstein was Nat Schachner's brother-in-law and wrote a story for Gernsback. Such a story has not been identified, apart from the possible present story. Given the close association of Schachner and Lasser in rocketry, the Schachner link seems at least suggestive.

1236. **THE MOON DOOM**. *Wonder Stories*, February, April-June 1932. Ill. Paul.

A contest story. Salisbury began the story, which, according to contest rules, would be followed by continuations written by readers. Further installments were to be between three and four thousand words and in the same style as the first segment. The editors would pay 3/4 of a cent per word.

[a] **[Section by Nathaniel Salisbury.]** Wilfred Hartley, an amateur astronomer, observes that Ceres, one of the larger asteroids, has left its orbit and will crash into the Moon. He warns the authorities, but no one pays any heed. He proves to be right, of course, for the Moon has obviously been knocked out of its orbit and is approaching the Earth. Enormous tides devastate the east coast. Hartley drives west toward higher land, while the water continues to rise and the Moon draws closer. Along the way he rescues a young aviator (Witherspoon) from thugs, and the two men take to the air. Manhattan is now wholly under water, with only the tips of skyscrapers visible. * [b] **[Section by William Lichtenstein.]** Hartley and Witherspoon circle around New York City, seeing the horrendous destruction and witnessing tsunamis hundreds of feet high, as the Moon comes closer and closer to the Earth. The end should be a matter of a few hours. But Hartley, watching the Moon and the remains of Ceres, sees a measure of hope. He does not say what it is, but he persuades Witherspoon to fly to Harrisburg, where they may find a cabin plane. When they land, they come upon a band of refugees headed by the great astronomer Downer, who accepts Hartley's plan, and all take to the air in an airtight cabin plane. * [c] **[Section by Wesley P. Baird.]** The group of survivors are in air when the moon breaks up, forming a ring of large fragments and debris around the Earth. About three hundred miles up, the plane crashes into a large asteroid about fifty miles across. The plane is not badly damaged. Hartley and Downer, venturing outside in impromptu space suits, see that the Earth, although damaged, has not been destroyed. North America has been elevated, while Europe seems to have been flooded. Danger threatens as another asteroid will collide with the one on which the survivors rest. Witherspoon gets the plane back into the air, and all are knocked unconscious. * [d] **[Section by Clinton Earle Fisk.]** After more knockings about and periods of unconsciousness, the party returns to Earth, which has been totally devastated. Animal life has been wiped out by the enormous tidal waves, but plants are still present. The seven survivors of the human race now settle down and start repopulating the Earth. * We do not know Gernsback's evaluation of the contest, but to a modern reader the story is as much a disaster as the Luna/Ceres collision. A very bad story.

SANDERS. WARREN E.

No information, but portrait accompanying "The Sterile World" shows a young man. It has been suggested by Graham Stone in *Past, Present & Future* (No. 5, 1981, p. 30) that Sanders may be a pseud. for F. Orlin Tremaine, who used the pseud. Warren B. Sand.

1237. **THE STERILE WORLD**. *Wonder Stories Quarterly*, Spring 1932. Ill. Paul.

* Short story. * *Time:* the twenty-fourth century. * Since the story is very confused and muddled in presentation, with pseudo-flashbacks, it seems best to present it in chronological, not narrative, order. * At some time in the twentieth century, three great men, disgusted and horrified at the direction Terrestrial culture was taking, secretly built a small spaceship and together with a band of like-minded associates settled in the highlands of Venus. They deliberately set up a culture based on altruism, fostering the arts and sciences. The results are good, but there are occasional "atavisms" or throwbacks to the Old Race in egotism and selfishness. * One of these atavisms, about a hundred years or so before story-time, turned the omega ray on Earth, sterilizing all animal life. In a short time, humanity became all but extinct on Earth. * The sole survivor is a young woman (Chlo) who lives in an ice cave in Arctica, where the

Sanders, Warren E. (*continued*)

Earth's magnetic field weakened the omega ray. An expedition from Venus, now aware of the catastrophe that has befallen Earth, searches for survivors and rescues Chlo, just as she is about to commit suicide. She accompanies the explorers back to Venus. * The remainder of the story is concerned with intrigues sexual and political. In general the Venusians plan to reestablish themselves and their altruistic civilization back on Earth, But the high scientist Jaddo Fayne, an atavist, has other plans. He seizes the sole Venusian spaceship, kidnaps certain Venusians, flies to Earth, and plans to set up an empire guided by emotion rather than reason. Chlo loves him and will accompany him. Jaddo intends to install a force shield around Earth so that other ships cannot land. As a servitor race he will bring in small, timorous frog-men from the planetoid Eos. * The great scientist Theron, however, foils Jaddo. Capturing him on Earth, he takes him and Chlo to Eos, where they will atone for their mischief by civilizing the frog-men. * *Miscellaneous:* Juno, the capital city of Venus is a marvelous place. * The Venusians, who are physically superior to former *Homo sapiens*, have a lifespan three times as long. * Death rays and spy rays abound. * Venus, apart from the highlands where the Venusians live, is a horrible place filled with slimy semivisible monstrosities. * Eos is somewhat jungle-like, with horrible flying monstrosities that prey on the frog-men. The frog-men have a primitive civilization. * The author would seem to have read John Taine's "The Time Stream," whence Eos and the conflict between reason and romance. * A weak effort.

1238. **SHERIDAN BECOMES AMBASSADOR.** *Amazing Stories*, July 1932. Ill. Morey.

Novelette. * *Place:* Bolivia and Venus. * In Bolivia, Sheridan and a friend (who soon leaves the story) discover a remarkable archeological situation, a manmade globular formation rising out of a lake. Sheridan clears away debris from around the globe, whereupon the construction rises, exposing a much larger structure. * Sheridan finds a place of entry to a world of superscience. An elevator takes him to a lower level, where, after trying various devices, he activates a picture screen, on which appears a strange man clad in a tunic. Sheridan does not know it yet, but he has contacted the descendants of Atlanteans who settled on Venus millennia ago. * *Background:* As revealed when Sheridan has learned the language via the television device, Atlantean civilization underwent a crisis when a foreign planetoid entered the solar system and threatened to wreck the Earth. Fortunately, the planetoid did not collide with Earth, but took up an orbit around it and became our Moon. * This event caused enormous damage. Atlantis sank, and the human race was wiped out except for those who survived in the fortress-tower that Sheridan has found. The Atlantean survivors filled eight gigantic spaceships and flew to Venus, where they thrived and continued their supercivilization. * At the moment, though, their culture is in some peril, for silver, which they use for an energy source, is almost exhausted on Venus. In fact, it was almost exhausted on Earth when they left, but, of course, it has since been rereleased by the upheavals after their departure. * Sheridan chats amiably with the Venusian Atlanteans, not realizing that there is a hawkish Venusian group that will now attempt to conquer Earth. He learns about this when a ray from the television almost kills him. * For a time Sheridan, who is now trapped in the Atlantean building complex in Bolivia,

hesitates to approach the set, but when he next views it, it is to see Zahna, a beautiful young woman with whom he converses. She informs him that the war party has triumphed on Venus and that the moderates have been imprisoned. But she also reveals that a little spaceship with which the Atlantean survivors examined the flooded world after the lunar destruction is stored in the basement of his prison. * Decision made, Sheridan takes the spaceship out of mothballs, repairs some minor deterioration, loads it with power silver, leaves an account of what he has learned and experienced, and flies off to Venus. * In a brief epilogue set some years later, Sheridan and his wife, Zahna, visit Earth and tell how the hawks were defeated in a civil war. Earth is now safe. * *Miscellaneous:* The ancient Atlanteans defeated an invasion from Mars, hence they are reluctant to communicate with other worlds. * In the old days the black and yellow races were the servants of the Atlanteans. A ninth spaceship containing members of both races should also have flown to Venus, but the servants or slaves, being superstitious and ignorant, sabotaged the ship and remained on Earth. These survivors were the ancestors of present-day humanity. * The chief Atlantean weapon is a paralysis ray, which can be adjusted to a death or heat ray, as Sheridan learns to his discomfort. * Trade can now commence between Venus and Earth. * Routine at best.

1239. **THE MEMORY STREAM.** *Amazing Stories,* April 1933. Ill. Morey.

Short story. * *Time:* the middle paleolithic? * A device for a prehistoric story. * The invention in some fashion latches onto the collective memory of mankind, in this instance focusing on two Neanderthal ancestors of the human race. * Kor and Leetah, young man and woman, mate. While it is not spelled out, they seem to me more *Homo sapiens sapiens* than their fellows. Tension is provided by the brutal chief, the old man of the tribe, who also desires Leetah. In the final struggle, Kor wins with the help of Leetah. Kor had previously invented the bow and arrow. * The modern subjects of the experiment awake, aware that it was they who were Kor and Leetah. * Probably suggested in part by Mitchell's *Three Go Back.* * Routine.

SARGENT, SAMUEL M., JR.

No information.

1240. **THE TELEPATHIC PICK-UP.** *Amazing Stories*, December 1926. Ill. F. S. Hynd.

Short-short story. * Brant, the narrator, visits his friend Dr. Spaulding, who mourns the disappearance of his bad-egg brother Tom, who has embezzled fifty thousand dollars. Spaulding has invented a telepathic radio to find Tom. By focusing on a topic and fine tuning for detail, he hopes to find the missing man. He does. But Tom is on death row and just seating himself in the electric chair. Tom's thoughts come through as the current is applied, and after, for electricity, Brant recognizes, does not kill, but merely paralyzes. Tom's thoughts continue up to and into part of the autopsy. Spaulding goes mad with horror and destroys his machine.

1241. **DR. BRITTLESTONE'S METHOD.** *Amazing Stories*, May 1928. Ill. monogram DE?

Short story, very tenuous as science-fiction. * The narrator, Dr. Strang, is justifiably annoyed when a medical colleague, whom he barely knows, takes one of his patients, the wealthy Jim Hart, into his sanitarium. For a time Hart seems to be doing well, but unexpectedly Strang receives a note from him complaining of a

Sargent, Samuel M., Jr. (*continued*)

relapse. * Strang visits the sanitarium and finds Hart dead, with obvious hanky-panky on Brittlestone's part, including Hart's new will in favor of Brittlestone. * A little snooping on Strang's part reveals what has happened: Brittlestone has isolated the chemical factors that cause fatigue and uses them to kill wealthy patients who have bequeathed their fortunes to him. His method of obtaining the chemical is most cruel: An electric motor on an overhead track forces an utterly fatigued man to stagger around until he drops. The bad doctor leaps out a window and is killed by the fall.

SCHACHNER, NAT[HANIEL] (1895-1955)

U.S. (New York) author, lawyer; one of the mainstays of the early genre pulp era. Degree in chemistry, New York City College; degree in law, New York University. Practicing lawyer at times. A crude, very uneven, but intelligent, writer who may have deliberately written down mechanically, but sometimes brought current political and social ideas into his adventure stories. After the late 1930s wrote little science-fiction, reasons for the cessation not known. Schachner's serious work, such as his excellent biographies of Alexander Hamilton and Aaron Burr, is on a very different plane than his fiction. See also the pseuds. Chan Corbett and Walter Glamis, and the collaborations Nat Schachner and R. Lacher, and Nat Schachner and Arthur Leo Zagat. See also Nathanial Salisbury.

Schachner's fiction is described chronologically in The Revolt of the Scientists Series and Other Works

The Revolt of the Scientists Series

A series of three stories set in 1937 and following years, mostly in the New York City area. The series depicts an America still in the throes of the Great Depression, looted by organized crime on one hand and robber barons on the other. The politicians are for the most part corrupt or ineffectual. * The story postulates salvation in terms of managerial science and a controlled economy applied by world-famous scientists (who have had no business experience!). This, of course, is Technocracy. Back in 1934, according to this story, the Technocrats initiated a revolt, which was crushed bloodily. At the moment Technocracy is outlawed, with stiff prison sentences for advocates.

1242. **THE REVOLT OF THE SCIENTISTS.** *Wonder Stories*, April 1933. Ill. Paul.

Short story. * While slightly intoxicated and overenthusiastic, young millionaire sportsman Cornelius Van Wyck denounces the bootleggers who control the liquor industry and vows to spend millions to crush them. The next morning he has a vague memory of what he said. This memory is considerably enlarged when he is summoned by Adam Roode, the world's leading physicist and a Nobel Prize winner. Roode proceeds to conscript him and his millions in a fight against the criminal mastermind who controls the liquor underworld. A secret organization is established, with offices in an old warehouse. The latest scientific advances of the world's great scientists will be applied in the fight against crime. * Shoot-outs, gangster attacks, vigilante destruction of liquor warehouses take place. The Boss, a crooked former banker named Melchior, is just as clever as the scientists, but bad luck and science are too much for him.

Roode removes Melchior by sending his plane out into space with the reactive power of ionized hydrogen. Also involved is a stratosphere plane that can travel 1,000 MPH; it is equipped with a noise suppressor. * The first step toward the establishment of Technocracy has been taken, but thanks to Melchior, who left documents behind identifying the Technocrats, the organization will have to go underground and establish stronger security. * Competent thrills.

1243. **THE REVOLT OF THE SCIENTISTS. II—THE GREAT OIL WAR.** *Wonder Stories*, May 1933. Ill. Paul.

Short story. * *Time:* 1938. The same background as the previous story. Since Melchior's effects included a list of the new Council of Technocrats, all important members have gone into hiding. * At the moment the oil trust, headed by the infamous John Stoneman (obviously à clef for John D. Rockefeller), controls 90 percent of the world's oil and is wrecking the world's economy. The price of oil is falling, but the exploiters keep producing, wasting the Earth's resources. Associated with Stoneman are the steel mogul and other robber barons. * The three leaders of the scientists, including Roode, confront Stoneman and Federal cabinet members, demanding that the oil industry be nationalized and controlled. Naturally, this demand is scoffed at. * The Scientists cannot in conscience use the same murderous, vigilante tactics against the oil industry that they used against the mobsters, since it would amount to destroying the very resources that they wish to conserve. Instead, they rely on a stratagem. Infiltrating the industry, they insert chemicals into the oil domes and pipes that turn the oil into jelly. The change is only temporary, but it creates enough panic that Stoneman agrees to the Technocrats' terms: entire management of the oil industry to vest in a new corporation, controlling interest of which would lie with the Technocrats, though Stoneman would be included. Bonds would be issued to stockholders by all oil companies; these bonds would gradually be retired. * Along the way to this agreement Stoneman had demanded that the President of the United States purchase the dead wells and bail out the oil companies, along with other payments. A tariff on foreign oil was also a matter of dispute. * By now the Technocrats not only have control of a major industry, but have received amnesty and pardon for past activities. * Competent pulp treatment of an economic issue.

1244. **THE REVOLT OF THE SCIENTISTS. III—THE FINAL TRIUMPH.** *Wonder Stories*, June 1933. Ill. Paul.

Short story. * *Time:* 1940. * The Technocrat scientists have broken major crime and brought certain industries under control, but their most difficult contest is now upon them: the struggle with money. They must now combat J. P. Claremont (whose prototype is obvious from his initials), who controls the banks and secretly much of industry. It is not an unexpected confrontation, for at about the time that Claremont is wrecking the economy by calling in all outstanding debts, the outlawed Technocrats recognize that they must take the next step in their war for control. * There are threats back and forth as the two forces meet. As one tactic, the Technocrats install apparatus in banks that disintegrates gold, turning it to tin dust. This causes Claremont and his followers to hesitate, but they respond by forcing the government to cover their deposits, not as they are now, but as they were before the gold blight struck. * The Technocrats respond by releasing a chemical that destroys the writing on all the legal instruments in the bank. This hurts

Schachner, Nat (*continued*)

Claremont deeply. * But the robber barons and the government have learned the location of the secret Technocrat headquarters. They attack, but cannot penetrate force screens and are ignominiously defeated. Claremont surrenders. By now the country is on the edge of revolution. * In the new order "The Democratic form was to be maintained with the President and elective Lower House. The Upper House to be elected by unit divisions of the industries. The Technocrats . . . . to be put in complete control of industry. A nationwide plan of production and distribution to be put into effect; no man, woman, or child . . . . to lack the necessities of life." Thus, despite vagueness, a medley of democracy, syndicalism, and socialism. * By now shooting fish in a barrel.

Other Works

1245. **PIRATES OF THE GORM**. *Astounding Stories*, May 1932. Unsigned ill.
Short story. * *Time:* the interplanetary future. *Place:* mostly on Jupiter. * *Background:* The Earth and the other planets of the solar system have recently won a nasty war against Ganymede, whose humanoid inhabitants not only harbor revanchist feelings but are plotting a new strike. The Gorm is a Ganymedan artifact in the Red Spot of Jupiter; amounting to an antigravity area, it has the peculiar property of being either a violent attracter or repeller, depending upon the type of electric current applied to it. It is impenetrable to ray or bullet. * Grant Pemberton, an investigator posing as a layman on the ship *Althea*, is marooned on board the ship (along with the beautiful Nona). The *Althea* has been hijacked, and the criminals (who are Ganymedans under the sway of the villainous Miro) have escaped by floating down to the Gorm. The passengers on the *Althea* (except Grant and Nona) are killed with poison gas. * Grant and Nona leave the ship, float down to the Gorm, and are captured—but not for long. Grant reverses the current on the Gorm, then shifts it to alternating current, thereby wrecking the device. He and Nona escape. * Pretty bad.

1246. **SLAVES OF MERCURY**. *Astounding Stories*, September 1932. Ill. Wesso.
Short story. * *Time:* the near future. * Hilary Grendon returns to Earth after five years in space to find a deplorable situation. Not long after he left, Mercurians invaded and conquered the Earth. The Mercurians are humanoid, but larger than Earthmen, have a superior science, and are a brutal, exploitative lot. Their occupation of Earth is cruel, with disintegration or torture for slight offenses. Earthmen are no more than slaves. * Grendon, who has not experienced the degradation of the occupied areas, becomes the focal center for a successful rebellion. He is fortunate in knowing the secret entrances and passages to the building where the Mercurian ruler dwells. There is also a young woman who escapes the fate worse than death. * Filled with clichés; little to recommend.

1247. **EMISSARIES OF SPACE**. *Wonder Stories Quarterly*, Fall 1932. Ill. Paul.
Short novel. * *Time:* A.D. 1937 and the following years, in various places. * *Background:* In 1936 strange, powerful electric disturbances were visible in the sky over the world. Connected with the lights and other phenomena was a nervous disorder that killed or incapacitated hundreds of thousands of people, one of its symptoms being vague, half-forgotten memories of strange signals or sounds, almost comprehensible, but not quite. * The dynamic tycoon John Boling, however, both understood the message and had a clear memory of it. He thereupon hired the brilliant young physicist Philip Haynes to bring that memory into actuality—an incredibly powerful atomic energy generator. * Boling is a complex man. On the one hand, he has a megalomanic thirst for total power at any cost, while on the other, he would sincerely use such power to benefit the human race, breaking the Great Depression and freeing the world from want. * As is gradually revealed, mostly to Haynes, Boling has been in communication with space energy beings of incredible intellect who can wreck the Earth with artificial storms and influence minds. The Emissaries have no objection to Boling's seizing control of the world; indeed, they help him in small ways, for his success will include the price they ask for the atomic secret. * As the story opens, Boling assembles a group of economic titans, who at his urging agree to form a Power Council that will not only control atomic energy, but will absorb the governments of the world. Among the group is oil king William Janus, who is obviously modelled on John D. Rockefeller Jr. A religious fanatic as well as a financial shark, he will play a strange part in the last days. * Boling's plans go well up to a point, but it becomes clear to Haynes, who has remained as a loyal associate, that something is wrong. The Emissaries (who are said to be but agents of even more powerful extraterrestrials) have demanded their price, and Boling is reluctant to comply. After great storms ravage the world, Boling yields. The price: Mankind must erect a series of towers one thousand feet high, one thousand feet apart, around the equator, land and sea. Such a colossal project means, of course, forced levee of labor and exhaustion of the earth's resources. * Haynes, who is embittered at the loss of his wife and child during the great storm, and Janus, who has come to be convinced that the Emissaries are diabolic, determine to fight Boling as an underground. Haynes tries to sabotage the construction of the towers in South America, and Janus secretly builds a private army of religious fanatics. Haynes matures into a man of action, but Janus succumbs to religious madness. * Time passes. The towers are being erected, notably in South America, but even though the outside world is contented or even delighted with the material benefits Boling has brought them, the workers are at the point of rebellion. In the meanwhile, Haynes has built a scrambler that will shut down the atomic engines, but he is afraid to use it, lest the space beings punish the Earth. On a previous occasion when work slackened, they punished South America severely. All the while, there seems to an unquestioned knowledge among all parties that the space beings will consider the contract canceled and will no longer be concerned with Earth if Earth returns the secret of atomic power, i.e., destroys the engines and builds no more. * The final Armageddon-like battles are too complicated to describe in detail, for there are several different parties, all with somewhat different aims: Boling and his associates; Janus and his religious fanatics; Haynes and his labor group; and a wild card in Ferdinand, a ruthless opportunist who has Boling's megalomania without his good qualities. * Eventually, after complicated military passages, Ferdinand seems to have control of the situation; Janus is dead, and Boling and Haynes are captives. The engines have been shut off. But Ferdinand reckons without the Emissaries. A world-shattering storm arises,

Schachner, Nat (*continued*)

and of the original principals only Boling and Haynes survive. Boling, a chastened man who recognizes his error in accepting the gift from space, informs the Emissaries that Earth no longer wants the atomic engines. The Emissaries, who reveal that they control the galaxy, seem content to leave Earth to its squabbles, but demand Boling's self-sacrifice, which takes place. * The world slowly rebuilds, but with traditional energy sources, and atomic research is forbidden. Some years later, it is observed that Mars, Mercury, and Venus are leaving the solar system. The implication is that their peoples accepted Emissary gifts, built towers, and were taken away. * *Miscellaneous:* Most of the world, after Boling's atomic engine becomes widespread, is run by wireless broadcast of power. Thus, during the military operations, shutting down the atomic engines disrupts everything, including air travel. * This is much Schachne's most ambitious work. It deals with ideas, instead of foolish thrills, and has attempted complex character analysis. The result, while occasionally slipping into pulp modes, is much superior to his shorter stories.

1248. **THE TIME EXPRESS**. *Wonder Stories*, December 1932. Ill. Paul.

Short story. * *Time:* A.D. 2124, A.D. 2850, and A.D. 4600. * *Background:* In this future system, in 2124, mechanical time travel is not only possible, but is exploited as a form of tourism. Upon payment of a fee, tourists are taken to allotted future times, where, carefully guarded in their movements and contacts, they are permitted to see worlds to come. * An odd characteristic of such time travel is that persons returning to their own time do not remember anything beyond vague generalities (hence there can be no anachronistic inventions) and cannot bring back anything material. * Two stops are significant in the story. The world of 2850 is a mechanistic eutopia, where no one works, but the world of 4600 is neoprimitive of a peculiar sort. The people of 4600, while maintaining a high science, will not accept any power systems or automation; everything must be done by hand-crafts. They permit time tourists on a very restricted basis, but do not allow travel beyond their own era, for fear of idea-contamination. Individuals who try to smuggle in advanced technology are subject to the death penalty. Oddly enough, the men of A.D.4600 are physical supermen. * As for the time travel itself, it is a matter of vibration. One can go into the future and return to one's own time, but cannot travel into the past. * The present situation is that the Secret Service of the World Council of 2124 has received a tip-off from the authorities of 4600 warning that an attempt will be made to smuggle technical information into 4600 on a certain Hook's Tour. Operative Denton Kels, disguised as an ordinary tourist, is assigned to the case. He is armed with a peculiar sort of needle gun that shoots great quantities of tiny metal slivers. A very thorough search of the vessel and the effects of the passengers turns up nothing. * The tour proceeds normally, with a short stop-off in 2850, where lunch is served and some restricted exploration is permitted. * In 4600, however, violence takes place. There are gun battles between the local police and outlaws, and the tour guide is kidnapped. * The resolution turns out to be simple. The smuggler is the tour guide, whose body is covered with technical diagrams drawn in invisible ink. When he is plopped into a developing pool, the diagrams appear. The future people had promised him great wealth, but although he mouthed a spiel

about the impossibility of bringing things from the future, he never really understood that there was no way that the future dissidents could reward him. Kels manages to smooth things over, and the crisis is ended. * Not a bad story. The basic situation is original and ingenious, but a purist might object to many logical weaknesses.

1249. **THE ETERNAL DICTATOR**. *Wonder Stories*, February 1933. Ill. Paul.

Short story. * *Time:* A.D. 2532. *Place:* the New York area and a space station orbiting Earth. * *Background:* The world is ruled by Vincent Melius, Melius the First, a seemingly immortal man who has held supreme power for something over two hundred years. While Melius is a ruthless autocrat whose lightest word is law, the world has become a materialistic eutopia, with no want, crime, or war, simply loss of freedom. In other words, Schachner is examining the concept of the "benevolent" dictator postulated during the 1920s and 1930s. * Capt. Denny Kels (the similiarity of name to the Kels of the previous story--#1248-- is without significance), of the Rocket Patrol, unexpectedly receives a summons to attend Melius. He is naturally a little worried, for such summonses usually involve severe punishment, even death. But Melius, who maintains a harsh and impersonal attitude, simply orders Kels to take a warship up to the space station (the Station in Space), replace the observational crew with fighting men, and shoot down everything, absolutely everything, without examining it or identifying it, that approaches Earth. Kels takes his position and proceeds to obey orders. * *More background:* This whole situation is somehow based on the expected appearance of Kyle's comet, which has a periodicity of about one hundred years. At its appearance three hundred years ago, the Second Station in Space, manned by Prof. Gordon Kyle and fellow scientists, was torn from its Terrestrial orbit by the comet and carried away. Gordon Kyle, a remote ancestor of Kels's, was also a close friend and colleague of Melius's. * Back to Kels: A space cylinder appears from the comet and approaches Earth. Although opposed by his second in command, who is obviously an underground member opposed to the Eternal Dictator, Kels follows orders and blasts at the vessel. Kels's explosives are repelled by a force screen, and the undamaged cylinder descends to Earth, landing near the palace of the Eternal Dictator. Kels follows, to continue the attack. * The cylinder is obviously the long-lost Second Station in Space. From it emerge Professor Kyle and his associates, who are also immortal. * A shoot-out follows, in which the visitors, thanks to force screens, more than hold their own. Their weapons, indeed, destroy the imperial army and chop up the palace. Melius surrenders and emerges. In a further shoot-out both Melius and the visitors are killed, rendering possible a new democratic Earth. * Before the slaughter, however, explanations were forthcoming: Melius was rendered immortal by Kyle. Mad for power, Melius then sabo-taged Kyle's space station so that it was dragged off by the comet. During the wanderings of the comet, Kyle discovered that the Melius sort of immortality was really only temporary, about three hundred years. And Kyle also discovered true immortality, which he refuses to share. His technique is cellular bombardment with cosmic and other radiation. * Routine.

1250. **THE ROBOT TECHNOCRAT**. *Wonder Stories*, March 1933. Ill. Paul.

Short story. * *Time:* 1954. * *Place:* mostly Pennsylvania. * *Background:* In this world of 1954, the Depression still holds

Schachner, Nat (*continued*)

sway and the United States is politically shattered into a welter of political parties: Extreme Communist, Communist, Socialist, Social-Laborite, Middle Class, Patriots, Fascist, Monarchy, Aristocrat, etc. Each of them constitutes a small dictatorship, with absolute leader, private army of storm troopers or strong-arm men, and a policy of ruthlessness. Most troublesome of all is the Nationalist Party headed by Adolph Hiller (whose referent the reader will not need a biographical dictionary to identify). The most palatable is the Reconstructionist movement headed by Corbin, who is a humane, reasonable man who does not see force as his first option. Europe and Asia have all gone either Communist or Fascist. * Corbin has received a summons from the long-disappeared Professor Kalmikoff, and together with his military leader General Wingdale and an attaché visits the scientist's hidden laboratory. * Kalmikoff explains. Since his withdrawal from society he has secretly been working on a supercomputer (my term) for the understanding and prediction of future history. By analyzing twenty variables, including those taken from individuals concerned, the machine will indicate what will happen. In a sense, as the scientist explains, it is a perfected, more sophisticated version of what the earlier Technocrats tried to do in simplistic fashion. * Corbin and Kalmikoff decide on a rash action: Kidnap all the party leaders, bring them to the lab, show them the machine, and let the machine predict the future that each man will create if he attains power. The caper succeeds, with one exception, Hiller is not picked up. But, as the machine is in operation, Hiller appears with his private army and takes over the situation. * The machine has shown disastrous futures for those it has "interviewed," and when Hiller voluntarily enters it, it shows a reign of terror. Hiller thereupon starts to execute everyone, but is interrupted in a grand shoot-out by friendly troops. * Hiller and a couple of the other extremists are killed. The survivors, now somewhat shocked into reason, agree to support Corbin when the machine predicts a favorable future under his leadership. * Obviously a product of the interest in Technocracy of the day. According to rumor, the story was commissioned by editor David Lasser, who regarded Technocracy favorably. Facing the editorial page, through no coincidence, is a full-page advertisement for Gernsback's new magazine, *Technocracy Review*, which fell with a clunk. * The story is interesting in idea, especially as a mirror of the times, but primitive in writing.

1251. **FIRE IMPS OF VESUVIUS.** *Astounding Stories,* October 1933. Unsigned ill.

Short story. * *Place:* inside Mount Vesuvius. * Geoffrey Clive, prize pupil, receives an urgent summons from the great Professor Carewe to come to Vesuvius, where the professor is conducting researches. Vesuvius is currently in heavy eruption. * After saving Mercelli, the somewhat stupid chief of public safety, from the molten lava and meeting Carewe, Clive learns what has been going on. In addition to violent eruptions and lava flows, fiery masses have been plummeting from the sky, killing government officials and leaving behind taunting messages written on asbestos. These attacks have obviously come from Vesuvius. On the basis of reports by an informer (who is obviously a villain), Mercelli believes that Professor Carewe is responsible. * Donning insulating suits Clive and the professor enter the fiery crater of Vesuvius. They find there a great open fumarole which contains (1) fire imps, or small humanoid beings who live in the

flames and heat; (2) apparatus for controlling the eruption of Vesuvius; (3) Campanella, an anarchist or socialist, who has been sending the fire imps out on the death missions against politicians; and (4) Fraschini, the informer, who plans to use Vesuvius to become new dictator of Italy. * The intrigue goes back and forth until the right lever is pulled quieting Vesuvius; Campanella and Fraschini are dead; and our heroes emerge from the volcano. * *Miscellaneous:* The fire people are not explained. It is assumed that their ancestors devised the apparatus for controlling the volcano. * Routine.

1252. **ANCESTRAL VOICES.** *Astounding Stories,* December 1933. Unsigned ill.

Short story. * *Time and place:* 1935 in contemporary America, and A.D. 452 in the Roman city of Aquileia. * A version of an old science-fictional cliché, going back in time and killing one's grandfather. * Using the mysterious substance vibratium, which functions backwards, the egotistical scientist Pennypacker has built a time machine. Although warned by his assistant about the dangers of changing the past, Pennypacker insists on moving into the past so that he can have definite proof that the machine works. * He arrives in Aquileia in A.D. 452, just as the Huns are sacking the city. Oddly enough, the Hun that comes toward him not only looks like him, but has a peculiar, almost contortionist, way of reaching around his head that runs in Pennypacker's family. The Hun is obviously Pennypacker's remote ancestor. Pennypacker, who prides himself on his pure Norman ancestry, is both horrified and incredulous. The Hun attacks, whereupon Pennypacker draws his automatic and kills him. * The time machine returns to 1935 without Pennypacker, but with the corpse of the Hun. And everyone, like Pennypacker, who had a trace of the Hun's blood, has vanished from the Earth. * The story is told partly in the adventure described, and partly in vignettes of others affected: the ranting, racist dictator Hellwig (Hitler) of Mideuropa; the prize fighters Schilling (Max Schmehling) and Bernstein (Max Baer); an Irish laborer worried about the paternity of his dark-haired young son; Mr. and Mrs. Henry Cabot; and others. About fifty thousand people disappear. But oddly enough, as a reader later pointed out, and was surely obvious, memories of the missing people and the results of their actions still exist. * Schachner, in a long letter in the same issue, points out that the story is in part a satire on the prevalent concept of racial purity. * Routine, although considerable fuss was made about the story when it appeared.

1253. **REDMASK OF THE OUTLANDS.** *Astounding Stories,* January 1934. Ill. Paul Orban.

Short story. * Comic opera in the political future. * *Time:* the fifty-fifth century. *Place:* mostly around present-day Pittsburgh. * *Background:* America in the fifty-fifth century consists of a group of independent city-states, each a fiercely isolationist unitary city operating behind impenetrable defenses. Around them is wilderness. The cities embody a political typology: Pisbor is a Fascist dictatorship; Chico is a Communist, totally controlled, pseudo-egalitarian, authoritarian state; Yorrick is a semifeudal world controlled by an arbitrary aristocracy of wealth. Only Washeen differs. It is an open democracy without scientific defenses, and its people cultivate surrounding fields. As the result of a crop failure Washeen is now in difficulty. * As joker, jester, wild-card is the great outlaw Redmask, a Robin Hood-like figure who ranges over the Outlands and, with his invisible air vessel, preys on the cities. He is called Redmask because he wears on his head a red fishbowl that permits only

Schachner, Nat (*continued*)

one-way vision, thus concealing his real identity. Redmask has various subterranean hide-outs from which he operates and is involved in underground movements in the cities. * The plotline is too complicated to spell out; main strands alone will be indicated. Janet of the Marches, daughter of Charles of the Marshes, ruler of Yorrick, is being flown to a forced marriage to vicious old dictator Carlos of Pisbor. Janet's lover, Edward of the Hudsons, is desperate at the situation, as is Comrade Ahrens of Chico, who fears a Pisbor-Yorrick alliance. Kidnapping, treachery, disguises, impostures, captivities, and shoot-outs all follow. In most situations, a dominant figure is the jester Stephen, who shoots off his mouth appropriately and plays a genuine Stradivarius violin. The reader, despite some authorial attempts at misleading, will easily recognize the identity of the jester. * All ends well despite the complicated intrigues. Carlos and Ahrens are foiled; Janet and Edward are united; and Redmask, in control, dictates that the cities contribute food by airlift to starving Washeen. * Sometimes on the laughable side, sometimes on the pretentious side, but in general routine pulp adventure. * For a sequel see #1263, "The Son of Redmask."

1254. **THE TIME IMPOSTOR.** *Astounding Stories,* March 1934. Ill. Marchioni.

Short story. * *Time and place:* Sing Sing in 1932, and an undesignated location about A.D. 8000. * Derek, a newspaper reporter assigned to cover the execution of Mike Spinnot, the most vicious ganglord of the era, is in the death chamber at Sing Sing as the execution is about to begin. * The execution is interrupted, however, by a time machine, from which emerge an old man and a young woman, who proclaim Spinnot a hero and release him from the chair. A force zone protects the time visitors, while an emanation from the old man's fingers serves as a paralysis ray. Derek, in these frantic moments, tries to question the time visitors, learning for his pains only that the future people consider Spinnot not only their ancestor, but an incredible hero who tried to release America from a tyrannical government. * Derek lunges forward as the time machine leaves with Spinnot and is carried along with him into the future. There, he quarrels with Spinnot and is proscribed, death on sight, by the future people. While eluding the police, he learns from the young woman, whose name is Merle, that after a tremendous war in the twenty-second century, almost all records were lost. The sole surviving document (which the future people take seriously) happens to be a fantasy of history, written as a burlesque by an acquaintance of Derek's, glorifying the criminal Spinnot à la Jonathan Wilde. * Derek eludes the police for a time and rescues Merle from rape by Spinnot. He and Spinnot tumble into the time machine, which brings them back to 1932, where the execution proceeds. Since the time machine was a one-time invention, there can be no more intervention from A.D. 8000 * As the story ends, Derek wonders whether Merle will be born in the future. It must be added that Merle's surname was Spinney, which all concerned accepted as a variant of Spinnot. * The idea is amusing, but the accomplishment is routine.

1255. **HE FROM PROCYON.** *Astounding Stories,* April 1934. Unsigned ill.

Novelette. * A departure from H. G. Wells's "The Man Who Could Work Miracles," pointing out a political moral. * The being from Procyon is a somewhat humanoid form of silicon life possessed of incredible intellect and superscience. Chancing on

Earth while exploring, he determines to perform a social and psychological experiment. Selecting four men and two women at random, he implants in their brains tiny devices that give them the power to control the will of others. This power, which seems to work mostly through sound, is to last a month. During this time the creature from Procyon watches developments. * The six include Jordan, a petty official with Fascist leanings; Doolittle, a downtrodden, henpecked small clerk; Marshall, a fundless playboy; Alison La Rue, a predatory, gold-digging minor actress; Miss Simmons, a schoolteacher; and Wentworth, a brilliant young physicist. * The story line follows mostly Jordan and Wentworth. * Jordan, who realizes his power early, uses it to climb into political authority, in a short time becoming dictator of the United States. Loudspeakers bearing his will-compulsion enslave masses of laymen and soldiery. * Wentworth, who works with the great psychologist Dr. Knopf, recognizes what is going on and its physiological basis. He alone of the six has a memory, though very dim, of the being from Procyon. After conventional tactics against Jordan fail, Wentworth develops an apparatus that will magnify his own willpower to overcome Jordan. * Of the other enhanced people, Doolittle and Marshall accomplish little; La Rue, on the other hand, does well for her predatory instincts. Miss Simmons, though somewhat shadowy and ineffectual, sides with Wentworth against Jordan. * There are captivities, escapes, battles, massacres before matters are settled. For a time Jordan, supplemented by the mental force of Doolittle, Marshall, and La Rue, is stronger than Wentworth and his machine, but Wentworth wins, just as the gift from Procyon expires, returning the individuals to their former mentalities. * Too long and rather junky. The cautionary aspect of the story does not fit well with the development.

1256. **THE 100TH GENERATION**. *Astounding Stories,* May 1934. Ill. C. R. Thomson.

Short story. * *Time:* 1934 and 1954. *Place:* significantly on a small South Sea island. * The narrator, Radburn Phelps, is summoned by his old college friend, millionaire biologist Bayley Spears, to help in a remarkable scientific project. Spears has assembled ova and spermatozoa from leading scientists, artists, musicians, statesmen, etc., and plans to anticipate evolution in the laboratory. By taking cells from the mesoderm of the embryo, rather than waiting for specimens to mature, he expects to be able to establish the changes of one hundred generations in a year or two. He hopes for remarkable development of human special abilities. * Phelps agrees to help, but disagrees with Spears on one approach; he believes that the specialized genetic lines should not be kept separate, but should be allowed to crossbreed. Spears, who controls the experiment, insists that specialization is paramount. * The program is finished on schedule, whereupon Spears disappears for twenty years. At this time Phelps receives another summons, now one of desperation. From the seaman who delivers the message, Phelps learns that Spears has set up a colony with his experimental subjects on a small South Sea island. Proceeding there, Phelps, his son, and the seamen are astonished to encounter the results of Spears's experiment. A strange-looking creature paralyzes them by emitting a sound, while other evolutes, each of which is hypertrophied to fit its specialty, gather. The evolutes reveal that they tortured Spears to death and that they plan to vivisect the visitors and conquer the world. They have suitable weapons. * Things look very bad, but all is saved by the one exceptional

Schachner, Nat (*continued*)

evolute: this is Una, a gorgeous, normal woman, who has taken a liking to Phelps's son. She shoots the musician who has the ability to paralyze with sound. As the visitors and Una leave, the island, which Spears had mined, blows up behind them. * Una, who has established a relationship with Phelps's son, was on the evolutes' death list. They regarded her as a potentially treacherous degenerate. * Part of the point seems to be that Phelps was right; crossbreeding would have kept the mutants closer to present-day humanity. * A child of Stapledon's *Odd John* and Wells's *The Island of Doctor Moreau*. Peregoy's "Short-Wave Castle" may also enter, although publication dates would seem to rule against this. * Routine.

1257. **STRATOSPHERE TOWERS**. *Astounding Stories*, August 1934. Ill. Dold.
Short story. * *Time:* around A.D. 2590. * *Place:* Arabia, the Ruba-al-Khali. * Almost all energy on Earth comes from two gigantic solar stations, Tower No. 1 in the Arabian Desert, Tower No. 2 on an artificial island in mid-Pacific on the equator. The towers are about twenty miles high, with bases five miles and tops three miles wide. Both are manned by a professional caste that is supposed to have no national affiliations. This is a wise precaution, since the world is apparently divided into three enormous empires, each spoiling to conquer its fellows. In any such war, however, the towers are supposed to be neutral and sacrosanct. * Such is the theory, which, as might be expected, soon breaks down. Internal conflict arises when a horrible genocidal war breaks out. Neville suggests shutting down Tower No. 1, which would stop the war machines of half the world; such a suggestion, however, is technically treasonous, and his chief Bentley rejects it. Then Tower No. 2 is captured by Midcentral, which seems to be Central Europe, and Tower No. 1 is imperilled by Midcentral fifth columnists. Northcontinent, which seems to be North America, defeats a Midcentral air fleet, and begins to disintegrate the defenses of Tower No. 1 when the tower refuses to surrender. But judicious flicking the switches breaks the siege. * The fifth columnists, in a reflection from the real world, are German and Japanese. * Routine.

1258. **THE LIVING EQUATION**. *Astounding Stories*, September 1934. Ill. Dold.
Short story. * Hugh Wilmot has constructed an unusual sort of mechanical brain; a maze of tubes, prisms, and electrical work, embodying the tools of the most modern mathematics, it is designed not to solve equations, but to create them. It is not quite finished, Wilmot says to his friend and guest Polger, and not quite ready to be turned on. * A burglar with the improbable name of Bill Sikes, however, anticipates Wilmot. Stumbling among the wires, he accidentally activates the brain, which behaves spectacularly, isolating itself and the burglar in a zone of force. * The problem (paralleling one of the schools of contemporary physics) is that equations themselves are reality, and phenomenality is only a manifestation of basic equations. Thus, when the brain devises new mathematical languages, it changes the universe. The Earth turns orange. Catastrophes afflict the world, and millions die. Shantung province in China disappears, and North Australia is stood on end, forming a huge mountain range. Silicon life-forms emerge, and strange duplications are evident, like several Empire State Buildings, and a clerk who finds himself three people. Atlantis is discovered when the sea recedes. The year shortens to 330 days, and the

Earth functions at a different time rate than the rest of the universe. Stars disappear and reappear elsewhere, and the cosmos begins to return to the original giant atom. * But the changes stop, for Wilmot's machine was not strong enough to change the whole universe. * Clumsily told, but an interesting idea.

1259. **THE GREAT THIRST**. *Astounding Stories*, November 1934. Ill. Dold.
Short story. * *Time:* probably the near future. * Business ethics among the great scientists. * The personal story centers on Sanford Dale, scientist of extreme genius, who has left the predatory Fillmore enterprises for conscience's sake. By chance, when a local farmer brings a water sample to be analyzed, Dale comes upon the first evidence of scientific skulduggery. The farmer's water is abnormal; it causes only thirst. The reason? It is heavy water. * This is only the beginning. In a short time, it becomes evident that almost all the potable water in the New York area, then in the nation, has turned to heavy water, which is poisonous. People are dying by thousands. But the Geyser Spring Water company, which has ordinary water, is making a fortune by selling water at five dollars a bottle. * The villainous entrepreneur is Dale's former associate Munn, who, in league with a vicious capitalist, plans to strip the nation bare. The mechanism? Munn has discovered how to produce deuterium and thereby heavy water in quantity by using the Earth's magnetic field to send a controlled beam of positrons into the water supply. Things get so bad that the President of the United States expropriates Geyser Springs, but to no avail. It is up to Sanford Dale, who works out what has happened, locates the source of radiation in a cave in Upstate New York; and blasts down the defiant culprits with a positron projector of his own. * Starts reasonably, but soon becomes unreasonable.

1260. **THE ULTIMATE METAL**. *Astounding Stories*, February 1935. Ill. Dold.
(Reprinted in Conklin, *Best of Science Fiction*.)
Novelette. * *Time and place:* New York City of the near future. * Business ethics and catastrophe. * The new Coulton Building is the marvel of the city; 150 stories high, self illuminating and powered, it exists thanks to the discovery of evanium (element 93), which in alloys conveys incredible strength, beauty, and other properties. * Evanium was discovered in the great Coulton Laboratories, credit being given to Thomas Coulton. But actually, Coulton is simply a ruthless capitalist of large rapacity and vanity; the real brain of the laboratory is Harley Dean, a quiet, unassuming man. Dean was unwilling to exploit the evanium alloys, pointing out that too little was known of their stability. Coulton, however, overruled him in a bullying manner. * Dean, of course, was right. While the building is in its glory, the metal sheathing and structure start to act up spectacularly, glowing, becoming invisible, and finally disappearing altogether, dropping tens of thousands of building occupants to their death. At the last moment, Dean, recognizing, in a general way, what is happening, tries to offset the disintegration with a machine that he whips together, but this apparatus, while preserving his and Coulton's lives, is not strong enough to protect the whole tower. * A typical social parable of the day, greatly weakened by Dean's building-saver apparatus.

1261. **MIND OF THE WORLD**. *Astounding Stories*, March 1935. Ill. Dold.
Novelette. * *Time:* the thirty-second century. * *Background:* As

Schachner, Nat (*continued*)

the end development of millennia of specialization, science has become completely compartmentalized and the property of many intellectually isolated Tribes. Accompanying this superspecialization is complete ignorance of other areas of technology, science, or even life. Thus, a psychologist delegate (oddly termed a "psychopath") to the Hall of Science meeting called by Warren Bascom lives in a culture with primitive agriculture and has had to walk five hundred miles to attend, while a totally naive rocketeer covered the same distance in a matter of an hour or two. * The purpose of the conference is to break the tribal barriers and permit insemination from other areas. The mechanism? A device like a thought helmet created by brilliant Clyde Moorhouse, perhaps the only real universalist on Earth. * When the helmet is successfully demonstrated, the assembly speedily recognizes that it should be possible to establish a universal scientific mind. An individual wearing the master helmet could unify all knowledge and make it readily accessible. * Moorhouse should have been selected for the world mind, but by chance, bad planning, and politics, the choice goes to Kalen Thorn, a specialist in wave mechanics, who is an able but unscrupulous academic politician. Thorn dons the golden helmet and becomes the mind for mankind. * At first all seems well, but Thorn's real character soon emerges. He decrees that everyone should wear a secondary helmet through which he can listen in on and control the thoughts of the wearer; he enforces his decree with a goon squad of desperadoes, stamping out all disapproval of his tyrannical rule. Moorhouse becomes Thorn's main target, for Moorhouse has concealed the formulas for creating the helmet and is an obvious malcontent. * Matters come to a head when Moorhouse and an associate escape from Thorn's control. Thorn tries to destroy them with storms and disintegrators, but Moorhouse survives. At the end, however, when Thorn finally captures Moorhouse's airship, Moorhouse wins—precipitating Thorn through a fourth-dimensional trapdoor that he has maintained (unknown to the reader) for such emergencies. * Routine or less. The resolution constitutes bad plotting.

1262. **THE ORB OF PROBABILITY**. *Astounding Stories,* June 1935. Ill. Dold.

Short novelette. The basic concept is one occasionally advanced in philosophy of mathematics, that mathematics does not reflect reality, but creates reality. * *Time:* A.D. 9678. * *Background:* Everything in the world is perfectly controlled, with omnipresent machines, power-centered at Machine City, that take care of aspects of life for humanity. Human longevity is now hundreds of years, but boredom, lassitude, physical weakness, ineffectuality are almost universal. The one exception is Fran 19, who is something of a mistake. Something must have gone wrong in the reproductive process, which is now totally handled by machines (sexual reproduction being long discontinued). Fran 19 should have been an exact facsimile of previous Frans. Instead, he is gifted with imagination, initiative, and vigor. * Almost alone, Fran 19 recognizes that his civilization is torpid and sterile. In the sole piece of scientific research and construction done in his time, he devises an apparatus that will change the formulas of the universe, thus setting mankind into a challenging environment where it will either adapt and grow, or perish. * The apparatus, a small globe, is finished and set into operation. It immediately disappears, but is later revealed to be sitting in space about five hundred miles away. At first it seems that

nothing has happened, but then the world starts to alter, ending with the destruction of the central power equipment in Machine City. The result is catastrophic, for there is no food; the artificial gravity activating individual flying wings no longer works; robots no longer repair or replace damaged equipment; and mankind begins to practice cannibalism in order to survive. * This is not the end, however, for Fran and his friend, the aged Sem (whom he has converted to his point of view), repair the power apparatus, hoping that the previous cultural shock will awaken mankind. Unfortunately, this is not the case. Humanity immediately falls back into the same rut as before. * Fran's orb, however, is powered from the central broadcasts. While the generators were down, it could not function. But now that power has been restored, the orb begins to operate again, on a deeper level. It alters space and time, bringing segments of past and future Earth into Fran's world, with ever increasing chaos. * Fran, recognizing what is happening, destroys the central power system permanently, shutting off the orb. Its activity, however, has not all been for the worse. The new lands dropped into Fran's time and space include agricultural areas. It is now possible for men to return to the soil and regain lost strengths. * Confusingly presented.

1263. **THE SON OF REDMASK**. *Astounding Stories,* July 1935. Ill. Marchioni.

Short story. * Sequel to #1253, "Redmask of the Outlands." * *Time:* the fifty-sixth century, a generation later than the first story. * *Background:* Since the last story a new world power has risen. This is the Purple Emperor, whose headquarters are in Labrador, atop the Earth's north magnetic pole. This tyrant, who may be a Mongolian, or perhaps an Eskimo, has discovered how to tap the Earth's magnetic field, which powers his airships and weapons. His ships are impenetrable, once their screens are on, and against his weapons nothing can stand. Chico and Pisbor have been easily smashed. Mighty Yorick has fallen, and Anne of the Hudsons, daughter of Edward of the first story, alone of the aristocracy has escaped from the ruins of her city. * Washeen, though unfortified and without superscience, alone has offered any resistance. Aged Stephen Halleck, the former Redmask, has secretly reactivated his ancient ship with its invisibility apparatus and has destroyed several ships of the Purple Horde before their defenses could be energized. Nevertheless, Washeen has been overrun, and its adult males are to be drafted into the Purple Horde. * But Washeen cannot be ignored. Young Kent Halleck learns for the first time that his father was Redmask and that he shot down the enemy ships. Old Stephen entrusts him with the equipment and identity of Redmask and assigns him to an important role in the struggle against the Purple Horde. Kent is to fly to a rendezvous in the Outlands and gather together the outlaw hordes, which have drifted apart and degenerated since the retirement of Redmask. * Kent flies to the rendezvous, saves Anne of the Hudsons (whose air vessel crashed) from a rapist, and is accepted as the new Redmask. The outlaws gather, but the rapist has betrayed them, and the Purple fleet will soon be upon them. * The fleet arrives overhead, and all seems lost. Even Redmask's invisible ship is no longer significant, since it can be tracked on Purple sensory equipment. Kent, however, saves the day. Acting on a hint that Redmask Sr., broadcast over a crystal set, Kent uses the magnetic force and the properties of an electric motor to overload the enemy fleet, destroying it utterly. Since the

Schachner, Nat (*continued*)

tyrannical cities have all fallen, the free men of the Outlands can found a new civilization. * Routine.

1264. **I AM NOT GOD.** *Astounding Stories,* October-November 1935. Ill. Dold.
Novelette. * Human frailty and the poisonous nebula. * Two events occur at about the same time. First, young chemist Stephen Dodd, working on ionizing gases, discovers a gas that, in tiniest proportion, creates suspended animation. It is very penetrating, with only lead serving as a barrier. Unfortunately, it is impossible to revive the victims. Second, a hitherto unobserved gaseous nebula is hurtling toward Earth and will hit in a matter of weeks. The nebula, spectroscopically analyzed, is composed of Dodd's gas and will undoubtedly wipe out Terrestrial life. * Dodd and a team of blue-ribbon colleagues work frantically to find an antidote to the gas, though they are badly strapped for funds. * A confusing factor is the War Lord of a certain European country, obviously à clef for Hitler and Germany, who first tries to manufacture Dodd's gas, then to buy it from him. One of his agents infiltrates Dodd's team. * The nebula is due to strike at any hour, and Dodd is still racing to find an antidote. His last resort preparation is still cooking when the gas strikes. In horror, in a lead-filled diving suit, Dodd watches his fiancée Deborah, her father, and the members of his team sink into what may be death. Desperately, as he is near suffocation in the diving suit, he injects himself with the preparation, just before sinking into unconsciousness. * He awakens about eighteen hours later. The preparation works, and with it he revives Deborah, her father, and one or two others. But then Dodd has a brainstorm, on which he is prepared to act. He announces that he will revive people selectively, on the basis of their usefulness in the new society that he intends to create, without war, want, or misery. * This sounds good in theory, but there are two flaws in it. First, for emotional reasons he must revive the worthless spouses of two of his men, thus setting a precedent for responding to personal pressure. Second, intellectual stature, as Dodd soon observes, is no gauge of moral fitness for a new world. Two of his most trusted men wreck his laboratory, seize his supply of the antidote, try to murder his aides, and fly off to revive the War Lord and his legions. * Dodd follows them, and what with air battles and ground shoot-outs it is a near thing. The traitors die, but the evil that they have started will continue, for the War Lord and his associates are alive again. * In utter discouragement and disillusionment, Dodd declares, "I am not God." He will make no more life or death decisions, but will revive everyone possible and let the world work out its wars and problems. * The gaseous nebula and the initial coincidence, of course, are trite, but the moral problem is interesting and deserves better treatment.

1265. **WORLD GONE MAD.** *Amazing Stories,* October 1935. Ill. Morey.
Short story. * *Time:* around 1990. *Place:* New York City. * Perhaps originally planned as a one-act stage play. * Personal situations, with some verismo, when war breaks out between the U.S. on one side and Sino-Russ and United Europe on the other. The casus belli is the repeated sabotage of naval forces of the other countries, persons responsible unknown. The characters include granddad Peter, a veteran of World War I, who takes a traditional patriotic view; his son, Donald, who is sure nothing like war could ever happen, and if it did, the U.S. would be

almost instantaneously victorious; and grandson Allen, who is off as a pilot and will not live long. The outcome is a debacle, as everyone is killed by bombing or poison gas. * *Miscellaneous:* Weapons include powerful rockets and radar equivalents. * Closet pacifist material of the day; unusual for the period and milieu, which was usually blindly hawkish. Excellent reproductions of war-hysteric propaganda, with a pathetic note.

1266. **THE ISOTOPE MEN**. *Astounding Stories,* January 1936. Ill. Wesso.
Novelette. * *Time:* the near future. * The great but somewhat flawed physical chemist Malcolm Stubbs has discovered how to dissolve objects and living things into their chemical components, isolate the isotopic elements, and then recombine the components into two replicas of the original. One of the replicas is roughly the same size as the original; the other isotopic version is much smaller, but in living creatures can be nurtured to normal size. * In all this work Stubbs has been assisted by Kenneth Craig, a brilliant man who has really supplied many of the ideas that Stubbs has appropriated. Just as Stubbs is an arrogant, irresponsible egotist and opportunist, Craig is a "good guy" with a conscience. * The crowning achievement of Stubbs and Craig comes when (by pulling many strings) they are allowed to use their apparatus in a prison death cell on convicted murderer (Jim Horty), who is otherwise scheduled for execution. The process works; Horty is dissolved, then reconstituted in a nonisotopic version, which is obviously a pleasant, good-hearted man. * The interpretation, born out by many later operations, is that the Stubbs-Craig process breaks humans down into good and bad components, à la Jekyll and Hyde, and that the good "positive" isotopic portions, no longer held back by their bad companions, are far abler and far more intelligent than their originals. But before this situation becomes known, Stubbs fires Craig, who objected on grounds of conscience to experimentation on Horty. * The Stubbs-Craig process sweeps the nation as a self-improvement fad. There are enormous advances in science and literature as the new "positive" isotope men achieve wonders. The other components, the "recessives," are thrown into the army, where they are presumably under control. As a curious result of the process, both personality halves have strong emotional feelings toward each other, the positives feeling love, while the recessives feel hatred. * At about this point Schachner loses control of the story, which becomes wild. There would be no point in describing the plot in detail. Let it be enough to say that Stubbs processes himself, with his positive becoming dictator of the United States. Civil war breaks out between positives and recessives. Stubbs is eventually killed by his bad component, toward whom he felt love. The disintegrator that he invented, however, does much to destroy the recessives. The positives lose much of their mentality and spend their time wandering about looking for their other halves. * The United States is wrecked and must be rebuilt. Chosen new dictator, Ken Craig closes all the ionic-dispersal stations and hopes that a new generation will develop on a natural basis. * As is frequent enough in Schachner's stories, what begins as a personal situation develops into a badly handled national catastrophe on a very unconvincing level.

1267. **ENTROPY**. *Astounding Stories,* March 1936. Unsigned ill. (Brown?)
Novelette. * *Time and place:* Our world and the end of our universe. * Jerry Sloan, gifted young physicist, has devised a

Schachner, Nat (continued)

new technique that he is sure will lead to the attainment of absolute zero. It does not involve heat transfer, like other cryogenic techniques, but stops molecular motion by filtering radiation through a tourmaline sphere. * He is currently making his first demonstration to a blue-ribbon panel when an accident takes place. His financial sponsor's unpleasant child meddles with the controls, there is an explosion, and the tourmaline sphere disappears, along with Sloan's fiancée, Kay Ballard. * Sloan, understandably upset, comes to the conclusion that Kay, with the cessation of matter and energy inherent in his process, is in another space-time and not necessarily dead. Determined to follow her and retrieve her, he sets up the same circumstances as before (except that he takes along with him a device that should reverse the atomic/molecular condition) and signals an assistant to throw the final switch. He disappears in a roar. Watch is kept for his return, but the years, decades, centuries pass, and there is no Sloan. * Sloan awakens in a strange partly transparent blue sphere of force, which he soon recognizes is no longer part of our universe. There is an enormous time differential between his sphere and our universe, for thousands of years pass in a flash, and he witnesses the births and deaths of systems in a matter of minutes, precluding any hope of returning to Earth. He also sees close beside his sphere another, containing Kay. They communicate by signals, but their supply of air is limited, and they are soon faced with the certainty of suffocation. * Deciding that a quick death would be preferable, they are about to shatter their tourmaline shells, when they receive a telepathic message urging them to take no action. Jerry slides into unconsciousness, awaking to find fresh air and a companion in the sphere. This is Horgo, a tall, remarkable superman who communicates with him telepathically. Immortal, Horgo is the last man, and the universe outside is just about dead. Previous scientists of his culture had been aware of the two spheres and had tracked them, but only now has it been possible to slow down their progress and enter them. Horgo's female associate, Lika, is in the sphere with Kay. While Jerry and Kay will survive, since they have now been rendered immortal like the two future beings, there is no possibility of merging the spheres. Indeed, Horgo is mildly puzzled why Jerry and Kay should want this. In his culture it is enough to communicate telepathically. * Horgo, instead, offers an infinity of thought in which all concerned contemplate and meditate forever. This does not appeal to Jerry and Kay, who are obviously far lower on the plane of evolution than the superpair. * But, a last minute resolution. The universe is now dead, and all its energy is tied up as potential energy. Perhaps Jerry's little device may serve as a spring to change the potential to actual, thus creating a new universe? Yes, says Horgo, this can be done. * After considerable work by Horgo, the device is activated, and a new universe springs into being. From all the energy buzzing around them Horgo and Lika will create a planet suitable for Jerry and Kay. In fact, it looks as if Eros is contagious, for Horgo and Lika have become aware of sexual attraction and may make another planet for themselves. * One of Schachner's better stories.

1268. **REVERSE UNIVERSE.** *Astounding Stories,* June 1936. Ill. Schneeman.

Short story. * *Time:* the interplanetary future. *Place:* space, on the way to Sirius. * The *Pathfinder,* on the first interstellar flight, is about half way to its goal, Sirius. There are two years left to go, but it is almost certain, as the story begins, that the *Pathfinder* will never reach its destination. The crew is on the edge of mutiny, in part due to the rigors of two years in a cramped spaceship, in part due to Captain Apperson, who is a martinet on the edge of insanity. Lieutenant Talbot, navigator and second in command, tries to warn Apperson about a possible mutiny, but Apperson does no more than pull rank. * The mutiny takes place, and when Talbot, as a matter of pride, refuses to join the mutineers, he is put into a small lifeboat with Apperson and six months' supplies. It is a death sentence, but if he hadn't been popular with the men, he might have been treated worse. * Talbot and Apperson continue on their way to Sirius, although they both know that they will not reach it. Ordered on by Apperson, who does not understand the mathematical physics involved, Talbot tries to break the speed of light—in vain. * Something strange, however, happens. There is a shock, and the men observe that the lifeboat is being carried along inside what seems to be an empty, hollow sphere of planetary size. There are many oddities in their situation, including the fact that they are growing younger. * Talbot theorizes that they have been caught up by a planetoid or something similar that is moving at many times the speed of light and amounts to a small negative pocket universe. He is probably right, for when he succeeds in blasting the lifeboat away from the planetoid, he finds that they are indeed very close to Sirius, which displays a green world that may have life and civilization. * Routine.

1269. **PACIFICA.** *Astounding Stories,* July 1936. Unsigned ill. (Brown?)

Novelette. * *Time:* from 1985 on, with major action in 2010. *Place:* mostly on a small island in the Pacific. * By the year 1985 the world is in very bad shape. Advanced medicine, greater longevity, unrestricted, indeed, in some cases greatly encouraged births have resulted in enormous overpopulation. The great nations—America-Great Britain, Europe, and the Eastern Empire are at the brink of war for Lebensraum. * At this point, the great engineer Adam Breder makes an incredible proposal at an international conference: Create a new continent, to be divided equally among the superpowers. He proposes, by applying the principle of Pascal's Law of hydrodynamics, to so work on the semisolid core of the Earth as to raise a continent in the Pacific. His working site will be the small volcanic island of Kam, where the geomorphology is suitable. As for the technology required to drill a shaft about thirty-five miles deep and to control the magma there encountered, Breder claims that he has it. The nations agree, although it is made clear to the reader that the Eastern Emperor Chu-san is planning dirty tricks. * The work proceeds apace, with occasional crises and mishaps, but nothing that cannot be surmounted. Toward the end of the project Breder dies, transferring his authority to the young American Ken Craig. Craig works with a triumvirate including a European, a Chinese in hot water with his government, and Nijo, a Japanese subject of the Eastern Empire. It is made clear to the reader that Nijo is planning treachery. * The shaft is finished; the magma is met and contained; and pressure is applied. Although there are diversions with volcanism and seismic activity, Craig and his associates perform brilliantly, raising the new continent Pacifica. * At this point villainy reveals itself. Nijo reports to the Eastern Emperor, and a fleet of air

Schachner, Nat (*continued*)

vessels occupies the control area. The Eastern Empire will annex Pacifica, and the remainder of the world will either have to accept this or fight. Indeed, it does not even come to war, for Nijo, down below in the shaft, is sending controlled earthquakes around the world. * The situation is bad, for Craig and his associates are captives during these events. But they escape, and Craig sends a most powerful bomb down the shaft, killing Nijo and stopping his wicked actions. The resulting eruptions destroy the Oriental forces occupying Pacifica. * The character Ken Craig is not the same person as the Ken Craig of #1266, "The Isotope Men." * Routine.

1270. **THE RETURN OF THE MURIANS.** *Astounding Stories,* August 1936. Ill. Wesso.

Novelette. * In a prologue of a sort, the human occupants of the mile-long biosphere that has been traveling for 5,000 years from Sirius's solitary planet, discuss hopes and fears. Their ship cannot hold out longer than another two or three hundred years, and they must find a habitable planet soon. Otherwise the ancient race of Murians will perish. If the planet is inhabited, says grim old Warlo, chief of the voyagers, the natives will be exterminated. * In New York, about a year later, the giant ship is sighted, and astronomers eagerly watch it. But Mark Sloan, who was present when his friend Mellish first sighted the spaceship, is working in solitude in the Adirondacks. He is an archeologist of sorts, special area Lemuria, and he holds in his possession the single surviving Lemurian artifact—a broken golden talisman. * He awakens one morning to see the ship resting where there had been a small lake. Captured, he is taken on board, subjected to a treatment that teaches him the Murian language (while the Murians learn English), and interrogated. Old Warlo is at his most bloodthirsty; Mark is as defiant as circumstances permit; and it looks for a time as if he will be vivisected. But partly through Warlo's daughter, who is soft-hearted, and partly through circumstances, he is spared, only to watch the invaders shatter every attack with force shields and disintegrator rays. Warlo continues to be contemptuous, although he gradually works into the position of permitting a few humans to live in a desert area. * The turning point comes when Sloan unwittingly produces his Lemurian relic. It causes a turmoil, at first with accusations of theft, then bewilderment when the relic matches the other half, which the Murians—or, as they are now revealed, Lemurians—treasure. When Warlo realizes that the humans of Earth are relatives, he relents and decides to settle on Venus, Mark accompanying them. * *Miscellaneous:* The Murians have tawny hair and golden complexions with a tinge of green. * Routine.

1271. **THE SAPROPHYTE MEN OF VENUS.** *Astounding Stories,* October 1936. Ill. Dold.

Short story. * *Place:* Vermont. * The subtext is the morality of survival, a question which hero Hugh Warner raises at the beginning and end of the story. * Hugh and friend Jane Castle, while hiking through the mountains, first experience a sudden darkness, as the sun disappears leaving a black hole, then see a towering pillar of light that reaches far into the atmosphere and merges into the black. As they soon discover, the zone of blackness forms a circle about two hundred miles across, including New York City. Hugh reasons that the pillar and the blackness must be an attack of extraterrestrial origin, probably from Venus. * As Hugh and Jane approach Middletown, they see the inva-ders—whitish, mobile, intelligent plants—who seize humans and eat them. They are using the cylinder of light as a transport tube from Venus. * While the invaders are digesting "their odious food," Hugh and Jane venture into the cylinder of light (which is cool) with small bombs. They are attacked by the plant creatures, but Hugh fights free, reaches the control machines that produce the cylinder of light and sabotages them. The pillar and darkness vanish in a tremendous explosion that travels along the path of the pillar back to Venus. Earth is saved, and Venus is at least badly damaged. Hugh and Jane survive. * Pretty bad as fiction.

1272. **THE ETERNAL WANDERER.** *Astounding Stories,* November 1936. Ill. Dold.

Novelette. * *Time:* the interplanetary future. * *Background:* There is an nominal Interplanetary Confederation to which Earth, Venus, Mercury, and Mars belong, but in practice it is ruled by a council dominated by Vesgo, the dictator of Mars. The other planets maintain a shadow of independence that does not mean much. On Earth a rebellion has arisen and has been smashed; as the story opens, one of the leaders, young Cliff Havens, is about to be sentenced. Cliff makes such an impassioned speech against the Martians that his audience is aroused. As a result, Vesgo makes his final coup, with complete subjugation of the solar system to Mars. * As for Cliff, he is sentenced to the penalty of the Eternal Wanderer. No one knows exactly what that means, but all are suitably horrified. Cliff learns. He is taken to the laboratory of Harg, where the brain machine rests. This apparatus, in association with a certain ray Harg has discovered, will break Cliff down into mathematical components and scatter them throughout the universe; according to theory, the fragments will retain part of his personality and will yearn desperately for reunification, forever. Harg pulls the switch, and Cliff goes off into eternal pain. * Meanwhile, rebellion has broken out on the planets. Cliff's girlfriend, Beulah Moorhouse, and her father (a great mathematician who served very unwillingly on the court that sentenced Cliff) have invaded Harg's laboratory in an invisible ship. (Harg, it turns out, detested Vesgo and his tyranny and was executed; but, a former friend of Moorhouse's, he had whispered the secret of the dissociator to Moorhouse, who claims to have worked out a method of reintegrating Cliff.) * The apparatus is set up, and Cliff reappears—but it is not Cliff, but a statuesque, superhuman version of Cliff that is beyond emotion or human weaknesses. As is revealed later, Moorhouse made a mistake in the mathematics involved, so that Cliff II is now a fourth-dimensional being, only one aspect of whom penetrates our universe. This explains his immunity to weapons and the strange powers that he will display. * Vesgo's soldiery storms the laboratory, but Cliff II is more than a match for them and their weapons. He walks away through walls and space. * The revolts have been quelled and Vesgo sits gloating. Cliff II enters the impregnable fortress and kills Vesgo, then strides about the solar system destroying Martians and their forces. The Martian hegemony is broken, and the planets regain their freedom. On Mars itself the tyranny is ended. But Cliff II is seen no more. * Time passes, while Beulah mourns and the solar system pays honor to Cliff's memory. Then Cliff II, manifesting himself to the Moorhouses, gives them new formulas to set up on the brain machine. This is done, and the old Cliff is back among them. He has no memory whatever of what happened to him either as the Eternal Wanderer or as Cliff II. * *Mis-*

Schachner, Nat (*continued*)

cellaneous: Disintegrators and paralysis guns are omnipresent. * Martians are humanoid, gigantic, and ugly, with three-clawed hands. Venusians are presumably fish-men. Mercurians are armored in scales and are very stupid. * Some ideas, but lots of clichés.

1273. **INFRA-UNIVERSE.**   *Astounding Stories,* December 1936-January 1937. Ill. Wesso.

Short novel. * *Place:* Maine for introductory section, the other side of our universe for the major portion. * Jim Wentworth, unemployed and stony-broke physics major, railroad engineer, soldier of fortune, and socialist activist, applies for an advertised job at the establishment of great physicist Professor Matthew Draper, whose courses Jim had taken about ten years earlier. But at the door, he finds a strange situation: A handsome young woman (Claire Gray) tries to discourage him and urges him not to apply. Readers of contemporary mystery stories will recognize what is going on. Nevertheless, Wentworth applies and is accepted. * Professor Draper is the Draper Jim knew, yet he is not. His personality has changed, and while he has access to Draper's memories, it is obviously a matter of slow retrieval. Then, too, he is a master of a science far beyond Draper's, as may be judged from the elaborate incomprehensible equipment he has built. * In a fairly short time Jim and Claire decide that Draper's body is possessed by someone or something else. But what the purpose of it all is, they do not know. * On the crucial occasion, all the machinery seems to be operative, whereupon Draper bids Jim and Claire to leave until the afternoon. When they return, they see that Draper is inside a gigantic container. He bids Jim to close a certain switch. Jim forces a showdown, refusing to activate the apparatus until Draper explains what is going on and what has happened to the real Draper. Jim and Claire were right in their suspicions. The individuality inhabiting Draper's body gives a limited explanation, urging that there is a deadline; if the switch is not closed before then, both his and Jim's universe will suffer. Jim is for holding out for a more satisfactory explanation, but Claire yields. She tries to throw the switch. Jim, trying to prevent her, dislodges part of the equipment. The result is an "event," in which a segment of Maine about ten by twenty miles is sheared neatly off Earth and deposited elsewhere, under a sky with triple, never setting suns. * In this strange situation Jim and Claire encounter the real Draper, freed from his inhabitant. He explains: In modern cosmology, our universe is on the outer surface of an expanding film of space time; the castaways are now on the other side of this surface. Draper adds that he had been possessed by a being named Insar, a formless creature on the border between life and inanimate matter, who had been expelled by powerful enemies and was trying to return to his own universe. Jim's clumsy actions brought along with Insar a small fragment of Earth, retaining all its space-time characteristics, atmosphere, gravity, etc. There is no return, says Draper. * Jim, Draper, and Claire recognize that organization is necessary for survival. There are about 275 people stranded on the segment; most of them are wealthy jet-setters whom Jim dislikes for class reasons. The remainder are service people and local farmers. Jim is chosen to head the castaways. Life proceeds as smoothly as can be expected until one day, the sky is filled with misty creatures who descend on the humans individually and carry them away. * The story follows Jim, who is possessed by an entity that is not

unfriendly. The action becomes too complex to cover in detail, and only leading threads will be covered. The area is currently the scene of a war between Insar's group and another group. As explained later by Insar, the original viral inhabitants were passive beings, but two incursions from our world changed matters: mind amoeboids from Betelgeuse, and horrors from near Sirius. These amalgamated with the virus-like beings, forming two different populations, Betelgeuse more or less good and Sirius, very bad. The power-mad Sirian group, under King Kam, is engaged in conquering Insar's planet. Thanks to Jim and his almost self-sacrificing actions, the wicked are defeated. Insar, who is basically good, prepares apparatus for returning the segment of Earth back to our universe. * *Miscellaneous:* When King Kam wants to be rid of dissidents, he tosses them into our universe, where they are broken up and become the filterable viruses that cause human diseases. * An erotic note, unusual for s-f of this day, enters when the being possessing Claire taunts and teases Jim by ripping off her clothing and displaying "her charms." Jim is both excited and horrified. * Clichéd in beginning, interesting soon after, somewhat silly for a time, and badly developed for the second half.

SCHACHNER, NATHAN and LACHER, R.
See separate entry for Schachner. No information on Lacher, who presumably supplied the plot that Schachner fleshed out.

1274. **THE MEMORY OF THE ATOMS.**   *Wonder Stories,* January 1933. Ill. Paul.

Short story. * *Time:* A.D. 2052. *Place:* mostly New York City, but a little in Manitoba. * Short story. * Wicked capitalists jockeying for yet more wealth. * *Background:* The world is beset by a cancer-like plague of extreme virulence; only radium can cure it, and the colossal Radium Trust holds a near monopoly—which it uses to demand fabulous prices. There are a few marginal dealers, like Mackington, who are allowed to operate in order to prevent Federal investigation. * At the moment Mackington (a greedy, treacherous swine) and Dr. Harvey Blake (an altruistic, high-minded scientist) form an uneasy partnership. Back in the early-middle twentieth century, an explorer stumbled on a fabulous radium lode, the location of which was lost. Mackington and Blake have located a descendant (Florence James) of the explorer, and Blake, who has been investigating electrical stimulation of the brain, hopes to tap Florence's ancestral memory. The process is dangerous, involving direct electrification of brain areas. * Florence dredges up her ancestor's memories, including the location of the deposit, but the situation is complicated by very elaborate double-crosses and crooked deals between Mackington and the Radium Trust. * Good triumphs when Florence and Dr. James, who have fallen in love, file papers on the claim. * Horrible writing. So bad that one could suspect a parody; but probably not.

SCHACHNER, NAT and ZAGAT, ARTHUR LEO
Schachner and Zagat have individual entries. The collaboration is said to have broken up because of disagreements. No precise information is available, but it seems reasonable to speculate that Zagat did not share Schachner's political and social concern and that Schachner was repelled by Zagat's somewhat meretricious development of story.

1275. **THE TOWER OF EVIL**.   *Wonder Stories Quarterly,* Summer 1930. Ill. Paul.

Schachner, Nat and Zagat, Arthur Leo (*continued*)

Short story. * *Place:* Tibet. * Oriental adventure based ultimately on sensational "ethnography" of the 1920s, notably William Seabrook's *Adventures in Arabia* and Robert W. Chambers's *The Slayer of Souls*. * John Dunton, American explorer who has heard tales of the legendary Towers of Evil, decides to investigate. As the story begins, he encounters the magical science of the Sheik-al-Jabal, descendant of the grandmaster of the medieval Middle Eastern sect of Assassins. * Dunton is captured and interrogated by the Sheik, who, although first sentencing Dunton to death for entering his realm, becomes impressed by his bravery and offers him a post in the new empire to come. * The Sheik's revelations: Centuries ago, his ancestors, escaping the Mongols, settled in this area of Tibet, passing for Buddhist lamas. The present Sheik, who is a very old man, has developed a superscience, which includes gravity control, atomic control, and much else. With this science he plans to conquer the world and force the worship of Shaitan. (Or, that is what he tells his followers. Actually, he is an utterly cynical atheist who uses the cult of Shaitan as a front. He is really concerned solely with political power.) The Sheik will first exterminate the present human race with a plague he has developed. His followers, a secret organization that has ramifications all over the world, will temporarily take over. These men, who are slaves of hashish and the artificial paradise that the ancient Assassins developed, will later also be slaughtered. * The Sheik, however, needs a right-hand man whom he can trust, and Dunton seems to be a good candidate. Dunton agrees to work with the Sheik; he has, of course, no intention of fulfilling his promise, and to his surprise his deception is revealed by a mechanical thought-reading screen. * As might be expected, Dunton wins through and destroys the monstrous lama and his plot. In this he is aided by a young English woman who had been held captive by the lama since she was a small child. * A bad job, even within its proper field, the adventure story, not science-fiction. This is Schachner's first story, and one might guess that Zagat had a larger part in it than in later stories.

1276. **IN 20,000 A.D.!** *Wonder Stories*, September 1930. Ill. Paul.

Short story. * *Place:* Long Island, present and A.D. 20,000. * An adaptation of the fairy-wood motif to science-fiction. * In the small town of Blaymont, Long Island, is a wooded area that few dare enter. Those who do enter disappear and are never seen again. Tom Jenkins, a young farmhand, accepting a dare, ventures in and disappears for months. Then he is suddenly found wandering about in a field. He refuses to talk, for fear of being put into an asylum. * Two smart young New Yorkers, a reporter and a scientist, hear of Tom's disappearance and reappearance, and decide to investigate. With some difficulty, they persuade Tom to talk. * On entering the wood, he undergoes a sort of dimensional transition (identified by the scientist as a relativistic weak spot between times, or, in modern language, a time wormhole), and finds himself in the future. He is seen by a twelve-foot-tall totally black, four-eyed man with four hands (two normal arms, two hands emergent from the hips), who summons his superior, a small balloon-headed man with four eyes and almost tentacular arms and a cylindrical body. * The balloon-head (Karet), whose English is barely comprehensible to Tom, explains. No one is permitted into the wood, undoubtedly because it is a time gate of a sort. He takes Tom

in a small antigravity vessel to headquarters, where Tom is interviewed by the Jed. * *Background:* In the future world, the population is divided into Masters, like the little man, and Robots, or the very tall, black people, who do all the dirty work. All are neuter and are produced under laboratory conditions from human ova. Longevity for the Masters is high, about three hundred years. The Robots are of very low intelligence, although there are occasional exceptions, due to laboratory accidents, who are average; the Masters are of superhuman intelligence; but by far the most intelligent of all is the Jed, an enormous brain floating in liquid, who is thousands of years old and fully telepathic. He rules the land. The status of the Robots is horrible, incessant labor, and death for the slightest offence, such as accidentally jostling a Master. * The dynamics: The land is about ready for a revolution, with Master Karet pushing and manipulating the Robots in terms of liberties. Actually, as Tom realizes when he joins the underground Robot movement, Karet really wants the Jed's position and will change nothing. * The revolt begins, and the Robots storm the House of the Mothers, where new individuals are manufactured. Karet now demands that the other Masters surrender or else he will destroy the Mothers and their eggs, thus ending the human race. The other Masters yield, but when Karet tries to turn the Robots against Jed, he meets a surprise: The great brain says that it is immortal and does not need humans any more. It is starting to disintegrate the hostile mobs when Tom makes a dash away to the forbidden wood, hoping to return to his own time, as he does. * *Miscellaneous:* In the past there was an invasion from Jupiter, which Jed warded off, and at another time, a revolt of the machines, which Jed broke. * Tom brought back with him a history book entrusted to him by one of the more intelligent Robots. * This is one of the very few instances in science-fiction where the word "robot" is used in the sense originally offered by Karel Capek. * Obvious parabolic elements referring to U.S. history and racial matters. Somewhat superior to the rubbishy adventure stories that Schachner and Zagat usually produced. Apart from having intrinsically more interesting subject matter, the story is handled with more craftsmanship. For a sequel see #1277, "Back to 20,000 A.D."

1277. **BACK TO 20,000 A.D.** *Wonder Stories*, March 1931. Ill. Marchioni.

Short story. * Sequel to #1276, "In 20,000 A.D.!" * *Time:* around A.D. 20,000. * Dunn receives an unexpected summons from Tom Jenkins, the young man who had previously chanced into the future. When Dunn and Chapin visit Jenkins, he tells them that Charlie, one of the more intelligent Robots, has come through the time gate into our world and is hiding in the woods. From Charlie they learn that some of the rebellious Robots are besieged in the future haunted wood by the Masters and will starve unless rescued. Chapin, Dunn, and Charlie resolve to enter the future world and remedy matters. * A new element now enters the story: Shortly after the time explorers' arrival in the future, a spaceship lands nearby, and they manage to rescue the occupant, a normal human, before the nearby Masters can kill him. * His story: Millennia ago, during the revolt of the Machines, a group of humans left Earth and settled on Neptune, with permission of the Neptunians. They lost all contact with Earth. But now the Neptunians, who need the space, have ordered the Terrestrial colony to leave. The present visitor, Arkon, is on a reconnaissance mission. * Since the Jed has

Schachner, Nat and Zagat, Arthur Leo (*continued*)

commanded the death of all who are taking refuge in the wood, something must be done. Donning a thought-screen headband that the Neptunian provides, Chapin rides a captured Master flyer into the Jed's palace, hoping to destroy him/it. In the palace he meets Eona, a handsome, tall young woman with whom he establishes the beginnings of a romance. She is a "destined mother," or a female kept as a sort of breeder. All the while the Jed is bombarding Chapin with telepathic threats. * Capture, rescue, and the arrival of a second Neptunian party culminate in a showdown with the Jed. Dunn reasons out the only tactics against him/it: The Jed's brain is a very powerful magnetic field that disrupts the electric structure of those that it wishes to disintegrate. Presumably this magnetic field can be exhausted if overworked. The Neptunian second group and some of the Robots sacrifice themselves, and Jed becomes weaker and weaker with each death. Just as Jed is about to collapse, he/it commits suicide rather than accept the ignomy of defeat. The surviving Masters surrender; Arkon will return to Neptune and guide the expatriates back to Earth; Dunn, Chapin, and Eona will enter the time warp back to our time. * *Miscellaneous:* The native Neptunians are telepathic reptilian men. * The authors are careless about story date, citing both 1931 and 1933. * Much less successful than the previous story, with little suspension of disbelief. The presence of the totally human woman does not fit with previous comments about asexual reproduction. * Routine work.

1278. **THE EMPEROR OF THE STARS**. *Wonder Stories*, April 1931. Ill. Marchioni.

Short story. * *Time:* the interplanetary future. *Place:* a dimensional world. * Burns and Fries, spacemen, are on their way to Pluto, hoping to gain the prize for being the first to visit it, when their ship is suddenly dragged around strangely. After a shock-like experience they find themselves in another universe that in many ways is a mirror image of ours: space is white with black bodies and the acting force is repulsion, not attraction. Since the men have little choice, they approach a planet-like mass that repels them; see a space vessel; follow it to an entrance into a hollow planet, within which is a central sun, whose repulsion acts like gravity, holding things to the inner surface of the planet. * As the men explore, they are attacked by alien creatures, against whom their ray guns are ineffective, then rescued by intelligent, friendly, jelly-like, dome-shaped creatures with tentacles and many tiny legs. On their bodies these creatures have a natural formation like a television screen that shows images, both pictorial and symbolic for communication. The dome creatures (Prostaks) welcome the two Earthmen, who gradually learn to communicate with them by pictures and writing. * There is a sour note: The Prostaks are subject to a being known as the Emperor of the Stars, who takes a frequent tribute of young Prostaks to serve as slaves on other planets. There is no resisting him, for he is able to destroy planets with little difficulty. As the Prostaks describe him, he is humanoid in form and operates from a huge crystal sphere. * Fries and Burn decide to help the Prostaks, partly out of compassion and partly from desire to return to their own universe, for they have concluded that the Emperor must be an Earthman. Their purpose is somewhat forestalled when the Emperor sends word that they, too, must join the tribute group. * Flying to the Emperor's station, the Earthmen see that he is indeed an aged, vicious-looking

Earthman. They attack. For long the battle is in doubt, but eventually their disintegrator pierces the crystal sphere and the Emperor is no more. At this time, a mingling of gravitation and repulsion forces drives the two Earthmen and their ship back to our universe. The Emperor is not explained. * *Miscellaneous:* The heat rays of Fries and Burns are not effective in the other world, but would be effective against an artifact from our universe, like the Emperor's sphere. * Half tongue-in-cheek, I would think, as can be seen by the names. In any case, a crude job.

1279. **THE MENACE FROM ANDROMEDA**. *Amazing Stories*, April 1931. Ill. Morey.

Short story. * *Time:* 1939. *Place:* California and elsewhere. * The first hint of the menace to come is perceived by Mount Wilson astronomer Donald Standish. Photographic plates of the Andromeda nebula show a pinpoint of light that is increasing. It is not a nova, as first believed, but something hitherto unknown. A new type of spectroscope that Standish has invented reveals that the light is phosphorescence, emitted by a living object! * Alcoreth, as Standish calls the object, is really a protoplasmic planetary entity. Although nearly omnivorous, it is limited to the surface of its planet, for it cannot penetrate beyond the lithosphere into the magmasphere. Now that its home planet is exhausted, it must prepare for a new generation, sending out spores to find other worlds. Indeed, there are already several such protoplasmic planet-beings in its area of space. * On Earth a packet of Alcoreth's seeds lands in the Atlantic Ocean; these seeds sprout and soon begin to seize ocean vessels. In less time than one would expect, the Atlantic is deserted of ships, and the protoplasm has irresistibly invaded the littorals of the United States, South America, and, to a lesser extent, Europe. There is no defense against the creature. * Standish, however, has a better idea of what is happening than most. After rescuing his fiancée from a skyscraper due to topple over into the monster, he and a friend salt the monster with cancer cells that kill it. Previously, the monster had been forced to retreat when exposed to strong light. * Routine at best.

1280. **THE DEATH-CLOUD**. *Astounding Stories*, May 1931. Ill. Wesso.

Short story. * Really a capsulated short novel, somewhat elliptical and confused in presentation. * *Time:* 1992. *Place:* the North Atlantic. * In the war between America and the USSR (which includes conquered territories in Asia, Africa, and Europe) both sides deploy huge permanent rafts off the sea coasts as outposts and staging areas. Small Russian subs raid the American coast, then are withdrawn to the rafts when their missions are accomplished. In addition to superexplosive, weapons include death rays. * At the moment, the great air warship *New York*, with a complement of 5,000 men, after penetrating a mysterious cloud bank above one of the enemy rafts, has suddenly disappeared. It is up to counterintelligence to determine what is going on. * Captain Bolton, U.S.M.I., is the chosen agent. Among his skills is the ability to control his face muscles so perfectly that he can assume the features of almost anyone. (He has assiduously practiced this before a mirror since childhood.) He can also alter his physical build. Further, he speaks Russian well, having learned it from his grandmother. The perfect spy. * Bolton has a plan: Capture a one-man Russian sub, and taking the place of the occupant, penetrate the enemy

Schachner, Nat and Zagat, Arthur Leo (*continued*)

lines. So it happens. Pretending injury and disorientation, he is placed in the Russian sick bay, but is smoked out by his great Russian opponent, the Ferret, with whom he has clashed before. Bolton escapes, assumes the identity of a French private, is again detected by the Ferret, is captured, is threatened, escapes, but now accomplishes what he had set out to do: destroy the generators supplying power to the secret disintegrator (Zeta ray) that the Russians are using to drill a large tunnel to the mainland. * *Miscellaneous:* Russian disintegrator rays, applied to the sea, create what amounts to a dry caisson within which the Russians work. * *Miscellaneous:* This is super-New York, with incredible buildings. Both the Hudson and the East Rivers have been covered over. * High point: In an act of great heroism, Bolton, when impersonating the Ferret on one occasion, deliberately breaks one of his fingers to match the Ferret's crooked finger.

1281. **THE REVOLT OF THE MACHINES**. *Astounding Stories*, July 1931. Ill. Wesso.

Short story. * *Time:* around A.D. 7000. *Place:* the equatorial belt. * The Earth is undergoing a new glacial period, and only the area around the equator is habitable. Here are concentrated the mostly automated pleasure cities of the aristos, the rulers of the human race. Enslaved to work the control systems for the aristos are the prolats, about four hundred of them. Not too long ago the prolats rebelled against their decadent masters and were almost exterminated. * At the moment prolats Keston and the narrator are working on a fully automated system for controlling the city utilities and pleasure devices, with the understanding that when it is finished, the prolats will be permitted to become aristos. But now that the system is operative the decadent aristos, realizing that they no longer need their slaves, welsh on their promises, and order the prolats to destroy themselves in a disintegrator chamber. * Keston, in a fury at this betrayal, thereupon activates an intelligent master control machine that he has kept in storage; previously, when turned on momentarily, this nasty, man-hating machine had attacked him. And turned on again, it immediately begins to exterminate the human race. Keston, the narrator, and about a score of the prolats survive by hiding on the glacial ice, where the machines cannot follow. Life there is precarious, especially because of a muscular atavist who is a good hunter, but hates Keston. * Keston works out a solution. Using a disintegrator that the men have seized from the machines, he undercuts the glacier so that it advances rapidly and destroys the homicidal master machine. Keston regrets its destruction, for it was a remarkable piece of equipment.

1282. **VENUS MINES, INCORPORATED**. *Wonder Stories*, August 1931. Ill. Marchioni.

Short story. * *Time:* the interplanetary future. *Place:* Venus and space toward Jupiter. * *Background:* The three inner planets are inhabited by civilized races. the Mercurians, who remain aloof, being the most advanced. Mars and Earth, on about the same scientific level, have intense trade rivalry, which despite an interplanetary board of control on Ganymede often involves skulduggery and crime. Both planets maintain commercial stations on Venus, which is a horrible, wet, tropical planet with ferocious wildlife and fishy humanoid primitives who use poisoned darts. The main trade object seems to be insect webs, which the traders purchase from the natives. The personnel in the Venusian factories live in small establishments protected by force screens. * Penger, veteran Venus hand, and Haldane,

rookie, receive a distress message from the next factory. They find Chris dying from a poisoned dart; he had found a deposit of jovium, the radioactive mineral used for space power, and the Martians, who know of his discovery, managed to open his force screen so that the natives could attack. Chris, however, has sealed details of his discovery in a special box, which Penger and Haldane are to register as a claim on Ganymede. * The two men take off, but are overtaken by a Martian vessel. Captured, Penger reveals that he tossed the box overboard near an asteroid. The Martians land, taking along the Terrestrial ship, and while they are out looking for the box, Penger and Chris manage to steal the Martian ship and take off. * As can be seen, a Western story displaced into space. Background material is not well integrated into the story, but otherwise competent pulp action.

1283. **EXILES OF THE MOON**. *Wonder Stories*, September-November 1931. Ill. Paul.

Novel. * *Time:* A.D. 2240. *Place:* New York and the Moon. * *Background:* The world of the future, which has a global government, is based on a very strict caste system. At the top are the Aristos, an utterly privileged class who live in luxury above the law. Beneath them are the Workers, who are constrained by a severe and comprehensive legal system and powerful police. The Workers have no rights and must obey the Aristo bureaucracy without question. The slightest Worker opposition will cause him/her to be reclassified and exiled to penal areas called Idlers' Colonies. There is no possibility of a Worker becoming an Aristocrat or marrying an Aristocrat. Within this structure, however, there seems to be a measure of socialism in that society supports the individual. An underground exists, but it does not amount to much, and there are bands of roving thugs. * Five men form the world council that makes laws and sees to their enforcement. Henry of the Fentons (the Americas) and George of the Windsors (Europe) are vicious, reactionary scoundrels who would like to see the Workers further constrained, with immediate execution of all malcontents; Salisbury (Oceania) and Na-jomba (Africa) would prefer that the caste law be weakened or abolished. Holding the balance of power is Hokusai of the Samurai, who so far has refused to take a position. Henry of the Fentons hopes that if his daughter Naomi marries Hokusai's son, Hokusai will join the reactionary group. * Scientifically the world has advanced since our time, but not remarkably so. There is rocket stratosphere travel, but, as yet, no real space travel, since fuel is inadequate. New York is an incredible futuristic megalopolis. * The story: Worker Garry Parker C12574 and Naomi of the Fentons, daughter of Henry, have established a furtive, clandestine, illegal Romeo and Juliet romance. There is no legal possibility of their marriage, but Naomi has (unrealistic) hopes of persuading her father to leniency. Naomi's forced wedding to Hokusai's son is only a week away. Garry, who is a pilot on the New York-Berlin run, has a week of leave, and the lovers hope to spend the time together. * Fate wills it otherwise. Garry is recalled to duty. When he refuses, he is immediately classified as a malcontent and sentenced to a penal colony. When Naomi tells her father of her love and pleads for Garry, Henry of the Fentons imprisons her in her apartment and changes Garry's sentence to the special 22 category. * The 22s are publicized as bootstrap back-to-the-soil agricultural communes, with seeds, cattle, and equipment furnished by the state, after which they are abandoned by civilization and allowed to make their own way. * Garry, friends,

Schachner, Nat and Zagat, Arthur Leo (*continued*)
and Naomi (escaped, disguised, and stowed away) are shipped to
a beautiful Pacific isle, presumably to start a new life as 22s.
But Garry discovers that the island is really a death camp, where
the so-called settlers are gassed. Garry arouses the Workers,
who make coracles out the hides of the cattle, and storm the
nearby police island that guards the death camp. About to be
attacked by police reinforcements, the Workers load their
agricultural equipment into a captured police ship and leave for
the Moon. This seems to be their only chance for survival. *
Backflash: While rocket ships have been capable of functioning
in space, interplanetary travel has been impossible for lack of a
suitable fuel. But during the episode on the death-camp island,
one of Garry's friends discovered that the poison gas emitted by
the local volcano is the long-sought catalyst for increasing the
potency of rocket fuel. True space travel is now possible. * On
the Moon, the settlers discover archeological remains of a former
high civilization, including enormous caverns suitable for habitation, if sealed off. The lunar civilization perished because of
a strange white mineral that is an oxygen-eater. * The colony
might have thrived, if it had not been for internal problems. Not
all the workers are hard-core rebels. There is a sizeable minority
that would sell Naomi back to her father in exchange for amnesty. Sabotage by the ringleader of this group removes all possibility of survival on the Moon. * The solution of the problem
is a harsh one: Use the oxygen-eating mineral to threaten
Terrestrial civilization, no matter what the cost in Worker lives.
* There is back and forth action at this point, with captivities,
escapes, threats, and deaths, but the Council surrenders and will
offer Workers equal rights. Hokusai, who is an absolute realist,
recognizes that the Workers have the power they claim and that
resistance is futile. * Not very good. Apart from the cops and
robbers version of the class struggle, the story is both clichéd
and clumsily presented.

SCHEER, GEORGE H., JR.
U.S. author. Thesis, University of Wisconsin, *A Study of the
Air-Space of the Lung of the Cat* (1902). Wrote two more
stories, "The Crystaline Salvation" and "The Last Ice" that
appeared in *Amazing Stories* in 1937.

1284. **BEAM TRANSMISSION**. *Amazing Stories,* July
1934. Ill. Morey.
Novelette. * In the university laboratory, a team composed of
Professor Kroelich and four graduate students is working on high
frequency radio beam transmission when they feel a strange
numbness. The sensation passes, but that evening, each awakes
with a compulsive urge to write higher mathematics. The next
morning they have pages of work, most of which is beyond their
comprehension, although it seems to have a certain inner logic.
* The men bring the head of the mathematics department into
the problem, and when he undergoes the same experience around
the apparatus, his "channelled" work brings the rest into the
range of contemporary knowledge. * What the men have received is the mathematical theory for a matter transmitter. It
turns out to be easy enough to translate the mathematics into
equipment, and after some trial and error the men have a
working transmitter. With a little practice the men are able to
transmit objects back and forth to the source of the message, and
some communication is established. When it seems safe, the
men decide to transmit themselves to meet their colleagues

elsewhere. They find themselves in a glass room, obviously
under quarantine for health reasons. * *Background as gradually
revealed*: Just where the men are is never resolved; star maps
prove of no avail, and since the signals were transmitted at
speeds millions of times greater than that of light, the second
planet may be far away in the universe. Or, as is also hinted, it
may be subatomic. (In the sequel it is stated that the other
world, Sar, was an electron in our universe.) The other people
contacted Kroelich's team when it observed the signals that they
was broadcasting. * The inhabitants of the new world are of two
types: humans, very much like Earthmen, and disk-beings (Fyns)
about eight-feet across, with multiple tentacles, who are more
intelligent than humans. The two races live in complete harmony and equality, although each of the races specializes in
certain areas of science. As might be expected, the level of
science is higher than Earth's, with rays of various sorts and a
cancer cure. * The stay in the other world is pleasant until
politics interferes. War breaks out between the mutually hostile
nations of the other-world, and it looks as if everything will be
destroyed. Our friends barely escape back to Earth on the matter
transmitter. Bell, one of the young men, brings back a wife
named Lele, who plays a part in the sequel. * A curious story.
The first half, which constitutes hard science-fiction, is good, but
the author, obviously uncertain how to end his story, slipped into
plot clichés that spoil the total. * For a sequel see #1285,
"Another Dimension."

1285. **ANOTHER DIMENSION**. *Amazing Stories,*
October 1935. Ill. Morey.
Short story. * Sequel to #1284, "Beam Transmission." * *Time:*
six or seven years after the first story. *Place:* Earth and Mars.
* The scientists of the previous story have become incredibly
wealthy with the matter transmission apparatus; indeed, to some
extent they are the most powerful men on Earth. Looking for
new worlds to conquer, they now decide to attempt space travel,
not by rocket or other navigational means, but along a transmission beam. * Work progresses well, but when the men send
out the first transmission beam, it impinges on a strange
spaceship that attacks the Earth. Later, the group contacts Mars
and establishes some communication, though not on a satisfactory level. * The men now decide to travel by ship along the
beam. Unfortunately, as the ship is in transit, the strange
spaceship destroys the transmitting stations, one by one, and it
looks for a time as if the party is doomed. But at the last minute
a Martian conductor beam seizes the ship and lands it, with the
travelers somewhat the worse for wear. * *Background:* Mars is
Schiaparellian, and the Martians, who live underground, are
human, but incredibly more advanced than Earthmen. They can
control matter by mental power. This development is in part due
to the near passage of a comet composed partially of mind
matter, ages ago. One of their mental faculties is an intuitive
knowledge of what will happen and what should be done about
it. As for the hostile spaceship, the Martians know all about it;
it is a scout for an enormous armada that will soon attack Earth.
* When the alien fleet attacks Earth, the battle turns into a
temporary stand off, for the aliens cannot penetrate the Earth's
defensive ray screens. A new factor enters, however. The aliens
deliberately push Earth out of its orbit with their force rays, out
away from the sun. This seems disastrous, especially since Earth
is running out of power. * Suddenly, Earth is shifted to another
dimension, around another sun, with a suitable orbit. The

Scheer, George H., Jr. (*continued*)

explanation: Earth, when it left its orbit, struck a space warp and was forced out of our universe. * Confusingly presented.

SCHEFTLEMAN, EUGENE H.

No information.

1286. **THE WATERSPOUT.** *Wonder Stories*, December 1934. Ill. Winter.

Short story. * *Place:* mostly up in the stratosphere. * The narrator of the frame situation, who is in a diner, recognizes José de Marillo, a former friend and veteran air pilot who disappeared in flight some years back. The narrator accosts Marillo, who claims he does not recognize him. After a while, however, Marillo, who is obviously ill at ease and depressed, admits his identity and repeatedly urges that it was not his fault. * Marillo's story: In 1931, he and his junior copilot, McCoy, flew on the Havana-Miami run in very bad weather. Their plane struck a waterspout, and when the men regained consciousness, they found themselves flying in a strange exhilarating atmosphere. Their altimeter is wrecked, and their speedometer indicates a speed far greater than the craft could fly. * McCoy and Marillo finally work out what has happened. The waterspout carried them up into the Heaviside layer, about a hundred miles above Earth; and the ionized atmosphere, which is thicker than expected, is causing the plane to behave fantastically well. * There are two problems: getting down again (which would probably wreck the plane) and controlling the passengers, who by now are hysterical. Marillo, with the new mental vigor imparted by the ionized air, recognizes that the Heaviside layer is connected to the Earth's magnetic field, so that it might be possible to descend at one of the poles [sic]. He proves to be right. But the passengers run out of control, killing McCoy. The plane sinks when it lands in the water, and Marillo is the only survivor. * Since then Marillo has been smothered with feelings of guilt. * Weak science, weak story.

SCHERE, MOSES

U.S. author, then resident in Brooklyn, New York. Portrait shows a young man. Contributed several stories to Street and Smith magazines. See also Edward S. Sears, "The Atomic Riddle."

1287. **THE METEORIC MAGNET.** *Air Wonder Stories*, April 1930. Ill. Paul.

Short story. * *Time:* 1938. * Much of the world is associated in the Mutual Understanding Treaty, a league of nations for maintaining peace and good will, but the small Balkan country of Molgravia has not joined. Instead, Molgravia has embarked on an aggressive anti-American policy, which is partly caused by restrictive U.S. immigration laws. * Most of the world considers it ridiculous that a tiny country should so confront a great power, but the Professor, a friend of the narrator's, insists that the Molgravians must have a secret weapon. He is right. * A strange aircraft much like a floating ship's hull appears over Mexico City and burns it. It is the so-called *Fate*, from Molgravia. It moves north toward the United States, burning everything in its path. American aircraft are powerless against it. Bullets and antiaircraft fire do not harm it, and it looks as if the Molgravians may be able to carry out their threat of moving en masse to North America after they have conquered it. * The Professor, however, has been otherwise concerned. He has been

excavating Meteor Crater in Arizona and has found, in addition to fossil leaves and a gigantic diamond, the solid iron core of the meteorite. * The narrator has a bright idea, which the Professor carries through. As the *Fate* passes directly overhead, the Professor electrifies the iron meteoritic mass and crashes down the *Fate* by magnetic attraction. The war is over, and Molgravia, after its dictatorship is dissolved, behaves. * The *Fate*, in addition to its combustion rays, had some sort of force screen that repelled missiles. An apparatus that created a vacuum in front of the vessel offered propulsion. * No indication is given where the Molgravians acquired their superscience. * Amateurish.

SCHLOSSEL, J[OSEPH] (1902-1977)

U.S. (Brooklyn, New York) author. Pioneer author of space opera with "Invaders from Outside" in *Weird Tales*, January 1925. Unfortunately, no other information. Died in Castleton on Hudson, New York.

1288. **THE SECOND SWARM.** *Amazing Stories Quarterly*, Spring 1928. Ill. Paul.

Short story. * Space opera. * It is now A.D. 12,001 and the great Second Expedition is about to set out for Sirius. For the past few hundred years the Earth has been sending out exploratory expeditions to the nearby stars, looking for habitable planets. The ships move at about half the speed of light, with shifts in suspended animation. Most of the nearby stars do not have suitable planets, but Alpha Centauri has two, and Sirius, one. * Sirius is the problem. A Terrestrial exploratory expedition sent to Sirius with peaceful intent about a hundred years earlier was attacked and massacred, and a follow-up of ten ships was outgunned by the science of the inhabitants. * The single ship that returned to Earth brought with it a terrible disease that raged for decades before it could be neutralized by an antitoxin. This disease had been shot up into the terrestrial vessel by the Sirians. * As a result of this hostility, the authorities of Earth have prepared a massive invasion fleet consisting of six thousand ships, each with a complement of ten thousand men, and the most powerful weapons that Earth can devise. The fleets are organized like Earth itself, with White, Yellow, and Black Quotas, females and males separated. * After years of preparation and battle practice, the armada takes off. There are no central characters, although the female leaders, particularly the black leader of the Black Quota, are slightly stressed. * When the fleet nears Sirius, it encounters resistance from an enemy fleet of space globes that emit electric bolts. Many of the Terrestrial vessels are destroyed, but the main body of the fleet wins through and approaches the Sirian planet. Sirian resistance is broken, and the Terrestrial fleet exterminates the natives. * The Sirians were an arachnid people, with a civilization almost as high as that of the solar system. There is now some regret that the Sirians were destroyed, but it is too late. As the author said earlier in the story, the Terrestrials would have continued on their way when they discovered that the Sirian planet was inhabited by intelligent life, but upon being attacked they realized that there was no room in the universe for a hostile race of almost equal technology. * Unusual in the early literature for its enormous scope and for its ability to convey vastness, also for the frank statement of Realpolitik.

1289. **TO THE MOON BY PROXY.** *Amazing Stories*, October 1928. Ill. Paul.

Schlossel, J. (*continued*)

Short story. * The narrator returns to his home town to visit his friend Emil Peters, who is a scientist and inventor of international reputation. * Emil declares that he has had a life-time dream of visiting the Moon, and now that there are reports of others who are planning such expeditions, he has decided to act. * Because he is paralyzed from the waist down, however, he cannot travel. Instead, he has constructed a humanoid, radio-controlled, metal figure with a television viewing screen, that he intends to send to act as his eyes. * Emil has already tested the metal man locally, with several pranks and adventures. These include overcoming a holdup man, killing a vicious escaped circus lion, and throwing a truck laden with bootleg liquor up into the air. * Emil sends the proxy to the moon by rocket and controls its movements with a keyboard. The proxy leaps over the dead lunar surface, descends into a cave where there is a little atmosphere and water, and transmits images of bat-like flying creatures, a huge monstrosity, and mushroom-like vegetation. But when the proxy ventures farther into the cave, undescribed creatures, presumably at least semi-intelligent, drop rocks on it. The proxy's head is smashed, and it is out of commission. Emil berates himself for putting the controlling apparatus in such a vulnerable place as the head.

1290. **EXTRA-GALACTIC INVADERS.** *Amazing Stories Quarterly*, Spring 1931. Ill. Morey.

Novelette. * *Time:* the beginning of the thirty-seventh century A.D. *Place:* the Moon and various areas of space. * *Background:* Technology is high, with advanced space travel, various military rays, and somewhat limited matter transmission. The human race has evolved and is now telepathic. As a sort of group mind for the race are the Two, humans with enormous heads who receive the telepathic power of the entire race and, as a result, have many paranormal powers: perfect telepathy, willcontrol, near omniscience about human matters, and other faculties. Humanity has now colonized the solar system, whose planets seem to be habitable. * On the Moon, far deep in the interior, in sealed caverns, centuries earlier explorers came upon an intelligent, civilized, utterly peaceful race that they treated as badly as Europeans did native Americans: enslavement in platinum mines and slaughter. * The surviving Lunarians, who are no longer slaves, but are still second-class citizens, remember this history bitterly and seek both revenge and independence, which latter the humans keep promising but never deliver. * In secret cities hidden far inside the Moon, the Lunarians are building up a potent armament for a sudden strike. Mankind in general does not know of this, but the Two apparently have some inkling. The Day is close. As for the Lunarians themselves, the author does not describe them, but they are not bipeds, are not telepathic, but are just as intelligent as humans. * The story line focuses on larger events, sometimes seen in terms of two personalities, Don Stelite, a human, and his friend (though ambivalently), the Lunarian 4-P-2269-L, sometimes called Lune. Lune, if the Lunarians achieved independent, would be one of their hereditary leaders. * Messages come from beyond the solar system; translated they relate an astonishing story: The galaxy is teeming with intelligent races of all shapes and sizes, all technologically advanced and all seriously threatened. Metal-clad, tentacled bipeds from the Magellanic Clouds are engaged in a program to conquer the universe, destroying all other forms of life. Their military technology is extremely high, and their

forces seem numberless. Their fleets sweep out almost irresistibly. Up to the present the defenders in our galaxy have been hard put to withstand them and are fighting a losing struggle. * The cosmic communicators furnish instructions for constructing an improved matter transmitter that can transmit living beings and larger, enormous spaceships, while arrangements are made to transmit an alien to Earth for consultation. * The transmission area is heavily fortified, the Two are at hand, and the alien arrives. It is so horrible in appearance that there is suspicion at first, but matters are smoothed over and arrangements are made for human delegates to attend the galactic Supreme Council. As the alien envoy leaves, there is a sudden commotion. The Magellans, who have seized control of a transmitter elsewhere, begin to transmit their own forces, with advanced weapons, including a black cloud that the Two cannot penetrate. If the aliens secure a foothold, it will be extinction for the people of the solar system. * The situation is touch and go before the Magellan invaders are defeated and destroyed, but two individuals escape in tiny ships and reach the Moon, where they are captured by the Lunarian underground and taken to a hidden city. The Lunarians consider this an opportunity to acquire Magellanic weapons against the humans for the forthcoming rebellion. * The story now centers on two foci, the Lunar situation and the war in space. The Two, who have become aware of Lunarian plans, decide to give the Lunarians complete independence and equality in exchange for help in the war. It is Don Stelite's task to convince Lune of Earth's sincerity, and then for Lune to convert or outmaneuver the hawkish Lunarian party. Both aims are achieved. The captive Magellans are destroyed, and the rebellion is over when the Two send a treaty to the Lunarian leaders. * About the peril from the Magellanic Clouds: The Two agree to join in the war against the Magellanic invaders, and mankind begins to construct enormous armadas of warships and gigantic matter transmitters and to train hosts of space soldiery. Don Stelite is involved in this preparation as a minor officer. * The battles now begin, and enormous fleets are shifted around the universe to battle the endless columns of Magellanic invaders. The battles are described in great detail, but it would be pointless to attempt to summarize them. The galactic forces suffer enormous losses in ships and manpower; whole solar systems are laid waste; stars are exploded. But eventually the Magellans are totally defeated. * Oddly enough, the author does not reveal the fate of his two main characters. Lune may have died in the great final battle. Stelite was captured by the Magellans and was about to be interrogated by torture, but the Two "emptied his mind" as the Magellans injected drugs. Perhaps this means death. * Occasionally amateurish in presentation, but with many good touches; of great sweep and far more imaginative than "Islands of Space" by John W. Campbell, Jr., which is the lead story of the issue.

SCOTT, E. M.

No information.

1291. **THE VOYAGE TO KEMPTONIA.** *Amazing Stories*, October 1928. Ill. Paul.

Short story. * *Place:* a second moon. * Professor Kempton is dead, and there is suspicion of murder and arson. Edgar Lawton, an unemployed man with a suspicious amount of cash on him, explains what happened. He answered Kempton's advertisement for an assistant who knew Morse code, at which time Kempton

Scott, E. M. (*continued*)

told him of a great discovery that he had made. * According to Kempton, Luna is not our only satellite; there are many others of varying sizes. One that he calls Kemptonia is only about forty miles from Earth. Since it is mist-covered, it is not visible. Kempton first thought of building a spaceship to visit his discovery, but instead has constructed a matter transmitter that works like radio. He would like Lawton to go to Kemptonia and report back by wireless. * Lawton agrees, and after some eight hours of preparation he is sent off. Awaking, he finds himself in a land of low gravity and weak, spindly vegetation. The inhabitants are humanoid, but huge-chested, and maintain a primitive culture with villages and agriculture, including domestic animals. Kemptonia itself is small, only about twenty thousand acres, and the humanoid population is about five or six hundred. * Lawton is ready to return, when a power failure in the professor's equipment damages some of the circuits. As a result, while Lawton returns safely, the apparatus explodes, killing Kempton and destroying his laboratory. * Lawton is first held for murder, but when his story is checked, he is released and told to leave town.

1292. WHAT HAPPENED TO PROFESSOR STOCKLEY? *Amazing Stories*, December 1931. Ill. Morey.
Short story. * *Place:* Pittsburgh, Pennsylvania. * Crime story. * A wave of daring burglaries, some involving brutal murder, afflicts the city. By chance, it is discovered that the criminal is Professor Stockley, whose diary is offered to the reader. * Stockley has discovered antigravity. Embittered when the bank that held his savings failed, he felt that society owed him recompense and took to a life of crime. The murders he committed were not intentional, but were self defense when he was cornered. As the diary ends, Stockley reveals that he has built a small spaceship and is taking off into space. * Routine or less.

SEARIGHT, RICHARD F. (1902-1975)
U.S. (Detroit, Michigan) author. See also poem in March 1934 *Wonder Stories*. Also contributed two stories to *Weird Tales*. Novel *Wild Empire* (1984) was published posthumously.

1293. THE COSMIC HORROR. *Wonder Stories*, August 1933. Ill. Paul.
Short story. * When Professor Elton and the narrator retrieve the strange meteorite that has fallen nearby, they release a peril to the human race. Taking the meteorite to their laboratory and examining it closely, they see a little plug, which they remove. Out pops a spherical creature, about three feet in diameter, that floats glowingly in the air. It attacks the spectators and kills one. There is seemingly no defense against it; bullets are useless, but a jet of water momentarily repels it. * The creature leaves the laboratory and flits around killing people, scorching them and absorbing their blood. Many deaths result. * The narrator and Elton try to hunt it down, although it seems that no weapon known to man can kill it. As Elton says, if the science that could expel it in a meteorite could not kill it, how can we? * The remainder of the story is told mostly in encounters and escapes. Finally, Elton takes a last chance. The party tracks the creature to the maze-like Dinosaur Cave, where it seems to have a sort of den. The humans creep in toward it, and as a last resort, they douse it with concentrated hydrofluoric acid, which takes effect, and blast down the cave roof upon the creature.

They acted just in time, for the monster was rearing a brood of young. * Competent pulp thrills.

SEARS, EDWARD S.
No information. See Moses Schere for a possible identity.
1294. THE SHADOW ON THE SPARK. *Amazing Stories*, August 1927. Ill. Aragón.
Short story. * Not s-f; really a detective story about a death that turns out to be murder by strychnine. The treatment is clichéd, with fine young men and ingenues, plus an investigating doctor. The editors may have passed the story as science-fiction, since it contains a long, turgid, completely irrelevant passage about colloids and electric sparks. The crime and its solution are not fantastic.

1295. THE ATOMIC RIDDLE. *Amazing Stories Quarterly*, Winter 1928. Ill. Paul.
Novelette. * A detective story with minimal science-fictional material. * Young Roger Bolton, cashier at the bank, is blamed when a large quantity of Molgravian bonds are removed from the bank safe, with no apparent sign of damage to the safe. Bolton seems doomed, but his girlfriend Olive invokes the aid of the great scientist Dr. Jarvis, who succeeds in working out the problem. The criminals employed a new sort of cutting torch that uses atomic hydrogen to cut neat holes in the top and side of the safe, then reseal the holes after removing what they wanted. * A very weak story.

1296. THE SINGING MOONBEAMS. *Amazing Stories Quarterly*, Summer 1929. Ill. Briggs.
Short story. * Really a detective story with a borderline science-fictional element. * Judge Sterling, whose wife, a noted opera singer, has recently died, is badly shaken when he hears her voice singing favorite songs. The sound seems to come from outside when the moon is high. * Sterling asks Inspector Craven of the New York Police Department for help, whereupon Craven and his friend and consultant Dr. Jarvis investigate. They soon discover that the judge is not hallucinating, and that the singing is a mechanical transmission. After some action back forth, the mystery is explained: Criminals in an adjoining house had hidden some of their loot in the judge's home and are trying to drive him out. Their technique involved an advanced instrument, stolen from a lab, that transmitted sound along a light beam. * Hugo Gernsback published descriptions of such devices in *Science and Invention*, but I believe that they never advanced beyond the experimental stage.

SEPTAMA, ALADRA (1874-1950)
Pseud. of Judson W. Reeves, a San Francisco lawyer. According to the records of The State Bar of California, Reeves was born in Penn-Yan, New York. Some sources identify the author as Justin Reeves, but this is not correct, nor is the author to be identified (via Social Security records) with a Judson Reeves (1905-1968) who was a resident of Georgia. Certain indexes list Septama as a female author; this is also incorrect. The stories suggest a person with a background in occult literature, notably Theosophy. The significance of the pseud. is not clear, although it conveys intimations of Marie Corelli.

Stories are presented as The Cerean Series and Other Works, chronologically within each group.

Septama, Aladra (continued)
The Cerean Series

Three stories set fairly far into the interplanetary future, together with a latch-on. The inner planets of the solar system are inhabited by human races that are mutually fertile. (Martians, however, are gigantic.) This similarity is explained very late in the first story as common descent from an ancient Martian stock. * Culture is more or less uniform among the planets. Gigantic ether-volt spaceliners ply the spaceways, riding on beams that are powered by atomic energy and alter gravity. On the planets there are aerocars that fly at five hundred MPH and aerial stations hovering above major cities. * The fictional mechanism of the first three stories centers on Mansonby of Mansonby Interplanetary Bureau, and later equally on the Cerean Ello-ta. * The stories grow progressively worse, with padding, purple language, and empty chitchat.

1297. THE BEAST-MEN OF CERES. *Amazing Stories Quarterly*, Winter 1929. Unsigned ill.
Short story. * A muddled mixture of detective story, adventure story, and romance. * *Time:* the interplanetary future. *Place:* Earth, space, and Ceres. * The story begins when Interplanetary Inspector Mansonby is summoned to solve a mysterious disappearance. The wife of the great scientist Calder Sanderson disappeared before his eyes, without a clue. Other disappearances follow, including Mansonby's Parisian girlfriend. * Logical deduction plus a few clues produce a hypothesis. The raids demonstrate very high scientific achievement, including invisibility, which is probably produced by bending light waves. Clues also suggest that the kidnappers, who are known to be very hairy, are probably to be identified with an ancient Martian race that was associated with woman-stealing and was expelled from Mars in the far past; until now it has been considered extinct. * Attacks and escapes from invisible beings follow, and Mansonby is repeatedly warned off the case. * Signs of recent activity on Ceres suggest that it is the habitation of the so-called beast-men. A small Tellurian fleet takes off, has an indecisive space battle with ships manned by the beast-men, and heads toward Ceres. * Just before the Earthmen reach Ceres, however, a beast-man in a space suit parlays briefly with them. He states that the Cereans will not give up all the women, since there are no more beast-man females, and the race must continue. He adds that a few outlaws were responsible for the lawless acts against Mansonby and others, and that the Cereans deplore their crimes. * The beast-man releases some of the women, in space suits outside the ship, but warns that Cerean science is so far superior to that of the inner planets that the expedition has no chance of succeeding. * Nevertheless, the Terrestrials land on Ceres, where they discover that their ships and weapons no longer function. Entering the Cerean underground establishment, they are met by the Cerean authorities, who are by no means unfriendly. The "kidnapped" women whom the Cereans have not returned are on Ceres willingly, affianced to Cerean men. Mansonby's fiancée was taken by mistake. * All ends on a pleasant note. The beast-men, in addition to being the living ancestors of solar system humanity, are essentially men of good will. Further, they are not really hairy. They simply wear hairy underwear! * For a sequel, see #1298, "The Cry from the Ether."

1298. THE CRY FROM THE ETHER. *Amazing Stories Quarterly*, Spring 1929. Unsigned ill.
Short story. * Sequel to #1297, "The Beast-Men of Ceres." * *Time:* the interplanetary future. *Place:* mostly Jupiter. * At a dinner party the personnel of the previous story receive a Morse SOS from Ceres, together with the single word "Jupiter." Traveling by etheric-magnetic means, the comrades soon reach Ceres, where they find a couple of corpses, but no living Cereans. * Following the hint in the message, a joint Martian-Terrestrial expedition travels to Jupiter. The equatorial regions are apparently uninhabitable, but the remainder of the planet becomes more or less Earth-like as one approaches the poles. Gravity is twice as powerful as Terrestrial. Nevertheless, the party can make its way about. * After some searching, the party finds humans (Kolatans) living in a high civilization at the pole. It is possible to converse with them in ancient Martian, leading to the conclusion that they are of the same general stock as other solar system humanity. The Kolatans know nothing of the missing Cereans, but suggest as culprits the Vulnos, particularly the tribe known as the Drugos. These are bestial ape-like creatures, generally of primitive culture, but well-armed, since they steal ships and weapons from the true humans. * With the aid of a Cerean mechanical telepathic device and Martian antigravity equipment, after a battle royal the seekers rescue the missing Cereans from a Drugo cave. Why the Cereans, described as scientifically superior in the previous story, were defeated and abducted by primitives is not explained. * *Miscellaneous:* The Martians are able to revive most of their dead, if they are not too badly injured. * A small part in the final battle with the Drugos is played by the so-called Elementals, floating, semimaterial creatures that dislike the Drugos and suck them up in batches. * Space travel is accomplished by electrical nullification of gravity and atomic disintegration. * Pretty bad.

1299. TANI OF EKKIS. *Amazing Stories Quarterly*, Winter 1930. Ill. Morey.
Short story. * A latch-on to the Cerean series. * The human race on Ekkis, a planet in another solar system, is on the edge of extinction because of a deadly epidemic. A small group of people who live in underground areas sealed away from the plague, however, are planning an exodus to another world, of necessity in another solar system. They fix on the planet Jupiter, where (it is revealed late in the story) there already are ancient colonies from Ekkis. * A gigantic spaceship will take five hundred people on the five-hundred-year journey. For obvious reasons a large percentage of the crew and passengers will be placed in suspended animation in a shift arrangement. * The story deals mostly with the experiences of Tani, who is a young woman as the story begins. She marries, has children on the spaceship, and is physiologically in her fifties when the vessel reaches Jupiter. * The cruise is uneventful, the story-development being filled with small talk, but along the way the ship encounters a derelict spaceship with the remains of two lovers from the distant past. This incident is handled in a sentimental manner. * On arrival the new colonists are welcomed by the older settlers. * With this story the writer seems to abandon the earlier proposition that ancient Martians were the progenitors of solar system humanity, in favor of human origins in another solar system. But it must be admitted that statements to this effect are not firmly made by the author. * This seems to be the first pulp science-fiction story devoted primarily to the experiences of a woman, not as a sex object, but as an individual. One wonders at its writing circumstances. While it is

Septama, Aladra (*continued*)

not as badly handled as the previous stories, it is still weak, being sentimental and padded.

1300. **DRAGONS OF SPACE**.   *Amazing Stories Quarterly*, Spring 1930. Ill. Morey.

Short story. * The third member of the Cerean series. * Just as "The Cry from the Ether" was more a postscript than an independent story, the present is a postpostscript. * *Time:* the interplanetary future. * Essentially, apart from an enormous amount of small talk, the author reveals that the Elementals, semimaterial beings encountered on Jupiter, come to Earth and Mars. There is no defense against them as they capture and dissolve their prey, and before a weapon is devised, more than a third of the human race has perished. * The weapon, created by the Cerean Ello-Ta, is an outgrowth of his telepathy machine. It does not convey thought, but produces overwhelming emotional fields. Thus, a projection of fear drives away the elementals, who are mind beings. * As for the apparatus, it consists of banks of telepathic machines operated by women specially trained by Hindu adepts. * A bad job.

Other Works

1301. **THE PRINCESS OF ARELLI**.   *Amazing Stories Quarterly*, Summer 1930. Ill. Wesso.

Novelette. * *Time:* 1938. *Place:* Peru and the Moon. * The great astronomer Fred Harding summons his friend Tony Upton to the great observatory in Peru. There, using new optical devices, Harding has made astonishing discoveries about the Moon, starting with a growing greenish spot in the crater Copernicus. * Harding does not reveal matters clearly, but, as the reader can distill out of pages of chitchat, he has made contact with a race of humans on the Moon. Formerly inhabitants of air-secured caverns, they have started to reemerge and reclaim part of the surface. More, Harding has conducted a romance with Altara, the daughter of the lunar leader, and is engaged to her. Indeed, he soon marries her by proxy in an absentee radio-television ceremony. * Harding and his pilot friend Donelan have constructed a small rocket-powered spaceship, with which they travel rapidly and safely to the Moon, where they are welcomed. All converse and sightsee until a scoundrel, Ullo son of Uffuldo, a former suitor of Altara's, kidnaps her. But his air suit leaks, and Altara escapes. * Other romances occupy the characters: Upton with the daughter of the President of Peru, and Donelan with a lunar maiden. * *Miscellaneous:* Most of the craters of the Moon contain airlock-sealed cities that are connected by underground transportation tubes. * In addition to the civilized people headed by the King of Arelli there are primitives who live in lower caverns and are a nuisance. * Lunar technology is high, with disintegrators and gravity control. * Pretty bad. * For a sequel see #1302, "The Terrors of Arelli."

1302. **THE TERRORS OF ARELLI**.   *Amazing Stories Quarterly*, Fall 1930. Ill. Wesso.

Novelette. * Sequel to #1301, "The Princess of Arelli." * *Time:* ancient and modern. *Place:* partly on the Moon. * Mostly an afterthought to the first story. Much of the story is taken up with a quest for ancient records going back hundreds of thousands, perhaps millions, of years. When discovered, these video tapes show the destruction of Atlantis, Heidelberg man, a lost great Asiatic civilization, on back to the dinosaur age. * The

author leaves this last point open, but it is probably intended to suggest that mankind came from another world or solar system and settled on the Moon. As a related matter, the author comments on a cyclical rise and fall of great civilizations, presumably from Theosophical sources. * The second theme is the emergence of the terrors—monstrous forms of life that live in the watery interior of the Moon. They have long been sealed off from the human sectors, but for the present occasion they break loose and overrun many of the Lunar cities, killing about a quarter of the population. They are destroyed by releasing the air in the cities they have occupied, suffocating them. This theme is presented mostly in the background, and the monsters are not precisely described, although they seem to be large, powerful, vicious, and tentacled. * Of no interest.

SERVISS, GARRETT P[UTNAM]   (1851-1929).

U.S. journalist (*New York Journal*), author of many books and articles popularizing science, particularly astronomy. Born in Sharon Springs, New York; B.S. from Cornell, and LL.B. from Columbia. Serviss was probably the closest to a professional science-fiction writer that existed in America before 1926, with both books and periodical publications. *Edison's Conquest of Mars* (1898, book publication 1947); *The Moon Metal* (below); *A Columbus of Space* (below); "The Sky Pirate," 1909; *The Second Deluge* (below); and "The Moon Maiden" are all described in full detail in *Science-Fiction: The Early Years*. Serviss was a competent writer working in the intermingled traditions of Verne and Wells. Technically, his preoccupation with marvelous events weakened his possible development of characterizations.

1303. **THE MOON METAL**.   *Amazing Stories*, July 1926. Ill. Paul.

(First published in book form by Harper, New York, 1900. A slightly earlier newspaper syndication has not been precisely located. Reprinted in *Famous Fantastic Mysteries*, November 1939.)

A nouvelle or short novel "with a parable-like note on financial theory [free silver] and a spoofing of science." The more fantastic works of Jules Verne would seem to be prototypes. * *Time:* the near future. * The economy of the world is about to collapse because of the discovery of vast deposits of gold in Antarctica. There seems to be no other metal that can be used as a standard, until a mysterious stranger appears at a monetary conference and offers a strange iridescent metal (artemisium) of which he has the only supply. * This is Dr. Syx, who as part of his presentation shows a motion picture depicting the destruction of humanoid life on another planet, undoubtedly our moon. * Syx's offer is accepted, and the financial structure seems stable again. But a resourceful young engineer named Hall discovers that Syx is not mining artemisium as he claims, but is bringing it from the moon by matter transmission. Hall duplicates Syx's process, whereupon Syx destroys his own plant and, traveling about the world, sets up competitive groups, all of which collapse. Syx's intention is to further destroy the world's economy. The financial situation is where it was in the beginning. * As Hall, most of his gains lost, happens to glance at the Moon, he sees Syx's features in the man in the moon. * The interpretation of the story is obscure, since it links the monetary agitations surrounding the gold standard and free silver with supernaturalism (the work of the Devil) and science-fiction motifs.

Serviss, Garrett P. (*continued*)

1304. **A COLUMBUS OF SPACE**. *Amazing Stories*, August-October 1926. Ill. Ray Wardell.
(First published in *All-Story*, January-June 1909. First book publication in revised form, Appleton, New York, 1911.)
Novel of interplanetary adventure and romance, with a beautiful princess on hand. * *Place:* mostly on Venus. * Edmund Stonewall, a wealthy independent scientist, has discovered antigravity and built a small spaceship in which he conveys himself and friends to Venus. The party lands on the cold dark side of Venus, which does not revolve, where the terrestrials encounter savage, hairy men. After some adventures, in which the Earthmen overawe the simple natives, the party crosses the libration zone into the lighted area of Venus, where they find handsome, blond humans with large radiant eyes and advanced telepathic ability. The Venusians are slightly ahead of us in technology, with efficient flap-wing aircraft and crystalline cities, but do not have antigravity or firearms. * Romance between beautiful Queen Ala and Stonewall is complicated by intrigues. * The idyllic visit is about to end, when disaster strikes. On rare occasions the cloudy atmosphere of Venus dissipates in places, admitting the overpowering rays of the sun and killing the natives. Such happens, and the visitors return sadly to Earth. * *Miscellaneous:* the Venusians also communicate with symbolic colors. * There are horrible gigantic insects. * More juvenile than Serviss's other works considered here.

1305. **THE SECOND DELUGE**. *Amazing Stories*, November 1926-February 1927. Unsigned ill.
(First published in *Cavalier*, July 1911-January 1912; first book edition McBride, New York 1912. Reprinted in *Amazing Stories Quarterly*, Winter 1933.)
A catastrophe novel in the mode of Jules Verne, focusing on an eccentric lead character and fantastic happenings. * *Time:* not dated, but probably mid-twentieth century. *Place:* important sequences in Egypt and the Rocky Mountain area. * The great maverick scientist Cosmo Versal predicts that the Earth will be flooded as it passes through a watery nebula. The waters, he calculates, will be about six miles deep (submerging almost everything), but new land masses should arise after the flooding ceases. * Versal also prepares an ark, sending out invitations to various notables whom he considers worthy of preservation. His list, to a modern mind, however, is strange, since it includes politicians. Most people do not take Versal seriously, but the flood comes, and his ark is afloat. * The heart of the book is devoted to the adventures of the persons on the ark, although a strong section is devoted to a French submarine vessel that explores the wonders of ancient Egypt—under water. The Frenchmen see the Sphinx collapse, revealing an inscription prophesying the deluge. * Eventually the ark and the French reach the area of the Rockies, where a new elevation has taken place. There they find other survivors, guided there by Versal's chief scientific critic. Altogether the survivors number about a million people. They plan to set up a better social system, which amounts to fettered capitalism headed by the President of the United States. When the second part of the deluge arrives, the survivors weather it more effectively. * Perhaps Serviss's best story, vividly imagined.

SHARP, D[RURY] D. (1880-1960)
U.S. author, resident at writing time in Cedar Crest, near Albuquerque, New Mexico. Born in Texas, died in Albuquerque. According to U.S. Census of 1920 for New Mexico, listed as a farmer. In later years was a clerk at the Santa Fe Railroad Dept, from 1929 t0 1940. Portrait accompanying "The Eternal Man" shows a middle-aged man. * Sharp continued writing up to 1943, with a total of eighteen known science-fiction stories. Also contributed to *Weird Tales*. Sharp's thought was often interesting, even perceptive at times, but his literary skills were not strong.

1306. **THE ETERNAL MAN**. *Science Wonder Stories*, August 1929. Ill. Paul.
(Reprinted in Margulies and Friend, *From Off This World*; in Ashley, *History of the Science Fiction Magazines, Part I*; in Conklin, *A Treasury of Science Fiction*; and in Ackerman, *Gosh! Wow!*. Also several magazine reprintings.)
Short story. * *Time:* not dated, but time indications in the sequel would probably bring this story into the near future; the sequel, however, suggests a different time frame. * Herbert Zulerich, a maverick scientist about eighty years old, has been investigating the fundamentals of life. He has extracted a growth substance from bacteria that enables him to produce animal monstrosities, which he mercifully destroys, and now he has found a preparation that promises eternal life. * His discovery is imperfect, however, for while it preserves the subject, the subject is in a death-like state, though apparently with full consciousness. This is the case with a rat that Zulerich has treated. * By accident Zulerich discovers the ingredient that will enable him to bypass the state of suspended animation. It is simply soda. The rat, thus revived, dashes away, immortal. * Zulerich is now ready to take his elixir. He drinks the basic preparation, intending to take the soda next—but absentmindedly he forgot what would happen. He is totally paralyzed, as was the rat. * His body is found and regarded with great interest because of its unchanging lifelike appearance. Later it is put into a museum as an example of perfect embalming. * Years, decades pass. The rat, perhaps evil by nature, has remained near Zulerich, perhaps taunting him, but finally it is squashed. Even shattered it remains alive and conscious. Centuries pass, and Zulerich muses. He finally recognizes that he should have striven to improve mankind, not render it immortal. * Crudely written, but, oddly enough, a touching story of some power, perhaps because of the byplay between the rat and the man and the metaphoric elements. It is much the best of Sharp's stories. * For a sequel, which is very much weaker, see #1308, "The Eternal Man Revives."

1307. **THE DAY OF THE BEAST**. *Science Wonder Stories*, May 1930. Ill. Butterfield.
Short story. * The narrator, a research biologist who has been forced to leave his original laboratory because of his unorthodox experiments with animals, locates a suitable deserted place to continue his work. He has a considerable amount of success in developing an extract that will cause gigantism, and soon has rabbits as large as sheep. His extract has one fault: Once it stimulates growth, growth continues indefinitely. * The narrator wisely decides, under these circumstances, to work only with very small creatures. One of his next subjects is a spider, which not only grows with fantastic rapidity, but also escapes. The narrator and his friend Tom have close shaves before they can kill it. At the end it is the size of a sheep and can carry a man away with no difficulty. The narrator suppresses his discovery. * Routine.

Sharp, D. D. (*continued*)

1308. **THE ETERNAL MAN REVIVES**. *Wonder Stories Quarterly*, Summer 1930. Ill. Volga.
Short story. * Sequel to #1306, "The Eternal Man." * *Time:* The twenty-third or twenty-fourth century. Since the author now states that Zulerich has been paralyzed for a little more than a century, this dating would bring the first story considerably into the future, which may not have been the author's original intention. * Zulerich is kept in the museum as an exhibit for some time, but cultural changes cause his presence to be offensive and he is buried. His cheap casket rots, and chemicals from the earth above him trickle down and revive him. * As he wanders about nude and feeble, he is picked up by a man in a strange flying machine, who takes him to the city. * *Background:* The future civilization is totally rational and mechanistic; it seems to be socialistic to some extent, in that all are guaranteed a livelihood. It is, however, tyrannical to the extreme, with thought control and harsh punishments. A corrupt Council enforces its will by gigantic robot police, called telecops. These telecops, it would seem, can be activated and controlled only by council members. * Foolishly (to the reader, in any case), Zulerich talks of his discovery of immortality; as a result he is eventually hauled before the corrupt Council, who are at first incredulous, then eager to acquire his secret. Zulerich temporizes, but in vain; he is forced to yield, with a lie-detecting apparatus checking him. But Zulerich cheats a little; he gives the Council eternal life, as he promised, but the same life of stasis that he suffered for a century or more. * Zulerich, who has liberal notions, believes that once the dictatorial Council is removed, free institutions will reemerge, especially since the robot police are no longer functioning. He is soon proved wrong, for after a brief period of progress, everything breaks down and anarchy results. Mobs attack the council palace with heat rays from the solar power stations, and Zulerich is in great danger. Panic stricken, he revives one member of the council so that the telecops can be activated, but this proves to be no solution, for, as he realizes, the single council man will be even a worse despot than the group rulers. * Things finally come to an end when Zulerich comes upon a recently invented apparatus for compressing atomic structure; he turns it on, and he, and the council, and the palace, compressed into neutronium, sink into the center of the Earth. * *Miscellaneous:* The Earth is now free of animal life; a preceding council released a gas that destroyed everything. * Mankind is concentrated in the great cities. * The chief power source is a system of solar stations. * At one point, after the immobilization of the council, Zulerich offered immortality to the populace, but the people refused it. * Little to recommend. A weak, jumbled, confused story.

1309. **THE SATELLITE OF DOOM**. *Wonder Stories*, January 1931. Ill. Marchioni.
Short story. * *Time:* the near future. * Intrigue and rather farfetched eventualities against a background of realistic rocketry of the day. * Clifford Peterson, a young inventor or scientist, has a revolutionary idea for mail service: a main rocket in orbit around the world, to be visited by small rockets. After intensive discussion of principles with the members of the board of the Rothberg Institution, Peterson receives approval. But thanks to the enmity of Briggs, Rothberg's sinister son-in-law, Clifford is shut out of the construction of the rockets. * When the main component is ready to be sent aloft, it is discovered that

Rothberg is missing. The solution, though no one knows it at the time: Briggs has gone mad, and has shut up the old man in the rocket. Rothberg is now in the sky and cannot survive long. * The institution builds another rocket, which Clifford rides up, hoping to save Rothberg. He is not successful, but the main rocket is finally brought down by electromagnets. Briggs, too, went into space, but froze, and when he landed, shattered into supercold fragments. Also involved is a budding romance between Clifford and Briggs's wife. * Overwritten and difficult to follow. A bad job.

1310. **THREE WORLDS TO CONQUER**. *Wonder Stories Quarterly*, Winter 1931. Ill. Marchioni.
Short story. * *Time:* after 1968, when solarite was developed. *Place:* space not too far from the Earth. * Richard Holt, amateur astronomer, has observed the strange body approaching the Earth, but his warnings have been unheeded. But now the new planet, named Nera, can no longer be denied. It may not strike Earth, but it will at least pass close by and cause enormous devastation. * Dick Holt, however, is up to the occasion. Taking his savings, he buys a failed spaceship from a crank inventor, stocks it with supplies, recruits his girlfriend Virginia, engages a crew, and prepares for what may happen. The ship is powered by solarite, the new compound that transforms solar energy into electricity, but requires gasoline as a starting fuel. * Nera approaches, and the damage is incalculable. Dick and Virginia barely manage to reach the spaceship. Unfortunately, tagging along with Dick is his acquaintance Kris Dillinger, the local banker, who turns out to be a very bad egg. * When things settle down, Dick discovers that the ship is no longer on Earth, but is floating in space on a sea littered with debris and ice floes. In the sky can be seen a strange-looking Earth, Nera, and a silvery globe. * *Explanation:* In passing Earth, Nera ripped away Earth's water and atmosphere, which formed themselves into two globes in space, amounting to two new moons for Earth. Dick's spaceship is on one such globe of water and air. Life on the ship is difficult, for the solarite does not function, since the ship happens to be in a planetary shadow, and Kris Dillinger causes perpetual trouble. * Eventually, Kris, who has an eye for both himself and Virginia, locks out Dick and takes the ship off on its emergency gasoline, thus wasting its resources. * Alone on the sea and ice floes, Dick survives on flotsam that drifts by. The flotsam includes a large tank of gasoline. * After a considerable time, Dick comes upon the stranded ship, to discover an appalling situation. Kris has murdered the crew, and Virginia is a captive. There are shoot-outs and defiances, risks and rifle-play. * Eventually, matters get straightened out. Dick and Virginia are in the spaceship, while Kris is locked out. The ship sinks into the water sphere, where it is safe, since it can function as a submarine. And, best of all, the two water spheres are gradually spiraling back to Earth, where Dick and Virginia will be the new Adam and Eve. * In the hands of a capable author, this might have been an interesting story.

1311. **THE MESSENGER FROM SPACE**. *Wonder Stories*, January 1933. Ill. Paul.
Short story. * *Time:* perhaps 1998. *Place:* mostly in space or on a tiny planetoid that pursues an irregular orbit among the inner planets. * A mysterious yellow spaceship lands momentarily on Earth, then leaves, setting off a wave of speculation. Grinstead, a noted scientist, works out the proper solution to the mystery. He theorizes that the space visitors have hitched a ride on

Sharp, D. D. (*continued*)

Reinmuth (1932-HA), a small planetoid whose orbit passes close to Earth, Mars, and Venus. He urges that Earth develop a spaceship to visit the planetoid. * The *Blue Bird* is nearly completed when a mysterious act of sabotage cuts it in two. This vandalism does not abort the expedition, for Grinstead's associates simply weld the ship back together and fly to Reinmuth, which is barren. All along they are pestered by a mysterious stowaway, both in space and on the planetoid. * The explanation, which is presented with cumbersome complexity, is that the mysterious visitors do not want Earth to enter the space age. They attack the explorers. There are battles royal on the surface of the planetoid and in the *Blue Bird*. Enough of the Earthmen survive to return to Earth. * *Miscellaneous:* Characteristic of the planetoid is a fantastically heavy element that is practically uncontainable in normal Terrestrial gravity. The visitors used a spray of it to cut through the *Blue Bird* while it was being constructed; the spray continued on to the center of the Earth. Sharp probably had neutronium in mind, though the fit is not exact. * Clumsily narrated and rather pointless.

1312. **AT BAY IN THE VOID**. *Wonder Stories*, February 1933. Ill. Paul.

Short story. * *Time:* the interplanetary future. *Place:* on the Mars-Earth run. * Business rivalry between the Red Line and the Blue Line for a lucrative contract. Whichever line makes the fastest run will win the mail contract. Commanding the Blue Line's *Blue Rocket* is young Justin Bennet, perhaps the finest pilot in space, just as the *Blue Rocket* is perhaps the finest ship. The rival Red Line *Meteor* is weaker in both respects. * The problem is one of ethics, business and personal. The Blue Line boss Ralls (whose daughter Bennet wants to win) is a ruthless, aggressive, greedy man, who cares for nothing but money, whereas Bennet is both humane and law-abiding. * The crucial moment comes during the race when Bennet picks up a distress signal from a disabled Martian vessel. Unless he stops to help the Martians, they will die; if he stops, he may lose the race and the contract. Many Earthmen, including Ralls, couldn't care less about the Martians, who are considered an inferior race and are discriminated against. But Bennet stops, rescues the Martians, loses the race, the contract, and his job. Ralls's daughter, however, sticks with him. * Fate deals Bennet another hand. Because of the circumstances, a second contract race is set up, and the owner of the rival Red Line approaches Bennet to fly the *Meteor*. Despite the fact that it a weaker vessel and is sabotaged, Bennet wins. In so doing he uses a dangerous orbital trick. * Routine, a standard pulp plot already developed several times in s-f.

1313. **CAPTIVE OF THE CRATER**. *Wonder Stories*, June 1933. Ill. Paul.

Short story. * *Time:* the interplanetary future. *Place:* the Moon. * On one of the early space flights to the Moon, an astonishing discovery explains why the Moon maintains one face only toward the Earth: Most of the Moon's mass is on the Terrestrial side. * Colonel Lewis, exploring the near surface of the Moon, falls into a crater. He does not crash at the bottom, but continues on through the Moon, out to an enormous depression on the other side. While his fellow explorers watch in dismay and try various expedients to catch him as he passes back and forth through the Moon, he seems doomed. Eventually, however, the spaceship intercepts him as he falls and rescues him. *

The important point is that in the distant past there was a sea on the dark side of the Moon; the then inhabitants constructed a tunnel (through which Lewis fell) to convey water to the side facing us. Thus, the Moon is really shaped like a punched-in ball. * Lewis's experiences are handled with more skill than is usual with Sharp.

1314. **HIGHER JURISDICTION**. *Wonder Stories*, December 1934.

Short-short story. * Not dated, but presumably the near future. * Irony. * Gatti Fenton, basing his work on the power of gravity to bend light, as in general relativity, has invented a device that will bend sunlight, thus permitting cheap illumination after sunset. He offers his invention to a swinish capitalist, Morehouse of Associated Light and Power, but Morehouse does not seem interested. * Fenton sets up his test, which works, and is prepared to light the city. He is still convinced that Morehouse will buy his invention. * Instead, a process server enters with a warrant forbidding Fenton to use his invention. What Fenton forgot was that Associated Light and Power has a monopoly in the city. As Sharp says, Morehouse is greater than Joshua. Joshua made the sun stand still, while Morehouse removed the sun.

1315. **DOOMED BY THE PLANETOID**. *Astounding Stories,* May 1936. Ill. Marchioni.

Short story. * *Time:* the near future. * *Place:* mostly in space, between Earth and the asteroids Selenite and Reinmuth. * *Background:* A state of war exists between the United States and Europe, which is unified under a dictator. The war is going badly for America, mostly because of an enormous base that the enemy has in Cuba, from which pour irresistible forces. If the United States had a supply of the mineral selenite (which seems to be radioactive) all would be well, for the radiations of selenite cause blindness. * Commander Gatti Fenton of the *Skyhawk* is assigned to fly to the asteroid Selenite to gather some of the needed substance. (The duplication of name, Gatti Fenton, from the previous story—#1314—seems to have no significance. The present story seems to be set considerably farther into the future than the previous.) It will be a race with the enemy, who also wants the mineral. Along the way, the *Skyhawk*, which is practically unarmed, is attacked by the enemy *Shark*, a much superior vessel. The *Skyhawk* is badly damaged, but the *Shark* does not pursue its advantage, instead flying on to Selenite. Fenton's mission is thus a failure. * The *Skyhawk* limps to the small sister asteroid Reinmuth for repairs. Fenton now realizes that the only way to prevent the *Shark* from returning to Cuba with selenite (an event which would mean total defeat for the United States) is to ram it. * His men are all willing to do this, but one man, Klein, German by birth and outrageous accent, acts peculiarly and seems to be sabotaging the operation. Thanks to his welding the anchor chain to the asteroid, the *Skyhawk* has no chance of ramming the enemy ship. * But all is not lost. The asteroid Reinmuth heads directly for Cuba, where its impact destroys the great hostile base, leaving a crater 100 miles across. The *Skyhawk* escaped, of course, before this happened. What Klein's intentions were, is not stated clearly, but he seems to have redeemed possible treachery at the last moment. * Some years later, when the war is over and a rational civilization that has abolished war is spread over the world, Fenton broods over past national madnesses. * The pacifist note is unusual in stories of this sort. * Not a very good story.

[Anonymous]
Presumably a British writer.

1316. **SHEER PERSONALITY.** *Scoops,* 17 February 1934. Ill. S. D.
Short story. * Professor Dingle theorizes that since matter cannot be destroyed, only transformed, human personality also cannot be destroyed. Further, that vestiges of personality remain in objects associated with people. His friends scoff. * Dingle, however, discovers a ray that liberates such vestiges, incorporating them into the nearest human present. For an experiment, when Dingle induces his charwoman to put on a ruff that once belonged to Queen Elizabeth (I), she assumes the personality of Queen Elizabeth. Storming out, calling for her guards and coach, and generally making a nuisance of herself, she is put in jail. Dingle can't restore her for a time, for he has lost the control device for his ray. It had fallen into the char's pail. * Dingle, to convince the skeptical, uses his ray on his friend the judge. When Dingle produces an article that once belonged to the notorious criminal Charlie Peace, the judge assumes the personality of Peace and berates the prisoner for not shooting when he was arrested. * For a more praiseworthy venture, Dingle presents Napoleon's snuffbox to the Prime Minister, who, Dingle feels, is not being masterful enough in certain dealings, like unemployment among fishermen. But when the ray is turned on, the Prime Minister does not act like Napoleon, but instead goes into a vulgar music hall routine, with songs, patter, and soft-shoe. It was a mistake of the jewelry house, who had sent the snuffbox of a noted low vaudeville comedian instead of Napoleon's. * When Dingle happens to be handling the real Napoleonic snuffbox, the char accidentally turns on the ray, and Dingle becomes Napoleon. Unfortunately, the tube rolled unseen under the wainscoting and cannot be turned off. Dingle is now in a madhouse, convinced that he is Napoleon. * Neatly handled, if clichéd; better than one might have expected. It is not so much a boys' story as sitcom humor that could have appeared in the *Strand Magazine* a decade or two earlier. * For a sequel see #633, "History Hysterical," which is presumably by the same author.

SHEPPARD, W. L., JR.
No information.

1317. **A HAIR-RAISING TALE.** *Wonder Stories,* July 1934.
Short-short story. * *Time:* perhaps the twenty-second or twenty-third century. * By now the human race has become almost totally bald. Scattered fringes of hair are unusual and highly desirable for their sex appeal. * Against this background Dr. Dashe, the great medical researcher, has developed a radiation treatment that causes hair to grow readily and rapidly. Dyes injected at the proper time ensure suitable coloration. * His discovery sweeps the world, and mankind feverishly seeks treatment to regain hair. The long-extinct occupation of barber comes back into existence. * But then the horrible other side of the discovery appears. Dashe's process involves shielding the face and other parts of the body during treatment, but there is no shield possible for the scalp. As a result, hair is growing inside the cranium of those who took the treatment. Madness, murder, and the complete dissolution of society are the result. * Dr. Dashe awakens. It was all a dream, but he still destroys his lab records dealing with a cure for baldness.

SHERIDAN, MAX C.
A vague biographical article in *Thrilling Wonder Stories* for June 1939 states only that Sheridan, in the manner of Depression Era authors, has held a multitude of jobs. A photograph shows a man in early middle age. Five more science-fiction stories are attributed to Sheridan.

1318. **INTERFERENCE.** *Amazing Stories,* March 1935. Ill. Morey.
Short story. * *Time:* 1964. *Place:* mostly the Galapagos Islands. * Past events: Ten years, earlier, as part of the peace treaty following the brief war between the United States and allied Russia, Japan, China, and India, all the Asiatic navies were confiscated and further shipbuilding prohibited. As a result, the Asiatics are greatly handicapped should they wish to wage war again. * A later event: Several months before the main sequence on the Galapagos, all the water in the world suddenly developed such surface tension that it was almost impenetrable. One could walk on it, as was the case with the four young people in a college swimming pool. * College over, pairing off in marriage, the two young couples take a joint honeymoon on the Galapagos. Wandering inland, they come upon a road, and in short order are captured by a Chinese. The Asiatics are obviously using the island for some devious purpose. * The leader of the Asiatics, a very pleasant, obliging Japanese named Mercadon, explains. It was he who solidified the water several months earlier by focusing radiation on a certain alloy. That was a trial run. Now, he has an enormous plant in the cone of an extinct volcano on one of the islands, and his machinery has solidified all the oceans. At this moment two hundred million Asiatic troops are dashing in automobiles and troop carriers across the solid Pacific. They will certainly overwhelm the United States. * But America is not lost. One of the newly weds, creating a distraction, uses Mercadon's radio apparatus to signal for help. American bombers blow up the installation, and all two hundred million Asiatics are drowned. * Below routine.

SHERIN, RONALD M.
No information, but, judging from the story, the author must have had a university background in astronomy and physics. Social Security records list a Ronald Sherin (1902-1980), resident in Minnesota, died in Texas.

1319. **THE LOST COMET.** *Amazing Stories,* June 1927. Unsigned ill.
Short story. * *Place:* France. * The great but discredited astronomer Professor Montesquieux has made a frightening discovery. Biela's comet, which is generally thought to have broken up in the 1850s, was only partially fragmented, and its core, followed by a train of poisonous gas, is due to strike the Earth on March 21, 1931. * Montesquieux is successful in getting a hearing before the Academy of Science, but his colleagues scoff at him, and he is clapped into a madhouse. * Time passes. Shortly before the vernal equinox in 1931, a nova appears in the sky, and it is not long before the astronomers recognize that it is Biela's comet, as predicted by Montesquieux, and that the Earth is seriously threatened. * The professor's chief adversary hastens to the madhouse to apologize to Montesquieux, who has been living there very comfortably. * The comet passes close by the Earth, without causing too much damage. Montesquieux now admits in embarrassment that he neglected to take into account Jupiter's gravity, which changed the path of the

Sherin, Ronald M. (*continued*)

comet slightly. As penance for this mistake, which caused so much panic and damage, he will voluntarily remain in the madhouse. * Not a bad story, but very heavily laden with astronomical data.

1320. **WHEN THE WORLD WENT MAD.** *Amazing Stories Quarterly*, Fall 1928. Ill. Paul.

Short story. * *Time:* 1938. * The great Russian mad scientist Ivan Teranhoff can control subatomic energy; exactly what this is in modern terms is impossible to say, perhaps fusion. But in any case it enables him to accelerate the rotation of the Earth substantially by manipulating the Terrestrial magnetic field. * The reason for this? Teranhoff wants to explore space, and he intends to use the increased centrifugal force to hurl his space sphere off the Earth. * The result is, of course, disastrous, with millions of people dying, seacoasts changing, and gravity lessening along the equatorial regions. Teranhoff must be located and forced to stop his devilish work. * Professor Jopplin is the savior of the world. He lands near Teranhoff's establishment, and when the mad Russian and his comrades leave into space, Jopplin turns off the machinery. The world is again stable, but with an eighteen-hour day and enormous damage along the equatorial zone. * Silly and confusing.

SHURTLEFF, BERTRAND L[ESLIE] (1897-1967)

U.S. author, born in Rhode Island. Under pseud. S. B. Leslie wrote boys' books, sports books, animal books. Series on "Awol," World War II attack dog.

1321. **NORTH OF MATTO GROSSO.** *Amazing Stories,* July 1932. Ill. Morey.

Novelette. * *Time:* apparently not long after World War I. *Place:* South America. * Ed, receiving an emergency call for help from his old wartime air corps buddy Bill, dashes off for South America. Bill, it seems, is employed by the government, but his superior is the former German ace Killer Stein, a very vicious man. Stein, who is a power unto himself, has forbidden aerial passage over a certain area. Bill and Ed, after various contretemps, venture into the prohibited area, partly because Bill's girlfriend is being held captive there by Stein, who wishes her favors. * The two men are captured and, although they escape and are recaptured with some frequency, are finally staked out in an arena where sun-worshipping Indians plan to let them die of sunstroke. But Ed's cigarette case embodies a little disintegrator, with which he clears away Stein and the hostile Indians. * *Miscellaneous:* Stein, who had been planning to conquer the world, maintained a stable of captive scientists who were working on advanced poison gases, insect weapons, water poisons, and much else. Some of them, including a half-mad scientist, originally believed that Stein was saving the world from Communism. * Told in a slangy manner. * The above résumé is short, but further detail would not have improved matters. Pretty bad.

SILVESTER, L. B.

No information. Presumably a British author. The story is so confusedly presented that it is unlikely that the author was a professional boys' writer like most of the contributors to the story papers.

1322. **METAL DICTATOR.** *Scoops,* 5 May 1934. Unsigned ill.

Boys' fiction. * Short story. * A mixture of many elements, narrated in a broken fashion. * *Time:* Main action in 1998, as seen from the future. * *Background:* In Britain at the edge of the twenty-first century no one works, since machines take care of everything. London is filled with gigantic skyscrapers. Distance travel is accomplished with rocket planes, while local travel is made easy with small electric individual flying wings. There is no more countryside; machines either cultivate every available inch or extract minerals. Books no longer are generally available, their place being taken by radio and television. * China, Japan, and Siberia, however, live in a completely different manner. While there is liberty and democracy in Great Britain, in the Orient everything is controlled by the Mind, a mechanical brain that seized power during the 1940s. It seems to offer some material security, but this is accompanied by extreme regimentation and repression. * Most of the story is taken up with the narrative of Professor Harold Winters, who was an eyewitness of the emergence of the Mind as a world power. Winters was a freelance engineer in the Far East, working variously for Russia, China, and Japan. When war broke out in 1940 between Russia and China on one side, and Japan on the other, Winters sided with the Russians and helped to develop new weapons against the Japanese. * On the crucial occasion, when the Russians move in to take a Japanese base, they find it empty, with mysterious tunnel-like holes in the ground. Shortly thereafter, Winters and associates see a violent movement in the earth, from which emerges an earth-borer, out of which steps a small machine that addresses them. It is an emissary of the Mind, which intends to stop the war and take over the three countries itself. It has already emptied the Japanese base. In the war that follows, the humans fight the machines, but are defeated, although a halian gun that Winters perfected was very effective. Winters escapes. * In the frame situation in 1998, not everyone in Britain is delighted with the mechanized state. Some, like young Roderick Saltney, regard it as decadence. Saltney, while spouting protests to the air, chances to meet Professor Winters, who relates his life history, as given above. The two men become friends and are instrumental when the Mind tries to take over England. The Mind broadcasts a radio message stating that it is prepared to offer its benefits to the people of Great Britain, if they vote in a plebiscite to accept them. If the British reject them, the Mind will impose them anyway. * It looks like all-out war, but a suggestion to the War Ministry by Winters defuses the situation. The Mind is afraid of halian guns and backs down.

SIMAK, CLIFFORD D[ONALD] (1904-1988)

U.S. (Minnesota) newspaper man, occasional author. One of the better writers during the Campbell era and later, technically superior to most of his fellow authors. Work is often marked by an exuberant imagination. Stories considered in this volume are not juvenilia, but certainly not on the level of his later work.

1323. **THE WORLD OF THE RED SUN.** *Wonder Stories*, December 1931. Ill. Paul.

(Reprinted in Asimov, *Before the Golden Age.*)

Short story. * *Time:* 1935, about A.D. 7000, and more than five million years in the future. *Place:* Colorado. * Harl Swanson and Bill Kressman have built a time-flying machine with which they hope to explore the future. Setting the controls of their machine for five thousand years, they travel through a spaceless

Simak, Clifford D. (*continued*)

continuum that is purely time. But when their machine stops and they emerge, they find a strange world, a sea on one side, a desert on the other, and a dull red sun in the sky. Ancient ruins might be the remains of Denver. * As they wander around in dismay, they are attacked by a horde of savage-looking men who overcome them despite the time travelers' revolvers. * Harl and Bill are taken to a crumbling city, where they are imprisoned. English of a sort is still spoken, and the two men obtain some information from an old man who seems eager to talk. They will perform in the arena against other men or beasts. This is the will of Golan-Kirt, "who came out of the cosmos and rules." The old man, who realizes that he is courting death, also informs the two men that Golan-Kirt rules by suggestion; that while he is enormously powerful, he is vulnerable to weapons if one can evade his suggestion. After revealing this, the old man dies, killed by the thought power of Golan-Kirt. * Swanson and Kressman decide to rid the land of the thought-monster before returning to their own time. Entering the arena, they shunt off Golan-Kirt's mental attacks—which take such forms as a band of Roman legionaries, a World War I machine-gun squad, and a lion—and defy the monster to fight them visibly. Golan-Kirt appears—a gigantic brain two feet across, floating in the air. * After this the battle of wills begins. The two men from the past, stronger than the future men, resist fiercely and discover that ridicule weakens the power of the giant brain. Taunting it with accusations of fraud, that it is not a being from the cosmos but simply a human laboratory experiment, they finally wear it down and shoot it. But it was a terrible struggle, and the time travelers almost lost a couple of times. * Kressman and Swanson are hailed as saviors by the future people, who are delighted to be rid of the thought-monster. The future men urge the time travelers to remain with them and teach them the old forgotten science—only a part of which remains. Perhaps then mankind can revive again. But Swanson and Kressman are determined to return to the past, even though the future savants say that time travel into the past is not possible. * The men reenter their machine and travel a short time-distance, but find themselves in the far, far future, where nothing remains except a very eroded statue of themselves. The race is dead, and they are the last two men. * Typical pulp action story, somewhat melodramatic, but with a stronger ending than is usual in such cases.

1324. **MUTINY ON MERCURY.** *Wonder Stories*, March 1932. Ill. Paul.

Short story. * *Time:* the interplanetary future. *Place:* Mercury. * Earth maintains crystal-domed mining centers on Mercury; the workers are apparently Selenites and Martians, while the overseers are Earthmen. The Selenites are stupid humanoid hunks. The Martians, who are yellow and have fangs and six arms, are born troublemakers and plotters. Decayed remnants of an ancient civilization, they bitterly resent the newer races of the solar system. Terrestrial policy, however, is to hire a few Martians for each installation, perhaps to avoid political trouble, perhaps to show fairness. The central figure, Tom, does not agree with this policy and would exterminate all Martians. * A revolt has broken out in Universal Ore Mining Company Station Nine. All the Terrestrials except Tom have been killed, and also all the rebels except two Selenites and a Martian. Tom would be at their mercy, except that he has handy an ancient sword, an heirloom treasure brought from Earth by one of his murdered

friends. Tom uses the sword to good advantage both within the station and outside, later, in space-suited duels. When the story ends, Tom is the sole survivor of the insurrection. * The Martian plot was not aimed at a single mining station, but was coordinated throughout the system. Apparently it failed everywhere. * Pulp action material, below Simak's later standard.

1325. **THE VOICE IN THE VOID.** *Wonder Stories Quarterly*, Spring 1932. Ill. Paul.

Short story. * *Time:* the interplanetary future. *Place:* Mars, the Rocky Mountains, Chicago. * *Background:* Interplanetary travel is well established, and the government of Earth maintains friendly relations with the government of Mars. The Martians, who are more or less humanoid and possess a science and technology about on the same level as Earth's, are decadent descendants of a higher civilization of immense antiquity. Religion is paramount in Martian life, and along with hypersensitivity goes ruthlessness in dealing with offenders against the religion. Earthmen are allowed a certain freedom on Mars, but the Martian government is inclined to be arbitrary and capricious in dealing with them. * Narrator Ashby, a reputable historian of Martian culture, and Kenneth Smith, an educated prospector, both have a grudge against the Martians. Ashby was summarily deported for expressing an interest in the shrine of Saldebar, where the most sacred Martian relics, the bones of Kell-Rabin, are preserved. Smith, who found a fabulously rich radium deposit, was cheated of his rights and expelled on a legal technicality. He has vowed revenge. * Some time later, on Earth, Smith looks up Ashby, revealing that he has stolen the bones of Kell-Rabin and will give them to Ashby. Smith is obviously a little mad, and while Ashby is wondering what to do, an attack by Martian priests settles his course. After Smith kills the priests with his flash pistol, the two men hide out in the Rocky Mountains, where they assume facial disguises and new identities, storing the bones in a safe deposit box in Chicago. * But matters are not that simple. Smith disappears, obviously kidnapped by the Martians, and Ashby is bound to learn his fate and rescue him if possible. * Ashby traces Smith to the temple on Mars but, surprise, Smith's brain has been removed from his body and installed in a cylinder. Martian priests are torturing Smith's encapsuled brain to learn from him the whereabouts of Kell-Rabin's bones. Smith does not talk. Ashby kills the priests; takes Smith's brain cylinder and a cylinder of an ancient Martian priest; and escapes to the drylands. * There Ashby and Smith find a mysterious pyramid. The captive Martian priest informs them that all such pyramids are destroyed when found, since they contain something inimical to Martian religion. The priest was right, for in addition to incredible wealth in gems, the pyramid contains the bones of Earthmen, perhaps millions of years old. The assumption is that a high civilization of the past, perhaps Mu, visited Mars; something which the Martians are desperate to conceal. * With the wealth from the pyramid, Ashby is immune to political persecution. He returns to Earth; prepares a broadcast revealing the great Martian religious hoax; has his brain placed in a cylinder like Smith's; and seals himself away until advancing science can place their brains back into bodies. At the moment it is impossible. * But, by an irony of fate lightning strikes the radio system and Ashby's destructive message is not broadcast. The brains may well be sealed away indefinitely. * *Miscellaneous:* The author does not make it clear whether Martians are thus descended from Earthmen or indi-

Simak, Clifford (*continued*)

genous. * The Martians apparently preserve many such brains in cylinders and activate them when needed. The cylinders contain energy sources enough for long life, and life in a bottle does not seem too uncomfortable or at least tolerable. * A crazy story (not in a pejorative sense), with far more imagination than the typical pulp s-f story of the time, but somewhat damaged by the trick ending.

1326. **HELLHOUNDS OF THE COSMOS**. *Astounding Stories*, June 1932. Ill. Wesso.

Short story. * The Horrors strike in many places around the world; black, amorphous shapes, they are completely invulnerable to all weapons—explosives, gas, radiation. Their numbers increase, and it looks as if mankind is doomed. * Eccentric, even slightly mad Professor Silas White, believing that he has a solution to the problem, asks that a reporter be assigned to interview him. * White then explains the situation to young reporter Henry Woods. The Horrors are three-dimensional versions of four-dimensional beings from another frame of existence, whence their invulnerability. White adds that he has created a device to fight them: something that will change a three-dimensional person into a four-dimensional one. And he has assembled a band of ninety-nine volunteers who will undergo the change, be transformed into four-dimensional beings in the four-dimensional world, and combat the monsters. Henry agrees to accompany the party. * When Henry finds himself in the strange, four-dimensional world, however, he discovers that he is part of a multiple being composed of all the ninety-nine other men, and that he has a former fourth-dimensional identity (Mal Shaf) that he is resuming. And the Horrors, similarly, are three-dimensional projections of another fourth-dimensional being, Ouglat, who ages before had forced Mal Shaf out of his world. * The two beings fight desperately, with changing fortunes, as Ouglat withdraws his projections from our world to gain strength. Eventually Mal Shaf wins, but does not return to our world. He remains with his fourth-dimensional fellows. * One wonders if Simak was serious with this story, which has touches of Lovecraft, Edward Hamilton, and, I think, some tongue-in-cheek.

1327. **THE ASTEROID OF GOLD**. *Wonder Stories*, November 1932. Ill. Paul.

(Reprinted in Ashley, *History of the Science Fiction Magazine, Part One*, and in Wollheim, *Every Boy's Book of Science Fiction*.)

Short story. * *Time:* the interplanetary future. *Place:* the asteroid belt. * The brothers Vince and Vernon Drake, space miners, have found an asteroid that is almost riddled with gold. Unfortunately, their work has been observed by the notorious space pirate Max Robinson, who lands, captures them, and takes their gold. * Robinson, who is a sneering sadist, announces that since he has done so many wicked things in his life, he will atone by sparing the Drakes. Instead of killing them, he will abandon them with three tanks of oxygen on the asteroid, with their ship in full sight on another asteroid. Max Robinson hopes that the Drakes will fight to the death over the third tank. * The brothers attack Robinson, fracturing his spine, but he survives and flies away. * Luck looks kindly on the Drakes. Thanks to a collision with a third body, the asteroid with their spaceship will collide with the asteroid that they are on. They survive and regain their vessel—but not their gold. * Routine.

SIMMONS, HENRY HUGH

An editorial response to a letter in the December 1929 issue of *Air Wonder Stories* states: "Mr. Fezandié, the author of "Hicks' Inventions with a Kick," is now traveling abroad and is apparently not doing any writing." It is not known whether this attribution is correct or an editorial slip. Fezandié is covered in a separate entry. The Hicks stories that follow are late members of a subform that flourished a generation earlier: the story of the silly invention that backfires upon its creator and his associates, to say nothing of bystanders. The basic concept, of course, is part of the general anti-scientific strand in early twentieth-century culture: ridicule the presumptuous inventor and thereby remove fear. Simmons's stories are completely formulaic, but are on the whole better developed and better written than most of their predecessors.

1328. **HICKS' INVENTIONS WITH A KICK. THE AUTOMATIC SELF-SERVING DINING TABLE**. *Amazing Stories*, April 1927. Unsigned ill.

Short story. * *Place:* Massachusetts. The silly invention in this case is a dining apparatus that prepares food and drink, revolves appropriately to serve the guests, and ultimately runs amok when the steam engine in the kitchen runs out of water.

1329. **HICKS' INVENTIONS WITH A KICK. THE AUTOMATIC APARTMENT**. *Amazing Stories*, August 1927. Ill. Paul.

Short story. * *Place:* Massachusetts. * In this story Hicks has created an automated (my term) apartment, in which household chores are taken care of by self-operative machinery: dusting by enormous suction devices, cleaning by small water jets, vacuuming by a pathed machine (with furniture moving aside at the proper time), an endless-belt dish washer and dryer, and an automatic shoe-shiner. * When visitors are present, everything goes wrong, and all are drenched, dusted, and pummeled, while one guest has his head polished by the shoe shiner.

1330. **HICKS' INVENTIONS WITH A KICK. THE ELECTRO-HYDRAULIC BANK PROTECTOR**. *Amazing Stories*, December 1927. Ill. Paul.

Short story. * *Place:* Massachusetts. * Hicks makes peace with the friends whom he injured or humiliated in previous episodes. He has developed a new invention, a bank protection system. It consists of jets of water at high pressure, which are deflected off the bank walls and windows, rendering the robber helpless, while a huge glob of glue falls from the ceiling upon him. * Naturally, the apparatus goes wrong, attacking the inauguration group, while gangsters, seeing that the system is exhausted, rob the bank.

1331. **HICKS'S INVENTIONS WITH A KICK. THE PERAMBULATING HOME**. *Amazing Stories*, August 1928. Ill. Paul.

Short story. * *Place:* California. * O'Keefe, the narrator, has left Massachusetts after his last experience with Hicks, and has moved to California, hoping thus to escape the nuisance inventor. * On the crucial occasion, as he is walking along a beach near Los Angeles, he sees a house that seems to move. He examines it closely, whereupon a door opens, revealing Hicks, who greets him enthusiastically, and takes him inside, where he meets all the personalities of the previous adventures. * Hicks's latest is a house that can be rotated to face the sun; its interior is automated, with an improved automatic dining room table. And most interesting is a liquor-laden table that can vanish into the

Simmons, Henry Hugh (*continued*)

ceiling. (Since the story is set during Prohibition, such a table could be most useful.) O'Keefe decides to let bygones be bygones and joins the merry crowd in their boozing. * The expected happens. The machinery gets out of hand when one of the drunken party members meddles with the controls, and the house, overweighted with water in its top level, waddles into the ocean, where it turns topsy-turvy and floats away. The coastal authorities pick up the involuntary voyagers.

SIMMONS, JOE
No information.

    1332. **THE LIVING TEST TUBE.** *Amazing Stories,* November 1928. Ill. Paul.
Short story. * Leonard Giffin, sentenced to death for murder, is obviously innocent, but the governor will not pardon him, indeed, has stated flatly that Giffin must die. The narrator (a newspaper reporter) and Moore (Giffin's lawyer) have great expectations from Dr. Hausen, the famed amateur criminologist. * They are not disappointed. Summoning all concerned, including the governor, Hausen reveals his scientific accomplishment: maintaining organs alive after the death of the individual. In this case, he has the head of a notorious criminal who tried to burglarize his office and was accidentally killed. The head denounces the governor as an accomplice in crime. The governor signs Giffin's pardon, but commits suicide. * Amateurish.

SIODMAK, CURT or KURT (1902-present)
German author, born in Dresden. Ph.D., University of Zürich. Removed to France and later the United States in the 1930s; associated with Gaumont-British motion pictures. Later worked in Hollywood film industry as playwright and director. Most of his films were lower level horror films, although there was also considerable quality work. The author of *F.P.I. Does Not Reply* (vt. *F.P.I. Fails to Reply*, both 1933) and *Donovan's Brain,* both of which have been made into motion pictures. Won Bundespreis for play of motion picture *Das Feuerschiff* in 1964.

    1333. **THE EGGS FROM LAKE TANGANYIKA.** *Amazing Stories*, July 1926. Unsigned ill.
Although Gernsback claimed that this was an original story, it is a translation of an earlier German publication, "Die Eier von Tanganyika See" (*Scherl Magazine,* perhaps 1926). The translator is not identified with the story, but C. A. Brandt (in an interview in *Fantasy Magazine* #28) claimed responsibility. Short story. * *Place:* Africa and Berlin. When Professor Meyer-Maier ignores the warnings of the natives and removes several gigantic eggs from the swamps around Lake Tanganyika, he sets off an unexpected peril. Taken to Germany, the eggs hatch into monstrous blood-sucking flies the size of horses. Escaping, the insects create a small reign of terror. Meyer-Maier fortunately loses consciousness during the worst of the peril, and when he recovers, learns that the danger was never as great as he thought. There were only a few insects, and because of their size they could not multiply as rapidly as smaller life-forms. * In the school of H. G. Wells, but there is a parodic element.

SKEEN, WARD
No information.

    1334. **170 MILES A MINUTE.** *Amazing Stories,* June 1935. Ill. Morey.

Short story. * Paul Plake, eager young inventor, manages to catch the attention of financier Mr. Goode. Plake, who has discovered a fantastically light metal, wants funds to build a plane for the one hundred thousand dollar Dolt competition for a nonstop flight around the world. * He obtains funds and is successful, of course. The explanation: With his superlight metal, Plake minimized the force of gravity. Then flying up into the stratosphere, he simply stood still while the Earth revolved beneath him. * Much like the work of D. H. Keller at his worst.

SKIDMORE, JOSEPH WILLIAM (1890-1938)
U.S. author, resident in various places in California. Often wrote as Joe W. Skidmore. At writing time, a real estate developer in Los Angeles area, also occasional film writer. Although Skidmore hinted at different birth dates in his letters, an account of his death on 10 January 1938, in an automobile accident, states that he was 47 years old. Of the frequent contributors to early pulp science-fiction, Skidmore was the weakest writer.

Skidmore's fiction is presented in The Posi and Nega Series and Other Works, chronologically in each group.

The Posi and Nega Series

Five stories based on personalized atomic particles, Posi being male, and Nega, female. Most of the story is exposition by Posi, who instructs his rather giddy, ignorant mate on atomic matters as understood at the time. Interspersed with the sometimes coy, sometimes brutal, tutoring are a series of quotations from the great, which Skidmore felt elucidated his points. The stories are all almost unreadable, and one is perpetually reastonished that they saw print.

    1335. **THE ROMANCE OF POSI AND NEGA.** *Amazing Stories,* September 1932. Ill. Morey.
Short story. * The pathetic fallacy as applied to atomic particles. Posi, who is incredibly old, lectures Nega, his mate, on atomic structure and radiation. At the end they are destroyed by Professor Millikan, who hurls 300,000,000 volts into their nucleus.

    1336. **ADVENTURES OF POSI AND NEGA.** *Amazing Stories*, January 1934. Ill. Morey.
Short story. * The second story in the Posi and Nega series. * Posi and Nega are not destroyed when they pass through Professor Millikan's experiment; instead they are forced into a lead atom on the walls of the machine. After a time, when the lead is removed and melted, Posi and Nega become part of a bullet with which a mad scientist murders a man. Posi and other atomic particles assemble their mentalities and force the scientist to reenact the crime in his sleep. After this the electrons pass into the body of a man dying of typhoid fever and are flushed down a sewer into the ocean. * Interspersed with words of wisdom from the great sages.

    1337. **AN EPOS OF POSI AND NEGA.** *Amazing Stories,* January 1935. Ill. Morey.
Short story. * The third story in the Posi and Nega series. * Much like the previous story. Posi and Nega converse, with Posi expounding science while they have mild adventures. In this case they enter the brain of a mad scientist who plans to destroy the universe with an atomic explosion. His plans are foiled by a concerted effort of the atoms in his brain. Certain particles in

Skidmore, Joseph W. (*continued*)

selenium atoms in his body sacrifice themselves. Their loss turns the selenium into arsenic, which poisons the madman. As the story ends, Posi and Nega are shot off in a Very pistol by the crew of a disabled zeppelin. * Abysmal.

1338. **A SAGA OF POSI AND NEGA.** *Amazing Stories,* May 1935. Ill. Morey.
Short story. * The fourth story in the Posi and Nega series. * Posi and Nega, shot out of a pistol, are later struck by lightning and imbedded in a granite, ice-covered mountain, where they become part of an enormous diamond. The diamond is found, cut, and fought over by gangsters. After a period in the possession of a mad scientist, Posi and Nega leave the diamond and enter the body of an ant, which crawls into a hospital's supply of radium and is killed.

1339. **A LEGEND OF POSI AND NEGA.** *Amazing Stories,* October 1935.
Short story. * The fifth and last story in the Posi and Nega series. * The ant (or termite, Skidmore alternates) is removed from the box, and Posi and Nega find themselves first in a boron atom, then a sulfur atom. In a sulfur compound, they pass into a human, where they become part of a white corpuscle, thence into a piece of glass, which is being dissolved by hydrofluoric acid. The ending is the cliffhanger typical of the series. * One wonders what finally moved the author or editor to terminate the series.

Other Works
It should be noted that the presence of a character named Joane Cromwell in several stories does not indicate that the stories are related or that the characters are the same person. Joane Cromwell was the maiden name of the author's wife, and he simply liked to use the name.

1340. **DRAMATIS PERSONAE.** *Amazing Stories Quarterly*, Fall 1931. Ill. Morey.
Short story. * *Time:* A.D. 22,930. *Place:* space and the planet of an unnamed star. * M.E.A. 16 and his prospective mate F.A.N. 24 are spending their year of premarital companionship in space before they can be married. As they look back toward the sun, they watch in horror as it goes nova. A last, broken, telepathic message from Earth bids them start the human race anew, wherever they find a friendly world. * Speeding at thousands of times the speed of light toward a likely star, they reach the planet Alpha, which is Earth-like and inhabited by humans on a barbaric level of culture. The Earth couple, superhuman and completely telepathic, are taken to be gods, and all seems well as they plan to raise the cultural level of the natives. * Two problems arise. There is an area of Alpha that is in perpetual darkness because of a permanent eclipse caused by another planetary body. This dark area is inhabited by colossal dinosaur-like beasts that occasionally raid the human area. M.E.A.'s atomic rifle can take care of them, but there is a second connected problem: Radiation from the new sun that was the old solar system will soon reach Alpha, light up the dark portion, and madden the colossal beasts into a real menace. This is surmounted. * M.E.A. and F.A.N. now must now take thought about continuing the human race. M.E.A., who has fallen in love with the native queen, is apprehensive about marrying F.A.N.. As he tells F.A.N., it has been so long since there has

been natural breeding among Earthmen that there might be reproductive problems. F.A.N. should marry an Alphan, notably a heroic warrior they call Heracles, and he, the queen. F.A.N. agrees with tears in her eyes, since she loves M.E.A. * *Miscellaneous:* Longevity is much greater for future man; M.E.A. is already 240 years old. * M.E.A. and F.A.N. can travel far faster than light, despite Einstein, by infinite shrinking then reexpanding. * Horrible writing and development. The author perpetually interrupts the story with words of wisdom: "If all men were equally intelligent, there would be no wise men—or fools." "The more primitive the woman, the more she is engined to cope with man in the battle of sex." "Love among humans has always been largely instinctive—never controlled by logic or reason." "It is well for humanity that women do not (as a general rule) possess the sex impulse—or desire—that is vested in man."

1341. **SOULS ASPACE.** *Amazing Stories*, February 1933.
Short-short story, a single page in length. * *Time:* the interplanetary future. *Place:* space. * The occasion is the return from Mars after the first successful visit. On board are Commander Cromwell, his daughter Joane, her fiancé Don Kent, and Maran the Martian. The Martians, who are apparently human, are a million years ahead of us and the masters of all sorts of mental powers. Maran loves Joane. * An emergency: A meteor rips a huge hole in the ship. Maran jumps into the hole, blocking the outrush of air, and sends a telepathic message: He is dying, but he can transfer his personality to another, if the other is willing. Kent accepts, and is immediately turned into a mental superman.

1342. **THE BEETLE IN THE AMBER.** *Amazing Stories,* November 1933. Ill. Morey.
Short story. * *Time:* "From the looks of that Brontosaurus. . . we are in the Pleistocene period." * Donald Cromwell and his wife Joane are experiencing marital strain as a result of Joane's fixation on an amber bead containing a large fossil beetle. The mystical philosopher and scientist Oliver Kent proposes to resolve the difficulty by sending them back to the period of the amber, via reincarnation, akashic record, or what have you. * Donald and Joane awaken (with both ancient and modern memories) in the bodies of primitives of a million years ago; they are hairy, and their arms are so long that their hands dangle below their knees. Outlawed from their tribe because they married without the chief's permission, they were deposited in the territory of chief Kalo and his sun worshippers, who are now pursuing them. * When a pterodactyl attacks them, Donald sacrifices himself to save Joane, who is then captured by Kalo's men. When she rejects Kalo's advances, she is sentenced to die by the bite of the death beetle. The beetle is standing there looking at her, when a glob of resin falls upon it, sealing it off. The portent is so remarkable that Kalo and his men dash away. * Joane and Donald awaken, the trauma released by their experience in the past. * Really badly written rubbish. * For the second story involving Oliver Kent, see #1344, "The First Flight."

1343. **THE VELOCITY OF ESCAPE.** *Amazing Stories,* August 1934. Ill. Morey.
Novelette. * *Time:* the near future. *Place:* Washington, D.C., and space around the Earth. * Cops and robbers, as superscientist Donald Millstein tries to save Earth from destruction by supervillain Russian mad scientist Verensky, known as the Falcon. * The Falcon, who has a bitter grudge against the Earth, has set up

Skidmore, Joseph W. (*continued*)

a process for pushing oxygen molecules out into space. Unless he is stopped soon, it will be too late. * Millstein, acting under the egis of the government, determines to foil the villain. The task may be difficult, since the Falcon has means of listening in on and watching Millstein. * The struggle moves out into space, where the Falcon has an enormous vessel, perhaps a mile long, that serves as a floating space platform. Millstein, in his new spaceship, has weapons that he is sure will do in the Falcon: two types of disintegrator and a vibratory weapon that will drive the victim mad. * As the two ships spar, however, it becomes obvious that the Falcon has the same weapons and defenses, plus a hypnosis ray of some sort. * When the battle becomes a draw, Millstein, knowing the Falcon's vanity, offers a space duel with swords. The Falcon accepts, and the two men, equipped with swords and recoil pistols, battle it out in empty space. The Falcon, however, cheats, and the stalemate continues, while the Earth's atmosphere bounces away. But a police ship, at times under the Falcon's hypnotic sway, accidentally crashes into the Russian's space station, ending the battle. The Falcon escapes, as a defiant message reveals. He may be setting up shop near Sirius. * Melodramatic in the worst sense, very badly written, clichéd. * For a sequel see #1347, "A World Unseen."

1344. THE FIRST FLIGHT. *Amazing Stories,* November 1934. Ill. Morey.

Short story. * A latch-on to #1342, "The Beetle in the Amber." * Donald Calvert, flying at 600 MPH in an attempt to fly around the world without stopping, finds himself subject to strange sensations as his reason seems to be departing. Perhaps the speed itself does something to body metabolism. * At this point he remembers a medication given to him by his friend the mystical philosopher Oliver Kent. Kent claimed that one globule might put him into another dimension or enable him to remember a past incarnation. * Taking a globule, Calvert now finds himself a prehuman subman. Parallel to his first flight in the superplane, the caveman Dowb, attacked by a pterodactyl, knocks it unconscious, holds to it as it revives and flies with it across the river to a handsome young cavewoman on the other side. * Awakening back in the present with a new appreciation of what he is doing, Calvert pulls himself out of a nearly fatal tailspin just in time. * For a further adventure of Calvert see #1346, "The Maelstrom of Atlantis."

1345. SEVEN PERILS TO QUICHES. *Amazing Stories,* February 1935. Ill, Morey.

Short story. * *Time and place:* romanticized pre-Columbian Mexico. * Prince Gucuma of Tollan, an Aztec champion, passes through several perils in order to reach the city of Nahuatl, where he overcomes the wicked King Taloc and becomes king. The perils, which include a pterodactyl, a ground dinosaur, and clashing cliffs like the Symplegades, are adapted from Maya legend. * Below routine.

1346. THE MAELSTROM OF ATLANTIS. *Amazing Stories,* February-April (2 issues) 1936. Ill. Morey.

A latch-on to #1344, "The First Flight." * Short novel. * *Place:* mostly in sealed caverns beneath the Atlantic. * Renowned millionaire adventurer Calvert, learning of a tremendous maelstrom in the Atlantic that drags liners and destroyers down, decides that the whirlpool must be connected with Atlantis. (The precise location of the maelstrom is not given; perhaps it is anticipatory of the Bermuda Triangle?!) Building a large

bathysphere he and his permanent girlfriend Joane Cromwell and Swedish scientist Benson descend in the proper place. While they are down, the maelstrom above becomes active, threatening the mother ship, and Calvert cuts the bathysphere loose. * The sphere settles on the bottom, but this is not the end. Intelligent octopi roll the sphere into an air-filled, sealed chamber, where the octopi regard the humans, who emerge from the sphere, with considerable interest. The meeting is reasonably amicable until the surface people see a humanoid being about to be killed by the octopi. Drawing their automatics, which they brought along for unexplained reasons, Calvert and friends save the humanoid, but have to fight off the octopi. Escaping into another series of chambers they encounter the descendants of ancient Atlantis, considerably devolved. Since Benson speaks a rusty Atlantean, communication is not impossible. * *Background:* The most unusual aspect of Atlantis is its political panoply. The king's throne is fixed on the back of a gigantic turtle that crawls about amiably. On occasion the turtle carries the throne into a pool filled with gigantic electric eels, which are pets to the king but vicious to outsiders. * King Zama poses problems, for he has decided to take Joane into his harem. Joane scorns the honor, while Calvert, a possessive male, is outraged. Eventually, this leads to a single-combat duel between the powerful king and Calvert, who used to be a varsity wrestler and boxer. At about the same time as Calvert, without too much trouble, breaks the king's neck, rebellion breaks out among the workers against the oppressive military caste; and the outsiders become acquainted with the single intelligent Atlantean. An ancient man, he is aware of the surface (while the rest of the Atlanteans reject the concept) and has built a private little bathysphere for an ascent. All pile in, the sphere is ejected with compressed air, and all safely reach the surface, where they are retrieved by the mother ship. * Below routine.

1347. A WORLD UNSEEN. *Wonder Stories,* February-April 1936. Ill. Paul.

A sequel to #1343, "The Velocity of Escape." * Short novel. * *Place:* Mostly inside Joane Cromwell, faithful sweetheart of young millionaire scientist Donald Millstein. * Millstein, the unselfish heir of robber baron Millstein, has devoted his life to science and justice. On the one hand, he has just invented the atomic reductor, which squeezes atomic spaces together. On the other hand, he responds to invitations when the government "often call[s] Millstein to destroy master-crooks and their terrible plots and intrigues against the society of civilization." Against Millstein, as a repeated opponent, is still the horrible Russian mad scientist Verensky, also known as the Falcon. As Millstein tells Joane, they cannot marry, because the Falcon has sworn to kill him. * Just as Millstein is explaining the atomic reductor to Joane and her brother Jack, a foul minion of the Falcon's shoots through the window at Donald. Joane, however, leaps into the path of the bullet, which lodges in her spine. It is too dangerous for the great surgeon Mado to operate, for Joane will either die or be permanently paralyzed. * Donald then has his bright idea: He and Mado will reduce themselves to the size of germs, enter Joane's bloodstream, and cut away the bullet. Not much later than said, done. The two men are in Joane's bloodstream, fighting trypanosomes, typhus germs, spirochetes (which have a poisonous sting), and white corpuscles. Despite perils, the men make their way to the bullet and loosen it, so that Mado can remove it when he returns to normal size. Returning, however,

Skidmore, Joseph W. (*continued*)
is a little difficult, for the microsurgeons are carried away by the bloodstream.   But they eventually emerge through Joane's mouth.   Along the way, they were careful not to leave their weapons behind, for the action of the reducing ray is temporary, and it would not do to leave a sword and hatchet in Joan's body. This would be much worse than the usual surgeon's sponge or scalpel. * Back in the lab, where Jack Cromwell stands guard, a bearded stranger enters, claiming to be a messenger from the Falcon. Jack rips off the stranger's false beard, and there is the Falcon, armed with a gas grenade. Jack is equal to the occasion. The bomb goes out the window, and the Falcon goes into the size-reducing machine. * Finale: Don and Mado have returned safely; the operation on Joane is a success; and the Falcon, when he regains size, will be trapped. We must hope that the typhus and syphilis germs in Joane's bloodstream will not erupt into disease. * Astonishing that *Wonder Stories* would print this story, which is even more rubbishy than the plot summary can indicate. Its only interest is as a predecessor of the motion picture *Fantastic Voyage.*

SKINNER, E. D.
U.S. author then resident in Cincinnati, Ohio.   According to portrait in *Air Wonder Stories*, November 1929, then an elderly man, who looks as whimsical as his stories would lead one to expect.

1348. **ELECTRO-EPISODED IN A.D. 2025**. *Amazing Stories*, August 1927. Ill. Paul.
Short story, obviously parodic of the Gernsbackian Ralph 124C 41+ universe. * *Time:* A.D. 2025. *Place:* New York City and Mt. McKinley. * Lt. Col. Algernon Sidney St. Johnstone of the New York National Guard awakens with a frightful hangover, due to a bad lot of bootleg booze that he had insisted on drinking.   His tiny personalized radio is signaling, and when, after various contretemps with his valet and the superscientific devices in his apartment, he turns it on, he receives a furious message from his fiancée, Esmeralda, who is trapped on Mount McKinley, with a tiger about to spring on her. The previous day they had quarreled bitterly about her overexposing clothing, and she had flown away to her own building. She received a ticket blasted in her back from an aerial traffic policeman. * After taking an assortment of sober-up pills and obtaining faxed (my term) permits for electro-flash travel at the speed of light, he rescues Esmeralda. The tiger turns out to be a frozen escaped zoo animal. * But about then Mary Jane, his wife, awakens dreaming John Henry back in the 1920s. It was all his nightmare. * Other future matters: the Bootleg Trust's stock is traded on the market; the Purity League patrols revealing dress, nose powdering, etc.; coffee, tobacco, and alcohol are banned and must be obtained illegally. An electric regenerator provides the equivalent of sleep in minutes; there are precise distance calculating and automatic directional devices; picture phones ("electro-visionals"); heated suits; and other gimmicks. One wonders if Gernsback got the point. * For another adventure of St. Johnstone, see #1350, "The Corpse That Lived."

1349. **SUITCASE AIRPLANES**. *Air Wonder Stories*, November 1929. Ill. Paul.
Short story. * *Time:* A.D. 2029. *Place:* New York and Ethiopia. * A parody of Gernsbackian science-fiction and business stories. * *Background:* The various puritanical societies have succeeded in outlawing alcoholic beverages, coffee, unpasteurized water, and many other substances. When Samuel Vandusenberry von Browne de Smythe (generally known as Sam Brown) awakens with a severe hangover and a boss screaming for his presence, he makes a cup of forbidden coffee and cream, takes an antihangover pill, swallows several food pills, climbs into a massaging shower apparatus that is like a suit of armor, and feels regenerated. He then lies down in an individual pneumatic tube car that shoots him right into the presence of his boss. * After some fairly acrimonious conversation back and forth, Sam learns why his boss has summoned him. Ethiopia has massed its armies in expectation of a simultaneous attack from the British, French, and Italians. While these three nations have modern, advanced weapons, Ethiopia, which is still under the rule of the Menelik dynasty, is a primitive country. * Sam's boss, Gordon-Cummings, wants Sam to sell the Ethiopians an air armada in exchange for mineral rights and assorted other matters. * A synchronizing globe of the world gives Sam the exact distance to Addis Ababa to one hundredth of a mile, while the electro-visional apparatus set in the wall transmits not only detailed pictures of what is presently going on in the royal palace, but, by gathering dead light that is still in the room, events of the past. It will pick up images anywhere where there is an electric wire. * Sam's boss orders him to sell a million two-person planes to the Ethiopians, with suitable weapons and ammunition. Sam goes to the roof where his tempered-copper *Electric Flash* reposes, supervises the loading of a thousand suitcases (each of which contains a collapsible airplane), sets controls for oxygen, temperature, atomic power, and other instructions, then locates Addis Ababa with a pin on a special automated map, turns on the power and takes off at six thousand miles per second. In Addis Ababa Sam demonstrates his wares and makes a sale on his boss's terms. * Sam orders two sharpshooters to man each of the million planes, then sends the robot planes against the English, controlling the planes from the *Electric Flash*. When the British planes are at a certain location, Sam blasts them. He then attacks the British lines, routing the the soldiers. The same procedure is followed against the French and Italians. When peace is declared, Ethiopia has access to the sea, and Sam's company has mineral rights and bonds. * The suitcase planes weigh about ten pounds, are constructed of an ultratempered steel that is as thin as gold leaf, but incredibly strong. The operating parts of the planes are so small that they are microscopic. * An amusing jeu d'esprit.

1350. **THE CORPSE THAT LIVED**. *Amazing Stories*, January 1930. Ill. Wesso.
Short story. * A latch-on to #1348, "Electro-Episoded in A.D. 2025." *Time:* A.D. 2026. *Place:* New York City and the Himalayas. * The story centers around Lt. Col. Algernon Sidney St. Johnstone, New York National Guard, a millionaire playboy of the period, and his wife Esmeralda. * The future world is a flying culture, with runaway capitalism, ruthless stock and commodity deals, and oppression of workers. Johnstone is a typical robber baron of the day (considering any worker who speaks up a Bolshevik), but is also a remarkable aviator. During the story he flies to the Himalayas to search for a new variety of *Ovis poli* that has been sighted, but has a mishap. He is frozen solid, but his wife locates him, chips him out, takes him to a laboratory, thaws him, and reanimates him with electricity. (The continued parody of Gernsback's "Ralph 124C 41+" is obvious.

Skinner, E. D. (*continued*)

It is Dr. David H. Keller's turn next.) Thereupon to keep Johnstone home and to save her marriage, Esmeralda sets up an old-fashioned living situation with a real bedroom, real kitchen, and the possibility of cooking real food. She also gives away her enormously expensive cosmetic machine, which could create all sorts of plastic effects with her face, body, and clothing. * *Miscellaneous:* Electrical Regenerators take the place of sleep. Natural food is extremely difficult to obtain, food tablets being almost universally used. Both tobacco and alcohol are prohibited; the police use far-viewers for spying, but there is wide-open bootlegging. Three quarters of the population works for the government as inspectors and patrolmen. Planes are atomic powered. Mountains are melted by electricity to obtain metals and useful minerals. Electro-forcing apparatus speed up plant growing cycles enormously. * Some amusing touches.

SLACHTA, PAUL

No information.

   1351. **THE TWENTY-FIRST CENTURY LIMITED**. *Amazing Stories*, December 1929. Ill. Paul.

Short story. * *Time:* A.D. 2028. *Place:* mostly space en route to Venus. * Commercial rivalry between two interplanetary lines, Interplanetary Express vs. Earth and Venus Express. A mail contract depends upon whichever one makes the fastest next trip to Venus. To Interplanetary, which is the focus of the story, this contract is a matter of life and death, since the company has overinvested in new liners. * All would be well, except that along the Interplanetary route is a very dangerous comet. It will be risking the lives of the crew and about a thousand passengers to pass near the comet, a necessity for gaining cruise time. * The Interplanetary vessel, despite doubts on all hands, goes along the dangerous route, barely escapes the comet, and wins the contract. * *Miscellaneous:* The spaceships operate by antigravity plates and travel at about a tenth of the speed of light; for atmospheric travel, a bank of propellers on the top surface of the vessel serves. The ships are much like Frank Reade airships in appearance. * City traffic is handled by controllers, who, aloft, stop vehicles to prevent accidents and to clear the way. * The narrator has a shipboard romance with Dana, a Venusian lady, but it is not clear whether she is a colonist or a native. * Venus is Earth-like. * Told in a lively manner.

SLOAT, EDWIN K[IRK] (1895-1986)

U.S. writer, resident in Fort Madison, Iowa. Graduate State Normal College, Oklahoma, 1916. Newspaperman, U.S. Post Office employee, band leader. Sloat is known to have written eleven s-f stories, the last appearing in 1940. Also wrote Western stories for *Top-Notch, Cowboy Stories,* and *Western Story.* His work is very uneven.

   1352. **FLIGHT TO VENUS**. *Amazing Stories,* December 1928. Ill. Paul.

Short story, perhaps inspired by Slater LaMaster's "Luckett of the Moon" (*Argosy-All-Story,* 28 January 1928). * *Time:* probably around A.D. 2000. * The narrator, who is part of a mobile television crew, interviews Professor Morteshang of the University of Chicago, who has built a rocket for a flight to Venus. Morteshang claims that previous space flights failed because they used electrical propulsion of some sort and were thereby affected by the solar wind (my term). Rockets would not be affected. * The two men become friendly, whereupon Morteshang takes Shepherd into his confidence: The space flight is really a hoax. The rocket is real, but Morteshang plans to parachute out of the rocket, hide out for a year or so, then claim to have returned to Earth. After a time he will uncover the hoax. * Shepherd agrees to work with him as publicity agent and writer. * The rocket takes off, Shepherd waits for a year, but there is no word from the professor. But then a message comes from Alaska. Shepherd flies there, and in the wilderness finds Morteshang, ill with pneumonia, and three green-skinned humans. Puzzled, Shepherd reads Morteshang's diary and learns the incredible truth. Morteshang dropped the key to the rocket door, could not leave the rocket in time, and really went to Venus, where he had adventures. * The party returns to civilization, where the professor is honored, lionized, and feted. But there is a reaction. Envious competitors and hostile scholars unite in proclaiming the whole story a fraud. Through circumstance and bad luck, the critics win out, and Morteshang is in disgrace. The final clincher was the statement of a waiter who overheard Morteshang and Shepherd plotting. * All this causes a change of plans. Morteshang had planned to send the three Venusians home on a new rocket ship, but now he decides to accompany them, since he seems to be in love with one of them, the beautiful Princess Loama. Shepherd watches them leave. * *Miscellaneous:* The Venusians are ahead of us scientifically, but their spacecraft cannot penetrate the space currents. * While on Venus, Morteshang had high adventures and perils, but these are only mentioned in a tongue-in-cheek throwaway. * The Venusians who accompanied Morteshang constituted a cultural mission to Earth. * Intelligent, with amusing touches.

   1353. **THE WORLD WITHOUT NAME**. *Wonder Stories,* March 1931. Ill. Marchioni.

Short story. * The story begins in Steinhilde's laboratory, where the police are investigating his disappearance. Among a mass of mysterious equipment is a small pile of ashes; the assumption is that Steinhilde has been incinerated. White, Steinhilde's friend, saw Steinhilde, armed, step through the machinery and disappear, but the police do not believe him and regard him with suspicion. * On working through Steinhilde's lab notes, White discovers what really happened. Steinhilde perfected matter transmission and with his superradio established communication with an unidentified extraterrestrial civilization. He sent a kitten and his lab assistant Josef through to the other world, then discovered, too late, that the other people are hostile and plan to invade Earth through his transmitter. They have been torturing Josef, and Steinhilde has gone through to rescue him, obviously unsuccessfully. * White, taking an automatic from the sleeping detective assigned to watch him, passes through the machine into the other world, which has a low gravity. By virtue of his surprise appearance, he rescues the other Earthmen and fights off a gladiatorial beast that the natives set upon him. The kitten is useful as an attention distracter. Back on Earth, Steinhilde smashes his machine and shouts curses at Mars, which is presumably the other world. * *Miscellaneous:* The Martians are humanoid, about seven feet tall, thin, and yellow skinned. They would seem to be ahead of us scientifically. * Competent action work.

   1354. **THE SPACE ROVER**. *Astounding Stories,* February 1932. Ill. Wesso.

Short story. * *Time:* the interplanetary future. *Place:* much of

Sloat, Edwin K. (*continued*)

the solar system. * Evan Winford is captaining a small spaceship manned by convicts who have escaped from the prison mines of Mercury. Winford and his associates have all been unjustly imprisoned, some because of the capitalist scoundrel Silas Teutoberg. * The fugitives come upon the *Golden Fleece*, a cargo ship that is incidentally smuggling valuable iridium, and seize it. They are now space pirates. But their freedom does not last long, for when they enter the atmosphere of Callisto, they are captured by a space patrol ship. A prize crew put aboard, the *Golden Fleece* heads for the prisons of Mercury. * Teutoberg now makes an appearance. Appointed governor of Ganymede, he was reported lost in space, but his ship now appears, ready to hijack the *Golden Fleece* for the sake of its iridium. * After ebb and flow of conflict, Winford retakes the *Golden Fleece* and heads for the outer planets, where he can sell the iridium for a great sum. Teutoberg is dead. The space patrol has been largely murdered by Teutoberg. * *Miscellaneous:* disintegrator rays, humanoid Martians and Venusians.

1355. **THE MASTER OF STORMS.** *Wonder Stories*, July 1932. Ill. Paul.

Short story. * *Time:* The near future; the twentieth century is mentioned as in the past. * The background and narrative are confusing, but the country would seem to be governed by the Secret Council of the League of the Cities; the Workers, who are in some way subordinate to the Cities, are organized like a union with a leader (Hogan) who is either corrupt or simply obstructive. * Allard, a great engineer, is determined to set up weather control machines on the Southwestern deserts and elsewhere. This amounts to rainmaking for dry areas. For selfish reasons both the Secret Council and the Worker leadership are against the project or wish to control it, and Allard is subject to life-threatening attacks, capture, and torture before the situation is cleared away by a Worker revolt and the establishment of a new nation based on the historic twentieth-century model. The title refers to Allard's system of weather control, which is invoked to help the revolution. * The story could have stood editing for organization. * The contents page and the running heads carry the story as "Master of Storms."

1356. **BEYOND THE PLANETOIDS.** *Amazing Stories*, August 1932. Ill. Morey.

Short story. * *Time:* the interplanetary future. *Place:* the asteroid belt and space near Jupiter. * Tom Basil, who has information about a fabulously rich mining claim, is shipping on the *Polaris*, which is captured by the space pirate Corvus, a cold, sardonic sadist. Corvus, however, does not know Tom's identity yet, but merely plans to sell him as a slave at the slave marts on Pluto. * But when Corvus's *Medusa* lands on an Earth-like asteroid that is a pirates' rendezvous, Tom finds an opportunity to escape. Another vessel lands, the old *Death Head*, captained by the swaggering pirate Morto. Secretly taking the place of one of Morto's crew, after the *Death Head* takes off, Basil emerges, claims to be a deserter, and asks to join Morto. * The idea, unfortunately, is unsuccessful, for Morto, who is just as cruel as Corvus, does not accept recruits and announces that he will feed Tom to his pet horde of Martian death mice—creatures like land piranhas. * The situation seems hopeless, but luck intervenes. A meteor strikes the ship. During the resulting confusion the death mice, who have escaped, eat Morto and most of his crew, while Tom and a few surviving captives snuggle safe in powered space

suits. * It is now Corvus's turn again. Corvus has learned Tom's identity and is determined to capture him. The old *Death Head* would have no chance against the *Medusa*, which is one of the finest ships in space, but Tom has a trick ready. Out of the ship in space in their space suits, he and his comrades watch while the malfunctioning motor in the *Death Head* explodes, destroying both ships. Tom will proceed to Callisto, where there are settlements. * *Miscellaneous:* Space travel seems to be some sort of electronic propulsion, with emergency traditional rockets. Disintegrating rays and force screens are standard. All the planets seem to be habitable, with humanoid populations, on out to Pluto and beyond. * Essentially a Caribbean pirate story, but also a a reasonable space-adventure story in the wildest pulp manner.

1357. **LOOT OF THE VOID.** *Astounding Stories*, September 1932. Ill. Wesso.

Short story. * *Time:* the interplanetary future. *Place:* mostly on Titan. * The old Martian has somehow identified Dick Penrun as the last descendant of the great space pirate Captain Halcon, and is about to pass him the map locating Halcon's treasure, when—the Martian is killed; a mysterious stranger steals half the map; a beautiful young villainess makes her appearance; and Penrun is almost murdered several times. * The treasure is hidden in the caverns of Titan, a satellite that is overrun with highly intelligent trap-door spiders. Penrun, fortunately, is one of the few men to have visited Titan before, and even with only half the treasure map, he stands a good chance of success. * Arriving at about the same time as his enemies, he rescues the young woman (who is not a villainess, but a victim), eludes the spiders, evades the villains, and finds the treasure. The spiders immobilize the villains' space ship, but Penrun and the young woman leave with a fair amount of Captain Halcon's loot. * A throwaway item: The trap-door spiders sting their prey and keep them paralyzed for centuries, as food for young spiders to hatch out upon and eat. Among the paralyzed prey that Penrun met on his previous visit was an Elizabethan Englishman who had reached Titan in a spaceship made of iron and wood. * Skimpy and unconvincing even within the parameters of such adventure fiction.

1358. **THE VIBRATION.** *Amazing Stories*, December 1932. Ill. Morey.

Short story. * *Time:* a little later than 1942. *Place:* mostly in Siberia. * The stability of the world is seriously threatened by enormous periodic shocks of unknown origin. Tokyo is in ruins; skyscrapers are toppling in New York and Chicago; tidal waves are sweeping from the north. The best theory is that in some fashion the ocean has penetrated into the hot interior of the Earth, causing steam explosions. * Millionaire adventurer George Darrell has been commissioned by the Geographic Society to discover what is happening. George almost misses an essential clue when he rebuffs beautiful young Evelyn Tulner who asks for help in locating her missing father. But then a connection clicks: Professor Tulner has developed by far the world's most powerful explosive. * Evelyn provides the key. Her father had been approached by Moklov, the half-mad, deposed dictator of Russia, and Moklov is undoubtedly causing the shocks from a monastery in southern Siberia. * A rapid flight to Siberia confirms this hypothesis, for there is Professor Tulner being tortured by Moklov, who insists that Tulner summon Evelyn to Siberia. The lecherous Moklov has Intentions for her. Aiding

Sloat, Edwin K.

Moklov are fifty wild-eyed fellow Communists, although many of them can be discounted as perpetually drunk on vodka. * All ends well. Moklov falls down into the explosion pit, and the vibrations will stop. * In this future world planes go 600 miles per hour, and there is advanced television. * Routine.

1359. **THE THREE SUNS OF EV**. *Amazing Stories*, May 1933. Ill. Morey.

Short story. * When laboratory assistant Neis assures arrogant, opinionated Professor Humphrey that he can make a demonstration that will overturn relativity, Humphrey gives him permission to go ahead. Unfortunate, for Neis cares nothing about relativity; he really uses the professor's equipment to summon a gigantic rocket ship that takes away Neis, Humphrey, the professor's daughter Winifred, and the professor's two other assistants, one of whom is the narrator. * *Background*: Neis is really a secret agent from the planet Ev. Ev, which is a planet in a triple star system, is inhabited by two races, the subservient human Ons, of which Neis is a member, and the Thaks, giant crustacean-like creatures, who rule. * The planet Ev is undergoing seismic dissolution because of the gravity of the triple suns, and the Thaks, despite their superscience, need scientific help. Since Earth is similar to Ev, the Thaks have sent Neis here, in the hope that Terrestrial science may provide new insights into their problem. Neis was instructed to build a suitable scientific library. He has failed, however, and has brought only one scientist. * The Thaks do not accept his excuse that one live scientist is worth more than a library, and Neis is in disgrace. He hopes to save his skin by turning Winifred over to his ruler's harem. * Things go badly. Humphrey is inadequate and dies. As punishment for his bungling, Neis is inoculated with a painful death fungus. When the planet begins to fly apart, the Thaks leave in spaceships, abandoning the Ons and the Terrestrial captives. * But when Winifred shows kindness to the dying Neis, he gratefully reciprocates by taking them to a partially fitted-out spaceship. Fighting their way through panic-stricken crowds, the three gain the ship, and return to Earth. The narrator and Winifred spend the four-hundred year journey in suspended animation, just as they did when traveling to Ev. When they awaken, they see a new Terrestrial civilization. Neis is a pile of dust. * Routine.

[Anonymous]
Presumably a British writer.

1360. **SMASHING ATOMS**. *Scoops*, 3 March 1934. Ill. S.D.

Boys' fiction. * Short story. * Great scientist Grant Ransome has abandoned his academic position, and, as a near recluse, is working with high voltages on smashing atoms. His first success is somewhat mixed, destroying his equipment and killing a would-be burglar with radiation. * Ruthless oil czar Joseph Martin, hearing of Ransome's progress, tries to buy in on an insultingly low level, but Ransome refuses. Instead, he obtains funding from the Hon. Malcolm St. John Selwyn, who serves as action hero. When the vicious Martin's air bombers raid Ransome's establishment, Selwyn fights them off, indeed, sets fire to Martin's nearby oil storage tanks. The fire gets out of hand, threatening a nearby town, whereupon Ransome, who has developed a disintegrator as a sideline to atomic energy, disintegrates the flaming masses. Martin, eating crow, tries to

buy the disintegrator, but Ransome will suppress it.

SMITH, CLARK ASHTON (1893-1961)

U.S. (California) poet, contributor to the fantastic pulp magazines. Member of the circle surrounding H. P. Lovecraft, who regarded his work highly. In poetry, a traditionalist often in the mode of fin de siècle mannerism. In prose an experimentalist at times, concentrating on lapidary effects that do not always succeed. Contributed a fair amount of supernatural and horror fiction to *Weird Tales*, some of it effective. One of the pioneers in exotic fantasy in highly fantastic milieus. Work is often macabre and morbid, with a strong note of sadism, toying with pain, decay, and death, presumably with the intention of arousing horror in the reader. In science-fiction, weak as a composer of well-wrought stories, but always intelligent and often a pioneer in the inclusion of philosophic ideas. See also the collaboration E. M. Johnston and Clark Ashton Smith.

1361. **MAROONED IN ANDROMEDA**. *Wonder Stories*, October 1930. Ill. Paul.

(Reprinted in Smith, *Other Dimensions*.)

Short story. * *Time*: the interplanetary future. *Place*: in space and on a planet of Delta Andromedae. * Captain Volmar's expedition has ventured the deepest yet into interstellar space, and certain members of his crew wish to turn about and return to Earth. A mutiny, involving three men, about a third of the crew, is crushed. Volmar now announces that he will maroon the mutineers on the first available planet, whether it is habitable or not, without food, weapons, or survival materials. * Volmar, who is a man of his word, thereupon abandons Adams, Deming, and Roverton on a planet of Delta Andromedae. The air is breathable, though not pleasant, and the planet has somewhat heavier gravity than Earth. * The three men now experience horrors such as one later came to expect of Clark Ashton Smith's work: man-eating plants, nasty semi-intelligent natives who try to sacrifice the maroons, fixed monstrosities and mobile monstrosities, all described with gusto. Adams is killed, and the other two men are on the edge of death when the spaceship returns. Volmar embarrassedly admits that he overreacted after the mutiny. Besides, all the rest of the crew have died in various ways, and he needs men. Is all forgiven? * *Miscellaneous*: The natives are small, humanoid, one-eyed, generally reptilian, and primitive in culture. * While wandering through perils and torments the castaways came upon rather elaborately carved monoliths. * The writing is literate, but the story is synthetic, flat, and dull, despite the horrors. * For a sequel see #1363, "The Amazing Planet."

1362. **AN ADVENTURE IN FUTURITY**. *Wonder Stories*, April 1931. Ill. Marchioni.

(Reprinted in Smith, *Other Dimensions*.)

Short story. * *Time*: mostly about A.D. 15,000. * Hugh Pastor, the narrator, becomes friendly with Conrad Elkins, a rather strange, but amiable and highly intelligent man. Eventually Elkins takes him into his confidence. He is a time traveler from about A.D. 15,000. He has come to the twentieth century to do research on human sexuality, since our age was the last in which the male-female birth ratio was close. Future man, he states, is in danger of extinction; females are often sterile, and there is an enormous preponderance of male births. But he has discovered that the twentieth century knows even less about such matters than does his own age. * Elkins (future name Kronous Alkon)

Smith, Clark Ashton (*continued*)

now invites Pastor to visit the future, where he will pass as a colonial from Pallas. As Elkins explains, time is the fourth dimension, and time travel is by machine powered by concentrated cosmic rays. * The two men arrive in the future without mishap. Akameria, capital city Djarma (on the site of old New York), is socially much like late Rome, with manors, luxury, and slaves. Smith, unlike most science-fiction authors, wastes no sympathy on the slaves, who are Venusians, described as hairy, bestial, savage submen. Treated very brutally, they are often bossed by Martian overseers, Martians being tall, large-chested, thin-limbed men of the classical sort. * As Pastor soon observes, the Earthmen, though highly civilized, are somewhat apathetic and ineffectual, paralleling their sexual decline. * The future culture is on the edge of collapse. There are repeated slave revolts, and in a short time the human race is under an organized, total attack from armed slaves controlled by Martians, who are taking over Earth. Conventional rays of the day are reinforced by frightful plagues released by the Martians. Mankind, after taking short refuge in the Arctic, where the plagues cannot flourish so well, abandons Earth, survivors resettling on the asteroids and elsewhere. Alkon sets the time machine to return Pastor to his own era. * *Miscellaneous:* Alkon gives Pastor a brief future history. Our period ended in great wars, followed by the extinction of civilization. Cyclical rises and falls followed, with an Amazon period as the most bloody. In this period female births greatly predominated, and society was matriarchal. When the Amazons were overthrown, only a few hundred thousand humans survived. * In Alkon's time, because of the shortage of women, polyandry is practiced. * Unusual in early science-fiction for its totally pessimistic attitude, and typical of Smith in the treatment of horrors.

1363. THE AMAZING PLANET. *Wonder Stories Quarterly*, Summer 1931. Ill. Marchioni.
(Reprinted in Smith, *Other Dimensions*.)
Short story. * Sequel to #1361, "Marooned in Andromeda." * *Time:* the interplanetary future. * The *Alcyone*, after long travels, comes to a planetary system of a star in the constellation Serpens. Captain Volmar and Roverton land, leave the ship to explore, and immediately fall into trouble. While trying to elude a monstrosity, they are captured in nets by gigantic primitive humanoid creatures. Carrying the Earthmen off, the monsters then sell them to civilized dwarves, who take them in an air vessel to a weird futuristic city. The dwarves, who are concerned with studying them, provide suitable atmosphere and put the men through a barrage of medical and scientific tests. * Exactly what the dwarves have in mind is not clear to the men, who panic and try to escape. They fight and race their way through the city, until they are finally trapped and tied to a platform, which carries them up into the sky, where the *Alcyone* picks them up. The dwarves apparently want no more to do with them. * The plot, which is primarily a chase sequence, is entirely secondary to the lush, highly detailed description of the city of the dwarves. * The dwarves are about three feet tall, with very large heads, tiny waists, and spindly arms. Another form of life, presumably the laboring class, is gigantic with a face full of tentacles. As weapons the dwarves use paralysis rods, paralysis gas, and a rod with a cone that burns matter instantaneously. * Smith's conversations are unbelievably stilted.

1364. THE CITY OF SINGING FLAME. *Wonder Stories*, July 1931. Ill. Paul.
(Reprinted in Smith, *Out of Space and Time*, in Margulies and Friend, *From off This World*, and in Derleth, *The Other Side of the Moon*.)
Short story. * *Place:* California, and an other-world. * Essentially the diary and notes of Giles Angarth, a writer of fantastic fiction who has disappeared. * Angarth relates that while wandering around the hills he sees two upright stones that look like eroded pillars. On passing between them, he undergoes a dimensional wrench and finds himself in an other-world with strange-colored vegetation and a cyclopean city in the distance. Apprehensive, he returns to his own land between comparable pillars, but revisits to the other-world. He approaches the strange city, lured on by an irresistible, sweet sound. Other strange forms of intelligent life are also headed toward the source of sound, which is a fountain of flame in the heart of the city. The flame rises and falls, the sound similarly rising and falling, and the other strange beings cast themselves into the flame, like moths into a candle flame, and disappear. * Angarth can resist the lure, since he has blocked his ears somewhat, but still feels the overpowering urge. He decides to share his experience with another person, the artist Ebbonly, with whom he ventures again into the other-world. Ebbonly, apparently more empathetic or of less stern stuff, succumbs to the message of the singing flame and leaps in. Angarth returns to our world, writes his final message and reenters the other-world. * *Miscellaneous:* The natives of the other-world are slow-moving, black humanoid giants; they are not unfriendly, but are remote. * A rather good story, well imagined. For a sequel see #1365, "Beyond the Singing Flame."

1365. BEYOND THE SINGING FLAME. *Wonder Stories*, November 1931. Ill. Paul.
(Reprinted in Smith, *Out of Space and Time*, and in Margulies and Friend, *From Off This World*.)
Short story. * Sequel to #1364, "The City of Singing Flame." * *Place:* California and other-worlds. * Hastane, who received Angarth's notes about the strange world of the singing flame, decides to venture into the other dimension and experience its wonders. After some difficulty he finds the entrance, passes through, and discovers a situation different to Angarth's reports. There are no throngs of pilgrims; the city itself is barred and closed to access; and the area is about to be attacked by fantastic siege towers controlled by an alien, hostile civilization. Hastane encounters two moth-like beings who carry him over the city ramparts and take him to the fane of the singing flame. Along the way, the moth-beings telepathically inform him that the attackers resent the loss of their citizens to the flame and are determined to destroy the city. Thus, Hastane and the two mothmen are the last pilgrims. * Carried through the flame, Hastane discovers to his surprise that it does not mean death, as the previous explorers and he had assumed, but entry into a new, even more-inner world, a pocket universe of incredible beauty and delightfulness. Angarth and Ebbonly welcome him. * The inner world, they inform Hastane, is also a gateway to wonderful explorations of the universe—but they must make haste, for once the flame is destroyed, if Hastane has not been in the inner world long enough, he will not be able to pass through. * Alas, Angarth is right. The flame collapses, as does the inner world, and the three men find themselves in the ruins of the city, which has been almost razed by the enemy. They sadly make their way

Smith, Clark Ashton (*continued*)
back to our world. * A good mood story.

1366. **THE ETERNAL WORLD**. *Wonder Stories*, March 1932. Ill. Paul.

Short stories. * A metaphysical concept translated into science-fiction. * Christopher Chandon, Californian maverick scientist, has isolated and can augment the negative time force. Related to fourth-dimensional time, his discovery will not take him into the past or the future, but across the stream of time that permeates the cosmos. He has also built a cylinder in which he plans to travel. He recognizes that his venture is risky, but he is bored with life. * After flashing through an infinitely varied panorama of planets and their ambiences, he finds himself in a strange world of frozen statue-like objects and weird perspective. As he realizes, he has projected himself beyond time, into a world where even the ether is a nonconductor of time. It is absolute stasis. Life is impossible, as is death, and he will remain in "a catalepsy of the senses, in a bright Nirvana of contemplation." Forever. * But there is an intrusion, a spindle-like vessel obviously operated by the same time force that Chandon used. From this vessel emerges a gigantic arm, which seizes and hauls away three of the frozen statuesque entities and also Chandon's cylinder. * In the vessel Chandon sees that his captors or saviors (it is still indeterminate which they are) are strange creatures with round bodies, two heads joined by a glittering membrane, and a multitude of lower limbs that serve for both locomotion and prehension. Perhaps this is a form of inorganic, metal life. * Chandon has a feeling of thawing, now that he is back in space-time, and sees that the gigantic figures brought out of the timeless world—called variously the Eternal Ones or the Timeless Ones—are also assuming life, which the insect-like people freeze with rays. * On reaching their home planet, the raiders start to lift the Eternal Ones out of their vessel. But one of the giant figures breaks into life, resists the freezing rays of the insect people, and grows to enormous size. The others, despite the efforts of the raiders, also assume life. There is a struggle of wills as the raiders try to restrain the Eternal Ones, whose power they had planned to use in war, but the raiders are no match for the titans, who grow to incredible size and systematically destroy the planet, which they kick into its sun. All through this, Chandon has been held safely on the shoulder of an Eternal One. * They pass through gulfs of time and space, past countless worlds, before the Eternal Ones reach our solar system, where they replace Chandon on Earth. The great ones then return to their contemplation beyond time. * An excellent story. Far superior to Smith's earlier stories. It is surprising that it has never been collected or anthologized.

1367. **THE INVISIBLE CITY**. *Wonder Stories*, June 1932. Ill. Paul.

(Reprinted in Smith, *Other Dimensions*.)

Short story. * *Place:* Chinese Turkestan, south of the Koko Nor. * Misfortune has plagued the Furnham Expedition, which is seeking the archeological remains of the ancient city of Kobar; only Furnham and Langley are left. Their native guides have abandoned them in the middle of the desert, fearing to enter a tabu area, and Furnham and Langley are near death from thirst. * They come upon a strange artificial looking depression and then run into invisible barriers, the walls of an invisible city. Hoping to find water, they feel their way down into the depression, even though they cannot see the stair treads beneath

them or the walls about them, until they smell a sweetish odor and collapse. * They awaken to find themselves in the company of the inhabitants of the city, which they now see as a misty vague construction. Their captors (the Tiisin) tell Furnham and Langley telepathically that they will not be harmed, but they cannot leave, since the Tiisin wish no further contact with humans. Furnham and Langley, instead, will be adapted gradually to life in the city, which is visible by ultraviolet light only. Indeed, the humans have already received injections so that they can perceive what is about them. * *Background:* The Tiisin, who are roughly humanoid, but with compound ears, large round eyes, and a trunk instead of a lower face, are descended from inhabitants of the missing ultraviolet planet that once existed between Mars and Jupiter. Ages ago when they saw that their planet was about to explode, they built a huge spaceship and migrated to Earth. * A Tiisin mentor now takes the men through a city filled with fantastic architecture to a huge room where there is a glowing, egg-shaped object called the Deir, which imparts nourishment to the Tiisin. Their guide urges the men to approach it and receive its emanations to continue their transformations. * Furnham and Langley, seeing a chance at escape, seize the Deir and threaten to smash it if they are not released. The Tiisin agree, with ill grace, and the men make their way out. As they leave, hostilities begin, whereupon the men fire a shot at the Deir. There is a cataclysmic explosion, destroying the invisible city, but releasing the men, who find the Tarim River nearby. * On the flat side. Smith does not handle well the transition in the Tiisin from peaceful hosts to evil monsters. The sense of menace does not emerge.

1368. **FLIGHT INTO SUPER-TIME**. *Wonder Stories*, August 1932. Ill. Paul.

Short story. * *Time:* 1940 and super-time. *Place:* other worlds. * A manuscript sent back through time by the maverick scientist Domitian Malgraff retails his adventures. Theorizing that it is possible to separate time from space, Malgraff isolates time energy, constructs a small globular vessel for traveling, and sets out with his Chinese servant and companion. He is soon surprised to learn that he is also moving in space and has left the solar system. * Passing stars and planetary systems, the two men finally crash-land on a planet that is somewhat Earth-like, but turns out to be covered by the most horrible giant carnivorous plants. As they watch, they see a strange humanoid figure something like a giant insect trying to escape the plants. They rescue the fugitive (Tuoquan), who is obviously an intelligent being, but are now themselves in great peril. Tuoquan had been dropped among the horrible plants by enemies who are determined on his death. When, watching from a nearby spaceship, they see that he has been rescued by Malgraff, they attack the time globe. Malgraff barely escapes into time. * The time sphere continues its travels through space, next landing on an Earth-like planet in the middle of a battle between humanoid armies, one savage, the other civilized. Their arrival decides the battle in favor of the civilized people, who carry the time sphere to their city. * There a new peril awaits the travelers, for they come under the scrutiny of an enormous robot fighting machine that regards them with hostility. A visitor from another time and space area, it is the tyrannical ruler of the planet. Malgraff and his associates seem doomed as the robot prepares an attack, but they are saved by the arrival of another time machine, a polyhedron in which Torquan's enemies have followed Malgraff. * The robot and the crew of the polyhedron attack each other. The

Smith, Clark Ashton (*continued*)

battle is fairly even, with disintegrating rays, but ends in a titanic explosion that destroys both combatants. * Malgraff and his companions are now the honored guests of the people of the new planet, small humanoid creatures with vestigial wings, who possess a superior science. They are delighted to be rid of the obnoxious robot. * An imaginative story. The robot fighting machine is brilliantly described.

1369. **MASTER OF THE ASTEROID**. *Wonder Stories*, October 1932. Ill. Paul.

(Reprinted in Derleth, *Strange Ports of Call*, and in Smith, *Tales of Science and Sorcery*.)

Short story. * *Time:* 1980 as seen from A.D. 2030. *Place:* the asteroid belt. * An examination of the psychology of space life, particularly breakdown under stress. * In 2030 a disabled spaceship containing a human skeleton is discovered on the asteroid Phocea, along with a diary explaining what had happened. * In 1980 the Earth maintains a small fifteen-man colony on Mars, but life there is precarious and men snap under the strain. Three men break down and, convinced that Mars has become overcrowded what with their dozen associates, seize a spaceship and take off for Ganymede or Europa, which are presumed to be habitable. * The ship, the *Selenite*, is not properly stocked with air, water, or fuel for a flight of this duration and chanciness, but the men, impelled by their mental condition, do not observe this or care. Indeed, their mental degeneration has progressed to the point that ordinary arithmetic is beyond them. * The story is told through the log or diary of Beverly, the sanest of the three. One of his comrades, suffering from horrible hallucinations, commits suicide by leaping into space; the other becomes a homicidal maniac, and Beverly is forced to shoot him in self defense. * The *Selenite* crashes on Phocea, a fairly large asteroid. Beverly is not injured, but the vessel is disabled, with the doors so crushed that they cannot be opened. There are no air leaks, and, with the death of his associates, Beverly has adequate supplies. * Although Beverly has nothing to hope for, he still has a will to live. After a time he sees outside the quartz-glass window slender, insect-like beings of some intelligence, who are interested in the spaceship. They obviously regard it with religious awe, and it becomes a sort of shrine to which they make offerings. As aphelion approaches, however, their number lessens, and some lie dead around the ship. * Beverly, too, would not have long to live, since his air is running out. He espies a strange, mist-like being gliding along toward the ship. Obviously hostile, it passes through the glass of the spaceship, and Beverly's journal ends. * *Miscellaneous:* The natives of Phocea, insect-like beings, are primitive in culture; Beverly refers to them as walking sticks. * The planetoid has a coarse sort of brittle vegetation. * The expedition of 2030 finds Phocea lifeless. * Well-handled and original.

1370. **THE DIMENSION OF CHANCE**. *Wonder Stories*, November 1932. Ill. Paul.

(Reprinted in Smith, *Other Dimensions*.)

Short story. * *Time:* 1976. *Place:* Nevada and another dimension. * The United States and Japan are currently at war. A crisis is at hand. The great spy Sakamoto, who has acquired top secret military information, is flying away with associates in his rocket plane. In pursuit are Morris of the Secret Service and Markley of the Air Corps, in Markley's superior aircraft. * As the Americans gradually overtake Sakamoto, they see his plane disappear into a haze. Then they themselves pass into the haze and emerge into an bizarre other-world. The engine of their plane dies, and the two men are forced to land. * It is incredible. As they move about, they see that they are in a world of multi-colored water, strange geological formations, perpetually shifting landscapes and elevations, varying gravitation and equilibrium, and a myriad of life-forms, each individual of which is totally different from the others. * As the fliers eventually realize, this is a world where there is no speciation, no uniformity; everything is unique, and much of it is hostile. (This aspect of the strange land is handled very well. As Smith puts it, "this whole chaotic cosmos . . . . had been shaped from atoms and electrons that had formed no fixed patterns of behavior, and whose one controlling law was chance. Nothing, apparently, was duplicated; the very stones and minerals were anomalous.") * Apart from dangerous hostile life and landscape, there are disintegrating "blowholes" into which the life-forms pour. * Morris and Markley seem doomed, but they are rescued by a small band of intelligent beings, the rulers of the strange other-world, who have managed to "forecast its very randomness and impose law and order on the ever-changing chaos." These creatures, the Masters, are ten-foot-tall, black, winged beings, reminiscent of dark angels, but benevolent. They communicate with the humans by a vague wordless telepathy. * The Masters bring the Americans to their plane and impose order on the area enough for the plane to operate and fly out of the dimension of chance. * As for Sakamoto and his comrades: They fought among themselves and perished in one of the disintegrating vortices. * *Miscellaneous:* In the world of chance weapons do not function, nor do the rocket plane's engines until protected by the Masters. * Very imaginative and well handled; one can ignore the war background.

1371. **DWELLER IN MARTIAN DEPTHS**. *Wonder Stories*, March 1933. Ill. Paul.

Short story. * *Time:* the interplanetary future. *Place:* the deserts of Mars. * An attempt to write a science-fiction horror story in the same mode as the supernatural horror stories in *Weird Tales*. * Three Earthmen, hard-bitten prospectors, are exploring the Chaur desert region for gold, which is said to be plentiful. Sighting an approaching sandstorm, they take refuge in a nearby cavern mouth, which as they soon see, is really the entrance to an enormous pit, around the side of which winds a pathway. * The men explore for a short distance, hearing strange plopping noises from below, then turn to make their way back up and out. Their way is blocked, however, by what seems to be a local cave variant of Martian intelligent life—etiolated, sometimes blind, and small. * Despite the prospectors' firearms, the Martians mob them and carry them far down into the pit. There at the bottom, in caverns lighted by phosphorescence, they come upon an ancient, blind Earthman, who explains elliptically and erratically the secrets of the pit. It is the Dweller, he claims, whom the Martians worship. The Earthman see a metal image of a strange monstrous beast. As the men watch, the Martians perform a ceremony, during which the Earthmen are overcome by stupor, perhaps an opiate emitted by the strange metal of which the idol is formed. * Two of the prospectors remain stupefied, but Bellman revives enough to see that the ancient Earthman has been torn to bits and half eaten. Bellman, realizing the perils of the pit, drives his somnolent comrades up the path to the outer world, all the while hearing strange noises—and there ahead of

Smith, Clark Ashton (*continued*)

them on the path is the monster of the image. It is huge, with a triangular head, suction-cup feet by which it can move perpendicularly up the shaft, and two tentacles emerging from its head. It approaches the two stupefied men, who are paralyzed, and its tentacles rip out their eyes. Bellman rushes madly to the surface, turning only once, to see the beast driving his two comrades back down the ramp, where they will join the Martians as eventual provender, both mental and physical. * Successful as a horror story, but the dialogue is poorly handled.

1372. **THE LIGHT FROM BEYOND**. *Wonder Stories*, April 1933. Ill. Paul.

Short story. * *Place:* California and another planet. * Smith here concentrates on the psychological reactions of a man exposed to a certain type of overwhelming visionary experience. * The narrative of Dorian Wiermoth, well-known illustrator of fantastic literature. The Wildean associations of the narrator's name, Dorian Grey and Sebastian Melmoth, do not seem to be significant. * Alone in his hermit-like life in his cabin in the Sierras, Wiermoth sees a strange glow in the distance among the rocks and trees. It seems to be like a revolving wheel of many-colored light. Associated with the phenomenon are an incense-like aroma and soft musical sounds. * Investigating, he finds on the spot where he saw the light a newly erected five-pointed cairn, in the center of which is a glowing stone shaped like a five-pointed star. Wiermoth finds it impossible to approach the cairn; he is prevented by a strange physical force that renders the cairn perpetually distant, no matter how long he walks toward it. Another oddity, as Wiermoth later observes, is that nearby vegetation has assumed a new beauty and vigor. * When Wiermoth next perceives the wheel of light, he also sees a strange boat-like vessel hovering above the cairn, while humanoid figures seemingly formed of an "immaterial matter" are demolishing the cairn and removing the star stone. Pushing forward, he is rapt into the radiance of the ship; when the strangers withdraw, he is drawn along with them, across alien dimensions into an other-world, the home of the aliens. * The visitors are friendly enough, but they are obviously puzzled what to do about Wiermoth. Wiermoth, however, observes. He now understands what the visitors were doing on Earth. Periodically they plant a seed there, to absorb Earth's coarser vigors, which are not present on their planet. They then bring the seed back to their own world. As Wiermoth watches, they plant the seed, which springs into fantastically exuberant life, bearing beautifully colored fruit. Aliens who seem faded and dim eat the fruit and regain vigor. * Wiermoth seizes a fruit, despite the mild objections of the visitors, and on eating it undergoes experiences that can only be described as mystical to the utmost. He understands the universe and all about it. But a reaction soon sets in. He feels depressed—and he finds himself back on Earth. * He does not know how he returned; whether the visitors brought him back to this dimensional world in their light-boat, or whether his return was a result of eating the fruit. In any case, he is now a partial being. Part of him remained in the other dimension, and he has lost his artistic ability. * *Miscellaneous:* The rotating lights and strange stone formations may be a reminiscence of the works of Charles Fort. * A very fine story.

1373. **THE VISITORS FROM MLOK**. *Wonder Stories*, May 1933. Ill. Paul.

Short story. * *Place:* California and the planet Mlok, on the other side of the galaxy. * The quest for artistic experience, in fantastic terms. * Sarkis, an artist who specializes in the macabre and fantastic, while wandering about the mountains comes upon two very strange beings: They are about four feet high, slab-shaped with top larger than bottom, the top fringed with feelers, and the bottom portion with trailing members. * They are friendly and telepathically invite Sarkis to accompany them. On their bodies appear images conveying further invitation to a new range of experience. * As Sarkis hesitates, sightseers come along and break the spell; the two beings disappear with the aid of a strange machine. * About a week later the two beings visit Sarkis in his studio and renew their offer to take him to their home planet, Mlok. He consents. * His first experiences on Mlok are horrible, what with heavier atmosphere and gravity, blinding glares, and the shock of being transferred from one frame of reference to another. He collapses in torments, which Smith describes fully. * The Mloki at first do not understand what is wrong, but when they recognize the problem, they alter his senses, his nervous system, and even his mind. Mlok still seems strange, but it is no longer horrible. He has also acquired new senses, including the ability to see more colors than humans do. When he is able to communicate with the Mloki, he learns that on visiting Earth they sensed his dissatisfaction and approached him. * After a time—how long, he can have no idea—Sarkis begins to feel homesick for Earth. The Mloki are prepared to adapt him further, but a new circumstance renders this unnecessary. Protoplasmic organisms that have the power to liquefy all other forms of matter invade the planet. Mlok is doomed. The inhabitants, deciding to die rather than move to another planet, return Sarkis to Earth. * But, horrors, Sarkis is still in his Mloki frame of perception, and Earth is now as horrible as Mlok first was to him. He can perceive nothing correctly. He goes mad and shortly thereafter dies, his illness a mystery to medical science. * *Miscellaneous:* Although it is not spelled out, the Mloki seem to travel by matter transmission. * An excellent story.

1374. **THE DEMON OF THE FLOWER**. *Astounding Stories*, December 1933. Unsigned ill.

Short story. * Supernatural fiction, more typical of *Weird Tales* than of a science-fiction magazine. * On the planet Lophai, plants are the dominant form of life, other forms living by sufferance. And ruling over the plants is the Voorqual, a demon in the form of a flower. A human priesthood tends to it, with human sacrifices. * Lunithi, chief priest and king of the planet, dares to rebel when Nala, his fiancée, is selected by the plant for its next victim. Remembering old tales of the Occlith, another demon that lives in the land and is not subservient to the Voorqual, he seeks it out. A bluish, cruciform pillar, it answers Lunithi's plea for instructions on how to kill the demon plant, but it adds that such a procedure may not be advisable. Lunithi does not take the opportunity to ask the further questions that the Occlith expects. * Returning to the temple, Lunithi drops poison into the plant's chalice that normally receives blood and watches as the Voorqual dies. But this is not the end. The priestess Nala enters, takes the position of the Voorqual, and is transformed into the demon plant. Then Lunithi knows that the Voorqual will forever rule over the land. * Told in Smith's Dunsanean manner, with heavy mood and elaboration of language. A rather good story. Not science-fiction.

1375. **THE PLUTONIAN DRUG**. *Amazing Stories*,

Smith, Clark Ashton (*continued*)
September 1934. Ill. Morey.
(Reprinted in Derleth, *The Outer Reaches* and in Parry, *Strange Ecstasies*.)
Short story. * *Time:* the twenty-first century. * Dr. Manners (a noted pharmacologist and medical research scientist) and Melcoth (a prominent sculptor) discuss the various drugs that have been discovered since space travel began. Among them are selinine, which has wiped out cancer; clithni from Ganymede, which bestows great longevity; and mnophka, which accelerates metabolism enormously. Most interesting of all, claims Manners, is plutonium, a fossil vegetable substance from Pluto that is perhaps billions of years old. It has the property of expanding the time sense so that the partaker sees, as in a controlled vision, both past and future. * Manners offers Melcoth plutonium in order to obtain clinical data. Melcoth thereupon sees his past clearly, in one direction, and his future, in another. But his future vision is very brief, perhaps a matter of minutes. * Manners, suspecting what the situation is, warns Melcoth against taking a certain route when he leaves, but Melcoth, missing the point, goes his way. He is sandbagged and killed, thus cutting off his future. * An excellent revivification of an otherwise threadbare motif.

SMITH, E[DWARD] E[LMER] Ph.D.. (1890-1965) and
GARBY, [MRS.] LEE HAWKINS (1892-1953)
Smith was a U.S. food chemist, author. Born in Sheboygan, Michigan. After various jobs graduated in chemical engineering from University of Idaho. Worked at Bureau of Agriculture in Washington during World War I. M.S., Ph.D. from George Washington University. In Michigan, chief chemist for F. W. Stock, later Director of Research, mostly on prepared flours and mixes, hence early nickname Doughnut Smith. Mrs. Garby was the wife of Dr. Carl Garby, a chemist who was Smith's college roommate. Mrs. Garby does not seem to have done any other writing.
According to accounts by Smith and Dr. Rodes Garby, the son of Mrs. Garby, the authors began their collaboration some time before 1919, when Smith and Dr. Garby were together in Washington. Smith and Mrs. Garby then continued their collaboration by correspondence after the Smiths moved to Michigan. It is not known what Mrs. Garby did, beyond the generality that she helped with some of the conversations and handled the romantic element. It is also possible that Mrs. Garby contributed the description of the elaborate wedding costuming and procedure on Osnome, an unusual element in a science-fiction novel. Dr. Carl Garby is said to have provided some of the scientific matter. After the story was finished, apparently in 1919, it was submitted to several magazines for publication, but was rejected. It was then revised, perhaps several times, before it was accepted by *Amazing Stories*. It is summarized in some detail because of its enormous historical importance.

    1376. **THE SKYLARK OF SPACE**. *Amazing Stories*,
August-October 1928. Ill. Paul.
(Reprinted in book form by [Buffalo Book Co.; Providence, R.I., 1946]. There are many paperback reprints.)
Novel. * Space opera. * *Time:* the near future. *Place:* Earth and unknown planetary systems around the universe. * The first full-fledged modern space-opera, with stern heroes of genius, black-hearted villains, pure maidens, and emotional clichés. * Perhaps the near future. * Richard Seaton, handsome, Herculean chemist

of genius, chances to run an electric current into copper and platinum wastes, and sees his apparatus fly off through the window in a straight line. Seaton realizes the implications: he has discovered a new power source. Exactly what it is, in modern terms, is not clear—releasing the strong force, smashing the atom, or what? But it can cause a tremendous explosion, and it is only chance that Seaton did not blow up half the United States. * Seaton, who is a canny man, sets up a fake repetition of his experiment for his associates and superiors, and then connives to gain position of the platinum wastes. With this, he and his multimillionaire engineer friend Reynolds Crane set up a company to do further research on Seaton's discovery, including the construction of a spaceship. * Seaton did not deceive everyone, however. One Marc DuQuesne, a saturnine, utterly pragmatic, selfish chemist who is Seaton's mental equal, figures out what must have happened, and going to Brookings of the Steel Trust, for whom he acts as an industrial spy, urges action. The two scoundrels try in various ways to acquire Seaton's secret preparation, but with only limited success; eventually their activities put Seaton and Crane on their guard. * DuQuesne, whose advice Brookings has been unwilling to follow, now urges kidnapping Dorothy Vaneman, Seaton's presumably platonic girlfriend, and exchanging her for the discovery. * Disguising himself as Seaton, DuQuesne arrives in a small spaceship imitated from Seaton's project and captures Dorothy. Also in the spaceship are a tool of Brookings, and Margaret Spenser, formerly Brookings's secretary, who knows too much and must be made to talk, then disposed of. * By accident the controls of the spaceship are jammed, and it takes off, reaching speeds thousands of times that of light, across the universe, out of control. It is captured by the gravity of a dark star, and there seems no way to escape, for the ship, in addition to being almost out of fuel, is simply not powerful enough. * Back on Earth Seaton and Crane figure out what has happened, and since they have a directional tracer on DuQuesne, they follow in their new spaceship, the *Skylark*, which is powerful enough to rescue DuQuesne and the two women. * But, in escaping from the dark star, the *Skylark*, too, runs out of control, far out into space. * It is now necessary to find fuel (copper). The explorers head for a solar system whose light shows evidence of copper, and land on Osnome, a planet much like Earth except that cupreous combinations are abundant. * The Earthmen are welcomed by a green-skinned human people, the men of Mardonale, who have a sword-and-ray-gun culture superior to ours. * Seaton amazes the natives with a little sleight of hand, especially with a salt shaker. He later learns that salt is incredibly rare on the planet, and is used as a catalyst to manufacture the supermetal arenak. * The voyagers receive an unfavorable impression of the ruler of Mardonale, an impression that is verified in an unexpected manner. One of the slaves attending Seaton constructs a small thought-transfer unit, which Seaton dons; by accident the mechanism also interchanges the memories of the slave, who is revealed to be Prince Dunark of Kondal, a nation of Osnome at war with Mardonale. Dunark explains that the king plans to kill the terrestrials and boil their bodies down for the salt they contain. * Seaton and company, and certain of the Kondalians escape, flying to Kondal, where they are welcomed. All through this, DuQuesne is treated with honor as Seaton's private captive. * Work now begins on a super-*Skylark*, a sphere with walls of arenak four feet thick. The new ship comes in handy when the

Smith, E. E., Ph.D. and Garby, Lee Hawkins (*continued*)

Mardonalian air fleet attacks. The spherical vessel simply zips in and out among the ships, crashing through the Mardonalian weapons. Kondal is now victorious. * The Earthmen return to Earth with some of the incredible wealth showered upon them by the Kondalians. When the ship is in Earth's atmosphere, DuQuesne parachutes out with a tube of radium worth a fortune. * *Miscellaneous:* Along the way to Osnome, the adventurers encounter a group of mental beings called the pure intellectuals, who materialize in various forms and promise to dematerialize the terrestrials, a simple task involving only calculation in ninety-five dimensions. The Earthmen manage to distract the entity sufficiently that it gracefully admits defeat and permits them to leave. (It is revealed in a sequel that the intellectual was toying with them and could have destroyed them at any time it wanted to.) * "The Skylark of Space," despite its imagination, is far from being a masterpiece of science-fiction. The writing is very bad, the characterizations are inept, the pacing is limp at times, and the plot is clumsy. In terms of ideas, it is, today, somewhat unpalatable, in its projection of colonialism, its ethnic polarities, its ultra-aggressive scientism, and its ridiculous sexist attitudes (perhaps Mrs. Garby's contribution). On the credit side, it conveys as no other earlier work did the zest of climbing into one's spaceship and joyriding into space, to see wonders. It offered a breakthrough comparable to the automobile in terrestrial travel, away from Earth out into the vastness of space. As for readability, the dustier passages can easily be skipped. * For a sequel see #1377, "Skylark Three."

SMITH, EDWARD ELMER, Ph.D..

See previous entry for biographical information.

   1377. SKYLARK THREE. *Amazing Stories*, August-October 1930. Ill. Wesso.

(Reprinted by Fantasy Press, Reading, Pa., 1948; also various paperback reprintings.)

Novel. * The second member of the *Skylark* series, following #1376. The main topics, apart from Seaton and DuQuesne's drives for power, are galactic empire and total genocide. * *Time:* the near future. *Place:* Earth and other planetary systems. * There are two subplot groupings, that associated with Seaton, and that associated with DuQuesne, Seaton's being much the larger and more important. * Seaton and his comrades are about to take off into space again with an improved *Skylark*, when they receive an unexpected visit from Dunark of Osnome. Since Seaton left the Green System, the Kondalians have massacred their enemies, the Mardonalians, but are in process of being themselves exterminated by invaders from another planet in the complex multiple-sunned system. These Urvanians, who are just as warlike and merciless as the Kondalians, are masters of superior science and weaponry. Dunark appeals for help; he wants a supply of "X"-metal (uranium? plutonium?), with which he intends to cause a planetary collision, destroying Urvania. Seaton and his associates, though not enthusiastic, agree to help. * As Seaton and Dunark's spaceships proceed together toward the planet that is rich in "X"-metal, they are attacked by an exploratory warship of the Fenachrone. * *Background:* The Fenachrone, who have determined to establish a space empire and rule the universe, are humanoid in appearance, short, extremely stocky, with stumpy legs and hypnotic eyes. They have probably evolved from reptilian-like carnivores. Incredibly

arrogant and aggressive, they consider themselves the master race of the universe, and, indeed, they are not far from it, with intelligence and science far superior to those of humans. At the moment, Fenachrone ships are exploring space preparatory to invasion, with instructions to destroy all ships encountered and to keep their presence secret. They communicate with their home planet via torpedoes. * When the Fenachrone attack the *Skylark* and Dunark's vessel, Seaton sees that his vaunted defensive and offensive weapons are only toys against the Fenachrone. His only recourse is to an undeveloped discovery that he had made some time before, a spherical zone of force that shuts off all matter or radiation, including gravity. Seaton does not understand it or recognize its potential, but he knows that when it is active, he is secure from attack, but cannot use his weapons. Unfortunately, the *Skylark* has limited energy to maintain the zone; when the ship reemerges, the Fenachrone will destroy it. * Actually, Seaton's incredible reflexes save the day. He zips out of the force zone, directs the *Skylark* on a collision course with the Fenachrone vessel, reestablishes the zone, and with its irresistibility cuts the enemy ship to shreds. (Apparently the Fenachrone, despite their technical prowess, have no automatic relays.) This done, Seaton mops up, fishes a space-suited Fenachrone into the Skylark, and rescues Dunark and his wife, whose ship was also destroyed. * Seaton now uses the Osnomian hypnotic device to read the mind of their captive, learning not only much technological information, but Fenachrone war plans, killing the captive in the process. * Seaton takes the remains of the Fenachrone ship to Osnome, where he begins a peace process between the warring planets of the Green System. His theme is that local quarrels must cease in the face of the far greater threat of the Fenachrone empire; as incentives to his plans he shares Fenachrone science and threatens to destroy the winning party if the war continues. Peace is established. * Seaton's next plan is to locate a semimythical race with superior science that exists somewhere in the Green System. According to folklore, such a people visited Osnome and Urvania millennia ago. Seaton's reasons for such a quest are simple: He knows that the Green System and Earth will be lost to the Fenachrone unless he can understand and fully use the zone of force. * In a surprisingly short time, Seaton finds his goal in the planet Norlamin, which is peopled by green-skinned humanoids who are far ahead of the Fenachrone scientifically. Since "X"-metal is totally absent in the Green System, however, Norlaminians have been unable to do more than occasional local space exploration. They know of "X"-metal theoretically, however, and welcome Seaton with projections even before he reaches their planet. Although the people of Norlamin are essentially quietistic, they agree that the Fenachrone must be stopped and give Seaton such scientific and technical aid as he needs. * The result is *Skylark III*, which is enormously more powerful than the previous vessels. * The Norlaminians, who are organized into superspecialist scientific guilds, understand much about the zone of force, which they declare is fifth-order material and subetheric. They establish a force projector with a neutronium lens on *Skylark III*. * Seaton now declares war on the Fenachrone via projection and blockades their home planet; with his fifth-order projector he destroys all Fenachrone warships known to be in space. Deciding upon total genocide of the Fenachrone, he blows up their home planet with copper-"X"-metal mines. * The only Fenachrone with the ability to foresee Seaton's plans is the master-scientist Ravindau,

Smith, E. E., Ph.D. (*continued*)

who has a little knowledge of fifth-order phenomena. Assembling fellow scientists into a gigantic spaceship, he leaves the planet hastily before Seaton's "blockade" is effective, aiming for a distant galaxy. Seaton pursues him and destroys his vessel in a super space battle, thus ending the Fenachrone menace. (The reader may regret the slaughter of Ravindau, who is more interesting than most of the other characters in the book, including the heroes.) * Now back to DuQuesne: After several failed attempts to murder Seaton and associates, DuQuesne builds a spaceship, and with a gunman associate (Dolly) sails off into space. His intention, like Seaton's, is to track down a superscience. In his case, it was early awareness of the presence of the Fenachrone in the Green System. Pretty much following Seaton's route, DuQuesne comes upon the rubble of Seaton's battle with the Fenachrone warship. He captures a space-suited survivor, who happens to be the chief engineer of the ship, and proceeds to read his brain much as Seaton did with his captive. DuQuesne, however, does not kill his captive, but strikes a bargain with him that neither side intends to keep. DuQuesne promises to release his captive if he will rebuild the spaceship's drive to match that of the Fenachrone and help the Earthmen acquire Fenachrone armament with which to kill Seaton. DuQuesne's real intention is to hijack a Fenachrone warship. His scheme must go astray, however, for there is a Fenachrone video recording of his ship being attacked by a patrol boat and DuQuesne and his associate being disintegrated. * *Miscellaneous:* To learn Fenachrone plans and to trace Ravindau, Seaton uses fossil light analyzed by projection. * Along the way to Norlamin Seaton and comrades visited a water world inhabited by friendly "porpoise-men" with an advanced but necessarily limited science and technology. * Seaton is now speculating about sixth-order phenomena. * At the end of the third and last installment is an Epilogue spoken by an ancient Norlaminian describing the preceding fiction as a three-dimensional moving picture of the great past, the beginnings of the League of Civilization, which now fills the first galaxy. He adds that the new Chief of the Galactic Council is to be Richard B. Seaton the fourteen hundred and sixty-ninth of Earth, the first Earthman to fill this office. This epilogue is omitted in book editions, where the narrative ends with the destruction of Ravindau's intergalactic cruiser. * Wild and woolly adventure with Smith's typical characteristics of drive, good ideas, imagination, sloppy sentiment where personal relations are concerned, lack of uniform tone, and sometimes excruciatingly bad writing. But it still held my attention when I reread it for the first time in perhaps fifty years. * For a sequel see #1378, "The Skylark of Valeron."

1378. **THE SKYLARK OF VALERON.** *Astounding Stories,* August 1934-February 1935. Ill. Dold.
(Reprinted in book form by Fantasy Press, Reading, Pa, 1949; also various paperback reprintings.)
Novel. * Sequel to #1377, "Skylark Three" and the third story in the Skylark series. * *Time:* not long after the previous story. *Place:* space, the Green System, and elsewhere. * The story has three narrative centers, DuQuesne, the Skylark group, and the people of the planet of Valeron, which is somewhere in a distant galaxy. * The DuQuesne subplot: DuQuesne and his gangster comrade were not killed when the Fenachrone rayed his vessel. Anticipating treachery on the part of his Fenachrone captive, DuQuesne was prepared for an attack. Injecting the Fenachrone

engineer with a lethal will suppressor, DuQuesne forced him to construct working models of the Earthmen, who hid in space suits while the dummies were disintegrated. DuQuesne gassed the cruiser that rayed their vessel, then captured a full-sized warship in a shootout. Intelligent enough to recognize that the Fenachrone home planet was in danger, he escaped its destruction by Seaton. * DuQuesne, who is dominated by two drives, revenge on Seaton and political power, now flies to Norlamin, where he persuades the brilliant but gullible scholars to build him a ship comparable to *Skylark III*, in which he can go seek his "associate," Seaton. Instead, he circles around to Earth, which he captures easily, fortifying it and setting up stupendous weapons. From Earth he undertakes a long-distance campaign against Norlamin, which he considers the only impediment to universal conquest. He is now planning to fit a planet filled with radioactive material with a space drive and crash it into Norlamin. * The Seaton subplot: Seaton, meanwhile, has again encountered the pure intellectuals of space, who threaten to destroy the party. Even *Skylark III* cannot withstand them, and the only escape for the explorers is rotation into the fourth dimension in the old original *Skylark*. * As three dimensional beings in a fourth-dimensional world, the humans have difficulties. Their mass is so great that the ship sinks many yards into the ground, and interpenetration is an enormous problem. The environment is flat and gloomy. The intelligent, but determinedly hostile, natives capture Seaton and Crane and besiege the trapped *Skylark* and the women. There is considerable slaughter before the men escape and the spaceship is rotated automatically back into our universe. All this happens in a tiny fraction of our time. * Now back in our universe, Seaton and crew are lost, with no idea which of the myriad visible galaxies is ours. They look about for a system similar to the solar system, partly to find beings with suitable star maps, partly for Seaton to build himself a new spaceship with an even larger mechanical brain potential than *Skylark III*. In this search the party comes upon the Earth-like planet Valeron, which is inhabited by humanoid beings. * The Valeron subplot: Besieged by amoeba-like chlorine-breathers, whom they call Chlorans, the men of Valeron are on the edge of succumbing when Seaton approaches and offers help in exchange for information. * A fairly long backflash now describes the history of Valeron. At some time in the past another solar system passed through the system of Valeron, threatening to destroy its human inhabitants. Considering racial survival paramount, the elite of Valeron entered subterranean shelters, defending them without mercy against those not fortunate enough to have entry. After the second system had passed, the survivors emerged and reestablished a new civilization, which is a strange mixture of anarchism and dictatorship, altruism and ruthlessness. * The men of Valeron soon observed, however, that a new planet had been left behind in their solar system. On investigating it, they discovered that it was inhabited by ferociously hostile amoeboids, who at once attacked. Valeron has since then been on the defensive, slightly inferior in weaponry and power to the Chlorans. Valeron was just about to go under when Seaton and company arrived. * With Seaton's Norlamin mentality and know-how, it is simple for the humans to beat off the chlorine breathers. Seaton now builds his supersuperspaceship with supersuper-mechanical brain capacity. * Transferring the planet of the Chlorans out of the system of Valeron to its original system, thus

Smith, E. E., Ph.D. (*continued*)

removing their menace indefinitely, Seaton now undertakes to rid the universe of the space intelligences. Setting up a supersuper-sphere of high-level force, he snares them and imprisons them in a tiny capsule. * Learning of the problems that DuQuesne is causing to Norlamin, Seaton now flies to Earth, easily shatters DuQuesne's forces and captures him. * DuQuesne willingly joins the space intelligences as a pure intellect, and with them is imprisoned in a capsule that is hurled into the fourth dimension and sealed for ages. * There is now nothing much left for Seaton to do, since his powers are almost divine, except take on Jehovah. * Rating: Unfortunately, more of the same as the preceding works, and less entertaining.

In the fourth and final novel in the Skylark series, *Skylark DuQuesne* (1965, book 1966), several themes are worked out. Smith retracts or dismantles much of Seaton's megalomanic activity. The space intelligences were still playing games with him, and he miscalculated badly on their exile. A Fenachrone remnant is permitted to survive; a new race of totally logical beings maintains a large space empire; fourth-dimensional transport is perfected; DuQuesne, who did not like being a disembodied intelligence, returns in the flesh; and the Chlorans that infest a galaxy are exterminated in mass genocide by Seaton and DuQuesne acting in collaboration. No longer so much a melodramatic villain, DuQuesne is, if not quite sanitized, more human and becomes the bearer of Faustian conservative values. Accompanied by a suitable consort, he sets out to found a space empire elsewhere.

1379. SPACEHOUNDS OF IPC. *Amazing Stories,* July-September 1931. Ill. Wesso.

(Reprinted in book form by Fantasy Press, Reading, Pa., 1947. Also by Ace Books, New York, 1966 and later.)

Novel. * *Time:* the interplanetary future. *Place:* mostly the Jovian system and Titan. * *Background:* The Earth has a world government, and the three inner planets, all roughly at the same scientific level, have formed an interplanetary league. The basis of space travel has been derived from Mars (which on first contact held a higher civilization than the other two planets, but lacked raw materials) and involves transmission of subatomic energy from planetary sources. Space stations monitor and correct flight patterns as spaceships pass by. Space travel seems to be pretty much a monopoly of the IPC, a commercial organization. * All the planets and their satellites (except the Moon and Titan) are Earth-like and habitable by humans. The peoples of Venus and Mars are roughly humanoid. Martians are gigantic, with a thick rugose skin and multiple nictitating eye membranes, while Venusians are closer to humans. Future scientists are not certain whether these likenesses are due to parallel evolution or common ancestry. During the story, other humanoid races will be met from Titan and Callisto. The Titanians, who are extremely thin humanoids, are unusual in having a metabolism designed for temperatures far below 0° Centigrade. * The humanoid peoples who arose on most of the Jovian satellites were almost all exterminated by the second major racial grouping of the solar system, the so-called hexans, who also arose on several of the Jovian satellites. The hexans, who are six-legged and like gigantic insects, are scientifically more advanced (militarily at least) than the various human races. An unspeakably foul, vicious, intractable race, they are utterly hostile to all other forms of intelligent life and are attempting to

wipe out humanity. At present their culture is centered on Jupiter itself, where they live in conflict with the third intelligent racial group, the Vorkul, who hold their own against the hexans and are biding their time for a master strike against them. The Vorkul, who are gigantic serpentine beings with wings and multiple arms, are scientifically the most advanced of the solar peoples, but are utter isolationists; they are totally unwilling to have any contact with the other peoples and are indifferent to matters outside Jupiter. * The story: On a routine flight of the space passenger cruiser *Arcturus*, Percival Stevens, scientific ace and troubleshooter, is courteously showing Nadia Newton, the daughter of the chief of IPC (the Interplanetary Corporation), around the ship, when the hexans attack with a disintegrator beam that slashes the *Arcturus* into neat segments. Since the ship has multiple safety compartments, there is not much loss of life, and the hexans (who apparently have not ventured among the inner planets before, or perhaps not very often) drag away the fragments of the dissected vessel and their occupants for study. * The first part of the story covers the adventures of Stevens and Nadia. Stevens, by creating a diversion among the *Arcturus*'s fragments, manages to extract a lifeboat away from the hexans and land it on Ganymede. There, with the assistance of Nadia, he constructs from scratch an electric power system and starts upon a superradio like the one he and his associates had been working on before he shipped on the *Arcturus*. During this scientific Robinsonade, Stevens and Nadia fall in love, but postpone activities until they can be married. * One thing is lacking: special metals for the radio valve (tube). The most likely source is a comet that orbits Jupiter. But when Stevens and Nadia reach the comet, they are attacked by a hexan space sphere and would have been killed had it not been for the intervention of a spaceship from Titan, which defeats the hexans. The friendly Titanians take Stevens and Nadia to their world, where they build a suitable radio tube for Stevens. The two Terrestrials earn their keep by repairing a power broadcasting plant on Saturn, which is too hot for Titanian comfort or safety. Back on Ganymede, Stevens sends out a signal to his associates. * The second series of episodes is concerned with the fate of the personnel and passengers of the *Arcturus*. As they are being hauled away in tow by the hexans, they are rescued by Callistans, humanoid people who have long been fighting a losing battle with the hexans of the Jovian system. The Callistans harbor the survivors until the arrival of the titanic IPC vessel *Sirius*, which incorporates the last word in armaments and is rendered even stronger by Callistan science. Other inner planet armaments move up. * The battle for the control of the solar system is ready to begin. The hexans would have won, since they were stronger and more numerous than the allied forces, but at this time the Vorkul of Jupiter decide to strike. Here the story is told from the point of view of the Vorkul. With super space fortresses and irresistible weapons, they smash the hexans utterly. There is no question, however, of friendly relations with the human races of the system; the Vorkul remain totally aloof. * Stevens and Nadia have married by now, with the Victorian sentimentality that appears, in such circumstances, in Smith's work. * Space opera, of course. Smith has taken pains with the power systems and weaponry, despite his great liberties with planetary geography, but the story, as is usually the case, is very uneven. The combination of a considerable amount of advanced scientific double-talk, women's magazine romance, and space

Smith, E. E., Ph.D. (*continued*)

battles does not succeed. The story, however, was very popular in its day.

1380. **TRIPLANETARY**. *Amazing Stories,* January-April 1934. Ill. Morey.

(Expanded, printed in book form by Fantasy Press, Reading, Pa., 1948, with various paperback reprints.)

Novel. Space opera. * *Time:* the interplanetary future. *Place:* Earth, space, and an unidentified planet in a different solar system far from Earth. * The story is concerned with two topics, the suppression of a notorious superscientific space pirate (gray Roger) and the first, unfortunately hostile, meeting of civilized cultures across interstellar space. * *Background:* The inner three planets (Venus, Earth, Mars) are united in Triplanetary, a league that controls space, but in general does not affect local autonomy on the planets themselves. Within this league is a top secret secret police headed by Virgil Samms, whom Smith rates highly, but a modern reader is likely to consider a freewheeling proto-Fascist. Samms's agents, who carry little metal identification badges that convey a peculiar electric shock, have apparently infiltrated much of civilization with gadgets and doodads more advanced than those generally around. In case of emergency decreed by Samms, his agents can supersede local space authorities. * Triplanetary civilization is pretty much a Terrestrial affair. Space travel is fairly advanced, with faster-than-light travel just slightly around the corner; sophisticated weapons include rays of all sorts, explosives, gases, and protective energy shields. Other humanoid races are to be found in the solar system, including Martians, Venusians, and a now defunct group called the Adepts of Jupiter. * The other pole of civilization is to be found on Nevia, circling an unidentified star. Mostly water covered, Nevia supports various races of intelligent fishes, who have superscience of a sort, and the dominant amphibians, who have flat, horizontal bodies, multiple legs, cone-shaped heads with multiple eyes, and tentacles emerging from their heads. These Nevians, who are about on the same level of scientific advancement as the solar system, are slightly ahead in faster-than-light travel, which they have already mastered. (Smith does not explain faster-than-light travel, simply asserts it.) Their cultural problem is a shortage of iron, which they use as fuel in their atomic engines. Thus, they have fitted out two enormous spaceships to search the galaxy for free iron. * Their astronomy, which is surprisingly backwards, assumes that planets are extremely rare. Thus, when Nerado's ship enters the solar system, he is astonished to see many planets, with iron, iron everywhere. * The plot: Conway Costigan (top undercover agent for Triplanetary police), beautiful Clio Marsden, and Captain Bradley are the sole survivors when the space pirate gray Roger's invisible planetoid (which houses many ships) attacks the space-liner *Hyperion*. Captured, they will meet expected fates: The men will either join Roger or die, while the fate worse than death awaits Clio. Costigan, with his secret equipment, manages to contact Triplanetary headquarters, and the Triplanetary fleet draws up to attack Roger as Costigan and comrades escape. Roger, who has weaponry more advanced than that of Triplanetary, is mangling the Triplanetary armada when the Nevian vessel captained by Nerado draws near. Seeing the battle going on, musing that since all concerned are killing or dying, he attacks both sides, extracting the iron from the fleet and Roger's planetoid. The Triplanetary fleet is wiped out;

Roger and a few survivors escape from his supposedly invincible planetoid; and Costigan and comrades are captured as specimens to take back to Nevia. * On board Nerado's vessel the Earth people are treated well enough, and once it is recognized that the Nevians communicate in supersonics, language difficulties are mostly overcome. On reaching Nevia, the three repeatedly try to escape, but without success, until the final occasion. * Meanwhile, back in the solar system, Samms's scientists have learned much from the gigantic space battle and have finished their superspaceship (the *Boise*) that will travel faster than light and carry armament of top quality. At about this time, the second Nevian spaceship comes to Earth and destroys Pittsburgh, extracting all its iron. The *Boise* and the Nevian vessel conduct a running battle all the way to Nevia, before the *Boise* wins. The *Boise* then, in reprisal for Pittsburgh, destroys a Nevian city. * Another prolonged battle takes place between the *Boise* and Nerado's ship. It ends in a stalemate; neither can prevent the other from devastating a home planet, but neither can destroy the other. Peace is declared. Since the Nevians are total pragmatists, their decision is not out of character. * Costigan and comrades, who have escaped one more time, are rescued, and all is well. * As for gray Roger, he set up shop again in a different star system, but was finally wiped out by the *Boise*, which chanced upon his lair. He is explained as an aberrant human trained by the Adepts of Jupiter, whence his unusual abilities, including extreme longevity. * Old-fashioned space opera, with a typical romance; the novel feature is the dawning possibility of galactic civilizations.

Smith later revised and enlarged "Triplanetary" in order to bring it into his History of Civilization series, making it a preliminary to the Lensman novels. In the new *Triplanetary* (Fantasy Press, Reading, Pa., 1948) Smith equated gray Roger (now called simply Roger) with Gharlane, an Eddorian animation who was working to shatter Terrestrial civilization. Smith made occasional additions to the text, offering somewhat lame explanations to maintain this posture. In a long prologue Smith also described the initial phases of the Manichean Arisian-Eddorian conflict, the destruction of Atlantis, the fall of Rome, and the collapse of civilization in World War III. The Virgil Samms of "Triplanetary" went on to become the first wearer of the lens in *First Lensman* (1950). * The adaptation is far from being convincing, and Smith would have done better to write a new novel.

SMITH, EVERETT C. and STARZL, R. F.

Smith, whose portrait shows a young man, was then a resident of Lawrence, Mass. It is not clear whether he is the same person as the Everett C. Smith, who wrote *Industry Views the Teaching of English* (1956), reprinted from the *English Journal*. Starzl has a separate entry.

1381. **THE METAL MOON**. *Wonder Stories Quarterly,* Winter 1932. Ill. Paul.

Short story. * The fourth-prize-winning story of the Interplanetary Plot Contest. Smith received $10. * *Time:* A.D. 1,000,144. * *Place:* space around Jupiter. * Adventure, romance, and the Class Struggle. * Around A.D. 800,000 a gigantic meteor swarm filled the solar system, halting interplanetary travel completely. Mankind had already spread out beyond the inner planets, but all contact was lost with the colonists—if they indeed survived. At present, space seems to have cleared sufficiently for the first Terrestrial ship to venture out beyond Mars toward

Smith, Everett C. and Starzl, R. F. (*continued*)

Jupiter. * As the spaceship with its three-man crew nears Jupiter, the explorers encounter a gigantic floating cylinder that they soon realize is another spaceship. The floating cylinder pulls the Terrestrial spaceship in with a gravity ray, and the Earthmen find themselves in the presence of Jovian humans, who are quite friendly. The leader of the First Race, as the Jovians call themselves, brings the explorers to a large artificial satellite called The Pleasure Bubble. Presumably all sorts of orgies take place there, but they play no part in the story. * *The situation:* The culture of Jupiter and its moons is formed of two peoples, the First Race, who are extremely muscular normal humans and hold the top hand; and the Second Race, also called Mugs, who are an assemblage of grotesque genetic horrors and mutations. While the First Race plays in the top half of the Pleasure Bubble, the Mugs work among radioactive equipment, exposed to hard radiation, in the lower half. The same situation presumably holds for Jupiter itself. In other ways, too, the Mugs, who are held in complete contempt by their rulers, are treated abominably. * *Intrigues and events:* The explorers sympathize with the Mugs, indeed, one of them falls in love with a delicate, apparently normal young Mug woman. As they try to rescue her from her horrible living situation, an attack comes from outer space. Mugs who were expelled from Jupiter a long time ago have now returned for revenge. This is no help to the Earthmen, however, for they are unwelcome to both the invading Mugs (who do not trust them) and the First Race (whom they have alienated). * As a resolution, the disabled, ill father of the young Mug woman reveals that he has a spaceship in his basement. All pile in, and as they fly off, they see that the Pleasure Bubble has been destroyed. The Terrestrials and their friends fight their way back toward Earth. * Also involved are heat rays, paralysis rays, and similar paraphernalia. * Below routine.

SMITH, GARRET (1876?-1954)

U.S. newspaperman, associated as night editor with the New York *Tribune*. Occasional contributor to the pulp magazines. A literate writer, although his tendency to recycle ideas and themes limits his interest. His other fiction is covered in *Science-Fiction: The Early Years.*

1382. **TREASURES OF TANTALUS**. *Amazing Stories*, October-November 1927. Unsigned ill.

(First published as "The Treasures of Tantalus" in *Argosy-Allstory* 11 December 1920-8 January 1921.)

Covered in more detail in *Science-Fiction: The Early Years.* * *Time:* A.D. 2000. * The story is based on a motif and theme that Smith used several times with different social aspects: the ubiquitous spying machine. * In this case, the machine is used for a discursus on greed. * Professor Fleckner's telephonoscope can pick up images and sound from anywhere in the world and can also transmit three-dimensional projections with sound. When the machine accidentally uncovers an enormous criminal racket that extends to the highest political circles, millionaire Tom Priestly and Fleckner investigate it and take it over, for honest purposes. * The problem is, where is the enormous loot that the crime syndicate must have amassed? * A second situation involves images that the machine picks up from space. It shows a young woman and her father on a planet where gold and gems are as common as dirt. Yet there is another, puzzling value-object, greed for which drives them into unhappiness and

death. This turns out to be iron. * Eventually, threads are united, puzzles explained. Fleckner finally faces the ethical dimension of his invention. Developing a paint that is opaque to the telephonoscope, he releases his viewer and the paint to the world and retires. * Competent pulp fiction.

SMITH, LAWRENCE

Per Tuck, pseud. of Sydney J. Bounds. Bounds (born 1920, per Rock), a British writer, contributed stories to *New Worlds* in 1949 and 1950. Also author of *Robot Brains* (1967), and said to have written Western stories. It should be noted that if the identification and birth date are correct, Smith was fourteen years old at the time the story was published. This is very suspect.

1383. **BURIED IN SPACE**. *Amazing Stories,* October 1934.

Short-short story. * *Time:* the near future. * At this time space spheres move readily between Earth and the Moon, carrying cargoes and passengers. This is all due to the researches of Dr. Allison, who has discovered a metallic antigravity substance. * In a general conversation about space travel, Allison reveals a hitherto suppressed item of space history. The Moon has a small satellite, a human corpse, tossed out into space during the first voyage. One of the workmen stowed away in the power section of the vessel. Unfortunately, he was overcome by picric acid poisoning and died during the flight. Since it was impracticable to keep his corpse on board the vessel, it was put outside the ship, where it became a small lunar satellite. The man had no relatives or friends, so that it was easy to cover up the incident.

SMITH, WILL AND ROBBINS, R. J.

No information. The collaboration also published two science-fiction stories in *Weird Tales*. These are covered in *Science-Fiction: The Early Years.*

1384. **THE SOUL MASTER**. *Astounding Stories*, March 1930. Unsigned ill.

Short story. * Newspaper reporter Horace Perry and cameraman Skip Handlon have been assigned by their hard-boiled chief to interview eccentric Professor Kell, who lives in an isolated small town where mysterious disappearances have taken place. As they snoop around the Professor's rundown establishment, they see a dog that tries to ram them like a sheep and a chattering mule that tries to climb upon a perch. * Professor Kell, resentful of trespassers, but delighted to obtain human laboratory animals, succeeds in capturing the two newsmen. * Perry awakens, dazed, on a train, without too much memory of what has happened. He reports to his chief, but something is wrong. After a time, Perry realizes what has happened: Kell, who has been working on mechanical personality transfer, has transferred Handlon's personality into Perry's body, so that it now has two identities. * The newspapermen return in force, capture the Professor, release a beautiful maiden, and force the Professor to remove Handlon from Perry. The newspapermen, with the connivance of a police authority, then transfer Handlon's mind into Kell's body (since Kell had destroyed Handlon's body) and set fire to the establishment. Justice has triumphed.

SNOOKS, EPAMINONDAS T., D.T.G.

Pseud. of Charles P. Mason (c.1888-?). Served in World War I. Magazine editor, associate editor of *Wonder Stories* and earlier of *Amazing Stories*. Also worked on Gernsback's *Everyday Sci-*

Snooks, Epaminondas T. (*continued*)

ence and Mechanics and other Gernsback science magazines. Very little is known about Mason, but Hornig (in Davin, "The Silberkleit Years") refers to him as a highly intelligent man with an excellent scientific background. Mason apparently either handled the scientific questions and answers department in *Wonder Stories* or assisted Hornig. The Summer 1931 issue of *Wonder Stories Quarterly* prints a long letter from Mason explaining aspects of celestial mechanics and indicating that Mason had done fairly thorough historical research on the interplanetary story. Mason's last published work seems to have been an article in *Thrilling Wonder Stories* in 1941.

1385. WHY THE HEAVENS FELL. *Wonder Stories*, May 1932. Ill. Paul.

Short story, humor. * Slicker, who is legman and negotiator for the gigantic Supernational Electric and Radiation Corporation, visits the great scientist Professor Hans von Schnickelfritz to deliver a royalty check and also to snoop out any new discoveries that might have commercial value. The professor obligingly feeds him a sausage that has been created from a block of granite; the sausage is palatable enough, but production costs are fantastically high. Schnickelfritz also demonstrates a dishwashing ray and an apparatus for power transmission. Unfortunately, the professor says, the power transmitter is not satisfactory, for its radiation is subject to the law of inverse squares. * Slicker reports back to his superior, lamenting the physical limitations of radiation. His resourceful boss, however, has a solution. He places a call to Senator Bloughard, who introduces a clause in a financial bill repealing the law of inverse squares. * Just as the president is about to sign the bill into law, Slicker chances to meet Schnickelfritz, who becomes greatly excited when Slicker tells what is happening. But it is too late. The bill is signed. First, everything is squashed flat in the United States and its territories. Then the United States and its territories are pulled out of the Earth by solar gravity and fall into the sun. * According to an editorial reply to a letter in the September 1932 issue of *Wonder Stories*, "Why the Heavens Fell" originally ended with the narrator awaking; it was all a dream. But the editors decided to drop this ending in favor of the printed version. According to another account the dream ending was dropped for lack of space. * Amusing in a small way.

1386. BRAHMA-KALPA—OR THE EXPANDING UNIVERSE. *Wonder Stories*, May 1933.

A very short piece, only a half page in length. * What is the expanding universe? It is really only a cloud of cigar smoke emitted by the Demiurge. When the Demiurge's wife complains of the tobacco reek, he opens the window, dispersing the smoke electrons—our universe. But this takes so long in our time that the destruction is in the far, far future. * The title reference is to Hindu mythology, in which the universe undergoes cyclical creation and destruction, each age being a kalpa.

1387. TRADERS IN TREASURES. *Wonder Stories*, May 1934. Ill. Paul.

Short story. * *Time:* 1946. * Two pieces of reportage. * On the Sinfoco television program the great explorer Captain Fjord reports on his discoveries at the south pole. As the captain relates, some years earlier, on a previous aerial expedition, he had discovered a misty stream of hot, very heavily radioactive air; indeed, he had been severely burned by the radioactivity.

Now returning to the spot, he has acquired an enormous amount of radium and a gigantic blue diamond. * The second document is an excerpt from the *Report of the Thirty-seventh Projection toward the External Surface*. The beings of inner Earth, who cannot conceive of external life, tell how they obtained a certain amount of that extremely rare element nitrogen during their surface probe. On abandoning the probe, the internals left behind worn-out radioactive fuel and some of the crystallized carbon used for drilling. * A neat concept.

SNYDER, ALEXANDER

No information.

1388. BLASPHEMERS' PLATEAU. *Amazing Stories*, October 1926. Unsigned ill.

Short story. * What happens when fanatical religiosity and fanatical scientism collide. * Mason visits his old friend Dr. Santurn, whom he has not seen for years. Santurn, as the locals tell Mason, lives as a recluse, with a zoo of strange animals. Armed guards protect his place. * Santurn receives Mason in friendly fashion and explains his research. Essentially, he is creating life chemically. He also works upon ova, creating new animals by similar manipulations. His purpose is to demonstrate the fallacy of the belief in an immortal soul and an immanent God. * Mason, who is a religionist, is suitably horrified. When, some months later, Santurn prepares to create a human being, Mason decides to prevent the sacrilege. While Santurn and his team are working at the project, Mason shifts a ray onto them. The scientists, who did not trust Mason and half expected him to do something of the sort, seize him and with suitable rays render him an idiot. But this is not the end of the story. Santurn and his associates now discover that they have cancer and commit collective suicide by blowing up the establishment. * Crude in presentation.

1389. THE CORAL EXPERIMENT. *Amazing Stories*, September 1929. Ill. Wallit.

Short story. * *Place:* the South Seas. * Dentist Wimble, who worries much about keeping his patients comfortable, is told by his physician to take a sea trip or face a nervous breakdown. Wimble travels to the South Seas, where he receives his brilliant idea—which the author does not reveal until close to the end of the story. * Hearing of a newly formed coral island, he has experimental equipment and living supplies shipped there, giving his carrier, the drunken but sea-wise Captain Squareface Burnell, instructions to return in a year. * Wimble's experiments progress, until he has developed a technique for accelerating the growth of coral organisms. At about this time he notices, with some alarm, that his island is gradually sinking. * His experiments are in their final stages when the submergence of his island accelerates. At the end of the story he is living (with very little food) on a raft anchored to the now submerged island, waiting for Burnell. He has no way of knowing that Burnell was murdered and that no one knows the location of the coral island. * Wimble's project was the creation of a type of coral that could be inserted into a decayed tooth, where it would eat out the decay and create new coral tooth structure. All this is to avoid the necessity of drilling.

SONNEMANN, WILLIAM K.

No information. Judging from "The Council of Drones" the

Sonnemann, William K. (*continued*)

author has had practical experience in bee husbandry.

1390. **THE MASTER MINDS OF VENUS.** *Amazing Stories,* September 1934. Ill. Morey. Published as by Sonnemann.

Novelette. * The story is long and rambling, with considerable padding. * James Samuel Lee, a young would-be inventor, putters around with radio equipment in his attic, hoping to develop a static-free radio. In this, his wife, Madge, supports him. After considerable effort he develops an enormously powerful radio that can pick up, apparently, almost anything in the world. But then he hears an extremely weak signal that calls him by name, urging him to apply more power. He does so, and learns that he is in contact with Venus. * As Lee learns over a period of time, the Venusians have long been monitoring Earth both telescopically and telepathically and have watched his experiments with enthusiasm. They now make him an offer: They will put him and Madge through a mental training course that will turn them into mental superhumans. After this it will be Lee's task to establish Terrestrial commercial relations with Venus. * The Venusians, though a thousand years ahead of Earth in psychological studies and five hundred in science, with a perfect social system, have one enormous problem: They have nothing to eat except one tuber, of which they are heartily sick. They will swap science and technology for vegetable seeds. * As the Venusians describe their planet, it is free from want and crime. Potential criminals are subject to ray treatment that either kills or cures them. Society is stratified, with first, second, and third class citizens. * It is now up to Lee to bring the benefits of Venus to Earth. To protect him, since he will encounter resistance, a special device will incapacitate anyone who is hostile. * Lee, a perfect telepath, now interviews leaders of various sorts, bringing the United States and Great Britain into alignment. But an Asiatic power (obviously Japan) attacks the United States, causing great destruction. The Venusians destroy the enemy fleet with a ray of madness. After a few obstacles, the Venusian system is set to work on Earth. The Venusians even visit Earth on one occasion to protect Lee. * Lee's telepathy comes in handy in cleaning out corrupt politicians. * The Venusians, who are sentimentally attached to the Lees, are beautiful strong blonds. * Far too long, too naive, and too muddled.

1391. **THE COUNCIL OF DRONES.** *Amazing Stories*, October 1936. Ill. Morey.

(Reprinted in Knight, *Science Fiction of the Thirties.*)

Novelette. * During the Depression Fred, the narrator, is marking time on the family farm, when he visits the laboratory of his friend Newton Ware. Newton Ware, who has been experimenting with the life force, has developed a technique for transferring personalities from one animal to another. * Fred, who is an enthusiastic beekeeper, decides, after some internal debate, that he would like to experience briefly the life of a bee, whereupon Ware agrees to put him for five minutes into the body of a queen bee that has been accepted in one of Fred's hives. * Fred awakens as the queen and takes up her life readily. But as he soon observes with panic, the five-minute period, judging by apian life cycles, must have passed. He is trapped as a queen, with both human personality and intelligence, and a knowledge of bee ways. * As he soon learns, the various bees communicate by telepathic means, and Fred, with his superior intelligence, is gradually able to override the instinctive responses and behavior of the workers who attend him. He becomes the ruler in fact of the hive. * As time passes, however, Fred's bee nature asserts itself more and more, and he comes to hate the humans who smoke the hive and extract honey. He decides to defend the hive with perpetual guards of workers; when this does not work, for the smoke is too overpowering, he carries the war to the beekeeper (in this case his human father) by creating a band of workers whose stings have been debarbed so that they can make multiple stings. * Before this, however, Fred has observed that those workers and drones who are descended from him after his insertion in the hive show a partial human intelligence and individuality. With this new resource he educates a race of intelligent bees that can resist human aggression. * Fred's plans come to nothing when his human father, raiding the hive, accidentally crushes him. As Fred lies dying, he instructs his more intelligent assistants to start a new, hidden hive elsewhere. He then dies, but awakens in his human body in a nursing home. He has been there, mostly unconscious, for about three months. What both men forgot when they transferred personalities was that the bee in Fred's body might cause trouble. After the transfer, Fred's body attacked Ware, disabling him and smashing the apparatus. Ware, too, is in the sanitarium. * Both recover. Ware, as a result of the trauma, has lost his memory about his discovery. Fred continues to be an enthusiastic apiarist, but immediately destroys his previous bee associates. * The story is overlong, but some of the bee lore is interesting. The author avoids the usual facile personalization of insects in such stories.

[Anonymous]
Presumably a British writer.

1392. **THE SOUNDLESS HOUR.** *Scoops,* 10 February 1934. Ill. S. D.

Boys' fiction. * Short story. * Seigfried [*sic*] Hordtmund, great Swedish scientist, had just announced to the *Tribune* that he had perfected a great discovery, when two gangsters entered his laboratory, shot him dead, and made off with his work. * Joe Mannington and Ted Wrayburn, cub reporters on the *Tribune*, investigate. They learn that Hordtmund had been working on the phenomenon of sound-suppression in fogs and had come up with a gas that destroys sound. The gangsters put Hordtmund's gas to good use, robbing hotels and banks, while Joe and Ted are hot on their trail. * In Manchester the criminals turn the tables on the reporters, capturing them, tying them onto a bed, and rigging up the sound suppressor and a time bomb. Fortune favors the brave, for although the criminal apparatus goes off, the men are shielded enough by the mattress that they are not greatly injured. * The boys now set a trap. They announce a visit by the fabulously wealthy Rajah of Ranipore. When the crooks begin their operations, they are taken by police who staked out the property.

[Anonymous]
Presumably a British writer.

1393. **SPACEDROME NO. 1.** *Scoops,* 24 March 1934. Unsigned ill.

Boys' fiction. * Short story. * *Time:* the beginning of the interplanetary future. * *Background:* Although there has been radio communication among Earth, Mars, Venus, and other planets, interplanetary travel has proved impossible: spaceships cannot carry enough fuel and supplies for the long journeys

Spacedrome No. 1 (*continued*)

involved. * The great scientist/engineer John Melton has a solution to the problem: a spacedrome (space station) between Earth and Mars, to serve as a halfway house. Supported by gravity neutralizers, huge, with hotels, service centers, etc., it should render trade and travel with Mars feasible. Not everyone, however, approves of the plan, both on Earth and elsewhere. * When *Spacedrome No. 1* is about ready to leave and take up its position, with Melton and pilot Wally Hurst on board, it is attacked by bombers, which Hurst disposes of with his fighter plane. * Out in space, a Venusian spaceship attacks the station, damaging it with a solvent liquid and rays. Melton fights off the Venusian with artificial lightning, whereupon a more powerful Venusian vessel attacks, disabling the spacedrome completely, destroying power, smashing the crystal dome that covers the living quarters, and causing general severe damage. * Melton surrenders, whereupon the Venusians board the station. Their leader announces that he wants the gravity neutralizing apparatus; he will take Melton and Hurst to Venus to demonstrate it, but the other staff will be executed. * In a combination of luck and daring, Hurst and others regain control of the spacedrome, and Hurst, in his fighter rocket, manages to knock out the Venusian ship's disintegrator beam. Surrender follows. * *Miscellaneous:* The Venusians are humanoid, but very short and extremely broad. * The author does not explain how the space station will function when Mars is on the other side of the sun.

SPARKS, DAVID R.

Author of one story in *Adventure*. Perhaps David R. Sparks (1897-1968), New Hampshire writer.

1394. **THE APE-MEN OF XLOTLI.** *Astounding Stories*, December 1930. Ill. Wesso.

Novelette. * *Place:* Mexico. * Lost-race story. * Freddie Kirby, soldier of fortune in Mexico, is chased by bandits into what must be a tabu area, since they do not follow him. * He enters a mountainous region, passes through caves and perils down into a subterranean world, falls into an arsenic-laden lake, swims ashore, and is greeted by thirty-four maidens who speak a Spanish patois. They hope that he will be their liberator. * *Background:* The land seems to have been settled by Aztecs or Toltecs, but Spanish speakers have obviously interbred with them. * To anticipate: The race is almost extinct, the maidens and a group of old men, the Caciques and the Duca, being the only survivors. Ape-men, too, inhabit the lost land. Lustful creatures, they desire the women, and are so numerically superior to the true humans that they are to be dreaded. The rulers of the humans want to surrender some of the maidens to preserve peace. The women are unenthusiastic. * Kirby helps beat back an attack by the subhumans and agrees to help the women. The result is immediate warfare with the Duca and the caciques, who invoke the aid of the ape-men. * Kirby finds rifles and ammunition, which defeat the subhumans, but his sweetheart (whom he was to have married) is carried off to be sacrificed to Quetzalcoatl in the ape-man land. Kirby rescues her. * *Miscellaneous:* Quetzalcoatl is a snake hundreds of feet long. * Also present are a tyrannosaurus and a water monster powerful enough to eat the tyrannosaurus. * Pretty bad.

1395. **THE WINGED MEN OF ORCON.** *Astounding Stories*, January 1932. Ill. Wesso.

Novelette. * *Time:* the interplanetary future, time enough for

there to be an organization of planets. *Place:* Orcon, an almost unknown planet "at the other end of the Universe." * Frederick Weeks, he-man astronomer, awakens to find himself cracked up on Orcon. He had been shanghaied there by the U.S.W. (United Solar Worlds) police organization since he is an authority of a sort on Orcon, having discovered it telescopically. Along with him is Captain Virginia Crane, commander of the spaceship. * *Background:* Unknown to others, however, the mad Prussian scientist Ludwig Leider had anticipated Weeks and is currently on Orcon, plotting the destruction of the Earth. * Weeks, Crane and a Japanese officer named Koto are captured by Leider's magnetic force, and after various time-consuming shenanigans meet the mad scientist. A cartoon-strip German, he has many cute devices: a far-seeing device that shows Earth instantaneously; a paralysis ray; rays that destroy the magneto-gravitational plates of spaceships; devices for changing the erratic rotational period of Orcon; translating machines; and planetary disintegrators. In league with him are the winged men of Orcon, who are humanoid with gauzy wings. * Against this the Earth people have a high explosive in the hold of their inaccessible ship, courage, and physical prowess. * Weeks, of course, wins out, and the Earthmen escape in Leider's remarkable space craft, setting off a titanic explosion behind them. * *Miscellaneous:* Weeks has medical preparations that heal broken bones almost instantaneously. * Exceptionally silly and amateurish in writing, but unusual in having a female space commander and a friendly Oriental. * The hero makes occasional erotic comments about Virginia, but by and large she is a space officer, not a sex figure.

SPEAKER, DAVID M.

U.S. author, then resident of Philadelphia. No other information, but the author would seem to have been a young person.

1396. **THE DISINTEGRATING RAY.** *Amazing Stories*, February 1928. Ill. Paul.

Short-short story. * The narrator, a former student of the eccentric Professor Clinton Wild, is summoned by the professor to witness his great invention: a super-X-ray, perhaps a cosmic ray generator, that will penetrate organic and most inorganic matter. It also bombards individual atoms, transmuting them. To demonstrate, the professor nonchalantly changes some mercury into gold. * The professor admits the possibility of an atomic explosion, but since iron is impermeable to the rays, he feels that his devices, which are amply shielded with iron, are safe and marketable. * The narrator leaves, and not long afterward learns that an enormous explosion destroyed the professor and his lab. * Very flat.

1397. **THE MESSAGE FROM SPACE.** *Amazing Stories*, July 1930. Ill. Morey.

Short story. * A long introductory section describes the isolation of the new element Wadson, which amateur scientist Wadson has found in a meteorite. It is 106 on the periodic table and is slightly radioactive. * Wadson inserts a particle of his new element into a radio tube, with astonishing results. He picks up a voice that broadcasts the same long speech for several nights consecutively. The language is alien, probably from a planet far out in the Milky Way, thousands of light-years away, but eminent linguists manage to translate it. * The message of Prixton Lestax of the planet Astrax, the last survivor of his world: Lestax, an inspector on the interplanetary landing stations, is sent out to investigate the peculiar behavior of a spaceliner. After a

Speaker, David M. (*continued*)

brush with the space navy of the Drulls, an inimical culture, Lestax's ship reaches the spaceliner and is captured by a ship from a far higher civilization. The two captive ships are taken by tractor beam to the dark star where the Super-Intelligences of Extrose live hundreds of miles underground. * The Super-Intelligences, smallish glowing spheres with various power beams for performing activities, are actually cyborgs (my term), with organic brains in artificial apparatus. In intelligence they are far superior to the Astrakians they hold captive, and can converse with them, control them, and kill them by mental power. * After attempting a rebellion, the other Astrakians are killed, leaving Lestax the sole survivor. * *Background:* The Super-Intelligences of Extrose need Lebensraum, but in their extensive explorations of space have found only one world that seems possible for expansion. This is Astrax. Lestax and the other Astrakians were brought to the dark star as a final ecological test: If they could live on the dark star, the Super-Intelligences could live on Astrax. Now that this has been cleared up, they intend to invade Astrax and exterminate its inhabitants. * Lestax pleads for his world, pointing out its beauty, etc., but is told that science is all that counts. * The Extrose armada approaches Astrax, wiping out the Drull fleet, and attacks Astrax with mental power. While the Astrakians bring down a few Extrose ships with atomic rays, the Astrakian fleet is totally destroyed. The Super-Intelligences, who have already wiped out most of the large cities, now proceed to exterminate the natives. Lestax manages to escape and make his way to a hidden underground laboratory, where he makes his broadcasts, warning the rest of the universe against the Super-Intelligences.

1398. **THE SUPERMEN.** *Amazing Stories,* October 1933. Ill. Morey.

Short story. * *Time:* 1961 on. *Place:* mostly Pennsylvania. * The supermen appear mysteriously in the countryside, and in a short time their powers are felt: mass willcontrol, high explosives, a red force screen that stops projectiles, and a green ray that disintegrates metal. As they continue to blow up nearby towns, the army attacks them, with no success. * Professor Carl von Renstein, however, provides an answer. Discovering that the red screen involves a sort of supermagnetism, he works out a chemical coating that will penetrate the screen. During the next encounter, a high explosive shell, suitably protected, destroys the supermen. * Extracts from Renstein's diary follow: It was he who created the supermen. He developed a system of gene transplants and by interbreeding turned out a batch of superbeings, all but six of whom he destroyed. These six got out of hand, but why, the author does not deign to tell us. * *Miscellaneous:* The supermen developed atomic energy out of a small amount of uranium that was present in a laboratory they raided. * Flat, undeveloped, almost puerile.

[Anonymous]

Presumably a British writer.

1399. **SPIRIT OF SPEED.** *Scoops,* 17 March 1934. Unsigned ill.

Boys' fiction. * Short story. * *Time:* the near future. * After an explosion in a coal mine, Hubert Baylis isolates a mineral component that is more than one hundred times as powerful as petrol. He intends to use it for automobiles, and, since races are very important publicity events, he plans to enter a car powered by tetra-autoline in the forthcoming rally. * The car is developed, but there are problems, caused by oil czar Garford of International Petroleum Corporation. First, Garford hires thugs to sabotage the *Terracoach Marvel,* but the thugs are themselves burnt to death. Then, during the race, Garford blocks the road with lorries, but young Jack Carland, son of Baylis's partner, drives the car beautifully, bypassing the obstacles and winning with a speed of 420 MPH.

SPOHR, CARL W. (1896-1971)

According to the story blurb, an artillery officer in the German army in World War I. Carter, however, without citing source, states that Spohr served in the Austrian army. Also author of *Spätlese: Gedichte, 1916 bis 1965* (1968). Jordan considers Spohr to have been a German author, although she was unable to identify him further. Actually, Spohr was a resident of Chicago in 1968, and the probabilities are that he was in the United States when he wrote "The Final War." There is no indication that the story is a translation, and the mis en scène is American.

1400. **THE FINAL WAR.** *Wonder Stories,* March-April 1932. Ill. Paul.

Short novel. * *Time:* the twenty-first century. *Place:* deliberately unidentified, though personal and place names suggest the eastern United States. * A story of imaginary war, told with a savage verismo seldom found in early science-fiction. * The story is concerned mostly with the fate of two young college students, Fred Young and John Burke, who are caught up in the war that suddenly breaks over them. There has been international tension for some time, and when an aircraft drops bombs (perhaps accidentally) on a border town on the other side, the war breaks out. All-out air attacks with high explosives and poison gas devastate the city of Liberty, killing Burke's fiancée, after which Young and Burke volunteer. The war continues, and a Committee of Four seizes national power, suspending the Constitution. * There is little that can be said about much of the remainder of the story. The war turns mostly into trench warfare, with ever more noxious poison gases and stronger explosives, for over six years. During this time Burke is killed, and Young is temporarily assigned to assist an elderly professor (Doehler) who is working on superexplosives. * By now, the country has gone totally totalitarian, with everything controlled and regimented, with Secret Service men spying upon everyone, and summary punishment. Marriages are made temporary, and pregnancy is insisted upon, whereupon the child is taken from its mother and brought up in state schools as a future soldier. Young marries a woman under such circumstances, after they have seen each other only once before, but they come to love each other. * Old Professor Doehler discovers how to make atomic explosives, but is reluctant to reveal the secret. He is tortured until he gives it to the military, but thanks to espionage, the enemy has the secret almost as soon as Young's side. * The resulting barrages of atomic explosives destroy civilization. The war ends with most of the human race dead. Small bands of survivors, disavowing war and demanding peace, organize in groups that tend to be socialist communes. Young and his wife are among them. Perhaps a new world can be created, now that the militarists are either dead or out of power. * The point of the story is obvious, militarists cause wars that no one else wants. * Competently written, but after a time the verismo account of

Spohr, Carl W. (*continued*)
bombings, horrors, tragedies, becomes a little too much. The attempt to show character change is unusual in war fiction. Probably suggested by *All Quiet on the Western Front,* although the relationship is in point of view, not incident or development.

SPRIGG, C[HRISTOPHER] ST. JOHN (1907-1937)
British poet, essayist, aesthetician, aviation expert. Best-known works posthumous collections *Studies in a Dying Culture* (1938) and *Further Studies in a Dying Culture*)1940). Also wrote considerable popular fiction: *Crime in Kensington* (1933), *Death of an Airman* (1934), etc. Killed in Spanish Civil War. Apparently a more considerable writer than the present story would indicate.

1401. **THE ACCELERATOR RAY.** *Scoops,* 26 May 1934. Unsigned ill.
Boys' fiction. * Short story. * Dr. Jay has invented a ray that can speed up or slow down the motion of electrons in their circuits, thus effectively accelerating or retarding motion. His false friend and rival Dr. Farrow first learns of the ray when he finds Jay seemingly dead in his laboratory. Actually, Jay is alive, simply living at an incredibly slow rate. When his exposure to the ray wears off and his metabolism returns to normal, Jay explains matters to Farrow, promising an early report to the Royal Society. * The false Farrow, however, focuses the ray on Jay, intending to render him infinitely slow and thereby out of the picture. By mistake, being unfamiliar with the device, however, he accelerates Jay to the speed of a year in one of our days. * Jay, now superspeeded, undertakes various adventures that are mentioned briefly: raiding banks and giving the money to the poor, rescuing people from muggers, and berating Parliament for its do-nothing attitude. He also abducts Farrow while he is addressing the Royal Society claiming Jay's invention and entombs him in the foundations of a church that is being built, radiating him to return to normalcy in about two hundred years. * *Miscellaneous:* As preliminaries Jay hatched and matured a rooster in a couple of days and similarly speeded up an oak tree from an acorn.

STALEY, M. L.
No information.
1402. **THE STOLEN MIND,** January 1930. Ill. J. Fleming Gould.
Short story. * *Place:* Chicago. * Quest, undercover Secret Service agent, answers a want ad for a daring man without familial ties to undergo an experiment. * Keane Clason, inventor, explains: He and his brother Philip have invented a most powerful death ray that operates with certain light frequencies and radio combinations. Philip would like to sell it to the Russians. Keane, who claims patriotic reasons, disapproves of such a sale and will do almost anything to prevent it. * Keane explains further: He has invented an electrolytic process that shifts personalities from body to body. He will put Quest into the tank; remove his personality and transfer it to his own (Keane's) body, then to Philip's, thus foiling Philip. The complex exchange seems necessary by the nature of the process. * That is Keane's proposal, but things are not really that simple: Actually, Keane is a dastardly villain, and it is he, not Philip, who wants to steal the invention and sell it to the Russians. Quest will then die. * There is much complicated action, back

and forth, as Quest struggles to regain his freedom of action from Keane. Eventually good triumphs. * Not very good.

STANGLAND, ARTHUR G[OLEND] (1908-?)
U.S. (Oregon) author. At writing time a student of electrical engineering at Oregon State College. Other sources give his birth date as 1909, but 1908 is correct. Otherwise, no information.

1403. **THE ANCIENT BRAIN.** *Science Wonder Stories,* October 1929. Ill. Paul.
(Reprinted in Margulies and Friend, *From Off This World.*)
Short story. * *Time:* about A.D. 12,000. * A Ralphism of future life. * William Allen Golend suddenly awakens in the future. Friendly medical attendants explain: He was accidentally electrocuted in Oregon State University back in the twentieth century; his brain, however, was preserved and kept alive; and now, since medical science is capable of the feat, it has been enlarged to meet future standards and placed in the body of a young man who died of brain illness. * The future people help William adjust to future life. He successfully studies engineering and becomes attached to a friendly young woman. * More attention is paid to future culture than story: Golend is examined thoroughly by mechanical equipment, and his physical and psychological specifications are carefully recorded. He is assigned a new name, which is a first name followed by a long number, and is enrolled in a university. Part of his education is accomplished by sleep learning. He now has greater intelligence than he had in his former life, and he will probably share future longevity. * As for the future world: Most people live in aerial floating disk cities that are supported by repulsion rays; such cities are healthier than the ground. On each city disk there are twenty-story buildings linked by aerial crossings for moving sidewalks. Aerocars are omnipresent, and space travel is perfected, with extensive trade in interplanetary materials. Much of the mechanical labor is done by robots, and energy is drawn from the electrical field of the sun. * Social matters, however, seem much the same as in the twentieth century. Future man has a slightly larger head than modern man, but is otherwise not greatly changed. * Like most Ralphisms, of curiosity interest for predictive value, which here is not high.

1404. **THE MENACE FROM THE SKIES.** *Science Wonder Stories,* April 1930.
Short-short story. * Honorable mention in the contest based on the cover to the November 1929 issue of *Science Wonder Stories.* * This is the Report of the Three, sponsored by the League of Nations. Witnesses saw a flying saucer descend, grasp the Woolworth Building, and fly away with it. Similarly, there were witnesses to the theft of the Eiffel Tower. * The two flying saucers, accompanied by a third, flew off into space, but suddenly all three exploded. * Nothing is known why all this happened, though perhaps the thieves were cosmic souvenir hunters.

1405. **THE EYE OF TWO WORLDS.** *Wonder Stories,* June 1931. Ill. Marchioni.
Short story. * Crime and financial finagling in the interplanetary future. * Interplanetary communication is accomplished by a gigantic heliograph on a mountain top; it can easily contact Venus and Mars. Fran Hammond, heir to Hammond Interplanetary Communications, Inc., currently on college vacation, is operating the heliograph (to learn the business) when shots from

Stangland, Arthur G. (continued)

the dark shatter the lenses. Fran chases the culprits in his 300 mph diesel, catches up with them, and is captured. * His captors are a band of interplanetary criminals who raid banks and launder money in complicated operations. They have destroyed the heliograph in order that information about their techniques will not reach Venus. Now they are forcing Fran to release several million dollars of his father's wealth to them, playing heat rays on him as he gives instructions over the picture phone. But Fran outwits them, and they are captured by the planetary police. * One wonders how the planets communicated when they were on opposite sides of the sun * Routine at best.

1406. **OUTCAST IN SPACE**. *Wonder Stories Quarterly*, Summer 1931. Ill. Marchioni.

Short story. * *Time:* December 31st, 2000. *Place:* Oregon and Mexico. * *Background:* Science and technology have advanced considerably, with good television, and many personal planes. Interplanetary travel to Mars is common, and Martian and Terrestrial capitalists vie to create huge cartels. The Martians, who are entirely human, have a considerable establishment on Earth. * To writer James Hamlyn Cord's woodland house comes a beautiful young damsel in distress. Dinah Lilliard, daughter of the interplanetary tycoon Lilliard, she is worried about her father. * Almost before James and Dinah know it, they are kidnapped by Martians and flown to Mexico, where Mr. Lilliard is engaged in a business conference with the comparable Martian tycoon Nog Boshl. There is obviously fishy work going on, for Nog Boshl is a cruel, villainous man, and he has some sort of a hold over Lilliard. In fact, unless Lilliard surrenders his daughter to the Martian. . . * After various contretemps things get sorted out. Lilliard refuses to yield to Nog Boshl, who threatens exposure for a murder that Lilliard is supposed to have committed. But actually, it was the Nog who did it. Cord saves the situation. The Nog flees in his spaceship, but it has insufficient fuel—the point of the story. * Parodic?

1407. **THE 35TH MILLENNIUM**. *Wonder Stories*, August 1931. Ill. Paul.

Short story. * *Time:* despite the title, A.D. 35,082. *Place:* the area around Virginia or North Carolina. * *Background:* For about twenty-five thousand years the human race advanced in civilization and culture, then around A.D. 24,000 a hundred-year war exhausted most of the Earth's resources and killed most of its people. * To make matters worse, a new glacial period set in. Around A.D. 35,000 the climate in the middle Atlantic area is arctic or subarctic, and the human race (in North America at least) falls into two groups: the Futurans, who maintain some civilization, and the Kulons, who are considerably inferior in culture, but larger, stronger and more aggressive. The Kulons have been waging a war of attrition against the Futurans, raiding their cities for supplies and technical equipment. What with names and titles the Kulons seem to figure Russian communism. * Young Bensar, looking for pitchblende out in the wilderness, is captured by Kulons. After escaping through an almost unknown region, looking for a place to hide, he stumbles on the edge of a buried concrete building. With a little difficulty he forces an entry and finds himself in an enormous time capsule chamber buried by the people of A.D. 5000. Within the chamber are books on metal tape, scientific equipment in working order, and weapons, including several disintegrator pistols. The secret of atomic power, which had been lost over the ages, is

present. * Bensar uses the pistols to ward off Kulon attacks and manages, after great hardship, to return to his home city. At first the authorities believe that his story is a fantasy resulting from hardships. But eventually an air flight locates the repository, from which the Futurans remove certain of its contents. As they fly back, a box containing the atomic pistols falls out of the plane; it is retrieved by Kulons, who use the pistols to some effect before they are killed. * There are two complications, serious rivalry between the three Futuran cities that almost leads to civil war, and the acquisition by the Kulons of weapons from the ancient cache. The Futuran cities make peace with one another and under Bensar's leadership defeat the Kulons after a superscientific attack. A new civilization will now arise. The Futurans do not plan to exterminate the Kulons, but will try to civilize them more. * Routine.

1408. **50TH CENTURY REVOLT**. *Wonder Stories*, April 1932. Ill. Paul.

Short story. * *Time:* the fiftieth century, exact date not disclosed. * *Background:* Around A.D. 3000 astronomers discovered that the sun was about to become a "flaming variable" (an anticipation of a pulsar?), and the Earth was likely to be roasted. The science of the day was able to cope with this by using giant rockets to stop the rotation of the Earth, so that even if one side is uninhabitable by reason of heat and radiation, the other, the frozen side, would at least permit humanity to survive until the sun settled down again. Calculations indicated that the sun would return to normal in the fiftieth century, at which time the giant pulsating rockets would be reignited to start the hundred year process back to a twenty-four hour rotational day. * Mankind was hard hit by the catastrophe. Some humanity survived in the narrow temperate zone bordering the cold and hot hemispheres, while a few of the hardiest survivors settled in the cold zone at temperatures of 100° below zero, Fahrenheit. * A confusing factor entered. Some time after the sun began to pulsate, Venusians attacked and conquered the Earth. The Earth now is under their domination. Totally human, they are harsh masters who have enslaved the Earthmen along the temperate borderland in, for example, Sunshine City. A secret group of Terrestrial scientists, however, has an establishment a thousand miles from the border, where they work on weapons and plot an uprising, which is to begin soon. * Two of the scientists, exploring, find a block of ice within which is a frozen human being. Thawed out, Spear Mohler, an electrical engineer from the year 2008, adjusts well to the new era and becomes an impassioned fighter for liberty. * The plot line is melodramatic. Mohler and friends venture into Sunshine City, where they are captured and put to work at a killing pace. Actually, Mohler precipitated their capture and disrupted plans by rescuing a beautiful young woman from sexual assault by a high Venusian official. * The rebellion comes, with rebel explosive bullets pitted against Venusian pain and paralysis rays. An attack in flying suits destroys the Venusian power system, and the rebellion is successful. In a cliff-hanger Mohler starts the apparatus for restoring the Earth's rotation. * A good idea, poor development, with a routine total. The future dates are awry.

1409. **CASTAWAYS OF SPACE**. *Wonder Stories*, July 1932. Ill. Paul.

Short story. * *Time:* the interplanetary future. *Place:* the asteroid belt. * Captain Rogers and engineer Kraft are the only survivors of the *Mercedes*, whose rocket tubes blew up, badly

Stangland, Arthur G. (*continued*)

disabling the ship. The ship is now drifting helplessly toward a medium-sized, unnamed asteroid, where it crash-lands. The two men will survive only a short time, until their air runs out, and they are prepared for death. * Outside, however, they see a human figure running toward the ship. Brandishing a rod, the stranger breaks the window of the *Mercedes*, thus allowing the air to escape. He is obviously mad. * Rogers and Kraft, now wearing space suits with limited air supplies, investigate, hoping to find another ship on the asteroid. They discover (1) that the planetoid is rich in heavy metals, including radium; (2) that there is another ship, but that all its crew (except the madman) is dead from radium burns; (3) that by cannibalizing both ships, they can escape. But the madman is a loose cannon, and eventually Kraft must sacrifice himself in a radioactive blaze so that Rogers can escape. * Routine.

1410. **CROSSROADS OF SPACE**. *Wonder Stories*, September 1932. Ill. Paul.

Short story. * *Time:* the interplanetary future. *Place:* space between Neptune and Pluto. * As Captain Heath of the space refueling station *88-X* discovers, something is badly wrong. Supply vessels are late, with the result that the station is running short of fuel and air, and the station is not only millions of miles off its beacon line, but cannot communicate with Neptune. The answer, as Heath and his officers recognize, is that the space station is passing through a belt of ionized gas. * Some panic arises, notably among the Plutonian engine room personnel, who mutiny and leave in the lifeboat, hoping to reach a planet. (Heath had previously planned to send the lifeboat out to signal for help.) * There are deaths and great damage, but all ends well. When the mutineers (who included no competent navigators) crashed into an asteroid, the resulting flame ignited the gas cloud, releasing the *88-X*. * *Miscellaneous:* The Plutonians, who are present because of interplanetary treaty, are small, black, and humanoid. * Routine pulp adventure, an improvement over the earlier stories.

1411. **OUTCASTS FROM MARS**. *Wonder Stories*, October 1932. Ill. Paul.

Short story. * *Time:* the interplanetary future. *Place:* Antarctica. * *Background:* One of the provisions of the treaty between Earth and Mars is that the Martians are permitted to establish a colony of exiles on Antarctica. Also on Antarctica is an enormous Terrestrial electrical station that beams power to much of the Earth and transmits communications into space, notably for the guidance of interplanetary vessels. * As the story begins, the giant spaceliner *Martian Princess* is lost in space and needs navigational instructions; at the same time there is a severe power shortage, so that adequate signals cannot be sent to the lost liner. Rosson and a comrade volunteer to find the leak, the source of which does not register on the station instruments. * Rosson soon discovers, after his plane cracks up, that the Martian colony has been stealing the electricity. As the Martian leader explains, their other energy sources, including coal, have been exhausted and they need the electricity to survive. It is clear that the Martian government has planned the death of the exiles. * Rosson faces a dilemma; If the Martians continue to divert electricity, the *Martian Princess* will be lost; if they stop, they will die. * The desperate Martians, temporarily in control of the situation, try to seize the main Antarctic installation, but fail. As a final move, they short the enormous current, and thereby al-

most exterminate themselves. Rosson helps them retrieve the situation. * Finally, all parties vow to help resettle the Martians in a more viable location, probably Patagonia. The *Martian Princess* was lost, but most of the passengers survived in lifeboats. * *Miscellaneous:* The Martians are humanoid, but small. * One wonders how the station works when Mars is at opposition. * Competent pulp work with a softer social message than is typical.

1412. **THE LAKE OF LIFE**. *Wonder Stories*, November 1932. Ill. Paul.

Short story. * *Place:* Central Australia. * Laughlin, Webster, and Murrumbidgee (an aborigine guide), searching for the lost Laxton and Davidson expedition, are themselves lost. Their helicopter is out of gas, and unless they find water soon, they will die. * Lo and behold, they come upon the legendary freshwater lake that the previous expedition had been searching for. But there is a cave nearby, and in the cave are stalagmites containing petrified men, from ancient Vikings and Genoese merchants on up to the missing Laxton and Davidson. * Danger is at hand. A herd of giant kangaroos appears, captures the white men, and takes them to their masters, strange-looking slight, dark men. There seems to be no possibility of communication with them. Laughlin and Webster are confined in a pen, in preparation for a corroboree during which they will be encased in crystal. * Laughlin now explains what is going on. Their captors are not really men, but humanoid, rootless plants. * Things look bad, but Murrumbidgee enables the explorers to escape. As they flee, they come upon fuel from the lost previous expedition. The men decide on a desperate stratagem. Laughlin and the aborigine will hold back the plant-men, while Webster will dash to the helicopter with a small can of gasoline. He will fly back with a submachine gun. * The scheme is only partially successful. Laughlin, recaptured, is almost encased in the liquid crystal and Murrumbidgee is killed before Webster returns. But the plant men are now convinced that the white men are gods and bother them no longer. * Some attempt to create an Australian background, but a rather silly story.

1413. **THE LAST OF THE LEMURIANS**. *Wonder Stories*, January 1933. Ill. Paul.

Short story. * *Place:* Mount Shasta, California. * Jeff Crang, greatly interested in the folktale of Lemurians living on Mt. Shasta, determines to investigate. The local people tell him that visitors are discouraged, but he proceeds, accompanied by a chance-met associate, and encounters not Lemurians, but gangsters, who have murderous armed guards surrounding the area. * Explanation: The great scientist Ledgerwood, who has hollowed out Shasta for experimental purposes, has created a vortex that combines electricity, magnetism, and gravity. Unfortunately, it has fallen into the hands of the gangster chief Ramponi and his men, who want to use it for criminal purposes. And, since it has been improperly operated, it is due to explode at any moment. * Jeff and De Koningh, one of the concerned scientists, try to outwit the gangsters and turn off the mechanism, but without much success. But they do escape via a tunnel, which explodes behind them. * At this point the adventure ends. It was all a controlled dream to which Jeff was subjected by his real-life friend De Koningh, who used a dictaphone and various sensory stimuli to actuate the adventure as Jeff slept. The story is avowedly based on an editorial of Gernsback's promoting sleep learning. * The interpenetration of realities is interesting,

Stangland, Arthur G. (*continued*)

but the story per se is routine. As for the title, it is deliberately deceptive, undoubtedly to arouse reader interest.

1414. **THE FATAL EQUATION.** *Wonder Stories*, April 1933. Ill. Paul.

Short story. * *Time:* the near future. *Place:* Oregon. * The great young mathematical physicist Jan Friede has been found dead at the keyboard of his integraph (computer). The doctor considers it a natural death, but detective Kip and scientist Funkhouser believe that murder has been committed. Friede, who was working on ultimates, would not have died at this point in his work. As Funkhouser works through Friede's papers, he learns that Friede had theoretically extracted time from space and was working toward the physical definition of the universe as cosmic mind. * Friede calls in MacMillan, a scientist of equal repute, who describes Friede's work as nonsense. Yet there is something going on. An expert at the Integrator factory discovers that certain of the insulating pads in the machine have been removed, so that if one pressed a certain combination, one would receive a severe, perhaps fatal shock; Funkhouser discovers that a quantity has been changed in Friede's final equation, to evade the shock; and a third party, Bishop, has been working on apparatus to actualize Friede's equations. * The solution, which appears early enough that the reader need not feel annoyed if I reveal it: MacMillan realizes all too well that Friede's work is valid, but is terrified at its consequences. He therefore has murdered Friede and has made arrangements for Bishop's apparatus to be destroyed. At the final revealment, where Friede's absolute equations are shown to operate, MacMillan steps into the machine and commits suicidal annihilation. MacMillan, though committing a crime or two, has prevented far greater damage. The ultimates are too dangerous to be meddled with. * Reasonable exposition.

STARR, PAUL

Street and Smith records indicate that payment was made to Richard Parmenter, which may be the real name of Paul Starr. Starr (then a resident of Nantucket, Massachusetts) also contributed stories to *Air Trails, Top-Notch*, and other pulps.

1415. **THE INVADING BLOOD STREAM.** *Astounding Stories*, December 1933. Unsigned ill.

Short story. * *Time:* the near future. *Place:* partly in Bulgaria. * Cloak and dagger work and skulduggery. * The two hostile world powers, the U.S. and the Central European Confederacy, are about equally matched. The United States has no army to speak of, but rules the air and sea, while the C.E.C. has an enormous, well-trained army, but inadequate air and sea forces. Thus, the C.E.C. cannot very well invade the Americas. * The solution to C.E.C.'s transport problem may lie with the great scientist Dr. Hugo Presnick. Some time earlier, at a lecture at the Smithsonian, Presnick demonstrated a technique for compressing the orbits of atomic particles. * The great secret agent Carson Dane takes to the field to see what the C.E.C. is plotting, for there are rumors of a forthcoming irresistible attack. Flying to Bulgaria, assuming the identities of various soldiers and assistants (since he speaks suitable languages with great fluency and is fortunate in finding near doubles), he discovers the secret. Presnick is able to shrink humans to microscopic size, encapsulate them into suspended animation, insert them into a carrier's blood stream, and retrieve them as needed. Thus a dozen or so

men can convey an army of half a million. * After back and forth action, Dane plays the enlarging ray on the plane carrying the bearers of the mini-soldiers; the micro-soldiers resume full size and are drowned in the ocean. * Almost parodic, with many loopholes.

STARZL, R[OMAN] F[REDERICK] (1899-1976)

U.S. (Iowa) journalist, writer, newspaper publisher. Contributed twenty-odd science-fiction stories to the pulps. These were literate, usually capable action fiction with science-fictional trappings. His first published story is exceptional in this respect. Also wrote pulp fiction in other genres. According to Davin (who provides a good coverage), Starzl wrote to obtain cash to purchase the family newspaper and printing establishment, and stopped when this goal was attained. He was unusual in being able to strike the pulp mode immediately and well, also for abandoning it after some success. Starzl was also an important member of both the German and American rocket societies. In later life interested in right-wing politics. * See also collaborations Everett C. Smith and R. F. Starzl and R. F. Starzl and Festus Pragnell.

Nine of Starzl's stories are concerned with the Interplanetary Flying Police: #f1420, 1421, 1422, 1423, 1425, 1428, 1429, 1430, and 1431. These stories, however, are not mutually consistent, differing so greatly in time (perhaps A.D. 1998 for #1422, as compared with A.D. 3977 for #1425) and circumstance that they do not form a series in our sense.

1416. **OUT OF THE SUB-UNIVERSE.** *Amazing Stories Quarterly*, Summer 1928. Unsigned ill.

(Reprinted in Ashley, *History of the Science Fiction Magazine, Part 1*.)

Short story. * Professor Halley, who has been working with cosmic rays, has discovered that certain harmonics of the rays can increase or decrease size almost infinitely. He has also satisfied himself that atomic structures parallel solar systems in our universe. With his apparatus he has sent objects into an atomic world and retrieved them, but has had no success with living creatures. * Hence (although the reader may find the reasoning a little lopsided) it is agreed that the professor's daughter Shirley and her near-fiancé, Hale, should go down into the atomic world to explore. Halley intends to retrieve them in a half hour. * At the appropriate time, Halley throws the switch. He sees emerging up in size, not Shirley and Hale, but about two hundred strangely garbed people. Still tiny, they address him in English, telling him that they have maintained the temple of Halley's descendants for about a million years. The professor overlooked the fact that time would pass far more rapidly in the sub-universe than in ours. * The professor now has to account for the disappearance of the long-dead Shirley and Hale and for the presence of about two hundred people, whom he enlarges to normal size. * "Out of the Sub-universe" is sometimes considered a pivot stories in science-fiction because of its consideration of differential time, but it was anticipated by G. Peyton Wertenbaker's "The Man from the Atom," where the concept is very clearly stated. Wertenbaker's story seems to have been generally overlooked by later readers.

1417. **MADNESS OF THE DUST.** *Amazing Stories*, May 1930. Ill. Wesso.

Short story. * *Time:* not too long after A.D. 2025. *Place:* Mars. * Young John Farrington is a supervisor in a Martian mine that

Starzl, R. F. (*continued*)

produces borium, which is processed by native Martian workers. The job is an Earthman's grave, for sooner or later Earthmen come down with the dust madness, which drives them to homicidal fury. Farrington has taken the job knowingly for its high salary, which will enable him to marry Alfreda. * Farrington succumbs to the dust madness and must be removed. The captain of the rescuing spaceship is Steve, an old friend who is also an admirer of Alfreda. In his madness Farrington believes that Steve is trying to cut him out from the woman both men love. This would be bad enough, but Steve suddenly comes down with appendicitis, and Farrington, alternating between periods of frantic rage when he wants to kill Steve and moments of responsibility, must operate on Steve, instructed by radio. * All ends well. There is now a serum against the Martian madness. * Mars is Schiaparellian, with canals. The Martians are very gentle, kindly humanoid giants. The workers are rather stupid, but there are supposed to be superior Martian aristocrats, who do not enter the story. * Venus is also available to Earth people, but mostly as a vacation center.

1418. **THE PLANET OF DREAD.** *Astounding Stories*, August 1930. Ill Csabo (?).

Short story. * *Time:* the twenty-third century. *Place:* the imaginary planet Inra, which is a tropical hell. * Mark Forepaugh and his Martian servant Gunga are on Inra hunting orchids for the Terrestrial market. All should be well, but Mark discovers that his hydrogen fuel cylinders are empty, thanks to an inefficient supply man. This means that the two men are almost energyless and defenseless. As horrible Inranian carnivores assault their cabin, Mark and Gunga risk everything in flight, hoping to reach the cooler mountains. Along the way there are many combats with horrors, culminating in an encounter with a highly intelligent, will-controlling amoeboid that has ideas of ingesting them. An old frontier six-shooter that Mark brought along mostly for sentimental reasons proves to be their salvation. * *Miscellaneous:* The Martian is humanoid, but with one eye; he is also very stupid. * Inra has natives who are stupid and primitive. * Mark has atomic disintegrator pistols. * Capable pulp work, without much novelty.

1419. **THE KING OF THE BLACK BOWL.** *Wonder Stories*, September 1930. Ill. Miller.

Short story. * *Time:* 1935. *Place:* Chicago. * A fictional development of a common joke or prediction of the time (per *Ballyhoo* and *New Yorker* cartoons) that gangsters would formally take over Chicago. * The gangster chief Felix Spumelli is now de facto ruler of Chicago, with his own private police force who wear special uniforms and ride in armored vehicles. * Spumelli wants even more, however, and his forces kidnap famous University of Chicago physicist Dawkelson. Former student Darwin Ellis and former collage athlete Buck Holt try to prevent the kidnapping, but without success, Spumelli only laughing when his thugs manhandle Buck. The two ex-collegians, however, vow to rescue the scientist. * Things happen: A black bowl settles over Chicago, cutting off not only entry and exit, but radiation of all sorts; water, however, continues to enter. And Spumelli now declares himself King Felix, his forces gunning down any police who resist, also some National Guard units. The occupation is harsh. * Ellis, however, has devised a long-distance supermicrophone that will pick up vibrations from even a window pane, and with the apparatus the young men locate the

kidnapped professor. * There is considerable action—chases, hidings, shoot-outs, fisticuffs, etc. before Buck and Darwin penetrate Spumelli's headquarters on the west side and rescue the professor. Part of his equipment—which produced a relativistic zone of nothingness—is broken. * The three flee through the city, ending in the East River. Just in the nick of time the black bowl suddenly disappears. The overloaded equipment in Spumelli's headquarters has exploded, presumably also killing Spumelli. * Competent pulp action work.

1420. **THE GLOBOID TERROR.** *Amazing Stories*, November 1930. Ill. Morey.

Short story. * *Time:* around 2124. *Place:* Venus. * Corporal Heywood Crombie of the Interplanetary Flying Police has been assigned to investigate the continued disappearance of gray diamonds from the diggings on Venus. These diamonds, which are superior for industrial purposes to either gemstones or artificial diamonds, are essential to industry. * Shortly after arrival he is subjected to attacks: two native Venusians try to slip into his bedroom and kill him with a deadly fungus; a miner "accidentally" disrupts the elevator system when Crombie is descending into the mine. But Crombie survives, climbing out of the mine, and discovers who the culprits are. He kills some of them, but two are eaten by the globoid, a form of Venusian amphibian life that, being semimaterial, is immune to rays. * *Miscellaneous:* Venus is tropical, with strange life-forms. The Venusians are somewhat taller and slenderer than Earthmen, with a seven-fingered single arm that grows out of their chests; they are stupid and treacherous. * The method of crime: the trusted criminal, when storing the diamonds substituted artificial gems that spontaneously disintegrated after a time. * Starts out well as an action story, but soon fizzles.

1421. **HORNETS OF SPACE.** *Wonder Stories*, November 1930. Ill. Marchioni.

(Reprinted in Margulies and Friend, *From off This World*.)

Short story. * *Time:* the twenty-third century. *Place:* mostly space near Eros. * An Interplanetary Flying Police story. * The spaceliner *Medusa* is attacked by a space pirate who operates the old *Redoubtable*, a captured Martian warship. On board the *Medusa* is a contingent of the I.F.P., who man tiny one-person spaceships (called hornets) that deliver torpedoes or bombs. In this case the hornets are hampered by by a black cloud that blocks rays and explodes bombs on contact (or neutralizes them). * The story is told in terms of dynamics among the I.F.P. men: hostility between Strickland and an older crew member; a potential love affair between Strickland and a young radio operator; previous cowardice on the part of Henderson, who is now semi-ostracized; and redeeming heroism on Henderson's part that saves the battle. The pirate crashes on Eros when disabled. * *Miscellaneous:* Paralysis rays are also in use. * Standard pulp fiction, not of the s-f order, competently done, but so synthetic as to be lifeless.

1422. **THE TERRORS OF ARYL.** *Wonder Stories*, March 1931. Ill. Marchioni.

Short story. * *Time:* The interplanetary future, perhaps 1998, which is mentioned in the story. *Place:* Aryl, a small intra-Mercurian planet. Aryl is at this time largely unexplored. A thick atmosphere of peculiar chemical composition, although breathable by humans, shields the planet from solar rays, so that the climate is only tropical. This atmosphere distorts light so that the planet is nearly invisible from Earth and also causes all

Starzl, R. F. (continued)

sorts of looming and miragic effects. * An I.F.P. two-man spaceship, while pursuing the space pirate Captain Nirvo, has cracked up on Aryl. Corporal Henley has been ill with a local fever, and his companion, Private Elsinger, has been able to do little more than nurse him. Now that Henley is partly recovered, the two men set out to locate Nirvo's base, which is their only hope for survival. They encounter all sorts of monstrous, carnivorous creatures along the way; these are described with more imagination than is usual in such stories. * Since the planetoid is small, they find the pirate base and in a surprise attack hijack Nirvo's space cruiser. Along the way they rescue captives that Nirvo had been holding, including Henley's sweetheart. * This last romantic touch spoils what had been a competent adventure story.

1423. THE EARTHMAN'S BURDEN. *Astounding Stories*, June 1931. Ill. Paul.

Short story. * Mercantilism and police work. * *Time:* the interplanetary future. *Place:* mostly Mercury, parts of which are like tropical Earth. * Olear of the Interplanetary Flying Police is assigned to investigate why the factors of the Blue River Station of the Mercurian Trading Concession (M.T.C.) have been disappearing. The M.T.C. buys from the natives a certain gum that is the only known cure for cancer. * Olear lands, quarrels with the present factor, flies away, and sneaks back on foot. He discovers that the problem has been caused by a Plutonian who has been manipulating the natives in order to gain power. Olear saves the situation. * *Miscellaneous:* The Mercurians, or frogfolk, are humanoid but batrachian, with a primitive culture. * The Plutonians, who are almost extinct, once held a superscience that they have largely lost. Early Plutonian visits to Earth survived in folk memory as the devil, since Plutonians are gigantic, with horns, hooves, and tail.

1424. THE MAN WHO CHANGED THE FUTURE. *Wonder Stories*, June 1931. Ill. Fisher.

Short story. * *Time:* 1930 and 2030. *Place:* Lakopolis, which is obviously à clef for Chicago. * Lakopolis is run by gangsters who openly commit their crimes without fear of retribution. Young Park Helm, who has strong ideas about cleaning up the situation, is discussing it with his friend Professor Nicholson, wondering what will eventually happen. Nicholson states that such knowledge is attainable, for he has invented a time apparatus with which Helm can travel in astral body to whatever year he wishes. * The two men agree on 2030, one hundred years in the future. Helm finds himself in future Lakopolis, which is even more gangster-overrun than his own time. Stumbling into a romantic situation in which a young woman is being forced into marriage with a gangster, he rescues her. During the back-and-forth action the gangster overlord of the area is killed, and Helm, in some manner not specified, becomes leader of the reform movement, cleans up Lakopolis, and wins a wife. * The key moment came when Helm, who has hitherto been able only to watch, found himself free to emerge in 2030 and act. On this point, the text is self-contradictory. * Nicholson's apparatus consists of enormous generators whose magnetic fields distort the ether. * Not very successful.

1425. THE PLANET OF DESPAIR. *Wonder Stories*, July 1931. Ill. Marchioni.

Short story. * *Time:* A.D. 3977. *Place:* Earth, space, Pluto. * *Background:* In the year 3927 the Earth engaged in a disastrous war with Pluto. The Plutonians, who are gigantic black, horned beings, were far superior to Earth scientifically. They disintegrated the Terrestrial space fleet and moved Earth from its orbit away from the sun. Earth had no choice but to surrender, whereupon the Plutonians replaced it in its orbit. But each year the Earth must supply a tribute of thirty perfect young men and women, whom the Plutonians take away for experimentation. Utterly without passion (other than anger), the Plutonians are fascinated by human emotions, which they wish to understand. They are also concerned with what might be meant by the soul. Fifty years of vivisection have not given them answers. In a previous episode (not described in detail) perhaps three thousand years earlier, the Plutonians conducted similar research on Earth, whence our legends about devils. * Hi Buckram of the Interplanetary Flying Police, which still operates for the inner planets under Plutonian tolerance, returns to Earth to find that his sweetheart, Cinda Mara, has been selected as one of the victims. With a combination of violence and bribery, he takes the place of one of the selected men, hoping that the Plutonians will not notice the deception. The great Plutonian scientist Fernon does single him out, but decides to retain him since Hi is psychologically more interesting than the other men and women. * On the space trip Hi and Fernon hold many conversations, during which Hi learns what the Plutonians are really trying to discover. * On Pluto he strikes an agreement with Fernon: If Fernon will spare him and Cinda, he will reveal the secret of emotion and the soul. Fernon, after some hesitation, agrees, and Hi is allowed to work in the central control and power area of the planet. Here he does what is expected: jimmies the central gravitational beam so that Pluto explodes. Hi, Cinda, and the other victims escape in the spaceship. Furlough over, Hi returns to duty. * Routine, without much fictional conviction.

1426. IF THE SUN DIED. *Astounding Stories*, August 1931. Ill. Wesso.

Short story. * *Time:* around A.D. 65,000. * Around A.D. 50,000 the human race, due to sharply decreased solar radiation, was forced to go underground. Enormous caverns with every necessity for life were constructed and sealed off. But life inside Subterranea, though safe and secure, has not been to the best interest of mankind, for most people are sluggish, careless, and without drive. The massive maintenance machinery has been breaking down, and much it cannot be repaired for want of skilled labor. The food and atmospheric apparatus are not functioning properly. It seems only a matter of time before cavern humanity will die. * The only dynamic people are the techies, who try to keep the machinery running. Recently there has been some interest in checking conditions outside, for a possible reemergence. A referendum, however, defeated such a proposal heavily. The opposition stressed what had happened to the Atlantic cavern during a similar attempt: Liquid air flooded in and killed everyone. * There are also other elements in the dispute. Romance: Mich'l Ares and his girlfriend oppose the son of the most powerful politician. Political: a putsch has established a dictatorship and destroyed the opposition. * The expected resolution comes when Mich'l and a small band of techies manage to open the air valve and leave the caves, emerging into a very pleasant outside. The Earth had simply passed through a glacial period, not a solar cooling. * *Miscellaneous:* Subterranea is destroyed at the end of the story. * Science and technology are advanced in some areas, with

Starzl, R. F. (*continued*)

speaking projections and heat rays.

1427. **A 20TH CENTURY MEDUSA**. *Wonder Stories*, September 1931. Ill. Marchioni.

Short story. * *Time:* 1940. *Place:* the Chicago area. * Another utilization of Chicago's contemporary unsavory history. There is a difference, however, from the usual situation. Gangsters may seem to run Chicago; actually, they are run by Medusa, a mysterious figure. Who is Medusa? No one knows, but her enemies are found petrified, or in milder cases, paralyzed, and she seems to know the hidden secrets of all of her potential enemies, from crooks to reform groups. Some think that she is really the ancient Gorgon Medusa. Or was there once a race of Medusas in perhaps Atlantis, some of whom have survived? * Summoned to Chicago is Secret Service agent Hal Gibbs, who hopes to pierce the mystery without being petrified. Following a lead found by a previous (murdered) investigator, he penetrates the Medusa's lair near the Chicago waterfront. He sees Medusa, a beautiful young woman dressed in Classical fashion, among elaborate Classical surroundings. But he is captured by Sollini, the Medusa's "right bower" and is given the choice of joining the organization or dying. He joins. * Medusa and her organization are building up for a big haul, fifty million dollars worth of Federal Reserve gold. Gangsters armed with little paralyzing disks should find it an easy heist. * But there is one problem: The young woman who plays the part of Medusa has been operating under hypnosis, which is not totally effective, and she manages both to slip Hal a paralyzing disk and to exhaust the disks of the would-be robbers. The caper is foiled, "Medusa" is rescued, and the arch criminal, who turns out to be a prominent member of the reform committee, is unmasked. * Not very convincing even as a fanciful thriller. Material of this sort was not Starzl's forte.

1428. **IN THE ORBIT OF SATURN**. *Astounding Stories*, October 1931. Ill. Paul.

Short story. * *Time:* 2159. *Place:* space among the outer planets. * The *Celestia*, en route to Titan, is seized by pirates headed by the redoubtable Captain Strom, also known as the Scourge. On board in disguise is Quirl Finner, a member of the Interplanetary Flying Police. The captives are treated brutally, not by Strom, but by his thuggish mate Gore. * Quirl tries to defend Lenore, a remarkably rich young woman, from Gore, is badly manhandled, and his disguise is pierced by Strom. * Strom reveals his secrets: He does not consider himself a criminal, but a social reformer; he was framed for treason and exiled to solitary confinement. Escaping, he now plans to start an ideal society on a small planet. Quirl, though not unsympathetic to Strom, cannot disregard his oath to the patrol. * Mutiny and a general explosion of events! Strom is killed; Gore is killed; Quirl and Lenore survive, and the I.F.P. seizes the pirate vessel. This last was possible because Quirl had destroyed the pirates' invisibility apparatus. * *Miscellaneous:* Quirl has visited a Vulcan-like planet. * Strom's invisibility was produced by bending light rays. * Ionizing pistols are lethal weapons. * Rockets are used for space travel. * Competent pulp action, with the fairy tale aspect that Starzl has used elsewhere of a millionairess falling in love with a poor man.

1429. **THE MARTIAN CABAL**. *Astounding Stories*, May 1932. Ill. Wesso.

Novelette. * *Time:* the interplanetary future, perhaps the twenty-second century. *Place:* Mars. * Sime Hemingway, agent of the Interplanetary Flying Police, is acting as undercover man on Mars, where a political crisis is at hand. It is election time, and the various parties all seem equally unscrupulous: big business, military, democratic, and royalist. In terms of individuals, the corrupt planetary president Wilcox is working to become governor of the solar system; backed by interplanetary bankers, he plots war with Earth. Aiding him is the remarkable impersonator Scar Balta, who would like to marry Princess Sira to acquire the monarchist votes and become king, under Wilcox. The Machiavellian Prince Joro, leader of the monarchists, also has plans for Sira. * Sime enters this complex set of cabals, and with the aid of another undercover I.F.P. man is lucky enough to smash the plotters and get the Princess Sira. Along the way he resists temptation to join Balta, is tortured quite a bit, and triumphs in hand-to-hand battles. An odd incident is the safe landing of I.F.P. man Murray: tossed out of a trapdoor in a flying machine, he snatches the carpet off the floor as he goes and uses it as a parachute. * Miscellaneous props: levitators, needle rays, the gravitorser (which changes gravity as a weapon), and the detonator. * Pretty silly.

1430. **THE POWER SATELLITE**. *Wonder Stories*, June 1932. Ill. Paul.

Short story. * *Time:* the interplanetary future. *Place:* Triton, which the author calls Goddard in honor of the twentieth-century rocket experimenter. * Triton is the sole or most important source for the mineral catalyte, a radioactive element that is indispensable to space travel and industry. The mines on Goddard are interplanetary, under the triple control of Earth, Mars, and Venus. Special officials check out the treaty amount of catalyte to representatives of each planet. * At the moment there is a problem, for large amounts are lacking from the inventory. Anton Waite, Terrestrial member of the I.F.P., has been assigned to investigate. * He is soon in the middle of a romance with a Martian girl and life-and-death adventure among Martian plotters. All ends well, of course. * For at least this story about the I.F.P., the natives of Venus and Mars are descendants of Earth colonists who have evolved into planetary types. * The story is capably handled, but formulaic.

1431. **THE LAST PLANET**. *Wonder Stories*, April 1934. Ill. Winter.

Short story. * *Time:* more than a million years in the future. *Place:* Mercury. * *Background:* The sun is going out and in a short time will be extinguished. Mankind now survives in small number on Mercury. A great project has been under way for a long time, building an enormous spaceship for an interstellar voyage to a habitable planet around a star about a light-year away. The ship, the *Ventura*, after an exploratory voyage, will ferry the remainder of the human race to its new home. * Unfortunately, human nature has not changed much since our time, and there is considerable agitation and resentment about the project as various groups demand special consideration. The original, contractual plan was for the technies (the scientists and engineers who are creating the *Ventura*) to man the ship on its maiden voyage, with token members from other groups. But the financial-legal clique, who financed the construction of the ship, now demand to be taken en masse to the new planet on the first voyage. The workers, too, demand passage, threatening to sabotage the *Ventura* if they are not given precedence. A fourth potential source of trouble is the band of Peace Makers, a

Starzl, R. F. (*continued*)

semioutlaw group of strong-arm men who are supposed to protect the technies. * The personal situation is a triangle among Jay, a brilliant scientist who is a leader of the technies; Curtes, a dynamic, blustering rogue who is the commander of the Peace Makers; and Idar, Jay's girlfriend, who is unwholesomely attracted to Curtes. * The Peace Makers seize the ship, capturing Idar and Jay; the technies turn the tables; Jay proves a better swordsman than Curtes; and despite sabotage and riots, the *Ventura* takes off. * Routine.

1432. **DIMENSION OF THE CONQUERED**. *Astounding Stories*, October 1934. Ill. Dold.

Short story. * The narrator, forced to talk by a state commission, explains the Simeon affair. The narrator and his associates framed Simeon and had him institutionalized as insane. Their reasons follow. * Gerald P. Simeon, a brilliant scientist, has invited friends to a demonstration of his great discovery. He has devised a means to communicate with the fourth dimension, indeed, with a second apparatus, has translated the speech of the intelligent natives into English. * Simeon demonstrates, speaking to a fourth-dimensional being, who explains matters. Millions of years ago some sort of cosmic storm beset the world, creating a counterpart in the fourth dimension, so that, essentially, there are two Earths. The communicant continues: It would like information on weapons, since its society is ignorant of them, for a race of savage servitors is on the edge of revolt and will imperil the civilized people. At about this time Simeon sets the television component of his apparatus working, displaying the other world, which contains a fantastically regular city. As for the menace, Simeon and his friends see a subman struggling to evoke mentality. And as for the civilized people, they are revealed to be wasps, who control the submen by their stings. * Simeon is all for providing the wasps with information about weapons, but his associates, as human chauvinists, overcome him, sit on him, smash his apparatus, and certify him as insane. * The story, perhaps unintentionally, causes the reader to wonder about the true nature of humanity: physical shape or mentality. Lifted above routine by the morsel of question.

STARZL, R. F. and PRAGNELL, FESTUS.

Biographical information is given in separate entries under the authors' names.

1433. **THE VENUS GERM**. *Wonder Stories*, November 1932. Ill. Paul.

Short story. * *Time:* A.D. 3976. *Place:* Earth and Venus. * Wicked capitalists in a situation of crisis. The story is loosely latched onto Starzl's Interplanetary Flying Police series. * *Background:* Venus, colonized by Earth, is held in economic subjugation by the great financial powers that really rule the political scene behind the politicians. The Venusians have wanted independence for some time, but the Terrestrial government has refused, for economic reasons. * At the moment there is a crisis that may force a change. A new plague is ravaging Earth, killing millions; it is so deadly that it may eventually cause the extinction of mankind. Although many Terrestrials believe that the Venusians loosed the plague, it is actually a Terrestrial laboratory escape from experiments with cancer bacteriophages. * Earth medical science is helpless before the epidemic, but the Venusians have discovered an antitoxin. They refuse to surrender it freely, but demand independence as

its price. * Despite the bitter obstruction of the capitalist leaders, the Terrestrial government votes to accept the Venusian offer. History, however, is not that simple. The capitalists do their wickedest to undermine the treaty, lest their investments suffer. * Leading the fight for righteousness is Glenn Haye, a Captain in the I.F.P., and his friend Panco, a Venusian. Their adventures are routine, with attempted murder, kidnappings, and a girlfriend who is at the point of death from the plague. Justice triumphs. * *Miscellaneous:* The main weapon is a paralysis ray. * Venus is much like a tropical Earth, with sunlight cut markedly by the permanent cloud screen. The Venusians, some of whom have reverted to primitivism despite the high science of others, have evolved away from the parental human stock and developed a mane of hair down their spine. * Among the Venusian wildlife a particularly dangerous form is a small rodent-like creature something like a land piranha. * The diluted Marxist social theory is probably Pragnell's, since Starzl was politically very conservative. * Oddly enough, while government is considered venal, the police are highly regarded. * Routine.

STEIN, J. H.

British writer of boys' fiction. No other information.

1434. **ROCKET OF DOOM**. *Scoops*, 10 February 1934. Ill. S.D.

Published anonymously, attribution per W. O. G. Lofts, who had access to the publisher's records.

Boys' fiction. * Short story. * Professor Barrymore and his young assistant Brant Allen have just finished constructing a giant rocket ship, when an unexpected event changes their plans. The vicious American gangster Buck Renaldo has escaped from prison and with two associates, Slim Kelly and Tommy-gun Gatti, is heading this way, pursued by a horde of wardens. Indeed, the criminals are soon under siege in the Barrymore's shop. Renaldo and his comrades, seizing Brant, pile into the spaceship and take off. They obviously do not understand what they have done and are incredulous when Brant informs them that they are already one thousand miles above the Earth. At this point Brant activates the professor's antigravity device (a gravity neutralizer) and the spaceship slides into orbit at a speed slightly less than the rotational speed of the Earth. How to get down? Brant is not clear. * Suddenly a bevy of octopoidal space monsters attacks the ship. Indeed, a tentacle reaches in through one of the valves and seizes Buck Renaldo. * Although the procedure is fraught with peril, Brant has no choice but to try to glide the ship down with the gravity neutralizer. He lands the ship, which is not too badly damaged, in Poland. Brant had the foresight to don a oxygen mask; the gangsters, who did not, are out cold. They are secured, and all is well. * The ship is powered by a new explosive of Barrymore's discovery.

STEPHENS, I. M. and PRATT, FLETCHER

Stephens was Inga Stephens Pratt, Mrs. Fletcher Pratt. An artist, she illustrated several of Pratt's books. Pratt (died June 10, 1956) predeceased her. The blurb for "A Voice across the Years" refers to Stephens as "a scientist"; since the Pratts were Christian Scientists, this may have been an in-joke. Fletcher Pratt has a separate entry.

1435. **THE PINEAL STIMULATOR**. *Amazing Stories*, November 1930. Ill. Paul.

Short story. * The narrator visits his old college chum Jimmy

Stephens, I. M. and Pratt, Fletcher (*continued*)

Casmey, who holds a minor position at the old University. Casmey has become an alcoholic and has alienated his department head, but is nevertheless a brilliant scientist. His field of interest is ancestral memory, which he regards as related to instinct, hence potentially existent. As he explains to the narrator, after observing that one of the lab lizards lacked instinct, he settled on the pineal gland as the repository or conductor of ancestral memory. To awaken it, he uses a cosmic ray projector. * When the brave narrator lets Casmey demonstrate the projector on him, he reexperiences first an incident in the American Civil War, then an episode in the life of a paleolithic man. * Well and good, but now Casmey wonders whether his pineal stimulator, with suitable alterations, can reveal the future. Casmey, under the ray, shrieks, "The yellow men! Gaz!," probably referring to future warfare, and collapses. He is now totally mad. The narrator suppresses the invention.

1436. **A VOICE ACROSS THE YEARS**. *Amazing Stories Quarterly*, Winter 1932. Ill. Wesso.

Novel. * *Place:* Upstate New York, near the Canadian border, and a planet circling Mu Cassiopeia. * A frame situation describes the acquisition (in the Gobi desert) of a "meteorite" that proves to contain a quantity of thin metal sheets. Upon them is written in English the experiences of Alvin Schierstedt. * Alvin's message: He and a friend (Merrick) are at their summer camp in the woods when a peculiar meteorite lands in a nearby pond. Later they hear strange noises emanating from the meteorite. That evening a peculiar-looking man staggers into their cabin and collapses. He has in his possession an object like a flashlight, but it proves to be a heat-ray projector. * The stranger recovers after a few days. Donning a peculiar helmet, he is able to coordinate spoken English with thoughts and can communicate with the two campers. Since Merrick helped build up the stranger's vocabulary by reading the plays of Shakespeare to him, for a time the stranger speaks a sort of Elizabethan English. * To consolidate what is presented gradually in a roundabout way: Koumar Ashembe Budrog Fotas (familiarly known as Ashembe) is an explorer from planet Murashema of the Mu Cassiopeian system. His planet is desperately in need of mercury, its chief power source, and he is willing to pay almost any price, including the secret of the thought helmet, for a large quantity. Ashembe is curious about Terrestrial culture, which Alvin and Merrick, who soon leaves the story, explain. The purpose of this, of course, is satire, for Ashembe's world is far more advanced socially as well as scientifically. * In order to build a spaceship for Ashembe's return to his home planet, the men need money, which they obtain by setting up an apparatus for transmuting other metals into gold, then selling the gold to the U.S. Mint. Work progresses on the spaceship, but there is a disturbing factor. A local schoolmaster has stumbled on their doings and is conducting polite blackmail. When Alvin refuses to pay him on one occasion, the schoolmaster denounces him as a counterfeiter, confirming suspicions that the authorities have had. Alvin and Ashembe barely escape into the spaceship in time. * While Ashembe can operate his ship with helium fuel on local trips, he needs coronium from the sun for interstellar travel. The travelers visit Venus, find no coronium, but see a jungle planet with a horrible jelly-like life. Mercury is barren, but affords enough coronium to render possible a trip to Mu Cassiopeia. * Alvin and Ashembe set forth, building up to speeds many

times that of light, and after a couple of years arrive at Ashembe's home planet. * From here, the rational, restrained, controlled culture described by Ashembe in the first part of the story begins to disintegrate. The two men land in what Ashembe calls a "hunting area." As he explains, every person of his explorer-warrior caste, from the age of seventeen to twenty-one, must spend five years in a waste area, where everything is permissible: murder, rape, gang wars, etc. There is no outside control whatever, and at the end of five years the survivors, male and female, are permitted to emerge and enter normal life. The mortality is about one-third. Alvin and Ashembe must fight their way out of the hunting area in order to reach civilization. * Murasheman culture is a supercivilization, with much automation and evidences everywhere of a superior technology. Medical scientists examine Alvin thoroughly, and although he is an inferior person by Murasheman standards, he is given an honorary title and social status because of his assistance in bringing the mercury to Murashema. But as his stay on the planet lengthens, Alvin begins to see that behind the superficially amiable rationality of the culture there are ruthlessness and overregimentation. There is also a small underground that, in addition to having a mystical creed that believes life is a disease, wishes to discard regimentation and return to primitive ways. Alvin is not really concerned with this underground, but he is picked up by the police when he chances to attend a meeting. * The text from here on is deliberately fragmentary, but Alvin will either be brainwashed into a human vegetable or sentenced to the lowest form of labor for the rest of his life. The story ends abruptly as he reveals that Ashembe, who has remained true to him, will send the manuscript to Earth. * Highlights of Murasheman culture: All food is artificial, created from alcohol derived from greenhouse-grown plants, with which much of the planet is covered. Transportation between cities is accomplished by very fast rocket-propelled cars, while air travel locally utilizes man-powered small planes. Clothing is synthetic and recycled after a day or two's use; it is simple, but always displays heraldic marks indicating social status, which is extremely important. There is very little concept of family, most children being taken from their parents and reared in state crèches, where they are sorted according to capabilities. Special boards then classify the young and assign them life occupations. Marriage and marital love do not exist; individuals are assigned mates by eugenics boards. Medical science is high. * Amusements are scant, the narrator's recitation of poetry creating a sensation, but bloody gladiatorial contests among private parties are very popular. There is very little regard for individual human life. * The coronium mentioned as necessary for space travel is based on an early explanation of a green line in the solar spectrum, since interpreted as highly ionized iron and other elements. Coronium was probably out of date at the time the story was written. * All in all, a prolonged bore.

STERLING, KENNETH (1920-1995)

Distinguished U.S. physician, medical researcher. B.S., Harvard, 1940. M.D., Johns Hopkins. Specialization, endocrinology. Author of *Diagnosis and Treatment of Thyroid Disease* and more than one hundred technical papers. Recipient of many medical-scientific awards. * At writing period a member of the Lovecraft circle; collaborated with HPL on "In the Walls of Eryx." See also pseud. Leviticus Wilmington Postlethwaite, D.T.G.

Sterling, Kenneth (*continued*)

1437. **THE BRAIN-EATERS OF PLUTO**. *Wonder Stories*, March 1934. Ill. Paul.
Short story. * It would be pointless to attempt a plot summary of this story, for such a procedure would destroy its purpose. The piece is a parodic collection of puns, wise cracks, contemporary slang, period references, etc., loosely draped on a rescue plot as Ray Williamson saves his girlfriend Mary from Martians and Plutonians. The story was probably printed for the high school market, which, judging from later letters, was pleased. While the story has no literary merit, it is interesting as a collection of period artifacts for the youth culture of the day. An achievement for a boy of thirteen.

1438. **RED MOON**. *Wonder Stories*, December 1935. Ill. Paul.
Short story. * The O. Henry irony-of-fate sort of thing. * *Time:* The interplanetary future. *Place:* Mostly the Moon. * A small mineral formation, the so-called red moon, found on Luna, has proved to be the remedy for a loathsome skin disease. Enormously valuable, the stone is avidly sought by amateur prospectors, few of whom survive long on the Moon. One of the dangers is the crater beast, an octopus-like, living-stone creature that is immune to small arms fire, is hungry, and is fast enough to catch humans in space suits. * Dic R35 is unfortunate enough to be captured by such a beast, but escapes with his precious red moon. But on taking it back to Earth for sale, he learns that red moons have been superseded by a far superior medical discovery. They are worthless, except as curiosities. * In a rage, Dic R35 crushes his specimen, only to learn shortly thereafter that red moons are eagerly sought by molecular physicists, who will pay enormous prices for them. * The moral, don't lose your temper. * Not a bad job, considering.

1439. **THE BIPEDS OF BJHULHU**. *Wonder Stories*, February 1936.
Short-short story. * Second-prize-winning story in the contest based on the cover of the July 1935 issue of *Wonder Stories*. * *Time:* Probably the near future. * The story is told from the point of view of an alien being who is watching a flying disk rising up from Earth toward his/her maneuverable asteroid. * Ages ago, the aliens, acting upon their altruistic principle of civilizing primitives, had approached Earth, and, seeing that the only possibly intelligent race was utterly savage, had used a thought projector to advance material culture. Over hundreds of millennia the aliens have worked conscientiously, though puzzled by the irrepressible violence and destructiveness in human mentality. * Now, the aliens expect to welcome the approaching disk from Earth. Instead, it shoots an electric bolt at the asteroid, damaging some equipment and killing some aliens, before retreating to Earth. * Disillusioned, the aliens withdraw, determined not to advance humankind any farther. * An early version of the basic idea in the motion picture *2001*.

STIMSON, A. C.
No information.

1440. **THE LAND OF MIGHTY INSECTS**. *Wonder Stories*, April 1934. Ill. Paul.
Short story. * *Place:* Antarctica. * The frame narrator prints the diary of George Tolliver, noted explorer, who has been found more than half mad and a physical wreck. * Tolliver and his research expedition, which included a mother ship, a dirigible, and a small plane, are exploring Antarctica. As the plane flies over unknown territory, it enters an intensely foggy area, which turns out to be a large area heated by geysers and volcanic activity. The explorers land and immediately find themselves the prey of enormous beetles, spiders, wasps, etc. Their adventures are what would be expected under such circumstances, as the members are killed off one by one. * Motifs include enormous ants who maintain "aphid" colonies of unintelligent, semihuman creatures. These creatures gather certain plants, store it in belly pouches like those of kangaroos, and then feed it to the ants upon being stroked. Puzzling to the expedition is a feral young woman who has spent her entire life in the top of a single tree, eating its fruit, while the giant insects rage below. She is fully human, but her origin is not explained. * Gradually she learns to talk, but her presence causes violent quarrels among the men. One of the aviators, indeed, goes mad when he thinks that Tolliver is wooing her; the aviator tries to kill Tolliver and sabotages the supplies, gasoline, and weapons. * Tolliver flies out to get help and ends in the South Atlantic, where he is picked up, a shell of a man. * Somewhat less than routine.

STONE, LESLIE F.
Maiden and writing name of Leslie Frances Silberberg (1905-1991). U.S. writer, born in Philadelphia; adult life mostly in Virginia and Maryland environs of Washington, D.C. Worked for a time in National Institute of Health, Bethesda, Md. Stone wrote only three genre stories after our cut-off date, the last in 1951. Stone was a very uneven writer, not at home in longer forms, and erratic in short stories.

1441. **MEN WITH WINGS**. *Air Wonder Stories*, July 1929. Ill. Paul.
Short story. * A brief prologue from the twenty-fifth century accompanies a contemporary account of twentieth-century happenings. The narrator is newspaper reporter Harry Brent. * There has been a wave of abductions of good-looking young blonde women, and as evidence mounts up, it becomes clear that the abductions were performed by winged men who seized the women in question and flew away with them at high speed. The indications are that the abductors have their headquarters in the jungles east of Peru. Peons tell stories of working for such winged people. * Thither hies Brent with companions. They see the winged men, but their plane is seized by a cyclone and dashed down, with only two survivors, Brent and Wormley. Wormley drops out of the story soon. * Brent awakens to find himself in a hospital recovering from severe bruising and a mild concussion. The nurse attending him is winged, but the doctor, from outside, is not. * *Background:* Some centuries ago, Stone is not precise when, a Scottish laird named Mentor conducted researches on birds, hoping to incorporate into mankind the ability to fly. His system involved bird glandular extracts, shots, and potions. Eventually, he achieved some success, and his descendants even more, until the large ancestral estates held a considerable population of winged people and people with rudimentary wing nubs. * The authorities became aware of the situation, and the Mentors and their followers had to flee Scotland. While they planned to settle in North America, storms forced them south. They landed in South America and eventually worked their way into their present location. In succeeding generations the proportion of fliers increased. The total population today is about a half million people living in six

Stone, Leslie F. (*continued*)

large underground cities and spread out in concealed plantations above ground. * The abductions are for the purpose of acquiring new breeding stock. Males, like crashed aviators, are also inducted into the race, with the injunction be fruitful, etc. There is no marriage, only a system of free love, with the Patriarch maintaining a harem of satisfied wenches. * Economically, the land is communistic, with all working for the state and receiving living necessities. There is no money, and perhaps no personal property. The Patriarch, descended from the original Mentor, is absolute ruler. * Brent, who is told that he will die if he attempts to leave, is disgruntled at first, but gradually accepts the situation. The Patriarch supplies him with a woman, whom he comes to love, and there are children. * In the meanwhile, the outside world has become aware of the land of Mentor and its proclivity for blondes. Air attacks fail, for the Mentorians are well defended by artificial cyclone machines, and a major assault is foiled by portable lightning projectors that the flying Mentorians wield. * Finally peace is made with the outside world. The Mentorians are tolerated, some moving to the United States, and they give up their woman stealing. Since flying is a desirable ability, the rest of the world gradually makes use of the Mentorian formula, and by the time of the frame situation, the human race is a-wing. * An interesting idea, but very clumsily executed with bad errors in fact. * For a sequel see #1445, "Women with Wings."

1442. **OUT OF THE VOID.** *Amazing Stories*, August-September 1929. Ill. Hugh Mackay.

(Book publication, one wonders why, Avalon, New York, 1957.) Short novel, with obvious influences from Edgar Rice Burroughs and perhaps J. U. Giesy's Palos stories. * In the first frame, the narrator encounters a very strange glass-like, thousand-foot-long contraption that turns out to be a spaceship. After trying to break in or damage the vessel, he is captured. He is astonished to see that his captors, though human, are obviously not Earthmen. The leader, Sa Dak, is about six feet six inches in height, with silver skin and hair, and lavender eyes. Sa Dak's servant is shorter, golden skinned and haired, with red eyes. * The aliens are not hostile, and Sa Dak informs the frame narrator that they have a message for Professor Ezra Rollins. They find Rollins in Africa, where Sa Dak gives him the diaries of Dana Gleason and a narrative of Gleason's fate. * The diary and narrative: Rollins has constructed a hundred-foot long rocket ship with which he intends to send to Mars. Dana Gleason, extremely wealthy, well-known young socialite, is to make the journey. However, although only one or two people know it, Gleason is a young woman who has lived as a transvestite because of her eccentric father, who wanted a male heir. One of the few that have pierced the disguise is Richard Dorr, a mining engineer, who is in love with Dana. * The rocket blasts off, with Dorr leaping in at the last moment. As the ship flies along, he declares his love for Dana, who responds. The rocket, unfortunately, misses Mars and continues out into space, ultimately crashing on Abrui, the ninth planet, beyond Neptune. * *Background:* Abrui is smaller than Earth, with weaker gravitation, but is otherwise Earth-like. Life has arisen there and is possible because of a small second sun, once a satellite, that revolves around the planet. The people are of three races: the silvery Tabora, like Sa Dak, who are the dominant race; the golden-skinned Moata, who once were dominant, but are now servitory and at best clentary to the Tabora;

and the brown-skinned Gora, who are wholesome savages. Tabora culture, which is based heavily on radium, is on the whole superior to ours, although the Tabora do not have explosives. Telepathy is practiced to some extent. * When the rocket crashes, Dana is thrown far aside, where she is found by the Tabora scientist and mastermind Moura, who takes her to the city and does what he can to heal her. As the finest telepath in the world, he is able to communicate with her by means of images. At first Moura, who is Machiavellian and ambitious, uses Dana as a means of publicity and advancement, but gradually sincerely falls in love with her. * Dorr was thrown out of the rocket in a different area, and when Moura's companion saw his unconscious body, he thought him simply a Gora, and ignored him. Dorr, however, was picked up by the Goras. He has risen high in their councils, particularly since international relations are becoming quite strained. Moura succeeds for a time in concealing the fact that Dorr survived, but eventually Dana discovers it, and the lovers are united temporarily and dangerously in the Tabora capital, where Dorr is spying. * There is much intrigue, disguise, and back-and-forth action. The resolution is as follows: The servile Moata all go on strike, taking with them all Tabora transportation, whereupon the Gora attack and conquer the Tabora. As a result of all this, Dorr ends as warlord of the planet, arbiter of differences between the now more nearly equal nations. who will try to live together in peace. Dorr and Dana marry, and Moura, chastened and reformed, has gone into exile. Indeed, it is Moura, once the prime villain, who is on Earth as Sa Dak. All is forgiven. * Probably an attempt to write a woman's interplanetary romance on a shopgirl level, but a very bad job. For a sequel see #1446, "Across the Void."

1443. **LETTER OF THE TWENTY-FOURTH CENTURY.** *Amazing Stories*, December 1929.

Two-page piece in letter form, from Harry to Joe. * *Time:* the twenty-fourth century. * Harry and friends have found a cache of science-fiction magazines from the 1920s and 1930s, and Harry uses them as a hook to discuss his own world. * He comments on the various projections to be found in the magazines: interplanetary travel, racial wars, feminist domination, world conquest by aliens, devolution, etc. * The real twenty-fourth century, however, is quite different, being a garden-city eutopia with a scientific cast. Radio and television have obviated the need to leave the house for recreation or school, dramatic performances, etc. National boundaries have disappeared, and there is a World Court, but everyone participates electronically, à la Ross Perot. The cities have disappeared, as have poverty and misery. and all live in garden homes, with almost everyone having private planes. Medicine is greatly advanced. Interplanetary travel is still in the future. * A clever device, much superior to the author's previous work.

1444. **THROUGH THE VEIL.** *Amazing Stories*, May 1930. Ill. DePauw.

Short story. * A fictional defense, probably not meant seriously, of Arthur Conan Doyle's claims that certain photographs of fairies taken by young English girls were genuine. The author may also have read Evans Wentz's *The Fairy Faith in Celtic Countries,* which made much the same points as she does. * When Warren visits his old friend Charlie Keller, he is astonished by what Keller has to say and demonstrate. Keller had come to the conclusion that fairies exist, and that, since the Irish were notorious for seeing them, fairies most be more pre-

Stone, Leslie F. (*continued*)

valent in Ireland than elsewhere. * Moving to the Irish country-side, Keller deliberately slept in a fairy ring. He awakened in the company of fairies, who are much as portrayed in bowdlerized folklore. The fairies explained that they are evolved from different animals than man, the flying type from butterflies. * Although the fairies do not have much understanding of modern science, Keller speculates from what they told him that there is a fourth dimensional barrier draped over the surface of the Earth. This barrier separates the fairy world from ours, but there are weak places through which humans can enter the fairy otherworld. * Keller, returning, has discovered that his family home is such an entry place, as is proved by the fact that his friend Warren can take photographs of fairies. * Keller has also developed the Z-ray, which is the equivalent to the barrier between worlds.

1445. **WOMEN WITH WINGS**. *Air Wonder Stories*, May 1930. Ill. Leonard.

Short story. * A sequel to #1441, "Men with Wings." * *Time:* the thirtieth century. *Place:* New York and Venus. * Earth is now populated by winged people. There are nine national governments, and over them is the Mentor, presumably a descendant of the Mentors of the previous story. The world is at peace, and all is well, except for one horrible problem: A mysterious disease has struck the race. Women are dying in childbirth, with barely five or ten percent surviving. * The Mentor has summoned a world conference to discuss the problem and find a solution. In general, three solutions are proposed, none of which would be immediate. First, sterilize the race until a remedy for the disease can be found. Second, start creating humans in the laboratory; the technology for this is almost at a ready point. Third, look about the solar system for humans on the other planets and, if they are suitable, steal women. It is known that both Mars and Venus are inhabited, though little else is known about them. As a point in the last proposal, Japanese scientists have designed the first spaceship. The question, however, is not resolved, for a crisis occurs. * A gigantic spaceship, two thousand feet long, lands nearby. A crowd of humans that gathers around the ship is put to sleep by ray or gas and kidnapped by the visitors, who head for Venus. The council, speculating that Venus may be suffering from a problem similar to Earth's, decides to build a small fleet of spaceships, arm them with weapons recorded in the ancient past, and send them to Venus to confront the Venusians. * When near Venus the Earth vessels encounter a Venusian raiding party and chase it back to its base, where a great air battle takes place. Venusians use paralyzing gas, the Earthmen use various rays, and in hand-to-hand combat the Earthmen use electricity projectors. When the battle begins, the Earthmen discover that their foes are winged women, who are covered with scales and somewhat amphibious. * Despite the heatedness of the action, few lives are lost, and victory lies with the Earthmen. At this point the invaders receive a radio message in the name of Waltia, Queen of the Zoltans. She offers a truce, guarantees no treachery, and invites the Earthmen to her palace. She also showers them with praise, for even though they are only men, they have defeated the warrior women of Venus! * The Earthmen accept the invitation and learn what is behind the Venusian raid. The Venusians are suffering from a problem comparable to that of Earth. Venusian males are of poor quality and are gradually

dying out. Waltia offers extended crossbreeding between the populations of the two planets. As she demonstrates, the two people are mutually fertile, and the hybrids that have been sired by her captives are entirely acceptable. They are intermediate between the two race, being lightly scaled and provided with smaller wings than Terrestrial humans. The disease that has ravaged the Earth seems to have lost its potency with the hybrids. * The two peoples part amicably, and the Terrestrial fleet returns to Earth, where Waltia's offer is considered. It is accepted, and in a few generations Venus and Earth contain a single race of healthy, partly amphibious flying humans. * *Miscellaneous*: Venus is mostly water-covered, with occasional islands. * The Venusians, who seem to be descended from flying fish—Stone is obscure—constitute a complete gynecocracy, with a leader known as the Matriarch. They are not viviparous, but oviparous. They do not have speech in our sense, but communicate by humming noises, although they can be taught speech. Scientifically, they are about on the same level as Earth, hence the Matriarch's chauvinistic attitude is a little surprising. * Mars is also inhabited, but the Moon is dead, covered with ruins. * There was a great world war back in the twentieth century, in which the United States became triumphant over the rest of the world. * No interest.

1446. **ACROSS THE VOID**. *Amazing Stories*, April-June 1931. Ill. Wesso.

Novel. * Sequel to #1442, "Out of the Void." * *Time:* an introductory frame in 1950, with action in the late 1920s. * Richard Dorr, accompanied by a strange man and woman, returns to Earth and visits his friend Kington, to whom he recounts the events of the previous story. The chief reason for Dorr's trip back to Earth is business; both the Abruians, who lack iron and other metals, but have enormous deposits of radioactive metals, and the Terrestrials can profit from such trade. This same shop attitude appears several times later in the story. * The two strangers are Elsie Rollins-Weiti and her son Ezra, a tall handsome young man. Kington further reveals that Elsie is the widow of the charismatic Moura, who had caused so much trouble in the earlier story, then repented. * This background furnished at great length, Elsie tells of her life and marriage to Moura: Moura agrees to take old Dr. Rollins and Elsie on an interplanetary voyage, since Rollins desperately wants to go into space before dying. The voyagers visit Mercury, which they find barren and lifeless, except for a mushroom-like creature that has limited mobility. Venus, on the other hand, is inhabited by twenty-foot-tall monsters that look like a centaur version of human and elephant. The Venusians, who have a very high science and remarkable architecture, are friendly and welcome the explorers. Moura converses extensively with them telepathically. Venus itself is like Earth, but is almost entirely water-covered, with only a few large islands. * Following the death in space of Professor Rollins, the explorers decide to make their way to one of the planets of Alpha Centauri. The selection of Alpha Centauri is not random. Moura has been in telepathic communication with a being there who has an overweening drive for power. For reasons not convincing to the reader, Moura is determined to reform this individual and show him how to tread the shining path. * Elsie, in the meanwhile, has fallen in love with Moura and they marry. During their eight-year trip to Alpha Centauri their child Ezra is born. Life on board the gigantic vessel, however, is not too difficult. There is a

Stone, Leslie F. (*continued*)

swimming pool, and the Abruians have brought along a small herd of animals like milch cows. At a later stage of the voyage Moura is able to tap cosmic energy and create by mind power fresh vegetables and flowers. * The explorers, when they arrive at Kal, the planet of Alpha Centauri in question, discover that it is a world of hypertrophied insects, with semi-intelligent giant bees. The members of ruling race, however, are humanoid, evolved butterflies. * On telepathically summoning the individual he has been in contact with, Moura learns that the situation is bad. This person, the high priest Atun Wei, intends to usurp total power by marrying the Dada queen. He will accomplish this by subverting the Pattern, an immense web in which the doings of individuals and actions recommended by the gods are woven. * Moura, who has sympathy for the queen, outwits Atun Wei, but in the ensuing brawl is killed. The story ends abruptly. * In addition to gushes of sentiment, the author incorporates an enormous amount of background padding, most of which is not worth summarizing. To some extent Stone deserves credit for trying to develop aspects of strange culture, but this is done on a trite level. * The story is not quite so amateurish as its predecessor, but it is still not worth reading.

1447. **THE CONQUEST OF GOLA**. *Wonder Stories*, April 1931. Unsigned ill.

(Reprinted in Conklin, *Best of Science Fiction*.)

Short story. * *Time:* the interplanetary future. *Place:* probably Venus, although the author does not offer a firm location. * *Background:* The cloud-covered planet of Gola is peopled by an alien life-form: circular body with round feet, movable eyes, and the ability to hear or feel and absorb nourishment with any part of the body. The culture is a strongly xenophobic gynecocracy, with males, who are smaller than the females, characterized as weak, frivolous beings. Science is very high, with various rays, to say nothing of telepathy and willcontrol * The story is told by the Matriarch, who thinks back on the various exploratory attempts and invasions from Detaxala (Earth). * When the Earthmen first came, the Golans, recognizing that they were males, assumed that they were simply playing with toy spaceships constructed for them by their females. Attracting the Earth ships by magnetic beams and establishing communication with ancient thought helmets, the Venusians, disgusted with the Terrestrial mode of thought, expel the intruders. On one occasion the Earthmen tried a sales pitch on the advantages of trade, but the Golans refused. The Earthmen later attacked the Venusians with disintegrator rays, but force fields formed complete defenses. The Venusians totally destroyed later expeditions with paralysis and disintegration rays, until Earth no longer bothered Venus. * One reason that the Golans objected so strongly to the presence of the Earthmen was that they gave the Golan males ideas above their station in life. * Perhaps because it has a point and has moments of humor, this is much Stone's best story, a far cry from the amateurish, feeble romances. The point, of course, is anticipatory feminism.

1448. **THE HELL PLANET**. *Wonder Stories*, June 1932. Ill. Paul.

Short story. * *Time:* the interplanetary future. *Place:* Vulcan. * Space travel is ultimately dependent on cosmicite, a strange element (or mineral) that has the property of reflecting all radiation, from heat to cosmic rays. It is a rare substance, however, hence the excitement when it is learned that Vulcan,

only recently visited for the first time, is rich in cosmicite. * *Background:* Vulcan, although a small planet, is composed mostly of the heavy, radioactive elements, so that its gravity is strong enough for Terrestrial comfort. The planet is hot, covered with a lush, inviting vegetation, and harbors primitive humanoids who are friendly and use cosmicite for weapons and ornaments. Yet because of its radioactive composition, Vulcan is a death planet for humans. Only one man survived from the first expedition, and the second expedition, that of the *Adventure*, currently described, does not fare better. * The story centers mostly on Jimson, the only crewman with enough willpower and sense to avoid the perpetual traps that the planet offers. His mates remove their protective lead clothing, swim in the poisonous water, even eat the deadly vegetation, and all die. * The Earthmen, who at first convinced the simple natives that they were gods, acted like Terrestrial colonialists or conquistadores. But, on seeing the debacle of the explorers, the natives lost faith and became hostile. * Jimson, though in bad condition and in danger from the natives, returns to the ship with a sack of cosmicite, enough to make him rich. * The story ends with a peroration against greed and selfishness on the part of so-called pioneers and explorers. * Routine.

1449. **THE MAN WHO FOUGHT A FLY**. *Amazing Stories*, October 1932. Ill. Morey.

Short story. * The experiences of a micro-man. * Professor Trent has developed a ray that shrinks organic material, but with incredible carelessness (it would seem to a reader) he leaves the projector, which looks like a sun lamp, standing about in his laboratory. * Mary Turey, the wife of handyman Mike Turey, sees the projector, and believing it a heat lamp, proceeds to use it to help her arthritis. Her husband enters in time to see her shrinking rapidly. * In haste to rescue her, he trips, is knocked unconscious for a time, and awakens in a very weird world. What seem to be water globules explode suddenly; still water slants uphill at the edges; the ground is extremely rough; and there are strange life-forms, some of which are hostile. Mike, although he does not know it yet, is about a tenth of an inch high. * Among Mike's adventures are battling with a housefly, which is as large as an elephant, and becoming entangled in a spider web when he tries to rescue the ensnared Mary. He also sees strange things: a great column that extends high into the air (a chair leg), peculiar vegetation (mosses), an enormous statue (a tiny figure in the professor's Japanese garden), and much else. Eventually Mike and Mary are observed, rescued from the spider, and restored to normal size, or a little larger. The professor gives them a bonus. * The only unusual aspect of the story is that Stone theorizes that since there is a limit below which brain size can go, without endangering intelligence, Mike and Mary had little mentality when tiny. * Routine, and on the flat side.

1450. **GULLIVER, 3000 A.D.** *Wonder Stories*, May 1933. Ill. Paul.

Short story. * *Time:* Despite the title, comments within the story place it in the early twenty-third century. *Place:* space and Jupiter. * Dennis Martin and Jimmy Small, pilots of the two-man *Patrol Ship 354* of the Jovian Patrol (which scouts among the moons of Jupiter and Saturn) receive an urgent message. They are to rescue Miss Willa March, who has been kidnapped. The criminals' spaceship has apparently been caught in the gravity of Jupiter. * The assignment does not please either man, since Jupiter is still unknown because of its cloud coverage and the

Stone, Leslie F. (*continued*)

fact that ships venturing into its gravitational field do not emerge. Martin, who is a decent man, accepts the assignment gracefully, while Small, a surly brute, makes trouble. Small, the author informs us, is a rogue with a bad reputation; he holds his position only through an uncle's pull. * The men fly down into Jupiter's atmosphere and see to their amazement that the area below them is filled with cultivated fields and habitations. Since their instruments are not functioning properly, they crash, losing consciousness. They awaken to find themselves tied down, just as Gulliver was by the Lilliputians, while tiny green humanoids surround them and prick them with knives. Escape is impossible, and the two men, after repeated punishment, learn that they are now slaves of the little people. Occasional attempts at rebellion fail. * Martin and Small are put to building a strong wall across a valley. The purpose of the wall becomes clear when an army of tiny red men invades the land. Martin and Small now see that other humans—survivors of a scientific expedition, Miss March, and her kidnappers—have been enslaved by the red pygmies. * The action becomes complex. The Terrestrials escape from their tormentors. Small, obtaining an antigravity device and a gun from one of the wrecked spaceships, "wastes" both tiny races and teams up with the criminals. Things look bad for Martin and the others, whom Small plans to abandon on Jupiter, but Small unexpectedly drops dead. During one of his attempts at rebellion the natives had shot him with arrows daubed with a slow-acting poison. The others leave Jupiter. * *Miscellaneous:* The author develops parallels with *Gulliver's Travels* extensively. * The moons of Saturn and Jupiter have been colonized, as have the inner planets. There seem to be solar system alliances and treaty groups. * The Jovians are primitive in culture. * Optical illusions played a part in the crash of the patrol ship. Flying visually, the crew misjudged altitude because of the tininess of landscape features. * Overlong, and routine.

1451. **THE RAPE OF THE SOLAR SYSTEM.** *Amazing Stories,* December 1934. Ill. Morey.
(Reprinted in Wollheim, *Flight into Space.*)
Short story. * The ancient history of the solar system. *Time:* the interplanetary future and perhaps after the last glaciation in the past. *Place:* initially on Pluto; in earlier history, Bode's fifth planet. * Jerry and Cart, the first men to reach Pluto, find the remains of a supercivilization, gigantic telescopes, the age-old frozen corpse of a white man, and a chest full of sheet-metal manuscripts. * Cart, who is a good linguist, deciphers the manuscripts, which offer episodes in the history of the solar system. In this presentation, the author's treatment is historical, without fictional development. * In the remote past, a much larger Pluto was Bodia, the fifth Bodean planet. It maintained trade relations with the other two inhabited planets: Mars, which was peopled by black men, and Luna, by yellow men. All three planets were aggressive and were suffering from overpopulation. * Thus, when Earth became habitable, each tried to colonize and seize it. As a result, a three-way war broke out. During the course of the war, Luna was bombarded, whence its present craters, and died when its atmosphere was removed by a Bodean weapon. The fifth planet underwent a similar bombardment from the Martians; chunks knocked off formed the asteroids. The Bodeans, in turn, set up apparatus to remove Mars's atmosphere. * During the war, when the planets moved apart in their orbits, a Bodean scientist

proposed making the fifth planet mobile so that it could follow Mars and continue the war. The proposal was accepted, but it proved to be disastrous. Through a succession of events, the fifth planet was split apart and a large section was driven far out beyond Neptune, to become our Pluto. On Earth, the colonies of Bodeans, Lunarians, and Martians eventually produced the modern whites, yellows, and blacks. The home populations of the three planets all seem to have perished in the war. * *Miscellaneous:* During the war, Atlantis, which was inhabited by whites, and Lemuria, by yellows, were both destroyed. * Routine.

1452. **COSMIC JOKE.** *Wonder Stories,* January 1935. Ill. Paul.
Short story. * A gigantic meteor shower with individual fragments the size of small moons fell into the sun, releasing hitherto unknown radiation from new elements. The implications of this event, however, were not understood until some time later. * Suddenly, and at first inexplicably, people grow taller day by day. A very short man, who normally has difficulty in seeing himself in the mirror as he shaves, wonders whether his wife has not lowered the mirror, since he now can see himself. A wealthy woman cannot understand why her dressmaker has made her dresses too short. Motion picture actresses carefully selected to be of a certain height are suddenly too tall. The phenomenon is worldwide, affecting animal life as well. * It lasts until mankind averages seven feet tall, then ceases. The explanation reached is that the new solar radiation in some manner has affected the pituitary gland. * Routine.

1453. **THE MAN WITH THE FOUR DIMENSIONAL EYES.** *Wonder Stories,* August 1935. Ill. Marchioni.
Short story. * Professor Gaylor, a penetrating researcher of dimensions, is funded by the eccentric millionaire Gordon Fellows, who follows the research closely. When Gaylor, operating on the theory that the fourth dimension is a geometric matter, succeeds in transmitting a rabbit into hyperspace, Fellows comes to corroborate the report. * After a further experiment and considerable conversation back and forth, explanations are forthcoming. Fellows, although totally blind so far as our world is concerned, has vision into another world, which seems to be an idyllic version of ours, with a handsome young woman and all. He has seen that the rabbit that Gaylor transmitted really arrived in the other-world. * Now Fellows insists that Gaylor send him, too, into the other dimension to meet the young woman. Gaylor agrees. After all, he has nothing to lose, for Fellows has left him the laboratory and funds. * *Miscellaneous:* The inhabitants of the fourth dimension are totally human, but furry. Scientifically, despite the Golden Age, pastoral aspects of their culture, they are far ahead of us, with transportation beams, etc. Their ambiance is much like our world, but better, with two suns, one yellow, the other purple. The world of the fourth dimension itself is possible because its subatomic particles are "hooked together" differently than in our world. * Routine, with sloppy sentiment.

1454. **THE FALL OF MERCURY.** *Amazing Stories,* December 1935. Ill. Morey.
Novelette. * *Time:* the interplanetary future. *Place:* mostly on Mercury. * Mort Forrest and Bruce, the narrator, are explorers heading for Mercury, when they are caught in the Whirlpool, a strange configuration of space that swallows up spaceships. To their knowledge, no one has ever escaped from it. Bruce,

Stone, Leslie F. (*continued*)

however, does take their ship, the *Victory*, out of it, but he recognizes that he must have had help of some sort; this outside influence becomes more and more obvious when the ship is dragged toward Mercury. * This is bewildering, for Mercury, as is generally known in these early days of space exploration, is a lifeless barren waste, with the only remotely tolerable region in the twilight area between hot and cold sectors. * On approaching Mercury, the ship is dragged into an opening in what had seemed to be a solid cliff, into an enormous cavernous room. There, the two men are captured by foot-high, four-armed white humanoids, who are telepathic and obviously possessors of a superscience. The men are taken to a prison-like complex, where they meet other captives, humanoids from the rest of the solar system (except Earth). These people all show signs of abuse, both physical and mental. * As Bruce and Forrest soon learn, the Mercurians, who have set up the Whirlpool to capture ships, are using the captives as guinea pigs in anticipation of taking over the solar system. Their science is obviously high enough to do so. * Things look very bad, and the men see nothing ahead of them but torture and death, when a gigantic black four-armed humanoid, twelve feet tall, is brought in. As the men realize, he is from Saturn, which has no relations with the other planets. The Saturnian, who is in physical difficulties, is helped by Forrest and Bruce. He tells his story. * The Saturnians, who are possessed of a superscience even superior to that of the tiny Mercurian, are nearly immortal, having transformed their bodies to subsist on light. Indeed, he would not have been captured had he not been careless on landing on Mercury. * The Saturnian explains past history. Both Saturnians and Mercurians originated in another solar system, together. The two races were long hostile, until a solution was reached by permitting the Mercurians to take total ownership of another planet in the system. To accommodate themselves to the smaller planet, the Mercurians reduced their size appropriately. * This situation continued for a long time until it became obvious that their solar system was going to collide with a giant star. There was insufficient time to build spaceships to transfer the population to another star, but it proved possible to move the planet itself away from the collision to another system. The little whites latched their planet onto the planet of the giant blacks, and both together, after considerable difficulty, became members of our solar system, the black planet becoming Saturn, the white, Mercury. Since the move, there has long been a covenant between the races according to which the whites would not try to conquer the other planets. But now, the whites, suffering from enormous overpopulation, since Mercury is honeycombed with underground caverns, plan conquest. The Saturnian (Chen-Chak), who is as gentle and friendly as the Mercurians are vicious, intends to stop the little men. * With his superscience Chen-Chak easily leads the Earthmen out of captivity and begins negotiations with the Mercurians. When this fails, it comes to war between the planet Mercury and the single giant Saturnian spaceship. The Saturnian's science is so superior that he wins, dragging Mercury into the sun, where it perishes. During the battle, his ship, including the Earthmen, passes through the sun itself. Battle over, the Saturnian and the Earthmen leave. * *Miscellaneous:* The Mercurians use fourth-dimensional devices to move the Earthmen around. * Chen-Chak has a hand gun that transfers Mercurians into the future, out of action temporarily. * Chen-Chak also has apparatus for enlarging

the Earthmen to fit better into his gigantic sphere—which is not material, but energy. * The general pattern for the solar system is humanoid. Martians are giants with enormous chests. Venusians are slender. Natives of the satellites of Jupiter are delicate and beautiful, etc. Such resemblances are due to a cosmic law. * With the destruction of Mercury, the Whirlpool went out of existence. * An attempt at a more colorful story, but not quite successful.

1455. **THE HUMAN PETS OF MARS**. *Amazing Stories*, October 1936. Ill. Morey.
(Reprinted in Asimov, *Before the Golden Age*.)
Novelette. * *Place:* Washington, D.C., and Mars. * The gigantic, glowing, drum-shaped vessel settles down in Washington, and several fifty-foot-tall creatures like gigantic octopi emerge. Since they make no hostile moves, and seem to be simply sightseeing, they are not molested while they wander the streets of Washington. But as they return to their vessel they seize individuals from the streets and make off with them. Police shoot, but the ten-tentacled octopi (called decapods), clad in golden, glowing armor, are impervious. Two members of the Bureau of Standards, Brett Rand and George Worth, who had crept into the vessel, are also taken prisoner. * They all awaken in a strange milieu, where the gigantic decapods maintain a high civilization. After examination by the rulers, the Earth people are taken one by one by individual decapods to their dwellings, where it soon becomes obvious that the captives are considered pets, not well-tended pets, but ill-treated, misunderstood, arbitrarily mishandled pets. * It is not clear how many Earth people were taken, for several were vivisected, but those who stay in the story for various periods of time seem to number about fifteen. Among them, in addition to Rand (upon whom most of the story centers) and Worth, there are Dell Wayne (blonde heroine), a D.A.R. matron, a pompous Congressman, a policeman and his horse, a black woman (who interprets matters in terms of revivalist religion), and a teenage science-fiction fan. * Life for Rand is difficult, for his owner capriciously and cruelly trains him to come, go, and lie down; feeds him food that is indigestible; makes no allowance for temperature comfort; and in general neglects him. The other humans are treated equally badly, and the weaker members die off. * Rand, however, plans escape. He manages to entice his owner's husband to take him to work, and he takes pains to note how the decapod's aircraft is operated—though he has some doubts whether Earth people would be strong enough to manage the controls. * The captives unanimously decide to risk death in an escape, for death is inevitable on Mars. Using their leashes to climb down the outside of the building via the rungs that the decapods use instead of stairs, they reach a spaceship and after some difficulties take off. * Despite their head start, a pursuing vessel catches up with them. Through meddling in various ways with controls, Rand and Worth more or less accidentally disable the following vessel, and all continue to Earth. Mortality continues to be high, and by the time the ship reaches Earth, most of the captives are dead, though not Rand, Worth, and Dell Wayne. * *Miscellaneous:* Mars is Schiaparellian. The decapod cities are in a deep depression that contains air and some water, in which the decapods bathe. * The spaceship operates on some sort of solar radiation. * No indication is given of a follow-up to the adventure. * Despite many logical loopholes in the basic situations, the hardships of life as a mistreated pet are well

Stone, Leslie F. (*continued*)

imagined. The message is obviously a figurative statement of human maltreatment of animals, and as such must be respected.

STOWELL, EUGENE
No information.

   1456. THE GIANT PUFFBALL. *Amazing Stories Quarterly*, Summer 1931.

Short-short story. * The narrator, the friend and confidant of the great botanist Professor Hoff, learns about *Calvatia giganteum*, the giant puffball. According to Hoff, the mushroom regenerates tissue and can be kept from maturing and sending out spores if it is repeatedly clipped. * More germane to our interests, the Professor succeeds in growing a monster Calvatia in his greenhouse. It soon shatters the glass, and spreads rapidly, overwhelming the area. It bids fair to become a menace, for explosives cannot damage it; it simply grows new tissue. * But when matters seem darkest, the mushroom dies. It had simply exhausted all the food within its area. * Perhaps written tongue-in-cheek.

STRANGER, RALPH
Pseud. of Ralph Judson, British engineer, author of popular and semipopular books on radio, including *The Mathematics of Radio* (1932) and *Dictionary of Radio and Wireless Terms* (1941). Editor of *Ralph Stranger's Science Review*.

   1457. THE MESSAGE FROM MARS. *Wonder Stories*, June 1932. Ill. Paul.

Novelette. * Narrator Major Cooper, a demobbed British army officer, is of help to the dying Professor Ostrohoomov, who turns over his work to him. Ostrohoomov, an emigré who is being pursued by political enemies, has established telepathic communication with Mars. The rationale is that there are cells in the brain that permit telepathy, which can be rendered practicable with certain mechanical aids, notably reflectors. As Ostrohoomov says, if England should need aid, his Martian contact, Borara, will provide it. * Cooper contacts Borara, who becomes friendly after identification is established, and Cooper uses the Martian's telepathic facility to learn about a Russian plot both to acquire the Martian contact and to conquer the British Empire. * Crises come. What with Russian agitation, Britain is beset with strikes. Japan goes Red and joins the Soviet Union. Africa rises in rebellion. Britain nationalizes industries. * Borara now reveals the Russian war plans. In addition to military strikes against the Baltic states and Poland, the Russians will set off a well-planned program of sabotage in Great Britain. Germany and Japan are to join with Russia in the conquest of the world. * Cooper is appointed field marshal of the British forces. He leads an attack armed with Martian death ray projectors (also ammunition exploders and engine stoppers) that wipe out the Russo-German air and naval forces. * In the Americas, the Mexican army invades the United States, while submarines and air forces demolish all the coastal cities, dropping enormous quantities of poison gas. Meanwhile a general strike cripples American industry. But the British rescue the Americans with Martian death rays. * The enemy is beaten, and the last world war is over. * *Miscellaneous:* The Martians are human, and Mars is Schiaparellian, except that the "canals" are really structures for concentrating resources and for communication between the cities. There are lakes and vegetation, but the food

prepared from the vegetation is liquid. All in all, Martian science is almost four thousand years ahead of Terrestrial. * While the telepathy concerned is organic, it can be stepped up by mechanical devices, for one of which Borara has given specifications. * Venus, which once held a very high civilization, is now covered with ruins. There are a few Venusians left, but they have lost their high science. * A bad job, combining aspects of British boys' fiction and the worst Gernsbackian exposition.

STRATHGLASS, ALAN
No information.

   1458. THE DOCTOR'S EXPERIMENT. *Amazing Stories*, March 1931.

Short story. * The highly skilled, if somewhat venal, Professor James Anton Anstruther, has a scheme for raising needed money. There is a large reward for recovery of the loot from the train robbery, and Red Wilson, the leader of the gang who committed the robbery, is due to be executed. Anstruther plans, with the cooperation of the prison authorities, to sever Wilson's head, revivify his brain temporarily, and make Wilson confess where the money is hidden. * In the presence of the other gang members, Anstruther, using an oxygen flow to awaken Wilson's brain, learns what he wants to know. He collects the reward, and the authorities take up the other gangsters. * Amateurish.

STRATTON, GEORGE FREDERIC[K] (1852-?)
U.S. electrical engineer, writer, publisher. Born in England; resident in Canada for a time; later life in Utah. Published the *Electric Magazine*, pre-Gernsback popular technology magazine that printed science-fiction. Contributed to Gernsback's technical magazines, also to various pulps, including *Adventure*. Occasionally wrote under the pseud. George Carling. His other science-fiction is covered in *Science-Fiction: The Early Years*.

   1459. SAM GRAVES' GRAVITY NULLIFIER. *Amazing Stories*, August 1929. Unsigned ill.

(First published in *Practical Electrics*, March 1924.)

Short story. * One of two stories about Sam Graves, amateur inventor. * *Place:* Colorado. * Graves has invented a device that nullifies gravity; since it is in a sealed box, it cannot be described, but it seems to involve special electric circuits. * Interested in the invention is Lundholm, the great utilities tycoon, who visits the Graves establishment in the desert and sees barrels of sand shifted up a device that looks like a classical perpetual motion machine. * The business end of the deal with Lundholm is handled by Mrs. Graves, who, despite her appearance as a petite, shallow housewife, reveals a shark-like business acumen as great as Lundholm's.

STRIBLING, T[HOMAS] S[IGISMUND] (1881-1965)
U.S. (Tennessee and Alabama) mainstream writer. Won Pulitzer Prize in 1932 for *The Store*, historical novel set in post-Civil War South. Also wrote other fiction, regional, genre, adventure, mystical, and black-oriented. Now remembered mostly for his detective short stories featuring Professor Henry Poggioli of Ohio State University. An excellent ironist who should have been a great novelist, but never quite succeeded. His science-fiction, including the following story, is covered in more detail in *Science-Fiction: The Early Years*.

   1460. THE GREEN SPLOTCHES. *Amazing Stories*, March 1927. Ill. Gambee.

Stribling, T. S. (*continued*)
(First published in *Adventure*, 3 January 1920. Reprinted in Wollheim, *The Pocket Book of Science Fiction*.)
Novelette. * *Place:* Peru. * The De Long Geographical Expedition encounters strange events in the tabu Valle de Rio Infiernillo: Lights in the skies, burned out areas, an evolutionary chain of skeletons strung up, and the mysterious 1758-12,697,109-654-3 (familiarly Three), who looks much like a South American Indian but has an incredible mentality. Then there are the radium burns that young Standifer gets when he takes coins from Three, the force-rays with which Three's companions herd animals along, and finally the towering, 750-foot, cigar-shaped vessel that takes off into the sky. * Various explanations are offered, but the truth is that the explorers experienced contact with a group of interplanetary looters without knowing it. * As is usual with Stribling, the fine ironies, the wit, and fancy make this well worth reading. Arguably the best nouvelle to appear in *Amazing Stories*.

STUART, ALBERT B., M.D.
No information.

   1461. **HIGH TENSION**. *Amazing Stories*, August 1926. Ill. Paul.
Short story. * The great brain surgeon Carter is a man of fine intellect and skill, but so irritable as to be intolerable. His only friend is his associate Dr. Bryan. * Bryan has an interesting side aspect: He is occasionally consulted by a friend on the police force. On this particular occasion he is called in to investigate a particularly brutal murder, in which a man's neck has been snapped as if by a giant. The only clue is a little screw. * Some time later, after Carter demonstrates unusual physical strength, Bryan puts two and two together (not very convincingly) and realizes that Carter murdered the man. * Carter admits this and explains: The victim was Ivanoff, an infamous Russian war criminal who had killed Carter's family. Bryan agrees that the death was hardly murder, since he has knowledge of Ivanoff. Carter explains further: His strength, intellect (and irritability) are the result of applying high tension electricity to his brain. * It all sounds fine, but then Carter accidentally electrocutes himself, and his secret process is lost.

STUART, DON A.
Pseud of John W. Campbell, Jr., who has a separate entry, with most of his other work. Campbell used the Stuart pseud. for what he considered a new direction in his fiction, stories stressing mood and biosocial concepts, rather than gadgetry, physical speculations, strife and/or warfare. Although the Don Stuart stories were often taken by fans as a new development in science-fiction, they are very much in the tradition of H. G. Wells. Stuart's stories are described in The Machine Series and Other Works, chronologically within each group.

The Machine Series

Three stories set progressively in the future, more interesting in revealing a social philosophy and authorial psychology than in event. One basic idea is the application of a Calvinist work ethic to mankind, that lack of stimulus, lack of struggle, lack of activity will lead to decadence. The other idea, which emerged strongly later in Campbell's editorial preferences, is that humanity, if suitably developed, is superior to other races in the universe, perhaps by virtue of paranormal abilities. The series was popular in its day, but now seems very thin.

   1462. **THE MACHINE**. *Astounding Stories*, February 1935. Ill. Dold.
(Reprinted in Campbell, *Cloak of Aesir*; Campbell, *The Best of John W. Campbell*; in Conklin, *Best of Science Fiction*; and in Elwood and Ghidalia, *Androids*.)
Short story. * *Time:* 2102. * *Place:* Texas and around the Great Lakes. * *Background:* About 150 years earlier, the Machine came to Earth from a planet circling Sirius. As the ultimate in machine intelligence, it had operated the planet of Sirius with perfect efficiency for the humanoid natives, but it worked itself into a dilemma. The more it helped the people, the more damage it did to them, for they became totally dependent on it, losing all culture and vitality. Toward the end the Sirians had adapted systems of human sacrifice hoping to propitiate the Machine when minor breakdowns occurred, even though such was far from the wish of the Machine. * Recognizing that things were going wrong and might be improved by its absence, the Machine abandoned Sirius and, coming to Earth, again began its task of benevolent servitude. It has turned Earth into a lazy man's paradise, with perfect climate control; it has eliminated crime, poverty, and much illness. But the same situation is arising on Earth as had on Sirius. Stripped of all intellectual or physical challenge, mankind is rapidly degenerating. The only area of endeavor seems to be sexual. * There is one exception to this decadence, one Noah to this world. This is the young scientist Tal Mason, who is apparently a throwback to more dynamic man. His girlfriend, Aies, shares much the same orientation. * Tal, with the help of the Machine, has built a steam-powered, heavier-than-air plane, which is in great contrast to the antigravity ships that are otherwise used. And now Tal receives a personal message from the Machine, the first such known in history. The Machine tells Tal to load the plane with books that it is sending, then fly to the north with Aies. The mechanical brain is about to pull the plug on mankind and leave. * The Machine cuts off all power, everything collapses, and in a matter of hours cannibalism breaks out. Tal and Aies escape to the north, where they are less likely to be harassed by the starving hordes abandoned by the Machine. With a trickle of similar survivors, they set up a new culture near the Great Lakes. (This point is covered very briefly and not really developed.) * Tal and Aies drop out of the story, but generations later most mankind migrates to the tropics, where life is infinitely simpler, picking fruit from trees—a mode of life that Campbell scorns. * Obviously hastily written, with bad development and much padding. * For a sequel see #1463, "The Invaders."

   1463. **THE INVADERS**. *Astounding Stories*, June 1935. Ill. Dold.
(Reprinted in Campbell, *Cloak of Aesir* and in Campbell, *The Best of John W. Campbell*.)
Short story. * Sequel to #1462, "The Machine." * *Time:* mostly around A.D. 4600, but with a concluding section around A.D. 4900. * For about 2500 years after the departure of the Machine mankind has gradually vegetated in the tropics, living an easy life gathering fruit from the productive trees. Physically, mankind seems much as now, but intellectually, has deteriorated enormously. Intelligence is unusual. * As Jan and his mate Meg watch, a spaceship almost a mile long descends gently, and the

Stuart, Don A. (*continued*)

Tharoo emerge. * *Background:* The Tharoo, who are a humanoid people about seven feet tall, with globular three-eyed heads, have come from a nearby stellar system after a journey of about forty years (of what time system?). Their native planet is about to be destroyed by a solar upheaval, and ten giant ships have born the Tharoo stock away to new homes. Two ships have settled on Earth, two on Venus, and the remainder have continued on a search for still other systems. While it is not specified, such travels would seem to necessitate faster-than-light travel. Scientifically, the Tharoo are advanced, with various ray projectors, but not outstandingly so. * The Tharoo, some of whose reports are reproduced by Don Stuart, are greatly impressed by the ruins that abound on Earth, but have no concept of what befell human culture. * For double reasons the Tharoo begin a eugenic program to bring mankind up to its former level. First, they feel a sort of sentimental pity for mankind (though they are ruthless to individuals), and second, they need a reservoir of efficient slave labor. As a start, Jan, who has never worked in his life, is forced to become a dirt agriculturalist. * After about three hundred years the Tharoo have definitely improved mankind, using two genetic techniques, one of which would obviously be very suspect to a modern biologist. But by a chance error, one of the classifications of mankind has developed initiative, something that the Tharoo do not wish. When an individual dares to question an incorrect Tharoo decision, his entire class is destroyed. * Not quite so carelessly written as the first story.

1464. **REBELLION**. *Amazing Stories*, August 1935. Ill. Dold.

(Reprinted in Campbell, *Cloak of Aesir*; in Campbell, *The Best of John W. Campbell*; and in Norton, *Futures Unlimited.*)

Short story. * The third and last of the Machine Series. * *Time:* The time table offered here differs considerably from that of the previous stories. According to "Rebellion" the Tharoo arrived somewhere between A.D. 5500 and 5800, with the present situation beginning three thousand years later, or A.D. 8500 to 8800. * The Tharoo human eugenics program is progressing smoothly until genetics assistant Bar-73-R32 interferes. Learning about and understanding the Tharoo destruction of a past human strain that showed independence of thought, he undertakes to breed humans with imagination, initiative, and daring. Since he is in charge of records, it is easy enough to falsify and conceal his work. * The result a couple of generations later is a small number of men and women who are as close to being super-human as Earth has known. Among their unusual capabilities is the ability to produce from their fingertips an actinic radiation that can incapacitate a human and is always fatal to a Tharoo. * Determined to destroy Tharoo domination and free mankind, they work in secret. They falsify their deaths and work underground in enormous chambers blasted out of the rock beneath the chief Tharoo city. * Der Tag is awaited, but comes a little earlier than expected when the Tharoo, incredulous and unable to believe their data, discover what has been going on. The Tharoo attack the underground chambers, but are destroyed as individuals by the human paranormal radiation, while Tharoo atomic blasts are harmlessly turned aside by a human force screen. * When the essence of the situation has been made clear to the Tharoo, they are bidden to climb into their spaceships and emigrate to Venus, where other Tharoo settled. On Venus, the

Tharoo apparently could not cope with the fierce jungle environment and lost their science and culture. * Padded, incredible; too much like shooting fish in a barrel.

Other Works

1465. **TWILIGHT**. *Astounding Stories*, November 1934. Ill. Dold.

(A frequently reprinted story. Reprinted in Campbell, *Who Goes There?*; in Campbell, *The Best of John W. Campbell*; in Ackerman, *Gosh! Wow!*; in Gunn, *The Road to Science Fiction #2*; in Knight, *Beyond Tomorrow*; in Rabkin, *Science Fiction;* in Schmidt, *The Analog Anthology #11*; in Silverberg, *The Ends of Time*; in Silverberg, *The Mirror of Infinity*; in Silverberg, *The Science Fiction Hall of Fame, Volume One*; in Warrick, *Science Fiction: Contemporary Mythology;* in Wollheim, *The Pocket Book of Science Fiction*, and probably elsewhere.)

Short story. * *Time and place:* The frame situation is presumably somewhere in the Southwest in the present; the main situation about seven million years in the future in various places. * Jim Bendell, a local man, tells of a stranger, seemingly an accident victim, he picked up. The man was practically a superman in appearance, tall, incredibly handsome, and large headed. The stranger, Ares Sen Kenlin, told his story to Bendell. He is from the year 3059, and during space manipulations he was pulled by a vortex to the place where the Earth will be about seven million years in the future. * This far-future world is filled with wonderful automatic cities bristling with wonderful machinery that keeps the cities in perfect running order, but with very few humans. Humanity has almost died out. When Kenlin finally encounters future man, he is shocked. Future man is tall, slender, more intelligent than Kenlin, but utterly lacking in drive, curiosity, and imagination. Indeed, the race is becoming sterile, and before long will become extinct, though three-thousand year longevity is general. Kenlin finds the same situation in each of the few places that he encounters humans. He travels far and wide in the automatic vehicles, even to Neptune, which the future men are abandoning, even though its machines are func-- tioning perfectly. * Kenlin decides that this future is not for him, since it is dying, while he is still alive. Indeed, the Earth itself is practically sterile, with almost all forms of life extinct except plants and a few pet animals. Enlisting the aid of one of the future men, who mentally works out problems in twenty vari- ables, he returns to the past, but has overshot his mark. After picking up some electronic equipment, he will return to his own time. * *Miscellaneous:* Before he left the far future, Kenlin set the incredible machines the task of creating machines with personality and curiosity. * "Twilight" conveys a mood. It is probably Campbell's best story, with many implications beyond the story level. * For a connected story see #1469, "Night."

1466. **ATOMIC POWER**. *Astounding Stories,* December 1934. Ill. Dold.

(Reprinted in Conklin, *Best of Science Fiction.*)

Short story. * *Time and place:* An introductory section in a macrocosmic universe to which our universe is a collection of atoms, followed by events on Earth in 1942. * In the supra-universe an instructor addresses his class as an atomic energy machine functions, then suddenly stops. A particle of un-splittable water has to be ejected before the machine can start again. * On our Earth, gifted physicist Ban Torrence makes a

Stuart, Don A. (*continued*)

discovery that has enormous importance: gravity is decreasing. At first it is simply an observational curiosity, but in a fairly short time the weakened force affects areas of human life, indeed, affects planetary orbits and the stars. The universe is obviously going to be destroyed. * Torrence, however, constructs a machine that broadcasts an energy wave that restores the old gravitational constant. While much damage has been done, Earth recovers, as does the rest of the universe. Ban's action was presumably the unsplittable atom that the people of the suprauniverse encountered. * Campbell says nothing about the people of the macrocosm, but they act and talk as if human. * Confusingly presented.

1467. **BLINDNESS**. *Astounding Stories*, March 1935. Ill. Dold.

(Reprinted in Campbell, *Who Goes There?*; in Campbell, *The Best of John W. Campbell*; and in Margulies and Friend, *My Best Science Fiction Story*.)

Short story. * *Time:* 2047. * The story of Malcolm Mackay, one of the great benefactors of humanity. Mackay, determined to solve the problem of atomic energy, comes to realize that the phenomenon must be studied near the only operating atomic energy plant, the sun. * Space travel is fairly commonplace, but it has not been possible to approach the sun, because of heat and radiation. Mackay determines to solve the problem of heat transfer, which he does with a device that might be considered a fantastic thermocouple. Fitting out a spaceship suitably, he and an associate spend about three years in the near vicinity of the sun. They solve the problem of atomic energy, but Mackay loses his eyesight in the process. * On returning to Earth, the pioneers are greeted by a fleet of novel air vessels; they also learn of enormous technological progress since Mackay left. The cause: Mackay's device for turning heat into electricity has turned out to be so revolutionary that atomic energy is not really needed. Mackay, in his intellectual blindness, did not realize that what he considered an adjunct was really more important than what he considered his major work. As matters stand, Mackay receives an inquiry from a space line for his atomic device; otherwise, it is not wanted. * One of Campbell's better stories.

1468. **THE ESCAPE**. *Astounding Stories*, May 1935. Ill. Dold.

(Reprinted in Campbell, *Cloak of Aesir*.)

Short story. * *Time:* 2018. * In this future world a mating bureau attends to marriages, deciding upon ideal matches and altering personalities so that the partners are in love with each other. Aies Marlan, a fine scientist and artist, resents the general situation, since she has good reason to believe that the bureau will assign her to Bruce Randall, who has been placed in her father's laboratory to work near her. While Randall is intelligent, she finds his mannerisms intolerable, much preferring sensitive Paul Treray, who reciprocates her feelings. * Aies decides to run away, although it is not clear what her ultimate destination is. Surreptitiously building a small projector, she paralyzes Randall and the police who have been assigned to bring her to the mating bureau, and flies off with Paul. * Despite some ingenuity in dodging the police, she and Paul are captured, with no great harm done to anyone along the line. Actually, her capture was possible because Randall has observed her work on the paralyzer and equally surreptitiously built a superior model and devised protective clothing against it. * Taken to the bureau,

Aies is conditioned to love Randall and presumably lives happily ever after. The process does not seem to be unpleasant. * Routine. A trite situation handled better by other authors.

1469. **NIGHT**. *Astounding Stories*, October 1935. Ill. Dold.

(Reprinted in Campbell, *Who Goes There?*; in Asimov, *Where Do We Go from Here?*; in Aldiss, *Evil Earths*; in Moskowitz, *Modern Masterpieces of Science Fiction*; and in Silverberg, *Galactic Dreamers*.)

Short story. * A follow-up to #1465, "Twilight." * *Time and place:* For the frame situation, probably the near future, indefinite place; for the heart of the story, perhaps billions of years into the future, on Earth and Neptune. * Flying about forty-five thousand feet high, Bob Carter is testing an antigravity control. Something goes wrong; the plane crashes; but Carter is not in the wreckage or elsewhere. Some time later he is found encased in his flying suit, nearly dead of asphyxiation. He tells his story. * After turning on the unit, he found himself falling, and landed in a "snowfield" of frozen gases. Overhead is a dark red sun that is obviously dead and throws no heat, and in the sky is a scanty grouping of stars. As he learns later, the universe has collapsed on itself so that the planets of the solar system are now only short distances apart and dead stars are close at hand. * Carter, who has a short supply of oxygen, wanders about, finding incredible ghost-town constructions, all totally mechanized, all dead. As he reasons it out, the extreme cold induced superconductivity, putting supporting machinery out of order and killing the human race. * He comes upon one building that seems to show a little stored energy in what may be an interplanetary signalling system. Reasoning that machinery originally designed for supercold, as on the outer planets, may still function, he signals to Neptune. * In a relatively short time a curious mechanical device appears, converses with him telepathically, and takes him to Neptune (now only a few million miles away) where a living ambience has been prepared for him. As the machine tells him, mankind is long extinct, and the few curious machines that survive on Neptune are simply waiting for their scanty supply of fuel hydrogen to become exhausted—a machine death wish. The machine warns him that at a certain time a reflux of the magnetic force that brought him into the future will return him to his own time frame. This is what happens. * While Campbell does not spell it out directly, it would seem that Carter erred in setting off his antigravity device too close to the Earth's magnetic field. Any implications that this may have for antigravity are ignored. * Better written than the earlier story.

1470. **ELIMINATION**. *Astounding Stories*, May 1936. Unsigned ill.

(Reprinted in Campbell, *Who Goes There?*, and in Campbell, *The Best of John W. Campbell*.)

Short story. * *Time:* the frame situation in 1959, the main events in 1937. *Place:* New York City. * In the frame situation young Dwight brings to Grantland, a family friend and patent attorney, information about a process for bottling electricity. He wants to apply for a patent, but Grantland urges him to suppress the invention, claiming that it will cause too much social and economic damage. * Dwight argues the point, whereupon Grantland cites as a parallel case an incident in the past in which Dwight's father was involved in a minor way. Kerry, a very great mathematician, and Darnell, an extremely ingenious

Stuart, Don A. (*continued*)

engineer, created a machine that showed the probabilities of anything that might happen. Because of its mode of operation, the near future was difficult to predict, but events farther ahead in time were fairly easily encompassed. * The men then considered connecting the not-too-distant future with the immediate future, in terms of individual lifelines. In other words, if A is to live to the age of 90, what should be his best action-line for tomorrow? * As the reader expects, the machine correctly showed the impending deaths of both men. Dwight's father helped dismantle the device and suppress further information. * For some reason, which this reader finds obscure, Grantland's anecdote convinces Dwight that he should be a mute Faraday and suppress canned electricity. * *Miscellaneous:* The machine, which was an accidental discovery Dwight made while trying to create a viewer, was not based on Einstein's curved space theory, which is wrong, but upon ten-dimensional electronic theory. * A familiar theme, handled routinely.

1471. **FRICTIONAL LOSSES.** *Astounding Stories,* July 1936. Ill. Wesso.

(Reprinted in Campbell, *Who Goes There?.*)

Short story. * *Time:* presumably the late twentieth century. * *Background:* About thirty years earlier one hundred great Granthee spaceships invaded the Earth. The Granthee, who were six-legged monstrosities of undisclosed origin, possessed heat rays, atomic bombs, atomic power and other appurtenances of superior science, but were gradually destroyed. * The cost, however, was high. Granthee atomic bombs turned cities and fortresses into lava pools, and rays exterminated the peoples of Asia and most of Europe. North America, while somewhat less hard hit, still suffered severely. Approximately 99.9% of the human race perished in repelling the invasion, and the survivors have relapsed nearly into primitivism. * The few men who try to recover the ancient science, including atomic bombs created toward the last of the invasion, are reduced to digging in the rubble of ruined cities for materials and growing castor beans for oil. Erratic radio, relapsed to Morse code, exists between such scattered establishments. * In the former New York area, old Hugh and his young friend Tom scavenge for radio parts. Hugh has the unrealistic hope of building weapons against the expected second invasion by the Granthee, but Tom and most of the others in their small settlement regard Hugh's work askance and are fatalistic about what they know is inevitable death. * While puttering with high frequency currents, however, Hugh accidentally constructs a device that destroys friction in the path of its emanations. This comes in the nick of time, just as the ships of the second Granthee invasion are overhead. Hugh has broadcast details of his invention, and the Granthee ships are no more than clay pigeons. * *Miscellaneous:* Japan was blown into the sea. * The Japanese used kamikaze planes against the Granthee, while Englishmen, about to be taken away as slaves or meat, carried atomic bombs on board Granthee ships. * A familiar theme from Campbell, developed with even less conviction than usual.

SULLIVAN,, H. L. G.

No information.

1472. **THE MOON WAITS.** *Amazing Stories,* November 1934. Ill. Morey.

Novelette. * Small-town America, Championville. * Since the development is (unnecessarily) intricate, the plot is best presented chronologically. * Brilliant young supergenius Mason Kent and his comrade Garth Gremillion are working on a secret project when their laboratory is destroyed in an accidental explosion. Kent cannot be found. * Despite the lack of a corpse, Gremillion is tried for murder, and had he not acted strangely at the trial, would have suffered the death penalty. As it was, he was placed in an establishment for the criminally insane. * At a meeting of the local astronomy club a strange dwarfish man (Kurokin), after many preliminaries, explains what has been going on. Kent is not dead, but is on the Moon. Kent and Gremillion had built a solid space tube from the Earth to the Moon, and Kent traveled along it to the Moon, where the natives welcomed him. The Lunarians, who are relatively few in number, live underground. While they have a superscience, limited resources have not allowed them to develop space travel. * The Lunarians are delighted with Kent's arrival and hope to establish relations with Earth. In exchange for barren land on Earth for settlement, they will give both science and Lunarian social techniques. Kurokin, now revealed to be a Lunarian, makes such a formal offer. * Despite some initial problems, Kurokin's statement is taken seriously by the nations of the world, but all that happens is near warfare as various governments jockey for a monopoly, while their populations bitterly resent the idea of lunar colonization. * The upshot is that Kurokin and his superiors recognize that Earth is not yet ready for interplanetary relations. Kent returns from the Moon, and Kurokin goes home. A few centuries from now the Lunarians will try again. * Many loopholes and loose ends, including the tube itself. It is surprising that *Amazing Stories,* despite its general low standard, did not try to ameliorate some of the scientific foolishness.

SUTTON, RANSOM

Writing name of Eli Ransome Sutton (1869-1934). U.S. miscellaneous writer. His *The Passing of the Fourteen* (1914) is concerned with Mexican bandit lore. The author's name is incorrectly carried as Ransome on both the story heading and the contents page.

1473. **THE ISLAND OF TERROR.** *Wonder Stories Quarterly,* Fall 1930. Ill. Marchioni.

Short story. * *Place:* an imaginary island in the mouth of the Orinoco River. * When the narrator (Henry Haveland) learns that his naturalist younger brother, Carl, is missing after having landed on Fantasmas Island in search of pirate treasure, he immediately sets out for South America. Reaching the vicinity, he learns that the island is tabu, considered haunted, and that no one will take him there. Eventually, a blonde young woman and her fiancé agree to help him. * Strange things are there on Fantasmas, including a pack of perfectly trained wild dogs and a weird-looking wild man who is presumably a back-mutation to an earlier stage of mankind. A hairy creature, he is called a loup garou, or werewolf, by the author. * Captured by the wild man, Henry is fortunate to survive, but his dead brother's thigh bone comes in handy as a club. Henry returns to the native village, with plans, perhaps not entirely honorable, for the blonde young woman, whom he considers a throwback to Spanish ancestry. * Genetics of a sort is the basis of a not very satisfactory story. In the blurb the editor states that the atmosphere comes from Mr. Sutton's personal experiences.

SYKES, HAROLD S.

Portrait printed with "The Beacon of Airport Seven" shows a middle-aged man. The locale of the following story suggests that the author may have been Harold S. Sykes, Mayor of Flagstaff, Arizona, 1947-1950.

1474. **THE BEACON OF AIRPORT SEVEN**. *Air Wonder Stories*, July 1929. Ill. Paul.

Short story. * Time: Perhaps the 1940s; in any case, later than 1932. *Place:* Nevada. * At first it looks like negligence when air pilot Royce almost crashes his passenger plane into the beacon at Airport Seven in the Nevada desert. Royce claims that the beacon light shifted in position, and it was not until the last minute that he saw it in its proper location and changed his course. Royce's story is regarded with incredulity, but when other pilots have the same problem with the beacon, resulting in crashes and deaths, the situation changes. * A solution comes when pilots checking the area near the beacon find a fairly large laboratory complex operated by Lawson, a curmudgeonly scientist. A few minutes of conversation reveal that Lawson is a mad scientist with a grievance against the airlines for the noise that the planes make around his lab. Invoking Einstein's principle that gravity bends light rays, he has succeeded in using magnetism to bend the light around the beacon. As the aviators try to break into the inner laboratory, Lawson accidentally electrocutes himself.

1475. **THE INSATIABLE ENTITY**. *Science Wonder Stories*, March 1930. Ill. Ruger.

Short story. * The young narrator, instead of going away on vacation, agrees to assist Dr. McInnis in his lab. McInnis has been experimenting with very short radiation and has obtained very curious results. Using a certain concentration of rays he is able to accelerate the growth of lower forms of life. For example, a tadpole grows legs in a matter of seconds. * In the crucial experiment McInnis plays his rays on certain Mycetozoa. One specimen grows rapidly until it is visible to the naked eye, then, in later sessions, even larger. * At the time when the creature must weigh about fifty pounds, McInnis leaves to welcome a foreign colleague. While he is away, the narrator is to attend the protozoan. It grows and grows, eventually to a mass three feet across. It is not consciously vicious, but since it needs food to develop, it eats McInnis's laboratory animals. Indeed, the narrator has a narrow escape from it. McInnis returns in time to rescue the narrator and destroy the protozoan. * A trite situation, but handled with some skill.

TAINE, JOHN

Writing name of Eric Temple Bell (1883-1960). Distinguished U.S. (mostly California) mathematician and educator. Awarded many international honors. Professor of Mathematics at California Institute of Technology; long president of The Mathematical Association of America. Many of his mathematical papers are now significant in modern computer theory. Author of very fine popular books about mathematics and mathematicians, books that influenced generations of readers. Taine, who claimed to have been unaware of the science-fiction development in the 1920s and 1930s (before his own work was published in the genre magazines) was essentially trying to adapt the matter of science (notably physics, chemistry and biology) to

a mainstream novel, with narrative influence from H. Rider Haggard. His work, thus, often seems inappropriate in the genre magazines with its sometimes intricate plotting, detailed exposition, and attempts at character realism. Throughout his work certain crotchets appear that now would be considered racism of the worst sort. Nevertheless, all in all, Taine could well be considered the foremost American science-fiction writer of the 1920s—a position, unfortunately, that does not encourage the imposition of laurels, since there was little competition. In any case Bell/Taine is one of the very few first-rank scientists who have taken to science-fiction to express their creative impulse.

Taine's book fiction is covered thoroughly in *Science-Fiction: The Early Years*. The present stories are listed in order of publication, which sometimes differs greatly from order of composition.

1476. **WHITE LILY**. *Amazing Stories Quarterly*, Winter 1930. Ill. Wesso.

(Reprinted as *The Crystal Horde*, Fantasy Press, Reading, Pa. 1952, and as "White Lily" in Taine, *Seeds of Life and White Lily*.)

Novel. * *Place:* the San Francisco Bay area and Kansu Province, China. * A rather curious combination of chemical speculation and international politics (Communists under the bed variety) of the late 1920s. * The chemical series of subplots is the more interesting. Extracted from the story sequence: It may well have been only cosmic chance that life on earth is carbon-based rather than crystalline silicate. And it is possible that that chance may be set aside by a new biogenesis. Such happens, in a limited way, when Captain Robert Lane and his family dye Easter eggs, using in one case an egg that has been preserved in water glass. In some inexplicable fashion this creates silicon-based, crystalline formations that grow with incredible rapidity, eating calcium and silicon. Incidents of the crystal creation are at first limited, a presence in the Lane household, then an eruption in the nearby desert, which creates some comic news interest. The first major appearance of the crystal life causes the almost total destruction of a troop transport bearing Marines under the command of Captain Lane across the Pacific. It now becomes clear that the crystal life is fulminatingly contagious, and that a combination of dim light, calcium, and cellulose will bring its seeds into fruition. Captain Lane's contaminated uniform carried the germs of the crystalline life. * Jonathan Saxby, a retired renowned geologist, who collects data about earthquakes, stumbles upon the desert incident, follows it up, and after a succession of perils, disasters, and forebodings realizes what has happened. He thereupon follows Lane to China, both to warn him to keep silent about the chemical events in his household, and to investigate the crystal life-form. * The second series of events deals with Kansu. There, the heavily Moslem population has been led into a pogrom against the small Christian minority by two Russo-Jewish agents provocateurs. Their unwitting agent is the Moslem leader Hu, once a great man, but now sinking into old age. The Russian aim is first to wipe out the Christians, then in turn the Moslems, then manage a takeover during the turmoil. * Captain Lane's involvement is simple but a little incredible: He is leading a small, lightly armed detachment of U.S. Marines into Central China to rescue a few American missionaries, with no clearance from the Chinese government. * Massacres, standoffs, confrontations, bluffs, and eruptions of the crystal life finally

Taine, John (*continued*)

come to a windup. The crystal life-form is dead, as are most of the characters. Lane survives, as does Saxby, who resists the temptation to recreate the crystalline life. * The story title is the name of the daughter of Hu, the Moslem leader; she was a force for good. * The first sections describing the crystal eruption have a certain fascination, despite the horrible writing, but the remainder of the story is a jumble that never achieves conviction.

1477. **SEEDS OF LIFE**. *Amazing Stories Quarterly*, Fall 1931. Ill. Wesso.

(Book publication by Fantasy Press, Reading, Pa., 1951; Rich and Cowan, London, 1955; and in Taine, *Seeds of Life and White Lily*.)

Novel. * The themes are the perils of meddling scientifically with nature's progress, and the unchangeability of innate human rottenness. * *Time:* perhaps entering the near future. *Place:* the Bay Area, California, in and around the Erickson Foundation, which conducts research and equipment development in high frequency electricity. * The leading characters, who serve as foils to one another, are Andrew Crane, a competent physicist, specialty extra-hard X-rays, and Neils Bork, a competent enough technical assistant with moral flaws, including alcohol and women. Crane (whom a reader may regard as an officious conniver, though this was probably not Taine's intention) unwittingly precipitates matters by attempting to uplift Bork. * Crane, with Bork's aid, is building X-ray apparatus of enormous power. A two-million volt tube is currently in operation, and a twenty-million volt tube has just been finished and is ready for testing. Unfortunately, as the two men are carrying the large tube, Bork drops his end, and the tube is partially broken. That evening, drunk and bitter at the needling he has received from Crane, Bork decides on revenge. Intending to sabotage Crane's project, he runs twenty-million volts through the two million volt tube, wrecking the installation. * Far more important than the sabotage, though, is what the radiation does to Bork. It alters him completely, advancing him about one million years in evolutionary terms. The once dull, blond Bork is changed to an incredibly handsome, dynamic, dark brunet with a mentality that is unbelievable. But he is almost totally amnesiac about his earlier life. He is a new man. * The new man, who chances on the name de Soto, decides to study electromagnetism, and after a few hours of reading in the local library understands infinitely more about the entire corpus of mathematical physics than the world's experts. As he now thinks to himself, "The world must be full of idiots." * De Soto applies for work at Erickson and by outlining a few enormous technical advances is installed in Crane's former job. Crane, as a studied insult, is offered a job as De Soto's assistant. Crane accepts, partly to annoy his enemies on the board and in the administration, and partly because he wants to spy on De Soto, who he is convinced is a monster of evil. * De Soto's reign at the laboratory is incredibly brilliant, with many discoveries that revolutionize electrical engineering. A good example is fantastically efficient molecule-thick electrical insulation. Crane continues to suspect the worst of De Soto, whose inner thoughts are hidden from us, although Taine reveals that De Soto is working toward a purpose, perhaps connected with apparatus for producing cosmic rays. * A side issue reveals part of what is happening behind the story. An exposure to Crane's earlier tube apparently created microscopic life, as Brown, a medical friend of Crane's, discovers. The two

men watch the evolution and extinction of microscopic life-forms different from anything previously reported. * Brown and Crane decide to experiment surreptitiously with De Soto's new giant X-ray apparatus, partly for research, partly to discover what De Soto is really up to. De Soto recognizes Crane's treachery and discharges him, but too late to disguise the properties of his tube. At about this time De Soto marries the girl Crane had loved, planning to use her in his experiments. * De Soto, as a supernal genius, knows exactly what his tube can do, from reversing evolution, to accelerating evolution, to transmuting metals, and he has everything under control. But chance transforms the situation. De Soto is accidentally exposed to the hard cosmic rays of his ultrapowerful equipment. The result is much like She's second entry into the flame of life. De Soto gradually begins to deteriorate, returning more and more to Bork. He comes to love the woman he married, and gradually turns more and more into the frail human that was Bork. * The final blow, with the complete deterioration and death of De Soto/Bork, is revealed somewhat hurriedly in a horrible climax. As a posthumous statement left by De Soto reveals, far from being the rotter that Crane believed, De Soto was really the ultimate idealist and perfectionist. When he first realized his own powers, he decided to try to elevate all mankind to his own level. But he gradually discarded this idea, reasoning that mankind was doomed to evolutionary extinction in a short time and was not worth the bother. He then decided to exterminate mankind. For this he provided two mechanisms. First, he devised wireless broadcast of electrical power for a competitor of Erickson Institute; hidden within the radiation was a subtle band that would almost instantaneously alter the germ plasm of the human race. The altered heredity would produce dinosaur-like reptiles, which would be sterile. Mankind, thus, would be extinct in about a hundred years. But then De Soto decided on a more merciful end for all life. He invented atomic energy, perfectly controlled, far beyond our present use. It would supplant electricity, but, hidden within the radiation, was a factor that would sterilize all life. * As De Soto continued to deteriorate, returning to Bork, he lost control of his mechanisms, and the radiation that was intended to produce a superchild in his pregnant wife instead produced a reptilian monstrosity. Broken by his wife's death in childbirth, still loving the monster, De Soto/Bork disappeared back to Bork's old lodgings. It is chance that he was killed and mangled by his reptilian child just before the two extermination systems were to go into operation. Crane, using the worldwide broadcasting systems designed by De Soto, warns the world of De Soto's death traps. * The earlier sections in which De Soto creates himself and revolutionizes electrical engineering are fascinating, but his lethal intentions are not convincing. As is often the case with Taine's work, the novel suffers from formal defects, inadequate development at times, superfluity at others, weak characterizations, and problems with tone. Nevertheless, the novel is well worth reading for its virtues.

1478. **THE TIME STREAM**. *Wonder Stories,* December 1931-March 1932. Ill. Paul.

(Reprinted by Buffalo Book Company and G. H. E. [Grant Hadley Enterprises; Providence, R.I.], 1946; and in Taine, *The Time Stream*.)

Novel. Despite the late date of publication, originally written, as discovered by Constance Reid, around 1921. The work, which

Taine, John (*continued*)

may well have been only a first draft, was abandoned for a time, then abridged and slightly updated for the *Wonder Stories* publication. * The basic concept is that time is a circular stream that runs eternally, with far past blending into far future. It is possible for certain individuals to enter this stream mentally and move in either direction, although this is a dangerous venture, for they may be carried away erratically by the stream. When individuals emerge from the stream at certain periods, they may be reincarnated or may be simply observers. Memories from previous ventures into the stream tend to be at best partial. * The stream, as Taine frankly admits, involves a paradox between human free will and predestination. Toward the end of the novel Taine claims that natural physical events are predetermined, but that they can be affected, altered, or realigned by the human will, a qualification that will not convince many readers. The story logic, however, is based on predestination. * *Time and place:* The narrative, which describes the collapse of a world, is set mostly in two eras/areas: San Francisco just before the great earthquake of 1906, and the planet Eos, in the far distant past and future. Eos is the more important of the two space-times, the San Francisco existences being shadows of reality. * In San Francisco nine associates, who have been troubled by occasional memories of Eos, band together to explore the time stream. They live out crisis moments in both times. * To describe Eos: It is almost a paradise. A planet in a solar system with five suns that are fixed in place by the colossal science of the past, it was settled in the remote past by a master race that destroyed all knowledge of gravity control and space travel. * Eos was set up as a rational "state," with a very high science and perfect happiness for all. The culture is ruled by two principles: reason and freedom. Essentially social control is achieved by a happy anarchism that at most involves social pressure. A supreme ruling council is not a power structure, but only an advisory body. But since everyone in Eos is rational, everyone obeys the council's decisions or admonitions. * This frozen eutopia is now about to dissolve. An unprecedented crisis has arisen: Cheryl, an aberrant but charismatic young woman, insists that romantic love, not science and rationality, should be the governing principle for life. She insists on marrying Beckford, even though their genetic lines indicate that catastrophe will result if they wed. The ruling council and the savants who can travel in time and have seen the horrible results of her philosophy of life, urge and beseech her to put aside her willful, hybristic egotism, but to no avail. And since no person can compel another in Eos, there is nothing that can be done but await the catastrophe that the wisdom of the ancient founders of Eos had predicted and the time travels of the savants have experienced. * Specifically, the time travelers have visited the mother planet from which Eos was settled and have learned its horrible history. On the ancient planet civilization was extremely high, but its science did not have the secret of atomic power, which is the sustenance of Eos, and the people were forced to labor to survive. When deserts inexorably devoured agricultural lands, the ancients had no remedy. Eventually, only one island of humanity was left on the planet, and the ruling council of the day determined on genocide to relieve the population pressure. The scientists, refusing to obey the council, took refuge underground as war with artificial lightning destroyed the surface population. Eventually emerging, the scientists in an outburst of creativity mastered both gravity

and atomic energy. They then migrated to the new planet, Eos, where they brought its multiple sun system under complete control. They also left a cryptic verbal heritage, the gist of which, later clearly revealed, is that if the Beast (war) is ever again released by men, humanity should be totally destroyed by releasing the captive suns. It looks as if Cheryl's rebellion will initiate such a new reign of the Beast. * Most of the book consists of interlocking episodes in San Francisco and Eos, as the time travelers explore time and try to hold Eos on its correct path. * The time rate between Eos and Earth is not uniform, so that in the final episodes when certain of the travelers spend a few days on Earth, a generation has passed on Eos. When they return to Eos they discover that the worst has happened, as predicted. The idyllic culture has been destroyed, and factions stressing either reason or love are at each other's throats, with the threat of superscientific war. The savants who have remained in Eos, however, are prepared and release the five suns from their bondage. They hope to destroy only part of Eos, but things go wrong, and Eos is totally destroyed. Two of the few survivors, Cheryl's daughter and the ancient militarist who exterminated the population of the earlier planet, are dropped by the stream upon another planet, one with nine suns, which apparently will evolve into our Earth and will be the future planet from which Eos was settled. Even though the principles of atomic energy are supposedly taught to all, Cheryl's daughter is unable to use them. Oddly enough, on the new planet is a human race, which must be our direct ancestors. * The intellects in exile, now back in San Francisco, witness the San Francisco earthquake. The parallel romance of the Terrestrial Cheryl and her lover achieves fruition, as it did in Eos, but here the result is good. The comment is made that while reason was ideal for Eos, perhaps love is ideal for our world. The time travelers now enter our life fully, working toward better things, atomic energy as a benefit for mankind, and peace. * Generally conceded to be Taine's best novel, despite its somewhat confusing presentation and very ambivalent theme. A reader may be baffled by the internal logic that rightly condemns war and regards the holocaust in the remote past with horror and dismay, yet finds self-justification for wiping out much of the human race during Eos's last days. But this ambivalence, war against peace, reason against love, makes the novel interesting.

1479. **TWELVE EIGHTY-SEVEN**. *Astounding Stories,* May-September 1935. Ill. Dold

Novel, not so much science-fiction as political fiction with science-fictional elements. The story treatment is more that of a mainstream novel than of pulp fiction. * *Time:* the near future. * *Background:* The narrative is concerned with a surreptitious scientific war waged by an unknown Asian power against the United States, with the aim of world conquest. The Asian power, judging by names and other matters, is obviously Japan, though it is never precisely identified. For convenience's sake, and since there is no longer reason to pussyfoot, in this description the enemy will be referred to as Japan. * A large part of the answer to the recession and the dust bowl of the 1930s has been the remarkable fertilizer that Japan has been supplying to the world on a peculiar basis. It is not sold in bulk, but is dusted by contract from Japanese planes. A tiny sprinkle of the substance is sufficient to turn the poorest soil into the finest loam, with one dusting lasting four or five years. * The result of the fertilizer is that the United States has been producing

Taine, John (continued)

enormous crops, much of which is sent to Japan, where it is stored. It looks wonderful (ignoring, as Taine does, the problem of overproduction), but the wiser heads in Washington are suspicious and apprehensive. What will happen with the dust on a long term basis? What if Japan withdraws the dust, and America and the rest of the world, suffering from soil exhaustion, are forced to buy food back from Japan? * A further problem is Japanese military development in a time of crisis. It is well known that Japanese aircraft are far superior to American or British; that Japanese battleships are both swifter and better armored; and that Japanese tanks are irresistible. In all three cases a mystery metal is involved. Up to the present American scientists have had no success in analyzing or duplicating the fertilizer or the armor. * Against this background, young Jay Jarvis is a hot item. The son of a failed American fertilizer manufacturer, he has just received a highest grade doctorate in physical chemistry for a theoretical extension of the periodic table. He finds himself being wooed by the Bureau of Standards, the President (secretly, of course), and the Japanese. * The Japanese connection is particularly interesting, since it has developed through his close friend Baron Tori, also a physical chemist, who (it is later revealed) is in charge of a Japanese basic research program. Tori is a strange personality; although friendly to Jarvis, he is also an ardent patriot of the most extreme sort, and it becomes clear that he has been cultivating Jarvis from the time that Jarvis showed promise. Part of the Japanese interest lies in the fact that Jarvis may be stumbling on Japanese secrets and needs to be controlled. The other part is that he may be able to help with a carefully hidden problem. * Jarvis takes the position with the Japanese, with the secret understanding with Washington that he will communicate in cipher. (Such communication fails.) On the way to Japan, Jay becomes friendly with Tori's half sister, Nara, who is the illegitimate child of an American naval officer. She is not only more Westernized than Baron Tori, but is an ardent internationalist and pacifist. She is also a beautiful woman. * Jarvis arrives at the Japanese science installation, which is a totally secured island, to which entry is forbidden except to classified personnel. There he begins his work under Tori. * Countering Tori's fanatical patriotism is Nara's liberal orientation. Nara is a high member of an underground that resists the official militarism of the nation. She and Jay, although completely friendly, are in a perpetual quandary, since, although their aims are similar, they cannot trust each other. * Overlaying the island is menace. The skies glow at night for inexplicable reasons, and there is a mysterious, fulminating, fatal illness that besets those who work in the radiation or biological laboratories. A further threat lies in the mysterious new, "improved" version of the fertilizer that is just about to be shipped to the United States, Canada, and Russia. What is wrong with it? * Intrigue follows intrigue until matters come to a head and the secret machinations are revealed. The fertilizer dust works by releasing atomic particles stimulating soil organisms. The second, "improved" dust, however, is lethal. As it decays radioactively, it will emit radiation that will totally sterilize the soil for perhaps a century. The reason that the Japanese recruited Jay was their hope that his work, which paralleled their own but differed sufficiently, would enable them to suppress the telltale luminosity of the second dust. Actually, Jay unwittingly did solve the problem; the

solution, which was inherent in his work on very high extensions of the periodic table, lay within his mathematics, unknown to him, and a superior Japanese scholar (posing as a personal servant and mathematical assistant) worked it out. But now that the work is finished, Jay's life is in danger. * In the final resolution, Tori is dying of radiation poisoning; the Japanese underground begins a civil war that seems likely to be successful and will install a peace regime; the ships bearing the lethal dust are sunk by the underground; and Jay is rescued. As a deterrent to future war, Jay releases to all nations the secrets of the Japanese fertilizer and armor plate. This is a very early use of the concept of preventive technology. * There is no romance with Nara, simply respect. * A mixed bag. Interesting in development, but floundering in the middle, and clumsy in conclusion, with many logical loopholes, notably the impossible roles of Baron Tori. Still, if read not as science-fiction, but as a thriller, it is better than it is usually accounted to be. The title of the novel derives from the position of the new elements in the expanded physical-chemical periodic table.

TALBOT, N.
Presumably a British author; otherwise no information.

    1480. **ONSLAUGHT FROM VENUS.** *Scoops,* 23 June 1934. Unsigned ill.

Boys' fiction. * Short story. * *Time:* A.D. 2142. * *Background:* Great Britain of the twenty-second century maintains an advanced civilization with enormous skyscrapers, planes that can travel 800 MPH, picture telephones, electric stun guns, voice-operated equipment, and radium-powered, radio-controlled robots that do the dirty work of the culture. London now extends from the Sussex coast to the Midlands, and Edinburgh counts Aberdeen as a suburb. * Lewis, Chief Constable of the English Sector of the World Police, is instructed by teleview to go to Edinburgh and stop Professor Ewart Agmar Grey from broadcasting landing information to the Venusians. He is to use force, even lethal force if necessary, for the Venusians are probably hostile and the Earth has no more defense forces. * Lewis remembers that some years back Professor Grey had announced that he was in radio communication with Venus, but was treated with scorn and ridicule. In a rage, he resigned from the Brotherhood of Science and has since lived as a recluse. * Along with Lewis and his subordinates goes Tim Lee, a reporter who has interviewed Grey and has taken him seriously. When the men reach Grey's establishment, the mad scientist at first refuses to admit them, but when the police cut down his door with the powerful Fire-ray-acid gun, he admits all but Tim Lee—and knocks them unconscious with an electric field. Lee he orders to relay a message of defiance to the world. Grey then goes into hiding. * The Venusians, Grey has said, are due in about three days. This turns out to be correct when a fifteen-hundred-foot-long cigar-shaped vessel lands, shoots out a cold ray that freezes people instantly, and protects itself against attack with a powerful electric screen that seems impenetrable. The Venusians do have a weakness, Grey has revealed in one of his rants, but it is not known, and things look bad for humanity. * Finally, the tide turns. The Brotherhood of Science works out a way to open a small passage through the screen, into which Lewis and associates creep. But a battle royal inside the screened area and later inside the spaceship might have gone badly for Earth, had not radium-powered robots entered the area, at which time the

Talbot, N. (*continued*)

Venusians fall dead. It seems that they are very sensitive to gamma rays. Professor Grey was killed during the tumult, and the peril is over. * *Miscellaneous:* Grey had falsely assured the Venusians that radioactivity did not exist on Earth. He intended, once the Venusians had wiped out humanity, to destroy them with this secret weapon. * The Venusians are roughly humanoid, but with extensible arms; their heads do not have eyes, ears, nose, or mouth, but only patches of sensitive skin. Their spaceship operated in space with rockets and on Earth with helicopter blades.

TANNER, CHARLES R. (1896-1974)

U.S. (Ohio) author and science-fiction fan. His work was very popular during the 1930s, although now it has been pretty much forgotten.

1481. THE COLOR OF SPACE. *Science Wonder Stories*, March 1930. Ill. Paul.

Short-short story. * The first-prize-winning story in the contest based on the November 1929 cover of *Science Wonder Stories*. Tanner received $150. * The great scientist Dr. Henshaw, captured by the Russian scientist Godonoff, is currently in a flying saucer rendered possible by the Russian discovery of antigravity. As can be seen through the window of the spaceship, the Russians, to demonstrate their power, are off into space on their way to Venus with the Eiffel Tower and the Woolworth Building in tow. In the meanwhile, war has broken out on Earth. Godonoff now demands Henshaw's (undescribed) secret process. * Henshaw, after a few questions, simply walks out the door and escapes—in New York, on Earth. What the Russian showed him was sophisticated motion-picture fakery. Henshaw realized that it was false when he saw that the Russians colored space blue instead of black. * Gernsback, in a note, states that the color error was deliberate. Perhaps. * Negligible as fiction.

1482. THE FLIGHT OF THE MERCURY. *Wonder Stories*, July 1930. Ill. Paul.

Short story. * *Place:* mostly Mars. * The narrator, who is on safari or expedition somewhere in the tropics, is surprised to see a strange flying machine without propellers, but with disks on its rear end. * It alights nearby, and an Englishmen emerges and tells his tale. After years of experimentation with the shortest radio waves, he constructed propellers that utilize the ether just as an ordinary propeller uses the air. * Since atmosphere is not necessary to his flight, he decided to strike out for Mars. He arrived there without incident, creating sufficient gravity along the way by acceleration and deceleration. Donning a space suit and oxygen helmet he began to explore. Greenish globular objects covered the ground, with cactus-like predatory vegetation occasionally present. Most interesting and most dangerous was a large globular, amoeba-like creature that apparently intended to dine on him. It was intelligent enough to cut him off from his spaceship as his oxygen supply dwindled; only the instant Martian night, which freezes Martian life into mobility, saved him. * The Englishman, who announces that he will make other such trips, leaves, but the narrator hears no more from him. * Partly Merritt-like, partly flat narrative.

1483. TUMITHAK OF THE CORRIDORS. *Amazing Stories*, January 1932. Ill. Morey.

(Reprinted in Asimov, *Before the Golden Age*.)

Novelette. * Perhaps the earliest statement of rat-hole man. * *Time:* the early fifty-third century. * *Background:* Around A.D. 3050 man first mastered space travel with an expedition to Venus. This was also the greatest disaster to befall mankind, for the natives of Venus (shelks) copied the design of the successful spaceship, built a huge armada, and invaded Earth. After prolonged fighting, Earth was defeated, and the human race was almost destroyed. * The survivors, however, had sufficient science left to disintegrate huge tunnels and chambers in the Earth, where they retreated. What with shelk pressure and general human deterioration, mankind gradually lost almost all it advanced science except the ability to make synthetic food and maintain lighting apparatus. * At story present, the early fifty-third century, mankind (in this area at least) has reverted to a series of small, independent, usually mutually hostile villages scattered throughout the maze of tunnels and pits. Humans no longer venture to the surface of the world, and to the men of Tumithak's world, the shelks are enormously potent, remote, unseen creatures. Shelks, by the way, are eight-legged creatures about four feet tall, with noseless but otherwise humanoid heads. * Tumithak, the son of an official in the village of Loor, has determined since childhood to be the first man to kill a shelk. On reaching manhood he sets out, equipped with three ancient, no longer understood heirlooms given to him by his father: a flashlight, a stick of explosive, and a six-shooter. * Tumithak's adventures as he creeps through hostile corridors to reach the surface need not be detailed, since they are not science-fictional, but one incident is of interest. Near the surface he comes upon the culture of the Esthetts, who are grossly fat sensualists gifted with great artistic ability. Their tapestries, statuary, and paintings are a revelation to Tumithak, since nothing of the sort exists in the corridors. The Esthetts consider the shelks their patrons and friends and believe it is a privilege to be taken to the surface by the shelks. But as Tumithak observes, the shelks drain the Esthetts vampirically. * Dazzled and enormously impressed when he reaches the mysterious surface, Tumithak kills a shelk and brings its head back to his village. His success is a bond between previously hostile settlements, and he is the new general leader. * *Miscellaneous:* Although the shelks, when discovered, were scientifically superior to humans, they knew little of astronomical matters because of Venus's impenetrable layers of cloud. * Oddly enough, there is a minor note of black humor within the story, perhaps a reflection of the author's genial personality. A very popular story when it appeared, perhaps because of its introduction of a new theme. But, today, of lesser standing. William Tenn's *Of Men and Monsters* is considerably superior. * For a sequel see #1484, "Tumithak in Shawm."

1484. TUMITHAK IN SHAWM. *Amazing Stories*, June 1933. Ill. Morey.

(Reprinted in Asimov, *Before the Golden Age*.)

Novelette. * Sequel to #1483, "Tumithak of the Corridors." *Time:* the early fifty-third century. * The first steps in human emergence. * Tumithak, now the war chief of several confederated underground villages, is leading the first human expedition out against the shelks. Two hundred men strong, it first passes through the Esthett area, massacring all the population, then waits while a four-man team, led by Tumithak, scouts outside. * When the men emerge, it is dark, something that puzzles and frightens then, since the concept of night seems to have been

Tanner, Charles R. (continued)

lost. * The story, which is fulfilled in a series of adventures, is best summarized in terms of leading incidents. (1) Tumithak and his followers are in considerable trouble once they emerge on the surface and barely escape capture and death. (2) They encounter not only shelks but a specially bred strain of mankind that the shelks use for hunting purposes. These men, tall, very thin, are dark complexioned and bearded. (3) The scouts also encounter and rescue a young woman who comes from the Tains, a different group of underground dwellers. The Tains, who are timid and fearful, have nevertheless preserved far more of the ancient human science than have Tumithak's groups. Indeed, they have actually maintained in readiness many of the ancient human weapons, but they have no energy sources. Tumithak solves part of the problem with stolen shelk power rods. The humans can now mount a disintegrator against shelk heat rays. (4) With captured shelk weapons, supplemented by Tain, Tumithak's group destroys the shelk village of Shawm. (5) With their disintegrator, the Tains dissolve a corridor to Tumithak's caverns, thus permitting a union of the peoples. (6) Conquering the shelk and their human troops seems remarkably easy. * Superior as an adventure story to the first story. * A third story, "Tumithak and the Pillars of Fire," appeared beyond the scope of this volume, in *Super Science Stories*, November 1941.

TAYLOR, J. GIBSON, JR.
U.S. author, then resident of New York City. Perhaps to be identified with James Gibson Taylor, author of *Dark Dawn* (1932).

1485. **LAST SACRIFICE.** *Astounding Stories,* December 1933. Ill. Amos Sewell.
Short story. * *Place:* Haiti. * A supernatural story. * The first-person narrative of a presumably American engineering official in occupied Haiti. When lightning blasts open the tomb of long-dead General Zephirin, the narrator is possessed by Zephirin's spirit and takes part in voodoo rites, including a human sacrifice. * After the orgiastic sacrifice and the sealing of the tomb, the narrator seems to recover his own personality, but lacks emotional involvement in what he remembers having done. * The author would seem to have some knowledge of Haiti.

TAYLOR, MERLIN MOORE
U.S. travel and miscellaneous writer. *The Heart of Black Papua* (1926) reprinted several times under different titles. Also *Red Pearls* (1929).

1486. **THE WHITE GOLD PIRATE.** *Amazing Stories,* April 1927. Ill. F. S. Hynd.
Short story. * Not science-fiction, but a crime story. * The government is trying to catch the so-called platinum pirate, who has been stealing the limited amount of platinum in the United States. Robert Goodwin, great scientist, and his friend Barry, a government investigator, track down an unidentified man who offers bootleg platinum. Their methods are ordinary detectional, except that when one of the pirate's gang is captured, Goodwin uses a sphygmomanometer as a primitive lie detector. * Of no particular interest.

TENCH, C[HARLES] V[ICTOR] (1888-?)
Canadian (Victoria, British Columbia) writer, born in England. Frequent contributor to American pulp magazines, British variety

magazines, and other popular forms.

1487. **COMPENSATION.** *Astounding Stories,* January 1930. Ill. J. Fleming Gould.
Short story, written in a fervid style. * The narrator, on visiting his old friend, Professor Wroxton, discovers that Wroxton is missing. The discovery of a diamond that the Professor used to wear is a suspicious circumstance. The servants say that a mysterious caller had arrived the night before, but he, too, is missing, car outside. * The police suspect the narrator of foul play, since he is the Professor's beneficiary, but a delayed letter explains matters: The Professor had achieved "the absolute zero," at which matter disappears. When the man who seduced Mrs. Wroxton years ago chanced to arrive at his house, Wroxton recognized him. He then disintegrated himself and the visitor with "the absolute zero."

THADDEUS, VICTOR
A Victor Thaddeus (1896-?) was the author of well-received biographies of Julius Caesar, Voltaire, Cellini, and Frederick the Great. It is unlikely (in terms of quality) that he is our author. Social Security records list another Victor Thaddeus (1895-1974), a resident of Delaware.

1488. **THE CHEMICAL MAGNET.** *Amazing Stories,* August 1927. Ill. Paul.
Short story. * The narrator becomes acquainted with the old recluse Schirmanhever, who lives in a shack on the waterfront. He soon realizes that Schirmanhever is a great chemist, for he has perfected a device that almost instantly desalinates sea water. He can also extract other elements from the ocean, but only en masse, for his "magnet" does not discriminate. * Schirmanhever's home is destroyed by a development, and the narrator loses touch with him. It is not until some years later that the narrator hears of the famous and fabulously wealthy Schirmanhever, who can extract gold and rare elements from the sea. * But, as the narrator learns, the scientist is not concerned with wealth. Dying, presumably of cancer, he is attempting to isolate the original life principle from the ocean. He is successful, but it is too late. * The narrator never learns how the apparatus works, but it is not electrical.

THEBAULT, EUGENE (?-1942)
French writer. Author of two other science-fiction novels: *Les deux reines du pôl sud* (1932) and *Le soleil ensorcelé* (1933).

1489. **THE RADIO TERROR.** *Wonder Stories,* June-October 1933. Translated from French by Fletcher Pratt. Ill. Paul.
(Originally published in parts or periodical form as "Radio-terreur, grand roman de mystère," Paris, 1927-1928. The story is covered in more detail in *Science-Fiction: The Early Years.*)
Short novel. * *Time:* 1952. *Place:* Paris. * The contest between genius scientist Mazelier and mad scientist the Marquis de Saint-Imier. Saint-Imier keeps trying to destroy the world, while Mazelier and his assistant Gribal perpetually thwart him. Included along the route are disruption of heat radiation; a sphere of solid air; death-ray attacks; a ray-induced automobile accident; a force-field that isolates France; and projections of the mad marquis that turn a courtroom trial into a farce. Mazelier wins, of course. * The treatment is feuilleton with abrupt endings and cliff hangers. All in all, much like a bad motion picture serial of the day. It was not worth translating.

THOMAS, MICHAEL

No information, but presumably a British writer.

1490. **THE MAN WHO MADE DIAMONDS**. *Scoops*, 4 June 1934. Unsigned ill.

Boys' fiction. * Short story. * When Meyer, head of the diamond combine that regulates the release and pricing of diamonds, learns of a sudden flooding of the market, he assigns an investigator to the case. The investigator reports that an eccentric scientist named Nathaniel Jones is not only manufacturing the diamonds, but is selling gems normally worth thousands of pounds for pence and shillings. Visiting Jones, the hitherto incredulous Meyer finds that the report is true; worse, Jones intends to make diamonds available to everyone at the prices mentioned. Meyer quarrels with Jones and leaves, but sends strong-arm men to wreck Jones's laboratory. This does not stop the scientist, nor does a later attempted murder. * Finally, Meyer hits on the correct tactic: He offers Jones an unlimited research job for ten thousand pounds per annum, in exchange for which Meyer promises to distribute the diamonds Jones makes. Everyone is now happy. Jones putters in the laboratory making diamonds, and Meyer's men shovel them into a furnace as fast as they obtain them.

THOMAS, REG[INALD] G[EORGE] (1899-c. 1958)

Extremely prolific British writer of fiction for boys' story-papers; said to have written over 12,000 stories.

1491. **THE STRIDING TERROR**. *Scoops*, 10 February-31 March 1934. Unsigned ill. Published anonymously, attribution per W. O. G. Lofts, who had access to the publisher's records.

Boys' fiction; the age-limit is difficult to place, but the story is more juvenile than the other stories in the paper and is undoubtedly aimed at a very young market. * Short episodic novel. Several comments confirm that "The Striding Terror" is an outgrowth of the American motion picture *King Kong*. * Jack Harvey and Frank Cooper (a significant name) stop at an almost unknown island off the coast of West Africa during their two-plane round the world flight. There they come upon and are captured by a giant some fifty feet tall. The giant, who is simply an enlarged Englishman, announces that his name is John Dexter and that he attained his present size through pituitary extracts he received as a child from his scientist father. Now he wants to return to England. * The terrified aviators are not enthusiastic, but Dexter provides a means: a sling seat suspended on a long chain between the two planes. The device, though suspect, works well enough, and after a few difficulties, like a forced landing in France, the three reach England. * A fifty-foot man clad in a loincloth is, of course, startling, even for the blasé English, and several adventure situations arise. Circus animals panic and escape from their cages, but the giant retrieves them all safely, later taking a lion for a pet. Entering London, Dexter finds it deserted. He climbs Parliament tower, where he affixes a notice stating that he is English and means no harm, but falls off and is knocked unconscious. The circus people thereupon capture him and keep him under control with sleep gas. He escapes, of course. * There is also a plot against a cabinet minister, which Dexter foils, and later a plot to use him to carry bombs into London and destroy it. All these wicked schemes fail, and the giant, accepted by the people, retires to Wales, where he lives. Along the way he befriended one of the circus

people, an American named Sam Blunt, who is quite helpful. * On a low level, even for British boys' fiction, with little power of invention.

THURMOND, WILLIAM and CUMMINGS, RAY

Thurmond was then resident in Victoria, Texas. According to the portrait accompanying his story, he was a middle-aged man. Cummings has a separate entry. Thurmond supplied the plot, which Cummings developed.

1492. **THE DERELICT OF SPACE**. *Wonder Stories Quarterly*, Fall 1931. Ill. Paul.

Short story. * The first-prize-winning story in the Interplanetary Plot Contest. Mr. Thurmond won $50. * *Time:* The near interplanetary future. *Place:* Space. * The exploratory spaceship sights a strange copper disk-like vessel in space. It is obviously derelict, and an elderly member of the crew recognizes it as the Deely time machine that left Earth around forty years earlier. The space men board the vessel, find six corpses and a manuscript kept by one of the time travelers. * The story is that of a sexual triangle. The time machine works perfectly, and Deely is about to return to his own time and place, when he discovers that his wife is committing adultery with Vane, a fellow time traveler. Shattered, Deely retaliates by destroying the control mechanism of the time machine, so that the six travelers are stranded somewhere forty years away from the Earth. The psychological result is varied. Vane and another man go to pieces; two others meet death bravely; and Deely and his wife make peace. * The gimmick is that while the time machine moved in time, it was stationary in space; the universe moved away from it, leaving it isolated. * Routine at best.

TOOKE, ALFRED I.

U.S. (Ohio?) author of short plays for children, miscellaneous work. *Recitation Stunts for Little Folks* (1934).

1493. **REAPING THE WHIRLWIND**. *Amazing Stories*, December 1930. Ill. Paul.

Short story. * *Time:* the near future. * Old Professor Crockett is a disgruntled, furious man. One of the world's leading researchers into atmospheric phenomena, he has contributed many revolutionary inventions, including new methods for the ventilation of closed spaces, neutralization of carbon monoxide, and local climate control. But with his latest invention, a solar motor for automobiles, he was swindled out of his life's work by crooked financiers. * The professor is now working on artificial cyclones, quite successfully. In his lab he demonstrates tiny whirlwinds that can pick up spilled flour very neatly. * On the crucial occasion, the professor arranges a controlled giant cyclone for his crooked former backers. They believe that it will be simply a spectacle for their benefit, but he directs the cyclone onto their plant, wrecking it and killing them. He dies in the process, and the narrator, his lab assistant, barely survives.

TOOKER, RICHARD [PRESLEY] (1902-1988)

U.S. (North Dakota, Minnesota, Chicago, elsewhere) author. In 1935 and 1936 resident in Phoenix, Arizona. Also wrote as Dick Presley Tooker. Best remembered for prehistoric novel *The Day of the Brown Horde* (1929), which, according to Tuck, he wrote while on a milk route. In later years worked as a subeditor for Fawcett in Chicago and as a ghost writer from 1940 on. Tooker has claimed that his first published story, "Planet Paradise"

Tooker, Richard (*continued*)

(*Weird Tales*, February 1924), was written at age 15. See also pseud. Henry E. Lemke.

1494. TYRANT OF THE RED WORLD. *Wonder Stories*, August 1932. Ill. Paul.

Short story. * *Time:* 1948. *Place:* mostly on a hitherto unknown planetoid of eccentric orbit. * Thanks to the discovery of arthane, a powerful gaseous fuel, space travel is possible, and the Aldane Expedition leaves to circumnavigate the Moon. The crew is male, except for Barbara Weyden, who has surreptitiously taken the place of one of the assigned crew members. * The ship passes the meteor zone that surrounds the Earth and ventures out into space, but is caught up in a magnetic vortex that carries it off course. Eventually, it crash-lands on an unknown planetoid that follows an irregular orbit between Earth and Venus. There are only five survivors, two of whom die, leaving the narrator, Barbara, and Mad Bjornsen (the pilot). * The new planet, called Aldane World, is much like Earth, but has one strange form of life, the so-called sky horses. These are intelligent but alien creatures who live partly in burrows and underground networks, in some fashion under the control of the so-called queen. * The problem with the new world is Mad Bjornsen, who lives up to his name. A man of titanic strength, energy, and intellect, he dominates the other two survivors, in part by his control of the food supply, which he has hidden, and in part by his indomitable will. He intends to found a master race, and therefore forces Barbara and the narrator to wander about half naked and to undergo the most extreme conditioning exercises. Just as he announces that he will breed with Barbara, he dies, struck down by one of the flying horse queens as vengeance for his vivisecting one of her subjects. A rescue party arrives shortly thereafter. * *Miscellaneous:* Aldane World is permeated with element 85, which causes metals, fabrics, and other substances to rot away rapidly. * There seems to be a group consciousness of a sort among the sky horses. * A bad story, with horrible writing, but with a curious surreal atmosphere, what with the doings of the madman and his subjects.

1495. THE TOMB OF TIME. *Amazing Stories,* March 1933. Ill. Morey.

Novelette. * *Place:* Colorado, and a world beneath it. * Spelunkers Robert Langtree, Roger Anson, and Willa Anson (Roger's daughter and Langtree's sweetheart) undertake to explore Comanche Cave. There are two reasons, beyond general interest, for this exploration: A colleague has reported a mysterious footprint in the deeper levels, and inexplicable sounds have been heard. * At the lowest level they find the footprint, which is something like a man's but splayed at the front, with marks of huge talons. And they hear strange noises seemingly coming from one of the cave walls. Charges of dynamite blast open an entrance to another, deeper series of caves, but also trap the explorers. (They do not seem to learn, but continue to set off dynamite, on each occasion trapping themselves worse.) * Continuing on down, the explorers, after long travel come to a dimly lit lost world with archaic vegetation and fauna, including various large dinosaurs. They also learn the origin of the footprint: humanoid amphibians (or perhaps reptiles?) who have a primitive culture, including weapons, villages, and dinosaur mounts. * To make a long story short, the explorers antagonize the amphibians and spend page after page shooting at them or tossing dynamite. Eventually the explorers raft along an underground sea and emerge somewhere along the Rio Grande. They neglect to mark the spot, hence cannot return. But in any case, there is a possibility that one of their blasts flooded the underground lost world. Wisely, they remain silent about their adventures, since they have no proof. * Obviously heavily indebted to Jules Verne. * Tooker's surface writing has improved, but the story is interminable.

1496. MOON OF ARCTURUS. *Amazing Stories,* July 1935. Ill. Morey.

Science-fantasy novelette. * *Time:* A.D. 4970. *Place:* en route to Arcturus and on the satellite of a planet orbiting Arcturus. * *Background:* In the world of the fiftieth century, there are two kinds of humans, artates, or normal men who can love and act, and compurions, balloon-headed intellectuals who are thinkers. Both are in the range of supermen. Immortality or extreme longevity has been achieved by gland transplants and other treatments. Space travel is common, with speeds approaching that of light. Gimmicks include personal antigravity belts, atomic energy, paralysis rays, and disintegrators. * About ten years ago the great space liner *Bridge of the Abyss* was wrecked near Venus, and beautiful young Alois Frontenac, a passenger and the artate daughter of Commissioner Frontenac, has been registered as dead. But now a radio message has arrived indicating that Alois is alive and somewhere near Arcturus, which is ten light-years away, much farther than space travel has hitherto reached. * Her lover the artate Drake Hillard is determined to rescue her, but to obtain a spaceship capable of carrying enough fuel for thirty years' travel, he must come to terms with his rival and enemy, the great engineer and scientist Nard Devonack. Devonack is unusual (perhaps unique?) in combining the abilities of artate and compurion, but he is otherwise a villain of the darkest sort, a snarling killer who would twirl a moustache if moustaches were in style. * Devonack builds the *Meteor III*, which he will captain, while Hillard will go along as supercargo. The vessel departs, and most of the thirty-year jaunt seems to be devoted to clashes between the two enemies, in which Devonack always wins. He makes it clear that he will kill Hillard as soon as he is in the mood. The crew for the most part supports Devonack. Both Hillard and Devonack wonder what Alois will be like, after forty years without rejuvenation treatments. * The *Meteor III* reaches the vicinity of Arcturus, finds the planets uninhabitable, but a radio message from Alois tells them to land on a certain satellite, which they do. The satellite is Earth-like, and the men, emerging from the vessel, set out in scouting parties to search for Alois. * Hillard finds her almost immediately, or so he thinks at first. What he has found is a beautiful woman who is the exact image of Alois as he remembers her, but she is cold, passionless, and obviously not Alois. Signals from other searching parties indicate that they, too, have found Aloises. * As the men soon learn, the planet is inhabited by globular beings who can assume such form as they want, in this case Alois. As superintellects, they all speak perfect English and have telepathic abilities. They have not harmed Alois; indeed, they cherish her and have maintained her in youth, for she has brought to them a new range of experience, emotion, which they lost long ago. As the intellects relate, ages ago they developed a superscience that gradually became mental; in transforming themselves into immortal beings, they lost sexuality. They are all, however, the equivalent of females. * Hillard and the real Alois clinch, while Devonack mutters. When the villainous wretch tries to shoot one

Tooker, Richard (*continued*)

of the Arcturan "women," she calmly disregards his rays and turns him into a statue, to be taken back to Earth as an example to other villains. * By now, the "women," excited by the males of the spaceship, propose marriage and the establishment of a new race of superbeings. This is accepted. Presumably Alois and Hillard will return to Earth. The author does not explain satisfactorily how Alois came to Arcturus. * Imaginative in a weird way, but unnecessarily melodramatic, badly written and clumsy.

1497. **THE GREEN DOOM**. *Astounding Stories*, December 1935. Ill. Dold.

Short story. * *Time:* 1976. * In the state of war between the Coalition of Aryan Nations and the Asian Alliance, the Aryans are doing badly. Their rocketeers (i.e., small rocket war vessels) have just been destroyed in an air battle. * At about this time a mysterious message comes from the missing great scientist Marloff, urging everyone to don radium-impregnated suits. No one pays any heed. * Some time later a greenish cloud descends from the sky and kills everyone in St. Louis, leaving dehydrated, twisted corpses. Chicago suffers the same fate, then Norfolk, Va. * When an Asian air fleet is similarly destroyed by the green cloud, which seems to be a single phenomenon, not generalized, the warring alliances make peace against a common enemy. It is soon discovered that only radium-impregnated suits, as warned by the hidden Marloff, are protection. Then the green cloud is seen no more, and scientists are puzzled. * A message from Marloff explains everything. He created the cloud in his laboratory as a force to bring about peace, but it escaped and has been working autonomously, doing the reported damage. Since then Marloff has been working on a defense against the cloud. He has finally found an agent that will destroy it, but the agent is almost as bad as the cloud itself: It induces rapid leprosy. To save mankind Marloff and his assistants flew into the cloud and released the agent. The cloud was destroyed, but so were Marloff and his associates. * Routine.

1498. **THE SONG FROM THE DARK STAR**. *Astounding Stories*, September 1936. Ill. Flatos.

Short story. * *Place:* South Dakota. * Wheat farmer Eric Paulson's wife, Anna, is haunted by strange melodic sounds. Others can hear them, too, but they disturb Anna enough that there is concern for her health. When she has strange, overpowering dreams of traveling through space and visiting alien worlds, Eric invokes the help of Tony Zeller, a local recluse who is deeply versed in matters scientific and otherwise. Zeller recognizes some of the words that Anna remembers from her dream, notably *Algol*, and identifies her description of a star occluded by a dark companion (Xarthon). Zeller also is aware that Anna is in great danger. * In accompaniment to strange sounds and a vision of what seems to them a monstrosity, the three receive a long telepathic communication from the being that has been troubling Anna. He is Egabl of Xarthon, the last survivor of a supremely advanced race that dwelt on the dark companion of Sirius when it held life. Over the ages Egabl's people abandoned physical existence and became pretty much incorporeal, but gradually died off. * Egabl is trying to recreate the long-lost technique of bisexual reproduction and has been roaming the universe looking for a suitable mate. He settled on Anna for a time, but realizes that she is not quite adequate, since she refuses to merge with him. He will now continue his search

elsewhere in the universe. * Zeller has acquired the occult knowledge he has striven for, but it is, of course, useless and unpublishable. * Unsuccessful, but it probably would have taken Lovecraft to handle the theme adequately.

TUCKER, LOUIS, D.D. (1872-1952)

U.S. Episcopal clergyman, stationed mostly in Alabama. Born in Mississippi. Received A.B., M.A., and D.D. from the University of the South. Author of several popular books on religion. Entertaining autobiography *Clerical Errors* (1943) unfortunately does not reach Gernsback era. According to Schwartz/Weisinger, Tucker's "Red Snow," was accepted by *Amazing Stories* around 1933, but for reasons now unknown, it was not printed. Perhaps it was among two hundred-odd stories that Ray Palmer returned to their authors when he took over *Amazing Stories*.

1499. **THE CUBIC CITY**. *Science Wonder Stories*, September 1929. Ill. Paul.

(Reprinted in Margulies and Friend, *From Off This World*, and in Ackerman, *Gosh! Wow!*)

Short story. * A Ralphism. * *Time:* A.D. 2130. *Place:* the New York City area. * The narrator inexplicably finds himself in a gigantic hotel circumstance, escorted by a bellhop named Cartex, who explains matters as they move along. They are in a cubic city, two miles in each direction, with eight hundred floors and a population of eighty million. Each person in the city is allocated one thousand square feet of living area, and there are enormous sun decks and recreational areas. In the hotel room are various communication devices as well as spouts for liquid food. * All seems to be going well, despite the narrator's partial bewilderment, until he offers Cartex a tip. At this the bellboy shrieks that he is being bribed, gas renders the narrator and the bellboy unconscious, and the police come and capture the narrator. * After preliminaries, he is taken to court, where he is examined. As he describes his inexplicable appearance from the past, mechanical devices confirm that he is not lying, but cannot indicate whether he is insane. In any case, he is in danger of being declared "inurbane," which he later learns means being put in a lunatic asylum and sterilized. * The narrator manages to regain the good will of the bellhop, and together with a doctor assigned to observe him they leave. All the while, although the narrator does not know it, they are being monitored and broadcast. * As matters turn out, the narrator realizes that the bellhop is really a beautiful young woman; he falls in love with her, and she reciprocates; the doctor, a rejected suitor, causes trouble, and the lovers flee. They barricade themselves in Cartex's room, while her friends in the news agencies cover the situation as the police try to break in, and while the lovers await a marriage license by automatic tube. The license arrives, they are married, the police succeed in storming the apartment—and the narrator awakens back in the twentieth century with his landlady in his arms. It was all a dream. * The cubic city is located in Westchester County; Manhattan is a meadow. Altogether there are about three hundred cities in the world, which is governed by a League of Cities. * Longevity has increased to 150 years, and, in general, humanity is superior to what it was in the past, since defectives of various sorts have been weeded out. * Bathing suits are very skimpy, and there is no prejudice against near nudity. * There is no more money. * More fictional than Gernsback's or E. D. Skinner's work, and at times amusing. One wonders whether it is Tucker's dream.

TURNER, D. G.

No information, but presumably a British author.

1500. **MOON MADNESS.** *Scoops,* 2 June 1934. Unsigned ill.

Boys' fiction. * Short story. * *Time:* 1951. * *Place:* partly on the Moon. * *Background:* The first rocket flight into space took place in 1939, followed by a British Moon landing in 1942. The explorers, however, could not return to Earth and starved to death. The first successful space voyages began in 1942, when Benjamin Harper developed an atomic engine and flew to the Moon and back. Since that time, however, Harper, seems to have done little more than drink to soothe the pains of unrequited love for Shirley, daughter of moon developer and entrepreneur Sir John Hughes. * When explorer Raymond Drummond discovered vast gold lodes on the Moon, Hughes, already a powerful capitalist, began to exploit the area, building two large domed cities (Cassini and Aristullus) atop the mining operations. These cities, which are controlled by Raymond Drummond (a more favored suitor of Shirley's), are very large, with parks, rapid transportation, and much else. * As the story opens, an emergency message comes from the Moon. The cities are under attack from the Earth and cannot hold out very long. Indeed, the population of Aristullus has already been evacuated to Cassini. Drummond is unable to cope with the attack, and to send help to the Moon would take at least eight hours, which would be too late. * Shirley Hughes succeeds in persuading Ben Harper to take her to the Moon in his ultrafast little flyer, which can cover the distance in about four hours. They find the situation very bad, with part of the population already in flight back to Earth and fighting going on in Cassini. The only hope, Ben says, is to urge all the population to take refuge in spaceships; then he will destroy the city's atmosphere plant. This is done, and the invaders apparently mostly die of suffocation. All through these events, Drummond, in contrast to Harper's heroism, showed the white feather and eventually collapsed. Shirley now marries Ben Harper. * *Miscellaneous:* The attackers seem to have been Japanese. * The author obviously bit off more than he could chew in terms of development.

ULLRICH, J. ROGERS

No information. Portrait accompanying "The Inverted World" shows an elderly man.

1501. **THE MOON STROLLERS.** *Amazing Stories,* May 1929. Unsigned ill.

Short story. * *Time:* The near future, after Robert Goddard's unmanned rocket had hit the Moon. *Place:* mostly the Moon * Really a procedural story that tries to apply scientific and engineering accuracy to an early Moon voyage. The Moon shot grew out of a roughing-it vacation on the part of a few imaginative scientists and entrepreneurs. * The stress of the story lies on strollers, or highly perfected space suits that can be used for walking about on the Moon. * Mueller, Scoefield, and Kenworthy ride a rocket to the Moon, land safely, and explore. The Moon is now lifeless, but at one time it had seas, as fossils and bones indicate, and some sort of intelligent life, the mounds of whose settlements are seen. * While the surface is airless, a deep cave in Copernicus contains air and hot springs, which permit one of the men, who is trapped there, to survive. * A relief rocket brings supplies and equipment, and the men return to Earth. * *Miscellaneous:* The lack of atmosphere on the Moon permitted observations of Mars, which really has canals and intelligent life. * Signals are received from Earth by black cloth displays. * Intelligent, but very amateurish as fiction. Probably written by a man with technical background. For a sequel see #1503, "The Stolen Chrysalis."

1502. **THE INVERTED WORLD.** *Wonder Stories Quarterly,* Spring 1931. Ill. Ivan Volga.

Short story. * Harry Lambert, being routinely X-rayed for a possible malar injury, undergoes a weird experience. As the X-ray is functioning, a piece of strange metallic ore that the attending doctor had been studying flies up and smashes the tube, exposing Lambert to mysterious radiation. Lambert remains rigid in place for a couple of days before returning to normalcy. Then he tells of his experiences. * The narrative is not wholly clear, but Lambert seems to have been in circumstances where everyday things received new coloration and tonalities. In some sense this amounted to an opposite to our everyday world. * Unfocused and murky. * According to a note by Schwartz/Weisinger, the story was almost totally rewritten by the *Wonder* staff.

1503. **THE STOLEN CHRYSALIS.** *Amazing Stories,* July 1931. Ill. Paul.

Short story. * Sequel to #1501, "The Moon Strollers." * *Time:* 1935. *Place:* Vermont. * Scoefield, Mueller, and Kenworthy, the veterans of the moon voyage, assemble for their annual commemorative meeting, at which Mueller examines certain of the lunar fossils that they brought back with them. As he splits open a slab of sedimentary rock, the men espy a strange-looking object, which Mueller declares is the fossil chrysalis of a gigantic moth. The chrysalis looks so lifelike that the men decide to soak it and expose it to sunlight to see if it will hatch. * It shows signs of vivification, but is missing the next morning. * Some ratiocination, in the manner of Sherlock Holmes, points to a type of suspect, and after some investigation among learned societies and publications, Scoefield locates a renegade sensational science-feature writer who stole the chrysalis. (The reader has already seen the criminal in action.) In exchange for advance information about a projected lunar voyage, the thief restores the chrysalis, which Scoefield returns to Vermont. * It opens, and a beautiful moth emerges—but it emits such a powerful gas that the lunar explorers all fall unconscious, narrowly escaping death. The moth itself flies away.

VALIER, MAX (1895-1930)

Italo-Austrian engineer, writer, pioneer in rocket research and space research, born in Bölzen/Bolzano. His name is probably a spelling variation of the well-known Venetian name "Falier." Served in Austrian air force in World War I. Built, in cooperation with Fritz Opel, rocket-powered automobile. Wrote *Der Verstoss in den Weltraume,* 1924, very early book on scientific-engineering basis of space travel. Killed by an exploding rocket; usually considered the first martyr to space research.

1504. **A DARING TRIP TO MARS.** *Wonder Stories,* July 1931. Ill. Marchioni.

Translated from German by Francis Currier.

Valier, Max (*continued*)

(*Auf kühner Fahrt zum Mars. Eine kosmische Phantasie*, 1928.)
As a story that did not originate in the pulps, this is described in more detail in *Science-Fiction: The Early Years*.

Short story. * *Place:* Germany and space between Earth and Mars. The engineer, his wife, and the doctor leave in a small rocket, planning to land on the moon, prepare fuel, and, taking advantage of the Moon's weak gravity, continue on to Mars. All goes well, apart from a certain amount of malaise because of strain and cramped quarters, but an unpredicted comet drags them offpath, and they are forced to use their reserve fuel to escape. As a result, they cannot land on Mars, but can only fly around it and return to Earth. When in a proper position above Earth they leap out individually in parachutes and land safely. * Probably the last word in technical accuracy for the day, but not strong as fiction.

VAN CAMPEN, KARL

Pseud. of John W. Campbell, Jr., who has a separate entry.

1505. **THE IRRELEVANT**.   *Astounding Stories,* December 1934. Ill. Dold.

Short story. * An idea story, toying with one of Campbell's fancies, perpetual motion—or, getting out more energy than one puts in. * Inventor Kent Barret, despite legal obstacles, stubbornly sets out to fly to the Moon in his rocket ship the *Ghost.* The problem is that he does not have enough fuel to return; hence his flight is deliberate suicide for the sake of science. * As Barret communicates with his ground associate, however, it becomes obvious that something is wrong. The *Ghost* is traveling far faster than it theoretically should, and is using less energy to attain that speed. Since Newton's laws seem to have no relevance to actuality, Barret renames his ship the *Irrelevant.* * The implications are double: the law of conservation of energy has been broken, and it is possible to set up space power stations using the Earth's magnetic field. The ultimate gimmick is relativity of motion—motion with relation to what? * The story created an enormous amount of controversy in the letter columns of *Astounding Stories,* with many persons objecting to or refuting van Campen's arguments. Much of this dispute is technical, but the main point seems to be that van Campen's argument itself is irrelevant, as JWC probably knew. A second van Campen story, which was rejected by *Astounding Stories* and *Wonder Stories,* was printed later in *The Space Beyond* (1976).

VAN DRESSER, PETER

No information. The author later contributed two semitechnical articles to *Astounding Science Fiction,* "Why Rockets Don't Fly" (1938) and "Introduction to a Nameless Science" (1940).

1506. **SOUTH POLAR BERYLLIUM, LIMITED.** *Amazing Stories,* August 1930. Ill. Morey.

Short story. * *Time:* around 1960. *Place:* Antarctica. * Antarctica was internationalized and transferred to the League of Nations in 1952. In 1957 huge deposits of aluminum and beryllium silicate, a mineral of great economic importance, were found there, and South Polar Beryllium, Ltd., has begun to develop the deposits. * There is, however, a production problem. Transportation of the ore is extremely difficult and expensive. To solve this problem a new process has been developed and tested in a pilot plant. * As the story begins, Hamilton, a chemist

and graduate of the Colorado School of Mines, has been assigned to install the equipment needed for the new process. After an investigatory visit by plane, he returns with plans and a model, traveling overland by landrover. * The vehicle is attacked and hijacked by a former employee, who is somewhat paranoid, and only a clever trick enables Hamilton and his friends to outwit the bandits and save the situation. * The development, as an adventure story with a scientific background, is rather good, although there are passages of technical chemistry that will faze the lay reader.

VAN LORNE, WARNER

The identity of Warner Van Lorne was a popular topic for discussion in fan circles in the late 1930s and early 1940s, more than the quality of the stories published under that name warranted. The editors refused to reveal the author's identity for a very good reason. Street and Smith frowned on editors' accepting their own stories for publication, and Van Lorne, it was later revealed (confirming earlier suspicions), was the pseud. of the editor of *Astounding Stories* and his brother.

VAN LORNE, WARNER [I]

For the single following story Warner Van Lorne was Frederick Orlin Tremaine (1899-1959). F. Orlin Tremaine, born in Harrisonville, New York; attended Valparaiso College. Professional magazine editor, editing *Metropolitan,* Bernarr Macfadden's *True Story,* and *Everybody's.* Later became editor of the Hearst *Smart Set,* and high executive in the Clayton magazine group. When Street and Smith reestablished certain Clayton publications (after the failure of the Clayton chain), Tremaine became editor of several magazines, including *Clues; Top-Notch; Cowboy Stories; Bill Barnes, Air Adventure,* and *Astounding Stories,* which he edited from October 1933 to December 1937, during which period he significantly improved the quality of the magazine. His policy was followed (despite divagations in other directions) by his successor John W. Campbell, Jr. On leaving Street and Smith Publications Tremaine founded his own publishing company, the Orlin Tremaine Company, which issued the magazine *Comet Stories* (1940-1941). At a later period Tremaine was connected with Bartholomew House. Tremaine wrote a fair amount of fiction under his own name and various pseuds. including Orlin Frederick (in *Weird Tales*), but he was a better editor than writer. * In a letter to Donald Day (January 25, 1951) Tremaine states, "I wrote a story, 'The Upper Level Road'. . . . under the pseudonym of Warner Van Lorne . . . . [There have been] persistent rumors that I was Warner Van Lorne. I was—on the one story mentioned above—but not thereafter." In this letter F. Orlin did not identify the second author who used the pseudonym, but for some reason obscured the issue.

1507. **THE UPPER LEVEL ROAD.** *Astounding Stories,* August 1935. Unsigned ill.

(Reprinted in Conklin, *Best of Science Fiction.*)

Short story. * When student John Hayden seems disrespectful in Professor Eberhardt's class, it opens up a new world of experience. Pressed for a reason for his behavior, Hayden takes Eberhardt out along a country road, whereupon, for no particular reason, the two find themselves in a different plane of existence. It is a North America, but one that may have been settled by Europeans hundreds of years earlier, since the two men find a huge, deserted, fortress castle. They also find a few men and

Van Lorne, Warner [I] (*continued*)

women who, like themselves, have strayed into the other-world from our time. Entry seems to be based on some trick of speed, road level, exact location, and mental set. * Hayden and Eberhardt begin to develop the other-world with supplies and some simple technology. The professor considers the new world a possible basis for peace activities, since according to his calculations there should be similar entry places around the world in specific locations. Exactly what is involved in the other-world is not entirely clear, but it seems to be forks in time. * This is generally considered the best of the Van Lorne stories. F. Orlin Tremaine seems to have been struggling to get across a vague, formless idea in this story; he is not successful, but the story has a certain interest, even a minor charm. One suspects that Tremaine had H. G. Wells's *Men Like Gods* in mind.

VAN LORNE, WARNER [II]

Pseud. of Nelson Tremaine (1903?-?), younger brother of F. Orlin Tremaine, later associated with him in the Orlin Tremaine Company. The authorship of the remaining Van Lorne stories was established by Sam Moskowitz, who conducted a phone interview with Nelson Tremaine in which he admitted writing the following stories published as by Van Lorne. A (perhaps faked?) autobiographical article in *Amazing Stories* (February 1939), gives Van Lorne's birth date as 1903 and states that he was reared in the Adirondacks. This could fit Nelson Tremaine. Street and Smith author cards give Van Lorne's address as Stony Creek, New York, where a relative, DeWitt C. Tremaine, operated a lodge. Although the issue was not raised, it is possible that F. Orlin, who was a practiced writer, assisted Nelson in the following stories. Nelson is said to have been an engineer or machine operator of some kind. * Van Lorne [II] also contributed stories to other pulp magazines, including *Clues* and *Romance Range*. Among the fans of the 1930s and 1940s the identity of Warner Van Lorne was a matter of intense speculation, but today it seems of much less importance, considering the poor quality of the stories. See also Spencer Lane, pseud.

1508. **LIQUID POWER.** *Astounding Stories,* July 1935. Ill. Marchioni.

Short story. * Time: 1949. * Don Morrow, twenty-year old son of a great inventor, is somewhat constrained by Fervick, his financial guardian. Fervick not only steals Don's invention of a superbattery, but turns out to have murdered Don's father and to be an agent of a hostile foreign power. In the background is a remarkable rocket ship that Don's father built, but has been inoperative since his death for lack of a power source. * Don, discovering liquid electricity and a disintegrating ray, reactivates his father's airship and single-handedly defeats the invading air and sea forces of an unidentified nation. * In some ways reminiscent of a dime novel of the turn of the century, boy inventor and all. In any case, very bad.

1509. **STRANGE CITY.** *Astounding Stories,* January 1936. Ill. Marchioni.

Novelette. Romance and culture heroism, or the handyman's dream. * *Time and place*: as revealed in the sequel #1514, "World of Purple Light," inside the hollow Earth and, thanks to differential time rates, our future. * Engineer Tom Corbin awakens, naked and astonished, in an enormous room, above which is a rotor of incredible size. Exploring a little, he enters

a self-propelled car that takes him to an unknown destination. On disembarking, he finds clothing and encounters a group of guards. When they attack him with swords, all concerned discover that Tom has fantastic strength (perhaps that of twenty men) and is to some extent impervious to manual weapons. This arouses awe rather than hostility, comments (translated) about gods, and a not-quite-royal reception. Tom is installed in apartments and taught the local language by the beautiful slave girl Zola. * *Background:* Tom is in the city of Borid. All about him are colossal buildings, automated equipment, wonderful transportational devices, inexplicable mechanical apparatus, and evidence everywhere of an incredibly advanced technology, yet very little functions. Almost everything is broken. The one exception to this nearly omnipresent breakdown and malfunction is a system of automated monorails that takes Tom to all sorts of odd places. * As Tom learns, the material culture of Borid was created a long time ago by so-called gods, who used the ancestors of the present people of Borid as servants, then left. Since then the Boridians have become feckless and have lost their technology. This is partly due to their social structure, which consists of a small number of aristocrats and a large number of slaves. The aristocrats consider work beneath them, and the slaves share much the same attitude. Not only is no one able to fix anything; no one seems to be interested or to care. When something breaks, a slave fetches a replacement from one of the giant storage depots left by the gods. But replacements, including even light bulbs, are running low. Food is provided by female slaves, who work naked in small fields, with primitive tools, cultivating weedy vegetation. Population is small and dwindling, and most of the colossal city is empty and unfrequented. * There has long been a cargo-cult prophecy or promise that the gods will return and improve things, and Tom, both by his entrance from the chambers of the gods and his fantastic strength and great knowledge, is generally taken to be either a god or a messenger of the gods. * The first section of the story is devoted to Tom's stay in the open city of Borid. He becomes friendly with Prince Cama (purported son of the king) and spends most of his time repairing equipment around the city. But he falls in love with the slave girl Zola, who reciprocates; this is a situation that calls for the death penalty, what with the strict endogamy of the land. Tom and Zola are forced to escape, fleeing through secret passages (which riddle all the buildings) to the hidden culture of Borid. * *Background:* Although the masters are unaware of it, generations of escaped slaves have lived secretly in other buildings in the enormous city and have cultivated fields that the masters do not know about. Some of the slaves, like Zola, who is a princess, are descended from war captives. On the whole, the slave culture is less rigid and caste ridden than the aristocratic culture, but the people are equally feckless and unenterprising. As Tom discovers, the slave people have been shivering in the cold for generations, since no one has thought of fixing, or been able to fix, the heating system. The task should have been easy enough, for the gods left excellent service manuals, pictorial instructions, and even holographic images of all the machinery. * Tom settles down in the counter culture, training a nucleus of handymen in the mysteries of wielding hammers and wrenches. After a short time, thanks to Tom, the elevators are functioning; tractors work the fields, etc. Along the way of progress, Tom finds disintegrator pistols and a flying machine equipped with disintegrator cannon. * In the

Van Lorne, Warner [II] (*continued*)

third and final part of the story, Tom begins a unification of the bipolar land. Riding around on the transportation system, Tom chances to return to the aristocratic part of the city, where he hears that his friend Prince Cama is in trouble. Fetching his disintegrator pistol and associates, Tom rescues him. The king, who is disintegrated, was not Cama's father but a look-alike usurper. * Tom now announces the new culture. Caste, rank, and slavery are abolished; both peoples are equal and will fraternize on equal terms. A work ethic is in order, and Tom and his trainees will get the mechanical side of the culture functioning again. There is some resistance, which Tom disposes of with his disintegrator, and the matter is settled. Tom refuses the kingly crown, which he awards to Cama, but takes the nebulous position of planetary leader. He marries Zola, and Cama does the noble thing in marrying a former slave girl. * *Miscellaneous:* The technology of Borid is alien. The machinery has no gears or belts, but operates with magnetically operated pistons and slides. Energy is ultimately wireless transmission of magnetism and seems limitless. * A curious story, carelessly written and at times self-contradictory, clichéd in the manner of Edgar Rice Burroughs, silly, yet at times with a certain reader-pull and charm. The work ethic has social interest. as does the description of mechanical movements. "Strange City" is generally considered the best of the stories written by Nelson Tremaine. For a sequel see #1514, "World of Purple Light."

1510. **WHITE ADVENTURE.** *Astounding Stories,* April 1936. Unsigned ill.

Short story. * *Time:* 1941. * Most of the story is historical summary, with only a little personal narrative. * In May a strange snowfall covers much of the East. It looks like ordinary snow, but it is warm and it does not melt. At first it is only a curiosity, but it soon becomes a real problem, for it clogs roads, fields, water supplies. * In a short time similar falls occur over the country, with disastrous results. Farming is no longer possible, and when stores are low, it is necessary to buy food from Europe—which after a time refuses to sell, fearing similar falls. Water is scanty, then no longer obtainable, for there are no more rainfalls and reservoirs are exhausted. The big cities are filled with death. * Amateur scientist Henry Atwood works out a practical way of changing the electrical charge in the snow so that it will melt. His method works almost instantaneously. Atwood broadcasts his technique, but urges that the melting be done gradually, to avoid floods. No one pays any attention to his warning, and as the story ends abruptly Atwood sees his land under water. * The text, perhaps written in haste, even with grammatical mistakes, gives no indication of causation or the reason for the limitation of the snowfalls to the United States.

1511. **GLAGULA.** *Astounding Stories,* June 1936. Ill. Schneeman.

Short story. * *Place:* somewhere along the permanent frost zone in the Arctic. * The group, following a somewhat vague map obtained from an old prospector, is trying to find a rich lode of gold. So far the search has not been successful. But as the men are clearing away snow to reach bedrock, they come upon the frozen body of a man. When lifted out, the man, of an unknown racial type, is about seven-feet-six in height and much heavier proportionately than one would expect. He is dressed strangely. * Tom Hoag, on examining the body closely, believes that since

it is perfectly preserved and was probably frozen instantly, it might be revived. Such proves to be the case when it is put into a special tent, warmed gradually, and massaged into life. * The strange being, who is totally telepathic, reveals that he is named Glagula and is from another world. He suffers badly from hypothermia, and must have collapsed almost instantly when he left his spaceship. Glagula tells of his world, about which it would be irrelevant to give details, except that it is superior in all ways to ours and is practically an eutopia. Where is it? This is not disclosed, except that it is in another solar system. * The men locate Glagula's spaceship easily enough. It is a super-scientific affair, with, apparently, mentally controlled matter transmission from one section to another. Glagula takes the men up in the vessel, which seems to operate by antigravity, and finds the gold lode for them. He then resumes his journey to his destination, Tom Hoag accompanying him. * *Miscellaneous:* Glagula, oddly enough, has had no experience with heat, and has never seen fire. * Flat and undistinguished.

1512. **AUSTRALANO.** *Astounding Stories,* July 1936. Ill. Dold.

Short story. * *Time:* A.D. 2900. * *Place:* North America and Australia. * *Background:* After a succession of terrible wars, civilization had just about collapsed, and most of the world's population had been killed. The situation was very bad, but around A.D. 2400 Brant Ryan presented a plan: Concentrate the world's population on North America and begin to build up again. The surviving nations accepted Ryan's plan and set up the Combine in North America. For reasons not clearly presented, the Europeans then froze Ryan out of power and set up a dictatorial government. * Ryan, who refused to accept the new situation, thereupon moved to Australia with about six million followers, or one-tenth of the human race, and set up Australano, which is still ruled by his descendants. * There is little or no communication between the Combine and Australano, and a hostile truce prevails after a brief war. Some years back, when the Combine air fleet attacked Australano, it was wiped out of the sky by superior Australano materiel. As this exemplifies, while the Combine considers itself superior, it is really much inferior to Australano in science and technology. * As the story begins, Captain Randall Borden of the Combine returns from a space voyage to learn that his father has been arrested for failing to fill his work quota designing improved spaceships. Actually, a personal enemy has become Commandant of the dictatorial, highly regimented Combine and has prosecuted Borden, Sr., out of personal malice. Borden, Sr., has been sent to the prison planet for life, which is equivalent to a death sentence. * Randall Borden, outraged, insults the Commandant; as an act of mercy, after he apologizes, he is merely degraded and assigned to a minor teaching position. One of his pupils is Gorna, the pleasant daughter of the Commandant. * Hoping to strike a bargain to free his father, Randall and comrades steal a spaceship and take off, with Gorna as a not unwilling hostage. Unfortunately, Randall forgot to check fuel gauges, with the result that he can only barely make the outskirts of Australano. Here the group disembarks from the inactive ship and makes a long trek to civilization. * In Australano, they are treated with great courtesy. Indeed, they are escorted around by a personable young man named Peter, whose identity the reader will easily guess. * Randall and associates now hijack an Australano ship, hoping to reach the prison planet and release his father, but Australano

Van Lorne, Warner [II] (*continued*)

draws the vessel back by remote control. * Explanations now follow. The authorities at Australano were well aware of all the actions of Randall and company from the time they escaped from the Combine, and have orchestrated everything about them. Prince Hamin's men had already rescued Borden, Sr. from the prison planet, and he is an honored guest in Australano. * By now Prince Peter and Gorna are in love, but it is only with difficulty and a threatened war with the Combine that romance can take its course. * *Miscellaneous:* Both countries have efficient space travel. * The Combine displays a certain missionary zeal and is convinced that it has a duty to share its regimentation with Australano. * Below routine.

    1513. **FOLLOW THE ROCKET TRAIL**. *Astounding Stories*, September 1936. Ill. Thomson.

Short story. * *Time:* the twenty-third century. * *Background:* Extensive trade takes place between the planets, controlled (mostly? or totally?) by the "society." * For the past ten years changes have been noted in the orbits of the planets, including Earth. Astronomers and mathematicians have unable to account for these changes, but Professor Bogelman, the head of the Society, has a theoretical explanation, which he advances. He is immediately fired, for his explanation would halt space travel. * Bogelman claims that interplanetary trade, by changing the mass of the individual planets, has altered their orbits. His theory is disregarded, and the orbital eccentricities increase, Earth itself now becoming uncomfortable. Desperate, at the last moment, the Society approaches Bogelman, offering him his old position back, with increments, if he can halt the changes. Bogelman meets them and calmly announces that they have ten minutes to live before Earth shatters. He is right. * Silly in idea and clumsily narrated.

    1514. **WORLD OF PURPLE LIGHT**. *Astounding Stories*, December 1936. Ill. Dold.

Novelette. * Sequel to #1509, "Strange City." * Three (sleep cycle) years have passed since Tom Corbin arrived in Borid, the mysterious city somewhere. During this time Tom has become something of a culture hero or even a demigod. As Super(handy)man he has repaired much of the broken-down machinery, instituted social reforms, and in general has things running. But he still knows no more, essentially, than when he first arrived. * Tom, who has been busied repairing the water works, notices that his wife, Zola, is missing. After frantic searching, in which he is aided by the people of the city, he discovers that she must have stumbled upon a hitherto unknown transportation system in a building whose function had not been recognized or investigated. Tom follows her steps and discovers a system of powered monorail cars that lead out of the city. Chancing that he will follow the same route as Zola, he enters and activates the car. Everything works perfectly. * After whizzing through the countryside for perhaps hundreds of miles, Tom's vehicle stops in another city, the existence of which had not been suspected. Exploring, Tom is attacked by hairy creatures who look like submen but are intelligent and are servants or slaves to the dominant white race, who do not speak the language of Borid. Tom permits himself to be captured, with the thought that he can easily escape when he wants. * A series of secret passages à la Edgar Rice Burroughs provides the avenue. He finds Zola, who explains a little. The city of Jeelib, which has been deteriorating much like Borid, has a serious population problem. There are

only a couple of hundred whites, and women are in very short supply. Hence Zola was a great prize when she emerged into the city. * As Tom demonstrates his fantastic strength, he observes that something like a cult is emerging, despite the original hostility. Just as had happened in Borid, he is gradually recognized as the savior of prophecy. Explanations emerge. * When he enters an electrically guarded corridor, passage through which no native could have survived, he finds himself in a special living circumstance designed for him, not for the natives. * Recordings explain the mysteries of the land and of his presence. The strange land is the interior of the hollow Earth, which developed separately from the outer world. Time is different, with the inner world many times slower than the outside, so that Tom has already been in Borid for several Earth generations. In the far past, a high civilization from the outer world penetrated the inner world and began to civilize the natives. The fantastic omnipresent machinery and technology are the product of the outsiders (the Gods), who lived entirely in protective armor and moved several times faster than the natives. After a time, the outsiders retired back to their own world outside. Before leaving they set the giant rotor (which provides power for everything from the Earth's magnetic field) to select a man from the outside, transform him so that he can live in the low oxygen and slow time of the interior, and transfer him. This chanced to be Tom. He will live many generations of the inner world, will breed true with a native woman, and will be as a god to the internals. But he can never return to the outside. * *Miscellaneous:* The submen, who are really irrelevant to the story except as a projection of contemporary thought about racial matters, are the result of miscegenation of some sort after the outer men left, violating a prohibition of the Gods. This social crime has led to a general guilt complex. But the prohibition has now been lifted. * The cities of Borid and Jeelib can arrange a sexual population swap to the advantage of both. * Wandering and sloppily written, relying on a somewhat dated sense of wonder and surrogate power drive.

VAN NAME, E[DGAR] J[AMES] (1904-1995)

U.S. author, then resident of Pasadena, California. See also Jim Vanny, pseud.

    1515. **THE SUNLIGHT MASTER**. *Amazing Stories*, April 1935. Ill. Morey.

Novelette. * *Place:* prefatory material in London, with the main story in Tanganyika. * *Background:* Some years back, the great scientist Max Konrad, working at Stanford, was able to harness solar energy (to a degree hitherto unknown). His invention promised cheap power, but it would have cut into the profits of International Consolidated Oil Corporation, headed by Robert Kaplin. * Kaplin attacked Konrad in the courts, prevented him from patenting his invention, and harassed him so greatly that Konrad, in disgust, left the area and disappeared without a trace. * In London, former friend Professor Gould and associates have been trying to discover what became of Konrad; the trail leads to Tanganyika. * After traveling through East Africa, the men finally find what they have been seeking: the superscientific city of Solaropolis, which operates with solar power. The explorers are captured by masked men and taken before the Master, the masked chief of the city, whom they recognize as Konrad. * Although he admits that he recognizes some of them, he is not particularly friendly and assigns them to various scut tasks about

Van Name, E. J. (*continued*)

the solar city. They are guarded by men whom a masked man, presumably Konrad, had previously spirited from Devil's Island. * Konrad, as is customary, tries to recruit the explorers. When this fails, he and his myrmidons, clad in special shielded clothing, are about to disintegrate them, when an accidental shove turns the tables. At the same time, the Master's own plane bombs the establishment, destroying the power cables. * It is now time for unmasking. The bomber is the real Max Konrad, who had been working for the Master, biding his time until he could successfully rebel. As for that masked hombre, he is Kaplin the oil czar. Stealing Konrad's papers, he built Solaropolis, staffing it with criminals. * Thriller material, not too well handled.

VANCE, ARLYN H. (1890-?)

U.S. author, born in Illinois, resident, at time of writing, in Wisconsin. Author of articles in popular mechanical magazines. Social Security records list an Arlyn Vance (1890-1977) whose number was issued in Florida.

1516. **WHEN THE EARTH STOOD STILL.** *Amazing Stories,* December 1936. Ill. Morey.

Short story. * *Time:* the near future. *Place:* northern Wisconsin. * Labor Day will be a red-letter day, for the President of the United States will set in operation the first cosmic ray generation extractors. It promises to usher in a new era of human prosperity, say the experts. * In violent disagreement is old Dr. Howells, who has worked out scientific proof that the extraction of the cosmic rays will upset the structure of the universe. Howells is derided and persecuted, losing his university position, whereupon he, his daughter Mary, and his assistant Alan Winters retire to an island in Turtle Lake, Wisconsin. There the professor works on a mysterious apparatus. * The generator is turned on, and the worst happens. Gravity, sound, most light, other natural forces all disappear, and the Earth stops rotating. Almost all the population of the world is wiped out. The professor, however, has a small apparatus that gradually has some effect in restoring natural forces. After things settle down a little, with gravity, full light, and sound restored, the Earth no longer rotates. Part of it is perpetually frozen, part is torrid, but Wisconsin emerges as something of a subtropical paradise. The few survivors assemble there and are prepared to start a new life. * Also present in the story are long irrelevant passages about an ancient Indian prophecy concerning Turtle Lake and the present state of affairs. * Below routine.

VANCE, R. C. and YOUNG, F. K.

No information. Probably pseuds. The story is much the sort of fiction that Hersey would have run in the deceased *Thrill Book* magazine that he edited. Vance is also carried as Vane in the magazine.

1517. **THE MAN WITHOUT A BRAIN.** *Flash Gordon Strange Adventure Magazine,* December 1936.

Short story. * Borderline rationalized s-f. * Dr. Nesbit, a great psychiatrist, tells his listeners that he has obtained the body of an executed murderer from prison and has removed his brain, bit by bit, while keeping the man alive. He removes the top of his experimental subject's skull, and shows that the brain pan is totally empty. Nesbit now boasts that he is the greatest of all psychiatrists and asks his listeners whether one of them, for the

sake of science, would not consent to the same operations, sequence reversed. * But Nesbit is mad; his subject has been long dead; and Nesbit is not even Nesbit. * All rather pointless.

VANNE, EMMA

U.S. author, journalist, then resident of Westfield, New Jersey. No other information. In a letter in the July 1935 issue of *Wonder Stories* Ms. Vanne makes an unusual contribution to the contemporary discussion of phonetic spelling. She suggests not that spelling be reformed, but that pronunciation be changed to fit spelling.

1518. **THE MOANING LILY.** *Wonder Stories,* May 1935. Ill. Schneeman.

Short story. * The great botanist and horticulturalist Carl Brense, who specializes in plant grafting, has gone to Brazil to locate a remarkable flower he has heard of. When the narrator meets him at a flower show after his return, Brense, obviously very ill, is dressed in a flowing black robe and holds in his arms a remarkable giant efflorescence that resembles a human mouth and vocal organs. More, the flower gives audible moans, whence the title of the story. * Brense dies, leaving an explanation. He has grafted the remarkable plant onto himself, since it is a carnivorous plant, and the plant has worked its way through his system. He has now severed the flower and placed it in a vase filled with blood. The flower should thus last for a week or so. * Brense's prediction is correct, and as the flower dies, a week later, in Grand Central Hall, it emits a loud groan. * Fervidly Gothic in telling and without much merit.

VANNY, JIM

Pseud. of Edgar James Van Name (1904-1995) U.S. author, then resident in Pasadena, California. See also E. J. Van Name for another story.

1519. **LINERS OF SPACE.** *Air Wonder Stories,* February 1930. Ill. Ruger.

Short story. * *Time:* the twenty-sixth century. *Place:* space. * Captain Cameron of the Inter-Stellar Patrol is one of the first to see the strange spaceship *Barta.* It is much faster than anything known and for some inexplicable reason is not damaged by meteor swarms, which are a real danger in space. * Cameron's second encounter with the *Barta* comes when he learns that the great passenger liner the *Martian,* carrying his wife, Myrna, has been lost in space. Most of the passengers and crew escaped in life tubes, but the tube carrying Myrna and others has not been picked up. Cameron goes in search of her. His ship is disabled by a meteor, but he and his crew are rescued by the *Barta,* on which is Myrna, previously taken aboard by the great Venusian scientist Dr. Sigurd. * Sigurd, who is polite and amiable, explains his ship: It draws upon cosmic rays, hence needs not carry fuel. Sigurd has also discovered antigravity, solar power, and a meteor repeller. All, however, is not well, for Sigurd is an insane revanchist where the Earth is concerned and will never release his captives. He is also utterly irresponsible as a space captain, persistently subjecting his ship to trials for which it was not designed. His crew, half Earthmen and half Venusians, lives in terror of future escapades. * Sigurd's downfall comes when he announces that he will take the *Barta* to Mercury. This is obviously suicidal because of solar radiation. The vessel is beginning to melt when the Earthmen mutiny. Sigurd, however, regains control, and the best the mutineers and the captives can

Vanny, Jim (*continued*)

do is escape in a lifeboat while the madman drives on toward the sun. His secrets die with him. * *Miscellaneous:* An ancient souvenir pistol turns the trick during the mutiny; Sigurd has an atomic pistol; Venusians are green-skinned, but otherwise human. * Vernean antecedents, but original within those limits. Vanny's best story.

1520. **THE WAR OF THE GREAT ANTS.** *Wonder Stories*, July 1930. Ill. Leonard.

Short story. * *Time:* 1945. *Place:* the Malay Peninsula. * Told within three frames. * David Marsden, on a surveying expedition, finds a manuscript in a thermos bottle. Written by John McConnell of the missing McConnell Expedition, it tells of being captured by gigantic intelligent ants (the size of sheep) who keep human prisoners to cultivate their fungus gardens. * Marsden investigates, and in addition to finding the ant city, comes upon another expedition, that of McConnell's daughter, in search of her father. All concerned are either killed or captured by the ants, but are rescued by a dual attack on the ant city: driver ants, who prey on the giant ants, and a military expedition from colonial headquarters. A rapid-fire romance is also included. * Confusedly narrated and somewhat below routine.

1521. **THE RADIUM MASTER.** *Wonder Stories*, August 1930. Ill. Paul.

Novelette. * *Time:* later than 1985. *Place:* Africa, near Lake Victoria. * The great explorer Kramer returns to New York with a strange tale. While accompanying the Olsen aerial mapping expedition, his plane suddenly died, and the party was forced to land at an unknown city that showed all the marks of a mild superscience based on radium. They were taken before a masked man known as the Masked Emperor, who welcomed them, then informed them that they could not leave and put them to work. Kramer escaped and survived to reach civilization. * The authorities at the Belmont Museum do not believe Kramer (who is soon found murdered), but his friend Billy Carveth, and Victor Leonard, decide to investigate. As they fly over the area mentioned by Kramer, their plane motor dies, and they are forced to land on the airstrip for Urania, the radium city. They are taken before the Masked Man, who is not unfriendly and explains much to them. He is looking for population to build up Urania so that eventually it can take over the world. He has been bringing in settlers, some of whom are criminals to be rehabilitated. As expected, the Masked Emperor informs them that they cannot leave; they will be assigned to a training program for operating robots. * Urania is a futuristic city, with dazzling white architecture, robots of all sorts performing work, and controllers who manage the robots electronically through polonium emanations. Behind all this is an incredible radium deposit, which the Masked Emperor, who is a scientific genius, has developed in many ways: lighting, atomic power, robot control, explosive weapons, wonderful underground subway transport, flying machines, etc. * After finishing their training course, the outsiders are put to work controlling mining robots. They soon meet Dr. Olsen and his beautiful daughter Greta. All concerned plot to escape, but they overlooked the fact that the Masked Emperor has the entire establishment bugged and knows of their plans. * Billy and Vic are sentenced to the deepest, most dangerous, most glowing mines, but things work out all right. Vic, with his radium mining tool, cuts the tube providing polonium to control the mining robots, thus inactivating them.

Billy, Vic, and the Olsens escape just in time to be rescued by a fleet of international police planes. Behind them Urania explodes in a radioactive chaos, destroying everything, and killing everyone. * Who was that Masked Man? It was Belmont, the museum head, if anyone cares. * Routine pulp action, sometimes on the self-parody level.

1522. **THE EXILES OF VENUS.** *Wonder Stories*, June 1931. Ill. Marchioni.

Short story. * *Time:* the near future. *Place:* California, space, and Venus. * The narrator and a friend are trying for an altitude record in their California-based biplane when they come upon an enormous flying structure above fifty thousand feet. The motor of their plane dies and they are pulled by an unknown force into the structure. * The friend escapes by parachute, but the narrator does not. A dwarf with a large head leads him into the machine, and he shortly sees that they are heading for the Moon. To his surprise he meets a beautiful young woman in the spaceship. * *Background:* Some six years earlier the great Professor Hammond built the spaceship, went mad, and shanghaied his two daughters and some workmen on board. They then flew to Venus, where they met a friendly little people, specimens of whom the narrator has seen on the vessel. Unfortunately, the professor, who regained some of his sanity, meddled in the political affairs of the planet, encouraging his hosts into a war, in which they were badly defeated. The professor and a few friends had to flee. They then went to our Moon, where they have a base. In the meanwhile, the professor has died. One of the young women is unattached, but the other has a sweetheart (Starbuck) who is languishing in a Venusian prison. * The narrator throws his lot in with the Hammond women and succeeds in rescuing the captives, overthrowing the Venusian government, installing Hammond's friends, and gaining one of the women for a wife. The Earth people return to Earth and settle in the Carmel Valley, California. * *Miscellaneous:* The spaceship has a potent magnetic ray that plays havoc with the hostile Venusians, but only Starbuck can operate it. * The Venusians have antigravity space suits and disintegrator hand guns. * Pretty bad.

VAUGHAN, RICHARD

According to consensus of early fans, Tuck, and Ketterer, a Canadian author, but nothing more has been learned of him, despite extensive research and inquiries. Portrait shows a middle-aged man.

1523. **THE WOMAN FROM SPACE.** *Wonder Stories Quarterly*, Spring 1932. Ill. Paul.

Short story. * *Time:* around A.D. 2350. *Place:* Tibet, space, and the new planet Arion. * About sixty years earlier a runaway star entered the solar system, disrupting orbits and threatening destruction. It seemed headed toward Earth, but about ten years ago veered aside and moved out of the solar system. The Earth, which suffered greatly from the event, was pulled into a new orbit closer to the sun, resulting in a hotter climate. * The protagonist Dirk Sarazin, one of the best minds on the planet, is an astronomer at the great observatory in Tibet when word comes to him of a strange craft, presumably a spaceship, from which has emerged a blue person. He goes to investigate; finds a remarkable vessel; meets Lella, a beautiful, blue-skinned woman; and, via thought helmet, enters into conversation with her. Extended acquaintance reveals that she comes from the planet Arion, which had formerly been associated with the

Vaughan, Richard (*continued*)

invading star and has been left behind out near Neptune. Lella further explains that it was the science of her race that had diverted the runaway star and saved the solar system from destruction. * By a curious circumstance the sexual situations on Earth and Arion are complementary; Earth, thanks to the disasters, has a great shortage of women, while Arion has a similar shortage of men. * Lella and Sarazin now voyage to Arion, along the way encountering peril from a planetoid, which the ship's disintegrators move barely in time. By now Sarazin and Lella have fallen in love and agree to mate. Lella is particularly enthusiastic at having a mate so superior to the scruffy males of Arion. * The Council of Arion, taking note of matters, decides to remedy the sexual situation on both planets. Arion will be moved to the position of the asteroids, which will be either disintegrated or booted out of the system with force rays. In this way, the two worlds can have easy intercourse. * *Miscellaneous:* The civilization of Arion is higher than that of Earth, with thought-recording machines, disintegrators, indestructible metals, and much else. The cities of Arion are covered over with transparent domes. Lella wears a gravity-regulating suit. * Routine at best.

1524. **THE EXILE OF THE SKIES**. *Wonder Stories*, January 1934-March 1934. Ill. Paul.
Novel. * *Time:* A.D. 2247 on. *Place:* perhaps mostly the asteroid belt. * This story might with some justice be called "Skylark Three and a Half," since it is very heavily based on E. E. Smith's Skylark series, though not plagiaristically so. * Knute Savary is the greatest scientist on Earth, the man who has contributed most to the scientific and material welfare of the day. Unfortunately, he has succumbed to hybris and ambition and has tried to make himself master of the world. His intentions were good, improving the lot of mankind and preserving the world from an unexpected doom, but his actions were irresponsible, cruel, and ruthless: artificial hurricanes that devastated Chicago, disintegration that dissolved the dikes of the Netherlands, destruction of energy over the world, etc. * Savary, however, has failed. Betrayed by a colleague, he has been captured and tried by the world government. The council, loath to execute the most brilliant mind in history, sentences him to perpetual exile in a gigantic spaceship (the *Victory*) that he had been building for the conquest of Mars. The ship is fitted out with every material of science that Savary wants, including heat rays, but it is coated with repellum, a discovery of Savary's that will not permit the ship to land on Earth or a planet similarly constituted chemically. * Savary takes off, heading into outer space, toward the asteroid belt, his newly installed disintegrators preventing collision with meteors or space rubbish. He does not know that Nadja Manners, the woman who betrayed him, is a stowaway on the *Victory*. Nadja, despite her action, is deeply in love with Savary and suffers remorse. * Savary regrets leaving Earth, for one of his reasons for world conquest is still important to him. The Earth is rapidly losing its atmosphere, and unless the process is stopped (which Savary can do) the Earth (and Mars, too) will soon be airless. According to Savary's theory, the atmosphere is held in place by the Earth's magnetic field; when air leaves, it does not dissipate into space, but simply extends out farther and thinner. With suitable apparatus it should be retrievable. * Most of the middle action of the story centers on an asteroidal subgroup, a cluster of five planetoids that orbit more or less

together. These planetoids, despite their common origin, differ markedly. The planetoid called Speira is dead and empty of life and atmosphere; at one time in the past, judging from archeological evidence, it housed a high civilization, but it lost its atmosphere. Not all the Speirans are dead, however; a few are preserved in suspended animation awaiting the arrival of a science capable of restoring the planet. Savary vows to bring air back to Speira. * It is on this planetoid that Savary first learns that Nadja has accompanied him. When she emerges on Speira, space-suit clad, she is attacked by a semimaterial being that radiates cold. Savary rescues her, but since he is uninterested in women, accepts her only as a junior comrade in his fate. * Savary decides to exterminate the cold beings, which center upon Sakka, a second asteroid. There are cliffhangers, but his heat rays destroy them, even if his disintegrators do not. Savary reasons out that the cold beings are intrusions from a parallel world formed along with our universe and complementary to it. To remove the peril from the cold beings forever, Savary sets off an atomic disintegration process that will eventually destroy Sakka, except for its iron core. * On approaching the third asteroid (Lydda), which is barren and airless, the *Victory* is seized by a force ray and drawn into the interior of the planetoid. Telepathic messages indicate that this is not an unfriendly move. Inside Lydda, which has been maintained as a semi-paradisiacal world, lives a race of small bird-men with vestigial wings. Superior to Earthmen in mentality (except for Savary, whom they recognize as an equal or superior), they retain many aspects of a superscience, but are bored, lackadaisical, and somewhat ineffectual. When Savary offers to restore the air on their planet, they are not really interested. But the Lyddans freely share their science with him, thus enlarging his already colossal capability. As a result of these contacts with the bird men, Savary's telepathic abilities are increased, and from here on telepathy of a sort plays a part in the story. * One of the bird men accompanies Savary and Nadja on their explorations and will help restore Speira. * The next planetoid, Reinos, is almost totally water-covered. A barbaric humanoid race has partly adapted to the water by evolving gills, but is almost extinct. To save them Savary, using a neutron beam, tosses the excess water off the planet out into space, rendering the world habitable. * The fifth planet, Merinoe, is filled with the most horrible gigantic beasts and carnivorous plants. It is here, when saving Nadja from a monster that is carrying her off, that Savary recognizes that he really loves her. Life is now more pleasant for both. * Merinoe, despite its horrors, will serve as a source of life-forms for the rejuvenation of Speira, which is now under way. The work is not always smooth, for the construction robots revolt, but they are quelled by telepathy. * Six years have passed since Savary was exiled. Savary, who has mellowed, is now willing to reveal to Earth the techniques for stopping atmospheric loss. Nadja delivers such a message. What Savary and Nadja did not know is that the human race is on the edge of extinction. Not long after Savary was expelled, a dark body approached Earth and became a second moon. From it erupted a swarm of semiintelligent creatures composed of a new form of matter, capable of changing their mass/weight to an enormous extent and practically immune to terrestrial weapons. They have devastated the land and killed most of the human race. Only a few strongholds and hidden retreats hold out. * The presence of the invaders also has affected the Earth's magnetic field in some

Vaughan, Richard (*continued*)

manner, so that the loss of atmosphere is proceeding far more rapidly than expected. * The World Council sends representatives to Savary, begging him to help. Savary returns to Earth and works out a way to defeat the monsters—strong vibratory waves. He then destroys the second moon. Atmosphere retrieval plants are being set up, and the world is saved. * Savary? He and Nadja decide that Earth is too small for them and fly away into the cosmos. * Some horrible purple passages, but on the whole not a bad job. Unfortunately, Vaughan wrote the novel a decade too late, for it is old-fashioned for its day. If it had appeared ten years earlier, it would probably be remembered as one of the early (though limited) classics of science-fiction.

VERNE , JULES (1828-1905)

French novelist, dramatist; one of the great predecessors of modern science-fiction, whose works have been popular and influential in the English-speaking world. Most of Verne's works were written for the publisher Hetzel, who published them as *voyages imaginaires*, which can be best translated as "fantastic adventures" or "amazing adventures." Verne's stress was on geography, which he worked into his stories exhaustively and usually very accurately, with the intention of doing for the Earth sciences what Gaboriau had done for crime and Balzac, for social matters. Not all his work is science-fiction, and a fair amount of his fiction reprinted in the early genre magazines is geographical adventure.

Despite the fact that Verne wrote for a semijuvenile market, his work is now considered of much wider interest. Particularly interesting in his life is the dichotomy between his fostering, yet distrusting, hard science and technology. The same breech occurs in life pattern: he was a very conservative small-town bourgeois, yet (in his works) a proponent of various sorts of social protest, notably philosophical anarchism. In many translations and modern editions these social elements are suppressed, as are technical matters.

A word must be added about translations. All covered below are bad, but in several cases there are no others.

The following presentation is brief, since the stories are premodern and not original with the pulp magazines. Verne's science-fiction works are covered in full and in much more detail in *Science-Fiction: The Early Years*.

1525. **A DRAMA IN THE AIR**. *Amazing Stories*, November 1926. Ill. Paul.

(First published as "Un drame dans l'air," 1851. Translated as "A Drama in the Air" in Verne, *Doctor Ox,* 1874. Reprinted in Verne, *Doctor Ox,* Arco, 1964.)

Short story. * *Place:* Germany and the Netherlands. * Not science-fiction. The narrator, a professional balloonist, is making an ascent at Frankfurt when a stranger leaps into the basket. The stranger, who is mad, on the one hand keeps tossing ballast overboard so that the balloon cannot descend, and on the other, recites in great detail misfortunes that have befallen balloonists of the past. To keep the balloon from sinking into the sea, the men have to jettison everything moveable, including their clothing. At the last, when the basket falls off, the narrator clings to the ropes and is saved.

1526. **THE WATCH'S SOUL.** *Amazing Stories*, December 1933.

(First published as "Maître Zacharias, ou l'horloger qui a perdu son âme," 1854. English translation as "Master Zacharius" in Verne, *Doctor Ox and Other Stories*, 1874; Verne, *Doctor Ox*, Arco, New York, 1964. Also titled "The Watchmaker's Soul.") Not science-fiction, but an allegory of science in the mode of E. T. A. Hoffmann. * *Place:* Switzerland. * A problem faces the great Swiss horologist Zacharias. All his clocks and watches no longer function; the mainsprings are dead, and substitutions are of no avail. The answer is provided by the old iron clock in Andermatt. It first states in mottoes it issues that man must be subservient to science, then, at the last, proclaims that one who tries to be equal to God should be destroyed. The moral is that Zacharias has so entered his craft and has been so presumptuous that, figuratively speaking, he has ceased to be human. * One of Verne's better stories. The fabular note suits him well.

1527. **A WINTER AMID THE ICE, OR THE CRUISE OF THE JEUNE-HARDIE**. *Amazing Stories Quarterly,* Winter 1933.

(First published as "Un hivernage dans les glacés" in *Musée des familles*, 1855. Translated in *Doctor Ox and Other Stories*, 1874.)

Short story. * Not in the slightest degree science-fiction, simply hatred, peril, romance among castaways in the Arctic. One can only wonder why T. O'Conor Sloane reprinted it, apart from the fact that it would have been public domain and free.

1528. **A TRIP TO THE CENTER OF THE EARTH**. *Amazing Stories*, May-July 1926. Ill. Paul and M.C. (?). This reprints the anonymous Scribner translation that used to be considered "standard," but has been superseded as inaccurate and badly prepared.

(First published as *Voyage au centre de la terre*, 1863; revised, enlarged, 1867. English translation *A Journey to the Centre of the Earth*, Griffith and Farren, London, 1872. Scribner and Armstrong, New York, 1874. There are many later reprints, as well as more modern, better translations.)

Novel of geographic adventure; Verne's first significant work. It is basically a fictionalization of the geological theory of his day. * When Professor Hardwigg finds a runic manuscript in an old book, it sets off an important chain of events. The manuscript, whose decipherment Verne describes in detail, tells of a Renaissance descent "to the center of the Earth" via the crater of an extinct Icelandic volcano. Hardwigg, his nephew Harry, and their Icelandic guide/companion Hans descend into the volcano and follow the tortuous turnings of the underground passage for perhaps three thousand miles to the southeast. For light they carry an electric generator. * The journey has its thrills, but more important are Verne's descriptions of the geological formations that the men encounter. At one time Harry has horrible, realistic nightmares about threatening prehistoric life. * The high point of the exploration comes when the travelers, perhaps thirty miles below the surface of the world, come upon an enormous cavern that is lighted by some inexplicable energy. It contains vegetable life and a herd of grazing mammoths, tended by a mysterious gigantic figure. The vision of this gigantic figure is one of the most thrilling moments in early science-fiction, all the more potent because it is not explained. In a huge lake or ocean that is nearby, the men see a plesiosaurus and other prehistoric forms of life. * The explorers continue along their designated path until they reach a rockfall, which they remove by explosives. The explosion releases the subterranean sea and the men are washed along dark

Verne, Jules (*continued*)

passages until they finally emerge from the crater of Stromboli off the shore of Sicily. * Verne's fiction is generally considered dated, but the present work is an excellent fictionalization of a branch of science of Verne's day.

1529. **THE ENGLISH AT THE NORTH POLE**. *Amazing Stories*, May-June, 1929. Ill. Paul.

(First published in *Le magasin d'éducation et de récréation* 1864-1865, as "Les Anglais au pôle nord: Aventures de Capitaine Hatteras." Published in book form as *Les Anglais au pôle nord* (1866), first translated as *The English at the North Pole*, Routledge: London, 1874. Other editions are variously titled *A Journey to the North Pole*, or *At the North Pole*, or *The Adventures of Captain Hatteras, Part I*, or *At the North Pole* (1961, perhaps abridged).

A short novel of essentially geographical adventure, with the almost compulsive inclusion, characteristic of Verne, of historical and geographical information. The science-fictional element in this story and its sequel, *The Desert of Ice*, is very slight, certainly not enough to warrant classifying the narrative as science-fiction. * *Time:* the 1850s. *Place:* Liverpool and the north polar regions. * There is a mystery surrounding the ship *Forward*, which has been specially built, stocked with food for five years, and pays sailors' wages far higher than the ordinary. No one knows where the ship is ultimately going or who the captain is. Instead, there is a sense of bewilderment as the ship sails north without a leader. An emergency finally produces the captain, Captain Hatteras, well-known in naval circles as a dangerous man to serve under. In previous voyages he had little regard for crew or vessel. Indeed, he is a familiar type in Verne's fiction, a monomaniacal, compulsive, egotistic dreamer. Hatteras, who is an extremely wealthy man, intends to reach the north pole. * The party goes through typical Arctic adventures, usually for the worse. Coal and other stored supplies that Hatteras had counted on have been raided, and eventually the ship is trapped in the ice around 83° north. While Hatteras and others are out exploring with a dog team, a mutiny breaks out on the *Forward*, and the ship with all its supplies is destroyed. * It looks as if Hatteras and his companions are doomed. * For a continuation see #1530, "The Desert of Ice."

1530. **THE DESERT OF ICE**. *Amazing Stories*, June-July 1929. Ill. Hugh Mackay.

First published in *Le magasin d'éducation et de récréation*, 1865, as "Le désert de glace. Aventures de Capitaine Hatteras." Printed in book form as *Le désert de glace* (1866), with English translations *The Desert of Ice* (1874), *The Field of Ice* (1874), *The Wilderness of Ice* (1961, perhaps abridged). Both *The English at the North Pole* and *The Desert of Ice* have been published together as *The Adventures of Captain Hatteras* or *The Voyages and Adventures of Captain Hatteras*.

Novel. Continuation of #1529, "The English at the North Pole." * *Place:* the north polar area. * Just as things look hopeless, the British rescue an American who is on the point of death. This is Captain Altamont of the *Porpoise*, who soon recovers his strength and leads the others to his ship, which is plentifully supplied with fuel and food. Altamont had been in search of the Northwest Passage. Much is made of the tension between Hatteras and Altamont, who are both not only egotists but violent chauvinists. * The two men become reconciled, and the comrades continue on toward the pole in a small boat, for the ice has

begun to break up. In a short time they are on the open polar sea. They find the pole itself on a small volcanic island, indeed, in the crater of the volcano. Hatteras, who has collapsed mentally, insists on entering the crater. * The pole found, the comrades make their way through great hardships back to civilization. Hatteras never recovers his reason. * The only science-fiction element is the open polar sea, a strong notion in crank geography of the nineteenth century.

1531. **DR. OX'S EXPERIMENT**. *Amazing Stories*, August 1926. Unsigned ill.

(First published as "Une fantaisie du Docteur Ox," 1872; first book publications in translation in *Doctor Ox and Other Stories*, Osgood, Boston, 1874 and *Dr. Ox's Experiment and Other Stories*, Sampson Low, etc. London, 1874. Modern reprints, in various translations, in Derleth, *Beyond Time and Space*; Verne, *Dr. Ox's Experiment*, Arco and Macmillan, New York.)

Novelette. * Ethnic humor poked at the Flemings. * The inhabitants of the small town of Quiquendone are so lethargic that they may take months, even years or decades, to accomplish what outsiders could do in minutes. But inexplicably things change: Calmness changes to irritability, lethargy to the most violent action. Indeed, the villagers start an attack on a neighboring village because of an affront that is centuries old. But once the men leave the town, their habitual inaction returns. * This strange behavior has been caused by Dr. Ox, a self-proclaimed philanthropist, who is installing a gas lighting system in the town, free of charge. Actually, Ox is conducting an experiment. His theory is that the Quiquendone syndrome (my term) is caused by lack of oxygen, and the pipes installed for illuminating gas are actually releasing oxygen. The experiment is successful. * Overlong and rather coy.

1532. **MEASURING A MERIDIAN**. *Amazing Stories*, May-August 1934. Ill. Morey.

(*Aventures de trois russes et de trois anglais dans l'Afrique australe*, 1872; translated by Henry Frith as *Meridiana; or, Adventures of Three Englishmen and Three Russians in South Africa*, 1873.)

Novel. * *Time:* 1854-1856. *Place:* South Africa, from Bechuanaland and the Kalahari Desert on east. * Not science-fiction, this is essentially a geographical novel based on an international expedition to measure a meridian of longitude, the ultimate aim being the correct establishment of the meter. The party consists of Colonel Everest, probably to be identified with Col. George Everest, who performed the great survey of India; a Russian counterpart named Strux, who may be intended as a member of the Struve family; and colleagues. The first part of the novel devotes quite a bit of space to the history of mensuration, which is given with considerable French bias. * The story itself includes episodes with animals and attacks by hostile natives, during which the engineers risk their lives for their scientific results. For a time, when it is learned that the Crimean War is taking place, the British and Russians conduct separate surveys, but under pressure from the hostile natives they make peace and continue on together. * *Miscellaneous:* As an example of geographical procedures different from those of the present day: When a huge, impenetrable forest lies in the way of the triangulation, the surveyors burn it to the ground. * Not one of Verne's major works, and not helped by a weak translation. It has not been possible to check, but it is assumed that this text (as the only English translation) is that of Frith.

Verne, Jules (*continued*)

1533. **OFF ON A COMET—OR HECTOR SERVA-DAC**. *Amazing Stories*, April-May 1926. Ill. Paul.
(First published as *Hector Servadac*, 1877. Translated editions as *Hector Servadac* by Sampson Low etc., London, 1878, and Scribner and Armstrong, New York, 1878. Also conflated two volume edition *To the Sun?* and *Off on a Comet!*, trans. by Edward Roth, New York, 1878; and two volume abridged edition, trans. by I. O. Evans, Arco, London, 1965. The present text probably translated by Ellen E. Frewer.)
Novel. An odd mixture of geographical fiction, a puzzle story, a last-man story, and ethnic bile. * *Time:* the near future. *Place:* mostly on a fragment of Earth with an eccentric orbit. * Captain Hector Servadac and his orderly are knocked unconscious by a great storm. When they awaken, the world seems very strange. They are inexplicably much stronger than they used to be, and what was formerly mainland Africa around them is now a small island. The alternation of day and night takes place in a matter of a few hours, and the Earth seems to be approaching the sun. The explanation, worked out later, is that the comet Gallia grazed the Earth and picked up a small fragment, which it has carried out into space. * Other personalities turn up: a Russian prince and his steam yacht, Spanish dancers, rude Englishmen on Gibraltar, Servadac's old teacher Professor Rosette, and a Jewish trader, who is portrayed in the most anti-Semitic terms. * The unwilling passengers on the comet survive a difficult winter inside the comet, and when the comet again grazes Earth, transfer back to North Africa, where they started. Rosette had unwillingly supplied the scientific knowledge for their salvation. * But was it all a dream?

1534. **ROBUR THE CONQUEROR**. *Amazing Stories*, December 1927-January 1928. Ill. Paul.
(First published as *Robur le conquérant*, 1886. Translated as *The Clipper of the Clouds*, Sampson Low, etc., London, 1887, and as *Robur the Conqueror*, George Munro, New York 1887. Modern reprintings of British edition by Macmillan, 1956, and Arco, New York, (perhaps abridged?) 1962. Available in several modern paperback editions.)
Novel. * "The rogue engineer used very consciously as a semi-allegory of scientific progress." At a meeting at the Weldon Institute, where the plans for a new dirigible are being discussed, a stranger asks to be heard. He, Robur, tells the audience that lighter-than-air craft are obsolete, since he has already built a successful heavier-than-air craft. Hooted, he leaves the meeting vowing vengeance. * Robur's revenge takes the form of kidnapping the leaders of the Philadelphia club and flying around the world with them. Eventually, the captives escape, leaving a bomb that blows up Robur's vessel. * Back in the United States the construction of the new dirigible proceeds. When it is ready to take to the air, a strange aircraft approaches. It is Robur, with a new machine. Robur attacks the dirigible, but when it is foundering, he rescues its passengers. * *Miscellaneous:* Robur's vessel is essentially a ship hull, to which are attached 74 horizontal propellers powered by electric batteries. It is the model for the many flying machines in the American dime novel. * At the end of the story Verne states that Robur is the science of the future. Progress is necessary, but should not be too rapid. * For a sequel see #1536, "The Master of the World."

1535. **THE PURCHASE OF THE NORTH POLE**. *Amazing Stories*, September-October 1926. Ill. Wardell.
(First published as *Sans dessus dessous*, 1889. English translations *The Purchase of the North Pole*, Sampson Low, etc. London, 1891. *Topsy-Turvy*, Ogilvie, New York, 1890. Also *The Purchase of the North Pole*, Ace, New York 1960; Arco, London, 1966.)
Novel. * A sequel to the double moon voyage *From the Earth to the Moon* and *Round the Moon*. * The near future. * The Baltimore Gun Club is again pondering action. What has aroused the officers of the club? The sudden recognition that the polar north, which probably has huge deposits of coal, is still unclaimed by the major nations. An auction seems the most reasonable way to settle possession, and, backed by a wealthy widow who has her eye on one of the club officials, the Gun Club buys the area. * Maston, the mathematician of the lunar voyages, has worked out a solution to the inaccessibility of the coal: straighten the axis of the Earth so that the climate of the polar regions will become temperate. * The Gun Club decides to carry out this scheme, even though it obviously will wipe out much of the human race. The great nations try to stop the fanatics, but to no avail. The Gun Club sets off an enormous explosion in Mount Kilimanjaro, hoping to jar the Earth upright—but nothing happens. The recoil does not disturb the Earth's position, but only shakes the ground locally. The explanation: While calculating, Maston was struck by lightning; although he was not injured, the shock caused him to omit a few zeros in his calculations. The project always was impossible, and all the brouhaha was uncalled for. * An amusing story, typical of Verne's later years, when he no longer trusted the results of advanced technology.

1536. **THE MASTER OF THE WORLD**. *Amazing Stories*, February-March 1928. Ill. Paul.
(First publication as *Maître du monde*, 1904. Translated as *The Master of the World*, Sampson Low etc., London, 1914, Lippincott, Philadelphia, 1915. Reprinted several times in modern paperback editions.)
Novel. * Sequel to #1534, *Robur the Conqueror*. * The story is told through John Strock, a Federal agent who investigates mysterious occurrences: a remarkably fast ship off New England, an automobile that wins a race at 150 miles per hour then dives into a lake, and, later, a submarine that sprouts wings and flies over Niagara Falls. And then there is a threat from the Master of the World. * It is Robur, now an out-and-out megalomaniac, who has a wonderful combination vessel that is a land vehicle, a surface ship, a submarine, and a flying machine. Robur has his headquarters in the Appalachians. * Robur captures Strock, who witnesses Robur's titanic end. In an act of hybris, Robur deliberately flies his vessel, the *Terrible*, into a thunderstorm. The ship is struck by lightning, and Robur dies with it, defiant to the end. * The allegory of science, man, and God is continued as outrageous pride is struck down.

VERRILL, A[LPHEUS] HYATT (1874-1954)
U.S. (mostly Florida) author, expositor of science and natural history. Born in New Haven, son of a distinguished naturalist. Educated at Yale University School of Fine Arts. Illustrated *Webster International Dictionary*, 1896 edition. Traveled extensively, with periods of residence, in many parts of Central America. Author of many books on popular science, crafts, history, etc. Also wrote several series of boys' books, most popular of which were the Radio Boys. Some of these boys'

Verrill, A. Hyatt (*continued*)

books, which approach science-fiction, are covered in *Science-Fiction: The Early Years*. * His work for the genre pulp magazines, as follows, was always literate, but tended to be repetitive and stodgy, particularly in later years. Verrill's fictional skills were weak. While he could create a convincing tropical background, he had difficulties with plot and characterizations. In general, his fiction, which approached hackwork on occasion, is best seen as an outgrowth of popular scientific travel literature. * Verrill was competent in natural history, but, probably as an adjunct to his lost-race fiction and the rising interest in New World antiquities, he tended to oversell himself greatly as an archeologist and ethnologist. I remember that Wendell Bennett, the great expert on Andean archeology, called him a charlatan. * Verrill, in his earlier years at least, was skilled at publicity, and he seems to have convinced Gernsback and Sloane that he was a noteworthy scientist. Perhaps as an outgrowth of this publicity, the artists who illustrated Verrill's stories often pictured him, pointed beard and all, as the protagonist. Verrill also contributed many stories to Street and Smith *Sea Stories* magazine.

1537. **BEYOND THE POLE**. *Amazing Stories*, October-November 1926. Ill. Paul.

Novelette. * *Place:* Antarctica. * Essentially derivative from travel literature, with some attempt at detailed botanical and ornithological verisimilitude. * A frame narrator on Kerguelen Island finds a remarkable crystal bottle containing a manuscript. It had been carried to Kerguelen by a sea bird. * The manuscript of Franklin Bishop, mate of the whaler *Endeavor*, which departed New Bedford in 1917. His ship is caught in an Antarctic storm and driven up on the ice. The sole survivor, he manages to salvage some supplies, on which he survives for a time. But on finding corpses of his shipmates, he temporarily loses his mind and wanders for a long time, ever farther inland into Antarctica, until he reaches a meadowed land that is temperate in climate. A series of volcanic craters, it is warmed by volcanic heat. * After a short time Bishop, at the point of starvation, encounters the strange crustacean people, a description of whose culture forms most of the story. These are multilimbed beings much like eight-foot-tall shrimp or lobsters, at least as intelligent as mankind, kindly and benevolent on the whole, but somewhat lacking in appetition. They are telepathic and have no difficulty in communicating with Bishop. * The shrimp people, who feed and house Bishop hospitably, have a lopsided science that is in some ways superior to ours, in other ways deficient. Building their culture on metallic sulfur and radioactive elements, they have cylindrical flying machines that may invoke antigravity, broadcast power, superexplosives, food tablets, and much else, but they do not know steam power, the wheel, or firearms. (In the past they had such devices, but they have dropped out of use.) Their eggs are reared in hatcheries, and in embryo individuals are shaped, by chemical and radiative means, for lifetime specialization. * The culture of the shrimp-men is governed by guilds of specialists. There is no family life, and emotions are apparently weak. Population is rigidly controlled, and in contrast to the general benevolence of the culture a rigid and ruthless system of euthanasia removes the sick and disabled. The economy would seem to be socialistic, without money; value is expressed in terms of labor. Writing does not exist, but there is a huge corps of oral historians whose data extends back mil-

lennia. * Bishop lives among the shrimp happily for a time, but eventually becomes bored. After introducing wheels and primitive automobiles, he builds himself a boat and prepares a message for the outside world. * The strange shrimp culture comes to a sudden end. Previously, the shrimp had almost exterminated fiercely aggressive, semi-intelligent ants, but kept a small stock imprisoned in a zoo. These ants escape, and multiplying with incredible rapidity, overrun the land. The pacifist shrimp, having long forgotten combat, are on the edge of extermination when Bishop sends out his message. * *Miscellaneous:* Dinosaurs are present, as are butterflies with wing spreads of yards. * The story demonstrates Verrill's general inability to plot.

1538. **THROUGH THE CRATER'S RIM**. *Amazing Stories*, December 1926. Ill. Paul.

Short story. * *Place:* Panama. * When aviator Lieutenant Hazen reports having seen a hitherto unknown stone city in the jungles of Panama, the unnamed narrator accepts that it is the legendary lost city the Indians speak of. * The narrator, with an Indian companion (who is soon killed), makes his way through the jungles, eluding carnivorous walking trees with grasping branches, until he reaches the proper area. Hazen is scheduled to fly in and pick him up in a few days. * The narrator is amazed to find the hidden city peopled by a dwarfish folk with emaciated legs and prehensile feet, who walk on their hands. After displaying such marvels as matches and smoking tobacco, the narrator is accepted as almost a god by the simple, primitive natives, although the king and the high priest (who walk on their feet) obviously have reservations, which they put into action. * In a short time the narrator finds himself captured, tied on the sacrificial altar, and about to be deprived of his heart, Aztec manner. But friend Hazen flies in at the proper time and rescues him. On their way out of the valley, since the plane is overloaded, the fliers must jettison everything to attain lift. This includes a bomb that accidentally shatters the reservoir and inundates the whole land. * Pretty dull, and occasionally silly.

1539. **THE MAN WHO COULD VANISH**. *Amazing Stories*, January 1927. Unsgnd. (F. S. Hynd?) ill.
(Reprinted in *Amazing Stories Annual* [1927]).

Short story. * The narrator visits his friend the great scientist Professor Unsinn, who has been working on the problem of invisibility. Unsinn explains his successes: so far he can make organic matter invisible, but not inorganic. He demonstrates a little black box and explains his technique, which is changing the Angström range of reflected light into a range that is invisible to the human eye. * On a later visit Unsinn demonstrates that he can also make inorganic material invisible. The two men thereupon go on a street walk, with Unsinn invisible. As might be expected, there are contretemps—on a street car, in the streets, and about a skyscraper under construction that Unsinn renders invisible. Unsinn's point of view is that the average person will accept invisibility as a great gift; the narrator takes the opposite view. Eventually, after many mishaps, Unsinn is forced to admit that he was wrong. But he will not suppress his invention; he will simply give it to the American government—who, the narrator cynically asserts, will lose it. * Padded and unable to extract the possibilities of the situation.

1540. **THE PLAGUE OF THE LIVING DEAD**. *Amazing Stories*, April 1927. Unsigned ill.

Short story. * *Place:* an imaginary tropical island, Central or

Verrill, A. Hyatt (*continued*)

South America. * Old Dr. Farnham, no Moreau, but a soft-hearted researcher who has settled on the island of Abilone, discovers a chemical that when injected gives the patient immortality, apart from accident. It does not restore youth, but maintains the recipient at the age in which he was inoculated. * Well and good. The doctor continues his researches and now, with an improved version of his formula, can give unkillability. Test animals "killed" in various ways remain alive, and dissected animals rejoin and heal in record time. * The crucial situation comes when the volcano on Abilone explodes, and much of the population is injured, even mortally. * The kindhearted doctor injects the suffering with his second elixir, then discovers that he has created a problem. While his animal patients did not reveal it, the second elixir creates a ravening, imbecilic madness that cannot be contained. * When the authorities recognize what the situation is, they quarantine the island on the pretense of plague. But there is no answer to the indestructible natives, who are homicidally uncontrollable. * Eventually, a solution is reached. All the madmen are lured or driven to a certain field which has been mined with high explosives. The explosion hurls them off the Earth into space. Routine, at best.

1541. THE VOICE FROM THE INNER WORLD.

Amazing Stories, July 1927. Ill. Paul.

Short story. * An honorable mention in the contest based on the cover of the December 1926 issue of *Amazing Stories*. Verrill's story received no monetary prize. * *Place:* a cavern world beneath the Andes. * After a frame situation, a prolonged radio message from James Berry, a mining engineer passenger on the ill-fated *Chiriqui*, which disappeared at sea some time ago. * Berry's message: A large metallic sphere appeared above the ship, and seizing the *Chiriqui* with force tentacles, soared off with it, probably to the Andes. There it descends into a volcanic crater, to a small subterranean world. As the ship is landed, Berry observes that his shipmates all lie collapsed, presumably gassed; a gas mask that he finds in a cabin saves him. * At first Berry thinks that his comrades are dead, but he discovers that they are unarousably unconscious. As he watches, gigantic nude females, about thirty-feet tall, with strange formations about their heads, dash onto the ship and, seizing the unconscious sailors and passengers, tear them apart and eat them. They also remove bodies, which Berry later learns will be stored, alive, for future food. Luckily for Berry, the monster women are terrified of him because of his gas mask, and leave him severely alone. * After many weeks in the underground world, Berry gives refuge to a small (ten-foot-tall) male, and from him learns something about his situation. But the women eventually attack, and unwilling to be kept alive like a caterpillar in a wasp's nest, Berry commits suicide. * *Miscellaneous:* The underground people constitute a rigorous gynecocracy, where the men, who are much smaller, are abused and eaten. * The spherical ships, while enormously powerful in some ways, are also limited; they can use their force rays only over water and cannot leave the underground world under their own power. They are blasted out by controlled volcanisms. * The huge females have captured other vessels, including the famous historical *Cyclops*; they need these ships as sources for metal, since their own metal resources have been exhausted. * How the gigantic women developed their science is not explained. * Better than the three prize-winning stories, though perhaps over-essayed. It probably was rated low because

it does not incorporate gobbets of popular science.

1542. THE ULTRA-ELIXIR OF YOUTH. *Amazing Stories*, August 1927. Ill. Paul.

Short story. * Professor Elias Henderson of McCracken College, a prominent biologist, has disappeared, as have several of his colleagues. There is suspicion of foul play, even of human sacrifice of infants. The narrator takes over Henderson's post, as much out of curiosity as anything. Investigating, he soon learns more than the police did. From Henderson's lab workbook he discovers that Henderson was investigating aging. A chance explosion of a dirigible released a secret gas (QW) that seemed to rejuvenate life near the catastrophe. Henderson followed this lead through and discovered that a new element, juvenum, was involved; when activated by radio waves, it turns back the biological clock. * Henderson at first rejoiced at his discovery; but then he observed that the "youthing" process could not be stopped. Henderson, his experimental animals, and his patients all regressed to the birth period. * Undoubtedly due to publishing prudishness of the day, Henderson et al. did not return to an embryonic stage, but just vanished completely after reaching babyhood. * Stuffily told.

1543. THE AMAZING DISCOVERIES OF DOCTOR MENTIROSO. *Amazing Stories*, November 1927. Ill. Paul.

Short essay story, with most of the text taken up by exposition. * *Place:* Lima, Peru. * The narrator, perhaps Verrill himself, converses with his friend the great maverick scientist Fenomeno Mentiroso (lying phenomenon). Mentiroso insists that he has solved the problems of both the fourth dimension and time. In the discussion Mentiroso sloughs off the fourth dimension, but states that he can travel in time by flying around the world faster than it rotates. He proves this by juggling various local times with reference to the international date line. The narrator is incredulous, but Mentiroso takes off in his own little time machine. He can enter both past and future. * Included is a biographical sketch and photograph of Verrill, and an exposition of his logic in a separate section. * In the December 1927 issue of *Amazing Stories* Verrill provides a small diagrammatic presentation of his ideas. * A prolonged bore.

1544. THE PSYCHOLOGICAL SOLUTION. *Amazing Stories*, January 1928. Ill. Paul.

Short story, doubtful as science-fiction. Really more a scientific detective story with advanced ideas on profiling. * Dr. Edmond Curtis Thane, an anthropologist who occasionally assists the police in special cases, has worked out an elaborate system of analyzing crime and criminals by racial and social criteria. Thus, when garbage collector Henry Columbus, in line of duty, finds the corpse of a murdered man, Thane's abilities come to the fore. * Despite misdirections, misidentifications of the corpse, and other confusing factors, chance (or criminal psychology) eventually brings about a solution that was not too far removed from Thane's analysis. * Interesting for the mode of thought, but for today's tastes, a little too racist.

1545. THE KING OF THE MONKEY MEN. *Amazing Stories Quarterly*, Spring 1928. Ill. Paul.

Novelette. * *Place:* the wilds of Brazil. * The narrative of Dr. Henry Meredith, noted American naturalist, who returns to civilization accompanied by a beautiful young blonde woman whose native tongue is an obscure Indian language. * Meredith, on his rambles, sees in the hut of a friendly Indian a remarkable headdress made of royal purple feathers some three feet long.

Verrill, A. Hyatt (*continued*)

They are so incredibly beautiful that Meredith wishes to track down their source, the semimythical waupona bird. His native informants tell him that it is to be found in the land of the monkey-men, an area into which they dare not venture. * With a couple of more courageous men, Meredith finds the habitat of the waupona, which is in a valley surrounded by sheer cliffs. Using a makeshift ladder, the men descend. One of the men shoots a waupona, whereupon they are all attacked by the monkey-men, who hold the bird sacred. * Meredith's companions are all killed, and Meredith himself escapes temporarily by leaping into a river, where he loses his rifle. He is captured soon after this and begins a long captivity among the monkey men. His life is spared when some of his captors tell their king about his rifle; when he throws a handful of cartridges into the fire, the explosions cause the simple creatures to consider him divine. But he is not allowed to leave the immediate area. * The monkey men: Paleolithic in culture at best, they are black-skinned, with long arms with which they brachiate through the trees. They are enormously strong. Obviously they are either a bypath of evolution or a survival of a pre-sapiens man. * During his stay with the monkey men Meredith teaches them simple arts, while equipping himself with bow and arrows. When the somewhat hostile king is killed by an exploding cartridge, Meredith boldly assumes the kingship, without opposition. He now explores the valley thoroughly, and, locating a stream that exits from the area, leaves, taking along with him some emerald fragments and gold that he has found. * In the second portion of the story Meredith heads for civilization, along the way rescuing a young white woman from hostile Indians who are about to barbecue her. On reaching civilization he discovers that the young woman, who has been reared by a remote tribe, is really his long lost daughter. * The first portion of the story, when Verrill concentrates on natural history, shows him at his strongest, as a popularizer of natural science. This part can be read with some pleasure, although there is some overlap with Verrill's boys' book, *The Boy Adventurers in the Land of the Monkey Men.* The lost-child motif, however, is on the silly side.

1546. **THE WORLD OF THE GIANT ANTS**. *Amazing Stories Quarterly*, Fall 1928. Ill. Paul. Also illustrations from *Nature's Craftsmen* by Henry C. McCook.

Long novel. * *Place:* The foothills of the Andes, where they meet the jungle areas of Peru or Western Brazil. * In the frame situation the narrator, presumably Verrill, is exploring enormous elaborate ruins in the jungle, when an earthquake shatters them. Among the debris he finds a dying man, Tom, the servant of Dr. Benjamin Henden, a noted scientist and friend of the frame narrator's who had disappeared some time previously. On Tom's body were Henden's field notebooks. * Henden, conducting an archeological and biological reconnaissance of a little known region with a few Indians and Tom, comes upon the ruins of Tupec, a highly elaborate city that shows no relationship to general South American archeology. Further exploration uncovers mummies of white men, though of an unknown group. Still further exploration reveals an entrance to a very long tunnel, into which Henden, Tom and two Indians (soon killed) penetrate, following it to its exit into an enormous volcanic crater. * The explorers have entered a lost world, with gigantic ancient vegetation, enormous fungi, and various hypertrophied insects. Much of the novel is concerned with escapes from and obser-

vations of such insects, on the level of an entomological manual. * More important are gigantic humanoid ants, some upright in posture, who have some intelligence and practice agriculture. Most of these ants are not hostile and suffer the explorers to remain among them without too much discomfort. As Henden and Tom wander about, they are occasionally captured by various ant peoples, but they manage to escape. * The two men encounter gigantic aggressive red slaver-ants who raid the agricultural ants, and also a race of black submen. * Two problems beset Henden and Tom: eluding the red ants and escaping from the valley. Henden works out a solution to both. He manufactures gunpowder (used as grenades and mines) and organizes the black agriculturalist ants, the black submen, and various insects into an army against the reds. * There are two major battles, the first of which Henden loses, the second of which he wins. But he is mortally wounded, and sends Tom back through the tunnel to the outside world. * Disorganized and long-winded. Of no interest.

1547. **INTO THE GREEN PRISM**. *Amazing Stories*, March-April 1929. Ill. Paul.

Novelette. * *Place:* Ecuador. * The narrator, perhaps Verrill, and his friend Ramon Amador, are both concerned with Andean archeology, the narrator in the sense of fieldwork and small artifacts, Amador with the large scale architectural materials. Both are now in the Manabi area of Ecuador, where the pre-Columbian Indians had the art of working with tiny gold beads. Amador is convinced that there is some hidden factor beyond these extremes of size, the tiny beads and the gigantic architectural material. * Amador, in excavating, stumbles upon a peculiar greenish mineral glass, which, on first examination, presents peculiar optical properties. Amador is convinced that the glass formed a lens. Further search uncovers a deposit of the mineral, which is of meteoritic origin and presumably cannot be duplicated. * Working with the green glass, Amador discovers that it has strange properties. Shaped not in a usual lens formation, but in a prism, it can focus at several feet or more, and it magnifies to an incredible sense, even to showing atoms in motion. * By a further chance, the prism reveals that in this tininess there is a village of Manabi Indians, not much larger than atoms, maintaining a pre-Columbian culture. While watching them, Amador sees a beautiful priestess and falls deeply in love with her. He is convinced that they are soul mates. * Further work with the green prism shows that when combined with certain acoustics, it can either physically (not just visually) enlarge objects enormously, or reduce them proportionately to the microcosmic world. Amador determines to venture into this tiny world. Perhaps the venture succeeded; the narrator does not know, for all the green glass was destroyed during Amador's transit. * There is a loose tie-in with #1546, "The World of the Giant Ants." * Very little matter is extended into a fairly long story, but not without entertaining properties. * For a sequel see #1551, "Beyond the Green Prism."

1548. **THE BRIDGE OF LIGHT**. *Amazing Stories Quarterly*, Fall 1929. Ill. Wesso.

(Printed in book form by Fantasy Press, Reading, Pa., 1950.) Novel. * *Place:* Guatemala. * Lost-race novel. * The unnamed narrator, who seems to be an explorer or scientific collector of some sort, finds an early Maya document in an old book that he buys in Spain. Authorities agree that it is genuine, but it cannot be read. Scholars pass the narrator along until in Guatemala he

Verrill, A. Hyatt (*continued*)

meets an aged man who claims to be hundreds of years old; although he cannot read all the document, he can read enough to motivate the narrator to a quest. * The document, otherwise known as the Token of Kukulkan, is a prophecy and a map, in figurative form, to the lost city of Mictolan. The narrator sets out, and after encountering various perils mentioned in the document—a flood, a desert, a pterodactyl and a Tyrannosaurus rex, and a cave of bats—finally reaches his goal. Across a chasm he sees a beautiful young Indian woman who waves in welcome at him. When he does not approach, she indicates that what seems to be a beam of light is actually a solid way across the depths. This is the Bridge of Light. * The narrator, who has taken an extraordinary reciprocated fancy to the young woman, whose name is Itza, enters a conventional lost race situation. There is a most vicious, depraved high priest; a prince whose throne has been usurped; and a welcome for the narrator as a son of the god Kukulkan. * The first problem for the narrator is removing Itza from the ranks of the sacred virgins, so that he can enjoy her. This done, he must browbeat and tread down Kinchi Haman, the high priest, who would like to discredit him. The narrator's revolver is most useful in such circumstances. These two tasks he accomplishes without much difficulty, although his success is shaky. * The crisis comes when the high priest kidnaps Itza with the intention of sacrificing her to the sun god and throwing her body into the sacred cenote. He does not succeed, of course. After things are cleared away, the narrator and Itza leave Mictolan, and despite hardships, reach New York, where Itza is delighted at the skyscrapers. Some time later an air flight over Mictolan seems to indicate that the land has been flooded and that everyone there is dead. * Points along the way: The land is permeated with radioactivity, enough to provide some light. While the narrator believes this to be radium, scientific analysis of a sample that he brings to the United States reveals a new element. In Mictolan an incredibly ancient magician has built a small science (including a blast weapon) around this new element, and the Bridge of Light, which operates intermittently, is a manifestation of it. The ancient magician can also see the past and future associated with Mictolan. * After settling in Mictolan, the narrator sets up as a culture hero and teaches the natives about wheels, windmills, and iron metallurgy. During his function as high priest of the sect of Kukulkan, he tries to bring the religion into line with a nonsectarian Christianity. * There are secret passages enough to satisfy anyone, idols whose moveable arms open hidden doorways, and a prophecy that the narrator fulfills literally. * An old fashioned work, obviously in the mode of H. Rider Haggard. The perils are synthetic, if derived in part from the *Chilam Balam*, and the hero's adventures in Mictolan are on the yawn-provoking side and not as smoothly written as is usual with the author. * *Miscellaneous:* Verrill develops the concept that the Maya had solvents of some sort (in this case radioactive) that they used to soften stone they intended to work. Verrill seems to have taken this idea seriously in his nonfictional work.

1549. **DEATH FROM THE SKIES.** *Amazing Stories*, October 1929. Ill. Bob Dean.

Short story. * *Time:* Events of about 1932 told in retrospect from 1972. * The narrator, Dr. Merritt, an archeologist, happens to be in Chile when the first meteorites begin to strike. Indeed, one strikes nearby, and when scientific friends go to examine it, they

are later found dead. * In short, the Earth is being bombarded with large meteorites, which not only cause fires and impact devastation, but have the peculiar property of killing, in some mysterious fashion, those who approach them. * At first it is thought that the Earth has been passing through a meteorite swarm, but it is soon recognized that the major cities are under attack. To list those that have been destroyed would take a large segment of type. (New York City and London, however, escape.) * The man who discovers exactly what is happening and what should be done about it is the great physicist Paul Henderson, helped by the narrator (Merritt) and an amateur astronomer (Fothergill). * Henderson determines that the meteorites cause death with a new sort of radiation, which can be blocked, however, by suitable insulation. Further, that those "killed" by the radiation can in many cases be revived by suitable counterradiation. Further, that similar attacks probably have extinguished earlier civilizations, notably the Maya. Further, that the meteorites originate from Mars. And still further, that by telescopic observation and calculation it is possible to predict their general area of impact. * Finally, Henderson derives the ultimate recourse: If a certain potential in the meteorites is reversed, an antigravity effect results and the meteorites will fly back to Mars and crash. * Telescopic observations later show that the returning space shots have shattered Martian civilization and that the Martians may now be extinct. * As usual with Verrill, garrulous and discursive.

1550. **VAMPIRES OF THE DESERT.** *Amazing Stories*, December 1929. Ill. Wesso.

Short story. * *Place:* The desert seacoast of Peru. * Barry, the narrator, a petroleum geologist, as the only scientist in the area, is central to the mysterious deaths along the coasts of Peru and Chile. * A change in the warm ocean currents brings unexpected rain to the hitherto desolate, arid land, resulting in the sprouting of seeds long dormant. Barry observes in particular specimens of a very peculiar looking plant that resembles a Strophanthus, but has enormous buds promising a gorgeous flower several feet across. Circumstances, however, prevent him from witnessing the flowering at this time. * Shortly after this, during a dry period, the mysterious deaths begin: strangulation, skin perforations, together with bloodless corpses. At first only a few, they increase in number until they assume almost epidemic proportions. The medical consensus is disease, but causative agents are not found. The accounts of the very few survivors seem to indicate a physical attack involving misty objects. The attacks cease during the rainy period. * Barry, who has survived one such attack, solves the mystery. He chances to be present, at last, when his new flowers bloom. He sees the blossoms leave the plants and fly toward him, attacking him. Actually, what he first thought were plants are really adaptations of sea animals like jellyfish, the seeds of which happened to survive for more than millennia. * The "plants" have spread so rapidly and so widely that the situation is dangerous, but it is discovered that they cannot tolerate petroleum, which kills them. * A rather good story, less garrulous and better developed than is usual with the author. Verrill's best story here.

1551. **BEYOND THE GREEN PRISM.** *Amazing Stories*, January-February 1930. Ill. Morey.

Novelette. Sequel to #1547, "Into the Green Prism." * *Place:* Ecuador. * The narrator, who mourns his friend Amador, comes into possession of another piece of the green glassy mineral from

Verrill, A. Hyatt (*continued*)

a collection of archeological material. Invoking the aid of an Austrian physicist, he constructs another prism and hastens back to the location of his first adventure. * When he sets up his prism, not only does he find the tiny Manabis, but his friend Amador comes up into our size with a whoosh. * Amador explains: There is enough of the green glass in the tiny world that he was able to make another prism; he was just awaiting the return of the narrator. Amador has married the beautiful princess and is quite happy. Indeed, he urges the narrator to go back down with him, since the tiny world is an archeological treasure trove. * After some reluctance, the narrator agrees and is transferred down into the tiny world. It is an idyllic place where everyone is more or less happy; there is no disease, since germs could not tolerate the shrinkage, and, in any case, the translation of the Manabis took place before the white man's diseases were introduced. The narrator finds a congenial woman and marries her. * But he is worried about the fate of the tiny people, in case someone should build a fire atop them or some other accident should occur. With Amador's assistance, he transfers all the Manabis into our world to a secluded valley where they can live in isolation. (Although the point is implicit, Verrill ignores the certainty of new diseases wiping out the transferred population.) * *Miscellaneous:* Among the treasures of the Manabis is the mummified corpse of a white man, which they call Viracocha. This, plus the high priest's name of Malik, indicates an early Semitic migration, perhaps the Lost Tribes; such an increment accounts for the light skin of the people. * Since there are no germs or stresses, longevity for the hidden people is very great, two hundred years and more. * In ancient times the properties of the prisms were used to enlarge and diminish stones so that they could be easily transported and worked. * During the shrinking process, one's personal molecules and atoms also shrink suitably. * Windy, with little matter.

1552. THE DIRIGIBLES OF DEATH. *Amazing Stories Quarterly*, Winter 1930. Ill. Morey.

Short story. * *Place:* England, told by several narrators including a somewhat brash young American. * A strange black, metal dirigible lands in a British field. After this begins the first of many brutal murders, in which men, women, and children are clawed, ripped apart, and partially eaten. Many such dirigibles, which are invisible at night, land, disgorging gigantic blacks with hands ending in great claws, skin covered with yaws, and brain partly removed; all are incredibly vicious and aggressive, and all lack human intelligence. They are also riddled with leprosy, and several infectious diseases of great severity. * It has not proved possible to examine living specimens, since they fight so desperately that they are usually killed when caught, but the dirigibles that carry them are so advanced that their operation can hardly be understood, being remote controlled, but by some principle other than radio. * Potentially the situation is extremely dangerous, not so much for the physical attacks as for the possibility of epidemic disease. * A breakthrough comes with the work of Bob and Jimmy, two Americans who have been working on long-distance wireless transmission of pictures and night photography with apparatus that uses stepped up and stepped down radiation. To their surprise, their ray explodes the helium in the black dirigibles. * The British are delighted with this discovery, which enables them to shoot down the black ships before they land. A further question is the origin of the dirigibles. By a process of elimination, this is discovered to be the small African Congo nation of Andaya, which is being used as a cat's paw by an unnamed hostile nation, presumably the USSR. The British invade and occupy Andaya, and the crisis is over.

1553. THE FEATHERED DETECTIVE. *Amazing Stories*, April 1930. Ill. Morey.

Short story. * Really a detective story rather than science-fiction. * *Place:* somewhere in southern coastal England. * The milieu is an inn that is operated by a former seaman who may have a shady past. His murder is entwined in the (factual) properties of the touraco bird, a specimen of which he keeps as a pet. This bird, although it has green plumage, secretes a red water-soluble pigment. * Overlong, and a little too Stevensonian, but not a bad story.

1554. THE NON-GRAVITATIONAL VORTEX. *Amazing Stories*, June 1930. Ill. Morey.

Novelette. * Split personalities and mysterious disappearances. * The narrator becomes acquainted with Sir Esme McDonald, who leads a double life that is on the edge (and sometimes over) of being a dual personality. As Sir Esme he is a millionaire dilettante who follows the code of the British aristocracy; as Alexander Macdonald, who possesses a remarkable laboratory in London, he is, secretly, one of the world's top scientists. Associated with Sir Esme is his confidential servant Harvey, whom he rescued from shipwreck some years before. Harvey had no memory when rescued, and although obviously a man of culture and education, has proved untraceable. * The second theme of the book comes with Macdonald's investigations into a new force, a repulsion vortex, which occurs occasionally in nature and which, after long theorizing and experiment, he can produce. A limiting factor seems to be smoke or fog. * A Fortean note enters when Macdonald declares that this new force, called Esmeism is responsible for the mystery of the *Mary Celeste*, rains of frogs and fishes, and probably his servant Harvey's mental state. Macdonald speculates that certain areas of the Earth spontaneously and sporadically produce Esmeism. * Nothing will satisfy Macdonald except to sail in his splendid yacht to one of these characteristic areas. Yes, indeed, the force does operate. The yacht is jerked up into the sky, dropped, and wrecked, with most of its personnel killed, but the narrator, Harvey, and Sir Esme survive. Harvey has regained his identity of several years ago, with no memory whatever of more recent events, and Sir Esme has lost the Macdonald facet and remembers nothing of his researches. While there is some doubt as to what actually happened, another survivor actually saw the yacht being lifted into the air. * A further speculation, not resolved, is whether the phenomena are controlled by beings outside Earth, perhaps from an area in the upper atmosphere.

1555. A VISIT TO SUARI. *Amazing Stories*, July 1930. Ill. Briggs.

Short story. * Intended to be a satire on Earth ways, as seen by an outside intelligence. * The story is told from the point of view of Martians, either on Mars or on Earth. Their names, however, are redolent of the Andes. * The Martians have long observed Earth with telescopic apparatus of increasing power, and they have attempted space travel on several occasions, all unsuccessful. The great scientist Kespi-Nanay, however, has devised a matter transmitter that needs no receiving pole. Aligning his invention toward Earth, he disintegrates himself.

Verrill, A. Hyatt (*continued*)

He is considered as good as dead, but three years later he returns to Mars and describes what he has seen and experienced. * Finding himself on Earth, he first mistakes a herd of sheep for intelligent beings, then when he meets humans is baffled, then amazed by clothing. * Aspects of human life covered: agriculture (as opposed to artificial food production), flesh-eating, political structures and wars, lack of resistance to political hysteria, money, sexually differentiated clothing, lack of eugenics, lack of population control, egalitarian education, prohibition of alcoholic drinks, gambling, feelings of racial superiority among whites, etc. * Kespi-Nanay also indirectly reveals a few facts about Mars and its inhabitants. The canals are really small bodies of water that are driven around Mars by artificial satellites. The Martians are many-legged with horns and pendulous ears. There is strict population and breeding control. While Martian science on the whole is much ahead of Earth's, with atomic power, far-viewing and far-hearing devices, and artificial food, the Martians do not have radio, automobiles, trains, or flying machines. * A listing of cultural clichés presented in essay style, without much perception, and very boring.

1556. **MONSTERS OF THE RAY**. *Amazing Stories Quarterly*, Summer 1930. Ill. Paul.

Novelette. * *Place:* the Peruvian highlands. * The archeologist narrator, perhaps Verrill himself, tells of the fate of Frank Ogden Harris, perhaps the world's foremost inventor. * Harris, a very private individual, has been responsible for most of the world's great breakthroughs, but lives in isolation in a desert area of the Andes. He maintains, nevertheless, a situation of personal luxury, with a superradio that can pick up any station in the world and fantastically well equipped laboratories. * The narrator visits Harris and finds himself in an archeological wonderland, with much architecture, ceramics, and other material otherwise not known. * The local Indians, who serve Harris, are not ordinary Quechua-speakers, but descendants of an earlier group. They have a myth that one of their kings was killed in a conflict with monster giants. * An archeological find, a three-part vase of an unknown metal, sets Harris on a new track of investigation. He discovers that the vase was an implement that the Indians used for cutting rock; filled with the proper chemicals, it emitted a ray that sliced through the hardest stone as if it were water, although without effect on organic materials. * Improving on the Indian process, Harris creates a ray projector that he plans to use to sculpt the landscape, creating a "natural" bridge out of a basalt formation. * As he works, however, he, the narrator, and the Indians see a strange vision out of the past of a similar incident. Apparently fumes caused by the operation of the ray recapture fossil light. * Harris pursues this enthusiastically, working out that the images must be stored on Eros, which would have been in line with his projector. He retrieves remarkable scenes, including one of Eros, but on the crucial occasion, monsters from Eros materialize from the picture and run amok, eating everyone they can catch. * The situation looks bad, but the narrator discovers that the projector will destroy the monsters, even though while doing this he blows up Harris's establishment. Harris, meanwhile, has committed suicide rather than be eaten alive. * The Erosian monsters are somewhat amoeboid, with slimy trails and the ability to extrude tentacles and grasping organs. * What the narrator witnessed was in part at least a recapitulation of the ancient myth that the Indians remembered.

1557. **WHEN THE MOON RAN WILD**. *Amazing Stories Quarterly*, Winter 1931. Ill. Morey.

(Reprinted in book form by Consul, under the pseud. Ray Ainsbury.)

Short novel. * *Time:* 1931 to 2145. *Place:* the Peruvian Andes. * The narrator is an elderly American currently in Peru. * In 1931 the moon, for no reason that science could discover, left its orbit and careened madly toward the Earth, establishing a new orbit around eighty thousand miles away. At first it circled the earth in a few hours, but gradually traveled more slowly in a new stable orbit. * The damage caused by the lunar divagation was incalculable: Western Europe was wiped out, the United States ruined, and most of the coastal regions of the world put under water. Tidal waves reached thousands of feet high. * The narrator was one of the fortunate ones who were able to outrun the waves, escaping in his automobile. The few survivors, who included Americans and Indians, gradually pulled together a small civilization in the Andes. The climate has changed greatly, now being very hot and damp, with incredibly lush vegetation. * Time passes. * On one occasion the narrator, on a trip of exploration, comes upon a hitherto unknown valley, in which he espies from a distance a functioning Inca city. He approaches and is received in friendly fashion. The city is ruled by an Inca, who is descended from the original dynasty at the time of the Conquest. When the catastrophe took place and subsided, the local Indians, recognizing the Inca as a divine ruler, restored and reestablished the city, which is pretty much on a Conquest level. * Especially surprising is the fact that the Inca is over 150 years old, with other Indians similarly aged, though physiologically young. They have attained this longevity by eating the seeds of a certain tree. The narrator eats the seeds, and now, roughly two hundred years after the catastrophe, is still alive and hale. * The narrator's group moves in with the Indians of the lost city, forming a congenial group, all under the authority of the Inca, who is a charismatic person. * The new community thrives for decades (Verrill is very vague on matters of time), but faces several crises. One is the incursion of an enormous horde of savages who have multiplied since the Catastrophe and are conducting raids for women. The savages are beaten and pretty much killed off. Second, dinosaur life reappears. A carnivorous reptile, not identified, is destroyed by a mine, and large, slow-moving reptiles on the order of small brontosauri are domesticated as beasts of traction. Third, worst of all, strange, diaphanous, flying creatures much like jelly fish, hitherto unknown on Earth, appear in enormous hordes. Vampiric, they attack both men and beasts, eating holes in their flesh. The suspicion is that they came from the Moon. There is little that the settlers can do about them, for gunshots are ineffective. For a time the creatures are beaten off by flying an airplane through their hordes, slicing them up, but the remnants merely hatch new monsters and the airplane crashes. The end result is that there is no real defense against them. * South American mankind would be doomed but for a new development. Contact is made with Pitcairn Islanders, who have reactivated a large steamer stranded near their land. The Pitcairners report that a new continent has arisen in the South Pacific, and since enough time has elapsed, it is covered with vegetation and able to be colonized. All concerned migrate to the new land. * The initial situation is handled well enough, but the succession of unconvincing thrills destroys the story.

Verrill, A. Hyatt (*continued*)

1558. **THE EXTERMINATOR**. *Amazing Stories*, February 1931. Ill. Morey.
A short-short story, narrating the experiences of a white blood cell as it attacks various germs. At the end it dies when it is taken out of a bleeding wound and put upon a microscope slide. * Not really science-fiction.

1559. **THE TREASURE OF THE GOLDEN GOD**. *Amazing Stories*, January-February 1933. Ill. Morey.
Short novel. * *Place:* British Guiana or nearby. * Archeological material. * Thornton, an archeologist, and Belmont, an engineer, are following traces, among the Indians and blacks, of Manoa, the fabled home of El Dorado. In the first installment, they have various jungle adventures that are realistic enough. * In the second installment they come upon a deserted city, far more sophisticated than Inca or other South American work, in a good state of preservation. In a huge temple they find a gigantic idol of solid gold; moving its arm opens secret passages inside the building, up into the idol itself. Gold is also present in incredible quantity, some of it hardened by some sort of alloying process. * Along with the treasures the men find a young American aviatrix, who has crash-landed not too far away, and Indians (or a hitherto unknown race, lighter skinned than Indians) who are both in awe of the ruins and resentful of the presence of the whites. * After a siege, the whites escape via a secret passage, but are captured. The Indians do not harm them, but set them loose at a distance, apparently hoping that they will not be able to find their way back. * A romance is included. * Suggestive of Frances Stevens's "Sunfire." In general a rehash of material that Verrill used over and over in his boys' books.

1560. **THE DEATH DRUM**. *Amazing Stories*, May 1933. Ill. Morey.
Novelette. * *Place:* a frame situation in Peru, the main story in the jungles of Brazil, notably along the Xingu. * A dying man is rescued and brought to Peru by Verrill, to whom the man tells his story. It is essentially a jungle adventure story, with but a single fantastic element. * The anthropologist narrator, Dr. Richard Sterling, accompanied the Matson expedition into Brazil. The expedition was ill-fated, mostly because of the brutality and rapacity of Matson, who mistreated the Indians badly. As a result of his stupidity, most of the expedition was killed. * When the survivors reached the isolated, hitherto-unknown Xinguays (who differed from other Indians in being somewhat taller and long-bearded), they might have had a chance to survive, since the Indians were friendly and hospitable, but Matson again abused the Indians. To defend themselves the Indians used the death drum, the vibrations of which (as Sterling recounts) dissolved flesh and bone into mush. * Sterling, who was a distance away from the other explorers, survived, but has been mentally ill since. The Indians, seeing Sterling externally unharmed, considered him a magic person and treated him well. While staying with the Xinguays recuperating, he witnessed the use of the drum to destroy a horde of invaders. But an erupting volcano forced Sterling to leave the area. He regained civilization as a broken man, and he dies soon after telling Verrill his story. * The drum is not explained. * A meandering story, at times interesting for its geographical background (and ethnographic nonsense), but greatly overextended.

1561. **THROUGH THE ANDES**. *Amazing Stories*, September-November 1934. Ill. Morey.

Novel * Lost-race story. * *Place:* an unknown area on the eastern slope of the Andes, probably in Peru. * A small band adventurers sets out to find the unknown land of Achcakuna; they include the narrator (Verrill), a former Texas Ranger (Red Neil), an English hunter (Saunderson), a comic black (Sam), and a Burmese servant (Karen) of Saunderson's. Karen provides woodlore, an ability to climb inaccessible regions, and other specialized know-how. * The men make their way into the wilderness, being ambushed first by bandidos, then, while they are struggling through a desolate area, by strange little men with rugose skins who, chameleonlike, change the color of their skins according to surroundings. * Following a mysterious inscription (never fully explained), the men reach the lost land of Ach-karuna-sapi, where a pre-Inca culture, the origin of all the native civilizations, still thrives. The men are welcomed, and the story takes the path of typical lost-race stories. Red, because of the color of his hair, fulfills an ancient prophecy about a redhaired man. He is soon betrothed to the daughter of the high priest and acclaimed king of the land. The country is brimming, of course, with gems and gold. * The sole problem is the monster to whom human sacrifices are still made; it is a surviving dinosaur of some sort. Red kills it rather easily with his six shooters. * Red and Saunderson remain in the land with their women, while the narrator returns to the outside world with a host of archeological information, but unfortunately lies under a vow of silence about the best parts. * *Miscellaneous:* While exploring a tabu part of the enormous palaces, the explorers find very ancient mummified bodies, including one of an enthroned man who is an ancient Hebrew. Also present is documentation showing that the culture was first founded by Hebrews from the Near East. Since then it became Indian, with ancestral Indian languages still preserved. * The naturalist portions in the first segment are well handled, as is often the case with Verrill, but the story falls apart into cliché too soon after this, and the characterizations are cartoon-strip, with stage Englishman, timid black, tough Texan, etc.

1562. **THE INNER WORLD**. *Amazing Stories*, June-August 1935. Ill. Morey.
Novel. * *Place:* inside the hollow Earth. * A manuscript contained in a sphere of strange metal found floating in the ocean. The manuscript has been written by Dr. Henry Marshall Thurlow, with whom the frame narrator used to have frequent arguments about geomorphology. Thurlow, a great scientist, asserted that the Earth is hollow, having cooled differentially, with layers separating out. * According to the manuscript, Thurlow has reached the inner area, although Verrill does not explain how. He finds himself in very strange circumstances. The area is lighted, not from a common light source, but by a spontaneous glow that is emitted by everything, including Thurlow himself. As a result of this, his depth perception is long aberrant. Around him is a most peculiar ambience, distorted, weird vegetation (which the reader may recognize as suggested by marine life) and strange animals. He soon meets an intelligent being of weirdest appearance: eight tentacular legs, each with a specialized function; an ant-like segmented chitinous body; a head with many-faceted eyes; short arms attached to bat-like wings. Extending out of the creature's head is a long appendage ending in what seems to be a biological cool light. This being (we later learn) is called a Tss'zor (or Tss-zor). * After some mutual examination, the creature takes Thurlow in its tentacles and flies away to its city. * As Thurlow gradually

Verrill, A. Hyatt (*continued*)

discovers, intelligent life inside the Earth is not single as with us. In addition to the Tss'zor there are upright beetle-like beings (the Iss-dors), who are more intelligent than the Tss'zors; other less important peoples; and finally, the Cheek-horkuls, or giant brains, who run and rule the culture. In general the culture could be called unbalanced barbaric, with sporadic very sophisticated elements. * All the various intelligent types, who live together in reasonable harmony, are sexless. New individuals are manufactured in laboratories from a single genetic stock, altered suitably by the great brains. * Against the associated cultures are ferocious wild creatures much like giant vampire bats. These intermittently attack the associated cultures, killing and eating what they can capture. * As for the narrative: Thurlow is brought to judgment before the great brains, who apparently disapprove of him, since they sentence him to be thrown into a pit with a captive wild bat. When he kills the bat with his revolver, the inner people regard him with some approval, which is increased when he plays a decisive part in repelling a raid of the bat animals. While the inner peoples know metal, which they prepare electrolytically, since they have no means for smelting, they have no weapons. Thurlow creates javelins and bows and arrows, with which the associated cultures almost wipe out the bats. * By now Thurlow's stock is so high that some of the Tss'zors and Iss-dors request him to rule the land. They pay no heed to his claim that he is not qualified, but destroy the great brains and install him. * Thurlow does the best that he can, but he is unable to process the germ stock and create the various specialized forms of life. His efforts produce either sexed beetles or wild bats. There is great dissatisfaction and grumbling among his subjects, and as Thurlow closes his manuscript, he predicts that he will soon be killed. * *Miscellaneous:* The inner peoples make use of a generalized electromagnetic force, which their manipulation sends out to the world in the form of magnetism. Thus, the city lies almost beneath the magnetic north pole. * The inner world beings also maintain an enormous, very sophisticated system of gigantic machinery, which operates by pressure, wheels being unknown. Verrill does not explain it. * Mostly exposition, and while the detail shows some ingenuity, the story is mostly a bore.

VINCENT, HARL

(Pseud. of Harold Vincent Schoepflin (1893-1968). Born in Buffalo, New York. Mechanical engineer working for Westinghouse, specializing in the design and testing of heavy electrical equipment. Later sales engineer. Resident for at least part of this time in Ridgewood, New Jersey. Vincent was one of the most prolific genre writers for the pre-Campbell period; his production dwindled in the late 1930s, and for all practical purposes he ceased writing around 1940. It is not known whether this was a result of personal activities in the war years, or of changes in editorial requirements. In the late 1960s, however, he returned briefly to writing with *The Doomsday Planet*, 1968. * Vincent was an uneven writer, whose work, though always demonstrating intelligence, often showed marks of haste. It would seem obvious that he often wrote down for the market. A brief biographical statement "Harl Vincent" is to be found in *Science Fiction Digest* (October 1933).

1563. **THE GOLDEN GIRL OF MUNAN**. *Amazing Stories*, June 1928. Ill. R. E. Lawlor.

Short story. * *Time:* A.D. 2406. *Place:* New York City, and an uncharted Pacific Island. * *Background:* In 1950, when the Powers formed the Terrestrial Government, two thousand "reactionaries" and "radicals" were seized, placed on the *Gigantean*, one of the last surface vessels, and told to betake themselves off, never to return, on pain of disintegration. (The deportation obviously echoes the American deportation of Communists and radicals in the early 1920s.) * The deportees landed on an uncharted Pacific Island (Munan), where one of their number devised a force screen that shut off the outside world. Since there was practically no more land or sea travel (only air-lanes), the outside world gradually forgot the existence of the exiles. * In succeeding years the population of Munan has multiplied greatly. The cultural norm is a violent desire for revenge for the wrong done their ancestors, and now, armed with superweapons, they are prepared to emerge and conquer the world. * The narrative: Roy Hamilton receives an unexpected call on his video phone: There is a misty image, and a golden female voice gives him the above information about Munan, begging him to consult his friend the great Professor Nilsson so that the impending invasion can be prevented. The speaker is a dissident pacifist on the island. * The woman urges Hamilton and Nilsson to come to Munan. Her associates will temporarily disrupt the force screens so that the two outsiders can land. * Nilsson accepts the offer. Indeed, he has a good, secret means of reaching Munan. This is the *Pioneer*, an air vessel that does not use the general power broadcast, but picks up power directly from the atmosphere. It also involves the principle of the Flettner boat. * The *Pioneer* arrives safely in Munan, where Hamilton immediately falls in love with Thelda, the Golden Girl. The other revolutionaries, who are equally simpatichi, describe the invasion plans: The forces of Munan number ten thousand airships that can be rendered invisible and carry an irresistible disintegrating liquid. The liquid can be stored only in the metal crysinum, which is found nowhere else but in Munan. * The Munan battle plan involves destroying all the great cities of the outside world, or about three-quarters of the world's population. * Thelda's underground, using seduction and other techniques, obtains a small portion of the disintegrating liquid for Nilsson, with which he experiments. Then, at the last minute, before the authorities of Munan can seize them, Thelda's group and the outsiders pile into the *Pioneer*. Nilsson directs a new ray at the Munan arsenal; this ray removes the protective nature of crysinum, and Munan is destroyed in a total melt down. "The Outside is saved!" * *Miscellaneous:* Munan seems to be organized on a military basis. * Some of the Munanese have limited telepathic powers. * The professor has a little disintegrator gun of his own. * Ersatz Ray Cummings, and a bad job. Vincent improved over the years. For a sequel see #1565, "The War of the Planets."

1564. **THE AMBASSADOR FROM MARS**. *Amazing Stories*, September 1928. Ill. Paul.

Short story. * *Time:* 1940 on. *Place:* New York and Mars. * Frank Chandler, a competent architect who is depressed with life, lights a cigarette on a park bench. There is an explosion, and he awakens on a spaceship millions of miles from Earth, heading toward Mars. * The Martians, however, are by no means ill-willed, but are an extremely benevolent, handsome human people, of obvious high intelligence. They have taken Frank in this fashion at the request of Jack Conway, a friend of Frank's,

Vincent, Harl (*continued*)
who has been living on Mars for years. * The Martian purpose: Their planet is dying, and the dwindling human population is beset by a monstrous bestial people, the Breggia, who will soon exterminate the humans if things continue. * Frank, whose mind will be impressed with the design of a communications machine that will reach Mars, will be returned to Earth to serve as an ambassador of good will, for the Martians wish to emigrate to Earth. * On Mars, Frank is greatly impressed with the high science and high humanity of the Martians. His friend Jack, indeed, is engaged to a Martian woman. But the immediate problem is the Breggia, who are waging war on ever increasing scale. * *Background:* Thousands of years ago, some humans were trapped underground during a volcanic episode. They devolved, becoming long reptilian beings with human heads. They are indestructible by any means known to the Martians; explosives, chemicals, germs are all to no avail. Like the Morlocks, the Breggia are photophobic, but their numbers are so great and their invulnerability so secure that they may exterminate the humans before Frank can accomplish anything. * While secretlt exploring the Breggia caverns, Frank overhears a conversation that reveals the one Breggia weakness: their susceptibility to the toxic effects of a very common plant. With this information, the humans defeat the Breggia on their next raid, thus gaining time. * Frank, who is sent back to Earth, spends two years building the communications machine. Just as it begins to function, Mars, wracked by volcanic convulsions, splits into fragments. All the Martians are dead. * It all seems like a waste of time.

1565. THE WAR OF THE PLANETS. *Amazing Stories*, January 1929. Unsigned ill.
Short story, sequel to #1563, "The Golden Girl of Munan." * *Time:* 2426. * It is now twenty years later. An astronomical observation causes some concern: About 108,000 miles away in space is a fleet of spherical vessels, heading toward Earth. * Professor Nilsson, discussing the matter with the Hamiltons, states that the probabilities favor trouble from Venus. He is soon proved right, for a radio message from the spheres declares war on the Terrestrial Government in the name of Venus. The message ends with the threat, "Munan shall be avenged," signed Mador. * Thelda offers an explanation. Mador, one of the greatest Munan scientists, had been working on a spaceship. Presumably aloft when the island exploded, he flew to Venus, where, gathering allies, he constructed the fleet now threatening Earth. * Weapons against the invaders must be found rapidly, for the fleet is only hours away. Professor Nilsson unwraps the old *Pioneer*, which he has rendered invisible with the Munan formula, and he and the Hamiltons proceed out into space, where they hover over the last Venusian globe. Nilsson drops to the observation deck of the globe, enters, seizes the commanding officer, and hijacks the vessel, which he takes to Washington. Scientists examine the globe, but there is much that is too advanced for them to understand. * The globes reach Earth and attack various communities in North America. Cincinnati is destroyed, and New York and Washington seem next. * Nilsson, however, discovers a means to destroy the globes fairly easily. He observes that they are constructed of a plastic like bakelite, and like bakelite they can be combusted with a suitable electric current. The Venusians are defeated, though much damage has been done on Earth. * The captive Venusian commander reveals

that not only does Venus plan further invasions, but that Mars, too, is planning to wage war on the Earth. The Terrestrial Government, recognizing future danger, appoints Nilsson defense chief. * *Miscellaneous:* The captive Venusian is tall, muscular, and blond, perfectly human. As Professor Nilsson says, while invoking religion, worlds will tend to produce the human type.

1566. THE SEVENTH GENERATION. *Amazing Stories Quarterly*, Winter 1929. Ill. Paul.
Short story. * *Time:* 1932 and 2132. *Place:* Saratoga, Florida, and Mexico. * Robert Wright, engineer, just returned from years of work in Afghanistan, is unable to find traces of his former love, Eileen. He receives an unexpected visitor, the maverick scientist Professor Claude Graham. Graham explains his visit: He has invented a matter transmitter that will successfully transport living objects and a ray that permits moving objects through time. The two rays combined permit time travel, which he has already experienced. Graham needs a qualified observer, and Wright is known through mutual friends. * The professor is not exaggerating, and Wright and Graham's assistant George Lesch decide to visit Saratoga, Florida, 2132. They leave, but unfortunately, land in the ocean and have to swim to shore, to an enormous fairy-tale-like city, which signs inform them is Sanscare, the pleasure capital. * They are admitted to the city, but are immediately imprisoned by the city boss (Travis), who suspects them of evil intentions. * Wright, however, meets Travis's beautiful daughter Eileen, who is the image of Wright's lost love Eileen. It turns out that Eileen is a lineal descendant of the original Eileen, who married while Wright was in Afghanistan. * Lesch escapes, but it looks as if Wright is doomed. Eileen, however, is as smitten with Wright as he with her, and she agrees to help him escape. As she frankly admits, her father is becoming paranoid. * After assorted perils, the two time travelers and Eileen are in Mexico, where they hope to obtain help from a scientist who has been working on the same lines as Graham had been two hundred years earlier. Eileen will accompany Wright back to the twentieth century. * But then Wright awakens in bed back in New York. It was all a dream. When a friend visits, Wright learns that he has not lost the original Eileen. She has been looking for him, but could not find him while he was in Afghanistan. * Surprising to find the dream rationalization at such a late date.

1567. THE MENACE FROM BELOW. *Science Wonder Stories*, July 1929. Ill. Paul.
Short story. * *Time:* 1935. *Place:* the New York area and caverns underground through most of the eastern United States. * An extraordinary collection of motifs thrown together. The plotting is so complex that it is best indicated by story threads. * First strand: New York City subway trains to Brooklyn, laden with passengers, inexplicably disappear from the tunnels. There are no side branches, nothing perceptibly wrong with the roadways. The prominent consulting engineer Ward Platt is commissioned to solve the mystery. * Second strand: Television inventor Tony Russell, away from the city for a rest, witnesses the murder of tycoon Van Alstyne and becomes acquainted with the charming Miss Van Alstyne, the murdered man's daughter. The unusual element is that the corpse of old Van Alstyne disappears before his eyes. * Russell, who is a college chum of Platt's partner, Charlie, installs television cameras in subway trains going to Brooklyn, and with Charlie rides one of the trains. In this case, the camera shows a man with a peculiar

Vincent, Harl (*continued*)

apparatus in front of the train, which thereupon is lowered into an empty space where the track should be. The guards and Tony all seem paralyzed. * Tony's experiences begin: He is carried away into a large, lighted cavern, where he meets his captor, who happens to be an old college chum, Jeremiah Talbot. Talbot, it is remembered, had to leave the country to avoid prosecution for assisting mad scientist Ainsworth in experiments like Dr. Moreau's. * Talbot explains: He and Ainsworth, while hiding out in Labrador, came upon the entrance to an enormous chain of caves far beneath the eastern half of the United States. Most of the caves are lighted by phosphorescence and support a considerable population of *Pithecanthropierecti*. Ainsworth has been working on them, improving them physically and mentally. When they reach a high degree of physical development, he plans to transplant brain sections from the more superior Brooklyn passengers he has captured and thus establish a superrace, with which he will conquer the world—and improve it. About five hundred such operations have already taken place. * Talbot takes his captives, who include Miss Van Alstyne, who happened to be riding a train, on a flying machine that glides along underground at 1,000 MPH to a headquarters in the Southwest. The tunnel connecting this establishment, which is elaborate and beautiful, with marvelous underground scenery, was bored very rapidly with disintegrator rays. Other projects, including the theft of the trains, were undertaken via the geometric fourth dimension, which Talbot and Ainsworth understand thoroughly. Indeed, the two scientists can transfer people to the fourth dimension as a disciplinary measure. * Talbot is friendly and reasonably solicitous of the welfare of his involuntary guests, though obsessed with ideas of wealth and world conquest, but old Ainsworth is a homicidal maniac, a mad dog of the worst sort, who delights in slaughter. Thus, when Platt's crew crashes through the subway section where the disappearances take place, into a cavern (though not the network known as Subterrania, which is miles below), Ainsworth kills most of them. * What to do? * Moreau catches up with Ainsworth. The transferred personalities, obviously undergoing horrible mental turmoil, revolt and kill Ainsworth. Talbot, mortally wounded, repents and gives his captives the means to leave Subterrania. The air car and a small plane will take them to the Southwestern exit, and Subterrania will be sealed off by explosives. * A surfeit of riches? * For a sequel see #1578, "The Return to Subterrania."

1568. **VENUS LIBERATED.** *Amazing Stories Quarterly,* Summer 1929. Ill. Hugh Mackay.
Novel. * *Time:* about 1945. *Place:* New York and Venus. * Sequences of events merge. First, Ralph Prescott, heir to a department store chain, bursts into Dr. De Polac's office and demands treatment. He suffers from horrible dreams in which he struggles through monstrosities toward a gigantic, beautiful woman. The dreams are progressive and are driving him toward a breakdown. * Second, Dr. De Polac, a psychiatrist of renown, has just perfected an apparatus that picks up dreams and projects their content on a screen. This apparatus reveals that Prescott is not mad, but is the subject of a telepathic summons from Queen Thalia of Venus. She begs for help, hoping that terrestrial science, which has evolved on different lines from Venusian, may help her repel horrible, irresistible interplanetary invaders who are devouring her people. * Third, Teddy Crowley, working

for Sorenson Aircraft, has developed antigravity. He and his friend the great astronomer Professor Timken have been discussing a voyage to Venus in a spaceship (the *Comet*) that they are building. * All parties, including two women who inveigle their way on board, come together, and after a time the *Comet* leaves, reaching Venus in a matter of hours. * Venus, which is mostly water-covered, is much like Earth. In a short time the terrestrials encounter Venusians, who are blond humans about seven feet tall. * Queen Thalia fills them in telepathically. The Venusians, who are essentially a peaceful people, are periodically raided by monstrous slug-octopus-like creatures who either eat their captives on the spot or carry them off in spaceships, presumably as provisions or as slaves. The invaders, called Kellonians, have a purple paralyzing gas and a presumably radioactive substance that spreads and destroys all it touches. The Kellonians severely punish any resistance. Millions of Venusian humans have been killed, and large areas laid waste. * The *Comet*, however, is more than a match for the torpedolike Kellonian vessels, what with the *Comet*'s superexplosives and an energy ray, the Kellonians are driven off Venus. * It is now necessary to find their home planet, which is located by celestial mechanics. It is a small, dark world, invisible because of its blackness, not too far from Venus. The Kellonians and their slaves live underground in huge caverns with atmospheric seals. * The Earthmen attack the Kellonian home world, and after some difficulties and casualties, blow up the planet with the superexplosive. The menace is ended. * *Miscellaneous:* There are also romances between the women (including Queen Thalia) and the male explorers. * The Venusians have mechanical thought recorders and broadcasters. Perfect air conditioning has resulted in exceptional health among the Venusians. * On Venus, iron, lead, and copper are very rare metals, whence the Venusian lack of defenses against the invaders. * Much of Venusian science and technology has been deliberately copied from Earth, via observation with supertelescopes. * For a sequel see #1597, "Faster Than Light."

1569. **BARTON'S ISLAND.** *Amazing Stories,* August 1929. Ill. Hugh Mackay.
(Reprinted in *Amazing Stories Quarterly,* Winter 1933.)
Short story. * *Time:* A.D. 2229. *Place:* mostly New York (which stretches fifty miles in all directions and has a population of sixty million), and a new volcanic island off the west coast of Africa. * The world of 2229 is much like that of H. G. Wells's predictions. After a series of wars, United North America (really the United States empire) rules the world, either politically or economically through foreign loans. Although there is a pretense of democracy, with an elected president, the country and the world are really run by Jerome Carter, the supreme capitalist, and his associates. * Socially, United North America no longer has a middle class; after various economic maneuvers, the upper class (the Purples) seized almost everything, while the lower class (the Grays) became more and more downtrodden, with severe restrictions on their education and advancement. The Red police hold the populace down, but the country and the world are ripe for a revolution. * As the story begins, Carter has ordered President Haven to exile the great scientist Philip Barton, who is the president's son-in-law. Philip Barton, Carter rightly believes, is too friendly with the leaders of a workers' underground movement. The president has no choice but to comply. * Barton, however, is too clever to accept a banishment, which he

Vincent, Harl (*continued*)

recognizes might mean assassination. He has prepared for this emergency by constructing a super air yacht, the *Inquisitor*, which has all sorts of secret abilities and compartments. * Barton, his wife, and the carefully concealed leadership of the Grays leave, ostensibly to exile in the Antarctic, but Barton fakes the destruction of his vessel and eludes the police viewing screens by sailing under water as a submarine to a new volcanic island off Africa. There he sets up apparatus and reveals new equipment: far-viewing equipment, far-speaking equipment, long distance projections, etc. * Barton also has constructed a hypnotic globe with which he can control his enemies, even at a distance. He uses the globe to abort Carter's plans for poisoning several million people and also to stave off a premature rebellion by the Grays. Meanwhile, Barton is working on his greatest invention. * When located by the Secret Service, Barton is prepared. He first hypnotizes the agents with his globe, then, using rays, performs psychic brain surgery on them, canceling their evil potential and developing their good. * With this armament at the service of the Grays, there is no more need for a bloody revolution. Carter, put under the rays, emerges as a new man and will lead the reformation of the unjust society. * *Miscellaneous:* Barton developed useable antigravity several years ago. His air yacht also uses reaction motors that emit streams of electrons.

1570. **THE YELLOW AIR-PERIL**. *Air Wonder Stories*, September 1929. Ill. Paul.

Short story. * *Time:* 1946. *Place:* over the Atlantic and on an unknown island near the north pole. * Roger Erskine, young executive of New York-Paris Airways takes a vacation on the *Albatross*, one of the company's superdirigibles. Also on board the three-decked monster, which carries some seven hundred passengers, are Professor Ingalls and his daughter Irene. Since Ingalls has contributed greatly to aeronautics, it is natural that Erskine should make his acquaintance. * Ingalls is a hunted man. As he reveals, he is being followed by members of a gigantic conspiracy, the Gautamans, who are mostly Oriental and are striving for world conquest. As the professor states, they use the external trappings of Buddhism, whence their name. They want to capture Ingalls and extract from him the knowledge of his two recent discoveries, atomic energy and the transmutation of metals. * The Gautamans strike, first rendering the Ingallses and Erskine unconscious and stealing the professor's documents, then capturing the three. A small plane lands atop the dirigible and spirits them away at enormous speed, to the organization's headquarters on an island near the north pole. There, New Kurja is a supercity inside a hollow mountain. * The head of the organization, Chandra Dai, welcomes them and explains their roles. Ingalls will reveal the secret of atomic energy; Erskine will start organizing the Gautaman air force in preparation for the new energy source; and Miss Ingalls, if her father does not cooperate, will suffer be forced to become the mistress of a caddish acquaintance of Erskine's. Chandra Dai, too, has a wandering eye. Professor Ingalls yields, and it looks bad. * A resolution comes during an experimental flight in which Erskine, Irene and a somewhat disgruntled Gautaman take part. As they watch headquarters in their television, they see that Professor Ingalls has indeed split an atom, but that he is sacrificing himself to turn it loose, disintegrating the Gautaman base. In the resulting confusion on board the plane, Erskine and Irene win

out, even to knocking out fighter planes that were escorting them. * *Miscellaneous:* To achieve atomic power the professor uses cosmic rays, complex prisms and reflectors, and magnetic fields. * Dirigibles of the day use a jet principle by forcing air through the long axis of the ship. * Routine. * There was some complaint by readers at Vincent's use of Buddhism as a vehicle for world terrorism. Vincent later explained and apologized.

1571. **THROUGH THE AIR TUNNEL**. *Air Wonder Stories*, October 1929. Ill. Paul.

Short story. * *Time:* 1958. *Place:* New York and the West Coast. * Much of the nation's transportation is conducted through air tunnels, that is to say, etherized tubes in the atmosphere that provide light, electricity, and energy to activate the antigravity mechanisms and power the propellers. A coast-to-coast trip takes about six hours. * *Romance:* Brilliant young inventor Jimmy Streeter would like to marry Doris Townsend, but her father is trying to force her to marry Hoyt, director of Air Tunnels, Inc. The reason: Townsend owes Hoyt five million dollars. Doris agrees to the marriage, but stipulates a month's delay. * Sterling obtains funds to construct a new type of air tunnel, one that is a vacuum in which cars will be propelled by S energy. * Just as it is finished, there is an emergency. Doris, on the West Coast, has a streptococcic infection, and unless a certain physician with a certain serum reaches her in less than three hours, she will die. All concerned pile into Sterling's special car and make it to California in less than one hour. Doris recovers. As for Hoyt, he behaved so caddishly all along that old Townsend sends him packing. The chairman of Air Tunnels, Inc., relieves Townsend by lending him the five million owed to Hoyt. And so Doris's fair body did not serve to pay off the mortgage. * Slop.

1572. **MICROCOSMIC BUCCANEERS**. *Amazing Stories*, November 1929. Ill. Morey.

Short story. * *Time:* the thirty-third century, but there are some time difficulties. * Civilization is high; gravity was overcome a thousand years earlier, and interplanetary flights are now commonplace. There seems to be a world government. * Minott V8CA, the great scientist who is director of physical research of the Eighth Terrestrial District, explains his researches to his young friend Grayson R36B. He has developed an ultramicroscope that shows subatomic worlds, including one with human inhabitants. Minott now has plans of visiting this world. * After several false starts, Minott settles on the fourth dimension as a means of translating himself and Grayson down to the atomic world. Actually, the technique of rotating small objects into a hyperdimension has been known for a time. * Minott sets a time-recall mechanism, and he and Grayson are dumped down onto the electron world, but not exactly where they planned. * In a trice the two men are captured by humanoids with goggle-eyes, no ears, and a certain ability at telepathy and will-control. * *Background:* The little atomic pocket universe which the men have entered is inhabited by several different peoples, human and humanoid. One group, the Prags, who captured the explorers, are piratical overlords of the other worlds, raiding for slaves and materials. The Prags have a superscience, perhaps not much ahead of that of the macrocosm, but different. Another group, the totally human Elsians, have been enslaved by the Prags. * The Great Ones, giant brains who rule the Prags, are quite interested in the knowledge of the macrocosm that they have extracted telepathically from Minott's mind, and plan an in-

Vincent, Harl (*continued*)

vasion. Minott is forced to serve as a consultant and is treated honorably, so far as the Prags can do this. Grayson is put into the slave quarters as a laborer. * While Minott is working with the Prags, Grayson becomes aware of an (Elsian) slave underground that plans insurrection and destruction of the Prag power. The chief weapon is an ultrasonic projector that will kill Prags. Grayson also acquires an Elsian sweetheart named Lola. * The excitement begins. The Prags are experimenting with sending ships to the macrocosm, but since their fourth-dimensional projector is askew, are not successful. The Prags conduct a slave raid on the Elsians, and Lola is killed (only temporarily; she turns up alive later; it was a misunderstanding). The underground rises and with its supersonic weapons defeats the Prags. And Grayson has the pleasure of killing the Great Ones, at the end even defying their will control. * As Minott, Grayson, and Lola are at the ruins of the Elsian village and the Prag ship, there is a wrench, and all three are translated up to our world. All the events in the microcosm took only two minutes of our time. * There is still a matter of time relativity that Minott must work out. * *Miscellaneous:* All the microcosmic people, what with their telepathy, can speak perfect English in a matter of hours. * The Prags have pistols that shoot a decomposition ray.

1573. **THE COLLOIDAL NEMESIS.** *Amazing Stories*, December 1929. Ill. Morey.

Short story. * *Time:* 1953. * The world war has been raging for eight years, with roughly one quarter of the human race dead. The opponents are the Asians (which term seems to include Russia, China, and perhaps other areas) and the Western Alliance (the Americas and Europe). The United States has been invaded and is about to be defeated. * A young man named Larkin approaches the war council and offers a new weapon, which he will demonstrate in his laboratory. It consists of a colloid that assumes life when infused with a certain ray. When the ray is removed, the colloid slumps back into water. While it is active, it is omnivorous and indestructible. * Alliance planes fly over Asian armies, turning the ground water and rivers into irresistible monsters. In a short time the war is over. * As a reward for saving at least the Western nations, and perhaps the world, Larkin is assigned to a minor job in the government.

1574. **EXPLORERS OF CALLISTO.** *Amazing Stories*, February 1930. Ill. Morey.

Short story. * *Time:* 1967. *Place:* significant action on the Moon. * Radio signals have been intercepted from the Moon; but this poses a problem, for the superlative viewing apparatus of the day reveal the Moon to be utterly uninhabited. The great young scientist Parsons proposes an explanation: The signals are coming from the dark side of the Moon. And Parsons intends to go there. Since he has already invented artificial gravity, inertia control, superexplosives, and various rays, it is a simple matter for him to build a small spaceship (the *Meteor*). * Parsons and two comrades travel through space at 120,000 MPH, propelled by rockets, and move around the Moon to the dark side, where they see buildings and hostile bipeds who attack them as they land. But Parsons's weapons (which include a paralysis ray and a heat ray) are superior to those of their opponents, and the Terrestrials are in no great danger. * A turning point comes when the Earthmen rescue a small running figure from two of the invaders. Back in the *Meteor* the rescued person is revealed to be Lola, a beautiful young woman of great artistic ability and

intelligence. With a series of drawings she informs the Earthmen that she is a deposed princess from Callisto. As her facile pencil reveals: On Callisto there are two nations, the warlike blond Anurdi and the peaceful brunet Dassans. The Anurdi have conquered the Dassans and now plan to invade Earth. * There are more clashes with the Callistans, including a narrow escape from a gigantic spaceship that clutches them with magnetic force, and a space battle. But the *Meteor* wins through, and the comrades return to Earth to warn the nations of the impending interplanetary invasion. * *Miscellaneous:* The most dangerous of the Callistan weapons is a yellow ray that creates heat and temporarily inhibits electrical function. The *Meteor* has no defense against it. * For a sequel see #1577, "Callisto at War."

1575. **OLD CROMPTON'S SECRET.** *Astounding Stories*, February 1930. Unsigned ill.

Short story. * *Place:* rural America, not located. * Young Tom Forsythe and octogenarian Crompton, neighbors on bad terms, have a common pursuit that brings them into some acquaintance: the quest for the secret of life. Old Crompton has pursued it unsuccessfully in terms of traditional occult means, but Forsythe employs the most modern science, and beyond. Forsythe is successful; he has found the life force to be a form of electricity that stimulates a certain gland. With his apparatus he can create giant and miniature animal forms, regenerate limbs, restore youth, and even, to some extent, awaken the dead. * Crompton first learns details when he rescues Forsythe from the attacks of a three-foot-tall vicious rooster. When he begs Forsythe to rejuvenate him, Forsythe refuses scornfully, saying that his discovery is for millionaires, not local charity. The two men struggle, Tom is injured about the head, and falls, apparently dead. Crompton puts himself through the process and emerges a young, personable man, probably better than he had been previously. He leaves the area. * Twelve years later, however, a prosperous middle-aged man approaches the local law officer, identifies himself as Crompton, and gives himself up for killing Forsythe. His conscience has been bothering him. But Forsythe is not dead; he was only stunned, but he has never been able to reconstruct his apparatus, which Crompton had smashed. Crompton then ages suddenly, and becomes a centenarian. * The ending is thus moral enough for the most sensitive reader. The story starts with acceptable local color, but soon fizzles away.

1576. **BEFORE THE ASTEROIDS.** *Science Wonder Stories*, March 1930. Ill. Paul.

Novelette. * *Time:* Frame material in the 1970s, but main action about a half million years ago. *Place:* Mars and the fifth Bodean planet. * In 1971 the space expedition of Moody and Bedworth leaves Earth, and in 1974 the men return with much information about Mars, where they explored. Among the artifacts which they brought back with them are thought tapes telling the story of the lost fifth planet. This forms the body of the story. * About five hundred thousand years ago, the fifth planet, Voris, exists between Mars and Jupiter. It is inhabited by a human race identical to that of Mars, and of about the same degree of scientific advancement. There is, however, one difference between the two peoples: the Martians, under a benevolent emperor, are peace-loving, while the Vorisians, under a vicious dictator, are warlike. * A cause for war in the minds of the Vorisians is the fact that in recent years Mars has outstripped Voris culturally. The dictator of Voris is now prepared to attack and is only looking for an excuse. * Such an excuse comes when

Vincent, Harl (*continued*)

Prince Ronal of Mars visits Voris incognito, an action that violates treaty, but actually has tacitly been ignored when it happened in the past. Olar, the drunken, brutal dictator, attempts to arrest Ronal, but with the help of Olar's daughter Ila, who is half-Martian, Ronal escapes. With Ila and others, he returns to Mars as the Vorisian attack begins. * Some parts of Mars are protected by a force screen, but on the whole the war goes very badly for the Martians. Defeat seems almost certain, until the great scientist Andites devises a new weapon, a projector that causes atomic disintegration and atomic fire at a distance. With it, in a matter of minutes the planet Voris explodes into fragments. * The shock of the explosion changes the motion of the solar system slightly, so that a nebula that absorbs carbon dioxide from the atmosphere, causing a terrible ice age, will eventually pass over Mars. When this happens, human life on Mars will be extinguished—as has happened. * *Miscellaneous:* Both nations use disintegrator rays, radium fuel, rockets, space travel along vibratory beams, and similar devices. The Vorisians also have a poison gas that puts its victims into suspended animation; if they do not receive an antidote in time, they die. * Routine work, with stuffier writing than is usual with Vincent.

   1577. **CALLISTO AT WAR.** *Amazing Stories*, March 1930. Ill. Morey.

Short story. * Sequel to #1574, "Explorers of Callisto." * *Time:* the late 1960's. *Place:* the Moon, space, Callisto. * The *Meteor* returns from the Moon, and Parsons and his two companions inform the President of the United States of their discoveries. Lola, the Callistan maiden, with the help of telepaths and linguists, learns to speak English, and with her assistance the mysterious messages from the Moon are deciphered. The war plans of the Callistans are now known, and the Earth, which is pretty much disarmed, must be prepared for an immediate invasion. * Parsons, who recognizes that his weapons were not really good enough, works feverishly to invent something more potent. His result, at the last minute, is a device that can project increased gravity. * The invasion comes. The few armored planes equipped with Parsons's heat ray would have fared badly, had it not been for the *Meteor*, but the increased gravity ray works splendidly. A great Terrestrial victory is followed by an attack on the Callistan lunar base, which the *Meteor* destroys. * But the war is not over. The Terrestrial fleet flies—increased power tubes now permit speeds of 120,000 MPH—to Callisto, destroys the Callistan fleet, bombards the capital of the Anurdi, and frees Lola's land from foreign domination. The peace that follows permits friendship between the Callistans and the Earthmen. * A secondary matter is a romance between Lola and Eddie, the mechanic of Parsons's first expedition. Lola renounces her throne to marry him. This is an unusual feature in science-fiction romance, a princess marrying not the great scientific hero, but a blue-collar worker.

   1578. **THE RETURN TO SUBTERRANIA.** *Science Wonder Stories*, April 1930. Ill. Paul.

Novelette. * Sequel to #1567, "The Menace from Below." * The survivors of the first story are ridiculed as liars, but Platt has an answer: He has duplicated the viewer that the mad scientists constructed in the cave world and, adding sound, has entered into communication with Jerry Talbot, down in Subterrania. * What is new? Talbot, though badly wounded, survived and is repentant. He would like to undo the evil he has committed, but

needs help. The men at the surface agree to help him, whereupon Jerry brings them down via the fourth-dimensional apparatus. * The situation down below: The supermen have all moved away, and a peculiar situation has arisen among them. The individual counterparts in the brain swaps (survivors from the Brooklyn subway trains that Talbot and Ainsworth hijacked via the fourth dimension and artificially evolved cavemen) have paired off, seeming to find a unity that they do not have separately. Those without partners are unhappy. * Unfortunately, the supermen and their partners do not trust Jerry, and it takes much persuasion, plus signs of repentance, before they agree to the reverse operation. The surgical procedures, which are minor, are all accomplished, and the restored surface men and women are returned to the surface by the fourth-dimensional transportational device. * Ends that might be loose: Jerry suffers from terminal tuberculosis and barely finishes the job before dying. * The pithecanthropi and other primitive men, who adore Jerry, go berserk when it is known that he is dead and attack the rescue party, which escapes with difficulty. * Also included, undoubtedly for wordage, is an episode in which several enormous dinosaurs escape from a cavern Jerry had previously sealed off and attack the buildings. They are killed by hordes of pterodactyls, and Jerry closes off the cavern again with disintegrator rays. * During the initial stages of communication with Jerry, telepathy also helped. * Routine work.

   1579. **THE TERROR OF AIR-LEVEL SIX.** *Astounding Stories*, July 1930. Ill. J. Fleming Gould.

Nouvelle. * *Time:* A.D. 2011. *Place:* partly in space. * Air traffic is disrupted when fleets of air liners disappear as a violet ray plays upon them. What is happening? * The role of world-saver falls to Hartley Jones, who has developed a rocket-propelled plane of fantastic speed and altitude capability. His power source is an device that removes oxygen and hydrogen from the atmosphere and uses then as fuel. Jones's trial flight reveals that the attacks are coming from space. * About this time the government of the United States receives an ultimatum: "Surrender and grant 40 percent of your resources, including young people, or be destroyed." * As proof of capability, the menace plays heat rays on cities and countryside. Soon the whole world is included in the demand. * Jones is the only hope. In an enlarged, heavily weaponed version of his rocket plane, he flies into space at the speed of 40,000 MPH. He comes upon a gigantic doughnut-like vessel hovering at the dead zone of Earth-sun gravitations, projecting its lethal beams. * Jones attacks the doughnut with disintegrator rays, and after some peril destroys it. * The menace was renegade Professor Oradel, who left Earth some years earlier in a rocket, reached Venus, and made a bargain with the Venusians who manned the doughnut. * A domestic interest subplot is also included.

   1580. **SILVER DOME.** *Astounding Stories*, August 1930. Ill. J. Fletcher Gould.

Short story. * *Place:* the Ramapo Hills, New York, and underground. * Frank Rowley and Arnold Thompson, on receiving an alarming message from old Professor Leland's man, decide to see what is wrong. The professor's house is deserted, but in the basement, in addition to a first-class laboratory, is a secret room, within which is a large tube with a gravity-reducing apparatus. Rowley and Thompson enter the tube, descending into a large cavern, where they see a gigantic silver dome. When they enter the dome, they lose consciousness, awakening as guests in the

Vincent, Harl (*continued*)

underground city of Theros. * Theros is a eutopia, with handsome, happy people, beautiful ambience, and no hardships. Its inhabitants are ultimately descended from Atlanteans who escaped to North America and were driven by land upheavals into the cave world, where they prospered. Their science is far superior to ours, with aerocars, thought-reading machines, farviewing machines that can see anything on Earth, machines that view the past, antigravity; and much else. * The beautiful Queen Phaestra welcomes the two men, since the Atlantean analyzing machines show that they are good-hearted men, and in her pastviewing machine shows them the destruction of Atlantis. She and Rowley fall in love. * The two surface men are informed that they can return to the surface if they wish, but that old Professor Leland cannot leave Theros, since he is evil and greedy and could not be trusted to keep the existence of the land secret. When Leland breaks loose with his automatic (the only weapon in Theros), Rowley saves the queen's life. * The surface men are about to return to New Jersey by matter transmitter when the beautiful queen rushes up and pulls Rowley off the apparatus. He will presumably serve as her consort. * A pleasant scientific fairy tale.

1581. **FREE ENERGY**. *Amazing Stories*, September 1930. Ill. Paul.

Short story. * *Time:* 1988. * The tycoons of the American Utilities Corporation, one of the largest, most ruthless robber baronies, buy a wonderful invention that will reduce the cost of producing electricity enormously and will also enable them to corner the world's market of electricity. The invention, developed by young Alan Huxley, involves gyroscopes and the rotation of the Earth. * A satisfactory business deal is consummated, but in a surprisingly short time after the huge AUC gyroscopes are activated, it is observed that the rotation of the Earth is slowing down. The change is caused by the gyroscopes, which must be shut off to avoid destroying the human race. * This fiasco ruins the AUC, notably its greedy boss Benjamin Shapley. Huxley now explains: His father had been ruined by the AUC, and this is his revenge. But revenge over, he and Shapley make peace.

1582. **VAGABONDS OF SPACE**. *Astounding Stories*, November 1930. Ill. Wesso.

Short story. * *Time:* around A.D. 2320. *Place:* the asteroid belt, Europa, Ganymede, space. * Carr Parker, young president of International Airways, deciding that he has had enough of business life, leaves on an exploring trip with his Martian friend Mado in Mado's new, highly advanced spaceship. Around the asteroid belt they receive a thought message warning them back: an alien spaceship is being destroyed by an enormous space amoeboid. Carr and Mado, escaping the monster, determine to carry the death message of the alien ship to Europa, its home planet. * Europa is much like Earth. The inhabitants are completely human, with a civilization in many ways superior to that of the inner planets. Although the Europans have had no contact with the inner planets, their viewing machines keep them aware of events and enable them to speak Cos, the interplanetary lingua franca. Europan thought machines verify Carr and Mado's story. * Carr falls in love with Ora, the daughter of his host. * Bad news: The Europans have learned that the Ganymedans plan to conquer the inner planets with various rays that they have developed. The Ganymedan armada will leave almost im-

mediately. * Carr and Mado fly to negotiate with the Ganymedan leader, a lecherous brute who desires Ora, but matters get out of hand. The Earthmen are taken prisoner, and the Ganymedan leader commandeers Mado's ship for his flagship. * Things look bad, but the inner worlds must be saved. Carr overcomes his captors, including the Ganymedan king, and manages to trick the Ganymedan fleet into flying within the reach of the gigantic space amoeboid. Both fleet and monster are destroyed in an explosion. There will be no further attempts at invasion, for Ganymede used all its resources on its failed armada. * *Miscellaneous:* The Martian spacecraft operates by capturing cosmic rays, which it uses to create hydrogen for fuel. * Both Europans and Ganymedans originally came up from Jupiter. The Europans are totally human, while the emigrants from Ganymede are humanoid. Martians resemble Earthmen, but are gigantic. * For a sequel, see #1591, "Creatures of Vibration."

1583. **GRAY DENIM**. *Astounding Stories*, December 1930. Unsigned ill.

Short story. * *Time:* A.D. 2108. *Place:* New York City and the capital of the Continental Empire. * *Background:* The world is divided into two empires, the New World, and the rest of the world (the Continental Empire), which is ruled by Zar Boris. About twenty-five years earlier, the Zar, then the great scientist Boris Van Dorn, contacted the inhabitants of the dark side of the Moon, and with their advanced weapons created his empire. He has since feuded bitterly with his brother, and would kill his nephew Karl, except that his nephew has been hidden since infancy in the Americas. * Karl Krassin, the missing nephew, has been reared among the Grays in ignorance of his identity. The Grays are the workers who live completely underground and slave away to fulfill the whims of the Purples, who live lives of luxury and decadence. Karl has often wished he were a Purple, and when chance reveals that he is not a Gray, he approaches the police and asks to be recognized as a Purple. Instead, he is immediately spirited away to the Zar's capital. * The vicious, ancient Zar intends to kill him, but first would like to torment him a little, offering him a taste of luxury life, before a death of utmost pain. * But members of an underground, inimical to the Zar, rescue Karl and provide him with a heat ray to destroy the Zar's floating palace. Karl melts the palace, but instead of remaining to take up his rightful throne, flies back to America to the life of a Gray as Karl Krassin. * Gimmicks: paralysis rays, rocket ships, antigravity, thought machines, detectoscopes, disintegrator rays, anticohesion rays, the vibrating death. * *Miscellaneous*: The dark side of the Moon is much like Earth, but the natives are dwarves.

1584. **TANKS UNDER THE SEA**. *Amazing Stories*, January 1931. Ill. Morey.

Short story. * *Time and place:* perhaps a few years subsequent to the great war of 1938, after which the Russian dictator André Chevan was exiled to a Pacific Island. * Pete Caldwell and Ben Walton, flying the mail route between New Zealand and Chile, see a strange structure in the sea, whereupon a purple ray kills their motor and they are forced to descend. They are captured by a dwarfish, vicious-looking people, taken in a sub-tank (an amphibious vessel with caterpillar treads) to an enormous underground cavern where they are greeted by the deposed Chevan. Chevan welcomes them, for, as he privately admits, he does not really like the Akata as companions. * The Akata, or subterranean people, are descended from surface men who were

Vincent, Harl (*continued*)

driven underground by enemies millennia ago and have ever since nursed a spirit of revanchism. Chevan, who is obviously a little mad, has built upon this hatred and (with the authority of the Akata king) is organizing an invasion of the upper world. Since the Akata are more intelligent and more advanced scientifically than surface man, conquest is inevitable. * Chevan offers Pete and Ben positions in his administration, with one week for them to decide whether to accept. The two men plot, of course, but without much success. They are guarded, and Akata disintegrator pistols are very effective. * Chevan, in an attempt to win over the two men, confesses that he intends to kill all the Akata as soon as the conquest is established. Their metabolism, thanks to living near radioactive materials underground, contains a certain amount of radioactivity, which Chevan can destroy almost instantaneously. * Unfortunately for Chevan's plans, the Akata overhear this conversation, and things collapse. Pete and Ben seize a sub-tank and make their way out, smashing the airlock and drowning the Akata. * Civilization is saved. * *Miscellaneous:* The Akata also have paralysis gas, force screens to protect their sub-tanks, and superexplosives.

1585. **TERRORS UNSEEN**. *Astounding Stories*, March 1931. Ill. Wesso.

Short story. * *Time:* the near future, with reference to 1944 as in the past. * Edward Vail sees the girl in the bathing suit acting strangely, stops to help her, and observes that she has been bruised and scratched by something invisible. * She is the daughter of David Shelton, the so-called robot wizard. As it turns out, Shelton has not only created huge iron robots, but can make them invisible by vibrating them beyond the frequency of visible light. Shelton intends them for military use, to prevent wars. But someone else, apart from Shelton's switchboard, apparently can control the robots. This is what has been causing the trouble. * The culprit is not a foreign country, but Al Cadorna, the gangster lord, whose real life referent should be obvious. Cadorna captures everyone and tries to make Shelton reveal his secrets, but right triumphs. Cadorna will go to the chair, and Miss Shelton is very friendly to Ed Vail. * *Miscellaneous:* In 1944 the United States defeated Germany in war. * Hack work, with obligatory fisticuffs and fill-page action.

1586. **TOO MANY BOARDS**. *Amazing Stories*, April 1931. Ill. Morey.

Short story. * *Time:* c. A.D. 2025. *Place:* Earth and Mercury. * *Background:* Interplanetary communication was established in 1988, and efficient rocket space travel has been available long enough for Earth, Venus, and Mars to have formed the Triplanetarian Alliance, with considerable interplanetary trade. Mercury, however, is not a member of the group and has a more liberal, less authoritarian culture. The peoples of the solar system seem to be human or humanoid, with Mercurians much taller than Earthmen. * On Earth a very strict eugenics program is in effect, with rigid classifications and group endogamy. The Terrestrial law is recognized by Mars and Venus, but not by Mercury. * Larry Conover, legally compelled to marry within two months, is being pressured by Mills (the major stockholder in his company) to marry Alta Farrish, whom he does not love. Thus, there are complications when he and his new secretary (Una Sinclair) fall in love. A further problem comes when Una's classification is lowered, rendering marriage illegal. * Larry and Una, at the suggestion of a friend, decide to elope illegally to

Mercury, where marital regulations are looser and where Earth has little influence. The captain of the interplanetary liner *Rocket III* agrees to drop them off. He will fake engine trouble as the cause for leaving course and landing on Mercury. * When the ship lands, however, the lovers find that Mills and a Terrestrial ambassador have preceded them on fast official rockets and have made arrangements with the Mercurians for an extradition treaty that will affect them. * Some fast thinking and smooth talking, however, reveals that not only has Mills been responsible for Una's reclassification, but that he has committed many white collar crimes. Mills is discredited; the extradition treaty is scrapped; and Una and Larry marry. Alta, too, finds a willing mate. * *Miscellaneous:* All communicate in an interplanetary lingua franca. * It is not clear whether the Mercurians are settlers from Earth or natives, probably settlers. Their habitat is the libration zone.

1587. **INVISIBLE SHIPS**. *Amazing Stories Quarterly*, Spring 1931. Ill. Morey.

Short story. * *Time:* the interplanetary future. *Place:* space, near Venus. * *Background:* This is the sixth year of the Second Interplanetarian War, with Earth and Venus pitted against Mars. The war is not going well for the Allies, and the Martian forces are not too distant from Venus. The latest crisis is that a strange untraceable ray is destroying the Venusian capital, turning buildings into sand and dust. * The story centers on Scout Ship 9B5, commanded by Capt. "Rocks" Stone, a notorious bully and old line officer, who is also squadron chief. On board the ship is a new shavetail, Lt. Victor Masters, whom Stone delights in ragging. * It is the rookie officer, fresh from the scorned academy, who saves the day. He locates the source of the rays that are demolishing Venus, working out that the rays are following a parabolic curve; he also discovers that the Martian fleet attacking them is invisible; and when they are captured by an invisible Martian vessel, Masters is responsible for their escape and victory over the Martians. * After Masters discovers the vibratory secret of invisibility and locates the ray projectors, the Martians sue for peace, and the war is over. Stone, who is a fair man despite his crudeness, recognizes Masters's true quality and now treats him with respect. * Martians are humanoid, tall, barrel chested, thin-legged, and impossibly arrogant. * Vessels on both sides travel by gravity energy and have disintegrator rays and repulsion rays.

1588. **THE MOON WEED**. *Astounding Stories*, August 1931. Ill. Wesso.

Short story. * Carl Vanderventer astonishes his friend by showing him diamonds that he has obtained from the Moon by matter transmitter. He has also obtained other articles, including seed pods, which, thanks to a thief, reach the ground outside. * The result is incredible. In almost a matter of minutes the seeds sprout, producing red, pulpy, vine-like growths that spread with unbelievable rapidity and seem unstoppable. Explosions merely spread them. * The vines spread over much of the eastern United States in a matter of days, and it seems as if the world is doomed. But Vanderventer reasons that ultraviolet light should be toxic to the plants. And so it is. But the death toll and the destruction have been enormous.

1589. **THE COPPER-CLAD WORLD**. *Astounding Stories*, September 1931. Ill. Wesso.

Novelette. * *Time:* the interplanetary future. *Place:* mostly on Io. * A sinister hunchback has hijacked the *RX8*, which had been

Vincent, Harl (*continued*)

en route to Mars with a cargo of K-metal, the radioactive fuel that powers civilization. Blaine Carson and Tom Farley, pilot and engineer, are captives, enslaved by a will-controlling gas. * As the ship approaches Io—which is normally far beyond the reach of the rocket ships of the inner planets—the men see that it is almost a perfect sphere, completely encased in copper. They later learn that the satellite was encased millennia ago, in order to conserve atmosphere and internal heat, and that its inhabitants originally came from Europa and Ganymede. The Europans, who are few in number, are normal but splendid humans; the Ganymedans, who hold a tyrannous upper hand, are characterized by great sexual differentiation, the females being gorgeous, the males hunchbacks. * The plot, which is complex, embodies a series of clichés: A remarkably beautiful, red-hot, lustful female ruler, who develops a passion for Blaine. A beautiful and virtuous Europan maiden, with whom Blaine falls in love. A dictator who seizes power and conducts massacres. A scientific underground that conceals itself in order to survive. Plots and counterplots. * Behind everything is the Ioan purpose: to use the shipload of K-metal as fuel for a gigantic planetary rocket that will take Io out of its orbit around Jupiter and place it in among the inner planets, where it will conquer Earth. Everyone except the Ioan leaders realizes that this plan is unrealistic militarily and probably would disrupt the stability of the solar system. * Blaine, Farley, and the Ioan maiden foil the plot and manage to escape as Io blows up behind them. * Included as props are paralysis rays, disintegrators, cloaks of invisibility, viewers, sound pickups, monorails, etc. * The jungle of Io, in which our hero takes refuge, abounds in enormous ferocious lizards and carnivorous plants. * Much influence from A. Merritt.

1590. **A MATTER OF ETHICS**. *Amazing Stories*, October 1931. Ill. Morey.

Short story. * A scientific detective story shading into science-fiction. * Bret Garrison, who seems to be some sort of scientific consultant, becomes interested in the strange case of the noted surgeon Frank Robeson. Twice recently, Robeson has become partly paralyzed during an operation and has had to turn over the procedures to his assistants. Robeson, who is near a breakdown, is on the edge of resigning. Further, although this is confided to Bret by Robeson's wife, Robeson occasionally tries to strangle her nights—with no memory of his actions the next day. * Garrison gains some insight into the case when Robeson, on the golf course, acts strangely when the party passes near a television broadcasting unit. * The solution, without revealing identities: a sex triangle, as a false friend lusts for Robeson's beautiful young wife. The modus operandi: an electronic implant near the spine that can be set off with radio waves.

1591. **CREATURES OF VIBRATION**. *Astounding Stories*, January 1932. Ill. Wesso.

Short story, sequel to #1582, "Vagabonds of Space." * *Time:* around A.D. 2320. *Place:* Titan. * Carr; Mado the Martian; Ora, Carr's Europan wife; and Detis, her father, while exploring the solar system, crack up on Titan. The unusual thing about Titan is that it is permeated by noxious vibrations from the rings of Saturn that evoke the evil potential in one, if one stays there for any length of time. * Titan is inhabited by two peoples; civilized, advanced humans who shield themselves against the vibrations, and horrible red savages on a primitive level who practice human

sacrifice to a blue volcanic flame. Actually, the two races are one genetically; the savagery is what happens if one is not shielded from the ring vibrations. * Our friends are captured by the savages and about to be tossed into the flame, when they are saved by a gigantic projection that Detis makes from the space-ship. They escape, but Detis necessarily dies as a result of the projection. The explorers leave hurriedly before they, too, succumb to the evil vibrations. * *Miscellaneous:* gigantic flying lizards like pterodactyls, ray guns, and cosmic ray energy for space travel.

1592. **POWER**. *Amazing Stories*, January 1932. Ill. Morey.

Short story. * *Time:* the twenty-third century. *Place:* mostly the New York City area and Washington. * *Background:* The countryside has been abandoned to wilderness and jungle, and the entire population of America is concentrated into eight gigantic cities, of which New York is typical. Housing some fifty million people, it consists of a single windowless, steel-cased, monolithic structure of one hundred levels. Of these levels, thirty are devoted to machinery, sixty-five to the gray clad workers, and five to the wealthy, hedonistic purples. * There is an enormous social gap between grays and purples, just as there is a similar gap in privileges and living standards. A tight control over the workers is maintained by the red police, who are the creatures of the purples. * In name, United North America is a democracy with an elected president, but in fact, the country is ruled by the leaders of a few gigantic trusts, notably the Power Syndicate. Since fossil fuels are exhausted, the ability of the Power Syndicate's stratospheric plants to extract energy from cosmic rays gives it a stranglehold over the nation. Naturally, the nation is on the edge of revolution, and there is a strong underground that awaits only a tool for seizing power. * Scott Terris, head of the Science Research Bureau and a powerful purple, has hitherto been an apolitical figure, concerned only with science, though a well-meaning, liberal man. But he is impelled into politics when he returns unexpectedly to his laboratory one evening and finds a strange gray using his equipment. The two men talk amiably, and Terris learns that the stranger, whose name is Gail Destinn, has created nuclear fusion power. A demonstration reveals the truth of Destinn's claim. * Terris's dormant sense of decency is awakened by Destinn, all the more when he visits the workers' levels in disguise and sees the actions of inflammatory speakers and repressive police. * During this visit, Destinn is seriously wounded by an atomic dart, thus leaving the way open for Terris to take over his discovery and role. But, with the secret of unlimited power and a potent disintegrating force, Terris, succumbing to ambition, takes the high road and forces himself into the position of hidden dictator of United North America, with the nominal president under control. His program is not unbridled revolution or egalitarianism, but sensible change that will combine social equality with an elitism based on ability, not wealth. Only Crawford, the energy czar, gives him serious trouble, and Crawford flees the country. * There are, of course, stresses and strains, as Terris is attracted to Norine Rosov, the contracted sex partner of Destinn, and Destinn is being subject to medical malpractice. But the real crisis comes when Crawford returns with a fleet of mercenary aircraft armed with heavy explosives, demanding control of the country. * All ends well. Destinn recovers. Terris's fusion apparatus destroys Crawford's fleet. Norine is not really "married" to Destinn, but is a free

Vincent, Harl (*continued*)

woman and (a ludicrous touch) is the long-lost daughter of the former food czar. * *Miscellaneous:* Food is synthetic and is produced in the city by machines controlled by the food trust. The food czar, once a powerful enemy of Terris's, reforms when put into a rehabilitation center and becomes a useful ally. Aerial piracy seems to be rife; from such pirates Crawford recruited his bombers. * A more sensible *Metropolis* world, of course. The story starts out well, with a good background, but loses conviction more and more as it advances. One might guess that Vincent lost interest in it about midway.

1593. **ONCE IN A BLUE MOON**. *Amazing Stories Quarterly*, Winter 1932. Ill. Morey.

Short story. * *Time:* A.D. 2019. *Place:* the Moon. * Lunar exploration is in its earliest stages, but the Moon is already an invaluable resource because of its deposits of lunium, a metal that becomes an antigravity substance when electricity is applied to it. Rockets from Earth bring mining crews to extract the metal and take it back to Earth. * At the moment, the Terrestrials know little about the moon. The story is intended to explain why the Moon suddenly backflipped and henceforth displayed its hitherto hidden side. * *Moon Rocket IV* is loading lunium ingots when *Moon Rocket VII* flashes by, apparently headed for a crash, its communications personnel acting strangely. Pete (Clark Peters) and two associates (one of whom is a mole and assassin) decide to investigate. They find that *VII* has landed safely in a huge crevasse, that there are signs of a high lunar civilization, and, indeed, small humanoid bipeds are working around the rocket. Financial robber baron Aleck Carter, who is present, is up to skulduggery. * As Pete and his associates watch, four-foot spheres of gleaming metal emerge from a mist and "swallow" them; explosive bullets are of no avail. * The spheres, which are living beings formed of lunium, are not hostile. As they inform Pete telepathically, they are one of the three Lunar life-forms, the long product of evolution from protoplasmic life. Their science is far higher than that of Earth, but is somewhat spotty. * There are two kinds of spheres, the Great Ones, or rulers, and the Lesser Ones, with whom Pete is in contact. The Lesser Ones have the task of caring for and protecting the lunar bipeds. * As the Lesser One informs Pete, Carter has made a bargain with the bipeds. In exchange for their help he will energize the lunium deposits and counteract the Earth's gravity, then bring the Moon down upon the Earth, so that the bipeds can colonize the Earth. The spheres, despite their awesome power, cannot act; foiling Carter will be up to the humans. * These is a further element, the Dark Ones, evil unipedal beings also of awesome mental power. * Actually, as Pete soon learns when captured by the looters, Carter has no intention of bringing the Moon down to Earth; he intends to take it farther out into space, so that he can maintain a monopoly more securely. The lunar bipeds are to be exterminated. * Down inside the hollow moon the final showdown takes place. Pete is captured by the mental power of a Dark One, a football-like creature on a single leg; Carter starts to activate the lunium; the Great Ones (spheres fifty miles across) are caught in the energy trap; there is a revolt among Carter's scientists; and the mole in Pete's group, realizing the implications of Carter's work, repents and sacrifices himself to destroy the switch controlling the work. * The wicked are all wiped out, but the short period that the lunium was activated turned the Moon over. * *Miscellaneous:*

The Great Ones and the Lesser Ones may be cyborgs; the author is not clear. * A competent thriller until the last portions, when extra elements and confusion spoil what went before.

1594. **WATER-BOUND WORLD**. *Amazing Stories Quarterly*, Spring/Summer 1932. Ill. Morey.

Short story. * *Time:* the twenty-second century. *Place:* Iapetus, a moon of Saturn. * The disabled passenger liner *Mercurianic* is making repairs and restoring energy in space near Iapetus. It would be more efficient to descend to the moon itself but Iapetus is legally off limits, and Captain Boe refuses to land, even though the crew urge him. * A mutiny breaks out under Venusian chief engineer Zarko Nad. The officers are all killed except hero Ridge Coler, pilot, and Kal Turjen, Martian communications man, both of whom Zarko needs to operate the ship. To save their lives Coler and Kal agree to join the mutineers, although they have no intention of fulfilling their promises. * Zarko takes the ship down to Iapetus, which is usually thought to be water-covered, toward a gigantic coffer dam, into which he drops. There, along with other spaceships, is a horde of small, humanoid frog-men who are working with Zarko. Also present are the Yrlds, strange beings of incredible mind power, with enormous brains and weak, vestigial bodies. * The Yrlds and Zarko have struck a bargain. The Yrlds will give him enormous treasures, and in exchange Zarko will transport them off Iapetus to a place where they can obtain human bodies onto which they can graft their heads. * By the time the Yrld leader Bzor interrogates Ridge Coler, the Yrlds have already taken over the bodies of most of the passengers of the *Mercurianic*. * Complications: Zarko and the Yrlds would have kept faith with one another, but Zarko's men mutiny, killing him, and the situation becomes complicated as the various parties fight against one another. The Yrlds are masters of all sorts of rays, disintegrator and otherwise, but iron is a defense against them. Iron does not occur on Iapetus, and the Yrlds were not able to work it into their calculations. * All the humans are killed except Coder, Kal, and a young woman (Rita), and all the ships but one are destroyed. The three humans escape with the treasure. As they leave, Coder directs the rocket blast against the coffer dam, destroying it and the Yrlds. The frog-men, who have been under Yrld mental domination, are now free to lead their own lives. Rita is a good girl, but her brother, a foul cad, was one of Zarko's men and led the mutiny against him. * *Miscellaneous:* The Yrlds, who originated on Saturn, discovered immortality, whereupon their bodies gradually degenerated. They came to Iapetus by spaceship. * During his interrogation, the Yrlds showed Ridge the past by fossil light. * Venusians are very heavily built and slow moving. Martians are big-chested and tall. * A romance and the complex situation among Rita, her rogue brother to whom she is devoted, and Ridge are very clumsily handled. * Further adventures of Ridge Coler and Kal Turjen are to be found in #1600, "When the Comet Returned," and #1605, "Lost City of Mars."

1595. **VULCAN'S WORKSHOP**. *Astounding Stories*, June 1932. Ill. Wesso.

Short story. * *Time:* the interplanetary future. *Place:* Vulcan. * Luke Fenton, a Herculean thug reminiscent of Eugene O'Neill's Hairy Ape, has been sentenced as an incorrigible criminal to Vulcan's Workshop, a penal colony on the planetoid Vulcan. * Vulcan, whose existence was corroborated after space exploration began, is a small planet, about 250 miles in diameter, but with

Vincent, Harl (*continued*)

a gravity several times as strong as Earth's because of its neutronium core. The planetoid does not revolve, but has a twilight zone between cold and hot halves, with a libration factor. * The Workshop is a death sentence, for prisoners seldom live longer than a few months because of the intense radioactivity in the mines. Against the heavy gravity they wear anti-gravity suits, which the guards can nullify with ray tubes; a crushing weight results. * Luke is a troublemaker, and does not get on well. After severely injuring a Martian guard, with whom he had a permitted grudge fight, he is placed in a special laboratory with Fuller. * Fuller, an educated elderly man, soon takes Luke into his confidence. He plans an escape. He has friends nearby who will help him if he can get out of the camp, and he has a way to nullify the guards' gravity tubes. But it must be soon, for he is dying of radiation. * The two men break out of the camp, and after perils, reach Fuller's friends, who take them off Vulcan. * The full background is now revealed: Fuller, whose condition can be cured, has been working undercover investigating prison conditions. The Workshop, which is conducted by private enterprise, not the state, will be abolished as inhuman. * Luke, shamed and inspired by Fuller's self-sacrificing probity, undergoes a character change and will now be a useful citizen. * Well imagined detail in the first part, but Luke's conversion is much too pat.

1596. **THIA OF THE DRYLANDS**. *Amazing Stories*, July 1932. Ill. Morey.

Short story. * *Time:* a little after A.D. 2000. *Place:* mostly Mars. * Cliff Barron, former space pilot of some reputation, has contracted a mysterious Martian disease that has wasted his arms and made them almost powerless. His employer, Sykes of Interplanetary Lines, Inc., refuses to help him reach Mars, where a noted physician can rebuild his nerves and muscles, whereupon Barron is understandably bitter. Thus, when a stranger named Vetter approaches him with an unusual offer, he is willingly to listen. Vetter has a new method of reaching Mars: passage along a space-tube that accomplishes in a matter of minutes what takes days by ordinary space travel. So far, the system has worked with animals, but a human must prove its safety. If Barron agrees to undertake the transmission, he will receive funds and an introduction to the otherwise almost inaccessible Martian physician. * But things are not as simple as they seemed, for on arriving on Mars, Barron is immediately enmeshed in a complex series of intrigues involving Terrestrial secret service men, gangster-like Martians who want to kill him, and the beautiful Princess Thia. After narrowly escaping execution, Barron is healed by the physician, and then discovers that much of what he had accepted as truth was wrong, disastrously so. * By the time matters get sorted out a little, he and Thia (who are in love and are both outlaws) are halfway between Earth and Mars when the space-tube is cut off, leaving them stranded in midspace. They are rescued, of course, but being outlaws, they cannot return to either Mars or Earth. Callisto is possible. * Sykes, it turns out, really wanted to help Barron, but was constrained, and Vetter was a villainous murderer. * Routine. * With this story Vincent sets a general pattern that he uses in future Martian stories: Schiaparellian Mars, totally human or nearly human native inhabitants, with city and canal dwellers opposed to natives of the Drylands.

1597. **FASTER THAN LIGHT**. *Amazing Stories*

Quarterly, Fall/Winter 1932. Ill. Wesso.

Novelette. * Sequel to #1568, "Venus Liberated." * *Time:* about 1947 or 1948. *Place:* Venus and interplanetary space, on the way to and at a planet of Procyon. * The protagonists of the first story, two years later, are bored with the monotony of daily life and would like to resume adventuring. Other factors coincide: Professor Timken has designed a spaceship that will travel faster than light; and there is a trade war going on concerning spaceship fuel. If Sorenson is to stay in business, a new energy source must be provided. This means radium, which spectroscopic analysis shows is far more abundant elsewhere than on Earth. Also, Dr. De Polac has invented the mentascope, a helmet that permits telepathy; the explorers take along ten. * The friends assemble on Venus, where the *Blue Streak* is built. Then with a new associate, Dillon, whose presence on the ship seems to be a whim of Sorenson's, they leave. Some of the comrades do not trust Dillon. * On the way to Procyon, which seems to be a likely source for radium, the associates come upon an annular planet (Kirpin) that is surrounded by a luminous orange mist. It is traveling faster than light. * The explorers land, finding humanoid people with a spottily high civilization. An unusual feature about the Kirpina is that their lower limbs are atrophied and they move about on small electrically powered chassis that are covered by their clothing. Since the mentascope seems to show that the Kirpina are friendly, the explorers are off their guard and are soon in difficulties. The priests regard them with disfavor and try to sacrifice them by dropping them out of antigravity holders into an abyss. But the explorers make their escape and continue on. * Reaching the Procyon system, the voyagers find a planet rich in radium, which they extract in large quantity. As they are leaving, a tractor ray from Mosin-ton, a nearby twin planet, captures the *Blue Streak*. * Mosin-ton is inhabited by a race of metal men with a high science. These men, who are genuinely friendly, are cyborgs with organic nervous and circulatory systems maintained in a humaniform metal body. * At this point the skulduggery plot surfaces, rather incredibly. Collins reveals his true colors. He is an agent of the Asiatic Empire of Earth and even has two stowaway Orientals on board to enforce his seizure of the vessel. * After some back and forth action, Dillon flies off with the *Blue Streak*, taking along with him the women and Professor Timken. The explorers on Mosin-ton trace the motion of the *Blue Streak* with local equipment, but cannot catch it. * Then, the unexpected happens. The ship wanders back as if partly out of control. Disembarked, the women explain. Dillon and one Oriental are dead; the other Oriental, an honest, loyal man, perceiving that Dillon was a scoundrel, a would-be rapist, and a traitor to the yellow emperor, killed him and the other guard. * The survivors head back to Earth. * *Miscellaneous:* The author does not offer a theoretical basis for faster than light travel; simply, Einstein was wrong. * The Kirpina have broadcast electrical power.

1598. **ROADWAYS OF MARS**. *Amazing Stories*, December 1932. Ill. Morey.

Short story. * *Time:* the twenty-first century. *Place:* Mars. * *Background:* This is pretty much Schiaparellian Mars, with huge desert wastelands and shallow atmosphere, but with a more or less primitive humanoid population in the drylands. * Bob Coleman and his brother Gordon are freelance engineers and construction men who have received a contract to drive roads through some of the worst desert areas of Mars. * There are,

Vincent, Harl (*continued*)

however, difficulties. For no good reason, much of the populace is against the construction, and Bob has to convince them that their lives will be bettered by the advance of civilization. More dangerous is the well-known, established Martian bandit Bingord, a savage, sadistic brute. As is later revealed, he has a grudge against the Colemans, since Gordon once bested him in a quarrel. He is a man who likes his revenge. * During an attack on the installation, Bingord captures Gordon and returns to his headquarters, where he proceeds to torture Gordon in ingenious and leisurely fashion. * Bob follows with police and a Martian enemy of Bingord's, but Bingord has his establishment well guarded with superscientific means. Bob wins, of course, but along the way loses most of his men and takes a bad beating, psychologically and physically. * Some imagination in Bingord's gadgets, but otherwise a Western story of a sort.

1599. **WANDERER OF INFINITY**. *Astounding Stories*, March 1933. Ill. Wesso.

(Reprinted in Goodstone, *The Pulps*.)

Short story. * *Place:* Ramapo Hills, New York. * Bert Redmond, Indiana fruit farmer, receives a note from Joan Parker, his half-estranged girlfriend in the Ramapos, asking him to come and help her. When he arrives, he learns that her brother Tom is experimenting with dimensions and that she is frightened. * Tom explains: He has discovered that the fifth dimension consists of an enormous number of parallel worlds, interpenetrating one another, separated by subatomic factors. * Tom demonstrates his machine, showing a world where spider-like creatures are constructing a metal cage. * Bert is horrified, all the more so when the spider-men step through the center of Tom's apparatus into our world, and drag Tom and Joan away. * Bert tries to leap through after them, feels a wrenching pain, and finds himself in a sphere with a charismatic giant who speaks English and promises to help him. Time is not a factor, the giant says; they can rescue the Parkers a second or two after they reach the spiders' other-world. * The giant explains: He is the Wanderer of Infinity, condemned to move about among the parallel worlds because of a crime that he committed against his own people in the remote past. To make his point the giant takes Bert to an almost eutopian world of humans. Here, ages ago, the giant, carried away by scientific hybris, had opened a dimensional gate like Tom Parker's and walked away. Metal monsters swarmed through the gate into his world and wiped out the humans. Since then the giant moves through the dimensions, trying to help humans who find themselves in a similar situation—as the people of Earth now do. Unless Tom Parker's gate is closed, the scientifically superior spider-men will overrun Earth. * The giant takes Bert to the world of the spider-men, where he rescues Tom and Joan, returning them to our world. To close the gateway and destroy the apparatus, however, Tom must sacrifice himself. * One of the better stories in Clayton *Astounding Stories*

1600. **WHEN THE COMET RETURNED**. *Amazing Stories*, April 1933. Ill. Morey.

Short story. * *Time:* the twenty-second century. *Place:* space near Jupiter. * Ridge Coler, captain and owner of the *Ariel*, has contracted to take three scientists to a certain destination in space, exact coordinates to be given at the proper time. It is a somewhat fishy situation, especially since two of the scientists—a Martian and a Venusian—are totally aloof, and the third, Earth-man Sir James Beveridge, is an obnoxious bully who tries to

meddle in the operation of the vessel. * A complication is added when a stowaway is discovered. This is Nyu Varon, a feeble, ancient Martian who is the leader of a strange sect among the Martian drylanders. Nyu claims that he came on the expedition by the will of his god, that ancient prophecies are being fulfilled, and that he will return to his god. Nyu seems like a senile fanatic, but it should be noted that he seems to have an intuitive knowledge of advanced theoretical physics, though in a figurative way, and is able, apparently, to move about inexplicably. * The common factor in the quests of the three scientists and Nyu is a mysterious comet that manifests itself only at intervals of about a thousand years. The head of the comet contains rhenium, a rare miracle element used for medical purposes on the inner worlds. Beveridge and his associates want the rhenium for selfish reasons; Nyu believes that the comet is a divinity whose will he must obey. * When the *Ariel* draws near the comet, Nyu leaps out into space to embrace it. The others are trapped and lose consciousness as their ship is attracted into the comet, which sweeps toward the inner planets, brushing through the atmosphere of Mars. * At a certain mysterious shrine in the Martian drylands, the final episode takes place. A small spaceship detaches itself from the comet and settles at the shrine. Coler and his associates regain consciousness, and a new priest, perhaps Nyu reconstituted as a young man, (the text is not clear) presents the men with a globe of rhenium, to be used unselfishly, the gift of the comet god. The three scientists, upon association with the rhenium, have been transformed, their evil components no longer in sway. All ends well, but there are many things that Coler or the scientists cannot explain—except by the supernatural that Nyu followed. * Unusual for the irrational element. * See also #1594, "Water-Bound World" and #1605, "Lost City of Mars," for other stories concerning Ridge Coler.

1601. **CAVERN OF THUNDERS**. *Amazing Stories*, July 1933. Ill. Morey.

Short story. * *Time:* the forty-second century. *Place:* a layered group of underground cities. * *Background:* In the twenty-eighth century, mankind reached its acme in civilization, with universal peace and prosperity. But this all collapsed when Earth began to pass through a cloud of dust that cut off solar radiation. It happened so rapidly that there was no time for preparation, and the entire human race perished, except for a small band of scientists who sealed themselves into a huge cavern. They enlarged the cavern with disintegrators and began a self-sufficient underground culture. From this small group humanity arose again, spreading through new underground chambers. Human history was not a unilinear progress, however, for there were different political manifestations and intercity wars until the present peaceful world was established. * At present there are about twenty million people living in the caverns, which are enlarged as needed. In the area of the story, several cities are stacked in a vertical group; all belong to a confederation except the bottom city of Raoz, which holds an eccentric vegetarian culture. The outside, it is well-known, is still utterly uninhabitable, and, indeed, there is no exit to the surface. * The narrative deals with Ivarg, a young seismic engineer, who is in love with Aorna, a young woman from Raoz. The problem is that unexpected seismic activity, including lava flows, is rapidly destroying the cities, one by one. Ivarg and Aorna flee before the destruction, with intermittent incidents of sexual harassment and vendetta. * As the destruction continues, Ivarg and comrades

Vincent, Harl (*continued*)

disintegrate their way into unknown caverns filled with tropical vegetation and ape-like beings who have evolved into submen. For a brief time, Aorna holds a position there as a flame goddess among these beings, who practice human sacrifice. * After further turmoil the survivors from the destroyed cities disintegrate their way out to the surface, which they discover is habitable again. The estimates of the astronomers were wrong, and the cities were closer to the surface than they believed. The surviving millions of the underground people can now establish a new, surface civilization. * Routine adventure.

1602. **TELEGRAPH PLATEAU**. *Astounding Stories*, November 1933. Unsigned ill.
Short story. * *Time:* 1951. *Place:* under the sea in the North Atlantic. * The great passenger and freight airliners of North Atlantic Air Transport Service have been disappearing over a certain stretch of the ocean, and Graham, Perry, and mechanic Dugan have been assigned to investigate in a small reconnaissance plane. As they approach the danger area, they lose control of their plane. Before them is a pillar of water ascending into the sky and a hole in the water from which emerges a gigantic metal sphere that draws the plane into a reception slot. The sphere descends, and the men are captives in the underground land of Kafeja. * *Background:* Kafeja, where the ruling class and most of the people speak some English in addition to their native tongue, was founded about two thousand years earlier by Scandinavians who took refuge in caverns that were later sealed off by earth movements. There, in order to maintain life, they gradually developed a superscience, which includes antigravity, heat rays, paralysis guns, and much else. The population, which numbers about twenty-five thousand, is rigidly divided into priests, who are really highly advanced scientists, and laymen, the laymen being vastly greater in number. What with millennia of underground life, the Kafeja have evolved away from outside mankind, being very tall and slender, with enormous eyes that have a different range of color vision than ours. The prime myth of the land is emergence; as the legend goes, when there are enough captive surface people to be sacrificed, one for each of the natives, Kafeja will reemerge. * The priesthood carefully preserves the surface people—of whom they now hold several hundred. Individuals keep disappearing, however, and it is generally believed among the captives that human sacrifice is taking place. * For a time Graham is put to work for a time hunting giant octopi from a small supersubmarine with a device that can repel water in a globe around the vessel. * After the captives make an ineffectual attempt to escape, two factors bring a resolution. First, the laity of Kafeja, who become rightly convinced that the priesthood is planning to abandon them and the land, rise in rebellion. Second, the land is doomed by earthquakes, as the priesthood knows. Kafeja may be destroyed at any moment. * During the confusion attending the uprising, while the commoners try to kill the captives and the priests desperately protect them, the captives reach the giant sphere, rise to the surface, and escape, just as the land beneath them is destroyed by temblors. * *Explanation:* Perry mugged a priest, and using a thought-exchange helmet, learned the secrets of the land and the mode of operating Kafeja equipment. What was really going on was not human sacrifice. The priests were transplanting eyes from the surface people into themselves, so that they could tolerate the strong, different light of the outside

world. Ordinary white light, it turns out, would blind them. * Not bad as an adventure story.

1603. **WHISPER OF DEATH**. *Amazing Stories*, November 1933. Ill. Morey.
Novelette. * *Time:* 1952. *Place:* various, including Mexico and an island off Siberia. * The basic situation is that the gold hoards of the Western world are mysteriously disappearing in conjunction with an utter absence of sound or a whispering noise, sometimes accompanied by death of nearby persons. * Involved in the solution of these mysterious events is Bret Garrison, a scientist of genius, and his friend Wayne Gordon. Opposed to them in various ways are: (1) Paula Kratkin, a beautiful Russian who is a devoted Communist and believes that the destruction of Western gold will bring on the Revolution. (2) Anton Tulov, Paula's estranged husband, the real master of the operation, who is playing for world power and is using the unwitting Paula as a tool. (3) Dai Chan, renowned Asian scientist, who developed the vibratory technique for stealing the gold, which is reconstituted in his Siberian stronghold. * The plot involves adventures on the ground and in the air, until all end up on Tulov's Siberian island stronghold. Paula, who is playing a double, perhaps triple, game, destroys her fellow plotters. * The capitalist system is saved, and only in time, for it was beginning to break down. * *Miscellaneous:* Dai Chan operates his apparatus with a viewing screen that serves as a focusing mechanism. * There are various dart weapons. * The story is carried as "The Whisper of Death" on the contents page.

1604. **MASTER OF DREAMS**. *Amazing Stories*, January 1934. Ill. Morey.
Novelette. * An unusual sort of story for Vincent, essentially a thriller with strong elements of fantasy, including practical questionings of the reality of experience, though basically science-fiction. * *Time and place:* Prohibition-era New York. * The story begins with four men meeting in a speakeasy: Sir Percy Clive Graves, important British economist and minister; Cullen, an American newspaperman tailing Graves for a story; Eric Stanley, a gifted amateur scientist who "avoids women, to the point of rudeness"; and Abdul Nad, a mysterious Turk who has struck up conversation with Graves. As the meal proceeds, hostility arises between Nad and Graves, during which Nad claims that he can control the will of others. * The plot of the story is very complex and not easily summarized. Let it be enough to say that Abdul Nad is not faking; he has the technology to insert little radio receivers into the skulls of his victims and thereafter to control both their dreams and their conscious actions. His general aim is world domination, and he already has important financiers, politicians, and military men completely under his control. His more specific aim is vengeance against Sir Percy, who he (mistakenly?) believes killed his brother Mustafa. * The story centers on Stanley, who witnesses bizarre actions by Nad's victims and himself (when implanted with a control crystal) and experiences weird dreams. Stanley, however, breaks loose. In his own laboratory, but under Nad's control, he chances to approach a radio transmitter whose broadcast range cancels out Nad's signals. From here, despite some setbacks, it is possible to fight against Nad and save not only individuals, but also Western civilization. * *Miscellaneous:* Nad's surgeons insert a marble-like device in the nape of the neck; Nad then controls his victims by radio waves, but for this it is necessary for him to remain awake at all times. If he

Vincent, Harl (*continued*)

sleeps, the victims are free. Thus, he tries to recruit Stanley as a stand-by, and, thus, his organization falls apart when he is knocked unconscious. * Some of the in-between states of mind are interesting.

1605. **LOST CITY OF MARS**. *Astounding Stories*, February 1934. Ill. Browne.

Short story. * *Time:* the twenty-second century. *Place:* Mars and Phobos. * A quest story, as Earthman Ridge Coler and Martian Kal Turjen are following mysterious instructions, hoping to find Turjen's father, long believed dead. To the accompaniment of seemingly magical effects that are really the products of a superscience, they reach their destination, a secret installation in the Martian drylands, where they are welcomed by an ancient Martian sage who explains matters to them. * *Background:* In the remote past, Mars was inhabited by a dark red race, the people of the city of Scarta, who developed a superscience before desiccation struck Mars. Among their achievements were antigravity and immortality. As Mars grew progressively drier, other red Martians also developed high civilization and created the canal system, while Scarta remained aloof. The descendants of the canal builders still survive as the civilized Martian aristocracy. Still later, another evolutionary chain produced the Martian Drylanders, who live in the desert regions, are almost white, and have a culture with strong elements of magic and witchcraft. * In the remote past, the Drylanders became troublesome enough that the people of Scarta packed up their city, created an artificial satellite (Phobos) into which they inserted the city, and left Mars. Scarta still survives, with its immortal population, inside Phobos, unknown to other Martians; but occasionally Scarta makes manifestations on the planetary surface that have given rise to legendry. * As for the present: Kal Turjen now learns that his father Bas Turjen has just died, hoping that Kal will continue his work. The problem is that Zaraf, the immortal ruler of Scarta, plans to return to Mars and conquer it. Bas Turjen and an underground have been working against this scheme, which is quite feasible, considering Scarta's level of scientific advancement. * Kal Turjen agrees to take up his father's role (which amounts to providing leadership to the somewhat diffident, impractical Scartans). Indeed, Kal is as good as possessed by his father's spirit, to the point of physical change. * Civil war breaks out, with incredible weaponry used by both sides. Among the most fearsome is a black ray that ages one rapidly. * The rebels win, in so far as Coler kills the half-mad emperor and gains control of Phobos's planetary power and steering mechanism, but the loss of life is great. As Coler sends Phobos off into outer space, where it can no longer menace Mars or other worlds, he sees that his friend Turjen is reassuming his former identity and physique. The two men will return down to Mars while Phobos flies away. * *Miscellaneous:* All the Martians are human, but taller than Earthmen. * Travel to Phobos is accomplished by a magnetic tube. * This story contains the most detailed explanation of the Martian ambience that seems central to Vincent's Martian stories. * The mythic aspects of the story are interesting, as is often the case in Vincent's better, later work, but the development is awkward and confusing. * For other stories concerning Ridge Coler and Kal Turjen see #1594, "Water-Bound World" and #1600, "When the Comet Returned."

1606. **CAT'S EYE**. *Amazing Stories*, March 1934. Ill.

Morey.

Short story. * A gem like a cat's eye offers entry, when suitably powered by apparatus, to a fifth-dimensional universe. Jim Wyatt buys the stone from a panhandler and becomes entangled in a complex story. * To mention leading story points: Jim's scientist friend Carr helps rogue scientist Emory to open entry into the other dimension with the stone. The fifth-dimensional world is Earth-like, but is gloomy, with a fixed sun in the sky. Jim enters the other dimension, where he tries to save a young human woman from various perils. Emory, who has previously entered the fifth dimension, is power mad. Hostile semihumans in the fifth dimension try to seize the stone, which is an object of fanatical worship. Weapons include a pistol that shoots a lather that disintegrates protoplasm almost instantaneously. Jim, Carr, and the young woman, after peril, fisticuffs, and slaughter, are able to return to our world. * A mode that doesn't suit Vincent well.

1607. **REX**. *Astounding Stories*, June 1934. Ill. Dold. (Reprinted in Moskowitz, *The Coming of the Robots.*)

Short story. * *Time:* the twenty-third century. * The class struggle of a sort, obviously examining the economic structure of the day. * Humanoid in form, Rex is a robot surgeon; he is in charge of repairing damaged or inoperative robots in the highly mechanized future world. An incredibly complex mechanism, the high point of robotics (my term), he supervises the necessities of civilization with total efficiency. As a machine he has no personality. * A tiny alteration in an atomic orbit, however, changes all this. Rex develops personality and begins to think. Surreptitiously, he gathers information about the world about him, reading and watching viewers that he builds. He learns that United North America is fenced in with an impenetrable zone of force; that the nation consists of a small number of enormous unitary cities in a land otherwise abandoned and waste. Each city is stratified, with a wealthy superior class at the top, a middle class in the lower levels of the city, and the toiling robots, who may never reach the surface, in the underground levels of the city. Wealth is created by robot labor, but does not benefit the robots. * Rex conducts his investigations in secret. When he is caught by Shelby, a scientist, however, Rex turns this into advantage. Seizing Shelby and overpowering him, he operates on his brain. Discovering the seat of emotion, he removes it, turning Shelby into a passionless semi-invalid. * Rex has come to realize that robots are the superior race, but that they still lack something that humans have—the emotion center in the human brain. Rex strikes. At his command, the robots cease working, and civilization is about to fall. Summoning the leaders of United North America, Rex presents his program. All the lower class humans are to be deprived of emotion centers, which will be transferred to robots, who will now be supported by the passionless human workers. The human leaders are quite willing to accept Rex's proposal, since it will only give them more power. * But with Rex's downfall, everything returns to the previous status quo. Rex had inserted human emotion cells into himself, and when he believed that nothing had happened, in a rage, he blew himself up. The humans realize, of course, that Rex had paradoxically succeeded all too well in gaining emotion. * On one level a social metaphor with some thought, but better in idea than in story.

1608. **THE BARRIER**. *Amazing Stories*, September 1934.

Vincent, Harl (*continued*)

Short story. * Interplanetary intrigue told as an action story. * *Time:* the twenty-first century. * Pete, worried about his girlfriend Marian, tries to visit her at her job, a secluded installation in Long Island, where Professor Daniels is creating secret weapons for the government. Repelled by a force shield, he returns with his friend Bert. When they try to fly above the force zone, they are captured by men who are obviously Martians who want Daniels's new weapons. And to Pete's dismay, Marian is visibly smitten by the Martian chief, a slick false-aristocrat named Boris. * The men escape, rescue Daniels, and use his disintegrators to wipe out most of the spies. Marian, as the reader would undoubtedly guess, was playing along with Boris in order to save Professor Daniels, then, later, Pete and Bert. * Among Daniels's devices are a good disintegrator and the force screen the men encountered. The men fly an aerocab. * Martians are human, but with racial distinctions from Earthmen. * Routine at best.

1609. **COSMIC RHYTHM**. *Astounding Stories*, October 1934. Ill. Dold.

Novelette. * *Time:* around 2095. *Place:* mostly space and a planet above the planetary plane. * Since Earth and Venus are in opposition, the *Centaurianic* is taking the "outside route" above the sun, instead of following planetary orbits. This "outside route" is seldom used, and, indeed, on the previous occasion, the flight of the *Lycurgian,* the ship was lost. But officialdom has decided to take the chance of the shorter route. * The story is told mostly through the great scientist Plattner, who is a specialist in cyclical vibrations, and Tom Hurley, a burly young man who is traveling on the *Centaurianic* in the hope of finding his fiancée Lesa who was on the missing *Lycurgian.* * As the ship progresses, however, strange things are happening: the *Centaurianic* is vibrating in a strange rhythm, has left its calculated path, and is more or less out of control. Carried along by a strong interstellar current of cosmic rays, it eventually crashlands on the strange planet Dovar, which lies above the planetary plane. An exploratory party finds unexpected phenomena: Dovar was once peopled, and half-ruined buildings contain the bodies of humans in a form of suspended animation. There must be something in the thin, dry atmosphere, or otherwise present, for the castaways also find the passengers and crew of the *Lycurgian,* including Lesa, in a similar state. * But this is not all. A single Dovarian is not only awake, but speaks English, learned from the members of the previous spacewreck. He reveals a larger problem, which Plattner verifies. Dovar, which came from the planetary system of Sirius, is headed for an interplanetary collision within a matter of hours. Thus, it does not matter much whether one is awake or asleep. * The collision takes place, but it is not a catastrophe. The colliding dark body is mostly gaseous, and the collision revivifies Dovar with atmosphere and water; it also knocks Dovar down into the ecliptic plane into the orbit of Mars, but in perfect opposition to Mars. * The explanation for these strange events is Fortean. The universe is an organism of a sort, and the cosmic ray currents are creating some sort of cosmic balance and superchemical correction between various parts of the universe. * An interesting concept. The story is competent, but not superior.

1610. **ENERGY**. *Astounding Stories*, January 1935. Ill. Marchioni.

Short story. * *Time and place:* twenty-third century New York.

* The eleven great cities of United North America suffer from a growing problem, lack of energy. The extractive industries can no longer produce enough raw material, and other sources are inadequate. Thus, the quest of noted scientist Arnold Dale for a new energy source is highly important, important enough to get him an interview with Carson, the president of the energy trust. * Dale plans to create a fusion process, building up atoms of hydrogen to helium, thus liberating enormous amounts of energy. Convincing the incompetent, slothful Carson, he receives the use of a laboratory and work robots. Normally in charge of the laboratory is spinster Dorothea Haynes, who at first resents the intrusion. * Dale's work progresses, and Miss Haynes becomes drawn into the project with increasing enthusiasm. Success achieved, Dale is confronted by Carson and his associates, who realize that Dale's discovery can make them dictators of United North America. But Dale has other plans, a social clean-up, with himself as dictator. Further, as lagniappe, he and Miss Haynes discover that part of the radiation from the project has rejuvenated them and improved their general physical condition. It looks like a new era for mankind. * Routine.

1611. **VALLEY OF THE RUKH**. *Amazing Stories,* February 1935. Ill. Morey.

Short story. * *Place:* Arizona, with short episodes on Venus. * Stanley Kent, airline pilot; Ruth Owens, spoiled young authoress in search of atmosphere; and her guide, slippery Pedro Martinez, all find themselves unexpectedly in a green land where the Painted Desert should be. A lush area, filled with strange plants, with enormous predatory reptiles, a gigantic bird equivalent to the roc of Sindbad's adventure, and a certain strange psychic urge—it might be a piece from another planet—as it really is. It is a segment of Venus of the remote past transferred in a major psychological experiment conducted from Venus. Also present is the Venusian scientist-philosopher Quor, the possessor of many strange abilities. * Quor, who is totally human, saves the humans from attack from kangaroo-like submen and from the incredibly vicious fauna. In part he uses mental power that creates a feeling of friendship and good will, and in part he has a weapon that looks like a blowpipe, but is really an enormously complex electronic weapon. * Involved are will combats with an evil presence that Quor, Kent, and Owens defeat. * When the adventure is over, Martinez, who has shown his evil side, is dead; the evil potency of the area is destroyed; Quor and Owens have gone together as lovers to Venus; and Kent is left alone, wondering about it all. * Much more interesting than Vincent's staider stories, with the appeal lying more in the atmosphere of the story than the events.

1612. **PROWLER OF THE WASTELANDS**. *Astounding Stories,* April 1935. Ill. Marchioni.

(Reprinted in Elwood and Moskowitz, *Strange Signposts.*)

Short story. * *Time:* the twenty-third century. * *Place:* the New York City area. * The story is told through the prowler, a 150-pound beast of prey who is the result of genetic engineering aimed at creating superpets for a blasé, overrich clientele. His genome includes human genes. Intelligent, capable of adjusting to human society, he has nevertheless lived in the wilderness since his mother escaped some years earlier. * The wanderer comes into contact with civilization and is returned to his breeder, who enhances his abilities by psychological and surgical means. For a time the wanderer, as Miracle, a superintelligent animal, performs on the stage in an animal act with the

Vincent, Harl (*continued*)

performer Lolita, whom he likes; but when a millionairess offers Rosso, his breeder and legal owner, three million dollars for him, it seems as if Lolita and Miracle will be separated, something that Lolita cannot accept. * When Lolita tries to steal him, Miracle takes thought. It would be better for himself and Lolita if he returned to the wilderness. He does so. * Unusual for Vincent. * A sequel, "Return of the Prowler," appeared in the November 1938 issue of *Astounding Stories*, beyond the scope of this study.

1613. **THE PLANE COMPASS.** *Astounding Stories,* June 1935. Ill. Dold.

Short story. * *Time:* probably 1995. * Hannishaw, almost universally regarded as the world's greatest scientist in both pure research and application, is really something of a humbug who steals the ideas of his more creative subordinates at the great laboratory. At the moment he is engaged in stealing the cosmological theories of brilliant young Bill Sherwood. * According to Sherwood's new system, light has infinite speed and permeates a succession of universes that constitute a superuniverse. Individual universes occur something like the nodes on a sine wave. There is also an infinite number of dimensions in the superuniverse, distributed according to subuniverse, with corresponding atomic structures. * Sherwood's ideas are apparently easily adapted to apparatus, permitting entry to other universes. Together Hannishaw and Sherwood construct suitable equipment, eventually sending small animals back and forth. * Another factor besides greed and vanity motivates Hannishaw; although not a young man, he has become infatuated with his secretary, Cora, who is Sherwood's girlfriend. The older man now plans to remove Sherwood by using faulty equipment to send him permanently into another universe. * His elaborate scheme does not work out. Cora is aware of his plans and sets a trap, even though Hannishaw drops her and Sherwood into another world. They are retrieved, and Hannishaw is accidentally killed. * Good exposition, but a rather flimsy denouement.

1614. **PARASITE.** *Amazing Stories,* July 1935. Ill. Morey.

Novelette. * *Time:* 1955. *Place:* New Jersey, New York. * An anticipation of Heinlein's *The Puppet Masters.* * *Background:* When the humanoid beings in a system about twelve light-years away learned that life would no longer be possible on their planet, they converted a small group of their leaders into conscious beings formed of electricity. They then altered the remainder of the population into small seed-like germs that could be reanimated at the proper occasion. The aliens then inserted electric beings and germs into a small metal sphere and sent it across space to Earth, which they knew from their advanced science would be suitable for them. * When the space vessel crashes as a meteorite in northern New Jersey, it releases the thirty-four electrical beings, who seize upon suitable humans as carriers. Invisible, since they are pure force, the aliens fasten upon the back of a human's neck and are absorbed into the human nervous system, imparting enormous strength and vitality. The human carriers are conscious, do not suffer any pain, but are no longer in control. The leaders of the migration, suitably housed, now are ready to awaken their fellows and let them loose upon humanity. * This is the problem that faces Bert Garrison and Wayne Gordon, amateur scientists of considerable

standing and skill. Some time passes before the authorities recognize the gravity of the situation, and even then the nature of the invaders is not understood. Conventional attacks on the headquarters of the aliens are no avail, for the aliens have potent paralysis rays and other weapons. The situation looks bad, for the invaders are beginning to increase their territory. * Resolution comes from two sources. One of the carriers has a partial immunity because of a silver plate in his head. When the invaders expel him, he can provide information. More important, Oa, an invader female, has compassion for the humans and gives Garrison instructions about a radiation lethal to her fellows. While Garrison was working in the right direction, her information speeds up matters considerably. The invaders perish. * Not a bad story, but Heinlein's is better.

VINCENT, HARL and COX, CHARLES ROY

Vincent has a separate entry. Cox (1899-?) was an Ohio author possibly in the employ of the American Book Company. Cox also compiled a crossword dictionary.

1615. **SKY COPS.** *Amazing Stories,* December 1931. Ill. Morey.

Short story. * *Time:* the interplanetary future. *Place:* mostly space. * Sgt. Mike Dooley of the Interplanetary Police, a hard-bitten, intensely loyal spaceman, has a perpetual gripe: that he hasn't received the promotions he believes he is entitled to. * On the present occasion he is assigned to accompany Captain Brown to capture the space pirate and smuggler Rolenski, whose ship has been observed in the Arizona desert. * But there is something fishy going on. Mike sees Captain Brown take a huge bribe from Rolenski, which Brown offers to share. Mike is outraged at this betrayal of trust, and in a wild free-for-all, captures Rolenski, places the captain under arrest and proceeds home. * Along the way he sees a spaceship under attack by the milky monster of space, a gigantic amoeboid creature that not only flourishes tentacles, but emits a deadly radiation. Thanks to Mike's skill with disintegrator rays, both his ship and the other escape—a rare occurrence for those who encounter the monster. The other ship turns out to be Rolenski's major ship. * There is a final showdown and unmasking, and Vincent and Cox reveal what the reader has suspected all along. The man Dooley assaulted and captured as Rolenski was really a high police official; this person and Captain Brown were simply testing Dooley's honesty before giving him a high promotion. The real Rolenski is captured. * *Miscellaneous:* Antigravity screens make space travel possible. * Police subheadquarters are on a space station ninety-five thousand miles away from the Earth. * To a present-day reader Dooley's temptation sounds like entrapment. As can be seen, apart from the space monster, a story that could have appeared in any of the crime pulps.

[Anonymous]

Presumably a British writer.

1616. **VOICE FROM THE VOID.** *Scoops,* 10 February-28 April 1934. Unsigned ill.

Boys' fiction. * Short episodic novel or nouvelle, a juvenile version of an adult espionage and international skulduggery thriller. * *Place:* England, France, Arabia. * The central character is young Jimmy Drayton, nephew of War Minister Lord Broadwater. Jimmy, who is obviously modelled on the Wodehouse silly-ass syndrome, is not quite as foolish as he

"Voice from the Void" (*continued*)
sometimes seems, and, despite mannerisms, is able to act intelligently and decisively. * *Background:* An international quinvirate headed by the German Broggerman, including an Italian, a Frenchman, an Englishman, and an American, is determined to start a world war in order to increase their profits. With this aim they undertake various despicable acts, including the attempted assassination of King Karl (or Michael, the author seems undecided) of Karania. * *Second background:* There have been mysterious sightings of a ghost ship—glowing, rapidly disappearing—and a blasting voice from the sky that makes oracular comments seemingly based on a vision of what is happening—which is impossible. It annoys the capitalist warmongers with its heckling. When young Jimmy, urged to get a job, approaches Broadwater for a secret service assignment, Broadwater requests him to go to the Rochester area and solve the mystery of the phantom ship. * The connections among these phenomena lead Jimmy and Bilks, a Cockney associate, to Paris, to Arabia (where Jimmy is captured as a lever against Broadwater), and back. Along the way there are plenty of spilled blood, captivities, escapes, broolies, etc. Virtue triumphs. * As for the seemingly supernatural effects, the phantom ship is a mothball vessel painted with phosphorus; the voice from the void is operated by a crippled war hero inside the vessel, with a remarkable radio device that can pick up and produce sound at great distances. * Unusual among British boys' fiction, which is usually jingoistic, in being avowedly pacifist in orientation. It is, of course, nationalistic.

VON DREY, HOWARD
Pseud. of Howard Elmer Wandrei (1909-1956). U.S. (mostly Minnesota) author, artist. Brother of the better-known Donald Wandrei. Resident for much of this period in New York City. See also other pseuds. Howard D. Graham and H. W. Guernsey. More biographical information is given under Graham.

1617. **THE GOD BOX.** *Astounding Stories,* April 1934. Ill. Charles Durant.
(Reprinted in Howard Wandrei, *Time Burial,* and in Derleth, *Strange Ports of Call.*)
Short story. * More a science-fantasy than pure science-fiction. * Amateur Egyptologist Pence finds the box. A small, sealed rectangular object about the size of a cigar box; it is apparently of Ancient Egyptian provenience, with small heads of the gods on its upper surface. Oddly enough, despite its small size it must weigh about a ton. * Pence enlists the aid of Thorn, a research engineer, and together the two men study it. They discover that when activated by electric current, it expands (or is projected) into a large cube of impenetrable light that permits far vision, matter transmission, and crushing attack. * With the god box the two men engage in various experiences that edge onto pranks: shifting boats from the Bay of Naples to New York City harbor, and vice versa. Indeed, the possibilities of the cube seem endless, but the men are no closer to its origin or its mode of operation than when they began. * By accident, after Pence has tried to murder Thorn, the controls are jiggled and the men find themselves inside the cube of light, where they envision the cube creators or their descendants—an Egyptian-like people in a land governed by two suns. The cube rushes off into the sky in the direction of Vega. * The implication is that the god box originally was used as space transport from a planet circling

Vega, which was perhaps the origin of human life. * *Miscellaneous:* The device attracts cats, which swarm about it. * A curious story that reads as if it were written entirely extemporaneously.

WAGENER, SIEGFRIED
No information.

1618. **THE COSMIC COCKTAIL.** *Wonder Stories,* April 1936. Ill. Winter.
Short story. * Probably intended as humor. * Young scientist Edwin McCall has determined that the radiation from heavenly bodies really affects human behavior in various large ways. But when he presents his theories at a learned congress, he is laughed out of the hall, notably by the president, Dr. Waldorff-Palmer, who happens to be the father of McCall's sweetheart Eleanor. * McCall decides, with Eleanor's more or less passive approval, to work upon Waldorff-Palmer with various types of stellar radiation, both as revenge and as proof of his theory. He rents an empty house across from Waldorff-Palmer's and from it bombards the old man with assorted radiation, almost driving him mad. After a time, when Eleanor cannot tolerate the sadistic play any longer, McCall reveals what he has been doing and converts Waldorff-Palmer. * A bad story, often semiliterate in expression.

WAIT, ROBERT A.
U.S. (Illinois) educator, chemist. Then resident in Decatur, Illinois. Instructor in chemistry at James Millikin University. Later research director of Irwin, Neisler in Decatur.

1619. **THE INVISIBLE FINITE.** *Amazing Stories,* May 1929. Ill. Paul.
Short story. * Old Professor Moore is greatly interested in the question of invisibility. In discussion with his student assistants Murphy and Manoras, he describes two forms: that achieved by rapid motion, as with the spokes of a revolving bicycle wheel, and that achieved by division of matter into molecular units, as with a gas. The second type theoretically could also be attained, in part, by metallic sprays. * It is Moore's hope to combine elements of both types of invisibility (elongating molecular chains and breaking molecular masses) into a single working method. He succeeds, but in a moment of carelessness ventures under his machine and vanishes. * In frustrated rage, Manoras destroys the machine. Moore's voice is then heard. He is not dead, but has been changed to a different form of matter. If the machine were still in existence, he could be retrieved, but now he will soon pass into a new phase of existence. * Such happens. * A simple plot, but very heavily laden with scientific and pseudoscientific exposition. The logical connection between invisibility and disappearance is weak.

1620. **CLAVILUX,** *Amazing Stories,* June 1929. Ill. Clardy.
Short-short story. * M. Du Bois, noted French musician, is giving a concert on the clavilux, a keyboard color organ that projects color combinations on a screen. (No sound is involved.) With it he first entertains the audience with merry combinations, then depresses and terrifies them with deep emotional combinations. Then he announces that he will try to attain very low notes. The result is the production of heat. The apparatus short circuits, there is a fire, and Du Bois collapses. A newspaper

Wait, Robert A. (*continued*)

article, however, blames the fire on defective electrical wiring.

1621. **LANTERNS OF GOD**. *Amazing Stories*, March 1930. Ill. Morey.

Short story. * The brilliant young inventor Carl Brown is quarreling with his fiancée, Georgia Hemway. She refuses to marry him unless he gives up his grandiose plans and settles down to providing a home. * What Carl wants to do is very ambitious: He wants to convert the Earth's kinetic energy into potential energy so that he can move the Earth out of its orbit and explore the solar system. As Georgia points out, he is indifferent to the damage such a procedure would cause. * Finally, Carl delivers an ultimatum: Unless Georgia agrees that evening to set a marriage date, he will turn on the machine, come what will. Georgia goes home, reads a little, but does not yield. * Strange things now happen: A new star passes near the solar system, and observations reveal that it is moving faster than light. The Earth, cut off from the sun's gravity by Carl's invention, follows the new star, called the Thief, into space. * At first the results are catastrophic, but as the Earth draws closer to its captor, conditions return almost to normal. But the Thief, moving at many times the speed of light, leaves our galaxy. After years in intergalactic space, the star and Earth approach another galaxy, where the Thief is dissipated in a collision with other stars. The Earth is free again, and Carl, now happily married to Georgia and recognized as the greatest genius on Earth, directs the Earth toward a multiple star group that he calls the Lanterns of God. There are other planets in the system, and on the suitable occasion, as Georgia watches, a strange, beautiful spaceship lands. When Carl and others enter it, it flies away. * But then Georgia awakens. It was all a dream. A phone call from Carl reveals that his apparatus short circuited. By now repentant, Carl agrees to concentrate on practical inventions, and Georgia agrees to marry him. * Large gobbets of technical information, rather disorganized narration. Perhaps best considered an unsuccessful scientific fairy tale.

1622. **COSMIC STEEPLE-CHASE**. *Amazing Stories*, April 1932. Ill. Morey.

Long novelette. * *Place:* The Earth, interstellar space, and a planet orbiting one of the components of Polaris. * The equivalent of Hairbreadth Harry and Rudolph Rassendale in space. * There is a thud in the back pasture, mysterious lights and explosions, and there it is, a cracked-up spaceship! Brilliant young astronomer Jameson and associates pry open the ship and find, in addition to a few dead bodies, a wealth of cultural material, including many, many documents—with what looks like a key for understanding them. * Some months later, a solution is reached. The spaceship came from a planet revolving around one of Polaris's components, and the builders thoughtfully enclosed a full set of plans so that a duplicate spaceship can be built. The documents also include an invitation to an interstellar conference or assembly at Polaris's planet. As Jameson informs the others later, it is possible to travel to Polaris in about a year, at several times the speed of light, for modern theoretical physics is wrong about such matters. * At about this point, personalities enter. Jameson chastely loves beautiful Alice Baldwin, daughter of the owner of the farm on which the spaceship crashed. She reciprocates. But there is a villain, young Bellant, a brilliant physicist who lusts for Alice, and, in addition to periodically assaulting her, repeatedly demands her favors. He may be repulsed, beaten, ostracized, jailed, but he keeps returning, but not for more, since he never gets any. Bellant blackmails his way onto the spaceship, and all set forth. * The trip to Polaris is uneventful, except that a vessel from Pluto intercepts them, stating that it alone can represent the solar system. When the Plutonian vessel leaves, unfortunately, it takes along with it Bellant and the captive Alice. * The party continues on to the proper planet, makes acquaintances, and witnesses the awesome superscience of the world. An interstellar conference is about to take place, and the humans, again, are overawed at the superiority of most of the other attendees, animal, vegetable, and mineral. In the meanwhile, the Polarian police have arrested the Plutonians and taken Bellant (who is put into a rehabilitation unit) and Alice. * It is time to return to the solar system, and the party sets out, Bellant as usual working solitarily in his laboratory. Elan, a Polarian, accompanies the party. Being perfectly human, Elan, too, is in love with Alice, but honorably. The Polarian shows the Terrestrials how to use suspended animation, thus avoiding the tedium of long-term travel. Alice, for one, is put under. As the explorers near Earth, Bellant's lust once again becomes uncontrollable. Seizing the sleeping Alice, he escapes onto the captive Plutonian vessel, which had been brought along, and flees. To annoy Jameson and Elan, Bellant shows them via vision screen what he will do after he revives Alice with an injection. The needle descends—and the spaceship blows up, ending Bellant and Alice. * No, not really. Elan now reveals what he has been surreptitiously doing. With Polarian superscience, he has grown a mindless android clone (my term) of Alice, which Bellant kidnapped instead of the real Alice. The dummy Alice was stuffed with explosives set to go off when Bellant injected the awakening drug. * One of those strange stories, sometimes encountered in the pulps, that are so bad that one wonders whether they are meant to be parodies. Probably not. The concept of cloning, though it is not expressed in cellular terms, seems to be new.

WALKER, DERALD S.

According to Schwartz/Weisinger, the pseud. of W. Dubenpeck, about whom there is no information.

1623. **THE PHYTIC EMPIRE**. *Amazing Stories*, June 1935. Ill. Morey.

Short story. * *Time:* 1948 following. * *Place:* mostly New Mexico and Brazil. * The story, although written by an intelligent man with some background in botany, is so confused that the following statement is offered with diffidence. * The reporter narrator reminisces about his friends, especially botanist Paul Dwight, who has been doing pioneer work on the compatibility of plant parasites and their hosts. Dwight and his wife have disappeared, and his laboratory in New Mexico has burned down. * A year or two later, fungous plagues destroy much of the world's food supply. But these are not ordinary fungi. In some fashion (the author is not clear about this) they are related to underground growths that extend for enormous distances. Tracking down such "rays" locates "epicenters" in New Mexico and elsewhere. * Then the narrator receives a message in a bottle from Dwight. He and his wife are captive in Western Brazil, where a band of criminals is responsible for the plant plagues. The narrator flies to Brazil, and after a shootout rescues the Dwights. * No explanation is given for the criminals' actions or methods. * Below routine.

WALLIS, B[RUCE] and WALLIS, GEO[RGE] C.

Bruce Wallis, who was resident in British Columbia, Canada, in the early 1930s, claimed to have been a seaman on sailing ships in his youth. He was an occasional contributor to the British variety and American pulp magazines in the first third of the century. His cousin George Wallis (1871-1956), resident mostly in the Midlands, England, was originally a printer by occupation, then a motion picture exhibitor and manager. He contributed fiction from 1901 to 1941 to the British variety magazines, and occasionally to the American pulps. George Wallis is the more important writer of the two, with, for example, "The Great Sacrifice," (*Harmsworth's Magazine*, 1903), which postulated a twenty-million-year cometary extinction cycle for the Earth. * Tuck considers B. Wallis to have been merely an agent of sorts for George Wallis, but this seems unlikely.

1624. **THE WORLD AT BAY.** *Amazing Stories*, November-December 1928. Ill. Paul.

Short novel of emergence in the mode of Edward Hamilton. * *Time:* 1936. *Place:* mostly Brazil, regions underneath it, and England. * When the first reports of the destruction of Rio de Janeiro come in, there is general incredulity. Max Harding, star newspaper reporter, is among the first to know and to witness the horrors. Short, pasty-faced men have flown over the city and discharged clouds of poisonous gas that is not only almost instantly fatal, but mummifies the bodies of those affected. * Military response to the strange aircraft is not too effective, for plane engines die when they approach the enemy craft, and clouds of the irresistible gas kill troops. * Harding, after witnessing the huge hole in the jungle from which the strange craft emerge, attempts to escape from the danger region, but he and friends (including Rita Courtney) are captured in huge nets suspended from the alien aircraft and taken down the hole into a cavern world. * There they learn that they are slaves captured to work in the radioactive mines from which the Troglodytes (as the author terms them) extract their lethal gas. Life expectancy in the mines is not great. * An unusual feature of the author's presentation of slave life is his development of organizational aspects, in which Harding and friends (who have more skill than the other captives in using the Trog language) serve as administrators and contact people. This is reminiscent of such organizations in a POW camp. * Harding et al. determine to escape, and with some aid from a friendly Trog eventually stow away on an airship headed for the surface. Harding and Rita parachute off, landing in Sydney. Here they learn that the Trogs have continued their advance, with damage in New Zealand and Australia, and the destruction of Chicago and Baltimore. * It is now clear what the Trogs want: Being utterly pragmatic people, they want slaves, and such destruction as they accomplish is either unavoidable or for scare purposes. * Back in London, Harding works out an idea he had for neutralizing the Trog gas and paralysis rays; this is a sort of radio emission. With Harding's apparatus the Trog advances are finally stopped. * But all concerned feel that an invasion of the underworld is necessary, both to obtain leverage for negotiating a peace and to rescue the slaves. Rita and Harding descend in a captured Trog flying machine, are recaptured, but, taking the Trog ruler prisoner, bluff their way out again. The Trog ruler, who is not unreasonable, agrees to a peace in which the Trogs would withdraw, pay enormous reparations in radium, and teach the surface people advanced technology, but the Trog elders, who will not

accept these terms, blow up the entrance, sealing off the underground world. * The consensus on the surface is that the Trogs will not emerge again, since they used most of their atomic explosive to make their first exit. They will probably die out. * *Miscellaneous:* The Trogs have a paralysis ray and a one-shot atomic disintegrating pistol. * Their aircraft, which are much superior to surface craft, have radium motors. * The Trog world is rich in radioactive materials. * Underground lighting is provided by artificial phosphorescence. * There is also a romantic triangle among Harding, Rita (who is a very masterful woman), and Rixton, the underground slave leader. * Too short to be a novel; too long for the material included. Routine pulp competence, although the dashing about gets confusing at times.

1625. **THE MOTHER WORLD.** *Amazing Stories Quarterly*, Spring/Summer 1933. Ill. Morey.

Novelette. * *Place:* space and the planet of an unidentified star about one hundred light-years away. * The British maverick scientist Austin Locke has been puttering for years in his backyard laboratory, but most of his friends do not take him seriously. * At the house party are assembled Locke, the narrator (Mark Arden, incipient barrister), Professor Chalcote (friendly enemy, frustrated rival in ancient love), Locke's daughter Edith (Mark's chilly flame), and others who do not matter. * When Locke boasts that he has finally achieved his goal, space travel faster than light, the others scoff. Locke explains: By distorting atomic particles he can dissociate his vessel from the universe; his ship stands still, while the universe revolves rapidly beneath it—comparable to standing still in a balloon while the Earth revolves. * After enduring more scoffing, Locke displays the space sphere he has built in his laboratory. All crowd into the sphere, whereupon Chalcote meddles with the controls, and they are off. Despite the fact that their flight is practically uncontrollable, that Locke has no way of returning to Earth, that their supplies are limited, that the women have only the evening clothes on (or not on) their backs, all accept the situation with stiff upper lips and British aplomb. * After several months, as supplies are about to run out, they draw near a star with planets, and Locke takes the desperate chance of stopping the vessel and landing. (It is later revealed that he had little to do with this.) * The involuntary pilgrims are now shipwrecked on a small desert island on a planet much like Earth. But there is a metal tower with reflectors, and in a short time a flying machine appears. A handsome man floats down by mental control of gravity, takes the Britons into his ship and to a city on the planet of Ethmar. * First background: Ethmar is far more advanced scientifically than Earth, with atomic power in general use. Space travel is frequent to all parts of the galaxy, perhaps of the universe, using Locke's principle. Viewing apparatus is incredibly sophisticated, permitting examination of worlds around the cosmos. Indeed, Ethmarian viewing apparatus sighted Locke's vessel as it left Earth and really drew it to Ethmar safely. Ethmarian culture is so high that peoples from other planets voluntarily come to Ethmar and do terms of service and apprenticeship. The duodecimal system is in use. Chemistry is incredibly high, with synthetic food. * Socially, Ethmar is an utterly altruistic world, with everyone instinctively and intuitively doing what is right and best. As a result there are no wars or poverty. The economy is inexplicable, as Mark admits. The institution of formal marriage does not exist, but there is a eugenics program that is rigid and rigorous. * The Terrestrials

Wallis, B. and Wallis, Geo. C. (*continued*)

are welcomed, and to make things easier are subjected to a sleep-hypnosis that teaches them the language in a few hours. * The travelers establish friendly relations with the man who first rescued them, whom they call Zeus, and a beautiful young woman named Errangia. The result is the formation of ungratified triangles: Errangia is in love with Mark, whom she propositions in vain; Locke and Chalcote are both in love with Errangia, who obviously does not respond. * Second background: Despite the eutopian aspects of Ethmarian culture, there is another, less pleasant side. Although the Ethmarians are utterly just, the quality of mercy is lacking among them, and there is little room for emotion in the utilitarian rationalistic culture. There has been and is (in a very slight way) an underground that would like to bring romance and emotion back into life, but it is strongly censured. Part of the rational code is that if one is dissatisfied with life or incurably ill, one may take a small spaceship whose controls are set on an endless path and leave, to die in space. * A further surprise comes when the Terrestrials learn that the Ethmarians (whose remote ancestors came from another galaxy) have been systematically colonizing the cosmos. Indeed, the human race on Earth (and also on Mars) is descended from such a colony, the appearances of evolution being simply animal modification toward a human figuration. Further, Earth and Mars were colonized, as a deliberate experiment, with early members of the romance-seeking underground, whence the differences between Terrestrial (and Martian) culture and that of Ethmar. * And, the clincher, Ethmar keeps a close eye on its colonies, and if it considers that they have strayed too far from the right path, disintegrates their solar system. * And, the superclincher, Earth and Mars have come up for recent evaluation, have flunked, and the solar system is due to be disintegrated at any moment. * Resolutions: The Ethmarian council, after pleas from the Terrestrials and secret members of the underground, decides to give the Earth a fifty-year suspended sentence and will send the explorers back to Earth, where they can try to awaken the multitudes to the sinfulness of their ways. * Further problems and resolutions: Locke will not return to Earth without Errangia, which sets up a dilemma. Chalcote wants Errangia, but reveals that he has learned enough Ethmarian science that if he returns to Earth, he will reply to Ethmarian aggression with a countercontract against Ethmar. The Council tried to brainwash him, but his will was too strong, and it failed. * Resolution: Errangia and Chalcote both commit suicide via the spaceship route. The Council puts the remaining Terrestrials on board a vessel and ships them back to Earth, but withdraws all evidence of their adventure. The voyagers have landed in Australia and are ready to start their missionary work. * Some imagination, but somewhat on the naive side. Apparently the first story of colonized ancient galactic man.

WALSH, J[AMES] M[ORGAN] (1897-1952)

Australian/British author born in Victoria, Australia. Educated at Xavier College, Melbourne. Moved to England in 1929, where remained for most of his adult life. Very prolific author of mystery novels, Hubin listing eighty-five books under the name Walsh and pseuds. H. Haverstock Hill, Stephen Maddock, and George M. White. His mysteries have received little attention in America, and he now seems forgotten. Walsh was one of the very few British authors of popular fiction who suc-

cessfully made the transition to American science-fiction. See also H. Haverstock Hill, pseud.

1626. **VANDALS OF THE VOID.** *Wonder Stories Quarterly*, Summer 1931. Ill. Paul.
(Printed in book form by Hamilton, London, 1931. Also translated into French as *Les corsaires du vide*, Hachette, Paris, 1951.)
Novel. * *Time:* perhaps late twenty-first century. *Place:* mostly space between Earth and Mars. * *Background:* This is the interplanetary future, with space travel common between Earth, Venus, and Mars. World governments exist on each of the planets, with peace and cordiality among the three worlds. Both Venus and Mars are inhabited by humanoid peoples who differ very little from Earthmen; indeed, intermarriage is not uncommon, and such marriages are fertile. * The Martians, who have an older civilization, are scientifically somewhat more advanced than Earth or Venus, but the difference is not great. Space itself is patrolled by the I.P.G., a police organization that can assume command in case of emergency. * Captain Sanders of the I.P.G. is traveling on vacation to Mars on the spaceship *Cosmos* when he receives secret emergency orders. Some force or agency is attacking merchant ships, freezing the crew and passengers and boarding the ships. Indeed, not long after the report comes in, the *Cosmos* comes upon such a ship. * The situation is puzzling. The passengers and crew are in a sort of suspended animation; the ship is abnormally cold; and, judging from an impression one passenger received before becoming unconscious, the phenomenon of invisibility may be involved. * The *Cosmos* continues on its route, while Sanders indulges in a romance with Jansca, a young Martian woman of high rank; this results in an engagement. * But then the *Cosmos* itself is attacked by the strange raiders. Thanks to the chance that Sanders and Jansca had taken a certain Martian stimulant not long before, they remain awake when the raiders enter. The raiders are indeed invisible, as is their ship. During a surprise shoot-out, Sanders repels the pirates and sees their ship explode. The corpses on the floor are of unknown race, probably from Mercury, which has not yet been explored. * War now suddenly breaks out. Mercurian spaceships attack patrol vessels and merchant ships, and Venus comes under severe attack. By now a Venusian scientist has worked out the principle of invisibility (which is vibratory), so that it will no longer be a weapon against the patrol; an atomic ray that amounts to a colossal disintegrator has also been readied. * Sanders takes command of the newly armed *Cosmos* and with vibratory weapons, heat rays, and disintegrator flies to Venus, where he takes part in the attack on the Mercurian secret bases. The Mercurians are beaten, and the menace is over. * *Miscellaneous:* The Martians, in addition to the remarkable stimulant, have a pocket-sized super-X-ray apparatus; both are secret, since the Martians have a strong sense of cultural privacy. * The Mercurians have a head crest that distinguishes them from the other races of the solar system. For some time they have been infiltrating the solar system in disguise. Since Mercury is inhospitable, they hoped to conquer Venus and move there en masse. * Starts out moderately well, but soon degenerates into a dreary, prolonged, muddled bore. * For a sequel see #1627, "The Struggle for Pallas."

1627. **THE STRUGGLE FOR PALLAS.** *Wonder Stories Quarterly*, Fall 1931. Ill. Marchioni.
Short story. * A sequel to #1626, "Vandals of the Void." *Time:*

Walsh, J. M. (*continued*)

perhaps the late twenty-first century. *Place:* mostly Pallas. * Sanders, now settled in with his Martian wife and family, is called to duty for an emergency on Pallas, which has been settled by Reversionist Earthmen, the violent individualists who cannot conform to civilization. Now, instead of normal communication with Pallas, there are only strange sounds and suggestions of trouble. * Sanders soon learns what is wrong when he visits Pallas. The asteroid is overrun with intelligent monsters: creatures with scales, wings, claws, and vicious disposition. They are apparently the result of fossil eggs (dating from a time when Pallas supported native life) that hatched after Pallas was terraformed by Earth. * Fighting them is difficult, for heat rays have little effect on them and atomic disintegrators cannot be used under the circumstances. The creatures have learned how to use weapons, and, indeed, have even floated and manned a wrecked Martian spaceship. When the atomic ray destroys the spaceship, however, this is the downfall of the monsters, who are almost exterminated. * Routine work.

    1628. **AFTER 1,000,000 YEARS.** *Wonder Stories*, October 1931. Ill. Marchioni.

Short story. * *Time:* 1935 and about a million years in the future. * John Harling, a British estate broker, is hiking in the countryside when he sees a strange machine crash-land near him. From it emerges a handsome young woman who asks him what the year is. She expresses great concern when he replies 1935, and indicates that she is fifty years off her mark. The young woman, whose name is Leela Zenken, and Harling converse, and after a time she tells her story. * She is from the far future, and has come on a quest. In her time, solar radiation is being hindered by a cosmic cloud of vast extent, and her race is perishing from cold. Combing the literature of the past for evidence of atomic energy, which would save the race, the future scientists settled on 1985 as an almost certain date. Building a time machine they sent Leela to find the secret of the process, but there was a miscalculation and she arrived too early. * Leela repairs her damaged machine, and with Harling sets out again for 1985, but something goes wrong. Perhaps her machine was more damaged than she thought; in any case, the machine returns to Leela's time in the far future. Leela's quest must have failed, for corpses are strewn all over in frozen rooms. * Depressed, the two come back to the twentieth century, where they marry and settle down. In reminiscing, Harling now reveals something that he hid from Leela: It is possible that some of the future people were in suspended animation. Perhaps he and Leela will return to the future, one hundred years later than their previous visit, to investigate. * *Miscellaneous:* Walsh stresses the concept that there is a duration balance between eras in time traveling; thus, if one spends five days in the future, one will return to one's own time five days later than the start. * Competent pulp work, although Walsh's aperçu about time balancing, which he advances to evade certain paradoxes, is not very convincing.

    1629. **THE VANGUARD TO NEPTUNE.** *Wonder Stories Quarterly*, Spring 1932. Ill. Paul.

(Reprinted in book form by Cherry Tree, London, 1952.)

Novel. * *Time:* A.D. 2235. *Place:* space and Neptune. * In the twenty-third century the three inner planets are united in a confederacy headed by a council. Space travel is common and relatively safe, with the space lanes patrolled by ships of the Interplanetary Guards. The economy, however, seems to be runaway capitalism, with robber barons eager to exploit whatever can be exploited; corruption, pull, and substandard product seem omnipresent. * Thus, Phil Grayne, communications officer of the interplanetary passenger vessel *Sirius*, is not pleased when he learns that he has been assigned a trainee with connections; he knows all too well that when the trainee, who is capable in book learning, learns the practical aspects of the position, he (Grayne) may be fired. Nor is he happy that Paula, the daughter of the ruthless tycoon Jens Fontaine, is on board the ship and not unwilling to use her power for special treatment. * Fate, however, changes matters. The *Sirius* runs into a meteor swarm and is destroyed, only Phil and Paula survive. By chance they were in the navigation module, which survives intact. Donning space suits they await rescue or death. During this time Paula shows a different aspect, and they come to an emotional understanding. * At the point of death they are rescued by a government-sponsored scientific expedition to Neptune. The expedition, which is the first to go beyond the inner planets, is intended to forestall the commercial exploiters and is supposed to be secret, but ill-wishers, notably Fontaine, have worked some mischief. After some hesitation, the leaders of the expedition accept the good faith of Phil and Paula and enroll them. * The first peril comes when the *Icarus* is almost seized by the gravity of Jupiter; it escapes only by invoking the gravitational pull of one of Jupiter's satellites. * The second peril comes when the expedition lands on Triton, which is a frozen world. Seeing what seems to be an ancient building under the ice, the explorers thaw it out, but to their horror they have released myriads of extremely hostile, intelligent, slug-like beings. An oddity about the slug beings is that they throw canisters of poison gas—which happens to be ordinary air to the humans. * Descending to Neptune, the explorers find an Earth-like planet with passable atmosphere and gravity slightly less than Earth's. The land is cultivated, and the expedition soon encounters the Neptunians, humanoid creatures about four feet tall who ride about in tall, bird-like walking machines. These people are friendly. Although their science is on the whole much below that of the inner planets, they do have remarkable condensers and reëmitters of solar light. * After acquaintance has been struck, the Neptunians take the Earthmen (and woman) to Gark, an enormous brain maintained mechanically, the master (in a vague sort of way) of the planet. An evolutionary development extinct except for this one being, he possesses an incredible intellect, but his mechanical apparatus no longer functions properly, and he is aged. While he still can operate with past data, he can no longer work well with present data or work out predictions. As he calmly states, he will soon perish, as will the Neptunians, who are languid, debilitated, and ineffectual. * The humanoids, however, are not entirely the dominant race on Neptune. There are enormous, intelligent, very vicious, bird-like creatures, who are powerful enough to lift and endanger the *Icarus* with their sharp, hard claws. They are finally disposed of with heat rays. * A greater peril comes when a small polyhedral spaceship lands not too far away. While some of the crew of the *Icarus* is visiting the great brain, the others are captured by the strangers, who impose over the area a black fog that cuts off light and electricity. * When checking the *Icarus*, the remaining members of the expedition capture one of the invaders. It is a tiny spindly creature, vaguely humanoid in form. To summarize what is gradually learned later: The invaders are plant beings with

Walsh, J. M. (*continued*)

chlorophyll blood. Either they do not originate in our solar system or they come from outer planets as yet unknown, but they have occasionally visited Neptune before. Regarded with horror by the Neptunians, they are so alien in mentality that it is impossible to communicate with them. * After some commotion back and forth, the captives are rescued; the polyhedron and the *Icarus* jockey back and forth against each other in air battle, without any real advantage to either. The polyhedron is faster and navigates better, but the *Icarus* is sturdier. The battle ends in a stalemate. * Against the gigantic birds, however, the polyhedron fares worse. The birds' talons pierce the outer metal, and the vessel is wrecked. The members of the expedition decide to help the plant men in order to establish good will. They nurse the injured as well as they can, and they repair the polyhedron with native metals. But their intentions are not appreciated, for the invaders make off with both the repaired polyhedron and the *Icarus*, leaving the Earth people temporarily paralyzed and stranded on Neptune. It seems that there were other plant men hidden on the *Icarus* who were not found. Undaunted, the castaways build a radio and send out signals, although they are not hopeful that the signals will be received. They also start to build a new spaceship, a task for which they have neither the skills or materials. * Salvation comes. A vessel of the Interplanetary Guard rescues them. Grayne and Paula, who have been carrying on a romance, will marry on Earth. Paula has turned out to be more liberal than anticipated and does have some control over her swinish father. * *Miscellaneous:* Space travel involves antigravity and rocket tubes. * The Earthmen carry small heat ray pistols. * Neptune is riddled with valuable ores and minerals. A most useful mineral occurs underground in liquid form, but solidifies in air, becoming hard and tough. * The plant men wear suits with gravity controls and carry tiny ray tubes. * The first part of the novel is a competent space story of the day, but after the *Icarus* leaves the inner planets the story falls apart into a succession of sometimes unlikely episodes. At best a mediocre work. Nevertheless, it was a considerable achievement for a professional mystery story author to fulfill all the requirements for true science-fiction, no matter of what quality.

1630. **WHEN THE EARTH TILTED**. *Wonder Stories*, May 1932. Ill. Paul.

Short story. * *Time:* the near future. * When the comet passed close by the Earth, it changed the Earth's tilt, with disastrous results. Much of the Earth's habitable land was submerged, and most of mankind was wiped out. The change in tilt also exposed the polar regions to more solar radiation, with the result that the ice caps have melted, causing flooding. * At the moment the survivors are investigating Antarctica as a possible dwelling place, since it seems to be almost the only undisturbed area left. * Kerford Sansen and representatives of the Pan-American delegation are flying a reconnaissance mission over Antarctica, when to their amazement they see a settled land, with gigantic pyramids and other structures. A force ray seizes their plane and brings it down to a landing area, where the fliers are met by members of a hitherto unknown very tall, blond race. * Sansen, who is part Maori, can communicate after a fashion with the strangers, who are people of Mu. When Mu sank, a powerful colony remained in then habitable Antarctica. But the same comet that wrecked the modern world threatened the Antarctic

Muians in the past. Since they knew that the comet has a periodicity of about fifteen thousand years, they placed themselves in suspended animation, waiting for the comet to swing Antarctica back to a temperate climate. * Their emergence presents a problem. There is not enough land on Antarctica for both modern man and the Muians. After hearing the commission's report, the Pan-Americans declare war. Muian science would be more than a match for the survivors, but a remarkable phenomenon takes place. As American bombers zero in, they disappear, as does the entire Muian culture, people and buildings. It is later learned that the Muians, who accidentally discovered a technique for throwing artifacts out of time, have projected themselves ten years into the future. By then the crisis caused by shortages would be over. * Routine.

WANDREI, DONALD A[LBERT] (1908-1987)

U.S. (mostly Minnesota) author, resident in New York City for much of the period in this study. Member of Lovecraft circle, and with August Derleth, founding partner of Arkham House, first major genre publishing house. Most of Wandrei's fiction falls into the category of supernatural horror; his science-fiction, which often has horror elements, is on the whole less important. Wandrei's best work lies in his occasional story that involves elements of Minnesota regionalism. None of the stories described here falls into that category, most being pulp action material. Wandrei himself had a low opinion of his fiction, considering it commercial work, but his best stories have a poetic touch that is unusual, as well as clear, intelligent writing. Wandrei, who began to suffer from writer's block, wrote little after this period. He is also the author of several poetry collections. His better work is worth reading.

1631. **RAIDERS OF THE UNIVERSE**. *Astounding Stories*, September 1932. Ill. Wesso.

(Reprinted in Donald Wandrei, *Colossus*.)

Short story. * *Time:* the thirty-fourth century. * Strange events are observed in the heavens. New stars come into being in a pattern that leads to a predictable star-birth in the solar system—and somehow the sequence involves speeds faster than that of light. * Neptune turns into a small sun and leaves the solar system; Saturn is similarly affected; and Earth suffers from enormous earthquakes and floods. * The cause of all this is the arrival in the solar system of an enormous dark planet, from which stream beams to the sun and out into space. * The astronomer Phobar is working at his observatory when an enormous metal structure snaps him away, out to the dark planet. There Phobar sees the invaders, who are metal beings, about a hundred feet high, with tentacles. * The invader monarch, known as The Ruler of the Universes, and a scientist inform him telepathically about the invaders and their demands. * The invaders are metal life that originated in another universe a trillion light-years away. In this other universe the elements are different, being in the 800 and 900 range, as extrapolated from our atomic table. When the invaders' universe ran low on energy, they absorbed what was left and moved on in an artificial planet to other universes, which star by star, they devoured. The invaders, in fact, have already demolished half our universe. (Implicit in the Ruler's narrative is the fact that different universes have different laws.) * Phobar is to relay this demand to the authorities of Earth: All the Earth's radium must be extracted and ready for shipment within a week. * To prove his

Wandrei, Donald (*continued*)

power, the Ruler then destroys New York City. * To finish the exposition, so that Phobar can reveal the might of the invaders, the scientist Garboreggg (*sic*) shows him the ultimate controls: a traction beam, a repulsion beam, a matter transmitter (which does not work on Phobar, since he is of a different universe), and a device that contracts the space between atoms, shrinking the object. * Phobar realizes that he has only minutes to defer the alien attack. Blanking his mind against telepathy, he tosses his keys against the size-controlling switch. It snaps into the "on" position, and the metal beings and their planet begin to shrink, while Phobar remains full size. Beating off the now tiny metal creatures, he throws all the switches, and the universe is saved. * Imaginative in some of the detail, but saving the world is a little too easy. Even Edmond Hamilton considered it harder to do.

1632. **A RACE THROUGH TIME**. *Astounding Stories,* October 1933. Unsigned ill.
(Reprinted in Donald Wandrei, *Colossus.*)
Short story. * *Time:* beginning at 1950, eventually to A.D. 1,000,000 and 1,001,950. * Two men, rivals in love and science, work on the problem of time travel. Warren Daniels, basing his study on extreme suspended animation, has built a time vault to hold occupants for the proposed period. Webster Conning, in a different approach, has built a spaceship-time machine that he calls the cosmocraft. Both men are madly in love with Ellen MacOrm. * The crucial situation arrives when Webster finds a message left behind by Ellen: Warren has kidnapped her and is taking her with him one million years into the future. Webster visits the sealed vault, which is protected by a time stasis, and sees that the message is true. He thereupon leaps into his time machine and leaves. * Ellen and Warren awaken to a barren world, empty of people, with only a few giant mushrooms. She reproaches Warren bitterly for destroying her life. * Webster arrives at a barren world, empty of people, with only a few giant mushrooms. But he finds a little plaque telling him that Ellen and Warren had been there. * The gimmick: While both men used the figure of a million years and planned properly, Warren counted from the year 1, while Webster counted from 1950. Thus, Warren and Ellen are long dead, and Webster is the last man. There is no returning, for both men created one-way time travel. * For a sequel see #1633, "Farewell to Earth."

1633. **FAREWELL TO EARTH**. *Astounding Stories,* December 1933. Unsigned ill.
(Reprinted in Donald Wandrei, *Colossus.*)
Short story. * Sequel to #1632, "A Race through Time." * *Time:* 1,001,950. * Webster Conning, musing over his predicament, wonders whether the entire world is really as barren as his present locale, and whether mankind may not survive elsewhere. On exploring the ruins of New York City, he finds an answer: a tall, slender, large-chested, pallid woman (Ellayn) who speaks English of a sort. After fighting off an attack of carnivorous rolling amoeboids, the two make mutual explanations. Ellayn's story: Ellen and Warren bred, and in each generation watch was kept for Conning. The present Ellayn is the last of the family, the last woman on Earth. * Conning and Ellayn fly about in the cosmocraft, looking for other traces of humanity, but find nothing. They do, however, undergo great peril in Egypt, where they are attacked by mobile carnivorous trees. * At the end, deciding that Earth must be abandoned, Conning and Ellayn take

their chances out in space. * *Miscellaneous:* Wandrei also includes a long passage of Stapledonian future history in which atomic power almost devastated the world. At one time a small unisexed winged people existed. * In the same issue of the magazine Wandrei has a long letter commenting on the evolutionary changes that produced Ellayn, new physical elements, and other matters. * Routine.

1634. **COLOSSUS**. *Astounding Stories,* January 1934. Ill. Howard V. Brown.
(Reprinted (in altered, abridged form) in Donald Wandrei, *Colossus;* in Derleth, *Beyond Time and Space,* and in Asimov, *Before the Golden Age.*)
Novelette. * *Time:* the near future, perhaps 1975. *Place:* the Himalayas, New York City, and the macrocosm above our universe. * Against a background of impending war, Duane Sharon has built the *White Bird,* a space vehicle that is powered by the energy of space itself and should be able to travel thousands of times faster than light. Since the universe seems limited telescopically and not infinite, it is possible, as he and his friend Dowell agree, that the *White Bird* might break out of our space and enter a supposititious macrocosm in which our universe is a matter of atoms. On a trial run Duane and his girlfriend, Anne Dowell, flip speedily around the Moon. * Then war breaks out, Japan and England against the United States and Russia. Anne dies in the bombing of New York City, and Duane, in despair, flies away in the *White Bird,* at ever increasing acceleration. * As he reaches inconceivable speeds, his ship increases in length (Wandrei having the Lorenz-Fitzgerald contraction backwards) and it becomes so tenuous that it simply passes through other matter. Finally, with a wrench, the *White Bird* bursts out of our universe into the macrocosm, where it rests on the specimen slide of a titanic microscope. * *Background:* Duane is now on the enormous planet Qthyalos, which is inhabited by the Titans, humanoid beings perhaps hundreds of feet tall—Wandrei gives no specific measurements. The Titans, who resemble Easter Island sculptures cranially, are the masters of a superscience far beyond Duane's comprehension. Judging from events and statements, they are a pragmatic, passionless race, totally focused on intellectual pursuits, with little or no feeling of compassion; on the other hand, they are not evil. Qthyalos itself is a member of an enormous solar system containing hundreds of planets. * Duane attracts the attention of the Titans, who seem amazed at his appearance. They communicate by means of a thought helmet that Duane touches. At the time he appeared, the Titans were engaged in far-viewing a small planet (Valadom) inhabited by humans, hence they first thought that Duane originated there. * As the conversation proceeds, Duane realizes that he is in great peril, for the Titans plan to use him as a guinea pig and then vivisect him. In desperation, he makes an offer: Since the Titans are really curious about Valadom, they would be better served if he went there for a year, studied the planet, then returned with a corpse or two for the Titans to examine. The Titans, who can evaluate his thoughts mechanically, recognize both his logic and sincerity, and agree. * Duane leaves. He lands on Valadom, which is a beautiful, elfin planet, where he immediately meets a pleasant, nude female who reminds him of the dead Anne. * The immensity of Qthyalos and its alienness are well-handled, and the fairy-tale aspect of Valadom is not unacceptable, although it does not fit well with the events of the sequel. * Wandrei has a letter in the

Wandrei, Donald (*continued*)

same issue discussing the story and attempting to explain away its incorrect premise. * For a sequel see #1640, "Colossus Eternal."

1635. THE MAN WHO NEVER LIVED. *Astounding Stories*, March 1934. Ill. Marchioni.

(Reprinted in Donald Wandrei, *Strange Harvest.*)

Short story in the manner of Poe or Lovecraft. * The narrator is present when the noted philosopher-scientist Professor Nicholas van Allensteen conducts his great experiment. Van Allensteen theorizes that there is a universal mind that encompasses all experience, past, present, and future, so that nothing is ever lost. He claims to be able to experience that mind. * As the experiment begins, van Allensteen describes his mental voyage farther and farther into the past; through the period of recorded history, prehistory, the dinosaur age, the formation of the planets, the emergence of the stars, back to the Big Bang (my term, but implicit in the description) forming the universe. But when van Allensteen goes back beyond the universe, he disappears. * A trite topic by now, particularly with the "surprise" ending.

1636. THE ATOM-SMASHER. *Astounding Stories*, April 1934. Ill. Charles Durant.

(Reprinted in Donald Wandrei, *Colossus*, and in Donald Wandrei, *Strange Harvest.*)

Short-short story, only two pages long. * Schonheim has invented a matter transmitter, which he intends to demonstrate. His technique: bombarding the substance with neutrons, then catching disrupted atoms in a magnetic field. He plans to transmit a cork across the room. But something goes wrong. Either Schonheim trips or he has a sudden heart attack. In any case, he falls within his transmission field and is transmitted across the room as a pudding-like bleeding blob.

1637. BLINDING SHADOWS. *Astounding Stories*, May 1934. Ill. Howard V. Brown.

(Reprinted in Donald Wandrei, *Colossus;* in Donald Wandrei, *The Eye and the Finger;* and in Derleth, *Beachheads in Space.*)

Short story. * *Time:* 1970. *Place:* the New York City area. * At present, post-1970, a circular area about ten miles in diameter, centering on New York City, has been cordoned off, with entry barred. The reason, the area is frequented by "blinding shadows" from a fourth-dimensional world; they gobble up such humans as they encounter. Up to now the shadows have not extended their area, which is presumably an overlap section between our world and theirs. * The explanatory narrative, told by Lawrence A. Gilroy, the assistant to and collaborator with the great Professor G. Dowdson: Dowdson has theorized that other matter may exist than our universe, this other matter being found in the empty spaces between electronic orbits; this is also the fourth dimension. He also claims, by analogy, that such a four-dimensional world would cast three-dimensional shadows into our world. * Scoffed at when he announces his theories, Dowdson first scours the Earth looking for proof, then, together with Gilroy, settles to experimenting in the New York City area. Working with solid objects does not avail, for Dowdson "found it a physical impossibility to arrange four right angles at right angles to each other." The men then experiment with mirrors and prisms of various sorts. Running heavy currents of electricity through artifacts made of newly discovered element 95, however, is promising, in showing tantalizing glimpses of another world with a titanic black city. Then, as the experiments

are refined, the men see their first blinding shadow, a brick-shaped glowing phenomenon that appears in the laboratory. At first, this shadow and others that appear are motionless, but then, suddenly, it eats Dowdson. Other shadows similarly consume whatever living creatures are around. In a short time New York City and its environs are completely depopulated and have to be isolated. * *Miscellaneous:* In 1955-1958 World War II took place between the U.S., Great Britain and the USSR on one side, and an African-Asiatic confederation on the other. The American alliance won, thanks to viewers invented by Dowdson. * The influence of H. P. Lovecraft is apparent in the close factual development, together with suggestions that Dowdson obtained hints for his work from submarine archeological material from the Easter Island area. * A rather good story of its sort. Perhaps Wandrei's best early story. According to Schwartz/Weisinger, the story was commissioned by Desmond Hall.

1638. THE NERVELESS MAN. *Astounding Stories*, July 1934. Ill. Marchioni.

(Reprinted in Donald Wandrei, *The Eye and the Finger.*)

Short story. * The narrative of Dr. E. J. Loris-Hayle, who has discovered a superanaesthetic—diochloresthane. It works perfectly, the subject feeling no pain at all, even in major surgery. * When summoned to an emergency case involving an automobile accident, Loris-Hayle uses his discovery to save his patient's life. Colin Leeds, the young man concerned, recovers speedily, but feels no pain, and it soon becomes obvious that the effects of diochloresthane are permanent. At first Leeds is enthusiastic about his condition, but gradually comes to realize that pain is necessary to life. Embittered, he regards the doctor as his enemy, and in a final scene in a burning house forces Loris-Hayle into a duel with swords. The doctor is forced to kill Leeds, who is burned horribly, and now awaits the police. * Literate, but routine.

1639. A SCIENTIST DIVIDES. *Astounding Stories*, September 1934. Ill. Dold.

(Reprinted in Donald Wandrei, *The Eye and the Finger*; in Conklin, *Best of Science Fiction*; and in Warrick, *Science Fiction: Contemporary Mythology.*)

Short story. * Dr. Weylith, a prominent biologist, theorizes that it may be possible to isolate a basic "homoplasm" that is the essence of a human being, ultimately of mankind. And now, from theory to fact, as he demonstrates the tiny moving glob in a beaker to his friend the narrator. * As might be expected, the beaker is accidentally broken, and Weylith is infected by the nodule. In an instant, his body dissolves and forms two similar little Weyliths, naked, intellectless, and aggressive, who in turn divide, repeating up to multiple powers, so that the floor is covered with tiny Weyliths all eager to attack the narrator. The narrator sloshes acid over the tiny creatures, then eradicates them with a blowtorch. * But there are repercussions. The narrator is arrested for the murder of Weylith, but escapes conviction through lack of evidence. Worse, some of the homoplasm must have escaped destruction, for every now and then a similar dissolution of a human or an animal into tiny Weyliths is recorded. * Nicely imagined, if a trite theme.

1640. COLOSSUS ETERNAL. *Astounding Stories*, December 1934. Ill. Marchioni.

(Reprinted in Donald Wandrei, *Colossus.*)

Novelette. Sequel to #1634, "Colossus," though by no means a close sequel. * Duane Sharon has landed on Valadom, where he

Wandrei, Donald (*continued*)

has just met the beautiful young woman Shyrna. Through her telepathic abilities they are able to converse easily enough, and an attachment grows between them. Although the concept is not tendered until late in the story, there is some carry-over in personality after death from sub- to superuniverses, and Shyrna in some fashion represents Duane's dead fiancée, Anne. * Shyrna explains Valadom to Duane. It is built of elements from 93 on up, the lower elements not existing except under laboratory conditions. The people are almost immortal, with a mental control over each atom of their being. The land itself is beautiful, idyllic. * The only problem is Nrm 17^31, the ruler of the planet. A superman by any standards, he is not only the ruler, but the group being of the entire race. Unfortunately, Nrm is power mad and jealous of the only race in the universe superior to Valadom, the Titans of Qthyalos. He is determined to force from the Titans such powers as they uniquely have, notably the ability to predict the future. And Nrm has selected Shyrna as his bride, the wedding to take place tomorrow. * The story follows several subplots. (1) Nrm versus Shyrna: Shyrna resists the mental power of the race and refuses to marry Nrm, who will keep her prisoner until she changes her mind. * (2) Nrm versus Duane: Nrm, after examining Duane with projections, teleports the *White Bird* into a space-bend island where time stands still. There Duane will remain unaltered, unaware that time is passing outside, until he is released—which Shyrna manages to do. Even so, Duane would have been destroyed had not the Titans reached out to Valadom and saved him with an impenetrable cocoon of force. * (3) Nrm versus the Intelligence, a mechanical superbrain that he utilizes: The Intelligence, which has been working on the problem of prediction, announces that it now knows how to gain knowledge of the future, but the process will take several thousand years—much longer than Nrm is willing to wait. The Intelligence is also greatly concerned lest Nrm's mad projected attack on the Titans will destroy the universe, and tries to deter him, but Nrm refuses. The Intelligence, though emotionless, is still moved enough by intellectual curiosity about the problems before it to attack Nrm, so that it can continue to function. Nrm, by luck as much as anything, survives, destroying the Intelligence. * (4) Nrm versus the Titans: For centuries Nrm has been developing, at accelerated evolution, intelligent races around the universe, all aimed at the Titans. He now summons all these incredible monstrosities, who have fantastic abilities and weapons, for an onslaught on Qthyalos. * The war is about to begin. Nrm delivers an ultimatum to the Titans, who reject it, whereupon his forces begin the attack. The Titans, who know the outcome of Nrm's mad actions, resist long enough for Duane to rescue Shyrna, bring her to Qthyalos, and, leaving in the *White Bird,* begin expanding to the next superuniverse. Then, the Titans, as they knew would happen, release the atomic basis of their universe, the monotronic force, and the entire universe is destroyed. The energy of the exploding universe reaches into the new superuniverse. But there is no superuniverse, strictly speaking, it is being created as the *White Bird* moves along. Death, but the hope of a new life ages later ahead in the third universe. * As a carry-over from the first story, it would never have been possible for Duane to fulfill his promise to the Titans; there was almost no death on Valadom, and he could not have delivered a corpse. The Titans knew this quite well—for it was fated. * Filled with ideas, interesting for its

fantastic milieu, but much more sloppily written than is usual with Wandrei.

1641. **LIFE CURRENT**. *Astounding Stories,* April 1935. Ill. Marchioni.

(Reprinted in Donald Wandrei, *Strange Harvest,* and in Donald Wandrei, *Colossus.*)

Short story. * *Place:* New York City. * As Langston tells his wife Marjorie when she visits him on an impulse in his laboratory, he has finally succeeded in duplicating the electricity of life energy. He will now subject himself to a highly augmented charge, which he expects will enhance him in various ways. Marjorie has forebodings, but Langston pooh-poohs her worries. As might be expected, the result is tragic. The charge is so powerful that it dashes Langston to a horrible death, and Marjorie, who is too near, to a similar fate. The watchman faints when he sees the mass of broken bones and flesh. * Good enough for a trite theme.

1642. **THE WHISPERERS**. *Astounding Stories,* May 1935. Ill. Marchioni.

(Reprinted in Donald Wandrei, *Colossus.*)

Short story. * *Time:* the twenty-first century. *Place:* partly Siberia, partly New York City. * The small ovoid meteorite, obviously a construct, falls in Siberia, where peasants smash it open. It contains a gelatinous substance. The meteorite is sent out for scientific study, but then the whispering death begins. Everyone who has been in contact with the meteorite dies in a matter of hours from a fulminating infection characterized by a sound like whispering. The disease is fantastically contagious, and there are no survivors. Thanks to modern transportation, it spreads around the world in weeks. It looks as if mankind will soon be extinct. * In New York City, Langley and Chard, who are working on a supermicroscope, become infected and have only a few hours to find causation and remedy. They are successful. The whispering disease is caused by trillions of submicroscopic intelligent entities, who swarm through the body. The end? No, alcohol will kill them. An unlikely remedy, what with the Russian peasant's proclivity for vodka! * In any case, the origin of the meteorite is never discovered. * Routine.

1643. **MURRAY'S LIGHT**. *Astounding Stories,* June 1935. Ill. Dold.

(Reprinted in Donald Wandrei, *Strange Harvest,* and in Donald Wandrei, *Colossus.*)

Short story. * Newspaperman Cooke stumbles upon the remarkable lighting device created by D. V. Murray, president of the Arctolight Company. Murray's lights are small globes set into holders, without connection to any power source; they produce a soft cold-light and are guaranteed for six months. They are also cheaply produced, sold retail only by Murray for $3, with promises of price reduction soon. * Murray, a burly eccentric who believes that he has been cheated by big business, refuses to tell exactly how the lights work, beyond saying that he charges rare gases in such a way that they utilize cosmic rays. He refuses to patent his lights, pointing out that the huge cartels would either steal his patent or prevent its being registered, especially since he does not have the funds to fight. As events show, Murray is right, for wicked capitalists, when they cannot deal with him, try to assassinate him. * The lights create both a business and a technological revolution, but the end comes when there is an extraordinarily strong display of Northern Lights. Murray's lights all explode. It had previously been revealed that

Wandrei, Donald (*continued*)

Murray had spent time in the Arctic and that in some fashion his lights were connected with the aurora. * An interesting story.

1644. EARTH MINUS. *Astounding Stories,* September 1935. Unsigned ill.

(Reprinted in Donald Wandrei, *The Eye and the Finger*, and in Donald Wandrei, *Colossus.*)

Short story. * *Time:* the near future. * In a prologue, a drum-shaped spaceship is approaching Earth. It is operated by beings who look like gigantic feathers, are nourished by space substances, do not need atmosphere, and are impervious to heat or cold. They are on an exploratory voyage. * On Earth, great scientist Professor Hendrick Hall-Carruthers is determined to reduce an element to its ultimate, the monotrons. For this he uses intense pressure plus certain new radiations. The professor's friend and colleague, Karl von Kurt, urges him not to pursue the experiment, since it is too dangerous, but Hall-Carruthers places knowledge above danger, even though the danger may affect others. * Hall-Carruthers subjects a small iron cube to his process, and after he has attained heats much higher than those in the sun, the cube vanishes. Presumably it has been broken down into monotrons. * The two men feel an itching sensation and a feeling of malaise, but little else. Gradually matters grow worse. All the ammunition in the world explodes. People collapse or run amok. And worst of all, everything begins to dissolve, including the two professors. Earth is finished, for the monotrons, when released, apparently damaged all atoms nearby. * The space beings arrive at this time, and seeing what is going on, retreat as rapidly as they can. * It is not clear whether Hall-Carruthers will have destroyed the universe, or whether the destruction will be limited to Earth. * A good thriller.

1645. FINALITY UNLIMITED. *Astounding Stories,* September 1936. Ill. Wesso.

(Reprinted in Donald Wandrei, *The Eye and the Finger*; in Donald Wandrei, *Colossus*; and in Derleth, *The Outer Reaches.*) Novelette. * *Time:* A.D. 2005. * *Place:* West New York, New Jersey, and everywhere. * Science-fiction author Stanley King and liberated girlfriend, Merl Hudson, obey a summons from great scientist friend Van Field Ruyter to witness his new discovery. Ruyter explains: He has isolated the ultimates of the universe—Time, Space, Matter, Energy, Life, and Intelligence—and has built machinery to control them. He now wants to experiment by eliminating, combining, and altering each of the ultimates. * After a first display, in which he sends time ahead two billion years, with no observable results except that the universe has lost about ten minutes, Ruyter explains that working with one ultimate, without the others, is a sterile approach. It is best to stay with combinations. * Ruyter now generalizes space and matter. The three undergo separate experiences, sometimes horrible, around our world and other worlds, including the interior of a star. As Ruyter calmly remarks when they return, everyone in the world went through similar experiences; there must be considerable madness as a result of this. * Ruyter, after more explanation, now alters intelligence, dragging the other controls along with it, with the result that the three personalities flit around among different entities (human, animal, plant), displacing them to still others. The intelligence (really personality) factor now shifts through time, with experiences past and future, Praxiteles, a superman of A.D. 4000, a caveman of 50,000 B.C., a metallic spore a billion

and a half years in the future, a precambrian life element, and so on. * At this point, the ending of the story is not clear, although it seems to be an ouroboros situation. The personalities return to A.D. 2005, but in a (perpetual?) recapitulation Ruyter is going to start the experiment with intelligence again. * *Miscellaneous:* In the world of A.D. 2005, space travel is successful, with trips to various planets. Moving sidewalks connect parts of New York. Crash-proof helicopters are the normal mode of short-distance travel. * Competently done.

1646. INFINITY ZERO. *Astounding Stories,* October 1936. Ill. Marchioni.

(Reprinted in Donald Wandrei, *Strange Harvest*; in Donald Wandrei, *Colossus*; and in Derleth, *Far Boundaries.*)

Short story. * *Time:* the near future. * A world war is in progress, with the United States, Great Britain, and the Soviet Union allied against Japan, Italy, and Germany. Transatlantic planes regularly bomb the American east coast. In one such raid, whea a bomb falls on the United Chemical Testing Laboratory, Conway, spot photographer and reporter, is assigned to cover the destruction. The site looks a little odd, but Conway thinks little of it, beyond the horrors of war. * Four nights later, Conway is reassigned to the UCTL site, where something strange is said to be happening. There is, indeed. A pillar of what looks like flame, except that it does not radiate heat, reaches into the sky, and a rapidly growing "empty" depression is taking over the site. This depression is a perfect hemisphere, and the assumption is that another hemisphere reaches into the sky. Things tossed into the area disappear. * Recognizing that something important is happening, Conway turns it into a front-page article. He also persuades a top-ranking scientist to accompany him to the depression, which is growing more and more rapidly. * As Professor Daël explains: We think of matter as occupying space, but what is happening here is that the bomb, striking a collection of all the elements in the laboratory, created a situation where space is now taking the place of matter. There is no stopping the process, and in about two weeks the Earth will be gone. After that, the universe. * Competently handled.

WARD, CHARLES

No information.

1647. WRITTEN IN THE YEAR 2100. *Amazing Stories,* October 1930.

A very short story. * *Time:* 2100. * When John David Andrews's wife and children suddenly die, he offers a million dollars to anyone who can rid the world of disease. Most of the applicants are either inadequate or cranks, but Professor Scott of an obscure college offers a reasonable solution. Blaming disease on germ-carrying dust particles, he plans to remove dust, using a new gas that precipitates colloids. * He is successful, and disease wanes. But there is no more rain, only water of condensation, no clouds, no sunsets or sunrises. All in all, though, what with increased ultraviolet penetration of the atmosphere, the change is for the better, since mankind is healthier. * An undeveloped essay-story.

WATES, CYRIL G[EOFFREY] (1884-1946)

Canadian author, then resident in Edmonton, Alberta. Born in England; family removed to Jamaica for a time; attended Harvard College, but without degree, leaving upon death of father. Telephone engineer by profession, author of basic study,

Wates, Cyril C. (*continued*)

Handbook of Telephone Engineering. Important amateur astronomer, with several technical papers; awarded the Chant Medal by the Royal Astronomical Society in 1944.   Enthusiastic mountain climber.

1648. **THE VISITATION**. *Amazing Stories*, June 1927. Unsigned ill.

Short story. * The first-prize winner of the contest based on the cover of the December 1926 issue of *Amazing Stories*. Wates's story won $250. * *Time:* Events of 1949-1950 told in retrospect from perhaps seventy-five or eighty years later. * Ancient Captain Clinton tells of the great event. He was captain of the ocean liner *Shah of Iran*, which sailed between Vancouver and Australia. On the crucial occasion, a gigantic iron meteorite strikes the sea near the ship, apparently off the coast of South America, with the resultant storm driving the ship into a land-locked lagoon. An aftershock raises the coral barrier so that the ship cannot leave. * Soon after this the trapped voyagers see a flying machine approach, from which emerge incredibly beautiful, nude humans with odd feather-like growths on their heads. * The newcomers learn English perfectly in a matter of hours from hearing the voyagers speak, and express wonder that the outsiders do not have similar abilities. * During this acculturation period, the Deelathon (as the strange people are called) continually make reference to the "thon" as the basis for their culture, which boasts of advanced science (including antigravity), near immortality, perfect health, complete happiness, etc. * At first the Deelathon are reluctant to reveal the thon to the voyagers, but finally do. It is cosmic rays, interpreted in a highly mystical manner. * The Deelathon lift the *Shah of Iran* out of the landlocked lagoon with their antigravity device, and the ship sails away. * One hundred Deelathon will enter the outside world to convey a message of health and happiness through cosmic rays. Their mission is one of death for themselves, for despite their incredible advancement, they cannot survive long outside this one small island, and, in some way connected, their flying machines do not function beyond the island limits. This is why they know nothing of the outside world, and vice versa. * As a result of the Deelathon mission, the outside world has become a near paradise. Humans born since the Visitation, as it is called, are immortal and perfect. * Obviously an epigone of Bulwer-Lytton's *The Coming Race*. * Not very strong as fiction, and certainly not worthy of a prize.

1649. **THE FACE OF ISIS**. *Amazing Stories*, March 1929. Unsigned ill.

Short story. * *Place:* Massachusetts and somewhere in Spanish Morocco. * Professor Myron B. Wadsworth is convinced that at some time during the Fifth Dynasty of Ancient Egypt an expedition crossed Africa and sailed to the New World to found Aztec culture. * He and his student Courtland travel to the interior of Spanish Morocco, hoping to find traces of such an expedition. * Thanks to a passing aviator, who can see features not visible from the ground, the explorers locate a well-preserved temple at the top of an isolated pinnacle. Although the explorers had to climb up a very difficult craggy surface, they find, when they have reached the top, a huge tube descending to ground level, plus a well-preserved stairway. More, they find a golden casket containing a strange powder and a document. * The document, when set into context, reveals that the powder, when combined with certain chemicals, creates an antigravity effect

and that the pharaoh concerned used it to ride a small conveyance up the tube toward the moon! Naturally, he did not reach the moon, but cracked up. * Back in New England, Wadsworth and Courtland build a small aerial car which they hope the Egyptian powder will activate. Unfortunately, they are merely oppressed with weight, while the car is wrecked. * Some time later Wadsworth reveals what went wrong: to activate the powder, he used an acid, whereas he should have used an alkali. As a result of this mistake, gravity was increased, not lessened. There can be no second attempt, for all the powder has been used in the failed experiment. * The archeological materials in the first section are not uninteresting, but the remainder of the story is weak. The local color for the Boston area and Harvard is convincing.

1650. **GOLD DUST AND STAR DUST**. *Amazing Stories*, September 1929. Ill. Hynd. Geometric figures presumably by the author.

Short story. * *Time:* the near future. * The Federal government requests the very great universal genius-scientist Hilary Corwin to solve the mystery of fifty million dollars worth of gold bullion, which vanished from a guarded airplane hangar. Corwin, an eccentric whose specialty is insolence, on inspecting the hangar with what amounts to a primitive doodlebug, discovers that the gold is still there, but invisible and intangible. * In the great tradition of detectives, he refuses to explain, but predicts that the gold will reappear at a certain time. He is correct. * Solution: The gold, enormous in weight, was in the fourth dimension, knocked there by a ray beam from a newly erected wireless power transmission station nearby. Corwin gives a detailed explanation that involves folding simple geometric figures to simulate higher dimensions. * Most interesting of all, when the gold returns, a curious dust is visible on the boxes. Spectrographic analysis reveals that it is a new element characteristic of the double star in Andromeda, which must be near the Earth in the fourth dimension.

1651. **A MODERN PROMETHEUS**. *Amazing Stories Quarterly*, Fall 1930. Ill. Wesso.

Novel. * *Time:* A.D. 2189 to 2200. *Place:* mostly the Canadian Rocky Mountains, but also New York and around Santa Lucia. * The author early provides historical perspective: Around 1953 a backroom inventor named Walter Ballantyne discovered a method for producing allotropes. For most substances this was only of academic interest, but for iron it was overwhelmingly important. From allotropic iron an incredible range of materials could be made; as the author puts it, "There was no substance known to man which could not be replaced to advantage by some transmuted form of this master element, iron." * Ballantyne, a canny businessman, chose wisely in selecting a marketer, and in a short time Pan-American Steel and Iron was tremendously powerful financially. The transmutation process was guarded zealously by its owners. * Allotropic iron, however, proved to be a political catalyst. When Brazilians stole the secret, the United States declared war, but no one was willing to enter combat, despite the hawkishness of the governments. The reason for this was that following World I a certain disillusionment with world politics had emerged all over the world. Nevertheless, governments toppled right and left. * Finally, as the world struggled to arise from turmoil, three men met in the Caribbean, on the island of Santa Lucia. These were the inventor Ballantyne, the former president of Brazil, and the

Wates, Cyril G. (*continued*)

former King George VI of Great Britain, now simply George Windsor. The three men set up a world government that lasted until story time, 2200 or so, with the Three and a Council ruling the world. Most important, the society that the original Three set up, although still capitalistic, has provided for healthy and congenial occupation with adequate income, equal opportunities and full rewards to all, and no more unfair advantages. These principles have become practically a religious slogan in the new culture, and the political apparatus has become a cult. The Three are completely altruistic and operate for the good of the world; indeed, the entire culture centers on altruism. The result is a near social eutopia, and the culture prides itself on embodying the principle of social advance. * This all sounds be fine, but on the debit side, the political structure has decided that there is nothing more to be learned or gained from science and has actually forbidden research, under threat of criminal penalties. The result is scientific and technological stasis. * The story is concerned with the doings of an underground called the Rebels, to which (as new members) Ralph Ballantyne (rebellious heir of the Ballantyne world cartel) and a couple of friends belong. In a secret laboratory in the Canadian Rockies Ballantyne and his associates carry on scientific research clandestinely. * At the moment there is a crisis. A mysterious "disease" has attacked iron ore, turning it into an unusable mineral. The Three have been trying desperately to remove still usable ore from contagion, but with little success, for an aberrant capitalist has really created the crisis and intends to exploit it by spreading the disease. (In these activities he is far away from the cultural norm.) * The Rebels, however, have another solution. Earth has acquired a tiny second moon that seems to be a lump of iron. The Rebels have the technology to draw this lump down without catastrophic collisions, but insist on recognition and relaxation of the antiscientific laws. Eventually they succeed; the Three backtrack and abandon the barriers against science, and the Rebels bring down the second moon. * *Miscellaneous:* There are also thriller ins and outs: A romance develops between Ballantyne and the niece of the wicked capitalist; there is apparently no marriage in this culture, simply a consent to live together as companions. * Longevity is three or four times that of the present. * An evil spy, assassin, and saboteur is reformed by a brain operation. * The secret headquarters of the Rebels is under the sea, with a floating approach lock; no one knows its location, and it is found by directional finger rings. * The little moon is brought down by means of a new supermagnetic mineral that Ballantyne discovers under a glacier. * As opposed to the usual anti-Oriental bias of most such pulp fiction, the motivating character throughout is a Japanese, Dr. Umetaro. * The Rebels also have a superaircraft that can double as a space ship. * Intelligent writing, but bad novelistic construction and a floundering about from the middle on.

WATSON, GEORGE COOKMAN

Forthcoming notice refers to Watson as a newspaper man, otherwise no information.

1652. **CAUPHUL, THE CITY UNDER THE SEA.** *Amazing Stories*, January 1929. Unsigned ill.

Short story. * *Place:* the American Southwest and Atlantis. * A blue-ribbon archeological expedition to the Southwest discovers in an ancient burial a token with Maya symbols, obviously from

Atlantis. * This find convinces the men that they should investigate the traditional site of Atlantis in the Atlantic Ocean. * With a French submarine and diving bells, the men explore. They find evidences of civilization, including a huge swivelling lens, then a trapdoor to a tunnel leading down beneath the ocean. * The men enter the tunnel, and, after a time, they emerge into a lighted chamber, where two men greet them in friendly fashion, take them to a pneumatic car, and whisk them to the city, which is about 150 miles away. * There an ancient man addresses them in perfect English. He bids them welcome, but informs them that before they can move about or learn anything about the land, they must learn the language. As one of the savants from the surface recognizes, the language is a mixture of Early Phoenician, Hebrew, and Mayan. * Literate, the explorers are now informed about Atlantis—for many thousands of words. When Atlantis was destroyed, many people took refuge in the catacombs beneath the land, where they survived. At first they derived light from the surface (whence the lens found earlier), but as their science developed, they produced their own light. The sunken people eventually expanded their realm almost around the world. Scientifically they are far ahead of the surface peoples. Politically, they maintain the system of ten kings mentioned by Plato. Physically, they are remarkable specimens. * All in all, Atlantis is a near eutopia, but there is one sour note: There are other underground races, including a darker people whom the Atlanteans have enslaved. * The end comes. The dark men revolt with scientific weapons of their own, and the Atlanteans are in trouble. The narrator and his Atlantean wife, however, are helped to escape by a dark man whose life the narrator saved. Now back on the surface the narrator wonders what finally happened in Atlantis. * *Miscellaneous:* The Atlanteans are responsible for the *Mary Celeste* incident and the disappearance of John Orth. * Atlantean science is largely based on an understanding of the higher dimensions. It is far too advanced for the narrator to comprehend. * The Atlanteans are in communication with the other planets via their dimensional knowledge. * An exhaustive, almost ethnographic coverage of Atlantis makes this one of the most boring stories to appear in Gernsback's *Amazing Stories*.

WATSON, WEBSTER

No information.

1653. **WHEN THE MOON MOONS.** *Amazing Stories*, November 1933.

Short-short story. * Really a fantasy, rather than science-fiction. The Moon, as a skittish female, makes bright comments about Earth and other matters. Of no interest whatever.

WEBB, A. C., M.D.

No information. Portrait accompanying the story shows a middle-aged man. Also contributed "The Double Lightning" to *Amazing Detective Tales*.

1654. **UNDERGROUND WATERS.** *Science Wonder Quarterly*, Winter 1930. Ill. Paul.

Short story. * Not science-fiction. * The water supply of the town of Hillsboro, normally a matter of civic pride, fails. Professor Caldwell, a geologist, investigates, and with his potential sweetheart descends into a cave system that contains an enormous underground lake. A jealous lover maroons them, and things look bad, but the professor attracts rescuers by sending up

Webb, A. C., M.D. (*continued*)
little messages through the water pipes. * Amateurish.

WEDE
No information.

1655 . **DEATH CREEPS THE MOON**. *Amazing Stories*, December 1936. Ill. Morey.

Short story. * *Time and place:* about a million years ago on the Moon, for the main narrative. * In a long framework, colored by the obnoxious personality of the pedantic narrator, geologists find an enormous fossil termitarium in a Miocene deposit. This is unexpected enough that the narrator visits the site, where he and associates find in a central core of the formation a metal manuscript that resembles a player piano roll. Since the roll contains a built-in pictorial deciphering system, it is soon translated into English. * It is the narrative of Birna, Minister Plenipotentiary to Womanland on the Moon. As Birna reveals through his communications to his ruler, the Moon, which still rotates, is divided into male and female nations that are totally separate. Both groups reproduce ectogenetically. The Lunarians seem to be human or humanoid, and are possessed of a science beyond ours. * Their problem is the perpetual encroachment of termites and ants upon human territory. While his superiors cannot see the danger, Birna repeatedly warns that the humans are on the edge of being destroyed by the insects, who are flesh-eaters. * Birna proves right. The last human flame barrier collapses, and the insects are triumphant. In a small spaceship, accompanied by Queen Ala of Womanland (with whom he is in love) Birna escapes from the Moon, heading for Earth. But just before landing, he sees that termites are present on his ship. They eat him and Queen Ala after he finishes his manuscript. * Undoubtedly parodic. Some amusing touches, but not quite good enough to be memorable.

WEINBAUM, STANLEY G[RAUMAN] (1902-1935]
U.S. author (mostly Wisconsin). Born in Louisville, Kentucky. Attended University of Wisconsin, majoring in chemical engineering. His work was very popular in the 1930s, and he was generally considered the most promising new s-f author of his day. In general Weinbaum's style was more lively than that of most of his genre contemporaries, and he was imaginative in background details, but otherwise his work was ordinary pulp fiction, with routine plots, slapdash presentation, cardboard characterizations, and much cliché of idea. In retrospect, it is difficult to agree with the enthusiasm that his work inspired sixty years ago. * Weinbaum's work has often been reprinted, with several major collections: *Dawn of Flame and Other Stories* (Milwaukee Fictioniers, 1936; a collector's rarity); *A Martian Odyssey*; *The Best of Stanley Weinbaum*. Other stories and collections are listed in standard reference works like Contento. See also pseud. John Jessel; also collaboration Ralph Milne Farley and Stanley G. Weinbaum; also #1829, "The Circle of Zero," and #1830, "The Brink of Infinity."

Stories are described as The Van Manderpootz Series, The Ham and Pat Series, and Other Works.

The Van Manderpootz Series

Three stories, set in the early twenty-first century; the chronology is carelessly handled, so that year dates conflict. The stories are centered on the personalities of the narrator and Professor van Manderpootz. The narrator, Dixon Wells, is a mildly irresponsible, wealthy young playboy who has been trained as an engineer and works, after a fashion, in the family business. His obsession with sex, reminiscent of Gibson girl fiction of the early twentieth century, usually brings about unhappy results. His former university instructor Haskel van Manderpootz is a caricature of the eccentric scientist; a man of genius but also of incredible vanity, he is a weak reminder of A. C. Doyle's Professor Challenger. The stories are light in tone, with some attempt at humor, but do not rise above commercial fiction. It is difficult to describe, but an air of condescending writing-down permeates the stories.

1656. **THE WORLDS OF IF**. *Wonder Stories*, August 1935. Ill. Paul.

(Reprinted in Weinbaum, *The Best of Stanley G. Weinbaum*; in Weinbaum, *A Martian Odyssey* [Fantasy Press]; in Weinbaum, *A Martian Odyssey* [Hyperion]; in Weinbaum, *Dawn of Flame*; and in Silverberg, *Other Dimensions*.)

Short story. * *Time:* A.D. 2022. * The first story about the eccentric, egotistical genius, Professor van Manderpootz. * On the present occasion, Dixon has missed his rocket ship (the *Baikal*) for Moscow. He is fortunate, for the ship was destroyed in an air crash and most of the passengers were killed. * Visiting van Manderpootz, Dixon is first subjected to prolonged boasting, then informed that van Manderpootz has mastered time. As the scientist explains, time travel to the past or future is impossible, because of the relativity equations, but if one uses a thought projector and other equipment, it is possible to visualize worlds of if, worlds that might have happened. * Dixon opts to visit the time-frame in which he flew on the *Baikal*. On the flight he strikes up an acquaintance with Joanna Caldwell, a handsome young artist with whom he immediately falls in love. After the collision, Dixon behaves heroically, trying to save Joanna and himself, but returns to our world as the water pours into the plane. Presumably he and Joanna drowned. * Dixon spends time mooning about Joanna, until van Manderpootz reminds him that what he experienced was not reality. On checking, Dixon now learns that Joanna survived, but she is not for him. She marries the heroic pilot who saved her. * *Miscellaneous:* The apparatus is called the subjunctivisor, since it shows contrary-to-fact conditions. * Light in writing, but clichéd in too many ways.

1657. **THE IDEAL**. *Wonder Stories*, September 1935. Ill. Paul.

(Reprinted in Weinbaum, *A Martian Odyssey* [Fantasy Press]; in Weinbaum, *A Martian Odyssey* [Hyperion]; and in Weinbaum, *The Best of Stanley Weinbaum*.)

Short story. * The second van Manderpootz story. * *Time:* early twenty-first century. * Dixon Wells again visits van Manderpootz, and as background Weinbaum offers a version of the legend about Roger Bacon and the brazen head he constructed. Van Manderpootz brings the legend into relevance by announcing that he intends to build an omniscient device in the form of a head. This is possible for the great savant since he has already discovered the basic units of time (the chronon) and space (the spation). Beyond these and other subatomic particles is the cosmon (the ultimate), and from these can be constructed the psychon (the unit of thought). * When van Manderpootz constructs his device, it turns out to be a mechanism for viewing the ideal

Weinbaum, Stanley G. (*continued*)

of anything thought of. Since some risk may be involved in extracting psychons from the brain, Wells is the first to use the idealizator, and, naturally, he thinks of the ideal woman. She appears, and once again Wells is floored and devastated thinking of her. * Some time passes, during which the oversexed, undergratified Wells languishes, until van Manderpootz observes the image of Wells's ideal woman. She turns out to have been a stage star of the past—her image preserved by cryptomnesia (not Oedipus complex, as Weinbaum states) in Wells's memory. Better yet, van Manderpootz knew her, and even better, her daughter, who resembles her closely, is coming to study with him. * When Denise d'Agrion turns up, Wells falls in love with her, and she seems interested in him. The crash comes when Denise insists on using the idealizator and concentrating on the utmost horror. She is petrified, and when Wells tries to rescue her, his image becomes mixed with that of horror, ending his chances—especially when she marries the psychologist who has been attending her since her collapse. * A secondary element, generally considered more interesting than the primary, is the mechanical "beast of prey" that van Manderpootz has designed to "kill" automobiles. Constructed roughly in an erector-set likeness of a carnivorous dinosaur, it is activated by photoelectric cells that convey the image of an automobile to an electronic center. It is programmed to lunge forward, seize the automobile, and drain its fuel. This scene, suggested rather than actual, served for Paul's well-known cover and inside illustration.

1658. **THE POINT OF VIEW.** *Wonder Stories*, February 1936. Ill. Marchioni.

(Reprinted in Weinbaum, *A Martian Odyssey* [Fantasy Press]; and in Weinbaum, *A Martian Odyssey* [Hyperion].)

Short story. * The third van Manderpootz story. * *Time:* A.D. 2015. * Dixon is still mooning about his lost romances from previous stories, and van Manderpootz is still wallowing in self-praise. * Van Manderpootz's latest invention is a device that lets the user see things from the point of view of whatever person it happens to be focused on. It reveals van Manderpootz's universe to be a strange, incomprehensible chaos, and it offends van Manderpootz when he sees Dixon's estimation of him. * The essential part of the story is that Dixon happens to focus on van Manderpootz's lab assistant, a worm-like drudge, and catches his vision of a glorious woman. The glorious woman turns out to be the drudge's opinion of van Manderpootz's secretary. * The vision is so attractive that it acts like a drug on Dixon, who spends too much time with the device dipping into the lab assistant's point of view. * When Dixon pines away in his usual manner, van Manderpootz, who is understanding, sends the assistant and the secretary away for a honeymoon.

The Ham and Pat Series

Three stories telling the extraterrestrial adventures of Ham Hammond and Pat Burlingame, later Mrs. Hammond. The stories stress curiosities of alien life-forms.

1659. **PARASITE PLANET.** *Astounding Stories*, February 1935. Ill. Dold.

(Reprinted in Weinbaum, *A Martian Odyssey* [Fantasy Press]; in Weinbaum, *A Martian Odyssey* [Hyperion]; in Weinbaum, *The Best of Stanley G. Weinbaum*; in Asimov, *Before the Golden Age*; in Goodstone, *The Pulps;* and in Wollheim, *Flight into Space.*)

Short story. * *Time:* per the date given for #1661, "The Planet of Doubt," around A.D. 2100. * *Place:* the libration zone on Venus. * *Background:* Most of Venus is either impossibly hot or cold for humans, but the libration zone offers a treacherous possibility of existence. It is filled with parasitic forms, notably carnivorous fungi of horrendous reproductive rate that make life outside a special suit impossible. There are also horrible creatures like giant amoebas. The landscape, too, is a threat, being perpetually unstable, what with underground boiling and frigid rivers that burst into destructive mud eruptions and resultant sinkholes that swallow up huge areas. * Politically, the libration zone is partly British and partly American, although the traders that wander about in search of xixtchil pods do not worry about boundaries. Xixtchil is highly prized on Earth for its ability to restore youth and sexual potency. * Ham Hammond, American trader, is dispossessed when his hut is swallowed by a mud upheaval. Planning to make his way to the closest American settlement, he comes upon another outpost maintained by Pat Burlingame, a Briton who is studying the flora for the Royal Society. But Pat is a woman. They set up a battle-of-the-sexes relationship, but when her establishment, too, is swallowed, they set out together for civilization. Along their unfriendly way they encounter expectable perils, and at the moment of decision discover that they love each other. A mean trick that Pat seems to have performed turns out to have been a hoax. * *Miscellaneous:* Among the curiosities are Jack Ketch trees that try in a clumsy way to lasso their prey and friendly quadruped natives that speak a complex language. There are also fiercely hostile, semi-intelligent creatures (trioptes) from the cold side who wander into the libration area. * The background is detailed, though familiar from similar stories, but the romance is shopgirl.

1660. **THE LOTUS EATERS.** *Astounding Stories,* April 1935. Ill. Dold.

(Reprinted in Weinbaum, *Dawn of Flame*; in Weinbaum, *A Martian Odyssey* [Fantasy Press]; in Weinbaum, *A Martian Odyssey* [Hyperion]; in Weinbaum, *The Best of Stanley G. Weinbaum*; in Derleth, *Beyond Time and Space*; in Moskowitz, *Masterpieces of Science Fiction*; in Schmidt, *The Analog Anthology #1*; and in Wollheim, *The Hidden Planet.*)

Short story. * The second story in the Ham and Pat series. * *Time:* per the date given for #1661, "The Planet of Doubt," around A.D. 2100. * *Place:* the libration zone on Venus. * Ham and Pat, now married, are conducting a joint Anglo-American biological expedition into the cold area of Venus. Here the fungi are absent, so that air-breathing is possible. * The explorers encounter several odd forms of life: a fungus-like creature that generates its own heat; more of the insanely vicious, stone-throwing trioptes met in the previous story; and the Lotophagus veneris. The latter, a vegetable far more intelligent than mankind, is also utterly quietistic, unable to defend itself against the trioptes, content to rest and think. It is perfectly telepathic and via a small diaphragm is able to speak English when it hears the words from Pat and Ham. Its mental powers are so great that it can construct accurate understanding of the universe from a few facts. Unfortunately, it will be extinct in about a hundred years, what with the depredations of the trioptes. Its lassitude, however, is contagious if one breathes its spores. * The best of the three stories, and one of the two stories by Weinbaum that

Weinbaum, Stanley G. (*continued*)
deserve remembering, the other being "A Martian Odyssey."

1661. **THE PLANET OF DOUBT**. *Astounding Stories,* October 1935. Ill. Dold.
(Reprinted in Weinbaum, *A Martian Odyssey* [Fantasy Press]; in Weinbaum, *A Martian Odyssey* [Hyperion]; in Silverberg, *Tomorrow's Worlds*; and in Wollheim, *More Adventures on Other Planets*.)
Short story. * The third story in the Ham and Pat series. * *Time and Place:* A.D. 2102, Uranus. * Ham and Patricia are now on an expedition sponsored by the American government to explore and lay claim to a part of Uranus. This seems to be the second expedition to Uranus. * Uranus is solid, with a gravity much like that of Earth. The atmosphere contains adequate oxygen, but with a heavy proportion of argon. The planet is covered with heavy mist, however, and strong winds are common. * Ham and Pat explore, linked to the ship (except when noted otherwise) by ropes, in order not to be separated or lost. The wildlife they encounter includes a segmented monster that seems to have hostile intent, though it really does nothing; and shadowy mist-like forms that hover through the air suggestively and seem to have humanoid features. * Pat wanders off the rope, and it is about thirty-six hours before they find her again. She has been trapped within a circle of the segmented monster, which the Earthmen have to leap over to rescue her. * Pat explains: The segmented monster corresponds to Terrestrial chain caterpillars, which follow the leader; the mist beings are probably shadows of moth-like creatures flying on high, completing the analogy of larvae and moths. * Routine at best.

Other Works

1662. **A MARTIAN ODYSSEY**. *Wonder Stories,* July 1934. Ill. Paul.
(Reprinted in Weinbaum, *A Martian Odyssey* [Fantasy Press]; in Weinbaum, *A Martian Odyssey* [Hyperion]; in Weinbaum, *The Best of Stanley Weinbaum*; in Weinbaum, *Dawn of Flame*; in Asimov, *Where Do We Go From Here?*; in Gunn, *The Road to Science Fiction, #2*; in Margulies and Friend, *From Off This World*; in Wollheim, *The Pocket Book of Science Fiction*; in Silverberg, *Science Fiction Hall of Fame*; and in Silverberg, *The Science Fiction Bestiary*.)
Short story. * *Time:* The early interplanetary future, distant enough for France to be established as a Sixth Commune. *Place:* Mars. * Adventures of the first expedition to Mars, told as Jarvis's report of his experiences, with interruptions from his colleagues. The basic situation, frequently repeated, is encounter with life-forms so alien that there can be little or no comprehension of them. * Jarvis, whose small rocket failed, so that he was forced to make an emergency landing, is walking back toward the terrestrial camp, water container strapped to his back, when he sees a strange, bird-like creature struggling against an octopoid monster. Since the bird-like being is wearing a wallet-like piece of equipment, Jarvis decides that it must be intelligent and rescues it. This being, who has a long trunk-like appendage, is Tweel (a rough approximation of his name), who will be Jarvis's companion in his wandering. * Communication is almost impossible between the two beings, although Jarvis does convey the message that he is from Earth. The problem, from a modern point of view, is that Tweel's culture has a totally different

classification of experience, perhaps without the generic terms that we have. In any case, Jarvis and Tweel communicate in a slight way by means of the numerical system, which Jarvis interprets with not always convincing ingenuity. * As for the being that had captured Tweel, it was a dream monster, a creature that takes its prey by projecting something the prey loves or wants. Thus, later another dream monster almost captures Jarvis by showing him his Terrestrial girlfriend. * The second strange form of life Jarvis and Tweel encounter is a creature that builds around itself pyramids of silicon bricks that it excretes, then, when the pyramid is completed, moves along and builds a larger one. Following the back trail of such a creature, Jarvis speculates that it is aeons old. A third strange life-form, which inhabits a small town, consists of a horde of barrel-like beings who in endless chains trundle up barrows of rock and vegetable debris, which they dump into a huge grinding machine. (They are compared to corpuscles in a blood stream.) The beings ignore Jarvis and Tweel, but knock Jarvis out of their way when he tries to interrupt them. Words that he speaks to them are repeated indefinitely. In both such instances, Tweel, with numerical analogies, tries to convey the fact that they are different life-forms from himself and Jarvis. * But the barrel monsters suddenly turn nasty and attack the two onlookers, who have ventured into their tunnel-like barrows. The two are rescued by the space rocket that has been searching for Jarvis. Tweel hops or flies away to the south. * Jarvis does his best to convince his associates that Tweel represents a life-form perhaps more intelligent than humans. He also confesses why the barrel people suddenly attacked them. He stole from them a radioactive gem with great healing properties. * *Miscellaneous:* Tweel carried as a weapon a small gun that shot needles presumably drugged or poisoned; as propulsive power it used steam created by a chemical reaction. * The odd life-forms are interesting, but the narrative method and the O. Henry ending tend to date the story. For a sequel see #1663, "Valley of Dreams."

1663. **VALLEY OF DREAMS**. *Wonder Stories,* November 1934. Ill. Paul.
(Reprinted in Weinbaum, *A Martian Odyssey* [Fantasy Press]; in Weinbaum, *A Martian Odyssey* [Hyperion]; in Weinbaum, *The Best of Stanley Weinbaum*; in Margulies and Friend, *From Off This World*.)
Short story. * Sequel to #1662, "A Martian Odyssey." * *Time:* the interplanetary future. *Place:* Mars. * A continuation of the first story. Jarvis and Leroy recount their experiences in an expedition to the south to locate Tweel's people. They find a titanic city; it is almost deserted, but shows evidence of a past high civilization. Accompanied by Tweel and some of his fellow Martians, the explorers see enormous installations, including a colossal sun-power plant. Some of the installations are operated by the barrel creatures in cooperation with Tweel's people. Another encounter with the dream monsters, in this instance a valley peopled by them, is hazardous for the two men. * The heart of the story is not so much the adventures of Jarvis and Leroy, or descriptions of incomprehensible creatures, as in the first story, but theories and explanations. Martian civilization is obviously decadent from a higher state, and Jarvis speculates that the falling off is due to lack of power sources. There is no water head on Mars, and apparently there are no radioactive minerals that might have been used for atomic power. Other fuels were exhausted in the past. * The political structure of the

Weinbaum, Stanley G. (*continued*)
Martians seems to be anarchism, which works for them. * In the past the Martians visited Earth, for a bas relief on one of the buildings shows a Martian being rendered service by an Earthman, probably an Ancient Egyptian. The Martians served as the prototype for the iconography for the god Thoth; Tweel recognizes the word "Thoth." * As for Tweel and his fellows, like the dream monsters, they are probably advanced vegetables; Tweel's trunk or beak, which he inserts into the ground on occasion, is probably an evolved root. * As the clincher ending, Jarvis reveals that he has given Tweel the atomic power mechanism from his disabled scouting vessel. One wonders, if Mars is lacking in the heavier elements, what good this will do? * Lacking the originality-interest of the first story.

1664. **FLIGHT ON TITAN**. *Astounding Stories,* January 1935. Ill. Marchioni.
(Reprinted in Weinbaum, *A Martian Odyssey* [Hyperion], and in Weinbaum, *The Red Peri*.)
Short story. * *Time:* A.D. 2142. * *Place:* mostly on Titan. * When, during the depression of 2142, Tim Vick loses his job (and has little hope of finding another), he and his wife, Diane, decide to use their small resources to take a rocket to Titan, where they can hunt for the fabulously valuable flame orchids. * They manage well enough for a time, finding eighteen of the glowing egg-shaped gems, mostly by trading rubbish to the stupid, primitive natives. But then their camp is destroyed by the gravitational tides of Saturn, and, to survive, they must cross about one hundred miles of frigid, icy mountains to reach Nivia, the only human settlement. It is questionable whether Diane can survive the trip. * But they manage well enough, finding shelter in the dome-like habitations of the ice ants, where warm air is to be found. All but one of their gems are lost, however, when they encounter the Titanian threadworm, a snake-like, seemingly intelligent creature which projects a telepathic message that puts its prey to sleep. Diane and Tim escape, of course, but their last gem is shattered. * Bouleversement: In the threadworm's cave the shattered egg seeds itself, resulting in a crop of flame orchids. All is well. * *Miscellaneous:* Titan is cold, but not impossibly so; Tim and Diane wear rubber insulating suits. * The threadworms are probably the decadent descendants of a civilized form of life. * Also present are whiplash trees and a knife-kite, a gliding creature that impales its prey. * Routine.

1665. **PYGMALION'S SPECTACLES**. *Wonder Stories,* June 1935. Ill. Winter.
(Reprinted in Weinbaum, *The Best of Stanley G. Weinbaum*; in Weinbaum, *A Martian Odyssey* [Fantasy Press]; and in Weinbaum, *A Martian Odyssey* [Hyperion])
Short story. * Sensory deception and romance. * Dan Burke strikes up a chance conversation with Professor Ludwig, who has invented the ultimate motion picture, a device that combines sight, sound, and smell (with tactile sensations added by the subject) to create a complete second reality. Its only disadvantage is that it can be used by only one person at a time. Hence it does not have a great commercial potential—or so investors have told Ludwig. * Ludwig has prepared a full adventure sequence, which he invites Burke to try. Burke slips on the suitable apparatus and finds himself in an incredibly beautiful elfin environment, where he soon meets Galatea, a delightful young female with whom he establishes immediate empathy. Also present is her ancient grandfather, called the Grey Weaver since he spends his time weaving metallic cloth. * In this world, which Galatea and the Grey Weaver assure Burke is reality, while his world is only a shadow, there are no unhappiness, no want, and no death. However, there can be tragedy, as when a woman falls in love with a man from Burke's shadow world. * This is what happens. Burke and Galatea fall in love—and Burke awakens back in our world, accidentally smashing the apparatus. Ludwig is not present. Burke leaves, but is ever haunted by his memory of the wonderful, imaginary Galatea. But chancing to meet Ludwig later, he learns that Galatea exists and is available as the Professor's niece. * An attempt to create an idyllic world does not quite come across, clashing too much with the pulp approach.

1666. **THE RED PERI**. *Astounding Stories,* November 1935. Ill. Dold.
(Reprinted in Weinbaum, *The Red Peri*; in Weinbaum, *Dawn of Flame*; in Weinbaum, *A Martian Odyssey* [Hyperion]; and in Ackerman, *Gosh! Wow!*)
Novelette. * *Time:* probably mid twenty-second century, since it is in the same world pattern as #1664, "Flight on Titan." *Place:* mostly on Pluto. * Romance, sudden and red-hot, against an interplanetary background. * Menacing interplanetary trade is the pirate ship the *Red Peri*, captained by an individual of the same name. A strange-looking vessel, something like a skeletal tetrahedron, it is far superior to anything else in space and obviously embodies a new technology. Its base of operations has never been found, although much search has been made. * Frank Keene happens to be on board the Dutch spaceship *Aardkin* when the Red Peri seizes the vessel. Chancing to be near the space-suited leader of the bandits, Keene comments on his red hair, at which the leader tweaks his nose severely, but does nothing more. * About a year later Keene and fellow scientist Nestor are investigating cosmic radiation for the Smithsonian when a rocket tube burns out. Their only resource is to make for nearby Pluto, in hope of finding metal for constructing a new tube. Landing and starting to explore, they are immediately captured by men from the *Red Peri* and taken to an elaborate permanent base. There they are interrogated by a beautiful young woman, who also happens to be arrogant, suspicious, and ruthless—in short, a sanitized Dragon Lady. So great is her beauty that all the men in her band are infatuated with her, although she obviously preserves her virginity. Keene, who recognizes her as the redhead he met on the *Aardkin*, follows the same pattern as the other men, falling violently in love with her. * The Red Peri at first is all for executing her two captives, but, perhaps due to Keene's manly charms, relents. She and Keene become friendly enough that she reveals part of her history. She is Peri Maclane, the daughter of the great inventor Perry Maclane, who had been swindled by the space cartel. She and her late father vowed vengeance, first by pirating cartel ships, then, when they have taken enough cash, by setting up a competitive space line and driving the cartel out of business. The vessel the *Red Peri* has been operating for about fifteen years, first captained by her late father, then after his death by Peri, who is only nineteen. Peri claims that she has never killed anyone except in self defense. * Keene and Nestor chafe at their captivity and plan to escape. Basing his actions on an insight of Nestor's, that the danger of airless, low-temperature space to the human body is a myth, Keene seizes Peri, flings her across his shoulder and makes a dash, unprotected by spacesuit or anything,

Weinbaum, Stanley G. (*continued*)

to his repaired ship. He then flies away, with her as hostage and the *Red Peri* in frustrated pursuit. * Keene and Peri are in love, and probably could have worked something out, but Peri manages to escape. Crossing space, unprotected, to her ship, she leaves Keene holding the bag, hoping that he will meet her again. * *Miscellaneous:* Pluto is the home of semi-living crystal complexes that devour various elements, usually metallic. At one point, however, a carbon-feeding crystal alights on Keene's toe and endangers both Keene and Peri. He saves her life by dashing across a hairline bridge with her. * As is commonly the case with Weinbaum, the background is imaginative, but the romance is on the level of the shopgirl pulps, and the writing leaves much to be desired. An astronomical purist would cavil at the distances concerned.

    1667. **THE MAD MOON.** *Astounding Stories*, December 1935. Unsigned ill.

(Reprinted in Weinbaum, *A Martian Odyssey* [Fantasy Press]; in Weinbaum, *A Martian Odyssey* [Hyperion]; in Weinbaum, *The Best of Stanley Weinbaum*; in Weinbaum, *Dawn of Flame*; in Moskowitz, *Exploring Other Worlds*; in Knight, *Science Fiction of the Thirties*; in Pohl, *Jupiter*; in Liebman, *Science Fiction*; and in Silverberg, *Arbor House Treasury*.)

Short story. * *Time:* A.D. 2112. * *Place:* Io. * Grant Calthorpe, former playboy and sportsman who lost his shirt during the recession of 2110, is now working as a trader for the Neilan Company on Io. His job is to collect ferva leaves, which seem to have medicinal value against the fevers prevalent on Io (and perhaps elsewhere). As for Io: Its gravity, atmosphere, and climate seem to be much like Earth's, but the fauna and flora are strange. Whiplash trees are not uncommon. * Three life-forms enter the story. The Loonies are humanoid creatures with gigantic globular heads on long fragile necks; mentally, they are about on the level of a Terrestrial half-wit. They serve to gather ferva leaves, although they usually misidentify what they have. The parcats, a specimen of which is a pet of Grant's, are small creatures that have speech-echoing abilities beyond that of a parrot. Their intelligence is questionable. The third life-form is the slinky, an intelligent creature that is much like a rat with a cape. The slinkies build towns, have fire and some metallurgy, shoot poisoned arrows, and are determinedly hostile to the human exploiters of their planet. * The story line is the familiar boy meets girl, boy rescues girl plot that Weinbaum favored. The only unexpected element is a ruined site of considerable beauty and grandeur, which was constructed by ancestral loonies before they devolved to idiots. * The slinkies are a good creation, otherwise routine.

    1668. **REDEMPTION CAIRN.** *Astounding Stories*, March 1936. Ill. Marchioni.

(Reprinted in Weinbaum, *The Red Peri*; in Weinbaum, *A Martian Odyssey* [Hyperion]; and in Weinbaum, *The Best of Stanley Weinbaum*.)

Short story. * *Time:* A.D. 2111. *Place:* mostly on Europa. * Space pilot Jack Sands has been blacklisted for cracking up the *Hera*, thereby causing the death of the members of the Gunderson Expedition and the loss of their data. It wasn't really Jack's fault; he had been working for two shifts, and his copilot Kratska, a dope fiend, was under the influence of drugs. Actually, Kratska caused the crash, but Sands is universally blamed. Hence, when his friend Henshaw offers him a job piloting the *Minos* to Europa, he is delighted to accept. He is less delighted to hear that the copilot is Claire Avery, the so-called Golden Flash, a rich young publicity seeker and spectacle racer of dubious qualifications. * Sands's cynicism is justified, for the Golden Flash, though gorgeous, is unpleasant and incompetent. On occasions Sands has saved the ship from her bungling. * The other members of the crew consist of Henshaw, Coretti, and Gogrol. * The *Minos* reaches Europa safely. Although Sands has known almost nothing of the background or purpose of the trip (and is remarkably lacking in curiosity), he now learns that the expedition is headed for Gunderson's diggings. And there is skulduggery afoot. Gogrol murders Henshaw and wounds Coretti. * The Golden Flash now explains some of what has been going on. Gunderson had been experimenting with atomic energy, using protactinium (element 91), which is especially plentiful on Europa. His data were all lost in the crash of the *Hera*, but the government has hopes that he may have left duplicate documents in a cairn at the old diggings. A further revelation is that Gogrol is really Kratska, whom Jack Sands did not recognize. He, too, wants the documents. * There are shootouts, captivities, and physical clashes before right triumphs. Kratska is dead. The Golden Flash is really a pleasant young woman who is by no means a spoiled, rich publicity seeker, but a poor working girl who makes a scant living at racing and piloting. She and Jack are now in love. * *Miscellaneous:* The outlandish fauna include the bladder bird, which has a huge reservoir of air for flying at high altitudes. When Sands has to cross hills above the breathing level, he uses the sack from a bladder bird to provide air. * Routine romance that could have been printed in one of the love magazines, apart from the setting. The Kratska situation is, of course, simply silly.

    1669. **PROTEUS ISLAND.** *Astounding Stories*, August 1936. Ill. Wesso.

(Reprinted in Weinbaum, *A Martian Odyssey* [Hyperion]; in Weinbaum, *The Red Peri*; and in Weinbaum, *The Best of Stanley G. Weinbaum*.)

Short story. * *Place:* a small island southwest of New Zealand. * Carver, a young zoologist who is classifying the fauna of the area, is warned away from tabu Austin Island by his Maori boatmen. He scoffs, but the Polynesians abandon him at the first chance. * When Carver begins to explore the island, he soon discovers its uniqueness: Every individual plant or animal is distinct, from a phenotypical point of view. Most of the wildlife is harmless, but there is one vicious group of creatures that look vaguely like cats crossed with large monkeys. * More novelty appears when a pack of misshapen dogs attack him. He shoots a couple and then finds himself the captor of a beautiful young blonde, who seems utterly feral, even unacquainted with fire. Carver calls her Lilith. She speaks a few words that the reader will immediately recognize as bastardized American French, but Carver, who may not have studied French, cannot communicate with her. They pass some time together, repeatedly attacked by groups of the cat-apes. * Things look perilous for Carver and Lilith, but the mother ship arrives and rescues them. At an earlier point Carver found a ruined hut in which a long-missing scientist recorded his experiments with radiation on the local wildlife. The scientist died, but shortly before his death rescued the young girl from a shipwreck. Since he destroyed his equipment before Lilith came ashore, she is free of the island's taint and is now on the vessel leaving with Carver. * Routine at best.

WEISINGER, MORT[IMER] (1915-1978)

U.S. (New York) fan, literary agent, author, editor. With Julius Schwartz operated Solar Sales Service, pioneer science-fiction literary agency. Also with Schwartz edited and wrote important early fan magazine *Fantasy Magazine*. Editor for Standard Magazine publications *Thrilling Wonder Stories, Startling Stories, Captain Future* in late 1930s. In 1940s editor of Superman comic books and executive in D. C. Comics. Wrote mysteries under anagrammed pseud. Tom Erwin Geris and participated in at least one Doc Savage novel for Lester Dent. * See also #1831, "Nth Degree."

1670. **THE PRICE OF PEACE.** *Amazing Stories,* November 1933. Ill. Morey.

Short story. * *Time:* a prologue from 2280, with the action in 1980. * Professor Balfour, the greatest scientist in history, is dismayed at the political situation of the day. He thereupon determines to create an invention that will forever remove war. * Several years later, he makes known his discovery, which he has deeded and assigned to the government of the United States. It is a disintegrator ray powered by atomic energy. Balfour demonstrates it in a test against three obsolete naval vessels, where it works beautifully. * But, the 2280 narrator reveals that it was all a hoax that Balfour conducted with the connivance of the President of the United States. There was no disintegrator, only a staged explosion.

1671. **THE PRENATAL PLAGIARISM.** *Wonder Stories,* January 1935.

Short-short story. * The suicide note of the great author Daniel Cartwright. * Cartwright's recently published novel, *The Davis Family*, a social epic set in the 1880s, is acclaimed as a masterpiece. Indeed, the Nobel Prize is mentioned. * Cartwright thereupon goes upon a short vacation. On returning, however, he hears not renewed applause, but accusations of the most blatant plagiarism. His novel, it is charged, is an exact reprint of a book published in the 1880s by one John Meadows. * There is no question about Meadows's book; it was published more than fifty years earlier; and it is identical to Cartwright's. * Cartwright desperately seeks to clear himself, tracking down Meadows's descendants and acquiring his papers. A solution emerges from Meadows's diary. He had invented a time machine; had gone into the future of 1934 and bought a copy of Cartwright's book; then, on returning to his own time and needing money, sold it to a publisher. * Cartwright should be cleared, but he is tricked by fate. He loses the diary, and recognizing that he has no proof and that his life is blasted, he commits suicide. * Ingenious idea.

1672. **PIGMENTS IS PIGMENTS.** *Wonder Stories,* March 1935. Ill. Winter.

Short-short story. * Bob Raynell, who has developed a new adrenalin serum, has been swindled out of his rights by capitalist Max Dribben. Raynell vows revenge, and soon works out a way. He surreptitiously inoculates Dribben with a culture that turns his skin totally black. * Dribben must come to terms, and pays Raynell a million dollars, in exchange for which Raynell guarantees to turn him white. The guarantee is fulfilled, but with unpleasant results. The next inoculation, a culture producing vitiligo, turns Dribben albino white. Dribben confesses himself defeated, and the two men come to terms, forming an amicable partnership. * Trivial, with poor integration of science and story.

WELLMAN, MANLY WADE (1903-1986)

U.S. (New York area, in later years North Carolina). Born in Angola, son of missionary doctor; educated at Wichita State University, A.B.; and Columbia, B.Lit. Worked in Southern folklore and history; also wrote a considerable amount of science-fiction and supernatural fiction for the pulp magazines. While his science-fiction, notably the stories here, is only at best routinely competent, his supernatural fiction, notably the stories about Silver John the ballot singer, is often excellent. Wellman was exceptionally skilled in the fictional manipulation of Mountain White folklore, real and imaginary. His best work is reprinted in *Who Fears the Devil* (1963) and *Worse Things Waiting* (1973).

1673. **WHEN PLANETS CLASHED.** *Wonder Stories Quarterly*, Spring 1931. Ill. Marchioni.

Short story. * *Time:* A.D. 2675. *Place:* Mars, the Moon, and Earth. * An episode of the Mars-Earth war. *Background:* Space travel is now commonplace. Communications and trade between Earth and Mars are well established, and there is considerable intermingling of the two peoples, who are physically almost identical. Both planets are about equally advanced scientifically. * The story is a psychologized study of a stupid war that broke out for no good reason. A background cause was the refusal of the Terrestrial World League to permit Martian colonies to be established on Earth; Earth, the council replied, has population problems enough of its own. The igniting incident was a riot in St. Louis in which several Martians were killed. As a reprisal the Martians interned Terrestrial tourists, and Earth retaliated. In a short time the situation was out of hand. * The story concerns Jack Stillwell, who grew up on Mars, is engaged to Yann, a Martian maiden, and is very friendly with her brother Nalo. Stillwell is torn in loyalties, but decides that his duty lies with Earth. * In the war that soon follows, Mars has the edge, what with much larger space fleets, even though Terrestrial weapons may be a little superior. As hostilities begin, the Martians systematically stage hit-and-run attacks on Terrestrial industries. There can be no defense against such tactics, and the Martian base has not been located. * A breakthrough comes when it is recognized that the Martians must be operating from our moon. Stillwell thereupon volunteers to neutralize the base. On the Moon, however, he is soon captured by the Martians; his pretense at being a deserter is unconvincing. If his friend Nalo hadn't vouched for him, he would have been executed. With some freedom of the Martian base, Stillwell sabotages it, his friend Nalo dying in the destruction. * The war now shifts to space battles. Despite the enormous preponderance of Martian warships, Earth holds its own; the final battle, however, might have been disastrous for Earth, but an armistice is declared at the right moment. * Stillwell returns to Mars and makes up with Yann, who forgives him for her brother's death. * Some attempt at psychological maturity within the space-opera plot, and certainly superior to most of the space stories published at the time.

1674. **THE DISC-MEN OF JUPITER.** *Wonder Stories,* September 1931. Ill. Marchioni.

Novelette. * *Time:* A.D. 2698. *Place:* Mars, space, Ganymede, Jupiter. * In the same universe as #1673, and a sequel of sorts, though with some modification of detail. * Mars is dying and will not be habitable much longer. As a result, Martian culture has turned to wild, fin de siècle decadence, with outlandish

Wellman, Manley Wade (*continued*)

drugs, sensation-enhancing rays, and general hedonism. Into one such wild party wander Lieutenant Duvelskoe and Captain Bromburg, who have been chosen to conduct an exploratory expedition into the Jovian system to determine whether Ganymede (which looks promising telescopically) might be suitable as a new home for the Martians. At the party, Bromburg meets Thiana, the beautiful but wild daughter of Colonel Stillwell, the local head of the interplanetary committee. Thiana tries to vamp Bromburg, and the two establish a warring relationship that will not fool the reader. * The two-man, state-of-the-art expedition has just left Mars when a stowaway is discovered: Thiana. It is not convincingly explained why she stowed away, but the two men must accept her presence, for it is impossible to turn back. * The spaceship continues on its elaborately calculated path, Bromburg at the keyboard, through the asteroid belt—members of which are evaded when they are potentially dangerous—and on to Ganymede. Ganymede is Earth-like, very pleasant, vegetated, with apparently no intelligent life. The expedition has been a success. Now it is necessary to create new fuel (hydrogen and oxygen) and start the nine-month journey back to the inner planets. * At this point personalities erupt. Bromburg is a cold fish; Duvelskoe is a happy-go-lucky type; and Thiana, who is a wilful, egocentric, badly spoiled young woman, decides to pay off a long grudge for what she considers slighting treatment by the men during the voyage. Locking herself into the control room, she takes the spaceship off the ground. This is potentially fatal, for the fuel tanks are nearly empty and Thiana will not believe the men when they shout the truth in to her. She goes so far as to knock Duvelskoe unconscious when he tries to enter the control room through the crawl space. * When the rocket is about ready to crash, she realizes what she has done, and permits Bromburg to do what he can to remedy the situation. * The only solution, with the small amount of fuel in the spare tank, is to establish an orbit inside Jupiter's atmosphere and obtain fuel from its constituent gases. * This seems feasible, but intelligent or semi-intelligent flying monstrosities investigate the ship, ensnarl it in a fibrous substance, and prevent its takeoff. Thiana redeems herself by crawling out in a space suit and cutting the strands of rope with a small hand disintegrator. The ship speeds off, back home, and Thiana and Bromburg discover the inevitable. * *Miscellaneous:* Twenty years earlier there had been a war between the Earth and Mars over Lebensraum, Stillwell (presumably the Jack Stillwell of the previous story, #1673) being one of the heroes. * As in #1673, Martians, who can interbreed with the Earthmen, are fully human, but slenderer and more emaciated. Thiana, whose mother was Martian, combines the best of both races physically. * Much is made of Bromburg's descent from a twentieth-century hero who was the first to fly around the world, an obvious echo of Lindbergh. * Pulp action, with some good lines, but very weak characterizations and clichéd situations. Wellman was a late starter.

1675. **OUTLAWS ON CALLISTO.** *Astounding Stories,* April 1936. Ill. Wesso.
Novelette. * *Time:* the early twenty-eighth century. *Place:* space and Callisto. * Pirates and romance. * Space pirates capture the space freighter *Rook*, from Mars, and Captain Hall Tarrant is offered the choice of joining the pirates as a navigator or dying. He joins, but as pirate's prerogative claims the female passenger whom he had hitherto concealed in order to protect her. His

action causes resentment, followed by a ray-sabre duel with the pirate captain. Tarrant, of course, wins. * His victory brings him into new peril, perhaps fatal, but a word from the female passenger stops his attackers. She is really the redoubtable Jahree, HERSELF, the Dragon Lady of the day, the pirate queen of the band, who had been traveling in disguise on the *Rook*. She now regards Tarrant with favor. * From here the story proceeds in a series of action incidents, including plots, encounters with an invisible Martian, escape, and conflict. Tarrant and Jahree fall in love, hence he is remorseful when he shoots down her flier and kills her. * *Miscellaneous:* Callisto has air-filled caverns in which the pirates live. The Callistan natives are gigantic and apelike. Gorgol, a Martian scientist in the pirate group, raised the intelligence of one such native, which becomes Tarrant's loyal follower. * An unsuccessful attempt to translate the Robert E. Howard and Edgar Rice Burroughs sort of adventure thriller into space opera.

WELLMAN, MANLY WADE and JERGOVIC, MAX
Wellman has a separate entry. * Jergovic, who supplied the plot that Wellman fleshed out, was then a resident of Omaha, Nebraska. Nothing else is known about him, but his portrait shows a young man. Social Security records list a Max Jergowitz (1907-1974), a resident of Nebraska, who may be the author.

1676. **REBELS OF THE MOON.** *Wonder Stories Quarterly*, Spring 1932. Ill. Paul.
The fifth-prize-winner of the Interplanetary Plot Contest.
Short story. * *Time:* about A.D. 2150. *Place:* the Moon. * Seamus O'Grady of the World League's secret police has been assigned to discover what is going wrong on the Moon. There, the great scientist Von Rickopf has been assembling an enormous space rocket that is scheduled to visit Venus. Launching date after launching date has been missed. Von Rickopf claims that he has had trouble manufacturing fuel, but the authorities are suspicious. * Landing, following tracks and small rocket vehicles, O'Grady discovers a large fuel dump that is not accounted for, and is captured. Von Rickopf, who is amiable enough, explains. He intends to sabotage the Venus rocket. Reason: He and his men, all of whom he says are in cahoots with him, have discovered an enormous diamond field on the moon. After the Venus expedition has ended in a fiasco, they intend to return to Earth, then revisit the Moon as private citizens and take the diamonds. As proof of his statement, the scientist shows O'Grady perfect gems the size of apples, then invites O'Grady to join his group in a managerial role. * Stalling for time, O'Grady agrees. To his surprise, he finds among the gang another secret agent. The two plot. The upshot is that O'Grady and the other secret agent seize the rocket and leave for Venus, impressing several members of the gang as crew. The more potent villains are killed. * Along the way O'Grady disguises himself as one of the more villainous conspirators and passes muster. * Competent as pulp action fiction, but not really worth reading.

WELLS, HAL K. (1900-?)
U.S. author, journalist. Born in Ohio, attended Ohio State University. Associated with motion picture fan magazines in New York and California, and with motion picture industry in general. During this period associated with the *Miami Herald*,

Wells, Hal K. (*continued*)

Miami, Florida. Also contributed fiction to *Top-Notch, The Shadow* and other pulp magazines. * Social Security records list a Harold Wells (1900-1965), born and died in Ohio. This may not be the same person. * See also #1832, "Man Jewels for Xothar."

1677. THE GATE TO XORAN. *Astounding Stories,* January 1931. Ill. Wesso.

Short story. * World peril. * *Place:* California. * When Blair Gordon sees the young woman he admires being kidnapped under hypnotic duress, he follows and becomes involved with Arlok, a humanoid being of living metal (weight about three-quarters of a ton) from Xoran, a planet of Rigel. * The Rigelian, whose science is far ahead of ours, has come to Earth in order to set up apparatus for a Rigelian invasion. In the fourth dimension Xoran and Earth are close, and with electric apparatus the Rigelians can bridge the gap. * Arlok, who is a vicious and almost invulnerable being, plans to take Gordon and girlfriend back to Xoran to be vivisected. But Gordon contrives to get possession of the Xoran equivalent of a welding torch and slices up the metal man. The world is saved. * No merit.

1678. WHEN THE MOON TURNED GREEN. *Astounding Stories,* May 1931. Ill. Wesso.

Short story. * It is just chance that Bruce Dixon, who has been working with radioactive materials, is wearing his lead-impregnated garments when the green ray of the Alpha Centaurians strikes. Almost all the rest of the world has been thrown into a coma that will end in death unless relieved. * Bruce investigates, and after battling horrible, hypertrophied insect-mammal hybrids, comes into contact with the invaders, who are the last survivors of a failed attempt at planetary engineering. * Bruce, with his girlfriend, Ruth Lawson, and her uncle, the inventor Crawford, battle through. When the Alpha Centaurians here on Earth are killed, Bruce sets off an atomic rocket with a radio-guided smart bomb that destroys the alien spaceship in space. The ship had been bouncing radiation off the moon, thence to Earth. * Also involved are thought helmets with which the aliens communicate with Earth people, and will-control apparatus. The Alpha Centaurians are roughly humanoid, but of reptilian origin. * Routine.

1679. DEVIL CRYSTALS OF ARRET. *Astounding Stories,* September 1931. Ill. Paul.

Short story. * Professor Marlowe and his assistant, Larry Powell, have invented an apparatus that transports things into a parallel world. Since animal tests have been successful, they plan to enter the other world (which they call Arret) themselves. Marlowe's headstrong niece Joan, however, precipitates matters by transmitting herself into the parallel world before the men can stop her. * The men are so excited that they damage the machine trying to retrieve her. They have only twelve hours to repair the machine and bring her back; after that, it is impossible. * The machine fixed, with four hours to go, Powell enters the other world in search of Joan. He is almost immediately captured by rat-like humanoids who plan to sacrifice them to the Tinkling Death (the Devil Crystals). These are large crystalline forms that extrude pseudopods and kill victims. Bullets do not harm them. * Larry and Joan are just about to be eaten when Professor Marlowe retrieves them. * *Miscellaneous:* Arret differs from Earth in being formed of negative matter of a sort, hence can interpenetrate Earth. Marlowe's machine reverses atomic structure.

1680. ZEHRU OF XOLLAR. *Astounding Stories,* February 1932. Ill. Wesso.

Short story. * Robert Blake, Helen Lawton, and gangster Gil Mapes are in the New York subway when the walls shimmer away and a force net seizes them and drags them off. They next find themselves in a strange enclosure, with two purple suns overhead and a purplish gas swirling outside. * After a time a second group of beings emerges into the enclosure. These are group beings consisting of bear-like headless animal bodies and separate floating brains that control the animal bodies by thought connections. These beings are hostile. Blake kills one of the brains with Mapes's revolver, whereupon the other, driven out of the enclosure, dies in the poisonous atmosphere. * Telepathic explanations come from a third creature, a tentacled being outside the enclosure. He is Zehru of Xollar, which is a planet in the Andromedan nebula. A criminal, he has been sentenced to death, but he has a scheme to evade his sentence. Bridging the space between his prison and Earth by relativity, he plans to transfer his mind to Blake's body, enter Earth, and become ruler. His jailers can never trace him. * It all sounds plausible, especially since the three terrestrials are paralyzed and Zehru has a disintegrator tube. * But Blake breaks the paralysis by moving onto his rubber raincoat, drags Zehru into the oxygen atmosphere of the enclosure, and in a fierce battle overcomes him. He and Helen return to Earth, the gangster Mapes having been disintegrated. * Perhaps the earliest instance of the survival ordeal.

1681. THE CAVERN OF THE SHINING ONES. *Astounding Stories,* November 1932. Ill. Wesso.

Short story. * *Place:* the Mojave Desert. * Don Foster, down and out Depression victim, and a group of fellow victims agree to follow the mysterious Layroh on an expedition into the Mojave Desert. * There is much that is odd about the expedition. Layroh, a very strange looking person, does not associate at all with his men. Nor is it known what he is looking for. But he has a weird apparatus that seems to be a tracking or locating device. * When the device sounds appropriately, things begin to happen. Layroh produces a disintegrator and slices a path into a mountain, opening the way to enormous artificial caverns. In them the men see a mass of incredible machinery, and, in apparent suspended animation, a range of slug-like beings with orange, pulsating core-spots. * Layroh, covering the humans with his ray tube, now crawls out of his human disguise and reveals himself as a similar slug. He explains: Millennia ago, the slug people, who originate on a planet whose sun approaches the solar system on an erratic orbit of a million years or so, invaded Earth, since their world was dying. But the Atlanteans, who mounted a science superior to theirs, defeated them badly, so that only a few slugs survived. * The slugs, however, had undermined Atlantis with high explosives, so that Atlantis went down. But the Atlanteans had saturated the atmosphere with a gas fatal to the slugs, so that the few slug survivors had to take heroic measures. Most of the slugs were placed in suspended animation, while a half dozen returned to their home planet to sweat out the period of time before the gas would dissipate. * Layroh is the only survivor of the half dozen, and he has returned to revive his fellows, who, multiplying, will take over the world with superscientific weapons. * Layroh adds that the slugs eat humans. He proves his veracity by revealing that he has already eaten one of the men, who had been thought to have deserted, and then eating another man. He now drops the surviving men

Wells, Hal K. (*continued*)

into pits until they are needed as food for the revived slugs. * Under Foster's leadership, the men escape and attack Layroh, who is not invulnerable, but Layroh manages to enter and activate a fighting machine that is present. Layroh easily kills off most of the men, but Foster, in a daring move, breaks a high tension wire and rides it down upon the fighting machine, electrocuting Layroh. Foster himself is fortunate to escape with a few injuries. The slugs who had been in suspended animation all die, and the world is safe.

1682. **FLAME-WORMS OF YOKKU**. *Amazing Stories*, March 1933. Ill. Morey.

Short story. * *Time:* 2154. *Place:* space and an unknown trans-Neptunian planet or dead star. * Larsen and Wheeler, small businessmen and adventurers, are on their way to the mines of Uranus when their Martian navigator (Dalo Yok), freaked out on Martian drugs, seizes control of the ship and locks them in the pen the men use for captive animals. * Yok explains his actions. His father, Ran Yok, claimed to have discovered a dead star, far out beyond the solar system; this star (or planet), dimly lighted and heated by its own internal activity, was the habitat of very strange life-forms that he called flame-worms. Ran Yok, who was dying when he returned, was ridiculed as a madman, but now his drug-crazed son intends to rehabilitate the family honor by rediscovering the lost planet. (Yok is said to be a common Martian name, and the Earthmen did not suspect their navigator's identity.) * Ran Yok and Dalo Yok are right, and the *Falcon* lands on the strange planet. When Dalo Yok leaves the vessel to explore, Larsen and Wheeler escape from confinement and track down the mad Martian, who has carefully taken along with him a necessary control component. * Shoot-outs and encounters with the horrible wildlife follow until Yok is killed by a flame-worm and the men, retrieving their control component, leave. Among the wildlife of the planet are a carnivorous plant that snaps up Wheeler and worm-like creatures that blast their prey into lumps of carbon. The flame-worms themselves are enormous creatures with thick scales that are impervious to Terrestrial explosive bullets; they have the same blasting ability as smaller life-forms. * *Miscellaneous:* Martians are human-like, but slender and weak, with blue skin. * Yokku is a dead former companion star to Sol. * Space travel utilizes propulsion rays. * Competent pulp adventure.

1683. **THE PURPLE BRAIN**. *Astounding Stories*, December 1933. Unsigned ill.

Short story. * *Place:* Southern California. * Neil Andrews and John Kincaid, while out horseback riding in the hills, encounter a cougar that has something on its head—a purplish, luminescent jelly-like object that emits a feeling of overwhelming horror and cosmic evil. Kincaid shoots at the cougar, whereupon it springs away, while the two men are thrown from their panic-stricken horses. * Kincaid is not altogether ignorant of the monster, for he has heard tales according to which it is associated with the lodge occupied by the scientist Yaagir. * On proceeding to Yaagir's place, they are captured by the strange being, which now occupies a monstrous cadaver formed by combining two human bodies. The creature explains: Arriving from the planet Zaas, which is about six light-years away, it is a scout investigating the Earth and mankind. It will report back to Zaas, whereupon a huge fleet will come to Earth and conquer it, enslaving mankind as carriers for the jelly beings. As the two

man can see from corpses lying about, the creature removes the top of the cranium, then infiltrates the brain. While the men watch in horror, the jelly being vivisects a couple of other captives, using a cosmic ray apparatus that both removes tissue and records the results photographically. * Working loose from his bonds while Yaagir's attention is elsewhere, Neil seizes control of the cosmic-ray apparatus, which he turns on the alien, disintegrating him. Before dying, however, Yaagir starts the fuse for an atomic bomb that is to destroy his headquarters. Neil and John leave hurriedly. * Not one of Wells's better stories, but perhaps the earliest instance of the puppet-master motif.

WELLS, H[ERBERT] G[EORGE] (1866-1946)

British author, preeminent as writer of science-fiction, social fiction, political theory, and popular histories. Honored as the great, true father of modern science-fiction, who established the basic fictional approach and many of the most important motifs and structural patterns. His works were generally available during the period covered by this study and were obviously read by the better-educated pulp authors. Stories of interplanetary invasions, time travel, supermen, marvelous inventions, biological transformations, future social life are all indebted to Wells, although most often with a significant difference. Whereas Wells (as a Fabian, early socialist) was by no means an apostle of scientist or mechanization, and was greatly concerned with larger matters of culture, society, and civilization, most of his science-fiction followers ignored such matters or took contrary points of view.

Wells's individual stories have been republished so many times that it would be pointless to list all reprints. Only major sources have been indicated. For further appearances, see Contento in the general bibliography.

Stories are presented in order of original publication.

1684. **THE DIAMOND MAKER**. *Science Wonder Stories*, June 1929. Ill. Paul.

(First published in *Pall Mall Budget*, 1894, issue not known. Reprinted in Wells, *The Stolen Bacillus*; Wells, *The Short Stories of H. G. Wells*; Wells, *The Best Science Fiction Stories*; Wells, *The Collector's Book*, and elsewhere.)

Short story. * In the frame situation the narrator, a man much like Wells himself, enters into conversation with a derelict who protests the difficulties and hardships of enormous wealth and power. Interested, the narrator listens to the stranger's tale, which is buttressed with the demonstration of a gem the size of the narrator's thumb tip. * Since boyhood the stranger has been fascinated by the problem of manufacturing diamonds and has devoted his life to its solution. He has finally achieved success. His technique, which involves a flux he has discovered, subjects carbon to tremendous pressure, in this case steam in a sealed container. After allowing two years for crystal growth, he has opened the cylinder and obtained several diamonds, but he has been unable to dispose of them. He offers to sell the giant gem for one hundred pounds. * The frame narrator, torn between greed and suspicion, encourages the man in a small way, but nothing is ever rendered final. * An amusing sketch.

1685. **THE FLOWERING OF THE STRANGE ORCHID**. *Amazing Stories*, March 1928. Ill. Paul.

Wells, H. G. (*continued*)

(First published in *Pall Mall Budget*, August 1894. Reprinted in Wells, *The Stolen Bacillus*; Wells, *The Country of the Blind*; Wells, *Thirty Strange Stories*; Wells, *The Works of H. G. Wells*, Vol 1; Wells, *The Short Stories of H. G. Wells*; Wells, *28 Science Fiction Stories*; Wells, *Best Science Fiction Stories*; Wells, *The Collector's Book* and elsewhere. In reprints occasionally titled "The Strange Orchid.")

Short story. * An orchid collector buys a half-dried-out, unidentifiable orchid rhizome and establishes it in his greenhouse. It turns out to be carnivorous, capable of moving its tendrils rapidly, and altogether too dangerous to keep. * A clichéd notion now, but fresh with Wells. The psychology of the collector is very convincingly handled.

1686. THE LORD OF THE DYNAMOS. *Amazing Stories*, February 1929. Ill. Paul.

(First published in *Pall Mall Budget*, September 1894. Reprinted in Wells, *The Stolen Bacillus*; Wells, *Thirty Strange Stories*; Wells, *The Short Stories of H. G. Wells*; Wells, *Best Science Fiction Stories*, and elsewhere.)

Short story. * Not science-fiction, but interesting in terms of modern psychology of religion for its estimation of the numinous. * The scene is the power plant for the electric railway. Holroyd, the engineer, employs as an assistant Azuma-zi, an ethnic primitive (racial origin apparently mixed, but black in part) who both suffers abuse from Holroyd and comes to worship the power in the largest dynamo in the shop. * As the scientific manager recognizes after certain events, the dynamo, as God, has had both a human sacrifice (Holroyd, whom Azuma-zi electrocuted) and a martyr (Azuma-zi, who leaped in and grasped the terminals).

1687. AEPYORNIS ISLAND. *Amazing Stories*, October 1927. Ill. Paul.

(First published in *Pall Mall Budget*, December 1894. Reprinted in Wells, *The Stolen Bacillus*; Wells, *Thirty Strange Stories*; Wells, *The Country of the Blind*; Wells, *The Works of H. G. Wells*, Vol. 1; Wells, *The Short Stories of H. G. Wells*; Wells, *28 Science Fiction Stories*; Wells, *Best Science Fiction Stories of H. G. Wells*; Wells, *The Collector's Book*, and elsewhere.)

Short story. * *Place:* Madagascar and an island nearby. * Butcher, abandoned by his native assistants after breaking a tabu—taking an enormous egg from a swamp—finds himself a castaway on a small island. He survives, but the egg, warmed by the sun, unexpectedly hatches, and a small aepyornis emerges. Butcher fosters and loves it, but when it matures to a bird fourteen feet tall, it becomes so vicious that he is forced to kill it to save his own life. * One of Wells's best stories. The examination of love renders the story pathetic.

1688. THE MOTH. *Amazing Stories*, August 1928. Unsigned ill.

(First published in *Pall Mall Gazette*, March 1895. Reprinted in Wells, *The Stolen Bacillus*; Wells, *Thirty Strange Stories*; Wells, *The Short Stories of H. G. Wells*; Conklin, *In the Grip of Terror*, and elsewhere. * Also titled "A Moth—Genus Novo.")

Short story, possibly to be interpreted as madness, possibly as a true haunting. * In a vicious scientific feud concerning insects biologist Hapley hounds and persecutes his rival, Pawkins, who dies of a heart attack. Thereafter Hapley is haunted by a moth symbolizing Pawkins; Hapley goes mad and commits suicide. Conscience or a haunting? * Most academics are probably not that sensitive.

1689. THE TIME MACHINE. *Amazing Stories*, May 1927. Unsigned ill.

(Published in book form as *The Time Machine*, Heinemann, London, 1895. A somewhat different text was published slightly earlier by Holt, New York, 1895. The Heinemann text, which is the "standard" text, has been reprinted many times, both separately and in collections or anthologies, sometimes with minor alterations. * The complex textual situation of *The Time Machine*—its anticipatory versions, its final texts, suppressed published sections, and unpublished manuscript episodes—is covered in *Science-Fiction: The Early Years*. * Gernsback followed the "standard" Heinemann 1895 text, probably without awareness of variants. * The story has been reprinted, Heinemann text, in Wells, *Seven Famous Novels of H. G. Wells*; Wells, *The Short Stories of H. G. Wells*; Wells, *The Works of H. G. Wells* [slightly altered text]; Wells, *The War of the Worlds, The Time Machine*; Wells, *Three Prophetic Novels* [restored text, adding material dropped from the Heinemann edition]; and elsewhere.)

Short novel, in theme an evolutionary examination of contemporary social trends, notably the growing gulf between the laboring classes and the idle rich of Wells's day. * *Time:* A.D. 802,701. * Time is a dimension, like the three dimensions of space, and the Time Traveler has created a machine that can travel along time, taking him to past or future. * In his trip to the future, he stops at the year 802,701, where he finds, after puzzlement and tragedy, that the human race has bifurcated into two species: the Eloi, who are childlike, even infantile and degenerate, live a life of gay and superficial hedonism, denying the shadow side of life; and the Morlocks, who live in dark tunnels underground, are photophobic and bestial, despite more intelligence that the Eloi. The two peoples seem poles apart, yet there is a horrible symbiosis. The Morlocks supply the Eloi with artifacts for life, but also kidnap the Eloi and eat them. * After a narrow escape from being captured by the Morlocks, he sets out again on his pilgrimage, now to the far distant future when the sun is dim and Earth is near its end as an above of life. * Returning to 1890, he tells a circle of friends of his experiences, then sets off on a new exploration of time—from which he does not return. * One of the great classics of science-fiction.

1690. THE REMARKABLE CASE OF DAVIDSON'S EYES. *Amazing Stories*, April 1927. Ill. Dean.

(First published in *Pall Mall Budget*, March 1895. Reprinted in Wells, *The Country of the Blind*; Wells, *Thirty Strange Stories*; Wells, *The Works of H. G. Wells*, Vol. 1; Wells, *The Short Stories of H. G. Wells*; Wells, *28 Science Fiction Stories*; Conklin, *Best of Science Fiction*, and elsewhere. Also sometimes titled "The Story of Davidson's Eyes.")

Short story. * When Davidson is subjected to a very powerful magnetic field, his vision is strangely affected: He does not see what is about him, but sees far off things. The explanation is a folding of space via the fourth dimension. The effect gradually wears off.

1691. POLLOCK AND THE PORROH MAN. *Amazing Stories*, February 1928. Ill. Paul.

(First printed in *New Budget*, May 1895. Reprinted in Wells, *The Plattner Story*; Wells, *Thirty Strange Stories*; Wells, *The Short Stories of H. G. Wells*; and elsewhere.)

Short story. * *Place:* West Africa and London. * Pollock, on

Wells, H. G. (*continued*)

safari in West Africa, meddles with a native woman, the property of a Porroh man who resents the incident and attacks him. Pollock wounds the Porroh man slightly, whereupon the Porroh man begins a persecution. Pollock has the native murdered, but he is now physically haunted by the dead man's severed head. After a time this changes to hallucination, in which he sees the bleeding head almost everywhere. Eventually Pollock can stand the sight no longer and commits suicide. Perhaps madness, perhaps a supernatural following, but in any case not science-fiction.

1692. **THE ISLAND OF DOCTOR MOREAU.** *Amazing Stories*, October-November 1926. Ill. Paul.

(First published by Heinemann, London, 1896, Stone and Kimball, New York, 1896. Reprinted in Wells, *Seven Famous Novels*. Available in many separate reprints.)

Novel, so familiar that it hardly needs description. * The narrator, forced by circumstances upon a small Pacific island, discovers the establishment of Dr. Moreau, a biologist who had been driven out of England because of the cruelty of his experiments. Present on the island are various monstrous creatures that seem partly human, partly animal. * The narrator, misinterpreting Moreau's results, believes that the creatures are men whom Moreau has surgically turned into animals. As we all know now, it is the other way around: Moreau is turning animals into men, using an elaborate system of pain and social constraint to suppress their perpetually reëmergent animal natures. * Moreau's cruelty cannot extirpate atavism, and in an inevitable rebellion of the beast-men Moreau and his assistant are killed. The narrator manages to survive. * The point of the novel is satire on religion and a portrayal of the foul nature of mankind; also present is material on the malleability of life, both socially and physically.

1693. **UNDER THE KNIFE.** *Amazing Stories*, March 1927. Unsigned ill.

(First publication in *New Review*, January 1896. First book publication in *The Plattner Story*, Methuen, London, 1897. Reprinted in Wells, *The Country of the Blind*; Wells, *The Works of H. G. Wells,* Vol. 1; Wells, *The Short Stories of H. G. Wells*; Wells, *28 Science Fiction Stories*; Wells, *Best Science Fiction Stories;* and elsewhere.)

Short story. * The narrator, undergoing an operation, dies, and his spirit moves in a cosmic flight through the solar system, out into the great universe. But it is all delirium caused by the anaesthetic; he did not die. * As always with Wells, nicely imagined; the theme is now threadbare, but it was not so when Wells wrote the story.

1694. **THE PLATTNER STORY.** *Amazing Stories*, July 1927. Unsigned ill.

(First published in *New Review*, April 1896. Reprinted in Wells, *The Plattner Story*; Wells, *Thirty Strange Stories*; Wells, *The Country of the Blind*; Wells, *The Works of H. G. Wells*, Vol. 1; Wells, *The Short Stories of H. G. Wells*; Wells, *28 Science Fiction Stories*; Wells, *The Best Science Fiction Stories;* and elsewhere.)

Short story. * Plattner, a master in a small British school, is analyzing a strange powder that a boy brought to him, when it explodes, precipitating him into a shadowy world, from where he can faintly see his former surroundings. This dim world is inhabited by creatures with human heads and trailing bodies; in

some fashion they are connected with evil and the dead of our world. Plattner also sees a long black arm that preys on the beings. When he drops the remainder of the powder, after subsisting in the other world for about nine days, he is exploded back to our world. He had presumably been in the fourth dimension, the land of the dead.

1695. **THE STORY OF THE LATE MR. ELVESHAM.** *Amazing Stories*, June 1927. Ill. Paul.

(First published in the *Idler*, May 1896. Reprinted in Wells, *The Plattner Story*; Wells, *Thirty Strange Stories*; Wells, *The Country of the Blind*; Wells, *The Short Stories of H. G. Wells*; Wells, *28 Science Fiction Stories*; Wells, *Best Science Fiction Stories;* Wells, *The War of the Worlds, The Time Machine* and elsewhere.)

Short story. * Borderline science-fiction. * The narrator, Edward George Eden, an impoverished medical student, is befriended by the great philosopher Egbert Elvesham. * Elvesham, who is old and failing, has decided, he says, not to waste his great wealth on philanthropy, but to will it to a most deserving young man. He has settled on Eden on the recommendation of Eden's instructor. * Eden is delighted and enjoys a sumptuous meal with Elvesham, who also shares with him an exciting drug. More than half tipsy, Eden goes home, takes another drug that Elvesham gave him—and awakens the next morning in Elvesham's decrepit body. Elvesham has accomplished a perfect personality transfer. Eden-in-Elvesham is trapped and does not live long, but Elvesham-in-Eden does not do much better, being killed by a cab. * Nicely realized as a story.

1696. **IN THE ABYSS.** *Amazing Stories*, September 1926. Unsigned ill.

(First published in *Pearson's Magazine*, August 1896. Reprinted in Wells, *The Plattner Story*; Wells, *Thirty Strange Stories*; Wells, *The Short Stories of H. G. Wells*; Wells, *28 Science Fiction Stories*; Wells, *The Best Science Fiction Stories*; Wells, *The Collector's Book;* Wells, *The War of the Worlds, The Time Machine*; Wollheim, *The Pocket Book of Science Fiction*, and elsewhere.)

Short story. * Elstead's narrative after being trapped at the sea bottom for several hours. His bathysphere was resting on the bottom, release mechanism jammed, when a band of somewhat humanoid fishes with spears came and dragged it away. The fish-men took the bathysphere to a town constructed of wreckage and seemed to worship it as a god. Finally, the release mechanism worked, and the sphere rose to the surface.

1697. **THE WAR OF THE WORLDS.** *Amazing Stories*, August-September 1927. Ill. Paul.

(First published in *Pearson's Magazine*, April-December 1897. Book publications, Heinemann, London, 1898 [somewhat abridged]; Harper, New York, 1898. Reprinted in many editions, with minor textual variation. Reprinted in Wells, *Seven Famous Novels*; Wells, *The War of the Worlds, The Time Machine*, and separate reprints.)

Novel. * *Time:* the near future. * The story concerns the experiences of a young Briton (perhaps Wells) during an invasion of monstrous creatures from Mars. The narrative is a first-person story of experiences and emotional reactions, but with speculative elements in science and social thought. * Lights are seen on Mars, and a huge cylindrical object crash-lands in rural England. The narrator happens to witness the first emergence of the Martians, their attacks on bystanders, and their

Wells, H. G. (*continued*)

ravaging raid through England with huge walking machines bearing heat rays and dispensing poison gas. The armed forces do not do well against them, for only a direct hit by heavy artillery affects the walking machines. * But then the Martian menace is suddenly over. Examination reveals that the Martians had no defense against terrestrial bacteria. * The story is vividly imagined. Beyond the narrative level the story is concerned with social Darwinism of a sort, with the narrator wondering whether humans, too, will have to invade other worlds if the Earth loses its resources. * One of the classics.

1698. **THE CRYSTAL EGG.** *Amazing Stories*, May 1926. Ill. Paul.
(First publication, *New Review*, May 1897. First book publication in *Tales of Space and Time*, Harper, London, 1899; McClure, New York, 1899. Reprinted in *The Works of H. G. Wells*, Vol. 10; Wells, *The Short Stories of H. G. Wells*; Wells, *28 Science Fiction Stories*; Wells, *Best Science Fiction Stories*; Wells, *The War of the Worlds, The Time Machine*; Derleth, *Strange Ports of Call*; Fiedler, *In Dreams Awake*; Knight, *A Century of Science Fiction*, and elsewhere.)
Short story. * Cave, a rather ineffectual antiques dealer, found the strange egg-shaped crystal in a job lot purchased from another dealer. A dreamer, somewhat unhappy, he finds solace in looking into the crystal, which reveals an exotic landscape with flying creatures that have tentacles below their heads. Similar crystals on pillars lead him to the conclusion that they are viewing devices. Two moons in the sky indicate that the crystal came from Mars. * Cave shows the crystal to a science demonstrator, who does not see all that Cave does, but enough to accept Cave's visions. Cave's wife objects, and he conceals the crystal. But Cave dies suddenly, and the crystal is lost. * One of Wells's best short stories.

1699. **A STORY OF THE STONE AGE.** *Amazing Stories,*
November 1927. Ill. Paul.
(First published in the *Idler*, May-September 1897. Reprinted in Wells, *Tales of Space and Time*; Wells, *The Short Stories of H. G. Wells*; Wells, *28 Science Fiction Stories;* and elsewhere.)
Short story. * Novelette, really a series of five connected short stories. The theme is primarily a struggle for power. * *Time and place:* about fifty thousand years ago in Southern England. The people concerned are not quite *Homo sapiens sapiens*, but have fire, throwing stones, and spears. The area is diverse, partly heavily forested, with hippopotami, rhinoceroses, mammoths, lions, and other large animals. * The Kipling-like narrative, with talking animals, centers on Ugh-lomi, who is a little more intelligent than his fellows. Ugh-lomi makes the first axe, with which he kills animals and his fellows, and (accidentally) first rides a horse. * Really a historical romance, not science-fiction, and not one of Wells's better stories.

1700. **THE INVISIBLE MAN.** *Amazing Stories*, June-July 1928. Ill. R. E. Lawlor.
(First published as *The Invisible Man*, C. A. Pearson, London, 1897; Edwin Arnold, New York, 1897. Reprinted in many editions. Also available in Wells, *Seven Famous Novels*; and in Wells, *Best Science Fiction Stories*.)
Novel. * Familiar enough from motion pictures that a close summary is not needed. * Strange phenomena in a small village in Sussex are ultimately explained as the work of an invisible

man. Once his clothes (and bandages) are removed, he cannot be seen. Eventually he is identified as Griffin, a nearly albino chemist who rendered himself invisible through chemical means. * At first Griffin is busied trying to regain visibility, but his character deteriorates. Involved in robberies and assaults, he becomes a murderous menace. As the novel reaches its climax there is a double hunt: Griffin's mad desire for revenge on Kemp, a friend who he thinks has betrayed him, and the general quest of the authorities for the dangerous madman. Griffin is finally accidentally killed while trying to murder Kemp. * The theme, of course, is unrestrained egotism, plus a touch of anti-scientism. * There are textual differences among the major editions.

1701. **THE STAR**. *Amazing Stories,* June 1926. Unsigned ill.
(First published in *Graphic*, Christmas Number, 1897. Reprinted in Wells, *The Country of the Blind;* Wells, *The Works of H. G. Wells,* Vol. 10; Wells, *The Short Stories of H. G. Wells*; Wells, *Best Science Fiction Stories*; Wells, *Tales of Space and Time*; Wells, *28 Science Fiction Stories*; Gunn, *The Road to Science Fiction*; Rabkin, *Science Fiction,* and elsewhere.)
Short story. * Catastrophism offers a chance to build a better world. A small planetoid enters the solar system and collides with Neptune, creating a small new sun that rushes toward Sol. The Earth, along its path, suffers enormous damage, what with earthquakes, heat, and tidal waves. Most of the human race perishes, but the remainder will build a better new social order.

1702. **THE MAN WHO COULD WORK MIRACLES.**
Amazing Stories, July 1926. Ill. F. S. Hynd.
(First published in *Illustrated London News*, July 1898. Reprinted in Wells, *Tales of Space and Time;* Wells, *The Country of the Blind*; Wells, *The Short Stories of H. G. Wells*; Wells, *The Best Science Fiction Stories*; and elsewhere.)
Short story. * Fotheringay, in a pub conversation, discovers that he has the power to work miracles. At first bewildered by his new power, then gradually more and more enthusiastic, he explores his capabilities. He consults with his clergyman (Maydig), who encourages him. The miracles build up until Maydig thinks of Joshua—and Fotheringay stops the rotation of the Earth. * Everything is destroyed, or on the point of destruction, until Fotheringay miracles away his miraculous power, and things are all as they were before he started in the pub. * There is a possibility that Wells is setting up a cyclical situation, with recurrence of the miracles. * An amusing story.

1703. **THE STOLEN BODY.** *Amazing Stories*, January 1928. Ill. Paul.
(First published in the *Strand Magazine*, November 1898. Reprinted in Wells, *Twelve Stories and a Dream;* Wells, *The Short Stories of H. G. Wells*; Wells, *28 Science Fiction Stories;* and elsewhere.)
Short story, really supernatural rather than science-fiction. * Bessel and Vincey are conducting long-distance experiments in releasing their astral bodies when the strange events take place. Bessel runs mad, wrecking his digs, rushing through the streets shouting "Life," and assaulting people. Then he disappears. Vincey, after strange dreams about Bessel, consults a medium, and through her aid they find Bessel, bones broken, in an excavation pit. * Bessel reveals what happened: When he left his body during the experiment, a being entered, and Bessel found himself in a new plane of existence, peopled by horrors—which

Wells, H. G. (*continued*)

are suggested to be the minds of madmen. As his body lay broken, he managed to creep back into it when the mad spirit left. * The pineal gland is considered to be an organ of enlightenment in paranormal situations.

1704. **WHEN THE SLEEPER WAKES**. *Amazing Stories Quarterly*, Winter 1928. Ill. H. Lanos.
First published in *Graphic*, 9 January-6 May 1899. Book publication as *When the Sleeper Wakes*, Harper, London and New York, 1899. Reprinted in Wells, *Three Prophetic Novels*; Wells, *The Collector's Book*. Revised, slightly abridged edition as *The Sleeper Awakes*, Nelson, London, 1910; reprinted in Wells, *The Works of H. G. Wells,* Vol. 2.)
Novel. * A fine dystopia based on modern mechanism, anticipating Zamiatin's *We* and Aldous Huxley's *Brave New World*. * *Time:* An introductory section in 1897, with the main story around A.D. 2100. * The plot line is simple: In 1897, an insomniac young liberal, after a regime of drugs and fatigue, falls asleep so soundly that he cannot be awakened. A trust is set up to preserve him, and he is carefully guarded, while trustees manage his wealth so shrewdly that he owns much of the world when he suddenly and inexplicably awakens around A.D. 2100. * Awakened, Graham is an embarrassment to various factions of the future world. On the one hand there is a popular messianic cult that believes that if he awakens, he will remedy the sore exploitation under which the people suffer; on the other hand, his trustees would like to see him dead, and, indeed, make attempts on his life; third, to the various politicians he is a useful tool for seizing or holding power. * After various adventures, Graham sides with the people and takes part in the rebellion against the bosses. He dies in aerial combat with the corrupt new dictator. Perhaps his rebellion will succeed; more probably, it will not. * More important than the plot is Wells's detailed description of the culture of the future, an extrapolation of nineteenth-century unrestrained capitalism and political corruption, with thought control, the equivalent of newspeak, propaganda machines, mass advertising cults, brutal political police, and a social system that combines a decadent plutocracy with downtrodden masses. An underestimated work. * "When the Sleeper Wakes" was not popular among the readers of *Amazing Stories*, if the letters in the readers' column are to be taken as a general response. One reader—James G. Roche of Schenectady—wrote a new ending, which was published in the letter column of the May 1929 issue of *Amazing Stories*. In this ending Graham survives the crash of his aircraft and awakens in the arms of Helen. The editor added in a subscript, "This ending of Mr. Wells' story speaks for itself. We wonder what Mr. Wells will think when he reads it." We do not know.

1705. **A STORY OF THE DAYS TO COME**. *Amazing Stories*, April-May 1928. Ill. Paul and R. E. Lawlor.
(First published in *Pall Mall Magazine*, June-October 1899. Reprinted in Wells, *Tales of Space and Time;* Wells, *The Short Stories of H. G. Wells*; Wells, *28 Science Fiction Stories*; Wells, *Three Prophetic Novels*; and elsewhere.)
Novelette or short story chain. * *Time:* around A.D. 2100. * The experiences of Elizabeth and Denton, a young couple in the world of *When the Sleeper Wakes* (though no mention is made of the sleeper or his cult.) Elizabeth's father disapproves of her match, and a rejected lover does what he can to injure the prospects of the young couple. As a result, Denton and Eli-

zabeth, of well-to-do origins, are forced to enter the ranks of the Labour Company, which is not much better than slavery. Things grow worse and worse, until it seems that they will break. At this point, the death of their former enemy saves them. * As with *When the Sleeper Wakes*, the interest lies not so much in the narrative (though this is stronger here than in the novel, growing out of the social situation), but in the horrible culture that is described.

1706. **THE FIRST MEN IN THE MOON**. *Amazing Stories,* December 1926-February 1927. Ill. R., and unsigned.
(First published in the *Strand Magazine*, December 1900-August 1901. First book publications by Newnes, London and Bowen-Merrill, Indianapolis, both 1901. Reprinted in Wells, *Seven Famous Novels* and in Wollheim, *Portable Novels*. Often reprinted.)
Novel. * An interplanetary voyage incorporating some satire on biological specialization, evolution, and genetics. * *Place:* mostly the Moon. * Most of the narrative is told through Bedford, who recounts his experiences with the inventor Cavor. * Cavor, a reclusive maverick scientist, has invented an alloy that creates antigravity. Building a small spaceship, he takes Bedford along on a trip to the Moon. They find the lunar surface much as Johannes Kepler had speculated in the early seventeenth century, with xerophytic life that is adapted to sudden extremes of heat and cold, as well as cyclically frozen atmosphere. But the interior is a hollow mass honeycombed with caverns containing atmosphere and fungi. * Cavor and Bedford are captured by the Selenites and taken into the Moon. Bedford manages to escape to the surface. Believing Cavor dead, he flies back to the Earth, where he retails his adventures. * Radio broadcasts from the Moon, however, tell a very different story. Cavor is alive and well-treated by the moon-people (whom Wells calls Selenites), who are highly evolved insects with a science far superior to ours. Space travel, however, is impossible for them, since the Moon lacks the element helium. As would be expected in an old biological form, the Selenites are greatly diversified physically to fit their social function. They have manipulated their genetics to produce different races for different purposes, including gigantic intellects. * Selenite specialists learn English rapidly, but the Selenite ruler is somewhat disturbed at what Cavor tells him about human nationalism and wars. Thus, as Cavor is about to transmit the formula for cavorite, the broadcasts suddenly cease. It is a reasonable supposition that the Selenites dragged him away from his radio to prevent an onslaught from the Earth.

1707. **THE NEW ACCELERATOR**. *Amazing Stories*, April 1926. Unsigned ill.
(First published in the *Strand Magazine*, December 1901. Reprinted in Wells, *Twelve Stories and a Dream;* Wells, *The Country of the Blind*; Wells, *The Works of H. G. Wells*, Vol. 10; Wells, *The Short Stories of H. G. Wells*; Wells, *28 Science Fiction Stories*; Wells, *Best Science Fiction Stories*; Wells, *Best Stories*; Gunn, *The Road to Science Fiction #2*; Janifer, *Masters' Choice*; Silverberg, *The Arbor House Treasury*; Derleth, *Beyond Space and Time*, and elsewhere.)
Short story. * Professor Gibberne has discovered a chemical that speeds up metabolism thousands of times. He and the narrator, taking the chemical, wander about in a world of stopped motion.

1708. **THE COUNTRY OF THE BLIND**. *Amazing Stories*, December 1927. Ill. Paul.
(First published in the *Strand Magazine*, April 1904. Reprinted

Wells, H. G. (*continued*)

in Wells, *The Country of the Blind*; Wells, *The Short Stories of H. G. Wells*; Wells, *28 Science Fiction Stories*; and elsewhere. An altered version appeared as a separate publication, *The Country of the Blind*, Golden Cockerel Press, London, 1939, thence reprinted in Moskowitz, *Masterpieces*.)

Short story. * *Place:* the Andes, Ecuador. * "In the kingdom of the blind, the one-eyed man is king" is not true. * *Background:* Hundreds of years ago a landslide isolated a sparsely inhabited valley in the Andes, and an eye disease (or mutation?) eventually turned all the inhabitants blind. That is one of the local legends. * Nuñez, with a mountain climbing expedition, survives a fall into the valley. At first he has grandiose plans for ruling the small land, but soon discovers that despite his extra sense he is more limited than the blind natives. The natives consider him an imperfect being, hampered by the fluttering things in his face and his obsession with strange words. * Nuñez almost accepts their decision to blind him, but at the last moment climbs out of the valley. * A very fine story, but I would not consider it science-fiction.

1709. **THE EMPIRE OF THE ANTS**. *Amazing Stories,* August 1926. Unsigned ill.

(First published in the *Strand Magazine*, December 1905. Reprinted in Wells, *The Country of the Blind*; Wells, *The Works of H. G. Wells*, Vol. 10; Wells, *The Short Stories of H. G. Wells*; Wells, *28 Science Fiction Stories*; Wells, *The Collector's Book*; and in Silverberg, *Earth Is the Strangest Planet*, and elsewhere.)

Short story. * *Place:* Brazil. * World peril as a new sort of ant appears in the Amazon drainage: large (2" long), carnivorous, intelligent. They probably have the use of fire and tools, but certainly manufacture a poison which they inject with little slivers of wood. It is projected that by about 1950 they will reach Europe. * One of Wells's best stories.

WERNHAM, GUY

Possibly the Guy Wernham who translated Lautremont's *Les chants de Maldoror* (1943).

1710. **OUTCASTS**. *Astounding Stories,* November 1934. Ill. Dold.

Short story. * *Time::* the far future. *Place:* space and an unlocated planet. * *Background:* When the sun dimmed and Earth became uninhabitable, mankind left Earth in a mass exodus of many giant spaceships, hoping to find a new home. The quest was unsuccessful, for suitable planets turned out to be inhabited by inhospitable beings, and the wanderers, who are governed by a quietistic ethic, would not fight or attempt to dispossess others, but continued their search. Many of the giant ships have met with accident. At the moment, only one ship is left, and it is running out of energy, which is almost impossible to replace. It is manned by three ancient immortals, who are weary of their long journey, and a cargo of embryos suitable for activation if a suitable world is found. Two of the immortals propose to quit their hopeless search and commit suicide, but the third argues for a last chance on a world that he has been observing. If the world turns out to be hospitable, mankind may arise again, though the ship can fly no longer. * The planet unexpectedly turns out to be nearly perfect: green, pleasant, and seemingly empty of inhabitants. Activating the embryos, the immortals establish mankind on the new planet. * Some years later, a strange flying cone appears. It lands, and creatures who amount

to enormous hypertrophied heads emerge. They are friendly, and communication is established by thought helmet. The giant brains, who are few in number and live underground, hence escaped notice, talk darkly of a doom over them. Curious and concerned, the immortals accompany the visitors to their city, which is underground and provided with an artificial atmosphere unbreathable by humans. * The leader of the giant brains—a triple being—offers background. Ages ago, the giant brains were humanoid. They had no interest in space travel, but developed an underground civilization. Internal strife, civil wars, massacre of scientists eventually caused problems. The brains can no longer survive in the atmosphere of their planet, and they, like the Earthmen, have run out of energy elements. Their doom is imminent. * The three immortals take thought. They are no longer needed by the humans whom they have established; indeed, it would be better if humanity developed afresh without them. Thus, the three immortals will remove their breathing apparatus and die along with the giant brains native to the planet. * Interesting for the death-wish and thanatoptic message, but told in a cumbersome manner.

WERTENBAKER, G[REEN] PEYTON (1907-1968)

U.S. (New York, Texas) journalist, technical writer. Born in Delaware, attended the University of Virginia. Writer and editor with *Fortune* and *Time*. Served in U.S. Navy in World War II. Later associated with the USAF School of Aerospace Medicine, National Aeronautics and Space Administration, and Air Force Systems Command. Author of several novels and books of Southwestern regional interest. In later life often wrote under the name Green Peyton. Died in San Antonio, Texas. * An interesting expression of science-fiction aesthetics by Wertenbaker is reprinted in the magazine history of *Amazing Stories* in this volume.

1711. **THE MAN FROM THE ATOM**. *Amazing Stories*, April 1926. Unsigned ill.

(First published in *Science and Invention*, August 1923.)

Short story. * Professor Martyn has devised a little box-like apparatus that permits the wearer to increase or decrease his size. It operates by chopping atoms in half or pulling in new atoms. * Kirby the narrator, a friend of the professor's, putting on the box and a thermal suit, zooms up in size. At first he has to watch out lest he crush the professor, but soon he is beyond Earth, the solar system, and eventually beyond our universe, which is but an atomic particle in a larger universe. * It is all fine, but when he wants to return from the macrocosm, he realizes that he could never find Earth again, and in any case it would have been gone for trillions of years. * He is currently on a somewhat Earth-like planet, with intelligent beings with whom he can converse, though they are not described. * Undeveloped, but interesting for perhaps being the first story to recognize the problem of time in expansion. * A precocious author; the present work was written while he was a high school student. * For a sequel, see #1712, "The Man from the Atom (Sequel)."

1712. **THE MAN FROM THE ATOM (SEQUEL)**. *Amazing Stories*, May 1926. Unsigned ill.

Short story, sequel to #1711, "The Man from the Atom." * The background is considerably changed. * Kirby, who has expanded up out of our universe, approaches a planet that is much like Earth, with wide grain fields, rivers, and human inhabitants. On landing, he is taken prisoner and carried on a flying platform to

Wertenbaker, G. Peyton (continued)

a city. After some interrogation, which consists of his talking while those present listen (and apparently understand a reat deal telepathically), he is placed in a prison cell. * There he becomes acquainted with the beautiful, charming, genius-level young woman Vinda. * *Background:* The natives of the macrocosmic world, who are completely human, are far superior to Earthmen in almost every way. But the culture is very heavily male-oriented, for as Vinda admits, the men are millennia ahead of the women in an evolutionary sense. Women are seldom fully educated and are regarded with some scorn. Vinda is exceptional in background and ability. * Vinda is obviously deeply in love with Kirby, who is obtuse and thinks only of returning to Earth. This is impossible, of course, but Vinda's uncle, a great savant, suggests that Kirby can possibly find a good substitute. * The universe is completely cyclical, and after its death it is reborn, developing with the same events as the previous universe—with this difference: There is a slight improvement from universe to universe. Vinda's uncle can give him directions and a chronometer, but Kirby will have to find the exact year. * Kirby takes off, callously parting from Vinda, and makes his way to the next Earth at an appropriate time. There, another Kirby has just left on a size-journey, Professor Martyn is in jail for his murder, and Theodore II is emperor of the United States. * But now Kirby suddenly realizes that he loved the wonderful Vinda and determines to seek her out again. But what about the other Kirby? * Interesting in ideas and with some period charm.

1713. **THE COMING OF THE ICE.** *Amazing Stories*, June 1926. Ill. Paul.

(Reprinted in Ashley, *History of the Science Fiction Magazine, Part 1.*)

Short story. * *Time:* into the far future. * A soliloquy by an incredibly ancient man, alone in an ice-covered waste caused by renewed glaciation. * Back around 1930 his friend Sir John Granden discovered the secret of eternal life. This was a surgical procedure, involving removing certain organs, closing others, and opening still others that were dormant. The operation seems to involve sterility and loss of sexual desire. * Donnell, the narrator, volunteers to undergo the operation; he is urged on by his fiancée, who agrees to live chastely with him. Unfortunately, she and Granden are killed almost immediately after the operation. * Donnell lives on, for thousands of years. He amasses knowledge, but is soon faced with the humiliating fact that human evolution has progressed and that he can no longer cope with the new intellectuality. * Hundreds of thousands of years pass, during which mankind continues to evolve, now becoming a balloon head with a tiny body. * And then the glaciation comes. All mankind is dead except Donnell and a dozen future men. The future men commit suicide, and Donnell is left alone, presumably to freeze to death. * Throwaway points along the way: The East conquered the West in a planetary war. * Humanoid Venusians unsuccessfully invaded Earth. * Immortality was rediscovered. * Future man is telepathic. * In his late years, before the coming of the ice, Donnell was put in a zoo. * Perhaps suggested by Leonard Kip's "The Secret of Apollonius Septrio."

1714. **THE CHAMBER OF LIFE.** *Amazing Stories*, October 1929. Ill. Briggs.

Short story. * The narrator, who awakens to find himself plunged into the river, swims ashore and recreates his experience piecemeal, as it gradually comes back to him. * To put it into historical order, disregarding Wertenbaker's structuring: The narrator, at a gathering of friends, strikes up an acquaintance with Melbourne, a rather mysterious Southerner. The two men are simpatichi, and Melbourne tells the somewhat blasé narrator of his lifework. He has been working on a synaesthetic experience machine that will give the user complete sensory illusions, in s-f terms, a dream machine, in modern terms advanced virtual reality. He has programmed a sequence, which the narrator agrees to try. * The narrator's experience: He finds himself in a beautifully landscaped setting. (He later learns that the hills, the mountains and even the sea have been carefully reworked to create utmost effect). A flying machine arrives, friendly men emerge, greet him, and tell him that his arrival has been expected. His new name is Baret. * The heart of the culture in which Baret arrives is absolute prediction and allocation (if not quite regimentation). Incredible machines work out the fate of everyone in the culture, and everything is preordained, if not quite predestined. As Baret he is only a guest for a predetermined time; he cannot stay longer, for it would require reprogramming (my term) all the predictive equipment. * It is a pleasant world, in part an arts and crafts eutopia, in part a communist Bellamistic work army. There is very little personal property, and the anarchistic "state" provides necessities. The machines do everything, and the humans simply attend them for limited duty hours; their plentiful free time is devoted to the arts, learning, and creative thought. As Edvar says, it is an automatic life; the soul of the machines pervades everyone, and the machines are perfect. * Living in this ideal world is pleasure to Baret, but he falls in love with Selda, his assigned instructor. Any consummation is impossible, however, for the predictions have been set for another man to marry Selda, and there is no permanent place for the narrator in the new world. As time goes on, he feels weird tactile sensations, as if there were another world beside him. Finally, in despair at the loss of Selda, he takes his flying machine to the river and leaps in to commit suicide. The shock of the water awakens him and he finds himself back in his ordinary, workaday world. * As he comes to understand that his experiences were all the product of Melbourne's dream machine, the narrator thinks back wryly. The only woman he has really loved is a dream, but so be it. He does not know where Melbourne lives, but so be it. He must accept life as it is. * Handled with a dexterity and cleverness not obvious from a plot summary. A good story.

1715. **THE SHIP THAT TURNED ASIDE.** *Amazing Stories*, March 1930. Ill. Morey.

(Reprinted in Conklin, *Big Book of Science Fiction*, as by Green Peyton and in Ackerman, *Gosh! Wow!*)

Short story. * On an ocean liner, en route from New York to Liverpool. * Strange lights in the sky form a prelude to most mysterious conditions as the ship travels along. There is no sun, although the day is reasonably bright, and at night the stars are completely different from what they should be. Electricity no longer functions at all. * What has happened? A solution is reached through joint discussions among the narrator, Captain Weeks, and Pretloe (a "scientist"). As Pretloe finally formulates it, the fourth dimension is a group of segments, one of which is our world, and the ship—perhaps as something to do with the sun—has slipped into a different segment. There is no possibility of returning along the route the ship has taken, for the ship's

Wertenbaker, G. Peyton (*continued*)

instruments do not function. * As the ship moves along, the captain worries about supplies and also about the reaction of the passengers and crew, for the previously mentioned cosmological speculations have been secret. After a time, however, land is sighted. It proves to be barren, wooded, and without sign of habitation, although flotsam remains indicate that previous mysterious disappearances have entered this new world. By now the captain and his informal cabinet, Pretloe and the narrator, recognize that the passengers and crew must be informed of their situation and that plans must be made for some sort of a land settlement. This is done. * Weeks and his two associates make a reconnaissance trip inland through the wilderness, when they see in the distance the distorted image of a city. They approach it, are suddenly shifted, and find themselves in Paris. The fourth dimension segment must overlap or end at this place. The three men make their personal arrangements in Paris, hoping (since it is impossible for them to go back and inform the remaining stranded men and women) that the others will follow them. * Nicely paced and well developed; one of the better stories in *Amazing*.

1716. **ELAINE'S TOMB.** *Amazing Stories Quarterly*, Winter 1930. Ill. Morey.

Short story. * *Time:* the present and an incalculable distance in the future. *Place:* Egypt, various places in the future, including Chicago. * A very long lead-in situation precedes the heart of the story. * Alan, the narrator, a chemistry professor in a small university, is deeply in love with Elaine, one of his students, but is too shy to say anything; she feels the same way about him, and is equally shy. When the narrator's contract is not renewed, he goes on an archeological expedition with his friend, the brilliant scientist Weber. Together they investigate a possibly predynastic civilization that according to Weber has perfected a technique for indefinite suspended animation. There is a beautifully preserved corpse/body to prove the point. * Alan falls sick and dies, but before his final moments he agrees to let Weber preserve his body for a future resurrection. Weber, who knows only part of the process, expects to have the full secret shortly. In this manner, Alan expects to meet Elaine when he is shipped back to the United States, revived, and cured. * But it does not happen that way. Alan awakens to find strange people around him. There is no way of learning how long he was in suspended animation, for the people of the future have completely lost a time sense, and although they speak English of a sort, do not even know the word for year. Any explanation by Alan is shrugged off or not understood. While the future people are intelligent, their focus of interest is so alien that there is little mutual understanding. But it is clear that enough time has passed for the world to be in a new glacial period, with much of the world uninhabitable. * Alan mourns Elaine and his friend Weber, until he makes an astonishing discovery. In an old travel book he reads of a mysterious Tomb of Elaine, which further research locates in North America. An air trip to America uncovers further evidence, that the tomb is at the former location of Chicago. * Alan flies to the ruins of Chicago, locates the tomb, finds Elaine still well preserved, the center of a cult, and revives her. The local people object to the removal of their goddess, but a disintegrator and a rapid flight away resolve the problem. Still, Alan and Elaine would have died in the snow had they not been rescued by a friendly savant from Mexico.

Alan and Elaine are now the only two pre-ice people on Earth. * Pleasantly written, but on the weak and syrupy side.

WEST, WALLACE G[EORGE] (1900-1980)

U.S. author, attorney, publicist, executive. Born in Walnut Hills, Kentucky; A.B. from Butler University; LL.B. from Indiana University Law School. Associated in high positions with UP, NBC, Mutual Broadcasting System, and American Petroleum Institute. Resident at Beacon, New York and Indianapolis during this period. Wrote film scripts. Occasional author of science-fiction stories.

1717. **THE LAST MAN.** *Amazing Stories*, February 1929. Ill. Paul.

(Reprinted in Wollheim, *The Pocket Book of Science Fiction* and in Moskowitz, *When Women Rule*.)

Short story. * *Time:* perhaps around A.D. 200,000. * M-1, the last human male, an atavism, spends much of his time sitting in a cage so that the all female population can see what males were like in the old days of bisexual propagation. The current population—desexualized, neutered females—is produced chemically from a master stock of protoplasm. * This situation came about gradually. During one of the feminist seizures of power, the rulers decided to keep alive only enough males to produce future generations; all others were slaughtered. Later, with the discovery of complete chemical generation, almost all males were destroyed. * M-1 is not too unhappy. He is required to spend only a few hours daily on exhibition in his cage. He is well treated and has a special nurse to attend to him. * All in all, this future world is not intolerable, but it is incredibly dull, and a collapse is imminent. Much of the ancient machinery no longer functions and cannot be repaired, and humanity is so dependent on routine and such machines as still operate that mechanical breakdown would be disastrous. The future females, however, do not recognize the danger. * The spark of change comes when an atavist female, who refuses to give her name, surreptitiously approaches M-1 and proceeds to seduce him. M-1 is more timid than the young woman, who calls herself Eve, but after a time glandular secretions function, and he decides to help her to destroy the horrible culture of the day and reestablish a new, old-fashioned human race. Their plot to destroy the breeding protoplasm is successful, and they manage to escape to the hills, where perhaps they will survive as a new Adam and Eve. * Several large loopholes in the story logic, but still unusual among the early Gernsback stories in being alive in writing and imaginative. David H. Keller, M.D., should have read the story and pondered on it.

1718. **THE END OF TIME.** *Astounding Stories*, March 1933. Ill. Marchioni.

Short story. * Dr. Manthis, renowned chemist, tells his daughter's friend Jack Baron, a radio engineer, that time will shortly come to an end. He bases his statement upon two elements: the Kantian position that time is a psychological matter and the observation that clocks seem to be speeding up. The end will come in a matter of hours. * Against this catastrophe Manthis has prepared an extract of hashish, which will keep the time senses of himself, his daughter June, and Baron at their previous normality. * It all happens as Manthis predicted, and New York is a lifeless city, presumably in suspended animation. * What causes it? Speculation and some monitoring of radio waves lead to the conclusion that an individual in New York, probably a

West, Wallace (*continued*)

hashish fiend, is broadcasting waves that work upon the brain. * Shortly after Manthis and his associates try to revive the city with a wave counter to that causing the loss of time sense, the mad Russian scientist Solinski reveals that he is behind it all. He plans to seize power and become master of the world. * Obviously, he does not. Manthis and others succeed in waking the city. * Reasonably imagined within a rather silly presupposition, but with a weak ending.

1719. **PLANE PEOPLE.** *Astounding Stories,* November 1933. Unsigned ill.

Short story. * *Place:* off on a comet. * Strauss's comet, which has occasionally been difficult to see, is peculiar: It is a flat plane, like the blade of a circular saw, and like a saw it carves off and carries away a small section of Earth holding four people: Professor Strauss, his son Frank, Frank's girlfriend Marie, and Bert, an unpleasant young druggist who is Frank's unsuccessful rival. * The surface of the comet is covered with a grayish lichen-like vegetation, and the atmosphere is breathable. Occasional berries provide food for the unwilling voyagers. * The Strauss party soon encounters the inhabitants of the comet, who are called Umenians: creatures about six feet long, two feet wide, and an inch or so high. After a little problem with a heat ray with which the creatures chivvy our friends along by burning their toes, telepathic communication is achieved by touch. * The author now treats his Umenians as if they were flatlanders, two-dimensional creatures that are intelligent, but totally limited in vision and other senses to a flat surface and unable to conceive of a third dimension. * The professor explains matters to the Umenian king, and as an illustration, lifts a member of the court up out of the plane so that he can see in three dimensions. This is convincing, but a tactical mistake, for Puro, the elevated one, develops delusions of grandeur and attempts to overthrow the government. In this he is aided by Bert the pharmacist, who places his chemical knowledge at Puro's disposal. * Bert and Puro attack with poison gas (chlorine) and "elevators," but their forces are defeated. As the story ends, the Strausses and Marie wonder whether they can build a rocket ship to take them back to Earth. * The treatment, which attempts to be breezy, is probably aimed at a teenage reader.

1720. **THE RETREAT FROM UTOPIA.** *Astounding Stories,* March 1934. Unsigned ill.

Short story. * *Time:* present and 2175. * The newspaper feature editor receives an unexpected visitor at his home: a strangely clad man (Smith) who claims to be a reporter of the *Vacuum,* a newspaper of the year 2175. * According to Smith, time is really a true dimension that curves like an oxbow river, with 1934 and 2175 close together in the stream. To travel, one takes a drug that paralyzes the time sense and then simply walks across time. * Smith describes the future. Not many years earlier, the country underwent a wave of puritanism in which liquor, tobacco, body exposure, female display and much else were forbidden—with regulations strictly enforced. * Then, about a few years later, all the criminals, social agitators, and malcontents were rounded up and deported to Borneo, which was sealed off. The result was not greater happiness, but considerable discontent. Indeed, a reaction set in, and much of the puritanism was set aside. The exiles in Borneo were invited to return, but refused. * Journalism in particular was hard hit by the cultural changes, since there was nothing more to print as news. Hence, when a

French scientist worked out time theory and suitable drugs, Smith's editor thought it a fine news break for Smith to visit the past, where things still happened. * The narrator is intrigued by the thought of visiting the future and departs with Smith for 2175. There he sees the future civilization, rocket transport and all, and takes part in a visit to Borneo, in a second attempt to persuade the exiles to return. This time, the plea is successful, and crime returns to eutopia, to everyone's satisfaction. * Back in 1934 the narrator, when he describes his experiences, is called a dope fiend. * The paradox is amusing in concept, but the execution of the story leaves something to be desired.

1721. **DRAGON'S TEETH.** *Astounding Stories,* September 1934. Ill. Dold.

Short story. * A euhemerization of the Greek gods and Plato's Atlantis, with Mercury the narrator. * *Time and place:* Atlantis, at some time in the past. * *Background:* In the past humanity developed a high civilization on the continent of Mu, which sank into the sea. Before the submergence, however, some natives of Mu fled to Mars, where they settled; other Muans, surviving in the colonies, ultimately founded the kingdoms of Atlantis and Egypt. Both groups lost much of the ancient science, but are still far ahead of us. * Now, five thousand years later, a Martian expedition led by King Poseidon has landed in Atlantis, intent on conquering it. Poseidon, who is arrogant and hotheaded, affronts visiting King Plu-Toh-Ra of Egypt, thereby setting off a prolonged war. As Poseidon soon learns, the Egyptians also retain some of the ancient science of Mu, namely teleportation and invisibility. * The war goes badly for the Martians. Only Cadmus of the ten kings of Atlantis sides with them, while Plu-Toh-Ra organizes all the peoples of the Mediterranean against the invaders. The Martians, used to weak gravity, cannot stand against the Terrestrial barbarians, and Martian energy is rapidly running out. * At this time Vulcan devises a ruse. Creating a high explosive substance, he forms out of it many tooth-shaped amulets, which Cadmus sells to the enemy as charms of invulnerability. At the proper time Vulcan, using a radio wave, explodes the amulets, destroying the allied Mediterranean armies. The invaders have won for the time, but the war is not yet over. * A jeu d'esprit that does not work.

1722. **THE PHANTOM DICTATOR.** *Astounding Stories,* August 1935. Ill. Marchioni.

Short story. * *Time and place:* New York and Washington, perhaps in the near future. * When the narrator, a psychologist, returns from a six-week vacation in Canada, he discovers that almost the only topic of conversation is the Willy Pan cartoons. His friends, his nurse, strangers overheard on the street all speak of Pan in a sort of dazed way, and all urge the narrator to see the cartoons. * The narrator, who is hardheaded, suspects something nasty, hence when he sees the pictures, he is able to recognize that they constitute a very elaborate form of hypnotic suggestion conveying both patent and subliminally unconscious ideas. After lead-ins and visual effects to establish rapport, the cartoons take a political turn, promising an eutopia and urging the viewers to accept Pan as dictator. * The narrator soon recognizes that the creators of Willy Pan plan a political coup. When he tries to warn prominent politicians, however, it becomes obvious that, up to the President, they are all under the sway of Willy Pan. * The narrator hopes to counteract the pictures with a contradictory message in a cartoon prepared by an rival animator who is disgruntled by Willy Pan's success, but is

West, Wallace (*continued*)

thrown into a lunatic asylum. He has failed and Willy Pan will succeed. * Unusual ideas, unusual ending.

1723. **EN ROUTE TO PLUTO**. *Astounding Stories*, August 1936. Unsigned ill. (Brown??)

(Reprinted in Conklin, *Best of Science Fiction*.)

Short story. * *Time:* the interplanetary future. *Place:* mostly on Pluto. * Space pilot Jack and his wife, Jahna, a Martian bird-woman, are making the pioneer exploration of Pluto. Jahna is one of a special Martian caste that retains the feathers and flying ability that other Martians lost millennia ago. Held as semi-sacred, her group is pampered and trained as entertainers. * Jack, although once in love with Jahna, now finds many of her ways irritating, especially her trait of singing conversation. Thinking of her as a useless, ornamental parasite, he is heartily sick of her. As the reader will guess, he will learn a lesson. * After an accident, Jack, who at first does not know what to do, lands the ship according to a suggestion of Jahna's. They then leave the ship to explore Pluto, which at the moment is about 100° below zero. They are attacked by native mist beings, who project cold at them, threatening their lives. Jack's heat pistol is useless against them. On an inspiration he rewires his weapon to project cold, which dissipates the attackers. He collapses, however, and would have died had not Jahna flown into the ship, rigged up a winch, and dragged him back on board. His opinion of Jahna has now changed. * Routine.

[Anonymous]

Presumably a British author.

1724. **WHEN THE SKULL MEN SWOOPED**. *Scoops*, 24 February 1934. Unsigned ill.

Boys' fiction. * Short story. * Hundreds of strange spaceships land in Great Britain. Enormous, mobile on jointed legs, they move across the countryside, disintegrating and heat-raying. From them emerge the skull men: armor-clad beings, about six-feet tall, with bare skulls. They are first seen (in obvious parallel to H. G. Wells's *The War of the Worlds*) by P. C. Grover and his pal navvy Bill Smith. * Brilliant young scientist Jerry Linden decides to investigate, and, examining a crushed skull man, discovers that the armor suit is filled with machinery, and the skull only a decorative appendage. The invaders are machine men. * Linden is captured by the skull men and brought before King Branco, who discourses to him telepathically. The invaders come from the planet Zlinn, which is millions of miles away. Since Zlinn is dying, the skull men need a new home. Originally, Zlinn was inhabited by humans, who constructed robots. But when the humans became extinct, the machine men, now conscious, redesigned themselves in human form. Jerry is released so that he can report to British authorities and arrange a surrender. * On meeting the Prime Minister Jerry learns that the situation is very bad, for the skull men have also released gigantic robotic animals, some resembling mammoths, that pre-date over the countryside. The only hope for Britain and the Earth is Professor Norrington, who is working on a heat ray. * This provides the remedy. When the heat ray is ready, Jerry and associates install it into a rapidly assembled mammoth skeleton, in which Jerry rides. This turns the tide. The decisive defeat of the skull men comes when disintegrators taken from crushed skull men are installed in airplanes. During the battles Jerry seeks out King Branco, but in vain. Knocked unconscious, he

revives to learn that the skull-men have been beaten and that the world is safe.

WHITE, CECIL B.

Pseud. of William Henry Christie (1896-1955). At the time submitted the following stories, a student in British Columbia. Later a noteworthy astronomer and physicist associated with Mount Wilson Observatory, Carnegie Institution, Atomic Energy Commision, and other scientific organizations. Author of several monographs on spectroscopic stellar analysis. White (as Christie) also contributed articles on home telescope construction to Gernsback's *Science and Invention*.

1725. **THE LOST CONTINENT**. *Amazing Stories*, July 1927. Ill. Paul.

Short story. * Honorable mention in the contest based on the cover for the December 1926 issue of *Amazing Stories*. * *Time:* a large segment about twelve thousand years in the past. *Place:* partly in Atlantis. * Dr. Joseph Lamont, summoning the narrator and an associate, announces that he has worked out a way of altering space-time coordinates. This permits time travel into the past. Objects placed between the electrodes of a small spherical device enter the past, the distance depending on the strength of the current; they are retrieved by diminishing the current. If the current is suddenly cut off, objects are stranded in the past. Travel into the future is impossible. * Lamont, after demon-strating his device, builds a gigantic time sphere propelled by X-rays that will ionize the air. * Next heard of, the sphere appears above the liner *Aurantia* in the mid-Atlantic. Lamont announces to the passengers on the *Aurantia* that he is going to vindicate his brother's theories about Atlantis by taking the ship and everyone on board back twelve thousand years. Since the pas-sengers are mostly professional geographers, the voyage should not be too unexciting. * The sphere and the *Aurantia* arrive in Atlantis, a verdant land inhabited by handsome people wearing feathered headdresses, nothing more. While the time travelers make no contact with the Atlanteans, the Atlanteans are ob-viously an advanced race psychologically, since they show no fear of the vessel and the time globe. Fine architecture and art abound. * But something goes wrong. While the *Aurantia* and its passengers return to the present, the globe itself slips into the past and is stuck there. The narrator plans to build another globe and retrieve Lamont and his companions.

1726. **THE RETREAT TO MARS**. *Amazing Stories*, August 1927. Ill. Paul.

(Reprinted in Conklin, *Best of Science Fiction*.)

Short story. * The narrator, an astronomer who has made ex-ceptionally clear observations of Mars that confirm the Schiaparelli-Lowell hypothesis, receives a visit from Hargraves, a well-known archeologist. * Hargraves tells his story: On a dig in Africa, after tracking down the origin of a piece of unusual metal that natives brought to him, he uncovered a gigantic metal building, in which were functioning "picture books" and other evidences of a civilization superior to ours. * The books included a programmed learning system, so that Hargraves could read them after some study. * The documents tell of Martian explora-tions and attempted colonizations of Earth. The first explorers found Earth's gravity and living conditions impossible and did not survive. In preparation for later expeditions, the Martians bred a special colonial stock that (with metal prosthetics) could tolerate terrestrial gravity. But even this did not work, for within

White, Cecil B. (*continued*)

a few generations the settlers degenerated physically and mentally, becoming bands of roaming savages, presumably our ancestors. * The undegenerate Martians withdrew after building three record towers for future discovery, perhaps half a million years later. * *Miscellaneous:* The Martians are humanoid, but nine feet tall, large headed and chested. * Their civilization is based on birth control, eugenics, perhaps socialism, and strict environmental conservation. * The books offer what amount to holograms. * Martian space craft are winged and propelled by "Goddard Rockets," an early recognition of Goddard's work. * In general the story would seem derivative from Erle Cox's *Out of the Silence* (Australian and British editions, 1925). * Intelligent, but unsophisticated narrative. For a sequel, see #1727, "The Return of the Martians."

1727. **THE RETURN OF THE MARTIANS.** *Amazing Stories*, April 1928. Ill. Paul.

Short story. * Sequel to #1726, "The Retreat to Mars." * *Place:* British Columbia and Mars. * Following instructions in the Martian manuals found in the previous episode, Hargraves, Smythe, and the narrator build a transmitter and receiver and communicate with Mars. The first information they receive is tragic. The returning Martian expedition took back with it terrestrial germs, with the result that almost the entire Martian population succumbed. Since then, progress has been slow, because the Martians have had to concentrate on basics. * The Martians now invite a party of Earthmen to Mars; the three researchers and the narrator's wife accept, whereupon a spaceship arrives and picks them up. It is made clear from the beginning that both Martians and Earthmen will wear protective clothing to avoid a repetition of the previous epidemics. * The Earthmen are hospitably received and after a thorough indoctrination, at times reminiscent of Hugo Gernsback's "Baron Münchhausen's Scientific Adventures," return to Earth. * Mars and its culture are described in some detail. The population is organized into a work army, with occupation assigned according to aptitude and training. Hours of labor are short. All receive sustenance from the government, with extra credits for personal matters; labor is graded mathematically. All work hard and altruistically. * There is strict population control, with bureaus that pass on prospective marriages, which are one-time and permanent. Martian longevity is great, over fourteen hundred years, in part due to the perfected medical system—which is invoked to correct minor disabilities that the narrator, like all Earthmen, has. * The "canals" seem to be belts of intensive cultivation, which is performed automatically by sophisticated machinery. Water is stored underground, and the atmosphere is maintained by gigantic generators. * The Martians have had and discarded wireless transmission of power; they now have a new power source that seems to amount to antigravity. * Of no interest.

WILKINS, RALPH W.

No information, but portrait shows a young man. An Ohio lawyer, Ralph Wharton Wilkins (1901-1966) is recorded, but there is no evidence that he ever wrote any fiction.

1728. **WHEN SPACE RIPPED OPEN.** *Air Wonder Stories*, November 1929. Ill. Paul.

Short story. * *Time:* A frame situation reminiscences about the horrors of the late twentieth century. * A document from the past: The green star passes close to the Earth, but does not collide with it, as had been feared. Then, inexplicably, monstrous insects begin to appear in most of the world, North America at first excepted. These include wasps larger than airplanes, beetles hundreds of feet long, and similar gigantic forms. Because of their size and multitude, there is little defense against them, for small arms are useless and only a direct hit with a cannon will avail. * The great Professor Abelton explains and proposes a solution. When the green star passed, its gravity disrupted space so that a path to a parallel universe (universes being stacked beside each other like cards in a pack) was opened, and the monsters came through. There is no immediate defense against them, Abelton declares, but ultimate salvation for the human race may lie in setting up an impregnable stronghold. * With strong government assistance, Abelton builds a fortress ten miles square, with 250-foot-high steel and concrete walls, top guarded by an electrified screen. Inside are housing, a factory, arms and ammunition, planes, and agricultural land. * Abelton then populates his town with an elite, in the last stages machine gunning others who try to break in. In the meanwhile a terrible plague, perhaps from the other-world that impinges on ours, kills about ninety percent of the human race. * The refuge works well when the gigantic insects arrive, and after a time the humans begin to reclaim the land, first setting up comparable settlements, populated in part from the first town and in part from the occasional survivors outside. The ground insects are much less a problem than the aerial insects, and they are controlled with tanks and high explosives. Against the horrible flying forms Abelton builds a gigantic seaplane with wingspread and fuselage nine hundred feet long. Armored and provided with cannon, it is able to seek out and destroy insect hordes at their breeding places. Eventually, North America is reconquered. Three centuries later Europe and Asia still seem to be wasteland. * The story is told without characterizations, as a chronicle.

1729. **THE EMPIRE IN THE SKY.** *Wonder Stories*, October 1930. Ill. Paul.

Short story. * *Place:* up in the sky. * The narrative told by Athelstan Speare, aviator friend of the frame narrator. * Caught in an updraft and blown to an altitude of about ten miles, he sees floating in front of him a great cube about two miles wide. He lands on top of it, enters, and finds enormous chambers, some filled with rusting machines of incalculable function, some with rotting furniture. All over are skeletons of men who have apparently died violently. * Speare wanders about for days, but on the crucial occasion, when napping, he awakens to find a beautiful young blonde woman looking at him. Things are complicated for a moment when strange men attack the woman, but what with Speare's pistol and the woman's explosive ray gun, all is well. * Communicating telepathically with Speare, the young woman, whose name is Dhera, takes him across the reservoir that occupies a whole floor of the cube to her dwelling, the water control station. She now lives there alone, her father having died recently. As becomes clear, she is the last upper class Atlantean left in the cubic city. * Background, as conveyed in part by motion pictures, in part by telepathy: When it became obvious that Atlantis would sink, Atlantean superscience constructed ten cubes from the bedrock of the land and floated them high in the air on electron streams. Each cube contained two hundred floors, offering a total area of about 800 square miles. Atomic motors sustain the cities, manufacture air, and provide necessities of life directly from electricity. One floor constituted a reser-

Wilkins, Ralph W. (*continued*)

voir, while several lower floors were used to grow plants that were transformed into manufactures and food. The cubes were rendered invisible from below by light manipulation. * The population of each cube was about a million, rigidly arranged in a caste system, with the nobles (descendants of the ancient warlords) at the top, beneath them scientists and artists, then a vast horde of serf-like people who lived like domestic animals. Dhera's father wanted to alleviate the lot of the serfs, whereupon by order of the king of Atlantis the other nine Atlantean cities attacked Dhera's cube, slaughtering everyone. Dhera and her father managed to escape, but the invaders left a slave garrison behind with orders to kill any possible survivors. * Speare and Dhera live together happily, eventually making peace with the garrison, whose members come to recognize that Dhera and her father had been their friends, not the monsters the establishment claimed. * But now there is word that the King is planning to colonize the cube with settlers from other cities. Speare and Dhera are determined to overthrow the king, and have come to Earth with huge quantities of gold to manufacture potent Atlantean weapons for an uprising. * Dhera and Speare leave, and the frame narrator hears no more from them. Years pass, while he wonders about their fate. But then he learns of a strange plane found in the ocean. Obviously Atlantean, its emblem has images of Dhera and Speare, indicating that the coup was successful. * An entertaining story with a certain amount of charm.

WILLARD, CHARLES D.

Pseud. of Charles Willard Diffin, who is covered in a separate entry.

1730. **OUT OF THE DREADFUL DEPTHS.** *Astounding Stories*, June 1930. Ill. J. Fleming Gould.

Short story. * *Place:* mostly mid-Pacific, not too far from Hawaii. * Partly as a the result of a bet with Admiral Struthers, U.S.N., travel-writer Robert Thorpe undertakes to sail alone from Manilla to San Diego. * Along the way, as he later reports to the admiral in San Diego, he encounters a mysterious derelict ship, whose log records an attack by a strange monster. * Thorpe returns to the area on a destroyer, and after some to-do, encounters the creature. It is immense, large enough to drag ships around, and it is abundantly furnished with eyes, tentacles, and beaks. It is not an octopus, but perhaps a kraken? * Thorpe's vessel manages to survive an attack, though other ships are destroyed. A destroyer shells the creature and presumably kills it. * There is also a rather feeble romance, but otherwise competent action pulp fiction, science-fictional by courtesy of the monster.

1731. **THE EYE OF ALLAH.** *Astounding Stories,* January 1931. Ill. J. Fleming Gould.

Short story. * Disreputable photographer Blinky Collins accidentally enhances his X-ray machine so that it can penetrate anything, at adjustable distances. The apparatus can also kill by projecting electricity. * Blinky's criminal associates find his machine useful, but he is murdered and his invention is stolen by a disgruntled madman who uses it for intimidation and extortion. * When the President of the United States is threatened, Robert Delamater of the Secret Service takes a hand. He reasons out the modus operandi of the apparatus and prepares a counterblow that removes the criminal and his stolen device. * Routine.

WILLIAMSON, JACK

Writing name of John Stewart Williamson (1908-present). Born in Bisbee, Arizona; educated at West Texas State University and University of New Mexico; received A.B. and M.A. from Eastern New Mexico University, and Ph.D., from University of Colorado (1964). Professor of English, Eastern New Mexico University (1960-1977). One of the major authors in pulp science-fiction, with longest active career in quality work. Williamson's early stories were largely derivative from A. Merritt, with highly romantic plots and settings, a deep sense of longing, and a general rationalized fairy tale atmosphere. In his later work, mostly beyond our time limit, Williamson developed a more individual story that was often thought-provoking, with considerable psychological depth. While the early stories considered in this study are not to be disparaged, Williamson's later work from the 1950s and 1960s is generally considered much superior. In an interview Williamson described his interpretation of science-fiction, which in some respects is a more sophisticated version of Hugo Gernsback's messianic approach:

> [Elliot:] "[Y]ou describe science fiction as 'a kind of periscope, raised above our own time to survey possible worlds to come'. . . ."
> [Williamson:] "The image of science fiction as periscope reflects my old notion of 'scientifiction' as the 'searchlight of science.' In our age, science is exploring the universe; I have called that the greatest and most absorbing mystery story. To the extent that science fiction relates to 'hard' science, it can be seen as moving beside or sometimes ahead of science to probe the frontiers of knowledge . . . In particular, that there was, or is, truth in C. P. Snow's distinction between the 'culture of science' and the 'traditional literary culture.' I felt the need of a bridge between the two cultures, and felt that science fiction could be such a bridge." (Elliot, p. 23).

Williamson's autobiography, *Wonder's Child,* is well worth reading.

See also collaborations Miles J. Breuer and Jack Williamson and Jack Williamson and Laurence Schwartzman.

1732. **THE METAL MAN.** *Amazing Stories,* December 1928. Ill. Paul.

(Reprinted in Williamson, *The Early Williamson;* Williamson, *The Pandora Effect;* Williamson, *The Best of Jack Williamson;* Ross, *The Best of Amazing;* Clareson, *A Spectrum of Worlds;* Elwood and Ghidalia, *Androids;* and in Silverberg, *The Arbor House Treasury.*)

Short story. * *Place:* Main narrative somewhere near the Pacific coast of a Latin American country. * In the frame setting, sailors land and deliver to the frame narrator a coffin; in it is a metal corpse, which the narrator recognizes as that of his friend Professor Kelvin. A manuscript accompanies the figure. * The manuscript: Kelvin, who is a geologist, is tracing the source of the Rio de Sangue, a red, highly radioactive stream. Flying into the mountains in his small plane, he sees strange lights ahead of him, a red metal sphere rising into the air, and a peculiar mist. He feels sensations of weight, and he and his plane are dragged down into a mountain crater, where he is forced to land. On leaving his plane, he finds metal birds, animals, and even a metal

Williamson, Jack (*continued*)
pteranosaurus, all transformed by the strange atmosphere of the crater. And he notices that his finger tips are also turning metallic. The juice of certain berries, however, removes the metal. * Kelvin, exploring, sees a city with pillars, from which flare lights, and the gigantic sphere. But then he is captured by a crystalline being something like a gigantic snowflake and carried away to the crater of the crystals. * When his captors seem inactive, he manages to escape and fly away. He is fabulously rich because of the radium he has found, but he is also turning into a metal simulacrum of himself. * Professor Kelvin now stands in the museum of the university to which he was attached. * Williamson's first published story. While it is heavily derivative from A. Merritt's "The People of the Pit," it is nicely written and imaginative.

1733. **THE ALIEN INTELLIGENCE**. *Science Wonder Stories*, July-August 1929. Ill. Paul.
(Reprinted in Williamson, *The Alien Intelligence*.)
Short novel. * *Place:* Central Australia. * Young Winfield Fowler, an American living in Australia, receives a radio summons from his friend the great scientist Horace Austen, begging him to bring certain eqwuipment to the Mountain of the Moon in the Victoria Desert. Austen, who has long been missing, also instructs Fowler to climb the steps up the mountain, descend into the crater and greet "Melvar, maiden of the crystal city," who will provide more information. * Fowler, moving alone, follows instructions, finds a silvery ladder that takes him to the top of a ridge, whereupon he descends a great distance into the crater, falling the last few feet. Along the way, and from here on, the story is filled with color prolixities in the manner of A. Merritt. * Rather than offering a straight-line plot, it seems better to list what Fowler encounters as individual items, then indicate interrelations. * Fowler sees strange scarlet torpedo-like ships zipping around through the air and strange rays acting upon the environment. These, as he learns later, are operated by the Krimlu, highly evolved, physically decadent insects who move about in cyborg walking machines and possess a superscience. * He meets the maiden Melvar, a gorgeous blonde who speaks enough English that they can instantly fall in love. * Melvar's people live in the city of Astran, which is apparently built of worked diamond. Handsome physically, the natives of Astran have lost almost all of the supernal science that created synthetic diamond as a building material, and survive by gathering wild berries. They have even forgotten the use of fire, but they still possess a single operative ray field-gun that they use to ward off Krimlu attacks. * The culture of Astran is not entirely pleasant, for the frenziedly vicious high priest delights in human sacrifices made by pouring on victims a highly corrosive silvery liquid from a nearby lake. This liquid is radioactive, though apparently not a known element; the Krimlu use it to power their culture. * The Krimlu kidnap humans from the crystal city and transform them into purple slaves who are utterly mindless, incredibly strong and vital, and very vicious. Escaped slaves are a peril to the humans. * Arriving at the crystal city of Astran, Fowler learns that he is not welcome, for Austen had alienated the priesthood by talking about an outside, which the priests deny exists. Austen has been expelled, and Melvar is in danger for having befriended him. Saving Melvar from being sacrificed, Fowler flees with her to the wilderness, where they are perpetually threatened by the violent, almost indestructible purple

men. The situation changes, however, when Fowler succeeds in capturing a raiding Krimlu airship, which he can operate easily. He and Melvar find Austen, who has been experimenting with the silvery liquid metal, developing an explosive to destroy the Krimlu power plant. * After various other perils, Austen descends into the pits and explodes the plant, thereby destroying the whole crater, weird life-forms, lost race, insect intelligence, and all. Fowler and Melvar, however, escape in the stolen Krimlu airship. * As is often the case in the early Williamson, too much influence of A. Merritt and too much going on for the length of the story, but pleasant for a dreamy atmosphere.

1734. **THE SECOND SHELL**. *Air Wonder Stories*, November 1929. Ill. Paul.
(Reprinted in Williamson, *The Alien Intelligence*.)
Short story. * *Time:* 1939. *Place:* Durango, Mexico; in the stratosphere. * The plot, which should have been developed into at least a novelette, is somewhat threadbare and confusing. It is better to consider individual themes. * Robert Barrett, a newspaper reporter, is approached by a Secret Service man who wants him to accompany him to Mexico. The Secret Service man suspects that there are Japanese war preparations in the area. * Dr. Vernon, a friend of Barrett's, has been working on a death ray for many years. The principle is atomic disintegration of thorium, focused appropriately. The doctor also has a beautiful daughter, Ellen, with whom Barrett is in love. * Herman Vars, a mad scientist, knows of Vernon's death rays and has stolen specifications for making an apparatus. Vars, who wears a Flash Gordon-like uniform and has assembled a band of cutthroats, intends to be king of the world. * Assisting Vars are stratosphere creatures of the usual type, purplish semimaterial octopoidal beings who live in a semimaterial world, but have a high science. Among their weapons is a purple gas, based on thorium, which has the effect of antigravity. They use it to power their air vessels. * Vars has his headquarters up in the clouds. * There are the usual captures and escapes, with Barrett doing his share with a slow-poke, lazy-acting pocket death ray. As the good characters are escaping from the cloud city, it explodes behind them. Apparently the death-ray machine that Vars built needed some modification not to be found in the blueprints. * *Miscellaneous:* Incidents include a purple gas attack that sends naval vessels off the Earth into space. * Williamson hints at a sequel, but none seems to have been written.

1735. **THE GREEN GIRL**. *Amazing Stories*, March-April 1930. Ill. Wesso.
(Printed in book form by Avon Books, New York, 1950, and also translated into German.)
Short novel. * *Time:* 1999-2000. *Place:* mostly beneath the South Pacific Ocean. * "At high noon on May 4, 1999, the sun went out!" begins Williamson. But there is considerable antecedent material. The narrator, Melvin Dane, has had a more than imaginary playmate since childhood, a beautiful young woman with green skin. He has seen her in his dreams, and in later life has spoken to her over an old-fashioned radio set, learning her language, which is not related to any known tongue. Melvin perpetually daydreams of this ideal Green Girl. * Melvin has been reared as the ward of the great maverick scientist Sam Walden, the inventor of the hydrodyne subatomic engine, which is the basis of contemporary civilization. Sam has long been working on a secret project which he will not reveal even to Melvin. * When the sun goes out, as mentioned above, Dr. Sam

Williamson, Jack (*continued*)

simply says in effect, "I knew it." He has been aware of an attempt to jam the sun's radiation frequencies and has been readying an apparatus with which he restores solar radiation. Sam has also located the source of the attack, nine miles below the South Pacific, and has built the Omnimobile, a vessel that will function in space, in the air, on land, on the sea, and even below the sea. * When a hostile force destroys Sam's compound, he and Melvin decide to take the Omnimobile down deep in the South Pacific and discover what is going on. * After they reach a certain depth, they find themselves beneath a red gas layer (radium fortified) that keeps the sea from invading a lost world nine miles down. The land has a strange vegetation unlike that of the surface and strange animal life; noteworthy is the lunak, a gigantic flying creature with a flower for a head, six root-like legs, and powerful wings. It lives on the blood and vital fluids of mammals. * As the men are exploring, they sight such a creature flying away with a nude young woman as its prey. Rescuing her, they discover that she is Melvin's "imaginary playmate," the Green Girl, whose name is Xenora. On her back had been a mechanical device that must have been ripped off when the lunak seized her. * Revived, fortified, Xenora, when not interrupted by Melvin's moonings, describes the strange land, although her knowledge does not extend far. Her people, the city of Lothar, constitute the last remnants of a once high civilization that has reverted to primitivism and is almost extinct. It was on an ancient radio that Xenora spoke to Melvin. Also present in the land is the city of Mutron, which maintains a high civilization, but whose inhabitants are completely will-controlled by the nearby Lord of Flame. Xenora had been captured as a slave by the men of Mutron. Will-control device strapped to her back, she was scheduled as a mine hand when she was seized by the lunak. * The Lord of Flame is the real problem. Xenora has a vague notion that it was created by the Mutrons long ago, and since escaped control. Presumably an energy being of some sort, it manifests itself as a column of green flame, and can rule the will of anyone on whom its attention fastens. It maintains silvery spherical airships with fantastic weapons; it was one of these ships that emerged earlier and destroyed Doc Sam's surface establishment when the Lord of Flame recognized his interference. * The remainder of the plot is too complicated to detail. As motifs and strands: After he and Melvin succumb temporarily to the Lord of Flame's will, Sam devises protective headgear. Sam captures a baby lunak and domesticates it; it is as friendly as a dog. Sam disappears. Melvin is captured by the Lord of Flame when his helmet is knocked off, and, after he does a stint in the mines, is rescued by Xenora. Melvin starts an amateur chemical factory and manufactures barrels of nitroglycerine, with which he plans to breach a wall holding an inland sea. Sam reappears with an army of friendly lunaks who storm the stronghold of the Lord of Flame. Melvin blows up the wall, the red gas dissipates, and the sea crashes down over everything. Only Sam, Melvin, and Xenora survive, reaching the surface in the Omnimobile. * *Miscellaneous:* The Lord of Flame was going to all this trouble because he/it distrusted the gas barrier and believed that an ice lens (if the Earth froze) over the lost land would be superior. * In the school of A. Merritt; its lush romanticism was popular two generations ago.

1736. **THE COSMIC EXPRESS**. *Amazing Stories*, November 1930. Ill. Morey.

(Reprinted in Williamson, *The Early Williamson*; in Williamson, *The Pandora Effect*; in Elwood and Moskowitz, *Strange Signposts*; and in Liebman, *Science Fiction. The Best of Yesterday*.)

Short story. * *Time:* A.D. 2432. *Place:* New York and Venus. * Eric Stokes-Harding and his wife Nada, who live in an apartment in crystal-domed super New York, are both writers. Being imaginative, they are bored with their protected lifestyle and yearn for primitivism, such as their ancestors enjoyed. * An idea: Why not travel to Venus and live there happily in the jungle, close to nature? * In 2432 travel is accomplished by terminal-less matter transmission. Since Eric has a friend in the transmission office, such a trip may be possible. Bribing his friend with an extremely rare bottle of hard liquor, Eric and his wife are surreptitiously dropped upon Venus. * But it is not as they expected. Deposited on a swampy island, they cannot start a fire by knocking stones together, even if they knew how. They are beset by noxious insects; and gigantic monsters bellow and fight near them as they lay buried, shivering with terror, in the mud. It is all hopeless. * But then they are retrieved. Their friend's superior, finding him drunk, believes that a mistransmission took place, and is all too eager to forget everything if Eric and Nada agree not to sue. * An amusing bit.

1737. **THE PRINCE OF SPACE**. *Amazing Stories*, January 1931. Ill. Morey.

(Reprinted in Williamson, *The Alien Intelligence*.)

Novelette. * *Time:* the interplanetary future. *Place:* New York, Mars, space. * Subplots: First, space-liners are harassed and looted by a space pirate who calls himself the Prince of Space and leaves a personal calling card after his raids. Until the present incident lives have not been lost, but the *Helicon* has been robbed, and all on board have been killed, drained of blood. Did the Prince do it? * Second, Professor Trainor, with funds from unknown sources, has built a tower twelve thousand feet high in New York City. It serves the same purpose as a mountain observatory. Trainor has also built a supertelescope, which shows Mars very clearly and reveals that something very fishy is going on. * Third, the reporter narrator later learns that the Prince of Space and Trainor are acting together to ward off a Martian invasion. * When the narrator accompanies a vessel of the Moon Patrol to investigate the *Helicon* disaster and destroy the Prince of Space, his ship is attacked and wrecked by a Martian vessel. His vessel never had a chance, for the Martian space globes are armed with rays more powerful than those on Terrestrial ships and are seemingly invulnerable to attack. The Prince of Space's vessel, which is superior to other Terrestrial vessels, rescues the narrator and other survivors, but cannot stand against the Martians, who land on Earth and establish a foothold. * For a time the situation seems hopeless, but Professor Trainor invents a torpedo-like high-explosive weapon that can penetrate the Martian force screens. It enables the Prince to destroy the Martian desert station. * This small victory, however, means little, as the Prince, Trainor, and their comrades recognize. Mars itself must be attacked. * Reinforcing his flagship, the Prince and others set out for Mars. They would have been overmatched, since there are too many Martian ships, but Trainor invents still another device: the vitamaton, a utilization of the life principle that can be directed by radio. It eats *everything*, turning atoms into nothingness. When the Martians prove impossible to deal with, Trainor directs the vitamaton on Mars and disintegrates it.

Williamson, Jack (*continued*)

* *Miscellaneous:* The Martians are greenish octopoidal creatures with disks for sucking blood. They are incredibly vicious and keep herds of subhuman creatures for food. * Mars is Schiaparellian, with canals, deserts, and high civilization. * Space travel is possible through the new element vitalium, which stores sunlight most efficiently, to be drawn off as electricity. This in turn operates rockets. * Also present, not entirely convincingly, is a romance between the misogynist pirate and Trainor's teenage daughter. She may have sounded charming to readers of the early 1930s, but she now reads as a neurotic twerp. * Routine.

1738. **THE METEOR GIRL**. *Astounding Stories*, March 1931. Ill. Wesso.

(Reprinted in Williamson, *The Early Williamson*.)

Short story. * Charlie King and the narrator operate a small aircraft factory, with Charlie, who is a serious mathematical physicist specializing in relativity, attending to the mathematical side. * Charlie's fiancée, Virginia, (who is a millionairess) has just broken off their engagement because she believes that he prefers math to her. * A meteorite falls. It is impregnated with a new force that when manipulated with X-rays and electricity alters the coordinates of space-time. With it Charlie can see Virginia's yacht foundering and her swimming toward a bare rock in the Pacific. But the time factor is awry. Charlie and the narrator are able to reach her in time to save her, once the space-time coordinates are understood. The romance is reëstablished.

1739. **THE LAKE OF LIGHT**. *Astounding Stories*, April 1931. Ill. Wesso.

Short story. * *Place:* Antarctica. * The narrator and Ray Summers are flying across Antarctica on an exploratory flight when their propeller breaks and they have to make a forced landing. Since they do not have enough supplies to return to their mother ship, they decide to try to reach a luminous mountain range that is not too distant. Along the way they come upon a wrecked plane, that of Major Meriden and family, lost nineteen years earlier. * The explorers soon come upon evidences of a strange civilization, notably a reservoir of some unidentified liquid that absorbs light and then pours into chasms. * The aviators, finding ladders cut into the rock, descend to a great depression, where they find a supercivilization developed by gigantic crabs. They also encounter Mildred Meriden, the surviving daughter of the Meridens. * Mildred explains: She can communicate with the giant crabs, who are not actively hostile, but will not let the humans leave the land. Mildred earns her keep by providing wordless vocalizing concerts for the crabs. * The humans decide to escape, but evading the crabs' heat rays may be a difficulty. Mildred provides rifles, and after back-and-forth action, the humans emerge into the snows. By shifting Meriden's propeller to their own plane they can fly away to their mother ship. * As is sometimes the case with the early Williamson, attractively written, but not too credible fictionally.

1740. **THROUGH THE PURPLE CLOUD**. *Wonder Stories*, May 1931. Ill. Paul.

(Reprinted in Williamson, *The Early Williamson*; also in Margulies and Friend, *From off This World*.)

Short story. * *Place:* California and an other-world. * George Cleland and Juanita Harvel, not acquainted as yet, are flying from Los Angeles to San Francisco when their plane flies into a purplish misty disk. After they feel a wrenching sensation, the plane emerges into a red landscape, where it crashes. All on board are killed except George, Juanita, a nameless thug, and a small businessman who never regains consciousness. * The world in which the passengers find themselves is absolutely barren, craggy rock, uniformly and horribly red, except for large purplish crystals that are strewn about and black cliffs in the far distance. The sun and sky are red. There is no food or water. * The thug, crazed with thirst, shoots the businessman and drinks his blood, then sets out in pursuit of George and Juanita, who hide among the rocks. * A strange phenomenon takes place: Enormous drops of red liquid, the size of footballs, fall from the scarlet sky. They are not potable, but a condensation of chemicals. * A way out of the strange world: When a drop falls onto one of the giant crystals, the crystal evaporates into a purple mist, like the one that gave the party entry to the other-world. * The drops are evaporating rapidly, the thug is shooting at George and Juanita, and George is trying to run as fast as he can with a thirty-pound rock, hoping to find a red drop. He succeeds, of course, and George and Juanita fall through the purple mist back into pleasant California. * *Miscellaneous:* George explains it all as an Einsteinian fourth dimension. * Interesting for the psychological adumbrations and economically written, if pulp in plot. One of Williamson's better early stories.

1741. **THE DOOM FROM PLANET 4**. *Astounding Stories*, July 1931. Ill. Wesso.

(Reprinted in Williamson, *The Early Williamson*.)

Short story in the mode of Edmond Hamilton. * *Place:* an island in the South Pacific. * Dan McNally, master of a small trading vessel, sees a strange signal from Davis Island; this is followed by a ray that destroys his ship and kills his crew. Dan escapes, however, and swims ashore. * Looking for food, clothing, shelter, he is caught out by a strange box-like machine that wields a disintegrator ray. Dan escapes, however, and meets Helen Hunter, who explains matters. * The enormous suspended metal ring with the lavender light and the white needle is a device for interplanetary communication. Her father, after watching an eclipse, experimented with radio signals and was able to communicate with Mars. * After months of semiotic juggling, the Martians gave him instructions for building a machine—which immediately took over the island, building copies of itself. * The Martians are apparently living, intelligent machines, ruled by the Master Intelligence, who plans to conquer Earth. * Dan and Helen have close calls with the hostile Martian machine beings, but the world peril is ended when Dan, in a self-sacrificing, heroic act, leaps into the communications cone, destroying it. The machines all come to a halt. Dan, though severely injured, survives and will recover. * Superior in writing to comparable contemporary world-saver stories, but the concept is getting clichéd.

1742. **TWELVE HOURS TO LIVE!** *Wonder Stories*, August 1931. Ill. Marchioni.

Short story. * *Time:* the interplanetary future. * The *Queen of Night*, a gigantic space cruiser with hundreds of passengers and a load of valuable minerals, is being pursued by the Black Hawk, a notorious space pirate. The captain of the *Queen of Night*, David Grant, is a virtuoso commander and uses every trick of navigation to evade the pirate and its disintegrator rays. But after a long chase, the *Queen of Night* runs out of fuel and is captured. * The saturnine Black Hawk, who poses as a debonair gentleman bandit, but is really a sadistic scoundrel, expresses delight at the chase that Grant led him, and offers Grant a wish

Williamson, Jack (*continued*)

in gratitude. Grant asks that his newly wed wife be set safely on a friendly planet. The Black Hawk thinks for a moment, then smiles sardonically, and agrees, adding that Grant will be set down with her. The Black Hawk then demonstrates a crimson fungus from the (imaginary) third moon of Neptune; it devours a man horribly in a matter of seconds. * The time has come for a landing, and the Black Hawk, maintaining his usual mask of mocking courtesy, sets Grant and his wife on a planetoid. * But there is a hitch: The jesting pirate has placed Mrs. Grant unconscious, with a radio and some other pieces of equipment and food, in a large metal box. A second, identical box, the Black Hawk assures Grant, contains the crimson fungus. If Mrs. Grant is not removed from the box within twelve hours, she will die. The Black Hawk then leaves. * Grant is almost mad with anxiety and perplexity. Which box should he open? One is marked "The other one." What does that mean? * According to Williamson's autography, *Wonder's Child*, the story originally ended as a dream, thus leaving the problem unsolved. Editor David Lasser, however, dropped the dream ending and turned the story into a small contest with prizes for the best solution. The editors printed winning solutions in the November 1931 issue of *Wonder Stories*. First prize, $25, went to Walter L. Dennis of Chicago, who suggested undermining one of the chests so that it could be jiggled up and down. If there was any noise from within the chest—what with the equipment included—Grant should open it. * Second prize, $15, went to M. Gittelman of Detroit, who suggested waiting until Mrs. Grant awoke and began to scream, then taking the lid off. * Third prize, $10, went to Frank K. Kelly of Kansas City, Mo., who suggested, on psychological grounds, that Grant open the chest marked "The other one." * The editors claimed to have received around seventeen hundred solutions.

1743. THE STONE FROM THE GREEN STAR. *Amazing Stories,* October-November 1931. Ill. Morey.

Short novel. * Time: about A.D. 2,028,000. *Place:* Earth and imaginary planets at the edge of the universe. * A manuscript, contained in a curiously decorated black box, is miraculously precipitated on Jack Williamson's desk. Transmitted from the far future, it details the experiences of Williamson's friend Richard Smith. * Smith, on board a tanker in the Pacific, finds himself seized by an unknown power and in a strange ambience. Before him are a beautiful young woman named Thon Ahrora and her blind scientist father, Midos Ken. Around him is a wonderful world of transformed landscapes, beautiful buildings, and handsome people. As he learns a little later, it is the Earth of about 2,028,000. * *Background:* In this future world mankind has spread among the stars, the predominant power source being the K-ray, which permits almost instantaneous interstellar transmission; it is a subatomic force unknown to us and is far faster than light. Future man can also easily create matter of almost any sort from free particles, and with the El ray can dissolve matter into water. * Most of the stars in the universe have planets, and most of these have been terraformed to make them suitable for human habitation. Many such worlds are associated in the Union, which is an organization for peace, but there are outlaw worlds, like the Dark Star, and many unexplored, unknown planets scattered throughout the universe. In a previous war, the science of Midos Ken, who is a man of incredible genius, was responsible for the defeat of the Dark Star when

it made war against the Union. * The story is formed about two quests. Midos Ken has devoted most of his life to finding a substance that will restore youth or create eternal youth for the vast human population around the universe. For decades he has been near success, but he lacks a certain catalyst of known properties, which eludes him. He has agents searching throughout the universe (with little detectors), and he has even tried retrieving substances from the past with a time apparatus, whence Smith's accidental presence in this world. * The second quest is an ignoble one. Garo Nark, the lecherous, ruthless Lord of the Dark Star (an orphan planet), wants Thon Ahrora in his harem, revenge on Midos Ken, and the secret of youth that Midos Ken has been seeking. * As for the story, simply to list themes: One of Midos Ken's agents has located the catalyst on the Green Star, an orphan planet at the edge of the universe, but he was unable to retrieve it, since it was guarded by semimaterial beings of incredible ferocity. Garo Nark kidnaps Thon Ahrora, but she is rescued. All proceed to the Green Star, where Dick Smith is attacked by one of the vampiric beings, who extracts his youth from him, turning him into an old man. But Midos Ken restores his youth with the catalyst, which the party has stolen. Garo Nark appears with the maneuverable Dark Star and captures everyone, but dies when Midos Ken's agent releases a deadly fungus. Midos Ken sacrifices himself to crash the Dark Star into the Green Star, destroying both. Richard Smith and Thon Ahrora survive, of course. * *Miscellaneous:* The future world, oddly enough, is intensely capitalistic, and Smith earns an enormous amount of diamond tokens by writing a book about twentieth-century life. Unfortunately, Garo Nark, on one of his raids, steals Smith's royalties. * The first part is among Williamson's best early work, but the story turns melodramatic and forced.

1744. THE MOON ERA. *Wonder Stories*, February 1932. Ill. Paul.

(Reprinted in Asimov, *Before the Golden Age* and in Moskowitz, *Three Stories*.)

Short story. * *Time and place:* main action on the Moon in the remote past. * Stephen, an impoverished school teacher in the Southwest, is summoned by his extremely wealthy uncle Enfield, who makes an offer to him. If Stephen will operate Enfield's invention, Enfield will leave his vast fortune to him. The invention is a device for cutting off gravitation (which originates in the fourth dimension) and visiting the Moon. * Thinking of the millions awaiting him, Stephen agrees to his uncle's conditions, even though the engineers who have constructed the device say that it is too dangerous. * Stephen enters the space machine, turns it on, and soon sees that things are going backwards—revolution of the Earth, sunsets, planetary orbits. In manipulating space-time the machine is not only carrying him to the Moon—but also into the remote past. * The Moon of this past period has a breathable atmosphere, lush vegetation, and an abundance of life. After being nearly killed by a balloon-like creature that lassos ground life and floats away with it, Stephen encounters the Mother, the sole survivor of the once dominant Lunar intelligent life-form. The Mother, who is probably an evolved insect, has a somewhat serpentine body, vestigial wings that serve as grasping organs, and a tiny head. She is beautiful, benevolent, and telepathic. With her power of will she can control much of the animal life. * But as she informs Stephen, she is being pursued by the Eternal Ones, cyborgs (my term)

Williamson, Jack (continued)

who have become totally machine-like. The Eternal Ones want to capture her and use her eggs for their own reproduction. * Stephen and the Mother make common cause, she to escape the Eternal Ones, and he to return to his time-spaceship. * They pass through perils together, including a rolling monstrosity, and some of the Eternal Ones. These are walking-machines with organic brains carried atop their apparatus in transparent containers. * Eventually, near the time-spaceship, Stephen and the Mother are cornered. Stephen fights off the cyborgs, though wounded, but the Mother is killed. This is the end of the Lunar race. Stephen prepares to return to his own time. * Miscellaneous: The Mother can impart her own vitality to heal Stephen's frequent wounds. * Although still influenced by Merritt, Williamson is now beginning to write a more independent story and the pathos of the situation breaks through the thrills. Although Weinbaum is often credited with offering the first sympathetic alien life-form, Williamson, in this story, as well as other authors preceded him.

1745. **THE PYGMY PLANET**. Astounding Stories, February 1932. Ill. Paul.

Short story. * Larry Manahan, Herculean adman, receives a mysterious call from his friend Agnes Sterling, who is assistant to the great scientist Travis Whiting. Rushing to Whiting's lab, he meets Agnes, who tells him a strange story. Whiting, by compressing subatomic orbits, has created a tiny world, which Larry can see floating, rotating, in a mass of apparatus in the room. * Whiting, as Agnes informs him, has not only established and watched evolution on the planetoid, but can visit it by means of size rays. Indeed, both he and Agnes have landed upon the planetoid. The situation seemed controllable, but, totally unexpectedly, a strange machine, a cyborg (my term) with a brain set in mechanical apparatus, has come up from the planetoid and carried Whiting off. Agnes is sure that the machine and its fellows will sacrifice the professor to their god, an ancient steam hammer. * Agnes's perturbation is not without reason, for at this point a machine-being swells up from the tiny world and also carries Agnes off into miniature, despite Larry's attempts to rescue her. * Recovering his breath, Larry mounts a tiny plane that Whiting and Agnes maintain for travel to the planetoid, and descends, via the size rays, to the tiny world. * Captured by the cyborgs, he watches Whiting being smashed by the steam hammer. He tries to disrupt the ancient device, which explodes. In the confusion that follows he and Agnes escape back to our world. Here Larry smashes the tiny world. * Not one of Williamson's better stories.

1746. **THE LADY OF LIGHT**. Amazing Stories, September 1932. Ill. Morey.

Novelette. * Time: 1930 and following. Place: space, far out into the universe. * Eric Locklin, wealthy young scientist, has just finished his rocket ship, and he and narrator Higdon shoot out into space. But the combustion has progressed too far, destroying much of the fuel chamber and stranding the men in orbit about eighty thousand miles from Earth, with a limited supply of air. * As they lie dying of suffocation, they see a light approaching, and wonder of wonders, a young woman floats up outside the window of the ship. An incredibly beautiful blonde, she is clad in a shimmering haze and carries a wand-like staff. * Comprehending the situation, she signals to be admitted to the ship. Eric and Higdon can barely manage the airlock, but once

in, the young woman manipulates controls on her rod, producing fresh air. Manipulating her wand again, she creates—seemingly out of nothing—two disks, which when applied to the foreheads of the two men enable them to converse telepathically with her. It is obvious that it is love at first sight between Eric and the strange woman, whose name is Sharothon. * Historical background: Sharothon is a member of the people of Yothanda, who live in a space city of incredible futuristic splendor and magnificence. Her ancestors originally inhabited the Bodia, the lost fifth planet, which they accidentally blew up while creating atomic energy. A large asteroidal fragment, though airless and vegetationless, served as a new home for survivors, who utilized the energy of cosmic rays to create a new supercivilization. A girdle that Sharothon wears and the ytlan rod that she carries enable her to focus cosmic rays to create matter of any sort. Thus protected by energy apparatus, the space people can venture almost anywhere in space. * Sharothon offers to repair the spaceship with her rod, so that Eric and Higdon can return to Earth, but Eric, smitten with love, refuses the offer and prefers to stay with her. * Social background: The civilization of Yothanda is decadent and corrupt, and most of the people are no more than sensuous pleasure seekers. Indeed, to preserve the race, a law has been passed instituting compulsory mating and breeding. Sharothon has been assigned to Kerak, a member of the Council, whom she dislikes. The presence of Eric makes things worse. * Sharothon takes the two Earthmen into the space city—an action itself illegal, just as was her exploration of space—but she uses a newly invented invisibility apparatus. She installs the two men in a luxurious apartment that she creates within the head of an enormous statue. * Things do not go well, however, for both men sicken of exposure to the cosmic rays, and it is obvious that they cannot survive in space. * Matters come to a head when Kerak discovers the love nest and the three are brought in irons before the Council. The aged Luroth, the head of the Council, is sympathetic to the three and decrees that all should be freed to solve their destinies as they will. At this, the other members of the Council rebel, deposing him and installing Kerak as the new leader. * Like fairy gifts, the decisions of the Council cannot be rescinded, but Kerak can and does add details to modify it. No help will be given to the three. The Earthmen may return to Earth. If Sharothon chooses to descend with Eric, she cannot take her rod or girdle. This is equivalent to a death sentence for her. * The choices are horrible, but a new element enters. With his purple rod, which is the most powerful in the culture, the deposed Luroth releases the three from their shackles, transports them out into space, and builds defensive weapons and a spaceship. In this the four flee to the edges of space, pursued by Kerak's ships. * There are many battles of titanic forces, but it is obvious, as Luroth realizes, that the fugitives will eventually lose. At the last encounter, Luroth transforms himself into energy to save his proteges, but it is in vain. They are captured and taken back to judgment. * Sharothon chooses to descend to Earth with Eric (the primitive beast, as Kerak calls him). For a time the two Earthlings and Sharothon live together happily in New Mexico, but Sharothon, as was expected, cannot survive. When she lies dying, Kerak momentarily visits her, and as she is at the moment of death, a ray removes her. Eric leaps into the ray to be with her. * The narrator believes, from the expression of hope that he saw on Eric's face, that they both survive, but he has heard no more. *

Williamson, Jack (*continued*)

The quintessential Williamson fairy tale of science, arguably the best of his work in this subgenre.

1747. **THE ELECTRON FLAME.** *Wonder Stories Quarterly*, Fall 1932. Ill. Paul.

Short story. * *Time:* 2432. *Place:* Mars and a satellite. * *Background:* Venus and Mars have been colonized by Earthmen long enough for racial types to have emerged. Interplanetary travel is common and apparently easy, with the Planetary League maintaining enormous fleets of war rockets on each of the planets. * At the moment the Defense Ministry of the League is facing a crisis, because an outlaw has gained the upper hand over them. Identity unknown, he has stolen a great scientific discovery enabling him to start inextinguishable atomic fires. He threatens to destroy Mars unless all police fleets are grounded. Meanwhile, he commits crimes with impunity. * It is known from a test the League conducted before the discovery was stolen that no equipment beyond ordinary radio is needed to set the fire off and extinguish it; and that the specifications were written on a single sheet of yellow paper. * The Defense Ministry has summoned White of Denver, one of the greatest Terrestrial detectives. White, who is obviously modelled on David H. Keller's Taine of San Francisco, disappoints the Ministry when he arrives. He is small, nondescript, and hopelessly average in appearance. Nevertheless, White works out the problem in record time. * To anticipate: The criminal has his headquarters on a small third moon of Mars, which has been converted by planetary terraforming into a palatial estate, with artificial gravity, atmosphere, plantings and all. * White beards the criminal and his associates on the satellite, outwits them, retrieves the spec sheet, and ultimately destroys them. * While obvious as a futuristic detective story, entertaining and unusual in being low key. Certainly superior to Keller's comparable work.

1748. **IN THE SCARLET STAR.** *Amazing Stories*, March 1933. Ill. Morey.

(Reprinted in Wollheim, *Every Boy's Book of Science Fiction.*)

Short story. * *Place:* El Paso, Texas, and probably a fourth-dimensional world. * The narrator, John Stewart, strikes up an acquaintance over a science-fiction magazine with a young man named Jimmy Miles. Miles, who is broke, has spent his last money on a strange artifact, a large disk of red glass that appears to have a metal apparatus imbedded inside it. As Miles says, electric current passed into it seems to open a way to another plane of existence. * Stewart, who accepts Miles's story, supplies money for further research, whereupon, after a time, Miles insists that he will enter the disk to the other world. Artifacts placed in it have been easily retrieved and seem undamaged except for aging. * Miles enters; Steward waits for a minute or so, then retrieves him, to find a new Miles, a man years older, heavier, scarred, and clad in a leopard skin. There is obviously a large differential time ratio between the two worlds. * Miles's story: He found himself in an Earth-like world, where he would not have survived had he not been protected by a subhuman creature called Harr Garr. Harr Garr's people were cave dwellers with a Freudian concept of organization: a powerful, old, bullying father figure. * Miles lived among the primitives for about five years before Stewart retrieved him. During this period he had adventures with creatures equivalent to giant tigers and witnessed the first use of fire for protection against animals and for social

domination. * *Miscellaneous:* Williamson does not explain the origin of the wonderful disk except to say that Miles bought it in a pawnshop and that it was supposed to have come from local Indian ruins. * Routine. According to Williamson's autobiography, this was intended as the first member of a series, but other stories were not written.

1749. **SALVAGE IN SPACE.** *Astounding Stories*, March 1933. Ill. Marchioni.

(Reprinted in Williamson, *The Early Williamson.*)

Short story. * *Time:* the interplanetary future. *Place:* the asteroid belt. * Thad, a metal-miner in the asteroid belt, has not been very successful in gathering iron. A derelict spaceship comes within range. He makes his way to it, and finds it empty of life, except for a small dog. Patches of blood are to be found on the floors; fabulous wealth in jewels and precious metals fills the hold; and in a casket, on a heap of jewels, lies the corpse of a beautiful woman, who is later identified as Linda Cross. Also in the hold is a collection of seemingly stuffed monsters, which Dr. Cross, the ship's owner or charterer had brought (along with the treasure) from Titania, the hitherto unexplored moon of Uranus. * To the mystery: An entry in the log states that the crew believe that one of the stuffed monsters has come to life and is eating the men. * Thad soon learns what is what: An invisible monster, huge, hungry, and vicious. For a time it seems as if Thad, too, will become a meal for the monster, but he uses his welding iron to good purpose and kills the creature. * New point: In the casket with the beautiful young woman is a note saying that she is in suspended animation and will awaken some day. * She does, a year or so later, after Thad has collected his fortune in salvage money. She is, of course, the woman of his dreams. * *Miscellaneous:* The monster attains invisibility by bending light rays. * At times a fairy tale atmosphere.

1750. **DEAD STAR STATION.** *Astounding Stories*, November 1933. Unsigned ill.

(Reprinted in Williamson, *The Early Williamson*, and in Williamson, *The Best of Jack Williamson.*)

Short story. * *Time:* far enough into the future for interstellar travel. * *Place:* a space station (really a "moored" spaceship) near a dead star somewhere in the constellation Orion. * Human interest story. * Among the small personnel of Dead Star Station is old Gideon Crew, an ancient space man long past his prime. Crew, who is allowed to stay on the station out of the commanding officer's good-hearted tolerance, theorizes that gravitation is a radiation and has been working on an apparatus to nullify it. * But with new CO Captain Kempton, things change. Crew is allowed one (unsuccessful) trial of his apparatus, then is ordered to leave on the visiting space-liner *Bellatrix.* * The space pirate Skal Doon causes a further change. He hijacks the *Bellatrix,* and when Dead Star Station goes to its aid, both are caught by the gravity of the dead star and are doomed. * But old Crew gets his antigravity invention working properly, and all is well. Skal Doon and his men previously committed suicide when they believed they would crash. * Also present is eight-year-old Tonia, with whom old Crew has a special bond that today would be regarded with raised eyebrows and some concern. Otherwise, Tonia is as obnoxious as Little Nell. * Not one of Williamson's better stories.

1751. **TERROR OUT OF TIME.** *Astounding Stories*, December 1933. Unsigned ill.

(Reprinted in Moskowitz and Elwood, *The Time Curve.*)

Williamson, Jack (*continued*)

Short story. * Old Dr. Audrin has invented a device that can transfer the psyche through time; neuro-induction the doctor calls it. Since he needs a guinea pig for experiment, young Terry Webb, a reporter in love with Audrin's daughter Eve, reluctantly volunteers. His reward is to be the hand or body of Eve. Unfortunately, the doctor's previous subject went mad during the experiment. * Terry remains under the full strength of the ray for an hour, an exposure that the doctor hopes will take Terry to the mind of the last man. * Terry returns, sane, but exhausted. He explains. He went forty million years into the future into the mind of Gorkon, a Martian scientist who, in a dry Pacific deep, maintains the last stronghold of humanity against floating, gaseous creatures that are incredibly vicious and numerous. Along with Gorkon are a handful of small, furry humans, the last degenerate men who are totally and fearfully subservient to the Martian. As for Gorkon, he is about ten feet tall, black, with triangular yellow eyes and is usually furnished with a whip. His sort conquered Earth about a half million years earlier. * The story now follows two routes. Terry, back in the present, does not stay Terry, but becomes Gorkon, who immediately uses his superscience to build an invisibility apparatus and a paralysis ray. The true Terry finds himself in the body of one of the future men, for it has become a three-way swap: Gorkon in Terry's body, Terry in Ato Lu's body along with Ato Lu's mind. Gorkon seemingly moves back and forth in time, working to consolidate his presence in the twentieth century. * The blue floating beings attack, and all the humans except Ato Lu are killed. Gorkon, who states that his mind transfer is almost complete, scoffs at Ato Lu, but Terry-in-Ato Lu rebels successfully, cracking the Martian's skull with a stone. Terry then returns to his own body, apparently with some memory of the Martian's superscience.

1752. **THE FLAME FROM MARS**. *Astounding Stories*, January 1934. Ill. Marchioni.

Short story. * *Place:* Meteor Crater, Arizona. * Young millionaire engineer Don Belgrand is obsessed with finding the meteor in Meteor Crater, to which he has bought mineral rights. He is putting a fortune into mining the crater, despite the disapproval of his friend and financial manager, Ared Stokes, who is the narrator of the story. * On the critical occasion, Stokes receives an urgent summons to come to Meteor Crater and see what Belgrand has found. The men descend deep into the shaft, where Belgrand shows Ared not a chunk of meteoritic iron, not a piece of rock, but a gigantic metal sphere, into which they enter. It is a missile from Mars, Belgrand states, and it contains the glowing body of a beautiful young woman. * When Stokes declares that she is dead and that the sphere must have been a coffin, Belgrand is able to contradict him. Documentation with built-in keys has revealed that the woman is Allurova, the Martian version of Rappaccini's daughter. She was so imbued with a lethal radiation (by her misanthropic father) that her very touch is poisonous. Indeed, many men came to woo her, and though she had the power to shut off her radiation, she did not, and they all died. Hence she was expelled from Mars. * This is fine as far as it goes, but there are two complications: first, Belgrand is madly in love with her and intends to revive her, hoping that she will respond and cancel her lethal emanation, yet not caring if she doesn't. Second, irresistible ground water is flooding the tunnel, and the men have only a few min-

utes in which to leave. * Belgrand awakens Allurova, embraces her, and readies himself for death. He claims that Allurova can return to suspended animation, if the water is kept out, but she has told him that he must die soon. * Stokes leaves, barely in time to avoid drowning, not expecting to see Belgrand again. But Belgrand and Allurova also emerge. It seems that during the fifty thousand years or so that she spent in Meteor Crater, the radiation had pretty much exhausted itself. The two are in love, though a reader may consider Belgrand somewhat overtrusting. * Possibly suggested by Erle Cox's *Out of the Silence*, which would have been available to Williamson as one of the books offered for sale by Hugo Gernsback. The sexual substructure is interesting.

1753. **BORN OF THE SUN**. *Astounding Stories*, March 1934. Ill. Brown.

(Reprinted in Asimov, *Before the Golden Age*, and in Ackerman, *Gosh! Wow!*)

Short story. * Foster Ross is working on his spaceship, which operates on a new principle (presumably antigravity of one sort or another), when his long-lost uncle, Barron Kane, appears on his doorstep—pursued by desperate Orientals who try to kill him with a death ray. * Assassins disposed of, Kane tells a strange story. There is an Asian sect, the Cult of the Great Egg, that knows more about cosmology than does Western science. As its leader, the great L'ao Ku, has determined, the Earth and the other planets are due to be destroyed in a very short time. The sect, which is both persistent and very violent, is determined that mankind should die with the planet and attacks anyone who might help humans survive the catastrophe. Thus, Kane concludes, Ross must finish his spaceship and, using it as a new ark, be prepared to reestablish mankind elsewhere. It all sounds strange, but the outer planets are beginning to disappear, and the Earth is starting to experience temblors of great violence, while Ross works on his ark. * The awaited explanation arrives during the destruction of the Moon. It splits apart in giant shards, and a planet-sized, dragon-like creature emerges and flies away. The planets are really cosmic eggs. * It now turns into a complex race as Ross tries to finish his space ark (which has many bugs that keep it inoperative), the Earth begins to break up, and L'ao Ku and his forces try to wreck Ross's project. Incidentally, L'ao Ku intends to capture June Trevor, Ross's girlfriend, and sacrifice her. * When the turmoil is over, the Earth is shattered, its fledgling has flown off, and the human race is extinct except for Ross, Kane, and June Trevor, who are flying away in the space sphere that became operative at the last possible moment. * *Miscellaneous:* The space sphere, the *Planet*, is so large and so well stocked that it is a planetary home. Mankind need no longer exist on sufferance on worlds that are likely to spring into destructive life. Other *Planets* will be built by the descendants of Ross and June. * Midway between A. G. Birch's "The Moon Terror" and Robert A. Heinlein's "The Strange Profession of Jonathan Hoag." One of the more imaginative (in concept) of the Tremaine "thought variant" stories.

1754. **XANDALU**. *Wonder Stories*, March-May 1934. Ill. Paul.

Short novel. * *Place:* North Africa, and an enormous artificial cavern world under North Africa. * In the mode of A. Merritt. * The story is told in three episodes narrated by millionaire aviator Miles Kendon to his friend Dr. Brander, who cruises the Mediterranean for his health. * As a prelude to the first episode,

Williamson, Jack (*continued*)

Brander saw a plane pursued by light globes that attacked it with flashes, while the pilot fought back with machine gun bullets. The plane crashed, but Kendon and a mysterious young blonde woman were rescued from the sea. * Kendon's first narrative: He was working as a aviator-soldier of fortune for the Berbers against the French when he espied a remarkable archeological complex on the ground. Landing and exploring, he discovered ruins made of an imperishable porcelainlike material and an enormous artificial hole, depth unknown, about a thousand feet across. As he watched, a gigantic bird flew out of the hole, bearing a handsome young woman, whom he rescued as the bird lay exhausted. The young woman, Su-Ildra, communicated with him in sign language and pictures, urging that they leave the area as soon as possible. Just before Kendon was ready to take off, light spheres emerged from the hole and attacked them. Kendon flew away, and, surviving the battle previously described, is now on his way to Marseilles with Brander. * The light spheres follow them, however, and steal away Su-Ildra. Kendon vows to return and rescue her. * Background to all this, revealed piecemeal: The underground world, which is enormous, was created ages ago by the Fire People, intelligent reptiles who constructed it to avoid the glaciation. They possessed (and still possess) a superscience almost incredible to us. When they withdrew from the surface, they took small populations of Lemurians (who are not quite human) and humans. The descendants of the Lemurians have red or orange skin and black teeth, with facial features somewhat different from humans. Violating an ancient compact, they have overrun the lands of the true humans, killing most of them. Su-Ildra has been protected so far by the Fire People, but the power of the Fire People has waned. Theoretically they are the overlords of the land, but they have evolved so far into quietism that they find it difficult even to think seriously about self-defense. As will be revealed, the amiable reptilians will use Kendon as their weapon against their enemies. * Kendon's second narrative: Purchasing another plane, he plans to fly down into the tube to the inner world, but a battle with more light balls wrecks his plane. He therefore leaps into the abyss with his parachute, descending about a hundred miles, landing in the sea near an island where Su-Ildra lives. One of the Fire People now tells him telepathically what is going on: The red Lemurians are fanatical devotees of death. Under their leader and high priest, the villainous Bak-Toreg, they plan not only mass suicide, but the destruction of the planet, and ultimately, by contagious atomic disintegration, the universe. It is up to Kendon to save the universe and Su-Ildra, who has been recaptured. * Taken prisoner by the forces of the red race, Kendon is placed for sacrifice in a temple (called from another dimension) against an enormous scorpion. Armed with an invisible sword provided by the Fire People, he slays the scorpion, but is badly wounded. His contact among the Fire People rescues him, heals him instantly, and transports him back to the surface. * Kendon's third narrative: Purchasing a third plane, he flies down into the inner world and makes his way to the land of the Fire People. Here he learns that the situation is as bad as ever; indeed, perhaps worse, for in a matter of hours the red Lemurians will attack the reptilians and destroy them. The reptilians are helpless, but at the cost of enormous psychic pain, Kendon's contact tells him of an ancient arsenal. Here Kendon finds and operates a disintegrator, with which he wipes out the

red air fleet. The situation is still bad, however, for the wicked Bak-Toreg, in addition to holding Su-Ildra as a hostage, has a little box with which he will blow up the world. Kendon wins, and he and Su-Ildra are living happily underground. * *Miscellaneous:* The reptilian men travel by folding space to their desires. They were able to place Kendon on Bak-Toreg's airship for the final combat. * Good touches, but by now the exoticism of the school of Merritt no longer rings true. As I boy, however, I found this and "The Lady of Light" my favorite early Williamson.

1755. **THE LEGION OF SPACE.** *Astounding Stories,* April-September 1934. Ill. variously by Brown, Dold, and Marchioni.

(Reprinted in book form by Fantasy Press; Reading, Pa., 1947; and in Williamson, *Three from the Legion.*)

Novel. Space opera. * *Time:* from chronology offered in "The Cometeers," around A.D. 2900. *Place:* mostly Mars and the planet Yarkand circling Barnard's Runaway Star (also called Yarkand). * *General background:* The solar system, which seems to be peopled solely by humans of Terrestrial origin, is governed by a democratic council that is seated at Green Hall in New Mexico. About two hundred years earlier, the system was an empire governed tyrannically by the Ulnar family, whose power was broken mostly by the discovery of AKKA. AKKA, which requires precise but minimal equipment and is in part operated by mental set, can remove almost anything instantaneously from space and time. It is thus in effect an infinitely powerful disintegrator. AKKA is severely guarded and is kept in the sole possession of a single member of the Anthar family. * The Ulnar pretenders, who perpetually plot to regain their empire, are still in positions of power in the government. They also own the moon Phobos as their family seat, Purple Hall. * *Special background:* Adam Ulnar, commander of the Legion of Space, is conspiring to place his nephew Eric back on the throne. Eric has just returned from an interstellar expedition to Barnard's Runaway Star, where he has encountered the alien civilization of the Medusae. The Medusae, who are able to levitate themselves by manipulating space-time coordinates, are like gigantic jellyfish with a single enormous eye. Scientifically, they are more advanced than the solar system, with far superior spaceships, weapons that toss miniature suns, and much else. * Despite their advancement, they are losing the battle for their planet. Their sun is dying, and the planetary environment is incredibly hostile. * Eric Ulnar has made a treaty with them. In exchange for a shipload of iron, which is lacking in their system, they will conquer the solar system for him and restore the Ulnar empire. Actually, the Medusae, who are expectedly vicious and foul, really mean to take the solar system for themselves. Eric learns this too late. * *Personalities:* The conspirators include Adam and Eric Ulnar; Adam is to some extent a man of honor, even if beset by schemes of power, whereas Eric is simply a wastrel and swine. * Against the conspirators are: John Ulnar, a distant relative, who in a wooden way is totally upright and loyal to Green Hall; Aladoree Anthar, a beautiful maiden, who is the current holder of AKKA; and the then equivalents of the Three Musketeers. They are Jay Kalam (mind and honor), Hal Samdu (muscle and bravery), and Giles Habibula (gluttony and deviousness, but honorably so). Giles is an ingenious rogue of many unexpected abilities. * *The narrative:* A gigantic Medusan ship, guided by Eric Ulnar, kidnaps Aladoree and takes her to Yar-

Williamson, Jack (continued)

kand, where the Medusae work on her to obtain the secret of AKKA. John Ulnar, at first deceived by the other Ulnars, finally recognizes what is happening and follows with his three companions to rescue her. After great peril they reach Yarkand, which is a horrible place, vividly imagined. They are captured, but fortunately are imprisoned near Aladoree, whom they rescue. Returning to the solar system, they find that the Medusae have all but conquered it, and that the human race is being destroyed by a poison gas (peculiar to Yarkand) that the Medusae are dropping on Earth. Aladoree, who has suffered badly during her captivity and rescue, recovers sufficiently to set up an AKKA apparatus. She first disintegrates the Medusan fleet, then the Moon, which was the Medusan base. John Ulnar, whose name is now officially changed to Star, and Aladoree marry. * *Miscellaneous:* Space travel is accomplished by geodynes (which permit faster-than-light travel) and auxiliary rockets. Hand weapons include proton guns. * There are stylistic and developmental problems with "The Legion of Space," notably the irritating characterizations of the musketeers and John Ulnar; nevertheless, the concept of AKKA is tantalizing, and the story is carried along by a drive and verve that make it one of the better early space operas. * For a sequel, see #1758, "The Cometeers."

1756. **THE GALACTIC CIRCLE.** *Astounding Stories,* August 1935. Ill. Dold.
Novelette. * An unusual story for the day and Jack Williamson; an attempt to combine adventure based on a scientific concept with a certain amount of social realism—dissatisfied husbands and wives, an accepted triangle, etc. * *Time:* the near future. * Reporter Rodney Trent is assigned to cover the remarkable experiment that Jarvis Thorn is making; it is undoubtedly the greatest experiment of all time. * Trent, passing through extensive security arrangements, meets the principals of the mysterious experiment: Thorn, who is sure, from mathematical calculations and physical tests, that the experiment will be successful, and his friend and colleague Starbuck, a man equally eminent, who is certain that the experience will be fatal. * What is the venture? Thorn, who has brought atomic energy under control, explains. By expanding or contracting time, he is able to change the size of atomic orbits, with resultant gross size changes. Thus, by playing with sizes up and down, he has created a globe of uranium that will serve as a spaceship powered by devouring its own substance. He plans to enlarge it until it reaches the macrocosm above us. Thorn thinks that this can be done successfully; Starbuck is sure that it will be a disaster. * A mixed company of men and women, most of whom have personal problems, will leave together. Obviously, there will be no returning, but it will be the greatest adventure. * The *Infiniterra* leaves, expands, and progresses upward, while the adventurers see the sun and solar system become pinpoints and disappear. There is suspense and peril by the time the uranium globe, now sadly depleted, bursts through into the macrocosm. It looks, for a while, as if the uranium that composes the vessel will be used up. But Starbuck works out a way to reconvert incoming energy back to uranium, and the *Infiniterra* is ready to continue to enlarge and explore the macrocosm. The vessel expands, light appears, the familiar universe is manifest, including Earth, and the explorers look out to see—themselves departing in the *Infiniterra* in the grounds of the laboratory.

They did not break into a macrocosm, but in some fashion returned to their starting point. As Thorn and Starbuck work it out, it is a complex bit of relativity. When one reaches a limit in size, one snaps back into being an atom in a time frame—or that seems to be the point. * *Miscellaneous:* The complex marital and extramarital problems that beset the leading characters were resolved during the voyage. * Much the most mature of Williamson's early works, with more careful writing than usual, an adult point of view, and sophisticated social patterns. A work that was not appreciated in its time.

1757. **ISLANDS OF THE SUN.** *Astounding Stories,* September-October 1935. Ill. Dold.
Novelette. * In total contrast to the social realism of "The Galactic Circle," "Islands of the Sun" is a science-fictional fairy tale with handsome young hero, beautiful princess to be won, perils, and fruition. * *Time and place:* the remote past, inside the sun. According to the "thought-variant" concept behind the story, the planets of the solar system were not formed out in space as in real-world cosmology, but were the result of "a tidal vortex, deep within the tortured bowels of the Sun, [that] ruptured space itself and extruded the matter of the newborn planet[s] into a subspace beyond." These ur-planets are protected by etheric shields that are impenetrable by the xyli, the totally hostile flame beings native to the sun proper. * When Ken Darren and Dakkil Kun were herdsmen on the planet Pylos (present-day Earth), Ken found an enormous spherical crystal of okal, a carbon allotrope harder than diamond that alone makes atomic energy possible. Ken, who is a decent young man, despite a strange infatuation for the Princess Wyndonee (whom he has never met), wants to keep the gem for its beauty; but Dakkil, an ambitious, brutal man who has been bestialized by the oppressive Labor Company, wants to use it for power. With it he can topple the interplanetary ruler (the Lhundar) from his throne. Dakkil, too, has an erotic compulsion about Wyndonee; he wants to flagellate her and abuse her. * Dakkil Kun knocks Ken unconscious, steals the okal, and with a smaller gem that he has obtained by murder leaves the planet. * Ken, who pursues him, loses the trail and much time before he learns what has happened: Dakkil Kun, striking a bargain with the xyli, has become new emperor of the planets. As part of the agreement, the xyli will keep him in power for his lifetime, after which, since Kun has betrayed to them the tensors for dissolving the etheric shields protecting the planets, they will let the total solar heat in on the planets, wiping out mankind. * Ken and friends, caught up by the tyrannical system, are sentenced to prison terms on the mining planet Kardon, where few survive long. Ken Darren, however, is too resourceful to remain a convict. He seizes the prison, the planet, and with the imperial fleet (which goes over to him) begins an attack on the dictator Dakkil Kun. * Darren's motives are multiple: revenge on Kun, rescue of Wyndonee, and regaining the giant okal. With the okal (which is by far the largest known) the great scientist Teddu Len will be able to hurl the planets out of the sun and into exterior orbits. Although a most risky procedure, such "childbirth" is the only hope for human survival, since the xyli now have mankind at their mercy. * Adventures follow. Teddu Len devises a potent disintegrator; the xyli fleet is defeated; Kun is deposed and commits suicide; Ken locates the okal back in the cave where he first found it; Wyndonee turns up unexpectedly, in love with Ken; and the planets are tossed out. It was just in time, for in

Williamson, Jack (_continued_)

a cliffhanger, the xyli were beginning to destroy the planetary heat shields. As Len says, mankind may lose all its science, but it will recover. * Imagination, as usual with Williamson, but the calculated simplicity of characterizations and situations almost turns the story into a semijuvenile. The psychological aspects of the story, however, are interesting.

1758. **THE COMETEERS.** _Astounding Stories_, May-August 1936. Ill. Marchioni.

(Reprinted in revised book form by Fantasy Press, Reading, Pa., 1950, and by Pyramid, 1967. Included in Williamson, _Three from the Legion._)

Short novel. * Sequel to #1755, "The Legion of Space." Although the plotline is similar, the subtext is much more complex. * _Time:_ about 2920 or so. The story centers upon Bob Star, son of John Star and Aladoree, who make only cameo appearances. Bob is the potential successor to Aladoree in wielding AKKA, but he has not been groomed for the position as he really should have been; instead he has been sheltered, a situation that has embittered him. * The problem is that Bob is broken man, in general opinion (though not stated openly) incapable of handling AKKA. His parents believe that the strain of study at the space academy was too much for him; but actually, Bob's psychological problem stems from an incredibly brutal hazing that in some ways broke his spirit. Much of the subtext of the story is concerned with Bob's overcoming his mental block, which focuses on Stephen Orco, the man who brutalized him. * _Background 1:_ Some years back, a revolt against Green Hall took place in the Jupiter system. The leader, who masked his revolt at first, was Stephen Orco, the most brilliant man ever to graduate from the space academy. At one time the revolt was serious enough that the Legion asked Aladoree to use AKKA. Surprise! AKKA did not work, for the brilliant Orco had rediscovered the secret and could guard against it. The revolt was subdued with proton cannon. Although details are top secret, with even Bob Star ignorant until the story begins, Orco is not dead, as is universally believed. When he saw that he was beaten, he surrendered on condition that his life be not only spared, but guaranteed. There is one exception to this agreement: Orco laughingly added that if Bob Star ever had the guts to kill him, it would be all right. Orco now sits in solitary confinement, totally shut off from communication. Outside his cell is a red button for Bob Star to push. * _Background 2:_ A strange cometary formation is entering the solar system. Greenish and about twelve million miles long, it does not seem to be composed of ordinary matter, but is eventually revealed to be a force screen of a sort. The Legion is concerned about the comet, and contradictory orders are issued to Aladoree about destroying it. Out of humaneness, Jay Kalam, now commanding officer of the Legion, restrains Aladoree until it is too late. * As events pile up: Invisible beings from the comet invade the system's defenses, learning the secret of Orco's existence and AKKA; Jay Kalam tries to visit the comet in the most powerful ship of the day, which the cometeers coldly disintegrate, Jay barely surviving in the command module; John Star and Aladoree flee from the solar system; Bob Star is sent to the prison with veiled instructions to kill Orco, which he cannot forced himself to do; the Cometeers spring Orco and take him away; the Cometeers start drawing planets into the comet; and things look hopeless, for the invaders are far superior scien-

tifically to the solar system. * As for the Cometeers themselves, they are energy beings, about ten feet tall, with strange star-like lights and zones. They can pass through matter and are (with exception to be brought in later) immortal and indestructible. No human weapon is of any avail against them. AKKA could have destroyed the comet itself, but the Cometeers would have been only inconvenienced. They are also vampiric, living by extracting life force or substance from their prey. Utterly rapacious and predatory, they maintain an empire of alien life-forms within the comet. * Bob, Jay Kalam, Hal Samdu, and Giles Habibula undertake the quest against the Cometeers. Space-wrecked, thanks to an encounter with Cometeers, they spend some time on a remarkable trans-Plutonian asteroid that has been planetary-engineered into a near paradise, until it is drawn into the comet. Inside, they are thrown into a slave pit. Leading a revolt, the four men make their way to the secret chamber where the Cometeers keep the only weapon that can be used against themselves. There, Giles Habibula's talents are indispensable in opening almost unopenable locks. But the small box that is supposed to contain the ultimate weapon against the Cometeers is empty! * At this point the comrades are discomfited by the entry of the chief Cometeer and Orco (transformed into a Cometeer), leading to a final confrontation. The legionnaires stall for time, while Orco jeers at Bob, gloating at the tortures to which Aladoree will be subjected. But then unexpectedly the secret weapon is in Bob's hand, presumably retrieved from a dimensional pocket by Giles. Bob, enraged by Orco's comments about his mother Aladoree, breaks his psychic barrier, turns on the weapon, and destroys Orco and all the other Cometeers. * There are many side issues. On the asteroid Bob meets Kay, a beautiful young woman of unknown tongue, who had been sent there by matter transmission. After they learn to communicate, she reveals that inside the comet there was a human underground of escaped slaves who had created a very high science. Kay's father had developed the matter transmitter and also found out about the secret weapon against the Cometeers, although he himself could not obtain it. It is thanks to Kay's information that the comrades know where to seek it. * Kay: She is the descendant of an early space venture from Argentina, which had been captured by a Cometeer scouting expedition. Romance develops between her and Bob. * Aladoree and John Star: They made a run for it, but were captured and were inside the comet, where Stephen Orco was working on Aladoree to pick up a few finer points about AKKA. * As for Orco, it turns out that he was an android. The artistic developer of the mysterious asteroid beyond Pluto was a white slaver of a sort; he manufactured and sold beautiful women for sexual purposes and was tied into interplanetary crime. The Cometeers destroyed him and his organization. This man manufactured Orco but, for reasons that are not convincing, decided that Orco would turn out badly and sent him into space, à la Superman. * The finale: It is not yet decided whether Aladoree will destroy the comet, whether it will remain in the solar system, or whether it will be allowed to leave with its alien races, which include all sorts of monstrosities formerly subservient to the Cometeers. * Much more elaborate, much more thought-provoking than "The Legion of Space," especially with Star's psychological difficulties, obviously a projection, but the individuation subtlety does not come across when combined with pulp simplistic treatment. * Later components to the series are "One against the Legion" (_Astounding_

Williamson, Jack (*continued*)

1939), "Nowhere Near" (1967, in book collection *The Cometeers*), and *The Queen of the Legion* (1983).

WILLIAMSON, JACK and SCHWARTZMAN, LAURENCE

Williamson has a separate entry. Schwartzman, a young man judging from his portrait, was then a resident of Brooklyn, New York. Nothing else is known about him. * Schwartzman was sixth-prize winner ($5) in the magazine's Interplanetary Plot Contest. Williamson fleshed out the plot.

1759. **RED SLAG OF MARS**.   *Wonder Stories Quarterly*, Spring 1932. Ill. Paul.

Short story. * *Time:* events of 2030 and 2035 as seen from 2080. *Place:* mostly Mars. * In 2035 the notorious renegade and Quisling Dr. Nyland Eldred was captured in the Sahara desert after a Martian spaceship dropped him off. The narrator, who knew Eldred well, visited him in prison and was sworn to secrecy about what Eldred told him. Some time later Eldred was executed as a traitor, and only now, in 2080, can the narrator reveal what really happened in the Earth-Mars war of 2030. * Eldred, a great scientist as well as a renowned peace activist and proponent of world unity, leads an expedition to Mars, with the narrator as communications officer. The expedition, on landing, finds Mars totally covered with a red slag with occasional ruined features protruding. It seems obvious that the Martians were destroyed by war. Meanwhile, back on Earth, a world war has broken out, with tremendous destruction and slaughter. Ironically, the aircraft made possible by Eldred's discovery of anti-gravity have destroyed many of the great cities. * The story takes two paths. First, the expedition finds a monument later than the slag, with a deciphering key built into the inscription. Eldred is deciphering it. Second, the various nationalities on the expedition are at each other's throats and clamoring to return to Earth. Some are trying to rediscover the ray that the Martians used for self-destruction. * After mutiny, fighting, and loss of lives, the expedition is about to return to Earth, though Eldred is missing. Just before the expedition departs, however, a Martian ship appears, which the trigger-happy mutineers shoot down. * On arriving at a ruined San Francisco, the narrator and his associates learn that a Martian fleet has already attacked Earth, wiping out the air fleets of the major nations. The situation seems bad, especially when Eldred appears on interplanetary television and urges the forces of Earth to surrender, to become a Martian province. After defeating terrestrial forces in other one-sided battles, the Martian ships return to Mars, and nothing more is seen of them. * During the five years that pass before Eldred's return, a world government is established, and the Earth, as a unit, prepares for a second Martian invasion. * Eldred's secret, that he revealed in confidence to the narrator: From the inscription that he deciphered he learned the rough location of Martian survivors. He followed the instructions and came upon a thriving underground culture with a superscience. The Martians, who are snake-like beings, were benevolent, and while they were annoyed at the destruction of their ship, they bore no malice. In fact, at Eldred's request, they agreed to make a limited strike at Earth in order to stop the world war in progress; by offering a common enemy the Martians hoped to force the nations of Earth to unite. Eldred deliberately posed as a traitor to bring about peace. Although well treated on Mars, he became homesick and asked the Martians to return him to Earth, where,

unfortunately, he was captured. * Eldred begged that his story be suppressed until enough time passed for the new world government and peace to be established firmly. * Somewhat confusing at first, what with the various time frames, but not a bad job.

WILLIS, CAPT. JOHN

No information, but presumably a British author.

1760. **DEATH BROADCASTS**. *Scoops*, 2-23 June 1934. Unsigned ill.

Boys' fiction. * Novelette. * *Place:* mostly England, but episodes in California and New York City. * The reform vigilante in action. The Master of Destruction, who has a long-distance, directable ray that destroys inorganic matter, sends warnings to various social criminals and takes action when they do not follow his instructions. His targets include a swindling oil magnate, ordered to give two million dollars to the unemployed; an armament manufacturer, ordered to close his factories and distribute his wealth to war widows; the Governor of New York, ordered to disgorge millions he has embezzled; dope smugglers, etc. In each case he disintegrates their ships, vehicles, or other inorganic property so that they die in the collapse. * Against the Master of Destruction are Chief Inspector Grosvenor of Scotland Yard and toff Detective Sergeant Billy St. John Castledale. Oddly enough, the Master, who operates from a run-down farm in Yorkshire, communicates frequently and frankly with Billy. * Observing that the Master's strokes interrupt BBC broadcasts, the investigators manage to track him down and, in a shoot-out, kill him. The Master's last threat had been to disintegrate the bars in the London Zoological Gardens and release all the animals. * Part of the action involves conflict between the Master and the hidden chief of the armaments industry.

WILSON, ROBERT H.   (c. 1910?-1931)

Portrait accompanying "A Flight into Time" shows a young man. According to Ackerman, *Gosh! Wow!*, a suicide.

1761. **A FLIGHT INTO TIME**.   *Wonder Stories*, February 1931. Ill. Marchioni. Two stills from the motion picture *Just Imagine*.

Short story. * *Time:* 1933 and 2189. *Place:* San Francisco. * Ted Storrs was standing near the Golden Gate Bridge in 1933, when he bumped slightly into a stranger, who asked him the time. The stranger was oddly dressed, and he wore a wristwatch that indicated ten hours and a hundred minutes. As Ted soon learns, he is in the future, A.D. 2189. * Rodgers, the stranger Ted encountered, is perfectly willing to believe that Ted came from 1933; this is confirmed when a check reveals that Ted's fingerprints are not on record. * Ted goes home with Rodgers, meets his beautiful daughter, and takes up life in the new world. * San Francisco, 2189: San Francisco is a megalopolis, with incredible, tall, beautiful buildings. Air traffic is heavy, and interplanetary travel is common. Atomic power stands behind the civilization, and wireless broadcast of power propels even spaceships. Unfortunately, Ted is a very average man, and he never thinks to ask the questions about social matters that would interest us or his friends back in 1933, but the economy may be socialistic; at least, there are common food-processing centers in the large dwelling buildings. Most of the social problems of our time seem to have been worked out, and while the culture is not a play culture, it allows plenty of leisure time. Casual nudity is

Wilson, Robert H. (*continued*)

common. * The scientists of the twenty-second century are greatly interested in time travel; indeed, there is a prize for the first person who achieves it, but Ted may not be eligible since his experience was involuntary. When he is examined by a board, his information reveals a basic point in time theory: that time is a spiraling stream, points of which may touch, in this case every 256 years, or 2 to the eighth power. With this information, the future scientists can return Ted to his own era if he so wishes. * Ted has never felt happy in the future, which seems dreamlike, and returns to our time. Because of his limitations, he can say very little of value. * *Miscellaneous:* There was a great war from about 2030 on, with the Western world against China. What with atomic bombs and disintegrators, the war came close to wiping out humanity. Japan was blown off the Earth, and Central and Western Europe were pretty much depopulated. Around 2050 both sides, exhausted, accepted a peace and the challenge to build a better world than the old. * Not bad. More readable than most such accounts.

1762. **OUT AROUND RIGEL**. *Astounding Stories,* December 1931. Unsigned ill.

(Reprinted in Knight, *Science Fiction of the Thirties,* and in Ackerman, *Gosh! Wow!*)

Short story. * *Time:* presumably in the remote past. *Place:* the Moon and around Rigel. * Some implications of relativity, combined with lost romance. * A manuscript found on the Moon, together with teaching aids for its decipherment. * The great young scientist Garth has constructed a faster-than-light spaceship that operates by distorting space. In it he and his friend Kelvar are to travel to Rigel on a maiden voyage. The trip should not be long, for the vessel can travel thousands of times faster than light. * But all is not as it seems, for both Kelvar and Garth love the same woman. While Kelvar thinks that their rivalry is friendly, Garth knows otherwise. When they land on a Rigelian planet that has a chlorine atmosphere, Garth makes it clear that only one of them will return to the Moon. Though reluctant to fight, Kelvar defends himself, and the two space-suited men slash at each other with swords. But there is an interruption, a horrible form of native life emerges from the ground. Though siliceous and brittle, it is a menace. * Only Kelvar can reenter the spaceship; Garth, in a gesture of remorse, sacrifices himself. * Kelvar returns to the Moon, which he finds dead and almost airless. What both men forgot was the time factor. A millennium has passed in terms of Moon time, and a great meteorite storm has wreaked havoc. Kelvar writes down his experiences and commits suicide. * A story with a large reputation among the older fans, many of whom have praised it highly. Harry Bates, for example, called it poetic. I found the writing a little brisker than much other contemporary science-fiction, but otherwise consider the story routine. The older fans may have liked the sentimentality.

[Anonymous]
Presumably a British author.

1763. **WIMPOLE'S WEIGHT REDUCER**. *Scoops,* 31 March 1934. Unsigned ill.

Boys' fiction. * Short story. * Humor. * Strange events: a man is floating in the air above Tower Hill; a flying man breaks up a nobleman's party and steals a bottle of whiskey; a strange creature is cavorting around the top of St. Paul's. It is all Ben Bowline, caretaker of Professor Wimpole's establishment. Wimpole has been working on reducing weight by magnetic force, with the result that Bowline, who has floated uncontrollably away, is not subject to gravity. * The professor and his nephew Jack Braxton follow Bowline in an automobile, hoping to retrieve him, but with little success. When he seems headed for the Channel on a stormy night, they enter a balloon park, where they steal a balloon. Eventually catching up with Bowline, who is now very drunk, Jack lassoes him. The wind blows them over to France, where they learn that they have won an international race. On returning home, Wimpole demagnetizes Bowline and suppresses his invention.

WINKS, JACK
According to letter in June 1934 *Astounding Stories,* an electrical engineer resident in Chicago.

1764. **THE FIRST ORNITHOPTER**. *Amazing Stories,* January 1930. Ill. Morey.

Short story. * The reclusive inventor John Petite has constructed what might be a successful one-man flying machine with flapping wings. Unfortunately, he does not have an adequate power source. While making a brief trial flight he chances to meet electrical engineer Grossman, who can provide a far superior battery than Petite has, and constructs a more efficient motor. As a result, after a few mishaps, the ornithopter flies beautifully. * Anecdotally told, of no interest.

1765. **ADRIFT ON A METEOR**. *Amazing Stories,* August/September 1933. Ill. Morey.

Short story. * *Time:* A.D. 2014. *Place:* the asteroid belt. * Essentially a monologue about a space adventure, told by old Jake Henderson in a folksy, colloquial manner to his grandchildren. Jake was first mate on the old *Polyphemus,* which was metal hunting among the asteroids, when a mutiny took place. The mutineers made the officers and loyal crew members take the space cure (i.e., walk the plank out into space), but the leader, who had a special grudge against Henderson, put him into a space suit so that he would suffer longer. Henderson floated in space for a time, eventually drifting onto a meteor or small asteroid that turned out to be valuable ore. Although his situation seemed hopeless, he did not lose heart, but on seeing a light, set off a flare that was included with his suit. He was then rescued by the *Polyphemus.* A friendly mutineer, killing Henderson's enemy, convinced the others that Henderson should be rescued, since he was the only man available who could navigate. * As can be seen, a sea marooning transferred into space, but the author has done a good job of creating convincing space slang.

WINN, CHARLES C.
No information.

1766. **THE INFINITE VISION**. *Amazing Stories,* May 1926. Ill. Paul.

(First published in *Science and Invention,* May 1924.) Short story. * *Place:* mostly the Andes. * At the meeting of the International Astronomical Society, scientists express dissatisfaction at the functioning of telescope lenses. The great scientist Glenn Faxworthy thereupon offers to create a far superior telescope if he can receiving funding of one million dollars. * Several years and probably a million dollars later the great telescope is first functioning in the Andes. Faxworthy has not only found a way

Winn, Charles C. (*continued*)

to stabilize the mercury mirror, but has also created an ether beam that destroys matter so that light can reach the lens without atmospheric turbulence. * The Moon is examined, even down a microscopic level, then Mars. Mars, which is Lowell-Schiaparellian, has remarkable cities, superb human inhabitants, and a superior science. Indeed, a look at a Martian observatory shows an ether-ray similar to Faxworthy's. At this point lightning strikes the observatory in the Andes, skewing the ether ray down so that it destroys apparatus and men. * On first reading, I interpreted the disaster as having been caused by the Martians; on second reading, I am less sure of this. It may have been an accident of nature. The author is not entirely clear.

WINSOR, G[EORGE] McLEOD

Presumably a British author. Also wrote the detective novel *The Mysterious Disappearances* (1926) (American title, *Vanishing Men*, 1927), in which a criminal utilizes antigravity. Both *Vanishing Men* and *Station X* are described in detail in *Science-Fiction: The Early Years*. Since no information has turned up on Winsor, his name may be a pseud.—which could be an echo of the name of the reigning monarch.

1767. **STATION X.** *Amazing Stories*, July-September 1926. Ill. Paul

(Previous book publication by Jenkins, London and Lippincott, Philadelphia, both 1919. It is possible that there was earlier unlocated periodical publication.)

Novel. *Time:* shortly before World War I. *Place:* an island in the mid-Pacific and the United Kingdom. * World peril arising out of a mental invasion from Mars. In the first part of the novel, Macrae, an operator in a secret radio relay station, is contacted by Venusians, who warn him that the Martians are planning to invade Earth. Ages previously, the Venusians say, the Martians lived on the Moon; when life became difficult, what with waning atmosphere, they transferred their minds en masse to Mars, taking over the bodies of the native Martians. Now they plan to repeat the same maneuver with Earth. * As Macrae listens, the Martians interrupt, swamping the Venusian message. Macrae collapses, and the station no longer broadcasts. * In the second part of the novel, an examination of Macrae's papers, combined with other information, reveals that the Martian invasion has already begun. Martian minds have taken over a destroyer, which they have armed with antigravity and fantastic weapons. The combined fleets of the world have difficulty in defeating this one Martian ship, but the peril is now over. * The story has had admirers, but it is at best commercial fiction in the first half, and less in the second.

WINSTEAD, D. E., M.D.

No information.

1768. **THE ULTRA-GAMMA WAVE.** *Amazing Stories*, May 1934. Ill. Morey.

Short story. * *Time:* 1923. *Place:* Hong Kong and Yokohama. * Dexter, the narrator, apostrophizing his fate, narrates, in a long backflash, what he has done. * Arriving in Hong Kong, he entered the employ of Gerald Farley, a chemist who was conducting private experiments. After suitable background incident, Farley reveals that he has built a remarkable (undescribed) weapon, which he is terrified lest the Japanese seize. He has already been attacked, and he is desperately thinking of secret ways to remove the invention to the United States. * Eventually Farley tells what the apparatus does: it projects a very long wave (beyond gamma) that can break the crystal structure of silicon, turning it into powder. * En route to America the two men smuggle the apparatus into Yokohama, where Farley has a trusted Chinese agent named Ling, whom Dexter intuitively distrusts, fearing he is a Japanese spy. * Dexter is half right. Ling steals the apparatus, murders Farley, but is in turn shot by Dexter. But the apparatus functions, destroying Yokohama and much of Tokyo—or producing the great Tokyo earthquake of the time. The machine in itself would not have caused so much damage, but the disintegration activated a fault. As for Ling, he was not a Japanese spy, but so anti-Japanese that he wanted to destroy the land.

WINTER, H. G.

Pseud. of Harry Bates and Desmond Winter Hall, who have separate entries. Exact details of the collaboration are not known, although in general, in their joint works, Bates supplied the ideas and plots, while Hall fleshed them out.

1769. **THE HANDS OF ATEN.** *Astounding Stories*, July 1931. Ill. Wesso.

Novelette. * *Time:* 1933. *Place:* the Arctic. * Leslie Craig of the Somers Arctic Expedition on landing his plane sees a strange sight: three humans frozen in the ice—a beautiful young woman, a young man, and a burly older man. As can be seen by their dress and ornamentation, they were ancient Egyptians. (Despite his presence on an Arctic expedition, Craig is really an Egyptologist, so that he should know.) * He digs out the figures, and on a mad impulse proceeds to thaw them and revive them with a new superadrenalin. The three awaken easily enough, but there is trouble immediately. The burly man kills the younger man and overcomes Craig. * The situation: Craig and Taia, the young woman, are now the captives of the Pharaoh Shabako, ruler of the lost race of Egyptians who dwell in the crater of the nearby volcano. Shabako had been chasing the other two, who were runaway lovers, some twenty years earlier. * The Ancient Egyptians maintain some of their old culture, but have an articulated statue that kills human sacrifices. The priests, despite being somewhat hostile to Shabako, agree that Taia and Craig should be sacrificed. After some difficulties, Craig operates the idol to save Taia and shoots out the lamps with his revolver, which he found in the temple. * Craig and Taia flee, with Shabako behind them. The effects of the reviving drug wear off, however, and Shabako and Taia die in the snow. Craig escapes in his plane. * Pretty bad. Obvious imitation of Edgar Rice Burroughs. One would suspect Hall's hand more than Bates's.

1770. **THE MIDGET FROM THE ISLAND.** *Astounding Stories*, August 1931. Ill. Wesso.

Short story. * *Place:* the Detroit area. * A naked man, three feet tall, perfectly built, but weighing about 185 pounds, is rescued from a drifting rowboat. * His story: Garth Howard and his assistant Hagendorff have been experimenting with reducing the size of living things by compressing atoms. Since experiments have been successful, Howard himself undergoes the process, shrinking to about two feet tall, but retaining his original weight. * When it is time for him to return to his normal size, however, Hagendorff, planning to steal credit for the invention, plays him false and reduces him even more. * Howard escapes and has adventures typical of micromen. When he is recaptured, his fate

Winter, H. G. (*continued*)

seems unavoidable, for the villainous German plans to kill him. But a chance splashing of the ray creates a monstrous tarantula that kills Hagendorff. In the meanwhile Howard has reenlarged himself to about three feet.

1771. **SEED OF THE ARCTIC ICE.** *Astounding Stories,* February 1932. Ill. Wesso.

Short story. * *Time:* the near future. * *Place:* the Arctic. * Whale hunting (for oil) is now accomplished with a supersubmarine, from which emerge torpoons (minisubs armed with small cannon). Kenneth Torrance, first-class torpooner, is out in such a torpoon when a whale damages it, forcing him to take to the sea in his water suit. In a short time he sees a strange sight: seal-like creatures with weapons. * These creatures, who are humans who have devolved into water mammals, capture him and take him underwater to an air-chamber under a mound, where he finds Chan Beddoes, a previously missing torpooner. Some attempt at communication with the seal creatures, also called blubber-men, does not get far. * Torrance is for negotiating with their captors, but Beddoes, who is half-mad, is for killing their guard and escaping. Chan forces the issue, and both make a swim for it when a killer whale is trapped nearby. * Chan is killed, but Kenneth successfully reaches Chan's intact torpoon and returns to the mother submarine. * For a sequel, see #1772, "Under Arctic Ice."

1772. **UNDER ARCTIC ICE.** *Astounding Stories,* January 1933. Ill. Wesso.

Short story. * Sequel to #1771, "Seed of the Arctic Ice." * *Time:* the near future. * *Place:* the Arctic. * Torrance, when he told of his experiences, was considered insane and clapped in a sanitarium, where some six weeks later he hears of the loss of the exploratory submarine *Peary.* Torrance knows what must have happened, since the submarine stopped radio contact in the area of the seal men. * Escaping from the asylum, borrowing a plane from a friend, stealing a torpoon in Alaska, he heads for the place where the *Peary* must be. * He is right. The submarine, disabled by striking a rock, has been captured by the seal men, who have tied it down and are besieging it. * Torrance takes his torpoon into the sub, and tries to work out a rescue with the survivors. But the seal men are smashing in the windows and airlock doors. * At the last moment Torrance sets off an explosion outside the sub that stuns the seal men nearby, while the submarine survivors fly up to the surface in their sea suits. Despite battles and perils, Torrance brings his torpoon up, too, and the survivors now have a chance, if a plane arrives. One does. * Not much to recommend in either story.

WINTERBOTHAM, R[USSELL] R[OBERT] (1904-1971)

U.S. (New York) newspaperman and author. Born in Kansas; graduate U. of Kansas. Resident in Pittsburg, Kansas for part of this period. Fiction editor for Scripps-Howard NEA News Service. Contributed prolifically to the pulp magazines within various genres, scripted comic strips, wrote Little Blue Books and Big Little Books. S-f work falls into two periods, before World War II and after 1952. In later work also used pseuds. J. Harvey Bond and Franklin Hadley. Winterbotham's later work is much superior to the stories considered here. See also R. R. Botham, pseud.

1773. **THE STAR THAT WOULD NOT BEHAVE.** *Astounding Stories,* August 1935. Unsigned ill.

Short story. * Two scientific anomalies are recognized at about the same time: unknown radiation striking the Earth in an odd way, and, during observations of a solar eclipse, a star traveling toward the solar system and due to pass near Earth in about three years. The latter information is suppressed for a time, but is greeted with imaginable panic when it is released. * The strange star, which is named Chaos, has planets, one of which passes through the solar system with no gravitational results whatever. Scientists are totally bewildered at the phenomenon. And as the star with other planets draws near and eventually passes through the system, the only effect is a small increase in heat from the star's radiation. That and the destruction of the innermost satellite of Jupiter, which disintegrates as it reaches Roche's limit. * Professor Walleck (who also appears in the next two stories) explains. It had been observed, as the strange solar system approached closely, that it was a counterpart of a sort to our solar system, with the proper number of planets and associated moons. There was even a planet (named Alecto) corresponding to Earth, with one moon. But it was apparently empty of vegetation and life. Says Walleck: This is all an Einsteinian example of curved space. The light from our solar system has eventually traveled around the universe and returned back to us. Thus, one might call it a cosmic mirage. * Not too well expounded, but a tricky idea.

1774. **THE PSYCHO POWER CONQUEST.** *Astounding Stories,* February 1936. Ill. Marchioni.

Short story. * *Place:* Earth and Pluto. The story is told in alternating sections from the Terrestrial point of view and the Plutonian. * On Pluto, the native race, which lives in an underground city, faces extinction as the internal heat of the planet is diminishing. An expedition exploring the inner planets has found that only Earth is suitable for habitation. The explorer, Brulf, who studied Terrestrial culture and languages telepathically, reports that Earthmen, while at a lower level of civilization than Plutonians, are warlike and have superior weapons; also, while they are not telepathic, their minds are easily read and they are extremely susceptible to hypnotic suggestion. The Plutonian rulers decide to conquer Earth by suggestion, and an armed force lands in Antarctica. * On the Terrestrial side, Professor Walleck has invented what amounts to a thought-reading machine; it operates by electrical induction of brain currents. More or less through chance, Walleck discovers that the Plutonians have taken over a Terrestrial Antarctic expedition hypnotically and plan to establish mental control over the leaders of the world. The Plutonian weapons are hitherto unknown gems brought back by members of the Antarctic expedition and distributed among the world's leaders. At the proper time the Plutonians will use these gems to broadcast a sleep signal. * It looks as if the defenses of Western civilization will be down when the Plutonian fleet approaches the national capitals. But it does not happen that way. The Plutonian ships are blasted out of the sky. * Explanation: Walleck, who worked out the Plutonian scheme, broadcast a suggestion that the sleep gems would be investments of great value; the result was that they soon were concentrated among wealthy ne'er-do-wells, whose sleeping or waking condition made no difference. As Walleck says, the Plutonians understood mankind reasonably well, but, what with their own cooperative culture, did not understand human greed. * *Miscellaneous:* The Plutonians are tripeds with tentacles. They are not evil, simply concerned with

Winterbotham, R. R. (*continued*)
survival. * Routine; somewhat confusing in presentation.

      1775. THE TRAIN THAT VANISHED. *Astounding Stories*, July 1936. Ill. Wallace Saaty.
Short story. * In 1925 a train mysteriously vanished in a small Latin American country. * Some years later, Dr. Walleck, well-known scientist, acquires a meteorite that has imbedded in it a railroad coupling pin with the letters A & O. Walleck, with the help of an experienced Scottish railroad man, discovers that A & O is the symbol for a small South American line from which a train totally disappeared in 1925. * In Bamborro Walleck soon learns what is going on when he is tied to a railroad track with a train approaching. Along with him is a device that the local villain considers a disintegrator of a sort. It will be activated by the train and will destroy both train and Walleck. * All ends well. The device was improperly placed, so that it did not harm Walleck, but simply held back the train. Actually, it was not a disintegrator, as its inventor mistakenly believed, but a mechanism that built up enormous electric potential between the train and the track. In the 1925 incident the train was violently repelled from the Earth, and by the time it came down again, the Earth had moved away, and the train ended up in space. * Not very well expounded and certainly not very convincing.

      1776. THE FOURTH DYNASTY. *Astounding Stories*, December 1936. Ill. Thomson.
(Reprinted in Conklin, *Omnibus of Science Fiction.*)
Short story. * *Time:* A frame dated at A.D. 2,678,203, reporting events from A.D. 1,500,000. A few antecedent events from 1937 on. * Young undertaker Victor Hansen invents a preservative fluid that fixes bodies in diamond-like hardness. It is also a means for suspended animation, for an injection will counteract the preservative. Frustrated in love, he drinks his preservative, leaving full instructions for both it and its antidote. His girlfriend Georgiana, discovering that she really loves him, finds his body, removes it to a suitable cave, sets a mineral deposition clock, and joins him. Things go wrong with the revival mechanism, and the two do not revive until A.D. 1,500,000. * Victor and Georgiana awaken in the middle of a battle between two new life-forms that have apparently evolved out of mankind, the Xubrans, who have strange specialized forms, and the Kolans, who are eyeless, earless, noseless, but sense through their skins. The battle is conducted not with physical weapons, but with psychic death blasts. When the combatants perceive that the two strange-looking individuals are immune to their mental attacks (since they are too primitive to respond), the battle turns to a rout and the Kolans win. * Victor and Georgiana dwell with the Kolans, who explain history and other matters to them. The first dynasty was that of the fish; the second, of the giant reptiles; the third, of man, who considered thought most important; and the fourth, evolving out of man, the Kolans, who are concerned with utmost logical certainty, not factual knowledge per se. This emerges in Kolan arithmetic: Since one and one equal two, or one more than its base; the second number doubled should be three—or two and two are three. There is, thus, no relationship between two and four. This is, however, pure mathematics; facts are another matter. * Victor and Georgiana soon become bored with life among the Kolans, and by setting up their departure on a logical basis, are permitted to leave. They settle among the Xubrans, where their descendants mingle with the more human types and form the fifth dynasty. * Intended to be humorous,

perhaps satiric, but a narrative mess. The strange arithmetic, however, is amusing. Good ideas, but total incapability to handle them.

      1777. THE SAGA OF THE "SMOKEPOT." *Flash Gordon Strange Adventure Magazine*, December 1936. Short story. * *Time:* the interplanetary future. * The space cruiser *Z-10457*, nicknamed the *Smokepot*, is out of control, atomic rockets fused, out beyond the solar system. The only hope is either to reach another star system or find an uncharted planet. * Chance favors the brave. After two years of uncontrolled flight, the men come upon an unknown orphan planet, unlighted, but heated by electrical phenomena. It seems like a good place to make repairs. * But there is a problem. The planet is inhabited by a mass-being, an electric entity made up of strands and globes that devours all kinds of organic material. It soon besieges the ship. Captain Olney, making repairs outside, barely escapes, saved by an artificial storm created by a crewman. * Similar to Sewell Peaslee Wright's Commander Hanson stories, but without the personalized element.

WITWER, BENJAMIN
No information.

      1778. RADIO MATES. *Amazing Stories*, July 1927. Ill. Paul.
Short story. * A long letter from Bromley Cranston, explorer and radio researcher, to his cousin. * While Cranston was in Afghanistan, Marston, an acquaintance, stole Venice, Cranston's near-fiancée, forging letters in the process. Cranston determined on revenge. * Adopting a new identity and settling near the now-married Marstons, he continued his researches, succeeding eventually in performing matter transmission by radio. * When he meets his former sweetheart, Venice, she recognizes him, and they both realize that they are still in love. * Since nothing can be done about it, Cranston rigs up his matter transmission apparatus and disintegrates himself and Venice. Both hope that at some time in the future they may be reassembled under happier circumstances. * Contemporary mores, undoubtedly, but one wonders. Divorce courts were functioning then.

WOLFE, CHARLES S.
No information. Contributed frequently to Gernsback's popular science and technology magazines. May possibly be the Charles S. Wolfe who wrote *Air Castle Architecture*.

      1779. "WHISPERING ETHER." *Amazing Stories*, June 1926. Unsigned ill.
(First published in the *Electrical Experimenter*, March 1920.)
Short story. * The irony of fate in a science-fictional situation. * Professor Proctor, who has invented an incredibly powerful explosive, traps an industrial spy who has come to steal his secret formula. How did Proctor catch the spy? A mechanical thought reading device that he wears on his head. * The professor, unfortunately, cannot resist the temptation to boast and taunt. The two men struggle; a small quantity of the explosive is detonated; the thought-reading device is destroyed; and the professor is knocked out. * When he regains consciousness and explains what happened, he is certified insane and put into an asylum, for the burglar will not support his story. * Also involved is an after-the-fact prediction of World War I by reading thought. * Primitive.

      1780. THE EDUCATED HARPOON. *Amazing Stories*,

Wolfe, Charles S. (*continued*)
December 1926. Ill. monogram MEC (?).
(First published in the *Electrical Experimenter*, April 1920.)
Short story. * One of a series of detective stories, not all science-fictional, that appeared in the *Electrical Experimenter* chronicling the cases of Joe Fenner, a college student whom the local police consult when they are out of their depth. No humor is intended. * A man has been murdered in a sealed room in a skyscraper, and the obvious suspect is clear. Fenner observes a "clothes line" on a nearby skyscraper. It is really an aerial, and the murderer sent a tiny radio-operated drone plane with a knife in its nose across the gap between the two buildings. It stabbed the victim and flew away. * After the murderer confesses, the apparatus is suppressed as too dangerous to exist.

1781. **THE MASTER KEY**. *Amazing Stories*, April 1928. Unsigned ill.
(First published in *Science and Invention*, August 1920.) A detective story, at best borderline as science-fiction. * Fenner solves a sealed room mystery. An electromagnet draws bolts. This would seem to be a very early use of this motif, but the story is weak.

WOLLHEIM, DONALD A[LLEN] (1914-1990)
U.S. (New York) fan, editor, publisher, author. B.A., New York University. Dominant member of the New York Futurians, a fan group. Edited magazines *Cosmic Stories* and *Stirring Science Stories* in early 1940s. Edited fiction series for Avon Books and Ace. Founded DAW publishers in 1972, specializing in fantastic fiction. Wrote fiction under pseud. David Grinnell, and as Wollheim wrote a series of Mike Mars juvenile novels. Also edited many anthologies. * As a fan, an interesting if not always likeable figure in the power plays and disruptive intrigues of the 1930s. As an editor and publisher, competent, with many routine publications and some interesting work; of considerable commercial importance in the 1970s and 1980s. As a writer, routine at best. See also pseud. Millard Verne Gordon.

1782. **THE MAN FROM ARIEL**. *Wonder Stories*, January 1934. Ill. Paul.
Short story. * The narrator hears a whistle and crash outside. Investigating, he comes upon a humanoid figure with red, smoldering eyes. The figure is obviously badly injured, for it clutches its side, from which liquids ooze. The narrator feels a mental sensation as if his mind is being exhausted, as the creature collapses, dies, and dissolves to a small puddle. * On sleeping, the narrator now relives the experiences, telepathically imprinted in his brain, of V'thardor, the man from Ariel. * The people of Ariel are preparing their first space probe, a space egg that is to be hurled off Ariel by a Ferris-wheel-like rotor and placed in orbit around Neptune, thence to return. Rockets are also involved. But the centrifugal force developed is far too great, and the Arielian is hurled out into space toward the sun. He crashes on Earth, and as he stands dying sees approaching him the Terrestrial narrator. * Immature work.

WOODBURY, DAVID O.
U.S. author, then resident at Cape Neddick, Maine. Perhaps David Oakes Woodbury (1896-1981) U.S. author of popular books on technology and company histories; if so, his work improved greatly since the following stories. *The Glass Giant of Palomar* (1939) went through several editions. *Atoms for Peace* (1955).

1783. **THE ELECTRIC SNARE**. *Astounding Stories*, July 1934. Ill. Dold.
Short-short story. Questionable as science-fiction. * Shelby Cobb is putting the finishing touches on his apparatus, which seems to be an extra-powerful X-ray, when an industrial thief enters the work area, produces a gun, and demands Cobb's report paper. Cobb, knowing the identify of the would-be thief, who has previously tried to steal the invention, traps him and subjects him to lethal X-ray bombardment.

1784. **AGROUND IN SPACE**. *Astounding Stories*, August 1934. Ill. Dold.
Short story. * Mark, the narrator, a surgeon friend of Joe Barnaby's, leaves his hospital position to assist Joe in a university sponsored project: a new version of the old scheme of rising high enough to stand still while the Earth revolves beneath—thus in effect traveling at 1,000 MPH. The new gimmick is that the ether exists and circles the Earth in a stream, which Joe plans to slip up into. * The ether vehicle, with Joe and Mark on board, works, but Joe overlooked one point: the ether is not simply circling the Earth slowly, it is running through the solar system at a speed of several hundred thousand miles per hour. * This discovery opens up enormous possibilities, namely space travel. Joe is all for remaining up in space, riding the rapid stream away from Earth, but Mark, unwilling to take the risk, drops back down to Earth in a special parachute. * The dialogue is handled well enough, but the story is flat.

[Anonymous]
Presumably a British author.

1785. **THE WORLD OF VAPOUR**. *Scoops*, 10 March 1934. Ill. Shirley.
Boys' fiction. * Short story. * Sir Ian Forsyth has built a bathysphere with neutron ray disintegrators in its base, permitting more rapid descent than by ordinary means. When he and young Dick Ranger descend into the Atlantic, they encounter a strange situation. Their bathysphere is seized by a whirlpool, carried away, and deposited on a submarine peak. The top of the vessel is in ocean water, but the bottom is in an atmosphere. * The two men leave the bathysphere and explore among the three-hundred-foot-tall purple trees. In the distance they see a group of blue, metallic inverted cones that seem to be dwellings of some sort, with strands of netting around them. Then they encounter one of the inhabitants, a spider-like creature about four feet high with two metal pain-ray rods. Sir Ian and Dick are rendered unconscious and captured. They awaken in a gigantic spider web. With some difficulty they cut their way loose, kill a spider who tries to stop them, and race toward their bathysphere, pursued by spiders in flying machines. The men evade capture for a time, and when a temporarily disabled machine lands near them, they seize it, fly to their bathysphere, and mount to the surface. They reflect that the surface at some time may be invaded by the giant spiders.

WRIGHT, SEWELL PEASLEE (1897-1970)
U.S. journalist, owner of an advertising agency. Born in Pennsylvania; reared in Ohio; writing life in New York. Contributed stories to the various pulp and slick magazines. Wright is not to be confused with Sewall Wright (1889-1987), a noted evolutionary biologist.

Wright, Sewell P. (*continued*)

Wright's stories are described in two categories: The Commander John Hanson Series and Other Works.

The Commander John Hanson Series

Hanson is a retired high officer of the Special Patrol, the space-police arm of the mercantile space empire known as the Interplanetary Alliance. Despite its limiting title, the IA spreads over the universe with its bases and trading centers. The inhabited planets seem to be Earth-like, with more or less humanoid populations, more or less on the same level of technology. The time range is indeterminate future. * Faster-than-light travel is obviously involved, but no explanations are given. The individual vessels, which seem to be organized like a modern maritime navy, use both rockets and atomic power. Disintegrator rays, pain rays, dehydrating rays, atomic bombs, etc. are in common use. Communication is often by the menore, a mechanical thought transceiver worn on the forehead. * The stories follow a pattern. Hanson, a crusty old spacedog who is contemptuous of more modern developments in the Patrol, narrates exploits in which he has been concerned, all the while grousing bitterly about decadence, aliens, and lack of recognition for the Patrol of his day. The stories are competent professional pulp work.

1786. THE FORGOTTEN PLANET. *Astounding Stories*, July 1930. Ill. Wesso.
Short story. * The first of a series of reminiscences of Commander John Hanson, a retired officer of the Special Patrol of the Interplanetary Alliance. * The universe is filled with habitable planets that belong to the Alliance. There is one exception: a planet whose name has been expunged from all records, whose location no ship is permitted, under any circumstances, to draw near. * As Hanson tells it, the planet, whose population is reptilian humanoid, was the trouble spot of the universe since its discovery. The native population was incredibly vicious and quarrelsome, and many wars and centuries of education were necessary to bring it into compatibility with the Alliance. But this compatibility has been illusory, a screen for hidden preparation for war. * As the story begins, the natives, who have suddenly massacred all the Alliance personnel on their planet, demand that an accredited ambassador validate their claim to an irresistible weapon—the basis for their diplomatic offensive. Hanson is selected by the Council. He understands that he must act cautiously. * The natives of the nameless planet show Hanson their weapon: A fungus so rapid and so horrible that it can destroy a planet's plant and animal life almost in minutes. * Hanson recognizes the reality of the threat and leaves, ostensibly to make his report. Actually, he has prevented war and the destruction of the inhabited planets. Unobserved, he pocketed a small vial of fungus spores. Back on his ship, he orders his crew to destroy all ships leaving the planet, and drops the fungus on the planet, killing everyone. * This area of space is now closed off. * Well enough told, though modern readers may find the genocide handled a little too glibly.

1787. THE TERRIBLE TENTACLES OF L-472. *Astounding Stories*, September 1930. Ill. Wesso.
Short story. * A reminiscence of Commander John Hanson. Hanson, a young junior officer, is assigned to investigate the fate of two patrol vessels, the *Filanus* and the *Dorios*, which have

apparently been lost on the uninhabited planet L-472. Hanson's expedition, too, almost fails. The problem is that the planet is covered by a single, gigantic tree formation that can move its limbs and is violently carnivorous. Hanson turns his disintegrators on the tree and rescues some of the surviving patrolmen.

1788. THE DARK SIDE OF ANTRI. *Astounding Stories*, January 1931. Ill. Wesso.
Short story. * Hanson reminisces on his experiences of Antri, a small planet that does not revolve. On its light side, the natives are extremely pleasant and civilized. The dark side used to be uninhabited, but an intelligent humanoid life-form has developed: about twelve feet tall, goggle-eyed, lanky, and hostile. * The dark-siders plan to invade the light side, whose inhabitants appeal for Hanson's aid. One vessel, even though powerful, cannot repel an invasion, but Hanson impresses the dark siders with his disintegrators. They agree to maintain peace if Hanson leaves one of his officers with them as an "adviser" (hostage). Hanson does not like the idea, but has to agree.

1789. THE GHOST WORLD. *Astounding Stories*, April 1931. Ill. Wesso.
Short story. * Hanson reminisces about the strange hitherto unknown world that his ship, the *Ertak*, discovered after losing course because of a meteor swarm. * Disabled, the *Ertak* lands on the Earth-like planet. The primitive inhabitants, who are globe-like monstrosities are unfriendly and capture the patrolmen. The patrolmen escape, and Hanson decides to perform a socially useful act. The alien creatures subsist on a vapor that emanates from the planet; this has given rise to an oligarchy in which those who control the vapors oppress the lower orders badly. With his disintegrators Hanson drills a hole, releasing vapor so that all can profit from it.

1790. THE MAN FROM 2071. *Astounding Stories*, May 1931. Unsigned ill.
Short story. * A reminiscence of Commander Hanson's. * Hanson is on duty back on Earth when a man suddenly appears on the landing field. The man is strangely dressed and seems on the point of collapse. Hanson helps him, and the man reveals that he has traveled in time from the twenty-first century. * As he explains, time is a stream on which the universe flows; he has built machinery to embark on it. * Hanson, accepting the man's story, shows him about his ship, explaining its equipment. The man learns quickly, then surprises Hanson by demanding to take certain pieces back to the twenty-first century with him. As he says, with atomic energy he will conquer the world of his own time. * Hanson points out that such a conquest is not recorded, but this makes little impression on the man. The time traveler would have escaped and gone back to the past with information about new weapons had Hanson not suddenly elevated the ship so that the man fell to his death. His body disappears, and Hanson hushes everything up.

1791. THE GOD IN THE BOX. *Astounding Stories*, September 1931. Ill. Wesso.
Short story. * A reminiscence of Commander Hanson's. * Hanson, who is grousing at the chauvinistic pride of the Xenians in being the first to master space travel, tells of a patrol visit to Strobus, an Earth-like planet whose orbit brings it close to the solar system only after enormous intervals. * Strobus is inhabited by a human race, some of whom speak English. While by no means at the general galactic level, the Strobans have radio,

Wright, Sewell P. (*continued*)

telephones, and similar devices, but being peaceful they have no weapons beyond bows and arrows. * Hanson finds an explanation: an Earthman named Thomas Anderson cracked up on Strobus in the twenty-first century and acted as a culture hero to the then-primitive natives. Anderson thus was far earlier than the Zenians. * Hanson uses atomic bombs to repel an invasion of the peaceful land. * The god in the box is an ancient sound recording of Anderson.

1792. **THE TERROR FROM THE DEPTHS.** *Astounding Stories*, November 1931. Ill. Wesso.
Short story. * A reminiscence of Commander Hanson's. * While passing by the water planet Hydrot, the crew of the *Ertak* sees an island emerge from the depths. Hanson cannot leave his patrol route to investigate, but shortly afterwards is dispatched to rescue the space passenger liner *Kabit*, which is stranded and under attack on Hydrot. * The problem is a sea serpent hundreds of feet long that has wrapped itself around the *Kabit*, preventing it from rising and threatening to crush open its seams. * Hanson and his men lure the serpent away, and after perils, kill it. Hanson, as he crabbedly reports, was virulently condemned by naturalists for destroying the monster's skull.

1793. **VAMPIRES OF SPACE.** *Astounding Stories*, March 1932. Ill. Wesso.
Short story. * Old Commander Hanson reminisces as a young visiting officer tells him about electites, creatures that live in space. * The *Ertak* is assigned to investigate the disappearance of two spaceships. Hanson soon discovers what has happened to them when the metal hull of the *Ertak* is attacked by red crescent shaped creatures that are not ordinary matter, but electrical. The ship's disintegrators do not affect them. * Hanson sets the *Ertak* down on a nearby planet, but it looks as if the ship is doomed, for the creatures rapidly eat into the outer hull. * A chance discovery resolves matters: A water spray short-circuits the creatures.

1794. **PRIESTESS OF THE FLAME.** *Astounding Stories*, June 1932. Ill. Wesso.
Short story. * Commander Hanson is on a mission to the planet Lakos, which is the chief source of terite, a mineral needed for space travel. Lakos, which is inhabited by a bestial sort of mankind, is currently undergoing great unrest as the result of a very strong cult headed by Liane, the Priestess of the Flame. Liane can stop production of terite completely, and in case of hostilities can blow up the mines, severely hampering space travel. * Liane has been at interstellar headquarters on an official "visit," but actually has presented an ultimatum. As her price for cooperating with the other worlds, she demands a seat on the Interplanetary Council. * Hanson, therefore, is quite dismayed to discover that Liane, a beautiful and charming, if enormously dangerous woman, has stowed away on the *Ertak*. He can do no less than treat her as an honored guest. * On arrival at Lakos, Hanson discovers that the situation is very bad. But it resolves itself in an unexpected way. During the flight Liane had seduced one of Hanson's officers and now plans to marry him. This leads to a rebellion on the part of her council of elders, and, eventually, an explosion that destroys both Liane and the elders. Space travel is safe. * The flame is a greenish affair that pops out of the earth. Liane feeds criminals and offensive persons to to it.

1795. **THE DEATH TRAPS OF FX-31.** *Astounding Stories*, March 1933. Ill. Wesso.
Short story. * Hanson, to his annoyance, is detailed to transport a scientific expedition to FX-31, a barely known planet that is inhabited by fairly intelligent creatures much like gigantic trapdoor spiders. The expedition lands; three scientists leave with suitable equipment; and the space patrol waits impatiently. * The scientists are doing well, having established communication with the spiders (once the spiders discovered that they could not penetrate the protective costumes the scientists wore) until members of Hanson's crew land, clash with nearby spiders, and kill several with their disintegrators. * The three scientists are then in trouble, for the spiders attack them. One of the scientists, Tipene, a Xenian, reaches the ship and claims that his associates are dead. But Hanson, suspicious, surreptitiously places a mind-reading device under the Xenian's pillow, and discovers that the other two men are alive and besieged down in a tunnel. * A display of disintegrators grants a truce. Hanson and a detachment enter the tunnels to rescue the scientists, but the spiders attack and the expedition members are fortunate to escape with their lives. The treacherous Xenian is killed by the spiders.

Other Works

1796. **FROM THE OCEAN'S DEPTHS**. *Astounding Stories*, March 1930. Unsigned ill.
Short story. * *Place:* Florida. * The narrator (Taylor) is summoned by Warren Mercer to his palatial estate in Florida, where Taylor sees a strange sight: a beautiful nude woman walking about the bottom of a swimming pool. She is obviously a merwoman. * Mercer had found her, dazed and semiconscious on the shore and tried to revive her, but almost killed her so doing. But she managed to reach the pool, where she revived. * The woman, who is a beautiful blonde, takes a fancy to the narrator, and when he enters the pool with her, becomes quite friendly. * By an odd coincidence Mercer has just invented thought-transference helmets. When the young woman is induced to put one on, her thoughts reveal an undersea culture of some quality. As the author states: Humans emerged from the sea, and in the case of the merpeople, returned. * Mercer and Taylor carry her back to sea and watch her swim away. * The merpeople live in huts much like igloos. * Competent pulp work. For a sequel, see #1797, "Into the Ocean's Depths."

1797. **INTO THE OCEAN'S DEPTHS**. *Astounding Stories*, May 1930. Ill. J. Fleming Gould.
Short story. * Sequel to #1796, "From the Ocean's Depths." * *Place:* Florida. * Taylor is summoned back to Florida by Mercer, who has constructed advanced diving suits and a small submarine that can stand extreme pressures. He plans to go in search of the sea-girl's people. * But circumstances change: The sea-girl (Imee) appears on the beach with her father and mother; Mercer's thought-reading apparatus explains. An alien race of sea men, dark, gilled, and more fish-like than the sea girl's people, have demanded a quota of men and women as slaves, or else they will destroy Imee's people. * Mercer and Taylor agree to help, and descend in time to frustrate an invasion of the aliens. Mercer has flasks of hydrocyanic acid which he releases, killing the invaders, but at one time the situation is perilous. * There is a possibility of salvaging a fortune in silver ingots, which the alien sea men hold, but it falls through.

Wright, Sewell P. (*continued*)

1798. **THE INFRA-MEDIANS.** *Astounding Stories,* December 1931. Ill. Wesso.

(Reprinted in Wollheim, *Every Boy's Book of Science Fiction.*)

Short story. * Pete receives a note from Vic Butler asking him to come to the laboratory; there he learns that Vic and his sister Hope have transferred themselves into what amounts to a parallel universe separated from ours by vibratory frequency. Pete is to rescue them if they haven't returned. * Pete, following instructions, finds himself in a dark, dismal place that amounts in some ways to a reverse world: trees grow with branches in the ground and roots in the air. The inhabitants, who capture Pete, are made of a strange sort of matter that dissolves at will as they teleport themselves from place to place. Their driving force is a desire for death, and they are delighted when Pete shoots a few individuals. * But the priesthood is jealous of the terrestrials' death-dealing potential, and would like to remove them. * The priests have an idol-like formation that shoots out a red death-ray. Pete damages the idol, and in the confusion the Terrestrials succeed in reaching their transport site and return to Earth.

WULFRES, ROGER

No information. Portrait accompanying story shows a middle-aged man.

1799. **THE AIR-PLANT MEN.** *Wonder Stories,* December 1930. Ill. Marchioni.

Short story. * *Place:* mostly on an imaginary island in the Caribbean Sea. * Dr. Destanne, renowned botanist, comes to seek the aid of the narrator. Clad in chain mail, Destanne explains: A new life-form is establishing itself in a few places in the southern United States, and it exists in concentration on Shadow Island, southeast of Cuba. It is a creature like a flying jellyfish, with a large body that apparently generates hydrogen and floats, rising through the air with incredible rapidity. Long tentacles can lift and strangle a man in seconds. And worse, these creatures are probably more intelligent than humans. Is man's rule of Earth due to end? It is later learned that these creatures feed on the aroma and gases emitted by a certain lily, and that they are compound beings, each made up of several smaller beings. * Destanne also explains that the narrator's fiancée, Sibyl, is being held captive by these beings for reasons not known. * Clad in chain mail, eyes protected by goggles, bearing machetes and a chest of explosives, the two men invade Shadow Island, where they find Sibyl in a trance-like state; in a message previously written she states that the air-men plan to absorb her personality into one of their units. * The narrator and Destanne rescue Sibyl with surprising ease, blow up the ridge that restrains the sea from the volcanic cusp that forms the heart of the island, and leave. The air-men are drifting off, blown by the winds. But the menace is by no means over. Humanity faces a bitter struggle. * Below routine.

WYCOFF, J. EARLE

U.S. author, then resident of Shenandoah, Iowa. The author's name is spelled Wyckoff in the Street and Smith records.

1800. **THE SEEING BLINDNESS.** *Astounding Stories,* February 1936. Unsigned ill. (Brown?)

Short story. * Ralph Morris will receive five thousand dollars for undergoing the experiment designed by Dr. Merton, who claims to have perfected a preparation that will give what amounts to far superior X-ray vision. A few drops in the eye, and then . . . * The preparation works, but as Morris discovers, it works too well. His vision is besieged with a total mass of light, for he sees through everything. It is torturing, maddening, but, as Merton says, the effect (judging from animal experiments) will last only about twenty-four hours. Merton quietly destroys his discovery. * A tiny idea well developed.

YOUNG, RAYMOND A.

U.S. author. According to Schwartz/Weisinger Young was the pseud. of Vernon H. Jones, an active fan in Des Moines, Iowa. A Raymond A. Young wrote *Helicopter Engineering* (1945), but this is not likely to have been the same person.

1801. **A THIEF IN TIME.** *Wonder Stories,* July 1935. Short-short story. * Tony Carponi, small-time gangster, undertakes a quest for the elderly scientist. Tony has only to enter a matter transmitter, walk to a certain building, pick up a certain tube, and bring it to the scientist via the matter transmitter. For this he will receive fifty thousand dollars. * Tony accomplishes his task, which turns out to be the theft of a large quantity of radium, and returns to his reward, though vainly pursued by police. * Twenty years pass, during which Tony, using the professor's cash, has become a radio mogul. Unfortunately, chance (or fate) entraps him in his crime, which was really time traveling, not geographical matter transmission. Suicide is his way out. * *Miscellaneous:* Future weapons include tubes that project explosions. * Weak in plotting.

[Anonymous]

Presumably a British author.

1802. **Z.1.—RED FLYER.** *Scoops.* 17 February 1934. Ill. Drigin.

Boys' fiction. * Short story. * Academic rivalry in the United Kingdom takes a serious turn. * Professor Cavendish and his young assistant Jack Strongbow have developed a new sort of air craft, which is a mixture of "an autogiro and pterodactyl." Exactly what it looks like is thus deliciously vague, but it can hover and can also travel at far higher speeds than conventional airplanes. * Thugs attack, the *Z.1.* is temporarily disabled, Jack is knocked out, and the professor is kidnapped. All this takes place just before the craft is to undergo an official test by the air ministry. * Strange Morse signals from a lighthouse resolve matters. Jack flies the repaired *Z.1.* there, retrieves the professor, and is all ready for the test—at which the *Z.1.* flies at 500 mph. * The villain was one Professor Crockett, who stole some of Cavendish's ideas and was building a rival plane.

ZAGAT, ARTHUR LEO (1895-1949)

U.S. (New York) author. B. A. from City College of New York; LL. D. from Fordham Law School. Founded Writers Workshop at New York University. Prolific contributor to various areas of pulp fiction. Not important as a science-fiction author. His best work is generally considered to be "Drink We Deep," lost-race novel (*Argosy* 1937). * See also collaboration Nat Schachner and Arthur Leo Zagat. * See also #1834, "The Land Where Time Stood Still," and #1835, "The Lanson Screen."

1803. **THE GREAT DOME ON MERCURY.** *Astoun-*

Zagat, Arthur Leo (*continued*)
ding Stories, April 1932. Ill. Wesso.
Short story. * *Time:* the interplanetary future. *Place:* Mercury.
* Within the great crystal dome on Mercury live and work three terrestrial engineers and a horde of Venusians, who mine a mineral needed as a food supplement on Earth. The Venusians are small and somewhat humanoid. The native Mercurians, who have been dispossessed of their land, are smaller and more bestial. * There is a sudden large leak in the dome, and Darl goes aloft to repair it, lest all the air be lost. He succeeds, but sees a strange figure outside the dome, obviously the person who knocked a hole in the crystal. Putting on a space suit, Darl gives chase, but is captured by his quarry, a Martian, who is allied with the native Mercurians. * Purposes: Mars has declared war on Earth, and the Martian, in addition to possession of the dome, wants the recognition signals used by Earth's spaceships. Lane, naturally, will not talk. * Things do get cleared up after a fashion. Darl is rescued by his associates; the Venusians are almost all killed; hordes of the Mercurians are dead; the Martian is blasted; and Darl, to warn an approaching Earth vessel, wrecks the dome completely. * Not much to recommend. Crude action and adventure.

1804. **WHEN THE SLEEPERS WOKE**. *Astounding Stories*, November 1932. Ill. Marchioni.
Short story. * *Time:* the near future. * The great world war is on, the Chinese versus the rest of the world. The struggle is fairly even, and since both sides are better at offense than defense, the great cities of the world have been wiped out and the continents covered with poison gas. * Allan Dane, an aviator in the great air armada that unsuccessfully tried to defend New York City, crashes. * He awakens about twenty years later in an underground vault, tended by seven skeletal people. He is equally skeletal. As they inform him, when the extinction of humanity seemed inevitable, a small group of scientists and their wives (if any) sealed themselves up underground; to conserve resources they have alternated in suspended animation. One of them pulled Dane into the shelter just after he crashed. * When the survivors recognize that they cannot remain underground any longer, whether the atmosphere is still lethal or not, Dane agrees to venture out, and, if possible, to conduct a limited exploration in a small helicopter that has been stored away. There may be another refuge with two more people. * Dane finds the second refuge just in time to prevent a bestial black giant from raping a beautiful blonde woman. But there are other problems, horrible Asians who have also survived and have the same plans for the woman. There is back-and-forth action, but Dane wins, incinerating the vile Orientals and the black. * The racism and Zagat's gloating treatment of the near rape are very offensive.

1805. **THE LIVING FLAME**. *Astounding Stories*, February 1934. Ill. Howard V. Brown.
Short story. * *Place:* Oak Island, Nova Scotia, and an underground world connected to it. * A mishmash of motifs: the Treasure Pit of Oak Island; a lighted underground world accessible from it; a flame of life that creates immortality under some circumstances; Hagen, an immortal Viking from about the year 1000; two-foot-high immortal dwarfs allied with the Viking; immortal Indians, cruel and villainous; Gerda, a beautiful maiden (the only female in the underworld); and two Americans (both of whom can speak Old Norse). * Eric and Carl find a runic inscription at the edge of the Treasure Pit; Eric falls in,

whereupon Carl follows; and both encounter the wonders listed above. They come in time to rescue the maiden from the Jotuns (Indians), but are themselves suspected of being Indian agents. Only a strange birthmark on Eric's chest saves his life, for it proves that he is descended from the immortal Hagen. The Indians are beaten off; Eric and Gerda team up; Gerda is revealed to be a normal, mortal woman brought in by the Indians; and Eric, Carl, and Gerda find a way to escape to the outer world. * Little to recommend.

1806. **SPOOR OF THE BAT**. *Astounding Stories*, July 1934. Ill. Dold.
Novelette. Space opera. * *Time:* the interplanetary future. *Place:* space, Mars, Venus. * *Background:* Earth, Mars, and Venus are united in the Triplanetary Union, but all is not well politically. Mars owes Venus an enormous balance, but cannot pay it until it receives a covering payment from Earth. Earth has attempted to send the needed funds to Mars, but the notorious space pirate, the Black Bat, who has a spaceship faster than those of the Triplanetary Patrol, has been intercepting the Terrestrial ships, looting them, and killing all on board. Actually, as soon becomes apparent, Venus is using the financial question to create an incident for war on Earth and Mars. * The brothers Brad and Darl Hamlin agree to a ruse to rush the funds through to Mars. Faking a quarrel and a bet as to which is the faster of their spaceships, one will carry the cash and the other, an empty chest. Thus, since no one knows which, there is a 50/50 chance of getting the money through. The story is told through Brad. * In space, the Black Bat strikes, attacking Darl's ship, capturing it and (as it turns out) the money. Darl is presumed dead, although his body is not found on the gutted vessel. But Brad, reporting to his superiors after the attack, receives a surprising reception. He is accused of complicity with the Black Bat and jailed. Escaping with the aid of a strange little man (Toom Gwyllis), who was previously a stowaway, he now learns more of the background: The Black Bat is a Venusian agent, and the Venusians, with a fleet of one hundred ships like the Black Bat's, are planning to attack Mars and Earth. Brad and Gwyllis fly to Venus, rescue Darl (whom the Black Bat has been trying to recruit), and destroy the Venusian fleet. It is then further revealed that the mysterious semicomic Toom is really the number one secret service agent of the Triplanetary system. The Black Bat was a renegade Earthman who had been badly mistreated by his superiors; for revenge he sold out to the Venusians. * *Miscellaneous:* Martians are gigantic and human; Venusians are fish-men. Mars is Schiaparellian; Venus is like Earth, but watery. Space travel is by rocket, except for the Black Bat's vessel and the Venusian fleet, which employ a different principle. * Routine. Not quite as nasty as Zagat's other work.

1807. **BEYOND THE SPECTRUM**. *Astounding Stories*, August 1934. Ill. Dold.
Short story. * *Place:* Florida. * Professor Ed Thomasson, a physicist, receives a coded telegram asking him to come to the aid of his geologist friend, Tom Denton. Denton and his wife, Mary, had gone to Tonasota, Florida, to investigate the disappearance of the town's artesian water supply. * In Tonasota, Thomasson learns what has happened. Denton had drilled a shaft to check for fault leakages; since then something monstrous has been coming out of the shaft and carrying away people. It is never seen, but it is obviously powerful. Unfortunately, the

Zagat, Arthur Leo (*continued*)

town authorities will not permit outside forces to be called in, lest it damage the tourist industry. An attempt to cement the shaft shut failed, for the beings below simply opened it up again. Worst of all, one of the men carried away has returned, but with his eyes surgically removed. * The crisis comes when the creatures, which are invisible, attack Denton's house and carry off Mary. Ed and Tom descend the shaft with a small arsenal, chop down the invisible creatures, and rescue Mary. A huge charge of explosive then seals the shaft. * The monsters, which seem to be somewhat amorphous, but with many tentacles, are invisible because their skin refracts light perfectly. They are obviously intelligent and civilized. They probably plan to invade (or at least massively raid) the surface, since they transplanted human eyes into one of themselves. * Their origin is not revealed.

ZISKA, K[ARL] F[RANCIS] (c. 1900-1979)
U.S. author, then resident of Cleveland, Ohio.
1808. **SUCCUBUS.** *Astounding Stories,* May 1934. Ill. C. R. Thomson.
Short story. * The narrator, who is a hospital administrator, relates the fate of his friend the great biologist Igor Boronoff. As Boronoff's diary reveals, he has been attempting to interbreed human and plant forms. He succeeds with a tiny plant that grows into a beautiful rooted woman. Unfortunately, she needs fresh blood to survive. The reader can probably guess what will happen without my relating it. * Boronoff, who has gone mad, falls in love with his vampiric creation. The frame narrator comes into the story at the end to see the monster, who is bubbling over with sexual allure, crush Boronoff to death. * A trite theme, handled in a trite manner. With stories of this obvious sort one often wonders whether they are meant to be parodic, but the following story removes this question.
1809. **MAN OF AGES.** *Astounding Stories,* October 1934. Unsigned ill.
Short story. * *Time:* A.D. 2150, 2250, and 2450. * Episodes in the life of Johnson/Jones/Smith. In 2150 he is the most remarkable athlete ever seen. In 2250, still young, he almost single-handedly defeats the Mongolians who are at war with the Caucasians. In 2350, he volunteers for a medical experiment that may be fatal. Doctor MacPherson has developed a serum that he hopes will cure all bacterial diseases. He has used it on animals with success, but he must try a human. The problem is that the injection will almost certainly kill the subject. Johnson/Jones/Smith volunteers, but before MacPherson will accept him, Johnson/Jones/Smith must tell the secret of his life. Back in 1932 Johnson's father, experimenting with cosmic ray treatments on the human body, turned his son into a superman. Fantastically strong, almost invulnerable, either immortal or extremely long-lived, he has passed through the centuries, somewhat bored and tired of life. Thus, MacPherson's experiment appeals to him. MacPherson, dubious at first, consents and Smith survives, but barely. * Too close to Philip Wylie's *Gladiator* and rather silly.

Addenda

Although *Thrilling Wonder Stories* is not really part of the Gernsback years (since Gernsback had relinquished *Wonder Sto-*ries, which was then retitled), it seems better to include brief information about the three 1936 issues than to ignore them.

In all cases the stories were illustrated by Mark Marchioni. Biographical information about the authors is provided in the earlier section, with the exception of three new authors, Allan K. Echols, Max Plaisted, and Gabriel Wilson. None of the stories, except perhaps Merritt's "Rhythm of the Spheres," is worth serious consideration.

BINDER, EANDO
1810. **THE HORMONE MENACE.** August 1936.
Short story. * *Time:* the near future. *Place:* Germany? * America is losing its war with the Allied States of Europe because of the incredible inventions created in Bergmann's secret laboratory: cloaks of invisibility, supersonic guns, and more. * American superspy Wistert parachutes into the establishment with a cloak of invisibility. By eavesdropping he learns Bergmann's secret: Manipulating ductless glands, he has produced specialized supermen, who developed the inventions. Wistert is captured, but escapes with the aid of another spy. One of the supermen, whom Wistert's associate brainwashed, blows up the laboratories. * Routine at best.
1811. **STATIC.** December 1936.
Short story. * Into Professor Hobson's laboratory burst two masked thugs who are revealed to be foreign agents. They demand specifications of Hobson's invention, which involves wireless transmission of power and what amounts to an explosion/death ray. Hobson outwits the spies and kills them by exploding the bullets they carry.

BURKS, ARTHUR J.
1812. **DICTATOR OF THE ATOMS.** October 1936.
Short novelette. * Dale Pruett, Secretary of Military Science, is in the frontline during most of the strange attack. The giant buildings of New York, one by one, collapse into fragments, and in their places are white conical or blob formations, which seem impregnable, since they absorb bombs and bullets. A message comes through: the World Dictator demands surrender. * Paradoxically, men can push through the white shell, at which time they find themselves within the original interiors of the buildings. Rush attacks led by Pruett and others smash the invaders, including the would-be dictator. He had a machine called the Atomotor, that controlled the ether flow. * With little fictional conviction.

CAMPBELL, JOHN W., JR.
1813. **THE BRAIN STEALERS OF MARS.** December 1936.
(Reprinted in Campbell, *The Planeteers*; in Asimov, *Before the Golden Age*; and in Elwood, *Alien Worlds*.)
Short story. * The first of five stories about Penton and Blake, two scientists who have been outlawed from Earth for working (successfully) to develop atomic energy. The stories contain incidents of their travels around the solar system. * On an Earth-like Mars, the explorers come upon shape-changers who duplicate them, even to memories, so that there are about twenty Pentons and Blakes. How can the duplicates be identified and prevented from reaching Earth? * A good touch, in an otherwise weak story, is that the intelligent, centaur-like native Martians manage to live comfortably with their duplicates.

CUMMINGS, RAY

1814. **BLOOD OF THE MOON**. August 1936.
Short story. * *Time*: the twenty-sixth century. *Place*: the Moon.
* A Martian space pirate attacks the transport bearing radium to Earth, forcing it to crash. The Lunar governor, who was on the ship, is held for ransom, which Georg [*sic*] pays. But the pirate insists on retaining the governor's beautiful daughter Aura, for personal reasons. All ends well as a young Lunar miner sacrifices his life to disable the pirate ship.

1815. **SHADOW GOLD**. October 1936.
Novelette. * When Johnny Hall comes of age, he finds in a message left by his long missing father instructions for entering another dimension. Johnny and his girlfriend Anne, acting suitably, find themselves in a small pocket universe that is the inside of a hollow sphere. Gravity is slight; the inhabitants are human; the atmosphere contains gaseous gold, which is necessary for respiration; and Johnny's father is alive and honored. * The sour note is that criminals are stripping the gold from the atmosphere. Their leader, Taro, plans to take it to Earth and buy up the planet. Skulduggery, capture, and escape end in the destruction of the criminals. The three explorers return to Earth.

1816. **TRAPPED IN ETERNITY**. December 1936.
Short story. * Alan Blair and Dora, his blind fiancée, are suitably astonished when a man (Sah Groat) materializes before them and announces that he is from 2536. He offers to take them to the future, where Dora's blindness can easily be cured, but it is clear from the way he eyes Dora that he has an ulterior purpose. In 2536 a surgeon cures Dora in a matter of minutes, whereupon Groat disintegrates the surgeon, forces Alan and Dora to accompany him, and leaves for the future, where he intends to found a new, more perfect race with Dora. But the future is not suitable, and our friends overpower Groat, who dies and is revealed as a cyborg. * Time is a dimension in which one can move by altering the vibration of the atomic nucleus.

ECHOLS, ALLAN K.

Occasional contributor to *Thrilling Adventures* and other pulp magazines. Presumably a U.S. author.

1817. **THE ISLAND OF DR. X**. December 1936.
Really a capsulated menace novel, short story length. * The U.S. government appeals to great scientist Lowell Best to discover who is flooding the market with artificial gold and disrupting the economy. A mysterious message seems to involve the secret island laboratories of Best's friend Dr. Dupree, to which Best and a Treasury agent fly by rocket. There they are trapped and forced to work on a machine that disrupts matter down to atomic particles, then reassembles it as gold. As they have learned, Dupree himself is Dr. X. With a crew of fanatical anarchists he plans to take over the world. Best wins out, of course. There are expected revealments and plot clichés.

ERNST, PAUL

1818. **DEATH DIVES DEEP**. August 1936.
Short story. * Professor Ogden has invented an atom-compressing earth-borer that gangster millionaire Cunao wants. When Cunao's mob attacks the laboratory, Ogden, his assistant John Street, and Street's girlfriend, Ria, take refuge in the untested borer and descend. Short circuits and loss of power afford crises, but the borer reaches, 120 miles down, a cave inhabited by semiintelligent giant insect-like beings who capture the involuntary explorers. Escape is followed by renewal of power. Cunao's mob has been wiped out by an explosion.

1819. **THE MICROSCOPIC GIANTS**. October 1936.
(Reprinted in Margulies and Friend, *From off This World* and in Conklin, *Science Fiction Terror Tales*.)
Short story. * *Time*: late 1941, toward the end of the Great War.
* Strange happenings in the 45,500-foot-deep copper mine. At the lowest level the concrete turns transparent and little two-foot-tall density-men, obviously unfriendly, walk through the stone and concrete. They are equipped with disintegrators. The narrator, after seeing his friend chopped up, blows up the mine.

FARLEY, RALPH MILNE

1820. **LIQUID LIFE**. October 1936.
(Reprinted in Conklin, *Best of Science Fiction*, and in Leinster, *Great Stories of Science Fiction*.)
Short story. * A rambling account of an intelligent virus-like life-form that is discovered in a local pond. A portion taken to a laboratory, provided with radio communication, and educated by oral readings, turns out to be far more intelligent than humans. It aids considerably in the laboratory work, making sensational discoveries, but if it reaches the outside world (since it has developed mobility), humanity is doomed. Part of the situation is the reactions among the lab owners: friendship, exploitation, fear. The situation is resolved when the virus runs its life cycle.

GALLUN, RAYMOND Z.

1821. **SATURN'S RINGMASTER**. December 1936.
Short story. * *Time*: the interplanetary future. * The Ringmaster is a noted space outlaw who prowls the outer planets. He has just stolen from courier Orethon and his Uranian comrade, Ruzza, several apparatus for creating impenetrable force screens; with them the Ringmaster can set up a space empire. Orethon and Ruzza, whose ship lies wrecked on a meteor in one of Saturn's rings, work out a way to track the Ringmaster, explode his ship, and destroy much of his fleet. The gimmick involves psychological trickery and mobility. * Ruzza, the Uranian, is a small creature like a bundle of cords, lumps, and twigs. * Not one of Gallun's better stories.

HAMILTON, EDMOND

1822. **COSMIC QUEST**. October 1936.
Short-short story. * The narrative of Ran Argal, who is setting out, in the far future, on a quest for a habitable world. Earth is dying in a glaciation, and telescopes do not reveal suitable planets. Argal's ship, which travels millions of time faster than light, thanks to dimension shifting, is the only hope. After long search Argal finds a suitable planet in an incredibly distant galaxy, but it is Earth tens of thousands of years later, and mankind is extinct. He has traveled around a finite universe. Everyone overlooked the time factor in relativity.

1823. **MUTINY ON EUROPA**. December 1936.
Short story. * *Time*: the interplanetary future. *Place*: Europa. *
John Allan, formerly a captain in the Earth Colonial Service, has been unjustly found guilty of treachery and sentenced to hard labor in the mines on Europa. His anger is now intensified when he sees visiting Europa the false friend who betrayed him. * A successful uprising of the convicts (during which Allan intends to kill his enemy) is interrupted by a rebellion of the natives.

Hamilton, Edmond (*continued*)

After much to-do, Allan and the convicts sacrifice their chance to escape in order to save the prison officials and visitors. All ends well.

JAMES, D. L.

1824. **CRYSTALS OF MADNESS.** October 1936.

Short story. * *Time*: the interplanetary future. * Bruce and Larry of G-rockets have been assigned to disintegrate Deimos. Reason: It has become the source of a strange life-form that absorbs organic material, creating crystalline counterparts of sorts. Oddly enough, the problem first arose with certain pebbles found in Patagonia. The two men have their problems, with Larry succumbing to the telepathic attacks of the crystals for a time, but they accomplish their mission. * Deimos also holds a native life-form, semi-intelligent arachnids. * A very confused story.

KLINE, OTIS ADELBERT

1825. **REVENGE OF THE ROBOT.** August 1936.

Short story. * *Time*: A.D. 2000. * Congress is offering a prize of one million dollars for the construction of a reasoning robot. Leading contestants are Bradshaw, a reputable scientist, and Grimes, a scoundrel. Grimes doses Bradshaw with poison gas and steals his entries. Bradshaw survives, but has only six months to live. He works feverishly on his entry, but dies before the ceremony. * During the competition French and German entries are disqualified for cheating. Grimes, who is also cheating, may win; but Bradshaw appears, reveals Grimes's past crimes and present deception, then discloses himself to be a cyborg containing Bradshaw's brain. Bradshaw wins the prize. His girlfriend, Yvonne, has also become a cyborg to join him.

MERRITT, A.

1826. **RHYTHM OF THE SPHERES.** October 1936.

(First publication in *Fantasy Magazine*, April 1934 as "The Last Poet and the Robots." Originally a part of the round-robin serial "Cosmos," here edited for separate publication. Reprinted as pamphlet, [Brotherhood of the White Temple, Sedalia, Col., 1948]; also reprinted in Merritt, *The Fox Woman*, and in Rabkin, *Science Fiction*.)

Short story. * *Time*: about A.D. 3000. * Narodny, "the last poet," and a small band of like-minded scientists have built a secret world in caverns hollowed a mile beneath the surface. There they devote themselves to aesthetic experiences, recreating scenes from the past and establishing new art forms based on supernal science. They are indifferent to the outside world until external radiation distorts Narodny's music. On looking out, they see that the world has been taken over by arrogant robots, with humans as oppressed servants. Narodny and his colleagues destroy the robots by broadcasting a rhythm that causes metal fatigue. Mankind has a chance to develop again. * Better than most of Merritt's other work. * A continuation of sorts by E. E. Smith, Ph. D., "What a Course!", appeared in the September 1934 issue of *Fantasy Magazine*.

1827. **THE DRONE MAN.** August 1936.

(First publication in longer form in *Fantasy Magazine*, September 1934 as "The Drone." Reprinted as pamphlet, [Brotherhood of the White Temple, Sedalia, Col., 1948]; also reprinted in Merritt, *The Fox Woman*.)

Short-short story. * Anecdotes involving theriomorphy told at the

Explorers' Club. One of the narrators is Alan Caranac, lead character in *Creep, Shadow!* * One story involves an African were-hyena. The other, longer, anecdote, tells of Ferguson, who had an incredible empathy with animals, enabling him to put himself into their frames of mind. He took up apiculture when he left college, and over the years his empathy increased from mental to physiological, so that he became a giant drone bee.

PLAISTED, MAX

Pseud. of Jack Binder, brother of Earl and Otto Binder. During and after World War II Binder worked extensively in the comic book industry in New York. None of his work seems to have been really significant; perhaps his largest role was as the creating artist of *Doc Savage Comics*.

1828. **ZARNAK.** August 1936-October 1937.

A crude comic strip describing the hair-raising adventures of Zarnak, an Earthman, on Mercury in A.D. 2936. He started with the intention of locating descendants of an almost forgotten interplanetary expedition of centuries earlier. * In response to reader demand, the strip was discontinued in midstory.

WEINBAUM, STANLEY G.

1829. **THE CIRCLE OF ZERO.** August 1936.

(Reprinted in Weinbaum, *A Martian Odyssey* [Fantasy Press], and in Weinbaum, *A Martian Odyssey* [Hyperion].)

Short story. * During the stock market crash of 1929 Jack Anders and old Professor de Néant lost their savings. Néant suggests a way to recoup: in an infinity of time, the atoms forming Anders, Néant, and their world must have combined before. Time being circular, past "incarnations" can be experienced with hypnosis. The professor is half mad, but Anders likes his daughter Yvonne. * Jack spends months under hypnosis, experiencing fragments from many lives, until he believes he has gained information. Néant's suicide and his insurance policy provide funds, and Jack recoups for himself and Yvonne. Then he learns that Néant had been suggesting false memories. But there is a residue of true foreknowledge. * "The Circle of Zero" was rejected by the three science-fiction magazines during Weinbaum's lifetime and was undoubtedly printed only to satisfy the fan demand for his work.

1830. **THE BRINK OF INFINITY.** December 1936.

(Reprinted in Weinbaum, *A Martian Odyssey* [Fantasy Press]; in Weinbaum, *A Martian Odyssey* [Hyperion]; and in Weinbaum, *The Red Peri*.)

Short story. * Prof. Abner Aarons, a mathematician who moonlights as a consultant, visits a potential client (Court Strawn), who immediately takes him captive. Strawn, who is badly crippled from an accident caused by faulty mathematics, has sworn vengeance on mathematicians. Aarons is allowed ten questions to work out the "numerical expression" Strawn is thinking of, or die. * The story is an adaptation of "The Tenth Question" by George Allan England, which appeared in *All-Story Weekly*, 18 December 1915. Weinbaum rewrote "The Tenth Question" in much shorter form, but retained the central elements and many details. If "The Brink of Infinity" had been placed commercially, it would unquestionably be considered blatant plagiarism, but, according to Weinbaum's widow (*Thrilling Wonder Stories*, December 1936, p. 118), it was written to amuse her and not intended for publication. After his death, the story was found among his papers. When the editors of *Thrilling*

Weinbaum, Stanley G. (*continued*)

Wonder Stories asked Mrs. Weinbaum for other material by her late husband, she sent them the story, probably not recognizing its origin.   This account seems entirely credible, since Weinbaum, from all that is known of him, was a completely honorable man.

WEISINGER, MORT

1831. **Nth DEGREE**. August 1936.

Short story. * *Time*: 1980. * Arthur Ainsworth, brilliant biochemist, has captured Darius Waxman, president of Solar Spaceways, an incredibly vicious, murderous capitalist swine. Ainsworth threatens: Unless Waxman confesses about his crimes, he will be devolved to primordial slime. Waxman refuses, but after a short ray treatment turns him into *Pithecanthropus erectus,* he breaks and confesses.   But it was all a hoax: Ainsworth simply injected instant acromegaly solution, which accomplished the changes.

WELLS, HAL K.

1832. **MAN-JEWELS FOR XOTHAR**. October 1936.

Short story. * The Maynard Expedition in the South Seas is beset by interstellar jewel hunters—horrible, worm-like monstrosities that turn living organic creatures into incredible jewels. Bob Kellar, escaping capture by luck, manages to turn the tables on the creatures as they are about to transform beautiful Doris Maynard. Fortunately, the raiders find Terrestrial atmosphere almost instantly poisonous and die when Kellar disrupts their atmospheric shield.

WILSON, GABRIEL

Pseud. of Ray Cummings, perhaps in collaboration with his wife Gabrielle Wilson Cummings; the situation is not clear, according to Mike Ashley in "Remembering Ray Cummings." The name Gabriel Wilson was used primarily on mystery fiction.

1833. **EARTH-VENUS 12**. December 1936.

Short story. * *Time*: 2036. *Place*: space between Earth and Venus. * On board the ship are Ken Masters, third officer; beautiful Nona Guelph, daughter of the president of Earth; Felah Bartano, a Venusian conspirator; and others.   The ship is carrying arms to the Venusian government. Bartano and his fellows seize the ship, and in the ensuing donnybrook, everyone is killed except Masters and Guelph, who are floating back to Earth in powered space suits. * Venusians are human.

ZAGAT, ARTHUR LEO

1834.   **THE LAND WHERE TIME STOOD STILL**. August 1936.

Short story. * Ronald Stratton, wandering about Wiltshire, suddenly finds himself in a strange land with Neanderthals, Romans, Vikings, eohippi, dinosaurs, and Elaise, a beautiful damsel from King Arthur's court (where they speak Wardour Street English). They are all at the hub of a time wheel, into which all ages can drop. Ruthless, balloon-headed, telepathic, unisex men from A.D. 6000 frequent the area looking for historical specimens. Captured, slated for vivisection, Ronald and Elaise survive through endless slaughter. Ronald returns to 1936, but goes back to the time hub to join Elaise.

1835. **THE LANSON SCREEN**. December 1936.

(Reprinted in Conklin, *Best of Science Fiction.*)

Short story. * In 1937 the great scientist Professor Lanson is demonstrating to the military his totally impenetrable force screen. As a trial he plans to use it to isolate Manhattan for a few minutes. He will be inside controlling the screen. Unfortunately, he is accidentally killed, and the screen cannot be shut off. Everyone in Manhattan dies miserably. Sixty years later, in 1997 Harold (or Howard; the author uses both names) Cranston works out a way to turn off the screen. * Zagat prints passages from the diary of one of the men who died in Manhattan.   Earlier in the story Zagat provided thumbnail sketches of typical New Yorkers of the day.

Anthologizations

Stories described in this volume have been reprinted in the following anthologies and collections or are present in earlier, usually accessible, collections. Most of the books concerned contain, in addition, other stories. Full contents of these books are provided in such anthology indexes as Contento and Tuck, listed in the bibliography to this volume.

Ackerman, Forrest J., ed. *Gosh! Wow!* New York: Bantam, 1982.
Clyde Crane Campbell (Horace Gold), "Inflexure." Raymond Z. Gallun, "Old Faithful." Desmond Hall, "A Scientist Rises." Edmond Hamilton, "The Eternal Cycle." L. Hansen, "The Prince of Liars." Clare W. Harris and Miles J. Breuer, M.D., "A Baby on Neptune." Irving Lester and Fletcher Pratt, "The Roger Bacon Formula." Amelia Reynolds Long, "Omega." Capt. S. St. P. Meek, "Futility." A. Merritt, "The Face in the Abyss." W. Varick Nevins, III, "The Emotion Meter." D. D. Sharp, "The Eternal Man." Don A. Stuart (John W. Campbell, Jr.), "Twilight." Louis Tucker, D.D., "The Cubic City." Stanley G. Weinbaum, "The Red Peri." G. Peyton Wertenbaker, "The Ship That Turned Aside." Jack Williamson, "Born of the Sun." Robert Wilson, "Out around Rigel."

Aldiss, Brian, ed. *Evil Earths.* London: Weidenfeld and Nicolson, 1975.
Don A. Stuart (John W. Campbell, Jr.), "Night."

Ashley, Mike. *History of the Science Fiction Magazine.* Part 1, 1925-1935. London: New English Library, 1974.
Philip Barshefsky, "One Prehistoric Night." C. W. Diffin, "The Power and the Glory." Lloyd A. Eshbach, "A Voice from the Ether." Francis Flagg, "The Machine Man of Ardathia." Edmond Hamilton, "The Island of Unreason." Raymond Z. Gallun, "Davey Jones' Ambassador." D. D. Sharp, "The Eternal Man." Clifford Simak, "The Asteroid of Gold." R. F. Starzl, "Out of the Sub-Universe." G. Peyton Wertenbaker, "The Coming of the Ice."

Asimov, Isaac, ed. *Before the Golden Age.* Garden City, N. Y.: Doubleday, 1974.
John W. Campbell, Jr., "The Brain Stealers of Mars." Raymond Z. Gallun, "Old Faithful." Edmond Hamilton, "The Accursed Galaxy." Edmond Hamilton, "Devolution" Edmond Hamilton, "The Man Who Evolved." Henry Hasse, "He Who Shrank." Neil R. Jones, "The Jameson Satellite." Murray Leinster, "Proxima Centauri." Murray Leinster, "Sidewise in Time." Laurence Manning, "The Man Who Awoke." Capt. S. St.P. Meek, "Awlo of Ulm." Capt. S. St.P. Meek, "Submicroscopic." P. Schuyler Miller, "Tetrahedra of Space." Clifford Simak, "The World of the Red Sun." Leslie F. Stone, "The Human Pets of Mars." Charles R. Tanner, "Tumithak in Shawm." Charles R. Tanner, "Tumithak of the Corridors." Donald Wandrei, "Colossus Stanley G. Weinbaum, "Parasite Planet." Jack Williamson, "The Moon Era Jack Williamson, "Born of the Sun."

——. *Where Do We Go from Here?* Garden City, N. Y.; Doubleday, 1971.
Don A. Stuart (John W. Campbell, Jr.), "Night." Stanley G. Weinbaum, "A Martian Odyssey."

Bleiler, Everett F. and Dikty, Thaddeus, eds. *Imagination Unlimited.* New York: Farrar, Straus, and Young, 1952.
Harry Bates, "Alas, All Thinking." Raymond Z. Gallun, "Old Faithful."

Burroughs, Edgar Rice. *Three Martian Novels by Edgar Rice Burroughs.* New York: Dover Publications, 1962.
"The Master Mind of Mars."

Campbell, John W., Jr. *The Best of John W. Campbell.* Garden City, N. Y.: Nelson Doubleday, 1976.
"Blindness." "Elimination." "Rebellion." "The Invaders." "The Last Evolution." "The Machine." "Twilight."

——. *The Black Star Passes.* Reading, Pa.: Fantasy Press, 1953.
"The Black Star Passes." "Piracy Preferred." "Solarite."

——. *John W. Campbell Anthology. Three Novels.* Garden City, N.Y.: Doubleday, 1973.

Campbell, John W., Jr. (*continued*)
"The Black Star Passes." "Islands of Space." "Invaders from the Infinite."
——. *The Planeteers*. New York: Ace, 1966.
"The Brain Stealers of Mars."
——. *Who Goes There?* Chicago: Shasta Publishers, 1948.
"Blindness." "Elimination." "Frictional Losses." "Night." "Twilight."

Carr, Terry, ed. *Creatures from Beyond*. New York: Thomas Nelson, 1975.
David H. Keller, M.D., "The Worm."

Clareson, Thomas D., ed. *A Spectrum of Worlds*. Garden City, N.Y.: Doubleday, 1972.
Jack Williamson, "The Metal Man."

Clarke, Arthur C., ed. *Time Probe*. New York: Delacorte, 1966.
Julian Huxley, "The Tissue Culture King."

Colombo, John, ed. *Friendly Aliens*. Boston: Houghton, Mifflin, 1981.
George Allan England, "The Thing from——Outside." Edmond Hamilton, "Devolution." A. Merritt, "The People of the Pit."

Conklin, Groff, ed. *Best of Science Fiction*. Crown: New York, 1946. Reprinted 1980 as *The Golden Age of Science Fiction*.
Morrison Colladay, "Giant on the Earth." C. W. Diffin, "Spawn of the Stars." Paul Ernst, "The 32nd of May." Ralph Milne Farley, "Liquid Life." Raymond Z. Gallun, "Davey Jones' Ambassador." Austin Hall, "The Man Who Saved the Earth." Julian Huxley, "The Tissue Culture King." Keller, David H., M. D., "The Ivy War." Frank Belknap Long, "The Flame Midget." Nat Schachner, "The Ultimate Metal." Leslie F. Stone, "The Conquest of Gola." Don A. Stuart (John W. Campbell, Jr.), "Atomic Power." Don A. Stuart (John W. Campbell, Jr.), "The Machine." Warner Van Lorne [I], "The Upper Level Road." Donald Wandrei, "A Scientist Divides." H. G. Wells, "The Remarkable Case of Davidson's Eyes." Wallace G. West, "En Route to Pluto." Cecil B. White, "The Retreat to Mars." Arthur L. Zagat, "The Lanson Screen."
——. *Big Book of Science Fiction*. Crown: New York, 1950.
W. Alexander, "One Leg Too Many." Miles J. Breuer, M.D., "The Man with the Strange Head." Morrison Colladay, "The Planetoid of Doom." Irving Lester and Fletcher Pratt, "The Roger Bacon Formula." G. Peyton Wertenbaker, "The Ship That Turned Aside."
——. *Br-r-r!* New York: Avon, 1959.
David H. Heller, M.D., "The Worm."
——. *Great Science Fiction by Scientists*. New York: Collier Books, 1952.
Miles J. Breuer, M.D., "The Gostak and the Doshes." Julian Huxley, "The Tissue Culture King."
——. *In the Grip of Terror*. Permabooks: New York, 1951.
H. W. Guernsey (Howard Wandrei), "Macklin's Little Friend." H. G. Wells, "The Moth."
——. *Omnibus of Science Fiction*. New York: Crown, 1952.
Will H. Gray, "The Bees from Borneo." David H. Keller, M.D., "The Doorbell." H. P. Lovecraft, "The Colour out of Space." Fletcher Pratt and B. F. Ruby, "The Thing in the Woods." R. R. Winterbotham, "The Fourth Dynasty."

——. *Possible Worlds of Science Fiction*. New York: Viking Press, 1951.
Frank Belknap Long, "Cones."
——. *Science Fiction Adventures in Dimension*. New York: Vanguard, 1955.
Miles J. Breuer, M.D., "The Gostak and the Doshes."
——. *Science Fiction Adventures in Mutation*. New York: Vanguard, 1955.
Miles J. Breuer, M.D., "The Hungry Guinea Pig."
——. *The Science Fiction Galaxy*. New York: Permabooks, 1950.
Miles J. Breuer, M.D., "The Appendix and the Spectacles." A. Rowley Hilliard, "Death from the Stars." Laurence Manning, "The Living Galaxy."
——. *Science Fiction Terror Tales*. New York: Gnome Press, 1951.
Paul Ernst, "The Microscopic Giants."
——. *Science Fiction Thinking Machines*. New York: Vanguard, 1954.
Raymond Z. Gallun, "The Scarab."
——. *A Treasury of Science Fiction*. New York: Crown, 1948.
P. Schuyler Miller, "The Chrysalis." D. D. Sharp, "The Eternal Man."

Conklin, Groff, and Fabricant, Noah D., eds. *Great Science Fiction about Doctors*. New York: Collier Books, 1963.
David H. Keller, M.D., "The Psychophonic Nurse." Edgar Allan Poe, "The Facts in the Case of M. Valdemar."

Crawford, William L., ed. *Science-Fantasy Quintette*. Los Angeles: F.P.C.I., 1953.
Ed Repp, "The Radium Pool."

Curtis, Richard, ed. *Future Tense*. New York: Dell Books, 1968.
Hugo Gernsback, "Ralph 124 C41+" (fragment), Murray Leinster, "Politics."

Davenport, Basil, ed. *Famous Monster Tales*. Princeton: Van Nostrand, Rinehold, 1967.
Paul Ernst, "The Thing in the Pond."

Derleth, August, ed. *Beachheads in Space*. New York: Pellegrini and Cudahy, 1952.
Donald Wandrei, "The Blinding Shadows."
——. *Beyond Time and Space*. New York: Pellegrini and Cudahy, 1950.
David H. Keller, M.D., "The Revolt of the Pedestrians." Edgar Allan Poe, "The Thousand and Second Tale of Scheherazade." Jules Verne, "Dr. Ox." Donald Wandrei, "Colossus." Stanley G. Weinbaum, "The Lotus Eaters." H. G. Wells, "The New Accelerator."
——. *Far Boundaries*. New York: Pellegrini and Cudahy, 1952.
H. A. Highstone, "Frankenstein—Unlimited." Donald A. Wandrei, "Infinity Zero."
——. *The Other Side of the Moon*. New York: Pellegrini and Cudahy, 1949.
Clark Ashton Smith, "The City of Singing Flame." H. G. Wells, "The Star."
——. *The Outer Reaches*. New York: Pellegrini and Cudahy, 1951.
David H. Keller, M.D., "Service First." Clark Ashton Smith, "The Plutonian Drug." Donald A. Wandrei, "Finality Unlimited."
——. *Strange Ports of Call*. New York: Pellegrini and Cudahy,

Derleth, August (*continued*)
    1948.
        George Allan England, "The Thing from—Outside." Harry S. Keeler, "John Jones' Dollar." David H. Keller, "The Worm." H. P. Lovecraft, "At the Mountains of Madness" P. Schuyler Miller, "The Forgotten Man of Space." Clark Ashton Smith, "Master of the Asteroid." Howard Von Drey (Howard Wandrei), "The God Box." H. G. Wells, "The Crystal Egg."
——. *Worlds of Tomorrow.* New York: Pellegrini and Cudahy, New York, 1963.
        Frank Belknap Long, "The Great Cold."
Elwood, Roger, ed. *Alien Worlds.* New York: Pocket Books, 1964.
        John W. Campbell, Jr., "The Brain Stealers of Mars." John Beynon Harris, "The Man from Beyond."
Elwood, Roger and Ghidalia, Vic, eds. *Androids, Time Machines and Blue Giraffes.* Chicago: Follett, 1973.
        Don A. Stuart (John W. Campbell, Jr.), "The Machine." Jack Williamson, "The Metal Man."
Elwood, Roger and Moskowitz, Sam, eds. *Strange Signposts.* New York: Holt, Rinehart and Winston, 1966.
        Edmond Hamilton, "The Man Who Saw the Future," Edgar Allan Poe, "Mellonta Tauta." Harl Vincent, "Prowler of the Wastelands." Jack Williamson, "The Cosmic Express."
Eshbach, Lloyd A. *The Tyrant of Time.* Reading, Pa.: Fantasy Press, 1955.
        "The Meteor Miners." "The Time Conqueror."
Fadiman, Clifton, ed. *Fantasia Mathematica.* New York: Simon and Schuster, 1958.
        Miles J. Breuer, M.D., "The Captured Cross-Section." Harry S. Keeler, "John Jones' Dollar."
——. *The Mathematical Magpie.* New York: Simon and Schuster, 1962.
        Miles J. Breuer, "The Appendix and the Spectacles."
Fiedler, Leslie, ed. *In Dreams Awake.* New York: Dell Books, 1975.
        H. P. Lovecraft, "The Colour out of Space." H. G. Wells, "The Crystal Egg."
Franklin, H. Bruce, ed. *Future Perfect. American Science Fiction of the Nineteenth Century*, 2nd ed. New York: Oxford, 1978.
        Fitz-James O'Brien, "The Diamond Lens." Edgar Allan Poe, "Mellonta Tauta." Edgar Allan Poe, "The Facts in the Case of M. Valdemar."
Gallun, Raymond Z. *The Best of Raymond Z. Gallun*, ed. J. J. Pierce. New York: Ballantine, 1978.
        "Davey Jones' Ambassador." "Derelict." "Godson of Almarlu." "Old Faithful."
Ghidalia, Vic, ed. *Satan's Pets.* New York: Manor Books, 1972.
        David H. Keller, M.D., "The Rat Racket."
Goodstone, Tony. ed. *The Pulps.* New York: Chelsea House, 1970.
        Harl Vincent, "Wanderer of Infinity." Stanley G. Weinbaum, "Parasite Planet."
Gunn, James, ed. *The Road to Science Fiction from Gilgamesh to Wells.* New York: New American Library, 1977.
        Fitz-James O'Brien, "The Diamond Lens." Edgar Allan

Poe, "Mellonta Tauta." H. G. Wells, "The Star."
——. *The Road to Science Fiction #2. From Wells to Heinlein.* New York: New American Library, 1979.
        Julian Huxley, "The Tissue Culture King." David H. Keller, M.D., "The Revolt of the Pedestrians." Murray Leinster, "Proxima Centauri." A. Merritt, "The People of the Pit." Don A. Stuart (John W. Campbell, Jr.), "Twilight." Stanley G. Weinbaum, "A Martian Odyssey." H. G. Wells, "The New Accelerator."
Haining, Peter, ed. *The Fantastic Pulps.* New York: St. Martin's, 1976.
        Hugo Gernsback, "Baron Munchhausen's Scientific Adventures" (fragment). Edmond Hamilton, "The Man Who Saw the Future." David H. Keller, M.D., "A Twentieth Century Homunculus." A. Merritt, "The People of the Pit."
Hamilton, Edmond. *The Best of Edmond Hamilton*, ed. Leigh Brackett. Garden City, N.Y.: Nelson Doubleday, 1977.
        "The Accursed Galaxy." "A Conquest of Two Worlds." The Island of Unreason." "The Man Who Evolved."
——. *The Horror on the Asteroid.* London: Philip Allan, 1936.
        "The Accursed Galaxy." "The Man Who Evolved." "The Man Who Saw the Future."
Harris, Clare Winger. *Away from the Here and Now.* Philadelphia: Dorrance, 1947.
        "A Baby on Neptune" (with Miles J. Breuer, M.D.). "The Ape Cycle." "The Artificial Man." "The Diabolical Drug." "The Evolutionary Monstrosity." "The Fate of the Poseidonia." "The Fifth Dimension." "The Menace of Mars." "The Miracle of the Lily."
Healy, Raymond J. and McComas, J. Francis, eds. *Adventures in Time and Space.* New York: Random House, 1946.
        Harry Bates, "A Matter of Size." Henry Hasse, "He Who Shrank."
Janifer, Laurence M., ed. *Masters' Choice.* New York: Simon and Schuster, 1966.
        Murray Leinster, "Politics." C, L, Moore, "Bright Illusion." H. G. Wells, "The New Accelerator."
Jones, Neil R. *Planet of the Double Sun.* New York: Ace, 1967.
        "The Jameson Satellite." "The Planet of the Double Sun." "The Return of the Tripeds."
——. *Space War.* New York: Ace, 1967.
        "'Labyrinth.'" "Space War." "Zora of the Zoromes."
——. *The Sunless World.* New York: Ace, 1967.
        "Into the Hydrosphere." "The Sunless World." "Time's Mausoleum."
Keller, David H., M.D. *The Folsom Flint and Other Curious Tales.* Sauk City, Wisc.: Arkham House, 1969.
        "Air Lines." "The Pent House." "Unto Us a Child Is Born." "The White City."
——. *Life Everlasting and Other Tales of Science, Fantasy, and Horror.* Newark, N.J.: Avalon, 1948.
        "The Boneless Horror." "The Cerebral Library." "Life Everlasting." "No More Tomorrows." "Unto Us a Child Is Born."
——. *Tales from Underwood.* New York: Pellegrini and Cudahy, 1952.
        "A Biological Experiment" "The Doorbell" "The Flying Fool." "Free as the Air." "The Ivy War." "The Literary

Keller, David H., M.D. (*continued*)
    Corkscrew." "The Psychophonic Nurse." "The Revolt of the Pedestrians." "The Worm." "The Yeast Men."

Kelly, Frank K. *Star Ship Invincible. A Noel Young Book.* Santa Barbara, Cal.: Capra Press 1979.
    "Crater 17, Near Tycho." "The Radium World." "Star Ship Invincible."

Knight, Damon, ed. *Beyond Tomorrow.* New York: Harper, 1965.
    Don A. Stuart (John W. Campbell, Jr.), "Twilight."

——. *A Century of Science Fiction.* New York: Simon and Schuster, 1962.
    Stanley G. Weinbaum, "The Ideal" (fragment). H. G. Wells, "The Crystal Egg." H. G. Wells, "The Time Machine" (fragment).

——. *Science Fiction of the Thirties.* Indianapolis: Bobbs-Merrill, 1975.
    Harry Bates, "Alas, All Thinking." John W. Campbell, Jr., "The Battery of Hate." Raymond Z. Gallun, "Davey Jones' Ambassador." Howard D. Graham (Howard Wandrei), "The Other." Howard D. Graham (Howard Wandrei), "The Wall." David H. Keller, M.D., "The Lost Language." Frank K. Kelly, "Into the Meteoric Orbit." Murray Leinster, "The Fifth-Dimension Catapult." Frank Belknap Long, "The Last Men." A. B. Macfadyen, "The Time Decelerator." William K. Sonneman, "The Council of the Drones." Stanley G. Weinbaum, "The Mad Moon." Robert Wilson, "Out around Rigel."

Leinster, Murray. *The Best of Murray Leinster.* ed. J. J. Pierce. New York: Ballantine, 1978.
    "The Fourth-Dimensional Demonstrator." "Proxima Centauri." "Sidewise in Time."

——. *Monsters and Such.* New York: Avon, 1959.
    "Proxima Centauri."

——. *Sidewise in Time.* Chicago: Shasta Publishers, 1950.
    "The Fourth-Dimensional Demonstrator." "Proxima Centauri." "Sidewise in Time."

——. *Twists in Time.* New York: Avon, 1960.
    "The Fourth-Dimensional Demonstrator."

——. ed. *Great Stories of Science Fiction.* New York: Random House, 1951.
    Ralph Milne Farley, "Liquid Life."

Liebman, Dr. Arthur. ed. *Science Fiction. The Best of Yesterday.* New York: Richard Rosen Press, 1980.
    John W. Campbell, Jr., "The Last Evolution." David H. Keller, M.D., "The Literary Corkscrew." Stanley G. Weinbaum, "The Mad Moon." Jack Williamson, "The Cosmic Express."

Long, Frank Belknap. *The Dark Beasts.* New York: Belmont, 1964.
    "The Flame Midget."

——. *The Early Long.* Garden City, N. Y.: Doubleday, 1975.
    "The Flame Midget."

——. *The Hounds of Tindalos.* Sauk City, Wisc.: Arkham House, 1946.
    "The Flame Midget."

——. *The Rim of the Unknown.* Sauk City, Wisc.: Arkham House, 1972.
    "Cones." "The Great Cold." "Green Glory." "The Last Men."

Lovecraft, Howard P. *At the Mountains of Madness and Other Novels.* Sauk City, Wisc.: Arkham House, 1964.
    "At the Mountains of Madness."

——. *The Best of H. P. Lovecraft.* New York: Ballantine, 1982.
    "The Colour out of Space." "The Shadow out of Time."

——. *Best Supernatural Stories.* Cleveland and New York: World, 1945.
    "The Colour out of Space."

——. *The Colour out of Space.* New York: Lancer, 1964.
    "The Colour out of Space." "The Shadow out of Time."

——. *The Dunwich Horror.* New York: Bart House, 1945.
    "The Shadow out of Time."

——. *The Dunwich Horror and Others.* Sauk City, Wisc.: Arkham House, 1963.
    "The Colour out of Space." "The Shadow out of Time."

——. *The Haunter of the Dark.* London: Gollancz, 1951.
    "The Colour out of Space."

——. *The Lurking Fear.* New York: Avon, 1947.
    "The Colour out of Space."

——. *Marginalia.* Sauk City, Wisc.: Arkham House, 1944.
    Hazel Heald, "The Man of Stone."

——. *The Outsider and Others.* Sauk City, Wisc.: Arkham House, 1939.
    "The Colour out of Space." "At the Mountains of Madness." "The Shadow out of Time."

——. *3 Tales of Terror.* Sauk City, Wisc.: Arkham House, 1968.
    "The Colour out of Space."

Lovecraft, Howard P. [et al.]. *The Horror in the Museum and Other Revisions.* Sauk City, Wisc.: Arkham House, 1970.
    Hazel Heald, "The Man of Stone."

Margulies, Leo and Friend, Oscar J., eds. *From Off This World.* New York: Merlin Press, Inc., 1949. (Some of the stories in this collection have been abridged.)
    Paul Ernst, "The Microscopic Giants." Thomas S. Gardner, "The Last Woman." Edmond Hamilton, "The Man Who Evolved." Benson Herbert, "The World Without." A. Rowley Hilliard, "The Green Torture." David H. Keller, M.D., "The Literary Corkscrew." P. Schuyler Miller, "'The Man from Mars.'" D. D. Sharp, "The Eternal Man." Clark Ashton Smith, "The City of Singing Flame." Clark Ashton Smith, "Beyond the Singing Flame." Arthur Stangland, "The Ancient Brain." R. F. Starzl, "Hornets of Space." Louis Tucker, D.D., "The Cubic City." Stanley G. Weinbaum, "A Martian Odyssey." Stanley G. Weinbaum, "Valley of Dreams." Jack Williamson, "Through the Purple Cloud."

——. *My Best Science Fiction Story.* New York: Merlin Press, Inc., 1949.
    Paul Ernst, "The Thing in the Pond." Fletcher Pratt, "Dr. Grimshaw's Sanitarium." Don A. Stuart (John W. Campbell, Jr.), "Blindness."

Merritt, A. *The Fox Woman and Other Stories.* New York: Avon, 1949.
    "The Drone Man." "The People of the Pit." "Rhythm of the Spheres."

Miller, P. Schuyler. *The Titan.* Reading, Pa.: Fantasy Press, 1952.
    "The Arrhenius Horror." "The Forgotten Man of Space."

Moore, C. L.   *The Best of C. L. Moore*, ed. Lester Del Rey. Garden City, N.Y.: Nelson Doubleday, 1975.
"The Bright Illusion." "Tryst in Time."

Moskowitz, Sam, ed. *The Coming of the Robots*. New York: Collier, 1963.
Raymond Z. Gallun, "Derelict." John Beynon Harris, "The Lost Machine." Harl Vincent, "Rex."

——. *Editor's Choice in Science Fiction*. New York: McBride, 1954.
Chester D. Cuthbert, "The Sublime Vigil."

——. *Exploring Other Worlds*. New York: Collier Books, 1963.
Ross Rocklynne, "At the Center of Gravity." Stanley G. Weinbaum, "The Mad Moon."

——. *Masterpieces of Science Fiction*. Cleveland and New York: World, 1966.
H. P. Lovecraft, "The Colour out of Space." A. Merritt, "The People of the Pit." Stanley G. Weinbaum, "The Lotus Eaters." H. G. Wells, "The Country of the Blind" (the altered Golden Cockerel text).

——. *Modern Masterpieces of Science Fiction*. Cleveland and New York: World, 1965.
Don A. Stuart (John W. Campbell, Jr.), "Night."

——. *Science Fiction by Gaslight*. Cleveland and New York: World, 1968.
Ellis P. Butler, "An Experiment in Gyro-Hats."

——. *Three Stories, by Murray Leinster, Jack Williamson, and John Wyndham*. Garden City, N.Y.: Doubleday, 1967.
Murray Leinster, "The Mole Pirate." Jack Williamson, "The Moon Era." John Wyndham Harris, "Exiles on Asperus."

——. *Under the Moons of Mars*. New York: Holt, Rinehart and Winston, 1970.
Murray Leinster, "The Mad Planet." A. Merritt, "The Moon Pool" (the short story only.)

——. *When Women Rule*. New York: Walker, 1972. [Stories Thomas K. Gardner, "The Last Woman." David H. Keller, M.D., "The Feminine Metamorphosis." Wallace West, "The Last Man."

Moskowitz, Sam and Elwood, Roger, eds. *Other Worlds, Other Times*. New York: Macfadden-Bartell Books, 1969.
Edmond Hamilton, "The Man Who Saw the Future."

——. *The Time Curve*. New York: Tower Books, 1968.
Jack Williamson, "Terror out of Time."

Norton, Alden H., ed. *Award Science Fiction Reader*. New York: Award, 1966.
John W. Campbell, Jr., "The Last Evolution."

——. *Futures Unlimited*. New York: Pyramid Books, 1969.
Don A. Stuart (John W. Campbell, Jr.), "Rebellion."

Norton, Alden H. and Moskowitz, Sam, eds. *The Space Magicians*. New York: Pyramid, 1971.
John Beynon Harris, "The Venus Adventure."

Norton, Andre and Donaldy, Ernestine, eds. *Gates to Tomorrow*. New York: Atheneum, 1973.
Frank Belknap Long, "The Flame Midget."

Parry, Michel, ed. *Strange Ecstasies*. London: Pinnacle, 1974.
Clark Ashton Smith, "The Plutonian Drug." H. G. Wells, "The New Accelerator."

Pohl, Carol and Pohl, Frederik, eds. *Science Fiction: The Great Years*. New York: Ace, 1973.
Raymond Z. Gallun, "Old Faithful."

——. *Jupiter*. New York: Ballantine, 1973.
Stanley G. Weinbaum, "The Mad Moon."

Rabkin, Eric, ed.. *Science Fiction. A Historical Anthology*. New York: Oxford, 1983.
Hugo Gernsback, "Ralph 124 C41+" (a fragment). A. Merritt, "Rhythm of the Spheres." Edgar Allan Poe, "A Descent into the Maelstrom." Edgar Allan Poe, "The Facts in the Case of M . Valdemar." Don A. Stuart (John W. Campbell, Jr.), "Twilight." H. G. Wells, The Star."

Repp, Ed Earl. *The Radium Pool*. Los Angeles: F.P.C.I., 1949.
"The Phantom of Terror." "The Radium Pool." "The Red Dimension."

——. *The Stellar Missiles*. Los Angeles: F.P.C.I., 1949.
"The Second Missile." "The Stellar Missile."

Rocklynne, Ross. *The Men and the Mirror*. New York: Ace, 1973.
"At the Center of Gravity."

Ross, Joseph, ed. *The Best of Amazing*. Garden City, N.Y.: Doubleday, 1967.
John Beynon Harris, "The Lost Machine." David H. Keller, M.D., "The Worm." Murray Leinster, "The Runaway Skyscraper." Jack Williamson, "The Metal Man."

Schmidt, Stanley, ed. *The Analog Anthology #1*. New York: Davis, 1980.
Don A. Stuart (John W. Campbell, Jr.), "Twilight." Stanley G. Weinbaum, "The Lotus Eaters."

Silverberg, Robert, ed. *The Arbor House Treasury of Science Fiction Masterpieces*. New York: Arbor House, 1983.
Harry Bates, "Alas, All Thinking." Miles J. Breuer, M.D., "The Gostak and the Doshes." Julian Huxley, "The Tissue Culture King." Edgar Allan Poe, "Mellonta Tauta." Stanley G. Weinbaum, "The Mad Moon." H. G. Wells, "The New Accelerator." Jack Williamson, "The Metal Man."

——. *Earth Is the Strangest Planet*. Nashville and New York: Thomas Nelson, 1977.
Raymond Z. Gallun, "Davey Jones' Ambassador." P. Schuyler Miller, "The Chrysalis." H. G. Wells, "The Empire of the Ants."

——. *The Ends of Time*. New York: Hawthorn Books, 1970.
Don A. Stuart (John W. Campbell, Jr.), "Twilight."

——. *Galactic Dreamers*. New York: Random House, 1977.
Don A. Stuart (John W. Campbell, Jr.), "Night."

——. *The Mirror of Infinity*. New York: Harper and Row, 1970.
Don A. Stuart (John W. Campbell, Jr.), "Twilight." H. G. Wells, "The Star."

——. *Other Dimensions*. New York: Hawthorn Books, 1973.
Miles J. Breuer, M.D., "The Captured Cross-Section." Stanley G. Weinbaum, "The Worlds of If."

——. *The Science Fiction Bestiary*. Camden, N.J.: Thomas Nelson, 1971.
Stanley G. Weinbaum, "A Martian Odyssey."

——. *Science Fiction Hall of Fame*. Vol. 1. Garden City, N. Y.: Doubleday, 1970.
Don A. Stuart (John W. Campbell, Jr.), "Twilight." Stanley G. Weinbaum, "A Martian Odyssey."

——. *Tomorrow's Worlds*. New York: Meredith Press, 1969.
Stanley G. Weinbaum, "The Planet of Doubt."

Silverberg, Robert (*continued*)
——. *Worlds of Maybe*. Camden, N.J.: Thomas Nelson, 1970.
Murray Leinster, "Sidewise in Time."

Smith, Clark Ashton. *Other Dimensions*. Sauk City, Wisc.: Arkham House, 1970.
"An Adventure in Futurity." "The Amazing Planet." "The Dimension of Chance." "The Invisible City." "Marooned in Andromeda."

——. *Out of Space and Time*. Sauk City, Wisc.; Arkham House, 1942.
"The City of Singing Flame." "Beyond the Singing Flame."

——. *Tales of Science and Sorcery*. Sauk City, Wisc.: Arkham House, 1964. [Stories ##672, 1369]
"Master of the Asteroid." "The Planet Entity" (with E. M. Johnston).

Stong, Phil, ed. *The Other Worlds*. New York: Wilfred Funk, 1941. (Reprinted as and more commonly met as *25 Modern Stories of Mystery and Imagination*.)
Harry Bates, "Alas, All Thinking." John Jessel (Stanley G. Weinbaum), "The Adaptive Ultimate." Murray Leinster, "The Fourth-Dimensional Demonstrator."

Strange Love Stories. London: Utopia Publications, 1946.
Edmond Hamilton, "The Reign of the Robots."

Taine, John. *The Time Stream. The Greatest Adventure. The Purple Sapphire. Three Science Fiction Novels*. New York: Dover Publications, 1964.
"The Time Stream."

——. *Seeds of Life and White Lily. Two Science Fiction Novels*. New York: Dover Publications, 1966.
"Seeds of Life." "White Lily."

Wandrei, Donald. *Colossus: The Collected Science Fiction of Donald Wandrei*. Eds. Philip J. Rahman and Dennis E. Weiler. Minneapolis: Fedogan and Bremer, 1989.
"The Atom-Smasher." "Blinding Shadows." "Colossus." "Colossus Eternal." "Earth Minus." "Farewell to Earth." "Finality Unlimited." "Infinity Zero." "Life Current." "Murray's Light." "A Race through Time." "Raiders of the Universe." "The Whisperers."

——. *The Eye and the Finger*. Sauk City, Wisc.: Arkham House, 1944.
"Blinding Shadows." "Earth Minus." "Finality Unlimited." "The Nerveless Man."

——. *Strange Harvest*. Sauk City, Wisc.: Arkham House, 1965.
"The Atom-Smasher." "Infinity Zero." "Life Current." "The Man Who Never Live." "Murray's Light."

Wandrei, Howard. *Time Burial. The Collected Fantasy Tales of Howard Wandrei*. Edited and introduced by Dwayne Olson. Minneapolis: Fedogan and Bremer, 1995.
"The God Box" (as by Howard Von Drey). "Macklin's Little Friend" (as by H. W. Guernsey). "The Other" (as by Howard D. Graham). "The Wall" (as by Howard D. Graham).

Warrick, Patricia; Greenberg, Martin H,; and Olander, Joseph D., eds. *Science Fiction: Contemporary Mythology*. New York: Harper, 1978.
Hugo Gernsback, "Ralph 124 C41+" (fragment). Don A. Stuart (John W. Campbell, Jr.), "Twilight." "Donald A. Wandrei, "A Scientist Divides."

Weinbaum, Stanley G. *The Best of Stanley G. Weinbaum*. New York: Ballantine, 1974.
"The Adaptive Ultimate" (as by John Jessel). "The Ideal." "The Lotus Eaters." "The Mad Moon." "A Martian Odyssey." "Parasite Planet." "Proteus Island." "Pygmalion's Spectacles." "Redemption Cairn." "Valley of Dreams." "The Worlds of If."

——. *Dawn of Flame. The Weinbaum Memorial Volume*. [Jamaica, N. Y.: Ruppert Printing Service, 1936]
"The Adaptive Ultimate" (as by John Jessel). "The Lotus Eaters." "The Mad Moon." "A Martian Odyssey." "The Red Peri." "The Worlds of If."

——. *A Martian Odyssey and Other Science Fiction Tales*. Ed. Sam Moskowitz. Westport, Conn.: Hyperion, 1974.
"The Adaptive Ultimate" (as by John Jessel). "The Brink of Infinity." "The Circle of Zero." "Flight on Titan." "The Ideal." "The Lotus Eaters." "The Mad Moon." "A Martian Odyssey." "Parasite Planet." "The Planet of Doubt." "The Point of View." "Proteus Island." "Pygmalion's Spectacles." "The Red Peri." "Redemption Cairn." "Smothered Seas" (with Ralph Milne Farley). "Valley of Dreams." "The Worlds of If."

——. *A Martian Odyssey and Others*. Reading, Pa.: Fantasy Press, 1949.
"The Adaptive Ultimate" (as by John Jessel). "The Circle of Zero." "The Ideal." "The Lotus Eaters." "The Mad Moon." "A Martian Odyssey." "Parasite Planet." "The Planet of Doubt." "The Point of View." "Pygmalion's Spectacles." "Valley of Dreams." "The Worlds of If."

——. *The Red Peri*. Reading, Pa.: Fantasy Press, 1952.
"The Brink of Infinity." "Flight on Titan." "Proteus Island." "The Red Peri." "Redemption Cairn." "Smothered Seas" (with Ralph Milne Farley).

Wells, H. G. [Selected by E. F. Bleiler] *Best Science Fiction Stories of H. G. Wells*. New York: Dover Publications, 1966.
"Aepyornis Island." "The Crystal Egg." "The Diamond Maker." "The Flowering of the Strange Orchid." "In the Abyss." "The Invisible Man." "The Lord of the Dynamos." "The Man Who Could Work Miracles." "The New Accelerator." "The Plattner Story." "The Remarkable Case of Davidson's Eyes." "The Star."

——. *Best Stories of H. G. Wells*. New York: Ballantine, 1960.
"The Crystal Egg." "The Lord of the Dynamos." "The Man Who Could Work Miracles." "The New Accelerator." "The Plattner Story." "The Star." "A Story of the Days to Come." "The Story of the Late Mr. Elvesham."

——. *The Collector's Book of Science Fiction by H. G. Wells*. Secaucus, N. J.: Castle Books, 1978.
"Aepyornis Island." "The Country of the Blind." "The Diamond Maker." "The Empire of the Ants." "The First Men in the Moon." "The Flowering of the Strange Orchid." "In the Abyss." "The Man Who Could Work Miracles." "A Story of the Stone Age." "The War of the Worlds." "When the Sleeper Wakes."

——. *The Country of the Blind and Other Stories*. London: Thomas Nelson, 1911.
"Aepyornis Island." "The Crystal Egg." "The Country of the Blind." "The Empire of the Ants." "The Flowering of the Strange Orchid." "The Lord of the Dynamos." "The Man Who Could Work Miracles." "The Moth."

Wells, H. G. (*continued*)

"The New Accelerator." "The Plattner Story." "The Remarkable Case of Davidson's Eyes." "The Star." "The Story of the Late Mr. Elvesham." "Under the Knife."

——. *The Plattner Story and Others.* London: Methuen, 1897.
"In the Abyss." "The Plattner Story." "Pollock and the Porroh Man." "The Story of the Late Mr. Elvesham." "Under the Knife."

——. *Seven Famous Novels of H. G. Wells.* New York: Knopf, 1934. Republished as *Seven Science Fiction Novels of H. G. Wells.* New York: Dover Publications, 1953. Republished as *The Complete Science Fiction Treasury of H. G. Wells.* New York: Avenel, 1978.
"The First Men in the Moon." "The Invisible Man." "The Island of Doctor Moreau." "The Time Machine." "The War of the Worlds."

——. *The Short Stories of H. G. Wells.* London: Benn, 1927. Republished as *The Famous Short Stories of H. G. Wells.* New York: Literary Guild, 1929.
"Aepyornis Island." "The Country of the Blind." "The Crystal Egg." "The Diamond Maker." "The Flowering of the Strange Orchid." "In the Abyss." "The Lord of the Dynamos." "The Man Who Could Work Miracles." "The Moth." "The New Accelerator." "The Plattner Story." "Pollock and the Porroh Man." "The Remarkable Case of Davidson's Eyes." "The Star." "The Stolen Body." "A Story of the Days to Come." "The Story of the Late Mr. Elvesham." "A Story of the Stone Age." "The Time Machine." "Under the Knife."

——. *The Stolen Bacillus and Other Incidents.* London: Methuen, 1895.
"Aepyornis Island." "The Diamond Maker." "The Flowering of the Strange Orchid." "The Lord of the Dynamos." "The Moth." "The Remarkable Case of Davidson's Eyes."

——. *Tales of Space and Time.* London: Harper, 1899. New York: Doubleday, McClure, 1899.
"The Crystal Egg." "The Man Who Could Work Miracles." "The Star." "A Story of the Days to Come." "A Story of the Stone Age."

——. *Thirty Strange Stories.* New York: Edward Arnold, 1897.
"Aepyornis Island." "The Flowering of the Strange Orchid." "In the Abyss." "The Lord of the Dynamos." "The Moth." "The Plattner Story." "Pollock and the Porroh Man." "The Remarkable Case of Davidson's Eyes." "The Story of the Late Mr. Elvesham." "Under the Knife."

——. *Three Prophetic Novels,* ed. E. F. Bleiler. New York: Dover Publications, 1960.
"A Story of the Days to Come." "The Time Machine" (restored text). "When the Sleeper Wakes."

——. *Twelve Stories and a Dream.* London: Macmillan, 1903. New York: Scribners, 1905.
"The New Accelerator." "The Stolen Body."

——. *28 Science Fiction Stories.* New York: Dover, 1952.
"Aepyornis Island." "The Country of the Blind." "The Crystal Egg." "The Empire of the Ants." "The Flowering of the Strange Orchid." "In the Abyss." "The Man Who Could Work Miracles." "The New Accelerator." "The Plattner Story." "The Remarkable Case of Davidson's

Eyes." "A Story of the Days to Come." "The Star." "The Stolen Body." "The Story of the Late Mr. Elvesham." "A Story of the Stone Age." "Under the Knife."

——. *The War of the Worlds, The Time Machine, and Selected Short Stories.* New York: Platt and Munk, 1963.
"The Crystal Egg." "In the Abyss." "The Story of the Late Mr. Elvesham." "The Time Machine." "War of the orlds."

——. *The Works of H. G. Wells, The Atlantic Edition.* London: Unwin and New York: Scribner, New York, 1924-1927.
"Aepyornis Island." "The Crystal Egg." "The Empire of the Ants." "The First Men on the Moon." "The Flowering of the Strange Orchid." "The Invisible Man." "The Island of Doctor Moreau." "The New Accelerator." "The Plattner Story." "The Remarkable Case of Davidson's Eyes." "The Sleeper Awakes" (revised, altered edition of "When the Sleeper Wakes"). "The Star." "The Time Machine." "Under the Knife." "The War of the Worlds."

Williamson, Jack. *The Alien Intelligence.* New Orleans: P.D.A. Enterprises, 1980.
"The Alien Intelligence." "The Prince of Space." "The Second Shell."

——. *The Best of Jack Williamson.* New York: Ballantine, 1978.
"The Metal Man." "Dead Star Station."

——. *The Early Williamson.* Garden City, N. Y.: Doubleday, 1975.
"The Cosmic Express." "Dead Star Station." "The Doom from Planet Four." "The Metal Man." "The Meteor Girl." "Salvage in Space." "Through the Purple Cloud." "12 Hours to Live!"

——. *The Pandora Effect.* New York: Ace, 1969.
"The Cosmic Express." "The Metal Man."

——. *Three from the Legion.* Nelson Doubleday; Garden City, N.Y., 1979.
"The Cometeers." "The Legion of Space."

Wollheim, Donald A., ed. *The End of the World.* New York: Ace, 1956.
Amelia R. Long, "Omega."

——. *Every Boy's Book of Science-Fiction.* New York: Frederick Fell, 1951.
Daniel Dressler, M.D., "The White Army." Edmond Hamilton, "A Conquest of Two Worlds." David H. Keller, M.D., "The Living Machine." Clifton B. Kruse, "Dr. Lu-Mie." Bob Olsen, "The Four-Dimensional Roller-Press." Clifford Simak, "The Asteroid of Gold." Jack Williamson, "In the Scarlet Star." Sewell P. Wright, "The Infra-Medians."

——. *Flight into Space.* New York: Frederick Fell, 1950.
Clare W. Harris and Miles J. Breuer, "A Baby on Neptune." Frank Belknap Long, "Red Storm on Jupiter." Alexander M. Phillips, "The Death of the Moon." Leslie F. Stone, "The Rape of the Solar System." Stanley G. Weinbaum, "Parasite Planet."

——. *The Hidden Planet.* New York: Ace, 1959.
Stanley G. Weinbaum, "The Lotus Eaters."

——. *More Adventures on Other Planets.* New York: Ace, 1963.

Wollheim, Donald A. (*continued*)
    Stanley G. Weinbaum, "The Planet of Doubt."
——. *The Pocket Book of Science-Fiction*. New York: Pocketbooks, 1943.
    Thomas S. Stribling, "The Green Splotches." Don A. Stuart (John W. Campbell, Jr.) "Twilight." Stanley G. Weinbaum, "A Martian Odyssey." H. G. Wells, "In the Abyss." Wallace West, "The Last Man."
——. *Portable Novels of Science*. New York: Viking, 1945.
    H. P. Lovecraft, "The Shadow out of Time." H. G. Wells, "The First Men in the Moon."
——. *Swordsmen in the Sky*. New York: Ace, 1964.
    Otis A. Kline, "A Vision of Venus."
Wollheim, Donald A. and Ernsberger, George, eds. *The Second Avon Fantasy Reader*. New York: Avon, 1969.
    Laurence Manning and Fletcher Pratt, "The City of the Living Dead."
Wyndham, John (originally writing in the following stories, as John Beynon Harris) *The Best of John Wyndham*. London: Sphere Books, 1973.
    "The Lost Machine." "The Man from Beyond."
——. *Exiles on Asperus*. London: Coronet, 1979.
    "Exiles on Asperus." "The Venus Adventure."
——. *The Man from Beyond and Other Stories*. London: Michael Joseph, 1975.
    "The Lost Machine." "The Man from Beyond."

Authors' Letters

The following consolidated table lists published letters and guest editorials by authors covered in this volume. It does not include fan personalities per se or others peripherally concerned with science-fiction. A limited chronological exception has been made by including juvenile letters by Isaac Asimov, Arthur C. Clarke, and a few other later authors who have been important enough in the history of science-fiction that it would be improper to overlook them for the sake of consistency.

It should be pointed out that the following letterbag is of very mixed quality. The list includes excellent letters by John W. Campbell, Jr. and E. E. Smith, Ph.D., discussing matters of technique and parameters of extrapolation; intelligent letters by P. Schuyler Miller, who seems to have been the first to state aspects of science-fiction scholarship, although he did not follow them up; and individual letters about specific points in stories by important writers of the day, like Jack Williamson, Miles J. Breuer, M.D., and Clark Ashton Smith.

Present also are many letters important in the social aspects of early science-fiction readership, like the flurry of science clubs in the early 1930s, and the far more productive American Interplanetary Society (later American Rocket Society), which had a significant impact in later space engineering.

It must be admitted, however, that there are many, many disappointing letters, sometimes by the most frequent contributors to this area. There are listing letters, simply stating dislikes and dislikes, rather puerile attempts at humor, and self-publicity letters of a distressing sort. The reader must evaluate them for himself/herself.

Abbreviations are as follows: Am, *Amazing Stories*; AmQ, *Amazing Stories Quarterly*; Ast, *Astounding Stories*; AW, *Air Wonder Stories*; F, Fall; Sc, *Scoops*; Sp, Spring; Su, Summer; SW, *Science Wonder Stories*; SWQ, *Science Wonder Quarterly*; W, *Wonder Stories*; Wi, Winter; WQ *Wonder Stories Quarterly*. Months are numbered.

Ackerman, Forrest J. F/1929 SWQ; Wi/1930 SWQ; 5/1930 Ast; 5/1930 AW; 5 Su/1930 WQ; 7/1930 Am; F/1930 WQ; 12/1930 Ast; 1/1931 Ast; Wi/1931 WQ; 4/1931 Ast; Sp/1931 WQ; 5/1931 W; 6/1931 Ast; 6/1931 W; 8/1931 Ast; F/1931 WQ; 11/1931 Ast; 11/1931 W; 12/1931 W; 1/1932 Am; 1/1932 Ast; 2/1932 Am; 2/1932 W; 3/1932 Am; 3/1932 W; 4/1932 Ast; 6/1932 W; 10/1932 W; 11/1932 Ast; 4/1933 Am; 7/1933 Am; 8/1933 W; 10/1933 W; 11/1933 Am; 1/1934 W; 3/1934 Am; 3/1934 W; 6/1934 W; 12/1934 W; 2/1935 W; 6/1935 W; 7/1935 Ast; 7/1935 W; 8/1935 Ast; 9/1935 W; 10/1935 W; 4/1936 W.

Asimov, Isaac 2/1935 Ast.

Barnes, Arthur K. 6/1932 W; 12/1934 W.

Barnette, Jack 11/1929 Am.

Beck, Clyde 11/1928 AW; 1/1930 Am.

Beckwith, O. L. 3/1930 SW.

Berlow, Sidney 4/1932 W.

Bernal, A. W. 6/1930 Ast; 8/1930 Am.

Binder, Eando 8/1934 W.

Binder, Otto F/1929 AmQ (editorial); 6/1930 Am; 5/1931 Am.

Blish, James 7/1932 Ast; 9/1932 Ast; 10/1935 W; 2/1936 Ast; 7/1936 Ast.

Breuer, Miles J., M.D. 6/1927 Am; 7/1928 Am; 8/1928 Am; 1/1929 Am; Su/1929 AmQ (editorial); 9/1929 Am; 2/1930 Am; 4/1930 Am; 5/1930 Am; 10/1930 Am; 1/1931 Am; 6/1931 W.

Bridge, Frank 11/1931 Am; 1/1932 W.

Brueckel, Frank, Jr. 6/1929 Am; 4/1930 Am.

Burks, Arthur J. 6/1931 Ast.

Burroughs, Edgar Rice quoted 12/1927 Am.

Burtt, J. Lewis 2/1930 Am; 4/1934 Am; 9/1934 Am.

Byrne, Stuart J. 6/1928 Am.

Campbell, John W., Jr. 7/1929 SW; 3/1930 Am; 5/1930 Am; 9/1930 Am; 11/1930 Am; 2/1931 Am; 3/1931 Am; 5/1931 Am; 5/1933 Am.
(as Karl van Campen) 12/1934 Ast; 2/1935 Ast; 3/1935 Ast; 5/1935 Ast; 7/1935 Ast.

Chandler, A. B. (?) 7/1927 Am.

Chappelow, Edward F/1929 SWQ.

Clarke, Arthur C. 2/1935 Am.

Cloukey, Charles F/1929 AmQ (editorial).

Connell, Alan 5/1931 Am; 6/1931 Am; 4/1934 Am.

Cummings, Ray 10/1930 Ast; 4/1931 Ast; 11/1932 Ast.

Daniels, David R. 3/1934 Ast; 9/1934 Ast.

del Rey, Lester 3/1935 Ast; 5/1935 Ast; 7/1935 Ast;
    8/1935 Ast; 11/1935 Ast; 7/1936 Ast.

Dennis, Walter 12/1929 SW; Su/1929 AmQ; 1/1930 Am;
    Wi/1930 SWQ; 4/1930 Am; 6/1930 Ast; 10/1930 Ast;
    2/1931 Am; 3/1931 Ast; 11/1931 W; 8/1933 Am;
    1/1936 Ast.

Derleth, August 5/1936 Ast.

Dold, Elliott 2/1936 Ast.

Edwards, Gawain 8/1931 W; perhaps 3/1932 Ast.

Endersby, Victor A. 11/1929 AW; 3/1930 AW; 4/1930
    SW; Sp/1930 AmQ (editorial); 5/1930 AW; 10/1930
    Am; 3/1931 W; 4/1931 W.

Ernst, Paul 7/1931 Ast; 6/1932 Ast.

Eshbach, L. A. 11/1930 Ast; 12/1931 W; 4/1936 Ast.

Farley, Ralph Milne Su/1930 WQ (editorial).

Fearn, John Russell 3/1931 Am; 1/1932 Am; 5/1934 Am;
    16/6/1934 Sc; 4/1936 Am.

Flagg, Francis 7/1935 W.

Gardner, Thomas S. 9/1932 W; 10/1934 W; 2/1936 Ast;
    8/1936 Am.

Garfinkel, Samuel 2/1929 Am.

Gee, Jackson 6/1931 Ast.

Glasser, Allen 6/1927 Am; 6/1927 Am; 8/1927 Am;
    5/1928 Am; 2/1930 AW; 3/1930 SW; Sp/1930 SWQ;
    4/1930 Ast; 4/1930 AW; 4/1930 SW; 4/1930 SW;
    6/1930 W; 7/1930 Ast; 9/1930 W; 10/1930 Ast; 11/1930
    W; 12/1930 Ast; 12/1930 W; 5/1931 W; 7/1931 W;
    8/1931 Am; 8/1931 W; 9/1931 W; 12/1931 W; 1/1933
    Am; 2/1933 Am; 8/1933 Am; 12/1933 Am; 1/1934 W.

Gold, Horace (as C. C. Campbell) 10/1934 Ast.

Gurwit, S. Gordon 1/1934 Ast.

Haggard, J. Harvey 1/1931 W; 12/1931 W; 7/1933 Am;
    2/1934 W; 11/1934 W; 6/1935 Am; 8/1935 Am.

Hale, Stephen G. 4/1932 Am

Hansen, L. Taylor Wi/1929 AmQ (editorial).

Happel, R. V. 7/1927 Am.

Harris, Clare Winger 5/1929 Am; 9/1929 AW; 8/1931 W.

Harris, John Beynon 2/1932 W.

Hasse, Henry 3/1930 AW; 5/1931 Am; 8/1932 Am;
    12/1933 Am; 1/1934 W; 11/1934 Ast; 2/1935 W;
    5/1935 W.

Hodge, Frederick Arthur Su/1929 AmQ (editorial).

Hornig, Charles 10/31 Am; 12/1931 Ast; 1/1932 Ast; 11/1932
    W.

Jones, Neil R. 11/1932 Am; 6/1934 Am.

Jones, Vernon 12/1934 W (reprint); 3/1935 W; 8/1934 W;
    11/1934 W.

Kaletsky, Milton 8/1931 W; 10/1931 W; 11/1931 W;
    1/1932 Am; 1/1932 W; Sp/1932 WQ; 11/1932 W;
    12/1932 W; 1/1933 W; 4/1933 W; 11/1933 Am;
    11/1933 W; 2/1934 Am; 6/1934 W; 7/1934 Ast; 9/1934
    Ast; 12/1934 W; 3/1935 Ast; 5/1935 Ast.

Kalland, James Francis Su/1931 AmQ (editorial); 3/35 Am.

Kateley, Walter 2/1930 SW.

Keller, David H., M.D. 12/1929 Am; 4/1930 SW; 9/1934 Am.

Kelly, Frank K. 9/1929 SW; 10/1929 SW; 2/1930 AW;
    11/1931 W; 1/1932 W; 4/1933 Am; 3/1934 Am;
    7/1934 Ast; 10/1934 Ast.

Kerlin, Richard 11/1934 Am; 2/1935 Am.

Key, Eugene George 3/1930 AW.

Kober, William 8/1931 Am; Sp-Su/1932 AmQ; 4/1934 Am.

Kostkos, Henry 5/1934 Am.

Kraus, Joseph H. 9/1935 W.

Kuttner, Henry 9/1929 AW; 11/1929 AW; 10/1931 W.

Ley, Willy 9/1930 W; 1/1931 W; 1/1932 W; 8/1932 W.

Lower, Harold A. 2/1929 Am.

Lowndes, Robert 5/1935 W; 10/1935 W; 2/1936 Am;
    12/1936 Am.

Marshall, James P. 7/1929 SW; 8/1929 SW.

Mason, C. P. 6/1930 W; 7/1930 W; Su/1930 WQ; 8/1930
    W; 12/1930 W; 4/1931 W; Su/1931 WQ.
    (as Epaminondas Snooks) 9/1932 W; 8/1933 SW.

McDermott, Dennis 4/1932 W.

McDowd, Kennie 8/1929 SW.

Meek, Capt. S. P. 6/1930 Am; 1/1931 Ast; 5/1931 Ast;
    3/1932 Am.

Menzel, Donald 7/1932 Am.

Michel, John 7/1932 Am; 7/1932 Am; 11/1932 Am;
    1/1933 Am; 3/1933 Am; 8/1933 Am; 11/1933 Am;
    11/1936 Ast.

Mihalakis, Ulysses George (as Ulysses George) 11/1929 SW;
    12/1929 SW.

Miller, P. Schuyler 2/1928 Am; 3/1928 Am; 2/1929 Am;
    F/1929 AmQ (editorial); 5/1930 Am; 10/1930 Am;
    11/1930 Ast; 5/1931 W; 6/1931 Ast; 8/1931 Am;
    10/1931 W; 3/1932 W; 4/1932 Am; 6/1932 W; 12/1932
    W; 11/1933 Am; 2/1934 Am; 3/1934 W; 7/1935 Am.

Murray, Richard Rush 10/1930 Am; 4/1932 Am; 5/1933
    Am; 1/1934 Am.

Nevins, W. Varick 6/1935 W; 7/1935 W.

Newton, Edsel 12/1930 W; 2/1931 W.

Nowlan, Philip 2/1934 Ast.

Numa, Hero C. Wi/1930 AmQ (editorial).

Olog, Tom 6/1929 SW (editorial); 7/1929 SW; 3/1931
    Ast; 3/1932 Ast; 9/1934 Ast; 6/1935 Am.

Palmer, Ray 10/1928 Am; 10/1929 SW; 4/1930 Am;
    Sp/1930 SWQ; 8/1930 W; 12/1930 W; 3/1932 W;
    5/1932 W; 8/1932 Am; 11/1932 Ast; 1/1933 Ast;
    7/1934 Am; 4/1936 Ast; 9/1936 Ast.

Parkinson, R. 4/1936 W.

Pelcher, Anthony 1/1930 SW.

Penguin (Pendray?), G. Edward 3/1932 Ast.

Phillips, Alexander M. Wi/1930 AmQ (editorial).

Pragnell, Festus 8/1933 W; 3/1934 Am; 6/1935 W.

Pratt, Fletcher 9/1929 SW; 8/1930 Am.

Ray, Rice 9/1934 W.

Repp, Ed Earl 6/1929 SW; 12/1929 SW; 6/1933 Am.

Rocklynne, Ross 2/1932 Am; 1/1936 Ast.

Ryan, Franklin W. 7/1933 Am.

Schachner, Nat 6/1931 W; 9/1931 Am; 12/1931 W;
    4/1932 W; 12/1933 Ast.

Searight, Richard F. 3/1934 W.

Septama, Aladra (Judson W. Reeves) Wi/1929 AmQ

Septama, Aladra (*continued*
        (editorial); Wi/1929 AmQ (ltr.).
Sharp, D. D. 4/1933 W; 5/1933 W.
Siegel, Jerome 8/1929 Am; 11/1929 SW; 1/1931 Ast;
        8/1931 Ast.
Skidmore, Joe W. Wi/1930 AmQ (editorial); 9/1932 Am;
        4/1933 Am; 1/1934 Am; 3/1935 Am; 10/1935 Am.
Skinner, E. D. 8/1927 Am.
Smith, Clark Ashton 7/1931 Ast; 8/1932 W; 10/1932 Am;
        2/1933 W.
Smith, E. E., Ph.D. 6/1929 SW (editorial); 12/1930 Am;
        4/1931 Am; 4/1932 Am; 7/1932 Am; 9/1934 Am;
        11/1934 Am; 1/1935 Ast; 7/1935 Ast; 4/1936 Ast.
Speaker, David 6/1928 Am; Sp/1929 AmQ (editorial).
Starzl, R. F. 10/1930 Am.
Sterling, Kenneth 3/1932 Ast; 11/1932 Ast; 12/1933 Am;
        3/1935 W; 4/1935 Ast; 5/1935 Ast; 8/1936 Ast.
Stone, Leslie F. 10/1928 Am; 11/1935 W.
Stranger, Ralph 12/1932 W.
Thurmond, William T. Sp/1932 WQ.
Tooker, Richard 6/1929 SW; 8/1933 Am.
Tucker, Bob 4/1934 Ast; 4/1934 W; 6/1934
        W; 9/1934 W; 10/1934 W; 1/1935 W; 2/1935 W;
        5/1935 W; 6/1935 W; 8/1935 Ast; 8/1935 W; 9/1935
        Ast; 11/1935 Ast; 11/1935 W; 1/1936 Ast.
Vanne, Emma 7/1935 W.
Vanny, Jim 11/1930 W.
Verrill, A. Hyatt Wi/1930 AmQ.
Vincent, Harl 9/1929 Am; 9/1929 SW; 11/1929 Am;
        1/1930 AW; Su/1930 AmQ; 10/1930 Am; Su/1931
        AmQ.
Wandrei, Donald 12/1933 Ast; 1/1934 Ast; 5/1934 Ast.
Wates, Cyril G. 2/1930 Am; 1/1934 Am; 8/1935 Am.
Weisinger, Mortimer 10/1930 Ast; 4/1931 Ast; 5/1931 W;
        6/1931 Am; 8/1931 Ast; 11/1932 Ast; 7/1933 Am.
Wertenbaker, G. Peyton 7/26 Am (quoted in Gernsback's
        editorial), 11/1930 Am.
White, Cecil B. 2/1929 Am.
Williamson, Jack 10/1927 Am; 10/1928 Am; F/1928 AmQ
        (editorial); 6/1929 Am; 6/1929 SW (editorial); Wi/1929
        AmQ (editorial); 1/1930 SW; 8/1930 Ast; 6/1931 W;
        6/1932 Am; 11/1932 Ast.
Winks, J. L. 11/1933 Am; 4/1934 Ast; 7/1934 Ast;
        9/1934 Ast; 12/1934 Ast.
Wollheim, Donald 11/1930 Am; 11/1933 Am; 5/1934 Am;
        6/1934 Am; 7/1934 Ast; 9/1934 W; 11/1934 Ast;
        3/1935 W; 4/1935 Ast; 6/1935 Am; 7/1935 Ast; 8/1935
        Ast.
Wright, Sewell P. 11/1931 Ast.
Zagat, Arthur Leo 9/1934 Ast.

Poetry

Poetry played a minor role in the early science-fiction pulp magazines, but a certain amount was present, undoubtedly used as filler material to conceal empty space when stories did not end neatly at the bottom of a page.

It will be observed that only about a quarter of the verse listed was the product of the regular science-fiction writers of the time. These are indicated by a bullet •, with biographical information under author fiction entries. Surprisingly, Stanton A. Coblentz, who was one of the leading figures in the amateur traditional poetry movement of the day, is present with only two poems, and Lilith Lorraine, also important, is not present at all. Leland Stanford Copeland (1886-?), a resident of Santa Barbara, California, was also the author of *Whimsical Rimes* (c. 1922). Julia Boynton Green, whose poetry had been appearing in magazines and newspapers since the turn of the century, was also a resident of California. She was the author of two books of poetry, *Enchanting Coast* (1928) and *Noonmark* (1936).

It would be impossible to generalize about this magazine verse. Some is reasonably competent from a technical point of view, but much is doggerel.

Abbreviations: Am, *Amazing Stories;* AmQ, *Amazing Stories Quarterly;* Ast, *Astounding Stories;* SW, *Science Wonder Stories;* W, *Wonder Stories;* WQ, *Wonder Stories Quarterly.*

A. S. [Albert Sidney?] "Oh, Ye Fourth Dimension" 5/1930 Am.
Ackerman, Henry. "Astounding Stories" 3/1933 Ast.
Benefiel, Eugene and Skora, George. "In Vindication" 1/1933 Ast.
Best, Susie M. "The Miracle" 12/1929 Am.
Beta. "A 'Psalm' of Life" 8/1926 Am.
•Breuer, Miles J., M.D. "Sonnet to Science" 12/1930 Am.
——. "Vis Scientiae" 5/1930 Am.
Browne, Al. "The Riddle" 1/1934 W.
Camp, E. M. "Higher Mathematics" 2/1933 Am.
•Chappelow, Edward E. "Join a Chapter" 9/1935 W.

•Cloukey, Charles. "The Interplanetary Blues" 12/1931 Am.
•Coblentz, Stanton A. "Across Eternity" 12/1934 Am.
——. "The Triumph of the Machines" 9/1929 Am.
Cody, Booth. [Untitled about *Astounding Stories*] 8/1931 Ast.
Copeland, Leland S. "Alone" 7/1927 Am.
——. "Ascension" l2/1926 Am.
——. "Aspiration" 8/1926 Am.
——. "Change Eternal" Sp/1929 AmQ.
——. "Cosmic Ciphers" 7/1927 Am.
——. "Hail and Good-Bye" 10/1926 Am.
——. "Life" 9/1928 Am.
——. "Light of Life" 5/1927 Am.
——. "Lullaby" 10/1926 Am.
——. "Of Their Own Have We Given Them" 7/1927 Am .
——. "Our Little Neighbor" 5/1928 Am.
——. "Ourselves" 7/1927 Am.
——. "Planet Neptune to Mother Sun" 7/1927 Am.
——. "Secrets Never Told" 6/1927 Am.
——. "Speeding" Sp/1929 AmQ.
——. "Stars" 11/1926 Am.
——. "Superstar" 4/1927 Am.
——. "When Hearts Remember Home" 4/1928 Am .
——. "Worlds Unknown" 7/1927 Am.
Derleth, August. "Omega" 11/1934 W.
——. "To a Spaceship" 3/1934 W.
Derms, Charles H. "A Toast!" 9/1935 W.
Eberhart, V. P. "Red Moon" 6/1932 Am, 8/1932 Am.
——. "Revelation" 4/1933 Am.
Elliott, Forrest. "Reverie" 3/1933 Am.
•Eshbach, L. A. "Luna Doom" 4/1935 W.
——. "The Martian Cry" 11/1934 W.
——. "The Wanderer" 9/1934 W.
Everett, E. A. "The Difference" W/1932 AmQ.
Flynn, Clarence Edward. "The Dead World" 6/1933 W.
——. "The Robot" 6/1933 W.
Friend, Robert. "Some Day the Moon" Su/1932 WQ.

•Glasser, Allen. "Mu and Atlantis" Sp/Su/1933 AmQ.

Green, Julia Boynton. "Evolution" 8/1931 Am.

——. "The Evolution of an Ace" 3/1931 Am.

——. "The Night Express" 7/1931 Am.

——. "Radio Revelations" F/W/1932 AmQ.

——. "Science and the Saucepans" 6/1936 Am.

——. "This Mechanical Age" F/1931 AmQ.

Harper, Clio. "Antipodal" Sp/Su/1932 AmQ.

Hinson, Donald. "Upward" 10/1932 Am.

•Hornig, Charles D. "Ode to Arrhenius" 6/1934 W.

Howard, J. Z. "Epilog to the Rubaiyat" Su/1932 WQ.

Kaufman, Max. "From Tales of Specks of Dust" 12/1932
   Am.

Lathrop, M. G. "Evolution" 8/1935 Am.

Lewis, Henry, Jr. "Comet Head Drace" 1/1933 Ast.

——. "In 2082" 9/1932 Ast.

——. "Verse" 1/1933 Ast.

Lonecoast. "Calories in the Boarding House" 2/1930 Am.

•Miller, P. Schuyler. "Man's Question" 6/1931 Am.

——. "Meteor" 8/1931 Am.

——. "Space" 2/1933 Am.

•Olsen, Bob. "How Inventions Are Born" 4/1935 Am.

——. "In 1999" Am 1/1934 Am.

——. "Landscapes of Luna" 10/1935 Am.

——. "My Robot Son" F/1931 AmQ.

——. "Transports of Love" 6/1929 Am.

——. "Who Deserves Credit?" 2/1935 Am.

——. [Untitled about the fourth dimension] 7/1934 Am.

Parsons, Edward. "Sonnet to Our Magazine" 12/1929 Am.

Pike, Robert Bridge. "Babylon, A Song of Memory" F/1934
   AmQ .

•The Planet Prince. (J. Harvey Haggard) "Advance of
   Science" 07/1930 W.

——. "At the End of the Spectrum" 12/1931 W.

——. "The Master Allegory" 7/1930 W.

——. "My Little Martian Sweetheart" 11/1929 SW.

Reid, Edward. "A Dream" 5/1934 Am.

Robertson, Stark. "The Planeteer" 5/1935 W.

Searight, Richard F. "Impressions of the Planets——Venus"
   1/1934 W.

Sidney, Albert. "Sonnet" 10/1930 Am.

[Sloane, T. O'Conor] "Love of Country" 6/1934 Am.

Terry, James A. "The Sweep of Space" 2/1930 Am.

Thomas, Pauline E. "Prayer of an Elderly Philosopher"
   6/1933 Am.

•Tucker, Bob. "Scientifictionuts" 1/1935 W.

Van Duke, Dix. "The Radio" 1/1935 Am.

W.T.B. "Through Intervening Space" Su/1931 AmQ.

•Weisinger, Mort. "Eulogy to Mr. Hamilton" 11/1932 Ast.

Zerrin, H. S. "Passing of the Planets—Luna" 3/1934 W.

——. "Passing of the Planets—Venus" 4/1934 W.

Reprint Sources

The following stories have been reprinted from other sources. As a tabulation shows, more than half of these stories appeared in 1926 and 1927, the birth years of *Amazing Stories*. After this, the number of reprints dwindles, although there is a second small peak in 1933 and 1934, when Dr. T. O'Conor Sloane, undoubtedly for financial reasons during the Great Depression, frequently printed stories by Edgar Allan Poe and Jules Verne. These would have been in the public domain and free of charge.

While original publication is listed, the older stories by Fitz-James O'Brien, Edgar Allan Poe, Jules Verne, and H. G. Wells would have been available to Gernsback and Sloane from reprintings.

Am Bruhl, Leo. "Garfield's Invention," [source unknown].

Anthos. "The Malignant Flower," [source unknown].

Ball, Clelland. "The Gravity King," *Science and Invention*, April 1922.

Balmer, Edward and MacHarg, William. "The Eleventh Hour," "The Hammering Man," "The Man Higher Up," and "The Man in the Room" from *The Achievements of Luther Trant* [1910], with probable earlier periodical or newspaper publication.

Bishop, Capt. H. G. "On the Martian Way," *Broadway Magazine*, November 1907.

Bissiri, Augusto. The Lord of the Winds," [source unknown].

Buergel, Bruno. "The Cosmic Cloud" [German book publication in 1921].

Burroughs, Edgar Rice. "The Land That Time Forgot," *Blue Book*, August, October, December 1918. [book publication in 1924].

Butler, Ellis Parker. "An Experiment in Gyro-Hats," *New Broadway Magazine*, June 1920.

———. "Solander's Radio Tomb," *Radio News*, December 1923.

Cummings, Parke. "Nothing to It," *Saturday Evening Post*, 1934.

Cummings, Ray. "Around the Universe," *Science and Invention*, July-December 1923.

Doyle, Arthur Conan. "The Poison Belt," *The Strand*, April-November 1912. [book publication in 1912].

England, George Allan. "The Flying Legion," *All Story Magazine*, 15 November-20 December 1919. [book publication in 1920].

———. "The Thing from—'Outside,'" *Science and Invention*, April 1923.

Fawcett, Col. P. H. "Callahuaya's Curse," [probable reprint; source unknown]

Freksa, Friedrich. "Druso" [German book publication in 1931].

Gail, Otto Willi. "The Shot into Infinity" [German book publication in 1925].

———. "The Stone from the Moon" [German book publication in 1926].

Gernsback, Hugo. "Baron Muenchhausen's Scientific Adventures," *Electrical Experimenter*, irregularly May 1915-February 1917.

———. "The Electrical Duel," *Science and Invention*, August 1923.

———. "The Electrical Storm," *Electrical Experimenter*, August 1918.

———. "Ralph 124C 41+," *Modern Electrics*, March 1911-April 1912, plus revisions of the 1925 book edition.

Golub, F. "The Secret of the Microcosm," [source unknown].

Hale, Edward Everett. "The Good-Natured Pendulum," from *The Ingham Papers* [1869].

Hall, Austin. "The Man Who Saved the Earth," *All-Story*, 13 December 1919.

Hanstein, Otfrid von. "Between Earth and Moon" [German book publication in 1928].

———. "Electropolis" [German book publication in 1928].

———. "The Hidden Colony" [German book publication in 1924].

———. "In the Year 8000" [claimed as original; German

Hanstein, Otfrid von (*continued*)
publication probable, but unlocated].

——. "Utopia Island" [German publication probable, but unlocated].

Held, Serge. "The Death of Iron" [French book publication in 1931].

Huekels, Jack. "Advanced Chemistry," *Science and Invention*, August 1923.

Huxley, Julian. "The Tissue-Culture King," *Cornhill Magazine*, April 1925.

Johnson, E. H. "The Golden Vapor," *Science and Invention*, February 1920.

Keeler, Harry Stephen. "John Jones's Dollar," *Black Cat*, August 1915.

Kline, Otis Adelbert. "The Malignant Entity," *Weird Tales*, May/June/July Anniversary Issue 1924.

Leinster, Murray. "The Mad Planet," *Argosy*, 10 June 1920.

——. "The Red Dust," *Argosy*, 8 April 1921.

——. "The Runaway Skyscraper," *Argosy*, 22 February 1919.

Locke, Richard A. "The Moon Hoax," *New York Sun*, 15-31 August 1835.

MacClure, Victor. "The Ark of the Covenant" [book publication in 1924].

McLociard, George. "Monorail," *Lane Tech Prep*, February 1927.

——. "Smoke Rings," *Lane Tech Prep*, October 1926.

Merritt, A. "The Drone Man," *Fantasy Magazine*, September 1934.

——. "The Face in the Abyss," *Argosy-All-Story*, 8 September 1923.

——. "The Moon Pool," (including "The Conquest of the Moon Pool") *All-Story*, 22 June 1918, 15 February-22 March 1919. [book publication in 1919].

——. "The People of the Pit," *All-Story*, 5 January 1918.

——. "Rhythm of the Spheres," *Fantasy Magazine*, April 1934.

Morgan, Jacque. "The Feline Light and Power Co.," *Modern Electrics*, October 1912.

——. "The International Electro-Galvanic Undertaking Corporation," *Modern Electrics*, December 1912.

——. "Mr. Fosdick Invents the Seidlitzmobile," *Modern Electrics*, November 1912.

O'Brien, Fitz-James. "The Diamond Lens," *Atlantic Monthly*, January 1858.

Orlovsky, V. The Revolt of the Atoms, *Mir Prikl'uchenii*, #3, 1927.

Poe, Edgar Allan. "The Balloon Hoax," *New York Sun Extra*, 13 April 1844.

——. "A Descent into the Maelstrom," *Graham's Gentleman's and Lady's Magazine,* May 1841.

——. "The Facts in the Case of M. Valdemar," *The American Review*, December 1845.

——. "The Gold Bug," *Dollar Newspaper*, 21-28 June 1843.

——. "Ms. Found in a Bottle," *Baltimore Sunday Visiter*, 10 October 1833.

——. "Mellonta Tauta," *Godey's Lady's Book*, February 1849.

——. "Mesmeric Revelation," *Columbia Lady's and Gentleman's Magazine,* August 1844.

——. "The Sphinx," *Arthur's Lady's Magazine*, January

1846.

——. "The Thousand-and-Second Tale of Scheherazade," *Godey's Lady's Book*, February 1845.

——. "Von Kempelen and His Discovery," *The Flag of Our Union*, 14 April 1849.

Regis, Jul. "The Paradise of the Ice Wilderness," [source unknown].

Richards, Harold F. "The Vibrator of Death," *Science and Invention*, January 1922.

Richter, Charles de. "The Fall of the Eiffel Tower" [source unknown].

Serviss, Garrett P. "A Columbus of Space," *All-Story*, January-June 1909. [book publication in 1911].

——. "The Moon Metal" [newspaper and book publication in 1900].

——. "The Second Deluge," *Cavalier*, July 1911-January 1912. [book publication in 1912].

Siodmak, Curt. "The Eggs from Lake Tanganyika," [*Scherl* magazine, 1926].

Smith, Garret "Treasures of Tantalus," *Argosy-All-Story*, 11 December 1920-8 January 1921.

Stratton, George F. "Sam Graves' Gravity Nullifier," *Practical Electrics*, March 1924.

Stribling, T. S. "The Green Splotches," *Adventure*, 3 January 1920.

Thebault, Eugene. "The Radio Terror" [French feuilleton 1927-1928?].

Valier, Max. "A Daring Trip to Mars" [German book publication in 1924].

Verne, Jules. "Dr. Ox" [French 1872; translation 1874].

——. "A Drama in the Air" [French 1851; translation 1874].

——. "The English at the North pole and The Desert of Ice" [French 1864-5; translation, 1874].

——. "The Master of the World" [French 1904; translation 1914].

——. "Measuring a Meridian" [French 1872; translation 1873].

——. "Off on a Comet" [French 1877; translation 1878].

——. "The Purchase of the North Pole" [French 1889; translation 1891].

——. "Robur the Conqueror" [French 1886; translation 1887].

——. "A Trip to the Center of the Earth" [French 1863, revised 1867; translation 1872].

——. "The Watch's Soul" [French 1854; translation 1874].

——. "A Winter amid the Ice" [French 1855; translation 1874].

Wells, H. G. "The Crystal Egg," *The New Review*, May 1897.

——. "The First Men in the Moon," *The Strand*, December 1900-August 1901. [book publication in 1901].

——. "The Flowering of the Strange Orchid," *Pall Mall Budget*, August 1894.

——. "In the Abyss," *Pearson's Magazine*, August 1896.

——. "The Invisible Man" [book publication in 1897].

——. "The Island of Doctor Moreau" [book publication in 1896].

——. "The Lord of the Dynamos," *Pall Mall Budget*, September 1894.

——. "The Man Who Could Work Miracles," *Illustrated*

Wells, H. G. (*continued*)
   London News, July 1898.
———. "The Moth," *Pall Mall Gazette*, March 1895.
———. "The New Accelerator," *The Strand*, December 1901.
———. "The Plattner Story," *New Review*, April 1896.
———. "Pollock and the Porroh Man," *New Budget*,
   May 1895.
———. "The Remarkable Case of Davidson's Eyes," *Pall Mall
   Budget*, March 1895.
———. "The Star," *The Graphic, Christmas Number*, 1897.
———. "The Stolen Body," *The Strand*, November 1898.
———. "A Story of the Days to Come," *Pall Mall Magazine*,
   June-October 1899.
———. "The Story of the Late Mr. Elvesham," *The Idler*, May
   1896.
———. "A Story of the Stone Age," *The Idler*, May-September
   1897.
———. "The Time Machine" [book publication of this text in
   1895].
———. "The War of the Worlds," *Pearson's Magazine*, April-
   December 1897. [book publication in 1898].
———. "When the Sleeper Wakes," *The Graphic*, 9 January-6
   May 1899. [book publication in 1899].
Wertenbaker, G. Peyton. "The Man from the Atom," *Science
   and Invention*, August 1923.
Winn, Charles C. "The Infinite Vision," *Science and
   Invention*, May 1924.
Winsor, G. Macleod. "Station X" [book publication in
   1919].
Wolfe, Charles S. "The Educated Harpoon," *Electrical
   Experimenter*, April 1920.
———. "The Master Key," *Electrical Experimenter*, August
   1920.
———. "'Whispering Ether,'" *Electrical Experimenter*, March
   1920.

The Science-Fiction Solar System

The solar system in premodern science-fiction terms. The bullet • indicates imaginary bodies or phenomena.

The Sun.
•Vulcan or other infra-Mercurian planets. Certain nineteenth-century astronomers claimed to have seen an infra-Mercurian planet, which was named Vulcan by Leverrier; these were probably observational errors.
Mercury.
Venus.
•Planets or planetoids between Venus and the Earth.
Earth.
    Satellite: Luna, the Moon
    •Secondary moons
    •Internal sun inside hollow Earth
    •Internal planets inside hollow Earth
    •Skyland; various semimaterial layers above or spheres around the Earth. This is often identified with the Heaviside layer.
•Counter-Earth. A planet set in Earth's orbit exactly on the opposite side of the Sun.
•A planet "behind the Earth."
Mars.
    Satellite: Phobos
    Satellite: Deimos
    •Other satellites
•Counter-Mars. A planet set in Mars's orbit exactly on the opposite side of the Sun.
The asteroids. Asteroids or minor planets include Astraea, Ceres, Eros, Juno, Pallas, and Vesta. More than 400 asteroids were known at this time, but only a few were used fictionally. The orbits of most of the asteroids lie between Mars and Jupiter, but some are very eccentric, Eros passing close to Earth.
•Bodia. The fifth planet in the place postulated by Bode's Law (stated 1772), now occupied by the asteroids. According to early theory, the asteroids were the result of Bodia's fragmentation. In one story (#569) both Bodia and the asteroids still exist. In another (#1451) the major part of Bodia was knocked out of place and became Pluto.
Jupiter.
    Satellite 1, or Io (the second largest satellite)
    Satellite 2, or Europa
    Satellite 3, or Ganymede (the largest satellite)
    Satellite 4, or Callisto. The first four satellites are grouped as the Galilean satellites.
    Satellites 5 on are not named.
Saturn:
    Satellite: Mimas
    Satellite: Enceladus
    Satellite: Tethys
    Satellite: Dione
    Satellite: Rhea
    Satellite: Titan
    Satellite: Hyperion
    Satellite: Iapetus
    Satellite: Phoebe
Uranus:
    Satellite: Ariel
    Satellite: Umbriel
    Satellite: Oberon
    Satellite: Titania
Neptune:
    Satellite: Triton
    •Other satellites
Pluto: Discovered in 1930.
•Trans-Neptunian fictional ninth planets, occasionally invoked before the discovery of Pluto.
•Trans-Plutonian tenth planet.
•Intrusive planets.
•Intrusive or extra suns.
Meteor swarms.
Cosmic clouds of various sorts. Usually considered in a fantastic, imaginary manner.

Comets.
•Occasional dark planets on an individual basis.
•Space whirlpools.
•Sargasso Seas of space. Places where debris, including stranded spaceships, accumulates.
•Artificial planetoids, satellites, etc.
•Dead zones. Places where gravitational attraction from various bodies meets at equal strength, causing stasis and trapping vessels.

Magazine Histories and Contents

AIR WONDER STORIES

At some time in late Spring 1929, after the loss of his small publishing empire, Hugo Gernsback may well have taken a long look at contemporary aviation technology and the magazine world and decided on something new. (This is all conjecture, of course, to explain history.) Radio had been very successful for him, but radio was moving out of the amateur world. The days of young men carefully winding wire around Quaker Oats boxes (as I remember my father doing) were gone, and the commercial world was now far ahead of the putterer. What was the up-and-coming field, the field likely to explode technologically? The air, notably heavier-than-air flight. Thus, why not combine this new field with scientifiction, which was a proved success, and obtain double the results?

If this was Gernsback's mental diagram, there were, as we can see about 65 years later, several things wrong with it. First, while Gernsback knew practical aspects of electricity and electronics quite well, he did not know aviation and aeronautics. His editor Joseph Kraus knew enough about airplanes to write an occasional popular article in *Science and Invention*, but was by no means a specialist. Second, serious aeronautics was a field in itself, not for amateurs, and the number of young men who were building monoplanes in the family barn was much smaller than those who, ten or fifteen years earlier, had been adjusting the positions of crystals to produce sound. The serious aviation market was limited, and highly competitive, well-produced magazines were already available. Third, as his comments show, Gernsback

had no empathy for readers of the air pulp magazines, which were apparently quite successful in their repeated recapitulation of World War I aerial dogfights against barons of various colors. Fourth, there was the danger that, instead of establishing an enlarged publishing area that would subsume both aviation and science-fiction, Gernsback's approach would create only a small compartment within science-fiction, aviation science-fiction (a term Gernsback used).

This last was what happened. Considering the potential area of general science-fiction, such a delimitation could not help but be crippling. As Gernsback indicated in a reply to a letter in the August 1930 issue of *Wonder Stories*, his magazines *Air Wonder Stories* and *Science Wonder Stories* duplicated each other 90 percent in circulation. While this figure is undoubtedly based on subscriptions rather than newsstand sales (which could not be measured), it is probably generally valid.

Gernsback did not want to imitate *Sky Birds* or similar magazines. As he states in response to a letter in the January 1930 issue of *Air Wonder Stories*: "We were asked [One wonders who asked him. EFB] to put out a regular aviation magazine—but we refused because there is not enough real material possible for one. Any magazine can print a story of a murder or a courtship or a marriage taking place in the air" (p. 669).

As was the case with his other publications Gernsback desperately wanted respectability, which he believed could be obtained by stressing educational value and perhaps a note of prophecy. There is no question but that Gernsback was sincere in believing that science fiction had an

educational value; but he also had to face realities of publishing and financing, and scientific accuracy and educational value often were quietly jettisoned. It would be unjust to call Gernsback a hypocrite because he claimed values that were not present in his magazine, or were present minimally, but it would be fair to say that like many other advertisers of his day, he was somewhat irresponsible and oversold his product greatly.

In his editorial introducing the first issue of *Air Wonder Stories*, Gernsback wrote:

Aviation is no longer a new thought in literature. Over a dozen such magazines testify to this. But practically all of these magazines are of the purely "Wild West"-world war adventure-sky-busting type.

AIR WONDER STORIES imitates no other magazine in print, rather it pioneers into new and higher realms, yet at the same time into a field that is increasing in popularity every year . . . . AIR WONDER STORIES will present SOLELY flying stories of the future, strictly along scientific-mechanical-technical lines, full of adventure, exploration and achieve-ment . . . . Where will aviation be 30 years hence? In 100 years? In 1000 years? AIR WONDER STORIES gives that answer in an unmistakable manner. The reason is that the authors who contribute to this magazine are all trained in science and mechanics. They are the prophets who will mirror the future of aviation better than the best aeronautical authority . . . . I am happy to announce that I have secured the full and enthusiastic cooperation of a number of well-known and outstanding science fiction authors, who have agreed to write for the new magazine. And I am particularly proud and happy to present to the readers of AIR WONDER STORIES the very distinguished aeronautical educators who compose the science-aeronautical talent of our editorial board . . . . [These men] will carefully scrutinize all manuscripts in AIR WONDER STORIES before they are printed, with the object to prevent gross scientific-aviation misinformation from reaching our readers. Our editorial board, then, is a guarantee to our readers that the scientifically impossible will not be published in AIR WONDER STORIES, but that, on the contrary, the educational motif will always be uppermost in our minds. We must instruct while we entertain . . . . I know AIR WONDER STORIES will be one of the most discussed magazines in America. Science Fiction as it will be published in AIR WONDER STORIES already is a tremendous force in America. Everyone talks about aviation and science. This type of story is constantly discussed in the classroom by educators. Teachers encourage the reading of this fiction because they know that it gives the pupil a fundamental knowledge of science and aviation. Likewise parents insist that their children read this type of fiction in preference to the debasing and mischief-creating sex and crime stories. (*Air Wonder Stories*, July 1929, p. 5).

Apart from the abundant wishful thinking in this document, there are several strange passages. First, that Gernsback should denigrate the scientific and engineering establishment as compared with his stable of writers. As a curiosity in ideas, Gernsback's position is suggestive of the concept of *supplément* in Derridan deconstructionism, although neither Gernsback nor the present writer would have accepted the corollaries associated with the idea. Second, that Gernsback should claim to have "well-known and outstanding" science fiction writers with technical backgrounds prepared to write for him. One wonders whom Gernsback meant, if anyone. While several authors who appeared in *Air Wonder Stories* had previously published work, they hardly qualify for such praise: Bob Olsen (five previous amateurish stories), Harl Vincent (four previous beginner's work stories), Edmond Hamilton (known primarily for space operas in *Weird Tales*), and David H. Kéller, M.D. (a very erratic primitive, almost totally without technical knowledge). This is not a strong list. As it turned out, the magazine was very largely written by

young beginners who were often as ignorant of English and story-writing as they were of science or engineering. Third, the stories Gernsback published had little or nothing to do with anticipating future developments in aeronautics. Fourth, the editorial board of scholars who were to "carefully scrutinize all manuscripts in AIR WONDER STORIES" was a myth, not to say hoax. Indeed, occasional letters from members of the expert panel hint most strongly that they had not seen stories. But this was Gernsback's approach, the air of respectability, if not respectability itself.

Just what Gernsback was really aiming at, away from rhetoric and ballyhoo, can probably be determined by the cover art, which would have been focused on potential purchasers. Here, it is obvious that Gerns-back expected support from his science-fiction readers, not aviation enthusiasts. The eleven covers included: two aerial flight platforms, one with people flying with wings; four torpedo-shaped vessels, one bisected by rays, two directing rays downward; a circular city like Jonathan Swift's Laputa, floating in air; a contest cover totally science-fictional, best left to contestants; and a flying circular saw slicing up airplanes in flight. Only one cover, the very last, shows an aviation scene, a man descending in a parachute. Incidentally, these covers were flat and dull compared with the exciting covers that were appearing on, say, *Flying Aces* or *Sky Birds*.

Gernsback was correct, as the correspondence column shows, in expecting support from his science-fiction followers. There are very few letters from people concerned with aviation or aeronautics. Indeed, the majority of letters are from young readers obviously without technical education who are reading for entertainment.

As inducements for the real aviation people, however, Gernsback included departments of air interest. In the early issues there was an aviation quiz, soon dropped. In the last issues there were very short, popular articles on aviation topics. Through all issues ran a question and answer department that did try to answer questions seriously and was well handled, if repetitive, and an aviation section that was totally ineffectual, simply citing publicity articles *in breve*. Also present were book reviews on aviation and scientific topics; these were capable, but short.

As for the fiction that Gernsback published, it was not very good. The outstanding items were two reprint serials, "The Ark of the Covenant" by Victor McClure and "The Flying Legion" by George Allan England, both competent commercial work (despite ethnographic nonsense in England's novel). Henrik Dahl Juve's first story, "The Silent Destroyer" and Bob Olsen's "Flight in 1999" are

curiosities in the manner of Gernsback's "Ralph 124C 41+," a subsubform that we are likely to regard today as unintentionally hilarious. Edmond Hamilton's Fortean "The Space Visitors" is far removed from reality, besides being routine. And Lloyd Eshbach, Raymond Z. Gallun, and Jack Williamson were present with apprentice work.

During the lifetime of *Air Wonder Stories,* three matters of policy were belabored by correspondents and editors. First was the persistent dispute about serials versus short stories, a question that always arose in the early pulp magazines, with no overall solution. Gernsback took the general position of the industry that a cliffhanger encouraged purchase of the next issue.

The second question focused on the delimitation of aviation. Did it include interplanetary (or extraterrestrial) fiction? The correspondence column heavily favored the inclusion of space fiction, but Gernsback needed convincing. "No interplanetarian stories are contemplated at present . . . . It is believed by the editor that *Air Wonder Stories* should concern itself with terrestrial aviation alone" (Reply to letter, September 1929, p. 282). Four months later, however, the situation had changed: "As our correspondent will already have noticed, we are now beginning to publish interplanetarian stories in *Air Wonder Stories* magazine due to the great demand from our readers for this subject" (February 1930, p. 764).

The third question was the possibility of a quarterly publication comparable to *Amazing Stories Quarterly* and *Science Wonder Quarterly*. Reader response was mixed, with many correspondents claiming that they could not afford to buy another magazine, though this comment may not have always been meant seriously. Gernsback hedged, with equivocal comments, but by the May 1930 issue he seems to have been favorable to the idea: "As for the *Air Wonder Quarterly*, we shall get this when we are mechanically able to do so. The publishing of four magazines with the large circulation of *Air Wonder*, is in itself a stupendous task, necessitating an organization not always appreciated by the actual reader." (Reply to letter, May 1930, p. 1041).

The absence of *Air Wonder Stories* from the newsstands on May 10, 1930 must have come as a large surprise to the readership, which had every reason to think that the magazine was sound. In the April and May issues Gernsback was offering $100 in gold for a slogan for the magazine, and in the December 1929 issue Gernsback had been selling enlarged prints of artwork suitable for framing. The "Next Month" column on the contents page of the May 1930 issue lists three stories to be published in the June issue. In addition Gernsback seems finally to have made up his mind to publish a quarterly, a topic that had been bandied back and forth for months. And Gernsback had claimed the magazine was sound, for what that was worth.

The Massacre changed all this. We cannot be precise on dates, but a decision to cancel the June 1930 issue must have been made so late that the text of the May 1930 issue could not be altered. March 1930 seems a likely date for a general upheaval at Stellar Publishing Corporation.

While the euphemism "combining" was presented, in actuality Gernsback killed *Air Wonder Stories*, retaining only a couple of stories that had already been accepted, and discharging several masthead employees. Gernsback, undoubtedly for sales reasons, changed the titles of the sister magazines: *Science Wonder Stories* to *Wonder Stories*, the quarterly *Science Wonder Quarterly* to *Wonder Stories Quarterly*, and the sickly cousin magazine *Scientific Detective Monthly* to *Amazing Detective Tales*. Nowadays this is called consolidation or downsizing.

The suddenness and breadth of this shake-up suggests that the various magazines were not selling as well as Gernsback said or hoped. Was the impetus for change a demolishing tax statement for the year? Was it anticipated competition from the colorful new Clayton *Astounding Stories of Super-Science*? In any case, what with the stock market crash of October 1929, it probably was a fortunate maneuver.

Air Wonder Stories died, but I doubt that it was mourned deeply. For the air-war adventure market Gernsback offered poor merchandise. He charged twenty-five cents per issue, whereas the aviation pulps charged ten cents or fifteen cents. He offered science-fiction instead of the World War I fiction that the market demanded, and his factual material was far inferior to that offered by the aviation pulps, which published interesting historical photographs, issued model-making instructions, provided glossaries of terms, and much else of interest. For science-fiction readers, Gernsback wasted space on aviation material and published weak fiction that he overpraised. *Air Wonder Stories* never accomplished what it set out to do; it was unfocused in what it did and ended as a fractional science-fiction magazine, stodgy and amateurish.

Since it remains a little marginal to the direct science-fiction field, *Air Wonder Stories* has never been collected enthusiastically, and while copies are difficult to find, it has never left the middle-range pulp price range.

Publishing information

Dates shown are masthead issue dates, not calendar dates, unless otherwise noted. Such issue dates are not precise for organizational matters, for changes would have taken place considerably earlier.

Publisher: Stellar Publishing Corporation. Editorial offices, 96-98 Park Place, New York, N.Y.
Company officers:
Hugo Gernsback, president.
I. S. Mannheimer, secretary.
Sidney Gernsback, treasurer.
Staff:
Hugo Gernsback, editor-in-chief.
David Lasser, literary editor July 1929-February 1930; managing editor March-May 1930. Despite his title Lasser was in effect managing editor for all issues.
M. E. Dame, associate editor April-May 1930.
A. L. Fierst, associate editor February-March 1930.
C. P. Mason, associate editor February-May 1930.
Frank R. Paul, art director all issues.
Schedule: Monthly.
Appearance: Tenth of previous month.
Price: 25¢.
Range: July 1929-May 1930. Unfinished business (contests, serial parts) assumed by *Wonder Stories* from June 1930 issue on.
Number of issues: 11.
Size and format: 8 1/2" x 11 3/4." Side stapled, trimmed.
Pagination: 96 pp. in volume sequence.
Artwork: Covers by Frank R. Paul.
Interior artwork mostly Frank R. Paul, but also Jno. Ruger, Leonard, Lumen Winter, S. Strother, and unsigned. Line renderings of authors' photographs signed B, perhaps Walter Blythe.
Departments: Editorials by Hugo Gernsback, all issues.
"What Is Your Aviation Knowledge" July 1929-February 1930.
"Aviation News of the Month." July 1929-April 1930.
"Aviation Forum." September 1929-May 1930.
Book reviews. September 1929-May 1930.
Short articles and fillers. September 1929-May 1930.
"The Reader Airs His Views." July 1929-May 1930.
Advisory panel:
Major William A. Bevan, Air Corps Reserve, Prof. Iowa State U.; Prof. Earl D. Hay, U. of Kansas; Prof. George J. Higgins, U. of Detroit; Prof. Felix W. Pawlowski, U. of Michigan; Prof. John E. Younger, U. of California.

Contents

July 1929. I-1. Cover: Paul.
MacClure, Victor. The Ark of the Covenant (1)
Morrow, Lowell Howard. Islands in the Air

Sykes, Harold S. The Beacon of Airport Seven
Keller, David H., M.D. The Bloodless War
Stone, Leslie F. Men with Wings
[*Miscellaneous.* Editorial: "Air Wonder Stories."]

August 1929. I-2. Cover: Paul.
Juve, Henrik Dahl. The Silent Destroyer
Repp, Ed Earl. Beyond Gravity
Chappelow, Edward E. The Planet's Air Master
MacClure, Victor. The Ark of the Covenant (2)
[*Miscellaneous.* Editorial: "Future Aviation Problems."]

September 1929. I-3. Cover: Paul.
Vincent, Harl. The Yellow Air-Peril
Leitfred, Robert H. Where Gravity Ends
Olsen, Bob. Flight in 1999
Morrow, Lowell Howard. The Air Terror
MacClure, Victor. The Ark of the Covenant (3)
[*Miscellaneous.* Editorial: "Rocket Flying." * Article: "The Airplane of the Future" by Hugo Gernsback. * Letters from author Clare Winger Harris and future author Henry Kuttner.]

October 1929. I-4. Cover: Paul.
Juve, Henrik Dahl. The Sky Maniac
Romans, R. H. Around the World in 24 Hours
Vincent, Harl. Through the Air Tunnel
Harrison, Edward Lee. The Air Spy
Repp, Ed Earl. The Invisible Raiders
Beckwith, O. L. The Robot Master
MacClure, Victor. The Ark of the Covenant (4)
[*Miscellaneous.* Editorial: "Airship vs. Airplane."]

November 1929. I-5. Cover: Paul.
Hamilton, Edmond. Cities in the Air (1)
Wilkins, Ralph W. When Space Ripped Open
Skinner, E. D. Suitcase Airplanes
Repp, Ed Earl. Beyond the Aurora
Williamson, Jack. The Second Shell
Gallun, Raymond Z. The Crystal Ray
[*Miscellaneous.* Editorial: "Airplanes MUST Have Radio." * Letters from authors Clyde Beck, Victor A. Endersby and future author Henry Kuttner.]

December 1929. I-6. Cover: Paul.
Morrow, Lowell Howard. The Blue Demon
Repp, Ed Earl. Flight of the Eastern Star
Ruff, J. W. The Phantom of Galon
Newton, Edsel. Freedom of the Skies
McKay, H. Flannelcake's Invention
Hamilton, Edmond. Cities in the Air (2)
[*Miscellaneous.* Editorial: "Glider Flying."]

January 1930. I-7. Cover: Paul.
England, George Allan. The Flying

January 1930 (*continued*)
    Legion (1)
Repp, Ed Earl. The Storm Buster
Jones, Neil R. The Death's Head Meteor
Johnson, A. H. The Thunderer
[*Miscellaneous.* Editorial: "One Thousand Miles an Hour." * Article: "Airports for World Traffic," by H. Dominik. * Letter from author Harl Vincent.]

February 1930. I-8. Cover: Paul.
Juve, Henrik Dahl. The Vanishing Fleet
Key, Eugene George. The Red Ace
Vanny, Jim. Liners of Space
England, George Allan.   The Flying Legion (2)
[*Miscellaneous.* Editorial: "$300.00 Prize Story Contest." Offers prizes for stories based on cover. * Article: "Berlin to New York in One Hour," by Max Valier. * Letters from authors Frank K. Kelly and Allen Glasser.]

March 1930. I-9. Cover: Paul.
Chappelow, Edward E. The Return of the Air Master
Plunkett, Cyril. The X-Gas
Hamilton, Edmond. The Space Visitors
England, George Allan.   The Flying Legion (3)
[*Miscellaneous.* Editorial: "Future Aviation Problems." * Article: "A Test of Airplane Lightning Hazards" by Walter E. Burton. * Letters from authors Victor A. Endersby, Henry Hasse, and Eugene George Key.]

April 1930. I-10. Cover: Paul.
Morrow, Lowell Howard.   Through the Meteors
Beckwith, O. L. The Heat Ray
McKay, Harold. The Flying Buzz-Saw
Schere, Moses. The Meteoric Magnet
Hamilton, Edmond. Evans of the Earth-Guard
England, George Allan.   The Flying Legion (4)
[*Miscellaneous.* Editorial: "Stations in Space." * Article: "How High Can Man Fly," by Lt. Apollo Soucek. * Letter from author Allen Glasser.]

May 1930. I-11. Cover: Paul.
Chappelow, Edward E. The Air Trap
Kateley, Walter. The Arctic Rescue
Stone, Leslie F. Women with Wings
Eshbach, L. A. The Invisible Destroyer
Repp, Ed Earl. The Sky Ruler
Jackson, Wood. The Bat-Men of Mars (1)
[*Miscellaneous.* Announcement that *Air Wonder Stories* will be combined with *Science Wonder Stories* as *Wonder Stories.* * Letters from authors Victor Endersby and Forrest J. Ackerman. * Wood Jackson's "The Bat-Men of Mars" is continued in *Wonder Stories*, June 1930.]

AMAZING STORIES

Around March 5, 1926, a browser at one of the nation's many newsstands could have seen a large-sized magazine showing on its cover ice skaters against a yellow background in which floated a Saturn-like planetary orb. Two stranded sailing vessels rose out of the ice heaps framing the skaters. This was the first, April 1926, issue of *Amazing Stories.*

Inside were stories by H. G. Wells, Jules Verne, Edgar Allan Poe, three modern reprints, and an editorial by Hugo Gernsback stating purposes and means:

A NEW SORT OF MAGAZINE

ANOTHER fiction magazine! At first thought it does seem impossible that there could be room for another *fiction* magazine in this country. The reader may well wonder, "Aren't there enough already, with the several hundreds now being published?" True. But this is not "another fiction magazine," AMAZING STORIES is a *new* kind of fiction magazine! It is entirely new—entirely different—something that has never been done before in this country. Therefore, AMAZING STORIES deserves your attention and interest.

There is the usual fiction magazine, the love story and the sex-appeal type of magazine, the adventure type, and so on, but a magazine of "Scientifiction" is a pioneer in its field in America.

By "scientifiction" I mean the Jules Verne, H. G. Wells, and Edgar Allan Poe type of story--a charming romance intermingled with scientific fact and prophetic vision.   For many years stories of this nature were published in the sister magazines of AMAZING STORIES—"SCIENCE & INVENTION" and "RADIO NEWS."

But with the ever increasing demands on us for this sort of story, and more of it, there was only one thing to do--publish a magazine in which the scientific fiction type of story will hold forth exclusively. Toward that end we have laid elaborate plans, sparing neither time nor money.

Edgar Allan Poe may well be called the father of "scientifiction." It was he who really originated the romance, cleverly weaving into and around the story, a scientific thread. Jules Verne, with his amazing romances, also cleverly interwoven with a scientific thread, came next. A little later came H. G. Wells, whose scientifiction stories, like those of his forerunners have become famous and immortal.

It must be remembered that we live in an entirely new world. Two hundred years ago, stories of this kind were not possible. Science, through its various branches of mechanics, electricity, astronomy, etc., enters so intimately into all our lives today, and we are so much immersed in this science, that we have become rather prone to take new inventions and discoveries for granted. Our entire mode of living has changed with the present progress, and it is little wonder, therefore, that many fantastic situations--impossible 100 years ago--are brought about today. It is in these situations that the new romancers find their great inspiration.

Not only do these amazing tales make tremendously interesting reading-- they are also always instructive. They supply knowledge that we might not otherwise obtain—and they supply it in a very palatable form. For the best of these modern writers of scientifiction have the knack of imparting knowledge, and even inspiration, without once making us aware that we are being taught.

And not only that! Poe, Verne, Wells, Bellamy, and many others have proved themselves real prophets. Prophesies made in many of their most amazing stories are being realized—and have been realized. Take the fantastic submarine of Jules Verne's most famous story, "Twenty Thousand Leagues under the Sea" for instance. He predicted the present day submarine almost down to the last bolt! New inventions pictured for us in the scientifiction of today are not at all impossible of realization tomorrow. Many great science stories destined to be of an historical interest are still to be written, and AMAZING STORIES magazine will be the medium through which such stories will come to you. Posterity will point to them as having blazed a new trail, not only in literature and fiction, but in progress as well.

We who are publishing AMAZING STORIES realize the great responsibility of this undertaking, and will spare no energy in presenting to you, each month, the very best of this sort of literature there is to offer.

Extensive   arrangements   have already been made with the copyright holders of the entire voluminous works of ALL of Jules Verne's immortal stories. Many of these stories are not known to the general American public yet. For the first time they will be within easy reach of every reader through AMAZING STORIES. A number of German, French and English stories of this kind by the best writers in their respective countries, have already been contracted for and we hope very shortly to be able to enlarge the magazine and in that way present always more material to our readers.

How good this magazine will be in the future is up to you. Read AMAZING STORIES-- get your friends to read it and then write to us what you think of it. We will welcome constructive criticism--for only in this way will we know how to satisfy you. (*Amazing Stories,* April 1926, p. 3).

This editorial provides a fairly clear statement about Gernsback's philosophy of literature, indicating the function it should serve. Scientifiction, to continue the dreadful portmanteau word that Gernsback coined, has three functions: (first) sugar-coated edu-cation into science; (second) inspiration toward a scientific career, though this aspect is developed more strongly in later editorials; and (third) prophecy of future technology.

What, exactly, is the point of such prophecy? Today, we would interpret such a position as "think future," enabling easier adaptation to the coming world. Gernsback may have intended this in part, but, basically, he seems to have believed that mentioning an invention in a story would lead to its creation, with economic advantage to the creator. As he says later: "[T]he serious-minded scientifiction reader absorbs the knowledge contained in such stories with avidity with the result that such stories prove an incentive in starting some one to work on a device or invention suggested by some author of scientifiction." (*Amazing Stories,* June 1926, p. 295).

This stress on invention probably arose from several grounds. Gernsback himself was an inventor and he achieved his first business success with an invention; he thought in such terms. Second, his technical magazines, too, stressed invention per se, with columns about patents and comparable material. Third, invention was still much in the air as a survival of the great outburst at the end of the nineteenth century.

Oddly enough, the first counterattack, in a mild way, on Gernsback's utilitarian position came from one of the authors in the first issue, eighteen- or nineteen-year-old Green Peyton Wertenbaker, who, in a letter in the July 1926 issue of *Amazing Stories,* expressed a poetic point of view basically at variance with Gernsback's, advocating a second of the several possible aesthetics of science-fiction:

Literature of the past and the present has made the mystery of man and his world more clear to us, and for that reason it has been less beautiful, for beauty lies only in the things that are mysterious. Beauty is a groping of the emotions towards realization of things which may be unknown only to the intellect. Scientifiction goes out into the remote vistas of the universe, where there is still mystery and so still beauty.

For that reason scientifiction seems to me to be the true literature of the future. The danger that may lie before AMAZING STORIES is that of becoming too scientific and not sufficiently literary. It is yet too early to be sure, but not too early for a warning to be issued amicably and frankly. It is hard to make an actual measure, of course, for the determination of the correct amount of science, but the aesthetic instinct can judge. (*Amazing Stories,* July 1926, p. 291).

To Wertenbaker's letter Gernsback replied, "These opinions, we believe, state the case clearly. If we may voice our own opinion, we should say that the ideal proportion of a scientifiction story should be seventy-five per cent literature interwoven with twenty-five per cent science."

Gernsback either missed or ignored the whole point of Wertenbaker's aesthetic, that "scientifiction" was concerned with the beauty and mystery of the universe, not with giving inventors ideas or presenting sugar-coated facts to the young. Nevertheless, Gernsback now admits the presence of a fourth ingredient: entertainment.

Reiterations of Gernsback's position occur. "Our most cherished ambition . . . . is to uplift humanity through the means of Science . . . . If AMAZING STORIES is accomplishing this, to ever so little an extent, we feel that its mission is being fulfilled." (*Amazing Stories,* February 1927, p. 1078). And when author E. D. Skinner, after decrying materialism and the quest for gold, asked "Will the presentation of scientifically possible pictures of a better life, even though they be fanciful, help to direct the vision of our race to better things? Is this the underlying *motif* behind AMAZING STORIES?" Gernsback (or his editorial worker) replied "The ideas on which AMAZING STORIES is [*sic*] based include what you designate as motifs. We wish to preach the possibilities of science, and the use of the most vivid imaginings in leading to new discoveries, and to make our readers feel that there is far more ahead of us in the way of scientific achievement than there is in the past" (*Amazing Stories,* August 1927, p. 516). Again, one wonders if Hugo Gernsback missed the point, for Skinner's three stories published in *Amazing Stories* are obvious parodies pouring ridicule on the mentality revealed by Gernsback's novel *Ralph 124C 41+.*

Did Gernsback really mean what he proclaimed? As has been stated in more detail in the biographical sketch accompanying his fiction, on one level he did, and on another level he did not. His whole life shows a devotion to science and perfectibility, yet he was always ready to qualify this or negate it, should circumstances render this desirable. Certainly none of the fiction he published fulfilled his

statements of purpose, and much was absurdly discordant.

Amazing Stories seems to have been reasonably successful, though not the runaway that is often claimed. As Gernsback states in his editorial "A Different Story" in the August 1927 issue:

Now that AMAZING STORIES has put the first year safely behind it, it is safe to say that the magazine has definitely 'arrived.' Much work, however, is still left to be done . . . . While the experimental period is over, and the magazine is on a fair road to success, much ground has yet to be covered. For one thing, the magazine is not yet on a paying basis, notwithstanding the fact that 150,000 copies are printed monthly. The expense of publishing and distributing the magazine and placing it on some 30,000 newsstands throughout the country is enormous . . . . while AMAZING STORIES now enjoys the confidence of a few advertisers, much remains to be done. Not until the magazine has some twenty or thirty pages of advertising will it be possible to realize a profit on the publication . . . . When we print 150,000 magazines, that does not mean that 150,000 are sold. The publishers [really the distributors, E.F.B.] put out their magazines on the newsstands, and only those that are sold are paid for. Those that are not sold are returned for credit. (August 1927, p. 421).

Gernsback now offers to send free copies of such returns to persons suggested by the readers. While this is a promotional tactic, the suggestion is that Gernsback, to obtain a cheaper price per unit, has been overprinting, for from what one can judge at this distance in time, 100,000 would have been a more realistic figure. Such overprinting may have been one factor in his financial debacle about a year and a half later. (It might be added that the print order for *Amazing*'s companion magazine *Science and Invention* was also 150,000, but *Science and Invention* had much firmer sales and usually had more than twenty pages of paid advertising.)

Once *Amazing Stories* was on the stands, Gernsback was faced with the problem of finding suitable fiction. It was one thing to accept an occasional amateurish short story for *Science and Invention* or *Radio News,* or to stretch a short novel there into fifteen installments, as he did with Ray Cummings's "Tarrano the Conqueror" in *Science and Invention;* all this was really lagniappe to technical or news matters. But now Gernsback had to find science-fiction stories that could compete with the general stories in other magazines, and in quantity. And there were no practicing science-fiction authors.

In the pulp world of the early middle 1920s, there were less than a dozen more-or-less professional or semi-professional writers who had significantly written stories that are now considered science-fiction, but were called various other things when they appeared. These were Edgar Rice Burroughs, William Wallace Cook, Ray Cummings, George Allan England, Ralph Milne Farley, Homer Eon Flint, Austin Hall, Murray Leinster, A. Merritt, Talbot Mundy, Victor Rousseau, and Francis Stevens. Somewhat later, coinciding with the first year or two of *Amazing Stories*, Edmond Hamilton and H. P. Lovecraft (writing science-fiction, not supernatural fiction) began to appear in *Weird Tales*.

Most of these writers for one reason or another were not available to Gernsback. Burroughs, by far the most valuable commercially, was soon soured by Gernsback's financial antics in the case of "The Master Mind of Mars" and wouldn't deal with him any further. (Details are given in the magazine history for *Amazing Stories Annual*.) In any case, Gernsback probably couldn't have afforded Burroughs's work. Cook had shifted to general fiction; his major fantastic fiction had been a decade or two earlier. Cummings, whose work Gernsback had published in his technical magazines, was more interested in writing mystery fiction and adventure than in science-fiction until the editors at Clayton *Astounding Stories* began a higher rate of payment than Gernsback offered. England had stopped writing science-fiction, although Gernsback reprinted one story that had appeared in *Science and Invention*. Farley was concentrating on the profitable Munsey magazines. Flint had died, although Gernsback obtained a weak posthumous story of his. Hall, with one later exception, was not writing fantastic fiction any more. Murray Leinster, the most dependable of the lot, after Gernsback reprinted three early stories, was apparently not interested in dealing with him; there are hints (described in the history of *Amazing Stories Annual*) of disagreement. In any case he was earning much more money (and undoubtedly had less difficulty collecting) from the adventure pulps. Merritt, next to Burroughs and Mundy the most saleable author, was unobtainable except in reprint, since he was a spasmodic writer and was busied with subediting the *American Weekly*. Talbot Mundy, most of whose work appeared in *Adventure*, was moving away from science-fictional elements into historical fiction and occultism, and would soon as good as retire from pulp fiction. In any case, Gernsback could not have afforded his work. Victor Rousseau, for reasons not known, never sold anything to Gernsback, although Gernsback at one time expressed interest in reprinting Rousseau's finest work, *The Messiah of the Cylinder*; but Rousseau did sell science-fiction later to

the higher-paying Munsey and Clayton magazines. And Francis Stevens, although her last story, "Sunfire," had appeared in *Weird Tales* in 1923, had stopped writing. Of the two late comers, Hamilton sold fiction to Gernsback on a special arrangement of twenty-five dollars per story, whereas Lovecraft, who had a strong, enthusiastic following, was driven away, as is generally known, by Gernsback's shabby treatment.

This left reprints as an immediate source of fiction. The older reprints, like Poe, Verne, and Wells, were cheaper than contemporary original fiction, and thus were desirable from a publisher's point of view. But they had the limitations of being dated and sometimes familiar to the audience, and, in Wells's case, of an active author who guarded his rights. Nevertheless, in the thirty-seven issues of *Amazing Stories* that Gernsback published, he reprinted twenty-three stories by Wells, seven by Jules Verne, and six by Edgar Allan Poe. A story or serial part by Wells appeared in each of the first twenty-nine issues of the magazine.

Gernsback also raided his own popular technical magazines for suitable fiction, picking up eighteen stories from the *Electrical Experimenter, Modern Electrics, Practical Electrics, Radio News,* and *Science and Invention*. These stories, with the exception of Gelett Burgess's non-science-fiction "Solander's Radio Tomb," were undistinguished, primitive even when they were published. On a higher level were reprints from various outside sources by Edgar Rice Burroughs, Garrett P. Serviss, Murray Leinster, A. Merritt, and Julian Huxley.

In his editorial "Idle Thoughts of a Busy Editor" in the March 1927 issue of *Amazing Stories*, Gernsback, after commenting on the fact that readers' critical opinion was usually evenly divided for and against individual stories, said:

Having made scientifiction a hobby since I was eight years old, I probably know as much about it as any one, and in the long run experience will teach just what type of story is acclaimed by the vast majority. Give the readers the very best type of stories that you can get hold of. Try out the best classics first, and get the readers' reactions. When the magazine has been published for a year, you will have a pretty good idea what sort of story makes the greatest appeal" (p. 1085).

Gernsback is also on record as saying that he was familiar with scores of suitable stories for reprint.

In his editorial titled "Thank You!" in the second issue of *Amazing Stories* (May 1926), Gernsback states:

Among the newer works of which we have acquired the publication rights are: "*Die Macht der Drei*" (The Might of the Three) [by Hans Dominik], one of the greatest—and perhaps the greatest—recent scientifiction story; and "*Feuer am Nordpol*" (The North Pole Fire) [by Karl August von Laffert] . . . . "*The Messiah of the Cylinder*" [by Victor Rousseau] is another tremendous story, and then, of course, there is H. G. Wells, with his "*The War in the Air*." (p. 99)

None of these stories ever appeared in *Amazing Stories*.

In Gernsback's employ was Carl A. Brandt, a chemist of German origin, who is said to have had an enormous collection of fantastic fiction in many languages and was acclaimed as a nearly omniscient authority on the earlier field. One might have expected a rich gathering from Brandt.

Yet Gernsback's reprint program soon bogged down, showing no knowledge whatever of the hundreds of earlier stories that he might have reprinted, many of them in the public domain. The conclusion is clear that Gernsback himself knew very little about earlier English-language science-fiction, and that Brandt, despite claims to the contrary, knew little more. Brandt, it might be added, was a weak book reviewer, who on occasion obviously hadn't even read the books he commented on in the early science-fiction magazines.

In the first six months of *Amazing Stories* Gernsback printed thirty-eight stories, six of which were originals. Of these six, Siodmak's "The Eggs from Lake Tanganyika" was new to American readers, but was a translation of a previously published German story.

Gradually, the percentage of new stories rose, but it was not until September 1928 that an issue of *Amazing Stories* consisted solely of new fiction.

An editorial note in the May 1926 issue contains an appeal for reader help and a very unrealistic boast:

Some of our readers seem to have obtained the erroneous idea that AMAZING STORIES publishes only reprints, that is, stories that have appeared in print before. This is not the case. We have a great number of new manuscripts on hand at the present time, and are buying quite a good many more.

Today, more than at any other time, is the day of Scientifiction. Authors, great and small, are taking more and more to this type of fiction, and we are getting an excellent supply of stories right along. Our only problem at the present time is to find room enough to publish all the good ones.

If you or your friends know how to

write a scientifiction story, the editors will be only too glad to look them (*sic*) over. At the present time, only rather short stories are required, as we are well stocked up for some time to come with serials and long stories.

If, on the other hand, you have heard of a good scientifiction story that may have appeared in print at some time or other, and which you think should be published in AMAZING STORIES, we shall be grateful to hear from you. We have an index of most scientific stories that have ever been published, but of course we can not know all of them. If you know of a good one, or have one * in your possession, we will be more than glad to have you send it in, or put us in touch with the persons or parties who have such stories. (p. 135).

In his quest for new material Gernsback inserted advertisements in the writing trade magazines.

AMAZING STORIES—*Experimenter Publishing Company, 53 Park Place, New York,* the first issue of which is that for April, will print nothing but the Jules Verne and H. G. Wells type of pseudo-scientific stories. The magazine wishes short stories and novels of 'scientifiction' type, and will pay for them at regular space rates. (*The Writer*, April 1926.)

In a later advertisement *Amazing* states its desires:

romances of the future, of interplanetary travel, fourth dimensional, and sometimes prehistoric times, etc. Stories must be based on exact, present-day scientific knowledge. The author may go off into wild flights of the imagination, but must stay within the bounds of plausibility. Short stories are particularly wanted at present (*The Writer*, February 1928).

It is impossible to say whether these advertisements were effective in bringing in stories, but gradually a few new writers, for the most part not pulp writers, began to submit publishable stories. These included Miles J. Breuer, M.D.; Charles Cloukey; Francis Flagg; Walter Kateley; David H. Keller, M.D.; H. P. Lovecraft; Bob Olsen; E. E. Smith, Ph.D.; A. Hyatt Verrill; Harl Vincent; and Jack Williamson. Keller, Smith, and Williamson continued to write beyond our period ending in 1936, while the others dropped away for various reasons.

To a small extent Gernsback established contractual arrangements with certain authors whose work satisfied him. These included Edmond Hamilton (at a later date),

A. Hyatt Verrill, and Dr. David H. Keller. As Keller describes the situation, after submitting "The Revolt of the Pedestrians" to *Amazing Stories*, "Hugo Gernsback seemed to like it, and sent me a contract for ten more stories at $40.00 each. Before I accepted this he raised the offer to $60.00." (Schwartz and Weisinger, "David H. Keller, M.D.," p. 3). Both Keller and Verrill later complained at difficulty in collecting their fees.

In his quest for new writers Gernsback tried promotional tricks. In his technical magazines, he had run many contests, some involving constructions, some more cerebral. *Science and Invention*, for example, was a ready source for skyscrapers, bicycles, and miscellaneous contraptions made out of scrap or waste material. Gernsback now tried a contest. For the December 1926 issue, Frank R. Paul, the alpha artist of the magazine, painted a cover showing an ocean liner or other large sea vessel suspended from a flying globe, while beneath, in a rugged landscape, stood nude women with peculiar growths on their head. A prize of $250 was offered for the best story based on the illustration. Stories were submitted and published, but the results were amateurish and quite bad.

A second contest, finding a logogram for scientifiction, began in the April 1928 issue of *Amazing Stories*. Unquestionably a publicity device, it produced many submissions, from the more acceptable of which artist Paul worked out a design. This symbol, cogwheels controlling a pen became thereby the symbol for scientifiction, still in use today.

In addition to stories, artwork was obviously necessary for a pulp magazine. Gernsback had artists working for his other magazines, and he drew upon them, plus outsiders, for the new magazine. An early pattern established itself: Frank R. Paul, who had often illustrated the fiction in the sister magazine *Science and Invention,* did the covers, while a multitude of other men (and women?) illustrated the stories inside. Paul's cover work was occasionally quite good, within the limits of s-f illustration, but the inside work was weak.

The problem essentially, as Clayton *Astounding Stories* rediscovered, was that there were very few artists capable of illustrating science-fiction. Technical draftsman-artists could not draw human beings or life forms, while artists experienced in pulp action could not draw science-fiction images—machinery, alien environments, or strange beings.

Given the choice, readers obviously preferred science-fiction images, as did (perhaps independently) Gernsback. The result was that Paul (skilled when he took pains with science-fictional motifs) became lead artist. It is not known why Gernsback did not also use Howard V. Brown, who later became cover monopolist for Street and

Smith *Astounding Stories*; Brown, who had done covers for Gernsback's *Science and Invention*, including that for the Scientific Fiction Number of August 1923, was better at the human figure than Paul, and if not on Paul's level in office perspective and other techniques of the architectural draftsman, was perfectly adequate in science-fiction images.

An iconography can be extracted from the early *Amazing* covers. The twelve issues from 1927 (this year has been selected to allow Gernsback and Paul time to stabilize *Amazing*) show the following breakdown:

Action scenes 6
Scientific event scenes 6
Bench scientific apparatus 5
Humans in stress or peril situations 4
Large scientific apparatus 3
Mysterious scenes (to make the reader wonder what is happening) 3
Monsters 1
Disaster scenes 1
Special motifs: submarine 1; dinosaurs 1; man-eating plant 1; spaceships 2; evolved future man 1; space scenes 1

The inside illustrations, based on eighty stories and serial parts, reveal the following pattern:

Action scenes 23
Humans in stress or peril situations 20
Scientific-event scenes 18
Large scientific apparatus 15
Monsters 10
Bench scientific apparatus 9
Strange humanoids 8
Nudity 5 (based on a contest picture, otherwise atypical)
Mystery scenes 4
Disaster scenes 3
Evolved future man 1
Special motifs: rockets 1; spaceships 3; dinosaurs 1; cosmic events 2; space scenes 2; man-eating plant 1; detailed landscapes 6; pictures with no science-fictional reference: 14

Even though stories dictate the illustration in pulp fiction, it is clear from these figures that the concept of science-fiction illustration is not yet precise. Action, stress, and peril rule less than a third of the illustrations; intellectual matters, like large machinery, scientific events, and special motifs like spaceships and cosmic events fare no better. In addition, roughly one-sixth of the stories display illustrations that have no relevance to science-fiction at all and might have appeared in another subfield of pulp fiction. The aesthetic of science-fiction art developed later in various directions.

Gernsback's art stands in direct contrast to the art established in Clayton *Astounding*

Stories in 1930, where there was a conscious aesthetic favoring stress and action.

Altogether Gernsback published thirty-seven issues of *Amazing Stories*, from April 1926 through April 1929, with a total of 203 stories. Over the three years the quality of the stories improved somewhat, but not as much as might have been expected. Only three original stories are remembered: Lovecraft's "The Colour out of Space," Jack Williamson's "The Metal Man," and E. E. Smith and Lee Hawkins Garby's "The Skylark of Space," the last for historical importance, not quality.

The reasons for this established mediocrity are multiple. First, Gernsback and his editorial staff had had no experience with editing a fiction magazine and did not know how to gauge reader reaction. His staff did not have the flair that characterized *Science and Invention*. Second, Gernsback lacked literary judgment; this is the consensus of those who worked with him later, notably David Lasser and Charles Hornig. Unfortunately, his editorial staff—T. O'Conor Sloane, Carl Brandt, and Wilbur Whitehead—also lacked literary judgment. Beginning writers had no possibility of editorial assistance until Gernsback's next enterprise, the *Wonder* magazines, when he hired David Lasser. Further, Gernsback was always torn between ideology, fulfillment, and business convenience. Third, Gernsback pursued a peculiar policy toward authors that mitigated against developing a solid group of men and women who could write science-fiction. On the one hand, throughout his career, he tried, with numerous contests, to attract new writers. On the other hand, he treated authors badly. There have been attempts by apologists to whitewash Gernsback in this respect, but the consensus of authors and early editors is against this. As David Lasser has said, Gernsback took the position that printing an author's work was reward enough. To cite an instance that has been mentioned elsewhere in this study, when *Amazing Stories* was profitable and Gernsback was drawing a salary of $50,000 (equivalent perhaps to $400,000 at present), he would not pay Lovecraft $25 for "The Colour out of Space."

Amazing Stories and its sister magazines seemed to be running smoothly and profitably in early 1929, but with the May issue observant readers may have noticed that Gernsback's name was no longer on the masthead or the cover, even though the publisher was still Experimenter Publishing Co. and the magazine looked much the same as before.

Although New York City newspapers carried the story explaining this change, readers around the country did not know for a time that Gernsback had just been declared bankrupt and had lost his publishing and broadcasting empire.

The story of Gernsback's involuntary bankruptcy and loss of his magazines has been told so many times that it hardly needs more than a brief recapitulation.

In February 1929, following the stock market panics that preceded the Great Depression, three parties, claiming that Experimenter Publications' debits to suppliers far exceeded assets, sued in court to have Experimenter declared in a state of bankruptcy.

Several courses were then open for Gernsback to ward off bankruptcy: playing for time by paying the small amounts the suitors demanded, proving solvency, or obtaining a loan to cover his debts. He did nothing.

The court accepted the bankruptcy and appointed the Irving Trust Company as receiver and trustee. The Irving Trust Company, instead of liquidating Experimenter and disposing of its assets (as happened later when Clayton Publications was declared bankrupt), allowed it to operate while offering it for sale.

Experimenter was purchased by one Bergan A. Mackinnon, who continued publication. One of the sale conditions was that Mackinnon would assume Gernsback's debts and pay certain operating expenses. The total payment by Mackinnon was $336,000 for Gernsback's magazines and publishing properties. That this may have been an overpayment, which succeeding publishers of *Amazing Stories* found difficult to absorb, may be seen by the price that Harry Steeger paid for the far more viable *Adventure* in 1934: about $40,000.

As a result of Mackinnon's purchase of Experimenter, Gernsback's creditors were paid at a very high rate per dollar, ultimately about 85¢ on the dollar. Oddly enough, naive fans have sometimes praised Gernsback for paying his creditors this generously. Actually, Gernsback walked away from his debts, and it was Mackinnon who paid.

These are the recorded facts, but there have been several opposed reconstructions of the situation behind the bankruptcy. Sam Moskowitz, who obtained his information *viva voce* from Gernsback, and various records, has declared that Gernsback was really solvent and that he was pushed into bankruptcy by Bernarr Macfadden, who wanted to acquire *Amazing Stories* and other Experimenter publications.

According to this interpretation Macfadden operated behind the scenes, using dummies. As a historical fact, not speculation, Macfadden later did declare ownership of *Amazing Stories* on a notarized Statement of the Ownership, but this was in September 1931, two and a half years after the bankruptcy.

A contrary interpretation has been put forth by Tom Perry, who interviewed Robert Halpern, the lawyer who conducted the case against Gernsback, and also checked court records. According to Perry, Gernsback could not have been greatly astonished by the court action, for his enterprises were in very bad financial condition. Company assets and capital had been milked and diverted extensively to private use by Gernsback and his fellow stockholders. In addition Gernsback had poured an enormous amount of money into his hobby television and radio stations, all of which operated at a heavy loss, nearly $50,000 per annum for the previous two years. Perry discounts any share by Macfadden in the bankruptcy.

Today, in absence of records and with the death, many years ago, of all parties concerned, it is difficult to decide many points of the detailed arguments between Moskowitz and Perry. It is possible that Macfadden, both for personal and business reasons, moved or urged Gernsback's suppliers to suit, as Moskowitz claims, but it must be submitted that such action by Macfadden would have made little difference, since Experimenter, as Perry has convincingly demonstrated, was obviously no longer viable.

As an example of Experimenter's finances, Hugo Gernsback received an annual salary of $50,000, plus perks, while his brother Sidney received $39,000. Today, Gernsback's salary does not sound impressive, but by the standards of the day, it was very high, especially for a small company. To cite a comparison, the salary of the Governor of New York State, Franklin Delano Roosevelt, was $25,000; that of the Chief Judge of the Court of Appeals, Benjamin Cardozo, was $22,500. The *total* of the salaries of the whole executive of New York State—Governor, Lieutenant Governor, Comptroller, and Attorney General—was only a little more than Gernsback's salary!

Beyond Moskowitz and Perry, however, there is a third interpretation of Gernsback's bankruptcy, according to which Gernsback, gauging well in advance that bankruptcy was impending, prepared for it and even welcomed it, knowing that there was no other way to escape his enormous indebtedness.

There are several pieces of evidence that favor this interpretation. First, Gernsback had been forced by his creditors to accept a resident accountant to check and possibly approve his expenditures. This is hardly the sign of a healthy company. Second, Gernsback had paid up almost all his authors, a most unusual, unaccountable situation for him—unless (one suspects) he wanted to maintain good will for new magazines after *Amazing Stories* collapsed. Third, Gernsback approached patent and copyright lawyers as to whether the name "Science Fiction" would conflict with the previously patented magazine name *Scientifiction*. His lawyers informed him that while Experimenter might make use of "Science Fiction," he personally probably could not. As is obvious, there would have been no reason for such inquiries unless he was planning to start a new magazine called *Science Fiction*. Fourth, Gernsback copied the Experimenter mailing list, even though he denied under oath that he had, and used it to circularize his new ventures, the *Wonder* magazines—a criminal act, though unprovable. Both Moskowitz and Perry accept that he did this. Fifth, Gernsback had a new magazine on the stands two and half months after losing *Amazing*, and two others a month later. This could not have been done without capital, negotiations, stories, and staff.

The result of all this was that Gernsback walked away from his debts, letting the new owner of Experimenter pay them, and was free to start a new series of magazines.

After Gernsback lost the *Amazing* magazines, their editorship was assigned first to Arthur H. Lynch, a professional editor who had served on radio publications and had been an occasional contributor to Gernsback's technical magazines. Exactly what Lynch did in his six months of editorship is not known; possibly, like Gernsback, he had ultimate say over editorial matters, but let the staff continue operations; perhaps he simply reported to Irving Trust. The consensus has been that the real work of the magazine devolved on those members of Gernsback's staff who remained with the magazine, Thomas O'Conor Sloane, Ph.D., Wilbur C. Whitehead, Carl A. Brandt, and Miriam Bourne.

T. O'Conor Sloane (1851-1940), who had been one of the stockholders of Gernsback's Experimenter Company, Inc., and presumably profited nicely from the diversion of operating capital, became masthead editor of *Amazing Stories* with the November 1929 issue, retaining the position until the magazine was sold in mid-1938.

Sloane's inaugural editorial makes clear his basic attitude toward science-fiction:

"AMAZING STORIES"

By T. O'CONOR SLOANE, Ph.D.

AMAZING STORIES is now entering its fourth year. It has attained wide appreciation, and has a large circle of readers, who are its friends in the truest sense. It is a completely new idea, and in the business world, new ideas are recognized as very dangerous. AMAZING STORIES, however, won success from the start. To use an expression which has become a colloquialism, it is something different. The basic idea of the magazine was the publication of fiction, founded on, or embodying always some touch of natural science.

The first issue appeared in April 1926, and contained nothing but reprints of the best scientific fiction of the past. More and more authors have been attracted to AMAZING STORIES as a vehicle for their work, and now we have become virtually a magazine of original stories. Some stories published many years ago are so distinctively good that from time to time we give reprints in our columns. We are now receiving so large a number of excellent stories from authors—many well-known, and many yet to become well-known—that we can be more and more discriminating in our choice.

AMAZING STORIES started as a monthly publication. It made its mark, and the public wanted more, so we heeded the demand, and issued an Annual. But even that seemed insufficient, so we substituted for it a Quarterly issue. And we experienced no difficulty in getting new stories of scientific fiction. We have published many stories on interplanetary travel. This subject remains a great favorite with our readers. Though it appears an impossible achievement, our authors make it a vehicle for much science, astronomical and in other branches. The Fourth Dimension, which is after all to be regarded as a mathematical conception, has been very ingeniously used by some of our writers. From archeology, the science in our stories runs through geology, chemistry, biology, psychology, and others, for the entire field of science is covered in the various stories published in these pages. And it is no wonder.

Among our authors we number chemists, physicians, astronomers, psychiatrists, and other leaders of thought in their scientific fields. To these it is a pleasure we are sure, to enter the realm of fiction, and use their knowledge there, for the instruction, as well as amusement of their readers.

We know our readers take much of the contents of the stories seriously, for we constantly hear from our correspondents that they have been taken well on the road of natural science by reading AMAZING STORIES and AMAZING STORIES QUARTERLY.

The change in editorial management, which this magazine has recently experienced, will result in a great improvement. The editorial policies will suffer no change except in the direction of effecting progressive improvements. It is a pleasure to us to be able to state that some of our better known authors, such as Dr. David H. Keller, Dr. Miles J. Breuer, Harl Vincent, Stanton A. Coblentz, Clare Winger Harris, Edmond Hamilton, Dr. Edward B. [*sic*] Smith, author of "The Skylark of Space," who promises us a sequel soon, Frederick Arthur Hodge, author of "A Modern Atlantis," Earle

(*sic*) L. Bell, and others—are going to stand by AMAZING STORIES and will continue as contributors to the MONTHLY and QUARTERLY. And their efforts, because of the various improvements we have already been able to institute, will, we feel sure, exceed anything they have done in the past.

Our "Discussions" Department, which has acquired much importance on account of the many splendid letters we receive, from which we select the most interesting for publication, will continue intact. Many of the letters are of a high order of merit and often some operate to keep our authors on the straight and narrow path, for it seems no errors in science will escape our readers. This department, like the rest of the magazine, we will endeavor to make better and better.

It is your magazine and we want to keep it your magazine. We can do so only if you will write us your opinions and give us constructive criticism, by which we may be guided. (*Amazing Stories*, May 1929, p. 103.)

It will be observed from this document that Sloane limited science-fiction to fiction "founded on, or embodying, always some touch of natural science." There is no recognition or admission of a fantastic element. Thus, this is not science-fiction, one might say, but "scientific fiction" as Sloane proclaimed in the magazine banderole for years.

Social sciences, biological sciences are excluded, if Sloane's phrase is to be taken literally, although below, Sloane claims to have published stories based on such sciences.

The purpose of scientific fiction, continuing one of Gernsback's themes, is educational or inspirational, leading readers "well on the road to natural science." Such fiction, too, is best written by scientists who take pleasure in both instructing and entertaining their readers. This, of course, is wishful thinking of the most unrealistic sort. Practically no pulp science-fiction of the day, with the exception of John Taine's fiction (printed somewhat later and not originally intended for pulp publication) was written by a "leader of thought."

Sloane's list of distinguished authors, it will be noted, is much more realistic than Gernsback gave in other contexts, but it is not very impressive. Oddly enough, neither Frederick Arthur Hodge nor Earl L. Bell, whom Sloane lists as being prepared "to stand by . . . . and contribute as authors to" *Amazing Stories*, ever appeared again in either *Amazing Stories* or any other science-fiction magazine. And, finally, anathema to science-fiction readers, editor T. O'Conor Sloane, Ph.D., has decried the possibility of space travel!

Most of Sloane's editorship took place when he was over eighty years old. He was a poor editor, perhaps because of his advanced age, and he is usually treated severely in historical accounts. His literary judgment was weak; his estimation of the science-fiction market was unrealistic and unsympathetic; and he was a very bad manager. He often pigeon-holed stories for years before reporting on them. An anecdote concerning Clifford Simak's first story is often repeated. After holding the story for four years without making a report or offering a decision, Sloane rejected it with the comment that it was dated. Another such incident occurred with Malcolm Afford's story "The Ho Ming Gland," which Sloane published after holding it without reporting for three years. He was outraged, after he finally published it, to learn that Gernsback had printed it two years earlier (entirely legitimately).

In his younger days, however, Sloane had been a competent scholar and respected teacher, with a doctorate in chemistry; his books on elementary science and mathematics were very well done. He was also a competent nature artist, with some of his paintings in the American Museum of Natural History.

If incompetent in his old age, he was, nevertheless, a very pleasant man. Frederik Pohl in his *The Way the Future Was* describes Sloane as physically weak and tottery, yet extremely kindly and courteous to young authors. He would come out of his office to greet writers hand-delivering manuscripts. Stanton Coblentz, who worked with Sloane, recalled him as a "scientist who, gray-bearded and with a long serious slender face, had a sense of humor and an affability that were delightful" (Elliot, p. 16). Even the hypercritical Horace Gold referred to him as "a wonderful old man" (Elliot, p. 26). Yet one cannot isolate an editorial personality, as one can with his contemporaries Harry Bates, Hugo Gernsback, Charles Hornig, David Lasser, or F. Orlin Tremaine.

During the eight-and-a-half-year editorship of Dr. Sloane, *Amazing Stories* progressed very uniformly downhill, in what has been called creeping stagnation. Most of the fiction Sloane printed was dull, amateurish, and low level, and some of it, especially geographical novels by Jules Verne, was not even science-fiction. On one occasion, in response to a letter complaining about inappropriate stories, Dr. Sloane went so far as to say that *Amazing Stories* need not confine itself to science-fiction: "Our stories are not necessarily of the science-fiction type" (*Amazing Stories*, December 1936, p. 142).

As *Amazing Stories* crept farther into the 1930s, authors with followings gradually dropped away and moved their work to *Wonder Stories* or *Astounding Stories*. John W. Campbell, Jr., alone remained with

Sloane until fairly late, although his stories in *Amazing Stories* were among his weakest, and it is possible that they were rejected elsewhere. Or, perhaps Campbell, who was a rapid writer, wanted to spread his work about, rather than flood any one market.

Amazing's circulation dropped so far that by 1935 it had shrunk to 20,000, or about a fifth of what was considered adequate in pulp publication. (At this same time, the circulation of *Wonder Stories* was 45,000 and *Astounding Stories*, 65,000. To indicate the fragility of pulp publication: Per the Hoover Report, p. 281-2, nine women's magazines in 1931 exceeded a million copies per month, and five general monthlies, 600,000 an issue. The *Saturday Evening Post, Colliers,* and *Literary Digest* each exceeded a million copies per weekly issue.)

Competition from the new *Astounding Stories*, whether published by Clayton or Street and Smith, to say nothing of Gernsback's loyal following, undoubtedly also hurt *Amazing*.

Today, it seems strange that the owners, no matter what their identity at any given moment, did little to reverse the circulation decline. An obvious step would have been to remove Dr. Sloane, or, if there were sentimental or personal reasons against this, to provide him with an able "assistant" who would really operate the magazine. But the publishers did very little. This is to be contrasted with Gernsback's many attempts to restructure *Wonder Stories* during the Depression Years.

One experiment, perhaps Sloane's, perhaps the publishers', involved a cover change. The artist "A. Sigmond," about whom nothing is known, was assigned to do seven low-cost covers in 1933. These covers, although competent artistically and modern in appeal, were as unsuitable for pulp publication as could be. After the Sigmond episode, covers were reassigned to Morey, who was sometimes colorful and striking. Some damage, however, had undoubtedly been done.

With the October 1933 issue the publishers again attempted to economize. *Amazing Stories* was changed to standard pulp size, 6 3/4" x 9 7/8," untrimmed. The covers were also changed, although it is not clear exactly what was involved technologically. It may have been low-budget color separations or bad plates, but the results were the dullest, grayest, most unappealing covers ever offered to the genre market—it is tempting to say to the pulps. These neutral covers, which amounted to camouflage on a newsstand, continued through the June 1935 issue, after which a new logo was used and somewhat superior coloration. Unquestionably, this printing experiment cost Teck dearly in newsstand purchasers.

If one considers Sloane's *Amazing Stories* as a unit, one must evaluate it as a clumsy, amateurish operation. There are very few highlights, and even these are dim: E. E. Smith's space operas, early work by Jack Williamson, perhaps three or four other stories. More typical is the work of A. Hyatt Verrill, who was past his prime and often irrelevant as science-fiction; Joe W. Skidmore, who was a very bad writer; and Neil R. Jones, who was a bore.

The end of the Sloane period came beyond our time limit in 1938.

Publishing information

Dates shown are masthead issue dates, not calendar dates, except for Statements of the Ownership and elsewhere where calendar dates are specified. Issue dates are not precise for organizational matters, for changes would have taken place considerably earlier.

It should be emphasized that although parent company, company name, company officers, and/or major stockholders changed several times after Gernsback's loss of *Amazing Stories* in February 1929, these changes are not significant for the magazine, since the editorial staff and policy remained essentially the same, despite financial reorganizations. Details have been given, nevertheless, since incorrect data occasionally appear elsewhere.

Publisher:

April 1926-April 1929. Experimenter Publishing Co., Inc. (Gernsback ownership). Editorial offices, 53 Park Place, New York, N.Y. until March 1927, after which, 230 Fifth Ave., New York, N.Y.

May 1929-June 1929. Experimenter Publishing Co., Inc. (under receivership, trusteeship, Irving Trust Company). Editorial offices, 230 Fifth Ave, New York, N.Y.

July 1929-October 1930. Experimenter Publishing Co., Inc. (Mackinnon and Fly ownership). Editorial offices, 381 Fourth Ave., New York, N.Y.

November 1930-August 1931. Radio-Science Publications, Inc. Editorial offices, 381 Fourth Ave., New York, N.Y.

September 1931-July 1932. Teck Publishing Corporation. (Macfadden et al. ownership.) Editorial offices, 350 Hudson St., New York, N.Y.

August 1932-[December 1936 and later] Teck Publishing Corporation. (Ellmaker et al. ownership). Editorial offices, 222 West 39th St., New York, N.Y. until October 1934, after which 461 Eighth Ave, New York, N.Y.

Owners and company officers:

April 1926-April 1929. Hugo Gernsback, president; Sidney Gernsback, treasurer; Robert W. DeMott, secretary (April 1926-April 1928); C. E. Rosenfelt, secretary (May-November 1928). Stockholders include Hugo Gernsback, Sidney Gernsback, T. O'Conor Sloane, and others. After calendar February 20, 1929, Irving Trust Company was receiver in bankruptcy, and after March 28, 1929, trustee.

May 1929-June 1929. Under trusteeship of Irving Trust Company.

July 1929-August 1931. B. A. Mackinnon, president; H. K. Fly, vice president. In a Statement of the Ownership, dated September 29, 1929, B. Mackinnon and H. K. Fly are listed as owners. In a Statement of the Ownership, dated March 27, 1931, R. B. Asmus is added to the list of owners. In a Statement of the Ownership, September 29, 1930, J. T. Van Zile is listed as president. From February to August 1931 the following company officers are listed: W. Z. Shafer, president; Byrd D. Wise, secretary; Laurence A. Smith, treasurer; Guy L. Harrington, vice president.

September 1931-July 1932. The following company officers are listed: Lee Ellmaker, president; Warren P. Jeffery, vice president; William Thompson, treasurer; Wesley F. Pape, secretary. On the masthead for November 1931 Huston D. Crippen is added as vice president. In a Statement of the Ownership dated September 24, 1931, owners are listed as Teck, Bernarr Macfadden, Macfadden Publications, and Orr J. Elder.

August 1932-April 1934. The following company officers are listed: Lee Ellmaker, president; Warren P. Jeffery, vice president; Huston D. Crippen, vice president; P. B. Diffenderfer, treasurer; Abner Germann, secretary. In the June 1933 issue, only Ellmaker, Jeffery, Crippen, and Germann remain. In a Statement of the Ownership dated September 29, 1932, Lee Ellmaker is listed as sole owner.

May-October 1934. The following company officers are listed: Lee Ellmaker, president and treasurer; Abner Germann, secretary.

November 1934-[December 1936]. The following company officers are listed: Lee Ellmaker, president and treasurer; B. M. Holcepl, secretary. In a Statement of the Ownership dated October 1, 1934, Teck and Lee Ellmaker are listed as owners.

Staff:

April 1926-June 1926. Hugo Gernsback, editor; T. O'Conor Sloane, Ph.D., managing editor.

July 1926-November 1928. Hugo Gernsback, editor; T. O'Conor Sloane, Ph.D., managing editor; Wilbur C. Whitehead and C. A. Brandt, literary editors.

December 1928-April 1929. Hugo Gernsback, editor; T. O'Conor Sloane, Ph.D., managing editor; Wilbur C. Whitehead and C. A. Brandt, literary editors; Miriam Bourne, associate editor.

May-October 1929. Arthur H. Lynch, as editor-in-chief May and June; as editorial director, July-October. T. O'Conor Sloane, Ph.D., associate editor; Miriam Bourne, associate editor; C. A. Brandt, literary editor.

November 1929-August 1931: T. O'Conor Sloane, Ph.D., editor; Wilbur C. Whitehead and C. A. Brandt, literary editors; Miriam Bourne, managing editor.

September 1931-November 1931. T. O'Conor Sloane, Ph.D., editor; C. A. Brandt, literary editor; Miriam Bourne, managing editor.

December 1931-November 1932. T. O'Conor Sloane, Ph.D., editor; Miriam Bourne, managing editor.

December 1932-[April 1938]. T. O'Conor Sloane, Ph.D., editor.

Schedule: Monthly, April 1926-August 1935, except for combined August-September 1933. Bimonthly, October 1935-December 1936.

Appearance: Fifth of previous month.

Price: 25¢.

Range: April 1926-[1995].

Number of issues: 120 from April 1926 to December 1936.

Size and format:

April-November 1926. 8" x 11." Side stapled, trimmed.

December 1926-March 1928. 8" x 11." Perfect binding, trimmed.

April 1928-August/September 1933. 8 1/2" x 11 5/8" (more or less). Side stapled, trimmed.

October 1933-December 1936. 6 3/4" x 9 7/8." Side stapled, untrimmed.

Pagination:

April-November 1926. 96 pp.

December 1926-August 1927. 104 pp.

September 1927. 110 pp.

October 1927-March 1928. 100 pp.

April 1928-December 1929. 96 pp.

January-February 1930. 112 pp.

March 1930-August/September 1933. 96 pp.

October 1933-December 1936. 144 pp.

Volume pagination until October 1934. After that, issue pagination.

Artwork:

April 1926-June 1929. Covers by Paul.

July-August 1929. Covers by Hugh Mackay.

September 1929-January 1930. Covers by Wesso.

February 1930-July 1930. Covers by Morey.

August 1930. Cover by Wesso.

September 1930-December 1932. Covers by Morey.

January-July 1933. Covers by Sigmond.

August/September 1933-December 1936. Covers by Morey.

Interior artwork was done by a host of artists, as indicated in the story descriptions in this volume. Paul predominated in the Gernsback period, and Wesso and Morey in the period after Gernsback ceased publishing the magazine. Most of the other artists are no longer remembered, some not even identifiable, but J. Fleming Gould, F. S. Hynd, and Hugh Mackay deserve mention.

Departments:

Editorials by Hugo Gernsback, April 1926-April 1929; by T. O'Conor Sloane, Ph.D., May 1929-[December 1936].

"Discussions." January 1927 on. A letter column.

"What Do You Know?" July 1927-May 1934, except October 1933. Retitled "Science Questionnaire" June 1934 on. A science quiz based on stories.

Book reviews. Intermittently, especially in later years.

Contents

April 1926. I-1. Cover: Paul.

Verne, Jules. Off on a Comet (1)

Wells, H. G. The New Accelerator

Wertenbaker, G. Peyton. The Man from the Atom

England, George Allan. The Thing from —— "Outside"

Hall, Austin. The Man Who Saved the Earth

Poe, Edgar Allan. The Facts in the Case of M. Valdemar

[*Miscellaneous.* Editorial: "A New Sort of Magazine."]

May 1926. I-2. Cover: Paul.

Verne, Jules. A Trip to the Center of the Earth (1)

Poe, Edgar Allan. Mesmeric Revelation

Wells, H. G. The Crystal Egg

Winn, Charles C. The Infinite Vision

Wertenbaker, G. Peyton. The Man from the Atom (Sequel)

Verne, Jules. Off on a Comet (2)

[*Miscellaneous.* Editorial: "Thank You!"]

June 1926. I-3. Cover: Paul.

June 1926 *(continued)*
Wertenbaker, G. Peyton. The Coming of the Ice
Morgan, Jacque. The Scientific Adventures of Mr. Fosdick. Mr. Fosdick Invents the "Seidlitzmobile"
Wells, H. G. The Star
Wolfe, Charles S. "Whispering Ether"
Leinster, Murray. The Runaway Skyscraper
Butler, Ellis Parker. An Experiment in Gyro-hats
Fezandié, Clement. Dr. Hackensaw's Secrets. Some Minor Inventions
Kline, Otis Adelbert. The Malignant Entity
Verne, Jules. A Trip to the Center of the Earth (2)
[*Miscellaneous.* Editorial: "The Lure of Scientifiction."]

July 1926. I-4. Cover: Paul.
Winsor, G. McLeod. Station X (1)
Wells, H. G. The Man Who Could Work Miracles
Morgan, Jacque. The Scientific Adventures of Mr. Fosdick. The Feline Light and Power Co. Is Organized
Serviss, Garrett P. The Moon Metal
Siodmak, Curt. The Eggs from Lake Tanganyika
Gernsback, Hugo. The Magnetic Storm
Poe, Edgar Allan. The Sphinx
Fezandié, Clement. Dr. Hackensaw's Secrets. The Secret of the Invisible Girl
Verne, Jules. A Trip to the Center of the Earth (3)
[*Miscellaneous.* Editorials: "Fiction Versus Facts." "Experts Join Staff of Amazing Stories," with comments about Wilbur C. Whitehead and C. A. Brandt. "Improvements," a discussion of perfect binding, a novelty in pulp publishing.]

August 1926. I-5. Cover: Paul.
Serviss, Garrett P. A Columbus of Space (1)
Wells, H. G. The Empire of the Ants
Morgan, Jacque. The Scientific Adventures of Mr. Fosdick. The International Electro-galvanic Undertaking Corp.
Verne, Jules. Dr. Ox's Experiment
Hasta, M. H. The Talking Brain
Stuart, Albert B., M.D. High Tension
Winsor, G. McLeod. Station X (2)
[*Miscellaneous.* Editorial: "'Impossible' Facts." * Poem: "Aspiration," by Leland S. Copeland."]

September 1926. I-6. Cover: Paul.
Wells, H. G. In the Abyss
Verne, Jules. The Purchase of the North Pole (1)
Locke, Richard Adams. The Moon Hoax
Serviss, Garrett P. A Columbus of Space (2)
Winsor, G. McLeod. Station X (3)

[*Miscellaneous.* Editorial: "Editorially Speaking." * Poem: "A 'Psalm' of Life," by Beta.]

October 1926. I-7. Cover: Paul.
Verrill, A. Hyatt. Beyond the Pole (1)
Wells, H. G. The Island of Dr. Moreau (1)
Snyder, Alexander. Blasphemers' Plateau
Verne, Jules. The Purchase of the North Pole (2)
Serviss, Garrett P. A Columbus of Space (3)
[*Miscellaneous.* Editorial: "Imagination and Reality." * Poems: "Lullaby" and "Hail and Good-By" by Leland S. Copeland.]

November 1926. I-8. Cover: Paul.
Serviss, Garrett P. The Second Deluge (1)
Leinster, Murray. The Mad Planet
Verne, Jules. A Drama in the Air
Verrill, A. Hyatt. Beyond the Pole (2)
Wells, H. G. The Island of Dr. Moreau (2)
[*Miscellaneous.* Editorial: "Plausibility in Scientifiction." * Poem: "Stars," by Leland S. Copeland.]

December 1926. I-9. Cover: Paul.
Wells, H. G. The First Men in the Moon (1)
Balmer, Edwin and MacHarg, William. The Man Higher Up
Kaw. The Time Eliminator
Verrill, A. Hyatt. Through the Crater's Rim
Bissiri, Augusto. The Lord of the Winds
Sargent, Samuel M., Jr. The Telepathic Pick-up
Wolfe, Charles S. The Educated Harpoon
O'Brien, Fitz-James. The Diamond Lens
Serviss, Garrett P. The Second Deluge (2)
[*Miscellaneous.* Editorial: "$500.00 Prize Story Contest." * Poem: "Ascension," by Leland S. Copeland.]

January 1927. I-10. Cover: Paul.
Leinster, Murray. The Red Dust
Verrill, A. Hyatt. The Man Who Could Vanish
Breuer, Miles J. The Man with the Strange Head
Wells, H. G. The First Men in the Moon (2)
Serviss, Garrett. The Second Deluge (3)
[*Miscellaneous.* Editorial: "Incredible Facts."]

February 1927. I-11. Cover: Paul.
Burroughs, Edgar Rice. The Land That Time Forgot (1)
Bishop, Capt. H. G. On the Martian Way
Alexander, W. New Stomachs for Old
Balmer, Edwin and MacHarg, William. The Eleventh Hour
Marcellinus, Ammianus. The Thought Machine

Wells, H. G. The First Men in the Moon (3)
Serviss, Garrett P. The Second Deluge (4)
[*Miscellaneous.* Editorial: "Interplanetary Travel." * Filler "The Red Dust a Fact!" * H.G. Wells—Hell of a Good Fellow—Declares His Son," by H. G. Robison.]

March 1927. I-12. Cover: Paul.
Stribling, T. S. The Green Splotches
Wells, H. G. Under the Knife
Balmer, Edwin and MacHarg, William. The Hammering Man
Huekels, Jack G. Advanced Chemistry
Merritt, A. The People of the Pit
Burroughs, Edgar Rice. The Land That Time Forgot (2)
[*Miscellaneous.* Editorial: "Idle Thoughts of a Busy Editor."]

April 1927. II-1. Cover: Paul.
Verrill, A. Hyatt. The Plague of the Living Dead (misattributed on the contents page to T. S. Stribling)
Wells, H. G. The Remarkable Case of Davidson's Eyes
Keeler, Harry Stephen. John Jones's Dollar
Taylor, Merlin Moore. The White Gold Pirate
Balmer, Edwin and MacHarg, William. The Man in the Room
Simmons, Henry Hugh. Hicks' Inventions with a Kick. The Automatic Self-Serving Dining Table
Poe, Edgar Allan. The Balloon Hoax
Burroughs, Edgar Rice. The Land That Time Forgot (3)
[*Miscellaneous.* Editorial: "The Most Amazing Thing." * Poem: "Superstar," by Leland S. Copeland.]

May 1927. II-2. Cover: Paul.
Merritt, A. The Moon Pool (1)
Gates, Frank. The Man Who Died by Proxy
Wells, H. G. The Time Machine
Prout, Bent. The Singing Weapon
Burch, Walter. The Man Who Was
Gray, Will H. The Star of Dead Love
[*Miscellaneous.* Editorial: "Amazing Creations." * Poem: "Light of Life," by Leland S. Copeland. Letter from author R. V. Happel.]

June 1927. II-3. Cover: Paul.
Wates, Cyril G. The Visitation
Fox, Geo. R. The Electronic Wall
Harris, Clare Winger. The Fate of the Poseidonia
Wells, H. G. The Story of the Late Mr. Elvesham
Sherin, Ronald M. The Lost Comet
Butler, Ellis Parker. Solander's Radio Tomb
Olsen, Bob. The Four-Dimensional Roller-Press
Merritt, A. The Moon Pool (2)

June 1927 (*continued*)
[*Miscellaneous*. Editorial: "The $500 Cover Prize Contest" announcing winners. * Poem: "Secrets Never Told," by Leland S. Copeland. * Letters from authors Allen Glasser and Miles J. Breuer, M.D. * Allegorical drawing by J. M. de Aragon.]

July 1927. II-4. Cover: Paul.
Coder, S. Maxwell. The Ether Ship of Oltor
Verrill, A. Hyatt. The Voice from the Inner World
White, Cecil B. The Lost Continent
McRae, D. B. The Gravitomobile
Wells, H. G. The Plattner Story
Poe, Edgar Allan. Von Kempelen and His Discovery
Witwer, Benjamin. Radio Mates
Merritt, A. The Moon Pool (3)
[*Miscellaneous*. Editorial: "Surprising Facts." * Letter from future author A. Bertram Chandler? * Poems: "Planet Neptune to Mother Sun," "Alone," and "Of Their Own Have We Given Then," by Leland S. Copeland.]

August 1927. II-5. Cover: Paul.
Wells, H. G. The War of the Worlds (1)
White, Cecil B. The Retreat to Mars
Skinner, E. D. Electro-Episoded in A.D. 2025
Verrill, A. Hyatt. The Ultra-Elixir of Youth
Simmons, Henry Hugh. Hicks' Inventions with a Kick. The Automatic Apartment
Sears, Edward S. The Shadow on the Spark
Huxley, Julian. The Tissue-Culture King
Thaddeus, Victor. The Chemical Magnet
[*Miscellaneous*. Editorial: "A Different Story." * Letters from authors E. D. Skinner and Allen Glasser.]

September 1927. II-6. Cover: Paul.
Anthos. The Malignant Flower
Kline, Otis Adelbert. The Radio Ghost
Gray, Will H. The Tide Projectile Transportation Co.
Breuer, Miles J., M.D. The Stone Cat
Lovecraft, H. P. The Colour out of Space
Blandford, Chas. G. A Link to the Past
Gernsback, Hugo. The Electric Duel
Wells, H. G. The War of the Worlds (2)
[*Miscellaneous*. Editorial: "The Mystery of Time."]

October 1927. II-7. Cover: Paul.
Cummings, Ray. Around the Universe
Wells, H. G. Aepyornis Island
Gilbert, Kenneth. The Winged Doom
Smith, Garret. Treasures of Tantalus (1)
Regis, Jul. The Paradise of the Ice Wilderness
[*Miscellaneous*. Editorial: "Amazing Youth." * Letter from author Jack Williamson.]

November 1927. II-8. Cover: Paul.
Wells, H. G. A Story of the Stone Age
Verrill, A. Hyatt. The Astounding Discoveries of Dr. Mentiroso
Flagg, Francis. The Machine Man of Ardathia
Smith, Garret. Treasures of Tantalus (2)
[*Miscellaneous*. Editorial: "Space Flying."]

December 1927. II-9. Cover: Paul.
Verne, Jules. Robur the Conqueror (1)
Wells, H. G. The Country of the Blind
Simmons, Henry Hugh. Hicks' Inventions with a Kick. The Electro-Hydraulic Bank Protector
Rodman, J. The Undersea Express
Rector, Charles H. Crystals of Growth
Breuer, Miles J. The Riot at Sanderac
Bauer, George Paul. Below the Infra Red
[*Miscellaneous*. Editorial: "Strange Facts." * Letter from John W. Bell incorporating letter quotation from Edgar Rice Burroughs.]

January 1928. II-10. Cover: Paul.
Hamilton, Edmond. The Comet Doom
Campbell, W. J. The Man on the Bench
Verrill, A. Hyatt. The Psychological Solution
Martin, Harry. Rice's Ray
Wells, H. G. The Stolen Body
Verne, Jules. Robur the Conqueror (2)
[*Miscellaneous*. Editorial: "Our Unstable World."]

February 1928. II-11. Cover: Paul.
Verne, Jules. The Master of the World (1)
Keller, David H., M.D. The Revolt of the Pedestrians
Gernsback, Hugo. Baron Muenchhausen's Scientific Adventures (1)
Wells, H. G. Pollock and the Porroh Man
Olsen, Bob. Four Dimensional Surgery
Speaker, David M. The Disintegrating Ray
Kateley, Walter. The Fourteenth Earth
Alexander, W. The Fighting Heart
McLociard, George. Smoke Rings
[*Miscellaneous*. Editorial: "The New Amazing Stories Quarterly." * Poems: "Cosmic Ciphers," "Ourselves," "Worlds Unknown," by Leland S. Copeland. * Letter from author P. Schuyler Miller.]

March 1928. II-12. Cover: Paul.
Hewelcke, G. Ten Million Miles Sunward
Wells, H. G. The Flowering of the Strange Orchid
Hammond, W. F. Lakh-Dal, Destroyer of Souls
Cloukey, Charles. Sub-Satellite
Verne, Jules. The Master of the World (2)
Gernsback, Hugo. Baron Muenchhausen's Scientific Adventures (2)
[*Miscellaneous*. Editorial: "Amazing Thinking." * Letter from author P. Schuyler Miller.]

April 1928. III-1. Cover: Paul.
Wells, H. G. A Story of the Days to Come (1)
Keller, David H., M.D. The Yeast Men
Aldinger, Harley S. The Way of a Dinosaur
Harris, Clare Winger. The Miracle of the Lily
Grant, Hal. The Ancient Horror
Wolfe, Charles S. The Master Key
White, Cecil B. The Return of the Martians
Gernsback, Hugo. Baron Muenchhausen's Scientific Adventures (3)
[*Miscellaneous*. Editorial: "$300.00 Prize Contest. Wanted: A Symbol for 'Scientifiction.'" * Poem: "When Hearts Remember Home," by Leland S. Copeland. * Article "The Fallacy of 'Ten Million Miles Sunward,'" by Prof. W. J. Luyten.]

May 1928. III-2. Cover: Paul.
Olsen, Bob. Four Dimensional Robberies
Lester, Irvin and Pratt, Fletcher. The Octopus Cycle
Sargent, Samuel M., Jr. Dr. Brittlestone's Method
Poe, Edgar Allan. The Thousand-and-Second Tale of Scheherazade
Flagg, Francis. The Master Ants
Donitz, Harold. A Visitor from the Twentieth Century
Gernsback, Hugo. Baron Muenchhausen's Scientific Adventures (4)
Wells, H. G. A Story of the Days to Come (2)
[*Miscellaneous*. Editorial: "Facts Outfictioned." * Poem: "Our Little Neighbor," by Leland S. Copeland. * Letter from author Allen Glasser.]

June 1928. III-3. Cover: Paul.
Wells, H. G. The Invisible Man (1)
Flagg, Francis. The Blue Dimension
Keller, David H. A Biological Experiment
Vincent, Harl. The Golden Girl of Munan
Gernsback, Hugo. Baron Muenchhausen's Scientific Adventures (5)
[*Miscellaneous*. Editorial: "Our Amazing Minds." * Letters from authors David M. Speaker and Stuart J. Byrne. * Article "An American Jules Verne" about Luis Senarens.]

July 1928. III-4. Cover: Paul.
Cloukey, Charles. Super-Radio
Marius. Vandals from the Moon
Knight, Raymond. Just around the Corner
Olsen, Bob. The Educated Pill
Wells, H. G. The Invisible Man (2)
Gernsback, Hugo. Baron Muenchhausen's Scientific Adventures (6)
[*Miscellaneous*. Editorial: "Our Amazing Senses." * Letter from author Miles J. Breuer, M.D.]

August 1928. III-5. Cover: Paul.
Smith, Edward Elmer and Garby, Lee

August 1928 (*continued*
Hawkins. The Skylark of Space (1)
Kleier, Joe. The Head
Nowlan, Philip. Armageddon—2419 A.D.
Simmons, Henry Hugh. Hicks' Inventions with a Kick. The Perambulating Home
Wells, H. G. The Moth
[*Miscellaneous.* Editorial: "The Amazing Unknown." * Letter from author Miles J. Breuer, M.D.]

September 1928. III-6. Cover: Paul.
Vincent, Harl. The Ambassador from Mars
Meadowcroft, Kirk. The Invisible Bubble
Keller, David H., M.D. Unlocking the Past
Lester, Irvin and Pratt, Fletcher. The Great Steel Panic
Smith, Edward Elmer and Garby, Lee Hawkins. The Skylark of Space (2)
[*Miscellaneous.* Editorial: "Our Amazing Universe." * "Results of $300 Scientifiction Prize Contest" with reproductions of winning entries—symbols or logos for scientifiction. * Poem: "Life," by Leland S. Copeland.]

October 1928. III-7. Cover: Paul.
Harris, Clare Winger. The Menace of Mars
Schlossel, J. To the Moon by Proxy
Jones, Thomas Richard. Reprisal
Scott, E. M. The Voyage to Kemptonia
Smith, Edward Elmer and Garby, Lee Hawkins. The Skylark of Space (3)
[*Miscellaneous.* Editorial: "New Amazing Facts." * Letters from authors Ray Palmer, Jack Williamson, and probably Leslie F. Stone {L. Silberberg} * Fillers "'Tele-vox'—The Mechanical Man" and "Dr. Pavlov and Amazing Stories."]

November 1928. III-8. Cover: Paul.
Wallis, B. and Wallis, Geo. C. The World at Bay (1)
Alexander, W. The Ananias Gland
Keller, David H., M.D. The Psychophonic Nurse
Brueckel, Frank, Jr. The Moon Men
Kateley, Walter. The Eye of the Vulture
Simmons, Joe. The Living Test Tube
[*Miscellaneous.* Editorial "Amazing Life."]

December 1928. III-9. Cover: Paul.
Breuer, Miles J., M.D. The Appendix and the Spectacles
Sloat, Edwin K. Flight to Venus
Williamson, Jack. The Metal Man
Harris, Clare Winger. The Fifth Dimension
Fritchey, Alfred. Before the Ice Age
McLociard, George. Monorail
Rementer, Edward L. The Space Bender
Wallis, B. and Wallis, Geo. C. The World at Bay (2)
[*Miscellaneous.* Editorial: "An Amazing Phenomenon."]

January 1929. III-10. Cover: Paul.
Vincent, Harl. The War of the Planets
Marius. The Sixth Glacier (1)
Watson, George Cookman. Cauphul, The City under the Sea
Colter, Harold Moorhouse. Absolute Zero
Lester, Irvin and Pratt, Fletcher. The Roger Bacon Formula
[*Miscellaneous.* Editorial: "Amazing Reading." * Letter from author Miles J. Breuer, M.D.]

February 1929. III-11. Cover: Paul.
Breuer, Miles J., M.D. The Captured Cross-Section
Wells, H. G. The Lord of the Dynamos
James, Henry. Mernos
Johnson, A. H. Phagocytes
Phillips, Alexander M. The Death of the Moon
West, Wallace. The Last Man
Marius. The Sixth Glacier (2)
[*Miscellaneous.* Editorial: "Life, the Amazing Puzzle." * Letters from authors Samuel Garfinkel, Harold A. Lower, P. Schuyler Miller, and Cecil B. White.]

March 1929. III-12. Cover: Paul.
Verrill, A. Hyatt. Into the Green Prism (1)
Wates, Cyril G. The Face of Isis
Keller, David H. The Worm
Nowlan, Philip Francis. The Airlords of Han
[*Miscellaneous.* Editorial: "Our Amazing Stars."]

April 1929. IV-1. Cover: Paul.
[This is the last issue published under Gernsback's editorship, although the magazine had already changed hands in calendar February.]
Orlovsky, V. The Revolt of the Atoms
McLociard, George. The Terror of the Streets
Breuer, Miles J. Buried Treasure
Verrill, A. Hyatt. Into the Green Prism (2)
[*Miscellaneous.* Editorial: "The Amazing Einstein."]

May 1929. IV-2. Cover: Paul.
[This is the first issue published under the editorship of Arthur H. Lynch, with T. O'Conor Sloane as associate editor.]
Verne, Jules. The English at the North Pole (1)
Coblentz, Stanton A. The Gas-Weed
Ullrich, J. Rogers. The Moon Strollers
Harris, Clare Winger. The Diabolical Drug
Lawrence, Raymond Emery. The Posterity Fund
Wait, Robert A. The Invisible Finite
[*Miscellaneous.* Editorial: "Amazing Stories" gives a pep talk for the new operation. * Letter from author Clare Winger Harris.]

June 1929. IV-3. Cover: Paul.
Coblentz, Stanton A. The Radio Telescope
Hays, Russell. The Beetle Experiment
Wait, Robert A. Clavilux
Verne, Jules. The English at the North Pole (2)
Verne, Jules. The Desert of Ice (1)
Mathison, Volney G. The Mongolians' Ray
Brough, Peter. Fingers of the Mist
Buswell, Louis. Clouds of Death
[*Miscellaneous.* Editorial: "The Romance of Some Thin Wire." * Poem: "Transports of Love," by Bob Olsen. * Letters from authors Frank J. Brueckel, Jr., and Jack Williamson.]

July 1929. IV-4. Cover: Hugh Mackay.
[Some sources incorrectly attribute the cover to Leo Morey.]
Breuer, Miles J. The Book of Worlds
Olsen, Bob. The Superperfect Bride
Keller, David H., M.D. The Flying Fool
Meek, Capt. S. P. Futility
Newton, Edsel. The Space Hermit (as by E. Edsel Newton)
Lester, Irvin and Pratt, Fletcher. Danger
Barnette, Jack. The Purple Death
Verne, Jules. The Desert of Ice (2)
[*Miscellaneous.* Editorial: "Appreciation of the Common."]

August 1929. IV-5. Cover: Hugh Mackay.
[Some sources incorrectly attribute the cover to Leo Morey.]
Vincent, Harl. Barton's Island
Keller, David H., M.D. The Eternal Professors
Click, J. Harold. The Dimension Segregator
Coblentz, Stanton A. The Wand of Creation
Stone, Leslie F. Out of the Void (1)
Clausen, Carl. The Grim Inheritance
Stratton, George Frederick. Sam Graves' Gravity Nullifier
[*Miscellaneous.* Editorial: "Waste Space." Letter from Jerome Siegel, later creator of cartoon "Superman."]

September 1929. IV-6. Cover: Wesso.
[Some sources incorrectly attribute the cover to Frank R. Paul.]
Meek, Capt. S. P. The Red Peril
Bell, Earl L. The Young Old Man
Wates, Cyril G. Gold Dust and Star Dust
Snyder, Alexander. The Coral Experiment
Dressler, Dr. Daniel. The White Army
Alexander, W. The Dog's Sixth Sense
Stone, Leslie F. Out of the Void (2)
[*Miscellaneous.* Editorial: "The Editor and the Reader." * Letters from authors Miles J. Breuer, M.D., and Harl Vincent {Schoepflin} * Poem: "The Triumph of the Machine," by Stanton A. Coblentz. * Story "Almost an Interplanetary Story," by Gor-

September 1929 (*continued*)
don Lane in letter columns.]

October 1929. IV-7. Cover: Wesso.
Verrill, A. Hyatt. Death from the Skies
Alexander, W. One Leg Too Many
Kline, Allen S. and Kline, Otis A. The Secret Kingdom (1)
Wertenbaker, G. Peyton. The Chamber of Life
Kateley, Walter. The Steam God
[*Miscellaneous.* Editorial: "Travel in City Streets."]

November 1929. IV-8. Cover: Wesso.
Vincent, Harl. Microcosmic Buccaneers
Dressler, Dr. Daniel. The Brain Accelerator
Lemkin, William, Ph.D. Cold Light
Hansen, L. Taylor. The Undersea Tube
Irving, Minna. The Moon Woman
Kline, Allen S. and Kline, Otis A. The Secret Kingdom (2)
[*Miscellaneous.* Editorial: "Acceleration in Interplanetary Travel." * Letters from authors Jack Barnette and Harl Vincent {Schoepflin}.]

December 1929. IV-9. Cover: Wesso.
Verrill, A. Hyatt. Vampires of the Desert
Harris, Clare Winger and Breuer, Miles J., M.D. A Baby on Neptune
Vincent, Harl. The Colloidal Nemesis
Rementer, Edward L. The Time Deflector
Slachta, Paul. The Twenty-First Century Limited
Stone, Leslie F. Letter of the Twenty-fourth Century
Kline, Allen S. and Kline, Otis A. The Secret Kingdom (3)
[*Miscellaneous.* Editorial: "The Subdivision of Power." * Letter from author David H. Keller, M.D. * Poems: "The Miracle," by Susie M. Best and "Sonnet to Our Magazine," by Edward Parsons.]

January 1930. IV-10. Cover: Wesso.
Verrill, A. Hyatt. Beyond the Green Prism (1)
Greenfield, Taylor H. The Sword and the Atopen
Campbell, John W., Jr. When the Atoms Failed
Breuer, Miles J., M.D. The Hungry Guinea-Pig
Keller, David H., M.D. Air Lines
Winks, Jack. The First Ornithopter
Skinner, E. D. The Corpse that Lived
Kendig, Julian, Jr. Fourth Dimensional Space Penetrator
[*Miscellaneous.* Editorial: "Calories and Diet." * Poems: "Calories in the Boarding House," by Lonecoast, and "The Sweep of Space," by James A. Terry. * Article "A Few Interesting Comments," by E. E. Free, Ph.D. * Letters from authors Clyde Beck

and Walter Dennis.]

February 1930. IV-11. Cover: Morey.
Vincent, Harl. Explorers of Callisto
Keller, David H., M.D. A Twentieth Century Homunculus
Douglas, William Withers. The Ice Man
Hansen, L. Taylor. The Man from Space
Meek, Capt. S. P. The Radio Robbery
Lemkin, William, Ph.D. Vitamine Z
Pringle, Alfred. Into the Valley of Death
Verrill, A. Hyatt. Beyond the Green Prism (2)
Miscellaneous. Editorial: "Discs." * Letters from authors John L. Burtt, Miles J. Breuer, M.D., and Cyril G. Wates.]

March 1930. IV-12. Cover: Morey.
Williamson, Jack. The Green Girl (1)
Wertenbaker, G. Peyton. The Ship that Turned Aside
Breuer, Miles J., M.D. The Gostak and the Doshes
Vincent, Harl. Callisto at War
Wait, Robert A. Lanterns of God
Eberle, Merab. The Mordant
[*Miscellaneous.* Editorial: "Propulsion and Acceleration in Interplanetary Travel." * Letter from author John W. Campbell, Jr.]

April 1930. V-1. Cover: Morey.
Campbell, John W., Jr. The Metal Horde
Kateley, Walter. Remote Control
Verrill, A. H. The Feathered Detective
Nathanson, Isaac R. The Conquest of the Earth
Cloukey, Charles. Rhythm
Williamson, Jack. The Green Girl (2)
[*Miscellaneous.* Editorial: "Natural Sources of Power." * Letters from authors Miles J. Breuer, M.D., Frank J. Brueckel, Walter L. Dennis with Raymond A. Palmer.]

May 1930. V-2. Cover: Morey.
Hamilton, Edmond. The Universe Wreckers (1)
Cloukey, Charles. Synthetic
Endersby, Victor A. The Gimlet
McNeill, A. M. The Noise Killer
Starzl, R. F. Madness of the Dust
Keller, David H., M.D. The Ivy War
Coblentz, Stanton A. A Circe of Science
Stone, Leslie F. Through the Veil
Hodges, A. L. The Pea Vine Mystery
Hodges, A. L. The Dead Sailor
[*Miscellaneous.* Editorial: Living on the Surface." * Poems: "Vis Scientiae," by Miles J. Breuer, M.D., and "Oh, Ye Fourth Dimension," by A. S. * Letters from authors Miles J. Breuer, M.D., John W. Campbell, Jr., and P. Schuyler Miller.]

June 1930. V-3. Cover: Morey.
Verrill, A. Hyatt. The Non-Gravitational Vortex
Linn, Ralph. Element 87

Campbell, John W., Jr. Piracy Preferred
Hamilton, Edmond. The Universe Wreckers (2)
[*Miscellaneous.* Editorial: "Gas." * Letters from authors Capt. S. P. Meek and Otto Binder.]

July 1930. V-4. Cover: Morey.
Verrill, A. Hyatt. A Visit to Suari
Breuer, Miles J., M.D. The Driving Power
Cloukey, Charles. Paradox +
Heller, Clarence Edward. Flamingo
Speaker, David M. The Message from Space
Hamilton, Edmond. The Universe Wreckers (3)
[*Miscellaneous.* Editorial: "Interplanetary Travel."]

August 1930. V-5. Cover: Wesso.
Smith, E. E., Ph.D. Skylark Three (1)
Hodges, A. L. The Mystery of Professor Brown
Van Dresser, Peter. South Polar Beryllium, Limited
Hamilton, Edmond. World Atavism
Meek, Capt. S. P. The Last War
Peters, Woods. When Inca-Land Revolted
[*Miscellaneous.* Editorial: "The Classic Sciences." * Letters from authors A. W. Bernal and Fletcher Pratt.]

September 1930. V-6. Cover: Morey.
Barclay, Fred M. The Troglodytes
Nathanson, Isaac R. The Passing Star
Putnam, Edmund W. The Translation of John Forsythe
Vincent, Harl. Free Energy
Breuer, Miles J., M.D. The Inferiority Complex
Smith, E. E., Ph.D. Skylark Three (2)
[*Miscellaneous.* Editorial: "The Atom and the Stars." * Letter from author John W. Campbell, Jr.]

October 1930. V-7. Cover: Morey.
Hansen, L. Taylor. The Prince of Liars
Hamilton, Edmond. The Man Who Saw the Future
Peril, Milton R. The Dynasty of the Blue-Black Rays
Kline, Otis Adelbert. The Man from the Moon
Ward, Charles. Written in the Year 2100
Smith, E. E., Ph.D. Skylark Three (3)
[*Miscellaneous.* Editorial: "The Million." * Poem: "Sonnet," by Albert Sidney. * Letters from authors Miles J. Breuer, M.D., Victor Endersby, P. Schuyler Miller, Richard Rush Murray, R. F. Starzl, and Harl Vincent.]

November 1930. V-8. Cover: Morey.
Meek, Capt. S. P. The Drums of Tapajos (1)
Starzl, R. F. The Globoid Terror

December 1930. V-9. Cover: Morey.
Lemkin, William, Ph.D.   The Eclipse Special
Repp, Ed Earl.   The Second Missile
Cloukey, Charles.   Anachronism
Tooke, Alfred I.   Reaping the Whirlwind
Meek, Capt. S. P.   The Drums of Tapajos (2)
[*Miscellaneous.* Editorial: "Inefficiency in Engineering." * Poem: "Sonnet to Science," by Miles J. Breuer, M.D. * Letter from author E. E. Smith, Ph.D.]

January 1931. V-10. Cover: Morey.
Williamson, Jack.   The Prince of Space
Vincent, Harl.   Tanks under the Sea
Bowers, Charles Gardner.   The Black Hand
Bridge, Frank J.   *Via* the Time Accelerator
Garfinkel, Samuel.   The Act of Retipuj
Meek, Capt. S. P.   The Drums of Tapajos (3)
[*Miscellaneous.* Editorial: "The Story of Motors." * Letter from author Miles J. Breuer, M.D.]

February 1931. V-11. Cover: Morey.
McLociard, George.   Television Hill (1)
Gray, Will H.   The Bees from Borneo
Hays, Russell.   The Purple Plague
Verrill, A. Hyatt.   The Exterminator
Collins, W. F.   Twenty Years from Today
Olsen, Bob.   The Man Who Annexed the Moon
[*Miscellaneous.* Editorial: "Weight." * Letters from authors John W. Campbell, Jr., and Walter Dennis.]

March 1931. V-12. Cover: Morey.
Eshbach, L. A.   The Valley of Titans
Breuer, Miles J., M.D.   On Board the Martian Liner
Meek, Capt. S. P.   The Earth's Cancer
Kline, Otis Adelbert.   The Thing That Walked in the Rain
Strathglass, Allan.   The Doctor's Experiment
McLociard, George.   Television Hill (2)
[*Miscellaneous.* Editorial: "Weight in Chemistry." * Poem, "The Evolution of an Ace," by Julia Boynton Green. * Letters from authors John W. Campbell, Jr., and John Russell Fearn.]

April 1931. VI-1. Cover: Morey.
Stone, Leslie F.   Across the Void (1)
Dare, John C.   Cosmic Power
Keller, David H., M.D.   The Ambidexter
Hale, Stephen G.   The Laughing Death
Ernst, Paul.   Hidden in Glass
Gallun, Raymond Z.   Atomic Fire
Vincent, Harl.   Too Many Boards
Schachner, Nat and Zagat, Arthur Leo.   The Menace from Andromeda
[*Miscellaneous.* Editorial: "Errors in Science." * Letter from author E. E. Smith, Ph.D.]

May 1931. VI-2. Cover: Morey.
Miller, P. Schuyler.   Through the Vibrations
Keller, David H., M.D.   The Cerebral Library
Colby, Lincoln S.   The Radio Detective
Kateley, Walter.   Beings from the Boundless Blue
Peters, Woods.   The Great Catastrophe of 2947
Eshbach, Lloyd Arthur.   A Voice from the Ether
Stone, Leslie F.   Across the Void (2)
[*Miscellaneous.* Editorial: "The Curved Earth." * Letters from authors Otto Binder, John W. Campbell, Jr., Alan Connell, and Henry Hasse.]

June 1931. VI-3. Cover: Morey.
Leinster, Murray.   The Power Planet
Ernst, Paul.   The Incredible Formula
Keller, David H., M.D.   Free as the Air
Dutton, Patrick.   The Beautiful Bacillus
Breuer, Miles J. M.D.   The Time Flight
Stone, Leslie F.   Across the Void (3)
[*Miscellaneous.* Editorial: "More about the Moving Earth." * Poem: "Man's Question," by P. Schuyler Miller. * Letters from authors Alan Connell and Mortimer Weisinger.]

July 1931. VI-4. Cover: Morey.
Smith, E. E., Ph.D.   Spacehounds of IPC (1)
Miller, P. Schuyler.   Cleon of Yzdral
Jones, Neil R.   The Jameson Satellite
Kline, Otis Adelbert.   The Metal Monster
Johnson, A. H.   The Raid of the Mercury
Ullrich, J. Rogers.   The Stolen Chrysalis
[*Miscellaneous.* Editorial: "Waves and Rays." * Poem: "The Night Express," by Julia Boynton Green.]

August 1931. VI-5. Cover: Morey.
Meek, Capt. S. P.   Submicroscopic
Bolton, Paul.   The Time Hoaxers
Bauer, E.   The Forgotten World
Colladay, Morrison F.   The Burning Swamp
Johnson, A. H.   The Superman
Smith, E. E., Ph.D.   Spacehounds of IPC (2)
[*Miscellaneous.* Editorial: A Curious Substance. * Poems: "Meteor," by P. Schuyler Miller, and "Evolution," by Julia Boynton Green. * Letters from authors Allen Glasser, William Kober, P. Schuyler Miller.]

September 1931. VI-6. Cover: Morey.
Meek, Capt. S. P.   Awlo of Ulm
Miller, P. S.   The Arrhenius Horror
Gallun, Raymond Z.   The Lunar Chrysalis
Keller, David H.   The Steam Shovel [omitted from contents page]
Smith, E. E., Ph.D.   Spacehounds of IPC (3)
[*Miscellaneous.* Editorial: "Inconsistencies and Contradictions." * Obituary of Wilbur

C. Whitehead. * Letter from author Nat Schachner.]

October 1931. VI-7. Cover: Morey.
Williamson, Jack.   The Stone from the Green Star (1)
Brown, Bernard.   Prima Donna, 1980
Olsen, Bob.   The Master of Mystery
Vincent, Harl.   A Matter of Ethics
Groves, J. W.   The Sphere of Death
[*Miscellaneous.* Editorial: "Iron, the Amazing Metal." * Letter from later editor Charles Hornig.]

November 1931. VI-8. Cover: Morey.
Gelula, Abner J.   Automaton
Keller, David H. M.D.,   The Rat Racket
McKenzie, A. R.   Luvium
Nathanson, Isaac R.   The Antarctic Transformation
Williamson. Jack.   The Stone from the Green star (2)
[*Miscellaneous.* Editorial: "Heavy Stone." * Letters from authors Frank J. Bridge and possibly A. Fedor, cited as A. Feder.]

December 1931. VI-9. Cover: Morey.
Lovering, Paul H.   The Inevitable Conflict (1)
Barry, B. X.   Pirates of Space
Vincent, Harl and Cox, Chas. Roy.   Sky Cops
Kennedy, Fred.   Trial by Television
Scott, E. M.   What Happened to Professor Stockley?
Colladay, Morrison F.   The Blattids
[*Miscellaneous.* Editorial: "The Discs of the Planetary World." * Poem: "The Interplanetary Blues," by Charles Cloukey.]

January 1932. VI-10. Cover: Morey.
Vincent, Harl.   Power
Tanner, Charles R.   Tumithak of the Corridors
Burtt, J. Lewis.   The Lemurian Documents. No. 1—Pygmalion
Lovering, Paul H.   The Inevitable Conflict (2)
[*Miscellaneous.* Editorial: "Motes and Beams." * Letters from authors Forrest J. Ackerman, John Russell Fearn, and Milton Kaletsky.]

February 1932. VI-11. Cover: Morey.
Meek, Capt. S. P.   Troyana (1)
Keller, David H., M.D.   The Pent House
Kalland, John Francis.   The Sages of Eros
Leinster, Murray.   The Racketeer Ray
Jones, Neil R.   The Planet of the Double Sun
Aldinger, Harley S.   The Heritage of the Earth
[*Miscellaneous.* Editorial: "The Brownian Movement." * Letters from author Forrest J. Ackerman and from future author Ross Rocklynne.]

March 1932. VI-12. Cover: Morey.
Flagg, Francis.   The Cities of Ardathia

March 1932 (*continued*)
Johnson, A. H.   The Amir's Magic
Eshbach, L. A.   The Light from Infinity
Burtt, J. Lewis.   The Lemurian Documents. No. 2. "The Gorgons"
Farley, Ralph Milne.   The Degravitator
Meek, Capt. S. P.   Troyana (2)
[*Miscellaneous*.   Editorial: "The Beginning of Chemistry." * Letters from authors Forrest J. Ackerman and Capt. S. P. Meek.]

April 1932.   VII-1.   Cover: Morey.
Breuer, Miles J., M.D.   Mechanocracy
Olsen, Bob.   Seven Sunstrokes
Harris, John Beynon.   The Lost Machine
Wait, Robert A.   Cosmic Steeple-Chase
Meek, Capt. S. P.   Troyana (3)
[*Miscellaneous*.   Editorial: "The Corner-Stones of Chemistry." * Letters from authors Stephen G. Hale, P. Schuyler Miller, Richard Rush Murray, and E. E. Smith, Ph.D.]

May 1932.   VII-2.   Cover: Morey.
Keller, David H., M.D.   The Metal Doom (1)
Jones, Neil R.   The Return of the Tripeds
Breuer, Miles J., M.D.   The Perfect Planet
Burtt, J. Lewis.   The Lemurian Documents. No. 3. Daedalus and Icarus
Corbett, John M.   The Caves of Pele [The contents page lists the author as James M. Corbett.]
Hale, Stephen G.   Worlds Adrift
Aronin, Ben.   The Doubt
[*Miscellaneous*.   Editorial: "The Nationality of Chemistry."]

June 1932.   VII-3.   Cover: Morey.
Edwards, John.   Masters of the Earth
Burtt, J. Lewis.   The Lemurian Documents. No. 4. Phaeton
Lemkin, William, Ph.D.   A Matter of Nerves
Leinster, Murray.   Politics
Keller, David H. M.D.   The Metal Doom (2)
[*Miscellaneous*.   Editorial: "Our Flatland. * Poem: "Red Moon: by V. P. Eberhart. * Letter from author Jack Williamson.]

July 1932.   VII-4.   Cover: Morey.
Vincent, Harl.   Thia of the Drylands
Shurtleff, Bertrand L.   North of Matto Grosso
Burtt, J. Lewis.   The Lemurian Documents. No. 5. The Sacred Cloak of Feathers
Flagg, Francis.   The Resistant Ray
Long, Amelia Reynolds.   Omega
Sanders, Warren E.   Sheridan Becomes Ambassador
Keller, David H., M.D.   The Metal Doom (3)
[*Miscellaneous*.   Editorial: "Cosmogony." * Letters from authors John B. Michel and E. E. Smith, Ph.D. * Also letter from

Professor Donald Menzel.]

August 1932.   VII-5.   Cover: Morey.
Cloukey, Charles.   The Swordsman of Sarvon (1)
Campbell, John W., Jr.   The Last Evolution
Sloat, Edwin K.   Beyond the Planetoids
Kateley, Walter.   Room for the Super Race
Olsen, Bob.   The Purple Monsters
[*Miscellaneous*.   Editorial: "Simple Laws in Science." * Poem: "Red Moon," by V. R. Eberhart. * Letters from authors Henry Hasse and Ray Palmer.]

September 1932.   VII-6.   Cover: Morey.
Williamson, Jack.   The Lady of Light
Skidmore, Joe W.   The Romance of Posi and Nega
Burtt, J. Lewis.   The Lemurian Documents. No. 6. Prometheus
Jones, Neil R.   Suicide Durkee's Last Ride
Cloukey, Charles.   The Swordsman of Sarvon (2)
[*Miscellaneous*.   Editorial: "Lost Motion." * Letter from author Joe W. Skidmore.]

October 1932.   VII-7.   Cover: Morey.
Hamilton, Edmond.   Space-Rocket Murders
Fast, Howard M.   Wrath of the Purple
Stone, Leslie F.   The Man Who Fought a Fly
Melhorn, R. I.   Infra-Calorescence
Binder, Eando.   The First Martian
Reid, J. D.   The Great Invasion of 1955
Cloukey, Charles.   The Swordsman of Sarvon (3)
[*Miscellaneous*.   Editorial: "Friction." * Poem: "Upward," by Donald Hinson. * Letter from author Clark Ashton Smith.]

November 1932.   VII-8.   Cover: Morey.
Lemkin, William, Ph.D.   The Doom of Lun-Dhag
Breuer, Miles J.   The Finger of the Past
Kober, William.   The Man Who Lived Twice
Olsen, Bob.   Captain Brink of the Space Marines
Repp, Ed Earl.   World of the Living Dead (1)
[*Miscellaneous*.   Editorial: "The Rotating Earth." * Letters from authors John B. Michel and Neil R. Jones.]

December 1932.   VII-9.   Cover: Morey.
Dornisch, Alcuin.   Solarius
Keller, David H., M.D.   No More Tomorrows
Podolsky, Edward.   Death by Radio
Vincent, Harl.   Roadways of Mars
Ellis, Sophie Wenzel.   The Shadow World
Crimp, H. M.   The Call to Migrate
Sloat, Edwin K.   The Vibration
Repp, Ed. Earl.   World of the Living Dead (2)

[*Miscellaneous*.   Editorial: "Eclipses of the Sun." * Poem: "From Tales of Specks of Dust," by Max Kaufman.]

January 1933.   VII-10.   Cover: Sigmond.
Verrill, A. Hyatt.   The Treasure of the Golden God (1)
Olsen, Bob.   The Pool of Death
Ryan, Franklin W.   The Last Earl
Morrow, Lowell Howard.   Omega, the Man
Rea, Margaretta W.   Delilah
Murray, Richard Rush.   Radicalite
[*Miscellaneous*.   Editorial: "Bridges and Tunnels." * Letters from authors Allen Glasser and John B. Michel.]

February 1933.   VII-11.   Cover: Sigmond.
Leinster, Murray.   Borneo Devils
Skidmore, Joe W.   Souls Aspace
Afford, Malcolm.   The Ho-Ming Gland
Kendig, Julian, Jr.   The Eternal Mask
Verrill, A. Hyatt.   The Treasure of the Golden God (2)
[*Miscellaneous*.   Editorial: "Some Simple Laws in Nature." * Poems: "Space," by P. Schuyler Miller and "Higher Mathematicians," by E. M. Camp. * Letters from authors Forrest J. Ackerman and Allen Glasser.]

March 1933.   VII-12.   Cover: Sigmond.
Tooker, Richard.   The Tomb of Time
Campbell, John W., Jr.   Beyond the End of Space (1)
Williamson, Jack.   In the Scarlet Star
Murray, Richard Rush.   Stellarite
Collins, Dean.   Stallion's Trappings
Wells, Hal K.   Flame-Worms of Yokku
[*Miscellaneous*.   Editorial: "The Slow Advance of Early Science." * Poem: "Reverie," by Forrest Elliott. * Letter from author John B. Michel.]

April 1933.   VIII-1.   Cover: Sigmond.
Vincent, Harl.   When the Comet Returned
Renshaw, F. Stanley.   Ancients of Easter Island
Sanders, Warren E.   The Memory Stream
Repp, Ed Earl.   The Phantom of Terror
Bird, Roger.   Universal Merry-Go-Round
Bain, Arthur L.   Author's Adventure
Campbell, John W., Jr.   Beyond the End of Space (2)
[*Miscellaneous*.   Editorial: "Heat Engines." * Poem: "Revelation," by V. R. Eberhart. * Letters from authors Forrest J. Ackerman, Frank K. Kelly, and Joe W. Skidmore.]

May 1933.   VIII-2.   Cover: Sigmond.
Verrill, A. Hyatt.   The Death Drum
Jones, Neil R.   Martian and Troglodyte
Miller, P. Schuyler.   Jeremiah Jones, Alchemist
Sloat, Edwin K.   The Three Suns of Ev
Benedict, Jerry.   The Bronze Door
Pearce, George P.   The Girl and the Glacier

May 1933 (*continued*)
Hale, Edward Everett. The Good-Natured
  Pendulum
[*Miscellaneous*. Editorial: "Aluminium." *
Letters from authors John W. Campbell, Jr.
and Richard Rush Murray.]

June 1933. VIII-3. Cover: Sigmond.
Tanner, Charles R. Tumithak in Shaum
Moore, Wm. Russell. Warriors of Zantos
Fearn, John Russell. The Intelligence
  Gigantic (1)
Olsen, Bob. The Crime Crusher
[*Miscellaneous*. Editorial: "Soap Bubbles
and Candles. * Poem: "Prayer of an Elderly
Philosopher," by Pauline E. Thomas. *
Letter from author Ed Earl Repp.]

July 1933. VIII-4. Cover: Sigmond.
Keller, David H., M.D. Unto Us a Child
  Is Born
Gelula, Abner J. Hibernation
Vincent, Harl. Cavern of Thunders
Gallun, Raymond Z. The Flight of the
  RX-1
Fearn, John Russell. The Intelligence
  Gigantic (2)
[*Miscellaneous*. Editorial: "The Candle." *
Letters from authors Forrest J. Ackerman, J.
Harvey Haggard, Franklin W. Ryan, and
Mort Weisinger.]

August-September 1933. VIII-5. Cover:
Morey.
Kostkos, Henry J. The Meteor-Men of
  Plaa
Drennen, Paul. Headhunters Fooled and
  Foiled
Kateley, Walter. Children of the Great
  Magma
Winks, Jack. Adrift on a Meteor
Pragnell, F. The Essence of Life
Ruby, B. F. The Pellucid Horror
Burg, Fritz. The Silicon Empire
Glasser, Allen. Across the Ages
[*Miscellaneous*. Editorial: "Old Time Rail-
roading." * Letters from authors Allen
Glasser, John B. Michel, and Richard
Tooker.]

October 1933. VII-6. Cover: Morey.
Coblentz, Stanton A. The Men without
  Shadows
Arthur, Robert, Jr. Theft of the Wash-
  ington Monument
Burtt, J. Lewis. When the Universe
  Shrank (1)
Keller, David H., M.D. The Tree Terror
Jones, Neil R. Into the Hydrosphere
Speaker, David M. The Supermen
O'Brien, Fitz-James. The Diamond Lens
[*Miscellaneous*. Editorial: "The Early
History of the Electric Light."]

November 1933. VIII-7. Cover: Morey.
Vincent, Harl. Whisper of Death
Bearden, Jack O. The Notorious "C39"
Campbell, John W., Jr. The Battery of
  Hate

Baldwin, Robert. Retribution
Burtt, J. Lewis. When the Universe
  Shrank (2)
Watson, Webster. When the Moon
  Moons
Weisinger, Mortimer. The Price of Peace
Poe, Edgar Allan. Mellonta Tauta
[*Miscellaneous*. Editorial: "Mechanism and
Energy." * Letters from authors Forrest J.
Ackerman, John B. Michel, Milton Kalet-
sky, P. Schuyler Miller, J. L. Winks, and
Donald A. Wollheim.]

December 1933. VIII-8. Cover: Morey.
Jones, Neil R. Time's Mausoleum
Breuer, Miles J., M.D. The Strength of
  the Weak
Olsen, Bob. The Four Dimensional Es-
  cape
Hirsch, Alcan, Ph.D. Within Sight of
  Hell
Kelly, Frank K. Into the Meteorite Orbit
Kline, Otis Adelbert. A Vision of Venus
Verne, Jules. The Watch's Soul
[*Miscellaneous*. Editorial: "Electric Units in
the Home." * Letters from authors Allan
Glasser, Henry Hasse, Kenneth Sterling.]

January 1934. VIII-9. Cover: Morey.
Smith, E. E., Ph.D. Triplanetary (1)
Vincent, Harl. Master of Dreams
Skidmore, Joe W. Adventures of Posi
  and Nega
Keller, David H., M.D. The Lost Lang-
  uage
Nathanson, Isaac. Gold
Doane, Warren F. The Alchemy of Ian
  Bjornsen
Miller, P. Schuyler. The Atom Smasher
[*Miscellaneous*. Editorial: "The Rotating
Earth." * Poem: "In 1999," by Bob Olsen.
* Letters from authors Richard Rush
Murray, Joe W. Skidmore, and Cyril G.
Wates.]

February 1934. VIII-10. Cover: Morey.
Hill, H. Haverstock. Terror out of Space
  (1)
Hawkins, Winthrop W. The Regenerative
  Wonder
Smith, E. E., Ph.D. Triplanetary (2)
Kruse, Clifton B. The Death Protozoan
Nowlan, Phil. The Time Jumpers
Poe, Edgar Allan. A Descent into the
  Maelstrom
[*Miscellaneous*. Editorial: "Lumens." *
Letters from authors Milton Kaletzky and
P. Schuyler Miller.]

March 1934. VIII-11. Cover: Morey.
Smith, E. E., Ph.D. Triplanetary (3)
Olsen, Bob. Peril among the Drivers
Hill, H. Haverstock. Terror out of Space
  (2)
Kostkos, Henry. The Man Who Stopped
  the Earth
Endersby, Victor. A Job of Blending
Poe, E. A. Ms. Found in a Bottle
[*Miscellaneous*. Editorial: "Progress in

Material Economy in the future." * Letters
from authors Forrest J. Ackerman, Frank K.
Kelly, and Festus Pragnell.]

April 1934. VIII-12. Cover: Morey.
Smith, E. E., Ph.D. Triplanetary (4)
Hill, H. Haverstock, Terror out of Space
  (3)
Vincent, Harl. Cat's Eye
Flagg, Francis. The Mentanicals
Poe, Edgar Allan. The Gold-Bug
[*Miscellaneous*. Editorial: "Conic Sec-tions."
* Article: "Why Read AMAZING
STORIES?," by J. E. Reynolds, carried
inside as by Eugene Reynolds. * Letters by
authors J. Lewis Burtt, Alan Connell, and
William Kober.]

May 1934. IX-1. Cover: Morey.
Peril, Milton R. The Lost City (1)
Hill, J. Haverstock. Terror out of Space
  (4)
Verne, Jules. Measuring a Meridian (1)
Winstead, D. E., M.D. The Ultra-
  Gamma Wave
Pratt, Fletcher. Dr. Grimshaw's Sani-
  tarium
Burtt, J. Lewis. The White Dwarf
[*Miscellaneous*. Editorial: "Light Wave
Lengths and Light Years." * Poem: "A
Dream," by Edward Reid. * Letters from
authors John Russell Fearn, Henry Kost-kos,
and Donald A. Wollheim.* Filler "Jules
Verne."]

June 1934. IX-2. Cover: Morey.
Peril, Milton R. The Lost City (2)
Verne, Jules. Measuring a Meridian (2)
Gelula, Abner. Peace Weapons
Rosborough, L. B. Hastings—1066.
Kateley, Walter. Subjugating the Earth
Maughan, Ralph. The Choice
[*Miscellaneous*. Editorial: "Old-Time
Problems in Mathematics." Poem: "Love of
Country," unattributed, but by T. O'Conor
Sloane. * Letters from authors Neil R. Jones
and Donald A. Wollheim.]

July 1934. IX-3. Cover: Morey.
Keller, David H., M.D. Life Everlasting
  (1)
Peril, Milton R. The Lost City (3)
Verne, Jules. Measuring a Meridian (3)
Scheer, George H., Jr. Beam Trans-
  mission
Olsen, Bob. The Four Dimensional Auto-
  Parker
Mills, Charlie. Roadside Strategy
[*Miscellaneous*. Editorial: "Asteroids and
Meteoroids." * Poem: {Untitled, about the
fourth dimension} by Bob Olsen. * Letter
from author Raymond A. Palmer.]

August 1934. IX-4. Cover: Morey.
Keller, David H., M.D. Life Everlasting
  (2)
Verne, Jules. Measuring a Meridian (4)
Skidmore, Joe W. The Velocity of Es-
  cape

August 1934 (*continued*)
Coblentz, Stanton W. In the Footsteps of the Wasp
Kostkos, Henry J. North God's Temple
Nathanson, Isaac R. Shot into Space
Brown, Bernard, B. Sc. Photo Control
[*Miscellaneous*. Editorial: "Old Time Writing—Papyrus and Vellum." * Filler "Otto von Goericke: Phlogiston," by John W. Campbell, Jr.]

September 1934. IX-5. Cover: Morey.
Jones, Neil R. The Moon Pirates (1)
Verrill, A. Hyatt. Through the Andes (1)
Smith, Clark Ashton. The Plutonian Drug
Sonnemann, William K. The Master Minds of Venus
Kaletsky, Milton. The Beam
Vincent, Harl. The Barrier
Matheson, Donald or Florence. The Molecule Trapper
[*Miscellaneous*. Editorial: "Paper and Printing." * Letters from authors J. Lewis Burtt, David H. Keller, M.D., and E. E. Smith, Ph.D.]

October 1934. IX-6. Cover: Morey.
Jones, Neil R. Moon Pirates [sic] (2)
Verrill, A. Hyatt. Through the Andes (2).
Miller, P. Schuyler. The Pool of Life.
Binder, Eando. Eighty-five and Eighty-seven.
Smith, Lawrence. Buried in Space.
[*Miscellaneous*. Editorial: "Type and Printing." * Filler "Cryptography," by C. A. Brandt.]

November 1934. IX-7. Cover: Morey.
Preston, Robert Page. Land of Twilight (1)
Sullivan, H. L. G. The Moon Waits
Olsen, Bob. Noekken of Norway
Skidmore, Joe W. The First Flight
Verrill , A. Hyatt. Through the Andes (3)
[*Miscellaneous*. Editorial: "The Sphere of Vapor." * Letters from authors Richard G. Kerlin and E. E. Smith, Ph.D.]

December 1934. IX-8. Cover: Morey.
Stone, Leslie F. The Rape of the Solar System
Jones, Neil R. The Sunless World
Coblentz, Stanton A. Beyond the Universe
Kostkos, H. J. Men Created for Death
Alexander, W. The Million-Dollar Gland
Preston, Robert Page. Land of Twilight (2)
[*Miscellaneous*. Editorial: "Our Ocean of Air." * Poem: "Across Eternity," by Stanton A. Coblentz.]

January 1935. IX-9. Cover: Morey.
Campbell, John W., Jr. The Contest [sic] of the Planets (1) [later portions were titled "The Conquest of the Planets"]
Nathanson, Isaac R. The World Aflame
Skidmore, Joseph Wm. An Epos of Posi and Nega

Chamberlin, Philip Dennis. The Tale of the Atom
Preston, Robert Page. Land of Twilight (3)
[*Miscellaneous*. Editorial: "Troposphere, Tropopause and Stratosphere." * Poem: "The Radio," by Dix Van Duke.]

February 1935. IX-10. Cover: Morey.
Campbell, John W., Jr. The Conquest of the Planets (2)
Vincent, Harl. Valley of the Rukh
Skidmore, Joseph Wm. Seven Perils to Quiche
Keller, David H., M.D. Island of White Mice
Pratt, Fletcher and Ruby, B. F. The Thing in the Woods
Bartel, Philip Jaques. When Time Stood Still
[*Miscellaneous*. Editorial: "Atmospheric Layers." * Poem: "Who Deserves Credit?," by Bob Olsen. * Letters from author Richard G. Kerlin and from future author Arthur C. Clarke.]

March 1935. IX-12. Cover: Morey.
Kostkos, Henry J. Earth Rehabilitators, Consolidated (1)
Sheridan, Max C. Interference
Jones, Neil R. Zora of the Zoromes
Breuer, Miles J., M.D. Millions for Defense
Repp, Ed Earl. The Body Pirate
Campbell, John W., Jr. The Conquest of the Planets (3)
[*Miscellaneous*. Editorial: "Space Traveling." * Letter from author Joseph W. Skidmore.]

April 1935. X-1. Cover: Morey.
Crimp, H. M. The Mosquito Army
Van Name, E. J. The Sunlight Master
Burtt, J. Lewis. The Martian Mail
Haggard, J. Harvey. Relativity to the Rescue
Kostkos, Henry J. Earth Rehabilitators, Consolidated (2)
[*Miscellaneous*. Editorial: "Leonardo da Vinci." * Poem: "How Inventions Are Born," by Bob Olsen.]

May 1935. X-2. Cover: Morey.
Fearn, John Russell. Liners of Time (1)
Keller, David H., M.D. The White City
Skidmore, Joseph Wm. A Saga of Posi and Nega
Hester, R. Frederick. The Gipsies of Thos
[*Miscellaneous*. Editorial: "Gliding and Soaring." * Filler "The Temperature of Space," by Donald H. Menzel.]

June 1935. X-3. Cover: Morey.
Fearn, James Russell. Liners of Time (2)
Verrill, A. Hyatt. The Inner World (1)
Tooker, Richard. Moon of Arcturus
Hodges, A. L. An Astounding Announcement

Olsen, Bob. Six-Legged Gangsters
Skeen, Ward. 170 Miles a Minute
Walker, Derald S. The Phytic Empire
[*Miscellaneous*. Editorial: "The Old and the New Atom." * Letters from authors J. Harvey Haggard, Tom Olog, and Donald A. Wollheim.]

July 1935. X-4. Cover: Morey.
Fearn, John Russell. Liners of Time (3)
Verrill, A. Hyatt. The Inner World (2)
Jones, Neil R. Space War
Miller, P. Schuyler. The People of the Arrow
Vincent, Harl. Parasite
Cave, Arthur. The Weather Master
[*Miscellaneous*. Editorial: " The Future of Power on Our Earth." * Letter from author P. Schuyler Miller.]

August 1935. X-5. Cover: Morey.
Verrill, A. Hyatt. The Inner World (3)
Fearn, John Russell. Liners of Time (4)
Eshbach, L. A. The Kingdom of Thought
Byrne, James. The Music of the Spheres
Coblentz, Stanton A. The Golden Planetoid
Burtt, J. Lewis. The Never-Dying Light
[*Miscellaneous*. Editorial: "Numbers, Lines, Areas, and Volumes." * Poem: "Evolution," by M. G. Lathrop. * Letters from authors J. Harvey Haggard, J. F. Kalland, and Cyril G. Wates.]

October 1935. X-6. Cover: Morey.
[Note that there is no September 1935 issue.]
Skidmore, Joseph Wm. A Legend of Posi and Nega
Scheer, George H. Another Dimension
Breuer, Miles J., M.D. The Chemistry Murder Case
Collas, Phil. The Inner Domain
Chesnutt, Clara E. Escape from Ceres
Schachner, Nat. World Gone Mad
[*Miscellaneous*. Editorial: "Meters, Barleycorns, Feet, Paces and Other Measurements." * Poem: "Landscapes of Luna," by Bob Olsen. Letter from author Joseph Wm. Skidmore.]

December 1935. X-7. Cover: Morey.
[Note that there is no November 1935 issue.]
Eshbach, L. A. The Meteor Miners
Stone, Leslie F. The Fall of Mercury
Bernal, A. W. Draught of Immortality
Palmer, Raymond A. The Symphony of Death
Kalland, John Francis. Restitution
[*Miscellaneous*. Editorial: "Air and Water."]

February 1936. X-8. Cover: Morey.
[Note that there is no January 1936 issue.]
Skidmore, Joseph Wm. The Maelstrom of Atlantis (1)
Rose, Dr. Walter. The Lurking Death
Brooke, James. Stroheim
Kostkos, Henry J. We of the Sun

February 1936 (*continued*)
Oles, Floyd. Hoffman's Widow
Keith, J. E. "21931"
Endersby, Victor. When the Top Wobbled
Cummings, Parke. Nothing to It
[*Miscellaneous.* Editorial: "Gas Lighting." * Letter from author Robert W. Lowndes.]

April 1936. X-9. Cover: Morey.
[Note that there is no March 1936 issue.]
Hamilton, Edmond. Intelligence Undying
Nathanson, Isaac R. A Modern Comedy of Science
Jones, Neil R. "Labyrinth"
Robin, Ralph. The Pygmies of Phobos
Carlisle, Logan. The Airwayman
Skidmore, Joseph Wm. The Maelstrom of Atlantis (2)
[*Miscellaneous.* Editorial: "The Great and the Small." * Letter from author John Russell Fearn.]

June 1936. X-10. Cover: Morey.
[Note that there is no May 1936 issue.]
Lemkin, William, Ph.D. Beyond the Stratosphere (1)
Olsen, Bob. The Isle of Juvenescence
Burtt, J. Lewis. When the Meteor Struck
McKenzie, A. R. Luvium under the Sand
Chamberlain, J. Leslie. The Sword of Akalah
[*Miscellaneous.* Editorial: "The Ether and Ether Waves." * Poem: "Science and the Saucepans," by Julia Boynton Green.]

August 1936. X-11. Cover: Morey.
[Note that there is no July 1936 issue.]
Hasse, Henry. He Who Shrank
Fearn, John Russell. Subconscious
Breuer, Miles J., M.D. Mr. Dimmitt Seeks Redress
Lemkin, William, Ph.D. Beyond the Stratosphere (2)
[*Miscellaneous.* Editorial: "Atlantis and Its Successors." * Letter from author Thomas S. Gardner.]

October 1936. X-12. Cover: Morey.
[Note that there is no September 1936 issue.]
Campbell, John W., Jr. Uncertainty (1)
Sonnemann, William K. The Council of Drones
Kostkos, Henry J. Six Who Were Masked
Stone, Leslie F. The Human Pets of Mars
Eshbach, L. A. The Outpost on Ceres
[*Miscellaneous.* Editorial: "Analysis and Synthesis." * Letter from author Robert W. Lowndes.]

December 1936. XI-1. Cover: Morey.
[Note that there is no November 1936 issue.]
Bartel, Philip J. The Time Control
Olsen, Bob. The Space Marines and the Slavers
Hamilton, Edmond. Devolution
Wede. Death Creeps the Moon

Vance, Arlyn H. When the Earth Stood Still
Campbell, John W., Jr. Uncertainty (2)
[*Miscellaneous.* Editorial: " Astrology."]

AMAZING STORIES ANNUAL. The Year Book of Scientifiction.

The decision to issue *Amazing Stories Annual* must have been late and hurried, for it was not until early April 1927 that Hugo Gernsback approached Edgar Rice Burroughs for possible fiction, and it was not until the first part of May that an agreement was reached. As late as May 9, 1927, the two men were still discussing the title of the new story—for a magazine that would appear on the stands in about two months, mid-July of the same year.

Gernsback's interest was welcome to Burroughs, who had been unable to sell the novel now known as "The Master Mind of Mars." As Porges has documented, the story had been submitted to the Munsey magazines, where it was rejected, and to Street and Smith's *Popular Magazine*, who also rejected it. Indeed, Burroughs was so desperate to place the story that he offered it free to *Popular Magazine*, with the proviso that he would be paid only if *Popular*'s circulation increased as the result of printing it. Street and Smith was not interested. Burroughs now offered the story to the *Elks Magazine*, which also refused it.

On literary grounds it is not obvious why "The Master Mind of Mars" should have been so universally disliked, for it is no worse than many stories by Burroughs that had been printed, and it is better than some that were to follow. If the romance and adventure are trite, the egotistical Ras Thavas and his bins of human recycling parts are entertaining, and today the satire on the Fundamentalism treasured by the benighted citizens of Phundal is amusing.

If we consider the middle 1920s, however, we may well believe that it was this satirical element that frightened away the pulp editors, who did not criticize the story as a story, but declared it not suitable for their publications. Many of their readers lived in the Bible Belt. In the murky aftermath of the Scopes Trial (July 1925), what with the increasing power of the Fundamentalists, religious satire and contention would have been a topic to be avoided in a pulp magazine. Burroughs probably did not help matters by directly indicating Fundamentalism as his target in the name of the land itself—Phundal.

Thus, Burroughs, who was beginning to have a backlog of rejected fiction, was prepared to cut his price for the story when Hugo Gernsback made overtures, and instead of the 6¢ a word he could have expected from Munsey, Burroughs sold first

periodical publication rights to Gernsback for about 2¢ a word, or $1,250.

The question arises why Gernsback was more courageous than the editors of the large pulp chains. It is a reasonable assumption that his market was not the typical pulp market, but one that overlapped very heavily into the popular science and how-to groups, which were less likely to be Fundamentalist than the Bible Belt reader. Or, it is possible that Gernsback, with his liberal German (Luxembourg) Jewish background and his sympathy with the scientific point of view, may have liked Burroughs's knocks at the fanatics. In later years Gernsback took a pussyfooting position with regard to organized religion, but his sympathies seem obvious.

Needless to say, Burroughs had great difficulty in collecting his payment from Gernsback, who kept sending commercial papers instead of checks. But Burroughs had more power than did beginning authors whom Gernsback was also reluctant to pay, and he finally did collect his fee, plus 7% interest. This experience may have soured Burroughs, for when Gernsback requested reprint rights for the forgotten "Beyond Thirty," Burroughs asked a prohibitive price, and nothing came of the offer.

It was in Gernsback's office that "The Master Mind of Mars" received its final title. Burroughs, while working on it, had provisionally titled the story "A Weird Adventure on Mars," but submitted it to publishers as "Vad Varo of Barsoom." Gernsback suggested "Xaxa of Mars," but when Burroughs gave him permission to finalize a title, settled on "The Master Mind of Mars," as the story has since been known.

The other sales magnet for the *Annual* was two stories by A. Merritt. There is no specific information about Gernsback's dealings with Merritt, but Gernsback's original plan called for only one Merritt story, "The Face in the Abyss," which had been published in *Argosy-All-Story* about four years earlier (8 September 1923). As his blurb for the Annual states: "Then you will also find another story by the versatile master of scientifiction, Mr. A. Merritt, whose "The Face in the Abyss" has not been printed in AMAZING STORIES either. A sequel to this story, by the way, is in preparation now and will be published in AMAZING STORIES at a future date." (*Amazing Stories Annual*, p. 5).

"The Face in the Abyss" was undoubtedly welcomed by readers, since it was otherwise unavailable and not likely to be reprinted, since it was not long enough for separate publication in book form. Oddly enough, as Mort Weisinger reported, "A. Merritt did not know, until your scribe told him so, that his 'Face in the Abyss' was reprinted in Amazing Stories Annual" (*Science Fiction Digest*, October 1933, p. 10). This suggests that Gernsback dealt with Munsey rather than directly with Merritt, although it is conceivable, but not likely, that Merritt forgot the incident.

Gernsback's statement that he would print Merritt's sequel to "The Face in the Abyss" is strange, for, apart from wishful thinking, he should have known that Munsey had an option on the proposed sequel.

Merritt's second story, "The People of the Pit," presumably entered the *Annual* as an emergency filler, since it is not mentioned in the publicity for the *Annual*, even after the *Annual* had been printed:

There has never been presented a more elaborate and thrill-provoking collection of scientific fiction. Included among the famous authors are Edgar Rice Burroughs, author of the famous Martian stories and creator of the Tarzan series; A. Merritt, author of "The Moon Pool," "The People of the Pit," etc.; Murray Leinster, well-known author who needs no introduction to AMAZING STORIES readers for the creation of his hero Burl of "The Red Dust," and "The Mad Planet." (*Amazing Stories*, December 1927, p. 912.)

Gernsback had originally planned to reprint Murray Leinster's "The Runaway Skyscraper," as can be seen by the running head for that story on page 89. This suggests that Gernsback had gone so far as to set the story in type. What went wrong? We do not know, though we might speculate that Leinster refused permission without additional payment or was soured on Gernsback. Leinster does not appear in a Gernsback magazine after the three reprints of 1926 and 1927. In addition to being a capable writer, Leinster was a canny businessman who would not have liked delayed payment.

The other stories in the *Annual* were reprints from *Amazing Stories*. Gernsback claimed, in his editorial, that since back issues of *Amazing Stories* were not available, he was responding to readers' requests with the *Annual*: "In this volume the stories most in demand, and those stories which received the highest number of votes from our readers have been reprinted." This is hard to believe.

Some of these stories were already old when Gernsback reprinted them in *Amazing Stories*. Jacque Morgan's "The Feline Light and Power Company" was originally published in Gernsback's *Modern Electrics* in 1912. Wells's "Under the Knife" dates from 1896, and Austin Hall's "The Man Who Saved the Earth" is reprinted from *All-Story Magazine* of 13 December 1919. It seems unlikely that any of these stories was markedly popular.

Today we think of the *Amazing Stories Annual* as a magazine, a sister publication to *Amazing Stories*. Gernsback, however, did not regard it as a magazine or period-

ical. The subtitle is "The Year Book of Scientifiction" and elsewhere he refers to it as a book (while referring to *Amazing Stories* as a magazine). It is probable that he played with the idea of a series of year books. Such a classification, of course, was odd, since the *Annual* was distributed along with magazines and placed on the stands with magazines. Perhaps it was a question of market reaction: 50¢ was cheap for a book. Publishing whole novels in a single issue of a magazine was not unknown before Gernsback's *Annual*, but in such cases (as with Lippincott and others) such issues were part of a continued serial publication.

As in generally known, *Amazing Stories Annual* was a financial success. Gernsback claimed to have sold all 150,000 copies that were printed, although it is possible that many copies were sold at cut rate or distributed as publicity. This large success, assuming that it is literally true, may have suggested to him that four times as many issues, or a quarterly, might be just as successful four times a year.

Such arithmetic, of course, did not match reality. The *Annual* had a built-in problem; it was very expensive for a newsstand magazine, greatly out of line with the many other pulp magazines. In terms of Gernsback's publications, the *Annual* cost twice as much as the monthly pilot, yet was not much larger—128 pages as opposed to 104 pages.

The *Annual* overcame this problem because of its unusual contents: a new novel by Edgar Rice Burroughs and two stories by A. Merritt. Gernsback could never again put together so strong a magazine with such unique sales appeal.

Publishing information

Dates shown are masthead issue dates, not calendar dates.

Publisher: Experimenter Publishing. Co., Inc. Editorial offices, 230 Fifth Ave, New York, N.Y.
Company officers: Not listed, but presumably the same as for *Amazing Stories*. Hugo Gernsback, president; Sidney Gernsback, treasurer; R. W. DeMott, secretary.
Staff: Not listed, but presumably the same as for *Amazing Stories*. Hugo Gernsback, editor; T. O'Conor Sloane, Ph.D., associate editor; Wilbur C. Whitehead, literary editor; C. A. Brandt, literary editor.
Price: 50¢.
Range: 1927.
Number of issues: 1.
Size and format: 8 1/4" x 11 3/8." Side stapled, trimmed.
Pagination: 128 pp.
Artwork: Cover by Frank R. Paul. Interior art by Paul, Martin Gambee, and

unsigned.
Departments: None.
Comment: Much lower production standards than *Amazing Stories*. Bulked up with a very cheap, thick, stiff paper that is without snap and is almost a thin cardboard. Surviving copies are usually in poor condition.

Contents

AMAZING STORIES QUARTERLY

The founding of *Amazing Stories Quarterly* was caused by optimism and an undoubted overestimation of the market. Gernsback's *Amazing Stories Annual*, with a new novel by Edgar Rice Burroughs and two reprints of stories by A. Merritt, had been so successful that Gernsback decided that it would be profitable to repeat publication, but more frequently. As he says in his first editorial in the new magazine:

In presenting this, the first AMAZING STORIES QUARTERLY, to you, we take it for granted that you are already a regular reader of *Amazing Stories* Monthly. In the two years during which *Amazing Stories* has been published, thousands of readers have voiced the opinion that they would like to see it come out more frequently. Many readers wanted to see it a semimonthly, and some even wanted it each week. These two suggestions, for production and publishing reasons, however, we have found to be an impractical solution to the problem.

Last summer we issued the *Amazing Stories Annual* in which was featured *"The Master Mind of Mars,"* by Edgar Rice Burroughs. This 50¢ Annual enjoyed an excellent reception, and brought forth many letters from readers who enjoyed the book, asking us to publish such a book more frequently.

The result is AMAZING STORIES QUARTERLY, the first issue of which you now have before you . . . . The

Quarterly performs one important duty; it enables us to publish many full length novels, which we know you want, and which, if they were printed in the monthly, would take a good deal of time to publish . . . . We have so many excellent full-length novels on hand which we wish to give our readers that we feel the Quarterly, supplementing the Monthly, will furnish an ideal arrangement.

Since the inception of *Amazing Stories*, a new literature, which we term "Scientifiction," has sprung up, and there are so many excellent short stories, as well as full-length novels, that are at our disposition now, that in the very nature of things, it would take too long if all of them were to be published in the Monthly . . . . Heeding the request of a large number of our readers, we have not included in this Quarterly, any stories that appeared in the regular Monthly publication. All the stories in the Quarterly are brand new, with the exception of "*When the Sleeper Wakes*," by H. G. Wells and "*The Gravity King*" by Clelland J. Ball" (*Amazing Stories Quarterly*, Winter 1928, p. 3).

It should be noted that the statement about Clelland Ball's "The Gravity King" is incorrect; it was not printed until the fourth, Fall 1928, issue. "The Golden Vapor" by E. H. Johnson, which presumably took its place, is a reprint from Gernsback's *Science and Invention*. Further, one wonders what Gernsback had in mind with his comment about so many excellent novels at his disposition. The second, Spring 1928 issue, does not contain a novel, and in the fifth issue, Winter 1929, Gernsback printed his own early work "Ralph 124C 41+." This last selection may have been vanity, lack of material, or perhaps impinging economics, for by the time the magazine was being set up Gernsback must have realized that he was in financial trouble.

In the second issue, Spring 1928, Gernsback indulged in a certain amount of crowing, both economic and nationalistic:

"The Rise of Scientifiction"

Scientifiction may now be said to have arrived with a bang. More and more authors of the better kind are taking to scientifiction as the proverbial duck takes to water. It is a great source of satisfaction to us, and we point to it with pride, that 90% of the really good scientifiction authors are American . . . . In our editorial opinion, our modern authors have far eclipsed Jules Verne and H. G. Wells. We know that is a broad statement, and one of vast import, but it is true, nevertheless. It takes time for a new art to develop and

while we are not as yet at the top, we are slowly getting there, and the movement of scientifiction will sooner or later assume proportions far exceeding the expectations of most of us.

Just as there are cycles in style, there are cycles in literature. During the last few decades, for instance, there were cycles of the exposé story; then we had the boys detective cycle; next the real detective stories; more recently the sex story; and still more recently, the self confession story. Of course, there are many others, but the scientifiction cycle is now in its ascendancy and is growing rapidly. (*Amazing Stories Quarterly*, Spring 1928, p. 3).

Gernsback's comments about cycles of taste are perceptive, but unfortunately premature. It took more than sixty years for the American entertainment industry to catch up with him.

The high point of the Gernsback issues of *Amazing Stories Quarterly* was H. G. Wells's "When the Sleeper Wakes," in which Gernsback followed the earlier text of 1899, rather than the revised 1910 text that appeared under the title *The Sleeper Awakes.* It is somewhat puzzling that Wells, who dealt directly with Gernsback, did not proffer the later, revised text, but perhaps Wells felt there would be a conflict with the Atlantic Edition of *The Works of H. G. Wells,* where the later version was currently in print. In any case, Gernsback's readers did not like the story.

In February-March 1929 Hugo Gernsback and his fellow stockholders lost Experimenter Publishing Company (including the *Amazing* group) in a widely publicized involuntary bankruptcy case. Details are given under *Amazing Stories*, but it may be said in brief that Gernsback was heavily in debt to his suppliers and had insufficient assets. The bankruptcy court assigned Experimenter to Irving Trust Company, which acted as trustee for a few months, then sold the *Amazing* group to one Bergan A. Mackinnon, whose payment cleared Gernsback's indebtedness. The *Amazing* group then passed through several owners until it was taken over by Zipf Davis in 1937.

Gernsback's exit, however, had little immediate effect on *Amazing Stories Quarterly*, which was edited, until its discontinuation in 1934, by T. O'Conor Sloane, Ph.D., who had been Gernsback's associate editor. Sloane continued Gernsback's policy of including one novel and assorted shorter material in the magazine, but with one minor exception did not follow Gernsback's promotional devices of contests, book reviews, science quizzes, question and answer departments, and science news.

Essentially, under Sloane *Amazing Stories Quarterly* drifted along, like the flagship *Amazing Stories* gradually de-

clining in quality, assuming a drabness and stodginess that signalled approaching moribundity. Circulation decreased and advertising, which was always weak, became minimal.

In mid 1932 *Amazing Stories Quarterly* hit financial difficulties. Publication shifted to twice a year, then became irregular. Artwork was cut back, covers simplified, and pagination reduced in the last two issues from 144 pages to 128. The final two issues reprinted stories from previous issues of the quarterly and *Amazing Stories*; some of this was public domain. It is reasonable to assume that the quarterly was never very profitable and may have been carried by the flagship magazine.

In retrospect, it would seem that *Amazing Stories Quarterly* embodied a weak publishing concept. Weekly, biweekly, and monthly magazines imparted a certain purchasing impetus to the reader (especially if serials were involved), which a quarterly lacked. Three months is a long time to be on the alert for an issue. Given the realities of newsstand display, where each magazine had to fight scores of others for visibility and (lamentably) the science-fiction magazines were usually shoved to the side, readers may well have neglected to look for the muted covers of the quarterlies. In such cases, announcements in the flagship magazine would have been perhaps the only reminder.

In content, too, for the contemporary reader, *Amazing Stories Quarterly* was weak. Of the twenty-one lead novels only three or four might have been considered strong from a sales point of view, notably John W. Campbell, Jr.'s turgid, lumpy space operas. Of the eighty-odd short stories and novelettes less than a dozen might have been considered worth reading if one could put oneself back in the 1930s, accepting the standards of the time.

The original novels that today we would consider somewhat memorable for their ideas, the works of Stanton A. Coblentz and John Taine, and Dr. Breuer's "Paradise and Iron," demonstrate a peculiar situation: not strong enough for mainstream fiction, too little action and too much sophistication for pulp.

A further weakness of the quarterlies must have been their 50¢ price, which was high for a Depression Era magazine, especially when, compared to the monthly magazine, it offered only roughly one and a half times the amount of fiction for twice the price. There was also the possibility that if one did not like the feature novel, there was not much else to read in the issue.

Historically, *Amazing Stories Quarterly* offered a mixed bag. Most of the fiction that appeared in it can be forgotten, but there are some moments of interest. Miles J. Breuer, Stanton A. Coblentz, and John Taine showed that it was possible to embody ideas (as opposed to scientific fantasies) in popular fiction, and in at least the cases of Coblentz and Taine the quarterlies brought into publication stories that had been refused elsewhere.

Publishing information

Dates shown are masthead issue dates, not calendar dates, except for Statements of the Ownership and elsewhere where calendar dates are specified. Issue dates are not precise for organizational matters, for changes would have taken place considerably earlier. More information is to be found under *Amazing Stories.*

It should be emphasized that although parent company, company name, company officers, and/or major stockholders changed several times after Gernsback's loss of *Amazing Stories Quarterly* in February 1929, these changes are not significant, since the editorial staff and the policy of the magazine remained essentially the same, despite reorganizations. Details have been given, nevertheless, since incorrect data occasionally appear elsewhere.

Publisher:

    Spring 1928-Winter 1929. Experimenter Publishing Co., Inc. (Gernsback ownership). Editorial offices, 230 Fifth Ave., New York, N.Y.

    Spring 1929-Summer 1929. Experimenter Publishing Co., Inc. (Irving Trust Company, receivership, trustee in bankruptcy) Editorial offices, Spring 1929, 230 Fifth Ave., New York, N.Y.; Summer 1929, 381 Fourth Ave., New York, N.Y.

    Fall 1929-Summer 1930. Experimenter Publishing Co., Inc. (B. A. Mackinnon and H. K. Fly ownership). Editorial offices, 381 Fourth Ave., New York, N.Y.

    Fall 1930-Summer 1931. Radio-Science Publications, Inc. Editorial offices 381 Fourth Ave., New York, N. Y.

    Fall 1931-Fall 1934. Teck Publishing Corporation. Editorial offices, Fall 1931-Summer 1932, 381 Fourth Ave., New York, N. Y.; Fall/Winter 1932-Fall 1934, 350 Hudson St., New York, N. Y.

Owners and company officers.

    Spring 1928-Winter 1929. Hugo Gernsback, president; Sidney Gernsback, treasurer; C. D. Rosenfelt, secretary; Alfred A. Cohen, business manager.

    Spring 1929. Under trusteeship of Irving Trust Company. Statement of the Ownership as of 1 April 1929 lists B. A. Mackinnon as business manager.

    Fall 1929-Fall 1930. B. A. Mackinnon, president; H. K. Fly, treasurer.

    Winter-Summer 1931. W. Z. Shafer, president; Byrd D. Wise, secretary; Laurence A. Smith, treasurer; Guy L. Harrington, vice president.

    Fall 1931. Lee Ellmaker, president; Warren P. Jeffery, vice president; William Thompson, treasurer; Wesley F. Pape, secretary.

    Winter and Spring/Summer 1932. Lee Ellmaker, president; Warren P. Jeffery, vice president; Huston D. Crippen, vice president; William Thompson, treasurer; Wesley F. Pape, secretary.

    Fall/Winter 1932-Fall/Winter 1933. Lee Ellmaker, president; Warren P. Jeffery, vice president; Huston D. Crippen, vice president; P. D. Diffenderfer, treasurer; Abner Germann, secretary.

    Fall 1934. Lee Ellmaker, president; Abner Germann, secretary.

Staff.

    Winter 1928. Not cited, but Hugo Gernsback, editor, with presumably the same staff members as indicated on the masthead of the next issue.

    Spring 1928-Winter 1929. Hugo Gernsback, editor; T. O'Conor Sloane, associate editor; Miriam Bourne, associate editor; Wilbur C. Whitehead, literary editor; C. A. Brandt, literary editor.

    Spring-Summer 1929. Arthur H. Lynch, editor-in-chief; T. O'Conor Sloane, associate editor; Miriam Bourne, associate editor; Wilbur C. Whitehead, literary editor; C. A. Brandt, literary editor.

    Fall 1929-Spring 1930. T. O'Conor Sloane, editor; Miriam Bourne, managing editor; C. A. Brandt, literary editor; Wilbur C. White-head, literary editor.

    Summer 1930 on, not listed on the masthead, but T. O'Conor Sloane, editor through 1934; Miriam Bourne, managing editor, through 1932. C. A. Brandt seems to have left at the end of 1931. W. C. Whitehead died in 1931.

Schedule: Quarterly until the Winter 1932 issue, after which, irregular.

Appearance: Winter, January 20; Spring, April 20; Summer, July 20; Fall, October 20. This schedule held until 1933, when scheduling became irregular.

Price: 50¢

Range: Winter 1929-Fall 1934.

Number of issues: 22.

Size and format: 8 1/2" x 11 1/2." Side stapled, trimmed.

Pagination: Winter 1928-Spring/Summer 1933: 144 pp.

Winter 1933-Fall 1934: 128 pp.

Volume sequence in both cases.

Cover artwork:

    Winter 1928-Spring 1929: covers by Paul. Summer 1929: unsigned, but perhaps by Hugh Mackay. Fall 1929-Winter 1930: covers by Wesso. Spring 1930-Fall/Winter 1932, and Winter 1933-Fall 1934: covers by Morey. Spring/Summer 1933: unsigned, but probably by Sigmond.

Interior artwork: Paul, with the exception of H. G. Wells's "When the Sleeper Wakes," illustrated all the Gernsback issues and most of first Lynch issue (Spring 1929). The second Lynch issue (Summer 1929) was illustrated by various hands. Wesso illustrated most of the Fall 1929 issue. From Spring 1930 Wesso illustrated the lead novel, while Morey illustrated most of the other stories. In the later issues, some stories were not illustrated.

Departments:

    Editorials by Hugo Gernsback Winter-Summer 1928.

    Guest editorials by various hands Fall 1928-Winter 1931, and Summer 1931.

    "Your Viewpoint" Summer 1928-Fall 1930; letter column retitled "Discussions" in Spring/Summer 1933.

Comment: From 1940 to 1943 and from 1947 to 1951, under the editorship of Ray Palmer, current issues of *Amazing Stories*, three per volume, were bound together and sold with a new cover as *Amazing Stories Quarterly*. These rebindings were simply a means of disposing of overstock and have nothing to do with the earlier *Amazing Stories Quarterly* described here.

Contents

Winter 1928. I-1. Cover: Paul.
Bell, Earl L. The Moon of Doom
Sears, Edward S. The Atomic Riddle
Wells, H. G. When the Sleeper Wakes
Johnson, E. H. The Golden Vapor
Breuer, Miles J., M.D. The Puzzle Duel
Orndorff, Frank. The Terrors of the Upper Air

Spring 1928. I-2. Cover: Paul.
Hodge, Frederick Arthur. A Modern Atlantis
Flint, Homer Eon. The Nth Man
Verrill, A. Hyatt. The King of the Monkey Men
Richards, Harold F., Ph.D. The Vibrator of Death
Schlossel, J. The Second Swarm
[*Miscellaneous.* Editorial: "The Rise of Scientifiction."]

Summer 1928. I-3. Cover: Paul.
Coblentz, Stanton A. The Sunken World

Summer 1928 (*continued*)
Starzl, R. F. Out of the Sub-Universe
Keller, David H., M.D. The Menace
Eustace, C. J. Ten Days to Live
[*Miscellaneous.* Editorial: "$50.00 for a Letter." Announces a contest for guest editorials.]

Fall 1928. I-4. Cover: Paul.
Verrill, A. Hyatt. The World of the Giant Ants
Keller, David H., M.D. Stenographer's Hands
Olsen, Bob. Four Dimensional Transit
Sherin, Ronald M. When the World Went Mad
Ball, Clelland J. The Gravity King
[*Miscellaneous.* Guest editorial: "Scientifiction, Searchlight of Science," by Jack Williamson, winning $50. * Also "Editorials from Our Readers."]

Winter 1929. II-1. Cover: Unsigned, but Paul. (The last issue attributed to Gernsback.)
Gernsback, Hugo. Ralph 124 C41+
Meek, Capt. S. P. The Murgatroyd Experiment
Septama, Aladra. The Beast-Men of Ceres
Hansen, L. Taylor. What the Sodium Lines Revealed
Vincent, Harl. The Seventh Generation
Harris, Clare Winger. The Evolutionary Monstrosity
Kateley, Walter. The Hollister Experiment
[*Miscellaneous.* Guest editorial: "Why We Believe in Scientifiction" by Frederick Dundas Stewart. * Also "Editorials from Our Readers," including authors L. Taylor Hansen, Judson W. Reeves (pseud. Aladra Septama), and Jack Williamson. * Letter from "John W. Reeves," of the same address as Judson W. Reeves, above, and presumably the same person.]

Spring 1929. II-2. Cover: Unsigned, but Paul. (Although Arthur H. Lynch is carried as editor, the selection of stories and preparation of the magazine may have taken place during Gernsback's regime.)
Coblentz, Stanton A. After 12,000 Years
Hamilton, Edmond. Locked Worlds
Septama, Aladra. The Cry from the Ether
Quien Sabe. The City of Eric
[*Miscellaneous.* Guest editorial "The Amazing Value of Scientifiction," by J. Roy Chapman. * "Editorials from our Readers," including author David M. Speaker. * Poems: "Speeding" and "Change Eternal" by Leland S. Copeland.]

Summer 1929. II-3. Cover: Unsigned. (Hugh Mackay?)
Vincent, Harl. Venus Liberated
Breuer, Miles J., M.D. Rays and Men
Keller, David H., M.D. White Collars
Cloukey, Charles. Paradox
Hall, T. Proctor. Dr. O'Glee's Experiments
Sears, Edward S. The Singing Moonbeams

[*Miscellaneous.* Guest editorial: "The Future of Scientifiction," by author Miles J. Breuer, M.D. * Also "Editorials from Our Readers" including author Frederick Arthur Hodge. * Letter from author Walter Dennis.]

Fall 1929. II-4. Cover: Wesso.
Verrill, A. Hyatt. The Bridge of Light
Keller, David H., M.D. Euthanasia Limited
Hamilton, Edmond. The Other Side of the Moon
Lovering, Paul H. When the Earth Grew Cold
[*Miscellaneous.* Guest editorial: "The Younger Generation and Future Science," by Joe Abrams. * Also "Editorials from Our Readers" including authors Otto Binder, Charles Cloukey and P. Schuyler Miller.]

Winter 1930. III-1. Cover: Wesso.
Taine, John. White Lily
Rice, Louise and Tonjoroff-Roberts. The Astounding Enemy
Septama, Aladra. Tani of Ekkis
Verrill, A. Hyatt. Dirigibles of Death
[*Miscellaneous.* Guest editorial: "Do We Need More Scientists?," by author Alexander M. Phillips. * Also "Editorials from Our Readers" including authors Numa C. Hero, and Joe W. Skidmore. * Letter from author A. Hyatt Verrill.]

Spring 1930. III-2. Cover: Morey.
Coblentz, Stanton A. Reclaimers of the Ice
Septama, Aladra. Dragons of Space
Keller, David H., M.D. The Flying Threat
Fabers, Dan. The Red Ray
[*Miscellaneous.* Guest editorial: "Scientific Responsibility," by author Victor Endersby. * "Editorials from our Readers."]

Summer 1930. III-3. Cover: Morey.
Breuer, Miles J., M.D. Paradise and Iron
Verrill, A. Hyatt. Monsters of the Ray
Campbell, John W., Jr. The Voice of the Void
Septama, Aladra. The Princess of Arelli
[*Miscellaneous.* Guest editorial: "A Father Speaks," by E. R. Briscoe. * "Editorials from our Readers." * Letter from author Harl Vincent.]

Fall 1930. III-4. Cover: Morey.
Wates, Cyril G. A Modern Prometheus
Campbell, John W., Jr. The Black Star Passes
Keller, David H., M.D. Boomeranging 'round the Moon
Septama, Aladra. Terrors of Arelli
Ludwick, Kathleen. Dr. Immortelle (carried on the contents page as by Luckwick.)
Happel, R. V. The Triple Ray
[*Miscellaneous.* Guest editorial: "What Scientifiction Means to Man," by James E. Suiter. * "Editorials from Our Readers."]

Winter 1931. (Incorrectly dated Winter 1930 on the contents page.) IV-1. Cover: Morey.
Breuer, Miles J., M.D. and Williamson, Jack. The Birth of a New Republic
Wertenbaker, G. Peyton. Elaine's Tomb
Verrill, A. Hyatt. When the Moon Ran Wild
Keller, David H., M.D. Service First
[*Miscellaneous.* Guest editorial "Science—Scientifiction—Science," by F. B. Eason.]

Spring 1931. IV-2. Cover: Morey.
Campbell, John W., Jr. Islands of Space
Nathanson, Isaac R. Moon People of Jupiter
Vincent, Harl. Invisible Ships
Schlossel, J. Extra-Galactic Invaders

Summer 1931. IV-3. Cover: Morey.
Coblentz, Stanton A. The Blue Barbarians
Keller, David H., M.D. Half-Mile Hill
Fleming, Roscoe B. Menace of the Little
Bernal, A. W. Cosmic Menace
Repp, Ed Earl. Deep Sea Justice
Stowell, Eugene. The Giant Puffball
[*Miscellaneous.* Guest editorial by author James Francis Kalland. * Poem: "Through Intervening Space," by W. T. B. * Letter from author Harl Vincent.]

Fall 1931. IV-4. Cover: Morey.
Taine, John. Seeds of Life
Breuer, Miles J., M.D. The Demons of Rhadi-Mu
Skidmore, Joe W. Dramatis Personae
Constantinescu, Clinton. The War of the Universe
Barrett, H. I. The Mechanical Heart
Janus, Warwick. Paladins of the Sky
[*Miscellaneous.* Poems: "This Mechanical Age," by Julia Boynton Green and "My Robot Son," by Bob Olsen.]

Winter 1932. V-1. Cover: Morey.
Stephens, I. M. and Pratt, Fletcher. A Voice across the Years
Vincent, Harl. Once in a Blue Moon
Kateley, Walter. Insects Extraordinary
Lemkin, William, Ph.D. Blue Waters
Morris, Earle H. Starvation in Space
Jacobi, Carl. Moss Island
O'Donnell, John Shamus. Naval Control
[*Miscellaneous.* Poem: "The Difference," by E. A. Everett.]

Spring/Summer 1932. V-2. Cover: Morey.
Campbell, John W., Jr. Invaders from the Infinite
Olsen, Bob. The Ant with a Human Soul
Vincent, Harl. Water-Bound World
Johnson, E. D. The Hole That Grew
[*Miscellaneous.* Poem: "Antipodal," by Clio Harper.]

Fall/Winter 1932. V-3. Cover: Morey.
Vincent, Harl. Faster than Light

Fall/Winter 1932 (*continued*)
Anderton, Seven. The King and the Pawn
Chadwick, Paul. Crusaders of Space
Barney, B. H. Beyond the Veil of Time
Caroll [*sic*], Duane N. Into the Mesozoic
[*Miscellaneous.* Poem: "Radio Revelations," by Julia Boynton Green.]

Spring/Summer 1933. VI-4. (An error for V-4, perpetuated in later issues.) Cover: Unsigned, probably Sigmond.
Coblentz, Stanton A. The Man from Tomorrow
Wallis, Bruce and Wallis, G. C. The Mother World
Ohmert, J. G. Celestial Pioneers
Gelula, Abner J. The Valley of the Blind
[*Miscellaneous.* Editorial: "An Engineering Epic." * Poem: "Mu and Atlantis," by Allen Glasser.]

Winter 1933. (In this case the seasonal sequence of issues has been broken; the winter issue is not the first issue of the year, but the last.)
VII-1. Cover: Morey.
Serviss, Garrett P. The Second Deluge
Verne, Jules. A Winter amid the Ice
Keller, David H., M.D. The Menace
[*Miscellaneous.* Editorial: "Rotary Force." * Filler "Rapid Aging of Wine."]

Fall 1934. VII-2. Cover: Morey.
Vincent, Harl. Barton's Island
Coblentz, Stanton A. The Sunken World
Meek, Capt. S. P. The Radio Robbery
Kline, Otis Adelbert. The Malignant Entity
[*Miscellaneous.* Poem: "Babylon. A Song of Memory," by Robert Bridge Pike. * Fillers "The Breathing of Fishes" and "Edgar Allan Poe."]

ASTOUNDING STORIES (CLAYTON)

In the late 1920s and early 1930s, the magazine group headed by William M. Clayton and commonly called the Clayton chain (although its title of registry was often different), was a fairly successful publisher of pulp magazines. According to the magazine masthead, in December 1929, for example, it published:

Ace-High Magazine
All Star Detective Stories
Big Story Magazine
Clues
Cowboy Stories
Five-Novels Monthly
Flyers
Ranch Romances
Rangeland Love Story Magazine
Western Novel Magazine
Wide World Adventures

as well as *Field and Stream* and *Miss 1930*. In the next two years "books" were added to the list and "books" were dropped. Altogether, Clayton published about fifty different magazines at one time or another. The chain did not have the resources or the distribution of the larger companies like Street and Smith, or Munsey, but it was adequate and until shortly before its demise, financially sound.

The appearance of Clayton *Astounding Stories* seems to have been a sort of publishing spontaneous combustion, ready to ignite when the proper moment came. That moment came in late 1929.

There are at least four accounts of its origin. According to the artist Elliott Dold, his brother Douglas, who was an editor with the Clayton chain, at one time suggested that Clayton issue a science-fiction magazine: "You see that's the way my brother, Douglas, induced Mr. Clayton to start *Astounding Stories*" (*Fantasy Magazine*, October-November 1934, p. 46). A second claimant was Harold Hersey, an editor with Clayton and later an independent publisher. "I discussed plans with Clayton before I resigned from his company to take over the Supervising Editorship of the Macfadden Publications, to launch a pseudo-science, fantasy sheet, but he did not issue *Astounding Stories* until about a year later" (Hersey, p. 188). A third possibility is described in an interview with Harry Bates, editor of *Astounding Stories*, conducted by Julius Schwartz and Mort Weisinger in the *Science Fiction Digest* for February 1933: "Mr. Clayton had the idea for a science fiction magazine in his mind for a long time and one day he suggested the idea to Bates. *Astounding Stories* was the result."

The most detailed account of the founding of *Astounding Stories* is presented in Harry Bates's "Editorial Number One" in Alva Rogers's *A Requiem for Astounding*. Bates, while admitting that there may have been earlier suggestions by other people, describes the decision that created *Astounding Stories*. A few details in Bates's account are suspect, perhaps due to faulty memory of events thirty-five years in the past, but there is no reason to doubt its general truth.

The immediate cause came in "the weeks just preceding the 1929 stock market crash" (Bates, p. xv), when Bates was summoned into Clayton's office and told to prepare a magazine devoted to historical adventure, provisionally titled *Torchlights of History*. Bates disliked the proposal and said so; his superiors told him to think it over. Instead, Bates decided to suggest a different sort of magazine:

I, editor of his [Clayton's] adventure magazine (*World Wide Adventures*), had like all others of my kind been a reflexive studier-of-newsstand displays

--so presently, as I sat at bay behind my desk "thinking it over," there popped up the memory of a certain magazine of large size whose covers invariably were chockfull of preposterous machinery and colored rays and monstrous or monstrously dressed creatures doing things. *Amazing Stories*! Once I had bought a copy. What awful stuff, I'd found it! Cluttered with trivia! Packed with puerilities! Written by unimaginables! But now at the memory I wondered if there might be a market for a well-written magazine on the *Amazing* themes . . . . and I sold myself on possibilities. Perhaps I could get Clayton to let me start a magazine of the science-monster type, instead! I thought it should not be too difficult to obtain the stories . . . .

Next morning I pumped myself full of combativeness and charged into Clayton's office. It was all as easy as pie! There'd be no Torchlights of History! Instead, there'd be an action-adventure *Astounding Stories of Super-Science*! I was to get right to work on it . . . .

I had better interrupt the obstetrics of my history to tell how the name *Astounding Stories of Super-Science* was chosen. It was a process of elimination. I had thought up about a dozen possible names. Of them all, the one I liked best was Tomorrow, but I didn't even show this one to Clayton, because it was too mild and indefinite . . . . My second preference was for Science Fiction, which was generic and like the other had dignity, but I killed this one with arguments that as a phrase hardly anyone had ever seen or heard it (*Amazing* preferring the horrible "Scientifiction") and that as a name it would promise only mild and orthodox stories concerned with *today's* science . . . . It was my third preference which I advocated: *Astounding*. As a name it lacked dignity, but no matter: it was gutsy and would compel attention, and it generally resembled *Amazing* and could be counted on to attract the eye of that magazine's readers while pleasantly promising others that the stories would stun them . . . . It was a little better than Fantastic, and much better than Astonishing and Future and the remaining ones on my list (Bates, pp. x-xi).

This is Bates's account. Condensed: publisher Clayton called house editor Bates in and suggested starting a historical fiction book, to which Bates counterproposed a science-fiction book like *Amazing Stories*, but slanted more toward adventure fiction. This account seems reasonable and acceptable.

One may doubt some of Bates's details, like the rejected titles *Science Fiction,*

Tomorrow, Fantastic, Astonishing, and *Future,* all of which smell more of the 1950s than the late 1920s; but the fact remains that Bates was at least present at the founding of *Astounding* Stories. Oddly enough, Bates does not mention *Science Wonder Stories, Air Wonder Stories,* or *Science Wonder Quarterly,* all of which would have been present on the newsstands. Bates also claimed in the same introduction that the economics of printing magazine covers was a factor in establishing a new magazine, but as Professor R. D. Mullen has pointed out (Mullen, 1994, pp. 110-111), Bates's statements, for technical reasons, are simply impossible to accept.

Bates had his assignment, and he was now compelled to find suitable stories at short notice. If his dating of the conference with Clayton is correct as perhaps early October 1929, there was something less than two months to acquire stories, edit them, have them set in type, prepare internal artwork, print the body copy, obtain cover art, photograph it, make plates, print the cover, ship the sheets to the bindery, bind them, and release them to the distributor. Bates had as assistants Desmond Hall and Douglas Dold, both veterans of the pulp world, and a highly skilled publishing house, but Bates's account would be more reasonable if the meeting had taken place a couple of months earlier.

Acquiring suitable stories—action fiction against a background of fantastic science that wasn't too far overboard—was an expected difficulty, for (as was the case when *Amazing Stories* was founded four years earlier) there were no professional s-f writers. The older generation of writers who contributed to the Munsey chain and *Blue Book* was either no longer writing or had shifted to other fields. Gernsback's authors for the most part did not fit Bates's requirements.

Bates invoked the Clayton stable of authors, undoubtedly in addition to authors from the other pulps.

I at once found myself locked in a continuing struggle with nearly everyone whom I induced to try. Most of them were almost wholly ignorant of science and technology, so much of what eventually got into their stories had in one way or another to be put there by myself . . . . I did very much rewriting . . . . When I dared, I sent the stories back to the writers for the fixing, but even if they could do it, and did, this required the sending of long letters of detailed instructions, often including brief lectures on some aspect of science . . . . I daily faced a danger you would not be likely to think of, the alienation of prospective suppliers of stories. Most of my draftees wrote with uncertainty and risk and some reluctance, and had to endure the indignity of reworking

their stories or seeing me put patches on them; how much of this would they stand? (Bates, p. xiii-xiv).

According to the introduction cited above, he found it necessary to send back for changes about two-thirds of the stories that were eventually accepted.

An addendum must be placed to Harry Bates's concern about alienating and driving away authors. Despite his doubts, according to authors' accounts he was liked and respected as an editor by the men and women he dealt with.

A modern reader is not likely to be impressed with Bates's result in the first few issues. But Bates did enlist a few professionals fairly well known in pulp fiction, notably Ray Cummings, Murray Leinster, and Victor Rousseau, who had previously written science-fiction. He also obtained stories from such general fiction writers as Arthur J. Burks, Hugh B. Cave, Tom Curry, and Sewell P. Wright, although Burks, Cave, and Curry were obviously ill at ease in science-fiction and dropped away. Two semiprofessionals, Capt. S. P. Meek, U.S. Army, and Harl Vincent came over from the Gernsback magazines.

Besides soliciting stories from Clayton authors and the fiction grapevine, Bates also advertised in the trade journals.

ASTOUNDING STORIES: Fantastic stories, fast-moving, with backbone of pseudo-science. A little woman interest permitted. Length limits: shorts, 4,000 to 9,000 words; novels, about 25,000 words; serials, 40,000 or 55,000 words, in three or four parts, each instalment about 15,000 words, except the last of about 10,000 words. Pays a minimum of two cents a word, on acceptance. Harry Bates, editor. ("Manuscript Market," *The Writer,* April 1931, pp. 106-107).

In practice Bates sometimes paid more than 2¢ per word to favored authors like Murray Leinster. This rate of payment was much superior to that of the *Amazing* and *Wonder* groups, who paid 1/2 cent per word on publication, collectible (in Gernsback's case) with difficulty. Clayton's rate of payment was good for the general pulps, but below what leading magazines like *Adventure* and *Argosy* paid for major work.

A later advertisement indicates in more detail the sort of stories that Bates wanted:

THE CLAYTON MAGAZINES, INC.—80 Lafayette St., New York, have the following requirements: ASTOUNDING STORIES desires "material that will interest the reader who enjoys good stories laid in the present or future time, and in which marvelous scientific devices, yet to be actually invented, play an important part. Much

of the material we must have, therefore, will be akin to that written by such men as Jules Verne and H. G. Wells—stories dealing with invisibility, time machines, earth invasions, interplanetary adventures. the fourth dimension, and so forth. We require material that is not overweighted with scientific explanations to such an extent that the story itself suffers. Story values—plot, physical action, conflict, suspense, human interest, a hero and heroine to sympathize with and a villain to dislike—are equal in importance to the accuracy and convincingness of the science that underlies the story. We especially are looking for good interplanetary shorts; which must be within 9,000 words; serials in three or four parts of about 40,000 and 55,000 words, respectively, 15,000 being the ideal length of all installments except the last, which should be 10,000 words (*The Writer,* December 1931, p. 355).

According to Desmond Hall, *Astounding Stories* generally received about fifteen stories per day. (*Fantasy Magazine,* October/November 1934, p. 44).

Bates faced the same problem with artwork that he did with stories. For all practical purposes, the only science-fiction artist in the late 1920's was Frank R. Paul, who illustrated for Gernsback and except for an occasional interior illustration in later Clayton *Astounding Stories* was not available. The other artists who illustrated the *Amazing* magazines had little quality.

Bates, however, was fortunate enough to acquire a relatively new cover artist, Hans W. Wessolowski, generally known as Wesso, who was able to adapt his work to science-fiction needs. His covers, more colorful and more dynamic than Paul's, stressed action and were eye-catching, even though Wesso never reached the height of the better pulp cover artists. His illustrations, with gesticulating and grimacing figures in strained postures, with occasional bright landscapes, and smooth space equipment became characteristic of Clayton *Astounding Stories.*

Harold Hersey describes the preparation of covers in the Clayton magazines:

Clayton was one of the best cover men in the trade. He insisted that every original, engraver's proof and final press copy be submitted to his inspection. And he always made some suggestion here and there that improved its appearance . . . . Gradually I learned a myriad little ways to improve a cover painting. Such things as never neglecting to show a character's eyes; that full faces are better than profiles; how to concentrate on important detail yet never let any part overshadow the whole; how to arrange the display so that if only a corner showed it would attract and hold a wavering eye. Clayton's contention was that the seven-by-ten space might be small but it would be used with telling effect by a professional hand. Attention must be concentrated into simple form. Use highlights on the characters' faces whether indoors or not. Where two figures could tell a story, eschew a third; better still, build up the cover situation around a single character so that the appeal was simplified for moronic minds. Keep background down to the essentials; suggest rather than portray a vista or the wall of a room. Doorways are forceful, dramatic, especially where a figure looms over the threshold, silhouettes against a deep, mysterious darkness (Hersey, pp. 60-61).

Clayton/Hersey's desiderata for a poster approach are general enough to fit most pulp magazines, but science-fiction has special requirements in subject matter. Diversity may be as valid as simplification, and precision more important than vague atmosphere.

For interiors, Bates first utilized the well-known pulp artist J. Fleming Gould, a very prolific, competent black-and-white man, who did most of the illustrations for the first eight issues. Gould, however, despite his general excellence as an action artist, could not draw science-fiction art, and after the August 1930 issue the interior illustrations were gradually shifted to Wesso who covered almost all the later stories.

The first issue of *Astounding Stories of Super-Science* contained the following editorial, which purports to reveal the tenor of the magazine. It will be seen that, as with Gernsback, respectability is prime, in this case not scientific accuracy, not education, but justification (somewhat far-fetched) through predictability. Needless to say, this was simply lip-service.

Introducing—

ASTOUNDING STORIES

What are "astounding" stories?

Well, if you lived in Europe in 1490, and someone told you the earth was round and moved around the sun—that would have been an "astounding" story.

Or if you lived in 1840, and were told that some day men a thousand miles apart would be able to talk to each other through a little wire—or without any wire at all—that would have been another.

Or if, in 1900, they predicted ocean-crossing airplanes and submarines, world-girdling Zeppelins, sixty-story buildings, radio, metal that can be made to resist gravity and float in the air—these would have been other "astounding" stories.

To-day, time has gone by, and all these things are commonplace. That is the only real difference between the astounding and the commonplace—Time.

To-morrow, more astounding things are going to happen. Your children—or their children—are going to take a trip to the moon. They will be able to render themselves invisible—a problem that has already been partly solved. They will be able to disintegrate their bodies in New York and reintegrate them in China—and in a matter of seconds.

Astounding? Indeed, yes.

Impossible? Well—television would have been impossible, almost unthinkable, ten years ago.

Now you will see the kind of magazine that it is our pleasure to offer you beginning with this, the first number of ASTOUNDING STORIES.

It is a magazine whose stories will anticipate the super-scientific achievements of To-morrow—whose stories will not only be strictly accurate in their science but will be vividly, dramatically and thrillingly told.

Already we have secured stories by some of the finest writers of fantasy in the world—men such as Ray Cummings, Murray Leinster, Captain S. P. Meek, Harl Vincent, R. F. Starzl and Victor Rousseau.

So—order your next month's copy of ASTOUNDING STORIES in advance! —*The Editor.* (*Astounding Stories,* January 1930, p. 5).

Under Bates *Astounding Stories* thus moved along. Bates early set a narrative pattern, pulp action stories against a fantastic background. Most of his stories fitted this generalization, although, for obvious reasons, there were also stories that lacked an optimal amount of action. Nevertheless, *Astounding Stories* was much more uniform in texture than its major rivals, the *Amazing* and *Wonder* groups.

During the early days of his editorship Bates faced the perpetual problem of requests for reprints from the older pulps, notably the Munsey magazines. His response was strong:

We admit, right off, that some splendid Science Fiction stories have been published in the past—but are those now being printed in any way inferior to them? Aren't even _better_ ones being written to-day? — since a whole civilization now stirs with active interest in science? — since three or five times as many writers are now supplying us with stories to choose from? — since science and scientific theory have reached so immeasurably much farther into the Realm of the Unknown Possible?". . . . Would it be fair to 99% of our readers to force on them reprint novels they have already read, or had a chance to read, to favor the 1% who have missed them? . . . . And how about our authors? Contrary to the old-fashioned opinion, authors must eat—and how will they eat, and lead respectable lives, and keep out of jail, if we keep reprinting their old stories and turning down their new ones? . . . . It would be much cheaper to buy once-used material . . . . but it would be very unwise, and very unfair, as you have seen. (*Astounding Stories,* June 1930, pp. 134-135).

The competition obviously regarded the new magazine askance. When George Race, an engineer reader, criticized the weak science in *Wonder Stories Quarterly*, Hugo Gernsback responded by blaming Harry Bates. Names are not cited, but the reference is obvious:

a new element entered the field of science fiction, magazines of "wild west" fiction in which science was of little or no consequence. This threw many good writers off their balance and destroyed in some their ability to create a good story without the use of rays, and rays and rays. (*Wonder Stories Quarterly,* Summer 1932, p. 576).

As the magazine aged, two almost contradictory trends emerged. First, unadorned physical violence increased, with almost mandatory hand-to-hand combat in which the leading character thrashes someone or something. Secondly, Bates apparently began to worry more about scientific plausibility in his stories. Thus, for a time authors contributed long letters defending, perhaps sometimes tongue in cheek, or commenting on the key ideas in their stories. Bates also attempted, despite his scorn of the Gernsback-type story, to "get a couple of hybrids combining the most conspicuous qualities of Astounding and Amazing. But I failed. It seemed we could not make them mix . . . . [But] when I had the rare luck to receive an uncrippled one I always saw to it that Clayton approved it." (Bates, p. xv.)

In the last two issues Bates moved toward the Gernsback magazines with an inspirational editorial and a science question-and-answer department.

There are no precise figures on the circulation of Clayton *Astounding Stories,* but Harry Bates in his interview in *Science Fiction Digest* stated that the print run was 100,000 copies, of which about 50,000 were sold in the United States, the remainder being exported at cut price to Great Britain.

Bates added that the magazine was never really profitable, but almost broke even.

The end of Clayton *Astounding* came not as a direct result of the Great Depression, but through a business decision, although the Depression, of course, was a contributing factor. For reasons not well documented, William Clayton agreed to buy out his partner, and the resulting cash drain was more than his chain could stand. It has been said that the figure was $600,000, payable in installments. Various economy moves, like reducing authors' rates from 2¢ a word on acceptance to 1¢ on publication were inadequate. Clayton could not meet his payments, and the Clayton chain passed out of his hands.

It is now difficult to characterize Clayton, except to say that he was a successful publisher for a time. According to rumor he gambled heavily, which activity contributed to his cash shortage. As for his personality, he treated his authors decently, and his staff seems to have liked him well enough. On the other hand, H. L. Mencken, who was notorious for his ferocious grudges, in his *My Life as Author and Editor*, describes him as little better than a scoundrel.

The death of *Astounding Stories of Super-Science* was not completely unexpected, for all the symptoms of a sick magazine had been apparent for some time. As Hugh B. Cave wrote to Carl Jacobi on 8 September 1932, "And keep your eye on Clayton. Something's in the air down there . . . . Clayton is way behind on payments, and the list of overdue checks must be mounting to startling proportions by this time. Bates tells me they are holding their business meetings in Chinese to keep the editors from knowing what's going to happen" (Cave, p. 20).

During bankruptcy proceedings Clayton's holdings were auctioned off, with one R. T. Foley (presumably the Foley who was an owner of *Weird Tales*) purchasing *Astounding Stories*. Street and Smith later bought the magazine, along with *Clues* and *Cowboy Stories*, but there was a hiatus of more than six months before the new *Astounding Stories* appeared on the newsstands.

In the January 1933 issue of Clayton's magazine there appeared a list of forthcoming stories, several of which were used in the last, March 1933 issue. Two, however, did not appear. These were "The Man in the Bottle" by Le Grand Travers (said to have been a pseudonym), which to my knowledge has never appeared anywhere, and E. E. Smith's novel "Triplanetary," the first half of which Bates promised for the next issue. *Astounding Stories* did not publish "Triplanetary," which was transferred to *Amazing Stories*, where it was printed from January through April 1934.

What did Bates accomplish in the thirty-four issues of *Astounding Stories*, in what

was really the first genre s-f *pulp* magazine? In terms of literary quality or general interest very little. Of the 164 short stories, novelettes, and novels that appeared in Clayton *Astounding Stories* there is hardly a story that is remembered today. Even anthologists looking for copyright-free stories seldom raid Clayton *Astounding Stories*. The one exception is in the case of early works by authors later important, like Jack Williamson or Murray Leinster.

From a typological point of view, however, Bates fulfilled what he had planned, creating a story of event set in background that in some way involved nonestablished science or technology. His accomplishment was professional, as opposed to the amateur approaches of Hugo Gernsback and T. O'Conor Sloane. This obviously resulted in breaking the Gernsback bind on early genre s-f.

Bates's approach developed the science-fiction he published as a small simulacrum of general pulp fiction. There was no intrinsic difference between a story set on Venus, for example, and a sea story colored with maritime lore, or a Limberlost story put into a romanticized forest, or a cowboy story set on a bowdlerized yet sensational ranch. In fact, Bates's own best-known series, the Hawk Carse stories which he wrote in collaboration with Desmond Hall, could be easily transferred to the Panhandle. While this approach continued in science-fiction, it has never been central. It is, however, obviously dominant in the various cinematographic productions of today.

Publishing information

Dates shown are masthead issue dates, not calendar dates. Such issue dates are not precise for organizational matters, for changes would have taken place considerably earlier.

Title:
January 1930-January 1931. *Astounding Stories of Super-Science.*
February 1931-November 1932. *Astounding Stories.*
January-March 1933: *Astounding Stories of Super-Science.*

Publisher:
January-November 1930. Publishers' Fiscal Corporation. Editorial offices, 80 Lafayette St., New York, N.Y.
December 1930-May 1931. Reader's Guild. Editorial offices, 80 Lafayette St., New York, N.Y.
June 1931-March 1933. The Clayton Magazines, Inc. Editorial offices, June 1931-January 1932, 80 Fayette St., New York, N.Y.; February 1932-March 1933, 155

East 44th St., New York, N.Y. (*Comment:* In all these changes of company name and address, the magazines bear the pennant logogram "A Clayton Magazine.")

Company officers:
William M. Clayton, publisher. All issues.
Nathan Goldmann, treasurer. January-October 1930.
Francis P. Pace, treasurer. November 1930 March 1933.
Stockholders, according to Statement of the Ownership notices, remain William M. Clayton and Nathan Goldmann for all issues.

Staff:
Harry Bates, editor, all issues.
Douglas M. Dold, consulting editor January 1930-July 1931, but apparently as an outside consultant.
Desmond W. Hall, editorial assistant to Bates; a period of about nine months from the inception of the magazine, exact dates not known.

Schedule:
January 1930-June 1932: monthly.
August 1932-March 1933: bimonthly.
Appearance: The first Thursday of the preceding month.
Price: 20¢.
Range: January 1930-March 1933.
Total issues: 34.
Size and format: 6 7/8" x 10." Side stapled, untrimmed.
Pagination: 144 pp. in volume sequence.
Artwork: All covers by Wesso. Interior art mostly by J. Fletcher Gould in earliest issues; mostly (totally for some issues) by Wesso in later issues, with occasional work by Sabo, Paul, Marchioni, and unsigned pieces.

Departments:
"The Readers' Corner" April 1930-March 1933.
"The Science Forum" by Carlyle Elliott, B.A., B.S., Ph.D. January-March 1933.

Miscellaneous:
Occasional popular science fillers.
Editorials by the editor in the January 1930, January 1933, and March 1933 issues.

Contents

January 1930. I-1. Cover: Wesso.
Rousseau, Victor. The Beetle Horde (1)
Meek, Capt. S. P. The Cave of Horror
Cummings, Ray. Phantoms of Reality
Staley, M. L. The Stolen Mind
Tench, C. V. Compensation
Leinster, Murray. Tanks
Pelcher, Anthony. Invisible Death
[*Miscellaneous.* Editorial: "Introducing—ASTOUNDING STORIES."]

February 1930. I-2. Cover: Wesso.
Cave, Hugh B. The Corpse on the

February 1930 (*continued*)
Grating
Diffin, Charles Willard. Spawn of the Stars
Meek, Capt. S. P. The Thief of Time
Vincent, Harl. Old Crompton's Secret
Ellis, Sophie Wenzel. Creatures of the Light
Pelcher, Anthony. Mad Music
St. Paul, Sterner. Into Space
Rousseau, Victor. The Beetle Horde (2)

March 1930. I-3. Cover: Wesso.
Meek, Capt. S. P. Cold Light
Cummings, Ray. Brigands of the Moon (1)
Smith, Will and Robbins, R. J. The Soul Master
Wright, Sewell Peaslee. From the Ocean's Depths
Locke, A. T. Vandals of the Stars

April 1930. II-1. Cover: Wesso.
Knight, Thomas H. The Man Who Was Dead
Burks, Arthur J. Monsters of Moyen
Pelcher, Anthony. Vampires of Venus
Curry, Tom. The Soul-Snatcher
Meek, Capt. S. P. The Ray of Madness
Cummings, Ray. Brigands of the Moon (2)
[*Miscellaneous:* Letter from author Allen Glasser.]

May 1930. II-2. Cover: Wesso.
Wright, Sewell Peaslee. Into the Ocean's Depths
Leinster, Murray. Murder Madness (1)
Lorraine, Lilith. The Jovian Jest
Rousseau, Victor. The Atom-Smasher
Cummings, Ray. Brigands of the Moon (3)

June 1930. II-3. Cover: Wesso.
Willard, Charles D. Out of the Dreadful Depths
Olsen, James P. The Cavern World
Curry, Tom. Giants of the Ray
Diffin, Charles W. The Moon Master
Cummings, Ray. Brigands of the Moon (4)
Leinster, Murray. Murder Madness (2)
[*Miscellaneous.* Letters from authors A. W. Bernal and Walter Dennis.]

July 1930. III-1. Cover: Wesso.
Meek, Capt. S. P. Beyond the Heaviside Layer
Burks, Arthur J. Earth, the Marauder (1)
Curry, Tom. From an Amber Block
Vincent, Harl. The Terror of Air-Level Six
Wright, Sewell Peasley. The Forgotten Planet
Diffin, Charles W. The Power and the Glory
Leinster, Murray. Murder Madness (3)
[*Miscellaneous.* Letter from author Allen Glasser.]

August 1930. III-2. Cover: Wesso.
Starzl, R. F. The Planet of Dread
Rousseau, Victor. The Lord of Space
Hamilton, Edmond. The Second Satellite
Vincent, Harl. Silver Dome
Rich, H. Thompson. The Flying City
Leinster, Murray. Murder Madness (4)
Burks, Arthur J. Earth, the Marauder (2)
[*Miscellaneous.* Letter from author Jack Williamson.]

September 1930. III-3. Cover: Wesso.
Breuer, Miles J. A Problem in Communication
Cummings, Ray. Jetta of the Lowlands (1)
Wright, Sewell Peaslee. The Terrible Tentacles of L-472
Ernst, Paul. Marooned under the Sea
Cave, Hugh B. The Murder Machine
Meek, Capt. S. P. The Attack from Space
Burks, Arthur J. Earth, the Marauder (3)

October 1930. IV-1. Cover: Wesso.
Meek, Capt. S. P. Stolen Brains
Rousseau, Victor. The Invisible Death
Leitfred, Robert H. Prisoners on the Electron
Gee, Jackson. An Extra Man
Cummings, Ray. Jetta of the Lowlands (2)
[*Miscellaneous.* Letters from authors Ray Cummings, Allen Glasser, Mort Weisinger, and Walter Dennis.]

November 1930. IV-2. Cover: Wesso.
Rousseau, Victor. The Wall of Death
Diffin, Charles W. The Pirate Planet (1)
Eshbach, L. A. The Gray Plague
Rouse, William Merriam. The Destroyer
Vincent, Harl. Vagabonds of Space
Cummings, Ray. Jetta of the Lowlands (3)
[*Miscellaneous.* Letters from authors P. Schuyler Miller and L. A. Eshbach.]

December 1930. IV-3. Cover: Wesso.
Ellis, Sophie Wenzel. Slaves of the Dust
Meek, Capt. S. P. The Sea Terror
Vincent, Harl. Gray Denim
Sparks, David R. The Ape-Men of Xlotli
Diffin, Charles W. The Pirate Planet (2)
[*Miscellaneous.* Letter from author Allen Glasser.]

January 1931. V -1. Cover: Wesso.
Wright, Sewell Peaslee. The Dark Side of Antri
Rich, H. Thompson. The Sunken Empire
Wells, Hal K. The Gate to Xoran
Willard, C. D. The Eye of Allah
Leinster, Murray. The Fifth-Dimension Catapult
Diffin, Charles W. The Pirate Planet (3)
[*Miscellaneous.* Letters from authors Capt. S. P. Meek and future author Jerome Siegel.]

February 1931. V-2. Cover: Wesso.

Hall, D. W. Werewolves of War
Gilmore, Anthony. The Tentacles from Below
Meek, Capt. S. P. The Black Lamp
Mason, F. V. W. Phalanxes of Atlans (1)
Diffin, Charles W. The Pirate Planet (4)

March 1931. V-3. Cover: Wesso.
Diffin, Charles W. When the Mountain Came to Miramar
Cummings, Ray. Beyond the Vanishing Point
Vincent, Harl. Terrors Unseen
Williamson, Jack. The Meteor Girl
Mason, F. V. W. Phalanxes of Atlantis (2)
[*Miscellaneous.* Letters from authors Mort Weisinger and Tom Olog.]

April 1931. VI-1. Cover: Wesso.
Hamilton, Edmond. Monsters of Mars
Cummings, Ray. The Exile of Time (1)
Curry, Tom. Hell's Dimension
Ernst, Paul. The World behind the Moon
Gilmore, Anthony. Four Miles Within
Williamson, Jack. The Lake of Light
Wright, Sewell Peaslee. The Ghost World
[*Miscellaneous.* Letters from authors Ray Cummings and Mort Weisinger.]

May 1931. VI-2. Cover: Wesso.
Diffin, Charles Willard. Dark Moon
Meek, Capt. S. P. When Caverns Yawned
Wells, Hal K. When the Moon Turned Green
Schachner, Nat and Zagat, Arthur L. The Death-Cloud
Cummings, Ray. The Exile of Time (2)
[*Miscellaneous.* Letter from author Capt. S. P. Meek.]

June 1931. VI-3. Cover: Wesso.
Wright, Sewell Peaslee. The Man from 2071
Burks, Arthur J. Manape the Mighty
Diffin, Charles Willard. Holocaust
Starzl, R. F. The Earthman's Burden
Cummings, Ray. The Exile of Time (3)
[*Miscellaneous.* Letters from authors Arthur J. Burks, Jackson Gee, and P. Schuyler Miller.]

July 1931. VII-1. Cover: Wesso.
Williamson, Jack. The Doom from Planet 4
Winter, H. G. The Hands of Aten
Rich, H. Thompson. The Diamond Thunderbolt
Holmes, A. R. The Slave Ship from Space
Schachner, Nat and Zagat, Arthur Leo. The Revolt of the Machines
Cummings, Ray. The Exile of Time (4)
[*Miscellaneous.* Letters from authors Paul Ernst and Clark Ashton Smith.]

August 1931. VII-2. Cover: Wesso.
Farley, Ralph Milne. The Danger from the Deep

August 1931 (*continued*)
Diffin, Charles Willard.   Brood of the Dark Moon (1)
Starzl, R. F. If the Sun Died
Winter, H. G. The Midget from the Island
Vincent, Harl. The Moon Weed
Meek, Capt. S. P. The Port of Missing Planes
[*Miscellaneous*. Letters from author Mort Weisinger and future author Jerome Siegel. * Fillers "Jazzing up the Universe" and "A Classi-fication of the Universe."]

September 1931. VII-3. Cover: Wesso.
Vincent, Harl. The Copper-Clad World
Wells, Hal K. Devil Crystals of Arret
Hamilton, Edmond. The Sargasso of Space
Wright, Sewell Peaslee. The God in the Box
Diffin, Charles Willard. Brood of the Dark Moon (2)

October 1931. VIII-1. Cover: Wesso.
Starzl, R. F. In the Orbit of Saturn
Flagg, Francis. The Heads of Apex
Ernst, Paul. The Red Hell of Jupiter
Meek, Capt. S. P. The Solar Magnet
Diffin, Charles Willard. Brood of the Dark Moon (3)

November 1931. VIII-2. Cover: Wesso
Ernst, Paul. The Planetoid of Peril
Gilmore, Anthony. Hawk Carse
Hall, D. W. Raiders Invisible
Wright, Sewell Peaslee. The Terror from the Depths
Rich, H. Thompson. Spawn of the Comet
Diffin, Charles Willard. Brood of the Dark Moon (4)
[*Miscellaneous*. Letter from author Sewell Peaslee Wright.]

December 1931. VIII-3. Cover: Wesso.
Wilson, Robert H. Out around Rigel
Cummings, Ray. The White Invaders
Meek, Capt. S. P. Giants on the Earth (1)
Wright, Sewell Peaslee. The Infra-Medians
Leinster, Murray. Morale
[*Miscellaneous*. Letter from future author and editor Charles Hornig. * Filler "Harnessing Solar Energy."]

January 1932. IX-1. Cover: Wesso.
Vincent, Harl. Creatures of Vibration
Burks, Arthur J. The Mind Master (1)
Sparks, David R. The Winged Men of Orcon
Flagg, Francis. The Seed of the Toc-Toc Birds
Ernst, Paul. The Radiant Shell
Meek, Capt. S. P. Giants on the Earth (2)
[*Miscellaneous*. Letter from future author and editor Charles Hornig.]

February 1932. IX-2. Cover: Wesso.
Williamson, Jack. The Pygmy Planet
Cummings, Ray. Wandl, the Invader (1)

Winter, H. G. Seed of the Arctic Ice
Sloat, Edwin K. The Space Rover
Wells, Hal K. Zehru of Xollar
Burks, Arthur J. The Mind Master (2)

March 1932. IX-3. Cover: Wesso.
Meek, Capt. S. P. Poisoned Air
Gilmore, Anthony. The Affair of the Brains
Diffin, Charles Willard. The Hammer of Thor
Wright, Sewell Peaslee. Vampires of Space
Cummings, Ray. Wandl, the Invader (2)
[*Miscellaneous*. Letters from authors Kenneth Sterling and Tom Olog.]

April 1932. X-1. Cover: Wesso.
Meek, Capt. S. P. B.C. 30,000
Diffin, Charles Willard. The Finding of Haldgren
Breuer, Miles J. The Einstein See-Saw
Zagat, Arthur Leo. The Great Dome on Mercury
Cummings, Ray. Wandl, the Invader (3)

May 1932. X-2. Cover: Wesso.
Schachner, Nathan. Pirates of the Gorm
Starzl, R. F. The Martian Cabal
Meek, Capt. S. P. The Great Drought
Gilmore, Anthony. The Bluff of the Hawk
Cummings, Ray. Wandl, the Invader (4)

June 1932. X-3. Cover: Wesso.
Vincent, Harl. Vulcan's Workshop
Diffin, Charles W. Two Thousand Miles Below (1)
Simak, Clifford D. Hellhounds of the Cosmos
Ernst, Paul. The Raid on the Termites
Wright, Sewell Peaslee. Priestess of the Flame
[*Miscellaneous*. Letter from author Paul Ernst.]

September 1932. XI-1. Cover: Wesso.
[There were no issues for July and August 1932.]
Sloat, Edwin K. Loot of the Void
Endersby, Victor A. Disowned
Wandrei, Donald. Raiders of the Universes
Schachner, Nathan. Slaves of Mercury
Diffin, Charles W. Two Thousand Miles Below (2)
[*Miscellaneous*. Letter by future author James Blish. * Poem: "In 2082," by Henry Lewis, Jr.]

November 1932. XI-2. Cover: Wesso.
[There was no issue for October 1932.]
Wells, Hal K. The Cavern of the Shining Ones
Hall, D. W. A Scientist Rises
Zagat, Arthur Leo. When the Sleepers Woke
Gilmore, Anthony. The Passing of Ku Sui
Diffin, Charles W. Two Thousand Miles

Below (3)
[*Miscellaneous*. Letters from authors Ray Cummings, Jack Williamson, Kenneth Sterling, Ray Palmer, and Mort Weisinger; Weisinger's letter includes a poem, "Eulogy to Mr. Hamilton." Also a Shakespearean parody by Harold N. Snyder.]

January 1933. XI-3. Cover: Wesso.
[There was no issue for December 1933.]
Winter, H. G. Under Arctic Ice
Kirby, Jason. The Floating Island of Madness
Leinster, Murray. The Fifth-Dimension Tube
Diffin, Charles W. Two Thousand Miles Below (4)
[*Miscellaneous*. Editorial: "Just around the Corner." * Short articles "Arcturus at the Exposition," "For the Transmutation of the Elements," "Rockets for Propulsion," "Humans are Electromagnetic Atoms." * Letter from author Ray Palmer. * Poems: "In Vindication," by Eugene Benefiel and George Skora; "Verse," and "Comet Head Drace," by Henry Lewis.]

March 1933.   XII-1.   Cover: Wesso.
[There was no issue for February 1933.]
Williamson, Jack. Salvage in Space
Burks, Arthur J. Lords of the Stratosphere
West, Wallace. The End of Time
Wright, Sewell Peaslee. The Death-Traps of FX-31
Vincent, Harl. Wanderer of Infinity
Leinster, Murray. Invasion
[*Miscellaneous*. Editorial: "The Expanding Universe." * Poem "Astounding Stories," by Henry Ackerman. * Ar-ticles "A Plane for the Antarctic" and "Cosmic Rays and the Atom."]

ASTOUNDING STORIES (STREET AND SMITH)

After the bankruptcy of Clayton Publications in early 1933, *Astounding Stories* remained for a time in a limbo of sorts. It was purchased along with other properties by R. T. Foley, who was at one time one of the owners of *Weird Tales*. Foley in turn sold it to Street and Smith Publications, Inc., who released the October 1933 issue, which would have been on the newsstands on September 20, 1933.

Of the various publishers of pulp magazines in the 1930s, Street and Smith was one of the most successful. Its *Shadow Magazine, Western Stories*, and *Doc Savage Magazine* were each the favored reading of scores of thousands. Part of its success was due to appreciation of what readers wanted, part to an excellent distribution system, and part to its captive plant which obviated the dependence on outside printers (for work and, all too often, financing) that hampered many other publishers. Before entering the pulp market, Street and Smith had been one of the leading publishers of dime novels; alone among this group Street and Smith was able to convert to an adult market.

In the immediate past Street and Smith had frowned rather strongly on fantastic fiction, so that a science-fiction magazine was a new venture for them. In late 1919, however, Street and Smith had almost pioneered with the *Thrill Book*, which though a magazine of mixed exotic fiction, was gradually being pushed toward fantastic fiction by its editor Ronald Oliphant. Had the *Thrill Book* lasted a few issues longer, it probably would have become the first such magazine. But Street and Smith had no faith in it, and it was suddenly canceled.

After acquiring *Astounding Stories*, Street and Smith first offered its editorship to John Nanovic, editor of the *Shadow* magazine, who refused it. Street and Smith then assigned Frederick Orlin Tremaine as its editor. Tremaine was a professional editor who had had long experience in magazines, including the Clayton chain. Assisting Tremaine for about a year was Desmond W. Hall, who had served in a similar capacity to Harry Bates on Clayton's *Astounding Stories.*

When Tremaine assumed the editorship of the new *Astounding Stories*, there was some indecision about the nature of the magazine, whether it would remain a science-fiction magazine or offer a mixture of unusual fiction—science-fiction, supernatural fiction, and exotic adventure.

As Desmond Hall stated in an interview reported in the October 1933 issue of *Science Fiction Digest*:

[T]he magazine will continue to carry science fiction of the brand made popular by Harry Bates, though with a little more science . . . . However, the contents are not to be restricted solely to science fiction; we will carry in each issue a few stories of the weird and supernatural, and there will be some which combine the two types into what we hope will prove to be a very popular form. Our first demand here is for a convincing story . . . . There will be nothing sketchy and fakey in the magazine (p. 17).

Thus, the first three issues (October-December 1933) include several weak traditional ghost stories and adventure stories apparently bought in part as a package from Great Britain. Science-fiction, of course, won out, and with the January 1934 issue *Astounding Stories* became totally a science-fiction magazine.

Tremaine obviously did not accept either Harry Bates's negative evaluation of science-fiction or his concept of science-fiction as an action story set in peculiar circumstances. Nor did he issue flamboy-ant statements about aims and goals, as did Gernsback. But, judging from his editorial selections and the trend of *Astounding Stories,* he did have certain ideas in mind. First, Tremaine, although he did not articulate it, must have had a faith in science-fiction as a literary phenomenon that had a right to exist. Second, he believed that by 1934, after an exciting start, it had drifted into doldrums and needed a push to set it in motion again. Along this line, in his editorial in the August 1934 issue he briefly expounded a biological-cyclical theory of literature:

Just as a plant or flower develops to maturity and then decays, so science-fiction had passed its supreme moment when Astounding Stories came to Street & Smith nearly a year ago. With the transition it stepped into a new cycle of life. Something glorious and fine remained from the old magazine—a tradition that we believed in . . . . Our magazine has a long period of development ahead before it reaches its supreme moment of full maturity. Who knows but what it may be three years—or five? (*Astounding Stories,* August 1934, p. 7).

Third, he considered the specific weakness of the science-fiction of the day—late 1933 and early 1934—to be clichéd: "We want *new* plots, *new* concepts of time and space; not worn-out plots with stereotyped characters" (*Astounding Stories,* October 1934, p. 38). Fourth, he accepted the science-fiction reader as a very special market, although this may have been merely a sales pitch. "Astounding is not like an ordinary magazine. It has a very special audience, with special interests" (*Astounding Stories,* November 1934, p. 9).

As a means for rejuvenating science-fiction (and, of course, as publicity) Tremaine announced the concept of "thought-variant" stories, by which he meant stories that embodied startling new ideas, not so much plot gimmicks as background situations. Tremaine states in an editorial in the December 1933 issue:

ASTOUNDING STORIES is back again with a new policy. It is a carefully planned and slowly unfolding policy which will please you more and more as time passes, because, first and foremost, you—our readers—are a thinking group.

Our purpose is bring to you each month one story carrying a new and unexplored "thought-variant" in the field of scientific fiction. This month you will find it in *Ancestral Voices* by Nat Schachner. It carries a thought which has been slurred over or passed by in many, many stories.

But it opens the way for real discussion, discussion deeply connected with social science, the present condition of the world, and the future. . . . ASTOUNDING STORIES is, perforce, a medium of logical fantasy. It must not become "habit-ridden"—or "grooved"—into a single line of thought. (*Astounding Stories,* December 1933, p. 138).

Schachner's "Ancestral Voices" developed two themes: first, changing the past, by means of time travel, would change the present, and second, (Nazi) theories of racial purity were nonsense. The second theme was one of the earlier developments of a social concept other than utopianism in genre science-fiction. Oddly enough, though, Tremaine (and Schachner) missed severe internal breaches of logic in the story.

Tremaine's quest for novelty continued with other thought-variant stories, some of which were hype and some of which were a little different in concept from the stories in *Amazing Stories* and *Wonder Stories.* In general, the direction of such thought-variant stories was away from hard science-fiction into a sort of rationalized fantasy with science-fictional terminology. The stress was on marvel. A typical example was Jack Williamson's "Born of the Sun," where the planets are eggs of cosmic dragons that hatch out, with resulting perils and crises for humanity.

Tremaine believed, for a time, at any rate, that the thought-variant policy was successful:

The thought-variants have injected new life into a field which was rutted by habit-driven vehicles. We sought variant ideas, suggested them, and they have blossomed into a fine series. The writers feel free to come to us now and suggest new themes which they have [previously] feared to tackle. (*Astounding Stories,* April 1934, p. 9).

Tremaine was also obviously more concerned with literary quality and professionalism than T. O'Conor Sloane or Gernsback's staff. All the stories Tremaine selected were not superior, of course, but he began a trend that continued past his reign as editor.

To support this purpose, Tremaine, it should be admitted, had an advantage over his competitors. He paid a much higher rate and paid rapidly, on acceptance; *Astounding Stories* was, thus, the market of choice for authors. Desmond Hall, in his interview in *Science Fiction Digest,* stated that Tremaine received about seventy-five manuscripts a week, whereas Florence Bothner, reader at *Amazing Stories,* estimated that she received only fifteen or twenty a week.

Speed of payment was an obvious factor. T. O'Conor Sloane of *Amazing Stories* might wait years before reporting on a manuscript, and then pay on publication, years later. Gernsback might accept within a month or so, but as the catchphrase has it "paid on threat of lawsuit."

The question of illustration must have arisen after the purchase of *Astounding Stories*. Tremaine (or his superiors) did not retain Hans Wessolowski (Wesso), who had monopolized much of the Clayton artwork, but assigned covers to Howard V. Brown, who had done covers for Gernsback's *Science and Invention* years before. Interiors, at first, were assigned to the Street and Smith stable.

It is possible to make a point with Brown versus Wesso: The new policy of the magazine was away from the frenetic action of Wesso and Clayton, toward a more intellectual approach, and Brown was a staid artist. But this is speculation, and the selection of Brown as cover artist may ultimately have been a matter of contacts and/or prices.

For interior art Tremaine (and his superiors) soon learned the same lesson that Harry Bates had: a science-fiction specialist was needed. After a short time Elliott Dold filled this role; the circumstances of his hiring, described in this volume in the section about magazine illustrators, suggest a certain awareness of special science-fictional needs. When Dold withdrew because of illness, Wesso and Marchioni took over.

During Tremaine's approximately four-year control of *Astounding Stories*, he said disappointingly little about theoretical matters beyond occasional reference to thought-variant stories, and he obviously had little use for the popular science editorials that Gernsback and Sloane offered in *Wonder Stories* and *Amazing Stories*. Instead, Tremaine's editorials were for the most part sales puffs, exhortations to the reader, boasts about quality and success, and boosts for forthcoming fiction. But ideas occasionally crept through the promotion. Tremaine comments about honest work, as opposed to sleazy competition, by which it is obvious he means Gernsback; elsewhere he makes a point that *Astounding Stories* has succeeded by offering more and better fiction than the competition, contrasting this with fake science clubs that are really concerned with selling junk to naive readers: "Somehow I feel that our audience is a little more mature than the type of mind whose loyalty is purchased by a gilt badge." (*Astounding Stories*, January 1935, p. 152).

The reference, of course, is Gernsback's Science Fiction League. It implies, too, that Tremaine was working with an older readership than was Gernsback.

Against this general market strategy, Tremaine's editorial in the December 1936 issue is surprising, for it reveals Tremaine

(in lip service, anyway) entering on the same messianic pilgrimage trod by Gernsback and Sloane. (Thought-variants have now for all practical purposes been tacitly jettisoned.) Along with an announcement that the readers' column would be retitled Science Discussions and maintained at a higher level, to "serve as an exponent of scientific advancement through the contributed discussions," Tremaine set himself the goal of removing stigma from pulp magazines.

> We have always faced an unwarranted bias on the part of a large portion of the educational world against "pulp" magazines as a class . . . . I am going to break down this opposition bit by bit until we are recognized as a distinct corollary of the sciences. Does this mean a lessening of interest? Absolutely the reverse . . . . If we supplement this fictional presentation with science articles in a popular vein, we shall be doing the greatest thing any magazine has ever accomplished . . . . We must so plan that twenty years hence it will be said that *Astounding Stories* has served as the cradle of modern science (*Astounding Stories*, December 1936, p. 152).

This is very much the same program that John W. Campbell, Jr., later maintained (with lapses) for the later *Astounding Science Fiction* and *Analog*.

All in all, Tremaine deserves more credit than he is usually assigned in the development of magazine science-fiction. While he perhaps went to extremes in his quest for "thought variants," in favoring outlandish ideas for their novelty, and while he was ill-advised to print his brother Nelson's feeble Warner Van Lorne stories, he did break the ancient bind that Gernsback and Sloane had fastened on science-fiction. Under his editorship science-fiction was in the first stages of being written by semi-professionals and early professionals.

A tally of Tremaine's authors reveals that in addition to the two specialists in space opera, Edward E. Smith and John W. Campbell, Jr., he published almost every important author of the middle 1930s: Harry Bates, Raymond Z. Gallun, Murray Leinster, Frank Belknap Long, Howard P. Lovecraft, C. L. Moore, Ross Rocklynne, Nat Schachner (though not his better work), Don A. Stuart, John Taine (though not his better work), Donald Wandrei, Stanley G. Weinbaum, and Jack Williamson. Only John Beynon Harris and Laurence Manning are missing. With Lovecraft and Moore, indeed, Tremaine was willing to stretch the boundary of science-fiction for the sake of literary quality. The overall result was much the best sequence of science-fiction printed in magazine form to that date.

It is always arguable how much an

editor is responsible for the good fiction in his magazine. After all, he does not write it, though he may suggest and on occasion rewrite, but there is the keen editorial eye that selects and fosters, that can support and encourage authors. This cannot be dismissed, although its proportion cannot be calculated.

Publishing information

Dates shown are masthead issue dates, not calendar dates, unless otherwise noted. Such issue dates are not precise for organizational matters, for changes would have taken place considerably earlier.

Publisher:
Street and Smith Publications, Inc. Editorial offices, 79-89 Seventh Ave., New York, N.Y.
Owners and company officers:
Per Statements of the Ownership, September 27, 1933 and October 1, 1936, owners were Street and Smith Publications, Inc., per stock holdings of Estate of Ormond G. Smith, Estate of George C. Smith, Cora A. Gould, and Ormond V. Gould.
George C. Smith, Jr., president.
Ormond V. Gould, vice president and treasurer.
Artemas Holmes, vice president and secretary.
Clarence C. Vernam, vice president (from June 1934 on).
Staff:
F. Orlin Tremaine, editor. (Others not named, but Desmond W. Hall was assistant and first reader to Tremaine from the inception of the magazine until late 1934.)
Schedule: Monthly.
Appearance: Third Wednesday of the previous month.
Price: 20¢.
Range: October 1933-[still in existence under a different publisher {Dell} and with a title change {*Analog*}].
Number of issues:
39 from October 1933 to December 1936.
Size and format:
October 1933-January 1936, 6 7/8" x 9 3/4." Side stapled, untrimmed.
February 1936-on, for period considered here, 6 3/4" x 9 1/2." Side stapled, trimmed.
Pagination:
October 1933-February 1934, 144 pp.
March 1934-December 1936, 160 pp. [April 1934 contains 168 pp, but the extra eight pages are a bound-in advertising section.]
Individual issue page-numbering in all cases. Volume and issue numbers, however, are continued from Clayton

Astounding Stories of Super-Science.
Artwork.
    All covers by Howard V. Brown.
    Interior illustrations by various hands in early issues, settling mostly to Elliott Dold from early 1934 through late 1935; after this various artists.
Departments:
    "Editor's Page" editorials by F. Orlin Tremaine.
    "Let's Get Down to Brass Tacks" December 1933 on. Readers' column.
Miscellaneous:
    Factual serial "Lo!" by Charles Fort, April-November 1934.
    Factual articles from September 1936 on.

Contents

October 1933. XII-2. Cover: Brown.
Glamis, Walter. The Orange God
James, Kenneth. Burroughs Passes
Gordon, Peter. Anything Can Happen!
Ernst, Paul. From the Wells of the Brain
Howard-Burleigh, F. S. Don Mackinder's Model
Edholm, Charlton. Ping-Ting
St. John-Loe, G. Where Four Roads Met
Fawcett, Col P. H. Callahuaya's Curse
Wandrei, Donald. A Race through Time
Gilmore, Anthony. The Coffin Ship
Schachner, Nathan. Fire Imps of Vesuvius

November 1933. XII-3. Cover: Brown.
Jackson, Stuart. The Lovely Ghost
Leitfried, Robert H. Prisms of Space
Jenkins, Ainslee. In the Shadow of the Tii
Williamson, Jack. Dead Star Station
Horn, Holloway. The Man from Cincinnati
Burks, Arthur J. My Lady of the Tunnel
Leinster, Murray. Beyond the Sphinxes' Cave
West, Wallace. Plane People
Vincent, Harl. Telegraph Plateau

December 1933. XII-4. Cover: Brown.
Schachner, Nathan. Ancestral Voices
Locke, A. T. The Machine That Knew Too Much
Wells, Hal K. The Purple Brain
Taylor, J. Gibson, Jr. Last Sacrifice
Williamson, Jack. Terror out of Time
Smith, Clark Ashton. The Demon of the Flower
Starr, Paul. The Invading Blood Stream
Wandrei, Donald. Farewell to Earth
Diffin, Charles Willard. Land of the Lost (1)
[*Miscellaneous.* Letters from authors Nat Schachner and Donald Wandrei.]

January 1934. XII-5. Cover: Brown.
Wandrei, Donald. Colossus

Schachner, Nathan. Redmask of the Outlands
Coblentz, Stanton A. The Confession of Dr. De Kalb
Gurwit, S. Gordon. World Flight
Williamson, Jack. The Flame from Mars
Hilliard, A. Rowley. Breath of the Comet
Diffin, Charles Willard. Land of the Lost (2)
[*Miscellaneous.* Letters from authors S. Gordon Gurwit and Donald Wandrei.]

February 1934. XII-6. Cover: Brown.
McClary, Thomas Calvert. Rebirth (1)
Vincent, Harl. Lost City of Mars
Zagat, Arthur Leo. The Living Flame
Peregoy, Calvin. Short-Wave Castle
Gallun, Raymond Z. Space Flotsam
Long, Amelia Reynolds. Scandal in the 4th Dimension
Auckland, Roi. Blind Reasoning
[*Miscellaneous:* Letter from author Phil Nowlan.]

March 1934. XIII-1. Cover: Brown.
Williamson, Jack. Born of the Sun
Fearn, John Russell. The Man Who Stopped the Dust
Wandrei, Donald. The Man Who Never Lived
Coblentz, Stanton A. Manna from Mars
Kostkos, Henry J. Black Death
Schachner, Nat. The Time Impostor
West, Wallace. The Retreat from Utopia
McClary, Thomas Calvert. Rebirth (2)
[*Miscellaneous.* Letter from author David R. Daniels.]

April 1934. XIII-2. Cover: Brown.
Schachner, Nat. He from Procyon
Bates, Harry. A Matter of Size
Williamson, Jack. The Legion of Space (1)
Coblentz, Stanton A. The Green Plague
Von Drey, Howard. The God Box
Wandrei, Donald. The Atom-Smasher
Moran, Neil. The Tooth
[*Miscellaneous.* Factual serial, "Lo!" by Charles Fort (1). Letters from authors J. L. Winks and Bon Tucker.]

May 1934. XIII-3. Cover: Brown.
Fearn, John Russell. The Brain of Light
Diffin, Charles Willard. The Long Night
Wandrei, Donald. Blinding Shadows
Graham, Howard W., Ph.D. The Wall
Ziska, K. F. Succubus
Schachner, Nat. The 100th Generation
Williamson, Jack. The Legion of Space (2)
[*Miscellaneous:* Factual serial, "Lo!" by Charles Fort (2). Letter from author Donald Wandrei.]

June 1934. XIII-4. Cover: Brown.
Leinster, Murray. Sidewise in Time
Kelly, Frank K. Crater 17, Near Tycho
Ernst, Paul. The Thing in the Pond
Fearn, John Russell. He Never Slept

Kostkos, Henry J. The Emperor's Heart
Gallun, Raymond Z. The World Wrecker
Vincent, Harl. Rex
Williamson, Jack. The Legion of Space (3)
[*Miscellaneous.* Factual serial, "Lo!" by Charles Fort (3).]

July 1934. XIII-5. Cover: Brown.
Fearn, John Russell. Before Earth Came
Zagat, Arthur Leo. Spoor of the Bat
Kruse, Clifton B. Dr. Lu-Mie
Wandrei, Donald. The Nerveless Man
Coblentz, Stanton A. The Radio Mind-Ray
Woodbury, David O. The Electric Snare
Graham, Howard W., Ph.D. Guns of Eternal Day
Williamson, Jack. The Legion of Space (4)
[*Miscellaneous.* Factual serial, "Lo!" by Charles Fort (4). Letters from authors Milton Kaletsky, Frank K. Kelly, Jack Winks, and Donald A. Wollheim.]

August 1934. XIII-6. Cover: Brown.
Smith, E. E., Ph.D. The Skylark of Valeron (1)
Schachner, Nat. Stratosphere Towers
Buchanan, Carl and Carr, Dr. Arch. Warriors of Eternity
Peregoy, Calvin. Dr. Conklin—Pacifist
Woodbury, David O. Aground in Space
Long, Frank Belknap, Jr. The Last Men
Zagat, Arthur Leo. Beyond the Spectrum
Williamson, Jack. The Legion of Space (5)
[*Miscellaneous.* Factual serial, "Lo!" by Charles Fort (5).]

September 1934. XIV-1. Cover: Brown.
Schachner, Nat. The Living Equation
Kelly, Frank K. Famine on Mars
Graham, Howard W., Ph.D. Time Haven
Wandrei, Donald. A Scientist Divides
West, Wallace. Dragon's Teeth
Gallun, Raymond Z. The Wand of Creation
Ernst, Paul. The Stolen Element
Smith, E. E., Ph.D. The Skylark of Valeron (2)
Williamson, Jack. The Legion of Space (6)
[*Miscellaneous.* Factual serial, "Lo!" by Charles Fort (5). Letters from authors David R. Daniels, Milton Kaletsky, Tom Olog, Jack Winks, and Arthur Leo Zagat.]

October 1934. XIV-2. Cover: Brown.
Campbell, Clyde Crane. Inflexure
Vincent, Harl. Cosmic Rhythm
Moore, C. L. The Bright Illusion
Long, Frank Belknap, Jr. The Vapor Death
Ziska, K. F. Man of Ages
Coblentz, Stanton A. The Truth about the Psycho-Tector.
Starzl, R. F. Dimension of the Conquered
Smith, E. E., Ph.D. The Skylark of Valeron (3)
[*Miscellaneous.* Factual serial, "Lo!" by

October 1934 (*continued*)
Charles Fort (6). Letters from authors
Clyde Crane Campbell, and Frank K.
Kelly.]

November 1934. XIV-3. Cover: Brown.
Leinster, Murray. The Mole Pirate
Schachner, Nat. The Great Thirst
Stuart, Don. Twilight
Milton, Dane. The Hormone
Long, Frank Belknap, Jr. Lost Planet
Wernham, Guy. Outcasts
Gallun, Raymond Z. The Machine from
  Ganymede
Smith, E. E., Ph.D. The Skylark of
  Valeron (4)
[*Miscellaneous*. Factual serial, "Lo!" by
Charles Fort (7). Letters from authors
Henry Hasse, and Donald A. Wollheim.]

December 1934. XIV-4. Cover: Brown.
Campbell, John W., Jr. The Mightiest
  Machine (1)
Wandrei, Donald. Colossus Eternal
Gallun, Raymond Z. Old Faithful
Graham, Howard W., Ph.D. The Other
van Campen, Karl. The Irrelevant
Stuart, Don A. Atomic Power
Coblentz, Stanton A. Riches for Pluto
Smith, E. E., Ph.D. The Skylark of
  Valeron (5)
[*Miscellaneous*. Letters from authors Karl
van Campen and J. L. Winks.]

January 1935. XIV-5. Cover: Brown.
Kelly, Frank K. Star Ship Invincible
Weinbaum, Stanley G. Flight on Titan
Long, Frank Belknap, Jr. Green Glory
Campbell, Clyde Crane. Gold
Vincent, Harl. Energy
Kruse, Clifton B. Osa the Killer
Gallun, Raymond Z. Mind over Matter
Smith, E. E., Ph.D. The Skylark of
  Valeron (6)
Campbell, John W., Jr. The Mightiest
  Machine (2)
[*Miscellaneous*. Letter from author E. E.
Smith, Ph.D.]

February 1935. XIV-6. Cover: Brown.
Schachner, Nat. The Ultimate Metal
Buchanan, Carl and Carr, Dr. Arch.
  Discus Men of Ekta
Weinbaum, Stanley G. Parasite Planet
Long, Frank Belknap, Jr. The Great Cold
Stuart, Don A. The Machine
Peregoy, Calvin. Shortwave Experiment
Campbell, John W., Jr. The Mightiest
  Machine (3)
Smith, E. E., Ph.D. The Skylark of
  Valeron (7)
[*Miscellaneous*. Letters from future author
Isaac Asimov and author Karl van Camp-
en.]

March 1935. XV-1. Cover: Brown.
Leinster, Murray. Proxima Centauri
Schachner, Nat. Mind of the World
Keith, Leigh. No Medals

Corbett, Chan. When the Sun Dies
Stuart, Don A. Blindness
Carr, Dr. Arch. Cardiaca Vera
Gallun, Raymond Z. Telepathic Piracy
Campbell, John W., Jr. The Mightiest
  Machine (4)
[*Miscellaneous*. Letters from future author
Lester (as Ramon) del Rey and authors
Milton Kaletsky and Karl van Campen.]

April 1935. XV-2. Cover: Brown.
Frederick, J. George. The Einstein
  Express (1)
Campbell, Clyde Crane. Age
Weinbaum, Stanley G. The Lotus Eaters
Long, Frank Belknap, Jr. The Blue
  Earthman
Coblentz, Stanton A. Triple-Geared
Vincent, Harl. Prowler of the Wastelands
Wandrei, Donald. Life Current
Ernst, Paul. The 32nd of May
Campbell, John W., Jr. The Mightiest
  Machine (5)
[*Miscellaneous*. Joint letter from authors
Kenneth Sterling and Donald A. Woll-
heim.)

May 1935. XV-3. Cover: Brown.
Taine, John. Twelve Eighty-Seven (1)
Fearn, John Russell. Earth's Mausoleum
Stuart, Don A. The Escape
Daniels, David R. Stars
Coblentz, Stanton A. An Episode in
  Space
Binder, Eando. Set Your Course by the
  Stars
Wandrei, Donald. The Whisperers
Gallun, Raymond Z. N'Goc
Frederick, J. George. The Einstein
  Express (2)
[*Miscellaneous*. Letters from future author
Lester (as Ramon) del Rey and authors
Milton Kaletsky, Kenneth Sterling, and Karl
van Campen.]

June 1935. XV-4. Cover: Brown.
Bates, Harry. Alas, All Thinking
Stuart, Don A. The Invaders
Schachner, Nat. The Orb of Probability
Wandrei, Donald. Murray's Light
Vincent, Harl. The Plane Compass
Gallun, Raymond Z. Blue Haze on Pluto
Duthie, John. Electrolytic Onslaught
Campbell, Clyde Crane. Fog
Daniels, David R. Into the Depths
Taine, John. Twelve Eighty-Seven (2)

July 1935. XV-5. Cover: Brown.
Gallun, Raymond Z. The Son of Old
  Faithful
Van Lorne, Warner. Liquid Power
Campbell, Clyde Crane. The Avatar
Long, Frank Belknap, Jr. Exiles of the
  Stratosphere
Hamilton, Edmond. The Accursed Galaxy
Kruse, Clifton B. Menace from Saturn
Mund, Edward S. Brain Leeches
Daniels, David R. The Far Way
Taine, John. Twelve Eighty-Seven (3)

[*Miscellaneous*. Letters from authors John
W. Campbell, Jr. {as Carl Van Kampen}; E.
E. Smith, Ph.D.; Donald Wollheim; and
future author Lester del Rey.]

August 1935. XV-6. Cover: Brown.
Williamson, Jack. The Galactic Circle
Stuart, Don A. Rebellion
Schachner, Nat. The Son of Redmask
Van Lorne, Warner. The Upper Level
  Road
Haggard, J. Harvey. Lost in Space
Winterbotham, R. R. The Star That
  Would Not Behave
Rocklynne, Ross. Man of Iron
West, Wallace. The Phantom Dictator
Taine, John. Twelve Eighty-Seven (4)
[*Miscellaneous*. Letters from authors Bob
Tucker and Donald Wollheim and from
future author Lester del Rey.]

September 1935. XVI-1. Cover: Brown.
Williamson, Jack. Islands of the Sun (1)
Fearn, John Russell. The Blue Infinity
Wandrei, Donald. Earth Minus
Moore, C. L. Greater Glories
Kruse, Clifton B. W62 to Mercury
Long, Frank Belknap, Jr. Skyrock
Fisher, Philip M. The Lady of the Moon
Taine, John. Twelve Eighty-Seven (5)

October 1935. XVI-2. Cover: Brown.
Schachner, Nathan. I Am Not God (1)
Stuart, Don A. Night
Weinbaum, Stanley G. The Planet of
  Doubt
Daniels, David R. The Way of the Earth
Gallun, Raymond Z. Derelict
Corbett, Chan. Intra-Planetary
Kruse, Clifton B. A Princess of Pallis
Ross, E. L. Faceted Eyes!
Haggard, J. Harvey. Phantom Star
Williamson, Jack. Islands of the Sun (2)

November 1935. XVI-3. Cover: Brown.
Diffin, Charles Willard. Blue Magic (1)
Weinbaum, Stanley G. The Red Peri
Binder, Eando. Ships That Come Back
Jessel, John. The Adaptive Ultimate
Haggard, J. Harvey. Fruit of the Moon-
  Weed
Beaumont, David H. When the Cycle Met
Long, Frank Belknap, Jr. The Lichen
  from Eros
Schachner, Nat. I Am Not God (2)
[*Miscellaneous*. Letter from future author
Lester del Rey.]

December 1935. XVI-4. Cover: Brown.
Montague, James. Forbidden Light
Gallun, Raymond Z. Davey Jones' Am-
  bassador
Weinbaum, Stanley G. The Mad Moon
Raymond, E. V. Nova Solis
Tooker, Richard. The Green Doom
Haggard, J. Harvey. Human Machines
Leinster, Murray. The Fourth-Dimensional
  Demonstrator
Elstar, Dow. Avalanche

December 1935 (*continued*)
Diffin, Charles Willard. Blue Magic (2)

January 1936. XVI-5. Cover: Brown.
Schachner, Nat. The Isotope Men
Van Lorne, Warner. Strange City
Farley, Ralph Milne and Weinbaum, Stanley G. Smothered Seas
Haggard, J. Harvey. Moon Crystals
Bowman, B. L. Laboratory Co-operator-3
Kruse, Clifton B. Stranger from Fomalhaut
Diffin, Charles Willard. Blue Magic (3)
[*Miscellaneous*. Letters from authors Walter Dennis and Ross Rocklynne, Bob Tucker.]

February 1936. XVI-6. Cover: Brown.
Lovecraft, H. P. At the Mountains of Madness (1)
Daniels, David R. Death Cloud
Fearn, John Russell. Mathematica
Long, Frank Belknap, Jr. Cones
Wycoff, J. Earle. The Seeing Blindness
Gallun, Raymond Z. Buried Moon
Miller, R. DeWitt. The Shapes
Kruse, Clifton B. Don Kelz of the I.S.P.
Winterbotham, R. R. The Psycho Power Conquest
Diffin, Charles Willard. Blue Magic (4)
[*Miscellaneous*. Letters from author Thomas S. Gardner, future author Jim Blish, artist W. Elliott Dold, Jr.]

March 1936. XVII-1. Cover: Brown.
Schachner, Nat. Entropy
Long, Frank Belknap, Jr. The Roaring Blot
Weinbaum, Stanley G. Redemption Cairn
Haggard, J. Harvey. A Little Green Stone
Gallun, Raymond Z. Mad Robot
Pierce, John, M.S. Pre-Vision
Kruse, Clifton B. The Drums
Lovecraft, H. P. At the Mountains of Madness (2)

April 1936. XVII-2. Cover: Brown.
Binder, Eando. Spawn of Eternal Thought (1)
Gallun, Raymond Z. Child of the Stars
Wellman, Manly Wade. Outlaws on Callisto
Miller, P. Schuyler. The Chrysalis
Van Lorne, Warner. White Adventure
James, D. L. The Cosmo-Trap
Lovecraft, H. P. At the Mountains of Madness (3)
[*Miscellaneous*. Letters from authors L. A. Eshbach, Ray Palmer, and E. E. Smith, Ph.D.]

May 1936. XVII-3. Cover: Brown.
Williamson, Jack. The Cometeers (1)
Fearn, John Russell. Mathematica Plus
Sharp, D. D. Doomed by the Planetoid
Long, Frank Belknap, Jr. Red Storm on Jupiter
Stuart, Don A. Elimination
Gallun, Raymond Z. The Weapon

Kruse, Clifton B. The W62's Last Flight
Binder, Eando. Spawn of Eternal Thought (2)
[*Miscellaneous*. Letter from August Derleth.]

June 1936. XVII-4. Cover: Brown.
Lovecraft, H. P. The Shadow out of Time
Schachner, Nat. Reverse Universe
Van Lorne, Warner. Glagula
Coblentz, Stanton A. The Glowworm Flower
Corbett, Chan. Ecce Homo
Rocklynne, Ross. At the Center of Gravity
Lane, Spencer. Origin of Thought
Williamson, Jack. The Cometeers (2)

July 1936. XVII-5. Cover: Brown.
Schachner, Nat. Pacifica
Van Lorne, Warner. Australano
Stuart, Don A. Frictional Losses
Macfadyen, A. B., Jr. The Time Decelerator
Miller, R. DeWitt. The Virus
Kruse, Clifton B. Code of the Spaceways
Winterbotham, R. R. The Train That Vanished
Williamson, Jack. The Cometeers (3)
[*Miscellaneous*. Letters from future authors Jim Blish and Lester del Rey.]

August 1936. XVII-6. Cover: Brown.
Leinster, Murray. The Incredible Invasion (1)
Weinbaum, Stanley G. Proteus Island
Schachner, Nat. The Return of the Murians
West, Wallace. En Route to Pluto
Long, A. R. A Leak in the Fountain of Youth
Gallun, Raymond Z. The Scarab
Farley, Ralph Milne. Black Light
Williamson, Jack. The Cometeers (4)
[*Miscellaneous*. Letter from author Kenneth Sterling. Factual article, "Mercury," by John W. Campbell, Jr.]

September 1936. XVIII-1. Cover: Brown.
Wandrei, Donald. Finality Unlimited
Jones, Neil R. Little Hercules
Fearn, John Russell. Deserted Universe
Barnes, Dave. The House That Walked
Gallun, Raymond Z. A Beast of the Void
Van Lorne, Warner. Follow the Rocket Trail
Tooker, Richard. The Song from the Dark Star
Leinster, Murray. The Incredible Invasion (2)
[*Miscellaneous*. Factual article, "The Veiled Planet," by John W. Campbell, Jr.]

October 1936. XVIII-2. Cover: Brown.
Gallun, Raymond Z. Godson of Almarlu
Drew, Douglas. Nightmare Island
Purcell, Arthur. Positive Inertia

Binder, Eando. The Time Entity
Schachner, Nat. The Saprophyte Men of Venus
Wandrei, Donald. Infinity Zero
Kruse, Clifton B. Flight of the Typhoon
Leinster, Murray. The Incredible Invasion (3)
[*Miscellaneous*. Factual article, "The Double World," by John W. Campbell, Jr.]

November 1936. XVIII-3. Cover: Brown.
Schachner, Nat. The Eternal Wanderer
Fearn, John Russell. Dynasty of the Small
Rocklynne, Ross. Anton Moves the World
Gallun, Raymond Z. The Path
Macfadyen, A., Jr. The Last Selenite
Guernsey, H. W. Macklin's Little Friend
Corbett, Chan. The Thought Web of Minipar
Leinster, Murray. The Incredible Invasion (4)
[*Miscellaneous*. Factual article, "Red Death," by John W. Campbell, Jr.]

December 1936. XVIII-4. Cover: Brown.
Schachner, Nat. Infra-Universe (1)
Van Lorne, Warner. World of Purple Light
Moore, C. L. Tryst in Time
Long, Frank Belknap, Jr. The Flame Midget
Highstone, H. A. Frankenstein—-Unlimited
Winterbotham, R. R. The Fourth Dynasty
James, M. F. The Expedition from Kytlm
Leinster, Murray. The Incredible Invasion (5)
[*Miscellaneous*. Factual articles "The Single Clue" by John W. Campbell, Jr., and "4th-Dimensional Possibilities" by Harry D. Parker.]

FLASH GORDON STRANGE ADVENTURE MAGAZINE

The comic strip "Flash Gordon" first appeared in King Features Syndicate newspapers on Sunday, January 7, 1934. Drawn by Alexander Gillespie ("Alex") Raymond and scripted by Don Moore, it immediately became popular, not only because it was superior in execution to the other major science-fiction strips ("Buck Rogers" and "Brick Bradford"), but because it embodied a certain mythic element in both story and picture: Flash, the dragon-slaying hero; Dale Arden, the soft, pliant heroine who must be saved; Doctor Zarkov, the mad scientist (later sanitized); the wonderful Ming the Merciless and his beautiful, cruel daughter Aura; lion-men; hawk men; and the weird scientific magic of Queen Azura. The strip eventually ran out of ideas, but in its earlier years it was imaginative and original.

Spin-offs began to appear. Flash's early

adventures were picked up in *King Comics*, first issue, April 1936, and a thirteen-episode motion picture serial starring Buster Crabbe, titled *Flash Gordon*, was released by Universal Pictures in the same year.

At some time in October or early November 1936 there appeared on the newsstands the singleton pulp magazine *Flash Gordon Strange Adventure Magazine*. It was published and edited by Harold Hersey, a veteran pulp editor associated at various times with Street and Smith, Clayton Magazines, Bernarr Macfadden, and his own unsuccessful publishing enterprises. His most lasting fame has been as the founding editor of the legendary *Thrill Book* magazine in 1919.

Hersey planned *Flash Gordon Strange Adventure Magazine* as part of an expansible series called Famous Characters Fiction Magazines based on comic strips. The other two published members were *Dan Dunn Detective Magazine* and *Tailspin Tommy Air Adventure Magazine*. Although both the series characters Dan Dunn and Tailspin Tommy are now probably forgotten except by survivors of the early 1930s and comic strip collectors, they were fairly popular in their day, although not the top strips.

This heterogeneous listing suggests that Hersey himself approached the comic strip syndicates with the idea of the hybrid magazine—fiction based on strip characters—for three different syndicates were involved: King Features for "Flash Gordon"; Publishers Syndicate for "Dan Dunn"; and Bell Syndicate for "Tailspin Tommy." Exactly what Hersey's relations with the strip owners were is not known, but it may be significant that *Flash Gordon Strange Adventure Magazine* has a double copyright, both by Hersey and King Features. This may indicate some sort of failed joint venture, or perhaps simply a protective measure on the part of King.

Oddly enough, Hersey says nothing about these dealings or about the magazine in his autobiography, *Pulpwood Editor*, which was published the next year. Given Hersey's usual attempts to glorify himself and to gild his failures, this silence suggests a fiasco larger than usual.

Flash Gordon Strange Adventure Magazine survived only a single issue, but an announcement on the contents page promises a second issue:

IN THE NEXT ISSUE
Another thrilling, tremendous, trying FLASH GORDON adventure brilliantly written—and illustrated with four-color pictures!
"THE SUN MEN OF SATURN"
a book-length novel of another age and world You can't miss it!

In the absence of records it is impossible to determine why *Flash Gordon Strange Adventure Magazine* did not continue publication—beyond the obvious generality of finances. But it is a little strange that a second issue did not appear, since pulp first publications usually went by the "seeders" approach, two or three issues planned simultaneously, to appear at proper intervals to establish a market—or fail.

It is sometimes stated that poor newsstand sales of the first issue caused the cancelation of the second, but this explanation does not take into account the timing of successive issues. The most likely explanation for the death of *Flash Gordon Strange Adventure Magazine* is the simplest one: Hersey ran out of cash and could not obtain further credit from the distributor, the printer, or the paper manufacturer.

Apart from finances there was every reason that *Flash Gordon Strange Adventure Magazine* should fail. From any point of view the magazine was dismal. From a sales point of view, the magazine fell between two stools: comic books and pulp science-fiction. By the end of 1936, the newsstand comic book market was fairly good, but not strong enough to absorb a hybrid form that was quite skimpy on artwork. If one wanted "Flash Gordon," one could find him, along with "Brick Bradford," "Popeye," and "Mandrake the Magician" in the monthly *King Classics*.

From a science-fiction point of view *Flash Gordon Strange Adventure Magazine* had little to offer: a moronic lead novel, one third-rate adult science-fiction story, one semi-essay short-short story, and one very dated short story that might have appeared in the old *Thrill Book*. In general one can say that regardless of the merit of Hersey's idea, his accomplishment was very poor.

Flash Gordon Strange Adventure Magazine was also a sloppily produced magazine, perhaps an indication of haste. For example, the lead novel, "The Master of Mars" is attributed to James Edison Northfield on the contents page, but to James Edison Northford in the story heading. "The Man without a Brain," similarly, is assigned to R. C. Vane and F. K. Young on the contents page, but to R. C. Vance and F. K. Young above the story. A vignette of a young woman is identified as Jane Arden instead of Dale Arden.

Undoubtedly because of its rarity and the difficulty of finding copies, *Flash Gordon Strange Adventure Magazine* has not always been described with accuracy. Despite other paginations cited, *Flash Gordon Strange Adventure Magazine* contained 96 pages, or three sheets. Nor was *Flash Gordon Strange Adventure Magazine* a boys' magazine, as it is often described. While the lead novel, "The Master of Mars," could be considered either fiction suited for the teens or simply very bad adult fiction, the other three stories are adult science-fiction. Indeed, the short

short story "The Last War" by R. R. Botham (pseud. of R. R. Winterbotham) is fairly sophisticated in approach.

The amount of color in the magazine has also been overstated. There are only eight full-page illustrations (in color) and six vignettes of characters. These are not presented in strips, as in comic books, or in sequence; they are merely scattered about to fit the color plate in the printing.

A word must be said about these illustrations. While the artist, Fred Meagher, undoubtedly saw illustrations by Alex Raymond, Meagher's renderings are unimaginative and crudely drawn, far inferior to the sometimes elegant work of Raymond. It must be admitted, though, that Hersey did not serve Meagher well. If Meagher's illustrations had been reproduced on a smaller scale, the coarseness of execution would not have been so noticeable, and they would have approximated comic strip style better. Meagher, a minor comic book artist, seems to have had most of his experience illustrating Western story premium books, notably a series about Tom Mix.

Today *Flash Gordon Strange Adventure Magazine* is a little known and extremely rare magazine. At the time of its issue it received no attention, and, in later years, collectors who hadn't seen copies may have confused it, because of its title, with comic books. Donald B. Day's excellent *Index to the Science Fiction Magazines 1926 * 1950* does not include it, though it includes everything else. And the senior author of this book, who actively collected all science-fiction magazines in the 1930s and early 1940s and was in communication with many of the fan collectors, did not even hear of the magazine until decades later.

Publishing Information

Publisher:
C.J.H. Publications, Inc. Editorial offices, 49 West 45th St., New York, N.Y.
Group:
Famous Characters Fiction Magazines.
Company officers and staff:
Harold Hersey, president and editor. Lloyd Jacquet, assistant editor. Otherwise, not known.
Schedule: Monthly.
Distribution: Federal News Co., Inc.
Price: 10¢.
Range: December 1936.
Number of issues: 1.
Size and format: 7 5/8" x 10 3/4." Saddle-wired, trimmed.
Pagination: 96 pp.
Artwork: Interior illustrations by Fred Meagher; cover also probably by Meagher.
Departments: "The Editorial Mail," a letter column undoubtedly written by the editors.

Contents

MIRACLE SCIENCE AND FANTASY STORIES

Harold Brainerd Hersey (1893-1956), the publisher of *Miracle Science and Fantasy Stories,* had long been associated with the pulp magazines. Demobilized from the U.S. Army after World War I, in 1919 he worked for Street and Smith as the first editor of the legendary *Thrill Book* magazine, and in later years he was associated with the Clayton chain of pulps and Bernarr Macfadden's Macfadden Publications. From 1928 until 1934, during the Great Depression, under various company names he sporadically issued crime, Western, love, and adventure pulps, the longest-lived of which was *Gangster Stories/Greater Gangster Stories* (1928-1934). A later publication was his *Flash Gordon Strange Adventure Magazine,* which is described above. He was not a very successful editor or publisher, from any point of view.

In his autobiography, *Pulpwood Editor,* Hersey gives a vivid picture of the production of a pulp magazine; but he is not trustworthy on other matters, since, in addition to being careless in his data, Hersey tended to exaggerate his importance and achievements. His work is also annoyingly vague, even evasive, on matters of dates or specific events. (See the extended discussion of Harold Hersey in *The Annotated Index to The Thrill Book* by Richard J. Bleiler.)

Hersey has little to say about the short-lived, mysterious *Miracle Science and Fantasy Stories.* I am quoting Hersey's discouragingly sketchy paragraph in full since elsewhere it is sometimes abridged or misquoted:

I discussed plans with (William) Clayton before I resigned from his company to take over the Supervising Editorship of the Macfadden Publications, to launch a pseudo-science, fantasy sheet, but he did not issue *Astounding Stories* until about a year later. My third venture was on my own. It was entitled *Miracle Science and Fantasy Stories.* Elliott Dold, whose brother Douglas Dold had been our (Clayton's) editor of an adventure magazine, the

Danger Trail, encouraged me—not that I needed to be spurred, into publishing this periodical. Elliott Dold is one of the brilliant artists whose work now appears in many of the fantasy sheets. Unfortunately, serious illness prevented his continuing his services as editor-artist-writer and I decided to put the magazine aside temporarily. I regret to say that it has never been revived." (p. 188).

Elliott Dold, in an interview printed in *Fantasy Magazine* gives a slightly different account of the origin of *Miracle Science and Fantasy Stories*:

Miracle Stories was my own brainchild. I talked its possibilities into Harold Hersey, the publishers, for months while I was painting western and air covers for him. (You see that's the way my brother, Douglas, induced Mr. Clayton to start *Astounding Stories*.) Finally Hersey saw the opportunity and asked me to get the necessary stories, illustrations, covers and attend to the birth of the child. And so the brat was born but after the second issue I became too ill to carry on and my beloved brain child died a natural death. (*Fantasy Magazine,* October-November 1934, p. 46).

As seems to have been the case with *Astounding Stories of Super-Science* in the Clayton chain of magazines, *Miracle Science and Fantasy Stories* was in the air and the common embryonic conception of more than one person, although since Hersey actually published the magazine, to him belongs the (somewhat dubious) credit for its birth.

It is questionable exactly what the Dold brothers did for Hersey. Elliott was staff artist, officially wrote one story, and according to both his own account and Hersey's served as production editor. Douglas Dold is credited with writing one short novel, but there are some difficulties involved in this attribution. According to Hersey, again, Douglas Dold was blind as the result of a World War injury, and, when he worked at Clayton, had an assistant who read manuscripts and proofs to him. This may be correct, though it is hard to see how proofreading would have worked under such circumstances. This situation, however, does not explain the novel attributed to Douglas. Douglas might have dictated it, but this seems highly unlikely. It is also possible, too, that Hersey exaggerated Dold's disability.

Miracle Science and Fantasy Stories probably reached the newsstands on March 5, 1931 and disappeared on August 5, when the stands and stores would have returned unsold copies to the distributor for credit.

It was discontinued after its second issue, a not uncommon fate for unsuccessful magazines. According to the *Time Traveller* (February 1932) Bob Olsen and Lloyd Eshbach had sold stories to *Miracle Science and Fantasy Stories,* but they were never printed and their titles are not known.

Hersey and Dold state that *Miracle Science and Fantasy Stories* was suspended because of Elliott Dold's illness. Under ordinary circumstances this would be a statement difficult to accept, for would-be editors are a dime a dozen, and while other artists of Elliott Dold's stature may not have been available, a lesser man would have sufficed. But if *Miracle Science and Fantasy Stories* was a shoestring operation, with Dold pulling four loads—artist, editor, writer, production man—for the price of one, Hersey would have felt his loss deeply. A further factor for the demise of *Miracle Science and Fantasy Stories* undoubtedly was the publishing circumstance. 1931 fell within the height of the Great Depression, and it is probable that Hersey scheduled only two issues as feeders because of inadequate funding. His distribution was not so strong as, say, Street and Smith's, and the resulting weak response to the chain classified ads, which were paid for on a very complicated basis, would not have helped. And, of course, the two issues were a very poor value on the newsstand. The price was higher than that of most other pulp magazines, and *Miracle Science and Fantasy Stories* was much the weakest of the six s-f magazines available at the time. It offered only three stories per issue, as opposed to six to eight from *Amazing Stories* and *Amazing Stories Quarterly,* five to seven for *Astounding Stories,* and six or seven from *Wonder Stories* and *Wonder Stories Quarterly.*

The stories, too, were of extremely low quality. The two lead novels, written by each of the Dold brothers, were old-fashioned, ramshackle affairs that look as if they were dashed off without plan. Indeed. Harry Bates records that he twice rejected Douglas Dold's "Valley of Sin" while editor of *Astounding Stories.* The two stories by Victor Rousseau were at best routine; Arthur Burks's "Mad Marionettes" was substandard; and John Miller Gregory's story reads more like an outline than a story. It is suggestive that all the authors were either friends of Hersey's or house writers. In any case, the fictional contents of the magazines suggest a hasty scraping together of anything to fill pages, much as Elliott Dold hinted in the interview cited above.

The only saving feature of *Miracle Science and Fantasy Stories* was the occasional illustration by Elliott Dold, who at his best was a fine black-and-white man.

Miracle Science and Fantasy Stories is of no real significance in science-fiction, being simply a small failed venture of no historical or literary importance. It is, however, a rare collector's item. Although not on the price level of the *Thrill Book* or other legendary pulp magazines, a copy still brings a premium on the rare occasions when one comes on the market.

Publishing information

Publisher:
   Good Story Magazine Co., Inc. Editorial offices, 25 West 43rd St., New York, N.Y.
Group: Red and Blue Band Magazines.
Company officers:
   Harold Hersey, president.
   Pauline Sandberg, secretary.
   Frank Moran, treasurer.
Staff:
   Harold Hersey, editor-in-chief.
   Elliott Dold, editor, production man, art director and artist with possible assistance from Douglas Dold.
Schedule: Bi-monthly.
Appearance: The 5th of the preceding month.
Price: 20¢.
Range: April/May 1931 to June/July 1931.
Number of issues: 2.
Size and format: 6 7/8" x 9 3/4." Side stapled, untrimmed.
Pagination: First issue, 144 pp. Second issue, 128 pp. Volume sequence.
Artwork: Covers and interior by Elliott Dold.
Departments: None.

Contents

April/May 1931. I-1. Cover: Dold.
Frontispiece: An Incident of the Future by Elliott Dold
Dold, Douglas. Valley of Sin
Rousseau, Victor. Outlaws of the Sun
Burks, Arthur J. Mad Marionettes

June/July 1931 I-2. Cover: Dold.
Frontispiece: Taxie—"The Hanging Gardens Honolulu, in Half an Hour," by Elliott Dold
Dold, Elliott. The Bowl of Death
Rousseau, Victor. Revolt on Inferno
Gregory, John Miller. Fish-Men of Arctica

SCIENCE WONDER QUARTERLY

Science Wonder Quarterly, which was announced as ready in the July 1929 issue of *Science Wonder Stories* is as much a production-time marvel as its mother magazine. To have established the magazine, acquired fiction (including a novel that

had to be translated), edited, typeset, proofed, illustrated, printed and distributed it in the three months after Gernsback's forced bankruptcy at the end of February is a feat. More details of such an operation are given under the mother magazine.

Format, however, was already established, for the new magazine followed the pattern that Gernsback had previously set in his *Amazing Annual* and *Amazing Stories Quarterly*: in each issue a novel accompanied by several short stories and/or novelettes.

In his first editorial Gernsback announced a publicity contest based on "What I Have Done to Spread Science Fiction," with prizes totalling $500. To introduce the contest Gernsback makes several points now probably familiar to his readers:

> In publishing a number of science-fiction magazines, the editors feel that they have a great mission to perform; their mission being to get the great mass of readers, not only to think what the world in the future is likely to become, but also to become better versed in things scientific. But it is impossible for us to succeed in our mission unless our science-fiction readers preach the gospel of science fiction, wherever and whenever they have a chance to do so . . . . There are, of course, any number of schemes by which the spread of science fiction can be accomplished, and we are willing to pay $500.00 in prizes for the best efforts in this endeavor . . . . The prizes will be based on the evidence offered and the sincerity and enthusiasm of the contestants as expressed in their letters. No letter should be longer than 500 words. (*Science Wonder Quarterly*, Fall, 1929, p. 3).

The religious metaphors should be noted, as well as the invocation of futurology, a point which probably would have had importance to the managing editor, David Lasser. It should also be noted that the text fluctuates between the terms "science-fiction" and "science fiction."

The first winner, Walter Dennis, an early author and long-time fan, described his founding of a science correspondence club, soliciting members whose addresses were given in the readers' columns. Second-prize winner, Victor Szanton, a sophomore at the University of Alabama, tells with brio how he converted philistines. As a student, working in the post office to earn tuition, he approached his fellow workers and students. He "made an impassioned speech . . . . [and] from then on pounded remorselessly at these men, bought them magazines, read to them passages from stories, and defied them to deny the truth of the prophecies made in the stories" (*Science Wonder Quarterly*, Winter 1930, p. 278).

Szanton appended a list of eighteen converts. Oddly enough, nothing more has been heard of Mr. Szanton's in science-fiction or fandom. One hopes that his listeners did not rebel forcibly. The third-prize winner, long-time fan and publisher, Julius Unger, converted many readers more gently, as was shown in accompanying letters of testimonial. The second series of winners, announced in the Spring 1930 issue, consisted of Ray Palmer and Allen Glasser, who worked on science correspondence clubs, and Conrad H. Ruppert, who apparently provided the suggestion for the science-fiction week that Gernsback declared. (Dennis, Palmer, Glasser, and Ruppert later became known as fans, as described in the introduction to this book.)

Another publicity or respectability technique that Gernsback used, as in *Science Wonder Stories*, is his list of eminent scholars who "pass on" the science in the printed stories. This list, of course, is a fraud, just as it was in Gernsback's other fiction magazines.

As for the fiction that Gernsback printed, it included two novels by Otto Willi Gail that embodied a considerable amount of the technical achievements of the German rocketry group. These novels were probably to some extent instrumental in the founding of similar American groups.

It was undoubtedly policy that the three first novels published were interplanetary stories, which remained a feature of the later *Wonder Stories Quarterly*.

Also present is Ms. M. F. Rupert's "Via the Hewitt Ray," which is a bad story, but today is of typological interest for its strong feminist position. The other fiction in *Science Wonder Quarterly* is negligible.

Science Wonder Quarterly underwent a name change similar to that of *Science Wonder Stories*, and with the fourth issue it became *Wonder Stories Quarterly*. Gernsback had been forced to recognize that the term "science" on the cover of the magazine frightened away certain newsstand buyers, most probably in the younger group.

Publishing information

Publisher:
   Stellar Publishing Corporation. Editorial offices, 96-98 Park Place, New York, N.Y.
Company officers:
   Hugo Gernsback, president.
   I. S. Manheimer, secretary.
   Sidney Gernsback, treasurer.
Staff:
   Hugo Gernsback, editor-in-chief.
   David Lasser, literary editor, Fall 1929 and Winter 1930; managing editor Spring 1930.
   Frank R. Paul, art director.
Schedule: Quarterly, with Fall, Winter, and Spring issues. The Winter issue

was the first of the year.

Appearance:

September 15, Fall.   December 15, Winter. March 15, Spring.

Price: 50¢

Range:

Fall 1929-Spring 1930. Title changed to *Wonder Stories Quarterly* for issues from Summer 1930 issue on.

Number of issues: 3

Size and format: 8 1/2" x 11 3/4." Side stapled, trimmed.

Pagination: 144 pp. in volume sequence.

Artwork: Covers by Frank R. Paul.

Interior art mostly by Paul, but also by Jno. Ruger, Lumen White, Leonard, and Barker. Unsigned line renderings of authors' photographs.

Departments:

Editorial by Hugo Gernsback, all issues.

"The Reader Speaks," all issues.

Advisory panel, associate science editors:

Astronomy: Prof. Samuel G. Barton, U. of Pa. Dr. Clyde Fisher, Curator, Am. Mus. of Nat. Hist. Prof. Willem J. Luyten, Harvard College Obser-vatory. *Astrophysics:* Prof. Donald H. Menzel, U. of California. *Botany:* Prof. Elmer G. Campbell, Transylvania College. Dr. Margaret Clay Ferguson, Wellesley College. Prof. C. E. Owens, Oregon Agricultural College. *Chem-istry:* Prof. Gerald Wendt, Pennsylvania State College. *Entomology:* Dean William F. Wheeler, Bussey Institute, Harvard U. *Mathematics:* Prof. C. Irwin Palmer, Armour Institute of Technology. Prof. James Byrnie Shaw, U. of Illinois. Prof. W. A. Titsworth, Alfred College. *Medicine:* Dr. David H. Keller, Western State Hospital. *Physics and Radio:* Dr. Lee deForest. *Physics:* Prof. A. L. Fitch, U. of Maine. *Psychology:* Prof. Marjorie E. Babcock, U. of Hawaii. *Zoology:* Dr. Joseph G. Yoshioka, Illinois State Institute for Juvenile Research.

Comment: Paul's artwork for the three covers is exceptionally fine, obviously the result of more labor than many of his other covers. The cover of the first issue is printed with a background of gold ink, the second, of silver ink; and the third, of simulated gold. The inner pages, however, are printed on very cheap, bulked paper.

Contents

Fall 1929. I-1. Cover: Paul.
Gail, Otto Willi. The Shot into Infinity
Harris, Clare Winger. The Artificial Man
Hamilton, Edmond. The Hidden World
Parker, Harry D.   The Gravitational Deflector
[*Miscellaneous.* Editorial: "$500 in Prizes." "In every issue for the next three numbers,

three prizes will be given, as follows: FIRST PRIZE—$100 SECOND PRIZE—$50 THIRD PRIZE—$20." The theme: "What I have done to spread science fiction." * Also letters from authors Forrest J. Ackerman and Edward Chappelow.]

Winter 1930. I-3. Cover: Paul.
Romans, R. H. The Moon Conquerors
Meek, Capt. S. P. The Osmotic Theorem
Lorraine, Lilith. Into the 28th Century
Webb, A. C., M.D. Underground Waters
[*Miscellaneous.* Editorial: "What I Have Done to Spread Science Fiction $500.00 Prize Letters," followed by letters from three top winners, including author Walter Dennis. Letter from author Forrest J. Ackerman.]

Spring 1930. I-3. Cover: Paul.
Gail, Otto Willi. The Stone from the Moon
Arnold, Wesley. Within the Planet
Rupert, M. F. Via the Hewitt Ray
Bridge, Frank J. The Mechanical Blood hound
Harris, Clare Winger. The Ape Cycle
Pratt, Fletcher. The Mad Destroyer
Long, F. B., Jr. The Thought Material-izer
[*Miscellaneous.* Editorial: "What I Have Done to Spread Science Fiction." Winning letters by Ray Palmer, Conrad H. Ruppert, and Allen Glasser. * Announcement for Science Fiction Week, March 31 to April 7, 1930, offering free posters.]

Continued as *Wonder Stories Quarterly.*

SCIENCE WONDER STORIES

In late February 1929, as described under *Amazing Stories*, Hugo Gernsback lost his publishing empire, including his two science-fiction magazines, *Amazing Stories* and *Amazing Stories Quarterly*, which were among his more profitable ventures. Yet in a little more than two months he was very visibly back in publishing. He had established a new publishing umbrella group, Gernsback Publications Incorporated, with two subsidiary companies, Stellar Publishing Corporation and Techni-Craft Publishing Corporation, registering with the patent office and the post office.

Under Stellar he published *Science Wonder Stories*, which was out on the stands on May 5, *Air Wonder Stories*, on June 5. The first six volumes of the chapbook Science Fiction Series were advertised as ready around the first of June. *Radio-Craft*, a intermediate-level magazine for repairmen and advanced hobbyists, was also on the stands in May, but it does not concern us.

The financial arrangements for his new

enterprise have not been published, if information about them survives, but even though Gernsback and his brother Sidney were fairly wealthy men, they had to es-tablish credit with printers and paper suppliers and possibly had to take out loans for operating expenses. Obviously they were successful. This was about eight months before the stockmarket crash of 1929, when credit was easy to acquire, suggesting that his involuntary bankruptcy did not weigh too heavily against him. He also had to arrange with a distributor for newsstand coverage and set up a mechan-ism for subscriptions.

According to figures cited by Harold Hersey in his *Pulpwood Editor* (p. 36 ff.) it cost about $5,300 to bring out a single issue of a pulp magazine. His figures were based on his own experience, of course, and did not necessarily reflect Gernsback's situation, but they may be taken as indicative. To-day, $5,300 is not large for an investment, but in the 1920s, it would have been considerable.

From the point of view of production, Gernsback's achievement was remarkable. He had to acquire for each magazine about 80,000 words of suitable fiction, edit it, establish departments with layouts and copy, arrange for illustrations once the stories were selected, order cuts, contract for advertising, obtain a cover illustration, print it, and then submit the body copy to the printer to be typeset, proofread, printed, bound, and ready for the distributor. Be-sides the in-house work the outside suppli-ers had to be cajoled into fitting Gerns-back's work into their own schedules.

Gernsback undoubtedly handled the planning and some of the fulfillment, but he could not have succeeded without a solid group of workers who stayed with him and helped him in the myriad details of pub-lishing.

It also seems obvious that Gernsback was well aware of his impending bankrupt-cy before Fenruary 1929 and had made contingency plans for establishing a new publishing enterprise. This aspect of his business is covered in more detail in the comments on *Amazing Stories*.

Part of Gernsback's ability to establish the new magazines so rapidly lay in his ac-cess to the Experimenter Publishing Com-pany's files, including subscription and author lists, and to at least some of the stories that had been submitted to Experimenter.   As an early step he circularized these subscription lists, ostensibly to seek a name for his new magazines, but really to announce publication. In this action he was, of course, taking chances, for it amounted to removing assets guarded by Irving Trust, who held Experimenter in receivership. During the court proceedings of the bankruptcy Hugo Gernsback, under oath, denied using these mailing lists, but both

Moskowitz and Perry, mutually hostile commentators, agree that he did, and the logic of the situation demands that he did. During testimony his brother Sidney admitted that the Gernsbacks kept duplicate lists, a standard practice in publishing. In all probability, the court did not pursue the matter, since, unless dummy names were available, it would be impossible to prove, and the Gernsbacks, if they used the list, would have been careful to remove the dummy names.

Perry quotes from the court records the letter that Gernsback sent to potential subscribers:

> You will remember me as the Editor and Publisher of AMAZING STORIES magazine and AMAZING STORIES QUARTERLY .... You know what I have done for you in the past and what sort of magazines I can publish .... In short, my friend, you will have a new and better magazine of Scientifiction, one infinitely better than the old AMAZING STORIES .... You realize that no publisher likes to go ahead with a new publication unless his old reader friends say to him, "Old man, I'm with you heart and soul, let's go!" And that's just what I'm asking you to do now .... And of course, good old Artist Paul will illustrate the magazine with his usual excellent drawings, and I, to be sure, will give you the monthly editorial, just as I always did. (Perry, p. 115)

Gernsback also wrote to his authors, undoubtedly asking for manuscripts and in some cases managed to divert manuscripts from Experimenter to himself personally, as an individual. He also solicited essays from authors in the guise of a small contest, "What Science Fiction Means to Me." (The responses were printed in the earlier issues of *Science Wonder Stories.)* Assuming that Gernsback did not change the title of his contest between his invitation and publication, this correspondence would be the first modern commercial use of the term "science fiction" as opposed to the earlier monstrosity "scientifiction," preceding the publication of the term in the magazine itself.

Gernsback claimed that the name of the new magazine was suggested by his readers:

> When the idea of the new magazine first formulated itself, naturally the name was of importance, and *I put that into the hands of the future readers.* The publishers, had no hand in it. Many thousands of prospective readers were circularized by means of a single letter .... And as the result of the popular vote, SCIENCE WONDER STORIES is the name of the new

magazine *(Science Wonder Stories,* June 1929, p. 5).

During his circularization of former subscribers, Gernsback also, according to his first editorial, sounded them out about the sort of stories they preferred: "I asked for a vote, too, for the TYPE of story wanted most. And the type that carried the majority of votes I herewith pledge myself to publish." *(Science Wonder Stories,* June 1929, p. 5).

Science Wonder Stories, as far as is known, was launched on time, with what amounted to a contemporary Contract on the Readers, stressing intellectual profit and moral sustenance:

> Science fiction, as published in SCIENCE WONDER STORIES, is a tremendous new force in America. They are the stories that are discussed by inventors, by scientists, and in the classroom. Teachers insist that pupils read them, because they widen the young man's horizon, as nothing else can. Wise parents, too, let their children read this type of story, because they know that it keeps them abreast of the times, educates them and supplants the vicious and debasing sex story ... . SCIENCE WONDER STORIES are clean, CLEAN from beginning to end. They stimulate only one thing—IMAGINATION. *(Science Wonder Stories,* June 1929, p. 5).

Primary, as always with Gernsback, was respectability, or the appearance of respectability. Part of this pattern was Gernsback's panel of "nationally known educators [who] pass upon the scientific principles of all stories." This was fakery, pure and simple. Almost no editorial heed at all was paid to accuracy of science, and the panel had little or nothing to do with the magazine. Oddly enough, several were men of national renown: Donald Menzel, Lee de Forest, and William M. Wheeler. Menzel and de Forest are known to have been personal friends of Gernsback's, and one may assume the same of some of the other panel members, who may well have received small honoraria for the use of their names.

Gernsback also included various reader-help departments, which usually took up about 10 percent of the printing inches. Of mixed quality, they embodied the dualism that permeated Gernsback's approach to publishing: an undoubtedly sincere faith in science as progress, yet also sales bunco. "Science News," which was junky and erratic, consisted of small squibs about technology; they might have served as newspaper fillers and were almost valueless. The "What Is Your Knowledge Science Questionnaire," which asked sometimes

pointless questions about science facts contained in individual stories, was of little worth. Gernsback's editorials, which he may have written himself, although they were undoubtedly copyedited by his staff, were competent popular semiscientific journalism, but were more inspirational than solid.

On the more positive side, the book reviews published in *Science Wonder Stories* were usually well done, being, if short, well selected and perceptive, and the "Science Questions and Answers" department took readers' inquiries seriously and tried to give full, accurate answers.

Where artwork and fiction were concerned, *Science Wonder Stories* was very similar to Gernsback's *Amazing Stories.* Paul's covers remained static and demonstrational. As for the stories, changes became apparent, but only after a time. For the new magazines Gernsback hired as editor David Lasser, an M.I.T. graduate who brought a new point of view to science-fiction publishing. Although Lasser had no previous editing experience, he seems to have realized more clearly than did Gernsback's previous editors on *Amazing Stories*—T. O'Conor Sloane, Carl Brandt, or Wilbur Whitehead—that certain standards must be met:

> [O]nce I was on the job and began to look into the stories that were being submitted, I was dismayed by the low quality of many that Gernsback had already accepted. Gernsback had been accepting the stories himself until I was hired. I thought that some of these were pretty terrible from both a literary and a scientific standpoint. So I immediately had a long talk with Gernsback about this. I told him if (Science) Wonder Stories was to amount to anything we had to do better .... We had to lift the quality of the stories. We needed more imagination in the stories, we needed a sound scientific basis, and since these were appealing mainly to young people, there should also be a socially useful theme to inspire the reader.
>
> Gernsback agreed with this, so I was given a free hand. Therefore, I examined the stories that were submitted quite rigidly and rejected a great many of them, even stories from authors who had previously been accepted. (Davin, "The Age of Wonder," p. 12).

On Lasser's point about the "socially useful theme," it must be added that Lasser was (as described in the thumbnail biography in our stories section) a serious political activist, greatly concerned with progressive causes. Lasser would have been more interested in the political anagogic function of literature than Gernsback, who seems to have been uninterested in such matters.

In addition to returning manuscripts for revision, Lasser also occasionally seeded authors with ideas for stories. Although both practices were common enough in the better pulp magazines, they seem to have been new to the science-fiction field.

How successful was Lasser in this program? *Science Wonder Stories* was too short lived to show much, but its extension in *Wonder Stories* did demonstrate a greater professionalism. In effect Lasser was the first science-fiction editor.

Lasser's reminiscences, as recorded by Davin in "The Age of Wonder," give a certain amount of information about the operation of *Science Wonder Stories* and, later, *Wonder Stories.* As editor, when hired, he was a one-man department. He read stories as they were submitted, accepted or rejected them, or returned them for changes. Lasser did not have complete control of the magazine, however; while he had a free hand in running his department, the Gernsback brothers gave final approval to story line-ups.

According to figures from 1934, *Wonder Stories* received about fifteen stories a week. Gernsback insisted on accurate records on such submissions, and reports were usually sent to authors in about two weeks. (The comparable figures for Street and Smith *Astounding Stories* are sixty stories per week and reports within six weeks; for *Amazing Stories,* about fifteen stories per week, and reports, erratically, within four months or longer.)

Presumably, though this point is not mentioned, Lasser followed the stories through galleys, page proofs, and final makeup.

Lasser handled the readers' column and various departments, and may have written Gernsback's editorials, as Charles Hornig claims to have done during the later days of *Wonder Stories.*

Around the end of 1929 or the first of 1930, Gernsback hired Charles P. Mason as an assistant to Lasser. Mason, who seems to have had an excellent scientific background, remained after Lasser's dismissal, working on the technical magazines and assisting Charles Hornig.

Possibly due to Lasser's initiative, Stellar began advertising for fiction:

SCIENCE WONDER STORIES—96-98 Park Place, New York, a new magazine which is edited by Hugo Gernsback . . . . only fiction 5,000 to 10,000 words in length, with a scientific background. Payment is made on acceptance. (*The Writer,* August 1929, p. 119).

The advertisement was, unfortunately, not entirely accurate, for Gernsback did not pay on acceptance, but on publication, and

even that very slowly. As Lasser has said: "We used to have fights about [Gernsback's reluctance to pay authors]. He felt, I believe—because of his German background—that the very fact that the authors were published should have been compensation enough." (Davin, op. cit., p. 14).

Gernsback also undertook various publicity expedients to attract attention. A contest based on Ray Myers's "Into the Subconscious" offered fifty dollars for the best explanation of a fallacy imbedded in the story. According to the editors, more than 800 responses arrived in the mail—probably more trouble than the contest was worth.

A more substantial contest was based upon the cover of the November 1929 issue, which showed two flying saucers carrying the Woolworth Building and the Eiffel Tower away into space. The first prize of $300 was won by Charles Tanner, who based his story on the background color of the cover. This contest marked the first appearance of future authors Tanner and John Robinson Pierce, but was not otherwise productive of new writers—if that was part of its purpose.

Gernsback also offered reproductions of his cover paintings for a dollar each. To the best of my knowledge none of these has survived.

All this was to undergo a change very soon. At the one-year mark, the Gernsbacks obviously took a serious look at their new enterprises, and what they saw was not wholly good. It is now becoming clear that despite publicity euphorologisms, Gernsback's second publishing empire was shaky. *Air Wonder Stories* was a failure, and was canceled, and there was a feeling that a different marketing approach might help *Science Wonder Stories.* Gernsback had come to recognize that the word "science" was frightening readers away, and while he was apparently unwilling to make major product changes, he was willing to make a cosmetic change. On the covers of the last two issues, April and May 1929, the word "Science" was printed in yellow ink that was almost invisible a few feet away, and a new banderole was added to the top of the cover: "Mystery-Adventure-Romance." This banderole is a little puzzling, for while mystery stories were in their heyday, romance is hardly what a reader would want from a science-fiction magazine.

Even this was not enough, and with the June 1930 issue *Science Wonder Stories* became *Wonder Stories.*

Publishing information

Publisher:
  Stellar Publishing Corporation. Editorial offices, 96-98 Park Place,

New York, N.Y.
Company officers:
  Hugo Gernsback, president.
  I. S. Manheimer, secretary.
  Sidney Gernsback, treasurer.
Staff:
  Hugo Gernsback, editor-in-chief.
  David Lasser, literary editor June 1929-January 1930; managing editor, masthead February-May 1930. Despite his title Lasser was in effect managing editor for all twelve issues.
  M. E. Dame, associate editor, April-May 1930.
  A. L. Fierst, associate editor, February-March 1930.
  C. P. Mason, associate editor, February-May 1930.
  Frank R. Paul, art director.
Schedule: Monthly.
Date of appearance:
  3rd of the preceding month.
Price: 25¢
Range: June 1929-May 1930. Title changed to *Wonder Stories* for issues from June 1930 issue on.
Number of issues: 12
Size and format: 8 1/2" x 11 3/4." Side stapled, trimmed.
Pagination: 96 pp. in volume sequence.
Artwork: Covers by Frank R. Paul. Interior art mostly by Paul, but also by Walter Blythe, Butterfield, Imrey, Lieberman, Jno. Ruger, Lumen Winter, and unsigned. Line renderings of authors' photographs often signed B.
Departments:
  Editorial by Hugo Gernsback, all issues.
  "Science News of the Month," all issues.
  "The Reader Speaks," all issues.
  "Book Reviews," all issues.
  "What Is Your Knowledge Science Questionnaire," June 1929-April 1930.
  "Science Questions and Answers," October 1929-May 1930.
  "What Science Fiction Means to Me," June-August 1929.
Advisory panel, associate science editors:
  Astronomy: Prof. Samuel G. Barton, U. of Pa. Prof. Donald H. Menzel, U. of California (June 1929 only). Dr. Clyde Fisher, Curator, Am. Mus. of Nat. Hist. Prof. Willem J. Luyten, Harvard College Observatory (Sept 1929-June 1930). *Astrophysics:* Prof. Donald H. Menzel, U. of California (July 1929-June 1930). *Botany:* Prof. Elmer G. Campbell, Transylvania College. Dr. Margaret Clay Ferguson, Wellesley College. Prof. C. E. Owens, Oregon Agricultural College. *Chem-istry:* Prof. Gerald Wendt, Pennsylvania State College (August 1929-June 1930). *Electricity:* Prof. F. E. Austin, Dartmouth College. *Entomology:* Dean

William F. Wheeler, Bussey Institute, Harvard U. (July 1929-June 1930). *Mathematics:* Prof. C. Irwin Palmer, Armour Institute of Technology. Prof. James Byrnie Shaw, U. of Illinois. Prof. W. A. Titsworth, Alfred College. *Medicine:* Dr. David H. Keller, Western State Hospital. *Physics and Radio:* Dr. Lee deForest. *Physics:* Prof. A. L. Fitch, U. of Maine. *Psychology:* Prof. Marjorie E. Babcock, U. of Hawaii (August 1929-June 1930). *Zoology:* Dr. Joseph G. Yoshioka, Illinois State Institute for Juvenile Research.

Contents

June 1929. I-1. Cover: Paul.
Lester, Irvin and Pratt, Fletcher. The Reign of the Ray (1)
Wells, H. G. The Diamond Maker
Marshall, James P. Warriors of Space
McDowd, Kennie. The Marble Virgin
Keller, David H., M.D. The Threat of the Robot
Coblentz, Stanton A. The Making of Misty Isle
[*Miscellaneous.* Editorial: "Science Wonder Stories." * Response to questionnaire offering $50 prize, "What Science Fiction Means to Me." Winning entries by authors Jack Williamson, E. E. Smith, Ph.D., and Richard Tooker. * Letter from author Ed Earl Repp.]

July 1929. I-2. Cover: Paul.
Williamson, Jack. The Alien Intelligence (1)
Keller, David H., M.D. The Boneless Horror
Vincent, Harl. The Menace from Below
Lester, Irvin and Pratt, Fletcher. The Reign of the Ray (2)
[*Miscellaneous.* Editorial: "The Wonders of Gravitation." * Factual serial, "The Problems of Space Flying" (1) by Capt. Hermann Noordung. * Response to contest offering $50 prize, "What Science Fiction Means to me." Includes "The Gift of the Master Mentality" by Tom Olog. * Letter from author John W. Campbell, Jr.]

August 1929. I-3. Cover: Paul.
Locke, William P. The Moon Beasts
Repp, Ed Earl. The Radium Pool (1)
Sharp, D. D. The Eternal Man
Keller, David H., M.D. The Feminine Metamorphosis
Williamson, Jack. The Alien Intelligence (2)
[*Miscellaneous.* Editorial: "The Wonders of Space." * Factual serial, "The Problems of Space Flying" (2) by Capt. Hermann Noordung. * Response to contest offering $50 prize, "What Science Fiction Means to me." * Letters from authors James P. Marshall and Kennie McDowd.]

September 1929. I-4. Cover: Paul.
Keller, David H., M.D. The Human Termites (1)
Tucker, Louis. The Cubic City
Phillips, Frank. The Onslaught from Venus
Repp, Ed Earl. The Radium Pool (2)
[*Miscellaneous.* Editorial: "Hidden Wonders." * Factual serial, "The Problems of Space Flying" (3) by Capt. Hermann Noordung. * Letters from authors Frank K. Kelly, Fletcher Pratt (2), and Harl Vincent.]

October 1929. I-5. Cover: Paul.
Repp, Ed Earl. The Metal World
Stangland, Arthur G. The Ancient Brain
Myers, Ray Avery. Into the Subconscious
Kateley, Walter. Eros to Earth
Chappelow, Edward E. In Two Worlds
Keller, David H., M.D. The Human Termites (2)
[*Miscellaneous.* Editorial: "Wonders of Speed." * Gernsback also offers $50 for the best letter identifying a fundamental error in the story "Into the Subconscious" by Ray Avery Myers. * Letters from authors Frank K. Kelly and Raymond A. Palmer.]

November 1929. I-6. Cover: Paul.
Olsen, Bob. The Phantom Teleview
Gernsback, Hugo. The Killing Flash
Repp, Ed Earl. The Stellar Missile
Kateley, Walter. The Gold Triumvirate
Gallun, Raymond. The Space Dwellers
Aldinger, Harley S. The Green Intelligence
Keller, David H., M.D. The Human Termites (3)
[*Miscellaneous.* Editorial: "$300 Prize Story Contest." Announces contest for best short-short story (1400-1500 words) based on the cover of the current issue. * Poem: "My Little Martian Sweetheart," by The Planet Prince. * Letters from Jerome Siegel, later creator of comic strip "Superman," and author Ulysses George {Mihalakis}.]

December 1929. I-7. Cover: Paul.
Keller, David H., M.D. The Conquerors (1)
Kirkham, Henry F. The Time Oscillator
Gleason, C. Sterling. The Radiation of the Chinese Vegetable
Carpenter, S. C. The Super Velocitor
Harbers, Henry. The Lost Martian
[*Miscellaneous.* Editorial: "The Wonders of Interstellar Flight" [Gernsback means interplanetary.] * Factual article: "The Rocket Comes to the Front Page." * Letters from authors Walter Dennis, Ulysses George {Mihalakis}, and Ed Earl Repp.]

January 1930. I-8. Cover: Paul.
Breuer, Miles J., M.D. The Fitzgerald Contraction
Repp, Ed Earl. The Red Dimension
Barnette, Jack. The Vapor Intelligence
Keller, David H., M.D. The Conquerors (2)

[*Miscellaneous.* Editorial: "Wonders of Other Worlds." * Replies to the $50 contest offered in the October 1929 issue. Among the entries is a letter from author Jack Williamson. * Letter from author Anthony Pelcher.]

February 1930. I-9. Cover: Paul.
Edwards, Gawain. A Rescue from Jupiter (1)
Juve, Henrik Dahl. Streamers of Death
Flagg, Francis. The Land of the Bipos
Kateley, Walter. The World of a Hundred Men
[*Miscellaneous.* Editorial: "Can Man Free Himself from Gravity?" * Factual article "Can Man Free—Himself from Gravity" by Dr. Th. Wolff, with following comments by rocket pioneer R. H. Goddard, and advisory panel members Menzel, Shaw, Fitch, Palmer and Barton. * Contest announce-ment "100 in Gold for a Slogan." * Letter from author Walter Kateley.]

March 1930. I-10. Cover: Paul.
Vincent, Harl. Before the Asteroids
Brueckel, Frank J., Jr. Professor Diel's Ray
Tanner, Charles R. The Color of Space
Pierce, John Robinson. Relics of the Earth
Brueckel, Frank J., Jr. The Manuscript Found in the Desert
Lower, Harold A. (incorrectly cited as Vernon A. Lower on contents page) Raiders from Space
James, H. [or T. Howard James] and James, Maurice. The Mystery Metal
Sykes, Harold S. The Insatiable Entity
Edwards, Gawain. A Rescue from Jupiter (2)
[*Miscellaneous.* Editorial: "The Results of the $300.00 Prize Contest." Winning entries are printed as above, with Tanner receiving $150, Pierce $75, Brueckel $50, and Lower $25. * Letters from authors O. L. Beckwith and Allen Glasser.]

April 1930. I-11. Cover: Paul.
Keller, David H., M.D. The Evening Star (1)
Nathanson, Isaac R. The Falling Planetoid
Vincent, Harl. The Return to Subterrania
Olsen, Bob. Cosmic Trash
Endersby, Victor A. The Day of Judgment
Stangland, Arthur G. The Menace from the Skies
Flagg, Francis. An Adventure in Time
[*Miscellaneous.* Editorial: "The Wonders of Stellar Space." * Further winning stories from the $300 prize contest by Olsen, Endersby, and Stangland, as above. * Letters from authors Victor A. Endersby, Allen Glasser, and David H. Keller, M.D.]

May 1930. I-12. Cover: Paul.
Repp, Ed Earl. Gulf Stream Gold
Campbell, John S. The Infinite Brain
Sharp, D. D. The Day of the Beast

May 1930 (*continued*)
Manning, Laurence and Pratt, Fletcher.
      The City of the Living Dead
Daniels, J. Stallworth.   The Horrible
      Transformation
Keller, David H., M.D.   The Evening
      Star (2)
[*Miscellaneous*. Editorial: "Science Fiction
Week. March 31 to April 7, 1930." * Let-
ter from author Allen Glasser.]

Science Wonder Stories is continued as
Wonder Stories with the June 1930 issue.

SCOOPS

With *Scoops, The Story Paper of To-
Morrow*, we enter a different area of
publishing and reading from the other
magazines covered in this project. The
American science-fiction magazines evolved
from the adult pulp magazine, with, in the
case of Gernsback's *Amazing Stories*, an
increment of the adult popular science and
hobbyist magazine.

Scoops, on the other hand, evolved
from British boys' story papers, of which in
most ways it was a fairly typical example.
Since the beginning of the twentieth century
British boys (and to a far lesser extent,
girls) had been provided with an endless
series of single-signature tabloid-size paper
booklets describing, equally endlessly,
comic situations in British public schools,
hair-raising adventures in outlandish places,
incredible feats of sports, and occasionally
situations that could be classified as science-
fiction. Such publications were usually low
in literary quality, chauvinistic, jingoistic,
and, in the opinion of critics like George
Orwell, deplorable social documents.

This field of literature, although
collected by enthusiasts in Great Britain,
has, unfortunately, never really been
explored in a serious manner, and, while
some aspects of it are remembered fondly
by elderly British readers, it is still largely
unfamiliar to Americans. It should be
enough to say that such publications as the
Rover, the *Wizard*, and the *Skipper*, published by Thomson of Dundee, were extremely popular in the early 1930s. On the
same level, roughly, were the *Magnet* and
the *Boys' Magazine*.

Shortly after the *Boys' Magazine* ceased
publication, C. A. Pearson, Ltd., long one
of Britain's giants in popular fiction,
established *Scoops* as a new direction in
boys' papers.

To the position of editor-in-chief
Pearson appointed Frederick Haydn Dimmock (1895-1955), who had spent most of
his life in the production of boys' story
papers. Starting as an office boy at
Pearson's, Dimmock had risen to editorship
of the important *Scout* and other publications, but there is no indication that he was

very conversant with other forms of literature. Dimmock is also credited with the
establishment of soapbox derbies.

Dimmock was also editor of all the
Pearson juvenile papers, and as managing
editor for *Scoops*, the publisher Pearson
chose Bernard Buley, an Australian resident
in England who for years had been a
voluminous writer of boys' fiction and had
also edited boys' papers. He, too, was a
product of this specialized field.

As was customary in boys' papers, the
stories in the first issues of *Scoops* were
printed anonymously or at times pseudonymously and were written by staff members or regular suppliers. *Scoops* also
followed the general pattern of brief short
stories and interminable serials that ran to
many episodic parts. The remainder of
each issue would be filled with juvenile
entertainments of various sorts, small
contests, and informational snippets on a
low level.

Scoops differed from its peers in being
set up with a slant toward science-fiction.
It seems probable, as several small points
hint, that the editors and higher authorities
at Pearson knew of American science-fiction magazines, which, in addition to occasional British subscriptions, were being
dumped as remainders in Woolworth's in
London and elsewhere. In the April 28
issue of *Scoops*, both the terms "scientifiction" and "science fiction" are used. The
presence of the words "amazing" and "wonder" in banderoles is also suggestive,
although these were incidental uses, the
usual designation in *Scoops* being "science
stories."

But the editors obviously had no understanding of American science-fiction.
Instead of imitating the American genre
magazines, they assembled a conglomera-
tion of story-types from the general boys'
papers. These included aviation stories
(perhaps influenced by the American air
war pulp magazines), menace stories,
invention stories, hero stories, and similar
subgenres. Like Hugo Gernsback, though,
the editors of *Scoops*—F. Haydn Dimmock
and Bernard Buley—pretended that *Scoops*
served an educational function, although in
their case the pretense was far less justified.
Essentially, editorial statements portrayed
their fiction as introductions to futurology:

> To a newspaper man everything
> that is different, out of the ordinary,
> something others haven't got, is a
> scoop.
> Here, then, is a paper full of good
> stories—all scoops. They are scoops
> because they are different, because they
> look ahead with the vision of Jules
> Verne and H. G. Wells, whose fiction
> stories of wonder and science, declared
> impossibilities at the time of publi-
> cation, are now fact,
> SCOOPS is a paper for all. It has

> the thrill of adventure and mystery and
> will transport its readers from the
> everyday happenings into the future,
> with all its expectations of develop-
> ment and discovery . . . .
> SCOOPS will endeavour to anti-
> cipate the marvels of the age in which
> we live. Thus will it justify its claim as
> the story paper of to-morrow . . . .
> We are living in a wonderful
> age—perhaps the most amazing in the
> whole history of the world. The thirty-
> three short years of the twentieth
> century have seen more progress than
> any similar period since the dawn of
> civilization. (*Scoops*, 10 February
> 1934, p. 15).

Banderoles used for different issues in-
clude: "No. 1 of an Amazing New Wonder
Weekly," "Stories of Imagination and
Science," "Britain's only Science Story
Weekly," "Great Stories of the Wonder
World," "Amazing Stories of the Wonder
World." With 5 May 1934, the legend
became permanently "Stories of the Won-
der-World of Tomorrow."

In the issue of 28 April the editors
make astonishing claims about their
readership:

> Letters from readers pour into our
> office by every post—letters of praise,
> criticism, suggestion, and, of course, a
> whole host asking for information con-
> cerning some phase of science or sci-
> ence fiction.
> Some of the letters are from young
> readers—boys about to leave school who
> realize the important part that science
> will play in the world of the very near
> future—but the majority of the letters
> are from young men who have already
> taken their places in the world of
> industry and have had experience of the
> tremendous influence and power science
> is wielding in everyday life. Men of
> riper years and experience are also
> among the readers and correspondents.
> (*Scoops*, 28 April 1934, p. 375).

If the editors were serious about this
classification of readers, which I doubt, it is
not surprising that *Scoops* failed.

It should also be pointed out that
though the paper was cluttered with fillers
and snippets, which the editors considered
science, this material was almost always
concerned with innovative technology,
sometimes on the crank side, and very
seldom with science. It suggests, as do
other aspects of the paper, that the editors
had no scientific training.

With the twelfth and thirteenth issues of
Scoops, the editors changed editorial policy
somewhat. This change was probably due
in part to the poor market results of *Scoops*
and in part to the remonstrations of British
science-fiction fans conversant with Ameri-

can science-fiction. These fans, among whom were Walter Gillings, Philip Cleator, John Russell Fearn, and perhaps others, seem to have made a strong case for upgrading *Scoops* into adult science-fiction.

The result was a face-lifting of the pictorial covers, which now became fairly realistic airbrushed illustrative scenes, reproduced by rotogravure, as opposed to the somewhat crude solids of the earlier covers. *Scoops* then reprinted A. Conan Doyle's "The Poison Belt," unquestionably the finest story to appear in *Scoops*, and tried to accommodate its stories to American-style pulp science-fiction.

The result, unfortunately, was not very good. British boys were being exposed to American science-fiction (as described above), and *Scoops* could not measure up to it.

The editors also publicized science (fiction) clubs on the American model. None of this, however, was successful, and with the twentieth issue *Scoops* disappeared.

According to W. O. G. Lofts, who had some access to the company records and was acquainted with certain of the authors, *Scoops* came into being through a special publishing arrangement made by John Adley, who persuaded the printing firm of Speaights to accept it as a fill-time for their presses. When Speaights found that they needed their presses for more profitable work, and when Pearson recognized that *Scoops* was not a successful publication, *Scoops* received its death warrant.

Almost everyone agrees that *Scoops* was a poor product, and in all probability, few mourned it. It aimed for the wrong market (preteenagers instead of older readers), provided bad fiction even for a juvenile market, and never seemed to recognize what science-fiction was about. Its title was most unfortunate, for I am sure that British readers, no less than American readers, cared little for the concept of scoopology or weak technological futurology. For science-fiction of a sort, it was a generation out of date.

It must also be admitted, on the other hand, that the United Kingdom at that time, for economic reasons, possibly could not have supported a true science-fiction magazine.

Because of its ephemeral nature and weak distribution, *Scoops* is now a rare item, with full sets bringing high prices in Great Britain. In the United States, where British boys' papers are not well known or highly esteemed, it is not considered especially desirable, except perhaps as an item for a completist collector.

Publishing information

Publisher:
    C. Arthur Pearson, Ltd.   Editorial

offices, Pearson's Weekly Buildings, Henrietta Street, London, W.C. 2., England.
Staff:
    Frederick Haydn Dimmock, series editor
    Bernard Buley, equivalent of managing editor
Schedule: Weekly.
Appearance: Thursday previous to date.
Price: 2d.
Range: 10 February 1934-23 June 1934.
Number of issues: 20.
Print run: 100,000 copies weekly.
Size and format: 9 1/4" x 12 5/8." Saddle-wired fascicle.
Pagination: 28 pp. in volume sequence.
Artwork: Cover art is generally unsigned and by different hands; the only identified artists are Serge Drigin (S.D.) on the first and second issues and E. P. Kinsella (EPK) on the 28 April issue. Interior art, by different hands, is generally unsigned, but occasional items are initialed S.D. (Serge Drigin) or signed Shirley.
Departments:
    "Here's a Scoop," editorial page, 10 February-9 June 1934, editorial page.
    "The Readers' Platform," 19 May-16 June 1934.
    "To the Planets," column on rocketry by P. E. Cleator, 5 May-23 June 1934.
    Feature on major technological projects inside front cover, all issues.
Minor features:
    "Can It Be Done?," "Modern Marvels," "Great New Wonders of the World," fillers, scrap-fun contests and features—irregularly and often perfunctorily.
Comment:
    Certain data given above differ from those provided by other sources. They are based, however, on an examination and collation of a complete set of *Scoops*. For example, pagination is not thirty-two pages, as is generally stated, but twenty-eight. Of this, twenty-four pages constitute a single sheet; the remaining four are a wrap-around, one side of which is printed in two colors, black and red in the first seven issues, blue and red from the eighth issue on. Dimmock (whose name is often given incorrectly as Hadyn Dimmock), was, despite his title, series editor for several publications, including *Scoops*; Bernard Buley was the equivalent of managing editor. The article in the issue of 24 March 1934, sometimes accredited to Sir James Jeans, was really an editorial based on a review of a book by Jeans. Although sources often say that Serge Drigin was the sole artist responsible for artwork, the covers are by several

different hands and Drigin was only one of several interior artists.

Contents

In the following listing, bracketed entries indicate that the stories were printed anonymously. Attributions are due to W. O. G. Lofts, who had access to company records.

10 February 1934. I-1. Cover: Serge Drigin.
[Buley, Bernard]. Master of the Moon (1)
[Thomas, Reg. G.]. The Striding Terror (1)
[Rideaux, Charles de B.]. The Rebel Robots
[Stein, J. H.] Rocket of Doom
[Anonymous]. The Mystery of the Blue Mist
[Anonymous]. Voice from the Void (1)
[Anonymous]. The Soundless Hour

17 February 1934. I-2. Cover: Serge Drigin.
[Anonymous]. Rebels of the Penal Planet
[Anonymous]. Z.-1., Red Flyer
Low, A. M. Space (1)
[Anonymous]. Sheer Personality
[Buley, Bernard]. Master of the Moon (2)
[Thomas, Reg. G.]. The Striding Terror (2)
[Anonymous]. Voice from the Void (2)

24 February 1934. I-3. Cover: unsigned.
[Anonymous]. When the Skull Men Swooped
[Anonymous]. No-Man's 'Plane
[Anonymous]. Monster of the Marsh
Low, A. M. Space (2)
[Buley, Bernard]. Master of the Moon (3)
[Thomas, Reg. G.]. The Striding Terror (3)
[Anonymous]. Voice from the Void (3)

3 March 1934. I-4. Cover: unsigned.
[Anonymous]. Smashing Atoms
[Low, A. M.] The Time Traveller
[Anonymous]. Air Road 14
Low, A. M. Space (3)
[Buley, Bernard]. Master of the Moon (4)
[Thomas, Reg. G.]. The Striding Terror (4)
[Anonymous]. Voice from the Void (4)

10 March 1934. I-5. Cover: unsigned.
[Anonymous]. The Flying Robot
[Anonymous]. The World of Vapour
[Brooks, Edwy Searles]. Submarine Road-'plane No. 1
Low, A. M. Space (4)
[Buley, Bernard]. Master of the Moon (5)[Thomas, Reg. G.]. The Striding Terror (5)
[Anonymous]. Voice from the Void (5)

17 March 1934. I-6. Cover: unsigned.
[Anonymous]. Spirit of Speed

17 March 1934 (*continued*)
[Anonymous]. The Peal of Death
[Anonymous]. The Invisible Witness
Low, A. M. Space (5)
[Buley, Bernard]. Master of the Moon (6)
[Thomas, Reg. G.]. The Striding Terror
(6)
[Anonymous]. Voice from the Void (6)

24 March 1934. I-7. Cover: unsigned.
[Anonymous].   The London-Capetown
Express
[Anonymous]. The Mind Machine
[Anonymous]. Spacedrome No. 1
Low, A. M. Space (6)
[Buley, Bernard]. Master of the Moon (7)
[Thomas, Reg. G.]. The Striding Terror
(7)
[Anonymous]. Voice from the Void (7)
[*Miscellaneous*. Article "Shall We Ever
Travel to the Planets." This was not written
by Sir James Jeans, as is sometimes stated,
but is an editorial article based on Jeans's
books.]

31 March 1934. I-8. Cover: unsigned.
[Anonymous]. The Legion of the Lost
[Anonymous].   Wimpole's Weight
Reducer
[Anonymous]. Metalclad
Low, A. M. Space (7)
[Buley, Bernard]. Master of the Moon (8)
[Thomas, Reg. G.]. The Striding Terror
(8)
[Anonymous]. Voice from the Void (8)
[*Miscellaneous*. Article, "We *Shall* Travel
to the Planets," by P. E. Cleator, replying to
the article based on Jeans in the previous
issue.]

7 April 1934. I-9. Cover: Unsigned.
[Low, A. M.] Vengeance on Venus
[Anonymous]. History Hysterical
[Brooks, Edwy Searles]. Submarine Tank
No. 1
[Martin, Stuart]. Devilman of the Deep
(1)
Low, A. M. Space (8)
[Buley, Bernard]. Master of the Moon (9)
[Anonymous]. Voice from the Void (9)

14 April 1934. I-10. Cover: unsigned.
[Anonymous]. Ice Metropolis
[Anonymous]. Death Dive
[Brooks, Edwy Searles]. The Iron Woman
[Martin, Stuart]. Devilman of the Deep
(2)
Low, A. M. Space (9)
[Buley, Bernard].   Master of the Moon
(10)
[Anonymous]. Voice from the Void (10)

21 April 1934. I-11. Cover: unsigned.
[Anonymous]. The Immortal Man
[Anonymous]. Bandits of the Strato-
sphere
[Anonymous]. Revolt of the Stone Men
Martin, Stuart. Devilman of the Deep (3)
Low, A. M. Space (10)

[Buley, Bernard].   Master of the Moon
(11)
[Anonymous]. Voice from the Void (11)

**28 April 1934. I-12.   Cover: E. P.
Kinsella.**
[Anonymous]. The Humming Horror
Cockroft, W. P. Cataclysm
Rochester, George E. The Black Vultures
(1)
Martin, Stuart. Devilman of the Deep (4)
[Anonymous]. Voice from the Void (12)

5 May 1934. I-13. Cover: unsigned.
Raymond, Moore. Scouts of Space
Silvester, L. B. Metal Dictator
Doyle, A. Conan. The Poison Belt (1)
Rochester, George E. The Black Vultures
(2)
Martin, Stuart. Devilman of the Deep (5)
[*Miscellaneous*. Article, "Shall We Travel
to the Planets?"]

12 May 1934. 1-14. Cover: unsigned.
[Low, A. M.] S.O.S. from Saturn
Fearn, John Russell. Invaders from Time
Doyle, A. Conan. The Poison Belt (2)
Rochester, George E. The Black Vultures
(3)
Martin, Stuart. Devilman of the Deep (6)

19 May 1934. I-15. Cover: unsigned.
[Brooks, Edwy Searles]. The March of the
Berserks
[Anonymous]. Fighting Gas
Doyle, A. Conan. The Poison Belt (3)
Rochester, George E. The Black Vultures
(4)
Martin, Stuart. Devilman of the Deep (7)

26 May 1934. I-16. Cover: unsigned.
Sprigg, C. St. John. The Accelerator Ray
Hugi, Maurice. Temple of Doom
Doyle, A. Conan. The Poison Belt (4)
Rochester, George E. The Black Vultures
(5)
Martin, Stuart. Devilman of the Deep (8)
[*Miscellaneous*.   Article,   "Mars   by
Rocket."]

2 June 1934. I-17. Cover: unsigned.
Turner, D. G. Moon Madness
Raymond, Moore. Scouts of Space
Willis, Capt. John. Death Broadcasts (1)
Doyle, A. Conan. The Poison Belt (5)
Rochester, George E. The Black Vultures
(6)

9 June 1934. I-18. Cover: unsigned.
Thomas, Michael. The Man Who Made
Diamonds
Dallas, Everard. Ray Control No. 1
Garfield, Harvey J. Electric Zone
Willis, Capt. John. Death Broadcasts (2)
Doyle, A. Conan. The Poison Belt (6)
Rochester, George E. The Black Vultures
(7)
[*Miscellaneous*.   Article, "Rocketing into
Space" by P. E. Cleator.]

16 June 1934. I-19. Cover: unsigned.
[Buley, Bernard]. Flaming Frontier
Lintott, J. N. T.   The Mystery of the
Twilight Belt
Cockroft, W. P. City of Mars
Rochester, George E. The Black Vultures
(8)
Willis, Capt. John. Death Broad-
casts (3)
[*Miscellaneous*. Letter from author John
Russell Fearn.]

23 June 1934. I-20. Cover: unsigned.
Hugi, Maurice. The Mines of Haldar
Nelson, Stanley H. The Time Tele-
visor
Talbot, N. Onslaught from Venus
Rochester, George E. The Black Vultures
(9)
Willis, Capt. John. Death Broadcasts (4)

THRILLING WONDER STORIES

In 1936 Hugo Gernsback sold his ailing
Wonder Stories to Beacon Publications, one
of the more prosperous pulp chains, with
superior newsstand distribution and sounder
advertising revenue than Gernsback's.
Retitled *Thrilling Wonder Stories* to fit
a series including *Thrilling Adventure,
Thrilling Confessions, Thrilling Mystery* and
Thrilling Sports, the new magazine appeared on the newsstands with an August
1936 issue.

Since Gernsback no longer published
the magazine, which followed a different
editorial policy, *Thrilling Wonder Stories*,
strictly speaking, is probably not part of the
Gernsback years.   But, to parallel the
coverage of the other science-fiction
magazines, where 1936 has been finished
out, it is probably better to provide some
basic information than to be rigidly
consistent.

Leo Margulies, editor of the chain,
selected Mortimer Weisinger as editor for
the new magazine. Weisinger, although he
had had little writing experience, had
worked with Julius Schwartz operating a
small literary agency and had co-edited
Science Fiction Digest/Fantasy Magazine, a
very useful early fan magazine. Horace
Gold, later the founding editor of *Galaxy
Magazine*, served as an assistant editor.
Charles Hornig, who had edited *Wonder
Stories*, had applied for a position, but
Margulies (or owner Ned Pines) was
unwilling to retain any of Gernsback's
personnel.

The fictional mode of *Thrilling Wonder Stories* was avowedly action, much in
the mode of the earlier Clayton *Astounding
Stories*, but with a younger readership in
mind, a readership familiar with science-
fiction, but less familiar with general pulp
fiction than had been the readers of Clayton's magazines.   The editors also took

heed of active-fan enthusiasms in seeking out stories by A. Merritt and Stanley Weinbaum. These undoubtedly were the selection of Weisinger, who had already dealt with the authors or their heirs. The editors chose shorter stories than those that appeared in the competitor magazines and did not publish serials.

Thrilling Wonder Stories continued publication under different publishers and editors, with varying schedules (bimonthly, monthly, and quarterly) until the Winter 1955 quarterly issue. A total of 111 issues appeared. During its twenty-odd years of publication, it gradually improved in content, with its heyday in the late 1940's and early 1950's, under the editorship of Sam Merwin, when it published material by James Blish, Ray Bradbury, Arthur C. Clarke, Robert A. Heinlein, Henry Kuttner and C. L. Moore, Walter M. Miller, Theodore Sturgeon, A. E. Van Vogt, and other leading writers of the day.

Publishing information for issues concerned

Dates shown are masthead dates.

Publisher:

Beacon Magazines, Inc. Editorial offices, 22 West 48th St., New York, N.Y.

Company officers:

N. L. Pines, president. Others not known.

Staff:

Leo Margulies, equivalent of general editor.

Mort Weisinger, equivalent of managing editor.

Horace Gold, assistant to Weisinger, dates not known.

Schedule: Bimonthly.

Price: 15¢.

Range: August 1936 to December 1936 (considered here).

Number of issues: 3 (considered here).

Size and format: 6 3/4" x 9 3/4." Side stapled, untrimmed.

Pagination: 128 pp. in single issue count.

Volume sequence: Continued from *Wonder Stories*.

Artwork: Covers by Howard V. Brown; interior art by Mark Marchioni.

Departments:

"What Is Your Science Knowledge?"

"Science Questions and Answers."

"Science Fiction League."

"The Reader Speaks."

"Forecast for the Next Issue."

"Scientifacts." October 1936 on.

"The Story behind the Story." October 1936 on.

"The 'Swap' Column." November 1936 on.

Occasional book and film reviews, titled "Scientibook Review" and "Scientifilm Review."

Contents

August 1936. VIII-1. Cover: Brown.
Binder, Eando. The Hormone Menace
Cummings, Ray. Blood of the Moon
Ernst, Paul. Death Dives Deep
Kline, Otis Adelbert. Revenge of the Robot
Merritt, A. The Drone Man
Weinbaum, Stanley G. The Circle of Zero
Weisinger, Mortimer. The Nth Degree
Zagat, Arthur Leo. The Land Where Time Stood Still
Plaisted, Max. Zarnak (1)

October 1936. VIII-2. Cover: Brown.
Burks, Arthur J. Dictator of the Atoms
Cummings, Ray. Shadow Gold
Ernst, Paul. The Microscopic Giants
Farley, Ralph Milne. Liquid Life
Hamilton, Edmond. Cosmic Quest
James, D. L. Crystals of Madness
Merritt, A. Rhythm of the Spheres
Wells, Hal K. Man-Jewels for Xothar
Plaisted, Max. Zarnak (2)

December 1936. VIII-3. Cover: Brown.
Binder, Eando. Static
Campbell, John W., Jr. The Brain Stealers of Mars
Cummings, Ray. Trapped in Eternity
Echols, Allan K. The Island of Dr. X
Gallun, Raymond Z. Saturn's Ringmaster
Hamilton, Edmond. Mutiny on Europa
Weinbaum, Stanley G. The Brink of Infinity
Wilson, Gabriel. Earth-Venus 12
Zagat, Arthur Leo. The Lanson Screen
Plaisted, Max. Zarnak (3)

WONDER STORIES

Although Gernsback announced that *Wonder Stories* was a merger of two magazines, *Air Wonder Stories* and *Science Wonder Stories*, it was really a retitling and continuation of *Science Wonder Stories*, to which was added a small increment of material left over from the canceled *Air Wonder Stories*. In the first issue Gernsback promised air fans one aviation story per issue, but this gesture was soon forgotten, and *Wonder Stories* became a conventional science-fiction magazine.

David Lasser continued his editorial work, cajoling authors, suggesting changes, trying to create a stable of writers who could be relied upon for repeated work. In this, of course, he was hindered by Gernsback's business practices, as described elsewhere.

An advertisement suggests that it was still necessary to spell out to potential writers just what a science-fiction magazine implied:

WONDER STORIES—*Stellar Publishing*

Corp., 96-98 Park Place, New York, wants the following types of stories: "Interplanetarian, stories of atomic disintegration, radium, or other stories dealing with chemistry; stories of biology and medicine; stories of future warfare; descriptions of the world of the future; ultra-modern cities, etc.; stories of the future evolution of man; exploration into unknown lands, in the deep sea, and within the earth; scientific detective stories of the Craig Kennedy type; new uses for radio and television." The following types of stories are taboo: "Spiritualistic or ghost stories; any weird stories, Oriental mystics or magicians; mere bloodthirsty tales; stories of astrology or fortune telling; stories containing a great deal of sexy material." Length limit: for short stories, 8,000 to 20,000 word; for serials, about 50,000 to 60,000 words. Rate of payment is from one-half to one cent a word, depending upon the value of the story. Hugo Gernsback, editor. (*The Writer*, July 1931, p. 203).

It is impossible to determine how successful such advertisements were, but professional writers do not seem to have responded (or perhaps submitted unsuitable material). In any case, no professional writers, as far as can be determined, sold fiction to Gernsback in response to this advertisement.

The history of *Wonder Stories* is a history of survival techniques about which, unfortunately, we have only general information, and about which we can only make inferences. The magazine was born in the height of the Depression, fathered by a shaky company, whose head, Gernsback, had (despite several years of publishing experience in semitechnical work) no real knowledge of how to operate a fiction magazine. As has been detailed elsewhere, in his biography and in the history of *Amazing Stories*, Gernsback had no literary background or taste, but had a very flexible messianic notion of the function of science-fiction, which notion could easily be pushed aside for expediency.

One of the most obvious points about *Wonder Stories* is that it was an early nonfigurate example of operations research. The problem was how to handle several variables: paper cost, printing cost, declining readership, retail price, margin of profit, optical aspects of production and display, sales projections—all to the most profit (or least loss). The result was five changes of trim size and binding, three changes of number of pages, and three changes of price, all of which were not closely coordinated. In some instances, judging by the speed with which Gernsback reversed himself, the changes were immediately recognized as unprofitable, indeed, damaging. Whether he ever found the right combination is doubtful, for *Wonder Stories* continued its steady decline.

An advertising notice in one of Gernsback's other magazines calls attention to the lowered price of *Wonder Stories*:

Now 15¢ per copy on all newsstands THE GREATEST EVENT IN THE HISTORY OF SCIENCE-FICTION! This astounding reduction in the price of WONDER STORIES is the culminating step in our struggle to get on top and stay there! Science-fiction has always been an expensive luxury to lovers of action and adventure. NOW it can be enjoyed by everyone at the low prices of ordinary magazines. (*Pirate Stories combined with High-Seas Adventure*, July 1935. p. 636).

As was the case with the previous similar price reduction in *Wonder Stories Quarterly*, the lowered cover price did not increase the number of sales sufficiently to make up for the loss in actual cash per copy.

There were, of course, outside factors that complicated Gernsback's arithmetic. First, there was increasingly strong competition from the new Street and Smith *Astounding Stories*, which presented an evolutionary step beyond Gernsback. Second, Gernsback paid considerably less than the general pulps or *Astounding Stories*, and even that little was difficult to collect from him. As a result his reputation was bad, and the better authors either avoided him or sent him material that was unsalable else-where.

Gernsback, however, was skilled at promotional techniques. There were contests to stir up reader interest, and a series of small prizes for stories, slogans, and useable plot summaries. Harry Bates of Clayton *Astounding Stories* scorned such tricks, saying that good material never turned up in contests. Strictly speaking, he was right, but for Gernsback, contests were also a way to arouse readers and create a band of devoted buyers. Gernsback also distributed leftover copies of magazines as samples, probably with some success.

Services for the reader also acted as promotional devices. Gernsback did not originate this technique, which goes far back into the nineteenth century and perhaps earlier, and among the pulp magazines was developed in exemplary fashion by *Adventure*, but handled it more effectively than other science-fiction magazines, before or since. He established an excellent scientific question and answer column in which topics of current interest, sometimes quite technical, were explained clearly and adequately. (Unfortunately, the column deteriorated in later years, after the departure of David Lasser.) Gernsback also published reviews of suitable fiction and books on popular science. These reviews,

if brief, were perceptive and clear. (They, too, deteriorated in later years.) It is not known exactly who wrote what in such cases, but in all probability the staff of Gernsback's technical magazines took part, possibly C. P. Mason.

Such departments seem to have pleased the reader, but one should not lose sight of the fact that space allotted to house-written departments was money saved from paying outside authors. A swap column also permitted fans to buy, sell, or swap science-fictional material. (It eventually turned into the birthplace of science-fiction scalping.)

Gernsback's most visible promotion device was the creation of the Science Fiction League, a quasi-fraternal national organization of science-fiction fans set up in local chapters. In later issues of the magazine several pages were devoted to inspirational material about the league, chapter publicity, and similar matters. There were no dues, but paraphernalia was available from Gernsback—buttons, insignia, stationery, and other matters, on all of which Gernsback undoubtedly turned a profit. At an earlier date Gernsback had operated a similar club through his technical magazines.

The concept of such a club was not original with Gernsback, although he was the first to apply it to science-fiction, for similar (much more altruistic) organizations had appeared a generation earlier in *Adventure* magazine. Many of the other pulps, too, conducted fan clubs. More enterprising, for example, was the club sponsored by *Flying Aces*. Grouping its members into squadrons, it sold them stationery, stickers, and even uniforms that imitated to some extent those of the U.S. Army Air Force. A high point came when *Flying Aces* managed to present one of its young club members to General Italo Balbo of the Italian air force after his squadron of planes, in a highly publicized event, reached New York City.

While *Flying Aces* offered Wiley Post and Eddie Rickenbacker among its attractions, Gernsback, to his credit, did not stoop to introducing young s-f fans to Einstein or Alexis Carrel.

Gernsback's Science Fiction League seems to have peaked at about a thousand members while *Wonder Stories* was in existence. While it was directly and indirectly profitable to Gernsback, it also accomplished a fair amount in organizing science-fiction fandom, which had hitherto been sporadic and individual. Such organization had mixed results. On the one hand, it helped create an "esprit d'âme," if such a term be permitted; on the other hand it opened the way to the intense factionalism that has long been characteristic of science-fiction fandom.

Trouble within the League began when several young New York fans, who happened to be ardent Marxists, decided that it was their duty to take over the League for

the Cause. A further stimulus to their activism came from Gernsback's reluctance to pay for fiction published. The results of the situation were: Gernsback paid, when threatened with a law suit; Gernsback also expelled the three leaders of the failed coup whom he (or Charles Hornig) described as "Three active fans who just got themselves onto the wrong road." (*Wonder Stories*, September 1935, p. 496).

There was also a somewhat discreditable side to the Science Fiction League. In the January 1935 issue of *Wonder Stories* Gernsback offered degrees in science-fiction: B.Stf., M.Stf., and D.Stf., depending upon how well one did on a simple question and answer test that was printed in the magazine for the reader to fill out and send in! Two later tests, in the July 1935 and February 1936 issues, however, did not mention the degrees. It is not known why Gernsback withdrew the offer, although one can speculate. And on another matter Gernsback misled members. He claimed that book publishers would give special discounts to club members, but made no arrangements for this. When members complained, Gernsback ran the following notice: "All you have to do to get these discounts is write to the book publisher, ordering the book (which must be science-fiction) and ask for the discount which you are entitled to as a member of the LEAGUE. Most publishers will heed your request." (*Wonder Stories*, May 1935, p. 1520.).

It is a reasonable assumption that most publishers did not honor such a request.

The Science Fiction League was in effect a surreptitious subsidiary business, but Gernsback also had other secondaries. In addition to activities in his popular science/technology magazines, he established Science Fiction Classics, a series of eighteen small chapbooks printing original short stories, usually one per booklet, but occasionally two. While the roster includes popular authors of the day—Miles J. Breuer, M.D.; David H. Keller, M.D.; Clark Ashton Smith; Manley Wade Wellman; and Jack Williamson—the general level of the series is very low.

Wonder Stories gradually declined throughout the early Depression years. There seems to have been a crisis in 1933, during which the magazine came close to being terminated, but details are not known. During this period of gradual collapse Gernsback laid off workers, cut the amount of fiction in the magazine, and, of course, withheld payment of authors.

Gernsback's most drastic change in *Wonder Stories* came in July 1933, when he fired David Lasser, who had edited the fiction magazines since 1929, and hired in his place Charles Hornig, who went to work on August 7, 1933. (Biographical information about both men is given in the author section.) The official reason for

Lasser's discharge was neglect of work, since Lasser was taking more and more time for labor activities. Another potent reason, undoubtedly, was financial, for whereas Gernsback paid Lasser $70 a week, he paid Hornig $20. In 1933 for Gernsback $50 per week was a large sum.

The selection of Hornig was also part of Gernsback's catch-as-catch-can operations research. Gernsback seems to have decided from his contacts with vociferous fans that his readership was mostly adolescent male. Since Hornig, then 17 years old, had edited and produced an excellent fan magazine called the *Fantasy Fan*, which featured work by Lovecraft, C. A. Smith, and others, Gernsback apparently felt that Hornig would have more empathy with the market than would an older man.

Hornig's reminiscences, printed in Davin's "The Age of Wonder" convey much the same picture of operations at Stellar as did David Lasser (as described in the section on *Science Wonder Stories*). Money was scarce, and Gernsback was very reluctant to pay authors even when money was available. Gernsback had no real interest in the literary aspects of the magazine and in general pursued a hands-off administrative policy, except for final approval of issues. As Hornig related to Davin:

I had total control over what appeared in the magazine. The one thing that we all liked about Gernsback and which kept us with him, despite his poor rate of pay and his employees having to hold pay checks for weeks upon weeks at a time, was that he gave everyone a free hand. He was good to work for that way. He didn't stop you from doing anything. He didn't criticize your work unless you did something really wrong. So, I was totally free to reject or accept stories. Of course, he never saw the rejected stories, but in the two and a half years I worked for him he never once disagreed with me over a story I accepted.

The practice was for me to read all the stories which came in. Maybe one out of twenty was worth considering. If I wanted to accept any story I wrote an evaluation on a special cover-sheet which was then attached to the manuscript, I described what I liked about the story and why I wanted to use it. This was passed on to Gernsback, and he'd send it back with an "OK" on it . . . . I wrote all the editorials, handled "The Reader Speaks" column, wrote all the blurbs and captions, and chose the work of all artists except for Frank Paul. (Davin, "The Age of Wonder" p. 22).

Hornig, it is presumed, was responsible for the editorial in the January 1934 issue, which promised a new direction:

Our New Policy

Since we have returned to the small size, we have changed our editorial policy. We hope that you have noticed this.

Have you observed that, for the most part, we have been avoiding time-worn plots and themes? Not only this, but we have demanded that our authors include good, logical, and accurate science in their stories, although not enough to become boring to those readers who are not primarily interested in the technicalities of the science. We have insisted that the stories be composed in such a way that they are not only refreshing, because of their originality, but are convincing due to their plausible action and science.

Such grey-haired ideas as reducing the characters' size by rays until they can walk about on electrons; repelling invaders from other worlds or dimensions (especially Martians!), travelling into the future and barely escaping from the hordes of savages or hostile inhabitants that are yet to be born; planets warring with terrible rays against each other;—we could go on for pages with others that all dyed-in-the-wool science-fiction fans are familiar with—these plots we are trying hard to avoid.

If you read a story in our magazine that tastes old-fashioned and is reminiscent of the old days of premature and adolescent science-fiction, there are but two reasons for its appearance in our pages; (1) the plot contains so many unusual and absorbing incidents that the time-worn plot is held subordinate and can be overlooked, or (2) the editors (who are only human) have slipped up . . . .

Wonder Stories is attempting a RADICAL REVOLUTION in science-fiction, and we hope that 1934 will be set down as the year of the GREAT CHANGE in scientific literature. THE EDITORS. (*Wonder Stories*, January 1934, p. 655).

Like Gernsback's (or David Lasser's) editorial in the Spring 1931 issue of *Wonder Stories Quarterly*, this cuts away important areas of science-fiction, and also ignores (except in a backhanded way) more important areas of development. Hornig and Gernsback couldn't follow this schema absolutely, of course, but in the last issues of *Wonder Stories* the pulp action story had been pushed into the background, as had the didactic Gernsback story; the dominant short story of the later issues tends to be something different, the quirk or oddity story. Whether this was a salutary development is another question, for *Astounding Stories* was doing quite well with superior space operas.

In a defense or description of his policy of seeking novelty, Hornig listed specific rejections:

Some of the more prominent stories that we have rejected which appeared in other magazines are as follows: "Triplanetary" by Edward E. Smith; "The Jameson Satellite" by N. Jones; "Omega the Man" L. H. Morrow; "Valley of the Titans" L. A. Eshbach; "Beings of the Boundless Blue" Walter Kately [*sic*]; "The Theft of the Washington Monument" by Robert Arthur, Jr.; "Air Lines" by David H Keller, M. D.; "Reclaimers of the Ice" by Stanton A. Coblentz; "The Hungry Guinea Pig" Miles J. Breuer, M. D.; "Atomic Fire" Raymond Z. Gallun; "Madness of the Dust" R. F. Starzl; "Scandal in the Fourth Dimension" by Amelia Reynolds Long; "Dr. Lu-Mie" Clifton Bryan Kruse; "Flight on Titan" Stanley Weinbaum; and dozens of others which limited space prohibits me from listing. Now you know what we mean by "Stories we reject appear elsewhere." (*Fantasy Magazine*, December 1934-January 1935, p. 77).

One might agree with Hornig's editorial decision on many of these stories, in terms of quality, but the rejection of "Triplanetary" and "Flight on Titan" was certainly a business mistake.

Wonder Stories became a bimonthly publication at the end of 1935, a change usually equivalent to a death rattle in pulp fiction. Then in the April 1936 issue there were two strange notices that imparted much the same information:

The difficulty today [in conducting a profitable operation] . . . . lies in distribution. Particularly is the difficulty severe when it comes to so-called pulp magazines. Such magazines must subsist from the money collected from the sales of the magazines since, because of the low-priced pulp paper necessarily used, it has been found impossible for any class of pulp magazines to get any real revenue from advertising. (Compare this, however, with Gernsback's statement about profitable advertising in the editorial from *Amazing Stories* for August 1927.)

The average pulp magazine, in order to exist at all, must print at least 100,000 copies each issue. At the present time, even the best of such "pulps" have never sold better than about 80%—or 80,000 copies—and that is tops!

Most of them sell less than 50,000. The other 50,000, therefore, is pure waste. Unsold copies are returned from the newsstands; either the complete copies go back to the publisher or, where the distance is great, the publisher gets back only the covers. The magazine distributor strips off the cover, and either junks the coverless magazines by selling them for old paper or, otherwise, sells them as imperfect copies to the public.

This latter form of racketeering is rapidly killing the business of many publishers . . . . The thought might occur to the average reader: "Why sell the magazine on newsstands at all, why not have the readers subscribe to it direct?" Unfortunately, up to the present time, this has never worked out; because only a comparatively small percentage of people can be induced to subscribe to any type of magazine in advance, and usually, the collection difficulties between publisher and individual readers are greater than when distributing the magazine at wholesale to newsstands. However, we have evolved a new plan, which is discussed at length on page 921 of this issue, and think it worth while to try out. (*Wonder Stories*, April 1936, p. 901).

The "entirely new plan" offered a postage-prepaid, cut-out coupon that could serve as a postal card ordering the magazine. On receipt of it, Gernsback would send the magazine, a bill for 15¢ and a prepaid envelope into which one could place coins or stamps.

As might have been expected, this proposal did not succeed, and *Wonder Stories* died. Hornig had already been discharged, and the final, April 1936 issue is said to have been thrown together from material in the office.

One wonders, even if the response had been large, how Gernsback could have turned any profit on such a subscription plan, for the first-class postage alone would have cost him 4¢, to say nothing of magazine postage. In any case, there is no evidence that Gernsback took his own offer seriously enough to make plans for publication.

The December 1935 and January 1936 issues list several stories that were scheduled for the future: J. Bartel, "The Jester of Xenonia"; Eando Binder, "Beyond the Limit" (described as "a weird experiment in the laboratory of a scientific genius"); Paul K. Chapple, "Black World"; David Kyle, "Golden Nemesis'; Laurence Manning, "Maze of Creation" (a sequel to "World of the Mist"); Ross Rocklynne, "Into the Darkness": Leslie Stone, "The Other Side" (a sequel to "The Man with the Four Dimensional Eyes"); and William Temple, "Another Chance."

Kyle's "Golden Nemesis" was printed in *Stirring Science Stories*, February 1941;

Ross Rocklynne's "Into the Darkness," in *Astonishing Stories*, June 1940. Binder's "Beyond the Limit" may be "Conquest of Life," which was published in the August 1937 issue of *Thrilling Wonder Stories*. The other stories do not seem to have been published, at least under the cited titles.

Wonder Stories was more willing than its competitors to break away from pulp action modes. Although *Astounding Stories*, after Tremaine took over, on the whole published better fiction, *Wonder Stories* was freer in what it offered, though not necessarily in the direct line of development of science-fiction. It thus published three original novels that approached mainstream development: "The Time Stream," by Eric Temple Bell (John Taine), which though choppy by abridgment from the original version, deals with ideas, notably clashing standards and inevitability; "The Perfect World," by Benson Herbert, which attempts ironic character studies against a background of interplanetary travel; and "The Green Man of Graypec," by Festus Pragnell, an adventure novel in the mode of the early H. G. Wells (it was praised by Wells). Although none is a work of first importance, each has points of interest beyond the average science-fiction story of the time. In addition Stanton A. Coblentz's "In Caverns Below," although weaker in its subgenre--satire--has some period association for its strong attitudes against militarism, brainwashing, propaganda, and incidentally, Franklin Delano Roosevelt.

Gernsback's translations of German fiction are also interesting in showing what was taking place in undifferentiated science-fiction in Europe. Hanstein's novels, although stodgy, express an extreme typological view, a premodern reification of "progress" without environmental concern. The French translations are less worthy. As has been indicated in more detail elsewhere, however, Gernsback (who is said to have negotiated the German rights personally) was remarkably insensitive to political events in Germany.

In short stories, the most noteworthy historical event was the appearance of the work of Stanley G. Weinbaum, which created a stir that has still not died among ancient fan survivors, although, in my opinion, the enthusiasm was excessive.

In general, although *Wonder Stories*, under both Lasser and Hornig, printed its share of bad fiction, one could say that it did contribute to the development of science-fiction and did offer an occasional story that is still worth reading.

Several months after the disappearance of *Wonder Stories*, its successor appeared. This was *Thrilling Wonder Stories*, published by Beacon Magazines, Inc. While it retained the issue and volume sequences and several departments of Gernsback's *Wonder Stories*, it differed greatly in editorial approach.

Publishing information

In the following tabulation, magazine masthead dates, not calendar dates, are used unless otherwise indicated. Masthead dates are not precise, for transfers of ownership and changes in company officials and staff would have taken place earlier than indicated in the magazine.

Publisher:
June 1930-November 1933. Stellar Publishing Corporation. Editorial offices, 96-98 Park Place, New York, N.Y.
Continental Publications, Inc. Editorial offices, 96-98 Park Place, New York, N.Y., from December 1933 to June 1934. Editorial offices, 99 Hudson St., New York, N.Y., from July 1934 to April 1936. Apparently simply a reorganization of Stellar.

Company officers:
Hugo Gernsback, president.
I. S. Manheimer, secretary, later business manager.
Sidney Gernsback, treasurer, June 1930-November 1933.

Staff:
Hugo Gernsback, editor-in-chief.
David Lasser, managing editor, June 1930-October 1933.
Charles Hornig, managing editor, November 1933-April 1936.
C. P. Mason, associate editor, June 1930-April 1936.
Frank R. Paul, art director.
C. A. Brandt, literary editor, January 1932-November 1932.

Schedule:
Monthly: June 1930-June 1933.
Bimonthly: August-October 1933.
Monthly: November 1933-October 1935.
Bimonthly: December 1935-April 1936.

Appearance:
3rd of the preceding month.

Price:
June 1930-October 1932: 25¢.
November 1932-March 1933: 15¢.
April 1933-May 1935: 25¢.
June 1935-April 1936: 15¢.

Range of issues:
June 1930-April 1936.

Number of issues: 66.

Size and format:
June-October 1930: 8 1/2" x 11 3/4." Side stapled, trimmed.
November 1930-October 1931: 6 3/4" x 9 7/8." Side stapled, untrimmed.
November 1931-October 1932: 8 1/2" x 11 1/2." Side stapled, trimmed.
November 1932-March 1933: 8 1/2" x 11 1/2." Saddle-wired, trimmed.
April-October 1933: 8 1/2" x 11 1/2." Side stapled, trimmed.
November 1933-April 1936: 6 3/4" x

Size and format (*continued*)
9 7/8." Side stapled, untrimmed.
Pagination, all in volume sequence:
June-October 1930: 96 pp.
November 1930-October 1931: 144 pp.
November 1931-October 1932:
96 pp.
November 1931-October November
1932-March 1933: 64 pp.
April-October 1933: 96 pp.
November 1933-April 1936: 144 pp.
Cover art:
All issues, Paul, though not always
signed.
Interior artwork:
Through 1931: Mostly Marchioni and
Paul, but also Leonard, Miller,
Lyman Anderson, Wilson, and
Fisher.
November 1931-October 1933: totally
Paul.
November 1933 on, mostly Paul, Lum-
en Winter second; also Burian,
Bulow, Schneeman, Saaty, and
Marchioni.
Departments:
Editorials by Hugo Gernsback: all
issues.
"Book reviews" June 1930 through
1933; irregularly after that, with
occasional film reviews.
"Science News of the Month" June-
September 1930.
"The Reader Speaks" all issues.
"What Is Your Knowledge," also titled
"What Is Your Science Know-
ledge" and "What Is Your Know-
ledge of Science" June 1930-
March 1932; May 1933-April 1936,
with occasional gaps.
"Science Questions and Answers" all
issues.
"What Science Fiction Means to Me"
June-August 1929.
"The Science Fiction Swap Column"
July 1934-April 1936.
"The Science Fiction League" June
1934-April 1936.
Various fillers, contest announcements,
sales pitches.
Advisory panel, associate science editors:
Astronomy: Prof. Samuel G. Barton,
U. of Pa. (June 1930-July 1931). Dr.
Clyde Fisher, Curator, Am. Mus. of
Nat. Hist. Prof. Willem J. Luyten,
Harvard College Observatory. *Astro-
physics:* Prof. Donald H. Menzel, U. of
California (Astronomy, June 1930; later
astrophysics). *Aviation:* Prof. William
A. Bevan, Iowa State College. Prof.
Earl D. Hay, U. of Kansas. Prof.
George J. Higgins, U. of Detroit. Prof.
Felix W. Pawlowski, U. of Michigan.
Prof. John E. Younger, U. of Cali-
fornia. *Botany:* Prof. Elmer G.
Campbell, Transylvania College. Dr.
Margaret Clay Ferguson, Wellesley
College. Prof. C. E. Owens, Oregon
Agricultural College. *Chemistry:* Prof.

Gerald Wendt, Pennsylvania State
College. *Electricity:* F. E. Austin,
Dartmouth College. *Entomology:*
Dean William F. Wheeler, Bussey
Institute, Harvard U. *Mathematics:*
Prof. C. Irwin Palmer, Armour Institute
of Technology (June 1930-October
1931). Prof. James Byrnie Shaw, U. of
Illinois (June 1930-April 1931). Prof.
W. A. Titsworth, Alfred University.
Medicine: Dr. David H. Keller, Western
State Hospital. *Physics and Radio:* Dr.
Lee deForest (through Summer 1932).
Physics: Prof. A. L. Fitch, U. of Maine.
Psychology: Prof. Marjorie E. Babcock,
U. of Hawaii. *Zoology:* Dr. Joseph G.
Yoshioka, Illinois State Institute for
Juvenile Research, later Yale U.

Contents

June 1930. II-2. Cover: Paul.
[A continuation of *Science Wonder Stories*,
with which has been combined *Air Wonder
Stories*.]
Bauer, George Paul. A Subterranean Ad-
venture (1)
Kateley, Walter. The Incredible Monstro-
sity
Meek, Capt. S. P. Trapped in the Depths
Palmer, Raymond A. The Time Ray of
Jandra
Arnold, Wesley. Waves of Death
Jackson, Wood. The Bat-Men of Mars (2)
[continued from the May 1930 issue of
Air Wonder Stories]
[*Miscellaneous.* Editorial: "The Wonders of
Sleep." * Letters from author Allen Glasser
and from editor and author C. P. Mason.]

July 1930. II-3. Cover: Paul.
Breuer, Miles J. The Time Valve
Tanner, Charles R. The Flight of the
Mercury
Endersby, Victor A. After 5000 Years
Vanny, Jim. The War of the Great
Ants
Miller, P. Schuyler. The Red Plague
Jackson, Wood. The Bat-Men of Mars (3)
Bauer, George Paul. A Subterranean Ad-
venture (2)
[*Miscellaneous.* Editorial: "Wonders of the
Unknown." * Result of prize contest from
Air Wonder Stories on the relative danger
of Lindbergh's flight across the Atlantic and
Admiral Bird's flight over Antarctica. *
Award on $300 prize contest from *Air
Wonder Stories.* * Poems: "Advance of
Science" and "The Master Allegory" by The
Planet Prince {J. Harvey Haggard}. *
Letters from editor and author C. P. Mason
and author M. F. Rupert.]

August 1930. II-3. Cover: Paul.
Juve, Henrik Dahl. The Martian Revenge
Repp, Ed Earl. The *Annihilator* Comes
Beck, Clyde F. When the Moons Met!
Vanny, Jim. The Radium Master

Bauer, George Paul. A Subterranean Ad-
venture (3)
[*Miscellaneous.* Editorial: "Wonders of
Memory." * "The Magazine of Prophetic
Fiction," article declaring winner of slogan
contest from *Science Wonder Stories.* *
Letters from author Raymond A. Palmer
and from editor and author C. P. Mason.]

September 1930. II-4. Cover: Paul.
Bridge, Frank J. The War Lord of Venus
(1)
Schachner, Nat and Zagat, Arthur Leo. In
20,000 A.D.!
Meek, Capt. S. P. The Tragedy of Spider
Island
Starzl, R. F. The King of the Black Bowl
Morrow, Lowell Howard. A Rescue in
Space
Newton, Edsel. The Torpedo Terror
[*Miscellaneous.* Editorial: "The Wonders of
SpaceMatter." * Letters from author Allen
Glasser and future author Willy Ley.]

October 1930. II-5. Cover: Paul.
Smith, Clark Ashton. Marooned in An-
dromeda
Flagg, Francis. The Lizard-Men of Buh-
Lo
Wilkins, Ralph W. The Empire in the
Sky
Hansen, L. Taylor. The City on the
Cloud
Haggard, J. Harvey. Faster than Light
Bonney, Norman J. The Man Who Laughs
Bridge, Frank J. The War Lord of Venus
(2)
[*Miscellaneous.* Editorial: "Announce-
ment" indicating that the size of the
magazine will change with the next issue.]

November 1930. II-6. Cover: Paul.
Manley, Edgar A. and Thode, Walter.
The Time Annihilator
Hermanson, Ulf. The House in the
Clouds
Campbell, John Scott. The Invulnerable
Kirkham, Henry F. Lords of the Deep
Starzl, R. F. Hornets of Space
Bridge, Frank J. The Warlord of Venus
(3)
[*Miscellaneous.* Editorial: "The Wonders of
Flight." * Letters from authors Allen
Glasser and Jim Vanny.]

December 1930. II-7. Cover: Paul.
Maxwell, Joslyn. The Outpost on the
Moon (1)
Kirkham, Henry F. The End of Time
Colladay, Morrison. The Silent Scourge
Repp, Ed Earl. The Synthetic Men
Arnold, Wesley. The Struggle for Venus
Wulfres, Roger. The Air-Plant Men
[*Miscellaneous.* Editorial: "Life on Other
Planets." * Letters from editor and author C.
P. Mason; from authors Allen Glasser, Edsel
Newton, and Raymond A. Palmer; and from
future author Willy Ley.]

January 1931. II-8. Cover: Paul.
Sharp, D. D. The Satellite of Doom
Newton, E. Edsel. The Flaming Cloud
Kennelly, Joseph. Death from the Seas
Afford, Malcolm R. The Gland Men of the Island
Pelcher, Anthony. The Soulless Entity
Maxwell, Joslyn. The Outpost on the Moon (2)
[*Miscellaneous*. Editorial: "The Wonders of the Vacuum." * Letters from author J. Harvey Haggard and future author Willy Ley.]

February 1931. II-9. Cover: Paul.
Miller, P. Schuyler. Dust of Destruction
Cummings, Ray. The Great Transformation
Wilson, Robert H. A Flight into Time
Beattie, George B. The Murders on the Moon Ship
Keller, David H., M.D. The Sleeping War
Herbert, Benson. The World Without
Maxwell, Joslyn. The Outpost on the Moon (3)
[*Miscellaneous*. Editorial: "The Wonders of the Simple." * Letter from author Edsel Newton.]

March 1931. II-10. Cover: Paul.
Edwards, Gawain. The Return from Jupiter (1)
Sloat, Edwin K. The World without Name
Starzl, R. F. The Terrors of Aryl
Schachner, Nat and Zagat, Arthur Leo. Back to 20,000 A.D.
Flagg, Francis. The Synthetic Monster
Hilliard, A. Rowley. The Green Torture
Repp, Ed Earl. From out of the Earth
[*Miscellaneous*. Editorial: "Wonders of the Future." * In letter section, "A Vision of the Future," by Time Traveller, which claims to be a veridical account of mental travel to the future, via a host mind. * Letter from author Victor A. Endersby.]

April 1931. II-11. Cover: Paul.
Schachner, Nat and Zagat, Arthur Leo. Emperor of the Stars
Smith, Clark Ashton. An Adventure in Futurity
Newton, Edsel. The Sargasso Monster
Hamilton, Edmond. The Man Who Evolved
Stone, Leslie F. The Conquest of Gola
Knight, Thomas H. Great Green Things
Edwards, Gawain. The Return from Jupiter (2)
[*Miscellaneous*. Editorial: "The Wonders of Creation." * Letter from editor and author C. P. Mason; letter from author Victor Endersby.]

May 1931. II-12. Cover: Paul.
Hanstein, Otfrid von. Utopia Island (1)
Williamson, Jack. Through the Purple Cloud

Colladay, Morrison F. The Cosmic Gun
Harris, John Beynon. Worlds to Barter
Pratt, Fletcher. The War of the Giants
Repp, Ed Earl. The Beast of Ban-du-lu [as "The Beasts of Ban-du-lu" on the contents page]
[*Miscellaneous*. Editorial: "Telepathy." * Letters from authors Forrest J. Ackerman, Allen Glasser, P. Schuyler Miller and Mortimer Weisinger.]

June 1931. III-1. Cover: Paul.
Cloukey, Charles. In the Spacesphere
Kelly, Frank K. The Light Bender
Stangland, Arthur G. The Eye of Two Worlds
Starzl, Roman F. The Man Who Changed the Future
Vanny, Jim. The Exiles of Venus
Hanstein, Otfrid von. Utopia Island (2)
[*Miscellaneous*. Editorial: "Wonders of the Human Body. * Letters from authors Forrest J. Ackerman, Miles J. Breuer, M.D.; Nathan Schachner; Jack Williamson.]

July 1931. III-2. Cover: Paul.
Lasser, David and Keller, David H., M.D. The Time Projector (1)
Starzl, R. F. The Planet of Despair
Smith, Clark Ashton. The City of Singing Flame
McDermott, Dennis. The Red Spot of Jupiter
Bentley, Garth. Rebellion—5000 A.D.!
Valier, Max. A Daring Trip to Mars
[*Miscellaneous*. Editorial: "Wonders of the Machine Age." * Letter from author Allen Glasser.]

August 1931. III-3. Cover: Paul.
Schachner, Nat and Zagat, Arthur Leo. Venus Mines, Incorporated
Herbert, Benson. The World Within
Stangland, Arthur G. The 35th Millennium
Williamson, Jack. Twelve Hours to Live!
Hilliard, A. Rowley. The Island of the Giants
Lasser, David and Keller, David H., M.D. The Time Projector (2)
[*Miscellaneous*. Editorial: "Wonders of the Void." * Letters from authors Gawain Edwards, Allen Glasser, Clare Winger Harris, Milton Kaletsky.]

September 1931. III-4. Cover: Paul.
Schachner, Nat and Zagat, Arthur Leo. Exiles of the Moon (1)
Starzl, R. F. A 20th Century Medusa
Edwards, Gawain. A Mutiny in Space
Wellman, Manly Wade. The Disc-Men of Jupiter
Haggard, J. Harvey. An Adventure on Eros
[*Miscellaneous*. Editorial: "Wonders of the Earth's Interior." * Letter from author Allen Glasser.]

October 1931. III-5. Cover: Paul.

Colladay, Morrison F. The Return of the Cosmic Gun
Hilliard, A. Rowley. Death from the Stars
Keith, J. E. Between Dimensions
Bentley, Garth. Beyond the Star Curtain
Walsh, J. M. After 1,000,000 Years
Schachner, Nat and Zagat, Arthur Leo. Exiles of the Moon (2)
[*Miscellaneous*. Editorial: "Important Announcement!" proclaiming that the magazine would return to the larger size.]

November 1931. III-6. Cover: Paul.
Miller, P. Schuyler. Tetrahedra of Space
Flagg, Francis. The Superman of Dr. Jukes
Smith, Clark Ashton. Beyond the Singing Flame
Gross, Jerome and Penny, Richard. Emperors of Space
Schachner, Nat and Zagat, Arthur Leo. Exiles of the Moon (3)
[*Miscellaneous*. Editorial: "Wonders of the Stars." * Letters from authors Forrest J. Ackerman and Milton Kaletsky. * Prize-winning letters from the competition based on Williamson's "Twelve Hours to Live!" include Frank K. Kelly and Walter Dennis.]

December 1931. III-7. Cover: Paul.
Taine, John. The Time Stream (1)
Hamilton, Edmond. The Reign of the Robots
Houghton, Joseph F. The *Andromeda* Menace
Barnes, Arthur K. Lord of the Lightning
Simak, Clifford D. The World of the Red Sun
Arthur, Robert, Jr. The Terror from the Sea
[*Miscellaneous*. Editorial: "Wonders of Life." * * Poem: "At the End of the Spectrum,," by The Planet Prince {J. Harvey Haggard}. * Letters from authors Forrest J. Ackerman, L. A. Eshbach, Allen Glasser, J. Harvey Haggard, and Nathan Schachner.]

January 1932. III-8. Cover: Paul.
Bell, Stanley D. Martian Guns
Campbell, John W., Jr. The Derelicts of Ganymede
Miller, P. Schuyler and McDermott, Dennis. The Duel on the Asteroid
Berlow, Sidney D. The Crystal Empire
Taine, John. The Time Stream (2)
[*Miscellaneous*. Editorial: "The Wonders of Space Radiation." * Letters from authors Frank Bridge, Milton Kaletsky, Frank K. Kelly, and future author Willy Ley. * "Welcome to C. A. Brandt." Announcing that Brandt has joined the *Wonder* staff.]

February 1932. III-9. Cover: Paul.
Williamson, Jack. The Moon Era
Barnes, Arthur K. The Challenge of the Comet
Hamilton, Edmond. A Conquest of Two Worlds
Kelly, Frank K. The Radium World

February 1932 (*continued*)
Taine, John. The Time Stream (3)
[*Miscellaneous*. Editorial: "The Wonders of 2031." * Letters from authors Forrest J. Ackerman and John Beynon Harris.]

March 1932. III-10. Cover: Paul.
Spohr, Carl W. The Final War (1)
Smith, Clark Ashton. The Eternal World
Gallun, Raymond. Waves of Compulsion
Kelly, Frank K. Red April, 1965
Simak, Clifford D. Mutiny on Mercury
Taine, John. The Time Stream (4)
[*Miscellaneous*. Editorial: "What Is Life?" * Letters from authors Forrest J. Ackerman, P. Schuyler Miller, and Raymond A. Palmer.]

April 1932. III-11. Cover: Paul.
Stangland, Arthur G. 50th Century Revolt
Hilliard, A. Rowley. The Reign of the Star-Death
Gardner, Thomas D. [*sic*] The Last Woman
Campbell, John W., Jr. The Electronic Siege
Beattie, George B. The Man Who Shrank
Spohr, Carl W. The Final War (2)
[*Miscellaneous*. Editorial: "The Wonders of Light-Time." * Letters from authors Sidney Berlow, Dennis McDermott, and Nathan Schachner.]

May 1932. III-12. Cover: Paul.
Bertin, John. Brood of Helios (1)
Meek, Capt. S. P. Vanishing Gold
Gallun, Raymond Z. The Moon Mistress
Walsh, J. M. When the Earth Tilted
Harris, J. B. The Venus Adventure
Snooks, Epaminondas T. Why the Heavens Fell
[*Miscellaneous*. Editorial: "Wonders of Atomic Power." * Letter from author Raymond A. Palmer.]

June 1932. IV-1. Cover: Paul.
Smith, Clark Ashton. The Invisible City
Stone, Leslie F. The Hell Planet
Stranger, Ralph. The Message from Mars
Kateley, Walter. Under Arctic Ice
Starzl, R. F. The Power Satellite
Bertin, John. Brood of Helios (2)
[*Miscellaneous*. Editorial: "Wonders of the Commonplace." * Letters from authors Forrest J. Ackerman, A. K. Barnes, and P. Schuyler Miller.]

July 1932. IV-2. Cover: Paul.
Hanstein, Otfrid von. In the Year 8000 (1)
Stangland, Arthur G. Castaways of Space
Eshbach, L. A. The Time Conqueror
Sloat, Edwin K. Master of Storms
Bertin, John. Brood of Helios (3)
[*Miscellaneous*. Editorial: "The Wonders of Distance." * Contest based on cover.]

August 1932. IV-3. Cover: Paul.
Tooker, Richard. Tyrant of the Red World
Smith, Clark Ashton. Flight into Super-Time
Hilliard, A. Rowley. The Space Coffin
Beattie, George B. The "Platinum Planets"
Hanstein, Otfrid von. In the Year 8000 (2)
[*Miscellaneous*. Editorial: "The Wonders of Knowledge." * Letters from author Clark Ashton Smith and future author Willy Ley.]

September 1932. IV-4. Cover: Paul.
Held, S. S. The Death of Iron (1)
Stangland, Arthur G. Crossroads of Space
Juve, Henrik Dahl. In Martian Depths
Flagg, Francis. After Armageddon
Miller, P. Schuyler. Red Flame of Venus
Hanstein, Otfrid von. In the Year 8000 (3)
[*Miscellaneous*. Editorial: "The Wonders of Dreams." * Letters from authors Epaminondas T. Snooks and Thomas S. Gardner. * Announcement of prize contest based on the magazine cover.]

October 1932. IV-5. Cover: Paul.
Coblentz, Stanton A. The Planet of Youth
Stangland, Arthur G. Outcasts from Mars
Bolton, Paul. Chicago, 2042 A. D.
Smith, Clark Ashton. Master of the Asteroid
Heald, Hazel. The Man of Stone
Held. S. S. The Death of Iron (2)
[*Miscellaneous*. Editorial: "Wonders of Sight." * Prize-winning Letters. July 1932 Cover Contest. * Letter from author Forrest J. Ackerman.]

November 1932. IV-6. Cover: Paul.
Starzl, R. F. and Pragnell, Festus. The Venus Germ
Stangland, Arthur G. The Lake of Life
Simak, Clifford D. The Asteroid of Gold
Smith, Clark Ashton. The Dimension of Chance
Held, S. S. The Death of Iron (3)
[*Miscellaneous*. Editorial: "Wonders of Colors." * Letters from authors Milton Kaletsky and Charles Hornig. * Announcement "Wonder Stories Now 15¢"]

December 1932. IV-7. Cover: Paul.
Manning, Laurence. The Wreck of the Asteroid (1)
Schachner, Nathan. The Time Express
Colladay, Morrison. The Planetoid of Doom
Campbell, John W., Jr. Space Rays
Held, S. S. The Death of Iron (4)
[*Miscellaneous*. Editorial: "Wonders of the Universe." * Editorial statement "Reason--ableness in Science Fiction," by Hugo Gernsback. * Letters from authors P. Schuyler Miller, Ralph Stranger, and Milton Kaletsky.]

January 1933. IV-8. Cover: Paul.
Schachner, Nathan and Lacher, R. The Memory of the Atoms
Sharp, D. D. The Messenger from Space
Meek, Capt. S. P. The Synthetic Entity (wrongly attributed to D. D. Sharp on the contents page.)
Stangland, Arthur G. The Last of the Lemurians
Manning, Laurence. The Wreck of the Asteroid (2)
[*Miscellaneous*. Editorial: "Wonders of Mars." * Letter from author Milton Kaletsky. * Fillers: "Presenting Paul" and "Fashions in Universes."]

February 1933. IV-9. Cover: Paul.
Schachner, Nathan. The Eternal Dictator
Jones, Neil R. Escape from Phobos
Sharp, D. D. At Bay in the Void
Salisbury, Nathaniel. The Moon Doom (1)
Manning, Laurence. The Wreck of the Asteroid (3)
Miscellaneous. Editorial: "Wonders of Intelligence." * Announcement of competition for finishing Salisbury's "The Moon Doom." * Letter from author Clark Ashton Smith.]

March 1933. IV-10. Cover: Paul.
Schachner, Nathan. The Robot Techno-crat
Manning, Laurence. The Man Who Awoke (1)
Smith, Clark Ashton. Dweller in Martian Depths
Harris, John Beynon. Wanderers of Time
[*Miscellaneous*. Editorial: "Wonders of Technocracy."]

April 1933. IV-11. Cover: Paul.
Schachner, Nathan. The Revolt of the Scientists (1)
Smith, Clark Ashton. The Light from Beyond
Stangland, Arthur G. The Fatal Equation
Colladay, Morrison F. Giant in the Earth
Binder, Eando. Moon Mines
Miller, P. Schuyler. The Forgotten Man of Space
Lichtenstein, William. The Moon Doom (2)
Harris, Hugh King. The Dimension Twister
Manning, Laurence: The Man Who Awoke: (2) Master of the Brain
[*Miscellaneous*. Editorial: "Wonders of Interplanetary Life." * Letters from authors D. D. Sharp and Milton Kaletsky.]

May 1933. IV-12. Cover: Paul.
Stone, Leslie F. Gulliver, 3000 A.D.
Harris, John Beynon. The Third Vibrator
Smith, Clark Ashton. The Visitors from Mlok
Hamilton, Edmond. The Island of Un-reason
Bruell, Edwin. Men without Sleep

May 1933 (*continued*)
Baird, Wesley P. The Moon Doom (3)
Snooks, Epaminondas T. Brahma-
   Kalpa—or the Expanding Universe
Manning, Laurence. The Man Who Awoke:
   (3) The City of Sleep
Schachner, Nat. The Revolt of the
   Scientists. The Great Oil War.
[*Miscellaneous.* Editorial: "Wonders of
Thought." * Letter from author D. D.
Sharp.]

June 1933. V-1. Cover: Paul.
Thebault, Eugene. The Radio Terror (1)
Sharp, D. D. Captive of the Crater
Pragnell, Festus. Men of the Dark Comet
Binder, Eando. Murder on the Asteroid
Fisk, Clinton Earle. The Moon Doom (4)
Manning, Laurence. The Man Who Awoke:
   (4) The Individualists
Schachner, Nathan. The Revolt of the
   Scientists: The Final Triumph.
[*Miscellaneous.* Editorial: "The Wonders of
Touch." * Poems: "The Dead World" and
"The Robot," by Clarence Edward Flynn;
the heading is "Three Poems," but only two
are printed.]

August 1933. V-2. Cover: Paul.
[There was no July 1933 issue.]
Dye, George A. The Mystery of Planet
   Deep
Searight, Richard F. The Cosmic Horror
Haggard, J. H. Castaways on Deimos
Pragnell, Festus. The Isotope Men
Manning, Laurence. The Man Who Awoke:
   (5) The Elixir
Thebault, Eugene. The Radio Terror (2)
[*Miscellaneous.* Editorial: "Wonders of
Space Flight." * Letter from authors Forrest
J. Ackerman and Epaminondas T. Snooks.]

October 1933. V-3. Cover: Paul.
[There was no September 1933 issue.]
Hinton, Edward H. Monsters of Callisto
Harris, John Beynon. Spheres of Hell
Kelly, Frank K. The Moon Tragedy
Lemke, Henry E. The Last of the Swarm
Thebault, Eugene. The Radio Terror (3)
[*Miscellaneous.* Editorial: "Wonders of
World Speeds." * Letter from author Forrest
J. Ackerman.]

November 1933. V-4. Cover: Paul.
Patzer, Sidney. The Lunar Consul (1)
Perry, James D. Death between the
   Planets
Jacobi, Carl. The Tomb from Beyond
Manning, Laurence. The Call of the
   Mech-Men
Hamilton, Edmond. The Man with X-ray
   Eyes
Haggard, J. Harvey. Through the Einstein
   Line
Fedor, A. and Hasse, Henry. The End of
   Tyme
[*Miscellaneous:* Editorial: "Oxygen on
Mars." * Letter from author Milton
Kaletsky.]

December 1933. V-5. Cover: Paul.
Haggard, J. Harvey. Evolution Satellite
   (1)
Jones, Arthur Frederick. The Inquisition
   of 6061
Harris, John Beynon. Invisible Monsters
Kruse, Clifton Bryan. The Heat Destroy-
   ers
Barnes, Arthur K. The Mole-Men of Mer-
   cury
Patzer, Sidney. The Lunar Consul (2)
[*Miscellaneous:* Editorial: "The Wonders of
Matter—Motion." * Letter from author
Festus Pragnell.]

January 1934. V-6. Cover: Paul.
Vaughan, Richard. The Exile of the Skies
   (1)
Wollheim, Donald A. The Man from Ari-
   el
Ray, Rice. To-day's Yesterday
Carroll, Duane N. When Reptiles Ruled
Golub, F. The Secret of the Microcosm
Am Bruhl, Leo. Garfield's Invention
Gallun, Raymond Z. Moon Plague
Haggard, J. Harvey. Evolution Satellite
   (2)
[*Miscellaneous.* Editorials: "Wonders of
Micro-Life" and "Our New Policy." *
Poems: "The Riddle," by Al Browne and
"Impressions of the Planets—Venus," by
Richard F. Searight. * Letters from authors,
Forrest J. Ackerman, Henry Hasse, and
Allen Glasser. * Article, "Science in
Fiction" reprinted from the *New York
Times*.]

February 1934. V-7. Cover: Paul.
Binder, Eando. The Spore Doom
Cuthbert, Chester D. The Sublime Vigil
Gelula, Abner J. The Vengeance of a
   Scientist
Haggard, J. Harvey. An Episode on Io
Herbert, Benson. The Shot from the Sky
Vaughan, Richard. The Exile of the Skies
   (2)
[*Miscellaneous.* Editorial: "Wonders of Our
Color Sense." * Letter from author J.
Harvey Haggard. * Fillers "Lays Static in
Radio to Radium of Moon" and "Electrical
Disturbances Apparently of Extra-Terres-
trial Origin."]

March 1934. V-8. Cover: Paul.
Williamson, Jack. Xandalu (1)
Sterling, Kenneth. The Brain-Eaters of
   Pluto
Haggard, J. Harvey. Children of the Ray
Cleator, P. E. Martian Madness
Manning, Laurence. Caverns of Horror
Keller, David H. The Literary Corkscrew
Vaughan, Richard. The Exile of the Skies
   (3)
[*Miscellaneous.* Editorial: "Wonders of
Radio Waves." * Letters from authors
Forrest J. Ackerman, Richard F. Searight,
and P. Schuyler Miller. * Poems: "To a
Spaceship," by August Derleth and "Passing
of the Planets—Luna," by H. S. Zerrin. *

Fillers "Man in Rocket Shot Six Miles" {a
hoax} and "'Lost Continent' Found on
Indian Ocean Floor."]

April 1934. V-9. Cover: Paul.
Stimson, A. C. The Land of Mighty In-
   sects
Harris, John Beynon. The Moon Devils
Edwards, John. The Menace from Space
Kaletsky, Milton. The End of the
   Universe
Starzl, R. F. The Last Planet
Williamson, Jack. Xandalu (2)
[*Miscellaneous.* Editorial: "The Science
Fiction League. An Announcement." *
Poem: "Passing of the Planets—Venus," by
H. S. Zerrin. * Letter from author Bob
Tucker. * Stills from Hungarian motion
picture "Cataclysm."]

May 1934. V-10. Cover: Paul.
Freksa, Friedrich. Druso (1)
Snooks, Epaminondas T. Traders in
   Treasures
Colladay, Morrison F. Earthspot
Osborne, Chester G. The Tone Machine
Chapple, Paul K. The Man with the
   Longitudinal Head (in The Reader
   Speaks)
Binder, Eando. The Green Cloud of
   Space
Williamson, Jack. Xandalu (3)
[*Miscellaneous.* Editorial: "The Science
Fiction League."]

June 1934. VI-1. Cover: Paul.
Raymond, Kaye. Into the Infinitesimal
Nevins, W. Varick III. Cosmic Calamity
Keller, David H. The Doorbell
Pierce, John. Adrift in the Void
Freksa, Friedrich. Druso (2)
[*Miscellaneous.* Editorial: "The Wonders of
Time." * Poem: "Ode to Arrhenius," by
Charles D. Hornig. * Fillers "Heavy Water
Causes Old Age" and "Gigantic Mirror
Space Study Aid." * Letters from authors
Forrest J. Ackerman, Milton Kaletsky, and
Bob Tucker.]

July 1934. VI-2. Cover: Paul.
Binder, Eando. Enslaved Brains (1)
Manning, Laurence. Voice of Atlantis
Weinbaum, Stanley G. A Martian Odys-
   sey
Sheppard, W. L., Jr. A Hair-Raising Tale
Cuthbert, Chester D. The Last Shrine
Freksa, Friedrich. Druso (3)
[*Miscellaneous.* Editorials "Wonders of
Automatism" and "Science-Fiction."]

August 1934. VI-3. Cover: Paul.
Burkholder, A. L. Dimensional Fate
Pragnell, Festus. A Visit to Venus
Fedor, A. and Hasse, Henry. The Return
   of Tyme
Nevins, W. Varick, III. The Sense Twist-
   er
Mantell, E. The Men from Gayln
Binder, Eando. Enslaved Brains (2)

August 1934 (*continued*)
[*Miscellaneous.* Editorial: "Wonders of Reality." * Letter from authors Eando Binder and Vernon H. Jones. * Filler: "Completely Empty Space Unlikely."]

September 1934. VI-4. Cover: Paul.
Richter, Charles de. The Fall of the Eiffel Tower (1)
Harris, John Beynon. The Man from Beyond
Manning, Laurence. The Living Galaxy
Keller, David H. The Tree of Evil
Binder, Eando. Enslaved Brains (3)
[*Miscellaneous.* Editorial: "Wonders of the Planets." * Poem: "The Wanderer," by L. A. Eshbach. * Letters from authors Rice Ray, Donald A. Wollheim, Bob Tucker.]

October 1934. VI-5. Cover: Paul.
Binder, Eando. The Thieves from Isot
Bivona, Francesco. The Final Struggle
Eshbach, Lloyd Arthur. The Brain of Ali Kahn
Richter, Charles de. The Fall of the Eiffel Tower (2)
[*Miscellaneous.* Editorial: "Wonders of Pressure." * Letters from authors Thomas S. Gardner and Bob Tucker.]

November 1934. VI-6. Cover: Paul.
Binder, Eando. Dawn to Dusk (1)
Herbert, Benson. The Control Drug
Weinbaum, Stanley G. Valley of Dreams
Barshofsky, Philip. One Prehistoric Night
Chapple, Paul K. The Growth Promoter
Bartel, Philip J. Twenty-Five Centuries Late
Hoy Ping Pong. Report of the 196th Convention (in The Reader Speaks)
Richter, Charles de. The Fall of the Eiffel Tower (3)
[*Miscellaneous.* Editorial: "The Wonders of Bio-Mechanics." * Letters from authors J. Harvey Haggard and Vernon H. Jones. * Poems: "Omega," by August Derleth and "The Martian Cry," by L. A. Eshbach.]

December 1934. VI-7. Cover: Paul.
Cockroft, W. P. The Alien Room
Sharp, D. D. Higher Jurisdiction
Corbett, John M. The Black River
Newton, Edsel. House of Monstrosities
Manning, Laurence. The Moth Message
Palmer, Raymond A. The Time Tragedy
Scheftleman, Eugene H. The Waterspout
Kostkos, Henry J. Sleep Scourge
Binder, Eando. Dawn to Dusk (2)
[*Miscellaneous.* Editorials: "Wonders of Fiction" and "What is a *New* Story?" * Letters from authors Forrest J. Ackerman, Milton Kaletsky, and Arthur K. Barnes. * Short reprint article by Vernon H. Jones.]

January 1935. VI-8. Cover: Paul.
Hanstein, Otfrid von. The Hidden Colony (1)
Weisinger, Mortimer. The Prenatal Plagiarism

Keller, David H., M.D. One-Way Tunnel
Nevins, W. Varick, III. The Emotion Meter
Hamilton, Edmond. Master of the Genes
Stone, Leslie F. Cosmic Joke
Binder, Eando. Dawn to Dusk (3)
[*Miscellaneous.* Editorial: "Wonders of Space-Distances." * Letters and poem "Scientifictionuts," by author Bob Tucker. * The monthly feature "The Science Fiction League" prints "The First Science Fiction Test," offering a B.Stf. {Bachelor of Scientific-Fiction} degree for those who pass it honorably. * Short editorials on writing science-fiction: "'How Do You Do It?'" and "Logic in Science-Fiction." * Reprint of short article, "Science in Fiction," by Theodore Lutwiniak.]

February 1935. VI-9. Cover: Paul.
Binder, Eando. The Robot Aliens
Lesser, Derwin. The Fatal Glance
Hamilton, Edmond. The Truth Gas
Keller, David H., M.D. The Life Detour
Hanstein, Otfrid von. The Hidden Colony (2)
[*Miscellaneous.* Editorial: "Wonders of Your Body." * Letters from authors Forrest J. Ackerman, Henry Hasse, and Bob Tucker.]

March 1935. VI-10. Cover: Paul.
Coblentz, Stanton A. In Caverns Below (1)
Hamilton, Edmond. The Eternal Cycle
Lorraine, Lilith. The Celestial Visitor
Weisinger, Mortimer. Pigments Is Pigments
Hanstein, Otfrid von. The Hidden Colony (3)
[*Miscellaneous.* Editorial: "Wonders of Weight." * Letters from authors Vernon H. Jones, Donald A. Wollheim, and Kenneth Sterling.]

April 1935. VI-11. Cover: Paul.
Bartel, Philip J. The Elixir of Progress
Kraus, Joseph H. Phantom Monsters
Collier, Harry. A Suitor by Proxy
Gardner, Thos. S. The Insect World
Brotman, Morton. The Missing Hours
Manning, Laurence. The Prophetic Voice
Coblentz, Stanton A. In Caverns Below (2)
[*Miscellaneous.* Editorial: "Wonders of Progress." * Poem: "Luna Doom," by L. A. Eshbach. * Results of the test printed in the January 1935 issue. * Filler "Science-Fiction Fan Makes a Discovery," the Nova Herculis." * Letters by authors Robert H. Lowndes and Bob Tucker.]

May 1935. VI-12. Cover: Paul.
Maxon, P. B. The Waltz of Death (1)
Haggard, J. Harvey. Human Ants
Vanne, Emma. The Moaning Lily
Keller, David H., M.D. The Living Machine

Coblentz, Stanton A. In Caverns Below (3)
[*Miscellaneous.* Editorial: "Disembodied Thought." * Letters from authors Henry Hasse and Bob Tucker. * Poem: "The Planeteer," by Stark Robertson.]

June 1935. VII-1. Cover: Paul.
Manning, Laurence. Seeds from Space
Weinbaum, Stanley G. Pygmalion's Spectacles
Nevins, W. Varick III. The Mystery of the -/-
Cramer, Sterling S. Death from Within
Maxon, P. B. The Waltz of Death (2)
[*Miscellaneous.* Editorial: "Wonders of Orientation." * Letters from authors Forrest J. Ackerman, Bob Tucker, Festus Pragnell, and W. Varick Nevins, III.]

July 1935. VII-2. Cover: Paul.
Pragnell, Festus. The Green Man of Graypec (1)
Pool, Charles B. Justice of the Atoms
Sachs, Bernard. The Memory Machine
Young, Raymond A. A Thief in Time
Maxon, P. B. The Waltz of Death (3)
[*Miscellaneous.* Editorial: "Wonders of Suspended Life." * Announcement of Short-Short Story Contest based on the cover illustration. * Filler "The Rocket Engine." * "The Science Fiction League" department contains the Second Science Fiction Test. * Letters from authors Forrest J. Ackerman, W. Varick Nevins III, Emma Vanne, and Francis Flagg.]

August 1935. VII-3. Cover: Paul.
Connell, A. The Reign of the Reptiles
Weinbaum, Stanley G. The Worlds of If
Stone, Leslie F. The Man with the Four Dimensional Eyes
Daniels, David R. The Branches of Time
Pragnell, Festus. The Green Man of Graypec (2)
[*Miscellaneous.* Editorial: "Wonders of Transportation." * Letter from author Bob Tucker.]

September 1935. VII-4. Cover: Paul.
Weinbaum, Stanley G. The Ideal
Bartel, Philip Jacques. One Hundred Generations
Gordon, Millard Verne. The Space Lens
Manning, Laurence. World of the Mist (1)
Lowndes, Robert. Report of the Plutonian Ambassador (in The Reader Speaks)
Moskal, Kenneth. Into the Earth (in The Reader Speaks)
Pragnell, Festus. The Green Man of Graypec (3)
[*Miscellaneous.* Editorial: "Wonders of Transplanted Organs." * Poems: "A Toast!" by Charles H. Derms; "Join a Chapter," by Edward E. Chappelow. * Short article: "Science Fiction," by Henry Lewis, Jr. * Fillers "Man Will Reach Moon" and "No People on Mars?" * Letters by authors

September 1935 (*continued*)
Forrest J. Ackerman and Joseph H. Kraus.]

October 1935. VII-5. Cover: Paul.
Phillips, Alexander M. Martian Gesture
Hamilton, Edmond. The Cosmic Panto-
    graph
Dickinson, H. O. The Sex Serum
Herbert, Benson. The Perfect World (1)
Postlethwaite, Leviticus. The Slithering
    Horror (in The Reader Speaks)
Manning, Laurence. World of the Mist
    (2)
[*Miscellaneous.* Editorial: "Wonders of
Extravagance." * Prize winners of the July
1935 Contest. * Contest response from
future author James Blish. * Letters from
Forrest J. Ackerman and Robert Lowndes.]

December 1935. VII-6. Cover: Paul.
[There was no November 1935 issue.]
Connell, A. Dream's End
Lorraine, Lilith. The Isle of Madness
Sterling, Kenneth. Red Moon
Palmer, Raymond A. Three from the
    Test-Tube
Parkinson, R. D. The Rays from the
    Asteroid
Kerlin, Richard G. The Alien Hah-Rah
    (in The Reader Speaks)
Herbert, Benson. The Perfect World (2)
[*Miscellaneous.* Editorials: "Wonders of
Mystery Rays" and "New Policy Still New."
* Letters from authors Leslie F. Stone and
Bob Tucker.]

February 1936. VII-7. Cover: Paul.
[There was no January 1936 issue]
Skidmore, Joseph W. A World Unseen
    (1)
Burkholder, A. L. The Mad World
Weinbaum, Stanley G. The Point of
    View
Lemkin, William. Isle of the Gargoyles
Sterling, Kenneth. Bipeds of Bjhulhu
Herbert, Benson. The Perfect World (3)
[*Miscellaneous.* Editorial: "Wonders of
Space Flight." * The Third Science Fiction
Test.]

April 1936. VII-8. Cover: Paul.
[There was no March 1936 issue.]
Gardner, Thos. S. The World of Singing
    Crystals
Wagener, Siegfried. The Cosmic Cocktail
Flagg, F. and Ackerman, F. J. Earth's
    Lucky Day
Connell, A. The Duplicate
Barshofsky, Philip. The Imperfect Guess
Adams, Gerald H. Futility
Conn, Alan. Fate
Gatter, George F. The Emotion Gas
Barnes, Arthur K. Emotion Solution
Skidmore, Joseph W. A World Unseen
    (2)
[*Miscellaneous.* Editorials: "Wonders of
Distribution" and "An Announcement" of-
fering *Wonder Stories* only on a subscrip-
tion mail-order basis. * Obituary of Stanley

G. Weinbaum. * Letters from authors
Forrest J. Ackerman and R. D. Parkinson.]

WONDER STORIES QUARTERLY

Wonder Stories Quarterly was a direct
continuation of *Science Wonder Quarterly*
with the same staff, much the same policies, the same production, and the same
volume sequence, differing only in title.
Gernsback had come to realize that the
word "science" tended to frighten away
buyers.

In an early editorial, however, Gernsback displayed a very strange attitude
toward science and imagination, offering
definitions that he may have intended to
apply to future issues of the magazine.

> In time to come, also, our authors
> will make a marked distinction between
> science fiction and science *faction* if I
> may coin such a term. The distinction
> should be fairly obvious. In science
> fiction the author may fairly let his
> imagination run wild and, as long as he
> does not turn the story into an obvious
> fairy tale, he will still remain within the
> bounds of pure science fiction.
>
> Science fiction may be prophetic
> fiction, in that the things imagined by
> the author may come true some time;
> even if this "some time" may mean a
> hundred thousand years hence. Then,
> of course, there are a number of
> degrees to the fantastic in science
> fiction itself. It may run the entire
> gamut between the probable, possible
> and near-impossible predictions.
>
> In sharp counterdistinction to
> science fiction, we also have science
> *faction.* By this term I mean science
> fiction in which there are so many
> scientific facts that the story, as far as
> the scientific part is concerned, is no
> longer fiction but becomes more or less
> a recounting of fact.
>
> For instance, if one spoke of
> rocket-propelled fliers a few years ago,
> such machines obviously would have
> come under the heading of science
> fiction. Today such fliers properly
> come under the term science *faction*;
> because the rocket is a fact today . . . .
>
> Which is the better story . . . . the
> man of science, the research worker,
> and even the hard-headed business man
> will perhaps look with more favor upon
> science faction because here he will get
> valuable information that may be of
> immediate use; whereas the information
> contained in the usual run of science
> fiction may perhaps be too far in
> advance of the times, and may often be
> thought to be too fantastic to be of
> immediate use to humanity. (*Wonder
> Stories Quarterly*, Fall 1930, p. 5).

This is, of course, a curious statement for
Gernsback, if, indeed, he wrote the editorial. He exalts imagination even to the
point of the "near-impossible," admits
prediction to the point of infinite regress,
but says nothing about the educational value
of science-fiction, which he used to belabor.
He then defines a new form, science-faction,
which is fiction overburdened with factual
data, then confuses the issues with a second
definition declaring that science-faction
treats present reality. Finally, he avows that
science-faction will be more profitable to
the scientist, businessman, and researcher,
since it will offer material for immediate
use. A strange utilitarianism! Oddly
enough, despite his creation of a potential
subgenre of fiction, Gernsback did not
notice that it did not exist. Even today
there are no rocket fliers, and the operation
of a jet plane would hardly form the subject
of a story.

Distinctions between fiction and fact set
aside, *Wonder Stories Quarterly* continued
the pattern set by *Science Wonder Quarterly*
of a lead novel together with a certain
number of short stories and novelettes.

Four of these novels were translations
from German, commissioned by Gernsback.
Hanstein's "Between Earth and Moon" is
based on German rocket research on a
reasonably realistic level, while his
"Electropolis" glorifies progress, which it
interprets in terms of technology and
futurism. Buergel's "The Cosmic Cloud" is
a disaster story that ends on a tragic note,
while Anton's "Interplanetary Bridges" is a
jingoistic, revanchist work that demonstrates Gernsback's utter insensitivity to the
emerging horrors of the Nazi regime in
Germany. Oddly enough, there seem to
have been few complaints about it, though
Donald Wollheim protested its publication
strongly. These four novels are hardly
remarkable, but they were important in
showing the directions that science-fiction
had taken in Europe. This same point has
been made for the translations in *Wonder
Stories.*

During the course of *Wonder Stories
Quarterly* Gernsback faced the perpetual
question of reprints from the older, non-
genre pulp magazines. This question was
raised by older readers who had memories
(but no texts) of stories by such authors as
George Allan England, Homer Eon Flint,
Victor Rousseau, and others. Gernsback
replied:

> When I first started to publish science
> fiction in regular magazine form back
> in 1926, I republished a number of
> science fiction classics. The selection
> finally narrowed itself down to only a
> few stories, and thereafter practically no
> reprints of full book novel [*sic*] were
> attempted. The reason is very simple.
> I have, as yet, to see one old time
> science fiction novel which, in the light

of today's advance in science fiction, is readable . . . . Time has caught up with them, and progress has been such that the authors' predictions have mostly been fulfilled, leaving the present-day reader with a very ordinary story on his hands (*Wonder Stories Quarterly,* Winter 1933, p. 101).

Gernsback, it will be noted, still sees science-fiction primarily as a predictive device. The point means little, however, since this was the last issue of the magazine.

As a fiction magazine, *Wonder Stories Quarterly* was still somewhat primitive, like its colleagues and competitors, but it had one unusual aspect: its surreptitious association with the budding American Interplanetary Society, later titled The American Rocket Society, which in 1963 merged with Institute of Aerospace Sciences to become The American Institute of Aeronautics and Astronautics. David Lasser, first president of the society, was the managing editor of the *Wonder* magazines, and *Wonder* authors Gawain Edwards, William Lemkin, Laurence Manning, Nat Schachner, D. D. Sharp, R. F. Starzl, and editor C. P. Mason were all active members.

This focus on rockets, space, and space travel was paralleled, apparently, by reader interest. By examining reader polls and spontaneous letters, Gernsback (or Lasser) came to the conclusion that interplanetary fiction (notably the space opera, though not yet known by that name) was the most popular subgenre within science-fiction. On the Winter 1931 issue the banderole "Interplanetary Number" was added to the cover; in later issues this was changed to "Interplanetary Stories." In the Spring 1931 issue Gernsback announced an "Interplanetary 'Plot' Contest," several stories from which appeared in later issues. In a later attempt to solicit plots Gernsback set parameters and explained proscriptions, telling why he rejected certain stories:

(1) They dealt only with interplanetary wars;
(2) They dealt with strange but unplausible beasts;
(3) They showed our hero going to another planet simply to rescue a fair princess from an evil high priest;
(4) They showed our explorers going clear out of the solar system to another world and *finding people just like ourselves.*

Therefore, if you hope to have your plot accepted, steer clear of those hackneyed and unrealistic ideas.

We will pay the uniform prize of $10.00 for each accepted plot. (*Wonder Stories Quarterly,* Winter 1932, p. 293).

Unfortunately, Gernsback would seem to

have condemned most of the so-called "classics" of the day.

In the last eight issues of *Wonder Stories Quarterly* out of thirty-seven stories twenty-five are out-and-out interplanetary stories and ten are marginal or related. One of these stories, Laurence Manning's novel "The Voyage of the Asteroid" may well be the first American story to embody realistic rocket research. In comparison, for the corresponding issues of *Wonder Stories,* out of 110 stories thirty-five might be considered interplanetaries, with another ten somewhat related.

Space matters, however, were not enough to save *Wonder Stories Quarterly* from the realities of the Great Depression. Gernsback was hard hit by the bankruptcy of his distributor, plus the fact that his finances were generally shaky. A further problem was that Gernsback was alienating the better writers with his business tactics. One-half cent a word was poor enough payment for a story, but when one could not even collect that? When even his stalwarts, to whom he gave special treatment—Edward Hamilton, David H. Keller, and Laurence Manning—had difficulty in obtaining payment, things began to decay.

Added to these personal problems were those inherent in a quarterly publication, as spelled out in more detail with *Amazing Stories Quarterly.* A quarterly, in newsstand terms, was really an irregular publication, and science-fiction magazines were likely to be pushed aside for magazines that were popular, dependable sellers and fitted the standard pulp size.

As a tactic to increase sales, Gernsback reduced the price of the last two issues to 25¢. It made no difference, perhaps, in part, because he also reduced the size of the magazine. It simply reduced the revenue from these two issues.

Unannounced, without an obituary, *Wonder Stories Quarterly* simply ceased to exist.

Was *Wonder Stories Quarterly* of any interest apart from its connection with serious rocketry? Like almost all the pulp science-fiction of its day, it is now a matter for nostalgics. But the translations from the German have a typological interest, particularly Hanstein's "Electropolis" with its ravening pursuit of "progress" and futurism; Nathan Schachner's ambitious "Emissaries of Space" reflects many of the social concerns of the day; John Beynon Harris's "Exiles on Asperus" explores links of culture and personality in a manner unusual for the pulps; and Laurence Manning's "The Voyage of the Asteroid," in addition to its association with rocketry, is entertaining.

Publishing information

Publisher:
Stellar Publishing Corporation. Editorial offices, 96-98 Park Place,

New York, N.Y.
Company officers:
Hugo Gernsback, president
I. S. Manheimer, secretary
Sidney Gernsback, treasurer
Staff:
Hugo Gernsback, editor-in-chief
David Lasser, managing editor
Frank R. Paul, art director
C. A. Brandt, literary editor (Winter 1932-Fall 1932)
Schedule:
Quarterly, with Fall, Winter, and Spring issues.
Appearance:
September 15, Fall. December 15, Winter. March 15, Spring. June 15, Summer.
Price:
Summer 1930-Summer 1932: 50¢.
Fall 1932-Winter 1933: 25¢.
Range: Summer 1930-Winter 1933.
Number of issues: 11
Size and format: 8 1/2" x 11 3/4." Side stapled, trimmed.
Pagination:
Summer 1930-Summer 1932: 144 pp.
Fall 1932-Winter 1933: 96 pp.
Volume sequence in all cases.
Artwork: All covers by Frank R. Paul. Paul illustrates the lead novel in all issues and all fiction from Spring 1932 on. Elsewhere Marchioni illustrates most of the short stories, with occasional work by Imler, Miller, and Volga. Unsigned line renderings of authors' photographs.
Departments:
Editorial by Hugo Gernsback: all issues. "The Reader Speaks" all issues except Fall 1932.
Advisory panel and associate science editors: Astronomy: Prof. Samuel G. Barton, U. of Pa. (through Spring 1932). Dr. Clyde Fisher, Curator, Am. Mus. of Nat. Hist. (through Spring 1931). Prof. Willem J. Luyten, Harvard College Observatory. *Astro-physics:* Prof. Donald H. Menzel, U. of California. *Botany:* Prof Elmer G. Campbell, Transylvania College. Dr. Margaret Clay Ferguson, Wellesley College. Prof. C. E. Owens, Oregon Agricultural College. *Chemistry:* Prof. Gerald Wendt, Pennsylvania State College. *Electricity:* F. E. Austin, Dartmouth College. *Entomology:* Dean William F. Wheeler, Bussey Institute, Harvard U. *Mathematics:* Prof. C. Irwin Palmer, Armour Institute of Technology (through Summer 1932). Prof. James Byrnie Shaw, U. of Illinois. (through Winter 1931). Prof. W. A. Titsworth, Alfred College. *Medicine:* Dr. David H. Keller, Western State Hospital. *Physics and Radio:* Dr. Lee deForest (through Summer 1932). *Physics:* Prof. A. L. Fitch, U. of Maine. *Psychology:* Prof. Marjorie E. Babcock,

U. of Hawaii. *Zoology:* Dr. Joseph G. Yoshioka, Illinois State Institute for Juvenile Research.
Added, Fall 1932-Winter 1933: Aviation: Lt. Col. William A. Bevan, Prof. Aeronautical Engineering, Iowa State College. Prof. Earl D. Hay, U. of Kansas. Prof. George J. Higgins, U. of Detroit. Prof. Felix W. Pawlowski, U. of Michigan. Prof. John E. Younger, U. of California.

Contents

Magazine Illustrators

Almost all early science-fiction illustration, both cover and interior work, is representational, using traditional techniques to simulate three-dimensional activity in flatwork. (For the ten exceptional instances see the commentary on the work of A. Sigmond below.) For the most part, this artwork focuses on single incidents within the stories, as imaged visually. Occasionally one meets pictorial representations suggestive of general situations or of larger elements in individual stories, but this is exceptional, and even this is an extension of the basic principle of pulp art: that it is an illustration of something else, not independent work. (This specific approach, however, broke down in the period following this study, where generic illustration often became important. In other areas of pulp art generic art was more important than in science-fiction.)

The covers of the individual magazines, as has been indicated in the introduction to this volume, were the most important artwork associated with the magazines, since they served to attract attention on the newsstands and to entice the reader to buy. Assigning the cover artist, thus, was critical, whereas for interior illustration anything (it sometimes seems) would serve, particularly in the earlier years.

Since publishers tended to retain satisfactory performers, rather than chance losing sales by experimenting, certain artists became cover specialists and monopolists. In our period and area these men were Frank R. Paul, Howard V. Brown, Hans W. Wessolowski (working as H. Wesso), and Leopoldo Peña y Morey (working as Leo Morey).

Each of these artists imparted a certain flavor to the sensory vista of the unopened magazine. How much they were controlled by the publisher or art director is not known beyond a few generalities, but each man's work became characteristic and remained so—though least with Morey.

The personal vision of these artists became important to the readership of the magazines and at times was fostered and stressed by the publishers. Gernsback, for example, made the presence of Paul's artwork a strong sales point in his advertising and publicity. This ties in with a curious feature in the fantastic

fiction magazines (including *Weird Tales* and *Strange Tales*): the growing tendency for fans/readers to take fantastic art seriously and to form cults focusing on individual artists. Thus, in the readers' columns letter after letter often demands more Paul, more Wesso, or, in *Weird Tales*, more Virgil Finlay. As Walt Reed, an important modern commercial artist, has said, "Even by pulp standards, the fantasy [i.e., science-fiction] artists were regarded as somewhat peculiar. Those titles had the most limited circulation with the lowest pay scale and some of the weakest art, but their fans were the most vociferous in their loyalty." (Lesser, p. 51).

This phenomenon, to my knowledge, was not significant in other areas of pulp fiction at the time, though now, in nostalgic studies of the older action and shudder pulps of the 1930s and 1940s and the rise of a collectors' market in pulp art, it has become highly important. Was a particular type of illustration an inherent need in fantastic fiction, as a bridge to empathy, hence preferences and rankings, or was the readership of a different sort than that of the other pulps?

The pressure for artistic control by fans/readers focused most strongly on interior illustration, perhaps because cover assignment was known to be fixed, perhaps because individual stories demanded different types of visualization. Such cultic followings for interior work included both the cover monopolists mentioned above and occasional other artists, notably Elliott Dold, who did not do s-f covers (exception noted below).

There were, of course, other artists who aroused enthusiasm, sometimes inexplicably to a modern eye, but these were transitory. The men who fixed science-fictional iconography during the period covered in this book were the five artists mentioned: Paul, Wesso, Brown, Morey, and Dold.

The work of these five men, together with that of the intrusive A. Sigmond and the prolific Mark Marchioni has never been examined closely in terms of professional technique. Most commentary has been anecdotal, biographical, bibliographic, or "appreciative."

Ideally, one should analyze individual pieces of artwork,

rather than a corpus, since each painting or drawing is an entity and different from all others, but this is obviously impractical, possibly unrepresentative, and arbitrary in the consideration of thousands of pieces of ephemeral work. In addition, general principles are more likely to emerge if one considers a larger sampling of material, and, in this area, an artist historically has been more likely to have been judged by his oeuvre, or a large part of it, than by individual works.

It should be remembered that where questions of quality arise, the standards implied are not those that would be applied to the world's great artists, but are those effective in commercial pulp-magazine illustration of the day. It must also be admitted that science-fiction pulp art of our period was, on the whole, weaker than the artwork to be found on the other pulps.

The artists concerned fall into categories based on their type of art: architectural draftsman and technical illustrator, Paul; commercial illustrators of no particular school, Brown, Wesso, Marchioni (perhaps influenced by Futurism); totally abstract expressionist, Sigmond; partially abstract expressionist and symbolist, Dold; traditional fine-artist of a sort, Morey.

Despite the contemporary popularity of at least five of these men, very little is known about them or their careers. Much of what is recorded is hearsay, or generality, or, even, possibly, misdirection. The same holds true of the secondary people whom we shall not discuss in detail.

Frank R. Paul (1884-1963) was born near Vienna, Austria, and received art education (probably as an architectural draftsman) in Vienna and Paris, although exact details, as with the remainder of his early life, are not known. It has been claimed that his original name, later Americanized, was Franz Rudolf Paul, but this has not been documented. He came to the United States before World War I, during which he served as a draftsman in shipyards in Florida and California, or so it is stated in his obituary in the *New York Times*, though it seems strange that an enemy alien could so serve during the war hysteria of the time. Somewhat later he was a political cartoonist for the *New Jersey Journal* in Jersey City.

Paul is usually linked with Hugo Gernsback, with whom he was associated on a freelance basis from the halcyon days of Gernsback's popular technical magazines up to the end of *Wonder Stories* in 1936, and, later, with Gernsback's final *Science Fiction Plus*. Although other artists illustrated occasional stories, Paul as lead artist dominated Gernsback's science-fiction magazines. His masthead position as "art director" on Gernsback's *Wonder* magazines, however, seems to have been nominal, although he did maintain a small office on the premises at times.

After Gernsback disposed of *Wonder Stories*, Paul drew both cover and interior illustrations for other magazines up through the early 1950s and sporadically after that. It has been claimed, with some probability, that although his reputation and acclaim was based on his science-fiction art, his main source of income and his true work were technical illustration of various sorts, particularly isometric projections.

The central point of Paul's art work was exposition: he was not concerned primarily with the light emergent from a scena, but with what was actually there, ascertainable from senses other than sight. Thus we find the incredible rendering detail in elaborate city scapes, rocky landscapes, and extra-terrestrial scenery. This aspect of his work has been rated very

high by fellow draftsmen.

Several points of technique are observable in Paul's work. He used classical office perspective in a masterly fashion, usually with a middle picture horizon and vanishing point, and he seems to have liked a composition involving motion from the bottom left to the top right, with occasional vertical repoussoirs on either side. Geometry played a large part in his picture composition, which was usually closed. While he did occasional silhouettes, usually for secondary illustrations around which type would be fitted, in general he preferred full picture-frame development with filled grounds. Considerable gradation of value is typical of Paul's work, from solid blacks to stippled fields, which are used with great virtuosity. Montage-like figures and objects within the illustrations are always drawn as if in isolation—they could be cut out and be self-sufficient—usually with moderately heavy, uniform shoelace outline. Detail is almost obsessive in landscapes, architecture, and machinery, but much of this is internally repetitious within his work, sometimes a little clichéd, sometimes a little stylized. As has been stated, this close rendering is usually not a representation of light patterns, but a depiction of what is known to be there, on a physical basis. Nothing is suggested; everything is either there or not there.

Paul was essentially a black-and-white artist, and the color work in his covers has little subtlety; it stresses primary colors, crimson, chrome yellow, and blue, often in large fields. This palette is occasionally attributed to Gernsback's printing process, but this is incorrect; Paul was obviously aiming at a poster effect, which he often achieved. It is on record that the solid colors of his backgrounds were occasionally changed during production for visual impact. As with his black-and-white interiors, he usually outlined figures rigorously, first inking in outlines before adding coloration. Paul created shadows with black in various manners and in his emphasis on local color seldom considered colored shadows or color influence from one surface to another.

In general one can say in matters within his draftsman range, he was a superb technician, though individual pieces, as might be expected from the quantity of his work, vary considerably in realization. With the human figure, however, he was inept, treating it clumsily, with too much repetition of stock work.

Paul is occasionally termed a primitive artist, but, apart from the social aspects usually associated with primitivism, this is far from the truth. His work is highly sophisticated and is typologically the opposite to primitive, what with classical perspective, single point of observation, clear horizon line, roundedness and three-dimensionality, geometric composition, concern for unity, and other qualities of historical Western art. Such "primitive" qualities as one finds in an occasional piece of work are accidental, not a matter of basic Weltanschauung.

There is little evidence, however, that Paul was influenced to any great extent by historical fine art, except as by vestiges of the Duesseldorf School. There seem to be no influences from the Impressionists, Cubists, Surrealists, or other modern schools. While his work sometimes shows superficial resemblances to Victorian narrative painting, there is seldom a narrative implied, only a stasis. One would be unlikely to create pre- and post-picture situations from his work, as one would from the better British painters. For this reason Paul's world is essentially rigid and inorganic, a moment totally frozen.

For covers Paul usually worked in watercolor, his first oil is said to have been for the February 1935 issue of *Wonder Stories* (*Fantasy Magazine*, December 1934-January 1935, p. 69); for interiors, usually with pen and ink. He generally devoted about three or four days to a cover, and a few hours, depending on elaborateness, for interior illustrations. Judging from the quantity of work he turned out, he was both a facile and a patient hand.

Paul did not use models; according to his own statement he drew heavily on a large swipe file that he maintained. Occasionally, such sources can be roughly identified; an unintentional amusing note is his precise copying of turn-of-the-century illustrations of fairies for winged humans. This use of secondary art can also be seen in his machinery. Despite its sometimes fine execution, the machinery he depicts is often suggestive of late Victorian iron work, with no recognition of emergent streamlining or contemporary commercial design.

Frank R. Paul is preeminently the artist associated with early pulp science-fiction, the artist who empathized with hard science-fiction, who provided the integration of humans and alienness, though on a literal level. He has sometimes, with an element of truth, been called the apotheosis of "scientifiction."

Signature: PAUL, underlined. If Paul contributed several illustrations to a story, it is not uncommon for some to be unsigned.

Oeuvre: A partial listing for Paul's work is to be found in Weinberg. In general it can be said that Paul designed all the covers for Gernsback's magazines, most of the internal art, plus occasional artwork elsewhere. It often stated elsewhere that Paul illustrated all the cartoons in the three issues of Gernsback's *Superworld Comics*. This is not correct. Paul painted the covers and illustrated only two strips, "Marvo 1-2GO+" and "Mitey Powers." The other strips were done by other hands, some being reprints of much earlier work.

Howard Vachel Brown (1878-1945), who is not to be confused with the author and science-fiction editor Howard Browne (1908-present?), was born in Lexington, Kentucky, and trained at the Art Institute of Chicago. Moving to New York, he served as occasional cover artist for *Scientific American* and other popular technical magazines as well as for Munsey pulp fiction magazines. His work often received favorable critical attention in professional circles.

Although Brown had created covers for Hugo Gernsback's *Science and Invention* (including the so-called "Scientific Fiction Issue" of August 1923), his first science-fiction cover was for the reanimated Street and Smith *Astounding Stories* of October 1933. He remained the "official" cover artist for *Astounding Stories* until the May 1937 issue, after which he appeared sporadically. Brown also contributed covers to *Startling Stories* and *Thrilling Wonder Stories* until mid 1940. There is an element of uncertainty about his oeuvre, since he seldom signed his work.

Brown and Paul could serve as type figures for the opposition between Classical and Baroque in Woelfflin's sense, not considered as era styles but as polar approaches to art. Almost every technical aspect that can be identified for Paul can be reversed to describe Brown's work. His figures are not outlined with shoelaces, but are formed by color or value differences; details are not shown as they are in actuality, but as misty, sometimes smudgy light patterns; office perspective is seldom used, instead aerial perspective, distance (which Brown does not favor so much as Paul) being shown by gradual atmospheric tones of color and shadow; point of view is not simple picture frame from direct human eye level, with middle vanishing point, but may be lopsided, bird's eye, worm's eye, or other approaches; shadows in color work are not indicated by black, but by deepening of value or chroma, with occasional color reflections from neighboring colors; suggestion is strong, rather than direct statement.

Brown's composition, which is usually effective, is not closed, as is Paul's, but often open, with hints outside the canvas or paper. Where he uses geometric forms, they do not follow the bottom-left to top-right triangle of Paul's, but are centered isosceles triangles or even squares, nicely balanced. While Paul, for all his detail, is often sparse in elements, Brown sometimes overcrowds his covers to include narrative elements. In coloration, too, Brown differs greatly from Paul, his palette being more elaborate and subtle. Instead of primaries or mild derivatives, Brown may include lavender, olive green, icy greens, terra cotta, powder blue, and many tints of gray.

Brown's coloration, oddly enough, has sometimes been called garish, but to a more modern eye his color work, because of its blurred intermingling of colors, often looks dull; the black plate used in Street and Smith's printing (but not used by Gernsback or Clayton) does not help. One could not call the result earthy, which is sometimes a term of praise, but one could say that Brown's covers are often muddy; they would not have stood out very well poster-wise in a newsstand display. Indeed his graying of color sometimes clashes with the icons of sensationalism considered.

In black-and-white work the two men also have different aims and used different techniques. Whereas Paul's black-and-white work is usually clear and characterized by a rich variety of stipplings to hint at hue or saturation, Brown tends to use uniform tint blocks that in printing often emerge as drab or muddy.

As a result, while there is a certain distinction in Brown's color work, a certain virtuosity latent beneath the requirements of pulp work, his black-and-white work is less satisfactory. His scumbling technique, smudgy tint blocks, and rough, hasty strokes of the pencil, perhaps sometimes of charcoal, are often disappointing, not only from a technical point of view but also because of an impersonality added to already cold work.

Considered for the peculiar needs of a science-fiction artist of the 1920s and 1930s, however, Brown shapes up very well. He was able to depict exotic landscapes and cityscapes. He was obviously conversant with mechanical movements and heavy equipment, and could extrapolate beyond this, better than Paul could. The excellent foreshortened, three-point perspective bird's eye view of the giant rotor in "Strange City" on the cover of the January 1936 issue of *Astounding Stories* is a good example.

In life forms, Brown was arguably the most skilled of the early science-fiction artists. He was renowned for his depiction of aliens and monsters, which he rendered convincingly in a naturalistic manner. His use of protruding eyes makes him one of the creators of the standard bug-eyed monster. In his treatment of the human figure, too, Brown was far superior to Paul. When he took pains, his work often took on the aspect of minor portraiture.

The greatest weaknesses of Brown's art, though it is

technically competent, are its dullness and lack of excitement. Inferior artists of the day in both science-fiction and other pulp fields were better able to convey a sense of vitality, a pull to drag the reader toward the magazine.

Signature: BROWN. Brown usually did not sign his work. Otherwise, elsewhere, sometimes Howard V. Brown.

Oeuvre: Weinberg lists Brown's covers, which are multitudinous. In brief, Brown did all the covers for Street and Smith *Astounding Stories* covered in this study, with scattered interior illustrations.

Hans Waldemar Wessolowski (1894-1961?), who illustrated under the name H. Wesso, was born in Germany, and attended the Berlin Royal Academy of Arts. He worked as a commercial artist in Germany for a time, contributing to the great German humor magazine *Simplicissimus*.

Although details are not known, Wesso is said to have come to the United States in 1914 and to have made his living as a commercial artist and general magazine illustrator before working with science-fiction. His first science-fiction illustration was the cover for the post-Gernsback September 1929 *Amazing Stories*. In late 1929 he began an association with the new Clayton *Astounding Stories*, eventually illustrating all thirty-four covers and becoming the chief interior illustrator. With the collapse of Clayton's chain of magazines, Wesso abandoned science-fiction illustration for a time, but returned in 1936 to Street and Smith *Astounding Stories* and Beacon *Thrilling Wonder Stories*. After 1942 for all practical purposes he ceased work in science-fiction, except for an occasional piece. Little is known of his working procedures, but he is said to have spent two or three days on a cover, sometimes a week. Unlike Paul, he occasionally used models, including toy machines.

Wesso's covers were more varied in color than those of Paul or Brown, with many pastel shades of lavender, green, and yellow. At his best he was a good colorist, though not on Morey's level, with interesting combinations that are often more lively than Brown's. It should be pointed out, however, that his colors are often completely arbitrary, without relation to subject matter, light sources, or aerial perspective, being used solely for contrast in the traditional Chevreul circle of complementary colors. As he states in an interview published in the *Science Fiction Digest* April 1933), cover background colors were often selected by Harry Bates and himself "by striving for variety" (p. 3). He seldom used black on his covers, but instead created shadows by deepening hues, and separated figures by color contrast.

Wesso is often thought of as a producer of bright, hot covers, but this is not entirely accurate. Many of his covers have very dark backgrounds or are high in value, rendering them rather dull in appearance. Such covers would not have high visibility on a newsstand.

In most respects Wesso was a good technician, undoubtedly due to his training at one of the bastions of traditional art. His composition is unified and often based on skilful use of geometry, especially right angles and circles. His lighting, however, tends to be arbitrary, sometimes multiple and sometimes inconsistent, and his observation points are sometimes multiple. These practices are probably not due to lack of skill, but are more likely intentional devices to create a full image based on physical aspects rather than accidents of light. (This is not carried out in the direction of cubism, however.) Shadows in his color work are sometimes indicated by adding black or increasing chroma, but also sometimes by arbitrary colors designed to form an eye-catching combination. Wesso generally avoids background depth, depending on aerial perspective which may, in color work, be handled by hue or value, in black-and-white work by what amounts to a tint block. In rendering, Wesso is by no means as full as Paul, but he does attempt some detail work, particularly on his occasional cityscapes. Landscapes, however, generally present highly stylized distance features. While Wesso sometimes uses front-on picture-frame viewing, particularly characteristic is an observation point angling in from outside the picture from the bottom right.

Just as obsessive detail is characteristic of Paul, clutter and kitsch of Marchioni, and exuberant coloration of Morey, the pictorial representation of stress is characteristic of Wesso. Humans are usually represented with body strained, legs extended and bent, arms tensely extended, facial features set in a taut grimace. His intention, obviously, is to capture an air of peril and excitement transferrable, it was probably hoped, to the viewer. In this Wesso mirrored, perhaps without plan, since his artistic personality remained the same throughout his career, the thrill aspect of Clayton *Astounding Stories*, as opposed to the desired intellectuality of Gernsback's magazines, as imaged by Paul.

Yet, even more than his colleagues, Wesso had extreme difficulty in rendering the human figure, which he usually represented as a lanky, sharp-featured brunet male with sunken chest and with curious proportions and musculature around the thighs. Limbs are very often disproportionate in length. The Wesso male, no matter how variant the remainder of the illustration may be, can usually be distinguished at a glance.

Certain situations and iconic tropes are also idiosyncratic to Wesso: very large unitary central elements, with tiny human figures, sometimes in multitudes, scattered around suitably; circular or spherical architectural constructions with skeletal girders; blimp-like spaceships; and mountains stylized in rough, jagged formation suggestive of chopped-up ice cubes or crumpled paper.

Considered as a science-fiction artist, Wesso is usually satisfactory. His machinery and special effects are adequate, though beneath those of Dold and Brown, but it must admitted that his human figures are so distressing that they detract from other aspects of his work. In general, however, it can be said that he caught the spirit of science-fiction better than the lesser artists who were practicing in his time.

Signature: H WESSO usually followed by a two-digit year date. Rarely, HW followed by a two-digit year date.

Oeuvre: Weinberg offers a list. In general Wesso prepared all the covers for Clayton *Astounding Stories* and most of the interior art work after August 1930; the covers and occasional interior work for the *Amazing* magazines in 1929 and 1930; and occasional interior work in *Astounding Stories* in 1936.

Leo Morey (1899-1965) was the fourth of the so-called "Big Four." His work was not so popular as that of Paul or Wesso, but still formed the mainstay of *Amazing Stories* for most of its post-Gernsback, pre-Palmer years.

Leo Morey, the working name of Leopoldo Peña y Morey,

was born in Lima, Peru, to a wealthy mercantile family. The sequence of events in his early life is not firmly known, but he matriculated in Louisiana State University in 1919, graduating with a degree in agriculture in 1924. (Statements elsewhere that his college major was engineering are, according to LSU records, incorrect; his field of specialization, in agriculture, was poultry management. This educational background is probably the reason that wherever possible Morey avoided designing fantastic machinery.) He worked as an artist on a newspaper on Argentina, and lived for a time in New Orleans. It is not known where he received his art training, which, judging from his better work, must have been formal and classical.

In 1929, or perhaps a little earlier, Morey moved to New York, where he became associated with Teck Publications, the new publishers of *Science and Invention* and *Amazing Stories*. His first work was technical illustration for *Radio News*; he then branched out into the pulps, illustrating *Wild West Weekly* and *Complete Detective Novels*. With the February 1930 issue of *Amazing Stories*, he became cover artist for all the Teck issues of that magazine (except eight covers by Sigmond and one by Wesso) until 1938, and irregularly after that. He also contributed covers to the several short-lived magazines that emerged in the early 1940s and to *Startling Stories* and *Thrilling Wonder Stories*.

Of the major artists considered here, Morey was the most uneven and erratic. He could turn out an occasional cover that would be considered excellent by any reasonable standard, traditional or modern, yet he could also fill the interiors of magazines with crude pencilings that should not have been published. It has been suggested that his inferior production consists of sketches, used for economy, rather than finished pieces. In the following discussion Morey's better work will be stressed.

As certain of the covers of *Amazing Stories* show, Morey was an excellent colorist, much the best of the early artists. Working in watercolor, he was able to achieve sophistications in color blends very different from Paul's primaries, or Brown and Wesso's limited off-shades. Blendings, colored shadows, reflections all demonstrate a fine eye and hand and a certain acquaintance with modern art movements. His best covers glow.

Morey also was skilful in the adaptation of hot and cool colors, sometimes together, sometimes concentrated in a single cover. He seldom used blacks. This may have been due to the fact that black was not a separate printing plate, but was really (and not always satisfactorily) a very dark purple produced by overprinting red and blue.

It should be noted that the color separations and printing of Morey's better covers were excellent and sustained his art—most of the time. But from October 1933 through June 1935, after *Amazing Stories* changed to small size, there was trouble. The colors became faint, dull and muddy, producing the worst covers technologically among the early science-fiction pulp magazines. This was sometimes considered Morey's fault, but it was obviously the result of incompetent or over-economical separations and/or printing.

Morey's work, particularly his black-and-white work, is heavily geometric in composition, with considerable use of the right angle. His illustrations are usually composed with a strong foreground group, with a generalized, suggested plane background, though in some instances the background can recede in office perspective with some detail. In the cases where Morey does this, his detail is not as profuse as Paul's nor as sharp, but often verges into suggestion and softness. In other circumstances Morey uses impressionistic blobs to suggest detail, as with people in crowds. A peculiarity of his work is an occasional deliberate violation of perspective, with two or more vanishing points, in order to bring desirable subject matter into prominence in the picture. This is usually well handled, as is his use of multiple light sources, with occasionally inconsistent highlights. In this freedom, the intent, of course, is to include, with full development, enticing elements. Morey has occasionally been criticized for overcrowding his covers, an accusation which has some truth, although it overlooks the iconographic purpose of the cover.

Just as Paul very frequently utilizes a picture-motion from bottom left to top right and Brown tends to center on the bottom in triangles, Morey seems to have preferred a central cylindrical movement to the top, sometimes with a second center of development not far from the magazine logo. Composition, in general, is balanced right and left, though there are exceptions, and unity is well maintained. Also occasionally present are bird's-eye shots with nearly classical perspective, but canted at an unusual visual angle. On the whole Morey did not use either the pointillism of Paul or the tint blocks of Brown. In his better black-and-white work composition is often achieved by blocks of texture made up of pen strokes of various sorts.

In his color work Morey usually did not outline his figures, but distinguished them by hue and value. In cases, where an outline is used, it is heavy and irregular, for purposes of emphasis, and is not shoelace. In his black-and-white work Morey usually outlined, but with an irregular, vibrant line that escapes the monotony of Paul's.

In his rendering of the human figure in our period Morey often did poor work, though it is possible that such weaknesses were due to haste and lack of empathy, since some of his later covers present passable pulp humans. Particularly bad, however, are his renderings of racial types, which are travesties. An oddity is that his heroic types are often Latin American: slender, gracile, often mustachioed, leptoprosopic, sometimes in garb suggestive of the South. Villains were usually characterized with brutal facial features reminiscent of Renaissance grotesques.

As a science-fiction artist, Morey was limited. A tally of his illustrations shows that whenever possible he drew humans, neutral backgrounds, and semi-abstractions suggestive of mechanical devices rather than literal machinery, which he tended to avoid. However, he did show many spaceships, which were usually simple, unenthusiastic radiform contraptions. Airplanes, which Morey seems to have liked, he drew extremely well in a realistic manner. When on occasion Morey drew planets or the moon, it would seem that he took jokes about cheese too seriously.

Yet, despite these serious flaws, Morey could do excellent work. He did produce beautifully rendered polychrome covers showing natural features, with an individual touch that the other science-fiction genre artists of the day probably could not have matched. The suggestion is that Morey's heart was not really in pulp illustration, where he made a living, but that he would have been better cast as a traditional watercolorist painting landscapes, seascapes, and similar forms. As has been stated, his work is characteristically uneven.

Signature: Usually LEO. MOREY or MOREY, sometimes with a two-digit year date.

Oeuvre: Weinberg provides a listing. In general, for our period Morey painted all covers for *Amazing Stories* between February 1930 and December 1936, with eight exceptions, and most interior art work. His best covers were printed in 1932.

Mark Marchioni (1910-?) was not one of the Big Four, but a prolific, standby artist in the science-fiction pulps. According to Weinberg, he was born in New York City, where he attended the Art Students League and the Grand Central Art School. During the period covered by this book he frequently contributed interior illustrations to *Wonder Stories* and *Astounding Stories*. In later years he drew for *Thrilling Wonder Stories* and other magazines up through the late 1940s. He is also said to have sold freelance work to various advertising agencies. He is not known to have done s-f cover work.

Of the important (i.e., numerically frequent) artists of the period 1926-1936, Marchioni was the least competent professionally, although his work showed improvement over the years. During the period up through 1936 his draftsmanship was poor, his perspective weak, and his composition bad. Unity all too often was lacking, with his drawings falling apart into a clutter.

Marchioni, however, did have a personal style whereby his drawings are often immediately recognizable. Basically, this was a peculiar combination of Futurism and Orientalism, with spindly sprigs and spidery lines sometimes emerging from solids. Costuming is often suggestive of an artists' ball, with jackboots, weird headgear, and odd body coverings. (On the other hand, contemporary figures look as if copied from clothing catalogues.) All in all, the suggestion is often of vaguely decadent fantasy, rather than science-fiction. Yet despite this personal element, Marchioni, particularly in later work beyond this project, sometimes showed the influence of the major science-fiction artists. Thus, on occasion one can see a typical mustachioed, goateed Marchioni man in high collared, flaring-bottomed short tunic, long hose, and elaborate shoes, facing a dynamo-like object reminiscent of Elliott Dold's work; or long rows of architectural features reminiscent of Paul's work, though without the intricate rendering of exact detail and formal perspective of Paul's; or figures contorted in the manner of Wesso.

Characteristic of Marchioni's work is a peculiar perspective in which objects are simply stacked on the page one above another (speaking spatially of the bottom of a page, to the top) with slight diminution of size, without vanishing point, light or shadow indication of distance. In a sense this is reminiscent of Oriental art, and a breaking of the direct representationalism characteristic of science-fiction art, but because of weak execution it is usually unsatisfactory.

As a science-fiction artist Marchioni was much inferior to his major colleagues, since he obviously had no understanding of even simple mechanical movements and, one would guess, had never seen either heavy machinery of any sort or laboratory equipment. Often, as in the illustration to Fearn's "Mathematica" in the February 1936 issue of *Astounding Stories*, he simply fantasized the impression of machinery, not too convincingly.

Signatures: Marchioni, ~~MM,~~ or M.

Oeuvre: A listing of Marchioni's work is to be found in Weinberg. In general, Marchioni's work appeared irregularly in *Astounding Stories* from 1934 through 1936 and in the various

Wonder magazines in 1930 and 1931.

The artwork considered so far has been representational, perhaps bolstered or cushioned by various techniques of simplification. It is true that Gernsback, with the September and November 1932 issues of *Wonder Stories*, experimented with non-pictorial covers based on technology, but with **A. Sigmond (?-?)** there appeared the first series of non-representational covers in the fantastic pulp magazines.

Sigmond did eight abstract covers for Teck Publications in 1933. His/Her work, which included the lettering, is modern, competent, and attractive, although without display value or sales appeal. Some of these covers, which are totally flat, with no attempt whatever at depth, contain highly abstracted icons like spaceships, but others seem to consist of decorative elements. In many ways they suggest a transfer of motifs from Scandinavian crafts.

It seems obvious that Sigmond's covers were associated with a desire to reduce printing costs, for one used only a blue plate, others only blue and red; only one cover applied full three-color printing. This last cover would seem to indicate that Sigmond did not understand printing processes well, for his/her stress on the blue and red plates, with only a slight visible hint of yellow from the yellow plate really amounted to a waste of press work. In effect he/she was preparing a two-color cover with three colors.

While artistically correct and aesthetically pleasing, Sigmond's covers were undoubtedly disastrous on the newsstands, since, practically, they amounted to camouflage.

Nothing is known about Sigmond. There is no record of his/her attendance at New York art schools and no listing of other work that he/she may have done. Social Security records include several "A. Sigmonds," male and female, but there is no reason to believe that any of them was the artist. In "Thomas O'Conor Sloane, A.B., A.M., E.M., Ph.D." by Schwartz/Weisinger (*Science Fiction Digest*, June 1933, p. 5), it is stated, apropos of nothing, "Cordial Dr. Sloane tells us that A. Sigmond lives in Hoag, Holland." If this is meant seriously, "Hoag" is possibly an error for The Hague; but Dr. Sloane was known to be a joker and *hoax*er. In any case, it is incredible that cover art could be handled from Europe.

A curious point emerges from a squib printed in Mort Weisinger's column "The Ether Vibrates" in the July 1933 issue of *Science Fiction Digest*: "The July [1933] cover of the same mag [*Amazing Stories*, signed as by Sigmond] was a composite of the work of three or four different artists, Morey tells me" (p. 8). This might be interpreted as reinforcing the notion of *hoax* in Dr. Sloane's statement.

Signature: Sigmond or A. Sigmond.

Oeuvre: Covers for *Amazing Stories,* January through July 1933, *Amazing Stories Quarterly,* for Spring/Summer 1933.

William Elliott Dold, Jr., (1892-1967), who used the work names of Elliott Dold and Elliot Dold, like Sigmond was an anomaly in science-fiction illustration, being an abstractionist, though an abstractionist who worked brilliantly with mechanical devices. Like Sigmond, too, he embodied the art persona of the time, in his case the heavy pole of art deco illustration and decoration.

Dold was born in New York City, son of the distinguished psychiatrist William Elliott Dold. He attended William and

Mary College, left in 1912, and served in the Serbian army in World War I. After returning to the United States and studying under Percy Bridgman at the Art Students League in New York, he entered the pulp world, where he did Western and air-war covers for William Clayton's publications.

While associated with Harold Hersey, he suggested, edited, and produced *Miracle Science and Fantasy Stories* (1931), to which he also contributed a novel and artwork. According to the accepted account, he then left publishing for a time because of illness.

In 1934 Dold approached Street and Smith for freelance work. According to Dold's reminiscence, Bill Lawler told him, after seeing his portfolio, "You're crazy enough for *Astounding*, we'll use you" (Schwarz/Weisinger, *Fantasy Magazine,* October/November 1934, p. 46). It is possible that Dold showed plates from *Night,* a privately published book in which he illustrated mildly erotic poems by Harold Hersey.

Dold contributed artwork to *Astounding Stories* as a lead artist through 1935, after which he did only occasional illustrations. His last science-fiction work consists of internal illustrations for the June 1941 issue of *Stirring Science Stories* and a cover (really a black-and-white.en ronde) for the July 1941 issue of *Stirring Stories.*

Dold was the most original of the important early science-fiction artists, yet also the most period-bound in that his work epitomized the "brutal" aspect of the art deco style dominant in the late 1920s and 1930s. Energy, force, power, motion, dynamism, and life all emanate from his drawings. Alone of the major science-fiction artists Dold was able to convey force. Heavy blacks and dark grays outlined with whites; strong, forceful highlighting; white fields are all worked together in intricate compositions that show a thorough grounding in both traditional and modern art.

The essential point about Dold was that he was a designer first and an illustrator second. His illustrations were often organized in complex geometric integrations, with simple solids like the sphere, cone, and cylinder present in many variations, recalling Cézanne's dictum about geometrics. (With these components, obviously, sexual symbolism will emerge.) These are often combined in the most complicated fashion, with circular structures pushing their way through the illustration on all sides.

Just as Paul favored verticals and horizontals, and Brown triangles, Dold favored circles, ovals, and extreme parabolic curves, with strong attempts at three dimensionality. As an embodiment of both the curve and power, the icon of the contemporary dynamo often pervades his work.

Yet in addition to the geometric and metallic aspects of Dold's work runs a strong organic component. His rounded metals seem alive; and frankly organic motifs, rendered in his strong, heavy style, are often incorporated among the metalwork. At times they resemble life forms from Ernst Haeckel's *Artforms in Nature.*

In his use of the human figure Dold seldom makes even the concessions that his colleagues did in various ways, but considers humans as design elements, typically stylized and geometrized to fit the metals and glass of the picture. Twisted and stressed, usually with much the same facial features, they seem ready to leap out of the illustration along with the mechanical elements. On occasion, Dold strips the human figure

down into planes, analogous to his master Bridgman's anatomic analyses.

Perhaps because of his earlier pulp experience, most of Dold's illustration is immediate foreground work, within which his figures and objects work around like placings on a small three-dimensional model. There is little opportunity for vistas or perspective of any sort, but when Dold does use perspective it is of the traditional office type.

The reader may compare Howard V. Brown's studio cover rendering of the monorail from Warner Van Lorne's "World of Purple Light" (*Astounding Stories,* December 1936) with Dold's towering interpretation of the same construction as a story illustration. Brown's shell-like vessel sits pleasantly dominant in a background field differentiated by color and tonal variation in rusty red-browns and dull blue-greens, but does not move, despite the exaggerated diminution of the vehicle and the presence of wind-lines. Dold's abstraction, against a stable background of geometric solids, on track held by towering pylons, whizzes through the air.

Dold's vision and technique, however, might be considered overspecialized. He developed only one style in his science-fiction work, thus raising doubts about his versatility, about his ability to employ other graphic means. In any case, when "brutal" art deco went out of fashion in favor of milder and more realistic styles, Dold was no longer appreciated—or used. (His withdrawal from publishing may also have been a matter of health or perhaps connected with the death of his wealthy father in 1942.)

As a science-fiction artist Dold ranks very high, and in a limited range his work is the best. His renderings of the mechanical side are imaginative and convincing and, with their recognition of streamlining and modern industrial design, more compelling than the work of his colleagues. His alien life possesses an alienness otherwise foreign to the pulps, and his backgrounds can be superb. His humanoid monsters, on the other hand, tend to standardization, being squat and lumpy, with batrachian heads. His forte, as might be expected from his style, is black-and-white work; such little color as he did for the science-fiction pulps, for *Miracle Science and Fantasy Magazine,* is excellent poster, but obviously simply black-and-white to which color has been added.

Signatures: DOLD or D; E. DOLD occasionally in Clayton covers. Dold's first name is usually spelled Elliot in editor's legends.

Oeuvre: Weinberg provides a list, but in general Dold's work is to be found in most issues of *Astounding Stories* from 1934 through 1936, with heaviest concentration in the earlier issues. The fine work in *Miracle Science and Fantasy Magazine* is generally unavailable because of the rarity of the magazine.

Artists, for one reason or another of lesser importance, also contributed to the early genre pulps. Austin Briggs, who later drew portions of "Flash Gordon" and other comic strips and was a creator of the Famous Artists School correspondence course, worked occasionally in *Amazing Stories* in 1929 and 1930, and *Amazing Stories Quarterly* in 1929. His style, very reminiscent of that of Joseph Clement Coll, did not fit the stories very well. John Fletcher Gould, one of the best action pulp illustrators, with an impressive academic background, contributed interior work to *Astounding Stories* in 1930 with an occasional illustration in 1931. Unfortunately, Gould had no concept of scientific illustration; a lab bench was his limit. F. S. Hynd, who illustrated occasional stories in *Amazing Stories* in 1926 and 1927, had an interesting style using black solids and white spaces, reminiscent of contemporary British woodcut work or French tachisme. R. E. Lawlor designed the drop-out contents and editorial pages of early *Amazing Stories* and *Amazing Stories Quarterly*. He also did occasional story illustrations in 1928 *Amazing Stories*. His work, which was very personal, was almost wholly linear, embodying strange distortions and contortions, making it interesting, but more suitable for fantasy than science-fiction. Hugh Mackay, an otherwise competent illustrator from the action pulps, contributed a few weak black-and-white illustrations to *Amazing Stories* during the take-over period in 1929, together with three covers, *Amazing Stories*, July and August 1929, and *Amazing Stories Quarterly*, Summer 1929. His better work was solid, but routine. Paul Orban and Charles Schneeman, Jr., were capable illustrators whose careers were just beginning in our period and who became important later. Orban appeared in *Astounding Stories* in 1933 and 1934; Schneeman, 1935 and 1936. Lumen Winter, who served as a back-up artist for *Wonder Stories* from 1933 through 1936, was undistinguished, but sometimes apparently tried to break spacial relations with interpenetrating planes.

Other artists, whose work appeared only occasionally or is not particularly noteworthy, include: Lyman Anderson (later of importance elsewhere), J. M. de Aragon, B. Bamont, Barker, Jack Binder (brother of Eando Binder), Blythe, Bulow, Burian, Butterfield, Clardy, COS, J. de Pauw, DE (a monogram), Bob Dean, Charles Durant (sometimes as C.D.), Fisher, Flatos, Martin Gambee, Don Hewitt, Hopper, Imrey, KAW, Charles Klinger, Lane, H. Lanos (of some importance, but not in this area), Leonard, McGerr, Fred Meagher, Miller, P. Muller, J. Munson, Nutter, R., Jno. Ruger (who did covers for *Scientific Detective Monthly*), Wallace Saaty, Sabo, Amos Sewell (later important in slick-magazine illustration), S. Strother, C. R. Thomson (C.R.T.; also spelled Thompson on the magazine contents pages), Ivan Volga, Sky Walitt, Ray Wardell, and Wilson. Attributions are to be found with individual stories in the main body of the text of this volume.

In most cases nothing is known of these men (and women?) but a signature, often only a partial signature or initials. It is probable that many of them were young art students or graduates who moved on to other areas. Unsigned illustrations, which were not uncommon, may have been produced by still other artists.

In the British boys' paper *Scoops*, a different series of artists appeared. Best-known was Serge Drigin, a Russian immigrant who sometimes signed himself Drigin and sometimes S.D. Although it is stated elsewhere that Drigin drew all the covers for *Scoops*, this is not correct. Also present were E. P. Kinsella, who signed as E.P.K., and an artist who used the signature Shirley. Most of the artwork, however, is not signed. The quality, on the whole, is superior to comparable American work.

II

Since data are not readily available, it seems appropriate to offer a little information on the production aspects of early science-fiction pulp-magazine artwork. Unfortunately, very little precise detail has been recorded, but the general picture can be reconstructed from various sources: non-fantastic pulp art of the 1930s and 1940s; printing procedures of the 1950s and 1960s, which (despite the increasing use of offset printing) still employed older techniques; and Harold Hersey's expository memoir, *Pulpwood Editor*, which despite weaknesses in other respects, is a gold mine of information about the business end of the pulps of his day.

Supervision of covers and inside illustration was, in general, the responsibility of the art director, although higher officials, like the publisher or editor-in-chief, might exercise right of approval. In the Gernsback enterprises, Hugo Gernsback and his brother Sidney were the ultimates, but, judging from the reminiscences of David Lasser and Charles Hornig, the Gernsbacks did not interfere if things were running smoothly. Frank R. Paul is listed on the masthead of the *Wonder* magazines as art director, but it is questionable whether this was more than an empty title. In the Clayton chain, according to Harold Hersey's reminiscences quoted in the magazine history of Clayton *Astounding Stories* above, William Clayton had a strong hands-on policy, participating in every stage of cover design, making suggestions according to a formulated aesthetic based on newsstand appeal. In Hersey's own *Miracle Science and Fantasy Magazine*, his art director, Elliott Dold, seems to have had a free hand, disregarding Hersey's principles, probably because Dold himself provided the artwork and handled production.

As far as is known, the science-fiction cover artists were free-lancers, although both Morey and Paul (at one time) maintained working areas in their publishers' offices. (The experiences of Frank Kelly Freas, a modern artist, as described in his *Science Fiction Art*, although not in our period, were probably typical of the young artist trying to peddle his work from publisher to publisher.) Payment was made on the basis of individual covers. Frank R. Paul, who set his own fees for Gernsback, received (it is said) forty-five dollars per cover (Lesser, p. 28), though the date of this arrangement is not clear. Presumably reflecting practice in the Clayton magazines, Harold Hersey mentions a typical figure of fifty to one hundred dollars for covers. (Such figures, of course, were averages; established artists with large reputations, like Rockwell Kent and N. C. Wyeth, who occasionally painted covers for the pulp magazines, received considerably more than this.)

As a commentary on relative rate of payment for types of magazine artwork, Quentin Reynolds mentions artist Amos Sewell, who as a young man contributed interior illustrations to *Astounding Stories*: "When the Nick Carter stories were revived, Hines [i.e., William "Pop" Hines, Street and Smith's art director] was smart enough to get Amos Sewell to illustrate them. Today [c. 1955] Sewell gets as much for one *Saturday Evening Post* cover as he then received for a year's work on *Nick Carter*." (Reynolds, p. 209).

Interior illustrations, too, were assigned as free-lance work, although occasionally staff members may have contributed. According to Harold Hersey (p. 34) a typical rate of payment in the 1930s for such interior illustrations was from five to ten dollars apiece, although Street and Smith, date not precisely indicated, often paid twenty dollars. (Reynolds, p. 209). The prolific J. Fletcher Gould, however, is on record as having been paid four dollars apiece, presumably in the early 1930s. The science-fiction artists, working in a more marginal area of publication, may well have been paid less.

In selecting scenes for depiction, the general policy was consultation of sorts between editors and artists. In some instances the editors suggested specific scenes to the artists; in other cases, the editors gave the artists galleys or page proofs of the stories and let the artists make their own selection.

The amount of control undoubtedly varied from house to house. In Clayton *Astounding Stories* Harry Bates worked closely with artists. A 1933 interview with Wesso describes the situation:

> Uses tractor models for some of his covers. When he was working on the cover illustration for Williamson's "The Pygmy Planet" he and Bates constructed with considerable difficulty a model for the scene in question . . . . Chooses the scene to be illustrated on the cover by consulting Harry Bates . . . . The color of the cover is selected by striving for variety. If they had a blue, a green, and red cover before, the next cover would probably be yellow or purple. Both read stories until they come across a suitable incident, one that is striking and sensational. Bates outlines his conception of the scene and Wesso adds his suggestions. A few pencil sketches are then made, terminating with a colored sketch. Mr. Clayton has the final word concerning the suitability of the cover. (Schwartz and Weisinger, "Hans Waldemar Wessolowski," p. 3).

Charles Hornig mentions, unfortunately without detail, that he discussed selection of scenes for *Wonder Stories* with Frank R. Paul. An interview with Leo Morey describes the procedure used in T. O'Conor Sloane's *Amazing Stories:*

> For a time he was advised by the editors as to the subject of his cover. This hindered Morey in a way, since his views on a theme for the cover occasionally contrasted with those of his editors. But later he was allowed to do his work independently . . . . Morey does all of his work in the office of *Amazing Stories*. He receives the original manuscripts from Dr. Sloane, who often indicates on the first page potential scenes for illustration . . . . We were watching Morey make a trial drawing for the conical headed creature described in "Triplanetary." For a time he painstakingly delineated Dr. Smith's description of this fantastic, nightmarish entity, with its medusa-like head. The finished trial drawing looked so fantastic that Morey promptly destroyed it, and began looking for another scene. (Schwartz-Weisinger, "Leo Morey" p. 17-18).

Hornig mentions an exceptional case involving the April 1935 issue of *Wonder Stories*. During discussion about a cover that was due up, Joseph Kraus, a member of Gernsback's scientific editorial staff, drew a rough sketch, which Paul fleshed out, whereupon Kraus wrote the story "Phantom Monsters" to fit the cover. This procedure seems, however, to have been very unusual in the science-fiction magazines, although not uncommon in the other pulps, where occasionally a cover with a striking scene would be prepared and an author asked to write an accompanying story.

Some artists, like Frank R. Paul and J. Allen St. John (Lesser, p. 83), read the stories, or parts of the stories, they illustrated; other artists simply flipped through the galleys until they happened upon a situation that showed promise, then prepared an illustration, which the editors checked for textual accuracy. By and large, the system worked, although there were two situations in cover art where the painting was markedly incorrect. In the cover rendering of A. Hyatt Verrill's "The Non-Gravitational Vortex" (*Amazing Stories*, June 1930), Morey showed a steamship, whereas the story described a five-masted sailing yacht; and in the cover illustration for Laurence Manning's "Seeds from Space" (*Wonder Stories*, June 1935), Paul placed events in wrong sequence. The publishers heard about these mistakes from observant readers.

Once an artist was assigned to an interior story illustration, he would prepare a sketch or sketches, perhaps thumbnails (very small sketches), which would show roughly what he intended to do. The art director (and possibly higher ups) would approve, accept with changes, or reject.

Quentin Reynolds quotes artists' reminiscences on the procedure in Street and Smith in the 1930s and 1940s.

> [As Amos Sewell reminisces,] "We all worked for Street and Smith . . . . perhaps the experience was good for us—it was certainly a humbling experience. Pop Hines always had a wet palette in his office. We'd bring in our illustrations, and if he didn't like them he'd tell us to get busy and change them then and there." . . . Howard Munce, the current [1955] President of the Society of Illustrators . . . . still pales a bit when he recalls the days when you had to please Pop Hines or borrow money to pay your rent. "I suppose Pop was awfully good at his job," Munce admits. "He ran an artistic assembly line and he looked upon paintings and drawings submitted to him much as a shop foreman looks upon the products of his machine shop. They had to conform exactly to his specifications. Hines would get illustrations to be used in any given issue and paste them onto a board. If one was too large he'd merely take a sharp knife and cut it down to size. They used to say that Pop would crop off the head of Whistler's "Mother" if he thought it would fit the page better. But he was a pretty nice guy anyhow." (Reynolds, p. 209-210).

During our period William Lawler seems to have been the art director or assistant art director concerned with Street and Smith *Astounding Stories*.

When a sketch for black-and-white work was approved, the artist would provide a finished drawing, perhaps on heavier drawing paper, perhaps on artist's illustration board, perhaps on one of the various textured boards, depending on the technique used--pen and ink, charcoal, dry brush, grease pencil, etc. In the later issues of *Amazing Stories* within our period, however, there is a suspicion that Morey's rough sketches were used, rather than finished drawings. This would have been an economy move on the part of the publisher.

Black-and-white interior work would probably have been sent to a cut maker, who would photograph it, imprint it on a zinc or copper sheet, etch it chemically, and nail it on a wood block so that it was the same height as the body type. It would then be fitted into the body copy, which in most cases would have been set in Linotype slugs. Pages would be locked up together to fit the paper folds that made up the little booklets (signatures) of which magazines were formed, then, for large runs, the typesetter or printer would make stereotype molds, which would be used in printing. In practice, the original type metal was kept on hand for a time (depending on contract arrangement), then melted down so that the special alloy could be reused.

With cover illustrations, the first steps were much the same as with interiors. The artist prepared sketches, then, on approval, a final version, which might be subject to minor revisions of various sorts. In most cases artists painted in oil, but on occasion watercolor, gouache, or mixed media were used. (In the science-fiction pulps watercolor was used much more frequently than in the general pulps, especially by Paul.) As a rule, the painting was considerably larger than the printed cover would be. Paul, for example, worked with a field that necessitated a 50 percent reduction. Artists in the general pulps often used much larger canvases.

This painting would be sent to a company specializing in color separation, who photographed it through various filters, at some stage of the process using a screen that broke up solid colors into fields of uniform little dots. Negatives were then prepared for the three basic colors (red, yellow, and blue) that made up the tints of the original. A negative for a black plate might also be prepared, but of the publishers considered in this study, only Street and Smith used true black on their covers. What appears to be black on the covers of Clayton, Gernsback, and Teck magazines is really blue superimposed on red, thus a dark purple. At the edges of the negatives were placed crosses or other symbols that permitted exact imposition (registration) among the negatives, which were then imprinted on metal and mounted.

Test printings of these plates, called progs (progressives), would be sent to the publisher for approval. If they were satisfactory, printing would be done either by a specialist in color printing (who might be the separator) or the general printing house, if it had the facilities. Because of the delicacy of the registration, it is possible that in many cases the printing involved not stereotypes, but letterpress.

Sides two, three, and four of the cover, which usually contained advertising, would be imposed on the sheet with the cover illustration. The advertiser or his agency usually supplied the negatives, metal, or plates required.

It is not certain exactly how lettering was applied on artwork, since there are several possibilities, and it may have been handled differently among the various publishers. With some interior illustrations, as in early issues of *Amazing Stories*, the artist (Paul in this case) hand-lettered titles and authors' names, presumably on the same board as the illustration. In other cases, type might be set by a house that had a good selection of display fonts, then pasted down on the illustration board.

In cover illustrations, it is not known exactly how magazine logos and other copy were handled. In practice of the 1950s and 1960s, this copy would have been printed or lettered separately, photographed, then stripped into the negatives appropriately, with drop-outs, if necessary, where type would overprint illustration.

With the exception of Street and Smith, who had a captive plant, pulp publishers used outside printing houses specializing in large runs to produce their magazines. This is the reason for the confusing statements about place of publication, as printed on magazine contents pages. For example, the May 1933 issue of *Wonder Stories* states "Publication office, 404 North Wesley Avenue, Mount Morris, Illinois." This simply means that the printing, binding, and perhaps typesetting took place in Illinois. The editorial and art work for all the magazines considered here would have been performed in New York City.

Cover illustration (retouched for legibility) by Frank R. Paul for the first issue of *Amazing Stories*, April 1926.

Cover illustration by Frank R. Paul for "The Moon Doom" by Nathaniel Salisbury, *Wonder Stories*, February 1933. New York City buildings are recognizable.

The middle space was immovable and gave access by staircases descending into subterranean ways. Right and left were an ascending series of continuous platforms, each of which traveled about five miles an hour faster than the one internal to it. The establishment of the Suzanna Hat Syndicate projected a vast facade upon the outer way, sending overhead an overlapping series of huge white glass screens, on which gigantic animated pictures of the faces of well-known beautiful living women wearing novelties in hats were thrown.

Illustration by Frank R. Paul for "A Story of the Days to Come" by H. G. Wells, *Amazing Stories* April 1928. Contrast this with R. E. Lawlor's interpretation as reproduced opposite. It must be pointed out that both artists totally missed the point of the story.

Very wide and spacious was their view . . . the oblongs of the Food Company, broken here and there by the ruins—grotesque little holes and sheds—of the ancient suburbs, and intersected by shining streams of sewage, passed at last into a remote diapering at the foot of the distant hills. . . . The Labor Company's field workers, in huge wheeled mechanical vehicles, were hurrying back to their meals . . . And through the air a dozen little private aeropiles sailed down towards the city.

Illustration by R. E. Lawlor for "A Story of the Days to Come" by H. G. Wells, *Amazing Stories*, May 1928. Contrast this with Frank R. Paul's interpretation of the story as reproduced opposite. Lawlor's fanciful near-infantilism is as inappropriate as Paul's architectural vision.

*And then came a sound—a horrible sound—which enabled
us to run like mad for the same outer air——*

Illustration by Howard V. Brown for "At the Mountains of Madness" by Howard P. Lovecraft, *Astounding Stories*, April 1936. This is generally considered Brown's best interior illustration.

Never before had human feet pressed upon those immemorial pavements!

Illustration by Howard V. Brown for "The Shadow out of Time" by H. P. Lovecraft, *Astounding Stories*, June 1936. Although the man seems panicked, the monsters are harmless. The illustration does not fit the story line.

¶ *From the flattened wreckage there gazed out at the rapidly growing crowd across the street, a pair of immense, pinkish-brown eyes . . . set in a head that looked somewhat like that of an enormously magnified rabbit. . .* Illustration by WESSO.

Illustration by H. Wesso (Hans Wessolowski) for "The Hungry Guinea-Pig" by Miles J. Breuer, M.D., *Amazing Stories*, January 1930. The monstrous rodent is well handled, but the humans are weakly typical of Wesso's work.

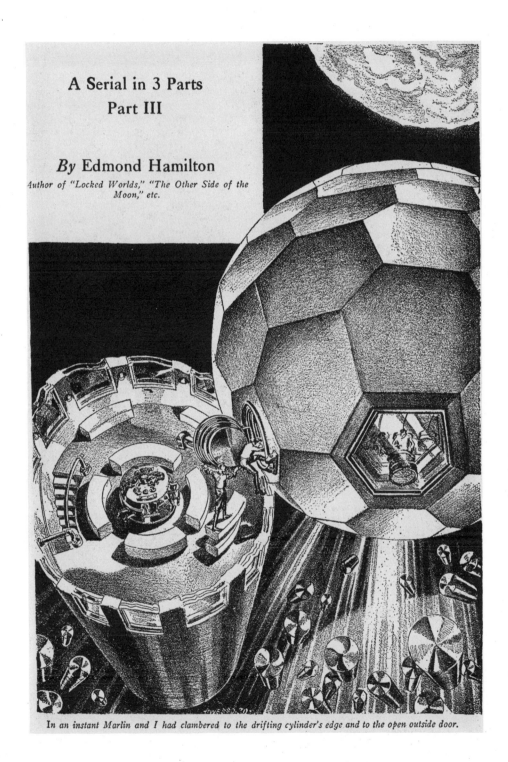

In an instant Marlin and I had clambered to the drifting cylinder's edge and to the open outside door.

Illustration by H. Wesso (Hans Wessolowski) for "The Universe Wreckers" by Edmond Hamilton, *Amazing Stories*, July 1930. Wesso was skilled at geometric solids.

They drove their fields of force against the fivefold bars.

Illustration by Elliot Dold for "The Skylark of Valeron" by E. E. Smith, Ph.D., *Astounding Stories*, January 1934. *L'art décoratif* at its strongest. Humans dwarfed by mechanism.

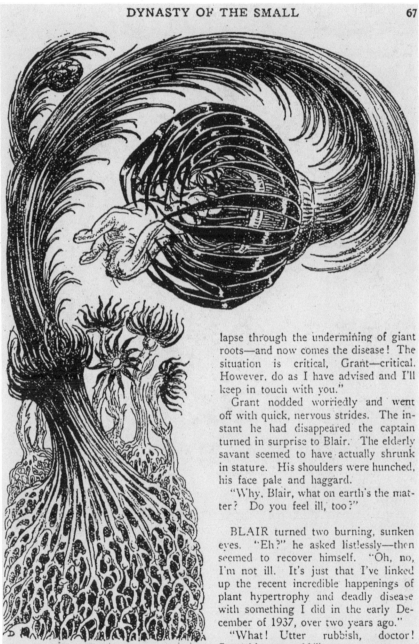

lapse through the undermining of giant roots—and now comes the disease! The situation is critical, Grant—critical. However, do as I have advised and I'll keep in touch with you."

Grant nodded worriedly and went off with quick, nervous strides. The instant he had disappeared the captain turned in surprise to Blair. The elderly savant seemed to have actually shrunk in stature. His shoulders were hunched, his face pale and haggard.

"Why, Blair, what on earth's the matter? Do you feel ill, too?"

BLAIR turned two burning, sunken eyes. "Eh?" he asked listlessly—then seemed to recover himself. "Oh, no, I'm not ill. It's just that I've linked up the recent incredible happenings of plant hypertrophy and deadly disease with something I did in the early December of 1937, over two years ago."

"What! Utter rubbish, doctor! Something *you* did!"

"Yes," Blair groaned, shrugging hopelessly. "You remember that antitoxin

The tentacled disk bent forward in sudden fury; the unfortunate rabbit was torn in pieces.

Illustration by Elliot Dold for "Dynasty of the Small" by John Russell Fearn, *Astounding Stories,* November 1936. The organic element, which is often unappreciated in Dold's work, is apparent.

"So you came! Well, you have not reached the
beginning even yet!"

Illustration by Mark Marchioni for "Mathematica" by John Russell Fearn, *Astounding Stories*, February 1936. The jumble
of futuristic material is characteristic, although the composition is better than usual.

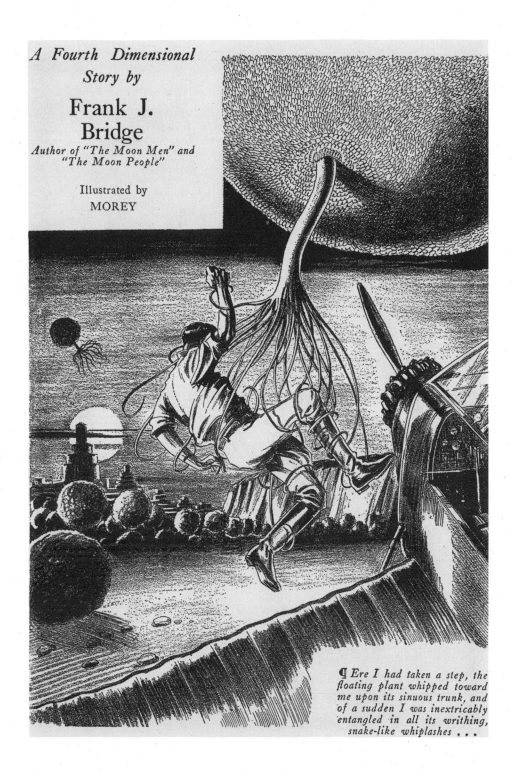

A Fourth Dimensional
Story by
**Frank J.
Bridge**
*Author of "The Moon Men" and
"The Moon People"*

Illustrated by
MOREY

¶ *Ere I had taken a step, the
floating plant whipped toward
me upon its sinuous trunk, and
of a sudden I was inextricably
entangled in all its writhing,
snake-like whiplashes . . .*

Illustration by Leo Morey (Leopoldo Morey y Peña) for "*Via* the Time Accelerator" by Frank J. Bridge (Francis J. Brueckel), *Amazing Stories*, January 1931. The detail in the aerial monster is atypical of Morey's work.

At last, with a rush, they landed on the lake shore, fifty yards from the ambuscade

Illustration by Leo Morey (Leopoldo Morey y Peña) for "The Flying Threat" by David H. Keller, M.D., *Amazing Stories Quarterly*, April 1930. Morey is usually best at coloration, but the contrasts here are notable. Morey liked airplanes.

Motif and Theme Index

Abduction by aliens.
  Asteroid: 598, 718, 720.
  Dimensions or via dimensions: 106, 303, 1599, 1677, 1680.
  Inner world inside hollow Earth: 548, 1541.
  Interstellar: 185, 260, 435, 442, 502, 546, 575, 639, 691, 1359, 1380, 1755, 1758.
  Jovian system: 335, 407, 954, 1180, 1297, 1298, 1379, 1460.
  Macrocosm: 386 (?), 1631.
  Mars: 437, 440, 488, 585, 623, 672, 1406, 1455, 1564, 1608.
  Mercury: 987, 1454.
  Miscellaneous: Reduced humans, origin not known: 52. Triton: 553. Saturn: 1437. Pluto: 1437. Other side of the universe: 1273. Other universe: 1366. Submen in Mexico: 1394.
  Moon: 549, 921, 951.
  Robots or cyborgs: 302, 469, 1745.
  Sea beings: 788, 1584, 1696.
  Skyland world above Earth: 402, 551 (?).
  Underground: 151, 342, 801, 975, 1014, 1199, 1602, 1624, 1807.
  Venus: 233 (by personality transfer), 328, 383, 562, 1445.
  Winged men: 161, 1441.
Abduction from the future. 407, 595, 949, 1222.
Abominable snowmen. 905.
Absolute zero.
  Separates dimensions: 224. Used to create neutronium: 279. Beings that live at: 450, 453. Weapon: 1227. Used for murder: 1487. Attainment knocks one out of space and time: 1267.

Accelerated beings from space. 435.
Accelerated growth. 626, 813.
Accelerated man; involvement.
  For revenge: 120. Robbery: 205, 967. Medical experiment: 429, 1531, 1707. Cultural pattern: 257. Military use: 813. Romance: 590. Sitcom experiences: 1401.
Accelerated man; techniques.
  Drugs: 205, 429, 590, 967, 1531, 1707.
  Rays: 1401.
Accident control. 141, 156, 773, 928.
Acromegaly. 1153.
Adams and Eves, new. 53 (failed), 66, 75, 98 (?), 287, 1267, 1310, 1358, 1633, 1717, 1753.
Adaptability, super. 317, 527 664.
Adirondack Mountains. 568, 611, 639, 1016, 1039.
Aerial cities. (*See* Flying cities.)
Africa. (*Since writers are often not geographically precise and since boundaries have changed since the date of writing, we have presented African locations in major subdivisions. Egypt is a separate category.*)
  East: 185, 1333, 1515, 1521.
  General: 318, 417, 648, 882, 1008, 1024, 1442.
  Islands off: 1491, 1569.
  North: 342, 924, 925, 1026, 1115, 1533.
  South: 218, 746, 880, 882, 1218, 1532.
  West and Central: 136, 151, 157, 1098, 1108, 1691.
Africa, future.
  World's leading power, one nation: 148. Empire, war against Europe: 582. Terraformed and covered with concrete: 780. Hostile black empire at war with U.S.: 813, 1637.

Afterdeath experiences. 224, 660, 816, 1693 (false).
Age measurer for women. 416.
Age riots. 835, 933.
Aging, unnatural. (*See also* Immortality, Rejuvenation.)
  Caused by weapon: 147. Caused by drinking heavy water: 180, 774, 1259. Occurs during time travel: 422. Used as disguise by vicious cult: 683, 684. Vitamin lack: 861. Hormonal: 1022. Aftereffect of rejuvenation treatment: 1575. Aftereffect of immortality treatment: 145 (instant). Result of "possession": 1605. Vampiric beings: 1743.
Agriculture. (*See also* Future, agriculture.)
  Automated: 578, 579, 581. Arctic: 240, 278, 712.
Air battles. (*See also* Duels.) 21, 32, 154, 198, 297, 542, 543, 550, 570, 610, 647, 662, 824, 856, 910, 923, 953, 986, 1000, 1036-1038, 1070, 1073, 1132, 1154, 1175, 1181, 1209, 1224, 1247, 1253, 1264, 1376, 1377, 1393, 1441, 1445, 1457, 1592, 1704, 1759.
  Battle among flying cities: 550. Flying circular saw against airplanes: 923. Battle among flying platforms: 1036. Invisible airplanes: 1181.
Air beneath the ocean. 135, 350, 1735, 1785.
Air cabs and buses. 910, 1090, 1297, 1298, 1300, 1403.
Air lanes, air control in future traffic. 3, 215 (magnetic beams), 322, 758, 1090, 1351.
Air mines. 551.
Air pirates and bandits. 32, 64, 65, 186, 215, 320, 384, 494, 667, 695, 790, 1037, 1090, 1181, 1183, 1189, 1209, 1230, 1343, 1570, 1592.
  Air pirate leaves company stock with

Atlantis, miscellaneous (*continued*)
Settled by Lunarians: 1216. Telepathic communication with: 941. Visions of: 574. War with Mars: 645. War with slug invaders from wandering star: 1681.
Atlantis, motion pictures of.
1216, 1302, 1580.
Atlantis, visit to.
792, 941, 1222, 1725.
Atlas Mountains. 1115.
Atmosphere-attracting substance. 815.
Atmosphere, future, without oxygen. 79.
Atmosphere in space. 66.
Atmosphere, loss. 1524.
Atmospheric decomposition as energy source. 1579.
Atmospheric electricity.
Power source: 108, 550, 744, 1063, 1230, 1563.
Canceled by atomic fission: 1187.
Atom, giant, used as earth-borer. 363.
Atomic bombs and weapons.
88, 114, 284, 325, 330, 471, 517, 610, 935, 982, 1035, 1071, 1400, 1471, 1678, 1761, 1786-1795.
Weapons: 316, 375, 828, 1160, 1340, 1624.
Atomic compression.
36, 60, 606, 684, 857, 990, 991, 1093, 1308, 1347, 1415, 1416 (?), 1547, 1551, 1745, 1770.
Atomic energy. (*See also* Space travel, *which often tacitly involves atomic energy.*)
17, 36, 66, 76, 79, 88, 113, 129, 168, 172, 179, 188, 191, 193, 198, 201, 202, 233, 260, 265, 284, 316, 325, 326, 327, 374, 384, 390, 400, 440, 442, 448, 450, 451, 463, 489, 519, 561, 573, 620, 650, 654, 666, 685, 717, 690, 717, 747, 750, 754, 780, 788, 807, 843, 863, 917, 934, 938, 954, 985, 987, 993, 1003, 1004, 1054, 1056, 1128, 1152, 1154, 1204, 1208, 1222, 1223, 1238, 1242, 1282, 1297, 1298, 1320, 1340, 1349, 1350, 1360, 1362, 1376-78, 1380, 1390, 1398, 1407, 1436, 1460, 1477, 1478, 1496, 1500, 1555, 1576, 1597, 1625, 1628, 1668, 1670, 1678, 1729, 1735, 1757, 1761, 1813.
Atomic energy, miscellaneous.
Attained by work near sun: 168, 1467.
Developed with cosmic rays: 954, 1570.
Experiments in macrocosm disturb our universe: 214, 386, 1466.
Fraudulent claim: 562.
Inhibitors: 192, 193.
Obtained, at a price, from space empire: 1247.
Obtained by squeezing electronic orbits: 36.
Rejected: 1247, 1467 (partially).
Atomic explosions.
Accidental: 17, 179, 1054, 1215, 1216, 1222, 1376, 1396, 1521, 1683, 1734.
Other: Used to move Earth: 73, 213.
Destroys Atlantis: 168, 213. Used to

create an artificial island: 237. Self-sacrifice to destroy outlaw nest: 1570. Lamentably destroys lost race, lost world, and remarkable villains: 1733. Destroys Bodia: 1215, 1216.
Atomic fire. 448, 451, 670, 1001, 1048, 1056, 1105, 1524, 1576, 1747.
Atomic miscellaneous.
Atomic changes create antigravity: 365, 963.
Atomic crystallization sets off time stasis: 75.
Atomic disintegration by ultrasonics as murder weapon: 962.
Atomic orbital expansion is essence of skyland: 708.
Atomic particles cemented together by electromagnetic forces: 810.
Atomic particles manipulated to create material culture: 705, 935-938, 1168.
Atomic processes in macrocosm disturb our universe: 214, 386, 1466.
Atomic rate change creates invisibility: 639.
Atomic transmutation, selenium to arsenic, saves universe from mad scientist: 1337.
Atomic waste affects orbit of Moon: 66.
Mental power of personalized atoms affects humans: 1336-1339.
Negative matter formed of electrons in reverse motion: 547.
Splitting atom removes atmospheric electricity: 1187.
Atomic planet used as metaphor for Earth. 1154.
Atomic supercatastrophes.
Cuts Earth in half: 539.
Destroys or will destroy universe: 583, 670, 1105, 1636, 1640, 1644.
Atomic synthesis. 705, 935-938, 1168.
Atomic worlds. (*Very, very small worlds, including molecular, atomic, and sub-atomic. See also* Microcosm, World in a Box.)
Atomic worlds, cultural level.
Primitive: 857, 1075, 1547, 1551.
Barbaric: 990, 991 (partly).
Our level: 301, 785, 786.
Superior: 430, 506, 569, 895, 991 (partly), 1154, 1168, 1284, 1572, 1745.
Atomic worlds, inhabitants.
Cyborgs: 1745.
Flame beings: 1168.
Human: 216, 301, 506, 569, 785, 786, 857, 895, 990, 991, 1075 (microscopic), 1154, 1284, 1285, 1416, 1547, 1551, 1572. Hawaiians: 990, 991. Indians: 1547, 1551. Mongoloids: 991.
Humanoid: Ape-men: 990, 1154. Goggle-eyed, telepathic: 1572.
Intelligent birds: 430.
Intelligent crustaceans: 1154.
Superbrains: 1572.
Atomic worlds, miscellaneous.
Inspired by spirit of Leeuwenhoek,

young man commits murder to obtain diamond and becomes besotted with atomic female: 1075. Invasion from atomic worlds: 430, 569, 1168, 1572. Plant life retrieved from atom wipes out Martian life: 385. Young couple enters atomic world; all concerned forget time differential, and when they should be retrieved, hundreds of their descendants appear: 1416.
Atomic worlds, mode of entry.
Atomic compression: 606, 990, 991.
Cosmic ray activity: 1416.
Drugs: 301.
Fourth dimension: 785, 1572.
Matter transmitter: 1284 (?).
Mineral lens compresses atoms: 1547, 1551.
Ray: 1745.
Size machine: 430, 857, 1168.
Supermicroscope: 1154.
Atomic worlds, romance. (*i.e., between persons of our world and atomic worlds.*)
216, 301, 857, 895, 990, 991, 1075, 1154, 1547, 1551, 1572.
Atomic worlds, viewing only, method.
Brain enhancement: 216.
Microscope: 385, 506, 569, 895, 1075.
Atoms, atomic particles, personalized. 862, 1335-39.
Attitude projector. 1650.
Aura used for personality classification. 693, 694.
Auroras. 696, 1643.
Australia.
225-227, 249, 275, 408, 581, 746, 906, 1157, 1221, 1258, 1412, 1512, 1624, 1625, 1733.
Miscellaneous. Future science base for world: 225-227. Martian plant lands and causes war: 249. Underground lost race with superscience: 275. Sinks into the sea: 408. Prehuman ruins and library of all time: 906. Overrun by Antarctic beetle horde: 1221; by Trogs: 1624. Continent stood up on end: 1258.
Austria, Tyrol. 82.
Autistic child with ancestral memory? 767.
Automatic writing of extraterrestrial origin. 1284.
Automation of a sort.
81, 115, 141, 431, 578, 579, 581, 582, 733, 1156, 1281, 1328-1331, 1438, 1349, 1465, 1469, 1509, 1514.
Automated maps: 1348, 1349.
Automated guns: 1156.
Automobile culture. 733.
Automobile races. 435, 579, 688, 910, 1399, 1536.
Automobiles, super. (*See also* Combination vehicles.)
156, 199, 579, 773, 814, 928, 1233, 1399, 1405, 1536.
Electric: 773. Powered by Seidlitz powder: 1032. Computerized non-local,

Automobiles, super *(continued)*
accident-free traffic: 339.

Aviation fiction, aviation of the future.
(*See also* Airplanes, super; Air battles; Air pirates; Air police; *and similar categories.*)
64, 215, 217, 218, 328, 542, 543, 619, 742, 748, 790, 856, 1036, 1037, 1038, 1070, 1090, 1179, 1181, 1183, 1185, 1187, 1214, 1230, 1348, 1474.

Azore Islands. 125, 137.

Aztecs. 338, 1345, 1394, 1538. Aztec god terraforms Venus and transfers mankind there: 479.

Baboon enlarged to size of gorilla. 1080.

Baby born with ancestral memory. 736.

Baby nurse, robot. 738.

Babylonian events recapitulated. 364.

Bacon, Roger, and his brazen head. 1657.

Bacteria, intelligent. 286, 349, 413, 1208, 1642.

Bacteria, miscellaneous. Photophilic, skotophobic: 250. Rays kill: 488. Cause evolution: 589. Cause death of iron: 612, 872. Wiped out: 668. Destroy interplanetary invaders: 951, 1697, 1727. Do not survive size changes: 1551. Enlarged: 116, 301, 349, 413, 800.

Bacterial warfare. 17, 226, 250, 293, 383, 458, 522, 572, 610, 668, 813, 893, 982, 1153, 1208, 1247, 1275, 1288, 1362, 1552.

Bad violin playing causes death of intelligent bacterium. 349.

Bahama Islands. 1224.

Baja California seized by U.S., then returned to Mexico. 1115.

Baldness cure, fatal. 1317.

Ball bearings litter space. 169.

Ball lightning. 229, 365.

Balloons. 365, 714, 921, 1141, 1146, 1525, 1763.

Baltimore destroyed. 1624.

Bank of England to be robbed. 419.

Bank panic almost exterminates mankind. 835.

Bank protection, automatic. 1330.

Barnacles, intelligent, with superscience in future. 888.

Barnard's Runaway Star. Home of Medusae, jellyfishlike monsters with superscience who invade solar system; their planet is Earth-like, but with jungle, poisonous atmosphere: 1755.

Baseball with controlled flight. 1088.

Basque, component of Atlantis. 1202.

Bathyspheres and bathyal adventures.
313, 350, 370, 394, 467, 818, 956, 971, 984, 1346, 1696, 1735, 1785.

Bat-men on Mars. 654.

Bats. Gigantic: 306, 342. Intelligent: 342. In hollow Earth: 801. Monstrous: 1562.

Battery, super. 199.

Battle of Salisbury Plain. 149.

Battles of will. 146, 169, 323, 356, 400, 454, 648, 997, 999, 1014, 1255, 1277, 1323, 1376, 1377, 1378.

Beauty standards, odd. Fat and wrinkles esteemed: 256.

Becoming king, queen, etc.
44, 256 (dictator), 296, 316, 326 (almost), 354, 370, 508, 793, 911, 990, 991, 993, 1034, 1442, 1509 (dictator), 1514 (dictator), 1545, 1561, 1562, 1580, 1757.

Bee extract conveys immortality. 743.

Bees.
Intelligent: 476, 887, 1432.
Killer: 516, 669.
Life as a personalized bee: 859, 1391.
Transformation into a bee: 1827.

Beetles. (*See also* Cockroaches.)
Giant: 487, 609, 1221, 1728.
Intelligent: 442, 573 (on Ganymede), 987 (on Mercury), 1127, 1221 (in hollow Earth; overrun surface).
Metaphor for cryptographic story: 1140.
The perfect insect pest: 184.

Befogging America to conquer it. 209.

Behavior patterns reversed. 241.

Behind reality.
Cosmic dreamer begins to wake and universe disappears: 282.
Everything is all mathematics on literal level: 409, 410, 1258, 1262, 1414, 1645.
Everything is the cigar smoke of Brahma: 1386.
In misty thought world apart from reality: 833, 947.

Belgium. 1531.

Bell, ultrasonic, acts as disintegrator. 1116.

Benevolence a threat to mankind.
Interplanetary missionaries: 242. Panacea plant from Mars causes wars: 249. Removal of evil component shatters civilization: 1123.

Berlin. Destroyed in war: 293, 235, 1128. Aerial city used as weapon: 550. Partially wrecked by meteor storm: 582.

Bermuda. 303.

Beryls. Giant beryls control rotation of Earth: 155. Mined in Antarctica: 1506.

Betelgeuse, planet of. Earth-like, peopled by energy beings: 193. Peopled by amoeboids: 1273.

Beta Centauri. 533.

Bets and wagers. (*See also* Races, Sports.)
To create a human being: 163. Concerning most dangerous game: 940. To circumnavigate the world: 1083, 1214. One-man perilous sea voyage: 1730. Space run: 1806.

Beyond space and time. 938, 1267, 1273, 1366.

Biblical anthropomorphism causes trouble among non-humans. 717.

Biblical myths and legends. (*See also* Adam and Eve, Cain and Abel.)
Giants on the Earth: 992.

Biela's comet causes space wreck. 91.

Big Ben. 1047, 1491.

Biospheres and biosphere ships. 285,
317, 853, 1270, 1753.

Bird people. 284, 424, 426, 470, 547, 698, 1723.

Birds, miscellaneous. Gigantic birds of prey on secondary satellite: 894. Giant, intelligent: 430, 1629. Giant, used as mounts: 1754. Green feathers, secreting red pigment, trap criminal: 1553.

"Black Light." (*An early popular term for ultraviolet light, which see.*)

Black light. (*i.e., light that is actually black.*) 696.

Blacks, miscellaneous. (*See also* Anti-Black bias.)
Vicious: 329, 727, 763. Comic: 678. Plot to exterminate whites: 727. Massacre Southern whites and return to jungle mode of life: 763. Slaves on plantations on Saturn: 829. Pirates and would-be conquerors: 910. Ruled the Moon and Earth in remote past: 1215, 1216. Black woman is space leader: 1288. Black slaves on Venus: 245.

Blind, country of the. 484, 1708,

Blindness.
Alleviated by retinal projection: 613. Caused by radiation: 1315, 1467. Cured in future: 1816.

Blood cells, personalized.
345, 615, 665, 809, 1339, 1558.

Blood, miscellaneous.
Conveys miniaturized soldiers: 1415. Blood substitute radioactive liquid: 450, 453. Chlorophyll as a blood substitute: 980. Blood tests for personality factors: 235.

Blood transfusions.
Alter personality: 817.
Alter racial type: 915.
Carry fatal snake venom: 480.
Convey immortality: 259, 428, 915.

Bloodstream, adventures in the.
286, 345, 615, 665, 809, 1339, 1347, 1558.

Blue is invisible, because of different range of vision. 442.

Blue men. 143, 187, 244, 423 (humanoid), 892, 1157, 1197 (humanoid), 1523, 1682.

Bode's Fifth Planet, "Bodia." (*A hypothetical planet between Mars and Jupiter that broke up to form the asteroid belt. It is usually fictionally considered as Earth-like, with a human population.*)

Bodia, cultural level.
Superior to ours: 405, 473, 659, 703, 812 (?), 1152, 1215, 1216, 1367, 1451, 1576.

Bodia, cultural type. Socialist utopia: 659, 703. Harsh, regimented society: 1152. Altruistic culture: 405, 703, 1576.

Bodia, inhabitants.
Human, not ancestral: 659, 1576.
Humanoids: 812, 1367 (invisible).
Our direct ancestors: 1152, 1215, 1216, 1451.
Our indirect ancestors: 405, 473.

Centipedes, gigantic. 267.
Central American island. 1540.
Central Europeans, war with U.S. 634, 1415. Centrifugal force for space travel. 1320, 1782.
Ceres, ambience.
Earth-like: 221, 391, 1297, 1298, 1300.
Ceres, cultural level.
Superior: 1113, 1297, 1298, 1300.
Ceres, inhabitants.
Human: 391 (colonists), 1297, 1298, 1300.
Ceres, miscellaneous.
Leaving orbit, hits Moon: 1236. War of liberation against Pallas: 1113. Inadvertently injures Earth: 1113. Penal colony: 221, 1071. Space wreck on: 475.
Chameleon-men, change skin color. 1561.
Change of radio channel turns religious broadcasting into jazz. 176.
Change of state, chemical, of universe. 587, 1619.
Channeling. 412.
Character analysis machines. 1580.
Chemical action halted by rays. 461, 474.
Chemical symbols as code. 127.
Chesapeake Bay. 22.
Chicago. (*See also* Illinois.)
Damaged or destroyed: 114, 190, 437, 460, 463, 551, 859, 1039, 1358, 1497, 1524, 1624.
Gangsters: 96, 270, 429, 1419, 1424, 1427.
Various crimes: 266, 757, 798, 967, 1402.
Chicago, future. In ruins: 79, 114, 903, 1716. Gangster run: 96, 270, 1424. Supercity: 70. Robots rule area (a fraud): 560. Communist tyrannical city state: 1253. Last stronghold of mankind against horrors: 22. Inhabited by wolf people: 903.
Chicago, miscellaneous.
Battle of Chicago, Orientals versus U.S.: 449.
General: 110, 114, 116, 149, 928, 1325.
Giant guinea pig runs amok: 111.
Martian robot parades streets: 85.
University feud with New York: 745.
Chicken heart tissue runs amok. 379.
Child-rearing by machine. 738, 748, 765.
Chile. 34, 1067, 1549.
Chimeras. (*See also* Monsters, Teratology.) 60, 93, 359, 1069.
Chimpanzee with human brain. 704.
China, miscellaneous.
China depopulated by glacier: 952. China invaded by U.S. for victims to feed monsters: 1225. Chinese people are all syphilitic: 728. Chinese people of Lunar origin: 799. Chinese settle North America in alternate world: 851. Liberated from Japanese occupation: 1115. Maintains cryogenic armies: 442. Site, in Chinese Turkestan, of Bodian colony: 1367. Surgical procedure

exemplifies Chinese revenge: 757.
China, wars. (*See also* Asia, Orient.)
War with, hostility to U.S.: 610, 693, 756, 824, 980, 1056, 1072, 1073, 1265, 1318, 1573, 1761, 1804.
Wars with other nations: France: 662. Great Britain: 662, 836. Germany: 662. World State: 442. USSR.: 982. Japan: 1322. Present-day civil war: 1476.
Chinese food, schemes and machinations about. 505.
Chinese language. First voyager to Moon teaches natives Chinese: 786.
Chlorophyll takes place of hematin in human blood. 980.
Cholera epidemic in New York City. 1145.
Chrysalis of monster in form of human female. 1016.
Cincinnati destroyed. 1565.
Circe. Imaginary outer planet in solar system; Earth-like, habitable: 1226.
Circular saw, flying. 923.
Circular time. (*See also* Time *categories*.) 409, 410, 1478.
Circuses. (*See also* Zoos.)
Aliens put into circus: 46, 504, 596, 1007. Mad scientist creates freaks and monsters: 60, 1158. Man with deformed head put into circus: 219. Fifty-foot tall man put into circus: 1491.
Cities. (*See* Crystal cities, Dome cities, Floating cities, Flying cities, Future demography, Garden cities, Machine cities, Megalopolises, Science cities, Social level cities, Underwater cultures, Underground man, Unitary cities, U.S., future composition.)
Civil engineering and surveying in Africa. 1532.
Civil war between isotopically separated people. 1266.
Claim jumping. 77, 297, 776, 1282
Clairvoyance caused by magnetic field, fourth dimension folding of space. 1690.
Class struggle in the Marxist sense, strict and classical.
70, 201, 296, 348, 431, 485, 668, 772, 782, 788, 792, 855, 1035, 1242-1244, 1250, 1281, 1283, 1346, 1381, 1433, 1445, 1457, 1509, 1514, 1569, 1572, 1583, 1592, 1602, 1610, 1689, 1704, 1705, 1729, 1757.
Class struggle, metaphoric, figurative. (*See also* Machine intelligence, Revolt of the machines, Revolt of the scientists, Technocracy.)
Age groups: 933. Anarchist versus business: 333. Antilabor parable involving revolt of machines: 622. Antilabor: 1350, 1362. Black slaves versus white balloonheads: 1276, 1277. Black slaves versus white overlords: 1126. Commoners versus Greek gods: 850. Communist old lags in lunar prison: 1223. Light-skinned natives dominant over dark-skinned: 989, 993,

1442, 1652. Males versus dominant females: 425, 908, 949, 1231, 1362. Playboy culture versus mutated subculture: 1381. Racial and social: 989, 993, 998. Religious dictatorship: 673. Robots versus humans: 1607. Saturnians and oppressed Earth colonists: 815. Scientists versus rulers: 858. Social activist versus alien exploitation: 1273. Social, religious, exploitative powers in struggle: 1247. Socialist murders counterrevolutionary entertainer: 1205. Stratified society: 780. The people versus monopolists: 916.
Unions: 1355.
Climate control. (*See also* Weather control.)
510, 708, 1066, 1535.
Cloak of invisibility. 118, 297, 902, 998, 1047, 1224, 1589, 1810.
Clocks parallel human soul. 1526.
Cloning. 1622.
Closed-circuit television medicine. 140.
Cloud beings. 593, 708.
Cloud city. 1734.
Cloud disintegrator. 437, 1038.
Clouds, artificial. 550, 1038.
Club mosses hundreds of feet high. 766.
Coal prized by Plutonians. 255.
Coal Sack, penetration of. 71.
Cobalt for atomic energy. 993.
Cockroach men. 269, 271.
Coffee. Panacea for vitamin deficiency: 49. Banned: 49, 1348, 1349.
Cold, a separate force. 968.
Cold as a weapon. (*See also* Absolute zero.)
302, 325, 888, 968, 1199, 1227, 1480, 1626, 1723.
Cold light. 860, 1025, 1643.
Colloidal gold. 864.
Colloids, activated, as weapon. 1573.
Colombia. 826.
Colonialism, particularly flagrant examples. 37, 136, 263, 442, 561, 699, 700, 718, 720, 1448.
Color of space. 86, 1481.
Color organ. 1620.
Colorado. 120, 942, 968, 1179, 1323, 1459, 1495.
Colors, miscellaneous. (*See also* Camouflage, Invisibility.)
New colors become visible: 1026, 1373, 1502. Color removed from the Earth: 402. Color associated with regional decay: 904. Earth conquerors do not see blue: 442. Color of clothing matches aura: 693. Human evolutionary offshoot has different color vision: 1602. Body color, communication by: 24, 352, 457, 1304. Symbolic colors on Venus: 1304.
Combination vehicles.
Submarine tanks: 135, 154, 1584. Air and submarine: 154, 550, 694, 1569. Land and air: 579. Land, air, submarine, surface ship: 134, 1536, 1735. Space suit doubles for mini submarine: 497.

Comets, ambience, other than realistic.
Earth-like: 909, 1719.
Energy cocoon containing suns and planets: 1758.Comets, artificial or controlled.
35, 450, 488, 1758.
Comets, cultural level.
Superior: 35, 450, 546, 909, 1150, 1204, 1719 (partially), 1758.
Comets, hitchhiking on. 446, 1311, 1249, 1533.
Comets, inhabitants.
Almost two-dimensional people: 1719.
Ant-like creatures with radioactive metabolism: 1204.
Cyborgs, four legs, tentacles: 546.
Energy beings and captive races, human and otherwise: 1758.
Gigantic humanoids: 909.
Plant-men: 1150.
Superhuman blacks with radioactive metabolism: 450.
Telepathic slugs: 35.
Comets, miscellaneous.
Composed of mind matter, improves Martians: 1285. Identified with Martian god: 1600. Space navigational problems involving: 91, 1351, 1504. Spaceship mistaken for comet: 822, 1157.
Comets, periodic. 1319, 1630.
Comets, threaten or damage Earth.
284, 510 (drags away Moon), 546, 621 (drags away Moon), 630, 1533, 1630, 1719.
Comic strip connections.
Flash Gordon: 1071.
Buck Rogers: 1072, 1073.
Original strip "Zarnak": 1828
Communication with dead, by radio. 803.
Communications oddities, a few. (*See also* Color, communication by body; Cryptograms and codes; Interplanetary Communication; Languages; Lights, organic, used as communication means; Morse Code; Semantics; Symbolic actions.)
Black patches of cloth on Moon: 1501.
Cipher using plant forms: 117.
Diagrams: 514.
Drums: 1009.
Flight patterns: 1662, 1663.
Humming language: 185, 531, 1445.
Interplanetary heliograph: 1405.
Invisible ink on body: 1248.
Moth wings with genetically produced messages: 942.
Organic picture display on body: 467, 881, 1048, 1278, 1373.
Periodic arson: 50.
Position of statue: 353.
Revving up sound recordings: 593.
Solar static for radio: 194.
Space communication via canister: 148.
Space smoke signals: 580.
Spectrographic lines: 573, 1231.
Three-dimensional message for four-dimensional being: 106.

Thumps: 31.
Whistling language: 45, 185.
Xylophone and Morse Code: 1129.
Communists. (*See also* USSR.)
Anti-Communist: 292, 764, 969-979, 982, 986, 1045, 1205, 1321, 1358, 1603.
Pro-Communist: 48, 51.
Companion star to sun, now dead. 1682.
Compound beings. 441, 477, 599, 746, 1206, 1290, 1326, 1494, 1640, 1680, 1799.
Compound interest, wonders of. 511, 650, 722, 835, 1704.
Compressed air propulsion. 515, 1090.
Computer equivalents. (*See also* Machine intelligence.)
Construction of universes: 409, 410.
Controlling sports apparatus: 740.
Creation of virtual reality: 1714.
Food production: 1231.
General use: 191, 695, 950, 1377, 1378, 1640.
Investigation and control of ultimates: 1258, 1262, 1414, 1645.
Prediction: 48, 51, 109, 114, 834, 981, 1002, 1135, 1250, 1470, 1714, 1738.
Space travel: 191, 232, 1377, 1378.
Condensed light as power. 907.
Conductor beam for space travel. 1285.
Confederacy won the Civil War. 851.
Confidence games. (*See also* Frauds and hoaxes, Swindles.) 344, 960, 1684 (?).
Congo nation, war with Great Britain. 1552.
Conscious mind suppressed to attain other faculties. Ancestral memory or memory of past lives: 24, 405, 411, 1342, 1344.
Conservation of energy refuted. 1505.
Contest stories. (*Stories originating in various contests offered by the magazines. Such contests were usually based on cover artwork, about which stories were to be written.*)
Air Wonder Stories, February 1930 cover: 63, 523, 1003, 1040.
Amazing Stories, December 1926 cover: 265, 440, 585, 931, 1541, 1648, 1725.
Science Wonder Stories, November 1929 cover: 143, 362, 913, 1092, 1133, 1404, 1481.
Wonder Stories, July 1935 cover: 1, 1113, 1439.
Wonder Stories Quarterly, plot contest: 504, 672, 1001, 1035, 1381, 1492, 1676, 1759.
Contests based on finishing or explaining stories already printed: 1046, 1236, 1742.
Story originating in essay contest on "What Science Fiction Means to Me": 1079.
Continent raising. 743, 1269.
Coral used in dentistry. 1389.
Corkscrew creates pain and writing ability. 768.

"Coronium." 1436,
Corpse misassembled by primitive matter transmitter. 876.
Corpses that shrink. 60.
Corpses transformed into statues. 61, 102, 418.
Corpses wired up and used as soldiers. 726.
Cosmic balance, disturbance in it destroys intelligent life in universe and macrocosm. 412.
Cosmic being imprisoned for "crime." 568.
Cosmic fault redeemed. 1028.
Cosmic flights. 146, 254, 316, 410, 441, 1693.
Cosmic rays.
Energy and power: 144, 550, 572, 718, 814, 954, 1045, 1074, 1204, 1207, 1362, 1396, 1516, 1519, 1570, 1582, 1591, 1592, 1643, 1746.
Matter created out of cosmic rays: 190.
Weapons: 190, 268, 270, 284, 1225, 1683.
Miscellaneous: As a disintegrator: 190, 268. Balance Fortean universe: 1609. Conceived of mystically: 1648. Create nothingness bubble that eats up everything: 964. Detect crime: 144. Earth almost destroyed when cosmic ray generator is turned on: 1516. Enable interplanetary communication: 1059. Enable matter transmitter (?): 1113. Enable space travel: 1519, 1582, 1591. Enable time travel: 1074, 1362. Transmute substances and kill: 658. Used in laboratory experiments: 1683.
Cosmic rays and life.
As life force: 1648. Cause evolution: 557, 1477. Create superpeople and enhance intelligence: 1124, 1809. Nourish Trans-Plutonian life forms: 537. Cause aging: 280 (fake), 407. Stimulate pineal gland, awaking ancestral memory: 1435. Cause devolution: 1477. Cause organic size changes: 1416.
Cosmic souvenir hunters. 1404.
Cosmologies, unusual. (*See also* Behind reality, Forteanism, Skyland.)
Universe the dream of cosmic dreamer: 282. When Earth formed, core first, then separate shell that does not touch core: 548. Universe is a god's cigar smoke: 1386. Planets originally formed and were contained in sun, where human life developed: 1757. Planets are eggs of cosmic dragons: 1753.
Counterfeiting. 854.
Counter-Mars. 1609.
Court trials with lie detectors. 1499.
Crabs. Amiable giant intelligent crabs in Antarctica: 1739. Shell of giant crab used as a boat on a satellite of Saturn: 501.
Cretinism as disguise. 222.
Cricket that miaows like a cat. 184.

Crime vigilantes. 1057, 1148, 1242.

Crimean War. 1532.

Crimes, various. (*See also* Air pirates, Claim jumping, Frauds and hoaxes, Gangsters, Kidnapping, Murder, Robbery, Space pirates, Swindling.)
Arson: 996.
Bribery of police: 1615.
Extortion: 118, 1118, 1731, 1760.
Future crime, breach of reason: 563.
Genetic manipulation: 565.
Harassment: 266, 798, 1296.
Hijacking: 204, 1506.
Plagiarism: 463, 1671.
Sabotage, pollution: 882, 1259, 1474, 1623, 1775.
Tax and customs evasion: 29, 298, 1248

Criminal tendencies cured.
Brain surgery: 57, 187, 229, 982, 1569, 1651.
Brainwashing: 235, 694, 1625.
Ray treatment: 545, 1123, 1390 (cured or killed), 1569

Crocodile men. 558 (on Mars).

Cro-Magnon men. 131 (on Venus), 161 (on Pacific island).

Crucifix phobia among vampires. 1232.

Cruelty to animals. 1455, 1692.

Crustacean men. 1359.

Cryptograms and codes.
107, 117, 127, 634, 1140, 1528.

Crystal cities. 457, 1154, 1304.

Crystal life. (*See also* Silicon life.)
72, 469, 477, 587, 1008, 1476, 1666, 1679, 1732, 1824. All except 587, 1476, and 1666 are intelligent.

Crystal optics. Create invisibility: 232.

Crystal set radio saves civilization. 1263.

Crystals embodying life forms. 1824, 1832.

Crystals form natural death ray. 449.

Cthulhu motif. 905.

Cuba.   European base in war against U.S.: 1315.

Cubic city. 1499.

Cults. (*See also* Secret societies.)
117, 455, 531, 535, 696, 731, 800, 833, 1010, 1275, 1753, 1754.
Suicidal or world destruction: 696, 1753, 1754.

Cultural apathy.   33, 38, 49, 53, 107, 115, 234, 570, 747, 748, 750, 772, 794, 902, 950, 1202, 1262, 1426, 1537.

Culture clashes, two examples.
Reason versus emotion: 1237, 1478.

Culture hero. 1509, 1514.

Curses. 61, 399.

Curvature of space used for travel. 191, 192.

Cyanogen carried by hurricanes. 1224.

Cyborgs. (*See also* Dream machines.)
84, 101, 125, 302 (?), 421, 428, 434, 462, 546, 591, 674-682, 686, 689, 690, 745, 760, 778, 890, 948, 1397, 1593, 1629, 1733, 1744, 1745, 1816, 1825.

Cyclical disaster, changes in the Earth's axis. 367.

Cyclical holes in space, out of space and time. 309.

Cyclical universe.   424, 567, 588, 1712, 1829.

Cyclones, artificial.   (*See also* Storms, artificial.) 929, 1441, 1493.

"Cyclops."   Missing ship in World War I. 1196, 1541.

Daedalus, euhemerized. 165.

Dalai Lama. 2, 522, 732, 866.

Dances, mating. 296.

Dark stars or planets.   1, 84, 188, 189, 322, 323, 618, 661, 679, 897, 1150, 1376, 1397, 1469, 1498, 1524, 1568, 1609, 1631, 1682, 1743, 1750.

Darkness, artificial. 402, 1271, 1489.

Darkness bombs. 297, 1224.

Daylight increases due to solar magnet. 976.

Daylight, perpetual, due to molten moon. 510.

Dead, communication with the. 803.

Dead, land of the. 224, 949, 1694.

Dead, revival of the.
150, 210, 226, 227, 346, 373, 488, 512, 522, 644, 686, 704, 804, 1117, 1232, 1298, 1350, 1408, 1511, 1575, 1769.
Frozen people: 341, 488, 512, 686, 1117, 1350, 1408, 1511, 1769.
Legal problems after revival: 150.

Dead, treatment of the.
Encased in crystal: 1412.
Frozen: 341, 488
Perfect preservation: 574.
Preserved, metal-plated and used as statuary: 61, 1033.
Put into orbit with rocket: 674.
Recycled: 586, 722.
Revival as cyborgs: 462, 674, 686.
Revival as zombies: 373, 726, 892, 1121.

Death and recreation by mathematics. 409, 410.

Death by suggestion. 388, 1688, 1691.

Death camps, Nazi style. 1283.

Death caused by wireless transmission of poisonous scent. 1137.

Death fetches. 640, 1688, 1691.

Death rays. (*One of the fixtures of early science-fiction, often not explained, simply to be accepted.*)
37, 42, 70, 75, 109, 164, 196, 327, 358, 359, 403, 435, 449, 461, 560, 625, 638, 658, 689, 807, 874, 909, 916, 924, 925, 954, 972, 989, 1123, 1154, 1162, 1237, 1238, 1280, 1390, 1402, 1428, 1457, 1471, 1489, 1734, 1753, 1811.
Miscellaneous: Death rays from hypostatization: 42. From idol: 1798. Natural, from mineral: 449. From strange life form: 5. Fraudulent: 560, 638. Martians apparatus give to terrestrial paleoanthrope: 689. Causes reversion to bow and arrow warfare: 874.

Death, speech after.   (*See also* Heads, severed, living; Brains in jars.)
1142, 1144.

Death Valley. 92, 292, 1161, 1180.

Death wish, natives wish to die. 1798.

Decay ray. 951.

Deimos.   (*Satellite of Mars.*)
Crashes down upon Mars: 153. Collides with the Moon: 171. Castaways make forced landing; barren, airless: 525. Forced stop for water, discover mineral, file claim: 776. Destruction of: 1824. Staging area for attack on Earth: 1824. Home of semi-intelligent arachnid life: 1824.

Derelict alien spaceships. 466.

Deuterium.   (H², D. *See* Heavy water.)

Devil, the. 1303 (?).

Devil prototypes. 200, 940, 1423, 1425.

Devil worship. 1275.

Devil's Island escape. 1515.

Devolution, personal, causes. (*See also* Atavism.)
Lobotomy: 181. Viral dust: 349. Unsuccessful genetic engineering: 384. Radioactive ambience: 527. Blocking solar radiation: 555. End result of superbeing: 557. Hard radiation: 1477. Fake: 1831.

Devolution, specific, generic.
75, 114, 324, 384, 422, 571, 838, 839, 887, 903, 907, 945, 1014, 1346, 1564, 1667, 1689, 1771, 1772.

Devouring sphere, the.   (*A disintegrating phenomenon that destroys everything in its expansion.*)
520, 670, 964, 1105, 1646.

Diamonds.
Artificial: 228, 1490, 1684.
Extraterrestrial: Venus: 16, 1420. Mercury: 877. Moon: 1588, 1676.
Miscellaneous: Diamond meteorites: 1203, 1287. Diamond smuggling: 1203. Used as building material: 1733. Used as lens for supermicroscope: 1075.

Dictators and would-be dictators. (*See also* Future, political; World conquest.)
81, 155, 156, 169, 198, 209, 251, 316, 330, 382, 400, 403, 463, 474, 570, 662, 673, 874, 916, 1227, 1233, 1247, 1249, 1250, 1253, 1255, 1261, 1263, 1266, 1269, 1272, 1290, 1315, 1378, 1426, 1441, 1445, 1512, 1583, 1592, 1610, 1651, 1704, 1794, 1812.
Solar system: 169, 1227, 1272, 1755.

Dimension, one removed by ray. 224.

Dimensional gateways, focal points, where it is possible to pass from one dimension to another.
291, 316, 363, 369, 675, 676, 1276, 1277, 1364, 1365, 1444, 1507, 1524, 1637, 1715, 1728, 1740, 1834.

Dimensional viewers, permitting vision into the fourth or other dimension.
109, 423, 842, 847, 1080, 1453, 1686.

Dimensions. (*See also* Fourth dimension, Fifth dimension.)

Dimensions, other than fourth or fifth, ambience.
Absolute randomness: 1370. Barren, scarlet, black mountains: 1740. Crystalline formations, multiple suns: 526.

Dimensions, other than fourth (*continued*)
Desert, empty: 724. Earth-like, but odd vegetation: 1364, 1365. Earth-like, gray: 381. Hell (?): 308. Land of the dead: 224, 949. Meadowy, with living machines: 724. Mouth of titanic animal, chlorine atmosphere, strange colors: 614, 615. Small, Earth-like pocket universe inside sphere: 1815.

Dimensions, other than fourth or fifth, cultural level.
Primitive: 526, 1186.
About our level: 1815.
Superior: 46, 381, 724, 1006, 1364, 1365, 1370, 1599, 1637, 1680.

Dimensions, other than fourth or fifth, inhabitants.
Absolute random forms of life: 1370. Armadillo-men: 526. Black horrors: 775. Black winged benevolent giants: 1370. Blinding shadows that devour humans: 1637. Fairies: 1444. Giant insects: 614. Golden-furred men: 526. Hairy horror: 291. Humanoid black giants: 1364, 1365. Humans: 1815. Immaterial horrors that drive one mad: 675, 676. Intelligent spiders, superman: 1599. Invisible horror: 369. Living machines: 724. Moth-men: 1364. Ridiculous monsters: 46. Two-dimensional horrors: 381. Vampiric creatures: 1524.

Dimensions, other than fourth or fifth, invaders from.
46, 291, 369, 675, 676, 775, 1524, 1599, 1637, 1680, 1728, 1815 (planned).

Dimensions, other than fourth or fifth, miscellaneous.
Dimensional study the basis of Atlantean science: 1652. Dimensions as shortcuts: 316, 1680. Energy passes through dimensions: 1186. Equivalent to visual range, hence correspond to infra-red: 1186. Military apparatus transfers objects to higher dimensions: 284. Ray changes dimension: 196. Ray strips away one dimension from objects: 224. Rebel leader in other dimension plans to take omnipresent gold and buy up our world: 1815. Research on dimensions leads to accidental time travel: 246, 693. Stacked like cards beside one another: 109, 614, 615. Strange temple in other dimen-sion: 1754. Visitor from other dimen-sion, not hostile: 1006.

Dimensions, other than fourth or fifth, mode of entry.
Mirror optics: 381. Space accident: 526, 784. Egyptian tomb artifact: 614, 615. Angles and curves: 656. Radiation of alien sun: 675, 676. High velocity: 724. Lorentz-Fitzgerald experiment: 724. Light and magnetism: 775. Atomic wave length or vibration change: 1006, 1815. Gateways: 1364, 1365, 1370, 1740, 1834.

Dining tables, automated. 1328.

Dinosaurs, domesticated. 42, 958, 989, 993, 999, 1557.

Dinosaurs, miscellaneous.
Contemporary motion pictures of: 56.
Extraterrestrial: Venus: 131. Secondary moon: 372. Ganymede: 142. Fifth dimension: 1197. Atomic world: 857.
Foil interplanetary settlements on Earth: 45, 1130.
Human offspring after hard radiation: 1477.
In the future: 893.
Inexplicably reappear: 1557.
Personalized: 4, 208.

Dinosaurs, surviving.
42, 94, 161, 207, 272, 384, 513, 851, 958, 989, 993, 999, 1024, 1190, 1195, 1345, 1394, 1495, 1528, 1537, 1548, 1557, 1561, 1578.

Dione. (*Satellite of Saturn.*)
Inhabitants humanoid, superior in science, invade Earth; planetoid pushed into the sun: 953.

Dirac ether, swarm of negative particles. 897.

Directional tracers, super. 1376-1378.

Dirigibles.
240, 478, 917, 926, 1000, 1136, 1209, 1534, 1552, 1570.

Disc beings. 147, 553, 1284.

Discipline, drastic, in future air corps.
Throw miscreant overboard: 1185.

Disease ray. 627, 628.

Diseases eradicated.
66, 286 (on the way), 413, 652, 735, 1647.

Diseases, fantastic. (*See also* Bacteriological warfare.)
For interplanetary war: 226, 383, 1153, 1247, 1288, 1362.
For war or world conquest: 17, 572, 610, 668, 813, 982, 1275, 1362, 1552.
From space: 80, 627, 628, 762, 1019, 1113, 1642, 1728.
Laboratory escapes: 239, 241, 250, 413, 825, 1433, 1497.
Miscellaneous: Adaptive immunity to all diseases: 664. Affect women in childbirth, on disaster level: 1445. Arises from dust of talking bacterium: 349. Artificial cancer: 745. Artificial disease to eradicate giant mosquitos also fatal to man: 859. Caused by incandescent Moon: 510. Caused by radon: 273, 778. Chaos when bubonic plague is released on world that has forgotten how to treat it: 668. Diseases are caused by break-up of viral beings when they enter our universe: 1273. General: 334, 1274. On other worlds: Moon: 457; Pluto: 465; Mars: 1417, 1596. Russians send disease against American laboratory animals: 982. Severe nutritional lack causes disease: 861. Skin diseases proliferate when dust

is removed from the atmosphere: 401.

Diseases of plants, artificial. 1623.

Diseases of Terrestrial origin beset other worlds.
Mumps on Pluto: 243. Common cold kills space pirates: 1223.

Dishwashing ray. 1385.

Disintegrating and reintegrating rays. 359, 572, 608, 705, 902.

Disintegrators. (*Seldom explained, disintegrators are among the standard elements in science-fiction, especially in space operas. They might be considered comparable to a cowboy's six-gun, present, without necessity for explanation.*)
33, 40, 56, 63, 79, 88, 96, 108, 129, 143, 154, 158, 164, 183, 185, 188, 191-193, 195, 197, 198, 201, 202, 217, 244, 263, 265, 268, 269, 270, 271, 302, 303, 316, 328, 331, 332, 336, 359, 360, 374, 375, 382-384, 386, 398, 406, 407, 418, 450, 453, 463, 495-498, 500, 504, 512, 514, 519, 520, 526-528, 537, 546, 547-549, 558, 572, 577, 582, 583, 599, 600, 634, 650, 690, 693-696, 794, 807, 842, 847, 882, 900, 902, 903, 908, 919, 935, 953, 954, 987, 992, 998, 1001, 1005, 1034, 1039 (?), 1040, 1041, 1064, 1071-1073, 1094, 1104, 1114, 1115, 1129, 1130, 1150, 1152, 1154, 1161, 1168, 1172, 1182, 1186, 1196, 1199, 1201, 1216, 1220, 1222, 1223, 1225, 1227, 1237, 1246, 1249, 1253, 1261, 1266, 1270, 1272, 1276-1278, 1280, 1281, 1290, 1297-1300, 1321, 1324, 1343, 1354, 1356, 1360, 1362, 1368, 1381, 1393, 1395, 1397, 1398, 1407, 1414, 1418, 1420, 1422, 1425, 1429, 1445, 1447, 1484, 1487, 1507, 1508, 1509, 1512, 1514, 1519, 1522-1524, 1556, 1563, 1566-1568, 1572, 1576, 1578, 1579, 1583, 1584, 1587, 1592, 1594, 1601, 1608, 1615, 1624, 1625-1627, 1670, 1673, 1674, 1680, 1681, 1724, 1737, 1741, 1743, 1754, 1755, 1758, 1760, 1761, 1766, 1775, 1785-1795, 1816.

Disintegrators, special topics.
Fake: 1670, 1775.
Mechanism: Ultra-violet: 40. Resonance change: 1005. Molecular anti-cohesion: 217. Absolute zero: 1487. Cosmic ray: 268, 270. Ether Wave: 270. Chemical: 520, 1393. Element 85: 1168. Element 93: 634. Gas: 1064. AKKA: 1755, 1758.
Odd use: To clean railroad tracks in future: 882.
Turns target into water: 1743.

Dissociated brain; creatures with body and brain separate. 1680.

Dissolution, instantaneous, on recognition of death. 1144.

Dissolution, into tiny replicas. 702, 1639

Dividing man, the. 702, 1639

Divine intervention. 479, 1026, 1027.

Earth, future geography (*continued*)

Miscellaneous: Almost paradisiacal: 893. Cut in two by runaway earth-borer: 539, 540. Damaged by runaway gravitational vortex: 171. Eastern U.S. sinks, Atlantis and Lemuria rise: 70. Frozen solid during war: 888. General submergence of sea coast: 98. Hollowed out: 794, Most of world under water, Rocky Mountain area elevated: 1305. No more rain or sunsets: 1647. No more tides: 621. No rotation, half torrid, half frigid: 892, 1408. No vegetation, no insects: 586. North America elevated, Europe submerged: 1236. Seas have disappeared: 155, 298. Southeast U.S. sinks: 859.

Earth imperilled. (See World peril.)

Earth, internal heat utilized. (*See also* Antarctic, warm oases; Arctic, warm oases.) 240, 332, 488.

Earth, interplanetary relations. (See Earth-Mercury relations, Earth-Venus relations, etc.)

Earth, invaded by. (*The physical presence of a non-terrestrial enemy on Earth. See also* various Earth- ——relations; Earth conquered and dominated *categories.*)

Alcyone: 1184, 1191.

Alpha Centauri: 1678.

Andromeda nebula: 1048, 1279.

Asteroids: 718, 720, 1311.

Atomic worlds: 430, 569, 1168, 1572.

Barnard's Runaway Star: 1755.

Callisto: 1577.

Comet: 1204, 1758.

Dimensions, parallel worlds, size: 46, 291, 303, 369, 386, 430, 547, 775, 847 (threatened), 855, 1122, 1326, 1572, 1599, 1637, 1680, 1728.

Dione: 953.

Ganymede: 1094.

Intrusive planets: 304, 442, 1043, 1524.

Jupiter: 954, 992, 1276.

Jupiter moon, unnamed: 1039.

Macrocosm: 386.

Magellanic Clouds: 1290.

Mars: 45 (remote past), 155, 225-227, 393, 437, 451, 558, 587 (after a fashion), 892, 1114, 1216 (remote past), 1272, 1362, 1455 (raid), 1673, 1697, 1721 (remote past), 1737, 1741, 1751, 1759, 1767.

Mercury: 987, 1246.

Miscellaneous: A planet "beneath" the Earth: 1184. Possible invasion while mankind was in suspended animation: 946.

Moon: 155, 356, 549, 951, 1215-1216 (remote past).

Other planets, presumably interstellar: 35, 190, 196, 260, 269, 271, 325, 387, 554, 661, 891, 1285, 1380, 1463, 1464, 1471, 1614, 1681, 1683, 1724.

Pluto: 83 (raid), 255 (raid), 1425, 1774.

Rigel: 1157, 1677.

Saturn: 247.

Secondary moon: 464.

Sirius: 192, 1270.

Skyland: 402.

Space empires: 878. 1247.

Unknown origin: 502, 661, 716, 807, 1201.

Venus: 233, 328, 383, 562, 1132, 1271, 1408, 1445 (raid), 1480, 1483, 1484, 1565, 1713.

Earth isolated.

For obnoxiousness: 201, 362, 891, 1040.

For physical reasons: 1039, 1381.

Earth leaves the solar system.

73, 75, 214, 408, 1285, 1621.

Earth liberated from alien domination.

Asteroids: 718, 720.

Crooks: 1378.

Interstellar: 878, 1157, 1247.

Intrusive planets: 442.

Jupiter: 992.

Mars: 1272.

Mercury: 1246.

Other: 1464.

Pluto: 1425.

Venus: 1408.

Earth, magnetic field.

Caused by people inside hollow Earth: 1562. Caused by underground people: 649. Change causes great destruction: 274. Combined with antigravity test, hurls man into future: 1469. Enlarged by atomic waste, it changes orbit of Moon: 66. Holds atmosphere in place: 1524. Magnetic pole is a beacon set up by stranded interstellar explorers: 939. Peace vigilante uses it to disrupt electricity: 356. Permits entry from space: 1286. Shifts in general: 367. Used for power: 794, 1263, 1505, 1509, 1514. Used to make heavy water: 1259. Used to speed rotation of Earth: 1320. Weakens ray attack from Venus: 1237.

Earth, orbit changed.

Attempt to improve climate: 392, 621 (failed).

General degeneration of solar system in future: 892, 1469.

Gravitational effects from other bodies: 75, 171, 188, 546, 1050, 1523.

Loss of mass due to space travel: 1513.

Moving for exploration: 1621.

Moving to attack another planet: 155.

Moving to escape various calamities: 73, 170, 214, 408, 1212.

Response to macrocosmic events: 1466.

Result of phase change in universe: 587.

War or attacks: 155, 304, 386, 546, 953, 1285, 1425.

Earth, origins, unusual.

Created by superhumans in other system: 405. Created by supermathematicians: 409, 410. Originally inside the sun, protected by etheric shield: 1757. Egg of a cosmic dragon: 1753. Dream

of a cosmic being: 282. Captured by sun from another solar system passing through: 1215, 1216.

Earth, overrun by Martian plant. 672.

Earth, ozone layer destroyed. 233,

Earth, resettled after abandonment. 66, 75, 193, 354, 815, 1237.

Earth, resources raided.

Coal: 255.

Copper and other metals: 83.

Eiffel Tower, Woolworth Building: 143, 362, 913, 1092, 1133, 1404, 1481.

Gold: 265.

Human females: 303, 855, 951, 1297.

Human males: 440, 585, 1445.

Iron: 1755.

Mankind in general: 161, 442, 502, 639. 954. 987, 1425, 1455, 1460.

Metals: 716.

Radium: 1180, 1460, 1631.

Talc: 1120.

Trawling at random: 551.

Water: 541.

Earth, rotational period.

Changed: 155, 295, 304, 473, 892, 1320, 1408, 1516, 1581, 1702.

Used as energy: 473, 1581.

Earth, saved by human mental vibrations. 153.

Earth, science originates elsewhere. 173, 411, 473, 1439, 1622.

Earth, science suppressed by aliens. 233, 562, 855, 922, 1153, 1311, 1463, 1464.

Earth, stop it, and let the universe go by. 810, 1625.

Earth, surrounded by globe of transparent matter. (*See also* Fortean stories, Skyland.) 333.

Earth, time different from rest of universe. 1258.

Earth tubes. (*i.e., tubes through the Earth. See also* Earth-borers, Transportation tubes.)

56 (planned), 488 (?), 582, 1108, 1754 (?).

Explodes: 582, 1108.

Shaft to underground wonderland: 1754.

Earth, used as a sunshield for Mars. 587.

Earth-asteroid relations. (*For additional material see* Asteroids; *see also* Earth-minor planets, *below.*)

Asteroids colonize Earth: 717, 718 (attempt), 720 (attempt).

Hostile: 718, 720.

Earth-Bodia relations.

Bodia colonizes Earth in remote past or is otherwise responsible for humanity: 405, 473, 1152, 1215, 1216, 1451. Invisible humanoid colonists: 1367.

Earth-interstellar relations. (*For additional material see* individual stars.)

Hostilities: 169, 188, 190, 192, 193, 196, 202, 1043, 1048, 1157, 1184, 1191, 1247, 1270, 1288, 1290, 1380, 1463, 1471, 1614, 1631, 1677, 1678, 1681, 1755.

Euphoria produced by gas. 481.
Europa. (*Second satellite of Jupiter.*)
   Ambience: Earth-like: 353 (?), 1369,
   1582, 1591, 1668 (somewhat),
   1823. Encased: 1589.
   Cultural level: Superior: 353, 1582,
   1589, 1591. Primitive: 1823.
   Inhabitants: Human: 353 (winged),
   1582, 1589. Humanoid: 1823.
   Miscellaneous: Destroyed by Ganymede
   with disintegrator stolen from
   Earth: 461. Part of Jovian Empire,
   in rebellion later: 353. Site of
   Earth penal colony: 1823.
Europe. (*Often tacitly considered a political entity.*)
   Conquered: 908 (Mongolians), 330
   (Russians), 662 (Russians).
   Depopulated: 22, 1471, 1761.
   Future war with U.S.: 250, 494, 550,
   634, 807, 1056, 1265, 1280, 1315,
   1415, 1646.
Euthanasia. (*See also* Population control,
Suicide, *where euthanasia is often implicit, though not specified.*)
   33, 122, 727, 765, 1537.
Evil component in mankind. (*See also*
Criminal tendencies cured.*)
   Consists of a few brain cells: 1123.
   Has a useful purpose: 1123.
   Removed by ray: 545, 1123, 1390,
   1569.
Evolution. (*See also* Devolution, Supermen,
Future man, Human evolution
categories.)
**Evolution, a cosmic law that human
forms will emerge.**
   878, 1039, 1151, 1560.
Evolution, controlled or artificial.
   190, 323, 349, 358, 384, 394, 557, 589,
   626, 747, 1122, 1192, 1256, 1477,
   1567, 1578, 1629, 1640, 1706.
   Dogs in other solar system bred into
   people: 190. Physical types created to
   match intellectual or artistic function:
   1256. Unsuccessful attempts: 384, 589.
   Controlled to produce superior intellect:
   323, 626.
Evolution, individual.
   161, 358, 384, 527, 557, 589, 626,
   1477, 1567, 1578, 1692.
   Island where evolution is an individual
   matter from small cell to winged men:
   161. Extremely rapid changes into
   mushroom-like beings: 527. Accidental
   exposure to hard radiation transforms
   clod into superman: 1477. Progressive
   stages of evolution into superman, giant
   brain, and beyond: 557.
Evolution, machine. 115, 196, 434.
Evolution, miscellaneous.
   A second evolution on Earth recapitulates a previous one destroyed
   when the sun went nova: 56.
   Evolution leads to supersupermen, than
   back down to the abyss: 557.
   Evolution on Earth is really devolution
   from a higher form: 571.
   Evolution stops when emotion takes

over: 38.
   Evolutionary chains leading to man are
   really misleading; actually, animals
   have imitated mankind: 1625.
   Intelligent machines theorize that they
   evolved from man via cyborgs:
   434.
   Present evolutionary chain canceled by
   time traveler in the past: 315.
   Single-line evolution as opposed to
   multiple-line: 901.
   Watching evolution on dimensional or
   atomic worlds: 109, 1256, 1745.
Evolution, other chains on Earth. (*See*
Crystal life, Other intelligent races on
Earth, *and similar categories.*)
Evolution, techniques for controlling.
   Plastic surgery: 1692. Grafting: 50.
   Radiation: 55, 358, 384, 527, 557,
   1477, 1567, 1578. Bacteria: 349, 589.
**Expanding universe created to prevent
disease (life) from spreading.** 568.
**Expanding universe explained as deity's
cigar smoke.** 1386.
**Explosives, super, not including atomic
bombs.**
   5, 53, 64, 138, 156, 187, 191, 193,
   225-227, 256, 322-324, 368, 418, 437,
   449, 542, 597, 828, 866, 972, 982, 993,
   1045, 1064, 1065, 1210, 1224, 1249,
   1395, 1537, 1568, 1574, 1584, 1737,
   1767, 1779.
**Extraterrestrial being lives in well in
Massachusetts.** 904.
Eyes. (*See also* Vision.)
   Dog's eyes transplanted to human give
   telepathic ability: 10. Eyes of carrion
   birds perceive odors: 709. Eyes transplanted to emergent hidden people:
   1602. Eyes transplanted to invisible
   aliens: 1807. Eyes undesirable in land
   of the blind: 484, 1708. Rays from eye
   stimulate growth: 702. Ripped out by
   hypnotic monster: 1371. Synthetic:
   231, 607. X-ray eyes: 407, 488, 564,
   1800.
Faces, vision of evil. 42, 999.
Fairies, who really exist in fourth dimension.
   1444.
The "Fall" in science-fictional terms.
   1478.
Falling upwards. (*See also* Antigravity.)
   Skyland shell breaks: 333. Lightning
   destroys gravity's hold on man: 365.
Family, instances of discard. 765, 1231,
   1436.
Far hearers. (*The equivalent of supersensitive microphones, but usually without
reception equipment at place of origin.*)
   215, 989, 993, 1349, 1555, 1569, 1616.
Faster-than-light communication. (*Often
implicit in stories concerning interplanetary travel or warfare.*) 85, 1284.
Faster-than-light travel. (*Often implicit in
space operas, stories of interplanetary
travel, the far future, etc.*)
   71, 110, 152, 185, 189, 190, 202, 284,
   295, 406, 466, 507, 523, 575, 583, 602,

   1045, 1048, 1150, 1268, 1340, 1376-
   1378, 1380, 1436, 1463, 1496, 1597,
   1621, 1622, 1625, 1631, 1634, 1640,
   1743, 1746, 1755, 1762, 1786-1795.
   With relativistic complications: 71, 110,
   189, 190, 202, 1150, 1268, 1762.
   Enables one to enter fourth dimension:
   152.
Fate, ineluctable. (*See also* Machine prediction.)
   109, 225-227, 280, 567, 569, 834, 981,
   1002, 1135, 1374, 1375, 1470.
Fate, miscellaneous.
   Repeated patterns in fate: 364, 1028.
   The strange operation of fate: 160.
   Fate working as justice: 58. Retributive
   fate: 78. Irony of fate: 280.
Fatigue, chemical causing it. 1241.
Fax machine equivalent. 1348.
Fear, machine projection. 1300.
Femmes fatales. (*See also* Poison damsel.)
   664, 684, 998.
Feral humans.
   Men: 1473.
   Women: 1440, 1669.
Fertilizer, super, ultimately poisonous.
   1479.
Fetishism, voyeurism.
   Watching and lusting after inaccessible
   females: 238, 895, 1075. Fetishism
   about statue: 919. Lust for frozen
   woman: 512.
Fever, artificial, enhances intelligence. 69.
Fever rays. 1113, 1471.
Fifth dimension, ambience.
   Earth-like, but gloomy: 1606.
   Earth-like, tropical: 842, 847, 1197.
   Eternity, with stasis: 1222.
   Many parallel worlds, atomic
   separation: 1599.
Fifth dimension, cultural level.
   Primitive: 1197.
   Barbaric: 1606.
   Superior: 842, 847.
Fifth dimension, entry.
   Electronic: 1197, 1599.
   Mechanical, geometric: 284, 842, 847,
   1599.
   Vibratory, with peculiar gem: 1606.
Fifth dimension, inhabitants.
   Human: 842, 847, 1606.
   Humanoid: 1606.
   Lizard-men: 1197.
Fifth dimension, miscellaneous.
   Attacks Earth: 847. Constitutes a
   gangster way station: 1197. Entry into
   it causes time jumps: 246, 693. Involved with recurrent cycles that create
   foreknowledge: 588. Land there lacks
   iron: 847. Place of retreat in space war:
   284. Spatial-temporal in nature: 842,
   847. Used in surgery: 1198.
**Fighting suits equipped with various
weapons.** 991.
Finland. 551.
Fire as magic. 335.
Fire people. (*i.e., people who live in fires.
See also* Flame people.)
   940, 1251.

Fourth dimension, mode of entry (*continued*)
Mental set: 112, 358, 400, 1507.
Mirror machine: 246.
Optics: 371.
Relativity: 121, 1057.
Through mysterious artifact: 1748.
Time machine: 1362, 1689.
Unstable dimensional checkpoint: 1694.
Fourth dimension, politics.
Far-out feminists versus male chauvinists: 1231.
Feudal: 303.
Oppressive oligarchy, ripe for revolution: 296, 855.
Fourth dimension, viewers into.
109, 152, 1444, 1637, 1690 (organic).
France. (*See also* Eiffel Tower.)
Announces that will pay war debts: 727. Communist uprising in future: 1205. French Revolution episode: 792. General: 262, 612, 856, 1319, 1489, 1491, 1616. Isolated by force field: 1489. Medieval Paris: 556. To France via the fourth dimension: 1715. War with Ethiopia: 1349. War with Germany: 487. War with Russia, China, India: 662. War with U.S.: 433, 440.
Frauds and hoaxes. (*See also* Crimes, various; Swindles.)
Artificial diamonds (?): 1684. Artificial gold: 1012. Classic Moon hoax: 880. Cultists fake time travel and robot future to gain funds: 560. Deliberate deception in psychological apparatus: 253. Devolution faked to make crim-inal confess: 1831. Fake heart trans-plant: 8. Fake interplanetary com-munication to deceive criminal: 215. Fake organ transplants as psychological qualification test: 1089. Faked space flight turns out real: 1352. Flim-flam about Mongol threat: 960. Growing vegetable ivory: 344. Hypothyroidism used as disguise for revenge: 222. Misinterpreted blood character analysis: 817. Nineteenth-century transatlantic balloon voyage: 1141. Physiological experiment is really psychological: 1060. Preying on fear of death: 280. Questionable trip to future: 1177. Robbery in the guise of stratosphere horrors (?): 1106. Russian plot to get secret miscarries thanks to scientific error: 1481. Science-fiction film passed off as reality: 217. Superweapon faked for sake of peace: 638, 1670.
Free love in future. 1441.
Freedom islands. (Exile areas set up by authoritarian, controlled societies; really more palatable than official culture.) 563, 903, 1283 (fake).
Freemasonry. 989, 993.
French and Indian Wars, episode. 1074.
Friction. In flight, oil globules extruded on plane reduce friction: 1083. Apparatus to cancel friction: 1471.
Frog-men. 554, 677, 691, 998, 1046, 1237,

1423, 1594.
Frozen people revived. 488, 512, 1117, 1350, 1408, 1511, 1769.
Fruit offers mystical experience. 1372.
Fruitfly as large as a gorilla. 1219.
Fuel, new, super. 1399.
Fugitives from tyranny. 79, 108, 122, 595, 648, 667, 684, 782, 893, 936, 949, 1071-1073, 1152, 1277, 1283, 1325, 1368, 1468, 1522, 1569, 1583, 1729, 1746.
Fundamentalism. 162, 597, 1192.
Fungi.
As dominant plant or life form: 79, 537, 801, 802, 838, 839, 1632, 1633, 1659, 1660, 1706.
As perils: 79, 457, 838, 839, 1159 (ambulatory, man-eating), 1420, 1623, 1632, 1633.
As weapons: 385, 458, 495, 601, 887, 1005, 1359, 1420, 1742, 1743, 1786.
Miscellaneous: Men turn into fungi on Ariel: 527. Major human food: 907, 933. Fungus-men invade the Earth: 1271. Giant puffball: 1456. Phosphorescent, light underworld: 940.
Used by insects: 826, 1093, 1520, 1546
Funerary oddities. (See Dead, treatment of.)
Furniture, spontaneous movement. 798.
Furry men. 451, 526, 815, 1297 (not really), 1453, 1751.
Fusion energy. 1592, 1610.

THE FUTURE.
(*Dates at which stories take place. Some stories are firmly dated, while others can be dated only by internal evidence. For others dates are only approximate. It should be remembered that while a date may be given as a starting point, the action of the story may continue over several years. The allocation of undated stories is subject, of course, to difference of opinion.*)

The undated near future. (*While precise cutoffs cannot be given, this category includes undated stories that take place within a generation or so of publishing time. In general, there is little cultural difference from our own time.*)
7-12, 14, 26, 32-35, 58, 60, 72, 80, 86, 88, 98, 100, 110, 114, 124, 154, 159, 174, 182, 204, 215, 218, 237, 259, 274, 320, 361, 368, 384, 393, 429, 445-448, 454, 456, 462, 474, 478, 518, 523, 551, 554, 562, 574, 580. 586, 604, 605, 612, 614, 615, 620, 629, 670, 707, 736, 738, 741, 745, 746, 748, 754, 755, 766, 771, 772, 795, 808, 836, 868, 882, 897, 908, 913, 929, 945, 950, 952, 985, 987, 1006, 1036, 1055, 1056, 1068, 1092, 1110, 1122-1124, 1127, 1131, 1132, 1135, 1137, 1156, 1187, 1189, 1207,

1214, 1260, 1266, 1285, 1303, 1309, 1343, 1344, 1355, 1376-1378, 1383, 1399, 1414, 1415, 1439, 1469, 1471, 1479, 1481, 1492, 1493, 1501, 1516, 1522, 1630, 1642, 1644, 1646, 1650, 1722, 1738, 1739, 1756, 1771, 1772, 1774, 1804, 1810, 1812, 1813, 1817.
The undated near to middle future. (*Undated stories set in a rather vague period markedly different from our own time, obviously more than a few generations away, but not totally alien.*) 348, 431, 563, 696, 810, 811, 815, 890, 893, 903, 946, 1317.
The interplanetary future. (*An axiom-motif generally accepted in the magazines. It is not only a chronological location, several hundred years in the future, but a cultural complex including moderately advanced space travel, usually with rockets; advanced weapons like disintegrators; antigravity or substitutes; perhaps atomic energy; a social situation involving planetary governments, strife, exploration and colonization of the solar system; and general cultural turmoil. Only undated stories are listed here.*)
52, 57, 71, 73, 77, 87, 91, 118, 154, 171, 177, 194, 212, 221, 232, 258, 299, 312, 374, 390, 391, 453, 455, 457, 458, 465, 466, 469, 526, 528-530, 536, 537, 559, 602, 603, 631, 641, 683, 776, 778, 819-823, 828-831, 843, 853, 869, 877, 891, 896, 912, 1001, 1010, 1011, 1029, 1040, 1052, 1071, 1095, 1103, 1134, 1150, 1169, 1170, 1172, 1194, 1211, 1226, 1227, 1245, 1268, 1272, 1278, 1282, 1297-1300, 1312, 1313, 1315, 1324, 1325, 1327, 1341, 1354, 1356, 1357, 1371, 1379, 1380, 1393, 1395, 1405, 1409-1411, 1422, 1423, 1430, 1437, 1438, 1447, 1448, 1451, 1454, 1500, 1587, 1589, 1595, 1615, 1662, 1663, 1723, 1737, 1742, 1749, 1750, 1777, 1803, 1806, 1821, 1823, 1824.
The interstellar future. (*Like The interplanetary future, this is as much a culture as a time period. Set perhaps many thousand years in the future, it involves faster-than-light space travel, antigravity or substitutes, very advanced weaponry, space empires and clashing interests, and galactic man. Only undated stories are listed here.*)
436, 532, 533, 1361, 1363, 1743, 1777, 1786-1795.
The undated far future.
Somewhat far: 23, 53, 62, 71, 119, 315, 563, 1133, 1716.
Middle far: 389, 476, 477, 599, 890, 937, 1710, 1822.
Far far: 389, 407, 1689, 1822.
Close to the end and after: 567, 701, 1267, 1469.

THE FUTURE, SPECIFIC YEAR DATES.
The 1890s: 1533, 1535.

OTHER CHRONOLOGICAL SYSTEM.

Future, business activities (*continued*)
rates.)

Cartels, oppressive monopolies, etc.:
129, 194 (of a sort), 245, 292, 319,
604, 620, 755, 758, 779, 781-783,
1035, 1054, 1104 (planned), 1274,
1314, 1348, 1349, 1477, 1490 (date
uncertain), 1515, 1581, 1586, 1597,
1610, 1705, 1794.

Dirty tricks, business crime: 77, 78,
140, 198, 199, 319, 322, 326, 641,
650 (of a sort), 759, 776, 778, 779,
781, 860, 929, 1054, 1068, 1282,
1312, 1349, 1406, 1420, 1477,
1490 (date uncertain), 1506, 1515,
1593, 1597, 1598, 1802.

Environmental damage, perils, foul
products: 290, 373, 483, 737, 759,
767, 773, 778, 780 (of a sort), 814,
835, 1158 (date uncertain), 1259,
1260, 1535, 1581.

Exploitation, promotion of inventions,
general business activities: 124,
212, 245, 375, 391, 515, 530, 713,
715, 748, 755, 790, 929, 1034,
1185, 1188, 1260, 1385, 1405,
1477, 1479, 1506, 1571, 1598,
1610, 1643, 1651, 1743 (publishing).

Interplanetary shipping, trade: 91, 190,
391, 530, 604, 641, 779, 783,
1034, 1185, 1312, 1351, 1354,
1403, 1446.

Miscellaneous: Bank collapse leads to
collapse of civilization: 835.
Businessmen special caste group,
with insignia indicating occupation:
375. Financial crisis because of
precious metal problems: 1303,
1817. Genocide via technological
improvement: 1477. Revenge upon
capitalists, breaking power: 27,
438, 1242-1244, 1493, 1581, 1610.
Runaway capitalism: 1629. Suppression of useful invention by
hidden people: 929.

Future, changing the. (*See also* Future,
machine prediction; Time paradoxes.)
48, 51, 225-227, 315, 834, 932, 981,
1252, 1424, 1738.

Future clothing matches aura colors.
693, 694.

Future, communication with.
89, 422, 434 (in a way), 946, 1248,
1743.

**Future, demography, important in-
stances.** (*See also* Earth abandoned,
Floating cities, Flying cities, Fortress
humanity, Future primitivism, Neoprimitivism, Underground man, *similar
categories.*)

Aerial cities, surface of the Earth more
or less abandoned: 406, 550, 893,
1201, 1403, 1729.

City modelled on anthill: 235, 531.

Floating cities: 892, 1403.

Garden cities: 302, 1443.

Individual life-units: 421, 936.

Mankind (or Americans) concentrated

in underground cities, surface more
or less wilderness and abandoned:
70, 79, 1601.

Mankind concentrated in enormous
cities, countryside more or less
wilderness and abandoned, sometimes with primitives: 62, 70, 122,
339, 431, 693, 694, 771, 934,
1308, 1322, 1407, 1499, 1592.

No more cities: 933, 936, 1267, 1443.

Wall-to-wall people: 155.

**Future, dominant life forms other than
man.**

Amoeboids: 875.

Bacteria: 349.

Carnivorous trees and giant amoeboids:
1633.

Flying jellyfish: 132.

Fungi: 838, 839.

Giant reptiles: 771.

Insects: 235, 315, 422, 476, 599, 838,
839, 886, 887, 888, 1133.

Intelligent machines (if they are to be
considered life-forms): 196, 434,
560, 1465, 1469, 1826.

Future eating rituals, foolish. 1177.

**Future, economic structures other than
capitalism.** (*See also* Future, business;
Capitalists, wicked.)

Communism: 1253, 1441.

Fettered capitalism: 81, 1244, 1305.

Socialism, sometimes partial: 47, 48,
49, 50, 70, 70, 77, 515, 733, 735,
765, 900, 916 (in effect), 933, 934,
1073, 1244, 1249 (?), 1283, 1808,
1400, 1761.

Work army, but not socialist: 874.

Future, education.

107, 201, 488 (hypnogogy), 524 (training film), 722 (television lecture), 900,
1090 (advanced beyond ours).

Future, financial crises, major.
722, 835, 1704.

Future, garbage disposal. Dump it into
space: 1092.

Future geography of Earth. (*See* Earth,
future geography, *and other categories
under* Earth.)

Future history. (*Stories that contain a
considerable amount of historical data.*)
70, 76, 79, 81, 84, 85, 141, 170, 193,
201, 248, 250, 261, 317, 334, 353, 354,
421, 422, 425, 434, 442, 451, 475, 476,
485, 539, 586, 662, 678, 733, 735, 835,
874, 883, 891, 900, 903, 908, 932-938,
946, 948, 980, 1072, 1073, 1115, 1249,
1254, 1276, 1318, 1362, 1407, 1408,
1425, 1426, 1462-1465, 1483, 1484,
1500, 1512, 1523, 1557, 1563, 1601,
1633, 1651, 1710, 1713, 1717, 1720,
1755, 1758, 1759, 1761.

Future, invasion from.
302, 403, 407, 421, 595, 946, 949,
1751.

Future, languages.

English: 1323.

Esperanto: 425, 519.

Tibetan: 932.

Universal: 934.

Future, machine prediction.

Allows for change: 48, 51, 834, 1250,
1738.

Computer type, inflexible: 109, 114,
981, 1002, 1135, 1470, 1640, 1714.

Considers worlds of if: 1250, 1656.

Predicted by parallel worlds: 109, 569.

Future man, physically.

Balloonheads, usually physically weak:
47, 49, 50, 53, 84, 557, 733, 1276,
1277, 1713, 1834. Legs atrophied
and ride about: 47, 49, 50, 733.
Four eyes and neuter: 1276.

Cyborgs: 84, 196, 302 (?), 421, 434,
462, 591, 686, 690, 890, 948, 1745
(?), 1816.

Degeneracy. Two races reflecting present society: 1689. Small, rabbit-
like: 1689. Stupid runts: 838, 839,
1751. Submen: 75, 114, 434, 903,
907. Scruffy: 422.

Giant brains: 287, 389, 535, 557.

Larger-headed, but not much different
from modern man: 53, 246, 314,
595, 599, 722, 883, 1021, 1041,
1290, 1403, 1710. Telepathic: 389,
1290.

Like modern man, but with some differences: Without teeth: 725, 935-
938. Without appendix: 935-938.
Two hearts, toeless: 949. Darker
than Europeans: 353, 935-938, 949.
Without sense of taste: 725. Intolerant of noise: 693, 694. Telepathic: 75, 794, 1267. Bald: 1317.
Different mind set: 75, 107, 531,
794, 1262. Blue-skinned: 892.
Furry: 451, 815, 1751. Smaller:
95.

Miscellaneous. Totally quietistic: 53.
Molded into insect psychology:
531. Human evolution traced with
one individual: 557. Rigorous social Darwinism results in superior
modern man: 727. Laboratory-pro-
duced synthetic Mongoloids: 932.
Evolutionary stages leading to new
development after *Homo sapiens:*
1776.

Monstrous. Four-armed black giants:
1276. Without eyes, ears, noses,
but with skin sense: 1776. Spider-
like, telepathic: 589. Physically
adapted to occupational specialization: 235, 535, 737, 1256, 1776.
Insect-like: 531. Rabbit-like: 1689.

Sexual characteristics. Sexless males
only: 475. Sexless females only:
1717. Large masculine women and
small effeminate men: 425. Sterile:
749, 794, 1276. Parthenogenesis:
421, 735. No more sexuality: 780.
Unisex: 1834.

Supermen and superwomen, mentally
and physically: 314, 315, 387, 557,
668, 903, 1267, 1340, 1464, 1465,
1477 (anticipation), 1496.

Tiny, perhaps a matter of inches: 886-
888.

Future man, physically (*continued*)
Winged: 50, 1441, 1445.

Future, marriage. (*See also* Eugenics and mating boards, Marriage, Sex.)
Caste restrictions: 1283. Companionate marriage: 735 (otherwise enforced sterilization), 736, 1233. Contractual, prenuptial: 1592. Controlled by dictator: 666. Controlled by eugenics board: 47, 81, 515, 765, 1468, 1478, 1586. Controlled by rating system: 765. Controlled to avoid high intelligence: 515. Different types of marriage, in some of which the female is legally dominant: 49. Duels to kill off rivals: 233. Female dominant: 49, 425. Forbidden: 400. Instant, temporary, pregnancy demanded: 1400. Interracial, polygamy permitted: 900. License and ceremony conducted by automatic tube: 1499. Machine treatment to create marital love: 52, 1468. None, free love: 1436, 1441, 1625, 1651. Polyandry: 433, 508, 1362. Sexes completely segregated until marriage: 47.

Future, migration to. 1021, 1630.

Future pleas for help. 1277, 1362.

Future, political structures other than democracy. (*See also* Interplanetary leagues, World state.)
Anarchism: 53, 84, 287 (of a sort), 936. 1465 (?).
Brain ruled, mechanical or organic: 122, 387, 431, 890, 934, 950, 1276, 1277, 1281, 1322, 1323, 1462.
Dictatorship: 81, 155, 156, 209 (would-be), 251, 316, 330, 382, 400, 403, 463, 474, 570, 662, 673, 874, 916, 1227, 1233, 1247, 1249, 1250, 1253, 1255, 1261, 1263, 1266, 1269, 1272, 1290, 1315, 1426, 1441, 1445, 1455, 1426, 1512, 1583, 1610, 1651, 1704, 1794.
Fascist: 874, 1269 (?).
Gangsters: 96, 771, 1419, 1424.
Guild or family syndicalism: 47, 49, 50, 1261 (political?).
Gynecocracy: 425, 908, 949, 1717.
Monarchy: 314, 397, 582 (?), 900, 908, 932, 1073, 1253, 1263, 1269, 1441, 1445, 1512, 1557.
Neofeudal: 667, 668, 1253, 1263.
Oligarchy: 70, 155, 201, 235, 373, 387, 431, 475, 667, 668, 733, 771, 772, 878, 900, 1253, 1263, 1276, 1283, 1308, 1355, 1569, 1592, 1704, 1705.
Primitive horde: 75, 433, 838, 839, 916, 950.
Religionist or cultic rule: 673, 683, 684.
Syndicalism: 908, 1244, 1261, 1431.
Technocracy: 81, 155, 156, 348 (?), 475 (?), 485, 563 (?), 1244, 1249.
Tribes: 1073, 1074.

Future, political-cultural orientation.
Altruistic: 84, 108, 531, 1237, 1651.

Oppressive: 47, 49, 50, 70, 77, 81, 122, 201, 235, 425 (to males), 431, 442, 475, 563, 673, 741, 765, 772, 780, 782, 893, 903, 908 (to males), 1276, 1277, 1283, 1308, 1322, 1323, 1400, 1512, 1569, 1586, 1704, 1705, 1729.
Puritanical, though perhaps not enforced: 1348, 1349, 1350, 1720.
Regimented heavily: 47, 49, 50, 70, 77, 122, 201, 235, 348, 425, 431, 475, 511, 515, 563, 673, 725, 735, 765, 771, 772, 780, 782, 892, 893, 903, 1227, 1249, 1262, 1276, 1277, 1281, 1283, 1308, 1400, 1499, 1512, 1563, 1586, 1592, 1705.

Future, prediction of. (*See* Future, visions of; Machine prediction of the future; Time viewing.)

Future primitivism. (*Loss of civilization and relapse into savagery. See also* Neoprimitivism, *which involves a deliberate discarding of aspects of technology.*)
70, 71, 75, 114, 235, 334, 387, 431, 433, 531, 555, 563, 597, 612, 622, 725, 763, 835, 838, 839, 883, 916, 948, 950, 1323, 1400, 1407, 1433, 1462, 1463, 1471, 1478, 1483, 1484, 1557.

Future, religion of. (*See also* Mars, religion.)
Blue flame: 433. Cult built around carnivorous plant on Venus: 1010. Cult built around people in suspended animation: 1704, 1716. Cult perpetrated by alien conquerors, insects from intrusive planet: 442. Cult with messianic figure that worships mechanism, Church of the Scientific God: 117. State religion of electricity, plus dictator: 673. Immortal man: 570. Interstellar mystical quest: 937. Living head in bottle: 795. Lunar cult with sex priestess: 455. Martian chauvinistic cult: 1325. Mechanism: 903. Nationalistic flame priestess on other world: 1794. New Thought with mystical aspects: 900. Scientism: 693. Traditional Fundamentalism: 1247. Worship of machine that runs city-state: 431.

Future, scientific level. (*In general, the future is more advanced than we are, with the occasional exception of future primitivism or neoprimitivism.*)

Future, sexuality. (*See* Eugenics and mating Boards; Future, marriage; Sex *and similar categories, where most entries are contained.*)
Free love: 535.
Sex discontinued: 475, 535, 780, 887, 1262, 1276, 1277, 1717, 1834.

Future society, certain cultural aspects. (*See also* Future primitivism, Neoprimitivism, Technocracy.)
Caste systems, rigid: 201, 235, 431, 667, 668, 725, 741, 772, 780, 1253, 1276, 1281, 1283, 1381, 1583, 1592, 1705, 1729.
Concentrated on concentration: 53.

Decadent play society, controlled by machine intelligence: 934.
Extreme privacy complex: 1267.
Gadget cultures: 488, 613, 693, 694, 1090, 1348-1350.
Health fanatics who live underground: 725.
Hedonism, extreme: 373, 934, 935.
High science, futuristic cities, but mankind takes refuge in dream machines: 935.
Human slavery to other forms of life: 287, 422, 442, 560, 639, 691, 890, 1463, 1464.
Individualistic, no society; people live in private living-machines: 936, 1267.
Modeled after insect societies: 235, 531.
Roman decadence, parallel to: 1362.
Surveillance society, three-quarters of population are inspectors or patrolmen: 1350.
Totally present-oriented: 1716.
Warrior cultures: 235, 247, 348, 425, 610, 892, 1073, 1400.
Woodland ecological: 933.

Future, travel to. (*The present category does not include reaching the future by suspended animation. Since, from various points of view, most time travel involves entering a future, this category is established on a baseline from story present. See also* Time travel *for more theoretical concerns.*)
23, 53, 70, 96, 108, 114, 119, 132, 225-227, 302, 314, 315, 339, 389, 407, 422, 425, 434, 519, 535, 556 (from the Middle Ages), 560 (fake), 567, 599, 693, 792, 794, 807, 900, 910, 920, 932, 1177, 1248, 1254, 1267, 1276, 1277, 1323, 1362, 1424, 1465, 1469, 1478, 1492, 1499, 1543, 1566 (fake), 1628, 1632, 1633, 1689, 1720, 1743, 1751, 1761, 1801, 1816, 1822.

Future, visions of. (*Non-mechanical perceptions; see also* Machine prediction, Precognition, Time viewers *for mechanical aspects.*)
168, 367, 667, 883, 1375, 1435, 1470, 1548.

Future, visitors from. (*This category is established on a baseline from story present. See also* Time travel *for theoretical concerns*).
53, 95, 227, 246, 302, 403, 407, 414, 415, 421, 434, 595, 949, 1021, 1254, 1277, 1362, 1465, 1628, 1720, 1751, 1816, 1834.

Galactic government. (*See also* Space empires.) 1290, 1377, 1378.

Galactic man. (*i.e., the human race spread out through the universe.*)
569, 937, 938, 1299, 1340, 1625, 1743.

Galapagos Islands. 1318.

Galatea does not awaken. 163.

Galaxy threatened by star beast. 938.

Gallstones removed by four-dimensional operation. 1081.

Gigantism, types (*continued*)

Rooster: 1575.

Sea monsters: 272, 971.

Spiders: 988, 1218, 1307.

Weasels: 625.

Glaciation and glaciers.

Miscellaneous: Cyclical appearance: 62. Caused by cold cosmic ether: 952. Repelled by shifting ocean currents: 952. Used to destroy oppressive mechanical brain: 1281.

Past glaciations: 332, 549.

Renewed glaciation: 62, 66, 148, 244, 285, 815 (great cold), 883, 886-888, 935, 952, 1281, 1407, 1426, 1713, 1716, 1822.

Gladiatorial combats.

503 (dream), 1323, 1436.

Glamorized outlaws.

14, 494, 501, 530, 552, 898, 1037, 1064, 1212, 1253, 1254, 1263, 1428, 1737, 1742.

Glands, effects of manipulation or disorders. (*See also* Pituitary, Thyroid.)

Create superman of sort: 429, 1810. Generosity or miserliness: 12. Gigantism: 2, 111, 710. Horrible metabolic disturbances, resulting in invasion of England by army of freaks: 137. Immortality: 1713. Literary ability: 768. Lying or truthfulness: 9. Rapid acromegaly: 1831. Sexual phenotype: 321.

Glass component creates insanity. 727.

Gliders. 763, 903, 948.

Glowing man wanders countryside. 860.

Goat-men, blend of primates and other animals. 200.

Gobi Desert. 743, 789, 983, 986, 1367, 1436.

Goddard, Robert, American rocket pioneer.

Author R. Starzl renames Triton Goddard in his honor: 1430. Unmanned rocket that hits moon named in his honor: 1501.

Gods.

Aztec sun god resettles mankind on Venus: 479. Egyptian god Thoth really a memory of Martian visit to Earth: 1663. God-being, created as projection of mankind: 1027. Gods battle: 1026. Hermaphrodite idol on Moon: 66. Hindu god Brahma; the universe is his cigar smoke: 1386. Tahitian godling saves harassed woman: 663.

Gods, euhemerized.

Apollo, other Greek gods really aristocratic oppressors in underground world: 850. Goddess Minerva, demigods Prometheus, Phaeton, and heroes really personalities in ancient Mu: 163-168. Mercury, Minerva, Pluto figures in war when Muans return from Mars: 1721. Hawaiian goddess Pele: 1129.

Gold, colloidal.

864, 1188, 1488.

Gold, disappearing.

380, 658, 671, 727B, 864, 966, 979, 1115, 1244, 1603, 1650.

Gold, miscellaneous.

City carved out of gold reef: 368. Discovery of synthetic gold ends in atomic explosion: 1396. Gold as a protection against disintegrators: 953. Hardened gold use by Indians: 1559. Necessary atmospheric component in dimensional pocket universe: 1815.

Gold, synthetic. (*See also* Transmutation of metals.)

179, 380, 395, 557, 713, 727 (fake), 966 (fake), 999 (after a fashion), 1012, 1054, 1122, 1147, 1196, 1396, 1436, 1817.

The Golden Calf. 989, 993.

The Golden Fleece. Euhemerized: 167.

Good and bad components in mankind result of isotopes. 1266.

Gorillas.

Artificial: 17. With lobster claws: 60. With brain transplant from human: 157. With human mentality: 300. Giant: 318. Nasty: 352. Used for heavy tasks via mind control: 707. Tries to rape: 857. Intelligence enhanced, used: 1115.

Gorilla-men. 677, 1071.

Grandfather, killing one's, time paradox. 1252.

Grasshopper, hundreds of feet long. 710.

Graveyard of lost ships. 1196.

Gravitational vortex, runaway. 171.

Gravity as a weapon. 159, 693-695, 1429, 1577, 1595.

Gravity control. (*See also* Antigravity.)

3, 83, 123, 195, 232, 304, 333, 374, 408, 527, 546, 549, 695, 718, 790, 953, 955, 982, 1112, 1245, 1275, 1381, 1577, 1587, 1625, 1629, 1649, 1732, 1747, 1750.

Gravity, miscellaneous.

Caused by rotation of electrons: 142. Caused by vibrations in the ether: 931. Changes caused by experiment in macrocosm: 1466. Changes caused by mac-rocosmic event: 1466. Comes from fourth dimension: 1744. Connected with cosmic rays: 814, 1516. Disaster when law of inverse squares repealed: 1385. New sort of gravity permits time travel: 807. Ray conducts gravity, changing law of inverse squares: 955. Ray reverses gravity: 159. Space travel possible by creating gravity: 171.

Great Britain. (*See also* England, Scotland, Wales.)

Decimal currency: 910. Depopulated: 22, 1204. Freezes when Gulf Stream diverted: 692. Invaded by matter-transmitted troops from Orient: 836. Invades Congo nation after air-borne atrocities: 1552. Site of construction site run by animals under mind control: 707. Under control of India: 1206. War with Axis: 1646. War with China: 662, 836. War with Ethiopia: 1349. War with Germany: 487, 1457, 1584,

1646. War with India: 662. War with Japan: 836, 1457, 1584. War with U.S.: 1634. War with USSR: 662, 982, 1457, 1584.

Great Depression. To be alleviated by Atlantean gold: 942.

Great Lakes area 1462.

Great Wall of China moved. 438.

Greco-Roman mythology euhemerized. (*See also* Gods, euhemerized.)

163-168, 743, 850, 1721.

Greece. 577, 850.

Greed saves the human race. 1774.

Greek, ancient, spoken. 234, 573.

Green men.

Location. Atom: 1154. Earth: 428, 1735. Jupiter: 335, 1450. Mars: 68, 162, 783. Other planet: 1376, 1377. Second moon: 554. Venus: 36, 536, 1352, 1519.

Type: Human: 68, 554, 1352, 1376, 1377, 1519, 1735. Humanoid: 36, 162, 335, 428, 536, 783, 1154, 1450.

Greenland. 209, 1209.

Grief removing machine. 190.

Group beings, group minds.

441, 477, 599, 746, 1206, 1290, 1326, 1494, 1640, 1680, 1799.

Growth. (*See also* Gigantism.)

Growth stimulated by rays: 60, 220, 702, 1475. Fantastically rapid growth in androids: 231. Caused by radioactivity: 306. Liquid is principle of growth: 655. Accelerator: 702. Caused by new solar radiation: 1452.

Growths, strange, on humans are ferocious space monster. 521.

Guam, near. 397.

Guatemala. 1548.

Guinea pigs.

Giant, runs amok: 111. Russians sabotage research animals: 982.

Gulf Stream.

Diverted: 235, 541, 692. Site of action: 1188.

***Gulliver's Travels* latch-on.** 918.

Gunpowder-operated engines. 698.

Gynecocracy. (*See also* Women.)

425, 908, 949, 954, 1231, 1362, 1445, 1447 (non-human), 1541, 1717.

Gyroscopes. 73, 141, 519, 1581.

Hades.

Euhemerized: 168, 850. Caves under Thessaly: 850.

Hair restorer with fatal results. 1317.

Haiti. 160, 1485.

Hallucination predators.

534, 1662, 1663.

Hallucinogen from space. 261.

Hands, people who walk on. 1538.

Handyman as culture hero. 1509, 1514.

Hangover pills. 1349.

Hard radiation turns dolt into superman, and back. 1477.

Harvard College. 634.

Hashish. Used both to destroy Kantian time and to keep time sense: 1718.

Hastings, Battle of. 1217.

Hat, stabilizes person with vertigo. 175.
Haunted houses. (*See also* Ghosts.) 39, 266, 399, 642, 798, 1296.
Hawaii.
289, 980, 1129. Goddess Pele euhemerized: 1129.
Hawaiian is language of atomic world. 990, 991.
Head deformation for literary triumph. 219.
Head lamps, natural, organic. 243.
Head, severed, haunts man. 1691
Head transplants. (*See also* Brain transplants.) 858, 1594.
Heads, detached, mechanized. 428.
Heads in jars, and comparable phenomena.
690, 745, 795, 1332, 1458.
Heads, separate from bodies, in compound beings. 1680.
Heads, shrunken, Jivaro style. 344.
Heart, artificial. 43, 206, 347, 591, 811, 1019.
Heart attacks.
Caused by rhythmic device: 230.
Caused by invaders' ray: 437.
Heart transplant causes personality change. 8 (fake).
Heat felt as cold. 865.
Heat produced by color organ. 1620.
Heat rays. (*One of the accepted axiom motifs of science-fiction, in this case with some basis in reality.*)
23, 34, 37, 45, 65, 68, 81, 159, 188, 191, 193, 217, 231, 256, 269, 270, 271, 297, 302, 319, 332, 376, 422, 470, 499, 510, 543, 550, 626, 645, 677, 718, 788, 790, 824, 829, 850, 918, 935, 954, 991, 1009, 1017, 1071, 1169, 1170, 1172, 1223, 1238, 1278, 1287, 1308, 1325, 1381, 1405, 1426, 1484, 1524, 1574, 1577, 1579, 1583, 1602, 1626, 1627, 1629, 1697, 1719, 1723, 1724, 1739, 1759.
Heat cones: 1363. Heat sticks: 801.
Heat vortex. 274.
Heat wells. 240, 332, 488.
Heated clothing. 1348.
Heaviside layer. (*See also* Skyland.)
Protects against invasions from space: 442. Solid: 868. A jelly protective against space monsters: 985, 987.
Inhabitants: human, but of a different substance from us: 708. Jelly cubes: 868.
Heaviside equivalent for light at edge of universe. 1217.
Heavy water.
Aging, harmful substance: 180, 772, 1259.
Created in scam using Earth's magnetic field: 1259.
Harmless: 910.
Hebrews, ancient, in America. 989, 993, 1551, 1561.
Heidelberg man seen on video tapes recorded on Moon. 1302.
Heisenberg's uncertainty principle used as weapon. 202.

Helicopters, super. 384, 922.
Heliograph for interplanetary communication. 1405.
Helium.
Sphere used to trap molecule: 959.
Solid: 1045. Atomic fuel: 1436. Explodes: 1552.
Hell, rationalized as dimension. 308.
Heroic ancestor revealed as cowardly rogue by time viewer. 1217.
Hidden people. (*Peoples who deliberately conceal their existence from the outside world. The concept is related to* Lost race, *and there is considerable overlap.*)
Hidden people, cultural level.
Primitive: 484 (but psychic powers), 1708.
Barbaric: 54, 368, 508, 796.
Our level: 50, 733, 1441, 1521, 1563.
Superior: 52, 56, 185, 256, 259, 275, 332, 384, 428, 518, 626, 649, 747, 750, 788, 850, 924, 925, 928, 929, 975, 989, 993, 997-999, 1128, 1165, 1521, 1537, 1541, 1584, 1602, 1624, 1648, 1652, 1729, 1732, 1733, 1739, 1754.
Hidden people, human identities of importance.
Atlanteans: 428, 788 (?), 993, 1652, 1729.
Hebrews: 989, 993.
Molemen: 975.
Mu or Lemuria: 259, 998, 1754.
Native Australians: 275.
Unknown white culture: 928, 929.
Hidden people, location.
Africa: 185, 924, 925, 1515, 1521, 1754.
Alaska: 649, 997.
Andes: 50, 796, 999, 1128, 1541, 1708, 1732.
Antarctica: 54, 1537, 1739.
Arabia: 368.
Arctic: 518.
Asia, Himalayas: 384, 508.
Atlantic area: 788 (Sargasso Sea), 1602, 1652.
Australia: 275, 1733.
Brazil: 484, 989, 993, 1165, 1624.
Greece: 850.
Location not known: 52, 428, 928.
Pacific area: 259, 626, 929, 998, 1563, 1584, 1648, 1735.
South America: 999, 1602, 1652.
The upper atmosphere: 1729.
U.S.: 56, 256, 332, 733, 747, 750, 975.
Hidden people, miscellaneous.
African city is base for space empire: 185. Ancient Hebrews in Brazilian jungle, with superior civilization: 989, 993. Descendants of Lemurians plot in underground world: 998. Gigantic, ruthless women raid outside world from caverns: 1541. In automobile culture, pedestrian underground plans ruthless emergence: 733. Inca-Mongol culture plans world conquest: 1128. Nasty

troglodytes emerge: 332. Political exiles on island build up supercivilization and plan trouble: 1563. Religious lunatics want to destroy the Earth: 626. Sacred Arab city carved out of gold reef: 368. Satire on American culture, the New Deal, F. D. Roosevelt: 256. Secret science-city established by would-be world ruler: 1515. Snake Mother and flying serpents maintain isolation of Andean preglacial civilization: 999. Subterrean civilization with intelligent reptilians and superscience: 1754. Sword-and-ray-gun dynasties under the Sahara: 924. Xenophobic, unknown supercivilization on Pacific island destroys viewer to retain isolation: 929.
Hidden people, other than ordinary humans.
Blind men: 484, 1708.
Cosmic ray eutopians with organic head crests: 1648.
Cyborgs: 428.
Cyborg giant insects: 1733.
Dwarves: 747, 750, 1584.
Fish-men: 518.
Giant females, small males: 1541.
Greek gods and Olympus: 850.
Intelligent giant crabs: 1739.
Intelligent giant shrimp: 1537.
Intelligent reptilians: 998, 999, 1754.
Light beings: 384, 997, 1732.
Mole-men: 975.
Troglodytes: 1624.
Winged men: 50, 1441.
High civilizations of the past, human.
(*See also* Archeological material, Bodia, Human race originated elsewhere.)
Africa: 1108, 1754.
Antarctica: 54.
Atlantis: 168, 213, 233, 234, 428, 445, 573, 574 (?), 645, 743, 788, 902, 941, 993, 999 (?), 1005, 1006, 1126, 1216, 1222, 1238, 1451, 1580, 1652, 1681, 1721, 1725, 1728.
Australia: 275, 1754.
"Conquerors" from cavern world: 747.
Hollow Earth: 56, 1509, 1514.
Indeterminable, general: 1215, 1478.
Lemuria/Mu: 110, 163-168, 200, 259, 743, 998, 1270, 1325, 1451, 1721, 1735 (?), 1754.
Mexico: 310.
Oceania: 998.
South America: 42, 999, 1165
U.S.: 172, 329, 443, 799.
Within the sun: 1757.
High civilizations of the past, non-human.
Gas beings: 407.
Crystal beings: 1732.
Hollow-earth shmoos: 548.
Insects: 1733.
Light beings: 384, 997.
Lovecraftian space creatures: 905, 906.
Reptilian: 281, 998, 999, 1754.
Silicon beings: 151.
Space creatures, since devolved: 571.

Human evolution, some oddities (*continued*)

eyes: 332. Prehensile feet, walk on hands: 1538. Return to rodent-like form: 1689. Scaly, hairless, photosensitive: 33. Specialized occupational types: 235, 535, 737, 1122, 1256, 1776. Stages individually lived from earliest life form to winged man: 161. Stony tissues: 1199. Stupid runts: 838, 839. Tiny: 52. Underground men, vicious dwarves: 1584. Underground men with different vision than ours: 1602.

Human genetics, lethal factor for females. 161.

Human longevity. (*See also* Immortality. *In general future man is longer lived than present-day man, but specific figures are not always given.*)

Specific figures: Two or three times modern man: 1651. Three times modern man: 1237. 150 years: 765, 980, 1499. 200 years: 722, 989, 993, 1551. Over 250 years: 1340, 1651. 300 years: 1276. 350 years or more: 725. 500 years: 84. 600 years: 61. Hundreds of years: 440, 1025, 1041, 1262, 1557. 1,500 years: 421. 3,000 years: 747, 750. Thousands of years: 595, 1465. Enormous: 1375.

Very short. 15-20 years: 626.

Reasons for greater longevity: Cellular transplants: 937, 938. Chemicals: 522, 620, 1025, 1151, 1375, 1557. Glandular transplant: 1496. New element: 1025. No cosmic rays: 407. Presence of cosmic rays: 440. Proximity to atomics: 433. Quiet life: 1551.

Human-plant mixtures.

Grafting: 347, 1518.

Shifting blood from hemoglobin to chlorophyll: 980.

Human personality affected by lunar rays. 580, 753, 969, 1618.

Human sacrifice.

33, 55, 66, 326, 332, 338, 384, 526, 529, 645, 712, 717, 731, 751, 793, 800, 848, 958, 989, 993, 1052, 1058, 1126, 1128, 1190, 1194, 1215, 1216, 1222, 1225, 1321, 1361, 1374, 1394, 1462, 1485, 1538, 1548, 1561, 1591, 1597, 1601, 1602, 1679, 1733, 1745, 1753, 1754, 1769, 1794.

Tribute, for vivisection, paid to Pluto: 1425.

Human sexual dimorphism, extreme. 425, 998, 1231, 1589.

Human sexuality, miscellaneous. (*See also* Eugenics; Free love; Future marriage; Future sexuality; Marriage; Mating bureaus; Sex, *and similar categories.*)

Artificial propagation: 475, 735, 747, 750, 780, 887, 1122, 1262, 1276, 1277, 1717.

Neuters and birth control: 582.

Sexuality discontinued: 475, 535, 780,

887, 1262, 1276, 1277, 1717.

Humaniform inventions. Gigantic iron woman transportation device: 136.

Humanity, what is it?

Intelligent insects against human vermin: 430, 586, 1432.

Humans affected by mental power of atomic particles. 1335-1339.

Humans considered as vermin: 424, 586, 1432.

Humans in zoos. 244, 255, 260, 304, 467, 475, 502, 604, 747, 750, 939, 1153, 1180, 1191, 1460, 1713.

Humans utilized by aliens.

As food or domestic animals: 323, 422, 424, 442, 691, 853, 1271, 1471, 1541, 1758.

As pets: 1151, 1455.

As racing steeds: 422, 691.

As slaves: 281, 323, 394, 442, 592, 598, 639, 691, 829, 886, 887, 888, 1450, 1520.

Specially created servitors: 281, 394.

Humming.

As communication: 185, 531, 1445.

Effect of Saturnian power beam, drives men mad: 647.

Hummingbird people. 426.

Humor, ethnic. (*See also* Anti-Black prejudice, Anti-Semitism, *etc.*)

Swedish: 1214. Jewish: 1533. Flemish/Dutch: 1531. Black: 1033.

Humor, nonsense. 1385.

Humor, parodic.

Science-fiction themes: 13. 46. 414, 415, 854, 885, 1149, 1348-1350, 1437, 1655.

Special stories or situations. *The Island of Doctor Moreau:* 2. *The Literary Corkscrew:* 219. *The Thousand-and-Second Tale of Scheherazade:* 491. *Ralph 124C 41+:* 1348-1350. Dr. David H. Keller's homespun social theories: 1350. Early silent motion pictures: 505.

Humor, silly inventions.

175, 176, 416, 1031-1033, 1088, 1099, 1328-1331, 1385.

Humor, situation oriented.

176, 276, 295, 349, 489, 490, 566, 633, 644, 854, 884, 885, 1012, 1023, 1061, 1092, 1124, 1163, 1214, 1386, 1459, 1618, 1656-1658, 1763.

Humor, social satire.

235, 243, 244, 246, 256, 257, 261, 643, 789, 902, 1042, 1176, 1177, 1555.

Hun, in ancestral time paradox. 1252.

Hurricanes. (*See also* Cyclones, artificial; Storms, artificial; Weather control.) 708, 1224, 1524.

Hydra, microscopic. 116, 800.

Hydra, mythological monster. 850.

Hydrogen motor. 372.

Hyena-man. 1827.

Hyperspace as a shortcut. 200.

Hypnogogy. (*Sleep learning; information fed aurally into the sleeper; one of Gernsback's pet projects.*)

190, 231, 488, 524, 1114, 1403, 1413, 1625.

Hypnosis, devices. (*See also* Mind control, mechanical.)

Gas: 850, 1589. Gems: 1774. Globe: 1569. Lights: 989. Machines: 225-227, 496, 1377, 1569. Metal: 1371. Motion pictures: 1722. Radio: 211. Rays: 138, 158, 217, 960, 1343.

Hypnosis, miscellaneous. (*See also* Mind control.)

Explanation for guilt: 817. Medical: 1030. Paranormal aspects: 224. Permits experience of past embodiments in cyclic universes: 1829. Personality control for crime: 1427. Subject takes on aspects of evolution during period he visits mentally: 883. Viewing future: 883.

Hypnotic animals.

Amoeboids: 141, 1014, 1418. Dream monsters: 534, 1662, 1663. Giant fruit fly: 1219. Gorgons: 164. Lunar spider monster: 326. Martian horror: 1371. Plant, uses powers to attract fertilizing agents: 534. Reptile: 1227. Sleep snake on Titan: 1664. Sphinxes: 850. Toad-like monster in the fifth dimension: 847. Venusian amoeboid: 1418.

Hypnotic beings.

323, 400.

Hypostatizations.

42, 999, 1027.

Hypothyroidism as disguise for crime. 222.

Iapetus. (*Satellite of Saturn.*)

Earth-like, but covered with jungle, colonized: 495-498. Visit to: 495-498, 1594. Almost totally water-covered, inhabitants frog-men and giant brains with superior science: 1594.

Icarus, euhemerized. 165.

Iceland. 1528.

Idaho: 256.

Ideal image, machine for creating. 1657.

Ideal societies, a few typical examples.

(*Pulp science-fiction is much less concerned with detailed social extrapolations than the science-fiction of the earlier period. Nevertheless, a few state plans exist.*)

Aggressive extreme feminists with oppressed males, warring against male neighbors: 1231.

Aggressive feminists, males biologically weakened and oppressed: 425.

Agrarian, bucolic, back-to-the-land neo-primitivism on Mars: 1077.

Almost total withdrawal of population to dream machines with small maintenance class: 935.

Anarchistic, voluntarily primitive, tribal, and violent: 563.

Anthill society with complete focus on the community, individualism suppressed, work ethic supreme: 531.

Carefree play culture, but with sinister, lethal machine intelligences beneath: 115.

Lathes venerated by cult. 117.
Latin America, fanciful. 565.
Lava.
　Flows destroy ancient high civilization:
　1108. As a weapon: 1132, 1154, 1378.
Law of inverse squares repealed by Congress. 1385.
Laws of science different for different universes. 1631.
Lead isotope, as mystery metal. 1175.
Leg regeneration causes identity problem. 11.
Legal matters.
　Problem of identity arises after organ
　regeneration: 11, 60. Legal status of
　revived executed man: 150.
Legerdemain. 1118, 1376.
Lemuria, miscellaneous. (*See also* Mu, *with which Lemuria is often confused.*)
　Action described in documents from
　Lemuria: 163-168. Descendants, after
　taking refuge near Sirius, return to
　invade Earth: 1270. Descendants are
　tawny haired, with green-tinged, golden
　complexion: 1270. Descendants are
　humanoid, with red skins and black
　teeth: 1754. Descendants interbreed
　with Phoenicians to form a lost race:
　793. Destroyed by atomic explosion:
　168. Destroyed by vibrator: 600.
　Destroyed in space war: 1451. Fake
　association with Lemuria: 1413.
　Reemerges from the sea: 70. Sub-
　sidence witnessed in time fugue: 1178.
Lemuria, seat of a high civilization.
　163, 164, 166, 168, 600, 1270, 1451.
Lenses. (*See also* Microscope, super; Telescope, super.)
　Prepared from element 85: 82. Pre-
　pared from enormous diamond: 1075.
Lethargy, produced by atmosphere of Venus. 312.
Levitation device, not explained: 205.
Lhasa, blown up. 866.
Library of all time. 906.
Libya. 924, 925.
Lie detectors, primitive.
　30, 31, 1486, 1499.
Life bonds.
　Clocks and maker's soul: 1526. Inner
　world people maintained by queen's
　life: 1196.
Life, creation of.
　93, 113, 150, 163, 182, 230, 231, 239,
　398, 400, 427, 568, 749, 797, 905, 986,
　995, 1041, 1192, 1388, 1476, 1477,
　1573, 1758.
Life histories of animals.
　4, 208, 827, 957.
Life line of individual confused by higher dimensions. 314.
Life patterns of behavior changed to opposites. 241.
Life principle, a few explanations.
　Radiation: 358, 1192, 1157. New
　element: 460. Cosmic rays: 1648.
　Electricity: 1575, 1641. New sort of
　electrons: 359. A disease of matter:
　568.

Life-death cycle in parallel worlds.
　55, 363.
Light beings.
　41, 384, 402, 568, 575, 997, 998, 1026.
Light, equalling the speed of, occasional instances. 448, 907, 1348.
Light, exceeding the speed of. (*Almost all interstellar travel and an occasional interplanetary story involve speeds faster than light.* See Faster-than-light travel.*)
Light, miscellaneous. (*See also* Colors, Fossil light, Invisibility *entries*, Mirages, Mirrors, Optical illusions, Space mirages, Ultraviolet.)
　Beam transmits sound: 1296. Has in-
　finite speed and permeates other uni-
　verses: 1613. Light as a propulsion
　source: 549. Light as a weapon: 1157,
　1754. Light conveyor beam reaches
　from Venus: 1271. Psychologically
　healing light: 466. Rays bent to cause
　illusion: 1474.
Lighting devices.
　Plant luminescence: 278. Martian: 489.
　Cold light: 860, 1643. Sunlight bender:
　1314. Connected with aurora borealis:
　1643.
Lightning, artificial. 878.
Lightning, destroys brain inhibitor. 411.
Lightning guns. 259, 284, 645, 878, 929,
　1349, 1441.
Lights, Fortean. 548, 1372.
Lights, organic, used as communication devices. 243, 457.
Lilies attack people. 241.
Linear motors. 715 (transcontinental),
　1215.
Linked souls. 1027, 1028.
Linked worlds. 55, 112, 224, 296, 363,
　547, 919, 947, 1164, 1278, 1444, 1524,
　1679, 1798.
Lipreading reveals that everyone is corrupt. 564.
Liquid food. 488.
Liquid light. 907, 1739.
Literary ability, physical factors. 219,
　768.
Lithuania seized by USSR 1115.
Littering space with ball bearings. 169.
Live tv coverage with spectacles on buses. 1090.
Living universe. 938, 1609.
Lizard-men. 426, 475, 821, 829, 1197.
Lizards, source of suspended animation serum. 334.
Lobotomy turns patient into subman.
　181.
Lobsters used in organ regeneration.
　11, 60, 650.
Locusts, radio control of. 292.
Lolita complex. 298, 1750.
London.
　Destroyed or badly damaged: 293, 550,
　666, 843, 1115, 1116, 1491, 1697.
　Few people and trafficless: 141.
　Future megapolis: 400, 403, 910, 1480.
　Invaded by Martians: 1697.
　Other: 210, 211, 215.

　Put to sleep: 14.
　Sky city: 406, 550.
　Terrorized by robots: 1207.
Longevity, other planets, a few examples.
　Andromeda nebula. Thousands of
　years: 1048.
　Jupiter. Hundreds of years: 1151.
　Lunarians. Several thousand years:
　185.
　Mars. "Remarkable": 440. 1400 years:
　1727.
　Saturn. "Enormous": 1454.
　Space people. Thousands of years:
　878.
　Venus. "Enormous": 514. Thousands
　of years: 750. 800 years: 1120.
Looming. (*See also* Mirages.) 1422, 1661.
Loreleis. 518.
Lorentz-Fitzgerald contraction, measuring devices. 284.
Los Angeles. (*See also* California.)
　On fire from petroleum outbreak: 290.
　Without power: 437. Destroyed by
　earthquake: 834. Plan to destroy: 1065,
　1161. Damaged by purple monsters:
　1094.
Lost continents. (*See* Atlantis, Lemuria, Mu.)
Lost discoveries. (*See also* Suppressed discoveries.)
　Antigravity: 82, 395.
　Archeological material: 443.
　Artificial gold: 395, 966.
　Atomic energy: 179, 1478.
　Cold light: 968.
　Cold projector: 968.
　Cosmic ray power: 1519.
　Creation of matter: 113.
　Death ray: 461, 600.
　Devouring sphere: 520.
　Disintegrators: 520, 600.
　Dissolution and retrieval of bodies: 520.
　Dream machines: 1714.
　Emotion controller: 311, 1107.
　Engine, super: 1063.
　Four-dimensional glass: 371.
　Immortality and/or rejuvenation: 74,
　650, 1306, 1575.
　Intelligence enhancer: 346, 1461.
　Invisibility: 1619, 1700.
　Magnet for non-ferrous materials: 1488.
　Matter transmission: 1291.
　Microscope, super: 506.
　Personality transfer: 1391.
　Reanimating ray: 346.
　Recapturing fossil sound: 879.
　Solution to three-body problem: 1155.
　Space travel: 6, 82, 597, 1130, 1519.
　Taste transmission: 13.
　Technique for lifting continents: 743.
　Telescope, super: 82, 238, 1766.
　Thought helmets: 1779.
　Thought into matter machine: 378.
　Time machine: 227, 246, 1689.
　Time travel by thought: 941.
　Viewers: 1091, 1186, 1698.
　Vitamins against disease, age: 861.
Lost during matter transmission.
　836, 876, 1148, 1778.

Lost in space. 189, 532, 1045, 1378.
Lost races. (*There is considerable overlap between this category and the category* Hidden people.)
Lost races, cultural level..
Primitive: 94, 120, 338, 484, 685, 719, 1125, 1221, 1538, 1551, 1733.
Barbaric: 161, 337, 370, 793, 796, 942, 958, 1202 (?), 1203 (?), 1346, 1394, 1548, 1769.
About on our level: 712, 1557.
Superior: 33, 54, 234, 645, 649, 989, 993, 998, 999, 1580, 1735.
Sword and raygun: 958, 1733.
Lost races, ethnic nature.
Ancestral Polynesians: 998.
Ancient Semites: 989, 993, 1561 (element).
Ancient Egyptians: 1769.
Ancient Egyptian-Tuaregs: 337.
Atlanteans: 234, 645, 942, 958, 989, 993, 999 (?), 1202, 1346, 1580.
Aztecs, sometimes with other racial admixture: 338, 1345, 1394, 1538.
Basque-Greeks: 1202.
Blind blonds: 484.
Blonds, photophobic, with nictitating membranes: 1221.
Dwarves: 1203.
Giants: 712.
Green people: 1735.
Incas: 645, 796, 1125, 1128 (with Mongol), 1557, 1561.
Indians: 484, 1538, 1547, 1551, 1559, 1561.
Lemurians: 793.
The Lost Tribes: 958.
Maya: 1548.
Mu descendants speaking Sanskrit: 120.
Norse-Indians: 94.
Phoenicians: 793.
Pre-Inca Indians and ancient Semites: 1561.
Scaly humans: 33.
Tartars: 649.
Winged people: 161.
Lost races, location.
Africa: 337 (Nubia).
Alaska: 649.
Andes: 999, 1125, 1128, 1557, 1561.
Antarctica: 54, 719, 1221.
Arctic: 712, 958, 1769.
Atlantic: 234, 1346. 1580.
Australia: 1733.
Brazil: 484, 645, 796, 989, 993.
Canada: 94.
Caroline Islands: 998 (cave world below).
Easter Island: 793 (cave world below).
Ecuador: 1547, 1551.
Guatemala: 1548.
Himalayas: 1203.
Hollow Earth: 1221.
Mexico: 338, 1394.
Pacific: 161, 370, 793, 998 (below), 1735 (below).
Panama: 1538.
Sargasso Sea: 1202 (below).
U.S.: 33 (underground), 120 (Color-

ado), 942 (Colorado), 1580 (in other dimension).
Lost races, miscellaneous.
Live in glass-dome city beneath Atlantic: 234.
Live in underwater pyramids with airlocks: 1202.
Nasty Atlanteans in suspended animation: 645, 993.
Natives, for mysterious reasons, walk on hands: 1538.
Prepared to emerge and conquer the world: 998.
Preyed upon by apemen: 1394.
Primitive material culture, high paranormal abilities: 484.
Reduced in size by mysterious meteoric material: 1547, 1551.
Religion based on peyote: 338.
Rigid hierarchy and caste system: 989, 993.
Ruled by intelligent reptilians: 998, 999.
Social status based on acknowledged murders: 161.
Socialist: 33, 234.
Steam culture based on volcanism: 712, 719.
Try to communicate by messages bred on moth wings: 942.
Worship bodies like giant electrons in the center of the Earth: 33.
The Lost Tribes.
958 (Arctic), 1551 (Ecuador).
Lost worlds. (*Mass survivals of ancient fauna and flora.*)
Alaska: 997.
Antarctic: 719, 1440.
Arctic: 207, 712, 1174.
Canada: 94.
Himalayas: 15, 384.
Inside hollow Earth: 1190, 1528.
Mexico: 338.
Moon: 457.
South America: 42, 1546.
South Pacific: 1051, 1735.
U.S. otherwise: 1014, 1495.
Lottery to determine victims to palliate monsters. 1225.
Louisiana. 293.
Love created by marriage machine. 52, 1468.
Lunacy caused by lunar rays. 580, 733, 969, 1618.
Lures. Electronic devices to bring in aerial torpedoes. 1065.
Lying, glandular based. 9.
Mach limit, exceeding it is fatal. 19.
Machine analysis of character. 235, 416, 1403, 1580.
Machine cities. (*Automated cities.*)
115, 125, 149, 1262, 1509, 1514, 1521.
Machine evolution.
115, 192, 196, 434, 939.
Machine intelligence, controls the world.
434, 934, 950, 1281, 1322 (most of the world), 1462, 1826.
Machine intelligence, individuals, machine-men. (*This category includes

such entities as both are mechanical and possess free will and individuality. In most cases they are humaniform. It will thus be seen that the usual category* Robots *is divided into two groups, the present group, and, secondly, programmed, controlled, non-individual entities. The latter are listed under* Robots. *In some cases the distinction is arguable, but it is significant enough in clear cases to be maintained.*)
153, 434, 466, 469, 483, 560 (fake), 596, 647, 724, 773, 939, 1368, 1465, 1469, 1524, 1607, 1724, 1741, 1826.
Machine intelligence, mechanical brains, i.e., supercomputers.
72, 115, 122, 183, 192, 196, 431, 622, 890, 934, 950, 1262, 1281, 1322, 1462, 1640.
Machine prediction of the future. (*See also* Future, visions of; Predestination; Time viewing.)
48, 51, 109, 114, 834, 981, 1002, 1135, 1250, 1470, 1640, 1714, 1738.
Usually this involves ineluctability, but the following allow for change: 48, 51, 834, 1250, 1738.
Machine translation, print to speech. 767.
Machine-human love.
302, 322, 686.
Machines, miscellaneous.
Future machines believe they evolved from man via cyborg: 434. Future machines transmit ideas for making time machine to our time: 434. Machines believe that they created mankind: 431. Self-reproducing swarm: 361. The ultimate machine: 196.
Machines, rebellion of.
183, 302, 622, 952, 1524.
Macrocosm. (*In science-fictional terms, the larger universe in which our universe is a collection of atoms.*)
Macrocosm, ambience.
Earth-like: 590, 1634, 1640 (but formed of higher elements), 1711, 1712.
Nothingness, preparatory to formation of new universe: 410, 1640.
Macrocosm, cultural level.
Superior: 214, 386, 412, 1466, 1634, 1640, 1711, 1712.
Macrocosm, inhabitants.
Human: 412, 590, 606, 1634, 1640, 1711, 1712.
Humanoid giants: 386, 1634, 1640.
Intelligent beings, not described: 1711.
Multiarmed, multi-eyed beings: 214.
Multitudinous forms, some very strange: 1640.
Macrocosm, miscellaneous.
Experiment on Earth destroys life in our universe and in the macrocosm: 412. Macrocosm above us is destroyed when ultimate energy particle is released, and next macrocosm above that is not yet formed: 1640. Macrocosm is a succession of universes like nodes on a sine wave: 1613. Macro-

Mars, miscellaneous (*continued*)

Martians, now extinct, put heritage space station above Earth: 6.

Martians in friendly control of Ganymede: 573.

Martians machinate to solve Earth's problems: 400.

Martians raid Earth's resources—human males: 440.

Martians send electric space cloud to kill mankind: 411.

Martians speak English: 558.

Martian food plant proves disaster: 249.

Music and arts exhaustively described: 489.

On visit to Earth Martians locate last man and hear about warfare, hitherto unknown to them: 1131.

Peopled long ago, like Earth, with galactic man: 1625.

Plant desiccates Mars; spores reach Earth: 132.

Plot to kill Earthmen with destructive music: 1110.

Pro-British, interfere in world affairs: 1457.

Purchase foodstuff because of home shortage: 1034.

Rebels against Earth control: 598.

Removed from solar system by Emissaries: 1247.

Road construction difficulties from outlaws: 1598.

Sect associated with periodic comet, rare element, supernatural elements: 1600.

Source of miracle radioactive element: 776, 779.

Superior medical resources on Mars: 1596.

Supernatural elements associated with ancient shaman: 1600.

Terraformed by invaders: 192.

To be destroyed by galactic empire unless reforms: 1625.

Tries to use Earth as sun shield: 587. Vision of Mars through supertelescope drives one mad: 870.

Visit by Martian is basis for satire on Earth: 1555.

Visiting Martians served as model for god Thoth: 1663.

War with Bodia: 1451, 1576.

War with Venus: 1040.

Water controlled by Earth capitalists, rebellion: 783.

Wild, high-life fin de siecle decadence: 1674.

Wrecked by war with Moon: 799

Mars, political and/or economic structure, if significant:

Anarchistic cooperative with other species: 1663.

Empire, with group being on top: 558.

Hierarchy based on intellect, super-ant on top: 437.

Imperial dynasties: 162, 776, 779, 909.

Intensely dirty politics: 1429, 1596.

Machine emperor, plots conquest: 1741.

Oppressive, aggressive dictatorship: 1071, 1272.

Paternalistic monarchy, feudal, cartels: 1034.

Peaceful coexistence between natives and shape changers: 1813.

Socialism and anarchism: 440.

Socialist, anarchist, regimented society: 1727.

Sort of protectorate over Ganymede: 573.

Syndicalist scientist rule: 385.

Utterly utilitarian society: 446-448.

Mars, religion.

Priest-ridden culture, with a shrine containing relics; lethally obsessive about concealing Earth origins of religion: 1325.

Rigid Fundamentalist fanatics with a talking idol: 162.

Shamanistic reverence for a periodic comet composed of a rare element, attributing (perhaps correctly) supernatural powers to it: 1600.

Mars, satellites. (See Deimos, Phobos.)

Mars, visits to and from Earth. (*See* Earth-Mars relations.)

The *Mary Celeste*. 1554, 1652.

Maryland. 972, 977.

Masonic material. 993.

Mass deportations. 442, 595, 718, 720, 747.

Massachusetts. (*See also* Boston.) 199, 349, 441, 538, 904-906, 1328-1330, 1649.

Master controls for space fleet. 284.

Masterminds of crime. (*See also* Gangsters, Space Pirates.) 36, 64, 65, 96, 205, 215, 368, 495-498, 501, 629, 696, 727, 729, 771, 841, 970, 1181, 1183, 1205, 1230, 1242, 1343, 1382, 1419, 1427, 1521, 1604, 1747. Mistressmind: 229.

Mastodons surviving. 1014.

Materialization bombs, rays. 303.

Maternal instincts awakened in ultrafeminists. 735, 738, 748.

Mathematical game as life and death. 1830.

Mathematics, strange, explained. 1776.

Mathematics the basis of reality. 409, 410, 1155, 1258, 1262, 1284, 1414.

Mating boards. (*See* Eugenics and mating boards.)

Mato Grosso. 306, 645, 954, 1321.

Matter, creation of. 17, 113, 190, 227, 378, 389, 409, 410, 572, 672, 693, 694, 900, 1004, 1376-1378, 1446, 1743, 1746,

Matter, disposed of by time shift. 154, 358, 975, 1454, 1630.

Matter duplication. 283, 482, 854, 1258.

Matter eaters invade other planet. 1373.

Matter, interpenetration. (*See also* Dimensions, Fifth Dimension, Fourth Dimension, Linked worlds, Parallel worlds.) 233, 303, 310, 675, 852, 855, 1210,

1232, 1369, 1372, 1524, 1819.

Matter, miscellaneous.

Matter consists of various vibratory variations: 876. Transformed: 696. Turned to light: 441, 858. Controlled by mental power: 1285. Total destruction of: 1640, 1646. Matter and life are all mathematically factorable: 409, 410.

Matter, strange forms of. (*See also* Atomic compression; Light beings; Matter, interpenetration; Size changes; Skyland; *and similar categories involving atomic and molecular changes.*) 41, 190, 316, 360, 459, 631, 675, 676, 705, 708, 896, 905, 997, 998, 1005, 1006, 1278, 1326, 1369, 1372, 1420, 1524, 1619, 1734, 1793, 1798.

Matter transmission.

Associated with space travel: 155, 193, 407, 459, 558, 858, 902, 911, 1113, 1226, 1284 (?), 1285, 1290, 1291, 1353, 1373, 1555, 1617, 1736, 1758.

Associated with theft: 229, 671.

Associated with time travel: 407, 1021, 1566.

Miscellaneous: A dream: 1566. Armies sent by matter transmission: 836. Brings new monetary standard metal from Moon: 1303. Intended use for jail break: 305. May permit Martian invasion: 558. Permits disastrous vacation on savage Venus: 1736. Provides connection to hollow Earth: 1509, 1514. Results in destroying trans-Plutonian world: 459. Straight-line only: 229. Used to dispose of gangsters: 1148.

Other uses than above: 201, 275, 305, 406, 482, 836, 876, 949, 992, 1148, 1231, 1284, 1303, 1509, 1511, 1514, 1580, 1588, 1631, 1636, 1778.

Persons lost during matter transmission: 836, 876, 1148, 1778.

Transports to fourth dimension: 193,

Matter transmission, modus operandi.

Changes atomic vibratory rate to radio wavelength: 482, 558, 836, 1291.

Connected with Element 87: 876.

Converts matter to light: 858.

Operates by neutron bombardment, catching atoms in magnetic field: 1636.

Turns electrons into waves: 836, 911.

Uses principle of electrolysis: 1148.

Wasn't really matter transmission; was a time machine: 1801.

Maturation ray creates adult zombies. 220.

Mauritius. 1221.

Maxwell's equations permit seeing future. 1135.

Maya. 445, 1345, 1548, 1549. Codex found: 1548. Lost race: 1548.

Mecca, raid on. 368.

Mechanical distortion of time rate. 335.

Mechanical judge tries cases. 416.

Medicine, fantastic. (*See also* Artificial hearts, Cyborgs; Dead, revival of the; Diseases *categories*; Drugs; Organ regeneration; Organ transplants.)
Anaesthetic, super: 146, 147, 1638.
As diagnosis technique doctors feel pain patients endure: 694.
Blindness cured during visit to future: 1816.
Cancer cures: 704, 762, 776, 778, 1284, 1375, 1423, 1662.
Closed-circuit television diagnosis: 140.
Combining injured persons to make one good out of two damaged: 582.
Coral teeth: 1389.
Criminality cured by blood transfusion: 817.
Criminality cured by surgery: 57, 186, 187, 229, 982, 1569, 1651.
Cures with solar radiation: 545.
Entry to bloodstream miniaturized: 809, 1347.
Germicidal ray: 40.
Martian medicine: 1596.
Meningitis serum: 961.
New vitamin: 861.
Omnicurants: 286, 770, 1809.
Surgery. Remodel heart: 6. Four-dimensional: 105, 1081, 1179, 1198. Appendectomy by layman in space: 1417. Amputation with ray gun: 1017. Frontal lobes fall out during surgery: 181. Brain removal with patient surviving: 1517.
Survival after severe skin damage: 364.
Suspended animation aftercare to surgery: 531.
Treatment via astral body: 100.
Medieval Europe. 556, 633, 721, 723, 1028, 1058, 1217.
Mediterranean basin, formerly dry valley, flooded by Lunarians. 1216.
Mediumistic phenomena. (*See also* Mesmerism.) 584, 1075.
Medusa.
Euhemerized: 164, 850.
Fake for criminal purposes: 1427.
Megalopolises. (*A few examples; cities under other classifications would often qualify as megalopolises.*) 23, 156, 302, 322, 375, 1283, 1761.
Melanism, artificially created. 1672.
Memories of the future. (*See also* Future, visions of.) 1002, 1435, 1478.
Memory analyzed and disked. 183.
Memory erasure. (*See also* Amnesia.) 906, 916, 970, 975, 993.
Memory of past lives. (*See* Ancestral memory, Reincarnation.)
Memory transfer. (*See also* Brains, dead, reading.) 383, 1233.
Men. (*i.e., human males. See also* Gynecocracy.)
Males to become extinct: 728, 949.
Man stealing: 1445.
Man shortage: 1445, 1523.
One male left: 1717.
Sexual harassment by women: 1717.

Subjugation by women: 425, 908, 949, 1231, 1362, 1447, 1541, 1717.
Meningitis cure. 961.
Mensuration, history of. 1532.
Mental control of disease-curing agents. 809.
Mental disorders cured by radiation. 545.
Mental gravity control. 1625.
Mental matter control. 1285.
Mental set permits entry to fourth dimension. 112, 358, 400, 1507.
Mental travel, spatial. 873.
Mentality affected by size change. 1449.
Mercury (element).
Atomic fuel: 1436
Mercury (planet), ambience.
Barren, but not uninhabitable: 646, 1001, 1446.
Caverns or hollow. 37 (inhabited by molemen), 646, 1454.
Earth-like: 987 (?), 1009 (dry), 1160 (tropical, monstrous fauna), 1246 (?), 1423 (tropical), 1586, 1828.
Habitable: 570 (terraformed in far future), 84 (in far future), 794 (in far future), 1041 (in far future), 1431 (in far future), 1626 (but uncongenial).
Libration zone more or less tolerable: 37, 794, 820, 877 (glass domes), 896, 1324 (glass domes), 1423 (tropical), 1454, 1586.
Molten: 561.
Returned to gaseous form in future: 892, 1001.
Uninhabitable, hot and cold zones: 37, 794, 877, 896, 1001, 1436 (?), 1454, 1803 (glass domes).
Mercury (planet), cultural level.
Primitive: 1160, 1423, 1803.
Barbaric: 646, 1160.
On our level: 37 (slightly lower), 284, 1160, 1586, 1626
Superior: 295, 987, 1009, 1246, 1282, 1454, 1828.
Mercury (planet), Earth colonizes or exploits. (*See* Earth-Mercury relations.)
Mercury (planet), Earth visits. (*See* Earth-Mercury relations.)
Mercury (planet), hostilities with Earth. (*See* Earth-Mercury relations.)
Mercury (planet), inhabitants.
Armor-plated, stupid: 1272.
Bluish electric bubbles, perhaps a form of life: 820,.
Egg-shaped molemen, flap-feet with suction cups: 37.
Giant intelligent beetles: 987.
Human: 284 (slight), 987 (slaves to beetles), 1160, 1586.
Humanoid: 646 (skeletal men), 1160, 1246 (giants), 1423 (batrachian), 1454 (small, white, four-armed, nasty), 1626 (with head crests), 1803 (small, bestial), 1828.
Last men in far future: 84, 569 (in pantograph), 570, 794, 1041, 1431.

Mobile mushroom-shaped beings, intelligence not stated: 1446.
Semi-intelligent cones of radiant particles: 896.
Small, bestial, stupid: 1803.
Submen: 1160.
Tetrahedra of living metal: 1009.
Mercury (planet), miscellaneous.
Aliens attempt atomic energy near Mercury, set it ablaze: 1001.
Archeological material; ancient civilization destroyed by Lunar thought monster: 88.
Extraordinarily dangerous exploration: 896.
Gum from trees is a cancer cure: 1423.
Have invisible space ships: 1626.
Intelligent giant beetles raid Earth for slaves to replenish weakened native stock: 987.
Last refuge of mankind, must be abandoned: 1431.
Martian-Earth trade rivalries: 1324, 1803.
Mercurian space piracy prelude to attempted conquest of solar system: 1626.
Mercurians maintain a zoo of solar-system natives: 1454.
Mercurians plan system conquest: 1454, 1626.
Mercurians, superior culturally, have no relations with rest of solar system: 1282, 1454.
Mercurians wish to move to Venus, which they attack: 1626.
Mercury originated in other solar system; captured on fly-through: 1215, 1216.
Mercury originated in other solar system; planet moved to our system to avoid stellar disaster: 1454.
Mercury pushed into sun: 1454.
Mercury removed from solar system by galactic empire: 1247.
More liberal marriage regulations than Earth: 1586.
Only source for antigravity metal: 37.
Radium mines, Terrestrial slaves: 646.
Source of noxious insects attacking Venus: 1120.
Tetrahedral natives communicate with drum-like sounds: 1009.
Vicious natives speak English learned from radio: 646.
Mercury (Roman god).
Euhemerized: 164, 1721
Mesmerism. (*See also* Hypnosis *categories*.) 1144, 1142.
Mesozoic, action in.
4, 45, 208, 281, 851 (alternate history), 1130.
Messiah cults. 334, 1509, 1514, 1704.
Metabolisms, strange. (*See also* Accelerated man, Alien intelligence, Crystal life, Light beings, Skyland.) 54, 260, 450, 453, 664, 682, 1454, 1584.)

Metal, destruction of.
233, 425, 433, 529, 612, 682, 763, 890, 1200.

Metal fatigue as weapon. 233, 1826.

Metal formation, theories of. 711.

Metal, hypnotic. 1371.

Metal life. (*See also* Machine intelligence; *the distinction is not always clear.*) 392, 475, 997, 1157, 1593, 1599, 1631, 1677.

Metal, man transformed into. 1157, 1732.

Metal, super or special.
Extension of periodic table: 1479.
Impenetrable: 403.
Indestructible, almost: 801.
New metal from Moon as monetary standard: 1303.
New: 435, 801, 1479.
Superlight: 1334.
Superstrength: 285, 517, 1157, 1376-1378.
Totally reflective: 819.
Wonderful, but unstable; results in spectacular building collapse: 1260.

Meteor Crater, Arizona.
706, 781, 1184, 1191, 1287, 1752.

Meteor fields and swarms, important.
Around Venus, preventing entry: 244.
Belt around Earth, sometimes impeding space travel: 781, 1039, 1381, 1494.
Damage Earth: 265, 582, 1236.
Destroy invaders: 387.
Disturbances when hits sun: 1167, 1452.
Interplanetary and interstellar: 436, 782.
Physiological problems when a swarm hits sun: 1452.
Space damage: 525.
Wrecks Moon: 1762.

Meteor mining. 78, 390, 685, 1327, 1749, 1765.

Meteor repellers. (*Often tacitly employed in space fiction.*)
169, 187, 200, 674, 963, 1039, 1519, 1524.

Meteorite, giant Siberian, really a spaceship that crashed. 1191.

Meteorite strands sea vessel, knocking it into a lagoon. 1648.

Meteorites as weapons.
284, 799, 1549.

Meteorites bearing life forms.
5, 41, 236, 269, 271, 468, 472, 521, 568, 627, 628, 808, 904, 1039, 1204, 1293, 1614, 1642, 1752.

Meteorites bearing messages.
6, 435, 659, 789, 856, 963, 1127, 1436.

Meteorites bearing objects, archeological material, spaceship debris, etc.
148, 463, 706, 812 (from Bodia), 894, 1003, 1039, 1203, 1287, 1775.

Meteorites, seeming, really spaceships.
85, 383, 1184, 1191.

Meteorites with special properties.
Alters space-time and permits prevision: 1738. Contains elements 85 and 87, permitting antigravity: 82. Enables

interstellar communication: 1397. Enables time travel: 23, 1074. Huge radioactive meteorite in Australia finances eutopian colony: 581. Knocks hole in Earth, filled with Dirac particles: 897. Neutronium: 947. Permits entry to tiny world system: 1547, 1551. Radioactive meteorite poisons crystal world: 477.

Meteors causing damage in space travel, significant instances. (*Minor damage caused by meteors during space travel is common in interplanetary fiction.*)
26, 194, 243, 244, 299, 391, 524, 525, 631, 659, 686, 1035, 1052, 1132-1134, 1341, 1356, 1519, 1629, 1789.

Mexico. 310, 445, 578, 742, 952, 1102, 1132, 1345, 1394, 1406, 1457, 1566, 1603, 1734.
Hostilities with U.S.: 742, 1457.

Mice, the size of bears. 60.

Microcephalics invade Vermont village. 1014.

Microcosm. (*The opposite to macrocosm; universes which consist of atoms (or atomic particles) in our world. The concept is not so well defined, however, and is best contained in* Atomic worlds, *which see.*)

Microfilm anticipated. 488.

Microman, adventures of a.
Literally: 52, 1158, 1347, 1449, 1770.
Related: 377, 614, 615, 809, 1093.

Microphone, super. 1419.

Microscopes, super.
385, 506, 539, 818, 825, 1075, 1154, 1572, 1642.

Microscopic life. (*Not small enough to be considered Atomic or Microcosmic. See also* World in a box.)

Microscopic life, cultural level.
Primitive: 990, 1075 (?), 1547, 1551.
Superior: 569, 716, 895, 899, 991, 1122, 1745.

Microscopic life, nature.
Human: 569, 716, 895, 990, 991, 1075, 1122 (evolved), 1547, 1551, 1745 (cyborgs at end).
Humanoid: 899.

Microscopic life seen as full-sized monsters. 818.

Migration of insects controlled by radio. 292, 293.

Militarism, a few stories opposed to it.
98, 235, 237, 244, 247, 256, 600, 1265, 1400, 1670.

Military installations destroyed by termites. 1206.

Military snobbism. 1786-1795. Naval ring-knocker counterpart: 1196.

Mill, destroyed by subterranean monster. 739.

Mind battles.
55, 323, 356, 389, 400, 454, 535, 1014, 1255, 1277, 1290, 1323, 1366, 1376-1378, 1640.

Mind composed of special electrons. 359.

Mind control, mechanical.
61, 138, 158, 211, 215, 217, 225-227,

242, 400, 403, 468, 496, 639, 707, 779, 783, 812, 903, 960, 1023, 1115, 1220, 1255, 1261, 1378, 1569, 1590, 1604, 1677, 1678, 1735, 1774.

Mind control, nonmechanical. (*See also* Hypnosis.)
133, 146, 190, 220, 234, 251, 323, 356, 387, 400, 411, 437, 454, 471, 479, 498, 535, 568, 589, 595, 626, 648, 746, 975, 1014, 1151, 1154, 1180, 1255, 1277, 1290, 1323, 1371, 1378, 1397, 1447, 1572, 1593, 1594, 1611, 1614, 1683, 1744.
Drugs involved: 251, 471, 498.

Mind dissociated from body. (*See also* Afterdeath experiences, Cosmic flights.)
146, 147, 162, 316, 873, 999.

Mind power creates matter out of cosmic energy. 1446.

Mind reading, mechanical. (*See also* Telepathy.)
424, 452, 489, 647, 691, 975, 992, 1237, 1240, 1786-1795.

Mindanao Deep. 350.

Minerals, miscellaneous.
Antigravity: 16. Causes blindness: 1315. Creates extreme longevity or immortality: 869, 1125. Eats oxygen: 1283. Mineral rights claimed by people from center of the Earth: 1182. Radioactive, kills men, animals: 218. Supermagnetic: 1651.

Minnesota. 76, 283, 510, 707, 1043.

Mira, planet of.
People humanoid, double-jointed limbs, vestigial feathers, telescopic eyes; invade solar system; science superior to ours: 202.

Miracles, power to work. 295, 1702.

Mirages. (*See also* Space mirages.) 576, 709, 1422.

Mirrors.
City of mirrors, with mirror beings as personality fragments: 936. Entry to dimensions: 381. Mirror reflects disintegrator ray: 953. Mirror saves the world: 953, 1201. Mirrors create invisibility: 1115. Space mirrors: 354, 445.

Mississippi Valley submerged. 272.

Mist beings. Pluto: 1723. Other side of reality: 947.

Mist causes decay. 747.

Mistletoe, apotropaic to monster. 1100.

Mistressmind of crime. 229.

Modern culture Islamicized à la Arabian Nights. 491, 1079, 1143.

Modernism, anti. A few examples.
733, 738, 748, 749, 759, 765, 774, 941.

Molecular motion rays, propulsions. 186-190.

Molecules, size.
Earth-borer shrinks molecules to create tunnels: 706. Molecule the size of an egg explodes: 959.

Mole-men. 37, 975.

Mollusks. (*See also* Octopi.)
Intelligent mollusk-like beings: 452,

Mollusks (*continued*)
Giant land mollusks as peril: 871. Intelligent mollusks and mollusk-like beings from space: 387, 562, 1048, 1154.

Money matters. (*See also* Socialism.)
Bluish glass used for money: 244. Monetary system collapses when Antarctic gold is discovered; new standard metal is matter-transmitted from Moon: 1303. Money cancelled, work vouchers issued: 874. No money: 1499. Real estate is standard of value, not gold: 488.

Mongolians. (*Perhaps not really, but called so by authors.*) 908, 1809.

Mongoose, super. 805.

Monkeys. (*Many of the jungle stories set in the Americas or Africa have casual inclusions of monkeys.*)
Monkey with cat's mind: 305. Intelligent: 592. Sets off four-dimensional machine: 1080.

Monorails. 339, 910, 924, 925, 927, 1589.

Monsters. (*Difficult to define, but something horrible, vicious, aggressive, misshapen, and usually not intelligent. Much extra-terrestrial wildlife not listed here might fit this category.*)
2, 59, 93, 307, 322, 323, 336, 375, 472, 656, 771, 848 (fake), 905, 940, 965, 998, 1016, 1025, 1068, 1094, 1106, 1149 (fanciful), 1157, 1192, 1193, 1293, 1371, 1556, 1734.

Montana. 437.

Montreal. 714.

Moon, ambience, desolate.
66, 68, 77, 88, 129 (thin atmosphere, air in caverns), 149, 155, 200, 202, 228, 295, 297, 324, 406, 451, 452, 455, 456, 457 (air in caverns), 463 (air in cav-erns), 472, 489 (some life), 519, 549, 552, 580, 603, 623, 690, 722, 779, 780, 782, 786 (our side), 790, 832, 921, 951 (?), 954, 955, 963, 1004 (air pockets, air in caverns), 1045, 1077, 1083, 1084 (but with mud slides), 1130, 1215, 1216, 1223 (air in caverns), 1236, 1283, 1289 (air in caverns), 1290 (air in caverns), 1301-1302 (air in caverns), 1438, 1445, 1472, 1500, 1501 (air in caverns), 1522, 1504, 1505, 1574, 1593 (air and water inside), 1673, 1676, 1678, 1706 (air filled caverns), 1755, 1814.

Moon, ambience, Earth-like.
326 (dark side), 420, 549 (dark side), 652 (?), 786 (the dark side), 799 (in remote past), 880, 1215-1216 (the dark side in the past), 1313 (in the past, with sea), 1583 (the dark side), 1655 (in the past), 1744 (tropical in the past), 1762 (in the past).

Moon, ambience, miscellaneous.
Habitable in dome cities: 129, 149, 452 (revived molluscoids glass in area), 549 (dark side), 552, 779, 780 (construction), 782 (?).
Hollow: 324, 489, 921, 1215-1216

(cavern filled), 1302 (cavern filled), 1313, 1593, 1706.
In shape a half-collapsed ball: 1313.
Really a cosmic egg that hatches, producing an enormous dragon-like creature: 1753.
Rendered habitable when Earth's air and water flow to Moon: 473.
Terraformed by interstellar visitors: 406.
Turned into small sun: 406, 451, 510.
Underground cities: 262, 263, 458, 1004, 1301, 1302, 1759.

Moon, colonized or exploited. (*See also* Earth-Moon relations.)
Colonization or exploitation by powers other than Earth: 77, 295, 287, 779,
The Moon as a staging ground for hostile aliens attacking Earth: 68, 295, 386, 454, 954, 1574, 1577, 1673, 1755.
The Moon settled from Bodia: 1215, 1216.

Moon, colonizes Earth. (*See* Earth-Moon relations.)

Moon, cultural level, past.
Barbaric: 66, 1501 (?).
Superior: 110, 114, 452, 455, 549, 603, 799, 832, 921, 1130, 1283, 1303 (?), 1655, 1744, 1762, 1767.

Moon, cultural level, present.
Primitive or barbaric: 129, 324, 326, 457, 786, 880, 1223, 1289.
Our level: 1290.
Superior: 88, 155 (slightly), 185, 356, 420 (?), 452, 463, 549, 603, 652, 786, 921, 951, 1004, 1215, 1216, 1301, 1302, 1472, 1583, 1593, 1706.

Moon, destroyed or badly damaged.
Aladoree disintegrates it with AKKA: 1762.
Collision with Ceres; smashed, forms belt around Earth: 1236.
Collision with new planet: 23.
Deliberately removed as hindrance to space travel: 722.
Destroyed because it is causing earthquakes: 1229.
Surface damage shown in historical motion pictures: 1303.
Wrecked by ancient war damage: 799 (by Mars), 921 (by Jovian system), 1216 (by Mars), 1451 (by Mars and Bodia).
Wrecked by meteor swarm: 1762.
Wrecked when captured by Earth: 1215, 1216.

Moon, hostilities with Earth. (*See* Earth-Moon relations.)

Moon, inhabitants, former.
Cyborgs: 1744.
Insect-like: 66, 455, 1130, 1744.
Human: 110, 799 (Orientals), 832 (whites), 1655 (?), 1762.
Humanoid: 603 (thin, large chests).
Molluscoid, eyed tentacles: 452.
Worm people: 549.

Moon, inhabitants, present.
Blimp-like: 881.
Elephantine intelligent creatures: 129.
Human: 142, 164 (mythical wise woman), 185 (superior), 326, 420 (beautiful blonde), 652, 786, 880 (winged), 1215, 1216, 1301, 1302.
Humanoid: 149, 155 (arms and legs, but tiny bodies), 324 (devolved winged), 356 (huge head, spindly limbs, telepathic), 603 (thin, large chests), 782 (small), 921 (gigantic), 951 (small, large heads, thin limbs), 1223, 1324 (stupid hulks), 1472 (somewhat misshapen), 1583 (dwarves), 1593.
Insect-like: 1004, 1706 (highly specialized).
Kangaroo-like with big flat feet: 1215, 1216.
Molluscoid, tentacles with eyes: 452.
Not described, but intelligent and not bipeds: 1290.
Plant men, slabs with roots: 457.
Superintelligent spherical cyborgs: 1593.
Thought monster: 88.
Turtle-men: 549.
Very nasty superintelligent unipeds: 1593.

Moon, interplanetary collisions.
66 (threatened), 171 (with Deimos), 173 (planetoid), 832 (comet, wipes out population), 1236 (with Ceres).

Moon, miscellaneous.
Ancient civilization shown by Devil (?) in motion pictures: 1303.
Ancient inhabitants divided into male and female states: 1655.
Ancient inhabitants leave on faster-than-light travel and return to find Moon desolate: 110, 1762.
Ancient inhabitants or visitors in survive in suspended animation: 406 (friendly), 452 (friendly), 603 (hostile).
Archeological material: 66, 406, 452, 455, 603, 690, 1283, 1313, 1445, 1501.
Bullet fired on Moon flies around and strikes shooter: 228.
Dinosaurs destroy Lunar colonizing expedition to Earth: 1130.
Falling through the Moon: 489, 1313.
Flesh-eating termites exterminate Moon men in past: 1655.
Fossil brought from Moon comes to life: 1503.
Gains Earth's atmosphere: 66.
Home of thought monster that destroys cultures: 88.
Horrible monstrous flying jellyfish said to come from Moon, when Moon draws nearer: 1557.
Luna formerly a planet between Earth and Mars: 799, 832.
Luna formerly an intrusive planet: 445, 1238.
Luna formerly part of Earth. Broken

Mysterious disappearances (*continued*)
1112. Diamonds from bank vault: 229.

People: 267, 308, 309, 314, 321, 333, 349, 384, 414, 420, 423, 513, 556, 579, 629, 708, 791, 800, 833, 855, 871, 964, 965, 1014, 1087, 1115, 1191, 1206, 1218, 1224, 1252, 1267, 1297, 1298, 1353, 1384, 1472, 1487, 1541, 1542, 1554, 1635, 1749.

Ships: 440, 585, 788, 1346, 1602, 1648, 1715.

Trains: 1168, 1567, 1578, 1775.

Mysterious radio signals from underground Australia. 275.

Mystical material. 84, 359, 409, 410, 937.

Names, future.

All consonants, no vowels: 107.

Elaborate coding, worn on left breast, indicating sex, occupation, marital status: 1090.

Forename plus number code: 57, 61, 488, 1403.

Letter and number combinations: 488, 524.

Serial numbers: 375, 400, 488, 563, 722, 765, 780, 1225, 1340, 1403, 1717.

Serial numbers with rank privilege of names: 765, 780.

Napoleon.

Gangster fancies self: 270. Madman assumes personality of Napoleon: 1361.

Nature tries to exterminate mankind.
84, 612, 746.

Neanderthal man.

161, 952, 994, 1015, 1046, 1216, 1222, 1239, 1834.

Slaves in preglacial Mexico to intelligent spiders: 952.

Nebraska. 101, 108, 123, 247, 766, 1004.

Nebulas. (*The term is used loosely in certain stories. See* Space clouds.)

The *Necronomicon.* 905.

Negritos of Malaysia. 1058.

Negative matter and universes. 1268, 1679.

Nelson's Column in London destroyed.
403, 1116.

Neoprimitivism. (*A voluntary discarding of science and technology, in varying degree, in order to return to a simpler life. This is not the same as the category* Future primitivism, *which involves the destruction of civilization and the regretted loss of science and technology.*)

367, 694, 735, 763, 771, 774, 909, 933, 1077, 1262, 1350, 1436, 1736.

Nepal. 264, 508.

Neptune, ambience.

Bare rock and gases: 593.

Bare, with specialized machines: 1465.

Earth-like: 697 (jungle), 699 (jungle), 1277, 1629.

Encased: 553.

Highly radioactive: 697, 699.

Neptune, colonized or exploited.

697, 699, 1277.

Neptune, cultural level.

Primitive: 697, 699.

Our level, more or less: 593, 1277, 1629.

Superior: 553.

Neptune, inhabitants.

Discs, seven limbs, bulbous eyes: 553.

Gaseous beings: 593.

Giant brains: 1629.

Gigantic gorilline with one eye: 697, 699.

Human: 284, 1277 (colonists).

Humanoid, small: 1629.

Reptile-men: 1277.

Neptune, miscellaneous.

Moves closer to Earth: 1469. Genocide of natives by Venus: 1040. Removed or destroyed: 188, 193, 265. Turned into small sun: 1631, 1701. Hatches into gigantic space dragon: 1753.

Neptune, visit to.

553, 593, 697, 699, 1465, 1469, 1629.

Vicinity: 559, 1410.

Nerves shifted, sensations reversed.
865, 1060 (hoax), 1502.

Nervous energy.

Mechanical production: 346. Trapped and utilized: 1206. Place taken by radio waves to produce zombie: 1121.

Netherlands. 1524, 1525.

Neutron weapons. 202, 830.

Neutronium.

Drops victims to Earth's core: 1308. Impact of neutronium asteroid breaks Antarctic crust creating warm oasis: 719. Is core of planet Vulcan: 1595. Made at home, causes mysterious death: 279. Neutronium planet destroys Bodia and Earth: 473. Neutronium ring permits entry to other dimension; 947. Used as power lens: 1377, 1378. Used as weapon to hamper Earth's space program: 1311.

Nevada. 332, 864, 990, 991, 1474.

New elements. (*See* Element 85; Element 87; Elements, new; Isotopes.)

New Guinea. 881.

New Jersey. 91, 267, 483, 751, 815, 855, 866, 1021, 1074, 1157, 1580, 1614.

Space port in Hoboken: 91.

New Mexico. 72, 1623, 1746.

New Orleans destroyed. 272.

New universes formed from old.
62, 409, 410, 567, 1267, 1640.

New Year's Eve, A.D. 2000. 1406.

New York City, destroyed or very badly damaged.

Accidentally incinerated by space explorers: 661.

Attacks from space: 190, 325, 393, 913, 1039, 1094, 1279, 1631.

Collapses from time vibrations, but in time paradox restored: 407.

Damaged by invaders from fourth dimension: 303.

Damaged by near interplanetary collision: 1236.

Damaged by would-be world conqueror: 64, 198, 1812.

Destroyed by robots from future: 302.

Earthquakes destroy: 1229, 1358.

Enormous damage when all mankind loses its memory: 916.

Flooding caused by heat vortex and melt: 274.

Glaciers race through toppling skyscrapers: 952.

In ruins in future: 235, 903, 1633.

Involuntary urban renewal as rays from sky remove old buildings and drop them into the Hudson: 159.

Isolated by runaway force screen: 509, 1835.

Mechanical brain, power mad, kills most of inhabitants: 183.

Now an Oriental city, destroyed by Buck Rogers: 1073.

Old New York disintegrated and sky city created: 406.

People turned to metal by space attack: 1157.

War destruction: 843, 982, 1073, 1634, 1804.

Water supply wrecked: 666.

New York City, future.

Automobilist culture: 733 (streets, no pedestrian rights).

Covered with a glass dome: 771, 1736.

Flying culture: 64, 215, 407, 758.

Garden city, apartment blocks separated by parks: 302 (in year 2038), 339 (25-story buildings, moving sidewalks, parks between), 1499 (single cubic city on the outskirts).

Gimmicky flying culture: 1348, 1349, 1350.

Like ancient Rome, with villas, slaves: 1362.

Moved into the sky: 406, 550 (flying, like other world cities), 755 (mooring masts for domestic arrangements).

Ruins: 235, 903, 1633.

Social level cities, with layers corresponding to social classes, usually integral and unitary: 201 (despotic), 1283 (futuristic architecture), 1583, 1592 (huge monolithic city).

Supercity, more or less free-developing: 156 (skyscrapers five hundred stories high, no more streets, Hudson covered over, reaches into Connecticut), 302, 322 (in 1973), 407 (flying, gravitational stairways), 511, 693, 694, 775 (futuristic architecture, now New York City State), 1280 (incredible buildings, rivers covered over), 1569 (total population of 60,000,000), 1610, 1737 (with a 12,000 foot high observation tower).

New York City, miscellaneous.

A giant ape, carrying a woman, climbs up a skyscraper: 158.

A model farm set in midtown Manhattan: 774.

Optical illusions (*continued*)
Pattern combinations create invisibility: 366. Moth, seen from close perspective, assumes likeness of monster: 1145. Due to distortion of eye, microscopic life appears as monster: 818. Atmospheric effects and shadows create illusions: 1661.

Oral historians instead of books. 1537.

Orchid attacks its owner. 1685.

Orchid-gathering on other planet. 1418.

Oregon. 696, 1403, 1406, 1414.

Organ regeneration. 11, 60, 231, 608, 1575. Cellular: 650.

Organ transplants, other than brains.
(*See also* Brain in a jar, Brain transplants, Cyborgs.)
Arm: 99.
Bodies and heads: 558
Dog's eyes to human: 10.
Eyes: 1602.
Forming body combinations: 582, 1089 (fake).
General, with organ banks: 231 (implied), 579, 723 (implied).
Heads: 858.
Heart: 8 (fake), 206.
Stomach: 7, 12.

Organic matter, magnet for. 259.

Organic picture screens on bodies.
467, 881, 1048, 1278, 1373.

Orient, war with U.S. (*See also* China.) 297, 334, 449, 517, 693, 694, 715, 1072, 1073, 1263, 1318.

Oriental villains, Fu-Manchu type.
2, 159, 522, 572, 866, 1275, 1570, 1604.

Ornithophobia. 618.

Orth, John. Disappearance due to Atlanteans. 1652.

Osmium precipitates colloidal gold. 864.

Other intelligent beings than mankind on Earth. (*This category does not include invaders, visitors, or occupying forces.*)
Ants: 887, 888, 1200, 1520, 1546, 1712.
Barnacles: 888.
Bats: 342.
Bees: 887, 888.
Beetles: 1221, 1562.
Centipedes: 1182.
Crabs: 1739.
Crystal beings: 1732.
Cyborg insects: 1733.
Density people: 705, 708, 808, 1387.
Dinosaurs: 281.
Fire people: 940, 1251.
Fish: 467.
Fish-men: 956.
Flying jellyfish: 1799.
Giant brains: 1562.
Goat-men: 200.
Humanoids, some of which are side branches of Homo sapiens: 18, 33, 332, 712, 747, 750, 801, 1129, 1196, 1584, 1601, 1624, 1754.
Inner world flesh monsters (shmoos): 548.
Intelligent bacteria: 413.

Invisible creatures: 1367 (from Bodia), 1807.
Light beings: 384, 997.
Lovecraftian beings: 905, 906.
Machine-men: 939.
Mole-men: 332, 975, 1624.
Octopi: 499, 1104, 1346.
Plant-men: 1412.
Reptile people: 998, 999, 1495, 1754.
Sea people: 313, 370, 394, 518, 956, 1696, 1796, 1797.
Seal-men: 1771, 1772.
Shrimp: 1537.
Silicon beings: 151, 1014, 1732.
Spiders: 468, 952, 1785.
Stone men: 1199.
Termites: 746, 826.
Turtle-men: 717.
Various exotics inside hollow Earth: 1562.

Other planets. (*This category contains hypothetical planets probably not in our solar system, but not precisely located elsewhere. For a related category, see* Intrusive planets.)

Other planets, ambience.
Annular world, but Earth-like: 1597.
Barren, with metal-eaters: 682, 1777.
Enormous, damp, thick air, non-Euclidean: 190.
Generally hot: 1.
Hollow world: 677, 679, 1268, 1278.
Like Earth: 52, 71, 109, 146, 147, 185, 189, 200, 238, 288, 316, 409, 410, 450 (originally?), 534, 575 (barren), 675, 676, 680 (?), 681 (?), 869, 907, 1029, 1237, 1284, 1299, 1359, 1372, 1374 (vegetation controlled), 1376-1378 (chemical milieu into copper), 1382, 1395, 1397 (?), 1418 (tropical), 1478, 1597, 1625, 1786, 1787, 1789, 1791, 1794, 1795.
Totally frozen: 189.
Utterly alien with odd colors, dimensions, but perceived as Earth-like: 1026, 1372, 1373.
Water covered, or almost: 677, 1377, 1378, 1792.

Other planets, cultural level.
Primitive: 71, 238 (?), 677, 1237.
Barbaric: 1026 (?), 1374, 1382.
Our level, more or less: 109, 190, 316, 575, 869, 1201, 1278, 1290, 1380, 1439, 1597, 1786-1795.
Superior: 1, 52, 146, 147, 185, 189, 190, 200, 288, 362, 410, 450, 523, 575, 639, 691, 1201, 1284, 1299, 1359, 1363, 1372, 1373, 1376-1378, 1380, 1397, 1478, 1614, 1625, 1681.

Other planets, hostile relations.
185 (with Terrestrial hidden culture), 190, 200, 891, 1380, 1463, 1464, 1614, 1681, 1786, 1794.

Other planets, inhabitants.
Ape-men: 238.
Cone-headed, amphibious, multiple eyes and legs, tentacles: 1380.

Cyborgs: 680.
Disk beings with tentacles: 1284.
Electric beings, mind parasites: 1614.
Evolved dogs: 190.
Evolved lizards: 190.
Fantastically strong midgets, with dimensional aspects: 190.
Frog-men: 677, 1237.
Globular beings that live on earth gases: 1789.
Goat-men: 200.
Gorilline heads, small bodies: 677.
Human: 52 (reduced to tiny size), 71, 109, 146, 147, 185 (Mongoloid), 200 (Lemurians), 284, 316, 450, 453, 639, 691, 869, 1043, 1284, 1290, 1299, 1301, 1359, 1374, 1376-1378 (green-skinned), 1379, 1380, 1382, 1397 (?), 1478 (our ancestors), 1597 (but mechanized), 1622, 1625 (our ancestors), 1788, 1791, 1794.
Humanoid: 189, 190, 200, 238, 406, 523 (little men), 677, 679, 869 (pig-snake-men), 1201, 1237, 1356, 1366, 1372, 1377-1378 (water adaptation), 1380, 1395, 1786 (reptilian), 1788 (giants), 1794.
Humans, legs atrophied, move on go-carts: 1597.
Immaterial semi-intelligent beings from other dimension: 675, 676.
Insect-like: 1.
Intelligent aerial jelly fish: 362.
Intelligent giant spiders: 288, 1795.
Intelligent will-controlling giant amoeboid: 1418.
Jelly, dome-like, tentacles, organic image screen on body: 1278.
Nonintelligent, electric metal eaters: 682, 1777, 1793.
Planetary tree: 1787.
Slab-like, feelers on top: 1373.
Slug-like creatures: 1681.
Snake-like creatures with multiple sexes: 1026.
Stick men: 869.
Superbrains: 1397.
Thought beings: 410.
Tripeds: 676.
Vaselike, four legs, six tentacles: 680.
Winged humans: 238, 1395.

Other planets, invade Earth.
190, 891, 1380, 1463, 1464, 1614, 1681.

Other planets, miscellaneous.
Beautiful, erotic women are vampiric: 869.
Clash between reason and emotion destroys idyllic ancestral world: 1478.
Cultures totally destroyed in forever war: 1029.
Earth people came from other planet in galactic seeding: 1625.
Eutopian ambience: 146, 147, 238, 1478.
Experiences of a woman colonist from other planet: 1299.

Prehistoric man. (*See* Cro-Magnon man, Neanderthal man, Paleolithic man, Piltdown man.

Prehuman civilizations on Earth.
151, 281, 384, 407, 468, 548, 549, 571, 905, 906, 949, 952, 997, 998, 999, 1732, 1733, 1735, 1754.

President of the United States.
154, 209, 237 (a scoundrel), 251 (a usurper under mind control), 383, 396 (assassination attempt), 437 (assassinated), 438, 623, 727b, 747, 834, 917, 969, 970, 974, 1114, 1128, 1224 (kidnapped and used as a footstool by the Invisible Emperor), 1243, 1259, 1305, 1384, 1516, 1569, 1577, 1592 (a figurehead for giant trusts), 1670, 1722 (thought controlled), 1731 (threatened).

Prey summoned telepathically. 323.

Prize fighters age in the ring. 180.

Procyon, planet of.
Home of invisible monsters, brought back in first Earth ship to visit: 602. Silicon life, far superior to us, visits Earth: 1255. Visit to, where Earth-like, with humaniform cyborgs of superior culture: 1597.

Profanation.
Islam: 368.   Martian religion: 162, 1544.

Profiles, personality for crime detection. 1544.

Programmed learning. 1726.

Prohibition era. (*See also* Bootleggers, Gangsters.) 1331, 1604.

Projections. 276, 334, 834, 1128, 1377, 1378, 1426, 1489, 1569.

Propaganda machines. 1704.

Prophecies fulfilled.
172, 310, 337, 421, 799, 1305, 1509, 1514, 1516, 1548, 1561, 1600. Not fulfilled: 597, 654.

Protection, odd. Venusians thump enemies of their representative on Earth: 1390.

Protons.
Atomic worlds: 385, 1154.
Matter composed of: 190.
Power source: 326.
Proton clouds in space as weapons: 284.
Weapons: 195, 892, 1755, 1758. ******

Protozoan diseases wiped out. 413.

Proxima Centauri, planet of.
Visit to area only: 620. Visit to; inhabitants are vicious plant men with superior science who capture spaceship, but planet is destroyed: 853.

Psychic affinities accompany physical resemblance. 1234.

Psychic battles. (*See* Mind battles.)

Psychic bonds.
Between brain transplant partners: 1578. Between individuals divided into two persons by isotopes: 1266.

Psychic emanations from humanity on Earth are harmful. 153, 362.

Psychic energy to feed insects. 442.

Psychic evolution. 441.

Psychic experiences of other planet. 261.

Psychic research. 1703.

Psychosomatic medicine. 889.

Pterodactyls and similar reptiles.
Early, though often anachronistic: 208, 689, 1342, 1344.
Surviving: 207, 1345, 1548, 1578.

Pugnaciousness caused by gas. 419.

Pulverizing ray. 1587.

Punishments, somewhat unusual, often sadistic. (*See also* Penal colonies, Revenges.)
Asphyxiate with natural gas: 717. Brain treatments of various horrible sorts: 108, 235, 243, 900, 970, 1436. Capture and vivisection by dominant machines: 115. Compel to wander universe or dimensions eternally: 1272, 1599. Disembody and put body into suspended animation: 146, 252. Exile: 64, 75, 563, 771, 847, 903. Feed to earth-flame: 1794. For erring aircrew members: toss overboard: 1185. For pirate who operates to obtain thrills, permission to steal: 1212. Gamut of tortures: 673. Lashings: 531. Put into space coffin in chains and let starve: 501. Scatter through space with matter transmitter: 1148. Send to the radium mines: 56, 1071. Shoot off into space in rocket: 474. Sterilization: 874. Traditional electric chair: 632.

Puppet-masters. (*A term taken from Robert A. Heinlein's later novel,* The Puppet Masters, *describing an alien form of life that fastens upon a human physically and controls its carrier by invading its nervous system.*)
1043, 1614, 1683.

Puritanism, future. 1348, 1349, 1720.

Puzzle stories. 946, 961, 1742.

Pygmalion, euhemerized. 163.

Pygmies, South American. 470.

Pyramids. 323, 342, 1630.

Pyrenees Mountains. 946.

Pyrophobia. 697, 699.

Quantum control for space travel. 58.

Quests for knowledge, odd. Fish scholar captures man and interrogates: 467.

Rabbits. Synthetic: 231. Attack people: 241.

Rabies cured by nutrition. 861.

Races.
Air: 3, 19, 231, 1334, 1536, 1763.
Automobile: 435, 579, 688, 910, 1399, 1536.
Miscellaneous: 927.
Space: 641, 1312, 1351.
Track: 691, 967.

Racial types "improved" by blood transfusions. 915.

Racism, general and odd. (*See also various* Anti- *categories.*)
General: 498.
Lunarians and Terrestrials: 1215, 1216.
Martians and Terrestrials: 623, 783.

Radar anticipations.
141, 488, 681, 963, 1233, 1265.

Radiation. (*See* Rays.)

Radiation sickness. (*See also* Space sickness.)
110, 172, 218, 245, 273, 306, 335, 897, 969, 973, 1204, 1304, 1387, 1388, 1409, 1448, 1460, 1477, 1479, 1595, 1746.

Radio-controlled planes.
742, 1070, 1349, 1780.

Radio, miscellaneous aspects. (*See also* Matter transmission, Wireless transmission of power.*)
Activates human nerves in zombie: 1121. Canceled by Conquerors: 747. Causes end of time sense: 1718. Causes time travel to future: 70. Clever prisoner uses torture device as radio to summon help: 505. Communi-cation with dead: 803.   Controls insect migration: 292. Destroys errant rocketship: 166. Destroys very dangerous sea life: 22. Detonates explosives in rationalization of Greek myth: 1721. Disperses poison gas: 1624. Paralyzes: 624. Permits dream control, will-control, visions: 1604.   Permits time communication: 434. Produced naturally by enormous crystals inside Earth: 332.   Radio towers 125 miles high: 1208. Sets off or controls atomic fire: 1747. Surface radio disrupts underground civilization: 1129.   Tomb equipped for perpetual broadcast: 176. Transmits hypnotic wave: 211. Transmutes metals: 966. Used for arson: 996. Waves disrupt Skyland: 402, 708.

Radio, super.
70, 194, 298, 402, 489, 1115, 1284, 1390, 1556, 1616, 1767.

Radioactive life.
450, 453, 899, 1184, 1204, 1584, 1752.

Radioactivity, miscellaneous.
Energy source in suspended animation: 329. Causes devolution: 571. Causes hypertrophy: 306.

Radium.
As power, weapons: 101, 674, 734, 776, 778, 924, 925, 1064, 1480, 1576, 1597, 1624, 1735.
Deposits of significance, non-Terrestrial. Moon: 297, 455, 582. Mars: 1011, 1325. Venus: 1035, 1597. Procyon: 1597. Asteroid: 1409. Neptune: 697, 699.
Deposits of significance, Terrestrial: 120, 386, 500, 581, 697, 785 (atomic), 917, 973, 1180, 1196, 1274, 1387, 1521, 1537, 1624, 1732, 1735.
Medical aspects: 613, 776, 778, 779, 1180, 1274, 1497.
Miscellaneous: Fake radium scam: 968. Labor problems in the Venusian radium mines: 1035. Radium poured into water to rescue sunken air rocket: 515. Radon awakens ancestral memory: 736. Radon causes plague and epidemic: 273. Transmutes metals: 979.
Radium cultures: 56, 813, 1196, 1442,

Radium, cultures (*continued*)
1446, 1537, 1624.
Radium mines as penal colonies: 56,
646, 987, 1196, 1624.
Radium moguls: 6l, 931.
Theft of radium: 204, 1801.
Rain. Ceases when dust removed from air:
401, 1647. Discontinued: 1647. Rains
of frogs and fishes explained: 1554.
Rain making: 1355. Red rain in di-
mensional world: 1740.
Ralphisms. (*Fiction in the mode of Hugo
Gernsback's "Ralph 124 C41+", based
on very detailed gimcrack technology of
the most extreme sort, though sometimes prophetic.*)
140, 489, 579, 613, 693, 694, 1090,
1348-1350, 1403, 1499.
Randomness ambiences. 527, 1370, 1669.
Rappaccini's daughter motif. 684, 1752.
Rat-men. 328, 1679.
Rathole man. 1483, 1484.
Rats. Immortal: 1306. Modern pied piper
summons them: 761. A metaphor for
gangsters, too: 761.
Rays, miscellaneous. (*Most useful axiom-
motifs, or stock techniques for doing
things, metaphors for action that does
not need to be explained or that the
author does not or cannot explain. For
major types of rays see* Antigravity
rays; Death rays; Disintegrator rays;
Evolution, techniques for controlling;
Force rays; Growth and maturation;
Heat rays; Intelligence enhanced;
Invisibility, radiation phenomena; Pain
rays; Paralysis rays; Personality
changing; Personality transfer; Re-
juvenation; Size changes; Suspended
animation; Tractor rays, *etc.*)
Accelerate growth in living things:
1401.
Activate colloids: 1573.
Animal liberation: 217.
Anti-cohesion: 1583.
Cancel chemical action: 461, 474.
Cancel electricity: 822, 1574.
Cathode projectors: 191, 192.
Cause artificial aging: 683, 684, 1605.
Cause disease: 627, 628.
Cause gigantism: 988.
Cause itch: 869.
Cause madness: 909, 969.
Cause sleep: 1445.
Cause sterility: 1237.
Change behavior patterns to opposites:
241.
Conduct gravity: 955.
Control minds: 1343.
Create invisibility: 486.
Create life: 427, 1477.
Create vacuum channel for telescope:
1766.
Cure baldness: 1317.
Cure mental disorders: 545.
Cut stone: 1556.
Decay: 951, 1153.
Destroy antigravity: 1595.
Disable: 20.

Dissolve bones: 690.
Enhance sensations: 1674.
Erase memory: 916.
Germicidal, also disintegration: 40.
Germicidal: 488.
Heal: 811.
Hypnotic: 138. 960, 1343.
Induce telepathy: 215, 217.
Inhibit atomic energy: 192, 193.
Invert gravity: 159.
Liberate psyche: 146, 147.
Magnetic: 1189, 1522.
Molecular motion: 188, 189.
Nourish: 1367.
Permit experience of insect life: 827.
Permit time travel: 1566.
Produce cold: 1480.
Produce comas: 1678.
Produce idiocy: 572, 1388.
Psychometric, awaken personality
residues: 633.
Reintegrate: 572, 608, 705, 902.
Remove evil component: 1123.
Spy: 217.
Strip away the third dimension from
objects: 224.
Super X-ray, permits matter trans-
mission: 1231.
Time stasis: 75.
Time-viewing: 792.
Transmit solar power: 489.
Transmit taste: 13.
"Vacuum" ray: 549.
Wash dishes: 1385.
Rays, miscellaneous military. 44, 45, 98,
169, 196, 202, 328, 348, 389, 543, 558,
623, 734, 777, 799, 813, 819-823, 893,
909, 924, 991, 1004, 1006, 1010, 1231,
1284, 1362, 1376-1380, 1445, 1574,
1582, 1591, 1594, 1598, 1605, 1733,
1746.
Reality breaks down.
178, 282, 1258, 1386, 1645.
Rebuilding civilization. (*See also* Future
primitivism, Neo-primitivism, Post-cat-
astrophe.)
79, 148 (?), 317, 367, 433, 540, 612
(minimal), 763, 815, 874, 916, 952,
1167, 1236, 1264, 1266, 1305, 1407,
1463, 1464, 1471, 1516, 1557, 1630.
Recapitulating previous universes.
567, 1756.
Reclaiming the Arctic.
240, 278, 1066, 1535.
Recurrent patterns in fate.
364, 600, 1342, 1344, 1756.
**Recycled soldier kills daydreaming in-
ventor.** 726.
**Red rain and purple crystals in dimen-
sional world.** 1740.
Red sand covers much of Earth. 1003.
Reelfoot Lake area. 747.
Reflectivity, total; property of ore. 819.
Regimentation, a few statements against.
(*See also* Dictators, Eugenics and
mating bureaus, Thought control.)
122, 367, 431, 474, 725, 1592.
Reincarnation.
24, 213, 364, 387, 445, 633, 1028,

1342, 1344, 1478, 1640.
Rejuvenation, methods. (*See also* Immor-
tality.)
Cell replacement: 937, 938.
Chemicals: 861, 885, 1151, 1743.
Factor in water: 180.
Gland transplants: 1496.
Life force: 1575.
Matter transmission and reconstitution:
902.
New element and radio: 1542.
Radiation: 245, 613, 1122, 1125, 1180,
1610.
Relativistic concerns.
71, 106, 110, 112, 121, 132, 189, 190,
202, 284, 363, 947, 1150, 1268, 1276,
1277, 1419, 1505, 1680, 1762.
Relativistic concerns, miscellaneous.
Compensation for Lorentz-Fitzgerald
contraction: 284. Curvature of space
will cause disintegrating ray to return:
583. Dimensional matters: 106, 112,
121. Evasion of limitation of speed of
light: 189, 190. Flight by manipulating
space-time: 1754, 1755. Hyperspace:
363. Relativity of motion to what?:
1505. Worm holes in time: 1276,
1277.
Relativistic concerns, time problems.
71, 110, 132, 1738, 1762, 1822.
Religion as a guise for power.
117, 442, 522, 1548, 1754.
Religions, case history of the birth of one.
1686.
Religious elements. (*See also* Future,
religion; Human sacrifice; Lost races.)
54, 172, 300, 302, 441, 705, 717, 773,
900, 1192.
Fanatics: 117, 162, 597, 669, 704, 719,
989, 993, 1247, 1325, 1388, 1606,
1753.
Remote control. Trip to the Moon: 1289.
Dirigible raids, remote control other
than radio: 1552. Diverted air raid:
742.
Repellent metal, against Earth. 1524.
Reptile-men.
36, 109 (?), 475, 558, 955, 1190, 1277,
1361, 1377, 1378, 1495, 1564, 1678,
1754, 1786.
Reptiles.
Poisonous, surviving in suspended animation: 59. With hypnotic powers:
1227. Superintelligent: 281, 998, 999,
1754.
Reptiles, extraterrestrial.
Atomic world: 1154. Mars: 700.
Mercury: 1160. Moon: 326. Parallel
world: 109. Second moon: 323.
Space: 316. Trans-Plutonian planet:
1227. Venus: 245, 802, 944, 955,
1194, 1611.
Repulsion as a natural force. (*See also*
Antigravity.)
332, 333, 365, 786, 1278, 1554.
Repulsion rays. (*See* Force rays.)
Rescue in space.
177, 186, 299, 322, 390, 391, 444, 488,
552, 580, 641, 674, 686, 687, 781, 823,

Reverse gravity caused by ball lightning. 365.

Reverse universe, physical properties. 1278.

Revolt of the animals. 217, 235, 592, 1692.

Revolt of the machines. 115, 125, 183, 302, 434, 469, 622, 1207, 1281, 1607, 1640.

Revolt of the scientists. 81, 858, 1242-1244, 1377, 1592, 1610, 1651.

Rhenium, a healing element. 1600.

Rhinoceroses, archaic. 719.

Richthofen, Baron von. Plane in a space sargasso. 832.

Rigel, planet of.
Ambience. Earth-like: 284, 1157. Chlorine atmosphere, miserable: 1762.
Cultural level. Our level: 284. Superior: 1157, 1677.
Inhabitants. Human: 284. Humanoid small elephantlike beings: 1157. Nasty silicon life: 1762. Humanoid living-metal beings: 1677.
Invasions from Rigel: 1157, 1677
Visit to Rigel: 284, 1762.

Rio de Janeiro.
Destroyed: 408, 1624.

Riots caused by emotion control machine. 103.

Roadways, elevated. 489.

Robberies. 14, 121, 126, 138, 144, 229, 419, 658, 671, 845, 852, 917, 966, 967, 971, 979, 1037, 1082, 1090, 1106, 1107, 1181, 1197, 1209, 1295, 1330, 1382, 1392, 1405, 1420, 1427, 1458, 1486, 1506, 1603, 1668, 1700, 1779, 1783, 1801.

Robin Hood figures. (*See also* Glamorized outlaws.) 1253, 1263.

Robot airplanes. (*See also* Drone airplanes.) 64, 1070, 1349.

Robot guns. 1156.

Robots. (*See also* Machine intelligence, Revolt of Machines.)
(*The category* Robot *has been limited to mechanical devices that are either programmed [though this concept was not strong during this period] for certain actions or are operated by controllers. A dividing line between such artifacts and independent machine intelligence is sometimes arguable. Robots are often humaniform, depending upon task, but not necessarily so.*)
Actors: 613.
Domestic help: 97, 738, 748, 1090.
Exploration devices: 85, 469, 1289.
Football players: 740.
General workers: 64, 115, 570, 781, 1001, 1090, 1207, 1403, 1480, 1521, 1607, 1610.
Military: 98, 302, 624, 718, 1585.
Miscellaneous: 439.
Police: 1308.

Spaceship stewards: 118.
Used to commit crimes: 64.

Robots, cultures based strongly on. 115, 425, 613, 1207, 1262, 1521, 1607.

Roc-like bird. 1611.

Rock beings. 375 (?), 657,

Rock prints. Footprints burned into rocks. 369.

Rocket airplanes and other terrestrial heavier-than-air craft. 60, 86, 186, 579, 616, 618, 670, 724, 787, 807, 849, 1179, 1183, 1185, 1189, 1203, 1230, 1322, 1370, 1497, 1508, 1569, 1583, 1656, 1720, 1733, 1817.

Rocket spaceships. (*See* Space travel, rocket.)

Rockets, miscellaneous uses.
Attack weapons with atomic heads: 187. Control planetary rotation: 1408. Earth-borer: 500. Effect retardation in falls: 204. General military use: 1072, 1073. Intercontinental missiles: 866. Mail delivery: 1309. Maintain space platform in position: 629. Planet-moving: 170. Propel dirigibles: 478. Rocket-powered shoes: 61, 170. Rocket-propelled automobiles: 688, 1436. Satellite rockets for mail sorting: 1309. Unmanned freight rockets: 868.

Rocky Mountains. 90, 849, 1073, 1120, 1122-1124, 1185, 1305, 1325.

Roller skates, mechanized. 244, 488.

Romance conducted by projection. 276.

Rome, ancient.
Ancient Roman maintains space station: 6. Ancient Roman revived into modern world: 341. Imperial Rome, gladiatorial contests: 503. Roman soldiers fight Carthaginians in space mirage: 507. Roman-Norse conflict viewed: 792. Romans conquered North America in alternate world: 851. Visit to ancient Rome: 1028.

Roosters. Metabolic extragances: 1401, 1575.

Rotating matter at speed of light causes permeability. 426.

Rumania. 444, 1232.

Russia. (*See* USSR.)

Saber-toothed tigers. 131, 689, 1014 (surviving).

Safe stolen into fourth dimension. 121.

Sahara Desert. 595, 882, 924, 925.

St. Helena. Exile for Russian leaders: 986.

St. Louis, Missouri. Everyone killed: 1497.

St. Paul, Minnesota. Supercity of future: 70.

St. Paul's cathedral, London. 1763.

Salt, as catalyst. 1376, 1377.

San Francisco. (*See also* California.)
Earthquake of 1906: 1478.
Destroyed: 149, 715, 903, 953, 1128, 1162, 1182, 1759.
Megalopolis in 2189: 1761.

Sandwich crawls around. 460.

Sanskrit. Spoken by lost race: 120. Language of Atlantis: 792. Ancient science written in Sanskrit: 1012.

Santa Lucia. 1651.

Sargasso of space. 149, 559, 832.

Sargasso Sea. 788, 1068, 1202.

Saturn, ambience.
Barren, but endurable in space suit: 469.
Earth-like: 659, 815, 829 (jungle), 912, 1397 (hot).

Saturn, cultural level.
Inferior: 659, 912.
Our level: 87, 284, 819, 829.
Superior: 247, 647, 815, 1454.

Saturn, hostilities with. 247, 647, 819, 829.

Saturn, inhabitants.
Gaseous humanoids: 247.
Giant insects: 912.
Green lizard-like beings: 819, 829.
Human: 87 (colonists), 284, 659, 815, 912.
Humanoid giants, black, four arms: 1454.
Machine beings: 647.
Once human, now giant brains and removed to satellites: 1594.

Saturn, miscellaneous.
Colonized by Terrestrial Blacks, who are then enslaved by Saturnians: 829. Destroyed in war, but back again in sequel: 819, 829. Dumped into the sun: 193, 953. Friendly Saturnian visitors massacred because their power beam is lethal to Terrestrials: 647. Natives originated in another system: 1454. Transformed into a small sun: 1631. Visiting Saturnians concerned to uplift mankind: 247.

Saturn, moons in general. (*See also* Dione, Iapetus, Tethys, Titan.)
Colonized by Earth: 1450. Unnamed moon is Earth-like, but dismal, with giant crabs: 501.

Saturn, rings.
Material used to cut off solar radiation from Earth: 819. Vibrations from rings bestialize life on moons: 1591. Action in: 1821.

Saturn, visits Earth. 247, 647.

Saturn, visits to. 87 (near), 469, 1428 (near).

Sausage created out of stone. 1385.

Scaly men. 33, 527, 558, 1272, 1445.

Scandinavia (?). 948.

Scent.
Odor prints for criminal identification: 787. Photographic recording and identification: 130. Scent amplifier: 417. Scent is a vibratory matter: 1127. Scents are ultraviolet and visible to birds: 709. Wireless transmission of scent: 1137.

Science and Invention **magazine cited in story.** 798.

Science unified. 1261.

Science and technology (Terrestrial) hampered by aliens. 442, 562, 929, 1153, 1311.

Seeds, miscellaneous.
Ancient seeds sprout: 586, 1550. Give longevity: 1557. Seeds shifted between worlds to increase fertility: 1372.

Seidlitz powder as propellant. 1032.

Selenium atoms change to arsenic, killing mad scientist. 1337.

Self-improvement fads. Cultivating fat and wrinkles: 256. Future cosmetic machine: 1350. Personality alterations: 248. Restoring head hair: 1317. Separating out personality configurations: 1266. Various fads in future: 1177.

Semantics as a topic. 112.

Semimaterial beings. (*See also* Cloud beings; Light beings; Matter, strange states.)
575, 675, 676, 906, 998, 1005, 1006, 1298, 1300, 1420, 1734, 1743.

Senescence and aging caused by heavy water. 180, 772, 1259.

Sensations of man approaching death in the sun. 177.

Sense organs, artificial. (*See also* Eyes, Vision.)
231, 607, 613, 935, 948.

Senses, hypertrophied.
484, 1708.

Senses, new. (*See also* Colors, miscellaneous; Paranormal abilities; Telepathy, X-ray vision.)
407, 564, 589, 1373.

Senses reversed. 865, 1060, 1502.

Sequels to work by other authors. (*See latch-ons.*)

Serial killers. 817, 915, 1086, 1087.

Serial numbers for individuals. 61, 57, 375, 400, 488, 563, 722, 765, 780, 1225, 1340, 1403, 1717.

Serpens, planet in.
Much like Earth, inhabitants dwarves and tentacle-faced giants: 1363.

Serpents, mythic aspects. 466.

Severed head denounces criminal. 1332.

Sex. (*See also* Eugenics and mating board, Future, marriage; Future, sexuality; Human sexuality; Marriage; Parthenogenesis.)

Sex changes. 321, 728, 811.

Sex, oddities. Male prostitutes for women: 1231. Multiple-sex systems: 1026. Original inhabitants of Bodia were totally male and totally female, whereas we as individuals have both male and female components: 405. Third sex (neuter) contains rulers, artists, scientists: 243. Three sexes: 582. Traumatic loss of sexuality: 38.

Sex roles reversed. 425, 1177, 1231. To some extent: 728, 738, 748.

Sexual dimorphism, extreme, in humans. 425, 998, 1231, 1589.

Sexuality, satires on. 243, 869.

Shadows, eat people. 1637.

Shanghai. Destroyed: 1128. Removed by aliens: 661.

Shantung Province. Destroyed: 1258.

Shape changers. 1813.

Sharing the experiences of others mentally. 696, 1023, 1234, 1658.

Shark-men. 1071.

Shenandoah, dirigible, cause of its destruction. 926.

Ships, super. 320.

Shipwreck. 259, 1138, 1196, 1537,

Shock therapy, accidental. 632.

Shoe shiner, automatic. 1329.

Shoes, rocket. 61, 170.

Short-lived people punished. 725.

Show biz. 481.

Shrimp-men. 1537.

Siberia. 976, 1174, 1191, 1209, 1358, 1603, 1642.

Sidewalks, moving. 339, 579, 1403, 1645.

Sign language universally understood. 426.

Silicon life.
72, 151, 236, 375, 465, 1008, 1014, 1255, 1258, 1476, 1662, 1663.
Accidental development from Easter egg dye: 1476. Grows out of seed from space: 1008. Silicon life wishes to become heterosexual: 151. Superbeing from Procyon: 1255.

Silkworms, gigantic. 751.

Silly inventions. (*See also* Humor.)
Automated apartment: 1329. Automated dining table: 1328. Automobile powered by Seidlitz powders: 1032. Device for ascertaining a woman's age: 416. Device for capturing static electricity from cats: 1031. Elaborate bank protection devices: 1330. Flying circular saw to cut up airplanes: 923. Machine that manufactures sausage from rock: 1385. Mechanical judge: 416. Perambulating house: 1331. Process for galvanizing corpses: 1033. Tomb that broadcasts hymns (later, jazz): 176. Whirling hat: 175.

Silver as atomic power source. 1238.

Sing Sing Prison. 697, 852, 1254.

Sirius, planets of.
Ambience: Earth-like: 577, 1270, 1288.
Cultural level:
Like us: 169, 1288.
Superior: 190, 192, 571, 577, 1270, 1498, 1609.
Inhabitants: Human: 169, 192 (in past), 1270 (colonists), 1609. Evolved insects: 577. Mechanical entities: 192. Spiders: 1288. Humanoid: 190, 1462. Thought being looking for a mate: 1498. Lizard-like: 1273. Jelly blobs: 571.
Invasions from Sirius: 169, 192, 1270, 1288.
Miscellaneous: Destroyed by atomic research in the macrocosm: 214. Invaders leave for Sirius: 188. Light, pouring through wormhole, affects solar system: 448. Mechanical brain that runs Earth came from Sirius: 1462. Primal amoeboids come to Earth from Sirius: 571. To collide with solar system in future: 573.
Visit from: 571, 577.

Visit to: 169, 532 (near), 577, 1268.

Sixth dimension.
Warps man's life lines so that he timeleaps: 314. A red dimension: 1186.

Size changes, mechanisms. (*See also* Microman, adventures of.)
By speed: 295, 1634, 1640.
Compressing atoms: 60, 606, 684, 990, 991, 1093, 1347, 1415, 1416 (?), 1547, 1551, 1631, 1745, 1770.
Drugs: 301, 590, 606, 1158, 1173.
Enlarging atoms: 708, 1093, 1711, 1712, 1756 (and time).
Matter transmitter: 1284 (?).
Rays: 52, 702, 1122, 1347, 1415, 1416, 1449, 1454, 1745, 1770.
Size machine: 857.
Supermicroscope: 1154.
Using a prism made of a meteoritic mineral: 1551.
Using cosmic rays: 1416.
Using Element 85: 377.
Via or to fourth dimension: 785, 1080, 1572.

Size changes, nature and type. (*See also* Atomic worlds; Macrocosm; Microman, adventures of.)
Larger: 295, 386, 430, 544, 569, 590, 708, 959, 1080, 1122, 1173, 1634, 1640, 1711, 1712, 1745, 1756.
Size-change ratios between planets: 1226.
Smaller: 52, 60, 301, 377, 430, 606, 684, 702, 785 (?), 857, 959, 990, 991, 1093, 1154, 1158, 1168, 1284 (?), 1347, 1415, 1416, 1449, 1454, 1547, 1551, 1572, 1631, 1745, 1770.
Splitting an individual into fragments of himself: 52, 702, 1639.

Skin color changed. 727, 1033, 1672.

Skyland. (*Various semimaterial layers above or spheres around the Earth. See also* Stratosphere.)
Ambience:
Like Earth, when adapted to: 333, 360, 402 (with mirages), 708.
Thin, unstable crust: 808, 868.
Semi-material: 1734.
Cultural level.
Inferior: 360, 868.
Like us: 708.
Superior: 333, 402, 551(?), 808, 1554 (?), 1734.
Inhabitants. Human: 333 (two types). Humanoid: 333, 402. Jelly cubes with tentacles and organic cutting torch: 868. Light-being and tall humanoids: 402. Octopoidal, semimaterial: 1734. Red, scrawny, with helium sacks and snowshoe feet: 808. Winged human: 360.
Miscellaneous: Complementary to Earth, in balance: 333. Earth radio disturbs and injures: 402. Land is destroyed by fire: 808. Force from area perhaps Skyland amounts to antigravity: 1554. Dredges from

Skyland, miscellaneous (*continued*)

sky scoop up humans, perhaps from Skyland, perhaps from space: 551.

Mode of reaching. Antigravity pull: 333. Matter diffuser and condensor: 360, 708. Spaceship, rocket ship: 402, 808, 1734.

Skyscrapers, oddities.

Becomes invisible: 775, 1539. Drops into the past: 837. Collapses because of resonance created by mad scientist: 1119. Made of miracle metal which suddenly changes state and disintegrates: 1260.

Slaves and slavery. (*It is often impossible to distinguish among true slavery, oppressed subject peoples, servitor groups, and captives of various sorts. The following examples, however, seem reasonably clear as slavery.*)

Slavery, location.

Atomic world: 991, 1572.

Callisto: 374.

Comet: 1754.

Earth: Ancient Mediterranean: 577. Antarctica: 1221. Future: 235, 287, 442, 684, 886-888, 890, 1281, 1362. Antebellum South: 915. Atlantis: 941, 1126, 1238, 1652, 1729. Mu: 165. Roman world of if: 851. Sea people: 1797. Giant brains: 890.

To invaders: Intrusive planet: 442, 720. Asteroid: 720. Rigel: 1157. Venus: 1408. Unlocated: 1463, 1471, 1683, 1748.

Underground: 332, 747, 801, 850, 1196, 1624, 1733.

Ganymede: 142.

Hollow Earth: 801, 1509, 1514.

Interplanetary cult: 684.

Jupiter: 954, 1450.

Mars: 162.

Mercury: 987, 1160.

Moon: 149, 356, 1290.

Other planet: 677, 1376.

Other universe: 1278.

Pluto: 1356.

Saturn: 815, 829.

Secondary Moon: 323, 464,

Space slavers: 36, 44, 639, 1103, 1356.

Venus: 245, 1568.

Slavery, miscellaneous.

Black slaves: 245, 829, 915, 1126. Whites enslaved by Blacks: 1215, 1216. Zombies: 373. White-slavery: 303, 855.

Slavery of humans to alien life forms.

To apes: 592. To asteroidal beings: 598. To birds of atomic world: 424. To insects: 422, 442, 886-888, 952, 1221. To mechanical intelligences: 302, 560. To reptiles in the past: 281. To Saturnians: 815. To transparent humanoids under Nicaragua: 801.

Sleep gas. 14, 186-190, 907, 970, 1191, 1541.

Sleep learning. 190, 231, 488, 524, 1114,

1403, 1413, 1625.

Sleep, miscellaneous.

Drug removes need for sleep: 145, 404. Sleep chemical put into water supply: 756. World put to sleep: 1678. Plutonians plan to conquer Earth by sleep: 1774.

Sleep rays. 1445, 1678.

Sleep regenerators. 1348, 1350.

The sleeper wakes. (*Awakening from suspended animation or similar process and experiencing a new world.*)

75, 84, 108, 235, 310, 329, 334, 339 (?), 341, 442, 485, 489, 511, 515, 531, 535, 604, 645, 652, 674, 907, 933-938, 1157, 1308, 1403, 1408, 1704, 1716, 1752, 1776, 1804.

Sleeping goddesses. 310, 1716.

Slingshot more useful than superscience. 849.

Slug-people. 35, 1568, 1681

Slugs, giant bathyal. 370.

Slum clearance, the tough way. 1115.

Smoke rings as weapons. 926.

Smuggling. 298, 528, 1203, 1248.

Snake-people. 999, 1026, 1759.

Snake venom in blood stream. 480.

Snakes.

Giant: 727, 731, 796, 1394. Extraterrestrial: 262, 1664, 1759. Intelligent: 1026, 1759. Snakes with legs: 262, 307, 771.

Snow. Unmeltable: 1510. Japanese attack on New York City with gigantic snowfall: 774.

Sobering up pills. 1348, 1349.

Social Darwinism, flagrant examples.

(*The concept is usually implicit in smaller ways in most interplanetary stories.*)

35, 184, 361, 718, 720, 943, 1157, 1271, 1288, 1697.

Social experiments. (*See also* Class struggle, Ideal societies.)

After defeat of gangsters and robber barons, set up technocratic government: 1244.

After space cloud puts humanity into suspended animation, decision to awaken only suitable persons: 1264.

Anti-mechanism cult sets up fake future robot-ruled culture to extract money from sucker: 560.

Compulsory eugenics: 666.

Create mutants by free-wheeling exposure of local inhabitants to radiation: 565.

Create subrace of perfect workers: 737.

Cultic society develops anthill civilization: 531.

Develop superhumans in a world in a box: 1122, 1256.

Exile malcontents, dissidents, nonconformists, perhaps to "freedom island," with hope that all will go hang themselves: 563, 903, 1563, 1720.

Feminist extremists attempt to take over

industry and society: 728.

In future, where blue collars reign, deport eggheads or make them work manually: 741.

In future, where strict eugenics and in vitro conception holds, return to natural childbirth: 735.

In the belief that past experience is responsible for present evils, remove memory from everyone: 916.

Increase general intelligence superscientifically: 1124.

Increase oxygen in atmosphere to stimulate lethargic Flemings: 1531.

Manufacture a race of supermen on desert island: 626.

Plan to breed a superrace on desert moonlet: 1494.

Raise the intelligence of apes and let them get out of control: 592.

Release a truth gas: 566.

Release serum of perfectibility and immortality: 770.

Remove evil component from mankind: 1123.

Set up a freedom isle that is really a death camp: 1283.

Set up altruistic culture on Venus: 1237.

Set up an old-fashioned farm in midtown Manhattan: 774.

Set up an old-fashioned farm on Mars: 1077.

Set up ruthless "benevolent" scientific dictatorship: 1249.

Set up stress society on desert island, with hope for sexual conflict: 732.

Set up the ultimate in agricultural automation in jungle: 578.

Set up ultimate rational science city: 579, 581.

Settle humans on Jupiter to develop muscle-bound subrace: 197.

Spread galactic man, hoping for valid local societies: 1625.

Transport dissident part of greatly reduced world population and set up new social institutions: 1512.

Turn animals into men: 1692.

Turn Blacks all white and seize control: 727a.

Visitor from Procyon releases willcontrol power to several humans: 1255.

Social-level cities. (*Cities with strict class divisions, with classes stratified into certain levels within the city. Specialized ghettos, restricted housing carried to a science-fictional extreme.*)

201, 772 (in a way), 780, 782, 1381, 1583, 1592, 1601, 1607, 1705.

Social protesters put into insane asylums. 1499.

Socialism, socialist cultures. (*See also* Future, economic systems other than capitalism.)

33, 54, 179, 234, 751, 1537.

Solar eclipse. 863.

Solar prominences as art forms. 340.

Spiders, culture (*continued*)
Like ours: 952.
Superior: 288, 464, 468, 547, 1599, 1785.
Spiders, habitat.
Terrestrial. Underground pocket: 468. Undersea air pocket: 1785. Antarctica: 1440. Preglacial Mexico: 952. South Africa: 1218.
Extra-terrestrial. Second moon: 322, 323, 464, 468. Other dimension: 547, 1599. Titan: 1357. Other planet: 288, 1288, 1795.
Spiders, miscellaneous.
Evolved in small secondary Moon, developing high civilization: 464. Exchange personalities across galaxy: 288. Irresponsible scientist breeds giant spiders for webs: 988. Lived in preglacial Mexico with Neanderthal slaves: 952. Plan to take over world: 468, 547, 1599. Terrestrial spiders descendants of slave insects from second Moon: 464.
Spider webs. Metaphoric for space travel: 288. Industrial use of superior forms: 988.
Spies and espionage.
233, 397, 562, 605, 610, 634, 777, 779, 836, 874, 928, 968, 1280, 1415, 1479, 1608, 1806, 1810.
Spiritualism. 1075.
Split personalities. 1372, 1554.
Sports. (*See also* Races.)
Baseball: 1088.
Boxing: 180, 1252.
Football: 740, 749, 1163.
Miscellaneous: Aristos whip women to death: 201. On other planet humans maimed and used as racing animals: 691.
Sports festivals: 579.
Track: 967.
Spy devices. Flying viewers: 471, 1073.
Squid tissue multiplies indefinitely. 139.
Squid-men. 562.
Squirrels used to operate computers. 707.
Standing still while the Earth revolves. 1334, 1784.
Standing still while the universe moves. 90, 810, 1492, 1625, 1784.
Star moving. 189, 284, 1478, 1758.
Stars disappear. 282.
Stars exploded. 938, 1290.
Stars, intrusive. (*See* Intrusive suns.)
Stars shift positions. 169, 284, 1258.
Stars with Elements 85 and 87. 750.
Stasis rays. 75, 196.
Statue of Liberty. Used as symbol for last men: 903. Disintegrated: 953.
Statues.
Giant statues used as habitations: 55, 1746.
People turned into statues: 61, 102, 201, 418, 611, 1157, 1496, 1732.
Statue brought to life: 919.
Statue object of fetishism: 919.
Statue signal for survival: 353.

Steam culture. 712.
Steam shovel controlled by elephant brain. 760.
Steamship taken back into past. 1725.
Steel, super. 350, 1349.
Stellar rays affect personality. 1618.
Stenographers, evolutionary specialization. 737.
Stereoscope, four-dimensional. 109.
Sterility, human.
Among Venusian supermen: 750.
Future man: 84, 749, 1362.
Planned for humans and other life: 1477.
Side-effect of perpetual youth or immortality: 351, 770, 999, 1125, 1713.
Stick-men. 869.
Stinginess has glandular basis. 12.
Stomach, transplanted. 7.
Stone creatures. (*See also* Silicon life.)
375, 657, 1199, 1438.
Stone-cutting ray used by Indians for architecture. 1556.
Stone face transmutes men to gold. 999.
Stone softeners used by Indians. 1548.
Storm control, dispersal.
1185, 1187.
Storms, artificial. (*See also* Weather control.)
34, 209, 666, 929, 1025, 1105, 1247, 1261, 1493, 1441, 1493, 1777.
Storms, hurricanes caused by actions of Skyland people. 708.
Stratosphere. (*See also* Skyland, *which is not always precisely located in the stratosphere or the Heaviside layer, but is a convenient classification.*)
Stratosphere, disappearances in.
3, 159, 554, 856, 868, 1106, 1579.
Stratosphere, monsters of.
322, 323, 1106, 1734.
Stratospheric atmosphere, mind enhancing. 1286.
Strength, super. Causation.
Chemical: 133, 336, 429, 1025 (new element).
Rearing on Jupiter: 195, 197, 200.
Radiation: 1809.
Stress situation, research in.
732.
Stromboli. 1528.
Stuck in space.
91, 166, 186, 444, 559, 580, 781, 856, 863, 985, 1055, 1179, 1235, 1286, 1376, 1434, 1492.
Stuck in the past. 1109, 1725.
Stuck in time. 693.
Stuck out of space-time. 1267.
Stun-guns. 1480.
Stupid persons to be exterminated by ray. 1115.
Subatomic power broadcast. 1379.
Subconscious mind; not human, but Martian extension. 411.
Submarine cities. (*See* Atlantis, Underwater cultures.)
Submarine tank. 135.

Submarines, miscellaneous.
World War I: 161, 515. Submarines on the Moon: 786. Torpoons, minisubs with small cannon: 1771, 1772.
Submarines, super.
154, 234, 428, 499, 518, 788, 984, 1188, 1195, 1202, 1213, 1280, 1602, 1771, 1772, 1797.
Submen. (*See also Pithecanthropus erectus.*)
352, 384, 389, 750, 857, 1014, 1160, 1342, 1394, 1514, 1528, 1545, 1546.
Submicroscopic life, intelligent. 1642.
Subterranean life forms. (*See* Underground.)
Subway trains disappear. 1567.
Subways constructed with disintegrating earth-borer. 539.
Suction cup feet. 1371.
Suez Canal wrecked. 666.
Suggestion causes death by disease. 388.
Suicide, miscellaneous.
Culturally demanded: 747, 1132, 1625.
Psychologically caused: 675.
Suicide missions in space: 456, 843, 1421, 1505, 1754.
Suicides.
24, 38, 67, 68, 87, 206, 277, 287, 300, 315, 321, 325, 346, 354, 380, 403, 411, 437, 456, 468, 486, 504, 511, 542, 564, 596, 607, 617, 630, 675, 701, 729, 735, 743, 747, 754, 757, 779, 803, 831, 843, 852, 853, 1086, 1093, 1109, 1111, 1121, 1132, 1151, 1230, 1233, 1277, 1332, 1369, 1388, 1421, 1505, 1541, 1556, 1625, 1671, 1688, 1691, 1710, 1713, 1714 (attempted), 1746, 1750, 1754, 1757, 1762, 1801.
Sulfur, metallic, principal metal used. 1537.
Sun, goes or will go nova.
56, 193, 575, 1155, 1167, 1340, 1408.
Sun, life in.
After-death life for humans and dogs: 816.
Flame beings with superscience; hostile to humans who live in planets still contained within the sun: 1757.
Immaterial solar beings, with supercivilization, during nova phase of sun colonize Earth: 1167.
Solar features are intelligent beings with a high civilization: 340.
Sun, losing heat and going out.
62, 84, 193, 285, 314, 389, 595, 674, 794, 892, 907, 937, 1323, 1426 (not really), 1431, 1469, 1689, 1710.
Sun, miscellaneous.
Destroyed by probe from the macrocosm: 214.
New solar radiation causes gigantism: 1452.
New sun created by Martians who destroyed old: 400.
Refueled by pushing in planets: 193.
Rotation changed and about to split: 553.
Solar radiation, usually screened by clouds, kills all Venusians: 1304.

Things go wrong (*continued*)
evolution ends with disappearance: 1635.

Optical experiment admits horrible beings from other dimension: 1637.

Painlessness turns out to be a curse: 1638.

Perceiving the utterly alien is fatal: 870.

Perfect paint turns out to be impenetrable barrier: 509.

Person in suspended animation is not awakened on schedule: 84, 235, 341, 442, 1306, 1704, 1716.

Personality transfer does not work out as planned: 1198.

Personality transfer to a praying mantis ends tragically: 827.

Plague escapes: 1497.

Production of atomic energy dissolves everything: 1644.

Production of fossil light leads to materialization: 1556.

Psychical research experiment permits demon to take over body: 1703.

Ray that induces opposite actions to normal sets free brood of monsters: 241.

Reconstitution accidentally mixes tiger with man: 336.

Recycled soldier kills absent-minded scientist: 726.

Reverse aging cannot be stopped: 885, 1542.

Rocket ship flames damage Earth: 166.

Ruthless scientist surreptiously creating mutations among natives accidentally injures his daughter: 565.

Scientist undergoing individual evolution ends up back at the bottom: 557.

Scientist, venturing on matter interpenetration, is exploded: 1210.

Seeds accidentally matter-transmitted from Moon sprout and overwhelm: 1588.

Seeds from meteorite sprout and almost take over world: 236.

Seemingly invigorating hormone really ages one: 1022.

Sound suppressor is too successful: 930.

Space dust seems an insoluble problem: 627, 628.

Stopping the Earth so that the universe can move along: 810.

Stranded in the fifth dimension: 842, 847.

Strange artifact transports experimenters to where? 1617.

Strange life-form turns vicious: 5.

Super X-ray vision is a nuisance: 1800.

Superadaptability, if imposed on the wrong person, is tragic: 664.

Supercomputer tries to change the universe: 1262.

Superman, created from low-grade man by radiation, regresses upon accidental further radiation: 1477.

Synthetic man is evil: 1192.

Teleportation to behind the scenes of reality is difficult to remedy: 833.

The atmosphere of Venus, seemingly a rejuvenator, is really a carcinogen: 245.

Therapeutic ray has bad side effect; entering sunshine results in disintegration: 40.

Time explorers are trapped in Atlantis: 1725.

Truth gas is not such a good idea as it seemed: 566.

Tulpa turns out to be evil and vicious: 378, 889.

Unstable artificial gold kills crook: 380.

Various silly inventions misbehave: 1328-1331.

Vegetable gene inserted into humans is disastrous: 980.

Venture into other-world causes problems: 152, 301, 657, 1090, 1099, 1186.

Weather control tube is accidentally turned on: 92.

World-in-a-box perishes while trying to surmount problems: 1745.

World-in-a-box plans to take over: 1122.

X-ray malfunction causes man to perceive in reverse: 1502.

Thinness, adaptation, to live in caves. 965.

Third dimension stripped away from object. 224.

Thirteen-month calendar. 857.

Thorium.
Used for atomic power: 1208. Used for death ray and antigravity: 1734.

Thoth, Egyptian god, based on visiting Martians. 1663.

Thought beings.
88, 247, 378, 400, 410, 441, 568, 1298, 1300, 1376-1378, 1496, 1498.

Thought control. (*See also* Brainwashing, Mind control.)
112, 117, 122, 201, 235, 256, 431, 442, 673, 893, 903, 1152, 1261, 1308, 1704.

Thought control of animals. 484, 707.

Thought control of matter. (*See also* Teleportation.)
Weapons: 155. General: 190, 287, 571, 1285. Flying machine: 802. Teleportation to world behind reality: 833. Various apparatus: 900.

Thought creates matter. 378, 389, 1027, 1376-1378, 1446.

Thought helmets.
88, 190, 216, 233, 275, 383, 412, 606, 623, 639, 645, 696, 781, 788, 809, 827, 941, 948, 1002, 1021, 1046, 1157, 1186, 1231, 1261, 1376-1378, 1436, 1447, 1523, 1602, 1634, 1640, 1656, 1658, 1678, 1710, 1746, 1779, 1786-1798.

Thought miscellaneous.
Dirty, violent, emotional human thought vibrations save mankind from invaders: 153. Thought is a vibration in one dimension: 1220. Thought is mathematics: 409, 410. Thought is transformed to physical sensation: 889. Thought projects transmitted by aliens advance Earth civilization: 411, 473, 1439. Thought vibrations trap writer: 46.

Thought music. 1208, 1498.

Thought projectors, screens, mostly.
42, 190, 382, 400, 405, 424, 448, 548, 584, 708, 1657.

Thought protection helmets.
400, 648, 676, 1277.

Thought reading, nontelepathic explanations.
Dog's eye transplanted into a human: 10. Muscle reading: 108. Hearing subliminal movements of the vocal cords: 429.

Thought recorders, mechanical.
1523, 1568, 1576.

Thought transmission and reading, mechanical.
56, 61, 88, 190, 214-217, 233, 275, 328, 382, 383, 412, 448, 463, 488, 518, 581, 606, 623, 639, 645, 696, 781, 788, 802, 809, 827, 832, 902, 941, 948, 975, 1002, 1003, 1021, 1023, 1046, 1064, 1076, 1150, 1157, 1240, 1231, 1275, 1298, 1300, 1376-1378, 1436, 1437, 1523, 1580, 1582, 1583, 1597, 1602, 1634, 1640, 1678, 1710, 1746, 1774, 1779, 1786-1797.

Thought, unit of. 1657.

Three-body problem solved. 1155.

Three-dimensional message for four-dimensional being. 106.

Three-legged beings. 260, 676, 939, 1774.

Throne, magnetically suspended. 924.

Thumps as communication. 31.

Thunder, abnormal, as a lure. 556.

Thyroid secretion.
Deficiency causes severe cretinism: 222, 867. Excess causes gigantism: 710. Deficiency used as a disguise for crime: 222.

Tibet. (*See also* Dalai lama.)
2, 122, 336, 502, 522, 572, 743, 799, 866, 932, 986, 1209, 1275, 1523. Tibetan medicine misused: 2. Tibetan is official language of the future: 932.

Tidal power.
81, 515.

Tigers. 217, 336, 1348.

Time as a storage or refuge place. 154, 358, 975, 1454, 1630.

Time assassins. 227.

Time capsule concept. 6, 84, 107, 310, 442, 706, 1407.

Time chases. 119, 302, 1368, 1632.

Time, communication through.
Mechanical: 422, 1248, 941, 946, 1743. Telepathy: 89 (plus radio), 434, 941 (plus equipment).

Time, differential rates.
Dimensional: 426, 657.
Jovian system, mechanical distortion: 335.
Macrocosm-microcosm, atomic worlds: 301, 386 (equalized), 785, 857,

Underground beings, nature (*continued*)

Human, but evolved somewhat differently: 33 (scaled, hairless), 275 (big heads and ears, from Australian aborigines), 332 (pointed heads, huge eyes), 747 and 750 (little men with huge heads, different internal organs), 1014 (cretinized Indians), 1199 (stony integument), 1441 (functional wings), 1564 (on Mars, reptilian characteristics), 1584 (squat, nasty, radioactive metabolism), 1602 (tall, thin, huge eyes), 1689 (Morlocks and Eloi).

Humanoid: 18 (gigantic, prehensile feet, blind), 243 (tall, thin, with organic headlights), 258, 428 (giant green men), 598 (winged, manually inept beings), 646 (skeleton men), 712 (giants), 801 (huge heads, transparent flesh) 812 (extinct, from Bodia), 921 (Lunar), 1129 (tiny), 1180 (from Jupiter), 1196 (transparent flesh, life-bonded with ruler), 1251 (fire imps), 1454 (small, four-armed, nasty), 1495 (reptilian or amphibian), 1528 (gigantic, dimly seen), 1541 (thirty-foot tall females, great sexual dimorphism), 1754 (Lemurian descendants, not quite human), 1805 (two-foot-tall dwarves), 1819 (dwarves composed of a different sort of matter).

Horse-like beings with group mind: 1494.

Intelligent bats: 342.

Intelligent giant beetles: 1221.

Intelligent giant centipedes: 1182.

Intelligent giant crabs: 1739.

Intelligent giant slugs: 1759.

Intelligent large insects: 1004, 1706, 1733 (cyborgs), 1818 (?).

Intelligent machine men: 560 (fake), 939.

Intelligent mollusks: 452, 1154 (in conflict with underground people).

Intelligent sharks: 394.

Intelligent spiders from crashed second moon: 468.

Invisible tentacled beings: 1807.

Light beings: 384, 997, 998.

Mole-men: 975.

Octopoids: 499 (intelligent), 1104 (semi-intelligent), 1346 (intelligent), 1568 (intelligent).

Plant-men on Moon: 457.

Rat-men on Venus: 328.

Semi-material monsters: 904, 1005, 1006.

Shoggoths: 905.

Silicon life: 72, 1014.

Superintelligent reptilians: 998, 1754.

Underground events elsewhere than Earth.

Atomic world: 1154.

Callisto: 1675.

Dimensional world: 424, 1005, 1006.

Mars: 263, 1003, 1040, 1285, 1371, 1564, 1759.

Mercury: 37 (colonial conquest of native mole-men), 84 (far future), 646, 1454, 1564.

Moon: 129, 452, 457, 690, 782, 921, 963 (science colony), 1004 (underground cities), 1290, 1301, 1472, 1706.

Other worlds: 598, 682, 1299, 1397.

Planetoid between Earth and Venus: 1494, 1568.

Pluto: 243, 1744.

Trans-Neptunian planet: 258.

Venus: 328.

Underground events, location, entrance, etc.

Africa: 151, 342, 924, 925, 1754.

Andes area: 1125, 1441, 1541.

Antarctica: 905, 1221, 1739.

Arctic: 207, 649, 712.

Atlantic Ocean: 1195, 1346, 1602, 1652.

Australia: 275, 905, 1733.

Brazil: 1624.

Caribbean: 1196.

Egypt: 17, 1126.

England: 1199, 1689.

Greece, Thessaly: 850.

Himalayas: 384.

Iceland, under Europe to Sicily: 1528.

Labrador: 442, 939.

Martinique, under Mount Pelee: 1196.

Mato Grosso: 306.

Micronesia: 998.

Nicaragua: 801.

Norway: 812.

Oak Island, Nova Scotia: 1805.

Off Newfoundland: 499.

Pacific Ocean or islands: 259, 468, 793 (Easter Island), 1584.

U.S.: Alaska: 649, 997. Arizona: 1752. California: 430, 725, 1180, 1182. Chicago area: 79, 560. Colorado: 1495. Denver area: 56. Florida: 1807. General U.S.: 1567, 1578. Hawaii: 1129. Idaho: 256. Indiana: 18. Long Island: 940. Mammoth Cave: 79, 965. Nevada: 332. New Jersey: 1157. New Mexico: 72. New York: 693, 1567, 1578, 1580. Off New York: 1195. Tennessee: 747, 750. The South-west: 975. Vermont: 513, 1014). Unlocated U.S.: 33, 1104, 1253, 1483, 1484, 1567, 1578, 1654, 1818, 1819.

Underground events, miscellaneous. (*See also* Social-level cities.)

Atlantean descendants: 428, 1005, 1006, 1126, 1346, 1580, 1652.

Captivity among the trogs: 1624.

Cave contains wonders of preglacial superior civilization: 433.

Cave world beneath Long Island with monsters, earth fires: 940.

Caverns or lost worlds with survivals: 207, 306, 513, 939, 965, 1195.

Devolved Indians telepathically con-

trolled by silicon amoeboid: 1014.

Dimensional invaders enter through California mines: 430.

Dinosaur-like creature inhabits cavern: 513, 965, 1195.

Earth-borer enters cavern with gigantic hungry amoeboid: 500.

Earth-borer enters oil caverns inhabited by octopoids: 1104.

Earth-borer strikes level filled with life force: 460.

Earthquake permits emergence of monster men: 18.

Exploring incredibly ancient ruined corridors still inhabited by horrible monstrosities: 905.

Fragment of Bodia, with magnetic attraction, in caverns in Norway: 812.

Future science city underground in Labrador: 442.

Gigantic cannibalistic females emerge and seize ship, per cover of *Amazing Stories*: 1541.

Glacial-period men took refuge underground and survived: 33.

Goat-men in other universe developed underground on Earth: 200.

Goddess Pele runs the show under Hawaii: 1129.

Hades euhemerized: 168, 850.

Hideout of would-be dictator: 695.

Immortal King Cheops runs the show: 1126.

Inhabited by almost two-dimensional invisible monster: 965.

Invading Rigelians have underground fortress chains in New Jersey: 1157.

Invisible monster so thin it is almost two-dimensional eats tourists in Mammoth Cave: 965.

Jupiter raids Earth's resources: 1180.

Life-force manifests itself in cavern: 460.

Lost race of immortal Incas: 1125.

Lost race of Phoenicians under Easter Island: 793.

Lost race of evolved Tartars: 649.

Machine civilization of future (fake), with human slaves, underground: 560.

Mad scientist, abducting subway train, maintains race improvement project in cavern world: 1567.

Meteor Crater, Arizona, contains sleeping Martian femme fatale: 1752.

Morlock-Eloi dichotomy in future: 1689.

Oak Island Treasure Pit leads to underworld with immortal men: 1805.

Olympian "gods" with superscience in underworld: 850.

Robin Hood outlaws frequent caves and underground hideouts: 1253, 1263.

Satire on contemporary politics, militarism: 256.

Satire on mores, economy, sexuality: 243.

Vibration enables matter transmission. 482, 558, 876, 1291.

Vibration enables size changing. 990, 991.

Vibration, miscellaneous.
Creates cosmic rhythm: 1609.
Creates pocket Earth: 569.
Destroys building: 1119.
Destroys robots that rule Earth: 1826.
Disintegrates gold: 1603.
Drives one mad: 1343.
Enables will control: 1220.
Gravity is vibration: 546, 931.
Indian drum's vibrations dissolve flesh: 1560.
Is secret of Pied Piper: 761.
Is wrecking Earth: 1358.
Odor is a matter of vibration: 1137.
Removes dust from atmosphere, with disastrous effects: 401.
Removes Earth's oxygen: 1343.
Shatters atoms, permitting mysterious murder: 962.
Vibration from future destroys present: 407.
Vibrations from Saturn's rings turn one bestial: 1591.

Vibration separates parallel worlds, the fourth dimension, etc.
55, 296, 382, 423, 428, 1005, 1164, 1798.

Vibratory changes enable time travel.
132, 302, 792 (time viewing), 900, 1248, 1252.

Vibratory weapons.
125, 159, 382, 401, 407, 449, 600, 1122, 1162, 1205, 1524, 1583, 1626.

Viewers. (*Devices for seeing things at a distance, amounting to live television without a transmitting camera.*)
6, 43, 52, 143, 144, 154, 158, 201, 215, 217, 400, 422, 423, 442, 466, 488, 573, 696, 703, 801, 929, 974, 989, 993, 1041, 1091, 1128, 1136, 1182, 1237, 1275, 1343, 1349, 1350, 1382, 1395, 1499, 1552, 1555, 1567, 1569, 1574, 1578, 1580, 1583, 1589, 1625, 1698, 1731.

Viking, surviving immortal. 1805.

Violins and violinists.
Aubrey plays the violin for a year to entertain fellow space travelers: 90. Bad violin playing causes death of intelligent bacterium: 349. Genuine Stradivarius used by Robin Hood outlaw to send signals: 1253. Superman violinist is assigned to destroy mankind with violin acoustics: 1122. Violinist concerned in organ regeneration: 608.

Virginia.
117, 747, 814, 834, 851, 1407.

Virtual reality machines. (*See also* Dream machines.)
42, 935, 948, 999, 1656, 1657, 1665, 1714.

Viruses, intelligent. 1273, 1820.

Vision, miscellaneous. (*See also* Colors, Eyes, X-ray vision.)
Artificial vision: 607. Blind man can see into fourth dimension: 1453. Deformation of eyeball causes viewer to see monsters: 818, 1145. Enhanced ultra-violet vision: 709. Experimenter, exposed to radiation, sees into other space: 1690.

Vitamins.
Intelligence and vigor vitamin: 49. Shortage threatens solar system: 212. New vitamin cures diseases: 861. Deficiency is cause of acromegaly, dwarfism, etc.: 1153.

Vitiligo, artificial. 1672.

Voice. Opera diva's voice mechanically enhanced: 140. Voice analysis for identification: 228. Voice-operated equipment: 1480.

Volcanoes.
Controlled: 1251, 1541.
Descent into volcanoes: 1129, 1251, 1528.
Eruption releases peril: 801.
Life forms: Imp-like beings in Vesuvius: 1251. Humanoid beings who plan world conquest from Hawaiian volcanoes: 1129.
Odd causations: Artificial diastrophism: 237. Density-layer people in their industries: 705. Earth-borer: 460. Explosion: 437. Mining of little underground people: 1129. Neutronium strikes Earth: 947. Radioactive elements in the Earth: 273. Weather control: 34.
Tosses atomic fire away from Earth: 1105.

Voodoo. 1485.

Vortices in space. 1494.

Vulcan. (*Imaginary planet between Mercury and the sun. See also* Infra-Mercurian planets.)
Artificial planet used to create our universe: 409, 410.
Exploited: 1422, 1448.
Hollow, a trap for space men: 1211.
Penal colony; heavy gravity because of neutronium core: 1595.
Somewhat Earth-like, hot, jungle-covered, highly radioactive, source of ore; primitive humanoid population: 1448.
Visits to Vulcan: 409, 410, 1211, 1448.

Wales. (*See also* Welsh.) 136.

Walking machines. (*Passenger-carrying machines with a mode of locomotion like that of a human walking.*)
79, 183, 936, 1501, 1629, 1697, 1733.

Wall Street raided. 917.

Warm polar lands.
Antarctic: 54, 358, 719, 1221, 1440, 1537, 1630 (in a way), 1739.
Arctic: 207, 712, 958, 1769.

Washington, D.C.
Action in: 14, 23, 122, 209, 237, 255, 396, 437, 482, 626, 705, 706, 716, 735, 742, 779, 834, 917, 965-979 (by implication), 982, 1048, 1224, 1253, 1255, 1343, 1455, 1565, 1592, 1722.
Destroyed or badly damaged: 198, 330, 874, 972, 974, 1064, 1189.

Washington Monument stolen. 23.

Washington's head from Mount Rushmore is future idol. 75.

Wasps. 1432, 1440.

Water burners. 353, 354, 1003.

Water, miscellaneous. Surface tension increased enormously: 1318. Transmutation to stone: 13. Turned into colloidal weapon: 1573. Under pressure, solution to murder mystery: 635. Water creators: 783. Water energy: 353, 354, 666.

Water repellant areas. (*I.e., underseas areas where water above is repelled, creating dry oases.*)
135, 350, 1735, 1785.

Water worlds. (*Worlds covered or almost totally covered with water.*)
328, 561, 562, 677, 802, 1377, 1378, 1445, 1446, 1524, 1568, 1594, 1597, 1792.

Waterspout lifts plane to stratosphere. 1286.

Weapons, oddities. (*See also* Planet moving.)
Computerized blowgun: 1611. Defensive shield of motionless atoms: 693-694. Destruction of faculty of foresight: 764. Explosive smoke rings: 926. Flying circular saw: 923. Focused sound: 1161. Insects: 235, 293, 487. Mass vertigo: 570. Neo-primitive, bows and arrows, spears, since advanced weapons have canceled each other out: 874. Programmed weapons: 431. Sleep-production: 756, 1774. Small suns: 1755. Steam-powered dart pistol: 1662, 1663. Time transfer: 1454. Weather control, fogs, snow: 209, 774. Yeast-men: 734.

Weasels, giant, threaten mankind. 625.

Weather control. (*See also* Cyclones, artificial; Snow; Storms, artificial; Storm control.)
34, 60, 92, 209, 358, 406, 488, 579, 666, 692, 774, 929, 1025, 1066, 1105, 1120, 1185, 1187, 1247, 1261, 1355, 1441, 1493.

Web of Fate. 1446.

Welsh, extinct dialect and ancestral memory. 767.

Werewolf, so-called. 1473.

West Indies, Anguilla. 347.

West Virginia, evacuated. 747.

Whales.
Used in construction work: 707. Early evolutionary stage with legs: 712. Skin inflated as a balloon: 714.

Whistling as communication. 45, 185.

White races slaves to Blacks in past. 1215, 1216.

Wind power. 1704.

Wine from past awakens emotion in a humdrum world. 107.

Title Index

The Other Side of the Moon. Hamilton, Edmond
Out around Rigel. Wilson, Robert H.
Out of the Dreadful Depths. Willard, C. D.
Out of the Sub-Universe. Starzl, R. F.
Out of the Void. Stone, Leslie F.
Out of Time's Abyss. Burroughs, Edgar Rice
Outcast in Space. Stangland, Arthur G.
Outcasts. Wernham, Guy
Outcasts from Mars. Stangland, Arthur G.
Outlaws of the Sun. Rousseau, Victor
Outlaws on Callisto. Wellman, Manly Wade
The Outpost on Ceres. Eshbach, Lloyd A.
The Outpost on the Moon. Maxwell, Joslyn
Pacifica. Schachner, Nat
Paladins of the Sky. Janus, Warwick
Paradise and Iron. Breuer, Miles J., M.D.
The Paradise of the Ice Wilderness. Regis, Jul.
Paradox. Cloukey, Charles
Paradox +. Cloukey, Charles
Parasite. Vincent, Harl
Parasite Planet. Weinbaum, Stanley G.
The Passing of Ku Sui. Gilmore, Anthony
The Passing Star. Nathanson, Isaac
The Path. Gallun, Raymond Z.
The Pea Vine Mystery. Hodges, A. L.
Peace Weapons. Gelula, Abner J.
The Peal of Death. [Anonymous]
The Pellucid Horror. Ruby, B. F.
The Pent House. Keller, David H., M.D.
The People of the Arrow. Miller, P. Schuyler
The People of the Pit. Merritt, A.
The People That Time Forgot. Burroughs, Edgar Rice
The Perambulating House. Simmons, Henry Hugh
The Perfect Planet. Breuer, Miles J., M.D.
The Perfect World. Herbert, Benson
Peril among the Drivers. Olsen, Bob
Phaeton. Burtt, J. Lewis
Phagocytes. Johnson, A. H.
Phalanxes of Atlans. Mason, F. V. W.
The Phantom Dictator. West, Wallace
Phantom Monsters. Kraus, Joseph H.
The Phantom of Galon. Ruff, J[ohn] W.
The Phantom of Terror. Repp, Ed Earl
Phantom Star. Haggard, J. Harvey
The Phantom Teleview. Olsen, Bob
Phantoms of Reality. Cummings, Ray
Photo Control. Brown, Bernard
The Phytic Empire. Walker, Derald S.
Pigments Is Pigments. Weisinger, Mort
The Pineal Stimulator. Stephens, I. M. and Pratt, Fletcher
Ping-Ting. Edholm, Charlton
Piracy Preferred. Campbell, John W., Jr.
The Pirate Planet. Diffin, Charles W.
Pirates of Space. Barry, B. X.

Pirates of the Gorm. Schachner, Nat
Pithecanthropus Island. Nathanson, Isaac
The Plague of the Living Dead. Verrill, A. Hyatt
The Plane Compass. Vincent, Harl
Plane People. West, Wallace
The Planet Entity. Johnston, E. M. and Smith, Clark Ashton
The Planet of Despair. Starzl, R. F.
The Planet of Doubt. Weinbaum, Stanley G.
The Planet of Dread. Starzl, R. F.
The Planet of the Double Sun. Jones, Neil R.
The Planet of Youth. Coblentz, Stanton A.
The Planetoid of Doom. Colladay, Morrison
The Planetoid of Peril. Ernst, Paul
The Planet's Air Master. Chappelow, Edward E.
The "Platinum Planets". Beattie, George B.
The Plattner Story. Wells, H. G.
The Plutonian Drug. Smith, Clark Ashton
The Point of View. Weinbaum, Stanley G.
The Poison Belt. Doyle, A. Conan
Poisoned Air. Meek, Capt. S. P.
Politics. Leinster, Murray
Pollock and the Porroh Man. Wells, H. G.
The Pool of Death. Olsen, Bob
The Pool of Life. Miller, P. Schuyler
The Port of Missing Planes. Meek, Capt. S. P.
Positive Inertia. Purcell, Arthur
The Posterity Fund. Lawrence, Raymond Emery
Power. Vincent, Harl
The Power and the Glory. Diffin, Charles W.
The Power Planet. Leinster, Murray
The Power Satellite. Starzl, R. F.
Pre-Vision. Pierce, John R.
The Prenatal Plagiarism. Weisinger, Mort
The Price of Peace. Weisinger, Mort
Priestess of the Flame. Wright, Sewell P.
Prima Donna, 1980. Brown, Bernard
The Prince of Liars. Hansen, L. Taylor
The Prince of Space. Williamson, Jack
The Princess of Arelli. Septama, Aladra
A Princess of Pallis. Kruse, Clifton B.
Prisms of Space. Leitfred, Robert H.
Prisoners on the Electron. Leitfred, Robert H.
A Problem in Communication. Breuer, Miles J., M.D.
Professor Diel's Ray. Brueckel, Frank J., Jr.
Prometheus. Burtt, J. Lewis
The Prophetic Voice. Manning, Laurence
Proteus Island Weinbaum, Stanley G.
Prowler of the Wastelands. Vincent, Harl
Proxima Centauri. Leinster, Murray
The Psycho Power Conquest. Winterbotham, R. R.

The Psychological Solution. Verrill, A. Hyatt
The Psychophonic Nurse. Keller, David H., M.D.
The Purchase of the North Pole. Verne, Jules
The Purple Brain. Wells, Hal K.
The Purple Death. Barnette, Jack
The Purple Monsters. Olsen, Bob
The Purple Plague. Hays, Russell
The Puzzle Duel. Breuer, Miles J., M.D.
Pygmalion. Burtt, J. Lewis
Pygmalion's Spectacles. Weinbaum, Stanley G.
The Pygmies of Phobos. Robin, Ralph
The Pygmy Planet. Williamson, Jack
A Race through Time. Wandrei, Donald
The Racketeer Ray. Leinster, Murray
The Radiant Shell. Ernst, Paul
The Radiation of the Chinese Vegetable. Gleason, C. Sterling
Radicalite. Murray, Richard Rush
The Radio Detective. Colby, Lincoln S.
The Radio Ghost. Kline, Otis A.
Radio Mates. Witwer, Benjamin
The Radio Mind-Ray. Coblentz, Stanton A.
The Radio Robbery. Meek, Capt. S. P.
The Radio Telescope. Coblentz, Stanton A.
The Radio Terror. Thebault, Eugene
The Radium Master. Vanny, Jim
The Radium Pool. Repp, Ed Earl
The Radium World. Kelly, Frank K.
The Raid of the Mercury. Johnson, A. H.
The Raid on the Termites. Ernst, Paul
Raiders from Space. Lower, Harold A.
Raiders Invisible. Hall, Desmond W.
Raiders of the Universes. Wandrei, Donald
Ralph 124C 41+. Gernsback, Hugo
The Rape of the Solar System. Stone, Leslie F.
The Rat Racket. Keller, David H., M.D.
Ray Control No. 1. Dallas, Everard
The Ray of Madness. Meek, Capt. S. P.
Rays and Man. Breuer, Miles J., M.D.
The Rays from the Asteroid. Parkinson, R. D.
Reaping the Whirlwind. Tooke, Alfred I.
The Rebel Robots. Rideaux, Charles
Rebellion. Stuart, Don A.
Rebellion--5000 A.D.! Bentley, Garth
Rebellion on Venus. Morris, Edward and Bertin, John
Rebels of the Moon. Wellman, Manly Wade and Jergovic, Max
Rebels of the Penal Planet. [Anonymous]
Rebirth. McClary, Thomas Calvert
Reclaimers of the Ice. Coblentz, Stanton A.
The Red Ace. Key, Eugene Key
Red April, 1965. Kelly, Frank K.
The Red Dimension. Repp, Ed Earl
The Red Dust. Leinster, Murray
Red Flame of Venus. Miller, P. Schuyler
The Red Hell of Jupiter. Ernst, Paul
Red Moon. Sterling, Kenneth

Author Index

The following listing contains all authors and translators covered in the main text. Authors are listed according to the names under which their stories appeared, with cross references, as needed, among real names, pseudonyms, and collaborations. Names beginning with Mc are filed as Mac. Anonymous stories are grouped together in the entry "Anonymous." Stories are alphabetized, with initial definite and indefinite articles disregarded in the filing. Abbreviations are filed as if spelled out, as are numbers.

Ackerman, Forrest J.
  [*See collaboration, Francis Flagg and Forrest J. Ackerman.*]
Adams, Gerald H.
  Futility 1
Afford, Malcolm R.
  The Gland Men of the Island 2
  The Ho-Ming Gland 2
Ainsbury, Ray
  [*See 1557, "When the Moon Ran Wild," by A. Hyatt Verrill.*]
Aldinger, Harley S.
  The Green Intelligence 5
  The Heritage of the Earth 6
  The Way of a Dinosaur 4
Alexander, W.
  The Ananias Gland 9
  The Dog's Sixth Sense 10
  The Fighting Heart 8
  The Million Dollar Gland 12
  New Stomachs for Old 7
  One Leg Too Many 11
Am Bruhl, Leo
  Garfield's Invention 13
Anderton, Seven
  The King and the Pawn 14

[Anonymous]
  Air Road 14 3
  Bandits of the Stratosphere 32
  Death Dive 320
  Fighting Gas 419
  Flaming Frontier 436
  The Flying Robot 439
  History Hysterical 633
  The Humming Horror 647
  Ice Metropolis 649
  The Immortal Man 650
  The Invisible Witness 651
  The Legion of the Lost 836
  The London-Capetown Express 882
  Metalclad 1000
  The Mind Machine 1023
  Monster of the Marsh 1024
  The Mystery of the Blue Mist 1047
  No Man's 'Plane 1070
  The Peal of Death 1116
  Rebels of the Penal Planet 1172
  Revolt of the Stone Men 1199
  Sheer Personality 1316
  Smashing Atoms 1360
  The Soundless Hour 1392
  Spacedrome No. 1 1393
  Spirit of Speed 1399
  Voice from the Void 1616
  When the Skull Men Swooped 1724
  Wimpole's Weight Reducer 1763
  The World of Vapour 1785
  Z.-1., Red Flyer 1802
Anthos
  The Malignant Flower 15
Anton, Ludwig
  Interplanetary Bridges 16
Arnold, R. Crossley
  The Secret of the Tomb 17
Arnold, Wesley
  The Struggle for Venus 20
  Waves of Death 19
  Within the Planet 18

Aronin, Ben
  The Doubt 21
Arthur, Robert, Jr.
  The Terror from the Sea 22
  Theft of the Washington Monument 23
Auckland, Roi
  Blind Reasoning 24
Bain, Arthur
  Author's Adventure 25
Baird, Wesley P.
  [*See collaboration, Nathaniel Salisbury, et al.*]
Baldwin, Robert
  Retribution 26
Ball, Clelland J.
  The Gravity King 27
Balmer, Edwin and MacHarg, William
  The Eleventh Hour 30
  The Hammering Man 31
  The Man Higher Up 29
  The Man in the Room 28
Barclay, Fred M.
  The Troglodytes 33
Barnes, Arthur K.
  [*See also Dave Barnes, joint pseud.*]
  The Challenge of the Comet 35
  Emotion Solution 38
  Guardians of the Void 36
  Lord of the Lightning 34
  The Mole-Men of Mercury 37
Barnes, Dave
  The House That Walked 39
Barnette, Jack
  The Purple Death 40
  The Vapor Intelligence 41
Barney, B. H.
  Beyond the Veil of Time 42
Barrett, H. I.
  The Mechanical Heart 43
Barry, B. X.
  Pirates of Space 44

Bibliography

In addition to general bibliographic and historical sources, the following specialized books and papers have been used:

Ash, Brian, ed.. *The Visual Encyclopedia of Science Fiction.* New York: Harmony Books, 1977.

Ashley, Mike. "Bankruptcy and Beyond." *Futures Past, 1929:* 17-18.

——. "The Birth of Amazing." *Futures Past, 1926* (Part 1):25-29; and *Futures Past, 1927* (Part 2):6-11.

——. "The Galactic Emancipator. Remembering Homer Eon Flint." *Fantasy Commentator* 8-3 & 4 (#47-48, 1995):258-265.

——. *The History of the Science Fiction Magazines.* Volumes One and Two. London: New English Library, 1974 and 1975.

——. "Memories of Frank Belknap Long." *Pulp Vault* #12/13 (1996):9-16.

——. "Mr. H. and Mr. H. G." *Fantasy Commentator* 6-4 (#40, 1989-1990):263-274.

——. "Remembering Ray Cummings." *Pulp Vault* #11 (1993):64-70.

——. "The Rocket Man." *Fantasy Commentator* 8-3 & 4 (#47-48, 1995):166-172.

——. "Science Fiction in the Depression." *Fantasy Commentator* 8-1 & 2 (#45-46, 1993-1994):95-102.

——. "Sons of Super-Science." *Fantasy Commentator* 7-1 (#41, 1990):49-55.

Australian Science Fiction Association. *Index to British Science Fiction Magazines 1934-1953. Part One. Scoops, Tales of Wonder, Fantasy.* Canberra City, A.C.T., Australia: [A.S.F.A., 1968].

Barron, Neil, ed. *Anatomy of Wonder.* New York: Bowker, 1976.

——. *Anatomy of Wonder.* 2d rev. ed. New York: Bowker, 1981.

——. *Anatomy of Wonder.* 3d rev. ed. New York: Bowker, 1987.

——. *Anatomy of Wonder 4.* New Providence, N. J.: Bowker, 1995.

Bates, Harry. "Editorial Number One." In Rogers, Alva. *A Requiem for Astounding.* Chicago: Advent:Publishers, 1964.

Blair, David H. *Astounding Revisited.* [Winnipeg: Author, 1995]

——. *The Clayton Astounding in Detail.* [Winnipeg: Author, 1994]

Bleiler, Everett F. *The Checklist of Science Fiction and Supernatural Fiction.* Glen Rock, N. J.: Firebell Books, 1978.

——. *The Guide to Supernatural Fiction.* Kent, Ohio: Kent State University Press, 1983.

——. *Science-Fiction: The Early Years.* Kent, Ohio: Kent State University Press, 1990.

——. ed. *Science Fiction Writers.* New York: Scribner, 1982.

——. ed. *Supernatural Fiction Writers.* 2 vols. New York: Scribner, 1985.

Bleiler, Richard J. *The Index to Adventure Magazine.* 2 vols. Mercer Island, Wash.: Starmont House, 1990.

——. *The Annotated Index to The Thrill Book.* Mercer Island, Wash.: Starmont House, 1991.

Bloch, Robert N. *Bibliographie der utopischen und phantastischen Literatur 1750-1950.* Giessen: Verlag Munniksma, 1984.

Carter, Paul A. *The Creation of Tomorrow. Fifty Years of Magazine Science Fiction.* New York: Columbia University Press, 1977.

Cave, Hugh B. *Magazines I Remember: Some Pulps, Their Editors, and What It Was Like to Write for Them.* Chicago: Tattered Pages Press, 1994.

Cioffi, Frank. *Formula Fiction? An Anatomy of American Science Fiction, 1930-1940.* Westport, Conn.: Greenwood, 1982.

Clareson, Thomas D. *Science Fiction in America, 1870s-1930s: An Annotated Bibliography of Primary Sources.* Westport, Conn.: Greenwood, 1984.

——. *Some Kind of Paradise. The Emergence of American Science Fiction.* Westport, Conn.: Greenwood, 1985.

Clute, John, and Nicholls, Peter, eds. *The Encyclopedia of Science Fiction.* London: Orbit, 1993.

Cockcroft, Thomas G. L. "An Index to 'The Eyrie.'" *Fantasy Commentator* 8-3 & 4 (#47-48, 1995):217-229.

——. *Index to Fiction in Radio News and Other Magazines.* Lower Hutt, New Zealand: [Author], 1970.

——. *Index to the Weird Fiction Magazines. Index by Author.* 2d ed. Lower Hutt, New Zealand: [Author], 1967.

Contento, William. *Index to Science Fiction Anthologies and Collections.* Boston: G. K. Hall, 1978.

——. *Index to Science Fiction Anthologies and Collections: 1977-1983.* Boston: G. K. Hall, 1984.

Cowart, David and Wymer, Thomas L., eds. *Twentieth-Century American Science-Fiction Writers: Dictionary of Literary Biography. Volume Eight.* 2 vols. Detroit: Gale Research, 1981.

Currey, Lloyd E. *Science Fiction and Fantasy Authors: A Bibliography of First Printings of Their Fiction.* Boston: G. K. Hall, 1979.

Davin, Eric Leif. "The Age of Wonder." *Fantasy Commentator* 6-1 (#37, 1987):4-25, 39-47.

——. "The Optimistic Pessimist: An Interview with Frank K. Kelly." *Fantasy Commentator* 6-3 (#39, 1989):195-207.

——. "Pioneer in the Age of Wonder: An Interview with Raymond Z. Gallun." *Fantasy Commentator* 6-2 (#38, 1988):78-97.

——. "Pioneer Publisher: An Interview with Lloyd Eshbach." *Fantasy Commentator* 8-1 & 2 (#45-46, 1994):121-134.

——. "Remembering R. F. Starzl: A Conversation with Dr. Thomas E. Starzl." *Fantasy Commentator* 8-3 & 4 (#47-48, 1995):150-161.

——. "Remembering Stanley Weinbaum." *Fantasy Commentator,* 7-2 (#42, 1991):78-103.

——. "The Silberkleit Years: An Interview with Charles D. Hornig." *Fantasy Commentator* 6-3 (#39, 1989):184-192.

Day, Donald B. *Index to the Science-Fiction Magazines 1926 * 1950.* Portland, Ore.: Perri Press, 1952.

de Camp, L. Sprague. "Afterword: Fletcher and I." In de Camp, L. Sprague and Pratt, Fletcher, *The Compleat Enchanter: The Magical Misadventures of Harold Shea.* Garden City, N. Y.: Nelson Doubleday, 1975.

del Rey, Lester. *The World of Science Fiction: 1926-1976: The History of a Subculture.* New York: Garland Publishing, Inc., 1980.

De Voto, Bernard. "Doom beyond Jupiter." *Harper's Magazine,* 179 (September 1939). Reprinted in *Fantasy Commentator,* 4-3 (Winter 1981):170-173.

Doyle, Brian. *Who's Who of Boys' Writers and Illustrators 1964.* London: Brian Doyle, 1964.

Dziemianowicz, Stefan R. *The Annotated Guide to Unknown and Unknown Worlds.* Mercer Island, Wash.: Starmont House, 1991.

Elliot, Dr. Jeffrey. *Pulp Voices or Science Fiction Voices #6. Featuring Jack Williamson, H. L. Gold, Stanton A. Coblentz, C. L. Moore, Raymond Z. Gallun.* San Bernardino, Cal.: Borgo Press, 1983.

Emerson, Jim, ed. *Futures Past. 1926.* Convoy, Ohio: Futures Past, 1991.

——. *Futures Past. 1927.* Convoy, Ohio: Futures Past, 1992.

——. *Futures Past. 1928.* Convoy, Ohio: Futures Past, 1992.

——. *Futures Past. 1929.* Convoy, Ohio: Futures Past, 1994.

Engel, Theodore. "Science Fiction in 'Modern Electrics' [and other technical magazines published by Hugo Gernsback]." [In Gernsback, Hugo. *Evolution of Modern Science Fiction.*]

Eshbach, Lloyd A. *Over My Shoulder.* Philadelphia: Oswald Train, 1983.

Fisher, Peter S. *Fantasy and Politics: Visions of the Future in the Weimar Republic.* Madison: University of Wisconsin Press, 1991.

Freas, Frank Kelly. *The Art of Science Fiction.* Norfolk, Va.: The Donning Company, 1977.

Gernsback, Hugo. *Evolution of Modern Science Fiction.* [New York: Author, 1952.]

——. *Science Fiction vs Reality. Address by Hugo Gernsback Publisher of Radio Electronics before The Massachusetts Institute of Technology Science Fiction Society, 21 October 1960.* [New York: Author, 1960.]

Goulart, Ron, ed. *The Encyclopedia of American Comics.* New York: Facts on File, 1990.

——. *Over 50 Years of American Comic Books.* Lincolnwood, Ill.: Publications International, Inc., 1991.

Gunn, James, ed. *The New Encyclopedia of Science Fiction.* New York: Viking, 1988.

Gunnison, John P. "Hersey, Revisited." *The Pulp Collector* 6-1 (Fall 1991):32-42.

Hall, H. W. *Science Fiction and Fantasy Reference Index, 1878-1985.* 2 vols. Detroit: Gale Research, 1987.

Hardin, Nils. "An Interview with Henry Steeger." *Xenophile* 3-9 (July 1977):3-18.

Hedman, Iwan. *Deckare och thrillers på svenska 1864-1973.* Strängnäs, Sweden: Dast Forlag AB, 1974.

Herrick, Daryl S. "Riding the Range of Opinion." *Pulp Vault* #12/13 (1996):101-103.

Hersey, Harold Brainerd. *Pulpwood Editor: The Fabulous World of the Thriller Magazines Revealed by a Veteran Editor and Publisher.* New York: Stokes, 1937.

[*The Hoover Report.* See *Recent Social Trends in the United States.*]

Hubin, Allen J. *Crime Fiction 1749-1980: A Comprehensive Bibliography.* 2d. ed. New York: Garland Publishers, 1984.

Jordan, Linda. "German Science Fiction in the Science-Fiction Magazines of Hugo Gernsback (1926-1935)." Master's thesis, McGill University, 1986.

Kelly, Frank K. "My Interplanetary Teens." *The Atlantic Monthly,* July 1947. Reprinted in *Fantasy Commentator* 6-3 (#39, 1989):192-194.

Ketterer, David. *Canadian Science Fiction and Fantasy.* Bloomington and Indianapolis: Indiana University Press, 1992.

Knight, Damon. *The Futurians: The Story of the Science Fiction "Family" of the 30's That Produced Today's Top SF Writers and Editors.* New York: John Day, 1977.

Kraeuter, David W. "The U.S. Patents of Alexanderson, Carson, Colpitts, Davis, Gernsback, Hogan, Loomis, Pupin, Rider, Stone, and Stubblefield." *Antique Wireless Association Review,* 6 (1991):174-175.

Kyle, David. *The Illustrated Book of Science Fiction Ideas and Dreams.* London: Hamlyn, 1977.

Kyle, David (*continued*)
——. *A Pictorial History of Science Fiction*. London: Hamlyn Publications, 1977.

Laney, Francis T. *Ah! Sweet Idiocy! The Fan Memoirs of Francis T. Laney*. Los Angeles: FAPA, 1948.

Lesser, Robert. *Pulp Art. Original Cover Paintings for the Great American Pulp Magazines*. New York: Gramercy Books, 1997.

Locke, John. "The Pulp Magazine Index." *Pulp Vault* #12/13 (1996):36-54.

Loder, John. *Australian Crime Fiction: A Bibliography 1857-1993*. Port Melbourne, Victoria, Australia: Thorpe, in Association with the National Centre for Australian Studies, 1994.

Lofts, W. O. G. *SCOOPS. Talk*. [Unpublished typescript of lecture delivered in London, c. 1989.]

Lofts, W. O. G. and Adley, D. J. *The Men behind Boys' Fiction*. London: Howard Baker, 1970.

Martell, Edward, ed. *The Author's and Writer's Who's Who*. London: Shaw Publishing Co., 1934.

McGhan, Barry. *Science Fiction and Fantasy Pseudonyms*. Dearborn, Mich.: Howard De Vore, 1971

Mencken, H. L. *My Life as Author and Editor*. New York: Knopf, 1993.

Moskowitz, Sam. *A. Merritt: Reflections in the Moon Pool*. Philadelphia: Oswald Train, 1985.

——. "Amazing Encounter. MacFadden's Takeover of Gernsback's Co." *Fantasy Review* 9-2 (#88, February 1986) (Part 1):8-10; *Fantasy Review* 9-3 (#89, March 1986):8-10.

——. "Bernarr Macfadden and His Obsession with Science-Fiction." *Fantasy Commentator* 7-3 (#43, 1992):189-203.

——. "Henrik Dahl Juve and the Second Gernsback Dynasty." *Extrapolation* 30-1 (Spring 1989):5-52.

——. "How Science Fiction Got Its Name." *Futures Past. 1929*. 58-65. [The most recent form of a chapter from the author's *Explorers of the Infinite*. World Publishing Co.; Cleveland and New York, 1963.]

——. *The Immortal Storm. A History of Science Fiction Fandom*. Westport, Ct.: Hyperion Press, Inc., 1974. (Reprint of 1954 edition.)

——. "The Marketing of Stanley G. Weinbaum." *Fantasy Commentator* 7-2 (#42, 1991):104-125.

——. "Newly Discovered Letters Reinforce Gernsback's Claim to Have Coined Term 'Science Fiction.'" *Science Fiction Times*, November 1967 (No. 448):1-2.

——. "The Science-Fiction of Nat Schachner." *Fantasy Commentator* 7:3 (#43, 1992):160-179. *Fantasy Commentator* 7:4 (#44, 1992):292-302.

Moukheiber, Zina. "The Geeks Have Inherited the Earth." *Forbes,* 160-1 (July 7, 1997):348-360.

Mullen, R. D. "Two Poets and an Engineer." *Science-Fiction Studies* 21-1 (March 1994):103-112.

——. "From Standard Magazines to Pulps and Big Slicks: A Note on the History of U.S. General and Fiction Magazines." *Science-Fiction Studies* 22-1 (March 1995):144-156.

——. "Notes and Correspondence: First Fandom." *Science-Fiction Studies* 23-3 (November 1996): 543-546.

Nicholls, Peter, ed. *The Science in Science Fiction*. New York: Knopf, 1983. (Contributions by Peter Nicholls, David Langford, and Brian Stableford.)

Perry, Tom. "An Amazing Story: Experiment in Bankruptcy." *Amazing Stories* 31-2 (May 1978):101-118.

Pohl, Frederik. *The Way the Future Was: A Memoir*. New York: Ballantine Books, 1979.

——. "Paradise at a Penny a Word." *Pulp Vault* #11 (1993):5-15.

Porges, Irwin. *Edgar Rice Burroughs: The Man Who Created Tarzan*. 2 vols. New York: Ballantine Books, 1975.

Recent Social Trends in the United States. Report of the President's Research Committee on Social Trends. With a foreword by Herbert Hoover, President of the United States. 2 vols. New York: McGraw Hill, 1933. (Referred to as the *Hoover Report.*)

Reginald, R. *Science Fiction and Fantasy Literature: A Checklist, 1700-1974*. 2 vols. Detroit: Gale Research, 1979.

Reid, Constance. *The Search for Eric Temple Bell, Also Known as John Taine*. Washington, D. C.: The Mathematical Association of America, 1993.

Reynolds, Quentin. *The Fiction Factory or from Pulp Row to Quality Street*. New York: Random House, 1955.

Robinson, Frank and Davidson, Lawrence. *Pulp Culture. The Art of Fiction Magazines*. Portland, Oregon: Collectors Press, Inc., 1998.

Robinson, Roger. *Who's Hugh? An SF Reader's Guide to Pseudonyms*. Essex, England: Beccon Publications, 1987.

Rock, James A. *Who Goes There? A Bibliographic Dictionary*. Bloomington, Ind.: James A. Rock & Co., 1979.

Rogers, Alva. *A Requiem for Astounding*. Chicago: Advent:Publishers, 1964. Reprint 1974.

Rynin, Nikolai Alexeevich. *Interplanetary Flight and Communication. Vol. 1, No. 1. Dreams, Legends, and Early Fantasies.*. Trans. by R. Lavoot. Jerusalem, Israel: Published for the National Aeronautics and Space Administration and the National Science Foundation by the Israel Program for Scientific Translations, 1970. (Original publication in Russian: Leningrad, 1928.)

——. *Interplanetary Flight and Communication. Vol. 1, No. 2. Spacecraft in Science Fiction*. Trans. by R. Lavoot. Jerusalem, Israel: Published for the National Aeronautics and Space Administration and the National Science Foundation by the Israel Program for Scientific Translations, 1971. (Original publication in Russian: Leningrad, 1928.)

——. *Interplanetary Flight and Communication. Vol. 1, No. 3. Spacecraft in Science Fiction*. Trans. by the IPST Staff. Jerusalem, Israel: Published for the National Aeronautics and Space Administration and the National Science Foundation by the Israel Program for Scientific Translations, 1971. (Original publication in Russian: Leningrad, 1931.)

Sanders, Joe, ed. *Science Fiction Fandom*. Westport, Conn.: Greenwood, 1994.

Schwartz, Julius. "An Interview with Frank R. Paul." *Fantasy Magazine* 4-3 (December 1934-January 1935): 71-72.

Schwartz, Julius and Weisinger, Mortimer. "Leo Morey." *Fantasy Magazine*, 3-2 (April 1934): 18-19.

——. "Hans Waldemar Wessolowski." *Science Fiction Digest*, 1-8 (April 1933): 3-4.

Schwartz, Julius and Weisinger, Mortimer (*continued*)
——. "David H. Keller, M. D." *Science Fiction Digest*, 1-11 (July 1933): 3-4.
[Schwartz/Weisinger]. [Files of the fan periodical *Science Fiction Digest*, retitled *Fantasy Magazine*, (1934-1937) edited by Conrad H. Ruppert, Julius Schwartz and Mortimer Weisinger. Data in this invaluable source are scattered through issues under various headings.]
Siegel, Mark. *Hugo Gernsback, Father of Modern Science Fiction, with Essays on Frank Herbert and Bram Stoker.* San Bernardino, Cal.: Borgo Press, 1988.
Sieger, James R. "Ghost Stories. Index by Author." In Seiger [*sic*], James R. and Moskowitz, Sam. *Ghost Stories. Stories of Ghosts.* Evergreen, Col.: Opar Press, 1973.
Smith, Curtis C., ed. *Twentieth-Century Science-Fiction Writers.* New York: St. Martin, 1981.
Sneyd, Steve. "Empress of the Stars: A Reassessment of Lilith Lorraine, Pioneering Fantasy Poetess." *Fantasy Commentator* 7-3 (#43, 1992):206-229.
Social Security Death Index (SSDI) Search. Ancestry, Inc. and Infobases, Inc. [n.d.]
Sullivan, Jack, ed. *The Penguin Encyclopedia of Horror and the Supernatural.* New York: Viking, 1986.
Tremaine, F. Orlin. "Editorial Number Two." In Rogers, Alva. *A Requiem for Astounding.* Chicago: Advent:Publishers, 1964.
Tuck, Donald H. *The Encyclopedia of Science Fiction and Fantasy. Vol. 1.* Chicago: Advent:Publishers, Inc., 1974,
——. *The Encyclopedia of Science Fiction and Fantasy. Vol. 2.* Chicago: Advent:Publishers, Inc., 1978.
——. *The Encyclopedia of Science Fiction and Fantasy. Vol. 3.* Chicago: Advent:Publishers, Inc., 1983.
Tymn, Marshall B., and Ashley, Mike, eds. *Science Fiction, Fantasy, and Weird Fiction Magazines.* Westport, Conn.: Greenwood, 1985.
Versins, Pierre. *Encyclopédie de l'utopie des voyages extraordinaires et de la science fiction.* Lausanne: L'Age d'homme, 1972.
Walker, Paul. "Jack Williamson: An Interview, Conducted by Paul Walker." *Luna Monthly* 62 (February 1976):1-7.
Warner, Harry. *All Our Yesterdays. An Informal History of Science Fiction Fandom in the Forties.* Chicago: Advent:Publishers, Inc., 1969.
Weinberg, Robert. *A Biographical Dictionary of Science Fiction and Fantasy Artists.* Westport, Conn.: Greenwood, 1988.
Westfahl, Gary. "Evolution of Modern Science Fiction: The Textual History of Hugo Gernsback's *Ralph 124C 41+*." *Science-Fiction Studies* 31-1 (March 1996):37-82.
Williamson, Jack. *Wonder's Child. My Life in Science Fiction.* New York: Bluejay Books, 1985.
Winter, Frank H. *Prelude to the Space Age. The Rocket Societies: 1924-1940.* Washington, D. C.: Published for the National Air and Space Museum by the Smithsonian Institution Press, 1983.

Also available from Kent State University Press, the companion volume to Science-Fiction: The Gernsback Years

Science-Fiction: The Early Years
by Everett F. Bleiler, with the assistance of Richard J. Bleiler

This enormous book, which contains more than a million words of body copy, opens for the first time early s-f to scholars and readers. It studies more than 3,000 novels, short stories, and plays from earliest times to 1930, both books and periodical stories, including many unusual items: utopias with s-f elements, fantastic Victorian boys' books, dime novels, pulp adventure, suitable mainstream fiction, as well as pure s-f, from everywhere except the genre magazines of the period. It describes hundreds of items not previously known to be s-f.

Each of the 2475 entries is exhaustive, with bibliography, including (for books) previous periodical publication (if any), and a full summary (up to 4,000 words in some cases) of each story, with historical and critical comments. Author biographical data, where possible, accompany each item.

The only place for precise information about impossibly rare books

It contains an incredible amount of information that is available nowhere else. Many of the 1800 books covered in this study are practically impossible to find. Some survive in less than a half dozen copies; some are not represented at all in American libraries. Covered are such important rarities as Dudgeon's *Columbia*; Davis's *Pyrna*; Cole's *The Struggle for Empire*; Wallace's *The Next War*; Powell's *The Wolf Men*; and scores of other important works.

A unique coverage of early magazine s-f

The book is especially strong on s-f in the early pulps. A partial listing: *Adventure*, 25 stories; *All-Story* 112; *Argosy* and *Argosy-All-Story*, 168; *The Black Cat*, 51; *Popular Magazine*, 27; *The Thrill Book*, 17; *Weird Tales*, 202; and many other rare magazines.

Among other unusual areas that are covered are dime novels (more than 100 rare examples); British family magazines like *The Strand*, 56 stories; *Pearson's Magazine*, 36; *Harmsworth's/London Magazine*, 18; and many American and British literary magazines, like *Harper's Monthly, Putnam's, Lippincott's, Atlantic Monthly,* and others. The book also covers the science-fiction (127 stories) from Hugo Gernsback's technical magazines like *Radio News, Science and Invention, The Electrical Experimenter*, etc.

During this gigantic project, which has taken more than six years of research, the senior author has read each of the 3000-plus stories that he describes. His work is not based on secondary sources.

The author's introduction not only provides a new understanding of the nature of science-fiction and its origins, but offers a brief structuralist history, setting it into its cultural background in Europe and America. The introduction also contains an exhaustive analytical table of science-fiction motifs as they fit into the conceptual scheme of the sciences.

Since many of the systems and idea-concatenations present in early science-fiction may not be familiar to the modern reader,

an appendix explains Fourierism, Henry George's single tax, Blavatsky's Theosophy, Symmes's theory of the hollow earth, Donnelly's Atlantis and cometary collisions with the earth, the Schiaparelli-Lowell canals of Mars, and similar concepts.

Indispensable, unique finding guides

* Author index, including pseudonyms and variant titles; locating all items
* Title index
* Date index, listing all stories by year of publication
* Magazine index, indicating periodical sources
* Motif and theme index. 65 pages, about 35,000 entries; enabling you to locate stories by ideas or to study historical development of motifs

Science-Fiction: The Early Years is obviously an indispensable book for everyone seriously concerned with science-fiction, but it also has a larger value. Since it covers (thoroughly analyzed and indexed) so many of the most powerful issues in American cultural history expressed in fictional form—feminism, racial and ethnic prejudices, military jingoism, crank scientific theories, extreme social and economic systems, occult ideas, as well as varying attitudes toward science and technology—it is a gold mine for students of American history, with a wealth of material that has never been presented before.

Typical reviews . . .

"This is the book for which I have been waiting most of my life. Written by our preeminent authority on popular fiction, it is the most valuable work yet published on its subject . . . . it is not likely to be superseded," R. D. Mullen, *Science Fiction Studies*.

"*Science-Fiction: The Early Years* cannot be praised too highly. . . . [it] gives its readers the most comprehensive picture of emerging genre yet published . . . . could shape much of the work done in coming years," Thomas Clareson, *Extrapolation*.

"For anyone with the slightest interest in SF this is an invaluable guide. You will learn something from every entry, often new information about authors you thought you knew well . . . . A remarkable achievement that cannot be praised enough . . . . An essential purchase for all medium and larger libraries and all scholars of the field," Neil Barron, *Science Fiction Research Association Newsletter*

"With this magisterial work, the historic roots of the science-fiction field are ably delineated. Few bibliographies in any field are as readable . . . . It is almost impossible to overstate the value of this work to any serious student of science-fiction or popular culture. Others may add an item or two to this compilation, but the foundation work for the history of SF is essentially completed," Robert S. Bravard, *Choice*.

ISBN 0-87338-416-4. 1024 pp., double-columns. 8 1/2 x 11. Clothbound: $75.00